The Nyingma School of Tibetan Buddhism
Its Fundamentals and History

HIS HOLINESS DUDJOM RINPOCHE

The Nyingma School of Tibetan Buddhism
Its Fundamentals and History

Section One: The Translations

Dudjom Rinpoche, Jikdrel Yeshe Dorje

Translated and edited by
Gyurme Dorje and Matthew Kapstein

WISDOM PUBLICATIONS Boston

First Edition 1991

Wisdom Publications
199 Elm Street
Somerville MA 02144 USA
wisdompubs.org

Library of Congress Cataloging-in-Publication Data
Available upon request.

ISBN: 0-86171-199-9

06 05 04 03 02
6 5 4 3 2
Cover by Gopa & Ted2
Interior by Character Graphics

Wisdom Publications' books are printed on acid-free paper and meet the guidelines for permanence and durability of the Committee on Production Guidelines for Book Longevity of the Council on Library Resources.

Printed in Canada.

This book is dedicated to
the continued enlightened activity of
HIS HOLINESS DUDJOM RIṆPOCHE
and to all those who maintain
the living traditions of
Tibetan Buddhism.

General Contents

SECTION ONE: THE TRANSLATIONS

List of Illustrations xv
Foreword by Shenpen Dawa Rinpoche xxv
Preface to the Second Edition xxxii
Credits for Illustrations and Maps xxxiii
Technical Note xxxv
Guide to Pronunciation xxxvii
Abbreviations for Section One xli

BOOK ONE: FUNDAMENTALS OF THE NYINGMA SCHOOL OF TIBETAN BUDDHISM

Detailed Contents of Book One 3
Translator's Introduction 11

THE TEXT

Verses of Invocation 45
Introduction 47

PART ONE: DOCTRINES OF SAṂSĀRA AND NIRVĀṆA

1 The Essence and Definition of Dharma 51
2 Doctrines of Saṃsāra 54
3 Doctrines of Nirvāṇa 70
4 Transmitted Precepts 73
5 Treatises 88
6 Quantitative Treatises 97
7 Treatises of Inner Science 108

PART TWO: THE NATURE OF THE TEACHER ENDOWED WITH THE BUDDHA-BODIES

Introduction 113
1 Samantabhadra, the Buddha-body of Reality 115
2 Vajradhara, the Emanation of Samantabhadra 120
3 The Two Buddha-bodies of Form 123
4 The Five Buddha-bodies and Five Pristine Cognitions 139
5 Distinctive Attributes of the Buddha-bodies and Pristine Cognitions 144

PART THREE: CAUSAL VEHICLES OF DIALECTICS

Introduction 151
1 The Three Promulgations of the Doctrinal Wheel 153
2 The Lesser Vehicle 156
3 The Greater Vehicle 160
4 The Superiority of Great Madhyamaka to Mind Only 178
5 The Provisional and Definitive Meaning of the Transmitted Precepts 187
6 The Enlightened or Buddha Family 191
7 The Two Truths According to Great Madhyamaka 206
8 Key to the Appraisal of Causal Vehicle Texts 217
9 A Recapitulation of the Causal Vehicles 223

PART FOUR: RESULTANT VEHICLES OF SECRET MANTRA

Introduction 241
1 The Superiority of Secret Mantra 243
2 The Essence and Definition of Secret Mantra 257
3 The Three Continua of Ground, Path and Result 263
4 The Four Tantrapiṭaka 268
5 Mahāyoga 275
6 Anuyoga 284
7 Key to the Appraisal of Secret Mantra Texts 290
8 The Superiority of Atiyoga, the Great Perfection 294
9 The Definition of Atiyoga 311
10 The Divisions of Atiyoga 319
11 A Recapitulation of the Resultant Vehicles 346

CONCLUSION

1 Concluding Remarks 375
2 Dedicatory Verses 376
3 Colophon 378

BOOK TWO: HISTORY OF THE NYINGMA SCHOOL OF TIBETAN BUDDHISM

Detailed Contents of Book Two 383
Translators' Introduction 393

THE TEXT

Verses of Invocation 403

PART ONE: THE ORIGIN OF THE PRECIOUS TEACHING OF THE CONQUEROR IN THIS WORLD

Introduction 409
1 The Coming of Buddha, Teacher of the Doctrine 411
2 The Collecting of Transmitted Precepts by Councils 428
3 The Patriarchs of the Teaching 432
4 The Preservation of the Teaching and Spread of the Greater Vehicle 440

PART TWO: THE RISE OF THE PRECIOUS TEACHING OF SECRET MANTRA

Introduction 445
1 The Turning of the Secret Mantra Wheel 447
2 The Collecting of Transmitted Precepts by Different Compilers 451
3 The Emergence of this Teaching in the Human World 452
4 The Lineage of Mahāyoga, the Class of Tantras 458
5 The Lineage of Mahāyoga, the Class of Means for Attainment 475
6 The Lineage of Anuyoga, the Perfection Stage 485
7 The Lineage of Atiyoga, the Great Perfection 490
8 Concluding Remarks 502

PART THREE: THE ORIGIN OF THE CONQUEROR'S TEACHING IN TIBET

Introduction 507
1 The Three Ancestral Religious Kings 510
2 The Decline and Expansion of the Doctrine during the Intermediate Period 523
3 The Revival and Later Expansion of the Teaching 524

PART FOUR: THE DEVELOPMENT OF THE THREE INNER CLASSES OF TANTRA IN TIBET

Introduction 531
1 Mahāyoga and Anuyoga 533
2 The Mental and Spatial Classes of Atiyoga 538
3 The Esoteric Instructional Class of Atiyoga, the Innermost Spirituality 554
4 Longcen Rapjampa 575

PART FIVE: THE DISTANT LINEAGE OF TRANSMITTED PRECEPTS

Introduction 599
1 The Lineage of Nyak 601
2 The Lineage of Nup 607
3 The Lineage of the Zur Family 617
4 Biographies of the Rong Tradition 650
5 Dotokpa's Lineage of the Zur Tradition 685
6 Biographies of the Kham Tradition 688
7 Miscellaneous Lineages of the Zur and Kham Traditions 700
8 Rongzom Chöki Zangpo 703
9 The Traditions of Vajrakīla 710
10 The Lineages of the Empowerment of the *Sūtra which Gathers All Intentions* 717
11 Later Lineages of the Transmitted Precepts 733

PART SIX: THE CLOSE LINEAGES OF THE TREASURES

1 The Nature, Purpose and Kinds of Treasure 743
2 Biographies of the Treasure-finders 750
3 Sangye Lama 751
4 Trapa Ngönshe 753
5 Nyang-rel Nyima Özer 755
6 Guru Chöki Wangcuk 760
7 Como Menmo 771
8 Orygen Lingpa 775
9 Ngödrup Gyeltsen or Rikdzin Gödemcen 780
10 Sangye Lingpa 784
11 Dorje Lingpa 789
12 Ratna Lingpa 793
13 Pema Lingpa 796
14 Karma Lingpa 800
15 Thangtong Gyelpo 802
16 Ngari Paṇcen Pema Wangyel 805

17 Rikdzin Jatsön Nyingpo 809
18 Rikdzin Düdül Dorje 813
19 Lhatsün Namka Jikme 818
20 The Fifth Dalai Lama 821
21 Rikdzin Terdak Lingpa, the Great Treasure-finder of Mindröling 825
22 Jikme Lingpa 835
23 Chogyur Decen Lingpa 841
24 Jamyang Khyentse Wangpo 849
25 Jamgön Kongtrül Lodrö Thaye 859
26 Mipham Jamyang Namgyel Gyamtso 869
Conclusion 881

PART SEVEN: A RECTIFICATION OF MISCONCEPTIONS CONCERNING THE NYINGMA SCHOOL

1 General Reply to Criticisms of the Nyingmapa Tantras 887
2 On the View of the Great Perfection 896
3 Response to Critics of the *Sūtra which Gathers All Intentions* 911
4 Response to Critics of the *Root Tantra of the Secret Nucleus* 914
5 The Continuity of the Nyingmapa Tradition and its Impact on the Other Schools 918
6 On the Validity of the Treasures 927
7 The Shortcomings of Refutation and Proof 929
8 On The Prophecies Found in the Treasures 934
9 The Relationship between the Nyingmapa and Pönpo Traditions 936
10 On the "Bad Luck of the Nyingmapa" 938

PART EIGHT: THE CHRONOLOGY OF THE DOCTRINE

1 Duration of the Doctrine 943
2 A Chronology of the Buddha's Life 946
3 From the Buddha's Final Nirvāṇa until the Beginning of the First Tibetan Sexagenary Cycle 948
4 From the Beginning of the First Sexagenary Cycle to the Present 951
5 Some Prophecies 960

CLOSING STATEMENTS

1 Primary Sources 965
2 Concluding Benedictions 967
3 Colophon 972

SECTION TWO: REFERENCE MATERIAL

Contents v
Introduction vii
Guide to Pronunciation xi
Abbreviations for Section Two xv

NOTES

1 *Fundamentals* 3
2 *History* 27

GLOSSARY OF ENUMERATIONS

Introduction 103
Glossary of Enumerations 105

BIBLIOGRAPHY

Introduction 191

Part One: Works Cited by the Author
Works Cited by the Author 199

Part Two: Works Referred to by the Translators
1 Indic Texts 293
2 Tibetan Texts 297
3 Secondary Literature 301
4 Addenda to the Bibliography 316

ARTIFACTS AND MATERIAL TREASURES

Introduction 320
Artifacts and Material Treasures 321

INDEX OF TECHNICAL TERMS

Introduction 331
Index of Technical Terms 333

INDEX OF PERSONAL NAMES

Introduction 391
Index of Personal Names 393

INDEX OF LOCATIONS

Introduction 453
Index of Locations 455

MAPS

Illustrations

PLATES

1 Samantabhadra, the primordial buddha-body of reality, with consort Samantabhadrī (*kun-bzang yab-yum*). Fresco at the Jokhang, Lhasa.

2 The peaceful and wrathful deities (*zhi-khro lha-tshogs*).

3 Vajrasattva (*rdo-rje sems-dpa'*), the buddha-body of perfect rapture.

4 Mahottara Heruka (*che-mchog he-ru-ka*), the central figure of the Deities of the Eight Transmitted Precepts (*bka'-brgyad lha-tshogs*).

5 Padmasambhava, flanked by his two foremost consorts, Mandāravā and Yeshe Tshogyel, and surrounded by his eight manifestations (*guru mtshan-brgyad*).

6 Maṇḍalas of the Eight Transmitted Precepts (*bka'-brgyad-kyi dkyil-'dhor*).

7 The three ancestral religious kings (*chos-rgyal mes-dbon rnam-gsum*), Songtsen Gampo, Trhisong Detsen and Trhi Relpacen. Statues in the Pelkor Chöde, Gyantse.

8 Jowo Rinpoche, the famous image of Lord Śākyamuni in Lhasa, brought to Tibet by Songsten Gampo's Chinese queen. Originally housed in the Ramoche Temple, it was later established as the central object of veneration in the Jokhang.

9 Image of King Songtsen Gampo in the Jokhang, flanked by those of his Nepalese and Chinese queens.

10 Gilded roofs of the Jokhang, the first temple of Lhasa and centre of Songtsen Gampo's geomantic design. Originally built by his Nepalese queen, Trhitsün, it has been enlarged and embellished over the years.

11 The stone-lion emblem of the Yarlung dynasty in the Chongye valley, looking towards the tumuli of Songtsen Gampo and Relpacen, with the town of Chongye in the distance.

12 The reconstructed central shrine (*dbu-rtse*) at Samye, Tibet's first monastery.

13 A realistic representation (*nga-'dra-ma*) of the peerless fourteenth-century scholar and treasure-finder (*gter-ston*) Longcen Rapjampa, now in the possession of Dilgo Khyentse Rinpoche.

14 Remains of the sacred juniper tree at Kangri Thökar, where Longcen Rapjampa's protector deities resided while he was composing his celebrated treatises, the *Seven Treasuries* (*mdzod-bdun*).

15 Tharpaling in Bumthang, Bhutan, founded by Longcen Rapjampa.

16 Katok Dorjeden Monastery in Kham, founded by Katokpa Tampa Deshek in 1159.

17 The imposing façade of Mindröling Monastery, the most influential seat of the Nyingma school in Central Tibet, founded by Terdak Lingpa in 1670.

18 The hidden valley of Rudam Kyitram, behind Dzokcen Monastery, with the Śrī Siṃha College in the foreground.

19 Pel Tshering-jong, the retreat of Jikme Lingpa in Tönkar valley near Chongye, where the Innermost Spirituality of Longcenpa (*klong-chen snying-thig*) was first revealed.

20 The restored Pelyül Namgyel Cangcup Ling Monastery, founded by Rikdzin Künzang Sherap in 1665.

21 The celebrated monastery of Dorje Trak, recently restored on the north bank of the Brahmaputra River, opposite Cedezhöl, where the Northern Treasures (*byang-gter*) tradition was preserved.

22 The deities of the *Combined Means for Attainment of the Three Roots*

(*rtsa-gsum dril-sgrub*), discovered by Tibet's first treasure-finder, Sangye Lama, and rediscovered by Jamgyang Khyentse Wangpo.

23 Painted scroll depicting Terdak Lingpa, with his handprints and footprints in gold. Preserved at Mindröling Monastery.

24 Dudjom Rinpoche (centre) surrounded by his previous emanations.

LINE DRAWINGS

Dignāga 101
Dharmakīrti 103
Samantabhadra and Consort 116
Vajradhara 121
Vajra on Lotus 134
Vasubandhu 157
Nāgārjuna 163
Āryadeva 165
Asaṅga 169
Maitreya 179
Vajrasattva 256
Śākyamuni 417
Śāriputra 424
Maudgalyāyana 426
Mahākāśyapa 433
Ānanda 434
Śāṇavāsika 436
Upagupta 437
Madhyāhnika 438
Samantabhadra and Consort 448
Vajradharma 450
Mañjuśrī, Avalokiteśvara, Vajrapāṇi 453
King Ja, Indrabhūti 459
Kukkurāja 461
Līlāvajra (or Vilāsavajra) 463
Buddhaguhya 465
Prabhāhasti 467
Padmasambhava 470
Hūṃkara 476
Yamāntaka 478
Hayagrīva 479
Vajrāmṛta 480

Vajrakīla 482
Mahākarmendrāṇī 483
Mahottara Heruka 484
Kambalapāda 486
Śākyamitra 488
Garap Dorje 491
Mañjuśrīmitra 492
Buddhajñānapāda 495
Śrī Siṃha 497
Jñānasūtra 499
Vimalamitra 500
Lha Thotori Nyentsen 508
Songtsen Gampo 511
Trhisong Detsen 512
Śāntarakṣita 514
Padmākara 517
Dorje Trolö 519
Pehar 520
Trhi Relpacen 521
Lhalung Pelgi Dorje 525
Lacen Gongpa Rapsel 526
Namkei Nyingpo 534
Gyelwa Choyang 536
Vairocana 539
Pang-gen Sangye Gönpo 541
Dzeng Dharmabodhi 544
Nyang Tingdzin Zangpo 556
Dangma Lhündrup Gyeltsen 557
Cetsün Senge Wangcuk 558
Zhangtön 559
Dorje Lekpa 560
Nyibum 562
Guru Cober 563
Trüzhi Sengegyap 565
Melong Dorje 566
Kumārādza 568
Ekajaṭī 570
Karmapa III, Rangjung Dorje 573
Longcen Rabjampa 576
Guru Trakpo 589
Nyak Jñānakumāra 602
The Sogdian Pelgi Yeshe 606
Nupcen Sangye Yeshe 608
Yamāntaka 611
Lharje Zurpoche Śākya Jungne 618

Yangdak Heruka 627
Zurcung Sherap-tra 636
Lekden Degü 644
Zur Dropukpa Śākya Senge 646
Zur Campa Senge 664
Yungtön Dorjepel 667
Tanak Drölmawa Samdrup Dorje 668
Zur Ham Śākya Jungne 670
Zurcen Chöying Rangdröl 680
Rāhula 682
Katokpa Tampa Deshek 689
Śrīdevī 690
Tsangtönpa 692
Campabum 694
Rongzom Chöki Zangpo 704
Yeshe Tshogyel 711
Vajrakīla 716
Rikdzin Lekdenje 718
Dorje Trak Rikdzin Pema Trhinle 719
Sangdak Trhinle Lhündrup 725
Locen Dharmaśrī 729
Dzokcen Pema Rikdzin 737
Rikdzin Künzang Sherap 738
Sangye Lama 752
Trapa Ngönshe 754
Nyang-rel Nyima Özer 756
Guru Chöki Wangcuk 761
Como Menmo 772
Orgyen Lingpa 776
Rikdzin Gödemcen 781
Rikdzin III, Ngagiwangpo 782
Sangye Lingpa 785
Dorje Lingpa 790
Ratna Lingpa 794
Pema Lingpa 797
Karma Lingpa 800
Thangtong Gyelpo 803
Ngari Paṇcen Pema Wangyel 806
Rikdzin Jatsön Nyingpo 810
Rikdzin Düdül Dorje 814
Lhatsün Namka Jikme 819
The Fifth Dalai Lama 822
Rikdzin Terdak Lingpa 826
Jikme Lingpa 836

Chogyur Decen Lingpa 842
Jamyang Khyentse Wangpo 850
Jamgön Kongtrül Lodrö Thaye 860
Mipham Jamyang Namgyel Gyamtso 870
Peltrül Rinpoche 875
The Author, Dudjom Rinpoche 888
Acintyaprabhāsa 897
Akṣobhyaprabha 904
Pel Jikpa Kyopei Yi 909
Düjom Lingpa 920
Rudrakulika 961

Trhadruk, possibly Tibet's first Buddhist temple

Samye, general view from Hepori

Lhodrak Khoting, a Border Taming temple

Lhodrak Kharcu, sacred site of Padmasambhava and Namkei Nyingpo

Karcung Temple of the Indesctructible Expanse, near Lhasa

Öncangdo Peme Trashi Gepel Temple,
with Longcenpa's retreat centre on the hillside behind

Foreword by Shenpen Dawa Rinpoche

His Holiness Dudjom Rinpoche, Jikdrel Yeshe Dorje, (1904-87) was appointed by His Holiness Dalai Lama XIV as the supreme head of the Nyingma tradition of Tibetan Buddhism. He was an enlightened yogin and meditation master, a discoverer of concealed treasure teachings (*gter-ston*) who was inseparable from Guru Rinpoche [Padmasambhava], the most prolific of contemporary Tibetan scholars, and an incarnate lama who had intentionally emanated for the sake of sentient beings through seventeen successive lives. In ancient India these emanations included: Buddha Śākyamuni's foremost disciple Śāriputra; the *mahāsiddha* Saraha; Kṛṣṇadhara, the religious minister of King Indrabhūti; and the *ṛṣi* Hūṃkara. In Tibet, they included: Khyeucung Lotsāwa, one of Padmasambhava's twenty-five disciples; Smṛtijñanakīrti whose lifetime demarcated the transition from the ancient to the new system of translation; Rongzom Paṇḍita who was among the first to compose major treatises within the Nyingma tradition; Katok Tampa Deshek (1122-92) who founded the monastery of Katok in East Tibet; Chögyel Phakpa (1235-80) who established a Sakya administration in Central Tibet; Rikdzin Düdül Dorje (1615-72) who is famous for his discovery of concealed treasure teachings (*gter-ma*) in the Puwo region of south-east Tibet; Gyelse Sonam Detsen, responsible for revitalising Katok; and the treasure-finder Düjom Lingpa (1835-1904) who discovered the "New Treasures" (*gter-gsar*).

Like many of his predecessors, His Holiness was also renowned as a great discoverer of concealed treasure teachings which are now widely practised and propagated. These are primarily the direct "treasures of intention" or "mind treasures" (*dgongs-gter*) of the awareness-holders (*vidyādhara*) concerning the inner tantras of the secret mantra vehicle, which can bring about the unsurpassed enlightenment of the rainbow body in one lifetime.

He took birth in the Pemakö region on the frontier of Tibet, on the twenty-third day of the fourth Tibetan month, 1904. This birth occured while his predecessor Düjom Lingpa was still alive. Düjom Lingpa himself gave the specific instructions of how to find his authentic emanation. His father was Tülku Jampel Norbu, who was Prince of Kanam, a direct descendant of King Trhisong Detsen, and his mother, Namgyel Drölma.

In his youth His Holiness received the transmissions and direct blessings of Guru Rinpoche, Yeshe Tshogyel and Mañjuśrī in person. He received all the lineages of the Nyingma school from his lamas: Phüngong Tülku Gyurme Ngedön Wangpo, Jedrung Trhinle Campa Jungne, Gyurme Phendei Özer, Namdröl Gyamtso of Mindröling, Gendün Gyamtso and Khenpo Aten, amongst others. He mastered every tradition of Tibetan Buddhism. Astonishingly, at the age of fourteen, he gave the full empowerment and oral transmission of the *Store of Precious Treasure* (*rin-chen gter-mdzod*), which are the collected treasure texts of the Nyingma lineage. From that time on, he gave major empowerments relating to different treasure cycles, and at the same time composed many means for attainment (*sādhana*) which elucidated the profound teachings of the *buddhadharma*. He wrote commentaries both on his predecessor's teachings and on his own revealed treasures. When he was seventeen years old he composed his first celebrated treatise on the Great Perfection (*rdzogs-pa chen-po*). He became widely renowned as a scholar and meditation master, and was followed by many students. Among his students in Tibet and throughout the Himalayan regions, many have shown the signs of full enlightenment.

He maintained the lineage of the Mindröling tradition in Central Tibet, and above all at Pema Chöling [Lamaling] and his other seats in the Kongpo and Puwo areas of south-east Tibet. Subsequently, forseeing the incipient Chinese invasion, His Holiness and family left Tibet for India in 1958, following the prediction of Düjom Lingpa that the lineage of his New Treasures would spread to all continents of the world, and especially to the West.

After his arrival in India, Nepal and Sikkim, he established many vital communities of Buddhist practitioners. These include Zangdok Pelri in Kalimpong, Düdül Rapten Ling in Orissa and the Buddhist monasteries in Tshopema [Rewalsar, Himachal Pradesh] and Bodhnath in Nepal. In addition, he actively encouraged the study of the Nyingma tradition at the Tibetan Institute for Higher Studies in Sarnath. In such locations, he continued to grant the empowerments and literary transmissions for the *Collected Transmitted Precepts of the Nyingmapa* (*rnying-ma'i bka'-ma*), the *Collected Tantras of the Nyingmapa* (*rnying-ma'i rgyud-'bum*), and the *Store of Precious Treasure*, among others. His prolific scholarship is attested by the recent publication in India of his *Collected Works*, and his edition of the *Collected Transmitted Precepts of the Nyingmapa*, a fifty-five volume work which he began at the age of seventy-four. At the request of the Dalai Lama, he also wrote a *Political History of Tibet (bod-kyi rgyal-rabs)*.

In the final phase of his teaching activity, His Holiness travelled widely throughout Asia, Europe and North America, where he brought many students to the *dharma*. He continued the buddha-activity of formal teaching, empowerment and personal supervision of meditation practice and retreat, which is the essence of the transmission of Vajrayāna Buddhism. Meditation and retreat centres were also established: the Vajrayāna Esoteric Society of Hong Kong, Dorje Nyingpo and Urgyen Samye Chöling in France, Yeshe Nyingpo and Orgyen Chö Dzong in the United States.

His Holiness passed into *parinirvāṇa*, dissolving his emanational body into the pure space of the buddha-body of reality (*dharmakāya*) on 17 January 1987, the eighteenth day of the eleventh month of the fire tiger year, shortly before the advent of a new Tibetan sixty-year cycle. This was at his residence overlooking the Vezère valley in the Dordogne, France. His passing was accompanied by miraculous signs of his enlightened realisation and buddha-attributes. His passing away in France is of great significance because it enacts the unification of East and West into a single maṇḍala of enlightened mind. His embalmed body was placed in a stūpa, constructed in Bodhnath, Nepal on 5 February 1989, in order to continue the Bodhisattva's activity of benefitting sentient beings. He was a Vajra Guru whose accomplishment is to be seen not so much in the outward form of elaborate monastic establishments, but in the direct, clear awareness of the mind, free from elaboration. This enlightened mind is displayed by many of his monastic and lay disciples. On this basis the purity of his lineage is established and maintained to this day in an unbroken succession.

The publication of this translation was originally conceived as a maṇḍala offering to His Holiness Dudjom Rinpoche and to those great teachers who, through their discriminative awareness and skilful method, lead sentient beings to the path of the *dharma* – what is to be abandoned and what is to be adopted. For twenty years Gyurme Dorje devoted painstaking and continuous effort to bring these translations to fruition. He is a modest and unswerving scholar who has accomplished a work of paramount importance for practitioners, scholars and those generally interested in Tibetan Buddhism. Matthew Kapstein has given invaluable assistance for the later stages of these translations. Our joy is that this work has now come to its final form – the seed having been carefully planted and tended throughout, its growth has borne fruit. It will bring inconceivable benefit to all those who come into contact with it through reading, contemplation or meditation. Our regret is that we could not complete the project in time to make an offering of it to His Holiness during his lifetime. It is a work which communicates the highest wisdom of the Nyingma lineage to the English-speaking world.

I dedicate the benefit of this profound work of my father to the long life of His Holiness Dalai Lama XIV, the incarnation of Avalokiteśvara, who is a benefit to the Land of Snows, and to the whole world. May all his actions be spontaneously accomplished. May the Tibetan people, under his lotus feet, never be separated from his enlightened discriminative awareness and compassion. May His Holiness the Gyelwa Karmapa manifest swiftly to raise the victory banner of the *dharma* which liberates sentient beings, and may the heads of the Kagyü schools continue to illuminate the path of those wandering in the six realms. May His Holiness the Sakya Trhizin powerfully safeguard and nourish the faultless tradition of the Sakyapa. May all other lineage-holders flourish, and their *dharma* activities increase like the waxing moon.

May His Majesty King Jikme Senge Wangcuk of Bhutan live long, bringing happiness, prosperity and spiritual growth to his people. May His Majesty King Birendra Bir Bikram Shah Dev of Nepal fulfil all the aspirations and wishes of his people. May the government and people of India, the land of the sublime ones, prosper and sustain their spiritual heritage.

May our *dharma* patrons, the Royal Grandmother of Bhutan, HRH Phüntsok Chödrön, M. Gerard Godet, Dr L. Y. Soo, Ms Emily Stevens and Jonathan Altman, enjoy both causal and wisdom merits and may their ability to benefit others never be exhausted. Tülku Pema Wangyel and Tülku Rangdröl selflessly served His Holiness – may their activities in the West be crowned with success.

To you, my physical and spiritual father and root guru, on behalf of my mother Rikzin Wangmo, my sisters Chime Wangmo and Tsering Penzom, my niece Lhanzey Wangmo, and my prophesied wife Sonam Chhuskit; on behalf of my sons Namgyel Dawa and Wangchen Dawa, and on behalf of all your disciples, I bow at your lotus feet and offer homage for your unrepayable kindness and guidance in making our lives wholesome and meaningful. May the victorious sound of the drum of the *dharma* penetrate all the levels of existence, bringing joy and happiness. May all be auspicious.

> Taking a humble position, rich with the treasure of
> contentment,
> Free from the binds of the eight worldly concerns,
> firm and strong-hearted in practice,
> Receiving the Guru's blessing, realisation becomes
> equal to space.
> May we attain the kingdom of the All-Good.

HIS EMINENCE SHENPEN DAWA RINPOCHE
Lineage-holder of the New Treasures
Dordogne, 1990

Preface

Two treatises form the present volume, namely, the *Fundamentals of the Nyingma School* (*bstan-pa'i rnam-gzhag*) and the *History of the Nyingma School* (*rnying-ma'i chos-'byung*). Among the most widely read of all His Holiness Dudjom Rinpoche's works, these treatises were composed during the years immediately following his arrival in India as a refugee. His intention in writing them, as the concluding verses of the *History* state, was to preserve the precise structure of the Nyingma philosophical view within its own historical and cultural context, in a period of great uncertainty and instability.

Since the early sixties, His Holiness had appreciated the growing interest in the meditation practices and philosophical views of the Nyingma tradition, which is now evident both in universities and in the large number of Buddhist meditation centres throughout the world. He knew that, despite the vastness of the Tibetan literature, very few texts had actually been translated into other languages, and he recognised an urgent need for the presentation in English of traditional works which precisely define, stage by stage, the entire range of Buddhist experience and thought, and the authentic history of its transmission from antiquity to the present. Therefore, in 1971, he authorised and encouraged me to translate into English his *History of the Nyingma School*, which constitutes the latter part of this volume. Then, in 1980, he further authorised the translation of his *Fundamentals of the Nyingma School*.

Prior to 1971, partial Chinese and Hindi translations of the *History* had already been published in Hong Kong and Nalanda respectively. Working from the original Tibetan and its Hindi version, I prepared an annotated English translation in manuscript form at the monastery of Orgyen Kunzang Chokhorling in Darjeeling and at the sacred place of the Nyingmapa known as Tshopema, or Rewalsar, in Himachal Pradesh, between 1971 and 1977. The typing of the first draft was completed by Sheona Gunn at Bodhnath, Nepal, during the winter of 1977 to 1978. In the summer of 1979, the Author asked Matthew

Kapstein to edit the manuscript, and consequently in 1981 we met to revise the edited translation and to standardise the English terminology. Then, between 1980 and 1982, I prepared a translation of the *Fundamentals* in the Dordogne region of France and met again with Matthew Kapstein in New York during the summer of 1983, where he helped edit the *Fundamentals*. Both texts were prepared for publication with the assistance of many volunteer typists at Orgyen Chö Dzong, Greenville, New York.

The *Fundamentals* is written in the terse, highly structured style of the *grub-mtha'* genre, and is by no means an easy text to comprehend. A synopsis of the treatise has been included in the Translator's Introduction so that the reader can form an overall view of its structure and become familiar with the English terminology. Those unfamiliar with even the basic categories of Buddhist thought are recommended to start by reading the *History*, Parts One and Two, where these concepts are introduced in the clear narrative context of the origins of Indian Buddhism, as understood in the Nyingma tradition.

The annotations, glossaries and indexes for both texts, which are published here in the second section as a resource for the reader, were compiled after consulting materials at the library of the School of Oriental and African Studies, University of London, between 1982 and 1983. The bibliographies were initially prepared in the Dordogne and London over the same period, and their sources thoroughly researched and documented at Brown University, Rhode Island, USA, from 1985 to 1986. All of this reference material was revised, updated and expanded into its present form with the help of our editor Sarah Thresher during the final editorial work in London, New York and Boston throughout 1989 and 1990.

The general problems of translation are compounded in the case of the Tibetan language. In the past, Tibetan scholars of the calibre of Vairocana and Kawa Peltsek could translate the Sanskrit Buddhist texts with great accuracy because they had fully realised the essence of enlightened mind. By contrast, in the present circumstances, despite our total absence of inner realisation, we are obliged to translate the great works of Tibetan literature in order to preserve and propagate them for the benefit of posterity. It is therefore hoped that the well informed reader will exercise some restraint in the knowledge that the translator accepts full responsibility for errors which inevitably exist. These in no way reflect on the realisation or scholarship of the Author.

At this juncture Matthew Kapstein and I wish to express our gratitude to all who helped bring about the publication of the English version of these texts. Above all, His Holiness Dudjom Rinpoche suggested the task and inspired the work of translation at every stage of its development. Specifically, he gave attention to many textual problems in the

Dordogne, France, during the summer of 1982 and in New York during the summer of 1983. His wife, Lady Rikdzin Wangmo (Sangyum Kusho), and his *dharma* heir, Shenpen Dawa Rinpoche, have also given constant support. The late Kangyur Rinpoche and his family facilitated the project during its formative years in Darjeeling from 1971 to 1976, and gave invaluable subsequent assistance. During this period, the project was also funded and staunchly supported by Eric and Joan McLennan. Then, from 1977 to 1983, Gerard Godet of the Kangyur Rinpoche Foundation sponsored the translation with dedicated generosity. Some financial support was also provided by Tom Stickland in 1978, Georgina and Etienne De Swarte in 1982, and Mr C. T. Chen of the Institute for Advanced Studies of World Religions during 1979 and 1980. Moreover, for the past twelve years enormous practical help has been given by Rigzin Dolma, who, keeping in the background, has sustained those working on the project.

Several scholars devoted many concentrated hours to clarify obscure points of *dharma* or translation. In chronological order, these were: Pema Dorje, the artist, and Khenpo Pema Sherab who dedicated themselves to the task at Clement Town during the winter and spring of 1978 to 1979; Khetsun Zangpo Rinpoche and Khenpo Tsewang Dongyel who offered similar assistance during the autumn and winter of 1979 in Nepal; and Lama Sonam Topgyel, Tülku Pema Wangyel, Khenpo Palden Sherap and Nyoshul Khen Rinpoche, who applied themselves to the editing problems in France from 1980 to 1982. I also wish to thank Professor David Snellgrove for his interest and support, Mr Hugh Richardson, Dr Michael Aris and Kalon Jikme Taring, who helped clarify specific points; and Mr Michael Farmer, who prepared our new maps with great thoroughness and care. Matthew Kapstein wishes to thank Khenpo Sangye Tenzin of Serlo Gumba, Nepal, for the profound kindness with which he introduced him to the historical and doctrinal traditions of the Nyingmapa.

Finally, we wish to express gratitude to all the staff of Wisdom Publications for their sustained efforts, editorial care and strong commitment to the preservation of the important works of Tibetan Buddhism. The publishers wish to thank Brian Boland for his assistance during the latter stages of production.

GYURME DORJE
London, 1990

Preface to the Second Edition

After H.H. Dudjom Rinpoche's *The Nyingma School of Tibetan Buddhism: Its Fundamentals and History* first appeared in English in 1991, many expressed to us the desire for a more moderately priced edition that would be readily available to the broad range of students of Buddhism in the West and in Asia. We are therefore grateful to Wisdom Publications for now undertaking to bring out a new edition that will fulfill this demand. Our thanks are also due to the Venerable Sogyal Rinpoche and to the Rigpa Fellowship, whose encouragements have greatly facilitated these efforts.

The present volume reproduces in full the text of the two volumes of the original publication, the Translations, and Reference Materials. It differs in that it offers a reduced selection of the photographic plates that illustrated the first edition; and it corrects, without comment, a number of errors and infelicities that were found in the text after careful review. A list of addenda to the bibliography of works referred to by the translators has also been added so as to reflect pertinent developments in Tibetan Buddhist Studies during the past decade.

As promised in the original version, an exhaustive Tibetan-English glossary of the material treated in volume two is being prepared, and we are happy to announce that it is nearing completion. Remarks on new researches concerning the identification and availability of primary textual sources, which we have not been able to incorporate here, will be included in that forthcoming work, intended as an aid to Tibetological scholarship.

In concluding our present task, we wish to honour once again the memory of our magnificent teacher, H.H. the late Dudjom Rinpoche. We have been greatly privileged to assist in bringing these treasures of his intention to interested readers throughout the world. *dge legs 'phel! May virtue and goodness increase!*

Gyurme Dorje and Matthew Kapstein
June 2002

Credits for Illustrations and Maps

PLATES

The following people and organisations kindly made available colour or monochrome photographs for inclusion in Section One:

Board of Trustees of the Victoria and Albert Museum, London, 5
Dudjom Rinpoche Collection, frontispiece, 6, 24
Gyurme Dorje, 1, 9, 11, 12, 16, 19, 20, 23,
Golbenkin Museum of Oriental Art, Durham, 2
Rigpa Meditation Centre, London, 3
Lama Yeshe Dorje, 4
Mathieu Ricard, 18, 22
Stone Routes, 10, 15, 17
Robin Bath, 8
Michael Farmer, 21
Richard Freling, 7
Ngawang Chödron, 13, 14

We would also like to thank Chris Conlon and all those who helped with the photo research.

LINE DRAWINGS

The series of line drawings in Section One was compiled from a number of sources and redrawn by Chris Conlon. The majority were commissioned and drawn under the guidance of Dudjom Rinpoche for the original publication of the *History* in its Tibetan version in 1962, and later redrawn by Gomchen Oleshey for publication in *Kailash*. We also acknowledge Professor Lokesh Chandra's *Buddhist Iconography of Tibet*, which was an invaluable resource, and thank all those who obtained or commissioned rare drawings, namely, Khenpo Pema Sherap, Nyoshul Khen Rinpoche, Tülku Pema Wangyel, Dr Yoshiro Imaeda, Dr Michael Aris, Chris Fynn and the Rigpa Meditation Centre, London. The completed line drawings were shown to Dilgo Khyentse Rinpoche in the summer of 1990, who then instructed Tülku Pema Wangyel to review them for accuracy. Several revisions were undertaken on the basis of the latter's valuable advice.

MAPS

The maps in Section Two were compiled by Michael Farmer and extracted from the Tibetan mapping database currently being used to generate the forthcoming Wisdom map of Tibet. He wishes to thank YRM plc for the extensive use of their Intergraph CAD system, without which the project would not have been possible; and also Robbie Barnett, Jeremy Schmidt, John Cannon, Bradley Rowe, Anders Andersen and Urgyen Norbu, who generously provided valuable and rare maps from their own collections.

Technical Note

The two treatises presented here are works of great breadth and complexity. For this reason, extensive annotations, glossaries and indexes have been compiled to assist the reader, and these constitute Section Two. The introduction to the second volume details the reference material at the disposal of the reader – this brief note is intended to introduce only those conventions commonly used within Section One.

Each book is preceded by a detailed list of contents which includes a complete breakdown of all the sections and subsections of the original work. For the benefit of the reader, chapter and section headings have also been inserted within the texts themselves whenever possible even though these do not always appear in the original Tibetan. None of the inserted headings have been enclosed within square brackets or parentheses.

Square brackets have been used in the text where the terse character of the Tibetan language necessitates short explanations by the translators. They are also employed where, at the beginning of each section of the translation, the pagination of the original Tibetan text is given for the convenience of scholars wishing to locate specific passages in the original. Parentheses have been used where technical terms and book titles given in the original text have been retained, either in their Tibetan or Sanskrit versions. In those instances where these conventions would require the running together of square brackets and parentheses only the former have been employed.

Tibetan and Sanskrit book titles have been given in English translation and after their first occurence are followed by the Tibetan title (in the case of indigenous Tibetan works) or a Sanskrit title (in the case of works of Indic origin). The translated title always represents the form in which it is given in the Tibetan text and so may not always correspond to the known Sanskrit title. Abbreviated bibliographical data for texts occuring in certain well-known collections, such as the *Kangyur*, has also been provided, along with precise identification of the original sources of citations from major Indian Buddhist works wherever possible. When the readings of the text and Sanskrit original diverge, the translators have remained faithful to the Tibetan. Full bibliographical information for texts cited by the Author or referred to by the translators is provided in Section Two.

Sanskrit has generally been used for the names of persons and places in India, and for the names of many of the deities. Sanskrit equivalents of Tibetan technical terms have also occasionally been given, though this is mostly reserved for the glossaries of Section Two. Where a technical term given in Sanskrit is not documented in the original Sanskrit sources that are presently available, this fact is indicated by the use of an asterisk (*) preceding the term in question. To avoid typographical clutter, however, we have not followed this convention with respect to personal and place names.

Numerical categories are not indicated in the body of the text and seldom in the Notes but are listed in the Glossary of Enumerations in Section Two, which should be directly consulted whenever enumerations occur. Similarly, Tibetan and/or Sanskrit equivalents for all the technical terminology employed in the body of the translations are given in the Index of Technical Terms.

Finally, readers are referred to the Guide to Pronunciation which follows, for an explanation of the system of romanisation and simplified spelling adopted for personal and place names in Section One. In particular, the conventions governing the use of the letters *c* and *e* may seem unnatural to an English speaker and so require special attention. Technical terms and book titles occuring parenthetically have been transcribed according to their proper Tibetan orthography.

Guide to Pronunciation

Readers should familiarise themselves at the outset with the following four rules of pronunciation for Tibetan and Sanskrit:

(1) A final *e* is never silent, but is always pronounced in the manner of the French *é*. Thus, Sanskrit *vane* is pronounced *vané*, and the Tibetan *Ghare*, *Kore* and *Dorje* are pronounced, respectively, *Gharé*, *Koré* and *Dorjé*.

(2) *C* is pronounced somewhat like the English *ch*, but without aspiration. Sanskrit *cakra* and *citta* thus resemble *chakra* and *chitta*, and Tibetan *Co-se*, *Campa* and *Koca* are rather like *Cho-sé*, *Champa* and *Kocha*.

(3) *Ph* is never pronounced like an English *f*, but like a *p* with strong aspiration, for example in Sanskrit *phala* and Tibetan *photrang*.

(4) *Th* is never pronounced like the English *th* in *think* or *that*, but always resembling a *t* with strong aspiration, for example in Sanskrit *tathāgata* and Tibetan *thuk*.

The following remarks explain the conventions adopted for the transcription of Sanskrit and Tibetan in greater detail:

SANSKRIT

The Sanskrit vowels in actual use here are as follows:

a, *ā*, *i*, *ī*, *u*, *ū*, *ṛ*, *e*, *ai*, *o*, *au*

A, *i*, *u*, *e* and *o* are pronounced as in Italian. *Ā*, *ī* and *ū* are not to be pronounced like the so-called "long vowels" in English, but like the *a* in *father*, the *ea* in *seat* and the *oo* in *boot* respectively. *Ai* is similar to the *y*-sound of English *by*, and *au* to the *ow* of *now*. *Ṛ* resembles the *ri*-sound of *brick*. Vowels may be followed by *ṃ* and *ḥ*, which respectively indicate the nasalisation and aspiration of the vowel to which they are affixed.

The transcribed Sanskrit consonants are:

k, kh, g, gh, ṅ
c, ch, j, jh, ñ
ṭ, ṭh, ḍ, ḍh, ṇ
t, th, d, dh, n
p, ph, b, bh, m
y, r, l, v
ś, ṣ, s, h

Of these, *k, ch, j, t, d, n, p, b, m, y, r, l, v, s,* and *h* indicate roughly the same sounds as they do in English, and *c, ph* and *th* have been explained above. The series *t, th, d, dh, n* is distinguished from the series *ṭ, ṭh, ḍ, ḍh, ṇ* in that the latter or "retroflex" series is pronounced with the tongue striking the roof of the mouth, and the former or "dental" series, with the tongue striking the upper incisors. *Kh, gh, jh, dh, ḍh* and *bh* are similar to *k, g, j, d, ḍ* and *b* respectively, but with strong aspiration. *Ṅ* resembles the *ng* in English *sing*, and *ñ* the *ny* in *canyon*. *Ṣ* and *ś* are both similar to the English *sh*-sound, but the tongue is positioned further back when pronouncing the former.

TIBETAN

The transcription of Tibetan in English introduces special problems owing to the fact that the pronunciation of the spoken language does not closely correspond to the orthography of the literary language. For this reason a transliteration of the Tibetan spellings is of little use to the ordinary reader, who will have no way of knowing that, for example, *bsgrubs* and *dbyings* are currently pronounced as *drup* and *ying* respectively. On the other hand, students of the classical Tibetan language usually prefer the literal transcriptions to simplified phonetic schemes. The solution adopted in the present work has been to give all Tibetan personal and place names occurring in the text in just such a simplified system, relegating the precise transliterations to the indexes. At the same time, book titles, technical terms and peculiarities of language which are given parenthetically or discussed in the annotations have been given in a formal transliteration of the classical Tibetan, the system used being based upon that of the late Turrell V. Wylie, which will be familiar to specialists.

Our simplified phonetic transcription approximates the pronunciation of modern Central Tibetan, but without the subtlety or precision of a formal phonetic transcription, such as that developed by Chang and Shefts. Our intention here is merely to minimise the difficulties with which Tibetan names confront the reader.

In addition to the five vowels *a*, *i*, *u*, *e* and *o*, which have the same values here that they do in Sanskrit, Tibetan introduces two more – *ö* and *ü* – which are pronounced as in German.

The following additional consonants are used, along with those also found in Sanskrit: *ng*, *ny*, *tr*, *trh*, *dr*, *ts*, *tsh*, *dz*, *w*, *sh*, *z*, *zh*. Of these, *ng*, *ny*, *tr*, *dr*, *w*, *sh* and *z* are similar to their English values. *Trh* is like *tr*, but with strong aspiration. *Ts* resembles the *ts*-sound in English *bets*, and *dz* the sound in *adze*. *Tsh* is the strongly aspirated version of *ts*. *Zh* is similar to the *s* in leisure, or the *j* of French words such as *jamais*.

Specialists will note that this system does not reflect tone, an important feature of modern spoken Tibetan, and that we have dropped the aspirate in cases where it is not usually pronounced, even if it occurs in the classical orthography. Following a vowel, *l* is often silent, the preceding vowel being lengthened by way of compensation.

Abbreviations for Section One

DZ	*Gdams-ngag mdzod. Store of Precious Instructions.* 12 vols. Delhi: N. Lungtok and N. Gyaltsan, 1971.
Fundamentals	Dudjom Rinpoche, Jikdrel Yeshe Dorje. *The Nyingma School of Tibetan Buddhism: Its Fundamentals and History*, Vol. 1, Bk. 1.
History	Dudjom Rinpoche, Jikdrel Yeshe Dorje. *The Nyingma School of Tibetan Buddhism: Its Fundamentals and History*, Vol. 1, Bk. 2.
Mvt.	*Mahāvyutpatti*. Ed. R. Sakaki, Kyoto, 1916-25.
NGB	*Rnying-ma'i rgyud-'bum. Collected Tantras of the Nyingmapa.* Thimpu: Jamyang Khyentse Rinpoche, 1973. 36 vols. Catalogue by E. Kaneko, Tokyo, 1982.
NMKMG	*Rnying-ma bka'-ma rgyas-pa. Collected Transmitted Precepts of the Nyingmapa.* Ed. Dudjom Rinpoche, Jikdrel Yeshe Dorje. 55 vols. Kalimpong, WB: Dubjung Lama, 1982.
NYZ	*Snying-thig ya-bzhi. Four-Part Innermost Spirituality.* 11 vols. New Delhi: Trulku Tsewang, Jamyang and L. Tashi, 1970.
P	*The Tibetan Tripiṭaka, Peking Edition.* 168 vols. Tokyo-Kyoto: Suzuki Research Foundation, 1955-61.
RTD	*Rin-chen gter-mdzod. Store of Precious Treasure.* 111 vols. Paro: Ngodrup and Sherap Drimey, 1976.
SK	*Sa-skya bka'-'bum. The Complete Works of the Great Masters of the Sa Skya Pa Sect of Tibetan Buddhism.* 15 vols. Tokyo: Toyo Bunko, 1968.
Skt.	Sanskrit
SP	*Śatapiṭaka Series.* Sarasvati Vihar, New Delhi.
T	*A Complete Catalogue of the Tibetan Buddhist Canons.* Ed. H. Ui et al. Sendai: Tōhoku University, 1934.
Tib.	Tibetan

Book One
Fundamentals of the Nyingma School

Dudjom Rinpoche, Jikdrel Yeshe Dorje

Translated and edited by Gyurme Dorje
Associate editor Matthew Kapstein

Note

This detailed list of contents has been compiled as a resource for the reader showing the entire structure and framework of the teachings as they are presented in Book One. Headings have been added which do not appear in the actual translation to give a more precise and full idea of the subjects mentioned in the text, and these have been included in square brackets. The actual nesting of subject categories within the original Tibetan treatise is indicated by the small figures in square brackets which follow each heading.

Detailed Contents of Book One

TRANSLATOR'S INTRODUCTION 11

THE TEXT

VERSES OF INVOCATION 45

INTRODUCTION 47

PART ONE: DOCTRINES OF SAṂSĀRA AND NIRVĀṆA [*1*]

1 THE ESSENCE AND DEFINITION OF DHARMA 51

[Essence] [*11*] 51
[Verbal Definition] [*12*] 51
[Classification] [*13*] 53

2 DOCTRINES OF SAṂSĀRA [*131*] 54

The Characteristics of Saṃsāra [*131.1*] 54
The Mundane Vehicle and the Brahmā Vehicle [*131.2*] 57
The Mundane Vehicle [*131.21*] 57
The Brahmā Vehicle [*131.22*] 61
Those of No Understanding and Those of Wrong Understanding [*131.3*] 62
Those of No Understanding [*131.31*] 63
The Apathetic [*131.311*] 63
The Materialists [*131.312*] 64
Those of Wrong Understanding [*131.32*] 64
Sāṃkhya [*131.321*] 64
Aiśvara [*131.322*] 65
Vaiṣṇava [*131.323*] 65
Jainism [*131.324*] 66
Nihilism [*131.325*] 66
Conclusion [*131.4*] 67

3 DOCTRINES OF NIRVĀṆA [*132*] 70

The Superiority of the Supramundane Vehicle [*132.1*] 70
A Detailed Account of the Supramundane Vehicle [*132.2*] 71
Realisation of the True Doctrine [*132.21*] 71
Transmission of the True Doctrine [*132.22*] 72

4 TRANSMITTED PRECEPTS [*132.221*] 73

[The Characteristics of Transmitted Precepts] [*132.221.1*] 73
[Verbal Definition of Transmitted Precepts] [*132.221.2*] 74
[Classification of Transmitted Precepts] [*132.221.3*] 74
Transmitted Precepts according to Buddha's Personality [*132.221.31*] 74
[*Those Given in Oral Teaching*] [*132.221.311*] 74
[*Those Given by Blessing*] [*132.221.312*] 75
[*Those Given by Mandate*] [*132.221.313*] 75
Transmitted Precepts according to Time [*132.221.32*] 76
[*The First Promulgation of the Doctrinal Wheel*] [*132.221.321*] 76
[*The Second Promulgation of the Doctrinal Wheel*] [*132.221.322*] 76
[*The Third Promulgation of the Doctrinal Wheel*] [*132.221.323*] 76
Transmitted Precepts according to Sections [*132.221.33*] 76
[*The Twelve Branches of Scripture*] [*132.221.331*] 76
[*The Nine Branches of Scripture*] [*132.221.332*] 76
[*The Three Piṭaka*] [*132.221.333*] 76
Transmitted Precepts according to their Function as Antidotes [*132.221.34*] 77
[*The Eighty-four Thousand Components of the Doctrine*] [*132.221.341*] 77
[*The Four Piṭaka*] [*132.221.342*] 78
Transmitted Precepts according to their Power [*132.221.35*] 80
[*One, Two, Three, Four, Five, Nine Vehicles*] [*132.221.351*] 80

5 TREATISES [*132.222*] 88

[The Characteristics of Treatises] [*132.222.1*] 88
[Pure Treatises] [*132.222.11*] 88
[Ostensible Treatises] [*132.222.12*] 88
[Verbal Definition of Treatises] [*132.222.2*] 88

[Classification of Treatises] [*132.222.3*] 89
Treatises according to the Standard of Composition [*132.222.31*] 89
[*The Four Kinds of Treatise*] [*132.222.311*] 89
[*The Nine Kinds of Treatise*] [*132.222.312*] 89
Treatises according to the Purpose of Composition [*132.222.32*] 90
[*Those Summarising Vast Meaning*] [*132.222.321*] 90
[*Those Rectifying Disorder*] [*132.222.322*] 90
[*Those Disclosing Profundity*] [*132.222.323*] 90
Treatises according to their Individual Composers [*132.222.33*] 90
[*Those on Teachings Given by Buddhas*] [*132.222.331*] 90
[*Those on Teachings Given by Arhats*] [*132.222.332*] 90
[*Those on Teachings Given by Bodhisattvas*] [*132.222.333*] 91
[*Those Composed after Prophetic Declarations*] [*132.222.334*] 91
[*Those Composed by Ordinary Paṇḍitas*] [*132.222.335*] 91
Treatises according to the Manner of their Composition [*132.222.34*] 91
[*Commentaries on Specific Transmitted Precepts*] [*132.222.341*] 92
[*Independent Commentaries on their Meaning*] [*132.222.342*] 92
Treatises according to the Transmitted Precepts they Explain [*132.222.35*] 92
[*Commentaries on General Transmitted Precepts*] [*132.222.351*] 92
[*Commentaries on Particular Promulgations*] [*132.222.352*] 93
Treatises according to the Meaning they Express [*132.222.36*] 96

6 QUANTITATIVE TREATISES [*132.222.361*] 97

Common Quantitative Treatises [*132.222.361.1*] 97
Uncommon Quantitative Treatises [*132.222.361.2*] 97
Outer Sciences [*132.222.361.21*] 97
The Arts [*132.222.361.211*] 98
Medicine [*132.222.361.212*] 99
Grammar [*132.222.361.213*] 99
Logic [*132.222.361.214*] 101
Minor Sciences [*132.222.361.22*] 103

Astrology [*132.222.361.221*] 104
Poetics [*132.222.361.222*] 104
Prosody [*132.222.361.223*] 105
Synonymics [*132.222.361.224*] 106
Drama [*132.222.361.225*] 106

7 TREATISES OF INNER SCIENCE [*132.222.362*] 108
Qualitative Treatises [*132.222.362.1*] 108
Treatises Teaching Liberation and Omniscience [*132.222.362.2*] 108

PART TWO: THE NATURE OF THE TEACHER ENDOWED WITH THE BUDDHA-BODIES [*2*]

INTRODUCTION 113

1 SAMANTABHADRA, THE BUDDHA-BODY OF REALITY [*21*] 115

2 VAJRADHARA, THE EMANATION OF SAMANTABHADRA [*22*] 120

3 THE TWO BUDDHA-BODIES OF FORM [*23*] 123
The Buddha-body of Perfect Rapture [*231*] 123
The Emanational Body [*232*] 127
Emanations of Natural Expression [*232.1*] 128
Emanations who Train Living Beings [*232.2*] 129
[*Those who Instruct by their Great Merit of Body*] [*232.21*] 131
[*Those who Instruct by Direct Perception of Mind*] [*232.22*] 131
[*Those who Instruct by Inconceivable Miraculous Abilities*] [*232.23*] 132
Diversified Emanations [*232.3*] 133
Emanations according to the Great Perfection [*232.4*] 134

4 THE FIVE BUDDHA-BODIES AND FIVE PRISTINE COGNITIONS [*241.1-242.5*] 139

5 DISTINCTIVE ATTRIBUTES OF THE BUDDHA-BODIES AND PRISTINE COGNITIONS [*25*] 144
[Distinctive Attributes of the Buddha-body of Reality] [*251*] 144
[Its Essence] [*251.1*] 144

[Its Characteristic] [*251.2*] 144
[Its Blessing] [*251.3*] 145
[Distinctive Attributes of the Buddha-bodies of Form] [*252*] 145
[Distinctive Attributes of the Buddha-body of Perfect Rapture] [*252.1*] 145
[Distinctive Attributes of the Emanational Body] [*252.2*] 145

PART THREE: CAUSAL VEHICLES OF DIALECTICS [*3*]

INTRODUCTION 151

[The Overall Meaning according to Classifications] [*31*] 151

1 THE THREE PROMULGATIONS OF THE DOCTRINAL WHEEL [*311*] 153
The First Promulgation [*311.1*] 153
The Second Promulgation [*311.2*] 153
The Third Promulgation [*311.3*] 154
Philosophical Systems of the Causal Vehicles [*312*] 155

2 THE LESSER VEHICLE [*312.1*] 156
Vaibhāṣika [*312.11*] 156
Sautrāntika [*312.12*] 158
Pious Attendants [*312.13*] 158
Self-Centred Buddhas [*312.14*] 159

3 THE GREATER VEHICLE [*312.2*] 160
Vijñānavāda [*312.21*] 160
[Sākāravāda] [*312.211*] 161
[Nirākārāvāda] [*312.212*] 161
Madhyamaka [*312.22*] 162
Outer Madhyamaka [*312.221.1*] 162
Svātantrika-Madhyamaka [*312.221.1*] 162
Prāsaṅgika-Madhyamaka [*312.221.2*] 164
Great Madhyamaka [*312.222*] 169

4 THE SUPERIORITY OF GREAT MADHYAMAKA TO MIND ONLY [*312.222.1*] 178

5 THE PROVISIONAL AND DEFINITIVE MEANING OF THE TRANSMITTED PRECEPTS [*312.222.2*] 187

6 THE ENLIGHTENED OR BUDDHA FAMILY [*312.222.3*] 191

7 THE TWO TRUTHS ACCORDING TO GREAT MADHYAMAKA [*312.222.4*] 206

8 KEY TO THE APPRAISAL OF CAUSAL VEHICLE TEXTS [*312.3*] 217

The Provisional and Definitive Meaning of the True Doctrine [*312.31*] 217
The Intention and Covert Intention of the True Doctrine [*312.32*] 218

9 A RECAPITULATION OF THE CAUSAL VEHICLES [*32*] 223

Vehicle of Pious Attendants [*321*] 223
Vehicle of Self-Centred Buddhas [*322*] 227
Vehicle of Bodhisattvas [*323*] 231

PART FOUR: RESULTANT VEHICLES OF SECRET MANTRA [*4*]

INTRODUCTION 241

1 THE SUPERIORITY OF SECRET MANTRA [*41*] 243

2 THE ESSENCE AND DEFINITION OF SECRET MANTRA 257

[The Extraordinary Vehicles of Secret Mantra] [*42*] 257
[The Overall Meaning according to Classifications] [*421*] 257
[*Essence*] [*421.1*] 257
[*Verbal Definition*] [*421.2*] 257

3 THE THREE CONTINUA OF GROUND, PATH AND RESULT 263

Classification of the Secret Mantra Vehicles [*421.3*] 263
The Three Continua of Expressed Meaning [*421.31*] 263
Continuum of the Ground [*421.311*] 263
Continuum of the Path [*421.312*] 265
Continuum of the Result [*421.313*] 266

4 THE FOUR TANTRAPIṬAKA 268

[The Four Tantrapiṭaka of Literary Expression] [*421.32*] 268
Kriyātantra [*421.321*] 269
Ubhayatantra [*421.322*] 271
Yogatantra [*421.323*] 272
Unsurpassed Yogatantra [*421.324*] 273

5 MAHĀYOGA [*421.324.1*] 275

The Ground or View of Mahāyoga [*421.324.11*] 275
The Path of Mahāyoga [*421.324.12*] 276
The Creation Stage of Mahāyoga [*421.324.121*] 279
The Perfection Stage of Mahāyoga [*421.324.122*] 280
The Result of Mahāyoga [*421.324.13*] 281
The Texts of Mahāyoga [*421.324.14*] 283

6 ANUYOGA [*421.324.2*] 284

The Ground of Anuyoga [*421.324.21*] 284
The Path of Anuyoga [*421.324.22*] 286
[Definitive Path of Skilful Means] [*421.324.221*] 286
[Liberating Path of Discriminative Awareness] [*421.324.222*] 286
The Result of Anuyoga [*421.324.23*] 287
The Texts of Anuyoga [*421.324.24*] 289

7 KEY TO THE APPRAISAL OF SECRET MANTRA TEXTS [*421.324.3*] 290

The Six Limits [*421.324.31*] 290
The Four Styles [*421.324.32*] 292

8 THE SUPERIORITY OF ATIYOGA, THE GREAT PERFECTION 294

[Atiyoga, the Great Perfection] [*421.324.4*] 294
[The Superiority of Atiyoga over the Lower Vehicles] [*421.324.41*] 294

9 THE DEFINITION OF ATIYOGA [*421.324.411*] 311

10 THE DIVISIONS OF ATIYOGA [*421.324.42*] 319

The Mental Class [*421.324.421*] 319
The Texts and Teaching Cycles of the Mental Class [*421.324.421.1*] 325
The Spatial Class [*421.324.422*] 326
The Texts of the Spatial Class [*421.324.422.1*] 329
The Esoteric Instructional Class [*421.324.423*] 329
The Texts of the Esoteric Instructional Class [*421.324.423.1*] 332
The View and Path of the Esoteric Instructional Class [*421.324.423.2*] 333
Cutting Through Resistance [*421.324.423.21*] 335
All-Surpassing Realisation [*421.324.423.22*] 337

10 *Fundamentals*

11 A RECAPITULATION OF THE RESULTANT VEHICLES [*422*] 346

Distinctions between Outer and Inner Tantras [*422.1*] 346
Outer Tantras of Austere Awareness [*422.2*] 348
Kriyātantra [*422.21*] 348
Ubhayatantra [*422.22*] 352
Yogatantra [*422.23*] 353
Inner Tantras of Skilful Means [*422.3*] 357
Mahāyoga [*422.31*] 359
Anuyoga [*422.32*] 363
Atiyoga [*422.33*] 369

CONCLUSION

1 CONCLUDING REMARKS 375

2 DEDICATORY VERSES 376

3 COLOPHON 378

Translator's Introduction

The Nyingma School of Tibetan Buddhism represents the original Buddhist teachings as they were translated, principally from Sanskrit but also from Burushaski and other languages into Tibetan, until the period of the Indian scholar Smṛtijñānakīrti (late tenth or early eleventh century) and prior to that of Locen Rincen Zangpo (958-1055). It is also known as the Ancient Translation School (*snga-'gyur*) in contrast to the other lineages of Indian origin such as the Kagyüpa, the Sakyapa, and the Kadampa, which subsequently arrived in Tibet and became known as the new traditions (*gsar-ma*) or the later translation schools (*phyi-'gyur*).

The original promulgator of the doctrines brought together within the Nyingma tradition is held to be Samantabhadra, who is the primordial buddha-body of reality (*chos-sku*, Skt. *dharmakāya*). However, there are also a considerable number of teachings which derive from Vajradhara and the Buddhas of the Five Families, who are the buddha-body of perfect rapture (*longs-spyod rdzogs-pa'i sku*, Skt. *sambhogakāya*), and from the emanational bodies (*sprul-pa'i sku*, Skt. *nirmāṇakāya*), such as Śākyamuni in the world of men, Munīndra in the god realms and so on.

All Buddhist teachings may be presented in accordance with the threefold approach of theoretical view (*lta-ba*), meditational experience (*bsgom-pa*), or conduct (*spyod-pa*). In the *Fundamentals of the Nyingma School,* His Holiness Dudjom Rinpoche precisely delineates the entire range of the Buddhist spiritual and philosophical systems from the standpoint of the view. It is traditionally held that once the view has been comprehended, it is then to be experientially cultivated through meditation, and practically applied in all everyday situations which arise during the aftermath of meditation.

The Buddhist spiritual and philosophical systems form what is essentially a dynamic gradation of experience from the most mundane level of cyclical existence (*saṃsāra*) to that of the Great Perfection (*rdzogs-pa chen-po*). As the text explains (p.80):

> When the transmitted precepts are classified according to their power, they form a vehicle, because it appears that therein higher and higher paths are traversed, in the manner of a "vehicle".

And again:

> Riding on that, which is the best of vehicles,
> Manifestly attaining to delightful bliss,
> All sentient beings pass into nirvāṇa.

The *Fundamentals* expands upon these systems, which are known in the Nyingma tradition as the nine sequences of the vehicle (*theg-pa'i rim-pa dgu*), in extraordinarily intricate detail. To facilitate the reader's understanding, a summary now follows.

SUMMARY OF THE TEXT

The *Fundamentals* consists of four parts. The first expounds the doctrines of cyclical existence or saṃsāra and the supramundane doctrines of nirvāṇa. The second explains the nature of the teachers who are endowed with the three buddha-bodies of reality, perfect rapture, and emanation. The third is an analysis of the causal vehicles of dialectics. And, finally, there is a detailed account of the resultant vehicles of indestructible reality (*Vajrayāna*) which are held to be supreme by all schools of Tibetan Buddhism.

Within these four parts the distinctions of entrance (*'jug-sgo*), empowerment (*dbang-bskur*), view (*lta-ba*), moral discipline (*tshul-khrims*), meditation (*bsgom-pa*), conduct (*spyod-pa*), and result (*'bras-bu*) are clarified as they apply to each stage of the Buddhist experience.

PART ONE: DOCTRINES OF SAṂSĀRA AND NIRVĀṆA

At the outset, the Author differentiates between mundane doctrines which do not transcend the suffering of cyclical existence and the supramundane doctrines which do so by relying on the continuum of enlightenment.

Doctrines of Saṃsāra

The basis of the mundane doctrines is held to be ignorance which, in three interrelated aspects, generates a sense of bewilderment. This, in turn, gives rise to consciousness of the ground-of-all (*kun-gzhi rnam-shes*, Skt. *ālayavijñāna*), the six conflicting emotions of ignorance, delusion, hatred, pride, desire, and envy, and also all sensory perception, the eighteen psychophysical bases, the five components and the twelve activity fields.[1] All these are said to be compounded internally by the mind, their apparent aspect and support being the five gross elements compounded by external objects. In this way, the three world realms of desire (*kāmadhātu*), form (*rūpadhātu*) and the formless (*ārūpyadhātu*) are nothing but apparitional modes of the bewildered intellect of living beings. They do not appear in the pure vision of the buddhas, and the sufferings sustained within them are prolonged by karma or world-forming deeds.

The Mundane Vehicle and the Brahmā Vehicle

The mundane vehicle which is followed by gods and human beings (*lha-mi 'jig-rten-gyi theg-pa*) is the basis on which the nine specifically Buddhist sequences of the vehicle develop. By regulating world-forming deeds, renouncing the ten non-virtues and observing good deeds with piety and humility, one is said to progress to the status of a god of the desire realm within cyclical existence. As the text says (pp.60-1):

> It either forms the foundation of, or is preliminary to, all vehicles, because the vehicle which is not retained by the correct view and which does not observe the deeds and path of the ten virtues as its actual foundation is nowhere to be found.

As an extension of this mundane vehicle, the vehicle of Brahmā (*tshangs-pa'i theg-pa*) generates the experience of all the twenty-one higher realms within cyclical existence. These include seventeen realms of form, which are experienced through the four meditative concentrations of form, and four formless realms at the summit of cyclical existence, which are to be experienced through the four formless absorptions. These meditative techniques employ both tranquillity (*zhi-gnas*, Skt. *śamatha*) and higher insight (*lhag-mthong*, Skt. *vipaśyana*), and are accompanied by the practice of the four immeasurables (loving kindness, compassion, sympathetic joy and equanimity). The chart on the following pages indicates the stages and overall structure of the three realms of cyclical existence with their subdivisions and their corresponding meditative states.

Since the vehicles of gods and human beings and the vehicle of Brahmā possess qualities which are basic to any Buddhist experience, they are regarded as a means of entering into the true vehicle of Buddhist experience.

Those of No Understanding and Those of Wrong Understanding

The sentient beings who are considered to be ensnared within cyclical existence and subject to continuous rounds of suffering are traditionally

THE SIX CLASSES OF LIVING BEINGS IN THEIR GRADATION TO THE SUMMIT OF EXISTENCE IN SAṂSĀRA

Class 6: God Realms

1. The Twenty-one Higher Realms (*khams gong-ma nyi-shu rtsa-gcig*)

1A. Four Formless Realms at the Summit of Existence (*gzugs-med khams-pa'i gnas-bzhi*, Skt. *Caturārūpyadhātu*, Mvt. 3110-3113)

4. Activity Field of Neither Perception nor Non-Perception (*'du-shes med 'du-shes med-min skye-mched*, Skt. *Naivasaṃjñāsaṃjñāyatana*)
3. Activity Field of Nothing At All (*ci-yang med-pa'i skye-mched*, Skt. *Akiṃcanyāyatana*)
2. Activity Field of Infinite Consciousness (*rnam-shes mtha'-yas skye-mched*, Skt. *Vijñānānantyāyatana*)
1. Activity Field Infinite as the Sky (*nam-mkha' mtha'-yas skye-mched*, Skt. *Ākāśānantyāyatana*)

1B. Seventeen Realms of Form (*lha gzugs-khams bcu-bdun*)

1Ba. The Five Pure Abodes (*gtsang-gnas lnga*, Skt. *Pañcaśuddhanivāsa*, Mvt. 3101-3108)

5. Highest (*'og-min*, Skt. *Akaniṣṭha*)
4. Extreme Insight (*shin-tu mthong*, Skt. *Sudarśana*)
3. Attractive (*gya-nom snang-ba*, Skt. *Sudṛśa*)
2. Painless (*mi-gdung-pa*, Skt. *Atapa*)
1. Slightest (*mi-che-ba*, Skt. *Avṛha*)

1Bb. The Twelve Ordinary Realms of the Four Concentrations (*so-skye'i gnas bcu-gnyis*, Mvt. 3085-3100)

FOURTH CONCENTRATION
12. Great Fruition (*'bras-bu che*, Skt. *Bṛhatphala*)
11. Increasing Merit (*bsod-nams 'phel*, Skt. *Puṇyaprasava*)
10. Cloudless (*sprin-med*, Skt. *Anabhraka*)

THIRD CONCENTRATION
9. Most Extensive Virtue (*dge-rgyas*, Skt. *Śubhakṛtsna*)
8. Immeasurable Virtue (*tshad-med dge*, Skt. *Apramāṇaśubha*)
7. Little Virtue (*dge-chung*, Skt. *Parīttaśubha*)

SECOND CONCENTRATION
6. Inner Radiance (*'od-gsal*, Skt. *Ābhāsvara*)
5. Immeasurable Radiance (*tshad-med 'od*, Skt. *Apramāṇābha*)
4. Little Radiance (*'od-chung*, Skt. *Parīttābha*)

FIRST CONCENTRATION
3. Great Brahmā (*tshangs-pa chen-po*, Skt. *Mahābrahmā*)
2. Priest Brahmā (*tshangs-pa mdun-na 'don*, Skt. *Brahmapurohita*)
1. Stratum of Brahmā (*tshangs-ris*, Skt. *Brahmakāyika*)

2. The Ten Higher Levels of the Desire Realm (*'dod-khams-kyi mtho-ris gnas-bcu*)

2A. Six Species of Kāma Divinities (*'dod-lha rigs-drug*, Skt. *Kāmadevaṣaṭkula*, Mvt. 3078-3083)

6. Mastery over Transformations (*gzhan-'phrul dbang-byed*, Skt. *Paranirmitavaśavartin*)
5. Delighting in Emanation (*'phrul-dga'*, Skt. *Nirmāṇarata*)
4. Joyful (*dga'-ldan*, Skt. *Tuṣita*)
3. Strifeless (*'thab-bral*, Skt. *Yāma*)
2. Heaven of Thirty-three Gods (*sum-cu rtsa-gsum-pa*, Ski. *Trayatriṃśa*)
1. Four Great Kings (*rgyal-chen bzhi'i ris*, Skt. *Caturmahārājakāyika*)

Class 5: Antigods — Antigods (*lha-ma-yin*, Skt. *asura*)[2]

Class 4: Human Beings — 2B. Human Beings of the Four Continents (*gling-bzhi'i mi*)
4. Surpassing the Body (*lus-'phags*, Skt. *Pūrvavideha* in the East)
3. Rose-Apple Continent (*'dzam-bu gling*, Skt. *Jambudvīpa* in the South)
2. Enjoyer of Cattle (*ba-glang spyod*, Skt. *Aparagodanīya* in the West)
1. Unpleasant Sound (*sgra mi-snyan*, Skt. *Uttarakuru* in the North)

3. The Three Lower Levels of the Desire Realm (*ngan-song gsum*)

Class 3: Animals — 3. Animals (*dud-'gro*, Skt. *tīryak*)

Class 2: Tormented Spirits — 2. Tormented Spirits (*yi-dvags*, Skt. *preta*)

Class 1: Hells — 1. Denizens of the Hells (*dmyal-ba*, Skt. *naraka*) divided into those who have no understanding (*ma-rtogs-pa*) and those who have wrong understanding (*log-par rtogs-pa*). The former include the apathetic who lack understanding of deeds and causality, and so fail to respond to any philosophical system, observing neither renunciation nor commitment; and the materialists (*Lokāyata*) who refer only to the present life and set their trust in the mysterious calculations of worldly wisdom.

Those of wrong understanding are traditionally said to comprise four schools of eternalistic extremism and one of nihilistic extremism. The former are the Sāṃkhya, the Aiśvara, the Vaiṣṇava, and Jainism. The Sāṃkhya hold all that is knowable to consist of twenty-five existent categories, which are said to be dissolved when sublimation of the self (*puruṣa*) occurs. The Aiśvara, who include the adherents of Nyāya logic and Vaiśeṣika analysis of substances, hold that an eternally existent lord or Īśvara controls the destiny of all beings regardless of deeds. The Vaiṣṇava uphold the authenticity of the Veda, along with the eternal status of Viṣṇu, Brahmā and other deities. And Jainism holds all the knowable to be divided into nine categories, among which animate substances (*jīva*) are eternally existent. The nihilistic extremists are the Bārhaspatya hedonists of ancient India who negate causality, past and future lives, the existence of invisible beings and the possibility of progress beyond suffering into nirvāṇa.

All these are said to lack a means of achieving liberation from the suffering of cyclical existence – those of no understanding because they are roused by no philosophical view and those of wrong understanding because they either cling to the concept of an eternal self or become totally negative. Even so, the Author maintains, there are certain circumstances when a buddha may teach in the manner of the eternalists for a specific purpose or in that of the nihilists when scepticism may be transmuted into Madhyamaka dialectic.[3]

Doctrines of Nirvāṇa

The true doctrine of nirvāṇa which transcends the suffering of cyclical existence is said to surpass mundane doctrines because it seeks refuge in the Buddha, the doctrines of Buddhism and the community of practitioners. There are four seals or hallmarks indicative of such transmitted precepts, namely, all that is compounded is impermanent, all that is corrupt is suffering, all things are without self, and nirvāṇa is peace. By the practice of the Buddhist teachings all cyclical existence and rebirth are opposed.

In general, the Buddhist teaching is divided according to realisation (*rtogs-pa*, Skt. *adhigama*) and literary transmission (*lung*, Skt. *āgama*). The former includes the realisation which has been achieved by buddhas, or the truth of cessation, as well as the active or dynamic means to attain that realisation – the truth of the path which removes obscuration and reveals the intrinsic awareness of buddhahood, bringing about the truth of cessation. The literary transmissions comprise both the transmitted precepts (*legs-bshad bka'*, Skt. *subhāṣitapravacana*) and the treatises (*bstan-bcos*, Skt. *śāstra*).

Transmitted Precepts

Transmitted precepts are the sūtra and tantra texts which originated from buddhas such as Śākyamuni. They comprise those given in the form of oral teaching, those given by the blessing or consecration of the buddha-body, speech and mind, and those given by a buddha's mandate (pp.74-6). They may also be classified according to the three successive promulgations of the doctrinal wheel, the twelve branches of the scriptures, the eighty-four thousand doctrinal components including the Vinayapiṭaka, Sūtrapiṭaka, Abhidharmapiṭaka, and Vidyādharapiṭaka,[4] or according to the nine sequences of the vehicle.

The Author indicates at some length that enumerations such as two vehicles, three vehicles, four vehicles, or five vehicles are merely different ways of categorising the single vehicle. In fact there may be as many vehicles as there are thoughts. As the *Sūtra of the Descent to Laṅkā* (*Laṅkāvatārasūtra*, T 107)[5] says:

> As long as there is perception
> The culmination of vehicles will never be
> reached.

In the Nyiṇgma tradition the vehicle is said to have nine sequences, which are differentiated according to the acumen of those who require training through them. Each lower sequence is also included in the higher. Thus the *All-Accomplishing King* (*kun-byed rgyal-po*, T 828) states:

> Existentially there is only one
> But empirically there are nine vehicles.

These nine sequences are the vehicles of the pious attendants (*nyan-thos*, Skt. *śrāvaka*), self-centred buddhas (*rang-rgyal*, Skt. *pratyekabuddha*) and bodhisattvas (*byang-chub sems-dpa'*); the vehicles of Kriyātantra (*bya-ba*), Ubhayatantra (*gnyis-ka*), and Yogatantra (*rnal-'byor*); and those of Mahāyoga (*rnal-'byor chen-po*), Anuyoga (*rjes-su rnal-'byor*) and Atiyoga, the Great Perfection (*rdzogs-chen shin-tu rnal-'byor*). However, it is emphasised that the transmitted precepts in the form of a vehicle are a means of attaining realisation, and that, in the words of the *Sūtra of the Descent to Laṅkā*:

When the mind becomes transformed
There is neither vehicle nor mover.

Treatises

Treatises are commentaries composed by sublime beings such as Nāgārjuna, Asaṅga and Longcen Rapjampa to elucidate the intention of the transmitted precepts.

In Buddhist terms, treatises are defined as compositions which are made so as to counteract the three poisons of delusion, desire and hatred, and to protect the mind from the suffering of cyclical existence (pp.88ff.). They require four special attributes, namely, a motivation based on compassion and discriminative awareness, expressive words in verse, an expressed meaning which reveals the means for those who desire liberation, and a purposeful composition. Treatises are then classified in six ways according to: the purpose of the composer, the qualitative standard of the composition, the status of the composer (i.e. buddha, bodhisattva, arhat or paṇḍita), the specific or general manner of their composition, the view, conduct and integration of view and conduct as revealed in each of the three successive promulgations of the transmitted precepts, and finally the meaning they express, which may be quantitative, qualitative or conducive to liberation and omniscience.

The quantitative treatises, in which diverse categories are enumerated, include general treatises on ethics, and specialised treatises on grammar, logic, art, medicine, astrology, poetics, prosody, synonymics and drama. Qualitative treatises include those on Madhyamaka philosophy which establish the selflessness of the individual and of phenomena. Finally, the treatises conducive to liberation and omniscience include esoteric instructions of five kinds, which are condensed in order to generate liberation from cyclical existence in those who require training through them.

PART TWO: BUDDHA NATURE ACCORDING TO THE BUDDHA-BODIES

Having distinguished between the doctrines which cause one to remain in cyclical existence and those which transcend such suffering, what then is the nature of the buddha or the teacher who is said to communicate the means of attaining liberation? This is the subject-matter of Part Two.

Buddha (literally, the "awakened one") is rendered in Tibetan as *sangs-rgyas*: *sangs* meaning purified of all conflicting emotions and *rgyas* meaning vast in enlightened attributes. Thus a buddha is one who has purified all sufferings of cyclical existence and is endowed with the enlightened attributes of buddha-body and pristine cognition. The buddha-bodies are held to number three or five, although they have many other aspects. Lower sequences of the vehicle speak of the two bodies of reality and form, or of three or four. Here in the Nyingma tradition there are five, namely, the buddha-bodies of reality, perfect rapture, emanation, awakening and indestructible reality.

The Buddha-body of Reality

The buddha-body of reality (*chos-sku*, Skt. *dharmakāya*), which is also known as Samantabhadra (*kun-tu bzang-po*), is considered to be the prime mover of the highest teachings of the Great Perfection or Atiyoga.

The Nyingmapa hold that buddhahood is attained when intrinsic awareness is liberated just where it is through having recognised the nature of Samantabhadra, the primordially pure body of reality. This buddhahood is endowed with the pristine cognition of the expanse of reality (*chos-dbyings ye-shes*, Skt. *dharmadhātujñāna*), for it is free from all conceptual elaborations, and the pristine cognition of sameness (*mnyam-nyid ye-shes*, Skt. *samatājñāna*) which remains pure through the extent of saṃsāra and nirvāṇa.

Reality (*chos-nyid*, Skt. *dharmatā*) in Buddhism refers to the emptiness which is the inherent nature of phenomena. The apparitional aspect of this reality is known as *chos-can* (*dharmin*), and that which is real (the phenomena themselves) are known as *chos* (*dharma*). Since it is held to be the foundation of all genuine experience, the body of reality is the basis of the buddha-bodies of form. It is also known as the youthful vase body (*gzhon-nu bum-pa'i sku*) because the pristine cognition remains inwardly radiant within it, in the manner of light within a crystal prism, even when it emanates as the buddha-body of form.

Through the blessing of this youthful vase body, the Buddha-field of the Bounteous Array (*Ghanavyūhabuddhakṣetra*) becomes manifest, and therein the Teachers of Five Enlightened Families, including the Buddha Vairocana, assume the body of perfect rapture. This is the great play of undifferentiated buddha-body and pristine cognition, which also acts out of compassion for the sake of sentient beings who are perceived to be bewildered without cause; for they wander in cyclical existence without recognising the nature of the primordial ground.

These teachers emanate all the buddha-fields within and around the body of Vairocana in order to guide beings to liberation. The fields are arrayed in three dimensions, namely, the Indestructible Nucleus of Inner Radiance (*'od-gsal rdo-rje snying-po*), Brahmā's Drumbeat (*tshangs-pa rnga-sgra*) and the Aeon of Great Brahmā (*tshangs-chen-gyi bskal-pa*), which correspond, respectively, to the body of reality, the body of perfect rapture and the emanational body. The last of these comprises all the realms of cyclical existence outlined in the chart above. It is said that in the space of a single atomic particle there are measureless fields of sentient beings being trained by the buddhas, and that on the surface of a single atom there are fields containing atoms of oceanic infinity.

As the *Great Bounteousness of the Buddhas* (*Buddhāvataṃsaka*, T 44) says:

> On the surface of a single atom
> There are as many buddhas
> As there are atoms.

However, as our text emphasises (p.119):

> These fields are said to be radiant apparitions, not existing in reality because, in the expanse of reality, relative appearances have not existed from the beginning.

The Buddha-body of Perfect Rapture

The buddha-body of perfect rapture (*longs-spyod rdzogs-pa'i sku*, Skt. *sambhogakāya*) is said to act within all those fields connected with Vairocana. It is endowed with seven attributes of natural expression, and the thirty-two major and eighty minor marks of the buddhas. These marks may appear outwardly, as the external form of the buddha-body; inwardly, as the network of energy channels, currents and seminal points (*rtsa rlung thig-le*) within the buddha-body; secretly, as present in the seed which is enlightened mind, or the nucleus of the tathāgata (*de-gshegs snying-po*, Skt. *tathāgatagarbha*); and, most secretly, as the rapture of the Great Perfection (*rdzogs-pa chen-po*) which is experienced when the energy channels and seminal points are naturally expressed as supreme bliss.

As such, the five components of mundane cyclical existence find their true natural expression in the Teachers of the Five Enlightened Families, namely, Vairocana, Akṣobhya, Ratnasambhava, Amitābha, and Amoghasiddhi; while the five elemental properties of space, cohesion, solidity, warmth and movement find their true natural expression as the five consorts: Dhātvīśvarī, Locanā, Māmakī, Pāṇḍaravāsinī, and Samayatārā. The four sensations of seeing, hearing, tasting and smelling, as well as the four sense objects, the four sense organs, the four temporal dimensions, the four aspects of sexual contact, and the four extremes of permanence, decay, self and character all find their true natural expression in the deities of the surrounding maṇḍalas. This pure vision, it is emphasised, lies within the perceptual range of the buddhas' pristine cognition alone, and remains invisible even to bodhisattvas of the highest level who are not liberated from all obscurations. It is maintained that all these elements of mundane cyclical existence are transmuted into the pure, divine nature through experiential cultivation of the Buddhist teachings. As the *Extensive Magical Net* (*sgyu-'phrul rgyas-pa*, NGB Vol.14) says:

> If there is no understanding of intrinsic awareness or genuine perception,
> The field of Sukhāvatī is even seen as a state of evil existence.
> If the truth which is equivalent to the supreme of vehicles is realised,
> Even states of evil existence are Akaniṣṭha and Tuṣita.

The Emanational Body

The emanational body (*sprul-pa'i sku*, Skt. *nirmāṇakāya*), which disciplines those who require training on the path to liberation, is of three types. First, there are the emanations of natural expression (*rang-bzhin sprul-pa'i sku*) who are the above-mentioned Teachers of the Five Enlightened Families appearing in their lower role before bodhisattvas of the highest level, in the manner of rainbow light. In this situation, when they are compounded by the minds of others, they are said to be endowed with a semi-manifest natural expression, half-way between the true body of perfect rapture and the emanational body.

Secondly, there are the supreme emanational bodies (*mchog-gi sprul-pa'i sku*) or emanations of the body of reality who train living beings through their twelve deeds in myriads of world systems. Within this world system of ours, which is known as the world system of Patient Endurance (*mi-mjed 'jig-rten-gyi khams*, Skt. *Sahalokadhātu*), the supreme emanational body appears as a sage embodying awareness of the true buddha nature in each of the six classes of living beings – gods, antigods, humans, animals, tormented spirits and hells. In the human world, for example, he appears as Śākyamuni Buddha, and, as the text explains (p.131):

> In these realms, the supreme emanational body projects the lamp of instruction for those requiring training in as many ways as they have psychophysical bases, sense organs and modes of conduct, and acts on behalf of sentient beings through four kinds of instruction.

These four are instruction by the great merits of the buddha-body's twelve deeds, instruction by the direct perception of the buddha-mind which is endowed with six supernormal cognitive powers (*mngon-shes drug*, Skt. *ṣaḍabhijñā*), instruction by inconceivable miraculous abilities which are the mysteries of the buddha's body, speech and mind, and instruction by knowledge conveyed in speech.

Thirdly, there are the diversified emanations (*sna-tshogs sprul-sku*) appearing as oases, food, and medicine, which are of benefit to living beings, and as the emanations of birth (*skyes-sprul*) and artistry (*bzo-sprul*) assumed, for example, by Śākyamuni Buddha in his previous lives and recorded in the *Jātaka Tales*.

The Nyingma tradition in particular holds that twelve teachers of the emanational body have appeared as the blessing of the body of perfect rapture in this world system to disclose the three emanational teachings of the buddha-body, speech and mind. A hand-sized vajra (*rdo-rje*) is said to be the actuality of the body of reality, a four-inch book is said to be the actuality of the body of perfect rapture, and the physical form, exemplified in those twelve teachers, is the actuality of the emanational body. The emanational body, in the Nyingma view, is endowed with sixty attributes; for each of those twelve teachers is connected with the five excellences of place, teacher, retinue, doctrine and time. A single emanational body also possesses ninety-six doctrines with respect to enlightened activity. Yet this enumeration is not regarded as a limitation because (p.138):

> The Sugata, learned in skilful means, manifests the body of form in ways which correspond to the number of atoms in the myriad fields of those requiring training, which are of oceanic extent.

The Buddha-body of Awakening

The buddha-body of awakening (*mngon-par byang-chub-kyi sku*, Skt. *abhisambodhikāya*), which is derived from the distinct apparitional functions of the aforementioned three bodies, possesses the four fearlessnesses, the eighteen distinct attributes of the buddhas, great compassion and the ten powers. These are all enumerated in the *Mahāvyutpatti*, the great glossary of technical terms composed by the Tibetan translators, probably during the reign of Senalek.

The Buddha-body of Indestructible Reality

Finally, the buddha-body of indestructible reality (*rdo-rje sku*, Skt. *vajrakāya*), which derives from the indivisible essence of the first three bodies, is the original unchanging expanse of reality in which all paths are concluded and all conceptual elaboration transcended. It is the taintless buddha nature pure from the beginning.

The Five Pristine Cognitions

The five pristine cognitions (*ye-shes lnga*, Skt. *pañcajñāna*), which are among the buddhas' attributes, are also discussed here. They are the pristine cognition of the expanse of reality (*chos-dbyings ye-shes*, Skt. *dharmadhātujñāna*), which is the perception of the buddha-body of reality; the mirror-like pristine cognition (*me-long ye-shes*, Skt. *ādarśa-jñāna*), which is the unbroken causal basis of all pristine cognition; the pristine cognition of sameness (*mnyam-nyid ye-shes*, Skt. *samatājñāna*), which continuously abides in tranquillity, loving kindness and compassion without falling into the extremes of cyclical existence or nirvāṇa; and the pristine cognition of discernment (*sor-rtogs ye-shes*, Skt. *pratyavekṣaṇajñāna*), which is unimpeded with regard to the knowable, and refers to contemplations, dhāraṇī and other attributes. These last three are the perceptions of the body of perfect rapture. Finally, the pristine cognition of accomplishment (*bya-grub ye-shes*, Skt. *kṛtyānuṣṭhānajñāna*) is diversified in all realms, within the emanations who act on behalf of living beings. Thus it is the perception of the emanational body.

The Author asserts that the nature of the buddhas who have purified obscurations and become vast in enlightened attributes of buddha-body and pristine cognition is to be experientially cultivated through the Buddhist teachings – both indirectly, through the sūtra texts, and directly through the mantra texts which are respectively a long and a short path to the same goal.

He concludes Part Two by distinguishing between the attributes of the buddha-bodies as they are revealed in the causal vehicles of dialectics, and in the resultant vehicles of secret mantra. The sūtras of the causal vehicles require one to undertake a long path of causal gradation, whereby conflicting emotions are abandoned, and merits and pristine cognition are accumulated. The resultant vehicles of the way of mantras, however, begin from the ultimate view of the buddha nature and insist that the whole of cyclical existence and nirvāṇa conform to the pattern of the three buddha-bodies.

PART THREE: CAUSAL VEHICLES OF DIALECTICS

The causal vehicles of dialectics (*rgyu mtshan-nyid-kyi theg-pa*, Skt. **hetulakṣaṇayāna*)[6] are classified either according to the three successive promulgations of the doctrinal wheel or according to the philosophical systems included within the lesser vehicle (*theg-pa chung-ba*, Skt. *Hīnayāna*) and the greater vehicle (*theg-pa chen-po*, Skt. *Mahāyāna*).

The Three Promulgations of the Doctrinal Wheel

In the first promulgation the Buddha expounded the four truths of suffering, its origin, the path and the cessation of suffering, with the intention that sentient beings should forsake cyclical existence. In the second promulgation he expounded the teaching on the transcendental perfection of discriminative awareness (*shes-rab-kyi pha-rol-tu phyin-pa/ma*, Skt. *prajñāpāramitā*) with the intention that the buddha nature should be comprehended through topics of emptiness, signlessness and aspirationlessness, and that consequently the ultimate truth which is referred to by synonyms in order to bring about the partial cessation of conceptual elaboration might become the foundation for those who enter the greater vehicle.

Then, in the third promulgation he excellently analysed all things from form to omniscience in accord with the three essential natures, namely, the imaginary (*parikalpita*), the dependent (*paratantra*), and the absolute (*parinişpanna*), and disclosed the nucleus of the tathāgata (*tathāgatagarbha*), intending that the ultimate truth for which there is no synonym should become the nucleus of the path of the greater vehicle. Such were the three promulgations delivered by Śākyamuni Buddha.

The Lesser Vehicle

Among the philosophical systems of the causal vehicles of dialectics, those which belong to the lesser vehicle are the Vaibhāṣika and the Sautrāntika systems.

Vaibhāṣika

The pious attendants of the Vaibhāṣika school classify the knowable into five categories: perceptual forms, mind, mental events, disjunct conditions unassociated with mental events, and uncompounded entities. They hold that consciousness ultimately exists as a series of time-moments and that the material substances composing the world are an association of indivisible atomic particles unified by vital energy. They claim the subject-object dichotomy to be created through the recognition of objects by consciousness, but that there is no intrinsic awareness apart from this consciousness.

Through the vehicle of the pious attendants (*śrāvaka*), the status of an arhat is realised by meditation on the sixteen aspects of the four truths, so that the obscurations of the three poisons and ignorance are destroyed. As it is said in the *Sequence of the Path* (*Māyājālapathakrama*, P 4736):

> If, without realising non-duality,
> Everything is viewed to exist substantially
> In terms of the four truths,
> And one resorts to renunciation and non-renunciation,
> This is the level of the pious attendants.

Sautrāntika

The self-centred buddhas and pious attendants of the Sautrāntika school hold ultimate reality to agree with consciousness, which is a series of time moments. They also hold that, although consciousness refers to objects, external objects are not actually perceived, a single, uncompounded sensum being transmitted in the manner of a reflection on a mirror. The subject-object dichotomy therefore becomes a subjective process, conventionally known as the recognition of objects. They are said to surpass the Vaibhāṣika in holding the conglomerate of atoms to be unknown and in their appreciation of an intrinsic awareness.

Through the vehicle of the self-centred buddhas (*pratyekabuddha*), the twelve modes of dependent origination are meditated on and reversed. Whereas pious attendants hold the individual self to be abandoned in ultimate truth, the self-centred buddhas hold external objects to be ultimately fallacious and subjective consciousness to exist genuinely. They are said to be realised in one and a half parts of what is implied by selflessness. This is because they realise selflessness with reference to the individual and understand that the atomic particles of external phenomena do not independently exist, but still hold time moments of consciousness or internal phenomena to be ultimately real.

The Greater Vehicle

Among the philosophical systems of the greater causal vehicle, there are the Vijñānavāda or proponents of consciousness, and the Mādhyamika or adherents of the middle path.

Vijñānavāda

The Vijñānavāda confirm the Sautrāntika view that objects are not perceived. All things are held to be apparitional aspects of mind, definitively ordered according to three essential natures: the imaginary which includes both phenomena and characteristics such as the concept of selfhood; the dependent which includes the five impure components of mundane existence and the pure attributes of buddha-body and pristine cognition; and the absolute which includes the unchanging abiding nature of reality and the incontrovertible absence of conflicting emotions.

The Mind Only school, which emphasises the ontological aspect of the Vijñānavāda, is divided into those who hold sensa to be veridical (*Sākāravāda*), and those holding sensa to be false, admitting only consciousness to be genuine (*Nirākāravāda*). These have many subdivisions. While the Vijñānavāda is held to surpass the Vaibhāṣika and Sautrāntika of the lower vehicle, it fails to understand the absolute nature, since it holds consciousness to exist absolutely in the ultimate truth.

Madhyamaka

The Mādhyamika or adherents of the middle path are either those who uphold the coarse outer Madhyamaka or the subtle inner Great Madhyamaka (*dbu-ma chen-po*).

Outer Madhyamaka

The Outer Madhyamaka include the Svātantrika (*rang-rgyud-pa*) who employ independent reasoning, and the Prāsaṅgika (*thal-'gyur-ba*) who employ *reductio ad absurdum*.

The Svātantrika surpass the previous philosophical systems which adhere to substantiality and subjective conceptual elaboration, and they avoid both extremes. All things which appear are said to exist in relative truth, which is either correct or incorrect in conventional terms, but are inherently empty and non-existent in the ultimate truth, which cuts through conceptual elaboration. All relative appearances can be refuted by logical arguments, but it is also proven that no scrutiny or judgement can be made in relation to ultimate truth.

The Prāsaṅgika distinguish between the unbewildered intellect or pristine cognition of the buddhas, in which relative phenomena never appear, and the bewildered intellect of sentient beings. Ultimate truth, the reality of the unbewildered intellect of the buddhas, is vitiated by bewilderment, and so mundane cyclical existence appears and is assigned conventionally to the relative truth, though not really admitted.

The Prāsaṅgika also employ the five kinds of logical axioms used by the Svātantrika, but unlike them do not seek to prove their conclusions positively with reference to relative appearances and conceptual elaboration, having refuted them. Rather they refute all possible views which lie within the range of the four extremes of being, non-being, both being and non-being, and neither being nor non-being. Ultimate truth is thus the pristine cognition of the buddhas, free from all conceptual elaboration of the subject-object dichotomy. It is said that the two truths form the Madhyamaka of the ground; the two provisions of merit and pristine cognition form the Madhyamaka of the path; and that the coalescence of the two buddha-bodies of reality and form is the Madhyamaka of the result.

Great Madhyamaka

The Great Madhyamaka (*dbu-ma chen-po*) is aloof from the reasoning of the Outer Madhyamaka which is based upon dialectics, and instead must be experientially cultivated in meditation. In accord with the analysis of all things made by Śākyamuni in the third promulgation of the doctrinal wheel with respect to the aforementioned essential natures, it holds the imaginary to imply that attributes are without substantiality, the dependent to imply that creation is without substantiality, and the absolute to imply that ultimate reality is without substantiality. Absolute reality is thus empty of all the imaginary objects which are to be refuted and all conceptual elaboration of cyclical existence, but it is not empty of the enlightened attributes of buddha-body and pristine cognition which are spontaneously present from the beginning.

The *Supreme Continuum of the Greater Vehicle* (*Mahāyānottaratantra-śāstra*, T 4024) says:

> The seed which is empty of suddenly arisen
> phenomena,
> Endowed with divisive characteristics,
> Is not empty of the unsurpassed reality,
> Endowed with indivisible characteristics.

The Great Madhyamaka therefore maintains that the conceptual area of the subject-object dichotomy is intrinsically empty (*rang-stong*), while the buddha-body of reality endowed with all enlightened attributes is empty of that extraneous conceptual area which forms the subject-object dichotomy (*gzhan-stong*). If enlightened attributes were themselves intrinsically empty of their own essence, the entire structure of the ground, path and result would be negated and one would be in the position of the nihilistic extremists who deny causality, progress on the path to liberation and so forth.

This expanse of reality, the ultimate truth, is said to pervade all beings without distinction and is known as the nucleus of the tathāgata (*tathāgatagarbha*) or the nucleus of the sugata (*sugatagarbha*). It is held to be only fully developed and qualitatively perceived according to its true nature by buddhas, and yet equally present in ordinary sentient beings and bodhisattvas who are partially purified on the path to liberation. It is when the obscurations covering this seed of the buddha nature are removed that liberation is said to occur. Now, there are two kinds of renunciation of obscurations which have been expounded, one that is a naturally pure, passive *fait accompli*, and another which actively removes the obscurations by applying an appropriate antidote. Although the nucleus of the tathāgata is held to be present from the beginning in all beings, it is not therefore claimed that all beings are buddhas free from all obscuration. Similarly there are two kinds of realisation, one that is naturally present and passive, and another that is dependently produced and active. They are equivalent to the truths of cessation and of the path described above in Part One.

While the second and the third promulgations of the doctrinal wheel give authenticity to the view of Great Madhyamaka, it is the third or final promulgation which extensively reveals the nucleus of the tathāgata. Certain scholars of the past have, as the Author states, erroneously linked the views of Great Madhyamaka and Vijñānavāda. However, the former is concerned with absolute reality, and the latter is directed towards consciousness. There is held to be a great distinction between the pristine cognition of the buddhas and the consciousness of the ground-of-all. The proponents of Mind Only maintain that consciousness is not transcended in ultimate truth, but this is a view which is bound within cyclical existence. According to Great Madhyamaka, the ultimate truth is the obscurationless pristine cognition, the uncorrupted expanse of reality transcending consciousness. This is because subjective consciousness is only dependently real, and pristine cognition is free from the subject-object dichotomy.

This view of the Great Madhyamaka is revealed in the compositions of Nāgārjuna,[7] Asaṅga and others, whether they belong to the second or third promulgation of the doctrinal wheel, for both refer to the three essential natures. Once Mind Only has been provisionally taught, the apparitionless Madhyamaka is taught, and when that has been transcended, the apparitional Madhyamaka is revealed. Without reaching that, the profound meaning of the greater vehicle is not perceived.

Those who actually and experientially cultivate the path to liberation do not differentiate the two modes of Madhyamaka (*rang-stong* and *gzhan-stong*), as is attested by the writings of Nāgārjuna, Asaṅga and other paṇḍitas who commented on the intention of the definitive meaning (*nges-don*). While the second promulgation is generally confined to an outright negation of conceptual elaboration, this is merely a step in the experiential cultivation of Madhyamaka, which must subsequently transcend the Prāsaṅgika and Svātantrika reasoning.

When meditational experiences have been established, it is the Great Madhyamaka, as taught in the third promulgation, which is profound and vast; and the vehicles of the secret mantra which are even more extensive. The purposes of the lower sequences of the vehicle are gathered within the higher. Otherwise the buddhas would not have given the three promulgations and nine sequences of the vehicle in that appropriate order.

Provisional and Definitive Meaning

Thus, in the Nyingma view, the first and second promulgations may be allocated provisional meaning (*drang-don*, Skt. *neyārtha*) because they are a basis for debate, respectively rousing the mind from cyclical existence by teaching impermanence and destroying by means of the three approaches to liberation the reductionist view which adheres to the selfhood of phenomena. The third promulgation, however, is allocated definitive meaning (*nges-don*, Skt. *nītārtha*) because it teaches that all relative appearances are intrinsically empty (*rang-stong*) and that all enlightened attributes are empty of those same extraneous appearances (*gzhan-stong*). The range of the buddhas' pristine cognition is thereby revealed and debate is surpassed by experiential cultivation. Yet, as the Author asserts, there is no difference between the transcendental perfection of discriminative awareness (*prajñāpāramitā*) revealed in the second promulgation and the pristine cognition revealed in the third. The distinction merely concerns the extent to which ultimate reality is revealed.

The Enlightened or Buddha Family

Since all beings are endowed with the nucleus of the tathāgata, the seed of the buddha nature, they are all part of the buddha or enlightened family. From the ultimate point of view, this family is one in which the natural expression of enlightenment is said to abide inherently, and from the conventional or dynamic point of view, it is one in which that natural expression is to be attained. The former is the ground of separation from obscuration (*'bral-rgyu*), in which the three resultant buddha-bodies arise. It is also known as the truth of cessation according to the greater vehicle. The latter is the truth of the path on which the provisions of merit and pristine cognition are accumulated in order that the obscurations covering the nucleus may be removed and the result be actualised (*bral-'bras*). The three buddha-bodies are thus said to abide primordially in the nucleus of the enlightened family, and are merely realised by the removal of the obscurations which cover them. They are not themselves compounded by the accumulation of causal provisions.

This indivisible essence of the enlightened family, the nucleus of the tathāgata, is extensively revealed in the writings of Nyingmapa authors such as Longcenpa, Rongzompa, Terdak Lingpa and Mipham Rinpoche, and also in the compositions of the great masters of other Tibetan traditions – Kadampa, Kagyüpa, Sakyapa and Gelukpa, as can be seen in the many quotations cited from their works.

The Two Truths according to Great Madhyamaka

During moments of meditative absorption, the outer and inner Madhyamaka do not differentiate the two truths since one then abides in the expanse of reality, the pristine cognition that is free from all conceptual elaborations of the subject-object dichotomy. During the aftermath of meditative absorption, however, they are distinguished differently by the Outer Madhyamaka, which allocates emptiness to ultimate truth and appearances to the relative truth; and the inner Great Madhyamaka, which determines ultimate truth to be the realities of nirvāṇa, in which the subject or pristine cognition and the object of its perception, as established by conventional logic, are harmonious, and relative truth to be the phenomena of cyclical existence, in which the subjective consciousness and the object of its perception, incapable of being established even in terms of conventional logic, are in a state of dichotomy. Ultimate truth is thus the expanse of reality in which pure appearances and emptiness are coalesced. Although this coalescence is even more elaborately revealed in the resultant vehicles of the secret mantra, it must first be established according to the view of Great Madhyamaka, on which the superior views from Kriyātantra to Atiyoga are all based. The Great Madhyamaka is therefore said to be the climax of the philosophical systems according to the causal vehicles of dialectics.

Through the vehicle of the bodhisattvas who uphold the Vijñānavāda and Madhyamaka philosophies, the ten levels and five paths are gradually traversed, and liberation is finally attained in the buddha-body of reality on the eleventh level (*Samantaprabhā*). Manifesting the two bodies of form, the bodhisattva then acts on behalf of others until all beings have been liberated from cyclical existence. It is therefore held that the vehicle of the bodhisattvas is the first of the nine sequences of the vehicle which may be conducive to total liberation.

Key to the Appraisal of Causal Vehicle Texts

Texts belonging to the causal vehicles of dialectics are firstly divided between those of the definitive third promulgation and their commentaries which reveal the full extent of the buddha nature, and those of the provisional earlier promulgations and their commentaries which partially reveal the buddha nature. There are also four kinds of intention with which buddhas deliver the teaching, unknown to the listener, and four kinds of covert intention which buddhas are said to employ in order for their precise meaning to be eventually understood by the listener.

Recapitulation of the Causal Vehicles

To facilitate comprehension of the above philosophical systems, Part Three is completed by a recapitulation of the three causal vehicles of dialectics, namely, those of the pious attendants, self-centred buddhas and bodhisattvas, within the context of their respective entrances, views, moral disciplines, meditations, modes of conduct and results.

PART FOUR: RESULTANT VEHICLES OF SECRET MANTRA

Part Four concerns the resultant vehicles of secret mantra, on which subject our text says (p.244):

> ...in the vehicle of dialectics, mind-as-such [or pristine cognition] is merely perceived as the causal basis of buddhahood. Since it is held that buddhahood is obtained under the condition whereby the two provisions increasingly multiply, and since the purifying doctrines which form the causal basis of nirvāṇa are made into the path, it is called the causal vehicle. Therein a sequence in which cause precedes result is admitted. According to the vehicle of mantras, on the other hand, mind-as-such abides primordially and intrinsically as the

essence of the result, identified as the buddha-bodies and pristine cognitions. Mind-as-such is thereby established as the ground which exists within oneself from the present moment as the object to be attained. It is then established as the path through its functions of bringing about recognition and removing the provisional stains which suddenly arise by means of inducing the perception of just what is, and it is established as the result through its function of actualising this very ground. Since a sequence in which cause precedes result is not really distinguished therein, it is called the resultant vehicle and the vehicle of indestructible reality.

Superiority of Secret Mantra

The resultant vehicles are said to surpass the causal vehicles in many ways. They are held to be unobscured, endowed with many means, without difficulties, and referred to by those of highest acumen; or to be swift, blissful, and endowed with skilful means. The *Tantra of Inconceivable Rali Cakrasaṃvara* (*Śrīcakrasaṃvaraguhyācintyatantra-rāja*, T 385) speaks of fifteen such superior qualities. Above all, the resultant vehicles are said to transcend all conceptual elaboration and logical reasoning, and to establish pristine cognition as the nucleus of the buddha-body of reality, the coalescence of appearance and emptiness, within one lifetime and so forth. Since a sameness with respect to all things is to be experienced, they are capable of making relative appearances into the path, without requiring them to be renounced as in the causal vehicles. Thus one meditates through the outer mantras of Kriyātantra, Ubhayatantra and Yogatantra with reference to the deity's body, speech and mind, and according to the inner mantras all things are realised and experienced as the maṇḍalas of the buddha-body, speech and mind.

Essence and Definition of Secret Mantra

Mantra is defined as an attribute of buddha-body, speech and mind which protects the mind with ease and swiftness. It also includes the deities in which emptiness and appearances are coalesced, symbolised by the seed-syllables E-VAṂ, because they too protect the mind from rebirth in the three realms of cyclical existence. Those who attain realisation through the mantras are known as awareness-holders (*rig-'dzin*, Skt. *vidyādhara*) and the texts which convey the mantra teaching are known as the Piṭaka of Awareness-holders. There are said to be three kinds of mundane awareness-holder and enumerations of either four or seven kinds of supramundane awareness-holder. The resultant vehicle is also known as the vehicle of indestructible reality (*rdo-rje theg-pa*, Skt. *Vajrayāna*) because pristine cognition or mind-as-such is imperishable and unchanging, despite the divergent apparitional modes of cyclical existence and nirvāṇa.

The Three Continua

Again, the resultant vehicle is also known as tantra, which is defined both as a means for protecting the mind and as the continuum extending from ignorance to enlightenment. There are said to be three such continua – those of the ground, path and result.

The continuum of the ground is another name for the nucleus of the tathāgata, the buddha-body of reality, the family in which the natural expression of enlightenment abides and the pristine cognition of the ground-of-all – which have previously been explained in the context of Great Madhyamaka. However, the same continuum of the ground is also spoken of in Kriyātantra as one's own real nature (*bdag-gi de-kho-na-nyid*), in Ubhayatantra as the blessing of that reality, which is the ultimate truth without symbols (*don-dam mtshan-ma med-pa'i byin-rlabs*), and in Yogatantra as a deity of the expanse of indestructible reality, who relatively appears (*kun-rdzob rdo-rje dbyings-kyi lha*).

Similarly, it is also spoken of in Mahāyoga as the superior and great body of reality in which the two truths are indivisible (*bden-gnyis dbyer-med lhag-pa'i chos-sku chen-po*), in Anuyoga as the fundamental maṇḍala of enlightened mind, the offspring of the non-duality of the expanse and pristine cognition (*dbyings-dang ye-shes gnyis-su med-pa'i sras rtsa-ba byang-chub sems-kyi dkyil-'khor*), and in the Great Perfection of Atiyoga as the ground conventionally known as essence, natural expression and spirituality (*ngo-bo rang-bzhin thugs-rje*).

The continuum of the path refers to the skilful means which purify the obscurations covering the ground, and cause all cyclical existence to be experienced as an array of deities and their fields of rapture. The continuum of the result is actualised when those obscurations have been removed, although it is essentially identical to the continuum of the ground. All accomplishments are therein actualised. It is said that when the ground and result are indivisible, the truth of the origin of cyclical existence appears as the truth of the path to its cessation, and that the truth of suffering appears as the truth of its cessation.

The Four Tantrapiṭaka

The texts in which the teachings of the resultant vehicles of the secret mantra are expressed are divided into four tantrapiṭaka, namely, Kriyātantra, Ubhayatantra (or Caryātantra), Yogatantra, and Unsurpassed Yogatantra (*Anuttarayogatantra*), which are taught as the means respectively for those of lowest, middling, superior and highest acumen who require training. According to the Nyingma tradition, the first three of these are known as the vehicle of austere awareness (*dka'-thub rig-pa'i theg-pa*) because they all, to a greater or lesser extent, include external observances of body and speech. The last one is known as the vehicle of overpowering means (*dbang-bsgyur thabs-kyi theg-pa*), in which skilful means and discriminative awareness are coalesced.

Kriyātantra

Kriyātantra (*bya-ba'i rgyud*), or the tantra of action, emphasises external observances of body and speech, while continuing the subject-object dichotomy. It holds that meditation is required alternately on an ultimate truth, which is one's own real nature, and on a deity of relative appearance endowed with pristine cognition, distinct from that reality, who externally confers the accomplishments. By aspiring towards accomplishment, regarding the deity as a servant would his master, and by practising ablutions, fasting and other austerities which delight the deity, one may be granted the realisation of a holder of indestructible reality (*rdo-rje 'dzin-pa*) within seven lifetimes.

Ubhayatantra

Ubhayatantra (*gnyis-ka'i rgyud*), or the tantra which gives equal emphasis to the view and conduct, includes both symbolic meditation on the seed-syllables, seals and form of the deity and non-symbolic meditation on ultimate reality, the blessing of which may confer accomplishment as a holder of indestructible reality within five lifetimes.

Yogatantra

Yogatantra (*rnal-'byor-gyi rgyud*), or the tantra of union, emphasises meditation. The blessing of ultimate reality relatively appears as a deity of the expanse of indestructible reality. Persevering in the acceptance and rejection of positive and negative attributes in relation to this deity, one may attain the accomplishment of a holder of indestructible reality belonging to the five enlightened families within three lifetimes. Symbolic meditation in this context includes the experiences of the five awakenings (*mngon-byang lnga*), the four yogas (*rnal-'byor bzhi*), and the four seals (*phyag-rgya bzhi*) associated with the deity, and non-symbolic contemplation concerns the real nature of the mind. External observances are not, however, rejected.

Unsurpassed Yogatantra

The Unsurpassed Yogatantra (*bla-na med-pa'i rgyud*, Skt. *Anuttarayogatantra*) emphasises the coalescence of skilful means and discriminative awareness, and is said to surpass the lower tantras which have not abandoned duality. The three poisons are carried on the path – desire as the essence of bliss and emptiness, hatred as the essence of radiance and emptiness, and delusion as the essence of awareness and emptiness – and the result may be achieved within a single lifetime. In the Nyingma tradition, the Unsurpassed Yogatantra is divided into Mahāyoga, Anuyoga and Atiyoga.

Mahāyoga

Mahāyoga (*rnal-'byor chen-po*) unites the mind in the superior body of reality, in which the two truths are indivisible. The continuum of the ground is established as the genuine view to be realised by means of four axioms. The continuum of the path has two stages, among which the path of skilful means (*thabs-lam*) carries the three poisons on to the path by means of practices concerning the network of energy channels, currents and seminal points (*rtsa rlung thig-le*) within the body. The path of liberation (*grol-lam*) comprises a ground of discriminative awareness, a path of contemplation and, as its result, the status of an awareness holder (*rig-'dzin*) is attained. Contemplation chiefly refers to the five contemplative experiences of the divine maṇḍalas in their creation and perfection phases (*bskyed-rim-dang rdzogs-rim*), which purify the rebirth process including the moment of death, the intermediate state after death (*bar-do*), and the three phases of life (*skye-ba rim-gsum*). At the successful conclusion of this practice one is said to become an awareness-holder and to actualise twenty-five resultant realities of the buddha level.

Anuyoga

Anuyoga (*rjes-su rnal-'byor*), or subsequent yoga, emphasises the perfection phase, and so forms a bridge between the creation phase of Mahāyoga and the Great Perfection of Atiyoga. The ground or view of Anuyoga is that the expanse of reality, which is the primordial maṇḍala of Samantabhadrī, and pristine cognition, which is the spontaneously present maṇḍala of Samantabhadra, are indivisible in the fundamental maṇḍala of enlightened mind.

The path of Anuyoga comprises these three maṇḍalas of the ground, along with all the nine sequences of the vehicle. Among them the specific Anuyoga practices include the definitive path of skilful means (*nges-pa'i thabs-lam*) in which the co-emergent pristine cognition of melting bliss is realised through the perfection of the energy channels, currents and seminal points within the body (see p.286); and the liberating path of discriminative awareness (*shes-rab grol-lam*) which establishes the view that all things are of the nature of the three maṇḍalas, and employs both a non-symbolic contemplation of reality and a contemplation of the symbolic deity. While the divine maṇḍalas of Mahāyoga and the lower sequences are gradually created or generated, those of Anuyoga arise spontaneously in a perfect manner. The result is that the five paths and ten levels known to Anuyoga are traversed, all the subtle propensities which lead to rebirth in cyclical existence are refined, and the rank of Samantabhadra is realised along with the twenty-five resultant realities of the buddha level.

Key to the Appraisal of Secret Mantra Texts

At this point, Dudjom Rinpoche discusses the criteria by which the texts of the resultant vehicles of secret mantra are to be appraised. The language of the texts is said to observe six limits and their styles of presentation are said to number four. Each line or verse of the teaching of indestructible reality (*vajrapāda*) is to be analysed in terms of these criteria before the meaning can be ascertained.

Atiyoga

According to the Nyingma tradition, the Great Perfection of Atiyoga (*rdzogs-chen shin-tu rnal-'byor*) or "highest yoga" is the climax of the nine sequences of the vehicle. The expanse of reality, the naturally present pristine cognition, is herein held to be the ground of great perfection. The eight lower sequences of the vehicle have intellectually contrived and obscured by their persevering activities the pristine cognition which intrinsically abides. Accordingly, the text says (pp.294-5):

> In this way the pious attendants and self-centred buddhas among the lower vehicles, with reference to the selflessness which they realise, hold consciousness and atomic matter to be the ultimate realities; and the proponents of consciousness who hold consciousness, self-cognisant and self-radiant in nature, to be the absolute characteristic of ultimate reality, do not transcend [the view of] mind and mental events harboured by mundane beings. The Mādhyamika adhere to a truth of cessation scrutinised by four great axioms and the like, concerning the absence of creation, absence of cessation, absence of being and absence of non-being, which are appraised according to the two truths, and they adhere to an emptiness which is, for example, like the sky, free from extremes and free from conceptual elaboration. The Kriyātantra among the lower ways of mantra hold that accomplishments are attained which delight the deity endowed with the three purities, by means of cleanliness and other such austerities. The Ubhayatantra are attached to superficialities in their equation of the higher view and the lower conduct. The Yogatantra, having regarded the blessing of ultimate reality as a deity, objectively refer to the yoga of the four seals. The Mahāyoga holds that pristine cognition is generated by incisive application of the creation stage, and

> [practices associated with] the energy channels, currents and seminal points according to the perfection stage. The Anuyoga regards the expanse of reality and pristine cognition as maṇḍalas of the deity which are either to be created or are in the process of creation.

Since these lower sequences are all drawn together by the intellect, they are said to be points of great deviation (*gol-sa*) from the Great Perfection, as the long quotation from the *Tantra of the All-Accomplishing King* (pp.295-7) clearly demonstrates. They are said to have been designed and so intended for the differing degrees of acumen in those requiring training through the vehicle, or as stepping-stones to Atiyoga.

The Great Perfection, on the other hand, refers not to consciousness but to pristine cognition. It is the intrinsic awareness of mind-as-such (*sems-nyid-kyi rang-rig*), transcending the mind, and buddhahood is said to emerge not through compounded provisions but through realisation of pristine cognition without activity. Thus the nucleus of all Buddhist teachings, in the Nyingma view, is pristine cognition, and the establishment of it through intrinsic awareness is the path of the Great Perfection. While the structure of the buddha level was revealed in the third promulgation by Śākyamuni, the path or means by which it is actualised was not revealed to the adherents of the causal vehicles. The lower mantras, too, are not considered to be definitive since they persevere with intellectually contrived activities. If the nucleus of pristine cognition is not realised in accordance with the Great Perfection, all aspects of the path, such as the six transcendental perfections (*pha-rol-tu phyin-pa drug*), the creation stage and the perfection stage, will not transcend the ideas and scrutiny of one's own mind. Yet these aspects of the path are not, it is emphasised, to be renounced, since they are spontaneously perfect in the ground. So the text declares (p.307):

> ...in this abiding nature that is free from all activity, all things belonging to the truth of the path are naturally complete, without effort, in the manner of a hundred rivers converging under a bridge.

Great Perfection is therefore defined as the naturally present pristine cognition, or as a sameness throughout the extent of cyclical existence and nirvāṇa, in which all lower sequences of the vehicle are perfected in a single essence.

The Divisions of Atiyoga

Within the teachings of Atiyoga, there are three modes of experiencing the goal of Great Perfection according to the nature of those who aspire to it. The text explains (p.319):

> There is the Mental Class (*sems-sde*), which teaches that all things are liberated from the extreme of renunciation, because they are not separated from mind-as-such. There is the Spatial Class (*klong-sde*), which teaches that all apparitions of reality are free from activity and liberated from the extreme of the antidote, because they are perfectly gathered in Samantabhadrī, the space of reality. And there is the profound Esoteric Instructional Class (*man-ngag-sde*), which teaches that the particular characteristics of truth itself are liberated from both extremes of renunciation and antidote, because they are established according to the modes of reality (*yin-lugs*).

The spiritual and philosophical goal of the Mental Class transcends the subject-object dichotomy. The compounded truth of the path as taught in the causal vehicles and lower mantras is determined in the great expanse of reality to be a pristine cognition of great purity and sameness. When the Mental Class is analysed, there are seven categories or areas of mind (*sems-phyogs*) in which this determination is made.

While the Mental Class holds the apparitions of reality to appear as the expressive power of mind-as-such, the spiritual and philosophical goal of the Spatial Class is the establishment of a great infinity of primordial liberation unscrutinised by mind. All that appears in the vast space of Samantabhadrī is an adornment of that array, free from all activities. The Spatial Class is divided into teachings concerning the Black Space propounded as Absence of Cause (*klong nag-po rgyu-med-du smra-ba*), the Variegated Space propounded as Diversity (*klong khra-ba sna-tshogs-su smra-ba*), the White Space propounded as the Mind (*klong dkar-po sems-su smra-ba*), and the Infinite Space in which Cause and Result are Determined (*klong rab-'byams rgyu-'bras la-bzla-ba*).

While the Mental Class, referring to mind-as-such, mostly achieves profundity rather than radiance, and almost clings to mental scrutiny because it does not recognise the expressive power of radiance to be reality, and while the Spatial Class almost falls into the deviation of emptiness although it achieves both radiance and profundity, the Esoteric Instructional Class is considered to be superior to both because it gathers all apparitions of reality within reality itself. It is classified into the three categories of the Random (*kha-'thor*), in which pristine cognition instantly arises without regard for formal structure, the Oral Tradition (*kha-gtam*), which naturally shatters the source of all conceptualisation and remains indefinite in character, and the Teaching which accords with its own Textual Tradition of Tantras (*rgyud rang-gzhung-du bstan-pa*), that is, the *Seventeen Tantras of the Esoteric Instructional Class* (NGB Vols.9-10), which turn to the origin of all transmitted precepts, without renunciation or acceptance, saṃsāra or nirvāṇa, or disputations regarding emptiness. These have their various subdivisions, and further subdivisions.

So in Atiyoga the awareness which transcends the mind is said to be a primordial liberation (*ye-grol*), a natural liberation (*rang-grol*), a direct liberation (*cer-grol*), and a liberation from extremes (*mtha'-grol*). Once this intrinsic awareness or pristine cognition has been ascertained to be the distinctive doctrine, there are said to be two means of realising it, which are known as Cutting Through Resistance (*khregs-chod*) and All-Surpassing Realisation (*thod-rgal*).

The former, Cutting Through Resistance, is oriented towards the emptiness-aspect, or primordially pure awareness without conceptual elaboration, and so causes the cessation of inherently empty phenomena. The latter, All-Surpassing Realisation, clarifies the apparitional aspect, which includes material objects, into inner radiance in a spontaneously present manner, and so causes the cessation of apparitional reality. It is said that when firm experience in Cutting Through Resistance has come about, one dissolves finally into a great primordially pure point of liberation. The coarse atoms of the four elements are transformed into pristine cognition and vanish. If, however, activity on behalf of others is resorted to, the dissolving atoms emanate as, and leave behind, relics of four kinds, while the awareness centred in the buddha-body of reality acts on behalf of beings through unceasing emanation.

While it is held that Cutting Through Resistance directly liberates the bewildering appearance of objects in fundamental reality, the All-Surpassing Realisation brings about the liberation of all apparitional aspects of the three world realms of desire, form and the formless (see chart, pp.14-15) in the inner radiance or luminosity of a seminal point of five-coloured light which is the natural tone of awareness. Thus, the expanse of reality and its appearances, which are known as indestructible chains [of light, *rdo-rje lu-gu rgyud*], are the mature awareness itself. At the successful conclusion of this practice, it is held that the outer and inner elements of the three world realms all dissolve into inner radiance through a succession of four visionary appearances (*snang-ba bzhi*), and so all cyclical existence is reversed. The awareness enters a formless disposition, as in Cutting Through Resistance, but the buddha-body of form continues to appear in the manner of rainbow light, and to act on behalf of sentient beings. As such, it is known as the body of supreme transformation (*'pho-ba chen-po'i sku*, Skt. **mahā-saṅkrāntikāya*), and this is recognised to be the buddha level attained by Padmasambhava, Vimalamitra, Śīlamañju and others. If, for the while, there is no one requiring to be trained, the buddha-body of supreme transformation is absorbed into the body of reality or the youthful vase body (*gzhon-nu bum-pa'i sku*), the emanational basis of all pristine cognition, and the intrinsic awareness abides radiantly within it.

Furthermore, according to the esoteric instructions (*man-ngag*, Skt. *āmnāya/upadeśa*) of the Great Perfection system, all things belonging to cyclical existence and nirvāṇa are established as a display of four intermediate states (*bar-do*, Skt. *antarābhava*), which are respectively known as the intermediate state of the birthplace, the intermediate state of the moment of death, the intermediate state of reality and the intermediate state of rebirth. Each of these transformations is provided with particular guidance, so that beings may be conveyed to the point of original liberation at any stage or in any circumstance. It is said that through the power of the descent of pristine cognition and the experiential cultivation of it in continuous yoga, the recollection of signs on the path, and the removal of obstacles, the result may be actualised within one lifetime.

Recapitulation of the Vehicles of Secret Mantra

Having detailed the overall meaning of the resultant vehicles of the secret mantra, Dudjom Rinpoche recapitulates them succinctly, categorising each sequence according to its entrance, view, moral discipline, meditation, conduct and result.

This concludes the summary of the contents of the *Fundamentals of the Nyingma School*. The history of their transmission in India by Garap Dorje, Mañjuśrīmitra, Jñānasūtra, King Ja, Kukkurāja, Līlāvajra and others, along with an account of their introduction to Tibet by Padmasambhava, Vimalamitra, Buddhaguhya and so forth, has been recorded by Dudjom Rinpoche, in his *History of the Nyingma School (rnying-ma'i chos-'byung)*, which is published here in conjunction with the *Fundamentals*.

The *History* elaborately traces the distant lineage of transmitted precepts (*ring-brgyud bka'-ma*) and the close lineage of concealed teachings or treasures (*nye-brgyud gter-ma*) from their first appearance in Tibet until the present century, and clearly indicates that the Nyingmapa for the most part remained aloof from the sectarianism which has so often been divisive in Tibetan history. Indeed, as the Author demonstrates, the destiny and propagation of all schools of Buddhism in Tibet have been interlinked from the earliest times.

THE LITERARY TRADITION REPRESENTED IN THE *FUNDAMENTALS*

The literary heritage of the Nyingma tradition includes both tantras and sūtras, along with the treatises or commentaries composed upon their intention over the centuries.

The tantras and sūtras which emphasise the particular Nyingma teachings of Mahāyoga, Anuyoga and Atiyoga are found in the canonical transmitted precepts of the *Kangyur* (*bka'-'gyur*) and in the *Collected Tantras of the Nyingmapa* (*rnying-ma'i rgyud-'bum*). Among them, those which focus on Mahāyoga are exemplified by the *Tantra of the Secret Nucleus* (*rgyud gsang-ba'i snying-po*, T 832, NGB Vol.14), those which focus on Anuyoga are exemplified by the *Sūtra which Gathers All Intentions* (*mdo dgongs-pa 'dus-pa*, T 829, NGB Vol.11), and those which focus on Atiyoga are exemplified by the *Tantra of the All-Accomplishing King* (*kun-byed rgyal-po*, T 828, NGB Vol.1). However, there are many other texts which elaborate on each of these three categories. Among those which refer to the entire nine sequences of the vehicle there are the *Tantra of the Great Natural Arising of Awareness* (*rig-pa rang-shar chen-po'i rgyud*, NGB Vol.10) and the *Miraculous Key to the Storehouse* (*bang-mdzod 'phrul-lde*, NGB Vol.2).

The treatises composed by Indian scholars of the past on those transmitted precepts include long commentaries on specific texts such as those on the *Tantra of the Secret Nucleus* by Līlāvajra (*Śrīguhyagarbhamahātantrarājaṭīkā*, P 4718) and by Sūryaprabhāsiṃha (*Śrīguhyagarbhatattvanirṇayavyākhyānaṭīkā*, P 4719). Yet they also include a tradition of short, pithy explanations of the nine sequences of the vehicle, among which one should note the *Garland of Views: A Collection of Esoteric Instructions* (*Upadeśadarśanamālā*, P 4726) by Padmasambhava, the *Sequence of the Path* (*Māyājālapathakrama*, P 4736) by Buddhaguhya, the *Lock of the Heart* (*Cittatālaka*, P 4758) by Śrī Siṃha, and the *Turquoise Display* (*gYu-thang-ma kras-dgu*, P 4729) attributed to Nāgārjuna.

When the Nyingma tradition was introduced to Tibet, the concise exegetical style was maintained by authors such as Kawa Peltsek who wrote the *Seventeenfold Appearance of the Sequence of the View* (*lta-rim snang-ba bcu-bdun-pa*, T 4356).

During the medieval period of Tibetan history which followed the persecution of the Buddhist doctrine by Langdarma and its subsequent restoration, long treatises were composed concerning these "ancient translations" by Rongzom Paṇḍita (eleventh century), Yungtönpa Dorjepel (1284-1365), Longcen Rapjampa (1308-63) and others. Longcenpa in particular was encouraged by his teacher Kumārādza (1266-1343) to compose the *Seven Treasuries* (*mdzod-bdun*) which definitively structured the entire Buddhist experience from the Nyingma point of view. These include his *Treasury of Spiritual and Philosophical Systems* (*grub-mtha'i mdzod*) which has had a profound influence on later interpretations of the nine sequences of the vehicle. Among his other works, one should note the *General Exposition [of the Secret Nucleus, entitled] Dispelling Mental Darkness* (*spyi-don yid-kyi mun-pa sel-ba*) which is a basic source-book for much of the present treatise.

Subsequently, Pema Trhinle (1641-1717) and Locen Dharmaśrī (1654-1717) have commented on the range of the Buddhist teachings in their respective *Collected Works*, and have explored in depth the distant lineage of transmitted precepts (*ring-brgyud bka'-ma*) and the meaning of the Anuyoga *Sūtra which Gathers All Intentions* (*mdo dgongs-pa 'dus-pa*, T 829, NGB Vol.11). The latter's *Oral Teaching of the Lord of Secrets* (*gsang-bdag zhal-lung*) is a primary source for the recapitulations found in Parts Three and Four of the present work.

In the eighteenth century, Jikme Lingpa (1730-98) intricately stated the view of the Nyingmapa tantras and the nine sequences of the vehicle in his nine volumes of *Collected Works*, particularly in the *Treasury of Enlightened Attributes* (*yon-tan mdzod*); and Gyurme Tshewang Chokdrup of Katok catalogued the *Collected Tantras of the Nyingmapa* in his *Discourse Resembling a Divine Drum* (*rgyud-'bum dkar-chag lha'i rnga-bo-che lta-bu*), the first part of which corresponds closely to our present text.

During the nineteenth century, under the inspiration of his teacher the great Jamyang Khyentse Wangpo, Jamgön Kongtrül (1813-99) compiled five anthologies (*kong-sprul mdzod-lnga*) which integrated the most important teachings from all schools of Buddhism.

More recently, Zhecen Gyeltsap and others have followed in this eclectic (*ris-med*) tradition, and Mipham Rinpoche (1846-1912) has composed elaborate exegeses on Madhyamaka, on the mind in its natural state (*gnyugs-sems*), and on the integration of the views of intrinsic emptiness (*rang-stong*) and extrinsic emptiness (*gzhan-stong*)[8] within the sphere of the causal vehicles of dialectics. These are all included in the four cycles of his *Collected Works*. His *Summary of the Spiritual and Philosophical Systems* from Longcenpa's *Wish-fulfilling Treasury* (*yid-bzhin mdzod-kyi grub-mtha' bsdus-pa*) has been partially translated into English by H.V. Guenther.[9]

These prominent texts and authors serve to illustrate the literary tradition which Dudjom Rinpoche has inherited. Looking back upon the development of the Nyingma exegetical tradition from the Indian period until the eclectic movement, he has produced a treatise, the *Fundamentals*, which conforms to contemporary circumstances and requirements. Many Tibetans who currently practise the doctrine do so in a refugee environment, and so lack the time and resources which were once available for the detailed study of vast commentaries. Capturing the elegance of traditional versification, and the scholarly insights which have gradually been acquired over the centuries, he has condensed the writings of past masters, presenting their reasoning in an immediate, contemporary manner, and at the same time has substantiated this summarisation with copious quotations from the concise exegetical tradition of both Indian and Tibetan origin, which epitomises the Ancient Translation School.

The formal title of this work is *An Abridged Definitive Ordering of the Nyingma Teaching, the Ancient Translation School of Secret Mantra, entitled Feast in which Eloquence Appears* (*gsang-sngags snga-'gyur rnying-ma-ba'i bstan-pa'i rnam-gzhag mdo-tsam brjod-pa legs-bshad snang-ba'i dga'-ston*). Its two hundred and thirty-two Tibetan folios were composed during the summer of 1966. The xylographs for the first edition of the text were prepared in Kalimpong, West Bengal, India, where they are preserved at the monastery of Zangdok Pelri. The text was subsequently reprinted in the *Collected Works of Dudjom Rinpoche* (Kalimpong, 1979).

GYURME DORJE

The Text

An Abridged Definitive Ordering of the Nyingma Teaching,
the Ancient Translation School of Secret Mantra,
entitled Feast in which Eloquence Appears

gsang-sngags snga-'gyur rnying-ma-ba'i bstan-pa'i rnam-gzhag
mdo-tsam brjod-pa legs-bshad snang-ba'i dga'-ston

Verses of Invocation

May you who are the indestructible reality
Of the speech of all conquerors,
Having attained supreme accomplishment,
A level whose wonder cannot even be grasped,
And arisen embodied as an awareness-holder,
Powerfully transforming the three spheres of existence,
Orgyen Dorje Chang,[10] confer your blessings.

May you who bind the entire network
Of the supreme skilful means,
Which appears as great bliss,
In the seal of discriminative awareness,
Which is emptiness in its natural state,
Heruka, completely present
In mobile and motionless creatures,
All-pervading lord and guru,
Grant protection until enlightenment.

When the brilliant, attractive lotus of eloquent discourse
Born from the taintless ocean of doctrinal tradition
Exudes honey drops of excellent meaning,
The feast of the discerning bee increases in all ways.

Introduction

[2b.3-3a.1] On the basis of the unsurpassed aspiration and enlightened activity of the three ancestral religious kings[11] who emanated in the land of snow mountains [Tibet], the field of the sublime and supreme Lokeśvara,[12] the Teaching of the Conqueror [Buddhism] was established. Its foundation was clearly made secure by the preceptors, masters, paṇḍitas, accomplished masters, bodhisattvas and translators who were representatives of the Teacher [Buddha] through their translations, exegeses, teachings, study, meditation, and attainment. Subsequently, an immeasurable number of accomplished awareness-holders manifestly equal to the Conqueror himself emerged, such as Nupcen Sangye Yeshe and his nephew [Nup Khulungpa Yönten Gyamtso], the generations of the Zur family, Nyang-rel Nyima Özer, Rok Sherap-ö, Rongzompa Chöki Zangpo and Longcen Rapjampa.[13] Therefore, I wish to summarise and briefly explain the fundamentals of that body of teaching renowned as the Nyingma tradition or Ancient Translation School of the secret mantra, the exegesis, attainment and enlightened activity of which continue to be maintained without decline until the present day.

Part One
Doctrines of Saṃsāra and Nirvāṇa

1 *The Essence and Definition of Dharma*

[3a.1-4b.5] At the outset, the doctrines of saṃsāra and nirvāṇa must be recognised in general and their characteristics established. This has three aspects: essence, verbal definition and classification.

The essence is as follows: Mundane doctrines are characterised as those which, when referred to objectively, cause one to wander in the three realms by the power of corrupt deeds, and as those whose nature is flawed in such a way that suffering alone is experienced. Supramundane doctrines are characterised as those which destroy the two obscurations when founded upon the continuum of the mind, and which are endowed with positive attributes affording protection from the suffering of saṃsāra. As it is said [in the *Rational System of Exposition*, *Vyākhyāyukti*, T 4061]:

> The true doctrine (*saddharma*) is that which removes all suffering and every obscuration.

The verbal definition is that the term *dharma*, which is derived from the root *dhṛ*[14] "to hold", holds or conveys ten meanings. The *Wish-fulfiller* (*Amaraṭīkākāmadhenu*, T 4300) explains:

> Because it holds everything
> It is the *dharma*.[15]

In the *Rational System of Exposition* the ten meanings emerge as follows:

> *Dharma* is that which is knowable, the path, nirvāṇa, an object of mind, merit, life, the scriptures, material objects, regulation, and the doctrinal traditions.

Accordingly, there are quotations from the sūtras illustrating the word *dharma* when it conveys the meaning of that which is knowable, for example:

> Some things (*dharma*) are compounded,
> Others are uncompounded.

And,

> All things (*dharma*) should be known in that way.

When *dharma* conveys the meaning of the path, it may be illustrated by the words:

> O monks, the wrong view is not the doctrine (*dharma*), but the correct view is the doctrine.

When it conveys the meaning of nirvāṇa, it may be illustrated by the words:

> He took refuge in the doctrine (*dharma*).

When conveying the meaning of an object of mind, it may be illustrated by the expression "activity field of phenomena" (*dharmāyatana*). When conveying the meaning of merit, it may be illustrated by the words:

> He practised the doctrine (*dharma*) in the company of a retinue of queens and maidens.

When conveying the meaning of life, it may be illustrated by the words:

> A childish person dearly holds to the things (*dharma*) which he sees.

When conveying the meaning of the scriptures, it may be illustrated by the words:

> O monks, that which is called the doctrine (*dharma*) includes for instance the piṭaka of the sūtras and the piṭaka of prose and verse combined.

When conveying the meaning of emergent objects, it may be illustrated by the words:

> As for compounded substances, this is their reality (*dharma*).

and:

> Even I have not transcended the phenomenon (*dharma*) of death and the reality of death.

When conveying the meaning of regulation, it may be illustrated by the term "four doctrines (*dharma*) of a spiritual ascetic",[16] and by the words:

> O monks, to kill is not the doctrine, but to renounce killing is the doctrine (*dharma*).

And so forth. When it conveys the meaning of tradition, it may be illustrated by "national traditions" (*dharma*) and "ethnic traditions" (*dharma*).

If one then wonders how these [ten definitions] relate to the sense of the term "to hold", then the things which are knowable hold both individual and general characteristics. Individual characteristics are held as illustrated, for example, in the following words:

> Earth is hard, water wet, fire hot
> And wind is light and mobile.

And the manner in which general characteristics are held may be illustrated by the words:

> All that is compounded is impermanent.
> All that is corrupt is suffering.
> All things are devoid of self.
> Nirvāṇa is peace.

By the path and nirvāṇa one is held from falling into saṃsāra. By the object of mind the mind is held. By merit one is held from falling into evil existences. By the life-span or life itself one holds the body or its appropriate stations. The scriptures hold the unmistakable truth. Emergent objects hold that which has a transient basis. Regulations hold the precise foundation. Traditions uphold an idiosyncratic conduct; and by awareness [of all these] one is held apart from the area of bewilderment. Such analogies may be inferred by reason.

The classification is twofold, consisting of the doctrine of saṃsāra and the doctrine of nirvāṇa. Concerning the distinction between these two, the *[Long] Mother* [i.e. the *Transcendental Perfection of Discriminative Awareness in One Hundred Thousand Lines*] says:

> Liberality is possessed by both mundane and supramundane beings. What, you may ask, is mundane liberality? That which, by the act of having made some offering, neither moves beyond, nor sublimates, nor transcends the world, is said to be mundane liberality. That which does move beyond, sublimate, or transcend the world, by the act of having made some offering, is called supramundane liberality.

According to such quotations, when one has reached a conclusion through any method, the result is distinguished by having or lacking the power to sublimate the world.

2 *Doctrines of Saṃsāra*

[4b.5-16a.3] First, the doctrines of saṃsāra are explained under three headings: (1) the characteristics of saṃsāra, (2) the mundane vehicle [and the Brahmā vehicle], and (3) an ensuing discussion of the views held by those of no understanding and by those of wrong understanding.

THE CHARACTERISTICS OF SAṂSĀRA

The doctrines or phenomena of saṃsāra are originally caused by ignorance which arises in three interrelated aspects. Firstly, the ignorance of individual selfhood (*bdag-nyid gcig-pu'i ma-rig-pa*) arises as consciousness, but it is not recognised as such. Secondly, through the co-emergent ignorance (*lhan-cig skyes-pa'i ma-rig-pa*), the unconsciousness of the true essence and that consciousness emerge together. Yet it is thirdly, through the ignorance of the imaginary (*kun-tu brtag-pa'i ma-rig-pa*), that one's own perceptions are externally discerned. Since these three aspects arise diversely from a single essence, they arise from the ground as the appearance of the ground; and since this is not known to have been self-originated, the threefold ignorance which subjectively discerns objects is the causal condition [of saṃsāra]. The objective appearances, which arise like one's own reflection in a mirror, through clinging to externals apart from oneself, are the referential condition [of saṃsāra]. The consciousness which holds to the [concepts] of "I" and "mine" is the possessive condition, and since these three [conditions] are simultaneous, they form the immediate condition. Bewilderment originates from the impure referential aspect containing these four conditions [of saṃsāra] and is maintained by divisively clinging externally to objective phenomena, and internally to subjective consciousness. As it is said in the *Penetration of Sound* (*sgra thal-'gyur*, NGB Vol.10):

> The basis of bewilderment is ignorance.
> Ignorance has three forms.

And:

> Owing to that root which is the single indivisible[17] cause,
> The true essence is not perceived;
> This, therefore, is the beginning of saṃsāra.

And in the *Great Array* (*bkod-pa chen-po*):

> Spontaneous presence arises as an object,
> Which is emptiness.
> At that time, from the cycle of bewilderment
> Which has four conditions,
> The snare of clinging comes into being.

From the very moment of bewilderment, that same bewilderment arises as the ground-of-all (*kun-gzhi*, Skt. *ālaya*) in its role as the ignorance, the naturally obscuring expressive power, which is the unconsciousness of the true essence. Dependent upon that [ground-of-all] is the mind which is the consciousness of the ground-of-all and the six conflicting emotions which originate from it. These are [ignorance, the basis on which bewildering thoughts are grasped];[18] delusion, the bewilderment in the area of discriminative awareness; hatred, the bewilderment in the area of creative phases;[19] pride, the bewilderment in the area of the view; desire, the bewilderment in the area of appearances; and envy, the bewilderment in the area of non-understanding [in relation to these]. Eighty-four thousand phenomena (*dharma*) then emerge through the gradual accumulation of ideas, beginning with the mind which apprehends emotionally conflicted thoughts such as the above, the intellect which apprehends all memories, the ideas which form the ground of connecting propensities and doubts, and that area [of mind] which clings to objects and entities.

In this way then, the five sensory perceptions originate together with the consciousness of the intellect wherein the twenty-one thousand phenomena [in each of four categories], namely, the three poisons and their equal combination, arise dispositionally.

The object which maintains the continuity of any of these six active consciousnesses[20] at the moment of objectification, the immediate consciousness which at the same instant apprehends the object and its form, and any of the three subsequent feelings of pleasure, suffering or neutrality, are together called the sensation of contact. So it is that the eighteen psychophysical bases originate, divided into three groups of six.[21]

[Thereupon, the evolution of] the five components, the twelve activity fields, the six sense organs and karma or [world-forming] deeds ensues. The five components are, namely, the component of form, which is an accumulation of atoms and is capable of being destroyed and split; the component of feelings, which are the source of enjoyment and desire; the component of perceptions, which are dynamic and object-oriented; the component of habitual tendencies which create and accumulate propensities; [and the component of consciousness which is aware and objectifying].[22]

As for the twelve activity fields which cause any accumulation of ideas to be sensed, there are six objective modes, such as form, the object apprehended by the eye, which causes both the continuity [of the object of perception] in the subsequent instant and the apprehending consciousness to be sensed; and there are also six subjective modes, such as the consciousness of the eye,[23] which arises in that subsequent instant and perceives as form that form which may be objectively sensed. There are five organs of sense, such as the eye, which have the power to apprehend objects, or six with the inclusion of the sense organ of the intellect, which originates from the possessive condition of the initial apperceptive consciousness.

Deeds may be of three types: virtuous, unvirtuous or neutral. The first includes the ten virtues which produce worldly happiness as their result. The second comprises the contrary deeds which cast [beings] into evil existences. The third refers to those [neutral] deeds[24] which cast beings into higher realms.

Although all these phenomena are compounded internally by the mind, their apparitional aspect and supporting foundation are the five gross elements of which external objects are compounded, and which are caused, conditioned, supported and substantiated by the fourfold process of creation, duration, destruction and dissolution. As the number of mental propensities through which they appear as objects expands, the world realm of desire containing the four continents, Mount Sumeru and perimeter appears like a dream, along with the realm of form, like self-radiating rainbow light of five colours, and the formless realm, which originates from the contemplation of the summit of existence, and so on.[25] In brief, the entire array of the inanimate container and animate creatures, mobile and motionless, subsumed by the three world realms, does not appear in the ultimate vision of sublime beings. Rather, it is an apparitional mode of the bewildered intellect of sentient beings, which appears by the power of the subject-object dichotomy lapsing into delusion, like water in a mirage, and into erroneous perception, like seing a multicoloured rope as a snake. As it is said in the *Pearl Necklace* (*mu-tig phreng-ba*, NGB Vol.9):

> In this way, the diverse appearances
> Resemble a rope when seen as a snake.
> Though not so, by clinging to them as such
> The outer container and inner essence
> Are established as a duality.
> The rope itself, on further investigation,

Is primordially empty of container and essence.
The ultimate takes form as the relative.
That perception of the snake is visually true,
The perception of the rope is genuinely true.
Enduring, for example, as a bird relates to a scarecrow,
The independent existence of the two truths
Refers only to the relative world.
It has no relation to genuine reality.
Because of the expanse of emptiness
The essence of that [reality] is that all is free.

And in the *Oral Instructions of Mañjuśrī* (*Mañjuśrīmukhāgama*, T 1853-4) it says:

All things of saṃsāra are held to be non-existent
Like the multicoloured rope when perceived as a snake.

Moreover, the creator of the happiness and suffering of saṃsāra, the high and the low and all such apparitional modes, is karma or [world-forming] deeds, corrupted by all-conflicting emotions, which are of three types. Without exception these modes are created by deeds, emanated by deeds, matured by deeds, and they appear through the power of deeds. Accordingly, it is said in the *Hundred Parables on Deeds* (*Karmaśatakasūtra*, T 340):

The diversity of the world is developed through deeds.
Happiness and suffering are created by deeds.
Deeds originate from an accumulation of conditions
And by deeds happiness and suffering are made.

And in the *Introduction to the Madhyamaka* (*Madhyamakāvatāra*, T 3861, Ch.6, v.89) it explains:

By mind itself the diverse
Sentient and inanimate worlds
Are allocated their share of deeds.
Living creatures without exception
Are said to be created through deeds.

THE MUNDANE VEHICLE AND THE BRAHMĀ VEHICLE

The Mundane Vehicle

[7b.2-10a.3] The mundane vehicle or the basic vehicle followed by gods and human beings is explained under three headings: essence, verbal definition and classification.

The essence is any method of progressing to the conclusive happiness of gods and human beings which lacks the power to sublimate saṃsāra.

It is verbally defined as a vehicle because it can merely unite with, and progress towards, the result of happiness experienced by gods and human beings. Its classifications are sixfold, namely, entrance, view, moral discipline, meditation, conduct and result.

Firstly, concerning the entrance: After having seen the three evil existences, which are naturally endowed with suffering, one enters by means of renouncing the unvirtuous deeds, which are the cause of birth therein. As it is said in the *Heruka Galpo* (*he-ru-ka gal-po*, NGB Vol.25):

> Non-virtue is renounced by the vehicle of gods and humans.

In this context the ten non-virtues consist of three physical deeds – to kill, to steal and to commit sexual misconduct; four verbal deeds – to lie, to slander, to talk irresponsibly and to utter abuse; and three mental deeds – to covet, to be malicious and to hold wrong views.

Secondly, concerning the view: The correct view is the conviction that there are such things as a future world and the cause and fruition of deeds. It says in the *Collection of Meaningful Expressions* (*Udānavarga*, T 326, Ch.4, v.9):

> The great one who possesses
> The correct view for a mundane being
> Even in a thousand lifetimes
> Will not turn to evil existences.

Conversely, with a wrong view, even though one may have practised other virtuous deeds, such as abstaining from murder, one will reap the fruit of suffering. As it is said in the *Letter to a Friend* (*Suhṛllekha*, T 4182, v.46):

> Even though an individual may have practised well,
> with a wrong view
> All that matures will be unbearable.

Therefore, it is important that the correct view be retained.

Thirdly, moral discipline is nothing but the moral discipline of renouncing the ten non-virtues. It has been said in the above-mentioned [*Letter to a Friend*, v.11]:

> The [eight vows of the] purificatory fast
> Cause the pleasant body of the gods who act as they desire
> To be bestowed upon lay people.

This being the case, is not the moral discipline derived from correct commitment explained to be necessary for one who would progress to the rank of the gods? Though indeed mentioned, it is spoken of only with reference to [the attainment of] the extraordinary [form] realms. For the ordinary [form] realms, its necessity is uncertain.[26] Therefore, these latter realms are held to be attained simply by enacting the deeds and path of the ten virtues, along with their concomitants, which are retained by the correct view.

Furthermore, concepts such as purity of the grasping components are adhered to, and one who has been motivated by the possession of conscience and humility is called a holy or superior being for performing his or her duties of body and speech with propriety. And the converse is true for an evil or inferior being. The *Treatise on Behaviour entitled the Holy Ornament* (*lugs-kyi bstan-bcos dam-pa'i rgyan*) says: [27]

> To honour well those who are worthy of reverence,
> To be especially benevolent to those who are unprotected,
> And not to forget to repay kindness
> Is the conduct of a holy being.
> The holy person actually chooses death,
> Rather than a life which has forsaken conscience,
> Experiences which are tainted with sin,
> And power gained by the deception of friends.

And again:

> An evil creature delights in sin,
> Shows ingratitude and casts away
> Conscience like an enemy.
> That one will do anything
> To achieve his or her own purpose.

And in the *Short Chapter on Discrimination* (*'byed-pa le'u chung*) sixteen pure human laws (*mi-chos gtsang-ma bcu-drug*) are taught as follows:

> Develop faith in the Three Precious Jewels without sorrow or weariness; search ultimately for the true doctrine; skilfully study the excellent sciences; first recollect and then appraise anything that is to be undertaken; do not hanker after unassigned work; look to a higher level and emulate the ancients and those of superior conduct; repay kindness to one's parents of the past, present and future; be broad-minded and hospitable in one's dealings with elder and younger siblings and paternal relatives; ensure that the young respect their elders by degrees; show loving kindness to one's neighbours; arduously assist one's acquaintances who are spiritual benefactors; perfectly fulfil the needs of those nearby who are connected through the worldly round; help others through one's skill in science and the arts; provide a refuge with kindness to those who depend upon it; resist bad advice and establish advice which will increase the happiness of the country; and, entrusting one's deeds to the doctrine, one

> should bring one's spouse to obtain the ground of enlightenment in future lives.

Fourth, meditation: There is training until one has the power to bring about the proper result.

Fifth, conduct: One enacts the deeds and path of the ten virtues "endowed with corruption" along with their concomitants, which [virtues] are so named after their function which is [merely] to renounce the ten non-virtues. The positive virtues of such physical actions as prostration, verbal actions as praise and mental actions which benefit others by virtuous thoughts are also included. However, one might object, is it not said in the *Heruka Galpo* that on the vehicle of gods and humans, the ten modes of doctrinal conduct such as writing [scriptures] and making offerings are necessary? Here, as before, there is a distinction between [the attainment of] the extraordinary realms, and the ordinary realms.

Sixth, the result is as follows: By the extent of the power of one's virtuous deeds, one is born in the ten higher levels of the desire realm, namely, among the human beings of the four continents or among the six species of Kāma divinities. Accordingly, the *Tantra of the Extensive Magical Net* says:

> The practice of the ten virtues and the renunciation of non-virtues
> Are the basis for birth among the gods and humans of the desire realm.

And in Buddhaguhya's[28] *Sequence of the Path* it says:

> By emphasising the ten virtues
> And not equating virtue with non-virtue,
> One is born among the gods and human beings.
> Without understanding sameness, one wanders in the desire realm.

Since this vehicle progresses to the culmination of the happiness desired in this life either as an emperor among men, or as a master of the Paranirmitavaśavartin[29] realm of the gods, the *Sūtra of the Descent to Laṅkā* speaks of it as the divine vehicle, after the name of the highest realm to which it progresses. It has been said of this vehicle in the *Sequence of the Path*:

> It is definitively arranged
> As the first of the fundamental vehicles.

Accordingly, it either forms the foundation of, or is preliminary to, all the vehicles, because the vehicle which is not retained by the correct view and which does not observe the deeds and path of the ten virtues as its actual foundation is nowhere to be found. The *Hevajra Tantra* (T 417-18, Pt.2, Ch.2, v.18cd) also states:

> Having commenced from the ten virtues
> His doctrine is disclosed.

The Brahmā Vehicle

[10a.3-11b.3] The *Sūtra of the Descent to Laṅkā* also speaks of the vehicle of Brahmā. Here Brahmā does not only apply to the three realms which begin with the Brahmakāyika,[30] but the meanings of chaste, clean and pure are also conveyed by the word Brahmā; for the conflicting emotion of desire is cleansed and purified. In this way the above sūtra refers to the whole range of the word Brahmā. All twenty-one higher realms, including the seventeen form realms of the gods and the four formless realms, are expressed by the word Brahmā, and the path, along with its concomitants, which progresses to these realms is called the vehicle of Brahmā.[31] It also says that one who has renounced the conflicting emotions of the lower level will be born in a higher realm by the power of having meditated with tranquillity, and with higher insight which perceives as coarse the level below one's own and perceives as subtle one's own level. Therefore, one will not be born in the higher realms without obtaining an actual foundation in the four meditative concentrations and the four formless absorptions on the path which removes attachment to the level below one's own. So it is that the meditative concentrations and absorptions are held to be the actual vehicle of Brahmā and the four immeasurables and five mundane supernormal cognitive powers to be the extraordinary path of enlightened attributes in the vehicle of Brahmā.

These attributes also require a view which accepts the [doctrine of] deeds and their result; an entrance and a moral discipline through which the ten non-virtues are renounced; a conduct through which the ten virtues are observed as before, but through which in addition the four immeasurables, namely, loving kindness, compassion, sympathetic joy and equanimity are practised; and a meditation which includes both formal and formless absorptions. The formal ones are the four meditative concentrations which are characteristically disillusioned with the sensations of desire. As the *Intermediate Mother* [*Transcendental Perfection of Discriminative Awareness in Twenty-five Thousand Lines*, *Pañcaviṃśatisāhasrikāprajñāpāramitā*, T 9] says:

> That which possesses both ideas and scrutiny is the first concentration. That which possesses no ideas but scrutiny alone is the second concentration. Mental action devoid of both ideas and scrutiny is the third concentration, and mental action united with delight is the fourth concentration.

The latter [i.e. the formless ones] are the four absorptions which are characteristically disillusioned with the cognition of the four concentrations. These are the absorptions into the activity field infinite as the sky, into the activity field of infinite consciousness, into the activity field of nothing at all, and into the activity field where there is neither perception nor non-perception. They are the culmination of the path to the summit of existence.[32] Concerning these, the *Tantra of the Extensive Magical Net* also says:

> One whose conduct is the four immeasurables
> And whose meditation is unwavering
> Will be born in the Brahmā realms and so forth.

The result [in this context] refers to both the form and formless realms. As regards the former, one takes birth in the three realms which begin with Brahmakāyika through having meditated respectively on the weak, middling, and strong aspects of the actual foundation of the first concentration, and [by applying the second, third and fourth concentrations] in the same way, altogether there are twelve such ordinary realms in which one revolves. During the fourth concentration the uncorrupted discriminative awareness of the sublime beings increases and one takes birth in the Five Pure Abodes beginning with Avṛha through meditation in five respective stages. Yet, one does not obtain freedom from attachment to form, and one continues to wander in saṃsāra through attachment to the flavour of concentration. As the *Sequence of the Path* says:

> Holding to individual selfhood through the stages
> Of the four immeasurables and four concentrations,
> And imputing self in all forms,
> One takes birth successively in the Brahmā realms.

As regards the latter [type of result], one takes birth as a formless god by clinging to [the idea of] self during the contemplation endowed with four nominal components[33] in which the discriminative awareness of higher insight is absent. The same text [*Sequence of the Path*] says:

> Without understanding sameness and that which is
> formless,
> One does not know the four names to be non-existent.
> When one abides in the four activity fields,
> One is born on the level of the summit of existence.

THOSE OF NO UNDERSTANDING AND THOSE OF WRONG UNDERSTANDING

[11b.3-16a.3] The ensuing discussion of the views held by those of no understanding and by those of wrong understanding is explained as follows: on this topic the opinions of past masters slightly differ. The master Sūryaprabhāsiṃha[34] claims that those of no understanding are the trio of the apathetic (*phyal-ba*), the materialists (*rgyang-'phen-pa*, Skt. *Lokāyata*) and the nihilistic extremists (*mur stug-pa*), while those of wrong understanding are the eternalistic extremists (*mu stegs-pa*, Skt. *tīrthika*). Master Līlāvajra[35] claims that those of no understanding are the apathetic and those of wrong understanding the extremists, both eternalistic and nihilistic. Vimalamitra[36] has said:

> The apathetic and materialists
> Have no understanding,
> The nihilistic and eternalistic extremists
> Have wrong understanding.

Since a similar account also is found in the great master Padmasambhava's *Garland of Views: A Collection of Esoteric Instructions*, I shall adopt the same approach here.

Those of No Understanding

[12a.1-12a.4] Among those of no understanding and those of wrong understanding, the former are both interpreted and classified as follows. They are interpreted to be ordinary individuals whose attitudes have not been changed by a philosophical system. They are classified into two groups: the actual and the incidental.

The Apathetic

First, those who actually have no understanding, the mundane apathetic, are explained under three headings: essence, verbal definition and classification.

Their essence is that they are totally deluded because from the beginning they have not understood [the relationship] between the causes and results of deeds. The verbal definition is that they are called apathetic because they do not act in response to the existence or non-existence of doctrines concerning interdependent causes and results, and observe neither renunciation nor commitment. As the *Parkap Commentary* [*on the Secret Nucleus, Guhyagarbhamahātantrarājaṭīkā*, P 4718] says:

> He who understands nothing at all
> Is a mundane apathetic being.

Their classification is into an inferior type and a dubious type. The inferior type have a debased intellect which does not consider the attainment of positive attributes. The dubious type are both good and evil, and resemble those described below.

The Materialists

[12a.4-12b.4] Secondly, those who are incidentally classed with those of no understanding, the materialists, are also explained under three headings. Their essence is that without understanding the existence or non-existence of previous and future lives, they are inclined to achieve only the slight temporal and spiritual well-being of one lifetime. The verbal definition is that they are called materialists because, rejecting the future as remote, their achievements depend upon the mysterious expressions, oracles, dreams and calculations of mundane beings, such as those who are mighty and powerful in this life. Their classification is into two types: the cut-off and the perceptive. The former includes those cut off by nature and by conditions. Since [the view that there are cut-off beings] is not held by those who uphold the philosophy of the greater vehicle (*Mahāyāna*), they may be known in detail from other sources.[37] The perceptive type is fourfold. As a great sūtra (*mdo chen-po*) says:

> The four perceptive types,
> Known as the attached, the distracted,
> The fearful, and the aspiring,
> Appear as the field
> Capable of retaining the seed [of enlightenment].

Respectively, these four are unable to resist lustful attachment to objects of desire, distracted by the duties of man-made laws in this life, successful in power and wealth through evil means, and the type which aspires to renounce the ten non-virtues and attain liberation.

Those of Wrong Understanding

[12b.4-16a.3] Secondly, those of wrong understanding are interpreted and classified as follows. They are interpreted to be any receptive individuals whose attitudes have been changed by wrong philosophy. They are classified as the five sophistic schools of the extremist masters of the past, who turn outwards rather than inwards.[38] Included among them are four schools of the eternalist view, the first being the Sāṃkhya.

Sāṃkhya

[12b.5-13a.3] During the age when living beings had a life-span of twenty thousand years,[39] the sage Kapila attained accomplishment through the austerities of the eternalistic extremists and composed many treatises. There were two students who upheld his philosophical system, Bharadvāja and Patañjali. Those who follow the tenet of Bharadvāja, that all that is knowable is divided into twenty-five categories, are the Sāṃkhya. Those based on the tenet of Patañjali, that the abiding nature of the twenty-five categories is empty, are the Followers of Kapila

[*Kāpila*, the Yoga School]. As the *Compendium of the Nucleus of Pristine Cognition* (*Jñānasārasamuccaya*, T 3851) says:

> The Sāṃkhya speak of attributes;
> The Followers of Kapila maintain they are empty.

So it is that they are called the Sāṃkhya, the Followers of Kapila and Adherents of the Three Attributes (*Traiguṇya*).

Aiśvara

[13a.3-13b.1] The second school holding an eternalistic view is that of the Followers of Īśvara [Śiva]. The god Īśvara, the teacher of many tantrapiṭaka, had two students who attained accomplishment, namely, Akṣapāda and Kaṇāda. The adherents of Nyāya (*Naiyāyika*) depend on the *View of Reason* (*Nyāyadarśana*) which was composed by Akṣapāda, while the Vaiśeṣika depend on the *Clear Distinction* (*bye-brag gsal-ba*, Skt. *Vaiśeṣikadarśana*) which was composed by Kaṇāda. This school holds that all the bondage and liberation of sentient beings is created by Īśvara:

> Having no consciousness, these living creatures
> Lack control over their own happiness and sorrow.
> But when dispatched by Īśvara,
> They become creatures who exclusively inhabit
> The abyss [of evil existences]
> Or the higher realms [of gods and humans].[40]

Thus they are called Followers of Īśvara, Followers of the Owl (*Aulūkya*)[41] and Adherents of the Six Categories (*Ṣaḍpadārthavaiśeṣika*).

Vaiṣṇava

[13b.1-13b.6] The third school holding an eternalist view is the Vaiṣṇava. Viṣṇu composed the *Anthology of Vedic Treatises*. The four-faced Brahmā was born from the lotus of his navel, and, after emanating the entire world and its contents, he recollected the great *Four Veda*, namely, the *Ṛgveda*, the *Sāmaveda*, the *Yajurveda* and the *Atharvaveda*. Later his exegeses were compiled by the sages and the following five divisions emerged:[42] the grammarians (*Vaiyākaraṇa*) who rely on Viṣṇu's treatise entitled *Light Rays of Grammatical Speech* (*brda'-sprod ngag-gi 'od-zer*); the logicians including Aviddhakarṇa[43] who rely on the *ṛṣi* Agni's *Weapons of Expression* (*smra-ba'i mtshon-cha*); the mystics among accomplished meditators who rely on the *ṛṣi* Satya's *Nine Cycles of the Meditational Sequence* (*bsgom-rim skor-dgu*); those proponents of textual exegesis who emphasise ritual, relying on the *ṛṣi* Bhṛgu's *Clear Judgement* (*rnam-dpyod gsal-ba*); and the followers of Caraka who are physicians relying on the *Anthology of Caraka* (*Carakasaṃhitā*), which was composed by the *ṛṣi* Ātreya and others. All of these uphold the authenticity of the *Four Veda*. When classified, they are known as the Followers of Viṣṇu (*Vaiṣṇava*), the Followers of Brahmā and the Followers of the Veda.

Jainism

[13b.6-14a.2] The fourth school holding an eternalistic view is the Jaina (*rgyal-ba-pa*). In the *Ornamental Mirror of Categories* (*tshig-don rgyan-gyi snang-ba*)[44] it says:

> The great god [Ṛṣabha], holiest of conquerors
> Ascertains that which is knowable
> In the following nine categories:
> Animate substance (*jīva*), inanimate substance
> (*ajīva*)[45] and commitments (*saṃvara*),
> Rejuvenation (*nirjara*), bondage (*bandha*) and deeds
> (*karmāsrava*),
> Evil (*pāpa*), virtue (*puṇya*) and liberation (*mokṣa*).

Consequently, it is held that liberation has form and colour, while trees are animate. They are called the Followers of the Conqueror (*Jaina*), Adherents of the Nine Categories and the Naked Ascetics (*Nirgrantha*).

Nihilism

[14a.2-14b.3] The fifth school is the only one which holds a nihilistic view. In Trayatriṃśa, the heaven of the Thirty-three Gods, Bṛhaspati, who had become the accomplished guru of the gods, composed the treatise entitled *Essence of the View which Negates Everything* (*thams-cad-la skur-pa 'debs-pa'i lta-ba'i snying-po*)[46] in order that the gods might develop enthusiasm for their struggle against the antigods. Later it was propagated in the human world by Vālmīki. The treatise negates past and future births, saying [cf. *Sarvadarśanasaṃgraha*, Ch.1, v.1]:

> Act joyously, good lady,
> While you are not dead,
> For nothing is not in death's range.
> Even your body will vanish like powder.
> Where can there be rebirths?

It then negates the existence of invisible beings, saying:

> As many creatures as there are,
> They exist solely
> Within the range of the senses.
> Alas, whatever the learned say
> Resembles the tracks of a deceiving wolf.

It goes on to negate buddhahood as the result of progress on the path, saying:

> The intellect is the body's soul,
> It is the body's fruit and the body's attribute;
> Depending on three modes such as these
> There is no possibility of progress [to enlightenment].

It negates logic, saying:

> Because it exaggerates
> There is no logic.

And it also negates causality, with the words [*Summation of the Real, Tattvasaṃgraha*, T 4266, vv.111-12ab]:

> Who made the anthers of a lotus?
> Who designed the markings of a peacock?
> Who sharpened the point of a thorn?
> All things emerge substantially without cause.

So it is that they are called the Followers of Bṛhaspati (*Bārhaspatya*), the materialists, hedonists,[47] and those who hold that mind emerges from space.

CONCLUSION

Since these four views of no understanding and wrong understanding exclusively originate from ignorance, they are mundane views. Such has been said in the *Garland of Views: A Collection of Esoteric Instructions* from the passage beginning:

> The countless sūtras which gather together the erroneous views of sentient beings in the mundane realm fall within four categories, namely, the apathetic, the materialists, the nihilistic extremists and the eternalistic extremists.

down to:

> All these are ignorant views.

Among these, the two which have no understanding represent no philosophical view. However, they are explained to be associated with [such a view] because they are subsumed within the status of the mind. The two which have wrong understanding do represent views which change the attitude through a philosophical system, but by clinging to extremes which exaggerate and depreciate the reality free from extremes, they have become erroneous. Therefore, they are not the means of liberation from saṃsāra. This applies not only to the nihilistic extremists who are the worst among those professing philosophy, but to the eternalistic extremists as well, because, maintaining a self, they are bound by clinging to a self, which is the root of saṃsāra. Accordingly, the *Exposition of Valid Cognition* (*Pramāṇavārttika*, T 4210, Ch.1, v.193cd) says:

> As long as one actually clings to a self,
> One will turn to saṃsāra.

And in the *Sequence of the Path*:

> Anyone who inclines towards
> The duality of eternalism and nihilism
> Is said to deviate from the reality
> Of the genuine essence.

On this occasion, I have not written about the texts and so forth which they individually uphold. One wishing to know them should look elsewhere. Some may well ask at this point whether it is not most inappropriate to explain the philosophical systems of the Outsiders,[48] etc., while analysing the Conqueror's transmitted precepts. Yet there is no fault, because having recognised the downfalls and things to be renounced on the path with reference to the eternalistic extremists who follow their own independent course, one has reason not to delay [in following] our own path, which is the supramundane vehicle. It says in the *Heruka Galpo:*

> When the vehicle of the eternalistic extremists is well
> ascertained,
> It is explained to you so that
> You will not practise but renounce it.

Furthermore, with reference to those eternalistic extremists who are [the buddhas'] emanations, [there is no fault] because in addition to that aforementioned reason [for pursuing the path of the supramundane vehicle], they are said to represent the enlightened activity of the conquerors who train each in accord with his or her needs. It is said in the *Rite which Ties by the Rope of Compassion of the Gathering of the Sugatas* (*bde-'dus-kyi thugs-rje dpyang-thag gnas-kyi lung*, P 4781), which was composed by the bodhisattva Vajradharma:

> By the diverse inroads of compassion,
> Training in whatever manner may be suitable,
> The Teacher speaks of this [true doctrine]
> And whatever appears therein
> To the schools of the Outsiders.

In the very same way, one might well wonder how the development of such a negative view as that of the nihilistic extremists could appropriately be within the conquerors' skilful means, since it is an extremely terrible wrong view. None the less, it is appropriate because the nihilistic extremists, too, admit much that is reasonable. When one examines the scriptures or meets the arguments of those who established the pure Prāsaṅgika dialectic,[49] one is first of all sceptical, and subsequently having seen the pure proof to the contrary, one comes to develop the correct logic. Therefore [the nihilists] are nearer to developing the correct view than the fools who have never entertained philosophy.

Again, if one asks how these [views] are explained to form an ensuing discussion that is derived from the vehicle of gods and human beings, they are so called because the receptive individuals who make progress through the vehicle of gods and humans are both Outsiders and Insiders. With reference to the Outsiders, as Śūra says:

> The beings who do not side with your teaching are blinded
> by ignorance.
> Though they have reached the summit of existence,
> They will achieve a rebirth in which suffering re-emerges.

And with reference to the Insiders, even though they may hold to the refuge with a will to perform their duties on behalf of the Three Precious Jewels (*dkon-mchog gsum*), they are referred to as remaining only on the mundane path, unless their intellects aspire to liberation. As the *Supreme Continuum of the Greater Vehicle* (Ch.1, v.19) says:

> With reference to differing volitions,
> The threefold refuge is laid down.

3 *Doctrines of Nirvāṇa*

[16a.3-17b.3] Secondly, the supramundane vehicle is explained in two parts: its superiority over [the vehicle of] the Outsiders and a detailed account of its own nature.

THE SUPERIORITY OF THE SUPRAMUNDANE VEHICLE

The true doctrine of nirvāṇa,[50] which affords protection from the suffering of saṃsāra, is the best of all doctrines, supreme, perfect and more special than others. Therefore, it is expressed by the word "true". Grasping the Three Precious Jewels as the focus of refuge, it admits to, or is included within, four seals indicative of the transmitted precepts which concern the view. By the study of the three correct trainings, it has a superior result because it can surpass the summit of existence. These [attributes] do not exist in the path of the Outsiders.

Among these [attributes], going for refuge must be the foundation and support of the path since that is the basis of the vows which support the aspiration for nirvāṇa. Therefore, one who has not gone for refuge does not develop the vows, and if one has not been bound by the vows, the correct path does not exist. The *Seventy Verses on Going for Refuge* (*Triśaraṇasaptati*, T 3971) says:

> For the three kinds of layman,
> Going for refuge is the root
> Of [their] eight vows.

And:

> Though one may keep all the vows,
> None exist for one who has
> Not gone for refuge.

The four seals are [the axioms that] all that is compounded is impermanent, all that is corrupt is suffering, all things are without self, and nirvāṇa is peace.

The three trainings are superior moral discipline, mind,[51] and discriminative awareness, and it is the study of these through listening, reflection and meditation for which the doctrine is respectively termed "virtuous in the beginning, middle and end". As the *Sun Commentary* (*Śrāmaṇerakārikāvṛttiprabhāvatī*, T 4125) says:

> The learned realise that the Buddha's speech
> Teaches well the three trainings,
> Is correctly endowed with the three seals,
> And is virtuous in the beginning, middle and end.

The result, which can surpass the summit of existence, is described by Śūra as follows:

> One who follows your teaching,
> Even without obtaining the actual foundation of
> concentration,
> Opposes rebirths as if they were the vision of Māra.

A DETAILED ACCOUNT OF THE SUPRAMUNDANE VEHICLE

The detailed account of the nature of this [supramundane vehicle] has two parts. Master Vasubandhu says [in the *Treasury of the Abhidharma*, *Abhidharmakośa*, T 4089, Ch.8, v.39ab]:

> The two kinds of the Teacher's true doctrine
> Are transmission and realisation.

Accordingly, there is both the doctrine which realises his expressed meaning and the doctrine which transmits his expressive words.

Realisation of the True Doctrine

[17a.2-17b.3] The former, the doctrine of realisation, also has two parts. Firstly, there is that doctrine attained through the attributes of realisation, evenly absorbed in the expanse [of reality]. This is the truth of cessation to which the sublime beings have departed, the great nirvāṇa wherein all signs of dualistic appearance have vanished, which is beyond objects of conception and expression. Secondly, there is that doctrine which becomes the essence of realisation, the uncorrupted pristine cognition along with its concomitants. This is the truth of the path by which any [sublime being] departs, and which remedies the obscuration [covering] the naturally pure nucleus of inner radiance whose range must be realised by each one individually.

The first aspect is the desireless essence, or the unborn, pristine cognition in which the mind-streams of the four classes of sublime being have finished renouncing what must be renounced. And the second aspect is the natural expression of that pristine cognition or the antidote by which renunciation and desirelessness are achieved. As the sublime Ajita [in the *Supreme Continuum of the Greater Vehicle*, Ch. 1, vv.10-11] has said:

> The doctrine is that which is without thought,
> Without duality and without ideas,
> And which is pure, distinct and an antidote;
> Thus it is both that which is and by which
> There is freedom from desire,
> Endowed with the characteristic of two truths.
> The reality of freedom from desire is subsumed
> By the truths of the cessation [of obscurations]
> And of the [correct] path.

Transmission of the True Doctrine

Secondly, the doctrine which transmits the expressive words [concerning that realisation] also has two aspects: the transmitted precepts of [the Buddha's] excellent teaching and the treatises which comment upon their intention.

4 *Transmitted Precepts*

[17b.3-28a.4] Firstly, [the transmitted precepts] are explained under three headings: characteristic, verbal definition and classification.

The transmitted precepts are characteristically the conquerors' scriptures preserved in the sūtrapiṭaka and tantrapiṭaka which are endowed with four special qualities originating personally from our extraordinary Teacher, the Buddha. The doctrinal wheel of transmission means exactly this and is a synonym [for the term "transmitted precepts"]. The four special qualities are said in the *Sūtra which Encourages Superior Aspiration* (*Adhyāśayasañcodanasūtra*, T 69) to be the possession of expressed meaning, immaculate words of expression, a function of renouncing rather than engaging in the conflicting emotions of the three realms, and a result which teaches the benefit of peace. Accordingly, the *Supreme Continuum of the Greater Vehicle* (Ch.5, v.18) says:

> The speech which is closely connected
> With meaningful doctrine
> And causes the all-conflicting emotions of
> The three realms to be renounced,
> And that which teaches the benefit of peace,
> Is the Sage's[52] speech.
> Others are its opposite.

It is furthermore explained that the four [qualities] are to teach the three trainings as the expressed [meaning], to possess immaculate words as its expression, to possess the three kinds of valid cognition as proof, and to have a result that is virtuous in the beginning, middle and end. Therefore it is said:

> Teaching the three trainings with immaculate words,
> Endowed with the three kinds of valid cognition
> And virtuous in the beginning, middle and end:
> These are the transmitted precepts
> Which the Conqueror taught in the greater [vehicle].

> Their opposite should be known as
> The texts of others.

The verbal definition of the term *transmitted precept* is as follows: Derived from the [Sanskrit] *subhāṣita*, [the prefix] *su* conveys the five meanings of noble, beautiful, happy, best and excellent, among which in this context it means excellent. *Bhāṣita* means that which has been taught. It is because they are excellently taught that they are "transmitted precepts".

If one wonders how they are excellently taught, it is through ten aspects. As it is said in the *Rational System of Exposition*:[53]

> If one asks how they are excellently taught, they are so in ten ways, namely, through the nature of their genuine source, through the nature of their scope, through the nature of their approach, through the nature of their sound teaching, through the nature of their classification, through the nature of their support, through the nature of their causing comprehension, through the nature of their titles, through the nature of their time, and through the nature of their complete grasp of enlightened attributes.

The transmitted precepts are classified in five ways: (1) through the personality [of the Buddha], (2) through time, (3) through sections, (4) through their function as antidotes and (5) through their power.

TRANSMITTED PRECEPTS ACCORDING TO BUDDHA'S PERSONALITY

Firstly, when classified according to [the Buddha's] personality, there are three kinds of transmitted precept: those given in oral teaching, by blessing and by mandate.

Among these, [the transmitted precepts] given in oral teaching are also twofold. The teachings delivered impromptu by the Teacher at receptions are exemplified by the *Verse Summation of the Transcendental Perfection of Discriminative Awareness* (*Prajñāpāramitāsaṃcayagāthā*, T 13) in which it is said (Ch.1, intro.):

> Then, in order to delight correctly these four assemblies, the Transcendent Lord taught this further *Transcendental Perfection of Discriminative Awareness*, and at that time pronounced these verses...

The teachings which he gave at the request of an assembly are exemplified by the *Litany of the Names of Mañjuśrī* (*Mañjuśrīnāmasaṃgīti*, T 360). Therein it is stated (v.13):

> The *Great Tantra of the Magical Net* says that
> Immeasurable great Vajradharas, holders of secret
> mantra,
> Joyfully beseeched him to explain
> That which is the excellent teaching.

The transmitted precepts given by blessing are threefold. The transmitted precepts given by the blessing of his body are exemplified by the *Sūtra of the Ten Levels* (*Daśabhūmikasūtra*, T 44) which was taught by Vajragarbha and Vimukticandra who had developed the brilliance to explain and request it after the Teacher had placed his hand on the crowns of their heads. The transmitted precepts given by the blessing of his speech are exemplified by the *Transcendental Perfection of Discriminative Awareness in Eight Thousand Lines* (*Aṣṭasāhasrikāprajñāpāramitā*, T 12), which was explained by Subhūti after the Transcendent Lord had said:

> Subhūti, beginning from the transcendental perfection of discriminative awareness of the great bodhisattvas, spiritual warriors, may you develop brilliance in the manner of the great bodhisattvas, spiritual warriors, who become disillusioned [with saṃsāra] through the transcendental perfection of discriminative awareness.

The transmitted precepts given by the blessing of his mind are said to have three subdivisions. Those transmitted precepts given by the blessing of the contemplation of his mind are exemplified by the *Heart Sūtra of Discriminative Awareness* (*Bhagavatīprajñāpāramitāhṛdaya*, T 21), which was delivered through the dialogue of Śāriputra and Avalokiteśvara by the power of the Teacher's meditative equipoise in the contemplation of profound appearances. Then again, the transmitted precepts given by the blessing of the true power of his mind are exemplified by the sound of the doctrine which emerges even from the sky, and from birds, trees and so forth through the accomplished power of the Buddha. And the transmitted precepts given by the blessing of the power of his great spirituality are exemplified by the collected transmitted precepts of mantra syllables, which were spoken by pious attendants, yakṣas and others through the power of the Buddha and which are capable of granting extraordinary results.

Concerning the transmitted precepts given by mandate, the *Sūtra of Final Nirvāṇa* (*Mahāparinirvāṇasūtra*, T 120) says:

> Ānanda, when councils are convened after I have passed into final nirvāṇa, let the teachings be compiled and introduced with the words "Thus have I heard on a certain occasion", with connecting verses in the middle; and let them

be concluded with the words "Manifest praise to the teaching given by the Transcendent Lord".

In accordance with such advice, the compilers included the sayings which had been transmitted in that way.

TRANSMITTED PRECEPTS ACCORDING TO TIME

Secondly, when classified according to time, the transmitted precepts comprise the three successive promulgations of the doctrinal wheel.[54] The first of these promulgations was concerned with the four truths, the second with signlessness, and the third with the definitive meaning of ultimate [reality].

TRANSMITTED PRECEPTS ACCORDING TO SECTIONS

Thirdly, when classified according to sections, [the transmitted precepts] form the twelve or nine branches of the scriptures. The enumeration of twelve is cited in the *Great Commentary on the Transcendental Perfection of Discriminative Awareness in Eight Thousand Lines* (*Aṣṭasāhasrikāprajñāpāramitāvyākhyābhisamayālaṃkārāloka*, T 3791):[55]

> Sūtras, aphorisms in prose and verse, and prophetic declarations,
> Verses, meaningful expressions and narratives,
> Parables and legends,
> Extensive teachings and tales of past lives,
> Established instructions and marvellous events:
> These twelve are the twelve branches of the scriptures.

The enumeration of nine branches excludes the three sections of narratives, parables and established instructions. Such is also said in the *Clearly Worded Commentary* (*Mūlamadhyamakavṛttiprasannapadā*, T 3860):

> Including the sūtra section of the buddhas and so forth,
> The teaching dependent on the two truths has nine branches.

The twelve sections are also condensed into the three piṭaka. As it is said in the *Minor Transmissions* (*Vinayakṣudrāgama*, T 6):

> The five sections of the sūtras, aphorisms in prose and verse,
> Prophetic declarations, verses and meaningful expressions
> Are subsumed within the Sūtrapiṭaka.
> The four sections of legends and narratives,

Parables and tales of past lives
Are subsumed within the Vinayapiṭaka.
The three sections of extensive teaching,
Marvellous events and established instructions
Are subsumed within the Abhidharmapiṭaka.

As far as the secret mantra (*gsang-sngags*) texts are concerned in this context, most ancients claim that they belong to the section of extensive teaching because they are said to be the Bodhisattvapiṭaka of extensive teaching (*Mahāvaipulyabodhisattvapiṭaka*) in the Mahāyoga tantra entitled the *Magical Net of Mañjuśrī* [i.e. *Nāmasaṃgīti*, T 360]. The learned Nartön Senge-ö,[56] however, has said that [the secret mantra texts] belong either to the section of established instructions or to that of marvellous events.

TRANSMITTED PRECEPTS ACCORDING TO THEIR FUNCTION AS ANTIDOTES

Fourth, when classified according to their function as antidotes, [the transmitted precepts] consist of the eighty-four thousand doctrinal components. As the *Dialogue with the Four Goddesses* (*Caturdevīparipṛcchā*, T 446) says:

The Great Sage [divided] the doctrines into
Eighty-four thousand components.

It is also said that the antidotes for each of the twenty-one thousand kinds of desire, hatred and delusion, and for conduct which results from these three poisons in equal proportion, are respectively each of the twenty-one thousand components of the Vinayapiṭaka, Sūtrapiṭaka and Abhidharmapiṭaka, and of the Mantrapiṭaka of the Awareness-holders. As it is said in the *Revelation of Endless Treasure* (*mi-zad-pa'i gter bstan-pa*):

The antidote for the twenty-one thousand kinds
Of desire, hatred, and delusion,
And of conduct in which all three poisons
Are of equal proportion
Is said to be as many doctrinal components.

Elsewhere, in other [texts], the great paṇḍita Vimalamitra subsumed the mantras within the Abhidharmapiṭaka, saying in the *Great Perfection endowed with Conch-Syllables* (*rdzogs-pa chen-po dung-yig-can*, NYZ)[57] that among the piṭaka they belong to the Abhidharma. Accordingly, Kyi Nyima Dorje[58] and others also have claimed that the Abhidharmapiṭaka contains both outer and inner aspects, among which the mantras form the inner Abhidharma. Others such as master Śāntipā[59] and

Nartön Senge-ö have said that, subsuming the profound meaning, the Teacher included the mantras in the Sūtrapiṭaka; for the *Tantra of the Summation of the Real* (*Tattvasaṃgraha*, T 479) says:

> This sūtra is excellently explained.

And the *Vajravidāraṇā* (T 750) says:

> On listening to this sūtra.

Although our own tradition[60] does not contradict [masters] such as these, who subsumed [the mantras] within the Abhidharma[piṭaka] and the Sūtra[piṭaka] because they determined their positions in accord with one or another tantra text, still, with reference to the tantrapiṭaka in general, it is best if they are allocated an independent piṭaka, called either the Piṭaka of the Awareness-holders, or the Fourth Piṭaka. Therefore, the *All-Accomplishing King* says:

> That spoken of as the antidote which cures everything
> Is the Fourth Piṭaka teaching twenty-one thousand
> components.

And also in the *Tantra of the Dialogue with Subāhu* (*Subāhuparipṛcchānāmatantra*, T 805):

> Thirty million five hundred thousand teachings
> Were given by the conquerors
> In the Piṭaka of Awareness-holders.

Furthermore, the *Indestructible Peak* (*Vajraśekharamahāguhyayogatantra*, T 480) speaks of:

> The prātimokṣa, bodhisattva and inner vows
> Of the awareness-holders...

Hence, there is another way of subsuming [all the transmitted precepts] within three [sections], known as the piṭaka of the pious attendants, bodhisattvas and awareness-holders, which respectively teach these three vows.

The *Ornament of the Sūtras of the Greater Vehicle* (*Mahāyānasūtrālaṃkārakārikā*, T 4020, Ch.11, v.1ab) also says:

> The piṭaka appropriately number three or two
> Because they are compilations,
> And owing to nine basic conditions.

Accordingly, if all the doctrinal components are subsumed, it is appropriate to subsume them either under the three piṭaka of the Vinaya, Sūtra and Abhidharma, or under the two piṭaka of the pious attendants and bodhisattvas.

Here, with reference to the threefold subsumption, the reason for the precise number given is that the nine basic conditions are allocated between the three piṭaka, three for each, by attending to what must be renounced, studied and known. [The basic conditions] allocated to the three piṭaka by attending to what must be renounced are said to be the Sūtra as the antidote for doubt, the Vinaya as the antidote for involvement in the two extremes, and the Abhidharma as the antidote for holding to the supremacy of one's own view. By attending to what must be studied, [the basic conditions] are that the three trainings are explained by the Sūtra, superior moral discipline and mind are attained by the Vinaya, and superior discriminative awareness is attained by the Abhidharma. Then, by attending to what must be known, [the basic conditions] are that the doctrine and its meaning are explained by the Sūtra, attained by the Vinaya, and that, by the Abhidharma, one becomes skilled in the formulation of discourses.[61]

These nine basic conditions are allocated between the three piṭaka, but the importance of such a distribution is also that, by studying the three piṭaka, propensities are left in the mind, by reflecting upon them the meaning is realised, and by meditating upon them, conflicting emotions are pacified through tranquillity, and one is liberated by means of properly realising just what is, through higher insight. As it is said in the *Ornament of the Sūtras of the Greater Vehicle* (Ch.11, v.1cd):

> By understanding and pacifying propensities
> And by their proper realisation,
> These are the cause of liberation.

Incidentally, [the piṭaka] are verbally defined as follows: Aphorisms [or sūtras] are so named because they are derived from [the Sanskrit] *sūtra* [Tib. *mdo*]. As that same text [*Ornament of the Sūtras of the Greater Vehicle*, Ch.11, v.3ab] says:

> Because they describe situations and characteristics,
> The doctrines and their meanings,
> They are the Sūtra[piṭaka].

Hence the section of the sūtras.

[The Sanskrit word] *abhi* means manifest [or clear], and when added to other syllables such as [the Sanskrit] *mukhya*, comes to mean "growing manifest". As [the above-cited text, Ch.11 v.3cd] says:

> Because it is manifest or clear,
> Because it is repetitive,
> Because of its overpowering realisation,
> It is the Abhidharma.

Hence the Abhidharma [Tib. *chos mngon-pa*].

[The Sanskrit] *Vinaya* [Tib. *'dul-ba*] means discipline. By syllabic variation it comes to mean moral downfall (*vipatti*)[62] and so forth. As it is said [*Ornament of the Sūtras of the Greater Vehicle*, Ch.11, v.4]:

> It is the Vinaya
> Because it sets forth downfalls,
> The source of negativity,
> Its rejection and renunciation,
> Individuals and the affirmation of vows,
> And the classification and ascertainment of vows.

[The Tibetan] *sde-snod* derived from the [Sanskrit] word piṭaka conveys the meanings of a collection, [Sanskrit] *piṇḍaka*, and of a large measuring basket, [Sanskrit] *piṭaka*. The piṭaka are so called because they subsume all objects of knowledge in an expressible form, or gather many meanings within them.

TRANSMITTED PRECEPTS ACCORDING TO THEIR POWER

Fifth, when the transmitted precepts are classified according to their power, they form a vehicle because it appears that therein higher and higher paths are traversed, in the manner of a "vehicle". This notion is derived from the [Sanskrit] word *yāna* (*theg-pa*), which generally conveys the meaning of "transportation". Therefore it is said in the *Verse Summation of the Transcendental Perfection of Discriminative Awareness* (Ch.1, vv.21cd-22ab) also:

> This vehicle is the great celestial palace.
> Riding on that, which is the best of vehicles,
> Manifestly attaining to delightful bliss,
> All sentient beings pass into nirvāṇa.

When this vehicle is classified, one cannot say with absolute certainty that only such and such an enumeration is precise. This is because it was taught by the compassion of the Buddha in order to train each in accord with his or her needs, in a manner which suited the intellects of those requiring training. Such has also been said in the *Sūtra of the Descent to Laṅkā*, (Ch.2, v.203acd and Ch.10, v.445abc):

> In order to guide sentient beings completely,
> I have explained the entire vehicle.
> As such it is not an object of reference.

This is expressed more briefly in the *Lotus Sūtra* (*Saddharmapuṇḍarīkasūtra*, T 113, Ch.2, v.54ab):

> The vehicle is one.
> It is not divided into three.

According to such intentions, it is established that there is a single culminating vehicle. Yet, [other enumerations are also given]. There is a twofold classification into the lesser vehicle and the greater vehicle with its causal and resultant aspects;[63] and a threefold classification either into the vehicles of the pious attendants, self-centred buddhas and bodhisattvas or, as it is said in the *General Sūtra which Gathers All Intentions*, into the "vehicles of direction from the cause of suffering, austere awareness and overpowering means". Then, there is a fourfold classification which combines the three causal vehicles with the resultant vehicle, as stated in the *Magical Net of Mañjuśrī* (v.135cd):

> Attaining disillusionment through the three vehicles,
> One abides in the result through the single vehicle.

Five vehicles are also given when the single vehicle of the higher realms [of saṃsāra] is added as a path leading to these four vehicles. The *Secret Nucleus* (Ch.3, v.6) says:

> [Through] the vehicle of gods and humans,
> The vehicle of the pious attendants,
> The vehicle of the self-centred buddhas,
> The vehicle of the bodhisattvas
> And the unsurpassed vehicle...

Again, there are nine successive vehicles when the "vehicle of direction from the cause of suffering" is divided into the trio of the vehicles of pious attendants, self-centred buddhas and bodhisattvas; the "vehicle of austere awareness" into the trio of the Kriyātantra, Caryātantra and Yogatantra; and the "vehicle of overpowering means" into the Mahāyoga, Anuyoga and Atiyoga. Therefore it is said in the *All-Accomplishing King*:

> Existentially there is only one,
> But empirically there are nine vehicles.

In brief, it is said that the vehicle is inconceivable because its culmination cannot be reached until the degrees of the intellect have been exhausted. As it is found in the *Sūtra of the Descent to Laṅkā* (Ch.2, v.202ab and Ch.10, v.458ab):

> As long as there are perceptions,
> The culmination of the vehicles will never be reached.

From the standpoint of the essentially pure intellect, the path on which movement relies and the one by whom movement is made are not objective referents of even the word "vehicle". So [the same text, Ch.2, v.202cd and Ch.10, v.458cd] says:

> When the mind becomes transformed
> There is neither vehicle nor mover.

As for the following statement found in the *Commentary on the Nucleus of Indestructible Reality* (*Vajrahṛdayālaṃkāratantrapañjikā*, T 2515):

> For those who are Buddhists,
> Neither the fourth nor the fifth
> Are the Sage's intention.

There are some who affirm this to imply that only the enumeration of the three vehicles is valid. The actual meaning of this authoritative passage, however, is that the secret mantra texts are also subsumed within the vehicles of the pious attendants, self-centred buddhas and bodhisattvas and, on this occasion, only indicated in a general way. That statement, in particular, was purposefully made in order that the force of the verse beginning:

> For those who are Buddhists...

might refute any equation with the five basic philosophical systems of wrong view held by the Outsiders and other such enumerations. Indeed, if that passage were [considered to be] a refutation of precise enumerations other than three vehicles, how then could one understand the *Sūtra of the Descent to Laṅkā* (Ch.2, v.201 and Ch.10, v.457) which does speak of five vehicles?

> The vehicle of gods and the vehicle of Brahmā,
> And likewise the vehicles of the pious attendants,
> Tathāgatas and self-centred buddhas were explained by me.

The *Magical Net of Mañjuśrī* (v.135) also speaks of this [resultant] vehicle in the following words:

> One who strives to benefit living beings
> By means of the diverse vehicles
> Attains disillusionment through the three vehicles
> And abides in the single vehicle's result.

It is inappropriate to think that some pious attendant or self-centred buddha, who has achieved disillusionment from saṃsāra, starting from then develops the aspiration and application of the greater vehicle in his mind and attains omniscience, because [such texts] refer to the disillusionment of all three vehicles. Again, if one were to think that a bodhisattva who has attained disillusionment from the two extremes [of eternalism and nihilism] manifests the sublime buddha level through his own path of the causal greater vehicle, the above-cited statement [from the *Magical Net of Mañjuśrī*] that the single vehicle [of the result] follows after the three vehicles would be meaningless.

If one asks what system is followed here: Though the definitive ordering of many vehicles has been made provisionally, these vehicles, their circumstances and the varying degrees of their emphasis were revealed as a means of guiding those who require training. It is intended that when these vehicles have each arrived at the result of their respective paths, they are continued still higher in the supreme teaching of the vehicle of indestructible reality (*Vajrayāna*), the unique path on which all buddhas have progressed. Those others are revealed merely as paths leading to this vehicle, and the paths which are to be traversed until perfect enlightenment are positioned like the rungs of a ladder. Therefore Nāgārjuna has said:

> This method has been taught by the perfect Buddha in the manner of the rungs of a ladder.

And in the *Lotus Sūtra* (Ch.2, v.54):

> The teaching of the three vehicles of the sages
> Is the skilful means of the guiding [buddhas].
> Though apart from the single vehicle,
> A second does not exist,
> The three vehicles are taught for the sake of guidance.

And similarly in the *Sūtra of the Descent to Laṅkā*:

> Those who are worn out by the path of rebirth
> Will not find the meaning of respite therein
> [i.e. in lesser vehicles].

Furthermore, it is said in the *Pagoda of Precious Jewels* (*Ratnakūṭa*, T 45-93):

> Kāśyapa, there are two vehicles,
> The lesser and the greater.

According to such passages the arrangment of only three vehicles is not exclusively observed. In this [Vajrayāna] tradition of ours, there is a precise enumeration of four, namely, the vehicles of the pious attendants, self-centred buddhas, bodhisattvas and mantras, the last of which is classified into the three lower classes of tantra and the three aspects of creation and perfection belonging to the Unsurpassed Tantra (*bla-na med-pa'i rgyud*). Therefore, there is no room for contradiction in this orderly succession of the vehicle. It is appropriate either to apply the name "single vehicle" to all the doctrines subsumed by the buddha level, or to apply the names of the individual vehicles to each in particular, because they are the path which brings about progress towards all-knowing [enlightenment].

Among them, firstly the three outer vehicles of dialectics (*mtshan-nyid theg-pa gsum*) are called vehicles because they respectively reach the goal of an arhat, a self-centred buddha [whose enlightenment is attained] in the manner of a parrot [i.e. in a group] or in the manner of a rhinoceros [i.e. in solitude], and the eleventh level[64] which is called Universal Light (*Samantaprabhā*).

Secondly, the three vehicles of the outer tantras of austere awareness (*phyi-rgyud dka'-thub rig-pa'i theg-pa-gsum*) are vehicles because they respectively cause one to reach the level of a Holder of Indestructible Reality belonging to Three Enlightened Families (*rigs-gsum rdo-rje 'dzin-pa*), the level of a Sky-farer belonging to Four Enlightened Families (*rigs-bzhi mkha'-spyod-pa*), and the level of the Bounteous Array of Five Enlightened Families (*rigs-lnga stug-po bkod-pa*, Skt. *Ghanavyūha*).

Thirdly, the three vehicles of inner tantras of skilful means (*nang-rgyud thabs-kyi theg-pa gsum*) are explained by the word "vehicle" because they respectively cause one to reach the level of the Great Mass of Rotating Syllables (*yi-ge 'khor-lo tshogs-chen*), the level of Great Bliss (*bde-ba chen-po*) and the level of Unsurpassed Pristine Cognition (*ye-shes bla-ma*).

With an intention directed towards this, it is said in the *Sūtra of the Descent to Laṅkā* (Ch.2, v.202 and Ch.10, v.458):

> As long as sentient beings manifest
> There will be no end to the vehicles.

Therefore, it is said that there are as many approaches to the vehicle as accord with the number of thoughts in the mind.

In the context of this [tradition of ours] also, the higher and lower mantra vehicles are proportionately revealed to those of middling and highest acumen with an intention directed towards appraising the intellects of those requiring training, which are classified into three groups of three. In addition, in the fundamental path of each [vehicle] the view, meditation, conduct and result are completely explained, one by one, but only in the context of the individual capacity of their respective paths. Then, the culmination in which intellect and all things have ceased is established as the literal truth of the sublime path.

Furthermore, with regard to this point, the nirvāṇa of the vehicles of the pious attendants and self-centred buddhas does not reach the culmination except in a merely provisional way. Having actualised the result of their own paths, in order that the nirvāṇa of liberation might be attained, they are actually gathered in the greater vehicle because, starting from then, they are required to enter the greater vehicle.

In the causal aspect of the greater vehicle, and in the three lower classes of tantra, the definitive order of the result is taught as an enumeration. However, the distinctive attributes of profound hidden meaning [contained] in the path which causes progress toward this result are not revealed in them, and the actual result makes a great distinction between perfection and imperfection. For these reasons, it is in the unsurpassed vehicle that the skilful means is perfectly revealed. All the modes of the path and result contained in the lower [vehicles] are fulfilled and gathered in this unsurpassed vehicle because its uncommon doctrines are neither included nor represented in those [lower vehicles].

However, even within the unsurpassed [vehicle] there are some paths of both the creation and perfection [stages] in which the means of attainment is no more than an intellectual contrivance. Since the object of their attainment becomes compounded, they differ from the vision of pristine cognition in an extreme way. This being the case, the Great Perfection, where there is no room for contact with intellectually contrived doctrines, is the uncorrupted pristine cognition, the truth of the path subsumed by sublime minds and attained by the power of realisation, which accords with the abiding nature of the truth of reality. This is because the unerring reality, which the lower paths reveal through many enumerations as still to be actualised, is actually perceived here.

Because the vehicles, without exception, are gathered in this unsurpassed greater vehicle, it is also explained to be the "vehicle of pristine cognition". The *Sūtra of the Great Bounteousness of the Buddhas* says:

> Deeply involved in the vehicle of pristine cognition and in the greater vehicle, the mind dedicates the merit of those fundamental virtues.

And in the *Sūtra Requested by the Devaputra Suvikrāntacinta* (*Suvikrāntacintaparipṛcchāsūtra*, T 161):

> This vehicle of the greater vehicle,
> The inconceivable vehicle of the buddhas,
> Giving sentient beings a chance,
> Is the unsurpassed greater vehicle.
> Among all the vehicles that there are,
> This is intended to be supreme.
> So it is that, derived from the greater vehicle,
> All vehicles are well classified.

In the *Sublime Seal of Great Realisation* (*'phags-pa rtogs-chen phyag-rgya*, T 265)[65] it is said:

> Certainly there is only one vehicle.
> It does not exist as two or three.

And in its commentary:

> [The vehicles] of the pious attendants, self-centred buddhas, and the greater vehicle, are revealed in order to discipline those who require training by the three vehicles. In reality, there is but a single vehicle, the resultant vehicle of the indestructible reality.

And also in the *Intermediate Mother*:

> Subhūti, there is only one vehicle,
> The unsurpassed vehicle of the buddhas.

And in the *Sūtra of the Descent to Laṅkā*:

> Apart from the single vehicle, no second exists,
> And the third never exists except in the world
> When diverse living beings are trained.

Thus, on certain occasions such as these, the single vehicle is mentioned.

None the less, in certain [passages] there are also statements in which no limits such as two, three or five [vehicles] and so forth are enumerated. As it is said [in the same text, Ch.2, v.203cd and Ch.10, v.445cd]:

> In order to guide the childlike,
> I have explained the different vehicles.

Or:

> The vehicle of the gods and the vehicle of Brahmā...

And they are sometimes also said to be countless, for example [in the same text, Ch.2, v.202b and Ch.10, v.458b]:

> As long as the mind manifests....

Then, with an intention directed toward the individual who sees the unbewildered abiding nature of reality, it is also said that there is no vehicle. As the same *Sūtra of the Descent to Laṅkā* (Ch.2, v.202cd and Ch.10, v.458cd) says:

> When the mind becomes transformed
> There is neither vehicle nor mover.

Therefore, one should know that the statement of an exact, definitive order, saying "all such teachings necessarily have this but not that as their sole limit" is an indication that the manifestations of the intellect have not been turned in the direction of the genuine abiding reality.

In this [Nyingmapa tradition], for the while, the vehicle is precisely enumerated in nine sequences. Accordingly, the *Tantra of the Great Natural Arising of Awareness* says:

> There are sūtras and extensive teachings
> And extremely extensive teachings.
> The extremely extensive teachings
> Are the inconceivable eighty-four thousand
> [components],
> An exceedingly vast number,
> Inconceivable and immeasurable,
> Ineffable and most unthinkable.
> The extensive teachings, in the same way,
> Are held to have nine divisions:
> Those of pious attendants and self-centred buddhas,

> And similarly bodhisattvas,
> The Kriyā and the Ubhaya
> And likewise the Yoga vehicles are explained;
> Then the Mahāyoga and the Anuyoga
> And likewise the Great Perfection, Atiyoga.
> Explained in nine such divisions
> Is the great teaching of the doctrine.

So this is the way that the vehicle which disciplines those requiring training was proportionately revealed, divided into three groups of three for situations involving those of lowest, middling and superior acumen.

It is said in the *Great Array of the Highest*:

> The doctrines of my teaching
> Were revealed in two stages
> Through greater and lesser distinctions
> Among the intellectual degrees of sentient beings.
> Each has its own view and basic position.

These respective views are classified into the erroneous and the genuine, the latter of which is outlined as follows in the same text:

> The genuine [view] has three stages.
> For those of lesser and greater intellect,
> And likewise for those of middling intellect,
> It is revealed in three stages.
> The three lesser kinds
> Are the doctrines corresponding to the following intellects:
> That of the pious attendants for those polluted by ideas,
> That of self-centred buddhas for the perceptive,
> And that of bodhisattvas for those who penetrate ideas.
> As for the teaching given to those of the three middling [intellects],
> The Kriyātantra is for the lowest,
> The Caryātantra is for the low,
> And the Yogatantra for those endowed with [higher] consciousness.
> For those endowed with the three greater degrees [of intelligence],
> The creation [of Mahāyoga] is for those who have transcended mind,
> The perfection [of Anuyoga] is for those having the essence of mind[-as-such],
> And Great Perfection is for [those intent on]
> That which is supreme and most secret.

5 *Treatises*

[28a.5-41a.6] The definitive order of the treatises which comment on the intention [of these transmitted precepts] is explained under three headings: characteristic, verbal definition and classification.

Primarily, for one who is motivated by the thought of composing treatises, a mere treatise is characterised as an authoritative doctrine set forth in order that the philosophical system of one's own inclination might be revealed to others. Some which possess four special attributes are characterised as pure treatises, while those lacking any of the four special attributes are characterised as ostensible treatises.

The four special attributes are the attribute of motivation, when a composer of undistracted mind is motivated by discriminative awareness realised in words and their meaning, and by compassion which desires to benefit others; the attribute of expressive words which form refined metrical verses; the attribute of the expressed meaning which teaches the essential means for those requiring training, who aspire to liberation; and the attribute of purposeful composition which has the power [to inspire] the attainment of liberation by study of and reflection upon those words. The *Supreme Continuum of the Greater Vehicle* (Ch.5, v.19) says:

> There are some who teach with undistracted mind,
> Referring solely to the Conqueror, the Teacher,
> Conforming to the path which attains to liberation.
> Let them be reverently accepted
> Like the Sage's transmitted precepts.

Concerning the verbal definition, the [Tibetan] word *bstan-bcos* [or treatise] is derived from [the Sanskrit] *śāstra*, which is a compound of *śāsana*, to refine [or instruct], and of *trāya*, to protect. A treatise is so called because in its causal aspect it refines the three poisonous conflicting emotions into the possession of the three trainings, and in its resultant aspect it offers protection from the suffering of evil existences and rebirth. In other words, because it possesses the attributes of refinement and protection, it is a treatise. Such is said in the *Rational System of Exposition*:[66]

> That which refines the enemies, conflicting emotions,
> without exception,
> And affords protection from rebirth in evil existences,
> Is a treatise, for it has the attributes of refinement and
> protection.
> Treatises having both these attributes do not exist in
> other traditions.

The treatises are classified in six ways according to: (1) the standard of their composition, (2) the purpose of their composition, (3) their individual composers, (4) the manner of their composition, (5) the transmitted precepts which they explain, and (6) the meaning which they express.

TREATISES ACCORDING TO THE STANDARD OF COMPOSITION

Firstly, when classified according to the standard of their composition, there are four kinds of treatise. As the *Binding of the Chapters of the Gathering of the Sugatas* (*bde-'dus-kyi sa-gcod tshoms-kyi chings*) says:

> One should know that there are four kinds of treatise: The meaningless, the low in meaning, the erroneous, and the meaningful.

The meaningless [treatises] are exemplified by a treatise on dentistry for crows (*Kākadantaparīkṣāśāstra*),[67] those which are low in meaning by the treatises of the four common sciences, the erroneous by the treatises of the eternalistic extremists who are Outsiders, and the meaningful by the treatises of the inner science of the Buddhists.

Then, in the *Yogācāra Level* (*Yogācārabhūmi*, T 4035), nine kinds [of treatise] are explained:

> The meaningless, erroneous and the meaningful;
> The hypocritical, the merciless and those which renounce
> suffering;
> Those devoted to worldly study, polemics and attainment:
> These are the nine kinds of treatise.

When divided into these three groups of three, the first two members of each group are ostensible treatises of low standard, while the last member of each group is a genuine treatise of high standard.

TREATISES ACCORDING TO THE PURPOSE OF COMPOSITION

Secondly, when classified according to the purpose of their composition, there are three sorts of treatise: those which summarise the vast meaning of the transmitted precepts, those which rectify disorder [concerning the doctrine], and those which disclose profundity. Basic examples of these three are respectively the *Compendium of the Abhidharma* (*Abhidharmasamuccaya*, T 4049), the *Root Sūtra of the Vinaya* (*Vinaya-mūlasūtra*, T 4117), and the *Supreme Continuum of the Greater Vehicle*.

TREATISES ACCORDING TO THEIR INDIVIDUAL COMPOSERS

Thirdly, when classified according to their individual composers, there are five kinds. The treatises composed upon the teaching given by perfect buddhas are exemplified by the *Five Transmissions of the Gathering of the Sugatas* (*bde-'dus-kyi lung-lnga*), which were composed by Vajradharma,[68] and the *Five Doctrines of Maitreya* (*byams-chos sde-lnga*).

The treatises composed upon the teaching given by arhats are exemplified by the *Seven Sections of the Abhidharma (mngon-pa sde-bdun)*. Concerning the *Seven Sections*, the *Commentaries on the Treasury of the Abhidharma* (*Abhidharmakośabhāṣya*)[69] says:

> It is reported that the *Components of the Doctrine* (*Dharmaskandha*) is by Śāriputra,
> The *Treatise on Description* (*Prajñaptiśāstra*) is by Maudgalyāyana,
> The *Body of the Elemental Bases* (*Dhātukāya*) is by Pūrṇa,
> The *Body of Consciousness* (*Vijñānakāya*) is by Devaśarman,
> The *Entrance to Knowledge* (*Jñānaprasthāna*) is by Katyāyanaputra,
> The *Dissertation* (*Prakaraṇapāda*) is by Vasumitra,
> And the *Enumeration of Classes* (*Saṃgītiparyāya*) is by Mahākauṣṭhila.[70]

According to the tradition of the Vaibhāṣika, since the teachings given in fragments by the Teacher in different places and times to different individuals were compiled by the likes of Śāriputra, they are transmitted precepts similar to the *Collection of Meaningful Expression*. Therefore, they say that the *Treasury of Detailed Exposition* (*Vibhāṣākośa*) is earliest among the commentaries. According to the Sautrāntika, however, the *Seven Sections of the Abhidharma* were formulated by ordinary pious attendants. They hold the compilation of these words of the Teacher by arhats to be an ill rumour and say therefore that the *Seven Sections* are earliest among the commentaries. But this is doubtful for the following reason: Just as there is a distinct Abhidharmapiṭaka in the greater vehicle, so also the pious attendants must have had one, and the doubt arises that there is surely no reason for [the pious attendants] to have had the other two piṭaka in their separate volumes but not the Abhidharma. Hence, the tradition of the Vaibhāṣika would seem to be correct.

Supreme scholars say that the great master Vasubandhu[71] maintained the Sautrāntika view and therefore held these [*Seven Sections*] to be basic examples of treatises composed by arhats. Elsewhere, there are some who talk meaninglessly, saying the *Seven Sections* are not transmitted precepts because they contain many errors, and that rather they were composed by the likes of Śāriputra. Such talk would seem to be extremely foolish, for if such great arhats as the Supreme Pair [Śāriputra and Maudgalyāyana] who had been produced by the Teacher himself, through his emanational power, had misinterpreted the transmitted precepts, there would be no referential basis for recognising any genuine witness [to the Buddha's teaching] because the genuine witness would have all but come to an end. And if even the arhats had not seen the truth, it is implicit that there would have been no individual who saw the truth in the tradition of the pious attendants.

Furthermore, the treatises composed upon the teaching given by sublime bodhisattvas are exemplified by the extensive treatises of the *Five Sections of the Levels*,[72] and the abbreviated treatises known as the *Two Summations*, namely, the *Compendium of the Abhidharma* and the *Collection of the Greater Vehicle* (*Mahāyānasaṃgraha*, T 4048), all of which were composed by the sublime Asaṅga who was abiding on the third level.[73]

The treatises which were composed after prophetic declarations had been obtained from the meditational deities are exemplified by Dignāga's[74] *Compendium of Valid Cognition* (*Pramāṇasamuccaya*, T 4203) and the *Seven Treasuries of the Scriptures* (*gsung-rab mdzod-bdun*) by the great all-knowing Longcen Rapjampa.

The treatises which were composed by ordinary learned paṇḍitas to advocate their own philosophical systems and to reject the wrong ideas of others are exemplified by the *Eight Dissertations* (*Aṣṭaprakaraṇa*)[75] composed by the best of scholars Vasubandhu.

Therefore, when the treatises are classified according to the individuals who composed them, they are gathered into these five divisions.

TREATISES ACCORDING TO THE MANNER OF THEIR COMPOSITION

Fourth, when treatises are classified according to the manner of their composition, they fall into two categories: those which are labelled as commentaries on the transmitted precepts themselves, and those which are composed independently on the meaning of the transmitted precepts.

The former treatises are also of four kinds. Those which establish both word and meaning in detail are the extensive commentaries such as the *Commentary on the Prātimokṣa Sūtra in Fifty Sections* (*Prātimokṣasūtraṭīkā*, T 4106), and the great commentary on the *Kālacakra Tantra* entitled the *Taintless Light* (*Vimalaprabhā*, T 845). Those which explain the words in conjunction with annotations are verbal commentaries such as the *Commentary on the Collection of Meaningful Expressions* (*Udānavargavṛtti*, T 4100), and the *Commentary on the Secret Nucleus entitled Dispelling Darkness in the Ten Directions* (*snying-'grel phyogs-bcu mun-sel*). Those which disclose points which are hard to understand are the commentaries on difficulties such as the *Commentary on the Verse Summation of the Transcendental Perfection of Discriminative Awareness* (*Sañcayagāthāpañjikā*, T 3798 or T 3792). And those which subsume and establish the primary meaning are the commentaries of summarised meaning such as Vimalamitra's *Condensed Commentary on the Secret Nucleus* (*Guhyagarbhapiṇḍārtha*, P 4755), and the *Chapterless Commentary on the Supplementary Magical Net* (*le-lag-gi sa-ma 'grel*) by the great Rongzompa.

The latter category of treatises composed independently on the meaning of the transmitted precepts are of three kinds. Those which completely teach the meaning of one transmitted precept are exemplified by the *Root Sūtra of the Vinaya*, the *Ornament of Emergent Realisation* (*Abhisamayālaṃkāra*, T 3786), and Buddhaguhya's *Sequence of the Path of the Magical Net*. Those which teach the meaning of a fragmentary transmitted precept are exemplified by the *Stanzas on the Novitiate* (*Śrāmaṇerakārikā*, T 4124). And those which teach the meaning of many transmitted precepts are exemplified by Śāntideva's[76] *Compendium of Lessons* (*Śikṣāsamuccaya*, T 3939-40) and the all-knowing Jikme Lingpa's[77] *Precious Treasury of Enlightened Attributes* (*yon-tan mdzod*).

TREATISES ACCORDING TO THE TRANSMITTED PRECEPTS THEY EXPLAIN

Fifth, when classified according to the transmitted precepts which they explain, those treatises which comment on the transmitted precepts as a whole include commentaries on their verbal structure such as the grammatical treatises of the *Kalāpasūtra* (T 4282) and the *Grammar of Candragomin* (*Candravyākaraṇa*, T 4269), and commentaries on their meaning such as the *Seven Sections of Valid Cognition* [by Dharmakīrti][78] and the *Sūtra* [i.e. the *Compendium of Valid Cognition* by Dignāga].

Then, there are those which comment on the intention of the different particular promulgations of the transmitted precepts. Commentaries on the intention of the first promulgation of the doctrinal wheel are divided into those which establish the view, those which establish conduct and those which establish the integration of view and conduct.

The first [those which establish the view] are exemplified by the *Treasury of the Abhidharma*. After an introduction which gives the definitive order of the body [of the text], the first of its eight chapters teaches the objects of perception, the components, psychophysical bases and activity fields. The second teaches the nature of the sense organs and the manner in which things that are compounded arise, along with their causal basis, conditions and results. The third teaches the truth of origination of the world, the container and its contents, [which experience] the truth of suffering. The fourth teaches of [world-forming] deeds, and the fifth the definitive order of the conflicting emotions. The sixth, teaching of paths and individuals, reveals how the path is experientially cultivated. The seventh reveals the manner in which complete knowledge of the result is attained; and the eighth teaches the definitive order of the concentrative absorptions and so forth, because they are necessary to support the truth of the path which is the antidote expounded previously in the sixth chapter.

Secondly, those commentaries which teach the aspect of conduct are exemplified by the *Root Sūtra of the Vinaya*. This text details the seventeen *pāda* [of the *Vinayavastu*, T 1], the first of which teaches the ordination of a renunciate (*pravrajyā*). Thereafter, based on the sixteen remaining *pāda* and the *Two Analyses* [*of the Vows of Monks and Nuns – Bhikṣuvibhaṅga*, T 3 and *Bhikṣuṇīvibhaṅga*, T 5], it explains the Vinaya instructions of the *Supreme Text* (*Vinaya-uttaragrantha*, T 7), the *Analyses*, and so forth, with suitable excerpts from the chapters of the *Minor Transmissions*. These commentaries are also exemplified by the *Flower Garland of the Vinaya* (*Vinayapuṣpamālā*, T 4123) which, based on the *Analyses*, explains the Vinaya in conjunction with various other quotations.

Thirdly, those commentaries which teach the integration of view and conduct are exemplified by the *Great Treasury of Detailed Exposition*, in which it is the meaning of the philosophy of the Vaibhāṣika that is explained in detail. This text is said to have been composed in the time of Upagupta[79] by all the arhats in common, and there are also some who hold it to be the work of Yaśaḥ, Sarvakāmin and others. The Tibetans have confused these two reports, claiming that it was composed by five hundred arhats such as Sarvakāmin and Kubjita at the Narttaka Vihāra in the Northern Vindhya Mountains. Actually, it would seem correct to say that the words of these arhats were transmitted by the elders (*sthavira*) from ear to ear in one continuous arrangement, and later written down.

Again, the commentaries on the intention of the intermediate promulgation of the doctrinal wheel are also divided into treatises which establish the view, those which establish conduct and those which establish the integration of view and conduct.

First, [those which establish the view] are exemplified by Nāgārjuna's[80] *Collection of Madhyamaka Reasoning* (*dbu-ma rigs-tshogs*). There are four such collections of reasoning which refute the elaborate extremes that others seek to prove, namely, the *Root Stanzas on the Madhyamaka entitled Discriminative Awareness* (*Prajñānāmamūlamadhyamakakārikā*, T 3824), the *Sixty Verses on Reason* (*Yuktiṣaṣṭikā*, T 3825), the *Seventy Verses on Emptiness* (*Śūnyatāsaptati*, T 3827), and the *Refutation of Disputed Topics* (*Vigrahavyāvartanī*, T 3828). Then, with the inclusion of the *Technique of Pulverisation* (*Vaidalyasūtra*, T 3826), a collection of reasons which refute the arguments of sophists, there are reputed to be five collections of reasoning; or six with the further addition of the *Vindication of Conventional Truth* (*Vyavahārasiddhi*) which teaches that, although ultimately there is no substantial existence, conventions are valid with reference to relative appearances. None the less, according to the intention of the *Clearly Worded Commentary*, the enumeration of five collections of reasoning is said to be correct.[81]

Secondly, those commentaries which teach conduct are exemplified by the *Introduction to the Conduct of a Bodhisattva* (*Bodhisattvacaryāvatāra*, T 3871) by Śāntideva. This text teaches in ten chapters: the beneficial attributes of the enlightened mind; the importance of the repentance of sins; the seizing of the enlightened mind; vigilance with respect to [the enlightened mind]; the guarding of awareness of the present; [the transcendental perfections of] patience; perseverance; meditation; and discriminative awareness; and the dedication of merit.

Thirdly, those commentaries which teach the integration of view and conduct are exemplified by the *Ornament of Emergent Realisation*. This text affirms (Ch.1, v.4) that:

> The transcendental perfection of discriminative
> awareness
> Is correctly explained through eight topics.

Accordingly, the eight topics are the three concerned with the entry into objective understanding [namely, understanding all aspects of omniscience – *rnam-mkhyen*, Skt. *sarvākārajñāna*; the understanding of the path – *lam-shes-nyid*, Skt. *mārgajñatā*; and understanding all bases of omniscience – *thams-cad shes-pa-nyid*, Skt. *sarvajñatā*]; the four concerned with the entry into the properties of the doctrine [namely, manifestly realizing all aspects of omniscience – *rnam-kun mngon-rdzogs rtogs-pa*, Skt. sar*vākārābhisambodha*; the reaching of the summit of existence – *rtse-mor phyin-pa*, Skt. *murdhābhisamaya*; the culmination of saṃsāra – *mthar-*

gyis-pa, Skt. *anupurvābhisamaya*; and the instantaneous perfect enlightenment – *skad-cig-ma-gcig-gis mngon-rdzogs byang-chub-pa'i sbyor-ba*, Skt. *ekakṣaṇābhisamaya*]; and the buddha-body of reality (*chos-sku*, Skt. *dharmakāya*) which is the result of these entrances. These eight topics are established through seventy points.

Then, the commentaries on the intention of the final transmitted precepts, the third promulgation of the doctrinal wheel, are also divided into treatises which establish the view, those which establish conduct and those which establish the integration of view and conduct.

First, [those which establish the view] are exemplified by the *Supreme Continuum of the Greater Vehicle* and the *Two Analyses* [the *Analysis of the Middle and Extremes*, Skt. *Madhyāntavibhaṅga*, T 4021, and the *Analysis of Phenomena and Reality*, Skt. *Dharmadharmatāvibhaṅga*, T 4022]. In the *Supreme Continuum of the Greater Vehicle* (Ch.1, v.1), it is stated that:

> Buddha, doctrine, community, seed and enlightenment,
> Enlightened attributes and finally activities of the
> Buddha:
> The body of this entire treatise when condensed
> Consists of these seven topics of indestructible reality.

Accordingly, this text establishes seven topics: the Three Precious Jewels, their causal basis or seed which is the nucleus of the tathāgata (*tathāgatagarbha*), its result which consists of enlightenment, the sixty-four enlightened attributes, and the enlightened activities of the buddhas. The *Analysis of the Middle and Extremes* dispels the extremes of existence and non-existence, or of eternalism and nihilism, and then teaches the middle path. The *Analysis of Phenomena and Reality* teaches the distinctions between the apparitional reality or phenomena of saṃsāra, and the reality of nirvāṇā.[82] In this way, these two are analytical texts or *vibhaṅga*.

Secondly, those commentaries which teach conduct are exemplified by the *Twenty Verses on the Bodhisattva Vow* (*Bodhisattvasaṃvaraviṃśaka*, T 4081). This text establishes the four root downfalls and forty-six transgressions which confront a bodhisattva of average ability.

Thirdly, those which teach the integration of view and conduct are exemplified by the *Ornament of the Sūtras of the Greater Vehicle*. Its twenty-one chapters, beginning with the "Proof of the Transmitted Precepts of the Greater Vehicle" (*Mahāyānasiddhyādhikāra*), establish [this integration] according to ten categories such as [the gradation of] the families (*gotra*), volition with respect to the doctrine (*dharmaparyeṣṭya*) and so on.

Similarly, with reference to the Fourth Piṭaka, or the Piṭaka of the Awareness-holders, also, there are treatises which comment on the intention of the four or six classes of tantra. For example, the master Padmasambhava's *Garland of Views: A Collection of Esoteric Instructions* and Kawa Peltsek's[83] *Seventeenfold Appearance of the Sequence of the View* are representative of those which teach the view. Līlāvajra's *Clarification of Commitments* (*Samayavivyakti*, P 4744) exemplifies those which teach conduct, and the master Buddhaguhya's *Sequence of the Path of the Magical Net*[84] exemplifies those which teach the integration of view and conduct.

TREATISES ACCORDING TO THE MEANING THEY EXPRESS

Sixth, when the treatises are classified according to the meaning they express, there are those which teach quantitatively, those which teach qualitatively, and those which teach the means for attaining liberation and omniscience.

6 *Quantitative Treatises*

The treatises which teach quantitatively are both common and uncommon.

COMMON QUANTITATIVE TREATISES

The common sort are exemplified by the treatise on worldly behaviour entitled the *Point of Human Sustenance* (*Nītiśāstrajantupoṣaṇabindu*, T 4330) and Cāṇakya's[85] *Treatise on the Behaviour of Kings* (*Cāṇakyarājanītiśāstra*, T 4334). Although these are actually the causal bases for birth in the higher realms [of gods and humans], one may still proceed through them to [a rebirth which is] receptive to liberation. It is said in the *Hundred Verses on Discriminative Awareness* (*Prajñāśatakanāmaprakaraṇa*, T 4328):

> If human traditions are well practised,
> Progress to the god realms is not far distant.
> If one ascends the stairway of the gods and men,
> One is close to liberation.

The common treatises also include the eight subjects of scrutiny, concerning which [Rongzompa][86] says:

> These are the scrutiny of precious gems, land,
> Garments, trees, horses, elephants, men and women.

UNCOMMON QUANTITATIVE TREATISES

The Outer Sciences

[34b.2-40b.4] The uncommon sort of [quantitative] treatises are those which emphatically establish the first four sciences. In the *Sūtra Repaid with Gratitude* (*thabs-mkhas-pa chen-po sangs-rgyas drin-lan bsab-pa'i mdo*, T 353) it is said:

> If a bodhisattva does not study the five sciences, he can never obtain all-knowing pristine cognition in the unsurpassed, genuine and perfect enlightenment. This being the case, in order to obtain unsurpassed enlightenment, the five sciences should be studied.

And in the *Yogācāra Level*:

> If one were to ask what are the five sciences, they are as follows: the sciences of medicine, logic, grammar and artistic crafts, in addition to the inner science [of Buddhism].

The necessity of training in the first four of these sciences is also mentioned by the regent Ajita [Maitreya, in the *Ornament of the Sūtras of the Greater Vehicle*, Ch.11, v.60c]:

> In this way they eradicate [the faults] of others
> And bring them into the fold.

Thus grammar and logic are the two sciences which respectively eradicate wrong understanding in the words and meaning of others, while art and medicine are the two which respectively bring into the fold seekers of many useful skills in general, and the advantage of sound health in particular.

The Arts

Since the arts gather within them the other three, it is opportune first to explain the science of the arts. If one were to wonder how this gathering comes about, then it has been said:

> Through emphasising the body, the speech or neither,
> The arts are divided into those of body, of speech and of mind.

Accordingly, those emphasising movements of the body and expressions of speech, which are related to the mind, are assigned to the arts of body and speech, while those in which the mind refers to thought alone, unrelated to those two, are called the arts of the mind. For this reason, the arts contain infinite means of attaining many useful skills such as the sixty-four crafts explained in the commentaries on the *Sūtra of Extensive Play* (*Lalitavistarasūtra*, T 95) and the *Minor Transmissions*, the thirty designated arts, the eighteen appendages of music such as dancing and drama, the seven harmonious tones beginning with the middle tone and the tone of the sages, and the nine dramatic airs such as erotic grace – all of which are explained in the *Mahāvyutpatti*

(T 4346);[87] the eighteen artistic techniques explained in the sūtras; and the eight subjects of scrutiny.

Supreme among the arts of the body, in particular, are the methods of constucting the receptacles and contents which represent the Tathāgata's body, speech and mind [i.e. images, books and stūpas]. Supreme among the arts of speech are the songs of praise in the form of offerings to the conquerors, and supreme among the arts of the mind are the extraordinary aspects of discriminative awareness[88] produced by processes of thought such as study, reflection and meditation. The textual tradition which teaches these art forms comprises the *Sūtra Requested by Śāriputra* (*Śāriputrāṣṭaka*, P 5812), scriptures such as the *Kālacakra Tantra* (T 362) and the *Emergence of Cakrasaṃvara* (*Śrī-mahāsaṃvarodayatantrarāja*, T 373), along with their commentaries, the *Notebook on Iconometry* (*Pratibimbamānalakṣaṇanāma*, T 4316) which was composed by the *ṛṣi* Ātreya, the *Alchemical Transmutation into Gold* (*Rasāyanaśāstroddhṛti*, T 4314) and other such artistic treatises.

Medicine

The second of the sciences, medicine, is exemplified by Yutokpa's *Commentary on the Intention of the Four Glorious Tantras of Medical Science* (*dpal-ldan rgyud-bzhi'i dgongs-pa bkral-pa*, SP Vol.72).[89] The *Exegetical Tantra on the Eight Divisions of Medicine* [*yan-lag bshad-rgyud*, the second of the *Four Tantras*] says:

> In order to maintain health and heal sickness in the
> human body,
> Superior among the six classes of living creatures,
> And to attain longevity, the wealth of the doctrine and
> happiness,
> The topics of medical science, when condensed,
> Are explained under these four headings:
> That which is to be healed and the remedy which heals,
> The mode of healing and the healer.

Accordingly, that which is to be healed includes the disease and the invalid, the remedy which heals includes regimen, medication and diagnosis, the modes of healing or therapy include the prolonging of life free from disease and the healing of sickness when it occurs, and the healer includes the doctor and the nurses. These are also subsumed and taught in Śūra's *Eight Divisions of Medical Science* [*Aṣṭāṅga-hṛdayasaṃhitā*, T 4310 by Vāgbhaṭa].[90]

Grammar

The third of the sciences, grammar, is exemplified by the eight great grammatical sūtras which, as explained in the *Commentary of Pāṇini*

(*Pāṇinivyākaraṇasūtra*, T 4420), were known in India, or, in particular, by the treatises and instructions of the *Kalāpasūtra* and the *Grammar of Candragomin* which are known here in Tibet like the sun and moon.

The common purpose of grammar is [the utilisation of] nouns, words and syllables. As the *Ornamental Flower of Speech* (*smra-ba rgyan-gyi me-tog*) says:

> The support for the teaching of both
> The essence alone and its distinctive attributes
> Comprises nouns, words and syllables.

Then, the distinctive meaning [of grammar] is stated in the *Clear Nucleus Grammar* (*brda'-sprod snying-po gsal-ba*):

> Natural stems, affixation and morphological changes
> Are the concepts to be expressed in grammatical texts.

Now, the basis on which various morphological changes (*rnam-'gyur*) are made by means of affixation (*rkyen*) is the natural stem (*rang-bzhin*). And when it is classified:

> There are natural roots and nouns among which
> The former contains the meaning of the verb.
> [The latter] comprises the three genders,
> With final vowels and consonants.

Both of these natural grammatical forms [roots and nouns] are subject to affixation or the adjuncts of grammar which cause nouns, words and phrases to be appropriately formed. There are in this respect seven kinds of affixation through which the root takes form as gender, the root takes form as an inflected word, the root takes form as a root, gender takes form as gender, nominal stems take form as nominal stems, gender takes form as a root, and gender takes form as an inflected word. Among them, the second and seventh [through which the root takes form as an inflected word and gender takes form as an inflected word][91] together are the common substratum (*samānādhikaraṇa*) of affixation and the declensions (*vibhakti*). Tense and meaning are differentiated by means of the second kind of inflection through which roots endowed with tense-affixes (*ti-ādi*) take form as words. Morphological change therefore includes strengthening and elision which result from the conjunction of natural stems and inflections, or of the interconnecting syllables. As the great Pang Lotsāwa [Lodrö Tenpa] has said:

> Strengthening and elision are morphological changes
> Which occur by conjunction of natural stems and affixes,
> Or by conjunction of the syllables alone.

Furthermore, the basic paradigms are revealed by the rules for euphonic conjunction (*sandhi*), the tables of nouns, the rules for syllabic quantity (*vṛtta*) and so forth, while their branches include the paradigms of the verbal roots, prepositional prefixes (*upasarga*) and suffixes (*uṇādi*).[92]

Dignāga

Logic

The fourth of the sciences, logic, is explained according to eight categories of dialectics. As the *Compendium of Valid Cognition* (*Pramāṇasamuccayavṛtti*, T 4204, Ch.1, v.2) says:

> Direct perception and inference,
> Along with their invalid forms,
> Are for one's own understanding.
> Proof and refutation
> Along with their invalid forms
> Cause others to understand.[93]

In this way, each of the four – direct perception, inference, formal argument and *reductio ad absurdum* – is ascertained to have both valid and invalid forms, [making eight categories]. When they are condensed, they are gathered under two headings: the means of comprehending that which is to be appraised by oneself, and the means of communicating that comprehension to others.

Now since the same text says:

> *The characteristic is one of infallible knowledge*[94]

logic is characteristically said to be reason which is infallible with respect to the objects of one's own experience as they newly arise. Therefore, it establishes an epistemic standard for making appraisals, in the manner of a measuring container or a scale-balance. There are three kinds of objects to be appraised, namely, the directly evident, the indirectly evident, and the indirectly evident to an extreme degree. As for their means of appraisal: There are three kinds of direct perceptions for appraising directly evident objects, namely, the direct perception of the sense organs, the direct perception of intrinsic awareness, and the direct perception of yoga. There are three logical axioms of implicit inference for the appraisal and proof of the indirectly evident objects, namely, the axiom of the result, the axiom of identity and the axiom of absence of the objective referent.[95] The axiom concerning those objects of appraisal which are indirectly evident to an extreme degree necessarily relies on scriptural authority of which the purity is established by three types of scrutiny, for it is not proven by the [other] two kinds of axiom – direct perception and implicit inference.

The treatises of logic are exemplified by the *Sūtra of Valid Cognition* which was composed by the master Dignāga, and the commentaries on its intention, the *Seven Sections of Valid Cognition*, which were composed by the glorious Dharmakīrti. Among them, the dissertations (*prakaraṇa*) of the *Seven Sections* include three treatises which are comparable to the main body [of the *Sūtra*], namely, the extensive *Exposition of Valid Cognition*, the intermediate *Ascertainment of Valid Cognition* (*Pramāṇaviniścaya*, T 4211), and the condensed *Point of Reason* (*Nyāyabindu*, T 4212). And they also include four treatises which proceed from them, comparable to the separate limbs, namely, the *Point of the Axioms* (*Hetubindu*, T 4213) and the *Inquiry into Relations* (*Sambandhaparīkṣā*, T 4214), which proceed from [the topic] concerning inference for one's own sake; and the *Proof of Other Minds* (*Saṃtānāntarasiddhi*, T 4219) and the *Reasoning of Polemics* (*Vādanyāya*, T 4218), which proceed from [the topic] concerning inference for others' sake.

Again, there are certain great scholars who say that the logical treatises are treatises of the inner science [of the true doctrine] because they belong to the Abhidharmapiṭaka, but this would appear to be incorrect.[96] We think as much because in many sources statements are found resembling the following quotation from the *Compendium of Valid Cognition* (Ch.6):

> By means of the true expression of logic and of objects which are to be appraised, the tenets of the extremists are [seen to

be] without essence. This [treatise] has been composed in order to oppose those who cling to their view. Yet, for this very reason, it is not concerned with providing an entrance to the Tathāgata's teaching; for his doctrine is not an object of sophistry.

And also [*Pramāṇasamuccayakārikā*, T 4203, Ch.6]:

The idea that one is lead to reality
By the path of sophistry
Is very remote from the teaching of the Sage.

Dharmakīrti

Minor Sciences

[38a.4-40b.4] There still remain five minor sciences which are designated as branches of either the artistic or the grammatical sciences. It has been said:

As for the quintet of astrology, poetics,
Prosody, synonymics and drama,
Their reputation in India as the "five sciences"
Resounded like a banner in the wind.

Astrology

Among these five, concerning astrology: There are ten planets demarcating celestial longitude, along with the moving band of constellations and lunar mansions[97] with reference to the objective basis [of space], and the years, months, days, and two-hour periods[98] with reference to time, on which basis celestial longitude is determined. Astrology is a procedure for correctly determining the degrees of celestial longitude demarcated by these [planets and constellations] and their quarterly aspects (*rkang-pa*). As a direct result of this, with reference to their cyclical motion, the calculations of the ascendent conjunctions in the sky are explained along with the calendrical cycle of the four seasons on earth, the rising and setting of the planets through their respective aspects, the eclipsing of the sun and moon through orbital direction, and the fading and rising of malign circumstances which occur in accordance with the respective celestial longitudes [of the planets and constellations].

When abbreviated, astrology is gathered under the two headings of that which is to be calculated and the calculation. Such are the astrological treatises which follow the *Commentary on the Kālacakra Tantra*, the *Commentary on the Four Seats* (*Catuḥpīthatantrarājasmṛtinibandha*, T 1607), and other such uncommon treatises of the Teacher's [doctrine], as well as those treatises which are held in common with the Outsiders, including the *Astrological Treatise entitled Martial Conquest* (*Yuddhajayanāmatantrarājasvarodaya*, T 4322).

Other than astrology, the science of elemental divination or geomancy (*'byung-rtsis*), also known as Chinese divination because it originated from China, is very necessary for the scrutiny of individual awareness. Among the cycle of texts concerning the five elements, which are the object of the calculation, there are two sets of techniques – those concerning the natural basic calculation, and those concerned with the appearances bewildered by ignorance which are subsumed within four *kaptse* or diagrams. The latter depict the discrete entities of the elements, the objective appearances, the acting intellect and the grasping mind. The method of calculation comprises nine topics:

> Bases (*khams*), years, numbers (*sme-ba*) and trigrams (*spar-kha*),[99]
> Months, days, two-hour periods, planets and stars.

The treatises which explain elemental divination are mentioned in the tantras, and would appear to be taught in their esoteric instructions such as the *Mother and Son of the Clarifying Lamp* (*gsal-sgron ma-bu*).[100]

Poetics

The treatises of poetics are exemplified by the *Mirror of Poetics* (*Kāvyādarśa*, T 4301) of Daṇḍin,[101] an exegesis which, in two special topics, subsumes the techniques through which the masters of the past formed the meaning desired in all poetical expressions, and embellished that body of verse, prose and mixed verse and prose. In the *Mirror of Poetics* (Ch.1, vv.10-11ab) it says:

> They excellently reveal the body
> And also the ornaments of poetics.
> The body is the string of words
> Determining the desired meaning;
> It consists both of verse and prose
> Or of a blend of verse and prose.

And (Ch.2, v.1ab):

> The features which embellish poetry
> Are well expressed as ornaments.

Accordingly, when classified, these ornaments include the uncommon sort, which is divided between the traditions [of Gauḍa and Vaidarbha],[102] and the common sort, which consists of thirty-five ornaments of sense (*arthālaṃkāra*) such as natural description (*rang-bzhin brjod-pa*), simile (*dpe*) and metaphor (*gzugs*), and of phonetic ornaments (*śabdālaṃkāra*) of which it is said:

> There are many such enumerations
> Of precise composition which are hard to execute,
> Such as alliteration and geometric poetry,[103]
> Assonance and so forth.

And there are sixteen ornaments of enigmatic innuendo (*gab-tshig*, Skt. *prahelikā*).

Prosody

The treatises of prosody are exemplified by the *Precious Source of Prosody* (*Chandoratnākara*, T 4303-4) of the master Śāntipā [Ratnākaraśānti], which in general is the basis for any metrical composition. There are those who, following the *Collection of Prosody* (*sdeb-sbyor-gyi tshoms*, SK Vol.5) which was composed by the doctrine master Sakya Paṇḍita,[104] disagree with the *Precious Source*, claiming that Sakya Paṇḍita does not cut the flow of composition into *pāda* or metrical lines. However, I think the intentions [of the two works] do agree, because it is said in the *Mirror of Poetics* (Ch.1, vv.80-1):

> When there are many compounded expressions,
> The text is sustained by passages of prose.
> Even in verse, with the exception of the southerners,[105]
> This custom alone is observed:
> Witness the heavy and light syllables,

The varying number of syllables,
The undulations in form,
Its expression and so forth.

Such an arrangement would appear to be a basis for investigation for those who have said that no such thing has been mentioned in this text on poetics [*Mirror of Poetics*], and it is clearly necessary to explain that the teaching in the *Precious Source* refers to the prosody of verse alone.

With reference to this text [*Precious Source*], verse is the basis of any metrical composition. When classified it consists of rules concerning syllabic quantity (*vṛtta*) and metrical feet [*jāti*, groups of morae]. As the text says [cf. *Mirror of Poetics*, Ch.1, v.11cd]:

These four *pāda* [i.e. lines] of verse
Are classified according to syllabic quantities
Or in metrical feet.
Vṛtta is the counting of syllables,
And *jāti* is the counting of morae.

Syllabic quantities are of three types: those in which the syllables form lines of equal length, those which form semi-equal lines, and those which form unequal lines. Metrical feet, on the other hand, form the *āryā* or sublime metre, the *mātrā* or morae metres, and lines of equal feet.

Synonymics

The treatises of synonymics are exemplified by the *Treasury of Amarasiṃha* (*Amarakośa*, T 4299). This text contains homonyms such as the [Sanskrit] word *go*, and synonyms such as the epithets for the sun which include "green-horsed", "hot-rayed" and more than a hundred others. As the text says:

There are single words conveying many meanings,
  clearly expressed.
The very word *go* has ten such meanings,
Including: a topic for discussion, light rays and
  cattle.
There are also many words conveying a single
  meaning:
The sun itself is known as "green-horsed" and
  "hot-rayed",
And as "gem of the sky", "friend of the lotus", and
  so on.

Drama

The treatises on drama are exemplified by the *Dramatical Treatise* (*Nāṭyaśāstra*) of Bharata and the *Utter Delight of the Nāgas* (*Nāgānan-*

danāmanāṭaka, T 4154). Drama means that certain works of verse, prose and a mixture of verse and prose are presented in a blend of the four languages [Sanskrit, Prakrit, Paiśācī, and Apabhraṃśa]. These works also include five sequences of dramatic juncture (*sandhi*) beginning with the introduction, along with four dramatic manners (*vṛti*) such as the dialogue, with their sixteen aspects such as the elucidation (*prarocanā*). Within these, there are interwoven [dramatic features] including the seven harmonious tones, the thirty-six characteristics such as embellishment and abbreviation, and artistic skills such as graceful song and dance (*lāsya*), the wearing of garlands, and aspects of other dramatic junctures.

7 *Treatises of Inner Science*

QUALITATIVE TREATISES

[40b.4] The treatises which teach qualitatively are exemplified by those of Madhyamaka which emphatically establish the two kinds of selflessness [of individuals and phenomena].

TREATISES TEACHING LIBERATION AND OMNISCIENCE

[40b.5-41a.6] The treatises which teach the means of attaining liberation and omniscience are exemplified by the *Bodhisattva Level* (*Bodhisattvabhūmi*, T 4037) and the *Introduction to the Conduct of a Bodhisattva*. If one were to wonder what sort of character the masters who compose such treatises have, the superior type includes masters who perceive the truth of reality, such as the glorious lord Nāgārjuna and the sublime Asaṅga. The middling type includes masters, such as Dignāga and Candragomin,[106] to whom permission has been actually granted by the meditational deities, and the lesser type includes those who are learned in the five sciences and possess the esoteric instructions of the lineage of the gurus, such as masters Śrīgupta and Śākyamati.[107]

Then, the instructions of the lineage which they possess have five aspects. As the *Rational System of Exposition* says (cf. BST 4, p.277):

> To those who wish to explain the sūtras
> I must give instructions.
> The following are the aspects of instruction
> Which are to be explained:
> One must give exegeses by relating
> The purpose and the condensed meaning,
> The words along with the meaning,
> And also with response to objections,
> And the outline which connects the text.

Alternatively, they are to be explained through five calculated approaches which conform to five headings given [by the Teacher]. As it is said in the *Clarifying Lamp* (*Pradīpodyotana*, T 1785):

> What is this tantra's title?
> For whose benefit is it composed?
> Who is the composer?
> What is its scope?
> And what is its purpose?

This completes the anthology through which the doctrines of saṃsāra and nirvāṇa are recognised in general and their characteristics established, the first part of this book, the *Feast in which Eloquence Appears*, which is a definitive ordering of the precious teaching of the vehicle of indestructible reality according to the Ancient Translation School.

Part Two
The Nature of the Teacher endowed with the Buddha-bodies

Introduction

[41b.1-41b.4] Having recognised the respective doctrines of saṃsāra and nirvāṇa, and generally outlined the structure of the true doctrine, now I shall reveal the structure of the Teacher endowed with the three buddha-bodies (*trikāya*), the Conqueror who is the ground from which that profound, true doctrine originated.

This is divided into four sections, namely, (1) the mode of awakening in the buddha-body of reality which is the Primordial Lord [Samantabhadra], (2) the manner in which his emanation Vajradhara attained the quiescence [of nirvāṇa] in this field [of the trichiliocosm],[108] (3) the manner in which the two buddha-bodies of form emanate from him, and (4) the distinctive attributes of the buddha-bodies and pristine cognitions as revealed in the causal and resultant vehicles.

1 *Samantabhadra, the Buddha-body of Reality*

[41b.4-45a.4] In general, it is the opinion of the lower vehicles that one such as this teacher of ours [Śākyamuni Buddha], after accumulating the provisions [of merit and pristine cognition] conducive to liberation over three "countless" aeons[109] as an ordinary person, in his final existence subjugated Māra at dusk in Vajrāsana, the Point of Enlightenment.[110] Developing the path of connection in his mind at midnight by means of the actual foundation of the four meditative concentrations, he manifested the six transcendental perfections at the very moment when the pale light of dawn appeared, and attained buddhahood endowed with the bodies of reality and form. Apart from his promulgation of the doctrinal wheel to [the five noble companions][111] – from Ajñātakauṇḍinya to Bhadrika and so forth – [these lower vehicles] do not admit the complete definitive structure of [the Teacher's] three buddha-bodies.

Then, in the sūtras of the greater vehicle the three buddha-bodies are taught, while the mantra texts also refer to the five outer and inner awakenings, as well as to the holder of indestructible reality who embodies cause and result, the emanational buddha-body (*nirmāṇakāya*) which comprises the physical form and energy channels [of that Teacher], the buddha-body of perfect rapture (*sambhogakāya*) which is his speech and vital energy, the buddha-body of reality (*dharmakāya*) which is his mind and seed in the form of nectar, the essential body (*svābhāvikakāya*) which is his nucleus and the vital energy of pristine cognition, and so forth. These, however, have all been revealed only according to the acumen of those requiring training and the volition of the yogin on the path.

In this [Nyingmapa tradition], however, it is explained in accordance with the uncommon transmission of the Indestructible Nucleus of Inner Radiance (*'od-gsal rdo-rje snying-po*),[112] supreme and unsurpassed among the vehicles, that pristine cognition itself, or intuitive awareness, is liberated right where it is through having recognised is nature as Samantabhadra to be self-manifesting – at the very moment when the ground arises as phenomena from the primordial ground. Samantabhadra is the teacher in whom both saṃsāra and nirvāṇa are indivisible, the antecedent of all, who holds sway over existence and quiescence in their entirety, and who is the expanse of reality and the nucleus of the sugata. Thus buddhahood is attained in the naturally present pristine cognition, without thoughts of the three times, beginning, middle, and end, or of all else that can be known. As the *Supreme Continuum of the Greater Vehicle* (Ch.2, v.38ab) says:

> Without beginning, middle, or end, and indivisible,
> It is neither two, nor three,[113] taintless and without thought.

Samantabhadra and Consort

And in the *Magical Net of Mañjuśrī* (vv.99cd-100ab):

> Spontaneously present without thought,
> Is the agent of the buddhas of the three times;
> Buddha without beginning or end,
> He is the original, impartial Buddha.

This buddhahood is supreme renunciation, because the two kinds of suddenly arisen obscuration [of conflicting emotions and that which is knowable], along with their propensities which are bewildering appearances non-existent in reality, are totally purified in that intrinsic essence. It is also supreme realisation because great pristine cognition, which does not divide consciousness and its object in two, sees existence and quiescence all-pervasively and without partiality. And it is supreme mind which naturally performs spontaneously present enlightened activity by means of [the aforementioned renunciation and realisation] for the sake of all living beings without qualification. As it is said in the *Ornament of Emergent Realisation* (Ch.1, v.43):

> Inasmuch as three supreme qualities are present
> In the trio of mind, renunciation and realisation,
> Which are supreme among all sentient beings,
> This purposeful activity of the self-emergent ones
> should be known.

Now, this buddhahood is the pristine cognition of the expanse of reality (*dharmadhātujñāna*), which is without object of reference and free from all elaborate extremes, and the pristine cognition of sameness (*samatājñāna*) which does not abide in the extremes of existence and quiescence because it sees neither good nor evil throughout the extent of saṃsāra and nirvāṇa equally. The hollowness of mere explanations through which the causal vehicles explain how all that is manifest abides in the expanse of reality, firm in the cessation of quiescent [nirvāṇa], is surpassed by mastery over that pristine cognition which qualitatively knows [the view, *ji-lta-ba mkhyen-pa'i ye-shes*].[114] The subtle natural expression of that pristine cognition continues to abide in the great field of the inwardly radiant youthful vase body (*gzhon-nu bum-pa sku*),[115] as if it were the light contained within a crystal. It is also unobscured when formally absorbed as the ground or causal basis of the range of objects perceived by the tathāgatas' pristine cognition of discernment. These are, namely: the buddha-body of form (*rūpakāya*) which appears before the eyes of the conquerors' sons or lords of the tenth level,[116] and of the host of those to be trained; the buddha-speech which is heard by their ears; the fragrance of sublime moral discipline which they scent; the savour of the doctrine which they relish; the bliss of contemplation which they feel; the appraisal of the doctrine which they make through their discriminative awareness endowed with ideas and scrutiny; and so forth.

Then, in the spontaneously present Realm of the Bounteous Array (*Ghanavyūha*), a field which is manifest in and of itself through the blessing or consecration of this [youthful vase body], far removed from objects of thought, expression and symbolism, and which is unlimited and without direction, the Teachers of the Five Enlightened Families abide in a great display of undifferentiated buddha-body and pristine cognition. These teachers are identified with the maṇḍala of the body of perfect rapture (*sambhogakāya*) which manifests in and of itself, is endowed with five certainties and is subsumed by the pristine cognition of buddhahood.

However, at other times, they perceive that when the expressive power by which the ground arises as phenomena from the primordial ground is not intrinsically recognised, there are dream-like sentient beings who, bewildered without cause for bewilderment, move in a cycle of ostensible suffering. Generating loving compassion for the sake of these beings, they emanate an extensive array of fields including those situated on the contemplative hand gesture of Vairocana the Great Glacial Lake (*gangs-chen mtsho*), who embodies the five kinds of pristine cognition and the self-manifesting body of perfect rapture.[117] This array also includes the great fields which extensively fill all the space in each of Vairocana's pores occupied by indivisible atomic particles of the four elements, and which are absolutely beyond all objects of expression such as shape, extent and altitude.

All these fields have distinct features; for the expanse of reality is filled with oceans of fields and buddha-bodies which do not intermingle, take birth or change into other forms, alter or decline, and which are not even slightly covered by extraneous matter. As it is said in the *Sūtra of the Arrayed Bouquet* (*Gaṇḍavyūhasūtra*, T 44, cf. Ch.34, v.28):

> Even on a single hair-tip,
> Is an unthinkable array of fields.
> Though they have various shapes,
> They do not differ,
> And they do not become intermingled.

And in the *Sūtra of Inconceivable Secrets* (*Tathāgatācintyaguhyanirdeśasūtra*, T 47):

> Śāntamati, all that is pervaded by space
> Is pervaded by the tathāgatas' fields and bodies.

Similarly, these fields are arrayed in three dissimilar dimensions which are respectively occupied by the buddhas' three bodies. In the dimension of the buddha-body of reality they are called Fields of the Indestructible Nucleus of Inner Radiance (*'od-gsal rdo-rje snying-po*). In the dimension of the buddha-body of perfect rapture, manifest in and of itself, they are called the Fields of Brahmā's Drumbeat (*tshangs-pa'i rnga-sgra*). And in the dimension of the emanational body they are called the Aeon of Great Brahmā (*tshangs-chen-gyi bskal-pa*). Oceans of buddhas who are emanations of the Primordial Lord [Samantabhadra] himself, appear in these dimensions throughout the three times, and there are also oceans of world systems of sentient beings which exist, but their entire extent, encompassed by the four elements and space, is confined within this Aeon of Great Brahmā.

In this aeon, diverse appearances of happiness and suffering are experienced; for example, the impure sentient beings transfer consciousness at death and emerge at birth, buddhas pass into nirvāṇa, the teaching endures and declines, the path is attained and so on. Similarly, in the space of each atomic particle, measureless fields containing mountains, continents and oceans appear, and in addition, each atomic particle of the world on the surface of a single atom consists of measureless world systems of sentient beings well furnished with causes and conditions. These include emanations of the sugatas, the most powerful of bodhisattva aspirations to purify lands [into buddha-fields], the accumulation of deeds manifestly gathered by the bewildered perceptions of sentient beings, and excellent attainments which spring from reality. As it is said in the *Great Bounteousness of the Buddhas*:

> Since the object of the buddhas' pristine cognition is
> unthinkable,
> So are these emanations of their blessing.
> Teaching in oceans of fields, without extreme or centre,
> Vairocana has totally purified them through the doctrine.
> In accord with enlightened mind, which is the thought of all,
> He has purified unthinkable oceans of aspirations.
> Since the oceans of deeds of sentient beings are
> unthinkable,
> All the oceans of fields in all directions emerge.
> The emanations of all the bodhisattvas and
> The approach to all-knowing reality
> Have been actually attained by all the oceans of aspirations,
> And in the expanse of space, infinite fields emerge.
> By oceans of conduct, beings without extreme or centre
> practise,
> And enter the range of measureless sugatas.
> Purifying all the oceans of fields in the directions,
> They purify each field for infinite aeons.
> All the oceans of fields of deeds
> Which are the thoughts of sentient beings,
> Inconceivable in expanse, emerge.

And in the *Aspiration of Good Conduct* (*Bhadracaryāpraṇidhānarāja*, T 44 and T 1095, v.29bcd):

> The three times are measured in the space of a hair,
> By oceans of buddhas in oceans of fields,
> Practising and manifesting for oceans of aeons.

Moreover, these fields are radiant apparitions, not existing in reality, because in the expanse of reality relative appearances have not existed from the beginning.

2 *Vajradhara, the Emanation of Samantabhadra*

[45a.4-46b.4] Secondly, concerning the manner in which Vajradhara attained buddhahood in this field [of the trichiliocosm]. For the sake of those requiring training in this field, the original buddha Samantabhadra gave teaching through his great emanation who is learned in skilful means, illustrating the manner in which ordinary, indifferent persons would generate the enlightened mind, and so he sent forth a display of the modes and actions of buddhahood. Such modes [of emanation] are also known in the ordinary vehicle. As it is said in the *Sūtra of the Meeting of Father and Son* (*Pitāputrasamāgamanasūtra*, T 60):

> Great Warrior, learned in skilful means,
> You have been the Conqueror in one billion aeons
> In order to mature sentient beings,
> And though you have revealed yourself as the Buddha,
> Even today, my Guide,
> You reveal yourself as manifold buddhas.

And in the *Sublime Great Bounteousness of the Buddhas*:

> Though they have well attained oceans of enlightenment,
> In order to mature fully oceans of sentient beings,
> They continually reveal their oceanic cultivation of
> enlightened mind,
> And at all times teach oceans of unobscured conduct.
> Such are the emanations of the sugatas.

Immeasureable aeons ago,[118] in the field which is called Array of Natural Expression (*rang-bzhin rnam-par bkod-pa*), the emanation of the Primordial Lord [i.e. Vajradhara, the emanation of Samantabhadra] offered a golden vajra to the Buddha Puṣpa Mahāroca (*me-tog mdzes-pa chen-po*), and so first aspired to supreme enlightenment. Then, after two such lifetimes in which he became the son of a householder, Sudāna (*legs-sbyin*), who was named Maṇimālya (*nor-bu'i phreng-ba*), he listened to the doctrine in the presence of the Buddha Sucaritacakra (*'khor-lo legs-par spyod-pa*); and thereafter, manifesting as the son of one Vidyutprabha (*glog-gi 'od*), who was named the brahman youth Sudatta (*bram-ze'i khye'u legs-byin*), he studied the doctrine under the Buddha Kalyāṇamati (*dge-ba'i blo-gros*) and abided in contemplation for seven years. Finally after seventy-five [years], on the summit of the mountain called Array of Gem Clusters (*rin-po-che'i phung-po rnam-par bkod-pa*), he revealed the way of manifest, perfect buddhahood and continued to abide in the intention of the buddha-body of reality for one great aeon.

Vajradhara

Then he naturally appeared as the buddha-body of perfect rapture in a cycle of ornaments and colours, and from its nature, self-manifesting maṇḍalas of the Conquerors of the Five Enlightened Families emerged of their own accord beyond number. However, among these apparitional forms, his emergence in the body of Vajradhara, perfectly endowed with the major and minor marks,[119] derived from that offering of the vajra, which was the supporting basis of his aspiration.

While these [deities] also have mastery over the thirty-six actions of the wheel of the inexhaustible ornaments of buddha-body, speech and mind, which form one aspect of the teaching on the Innermost Spirituality (*snying-thig*),[120] in reality, as explained above, they are no different from that magical emanation of the Primordial Lord, who is learned in skilful means. For there are numerous names which describe him, including: Vajradhara, who teaches most tantras of the way of secret mantra; Samantabhadra, who is the teacher of the profound abiding nature or indestructible reality of the utterly secret Innermost Spirituality; and elsewhere he is referred to as the Original True Buddha, Vajrasattva and so on. So it is that the *Collection of Realisation* (*Sarvakalpasamuccayasarvabuddhasamāyogottaratantra*, T 367) says:

> Supreme among all the purest,
> Primordially liberated tathāgata,
> Samantabhadra, the lord of all,
> Is certainly the enlightened mind itself.

And again:

> Spiritual warrior without beginning or end,
> Vajrasattva, supreme delight,
> Samantabhadra, the lord of all,
> Indestructible nucleus, highest of the high –
> Since he is primordial and without end,
> He is considered the first of the true [buddhas].
> Since he is the centre of all maṇḍalas,
> He is the true lord of the true [buddhas].

3 *The Two Buddha-bodies of Form*

[46b.4] Thirdly, there is the buddha-body of form (*rūpakāya*) which has two apparitional modes – namely, the body of perfect rapture (*sambhogakāya*) and the emanational body (*nirmāṇakāya*).

THE BUDDHA-BODY OF PERFECT RAPTURE

[46b.4-50a.5] As to the former, there is an explanation in Buddhaguhya's *Sequence of the Path*:

> The fields and celestial palaces
> With their thrones and ornaments,
> Which are the self-manifesting
> And spontaneously perfect awareness
> Appear as manifold light rays.

Accordingly, the great buddha-body of reality which abides within the nature of inwardly radiant reality, in the manner of the five-coloured light radiated within a crystal prism by the sun's rays, has an apparitional aspect of pristine cognition, which extends outward radiance to an object manifest [only] in and of itself. In this way it is experienced as measureless buddha-bodies and fields of rapture.

Among them, in this emanational array which comprises twenty-five different fields situated one above the other on the petals and anthers of a lotus stem growing on the palms of Vairocana the Great Glacial Lake, and in the sixteen different fields within the streams of fragrant water which flow beneath his crossed legs, uncountable [bodies of] rapture are projected in a constant cycle, endowed with oceans of major and minor marks. This natural expression of the Buddhas of the Five Enlightened Families, endowed with the five certainties, is the characteristic basis of the great body of rapture, the array of fields and buddha-bodies present within Vairocana, the Great Glacial Lake of Pristine Cognition (*ye-shes gangs-chen mtsho*).

It should be known that the indestructible play of these magical emanations is inconceivably secret. For example, it is by no means contradictory that fields containing atoms of oceanic infinity exist on the surface of a single atom, bodies of oceanic infinity are gathered in a single body and each body also covers an oceanic infinity of fields. Such is said in the *Tantra of the Secret Nucleus* (Ch.9, v.13):

> In the manner of the trichiliocosm
> Absorbed in a mustard seed,
> One should make offerings
> After inviting the maṇḍala from the expanse.[121]

And in the *Great Bounteousness of the Buddhas*:[122]

> On the surface of a single atom
> Are as many buddhas as there are atoms.

This buddha-body of rapture, the teacher who holds sway over these fields, is also endowed with seven particular attributes of natural expression. These are, namely: the natural expression which has fully matured in the nature of just what is; the natural expression which is spontaneously present without seeking for enlightened attributes; the natural expression which is pristine cognition without extremes or centre; the natural expression which, even though the result be mastered, does not reveal its true essence [i.e. it manifests only in and of itself]; the natural expression which, even when sameness has been disclosed, remains free from the range of objective qualification; the natural expression which is liberated from [concepts of] one and many; and the natural expression which is without conjunction and disjunction throughout the three times.

In the [buddhas] who greatly embody these seven [attributes of natural expression], spontaneous presence refers to the ordinary major and minor marks through which the diverse symbols of their body, speech and mind appear in accordance with the acumen of those requiring training. This transformation includes the thirty-two excellent major marks such as the wheel-marked hands and feet, and the eighty minor marks such as the copper-coloured nails which appear on their bodies, blazing with the major and minor marks. It also refers to the [major and minor marks], disclosed by the Teacher's mind through four kinds of pristine cognition, namely, the outer major and minor marks derived from his expressive power, the inner major and minor marks derived from the purity of his energy channels and centres, and the secret major and minor marks derived from the purified aspect of the seed that is the enlightened mind. Then, in the Great Perfection (*rdzogs-pa chen-po*),[123] the rapture of equal savour, experienced when the network of energy channels is naturally expressed as purified supreme bliss, is explained to be the supreme embellishment among the ornaments. The *Oceanic Magical Net* (*sgyu-'phrul rgya-mtsho*, NGB Vol.15) says:

Know that the twofold bliss of vowels and consonants
Intermingles and becomes one;
The sixteen [delights] by their dual movement
Possess the major marks.
One series of them is endowed with five pristine
cognitions,
And becomes the eighty minor marks.
Superior are they to the feeling of receptiveness and other
causal [teachings].[124]

The five components – namely, the one [component] which perceives the liberated and uncorrupted pristine cognition, utterly transcending accumulated ideas; the component of moral discipline; the component of contemplation; the component of discriminative awareness; and the component of liberation – are also naturally expressed as the Five [Conquerors] – Vairocana, Akṣobhya, Ratnasambhava, Amitābha and Amoghasiddhi, who are supreme embodiments of the tathāgatas' body, speech, mind, enlightened attributes and activities.

The five elemental properties [of space, cohesion, solidity, warmth, and movement], too, are naturally expressed as [the divine consorts of those conquerors] – Dhātvīśvarī, Locanā, Māmakī, Pāṇḍaravāsinī, and Samayatārā. Purified as such, [the components and elemental properties] abide in a coalescence of unchanging supreme bliss and emptiness endowed with all supreme aspects.[125]

In this way, the pristine cognition which transcends subject and object displays amazing maṇḍala arrays through its [rapturous] appreciation of all self-manifesting objects. These arrays include the maṇḍalas with their centre, periphery and clusters [of deities], their father consort and mother consort, body-colours, symbolic hand implements, passionate and passionless forms – male and female tathāgatas, male and female bodhisattvas, and male and female wrathful deities.

So it is that the four sensations of seeing, hearing, smelling, and tasting find their natural expression respectively as the four [bodhisattvas] Kṣitigarbha, Vajrapāṇi, Ākāśagarbha and Avalokiteśvara, and the four sense objects of form, sound, smell and taste as the four female bodhisattvas Lāsyā, Mālā, Gītā and Nartī. Similarly the four sense organs of eye, ear, nose and tongue find natural expression as [the bodhisattvas] Maitreya, Nivāraṇaviṣkambhin, Samantabhadra and Mañjuśrī, and the four temporal dimensions of past, future, present and indefinite time as Puṣpā, Dhūpā, Ālokā and Gandhā.[126]

Again, the common savour of supreme delight experienced through contact, the subject of contact, object of contact and sensation of contact, which interact when the secret [sexual] sense objects, organs and consciousness are united in meditative equipoise with the Vajra Queen,[127] is naturally expressed as the Four Mahākrodha [or "most wrathful male"] deities, "lords of death". The four [extremes] of permanence, decay, self and character are also naturally expressed as the Four Mahākrodhī [or "most wrathful female"] deities. Yet, the forms present in such infinite retinues are nothing but the display of the Teacher himself, the wheel of inexhaustible ornament which appears as the centre and periphery of the maṇḍala. So it is explained in the *Tantra of the [Secret] Nucleus*:

> The centre without extremes or middle is intrinsic
> awareness.
> The four pristine cognitions emanate around it in the
> manner of a wheel.

And in the *Illuminating Lamp of the Fundamental Text* (*khog-gzhung gsal-sgron*, P 4739):

> Having reached the culmination of the result in
> Akaniṣṭha,
> He abides as the centre and periphery of the maṇḍala.

The fields of these [maṇḍala deities] are present in every form because they are the pristine cognition of the buddhas manifest in and of itself and the display of the magical net, which is the nature of all forms. Their thrones are everywhere, their celestial palaces are everywhere, they arise everywhere, their zenith is everywhere, their nadir is everywhere, their spheres are everywhere, their squares are everywhere, their triangles are everywhere, their faces are everywhere, their hands are everywhere, their feet are everywhere, their eyes are everywhere, and they face in every direction. Each sense organ, too, performs the function of all sense organs, because the expanse of reality is infinitely covered and enveloped by the unimpeded expressive power of pristine cognition. Accordingly, the *Lion's Perfect Expressive Power* (*seng-ge rtsal-rdzogs chen-po'i rgyud*, NGB Vol.9) says:

> The face of Samantabhadra sees in all ten directions.
> The body of the all-seeing, all-positive [Samantabhadra]
> Has neither front nor back.
> With an eye which fills the ten directions,
> He sees form.

And also in the *Kālacakra Tantra*:

> With hands and feet everywhere,
> With eyes, head and face everywhere,
> Possessing ears everywhere,
> He who remains pervading all the world's limits...

Since these perceptual objects of the buddhas are subsumed by the minds of the buddhas alone, they are invisible even to the lords of the tenth level; for the latter are not liberated from all obscurations and have not attained the eye of pristine cognition, which, without even a mote [of obscuration], qualitatively knows [the view] and quantitatively knows [phenomena]. So the *Supreme Continuum of the Greater Vehicle* (Ch.2, v.69) says:

> Because it is not an object of speech,
> Is subsumed by ultimate reality,
> Is not within reason's domain,
> Is beyond exemplification,
> Is unsurpassed and is subsumed neither by existence nor
> quiescence,
> The objective range of the Conqueror is inconceivable,
> Even to sublime beings.

These perfect supramundane fields in which the cycle of myriad pure worlds and their contents arise, forming the apparitional aspect of the great inner radiance of the ground, manifest in and of itself, are equivalent to the purest of dreams. For, in situations where the subject-object dichotomy and its propensities are purified, there are not thought to be any material substances with independent attributes existing elsewhere apart from that apparition. As the *Tantra of the Extensive Magical Net* says:

> If there is no understanding of intrinsic awareness or
> genuine perception,
> The field of Sukhāvatī is even seen as a state of evil
> existence.
> If the truth which is equivalent to the supreme of
> vehicles is realised,
> Even states of evil existence are Akaniṣṭha and Tuṣita.

THE EMANATIONAL BODY

[50a.5-60a.3] The Teacher who instructs [sentient beings] appears as the emanational body (*nirmāṇakāya*) in response to the degrees of impurity, slight purity and utter purity of the stains which obscure the nucleus of the sugata within the minds of those to be trained. Without moving from the expanse of ultimate reality, for both saṃsāra and nirvāṇa have one great common savour in the utterly pure body of reality, his buddha-body of form sends forth a varied, unimpeded display of emanations of effortless, great spirituality. Among these, reality reflects as many aspirations as there are shapes of the moon in vessels of unsullied water, dependent on the ostensible dichotomy of those to be instructed and the instruction itself. As Ajita [in the *Supreme Continuum of the Greater Vehicle*, Ch.4, v.29] has said:

> Just as in the pure terrain of beryl
> The reflection of Surendra's body appears,
> So in the pure terrain of sentient beings
> The image of Munīndra's body is reflected.[128]

And in a sūtra:

> Having comprehended that the reality of the Conqueror
> Is without body, tranquil, not two, and without substantial existence,
> The body of form adorned with dignified marks continues to teach,
> Fulfilling the hopes of all living beings.

When classified, the emanational body is of three types: emanations of natural expression, emanations who train living beings and diversified emanations.

Emanations of Natural Expression

Firstly, concerning the emanations of natural expression: Just as the aforementioned teacher, the great buddha-body of perfect rapture who is an apparition of the expanse [of reality], appears to those lords of the tenth level who are somewhat pure among those to be trained, he also appears in the manner of a reflected image in clear crystal within the five fields of the emanational body of natural expression, namely, Akaniṣṭha in the centre, and Abhirati, Śrīmat, Padmakūṭa and Karmaprasiddhi respectively in the four cardinal directions.

Therein he appraises and teaches the doctrines through his body of measureless peaceful and wrathful transformations, in the form of the Five Teachers, who are identified by oceans of major and minor marks beginning with Tathāgata Vairocana, the king of form.[129] As an antidote to the five conflicting emotions of those who require training, he turns the inexpressible and unthinkable doctrinal wheel by means of his five great fields, five bodies, five doctrines, five pristine cognitions and so forth.

Since this Teacher, who is the body of perfect rapture and its retinue, is compounded by the minds of others, he is classified in the *Tantra of the Great Coalescence of Sun and Moon* (*nyi-ma dang zla-ba kha-sbyor-ba chen-po'i rgyud*, NGB Vol.9) as a semi-manifest emanation of natural expression. The Madhyamaka philosopher Dharmamitra has, in uniformity with this, given the following lucid explanation [in the *Clear Word*, *Prasphuṭapadā*, T 3796]:

> Manifestly perfect buddhahood is to be attained in only a single realm of Akaniṣṭha, which is disclosed to bodhisattvas as far as the path of insight by this body explained to be the imputed body of perfect rapture that appears to them, and by aspiration, the residual force of the accumulations, or mere intention. Therefore, the buddha-body of perfect rapture endowed with a multitude of forms has extensively appeared only as the emanational body in the Akaniṣṭha realms.[130]

And on the same subject, the *Sūtra of the Descent to Laṅkā* (Ch.10, v.774) says:

> In the desire and formless realms
> The Buddha does not become enlightened.
> In Akaniṣṭha among the realms of form,
> Without desire, you will attain buddhahood.

Through such quotations, authoritative passages do explain that the supreme emanational body attains buddhahood in Akaniṣṭha before becoming a buddha in the human world, and thus confirm the meaning expressed in this section.

Emanations who Train Living Beings

Secondly, concerning the emanations who train living beings: From the nature of this [Teacher], the emanational body who instructs living beings reveals inconceivable modes of display through skilful means in order to mature fully the mass of those to be trained in all world systems. The venerable Ajita [or Maitreya, in the *Supreme Continuum of the Greater Vehicle*, Ch.4, v.54] has said:

> Diversified in all realms,
> By measureless emanations beyond thought,
> He benefits all sentient beings.

Accordingly, the supreme emanational body simultaneously reveals the way of twelve deeds in myriad world systems of the ten directions, since it is skilled in remaining in the Tuṣita realm, in passing from that realm, in taking birth, renouncing the world, practising asceticism, reaching the point of enlightenment, vanquishing Māra's host, attaining perfect enlightenment, turning the doctrinal wheel, passing into final nirvāṇa, and teaching the duration and the decline of the doctrine. In each of these [world systems] it emanates as the Six Sages Embodying Awareness, who act on behalf of the six classes of beings to be trained, instructing them in accord with their differing sense perceptions and respective classes. So it is said in the *Sūtra which Resembles the Elephant's Expressive Power* (*Hastikakṣyasūtra*, T 207):

> Mañjuśrī, at this, when a great bodhisattva has become evenly absorbed in the contemplation named Great Lotus (*Mahāpadma*), he has taken into his following or takes into his following the hellish domains of sentient beings, and causes all these beings to experience the bliss of the gods, however slight. These sentient beings also perceive him as a denizen of hell in the hells, and through that guise he teaches the doctrine to the sentient denizens of hell in order that they might become free from the hells.

And in the *Great Bounteousness of the Buddhas*:

> Son of the enlightened family, the emanations of the tathāgatas are immeasurable. They act on behalf of living beings by training each in accord with his needs, and by their forms, colours and names.

Now, if one were to ask just how these sages act on behalf of beings in this realm with its six classes of sentient creatures, the *Superior Magical Net* (*sgyu-'phrul bla-ma*, NGB Vol.14, T 837) says:

> In the realms of the gods he is Lord Śakra,
> Among the antigods he is Vemacitra,
> Among men he is the Lord of the Śākyas who subdues
> Māra,
> In the domain of tormented spirits he is Jvālamukha,
> To animals he is called Siṃha,
> And in the hells he is Yama, lord of deeds.[131]

Such a sixfold classification of realms applies in this world system of Patient Endurance (*mi-mjed 'jig-rten-gyi khams*, Skt. *Sahalokadhātu*), the thirteenth among the series of twenty-five world systems which, as has already been explained, are situated one above the other upon the heart of a lotus on the palms of [Vairocana] the Great Glacial Lake of Pristine Cognition, at the centre of his buddha-fields which are as infinite in extent as atomic particles. In this context, the [Tibetan] word *mi-mjed* ["endurable"] is explained to mean patient or intrepid. The sentient beings of this field endure desire, endure hatred, endure delusion and endure fetters of conflicting emotion. Thus, it is so called because the [Sanskrit] word *saha* conveys the sense of endurance or capability.

The living beings [inhabiting this world] appear also to have their own respective world-forming deeds. The *Great Bounteousness of the Buddhas* says:

> The distinctions of deeds are inconceivable.
> The world of the hells slopes downwards.
> The world of Yama is topsy-turvy.

The animals and antigods move upwards and
downwards.

Or alternatively, the celestial beings face upwards, the animal beings face horizontally, and the hellish and tormented beings face downwards.

These six [classes of beings] are complete within a single trichiliocosm. As the *Short Commentary on the Secret Nucleus* (*Śrīguhyagarbhapiṇḍārthaṭīkā*, P 4755) says:

The six kinds of creatures in a single trichiliocosm
Are said to be the field of a single emanational body.

The world system of the four continents comprises everything from the energy field [below the earth][132] upwards as far as Akaniṣṭha. The chiliocosm has a circumference which encloses one thousand such world systems. The dichiliocosm is encircled by a second perimeter enclosing one thousand times that in extent. The trichiliocosm is encircled by a third perimeter one thousand times the dichiliocosm in extent. The frontier limits of one myriad world systems are one billion times that in extent; a series of myriad world systems one billion times that; a myriad oceanic world systems one billion times that; and one billion of these equals a single Buddha-field whose Foundation and Centre are Adorned with Flowers (*Kusumatalagarbhālaṃkārakṣetra*), which is explained to be the field of a supreme emanational body.

In these realms, [the supreme emanational body] projects the lamp of instruction for those requiring training in as many ways as they have psychophysical bases, sense organs and modes of conduct, and acts on behalf of sentient beings through four kinds of instruction. These four are instruction by the great merit of the body, instruction by the direct perception of mind, instruction by inconceivable miraculous abilities, and instruction by knowledge conveyed in speech.

Concerning the first of these [which instructs by the great merit of the body], it is impossible to enumerate exactly, or otherwise to qualify, the deeds of the Teacher's emanational body, for it is a topic beyond conception. In the sūtras of the greater vehicle, too, all manner of quantities are mentioned which contradict one another and do not lend themselves to summarisation; but here when his principle activities are subsumed, instruction through the great merit of the body refers to the deeds of taking birth, renouncing the world, practising asceticism, subjugating Māra, attaining buddhahood, turning the doctrinal wheel, displaying great miracles and passing into final nirvāṇa. It is so called because those requiring training who actually see them possess immeasurable merit.

Secondly, concerning instruction by the direct perception of mind, the pristine cognition [of the supreme emanational body], which is unhindered and unimpeded in respect of the three times, does not discriminate between the three times while entering into all that is knowable. Accordingly, there are six supernormal cognitive powers which accompany his mind. These are the supernormal cognitive power which knows time totally without obscuration, the supernormal cognitive power which knows the minds of others totally unobscured, the supernormal cognitive power of clairvoyance which totally perceives everything, the supernormal cognitive power of clairaudience which totally hears everything, the supernormal cognitive power which meaningfully enacts rites of total benefit to sentient beings, and the supernormal cognitive power with respect to the cessation of corruption, in which obscurations have been purified. Since these directly perceive and overpower all that is knowable, they are instruction by the direct perception of his mind.

Thirdly, concerning instruction by miraculous abilities, the supreme emanational body acts on behalf of those who require training through the totally inconceivable [mystery] of his buddha-body, the totally inconceivable [mystery] of his buddha-speech, and the totally inconceivable mystery of his buddha-mind. The mystery of buddha-body refers to his emanations who train living beings in accord with their class, such as Brahmā and Īśvara[133] among the gods, a universal emperor among men, and Vemacitra among the antigods;[134] and similarly as a woodpecker (*shing-rta-mo*) for the sake of birds,[135] Dṛdhasamādāna, the king of lions, for the sake of wildlife,[136] and so on. It refers, too, to the revelations of the maṇḍala of his visage which appropriately manifests in and of itself as the peaceful and wrathful deities, *piśācī* and so on, and to his revelations at various times, as when taking birth, transferring realms, living, passing away, and residing [in other realms], which accord with the respective fortunes [of those requiring training].

The mystery of his buddha-speech refers to the fact that the revelation of the doctrine, which manifests according to those requiring training and their intelligence, is also understood by means of different languages and symbols. As the *Great Bounteousness of the Buddhas* [i.e. the *Aspiration of Good Conduct*, v.18] says:

> In the language of gods, the languages of nāgas and yakṣas,
> In the languages of trolls and of humans,
> In as many languages as there are among living beings,
> I teach the doctrine in the languages of all.

The mystery of his buddha-mind refers to the pristine cognition, free from all corruptions, which manifests appropriately for all by qualitatively knowing the attitudes and minds of those requiring training. This threefold mystery is instruction through inconceivable miraculous abilities.

Fourth, concerning instruction by knowledge conveyed in speech, the supreme emanational body gives abbreviated teaching by means of the five vehicles which correspond to the perception of those requiring training, who are of five families or types (*gotra*). He gives detailed explanation, teaching the eighty-four thousand doctrinal components as an antidote for the eighty-four thousand conflicting emotions, and he concludes his teaching corresponding to the degree of acumen [in those who require training]. All these are instruction by knowledge conveyed in speech which conveys understanding beyond the attributes of mere sounds and words, to the realms of sentient beings in an appropriately intelligible form through the tathāgatas' blessing. As a sūtra of definitive meaning says:

> Concerning all these teachings,
> I did not teach a single syllable.

Diversified Emanations

Thirdly, the diversified emanations include all things basic to the greater well-being of sentient beings. As such, [the Teacher] reveals physical forms which originate both naturally and through deliberate efforts – emanations in the form of mansions, verdant meadows, *ghandhola* spires, and cities on the plains of suffering; as well as material objects such as the Wishing Tree (*Kalpavṛkṣa*), the Wish-fulfilling Gem (*Cintāmaṇi*), bridges, wagons, food, clothing and medicine. It also includes other diverse emanations of artistry and birth such as a great fish which appeared during a time of famine,[137] a noble creature which appeared [to cure] an epidemic,[138] the horse Ājāneyabalaha in the island of ogresses,[139] and a golden bee in a swampy marsh.[140]

Extensive descriptions [of these diversified emanations] are found, such as in the *Sūtra of the Lamp of Precious Jewels* (*Ratnolkānāmadhāraṇīmahāyānasūtra*, T 145):

> Everywhere I reveal many forms:
> As kings among bards composing verses,
> As dancers, drummers, athletes and musicians,
> As dancers wearing beautiful ornaments,
> adornments and garlands,
> And as masters of magical display.
> I become villagers, headmen and governors,
> And merchants, captains and landlords.
> I become kings, ministers, priests and messengers,
> Doctors learned in the rites of worldly treatises,
> And a vast oasis in a wilderness.
> I become unending treasures of medicine and
> precious gems,
> The Wish-fulfilling Gem and the Tree which Brings
> Forth Wishes;

And I reveal the path to those who deviate from the
path.

Emanations According to the Great Perfection

According to one method of explaining the emanational body, that of the uncommon Great Perfection in particular, twelve teachers of the emanational body have emanated from the apparitional buddha-body of perfect rapture in twelve different realms, and have acted on behalf of living creatures by simultaneously manifesting the three great emanational teachings of buddha-body, speech and mind.[141]

Vajra on Lotus

In this world [Jambudvīpa], the actuality of the teaching of the body of reality is a hand-sized vajra produced from a hundred precious gems, which is naturally arisen through the blessing conferred by the Great Perfection. The actuality of the teaching of the body of perfect rapture is a four-inch book, proclaiming the natural sound of reality, produced from one hundred and one precious gems, which is naturally arisen through the blessing of the *Naturally Present Teaching like an Only Son* (*rang-byung-ba bstan-pa bu-gcig-pa*, NYZ vol. 7). The emanational body is the physical form, equal in size to the body of a living being, naturally produced from one hundred and one precious gems, which naturally arises through the blessing of the twelve teachers. Since these three [actualities] are uncompounded, they are subject neither to creation nor destruction, and since they arise naturally through blessing, they have immeasurable miraculous abilities and enlightened attributes. Therefore, no matter who encounters them, they are the support which causes the teaching of the body, speech and mind of the emanational bodies of past and future buddhas to multiply in the world systems. They also embody the enlightened activities [of those emanations] which are seen, heard and felt, and which subsequently cause corporeal reality to vanish of its own accord.

As for the realms in which [these actualities] reside, while they are naturally expressed in a perpetual cycle, they reside in different realms according to the times for instruction through the teachings of buddha-body, speech and mind. The vajra, during the time for teaching through buddha-body, remains on an island in the country of Oḍḍiyāna and generates light, sound and countless emanational monks endowed with miraculous abilities. During the time for teaching through buddha-speech, the vajra is wielded by the yakṣa kings on Mount Malaya, the abode of Vajrapāṇi; and during the time for teaching through buddha-mind, it abides in space above the Vajrāsana.[142]

The book, during the time for teaching through buddha-body, is kept by the ḍākinīs in the sublime space five hundred *yojana* above the Vajrāsana; and during the time for teaching through buddha-speech, it remains with these same [ḍākinīs]. Then during the time for teaching through buddha-mind, the book remains in the Cave of the Most Wrathful Sage *(rab-tu khros-pa drang-srong-gi phug-pa)*.

The physical form, during the time for teaching through buddha-body, abides as the actual bodies of the buddhas, along with their emanations and further emanations through the blessing [of the aforementioned twelve teachers], and manifests the maṇḍala of their visage. During the time for teaching through buddha-speech, the physical form roams indefinitely throughout Jambudvīpa and becomes a focus of worship for all extraordinary assemblies of gods and humans. On occasions when harm comes to the teaching, the physical form emits light from its bodies, the syllable HŪṂ from their mouths and the fire of pristine cognition from their eyes. Then during the time for teaching which instructs through buddha-mind, it performs prostrations to the great glorious [Samantabhadra] whose natural expression remains the same, in the highest storey of Vajrapāṇi's palace in the celestial heaven of the Thirty-three Gods (*Trayatriṃśa*), and it is the embodiment of oceanic miracles.

Simultaneously, the twelve teachers of the emanational body, too, appeared within their twelve realms. During the first aeon inhabited by those who require training, in the place called Pagoda of Tuṣita (*dga'-ldan brtsegs-pa*), the teacher Acintyaprabhāsa [appeared] to a retinue of the Thousand Buddhas,[143] and revealed the *Penetration of Sound*, which is the basis of all teachings. It was compiled by the son of the gods Gaje Wangcuk assisted by the son of the gods Nyima Raptu Nangje during the period when sentient beings had a life-span of immeasurable years.

In the world system of Patient Endurance (*Sahalokadhātu*), the teacher Akṣobhyaprabha [appeared to] a retinue of two hundred thousand ḍākinīs, and revealed the teaching of the *Five Tantras of Buddha-body, Speech, Mind, Enlightened Attributes and Activities* (*sku-gsung-thugs yon-tan phrin-las-kyi rgyud lnga*) during the period when sentient beings had a life-span of ten million years.

In the realm of the Moisture Gathering Light Mass (*drod-gsher 'od-kyis spungs-pa*), the teacher Pel Jikpa Kyopei Yi [appeared to] a retinue of six hundred thousand bodhisattvas, and revealed the teaching of the tantras *Churner of Saṃsāra's Depths* (*'khor-ba dong-sprugs*), *Crossing the Peacock's Neck* (*rma-bya mjing-bsnol*, NGB Vol.2), and the *Glorious Tantra of the Cessation of the Four Elements* (*dpal 'byung-bzhi zad-pa'i rgyud*) during the period when the life-span was one hundred thousand years.

In the realm of Appearance in the Womb of Conception (*chags-'byung mngal-du snang-ba*), the teacher Zhönu Rölpa Nampar Tsewa [appeared to] a retinue of one thousand yakṣas and ogres (*rākṣasa*), and revealed the teaching of the *Five Basic Tantras and Six Branch Tantras of the Mental Class* (*sems-sde rtsa-ba'i rgyud-lnga-dang yan-lag-gi rgyud-drug*) during the period when the life-span was eighty thousand years.

In the realm of the Garden of Sustaining Youth (*'tsho-byed gzhon-nu'i ldum-ra*), the sixth teacher Vajradhara[144] appeared to a retinue including the Seven Generations of Buddhas, and revealed teachings such as the six transcendental perfections during the period when the life-span was seventy thousand years.

In the realm of the Blazing Fire Mountain Charnel Ground of Most Secret Display (*gsang-chen rol-pa dur-khrod me-ri 'bar-ba*), the teacher Kumāravīrabalin appeared to a retinue of seven including the bodhisattva Balāhaka, and revealed the doctrine of many tantrapiṭaka, including those of the Father Tantra (*pha-rgyud*) and Mother Tantra (*ma-rgyud*) during the period when the life-span was sixty thousand years.

In the realm of the Ogre Cave endowed with the Sound of the Rulu Mantra (*srin-phug ru-lu'i sgra-dang-ldan-pa*), the teacher Drangsong Trhöpei Gyelpo [appeared to] a retinue of ten million ogres, and revealed doctrines such as the *Ten Tantras on the Discipline of Coarse Defilements* (*rags-pa 'dul-ba'i rgyud-bcu*) during the period when the life-span was ten thousand years.

In the realm of Rājagṛha near Vulture Peak (*bya-rgod phung-po'i rgyal-po'i khab*), the teacher Arhat Suvarṇaprabhāsa (*gser-'od dam-pa*) appeared to a retinue of immeasurable sublime pious attendants endowed with miraculous abilities and revealed immeasurable myriads of true doctrines on the Vinaya (*'dul-ba*) during the period when sentient beings had a life-span of five thousand years.

In the realm of the Turquoise Eyebrow in Mongolia (*sog-po gYu'i smin-ma-can*) near the victorious tree of enlightenment,[145] the teacher Tsewe Rölpei Lodrö [appeared to] a retinue of eighth level bodhisattvas[146] and revealed the *Seven Tantras of Subtle Meaning* (*phra-rgyud bdun-pa*) and so forth during the period when the life-span was one thousand years.

In the realm of Vulture Peak (*Gṛdhrakūṭa*), the teacher, the elder Kāśyapa, appeared to a retinue of seven long-living *ṛṣi* and revealed true doctrines which included the sūtras, the Kriyātantra, and eighty thousand doctrines of the Anuyoga transmission during the period when the life-span was five hundred years.

In the realm of Vajrāsana, near the forthcoming Tree of Enlightenment,[147] the teacher Yab Ngöndzok Gyelpo appeared to a retinue of the Lords of the Three Families and revealed only doctrines of definitive meaning during the period when the life-span was three hundred years.

Then in the realm of Anāthapiṇḍada's Pleasure Grove (*kun-dga' ra-ba*), the teacher Śākyamuni [appeared to] a retinue of the four orders, and promulgated the doctrinal wheel of the four truths twelve times during the period when the life-span was one hundred years.

Since these events in the twelve realms are each connected with the five excellences [of place, teacher, retinue, doctrine and time], an enumeration of sixty doctrines emerges.

Concerning the approach [of the Great Perfection] to enlightened activities also, many special attributes have been explained. The twelve deeds of the body are as follows: In the twelve different realms, the Teacher himself appeared, emanated in twelve forms endowed with different colours and symbolic implements. He came forth in order to propagate the teaching of the body, relying on the charisma of the buddha-body which is said to perform twelve different deeds of immeasurable benefit to different gatherings of those requiring training who belong to twelve dissimilar classes or types (*gotra*).

Then, while [emanating] these bodies, he delivered twelve different doctrinal wheels of speech and so came forth in order to propagate the teaching of speech, which is said to perform deeds which liberate living beings from the twelve different fetters of speech. During the time of that same speech, through the twelve different intentions of his mind, he came forth in order to propagate the teaching of mind which is said to perform deeds which liberate the different classes of living beings from their twelve thought patterns. So it is that a single emanational body who establishes the teaching in this way requires an enumeration of ninety-six doctrines. One who possesses these doctrines is said to be a master of the teaching, and if one does not possess them it is said that the partial teaching of the Buddha has appeared in the world; for these doctrines have emerged from the perfect generation of enlightened mind in the past.

It is said in the *Great Array*:

> Through nine aspects beginning with the outer,
> The details of his deeds must be distinguished.

Therefore, deeds are spoken of in many ways. For example, deeds of body, speech and mind are each classified into three outer and inner aspects and each of these is also classified into four. However, I shall not enlarge upon this here. They are all evident in one special area of [the Teacher's] intention, and the Sugata, learned in skilful means, manifests the buddha-body of form in ways which correspond to the number of atoms in the myriad fields of those requiring training, which are of oceanic extent.

Concerning the revelation of the buddhas' deeds, one should not think that there is a contradiction even if within one tradition there are differences. Since the emanational power of the buddhas is an inconceivable object, it is not even within the range of the intellect of great sublime [bodhisattvas], let alone ordinary persons. Since their times and those who require to be trained by them and so forth cannot be exactly enumerated, one should not, having seen one of their aspects, disparage the others. For this reason it is said in the *Sublime Sūtra which Genuinely Comprises the Entire Doctrine* (*Āryadharmasaṃgīti*, T 238):

> Sentient beings who will an aeon of dissolution to become an aeon of evolution can indeed transform an aeon of dissolution into an aeon of evolution; and they experience an aeon of evolution. Sentient beings who will an aeon of evolution to become an aeon of dissolution can indeed transform an aeon of evolution into an aeon of dissolution; and they experience an aeon of dissolution. But really the evolution and the dissolution do not change into one another; for it is the will which changes in this way. Similarly, sentient beings who will one aeon to become just one morning may experience one aeon in one morning. And sentient beings who will one morning to become one aeon may experience just that. This is called the miraculous ability born of the bodhisattva's will.

4 *The Five Buddha-bodies and Five Pristine Cognitions*

[60a.3-63a.5] When these three buddha-bodies [which have just been outlined] are classified according to the five buddha-bodies, there are two exegetical traditions. Scholars of the Zur tradition[148] claim that there are five buddha-bodies with the addition of the body of awakening (*abhisambodhikāya*), which derives from the distinct apparitional functions of the three bodies; and the body of indestructible reality (*vajrakāya*) which derives from the function of their indivisible essence. These scholars assert therefore that the three bodies of reality, perfect rapture and emanation are the characteristic nature of the buddha-body, while the other two are the conventional buddha-body because, among them, the former is determined by the function of the form of the three bodies and the latter by the function of their indivisible essence.

The all-knowing Longcenpa claims that the three bodies of reality, awakening and indestructible reality are the characteristic nature of the buddha-body that manifests in and of itself (*rang-snang*), while the bodies of perfect rapture and emanation are conventional because they are compounded by the external perception (*gzhan-snang*) of those who require training.

Though no contradiction is discerned whichever of these explanations one follows, none the less when the buddha-body is definitively ordered according to its characteristic nature, it is the original expanse, the naturally pure point of liberation, primordially pure, in which all buddhas are of a single expanse, the reality in which all paths are conclusively traversed, that is called the unchanging buddha-body of indestructible reality. This is because it is perpetual, stable, and uncompounded without changing or turning into all manner of forms. It is also called "natural purity" because it is taintless from the beginning, and "the buddha endowed with two purities" because it is utterly pure with respect to the two aspects of suddenly arisen obscuration. As the *Net of Pristine Cognition* (*ye-shes drva-ba*, NGB Vol.15) says:

> The pure expanse is the body of indestructible reality.
> It is unchanging, undecaying and beyond thought.

The buddha-body of awakening is so called because it possesses the attributes of knowledge, love and power such as the ten powers (*daśatathāgatabala*, Mvt. 119-29), the four fearlessnesses (*catur-vaiśāradya*, Mvt. 130-34), the eighteen distinct attributes of the buddhas (*aṣṭadaśāveṇikabuddhadharma*, Mvt. 135-53) and great compassion (*mahākaruṇa*, Mvt. 154-86). It abides as the basis for the arising of all distinct doctrines and its attributes are free from obscuration owing to the unimpeded expression of [all-]knowing pristine cognition which is the apparitional aspect [of the above-mentioned body of indestructible reality] endowed with the two purities. As the above-cited [*Net of Pristine Cognition*] says:

> Because it is taintless, it is pure.
> Vast in attributes, it is consummate.
> Permeated by non-duality, it is coalescent.
> Such is called the body of awakening.

Then, when the buddha-body is definitively ordered according to pristine cognition, it is explained that the pristine cognition of the expanse of reality (*dharmadhātujñāna*) is the pristine cognition which qualitatively knows [the view, *ji-lta-ba mkhyen-pa'i ye-shes*], and the four subsequent pristine cognitions through their functions of supporting and depending on [the former] comprise the pristine cognition which quantitatively knows [phenomena, *ji-snyed-pa mkhyen-pa'i ye-shes*]. The great scholars who taught the definitive meaning during the later period of doctrinal propagation [in Tibet][149] meant the same when they explained the pristine cognition of the expanse of reality to refer to ultimate reality and the four subsequent pristine cognitions to be intermingled with various aspects of relative appearance.

Moreover, among those pristine cognitions, the former is held to be [the perception characterizing] the buddha-body of reality. As the *Supreme Continuum of the Greater Vehicle* (Ch.2, v.38) says:

> Without beginning, middle or end, and indivisible,
> It is neither two, nor three, taintless and without thought.

The four subsequent pristine cognitions are respectively described in the following quotations from the *Ornament of the Sūtras of the Greater Vehicle* (Ch.9, vv.68-9):

> The selfless mirror-like pristine cognition
> Is completely unbroken and permanent.
> Undeluded with regard to all [things] that are knowable,
> It is never directed upon them.
> Since it is the causal basis of all pristine cognitions,

As if the supreme source of pristine cognition,
It is the buddhahood of perfect rapture.

And (Ch.9, vv.70-1):

The pristine cognition of sameness
Is held to be purity of meditation
With respect to sentient beings.
That which abides dynamically and at peace
Is held to be the pristine cognition of sameness.
At all times endowed with loving kindness
And pure, consummate spirituality,
The buddha-body is definitively revealed
For all sentient beings in accord with their devotion.

And again (Ch.9, vv.72-3):

The pristine cognition of discernment,
Ever unimpeded with regard to all that is knowable,
Is solely like a treasure store
Of the contemplations and the dhāraṇīs.
In all the surrounding maṇḍalas,
As the revealer of all excellent attributes,
It causes a downpour of the supreme doctrine,
Cutting off all doubts.

Thus these three pristine cognitions refer to the buddha-body of perfect rapture.

Then, [the pristine cognition of accomplishment] refers to the emanational body. As the same text says (Ch.9, v.74):

The pristine cognition of accomplishment
Is diversified in all realms.
Through measureless, unthinkable emanations
It acts on behalf of all sentient beings.[150]

In this context, the great all-knowing Longcenpa has explained that the two pristine cognitions of the expanse of reality and sameness are the pristine cognition which qualitatively knows [the view] because their function is to perceive the abiding nature [of reality], while the other three pristine cognitions are the pristine cognition which quantitatively knows [phenomena] because their functions are respectively to be the ground for the arising [of all forms], to discern objects and to act on behalf of living beings. As it is said in the *Penetration of Sound*:

By the actuality of qualitatively knowing [the view]
The abiding nature of reality is known for one's own
sake.

> By that of quantitatively knowing [phenomena]
> The mental condition of those requiring training is known.
> The body which instructs the different beings who require training
> Is none other than the reflection of such compassion.

The sūtras speak of the rank of the great [emanations] who possess these three buddha-bodies and five pristine cognitions as [being attained when] the empowerment of great light rays is conferred by the myriad tathāgatas of the ten directions on a bodhisattva. This happens as the bodhisattva attains buddhahood, having relied on the unobstructed path at the end of the continuum, culminating the five paths and ten levels according to the causal phase of the greater vehicle. Thereby the two obscurations [covering] the bodhisattva's own level are purified. However, it is variously explained in the Unsurpassed Tantras of the way of mantras and their commentaries that there is no method of purifying the subtle propensities which transfer consciousness to the three appearances of the variable [desire realm], the blissful [form realm] and the experiential [formless realm] through [the union of] the white and red seminal points [sperm and ovum] and the vital energy without relying on the empowerment of supreme desire.[151] The *Magical Net of Mañjuśrī* (v.135cd) is of the same opinion when it says:

> Attaining disillusionment through the three vehicles,
> One abides in the result through the single vehicle.

Thus, the necessity of attaining the culmination of the causal vehicle by relying on the mantras can be known from the very names given to the causal and resultant vehicles.

One might then object that the definitive structure of the result which is taught in the causal phase of the greater vehicle would become meaningless; and yet there is no fault. Though that [structure] has been revealed to those dull persons who aspire through the causal vehicle, it is in the mantras that the culmination of the sūtras' definitive meaning abides. It does not follow that the buddhahood of the mantras does not refer to the buddhahood of the path of sūtras. After the result had been spoken of in the sūtras under such generalities as the absolute nature, inner radiance of reality and the true self,[152] then the most extensive abiding nature of reality and the complete means which realise it were revealed in the mantras. Just as, when the end of the long path encounters the short path, wherever they originated, they are both identical in their purpose.

Again, if one were to object that the path of the sūtras would then become a meaningless teaching apart from the mantras, that is not the case. Just as none but a person of powerful physique and intelligence can set out on a path of deep ravines and precipices, even though the distance be very short, there are great risks for all those who require training through the mantras apart from those of highest acumen and most potent intelligence. Then, just as one feeble in body and intelligence sets out on a journey which, though long, is without the fear of deep ravines and the like, and so encounters few risks by proceeding slowly, such is the teaching of the long path of the sūtras. It is therefore a most essential point that one should know [the Teacher's] methods of teaching the doctrine to be unsurpassed; for the All-knowing One is learned in skilful means. If it were otherwise, the two vehicles of cause and result would deviate from his basic intention, they would not be gathered together in the single culminating vehicle, the definitive meaning would also be divided in two, and other great flaws such as these would exist. One must learn therefore that the Conqueror's enlightened activity is never to be wasted.

5 *Distinctive Attributes of the Buddha-bodies and Pristine Cognitions*

[63a.5-66b.2] As for the distinctive attributes of the buddha-bodies and pristine cognitions which are revealed in the causal and resultant vehicles: In order to classify intellectually the distinctive attributes of the causal and resultant vehicles, the great scholars of supreme discernment in the past have examined the distinctive attributes of the buddhas as assessed in the sūtra and the mantra texts in the following way.

The buddha-body of reality has three distinctive attributes of essence, characteristic and blessing, among which the first, the essence, is that the body of reality according to the vehicle of dialectics is sky-like unelaborate emptiness. As it is said in the *Introduction to the Madhyamaka* (Ch.11, v.16):

> When the dry brushwood of all that is knowable is
> burnt,
> The peace which results is the body of reality of the
> conquerors.
> At that time there is neither creation nor cessation,
> For the cessation of mind has been actualised by that body.

The buddha-body of reality according to the mantras, however, is the natural expression of the expanse [of reality] and pristine cognition, the coalescence of appearance and emptiness. As it is said in the *Tantra of the Extensive Magical Net*:

> In the world with its moving and motionless
> creatures,
> In the nature of all such appearances,
> There is no substantial existence.

Secondly, as for its characteristic: The body of reality according to the vehicle of dialectics has fallen into the extreme of emptiness, whereas the body of reality according to the mantras does not fall into extremes of eternalism and nihilism since there is no dichotomy between appearance and emptiness.

Third, the blessing which arises from the body of reality according to the vehicle of dialectics is nothing but the two buddha-bodies of form; but as for the body of reality according to the mantras, the five bodies and various other apparitions arise from its blessing, which is the expanse [of reality] and pristine cognition, the coalescence of appearance and emptiness.

The buddha-body of perfect rapture and the body of emanation similarly have their distinctive attributes, which are outlined as follows. The vehicle of dialectics holds that the two buddha-bodies of form are created by causes and conditions, while the body of form according to the mantras is not created by causes and conditions. As the above [*Extensive Magical Net*] says:

> For it does not depend on causes and conditions...

When classified, [the buddha-body of form] has two aspects, namely, the distinctive attributes of the body of perfect rapture and those of the emanational body.

The distinctive attributes of the buddha-body of perfect rapture are also twofold. Concerning the distinctive attributes of the rapture that is experienced, the body of perfect rapture according to the vehicle of dialectics experiences rapture in positive areas, but not in negative areas. The body of perfect rapture according to the mantras experiences rapture in both areas. Then there are distinctive attributes of the means of the experience. In the vehicle of dialectics there are no means of experiencing rapture in negative areas, whereas the mantras do have means of experiencing rapture in both positive and negative areas.

Then, the distinctive attributes of the emanational body are also twofold. The distinctive attribute of its object, the one who requires the training, is that, according to the vehicle of dialectics, the emanational body only instructs those requiring training who are positively disposed, but not those of a negative character; whereas the emanational body according to the mantras is impartial regarding the character of those requiring to be trained. The distinctive attributes of their methods of instruction are such that the emanational body in the vehicle of dialectics has no means of instructing those of negative disposition, whereas the emanational body of the mantras is endowed with the means of instructing those of both positive and negative dispositions who require training.

In addition, one should know that other distinctions also exist. For example, the body of reality is distinguished by utterly unchanging supreme bliss. The body of perfect rapture endowed with the five certainties is the apparitional aspect consisting of all the fields, teachers and retinues, which is spontaneously present in the great inner radiance of the ground, manifest in and of itself (*rang-snang*), but it is not compounded by external perception (*gzhan-snang*). The emanational body has power to act on behalf of those who require training, having mastered the myriad ways that are suitable for the four kinds of enlightened activity to be applied by means of the four kinds of instruction.

Then, as for the actions performed on behalf of living beings by this [emanational] body: Whenever a tathāgata manifests his all-knowing level, the oceans of the myriad realms of the sentient beings who require training and all the distinctive attributes of the means of instruction, which are derived from his own essence, are nothing but the display of great compassion. All [those requiring training and the means of training] are of a common savour and are spontaneously present without effort, disregarding causes and conditions such as the provision of merit accumulated by those requiring training and distinctions of the Conqueror's aspiration. Therefore, the natural expression of the mind of all sentient beings, and the all-pervasive natural expression of reality, which is the pristine cognition of the buddhas and the nucleus of the sugata, are inseparable from each other, without coming and going, transferring and changing, as the oil that pervades the sesame seed. Enlightened activity is present therein, pervading the fundamental nature of reality, and its uncompounded essence is characteristically permanent, pervasive and spontaneous.

It says in the *Sūtra of the Introduction to the Development of the Power of Faith* (*Śraddhābalādhānāvatāramudrāsūtra*, T 201):

> Mañjuśrī, in all the myriad world systems of the ten directions, all the domains of the extremists and all the mundane and supramundane activities which occur originate through the spontaneously present pristine cognition of the Tathāgata. If you ask why it is so, it is because he possesses distinct attributes.

Commenting on the meaning of [the buddhas'] permanence, the *Supreme Continuum of the Greater Vehicle* (Ch.4, v.12) says:

> Since he is disillusioned with dependence,
> Perceives himself and sentient beings equally,
> And has not completed his deeds,
> He does not cease to act for the duration of saṃsāra.

Then, commenting on the meaning of his pervasiveness and spontaneous presence, it says (Ch.1, v.76):

> Ever spontaneously present to living beings
> Throughout infinite space,
> Endowed with unimpeded intelligence,
> He genuinely proceeds to benefit sentient beings.

And in the *Hundred Parables on Deeds*:

> The ocean domain of sea monsters
> May well pass beyond time,
> But for the sake of his sons requiring training,
> The Buddha will not pass beyond time.

Accordingly, this spontaneously present enlightened activity has regard for the awakening of the different minds requiring training in accord with their fortune, but is non-conceptual with respect to the effort amassed by the continuum of nirvāṇa. It is an encounter between the expressive power of the nucleus of the tathāgata and the phenomena which suddenly arise in the manner of saṃsāra. As a result, those who have matured the sprout of enlightenment, those who are in the process of maturing it and the means which brings about maturation are the amazing play of the sugatas' enlightened activity and compassion. These are, respectively, the spiritual benefactors who reveal the path of liberation, the adherents of the path and the antidotes which purify the stains arising on the path.

It is said in the *Tantra of the Extensive Magical Net*:

> Through the blessing of his great compassion
> In all the worlds of the ten directions,
> As many as there are atoms,
> The enlightened activities on behalf of living beings
> are inconceivable.
> Through body, speech, mind, attributes
> And activities which are spontaneously present,
> Those requiring training, inexhaustible in extent,
> Are purified of evil existences and enlightened.
> The perfect provision of pristine cognition is
> everywhere revealed.

It is additionally maintained that [the buddhas], without moving from the pristine cognition of meditative equipoise, act on behalf of sentient beings during the aftermath of their meditation. As has been explained [in the *Supreme Continuum of the Greater Vehicle*, Ch.2, v.7cd]:

> Both the non-conceptualising state
> And its aftermath are held to be pristine cognition.

Then, concerning the claim that the benefit of living creatures is basically caused by the increase in positive attributes of those requiring training, and conditioned by the former aspiration of the buddhas, the *Introduction to the Madhyamaka* (Ch.11, v.17) says:

> The fields and bodies are radiant like the Wishing Tree,

They are non-conceptualising in the manner of the
Wish-fulfilling Gem;
Ever remaining to guide the world until beings have
been liberated,
They appear to those who are free from elaboration.

Yet it is difficult to say that even these words reach the culmination of the definitive meaning, apart from their mere reference to a single aspect of the revelation [of buddha nature] for the sake of ordinary beings who require training.

This completes the anthology explaining the appearance of the Conqueror or Teacher endowed with the three buddha-bodies, the second part of this book, the *Feast in which Eloquence Appears*, which is a definitive ordering of the precious teaching of the vehicle of indestructible reality according to the Ancient Translation School.

Part Three
Causal Vehicles of Dialectics

Introduction

[66b.2-66b.4] Having briefly described the appearance of the Conqueror as the teachers endowed with the three buddha-bodies in the world system of Patient Endurance, now, among the promulgations of the doctrinal wheel delivered by these teachers, I shall first explain the definitive structure of the three turnings of the doctrinal wheel according to the causal [vehicles]. This includes a statement of the overall meaning according to classifications and a recapitulation of the meaning subsumed in their particular sections.

1 *The Three Promulgations of the Doctrinal Wheel*

[66b.4-68b.1] At the outset, the doctrinal wheel of the causal vehicle was promulgated in three successive stages by [Śākyamuni], the supreme emanational buddha-body and sage. The first commenced with the four truths, the second concerned the absence of attributes, and the third the excellent analysis [of reality].

THE FIRST PROMULGATION

The first is as follows: After discerning the utterly impure realms of sentient beings, the Teacher who promulgated the first turning of the doctrinal wheel intended to encourage these beings by the disturbing topics of impermanence, impurity, suffering, selflessness, ugliness, and so forth, and then cause them to forsake the attitude which actually clings to saṃsāra. For in this way they would achieve appropriate insight into ultimate truth and adhere to the path of the greater vehicle.

At the Deer Park of Ṛṣipatana in the district of Vārāṇasī, he repeated the four [truths] of suffering, its origin, the path and cessation [of saṃsāra] three times to an assembly consisting of his five noble companions.

The modes of the doctrine revealed in this context include the *Four Transmissions of the Piṭaka* of the pious attendants and self-centred buddhas who belong to the lesser vehicle.

THE SECOND PROMULGATION

Concerning the second: The Tathāgata's perseverance was not interrupted merely by that first promulgation of the doctrinal wheel. Subsequently, the Teacher promulgated the intermediate turning of the doctrinal wheel, intending that the realisation of the ultimate truth, which is referred to by synonyms in order to bring about the partial cessation of conceptual elaboration, should become the actual foundation for the path of the greater vehicle. In this way egotism would be averted once beings had comprehended the buddha nature through the extensive topics of emptiness, signlessness, and aspirationlessness in relation to all things.

In places such as Vulture Peak near Rājagṛha and chiefly to the communities of bodhisattvas, he revealed the Bodhisattvapiṭaka of the greater vehicle, which extensively teach the ineffable, unthinkable, inexpressible reality of just what is, whereby all things from form to omniscience are totally divorced from substantial existence.

The long versions [of these piṭaka] are the *Billion Lines on the Transcendental Perfection of Discriminative Awareness* (**Śatakoṭiprajñāpāramitā)* and the *Transcendental Perfection of Discriminative Awareness in One Hundred Thousand Lines*. The intermediate versions include the *Transcendental Perfection of Discriminative Awareness in Twenty-five Thousand Lines*, and the short versions include the *Transcendental Perfection of Discriminative Awareness in Eight Thousand Lines*; however, one should know there are an inconceivable number in addition to these.

THE THIRD PROMULGATION

Concerning the third: The Tathāgata's perseverance was not interrupted merely by that second promulgation of the doctrinal wheel. Subsequently the Teacher promulgated the final turning of the doctrinal wheel, directing his intention towards the nucleus of the path of the greater vehicle, and actually revealed the ultimate truth for which there is no synonym. This he did after opposing all bases for the views concerning being and non-being and the like by causing sentient beings to penetrate the objective range of the Buddha through the topics of that irreversible promulgation[153] and through topics concerning the utter purity of the three spheres [of subject, object and their interaction].

In places such as Mount Malaya, the Point of Enlightenment[154] and Vaiśālī, at indeterminate times and to the host of great bodhisattvas who required the essential training, he excellently analysed all things from form to omniscience in accord with the three essential natures of the imaginary (*parikalpita*), the dependent (*paratantra*) and the absolute (*pariniṣpanna*);[155] and having established the nature of the ground, path and result, he extensively revealed the abiding reality of the nucleus of the tathāgata.

Included in this promulgation are the *Billion Verses of the Great Collection of the Most Extensive Sūtras according to the Greater Vehicle* (**Mahāvaipulyamahāyānasūtrāntamahāsaṃgraha*), the *Great Bounteousness of the Buddhas*, the *Sūtra of the Descent to Laṅkā*, the *Sūtra of the Bounteous Array* (*Ghanavyūhasūtra*, T 110), the *Great Sūtra of Final*

Nirvāṇa and the *Sūtra which Decisively Reveals the Intention* (*Sandhinirmocanasūtra*, T 106).

The Vaibhāṣika hold that the doctrinal wheels in which these transmissions were given comprise exclusively the path of insight. The Sautrāntika hold that the three paths of insight, meditation and no-more-learning are comprised in the doctrinal wheels, while followers of the greater vehicle claim all five paths to be contained in the doctrinal wheels.

This causal vehicle, when classified according to its philosophical systems, has two divisions, namely, the lesser vehicle of the pious attendants and self-centred buddhas, and the greater vehicle of the bodhisattvas. The former also includes both the Vaibhāṣika and the Sautrāntika.

2 *The Lesser Vehicle*

VAIBHĀṢIKA

[68b.1-69a.6] The Vaibhāṣika, among the pious attendants, hold all that is knowable to be comprised in five categories. These are, namely, the basic category of apparent forms, the dominant mind, the concomitant mental events, the relational conditions and the uncompounded entities.

Of these five basic categories the first is as follows. Apparent forms are characterised as relatively true with reference to things, the idea of which can be lost when their gross material substance composed of indivisible atomic particles is destroyed, or when analysed by the intellect. They are characterised as ultimately true when the idea which apprehends them cannot be lost upon their destruction or analysis. As it is said in the *Treasury of the Abhidharma* (Ch.6, v.4):

> Whatever, on its destruction or intellectual analysis,
> Ceases to convey an idea, like a vase or water,
> Is relatively existent; all else is ultimately real.

The Vaibhāṣika hold that the relative truth, while not existing in an ultimate sense, is veridically existent; for they admit that all substances are exclusively veridical.

The second basic category, [that of the dominant mind], refers to the consciousnesses of the five senses, along with the mental faculty, which perceive external objects.

The third refers to all the fifty-one mental events, such as feeling and perception, which, together with the dominant consciousness, apprehend objects. When the sense organs regard their objects, [mind and mental events] are held to have the same reference, the same scrutiny, and to occur at the same time with the same sensory basis, and the same substance. In this way, the comprehension of objects by consiousness and the comprehension of the specific qualities of objects by mental events arise simultaneously with the objects which they apprehend. Therefore, there is held to be no intrinsic awareness but only mind and mental events, which are both aware of external objects.

The fourth basic category is that of the disjunct conditions including the meditative absorptions and including nouns, words, and syllables, which are held to exist substantially throughout the three times. For example, a vase exists during the past time of the vase, yet it also exists during the future and the present times. It is held that any action, even when completed, has inexhaustible substantiality.

Vasubandhu

Fifth, the uncompounded entities are three in number – space, cessation [of corruption] due to individual scrutiny, and the cessation [of the future arising of any object] independent of individual scrutiny. It is held that, together with the truth of the path and its concomitants and the consciousness of the mental faculty with its concomitants, these are free from corruption, whereas all the remaining entities [mentioned above] are corrupt.

SAUTRĀNTIKA

[69a.6-70a.3] Most of the Sautrāntika tenets are identical to those of the Vaibhāṣika, the distinctions between them being that, while accepting, for example, the imperceptible forms which maintain [a behavioural pattern resulting from] an attitude of renunciation[156] – which are held by the Vaibhāṣika to be form – the Sautrāntika hold they are merely given the name form because they originate from form, and they deny that the three times have substantial existence. The sense organs are held to have consciousness as their possessor and the sense objects, too, are held to be the referential condition by which a sensum is transmitted to perception. The basic categories of mind and mental events, which are the consciousnesses of the five senses and their concomitant mental events, refer to objects such as form, yet external objects such as form and sound are not actually perceived, a sensum being transmitted in the manner of the reflection on a mirror. Accordingly, the sensum of an object such as form transmitted prior to the present moment is covertly transmitted so that the sensum corresponding to the object such as form arises at the present moment. After that moment, when the present transmitter of the sensum is transmitted in the subsequent moment, an external sensum is perceived to arise, and is then referred to as an object. The subject-object dichotomy thus becomes a subjective process and is called the comprehension of objects. As it is said in the *Ascertainment of Valid Cognition* (Ch.1):

> An object is said to be experienced
> When its resemblance is experienced.

The Sautrāntika maintain that, while appearances are essentially consciousness, they are deceptive because the sensa which are transmitted are not externally existing [objects]. However the intrinsic awareness which clearly experiences all perceptual objects is not erroneous. They deny that relational conditions have substance apart from being mere functions of form, mind and mental events, and they profess that the three uncompounded entities are insubstantial like the son of a barren woman.

PIOUS ATTENDANTS

[70a.3-70a.6] Now, those who definitely adhere to these patterns of the pious attendants observe in their conduct all the appropriate eight *prātimokṣa* vows. And by meditating on the four moments as they each apply to the four truths, beginning with impermanence,[157] the individual is realised to be divorced from [the concept] of a substantially existing independent self.

As a result of this experience, the two kinds of obscuration, [that is, those of the three poisons with their seeds and of ignorance apart from conflicting emotions] are destroyed on the culmination of the five paths through the vajra-like contemplation (*vajropamasamādhi*)[158] on the path of meditation. Obscuration is abandoned in such a way that it ceases to be acquired. Then, the result of an arhat with or without residual [impurity] is actualised.

SELF-CENTRED BUDDHAS

[70a.6-70b.6] The self-centred buddhas, on the other hand, in addition to [the moments] beginning with impermanence as they apply to the four truths, meditate on the twelve modes of dependent origination. While their progression on the path is generally identical to that of the pious attendants, [the difference between them is that] the pious attendants hold self with respect to the individual subject to be abandoned but the indivisible atomic matter of objects to continue in ultimate reality. The self-centred buddhas, however, hold all these objects to be fallacious and non-existent in ultimate reality apart from mere mental phenomena. And they are partially identical to the Mind Only (*Cittamātra*)[159] position in their opinion that the internal subjective consciousness genuinely does exist. As it is said in the *Ornament of Emergent Realisation* (Ch.2, v.8):

> Since they renounce the idea of objects
> And since they do not renounce the subject,
> One must know the path genuinely subsumed therein
> Is that of a rhinoceros-like[160] recipient.

Having meditated in this way on selflessness as far as the great path of provisions, every attainment from the feeling of warmth on the path of connection to the path of no-more-learning is actualised in a single sitting.

Thus, the two vehicles of the pious attendants and the self-centred buddhas are differentiated according to the degree of [their adherents'] acumen, and yet there is no great difference in their pattern of thought and realisation, for which reason they possess the same piṭaka.

3 *The Greater Vehicle*

The greater vehicle or the vehicle of the bodhisattvas has two divisions which are made also on the basis of its philosophical schools, namely, the Vijñānavāda and the Madhyamaka.

VIJÑĀNAVĀDA

[71a.1-72b.3] The Vijñānavādin merely confirms that objects are not perceived and indeed that substance is covert in accordance with the Sautrāntika refutation which, on analysis, did not find the temporal parts of consciousness and the spatial parts of atoms postulated by the Vaibhāṣika. For this reason the *Sūtra of the King of Contemplation* (*Samādhirājasūtra*, T 127) says:[161]

> O sons of the Conqueror, this threefold realm is only mind.

This philosophical school is therefore called the Vijñānavāda [proponents of consciousness] because it maintains all things to be merely the apparitional aspect of mind.

The Vijñānavādin also admits, in conformity with the transmission of the final turning of the doctrinal wheel, that all things are definitively ordered according to three [essential natures] of reality, namely, the imaginary, the dependent and the absolute.

Among these, the essential category of the imaginary is classified into the nominal imaginary and the imaginary of delimited characteristics. The former, since it indicates the conventional, includes the essential features of, or the particular names and symbols applied to, all things, which are exaggerated by the intellect despite being nonexistent in reality. The latter is exemplified by the two [postulated] selves [of individuals and phenomena]. The essential nature of the dependent is also divided into both impure dependence and pure dependence. The former includes everything subsumed by the five basic components which arouse corrupt states, in accordance with the quotation beginning:

> All things originate interdependently.
> They are compounded by the conditions of ignorance.

And continuing down to:

> Thus only this great mass of suffering has arisen.

The latter includes the buddha-bodies, pristine cognitions and fields of the utterly pure conquerors. The former are so called because they depend on extraneous conditions of deeds and propensities, and the latter because they originate from the condition of obscurationless power.

Then, the essential nature of the absolute is classified into both the unchanging and the incontrovertible. The former consists of the nucleus of inner radiance, the unchanging natural expression of the expanse of reality, or the truth which is the abiding nature. As the *Sūtra of the Bounteous Array* says:

> This nucleus is well defined
> As the ground-of-all.

Concerning the latter, when the end of the uncorrupted path has been reached, it is explained that this same nucleus is incontrovertibly actualised because the conflicting emotions which cover the genuine, resultant ground-of-all are entirely purified.

This philosophical system of Mind Only (*Cittamātra*) is classified into both those who hold sensa to be veridical (*Sākāravāda*) and those holding sensa to be false (*Nirākāravāda*). The former profess that, to the consciousness of the eye which apprehends the colour blue, the blue exists as blue, just as it appears. The latter are slightly superior to the former in holding that everything such as the appearance of blueness has no substantiality of either object or intellect, and that nothing material exists apart from consciousness, through which the propensities of ignorance are exaggerated and appearances then vitiated or enhanced by the ignorance of the intellect.

When further classified, [those holding sensa to be veridical] are differentiated according to the categories of objects and consciousness, so that there are those claiming perception has an equal number of objective and subjective factors, those claiming there is a diversity of sensa but not of consciousness, and those claiming that [sensa and consciousness] resemble the two halves of one egg.[162] Those holding sensa to be false, too, are divided between the maculate and the immaculate since they hold that the essence of mind is either vitiated or not by the stains of ignorant propensities. Among those claiming perception entails an equal number of objective and subjective factors, there are adherents of the eight aggregates of consciousness, and adherents of the six aggregates of consciousness. And among those claiming there is diversity of sensa but not of consciousness, there are some who hold to the six aggregates of consciousness and others who hold to a single consciousness. Such classifications become limitless.

While this school is somewhat superior to the vehicles of the pious attendants and the self-centred buddhas, it does not correctly understand the nature of the absolute category which is the ultimate truth. This is because, although both those holding sensa to be veridical and those holding sensa to be false realise that the sensa of external objects are not true, they do admit the intrinsic awareness which is naturally radiant, non-dual perception to exist absolutely as the ultimate truth.[163]

MADHYAMAKA

Secondly, the Mādhyamika are divided into both adherents of the coarse, Outer Madhyamaka which claims there is no substantial existence, and the subtle, inner Great Madhyamaka of the definitive meaning. The former includes both the Svātantrika-Madhyamaka and the Prāsaṅgika-Madhyamaka systems.

Outer Madhyamaka

Svātantrika-Madhyamaka

[72b.4-73b.4] The philosophical systems of the Vaibhāṣika, Sautrāntika and Mind Only (*Cittamātra*) fall into the extreme of clinging to substantial existence, and so do not depart from conceptual elaboration, which is subjectively oriented. However, the Svātantrika system occupies the centre (*madhyama*) because therein all things are held to be of the nature of the middle way which does not fall into either of the two extremes.

Moreover, the tenet that all things exist in the perceptual aspect of the bewildered intellect of relative appearance, but are ultimately non-existent in the awareness of the unbewildered intellect is claimed by the Svātantrika-Mādhyamika.

When these [two truths] are classified, there is held to be both a correct relative (*tathyāsaṃvṛti*) in which appearances are causally effective, and an erroneous relative (*mithyāsaṃvṛti*) in which appearances are not causally effective. On the ultimate level, too, there is held to be an ultimate truth which is referred to by synonyms (*paryāyaparamārthasatya*) in order to cut through a single aspect of conceptual elaboration, such as the view that a shoot is not self-produced, and an ultimate truth without synonyms (*aparyāyaparamārtha-satya*) which cuts through conceptual elaboration of the four extremes, beginning with the view that a shoot is produced neither from itself, nor from another source and so on. Their characteristic nature is that the relative [truth] does not resist scrutiny inasmuch as it can be refuted by the scrutinising intellect, and the ultimate truth does resist scrutiny inasmuch as it cannot be refuted by the intellect.

Nāgārjuna

Accordingly, in order to realise that the relative or phenomenal appearances which cannot be denied are not [inherently] existent, one is made to perceive that they do not exist as veridical substances. The substances of external objects and of consciousness are held to be empty and only a pristine cognition undifferentiated into any of the exaggeration and depreciation of [views concerning] being and non-being is admitted. So it is that the *Short Commentary* (*Sphuṭārtha*, T 3793) begins:

> By the pristine cognition which is individual, intrinsic awareness...

The refutation of that which is to be refuted [i.e. the inherent existence of relative appearances] is also proven by reason and logical axioms, such as the Vajra Fragments (*rdo-rje'i gzegs-ma*) which scrutinises causes; the Refutation of Production from Entities or Non-Entities (*yod-med skye-'gog*) which scrutinises results; the Refutation of the Four

Limits of Production (*mu-bzhi skye-'gog*) which scutinises [both causes and results]; the Supreme Relativity (*rten-'brel chen-po*), arranged in syllogisms of implicitly affirmative negation (*ma-yin dgag*); and the Absence of the Singular and the Multiple (*gcig-dang du-bral*) arranged in syllogisms of explicit negation (*med-dgag*).[164]

As a result, illusion and so forth, which are the objects of proof [in this system], are not proven by means of implicitly affirmative negation which delimits their scope,[165] but they are adduced by means of explicit negation which excludes[166] through mere negation [the possibility of] genuine substantial existence. In this way, a hypothetically conceived unborn nature is claimed by the Svātantrika-Mādhyamika to be a characteristic of ultimate truth, unelaborate as the sky.

In addition, by proving that which does not ultimately exist to be relatively existent, this system continues the flaws of the eternalist-nihilist dichotomy. Their understanding of mere explicit negation, a hypothetically conceived freedom from conceptual elaboration, abides not in the definitive meaning, and even the intellectual reasoning which refutes conceptual elaboration does not transcend the details of conceptual elaboration.

Prāsaṅgika-Madhyamaka

[73b.5-77a.4.] Secondly, the Prāsaṅgika-Mādhyamika demarcate the two truths by distinguishing between the bewildered intellect and the unbewildered intellect. The dichotomy between subjective consciousness and objective data never appears within the range of the meditative absorptions of sublime bodhisattvas and the all-knowing pristine cognition of the buddhas, just as dreams are not perceived when one is not asleep. As the master Nāgārjuna says:

> Just as, for example, on falling asleep,
> A man sees by the power of dreams
> His son, wife, mansion and lands,
> But sees them not upon awakening,
> So it is that when those who know relative
> appearance
> Open the eyes of intelligence,
> Part from the sleep of unknowing,
> And wake up, they no longer perceive it.

The subjective entry into pristine cognition is also called quiescence, and when all the conceptual elaborations of mind and mental events have been interrupted and obstructed, that which abides in the cessation of supreme quiescence, the expanse of reality free from all thoughts and expressions, is called the reality of unbewildered intelligence. As Candrakīrti has explained [in his *Introduction to the Madhyamaka*, Ch.11, v.13]:

Thus, because reality is uncreated,
Intellects too are uncreated.
Therefore the reality known within the contents
of these [intellects]
Is known conventionally, in the manner,
For example, of the mind
Which correctly cognises its object
On the emergence of objective sensa.

Āryadeva

And also [Ch. 11, v.16]:

When the dry brushwood of all that is knowable is
burnt,
The peace which results is the body of reality
of the conquerors.
At that time there is neither creation nor cessation,
For the cessation of mind has been actualised by that
body.

So it is that this state is called the realisation of ultimate truth, and the object of this [realisation] is the fundamental abiding nature, the naturally pure expanse of reality.

However, the bewildered intellect of false perception vitiates [this reality] through its propensities of common ignorance. In the manner of a person with a certain eye disease clinging to the truth of darkness and the vision of combed-out hairs, the sensa of the bewildering subject-object dichotomy which appear as the various realms of the six classes of beings along with their experiences of happiness and sorrow, high and low, and the different sensa which appear to sublime beings during the aftermath of meditation, that is, the world and its contents as they are generally known, are both assigned to the two aspects of relative appearance, according to whether they are the sensa of impaired or unimpaired faculties. As the *Introduction to Madhyamaka* (Ch.6, v.24) says:

There are two kinds of false perception,
One endowed with clear sense faculties,
The other with impaired faculties.
The perception of the impaired faculties
Is deemed wrong observation by those of excellent
faculties.

By virtue of this, all the things of saṃsāra, along with mind, the mental events and their objective sensations, are relative appearances. This also applies to the attainment of the [bodhisattva] levels associated with the impure forms[167] which are within the unimpeded range of mind and mental events and to other such apparitions among the six aggregates of consciousness. In short, all that is renounced or undertaken is amassed on the side of relative appearance and established as bewilderment. Relative appearances are also divided into the erroneous relative which appears to those of impaired faculties, and the correct relative which appears as the object of unimpaired faculties. The former includes the perception of two moons and dreams which are reputed to be untrue even when they appear within the range of mundane perception. The latter includes the perception of one moon which is reputed to be true when it appears within the range of mundane perception.

Now, that which diversely appears to the bewildered intellect, ostensibly true under the circumstances of the bewildered intellect which clings to duality, is never referred to in the meditative equipoise of sublime beings or in a buddha whose bewilderment has ceased and to whom bewildering appearances never appear, just as the vision of combed-out hairs experienced by one of impaired eyesight never appears to one of good eyesight. Accordingly it is said in the above [*Introduction to the Madhyamaka*, Ch.6, v.29]:

Having investigated any erroneous objects
Such as the vision of hairs in blindness,
One should know the [relative truth] also to include
Anything seen by anyone of pure vision.

And in the *Destruction of Bewilderment* by Nāgārjuna [*Madhyamaka-bhramaghāta* by Āryadeva, T 3850]:[168]

> When genuine scholars have accordingly
> Destroyed all the propensities of ignorance
> By the sun of knowledge, without exception,
> The objective mind and mental events are not seen.

In this way, the ultimate truth is characterised as the essence free from all conceptual elaborations of the subject-object dichotomy, in which all the stains of the mind and its mental events are quiescent in the expanse of reality, and which is not extraneously perceived because it is not discursive thought, or words, phrases and other such particular existents. Ultimate truth is also characterised as the abiding nature of reality which is beyond thought, free from all conceptual elaborations, and untouched by philosophical systems. As explained in the *Root Stanzas on the Madhyamaka entitled Discriminative Awareness* (cf. Ch.25, v.24):

> It is characterised as quiescent
> Without being extraneously perceived,
> Unelaborated by conceptual elaborations,
> And not different from non-conceptualisation.

To sum up: The expanse that is characterised as the profound, calm mind of the sublimest of buddhas free from all obscurations, the all-knowing pristine cognition which realises that [expanse], the essence of the pristine cognition of sublime bodhisattvas' meditative equipoise, and the sensations of higher insight which appear during the aftermath [of meditation] are all the ultimate truth.

Although the Prāsaṅgika also appraise things to have no independent existence through the five logical axioms, they do not, in the manner of the Svātantrika, alternately prove relative appearances to be false having once refuted them, or prove freedom from conceptual elaboration having once refuted conceptual elaboration with respect to ultimate reality and so forth. Rather, this unbewildered intention of the Prāsaṅgika dialectic escorts the inexpressible, inconceivable abiding reality, in which no things are differentiated according to theories of being, non-being, both being and non-being or neither being nor non-being. It has refuted all the philosophical systems which have been upheld. Accordingly, the *Refutation of Disputed Topics* (v.29) says:

> If I were to possess some proposition,
> I would at that time be at fault.
> Since I am without propositions,
> I am entirely without fault.

And in the *Four Hundred Verses* (*Catuḥśataka*, T 3846, Ch.16, v.25):

> One who adheres to no standpoint,
> Of being, non-being, both being and non-being,
> Or neither being nor non-being,
> Over a very long period cannot be censured.

And also in the *Jewel Lamp of the Madhyamaka* (*Madhyamakaratna-pradīpa*, T 3854):

> Substances which are postulated
> Do not even subtly exist.
> Since they have been uncreated from the beginning,
> They are as the son of a barren woman.

If it is objected that [in the Prāsaṅgika view] the very definitive structure of the two truths would become non-existent, it is the case that in the abiding nature of reality all dualistic doctrines such as the two truths are transcended. The Prāsaṅgika do label the apparitional world according to its mere exaggerated status, but they do not adhere to it in the manner of those philosophical systems which cling to it as [inherently] true. As it is said in the *Introduction to the Madhyamaka* (Ch.6 v.18ab):

> Just as you hold substances to have dependent
> existence,
> I have not admitted even relative existence.

And in the *Sūtra of the King of Contemplation*:

> As for the unwritten doctrines [of emptiness],
> Those which are heard and revealed
> Are indeed heard and revealed
> After the unchanging [reality] has been exaggerated.

Therefore, when the provision of pristine cognition has been accumulated through meditation which coalesces meditative equipoise in reality, or discriminative awareness, and the great compassion of skilful means, and when the provision of merit has been accumulated by perceiving all things as an apparition during the aftermath of meditation, finally the buddha-body of reality and the two bodies of form are obtained. As it is said in the *Jewel Garland* (*Ratnāvalī*, T 4158, Ch.3, v.12):

> This body of form of the buddhas
> Originated from the provision of merit.
> The body of reality, to be brief,
> Springs from the provision of kingly pristine
> cognition.

Thus the Madhyamaka of the ground refers to the two truths, the Madhyamaka of the path to the provisions, and the Madhyamaka of the result to the coalesence of the two buddha-bodies.

Great Madhyamaka

[77a.4-84a.4] Secondly, concerning the subtle, inner Great Madhyamaka of definitive meaning, it is stated in the *Jewel Lamp of the Madhyamaka* by the master Bhavya (*skal-ldan*):

> The Madhyamaka of the Prāsaṅgika and the Svātantrika is the coarse, Outer Madhyamaka. It should indeed be expressed by those who profess well-informed intelligence during debates with [extremist] Outsiders, during the composition of great treatises, and while establishing texts which concern supreme reasoning. However, when the subtle, inner Madhyamaka is experientially cultivated, one should meditate on the nature of Yogācāra-Madhyamaka.[169]

Asaṅga

In this way, two Madhyamaka are spoken of, one outer and coarse, the other inner and subtle.

Concerning the latter, the regent Ajita [Maitreya] has extensively analysed the meaningful intention of the topics of vast significance which revealed all things in terms of the three essential natures. This he did by means of discourses connected with the irreversible intention of the final turning of the doctrinal wheel and with the utter purity of the three spheres [of subject, object and their interaction].

Whereas in the aforementioned tradition of Mind Only, the dependent nature is the ground of emptiness and is explained to be the absolute, empty of imaginary objects of refutation, here it is the absolute reality (*chos-nyid yongs-grub*) that is claimed to be empty of imaginary objects of refutation. Accordingly, the components, psychophysical bases and activity fields, which are dependently conceived, are said to be a ground which is empty of the imaginary self and its properties; and the ground which is empty of that dependent ground of emptiness is absolute reality. This ground of emptiness never comes into existence because it is empty of the phenomena of saṃsāra, which are characterised as suddenly arisen and which are divided according to essential stains and substantial faults. However this ground is not empty of the amassed enlightened attributes of nirvāṇa which spontaneously abide from the beginning.

Accordingly, it is said in the *Supreme Continuum of the Greater Vehicle* (Ch.1, v.155):

> The seed which is empty of suddenly arisen
> phenomena
> Endowed with divisive characteristics
> Is not empty of the unsurpassed reality
> Endowed with indivisible characteristics.

And in the *Commentary* [*on the Supreme Continuum of the Greater Vehicle, Mahāyānottaratantraśāstravyākhyā,* T 4025, p.76]:

> If one asks what is revealed by this passage, the reason for there being no basis of all-conflicting emotions requiring to be clarified in this naturally pure seed of the tathāgata is that it is naturally free from suddenly arisen stains. It contains nothing at all which can be established as a basis for purification, for its nature is reality, pure of divisive phenomena. So it is that the nucleus of the tathāgata is empty of divisions which may be removed and of the entire nest of conflicting emotions, but it is not empty of the inconceivable attributes of the buddhas which outnumber all the sands of the River Ganges and are non-divisive and inalienable.

Now it is also said that the imaginary implies that attributes are without substantial existence, the dependent that creation is without substantial existence and the absolute that ultimate reality is without substantial existence. The first two of these [indicate] that the conceptual aspects of the subject-object dichotomy, which are suddenly arising fictions, are empty of their own essence, and the latter refers to emptiness as the naturally expressed, fundamental essence itself which has no substantiality. Since this [ultimate reality] is naturally pure, it abides, through its function of emptiness, as the enlightened attributes of the buddha-body of reality, and through its apparitional function as the ground on which the buddha-bodies, fields, celestial mansions and so forth arise. Through its function of awareness, it is spontaneously present from the beginning, free from causes and free from results, because it is the supporting ground of the ten powers, the four fearlessnesses and the like. This natural expression of the buddhas, which is called the nucleus of the sugata, does not abide as the seed of creation, destruction, transformation, change, increase or decrease, cause or condition, and so forth, and it is ever uncovered, without being an object of metaphor, thought or expression. It is said in the *Play of Mañjuśrī* (*Mañjuśrīvikrīḍitamahāyānasūtra*, T 96):

> Sister, although suddenly arising conflicting emotions do emerge in relation to the natural inner radiance, the natural inner radiance cannot be defiled by those suddenly arisen all-conflicting emotions.

And the regent Ajita has said [in the *Supreme Continuum of the Greater Vehicle*, Ch.1, v.5]:

> Uncompounded and spontaneously present,
> Unrealised through external conditions,
> Endowed with knowledge, love and power
> Is the buddhahood possessing the two benefits.

If one were otherwise to apprehend all things as being exclusively empty of their own essence, in the manner of the proponents of intrinsic emptiness (*rang-stong-pa*), then it is said that according to the same extreme [argument] the buddha-body of reality would also be empty of itself. The buddha-bodies, pristine cognitions, fields and so forth would be non-existent, the accumulation of the provisions and purification of obscurations, which depend upon these, would also be non-existent, and indeed the teachings through which the causal and resultant vehicles reveal all the means of purifying stains, whatever their basis or path, would be diminished. The ground of purification being non-existent, there would be no need to effect purification. Being empty of pristine cognition, there would be no work on behalf of others and no [enlightened] understanding. There being nothing existent, even with respect to the relative appearances of the impure dependent nature, there would also be no enlightened attributes to transform these impurities into the pure dependent nature. There would be no self to become the ground of bondage and liberation, and there would be no doctrine to be realised by each one individually. Many such faults would persist and by nature give rise to the source of unbearable views. This can be known from quotations such as the following from the *Sūtra of the Dialogue with Kāśyapa from the Sublime Pagoda of Precious Jewels* (*Āryaratnakūṭakāśyapaparivartasūtra*, T 87):

> O Kāśyapa, whoever, referring to emptiness, relies upon emptiness deviates from this discourse of mine; theirs is said to be a great deviation. O Kāśyapa, it is better to abide in a view [which clings to] individual existence to the extent of Mount Sumeru, than with manifest egotism to adopt a view to emptiness. If you ask why, O Kāśyapa, I have explained that although that which arises from all views is emptiness, Kāśyapa, that which exclusively regards emptiness is untenable.

If one were, on the other hand, to object that this would not be emptiness, it is not the case, as the *Sublime Sūtra of the Descent to Laṅkā* says:

> If you ask what is the emptiness which is the ultimate reality of all things, the great pristine cognition of the sublime beings, it is as follows. The attainment of the pristine cognition of the sublime beings, which is one's own intrinsic awareness, is empty of the propensities of all views and faults. This is called the emptiness which is the ultimate reality of all things, the great pristine cognition of sublime beings.

This ultimate reality that is empty of extraneous entities (*gzhan-stong*), is similarly found in sūtras belonging to the intermediate promulgation of the doctrinal wheel. It is said in the *Transcendental Perfection of Discriminative Awareness in Twenty-five Thousand Lines*:

> In this context, if you ask what is the emptiness of other substances, it applies whether the tathāgatas have appeared or not. As the abiding nature of reality, as reality itself, the expanse of reality, the faultlessness of reality, the nature of just what is, the unmistakable nature of just what is, the unalterable nature of just what is, and as the genuine goal, it abides as just what is. Therefore, this reality, which is empty of extraneous entities, is called the emptiness of other substances. Subhūti, this is the greater vehicle of the bodhisattvas, great spiritual warriors.

And it is extensively mentioned in the *Supreme Continuum of the Greater Vehicle*, as cited above in the passage (Ch.1, v.155) which begins:

> The seed which is empty of suddenly arisen phenomena
> Endowed with divisive characteristics...

The nature of this expanse in the minds of sentient beings is like a treasure of precious gems within the earth, uncovered by stains in respect of its own essence, and yet it simultaneously assumes the suddenly arisen forms of saṃsāra, in the manner, for example, of water and ice. It says in the *Sūtra of the King of Contemplation*:

> Pure, clear and inwardly radiant,
> Undisturbed and uncompounded
> Is the nucleus of the sugata.
> It is the reality that abides from the beginning.

And in the master Nāgārjuna's *Eulogy to the Expanse of Reality* (v.23):

> The water that lies within the earth
> Remains immaculately pure.
> The pristine cognition within conflicting
> emotions, too,
> Remains similarly immaculate.

Such quotations maintain that the status of the nucleus [of the tathāgata] according to the definitive meaning is inconceivable.

This nucleus of the tathāgata, with respect to its own essence, is the same throughout saṃsāra and nirvāṇa, without good or evil. As it is said [in the *Ornament of the Sūtras of the Greater Vehicle*, Ch.9, v.37]:

> The nature of just what is, in all things, is
> undifferentiated.
> When purified, it is the nature of the tathāgata.
> Therefore all living beings possess that nucleus.

Such extensive quotations have an intention directed towards the absolute nature, which is unchanging reality. Therefore the *Supreme Continuum of the Greater Vehicle* (Ch.1, v.51) says:

> Subsequently just as it was before
> Is the unchanging reality.

When beings are circumstantially classified in relation to the stains which suddenly arise, they fall into three categories. As it is explained in the *Supreme Continuum of the Greater Vehicle* (Ch.1, v.47):

> According to their respective order of being impure,
> Purifying that which is impure and being utterly pure,
> They are called sentient beings, bodhisattvas and
> tathāgatas.

And in the *Commentary* [*on the Supreme Continuum of the Greater Vehicle*, p.40]:

> Therefore, those in the circumstance of being impure are called sentient beings, those in the circumstance of purifying that which is impure are called bodhisattvas and those in the circumstance of being utterly pure are called tathāgatas.

Similarly, everything appears according to distinctions such as the three vehicles, to differentiations based upon hierarchical classifications such as the ten levels and the five paths, and likewise to ethical hierarchies such as good and evil sentient beings, pious attendants and self-centred buddhas, and sublime bodhisattvas and buddhas. However, the natural inner radiance, which is the expanse of reality and the ultimate truth, pervades everything without [distinctions between] good and evil or decrease and increase, just as, for example, vases appear to be distinguished according to their quality, there being clay vases, wooden vases, vases of precious gems and so on, while the space within these vases is identical in that it is without qualities. Accordingly, the *Supreme Continuum of the Greater Vehicle* (Ch.1, vv.49-50) says:

> Just as space is omnipresent,
> Having a thoughtless nature,
> So the natural expression of mind,
> The immaculate expanse, is all-pervasive.
> Its general characteristic pervades the limits
> Of negative and positive attributes,
> In the manner of the space
> Within inferior, mediocre and superior material forms.

If one then asks what exactly the three circumstances just mentioned are, beings are separated between saṃsāra and nirvāṇa according to the distinction of whether they are liberated or not liberated from the stains that obscure the nucleus. As the same text says:

> One covered by the net of conflicting emotions
> Is truly called a sentient being.
> On becoming free from conflicting emotions
> One is called a buddha.

Regarding this threefold circumstance, ordinary persons who are obscured by the great darkness of obscuration have nothing but a portion of enlightened attributes. By contrast, the arhats among the pious attendants and self-centred buddhas are more sublime than them in enlightened attributes since they have gradually reduced the stains covering the nucleus by the greater or lesser potency of the antidotes which have power to remove them. Then, the bodhisattvas appear to be even more sublime, having attained the levels, and surpassed those who have not renounced all aspects of ignorance. Beyond that, the buddhas free from all obscurations appear yet more sublime.

Therefore, this ultimate truth which is the expanse [of reality] is not qualitatively perceived according to its abiding nature by the three lower kinds of sublime being, namely, the pious attendants, self-centred buddhas and bodhisattvas. It is not manifestly perceived by one who abides on the paths of provision and connection except as a mere volition of the scrutinising intellect. Again, although it is partially perceived on the paths of insight and meditation, the expanse cannot be perfectly perceived through these paths, apart from a mere proportion of its enlightened attributes, just as a small child does not perceive the all-encompassing sun apart from the mere glimpse of its rays through an aperture.

As has previously been cited [from the *Supreme Continuum of the Greater Vehicle*, Ch.2, v.68]:

> Because it is not an object of speech,
> Is subsumed by ultimate reality,
> Is not within reason's domain,
> Is beyond exemplification,
> Is unsurpassed and is subsumed neither by existence
> nor quiescence,
> The objective range of the Conqueror is inconceivable
> Even to sublime beings.

It is on the buddha level that the natural expression [of reality] is directly and perfectly perceived. As explained in the *Commentary on the Supreme Continuum of the Greater Vehicle* (p.77):

> Just as the sun in the sky appears
> Through an aperture in the clouds,
> In this situation you are not fully perceived
> Even by sublime beings endowed with pure eyes of
> Intelligence; for their intelligence is partial.
> However, Transcendent Lord, you who are the pure
> body of reality,
> Pervading the spacious expanse of limitless knowledge
> Are totally perceived by those whose intelligence is
> limitless.

Would it then be, one might object, that sentient beings become buddhas who have accumulated the two provisions and renounced the two obscurations by means of this naturally radiant expanse, which is effortlessly present in the nature of sentient beings? That is not so, because there are two kinds of renunciation, one that is naturally pure and the other that becomes free from the suddenly arisen stains. The former is the reality which, in respect of its own essence, abides without changing in the fundamental nature of great primordial purity. It is said in the *Sūtra of the Adornment of Pristine Cognition's Appearance which Penetrates the Scope of All Buddhas* (*Sarvabuddhaviṣayāvatāra-jñānālokālaṃkārasūtra*, T 100):

> Mañjuśrī, since the mind is naturally radiant, it is naturally undefiled by all-conflicting emotions, and is only [provisionally] defiled by all the subsidiary conflicting emotions which suddenly arise. That which is naturally radiant is the very absence of all-conflicting emotions. For one who is without all-conflicting emotions, there is no antidote through which all-conflicting emotions should be renounced.

And in the *Transcendental Perfection of Discriminative Awareness in Twenty-five Thousand Lines*:

> "Kauśika, what do you think of this? Are sentient beings created or do they expire?" He replied, "Venerable Subhūti, that is not the case. If you ask why, it is because sentient beings are pure from the beginning."

And also in the same text:

> Since form is naturally radiant, it is pure without all-conflicting emotions. Since feeling, perception, habitual tendencies and consciousness are naturally radiant, they are pure without all-conflicting emotions. Since all manifestations up to omniscience are naturally radiant, they are pure and without all-conflicting emotions.

According to such extensive quotations, natural renunciation is that which transcends the phenomena of consciousness and is a genuine liberation from all obscurations. It is complete from the beginning in ultimate truth because absolute reality is naturally pure.

The second kind of renunciation is the removal of the suddenly arising obscurations by an appropriate antidote. Although, as previously explained, the unactualised enlightened attributes which exist in the ground unrefined by the path are present in the situation of sentient beings, no defect is thereby introduced to this philosophical system because it is not claimed that sentient beings are buddhas free from all obscurations.

In the same way, there are also two kinds of realisation, namely, the naturally present pristine cognition realised through the intrinsic awareness of primordial reality, and the dependently produced pristine cognition realised through the power of meditating on the path. The former is characterised as supramundane, being the naturally present pristine cognition or discernment through individual intuitive awareness which realises the ultimate reality. Thus [the *Litany of the Names of Mañjuśrī*, v.155ab] says:

> It is awareness of itself, awareness of others,
> And awareness of all.
> It is the all-knowing sacred total awareness.

The two fundamental kinds of renunciation and realisation are complete in their own essence, which is the abiding nature of ultimate reality. As the venerable Maitreya [in the *Supreme Continuum of the Greater Vehicle*, Ch.1, v.154][170] says:

> Therein there is nothing to be clarified
> And nothing to be minutely established.
> Genuinely regarding that genuine reality,
> Genuinely perceiving it, one will be free.

The second kind of realisation is that pattern of realisation which is expanded by the power of meditating on the path. It is called the absolute which is incontrovertible because enlightened attributes of obscurationless power are actualised once the two provisions of pristine cognition have been accumulated through meditative equipoise and merit during the aftermath. As the *Ornament of the Sūtras of the Greater Vehicle Vehicle* (Ch.9, v.22abd) says:

> Though there is no distinction
> Between the former and the latter,
> It is the nature of just what is,
> Untainted by all obscurations,
> That is held to be the buddha.

4 *The Superiority of Great Madhyamaka to Mind Only*

[84a.4-92a.6] This system, according to which the relative is empty of its own essence and the ultimate empty of other entities, is variously revealed in both the intermediate and final promulgations. However, in particular, the presence of profound, radiant and non-dual pristine cognition, the nucleus of the sugata, as the ground of emptiness is extensively taught in the piṭaka of the final transmitted precepts, and in those which speak of all things as merely apparitional aspects of mind.

Derived from these [precepts], certain masters of the past have been obliged to admit that the mind is ultimately real and thereby originated the school of the Vijñānavāda [proponents of consciousness], which is one of those known at the present day as the four philosophical systems. While not reaching the genuine intention, that mind described as the mind of which all things are merely apparitional aspects partakes of two circumstances, one under which its intention is directed to the consciousness of the ground-of-all, and the other under which its intention is directed to the absolute reality (*chos-nyid yongs-grub*).

When the former is intended, it is said not to be the ultimate truth because it is impermanent, the bewildered subject and object being relative appearances. For example, the *Sūtra of the Adornment of Pristine Cognition's Appearance which Penetrates the Scope of All Buddhas* says:

> Śāradvatīputra, that which is called mind includes the consciousness of mind and intellect, the mental body, the faculty of the intellect and the base of the intellect. This is what is called the mind. If you ask how emptiness relates with it, Śāradvatīputra, the mind is empty of the mind. In it there is no actor. If there were some actor, then its actions would be experienced as such by others. The mind is not manifestly conditioned even by the mind.

Though it is taught that all things are merely apparitional aspects of mind, there is no occasion so to speak in connection with the ultimate truth, for the pristine cognition transcending mind, intellect and all aspects of consciousness is revealed in the ultimate truth. Accordingly, it is said in the *Sublime Sūtra of the Descent to Laṅkā*:

> One who has become without mind, intellect, the consciousness of the intellect, conceptualising thoughts and perception, will become receptive to the uncreated doctrine. O Mahāmati, since the doctrine which is apparitionless and divorced from conceptualising thoughts is revealed, this ultimate reality is without order or orderly intervals.

Maitreya

And also [Ch.3, vv.40-1]:

> Having renounced the mind and intellect,
> Consciousness, perception and thoughts,
> The pious attendants who have obtained the
> conceptualising doctrine
> Become the sons of the Conqueror.
> Through the distinctions of [buddha-]field
> and [bodhisattvas'] receptiveness,
> [They gain] the virtuous pristine cognition of the Tathāgata.

There are, in addition, proponents of the Mind Only philosophical system who hold that consciousness is not transcended in the ultimate truth. But this is simply a subjective perception of saṃsāra, unable to sublimate the world. The ultimate truth is characterised as the uncorrupted expanse, and as the obscurationless pristine cognition which realises it, namely, the supramundane, individual, intuitive awareness of the sublime beings.

The distinction between these two [views] has been extensively taught in passages such as the following from that [same] sūtra of the greater vehicle [*Descent to Laṅkā*, p.64]:

> In this context, Mahāmati, pristine cognition is of three kinds: mundane, supramundane and most supramundane. Of these, that which having been created is destroyed is consciousness; and that which is neither created nor destroyed is pristine cognition. Moreover, Mahāmati, that which falls into the dichotomy of being symbolic or non-symbolic, that which falls into the dichotomy of being and non-being, and that which is created from causes of diverse character, is consciousness; whereas that which is characterised as utterly transcending the dichotomy of symbolic and non-symbolic is pristine cognition. And yet again Mahāmati, that which is characterised as accumulating them is consciousness, and that which is characterised as diminishing them is pristine cognition.
>
> Now these three kinds [of pristine cognition respectively] generate the realisation of individual and general characteristics, the realisation of that which is created and destroyed and the realisation of that which is neither created nor ceases. The mundane pristine cognition is that of the extremists who manifestly cling to theses of being or non-being and of all ordinary childish persons. The supramundane pristine cognition is that of all pious attendants and self-centred buddhas who openly cling to thoughts which fall into individual and general characteristics. The most supramundane pristine cognition is the analytical insight of the buddhas and bodhisattvas into apparitionless reality. It is seen to be without creation or cessation, for they comprehend the selfless level of the Tathāgata who is free from theses concerning being and non-being.
>
> Furthermore, Mahāmati, that which is characterised as unattached is pristine cognition, and that which is characteristically attached to various objects is consciousness. And again, Mahāmati, that which is characterised as being produced from the triple combination [of subject, object and

their interaction][171] is consciousness and that characterised as the essential nature which is not so produced is pristine cognition. Then again, Mahāmati, that which is characterised as not to be attained is pristine cognition, since each one's own sublime pristine cognition does not emerge as a perceptual object of realisation, [but is present] in the manner of the moon's reflection in water. On this it must be said [Ch.3, vv.38-9]:

> *The mind accrues deeds and so forth,*
> *But pristine cognition breaks them down;*
> *By discriminative awareness, too, the apparitionless*
> *Reality and powers are well obtained.*
> *It is the mind which objectifies.*

And similarly it is said in the *Sublime Sūtra of Clouds of Precious Jewels* (*Āryaratnameghasūtra*, T 231):

> This doctrine genuinely transcends all written and spoken words. It genuinely transcends the entire range of expressions. It genuinely transcends all verbalisation. It is free from all conceptual elaboration and free from all that is accepted or rejected. It is free from all opening and closing, and free from all sophistry. It is not to be analysed and is not within the range of sophistry. It genuinely transcends the range of sophistry. It is non-symbolic, free from symbolism and genuinely transcends the range of symbolism. It genuinely transcends the range of the childish. It genuinely transcends the range of all demons, and genuinely transcends the range of all conflicting emotions. It genuinely transcends the range of consciousness. It does, however, lie within the range of the indeterminate, dynamic, quiescent and sublime pristine cognition. The individual, intrinsic awareness of these attributes is a topic which is taintless, uncovered, pure, bountiful, supreme, sacred, perfect, permanent, firm, enduring and imperishable. Whether the tathāgatas have appeared or not, this expanse of reality is exclusively present.

The inconceivability of the ultimate, sublime pristine cognition, extensively revealed by such quotations, does not lie within the path [followed] by the proponents of the Mind Only system. It is admitted that this naturally radiant, intuitive awareness, the perception free from the subject-object dichotomy, is itself the true basis of buddhahood, and it is held that the subject is dependently real. It is therefore difficult for anyone holding consciousness to exist substantially in ultimate reality to understand literally the selflessness of phenomena. In the same vein the *Sūtra of the Descent to Laṅkā* (Ch.10, vv.359 and 358) also says:

Being mind only, it is apparitionless.
Being apparitionless, it is uncreated.
These middle paths
Have been explained by myself, and others too.
Realising that there is only mind,
External substances are clarified.
By reversing the pattern of conceptualising thought,
That path becomes the middle one.

So it is that this intention of the final transmitted precepts, abiding in the Great Madhyamaka of definitive meaning, is clearly revealed in the commentaries of great bodhisattvas[172] and in the compositions of the two promulgators who were masters of the greater vehicle [Nāgārjuna and Asaṅga] along with their followers. Although certain masters may well have developed other systems and tenets elsewhere out of necessity, it is difficult to estimate whether they are ordinary or sublime beings. There may well be occasion to speak in the manner [of these masters] owing to various basic intentions once one has reached the level of the sublime ones, but childish persons like ourselves should understand the importance of not accumulating evil deeds which renounce the doctrine, having clung to a single extreme [view].

If this system [of Great Madhyamaka] were also to be described as Mind Only because the three essential natures are taught therein, then the three essential natures are extensively revealed, too, in the intermediate transmitted precepts such as the *Intermediate Mother*:

> Maitreya, regard any imaginary form as not substantially existent. One might regard any conceptualised form as substantially existent because thoughts exist substantially, but do not confer independent status upon it. Then you should regard the very form of reality as being disclosed by ultimate reality, for it is neither substantially existent nor not substantially existent.

And again in the *Epitome of the Transcendental Perfection of Discriminative Awareness in Eight Thousand Lines* (*Aṣṭasāhasrikāpiṇḍārtha*, T 3809, vv.27-9):

The transcendental perfection of discriminative awareness
Genuinely depends on three teachings:
The imaginary, dependent and absolute alone.
By negative expressions and the like
All that is imaginary is refuted.
By apparition and other such similes
The dependent is correctly revealed.
Through the fourfold purification[173]
The absolute is well known.

Other than the transcendental perfection
Of discriminative awareness,
The buddhas have no teaching.

Similarly, in the master Nāgamitra's *Introduction to the Three Bodies* (*Kāyatrayāvatāramukha*, T 3890), the three essential natures are also summarised as the causal basis for the attainment of the three buddha-bodies, and in the *Commentary* [*on the Introduction to the Three Bodies, Kāyatrayavṛtti*, T 3891] composed by the proponent of the Great Madhyamaka, Jñānacandra, the same point is explained. Despite all the definitive structures of the three essential natures which have been set forth in all such texts of Great Madhyamaka, those who propound that they belong not to the Madhyamaka tradition but just to that of Mind Only have not even seen these relevant texts. As the *Sūtra of the Descent to Laṅkā* (Ch.10, vv.256-7) says:

One who relies on Mind Only,
Does not discern external objects.
Relying on the apparitionless,
Mind Only should be transcended.
Relying on the genuine object of reference,
The apparitionless should be transcended.
A yogin who abides in the apparitionless
Does not perceive the greater vehicle.

Accordingly, after Mind Only has been provisionally taught and then genuinely transcended, the apparitionless Madhyamaka is taught; and when that too has been transcended, the apparitional Madhyamaka is revealed. If that is not reached, it is said that the profound meaning of the greater vehicle is not perceived. It is, in general, erroneous to describe everything expressed by the word *mind* as the Mind Only doctrine; for there are occasions when the abiding nature free from all extremes, [known] inclusively as the nature of just what is, the genuine goal, the natural nirvāṇa, the expanse of reality, the mind of inner radiance, and the intellect of Samantabhadra, is indicated by the word *mind*. The *Long Mother* says:

Subhūti, that mind is not the mind.
The nature of that mind is inner radiance.

One should not therefore mistake that which is spoken of as mind-as-such, the inner radiance transcending the mind of saṃsāra and its mental events, for the Mind Only system which does not transcend consciousness. The latter is characterised in the *Sūtra of the Descent to Laṅkā* (Ch.3, v.32 and Ch.10, v.486) as follows:

Connected with propensities of conceptualising thought,
The diversity which arises from the mind

And appears externally to mankind,
Is the mundane Mind Only [view].

There is indeed a distinction between the mundane and the supramundane Mind Only which is identical in meaning to the distinction between consciousness and pristine cognition, as previously explained. Similarly, those terms revealed in the most profound [sūtras] of the greater vehicle which are synonyms of mind should be likewise known. It would indeed be a grave error to equate the tenets of mundane Mind Only with the Great Sage's buddha-body of reality and the mass of its inseparable enlightened attributes, exceeding all the sands of the River Ganges, which are inclusively known as the uncorrupted expanse, the inconceivable expanse, ultimate virtue, unchanging and firm reality, truth in the ultimate abiding nature of reality, the primordially liberated buddha-body, freedom from all conceptual elaborations of the four extremes, and renunciation of the two concepts of selfhood. These are spontaneously present, utterly transcending the phenomena of consciousness.

In general, those whose intelligence is authoritative, without falling into prejudice, do not differentiate between the two modes of emptiness [*rang-stong* and *gzhan-stong*] when abiding in the Madhyamaka [view], which is the summit of the four philosophical systems dependent on different traditions of promulgation which have been precisely enumerated. This is clearly understood through the respective treatises of the two great masters, Nāgārjuna and Asaṅga, whom the Conqueror had prophetically declared would comment on the intention of the definitive meaning; and in conformity with them, it has been similarly explained by the all-knowing dialectician Ratnākaraśānti, the venerable Bhavya, the Guru of Suvarṇadvīpa,[174] the lord Atiśa and others. Even the master Haribhadra gives confirmation of it because, when explaining the intention of the *Ornament of Emergent Realisation* [in his *Mirror Commentary*, T 3791], he resolves that this non-dual pristine cognition alone is the genuinely existing essence. He then asserts this resolution to be made through the sequence of [discriminative awareness] produced by reflection, or through the yoga produced by the meditation of a yogin on the third level.[175] And he additionally confirms this by explaining the recognition of just what is to be pristine cognition, and by explaining, in his commentary on the essential buddha-body, that the remaining three buddha-bodies, through which it abides, are reality.

In this way, the emptiness directly revealed through the intermediate promulgation is claimed to have the definitive meaning of outright explicit negation in order that it might cut through the egotism that is coemergent with intellect in corporeal beings; as well as through the view of self, which is newly postulated by the philosophical systems of the eternalistic extremists; and through the subjective, conceptual elaborations of those of our own [Buddhist] philosophical systems which propound substantial existence.[176] Since [this intermediate promulgation] teaches that one meditates on emptiness when meditating on nothing at all, and realises just what is when nothing at all is perceived, that [reality] and its significance are indeed perceived. The view of this [promulgation] is therefore in the range of understanding or proper realisation of selflessness.

It is difficult to destroy attachment to superficial characteristics (*mtshan-'dzin*).[177] However, in order for the discriminative awareness born of study and thought to refute it, the Prāsaṅgika and Svātantrika reasoning which cuts through conceptual elaboration is sharp. But when the experiences of meditation are established, it is this tradition of the Great Madhyamaka, as taught in the third promulgation, which is supremely profound and vast. This naturally present pristine cognition, the ultimate truth of the naturally pure expanse, is the original abiding nature of all things, and it is the pristine cognition to be experienced by individual intuitive awareness. As it is said in Rāhula's *Praise of the Mother* [*yum-la bstod-pa*, T 1127, attributed to Nāgārjuna]:

> Homage to the Mother of the conquerors of the three
>   times,
> Who is the ineffable, unthinkable, inexpressible
> Transcendental perfection of discriminative awareness,
> Essential nature uncreated and unceasing as the sky,
> Within range of the individual intuitive awareness
> That is pristine cognition.

And [in the *Sūtra of Extensive Play*, Ch.25, v.1]:

> I have found a nectar-like doctrine
> Profound, calm, unelaborate, radiant and uncompounded.

By such quotations, the inconceivable pristine cognition has been illustrated, and through the vision of its nature the ultimate truth is perceived. It is wrong to refer to the mere emptiness, which is nothing at all, as the ultimate truth.

Thus, absolute reality is the pristine cognition of the non-dual nature of just what is. It is indicated by the words buddha-body of reality or essential buddha-body which genuinely transcends the phenomena of consciousness. Yet, also comprised within this doctrine, which is misrepresented as the philosophical system known as the Mind Only, are: the definitive order of the three continua as taught in the way of secret mantra;[178] the definitive order of the ground, path and result of purification and so forth which are adhered to by followers of the greater vehicle in both its causal and resultant aspects, and which include [the terminology] of deities, mantras, embodiments of indestructible reality, supreme bliss, emptiness endowed with all supreme aspects, the imperishable seminal point which is the fundamental support of body, speech and mind; and also the uncommon definitive order of the ground, path and result.

One should know that the intention of the final promulgation, even though not within the path upheld by the proponents of intrinsic emptiness (*rang-stong-pa*), is without contradiction by examining, one by one, the commentaries of the great lords of the tenth level and the teachings belonging to the tantrapiṭaka of the way of secret mantra.

Therefore, while the intention of the final transmitted precepts is not the same as that of the mundane Mind Only system in any of its forms, the purposes of the lower phases of the vehicle are gradually gathered within the higher, so that [Mind Only and the like] are not contradictory apart from their vindication of an extreme position. Indeed, one must truly comprehend that the great distinction of the higher over the lower phases is a feature of the precious teaching of the sublime Sugata. Otherwise, after one had been given teaching on suffering, selflessness, impurity and impermanence according to the first promulgation and everything had been established as emptiness according to the intermediate transmitted precepts, if one were then to grasp literally the meaningful intention revealed according to the final transmitted precepts concerning bliss, purity, permanence and true self,[179] without knowing how to accept them with an attitude confident in the four kinds of reliance, one would engage in conceptualising thoughts which would confuse those who require training and wrongly scrutinise the teaching.

With an intention directed toward this, the *Commentary on the Supreme Continuum of the Greater Vehicle* (p.74) says accordingly:

> To sum up, there are four kinds of individuals who do not possess the eye which perceives the nucleus of the tathāgata. If you ask who these four are, they are as follows: ordinary persons, pious attendants, self-centred buddhas and bodhisattvas who have newly entered the vehicle. As it has been said,[180] "O Transcendent Lord, this nucleus of the tathāgata is not within the range of those who fall into views concerning worldly existence, who openly delight in deception and whose minds waver towards emptiness."

This same point can also be proven thoroughly from all the transmitted precepts and treatises, but here one will suffice.

5 *The Provisional and Definitive Meaning of the Transmitted Precepts*

[92a.6-95b.6] When these teachings are allocated between the provisional meaning (*drang-don*) and the definitive meaning (*nges-don*), the three successive promulgations of the doctrinal wheel have the same common purpose, that is, to purify the stains covering the single nucleus of the tathāgata. They differ only in the greatness of their means which respectively purify the gross, subtle and very subtle stains that suddenly arise to obscure it. Thus, by teachings such as impermanence, the first promulgation arouses the mind from saṃsāra and causes it to approach nirvāṇa. In the second, the three approaches to liberation become an antidote to attachment to superficial characteristics, which include the mundane view of self; and the third intends that the extensive way of the sugatas be comprehended through the topics of that irreversible promulgation. This is extensively mentioned in passages such as the following from the *Sūtra of the Dialogue with King Dhāraṇīśvara* (*Dhāraṇīśvaraparipṛcchāsūtra*, T 147):

> Son of the enlightened family, it is in the same way as, for example, a skilled jeweller, who knows well how gems are refined, takes an impure stone from a species of precious gemstones and, after wetting it in dirty salt water, has it cleaned with goats' hair, and similarly after then wetting it in a beverage has it cleaned with a woollen cloth, and afterwards, in the very same way, wets it in a herbal solution and has it cleaned with fine clean linen; when it is well refined, the stainless gem is said to be "a great gemstone of the species beryl". Likewise, when a sentient being has first been induced to enter the Vinaya by the disturbing topics such as suffering and impermanence, and has then been made to realise the way of the tathāgatas by means of the three approaches to liberation, he subsequently is made to enter the objective range of the tathāgatas by the topics of the irreversible promulgation. To enter in this

> way and realise reality is to become an unsurpassed object of offering.

Thus, the three successive [promulgations] of transmitted precepts are classified into those of provisional meaning and those of definitive meaning. It says in the *Sūtra which Decisively Reveals the Intention* (*Sandhinirmocanasūtra*, T 106):

> The first promulgation of the doctrinal wheel by the Transcendent Lord, through which the four sublime truths were taught to those who enter the vehicle of the pious attendants, is surpassed, circumstantial, of provisional meaning and continues to be a basis for debate. Then, beginning with the Transcendent Lord's teaching that things have no essence, the second promulgation of the doctrinal wheel which teaches emptiness to those who correctly enter the greater vehicle is surpassed, circumstantial, of provisional meaning and continues to be a basis for debate. And then, beginning with the Transcendent Lord's teaching that things have no essence, the third promulgation of the wheel of the exceedingly wondrous and amazing doctrine, which is well distinguished, was revealed to those correctly entering the entire vehicle. That promulgation of the doctrinal wheel is unsurpassed, not circumstantial, of definitive meaning and does not become a basis for debate.

The allocation of provisional and definitive meaning is determined in ways such as these.

The intermediate promulgation has accordingly been allocated provisional meaning because in this turning of the doctrinal wheel the enlightened attributes of ultimate reality, such as the powers of the sugatas, are mostly revealed to be empty of their own essence (*rang-stong*), though they are not actually empty of their own essence, and because it does not teach that these attributes are well distinguished and without inherent contradiction. For such reasons it is said to be surpassed and so on. Definitive meaning, on the other hand, is allocated to the third promulgation because [therein] things of relative appearance are empty of their own essence and the ultimate reality is empty of extraneous entities, so that the nature of these [attributes] is qualitatively well distinguished and then revealed.

If there are those who say that definitive meaning is contained in the intermediate promulgation because it teaches the transcendental perfection of discriminative awareness, but that the final promulgation has an intention of provisional meaning because it teaches the contrary, then they have not made an accurate examination. The attributes, such as uncreated and unceasing original quiescence, which are terms relating to the transcendental perfection of discriminative awareness, are most extensively revealed in the final promulgation and very profoundly revealed in the vehicle of indestructible reality.

However, there is no distinction in the essence of the transcendental perfection of discriminative awareness, which is said to be distinguished as surpassed or unsurpassed depending on whether it is unclearly, clearly or very clearly revealed; for all the limitless [attributes] which are revealed by names such as the nucleus of the sugata, the expanse of reality, the mind of inner radiance, the naturally pure enlightened family, the genuine goal and the emptiness which is the essential nature devoid of substantiality, are identical in the naturally present, non-dual pristine cognition. This same [pristine cognition] is the transcendental perfection of discriminative awareness. Therefore the master Dignāga [in his *Epitome of the Transcendental Perfection of Discriminative Awareness*, v.1] has said:

> Being the transcendental perfection of
> Discriminative awareness,
> This non-dual pristine cognition is the Tathāgata.
> Since it possesses the meaning
> Which is to be accomplished,
> This term applies to the central texts and path.[181]

The final transmitted precepts are conclusively proven to be the definitive meaning by all [scriptural] transmissions and [logical] reasoning. The Conqueror himself made the classification of provisional and definitive meaning, and moreover, in his own words said:

> A monk who is called Asaṅga
> Learned in the meaning of these treatises,
> Will differentiate in many categories
> The sūtras of provisional and definitive meaning.

The final [transmitted precepts] were accordingly allocated conclusive definitive meaning by this sublime [Asaṅga], whom the Conqueror had prophetically declared would differentiate the provisonal and definitive meanings.

There are, on the other hand, no authoritative passages declaring the intermediate [transmitted precepts] to have definitive meaning and the final [transmitted precepts] provisional meaning. Indeed, even if the proponents of the Vijñānavāda could have composed these final transmitted precepts as such, they would have mistaken the correct sequence revealed by the above simile of the refinement of gemstones and by other similes which refer to the medical treatment of ill-health and the study of letters.[182] There would be no need even for the definitive order made by the Conqueror himself and the sublime [Asaṅga], and there would be limitless other such faults. In addition, after first teaching the provisional meaning and intermediately the definitive meaning to those who require training, the provisional meaning would then be repeated, so that one would be obliged to consider just what is the Buddha's intention *vis-à-vis* the teaching. It should be known that by proceeding in this way, there would be all kinds of unbearable evils, such as allocating the conclusive definitive meaning to philosophical systems which propound substantial existence, slandering the buddhas and great bodhisattvas as holders of a relative teaching, and abandoning this doctrine of the nucleus.

Furthermore, since the three vehicles have reference to the definitive meaning gathered in the final promulgation, the definitive meaning is conclusively proven. This is extensively mentioned in passages such as the following from the *Sūtra of the Irreversible Wheel* (*Avaivartacakra-sūtra*, T 240):

> Then, in reverence to the Transcendent Lord, the great bodhisattva Madhuranirghoṣa arose from his lotus posture and asked, "Transcendent Lord, what is the dimension of this world system of Patient Endurance?"
>
> He replied, "Son of the enlightened family, in the western direction of this world system there is a world system which outnumbers the sands of the River Ganges."
>
> Then he asked, "Transcendent Lord, in that world system which Transcendent Lord teaches the doctrine?"
>
> "He is called the Tathāgata Śākyamuni."
>
> "What manner of doctrine does he teach?"
>
> "He begins from the three vehicles."
>
> "What are the three vehicles?"
>
> "He reveals the doctrine beginning with the three vehicles, which are the vehicle of the pious attendants, the vehicle of the self-centred buddhas and the greater vehicle."
>
> "Do these conform to the doctrine revealed by the Transcendent Lord Buddha?"
>
> "Son of the enlightened family, the doctrines revealed by the [different] Transcendent Lord Buddhas do conform."
>
> "Just in what respect do the doctrines revealed by the Transcendent Lord Buddhas conform?"
>
> And he replied, "The doctrines revealed by the Transcendent Lord Buddhas conform to the irreversible promulgation."

6 *The Enlightened or Buddha Family*

[95b.6-106b.4] When this buddha family of the unsurpassed greater vehicle is classified, the *Supreme Continuum of the Greater Vehicle* (Ch.1, v.149) says:

> One should know this enlightened family to be twofold:
> One similar to treasure and the other to a fruit tree.
> The [first] is that which naturally abides from the beginning,
> And the [second] is supreme through having been genuinely nurtured.

So there is both an enlightened family which naturally abides and an enlightened family which is nurtured. Concerning the former, the *Sūtra of Final Nirvāṇa* says:

> Son of the enlightened family, the reality of the mind which is natural, inner radiance, and naturally without essence is not differentiated by the naturally pure mind as it appears, decorated with the enlightened attributes of blazing major and minor marks, but it is differentiated by its nature of appearance and emptiness.[183]

Therefore, when this enlightened family is classified, it is threefold owing to its function of being the ground in which the culminating three buddha-bodies of the result arise. It consists of [firstly] the enlightened family in which reality naturally abides, which resembles an image made of precious gems in that it is the spontaneously present causal basis or ground separating (*bral-rgyu*) the essential buddha-body (*svābhāvikakāya*) or the uncorrupted expanse [from obscuration]; [secondly] the enlightened family in which the apparition of this reality naturally abides, which resembles a universal emperor in that it is the causal basis separating the buddha-body of perfect rapture from obscuration; and [thirdly] its apparitional reflection, which resembles a golden image in that it is the causal basis separating the emanational body from obscuration. In actuality, however, the reality in which these three are of an inseparable essence is the great, naturally present, uncompounded buddha-body of reality, the pristine cognition of supreme sameness, coalescing appearance and emptiness without conceptual elaboration. Since it is the great, indivisible reality in which the ground differentiating appearance and emptiness has ceased, it is exemplified by the nature of the Tathāgata. As the *Supreme Continuum of the Greater Vehicle* (Ch.1, v.146) says:

> Since it is supramundane, in the world
> There are no examples to which it may be referred.
> Therefore the nature of the Tathāgata
> Is revealed to be similar to the seed [of buddhahood].

When this enlightened family is actualised without obscuration, the conclusive truth of cessation according to the greater vehicle is the essential buddha-body endowed with two purities.

The [second] enlightened family, the one in which [reality] is nurtured, includes those who awaken to the [aforementioned] twofold family, in which the expanse, or reality, and pristine cognition, or [reality's] apparition, naturally abide, and those who consequently study to integrate the two provisions of skilful means and discriminative awareness. These two provisions in turn are subsumed by the provisional path of learning (*śaikṣamārga*)[184] which includes the generation of enlightened mind, in order that the suddenly arisen stains covering [the nucleus] might be removed. The *Sūtra of the Arrayed Bouquet* says:

> Sons of the Conqueror, this which is called the enlightened family is devoted to the expanse of reality. It is one in which, having seen the natural, inner radiance vast as the sky, studies are pursued in furtherance of the great provisions of merit and pristine cognition.

So the former enlightened family is the ground of separation from obscuration and the latter is the path which removes the stains covering [the nucleus]. It is said that though the truth of the path depends on the ground-of-all and is subsumed in the causal basis of separation from obscurations, it does bring about the basis of unchanging authentic liberation. This is because its function of attainment which effects the result of separation [from obscurations] depends on the enlightened family or the nucleus.

For anyone to know that this enlightened family, which naturally abides, does exist, it is inferred to exist through the signs [visible in those who] awaken to it, just as one, in general, infers fire from smoke. The signs that one has awakened to the natural enlightened family of the buddha-body of reality are indicated in the *Introduction to the Madhyamaka* (Ch.6, vv.4-5c):

> One who, having heard about emptiness even as an
> ordinary person,
> Experiences within, sheer delight again and again,
> And who, owing to this delight, is brought to tears,
> And whose body-hair stands erect,
> Has the seed of intelligence which attains to perfect
> buddhahood.
> That one is a vessel for this very instruction,
> To whom the ultimate truth should be revealed.

The signs that one has awakened to the enlightened family of the buddha-body of form, which is the apparition of reality, are indicated in the *Ornament of the Sūtras of the Greater Vehicle* (Ch.3, v.5):

> Even prior to practice,
> Correct conduct with respect to compassion,
> Volition, patience and virtue,
> Is truly explained to be a sign of that family.

Then, the benefits which result when one awakens to that enlightened family are mentioned, too, in the same text (Ch.3, v.8):

> Though a long time has been passed in evil existences,
> Liberation will swiftly be attained;
> There, too, less suffering will be experienced,
> And being disillusioned, one will mature sentient beings.

As long as one has once awakened to this enlightened family, one will not be born in evil existences, and even if one is so born, one will be liberated in merely the time it takes to bounce a ball of yarn. There, too, suffering will diminish, and through strong disillusionment [with saṃsāra], one will indeed bring sentient beings to maturity. In this way it is said that when the Teacher himself [Śākyamuni] became the strongest of charioteers in the hells, he was instantly liberated by awakening to that enlightened family which embodies great compassion, and was born as a god in Trayatriṃśa.[185] He subsequently became the boy Bhāskara, the son of a potter, in Jambudvīpa and aspired to enlightenment in the presence of the Tathāgata Śākyamuni.[186] Similar things are said about the series of his [ordinary] lives in which he took birth as the daughter of a friend and so on.

If living beings were without this enlightened family, those who experience suffering would not even feel regret. It would be reasonable for some not to think that saṃsāra should be rejected and nirvāṇa acquired, and even the desire for liberation would not arise in their minds. However, untaught by anyone, some persons feel compassion when others experience suffering, and are disturbed by the experience of suffering. One should know such phenomena to be the virtuous power of the seed of beginningless reality. It says in the *Supreme Continuum of the Greater Vehicle* (Ch.1, vv.40-1):

> Without the seed of buddhahood,
> One would not feel regret for suffering;
> One would have neither the desire,
> Nor the prayer, nor the aspiration for nirvāṇa.
> This perception of suffering as a negative
> And happiness as a positive attribute,
> In relation to existence and nirvāṇa,
> Is present owing to the existence of the enlightened family;
> For it is not found in those lacking that family.

Passages which speak of beings belonging to no family or to a cut-off family are rhetorical devices which indicate through negation the baseness in those who have not awakened to the enlightened family. Indeed, there are no living beings who do not belong to the enlightened family which naturally abides. The *Sūtra of the Nucleus of the Tathāgata* (*Tathāgatagarbhasūtra*, T 258) says:

> Son of the enlightened family, this is the reality of all things. Whether the tathāgatas have appeared or not, these sentient beings always possess the nucleus of the tathāgata.

And in the *Sūtra of Queen Śrīmālā* (*Śrīmālādevīsiṃhanādasūtra*, T 92):

> The nucleus of the sugata
> Completely pervades living beings.

Therefore, the mind is developed in the enlightened attitude of the greater vehicle consequent on awakening into the [first] enlightened family, which has two aspects and is the causal basis. Subsequently, the stains which obscure the buddha-body of reality are removed by experiencing, above all, the non-conceptualising pristine cognition during meditative equipoise; and the stains obscuring the two buddha-bodies of form are skilfully removed by conduct that is relevant to the two provisions with the assistance of illusion-like compassion during the aftermath [of that meditation].

Then, there is obtained the culminating result of this separation from obscuration (*bral-'bras*), the essential buddha-body. It is defined as an expanse encompassed by inconceivable, uncorrupted, enlightened attributes, or the ground in which the buddha-body of form that appears to others is reflected like the moon in the sky. It naturally manifests as pristine cognition itself, without being extraneously sought, and is endowed with the three bodies of the buddhas manifest in and of themselves. The *Supreme Continuum of the Greater Vehicle* (Ch.2, v.3) says:

That which is called natural inner radiance is as the sky.
It is unobscured by the dense clouds
Of suddenly arisen conflicting emotions
And ignorance of the knowable.
This buddhahood endowed with all enlightened
attributes of the taintless Buddha,
Constant, steadfast and eternal, is attained
Dependent on the pristine cognition which discerns
things non-conceptually.

And [Ch.2, vv.38-9]:

Without beginning, middle, or end and indivisible,
Neither two, nor three, taintless and non-
conceptualising,
That realisation, which is the natural expanse of
reality,
Is perceived by the yogin during meditative
equipoise.
Endowed with enlightened attributes that are
immeasurable,
That outnumber the sands of the Ganges, limitless
and without peer,
This taintless expanse of the Tathāgata
Has renounced the entire range of faults, along with
their propensities.

Arising from that [essential body], the two buddha-bodies of form have the same uncorrupted pristine cognition. They become naturally present through a co-emergent cause, consisting of the basis of the pure vessel of the beings requiring training, as well as the conditions of their former aspirations and their experience of the two provisions. The maturing result *(smin-'bras)* of these bodies of form is then established through their function of teaching in forms manifest to others who require training, in the manner, for example, of the moon reflected in water. As the above [*Supreme Continuum of the Greater Vehicle*, Ch.2, vv.40-1] says:

With a buddha-body which manifests the diverse rays of the
true doctrine,
Persevering so that the liberation of living beings be
achieved,
Their deeds, like the king of wish-fulfilling gems,
Are without inherent existence despite their diverse forms.
All their forms which cause [beings]
To enter into, ripen and prophetically declare the path
by which the world is pacified

> Also constantly abide therein,
> Just as form occupies space.

And as Nāgārjuna [in the *Eulogy to the Expanse of Reality*, v.101] says:

> Since within the taintless body of reality
> An ocean of pristine cognition abides,
> The benefit of sentient beings emerges therefrom
> In the manner of diverse gemstones.

In short, as [Longcenpa has said] in the *Great Chariot* (*shing-rta chen-mo*):

> In this context, one should know that, among the three buddha-bodies, the body of reality, which is an expanse invisible to those requiring training outside the range of the Buddha alone, is present as subtle pristine cognition, the inner expanse that is unique and of a single savour. The two buddha-bodies of form endowed with pure enlightened activity, which are the pristine cognition that manifests to others, outwardly radiate through its blessing and the aspiration of those requiring training. They appear in the manner of the moon in the sky [body of perfect rapture] and the moon in water [body of emanation].

And in the *Treasury of Philosophical Systems*:

> Since the three buddha-bodies are primordially present as the twofold enlightened family, the apparitional aspect of the buddha level or [the enlightened family] of inner growth is the body of perfect rapture and its empty aspect or [the enlightened family] which naturally abides is the body of reality. From the indivisible blessing of these two, the emanational body gives teaching in form manifest to others who require training, and is exemplified as the reflection of a universal emperor (*cakravartin*) shining on a golden mountain.

One who, without knowing this, is attracted to the concept that a single uncompounded emptiness of explicit negation is the enlightened family which naturally abides, and that the enlightened family of inner growth is exclusively compounded and newly produced by the path, is found to interrupt the realisation which belongs to the paths of learning as a conclusive result and so to adhere to the cessation of the pious attendants' tradition, which resembles an expired butter lamp in that it establishes no order of buddha-body, pristine cognition and so forth. If one were to take this view, one would not even savour the fragrance of the truth of cessation according to the greater vehicle. In the ground, one would fall into the extreme of conceptual elaboration.

On the path, one would not require the two provisions of the greater vehicle. In the result, one would not distinguish between the nirvāṇa of the three vehicles; and as a conclusive result, one could not cross beyond the abyss of nihilism. The refuge of ultimate reality would never be found.

It was with an intention directed toward this mode [of the nucleus] that the all-knowing doctrinal master [Longcenpa] said in the *Precious Wish-fulfilling Treasury* (*yid-bzhin rin-po-che'i mdzod*):

> One who without knowing this mode [of the nucleus]
> determines emptiness verbally
> As free from extremes of being and non-being
> Harbours the view of the summit of existence,
> Ignorant of the causal basis of separation from obscuration.
> Since he is outside this teaching,
> He may as well cover himself with ashes,
> Like those who hold the mind to emerge from space.[187]

Such a wrong view is gathered within [the nihilism of] the Followers of Bṛhaspati [Bārhaspatya]. The *Dohā* also says:

> The Archer[188] says:
> "Those who hold the mind to emerge from space
> Never attain to liberation."

If one were to think that on the paths of learning one develops anew, by the two causal provisions, what was previously non-existent, then the body of reality, or essential body of the buddha, and the body of perfect rapture would be compounded and impermanent. If one were to hold this view, it is said one would harbour the immeasurable defects of looking upon the continuum [of enlightened mind] as an ephemeral compound; the suffering of change as something unrenounceable; the possession of the body of indestructible reality, which is pristine cognition vast as the sky, as non-existent; and the body of indestructible reality itself as impermanent. Because of such limitless faults, one would deviate from the meaning of the greater vehicle.

So, rather than merely differentiate the twofold enlightened family as being the apparitional and emptiness aspects of a single expanse, it is the flawless intention of the all-knowing doctrinal master [Longcenpa] to establish it to be this supreme essence or natural expression which is indivisible, uncorrupted and uncompounded. In the *Great Chariot* he says:

> There are nine similes which reveal as spontaneously present the enlightened attributes of the Buddha's body of form, deriving from the naturally radiant apparitional aspect of the taintless mind-as-such, the naturally pure essence, the mind in which the genuine pristine cognition of the Buddha ori-

> ginally abides. And the comparison of its emptiness aspect, the enlightened attributes of the body of reality, with the sky is explained in all the sūtras and tantras. However, these two are inseparable in the virtuous seed of beginningless reality. This [seed] firstly is called the enlightened family which naturally abides because it is unchanging, and secondly is called the enlightened family of inner growth because enlightened attributes are extensively manifest after the stains have been purified. Yet its root is inner radiance, the pristine cognition which is intuitive awareness.

Similarly, in the *Extensive Sūtra of the Commitments (dam-tshig mdo-rgyas)*, a teaching of the all-seeing Rongzompa, the naturally present pristine cognition in which the ground, path and result are inseparable, is said to be the mind or family of enlightenment:

> That which is imperishable like a vajra is the mind of Samantabhadra, unchanging like a vajra, because it naturally contains no distinction between [firstly] the enlightened mind of beginningless time [i.e. the ground], [secondly] the provisional mind which is the causal situation [of the path extending] from the development of enlightened mind to the attainment of the vajra-like contemplation, and [thirdly] the mind of the body of reality along with its actions which is the essence of the result, similar to the Wish-granting Tree and the precious Wish-fulfilling Gem.

These quotations serve to illustrate that all the paṇḍitas and accomplished masters of the Ancient Translation School, including the king of the doctrine Terdak Lingpa[189] and his brother, have affirmed the same system exclusively. This can be known in detail from the *Lecture Notes on the Nucleus of the Sugata* (*bde-gshegs snying-po'i stong-thun*), the *Lion's Roar in Affirmation of Extrinsic Emptiness* (*gzhan-stong khas-len seng-ge'i nga-ro*) and the *Proof of Mind in its Natural State* (*gnyug-sems sgrub-pa*) along with its branches, which are all teachings of the all-knowing Mipham Jampel Gyepa.[190]

The lord of living beings Atiśa,[191] too, has determined in conformity with them that the uncompounded expanse of reality, the coalescence of appearance and emptiness, which is empty of imaginary deeds and defilements, and inseparable from the uncorrupted enlightened attributes is the enlightened family [or the nucleus of the tathāgata]. In his *Song with a View to the Expanse of Reality* (*Dharmadhātudarśanagīti*, T 2314) he says:

> Just as the son of a pregnant woman is within her womb
> But is not perceived,
> So, covered by conflicting emotions,

The expanse of reality is also unperceived.
Since the expanse of reality is not a self,
It [resembles] neither woman nor man;
One should examine just how one clings subjectively
To that which is liberated from all objects.
When the mind is purified by all three actions,
Namely, [the meditations on] impurity, impermanence
and suffering,
The sūtras which point out emptiness
Are accordingly spoken by the Conqueror.
Conflicting emotions are reversed by all these topics,
But this seed [of reality] is not diminished.

And also:

The natural expression of reality's expanse,
Like space is without cause or condition:
Without birth, old age, duration and destruction,
Without being compounded,
The inseparable attributes of the Buddha
And, similarly, the attainment of this enlightened family
Are not false, deceptive or harmful.
They are the original, natural quiescence.

Then, among the esoteric instructions of the ḍākinī entitled *Valid Cognition of the Transmitted Precepts* (*Ājñāsamyakpramāṇa*, T 2331) which were introduced from Akaniṣṭha by Tilopā,[192] it is said:

Just as a butter lamp within a vase
Does not appear outside,
But if the vase is broken,
The lamplight is visible thereafter,
So is one's own body like the vase
And inner radiance like the butter lamp:
When well broken by the guru's instruction,
The pristine cognition of the buddhas becomes radiant.

And in the *Ganges Great Seal* (*phyag-chen gaṅgā-ma*, T 2303) which Tilopā imparted to Nāropā:[193]

Just as, for example, the nature of space transcends
colour and form,
And is uncovered and unchanged by positive and
negative values,
So does the nucleus of one's own mind transcend
colour and form,
And is uncovered by positive and negative doctrines
of virtue and sin.

As the nucleus of the sun, for example, radiant and clear,
Is not obscured by the darkness of a thousand aeons,
So the inner radiance of the nucleus which is one's own
mind
Cannot be obscured by the saṃsāra of aeons.

Then, in the *Teaching Cycle of Lord Maitripā* (*mnga'-bdag mai-tri-pa'i gdams-skor*) there is the *Ten Verses on the Real* (*Tattvadaśaka*, T 2236) composed by master Advayavajra,[194] which says:

Since you desire to know, the nature of just what is
Is neither represented nor representationless;
Unadorned by the guru's speech,
Even the Madhyamaka is mediocre.

The great brahman [Saraha][195] in his *Song of Instruction Given to Lord Marpa*[196] (*mnga'-bdag mar-pa-la gdams-pa'i mgur*, DZ Vol. 5) has also said:

Emptiness and compassion are indivisible.
The uninterrupted mind in its natural state
Is the original purity of just what is:
Space is seen in union with space.

The venerable Milarepa[197] has also revealed this in general in *Illuminating the Substance of the Aural Lineage* (*snyan-brgyud dngos-po gsal-byed*, DZ Vol.5, pp.443-55) which he gave to Nyiwa Rincen [Gampopa]:[198]

In every corporeal being
This truth of the nucleus originally abides.
Through it sentient beings have the basis of buddhahood.
When one arrives at the result from the cause,
It is reached primordially, not just presently.

Then, particularly in his *Song of Indestructible Reality in Answer to Questions Posed in a Trilogy by the Goddess of Longevity, which is the Root of the Aural Lineage of Ngamdzong* (*ngams-rdzong snyan-brgyud rtsa-ba tshe-ring skor-gsum-gyi zhus-lan rdo-rje'i mgur*, *mgur-'bum*, Ch.29),[199] he differentiates between the two truths, which provisionally have synonyms, beginning as follows:

With reference to the ultimate truth,
Due to negation there is not even buddhahood...

And:

With reference to the relative truth,
The Sage has said everything exists,
Both saṃsāra and nirvāṇa.

He then conclusively evokes the expressive power of ultimate reality for which there are no synonyms as follows:

> Since appearances in the form of existing substances
> And reality which is non-existing emptiness
> Are essentially inseparable and of a single savour,
> There is not just intrinsic awareness or extrinsic
> awareness,
> But a vast coalescence of everything.

And finally, he literally reveals the way in which the taintless, sublime, pristine cognition is directly perceived in the following verses:

> So, one skilled in realisation
> Perceives not consciousness but pristine cognition,
> Perceives not the apparition of reality, but reality itself,
> And thence the force of compassion emerges.
> The enlightened attributes of the buddhas,
> Including power, fearlessness and retention,
> Emerge in the manner of a precious gemstone.
> They are the measure of my realisation as a yogin.

Zhang Rinpoche[200] in his *Culmination of the Supreme Path* (*lam-mchog mthar-thug*, DZ Vol.5, pp.744-77) has said:

> The buddha-body of reality, or the nucleus
> Which is the culmination of definitive meaning,
> Is the essentially pure expanse of inner radiance.
> Whether the conquerors of the three times appear or not,
> Whether it is realised by the sublime assembly or not,
> Whether it is spoken of by the sages or not,
> Whether it is delivered by learned commentators or
> not,
> This reality which is pure unelaborate inner radiance,
> Abides from the beginning, spontaneously present,
> Without increase or decrease.
> Though the skies have been ravaged over many
> immeasurable aeons
> By the conflagrations, whirlwinds and the like
> Which create and destroy the world,
> The sky is unharmed, without increase or decrease.
> Similarly, the radiant sunlight obscured by clouds
> Ostensibly varies in the intensity of its radiance
> When the thick darkness and cloud mass dissolve,
> And yet the nucleus of the sun neither increases nor
> decreases.

This unchanging buddha-body of reality, which so abides,
Is nothing other than one's own mind.
The diversity of saṃsāra without exception arises from the mind.
When one's own mind is not realised,
The suffering of the world of saṃsāra and its contents increases
Through the confusion [caused] by erroneous, bewildered appearances.
When one's own mind is genuinely realised,
The limitless pristine cognition of nirvāṇa arises as supreme bliss.
Thus, everything without exception issues from one's own mind-as-such.
If one knows reality in relation to oneself,
One will know reality in relation to all sentient beings.
One who knows that knows all things including nirvāṇa.
One who knows all things completely transcends the three realms.
If that one thing is known, one becomes learned in all things.

The Lord of Conquerors, the venerable Karmapa [III], Rangjung Dorje,[201] has additionally given an extensive explanation of the classification of the enlightened family in accordance with the transmissions of the *Supreme Continuum of the Greater Vehicle* and the *Collection of the Greater Vehicle* in his autocommentary on the *Profound Inner Meaning* (*zab-mo nang-don*). Therein he says that the enlightened family of inner growth is not to be regarded as newly arising, as is the opinion of some. In such ways he clearly reveals [the family] to comprise both the expanse [of reality] and pristine cognition. That is, the expanse of reality is the enlightened family which naturally abides, and the pristine cognition, pure in respect of the eight aggregates [of consciousness], is the enlightened family of inner growth. Indeed, he proves both of these to be naturally pure in accord with the transmission of the *Analysis of the Middle and Extremes* (Ch.1, v.17) which he quotes as follows:

Just as water, gold and the sky are pure,
So are [these families] held to be pure.

The same point is also clearly revealed in his *Two Short Treatises* (*gzhung-chung gnyis*).

The venerable Karmapa VII [Chödrak Gyamtso][202] asserts, too, that the expanse or emptiness in which the sixty-four enlightened attributes are inseparable is the emptiness endowed with all supreme aspects. These and the statements made by the All-Knowing Situ [VIII, Dharmākara][203] and others are renowned among the Kagyüpa traditions.

Again, in the *Commentary on the Eulogy* [entitled *Taintless Gem Rosary*, i.e. *bstod-'grel*, SK Vol.5][204] which is his culminating personal statement, Sakya Paṇḍita first establishes the way in which the character of the mind is obscured by suddenly arisen stains despite the mind's naturally pure reality. He then establishes the ways in which the stains can be purified since they are suddenly arisen and buddhahood attained by their removal. At this point, he sets forth the intention of the *Collection of Madhyamaka Reasoning* (*Yuktikāya*, T 3824-8) that, with reference to reality, there is no transformation at this moment [of buddhahood], and the intention of the *Collection of Eulogies* (*Stavakāya*, T 1118-36) which is that, with reference to the apparitional mode of enlightened attributes, there is transformation [of consciousness into pristine cognition]. Then, after setting forth the viewpoints, one of which holds that these two [intentions] are essentially not contradictory and the other of which holds that there is no pristine cognition in buddhahood, he offers his personal statement, refuting the assertions that there is neither the pristine cognition nor the body of buddhahood, and says that these two [intentions] are inseparable.

Furthermore, in his *Answers to the Questions of Nyemo Gomchen* (*snyi-mo sgom-chen-gyi dris-lan*, SK Vol.5)[205] it is said by way of illustration:

> When the mind is realised to be empty, it cannot be estimated according to [the standards set in] the three piṭaka and the four tantrapiṭaka, for that is equivalent to the cessation of the pious attendants; but when it is realised to be coalescence, such an estimation can be made. In the exclusively empty aspect of mind, the Three Precious Jewels are incomplete. In the coalescence of awareness and emptiness, the seed [of buddhahood] is complete, and if the meaning of that coalescence is well realised, [buddhahood] is actualised completely.

He then states that:

> After freedom from conceptual elaboration has been established, the coalescence is experientially cultivated.

And also that:

> The view assumed during the causal phase is
> poisonous,
> The view assumed during the resultant phase is
> poisonless...

Regarding this passage, he claims that the former refers merely to freedom from conceptual elaboration, or the emptiness which is analytically appraised by study and thought. The latter, having no use for that, is identical in essence to the pristine cognition of the buddha level, which arises from the empowerment and the two stages [of creation and perfection] and results in the coalescence of bliss and emptiness, and of awareness and emptiness. Such statements are renowned among the glorious Sakyapa.

Again, in the *Three Emphases of the Path* (*lam-gyi gtso-bo rnam-gsum*, P 6087) of the great being Tsongkapa,[206] the expressive power of ultimate reality without synonyms, in which appearances and emptiness are coalesced, is brought into relief as follows:

> Whoever perceives the cause and result
> Of all things of saṃsāra and nirvāṇa,
> To be always infallible,
> And destroys all their referential bases,
> At that time enters the path pleasing to the buddhas.
> As long as one continues to differentiate
> Between the two understandings of
> Appearances which are infallibly interdependent
> And emptiness which is free from assertions,
> One will not yet realise the Sage's intention.
> But when [these understandings] are simultaneous, without alternation,
> And if, having merely seen interdependence to be infallible,
> True conviction has destroyed all postures of objective clinging,
> At that time, the scrutiny of the view is perfected.

Similar passages are found in the all-knowing Tölpo Sangye's[207] *Ocean of Definitive Meaning on Retreat Practice* (*ri-chos nges-don rgya-mtsho*), and in other works.

Despite the mere subtle distinctions provisionally asserted in these [various] philosophical systems, such as concern the degree to which appearances and emptiness are respectively emphasised, and the different delineations of the two truths, in actuality the secret activities[208] which are the intention of great sublime beings who perceive the truth of reality are of a common savour. They are inseparable like water and salt; for, within the space of the supreme pristine cognition, the conclusive ultimate reality which is without synonyms and free from the intellect, the two truths have a common savour. Therefore, [their systems] are not objects to be appraised by the childish intellects of inhibited perception.

The lord Atiśa has said:

> Since, in the manner of an ocean,
> Its depths and other shores are not found
> By words, examples and the intellect,
> It is the great, profound reality.

And also:

> Do not be critical of the doctrine;
> One should aspire to what one reveres.

Remembering this, as well as the points expressed in the *Short Tantra of Cakrasaṃvara* (*Tantrarājaśrīlaghusaṃvara*, T 368), the *Texts of Maitreya*, the *Jewel Garland*, and other sources, it is clearly of extreme importance that one personally preserve this [understanding].

7 *The Two Truths according to Great Madhyamaka*

[106b.4-116b.1] Nothing that is explained in accordance with the lexical, general, concealed or conclusive [exegetical styles, see pp. 292-3] is erroneous. Yet when the crucial meaning is briefly expressed: In the situation of the coarse, Outer Madhyamaka of the Prāsaṅgika and Svātantrika, one establishes, in accord with the provisional emphasis revealed in the intermediate promulgation, that there is no contradiction between all things being without independent existence and the modes of relative appearance, which are dependently originated; and then one is united in the conclusive ultimate reality for which there is no synonym. During the subtle, inner Madhyamaka, however, the only distinction made over and above this same basic structure is that the objective expanse of reality, established by the view revealed and realised in the final promulgation, is not merely the bare emptiness of one-sided explicit negation, but is the naturally present, uncorrupted, uncompounded [abiding nature] which is not differentiated from the appearances adorned by the buddha-body and pristine cognition. During meditative absorption, when balanced in the expanse of reality without conditions to be clarified or established, both modes of Madhyamaka make no distinction regarding the cessation of all elaborate signs of the subject-object dichotomy therein. However, during the aftermath of meditative absorption, they are distinguished between the former [Outer Madhyamaka] which classifies the two truths, allocating emptiness to the ultimate and appearances to the relative, and the latter [Great Madhyamaka] which determines the two truths to be [respectively] the harmony and disharmony of the abiding and apparitional natures (*gnas-snang mthun mi-mthun*).

None the less, since the reality of the latter cannot be established unless the former has been established, the conclusive ultimate reality without synonyms is to be established at the outset in accordance with the Prāsaṅgika intention of the *Collection of Madhyamaka Reasoning*. This reality lies within the range of the coalescent, sublime, pristine cognition, and in it things are uncreated, unimpeded, peaceful from the start and naturally beyond sorrow [i.e. in nirvāṇa].

Once this has been determined, then in accordance with the intention of the *Texts of Maitreya*, the *Collection of Eulogies*, and other works, there is no longer reason to deny that the uncorrupted appearances, including the buddha-body and pristine cognition, are naturally present and uncompounded, because they do not essentially differ from the expanse of reality.

This conclusive reasoning, which scrutinises the two truths, proves that the expanse of reality is the coalescence of appearance and emptiness without contradiction. If it were otherwise, the Prāsaṅgika view itself would be disproved. Therefore it is proven, according to the logic of conventional truth, that the actual appearance of this reality is invisible to sentient beings at the present but visible on the buddha level, and the manifestation of this bewildering apparition of present propensities is visible to sentient beings but invisible to buddhas. The former is similar to that which appears respectively when one is asleep and when one is not asleep, and the latter resembles the dreams which respectively occur when one is not awake and do not occur when one is awake. As such, this subsequent delineation of the two truths can easily be known.

One should know that because this allocation of truth and falsehood and so forth is made conventionally, it is not proven to have veridical existence when the truth is investigated according to the essential view of the apologists for extrinsic emptiness (*gzhan-stong-pa*).

This system also holds that the ultimate reality without synonyms, the expanse of reality in which appearances and emptiness are coalesced, is the ground attained in the single, conclusive vehicle. Therefore it is spoken of in the mantra texts as E-VAṂ, the continuum of the basis, the embodiment of indestructible reality, the great seal, the emptiness endowed with all supreme aspects, the mind in its natural state, the naturally present pristine cognition and so forth. If known as such, no one can contradict that this reality is the conclusive definitive meaning.

This mode [of ultimate reality] is identical in meaning to those modes mentioned in the outer tantras of the way of mantras, namely, one's own real nature (*bdag-gi de-kho-na-nyid*), the blessing which is the ultimate truth without symbols (*don-dam mtshan-ma med-pa'i byin-rlabs*) and the deity of the expanse of indestructible reality (*rdo-rje dbyings-kyi lha*).[209] It is also identical to those modes of the inner tantras, namely, the indivisible truth free from the range of the intellect according to Mahāyoga, the indivisible pristine cognition and expanse of reality according to Anuyoga, and the original ground in which primordial purity and spontaneous presence are coalesced according to the conclusive Great Perfection (*rdzogs-pa chen-po*).

If, at the outset, this mode of ultimate reality is not established, these subsequent modes will not become established. But if this mode is well understood, one acquires the power to discern that the later modes are gradually established without difficulty. Therefore, it is important to know this mode [of ultimate reality] by whatever means.

If a thorough examination is made in this way, the character of the two truths is well distinguished by relying on the coarse Outer Madhyamaka, which is the basis of discriminative awareness. Then, once the meaning of the two kinds of selflessness has been ascertained, and if a certainty free from the darkness of doubt is developed, one is gradually united with and experiences the truth of the great non-dual pristine cognition of the subtle inner Madhyamaka, which is the result of coalescence, during periods of meditative equipoise. Thus, there is not the slightest disharmony between the two kinds of Madhyamaka of definitive meaning with respect to the conclusive intention [of the buddhas].

The Prāsaṅgika do not claim that the ultimate reality referred to by synonyms, which lies within the range of the dualising intellect or consciousness, is conclusive other than as a provisional introduction. They do, however, say that the coalescent ultimate reality without synonyms, which is within the range of the genuine pristine cognition of individual intuitive awareness, is the unique ultimate truth, characterised as the ineffable, unthinkable and inexpressible perfection of discriminative awareness.

The proponents of extrinsic emptiness, in the same way, conventionally assign consciousness and its objects to the deceptive, false, relative appearance, making them as false on the conventional level as lightning and clouds. Yet they assign pristine cognition and its objects to the ultimate truth by virtue of their infallible conclusive reality, which is free from conditions to be clarified and established because it is permanent, steadfast and unchanging.

Therefore, when one meditates [according to these two kinds of Madhyamaka], they are found to make the same essential point. When the pristine cognition or ultimate reality experienced during sublime meditative equipoise according to the greater vehicle, which the all-knowing great Longcenpa expressed within our own [Nyingma] tradition, is objectified, it is impossible for conceptual elaborations such as the postures of clinging to explicit negation and implicitly affirmative negation to exist therein, regardless of the concepts of being and non-being upheld by philosophical systems.

There is no philosophical system to be upheld during this great sameness, which is a coalescence free from conceptual activity. However, when the aftermath of that meditative equipoise is conventionally objectified, the structure of the ground, path and result and so forth is differentiated in accordance with quotations from the authentic literary transmissions.

This essential point which is indubitably upheld is not contradicted in either of the two kinds of Madhyamaka [for the following two reasons]. Firstly, both of them refute all signs and ideas of conceptual elaboration, including being and non-being, in relation to the experience of meditative equipoise or the investigation of the truth, and afterwards are determined and balanced in a great sameness free from conceptual elaborations, without conditions to be clarified or established. Secondly, they both differentiate and uphold the two truths professed according to their respective philosophical systems in the situation of the relative or conventional truth during the aftermath of that meditative absorption. One should not, therefore, be exhausted by the conceptual elaboration of refutation and proof, pursuing mere words instead of relying on their meaning.

One who is attracted and adheres to any agreeable standpoint concerning appearances and emptiness cannot reverse the evil view of clinging to extremes. This is why the expanse of reality, the conclusive ultimate truth without synonyms in which appearances and emptiness are coalesced, should be well established as sameness throughout the extent of existence and quiescence.

The mode of establishing this [sameness] is also taught in the eighteenth chapter of [Longcenpa's] *Wish-fulfilling Treasury*. Accordingly, though all relative things that conventionally appear are non-existent in fact, bewildering apparitions appear by the power of the bewilderment of propensities, without past, without future, without existence during the present interval between them. However, these are empty forms which have never existed in reality, like the combed-out hairs that appear to the vision of one drugged by datura. Appearances and emptiness are not differentiated because the ground that differentiates between appearances and emptiness has ceased to exist, and attributes such as the naturally radiant buddha-body and pristine cognition of ultimate reality are free from the flux of the three times. For they are an uncorrupted expanse and original sameness, neither different nor distinct by nature.

One should know that even the two truths designated by the intellect are of a supremely pure, indivisible sameness, throughout the extent of existence and quiescence, because they are merely names and words, not existing independently in reality. As the text [*Wish-fulfilling Treasury*] says:

> Since it is beyond the interrupted and classified
> objects of relative appearance,
> And transcends the two designated truths,
> All elaboration is pacified.
> The indivisible truth is neither proven nor
> disproven;
> Since, in the expanse, appearances and emptiness
> are naturally without duality,
> This truth is also said to be indivisible.

And when the two truths are allocated through their abiding and apparitional natures, which depend on the universal logic of conventions, the text says:

> Thus all things of saṃsāra which are bewildering appearances
> Are the relative truth because they are false and fallacious.
> The reality of nirvāṇa which is profound, calm inner radiance,
> Is held to be the ultimate truth of unchanging natural expression.

So it is that, after precedence has been given to the establishment of the two truths as an indivisible great sameness without conceptual elaborations, as described above, the objects and subjects, in which the abiding and apparitional modes are in total harmony, are then both allocated to the ultimate reality, and the objects and subjects in which the abiding and apparitional modes are in a state of disharmony, are both allocated to relative appearances. This determination should be made according to their infallibility in conventional terms; otherwise, the whole structure of conventional truth would be deranged, because one would not know whether the apprehension of a conch-shell as white or yellow would be veracious.

It is appropriate, therefore, that all things of nirvāṇa attained through the power of the abiding and apparitional modes in harmony be assigned to the ultimate reality, and all things of saṃsāra which originate through the power of their disharmony, to the relative appearance. If scrutinised according to conventional analysis, all the apparitions of buddha-body and pristine cognition are uncreated by the bewilderment of deeds and defilements, and are proven to be true and not fallacious because they originate from the power of genuine pristine cognition, and are unpolluted by obscurations. The things of saṃsāra, on the other hand, are said not to be true because they are the opposite. Their respective truth and falsehood is proven by the logic which conventionally analyses them to be fallacious or not. In this respect, the subject in which the abiding and apparitional modes are in harmony is called pristine cognition because it is without the dichotomy of apprehending subject and apprehended object. The subject which apprehends them as disharmony is called consciousness because it is endowed with the dichotomy of subject and object. The object of which the abiding and apparitional modes are in harmony is reliable because it is never reversed by revelations of invalid cognition. To give a mundane example: It resembles the intellect which apprehends a rope as a rope. The object of which the abiding and apparitional modes are disharmonious, on the other hand, is not reliable because, like the intellect which apprehends a rope as a snake, it is reversed on being perceived as an invalid cognition. This is the point expressed in the *Sūtra Revealed by Akṣayamati* (*Akṣayamatinirdeśasūtra*, T 175) when it says:

Pristine cognition is permanent
And consciousness is impermanent.

In this way, this expanse and non-dual pristine cognition are permanent because they are no different from reality. The *Sūtra of the Arrayed Bouquet* says:

Though a multitude of world systems,
Inconceivable in number, have been incinerated,
The sky remains undestroyed:
Such is the naturally present pristine cognition.

And in the *Tantra of the Supreme Radiance of Truth without Conceptual Elaborations* (*spros-bral don-gsal chen-po'i rgyud*, NGB Vol.6):

In all the tantras and transmissions I have revealed,
When the words "unchanging" and "uncompounded"
And "like indestructible reality" are expressed,
They are explanations of the naturally present, pure,
  pristine cognition.

And in the *Commentary on the Nucleus of Indestructible Reality* [*rdo-rje snying-'grel*, T2515; or the *Commentary (on Hevajra) by Vajragarbha*, T1180]:

Just as, though a vase has been destroyed,
The space [within] remains undamaged,
Similarly, though the mind has been destroyed,
Pristine cognition remains undamaged.

Then, [in the *Eulogy to the Expanse of Reality*, vv.20-1] the sublime Nāgārjuna has said:

As cloth that may be purified by fire,
When soiled with various stains,
Is placed in the midst of fire,
The stains are burnt, but not the cloth,
So, too, when the mind that is inner radiance
Possesses stains such as attachment,
These stains are burnt by the fire of pristine cognition,
But not so its inner radiance.[210]

With reference to this apparition of reality, though creation and cessation are indeed ostensible, they cannot harm the ultimate, unbewildered, fundamental nature which is reality itself, because they are apparitional modes in relation to the bewildered consciousness. For example, though space ostensibly expands and contracts depending on the [size of the] vessel, it cannot be proven that space is compounded and impermanent. In its own essence, this reality or pristine cognition possesses four enlightened attributes of hidden meaning beyond the range of the childish intellects of inhibited perception. Namely, it is pure because it is originally uncovered by minute blemishes, permanent because it is naturally without change, blissful because it is never oppressed by suffering, and true self because it pervades all saṃsāra and nirvāṇa and pacifies elaborate concepts of self and selflessness. The lord Maitreya has said in the *Supreme Continuum of the Greater Vehicle* (Ch.1, v.35):

> Owing to its purity, self, bliss and permanence,
> The transcendental perfection of enlightened attributes
> is the result.

And in the *Litany of the Names of Mañjuśrī* (v.46) accordingly:

> Purest of the pure by nature,
> It is beginninglessly
> The self free from elaborations.

Furthermore, all the outer and inner phenomena subsumed by the components, psychophysical bases and activity fields are apparitions which arise from reality, and yet, by the power of its natural purity, with reference to the conclusive abiding mode, they do not stray from the natural sameness of the Original Buddha [Samantabhadra] and are of the nature of the buddha-body and pristine cognition. They are seen as such by the conclusive buddha-eye which is free from all obscurations. Therefore it says in the *Sūtra of the Arrayed Bouquet:*

> Those who well abide in natural sameness
> With respect to self and sentient beings,
> And are dynamic and non-acquisitive,
> Are said to be the sugatas.
> With purity of form and feeling,
> Of perception, consciousness and attention,
> The countless tathāgatas
> Become the supreme sages.

And in the *Kālacakra Tantra*:

> Sentient beings are buddhas.
> There are no other great buddhas
> In this world system.

And in the *Tantra of the Secret Nucleus* (Ch.2, v.4):

> Emaho! The chiliocosms of the ten directions are originally
> void.
> The three spheres of existence are pure buddha-fields.
> The reality of the five impurities is the blissful abode.

The reality of the five components is the perfect Buddha.
Since he possesses the nucleus of all that is supreme,
The Conqueror does not search elsewhere for the doctrine.
A doctrine which is said to be other than that,
Though searched for, is not found by the Conqueror.

If one were, on the other hand, to think that the Buddha would not even speak of the characteristic bases of suffering and its origin, such as the components, he does, by dint of necessity. As Maitreya says:[211]

Self is revealed,
And selflessness is also taught.
The conquerors reveal both self
And the total absence of self.

Accordingly, while buddhas have no thought of self, it is not contradictory, as known in the greater vehicle as a whole, for them to enter into the mundane consensus that speaks of an ego and its possessions, or to perceive that a personal self, though not really existing, appears as such to the childish. Although they perceive phenomenal existence as buddha-body and pristine cognition, it is not contradictory for them to teach in that way having seen that ostensible suffering and its origin are unimpeded in the face of the impure bewilderment of sentient beings.

It is similarly not proven that, if sentient beings are buddhas, a buddha implicitly suffers when a sentient being suffers in the hells and so forth. There is no flaw because ultimately saṃsāra does not exist, and one who is born therein, in the relative apparitional mode, not being a buddha whose obscurations have been purified, experiences bewildering dream-like appearances by the power of obscuration which inheres in one's own mind. In the abiding mode, on the other hand, suffering and so forth do not exist. It says in the *Tantra of the Extensive Magical Net*:

If there is no understanding of intrinsic awareness or genuine
perception,
The field of Sukhāvatī[212] is even seen as a state of
evil existence.
If the truth which is equivalent to the supreme of
vehicles is realised,
Even states of evil existence are Akaniṣṭha and Tuṣita.

One should know that these two [modes] are proven exclusively by the logic of convention, since all the appearances of impure saṃsāra are bewildering appearances which do not correspond to [the buddhas'] perception, and all the appearances of pure nirvāṇa such as the buddha-body and pristine cognition are unbewildered.

Now, concerning all these appearances of impure saṃsāra, including the hells which appear to one's own bewildered perception by the power of having an evil mind, it is said in the *Introduction to the Conduct of a Bodhisattva* (Ch.5, vv.7-8):

> Who made the [hellish] core of molten iron?
> Whence originated these infernos?
> The Sage has said that all these
> Are [products of] an evil mind.

The intentions of the sūtras and the tantras agree that the pure array of the buddhas' fields and bodies and so forth appears through the purity of one's own mind. This can also be known from the debate between Brahmā Śikhin and Śāriputra concerning the purity of this field [which contains our own world].[213]

It is said particularly in the tantrapiṭaka of the unsurpassed way of mantras that [the buddha-bodies and fields] originate through the purity of the internal structure of the energy channels, currents and seminal points and of mind-as-such. Therefore, while all things are not truly existent apart from being mere labels designated by the ideas of one's own mind, the infallibility with which these very objects designated by thought appear in circumstances dependent on different intellects, is called proof by the logic of convention. Not one of us at the present time, who has gathered the appropriate deeds and awakened to the appropriate propensities, can contradict in the case of fire, for example, the statement that fire is hot, since it is validly proven that the nature of fire does appear to be hot; and the same would appear to be true for virtue, evil and the like. Ultimately, however, no such one-sided determination can be made. This is known because fire does not appear to be hot to the creature Agniśuci[214] and so forth, and because empowered beings can display various emanations and transformations of substances.

It is said [in the *Collection of the Greater Vehicle*, Ch.8, para.20, v.a]:

> Since a single substance is differentiated by minds,
> It appears to be non-existent in reality.

Therefore, on thorough scrutiny, when this, one's own unique body, is observed by the organisms within it, by vultures without, by those who desire it and those who do not, by oneself and others, and by many such enemies and friends, it is said to be seen and apprehended in different ways – as a dwelling place, as food, as purity or impurity, as the possession of oneself or of another, as ugliness, beauty or an object of indifference and so on. If it is perceived by sublime beings the body is said to be without independent existence and so forth, and on the conclusive buddha level it is said that the pure physical component is the essence of Vairocana. Statements of this kind are not contradictory.

Then, if scrutinised even further, when one searches for that which is called the body, it can be known by penetrating analysis even now that it is not an object of reference and that it does not inherently exist even to the extent of the minutest atomic particle. Therefore, when this [analysis] is applied to all outer and inner phenomena, including the bodies of others, they can be established to be without independent existence. In ultimate reality, all things should be known as the great sameness of reality, naturally without divisions and [the need for] clarifications. Conventionally, however, one ought to ascertain that the phenomena which appear to ordinary sentient beings at the present time are false in comparison with those which appear in the face of that [ultimate reality], because they are impure, bewildered appearances. One also ought to ascertain that even the appearances [discerned by] bodhisattvas on the path are impotent in the face of that [ultimate reality], because there is a pure basis for perception which is progressively higher than theirs. The abiding mode is conclusively proven because nothing is to be gained beyond the perception of the conclusive buddha level. In short, the goal of that which is expressed is inexpressible, the goal of ideas is non-conceptualising, the goal of consciousness is pristine cognition, and the goal of the apparition of reality is reality itself. Therefore, the inconceivable pristine cognition that is reality is a great purity of natural expression, transcending the symbolic range of the subject-object dichotomy.

However, if one were to object that there would then be no point in meditating on the path, this is not the case. Since sentient beings meditate on the path in order to purify these bewildering appearances which arise suddenly as in a dream through their lack of realisation, and the propensities of the bewildering thoughts which cling to them, there need be no clinging to the idea that the doctrines of the path and result are truly existent. It is as when a sorceror removes fears on the path by an army of his emanations, or when a phlegmatic eye disease is cured.

Therefore, with reference to the conclusion that is to be realised, all things subsumed by the relative and ultimate truths should be established as naturally indivisible, in the great pure sameness free from conceptual elaborations, the original natural expression of the buddhas. Yet one should not be attracted to or fall into any elaborate viewpoint regarding dualistic concepts such as being and non-being, appearance and emptiness, or purity and impurity, as are partially appraised by childish intellects of inhibited vision.

To sum up, the Transcendent Lord has said:

> Rely not upon individuals but upon the doctrine,
> Rely not upon words but upon their meaning,
> Rely not upon the provisional but the definitive meaning,

> Rely not upon consciousness but upon pristine cognition.

This is why, in the context of the abiding mode of the two truths which are to be known, the result is incontrovertibly appraised by the logic of scriptural authority, reason and esoteric instructions. One should know that the entire intention of the sūtras and the tantras, which are the scriptures of the Tathāgata, is subsumed in a single nucleus, just as butter is condensed from milk, and cream from butter, so that the climax of the philosophical systems, according to the causal vehicle of dialectics, is this Great Madhyamaka, supreme among vehicles. Its meaning is revealed in the texts of Maitreya, such as the *Supreme Continuum of the Greater Vehicle*, and in the sublime Nāgārjuna's *Collection of Eulogies*, which subsume the essence of the definitive meaning of both the intermediate and final promulgations of the transmitted precepts.

It says in the *Sūtra of the Descent to Laṅkā* (Ch.6, v.5):

> In the five doctrines and three essential natures,
> In the eight aggregates of consciousness
> And in the two kinds of selflessness,
> The entire greater vehicle is subsumed.[215]

And in the *Intermediate Mother*:

> Maitreya, regard any imaginary form as not substantially existent. One might regard any conceptualised form as substantially existent because thoughts exist substantially, but do not confer independent status upon it. Then you should regard the very form of reality as being disclosed by ultimate reality, for it is neither substantially existent nor non-existent.

8 *Key to the Appraisal of Causal Vehicle Texts*

[116b.3] Having distinguished between the relative truth or apparitional nature, and the ultimate truth or abiding nature, the definitive order of the precious treasure store of the true doctrine that is to be appraised has been established. The precious key to its appraisal is structured in two parts, of which the first concerns the provisional and definitive meanings.

THE PROVISIONAL AND DEFINITIVE MEANING OF THE TRUE DOCTRINE

[116b.3-118a.2] The reality of all things, the expanse of just what is, the inner radiant intention of mind-as-such, which is of the essence of space, naturally pure and unchanging, beyond creation, cessation and duration, is the definitive meaning; and all the transmitted precepts and treatises which reveal it are subsumed within the definitive meaning. All the apparitions of reality that appear, dream-like and manifesting as the diverse, successive forms such as those of creation, cessation, coming and going, purity and impurity, components, psychophysical bases and activity fields, which are all appraised and exaggeratedly indicated by a succession of words, thoughts and expressions, are called the provisional meaning; and all the transmitted precepts and treatises which reveal them are subsumed within the relative truth. For example, those which boast in word, expression and thought that mind-as-such resembles space are relative, whereas the fundamental nature of ultimate reality, being the definitive meaning, is genuine. Such is said in the *Eulogy to the Inconceivable Madhyamaka* (*Madhyamakācintyastava*, T 1128, vv.56c-57c):

> The emptiness of all things
> Is indeed revealed as the definitive meaning.
> That in which creation, cessation and so on,

> And living beings, life itself and so on are revealed,
> Is the relative truth of provisional meaning.

The *Sublime Sūtra of the King of Contemplation* says:

> As spoken by the Teacher, the Sugata,
> Know the details of the sūtras of definitive meaning;
> All doctrines which teach of sentient beings,
> Individuals[216] or creatures
> Should be known as the provisional meaning.

And in the *Sublime Sūtra Revealed by Akṣayamati*:

> If one asks what are the sūtras of definitive meaning and what are the sūtras of provisional meaning, those sūtras which are taught in order that one might enter the path are called the provisional meaning, and those sūtras which are taught in order that one might enter the result are called the definitive meaning. Those sūtras which teach of self, sentient beings, life itself, creatures, individuals, personalities, personal selves, actors, subjects of sensation, explanations according to diverse terms, and of that which is not a possessor as a possessor, are called the provisional meaning. The sūtras which teach of emptiness, of that which is signless, aspirationless, not manifestly conditioned, uncreated, unoriginated, insubstantial, without self, without sentient beings, without life itself, without individuals, without a possessor and without any properties even as far as the approach to liberation, are called the definitive meaning. This text is said to rely on the sūtras of definitive meaning, but not to rely on the sūtras of provisional meaning.

In short, the fundamental abiding nature and the sūtras which reveal it are said to be the definitive meaning and its sūtras, while all those doctrines which guide the intellect of sentient beings by many methods to the means of entering that fundamental nature, and reveal the impure bewilderment, its classifications and so on, are called the provisional meaning and the doctrine of the provisional meaning.

THE INTENTION AND COVERT INTENTION OF THE TRUE DOCTRINE

[118a.2-121a.4] The second part concerns the [buddhas'] intention (*dgongs-pa*, Skt. *abhiprāya*) and covert intention (*ldem-dgongs*, Skt. *abhisandhi*). The former, intention, applies to those teachings which are included within slightly exaggerated explanations and reveal indirect methods and purposes. The *Ornament of the Sūtras of the Greater Vehicle* (Ch.12, v.18) says:

> Passages directed towards sameness and other
> meanings,
> And similarly towards other times,
> And towards the thoughts of individuals
> Should be known as the four kinds of intention.

Accordingly, the [buddhas'] intention is directed towards sameness, as is exemplified in the following words spoken with an intention directed towards the sameness of the body of reality:

> At that time, I became the Tathāgata Vipaśyin.

When this intention is directed towards other meanings it is exemplified by the following words which were spoken with an intention directed towards the three essenceless natures:

> All things are without essence.

Now, the imaginary is without essence in respect of attributes, because in truth it definitely does not exist. The dependent is without essence in respect of creation, because creation from the four alternative limits does not exist: Things are not created from themselves because both that which was created and creation itself consist of instantaneous time moments, which renders them mutually exclusive substances. Nor are things created from something else, because the specific characteristics of that something else do not, on analysis, exist. Then, things are not created from both [themselves and other causes], because they are mutually exclusive substances; and, [finally], without a cause, creation is impossible. The creation of whatever is apparitional and so forth instantly appears inasmuch as it is dependently originated, in the manner of a mere dream or illusion. Such is said in the *Sūtra of the Adornment of Pristine Cognition's Appearance* from:

> Mañjuśrī, dreams appear but do not exist. Similarly all things, too, appear but do not exist.

down to:

> They are illusory, like a mirage, a castle in the sky, the moon in water, a reflected image and an emanation.

Then, the absolute is without essence in respect of ultimate reality because therein [the views that] ultimate reality exists, or that the self is impure, and other such conceptual elaborations are essenceless. Such is said in the *Sūtra which Decisively Reveals the Intention*:

> With an intention directed towards essencelessness of attri-

> butes, essencelessness of creation and essencelessness of ultimate reality, I reveal all things to be without essence.

The [buddhas'] intention is also directed towards other times, as exem- exemplified in the words:

> By merely grasping the name of the Tathāgata Vimalacandraprabha, you will attain buddhahood.

Although buddhahood is not attained by that alone, [the intention is that] one who has accumulated many provisions in the past will at some time become a buddha.

The intention directed towards the thoughts of individuals is exemplified by [the buddhas'] downgrading of moral discipline and praise of liberality in the presence of certain individuals who are conceited with respect to their own moral discipline.

Secondly, concerning the covert intention: It is explained that in order to induce another party, who delights in any view whatsoever, to enter into the correct path or meaning, [the buddhas] adopt a style conforming to the needs of that person by relying somewhat on that one's vocabulary and mannerisms, but their meaning does not so conform. It is said in the *Ornament of the Sūtras of the Greater Vehicle* (Ch.12, vv.16-17):

> The covert intention in respect of entry,
> And, in addition, the covert intention in respect of
> attributes,
> The covert intention in respect of antidotes,
> And the covert intention in respect of interpretation,
> Directed respectively towards pious attendants
> and the essence,
> And similarly towards the discipline of faults,
> And towards profundity of expression,
> Are the four kinds of covert intention.

The covert intention in respect of entry is illustrated as follows. In order that certain members of the family of the pious attendants who have not entered the greater vehicle out of fear of emptiness may so enter, [the buddhas] would say that form does exist therein, and thereby the listener would enter assuming that [form] really exists, while the speakers [the buddhas] would intend that all appearance is like a dream.

The covert intention in respect of attributes is exemplified as follows. In order that the essenceless abiding nature [of reality] may be known, [the buddhas] reveal all things to be essenceless. The three essenceless natures, namely, the imaginary, the dependent and the absolute, have previously been explained.

The covert intention in respect of antidotes is exemplified by the following words which were spoken with an intention directed towards those beings who would think that, "Śākyamuni is inferior to other teachers because he is smaller in body, shorter in life-span and so on":

> At that time, I [Śākyamuni] became the Tathāgata Vairocana.

In this way, the listener understands their buddha-bodies of form to be the same, while the speaker [Śākyamuni] intends that their provisions are equally perfect, that their attainments of the body of reality are equal, and that their deeds on behalf of living beings are equal. As it is said in the *Treasury of the Abhidharma* (Ch.7, v.34):

> All buddhas are identical in their provisions,
> Their body of reality and their conduct
> On behalf of beings,
> But not so in their life-span,
> Race and physical stature.

The covert intention with respect to interpretation refers to teachings given in a form which is extremely difficult to understand in order to pacify the faults of those who think:

> This doctrine is inferior to others
> Because it is easy to understand.

For example, it is said in the *Collection of Meaningful Expressions* (Ch.33, v.62):

> He should kill his father and mother,
> And if he destroys the king and the two purities,
> The country and its surroundings,
> This man will become pure in nature.

Now, the father and mother are lust and acquisition because they compound saṃsāra. The king is the ground-of-all because this becomes the support or ground of diverse propensities. The two purities are the Brāhmaṇa view of mundane aggregates,[217] and the view of those who are conceited with respect to virtuous moral discipline and ascetic discipline. The country and its surroundings are the eight aggregates of consciousness, along with the subject-object dichotomy of the inner activity fields. If all these are destroyed and purified, one becomes a buddha.

The various kinds of intention and covert intention [of the scriptures] are identical in essence. Yet they do differ in details. On the distinction between the two, the translator [Ngok] Loden Sherap[218] claims that intention implies that another meaning apart from the meaning thought by the speaker is understood by the listener from the speaker's words, and covert intention implies that the very meaning thought by the speaker is [subsequently] understood by the listener. And it is said in the *Exegetical Commentary on the Collection of the Greater Vehicle* (*Mahāyānasaṃgrahopanibandhana*, T 4051):

> Intention is not held to refer to apprehension by another party, but only to a determination in the mind. Covert intention does refer to apprehension by another party.

These two are indeed known to be without contradiction. That which is partially explained with reference to something is intention, disregarding whether it is apprehended by another or not; and it is called intention because at times when it is questioned by others all incompletely [understood] meanings still remain in the ground of the intention. That which is revealed in order to benefit others, relying somewhat on intimation, and in conformity with the perception of other persons is called [the buddhas'] covert intention, because they understand the words of the speaker and, by entering thereafter [into the greater vehicle], now at last become receptive to the perfect understanding of other meanings and never turn to falsehood.

Such are the keys through which the scriptures are viewed. Since the profound texts possess many situations of word, meaning, intention and purpose, it is extremely important to know that they are disclosed in this manner.

9 *A Recapitulation of the Causal Vehicles*

[121a.4-121b.1] Having outlined the overall meaning [of the causal vehicles], I shall recapitulate the meaning that is subsumed in their particular sections. It is said in the *Tantra of the Secret Nucleus* (Ch.13, v.2):

> There are those of only partial realisation
> And those who do not [fully] realise genuine reality.

Accordingly, the lesser vehicle confers only partial realisation of the approach to the truth of liberation; and the bodhisattva vehicle, while acting in accord with the approach to inconceivable liberation, does not [fully] confer realisation of the genuine reality because the meaning of the vehicle of indestructible reality (*Vajrayāna*) is not understood therein. The former [the lesser vehicle or Hīnayāna] includes both the pious attendants and the self-centred buddhas.

VEHICLE OF PIOUS ATTENDANTS

[121b.1-124a.6] Firstly, the vehicle of pious attendants is explained under the three headings of essence, verbal definition and classifications. The essence is that with an intellect desirous of liberating itself from saṃsāra one resorts to the means of realising selflessness with reference to the individual.

The verbal definition is that the [Sanskrit] *śrāvaka* is rendered [in Tibetan] as *nyan-thos* or pious attendant because it means both to listen (*nyan-pa*) and to hear attentively (*thos-pa*), while in one respect, it is also rendered as *thos-sgrogs* [or preacher of what has been attentively heard] because, having attentively heard (*thos-pa*) one object [i.e. the teacher], the pious attendant preaches (*sgrogs*) to another.

Thirdly, [the vehicle of pious attendants] is classified according to six topics, namely, its entrance, view, moral discipline, meditation, conduct and result. Concerning the entrance: The pious attendants, being disillusioned by the suffering of saṃsāra, enter through the four truths with the thought of aspiring towards their own peace and happiness. As it is said in the *Tantra of the Great Natural Arising of Awareness*:

> Concerning the entrance, the four truths
> Are the entrance for pious attendants in general.

Now the truth of suffering resembles a disease, the truth of its origination resembles the cause of a disease, the truth of cessation resembles the happiness when one is freed from a disease, and the truth of the path resembles the medicine which is the antidote for a disease. Therefore:

> Suffering is to be known,
> Its origin is to be renounced,
> Cessation is to be obtained,
> And the path is to be relied on.

Therefore, the pious attendants enter by renouncing and accepting the causes and results to which the four truths refer.

Secondly, concerning the view: Selflessness with reference to the individual is realised [firstly] because the apprehended object which appears as coarse substances can be broken down and destroyed by an antidote or the intellect, [secondly] because the continuity of the apprehending subject which is the mind can be broken down by the three temporal dimensions, and [thirdly] because this coarse subject-object dichotomy has no independent existence apart from its mere relative appearance.

However, [the concept of] self with reference to phenomenal things is not understood because they hold that the substratum of indivisible atomic particles, which compose the objective appearance of coarse substances, cannot be destroyed by an antidote or by the intellect, and that the subjective mind is inseparable[219] from the series of indivisible time moments. The subtle subject-object dichotomy is therefore held to be ultimately real. As it is said in the *Garland of Views: A Collection of Esoteric Instructions*:

> All things are considered imaginary since they are exaggerated and depreciated by eternalistic extremists and the like. The nihilist view of no origin and the views concerning permanence and so forth are [considered] as non-existent as the snake which is perceived in place of a rope. Yet the indivisible atomic particles of the four gross elements, including the components, psychophysical bases and activity fields, and consciousness also, are viewed to have ultimate reality.

When [this view of the pious attendants] is classified, it is as Kawa Peltsek says in his *Seventeenfold Appearance of the Sequence of the View*:

The pious attendants who consider merely phenomena
Are both the Sautrāntika and the Vaibhāṣika.
They dispute the nature of external atoms
And agree that consciousness appears
As a series of time moments.

The Vaibhāṣika hold that though this coarse relative truth appears as a single aggregate in the manner of an alpine meadow, ultimately it consists of minute particles because indivisible atomic particles are surrounded without intervening spaces. In his *Turquoise Display*, Nāgārjuna says:[220]

Concerning the relative, the Vaibhāṣikas' central tenet is
That these material substances composing the world
Are an association of atomic particles,
But that [undivided] they appear in the manner of an
alpine meadow.

[These coarse substances] are held to be compounded by the force or power of the active vital energy of sentient beings. Then:

Concerning the ultimate, consciousness is held
To exist as a series of distinct time moments.

The Sautrāntika, on the other hand, hold that indivisible atomic particles are without cohesion but have no intervening spaces between them, in the manner of a heap of grain. As the above text [the *Turquoise Display*] says:

Sautrāntikas, concerning the atoms of relative appearance,
Hold them to form a single, compounded sensum.
And they claim that ultimate reality is agreement of
consciousness [with its object].

Thus they are superior to the Vaibhāṣika because they realise that the conglomerate composed of atoms is indeed partless, and so are similar to those who do not admit the existence of atoms on the grounds that they are not actually visible.[221]

In short, one is a pious attendant if one views the subject-object dichotomy in relation to the self of phenomenal things to be ultimately real, and adheres to the rejection and acceptance of causes and results comprised by the four truths which refer to saṃsāra and nirvāṇa. As it is said in the *Sequence of the Path*:

If, without realising non-duality,
Everything is viewed to exist substantially
In terms of the four truths,
And one resorts to renunciation and non-renunciation,
This is the level of the pious attendants.

Thirdly, concerning moral discipline, one should rely on the eight classes of *prātimokṣa* vows, or particularly the supreme vows of a monk, because training which follows [the example of] the Buddha is essential. It says in the *Treasury of the Abhidharma* (Ch.4, vv.14-15):

> The eight classes [of vow] called *prātimokṣa*
> Substantially refer to the four orders.
> Since their titles vary, depending on the [adherent's] sex,[222]
> It is no error to differentiate [the four into eight].
> Dependent on the vows which renounce
> Respectively five, eight, ten and all things that are to be renounced [223]
> Are the lay vows (*upāsaka*) and the vows of the purificatory fast (*upavāsa*),
> The novitiate (*śrāmaṇera*) and the actual vows of a monk (*bhikṣu*).

Fourthly, concerning meditation, the same text says (Ch.6, v.5ab):

> One who abides in moral discipline
> And has studied and pondered
> Should properly undertake meditation.

Relying in this way on the pure basis of moral discipline, one is required to study the piṭaka of the pious attendants under [the guidance] of a spiritual benefactor. Then, the meaning that has been studied should be pondered, and the meaning that has been pondered should be meditated upon.

Now, meditation initially requires that one makes the mind capable of action through tranquillity, which begins with meditation on ugliness as an antidote for attachment; and subsequently, one meditates with higher insight on the sixteen minor truths, four of which are differentiated in each of the four truths.

On this basis, one begins with renunciation by perceiving the conflicting emotions of the three realms, and then the mode of renunciation is effected in a succession of sixteen moments of pristine cognition. The sixteen minor truths are the four which are aspects of the truth of suffering, namely, impermanence, suffering, emptiness and selflessness; the four which are aspects of the truth of origination, namely, causal basis, origin, production and condition; the four which are aspects of the truth of cessation, namely, cessation, quiescence, excellence and disillusionment with saṃāra; and the four which are aspects of the truth of the path, namely, the path, reason, attainment and the act of becoming disillusioned with saṃsāra; sixteen in all. Then, the sixteen moments of pristine cognition are the perception of the doctrine (*dharmajñāna*), receptiveness to the perception of the doctrine (*dharma-*

jñānakṣānti), the after-effect of this perception (*anvayajñāna*) and receptiveness to the after-effect of this perception (*anvayajñānakṣānti*), as they apply to each of the four truths, making sixteen in all.

Fifth, concerning their conduct: Pious attendants perform acts which emphasise their own benefit by abiding in the twelve ascetic virtues. It says in the *Turquoise Display*:

> Their conduct is exclusively for their own benefit.

Sixth, as for the result: Pious attendants obtain the provisional results of entering the stream [to nirvāṇa], of being tied to a single rebirth and of not returning [to saṃsāra]. And then, as the culmination, they become arhats either with or without a residue, who are endowed with the twofold pristine cognition, which perceives the cessation [of corruption] and perceives that it is not recreated.

There is also an enumeration of eight results when each of these four is distinguished according to those who enter it and those who are firmly established in it. It is said that there are four pairs of sacred beings with reference to the ground of this classification, and eight kinds of individual [pious attendant] with reference to the properties so classified. Of these, the *Tantra of the Extensive Magical Net* says:

> One who is well pacified by training
> In the sixteen-faceted pristine cognition,
> Which understands the meaning,
> And is well renounced in respect of the four truths,
> And who has been trained through the succession of
>   [results],
> Such as entering the stream,
> Proceeds to the level on which the enemy,
> Conflicting emotion, is pacified.

VEHICLE OF SELF-CENTRED BUDDHAS

[124a.6-127a.2] Secondly, the vehicle of self-centred buddhas is also classified under three headings of essence, verbal definition and classification. The essence is that, without relying on a master, during one's final life in the world, one meditates on the path of dependent origination as a means for attaining manifest enlightenment, through the realisation of one-and-a-half parts of [the concept of] selflessness.[224]

Secondly, the verbal definition: The [Sanskrit] *pratyekabuddha* is rendered as self-centred buddha [Tib. *rang-rgyal*] because it implies that one's own enlightenment is realised by oneself. The enlightenment is attained individually, that is, for oneself alone.

Thirdly, there are six classifications as above, of which the first is the entrance. The *Tantra of the Great Natural Arising of Awareness* says:

> The entrance is through the twelvefold dependent origination.

In this way, a self-centred buddha enters through the twelve modes of dependent origination. As for dependent origination, it says in the *Heruka Galpo*:

> The doctrine of self-centred buddhas,
> In order to purify the intellect,
> Includes the doctrines of outer and inner
> Dependent origination.

Accordingly, the twelve modes of dependent origination are both outward and inward.

If one were to ask in what way these [twelve] revolve, the outward dependent origination [of physical elements] revolves quantitatively, and the inward dependent origination revolves as propensities in non-corporeal beings and concretely in respect of corporeal beings.

Concerning the procedure for entering therein: In general a self-centred buddha of the highest acumen, in the [solitary] manner of a rhinoceros, has accumulated the path of provisions over a period of one hundred aeons. One of mediocre acumen and great conduct in respect of the provisions has accumulated the provisions as far as the middling degree of receptiveness (*bzod-'bring*)[225] over a hundred human lives. And one who is of inferior acumen and low in conduct relating to the provisions has accumulated the provisions subsumed by the fifteenth moment [of pristine cognition] on the path of insight over thirteen human lives. Knowing that there is no chance of attaining enlightenment on this basis [alone], with prayers of aspiration they take birth in a world which is entirely unoccupied by buddhas and pious attendants. As the *Root Stanzas on the Madhyamaka* (Ch.18, v.12) says:

> If buddhas do not emerge
> And pious attendants have ceased to be,
> The pristine cognition of the self-centred buddha
> Is well developed without support.

On this basis and without preceptor or master, [the would-be self-centred buddhas] become natural monks. Going to a charnel ground, they become disillusioned with saṃsāra immediately after seeing the bones, and when they investigate the source from which these bones originated, it is realised that they originated from old age and death, that these in turn originated from birth, and in this way it is gradually realised that the root of saṃsāra is ignorance. Then, wondering how to attain liberation from this, they enter by realising the trend in which dependent origination is reversed, namely, that if ignorance is abolished, habitual tendencies cease and so on down to the cessation of old age and death.

Secondly, in their view [the self-centred buddhas] are similar to the pious attendants who realise selflessness with reference to the individual, but in addition they realise that the indivisible atomic particles which are the objective aspect of selfhood as it relates to phenomena do not independently exist. However, since they still regard the time moments forming the subjective mind to be ultimately real, and hold that the cause and result of saṃsāra and nirvāṇa are found in dependent origination, they are said to be realised in one-and-a-half parts of what is implied by selflessness. It says in the *Ornament of Emergent Realisation* (Ch.2, v.8):

> Since they renounce the idea of objects,
> And since they do not renounce the subject,
> One must know the path genuinely subsumed therein
> Is that of a rhinoceros-like recipient.

And in the *Sequence of the View*:

> Similarly, the vehicle of the self-centred buddhas
> Concerns the mere illusion of the twelve outer
> [links of dependent origination];
> It is superior in holding atoms not to exist
> In any spatial dimension,[226]
> But agrees that consciousness
> Is a series of time moments.

So also in the *Sequence of the Path*:

> If one does not perceive deeds and all the conflicting
> emotions
> To be in fact sameness,
> And entirely clings to the cause and result of
> dependent origination,
> This is the level of the self-centred buddhas.

Then this, one might object, contradicts the passage from the *Thirty Verses* (*Triṃśikākārikā*, T 4055, v.28d) which says:

> If there is no object, there is no subject.

There is, however, no flaw. This passage explains that, if that which is apprehended by direct perception is realised to have no independent existence, the subject is also necessarily understood [in the same way]. In this [vehicle], on the other hand, it is said that the object is realised to have no independent existence because objects which conceptually appear to the intellect are realised to be without independent existence, and because during such realisation, the ignorance which has become the root of the three poisons is reversed.[227]

Thirdly, in moral discipline, [the self-centred buddhas] are similar to the pious attendants. It says in the *Miraculous Key of Further Discernment* (*yang-'byed-'phrul-gyi lde-mig*, NGB Vol.2):

> The limits which pious attendants
> And self-centred buddhas sustain
> Are the two hundred and fifty disciplines of the Vinaya.

Fourth, on meditation, the *Yogācāra Level* says:

> It should be known to be just like that of the pious attendants,
> Because these two are similar in the nature of their paths.

Despite this claim that the [self-centred buddhas] meditate on the path referring to the piṭaka of the pious attendants, masters of the past have said that in the *Sūtra which Dispels the Grief of Ajātaśatru* (*Ajātaśatrukaukṛtyavinodanasūtra*, T 216) the piṭaka of the self-centred buddhas are briefly and distinctly explained in contrast to the piṭaka of the pious attendants. Also, in other texts, such as the *Ornament of Emergent Realisation* and its commentaries [*Abhisamayālaṃkāravṛtti*, etc. T 3787-9, 3791, 3793-6], their path is claimed to differ from that of the pious attendants. This is because, over and above the sixteen moments beginning with impermanence such as apply to the four truths, [the self-centred buddhas] obstruct the trend in which dependent origination arises and meditate in the correct order on the twelve [antidotes], that is, the emptinesses belonging to the trend in which it is reversed.

Fifth, in conduct, [the self-centred buddhas] communicate with those who require training through symbolic gestures, which are performed through the miraculous abilities of their bodies, and without teaching the doctrine by their speech. It says in the *Ornament of Emergent Realisation* (Ch.2, v.7):

> To those respective persons
> Who require training,
> Whatever they wish to hear,
> The respective meanings just appear,
> Without even a sound being uttered.

And in the *Turquoise Display*:

> By conduct that is the miraculous ability of their bodies,
> They variously act on behalf of others.

Sixth, as for the result, the self-centred buddha of sharp acumen who remains in solitude like a rhinoceros, after perfecting the five paths in a single sitting, becomes manifest, through the supreme bliss of his purpose, as an arhat who is conscious that the cessation [of corruption] has come about and that it will not be recreated. The *Treasury of the Abhidharma* (Ch.6, v.24) says:

> The Teacher and the self-centred buddha, similar to a rhinoceros,
> Become entirely enlightened on the sole basis of the final contemplation,
> And, before that, they are in accord with liberation.

Those of greater and lesser conduct with respect to the provisions, who flock together in the manner of parrots, respectively make manifest the first four and the first three paths.[228]

Again, on the subject of these self-centred buddhas, the *Extensive Magical Net* says:

> Knowing outer and inner dependent origination
> [To be] in the manner of an illusion and a mirage,
> They thoroughly penetrate substantial forms without impediment,
> They become realised through intrinsic awareness, untaught by a spiritual benefactor,
> And, with supreme bliss of purpose, proceed to an enlightened level.

VEHICLE OF BODHISATTVAS

[127a.2-131b.2] The latter of the causal vehicles, the vehicle of bodhisattvas, is explained under two headings: its superiority over the lesser vehicle and the particular nature of this sublime vehicle. First, [the bodhisattva] is superior through an ability to realise the two kinds of selflessness as the fundamental nature by means of great discriminative awareness, and an ability to act exclusively on behalf of others by means of great compassion. This is because these qualities are absent in the lesser vehicle. As stated in the *Tantra of the Array of Pristine Cognition (ye-shes rnam-par bkod-pa'i rgyud)*:

> That which refers to sentient beings with compassion
> And pervades the expanse of reality with discriminative awareness
> Is explained to be the greater vehicle.
> The others are its opposite.

And the master Aro [Yeshe Jungne][229] has said:

> The distinguishing features of the vehicles are
> Exclusively discriminative awareness and compassion;

> The distinction between the vehicles is made
> In accordance with their greater or lesser extent.

And in the *Verse Summation of the Transcendental Perfection of Discriminative Awareness*:

> One who has no skilful means
> And is without discriminative awareness
> Falls into the position of the pious attendants.

Secondly, the vehicle of bodhisattvas endowed with this particularly superior doctrine is explained under the three headings of essence, verbal definition and classification. The essence is that one realises all things to be without self and then firmly resorts to the means of performing great benefits on behalf of others through great compassion.

As to the verbal definition, a bodhisattva [spiritual warrior set on enlightenment][230] is so called because the [Sanskrit] *bodhisattva* indicates one who is totally unafraid to attain the unsurpassed enlightenment by means of great mental power.

Thirdly, among the six aforementioned classifications, first the entrance is effected through the two truths. The *Tantra of the Great Natural Arising of Awareness* says:

> The vehicle of the bodhisattvas
> Is entered through the two truths.

According to the texts of the Mādhyamika, after the intellect, which perceives unanalysed and unexamined appearances to be without real essence in the manner of an illusion despite their appearance, has been grasped by the enlightened mind of loving kindness and compassion, [a bodhisattva] enters the relative truth by inducing virtue and opposing non-virtue. But when the abiding nature of ultimate, fundamental reality is known to be free from conceptual elaborations, the bodhisattva enters by means of the coalescence [of the two truths].

Concerning the two truths, the *Heruka Galpo* says:

> The doctrine revealed by the buddhas
> Is genuinely gathered in the two truths.

Now, the extent of the knowable which forms the ground of this classification is polarised between the apparitional mode or relative truth, and the abiding mode or ultimate truth. Therefore, the same text says:

> In the appearances which form the knowable alone,
> The scope of the two truths indeed exists.

Of these, the relative truth refers to the symbolic apparition of reality which is the object perceived by the intellect. As [the *Heruka Galpo*] again says:

Deception and objectification of the intellect
Are the general characteristics of relative appearances.

Then, when classified, there is the correct relative which is causally effective in terms of phenomenal appearance, as when a man appears as a man, and the erroneous relative which is causally ineffective in terms of phenomenal appearance, as when a cairn of stones appears as a man. From the same text:

The divisions of relative appearance
Are called the correct and the erroneous relative.
The characteristics of each should be well explained:
The erroneous one is causally ineffective
In terms of what appears,
And the correct one is causally effective
In terms of what appears.

And also from the *Analysis of the Two Truths* (*Satyadvayavibhaṅgakārikā*, T 3881, v.12):

Since they are similarly apparent
And since they are respectively
Causally effective and ineffective,
The classification of the correct and erroneous
Relative has been made.

The ultimate truth, on the other hand, is free from all conceptual elaborations, as it is said in the *Heruka Galpo*:

Ultimate reality is characteristically
Free from all conceptual elaborations.

And in Jetāri's *Analysis of the Sugata's Texts* (*Sugatamatavibhaṅgakārikā*, T 3899):

Neither is it being, non-being,
Or neither being nor non-being,
Nor indeed an embodiment of them both,
But it is genuinely liberated from the four extremes.

When classified, there is the ultimate truth with synonyms which is partially free from conceptual elaboration, and the ultimate truth without synonyms which is free from all conceptual elaboration. As the *Heruka Galpo* says:

Its classifications are the ultimate truth with synonyms,
And that without synonyms which is free from the eight
extremes.

Then, one might ask, are these two truths the same or different? They are identical in their nature but different in their aspects, conventionally similar to the moon and the reflections of the moon in water, respectively. It says in the *Commentary on Enlightened Mind* (*Bodhicitta-vivaraṇa*, T 1800, v.57):

> Just as molasses is naturally sweet
> And fire is naturally hot,
> The nature of all things
> Similarly abides in emptiness.

Yet the ultimate reality can be expressed as neither an identity nor a difference. The *Dialogue with Maitreya* (*Maitreyaparipṛcchā*, T 85-6) says:

> The expanse, which cannot be expressed through the symbolic forms of habitual tendencies, is not this at all, and it is not anything else.

Although the Mādhyamika do not differ in their methods of determining the ultimate reality, with reference to the relative truth there are the Svātantrika who hold appearances to exist as a mere illusion, and the Prāsaṅgika who maintain that from the very moment of appearance there is freedom from conceptual elaborations.

The Mind Only (*Cittamātra*) system holds the objects and subjects which are dualistic appearances of the subject-object dichotomy to be the relative truth, and the intrinsic awareness, intrinsic radiance, or the consciousness which is without duality, to be the ultimate truth. When they are classified, there are those holding sensa to be veridical, who hold the sensa through which external objects are perceived to be veridical, and those holding sensa to be false, who claim that the status of appearances is exaggerated by consciousness.

Secondly, the view [of the bodhisattva vehicle] is the incontrovertible realisation of the two kinds of selflessness. Although relatively all things appear in the manner of [the reflection of] the moon in water, ultimately the abiding nature of the two truths is realised by understanding the quiescence of all conceptual elaborations. It says in the *Garland of Views: A Collection of Esoteric Instructions*:

> Ultimately all things, including all-conflicting emotions and pure [phenomena], are without independent existence, but relatively the attributes of each exist distinctly in the manner of an illusion.

And in the *Sequence of the Path*:

> Without knowing the meaning of sameness,
> The relative and ultimate truths are polarised;
> But if there is no self with respect to individuals,
> or phenomena,

This is the level of enlightenment.

Thirdly, on the subject of moral discipline, there are three aspects: the moral discipline of gathering the virtuous doctrine; that of acting on behalf of sentient beings; and that of controlling malpractices. The first refers to the attainment of the virtuous provisions of excellent conduct which are subsumed by the two provisions and six transcendental perfections; the second implies that all one's aspirations and applications are acted upon for the benefit of sentient beings. As for the third, though in the Madhyamaka tradition the necessity of holding *prātimokṣa* vows as a support for the cultivation of enlightened mind is uncertain, the moral discipline which controls malpractices on the level of the bodhisattvas includes the mind which aspires towards enlightenment, and the mind which enters into union with the provisions and necessary actions for that enlightenment, in addition to a basis in which training according to the seven classes of *prātimokṣa* vows[231] is established.

These aspects of [moral discipline] are adopted by the proponents of Madhyamaka and Mind Only in their rites, and training in them is pursued. Mind Only holds that there are four root downfalls. As the *Twenty Verses on the Bodhisattva Vow* says:

> These are to praise oneself and disparage others
> Out of attachment to profit and fame;
> Not to give the spiritual wealth of the doctrine, out of
> avarice,
> To one who suffers without protection;
> To find fault with others out of anger,
> Without heeding the repentance of others;
> And to renounce the greater vehicle
> And teach an imitation of the true doctrine.

According to the Mādhyamika, on the other hand, nineteen or twenty precepts are upheld. It is explained in the *Compendium of Lessons* that according to the *Sūtra of Ākāśagarbha* (*Ākāśagarbhasūtra*, T 260) there are nineteen root downfalls, namely, five which are certain for kings, five which are certain for ministers, eight which are certain for common people, and [the nineteenth] to abandon the mind of enlightened aspiration which is common to all. It is then said in the *Pagoda of Precious Jewels* that they number twenty when, in addition to these, the enlightened mind of engagement is abandoned and virtue not applied.

Concerning these bodhisattvas, too, the *Introduction to the Conduct of a Bodhisattva* (Ch.5, v.23) says:

> I fold my hands in the prayer
> That those wishing to protect the mind

> May guard mindfulness and awareness of the present
> Even at the cost of their lives.

Thus, a bodhisattva untiringly endeavours, with undiminished mindfulness and awareness of the present, to sustain [the precepts] by renouncing the four negative doctrines, accepting the four positive doctrines and so forth.

Fourth, in meditation, a bodhisattva generally meditates on the thirty-seven aspects of enlightenment during the four paths of learning. That is, he meditates on the four essential recollections during the lesser path of provisions, upon the four correct trainings during the middling [path of provisions], on the four supports for miraculous ability during the greater [path of provisions], on the five faculties during the feeling of warmth and its climax on the path of connection, on the five powers during the feeling of receptiveness and the supreme phenomenon [on the path of connection],[232] on the seven branches of enlightenment during the path of insight, and on the sublime eightfold path as far as the ninth level[233] during the path of meditation.

In particular, with reference to experiential cultivation from the beginning [of the path], as it is revealed in the sūtras of definitive meaning which belong to the final promulgation: When [a bodhisattva] has comprehended the nature of the nucleus of the tathāgata, and developed his mind in supreme enlightenment, being of the enlightened family, he meditates by combining tranquillity and higher insight. These are, namely, the tranquillity born of contemplation in which subjective thoughts concerned with unimpeded objective appearances are pacified, and the higher insight which views appearances according to the eight similes of illusion. This higher insight determines both the subtle and coarse subject-object dichotomies to be empty and then inspects reality as emptiness itself. It also includes meditative equipoise and absorption in the meaning of the Madhyamaka, free from extremes. As the *Introduction to the Conduct of a Bodhisattva* (Ch.8, v.4) also says:

> One should know that conflicting emotions are subdued
> By higher insight excellently endowed with tranquillity.

Fifth, in conduct, a bodhisattva acts on behalf of sentient beings, regarding others as more dear than himself during the aftermath [of meditation]. As the natural expression of his conduct, he acts according to the six or ten transcendental perfections in the manner of a mere illusion. The enumeration of six [transcendental perfections] which begins with liberality, and the enumeration of ten which adds skilful means, power, aspiration and pristine cognition, are all gathered within the transcendental perfection of discriminative awareness (*prajñāpāramitā*).

Sixth, concerning the result, when a bodhisattva has gradually traversed the ten levels and five paths, on the eleventh level of Universal Light (*Samantaprabhā*) during the path of no-more-learning, he is liberated for his own sake in the buddha-body of reality, and relying on the two buddha-bodies of form for the sake of others, he acts on behalf of sentient beings until saṃsāra has been emptied.

Furthermore, on this topic the *Extensive Magical Net* says:

> The yogin who has perfected the transcendental
>   perfections,
> Who has realised the two kinds of selflessness,
> And who has gradually traversed the ten levels,
> Will excellently attain, by means of the two truths,
> The path through which the buddha level is reached
> And its status is attained.

This completes the anthology which explains the definitive order of the causal vehicles of dialectics, the third part of this book, the *Feast in which Eloquence Appears*, which is a definitive ordering of the precious teaching of the vehicle of indestructible reality according to the Ancient Translation School.

Part Four
Resultant Vehicles of Secret Mantra

Introduction

[131b.2-131b.4] Having briefly described the structure of the causal vehicles of dialectics, now the definitive order of the piṭaka of the resultant secret mantra (*gsang-sngags*), the vehicles of indestructible reality, shall be expounded in two parts: the superiority [of the secret mantra] over the causal vehicles and an explanation of the nature of these extraordinary vehicles.

1 *The Superiority of Secret Mantra*

[131b.4-143a.6] This [vehicle] which makes the result into the path is superior to the vehicle of the transcendental perfections[234] which makes the cause into the path. There are adherents of the dialectical vehicle who object that, "When you proponents of the way of secret mantra make the result your path, it must either be a mature [result] which is made into the path, or an immature result which is made into the path. In the first case, this would lead to infinite regress because even after maturation, [the result] would be made into the path. You have accepted this logical entailment and it is proven that [the present instance] must be included therein, just as, for example, last year's fruit becomes the present's seed. So if this view is held, it is implied that the way of secret mantra is itself a long path. In the second case, it is not the result which is made into the path because this is immature. If this view were held, your own assertion would be refuted, and it is consistently proven that anything immature is not a conclusive result; witness for example a shoot and a stem."

If this argument were raised, the reply would be that, from the standpoint of being, the genuine essence which is to be obtained abides intrinsically, and yet, because it is not understood from the standpoint of realisation, it is merely the means of realising it which is said to be made into the path. As it is said in the *Sequence of the Path*:

> In this way, the pristine cognition
> Which intrinsically abides
> Is the essence of all the paths and results.
> In order that the connection with it may be purified,
> The supreme means which make it manifest
>   emerge intrinsically.

If it is said that when the intrinsically abiding result is manifested by the path, it must either have been produced on the basis of a previous result or not, then with reference to the essence, there is nothing to be produced. This is just as when a prince who wanders among the populace is recognised as a prince his status does not essentially improve. Yet with reference to the manifest clarity [of the essence], it *has* been produced, just as when [the identity of] the prince has been confirmed he can hold sway over the populace. This vehicle of secret mantra should be known as such. It says in the *Heruka Galpo*:

> Through the causal vehicle of dialectics
> Mind-as-such is perceived as the cause of buddhahood.
> Through the resultant vehicle of mantras
> Mind-as-such is meditated upon as buddhahood.
> So, too, one should know well the tendency
> Of any cause or result.

Therefore, in the vehicle of dialectics mind-as-such is merely perceived as the causal basis of buddhahood. Since it is held that buddhahood is obtained under the condition whereby the two provisions increasingly multiply, and since the purifying doctrines which form the causal basis of nirvāṇa are made into the path, it is called the causal vehicle (*rgyu'i theg-pa*). Therein, a sequence in which cause precedes result is admitted.

According to the vehicle of mantras, on the other hand, mind-as-such abides primordially and intrinsically as the essence of the result, identified in the buddha-bodies and pristine cognitions. Mind-as-such is thereby established as the ground which exists within oneself from the present moment as the object to be attained. It is then established as the path through its functions of bringing about recognition and removing the provisional stains which suddenly arise by means of inducing the perception of just what is, and it is established as the result through its function of actualising this very ground. Since a sequence in which cause precedes result is not really distinguished therein, it is called the resultant vehicle (*'bras-bu'i theg-pa*) and the vehicle of indestructible reality (*rdo-rje theg-pa*). It is said in the *Secret Nucleus* (Ch.12, v.14):

> From any of the four times and ten directions
> The perfect Buddha will not be found.
> Mind-as-such is the perfect Buddha.
> Do not search for the Buddha elsewhere.

And (Ch.13, v.19):

> The result, definitive and most secret,
> Has been turned into the path.

And also (Ch.9, v.29):

> This wondrous, marvellous, amazing reality
> Does not come into existence from elsewhere.
> But it emerges in those dispositions
> Which have the nature of discriminative awareness,
> Steadfast in skilful means.

Then, in the *Tantra of the Extensive Magical Net* it is said:

> Since cause and result are primordially without
> sequence,
> When the result has been turned into the path,
> They are simultaneously united.

Similarly, with reference to the outer tantras, the *Sequence of the Path* says:

> Through discriminative awareness
> And all branches of ritual
> According to the tradition of Kriyātantra,
> The Sugata made the result into the path.

And with reference to the inner tantras, the same text says accordingly:

> Other than this there is nothing to be obtained.
> When everything indeed has been ripened,
> There is nothing to be reached.
> This reality is the essence of the path.

Our predecessors, too, have claimed that there exists a distinction between [the resultant vehicle] which can make the relative appearances into the path and [the causal vehicle] which cannot. Through the transcendental perfections, the ultimate reality is to be attained and the relative appearances are to be renounced, but through the mantras relative appearances are also made into the path without being renounced, since sameness with respect to all things is experienced. Therefore, the mantra vehicles are superior because they do not fall into biased tendencies with respect to the two truths. The *Sequence of the Path* says:

> Within the unsurpassed vehicle, there are those
> Holding ultimate reality to be indivisible
> And relative appearances to include everything,
> Both the pure and the impure.
> The great vehicle of skilful means, however,
> Does not divide even relative appearances
> According to purity and suffering.
> The higher and lower views are just so.[235]

According to this system [i.e. the vehicle of skilful means] also, the result is made into the path because the essence of the result, in which all things are indivisible, is regarded as the buddha-body of reality in which appearances and emptiness are coalesced, and experienced by skilful means. It says in the *Tantra of the Extensive Magical Net*:

In the nature of appearances,
Including the animate and inanimate world,
There is no inherent essence.
This itself is the great body of reality.

The way of secret mantra is verbally defined as that which makes the result into the path and as the vehicle of indestructible reality because, through the outer mantras, one meditates with reference to the body, speech and mind of the deity and, according to the inner mantras, all things are realised and then experienced as the natural expression of the maṇḍalas of buddha-body, speech and mind. The *Miraculous Key to the Storehouse* says:

Concerning the resultant vehicle of indestructible reality:
When the maṇḍala of the seals[236] has been made into the path,
The result itself is then carried on the path.
One's own body, speech and mind
Are united in the indestructible reality of
Buddha-body, speech and mind.
Such is indicative of the vehicle of indestructible reality.

Yet [the way of secret mantra] also has other distinctive features, as it is said in the *Lamp of the Three Modes* (*Nayatrayapradīpa*, T 3707):

Though they are identical in purpose,
The vehicle of the mantras is superior;
For it is unobscured and endowed with many means,
It is without difficulty
And refers to those of highest acumen.

Although both the causal and resultant phases of the greater vehicle are identical in their purpose of seeking enlightenment with the aim of benefitting sentient beings, the mantras are superior through four distinctive features. [First,] they are unobscured in the area of skilful means which includes meditation on the deity and the recitation of mantras. [Second,] they are manifold because there are limitless approaches among the tantrapiṭaka, beginning with the Kriyātantra and Caryātantra, which correspond to the degrees of acumen [in those who require training], without being confined to a single methodical approach. [Third,] they are without difficulty because they are easily accomplished without requiring that three "countless" aeons and the like be arduously passed as in the causal path. [Fourth,] they are taught with an intention directed towards those of highest acumen who actually require training through the vehicle of these very mantras. So the mantras are superior in these four ways.

Moreover, if a somewhat detailed explanation is given according to the intention of the uncommon, inner tantras in this [Nyingma tradition]: When the profound and vast abiding nature of inconceivable reality[237] is appraised according to the dialectical vehicle, ultimate truth is established through the valid cognition of inference by means of perceptive judgements made according to logical syllogisms, and so is an intellectually created ground. Tranquillity is then secured by means of efforts directed to the birth of intellectual certainty, and it is the ideas and scrutiny in relation to that [ground] which are merely labelled as higher insight. The mere profundity [of this dialectical vehicle] refers to the result as that which lies in the direction of attainment through causes compounded of countless provisions over a long period of time, and its vastness comprises the components, psychophysical bases and activity fields. All of these, having been established as the relative truth, are nothing but the rigid ensnarement of the perception which accepts and rejects.

The mantra [vehicle], on the other hand, does not refer to logical syllogisms and the intellectually contrived discriminative awareness produced by thought. Pristine cognition uncreated by the intellect is established as the non-conceptualising reality or nucleus of the buddha-body of reality by the third empowerment,[238] by the irresistible descent of pristine cognition,[239] and by incisively applying oneself to [practices associated with] the energy channels, currents and seminal points which depend on the body of indestructible reality. Then enlightenment is actualised in one lifetime, and so forth, after the ultimate truth has been realised by the intellect abiding naturally in this state.

In this way, the continuum of the ground (*gzhi'i rgyud*) is established both through that actual development of profundity and also through the vastness which is the expanse [of reality], primordially abiding as a maṇḍala of inner radiance. Subsequently, it is revealed that the continua of the path (*lam-kyi rgyud-rnams*) are to be experientially cultivated by realising that the entire world and its contents, along with the components, psychophysical bases and activity fields, which are the ostensible relative appearances dependent on that [ground], are an array of deities, celestial mansions and buddha-fields free from acceptance and rejection. And the continuum of the result (*'bras-bu'i rgyud*) is thereby established, including the eight common accomplishments and the uncommon accomplishments which extend from the path of insight as far as the path of no-more-learning. Therefore, [the way of mantras] is unobscured with respect to profound and vast meaning.

In other respects also, the mantras are superior through their swiftness, bliss and skilful means. If one inquires into the quality of their swiftness, it is that enlightenment is attained through them within this life, sixteen rebirths, three aeons or eight aeons. And if one inquires into the reasons for their swiftness, it is that the mantras possess merit which originates from total enjoyment because, through their special rites, the offerings which are made are actually accepted by the deities; it is that by the power of mantras even a single drop of water is multiplied to the extent of the sands of the River Ganges and gives rise to as many merits; and it is that the contemplation of purifying [lands into] buddha-fields in which impure appearances have ceased is actualised by a novice. Moreover, through each particular quality of the mantras and contemplations, those extraordinary causes which bring sentient beings to maturity exist even in one who has just entered this vehicle, and through their range of contemplation, [the mantras] possess, from first to last, the discriminative awareness which refers to form as an aspect of the result in terms of the two truths.

If one inquires into the quality of their bliss, it is the absence of coarse physical and mental sensations. And if one inquires into the reasons for their bliss, it is that in this [vehicle] even a body which endures for six aeons may be achieved, that many miraculous abilities and contemplations are obtained, that through the power of the mantras the buddhas become actually present, and that through the application of the mantras and the tantras all the wishes of sentient beings are attained.

Then, if one inquires into the nature of their skilful means, [the mantras] include the training in moral disciplines such as the unchanging bliss, the training in contemplations which are both symbolic and non-symbolic, the training in discriminative awareness through which the two truths are realised to be primordially of indivisible nature, and they include all else that enters the range of experience.

Moreover, it is revealed in the *Tantra of the Inconceivable Rali Cakrasaṃvara*:

> In the lesser vehicle which includes the pious attendants,
> There are no esoteric instructions.
> The vehicle of the awareness-holders is superior
> Through fifteen distinctive features:
> The distinctions of its view, conduct and mind control,
> Of its cause, result, path and level,
> Of its time, rapture and yoga,
> Of its self- and other-oriented benefits, and its intention,
> Its renunciation of laborious extremes, and its ease,
> And its accumulation of the provisions.

Concerning superiority [of the mantras] through the view, mind-as-such is essentially and spontaneously present from the beginning as the ultimate truth, which has seven aspects of spiritual wealth, as follows. Through its function of being the naturally pure essence, it is the ultimate truth of the expanse. Through its function of abiding as the ground in which all things of nirvāṇa arise, clear and radiant without all obscurations and veils, it is the ultimate truth of pristine cognition.

Then, it is the ultimate truth of the result, which unimpededly abides, whatever enlightened attributes of buddha-body and pristine cognition arise. The resultant doctrines which are the great mystery of the buddha's fivefold body, speech, mind, enlightened attributes and activities, being spontaneously present within the latter, are the ultimate truth of natural, original cessation.[240]

The expressive power of this ultimate reality which is mind-as-such, otherwise [known as] the apparitional array of the world and its contents which, to childish persons, are ostensible relative appearances, is manifest in and of itself as a great maṇḍala of buddha-body and pristine cognition. Thus, the relative truth is perfect in that sameness where saṃsāra and nirvāṇa or good and evil are not distinguished. It is the great, superior body of reality wherein the truth is indivisible, and in which these two truths [both ultimate and relative] abide from the beginning as the identity of a single essence, coalesced in the manner of gold and the colour gold, or of a butter lamp and the light of a butter lamp, without alternating between acceptance and rejection. Only in conventional terms is [this body of reality] called the indivisible truth, transcending thought and expression. Indeed, it genuinely transcends the thoughts and expressions which apprehend it. It is neither improved by buddhas, nor worsened by sentient beings, because this doctrine of primordial origin, not being a contrived doctrine which suddenly arises, abides in the fundamental, natural state of mind-as-such. It is said in the *Sequence of the Path* by Buddhaguhya:

> Since it is neither created nor contrived
> By the conquerors or living beings,
> Its natural expression is intrinsically indivisible,
> And in order to loosen attachment to its descriptions
> It is unthinkable and inexpressible
> Within the two conventional truths.

Although this abiding mode of the two truths is the superior view of the mantras, certain scholars of Tibet hold that, in general, there is no distinction between the view of the vehicle of transcendental perfections and that of the way of secret mantra. In particular, they disapprove of relative appearances being held within the view, and profess instead that [the pure divine appearances] are similar to meditations on loving kindness, compassion, enlightened mind and so forth because they are the conceptual aspects of meditation [performed] by a subject with reference to a relative object. This, however, is the prattle of minds which are disinclined to the spiritual and philosophical systems of the vehicle of indestructible reality. It is of crucial importance that the above explanation be known as the view of the mantras, and it is also exceedingly important to meditate on it. This is because, concerning the view, when the meaning of the view appears to the unbewildered pristine cognition of sublime beings, through the eye of discriminative awareness which accords with the primordial abiding nature of all things, it is the abiding nature of all things, the measure of the ultimate truth. This is also because the things which appear as the objects of consciousness, which is the bewildered intellect of sentient beings, are false in that they are the apparitional nature or relative truth. For example, the six classes of living beings perceive the same water in many apparitional modes, but to the buddhas it appears as the expanse of the consort Māmakī.[241]

The abiding nature [of reality] is also exclusively free from the conceptual elaboration of any objective referent. If it is said in this context that there is no difference between the views of the sūtras and mantra texts because the dialectics explained in the sūtras are not erroneous, they are similar in the sense that it is the aspect of the buddha-body of reality, derived from the expanse free from all conceptual elaborations, which is made into the path according to the explanations in the causal phase of the greater vehicle. However, in that freedom from conceptual elaborations, which is exclusively one of explicit negation, the emptiness endowed with all supreme aspects, the ground in which all uncorrupted things arise, and also the enlightened attributes of supreme bliss distinguished by the way of mantras, are incomplete. Therefore it says in the *Taintless Light*:

> The emptiness of all aspects in space and the things which are uncreated are genuinely perceived in the manner of images on a mirror. This is remote from the emptiness of empty nihilism which scrutinises the properties of the self, comprising the aggregate of atomic particles, in order to equate the conceptual elaborations manifested by one's own mind with dreams. The inner bliss, a phenomenon of which one is intrinsically aware, is passionately adhered to, and the blissful phenomena of which one is aware through the external sense organs are totally abandoned.

And so it is explained in the *Brief Teaching on the Tenets of the View (Pradarśanānumatoddeśaparīkṣā*, P 4610):

> The emptiness which scrutinises the components,
> Coreless as a plantain tree,
> Is dissimilar[242] to this emptiness
> Which is endowed with all supreme aspects.
> Uncreated and unceasing,
> The knowable appearances discerned therein
> Are emptiness in the sense that they are substantially
>   empty,
> And not in the sense of a scrutiny of the components.

The proponent of dialectics, apart from merely establishing that the characteristics of relative appearance are non-existent, does not know the essence which abides from the beginning as great purity and sameness; and by not knowing that, he does not know the meditation which makes the precise aspects of the auspicious coincidence of the two buddha-bodies of form into the path.[243] By not knowing that, in turn, he does not know the means of accumulating the extraordinary provisions through which the desired qualities[244] are rapturously experienced, so that, being bound by the antidote of renunciation, he is obliged to aspire to a goal within three "countless" aeons. In the way of mantras, however, this utterly pure, original abiding nature of reality, in which the truest of results – that of the non-dual essence of the expanse and pristine cognition, the coalescence of bliss and emptiness – is spontaneously present from the beginning, is known as the object of the view. And thereafter meditation is the training which relates to this real disposition or enters into the experience of it. In this way, the intellect is purified by making that reality and its aspects into the path during the illusion-like creation stage (*utpattikrama*) and during the extraordinary perfection stage (*sampannakrama*) in which [practices associated with] the energy channels, currents and seminal points are incisively applied.

When all the apparitional modes of suddenly arisen deluded thoughts, originating from impure dependence – including the world, its contents, components, psychophysical bases and activity fields – have gradually vanished, the essence is present, in which the primordial abiding nature is actualised as a maṇḍala of utterly pure buddha-body and pristine cognition. So, it is because the view and meditation of the mantras are superior that it is proven to be the resultant vehicle. As it is said in the *Lotus Peak* (*Padmaśekhara*):

> Concerning the natural expression of the taintless expanse,
> Along with the three bodies and four kinds of pristine cognition:
> When, in that pure state,
> An image of actualised intrinsic radiance
> Is made into the path,
> It is correctly called the resultant vehicle.

As for the meditations of loving kindness, compassion and enlightened mind: There is no occasion to identify them with the uncommon view and meditation of the mantras because the subjective consciousness by which they refer to their appropriate appearances is a suddenly arisen, impure fiction. It can be simply realised even by childish intellects that these [meditations] are details concerning the development of enlightened mind according to the relative truth, which is taught in the sūtra texts. Therefore, as previously cited, the *Sequence of the Path of the Magical Net* says:

> Within the unsurpassed vehicle, there are those
> Holding ultimate reality to be perfect in sameness[245]
> And relative appearances to include everything,
> Both the pure and the impure.
> The great vehicle of skilful means, however,
> Does not divide even relative appearances
> According to purity and suffering.
> The higher and lower views are just so.

Still greater than that is the distinction between the following two kinds of view. First, there is the view that pristine cognition, the great intrinsic abiding reality which is the naturally pure inner radiance of the expanse, remains incontrovertibly as the abiding nature of immaculate awareness, transcending the three times and free from all conceptual elaborations, present as a naturally occurring fundamental nature, liberated from the bondage of created doctrines, and pure from the start without requiring to be artificially contrived by an intellectually applied analysis. The second view is laboriously created, adhering to extremes which accept or reject the mind and its mental events since, through the intellect and analysis, it claims to clarify eternalist and nihilist extremes. The distinction between these two views is similar to that between heaven and earth, and with reference to the abiding nature of the view, the former would appear to be genuine and the latter conventional.

Therefore, when a deity is observed [through the mantra vehicles]: according to the Kriyātantra, a deity of pure reality is realised; according to the Yogatantra, a deity blessed with great dynamic pristine cognition is additionally realised; and according to the Unsurpassed Yogatantra, in addition to both of these, [the deity] is realised within the spontaneously present maṇḍala. Otherwise, there would be no basis for purification in the abiding nature of the ground, there would be no need for the coincidence of the object of purification and of the act of purification, and one would instead cling to that which does not exist as if it did. It would be equivalent to meditation on the horns of a hare.

Now this refers to the distinction of the view [in the way of mantras]. Yet the master Indrabhūti has also explained that:

> There is a distinction of guru, a distinction of vessel, a distinction of ritual, a distinction of ritual action, a distinction of commitment, a distinction of view and a distinction of conduct.

And [in his *Point of Liberation, Muktitilaka*, T 1859], Buddhajñānapāda has also said:

> This vehicle is uncommon in three respects: the one who becomes accomplished through it, its path and its result.

In this way, the latter, who explains that [mantras] have distinctions in their view and result, also makes a distinction between the attainment of buddhahood in the causal and resultant [vehicles].

Elsewhere, [the mantras] are revealed to be superior through three distinctive features. These are elucidated in the *Definitive Order of the Three Vehicles* (*Triyānavyavasthāna*, T 3712):

> The vehicle pure in its visualisation,
> Its power of assistance and level of conduct,
> To those who are endowed with intelligence
> Is well known to be the greatest.

Accordingly, [the mantras] are revealed to be superior because therein one experientially cultivates three maṇḍalas[246] in which all things are indivisible, namely: a view pure in its visualisation, for it regards the natural buddha-fields and their utterly pure range of activity; a power endowed with the vows of uncommon commitment to assist it; and the deeds of the Tathāgata as conduct.

Again, it is revealed in the *Sublime Lasso of Skilful Means* (*'phags-pa thabs-kyi zhags-pa*, T 835):

> The mantras are superior through four greatest qualities, namely, the greatest of visualisations, and similarly, the greatest of attainments, the greatest of pristine cognitions and the greatest of skilful means.

And Ḍombī Heruka has also said:

> In this [tradition], the vehicle of mantras is superior
> Through the distinction of its recipients,
> Through the properties which mark its recipients,
> Through the distinction of its texts and paths,
> And through the distinction of its results.

Thus, the resultant view is one which realises the abiding nature of reality, and distinctions are revealed within it. For these reasons, it is proven that the view [of the mantras] holds distinction [over that of the causal vehicle].

Similarly, concerning [the second distinction of the mantras],[247] through their conduct: The proponent of dialectics continues to accept and reject in terms of a corruptible moral discipline because he abides in perceptions which abandon and obstruct the five poisons that are to be renounced. The mantras, however, are superior through their provisions, offerings, unchanging moral discipline and so forth because the source [of saṃsāra] is turned into the path by means of its [true] nature, which is one of apparitional purity and sameness.

Then, concerning [the third distinction of the mantras], through mind-control: The proponent of dialectics requires that the contemplations of tranquillity and higher insight be attained over a long period of time by the most exhaustive of efforts in mind-control. The mantras, however, are superior because pristine cognition is instantly realised through the extraordinary yoga of the two stages and their coalescence.

Concerning [the fourth distinction of the mantras], through their causal basis: The proponent of dialectics holds that ultimate reality is seen by one who has previously gone through the provisions and so forth, whereas the mantras are superior because the truth of reality is realised by one who has been forcibly introduced to pristine cognition, which intrinsically abides as the causal basis of separation from obscurations *(bral-rgyu)*.

As for [the fifth distinction of the mantras], through their path: The proponent of dialectics requires that the path be traversed over many great aeons by the alternation of meditative absorption and its aftermath once the provisions have been accumulated. The mantras are superior since one who enters the path in which meditative absorption and its aftermath are indivisible progresses swiftly.

Also, concerning [the sixth distinction of the mantras], through their result: In the dialectics [the result] is considered to emerge after a long period of time, whereas the mantras are superior because it is held that the ground and result are indivisible and spontaneously present here and now.

Concerning [the seventh distinction of the mantras], through their levels: In the dialectics [the levels] are held to number eleven by differentiating the successive renunciations and antidotes.[248] The mantras, however, are superior because [they progress] to the twelfth level of the Unattached Lotus Endowed *(ma-chags padma-can)*, the thirteenth level of the Holder of Indestructible Reality *(rdo-rje 'dzin-pa)* and so on.

As for [the eighth distinction of the mantras], that of time: The proponent of dialectics loiters for three great, "countless" aeons and the like, whereas the mantras are superior because one whose commitments are unimpaired achieves [the goal] in one lifetime and so forth.

Concerning [the ninth distinction], that of rapture: In dialectics attainment comes after desired qualities have been renounced, while the mantras are superior because the friendship [of desired qualities] is cultivated.

Concerning [the tenth distinction], that of yoga: The proponent of dialectics differentiates between meditative absorption and its aftermath, whereas the mantras are superior because the inconceivable yoga in which they are indivisible is made into the path.

Then concerning [the eleventh], that of their benefits which are self- and other-oriented: The proponent of dialectics does not achieve more than provisional, slight benefits, whereas the mantras are superior because through them one acts on behalf of oneself and others by many approaches which cut off [evil] and bring [others] into the fold, whichever deeds are appropriate.

Concerning [the twelfth], that of intention: In dialectics nothing is known apart from the mere causal vehicle, whereas the mantras are superior since they ascertain the great mystery of the result.

[By the thirteenth distinction] the mantras are superior to dialectics because the fault of fatigue is easily renounced, and [by the fourteenth] they are so because great benefit is achieved with little hardship.

Finally, concerning [the fifteenth distinction], that of the accumulation of provisions: The proponent of dialectics requires that the conduct of the six transcendental perfections, beginning with liberality, be extensively accumulated over countless aeons. In the mantras, though [the provisions] are somewhat smaller, they are vast because liberality is to be practised after [the provisions of offering] have been multiplied in the storehouse of space through the blessing or consecration of the mantras. All objects are perceived as buddha-fields, all raptures are transformed into feast offerings and conflicting emotions are naturally pure without having been renounced. The provisions of merit and pristine cognition are swiftly contracted and perfected. Therefore the mantras are superior.

Furthermore, according to the dialectics the appearance of the buddha-body has an illusory nature and, by means of the ordinary actions of the body, one does no more than enter into virtue. According to the mantras the mystery of the buddha-body is that all appearances within the world and its contents are deities and celestial mansions and, by perfecting the maṇḍala of buddha-body, the emanation and absorption [of light] from the deity's seal are not bypassed.[249] Therefore [the mantras] are superior.

According to the dialectics, buddha-speech is empty in the manner of an echo, and when ordinary speech is cut off one does no more than enter into virtue. The mantras, on the other hand, are superior because the mystery of buddha-speech is a raincloud of doctrine. It is perceived as the natural expression of a great, imperishable vibration of melody, and all sounds, words and tones arise as the natural intonation of mantras, because ordinary speech abides from the beginning in the maṇḍala of buddha-speech. Thereby all that is said is potent and unimpededly effective.

The proponent of dialectics seals the buddha-mind with the [view] that all recollection and thought are without independent existence, and, having obstructed the ebb and flow of thoughts in the ordinary mind, does no more than cling to the contemplations of tranquillity and higher insight. The mantras are superior because the mystery of buddha-mind arises as the natural expression of reality, where supremely unchanging great bliss and the emptiness endowed with all supreme aspects, which is essentially devoid of substantial existence, are coalesced. All recollections and thoughts of the ordinary mind are spontaneously present, without the duality of meditative absorption and its aftermath, in the maṇḍala of the non-conceptualising yoga, a continuous stream of contemplation, which is reality's display.

This alone serves to illustrate that one should know the other distinctive features [of the mantras] to be inconceivable. But if they are abbreviated, they should be condensed according to the following words from the *Prophetic Declaration of Intention* (*Sandhivyākaraṇatantra*, T 444):

> That which is known by the buddhas
> Over utterly countless aeons
> Is the perfect enlightenment attained in one moment
> And within one lifetime by the mantrins.

Vajrasattva

2 *The Essence and Definition of Secret Mantra*

[143a.6-147b.1] The extraordinary vehicles are expounded in two parts, one giving a detailed exegesis of the overall meaning according to their general classifications and the other recapitulating the meaning subsumed in their particular sections.

The first is outlined under the three headings of the essence, verbal definition and classification. First, [the essence] is that the Mantrapiṭaka of the greater vehicle, which was taught by the Teacher, Vajradhara, observes that the ground and result are indivisible and spontaneously present, owing to which the natural expression of the truth of the origin [of saṃsāra] appears as the truth of the path, and the natural expression of the truth of suffering appears as the truth of cessation. Thus, in respect of action, the result is swiftly accomplished by experientially cultivating the abiding nature of the ground, without rejection and acceptance.

Secondly, concerning the verbal definitions: The [Sanskrit] *mana(s)*, which conveys the meaning of mind, and *trāya*, which conveys that of protection, become "mantra" by syllabic contraction, and therefrom the sense of protecting the mind [*yid-skyob* in Tibetan] is derived. It says in the *Guhyasamāja Tantra*:

> Whatever has arisen through the conditions
> Of sense organs and objects is the mind.
> This mind is explained by [the term] *man*,
> And *tra* has the sense of granting protection.

And also, in the *Great All-Radiating Seminal Point which is an Ancient Translation* (*snga-'gyur thig-le kun-gsal chen-po*, NGB Vol.5):

> Concerning the verbal definition of the three kinds of mantra,
> They are so called because they protect consciousness.

According to such explanations, mantras are [so called] because they easily and swiftly protect the consciousness of the mind.

On the subject of protection by their ease, it says in the *Mahāmāya Tantra* (T 425):

As for the five sensual raptures:
It is by freely indulging therein
That accomplishment is attained.

And on the subject of protection by their swiftness: Without referring to provisions amassed over three "countless" [aeons] and the like, the result can be actualised through the skilful means [of the mantras] in one lifetime, and so forth. Hence they are established as the swift and resultant vehicle. As it is said in the *Glorious Seminal Point of Embrace* (*Śrīsampuṭatilaka*, T 382):

Though over many millions of aeons
There are buddhas who have difficulty in attaining this,
It is granted [by the mantras] in this very lifetime.
Hence they are called the resultant vehicle.

And in the *Buddhasamāyoga* (T 366-7):

Through countless millions of aeons
All the buddhas do not obtain actual [enlightenment];
The secret mantras, by the rites of this life,
Obtain it in this very lifetime.

Then again, the great seal of [the deity's] bodily form, reflecting the emptiness endowed with all supreme aspects (*rnam-kun mchog-ldan-gyi stong-gzugs phyag-rgya chen-po*), is introduced by [the experience] of a melting bliss, which is symbolised by [the syllables] E-VAṂ. This pristine cognition or unchanging supreme bliss, which coalesces in a single essence the emptiness and co-emergent bliss arising from the pulse of the seminal point of great desire, is obligatory for all buddhas.[250] It, too, is [defined as] mantra because it easily and swiftly protects the mind, and constrains the objects to be renounced, namely, the propensities, symbols and ideas which respectively transfer consciousness to the variable [desire realm] and the blissful [form realm]. It says in the *Kālacakra Tantra*:

The collection of vowels and consonants is not unchanging. The unchanging sound refers to Vajrasattva, the pristine cognition of supreme, unchanging bliss. Similarly, since they are the reality which protects the mind, the mantras, too, are called the supreme, unchanging pristine cognition.

And in the *Indestructible Peak* (*Vajraśekhara*, T 480):

The characteristic of all the mantras
Is the mind of all the buddhas.
Since they cause the nucleus of reality to be attained,
They are genuinely endowed with reality's expanse.

The collection of transmitted precepts which extensively teach this [way of mantras] is called the Piṭaka of the Awareness-holders or the Piṭaka of the Vehicle of Indestructible Reality. Derived from the [Sanskrit] *piṭaka*, which conveys the meanings of a container or a measuring basket, the most extensive piṭaka is so called because it establishes in accord with the abiding nature and reveals in detail all conditions which are knowable, from the doctrine concerning the components, psychophysical bases and activity fields to the buddha-body and pristine cognition. Because all the meanings of the three lower piṭaka are gathered and perfected in this, it is also called the source of all the piṭaka. The *Tantra of the Extensive Magical Net* says:

> Concerning the king of intrinsic awareness,
> Which realises the meaning of sameness:
> Just as all rivers flow into the great ocean,
> In these most skilful means,
> Which realise the unsurpassed meaning,
> The inconceivable vehicles of liberation are all gathered.

Then, concerning the expression "awareness-holder" (*rig-'dzin*, Skt. *vidyādhara*), [when referring to the realized exponents of secret mantra,] there are three [mundane] kinds. First, there is the lesser one who holds the awareness of the accomplishment of eight great activities. These are:

> Medicinal pills, eye-salve and swift feet,
> The penetration of matter
> And accomplishment of the enchanted sword,
> Sky-faring and invisibility,
> And that of immortality and the supression of disease.[251]

The middling one is the common sort who holds the awareness of the desire realms; and the greater one holds the awareness of the desire and form realms. The life-span, rapture and so forth of the latter endure for either six aeons or immeasurably.

The supramundane awareness-holders are either the coalescent beings (*yuganaddhasattva*) who abide on the level [of the paths] of learning beginning with the path of insight, or those who possess the taintless body of pristine cognition.

Also, there are those [awareness-holders] who are endowed with the rainbow body but do not possess a body of form belonging to the three realms, and these have seven distinctions of enlightened attributes, namely, they abide in contemplation, possess the five supernormal cognitive powers, act in various fields on behalf of living beings, are without desire or covetousness, enjoy limitless desires as supreme bliss, transcend the span of life, and abide in a mental body. However, those in whom the basket of the components [i.e. the physical body] has not diminished possess only the body of pristine cognition, and when it has been diminished by deeds and contemplation, it is called the awareness-holders' body of pristine cognition.

In the Mahāyoga, [awareness-holders] are classified into four kinds: those holding the awareness of maturation (*rnam-smin rig-'dzin*), those holding the awareness of power over the life-span (*tshe-dbang rig-'dzin*), those holding the awareness of the great seal (*phyag-chen rig-'dzin*), and those holding the awareness of spontaneous presence (*lhun-grub rig-'dzin*). And, in the *Buddhasamāyoga Tantra*, the [above] enumeration of seven is given.

The Piṭaka of the Awareness-holders is thus named either because it is the ground to be studied by these [awareness-holders] or because one who enters this vehicle comes to attain these common and supreme accomplishments. As explained in the *Commentary on the Tantra of the Dialogue with Subāhu* (*Subāhuparipṛcchātantrapiṇḍārtha*, T 2671):

> That which is called the Piṭaka of the Awareness-holders is the ground studied by the holders of gnostic mantras. Its teaching accords with this spiritual and philosophical system of transmissions concerning the view.[252]

Now this [way of mantras] is also known as the vehicle of indestructible reality (*rdo-rje theg-pa*, Skt. *Vajrayāna*). By definition, this term conveys the sense of "undivided" (*mi-phyed*) and "imperishable" (*mi-shigs*). That which is not divided into anything different never wavers from mind-as-such in the abiding nature of reality, despite the different apparitional modes of both saṃsāra and nirvāṇa. Therefore, as it is said [*Hevajra Tantra*, Pt.1, Ch.1, v.4a]:

> It is the undifferentiated nature that is expressed in the
> word *vajra*.

The mind of all the buddhas is imperishable because it is the essence of reality which cannot be destroyed by any symbolic doctrine. Since it is similar to a *vajra*, the so-called indestructible mind of all buddhas abides, as previously explained, as the essence of mantra. The term "vehicle" is used both metaphorically and literally because it is either the support for the attainment of this [reality] or else the [path] through which it is traversed. It is explained in the *Commentary on the Guhyasamāja*:

> Concerning that which is called the vehicle of indestructible reality: The entire greater vehicle is subsumed by the six transcendental perfections. They in turn are subsumed by skilful means and discriminative awareness, and the common

> savour of the enlightened mind subsumes these. Now, this is the contemplation of Vajrasattva [the spiritual warrior of indestructible reality] and this nature is the indestructible reality. The vehicle of indestructible reality, inasmuch as it is both the indestructible reality and a vehicle, means the same as the mantra vehicle. It is called unsurpassed because it is the supreme reality of all vehicles.

In the *Taintless Light* Avalokiteśvara says:

> That which is said to be the indestructible reality is the undivided pristine cognition, the indestructible reality of the inconceivable buddha-mind. Whatever possesses it is endowed with indestructible reality.

And:

> Indestructible reality is supreme indivisibility and inseparability, and the vehicle which leads to it is the vehicle of indestructible reality. The style of the mantras and the style of the transcendental perfections which [respectively] are identified as the result and the cause are blended together [in it].

And also:

> The vehicle of indestructible reality is the vehicle of the genuinely perfect buddhas. Since it cannot be changed by the vehicles of the extremists, pious attendants and self-centred buddhas, it is the vehicle of indestructible reality. Since one proceeds through it to liberation, it is the vehicle of indestructible reality.

In such ways [the definition of the vehicle of indestructible reality] has been extensively taught.

Furthermore, the [Sanskrit] *tantra* also conveys the meaning of protecting the mind, for *cetanā* has the sense of mind and *trāya* of protection. As the *Commentary on Difficulties entitled Endowed with Pristine Cognition* (*Śrībuddhakapālatantrapañjikājñānavatī*, T 1652) says:

> Tantra is so called because it protects the mind from
> conceptual thoughts.
> Tantrapiṭaka are so called because they form the
> collection or class of the tantras.

The word tantra also, in the manner of the strings of the lute, conveys the sense of continuity. It is so called because it subsumes the naturally pure reality of the mind from sentient being to buddha within the continuum of ground, path and result, continuously abiding without interruption. The *Guhyasamāja Tantra* says:

> Tantra is defined as a continuity.
> This tantra is of three kinds:
> It is divided according to the ground,
> Its natural expression and its inalienableness.
> Thus the natural expression is the causal basis,
> The ground is defined as skilful means,
> And similarly inalienableness is the result.
> The meaning of tantra is subsumed by these three.

And the *Subsequent Tantra of the Secret Nucleus* (*sgyu-'phrul phyi-ma*, NGB Vol.14) says:

> Tantra is explained as continuity:
> From its skilful means and causal basis,
> The result is derived.

3 *The Three Continua of Ground, Path and Result*

[147b.1-150b.5] [The way of secret mantra] is classified according to two divisions, one which generally reveals the definitive order of the three kinds of tantra or continuum comprising the expressed meaning (*brjod-bya rgyud-gsum*) and the other explaining, in particular, the divisions of the four tantrapiṭaka which form their literary expression (*rjod-byed rgyud-sde bzhi*).

The former consists of three kinds of continuum, namely, the continuum of the ground or basis which is to be realised, the continuum of skilful means or the path through which realisation and progress are acquired, and the continuum of the result wherein the goal is reached.

CONTINUUM OF THE GROUND

Concerning the first of these: The ground is that which is primordially present as the abiding nature without bondage or liberation. It is the enlightened mind of intrinsic awareness, the natural inner radiance wherein truth is indivisible and which is free from the range of the intellect. It is endowed with four extraordinary attributes, namely: it is distinguished by harmony with the resultant realities of buddha-fields, bodies, pristine cognitions and so forth; it is supreme bliss by nature; it is uninterrupted; and it is attained through [the nature of] reality.[253] Although it becomes the ground or basis of both saṃsāra and nirvāṇa depending on whether it is realised or not, it is defined as the continuum of the basis because its natural expression continues without change.

As the essence of the buddhas, [the continuum of the ground] is the nucleus of the sugata. As emptiness, it gives rise to the enlightened attributes of the buddha-body of reality, and as appearance, it gives rise to the buddha-body of form. Because [the continuum] is present in that way, it is the enlightened family which naturally abides. As the originating ground of both saṃsāra and nirvāṇa, it is the pristine cognition of the ground-of-all. It is one's own real nature according to

Kriyātantra. It is the blessing without symbols which is ultimate reality, and the deity of the expanse of indestructible reality which is relative appearance according to Ubhayatantra and Yogatantra [respectively]. It is the superior, great buddha-body of reality in which the two truths are indivisible according to Mahāyoga. It is the fundamental offspring maṇḍala of the enlightened mind in which the expanse and pristine cognition are non-dual according to Anuyoga; and it is the ground which is conventionally expressed as essence, natural expression and great spirituality according to Atiyoga.

It is explained, in particular, that the support for the continuum of the basis is the buddha-body of reality, the enlightened mind-as-such which is naturally present in the heart centre[254] of corporeal beings as an imperishable seminal point within a pure essence (*dvangs-ma*) of five colours. Furthermore, it emanates as the six pure essences, those of the five elements and the mind, which [are divided into three] groups of two, each with an identical savour, and as such it abides primordially in the nature of the three imperishable, indestructible realities of the most subtle three media [i.e. the body, speech and mind], without straying in any respect. It says in the *Vajra Garland* [*Vajramālā*, T 445]:

> That which abides in the heart of corporeal beings,
> As the form of the naturally present, uncorrupted
> pristine cognition,
> The imperishable seminal point which is supreme bliss,
> All-pervasive in the manner of the sky,
> Is the natural expression of the dynamic body of reality.

And in the *Glorious Kālacakra*:

> Just as, if water is poured into a vase, the space within it does not vanish, that which is endowed with the indestructible reality of all-encompassing space is similarly present within the body, without regard to any object.

As such passages extensively indicate, this ground of liberation, the spontaneously present reality that is the pristine cognition abiding in oneself, is definitively the basis which brings about the continuum of the result. Therefore, the *Blossom of Esoteric Instructions* (*Śrīsaṃpuṭatantrarājaṭīkāmnāyamañjariphala*, T 1198) says:

> The essence, which is the emptiness of substances, does not mean anything other than one's own nature or feature; it has the meaning of one's own essence. This is both the basis, and the holder of indestructible reality who effects [the result]. The same buddhahood, accomplished from beginningless time through the essential nature uncovered by stains,

> is the basis of that buddhahood which is characterised as an attainment of the immaculate [reality].

The ostensible phenomena of saṃsāra are the stains obscuring that ground of purification through which the continuum of the result is effected. They are to be purified because they are specifically designated and established by the erring consciousness which apprehends them, although they have no true existence as objects. Since it is obscured by them, [the ground] abides in the manner of a gemstone in a filthy swamp. As Nāgārjuna [in the *Eulogy to the Expanse of Reality*, v.23] has said:

> The water that lies within the earth
> Remains immaculately pure.
> The pristine cognition within conflicting emotions, too,
> Remains similarly immaculate.

CONTINUUM OF THE PATH

Secondly, the continuum of the path refers to the skilful means which purify these stains covering the continuum of the ground. Since it abides as the connecting activity between the ground and the result, causing the ground to be perceived through its downward connection and the result to be obtained through its upward connection, it is the continuum of the path. In the Great Master [Padmasambhava's] *Garland of Views: A Collection of Esoteric Instructions* it says:

> Concerning this, the goal is conclusively reached by means of three characteristics. Awareness, or the four kinds of realisation, is the characteristic of perception, the repeated experience of it is the characteristic of the entrance, and the actualisation of it by the power of experience is the characteristic of the result.

Accordingly, the basis [of the continuum of the path] is the view whose characteristic is perception, its condition is the contemplation whose characteristic is the entrance, and its result is characterised as the actualisation. The view is established with reference to the perception of the object which is to be entered by experiential cultivation, or to the object of meditation. Contemplation is established with reference to the actual entrance or act of meditation through experiential cultivation; and the result is established when the object of meditation is referred to as being actualised. The latter comprises both the conclusive result which has actualised all that is to be realised, and the result in which actualisation has been turned into the path only to a certain extent, of which the former is identical to the continuum of the result and the latter is the third characteristic during the continuum of the path. The definitive order of these shall be briefly explained below.

Having generally indicated the fundamentals of the path, the actual subject-matter of tantra, which is required for its implementation, is then revealed in accordance with its particular classifications. The path is said to be clearly divided into the following ten categories: a view of the real, determinate conduct, maṇḍala array, successive gradation of empowerment, commitment which is not transgressed, enlightened activity which is displayed, fulfilment of aspiration, unwavering contemplation, offering which brings the goal to fruition, and mantra recitation accompanied by the seals which bind [the practitioner to realisation].

CONTINUUM OF THE RESULT

Thirdly, concerning the continuum of the result: The result refers to the enlightened attributes which are qualitatively present in the ground and actualised after those stains which obscure the continuum of the ground have been purified by the power of meditating on the path. In the commentary on the *Secret Nucleus* entitled *[Illuminating Lamp of the] Fundamental Text* it is said:

> When accomplishment has been perfected
> It is called the result.

It is the result, therefore, because in it the thoughts of those who aspire to the unsurpassed, supreme result are entirely perfected, and it is the continuum (*tantra*) because its continuity is never broken.

Although within the piṭaka of the greater vehicle which concerns transcendental perfection, the result of supreme enlightenment is revealed in detail, there is a great distinction between the two kinds of buddhahood, one of which is explained therein and the other in the unsurpassed mantra texts. The former is attained through aspiration and conduct with respect to the two provisions and the latter is that in which the whole extent of the natural continuum of the ground is qualitatively actualised. Since it is incorrect [to say] that the uncommon result of this [buddhahood] is accomplished without relying on the uncommon path of the secret mantras, only the awareness-holder of spontaneous presence on the final path is conventionally described as a buddha. Indeed, the great adherents of the glorious Zur tradition[255] claim that the actual buddhahood of the mantra path must be obtained even after that.

When the doctrines of the result are classified, they are manifold, including the ten powers and [four] fearlessnesses which are generally known, and including the seven branches of union (*saptasampuṭa*) which are known only in the unsurpassed [mantras]. And then according to the text of the *Tantra of the [Secret] Nucleus,* there are said to be twenty-five resultant realities which gather within them the definitive structure of the supporting buddha-bodies, supported pristine cognitions and enlightened activities.

4 *The Four Tantrapiṭaka*

[150b.5-152a.2] Secondly, concerning the detailed explanation of the divisions of the four tantrapiṭaka which form the literary expression of the mantra vehicles, it is said in the *Tantra of the Array of the Nucleus of Indestructible Reality* (*rdo-rje snying-po bkod-pa'i rgyud*):

> The tantras intended by the Sugata
> Are correctly explained to be of four kinds:
> Kriyā, Caryā, Yoga and Unsurpassed Tantra.

While there are many dissimilar ways of dividing them, the reason for this division into the four tantrapiṭaka, which are well known, is that they are taught as the paths respectively for those of lowest, middling, superior and highest acumen [who require training], and as the means by which those beings are gradually led to the result. In the *[Indestructible] Tent* (*Vajrapañjaratantra*, T 419) it is said:

> The Kriyātantra is for the basest,
> And Caryātantra[256] is for those who are superior,
> The Yogatantra is for the supreme among sentient beings,
> And Unsurpassed Yoga is for those who are yet more superior.

The four tantrapiṭaka are also said to be taught with reference to the four temporal ages, as found in the following words [from the *Tantra which Genuinely Gathers All the Deities*]:[257]

> The Kriyātantra is [emphasised] during the first age or the *Kṛtayuga*,
> The Caryātantra is emphasised during the second age or the *Tretayuga*,
> The Yogatantra is emphasised during the third age or the *Dvāparayuga*,
> And the Unsurpassed Tantra is emphasised during the fourth age or the *Kaliyuga*.

It is with an intention directed toward the four ages[258]
That the tantras are explained to be of four kinds.

Teaching is also said to be given in the form of the four tantrapiṭaka because they instruct those to be trained who have four kinds of desire, but I shall not treat this separately because its import is actually included in this [analysis].[259]

The first three of these four tantrapiṭaka, which are specifically enumerated, are known as "the vehicle of austere awareness" and are established as the three outer tantrapiṭaka because their teachings respectively emphasise the external observances of body and speech, equate both external observances and the inner mind, and emphasise the inner mind without abandoning the external observances. The last piṭaka is superior to these and is therefore established as "the vehicle of overpowering means", the Unsurpassed Yoga of skilful means and discriminative awareness in coalescence.

The former comprises the three [vehicles] of the Kriyātantra, Caryātantra and Yogatantra, referring to which the *Commentary which Epitomises the Hevajra [Tantra]* (*Hevajrapiṇḍārthaṭīkā*, T 1180) says:

> If one has little ability to meditate on the real, there is the Kriyātantra which mostly teaches external conduct for those who openly delight in symbolic conduct.

And:

> For those who are devoted to the distinctions of activity but are disinclined to abandon the inner identification which indeed unites with the vast conduct of skilful means and discriminative awareness, there is the Ubhayatantra [i.e. Caryātantra] which is derived in common from both the Kriyātantra and Yogatantra.

And so on. Then in the *Commentary on the Tantra of the Awakening of Great Vairocana* (*Mahāvairocanābhisambodhitantraṭīkā*, T 2663) it says:

> The [Yogatantra] including the *Sublime Tantra of the Summation of the Real* emphasises inner union, and yet it is not without external conduct.

KRIYĀTANTRA

[152a.2-153a.4] The first of these [tantrapiṭaka], Kriyā, means action, because it emphatically teaches the actions of body and speech. Its view is that ultimately there are enlightened attributes through which one's own real nature is realised to be pure and without conceptual elaborations of the four extremes, and, distinct from these, there are relative appearances which have the characteristics of an utterly pure deity. Through this view, one resorts to skilful means, aspiring and striving towards an accomplishment externally [conferred by the deity]. It is explained in Buddhaguhya's *Sequence of the Path*:

> Since they are not known to be the same, without duality,
> The level of action requires alternate meditation
> On an ultimate truth which is simply the pure reality
> And a deity of relative appearance endowed with
> The enlightened attributes of pristine cognition.

Meditation in this context therefore refers to the yoga associated with three enlightened families of pure deities of relative appearance. By means of the deity's six modes, namely, the deity of emptiness, the deity of syllables, the deity of sound, the deity of form, the deity of seals and the deity of symbols,[260] whether one is oneself visualised as the deity or not, one aspires towards accomplishment, relating to the Being of Pristine Cognition *(jñānasattva)* as a master, and [considering] oneself as a servant. The *Tantra of the Great Natural Arising of Awareness* says:

> The deity and the pure yogin
> Are seen respectively as master and servant.

The deity is delighted by ablutions, cleanliness, fasting and other such austerities in conduct, and, by maintaining the appropriate ascetic discipline, the mind becomes immersed in the sound which is the reality of [mantra] recitation, in [the deity's] mind and in the ground. The reality of this concentration also has three aspects, as explained in the following passage:

> Abiding in the flame of secret mantra,
> Accomplishment is given;
> Abiding in its sound, the yoga is conferred;
> And at the limit of sound, freedom is granted.

As a result of having made these [meditations and conduct] into the path, one becomes provisionally accomplished as a sky-faring awareness-holder who is equal in fortune to a god of the desire realm, and, having practised the conduct of the mantras on that basis, the level of the Holder of Indestructible Reality belonging to the Three Enlightened Families *(rigs-gsum rdo-rje 'dzin-pa)*, which is explained in this Kriyātantra, is conclusively actualised. The *Heruka Galpo* says:

> Within seven lifetimes on the buddha level
> The Lords of the Three Families instruct living beings.

The piṭaka which reveals these [practices of Kriyātantra] includes the *Tantra of the Dialogue with Subāhu*, the *Tantra of the Emergence of*

Tārā (*Sarvatathāgatamātṛtārāviśvakarmabhavatantra*, T 726), the *King of the Three Commitments* (*Trisamayavyūharājatantra*, T 502) and the *Subjugation of Demons* (*Bhūtaḍāmaratantra*, T 747).

Then, when Kriyātantra is classified according to its enlightened families, there are six types, namely, those of the Tathāgata, Lotus, Varja, Wealth, Enrichment and Mundane enlightened families. Each of these is further analysed according to its central deity, master, female consort, *uṣṇīṣa*, male and female wrathful deities, male and female intermediaries, and male and female servants. Yet all [Kriyā tantras], when subsumed, are gathered within the two classes of the secret mantra and the gnostic mantra.[261]

UBHAYATANTRA

[153a.4-153b.5] Secondly, the Ubhayatantra [or Caryātantra] is practised in accordance with the view of Yogatantra and the conduct of Kriyātantra. Hence it is called the tantra of equal parts or the tantra of both, forming the connecting link between those two. The *Tantra of the Great Natural Arising of Awareness* says:

> The Ubhayatantra is as follows:
> The view is seen as in Yogatantra
> And conduct performed as in Kriyātantra.
> Therefore it is known as the tantra of both.

Once this view and conduct have been established as the ground, there is meditation. One should meditate definitively on the symbolic syllables, seals and deities of form, and then become steadfast in contemplation through one-pointed application. As the *Awakening of [Great] Vairocana* (*Mahāvairocanābhisambodhitantra*, T 494) says:

> When the syllables are conjoined with syllables[262]
> And the ground of reality is made into the ground
> [of meditation],
> With utmost mental concentration
> One should make a hundred thousand recitations.

Then when the yoga without symbols, in which the mind is absorbed in the nature of ultimate reality and so on, has been experienced, there are provisional results such as the accomplishment of the body of an awareness-holder. In addition, the level of a Holder of Indestructible Reality belonging to Four Enlightened Families (*rigs-bzhi rdo-rje 'dzin-pa*) is conclusively actualised by having practised the mantras on that basis either in five lifetimes, or, if one loiters, in three aeons, or in a single aeon. The *Heruka Galpo* says:

> One abides on the level of Vajradhara
> Endowed with the four enlightened families.

The piṭaka in which these [Ubhayatantra] are revealed, includes the *Awakening of Great Vairocana* and the *Empowerment of Vajrapāṇi* (*Vajrapāṇyabhiṣekamahātantra*, T 496).

YOGATANTRA

[153b.5-154b.5] Thirdly, concerning the Yogatantra (*rnal-'byor*), the master Ānandagarbha says:

> This Yogatantra emphasises meditation, for therein recitation is optionally revealed.

And in his *Epitome of the Illumination of the Real* (*Tattvālokāpiṇḍārtha*, T 2510) also:

> This tantra is called Yogatantra because it emphasises contemplative meditation.

The view of Yogatantra is therefore that the blessing of pristine cognition, which ultimately realises the natural inner radiance, free from the conceptual elaboration of all things, to be emptiness, is seen relatively as a deity of the expanse of indestructible reality. Consequently, the result is held to be attained by perseverance [in the acceptance and rejection] of positive and negative ideas in relation to that [deity]. The *Sequence of the Path* says:

> Since they are not realised to be spontaneously
>   present and the same,
> The blessing of pristine cognition, the purity of all
>   things,
> Becomes an emanational deity of the expanse of
>   indestructible reality,
> And the level of action is one of acceptance and
>   rejection.

The meditation of Yogatantra emphasises the yoga of skilful means. One meditates on oneself as a deity with his or her retinue through a sequence of five awakenings and four yogas[263] which are progressively connected with the four seals. Inner contemplations are also emphasised, including meditative equipoise in the pristine cognition or individual intuitive awareness, which actually realises the mind's reality.

Then, by relying on conduct such as cleanliness as an aid, in the manner of the previous [vehicles], there are provisional results, including that of a sky-faring awareness-holder. Then, conclusively, the Great Seal (*phyag-rgya chen-po*)[264] is accomplished within three or sixteen lifetimes, after which buddhahood is gradually attained on the level of the Bounteous Array of the Five Enlightened Families (*rigs-lnga stug-po bkod-pa*), in the essence of the five pristine cognitions and by means of the five awakenings. The *All-Accomplishing King* says:

> One who desires the Bounteous Array of Yogatantra
> Is held to be liberated within three lifetimes.

The piṭaka in which this [Yogatantra] is revealed includes the *Summation of the Real* and the *Glorious Paramādya* (*Śrīparamādya*, T 487-8). Then, if Yogatantra is classified according to its enlightened families, they comprise the Fundamental Enlightened Family, along with the following five: the Buddha, Vajra, Jewel, Doctrine and Activity enlightened families. Each of these is also subdivided into five minor families; and there is an additional eightfold division when [the major and minor families] are each divided into their four parts – nucleus, seal, secret mantra and gnostic mantra.

If these Yoga tantras are then condensed, they are gathered into skilful means and discriminative awareness. For example, the term "male consort" [i.e. skilful means] is expressed in the *Summation of the Real* and the term "female consort" [i.e. discriminative awareness] is expressed in the *Hundred and Fifty Verses on the Modes of Discriminative Awareness* (*Nayaśatapañcaśatikā*, T 17).

UNSURPASSED YOGATANTRA

[154b.5-156a.2] Concerning the vehicle of overpowering means or the Unsurpassed Yoga (*Anuttarayogatantra*): The three lower tantrapiṭaka are established as the three outer tantrapiṭaka, or the lower tantrapiṭaka. This is because they are mostly in harmony with the vehicle of dialectics, in that they are guided by the perceptions of purity and impurity which entail acceptance, rejection, renunciation, antidotes and so forth. They are deluded with respect to the abiding nature of supreme bliss by their separation of skilful means and discriminative awareness and so forth. This extraordinary path of Unsurpassed Yoga, on the other hand, is known as the short path and also the tantra of skilful means because, when one has entered into it, one is united in the result by this alone, without having to extend into other vehicles. Whereas in other vehicles the three poisons are to be renounced, here, by having driven in the nail of the view which is without objectification, the three poisons are carried on the path without being renounced – desire as the essence of bliss and emptiness, hatred as the essence of radiance and emptiness, and delusion as the essence of awareness and emptiness. In this way, the skilful means which achieves the extraordinary rank of coalescence in a single lifetime is amazing. The three outer tantrapiṭaka are therefore said to be a long path. Although they do belong to the path of mantra in general, and so are contained within the swift path, they are explained to be long in relation to this vehicle, because adherents of them are finally obliged to enter into this unsurpassed path.

The Unsurpassed Yoga is, in addition, superior through many distinctions. For example, it reveals the embracing union of the father and mother deities, which symbolises the coalescence of the naturally present pristine cognition that is skilful means and the emptiness that is discriminative awareness, and it reveals the extraordinary yoga of skilful means through which the five meats, the five nectars and so forth are rapturously enjoyed. It says in the *Guhyasamāja Tantra* (*Guhyasamājatantra*, T 442-3, Ch.18, v.32):

> The meditative equipoise in skilful means and
> discriminative awareness
> Is explained to be yoga.
> The non-substantiality of anything is discriminative
> awareness
> And substantiality is the characteristic of skilful means.

When the Unsurpassed Yoga is classified, it comprises the Father Tantra of Skilful Means (*thabs pha-yi rgyud*), the Mother Tantra of Discriminative Awareness (*shes-rab ma-yi rgyud*) and the Coalescent Non-Dual Tantra (*zung-'jug gnyis-med-kyi rgyud*). When these are classified according to their enlightened families, the Father tantras are sixfold, comprising the enlightened families of Akṣobhya, Vairocana, Ratnasambhava, Amitābha, Amoghasiddhi and Vajradhara. In the same way, the Mother tantras are assuredly classified into the six enlightened families of Vajrasattva, Vairocana, Vajrāditya, Padmanarteśvara, Aśvottama and Heruka. Thus there are twelve excellent divisions of the Unsurpassed Tantra. Then on further classification, there are said to be limitless enlightened families, and just as many tantras.

If [the Unsurpassed Yoga tantras] are subsumed, they are gathered into skilful means and discriminative awareness, and these, too, are without exception gathered within both the creation and perfection stages, which are then actually gathered into the Great Perfection. So it is that the unsurpassed vehicle of overpowering means is classified [by the Nyingmapa] into the three subdivisions of creation, perfection and great perfection, among which the first, the creation phase of tantra, is the Mahāyoga.

5 *Mahāyoga*

THE GROUND OR VIEW OF MAHĀYOGA

[156a.2-157a.5] Mahāyoga or Great Yoga *(rnal-'byor chen-po)* is so called because it unites the mind in the non-dual truth which is greatly superior to the outer Yogatantra. Although the specific enumerations of the Mahāyoga classes of tantra and means for attainment have been elaborated in many sources,[265] here they are expounded according to the general [Mahāyoga] *Tantra of the Magical Net*: The abiding nature of the continuum of the ground is established as the view which is to be realised, but it is not established by the ostensible reasoning of sophistry. Rather it is established by the three kinds of all-embracing valid cognition and should be realised by the direct perception of intrinsic awareness.

Now there are also four axioms which establish this [ground], namely, the axiom of the four kinds of realisation, the axiom of the three purities, the axiom of the four modes of sameness and the axiom of supreme identity. Among them, the first axiom is given in the following passage from the *Tantra of the [Secret] Nucleus* (Ch.11, v.2):

> The single basis and the manner of seed-syllables,
> The blessing and the direct perception:
> Through [these] four kinds of excellent realisation,
> All things are the great king, manifestly perfect.

Through the axiom of the single basis, all things are established as naturally present and uncreated; through the axiom of the manner of seed-syllables, all things are established as an unceasing display; through the axiom of the blessing, all things are established as the indivisible essence; and through the axiom of direct perception, all things are established to be without intellectual characteristics. Such are the axioms of the four kinds of realisation.

Concerning the second axiom, [that of the three purities,] it says (Ch.11, v.15):

> The world, its contents and the mind-stream
> Are realised to be pure.

So through the axiom of the three purities, the outer world, its inner contents and all the components, psychophysical bases and activity fields are established as a great purity.

Concerning the third axiom, [that of sameness,] it says (Ch.11, v.15):

> Through the two samenesses[266]
> And the two superior samenesses
> The maṇḍala is the field of Samantabhadra.

So through the axiom of the four modes of sameness all things subsumed by the relative and ultimate truths are established as a great sameness.

Concerning the fourth axiom, [that of supreme identity,] it says (Ch.9, v.35):

> The naturally present pristine cognition
> Appears without abiding.

Thus, through the axiom of supreme identity, all things are established as primordially abiding in the identity of a single, great, naturally present, pristine cognition, which is mind-as-such. The abiding nature of the natural continuum of the basis which is directly realised through these axioms of appraisal is the uncommon spiritual and philosophical goal of the Mahāyoga. Such is also said in the *Oceanic Magical Net*:

> In the manner of a clear reflection in the ocean,
> Without making an echo in the mind,
> The intrinsic awareness of direct perception
> That is without objective referent,
> Intrinsically radiant, without the three [times] and
> without wavering,
> Which is confident in its certainty,
> Concludes the view of study, reflection and meditation.

And in the *Flash of Splendour* (*Jñānāścaryadyuticakrasūtra*, T 830):

> If direct awareness is determined,
> The level of yoga is reached.

THE PATH OF MAHĀYOGA

[157a.5-158b.6] Having so established the definitive meaning of the view as the ground, the path comprises the two stages of skilful means and liberation, concerning the first of which it is said [in the *Oceanic Magical Net*]:

The path to liberation is taught as skilful means.

Through the path of skilful means, one who has practised deeds which bind one [to saṃsāra] obtains the result of liberation. Above all, the distinctive feature of skilful means is that if one has practised the discipline of conduct which directly overpowers the three poisons without renouncing them, one is endowed with the foundation of the view, and, in consequence, is not only unfettered but also swiftly obtains the result of liberation. If, on the other hand, one who is not so endowed were to practise [this discipline], liberation would not be obtained and there would indeed be a great risk of falling into evil existences, so that there is great danger, as in the [alchemical use of] mercury [for the sudden transformation of iron into gold].[267]

This path of skilful means (*thabs-lam*) is twofold, as it is said [in the above text]:

> Its oral instructions concern the upper
> And lower doors [of the body].[268]

Concerning the former: In a gradual manner the pristine cognition of supreme bliss is experienced through union [resulting from] the blazing and secretion [of seminal points].[269] This depends on [practices associated with] the six centres which form the "upper door of one's own body" (*rang-lus steng-sgo*), as indicated in the *Exegetical Tantra of the Oceanic Magical Net*.

And concerning the latter: In an immediate manner, the pristine cognition of bliss and emptiness is irresistibly generated in a single moment through the four unions of ritual service, further ritual service, rites of attainment and rites of great attainment.[270] These depend on [practices associated with] "the lower door of one's partner's body" (*gzhan-lus 'og-sgo*) in which the two secret [or sexual] centres (*mkha'-gsang gnyis*) of the male and female consorts are united, as indicated in the *Penetrating Exegetical Tantra of the Magical Net* (*bshad-rgyud thal-ba*, NGB Vol.15).

The second path, that of liberation (*grol-lam*), is above all established through the three kinds of discriminative awareness: After the bondage of one's own mind has been naturally cleansed by realisation, one is liberated in the space of reality. Though it contains no distinctive feature of speed, as does the path of skilful means, there is no difference inasmuch as one is united in the result, and the danger is less. It is similar to the Kaustubha gemstone [which gradually draws gold from ore].[271]

The path of liberation is also divided into two modes, one of which is immediately attained and the other gradually attained, according to the degree of acumen [of those requiring training]. The first is exemplified by Indrabhūti who attained liberation at the time of his empowerment. The latter is described as follows in the *Tantra of the [Secret] Nucleus* (Ch.12, vv.8-9):

> Retention which is endowed with the characteristics
> Of discriminative awareness and entrance
> Is the basis and condition
> Which brings the result to maturity.
> Those who transform it into a potent force
> Are known as awareness-holders
> In the fields of the Conqueror.

The path of liberation therefore has three aspects: the basis characterised as [discriminative] awareness is the view; the conditions characterised as the entrance are contemplation; and the result which has been brought about by the path is the awareness-holder. The first has been described above.

The second aspect of the path of liberation, the contemplation, includes meditation through devotion and definitive perfection. The former is referred to as meditation because it makes the general features of some [divine] object and devotion towards it into the path. The latter refers to training until the five contemplative experiences of the two stages [of creation and perfection] have been concluded. In Vimalamitra's *Meditative Absorption in the Mudrā* (*Māyājālamudrādhyāna*, P 4732) it is said:

> Wavering, attainment, skill, firmness and conclusion:
> These five are the modes in which the experience of
> meditative absorption arises.

Concerning the paths that are the object of this meditation, the *Tantra of the [Secret] Nucleus* explains:

> Through their maturation during the sequence of
> rebirth,
> The aspects of the entrance are established to be five:
> Because all that is substantial is intrinsic awareness,
> Death is [the moment of] the ultimate truth,
> The intermediate state before life is relative
> appearance
> And the three phases of life are the non-dual truth.

In this way, Mahāyoga perfectly reveals the paths through which the rebirth process including death, the intermediate state and the three phases of life, is immediately purified. Now, the path which corresponds to inner radiance at the moment of death is great emptiness (*stong-pa chen-po*), the path which corresponds to the intermediate state [after death] is great compassion (*snying-rje chen-po*), and the paths which correspond to the three phases of life are the single seal (*phyag-*

rgya gcig-pa), the elaborate seal (*phyag-rgya spros-bcas*) and the attainment of the maṇḍala clusters (*tshom-bu tshogs-sgrub*), making five in all.

The Creation Stage of Mahāyoga

[158b.6-160a.3] Within this [framework of meditation] there are two modes of purification, one through the coarse creation stage (*rags-pa bskyed-rim*) and the other through the subtle perfection stage (*phra-ba rdzogs-rim*). Concerning the first of these, when the consciousness of corporeal beings is transferred at the moment of death, after the outer and inner sequences of dissolution have been completed,[272] the condition of death arises as the inner radiance of the buddha-body of reality. In order that this [inner radiance] may be carried on the path, there is meditation on the contemplation of just what is, according to which all things subsumed in sensory phenomena (*snang-grags*) are the unelaborate buddha-body of reality.

If this nature of inner radiance is not recognised, there is the all-pervasive meditation on great compassion, the essence of contemplation on all that appears, without objective qualification, which purifies the provisional propensities of the apparitional mental body[273] during the intermediate state [after death].

So long as, on this basis, one is not liberated in the intermediate state, there are both the subtle and coarse aspects of the single seal which purifies the propensities from conception in the womb to the moment of birth. Now, the essence of the subtle contemplation of the causal basis, which purifies the rebirth situation immediately prior to entering into any birthplace conditioned by the growth of craving, is a training in the seed-syllables which have eight dimensions of radiance and constancy. And the coarse [contemplation], which purifies the situations from the moment [of conception], when [consciousness] intermingles with the male and female seminal fluids, to the moment when it awakens to the external sense organs and objects, is a training which, corresponding to the four kinds of birthplace, generates the body of a deity through the four awakenings (*mngon-byang bzhi*), the three kinds of rite (*cho-ga gsum*) and so forth.

Then there are four aspects of the training in the elaborate seal which purifies the propensities from the moment of birth to adult maturity. As explained in the *Sequence of the Path*:

> These are maṇḍalas, clusters, numbers,
> And faces and arms [of the deities].

The elaborate seal therefore comprises an emanation of maṇḍalas, an emanation of maṇḍala clusters, an emanation of a number [of deities] and an emanation of the [deities'] faces and arms. These four respectively comprise: the expansive, middling and condensed maṇḍalas of the peaceful and wrathful deities; a unit, trio or quintet of maṇḍala clusters; enumerations of one thousand, twenty-four thousand and a spontaneously present infinity of peaceful deities, and of one thousand four hundred and fifty, seventy-six thousand eight hundred and fifty, and a spontaneously present infinity of wrathful deities; and the faces and arms [of the deities] which also have extensive, middling and condensed formations.

[Finally], there is the attainment of the maṇḍala clusters, which purifies the propensities from adult maturity to old age. This has limitless subdivisions which are subsumed under the three headings: apprehending the ground attained through the five excellences; straightening the path by means of the four branches of ritual service and rites of attainment; and indicating the time for the accomplishment of the result as an awareness-holder.

Thus, these five paths connected with corrupt states downwardly correspond to saṃsāra so that it and its propensities are refined and purified. Upwardly they sustain the three buddha-bodies along with the power of their actions and conduct so that the result is perfected; and intermediately they establish a foundation through which those on a lower path can meditate on a higher path, for which reason they are a means of progressing to maturation.

The Perfection Stage of Mahāyoga

[160a.3-61a.4] Secondly, there are also five corresponding modes of purification according to the subtle perfection stage (*phra-ba rdzogs-rim*). The first is the training which brings to conclusion the [aforementioned] five experiences by experientially cultivating, through the fusion of day and night, the union of the daytime yoga, which is a training in non-conceptual contemplation by either of the two methods of absorption, and the inner radiance during the deep sleep of the night. The two methods of absorption are the immediacy of total awareness (*rig-pa spyi-blugs*), through which one endowed with the essential of the body (*lus-gnad*) becomes absorbed, during a concentration in which [the prick of] a thorn is not felt, in a state in which awareness is fresh and uncontrived, and the absorption which follows after insight (*mthong-ba'i rjes-la 'jog-pa*), in which one is absorbed in the state of that [awareness] after recalling the view which one has studied and pondered.

The second [mode of purification] is the sealing which is executed during this state of emptiness or inner radiance, by clinging neither to the formal images of emptiness derived from that disposition in which the mind has ceased [to operate] nor to all the appearances of inner radiance which arise by night.

The third is the sealing of whatever appearances arise by means of the single seal of the deity's body. This is connected with the melting bliss[274] [experienced] through the contemplation in which great compassion is projected to appearances without partiality.

The fourth is the entry into the experience of the deity's body, the maṇḍala centre, periphery and clusters, in which all appearances are coalesced, and which become distinct and perfect through the increasing magnitude of that divine apparition. And the fifth is meditation which relies on any maṇḍala cluster in harmony with either the elaborate creation stage or the unelaborate [perfection stage], in which the male and female yogins and the male and female central deities are assembled;[275] or on the extremely unelaborate phase in which there is the coalescent union of the father consort or unchanging, supreme bliss and the mother consort or emptiness endowed with all supreme aspects.

During these meditations, conduct consists of either the conduct of [overpowering] discipline during the path of skilful means, or the conduct of self-restraint during the path of liberation. The former is explained to be direct and the latter to have eight divisions, namely, the conduct of faithful perseverance, the conduct which is in harmony with discriminative awareness, that which is in harmony with compassion, the conduct which is one-sided, that which is elaborate, that which concerns the feast offerings, that which consists of miraculous abilities and that which is immediate.

Since these [methods of the Mahāyoga] are classified according to the superior, middling and inferior degrees of intelligence [in those who require training], one is united in the uncorrupted path of insight over a period of six months, one year and two months, or one year and four months. It says in the *Sequence of the Path*:

> The supreme accomplishment of empowered
>   awareness[276]
> Will be achieved in six or twelve months,
> Or in fourteen or sixteen.

THE RESULT OF MAHĀYOGA: THE AWARENESS-HOLDER

[161a.4-162a.6] As to the third [aspect of the path of liberation], the result, or the awareness-holder who is brought forth by the path: Through having meditated in this way, the four kinds of awareness-holder subsumed in the three uncorrupted paths of insight, meditation and conclusion are actualised. On the path of insight, through the greater or lesser power of intelligence, one becomes either an awareness-holder of maturation (*rnam-smin rig-'dzin*) whose mature body has not been transformed into a body of pure essence, or an awareness-holder with power over the life-span (*tshe-dbang rig-'dzin*) who has perfected the supreme path and transformed [the coarse physical body] into a body of pure essence. The remaining nine [bodhisattva] levels and the path of meditation are subsumed by the awareness-holder of the great seal (*phyag-rgya chen-po'i rig-'dzin*), who is subdivided according to deeds and conduct into the awareness-holder of indestructible reality (*rdo-rje'i rig-'dzin*) on the second to the fifth [bodhisattva] levels inclusively, the awareness-holder of the wheel (*'khor-lo'i rig-'dzin*) on both the sixth and seventh levels, the awareness-holder of precious gemstones (*rin-po-che'i rig-'dzin*) on the eighth level, the awareness-holder of the lotus (*padma'i rig-'dzin*) on the ninth level, and the awareness-holder of the sword (*ral-gri'i rig-'dzin*) on the tenth level. These subdivisions as far as the path to the liberation of the tenth level are all subsumed under [the awareness-holder] of the great seal. Then the path of conclusion or the path which is distinguished over and above the tenth level [results in] the awareness-holder of spontaneous presence (*lhun-grub rig-'dzin*), exemplified by the Lord of Secrets [Guhyapati Vajrapāṇi] who acts as the sixth regent,[277] assuming the guise of Vajradhara, the spontaneous presence of the five buddha-bodies.

Although the limits of the levels [traversed] by sublime [bodhisattvas] of the causal vehicle and the awareness-holders of this Mahāyoga are identical, the intentions [of these beings] differ greatly. This is because the first level of the causal vehicle and the awareness-holder of maturation are equal in their intention, as are the eighth level of the causal vehicle and the awareness-holder with power over the life-span, and the tenth level and the awareness-holder of the great seal. Furthermore, the level of Universal Light (*Samantaprabhā*), which corresponds to [the path of] no-more-learning, and the awareness-holder of spontaneous presence are also equal in their intention. As is explained in the *Lesser Path* (*sgyu-'phrul drva-ba lam rnam-bshad chung-ba*, DZ Vol.1, pp.12-13):

> Now the first [level bodhisattva] and first
> [awareness-holder] have the same fortune,
> The second holder of the enlightened family
> And the spiritual warrior of the eighth [level] have
> the same fortune,
> The third and [the spiritual warrior of] the tenth
> [level] have the same fortune.
> By oceans of conduct and intention, [the fourth
> and eleventh] are superior [to these].

After finally being united on the highest path, the rank of one who embodies the twenty-five resultant realities is actualised. These comprise: the five buddha-bodies, namely, the body of reality, the body of perfect rapture, the body of emanation, the body of indestructible reality and the body of awakening; the five modes of buddha-speech, namely, the speech of uncreated meaning, the speech of intentional symbols, the speech of expressive words, the speech of indivisible, indestructible reality and the speech of the blessing of awareness; the five kinds of buddha-mind, namely, the pristine cognitions of the expanse of reality, of sameness, of accomplishment, of discernment and the mirror-like pristine cognition; the five enlightened attributes, namely, the pure buddha-field, the dimensionless celestial palace, the radiant and pure rays of light, the exalted thrones and the rapturous enjoyment of acting as desired; and the five enlightened activities, namely, pacifying suffering along with its causes, enriching the excellent provisions, overpowering those who require training, forcefully uprooting those that are difficult to train and spontaneously accomplishing whatever emerges without effort.

THE TEXTS OF MAHĀYOGA

[162b.1-162b.4] The piṭaka in which these [Mahāyoga teachings] are revealed comprises both the class of tantras (NGB Vols. 14-19) and the class of means for attainment (NGB Vols. 20-33),[278] of which the former includes the *Eight Sections of the Magical Net* (*sgyu-'phrul sde-brgyad*, NGB Vols. 14-15), including the *Tantras of the Magical Net of Vajrasattva*, and the latter, the eight general and particular classes of means for attainment. These are [the cycles of]: Mañjuśrī the Body (*'jam-dpal sku*, NGB Vols. 20-2), Lotus the Speech (*padma-gsung*, NGB Vols. 23-4), Yangdak the Mind (*yang-dag thugs*, NGB Vol. 25), Nectar the Enlightened Attributes (*bdud-rtsi yon-tan*, NGB Vol. 26), Vajrakīla the Enlightened Activity (*phur-ba phrin-las*, NGB Vols. 27-9), Mātaraḥ the Liberating Sorcery (*ma-mo rbod-gtong*, NGB Vols. 30-1, 33), the Mundane Praise (*'jig-rten mchod-bstod*, NGB Vol. 32), and the Malign Mantra (*dmod-pa drag-sngags*, NGB Vol. 32).[279] In addition, there are Father tantras such as the *Guhyasamāja*, the *Red, Black* and *Bhairava Tantras of Yamāntaka* (*gshin-rje-gshed dmar-nag-'jigs gsum*, T 468-70, 473-5, 478), and those such as the *Hidden Point of the Moon* (*Candraguhyatilakatantra*, T 477), and Mother tantras such as the *Cakrasaṃvara* (T 368) and *Kālacakra*,[280] which should also be subsumed within [Mahāyoga].

6 *Anuyoga*

[162.b.4-163.a.2] Secondly, concerning the Anuyoga transmissions [which emphasise] the perfection [stage]: The [Sanskrit] *Anuyoga* conveys the sense of subsequent yoga. It forms the connecting link between the Mahāyoga of the creation [stage] and the vehicle of extremely perfect yoga [i.e. Atiyoga]. The view which is to be realised according to this [Anuyoga] is that all things are buddhahood from the very beginning in the fundamental maṇḍala of enlightened mind, characterised as a coalescence of the expanse [of reality] and pristine cognition, in which the three kinds of maṇḍala are indivisible. It says in the *General Sūtra which Gathers All Intentions*:

> Since everything is therein identical,
> The supreme bliss of primordial buddhahood
> Is the nucleus without creation or cessation.
> The three maṇḍalas, where there is no activity,
> Are accomplished from the beginning,
> spontaneously present.

THE GROUND OF ANUYOGA

[163a.2-164b.1] Now the three kinds of maṇḍala are, firstly, the primordial maṇḍala (*ye ji-bzhin-pa'i dkyil-'khor*) which gathers all things of phenomenal existence, saṃsāra and nirvāṇa, in the natural expressive power of the mind, and which is uncreated mind-as-such, free from all extremes of conceptual elaboration, the pure spacious expanse of the mother consort Samantabhadrī. The second is the spontaneously present maṇḍala of natural expression (*rang-bzhin lhun-grub-kyi dkyil-'khor*), the naturally present pristine cognition that is Samantabhadra, which all-pervasively arises manifest in and of itself, without partiality, unimpeded throughout the entire extent of this [expanse]. The third is the fundamental maṇḍala of enlightened mind (*rtsa-ba byang-chub-kyi dkyil-'khor*), the supreme bliss or offspring in whom there is no duality of the expanse and pristine cognition, and in whom both of these [maṇḍalas] abide in coalescence, essentially without differentiation.

These form the ground which is to be realised and, together with the path through which it is realised, are all subsumed and then explained under three yogas. The *General Sūtra which Gathers All Intentions* says:

> Friends! what, one might ask, is the inconceivable form? One unites with the form of all things, which is inconceivable, through three kinds of yoga. Just what are these three? They are the yoga which is an object of activity, the yoga which performs that activity and the yoga which is not an object of activity.

In the *Root Tantra of All-Gathering Awareness* (*rtsa-rgyud kun-'dus rig-pa*, T 831) these are also spoken of as the yoga of the basis, the yoga of conditions and the yoga of the result.

Subsuming and teaching the intention of both these tantras, the root and the exegesis,[281] in a single meaning, the *Summation of the Meaning of the Secret Sūtra* (*Guhyasūtrapiṇḍārtha*, P 4751) says:

> Derived from the definitive vehicle of ultimate reality,
> Which, with all-positive compassion on behalf of living beings,
> Instructs through the appearance of three vehicles,
> The truth of the sūtras and tantras,
> Which illustrate the secret approach,
> Should be known to be of three kinds:
> The yoga of the basis which is an object of activity,
> That of the conditions which perform the activity,
> And that of the result which is free from activity,
> Are explained to be the root of all things.

In this way, there are three yogas, namely, those of the basis which is an object of activity, of the conditions which perform the activity, and of the result which is free from activity, among which the first is as follows. The abiding nature of all things is the reality which abides, perfectly and distinctly, as the nature of the three maṇḍalas. This same [*Summation of the Meaning*] says:

> All things, as many as there are outer and inner distinctions,
> Primordially abide in the disposition of enlightened mind.
> This is the meaning of tantra which is to be known.

Concerning the second of these yogas: Rebirth in mundane existence is transcended by persevering on the path. This refers to the three vehicles of pious attendants, self-centred buddhas and bodhisattvas which cause one to enter into the provisional result of tranquillity. As the above text says:

> This vehicle, in which guidance is effected
> By conduct endowed with perseverance,
> Is the condition which performs the activity.

As for the third of these yogas: It refers to the outer and inner vehicles of the mantras which are without the hopes and doubts connected with the laborious attainment that seeks the result extraneously, because the reality of the mind is naturally pure from the beginning. This same text again says:

> Without hoping or striving for a result elsewhere,
> The path abides in that which is to be attained.
> So it is that this vehicle of supreme skilful means
> Is free from activity.

THE PATH OF ANUYOGA

[164b.1-165b.1] The two latter kinds of yoga are called the path which is common to all, and if, among them, the path of this extraordinary [Anuyoga] is classified, it comprises both the definitive path of skilful means (*thabs-kyi nges-pa'i lam*) and the liberating path of discriminative awareness (*shes-rab rnam-par grol-ba'i lam*). As the same text says:

> Its essence is of skilful means
> And discriminative awareness.

The former path is the skilful means whereby the supreme, unchanging bliss, or the co-emergent pristine cognition of melting bliss, is attained. It includes both esoteric instructions concerning the "upper door of skilful means" (*thabs steng-sgo'i man-ngag*) through which meditation connected with the four centres gradually leads to the co-emergent pristine cognition, and esoteric instructions concerning the "lower door of skilful means" (*thabs 'og-sgo'i man-ngag*) which immediately lead to the co-emergent pristine cognition by relying on the meditative absorption connected with the secret [or sexual] centre [of the consort]. That [*Summation of the Meaning of the Secret Sūtra*] says:

> Through skilful means of esoteric instruction,
> Such as concerns the "source of all display",[282]
> One enters therein.

Concerning the latter, [the liberating path of discriminative awareness], the above-cited passage continues:

Proceeding through study, thought and meditation,
One enters in three ways:
The mind [pursues] ideas and scrutiny,
Truth, and syllables.

First, [the mind] which pursues ideas and scrutiny establishes the view that necessarily precedes the path. The spiritual and philosophical system of this [Anuyoga] holds the apparitions of reality as the objects to be cognised, and, by a particularising analysis through the axioms of awareness[283] which cognise them, the abiding nature of all things is established as the ineffable, unthinkable, inexpressible nature of the three primordial maṇḍalas of reality.

Concerning the second [way of entering the liberating path of discriminative awareness]: The mind which pursues the truth abides in the non-symbolic, non-conceptualising contemplation. The meditating intellect is established just as it is in the corresponding disposition of reality which is the object of meditation. The *Sūtra which Gathers All Intentions* says:

Having established the intellect just as it is[284]
In the corresponding reality,
There is an unwavering recollection
Derived from that inexpressible disposition.

As for the third [way of entering the liberating path of discriminative awareness]: The mind which pursues syllables refers to contemplative meditation on the symbolic deity. The uncommon distinction of this path is that, by the mere recitation of the seed-syllables or mantras, which create the different supporting [celestial palaces] and supported [deities] in the manner of a fish leaping from the water,[285] there is an experiential cultivation which emphasises clear, distinct meditation on all worlds and their contents as the deity's celestial palace and the circle of the maṇḍala.

THE RESULT OF ANUYOGA

[165b.1-166a.6] Concerning the result which is accomplished through the attainment of these [paths]: Beings of great intellectual power become free from the effort involved in traversing the sequence of levels and paths because they have all at once reached the limit of all realisations and experiences. Those of middling and inferior intelligence, who have either gradually or all-surpassingly traversed the four paths of learning which correspond to the ten levels, are united with the conclusive result of the path of no-more-learning.

Now the first level, that of indefinite transformation (*'gyur-ba ma-nges-pa'i sa*),[286] and the second level, that of the basis of reliance (*brten-pa gzhi'i sa*), are subsumed by the yoga of the spiritual warrior who aspires on the path of provisions (*tshogs-lam 'dun-pa sems-'dpa'i rnal-'byor*) and bring the accomplishment of the divine body of devoted conduct, the clairvoyance of common accomplishment, supernormal cognitive power and so forth.

The next three levels [the third, fourth and fifth], which are called the level of important purification (*gal-chen sbyong-ba'i sa*), the level of the continuity of training (*bslab-pa rgyun-gyi sa*) and the level of supporting merit (*bsod-nams rten-gyi sa*), are subsumed by the yoga which reveals the great enlightened family of the path of connection (*sbyor-lam rigs-chen 'byed-pa'i rnal-'byor*), and bring accomplishment of the divine body [which coalesces] vital energy and mind.

After all corruption has then ceased and the coarse, transitory bliss which depends on progress in conduct connected with the provisions has been destroyed, the [sixth] level of superior progress through reliance (*brten-pas khyad-par-du 'gro-ba'i sa*) is subsumed by the yoga which confers the great liberating inspiration of the path of insight (*mthong-lam dbugs-chen 'byin-pa'i rnal-'byor*), and brings the accomplishment of the divine body in which bliss and emptiness [are coalesced] in inner radiance.

Then, there is the [seventh] level which gives birth to the result with reference to the aftermath of inner radiance on the path of insight (*mthong-lam 'od-gsal-las langs-pa'i rjes-la dmigs-pa 'bras-bu skye-ba'i sa*). This is subsumed by the yoga which obtains the great prophetic declaration of the path of meditation (*sgom-lam lung-chen thob-pa'i rnal-'byor*),[287] and brings the uninterrupted accomplishment of the divine body in which pristine cognition and the pure [path of] learning are coalesced.

The next three levels, that is, the [eighth] level of unchanging abode (*gnas-pa mi-'gyur-ba'i sa*), the [ninth] level of expanding reality (*bdal-ba chos-nyid-kyi sa*) and the [tenth] level of riding on perfection (*rdzogs-pa ci-chibs-kyi sa*), are subsumed by the yoga which perfects the great expressive power of the final path (*mthar-lam rtsal-chen rdzogs-pa'i rnal-'byor*).

Thereafter, the resultant empowerment is conferred according to the path of great desire (*'dod-chags chen-po'i lam*)[288] which depends on the unobstructed path at the conclusion of the path of no-more-learning, and the subtle propensities which transfer consciousness to the three appearances (*snang-gsum*) are also purified.[289] The rank of the glorious Samantabhadra, who is the identity of the four buddha-bodies and five pristine cognitions, is mastered. This is the essence in which the twenty-five resultant realities are indivisible and spontaneously present, coalesced in the path of no-more-learning, and it is thereby that deeds on behalf of those requiring training are performed through enlightened activity which is permanent, pervasive and spontaneously accomplished. It is said in the *Summation of the Meaning of the Secret Sūtra*:

Concerning the nature of the result:
The perfect Buddha is an infinity
Subsumed in the twenty-five aspects
Of body, speech, mind, enlightened attributes and activities;
This is a spontaneously perfect omniscience.

THE TEXTS OF ANUYOGA

[166a.6-166b.1] Now the piṭaka in which this [Anuyoga] is revealed includes the *Four Root Sūtras* (*rtsa-ba'i mdo bzhi*, NGB Vols. 11-12) beginning with *All-Gathering Awareness*, the *Six Tantras which Clarify the Six Limits* (*mtha'-drug gsal-bar byed-pa'i rgyud-drug*, NGB Vol. 13), the *Twelve Rare Tantras* (*dkon-rgyud bcu-gnyis*, NGB Vol. 13) and the *Seventy Literary Transmissions* (*lung-gi yi-ge bdun-cu*).

7 *Key to the Appraisal of Secret Mantra Texts*

[166b.1-166b.2] The uncommon tantras, literary transmissions, esoteric instructions and definitively secret tantras in which phrases of indestructible reality (*vajrapāda*) are most profoundly contained, are never established by the scriptural authority and reasoning of pretentious sophistry, but they are to be understood by means of the six limits and the four styles of appraisal.

THE SIX LIMITS

[166b.2-168a.1] It is said in the *Root Tantra of the Kālacakra (Kālacakramūlatantra*, T 362):

> Tantras are characterised by these six limits:
> There are those which employ the language of [hidden] intention
> And likewise those which do not,
> Those which are literal and likewise those which are not,
> And those of provisional meaning and of definitive meaning.

A single string of phrases of indestructible reality (*vajrapāda*) reveals different meanings with an intention directed toward those who lack and those who possess the fortune to understand the meaning of genuine reality. Among these [*vajrapāda*] there are those of provisional meaning which refer to skilful means and its aspects and introduce the inner structure of the maṇḍalas including those made of coloured powder, of offerings, symbols and hand gestures or seals, and of burnt offerings, the creation stage and the attainment of ritual feast offerings and so forth. There are also those of definitive meaning, referring to the texts which teach the binding of the energy channels, currents and "enlightened mind" [i.e. seminal points] according to the perfection stage, and the abiding nature of the naturally radiant mind which is the continuum of the basis, the nucleus of the tathāgata and the supreme, unchanging Great Seal. For example, it is said in the *Hevajra Tantra* (Pt.1, Ch.1, v.12):

> The great pristine cognition abides in the body;
> It has genuinely renounced all conceptions,
> And it pervades all substances.
> It abides in the body but is not born from the body.

Intention is explained to be that which is understood with reference to the intentional basis of the meaning, when bound by the use of [apparently] contradictory expressions. This is because there are different phrases of indestructible reality which express a single point pertaining to the creation and perfection stages. And there are also intentions of diverse meaning expressed in a single phrase of indestructible reality, with reference to which there is an intention directed towards time, an intention directed towards meaning and an intention directed towards thought. The first kind of intention is exemplified by the following words [from the *Litany of the Names of Mañjuśrī*, v.141c] which were spoken with an intention directed to events in future time:

> Perfect buddhahood is attained in an instant.

The second kind of intention [that which is directed towards meaning] is exemplified by the following quotation from the *Mahāmāya Tantra* which has an intention directed to the necessity of permanently enjoying the mother of all buddhas, Prajñāpāramitā, who, in the manner of a reflected image, is the emptiness endowed with all supreme aspects:

> Having been snatched away from all the buddhas,
> The daughter born from the supreme deity
> Should be enjoyed.

The third kind of intention [that which is directed towards thought] is exemplified by the following quotation from the *Hevajra Tantra*, which, with an intention directed toward the necessity of slaying egotism revealed under the name of the "vital energy of great life-breath" (*srog-chen-po'i rlung*) says:

> You should slay living creatures (*srog-chags*).[290]

However, there are other passages which are clearly understood through the mere revelation of their actual words of expression, without regard for the intentional basis of meaning. These are not intentional, and are exemplified in the following quotation:

> You should not slay living creatures.
> You should not speak words of falsehood.

Those texts which are literal are the rituals including maṇḍalas, burnt offerings and *torma* offerings, which are taught through the language familiar in treatises, and so forth, mundane in word and meaning. Those which are not literal are unknown in the mundane treatises and bound by the mysterious, symbolic language of the Tathāgata, as exemplified by *koṭākhyā* and so forth among the names for the ten kinds of vital energy, and by *ālikāli* ["vowels and consonants"], which is employed as a name for the rites concerned with sexual union and "liberation"[291] in the *Tantra of the Secret Nucleus*. Since all secret expressions and meanings do not bypass these, they are called the six limits.

THE FOUR STYLES

[168a.1-169.4] Secondly, concerning the four styles [employed in the exegesis of these texts], it is said in the *Tantra of the Compendium of the Indestructible Reality of Pristine Cognition* (*Vajrajñānasamuccayatantra*, T 447):

> The four styles of exegesis are the lexical,
> The general, the concealed and the conclusive.

The first among them, [the lexical style,] refers to the exegeses which appraise merely the meaning of the syllables: Arranged in conformity with the texts of grammar and logic, they are said to be lexical or, according to the *Heruka Galpo*, semantical.

The second, the general style, is of three kinds. The first of these counters the regret felt by one entering [the vehicles of] the sūtras and so forth. If one who first enters the sūtra [vehicles] or the Kriyātantra and Caryātantra without having entered into this easy and swift path of the inner mantras feels regret with the thought that, "This is not good", [according to the general style of exegesis] these [lesser ways] are supports for the path of this [way of inner mantras]. It is also said in the *Sūtra [which Gathers All Intentions]*:

> One endowed with the supreme skilful means
> Transforms conflicting emotions
> Into aspects of enlightenment.

This is said to be general because the sūtras and so forth also claim that, among other features of the easy and swift path, the provisions of many aeons can be amassed by a single wave of activity connected with the provisions if one is endowed with the extraordinary skilful means of sharp acumen.

The second [general style of exegesis] counters the regret felt by one entering the inner mantras. If one feels regret with thoughts that the conduct in this [vehicle] resembles that of dogs and pigs because it is without ablutions, cleanliness and other aspects of purity, and that it is an extremist doctrine because it propounds dangerous rites of sexual union and "liberation" within the doctrine, then these [rites and conduct] are said to be general because they are a common object of training; for the sūtras and so forth also claim that one who practises, thinking to renounce attachment, even after practising rites of sexual union and "liberation" with a virtuous mind, such as killing an evil, armed assailant[292] and sleeping with a merchant's daughter,[293] is uncovered by faults and that one's merit immeasurably increases. This is because, if attachment to filth and purity has not been renounced, the meaning of reality is not realised.

The third general style of exegesis is that of the creation stage. It is so called because meditation on the supporting celestial palaces, supported deities and other aspects connected with the creation stage are the common objects of training according to both the creation and the perfection stages.

Thirdly, the concealed style applies to concealed doctrines, such as those which display the action seal (*karmamudrā*) and rites of meditative absorption, because it is improper for them to emerge in public assemblies. There is also the concealed style of the relative truth, including that of the perfection stage, which refers to the energy channels, currents, and seminal points as a blessing for oneself (*svādhiṣṭhāna*). These are concealed because they are like a kernel, entering between the two extremes [of skilful means and discriminative awareness].

Fourth, [the conclusive style refers to] the perfection stage of inner radiance, the ultimate reality in which these [experiences] are sealed, which is the conclusion of the path. And [it refers to] the realisation in which the two truths are coalesced, that is, the conclusion of the result.

These four styles are known as the four styles of exegesis. They are utilised because a single phrase of indestructible reality has to be differentiated in accordance with the lower and superior degrees of acumen. Without possessing these esoteric instructions, however refined the ideas and scrutiny of one's thoughts may be, one cannot realise the crucial secret of genuine [reality]; and one who does possess them easily comes to realise the secret intention of the vehicle of indestructible reality.

8 *The Superiority of Atiyoga, the Great Perfection*

[169a.4-183a.6] Thirdly, [following Mahāyoga and Anuyoga,] there is the explanation of the definitive order of Atiyoga, the Great Perfection, which is the climax of all vehicles and the culmination of all [paths] to be traversed. This is revealed in two parts: its superiority over the lower [vehicles] and its divisions.

As to the first: This king among vehicles holds the expanse [of reality], the originally pure mind-as-such whose natural expression is inner radiance, and the naturally present, unchanging, pristine cognition that spontaneously abides in oneself to be the ground of great perfection. In the estimation [of Atiyoga], the vehicles of the eight lower sequences have intellectually contrived and altered that which is unchanging exclusively through their suddenly arisen ideas which never experience what in fact is so. They have applied an antidote to and abandoned that which is not to be renounced. They have referred to as flawed that in which there is nothing to be clarified, with an intellect which desires clarification. They have induced dissension with respect to that which is not to be obtained by their hopes and doubts that it is to be elsewhere obtained; and they have obscured the pristine cognition, which intrinsically abides, by their strenuous efforts, with respect to that which is effortlessly present. Hence, they have had no occasion to make contact with the reality of the fundamental nature.

In this way, the pious attendants and self-centred buddhas among the lower vehicles, with reference to the selflessness which they realise, hold consciousness and atomic matter to be the ultimate realities; and the proponents of consciousness (*Vijñānavāda*) who hold consciousness, self-cognisant and self-radiant in nature, to be the absolute characteristic of ultimate reality, do not transcend [the view of] mind and mental events harboured by mundane beings. The Mādhyamika adhere to a truth of cessation scrutinised by four great axioms and the like, concerning the absence of creation, absence of cessation, absence of being and absence of non-being, which are appraised according to the two truths. And they adhere to an emptiness which is, for example, like the sky, representative of freedom from extremes and freedom from conceptual elaboration and so forth. The Kriyātantra among the lower ways of mantra hold that accomplishments are attained which delight the deity endowed with the three purites, by means of cleanliness and other such austerities. The Ubhayatantra[294] are attached to superficialities in their equation of the higher view and the lower conduct. The Yogatantra, having regarded the blessing of ultimate reality as a deity, objectively refer to the yoga of the four seals. The Mahāyoga holds that pristine cognition is generated by incisive application of the creation stage and [practices associated with] the energy channels, currents and seminal points according to the perfection stage. And the Anuyoga regards the expanse [of reality] and pristine cognition as maṇḍalas of the deity which are either to be created or are in the process of creation.

In short, all these sequences [of the vehicle], from Anuyoga downwards, are exclusively spiritual and philosophical systems contacted through the intellect. All of them, on the surface of the intellect, produce such thoughts as, "this is non-existent, this empty, and this is true". Apart from this and their convictions and their boasting through ideas and scrutiny that reality lies within the subject-object dichotomy, they do not perceive the abiding nature of the natural state, just as it is.

Accordingly, it is said in the *Sūtra of the Nucleus of the Tathāgata*:

> The king assembled many blind men and, showing them an elephant, commanded, "Describe its particular characteristics." Those among them who felt the elephant's nose said that it resembled an iron hook. Those who felt the eyes said that they resembled bowls. Those who felt the ears said they resembled winnowing baskets. Those who felt the back said it resembled a sedan chair, and those who felt the tail said it resembled a string. Indeed, though they did not describe the elephant as anything else, they were lacking in overall understanding. Similarly, though the nature of the Buddha is diversely described as emptiness, as illusory, as inner radiance and so forth, there is no overall understanding.

These paths have obscured the meaning of the Great Perfection, and if one develops their realisations while abiding in the path of the Great Perfection, it is explained to be a point of deviation (*gol-sa*). The *All-Accomplishing King* says:

> The six vehicles of definitive attainment
> Are taught to be deviation points, according to the
>   Great Perfection.
> If one asks how this is the case,
> The sūtras of the bodhisattava [vehicle]
> Uphold the level of Universal Light.

Through ideas and scrutiny concerning the two truths
They hold reality to be empty as the sky.
The supreme bliss of Atiyoga, however,
Is the enlightened mind transcending ideas and scrutiny.
That which transcends ideas and scrutiny is obscured by the sūtras.
Ideas and scrutiny, according to the Great Perfection,
Are explained to be the deviation in the sūtras.

Kriyātantra upholds the holder of indestructible reality.
Having entered through the three kinds of purity,
The subject-object dichotomy abides in a pure object.
The supreme bliss of Atiyoga, however,
Is the enlightened mind transcending the subject-object dichotomy.
That which transcends subject-object dichotomy is obscured by Kriyā.
Objectification and subjectification, according to the Great Perfection,
Are explained to be the deviation in Kriyātantra.

Concerning the view and conduct of the Ubhayatantra:
The conduct is as in Kriyā and the attainment as in Yoga.
Since there is no point in [artificially] connecting view and conduct,
They do not realise the non-dual truth.
The supreme bliss of Atiyoga, however,
Is the enlightened mind without duality.
That which is free from duality is obscured by Ubhayatantra.
That which creates duality, according to the Great Perfection,
Is explained to be the deviation in Ubhayatantra.

The Yogatantra upholds the Bounteous Array.
Having entered it through symbolic and non-symbolic methods,[295]
The four seals are emphasised.
It cannot be entered without acceptance and rejection.
The supreme bliss of Atiyoga, however,
Is the enlightened mind without acceptance and rejection.
That which is without acceptance and rejection is obscured by Yogatantra.
Accepting and rejecting, according to the Great Perfection,
Are explained to be the deviation in Yogatantra.

The Mahāyoga upholds the Vajradhara.
Having entered through skilful means and discriminative awareness,

In the pure maṇḍala of one's own mind,
The four branches of ritual service and rites of attainment
are achieved.
The supreme bliss of Atiyoga, however,
Is the enlightened mind transcending perseverance.
That which transcends perseverance is obscured by
Mahāyoga.
Perseverance, according to the Great Perfection,
Is explained to be the deviation in Mahāyoga.

The Anuyoga upholds indivisibility.
Having entered through the expanse and pristine
cognition,
The things which accordingly appear include
The cause, which is the view of the pure expanse,
And the result, which is viewed as the maṇḍala of
pristine cognition.
The supreme bliss of Atiyoga, however,
Is the enlightened mind transcending cause and
result.
That which transcends cause and result is obscured
by Anuyoga.
To behold a duality of cause and result, according to the
Great Perfection,
Is explained to be the deviation in Anuyoga.

These [sequences of the vehicle] are created and fabricated by the mind, and yet [they hold that] the mind inclusive of the ideas present in all eight aggregates [of consciousness] is a stain to be rejected. This natural Great Perfection, on the other hand, refers to mind-as-such transcending the mind, the uncompounded inner radiance of pristine cognition which is the natural presence of awareness, in which all the enlightened attributes of fundamental nature are spontaneously present. Apart from that, its essential point is that the abiding nature, characterised in the manner of the sky as unchanging, does not need to refer to causes and results that are either to be created or are in the process of creation, or to extraneous conditions and such elements, because it is naturally free from them. Thereby, [the Great Perfection] teaches that the nature of the Primordial Lord, Samantabhadra, is the buddhahood attained without contrivance, by realising in one's own nature the naturally present pristine cognition, and that it does not otherwise emerge through extraneous conditions such as study, reflection and the accumulations of compounded provisions.

It is said in the *Sūtra of the Adornment of Pristine Cognition's Appearance which Penetrates the Scope of All Buddhas*:

> Nothing at all is seen by the buddhas, nor heard, nor intended, nor known, nor is the object of omniscience. Nothing has been said or expressed by the buddhas. The buddhas neither speak nor make expression. The buddhas will not resort to speech and they will not resort to expression. The buddhas do not become manifestly, perfectly enlightened. The buddhas have not caused anything to become manifestly, perfectly enlightened. The buddhas have not renounced conflicting emotions. The buddhas have not actually disclosed purity. Nothing at all is seen by the buddhas, nor heard, nor tasted, nor smelt, nor known, nor cognised. If you ask why this is the case, Mañjuśrī, it is because all things are utterly pure from the beginning.

The lord Maitreya [in the *Supreme Continuum of the Greater Vehicle*, Ch.1, v.51] has also said:

> Subsequently, just as it was before,
> Is the unchanging reality.

And also [Ch.1, v.5]:

> Uncompounded and spontaneously present,
> It is not realised through other conditions.

According to such quotations, the natural expression or abiding nature, the fundamental nature or the reality of all things is uncompounded and uncreated through causes and conditions. It is not dependent on others, is not realised through extraneous conditions, and does not abide in a goal that is attained by the intellect.

It is said in the *Sūtra of the Dialogue with Kāśyapa from the Sublime Pagoda of Precious Jewels*:

> That which is uncompounded is the enlightened family of the sublime ones. That which is the enlightened family of the sublime ones neither adheres to the training, nor transcends the training. That which neither adheres to the training, nor transcends the training neither moves, nor rests, nor rushes. That which neither moves, nor rests, nor rushes, has neither mind, nor the properties which emerge from mind. That which has neither mind, nor the properties which emerge from mind possesses neither deeds, nor the ripening of deeds. That which possesses neither deeds, nor the ripening of deeds knows neither pleasure nor pain. That which knows neither pleasure nor pain is the enlightened family of the sublime ones. That which is the enlightened family of the sublime ones possesses neither deeds, nor deed-forming volition.

Then, in the *Sūtra of the Greater Vehicle which Decisively Reveals the Intention* it is said:

> The inexpressible and manifestly perfect buddhahood which is attained by the Sublime Ones through their sublime perception and sublime vision, is called uncompounded because it is this inexpressible reality which is to be perfectly realised.

And in the *Root Stanzas on the Madhyamaka* (Ch.15, vv.1-2):

> It is incorrect that independent existents
> Emerge from causes and conditions.
> That which has emerged from causes and conditions
> Would be a created independent existent.
> In what way would it be admissable
> To speak of a created independent existent?
> For an independent existent must be uncontrived
> And not dependent on any other.

Extensive quotations, such as these, visibly set the tone in accordance with which the abiding nature of fundamental reality, the uncompounded pristine cognition transcending causes and conditions which is the spiritual and philosophical goal of the Great Perfection, is manifestly realised.

Concerning the way in which this reality is established to be free from extremes also, it is said [in the same text, Ch.15, v.6]:

> Whoever views independent existents, dependent existents,
> Substantiality and non-substantiality,
> Has not seen the reality
> Of the teaching of the Buddha.

And concerning the sequence of the path of the Great Perfection, glorious Nāropā's *Means for Attaining the Real (de-kho-na-nyid sgrub-pa'i thabs zhes-bya-ba rdzogs-pa-chen-po'i lam-gyi rim-pa)* says:

> Buddhas and sentient beings have a single nature.
> This mystery of the mind's pristine cognition
> Is more amazing than the truth of the nucleus.
> The body in which the naturally present greatness is identified
> Is the supreme, perfect bliss of intrinsic awareness.
> The emanational body in which spirituality appears
> Is the secret mind, not essentially existing.
> It is the indivisibility of the apparent and the invisible.

Then, concerning the fact that this [Atiyoga] does not objectively refer to a path as do the lower [vehicles], that same text says:

In the nucleus of perfect pristine cognition
The goal is reached without a sequential path.

Now, if one were to ask just what is the purpose of the teaching of these lower sequences [of the vehicle], it is intended either with reference to the intellectual degrees of those who require training, or as the means by which one on a lower [path], having trained the mind, gradually enters into this path [of Atiyoga], or else as a support for the path. The nucleus of all the Sugata's teachings, the culmination of meaning, is pristine cognition alone, the transcendental perfection of discriminative awareness, the natural state which is just what is; and the perfect establishment of it through the direct perception of intrinsic awareness is none other than the path of Great Perfection. The three vows, the six transcendental perfections, the creation stage and the perfection stage; all of these, indeed, are taught as the means of realising the Great Perfection and as mere rest-stations for those who progress towards it. The *Secret Nucleus* (Ch. 22, v.3) says:

Distinctions are indeed arrayed in the levels,
But these are paths which progress to the secret
nucleus.

And in Indrabhūti's *Esoteric Instructions on the Empowerment Circle* (*Ratnacakrābhiṣekopadeśakrama*, T 2472) it is said:

This is only spoken as the means to attain
That which is inner radiance by nature,
And the culmination of the Great Perfection,
The supreme among the supreme of all esoteric
instructions.

And Śāntideva [in the *Introduction to the Conduct of a Bodhisattva*, Ch.9, v.1] has also explained:

All these aspects were taught by the Sage
For the sake of discrimative awareness.

Now concerning this natural expression of the Great Perfection: The Sugata, during the intermediate promulgation of the transmitted precepts, did not reveal the structure of the fundamental reality, though he did extensively teach the inconceivable, abiding nature without referring to symbols of elaborate conception. And, during the final promulgation, though he did reveal the structure of the fundamental reality, he did not teach the characteristic path through which it is actualised. Therefore, the conclusive intention of the Two Promulgators[296] actually abides without contradiction in the nature of the Great Perfection. This intention comprises the unaltered intention of the *Collection of Madhyamaka Reasoning*, which consists of the commentaries on the intermediate promulgation by the sublime and supreme Nāgārjuna; and his [*Collection of Eulogies*] including the *Eulogy to the Expanse of Reality*, and the commentaries by the regent Maitreya, the sublime and supreme Asaṅga, and his brother [Vasubandhu] and so forth, which together form the intention of the final [promulgation]. If one were to ask why this is the case, it is because these masters did not claim anything other than the profound abiding nature of natural reality, and because the Great Perfection itself is none other than that.

Although the path through which this reality is actualised is superior only in the mantras, on further examination the lower ways of mantra consist of merely the symbolic and non-symbolic stages [of meditation]. The *Six-limbed Yoga of the Kālacakra* (*Kālacakraṣaḍaṅgayoga*, T 1367) which is renowned as supreme among the Unsurpassed tantras, the *Five Stages* (*Pañcakrama*, T 1802) and others,[297] too, merely explain the ten signs of inner radiance and the form of emptiness which is a reflection of the three spheres of existence within a black outline.[298] These are perceived by controlling the activity of the energy channels, currents and seminal points. As the experience of this perception increases and decreases, even one who has meditated appropriately cannot attain the body of indestructible reality in which the elements have dissolved into light. Thus, those of lowly fortune contact herein not the definitive meaning but merely the provisional meaning. So it is said by Nāropā:

> The single definitive means is the truth of the nucleus.
> The four successive seals and the six-limbed yoga,
> The diverse vehicles of thought,
> Have resorted to the provisional and not the definitive.
> The essential nature is neither high nor low.
> It ends the thoughts conceived by those who devoutly
> enter.

Furthermore, the meditation of the creation stage according to the lower [paths] merely effects the ripening of the perfection stage, and, through that meditation, nothing but [the result] of a sky-farer is accomplished by an awareness-holder of the desire realm or an awareness-holder of the form realm, whichever is appropriate in accord with the distinctions between the action seal and the seal of pristine cognition (*karmamudrā* and *jñānamudrā*).[299] Again, though one may desire to develop pristine cognition through the flexibility of the energy channels, currents and seminal points in accordance with the perfection stage, the conditions of tiresome efforts are not transcended. Even one who desires to develop the pristine cognition of bliss and emptiness in accordance with the third empowerment,[300] subsequent on the delight experienced when the two sexual organs are in union, is not liberated from the three realms [of saṃsāra]. Therefore, the supreme, unchanging pristine cognition which is the supreme, unfading bliss, is not taught to be realised by these methods, and the above practices explain merely the meditative absorptions in bliss. As it is said in the glorious Nāropā's *Means for Attaining the Real*:

> The naturally present mind,
> That is definitively free from elaboration,
> Is not known through the path of desire.
> This nucleus of naturally present, inner radiance,
> Through its non-symbolic natural expression,
> Is free from desire for discriminative awareness and
> skilful means.
> It is without the arduous emanation and absorption
> of desire connected with the seminal points.[301]
> Evenly absorbed in discriminative awareness and
> skilful means,
> It is the supreme blissful concentration.
> Without attachment to the savour of apparition,
> It is the perfect path of unattached pristine cognition.

Without realising the natural and utterly pure discriminative awareness, which is the abiding nature of the Great Perfection, by such attainments, the aspects of the truth of the path do not transcend the compounded fundamental virtues attained by the ideas and scrutiny of discrete recollections and thoughts. These aspects include the three vows, the six transcendental perfections and the creation and perfection stages which all refer to objects of the intellect, and their various means by which the mass of conflicting emotions are [respectively] renounced by pious attendants and self-centred buddhas, obstructed by bodhisattvas, and transmuted into the path by the secret mantra and so forth. Accordingly, it is said in the *Ornament of the Madhymaka* (*Madhyamakālaṃkārakārikā*, T 3884):

> The essence which is uncompounded
> Is not anything anywhere.

If, having had the opportunity to realise the reality of the abiding nature, one continues to cling to extremes of conduct such as renunciation and acceptance as they are applied to positive and negative attributes and to virtue and evil, it is explained to be a firm impediment in the way of the provision of pristine cognition and a point of great deviation. It says in the *Pagoda of Precious Jewels*:

> One should enter into this enumeration of the tathāgatas' intention. One should not actually cling to either virtuous

> or non-virtuous doctrines. One who actually clings to non-virtuous doctrines will continue to cling actually to non-virtuous doctrines. The phenomena of suffering and unease which emerge through actual attachment to non-virtuous doctrines are called the sublime truth of suffering. Thus the tathāgatas revealed them within the enumeration of non-virtuous doctrines. The absence of actual clinging to virtue and non-virtue, and the cessation of craving are to be realised as the renunciation of the origin [of suffering] and as the twofold sublime truth. Thus the tathāgatas revealed them within the enumeration of virtuous doctrines.

And in the same text:

> There, virtue is empty and non-virtue, too, is empty. Virtue is void and non-virtue, too, is void. Virtue is unadulterated by non-virtue and non-virtue, too, is unadulterated by virtue. There is neither basis nor cause for hankering after virtue and non-virtue.

And in the *Sūtra Requested by Jñānottara according to the Piṭaka of the Greater Vehicle* (*Jñānottarabodhisattvaparipṛcchāsūtra*, T 82):

> The bodhisattva Jñānaketu asked, "What is the provision of merit?" [The Transcendent Lord] replied, "It refers to the positive doctrines such as liberality, along with their symbols."
>
> "Then what is the provision of pristine cognition?"
>
> "It refers to non-symbolic [doctrines], such as discriminative awareness."
>
> "Then how should these two be accumulated?" he asked, and [the Transcendent Lord] replied, "As for the provision of merit, it is called the provision of the merit of saṃsāra, and is exemplified by the water contained in the hoofprint of an ox. If you ask why this is the case, it is quickly lost, exhausted and diminished, and, after the bliss of gods and humans has been experienced, it causes rebirth in evil existences. As for the provision of pristine cognition, it is called the provision of nirvāṇa and is exemplified by the water in a great ocean. It is not lost, not exhausted and is unfailing, and it causes attainment of nirvāṇa. Jñānaketu, you should accumulate only the provision of pristine cognition."

Furthermore, the ten categories (*daśatattva*) of the outer and inner mantras have also resorted to symbolism which obscures the truth of fundamental reality. It is said in the *All-Accomplishing King*:

> There is neither meditation on the view nor guarding
> of the commitments.

> There is neither purification on the levels nor
> progress on the path.
> There is neither perseverance in activity nor
> conferral of empowerment.
> There is neither perseverance in respect of the
> three media nor the creation of the maṇḍala.
> Cause and result are without duality, in the manner
> of space.

The sublime Mañjuśrī also says:

> The maṇḍalas and burnt offerings,
> The *torma* offerings and recitations counted on
> rosaries,
> The sedentary vajra-like and dramatic postures and
> so forth
> Are fallible with respect to this freedom from
> conceptual elaboration.
> For there is nothing to be done,
> And nothing either to obstruct.

And:

> Concerning activities, the yogin
> Apprehends them on the supreme paths,
> Just as a deer pursues a mirage:
> Though they always appear, they are not grasped.

And in the *Hevajra Tantra* (Pt.1, Ch.5, v.11):

> There is no meditation, nor meditator.
> There is no deity, nor mantra.

Again the *Secret Treasury of the Ḍākinī* (*mkha'-'gro-ma'i gsang-mdzod*) also says:

> The objects which accordingly appear
> Abide as apparitional male and female deities.
> There is nothing to be bound and there is no binding,
> Nor are there energy channels, currents and
> seminal points.
> Accomplishment comes about through emptiness.

And:

> Ablutions and cleanliness are not required here.
> Austerities and asceticism are not required here.

Such quotations extensively reveal [that the symbolism of the ten categories of mantra is not required in Atiyoga].

Now there are those of little intelligence who might ask whether the Kriyātantra and Caryātantra and so forth are not within the vehicle of indestructible reality or whether it is a contradiction that accomplishment is revealed through them by means of ritual and activity. Furthermore, they might ask whether, among the sūtras of the greater vehicle, those which emphatically teach the provision of merit including liberality to be the basis of omniscience, are in contradiction [to this supreme view]. However, all these teachings were intentionally given by the sugatas. They were given in order to embrace those of base, childish intellect, those who delight in conceptual elaboration and those who fear topics of utter profundity. Such is said in the *Introduction to the Real* (*Tattvāvatāra*, T 3709):

> One is liberated by the view of emptiness.
> That is the point of the remainder of
> meditation.
> All conduct of body, speech and mind
> Is taught within the lesser vehicles.

The master Nāgārjuna also says:

> Look for reality, and at the outset,
> One could say that everything exists.
> But when the objects are realised
> And there is no attachment,
> There is subsequently the truth devoid of them.

And in addition, the *Crest of Indestructible Reality* (*Vajroṣṇīṣakriyātantra*) says:

> If one evenly abides in the real,
> There is neither commitment nor the practice of
> mantra.
> It is not necessary to hold the vajra and bell.[302]
> One will become accomplished without the ten
> categories.

These and other literary transmissions have been extensively explained by the master Mañjuśrīkīrti [in his *Commentary on the Magical Net of Mañjuśrī*, *Mañjuśrīnāmasaṃgītiṭīkā*, T 2534], which clearly reveals that there is no mode of liberation by means of the creation and perfection stages or any other such doctrines of mental scrutiny unless there is realisation of the naturally liberated vast openness, in which saṃsāra and nirvāṇa are liberated as fundamental reality and of a common savour; and unless there is realisation of the inexpressible reality beyond the guarding of commitments and verbal and written objects. In the same vein, the *Magical Net of Mañjuśrī* says:

> Vajrapāṇi, I have revealed the distinctive features of the vehicle according to the differences in the intelligence of sentient beings and the distinctions of their class. Although it is revealed to some as the way of the Outsiders,[303] to some as the vehicle of the pious attendants, to some as the vehicle of the self-centred buddhas, and to others still as the vehicle of the transcendental perfections and the immeasurable tantras of the awareness-holders, it should be known that buddhahood is indivisibly attained through the great seminal point[304] which is unwritten and free from symbols.

These authoritative passages [belonging to the vehicle] of indestructible reality set the incontrovertible tone [of Atiyoga].

Nor is it the case that, through such teaching in the Great Perfection, the areas of skilful means according to the lower paths are renounced. With reference to the naturally present pristine cognition or the real nature of the Great Perfection, this reality does not require to be sought out and attained elsewhere because the great enlightened attributes of purity are spontaneously present, and the three buddha-bodies are effortlessly present. It is a fact that from the very moment of the realisation, through the guru's esoteric instructions, of this reality, the natural expression of the deities and mantras is also complete in a maṇḍala of great purity and sameness, which is present without conceptual elaboration. This is established totally without effort and without wandering from the disposition of this uncontrived, primordial reality. Indeed, even the area of conduct relating to the six transcendental perfections, which include liberality, becomes complete therein, as it is said in the *Sūtra of the Greater Vehicle which is a Dialogue with Brahmaviśeṣacinti* (*Brahmaviśeṣacintiparipṛcchāsūtra*, T 160):

> Without actual volition, moral discipline passes into
> nirvāṇa.
> Instantaneously, patience passes into nirvāṇa.
> Without acceptance or rejection, perseverance passes
> into nirvāṇa.
> Non-conceptually, concentration passes into nirvāṇa.
> Unimpededly, discriminative awareness passes into nirvāṇa.
> Since the expanse of reality is desireless,
> Desire is the limit of desirelessness.
> Since the expanse of reality is without ferocity,
> Hatred is the limit of genuine reality.
> Since real things are undeluded,
> Delusion is the limit of the undeluded.
> Without the transference of consciousness at death
> and without birth,
> Saṃsāra is also nirvāṇa.

> In a manner without manifest attachment,
> Nirvāṇa is also saṃsāra.
> By the view which is bound to conventions,
> The truth also becomes false.
> To those endowed with manifest pride,
> Falsehood also becomes the truth.
> So it is known.

And in the *Transcendental Perfection of Discriminative Awareness in Twenty-five Thousand Lines*:

> From this up to the unsurpassed, genuinely perfect enlightenment there is no earnest application. There is no earnest application in the purification of [lands into] buddha-fields. There is no earnest application in the maturation of sentient beings. There is no earnest application in regarding the buddhas. There is no earnest application in the generation of the fundamental virtues. If it is asked why so, Subhūti, it is because all things are empty of their own attributes. A bodhisattva and great spiritual warrior does not regard any of these things as genuine, whether one refers to the object in which earnest application is developed, that by which it is developed or that in which it is to be developed.

According to such extensive quotations, in this abiding nature that is free from all activity, all things belonging to the truth of the path are naturally complete, without effort, in the manner of a hundred rivers converging under a bridge. It says in the *Secret Nucleus* (Ch.12, v.14):

> The perfect Buddha is not found
> In any of the ten directions and four times.
> Other than the perfect Buddha which is mind-as-such,
> Do not seek the Buddha elsewhere.

And (Ch.2, v.4):

> Even though he would search,
> The Conqueror would not find it.

And in the *All-Accomplishing King*:

> Mind is the substance which is just what is.
> All things are accomplished in the nature of just
> what is.
> Do not fabricate that which is just what is.
> Do not attain anything but the essence.
> A conqueror who has sought it, will not find it
> Within the expanse [of reality].

Because it has already been done,
There is no need to do so now.
Because it has already been attained,
One does not attain it now.
Be equipoised without ideas and intentions.

And in the *Hevajra Tantra* (Pt.1, Ch.5, v.11):

In nature without conceptual elaboration
The deity and the mantra abide.

Furthermore, on the subject of the perfection of all things such as mantras, seals, commitments, and the emanation and absorption [of light] in the reality of awareness, the supreme king of recollection, it says in the glorious Nāropā's *Means for Attaining the Real*:

Unwritten, the speech of the nucleus
Abides in the true enlightened mind.

The king does not contrive commitments,
But keeps them unguardingly.

The unchanging seal
Is executed by the unchanging truth.

In the maṇḍala without extremes and centre,
Pristine cognition radiates without emanation or absorption.
This thoughtless natural expression,
That is the Conqueror's mind,
Does not transcend the enlightened mind.

In the same way, the area of conduct according to the causal vehicle, is revealed to be complete [in Atiyoga], as the same text says:

By possessing the truth of this nucleus
The mind is not induced to accumulate desires.
Likewise the six transcendental perfections
Abide in the naturally present, perfect mind.
The intention without thoughts and ideation,
Endowed with the six transcendental perfections,
Abides without thought and without apprehension.
The unwavering, uninterrupted awareness
Is the unqualified transcendental perfection of
discriminative awareness.

Although this is extensively propounded elsewhere in other texts, the above illustration should suffice here.

This being the case, the basis of the view concerning the abiding nature, which is just what is, is said to be a view of sameness throughout the three times. It uproots the seed of saṃsāra because it is devoid of conceptualisations which are disharmonious with respect to the unqualified essence. It is devoid of disharmonious, symbolic appearances with respect to the object, and it is free from disharmonious delusion with respect to the subject. It transcends the dominion of the eight aggregates of consciousness along with their thoughts, expressions, causes and results, and abides in the reality of awareness, the pristine cognition of the natural Great Perfection. In the words of the master Āryadeva [in the *Four Hundred Verses*, Ch.8, v.8]:

> That which is abandoned by mundane beings
> Is explained to be the ultimate reality.

And in the *Commentary* [*on the Four Hundred Verses*, *Bodhisattvayogācāracatuḥśatakaṭīkā*, T 3865, by Candrakīrti]:

> This incontrovertible reality has not been thought of by the ordinary, mundane being who has not realised it. It has not been conceived by the mind. It has not become an object of the sense organs. It has been abandoned unseen because it is darkened by a film of ignorance. The object seen by the pristine cognition of the sublime ones endowed with highest acumen is the ultimate reality.

The Great Perfection thus refers to the sublime truth which is to be experienced through the pristine cognition of individual intrinsic awareness, free from the subject-object dichotomy, and which is described under various names, such as: the ultimate truth, the genuine goal, the emptiness of emptiness and the great emptiness. Concerning that Great Perfection, which possesses the matrix (*spyi-gzugs*) of pristine cognition, corresponding to the buddhas' body of reality, it is said in the *Sublime Sūtra of Clouds of Precious Jewels*:

> This doctrine genuinely transcends all written and spoken words. It genuinely transcends the entire range of expressions. It genuinely transcends all verbalisation. It is free from all conceptual elaboration and free from all that is accepted or rejected. It is free from all opening and closing, and free from all sophistry. It is not to be analysed and is not within the range of sophistry. It genuinely transcends the range of sophistry. It is non-symbolic, free from symbolism and genuinely transcends the range of symbolism. It genuinely transcends the range of the childish. It genuinely transcends the range of all demons, and genuinely transcends the range of all conflicting emotions. It genuinely transcends the range of consciousness. It does, however, lie within the range of the indeterminate, dynamic, quiescent and sublime pristine cognition. The individual, intuitive awareness of

> these [attributes] is a topic which is taintless, uncovered, pure, bountiful, supreme, sacred, perfect, permanent, firm, enduring and imperishable.[305] Whether the tathāgatas have appeared or not, this expanse of reality is exclusively present.

Through these final words, the actual meaning, pure from the beginning, of the abiding nature of the Great Perfection is revealed just as it is.

9 *The Definition of Atiyoga*

[183a.6-190a.5] Now concerning that which is implied by the name Great Perfection: It is so called because it refers to the naturally present pristine cognition, without partiality or bias, in which the meanings of all the vehicles abide and are perfect in a single essence; or it is so called because all things are pure and are perfect in the instantaneous disposition of reality or awareness, without deliberate analysis by means of intellectual apprehension. The *All-Accomplishing King* says:

> Perfect in one, perfect in two, perfect in mind.
> Perfect in one, it is the perfection of mind's creations.
> Perfect in two, it is the perfection of excellent attributes.
> Perfect in all, it is the perfection of the enlightened mind.[306]

And in the *Sūtra of the Dialogue with Sāgaramati* (*Sāgaramati-paripṛcchāsūtra*, T 152):

> Those who are purifying these modes of the doctrine
> And those who direct the teaching
> Concerning perfect enlightened mind
> Are pure in the supreme enlightened mind,
> And never covered by the stains of conflicting emotions.
> Just as the sky can be overcast
> And yet subsequently become visible again,
> So, the perfect enlightened mind of natural, inner radiance
> Can never be obscured by conflicting emotions.

Therefore, the Great Perfection, the natural expression of enlightened mind, which is the inner radiance of reality, is revealed to be unbewildered with respect to its primordially pure attributes. The *Great Sūtra of Final Nirvāṇa* also says in the same vein:

> In addition, that which is said to be genuine is the mundane middle way, and that which is said to be perfect is known

> as definitively unsurpassed and genuinely perfect, if the middle way of the final path has been earnestly applied.

According to this teaching, the former is rationally established through the valid cognition of inference, and the latter, inasmuch as it is not an object of the intellect, actually abides in the intention of this, the sublime path.

As to the verbal definition of Atiyoga: [The Sanskrit] *ati* [Tib. *shin-tu*] means utmost, and also conveys the sense of supreme, best, perfect, climax and quintessence. [The Sanskrit] *yoga* [Tib. *rnal-'byor*] means union. Since it is the culmination of all yogas, it is the utmost or highest yoga, and since it is the nucleus of all aspects of the perfection stage, there is nothing else to be reached higher than Atiyoga. It is qualified by the word "great" [Tib. *chen-po*] because through it the reality unborn like the sky, which is most profound and difficult to analyse, is directly revealed. The Transcendent Lord [Śākyamuni] also directed his intention towards the verbal definition of this [vehicle] when he said:

> To teach the doctrine
> Which is inconceivable as the sky
> Is the greatest.

Furthermore, concerning the perfection of all things of saṃsāra and nirvāṇa in the naturally present awareness itself, Nāropā has again said:

> The contemplation of uncontrived awareness is
> radiant,
> Perfect in all meanings, without activity.
> It is the ground-of-all in its naturally present state.
> It is the spontaneously present path of yoga,
> not to be traversed,
> And it is the result itself in which everything
> whatsoever is perfect.
> It is the perfect treasure of the seminal point, free
> from activity,
> The blissful pristine cognition or non-conceptualising
> mind,
> Perfected immediately by fortunate individuals,
> And it comprises the thoughts of the six classes of
> beings in saṃsāra
> And the nirvāṇa that is the Conqueror's pristine
> cognition.
> The disposition of this unique awareness that is bliss
> supreme,
> And naturally present, uncontrived reality,
> Is a spontaneously perfect disposition without
> conceptual elaboration.

The master Buddhajñānapāda has also subsumed this in his *Oral Instructions of Sublime Mañjuśrī* as follows:

> Great Perfection, the matrix of pristine cognition,
> Is the utterly pure body, the great Vajradhara.
> Having obtained, through this second stage
> Which is the essence[307] of all the glorious ones,
> The enlightenment which conforms to the frustrating
> path of three aeons,
> And which is surpassed,
> Why does the yogin, having accumulated so little bliss,
> Not meditate on this [Great Perfection]?

Commenting on this [in his *Commentary on the Oral Instructions of Sublime Mañjuśrī, Sukusumanāmamukhāgamavṛtti*, T 1866], Vitapāda has eloquently said:

> That which is called the *Great Perfection* is the second stage of the second [i.e. perfection] stage. Its *pristine cognition* including the mirror-like one is fivefold, and the *matrix* is the purest utter purity of these [five]. So it is called the *utterly pure body*. This [matrix] is called *the great Vajradhara* [i.e. the great holder of indestructible reality] because it is the resultant buddha-body, which is just what is. The expression *all the glorious ones* applies to all the buddhas because they possess intrinsic discriminative awareness, and this [Great Perfection] is the *essence* of the ultimate and relative realities of them all. In the text, *this second stage* refers only to the stage of perfection. This, the supreme skilful means of the long paths, which is said to be meditation, is expressed by words such as *frustration*, and frustration is said to refer to the *paths* which endure for *three aeons* by means of such acts of liberality [as sacrificing one's own] head. Though one may have acted out of faith and *obtained the enlightenment which conforms* to countless aeons [of activity] – from the first to the seventh [level] and the eighth to the tenth[308] – that is said to be *surpassed* because the unsurpassed Buddha, the great Vajradhara, possesses a still higher [enlightenment]. The *bliss* of this [path], being *so little* in comparison with the union in supreme bliss, *why* does the *yogin* who *accumulates* it *not meditate on this* path through which the glorious and most auspicious beings become accomplished in a single lifetime? He should meditate on [the Great Perfection] alone.

The profound abiding nature of reality, which is just what is, does not abide as an object to be realised by the ostensible reasoning of logic and sophistry. On this topic, the *Sublime Sūtra which Decisively Reveals the Intention* says:

> That which is within the range of individual,
> intuitive awareness
> Is inexpressible and cut off from conventions.
> It is ultimate reality without disputation,
> And is characterised as transcending all sophistry.

And as it is said in the *Sūtra of the Descent to Laṅkā*:

> A puerile evil sophist
> Analyses it thus, in a corpse-like manner.

The discriminative awareness produced by sophistical reflection is designated through ideas connected with points of disputation, and with characteristics and objects that are characterised, as well as with substances and attributes, and logical contrariety and inclusion – which are entirely developed by the mind and mental events, thinking in terms of conventional and symbolic doctrines expressed in words and phrases. All things are therefore established to be without independent existence, to be without consciousness, without substance, without the ground-of-all, and so forth. They are established as emptiness by the intellect, and the inference which is made therein is asserted by the sublime master Nāgārjuna to be merely a childish train of thought. In the master's own words:

> Regarding creation and cessation,
> The condition is thought alone.
> That which emerges in consciousness only
> Has no substantial, independent existence.
> If the sophist who resorts to ideas
> Should meditate only on labels,
> The terms "no independent existence" and "no
> consciousness",
> "No substance" and "no ground-of-all"
> Could be applied as well by a child!
> They are entirely generated by evil sophists.

Therefore, with reference to the ultimate truth, objects of ideas, scrutiny and inference are utterly contradictory because it is a quiescence of conceptual elaboration, and an absence of symbolic doctrines. It does not abide in the path of verbalisation and conventions and it is not felt to pursue the imagination. For these reasons, if the occasions when meditative absorption in this pristine cognition or abiding mode of reality occurs are not recognised to be this same absorption in the spiritual and philosophical goal [of Atiyoga], which is effortless with respect to fundamental reality, then all that is studied pertaining to ideas and scrutiny becomes verbal chaff; thought and understanding become waves of conceptualisation; meditation becomes the apprehension of that; and experience the appraisal of it. It becomes extremely difficult even to approach the profound meaning of the abiding nature no matter how correctly it seems to arise in the face of the intellect. The *Sūtra of the Nucleus of the Buddha* (*Buddhagarbhasūtra*, T 258) says:

> The nucleus of the buddha is not seen as it is by those who are ordinary persons, pious attendants, self-centred buddhas or even bodhisattvas. For example, when one who is born blind asks another the colour of butter and is told that it resembles snow, he touches snow and so apprehends the colour of butter to be cold. Then, when he asks what the colour of snow resembles and is told that it resembles the wings of a goose, [hearing the sound of a goose's wings] he apprehends the colour of snow to be flapping. And then, when he asks what the colour of wings resembles and [is told that] it resembles a conch shell, he touches a conch and, inasmuch as it is smooth, he apprehends [the wings] also to be smooth. Just as one born blind does not know colour as it is, whatever is described, in the same way it is very difficult to perceive the Buddha's natural expression.

Similarly, it is said in the *Oral Instructions of Sublime Mañjuśrī for Attaining the Real*:

> How can an ordinary person know
> Such excellent, supreme pristine cognition?
> It is not known by the pious attendants.
> It is not even known by the self-centred buddhas.
> It is not known by the philosophers of Yogācāra,
> Or by the Madhyamaka philosophers among the
>   bodhisattvas.
> All the buddhas of the surpassed [levels], too,[309]
> Do not even slightly know this.

Such statements have been extensively revealed by the Conqueror and his sons.

The difficulty of realising [pristine cognition] is also that the grasping components of the mind and mental events, thinking exclusively with reference to effort, self-indulgence, ideas, scrutiny, causes and results, have divided and obscured it by hope and doubt, and apprehended it in terms of objects and subjects such as the diverse symbols of conceptual elaboration. Here, on the other hand, in the general path of the Great Perfection, all conceptual elaborations become quiescent in the intrinsic expanse through meditative equipoise, without wavering from this disposition in which the presence of fundamental reality, the abiding nature without bondage or liberation is established.

Other than that, nothing is contrived save that one abides constantly and naturally in the disposition of the supreme transcendence of intellect, which is free from all activities. All the suddenly arisen stains which appear through expressive power just become naturally pure, naturally clear and naturally liberated, without renunciation or antidote being applied, in the unchanging space of intrinsic awareness, the primal emptiness, in the manner of water and waves. Other than that, "meditation" and "meditative equipoise" are the labels conventionally applied to simple absorption in the intrinsic nature, just as it naturally occurs, without looking elsewhere, without purposefully meditating, without being fixed on one [point], without intellectualising, without conceptualising, without apprehending faults, without external clarifications and without internal attainment. Therefore the essence is emptiness, in that it is without thought or expression; signlessness, in that it is without conceptualisation; and aspirationlessness, in that it is without acceptance, rejection, hope or doubt. The three spheres naturally abide therein in an utterly pure character because there is no objective reference to the three times. This is extensively indicated, as in the following example from the *Piṭaka of the Bodhisattva* (*Bodhisattvapiṭaka*, T 56):

> In this connection, one might ask, what is the utter purity of the three spheres? It is the mind not entering into that which is past, the consciousness not pursuing the future and the intellect not entering into activity connected with present events. Since one does not abide in mind, intellect or consciousness, the past is not conceived of, hankering after the future is not active in the mind, and present events are not conceptually elaborated. Since this, the sameness throughout the three times, is the utter purity of the three spheres, the sentient beings who do not comprehend it should do so. Thereby the great compassion of the Tathāgata enters into sentient beings.

And in the *Sūtra of the Greater Vehicle which is a Dialogue with Brahmaviśeṣacinti*:

> All things are utterly pure of the past dimension. All things are utterly pure of the future dimension. All things are utterly pure of the present dimension. This is called the utter purity of the three times. This is an utter purity which never becomes impure, and by virtue of this, its natural utter purity is the purest of all. For this reason all things are said to be naturally radiant.

> What, one might ask, is it that is the nature of all things? The nature of all things is emptiness; they are without objective referent. The nature of all things is signlessness; they are free from idea and concept. The nature of all things is aspirationlessness; there is no acceptance, no rejection, no thought, no force and a total absence of substantial existence. It is naturally radiant. Whatever is the nature of saṃsāra is the nature of nirvāṇa. Whatever is the nature of nirvāṇa is the nature of all things. So it is that the mind is naturally radiant.

And in the *All-Accomplishing King*:

> Since it abides in that disposition,
> It is unwavering spontaneous presence.
> Since it naturally abides, it is not contrived by
> anyone.
> This abiding in uncontrived reality
> Is revealed as the supreme among actionless deeds.
> By regarding one as two, meditation is in error.
> The single essence is not obtained by two.[310]

And the master Nāropā has also said:

> Whatever abides in subjectivity
> Turns to the result of saṃsāra itself.
> Without concluding one's desired purpose,
> The secret, blissful level of pristine cognition
> Is neither accomplished nor obtained through desire.
> It emerges from its own desireless natural expression.
> The intrinsic manner of that perception is freshness.
> It is the intention of the All-Positive King.

In the Madhyamaka of the master Nāgārjuna, also, it is clearly revealed that the supreme transcendence of intellect is the truth which requires no meditation:

> How could things which do not exist
> Number two or three and the like?
> Free from the dogmatic conceptual elaboration
> Of appearances and mind,
> Reality, transcending intellect,
> Is not an object of meditation.

And the master Nāgabodhi [in his *Means for Meditation on Atiyoga*, *Atiyogabhāvanānāma*, T 2417] illustrates the teaching that the fundamental nature is accomplished just as it naturally occurs through its own presence:

Atiyoga is without intellectual appreciation;
It is just as it is presented.
In the non-dual mind there is no eternalist view,
Nor is there a nihilist view.

Through such presence, the sublime pristine cognition transcending the intellect, the reality which is neither to be clarified nor determined, is perfectly established in the direct perception of intrinsic awareness, and, at this moment of realisation, all the doctrinal approaches eloquently revealed by the tathāgatas are gathered and abide therein. In this context, the *Sūtra of Candrapradīpa* [i.e. the *Sūtra of the King of Contemplation, Samādhirājasūtra*, T 127] says:

In thousands of world systems
The sūtras which I have explained
Differ in words and syllables but have the same meaning.
It is impossible to express them all,
But if one meditates deeply on a single word,
One comes to meditate on them all.
All the buddhas, as many as there are,
Have abundantly explained phenomena.
But if those skilled in meaning
Were to study only the phrase:
All things are emptiness,
The doctrine of the Buddha would not be scarce.

10 *The Divisions of Atiyoga*

[190a.5-190b.3] Secondly, the esoteric instructions which possess these extraordinary properties are revealed in the divisions of the Atiyoga vehicle. There are three modes of appraising the spiritual and philosophical goal according to the degree of acumen [in those requiring training]. This is stated in the *Great Array*:

> Now, after I have passed into nirvāṇa,
> This will become manifest:
> For those who hold to the mind there will be the
> Mental Class;
> For those who hold to space there will be the Spatial
> Class;
> For those who do not strive after stages
> There will be the Esoteric Instructional Class.

In this way Atiyoga has three divisions. There is the Mental Class (*sems-kyi-sde*), which teaches that all things are liberated from the extreme of renunciation, because they are not separated from mind-as-such. There is the Spatial Class (*klong-gi-sde*), which teaches that all apparitions of reality are free from activity and liberated from the extreme of the antidote, because they are perfectly gathered in Samantabhadrī, the space of reality. And there is the profound Esoteric Instructional Class (*man-ngag-gi-sde*), which teaches that the particular characteristics of truth itself are liberated from both extremes of renunciation and antidote because they are established according to the modes of reality (*yin-lugs*).

THE MENTAL CLASS

[190b.3-195a.1] First, concerning the Mental Class: The spiritual and philosophical goal of the Mental Class is that the compounded truth of the path, which is endowed with corruption and guided by firm perceptions which cling to the sequence of the vehicle, the two truths, the six transcendental perfections, the two stages and so forth, is determined (*la-bzla-ba*) in the great expanse liberated from aspects of cause and result, virtue and evil, and acceptance and rejection to be the pristine cognition of great purity and sameness. This is the natural expanse of reality which is the enlightened mind in its natural state, or the fundamental reality of ultimate truth free from conceptual elaboration. In brief, all things which dualistically appear within the subject-object dichotomy are transcended. The following passages from the *All-Accomplishing King* also touch upon this:

> In mind-as-such, which is the essence
> Of the enlightened mind,
> There is neither meditation on the view,
> Nor the performance of conduct;
> There is neither attainment of the result,
> Nor progress through levels;
> There is neither the creation of a maṇḍala,
> Nor recitation, nor the perfection stage;
> There is neither the conferral of empowerment,
> Nor the keeping of commitments.
> The pure reality spontaneously present from the beginning
> Transcends the doctrines of cause and result
> Which adventitiously strive after sequences.

And:

> If one maintains that there is cause and effect
> For Atiyoga, the yoga of the Great Perfection,
> One has not realised the meaning of Great Perfection.
> If one maintains the relative and ultimate to be two,
> One's statements both exaggerate and depreciate;
> One has not realised that there are not two.
> The realisation of the buddhas of the three times
> Is gained in the sole determination that two are not seen.

And in the *Sublime Sūtra which Reveals the Relative and Ultimate Truth* (*Āryaparamārthasaṃvṛtisatyanirdeśasūtra*, T 179):

> Mañjuśrī declared: "O son of the gods, that which is just what it is, the expanse of reality, and the utterly unborn are ultimately equivalent; ultimately they are even equivalent to the five inexpiable sins. That which is just what it is, the expanse of reality, and the utterly unborn are ulti-

mately equivalent; ultimately they are even equivalent to opinionatedness."

While such teachings are insistently denied by the assertion which is made by some of narrow intellectual vision regarding the profound abiding nature, that the Great Perfection depreciates deeds, causes and results by allowing the area of skilful means to vanish, it can none the less be realised even from the above-cited passages that, though the childish intellect truly becomes afraid of the profound abiding nature, this doctrine which speaks of the dominion of pristine cognition, transcending the objects of conscious thought, and of the uncompounded expanse of reality that is the ultimate truth, is not developed through causes and conditions. It is held essentially not to abide in the three world realms or their elements, which are compounded by positive and negative deeds, and to be completely liberated from these.

If, however, one were to hanker for this [view of narrow intelligence], then as the master Nāgārjuna's *Root Stanzas on the Madhyamaka entitled Discriminative Awareness* (Ch.18, v.5) says:

> The conceptual elaboration of deeds and conflicting
> emotions,
> Which are elaborated through discursive thought,
> Comes to cease through emptiness.

Thus [Nāgārjuna], having said that all the causes and results of positive and negative deeds have emerged merely from the symbols of conceptualising thought, then says that all these are pacified by the emptiness which is without conceptual elaborations. Concerning that pacification, too, he says (Ch.18, v.9):

> Peace which is not extraneously known
> And absence of conceptual elaboration:
> These are the attributes of this [emptiness].

And also (Ch.17, v.33):

> Conflicting emotions, deeds and bodies,
> Actors and results are as
> Castles in the sky, a mirage,
> An optical illusion and the moon's [reflection] in
> water.

And then, in his *Transcendence of Existence According to Madhyamaka* (*Madhyamakabhavasaṅkrānti*, T 3840) he says:

> Empty and without any conceptualisation,
> Without activity in the mind, neither birth nor death,
> Apparitional in appearance, devoid of virtue and evil,
> Empty of saṃsāra and nirvāṇa,

And of emptiness and compassion,
The radiant reality that is inexpressible
Apparitional radiance and emptiness
Is without substance and ideas.

In accord with such passages, which indicate the realisation of the ultimate reality, [the Mental Class] has occasion to reveal directly that the realisation which occurs in the supreme common savour of good and evil, unfettered and unliberated by all compounded positive and negative deeds is, as previously stated, the reality in which the nature of all things is determined to be aspirationless in character. Such is said in the *Authentic Conduct of a Bodhisattva* (*Āryabodhisattvacaryānirdeśasūtra*, T 184):

Ratnadatta said:

Such must be declared:
Do not abandon desire.
Subdue not hatred.
Don't clarify delusion.[311]
Do not move so as to surpass your own body.
Practice vice.
Do not eliminate opinion.
Don't teach about the entanglements.
Grasp the components as whole.
Combine the psychophysical bases into one entity.
Indulge in the sensory activity fields.
Do not progress beyond an infantile level.
Think unvirtuously.
Renounce virtue.
Do not pay attention to the Buddha.
Do not reflect upon the doctrine.
Worship not the *saṃgha*.
Do not properly undertake the trainings.
Try not to pacify wordly existence.
Do not cross the river [of suffering].

Such are the instructions with which a novice bodhisattva should be instructed and advised. Why so? Because it is this abiding condition of the reality of things that alone abides.

And it is similarly said in the glorious *Guhyasamāja Tantra* (Ch.18, vv.194-5):

There is a sameness in sentient beings and buddhas:
Which is to be attained? Who is the attainer?
The lord of attainment, supreme identity,

Has slain all the buddhas.
How is he untainted by sin?
Yet if he were so tainted,
What result would there be?[312]

And (Ch.18, vv.197-8):

All substances are like an apparition.
One who acts to create and destroy them
Therefore incurs no sin.
Merits also are the same.
Whoever is without either sin or merit
Is said to have enlightenment.

According to the extensive teachings given in passages such as these, the area of skilful means is indeed allowed to vanish. None the less, reality appears as a dream-like ripening of cause and result to those who have not realised this abiding nature and perceive dream-like phenomena to be the truth. Therefore it is said in the Madhyamaka [cf. *Introduction to the Conduct of a Bodhisattva*, Ch.9, v.11cd]:

With reference to the nature of mere illusory
  subjectivity:
One who is endowed with an illusory mind
Incurs both merit and sin.
These therefore are false as a dream.

Now the Mental Class, if classified, consists of seven categories. The first is the area of mind which holds the result to be the mind's point of origin (*'bras-bu sems-kyi byung-sar 'dod-pa'i sems-phyogs*). The result is unchanging in the original expanse [of reality], and so the mind does not wander from this disposition, although it does arise in the manner of saṃsāra from the apparitional, spontaneously present aspect of the ground that is released from the same unchanging disposition. Therefore the mind is empty of impure particulars, and its emergence from the expanse, its abiding in the expanse and its dissolving in the expanse in the manner of a miraculous event in the sky, which are derived from that apparitional aspect, are determined to be primordial liberation, and effortless, natural presence (*ye-grol rang-gzhag 'bad-rtsol med-par la-bzla-ba'o*).

The second is the area of mind which has determined deviation and obscuration (*gol-sgrib la-bzla-ba'i sems-phyogs*). The eight sequences [of the vehicle] from Anuyoga downwards are deviations from the ground because they are designated by the intellect. In this [area of the Mental Class], on the other hand, cause and conditions have been determined by the naturally present pristine cognition free from the intellect, so that the great, primordial emptiness, which is reality, is unobscured in its fundamental nature, beyond recollection, thought, bias, emergent sensation and so forth.

The third is the area of mind which shatters the source of axioms (*gtan-tshigs khungs-rdib-pa'i sems-phyogs*). By realising the truth which is uncontrived with respect to the ground, or the supreme mind-as-such, free from conceptual elaboration, the essence is liberated without being created, and its unimpeded expressive power is evenly diffused in a vast openness. There is no support for propensities, and so there is no ripening of either positive or negative attributes. This is held to be liberation in sameness, throughout the extent of saṃsāra and nirvāṇa, by means of axioms [arising within][313] which concern the primordial emptiness of reality, its natural purity and great liberation from extremes.

The fourth is the area of mind which holds that there is no descent into partiality or bias (*rgya-chad phyogs-lhung-med-par 'dod-pa'i sems-phyogs*). Although mind-as-such, the naturally present pristine cognition, encompasses all of saṃsāra and nirvāṇa, it is impartial with respect to substantial appearances, impartial with respect to insubstantial emptiness, and, being without either, it does not even descend into bias with respect to their coalescence. Since its empty essence is liberated from the extreme of eternalism and its unimpeded expressive power is liberated from the extreme of nihilism, it is the reality without activity, transcending happiness and suffering.

The fifth is the area of mind concerning the level of dogmatic philosophical systems (*phyogs-'dzin grub-mtha'i sa'i sems-phyogs*). Without abiding and without existing anywhere, the essence of mind arises unimpededly in any appearance whatsoever. It is said in the *Superior Magical Net*:

> Appearing nowhere and everywhere,
> The uncreated, magical diversity appears.
> The diverse maṇḍalas of the Conqueror, too,
> Are the great miraculous display of mind.

Accordingly, [the mind] does arise, but it is unimpeded, unapprehending and non-conceptual.

The sixth is the area of mind which transcends dogmatism concerning that which is free from the intellect (*blo-bral phyogs-'dzin-las 'das-pa'i sems-phyogs*). The naturally present pristine cognition that is free from the intellect does not exist as any truth or falsehood, however it appears. It is a display of great liberation from the extremes of being and non-being.

The seventh is the area of mind which propounds actuality in reference to mind-as-such (*sems-kyi phyogs yin-tu*[314] *smra-ba'i sems-phyogs*). Although all these appearances appear diversely because they are the display of mind, the diversity of appearances is essenceless because mind-as-such is also essenceless; and although both the subjective forms of the mind which arise and objective appearances which emerge seem to differ, they are actually indivisible in reality, the naturally present pristine cognition, where there is no such thing. The duality of saṃsāra and nirvāṇa arises from the spontaneously present vibration of [mind's] natural expressive power, and yet that which arises is without essence. The distinctive doctrine of this [Mental Class] is therefore that [the mind] proceeds to natural liberation at the very moment when it arises. It says in the *All-Accomplishing King*:

> Phenomenal existence, the world and its contents,
> All buddhas and sentient beings,
> Are created by the mind,
> And are one in the disposition of mind.

The Texts and Teaching Cycles of the Mental Class (*NGB Vols. 1-3*)

[195a.1-195b.3] The tantras which express this Mental Class are said to number two million two hundred thousand verses. If these are subsumed, they comprise the Three Spaces (*klong gsum-po*) which are contained in six thousand three hundred sections (*bam-po*), namely, the Space in which Reality is Inexpressible (*chos-nyid brjod-du med-pa'i klong*), the Space in which the View is Not Absent (*lta-ba min-pa med-pa'i klong*) and the Space in which Conduct is Not Present (*spyod-pa yin-pa med-pa'i klong*). If further subsumed, these are gathered into the Three Vaults [or Appendices] (*'phyong-gsum*), namely, the Vault which Directly Reaches the Abiding Ground (*gnas-pa gzhi-thog-phebs-pa'i 'phyong*), the Vault into the Liberation of Appearances Right Where They Are (*snang-ba rang-sar grol-ba'i 'phyong*) and the Vault into the Equalisation without Differentiation (*ngo-mnyam tha-dad med-pa'i 'phyong*).

The texts of the Mental Class also comprise one thousand and three great tantra sections which are entitled the *Fifty Nails Undeviating with Respect to Reality* (*chos-nyid-la 'chugs-pa med-pa'i gzer-bu lnga-bcu*), the *Five Hundred and Eleven Situations in which Objects are Viewed as Mind* (*yul sems-la lta-ba'i gnas lnga-bgya-bcu-gcig*), the *Twenty Thousand Simultaneous Distinctions between Appearances and Mind* (*snang-sems cig-car-du shan-'byed-pa khri-phrag-gnyis*), the *Fifty Thousand Determinations Made in the All-Surpassing View* (*lta-ba thod-rgal-du la-bzla-ba lnga-khri*) and the *Thousand Situations which Cut Through the Idea of Being in Meditation* (*sgom-yod rtog-pa gcod-pa'i gnas cig-stong*).

If this spiritual and philosophical goal of the Mental Class is essentialised: All the apparitions of reality which appear are perfect in reality, the expanse of the enlightened mind, without having to seal all phenomenal appearances with the seal of reality. The awareness of appearances as the expressive power [of mind], or as a mere display [of mind], accompanies them without deliberate recognition. The glorious Nārotapa [Nāropā] also says:

> This nature of diverse appearances
> Is reality, and thus indivisible.
> Therefore, for the radiant mind-as-such or intention,
> In which [appearances and reality] are coalesced,
> Nothing even slightly appears that is not reality.
> This essence through which everything appears
> Is seen as the nucleus of pristine cognition itself.
> Essentially it is inexpressible.

THE SPATIAL CLASS

[195b.4-197b.4] Secondly, concerning the Spatial Class: In the vast space of Samantabhadrī, the reality of naturally present pristine cognition, all apparitions of reality which appear are merely adornments of that array which manifests in and of itself. Other than that, they do not exist as bondage and liberation, or as objects which arise and their actual arising. It is therefore not claimed, as in the Mental Class, that [the apparitions of reality] appear as the expressive power and display [of the mind]. The spiritual and philosophical goal of this Spatial Class is the establishment of a great infinity of primordial liberation, unscrutinised in terms of relational proof, explicit negation of existence, implicitly affirmative negation of existence, or purity and impurity. The master Nāropā's *Means for Attaining the Real* also says:

> The effortless, unconceived awareness,
> An uncontrived, blissful space manifest in and of itself,
> Arises as the spontaneously present space of pristine
> cognition.
> Naturally present and pervasive as the sky.
> This enlightened mind of self-manifesting display
> Is a blissful space of illusory pristine cognition.
> It actually radiates as the holders of the pristine
> cognition
> Of intuitive awareness, who are a naturally present
> illusion.

If classified, this Spatial Class consists of four categories [of teaching]. The essence of the first, the teaching of the Black Space propounded as the Absence of Causes (*klong nag-po rgyu-med-du smra-ba*), is that this naturally present pristine cognition, in its natural state, does not refer to either the apparitions of reality or reality itself because it is unchanging, naturally beyond causes and conditions, and without spatial parts. There are three subclassifications, namely, the Black Space of Deeds (*mdzad-pa klong-nag*), the Black Space of Spirituality (*thugs-rje klong-nag*) and the Black Space of Emanation (*sprul-pa klong-nag-gi sde*).

As for the essence of the second, the teaching of the Variegated Space propounded as Diversity (*klong khra-bo sna-tshogs-su smra-ba*): It is positively held that the appearances in the display of this naturally present pristine cognition are an adornment and display of reality, which appears as a naturally arisen diversity; and it is negatively held that the [same] display, which arises all-pervasively and without direction, is beyond refutation and proof. There are three subclassifications, namely, the Variegated Space which propounds Being in Conformity with the Mental Class (*yod-smra sems-sde dang mthun-pa'i klong khra-bo*), the Variegated Space which propounds Non-Being in Accordance with the Natural Position [of the Spatial Class, *med-smra rang-gnas dang mthun-pa'i klong khra-bo*], and the Variegated Space which propounds Both Being and Non-Being in Conformity with the Esoteric Instructional Class (*yod-med man-ngag dang mthun-pa'i klong khra-bo*).

According to the essence of the third, the teaching of the White Space propounded as the Mind (*klong dkar-po sems-su smra-ba*): It is held that everything which arises as outer appearance and inner awareness from the disposition of naturally present awareness is a display of mind, that appearances and conditions are pure from their basis with nothing to be done because they are liberated right where they are, and that there is nothing to be attained in the abiding nature. There are two subclassifications, namely, the White Space of the Inexpressible, Great Natural Arising (*brjod-med rang-shar chen-po'i klong dkar-po*), and the White Space of the Non-Duality of View and Meditation (*lta-sgom gnyis-su-med-pa'i klong dkar-po*).

Concerning the essence of the fourth, the teaching of the Infinite Space in which Cause and Result are Determined (*klong rab-'byams rgyu-'bras la-bzla-ba*): It is held that all things which arise from the disposition of the naturally present pristine cognition are known through mind inasmuch as they are apparent, and are known through the abiding nature inasmuch as they are not apparent. There are four subclassifications, namely, the Outer Infinity which concerns Freedom from Activity (*bya-ba dang bral-ba phyi'i rab-'byams*), the Inner Infinity which propounds the Spiritual and Philosophical Goal in accordance with the Texts of the Spatial Class itself (*grub-mtha' rang-gzhung-du smra-ba nang-gi rab-'byams*), the Secret Infinity which concerns the Dispelling of Obstacles (*gegs-bsal-ba gsang-ba'i rab-'byams*), and the Infinity of the Real which Unties the Essential (*gnad-bkrol-ba de-kho-na-nyid-kyi rab-'byams*).

If these [four kinds of Spatial Class] are then subsumed, they comprise the teaching of the Four Spaces (*klong-bzhi*) concerning display (*rol-pa*), adornment (*rgyan*), reality (*chos-nyid*), and freedom from activity (*bya-bral*). As to the first, [the Space of Display]: It is present because the display of mind-as-such does not change or alter from the disposition in which it unimpededly arises; and it is absent because this display which is without substantiality is not apprehended as an extreme. Its intention is openly directed in the manner of the sky.

As to the second, [the Space of Adornment]: Appearance, mind, natural presence and freedom from both artificiality and corruption, which successively arise as primordial adornments, arise unimpededly from that unborn disposition [of reality]. Appearances and mind are therefore neither refuted nor proven. Its intention is one of great natural rhythm and natural radiance.

As to the third, [the Space of Reality]: All things, whatever their source, neither come about, nor abide, nor cease. Though all the expressive powers of their display appear from the disposition of reality, they remain equipoised in the disposition of reality, just as the four elements do not wander from space.

Then, as to the fourth, [the Space of Freedom from activity]: Acceptance and rejection through strenuous efforts are not required with reference to anything whatsoever. Everything abides in an uncompounded realm, in the manner of the sky, because it abides not to be done but primordially completed, not to be liberated but primordially liberated, not to be purified but primordially purified, and not to be attained but primordially accomplished.

If these categories of the Spatial Class are similarly subsumed, they are gathered into Nine [Spaces], namely, the Space in which the View is Unchanging (*lta-ba 'pho-'gyur med-pa'i klong*), the Space in which Meditation is neither Present nor Absent (*bsgom-pa yin-min med-pa'i klong*), the Space in which there is neither Hope nor Doubt for the Result (*'bras-bu re-dogs med-pa'i klong*), the Space in which the Essence is neither Accomplished nor Clarified (*ngo-bo grub-bsal med-pa'i klong*), the Space in which Natural Expression is Unimpeded (*rang-bzhin ma-'gags-pa'i klong*), the Space in which Appearance and Mind are Liberated with respect to Characteristics (*mtshan-nyid-la snang-sems grol-ba'i klong*), the Space in which the Expanse is Unchanging (*dbyings 'pho-'gyur med-pa'i klong*), the Space in which Display Unimpededly and Naturally Arises (*rol-pa 'gag-med rang-shar-gyi klong*) and the Space which is the Total Presence of Spontaneous Sameness and Primordial Liberation (*lhun-mnyam ye-grol cog-bzhag-gi klong*).

If these, in turn, are subsumed, they are gathered into Three Spaces, namely, the Space of Supremely Vast Spontaneous Presence (*lhun-grub yangs-pa chen-po'i klong*), the Space of Effortless Intrinsic Radiance (*rang-gsal bya-rtsol med-pa'i klong*) and the Space which is Primordially Accomplished though Nothing is Done (*ma-byas ye-nas grub-pa'i klong*).

The Texts of the Spatial Class (NGB Vols. 3-4)

[197b.4-198a.4] There are eleven thousand chapters and six million four hundred thousand verses subsumed under the titles of the three thousand tantras, which extensively reveal these modes [of the Spatial Class]. These, too, are gathered into the *Eighty Thousand Aspects of Determination (la-bzla-ba khri-phrag-brgyad)*; these are then gathered into *Twenty Thousand Aspects of Distinction (shan-'byed khri-phrag gnyis)*; and these, in turn, are then gathered into *Nine Hundred Conclusions ('gags dgu-brgya)*. Along with *Two Thousand Essentials (gnad nyis-stong)* and the *Fifty Nails (gzer-bu lnga-bcu)*, all of these, if subsumed, are gathered into three categories, namely, Liberation from Activity (*byas-grol*), Liberation in the Establishment [of the Abiding Nature] (*bzhag-grol*) and Direct Liberation (*cer-grol*).

It is said in the *Dohā Composed by Lord Maitripā* (*Mahāmudrā-kanakamālā*, T 2454):

> Non-conceptual, without ideas,
> Transcending objects of ideas and scrutiny,
> Unthinking, without mind, utterly unthinkable,
> Without support or lack of support,
> Or going, coming and abiding,
> Awakening to the happiness and sorrows
> Of saṃsāra and nirvāṇa
> In the space of supreme bliss,
> Uncontrived, unwavering and naturally relaxed,
> Is the inner radiance, free from coming or going,
> In which mental events have been interrupted.
> Its appearance is ineffable and it is without any
> master.
> It is recognised to be reality,
> The intrinsically radiant awareness, and the body of
> reality.

Passages such as this, too, have arrived at the spiritual and philosophical goal of the [Spatial Class].

THE ESOTERIC INSTRUCTIONAL CLASS

[198a.4-200b.3) Thirdly, there is the Esoteric Instructional Class: This holds distinction over the two lower [Mental and Spatial Classes]. The Mental Class, by referring positively to the mind, has mostly achieved the area of profundity rather than radiance, and yet, by not realising the expressive power of radiance to be reality, it almost clings to mental scrutiny. The Spatial Class, though equally achieving profundity and radiance, rather than the mental scrutiny which apprehends reality, almost lapses into a deviation point within the range of emptiness. The Esoteric Instructional Class, on the other hand, is actually superior because it gathers within the expanse of reality that is free from conceptual elaboration, all apparitions of reality which appear through the self-manifesting, spontaneously present and natural, expressive power. As such [these apparitions] are the tone of the primordially pure, inexpressible essence, the supreme transcendence of intellect. It is said in the *Great Array of the Highest*:

> O holder of indestructible reality,
> If this is not established,
> There are those who cling to mental scrutiny
> And those who resort, in particular, to nothing
> at all.
> Therefore this definitive, secret nucleus,
> As a butter lamp amid the darkness,
> Or as an elephant among oxen,
> A lion among wild animals,
> Or a horseman among pedestrians,
> Is superior to them all.

The essence of this Esoteric Instructional Class is contrary to those bases and doctrines which refer to the dichotomy of bewilderment and non-bewilderment, or of realisation and non-realisation, by dividing the originally liberated and primordially pure reality into ephemeral objects that are to be inspected and the consciousness which makes inspection. From the position of the intrinsic essence, free from conceptual elaboration, both the subjective perception and objective focal point of perception are equal in their lack of authenticity, and, other than in mere conventional usage, the thoughts and expressions which apprehend that dichotomy are genuinely transcended. This class therefore resembles a geomantic centre which directly reaches the essential point, transcending intellect, thoughts of the mind, thinking processes and mental scrutiny. It is said by Mañjuśrī:

> Inwardly radiant by nature,
> Primordially pure as the sky,
> The primordial realities have abandoned
> characteristics.
> They are neither things nor reality:
> Similar to space which is without substantiality,
> They are liberated from all words and phonetic
> expressions.

As long as one refers to objects designated in views other than this, the posture of clinging to the subjective mind cannot be abandoned, and one who has not abandoned that comes to possess [corruptions] which are unceasing and [continually] arising, so that the root of worldly existence cannot be removed. As the same text says:

> The emptiness of the conquerors
> Is said definitively to remove all views.

If this [Esoteric Instructional Class] is classified, it comprises three categories, namely, the Random (*kha-'thor*), the Oral Tradition (*kha-gtam*) and the Teaching which Accords with its own Textual Tradition of Tantras (*rgyud rang-gzhung-du bstan-pa*, NGB Vols. 9-10). The essence of the first, [the Random category of esoteric instructions], is that the pristine cognition, which transcends the intellect, instantaneously arises without regard for extraneous classifications and clarifications. Its subdivisions are twofold: With reference to establishment [of reality], there are the Esoteric Instructions which Conclude the Path (*bzhag-pa lam-gyi mtha'-gcod-pa'i man-ngag*), and with reference to liberation, there are the Esoteric Instructions of Pure Power which Disclose the Path (*grol-ba stobs dag-pa lam mngon-gyur gyi man-ngag*).

The second [category of Esoteric Instructions], those given in the manner of an Oral Tradition, are essentially[315] free from the intellect and unbewildered. They naturally shatter the source of conceptualisation and, characteristically, they are free from deliberate recognition. Its subdivisions are twofold: the Oral Tradition which Permeates All Discourse (*gleng-ba yongs-la bor-ba'i kha-gtam*) and the Oral Tradition which is Divulged in Speech at No Fixed Time (*khar-phog dus-med-pa'i kha-gtam*).

The third [category of esoteric instructions], the Teaching which Accords with its own Textual Tradition of Tantras, is essentially the point of origin of all transmitted precepts. It is naturally effortless with respect to renunciation and acceptance because it is devoid of saṃsāra and nirvāṇa; and, characteristically, it is untouched by disputation concerning emptiness because it does not abide in sounds or words. Its subdivisions are fourfold: those transmitted precepts given in the manner of the Full Summation of the View (*lta-ba sgang dril-ba*), those given in the manner of Blood-letting which Removes Obstacles (*gtar-ga gegs-sel*), those given in a manner which Reveals the Hidden (*gab-pa mngon-du phyung*), and those given in the manner of Exegeses which are Naturally Clear (*bshad-pa rang-gsal*). These, too, are classified into many profound and vast subdivisions with respect to view, meditation and conduct such as: their Hidden Point (*gnad gab-pa*) and its Revelation (*mngon-du phyung-pa*); the Extent of their Warmth (*drod-tshad*); the Essence which having Penetrated the Essentials of Object and Consciousness Throws Open the Naked Awareness (*yul-shes gnad-la bor-nas rig-pa ther-la 'byin-pa'i gnad*); the Opposition to Bewilderment at its Ground (*'khrul-pa gzhi-la bzlog-pa*); and the Essential Penetration of the Seminal Point (*thig-le gnad-la dbab-pa*).

If these are subsumed, they comprise four [cycles], namely, the Outer Cycle which Resembles the Body (*lus-dang 'dra-ba phyi-skor*), the Inner Cycle which Resembles the Eyes (*mig-dang 'dra-ba nang-skor*), the Secret Cycle which Resembles the Heart (*snying-dang 'dra-ba gsang-skor*) and the Unsurpassedly Secret Cycle which Resembles the Perfection of All (*thams-cad rdzogs-pa-dang 'dra-ba yang-gsang bla-na med-pa'i skor*).

According to the first, or the Outer Cycle: Essentially, the five poisons are carried on the path because there are no conflicting emotions. Naturally, whatever appears arises as reality because there is no laborious accomplishment; and characteristically, emptiness is not divided into anything at all because there are no spatial parts.

As for the second, the Inner Cycle: Essentially, it is the signless reality because it has transcended formation. Naturally, it is the pristine cognition which permanently and continuously abides because it neither goes nor comes. And characteristically, too, it resembles roots in that it penetrates both saṃsāra and nirvaṇa; it resembles a tree trunk in that the intrinsic face [of awareness] turns in different [directions]; it resembles branches in that the appearance of expressive power is extensive on all sides; it resembles flowers in that the range of radiance is unimpeded; and it resembles fruit in that its diversity is ripened into one.

As for the third, the Secret Cycle: Essentially, it disregards the three kinds of discriminative awareness because introduction to reality (*ngo-sprod*) and realisation occur simultaneously. Naturally, it disregards the power of experience because the cessation of breathing[316] and liberation are simultaneous; and characteristically, it disregards the two causally based provisions because buddhahood and the emergence of spirituality are simultaneous.

Then, concerning the fourth, or the Unsurpassedly Secret Cycle: Essentially, it disregards the act of perception because there is nothing to be perceived. Naturally, this reality does not abide in mental scrutiny because it is directly perceived; and characteristically, vital energy itself is united in the expanse of the original ground through the four visionary appearances (*snang-ba bzhi*), without constructing the hope for a result in a future lifetime.

The Texts of the Esoteric Instructional Class (NGB Vols. 5-10)

[200b.3-202b.1] It is said [by the buddhas] in their transmitted precepts that the meanings and expressions contained in such [categories] of the Esoteric Instructional Class are equal to the limits of the sky. They include *Twenty Thousand Tantras of Expressive Words* (*rjod-byed tshig-gi rgyud khri-phrag gnyis*), *Thirty-five Thousand Chapters* (*le'u stong-phrag sum-cu rtsa lnga*), *Six Million Four Hundred Thousand Verses* (*śva-lo-ka 'bum-phrag drug-cu rtsa-bzhi*), *Five Thousand Essentials* (*gnad stong-phrag-lnga*), *Eight Great Vaults* [or *Appendices*, *'phyong-chen-po brgyad*],

One Hundred and Eighty Nails (*gzer-bu brgya-dang brgyad-cu*), *Nine Hundred Thousand Conclusions* (*'gags stong-phrag dgu-brgya*), *Seventy Thousand Distinctions* (*shan-'byed khri-phrag-bdun*), and *One Hundred and Fifty Thousand Determinations* (*la-bzla-ba 'bum-phrag phyed-dang gnyis*).

The four [cycles] of the Esoteric Instructional Class are also gathered in Three Spaces, namely, the Space of Unceasing Display (*rol-pa 'gags-pa med-pa'i klong*), the Space in which there is Nothing Unliberated in the Intellect (*blo-la ma-grol-ba med-pa'i klong*) and the Space in which the Essence is Neither Good Nor Evil (*ngo-bo-la bzang-ngan med-pa'i klong*). And the nucleus of the Esoteric Instructions is also fourfold: namely, that which Unties the Essential (*gnad-bkrol-ba*), that which Brings Final Closure [of Obstacles] (*'gag-bsdam-pa*), that which Introduces [Intrinsic Awareness] (*ngo-sprad-pa*) and that which Visibly Establishes the Intrinsic Essential (*mngon-sum rang-gnad-la dbad-pa*).

The View and Path of the Esoteric Instructional Class

According to this tradition of the Esoteric Instructional Class of the Great Perfection, which is the nucleus of all teachings, the individual intuitive awareness is an object to be experientially cultivated as pristine cognition. It transcends the mind which possesses the nature of the eight aggregates of consciousness, the corrupt grasping component. On this, indeed, it is said in the *Lion's Perfect Expressive Power*:

> Propensities of the mind and pristine
> cognition are insubstantial
> Though pristine cognition has been freed from all
> propensities,
> The diverse propensities are collected by the mind.
> If mind and pristine cognition are not differentiated as two,
> The root of objective appearances is not cut off.
> Although the unconditioned reality is pure,
> It is difficult to realise.

And also, in Nāropā's *Means for Attaining the Real*:

> When this intuitive awareness of the enlightened mind
> Is under the sway of the bewilderment of propensities,
> The diversity, although non-existent, is materialised by
> imagination.
> Though the propensities of the mind outwardly appear,
> The awareness is unchanging inner radiance.

And:

> Free from the movement of the conceptualising mind,

The inner radiance of intrinsic awareness is not
grasped.

In brief, all sensory appearances and objects of thought are the things of saṃsāra which appear through the mind and have the grasping mind as their particular characteristic. The *Sublime Transcendental Perfection of Discriminative Awareness in Eight Thousand Lines* makes the very same point when it says, concerning mind-as-such which transcends the mundane mind and its mental events, that:

> In mind there exists no mind. The nature of mind is inner radiance.

Furthermore, the *Sublime Pagoda of Precious Jewels* says:

> Free from mind, intellect and consciousness, the essential of contemplation, indeed, is not abandoned. This is the inconceivable mystery of the Tathāgata's mind.

And the sublime Nāgārjuna has also said:

> Inasmuch as there is no mind, there is nothing at all,
> There is neither body nor psychophysical base;
> Hence, according to the non-dual path,
> This is well explained as just what is.

Extensive quotations such as these also have an intention directed towards the awareness which transcends the mind.

This same awareness is also a primordial liberation (*ye-grol*) because its intrinsic face is uncovered from the beginning by the things of saṃsāra, so that the basis of the grasping components of worldly existence has ceased. It is a natural liberation (*rang-grol*) because, uncontrived by any antidote, all that arises [is liberated] without reference to other liberating activities, in the manner of a snake which has naturally uncoiled its knots. It is a direct liberation (*cer-grol*) because all the consciousnesses of the eight aggregates are naturally liberated with great suddenness in an instant, without a duality of subject and object. And it is a liberation from extremes (*mtha'-grol*) because it does not abide within the three times or within any perceptual object.

After this intrinsic awareness, the naturally present pristine cognition which abides in the dispostion of these four great modes of liberation, has been ascertained to be the distinctive doctrine of this path, in order that it might be appropriately realised, there exist two paths: Cutting Through Resistance (*khregs-chod*), which is oriented towards the emptiness aspect or primordially pure awareness without conceptual elaboration, and so causes the cessation of [inherently] empty phenomena; and All-Surpassing Realisation (*thod-rgal*), which clarifies the apparitional aspect or corporeal objects into inner radiance in a spontaneously present manner, and so causes the cessation of apparitional reality.

Cutting Through Resistance

[202b.1-204a.5] Concerning the first of these, Cutting Through Resistance, which establishes the primordially pure abiding nature: The intention of this supreme vehicle is directed towards awareness, the fundamental reality without bondage or liberation, the essence itself which is primordially pure, uncontrived and utterly impartial. It has not fallen into any direction whatsoever because it cannot be said that "the essence is intrinsically this". This naked, core-penetrating (*zang-thal*) awareness, transcending thought and expression, is itself emptiness in that it is free from the conceptualising intellect; it is signless in that it is not symbolised by verbal or written word during the path; and it is aspirationless in that from the standpoint of the result there is neither hope nor doubt concerning something that is to be obtained. Owing to that awareness, the attributes of enlightenment are perfected, and it is that awareness in which the [aforementioned] three natural approaches to liberation are present as inner radiance. In it, the things subsumed by consciousness which refers to the view, meditation, conduct and result either with or without thought,[317] do not exist. By looking for [awareness] it is not seen; by meditating on it, it is not realised; by conduct no benefit is incurred; and the result is not to be obtained. Because it is not [to be obtained], there is nothing to be done with respect to purification on the levels, progression on the paths, or referring to the results and their respective sequences. The glorious Saraha [in his *Song of Esoteric Instruction: An Inexhaustible Treasure Store*, *Dohākośopadeśagīti*, T 2264] says:

> Listen! do not regard cause and result as two.
> There are no causes and results which arise as substances.
> If this yogin's mind is maddened
> By the mind which hopes and doubts,
> The co-emergent pristine cognition will be bound therein.
> Listen! since that is without independent existence,
> Do not say it is an object of meditation.
> If, having realised both the object of meditation
> And act of meditating,
> One were to think of it as enlightenment
> With a dualising intellect,
> One would have committed a sin against oneself.

There are some who, not having comprehended such an abiding condition as this, depreciate the profundities of the perfection stage, holding that the resultant buddha-body of form is not achieved without the accumulation of the two provisions, including the causal creation stage and so forth. But their action is one which abandons the doctrine. According to this path [of Cutting Through Resistance] the body of reality itself is obtained because it is the culmination of the buddhas. Elsewhere it is accordingly said [in the *Diamond Cutter*, *Vajracchedikā*, T 16, para. 26, vv.1-2b]:

> Those who see me as form,
> Those who perceive me as sound,
> Those persons, who remain on the false path,
> Do not perceive me.
> It is the body of reality
> That is the Buddha's.

In this way, the nucleus of indestructible reality, the primordially pure awareness, enters into the qualitative experience of the original body of reality's modes (*yin-lugs*). In the manner of the naturally radiant sun, it is liberated from the obscuring action of conceptual elaboration, and it is held to be seen in the present moment, just like the sun, once the overwhelming ideas of the mind, which activate the eight sequences [of the vehicle] and cause obscuration through their dependence on the symbolic creation stage, have been purified of their obscuration. Since it possesses such distinctions, the naturally present pristine cognition, uncontrived by a conceptual view, meditation, conduct, and result, is determined in its natural establishment. This awareness is just present in its natural disposition, open, uncontrived, unconstructed, unmeditating, unwavering, unbewildered, without entering into ideas and scrutiny, aloof, naked, and relaxed; and it is only nominally called a view and a meditation. It says in the *Tantra of the Great Natural Arising of Awareness*:

> In the awareness that is without conceptual elaboration
> How could there be bewilderment and ignorance?
> In the pristine cognition that is without mind
> How could there be ignorance and propensities?

So it is that, through meditative equipoise, the fundamental, uncontrived abiding nature of great primordially pure awareness is directly introduced, and there can be no bondage through the subject-object dichotomy. The means of not contaminating it with objects of meditation or the act of meditating is excellently revealed by teachings such as the Twelve Great Laughs of Indestructible Reality (*rdo-rje gad-mo chen-po bcu-gnyis*).

If firm experience in this very path has come about, finally one dissolves into a great, primordially pure point of liberation. The coarse atoms of the four elements are transformed into the power of the fire of pristine cognition, and, having been so purified, they vanish accompanied by great miraculous events. If, on the other hand, activity on behalf of others is resorted to, the dissolving atoms emanate as, and then leave behind, relics of four kinds, while the awareness centred in the expanse of the body of reality then acts on behalf of living beings through unceasing emanational bodies.

All-Surpassing Realisation

[204a.5-211b.4] Concerning the second [path], the esoteric instructions of All-Surpassing Realisation which establish the spontaneously present visionary appearances: According to Cutting Through Resistance, the bewildering appearance of apprehended objects, without ground and without root, is directly liberated in fundamental reality. However, this [All-Surpassing Realisation] is superior to that lower path, because herein all those apparitional aspects of the three realms are liberated in the inner radiance of a great seminal point of five-coloured light, which is the natural tone of awareness. It is said in the *Penetration of Sound*:

> This [view] is that, upon the display of [subtle]
> objects
> By the disposition [of awareness],
> Without entering into the conditions of saṃsāra,
> Penetrating them to the very core,
> Transcending the [coarse] apparitional aspect
> Of objects and consciousness,
> They are directly liberated from their respective
> grounds.[318]

And the glorious Nāropā also says:

> All substances by nature
> Are the seminal point of the expanse of reality.
> Concerning the means for attaining this,
> The nucleus, awareness itself, arises,
> And so the darkness of extremes is purified by its
> disposition.
> Through this naturally present attainment,
> That is not to be attained,
> The three realms are proven to be inner radiance,
> the buddha-mind.

This explanation briefly indicates the path through which the visionary appearance of the expanse and the indestructible chains [of light] (*rdo-rje lu-gu rgyud*),[319] which are the nucleus or awareness, are matured. Finally, the outer and inner elements of the three realms dissolve into inner radiance through the visionary appearance of the cessation of their reality (*chos-nyid zad-pa'i snang-ba*).

Now this [path of All-Surpassing Realisation] is also subsumed in the Three Supportive Essentials of the Body (*bca'-ba lus-kyi gnad-gsum*), the Three Essentials which Guide [the Eyes] towards the Expanse (*'khrid-pa dbyings-kyi gnad-gsum*) and the Three Essentials of Objective Appearance (*snang-ba yul-gyi gnad-gsum*), which are to be experientially cultivated. And when [the essential of light] within the last of these groupings is classified according to the four lamps (*sgron-ma bzhi*), it consists of the watery lamp of the far-sighted [eyes] (*rgyangs-zhag chu'i sgron-ma*), the lamp of the expanse of awareness (*rig-pa dbyings-kyi sgron-ma*), the lamp of emptiness which is the seminal point (*thig-le stong-pa'i sgron-ma*), and the lamp of naturally present discriminative awareness (*shes-rab rang-byung-gi sgron-ma*).

The first of these lamps, [the watery lamp of the far-sighted eyes], senses the appearances which arise because it externally perceives the tone of awareness. The second, [the lamp of the expanse of awareness], is the ground from which the inner expanse arises as a tone of external radiance. The third, [the lamp of emptiness which is the seminal point], is the support which activates the arising forms. And the fourth, [the lamp of naturally present discriminative awareness], is the unerring abiding nature of higher insight, or the face of awareness, when it arises as a pure essence and not as a [gross] object.

Concerning these divisions, the *Tantra of the Great Natural Arising of Awareness* says:

> In the maṇḍala which is empty as the sky
> Four kinds of uncontrived lamp
> Radiate owing to the unimpeded reality.
> Concerning the lamp of the expanse of awareness:
> In the centre of space which is empty as the sky,
> The body of light, the natural expression of the
> expanse,
> Radiates in unimpeded, unceasing forms.
> The body of buddha-mind, endowed with five
> pristine cognitions,
> Arises as an indestructible chain [of light].
> Its coming and going
> And its movement, too, are indeterminate.
> Penetration of this lamp of the expanse of
> awareness,
> If awareness is not disturbed,
> Is well explained to be unchanging realisation.
>
> If the lamp of naturally present discriminative
> awareness
> Has cut off all exaggerations,
> If the lamp of emptiness which is the seminal point,

Has effortlessly arisen,
And if, by means of the watery lamp of the
far-sighted eyes,
It is regarded without wavering;
That is said to be the limit of conclusive meditation.

In this way, the awareness of higher insight regards the indestructible chains [of light], and becomes skilled in the four visionary appearances (*snang-ba bzhi*) through the succession of their experiences. The entrance to the buddha-fields is opened through the visionary appearance of the direct perception of reality (*chos-nyid mngon-sum-gi snang-ba*). Subsequently, the emanational body is seen through the visionary appearance of ever increasing contemplative experience (*nyams gong-'phel-ba'i snang-ba*) in which the seminal point is almost matured in the body. The body of perfect rapture is seen through the visionary appearance of reaching the limit of awareness (*rig-pa tshad-phebs-kyi snang-ba*) in which [the seminal point] is matured in the body. Then, all appearances are purified in the maṇḍala of a single, great seminal point. All the things that are designated by the intellect cease and the body of reality is seen through the visionary appearance in which [those things] cease to be even apprehended in reality (*chos-nyid-du 'dzin-pa tsam-yang zad-pa'i snang-ba*). Accordingly, it is said in the *Penetration of Sound*:

Through the vision that is direct perception of reality
The extremes which persist in mental scrutiny are
transcended.
Through ever increasing contemplative experience
Bewildering appearances vanish,
And the pristine cognition of the intermediate state
is actualised.
Through the visionary appearance of reaching the
limit of awareness
Appearances on the path which realises the three
bodies are transcended.
Through the visionary appearance of their cessation
in reality
The continuity of saṃsāra with its three realms
is broken.

An almost similar aspect of this maturation of the seminal point in the body is also referred to in the *Kālacakra Tantra*:

The mind which apprehends space in all directions,
And the unclosing eye which properly enters the path
of indestructible reality,
Out of emptiness come to perceive

> Apparitions of smoke, mirage, radiance, immaculate
> sky and butter lamps,
> Blazing flames, the moon, the sun, vajras,
> Supreme features and seminal points.
> And in their midst is the form of the buddhas,
> The manifold bodies of perfect rapture,
> Without objective appearance.

Therefore, in this unsurpassedly secret [vehicle] it is most essential for one who is learned in directly making into the path the naturally present awareness, which transcends the saṃsāra-based mind from the beginning, to reach the result swiftly and directly. If it were not so, the saṃsāra-based mind and mental events during the period of experiential cultivation would not be transcended. Their result would be saṃsāra itself. However, since cause and result are infallibly identical, there is no occasion for lapsing into deviation.

In particular, the instantaneous awareness itself, which regards this manifest inner radiance, reverses the mind and mental events of the three world realms along with the ground-of-all. It is the reversal of the realm of desire because it regards [inner radiance] with direct perception and is without the ebb and flow of internal imagination. It is the reversal of the realm of form because there is no antidote which allocates radiance to the radiant disposition. It is the reversal of the formless realm because there is no intellect which clings in the disposition of reality to one-pointed non-conceptualisation. It is the reversal of the ground-of-all because there is an awareness of the pure essences. It is the reversal of the consciousness of the ground-of-all because the naturally present, pristine cognition is determined. It is the reversal of the consciousnesses of the five senses because it does not appear to pursue ordinary [sensations] other than the objects of apparitional inner radiance; and, at that time, it is the reversal of the consciousness of the intellect and the consciousness of conflicting emotions because there is no idea which scrutinises and there is an absence of all thoughts of desire and hatred. In brief, the pristine cognition of the buddhas, liberated from the mind and mental events of the three world realms, is conclusive in that which is nothing other than quiescence [i.e. nirvāṇa]. Therefore, it is said in the *Enumeration of Doctrines which is the Great Pagoda of Precious Jewels*:

> Śāntamati, this mystery of the Tathāgata's mind is without mind, intellect and consciousness; nor is the essential of contemplation abandoned either. This is the inconceivable mystery of the Tathāgata's mind.

Those spiritual and philosophical systems of the secret mantra which hold the co-emergent pristine cognition to refer to the blissful, radiant and non-conceptual pristine cognitions, which are effected in the lower tantras by the entry of the vital energy from the right and left channels (*ro-rkyang*) into the central channel (*dbu-ma*),[320] do not reverse the consciousnesses of the eight aggregates. This is because [in those systems] the bliss of sensation is subsequently created by the intellect and by the intellect that is conscious of conflicting emotions. The range of non-conceptualising mind does not proceed elsewhere beyond the ground-of-all. In addition, they hold that the vital energy and the [white and red] seeds[321] enter from the right and left pathways into the central channel and liberate each respective knot in the central channel; and that by this power the renunciations and realisations of the ten levels arise. This is an essential point of deviation, because [according to those systems] the vital energy and the mind remain in the centres (*rtsa-'dab*) which correspond to the six classes of living beings, giving rise to impure, bewildering appearance.[322]

In this [All-Surpassing Realisation], on the other hand, the vital energies are absorbed in a natural quiescence, and apart from that, do not enter into the central channel and so forth. When the vital energy of the respective centres has become naturally pure, the vital energy of pristine cognition (*ye-shes-kyi rlung*) naturally radiates right where it is within a channel of light. Thus, there is no occasion for impure, bewildering appearances to arise from the natural expression of the buddha-bodies, fields and light, which are appearances of pure pristine cognition. The channels of light within the central channel multiply and become enlightened attributes in which the knotted forms of the channels (*rtsa-mdud*) gradually vanish into light; and therefrom the emergent realisations of the levels arise manifest in and of themselves.[323]

Now, by the vanishing of the first pair of knotted channels into light, a hundred buddha-fields arise within the light which externally appears. Therein, rays of light are diffused, motion occurs through their re-absorption in a self-manifest manner, and the hundred buddha-fields vibrate through the shaking of the body. Internally also, a hundred non-conceptual contemplations of reality are entered and risen from, and other such experiences occur.[324] Therefore, it should be known that the higher paths exemplified by these occurrences are superior to the lower vehicles.

At the time when these four visionary experiences are concluded, the body is dissolved into atoms by Cutting Through Resistance and yet the buddha-body of indestructible reality is not thereby achieved. Since it is not achieved, there is on that basis no means of attaining the great benefit for the sake of others which continues until saṃsāra has been emptied.

Therefore, [in All-Surpassing Realisation] the buddha body of form remains apparitional in the manner of the moon's reflection in water, while the awareness abides in a formless state. As such, immeasurable acts are performed on behalf of sentient beings. This is known as the buddha-body of great transformation (*'pho-ba chen-po'i sku, mahā-saṅkrāntikāya*), exemplified by [the attainment] of the great master Padmasambhava and Vimalamitra. If there is, for the while, no one requiring to be trained on this basis, the body of form itself, which is a coalescence of outer radiance, manifest in and of itself, is absorbed into the inner expanse, the disposition of the body of reality free from conceptual elaboration, and then the subtle pristine cognition of individual intuitive awareness is centred in the inwardly radiant youthful vase body (*gzhon-nu bum-pa'i sku*). In the dispositon of this [youthful vase body] and without wavering from the highest meditative absorption, reality is present as the basis for the emanation of pristine cognition, the great unimpeded spirituality which displays instruction for those requiring training. It is the culmination of the buddha-body of reality, in which the expanse and pristine cognition are without duality.

Therefore, it is asserted that enlightenment is the point of liberation in which primordial purity and spontaneous presence are without duality, the great primordial purity or abiding nature of the original ground. And it is equally asserted that [the view of] the Mādhyamika who propound non-substantiality, though indeed a freedom from all extremes of conceptual elaboration, is but one extreme of emptiness because they deny even the buddha-bodies and pristine cognitions which manifest in and of themselves on the grounds that all activities (*'jug-pa*) at this moment abide in the firm cessation of quiescence.

Though distinctive opinions are variously found concerning the non-conceptuality, in terms of subject and object, of the all-knowing pristine cognition, the intention of the Primordial Lord [Samantabhadra] is particularly established as such through the proper path of the Great Perfection. Within the expanse of emptiness free from all conceptual elaborations that derives from its primordial purity, the essence abides through its spontaneous presence in the manner of the light which is radiant within a crystal but not externally manifest. This [spontaneous presence] comprises: three subtle pristine cognitions, forming the ground in which the buddha-fields and the bodies of perfect rapture arise manifest in and of themselves; five pristine cognitions which are given character through the expressive power of these [fields and bodies]; and the aspect of the ground in which the pristine cognition that knows cognitive objects arises. Since it is endowed with this pristine cognition itself, the essence is the source of all buddha-bodies and pristine cognitions. From it there emerges the power by which, without wavering from the body of reality, the two bodies of form appear, along with their enlightened activities, to those who require training. If it were not so, the benefit of those requiring training and the immeasurable enlightened attributes of omniscience would not emerge through the possession of pristine cognition. This has been stated *ad infinitum* in such texts as the *Verse Summation of the Transcendental Perfection of Discriminative Awareness* (Ch.5, v.8cd):

> If there were no pristine cognition,
> The enlightened attributes would not increase,
> Nor would there be enlightenment
> Or the oceanic attributes of the buddhas.

And in the *Illuminating of the Lamp* (*sgron-ma snang-byed*):[325]

> So if there were no range of pristine cognition
> There would be no distinction [between this]
> And the outer space which is empty.
> Therefore, from the ground, pristine cognition is pervasive.
> If there were no pristine cognition
> There would be no distinction [between this] and nihilism.

This spontaneous presence of enlightened attributes is referred to in eloquent explanations, such as the following from the *Great Commentary on the Buddhasamāyoga* (*Buddhasamāyogaṭīkā*, T 1659):

> This body of supreme bliss, characterised as skilful means and discriminative awareness without duality, embodies the essence of yoga. The hosts of Māra and the like which symbolise dualistic ideas are destroyed by this disposition, and, inasmuch as it possesses all the arrays of excellent enlightened attributes, there are apart from it no other details of enlightened attributes. It is present through their natural spontaneous presence and disclosed through realisation.

The disposition of this body of reality gives rise to consecration or blessing which arises as the self-manifesting buddha-body of perfect rapture. Therefrom enlightened activities continuously emerge, such as those of the Five Enlightened Families of the Tathāgatas in the pure buddha-fields, and such as those of the supreme emanational body in the impure fields.

Subsequent to [these four visionary appearances of All-Surpassing Realisation] there are also the Esoteric Instructions of the Four Consolidations (*mtha'-rten bzhi*) which meaningfully draw [the practice] to its conclusion: The ground is determined in three unmoving states (*mi-'gul-ba gsum*), the limit [of awareness] is grasped by the three presences (*sdod-pa gsum-gyis tshad bzung-ba*), the nail is riveted by the three attainments (*thob-pa gsum-gyis gzer gdab-pa*) and the limit of liberation is revealed by the four assurances (*gding-bzhis grol-tshad bstan-pa*).

In brief, the abiding nature of the Great Perfection is absolute in its view, pure and equal with respect to cause and result, indivisible with respect to truth, naturally dissolved with respect to the subject-object dichotomy, and core-penetrating with respect to creation and cessation. It has not fallen into the extremes of either elaboration or non-elaboration, and it is uncontrived by the intellect. It neither radiates externally, nor is it apprehended internally, and nor does it lie in between. For it, the chaff-like words and conventions of the entire range of expression, and the entire range of thought and scrutiny have become only discursive designations. Thus, one determines that it does not abide in the extreme of self-affirmation. It is said in the *Mirror of the Heart of Vajrasattva* (*rdo-rje sems-dpa' snying-gi me-long*, NGB Vol.10):

> It should be known that all the doctrines of awareness are free from the intellect involved in egocentric ideas.

Now at all times, ancient and recent, there have been those who, boasting of attaining the profound reality through their intellectual creations, have been terrified by the profound discourses concerning reality which is free from the intellect. Also, on the basis of the ostensible rejection of the lower sequences of the path by [passages such as] this, there have been those in both ancient and recent time who have been enthusiastic to undertake perpetual labours due to envy, and in connection with their counterfeit, sophistical intelligence, which is extremely hostile to the [doctrine's] range of profundity and the vast abiding nature. However, as the sublime Mañjuśrī has said:

> Concerning activities, the yogin
> Apprehends them on the great paths,
> Just as a deer pursues a mirage.
> Though they always appear, they are not grasped.
> But more than that, all of these [vehicles]
> Are endowed with inauthentic intelligence.
> The intelligence of the lowest yogas
> Is surpassed by the highest.
> The intelligence of the lower
> Is rejected by the discriminative awareness of the higher.

One should therefore know this and be skilled in pacifying motivations connected with disputation in the inconceivable disposition of reality.

In addition, it is according to the esoteric instructions, which turn the instructions of the Great Perfection to practical application, that all things of saṃsāra and nirvāṇa are established as the display of the four intermediate states (*bar-do*). During the intermediate state of the birthplace (*skye-gnas-kyi bar-do*) exaggerated notions connected with study and reflection on the oral instructions are cut off in the manner of a sandpiper [decisively] entering its nest. During the intermediate state of the moment of death (*'chi-kha'i bar-do*) the oral instructions are clarified in the manner of a dancing girl [delightedly] looking in a mirror. During the intermediate state of reality (*chos-nyid bar-do*) there is [secure] conviction that [the deities] manifest in and of themselves, in the manner of a child [securely] nestling into its mother's lap. And during the intermediate state of rebirth (*srid-pa bar-do*) the residual effect of one's [wholesome] deeds is prolonged in the manner of a conducting pipe being thrust into a canal which is blocked. Relying on these oral instructions, fortunate beings are conveyed to the point of original liberation. By the mere affirmation of a view which approximates things as they really are, one never sees, or has the occasion to obtain, the essential nucleus which is the pristine cognition realised in the abiding nature. So it is said:

> Concerning the co-emergent pristine cognition of
> ultimate reality:
> Apart from the impression made by accumulating
> provisions and purifying obscurations
> And the exclusive blessing of the guru endowed
> with realisation,
> Reliance on other methods should be known as
> delusion.

And in the *Hevajra Tantra* (Pt.1, Ch.8, v.36):

> It should be known that
> The co-emergent is unexpressed by another,
> And it cannot be found anywhere,
> Save by relying on the guru's timely means
> And the provisions of one's own merit.

And as the glorious Saraha has said:

> One who takes to heart whatever the guru has said
> Resembles one who sees a treasure
> Lying in the palm of the hand.

If the auspicious coincidences of the guru, the student, the world and its contents accumulate, the great empowerment which pours out all the Conqueror's means (*rgyal-thabs spyi-blugs-kyi dbang-chen*), pristine cognition itself, is conferred by the power of [the guru's] blessing being transferred, and it manifestly and directly descends. Then the meaning of that descent [of pristine cognition] is experienced in continuous yoga which is the flow of the effortless state's presence. Relying on the recognition of the details of the signs and experiences occurring on the path, the removal of the obstacles of clinging to pleasant and coarse experiences, and the advantages granted by the enlightened attributes that are realised through experiential cultivation, the foundation is acquired, through which the result is actualised in this lifetime and in this very body, without aspiring towards it in the future.

11 *A Recapitulation of the Resultant Vehicles*

[211b.4] Having ascertained the exegesis of the overall meaning [of the secret mantra] according to their classifications, there now follows the second part [see p.257 above] in which the meaning subsumed in the particular sections [of the secret mantra] is recapitulated in order to facilitate understanding. This falls into two categories, namely, the vehicle of the outer tantras of austere awareness (*phyi thub-pa rgyud-kyi theg-pa*) and the vehicle of the inner tantras of skilful means (*nang-pa thabs-kyi rgyud-kyi theg-pa*).

DISTINCTIONS BETWEEN THE OUTER AND INNER TANTRAS

[211b.5-213a.5] Though many dissimilar claims have been made by those of the past concerning the distinctions between these two vehicles, in this [Nyingma tradition] there are said to be five [distinctions] derived from the master Dropukpa who subsumed the intention of the four "pillars", who were the spiritual sons [of Zurcungpa]:[326]

> Concerning the first distinction which refers to their views: The inner vehicle is that of the mantras in which mind-as-such is realised to be the supreme identity, and the outer vehicle is that in which there is no such realisation. It is said in Indrabhūti's *Array of the Path of the Magical Net* (*Māyāpathavyavasthāpana*, P 4737):
>
> *Since those who uphold*
> *The three enlightened families*
> *And the five enlightened families*
> *Do not realise the supreme identity,*
> *I have propounded them as equivalent*
> *To the common [vehicles].*[327]

Concerning the second distinction which refers to their modes of acquiring accomplishment: The outer [vehicle] is that in which accomplishment is requested by aspiring towards and attending upon a deity of pristine cognition, and the inner [vehicle] is that in which accomplishment is seen to be intrinsically present because, through realisation of the supreme identity, mind-as-such manifests in and of itself as a maṇḍala of buddha-body and pristine cognition. It says in the *Questions and Answers of Vajrasattva* (*rdo-rje sems-dpa'i zhus-lan*, P 5082):

> *In reply to the question, "What is the distinction between the yogins of the outer and inner mantras in their acquisition of accomplishment?" he said:*
>
> *As, for example, a king commands a minister,*
> *The outer way is the granting of accomplishment from above.*
> *And, as a king who holds sway having been offered the kingdom by the people,*
> *The unsurpassed way is that of the naturally present Great Perfection.*

And as it is said in the *Secret Nucleus* (Ch.2, v.6):

> *This wondrous, miraculous, and marvellous reality...*

Then, concerning the third distinction which refers to their empowerments: The outer [vehicle] is that in which the three higher, supreme empowerments cannot be obtained, and the inner vehicle is that in which these three are emphatically grasped.

As to the fourth distinction which refers to their conduct: The inner [vehicle] can accept conduct in which the twenty elements of saṃsāra are retained by skilful means, and the outer one cannot. And as to the fifth distinction which refers to their results: The outer [vehicle] can unite one with the result within seven, five or three human lifetimes and so forth, and the inner one can unite one with it in this very lifetime.

Lharje Kharakpa[328] and Lama Rok Sherap-ö have said that, with respect to the tantra texts, there is a distinction between the way in which the ten categories of tantra are interpreted in the outer and the inner [vehicles], and that, in particular, there are distinctions as to: whether, with reference to empowerment, the three profound empowerments can or cannot be revealed; whether, with reference to the view, the naturally present, pristine cognition can or cannot be propounded; whether, with reference to meditation, one can or cannot meditate on the [male and female deities] kissing one another; whether, with reference to conduct, the five sacramental substances can or cannot be enjoyed; whether or not an entrance can be made, having regarded the deity and oneself as identical; and whether, with reference to accomplishment, the acquistion takes a long or a short time, and is hoped for externally or internally.

Lharje Celpa [Künga Dorje],[329] too, has said that since these distinctions refer merely to specific aspects [of the vehicles], they are correctly classified, on this occasion, into three categories, namely, the distinctions concerning the ground which is to be known, the distinctions concerning the path which is the act of knowing, and the distinctions concerning the result which is to be obtained.

Lord Drölmawa [Samdrup Dorje][330] and Yungtönpa [Dorjepel][331] have both said that:

> The inner mantras are those which hold the view, conduct and contemplation to be indivisible, and the outer mantras are those which do not. Is there then, one might ask, no distinction between the causal vehicle and the outer mantras? Not so; there is a distinction between whether relative appearances can or cannot be made into the path.

OUTER TANTRAS OF AUSTERE AWARENESS

If, among these [vehicles], the vehicle of the outer tantras of austere [awareness] is first classified, then the *Tantra of the Great Natural Arising of Awareness* says:

> The outer tantras are of three kinds:
> Kriyā, Ubhaya and Yoga.

It is therefore divided into the vehicles of the Kriyātantra, the Ubhayatantra and the Yogatantra.

Kriyātantra

[213a.5-215b.5] The first, or Kriyātantra, is referred to under the three headings of essence, verbal definition and classification. The first of these, [the essence], is that, ultimately, the purity that is free from the four extremes is realised, and, relatively, one resorts to the skilful means which aspire and strive towards accomplishments externally [conferred by the deity]. It is said in the *Sequence of the Path*:

Since they are not known to be the same without duality,
The level of action requires alternate meditation
On an ultimate truth which is simply the pure reality
And a deity of relative appearance endowed with
The enlightened attributes of pristine cognition.[332]

Secondly, the verbal definition is that [the Sanskrit] *kriyā* conveys the meaning of activity [or action] because it emphasises external activity. Such is also said in the *Commentary on the Final Meditation* (*Ḍhyānottarapaṭalaṭīkā*, T 2670):

This tantra is called Kriyātantra because it emphasises
The activities of body and speech.

Thirdly, the Kriyātantra is classified according to six topics. Of these the first, the entrance, is twofold: There is the initial entrance [or empowerment] which effects maturation and the actual entrance itself. According to the former, the student is made into a worthy recipient [for the teaching] by the conferral of the water and crown empowerments along with their aspects (*chu-dang cod-pan-gyi dbang 'khor-bcas bskur-ba*).[333] It says in the *Seminal Point of Pristine Cognition* (*Jñānatilakatantra*, T 422):

The water empowerment and the crown
Are well known in Kriyātantra.

And as for the latter: The [actual] entrance is effected by means of ablutions, cleanliness, and the three purities (*dag-pa gsum*). The *Tantra of the Great Natural Arising of Awareness* says:

As to the entrance, it is entered
By the three purities, ablutions and cleanliness.

And on the subject of the three purities, it also says:

What, one might ask, are the three purities?
They are the purity of the deity and the maṇḍala,
The purity of substances and rapture,
And the purity of mantra and contemplation.

Secondly, the view of Kriyātantra refers to the two truths, as it is said in the *Sequence of the View* (*lta-rim*, T 4356):

According to Kriyātantra, living creatures are
  without bewilderment
When reality is regarded as the ultimate truth,
And when, relatively, maṇḍalas of three enlightened
  families of deities appear,
Endowed with enlightened attributes of intrinsic
  awareness.

Concerning the ultimate truth, it is held that mind-as-such, the pure pristine cognition [which coalesces] emptiness and radiance, is free from the four extremes of being, non-being, appearance and emptiness; as it is said in the *Determination and Distinction* (*la-zla-ba-dang shan-'byed-pa lta-ba'i sgron-me*, P 4727):

> Since the mind itself is awareness,
> Without the four extremes,
> It is none other than pristine cognition.

Now the relative truth [is held] to comprise both correct and incorrect modes, of which the incorrect one refers to all relative appearances which are considered to be both correct and incorrect [by those who adhere to the philosophical systems] from the Mādhyamika downwards, and the correct relative truth is held to refer to the enlightened attributes which are the realisation of reality and which appear as the maṇḍala of deities belonging to the three enlightened families. As the previous text continues:

> Through the pristine cognition of the appearances
> Which creatively arise,
> The sublime, gentle and rough phenomena which appear
> Are said to be pure when seen
> In the maṇḍala of the three enlightened families.[334]

Thirdly, on the subject of moral discipline, the *Miraculous Key of Further Discernment* speaks of eleven commitments:

> The Three Precious Jewels and the enlightened mind,
> The mantras and seals – do not abandon them;
> The vajra and bell should not be abandoned,
> And similarly the deity and the guru.
> These are the subsidiary commitments.
> As for the five basic commitments:
> One should not sleep on a [high] bed,
> One should neither eat meat nor drink ale,
> And one should not eat garlic or radishes.

Then, there is also the *Secret Tantra of General Rites* (*Sāmānyavidhīnāṃ guhyatantra*, T 806) which explains that there are three general commitments and thirteen particular commitments; and so forth.

Fourth, meditation is both symbolic and non-symbolic. Concerning the former, the *Heruka Galpo* says:

> The meditations are on [the deities] of reality,
> Sound, syllables,[335] form, buddha-mind,
> And the attainment of the perfect body of pristine
> cognition.

The Being of Commitment (*samayasattva*)[336] must therefore be created by means of the six real [sequential modes of] the deity according to the Kriyātantra, namely, the deity of emptiness (*stong-pa-nyid-kyi lha*), the deity of syllables (*yi-ge'i lha*), the deity of sound (*sgra'i lha*), the deity of form (*gzugs-kyi lha*), the deity of seals (*phyag-rgya'i lha*) and the deity of symbols (*mtshan-ma'i lha*). This is similarly stated in the following words from the extensive *Vajravidāraṇa Tantra*:

> The six are [the deities] of emptiness and syllables,
> Of sound, form, seals and symbols.

Thereafter, the Being of Pristine Cognition (*jñānasattva*) is invited; offerings, praises, recitations and so forth are performed; and accomplishment is acquired, having regarded [the relationship between the deity and oneself] as that of a master and servant. It says in the *Tantra of the Great Natural Arising of Awareness*:

> The deity and the yogin respectively
> Are regarded as a master and subject.

And in the *Tantra which Acquires the Accomplishment of All Families* (*rigs thams-cad-pa'i dngos-grub len-pa'i rgyud*):

> By regarding [the deity] in the manner of a lord,
> a master or a king,
> And perceiving oneself as a servant,
> The nucleus of accomplishment,
> That is attained through the mantras,
> Is accepted as the unsurpassed boon.

Concerning the second [or non-symbolic meditation]: There is alternate meditation on the two truths because absorption occurs in the pure disposition [of reality] free from the four extremes, without referring to those [aforementioned] appearances which are meditated on as symbolic deities, seed-syllables and the like. It says in the *Determination and Distinction*:

> Appearances and emptiness are successively
> established.

Fifth, conduct [according to the Kriyātantra] comprises six activities, namely, the activities connected with the time for entering [the vehicle], and with food, attire, cleanliness, visualisation supports and the recitation of mantras. It is further said in the *Heruka Galpo*:

> Concerning planets [or days], stars and seasons,
> And food, attire and cleanliness,
> The austerity of discipline is performed.

And in the *Garland of Views: A Collection of Esoteric Instructions*:

> Conduct concerns the images of [the deity's] body,
> The implements symbolic of his mind,
> Recitations and so forth.

Sixth, concerning the result, it is held that within seven human lifetimes the level of a Holder of Indestructible Reality of the Three Enlightened Families, endowed with the essence of the three buddha-bodies and five pristine cognitions, will be obtained. The *Heruka Galpo* says:

> Within seven lifetimes on the buddha level[337]
> The Lords of the Three Families instruct living beings.

Ubhayatantra

[215b.5-216b.3] The second, the vehicle of Ubhayatantra, is referred to under the headings of essence, verbal definition and classification. First, [the essence] is that one resorts to the skilful means which attain accomplishment by practising the view and meditation in the manner of Yogatantra, and conduct in the manner of Kriyātantra. It is said in the *Garland of Views: A Collection of Esoteric Instructions*:

> Accomplishment is attained by relying on both.

Secondly, [as to the verbal definition]: Ubhayatantra is so called because the [Sanskrit] word *ubhaya* ["both"] indicates that *both* the outer activities of body and speech and the inner yoga are equally performed. The *Tantra of the Great Natural Arising of Awareness* says:

> Ubhayatantra is as follows:
> The view is observed as in Yogatantra,
> And conduct is performed as in Kriyātantra.
> Therefore it is known as the Tantra of Both.

Thirdly, the Ubhayatantra is classified under the six topics, of which the first, the entrance, has two parts. The former is empowerment, which here refers to the three empowerments of the vajra, bell and name (*rdor-dril-ming-gsum*)[338] in addition to those of water and crown. As the *Seminal Point of Pristine Cognition* says:

> The vajra, the bell and likewise the name
> [empowerments]
> Are well clarified in the Caryātantra.

The actual entrance, along with the third topic, moral discipline, and the fifth, conduct, largely conform to Kriyātantra, whereas the second topic, or the view, and the fourth, meditation, largely conform to Yogatantra. It is said in the *Turquoise Display*:

> Those who uphold the Tantra of Both,
> Though conforming to Kriyātantra in their conduct,
> Do conform to Yogatantra in their view.
> Therefore their enlightened families and view
> Are superior to those [of Kriyātantra].

And in the *Sequence of the View*:

> Those who uphold the Tantra of Both
> Conform upwards in their view
> And downwards in their conduct.

The Ubhayatantra also appears to be somewhat superior [to Kriyātantra] because the view and meditation are directed towards four enlightened families of the conquerors.

Sixth, concerning the result: It is held that within five lifetimes the level of a Holder of Indestructible Reality belonging to the Four Enlightened Families is obtained. The fourth enlightened family to which this refers subsumes the Enlightened Family of Activity (*las-kyi rigs*) in the Enlightened Family of Precious Gems (*rin-chen rigs*). It is also said in the *Heruka Galpo*:

> One abides on the level of Vajradhara[339]
> Endowed with four enlightened families.

And in the *All-Accomplishing King*:

> It is a deviation which obscures
> Non-duality for five human lifetimes.

Yogatantra

[216b.3-219b.4] Thirdly, the vehicle of Yogatantra is considered under the headings of essence, verbal definition and classification. First, [according to the essence]: The blessing of the non-symbolic reality which is the ultimate truth is regarded as a deity belonging to the expanse of indestructible reality, which relatively appears, and it is held that the result is attained by perseverance in the acceptance of positive and the rejection of negative ideas [in relation to that deity]. It is said in the *Sequence of the Path:*

> Since they are not seen to be
> Spontaneously present and equivalent,
> The blessing of pristine cognition,
> Through which all things are pure,
> Becomes an emanational [deity]
> Of the expanse of indestructible reality,
> And the yogin acts in terms of acceptance and rejection.

Secondly, [the verbal definition]: Derived from [the Sanskrit] *yoga*, the Yogatantra is so called because it emphasises or teaches the inner yoga. The *Garland of Views: A Collection of Esoteric Instructions* says:

> Accomplishment is attained with emphasis on yoga.

Thirdly, the Yogatantra is considered under six topics. The first, the entrance, is twofold. The former is the empowerment which refers, in addition to the [previous] five empowerments of awareness (*rig-pa'i dbang lnga*), to the conferral of the empowerment of the master of indestructible reality (*rdo-rje slob-dpon-gyi dbang*), the sixth empowerment.[340] The *Seminal Point of Pristine Cognition* states:

> The empowerment of the irreversible vase
> Has been clarified in Yogatantra.
> This is a particular empowerment among the six
> And it is called the empowerment of the master.

The latter is the actual entrance which is effected by means of symbolic and non-symbolic contemplation. It says in the *All-Accomplishing King*:

> One who desires the Bounteous Array of Yogatantra,
> Having entered by symbolic and non-symbolic
> methods...

Secondly, the view [of Yogatantra] concerns the two truths. The ultimate truth refers to all things as inner radiance or emptiness, the nature of which is free from the signs of conceptual elaboration. The *Tantra of the Summation of the Real* says:

> Since all things are naturally radiant,
> They are essentially pure from the beginning.

The relative truth is polarised between an incorrect relative which is similar to that of the previous [vehicles], and a correct relative truth, which is held not to refer to the appearances discerned by living creatures in their own minds because everything that everywhere appears is within the maṇḍala of indestructible reality's expanse, which is the blessing derived from the realisation of reality. Such is also said in the *Heruka Galpo*:

> One who wishes to abide in the vehicle of Yogatantra
> Should look upon Akaniṣṭha as the expanse of
> indestructible reality.

And in the *Sequence of the View*:

> Within the pristine cognition of reality's expanse,
> Which is the purity of ultimate truth according to
> Yogatantra,

> The blessing of realisation appears as a deity.
> Accordingly, the perceptions of [mundane]
> Living creatures are bewilderment.

And also in the *Turquoise Display*:

> Derived from the pure pristine cognition of the expanse,
> In which both intrinsic awareness
> And the signs of its actual vision are indivisible,
> The blessing arises as a deity of indestructible reality's expanse,
> And the deity is regarded as a friend.

Thirdly, moral discipline includes the general commitments belonging to the five enlightened families, which are said to be the highest. The enlightened mind is first generated, and subsequently training in the three aspects of moral discipline is earnestly applied. Then there are said to be fourteen particular commitments, namely, three connected with Vairocana, four each with Akṣobhya and Ratnasambhava, one with Amitābha, and two with Amoghasiddhi. The *Miraculous Key of Further Discernment*, however, claims that they number thirteen when two uncommon commitments are added to the eleven commitments of Kriyātantra. In its own words:

> The limits guarded by the Yogatantra,
> In addition to the limits guarded by the above [Kriyātantra],
> Include [the commitments] not to drink water
> In a locality [inhabited by violators of commitments]
> And not to converse with such violators.

Fourth, meditation is both symbolic and non-symbolic. The former is meditation with reference to the yoga of the male and female deities, which applies the four seals (*phyag-rgya bzhi*) by means of the five awakenings (*mngon-byang lnga*) and four miracles (*cho-'phrul bzhi*). The *Garland of Views: A Collection of Esoteric Instructions* says:

> Without emphasising outer paraphernalia, and by means of contemplation in which the male and female deities that are uncreated and unceasing in ultimate reality and the mind-stream in which they are represented are entirely pure, one becomes accomplished by emphasising the yoga of meditation on the sublime body of form endowed with the four seals.

After the Being of Commitment (*samayasattva*) has been created and the Being of Pristine Cognition (*jñānasattva*) has been invited, [the deity] should then be regarded without the dichotomy of good or evil, and in the manner of a relative or friend. Offerings, praises, recitations and so forth should be made. So it is also said in the *Tantra of the Great Natural Arising of Awareness*:

> The deity and oneself, the yogin,
> Are held to relate as relatives or friends.

Now the five awakenings (*mngon-byang lnga*) are the awakenings which occur through emptiness (*stong-pa-nyid*), through the visualisation of a lunar throne (*zla-gdan*), through seed-syllables of buddha-speech (*gsung yig-'bru*), through hand implements symbolic of buddha-mind (*thugs phyag-mtshan*) and through the perfection of the [deity's] body (*sku yongs-rdzogs*). The four miracles (*cho-'phrul bzhi*) are the miracles of contemplation (*ting-nge-'dzin*), empowerment (*dbang-bskur-ba*), consecration or blessing (*byin-gyis rlob-pa*), and offerings (*mchod-pa*). Concerning these the *Heruka Galpo* says:

> Non-conceptualisation, moon, buddha-speech,
> vajra-emblem,
> And radiance of the [deity's] body during meditation
> On the emanation and absorption [of light];
> Contemplation, blessing, empowerment and offerings:
> Such are the five awakenings and four miracles.
> Though these are the activities of meditation and offering,
> They are to be performed in order that merit might be
> possessed.

The four seals (*phyag-rgya bzhi*) are so called because meditation ensues when the body, speech, mind and activity have been respectively sealed by: the great seal of buddha-body which secures the ground-of-all as the mirror-like pristine cognition (*me-long kun-gzhi sku phyag-chen*); the doctrinal seal of buddha-speech which secures the mental faculty as the pristine cognition of discernment (*sor-rtog yid gsung chos-rgya*); the commitment seal of buddha-mind which secures the mind of conflicting emotions as the pristine cognition of sameness (*mnyam-nyid nyon-yid thugs dam-rgya*); and the action seal of enlightened activity which secures the five senses as the pristine cognition of accomplishment (*bya-ba sgo-lnga phrin-las las-rgya*). Such are the four pristine cognitions which are to be actualised and with which they are connected. The [fifth] pristine cognition of the expanse of reality (*chos-dbyings ye-shes*), on the other hand, abides as the natural expression of them all.

The second [or non-symbolic meditation] refers to meditative absorption in the disposition where there is no dichotomy between the essential nature of ultimate reality which cannot be symbolised and the appearance of its blessing as a deity, which is the apparitional aspect of pristine cognition. It says in the *Emergence of Indestructible Reality* (*Vajrodaya*, T 2516):

The disposition of the non-dual expanse of reality
Is taken as the most sacred of unsurpassed
accomplishments.

Fifth, concerning conduct: With the assistance of external mundane practices such as cleanliness, conduct effects the benefit of oneself and others by maintaining, above all, the yoga of the deity. The *Indestructible Peak* says:

Abiding in the contemplation of the deity,
Do not dismiss all sentient beings.
Always be mindful of the buddhas.
Always hold offerings to the buddhas as supreme.

Sixth, as to the result: It is held that within three human lifetimes buddhahood is attained on the level of the Bounteous Array, endowed with the essence of the three bodies and five pristine cognitions. It says in the *All-Accomplishing King*:

One who desires the Bounteous Array of Yogatantra
Is held to be liberated within three human lifetimes.

And in the *Lock of the Heart*:

Having purified the five propensities of the subject-object dichotomy,
And, by the expressive powers of the five pristine cognitions,
Having overpowered the level of the Bounteous Array,
The result gathering the five enlightened families is obtained.
The pure uncreated body of reality then
Acts in an uncreated manner on behalf of living beings.
Its perfect rapture embodying the five kinds of seal
Fulfils the benefit of living beings as a bodhisattva,
And its ten thousand billion emanations
Teach everywhere in the presence of the six classes of beings.

INNER TANTRAS OF SKILFUL MEANS

[219b.4-221a.1] Secondly, there is the vehicle of the inner tantras of skilful means (*nang-pa thabs-kyi rgyud-kyi theg-pa*), concerning which it is said in the *Tantra of the Great Natural Arising of Awareness*:

> The inner [vehicle] is held to be threefold:
> Mahāyoga, Anuyoga and Atiyoga.

It therefore comprises the Mahāyoga tantras, the Anuyoga transmissions and the Atiyoga esoteric instructions.

Concerning the distinctions between these three, the master Zurcungpa said in reply to a request made by Lencap Parwa:[341]

> Mahāyoga appears as the miracle of awareness. Anuyoga appears as the expressive power of intrinsic awareness. Atiyoga is awareness, manifest in and of itself. Therefore, Ru Garap Dorje[342] said:
>
> > *They refer respectively to a miracle,*
> > *To expressive power and to the self-manifest.*

This means that [the three] are particularly distinguished according to their view: Mahāyoga realises all things to be the miraculous events of mind-as-such, in which appearance and emptiness are indivisible; Anuyoga realises all things to be the expressive power of mind-as-such, in which the expanse and pristine cognition are indivisible; and Atiyoga realises all things to be manifest in and of themselves as mind-as-such, the naturally present pristine cognition which is without creation or cessation from the beginning. This was asserted to be the most precious point by both Dātik [Cośāk of Nakmore] and Len [Śākya Zangpo of Chuwar].[343]

Kyo Kongbupa [Kyotön Śākye of Kongbu][344] also said that:

> They have a greater or lesser degree of emphasis:
> Mahāyoga lays great emphasis on conduct,
> Anuyoga lays great emphasis on contemplation,
> And Atiyoga lays great emphasis on the view.

Then, Lharje Rok Sherap-ö has said that:

> Mahāyoga is creative because the deity is gradually created by means of three contemplations. Anuyoga is perfecting because the deity is created in a perfect manner without relying on that [threefold creative phase]. And Atiyoga, the Great Perfection, is uncreatable because it is liberated from both the creation and perfection phases.
>
> Or else, Mahāyoga is greatly motivated with respect to the ten categories of tantra, Anuyoga is so motivated to a lesser extent, and Atiyoga is liberated from motivation.

And in the words of Menyak Jungdra [or Khyungdra]:[345]

> Though the three aspects of creation and perfection are present in them all, Mahāyoga emphatically teaches the creation

> stage, Anuyoga emphatically teaches the perfection stage, and the Great Perfection is effortless in both respects.

Cel Lotsāwa Künga Dorje also eloquently asserted this to be the distinction between their verbal definitions.

[Finally], the great, all-knowing Longcenpa [in his *Great Chariot*] has said:

> The Father tantras of Mahāyoga are the natural expression of the skilful means of appearance, intended on behalf of those requiring training who are mostly hostile and possessed by many ideas; the Mother tantras of Anuyoga are the discriminative awareness of the perfection stage which is the reality of emptiness, intended for the benefit of those who are mostly desirous and delight in the tranquillity of the mind; and the Atiyoga is revealed as the natural expression of their non-duality, intended for the benefit of those who are mostly deluded and who are energetic. Therefore the *Great Array* says:
>
> > *For one who would transcend the mind*
> > *There is the creative phase,*
> > *For one who would possess the essence of mind*
> > *There is the perfecting phase,*
> > *And for those who are supreme and most secret*
> > *There is the Great Perfection.*

And also in *Mind at Rest* (*sems-nyid ngal-gso*), he has said:

> Mahāyoga emphasises vital energy and the skilful means of the creation stage.
> Anuyoga emphasises the seed and discriminative awareness of the perfection stage.
> Atiyoga emphasises the pristine cognition in which everything is without duality.

Mahāyoga

[221a.1-224a.2] Among them, first the vehicle of Mahāyoga is considered under the three headings of essence, verbal definition and classification. As to [the essence]: Its nature is such that liberation is obtained through a union of realisation and experience in the indivisible meaning of the superior truth, by emphatic reliance on the creation stage of skilful means.

Secondly, [as to the verbal definition]: The [Tibetan] *rnal-'byor chen-po* is derived from the [Sanskrit] *Mahāyoga* which means great union. It is so called because it unites the mind with the non-dual truth and is thus superior to the outer Yogatantra.

Thirdly, Mahāyoga is classified according to the six topics, of which the first, the entrance, is twofold: The former refers to the empowerment. There are four empowerments which are to be conferred because three higher, supreme uncommon empowerments (*thun-min mchog-dbang gong-ma gsum*)[346] are added to the common vase empowerment (*thun-mong-pa bum-dbang*). It is said in the *Subsequent Root Tantra of the Magical Net*:

> There are the master, the secret,
> And the discriminating [empowerments],
> And, immediately afterwards, the fourth.

Five empowerments are also enumerated when the vase empowerment (*bum-dbang*) is divided into its aspects of beneficence and ability (*phan-nus gnyis*).[347] The *Sequence of the Activity of Indestructible Reality* (*Vajrakarmakrama*, P 4761) says:

> Its aspects become fivefold
> Because [the vase empowerment]
> Confers beneficence and ability on one.

The latter is the actual entrance which is effected by means of three contemplations, namely, the yoga of great emptiness which is discriminative awareness (*shes-rab stong-pa chen-po'i rnal-'byor*), the illusory compassion which is skilful means (*thabs snying-rje sgyu-ma*), and the seals which are subtle and coarse (*phyag-rgya phra-rags*). Therefore, Mahāyoga is the path which emphatically teaches the creation stage. In this respect, it is also said in the *Tantra of the Great Natural Arising of Awareness*:

> The entrance is the threefold contemplation.

And in the *Miraculous Key of Further Discernment*:

> The entrance of Mahāyoga
> Is effected by the threefold contemplation.

Secondly, the view [of Mahāyoga] refers to the ultimate truth as that in which awareness, appearing without conceptual elaboration, is held to be spontaneously present as the essential basis; and all the ideas which are the expressive power of this awareness itself are held to be the relative truth, manifest in and of themselves as a maṇḍala of buddha-body and pristine cognition. Neither of these truths refers in a biased manner to either appearance or emptiness because their essence is an indivisible sameness. If it is conventionally expressed by the term "indivisible", its indivisibility is free from the range of perception because it transcends the objects of thought and expressions which apprehend it. In this respect, the *Array of the Path of the Magical Net* says:

The superior, indivisible truth of sameness,
Though revealed everywhere by synonyms,
Is in truth beyond objects of speech and thought.

And in the *Sequence of the Path*:

And in order to loosen[348] attachment to that description,
It is unthinkable and inexpressible
Within the two conventional truths.

Thirdly, as to moral discipline: The later translations of the secret mantra claim it refers both to the conduct based on the knowledge of the fourteen basic violations of the commitments which are to be guarded (*bsrung-bya'i dam-tshig rtsa-ltung bcu-bzhi*) and to the conduct based on the knowledge of the nature of the commitments of the five meats and the five nectars which are to be practised (*spyad-bya'i dam-tshig sha-lnga bdud-rtsi lnga*).

In the terminology of the ancient translations, the commitments of Mahāyoga are said to number twenty-eight.[349] The *Miraculous Key of Further Discernment* says:

Concerning the limits guarded by Mahāyoga,
There are three basic commitments
And twenty-five ancillary ones which are kept.

Now, the three basic commitments are those of buddha-body, speech and mind (*sku-gsung-thugs-kyi dam-tshig gsum*). As for the ancillary ones, the above text says:

There are those to be practised,
Those not to be renounced,
And those to be adopted.
There are those to be known
And those to be attained.

Fourth, concerning meditation: There are two traditions, one emphasising the class of means for attainment (*sgrub-sde*), and the other emphasising the class of tantra (*rgyud-sde*). The former includes five classes of means for attainment of the deities of pristine cognition, namely, the Means for Attaining the Body of the Sugatas by Relying on the Four Centres of Mañjuśrī the Body (*'jam-dpal-gyi sku 'khor-lo bzhi-la brten-nas bde-gshegs sku'i sgrub-pa*); the Means for Attaining the Lotus Speech by Relying on the Three Neighs of Hayagrīva (*rta-mgrin-gyi rta-skad thengs-gsum-la brten-nas padma-gsung-gi sgrub-pa*); the Means for Attaining the Indestructible Reality of Mind by Relying on the Genuine and Unique Accomplishment, the Awareness and Naturally Present Pristine Cognition which is Yangdak the Mind (*yang-dag-gi thugs rig-pa rang-byung-gi ye-shes yang-dag grub-pa gcig-pu-la-brten-nas thugs rdo-rje'i sgrub-pa*); the Means for Attaining Nectar Attributes which Perfectly Reveal All Things of Saṃsāra and Nirvāṇa as the Enlightened Attributes of Mahottara (*che-mchog-gi 'khor-'das-kyi chos-thams-cad yon-tan-du rdzogs-par ston-pa bdud-rtsi yon-tan-gyi sgrub-pa*); and the Means for Attaining the Enlightened Activity of Vajrakīla which Emphatically Teaches the Skilful Means for Training Malicious Beings by the Rites of Sorcery of Vajrakīla (*phur-pa'i mngon-spyod-kyi las-kyis gdug-pa-can 'dul-ba'i thabs gtso-bor ston-pa phur-ba phrin-las-kyi sgrub-pa*). Also included in this section are the three common classes of means for attainment, namely, the Means for Attaining the Liberating Sorcery of Mātaraḥ (*ma-mo rbod-gtong*), the Malign Mantra (*drag-sngags dmod-pa*) and the Mundane Praise (*'jig-rten mchod-bstod*).

Concerning the latter [i.e. the class of tantras]: Mahāyoga is generally classified according to three kinds of tantra, namely, Father, Mother, and Non-Dual. In the Father tantras such as the *Guhyasamāja* there is held to be experiential cultivation in a manner which is non-conceptual with respect to radiance and emptiness because they emphasise the area of skilful means according to the creation stage and also the vital energy according to the perfection stage connected with it.

In the Mother tantras such as *Cakrasaṃvara*, *Hevajra* and *Yangdak* (NGB Vol. 25), the conceptual elaboration of the creation stage is diminished, and there is held to be experiential cultivation in a manner which is non-conceptual with respect to bliss and emptiness, and in which the perfection stage of discriminative awareness emphasises the seed or seminal point of enlightened mind.

Then in the Neutral tantras such as the *Magical Net* (T 832-7, NGB Vols.14-16) the phases of creation and perfection are coalesced and there is held to be experiential cultivation in a manner which emphasises the blissful, radiant and non-conceptual pristine cognition that is developed through the energy channels, currents and seminal points according to the perfection stage, and above all, the supreme pristine cognition of inner radiance.

In this context, [meditation] is explained with reference to the *Root Tantra of the Secret Nucleus*. Accordingly, the *Three Stages* (*rim-gsum*, P 4742)[350] says:

> There are said to be the two particular kinds of
>   meditation:
> The sequence of symbolic meditation
> And the nature of just what is.

Thus there is both symbolic and non-symbolic meditation.

The former comprises both the creation and perfection stages. As for the creation stage: It refers to the experiential cultivation in which the deity and ideas are meditated on as indivisible by emphasising the gradual creation of the maṇḍala through the three contemplations. It is subdivided into the devotional meditation (*mos-bsgom*) and the definitive perfection (*nges-rdzogs*). The former is exemplified by the experiential cultivation which, though firmness in contemplation has not been obtained, completes the ritual branches of the creation stage during the course of a single evening session of meditation on a [particular divine] form.[351] The latter refers to the five yogas belonging to [the paths of] provision and connection which are endowed with corruption, and the four kinds of awareness-holders who are without corruption.

The perfection stage refers to both the esoteric instructions through which [the energy channels, currents and seminal points] are grasped and trained within the "upper door of one's own body" (*steng-sgo 'ju-'dul-gyi man-ngag*), and the esoteric instructions which concern the display of the three realms through "the lower door" [or sexual centre of one's partner's body] (*'og-sgo khams-gsum rol-pa'i man-ngag*). Therefore it says in the *Three Stages*:

> There are oral instructions
> According to the upper and lower doors.

Secondly, non-symbolic meditation refers to the contemplation of reality, just as it is.

Then, fifth, as to conduct: Anything belonging to saṃsāra can be practised without attachment since it is retained by the foundation of skilful means. It says in the *Miraculous Key to the Storehouse*:

> The Mahāyoga of the creation phase
> Engages in the rites of "liberation" and sexual practices[352]
> And the five nectars which are sacramental substances,
> Through the conduct which observes great skilful means.

Sixth, as to the result: In this lifetime or in the intermediate state [after death], the embodiment in which the five buddha-bodies are spontaneously present is actualised. It says in the *Guhyasamāja* (Ch.13, v.118):

> This, the supreme nature of the Transcendent Lord,
> Originating from the undivided three buddha-bodies,
> Adorned with the ocean of pristine cognition,
> Will be obtained in this very lifetime.

And in the *Seminal Point of Pristine Cognition*:

> Otherwise, immediately after abandoning [this body],
> The result will be accomplished without any effort.

Anuyoga

[224a.2-228a.3] The vehicle of the Anuyoga transmissions (*lung anu-yoga*) is considered under the three headings of essence, verbal definition and classification. As to [the essence]: Its nature is such that liberation is obtained through a union of realisation and experience of the truth in which the expanse [of reality] and pristine cognition are without duality, by emphatic reliance on the perfection stage of discriminative awareness.

Secondly, [as to the verbal definition]: The [Sanskrit] *Anuyoga* is rendered [in Tibetan] as *rjes-su rnal-'byor* or subsequent yoga because it emphatically reveals the path of desire in pursuit of discriminative awareness (*shes-rab rjes-chags-kyi-lam*).

Thirdly, Anuyoga is classified according to the six topics, of which the first, the entrance, is twofold. The former is empowerment, which refers to the thirty-six empowerment ceremonies subsumed by the four categories of outer, inner, attaining and secret [empowerments] in the maṇḍalas of Anuyoga (*phyi-nang-sgrub-gsang-bzhis bsdus-pa'i dbang-chog sum-cu-rtsa-drug*). It says in the *All-Gathering Awareness*:

> The outer empowerment and the inner empowerment,
> The attaining empowerment and the secret empowerment
> Are respectively complete with ten aspects,
> With eleven, with thirteen and with two aspects.

According to some, the eight hundred and thirty-one ancillary empowerments,[353] which are derived from the basic thirty-six just mentioned, are the empowerments of the nine vehicles. Therefore, it is said in the *Summation of the Meaning of Empowerment* (*dbang-don bsdus-pa*):

> Derived from the six vehicles including Yogatantra,
> The outer empowerment is to be conferred as a continuous stream.

And in the *Analysis of the Meaning of Empowerment* (*dbang-don rnam-par 'byed-pa*):

> The ten empowerments bring about
> Possession of the enlightened family,
> The eleven empowerments bring about
> The inner secret meaning,
> The thirteen empowerments are known
> As those of the "great guru",
> And the two empowerments perfect
> The empowerment of the nine vehicles.

How is it, one might then object, that these become the particular empowerments of Anuyoga [which is only one of the nine vehicles]? There is indeed no contradiction because, in accord with the claims of learned gurus, they are called the empowerment of the nine vehicles (*theg-dgu'i dbang*) in so far as they correspond to nine sequences of the vehicle. There is no basis, however, for the opinion expressed by ordinary exponents of the empowerment for the *Sūtra which Gathers All Intentions* [that they actually are the empowerments of the nine vehicles]. If they were, it is absurdly implied that one would have to admit the higher Atiyoga empowerment to be gathered within the Anuyoga empowerment. By way of illustration, the uncommon doctrinal terminology of the inner [tantras] is not found in the outer tantras. The great awareness-holder Terdak Lingpa has therefore said:

> If one must refer to the fusion
> Of the basic rites of Anuyoga
> With the details of the particular doctrines of the eight [other] vehicles,
> How would these [other vehicles] then define the illustrative basis of Anuyoga [in particular]?

There is therefore no contradiction inasmuch as he is of the former opinion [expressed by learned gurus].

The latter [aspect of the entrance into Anuyoga] is the actual entrance, which is effected by means of the non-duality of the expanse and pristine cognition. It says in the *All-Accomplishing King*:

> Having entered into the expanse and pristine cognition
> Which, according to Anuyoga, are held to be indivisible...

What, one might ask, is the nature of the entrance? It is effected in the manner not of the creation but of the perfection stage. It says in the *Lock of the Heart*:

> The uncreated expanse itself is pristine cognition.
> Pristine cognition, awareness, is the expanse itself.
> The supreme bliss of this non-dual display
> Is not entered gradually.
> In all the [divine] seals of apparitional existence,[354]
> The great seal of apparitional existence is immediately encountered
> In the manner of a fish leaping from the water.

Secondly, as to the view: All things are one's own mind, and that itself is the pure celestial space of the mother Samantabhadrī, whose nature is uncreated and free from conceptual elaboration. It is also called the primordial maṇḍala (*ye ji-bzhin-pa'i dkyil-'khor*). In this respect, the *General Sūtra which Gathers All Intentions* also says:

> Since that which has emerged from the mind is emptiness,
> All that has emerged from it is empty.

This uncreated [reality], unceasing in all respects, is the awareness which radiates as a maṇḍala of naturally present light. It is called the pristine cognition that is Samantabhadra or the spontaneously present maṇḍala of natural expression (*rang-bzhin lhun-grub-kyi dkyil-'khor*). The same text says:

> Unseen upon inspection,
> It itself appears everywhere.

The essence of these two maṇḍalas, which radiate without differentiation, is the supreme bliss of their offspring wherein the expanse and pristine cognition are without duality, the fundamental maṇḍala of enlightened mind (*byang-chub sems-kyi dkyil-'khor*). As the above-cited text again says:

> That which is called the way of secret mantra is the real nature, in which appearance and non-appearance are without duality, which is liberated from the essence of that dichotomy, and does not objectively refer to the middle [ground].

Therefore, all things are regarded as primordial buddhahood in the fundamental maṇḍala of enlightened mind, the indivisible nature of the three kinds of maṇḍala. [The *General Sūtra which Gathers All Intentions*] again says:

> Since everything is therein identical,
> The supreme bliss of primordial buddhahood
> Is itself the nucleus without creation or cessation.
> The three maṇḍalas where there is neither activity nor agent,
> Are accomplished from the beginning, spontaneously present.

And in the *Turquoise Display*:

> From the celestial space of Samantabhadrī, or apparitional existence,
> The uncreated maṇḍala, Samantabhadra, arises.
> In its arising, there is nothing that arises.
> The supreme bliss of father, mother and offspring
> Is spontaneously perfect.

It is further held that the unimpeded expressive power of Samantabhadra's display arises as the body of a deity. The *All-Gathering Awareness* says:

> In the primordially evolved great perfection of Samantabhadra,

In this maṇḍala of the outer, inner and secret arrays,
Apparitional existence is an expanse of pure male and
female deities.

And in the *Miraculous Key to the Storehouse*:

According to Anuyoga, the perfection phase,
The components, psychophysical bases and activity fields
Are held to be uncreated, in a perfect manner,
In the maṇḍala of male and female deities.

Thirdly, concerning moral discipline, the *Summation of the Meaning of the Secret Sūtra* says:

It is commitment which apprehends the basis.
It guards and attains
The basic and ancillary aspects and so forth,
In order to discipline the three media.

In this way, there are basic and ancillary commitments and so forth which are to be guarded and attained by means of the three media [body, speech and mind].

When these commitments are classified, there are said, according to the sixty-sixth chapter of the *General Sūtra which Gathers All Intentions* to be nine enumerations, namely, four commitments definitive to the important sūtras (*gal-mdo nges-pa'i dam-tshig bzhi*), twenty-eight common commitments (*thun-mongs-gi nyi-shu rtsa-brgyad*), four superior commitments (*lhag-pa'i bzhi*), twenty-three relating to discipline (*brtul-zhugs-kyi nyer-gsum*), twenty concerning attainment (*sgrub-pa'i nyi-shu*), four relating to continuity of the path of conduct (*spyod-lam rgyun-gyi bzhi*), five Māras which are to be renounced (*bdud-lnga spang-ba*), four enemies to be destroyed (*dgra-bzhi gzhom-pa*), and the commitment of the view (*lta-ba'i dam-tshig*).

If, on the other hand, these are subsumed, they are gathered into the commitments which are acquired immediately with no limits to be guarded (*bsrung-mtshams med-pa cig-car-ba'i dam-tshig*) and the commitments which are acquired gradually and have limits to be guarded (*bsrung-mtshams-can rim-gyis-pa'i dam-tshig*). It says in the *General Sūtra which Gathers All Intentions*:

That in which there is no pledge to be guarded
Is the firm commitment of reality.

And:

This commitment is most amazing,
Since it is the most uncommon of all;
But for all those of weak volition
There are limits to be guarded.

Fourth, on the subject of meditation, the *Summation of the Meaning of the Secret Sūtra* says:

> Its essence is of skilful means
> And discriminative awareness.

Meditation therefore comprises both the path of skilful means (*thabs-lam*) and the path of liberation (*grol-lam*). The former refers to the yoga in which there is meditation connected with the four or six centres forming the "upper door" [of the body, *steng-sgo*], and to the skilful means which develops co-emergent, pristine cognition by relying on the meditative absorption associated with the two secret centres [of the male and female consorts] forming the "lower door" (*'og-sgo mkha'-gsang gnyis*). As the above text says:

> Through skilful means of esoteric instructions,
> Such as concerns the "source of all display",
> One enters therein.

As for the latter, [the path of liberation]: It comprises both the array of truth and the display of its signs (*don bkod-pa-dang rtags-kyi rol-pa*). The first refers to the non-conceptualising contemplation that is free from conceptual elaboration. It is an absorption derived from the disposition of the nucleus of reality, just as it is, uncontrived by the meditating intellect. In this respect, the *General Sūtra which Gathers All Intentions* says:

> Having established the intellect just as it is
> In the corresponding reality,
> There is an unwavering recollection
> Derived from that inexpressible disposition.

The second, [the display of its signs], refers to contemplation of the deity that is endowed with conceptual elaboration. It is the experiential cultivation which, by the mere recitation of mantra, emphasises immediate meditation in which the world and its contents distinctly radiate as the maṇḍala of deities, in the [immediate] manner of a fish leaping from the water. Such is also said in the *Miraculous Key to the Storehouse*:

> In the vehicle of Anuyoga
> There is uncreated meditation in a perfect manner,
> After merely the nucleus [of the mantra syllables] has been recited.

And in the *All-Gathering Awareness*:

> Pure apparitional existence is an expanse of male and female deities.
> The elements and elemental components

Are spontaneously perfect father and mother consorts.

Concerning the path of definitively perfect meditation in general, [the Anuyoga] includes both corrupt and uncorrupt forms. The former comprises the yoga of the spiritual warrior who aspires (*'dun-pa sems-kyi rnal-'byor*) and the yoga which reveals the great enlightened family (*rigs-chen 'byed-pa'i rnal-'byor*); and the latter comprises the yoga which confers the great liberating inspiration (*dbugs-chen 'byin-pa'i rnal-'byor*), the yoga which obtains the great prophetic declaration (*lung-chen thob-pa'i rnal-'byor*) and the yoga which perfects great expressive power (*rtsal-chen rdzogs-pa'i rnal-'byor*).

Fifth, as to conduct: The conduct of Anuyoga is one which, in general, emphasises sameness. The *Miraculous Key to the Storehouse* says:

The Anuyoga of the perfection phase
Is the perfect rapture of the expanse
And pristine cognition.

If classified in detail, there are three kinds of conduct, namely, consecration or blessing, overpowering and skilful means. The *General Sūtra which Gathers All Intentions* says:

The conduct which consecrates,
The conduct which overpowers,
And the conduct of skilful means
Are exemplified respectively by space and by a king,
And by the water which quenches a fire.

Sixth, concerning the result: Within one lifetime the essence is actualised, in which the twenty-five resultant realities are indivisible and spontaneously present. This is the body of supreme bliss, which is the embodiment of the four buddha-bodies. The *Tantra of the Supreme Seminal Point* (*thig-le mchog-gi rgyud*) says:

Mind-as-such or inner radiance is supreme bliss,
Without dividing the expanse and pristine cognition in two.
Whoever meditates on it will attain
The result of perfect buddhahood in this lifetime.

And in the *Miraculous Key to the Storehouse*:

The vehicle of Anuyoga,
Within one lifetime and without interruption,
Definitively proceeds to the buddha level.

Atiyoga

[228a.3-229b.6] The vehicle of Atiyoga, the esoteric instructions, is considered under the three headings of essence, verbal definition and classification. As to the first, [the essence]: It is the skilful means through which the truth of primordial buddhahood is directly liberated, and it is endowed with a nature which is free from renunciation, acceptance, hope and doubt.

Secondly, [the verbal definition] is that [the Sanskrit] *Atiyoga* is rendered [in Tibetan] as *shin-tu rnal-'byor* or highest yoga because it is the culmination of the perfection stage of both the creation and perfection phases, and because it is the summit of all vehicles.

Thirdly, Atiyoga is classified according to the six topics of which the first, the entrance, is twofold. The former refers to empowerment which here is the maturation effected by the empowerment of the expressive power of awareness (*rig-pa'i rtsal-dbang*) and so forth.[355] The latter is the actual entrance which is effected by not entering anything. The *All-Accomplishing King* says:

> Since with respect to the doctrine
> There is nothing to be done,
> It is entered effortlessly.

Secondly, as to the view, it is held that all things subsumed by apparitional existence, saṃsāra and nirvāṇa, are effortlessly the primordial buddhahood in the essence of a supreme seminal point, the body of reality, which is naturally present, supreme, pristine cognition. It is said in *Vajrasattva the Great Space* (*rdo-rje sems-dpa' nam-mkha' che*, NGB Vol.2):

> Having been effortlessly liberated
> Through the naturally present pristine cognition,
> The path of liberation is indeed revealed.

And in the *Great Garuḍa* (*khyung-chen*, NGB Vol.1):

> The naturally present pristine cognition
> Universally abides, without conception, just as it is.

Thirdly, on the subject of moral discipline, the commitments which include nothingness and plainness are not to be transcended. The *Miraculous Key of Further Discernment* says:

> The commitments of Atiyoga
> Are nothingness and plainness,[356]
> Uniqueness and spontaneous presence.
> Their meaning should not be transcended.

Fourth, as to meditation, the *Great Array of the Highest* says:

> For those who hold to the mind
> There will be the Mental Class;

For those who hold to space
There will be the Spatial Class;
For those who do not strive after stages
There will be the Esoteric Instructional Class.

In this way, there is the Mental Class (*sems-sde*) which pertains to the absorption in awareness and emptiness, the disposition of the buddha-body of reality. There is the Spatial Class (*klong-sde*) which pertains to the absorption in the disposition of reality without activity or effort; and there is the Esoteric Instructional Class (*man-ngag-gi sde*) which pertains to the absorption in the disposition of reality, primordially liberated and free from renunciation and acceptance.

In general, the meditation which accords with the tradition of the Great Perfection is gathered into two categories, namely, Cutting Through Resistance (*khregs-chod*) and All-Surpassing Realisation (*thod-rgal*). It is said in the *Pearl Necklace*:

Cutting Through Resistance
And All-Surpassing Realisation
Are experientially cultivated.

According to the former [Cutting Through Resistance]: There is absorption without wavering from the disposition of the primordially pure view. The *Great Garuḍa* says:

It is established because it spontaneously abides.

And the master Garap Dorje says:

The nature of mind is primordially buddha.
In the mind, as in the sky,
There is no creation or cessation.
Having realised the genuine truth
Of the sameness of all things,
If it is established without being sought,
That is meditation.

By meditating in that way there are four creative stages of the path:

There are the abiding and unwavering states,
Sameness and spontaneous presence.

As for the All-Surpassing Realisation (*thod-rgal*): Through reliance on the six essentials (*gnad-drug*), the four visionary appearances gradually arise, and thereby the goal is reached. These [four] are, namely, the visionary appearance of the direct perception of reality (*chos-nyid mngon-sum*), the visionary appearance of increasing contemplative experience (*nyams-gong-'phel*), the visionary appearance of reaching the limits of awareness (*rig-pa tshad-phebs*) and the visionary appearance of the cessation [of apparitional] reality (*chos-nyid zad-pa*).

Fifth, in conduct: There is conduct without acceptance and rejection because all that appears arises as the display of reality. It is said in *Vajrasattva the Great Space*:

> Since there is nothing to be done, actions are terminated.

And in the *Miraculous Key to the Storehouse*:

> Concerning the conduct of Atiyoga:
> The forceful conduct practised
> By one endowed with the vital force of view and
> meditation
> Resembles the conduct of a madman.
> Anything whatsoever is practised without impediment.

Sixth, as to the result: The goal is reached, abiding from the present moment on the level of the spontaneously perfect Samantabhadra. By reaching the limit of the four assurances (*gding-bzhi*), saṃsāra is liberated in nirvāṇa. This is also said in the *Miraculous Key of Further Discernment*:

> Concerning the result of Atiyoga, the Great
> Perfection:
> In the primordial nucleus which is enlightenment,
> The unattained result is mature in itself.

This completes the anthology which explains the definitive order of the resultant secret mantra, the vehicle of indestructible reality, the fourth and, for the while, the last exegetical part of this book, the *Feast in which Eloquence Appears*, a definitive ordering of the precious teaching of the vehicle of indestructible reality according to the Ancient Translation School.

Conclusion

1 *Concluding Remarks*

[229b.6-232a.4] With the hope of somewhat benefitting those persons who pursue the subject-matter of this book with fresh intellects, I have condensed and succinctly emphasised the words of the great, all-knowing doctrinal master Longcenpa, and those of Locen [Dharmaśrī] Chöpel Gyamtso of Mindröling, the paṇḍita Gyurme Tsewang Chokdrup of Katok, Jamgön [Kongtrül] Lodrö Thaye, Dodrup Jikme Tenpei Nyima and Zecen Gyeltsap Gyurme Pema Namgyel.[357]

Although the definitive order of the sūtras and the mantras may appear repetitive because it has been divided into two parts, one according to the overall meaning and the other according to the meaning subsumed in their particular sections, it is with a view to easy comprehension that the opportune recapitulations have been added in a way which will facilitate understanding.

As for those whose intellects are still unsatisfied by this mere [abridgement], who wish to thoroughly investigate the limits of study and reflection, the thousand petals of their intellects should be impartially liberated by relying on the extensive eloquent compositions of the prior learned and accomplished masters such as the following: the scriptures of the all-knowing Trime Özer [Longcenpa] which, in the manner of a treasury of precious gems containing the numerous extraordinary riches of a kingdom, excellently comment on all the definitive, profound essentials of tantra, transmission and esoteric instruction endowed with the six superiorities of the ancient translations, with an insight which perceives reality independently, just as it is;[358] his *Mother and Son Cycles of Innermost Spirituality* (*snying-thig ma-bu'i skor*);[359] the writings on the *Sūtra which Gathers All Intentions* and the *Cycle of the Tantra of the Magical Net* (*'dus-pa mdo-dang sgyu-'phrul skor-gyi yig-cha*) which were composed by [Locen Dharmaśrī], the brother of the great awareness-holder Terdak Lingpa; and the scriptures of Jamgön Mipham Mawei Senge [Mipham Rinpoche].

2 *Dedicatory Verses*

Again it might be said:

From the taintless ocean, profound and wide, of the tradition
Of the ancient translations which are the ultimate perfection
of the Conqueror's teaching,
I have extracted the essence, an excellent vase of exegesis,
A nectar stream satisfying the lot of those new students
who wish to know it.

The *Feast in which* the teaching's definitive order is
narrated
By relying on the sacred *Eloquence* of the past,
Approaching with smiles of superior aspiration, which
Appears,
Brings forth a springtime of supreme delight to a host of
fortunate beings.

If there are mistaken points herein, the fault is mine.
May those who are learned and honest be kind to
show restraint.
All that is eloquent, through the grace of the guru,
Is but my respect and service for the teaching.

May the grievous clouds which thunder with the verses
of indestructible reality,[360]
Profound essentials of the highest unsurpassed
vehicle,
And nakedly expose their mysteries and so forth,
Be dispelled by the whirlwind of the three roots'
blessing
In the inexpressible space of reality's expanse.

May all the merit obtained herein by my labour
Be dedicated to the expansion of the teaching.
Abiding long in the world, may the nucleus of the teaching
Adorn the lands with oceans of enlightened attributes.

May I, too, in all my lives,
In the manner of the spiritual warrior, Lord of Secrets,
Hold the secret repository of the Conqueror's teaching,
And, roaring the lion's roar of the profound truth,
May I churn the depths of existence by moving therein.

May fundamental reality in its natural state,
Free from the Fears (*Jikdrel*) of change,
Possessing the nucleus of *Pristine Cognition* (*Yeshe*)
Which encompasses all worlds, animate and inanimate,
Secure all things in supreme bliss
By the seal of imperishable mind's *Indestructible Reality* (*Dorje*).[361]

3 *Colophon*

This book, the abridged definitive ordering of the teaching of the Nyingmapa, or Ancient Translation School of the secret mantra, entitled *Feast in which Eloquence Appears*, begun by the vagabond Jikdrel Yeshe Dorje in his sixty-third year on Friday 3 June 1966 (fifteenth day of the fourth month (*sa-ga*) of the Fire Horse Year or *zil-gnon*), was composed with effort at all times; and it was brought to completion on Thursday 29 September (fifteenth day of the auspicious eighth month or *khrum-stod*) in the Citadel of Lotus Light (*padma 'od-kyi grong-khyer*) on the summit of Mount Rincen Pung, known as the supreme pilgrimage place of Kalimpong, which is an extension of the secret land of Sikkim. The first draft was prepared by the scribe Rikdzin Dorje, a venerable *mantrin* from Kurelung in Bhutan. May the nucleus of the teaching thereby secure the destiny of abiding long without decline. *Sarvadā maṅgala-śrī jayantu*! ["May glorious good auspices ever be victorious."]

> *Oṃ Svasti*:
> This definitive order of the ocean-like teaching
> Of the Ancient Translation School,
> Which reveals the extensive meaning with few words,
> Was prepared in its final xylographic edition
> Through the unending generosity to the doctrine
> Of the faithful Pelhün Yülgyel[362] of Tingri.
> By virtue of this merit may the precious teaching
> Multiply and increase until the end of time, without
> decline.
> May the great drumbeat of the doctrine
> Of definitively secret exegesis and attainment
> Resound throughout the whole world.
> Above all, may the father and mother
> Who gave birth to this benefactor,
> Along with his relations and all living beings,

Become naturally liberated of the two obscurations,
And then swiftly complete the two provisions
And actualise the two buddha-bodies.
May the two benefits resplendently blaze
With spontaneously present good auspices.

May these meaningful expressions of Jikdrel Yeshe Dorje be victorious. This xylograph is preserved at the monastery of Zangdok Pelri in Kalimpong.

Book Two
History of the Nyingma School

Dudjom Rinpoche, Jikdrel Yeshe Dorje

Translated and edited by Gyurme Dorje
with the collaboration of Matthew Kapstein

Detailed Contents of Book Two

TRANSLATORS' INTRODUCTION 393

THE TEXT

VERSES OF INVOCATION 403

PART ONE: THE ORIGIN OF THE PRECIOUS TEACHING OF THE CONQUEROR IN THIS WORLD [*1*]

INTRODUCTION 409

1 THE COMING OF BUDDHA, TEACHER OF THE DOCTRINE [*1.1*] 411

The Opinion of the Adherents of the Lesser Vehicle [*1.1.1*] 411
The Ordinary Opinion of the Greater Vehicle and of the Tantras [*1.1.2*] 412
The Special Position of the Nyingma Tradition [*1.1.3*] 413
The Body of Emanation [*1.1.4*] 415
The Life of Śākyamuni [*1.1.5*] 416

2 THE COLLECTING OF TRANSMITTED PRECEPTS BY COUNCILS [*1.2*] 428

The First Council [*1.2.1*] 428
The Second Council [*1.2.2*] 429
The Third Council [*1.2.3*] 429
The Councils of the Greater Vehicle [*1.2.4*] 430

3 THE PATRIARCHS OF THE TEACHING [*1.3*] 432

Mahākāśyapa [*1.3.1*] 432
Ānanda [*1.3.2*] 434
Śāṇavāsika [*1.3.3*] 435

Upagupta [*1.3.4*] 436
Dhītika, Kṛṣṇa, Sudarśana, Madhyāhnika and the Sixteen Elders [*1.3.5*] 437

4 THE PRESERVATION OF THE TEACHING AND SPREAD OF THE GREATER VEHICLE [*1.4*] 440

PART TWO: THE RISE OF THE PRECIOUS TEACHING OF SECRET MANTRA [2]

INTRODUCTION 445

1 THE TURNING OF THE SECRET MANTRA WHEEL [*2.1*] 447

The Intentional Lineage of the Conquerors [*2.1.1*] 447

2 THE COLLECTING OF TRANSMITTED PRECEPTS BY DIFFERENT COMPILERS [*2.2*] 451

3 THE EMERGENCE OF THIS TEACHING IN THE HUMAN WORLD [*2.3*] 452

The Symbolic Lineage of the Awareness-holders [*2.3.1*] 452
The Origination of the Symbolic Lineage among Non-Human Awareness-holders [*2.3.1.1*] 452
The Origination of the Symbolic Lineage among Human and Non-Human Awareness-holders [*2.3.1.2*] 454
The Aural Lineage of Mundane Individuals [*2.3.2*] 456

4 THE LINEAGE OF MAHĀYOGA, THE CLASS OF TANTRAS [*2.4*] 458

King Ja and Kukkurāja [*2.4.1*] 458
Līlāvajra [*2.4.2*] 463
Buddhaguhya [*2.4.3*] 464
Vajrahāsya [*2.4.4*] 466
Prabhāhasti [*2.4.5*] 467
Padmasambhava [*2.4.6*] 468

5 THE LINEAGE OF MAHĀYOGA, THE CLASS OF MEANS FOR ATTAINMENT [*2.5*] 475

Hūṃkara and the Transmitted Precept of Yangdak (Śrīheruka) [*2.5.1*] 475
Mañjuśrīmitra and the Transmitted Precept of Yamāntaka [*2.5.2*] 477
Nāgārjuna and the Transmitted Precept of Hayagrīva [*2.5.3*] 479

Vimalamitra and the Transmitted Precept of Vajrāmṛta [*2.5.4*] 480
Prabhāhasti, Padmasambhava and the Transmitted Precept of Vajrakīla [*2.5.5*] 481
The Revealed Treasures [*2.5.6*] 482

6 THE LINEAGE OF ANUYOGA, THE PERFECTION STAGE [*2.6*] 485

Kambalapāda or the Younger Indrabhūti [*2.6.1*] 485
The Successors of the Younger Indrabhūti [*2.6.2*] 487

7 THE LINEAGE OF ATIYOGA, THE GREAT PERFECTION [*2.7*] 490

Garap Dorje and Mañjuśrīmitra [*2.7.1*] 490
Buddhajñānapāda [*2.7.2*] 494
Śrī Siṃha, Jñānasūtra and Vimalamitra [*2.7.3*] 497

8 CONCLUDING REMARKS [*2.8*] 502

PART THREE: THE ORIGIN OF THE CONQUEROR'S TEACHING IN TIBET [*3*]

INTRODUCTION [*3.1*] 507

1 THE THREE ANCESTRAL RELIGIOUS KINGS [*3.2*] 510

King Songtsen Gampo [*3.2.1*] 510
King Trhisong Detsen and the Coming of Padmasambhava [*3.2.2*] 512
King Relpacen [*3.2.3*] 521

2 THE DECLINE AND EXPANSION OF THE DOCTRINE DURING THE INTERMEDIATE PERIOD [*3.3*] 523

3 THE REVIVAL AND LATER EXPANSION OF THE TEACHING [*3.4*] 524

PART FOUR: THE DEVELOPMENT OF THE THREE INNER CLASSES OF TANTRA IN TIBET [*4*]

INTRODUCTION 531

1 MAHĀYOGA AND ANUYOGA [*4.1/2*] 533

Mahāyoga, the Stage of Creation [*4.1*] 533

The Mahāyoga Class of Tantras [*4.1.1*] 533
The Mahāyoga Class of Means for Attainment [*4.1.2*] 534
Anuyoga, the Stage of Perfection [*4.2*] 537

2 THE MENTAL AND SPATIAL CLASSES OF ATIYOGA [*4.3.1/2*] 538

Vairocana [*4.3.1/2.1*] 538
Pang-gen Sangye Gönpo [*4.3.1/2.2*] 540
Ngenlam Cangcup Gyeltsen, Zadam Rincen-yik and Khugyur Selweichok [*4.3.1/2.3*] 541
Nyang Cangcup-tra and Nyang Sherap Jungne [*4.3.1/2.4*] 542
Bagom [*4.3.1/2.5*] 542
Dzeng Dharmabodhi [*4.3.1/2.6*] 543
Dzeng Co-se [*4.3.1/2.7*] 550
Master Künzang and Trülku Öbar Senge [*4.3.1/2.8*] 551
Other Lineages Stemming from Dzeng [*4.3.1/2.9*] 552

3 THE ESOTERIC INSTRUCTIONAL CLASS OF ATIYOGA, THE INNERMOST SPIRITUALITY [*4.3.3*] 554

The Tradition of Padmasambhava [*4.3.3.1*] 554
The Tradition of Vimalamitra [*4.3.3.2*] 555
Vimalamitra [*4.3.3.2.1*] 555
Nyang Tingdzin Zangpo [*4.3.3.2.2*] 555
Dangma Lhündrup Gyeltsen [*4.3.3.2.3*] 556
Cetsün Senge Wangcuk [*4.3.3.2.4*] 557
Zhangtön [*4.3.3.2.5*] 559
Nyibum [*4.3.3.2.6*] 561
Guru Cober [*4.3.3.2.7*] 563
Trhüzhi Sengegyap [*4.3.3.2.8*] 564
Melong Dorje [*4.3.3.2.9*] 566
Kumārādza [*4.3.3.2.10*] 568
Karmapa III, Rangjung Dorje [*4.3.3.2.11*] 572

4 LONGCEN RAPJAMPA [*4.4*] 575

PART FIVE: THE DISTANT LINEAGE OF TRANSMITTED PRECEPTS [5]

INTRODUCTION 599

1 THE LINEAGE OF NYAK [*5.1*] 601

Nyak Jñānakumāra [*5.1.1*] 601
The Sogdian Pelgi Yeshe [*5.1.2*] 605

2 THE LINEAGE OF NUP [*5.2*] 607

Nupcen Sangye Yeshe [*5.2.1*] 607
Khulung Yönten Gyamtso [*5.2.2*] 614
Yeshe Gyamtso, Pema Wangyel and the Later Successors in the Lineage of Nup [*5.2.3*] 615

3 THE LINEAGE OF THE ZUR FAMILY [*5.3*] 617

Lharje Zurpoche Śākya Jungne [*5.3.1*] 617
Zurcung Sherap-tra [*5.3.2*] 635
Zur Dropukpa Śākya Senge [*5.3.3*] 645

4 BIOGRAPHIES OF THE RONG TRADITION [*5.4*] 650

Cetön Gyanak [*5.4.1*] 650
Yöntenzung [*5.4.2*] 651
Tampa Sedrakpa [*5.4.3*] 651
Zhikpo of Central Tibet [*5.4.4*] 652
Zhikpo Dütsi [*5.4.5*] 653
Tatön Co-ye [*5.4.6*] 656
Tatön Co-sö [*5.4.7*] 659
Tatön Ziji [*5.4.8*] 660
Pakshi Śākya-ö [*5.4.9*] 660
Zur Campa Senge [*5.4.10*] 663
Yungtön Dorjepel [*5.4.11*] 666
Tanak Drölmawa Samdrup Dorje [*5.4.12*] 667
Zur Zangpopel and Zur Ham Śākya Jungne [*5.4.13*] 669
Sangye Rincen [*5.4.14*] 672
Gölo Zhönupel (Yezang Tsepa) [*5.4.15*] 674
Ce-nga Rinpoche, Zharmarpa IV [*5.4.16*] 675
Drigung Zurpa Rincen Phüntsok [*5.4.17*] 676
Khöntön Peljor Lhündrup [*5.4.18*] 677
Zurcen Chöying Rangdröl [*5.4.19*] 679
The Fifth Dalai Lama [*5.4.20*] 683

5 DOTOKPA'S LINEAGE OF THE ZUR TRADITION [*5.5*] 685

Dotokpa Sangye-tra and Kyi Chöki Senge [*5.5.1*] 685
Menlungpa Śākya-ö [*5.5.2*] 686
Dorje Gyeltsen and his Successors [*5.5.3*] 686

6 BIOGRAPHIES OF THE KHAM TRADITION [*5.6*] 688

Katokpa Tampa Deshek [*5.6.1*] 688
Tsangtönpa [*5.6.2*] 691
Campabum [*5.6.3*] 693
The Successive Regents of Katok [*5.6.4*] 694

Khedrup Yeshe Gyeltsen [*5.6.5*] 696
The Lineages of Katok [*5.6.6*] 698

7 MISCELLANEOUS LINEAGES OF THE ZUR AND KHAM TRADITIONS [*5.7*] 700

The Empowerment of the *Sūtra which Gathers All Intentions* in Kham [*5.7.1*] 700
The Lineage of Rok Sherap-ö [*5.7.2*] 701
The Lineage of Yatö Zurpa [*5.7.3*] 702

8 RONGZOM CHÖKI ZANGPO [*5.8*] 703

9 THE TRADITIONS OF VAJRAKĪLA [*5.9*] 710

The Transmissions of Vajrakīla [*5.9.1*] 710
Langlap Cangcup Dorje and Other Masters of Vajrakīla [*5.9.2*] 713
Darcarupa and the Terma Tradition of Vajrakīla [*5.9.3*] 714

10 THE LINEAGES OF THE EMPOWERMENT OF THE *SŪTRA WHICH GATHERS ALL INTENTIONS* [*5.10*] 717

The Lineage of Zur Ham Śākya Jungne [*5.10.1*] 717
  Dorje Trak Rikdzin Pema Trhinle [*5.10.1.1*] 719
The Lineage of Zur Ham's Sister, Zurmo [*5.10.2*] 720
The Lineage of the Son, Sangye Rincen [*5.10.3*] 720
  Zhangtön Namka Dorje [*5.10.3.1*] 720
  Rikdzin Yudruk Dorje [*5.10.3.2*] 721
  Khedrup Lodrö Gyeltsen Pelzangpo (Sodokpa) [*5.10.3.3*] 722
  Kong-ra Locen Zhenpen Dorje [*5.10.3.4*] 723
  Sangdak Trhinle Lhündrup [*5.10.3.5*] 724
  Locen Chögyel Tendzin [*5.10.3.6*] 726
  Locen Dharmaśrī [*5.10.3.7*] 728

11 LATER LINEAGES OF THE TRANSMITTED PRECEPTS [*5.11*] 733

The Mindröling Lineage of Transmitted Precepts [*5.11.1*] 733
The Mindröling Lineage of Atiyoga [*5.11.2*] 734
The Lineage of the *Collected Tantras* [*5.11.3*] 734
Lineages in Kham [*5.11.4*] 735
  Katok [*5.11.4.1*] 736
  Dzokcen [*5.11.4.2*] 736
  Pelyül [*5.11.4.3*] 738

PART SIX: THE CLOSE LINEAGES OF THE TREASURES [*6*]

1 THE NATURE, PURPOSE AND KINDS OF TREASURE [*6.1*] 743

The Nature of the Treasures [*6.1.1*] 743
The Purpose of the Treasures [*6.1.2*] 744
The Lineages of the Treasures [*6.1.3*] 745
The Concealment of the Earth Treasures [*6.1.4*] 746
Pure Visions and Treasures of Intention [*6.1.5*] 747

2 BIOGRAPHIES OF THE TREASURE-FINDERS [*6.2*] 750

3 SANGYE LAMA [*6.3*] 751

4 TRAPA NGÖNSHE [*6.4*] 753

5 NYANG-REL NYIMA ÖZER [*6.5*] 755

6 GURU CHÖKI WANGCUK [*6.6*] 760

7 COMO MENMO [*6.7*] 771

8 ORGYEN LINGPA [*6.8*] 775

9 NGÖDRUP GYELTSEN OR RIKDZIN GÖDEMCEN [*6.9*] 780

10 SANGYE LINGPA [*6.10*] 784

11 DORJE LINGPA [*6.11*] 789

12 RATNA LINGPA [*6.12*] 793

13 PEMA LINGPA [*6.13*] 796

14 KARMA LINGPA [*6.14*] 800

15 THANGTONG GYELPO [*6.15*] 802

16 NGARI PAṆCEN PEMA WANGYEL [*6.16*] 805

17 RIKDZIN JATSÖN NYINGPO [*6.17*] 809

18 RIKDZIN DÜDÜL DORJE [*6.18*] 813

19 LHATSÜN NAMKA JIKME [*6.19*] 818

20 THE FIFTH DALAI LAMA [*6.20*] 821

21 RIKDZIN TERDAK LINGPA, THE GREAT TREASURE-FINDER OF MINDRÖLING [*6.21*] 825

22 JIKME LINGPA [*6.22*] 835

23 CHOGYUR DECEN LINGPA [*6.23*] 841

Chogyur Lingpa's Seven Successions to the Transmitted Precepts [*6.23.1*] 844

24 JAMYANG KHYENTSE WANGPO [*6.24*] 849

Khyentse Wangpo's Seven Successions to the Transmitted Precepts [*6.24.1*] 855

25 JAMGÖN KONGTRÜL LODRÖ THAYE [*6.25*] 859

26 MIPHAM JAMYANG NAMGYEL GYAMTSO [*6.26*] 869

CONCLUSION 881

PART SEVEN: A RECTIFICATION OF THE MISCONCEPTIONS CONCERNING THE NYINGMA SCHOOL [7]

1 GENERAL REPLY TO CRITICISMS OF THE NYINGMAPA TANTRAS [*7.1*] 887

2 ON THE VIEW OF THE GREAT PERFECTION [*7.2*] 896

3 RESPONSE TO CRITICS OF THE *SŪTRA WHICH GATHERS ALL INTENTIONS* [*7.3*] 911

4 RESPONSE TO CRITICS OF THE *ROOT TANTRA OF THE SECRET NUCLEUS* [*7.4*] 914

5 THE CONTINUITY OF THE NYINGMAPA TRADITION AND ITS IMPACT ON THE OTHER SCHOOLS [*7.5*] 918

6 ON THE VALIDITY OF THE TREASURES [*7.6*] 927

7 THE SHORTCOMINGS OF REFUTATION AND PROOF [*7.7*] 929

PART EIGHT: THE CHRONOLOGY OF THE DOCTRINE [*8*]

CLOSING STATEMENTS

Translators' Introduction

In the traditional view, the Buddhist religion made its first appearance in Tibet during the reign of Lha Thotori Nyentsen at some time prior to the mid-fifth century of our era. According to some, a collection of scriptures and symbols consecrated to Avalokiteśvara, the bodhisattva of compassion, simply fell onto the roof of the palace, but others maintain that an Indian or Central Asian Buddhist monk made his way to Tibet with a translator. The country, however, was not yet ripe for the teaching of the Buddha's doctrine. Tibet was still not literate, much less prepared to import an alien civilisation.

The fact of the matter was that in the middle part of the first millenium Tibet was an island in the midst of a Buddhist sea. In India the great monastic universities of the Gangetic plain were at the height of their development. In China Buddhist learning and devotion had acclimatised themselves to an East Asian environment, and, all along the great trade routes linking China to India and to the West, wealthy oases patronised the spread of the genuine doctrine (*saddharma*). So during the seventh century when Tibet, under the leadership of King Songtsen Gampo, burst onto the international scene as a full-fledged empire, she found the unifying feature throughout the known civilised world to be Buddhism.

Songtsen Gampo is revered in Tibet as the father of Tibetan civilisation as we know it. He gave his people law and literacy, an improved technology and a new range of occult skills. Most of all, however, he gave them the basis for the growth of the universal religion of the Tathāgata, which reached its first fruition during the reign of Songtsen Gampo's descendant Trhisong Detsen. He and his grandson Relpacen generously sponsored the missionary work of Indian, Chinese and Central Asian Buddhist masters, who, in collaboration with a growing Tibetan Buddhist clergy, refined the literary Tibetan language into a precision instrument for the expression of the profound depths of scripture and commentary. Their achievement in translating, with astonishing accuracy, a vast literary corpus into Tibetan is certainly to be ranked among the great intellectual and spiritual monuments of mankind. Moreover, the Tibetans were not content to make of their new religion an intellectual exercise alone: yogin, monk and layman alike undertook to realise through meditative experience the perennial truths which the Buddha taught.

These new developments did not, however, meet with the approval of all factions of Tibetan society and a reaction set in. Relpacen was assassinated in 841 (or 838) and his elder brother Langdarma, who detested Buddhism, ascended the throne. The latter persecuted the monastic establishments until, not long after, he himself was assassinated. The ensuing chaos culminated in the final collapse of the dynasty and the end of the Tibetan empire.

Despite the hardships a few dedicated Tibetan monks did manage to keep their faith alive during that troubled age. Also, married yogins, who lived within the community and had suffered less in the persecutions, preserved all they could of Buddhist learning and lore. By the mid-tenth century Buddhism was in an ascendant phase once more: Tibetans in search of the doctrine began to travel to Nepal and India for instructions, and, perhaps encouraged by the eastward spread of Islam and the resurgence of Hinduism in India, Indian Buddhist masters began to journey to Tibet to instruct enthusiastic young disciples, who lived in communities largely supportive of their spiritual endeavours.

In the story related thus far there appears a major boundary, one that it is crucial to be aware of in order to appreciate the special position of the Nyingma or Ancient Translation School of Tibetan Buddhism, the history of which constitutes the subject-matter of the present book. On the one side there is the Buddhist religion of the imperial period, transmitted and redacted under royal patronage when Tibet was at the peak of its political and military stature, and when Buddhism itself was at its zenith as the religion of pan-Asian civilisation. On the other side of the boundary we see a politically disunified and weakened Tibet finding its own refuge in, and providing at the same time a refuge for, an enlightened doctrine tenuously existing in a fundamentally inhospitable world.

While all schools of Tibetan Buddhism trace some of their roots back to the earlier period, the Nyingmapa distinguish themselves by their assertion that they alone represent the complete unadulterated teaching of Padmasambhava, Vimalamitra, Śāntarakṣita and the other accomplished masters of India who, under the patronage of King Trhisong Detsen, transmitted the whole of their spiritual knowledge to Tibetan disciples of such remarkable calibre as Vairocana, Yeshe Tshogyel and the king himself. The Buddhist teachings which have been transmitted within the Nyingma school are elaborated in some detail by Dudjom Rinpoche, in his *Fundamentals of the Nyingma School* (*bstan-pa'i rnam-gzhag*) which constitutes the first part of this volume.

As Tibet passed through the first of its sixty-year calendrical cycles (1027-87), the political fragmentation of its society was mirrored in the development of a number of new independent Buddhist schools, each adhering to its own special system of meditative experience and tracing its lineage back through different masters. Most important among them were the Kadampa school, which based itself on the teachings of the saintly and accomplished Bengali scholar Atiśa, who came to Tibet in 1042 and remained there until his death in 1054, and whose teaching emphasised the cultivation of the pure enlightened attitude of the greater vehicle (*Mahāyāna*); the Path and Fruit (*lam-'bras*) school, which was introduced by the Tibetan translator Drokmi and rooted itself in the esoteric teachings of the accomplished master Virūpa; and the Kagyü school, derived from the precepts of Marpa Chöki Wangcuk, who had mastered the innermost instructions of the yogas taught by the Indian adepts Nāropā, Maitripā and others. These schools in their turn gave rise to numerous sub-schools. The Kagyü, for instance, is usually said to have four great and eight minor subsects within its aegis. At the same time other small and distinctive traditions flourished, the foremost among them being the Shangpa Kagyü, founded by Khyungpo Neljor; Pacification and the Object of Cutting, both tracing themselves back to the Indian master Phadampa; and various schools emphasising the *Kālacakra Tantra*. In the midst of these developments the Nyingma teaching maintained its own identity and its unique and treasured precepts.

The pattern of religious development in Tibet gradually yielded four major Buddhist schools: the Nyingma, Kagyü, and Sakya schools, and, in addition, the Gelukpa, founded by the great Je Tsongkapa (1357-1419), which based itself to a large extent on the teachings of the older Kadampa school. The first of these is here treated in detail, but like a gem in Indra's Net it reflects all the others as well.

In the conflicting and often violent political currents of post-imperial Tibet the various spiritual traditions, for better or worse, could not but become to some extent entangled in mundane power struggles. Thus, it was for the better that the Khön family, rising to prominence in Sakya, took a special interest in the Path and Fruit tradition, which has been preserved primarily by their school, the Sakyapa. But it was certainly for the worse that the hierarchs of Drigung, one of the Kagyü subsects, involved themselves in thirteenth-century Mongol politics only to bring about their own destruction at the hands of the Sakyapa's Mongol patrons. For some centuries Tibetan life was to be dominated by shifting alliances of religious and political parties. An unfortunate outcome has been a legacy of sporadic, bitter sectarianism.

At the same time greater minds saw beyond the rivalries and factionalism. Maintaining the integrity of their own traditions, they freely learned from and taught adherents of other traditions as well. All of the Tibetan schools can boast of such figures. In the pages of the present history we will encounter the likes of Rongzompa, Longcenpa, Terdak Lingpa and others who exemplified Nyingma ideals while affirming the common ground shared by all Buddhist traditions.

None the less, the Nyingmapa did suffer in the temporal sphere owing to their determined aloofness from the political scene. The distant lineage of the transmitted precepts (*ring-brgyud bka'-ma*), which was traced back in a direct succession to the ancient period, grew increasingly fragile with each new generation. This state of affairs, however, had been foreseen by the ancient masters: Padmasambhava, in particular, had responded by filling the land of Tibet with spiritual treasures which awaited rediscovery by individuals of appropriate vision. So it was that as the distant lineage waned there arose a close lineage of rediscovered spiritual treasures (*nye-brgyud gter-ma*) to meet the needs of a new age. Since this proved to be a perfect medium for maintaining the continuity and blessing of the ancient translations, most practising Nyingmapa at the present time adhere to meditative cycles which were revealed in this way. Moreover, from the seventeenth century onwards major Nyingmapa monasteries were founded and restored to preserve the vast array of such treasures as well as all that survived of the distant lineage, thereby guaranteeing the ongoing vitality of the tradition.

Thus there are now two methods of transmission through which the Nyingma teachings have been handed down. The distant lineage of the transmitted precepts (*ring-brgyud bka'-ma*) has synthesised the major texts and teaching cycles of Mahāyoga, Anuyoga and Atiyoga under the heading *Trio of the Sūtra, Magical Net and Mental Class* (*mdo-sgyu-sems-gsum*). These are respectively the Anuyoga *Sūtra which Gathers All Intentions*, the Mahāyoga *Tantra of the Magical Net*, and the *Mental Class* of Atiyoga. In addition, the close lineage of treasures or rediscovered teachings (*nye-brgyud gter-ma*) has transmitted the doctrines known as the *Trio of the Guru, Great Perfection and the Great Compassionate One* (*bla-rdzogs-thugs gsum*), which synthesise the teaching cycles relating to Guru Padmasambhava (*bla*), the Great Perfection (*rdzogs*) and the Great Compassionate One, Avalokiteśvara (*thugs*).

BRIEF SUMMARY OF THE TEXT

The *History* is divided into eight parts. The first of these is a general account of the origins and development of Buddhism in India, emphasising the life of Śākyamuni Buddha, the patriarchs of the teaching, its preservation, and the expansion of the greater vehicle.

Part Two describes the origins of the three inner classes of tantra – the Mahāyoga, Anuyoga and Atiyoga. These are the characteristic teachings of the Nyingmapa *par excellence*, and here the beginnings of their three main lineages are surveyed: the lineage of the intention of the Primordial Buddha, Samantabhadra, the symbolic transmission of the awareness holders, and the aural transmission of individual human beings.

Part Three gives an account of the introduction of Buddhism to Tibet during the reigns of Songtsen Gampo, Trhisong Detsen, and Trhi Relpacen by Padmasambhava and Śāntarakṣita, along with an account of the continuation of the Nyingmapa tradition through to the restoration of monastic Buddhism in Central Tibet during the late tenth and early eleventh centuries.

Part Four treats the introduction into Tibet of the three inner classes of tantra, but deals primarily with the lives of the masters of the Great Perfection, from Vairocana (*circa* eighth century) through to Longcenpa (1308-63).

In Part Five the subject-matter is the previously mentioned distant lineage of transmitted precepts, which was maintained at an early date by Nyak Jñānakumāra (*circa* late eighth century), Nup Sangye Yeshe (mid-ninth century) and the masters of the Zur family (eleventh century onwards). The lineage was continued by the Rong tradition in Central Tibet and the Kham tradition in the Sino-Tibetan border regions until the time of Terdak Lingpa (1646-1714), and descended to the present Author in an unbroken line.

Part Six outlines the history of the close lineage of the rediscovered spiritual treasures, providing an account of their meaning and purpose along with brief biographies of the most important treasure-finders down to Mipham Rinpoche (1846-1912).

Part Seven considers the polemical attacks which have been launched against the Nyingma tradition in the past and summarises the responses to these in order to introduce the reader precisely to the view that the Nyingmapa have traditionally held.

The eighth and final part provides a chronology for the book as a whole and an account of the prophecies concerning the future development of Buddhism.

THE LITERARY TRADITION OF THE *HISTORY*

It will be seen from the above that the central parts are the fourth to the sixth, which comprise some three-quarters of the work as a whole and which provide the actual accounts of the history of the peculiarly Nyingma teachings in Tibet. The historical traditions of the Great Perfection, considered in Part Four, were redacted in much of their present form as early as the fourteenth century by Longcenpa and his disciples. Those of the distant lineage of transmitted precepts, abridged in Part Five, were fairly well established by the time Gölo Zhönupel composed his *Blue Annals* (1478) and reached the form in which they are found here in the works of such seventeenth-century authors as Rikdzin Pema Trhinle and Locen Dharmaśrī. Finally, the contents of Part Six were established by a succession of masters, the most recent being Jamgön Kongtrül Lodrö Thaye (1813-99). There were therefore three major historical traditions connected with the lineages of the Nyingma school in Tibet, and these have been masterfully anthologised by Dudjom Rinpoche in this work.

The similarities at certain junctures between this and earlier histories have been noted by a number of contemporary scholars: Parts One to Five, for example, often correspond to the second part of Gyurme Tshewang Chokdrup's *Catalogue of the Collected Tantras*, and Part Seven to the third part of the latter, which similarly borrows from earlier works. It is important to recognise that Tibet was free from the concepts of ownership of the written word which form the bases for our copyright laws, and so Tibetan authors borrowed from one another with perfect freedom, the guiding principle being that the insights of enlightened masters of the past are always worthy of repetition. The works upon which Dudjom Rinpoche has drawn have, in accordance with tradition, been listed in a special section at the end of the book (pp. 965-6).

As the foregoing remarks suggest, the Tibetan historian acts very much as a compiler or anthologist of material that has been handed down by his or her tradition. It would be wrong, however, to see in Tibetan religious historiography merely an uncritical repetition of old stories; for its canons are most certainly not those of modern western historiography, and any attempt to judge the former in terms of the latter will always lead to the conclusion that Tibetan historiography is defective in the manner of its pre-Renaissance counterpart in the West.

As we read the biographies found in Dudjom Rinpoche's *History*, however, another observation forces itself upon us: many of these stories, which certainly do treat of historical figures, their studies, meditations, and actions on behalf of the Buddhist religion, function as allegorical accounts of the specific spiritual traditions in which they are written. Nyak Jñānakumāra (pp. 601-5), for example, appears motivated in his practice by a search for vengeance, but "his intention turned to reality itself and he was completely unable to perform the [wrathful] rite". Rikdzin Terdak Lingpa (pp. 825-34) lives different stages of his life according to the different stages of esoteric empowerment. The examples could be multiplied indefinitely. Viewed with sufficient sensitivity to the tradition it becomes clear that the spiritual paths taught abstractly in doctrinal texts are here mapped concretely through the lives of individuals. These accounts thus tell us as much of Tibetan religious beliefs, values and insights as can any other available sources. History, as understood in the contemporary West, is here clearly subservient to a spiritual end, but this should not prevent our appreciating these biographies as sources of inspiration and practical guidance for those who pursue the spiritual path outlined in them, and equally as a record of their world.

The historian, too, can find a wealth of data concerning the background, education and teaching careers of many Nyingma masters as well as information on the major monasteries and retreat centres. The text should therefore be explored with receptivity to the many levels on which it is written, abandoning rigid preconceptions of what history should or should not be.

The hard facts given in the *History* – names, places, titles and dates – are reproduced with fidelity to the sources upon which it is based. The translators have endeavoured to identify the persons, locations and literary works concerned and to provide the reader with the results of their researches. This material is occasionally given in the Notes in Volume Two, but the reader should also refer to the Glossary of Enumerations, Bibliography and indexes. We have avoided the temptation to fill the work with endless annotation, where specialised studies are in fact required. Accordingly, the annotations we have provided are intended primarily to clarify obscurities and problems in the text, to point out rare lexical items, and to direct the reader to secondary sources which treat specific topics in detail.

We have also endeavoured to convert all Tibetan dates to the western calendar. Here some difficulties arise of which the reader should be aware. The Tibetans only fixed the use of their characteristic sixty-year cycle to begin in 1027, the year given for the translation of the *Kālacakra Tantra* into the Tibetan language. Hence, for the whole period following 1027 Tibetan chronology is a relatively straightforward matter, and where errors do occasionally occur they may, for the most part, be readily corrected. For the period preceding 1027, however, the Tibetans often utilised only a twelve-year cycle, which was not well suited for the calculation of long spans of time. When Tibetan historians of the thirteenth century onwards attempted to convert the records of the imperial period into the sixty-year reckoning many discrepancies and errors arose, and it is not always a simple task to detect and correct them. Contemporary scholars have made admirable use of Chinese, Arabic and other chronicles in bringing light to bear on the problem, though many difficulties do remain. The course adopted by the translators, then, has been to leave the traditional dates for the pre-1027 period as they are given in the text, and to provide the alternative dates suggested by recent scholarship in the Notes. For the post-1027 period occasional errors in dating have been corrected in the body of the text with the Author's consent.

In addition, the precise chronological tables drawn up by Dieter Schuh in *Untersuchungen zur Geschichte der Tibetischen Kalenderrechnung* have permitted us to give exact calculations of dates following 1027 which include the day and month. A word of caution is in order, however, because Schuh has provided us with the calculations not of one, but of four calendrical systems, and as he himself has noted it is essential that one exercise discretion in deciding, in any given case, which system is to be used. The four systems are Phakpa, originating in the thirteenth century; Tshurpu, from the early fourteenth century; old Phukpa, from 1447 onwards; and new Phukpa, which became the official system of the Tibetan government in 1696. Our procedure has been to follow old Phukpa for the period from 1447 until 1695 and new Phukpa for the period which follows unless there are very strong reasons for preferring one of the other systems. For the period from 1027 until 1446 the choice of Phakpa or Tshurpu must be made on a case by case basis, and in some instances neither one seems quite right. When this problem occurs old Phukpa has been used even though it is anachronistic to do so, the maximum error possible being seldom more than one month. Future research may eventually resolve these difficulties.

The formal title of this volume is *A Clearly Elucidated History of the Precious Teachings of the Vehicle of Indestructible Reality according to the Earliest of All Teachings of the Conqueror in the Land of Snows, the Ancient Translation School, entitled Thunder from the Great Conquering Battle-Drum of Devendra* (*gangs-ljongs rgyal-bstan yongs-rdzogs-kyi phyi-mo snga-'gyur rdo-rje theg-pa'i bstan-pa rin-po-che ji-ltar byung-ba'i tshul dag-cing gsal-bar brjod-pa lha-dbang gYul-las rgyal-ba'i rnga-bo-che'i sgra-dbyangs*). Devendra is said to be the form taken by the Buddha when dwelling among the gods. His drum not only ensures divine victory, but rouses the gods from the slumber of complacency and reveals to them the impermanence of even their celestial condition.

The text was composed in 1962 by His Holiness Dudjom Rinpoche, Jikdrel Yeshe Dorje, the late head of the Nyingma school, after his arrival in India as a refugee. It was intended, as the Author clearly states, to give stability to the Nyingma tradition during that particular crisis situation. It has now seen many editions, the present translation following the third, which comprises four hundred and twenty-three Tibetan folios (eight hundred and forty-six pages) and occupies the first volume in the Author's *Collected Works* (Kalimpong, 1979).

GYURME DORJE & MATTHEW KAPSTEIN

The Text

A Clearly Elucidated History of the Precious Teachings of the Vehicle of Indestructible Reality according to the Earliest of All Teachings of the Conqueror in the Land of Snows, the Ancient Translation School, entitled Thunder from the Great Conquering Battle-Drum of Devendra

gangs-ljongs rgyal-bstan yongs-rdzogs-kyi phyi-mo snga-'gyur rdo-rje theg-pa'i bstan-pa rin-po-che ji-ltar byung-ba'i tshul dag-cing gsal-bar brjod-pa lha-dbang gYul-las rgyal-ba'i rnga-bo-che'i sgra-dbyangs

Verses of Invocation

[2.1-10.6] Always frolicking in pristine cognition,
The pure, unchanging, peaceful expanse,
Where there is no trace of elaboration,
May the unequalled Guru conquer the world!

The sun of all-knowing pristine cognition alone
Is never obscured by elaborations:
May he protect us, for he sheds a thousand rays of spiritual and temporal well-being
On the illusory city of the world, which arises dependent on causes.[363]

Cool, soothing camphor and nectar do not compare
With this gift that cures delusion's unbearable fever,
The panacea that destroys the plague of the world:
May that jewel of true doctrine, transmitted and realised,[364] be our victorious crown!

I praise, above all, the supreme community,[365]
The banner of the teaching,
Supported by a golden shaft of superior aspiration,
Flying the exquisite cloth of the three correct trainings,
And beautified by the jewelled peak of exegesis and attainment.

Primordially pure, just what naturally is, the supreme body of reality, the all-embracing nucleus – this is the essence, awareness and emptiness, Samantabhadra;
Ceaseless transformation, pristine cognition's expressive play, arisen as a billowing, magical net – this is his natural expression, bliss and emptiness, Vajrasattva;
Loving compassion, teaching each in accord with his needs at appropriate times, with an unqualified intention – this is his spirituality, appearance and emptiness, Vajradhara;

In devotion I bow to the gurus of the six lineages – intentional, symbolic, aural, and the rest – the teachers of the supreme vehicle, who are inseparable from these three buddha-bodies.[366]

You embody everything, always delighting, in an authentic and secret great maṇḍala endowed with supreme bliss.
To your many disciples you respond appropriately, appearing in a blazing form before wild ones, and before the peaceful and passionate as is fit;
And from the limitless union of your forms and abodes, arrayed like great thunder-clouds, you bring a satisfying and fertile shower of the two accomplishments.[367]
O mighty warrior, glorious Heruka, favour me with acceptance! and grant that I accomplish the indestructible reality of your body, speech, and mind.

There is nothing at all, animate or inanimate, that is not bound in the seal of this beauty, emptiness; there is no buddha who has not relied on you.
In the guise of a passionate lover you entice those who lust after form, for it is said that the pristine cognition of unchanging, supreme bliss may be known by this means.
You are a messenger to those who desire supreme accomplishment, and the sole mistress of my circle, for I have good fortune, O Vajra Queen!
Before you I bow, in the realisation of co-emergence, the common savour of all.
Embrace me tightly in the alluring play of great bliss, and let us make love!

I give obeisant worship to the host of India's great scholars,
The agents of the Conqueror, who revealed the Conqueror's teaching,
And equalled the Conqueror himself, like Nāgārjuna, Asaṅga, and others,
Who commented on [the Buddha's] intention, and arrived at philosophy's limits.

To the numberless host of accomplished masters I bow:
To Saraha, Lūipā, Kṛṣṇacārin, Ghaṇṭapāda and the rest,
Who arrived at the indestructible level, by the indestructible path,
So that they equalled Vajradhara's intention.

O Lord of the World,[368] renowned as Songtsen Gampo,
You were the lord who ushered in the very first dawn of the Conqueror's teaching

In the dark Land of Snows[369] beyond the pale.
Who is it that would leave your feet, even on becoming enlightened?

Body complete with major and minor marks, released from a lotus bud in Sindhu Lake, containing the seed-syllable HRĪḤ, the pristine cognition that is the knowledge and love of the Lord of Sukhāvatī Field:[370]
You are neither born, nor do you die, while saṃsāra exists, but by the dance, the indestructible discipline of great bliss,
You cut off, or take into your following, all conscious beings within the three spheres.
This being the unobstructed expression of your power, you can be compared with yourself alone in this world.
Although all the conquerors equally love living beings, only you, Skull-garlanded Master,[371] have been so kind as to protect the afflicted Tibetans; so I revere you with all my heart.

You were the sole spiritual son of the Śākya King,[372] O heroic Lord of Secrets,[373] who strictly maintained his vows, and was renowned as the great Bodhisattva.
Endowed with unlimited brilliance, retention, and mastery of the ten powers, you wilfully lived for nine hundred years to illuminate the Land of Snows.
You planted well the banner of the Tripiṭaka's teaching as the ornament of Central Tibet, and gave birth to a line of the Conqueror's family that had no precedent.
Thinking of you, Śāntarakṣita, who had the meritorious fortune to become the first venerated priest in Tibet, I bow down in faith, time and time again.

In the Cold Land that was obscured by darkest ignorance, you, whose sceptre is discernment's sword,[374] assumed a kingly guise,
And lit anew the illuminating lamp of the Conqueror's precious teaching, so that this frontier land achieved even greater fortune than India.
If the mass of such wondrous grace were given form, the vast universe would be too small a vessel!
Knowing that here and now whatever enjoyment is found in this storehouse of profoundly significant, wish-granting gems is thus due to your power alone, lord Trhisong, I have faith.

A hundred times I praise the Tibetan translators and Indian scholars,
Who flawlessly translated, revised and established
The immaculate scriptures of the Conqueror, and the commentaries on their intention,

And so opened for the Land of Snows a hundred doors of spiritual and temporal well-being.

I give my heart's faith to the host of supreme, accomplished masters, awareness-holders,
Who maintain the indestructible lineage of supreme transformation,[375]
Delighting in whatever appears in the maṇḍala of supreme bliss,
Intoxicated by the nectar of esoteric instructions, distilled from the intention of the three lineages.

Moreover, in devotion I here praise
All who appear as agents of our Guide, the Conqueror,
Who glorify the teaching and living beings without bias
By their liberating careers of learning, dignity and accomplishment.

Ḍākinīs and protectors of the transmitted doctrine, bearers of secrets!
Not wishing to divulge this profound history,
Please understand that the teaching now nears final rest,
And with joyful smile grant your consent.

In this most degenerate age the sun of the Conqueror's teaching is almost concealed by gathering black storm-clouds of disorder;
And the extraordinary tradition of the supremely secret vehicle, to which even accomplished persons take recourse, has virtually disappeared.
At the present time there are few who have mastered the lives of those who attained realisation, and those few rarely repeat the account.
For that reason I will endeavour to set this forth, so that some small part of the ancient tales, might be kept from disappearing.

Part One
The Origin of the Precious Teaching of the Conqueror in this World

Introduction

[10.6-12.3] It is my pleasure to relate briefly here, in pure and clear language, how the precious doctrine of the vehicle of indestructible reality – the unsurpassed, most secret nucleus of the entire teaching of our Teacher, the Sugata – originated and developed in the world at large and especially in the Land of Snows. So at the outset I must explain how, generally speaking, the precious teaching of the Conqueror came into the world.

The world systems of the universe, which are like vessels, supports created by the oceanic extent of the buddhas' compassion and the deeds of sentient beings, are spread throughout the infinite reaches of space. Therein, the place enjoyed by the buddha-body of perfect rapture, Vairocana the Great Glacial Lake, is the Buddha-field whose Foundation and Centre are Adorned with Flowers. Within each pore of the conqueror [Vairocana] residing there, there appear oceanic systems, numerous as grains of dust. Upon the lotuses which float in the perfumed oceans in the palms of his hands, there are twenty-five world systems situated one above the other. And here, in the thirteenth among them, the world of Patient Endurance,[376] there is a great trichiliocosm consisting of one billion worlds, each with four continents.

Of the four continents, each one of which has two subcontinents, the one to the south is Jambudvīpa, the Rose-Apple Continent, so called owing to the presence of the Jambu or rose-apple tree.[377] Its central country is Magadha, where there is the self-originated Indestructible Seat, Vajrāsana. Here one thousand supreme emanational bodies will come forth one after the other, as if forming a rosary, attain buddhahood and turn the wheel of the doctrine. Thus, they make of this Auspicious Aeon[378] an illuminated world. At the present time, the light of the precious teaching of the Fourth Guide[379] spreads throughout the world.

How this came to pass may be considered in four parts: (1) the coming of our Teacher, the Buddha; (2) the collection of his transmitted precepts by councils; (3) the line of patriarchs of the teaching; and (4) the preservation of the teaching and the expansion of the greater vehicle (*Mahāyāna*).

1 *The Coming of Buddha, Teacher of the Doctrine*

[12.4-13.3] Concerning this topic, the different philosophical systems hold many conflicting opinions, for they were conceived in accord with the varied intellectual capacities of those who required instruction.

THE OPINION OF THE ADHERENTS OF THE LESSER VEHICLE

Among these, the pious attendants of the Vaibhāṣika school[380] maintained that after developing a supremely enlightened attitude our Teacher gathered, for three "countless" aeons,[381] the provisions [of merit and pristine cognition] such as may be gathered on the path of provisions.[382] Then, as prince Siddhārtha, an ordinary individual who, in this his final birth, was still bound [to things mundane], he attained, on the basis of [his prior completion of] the greater path of provisions, the connecting path and the paths of insight, meditation, and no-more-learning during a single sitting at Vajrāsana; and thus he realised buddhahood. So it says in the *Treasury of the Abhidharma* (Ch.6, v.24ab):

> In the last stage of meditation
> The buddha and the self-centred buddha (*pratyekabuddha*)
> Obtain total enlightenment seated in one position.[383]

Thus, they claim that the buddhahood of the Teacher is like [the enlightenment of] the self-centred buddha, who is sharp-witted and enjoys solitude. Though they consider the Bodhisattva in his last birth to have been an ordinary individual, they refer to his previous births as having been "in accord with liberation";[384] and they say [*Treasury of the Abhidharma*, Ch.4, v.118]:

> Though they are not sublime,
> Parents, invalids, teachers of religion,
> And the Bodhisattva in his last rebirth
> Are said to be worthy beyond measure.

THE ORDINARY OPINION OF THE GREATER VEHICLE AND OF THE TANTRAS

[13.3-16.2] According to the usual opinion of the greater vehicle, however, after developing an enlightened attitude and gathering the provisions for three "countless" aeons, the holy Śvetaketu, a son of the gods and a bodhisattva of the tenth level[385] who was bound to take birth once more, was born as the prince Siddhārtha. He was a bodhisattva of the tenth level in his final birth, and he attained buddhahood in this world. In the *Sūtra of the Array of Attributes* (*Āryamañjuśrībuddhakṣetraguṇavyūhasūtra*, T 59) it says:

> From the time I first developed the unsurpassed enlightened attitude I gathered the provisions with great effort for a period of three "countless" aeons. Then, gazing upon the blind, unguided creatures of this age when life endures for one hundred years, I attained buddhahood here in Jambudvīpa, and turned the inconceivable wheel of the doctrine...

While some works concerning the way of secret mantra are in general agreement with this description, they maintain, in particular, that when Siddhārtha dwelt on the bank of the Nairañjanā River absorbed in fixed contemplation, he was roused and summoned by the tathāgatas. Leaving his conventional body behind, the body of his pristine cognition journeyed to the Akaniṣṭha heaven,[386] where he received empowerment from all the tathāgatas. Thus, he attained buddhahood by means of the five awakenings, and only afterwards did he demonstrate the attainment of enlightenment at Vajrāsana. Just so, the master Buddhajñānapāda [in the *Point of Liberation*] says:

> Though Śākyamuni gathered merit for three countless
>   aeons,
> He still did not realise this truth.
> At Nairañjana, then, he became absorbed
> In the contemplation of nothing at all,[387]
> When the sugatas of the ten directions
> Obstructed his impulsive desire,
> And bestowed the profound, clear, non-dual teaching[388]
> That is perfectly pure like the sky.
> At midnight he meditated on just what is,
> As have all the previous conquerors,
> And at dawn's first light he gained perfect realisation.
> Then, in order to teach living beings,
> He dwelt at the Point of Enlightenment[389]
> And vanquished the great host of Māra.
> To take sentient beings into his fold
> He then turned the wheel of the doctrine.

Moreover, the master Āryadeva [in the *Lamp which Subsumes Conduct, Caryāmelāpakapradīpa,* T 1803] says:

> Awakening is twofold:
> It is held to be outer and inner.

Āryadeva thus maintains that the outer awakening is the attainment of buddhahood by way of desirelessness, and the inner awakening is the attainment of the body of coalescence, which comes about when the body of reality, which is inner radiance, is made manifest by means of the four kinds of desire.

According to the special view of the greater vehicle, however, after attaining buddhahood in the Akaniṣṭha-Ghanavyūha realm the buddhas reveal the attainment of buddhahood in the Pure Abode[390] and at Vajrāsana, successively. In the *Sūtra of the Bounteous Array* it says:

> When the perfect buddhas attain enlightenment,
> They do not perform the buddhas' deeds
> In the realm of desire until they have attained
> Buddhahood in the supreme realm of Akaniṣṭha.
> But having journeyed to the Ghanavyūha realm,
> The buddhas create ten million emanations;
> And always absorbed in yoga they delight
> With each one of those emanations,
> Just as the moon shines on all lands.
> Thus, within their domains they come forth to teach
> Each one in accord with his or her needs.

And the *Sūtra of the Descent to Laṅkā* (Ch. 10, vv. 38ab; 39cd) says:

> Abandoning even the Pure Abode,
> The perfect Buddha attained buddhahood
> In the pleasant Akaniṣṭha-Ghanavyūha realm,
> And an emanation attained buddhahood here.

In short, all who are said to attain buddhahood in the realms of desire and form do so only to show the way to those who require instruction.

THE SPECIAL POSITION OF THE NYINGMA TRADITION

[16.3-18.2] Here, [our tradition favours] the unsurpassed teaching that is the essence of definitive meaning, according to which our Teacher realised enlightenment because, in the original expanse, or ground, pristine cognition that is intuitively aware has been free throughout beginningless time. In the radiant realm of reality [the Buddha] abides in that state in which the bodies [of buddhahood] and pristine cognition are free from both conjunction and disjunction,[391] his intention being of the same savour as that of all the buddhas of the three times. Without departing from this the Tathāgata appears, for the sake of sentient beings, as the inconceivable play of the emanational body. Thus, he trains those who require instruction as befits them individually, through infinite enlightened activity which establishes them in the three degrees of enlightenment. It says in the *Tantra of the Array of Wish-granting Gems* (*yid-bzhin rin-po-che bkod-pa'i rgyud*):

> The Buddha who preceded all,
> Vajradhara, Conqueror, Most Secret,
> Frolics in worlds beyond concept.
> At all times, without number, before and after,
> He benefits the world in various ways,
> In uncountable peaceful and wrathful forms,
> As a hunter, a whore, or some other.
> Now in this Auspicious Aeon
> He will become the Thousand Guides;
> And thus will he in various ways
> Benefit countless beings.

Also, it says in the *Root Tantra of the Secret Nucleus* (Ch.3, vv.1-2):

> The Six Sages Embodying Awareness,[392] who are said to be the "blessing of great spirituality", issue forth from the indestructible body, speech and mind of the tathāgatas. After issuing forth, each one of these great sages, transcendent lords, acts on behalf of the five classes of beings, by means of the four kinds of instructions, in each of the infinite great trichiliocosms in the ten directions of the six worlds, those of the lateral [cardinal points], zenith and nadir, which [exist] owing to the force of the [world-forming] deeds [of those beings].

This is not only said in the tantra texts of the secret mantra, but the profounder sūtras are in agreement. The *Lotus Sūtra* (Ch.15, v.1) says:

> Ten billion aeons, an inconceivable number,
> And even that does not measure those past
> Since I attained supreme enlightenment.
> Thus, I am always teaching the doctrine.

And the *Sūtra of the Meeting of Father and Son* says:

> Great warrior, learned in skilful means,
> You have been the Conqueror in one billion aeons
> In order to mature sentient beings,
> And though you have revealed yourself thus as the Buddha,
> Even today, my Guide,
> You reveal yourself as manifold buddhas.

THE BODY OF EMANATION

[18.2-20.2] Analysing the body of emanation, which responds to the natures of those requiring instruction, the *Ornament of the Sūtras of the Greater Vehicle* (Ch.9, vv.63-4) says:

> The countless emanations of the buddhas
> Are held to be the body of emanation.
> They have perfectly accomplished both goals[393]
> And abide in every form,
> Constantly demonstrating artistry and birth,
> Great enlightenment and also nirvāṇa;
> The buddhas' body of emanation
> Is the great means to liberation.

Thus, appearing in various guises, in the animate and inanimate worlds, [the forms of the body of emanation] are countless. None the less, if they must be summarised, three are said to be foremost, namely, those of artistry, of birth, and of supreme emanation.[394] Concerning the way in which the deeds of the great and supreme bodies of emanation are performed, the *Root Tantra of the Magical Net* (*sgyu-'phrul rtsa-rgyud*) says that they benefit beings by four kinds of instruction:

> They instruct by means of the great merits of the body, which reveals the activities from conception until the attainment of nirvāṇa.
> They instruct by means of knowledge conveyed in speech, which reveals the limitless mass of the doctrine.
> They instruct by means of direct perception of mind; for they benefit the world by intuiting directly all that is intelligible by means of the six supernormal cognitive powers.
> They instruct by means of inconceivable miraculous abilities, the enlightened attributes and activities which reveal inconceivable emanations of body, speech, and mind, as befits each and every one who requires instruction.

Among those deeds which "instruct by means of the great merits of the body" it is impossible to enumerate exactly, or otherwise to qualify, the deeds of the Teacher's emanational body. It is a topic beyond conception. In the sūtras of the greater vehicle, too, all manner of quantities are mentioned which contradict one another and do not lend themselves to summarisation, but here we are primarily concerned with the twelve deeds which the Buddha performed here in Jambudvīpa. Regarding this, the *Treatise on the Supreme Continuum of the Greater Vehicle* (Ch.2, vv.53cd-56) says:

> Not departing from the body of reality,
> Through the diverse nature of his emanations

He reveals these deeds to impure realms
For the duration of the world's existence:
He is actually born [among the gods],
And he descends from the Tuṣita realm,
Enters the womb and takes birth,
Becomes proficient in the arts,
Enjoys the company of his consorts,
Renounces the world, practices asceticism,
Reaches the Point of Enlightenment,
Vanquishes Māra's host, attains
Perfect enlightenment, [and turns] the wheel of the doctrine.
He then demonstrates [final] nirvāṇa.

THE LIFE OF ŚĀKYAMUNI[395]

[20.2-40.6] Our teacher appeared in the beautiful, divine Tuṣita heaven as the son of the gods, the holy Śvetaketu. He taught the doctrine to the gods and dwelt among them. Once, the courtyard [of the heavenly palace] spontaneously resounded with the music of verses inspiring him to fulfil the prophecies of Dīpaṃkara Buddha. The holy Śvetaketu then sat on the finest throne in the exalted mansion of the doctrine and, in order to demonstrate the act of taking birth in Jambudvīpa, made five special considerations of continent, family, father, mother, and time. Then he consoled the gods, saying, "Having been born from the womb of Māyādevī in Jambudvīpa, I will reveal the profound nectar [of the doctrine]. I will overcome eighteen sophists and establish many beings in liberation."

Then, in the form of a young, ash-gray elephant, as described in the Veda of the Brahmans, the Bodhisattva entered the womb of his mother Māyādevī while she was observing a purificatory fast (*poṣadhā*).[396] He transformed the womb into a celestial palace, beautiful to behold, free from the propensities of mundane existence, fit to be enjoyed by the sons of the conquerors, and there he taught the doctrine of the purification of the birthplace to many hundreds of billions of gods and men. He spent ten full months there to illustrate the certain succession of the ten [bodhisattva] levels.

When the time came for the Lumbinī Grove to receive the merit of the world, his body, enlightened in twenty ways and lustrous as a polished golden doorbolt, emerged painlessly from his mother's right side. Then, as a son of the royal family is anointed, or as an indication that he had awakened to the family of enlightenment and was identical to all the buddhas, such as Akṣobhyavajra, a host of deities appeared in the sky and they bathed him eagerly, all at once.[397] Celestial deities lauded him with songs of praise, and Brahmā and Indra made him comfortable with the robes they offered.

Śākyamuni

As soon as he was born, the Bodhisattva took seven steps in each of the four directions, in order to show that he was about to embark upon the path of the four immeasurables. It is said that lotus blossoms offered by the gods sprung from his footprints and shone brilliantly. At the same time, the flowers in the Lumbinī Grove bloomed spontaneously. In addition, five hundred Śākya princes, including Nanda, were born, as well as eight hundred maidens, including Yaśodharā, five hundred servants, including Chandaka, and five hundred excellent riding horses, including Kaṇṭhaka. The whole earth trembled and a brilliant light shone everywhere. Four minor kings boasted that these were signs heralding the birth of their own sons.

Furthermore, the Bodhi Tree appeared in the centre of the continent, along with five hundred gardens and five hundred treasures, so that all of King Śuddhodana's desires were fulfilled. Therefore he named his son Sarvārthasiddha, "All Aims Accomplished".[398] The oracles predicted that he would become a universal monarch conquering the four quarters if he were to remain a householder, but that if he were to renounce the life of a householder in favour of homelessness, he would become a buddha. His mother passed away seven days after he was born. The Bodhisattva was then entrusted to thirty-two nurses, including Mahāprajāpati, who raised him in infancy.

Afterwards he lived in the palace, during which time he studied and completely mastered many arts; for instance, writing and mathematics under [the tutelage of] Sarvamitra, Kṛmivarman and others, and elephant-riding under Mātulasulabha. His father then ordered three Śākya families, including that of Daṇḍapāṇi, to give their daughters to be his consorts. But they said, "Lord! girls of our families belong only to skilled athletes." His father was ashamed, but the prince said, "In the three world realms no one dares compete with me in archery or in the arts!"

With this assertion of his ability he rang the bell to announce a contest of skills with the fierce and impetuous Śākya youths, all of whom departed for the outskirts of the city. Then Devadatta, in a very jealous mood, killed an elephant which had been brought from Vaiśālī as an offering to the prince, with a single powerful blow of his palm. Nanda threw the elephant forcibly outside the gates. To match the strength of both, the Bodhisattva, without leaving his chariot, seized the elephant's tail with his big toe and hurled it over seven walls into the countryside. For this the gods in admiration praised him.

The contestants then competed to pierce seven palm trees, seven iron walls and seven cauldrons, one after the other, with a single arrow. Devadatta pierced three, Nanda pierced five, but the prince's arrow pierced them all. On the spot where his arrow alighted a fountain of water sprang forth, which possessed the eight qualities [of pure water] and was called the "Arrow-born Well". Similarly, in skilful contests of youthful prowess, elephant-riding, swimming like swans on the wide river, and in all the sixty-four crafts, no athlete could compete with the Bodhisattva.

The master among world-knowers sometimes trains people by following convention. Thus, in order to abandon the misdeeds which result from sensual dependence he married sixty thousand worthy ladies, namely, Gopā, Yaśodharā and Mṛgajā – who were free from the five defects of womankind and possessed the eight virtues – together with their respective retinues of twenty thousand. With them he enjoyed the sensual pleasures as if they were illusory. But even such enjoyment introduced him to perfect renunciation. His turn from mundane existence to the doctrine began when the sound of cymbals awakened the power of his former prayers. For consolation he went all around the city with Chandaka as his charioteer. On seeing the four omens of birth, old age, sickness and death his heart felt utterly distressed, and he said [*Buddhacarita*, Ch.4, v.86]:

> Old age, sickness, and death –
> If those three did not exist,

I would delight in the sense objects,
Which are exceedingly pleasurable.

Thus, having been disgusted by the reality of suffering, by which the most excellent succumb to impermanence; and accompanied by the suffering of change, embraced by the all-pervading conditions of mundane existence, and pursued by the suffering of pain itself, he vowed to renounce the world.[399]

At that time King Śuddhodana's retinue feared that the prince might become a monk. Therefore, they had the outskirts of the city vigilantly patrolled by the watchmen and gatekeepers, so that he could not go anywhere. On the final night he bowed to his father and, guided by his solemn vow, removed the obstacle posed by the [previous] lack of parental consent. Riding upon Kaṇṭhaka the prince galloped through the sky with the assistance of the four guardian kings. Then, near the Sacred Stūpa[400] he cut off his hair and thus shed the evidence that he was not a monk. He then exchanged his linen dress for the saffron robe.

In Vaiśālī and Rājagṛha, under Arāḍakālāma and Udraka, two sophists who were celebrated for their instructions, he studied the contemplations of nothing at all and of the pinnacle of existence,[401] and he attained states as high as those of his masters. But knowing that those contemplations and practices were not the path to liberation from the evils of mundane existence, he persevered in ascetic contemplation for six years with five noble companions on the banks of the wide Nairañjanā River. During each of the first two years he ate a single grain of rice. During each of the next two years he drank a single drop of water. And during the last two years he took nothing whatsoever.

Then the gods called to him in verse. The conquerors of the ten directions and their spiritual sons aroused him from the lower path and urged him to the Point of Enlightenment. Then, to remove his exhaustion, he enjoyed a little solid food, at which his five companions went off to Vārāṇasī in disillusionment.

He himself then set off for Vajrāsana in Magadha. On the way a brahman girl, Sujātā, served him with the honeyed cream of five hundred cows. Instantly his body became lustrous as a polished golden doorbolt, and he made Sujātā's merit inexhaustible. While on the road he received a handful of grass, as soft as a peacock's throat, from the grass-cutter Svāstika, and with it he proceeded towards the Indestructible Seat. At the Bodhi Tree in the centre of Vajrāsana, self-originated through the blessing of all the buddhas, he spread out the grass mat and, sitting upon it with his legs crossed, made this vow [*Sūtra of Extensive Play*, Ch.19, v.57]:

Let this body of mine dry up.
Let this heap of skin and bones decay.

I will not move from this position,
'Til the enlightenment, hard to gain,
After so many aeons, be attained!

Then in the evening twilight he composed himself in the contemplation which defeats Māra's host. He churned all the domains of Māra, and enveloped them with formidable rays of light. The evil Māra, appearing in the guise of a hunter, approached him and said, "Devadatta has seized power in Kapilavastu. He has destroyed the royal palace and the Śākyas have surrendered. Why do you sit here?"

"To become a realised buddha," he answered.

"But the perfect realisation of buddhahood is the result of immeasurable provisions [of merit and pristine cognition], and you have only lived the happy, joyful life of a prince."

The Bodhisattva replied, "By just one ephemeral offering you became lord of the realm of desire.[402] As I have completed the two provisions during limitless aeons, how can I not become a buddha?"

The lord of passion raised two fingers and reproached him, saying [*Sūtra of Extensive Play*, Ch.21, v.87]:

You bear witness to the ephemeral offering I made here,
But you have no witness yourself.
Without a witness you have already lost,
Whatever it is you say!

Then the Bodhisattva struck the earth with his hand, which had been formed by a hundred meritorious acts, and said [*Sūtra of Extensive Play*, Ch.21, v.88]:

This earth bears witness to all beings;
She is just and impartial to animate and inanimate alike.
This earth is my witness, I do not lie.
O Earth, come, be my witness here!

As soon as he had spoken, Sthāvarā, the goddess of the earth, raised her pure golden figure from the ground, and, taking in her hand a single particle, said, "I can count the whole earth [in fractions like this], but I cannot estimate the number of heads and limbs sacrificed by this worthy son. Thus, the time has come for him to become a perfectly realised buddha." With these words she became invisible, and the evil Māra weakened and departed for his own domain, in utter disgrace.

When he arrived there Māra mustered his army, one thousand trillion strong, striking fear and terror into those who lack the supreme understanding that [all appearances] are illusory, and he prepared for battle. But a military machine cannot crush one who has conquered the real enemy, the emotional defilements, and who perceives with a sky-like mind the insubstantiality [of all things]. Thus, without even a thought of anger or arrogance, the Bodhisattva remained absorbed in the contemplation of great loving kindness,[403] and, indeed, the swords and missiles hurled by Māra fell as a shower of flowers, and the harsh noises and battle-cries became songs of praise. In this way, the poisonous tree of desire was felled. The flowers of the Five-arrowed One wilted. The rocky mountain of pride crumbled. Martial spirit collapsed. The crocodile banner was lowered, and the chariot of Smara beat a hasty retreat.[404] Thus, the deceitful one and his army were scattered in utter confusion.

Māra then made his seven daughters attempt to seduce the Bodhisattva with the deceits of lust, having transformed them into seven beauties. They tried to ensnare him in the noose of a seductress' thirty-two wiles, with Puṇḍarīkā's coquetry, Menakā's dangling necklace, Subhūṣaṇā's tightly-bound girdle, Keśamiśrā's tinkling bracelets, and so forth.[405] But they stood not a chance of moving even the tips of the Bodhisattva's hair. When he transformed them into seven old women they repented and implored his forgiveness, whereupon he restored them to their original appearances.

Then the time of his awakening arrived. At midnight he became absorbed in the contemplation of the fourth meditative concentration.[406] At dawn, when the drum of victory was about to be beaten, he developed the supernormal cognitive powers of clairvoyance and of the exhaustion of corruption, and fully realised the four truths. As he became a perfectly realised buddha, the whole earth trembled and all the psychophysical bases which were to be purified of the subject-object dichotomy awakened to the pristine cognition free from duality, in the impeccable mansion of the body of reality, which is the "middle way"[407] and inner radiance. In this world there was a lunar eclipse. Rāhula and Ānanda were also born.

Seven weeks after he had attained buddhahood in this way the merchants Trapuṣa and Bhallika offered him honey. The great kings of the four directions offered him begging bowls made of everything from precious gems to stone. But he rejected [the precious ones] as being unfit implements for a renunciate and accepted only the worst. Then he gave his benediction [to these patrons]. To indicate that the profound nectar [he had realised] was beyond the grasp of sophists, he said [*Sūtra of Extensive Play*, Ch.25, v.1]:

> I have found a nectar-like doctrine,
> Profound, calm, simple, radiant and uncompounded.
> If I teach it no one will understand;
> I will remain right here in the forest, in silence.

Thus, he created a reason for the special merit of encouraging the turning of the wheel of the doctrine.

When Brahmā remembered the Tathāgata's former aspirations he approached him, and offered encouragement in verse [Ch.25, v.9d and v.11ab]:

> O Sun among teachers! Why remain indifferent today?
> I pray that you beat the great drum of the genuine doctrine,
> And blow well on the true doctrine's conch...

Scattering sandalwood powder he went off to his own domain to summon Indra. Afterwards, he and Indra together presented a precious gem to the Buddha and prayed [Ch.25, v.17]:

> Like the full moon released by Rāhu,[408]
> Your mind is liberated, O Sage.
> Arise, O victor in battle,
> And with the light of discriminating awareness
> Dispel the darkness of the world.

But the Buddha denied this request. Once again Brahmā considered that there would be great merit if he were to repeat the request. He offered a golden wheel with a thousand spokes, and reminded the Tathāgata in verse that he had previously learned the nature of defilement through contact with the impure religion of Magadha.[409] Thereupon the Buddha accepted the wheel and said [Ch.25, v.34]:

> Brahmā, I will open the portal of nectar-like instruction
> For those who live in Magadha,
> Who are attentive, faithful, and discriminating,
> Non-violent, and constantly attentive to the doctrine.

As soon as the Tathāgata had spoken, the word that he had agreed to turn the wheel of the doctrine was heard as far away as Akaniṣṭha. At that, the gods assembled, each with his or her own offering.

The Tathāgata considered that the first vessel for the profound nectar-like instruction should be easy to train, easy to purify, and endowed with unobstructed intelligence. He knew that Arāḍa and Udraka were [such vessels], but they had passed away. Then, remembering his former aspirations, the Tathāgata regarded his five noble companions and set out for Vārāṇasī. The five had rebuked him and agreed not to salute, saying, "The ascetic Gautama is lax. He has eaten much and has abandoned renunciation."

While the Tathāgata was on the way, a brahman named Upajīvaka carelessly and rashly said to him, "Gautama, who granted you the vow of celibacy?"

The Tathāgata replied [Ch.26, v.1]:

> I have no preceptor.
> I am without equal.

Alone, I have become a perfect buddha,
Whose [passions have] cooled,
Whose corruptions are exhausted.[410]

After three such exchanges he continued on his way to Vārāṇasī. When he arrived there, the agreement of the five companions spontaneously vanished, like the constellations by day. They said, "Long-living Gautama,[411] your senses are clear, and your complexion is pure. Is this a manifest sign that you have realised pristine cognition?"

As they regarded him still as an equal, he dispelled their ignorance, saying, "Do not call the Tathāgata 'long-living', or misfortune will surely follow for a long time. I have obtained a nectar-like doctrine. I have attained buddhahood. I have come to know everything!"

A thousand jewel thrones then appeared there. The Tathāgata bowed reverently before the thrones of the Three Buddhas of the Past, and radiantly sat down upon the fourth throne, whereupon the other thrones vanished. On behalf of the five noble companions and eighty thousand gods he turned the wheel of the doctrine of the middle way which abandons both extremes, and which concerns the four truths, repeating them three times and in twelve ways.[412] Then he fully ordained the five noble companions as monks, so that there arose the great monastic community, a matchless canopy over the world. All those assembled perceived the truth.

[The first wheel of the doctrine[413] emphasises] the Vinayapiṭaka [*Transmissions of the Vinaya, 'dul-ba'i sde-snod*, T 1-7], which, beginning with those sections which teach mainly the training of superior moral discipline, includes, among other topics, the Vinaya of the Vinayapiṭaka, which establishes and defines the transgressions and natural offences; the sūtras of the Vinayapiṭaka, which describe the sequence of yogic practice involving contemplation and purity of conduct; and the Abhidharma of the Vinayapiṭaka, which provides extensive analysis of the aforementioned topics.

Then on Vulture Peak,[414] which is a perfect location, the Tathāgata turned the wheel of the doctrine which concerns signlessness, the intermediate transmitted precepts, on behalf of the four ordinary assemblies – namely, those of the five thousand arhats such as Śāriputra and Maudgalyāyana, the five hundred nuns including Prajāpati, the host of laymen and laywomen including Anāthapiṇḍada and the laywoman Viśākhā, and a multitude of gods, nāgas, and gandharvas. In addition, he turned this [wheel] on behalf of a special assembly – a multitude of bodhisattvas who had attained the great levels, including Bhadrapāla, Ratnasambhava, and Jāladatta. This wheel of the doctrine emphasises the Sūtrapiṭaka, which teaches mainly the training of superior mind and includes the Vinaya of the Sūtrapiṭaka, which sets forth the bodhisattva's vows; the sūtras of the Sūtrapiṭaka, which describe profound and vast contemplations;

and the Abhidharma of the Sūtrapiṭaka, which contains analyses of the levels, paths, retentions, and contemplations.

Then in the sundry abodes of gods and nāgas, for the sake of innumerable monks, nuns, gods, nāgas and bodhisattvas, the Tathāgata turned the wheel of the doctrine of definitive meaning, which is the wheel of the final transmitted precepts. This doctrinal wheel emphasises the Abhidharmapiṭaka, which mainly teaches the training of superior discriminative awareness and includes the Vinaya of the Abhidharmapiṭaka, which concerns how to subdue the conflicting emotions easily, with little hardship; the sūtras of the Abhidharmapiṭaka, which show how to penetrate the nature of reality; and the Abhidharma of the Abhidharmapiṭaka, which contains analyses of the components, psychophysical bases, activity fields, sense organs, consciousness, and the nucleus of the tathāgata (*tathāgatagarbha*), which is naturally pure.

Concerning this, it says in the *Sūtra of the Array of Attributes*:

> Totally unspoken by me,
> The doctrine has spread among sentient beings.
> To all those who seek a gradual path

Śāriputra

It appears in just that way.
For those who penetrate it instantaneously,
The varied doctrine appears in full.
This is the greatness of speech
That fulfils every aspiration to the heart's content.

It is a special feature of that buddha-speech, which transcends the particulars of sound and word, that, depending on one's capacity, the three doctrinal wheels may be heard simultaneously or gradually by those beings whose fortune it is to penetrate them so. It is never possible for ordinary persons to imagine the extent of approaches to the doctrine, or the number of vehicles, the means of training, or the time sequences, associated with the Buddha's immeasurable activity.

So it was through the boundless ocean of the doctrine, which includes the three vehicles, that some were established in the teaching of the path and result;[415] some were secured in the happiness of gods and men; and others, too, were delivered and protected from great fears of a mundane sort.[416] In short, through the infinite play of enlightened activity, his great miraculous abilities and so on, the Tathāgata planted the seed of liberation and omniscience, like a catalyst in an alchemical transmutation, in all sentient beings who saw, heard, touched, or thought of him. Moreover, he made his actual disciples, even the gandharva Pramoda and the homeless mendicant Subhadra, enter into the precincts bounded by skilful means and great compassion. Then, considering his final act, he went to Kuśinagara.[417]

Concerning that final act: The Tathāgata's body, pleasant to behold, was free from such common attributes as the tendency to shout, laugh, or yawn. Once, when Prajāpati heard a sneeze emerge from his glorious throat, she prayed, "May the Buddha live for three countless aeons!" Her prayer, reverberating through space, was heard as far away as Akaniṣṭha, and the gods also echoed it. The Buddha said to Prajāpati, "You have done no good. Instead of praying for the duration of the doctrine, you have obstructed the spiritual practice of many lazy people!" So, as an act of penance, Prajāpati passed into nirvāṇa along with five hundred female arhats.

At about that time the Tathāgata's two supreme disciples, Śāriputra and Maudgalyāyana went to visit the hells. Teachers and preceptors of extremist doctrines,[418] who were reaping the fruits of their misdeeds, sent a verbal message through them to their followers, saying that they had erred in their philosophy. Śāriputra was the first to repeat the message, but the followers ignored him, showing no hostility. After that Maudgalyāyana said, "Your teachers sent this message to you because they have come to suffer in the Avīci hell."[419]

"This message insults not only ourselves", they said, "but also our teachers and preceptors. Crush him!"

Maudgalyāyana

So they beat Maudgalyāyana's body until it was as a broken reed. Śāriputra wrapped him in the fold of his robe and carried him into the city of Vṛkṣaraju. Knowing that Maudgalyāyana would not live, Śāriputra went on to glorious Nālanda, thinking, "I cannot bear even the news of a friend's death. How, then, the sight?" Thus, he entered nirvāṇa early in the morning along with eighty thousand arhats. That same evening Maudgalyāyana passed into nirvāṇa along with seventy thousand arhats. And so, like fires which have run out of fuel, did many other arhats enter nirvāṇa.

The Buddha then entrusted the teaching along with the four [monastic] assemblies to the elder Mahākāśyapa. Removing his upper garment, he said, "Behold, O monks, the body of the Tathāgata! It is as difficult to see a tathāgata as it is to see an *udumbara* blossom.[420] Be silent, O monks! Just as this body is subject to destruction, so too is all that is compounded."

In this way he encouraged lazy disciples to enter the doctrine with the motive for renunciation. Then, next to a pair of sal trees, his intention turned to final nirvāṇa.

When Mahākāśyapa arrived there from the nāga realm he prayed before the Buddha's remains, and the funeral pyre ignited by itself. The relics became fragmented and were suitably divided into eight parts, which came to form the cores of eight stūpas.[421]

Finally, it says in the *Great Treasury of Detailed Exposition*:

> The Sage, supreme being,
> Lived for one year each
> At [Vārāṇasī], the site of the wheel of the doctrine,
> And at Vaiśālī, Makkolam, and the god realms,
> Śiśumāra Hill, and Kauśāmbī,
> Āṭavī, Caityagiri,
> Veṇupura, as well as Sāketa,
> And the city of Kapilavastu.
> He passed twenty-three years in Śrāvastī,
> Four years in Bhaiṣajyavana,
> Two years in the Jvālinī Cave,
> And five years in Rājagṛha.
> He had spent six years practising austerity
> And twenty-nine years in the palace.
> So it was that the Conqueror,
> The supreme and holy Sage,
> Passed into nirvāṇa at the age of eighty.

2 *The Collecting of Transmitted Precepts by Councils*

[40.6-41.2] There are both ordinary and special explanations of the compilation of the true doctrines, the teachings delivered by the Teacher. According to the ordinary vehicle three successive councils were convened.[422]

THE FIRST COUNCIL

[41.2-42.3] Shortly before the Teacher's own nirvāṇa, when Śāriputra with eighty thousand other arhats, and Maudgalyāyana with seventy thousand arhats, passed into nirvāṇa, and again when the Transcendent Lord himself entered nirvāṇa along with eighty million arhats, the gods cried out, saying, "All the powerful monks have passed into nirvāṇa and the true doctrine has become like the smoke from a dead fire. The monks do not proclaim even the Tripiṭaka."

In response to this derision a council of five hundred arhats was convened in the Banyan Cave at Rājagṛha, during the summer monsoon retreat the year after the Buddha's nirvāṇa, under the patronage of King Ajātaśatru. During this council Upāli compiled the Vinayapiṭaka, Ānanda the Sūtrapiṭaka, and Mahākāśyapa the entire Abhidharmapiṭaka. As far away as Akaniṣṭha the gods perceived this and exclaimed, "The gods will flourish! The antigods will decline! The teaching of the Buddha will endure for a long period of time!" Likewise, it says in the *Minor Transmissions*:

> During the summer which followed
> the Teacher's nirvāṇa,
> In a secret cave in Rājagṛha,
> Ajātaśatru provided sustenance
> For a council of five hundred arhats,
> And the Tripiṭaka was compiled.

THE SECOND COUNCIL

[42.3-42.6] When one hundred and ten years had passed after the first compilation of the scriptures, the monks in Vaiśālī were indulging in the following ten transgressions [*Minor Transmissions*]:

> Permitting: [exclamations of] "*alas!*"; *celebrating* [the arhats];
> The *deliberate practice* [of agriculture]; [sipping "medicine" from] a *pot* [of ale]; [the misuse of the sacred stored] *salt*;
> [Eating while on] the *road*; [desecration of offerings with] *two fingers*; *stirring* [curd and milk together as an afternoon beverage]; [a new] *mat* [without an old patch];
> And [begging for] *gold* [or silver]. These are held to be the ten transgressions.[423]

In order to put an end to this, seven hundred arhats, including Yaśaḥ, held a council under the patronage of the religious king Aśoka, and the ten transgressions were rejected. They recited the complete Tripiṭaka once, and also observed a harmonious and auspicious purificatory fast.

THE THIRD COUNCIL

[43.6-45.6] Starting from the time of King Vīrasena, the grandson of King Dharmāśoka, and son of Vigataśoka, the monks Mahādeva, Bhadra, the elder Nāga and Sthiramati, all of whom had come under the influence of Māra, appeared in succession. They proclaimed five basic points:

> [Arhats may] answer others, remain unknowing,
> Harbour doubts and inquire discursively;
> And they may support themselves.
> This is the Teacher's teaching.

In this way, they taught a false doctrine, which caused dispute among the members of the *saṃgha*, during the latter part of King Vīrasena's life, throughout the lives of Nanda and Mahāpadma, and during the early part of the life of Kaniṣka; that is, during the reigns of four kings.[424]

Since the Teacher had not allowed the Vinaya to be written down, differences arose over a long period of time in the recitation of the *Prātimokṣa Sūtra* (T 2), owing to which there was a division into eighteen schools.[425] It happened in this way: Because the elder Nāga spread the dispute, the Mahāsaṅghikas, Sthaviras, and Sammitīyas split off from the Mūlasarvāstivāda tradition; and these then became the four basic schools. Later, Sthiramati spread the dispute widely and the four sects gradually divided into eighteen. It is said that the Mūlasarvāstivāda had seven branches; the Mahāsaṅghika, five; and the other two, three each. Afterwards, when the controversy had somewhat subsided, and the schools existed independently, the third council was held under the patronage of King Kaniṣka. At that council, it was proven that all eighteen schools were pure, on the basis of this passage drawn from the *Sublime Sūtra of the Teaching Given in a Dream* (*Āryasvapnanirdeśasūtra*, T 48):

> The perfectly realised Buddha Kāśyapa said to King Kṛkī,[426] "Your majesty, the dream in which you saw eighteen men pulling on a sheet of cloth means that the teaching of Śākyamuni will become divided into eighteen schools. But the cloth itself, which is liberation, will remain undamaged."

At that same council the Vinayapiṭaka was written down. They also wrote down those texts from the Sūtrapiṭaka and Abhidharmapiṭaka which had not been set down before, and corrected those which had been recorded previously. This was the purpose of the third council.

As this account is not given in the *Minor Transmissions*, there are many different opinions. The Kashmiri schools maintained that the council was convened in Kashmir in the Karṇikāvana Temple by the noble Pārśva and five hundred arhats, Vasumitra and four hundred supremely venerable monks, and five hundred bodhisattvas. And it is said that most of the Central Indian scholars claimed that five hundred arhats and five thousand supremely venerable monks assembled in the Kuvana Temple of Jālandhara Monastery. At present, the account best known in Tibet states that about four hundred years after the Teacher's nirvāṇa five hundred arhats and five hundred, or sixteen thousand, bodhisattvas assembled and held a council. And the *Flame of Dialectics* (*Tarkajvālā*, T 3856) says: "When two hundred years had passed from the Teacher's nirvāṇa, the elder Vātsīputra compiled the doctrine."[427]

The period of four hundred years [mentioned above] agrees with this if each solstice is counted as one year. But, after comparing this chronology with the succession of kings, it seems to me that the period of two hundred years may be too short.[428] It appears, therefore, that this must be further examined. Moreover, many different places are claimed as the venue of the council, for example, Śrāvastī, Kusumakūṭārāma in Jālandhara, and Kuvana Monastery in Kashmir.

THE COUNCILS OF THE GREATER VEHICLE[429]

[45.6-46.4] As for the special councils of the greater vehicle, it says in the *Flame of Dialectics*:

> The greater vehicle was taught by the Buddha, since the original compilers were Samantabhadra, Mañjuśrī, Guhyapati, Maitreya, etc.

In the *Sūtra of Inconceivable Secrets,* Vajrapāṇi is called the compiler of the teachings of the Thousand Buddhas, and an ancient annotation[430] says that one million sons of the Conqueror assembled on Vimalasvabhāva Mountain, which lies to the south of Rājagṛha. There Maitreya compiled the Vinayapiṭaka, Mañjuśrī the Sūtrapiṭaka, and Vajrapāṇi the Abhidharmapiṭaka. It also says in the piṭaka of the greater vehicle that the sections dealing with the profound view were compiled by Mañjuśrī, and the sections on the extensive conduct by Maitreya.[431]

3 *The Patriarchs of the Teaching*[432]

MAHĀKĀŚYAPA

[46.4-49.5] The Teacher appointed Mahākāśyapa to be his successor, indicating this by allowing him to be the one to fold the master's seat. Also, the teaching was entrusted to the great and exalted Sixteen Elders. Kāśyapa was born as the son of the brahman Nyagrodhaketu, in the brahman village of Nyagrodhikā in Magadha, in answer to a prayer addressed to the divinity of the Nyagrodha [Banyan] Tree. For this reason he was named Nyagrodhaja [Banyan-born], though his family name was Kāśyapa. He married a beautiful maid with a golden complexion, who was named Kapilabhadrī. But they regarded each other only as brother and sister; not even for a moment did the thought of lust arise.

When his parents died, Kāśyapa abandoned his possessions, which included nine hundred and ninety-nine hamlets, sixty million pieces of gold, and eighty golden granaries, as if they were mere grass. For himself he kept only two robes of Benares linen. He sent Kapilabhadrī to the Nirgrantha [Jains],[433] while he went to the Teacher, who was residing near the Bahuputraka Caitya shortly after attaining buddhahood. As soon as they met, he recognised his teacher, and three times made this request: "You, Lord, are my teacher! And I am the pious attendant of the Transcendent Lord!" The Lord responded thrice, saying, "Indeed, I am your teacher; and you are my pious attendant!" At this, he was fully ordained, and eventually he came to be revered as the supreme observer of the ascetic virtues.[434] He took the Teacher's robe, which had come from a trash heap, and offered to the Teacher his Benares linen. This happened about the same time as the Teacher descended from the realm of the gods, and many gods had arrived in Jambudvīpa to receive his nectar-like instruction.[435]

Kāśyapa compiled the transmitted precepts well and protected the teaching. For over forty years he advanced the teaching by establishing many disciples in liberation. Then he thought of entering nirvāṇa and said to Ānanda, "You should know that the Teacher entrusted the teaching to me before he passed into nirvāṇa. When I have passed into nirvāṇa, you must protect the teaching. You, in turn, should entrust it to Śāṇavāsika."

Then Kāśyapa worshipped the stūpas which held the remains and tooth-relics of the Buddha. He climbed Mount Kukkuṭapāda in the south, and spread out his grass mat in the centre of an open area. Wearing the robe of the Transcendent Lord, which had come from a trash heap, he consecrated his body so that it would not decompose

Mahākāśyapa

until Maitreya's attainment of buddhahood. And, with a display of many miracles, he passed into nirvāṇa. The gods then worshipped him and closed up the mountain; but they opened it when King Ajātaśatru came to see the remains.

On that occasion Ajātaśatru dreamed that the royal family on his mother's side had passed away forever. When he awoke he heard that Kāśyapa had entered nirvāṇa, whereupon he set out for Mount Kukkuṭapāda, together with Ānanda. A yakṣa opened up the mountain. The king bowed to worship the body and prepared for a cremation, but Ānanda said, "It is consecrated to remain until the teaching period of Maitreya. In Maitreya's first assembly he will come here with nine hundred and ninety million pious attendants and, holding Kāśyapa's body in his hand[436] and showing it [to all], he will say, 'This was the supreme observer of the ascetic virtues among Śākyamuni's pious attendants, and the robe he wears was that of the Teacher. There is no one here who maintains the ascetic virtues of a mendicant as he did.' Then Kāśyapa's body will display great miracles and dissolve entirely into space, and Maitreya's attendants will undertake the ascetic virtues and become arhats. Therefore, you cannot cremate this body."

In accordance with this advice, the king turned away and the mountain was resealed. On its peak, he erected a stūpa dedicated to the remains.

ĀNANDA

[49.5-51.2] Ānanda was the son of the Teacher's paternal uncle, Amṛtodana. He and Rāhula were both born at the time of the Teacher's attainment of buddhahood. In his sixth year, when the master met with his own son [Rāhula], Ānanda was entrusted to Kāśyapa, who possessed

Ānanda

the ten powers, and he received gradual ordination according to the current rite.[437] He became the Teacher's personal servant and was revered as supreme for his retention of what he had heard. He protected the teaching for more than forty years, and then said to Śāṇavāsika, "The Teacher entrusted the teaching to Kāśyapa and he, in turn, entrusted it to me. When I too have passed away you must protect the teaching."

Ānanda predicted that Naṭa and Bhaṇṭa, the sons of a merchant, would build a monastery on Urumuṇḍa Mountain, in the region of Mathurā, and that they would become its patrons. He directed Upagupta, the son of the incense-seller Gupta, to be ordained there and entrusted with the teaching. When King Ajātaśatru heard the news he came with his army [in order to take leave of Ānanda]. The people of Vaiśālī, who had been apprised of this by a deity, accompanied the army to meet him. When Ānanda reached the middle of the River Ganges, a *ṛṣi* with a retinue of five hundred requested ordination from him. Ānanda materialised an island in the middle of the Ganges and gave the ordination there. The *ṛṣi* immediately became an arhat, and so became known as arhat Madhyāhnika (Midday), or Madhyāntika (Midway).

Madhyāhnika requested permission to enter nirvāṇa before his preceptor, Ānanda, who answered, "The Teacher has predicted that you will spread the teaching in Kashmir; so do just that!" When he had promised to do so Ānanda displayed many miracles and passed away. Half of his relics were taken by Ajātaśatru, the other half by the people of Vaiśālī, and they erected stūpas at Vaiśālī and at Pāṭaliputra.

ŚĀṆAVĀSIKA

[51.2-52.1] Śāṇavāsika was an arhat who was learned in the Tripiṭaka. His patron was the religious king Aśoka. Concerning that king, the *Root Tantra of Mañjuśrī* (*Mañjuśrīmūlatantra*, T 543) predicted that he was to appear one hundred years after the Teacher's nirvāṇa, to live for one hundred and fifty years, and to worship stūpas for eighty-seven years.

Assisted by a yakṣa called Ratha, the king fulfilled the Teacher's prophecy by extracting relics from seven stūpas which held the Buddha's remains, and then by building eight hundred and forty billion stūpas of seven precious stones in all parts of Jambudvīpa.[438] The arhats praised his achievements saying:

> King Aśoka who lives in Pāṭaliputra
> Has vastly increased the seven stūpas.
> Mightily, too, he has adorned this earth
> With manifest objects of prayer.

Śāṇavāsika

After consecrating those stūpas and entrusting the teaching to Upagupta, Śāṇavāsika passed into nirvāṇa.

UPAGUPTA

[52.1-52.6] In the *Minor Transmissions* the Teacher had predicted:

> One hundred years after my nirvāṇa Upagupta, a son of the incense-seller Gupta, will be ordained as a monk. He will become a buddha who is without the marks of one,[439] and he will perform the deeds of a buddha.

Upagupta received ordination from Yaśaḥ and became an arhat learned in the Tripiṭaka. Once, while he was teaching the doctrine to a congregation, the evil Māra distracted his audience by displaying magical transformations and so prevented them from achieving the goal. Thereupon, Upagupta transformed three corpses into flower garlands and bound them round Māra's head. When Māra produced an evil thought, they appeared as corpses and exuded a foul stench; but when he produced a wholesome thought, they appeared to be flowers. It is said

Upagupta

that owing to this crown, which no one could cast off, Māra was subdued by Upagupta and promised to avoid evil thoughts thereafter.

So many became arhats through Upagupta's seven instructions that a cave, eighteen cubits long and twelve cubits wide, was completely filled with four-inch sticks, one for each of them. Since the Teacher's nirvāṇa there had been no larger gathering of arhats that this. Upagupta himself entered nirvāṇa after entrusting the teaching to Dhītika.

DHĪTIKA, KṚṢṆA, SUDARŚANA, MADHYĀHNIKA AND THE SIXTEEN ELDERS

[52.6-55.1] The sublime Dhītika was also an arhat learned in the Tripiṭaka. After entrusting the teaching to the sublime Kṛṣṇa of Pāṭaliputra (*dmar-bu-can*) in Magadha, he passed into nirvāṇa.

Kṛṣṇa, too, was an arhat learned in the Tripiṭaka. After protecting the teaching completely he entrusted it to Sudarśana and entered final nirvāṇa. Some include Madhyāhnika among the patriarchs as well, but in our opinion there were only seven patriarchs before Nāgārjuna.[440]

In particular, the great Sixteen Elders, who resided with five hundred arhats and others in various lands throughout the four continents and in the Trayatriṃśa heaven,[441] protected the precious teaching; and in so doing they visited China during the reigns of T'ang T'ai-tsung, Qubilai Qan, and the emperor Yung-lo. Some say that they could be seen by all, but others maintain that the common folk could not see them, their bodies being rainbow-like.[442]

Madhyāhnika

So it was that the teaching was propagated throughout sixteen great cities of Jambudvīpa during the Teacher's lifetime. None the less, because there were not yet cities in Kashmir, the Teacher had predicted that Madhyāhnika would establish the teaching in Kashmir one hundred years after his nirvāṇa, for it was a most restful place and one suited to meditation. Accordingly, nearly twenty years after Ānanda had passed into nirvāṇa, the arhat Madhyāhnika went to Kashmir, knowing that the time had come to fulfil the prophecy. In one cross-legged posture he covered nine valleys, which converged in a lake. The nāgas were furious. They caused an earthquake and a terrible rain storm, but they could not move even a corner of his robe. He transformed the shower of arrows and missiles which they hurled at him into flowers, whereupon the nāgas said in amazement, "What is your command?"

"I have come to this land to fulfil a prophecy of the Teacher. Please give this land to me."

"We will offer up the land covered by your sitting position. How many followers do you have?"

"Five hundred arhats."

"If even one of them is missing we will take back the land."

To this the elder replied, "Those depending on alms are supported in a place where there is sponsorship. Therefore householders must also be settled here."

Madhyāhnika had a sorcerer construct a magical city there, and he consecrated it to be both perfectly glorious and imperishable. He settled numerous people there and, having brought saffron from Gandhamādana Mountain, consecrated it so that saffron would grow there for the duration of the teaching. The place with its many towns became the delightful country that is renowned today as Kashmir.[443]

4 *The Preservation of the Teaching and Spread of the Greater Vehicle*

[55.1-60.4] After the Teacher's nirvāṇa a limitless number of great pious attendants, individuals who were like the Buddha himself, came forth to protect the teaching. Such were the host of arhats like Uttara and Yaśaḥ, the venerable monks like Kāśyapa, and the great brahmans like King Sujaya and Kalyāṇa. They were masters who served the teaching, who were illustrious for their learning, dignity and excellence, and who had attained the qualities of realisation. None the less, in the opinion of the pious attendants of the Sautrāntika school,[444] the first to compose [authoritative] treatises must have been the arhats who composed the *Great Treasury of Detailed Exposition*. But, according to the greater vehicle, the first to do so were Maitreyanātha and the master Nāgārjuna, since other commentators rely on treatises which follow their expositions of the path.[445]

According to the Teacher's own predictions, the three authors of fundamental texts were: Nāgārjuna, the Second Buddha, who was the disciple of the great brahman Saraha, and who set in motion the profound way of philosophical vision; the sublime Asaṅga, who was the disciple of the venerable Maitreya, and who spread throughout Jambudvīpa the extensive tradition of conduct; and the master Dignāga, who had been taken into the following of Mañjughoṣa and thus attained accomplishments which overcame all opposing forces, and who revealed the way of the knowledge [through logical analysis] of what is implicit in actuality.

Their three commentators were: the master Āryadeva, disciple of Nāgārjuna, who was born miraculously from a lotus; Asaṅga's younger brother, the master Vasubandhu, who committed to memory nine million and nine hundred thousand verses and thus crossed the ocean of learning; and Dignāga's [indirect] disciple, the glorious Dharmakīrti, who instantly broke the resolution of non-Buddhists, having followed in the footsteps of [Dignāga's pupil] the disputant Īśvarasena.

The masters and their disciples mentioned above are collectively known as the "six adornments of Jambudvīpa". Usually Nāgārjuna and

Asaṅga are esteemed as the "two supreme ones", and the six adornments are made up of the remaining four, with the addition of the masters Guṇaprabha and Śākyaprabha.[446] Śāntideva, the great son of the conquerors who was the subject of seven wonderful episodes, and Candragomin, who was learned in the sciences and their branches and achieved the accomplishments, are hailed as the "two marvellous masters". And there were innumerable other masters who attained full command of the meaning of the Buddha's scriptures, and who mainly elucidated the teaching of the Transcendental Perfections.

In general, as soon as the transmitted precepts of the dialectical vehicle, which deals with causes, had been compiled, the texts of the greater vehicle, which could not have been apportioned [their place in the Tripiṭaka], were introduced by devout men, gods, and spirits to their own domains. Those preserved in the human world were propagated gradually. Some of those preserved in the non-human worlds were introduced to the human world and propagated by holy personages.

Concerning the greater vehicle in particular: It transpired that shortly after the time of King Mahāpadma, Candrarakṣita became the king of Oḍiviśa. It is said that the sublime Mañjuśrī entered his house in the guise of a monk, taught some doctrines of the greater vehicle, and left behind a book. Adherents of the sūtra tradition believe that it was the *Transcendental Perfection of Discriminative Awareness in Eight Thousand Lines*, but followers of the mantra tradition believe it to have been the *Summation of the Real*. Regardless of which one it was, it is said that this was the first appearance of the greater vehicle in the human world after the Teacher's nirvāṇa. This must be held to have occurred before the third council. Therefore, the position universally adhered to by most contemporary scholars, namely, that all the transmitted precepts were committed to writing during the third council must be erroneous, for it is contradicted by this report.[447]

As for the tantrapiṭaka of the secret mantra: A discrepancy developed in the accounts of the ancient and new traditions [of Tibet], due to the changes that had taken place in India between the period when the doctrine was yet undiminished and the subsequent period of varied growth and decline. The opinion of our Ancient Translation School of the secret mantra texts will be explained below in detail.[448] In the opinion of the new tradition of secret mantra, the Teacher himself taught the tantras to Indrabhūti, the king of Oḍḍiyāna. It is also held that Vajrapāṇi entrusted them to him. In any case, whoever it was, the king had the tantras written down, and he taught them to the people. All the inhabitants of the land, even mere insects, became accomplished and vanished in the rainbow body. Then the land of Oḍḍiyāna became a desolate land, which the nāgas transformed into a lake. The Lord of Secrets [Vajrapāṇi] revealed the tantras to them and brought them to maturity. As a result they gradually changed into men, and, living in a village by the shore of the lake, they persevered in practice and became accomplished. When their sons and daughters became ḍākas and ḍākinīs, the land became renowned as "Oḍḍiyāna, the Land of the Ḍākinīs".

Eventually the lake dried up and a self-created temple of Heruka appeared. In its stores, the volumes of the tantras were preserved. Subsequently, most of the tantras were taken from it by accomplished masters: the *Guhyasamāja* by King Vasukalpa; the *Hevajra* by Nāgārjuna; the *Mahāmāya* and *Bhairava* tantras (T 468 & 470) by Kukkuripā; and so forth.

Similarly, there are many slightly different legends, for instance, that of Celuka and others obtaining the *Kālacakra Tantra* from the land of Shambhala, or from other lands, and propagating it. However it may have been, innumerable accomplished masters appeared: the glorious Saraha and the eighty-four accomplished masters;[449] Buddhajñānapāda and the twelve masters who were renowned at Vikramaśīla; the six paṇḍitas of the gates; and the elder and younger Kālacakrapāda. They secured innumerable fortunate beings in spiritual maturity and liberation, primarily by means of the secret mantra teachings of the greater vehicle.[450]

Thus it is not possible to describe here, in a few words, the numberless liberated careers of those who sustained the Conqueror's precious teaching, its transmission and its realisation, in India. Relying on the illumination of [other] well-known histories and elegant tales, may the lotus of reverence and enthusiasm [toward the doctrine] fully blossom!

This completes the general explanation of the origins of the Conqueror's precious teaching in the world, the first part of this book, *Thunder from the Great Conquering Battle-Drum of Devendra*, which is a history of the precious teaching of the vehicle of indestructible reality according to the Ancient Translation School.

Part Two
The Rise of the Precious Teaching of Secret Mantra

Introduction

[63.1-63.3] Now the rise of the precious teaching of secret mantra, or the vehicle of indestructible reality, will be explained in particular. This part has three sections: (1) where, and by whom, the doctrinal wheel of the secret mantra was turned; (2) how the transmitted precepts were collected by the compilers; (3) the emergence of this teaching in the human world.

1 *The Turning of the Secret Mantra Wheel*

[63.3-64.2] According to our special tradition there were three great descents of the teaching [of the secret mantra tradition]. It says in the *Exegetical Tantra of the Oceanic Magical Net*:

> The intentional, symbolic and aural lineages are respectively those of the conquerors, bodhisattvas and yogins.

That is to say, the three lineages to be explained are: the intentional lineage of the conquerors; the symbolic lineage of the awareness-holders; and the aural lineage of mundane individuals.

THE INTENTIONAL LINEAGE OF THE CONQUERORS

[64.2-69.2] Samantabhadra, who completely encompasses both saṃsāra and nirvāṇa, and who is the all-pervading lord, embodying the sixth enlightened family,[451] appears in the indestructible Great Akaniṣṭha realm, the utterly pure expanse that is manifest in and of itself,[452] in the form of Vajradhara, perfectly endowed with the signs and marks of buddhahood. There, his intention is the pristine cognition of just what is, the inconceivable abiding nature of reality, entirely free from verbal expression; and through its blessing he confers realisation upon the Teachers of the Five Buddha Families, the nature of whose assembly is no different from his own, and upon the assembly that appears as the countless maṇḍalas of self-manifesting peaceful and wrathful conquerors. This is conventionally referred to as the "speech of the buddha-body of reality". It says in the *Penetration of Sound*:

> Thus, in the celestial expanse of reality,
> There appeared the natural sound,
> Blessed by the speech of the Great All-Pervader...[453]

And in a *Commentary on the Secret Nucleus* (*snying-'grel*):

> The Teacher, who is the body of reality, communicates to the assembly, which is the ocean of pristine cognition, by unborn speech of genuine meaning.

Samantabhadra and Consort

In particular, according to the profound and extensive teachings whose perspective is that of the Indestructible Nucleus of Inner Radiance:[454] The doctrinal wheel is turned without straying from the single savour [of all that arises] in the vast equilibrium of reality, which transcends all objects of speech and of thought. This even transcends [sublime notions] such as that "the place, teacher, assembly, and doctrine have emanated from the infinite expanse of pristine cognition or naturally present awareness, whose nature is a spontaneous precious enclosure or vast self-manifesting array of the three buddha-bodies."

None the less, to the great sublime beings who have arrived at the end of the tenth level it appears that, in a special Akaniṣṭha realm,[455] where extraneous objects of rapture are fully enjoyed, [Samantabhadra], in the form of [Vajradhara] the Lord of the Sixth Buddha Family and those of the Teachers of the Five Buddha Families, keeps the doctrinal wheel of the inexpressible vehicle of Unsurpassed Yoga (*Anuttarayogatantra*) in perpetual motion, by means of intentional symbols, on behalf of an assembly of the great bodhisattvas who possess extraordinary awareness, such as Vajrapāṇi, Avalokiteśvara, and Mañjuśrī; beings who are themselves the products of purity of sense and sense object.[456] In the *Secret Nucleus* (Ch.6, v.14) it says:

> His body appears as Vairocana Buddha
> In the supreme realm of unsurpassed Akaniṣṭha.
> Without an utterance from his supreme speech,
> His body reveals all doctrines
> To the assemblies of bodhisattvas.

It is also said that this realm is the Akaniṣṭha of the Mahāvaśavartin, which lies beyond the Pure Abodes.[457] The *Magical Net of Indestructible Reality*, too, says:

> Abandoning the Pure Abode,
> In the supreme realm of Great Akaniṣṭha,
> Is the spontaneously present body of
> The lord of the buddha families, with his *mudrā*.
> Transcending unity and diversity, this is
> The common form of all buddhas.
> He is the original treasure of the greater vehicle
> Who appears at each instant to those disciples
> Who have abandoned all obscurations.

In the same way, in the ordinary Akaniṣṭha, which appears to bodhisattvas on the ninth level; and in the imputed Akaniṣṭha, which appears to bodhisattvas on the eighth level;[458] and in the palaces of great liberation, that are the expanse of reality, the glorious womb of the Vajra Queen,[459] there appear to the senses of Rudra,[460] Bhairava and other malicious disciples the forms of the foremost [Herukas], such as Mahottara Heruka, Kumāravīrabalin, Padmanarteśvara, as well as Hevajra, Cakrasaṃvara, and Kālacakra. These each reveal their indestructible realms and, through their transformations, emanate the maṇḍala of their respective assemblies. And, by means of the imperishable sound of pure vibration, each one turns the wheel of the doctrine. In the *Root Tantra of the Gathering of the Sugatas* (*bder-'dus rtsa-rgyud*, NGB Vol.31) it says:

> I am king of the great,
> And I am both teacher and listener.

And in the *Hevajra Tantra* (Pt.2, Ch.2, v.39ab):

> I am the teacher, and I am the doctrine.
> Endowed with my own assembly, I am even the listener.

Similarly, in conventional places such as Tuṣita, Mount Sumeru, Oḍḍiyāna, and Shambhala, [the Buddha] also taught the Kriyā, Caryā, and Yoga tantras, either in the guise of a passionless monk, or as a universal monarch. In the *Tantra of the Secret Nucleus* (Ch.6, v.13) it says:

> When he appears in various different forms
> Corresponding to the different [beings].
> He does not stray from just what is,
> But appears variously through the power of deeds.

Vajradharma

2 *The Collecting of Transmitted Precepts by Different Compilers*

[69.2-70.4] Although the compilers [i.e. recipients] of most Unsurpassed [Yoga] tantras were separate [from those who taught them], the compilers of the majority of the truly secret tantras, such as the *Tantra of the Secret Nucleus*, were none other than their respective teachers; for the teacher and his assembly were of identical intention. Accordingly, in the *Tantra of the Secret Nucleus* one finds the words, "Thus have I explained", and in the *Root Tantra of Cakrasaṃvara*, "Then, I will explain what is secret". The *Verification of Secrets* (*Śrīguhyasiddhi*, T 2217) also says:

> The teacher of tantra is the indestructible reality of mind.
> It is teacher as well as compiler.

Furthermore, most tantras on the Great Perfection, and related topics, were compiled by [bodhisattvas] like the Lord of Secrets [Vajrapāṇi] Vajradharma,[461] Vajragarbha, Mañjuśrī, Avalokiteśvara, and the emanation Garap Dorje; and by a host of ḍākas and ḍākinis like Pūrṇopaśānti; as well as by a host of disciples including devas, nāgas, yakṣas, and others of sundry genus.

It has been said that the Lord of Secrets collected all the tantras alone. But those who requested [the teaching of] particular tantras also became their compilers. Thus, the *Kālacakra* was compiled by Sucandra, the *Hevajra* by Vajragarbha, the *Emergence of Cakrasaṃvara* by Vajrapāṇi and the *Vajraḍāka* (T 370-1) by Varāhī.

3 *The Emergence of this Teaching in the Human World*

[70.4-5] This section has two parts: (1) the symbolic lineage of the awareness-holders; (2) the aural lineage of mundane individuals.

THE SYMBOLIC LINEAGE OF THE AWARENESS-HOLDERS

This comprises both: (1) its origination among non-human awareness-holders; (2) its origination among both human and non-human awareness-holders.

The Origination of the Symbolic Lineage among Non-Human Awareness-holders[462]

[70.5-72.4] Within the assemblies of bodhisattvas or sons of the conquerors, the Teacher appeared as the emanations who are [the Lords of] the Three Families [i.e. Mañjuśrī, Avalokiteśvara, and Vajrapāṇi]. They symbolically instructed and taught disciples who were, respectively, devas, nāgas, and yakṣas.

In other words, in the youthful and handsome form of Tīkṣṇavajra, Mañjuśrī instructed the deva Yaśasvī Varapāla in the realm of the gods. The latter, in turn, instructed the deva Brahmaratnaprabha. The teaching was then transmitted successively through Prajāpatibrahmā, Brahmasarvatāra, Brahmaśikhandara, and Indraśakra, who instructed a mass of one hundred thousand awareness-holders among the devas.

In the form of Amṛtabhaiṣajya, Avalokiteśvara instructed the nāga king Kālagrīva in the domain of the nāgas. The teaching was then transmitted successively through the nāginī Khandülma, the nāginī Dültsangma, the nāga Manorathanandin, and the nāga Takṣaka, who instructed a mass of one hundred thousand awareness-holders among the nāgas.

And in an awesome and menacing form, Vajrapāṇi instructed the yakṣa Samantabhadra in the domain of the yakṣas. Then, the teaching

Avalokiteśvara

Mañjuśrī

Vajrapāṇi

was transmitted successively through the yakṣa Vajrapāṇi, the yakṣa Yaśasvī Varapāla (*grags-ldan mchog-skyong*),[463] and the yakṣa Ulkāmukha (*skar-mda'-gdong*), who instructed a mass of one hundred thousand awareness-holders among the yakṣas.

All those instructed, in turn, instructed their own congregations, as a result of which they and their followers attained to the level of Vajradhara.

Concerning the Great Perfection: It is said that Adhicitta (*lhag-sems-can*), the son of the god Bhadrapāla, who resided in the Trayatriṃśa heaven, had four special dreams. Accordingly, Vajrasattva, being consecrated by all the buddhas of the ten directions and three times and by all the buddhas of the five families, bestowed upon Adhicitta, the son of the gods, the "empowerment of the vase that is the Conqueror's means"[464] and granted him the esoteric instructions of the Great Perfection. So it was that the Great Perfection spread in the realm of the gods. As it says in the *Point of Liberation* of Buddhajñānapāda:

> Starting from then the definitive meaning was taught,
> When this supreme truth was transmitted

From mouth to mouth, and from ear to ear,
To those who were endowed with good fortune.

The Origination of the Symbolic Lineage among Human and Non-Human Awareness-holders

[72.4-77.3] In the *Sūtra of the Declaration of Enlightened Intention* (*Sandhivyākaraṇatantra*, T 444) the Teacher is asked:

O Transcendent Lord! you have indeed taught
The three guiding vehicles.[465]
Why, then, do you not teach the definitive vehicle,
In which the spontaneous presence
Of the cause and the fruit is enjoyed,
And which cannot be requested from other buddhas?

To this he replied:

Having turned the wheel of the doctrine of causes
For those who are intent upon cause,
The short path of the vehicle of indestructible reality
Will make its appearance
In an age that has not yet come.

In accordance with this prophecy, twenty-eight years after the supreme emanational body of the Teacher in this world [Śākyamuni] had passed into nirvāṇa, five noble ones of the genuine enlightened family – namely, the god Yaśasvī Varapāla, the nāga king Takṣaka, the yakṣa Ulkāmukha, the ogre Matyaupāyika and the human awareness-holder Vimalakīrti the Licchavi[466] – each learnt by supernormal cognitive powers that, in this world, the Lord had passed into nirvāṇa. They then aroused themselves from their inner meditative absorptions and miraculously assembled on the peak of Malayagiri in Laṅkā. There, they cried out in twenty-three verses of lamentation beginning:

Alas! when the light from the Teacher's lamp
Is gone from the whole universe,
Who will dispel the world's darkness?

So they wept to the point of exhaustion.

The Transcendent Lord had predicted that the secret mantra would become renowned throughout the world at some future time and, as that time had arrived, Vajrapāṇi, the Lord of Secrets, appeared there in person; for he had been empowered by the Buddha to teach the secret mantra. He instructed the five noble ones, as well as most of the community of awareness-holders, repeating the teachings of the secret mantra vehicle which the Teacher had previously conferred in the Akaniṣṭha realm, and elsewhere. The ogre Matyaupāyika inscribed them in a golden book with melted beryl; and then by the seven powers of his intention the book was concealed, invisibly sealed in space.

The land of Laṅkā, where Malayagiri is situated, is not that Laṅkā also known as Cāmara, which is a subsidiary continent of Jambudvīpa. Rather it is an island isolated by the ocean on the south-east coast of Jambudvīpa, where, on the invitation of Rāvaṇa, the ten-headed lord of Laṅkā, the Transcendent Lord taught the extremely extensive *Sūtra of the Descent to Laṅkā* at the request of Mahāmati. Apart from that island, the teaching was propagated to some extent in both ancient and recent times on the islands of Tāmralipti, Yāvadvīpa [Java], Dhanaśrīdvīpa [Sumatra], Payigudvīpa [Burma] and so on.

Laṅkā, in particular, was so called because in ancient times it was under the sway of the ogre Rāvaṇa. Later the country was depopulated of ogres, and today it is called Siṅghala [Ceylon] because it was seized by the merchant Siṃha.[467] When the great master Kaṇhapāda went there he subdued a great ogress called Viśvarūpī, together with her five hundred followers, and propagated the mantra teaching. Later the master of the greater vehicle, Laṅkājayabhadra, was born there, and the master Candragomin also visited that land. When Śāntipā and the great scholar Vanaratna went there in turn, they also propagated the mantra teaching.

In antiquity, when the human king Rāma destroyed the ten-headed Rāvaṇa, he reached Laṅkā by building a stone bridge across the ocean from India to the island. Even today huge rocks are clearly visible in the ocean. Sometimes ships change course lest they collide with the rocks; and it takes a whole morning to walk along the outcropping of red stone, which is said to have been stained by the blood of the ten-headed ogre when he was slain.

In the centre of Laṅkā there is a ravine called Sumanakūṭa, "Mount Pleasant".[468] No ordinary person can reach it because it is surrounded by a chain of rocky hills. The great master [Padmasambhava] and his disciples went there and stayed for six years before returning to India. While that mountain is usually known by the aforementioned name, it in fact possesses all the qualities of the Malaya Mountain, which is a ferocious wilderness. It has been described as follows:

> On its peak dwells the king of powerful craft.
> On its face is a dog-shaped white rock.
> It's adorned with the likeness of a lion
> Leaping through space.
> At its base grow eight medicinal roots:
> Illness and disease do no harm here.
> On the summit there is the eyrie and nest
> Of the solitary Kalantaka bird,
> Which dwells apart from all others.

The peak is of easy access to those of good
fortune,
But to the unfortunate completely impregnible.

Laṅkā is more sublime than other islands by virtue of other praiseworthy qualities: Near the base of the mountain just mentioned, to the north of it, there are many stūpas containing relics of the Tathāgata, for instance, the great Caitya of Guṇavera. On its western side is a tree called Buddhaśaraṇa under which the Tathāgata remained in contemplation for seven days. That land, whose rivers are filled with pearls, treasuries with jewels, forests with elephants, and houses with voluptuous girls, is the very one famed by the name of Siṅghala.

In a dense forest called Kaṇḍala, in the north-east, there is a cavern which houses Śrīpāduka,[469] an enormous footprint of the Buddha. It is said that during the regular festival held at the footprint twelve thousand monks congregate; and that from ancient times up to the present day the teachings of both the lesser and greater vehicles have been widespread.

THE AURAL LINEAGE OF MUNDANE INDIVIDUALS

[77.3-78.4] After the third council, in the time of King Kaniṣka's son, five hundred masters who proclaimed the greater vehicle came forth. All of them received precepts transmitted by the Lord of Secrets and others and they all acquired miraculous powers. They were invited to the west by King Lakṣāśva, who built a temple on the summit of Mount Abu, and requested them to live there. He also caused five hundred intelligent members of his court to be ordained and to study the doctrine of the greater vehicle under those five hundred masters. The king thought that the piṭaka should be written down and he asked how large they were. The masters replied, "Speaking generally, they are innumerable, but these here comprise ten million [verses altogether]." To this, the king responded that they should be written down, despite the large quantity. And so he had them all committed to writing and then presented them to the masters. From this time on the greater vehicle was widely propagated. There were also a great many who secretly practised Kriyātantra and Caryātantra. Numerous tantra texts, concerning the way of mantras, were brought from different lands and propagated by those masters.

Concerning the Unsurpassed [Yoga]tantra: Until a later period, only a few supremely fortunate beings, those who had attained to all-surpassing [realisation], received teachings from their preferred deity or some other. They practised these teachings in solitude and attained accomplishment. Since neither the specific instructions were set forth, nor the sequence of the lineage established at all, no one ever knew their names; so how could there have been a public spread of their teachings?

4 *The Lineage of Mahāyoga, the Class of Tantras*

KING JA AND KUKKURĀJA

[78.4-85.2] When the Lord of Secrets turned the doctrinal wheel of the secret mantra for the five noble ones on Malayagiri, King Ja of Sahor,[470] who practised the outer tantras of the way of secret mantra, had, at the very same time, seven wonderful dreams, as follows:

> The signs of the buddhas' body,
> Speech, and mind dissolved [into his own];
> And a bejewelled book descended.
> He engaged in a doctrinal discussion.
> Everyone revered him as a saint.
> He performed a great rite of worship.
> Jewels fell down, as does rain.
> And it was prophesied that he would attain
> To the level of buddhahood.

King Ja was prophesied by the Teacher in all sorts of sūtras and tantras. The *Subsequent Tantra of the Emergence of Cakrasaṃvara* (*Saṃvarodayottaratantra*) says:

> One hundred and twelve years from now,
> When I have vanished from here,
> A quintessential doctrine,
> Renowned in the three divine realms,
> Will be revealed by the Lord of Secrets
> To one who is named King Ja,
> Who will appear by virtue of great merits
> At Jambudvīpa's eastern frontier.[471]

Similar quotations are also found in the *General Sūtra which Gathers All Intentions*.

Some say that King Ja was none other than Indrabhūti the Great, who had been empowered by the Teacher himself, but others maintain that he was that Indrabhūti's son. Some even believe him to have been an intermediate Indrabhūti.[472] Thus, there are various dissimilar opinions; but, because ordinary persons cannot imagine the emanations of great sublime beings, perhaps they are all correct! And yet, upon examining the chronology, we find he is described as the contemporary of master Kukkurāja. For this reason he may well be an intermediate Indrabhūti. Moreover, the great accomplished master Kambalapāda

King Ja, Indrabhūti

and this king are contemporary, whether or not they are in fact one and the same person. He is also the approximate contemporary of Vidyāvajra, Saroruha, and Jālandharipā.

In any case, while the king was sitting absorbed in the meditative cultivation of the yoga of the lower tantras, a volume containing the great texts of the way of secret mantra, including the *Buddhasamāyoga* and a one-cubit-tall image of the Lord of Secrets actually fell upon the royal palace, just as in his dream. Then, having performed prayers, he intuitively understood the chapter entitled the "Vision of Vajrasattva" and, relying on that and on the image of Vajrapāṇi, he practised for seven months. As a result he had a vision of Vajrasattva and received from him the empowerment of pristine cognition. Thus he came to understand the symbolic conventions and meanings of that volume in their entirety.

At the same time, the Anuyoga texts were revealed in Ceylon. As it says in the prediction found in the fifth chapter of the *Tantra which Comprises the Supreme Path of the Means which Clearly Reveal All-Positive Pristine Cognition* (*kun-bzang ye-shes gsal-bar ston-pa'i thabs-kyi lam-mchog 'dus-pa'i rgyud*, NGB Vol.3):

> The Mahāyoga tantras will fall onto the palace of King Ja.
> The Anuyoga tantras will emerge in the forests of Siṅghala.

Then King Ja taught the book to master Uparāja, who was renowned as a great scholar throughout the land of Sahor, but he could not understand their symbolic conventions and meaning. The king then taught them to the master Kukkurāja. He intuitively understood the chapter on the "Vision of Vajrasattva", from the *Tantra of the Magical Net of Vajrasattva*, and practised it, whereupon Vajrasattva revealed himself and predicted that the Lord of Secrets would reveal the meanings of this tantra thereafter. When he had practised more, the Lord of Secrets actually appeared and granted him the complete empowerment of the authentic teaching and of all vehicles. Then he told him to request the verbal teaching from the Licchavi Vimalakīrti. It is said that, following the transmitted precepts of the Lord of Secrets, master Kukkurāja divided [the Mahāyoga tantras] into the *Eighteen Great Tantrapiṭaka* (*tantra chen-po sde bco-brgyad*) and taught them to King Ja.[473]

In the king's own composition, the *Array of the Path of the Magical Net*, he says:

> In the eastern domain of Indrabhūti,
> At Vajrakūṭa in India,
> I, the noble Indrabhūti,
> Practised the *Magical Net*,
> Having been taught by the Lord of Secrets himself.
> I actually realised Vajrapāṇi,
> With his retinue of fifty thousand.
> Being empowered in wholesome action,
> By the practice of disciplined conduct,
> I was free from sin, and reached [an exalted] level.

Just so, although the king himself had attained realisation, he demonstrated the way of realisation by relying upon Kukkurāja. This was in order to prevent charlatans from entering this path at will.

Now, the renowned master Kukkurāja, whose name means "king of dogs", and who is also called Kuttarāja in some legends, taught the doctrine by day in the guise of a dog to a thousand warriors and yoginīs, and by night went to the charnel grounds with them to perform feast offerings and other sacramental practices. After practising in this way for twelve years he finally attained the accomplishment of the Great Seal.

Others say that while the master was abiding in such practice he went to Oḍḍiyāna and once more gave a detailed explanation of the *Five Inner Tantrapiṭaka* (*nang-rgyud sde-lnga*) including the *Buddhasamāyoga*; which were drawn from the *Eighteen Great Tantrapiṭaka* [of the Mahāyoga]. In this way, he finally attained the supreme accomplishment by following the *Tantra of the Hidden Point of the Moon* (*Candraguhyatilakatantra*, T 477).

This master was an adept of the *Buddhasamāyoga Tantra*. He wrote many treatises, including the *Six Arrays of Esoteric Meaning* (*Ṣaḍguhyārthadharavyūha*, T 1664-9), and the *Fivefold Rite for Entering into All Maṇḍalas* (*Sarvamaṇḍalānuvartipañcavidhi*, T 1670).

Now, in the peculiar terminology of the Ancient Translation School, the inner tantras are universally regarded as forming three classes: the Mahāyoga, [which deals primarily with] the stage of creation; the Anuyoga, [which deals primarily with] the stage of perfection; and the Atiyoga, [which deals primarily with] the Great Perfection.

Kukkurāja

The first of these, the Mahāyoga, has two divisions: the class of tantras [**tantravarga*] and the class of means for attainment [**sādhanavarga*, NGB Vols. 20-33]. Of these, the former, which consists of the great tantrapiṭaka, is divided into eighteen: the five great tantrapiṭaka of buddha-body, speech, mind, attributes, and activity – these are the ground and the roots; the five tantrapiṭaka concerned with the means for attainment – these are the branches; the five tantrapiṭaka concerned with conduct – these are also branches; the two supplementary tantras which make up the omissions; and the single tantrapiṭaka which summarises the meaning of all the others.[474] King Ja taught all of these to Kukkurāja. From the latter they were transmitted successively to Śakraputra, or Indrabhūti the younger, who was the king's son; Siṃharāja; Śakrabhūti, or Uparāja; and finally to the daughter Gomadevī. By practising the path on which the two provisions [of merit and pristine cognition] are achieved [rapidly], they and their respective retinues reached the level of Vajradhara. As it says in the *Sequence of the Path* :

> Then to the east of Jambudvīpa,
> Which rests on the Indestructible Seat,
> In a holy palace of precious gems,
> In an auspicious and sacred room,
> Kukkurāja and Indrabhūti,
> Together with Siṃharāja, Uparāja,
> Daughter Gomadevī, and others,
> Received the empowerment of the *Magical Net*.
> They actually attained the maṇḍala as an assembly,
> And manifestly reached the level of Vajradhara.

King Ja wrote the *Array of the Path of the Magical Net*, the *Two Stages* (*Śrīguhyagarbhakramadvayoddeśa*, P 4771), et cetera. He also composed many other definitive texts which bring out the most secret meaning: the *Commentary on the Root Tantra of Cakrasaṃvara* (*Śrīcakrasaṃvaratantrarājasambarasamuccayanāmavṛtti*, T 1413); the *Verification of Pristine Cognition* (*Jñānasiddhi*, T 2219); the *Verification of Co-Emergence* (*Sahajasiddhi*, T 2260) and so forth. Nearly all of the tantras and instructions that were widespread among the great accomplished masters of India came from this royal master. He gave the transmitted precepts on supreme bliss and on inner radiance to the accomplished master Bālapāda, or Jālandharipā, who in turn transmitted the lineage to Kṛṣṇacārin and his retinue of disciples. Tilopā and Nāropā and all their disciples came forth from this lineage.[475] It is also the source of the transmitted precepts concerning the action seal (*karmamudrā*), which were passed down from daughter Gomadevī to King Ja and Kukkurāja, and from them to the masters Līlāvajra and Buddhaguhya.

LĪLĀVAJRA[476]

[85.2-87.6] The master Līlāvajra was born in the country of Ṣaṃṣara. He was ordained in Oḍḍiyāna and studied the Tripiṭaka. He was particularly learned in the philosophical tenets of Asaṅga, and he also knew all of the ordinary sciences. On an island in Oḍḍiyāna called Madhima he practised the *Sublime Litany of the Names of Mañjuśrī*. When he was approaching accomplishment a ray of light emanated from the face of a painting of Mañjuśrī and illuminated the island for a long time, owing to which the master was called Sūryavat, "Sun-like".

Līlāvajra (or Vilāsavajra)

On another occasion, when a practitioner of perverse doctrines, who required the five sense organs of a Buddhist scholar as sacraments for his practice, came to kill the master, Līlāvajra appeared in various forms, such as those of an elephant, horse, boy, girl, buffalo, and peacock. Unable to recognise him, the fanatic went away. Owing to this incident, the master became renowned as Viśvarūpa, "Everyform".

Near the end of his life he vastly benefitted living creatures in Oḍḍiyāna. The master was learned and accomplished, generally speaking, in all the tantrapiṭaka, and in the *Magical Net* cycle, in particular.

He also lived for ten years at Nālandā, where he preserved the teaching of the way of mantras. He composed many treatises and expounded them in detail. [His works include]: a *Commentary on the Litany of the Names of Mañjuśrī* (*'jam-dpal mtshan-brjod-kyi 'grel-ba*, T 2533) according to the interpretations of the Unsurpassed [Yoga]tantra; the *Sequence of the Supreme Point* (*Mahātilakakrama*, T 1290), concerning the stage of perfection of Hevajra; a *Commentary on the Guhyasamāja Tantra*, based on the Guru's Instruction (*Śrīguhyasamājatantranidāna-gurūpadeśanavyākhyāna*, T 1910); the *Means for the Attainment of Co-Emergence* (*Śrīguhyasamājasahajasādhana*, T 1913); and other treatises dealing with sundry tantras. Concerning the system of the *Magical Net*, [he composed]: the *Parkap Commentary on the Secret Nucleus*;[477] the *Innermost Point* (*Cittabindu*, P 4723); the *Sixfold Sequence* (*Kramaṣaṭka*, P 4741); the *Clarification of Commitments*; the *Propensity for the Commitments* (*Samayānuśayanirdeśa*, P 4745) and so on. In the end he attained the body of indestructible reality. His ordination name was Śrīmad Uttamabodhibhagavat and his esoteric name was Līlāvajra. In the treatises, too, he is referred to as Līlāvajra, Sūryavat, or Viśvarūpa.

Under Līlāvajra the master Buddhajñānapāda studied the *Magical Net*, the *Buddhasamāyoga*, the *Guhyasamāja*, [the *Garland of Activity*, *Karmamālā*, NGB Vol.17][478] and the *Hidden Point of the Moon*, which are known as the *Five Inner Tantrapiṭaka* and are foremost among the *Eighteen Great Tantrapiṭaka*. He meditated upon them and attained mastery of pristine cognition. In the *Oral Instructions of Mañjuśrī*, he says:

> Then I went to Oḍḍiyāna, the birthplace of all virtues,
> Where there dwelt one famed as Līlāvajra.
> I learned much from him and pondered it...

While the venerable Līlāvajra was preserving the mantra teaching in Oḍḍiyāna, an outcaste boy met Āryadeva [in a vision].[479] By the latter's blessing the boy spontaneously understood the doctrine and expounded various texts concerning the way of mantras, which had been composed by the sublime Nāgārjuna and Āryadeva, [who were spiritual] father and son. Mātaṅgīpā and Rakṣitapāda of Koṅkana also heard them from Candrakīrti in person; and they were the first to copy down his book, the *Clarifying Lamp*. In the same way, it is said that the scholar Rāhula met Nāgabodhi[480] [and also received similar doctrines]. Thus, the sublime Nāgārjuna's cycle of teaching on the *Guhyasamāja* first appeared during this period.[481]

BUDDHAGUHYA

[87.6-90.2] The master Buddhaguhya was born in Central India and was ordained at Nālandā. He and master Buddhaśānti were both disciples of Buddhajñānapāda during the early part of the latter's life. When Buddhaguhya was propitiating the sublime Mañjuśrī in the Vārāṇasī region, it so happened that a picture of Mañjuśrī smiled; the clarified butter of a red cow, which was required for this practice, began to boil; and some flowers that had wilted blossomed anew. He realised that these were signs of accomplishment, but he hesitated for a while, not knowing whether he should first offer the flower, or drink the ghee. A yakṣiṇī obstructed him with a slap on the face and he fainted for a short time. Then, on regaining consciousness, he saw that the picture was covered with dust, the flowers had wilted, and even the ghee had boiled over. None the less, he wiped off the dust, adorned his head with the flowers, and drank what remained of the ghee. Thereupon, his body became free from all infirmity; and he became strong and sharp-witted, and acquired mastery of the supernormal cognitive powers.

At about that time, he went on to Oḍḍiyāna, where he met the master Līlāvajra, under whom he studied the Yoga tantras, and the *Five Inner Unsurpassed Tantrapiṭaka*. He became particularly adept at the *Magical Net*. On another occasion he went with Buddhaśānti to meet the sublime

Buddhaguhya

Avalokiteśvara on Mount Potalaka. There they met Ārya Tārā, who was teaching the doctrine to a host of nāgas at the foot of the mountain; Bhṛkuṭī, who was teaching the doctrine to a host of antigods and yakṣas on the slope; and sitting openly on the summit was the sublime Avalokiteśvara. All were as plainly manifest as they themselves were.

Buddhaguhya also attained accomplishments there, like the ability to walk without his feet touching the ground. It was Ārya Tārā, too, who advised him to go to Mount Kailash in the Himalayas, and to practise the means for attainment there.

Returning from Mount Potalaka, Buddhaguhya taught the doctrine in and around Vārāṇasī for many years. Then, once again, the sublime Mañjuśrī exhorted him to follow Tārā's former advice. He proceeded to Mount Kailash and practised the means for attainment, whereby he directly perceived the great Maṇḍala of the Indestructible Expanse (*Vajradhātumaṇḍala*) many times, and could speak to the sublime Mañjughoṣa, just as to another man. Non-human beings also acted as his servants.

The master composed a great many works, including: the *Analytical Commentary on the Tantra of the Secret Nucleus* (*gsang-ba snying-po-la 'grel-ba rnam-bshad-kyi 'grel*); the *Sequence of Indestructible Activity* (*Māyājālavajrakarmakrama*, P 4720); the *Significance of the Maṇḍala Doctrine* (*Dharmamaṇḍalasūtra*, T 3705); the *Holy Ornament* (*Tattvālokaparamālaṃkāra*, P 4735); the *Lesser Net* (*Sūkṣmajāla*, P 4734) and the *Greater Net* (*drva-chen*); the *Greater Sequence of the Path* (*Māyājālapathakrama*, P 4736) and the *Lesser Sequence of the Path* (*sgyu-'phrul lam-gyi rnam-bshad chung-ba*, DZ Vol.1); the *Stages of the Realisation of the Peaceful and Wrathful Deities* (*zhi-khro mngon-rtogs rim-pa*); the *Introduction to Yoga*, which is the means for the attainment of the Maṇḍala of the Indestructible Expanse according to the Yoga tantras (*Tantrārthāvatāra*, T 2501); the *Abridged Commentary on the Tantra of the Awakening of the Great Vairocana* (*Mahāvairocanatantrapiṇḍārtha*, T 2662); the *Expanded Commentary on the Later Stages of Meditation* (*Dhyānottarapaṭalaṭīkā*, T 2670), et cetera.

Buddhaguhya's great kindness to Tibet will be described later on.[482] At the end of his life, he vanished bodily.

VAJRAHĀSYA

[90.2-91.1] Again, King Ja and Kukkurāja expounded [the *Guhyasamāja*] to the "Zombie" Sukhasiddhi,[483] and to the *ṛṣi* Bhāṣita. The former taught the master Vajrahāsya, who composed the commentary on the *Guhyasamāja* entitled *Apprehending the Entire Intention* (*Śrīguhyasamājaṭīkā*, T 1909), as well as the *Means for the Attainment of Supreme Bliss* (*Mahāsukhasādhana*, T 1911), and other works. He was the master of these teachings and expounded them. It is maintained that in India there were twenty-four distinct teaching traditions of the *Guhyasamāja*, of which six were propagated in Tibet, the fourth of these being the *Guhyasamāja* tradition derived from Vajrahāsya's cycle of teachings.

Vajrahāsya bestowed the empowerment of *Cakrasaṃvara* on Vagīśvarakīrti, the "guardian of the western gate" at Nālandā, and expounded that tantra to him. He also conferred on him the instructions and further advice. By meditating on these esoteric instructions Vāgīśvarakīrti attained accomplishment; and in that very body he became a holder of the awareness of the Great Seal, the body of coalescence.

The master [Vajrahāsya] and the *ṛṣi* Bhāṣita both expounded the tantras to King Prabhāhasti of Sahor.

PRABHĀHASTI

[91.1-91.6] Prabhāhasti was born into a royal family in western India. He was ordained by master Śāntiprabha of Citavara, and by the great Vinaya master, Puṇyakīrti of Maru. He was given the name Śākya-

Prabhāhasti

prabha, and became learned in the entire Tripiṭaka. As the disciple of a great many holders of indestructible reality according to the way of mantra, for instance, master Vajrahāsya, he mastered all the tantras and obtained supreme accomplishment. His [esoteric] name according to the mantra tradition was Prabhāhasti. Śākyamitra, a disciple of this master, composed a commentary on the *Summation of the Real*, which is a Yoga tantra, entitled the *Ornament of Kosala* (*Kosalālaṃkāra*, T 2503). Both Prabhāhasti and Śākyamitra went to Kashmir where they vastly benefitted living beings. Master Buddhaguhya and the great master Padmasambhava studied under Prabhāhasti; but Padmasambhava also studied under King Ja himself.

PADMASAMBHAVA

[91.6-103.4] Concerning that great master [Padmasambhava]: There is a prophecy in the *Magical Net of Mañjuśrī* (vv.110cd-11ab):

> He is the glorious buddha, lotus-born,
> Possessing the store of all-knowing pristine cognition,
> A king displaying various magical feats,
> The great one endowed with the buddhas' gnostic mantras.

Actually, Padmasambhava is the emanation of the Buddha Amitābha, who embodies the indestructible speech of all the tathāgatas; but he seems to appear in different forms, because of the differences of fortune and acumen among those who are to be trained.

In the legend found in the transmitted precepts of Vajrakīla, and in some Indian versions, it is said that he was born as the son of either the king of Oḍḍiyāna, or of one of his ministers. Some say that he appeared in a lightning flash on the meteoric summit of Mount Malaya. But here, I will follow the well-known tale found in the revealed treasures, et cetera, which speak only of his miraculous birth.[484] According to them, the land of Oḍḍiyāna, which is to the west [of India], is surrounded by great oceans to the east, south, and north. In the southwest, towards the Land of Ogres, there is an island in a lake. There, in the bud of a multicoloured lotus, which had sprung up by the buddhas' blessing, a golden vajra marked with the syllable HRĪḤ emanated from the heart of Amitābha, the lord of the Sukhāvatī paradise. From it, there emanated forth an eight-year-old boy, who was adorned with the major and minor marks, and held a vajra and a lotus. The boy remained there teaching the profound doctrine to the gods and to the ḍākinīs of the island.

At that time the king of Oḍḍiyāna, Indrabhūti, had no son, so [in order to obtain one] he worshipped the Three Precious Jewels and exhausted his treasury by giving alms. He then ordered that the wish-fulfilling gem be brought from an island. His minister of righteousness, Kṛṣṇadhara,[485] [who had been sent to fetch the jewel] first saw the boy on his return journey. Then the king met him and brought him to the palace to become his adopted son. He received the names Padmākara (Lotus-origin) and Saroruhavajra (Vajra of the Lake-born Lotus), and was requested to sit upon a throne of precious stones, which appeared by the power of the wish-fulfilling gem. He satisfied the entire populace with a rain of food, clothing, and jewels. By his youthful play, he matured numberless disciples. He married the ḍākinī Prabhāvatī, and defended the kingdom of Oḍḍiyāna according to the doctrine. Therefore, he became renowned as King Śikhin (Crested King).

Then he realised that by governing the kingdom he could not be of great service to others. He asked his father for permission to leave, but was refused. Therefore, while performing a dramatic dance, he pretended that a trident slipped from his hand and thus he "liberated" the son of an evil minister.[486] As punishment for murdering the minister's son, he was banished to live in charnel grounds. He practised asceticism [in the charnel grounds of] Śītavana, Nandanavana, and Sosadvīpa, where he received empowerment and blessing from the ḍākinīs Mārajitā and Śāntarakṣitā. When he had brought the ḍākinīs of the charnel grounds under his sway he became known as Śāntarakṣita (Preserver of Peace).

Then he proceeded to the isle of Dhanakośa, where, by practising the way of secret mantra through the symbolic language of the ḍākinīs, he brought the ḍākinīs of the island under his sway. When he practised in the Paruṣakavana (Coarse Wood), Vajravarāhī appeared in order to bless him. He bound all the nāgas of the ocean, as well as the planets and stars of the sky under an oath of allegiance. Warriors and ḍākinīs of the three abodes conferred their accomplishments upon him, and he became renowned as Dorje Trakpotsel (Expression of the Ferocious Vajra).

After that he went to Vajrāsana, where he performed various miracles. When the people asked who he was, he replied,"I am a self-born buddha!" But, not believing this, they insulted him. Seeing that much power was required [in order to overcome their doubts], he went to the country of Sahor, where he received ordination from master Prabhāhasti, and received the name Śākyasiṃha (Lion of the Śākyas).

Having received the teaching of the Yogatantra eighteen times, the deities [of those tantras] appeared to him in that very place. Guhyajñānā, the ḍākinī of pristine cognition, appeared in the form of the nun Ānandā and, at his request for empowerment, she transformed him into the syllable HŪṂ, and then swallowed him. In her stomach he was given the complete outer, inner, and secret empowerments, and was then expelled through her vagina. In this way, the three obscurations were removed.[487]

Padmasambhava

He studied all the sūtras, tantras, and sciences under the many scholars and accomplished masters of India, of whom the foremost were: the eight great awareness-holders, from whom he received the Eight Classes of Means for Attainment; Buddhaguhya, from whom he received the *Magical Net*; and Śrī Siṃha, from whom he received the Great Perfection. Training himself thus, he fully understood all doctrines after studying them only once. He could see the deities even without propitiating them. In this way, he became renowned as Loden Chokse (Intelligent Boon-seeker), and he demonstrated the ultimate attainment of a holder of the awareness of spiritual maturation.

Then he gained influence over Mandāravā, the daughter of King Ārṣadhara of Sahor, who possessed the marks of a ḍākinī. He took her to the Māratika Cave,[488] to serve as the consort for his practice; and for three months they practised the means for the attainment of longevity. Lord Amitāyus actually came there and empowered them,[489] and he consecrated them to be no different than himself. He granted them one billion rites of longevity, whereby Padmasambhava attained the accomplishment of an awareness-holder endowed with power over the duration of his own life.

Having thus attained the body of indestructible reality that is beyond birth and death, Padmasambhava went to subdue the kingdom of Sahor. When the king and his ministers tried to immolate him, he performed the miracle of [transforming the pyre into] a lake of sesame oil, in the midst of which he remained seated on a lotus. Thus he secured them in faith and introduced them all to the doctrine, so that they reached the level of no-return.[490]

Again, in order to convert the kingdom of Oḍḍiyāna, he went there begging for alms, but he was recognised by the inhabitants. The evil minister [whose son Padmasambhava had slain] and his associates tried to burn the master in a fire of sandalwood, but, displaying his miraculous powers, both he and his consort remained seated on a lotus surrounded by a lake, the master wearing a garland of skulls to indicate that he released sentient beings from saṃsāra. Therefore, he became renowned as Pema Thötrengstel (Lotus whose Expression is a Garland of Skulls).

He acted as the king's venerated guru for thirteen years, securing the whole kingdom in the doctrine. By bestowing the [empowerments which cause] maturation and the [guidance which causes] liberation, for [the teaching called] the *Ocean of Doctrine, the Gathering of Transmitted Precepts* (*bka'-'dus chos-kyi rgya-mtsho*) he caused the king, queen, and all other fortunate beings to become holders of supreme awareness. Thus, he became known as Padmarāja (Lotus King).

According to a prophecy found in the *Sūtra of Magical Transformation of the Scope of Activity* (*Gocaropāyaviṣayavikurvāṇanirdeśasūtra*, T 146) he emanated as the monk Indrasena in order to convert King Aśoka. Having developed immutable faith, the king built ten million stūpas containing the relics of the Tathāgata throughout Jambudvīpa in a single night.[491]

Thereafter, Padmasambhava skilfully vanquished some powerful kings who were religious extremists, hostile to the teaching, by rites of exorcism. When one such king caused the master to eat poison he remained unharmed, and when he was thrown into the River Ganges the waters reversed their flow. He danced in the sky and became known as Khyeucung Khadingtsel (Youth who Flies like Garuḍa).

Moreover, he taught through countless other forms and manifestations: as Master Saroruha who introduced the *Hevajra Tantra*, the brahman Sarahapāda, and as Ḍombi Heruka, Virūpa, and the great Kṛṣṇacārin. He travelled to the great charnel grounds, such as Kuladzokpa, where he taught the doctrines of the secret mantra to the ḍākinīs. When he grasped the vital heart-mantras of all arrogant spirits, Buddhist and non-Buddhist, and charged them to protect the teaching, he became known as Sūryaraśmi (Sunbeam).

Once, when five hundred extremist teachers began to dispute the teaching at Vajrāsana, the master defeated them in a contest of debate and occult power. When they cursed him, he warded off their spells by using the wrathful mantra which had been given to him by the ḍākinī Mārajitā. He brought down a mighty thunderbolt which "liberated" those teachers and set fire to their city. When he initiated the remainder of them into the Buddha's teaching and raised aloft the victory banner of the doctrine, he became renowned as Siṃhanāda (Lion's Roar). By that time, he had traversed the supreme path which destroys the three corruptions and he lived as an awareness-holder, controlling the duration of his own life.

Then, in the Yangleshö Cave,[492] near the border of India and Nepal, he took the Nepali girl Śākyadevī, the daughter of Puṇyadhara, the king of Nepal, to serve him in his practice. While he was performing the means for the attainment of the glorious Yangdak Heruka [Śrīheruka], in order to obtain supreme accomplishment, three very powerful demons obstructed him. For three years it did not rain. Plague and famine were rampant. So he sent [messengers] to India to fetch from his gurus the doctrines which remove obstacles. They dispatched two porters carrying the transmitted text of the *Vajrakīla Tantra*, which caused the obstacles to subside by themselves. Rain fell and the plague and famine finally ceased. The master and his consort both obtained the supreme accomplishment and became holders of the awareness of the Great Seal.

Yangdak Heruka confers great accomplishments, but, like a merchant who has many obstacles, he must be escorted. The means for the attainment of Vajrakīla is his escort. Seeing this, Padmasambhava composed many practical means for attainment which combine Yangdak and Vajrakīla. The master bound all mundane spirits, both male and female, including the sixteen protectors of the *Vajrakīla Tantra* (NGB Vol. 19, 27-9, T 439), under an oath of allegiance and appointed them to protect the doctrine.

Moreover, at one time or another, he taught the doctrine in accord with the needs of disciples in Hurmudzu, Sikodhara, Dhanakośa, Rukma, and other districts of Oḍḍiyāna; in Tīrahuti and other Tharu kingdoms; and in Kāmarūpa, and elsewhere. By the common accomplishments, too, he helped many sentient beings. He made water flow from dry riverbeds. He diverted a wide river underground. When great harm came to the Buddhist teaching because images of extremist deities spontaneously appeared in the south, east, and centre of India, he annihilated all three by the power of Vajrakīla. When a Turkish king led his army by boat over the River Nīla to invade Kañcī, where the Buddhist community was widespread, the master raised his index finger in a menacing gesture and five hundred vessels sank in the water. Subsequently, the Turkish danger came to an end.

Though it is not clear exactly when he visited the land of Draviḍa (*'gro-lding-ba'i yul*), he did gradually convert the human and non-human beings of that country, the ḍākinīs and so on, and had a temple constructed there. Teaching, study and meditation on the four classes of tantra, and particularly on the tantras of *Hevajra*, *Hidden Point of the Moon*, *Yangdak*, *Hayagrīva* (T 839), *Vajrakīla*, and *Mātaraḥ* (NGB Vols.30-1)[493] according to the tradition of this master remained widespread until a later period. In the legends of these [tantras] it is said that he travelled thence to the Land of Ogres in the south-west.

The aforementioned accounts are well known from sources of Indian origin. While it is generally said that Padmasambhava remained in India for three thousand and six hundred years, acting on behalf of the teaching and living creatures, scholars believe either that the years referred to are half-years, or that the statement is hyperbole.

Moreover, to convert Turkestan and China, Padmasambhava emanated as a king with supernormal cognitive powers, and as a powerful yogin. And emanating as the self-born child Tavihṛca in Zhang-Zhung, he caused many fortunate beings to attain the body of light, by means of the instructions of the aural lineage of the Great Perfection.[494]

Thus, it is impossible to measure the extent of his activity, which, through varied actions befitting those requiring training, secured all beings, inhabiting diverse countries and speaking diverse languages, on the path to liberation. And all this merely refers to those biographies which describe specific manifestations and names. In fact, if we disregard the difference between his direct and indirect action, [then it may be said that] there is no place that is not to be trained by this emanation. Thus, no one at all can express a limit to the liberating activity of those who abide in the state of coalescence.

So it is that great accomplished masters may make themselves disappear from the view of ordinary disciples and then, after a long time has passed, they may make themselves reappear, and then remain present for a long time. They may be invisible in some places and visible in others simultaneously. In one place they may demonstrate transference [of consciousness at death], and in another, the act of taking birth. In these and other ways their manifestations are infinite. Thus, once upon a time, Virūpa thrice appeared bodily after disappearing; Jālandharipā similarly reappeared five times; and the great Kṛṣṇacārin, after passing away in Devīkoṭa and being cremated by his disciples, reappeared elsewhere in his former body and acted to benefit the world. At the same time, it is said that he took new births in yet other lands and demonstrated in them the attainment of supreme accomplishment. So, just as a commoner's status cannot be applied to a king, it is impossible to determine exactly the chronology and dwelling places of these accomplished masters according to the conventions of ordinary people. That is because they are empowered with miraculous abilities, which accord perfectly with the faculties of will and attitude among sentient beings. It says in the *Sublime Sūtra which Comprises the Entire Doctrine*:

> Sentient beings who will an aeon of dissolution to become an aeon of evolution can indeed transform an aeon of dissolution into an aeon of evolution; and they experience an aeon of evolution. Sentient beings who will an aeon of evolution to become an aeon of dissolution can indeed transform an aeon of evolution into an aeon of dissolution; and they experience an aeon of dissolution. But really the dissolution and the evolution do not change into one another; for it is the will which changes in this way. Similarly, sentient beings who will one aeon to become just one morning may experience one aeon in one morning. And sentient beings who will one morning to become one aeon may experience just that. This is called the miraculous ability born of the bodhisattva's will.

How master Padmasambhava came to Tibet will be described below.[495]

5 *The Lineage of Mahāyoga, the Class of Means for Attainment*

[103.4] Concerning the latter class of the Mahāyoga, that of means for attainment, there are two traditions, that of the transmitted precepts and that of the revealed treasures.

HŪṂKARA AND THE TRANSMITTED PRECEPT OF YANGDAK (ŚRĪHERUKA)

[103.4-106.1] As for the first: The transmitted precepts of Yangdak the Mind, including the *Heruka Galpo* and so on, which belong to the family of Akṣobhya, that of buddha-mind, fell to master Hūṃkara. This master was born into a brahman family in Nepal. He became very learned in the Veda and in the non-Buddhist textual traditions; and he also achieved spiritual power. Later, he developed supreme faith in the Buddha's teaching and was ordained at Nālandā in Central India by the master Buddhajñānapāda and the scholar Rāhulabhadra. He trained and purified himself by studying everything from the teachings of Transcendental Perfection to those of the outer and inner classes of the secret mantra.[496] He received empowerment and obtained all the instructions and further advice. In particular, when he was empowered into the maṇḍala of the glorious Yangdak Heruka, his flower fell upon the wrathful deity Hūṃkara.[497] After meditating [on that deity] for a long time he developed an excellent contemplation of the two stages. Realising that he would become accomplished if he were to practise the means for attainment for six months, he required an outcaste girl with the complexion of a blue lotus, a girl possessing all the signs of a *mudrā* belonging to the vajra family to be his action seal (*karmamudrā*).[498] He sought and eventually found such a girl in another district. He proposed to her parents, but they said, "You're a brahman master! Are you crazy? As we're an outcaste family, we'll surely all be punished!"

He replied, "I need her to serve my practice. So we will not be punished for violating the vulgar caste system."

"In that case, you must give us the girl's weight in gold and silver."

Immediately, the master extracted a treasure from the ground and gave it to them. The master and his *mudrā* then performed the ritual service, further ritual service, and the rite of attainment in a cave for six months.[499] At dawn on the eighth day of the light-half of the month, the mighty sound of HŪṂ thundered in the sky; and he actually saw the entire maṇḍala, with Vajra Heruka and the other deities. Then he attained the supreme accomplishment of the Great Seal by the path of

Hūṃkara

the rite of great attainment. This accords with the first [time period mentioned in] the *Sequence of the Path of the Magical Net*, which gives the following explanation:

> The genuine accomplishment of empowered awareness
> Will be achieved in six or twelve months,
> Or in fourteen, or in sixteen.

Master Hūṃkara benefitted many beings by [his teachings on] the three aspects of creation and perfection [together with their coalescence], and by other mantras and tantras as well. He also composed many treatises on the two stages, such as: the *Yangdak Rulu Golden Rosary* (*yang-dag ru-lu gser-phreng*), the esoteric instructions of the *Buddhasamāyoga* entitled *Elucidation of the Significance of the Four Limbs* (*Caturaṅgārthālokanāma*, T 1676), and the *Definitive Verification of the Means for the Attainment of the Great Heruka* (*Saṃsiddhimahāśrīherukasādhananāma*, T 1678).

In the end, Hūṃkara flew off bodily, like the king of garuḍa,[500] to the Buddha-field of Akṣobhya.

The masters Avadhūti and Buddhaśrīśānti of Oḍḍiyāna received the transmitted precepts of the stage of creation from Hūṃkara. In his turn, the great Sauripāda of Vajrāsana received teachings from them. The great master Abhayākaragupta[501] and his host of disciples arose in Sauripāda's following.

MAÑJUŚRĪMITRA AND THE TRANSMITTED PRECEPT OF YAMĀNTAKA

[106.1-108.4] The transmitted precepts of Yamāntaka, including the *Secret Tantra of Wrathful Mañjuśrī* (*Mañjuśrīkarmacatuścakraguhyatantra*, T 838), and so forth, which belong to the family of Vairocana, that of buddha-body, fell to the master Mañjuśrīmitra. This master was born in the village of Dvikrama in western India,[502] to Sādhuśāstrī and his wife Pradīpālokā. He became learned in the Veda and their branches, but received the empowerments of the outer and inner mantras, as well as all of the common and special instructions from the great master [Garap Dorje], the "Ashen Zombie", among others. It is said that he also studied the *Black Yamāri*, the *Six-faced One* (*Ṣaḍānana*, T 2015), and the *Vajrabhairava* (T 468) under master Lalitavajra. In any case, when he had acquired all the common accomplishments and was close to attaining the level of coalescence he went forth to give expression to enlightened conduct.

Once, while crossing a bridge, Mañjuśrīmitra encountered a king who was a very great patron of the extremists. The king was riding an elephant. Neither of them would make way for the other. The master just raised his index finger menacingly and the king and his elephant were split asunder, a half falling on either side of the bridge. When the king's retainers apologised and begged forgiveness, he revived the king and secured him in the Buddhist teaching. As the master himself said:

> Neither do I revere mundane lords,
> Nor do I step aside, though an elephant confronts me.
> I chant aloud the king of secret mantra,
> And my feet pass unhindered through rocky mountains.

At some point, Mañjuśrīmitra attained the exalted level of coalescence, and so became no different from the sublime Mañjughoṣa.

Yamāntaka

Mañjuśrī-Yamāntaka actually appeared, empowered him, and taught him all the tantras and their esoteric instructions. Many active emanations[503] of Yamāntaka circumambulated him and offered up their vital heart-mantras. He extracted from Mount Malaya a golden book which contained all the four rites written in beryl; and he understood it at just a glance. Using the mantras for subduing extremists he utterly demolished an extremist kingdom through wild activity. He concealed the book itself to the north of Vajrāsana, by making it invisible.

Because he was also known as the brahman Sārasiddhi, it is clear that Mañjuśrīmitra was the same venerable brahman Sāra who was the father of the great master Jetāri.[504] The latter also attained accomplishment through the gnostic mantra (*vidyā*) of Mañjuśrī. It is related that King Dharmapāla revered Jetāri as his guru. The king's own son received the empowerment of the sublime Mañjuśrī, through which he attained accomplishment.

The transmitted precepts which explain many of the tantras originate from Mañjuśrīmitra's disciples, the brahmans Jñānavajra and Bodhivajra, about whom there is a prophecy in the *Subsequent Tantra of Kālacakra* (*Śrīkālacakratantrottaratantrahṛdaya*, T 363). In particular,

Amoghavajra the elder received the complete cycle of Yamāntaka from this master, and the younger Amoghavajra received it from him and so on.[505] This is the origin of the *Yamāntaka* cycle, which is renowned in Tibet as the Kyo tradition.

NĀGĀRJUNA AND THE TRANSMITTED PRECEPT OF HAYAGRĪVA

[108.4-109.4] The transmitted precepts of the Lotus Speech tantras, including the *Play of the Supreme Horse* (*Aśvottamavīṇāsamata-mahātantra*, T 839), which belong to the family of Amitābha, that of buddha-speech, fell to the great master sublime Nāgārjuna.[506] Some say that he was the *baliṃācārya* [master of offerings] at Vikramaśīla, and hence not the same as the sublime Nāgārjuna. But the master of offerings was named Nāgārjunagarbha and is never called "sublime". Therefore, when the author of the treatises composed by the sublime master is styled *sublime* Nāgārjunagarbha, he should not be confused with the master of offerings.

Hayagrīva

According to the well-known biographies of Nāgārjuna, he introduced the *Eight Mahākāla Tantras (ma-hā-kā-la'i rgyud brgyad)*, the *Tantra of the Goddess Kālī* (*Śrīdevīkālīpraśaṃsārājatantra*, T 671), the *Realisation of Kurukullā* (*Muktakenatārodbhavakurukullesādhana*, T 3562), and a large number of other tantras. He obtained the oral instructions of the ḍākinīs of pristine cognition, and he is said to have introduced about sixty different means for attainment. He achieved many extraordinary feats in each of the eight common accomplishments. Finally, having remained at Śrīparvata[507] for two hundred years with a retinue of yakṣiṇī, all the while living in accord with the way of mantras, he attained the body of indestructible reality.

VIMALAMITRA AND THE TRANSMITTED PRECEPT OF VAJRĀMṚTA

[109.4-110.3] The transmitted precepts of Vajrāmṛta, including the *Eight Volumes of Nectar* (*Sarvapañcāmṛtasārasiddhimahodgatahṛdayaparivartāṣṭaka*, T 841), which belong to the family of Ratnasambhava, that of enlightened attributes, fell to the master Vimalamitra. This master

Vajrāmṛta

was born in a place called Hastivana in western India. He mastered all the sciences and their branches; and he also studied sūtras of the lesser and greater vehicles under masters of the piṭaka, and became learned in them. He studied all the tantras under many great holders of indestructible reality, such as Buddhaguhya, and by meditating upon them he realised the supreme accomplishment of the Great Seal. Vimalamitra was particularly learned in the *Magical Net*; and he composed many treatises, for instance: the commentary on the *Secret Nucleus* entitled *Illuminating Lamp of the Fundamental Text*; the *Removal of Darkness: A Commentary on the Superior Magical Net* (*sgyu-'phrul bla-ma'i 'grel-ba mun-sel*); the *Eye-opening Commentary on the Supplementary Magical Net* (*Vajrasattvamāyājālatantraśrīguhyagarbhanāmacakṣuṣṭīkā*, P 4756); the *Abridged Commentary on the Eighty Chapter Magical Net* (*brgyad-bcu-pa'i bsdus-'grel*); *Opening the Eye of Discriminative Awareness* (*Mahāyogaprajñāpraveśacakṣurupadeśanāma*, P 4725); the *Three Stages*; *Meditative Absorption in the Mudrā*; a *Ritual for Burnt Offerings* (*Māyājālahomasaṃkṣiptakrama*, P 4746); a *Cremation Ritual* (*Māyājālalaghudṛṣṭāntasvāśrayakrama*, P 4747); *Ritual Geometry* (*thig-rim*); the *Short Commentary [on the Secret Nucleus]*; et cetera.

PRABHĀHASTI, PADMASAMBHAVA AND THE TRANSMITTED PRECEPT OF VAJRAKĪLA

[110.3-111.2] The transmitted precepts of the *Vajrakīla Tantras*, which belong to the family of Amoghasiddhi, that of enlightened activity, fell to master Prabhāhasti. Also, when the great master Padmasambhava actually attained the realisation of a holder of the supreme awareness of the Great Seal, having relied on the maṇḍala of the glorious Yangdak Heruka while residing at Yangleshö, an irresistible impulse entered the minds of an obstinate nāga, a horse-headed yakṣiṇī, and the spirit of an atmospheric lightning-cloud. To subdue their evil design Padmasambhava practised the means for attainment based on the *Hundred Thousand Verse Tantra of Supreme Awareness* (*Vidyottama-la 'bum-sde*, NGB Vols.19, 27-9). Vajrakumāra[508] actually appeared and eliminated all traces of obstruction. Then the guru bound the twelve Mātaraḥ and four female earth spirits under an oath of allegiance. Later, he is known to have studied the *Vajrakīla Tantra* eighteen times under master Prabhāhasti, too; and thus he mastered all the transmitted precepts of Vajrakīla, who embodies enlightened activity.

The aforementioned transmitted precepts were all fully comprehended by those masters respectively, and they, in turn, explained them extensively to other fortunate disciples.

Vajrakīla

THE REVEALED TREASURES

[111.2-112.4] Second, the treasures: The bodhisattva Vajradharma did not perceive there to be anyone in the human world to whom the books containing the general and special means for attainment could be revealed for the time being, so he entrusted them to the ḍākinī Mahākarmendrāṇī. She inserted the five general tantras and the ten special tantras of the eight transmitted precepts concerning means for attainment into a casket made of eight kinds of precious gems. Having inserted the special tantras into separate caskets, she then concealed them all invisibly in the garden of the Śaṅkarakūṭa Caitya (*mchod-rten bde-byed brtsegs-pa*) in the Śītavana charnel ground.[509]

Later the eight great accomplished masters learned of this through their supernormal powers. They assembled there and devoted themselves to the formation of an enlightened intuition, whereby they liberated a host of mundane ḍākinīs and arrogant spirits by means of vows of truth and appropriate substances. The ḍākinī Mahākarmendrāṇī actually arrived, owing to the power of their contemplation, of which the intention was service to others. Bringing forth the caskets, she entrusted the gold casket[510] containing the tantra of *Mahottara* (NGB Vol.32, no.380) to Vimalamitra; the silver casket containing that of *Śriheruka* (NGB Vol.32, no.381) to Hūṃkara; the iron casket containing that of *Yamāntaka* (NGB Vol.32, no.382) to Mañjuśrīmitra; the copper casket containing that of *Hayagrīva* (NGB Vol.32, no.383) to Nāgārjuna; the turquoise casket containing that of *Vajrakīla* (NGB Vol.32, no.384) to Padmasambhava; the *bse*-stone casket containing that of *Mātaraḥ* (NGB Vol.32, no.385) to Dhanasaṃskṛta; the agate casket containing that of *Mundane Praise* (*Lokastotrapūja*, T 844) to Rambuguhya; and the *zi*-stone[511] casket containing that of *Malign Mantra* (*Vajramantrabhīru*, T 843) to Śāntigarbha. Each of them became adept in his own subject and attained the accomplishments of the way of mantras.

From the casket made of eight kinds of precious gems there emerged the transmitted precepts comprising the tantra and esoteric instructions of the *Gathering of the Sugatas* (*bde-gshegs 'dus-pa*, NGB Vols.31-2), which subsumes all the aforementioned means for attainment at once; and this fell to master Padmasambhava.

Mahākarmendrāṇī

Mahottara Heruka

6 *The Lineage of Anuyoga, the Perfection Stage*

KAMBALAPĀDA OR THE YOUNGER INDRABHŪTI

[112.4-116.6] Although King Ja, or Vyākaraṇavajra, had been empowered by the Lord of Secrets and had grasped the meaning of the entire teaching, even so, to prevent meddlesome onlookers from thinking he had entered the way of secret mantra at his pleasure, he relied on the human awareness-holder and layman, Vimalakīrti the Licchavi, from whom he received all the empowerments and verbal teachings [NGB Vols. 11-13]. The king also composed treatises like the *Commentary on the General Sūtra which Gathers All Intentions*. He gave empowerment in an emanational maṇḍala to master Uparāja, who had been his fellow student under the Licchavi, and to his own three sons – Śakraputra, Nāgaputra, and Guhyaputra; and he taught them the instructions. At the Śrī Dhānyakaṭaka Caitya, which is also called Śrī Dakṣiṇa,[512] he empowered Uparāja and entrusted the tantras to him. In the city of Kṣemākara (*skyid-pa'i 'byung-gnas*) he empowered his own three sons.

Among King Ja's sons, Śakraputra is renowned as Indrabhūti the younger. It is said that when he attained accomplishment he became renowned as the master Kambalapāda. This is also mentioned in the *Commentary on the Verification of Co-Emergence* (*Sahajasiddhipaddhati*, T 2261). In any case, because Indrabhūti introduced certain tantrapiṭaka like the *Cakrasaṃvara*, the brahman Ratnavajra and others are among the adherents of his lineage. Some later gurus of India say that the master Kambalapāda was a prince, and a native of Oḍḍiyāna. So, accordingly, he must be identified with Indrabhūti the younger.

At first, this master received empowerments from a great mantra master, and realised pristine cognition by meditating on the instructions. Then, at some other time, he went to Dhūmasthira, the city of the ḍākinīs in Oḍḍiyāna. There, he accepted a flower garland which some non-Buddhist ḍākinīs handed to him. The Buddhist ḍākinīs said, "Son, it was a mistake to take those flowers. Now you must follow the non-Buddhists."

Then, at midnight, when the master was sitting absorbed in contemplation, the extremist ḍākinīs caused stones to rain down upon him. But there was no damage on his side of the protective circle [created through the visualisations] of the stage of creation. It occurred to him that, as the stage of creation had such advantages, he should demonstrate the power of the stage of perfection as well. By abiding in a formless contemplation he caused all the stones to freeze in the sky. Even today, in the land of Oḍḍiyāna, in the sky above the master's meditation cave, there is a huge unsupported boulder; and many frozen stones are clearly visible on the rock-face, which is as smooth as a mirror.

Kambalapāda

Once upon a time, the master went to sleep right at the door of the royal palace. All those who entered the palace without prostrating themselves before him became paralysed in the legs; so everyone had to prostrate before entering. The duration of the master's sleep was twelve years, but to him it was only one session of absorption in inner radiance.

On another occasion five hundred sorceress spirits from the country of Oḍḍiyāna searched for the master with the intention of creating obstacles for him, but in the place of the master they found only a blanket. "Aha!" they said, "just look at the illusion conjured up by this monk! He has transformed his body into a blanket. Let's just tear it into shreds and eat them!" They divided the blanket into five hundred fragments and ate them.

Then, the master bodily appeared and cursed the five hundred sorceresses, who were transformed into five hundred sheep-headed demonesses. They went to the king and said, "The monk who is the lord of the charnel ground has done this to us. Please release us, your majesty!"

The king then petitioned the master, who stood up quite naked and said, "Your majesty's witches have eaten the blanket which is the only possession of this monk. Pray, summon those witches."

When they had all been summoned he pointed his index finger at each of them menacingly, and transformed them into creatures with various kinds of heads. Each one vomited up a fragment of the blanket. The fragments were sown together, but some parts were missing, "Three are missing", he said, "summon them!" Those three, who lived in the harem, were duly summoned, and he caused them to vomit, just as he had done to the others. The blanket was then completely restored, and the master wrapped it about his body. This is why he became renowned as the venerable Kambalapāda, the "Blanket Master".

There are a great many other stories about Kambalapāda. One describes how both he and King Indrabhūti revealed the signs of their accomplishment to the people. Another describes how, on a certain occasion, when master Lalitavajra had attained the common accomplishments, the two went to the country of Oḍḍiyāna together and waged a miraculous competition on Mount Muruṇḍaka.

It is said that at a somewhat later time everyone in the country of Oḍḍiyāna became an awareness-holder by following the instructions of both the king [Indrabhūti] and the master [Kambalapāda]; whereupon, even the vast land of Oḍḍiyāna was almost depopulated. It seems to me that this incident may be the same as that which occurred when Indrabhūti the younger, son of the aforementioned King Ja, became an awareness-holder along with the mass of his retinue.

THE SUCCESSORS OF THE YOUNGER INDRABHŪTI

[116.6-120.1] In the same way, the younger Indrabhūti empowered Siṃhaputra and the later Kukkurāja on the seashore; and he explained the [Anuyoga] tantras to them. The later Kukkurāja empowered the great master Sukha the "Zombie" and in turn explained the tantras to him. Sukha the "Zombie" is one of the names of the emanation Garap Dorje. Before him, all the masters in the lineage, along with all their respective followers, who numbered between ten and fifty thousand, obtained the body of coalescence and vanished, having practised the feast offerings, which involve elaborate activity.[513]

Śākyamitra

The master [Sukha the "Zombie"] empowered the master Vajrahāsya in Uttarasāra Forest, and explained the tantras to him. He, too, obtained supreme accomplishment by the path of supreme bliss. He composed a treatise entitled the *Sun of Yogic Awareness* (*rnal-'byor rig-pa'i nyi-ma*), which systematically explains the profound path of the *Sūtra which Gathers All Intentions*. On the bank of the Indus River, in the country of Gajane, he empowered the master Prabhāhasti and explained the tantras to him.

As has been previously mentioned, Prabhāhasti's ordination name was Śākyaprabha. He instructed the younger Śākyaprabha, who in turn taught Śākyamitra and Śākyasiṃha. Śākyamitra was very learned in the Yoga tantras. In the land of Kosala he wrote a commentary on the *Summation of the Real*, entitled the *Ornament of Kosala*. It is said that Śākyamitra received teaching from some eleven gurus, and that towards the end of his life he went to Kashmir, where he greatly served living creatures.

Śākyasiṃha is an epithet of the great master Padmasambhava. He explained the tantras to master Dhanarakṣita on the roof of the nine-storey Naivedyaśālā Pagoda [at Vajrāsana]. This Dhanarakṣita composed a treatise explaining the enumerations found in the *Sūtra which*

Gathers All Intentions. In the Vajra Cavern of Oḍḍiyāna he gave instruction to the master Hūṃkara, who wrote many treatises on the *Sūtra which Gathers All Intentions* such as the *Commentary on the Root Tantra entitled Seven Seals* (*rgya-bdun-ma*), and the *Lamp on the Levels of Yoga* (*rnal-'byor sa'i sgron-ma*). In the Asura Cave on the frontier of India and Persia (*Ta-sig*), he performed the means for attainment with the assistance of his consort Gagasiddhi; and he attained the body of an awareness-holder.

Though one can make one's body invisible by mundane methods, such as alchemy, seminal retention, and the exercises which circulate the lamp-like vital energy (*sgron-ma rlung-gi 'khor-lo*),[514] the aforementioned masters transformed their physical bodies, the products of their former deeds, into radiant light by relying on a mode of conduct which adhered to the non-discursive pristine cognition of the path of insight. We must recognise there to be a great difference between these methods.[515]

Dhanarakṣita [passed the teaching to Sthiramati],[516] and he gave empowerment to Sukhodyotaka in the city of Śrī Dakṣiṇa and entrusted the tantras to him. The latter also studied under master Hūṃkara and, after achieving success in the practice of his gnostic mantra, attained the body of an awareness-holder. He composed the *Eighteen Notes on the Sūtra* (*mdo'i yig-sna bco-brgyad*), the *Yogic Sequence which is a Lamp on the Greater Vehicle* (*rnal-'byor-gyi rim-pa theg-chen sgron-ma*), and so forth. He taught [the Anuyoga] to his four most fortunate spiritual sons, one of whom was Dharmabodhi of Magadha, a master of the *Sūtra [which Gathers All Intentions]*.

Dharmabodhi composed the *Compendium of the Sūtra's Meaning* (*Guhyārthasūtrapiṇḍārtha*, P 4751), the *Lamp of Discriminative Awareness* (*shes-rab sgron-ma*) and the *Sūtra Excerpts* (*bkol-mdo*). At glorious Nālandā, he empowered the preceptor Dhamarājapāla, and explained the tantras to him. He also gave empowerments and explanations on the tantras to Vasudhara, a Nepalese king, and to Tsuklak Pelge, in the city of Rājagṛha. It is reported that those last three mentioned also studied under the master Dhanarakṣita.

All of the lineage-holders just mentioned held the entire lineage [of Anuyoga], including the transmitted empowerments, exegesis, and esoteric instructions. These three masters, in turn, empowered the master Chetsenkye of Bru-sha [Gilgit] and explained the tantras to him in Central India.[517] Meditating on them he attained accomplishment and afterwards invited master Dhanarakṣita to Bru-sha where they began to translate the *Sūtra which Gathers All Intentions* and other texts. But because the people had little devotion Dhanarakṣita abandoned the translation and went to Nepal, where he instructed Vasudhara and Dharmabodhi. Later, in Bru-sha, the master Chetsenkye translated those texts into the Bru-sha language [Burushaski], under the supervision of Dharmabodhi and Dhanarakṣita.

7 *The Lineage of Atiyoga, the Great Perfection*

GARAP DORJE AND MAÑJUŚRĪMITRA

[120.2-127.2] When the Transcendent Lord of Secrets, Vajrapāṇi, was teaching the doctrine of the secret mantra to a host of ḍākas, ḍākinīs, accomplished masters and awareness-holders in the Blazing Fire Mountain charnel ground, to the north of Mount Sumeru, the island of Dhanakośa, in Oḍḍiyāna in West India, was inhabited solely by creatures called *koṣa*, who had bodies like those of men, the faces of bears, and claws all of iron. The island was encircled by many sublime types of tree, including sandalwood. This is why it was called Dhanakośa (Treasury of Wealth), or so it is said. In that country there was a great temple called Śaṅkarakūṭa, which was surrounded by six thousand and eight hundred small temples. It was a place perfectly endowed with splendour and wealth.

There, there was a king, Uparāja, and his queen, Ālokabhāsvatī. They had a daughter called Sudharmā. She was ordained as a novice and, shortly thereafter, as a nun. About one *yojana*[518] from Dhanakośa, on an island covered with golden sand, in a tiny thatched cottage, she practised yoga and meditation with her servant Sukhasāravatī. One night the nun had a dream in which an immaculate white man thrice placed a crystal vase sealed with the syllables OṂ ĀḤ HŪṂ SVĀHĀ upon the crown of her head.[519] The light radiating from the vase was such that she could clearly see the three world realms. Not long afterwards, the nun gave birth to a child, who was none other than the son of the Conqueror, Adhicitta (*sems-lhag-can*), the divine emanation of Vajrasattva who had propagated the Great Perfection in heaven. But the nun was ashamed, and saw [his birth] as a great impropriety:

To what race does this fatherless child belong?
Is he other than some mundane demon?
Is he a devil? Brahmā? or yet something else?

Is he a spirit – a Gyelpo, a Tsen or a Mu?[520]
In the three realms, who would desire him?
Though some gods and antigods may take diverse forms,
Still I see no precedent for this.
For whom does this unrighteous kingdom exist?
Alas! My conduct is pure and I wish to surpass the world,
But I will be blamed by perverse beings. What sin!

Garap Dorje

So she cried in great lamentation. But her servant said, "He is the son of the buddhas. It is improper to despair."

Without paying any attention to her, the nun cast the child into an ash pit, and at once sounds, lights, and other phenomena arose. Then, after three days had passed, she saw that the child was unharmed; so she knew him to be an emanation. When, with great respect, she brought him forth from the pit, celestial deities assembled and exclaimed:

O Master! O Teacher! Transcendent Lord!
O lord of the world, revealing true nature!
Protect us, Celestial Vajra!
We pray thus this day.

Then ḍākas, ḍākinis, gods, nāgas, yakṣas and other mundane protectors also honoured him with the many provisions of worship.

When seven years had passed the boy said to his mother, "Mother, I would like to converse with scholars on the doctrine. Please give me your consent."

To which she replied, "Dear child, you are still quite young. As the scholars are wise and learned men, it will be hard for you to succeed."

But, on his persistent request, she told him to discuss the doctrine with five hundred scholars, who were the priests of the aforementioned king Uparāja. The boy then went to Dhanakośa and sought an audience with the king, to whom he repeated his request. But the king thought, "The lad is but a child, so it will be too difficult for him to discuss the doctrine with scholars. And yet, there are many marks of a great individual upon his body. Perhaps he is an emanation."

The king consulted his priests, among whom there was no consensus. But one, who was very learned, said, "There is one mark that is most auspicious. Send the boy in and we shall find out if he is, in fact, an emanation."

When summoned into their presence the child prostrated before the

Mañjuśrīmitra

scholars. After lengthy discussions and critical dialogues he overwhelmed their brilliance, whereupon they bowed their heads at his feet. The scholars honoured him with great respect and gave him the name Prajñābhava (Source of Discriminative Awareness). The king, too, was astonished and delighted, owing to which he conferred on the child the title "Great Master" and the name Garap Dorje (Vajra of Highest Delight). Previously, his mother, who had been amazed to find him unharmed after being cast into the pit of ashes, called him Sukha the "Zombie", or the "Ashen Zombie".

Then, in the northern direction, on the precipice called Sūryaprakāśa, which was most fearsome, and where tormented spirits could actually be seen roaming about, Garap Dorje lived for thirty-two years in a thatched cottage, absorbed in contemplation all the while. At that time, the earth shook seven times and a voice came from the sky, heralding the decline of extremist teachings. Hearing it, an extremist king sent an assassin to murder the master; but when they saw Garap Dorje fly off through the sky, the king and his retainers acquired supreme faith and were initiated into the Buddhist teaching.

Now, Garap Dorje's memory contained all the scriptures of the outer and inner vehicles, and, in particular, the six million four hundred thousand verses of the natural Great Perfection [NGB Vols. 1-10]. So when Vajrasattva actually appeared to him and showed him how to realize the pristine cognition of [the path of] no-more-learning, having conferred on him the vase empowerment of awareness, he also ordered him to write down the verbal tantras. Then, on the summit of Mount Malaya, which abounds in precious gems, the master, together with the Vajradhātu ḍākinī (the Ḍākinī of the Indestructible Expanse), who relishes mundane bliss, as well as with the Pītaśaṅkarā ḍākinī (the Yellow Bliss-giving Ḍākinī) and the Anantaguṇā ḍākinī (the Ḍākinī of Limitless Virtues), spent three years recording these precepts in writing. They also correctly arranged them, without any error, along with the emanational writings, which were self-originated and naturally established. All of these they placed in a cave called the "Real Origin of the Ḍākinīs" (*mkha'-'gro-ma mngon-par-'byung-ba'i phug*).

On another occasion the master went to the great Śītavana charnel ground, to the north-east of Vajrāsana, where there is a great stūpa, and which is inhabited by many venomous ḍākinīs and savage beings. There, he continued to teach the doctrine to the ḍākinī Sūryakiraṇā and countless other beings. At that time, the sublime Mañjuśrītīkṣṇa declared to the master Mañjuśrīmitra, "O son of the enlightened family! if you wish to become a buddha in a single lifetime, go to the great Śītavana charnel ground."

Mañjuśrīmitra went to the Śītavana charnel ground, where he met master Garap Dorje and studied the doctrine under him for seventy-five years. After the great master Garap Dorje had given him all the instructions and further advice the master passed into nirvāṇa in the uncorrupted expanse, on the banks of the River Danatika. When that took place, Mañjuśrīmitra cried "Alas! Alas!" in distress three times. Then, in an aura of celestial light the master's body actually appeared; and the master dropped a casket of gold the size of a fingernail into Mañjuśrīmitra's hand. It contained his last testament, entitled *Three Phrases which Penetrate the Essential* (*tshig-gsum gnad-du brdeg-pa*, NYZ *bi-ma snying-thig*, Pt.1, Vol. *Ga*, pp. 304-18).

Afterwards, the great master Mañjuśrīmitra divided the six million four hundred thousand verses of the Great Perfection into three classes:

> The Mental Class is for those who abide in mind.
> The Spatial Class is for those who are free from activity.
> The Esoteric Instructional Class is for those
> Who are intent upon the innermost essence.[521]

From among the latter, in particular, he divided the concise version, the *Establishment of the Intrinsic Essential of the Innermost Spirituality* (*thig-le rang-gnad-du dbab-pa*),[522] into an aural lineage and an exegetical tradition. He annotated the aural lineage, but not finding, at that time, a vessel worthy to be entrusted with the exegetical tradition, that is to say, with the transmitted precepts of the Innermost Spirituality (*snying-thig*), he concealed it under a boulder to the north-east of Vajrāsana; and, sealing the boulder with a crossed-vajra (*viśvavajra*), he made it invisible. Then he went to the Sosadvīpa charnel ground, to the west of Vajrāsana, where he taught the doctrine to ugly ḍākinīs, countless animals, and to many practitioners who adhered to the conduct [of the secret mantra]. He remained there, absorbed in contemplation, for one hundred and nine years.

BUDDHAJÑĀNAPĀDA

[127.2-130.5] Mañjuśrīmitra's disciple was Buddhajñānapāda, a vajra master of the great maṇḍalas. At first he served many gurus, such as master Jālandharipā, master Līlāvajra of Oḍḍiyāna, and the yoginī Guniru. Under them he studied many aspects of the secret mantra. Jambhala and Vasudharā[523] provided him with the necessities of life. Once, when he had served the master Rakṣitapāda of Koṅkana for nine years, and had heard the *Guhyasamāja Tantra* eighteen times, he told his guru that he still did not understand reality. "Nor do I understand it," replied the guru.

Then, in Kupavana, a forest behind Vajrāsana, he practised for eighteen months, of which twelve were devoted to the four branches of ritual service and attainment, along with the rites for deriving the most success,[524] and six were devoted to the wrathful practice. Thereby, he

Buddhajñānapāda

received this injunction: "If you want to understand reality you must ask the sublime Mañjuśrī."

"Very well", he thought, "but Mañjuśrī resides on Mount Wu-t'ai-shan [in China]. I must go there."

He set out in that direction. Around midday, near a white house, he saw Mañjuśrīmitra dressed as a venerable old householder, wearing his robe as a turban, and ploughing the fields with the help of a filthy old peasant woman. Buddhajñānapāda was distrustful. Nearby, an ugly white bitch was sleeping.

At lunchtime, when Buddhajñānapāda went to beg for alms, Mañjuśrīmitra caught a fish from the canal and gave it to the bitch. The bitch vomited up the fish, and Mañjuśrīmitra offered it to the master, who, thinking it to be impure, refused to accept it. The venerable householder said, "The man from Jambudvīpa has a great many ideas and conceptions. Give him some good food." And he went off elsewhere.

When the master had eaten boiled rice and curd which the woman offered, and was about to leave, she said, "Now the sun is setting. You will not reach the village. Go tomorrow."

So he stayed there and read the *Guhyasamāja Tantra*. Whenever the master hesitated over a doubtful passage, the woman showed her displeasure. Then, realising that she knew the minds of others, he asked her to remove his doubts. "I don't know", she said, "but that venerable householder who just left is very learned in the *Guhyasamāja*. He will come back late in the afternoon and will put an end to your doubts."

Sure enough, late that afternoon the venerable householder arrived, staggering under the influence of wine. The master, knowing that he was a mantra adept, prostrated at his feet, and requested him to remove his doubts. "You must receive the empowerment," he answered.

"I have already received it from someone else."

"But I have to empower you myself, before I can teach you my doctrine." So saying, Mañjuśrīmitra went into another room.

At twilight, when the master was called inside, he saw the venerable householder with the woman and the bitch, all beside an emanation of the nineteen-deity maṇḍala of Mañjuvajra.[525] "From whom will you receive empowerment?"

"I will request it from the maṇḍala."

"Well, take it then!" replied Mañjuśrīmitra as he went into another room with the woman and the dog. But the maṇḍala also vanished. Then, in dismay, the master cried out, "Oh! you are the sole father of all sentient beings..."

At his distressful prayer, Mañjuśrīmitra rematerialised the maṇḍala and empowered him. He gave instructions on the Mental Class of the Great Perfection, whereupon Buddhajñānapāda's understanding became as vast as the sky. He compiled a work on the cultivation of the true nature of the two stages [of creation and perfection] entitled *Oral Instructions of Mañjuśrī* [as a summary of the teaching he received].

Buddhajñānapāda plumbed the profound depths of the entire doctrine. It is said that because he was at first distrustful of the food which the bitch had vomited and of the conduct of the venerable householder, he did not attain supreme accomplishment in that body, but realised the level of Vajradhara during the intermediate state [immediately after his death].

Also, Rakṣitapāda requested instructions from master Buddhajñānapāda and attained accomplishment.

Buddhajñānapāda composed a great many treatises, for instance, the *Point of Liberation* and the *Means for Attainment entitled Samantabhadra* (*Samantabhadranāmasādhana*, T 1855). The esoteric instructions of this master on the stage of perfection, that were translated into the Tibetan language in ancient times, are included among the purest tenets of the Mental Class. Therefore, it is implicit that the host of his followers and disciples belonged to the lineage of the Great Perfection. Some believe, too, that master Śrī Siṃha was one and the same as this great master. This seems quite conceivable if one examines the various histories.

ŚRĪ SIṂHA, JÑĀNASŪTRA AND VIMALAMITRA

[130.5-137.5] At about the same time [as Buddhajñānapāda], in the city of Shokyam in China, the householder Gewei Yicen (Virtuous-minded) and his wife Nangwa Selwa Raptukhyenma (She who Intuits what is Clearly Manifest) had a son, who was to become renowned as the master Śrī Siṃha, a possessor of the ascetic virtues. From his fifteenth year he studied the ordinary sciences, like grammar and logic, for three years under master Haribhala; and when he had become a great scholar, he set out for the city of Suvarṇadvīpa in the west. On the road, the sublime Avalokiteśvara appeared in the sky and made this prophetic declaration: "Fortunate one! if you really wish to realise the fruit of enlightenment, go to the charnel ground of Sosadvīpa in India."

The master was contented by this and thought, "Now, to understand the supreme fruit more easily, I should also master the other tantras of the way of secret mantra." On the five-peaked mountain of Wu-t'ai-shan, he studied all the outer and inner doctrines on mantra, without exception, under the outcaste master Bhelakīrti; and he thoroughly

Śrī Siṃha

mastered them. He became ordained and strictly observed the Vinaya vows for thirty years, acting as a monk who was learned in the piṭaka.

Then the sublime Avalokiteśvara again encouraged him by repeating his former prophecy. Śrī Siṃha thought that he should acquire some miraculous powers, in order to remove the hardships of the journey to India. He practised the means for attainment for three years and attained the body of an awareness-holder. Then, travelling with his feet about one cubit above the earth, he journeyed to the Sosadvīpa charnel ground, where he met the great master Mañjuśrīmitra; and propitiated him as his guru. He prayed to be accepted as a disciple. The guru delightedly granted his prayer. After giving instructions and further advice for a period of twenty-five years, the body of the great master Mañjuśrīmitra vanished in a mass of light. At that, Śrī Siṃha cried out in distress, whereupon the master's body actually appeared in the sky and dropped into his hand a casket made of precious stones, the size of a fingernail. It contained Mañjuśrīmitra's last testament, which was entitled the *Six Experiences of Meditation* (*sgom-nyams drug-pa*). Thereby, the master Śrī Siṃha understood the profound truth.

Later, at Suvarṇadvīpa in West India, master Mañjuśrīmitra reincarnated. When he had grown up, he became known as the younger Mañjuśrīmitra. He recited all the outer and inner mantra texts to master Padmasambhava. It is also said that the corrupt body of master Āryadeva vanished when he received teaching on the Great Perfection from him.

Afterwards, master Śrī Siṃha extracted the tantras which had formerly been concealed under the Indestructible Seat. He went to China and divided the Esoteric Instructional Class of the Great Perfection into four cycles: outer, inner, secret, and unsurpassedly secret. He collected the first three cycles together for those who required elaboration; and he concealed them as treasures in the balcony of the Bodhi Tree Temple. Then, in accordance with a prediction he received from the ḍākinīs, he concealed the unsurpassedly secret cycle in a pillar in the Auspicious Myriad Gate Temple; and he sealed it up with prayers. He himself then dwelt in the great Siljin charnel ground and, venerated by savage spirits, became absorbed in contemplation.

At that time, in Hastisthala in western India, the householder Sukhacakra and his wife Ātmaprakāśā had a son called Vimalamitra; and in the eastern city of Kamalaśīla the outcaste Śāntihasta and his wife Kalyāṇacittā had a son called Jñānasūtra. The glorious Vajrasattva actually appeared to them both and made this prophetic declaration: "O sons of the enlightened family! you have both been born as scholars five hundred times; and you have both practised the true doctrine. But you have not attained its fruit in past lives, nor will you in the present one [if you persist in the same course as before]. If you wish the corrupt body to vanish and to attain enlightenment, you must go to the Bodhi Tree Temple in China."

Vimalamitra arrived there carrying his begging bowl and met the master Śrī Siṃha. For twenty years he was given all the outer, inner and secret instructions of the aural lineage, but he was not given the books. Vimalamitra returned, contented, to India, and told Jñānasūtra what had happened.

Jñānasūtra

Jñānasūtra also made great efforts to go to China; and he met the master in the great Siljin charnel ground, exactly as the ḍākinīs had prophesied he would. For three years he delighted the guru by serving him appropriately. Finally, he made an offering of a golden maṇḍala and requested the guru to give him instruction. He was then given the instructions of the aural lineage, together with the books, over a period of nine years. When Jñānasūtra was contented with that and about to return to India, Śrī Siṃha asked, "Are you quite satisfied?"

"Yes, I am satisfied," he replied.

"But I have not entrusted you [with the succession]," said the guru.

Jñānasūtra understood and then asked for the most profound instructions. His guru said, "For this you must receive empowerment," and gave to him the complete outer empowerment, which involves elaboration, and then for three years imparted the esoteric instructions of the unsurpassedly secret cycle.

After that, when Jñānasūtra again asked for leave to practice, Śrī Siṃha conferred on him the complete unelaborate empowerment. When, on the summit of Mount Kosala, the disciple had performed the practice which divides saṃsāra from nirvāṇa,[526] he also conferred on him the very unelaborate, and, eventually, the extremely unelaborate empowerments. Then Jñānasūtra meditated on those practices for sixteen years.

Śrī Siṃha continued to perform many special activities. Once Jñānasūtra was invited to visit the king of Khotan.[527] On the seventh day of his visit there were wondrous sounds and great omens. Jñānasūtra saw the master sitting in the sky above, and knew that he would pass into nirvāṇa. He cried out in distress, at which Śrī Siṃha dropped into his hand the testament entitled *Seven Nails (gzer-bu bdun*, NYZ *bi-ma snying-thig*, Pt.1, Vol. *Ga*, pp. 318-25) and prophetically declared, "The books of the esoteric instructions of the [unsurpassedly] secret cycle of the Innermost Spirituality are hidden inside a pillar in the Auspicious Myriad Gate Temple. Take them and go to the Bhasing charnel ground."

Vimalamitra

Jñānasūtra then extracted the secret books and went to the Bhasing charnel ground in India, where he resided, turning the wheel of the doctrine of the secret Innermost Spirituality for mundane and supramundane ḍākas and ḍākinīs.

At that time Vimalamitra adhered to the conduct [of a mantrin]. The ḍākinīs declared to him, "Fortunate one! if you want the instructions of the Innermost Spirituality, more profound than before, you must go to the great charnel ground in Bhasing Forest."

Arriving there, he met Jñānasūtra and prayed that he might receive the most profound instructions. The master displayed various miracles, and conferred on him the elaborate and unelaborate empowerments. When, on the summit of Mount Bhāskara, Vimalamitra had performed the practice which divides saṃsāra and nirvāṇa, and had received the very unelaborate empowerment in its entirety, extraordinary understanding was born in him. The white syllable A appeared at the tip of his nose, as if on the verge of melting away. Then, he was given the whole extremely unelaborate empowerment, by which he perceived the naked reality of mind. The master gave him all the instructions and books on the four cycles of the Great Perfection, which correspond to those empowerments, and for ten years Vimalamitra thoroughly refined his understanding of them. Afterwards, when Jñānasūtra vanished in an aura of light, Vimalamitra cried out in distress. Then, the master's body actually appeared, and dropped into his hand a precious casket sealed with five kinds of precious stones. Inside, he found the testament entitled *Four Methods of Establishment* (*bzhag-thabs bzhi*, NYZ *bi-ma snying-thig*, Pt.1, Vol. *Ga*, pp. 325-31), by following which he acquired an undeluded comprehension of meaning, while neither abridging, nor enlarging upon its verbal content.

Afterwards, Vimala lived in the city of Kāmarūpa for twenty years as the guru and priest of King Haribhadra. Then he also served as priest to King Dharmapāla in the western city of Bhirya. Residing later on in the great charnel ground of Prabhāskara he observed the ascetic practice which overcomes all obstacles; and he taught the doctrine to a host of savage beings. He copied out the most secret books three times. The first copy he concealed on an island covered by golden sand in Oḍḍiyāna; the second he hid in a rocky hollow in the Suvarṇadvīpa district of Kashmir; and the third he deposited in the charnel ground of Prabhāskara, to be worshipped by the ḍākinīs. Finally the master Vimalamitra attained the body of supreme transformation[528] and lived for some time in India. His arrival in Tibet will be described later.

8 *Concluding Remarks*

[137.5-143.3] In general, the Indian adepts of the secret mantra strictly preserved secrecy. Until they attained accomplishment, no one knew them to be adepts of the way of secret mantra. And when they vanished in a most miraculous manner, or displayed extraordinary powers, people would exclaim, "Oh, my goodness! He was a mantra adept." So it was that they were only recognised later. This is why all those who practised the way of mantras attained at least some particular accomplishment.

Formerly, the Kriyā and Caryā tantras had been widely propagated, but no one practised even these openly. Afterwards, when the Unsurpassed [Yoga] tantras were propagated, the Kriyā and Caryā tantras seemed to decline gradually. While the Unsurpassed [Yoga] tantras had also existed earlier, only a few fortunate beings had practised them at all; and immediately afterwards they would simply vanish. Thus, there was no legacy of continuous teaching and instruction. Then, at the time of King Ja, the intermediate Indrabhūti, the greatest accomplished masters consulted the ḍākinīs of pristine cognition in Dhūmasthira in Oḍḍiyāna and elsewhere. From those places they brought forth some complete tantras, the summarised meaning of others, and the quintessential understanding of a few more. Secretly, they explained them to a few worthy recipients; and in this way the unsurpassed paths were extensively propagated. During that period many accomplished individuals appeared in all places. Their practices, though, could not possibly have had a great deal in common; and the books and treatises on mantra did not become widespread in the manner of ordinary texts.

Let us give an example: A long time after the master Nāgārjuna and the host of his disciples had passed into nirvāṇa, a volume containing the text of the *Clarifying Lamp* was discovered by Rakṣitapāda of Koṅkana. And then Mātaṅgīpā met the body of the pristine cognition of Āryadeva in a vision. It was only after these and other events had occurred that the *Ārya* cycle of the *Guhyasamāja Tantra* [i.e. the tradition stemming from Nāgārjuna] began to spread.

In the same way, after the emanation Garap Dorje taught the cycle of the extremely secret Great Perfection, the books were not even revealed except to the most fortunate masters of the aural lineage of direct verbal instruction, because on the demise of each master the books were concealed in an invisible form. The most profound instructions were only left behind in the form of testaments. Not even a fraction of them circulated in the ordinary way. Thus, the lineages of ancient tantras like the *Buddhakapāla* (T 424), those of the *Ārya* cycle, and those of the Great Perfection are similar.

No one but Vajradhara himself can perceive all the tantras of the way of secret mantra. Only a portion of them appeared in the human and non-human worlds; and it is apparent that, among them, those which appeared in the human world were very few indeed. Most of them came to India from Oḍḍiyāna. Today Dhūmasthira, the Place of Smoke, which was the central city of that country, is a very small town. There is not even a trace of King Indrabhūti's palace. The country is governed by barbarians. No one at all upholds the Buddhist or Hindu philosophies. But because the women belong to the ancient race of the ḍākinīs, they are still the ḍākinīs of that locale; and they have power over the arts of the magic gaze, transformation of objects by means of certain gnostic spells, and some minor sorcery. Even the palace of Dharmagañji, which housed the tantras of the mantra vehicle, cannot be actually perceived: people who see it just think that it is an ordinary town. But even today it contains some tantras of the way of secret mantra which have not yet appeared in India; for the ḍākinīs have kept them secured in the invisible sphere, so that they are not ordinary objects of perception.

Moreover, in Draviḍa, and in other lands, there are actually many tantras that were never well known in India.[529] This shows that the tantras appear in various human lands whose inhabitants are fit to be trained in the way of mantra. Therefore, those who try to maintain that there is exactly this or that precise number of tantras suffer from puerile conceptions. In short, we must understand that [the extent of the tantras] is inconceivable. This is also illustrated in the *Tantra of the Emergence of Cakrasaṃvara*, which says:

> That the number of Yoga tantras
> Is sixty million is certain.
> The number of Yoginī tantras
> Is known to be one hundred and sixty million.
> Excluding the greater vehicle, so it is said,
> The sūtras number eight hundred million.
> Likewise those of the Transcendental Perfection
> Number four hundred and ninety-nine million.
> All of these were proclaimed by the Lord of Sages,
> The embodiment of the three bodies.

Later in Central India the true foundation of the teaching declined. But to the east, in the border lands and in Kokī, which is a collective name for many small countries,[530] and in Dāmiḍodvīpa [the Tamil land], Dhanaśrīdvīpa and Candradvīpa to the south, and in Gujarat in the north, the teachings of the greater, lesser, and secret mantra vehicles continued without decline from before, and even regenerated. Thus, at the present time,[531] the teaching exists in those places in its original form. Of the adepts of the way of secret mantra, there are many who uphold the lineage of the great master Padmasambhava, but the majority are of the twelve orders of yogins who follow the great accomplished master Gorakṣanātha. And, in particular, there are a great many yogins who follow the great master of indestructible reality, Śāntigupta and his spiritual sons, who belong to the Nāṭeśvara suborder of the Nāthapaṇṭhas.[532]

At a later period, there was a kingdom in the district of Bhaṃdva in the Vindhyā Mountains of South India, which was ruled by the king Balabhadra, who was accomplished in some gnostic spells, and who gained power over most of the areas of the South. He adopted Śāntigupta and the host of that master's disciples as his gurus; and so he revived the precious teaching of the Sugata. It is said that the Indians declare that the Buddha predicted that the true doctrine would, in the future, be revived in the Vindhyā Mountains to the south.

This completes the special explanation of the development of the doctrine of the vehicle of indestructible reality, the way of secret mantra, the second part of this book, *Thunder from the Great Conquering Battle-Drum of Devendra*, which is a history of the precious teaching of the vehicle of indestructible reality according to the Ancient Translation School.

Part Three
The Origin of the Conqueror's Teaching in Tibet

Introduction

[147.2-151.6] Now [I shall explain] how it was that the teaching of the Conqueror spread in the Land of Snows.

In Jambudvīpa there were six great countries where the true doctrine was propagated, namely, India, China, Tibet, Khotan, Shambhala, and Kailash. Among them, one might wonder when it was that the teaching of the Buddha reached Tibet, the land of snow mountains. Concerning that, there is a prophecy in the *Root Tantra of Mañjuśrī*:

> When the lake in the Land of Snows has dried,
> A forest of sal trees will appear.

So at first there was a lake, which gradually dried up. When the country became enveloped by dense jungle, a monkey, blessed by the Great Compassionate One [Avalokiteśvara], arrived from Mount Potalaka; and from his union with an ogress of the rocks it is said that the Tibetan race evolved. Initially, the country was possessed by non-human beings. Humans developed there gradually, and were governed successively by [the lords of] twelve minor kingdoms and forty principalities.[533] Then Nyatrhi Tsenpo became the first human king to rule the whole of Tibet.

Canonical texts prove that the religious kings [of Tibet] were descended from the Licchavi race, and some believe Nyatrhi Tsenpo to have been the son of King Magyapa.[534] But, whatever actually occurred, a wonderful superhuman being appeared on Mount Lhari Rölpa in the Land of Snows. When he reached Tsentang Gozhi, the Pönpos called him a god because he had descended on a sky-cord. "Who are you?" they asked. To which he replied, "I am a king (*tsen-po*)." "Where have you come from?" they inquired. At this, he pointed to the sky.

Then the people carried him on their shoulders (*nya*), seated on a wooden throne (*trhi*). Therefore, he became known as Nyatrhi Tsenpo, the "King of the Shoulder-borne Sedan-chair". In his succession there appeared seven heavenly kings called *Trhi*, including his own son Mutrhi Tsenpo; two celestial kings called *Teng*; six earthly kings called

Lek; eight middle kings called *De*; and five linking kings called *Tsen*.[535] Throughout these ancient reigns Pönpos, who relied on legends and enigmatic riddles, governed the kingdom.

Now, it says in the *Prophecy Addressed to Vimaladevī* (*lha-mo dri-ma med-pa lung bstan-pa*):

> Two thousand and five hundred years after my final nirvāṇa the true doctrine will be propagated in the land of red-faced beings.[536]

Accordingly, when Lha Thotori Nyentsen, the twenty-eighth hereditary king, who was an emanation of the bodhisattva Samantabhadra, was residing in the Yumbu Lagang Palace, a casket fell down upon the palace roof. It was opened, and revealed the *Sūtra of the Rites of Renunciation and Fulfilment* (*spang-skong phyag-brgya-pa'i mdo*, T 267), a mould engraved with the *Dhāraṇī of the Wish-fulfilling Gem* (*Cintāmaṇidhāraṇī*), the *Sūtra of the Cornucopia of Avalokiteśvara's Attributes* (*Āryakaraṇḍavyūhasūtra*, T 116), the Six-Syllable Mantra, and a golden stūpa. The king did not know what they were, but understood them to be auspicious, and so called them the "Awesome Secret" (*gnyan-po gsang-ba*).

Lha Thotori Nyentsen

By the blessing that came from worshipping and venerating them the king, a man of sixty-one years, was rejuvenated and became a sixteen-year-old youth once more. He lived on for sixty more years, and so reached the age of one hundred and twenty. The king obtained a prediction that the meaning of the Awesome Secret would be understood after five generations. This was the beginning of the true doctrine in Tibet.[537]

But there are various other accounts of how it happened: Nelpa Paṇḍita [in his *History*] said:

> The Pönpos claim that the casket fell down from the sky because they adore the sky; but in reality those two books were brought by the scholar Buddhirakṣita and the translator Thilise. When they arrived in Tibet they found that the king could neither read, nor understand the meaning. So the scholar and the translator returned.

This account appears to be true.

At a later date Ba Selnang went to Nepal, where he met the preceptor Śāntarakṣita. The preceptor said to him, "While the Buddha Kāśyapa was teaching the doctrine, the king of Tibet, yourself, and I were the three sons of a woman poultry-keeper. We made a vow to propagate the teaching in Tibet. As the king had not been reborn and you had not come of age, I have been waiting here for nine reigns." Because this tale is said to occur in the "pure" *Testament of Ba* (*rba-bzhed gtsang-ma*),[538] and because it accords with known facts, some scholars hold it to be true.

1 *The Three Ancestral Religious Kings*

KING SONGTSEN GAMPO[539]

[151.6-154.4] There is a prophecy in the *Root Tantra of Mañjuśrī*:

> In the place called the divine land,
> Surrounded by snowy mountains,
> A king called "God among Men" will be born
> Into the Licchavi race.[540]

The fifth hereditary monarch after Lha Thotori was the religious king Songtsen Gampo, an emanation of Avalokiteśvara in the form of a mighty lord of men, who began to rule the kingdom at the age of thirteen. When he was fifteen the emanational monk Ā-kar Matiśīla brought him a self-created image of the Sublime One [Avalokiteśvara]. Then, the king commanded the religious minister Gar, an emanation of Vajrapāṇi, to invite the Nepalese princess Trhitsün, an emanation of Bhṛkuṭī, and the Chinese princess Wen-ch'eng K'ong-jo, an emanation of Tārā, both of whom were agreeable to the people, to be his two consorts.[541] This he did in order to introduce two images of the Teacher, representative of the Buddha himself, which were, respectively, the size of an eight-year-old, and that of a twelve-year-old.[542] The princesses came to be known as the two "Lotuses of the Lake".

While the Trhülnang Temple [i.e. the Jokhang, the "Cathedral of Lhasa"] was being constructed the building-work was disrupted by non-human beings. Therefore, the king and his two consorts went into retreat in the palace known as Maru, at Nyangdren Phawongkha in the valley of the Kyicu. They attained accomplishment by propitiating their meditative deity, on whose advice the king built the Border Taming, Further Taming, and District Controlling temples, which were situated on geomantic sites on the body of the supine ogress [that is Tibet]; and so it was that he exorcised the malignant earth spirits.[543] He then erected the Trhülnang and Ramoche temples and the images they housed.

Songtsen Gampo invited the master Kusara and the brahman Śaṅkara from India,[544] the master Śīlamañju from Nepal, and the master Ho-shang Mo-ho-yen from China. With others, they translated many sections of the Tripiṭaka and of the tantras, and thus introduced the teaching to Tibet. Though no actual teaching or study took place, the king himself secretly gave instruction on the peaceful and wrathful forms of the Great Compassionate One to many fortunate beings, who then practised these teachings. No one was ordained [as a monk] prior to the "seven men who were tested", but it is said that there were always

Songtsen Gampo

about a hundred long-haired yogins engaged in the practices of the Great Compassionate One at Nyangdren Phawongkha. At that time the scriptures which formed the king's testament were collected and hidden in three separate treasures. Later, these treasures were revealed by the accomplished master Ngödrup, Lord Nyang, and the teacher Śākya-ö. Today they are renowned as the *Collected Works of the King concerning the Mantra "Oṃ Maṇi Padme Hūṃ" (maṇi bka'-'bum)*, the first Tibetan doctrinal work.[545]

The king also sent Thönmi Sambhoṭa, an emanation of Mañjughoṣa, to India to study grammar and writing. On the basis of the Indian scripts he created the forms of the Tibetan letters, and he composed eight treatises on Tibetan grammar.[546]

Before Songtsen Gampo's time there had been no proponents in the Land of Snows of a code of conduct in accord with the doctrine, but thereafter the great door of the true doctrine and of theories in accord with the doctrine was opened for the first time. Thus, the king innovated the just spiritual and temporal laws, as illustrated by the ten divine virtues and the sixteen pure human laws.[547] In these ways, King Songtsen Gampo blessed the country of Tibet to become a prosperous and luxurious source of the true doctrine.

KING TRHISONG DETSEN AND THE COMING OF PADMASAMBHAVA

[154.4-166.5] In the fifth reign after Songtsen Gampo, King Trhisong Detsen, an emanation of Mañjughoṣa, appeared. His royal ancestor had inscribed a prophecy on a copper plate, to the effect that, "Five

Trhisong Detsen

reigns from now, in the time of my descendant, King De, the true doctrine will be propagated." He had concealed the copper plate in a confined place.[548]

Just so, when Trhisong Detsen was thirteen he began to govern the kingdom. At twenty he made a solemn resolution to propagate the true doctrine and he invited to Tibet the Bodhisattva, Śāntarakṣita, the preceptor from Sahor. The latter granted the eight vows to some, but when he taught the doctrines of the ten virtues and of the eighteen psychophysical bases, the savage demons and deities of Tibet became angry. Lightning struck Marpori [the "Red Mountain", site of the present Potala Palace] and the palace at Phangtang was swept away by a flood. The harvest was destroyed and great calamities befell the country. Evil ministers said, "This is due to the practice of the doctrine. The master should be banished to his own country."

The king offered much gold to the preceptor and told him of the situation. Śāntarakṣita replied, "The spirits of Tibet are displeased. I will go to Nepal for the time being. In order to subdue the savage spirits and demons of Tibet, there is a mantra adept called Padmasambhava, who is, at present, the most powerful in the world. I will send him an invitation, and Your Majesty should do the same." So they sent messengers consecutively.

Master Padmasambhava, however, already knew that the delegation, which included Nanam Dorje Düjom, was speeding on its way. In an instant he travelled to Kungtang, in Mangyül, where he met the group. He scattered their offering of gold in the direction of Ngari and said, "Everything I perceive is gold." In this way he turned Tibet into an abundant gold-producing land.

Then the Bodhisattva, Śāntarakṣita, set out for Tibet in advance, along with a skilled Nepali stonemason. Master Padmasambhava advanced from Kyirong, whereupon the gods and demons of Tibet launched a raging storm of snow and rain, which blocked the mountain passes. The master retired to a mountain cave, imprisoned the gods and demons by the power of his contemplation, and bound them under an oath of allegiance. From that time on, by his miraculous powers, he gradually covered the whole of Tibet on foot, from Ngari, Central Tibet, and Tsang [in the west], to Dokam [Kham and Amdo in the east]. He bound all the powerful spirits under oath, among whom the foremost were the twelve goddesses of the earth, the thirteen hunting gods, and the twenty-one *genyen*;[549] and he assumed control of their vital heart-mantras.

In the tamarisk forest of Trakmar he met the sovereign. While consecrating the Drinzang Temple at Trakmar, he invited the images of the deities to a place of feasting. That night the temple was empty. The next morning the deities were actually seen eating the offerings and conversing in the temple. That day all the musical instruments of

Śāntarakṣita

worship played by themselves and made a great din. At the same time the oracular mirror[550] was brought before some sensitive children who indicated the names, conduct, and residences of all the malignant gods and nāgas, who had formerly opposed the teaching of the doctrine in Tibet by the preceptor, Bodhisattva. With threats of intimidation the master bound those spirits under an oath of allegiance and secured them in the doctrine. He procured their vital heart-mantras, and the rituals for the propitiation of each of them; and he subdued those who still remained unconverted with burnt offerings, and so forth. Padmasambhava did this two times.

After he had subdued such nāgas as Zicen of Lake Manasarovar, Padmasambhava cultivated the king's friendship. He was offered fourteen mule-loads of powdered gold to erect a temple. The Bodhisattva inspected the land while the great master Padmasambhava went to Hepori [a mountain near Samye], where he overpowered all the local gods and demons. In a glorious voice he ordered them to sublimate their pride, and, by performing a dance of indestructible reality in the sky, he blessed the site. While laying the foundation lines he summoned by contemplation the two [spirits of healing], Cokro Pucungmen and

Lhabumen, to guide the ends of the measuring thread. The foundations were laid following the model of Odantapurī Monastery, in accord with the preceptor's orders.[551] Since the great master employed all of the arrogant spirits, the walls which were raised during the day by men were made even higher at night by the spirits. Thus, glorious Samye, the Temple of Unchanging Spontaneous Presence, which was designed to resemble Mount Sumeru, with its four continents, and its subcontinents, sun, moon, and iron perimeter, was entirely completed in about five years, along with the three shrines of the three queens.[552] During the consecration performed by the preceptor and the master, astonishing and inconceivable miracles occurred. For example, the deities enshrined in the central shrine (*dbu-rtse*) went outside.

Then the sovereign decided to introduce the foundations of the sūtra and mantra teachings by translating the true doctrine [from Sanskrit into Tibetan]. Intelligent Tibetan youths were instructed in the art of translation. Trhisong Detsen invited from India great scholars, who were learned in the piṭaka – monks such as the masters Jinamitra, Sarvajñādeva, and Dānaśīla; holders of indestructible reality such as Vimalamitra and Śāntigarbha; and twelve monks of the Sarvāstivāda order as well.[553]

To test whether or not Tibetans were suitable for monastic ordination, the king at first requested that those masters ordain his faithful minister, Ba Trhizi of the Zhang family. Under the supervision of the Bodhisattva, who officiated as preceptor, of Dānaśīla and Jinamitra, who acted as master of ceremonies and exposer of secrets, and of ten other paṇḍitas, who made up the quorum, Trhizi renounced the world and was fully ordained as a monk. He received the name Pelyang, and also became known as Ba-ratna, the "Jewel of the Ba Family"; for the king had praised him thus. Through meditation he acquired five supernormal cognitive powers.

After that, Ba Selnang, Pagor Vairocana, Ngenlam Gyelwa Choyang, Ma Rincen-chok, Khön Lüiwangpo Sungwa, and Lasum Gyelwa Cangcup gradually renounced the world. They were fully ordained as monks; and their names were changed to Yeshe Wangpo, and so forth. Together, they became known as the "seven men who were tested"; and they were the first monks in Tibet.

The king then decided that Tibetans were suitable for ordination. Trama, the minister of the Zhang family, and three hundred intelligent subjects were ordained. Scholars, such as the preceptor Śāntarakṣita and master Padmasambhava, along with the translators Vairocana, Kawa Peltsek, Cokro Lüi Gyeltsen, and Zhang Yeshe De translated the transmitted precepts of the sūtra, and mantra traditions, as well as the foremost commentarial treatises, into Tibetan. Vairocana and Namkei Nyingpo were sent to India, where Vairocana studied the Great Perfection under Śrī Siṃha, and Namkei Nyingpo studied the doctrines of Yangdak Heruka under Hūṃkara. When they had attained accomplishment they propagated these teachings in Tibet.

Moreover, the great master Padmasambhava gave numerous empowerments for the lower mantras, as well as the Unsurpassed [Yoga] tantras, to the king and some fortunate subjects. He taught the *Hundred Thousand Verses of the Vajrakīla Tantra*, the *Garland of Views: A Collection of Esoteric Instructions*, and other works.

On one occasion the master spoke to the king as follows, "Your Majesty should make this country prosperous. You should turn the sands of Ngamshö into groves and meadows. You should irrigate the barren regions like the three districts of Tra and Töl (*gra-dol-yul-gsum*). You should reclaim all the swamps for cultivation. You should obtain wealth from Vaiśravaṇa[554] and make the country a source of wealth. You should redirect the rivers, by means of canals, and make Tibet hold dominion over all the kings of China and Central Asia."

To this the king replied, "I beg you to do so!"

The master remained engaged in this intention for just a morning when water appeared in the desert of Trakmar. The sandy plain became an alpine meadow, in which was situated the so-called "Peacock Lake" (Tshomo Gülngön) of Trakmar. In Trak Daweidong a vast forest appeared instantly. And in Zurkar, a wide, flowing river sprang up without a source.

Then, though he was certainly about to complete all the rest according to his word, the remaining works and the performance of burnt offerings to increase the power of the royal dynasty were left undone, due to the common misfortune of the populace and, as a further circumstance, due to the harmful misconduct of hostile, evil ministers, who, because they could not endure the master's miraculous and supernormal cognitive powers, persuaded [the king] to delay. The deities and nāgas could not be bound under an oath of allegiance for yet a third time. At this point, Padmasambhava declared, "The result of the perverse aspirations of the ministers of Tibet will be the decline of happiness in Tibet. Although the great wheel of the doctrine will have made one complete cycle there will be great strife at an intermediate time. The nāgas and Gyelpo spirits will be ill-disposed and the dynasty itself will disintegrate, due to its neglect of the law." It is said that because he knew the future would be so, Padmasambhava suddenly departed to subdue the ogres [in Cāmaradvīpa], but only after he had first delivered many wrathful mantras and had concealed many books as treasures in Tibet.

Concerning the duration of Padmasambhava's stay in Tibet: Some maintain that it was but a short period, six or eighteen months. The moderate opinion holds that it was three, six or twelve years; and there are those who say that it was as long as one hundred and nine solstices, or fifty-four years and six months, altogether. The guru came to Tibet

Padmākara

when King Trhisong was in his twenty-first year; and the king passed away in his sixty-ninth. So it is evident that Padmasambhava stayed in Tibet for five years and six months after the king's passing. The learned masters of our tradition do not see any contradiction among these statements.[555]

The *Testament of Ba* and other works, which tell us that Padmasambhava stayed in Tibet for but a brief period, do so because the master emanated a second body to be seen by the evil ministers. Then, his escorts saw him fly into the sky from the summit of the mountain on the frontier of India and Tibet, across the narrow pass of Tongbap. He departed through the clouds, with his robe fluttering, and the rings of his staff jingling. But his real body remained in solitary hermitages, and in mountain caves in Zhotö Tidro, Chimpu, and elsewhere. In these locales he continued to turn the wheel of the unsurpassed, secret doctrine for the king and his fortunate subjects.

At one time the great master was perceived dwelling in such places of attainment; and when that rumour became widespread, the king, wishing to discover whether it was true or false, invited him to consecrate the Samye Monastery.

It is also said that in the interval between the lifetime of Trhisong Detsen and the reign of his son Mutrhi, the master departed into the sky, riding upon his horse from the summit of Kungtang Mountain. This is known from the lament, uttered by Mutrhi when he took leave of Padmasambhava:

> My one and only royal father has died.
> My guru is going to Oḍḍiyāna.
> O royal father! your life was too short;
> The happiness of your Tibetan subjects has passed.
> Why did I, Mutrhi Tsenpo, not die,
> While my father and my guru were present?[556]

Furthermore, we should not think that Padmasambhava could not have completed all the bountiful acts he desired during just a short visit. He was adept at inconceivable miraculous powers, like the ability to make his body manifest in all buddha-fields simultaneously. Similarly, when the Buddha himself performed miracles at Śrāvastī, as described in the *Sūtra of the Wise and the Foolish* (*mdo mdzangs-blun*, T 341),[557] and in the *Transmissions of the Vinaya*, some say that these miracles lasted for a few days, and some for many. In sum, whether his visit appeared to have been long or short depended upon the purity or impurity of his disciples' perception.

In this way, the master continued to consult with his patron, the king, in secret. He traversed the whole of Tibet on foot, down to the last hoof-sized patch of ground, along with Tshogyel and other fortunate companions. He inhabited each of the twenty mountain caves of Ngari; the twenty-one places of attainment in Central Tibet and in Tsang; the twenty-five great pilgrimage places of Kham and Amdo; and the secret lands of upper, lower, and central Tibet which are like three kings, along with five valleys, three districts and one parkland.[558] He blessed all of them, along with their glaciers, caves, mountains and waterways – which are as their roots, branches, flowers, and fruits – to be places of attainment. Since he knew that the teaching would be persecuted later by the king's grandson, an emanation of Māra, he gave many oracles and prophecies to the king. Then, intending that the teaching of the secret mantra should not vanish, nor the genuine blessing be weakened or adulterated by sophistry, and that disciples should gradually appear, he concealed countless treasures, both named and unnamed. The foremost of these treasures were the hundred treasures which were the master copies of King Trhisong, the five great mind treasures, and the twenty-five great profound treasures. For each one, he predicted the time of revelation, the discoverer, his fortunate spiritual successors, and so forth.

In thirteen places all called "tiger dens", such as Nering Sengedzong in Mönka [Bhutan], Padmasambhava assumed an awesome dis-

Dorje Trolö

figured, wrathful form, and bound all the arrogant deities and demons of Tibet, both great and small, under oaths of allegiance; and he appointed them to guard the treasures. At that time, the master became renowned as Dorje Trolö (Vajra Pot-belly). To induce faith in future generations, the guru and his consort left behind countless wonderful signs, such as handprints and footprints, in all the places of attainment. Such are the imprint of his body at Dorje Tsekpa in Bumthang, the handprint at Namtso Chukmo, and the footprint on the White Rock in Paro.

Once, the prince Murup Tsepo was sent [on a military expedition] and destroyed the hermitages of the Bhaṭa Hor.[559] When he was carrying away their property, the prince was pursued by the Gyelpo spirit Shingjachen.[560] Padmasambhava then assumed the form of Guru Trakpo (Wrathful Guru), bound the spirit under an oath of allegiance, and commanded him to guard the wealth of the temples.

The master founded many colleges to teach the dialectical vehicle and meditation schools for the way of secret mantra. The king and all his subjects acclaimed him as the most worshipful of renunciates; and the king established the twofold division of the religious community, consisting of the shaven-headed followers of the sūtras [the monks], and the followers of the way of mantras, who wore long, braided locks. He erected pillars [e.g. the Zhöl Pillar] inscribed with the great decree concerning protocol and with important edicts.[561] At that time the kingdom of Tibet reached the zenith of its power and held dominion over two-thirds of eastern Jambudvīpa. Because the kingdom was protected by the true doctrine, Tibet is known to have enjoyed the happiness of paradise.

When master Padmasambhava was about to leave to convert the ogres in the south-west, the king, ministers, and subjects of Tibet begged him to stay on. But he declined. To each of them he gave detailed instructions, and precepts concerning loving kindness. Then, riding on a lion, or on an excellent horse, he set out from the summit of Kungtang Mountain for Cāmaradvīpa, in the midst of an infinite mass of divine offerings. In Cāmaradvīpa, on the peak of the glorious Copper-coloured Mountain, he "liberated" the ogre Thötreng (Skull-garlanded), the king of ogres, and entered into his corpse. He materialised the inconceivable Palace of Lotus Light; and there he resides, ruling in his eight emanations over eight ogre islands, teaching

Pehar

the eight transmitted precepts concerning the eight means for attainment and other doctrines, and protecting the people of Jambudvīpa from deathly fears. He continues to dwell, even now, as the regent of the Sixth Conqueror, Vajradhara, the holder of the awareness that is the spontaneous presence of the final path; and so will he remain, without moving, until the dissolution of the universe.

Trhi Relpacen

KING RELPACEN

[166.5-168.5] The religious king, Trhisong Detsen, had three royal sons. The eldest was named Mune Tsepo, the middle one Murup Tsepo, and the youngest Mutik Tsepo, or Senalek Jingyön. They further propagated the teaching. In particular, Mune Tsepo founded the four great cycles of worship (*mchod-pa chen-po bzhi*) at Samye during his reign; and three times he alleviated the hunger of his Tibetan subjects.

Mutik Tsepo built the Temple of the Indestructible Expanse at Karcung. He had about five sons, among whom the most distinguished was Trhi Relpacen, an emanation of Vajrapāṇi, who was also known as Trhi Detsukten. Relpacen appointed seven householders among his subjects to serve each of the monks; and he is famed for having built a thousand temples and shrines. He humbly honoured and venerated the two orders – those of the traditions of the sūtras and mantras, with their gurus and venerable adherents – while placing at their feet the two silken ribbons which hung from his braided hair. Through these and other acts he displayed infinite veneration to the most precious teaching of the Conqueror.

In the lower valley of the Kyicu, Relpacen built the temple of Öncangdo Peme Trashi Gepel. He invited Surendrabodhi, Śīlendrabodhi, Dānaśīla, and many other scholars from India. He commanded them, along with the Tibetan preceptors Ratnarakṣita and Dharmatāśīla, and the translator Jñānasena, as follows:

> Formerly, when the doctrine was translated by scholars and translators in the time of my paternal ancestors, many terms were used which were unknown to the Tibetan language. Replace those terms among them which contradict the texts of the doctrine and grammatical usage, as well as those which are hard to understand, by searching [for alternatives] among the familiar terms of the colloquial language. Thus, you should revise the translations according to the texts of the greater and lesser vehicles.[562]

Therefore, at Kawa Namoche in Phenyül, they revised the translation of the *Great Mother* [the *Transcendental Perfection of Discriminative Awareness in One Hundred Thousand Lines*], and divided it into sixteen sections. They also established, in accord with the laws of contemporary language, the translations of most of the scriptures translated during the time of the king's paternal ancestors. But, owing to the strictness of the inner tantras of the way of secret mantra, whereby they cannot be grasped by ordinary persons who are not fit vessels for them, the translators preserved the ancient translations intact.[563]

So it was that the three ancestral religious kings [Songtsen Gampo, Trhisong Detsen, and Relpacen] made the greatest impact on the teaching of the Conqueror in the Land of Snows, and thus were most gracious to its inhabitants. Among those kings, Songtsen Gampo and Trhisong Detsen were particularly great in their kindness. The scholars Śāntarakṣita and Padmasambhava, and the translators Thönmi Sambhoṭa, Vairocana, Kawa Peltsek, Cokro Lüi Gyeltsen and Zhang Yeshe De were all most gracious and wonderful.

2 *The Decline and Expansion of the Doctrine During the Intermediate Period*

[168.5-169.6] At a later date, Langdarma Udumtsen, the elder brother of the sovereign Trhi Relpacen, was possessed by a demon because of his perverse aspirations, and he persecuted the doctrine. Not long after, the evil king was assassinated by Lhalung Pelgi Dorje.[564]

Still later, the kings Ösung and Pelkortsen revived the ancient customs and built temples and so forth out of devotion to the Three Precious Jewels.[565] At that time there were no monks, but householders who were devoted to the Precious Jewels carefully saved the temples, including those at Lhasa and Samye, from destruction. Ngari seceded [from the kingdom] and the royal dynasty disintegrated. Though the circumstances under which the whole of Tibet had been subject to the noble family of religious kings had changed, the mantra adepts, white-robed householders, maintained the exegesis and attainment of the profound stages of creation and perfection in their own homes, and in isolated hermitages. They insured that the continuity of the secret mantra according to the Ancient Translation School was never interrupted. By their devotion to the teaching in general, and their kindness in carefully preserving the texts of the transmitted precepts and [supplementary] treatises, which had been previously translated in the time of the three ancestral religious kings, most of the ancient translations of the sūtras and tantras exist for our use, even today.

3 *The Revival and Later Expansion of the Teaching*

[169.6-173.5] During the decline of the teaching following Langdarma's persecution, Mar Śākyamuni, a disciple of Ba-ratna, together with Yo Gejung and Tsang Rapsel, loaded the Vinaya texts onto a mule and set out for the Qarloq and Uighur country.[566] But, because they were unable to propagate the doctrine in that direction, they went to Kham. While they were meditating at Dorjei Trakra Encung Namdzong in Malung, or at the "Crystal Retreat" in Tentik, one Muzu Labar approached them, and in faith he asked for ordination. He was ordained as a novice by Mar Śākyamuni, who acted as the preceptor, and Yo Gejung, who acted as the master; and he received the name of Śākya Gewarapsel. But when he requested the complete ordination they did not have the quorum of five monks. They sought out Lhalung Pelgi Dorje in Den, who said, "Since I have killed the evil king, I cannot come to complete the group. But I will find another and send him."

He sent two Chinese monks, named Ke-wang and Gyi-phan, and ordination was granted by the group of five. For fifteen years Gewarapsel studied the Vinaya under his preceptor and master. Later, he studied Vinaya under Senge-trak of Korong, Transcendental Perfection under Kawa Ö-chokdra, and the Mental Class of the Great Perfection under Yudra Nyingpo. The exegesis of the *Tantra of the All-Accomplishing King*, which continued even at a later time, came through his lineage. This illustrates his most sublime, enlightened activity, and his great learning. For this reason he became renowned as Lacen Gongpa Rapsel, the "Great Guru whose Enlightened Intention was Utterly Clear".

Five years after Gewarapsel's complete ordination, the king Yeshe Gyeltsen and others sent five men from Central Tibet, including Lume Tshültrim Sherap, and five from Tsang, including Lotön Dorje Wangcuk, to Kham, so that they might revive the feeble doctrine in Central Tibet. Gewarapsel gave them all three levels of ordination in a single sitting, and they became learned in the Vinaya. Since he gave the full ordination simultaneously and not by precise stages over a period of ten years,[567] he became renowned as a bodhisattva whose practice was based on devotion. On that occasion Mar Śākyamuni, Yo Gejung, and Tsang Rapsel allowed him to give the ordination [although they were his seniors] because he was an extraordinary person and because there was a most urgent need to halt the decline of the teaching. Therefore, genuine authorities maintain that there was no fault [commit-

Lhalung Pelgi Dorje

ted during the aforementioned ordination]. Mar, Yo, and Tsang were alive at the time, but said they were too old to educate the disciples; and so they acted as masters of ceremony. The great guru [Gongpa Rapsel] appointed Lume as a preceptor, and when the ten men from Central Tibet and Tsang returned home they became the gurus and priests of their kings.

Lume had four disciples who were like pillars, eight like beams, thirty-two like rafters, and a thousand like planks. Thus, he restored the foundation of the feeble doctrine. He set up countless centres like those at Lamo, Ragye, Yerpa, Pare, and Tshongdü. The disciples, spiritual benefactors, and monks at Yamshü alone are said to have set up one hundred and eight centres. In this way, the centres of Lume and of his disciples covered the whole land. In fact, with each day the community of monks multiplied, and became known as the Lower

Tibetan Lineage of the Vinaya.[568] The ordained monks of the Ancient Translation School, and later the great translator Dharmaśrī, the emanation of Yudra Nyingpo, widely propagated its exegesis and practical application. The seminary of Orgyen Mindröling, the sole ornament of Tibet, and its branches preserved this Vinaya lineage.[569] Then, during the later propagation of the teaching, most of the early generations of the great men who adhered to the monastic vows, and also most of the spiritual benefactors in the ancient and new Kadampa schools adhered to this Vinaya lineage.

Furthermore, the scholar Jinamitra, the translator Kawa Peltsek, and others translated the *Treasury of the Abhidharma*, and the *Compendium of the Abhidharma* [from Sanskrit into Tibetan]. They instructed Nanam Dawei Dorje, Lhalung Pelgi Dorje and E Yeshe Gyelwa. The latter went to Kham and transmitted this teaching, which has been widely propagated until the present day.[570]

Lacen Gongpa Rapsel

Regarding the sūtras: Lang Khampa Gocha memorised the *Transcendental Perfection of Discriminative Awareness in One Hundred Thousand Lines*, and he propagated this and other sūtras of India, which belong to the intermediate wheel of the doctrine, by means of translation, exegesis, and study. All of the sūtras which belong to the final wheel of the doctrine were translated, and their exegesis established through teaching and study, by Kawa Peltsek, Cokro Lüi Gyeltsen, Vairocana and others. Their tradition of exegesis and attainment has continued until the present day.

It would be appropriate here to give a detailed account of the lives of the ancestral religious kings, who greatly promoted and propagated the true doctrine. But, owing to the immensity of the literature, I will not enlarge upon this brief description. Their lives may be ascertained from the other royal histories of Tibet.[571]

This completes the general description of the first illumination of Tibet by the lamp of the Conqueror's teaching, the third part of this book, *Thunder from the Great Conquering Battle-Drum of Devendra*, which is a history of the precious doctrine of the vehicle of indestructible reality according to the Ancient Translation School.

Part Four
The Development of the Three Inner Classes of Tantra in Tibet

Introduction

[179.1-3] Now, in particular, the development [in Tibet] of the three inner classes of the tantras of the way of secret mantra will be explained.

Although the Kriyā, Caryā and Yoga tantras of secret mantra were much studied and taught in the time of the religious king Trhisong Detsen and his master, Padmasambhava, the Unsurpassed [Yoga] tantras were propagated most of all. They have three divisions: Mahāyoga, which concerns primarily the stage of creation; Anuyoga, which concerns primarily the stage of perfection; and Atiyoga, which concerns primarily the Great Perfection.[572]

1 *Mahāyoga and Anuyoga*

MAHĀYOGA, THE STAGE OF CREATION

[179.4] Mahāyoga is divided into the class of tantras (**tantravarga*) and the class of means for attainment (**sādhanavarga*).

The Mahāyoga Class of Tantras

[179.4-182.1] The master Vimalamitra expounded [the eight tantras, known collectively as] the *Eight Sections of the Magical Net*, which form the cycle of texts associated with the *Magical Net of Vajrasattva*, the *Secret Nucleus* which is the root or most general of the *Eighteen Great Tantrapiṭaka*. He expounded them to Ma Rincen-chok, and translated them with the latter's assistance. Ma Rincen-chok instructed Tsukru Rincen Zhönu and Kyere Chokyong, who both instructed Zhang Gyelwei Yönten and Tarje Pelgi Trakpa. The former taught this tantra many times in Central Tibet and in Tsang. He also went to Kham and gave this teaching. The lineages of Zhang became known as "the transmitted precepts of Chimpu", or as "the lineage of esoteric instructions".

Moreover, the master Padmasambhava taught [this *Secret Nucleus*] to Nyak Jñānakumāra, along with his own celebrated composition entitled the *Garland of Views: A Collection of Esoteric Instructions*. Jñānakumāra instructed the Sogdian Pelgi Yeshe, and, with Zhang, he instructed Nup Sangye Yeshe.[573] At Mount Kailash the master Buddhaguhya also gave instruction on texts belonging to the *Secret Nucleus* cycle, such as the *Array of the Path of the Magical Net*, to disciples such as We Jampel and Trenka Mukti.

Similarly, the glorious *Guhyasamāja* was propagated according to master Vajrahāsya's exegetical tradition [T 1909], and the tradition of study, exegesis, and attainment derived from the commentaries of Viśvamitra. Also propagated were the commentaries on the *Buddhasamāyoga* belonging to the aural lineage of Kukkurāja [the *Six Arrays of Esoteric Meaning*] and of Hūṃkara [*Elucidation of the Significance of the Four Limbs, Caturaṅgārthāloka*, T 1676], and the lineage of its teaching, study, and attainment which follow the *Great Commentary on the Buddhasamāyoga*, by the accomplished master Indranāla, a king of Oḍḍiyāna.

Other fortunate beings were granted meditational deities based on the maṇḍalas of *Heruka* and of the *Supreme Horse*. Of these, King Trhisong Detsen propitiated Hayagrīva, with the result that the neighing of a horse was heard throughout Jambudvīpa.

Namkei Nyingpo

The Mahāyoga Class of Means for Attainment

[182.1-187.1] Generally speaking, the *Yamāri* cycle was propagated in Tibet by master Śāntigarbha. Master Vimalamitra propagated the *Vajrāmṛta* cycle, teaching it to Nyak Jñānakumāra and others. Most of the other cycles were propagated and disseminated solely by master Padmasambhava.

In particular, at Tregugeu, in glorious Chimpu, the great master answered the prayer of King Trhisong Detsen by granting complete empowerments in the outer, inner, and secret maṇḍalas of the Eight Great Classes of the Means for Attainment to a most fortunate group of eight, consisting of the king and his subjects. When they had practised the means for attainment and esoteric instructions for the deities on whom their flowers respectively alighted, each of them saw his or her deity in a vision.[574]

By propitiating Mahottara [Chemcok] Heruka, the king developed special contemplation; and owing to the development of discriminative awareness which is born of meditation, he composed works such as the *Treatise on the Proof of Authentic Transmitted Precepts* (*bka' yang-dag-pa'i tshad-ma'i bstan-bcos*, T 4352).[575]

By propitiating [glorious] Yangdak Heruka, Namkei Nyingpo ascended on the rays of the sun.

By propitiating Mañjuśrī [Yamāntaka], Sangye Yeshe drove a kīla into solid rock.

By propitiating Maheśvara [Hayagrīva], the head of a horse emerged from the crown of Gyelwa Choyang's head, and neighing resounded.

By propitiating Vajrakīla, Kharcen-za [Yeshe Tshogyel] could resurrect the dead.

By propitiating Mātaraḥ, Pelgi Yeshe employed the host of female protectors as servants.

By propitiating Mundane Praise, Pelgi Senge was served by the eightfold groups of spirits.

And by propitiating Malign Mantra, Vairocana acquired the eye of pristine cognition, and miraculous powers.

Moreover, regarding those disciples of master Padmasambhava who obtained accomplishment sooner or later by his empowerment, instructions and further advice: Nyak Jñānakumāra could extract nectar from dry rock.

Gyelmo Yudra Nyingpo could transform his body into a golden vajra.

Nanam Dorje Düjom could pass through a mountain of solid rock.

Master Yesheyang could actually travel to the realms of sky-farers.[576]

The Sogdian Lhapel could seize savage beasts of prey by the neck [with his bare hands].[577]

Nanam Zhang Yeshe De could fly like a bird in the sky.

Kharcen Pelgi Wangcuk, by merely brandishing his kīla, could "liberate" those at whom he brandished it.

Denma Tsemang obtained retention of all doctrines, such that he forgot none.

Kawa Peltsek intuited the minds of others without obstruction.

Shüpu Pelgi Senge could reverse the flow of a river.

Dre Gyelwei Lodrö could transform a zombie into gold.[578]

Drokben Khyeucung Lotsāwa could summon birds in the sky, merely through his gaze and a gesture of menace.

Odren Pelgi Wangcuk could swim like a fish in a wide river.

Ma Rincen-chok could crush and digest boulders as food.

Gyelwa Choyang

Lhalung Pelgi Dorje could pass unobstructedly through mountains of solid rock.

Langdro Köncok Jungne could hurl mighty thunderbolts like arrows.

And Lasum Gyelwa Cangcup could sit cross-legged in the sky, without any support.

There were also women who were accomplished masters: Mandāravā of Sahor obtained immortality, miraculous powers, and unsurpassed, supreme accomplishment.

Kharcen Yeshe Tshogyel achieved indestructible life, infallible recollection, miraculous powers, the abode of the sky-farers, and the supreme accomplishment of great bliss. The two noble ladies just mentioned were actually no different from Vajravarāhī, herself.

Tshenamza Sangyetsho vanished in a body of light.

Shekar Dorjetsho crossed rivers as if they were plains.

Tshombuza Pematsho's vital energy and mind matured into the body of her deity.[579]

Melgongza Rincentsho hung her silk gown on the rays of the sun.

Rüza Töndrupma used her gaze to employ the services of the twelve goddesses of the earth.

Shübuza Sherapma knew all the transmitted precepts of the buddhas, as well as the commentarial treatises, without having studied them.

While Yamdrokza Chöki Drönma taught the scriptures she was applauded by celestial deities.

When Oceza Kargyelma had a question about the doctrine she asked her meditational deity.

When Dzemza Lhamo needed food or drink she took them from the sky.

Barza Lhayang knew how to tame the minds of others.

Cokroza Cangcupmen could transform her body into fire and water.

Dromza Pamti Chenmo could fly like a bird in the sky.

Rongmenza Tshültrim-drön could ingest stones like food.

Khuza Peltsünma could cause the ritual kīla to vibrate.

Trhumza Shelmen could arrange flowers in the sky.

These and others were able to display various miracles to many people, and all of them attained the state of coalescence in their [human] bodies.[580] So it was that countless accomplished masters emerged: the twenty-five great accomplished masters of Chimpu; the fifty-five realised ones of Yangdzong; the [two groups of] one hundred and eight who attained the body of light at Yerpa and at Chuwori, respectively; the thirty mantra adepts of Sheldrak; the twenty-five ḍākinīs who attained bodies of light; et cetera.[581]

ANUYOGA, THE STAGE OF PERFECTION

[187.1-187.2] Dharmabodhi and Vasudhara, who were preceptors of the *Sūtra which Gathers All Intentions*, and the master Chetsenkye of Bru-sha instructed Nupcen Sangye Yeshe; and he brought the Anuyoga tantras to Tibet. This will be described later in detail.[582]

2 *The Mental and Spatial Classes of Atiyoga*

[187.3] Atiyoga is divided into three classes: [Mental, Spatial, and Esoteric Instructional]. The lineage of the first two is as follows:

VAIROCANA

[187.3-190.4] Scorning more than fifty-seven unbearable hardships, including the eight great fears, the master Vairocana, a native of Nyemo Cekar, journeyed to India, following the command of King Trhisong Detsen. He proceeded towards the Great Nine-Storey Pagoda (*ke'u-tshang chen-po dgu-brtsegs*), created by the miraculous power of master Śrī Siṃha in the cooling sandalwood forest of Dhanakośa. There, he introduced himself to a yoginī who was carrying water; but when she made no response he made her waterpot stick to the ground by means of his gaze. The yoginī then exposed her breast and in so doing revealed to Vairocana the Maṇḍala of the Indestructible Expanse.

In company with her he met the master Śrī Siṃha and, offering to him a golden maṇḍala, he requested teaching on the effortless vehicle.[583]

Śrī Siṃha said he would have to consider. The main points of the profound doctrine could be revealed in the morning, under the cloak of secrecy. But, without utmost secrecy, the master would run the risk of capital punishment, imposed by the local rājā. So he said to Vairocana, "Study the doctrine of cause and effect with other scholars during the day. I will have to reveal the doctrines of the esoteric instructions to you at night." In this way, and under these circumstances, others were kept ignorant.

During the night the master wrote down the *Eighteen Esoteric Instructions of the Mental Class* on white silk with the milk of a white goat; and he showed Vairocana how the letters became clear when fumigated by smoke. He made him swear an oath before the protectors of the teaching to maintain the utmost secrecy.

But even then Vairocana was not satisfied; so he remained there. Śrī Siṃha granted him all the empowerments and esoteric instructions of sixty tantrapiṭaka, along with the three branches of the Spatial Class – White, Black, and Variegated – which reveal that the goal is already naturally present.[584] Thus, Vairocana plumbed the very depths of all doctrines.

Still he remained unsatisfied. Śrī Siṃha said to him:

> The expanse of reality is infinite,
> But if you realise solely just what is,
> Everything is perfectly present in that
>   which lacks none.
> What accomplishment goes beyond that?

Vairocana

Then the master taught him the three ways to bring forth the fruit of the instructions, the four cases when the teaching should be granted, and the four cases when it should not.

Vairocana also met the master Garap Dorje in the great charnel ground of Dhūmasthira. He obtained the true lineage of the six million four hundred thousand verses on the Great Perfection and actually attained the great accomplishment of simultaneous realisation and liberation.

Relying on the accomplishment of swift-footedness Vairocana then returned to Tibet.[585] During the day he gave teaching to the king on the ordinary doctrines of cause and effect, but at night he taught only the hidden doctrines of the Great Perfection. He translated the five texts of the Mental Class which were the earliest translated.[586]

It was at this time that Vairocana was slandered by the Indians, who were jealous that the instructions had been lost to Tibet. And because one of the queens and her ministers became ill-disposed to the doctrine, master Vairocana was obliged to pass some time [in exile] in Tshawarong.[587] In the temple of the protector at Rongtrak in Gyelmorong, he accepted Yudra Nyingpo as his disciple, and caused him and others to be matured [by the empowerments] and liberated [by the instructions]. In the Taktse Castle at Tsharong, he taught the cycle of the Great Perfection to Sangtön Yeshe Lama. At Trakmar Göndzong in Tongkungrong he instructed Pang-gen Sangye Gönpo. And in Central Tibet Vairocana gave teaching to Nyak Jñānakumāra and to the Khotanese lady, Sherap Drönma. Thus, he is said to have taught five people in succession. The last mentioned also invited him to visit Khotan.

In the end, Vairocana attained the buddha-body of coalescence in Bhasing Forest in Nepal.

Gradually, one lineage developed from Nyak Jñānakumāra, which passed through the Sogdian Pelgi Yeshe, Tra Pelgi Nyingpo, and Lhalung Pelgi Dorje to Odren Pelgi Zhönu. One issued from the Sogdian Pelgi Senge to Nupcen Sangye Yeshe; and yet another from Tsang Śākdor, through P̂ang Rakṣita, Yatri Tarma Sherap, and Zermo Gelong to Marpa Sherap-ö. That lineage was subsequently transmitted to Zur Dropukpa.[588]

PANG-GEN SANGYE GÖNPO

[190.4-191.1] Moreover, there was the lineage of Vairocana's disciple Pang-gen Sangye Gönpo, in which everyone achieved the rainbow body. Pang Gönpo himself reached the age of eighty-five without having practised the doctrine during his youth. As an old man he was despised by his brothers and relatives. Owing to great age his body had a decrepit posture, but Vairocana gave him a meditation belt and a support [to prop up his chin], and showed him how to retain the teaching in his mind. By practising according to the transmission of master Vairocana he came face to face with naked reality, and an all-surpassing realisation was born within him. Becoming very joyful, the old man embraced his master about the neck and would not let go for a whole day. After attaining accomplishment he lived for over one hundred years more.

Pang-gen Sangye Gönpo

NGENLAM CANGCUP GYELTSEN, ZADAM RINCEN-YIK AND KHUGYUR SELWEICHOK

[191.1-192.2] Pang-gen Sangye Gönpo's disciple was Ngenlam Cangcup Gyeltsen, a monk from the three-valley district of Ngenlam in Uru. At the age of sixty-seven he went to Gyelmo Taktse Castle, where he requested instructions from Pang Mipham Gönpo [Pang-gen Sangye Gönpo]. The master granted them to him and told him not to go home, but to practise meditation at Wa Senge Trak. He went there obediently and meditated until his body vanished without a trace at the age of one hundred and seventy-two.

His disciple, Zadam Rincen-yik, came from upper Dokam. He requested instruction from Ngenlam and then sat absorbed in meditation, without leaving his guru, in the same rock cavern. His body vanished without a trace at the age of one hundred and forty-four.

Zadam Rincen-yik's disciple, Khugyur Selweichok from Yarlung Chö, was a monk of fifty-seven years. When he received instruction from Zadam Rincen he abandoned the idea of returning home and remained in meditation at Wa Senge Trak as well. His body vanished without a trace when he was in his one hundred and seventeenth year.

In this way, the bodies of the three masters and disciples vanished in the Wa Senge Cavern during the same year of the snake, one after the other, like mists, or rainbows, fading away.

NYANG CANGUP-TRA AND NYANG SHERAP JUNGNE

[192.2-193.2] Cangcup-tra, the disciple of the last mentioned, was a monk of forty-two years from upper Yudruk in Nyang. After requesting instruction from Khugyur Selwa he returned home. While practising meditation at Samye Chimpu he met an aged monk from Zha, in Uru, who was called Nyang Sherap Jungne, and who said, "I have been fully ordained for longer than you, but your teaching is greater. Please accept me as a disciple."

Nyang Cangcup-tra gave him instructions and then went to stay at Phukpoche, and at Yangdzong, where he revealed his power to transform the four elements to his disciple and grand-disciple. Finally, at Phungpo Riwoche, in Gyamnyeduka in Tsang, his body vanished without a trace, like a cloud disintegrating on a mountainside.

After that, Nyang Sherap Jungne lived in the glorious forest of Chimpu, at Yangdzong in Dra, and at Phukpoche. He experienced the naturally manifest, unbiased intention of the Great Perfection, and, after hanging his robe, rosary, and skull-cup on a juniper tree on the summit of Lhari in Phukpoche, his body vanished in the sky, just like a brilliant rainbow.

BAGOM

[193.2-195.6] Sherap Jungne's disciple was a native of Lomo, who became renowned as master Bagom, the meditator of Ba, after the name of his clan. While he was living at home a war broke out. His mother said, "This boy is my only son, and the brother of six sisters. I will entrust him to the master Sherap Jungne, and shall be content if he does not die." Therefore, in his sixteenth year he was entrusted to Nyang Sherap Jungne.

At that time, the aforementioned Nyang Cangcup Trakpa passed through Phukpoche, Yangdzong, and Chimpu, leading a stag. For this, he became famed as Nyang Shawacen, "Nyang with the Stag". On his next visit to Phukpoche, Nyang Cangcup said, "Look! I will put on a show for you both."

As master Sherap Jungne and Bagom looked on from the left and the right, the master, who was between them, became invisible. As their astonishment grew, he changed into a whirlwind one cubit high, which, after spinning to and fro, turned into a fire. The fire then turned into a bronze bowl for water offerings, filled to the point of overflowing. Then, in a fury, it turned abruptly into the master himself. When he had thus revealed his power over the activity field in which the four elements are overcome, he said, "From the time when the impurities of the elements are removed, and until their pure essences vanish, this may occur. Though one may perceive, through discriminative awareness, the significance of there being no basis for meditation, it is by adhering without distraction to symbolic content that one obtains such independence without difficulty. Therefore, it is most important to remain undistracted."

Once when Bagom went to gather wood in the forest of Pelbu, he saw the red glow of a fire around their thatched cottage; but the master had not lit a fire. Thinking the house was ablaze, Bagom went to investigate, but the thatched cottage appeared as before without a sign of fire. When he asked him what had happened, the master replied, "I became absorbed in the contemplation of fire. Do you not remember my guru, Nyang Cangcup-tra?" And, on another occasion, Bagom saw that his teacher's seat was covered with water.

Finally, the master said, "If I disappear, look at the summit of Lhari." But when the master did disappear Bagom thought that he had gone to the mountain for recreation and would return that evening. When the master failed to return Bagom went to investigate. He found his hat, his bodhiseed rosary, and so forth, hanging from a juniper tree, but Sherap Jungne's body had vanished without a trace. According to the natural Great Perfection, this is only one of the ways of death: ways resembling space, fire, sky-farers and awareness-holders are spoken of.[589]

In his twenty-fourth year Bagom had received instructions from Sherap Jungne. Bagom lived as a layman, and his proper name was Yeshe Cangcup. He possessed extraordinary realisation, whereby he could turn stone into clay and leave the imprint of his body in rock. In his ninety-eighth year he passed away without sickness. His wife, Como Kangmo, did not show the body to outsiders, but she cremated it in the household shrine. All of the people outside saw a pot-sized ball of light go off into the sky. No remains at all were left behind.

DZENG DHARMABODHI

[195.6-208.4] Bagom's disciple was Dzeng. Dzeng's mother was a nun from Thangcung in Yarlung. Her name was Tshargu Kyide. Dzeng was born from her union with the eldest son of the ruler of Thangcung. In his sixteenth year he went with a caravan of travellers to trade at Dong-na, in Töl. At Tshercung in Töl, he found a large gathering of

Dzeng Dharmabodhi

people. Going to investigate, he met Phadampa Sangye of India.[590] He followed Phadampa as a servant for fourteen months. When they reached the Zangcen district in Tsang, Phadampa gave him a blanket and, because Dzeng was very young, said, "You should return to your own country. Come and take apricots from Takpo. There is a caravan of travellers bound for Töl."

Then, while Dzeng was setting out on the journey Phadampa escorted him a little of the way. When Dzeng embraced him on the cheeks Phadampa said:

> That which is nothing at all transforms.
> In its transformations no duality is grasped.

They knocked heads together twice, and in Dzeng's astonished mind a sharp and clear understanding arose. His mouth grew moist.

So it was that he was blessed by Phadampa, who also predicted that he would encounter the *Vajra Bridge* (*rdo-rje zam-pa*, DZ Vol.1).[591] But later, he maintained that he did not understand all this at the time. Phadampa gave him some auspicious tokens and many essential points concerning the way of mantras. When he was given the instructions concerning the Six-Syllable Mantra[592] at Gyang-ro Tshelma, he obtained a great blessing by performing the practice. Then Phadampa prophetically said, "To the east of this great river lies a sandalwood forest. There lives your guru."

Afterwards, Dzeng went to Central Tibet, where he received teachings on Heruka and Pehar from Akhu Pelbar, and on Kriyātantra and the great *torma* offering of Jvālāmukhī from Nup Shangpoche. Having been sent to convey offerings to Lama Pari in Tsang, he received from him the means for attainment of Mañjuśrī and of Garuḍa. From Geshe Po he received teaching concerning the ancient translations.

In his thirty-fifth year he went to Cangtsik via Ngamshö. At the approach to the pass at Phukpoche, he heard that one Comowa had invited the spiritual benefactor Tsen Khawoche,[593] who had just returned from India, to visit and that there would be teachings, food, and entertainment. Early the next morning, when Dzeng was on his way there, a woman said to him, "If you go up on this side of the road from Trhap, you will meet a master called Bagom, who gives food most generously."

He proceeded in that direction, and a group of yogins also arrived. Bagom invited them to partake of a warm meal and gave to each a copper-ladleful of roasted barley flour as well. When he had served the group, he said, "There is also a novice among you," and sent him out to fetch a pot of water. He then performed the water offering and led Dzeng to a corner of his small cave and gave him a bowl of vegetables. The same evening he also provided him with food. Afterwards, Dzeng went to sleep at the foot of a rock.

In the morning Dzeng thought he would have to go, but Bagom again gave him food and said, "I have a young disciple who has gone to bring gold from Zotang, but owing to the heavy rain he has not returned. Gather some wood."

Dzeng brought a great bundle of wood from the forest. Bagom was delighted and gave him esoteric instructions on the symbolism of the Great Seal (*phyag-rgya chen-po brda'i man-ngag*) and the teaching called the *Seven Cycles of the Great Perfection which are Naturally Present* (*rdzogs-pa chen-po skor-bdun rang-chas*). At that time Bagom's disciple returned and said, "I thought the master would be troubled by my absence, but you have filled in. Stay for some more days." The disciple then made one more circumambulation of Yarlung and returned.

During the intervening period Dzeng had learned that Bagom was a special person. So he did not return to his own country, but went as far as Ön and Zang-ri, begging for alms. He bought a sack and then offered it, full of barley, to master Bagom. "It is enough that you serve me," said the master. "Keep this barley for your own provision. I have an esoteric instruction called the *Vajra Bridge*. By understanding its meaning in an instant one may attain buddhahood in a single lifetime, leaving no trace of the body. This has occurred in an unbroken lineage. I have mentioned it to no one until today. Now, I shall give it to you."

Dzeng earnestly offered the barley and prayed, "I have gathered it for you. Please confer the instructions upon me. I will return with new provisions."

Bagom placed his left hand on the crown of Dzeng's head and thumped him on the back with his right, saying, "Many thanks. Your commitments are strong. You deserve to benefit by my instructions."

Dzeng gave the means for the attainment of the Red Yamāri to a mantra adept from Locung, and received in return eight loads of peas and barley. Sometimes he would perform protective rites at Lomo and at Trhün, whereby he would receive sufficient provisions for the religious life. But still, he could not collect the requisites needed to request the blessing of the *Vajra Bridge*. The master said that if he were to grant the blessing just then, there would be obstacles later on.

Dzeng went to sell one pot of ale (*sir-mo*) to a friend in Kangbar and get payment for it, but instead he received a nun's robe. He divided up the woollen patches of which it was made, sold them and collected ale for offerings, *tormas*, five measures of barley, and a meat carcass. The master said that daylight would have to substitute for butter lamps, and bestowed fully on Dzeng the four empowerments of the path of liberation,[594] along with all the instructions. Even afterwards, Dzeng requested the blessing four times, and made offerings of barley and gold five times.

On one occasion Bagom said, "This world of appearances is completely false." Suddenly, he struck a blue "water-stone"[595] with his hand, whereupon his arm vanished up to the elbow. Then, with a twist, his body passed through the rock and left a distinct impression behind. In Phukcungrong he uprooted many juniper trees with his gaze, and said, "Here is the timber for building Como's shrine room." From such a master did Dzeng obtain the entire teaching of the *Vajra Bridge*.

Moreover, Dzeng obtained such teachings as those of the direct and circuitous paths of Transcendental Perfection according to the system of Atiśa.[596] Similarly, he received the *Six-limbed Yoga [of the Kālacakra]* from Yumo; the *Eight-Session Practice* (*thun-brgyad-ma*) from Khampalungpa; the *Three Cycles of the Intentional Object* (*dmigs-pa skor-gsum*) from a disciple of Neu Zurpa; the *Short Commentary* from Shongbu the translator; and Nāropā's *Path of Skilful Means* (*thabs-lam*) from the spiritual benefactor Drölgom. In return, Dzeng expounded the *Vajra Bridge*.

Dzeng also heard a great many other teachings: the *Emanation of the Lamp* (*sgron-sp[b]rul*) and the *Protective Cover* (*rgyab-sha*) from So-nyün Dang; the *Three Drops of Nectar* (*bdud-rtsi thigs-gsum*) from Dzaborwa; the *Three Verses on the Aural Lineage* (*rna-brgyud tshigs-gsum*) from Ritrö Lungcung; the esoteric instructions of the *Dohā* from Lung-ham Chenpo; the *Object of Cutting* (*gcod-yul*) from Lapdrönma, the sole mother;[597] the *Seven Cycles* (*sde-skor bdun-pa*) from Gyelwa Potön; the *Fifteen Doctrines on the Kriyātantra according to the System of Pari* (*ba-ri-pa'i kriya'i chos bco-lnga*) from Nup Shangcen; and various other teachings from Künga of Tingri.[598] He received the *Six Doctrines* (*Ṣaḍdharmopadeśa*, T 2330) and the *Yoga of Co-Emergence* (*lhan-skyes rnal-'byor*) from the physician of Takpo [Gampopa].[599]

Dzeng juxtaposed the various realisations [of the teachings he received] and became highly delighted. By practising the conduct of a mantra adept at the school of Ce-nga Neljor he became renowned as an exponent of the discipline [of the way of mantras]. His spiritual brothers included master Takshamcen, Lama Udrenpa, Lama Thü Khambar, Lama Tröjor, and Zhang Dronyön. Thus, he only associated with masters of yoga.

Dzeng went naked for five years in Tsang. Moreover, owing to his extremely great power over phenomenal appearances he left undone none of the many austerities such as bathing in icy water during the winter and in mid-stream during the summer, jumping into ravines of uncertain depth, bashing his head, and wounding himself with weapons. Therefore, he became renowned as Pawo Dzengcung, "Little Dzeng the Warrior".

When he instructed So Mangtsen on the Great Seal, the latter's delusions became pristine cognition. When he gave teaching on the Four Syllables,[600] and on the Great Perfection, to Ritrö Lungcung and Ngülmo Gyalecam, they became great destroyers of delusion; and finally their bodies vanished without a trace. In the same way, when he revealed the *Vajra Bridge* to a faithful nun and to a steadfast Khampa, their bodies vanished without traces, the nun at Lake Mönka Sermo, and the Khampa at the Lake Castle of Kongpo. They died according to the ways of space and of the sky-farers.

By merely giving instruction to Repa Gomtak, Shore, Gyare, Lungre, and others, Dzeng caused the inner heat to blaze up within them. Similarly, when he just pointed out reality, a great many of his followers gained liberation and realisation. Dzeng Dharmabodhi himself said, "About four translators have come to me, and also monks, great teachers, yogins, and yoginīs, who were arrogant, thinking only of themselves. A great many of them have correctly taken the teachings to heart. There were eleven housewives who practised a bit in Takpo. When the time of death grew near, they passed away painlessly, and rainbows enveloped their bodies. If anyone should practise these instructions of mine for five or six years, with the care of a spinner spinning wool, or of parents raising a sole surviving child, then his body will certainly vanish without a trace. He will leave no physical remains behind."

Because he had mastered an oceanic array of miraculous powers, Dzeng's body was sometimes enveloped by a rainbow. At other times he travelled without his feet touching the ground. By integrating his mind and phenomenal appearances he could travel to very distant places in just a moment. Through unimpeded, supernormal cognitive powers, such as the knowledge of other minds, he could foretell all future events. For example, being endowed with pure clairvoyance, he saw the son of Cosema Dorjekyi, who had fallen asleep, almost fall through a skylight at midnight. Since night and day were the same for Dzeng, he easily saw, even at night, a needle that had fallen into a pile of chaff.

Later on, after Dzeng had lived in Tsang for seven years, he returned to Phukpoche. Master Bagom said to him, "Comprehend fully [the implications of] space! When you realise fully that it has no basis, the great nail of non-meditation will have struck home!"

Thus, Dzeng developed profound certainty.

While residing at Takpo Zhu he received the instructions of the *Seven Cycles of the Peaceful Guru (gu-ru zhi-ba sde-skor bdun-pa)* from Lama Zheldam. By practising the *Four Symbols (brda-bzhi)*[601] for three years at Lhazur Monastery, he mastered all doctrines. His mind became as simple as space.

Again, Dzeng could endure great austerities: He practised the austerity of the deathless nectar[602] after he had received the *Vajra Bridge* at Phukpoche, owing to which he became immune to disease.

After performing the austerity of serving the guru Nup Shangpoche, that guru protected his mind wherever he went.

By the austerity of learning, under Phadampa Sangye of India, to examine [reality] critically, he mastered all things.

By practising the austerities of the Vajrakīla recitation at Kyikung, he was obeyed by mundane gods and demons.

From Atiśa's Kadampa school he learned the austerity of humility, owing to which people loved him wherever he went.

By performing the austerity of the "three movements with reference to the Four Syllables"[603] the inner heat blazed within him and he went naked for five years.

Having thus developed certainty he practised the austerity of propitiating Vajravarāhī, whereby he saw the venerable goddess in a vision to the west of Gurmo; and from her he received many symbols.

By following the discipline of the dream yoga in Nup Yülrong, he realised that all appearances are like dreams.

In the Crystal Cave of Zhotö Tidro, Dzeng had a vision of the wrathful Amṛtakuṇḍalin. A spiritual being served him with great veneration. Once he saw a venerable monk flying to and fro in the sky, but after making search could not find him. Dzeng said that he did not know whether it was a man or spirit.

At Zhu, in Takpo, he propitiated Aparājita (*A-dzi*), and had a vision during the morning. Then, while he was thinking of exchanging vows [with the deity], his consort Chale came in. The deity exclaimed, "He's married!" and vanished in a flash of light.

When Dzeng practised alchemy in Lhazur he had a vision of Amitāyus. The definitive order of many doctrines arose in his mind.

When Dzeng practised at Ökar Rock he had a vision of Cakrasaṃvara with consort.

Once, when he had decided to travel, Dzeng came to the town of Möngar. He boldly jumped onto a frozen pond, but the ice cracked and he fell into the water. When he felt ashamed, steam rose from the water and almost clouded the sky. The people said in astonishment that he resembled a red-hot iron image[604] entering the water in the bitter cold of winter. Dzeng merely said, "I was frozen!"

Then, on another occasion, Dzeng and his consort went to gather wood, and obtained a heavy bundle. Carrying it they reached the edge of a sheer precipice. Dzeng thought it was like a dream. He jumped and floated down like a bird. His consort exclaimed, "O extraordinary guru! are you human or not? You remind me of Phadampa Sangye!"

Until that time, Dzeng had not propagated the instructions much. He acted as a village priest and preserved his own practice in secret. But thereafter his disciples increased, as many came from afar.

Once, when he was invited by one Pelbudor, and gave instruction, many rainbow canopies and patterns appeared at the first moment of sunrise. When he finished his discourse he went up to the mountainside for recreation. Someone asked whether the rainbow was the unhappy portent of his death, but he replied, "At the very time my guru Bagom gave these instructions to the spiritual brothers Bartön and Sherap-tra, the valleys of Ngamshö and the slopes of Phukpoche were almost filled with light. The sign accompanies these instructions."

Again, while the guru was living at Dzeng his disciple Co-se arrived. Dzeng was sitting at an embankment beneath the base of a stūpa, so when Co-se reached the hermitage he could not see the master. But he did see an orb of light [at the stūpa]. When he drew near the light vanished. "How did this happen?" asked Co-se. Dzeng told him that it was a sign of meditative absorption, which he should not divulge to anyone.

Furthermore, Dzeng used to say, "When brother Ngödrup had leprosy, I tried to help him by reciting mantras, but the leprosy was not cured. Instead, *I* had a vision of Vajrapāṇi.[605] What a joke!"

Dzeng the meditator, [whose proper name was] Dharmabodhi, had fully mastered all the real goals of such instructions as the *Common Savour* (*ro-snyoms*), *Six Doctrines*, *Object of Cutting*, and *Five Stages*, which are renowned in the other traditions of the doctrine. When he was an old man, in his one hundred and second year, he fell ill and his followers feared their guru would pass away. But he said, "Last night I had an auspicious dream. I will not die. I dreamt that I was on the summit of Gyelpori, when the sun and moon rose together. On the roofs of many huts made of bone there were many women who said, 'Lama Dzeng! come after four years.'"

Then, on another occasion, Dzeng said, "I have reached old age; and certainly I have nothing to teach." This signified that he had inwardly reached the end of his intentions, because he was no longer attached to his own discursive thoughts. Then, when his followers requested that he perform acts of merit [to extend his life], he took no interest in conditioned merits. They then asked him to practise alchemy, but he said, "If I practise alchemy I can prolong my life for about ten years, but there is no need for longevity in bad times."

In this way, having encouraged others to practise true renunciation, Dzeng passed away. During his cremation the sky was filled with rainbows. Many relics[606] and stūpas were discovered [among his ashes]. Because he had continued to protect his disciples, his impure body did not dissolve into the rainbow body; but, in fact, he fulfilled all the signs of having passed into nirvāṇa on the primordially pure level which is beyond all phenomena.

It was from this time on that the aural lineage of the *Vajra Bridge* became widely propagated. Dzeng had a great many disciples: master Künzang, Dzeng Co-se, Tsentangpa Nyang Dharmasiṃha, master Serlungpa, Lama Tu Dorje Gyeltsen, Zik Yeshepo, and Yaktön Dawa Özer, to name just a few. And Dzeng passed away when he had reached the age of one hundred and seventeen. He was a contemporary, more or less, of masters such as Atiśa, Dromtön, Chapa Chöki Senge,[607] the venerable Milarepa, and their masters and disciples.

DZENG CO-SE

[208.5-210.3] Dzeng Co-se was born into the family of a mantra adept. During his childhood he studied writing and arithmetic. He requested Nyingma teachings, such as the *Magical Net* as well as [teachings of the new translation schools such as] the *Hevajra Tantra* and the *Litany of the Names of Mañjuśrī*, from an artist of Ölka. When his master, the artist, was about to die, he declared, "Though I know all these great texts, now, as I am about to die, nothing has been at all beneficial, except the *Seven Sessions of Aro* (*a-ro thun-bdun*, DZ Vol.1).[608] You should apply yourself to the instructions, without studying texts. Your guru is called Dzeng. He lives in Takpo. Go there."

Then, in Kangbar, Co-se passed three summers and three winters at the centre of master Zam, who was learned in the spontaneous presence of the Great Perfection; but they did not form a spiritual rapport. Without having first cut through his elaborate conceptions of the instructions, Co-se thrice requested teaching on the *Vajra Bridge* from master Dzeng in Pelung. Dzeng gave his blessing and said, "Go to Tsang for some time and study the texts. When you return from Tsang, stay at your ancestral hermitage."

Co-se realised that Dzeng would not give him the instructions. He asked who else knew them and was told, "There is one called Co-se Zhanglakyap of Traci who knows them." While he was thinking of requesting them from him, that guru passed away; so again Co-se went to Takpo and requested them from Dzeng, who again refused. Co-se then thought of asking one of Dzeng's disciples, and went to meet master Tu in Shokyam, who said, "This teaching will not come to you by such artificial hopes. Go back to Takpo and ask Dzeng."

Once more he went to Takpo and made his request. Dzeng said, "If you want the instruction above all else, you must persevere." And he gave him the complete instructions.

Co-se then stayed with the master for a number of summers and winters. During the course of six years he received even the most minor aspects of the teaching. He also acted as the master of ceremonies during the conferral of blessings [to others]. When about fifty disciples, including Rokpoga, the lama of Thöpa, and Majo Dowa, requested the *Vajra Bridge*, Dzeng said, "Let Co-se explain it! You others listen!" Co-se delivered the teaching from the master's own seat.

These two masters, Dzeng and Co-se, were associated over a period of about eighteen years. Co-se was appointed to be the lineage-holder, having received the transmitted instructions.

MASTER KÜNZANG AND TRÜLKU ÖBAR SENGE

[210.3-211.4] Similarly, the master Künzang was a disciple of both Dzeng Dharmabodhi, and of "mad" Co-se, the younger Dzeng. Künzang's father, Khuwo Phajo, was a brilliant meditator, who had been a disciple of the Central Tibetan, Phakmotrupa.[609] His mother, Ziza Tecok, used to listen to the doctrine from the ascetic woman "mad" Samdrup. Künzang's birth was augured by auspicious dreams. At the age of eight or nine he studied a little under the master Kortön Radza. When he was fifteen his master passed away and he received teaching on *Pacification* (*zhi-byed*) from master Tuwa over the next five years. During that period he served the master to the best of his ability. When he met master Tuwa at Serlung Monastery he dreamt that two stars were absorbed into the full moon. He requested the *Vajra Bridge* from the elder Dzeng once. Then, when Dzeng Co-se was invited to Pungring he requested the *Vajra Bridge* seven times. He went to Takpo for four winters and obtained the *Vajra Bridge* thirteen and a half times. He stayed with Co-se for eight years and received the *Vajra Bridge* seven more times. Afterwards, he received it twice in Sho, once in

Serlung, and also received parts of the teaching as it was being given to others. Altogether he obtained the *Vajra Bridge* thirty-five times from the two Dzengs, elder and younger. Künzang became the successor to the lineage of their transmitted instructions and also wrote two exegetical treatises, long and short.

Master Künzang had a son called Trülku Öbar Senge, who was endowed with intelligence and perfect discrimination. At the age of fourteen he was taught the *Vajra Bridge*. He transmitted it to the lineage-holder Cogön; and the latter transmitted it to Carme Tshülrin.

OTHER LINEAGES STEMMING FROM DZENG

[211.4-213.5] Dzeng also taught the *Vajra Bridge* to Nyang Dharmasiṃha of Tsentang in Yarlung, who received the blessing and developed all-surpassing realisation. He stayed at Turtrö Monastery and performed extensive acts of service to the world. Finally, he passed away in his seventy-seventh year. There is also an exegetical treatise according to his lineage. His disciple was Vajrapāṇi, and the latter's was Lama Lha.

Again, Dzeng taught Serlungpa. Serlungpa's disciple was the master Rangdröl, who gave the teaching to his son Chörin.

Dzeng also taught Tu Dorje Gyeltsen, who gave the teaching to Tutön Tepa Tsöndrü. There is also an exegetical treatise composed by one of his disciples.

Dzeng gave teaching to Zik Yeshe Wangpo, as well. He transmitted it to Khenpo Lhakawa; he to master Gönkyap; he to master Goriwa, who taught Sotön. And there is an exegetical treatise composed by Sotön.

Dzeng also taught Yaktön Dawa Özer of Pung-ring. He transmitted the teaching to Loktön Gendünkyap, from whose lineage there also originated an exegetical treatise. This Yaktön of Pung-ring lived for almost one hundred years. He also passed the teaching to Laru Pende of upper Önak, and it was duly propagated.

Finally, Dzeng gave teaching as well to Kyetse Yeshe Wangcuk. He passed it down to Zik Yeshe Wangpo; he to the great preceptor Ngurpa; he to Tutön Vajreśvara; he to the great preceptor Sonam Gyeltsen; he to the great preceptor Zhönu Sherap; he to the master Zhönu Trakpa; he to the great preceptor Sangye Zangpo; he to Lama Tsöndrü Wangcuk; he to Thazhi Trakpa Rincen; and he to master Śākya Gyelpo. When the latter was young he was ordained as a novice at Trhaplakha; and eventually he received the complete ordination. He became learned in the *Treasury of the Abhidharma* and the Vinaya, and became a scholar at the college of Kyorlung. His spiritual resolve steadily increased. In old age he grew blind, but continued to teach by explaining the texts after they had been read by another, so great was his enlightened aspiration. When he passed away at the age of almost one hundred years, numberless relics were recovered from his heart.

Śākya Gyelpo taught [the *Vajra Bridge*] to Gölo Zhönupel,[610] who gave [this and other teachings] to Ce-nga Chöki Trakpa; he to Chöki Lodrö of Sheldrak; he to Khyungtsangwa Lodrö Pelden; he to Pangtön Karma Gurupa; he to Pangtön Chöwang Lhündrup; he to Chöwang Künzang; he to Pangtön Künzang Chögyel. The latter gave these teachings to Rikdzin Terdak Lingpa.[611]

3 *The Esoteric Instructional Class of Atiyoga, the Innermost Spirituality*

[213.5] In the teaching of the Innermost Spirituality, which is most profound, and which belongs to the Esoteric Instructional Class, there are two traditions: that of the transmitted precepts of the great master Padmasambhava and that of the transmitted precepts of master Vimalamitra.

THE TRADITION OF PADMASAMBHAVA

[213.6-215.2] In general, since Orgyen [Padmasambhava], the Second Buddha, embodies the whole ocean of teachers who are endowed with the three buddha-bodies, he does not require an unbroken lineage; for his own characteristics are no different from those of the realms of the three bodies, which include both the realms themselves and the buddhas who inhabit them. None the less, he overtly received the succession of the transmitted precepts from Śrī Siṃha, Mañjuśrīmitra and so on, in order to guide others by his example.

In Tibet, after Vimalamitra had propagated the Innermost Spirituality which belongs to the Esoteric Instructional Class, and Vairocana had propagated the Mental Class, Padmasambhava taught [his own Innermost Spirituality] secretly to Khandro Yeshe Tshogyel at Zhotö Tidro, with the intention of greatly serving living creatures at a future time, when the other traditions would be confused and divorced from the essential instructions.

Then, the princess Pemasel, daughter of the royal consort Cangcupmen of the Drom family, died at the age of eight. Her father the king grew weary in sorrow.[612] To dispel his bereavement Padmasambhava wrote the syllable NṚ[613] on Pemasel's breast in vermillion – this took place at Chimpu – and he caught hold of her consciousness with the sharp hook of his contemplation. When she could again open her eyes and speak, he gave her the esoteric instructions of the *Innermost Spirituality of the Ḍākinī* (*man-ngag mkha'-'gro'i snying-tig*, NYZ Vols.2-3) by means of his power to transfer blessings directly; and he empowered her to reveal this doctrine in a future birth. Then he concealed it as a profound treasure. It is this teaching that was later revealed by Pema Lendreltsel,[614] and is known as the *Khandro Nyingtik*, the *Innermost Spirituality of the Ḍākinī*.

Longcenpa, the all-knowing lord of the doctrine, became the successor to this profound doctrine. A brief description of his life will follow. Moreover, most of the treasures [of Padmasambhava], which contain cycles for the attainment of the three roots, include esoteric instructions in which the fundamental points of the Innermost Spirituality are presented fully, without error.

THE TRADITION OF VIMALAMITRA

Vimalamitra

[215.3-216.3] When King [Trhisong Detsen] established the teaching in Tibet, Vimalamitra was nearly two hundred years old. At that time, there was one named Nyang Tingdzin Zangpo, who could sit without moving for seven years in one continuous session of contemplation and see the four continents all at once with his naked eye. He made a prediction and, at his insistence, the king sent the translators Kawa Peltsek and Cokro Lüi Gyeltsen along with gifts of gold to invite Vimalamitra to Tibet. Vimala saw that the time was ripe for conversion and set out with them. At this point, jealous Indians created discord, so he had to induce faith in the sceptical Tibetans by his amazing miraculous powers. He translated texts concerning the doctrines of cause and effect in general; and, with the help of the translator Yudra Nyingpo, he translated, in particular, the thirteen texts of the Mental Class that are known as the "later translations".[615] He gave teaching on the most profound esoteric instructions, those of the Innermost Spirituality, to the king and to Nyang Tingdzin Zangpo in secret, but seeing no other worthy recipients, he translated and concealed the books at Gegong in Chimpu. After passing thirteen years in Tibet, master Vimalamitra set out for Wu-t'ai-shan[616] in China. He promised to remain alive in that very body for as long as the teaching of the Sage endures, and to elucidate the teaching of the Innermost Spirituality by appearing once every century as an emanation in the land of Tibet.

Nyang Tingdzin Zangpo

[216.3-216.5] Fifty-five years after Vimalamitra went to China, Nyang Tingdzin Zangpo became one who had exhausted the corruptions. When [the deity] Dorje Lekpa devastated Kham with a hailstorm, he offered to Nyang the one hundred camel-loads of barley [he had received

Nyang Tingdzin Zangpo

for it], on the basis of which Nyang built the Zha Temple in Uru.[617] He concealed the books which contained the instructions in the entrance pillar of the three-tiered portico of the temple; and he gave the teachings of the aural lineage to Dro Rincen Barwa. Finally, in the Trak Lhalu Cave at Lhasa, Nyang Tingdzin Zangpo vanished in the rainbow body.

Dangma Lhündrup Gyeltsen

[216.5-218.1] Eight years after the great priest Nyang had dissolved into light, and in the time of Nyangmi Tarma, Uru Zhölma Gecok had a son, called the elder, Dangma Lhündrup Gyeltsen. He was known to be the emanation of Vimalamitra himself, but to the ignorant he appeared as an ordinary elder.[618] Following a prophecy he received from Dorje Lekpa, he discovered the treasures which had formerly been concealed. He also received the verbal lineage from We Lodrö, and then cultivated the experience of reality, without leaving [the teaching] to be merely academic. Fifteen years after obtaining the esoteric instructions he went in search of a worthy recipient, to whom to entrust the exegetical lineage. Then, in upper Nyang he found one Cetsün Senge Wangcuk, and conferred on him the instructions in seven stages.

Dangma Lhündrup Gyeltsen

He also entrusted them to Kharak Gomcung, who lived nearby; and through them the latter, too, attained liberation.[619]

Dangma told Cetsün to copy the books accurately and to take them away during the month of Uttaraphalgunī.[620] Later, when Cetsün was returning with a great many presents, he met Nyang Kadampa of Meldro at Nyetang. Nyang Kadampa informed him that Dangma had passed away. Therefore, Cetsün offered the presents to the monastic community in that place. Nyang, moreover, said to him, "Before, no one knew that Dangma was a remarkable person, and not just an ordinary elder. But when he passed away the sky was filled with rainbows. The remains and relics were innumerable. Everyone present became astonished and regretful. But you appear to have his special instructions, because you were bringing all these presents. Please bestow them upon me." Nyang Kadampa was given the instructions he requested. Then, by meditating for two years at Tidro Rock in Zho, his body vanished without a trace.

Cetsün Senge Wangcuk

[218.1-219.4] The great Cetsün was the son of Ce Thupei Wangpo of Nyangro Nyentso. From his youth he became conversant with many

Cetsün Senge Wangcuk

teachings. He met Dangma the elder in the valley of Rizar Göpo. When Dangma gave the instructions to Kharak [Gomcung], he obtained them all. After the death of his master, Cetsün concealed the books found in the ancient treasures as three separate treasures – one at the foot of the spring at Langdro Chepa Takdra, another at Uyuk, and the third in the upper valley of Cel. He traversed the mountain ranges from Uyuk to Shang practising meditation, at which time an *ācārya* appeared to him in a dream saying:

> O fortunate one! I am the learned Vimalamitra.
> If that which you seek is innermost quintessence,
> On the upper slope of Trakmar Gegong in Chimpu
> there is
> The heart-like, secret Innermost Spirituality.
> Take it and meditate for seven years,
> Not seen by anyone, at Oyuk Chigong.
> The corrupted body will then disappear.

On hearing these words Cetsün went to Chimpu, where a woman with teeth of conch and eyebrows of turquoise gave him the books.

Then, when he sat in meditation in a clay enclosure at Oyuk Chigong, Vimalamitra actually appeared and gave him the complete empowerment, guidance, and instructions in a fortnight. Then master Vimala returned to China.

After meditating for seven years Cetsün attained freedom from any trace of corporeality. He gave the complete instructions to Trülku Zhangtön and, at the age of one hundred and twenty-five, vanished in the sky in a mass of rainbow light. In the thirtieth year after Cetsün had concealed the treasures, Rongnangda Cegom Nakpo discovered some, which he practised himself and taught to many others. Similarly, Shangparepa is also known to have found those concealed at Langdro Chepa Takdra, and to have propagated them widely.

Zhangtön

[219.4-222.2] Zhangtön was born in Yamdrok Tonang in 1097 (fire female ox year). He was named Trashi Dorje. In his eleventh year he asked Lama Cegom for many teachings. From then until he was twenty-one he served many learned and accomplished gurus. By studying the

Zhangtön

Dorje Lekpa

Tripiṭaka and all the tantras, of both the ancient and new translation schools, the lotus of his discriminative awareness blossomed. While living at Khüyül in upper Nyang he had a vision of his guru, the Great Compassionate One, Tārā, and others, all in the sky; and he received prophecies from them.

Once he was guided by Dorje Lekpa, who appeared to him as a white man wearing a white hat and said, "Come with me to find accomplishment." Since there were many attendants of that deity in Patsap in lower Nyang, who provided him with food and drink, he thought that that might have been the accomplishment referred to. But the white man said to him, "Come on to another place for accomplishment," and guided him along the path with his light.

They slept that night in an empty house. But when told that it was a dangerous place they moved to a cave. At that moment the empty house collapsed.

The emanation of Dorje Lekpa also provided Zhangtön with food and drink. When they reached the Oyuk river-basin, a great battle was in progress, but Dorje Lekpa arranged it so that he was invisible to the armies. Then, when they reached the peak of a lion-shaped rock,

Dorje Lekpa disappeared. Zhangtön thought of returning, but there was no way of escape. While looking hesitantly around he discerned the grass-covered entrance of a cave facing north [or: which revealed the inventory of the treasures].[621] On exploring it he at first found many snakes and frogs. Then, when he had found the inventory, the white man came out with a lamp. For a moment Zhangtön heard a harsh piercing sound. When Dorje Lekpa explained that it was the voice of his sister, Ekajaṭī, she herself appeared, fearful to behold with her single eye boiling with blood, and her gnashing fangs. "She has given an oracle that you must undertake one hundred and eight feast offerings, and not teach anyone for three years." Zhangtön arranged for the one hundred and eight offerings by selling two turquoise stones which he found in the grass door of the cave.

In his twenty-fifth year Zhangtön journeyed to Central Tibet. At Chimpu he rediscovered the doctrinal treasures of Vimalamitra, after meeting the latter in person and in visions, and receiving his consent. Then, while returning to Shang Tanak he met the great Cetsün at Zamka, and received from him the complete instructions on the secret Innermost Spirituality.

When Zhangtön was older he had a son, Nyibum, to succeed him as the lineage-holder. Zhangtön used to say that if he had not maintained an assembly of disciples his body would have vanished without a trace. Since he had mastered the aspect of enlightenment known as physical refinement,[622] he sometimes appeared in the form of the Conquerors of the Five Families, and his body never cast a shadow. When he gave teaching on the doctrine of the Great Perfection there were many wonderful signs, such as the unfurling of a rainbow tent. On Saturday 13 May 1167 (twenty-second day, fourth month, fire female pig)[623] great claps of thunder resounded seven times in the eastern sky and the earth trembled three times. With a display of rainbows, light, music from heavenly cymbals, and the fragrances of divine incense, all the signs that he had attained manifest awakening in the original ground, Zhangtön passed away in his seventy-first year. After the cremation at dusk on the following day, five large remains and small relics in five colours, representing the Conquerors of the Five Families,[624] were left behind. A shower of flowers, a rainbow canopy, and other signs also appeared, owing to which many people developed firm faith and naturally entered into meditative absorption.

Nyibum

[222.3-223.5] Zhangtön's disciple was [his own son] Nyibum. When he entered the womb of his mother, Gyelmoyang, [she had a dream in which] many suns rose simultaneously. His father then predicted that he would illuminate the dark ignorance of sentient beings and therefore named him Nyimabum, "One Hundred Thousand Suns". Starting during his fifth year he gradually received the empowerments, guidance, and instructions of the secret Innermost Spirituality from his father; and he thoroughly mastered them as well. When, in his tenth year, he was enthroned, he expounded the *Seventeen Tantras (rgyud-bcu-bdun*, NGB Vols.9-10),[625] to the astonishment of all his fellow students. Until his twentieth year he persevered only at practice.

Nyibum

Having become familiar with the contemplation of the apparitional during the aftermath [of meditative absorption],[626] Nyibum went to study the new tantras, along with their esoteric instructions, under Ngok Gyeltse.[627] In his twenty-second year he took Como Gyagar to be his consort in the attainment of accomplishment. In his twenty-seventh, he served Khön Trakpa Gyeltsen[628] and Lama Taksowa; and he became learned in the *Three Continua (rgyud gsum)*[629] along with their instructions and in the Melgyo tradition of the *Cakrasaṃvara*. From Druktön Trakpa of Kharak he received the *Cakrasaṃvara*, *Bhaṭṭārikā according to the Tradition of Ra Lotsāwa*, and the *Protector of Pristine Cognition*.[630] He attended on many learned and accomplished gurus, such as Zhang Yudrakpa[631] and Ngok Dorje Senge of Zhung;

and under them he studied many sūtras and tantras with an unbiased mind. He even composed a treatise entitled the *Great Exposition of Words and Meaning* (*tshig-don chen-mo*). Then, in his fifty-sixth year Nyibum passed away. After the cremation remains representing the five buddha families were left behind. A canopy of rainbow colours appeared. *Khukcö* flowers[632] bloomed, even though it was the first month of the year, and so forth. It is well known that Nyibum has been identified with Vajraphala, an emanation of Vajrapāṇi foretold in the *Penetration of Sound*.[633]

Guru Cober

[223.5-224.6] Nyibum's disciple, Guru Cober, was the son of his younger brother, Dawabum. Until his seventh year he appeared to be

Guru Cober

dumb, but from his eighth year onwards discriminative awareness blazed like a fire within him. Until his eighteenth year he lived with his uncle, Nyibum, and received from him the complete empowerments, guidance, and instructions of the unsurpassed secret [i.e. Innermost Spirituality]. By listening to the explanations of the tantras his doubts were resolved. And by meditating on the meaning of the esoteric instructions he developed diligence in practice. From nineteen to twenty he studied the *Three Continua* along with their instructions under the Translator of Sakya [Sakya Paṇḍita][634] as well as the Melgyo tradition of the *Cakrasaṃvara*. He comprehended Madhyamaka and logic, and also the other sciences. Similarly, he received the transmissions of many scriptures and tantras from many learned and accomplished gurus before reaching his thirty-sixth year. Among them, he received the instructions of Mitrayogī from Trhopu Lotsāwa,[635] the *Compendium of Valid Cognition* from Chumikpa, and the *Dohā*[636] and the Great Seal opuscules from the Nepali, Trakbum. In this way Guru Cober became renowned for his sharp intellect and very great learning.

With each means for attainment he practised he had a vision of the meditational deity, but he never spoke of this because of his profundity. While worshipping the image of Lord Śākyamuni in Lhasa[637] he saw the sublime Padmapāṇi and Vajrapāṇi emerge from within an orb of light. One day at dawn, he had a vision of Amitāyus and said, "Though we do not have a lineage noted for its longevity, it is owing to his blessing that it has turned out all right for me."

Thus, being endowed with infinite learning and compassion, Guru Cober became like a caravan guide for living beings. He finally passed away at the age of sixty. There was a net of rainbow light around him which endured for seven days, and remains in the form of the syllables OṂ ĀḤ HŪṂ and many other relics were left behind.

Trhüzhi Sengegyap

[224.6-226.6] His disciple, Trhüzhi Sengegyap, was born under a canopy of rainbow light at sunrise, in the village of Phuso Getreng in Tra, Yoru. From his ninth year on, his affinity with the enlightened family was awakened, and pure vision and devotion arose boundlessly within him. In his tenth year he perceived this seeming solidity of appearances, like that of dreams, to be without true existence. At twelve, he became utterly disillusioned with the world, and became certain that nothing would help except the doctrine. At thirteen he had a dream in which the sun and moon arose simultaneously; and on waking he had a vision of the sublime Great Compassionate One [Avalokiteśvara], who said, "To attain liberation in one life, meditate on the meaning of Innermost Spirituality."

After that Sengegyap developed boundless compassion, and he regarded all beings as a mother does her only child. For this reason he vowed neither to seek out the company of the high and mighty, nor to avoid the lowly. His great compassion was such that he would not forsake any sentient being, even a louse on his own body. He possessed other special signs of the family of the greater vehicle too, like showing loving kindness to the blind, to beggars and to the poor.

Trüzhi Sengegyap

In his eighteenth year he realised that phenomenal appearances are without true existence and he began to rave like a madman. Once, he scattered his parents' offerings to the gods and offered them instead to Gyelpo, a malignant male spirit, and to Senmo, a malignant female spirit. His parents scolded him, saying, "Why did we have a son such as you?"

When Sengegyap was in his twentieth year he was ordained as a novice by the preceptor Deu Gangpa and the master Tre Gangpa. In his twenty-fifth year he went to Sengegyap [the place from which he would take his name] in Sizhel, and there he heard the Tshelpa cycle of doctrines from the middle Sengegyapa; *Crossing the Lion's Neck* (*seng-ge mjing-bsnol*, NGB Vol.2) from Lama Tsariwa; and many teachings of the way of secret mantra according to the ancient and new translation schools, as well as *Pacification*, the *Object of Cutting*, and the Great Seal, from such famous gurus as Repa Trimeö, Lharipel, Zhönubum, Töncar Cangyön, and Co-se.

In particular, as had been predicted by the Great Compassionate One, Sengegyap studied the Great Perfection under Guru Cober; and through it he developed all-surpassing realisation. He remained absorbed totally in his practice for many years in Trhowoma and other mountain retreats and desolate valleys. Thus, his mind reached the level of primordial purity. He secured many fortunate beings in spiritual maturation and liberation, and, manifesting the special signs that he had realised the fruit of the supreme vehicle, he passed away in his sixty-fourth year.

Melong Dorje

[226.6-229.6] Trhüzhi Sengegyap's disciple, the great accomplished master Melong Dorje, was born in the upper valley of Dra as the son of the yogin Samye. In his ninth year, he was ordained as a novice by the accomplished master Zalungpa, and the preceptor Selungpa. During that period, he would recite the long, medium, and short versions of the *Mother*, the *Transcendental Perfection of Discriminative Awareness* sūtras, at funerals and then, in his sixteenth year, he recited the *Transcendental Perfection of Discriminative Awareness in Eight Thousand Lines* one hundred times at Zhokteng in the upper valley of Dra. Thereby, he realised the meaning of the abiding nature of reality. When he

Melong Dorje

practised meditation at Zangtso, he blazed with spiritual experiences, and also developed supernormal cognitive powers to a slight degree.

Then, wandering without direction, he attended on Towarepa of Tshurpu, and on many other gurus. He visited many great pilgrimage places, such as Shawuk Tago and Kharcu. He could endure very great hardships, as when he sustained his life for one month and twenty days on a measure of barley. Indeed, his austerity cannot be imagined.

When Melong Dorje was in his eighteenth year, he met Sangye Önpo of Sengegyap [Trhüzhi Sengegyap] and received the esoteric instructions of Innermost Spirituality. He was inspired by the thought that his desire for esoteric instructions was now fulfilled; and he meditated upon them. Even while engaged in the preliminary practice he had a vision of Vajrasattva that continued for six full days. And during the actual ground of the practice he met the gurus of the lineage in a dream, and was blessed by them.[638]

In his twenty-third year he studied many treasure doctrines, including those concerning Vajravārāhī, under Sangye Repa; and after propitiating Vajravārāhī he actually met her in a vision. When he struck a rock with his "secret vajra" it actually penetrated the stone.[639] He also had visions of Hayagrīva, Tārā, Avalokiteśvara, the great master Padmasambhava, Samantabhadra, Vajrasattva, Vimalamitra, Zalungpa, Sangye Repa, and the lord of beings Phakmotrupa. At Tunglung he heard the most melodious voice of a ḍākinī declare that he had cut off the stream of rebirth. In Kawacen the Red Varāhī and the accomplished master Zalungpa appeared in the sky before him. When he visited Ngarcung, he saw Varāhī and her five attendants in a dream. And, on awakening, he actually saw her body of light. Then, at Kyapne Dzong, Vajrasattva empowered him into the Great Perfection during a dream.

In general, Melong Dorje attended on many gurus, but among them thirteen were particularly sublime. He obtained that which is of most central significance [i.e. the Great Perfection] from Zalungpa, an accomplished master of matchless compassion, from Towarepa of Tshurpu, and from Trhüzhi Sengegyap. Because of his very great discipline his conduct was impeccable, free from acceptance and rejection; so he was able to observe the commitments of the way of secret mantra to the letter. Like a young vulture soaring in the sky, he traversed the heavens by the sheer power of the discipline of awareness. And he made solid rock seem like clay. In the lands of Khenpajong, Khenpaling,[640] Sengedzong and Kharcu, he planted the banner of attainment and served living creatures.

Melong Dorje had been destined to live for thirty-seven years, but owing to the prayers of a worthy being named master Künga, he passed away at the age of sixty-one, in the charnel ground of Labar. At that time everyone saw a great light, accompanied by sound, which vanished in the western direction. During the cremation a blanket of five-coloured light stretched out in the sky over the crematorium (*pur-khang*), and innumerable other wonderful omens occurred. Remains indicating that he had realised the five bodies of buddhahood were left behind, just as they are described in the tantras.

This Melong Dorje was a contemporary of the accomplished master Orgyenpa, but Orgyenpa was ten years his senior and lived a longer life.[641]

Kumārādza

[229.6-236.5] The disciple of Melong Dorje was the awareness-holder Kumārādza.[642] He was born in a market town called Önbar Sardzingka in Yoru in 1266 (fire male tiger). He received the name Tharpagyen. From childhood he possessed many special qualities; for he was endowed with faith, compassion, discriminative awareness and the other aspects of sublime wealth. Thus, he learned how to read and to write without studying. In his seventh year he received the empowerments of *Hevajra* and of *Cakrasaṃvara* from Lama Gyedor of Orshö Thoteng Monastery in Kongpo. In his ninth year he was fully ordained as a layman by the preceptor Tsangpa, and practised the doctrinal cycle of

Kumārādza

Avalokiteśvara, the Churner of Saṃsāra's Hellish Depths.[643] In his twelfth year he was ordained as a novice by the preceptor Yerwapa of Phakmotru and the master Ngaripa. The name Zhönu Gyelpo [Kumārādza] was conferred upon him and he studied the Vinaya. He studied, too, the *Six Doctrines of Nāropā* and other teachings, over a period of five years under Rinpoche Trak-ye, and the *Hevajra Tantra* under Tshar Tengpa. Also, he trained as an artist under Ön Sangshe.

When Kumārādza recited the Six-Syllable Mantra he had a vision in which he saw the smiling face of the Great Compassionate One in a crystal room. He received many tantras, transmissions, and esoteric instructions belonging to the Ancient Translation School from Khyung Nakshadar; and, when he met Melong Dorje at Ngarpuk, he requested guidance on the Great Seal, through which he came face to face with the naked reality of mind.

Then Kumārādza went to serve the great, accomplished master Melong Dorje at Khandroling in Mön. He received the cycle of doctrines devoted to Vajravarāhī and others as well. When he performed the ritual service [of Vajravarāhī] he had a vision of Padmasambhava of Oḍḍiyāna, who appeared on the evening of the tenth day of the month and said, "O son of the enlightened family! Always practise the doctrine!"

Kumārādza went to Tshurpu, too, where he received the cycle of the Karmapa's doctrines from Nyenre and from Tarma Gönpo. When he went to Tingri and to Purang in Latö he met the great, accomplished master Orgyenpa and the venerable Karmapa Rangjung Dorje, who, in his seventh year, had just been ordained as a novice. Kumārādza received many instructions from Orgyenpa, and in a single month he obtained all the teachings of the Innermost Spirituality, which Orgyenpa had received from Nyenre over some years.

Also, Kumārādza received the secret cycles of the Great Perfection, for instance, the *Introduction to the Essence of the Secret Cycle* (*gsang-skor gnad-kyi ngo-sprod*) from Namkei Dorje of Gyamen, and the *Secret Mirror of the Essence* (*gsang-ba gnad-kyi me-long*) from Keldenpa Chöki Senge.

Again, in Kharcu he fully obtained the empowerments, guidance, and instructions of the Innermost Spirituality from the great, accomplished master Melong Dorje. Because he had nothing else to offer he served his guru with body and speech, and spent two whole summers painting for him. The master gave him four loads of barley, and two of these he used to buy paper, on which he copied books during the night. The other two provided butter lamps and his own food. Because of his austerities he contracted a severe case of lice; but extraordinary spiritual resolve was born within him.

His guru was delighted and advised him to act on behalf of living beings. Once, during an empowerment, he saw the four-armed

Ekajaṭī

Mahākāla above the guru's head, and the dark-blue Ekajaṭī in front of the door. She appeared twice the size of a man, wielding an impaling stake and holding a she-wolf, while outside the door the witch who served her, whose locks were drenched in blood, drank blood which she held in her cupped hands.

Kumārādza served the guru for eight consecutive years. He passed a full winter in the hollow of Nyuktsel, one of the places of practice hallowed by the precious master from Oḍḍiyāna; and there he had a vision of Vajravarāhī. His discriminative awareness became limitless.

He built a hermitage at Tsharteng in Yarlung and stayed there for some time. Later, knowing that his guru had passed away, he went to Kharcu and met the guru's two sons in Sakyak. On returning home he held a memorial ceremony on the twenty-fifth day of the month.

When Kumārādza travelled to Tsāri, five-coloured rainbows penetrated a stone image in the meadow of Trikmo-lha and he encountered many other omens as well. Then, when invited to Tshurpu by Karmapa Rangjung Dorje, the master of the doctrine, he offered to him the instructions of the Innermost Spirituality. He went to Shang and received the aural lineage of the Secret Cycles and the *Lamp for the Eye of Contemplation* (*bsam-gtan mig-gi sgron-me*) from master Gompa, a spiritual descendant of Cegom Nakpo. At Namar in Tingri he attended on Pönpo Cangdrup's discourses on Yang-gönpa's *Teachings for Retreat* (*yang-dgon-pa'i ri-chos rnams*). He also met Orgyenpa Rincenpel. On the return journey he received the *Black Yamāri* and other teachings from Lama Tralungpa.

Kumārādza mastered most of the teachings on the stage of perfection which were well known in Tibet: the *Secret Cycles* (*gsang-skor*); the *Cycle of Götsangpa's Guidance* (*rgod-tshang-pa'i khrid-kyi skor*); the *Cycle of Meaning, which is Aro's Great System of Guidance* (*a-ro'i khrid-mo-che don-skor*); and so on. These he received from many spiritual benefactors such as master Yegön and others.

He endured hardships for the sake of the doctrine: On one occasion he went to Tsāri Sarma and lived alone for eight months by the shore of Nyingmei Yutso, the Turquoise Lake. Because great miraculous powers arise when [one realises] the common savour with respect to the disposition of reality, Kumārādza held sway over the local divinities and invited them to his house, where they served and venerated him. Jambhala presented him with a precious gem. Once, he saw a bubble of five-coloured light, about the size of his thumb, dissolve into the lake.

Kumārādza's heart wept with disillusionment and sorrow [at the impermanence and suffering of the world] and, therefore, he always lived in mountain hermitages and totally desolate valleys like Shampo, with only a wind-break for shelter. Acting thus, he delivered many disciples from saṃsāra.

Because his foremost disciples in the Great Perfection were the indubitable emanation Karmapa Rangjung Dorje and the conqueror Longcenpa, Kumārādza's activity as a propagator of this teaching had no limit or end. Just so, the king of the doctrine Drigung Rincen Phüntsok has said, "The master of the teaching of this doctrine was the all-knowing Longcenpa. Its great expansion was effected in the time of the conqueror Rangjung Dorje."[644]

Kumārādza had thoroughly trained himself in the conduct of a bodhisattva and so, by the power of great compassion, he totally devoted himself to planting by skilful means the seed of liberation in many villages and districts. He gave safe passage to all who travelled on the terrifyingly dangerous trail from Kongpo to E; and he was truly endowed with loving kindness toward wild animals, fish, and other feeble creatures. Thus, he unstintingly exerted himself to form sanctuaries by the mountains, roads, and rivers; and he made the land happy and gentle. He alleviated the misfortunes of frost, hail, and infectious disease and so on, in all the districts, towns and countries in which he dwelt; and he was totally devoted to benefitting others.

Kumārādza was able to explain the instructions of the Innermost Spirituality without mixing them with other systems of the stage of perfection; and thus he created a philosophical system in the technical language [of the Great Perfection itself].[645] The tip of his nose was marked with the syllable A. Ekajaṭī, protectress of the way of secret mantra, Rāhula, the planetary divinity, and the oath-bound Dorje Lekpa obeyed his command,[646] and he could converse with them as with men. By supernormal cognitive powers he knew the thoughts of those requiring teaching and thus was skilled at teaching, and could bless the minds of others.

To all the fortunate ones who were his disciples special signs arose at the time of his passing. For all of these reasons he is said to have been an emanation of Vimalamitra. And there is a prophecy in the *Penetration of Sound* which refers to him as Gelong Pelden, the "Glorious Monk".[647]

After innumerable acts of service to living creatures, Kumārādza passed away during his seventy-eighth year, on Sunday 14 September 1343 (twenty-fifth day, eighth month, water female sheep).[648] His passing was attended by sound, light, a rainbow canopy and other wondrous omens. His attendant Gomdar and other close followers were consumed with fervent devotion at that time, and the master rose again. Sitting cross-legged and smiling, he said, "Do not grieve. I am not dead." And he gave them suitable instruction and advice. He prolonged his life for thirteen days and then, on the morning of the seventh day of the following month, his disciples asked, "What are we to do after your passing? Should we invite the all-knowing guru, Longcenpa?"

He answered, "Do not bother him. If even now you have not resolved your doubts regarding the doctrine, then go to him. But I have already given you much advice. Do not indulge in idle talk."

Then, crouching in the posture of a *ṛṣi* he smiled, with his eyes fixed in the gaze of the buddha-body of reality. At dawn, on the eighth, he journeyed to wherever it is that the primordial city may be found. After the cremation, which was held on the twenty-fifth of the month, his whole skull was left behind. It contained the maṇḍala of the Conquerors of the Five Families, a whole blue-coloured image of Bhaṭṭārikā above the right ear, and five kinds of remains and relics. And all around there was a dense canopy of rainbow light.

Karmapa III, Rangjung Dorje

[236.5-238.5] The lord among conquerors, Karmapa Rangjung Dorje, was the actual presence in the world of the sublime Avalokiteśvara. He was summoned from the expanse of reality by a song of indestructible reality [sung by] the ḍākinīs of pristine cognition. Gazing upon sentient beings with boundless compassion he entered the world by resurrecting the corpse of the dead son of an elderly couple from Tölung. But people said, "It is an ill omen for the eyes of the dead to see the living!" And they gouged out his eyes with a needle.

The Karmapa then abandoned that body, which was no longer perfect with respect to the eight liberties and ten endowments.He transferred his consciousness and took birth as the son of a yogin and a yoginī.

It is well known that with the exceptions of Śākyamuni Buddha in India and this great, accomplished master in Tibet, no one else possessed such recollection of past lives, without even a hair's breadth of obscuration, and was completely unpolluted by the taints of the womb. In India and Tibet respectively, they were unique life-giving trees of the Buddha's teaching.

Karmapa III, Rangjung Dorje

Karmapa obtained the treasure of the elixir of life at Samye Chimpu and Yamalung; and he used it to prolong the life of the Chinese emperor.[649] He saw Vimalamitra vanish in the circle of hair between his own eyebrows, whereupon the intention of the Innermost Spirituality was properly revealed to him. But, in order to show others how to attend on the guru in accord with the way of secret mantra, he surpassed pride and studied the complete esoteric instructions of the Secret Innermost Spirituality under the awareness-holder Kumārādza. When he realised that there had to be a lineage of this teaching coming from the great master Padmasambhava, he had a vision of that master, the Second

Buddha. He received the esoteric instructions of the Innermost Spirituality directly from him; but to preserve the verbal lineage he invited Gyelse Lekpa of Sho, and received the complete teaching from him at the New Tsāri Hermitage.

Moreover, Rangjung Dorje taught his own disciples to be adept in the Great Perfection. He gave to Menlungpa Śākya Zhönu and others an order saying that, in order to prevent the decline of this doctrine, it should be propagated in Tsang by Yungtön Dorjepel,[650] in Kham and Kongpo by Yegyelwa, in Mongolia and China by Yeshe Gyeltsen, and in Central Tibet by Trülkuwa.

There is a well-known prophecy referring to Karmapa Rangjung Dorje:

> This teaching will be propagated
> To the shores of the oceans,
> By a bodhisattva who abides on the [ten] levels.[651]

Samantabhadra was naturally manifest in the expanse of Rangjung Dorje's mind; and when he had mastered the great treasure of his intention he originated the instructions known as the *Innermost Spirituality of Karmapa* (*karma snying-tig*), which was also one fountain-head of the teaching.

4 *Longcen Rapjampa*

[238.5-277.4] The second conqueror, the all-knowing lord of speech from glorious Samye, Longcen Rapjampa, hailed from a line of noble descent – that of Öki Kyinkorcen, the ruler of Ngenlam – in the village of Tödrong, in the Tra valley of Yoru. His clan was Rok, and his father was of the twenty-fifth generation descended from the family of the *bhikṣu* Gyelwa Choyang, who had been a direct disciple of the great master Padmasambhava, and one of the "seven men who were tested". This figure was also known by the name Jñānendrarakṣita or, in Tibetan, Yeshe Wangposung.[652] Longcenpa's grandfather, Lhasung, had lived for one hundred and fifty years by achieving the alchemical transformation of deathless nectar; and his father, master Tenpasung, was adept at the sciences and the yoga of mantras. Longcenpa's mother, Dromza Sonamgyen, was descended from the family of Dromtön Gyelwei Jungne.[653]

When Longcenpa was conceived his mother dreamt that the rays of the sun shone upon the forehead of an enormous lion, illuminating the three world realms, and vanished into her body. On Saturday 2 March 1308 (tenth day, second month, earth monkey year of Phurbu, fifth cycle)[654] he was released from her womb. Namdru Remati raised the babe in her hand,[655] just as Devendra had done to Prince Siddhārtha, and said, "I shall protect him." She returned the child to the mother and vanished.

Because the bodhisattva was rich from the beginning in sublime wealth, the attributes of faith and compassion were clearly and unobstructedly present within him. From his fifth year he knew well how to read and write. He received many means for attainment and ceremonies from his father, such as those of the *Gathering of the Sugatas of the Eight Transmitted Precepts* (*bka'-brgyad bder-'dus*), *Vajrakīla*, *Hayagrīva*, and the *Text on the Rites of the Guru* (*bla-ma'i las-gzhung*). He also obtained a sufficient understanding of medicine, astrology and the other sciences. In his ninth year he memorised completely the sūtras of the *Transcendental Perfection of Discriminative Awareness in Twenty-*

Longcen Rabjampa

five Thousand Lines and in *Eight Thousand Lines*, by reciting them one hundred times. In his twelfth year he was ordained as a novice by the preceptor Samdrup Rincen of Samye and master Künga Özer; and he received the name Tshültrim Lodrö.

Longcenpa made a thorough study of the Vinaya of the true doctrine and was capable of explaining its meaning to others during his fourteenth year. At sixteen he received many empowerments, instructions and much guidance from master Trashi Rincen: those of the Path and Fruit (*lam-'bras*); the *Two Systems of the Six Doctrines* (*chos-drug gnyis*); the *Six Doctrines of Varāhī* (*phag-mo'i chos-drug*, T 1551-6); *Cakrasaṃvara according to the Tradition of Ghaṇṭāpāda* (*bde-mchog dril-bu-pa*, T 1432); and the *Great Assembly of Vajrapāṇi* (*phyag-rdor 'khor-chen*). From gurus such as master Wang-ye, Töntshül, and Trhopupa, he received many tantras of the way of secret mantra, including those belonging to the Kriyātantra, Caryātantra, and Yogatantra; and also the *Indestructible Tent*; the *Ocean of Ḍākas* (*Ḍākārṇava*, T 372); the *Buddhakapāla*; the *Vajra Garland*; and the *Kālacakra*. And from the precious Zalungpa and others he received the *Cycle of Instructions of Zhang Tshelpa* (*zhang-tshal-pa'i gdams-skor*); the *Guidance on the Path according to Götsangpa* (*rgod-tshang-pa'i lam-khrid*); the *Object of Cutting*; and *Pacification according to the Early, Middle and Later Traditions* (*zhi-byed snga-phyi-bar-gsum*).

In his nineteenth year Longcenpa entered the seminary of Sangpu Neutok, which had been founded by Ngok Lekpei Sherap, and which was the great academy for the study of logic in Tibet.[656] Under master Tsengönpa, the fifteenth to hold the seat of Lingtö [at Sangpu], and Labrangpa Chöpel Gyeltsen, the sixteenth to hold the seat, he studied the scriptural authorities and theoretical reasoning of the dialectical vehicle, including the *Five Doctrines of Maitreya*, the *Seven Sections on Valid Cognition*, Transcendental Perfection, and Madhyamaka. From Pang Lo Lodrö Tenpa he received such inner treatises as the *Five Profound Sūtras* (*zab-chos mdo-lnga*), which include the *Sūtra of the King of Contemplation*; the *Detailed Commentary on the Heart Sūtra of Discriminative Awareness* (*Āryaprajñāpāramitāhṛdayaṭīkā*, T 3821); and many other miscellaneous transmissions, along with all the outer and ordinary subjects: grammar, poetics, prosody, drama and so on. Thus, he reached the culmination of learning.

When Longcenpa propitiated Mañjughoṣa, Sarasvatī, Acala, and the White Varāhī he had visions of them all. In particular, Sarasvatī, the goddess of melodious sound, carried him in the palm of her hand and showed him around Mount Sumeru and the four continents in seven days. From her he received a prophecy [of his impending enlightenment].

He independently achieved the great accomplishment of unobstructed intelligence, and so, obtaining fearless brilliance in [the study of] the prolific scriptures and sciences, the great drum of his reputation resounded in all directions, conferring on him the titles "Samye Lungmangwa" (Samye's Recipient of Many Transmissions) and "Longcen Rapjampa" (Extensively Learned One who is Like Vast Space).[657]

Under four gurus, including masters Ten Phakpa, Zhönu Töndrup, and Nyötingmawa Sangye Trakpa, he studied teachings belonging to the Ancient Translation School of the vehicle of indestructible reality, in particular, the *Trio of the Sūtra which Gathers All Intentions, the Magical Net, and the Mental Class*, as well as the *Collected Tantras of the Nyingmapa* (*rnying-ma rgyud-'bum*). Under the master Zhöngyel and others he studied the complete tradition of the sublime Nāgārjuna, including the *Clearly Worded Commentary* and the *Introduction to the Madhyamaka* [both by Candrakīrti]. Under Zhöndor he studied [Śāntideva's] *Introduction to the Conduct of a Bodhisattva* and *Compendium of Lessons*, and so on, as well as the *Cycle of the Meditational Deities of Atiśa* (*jo-bo'i yi-dam-skor*), the *Six-limbed Yoga* (*Kālacakraṣaḍaṅgayoga*), and the *Six Doctrines* [*of Nāropā*, *nā-ro chos-drug*, T 2330]. Under his preceptor he studied the *Cycle of Trhopupa* (*khro-phu-pa'i skor*) and the *Doctrinal Cycle of Kharak* (*kha-rag chos-skor*), as well as the *Ocean of Means for Attainment* (*sgrub-thabs rgya-mtsho*, T 3400-644), the *Hundred Brief Doctrines* (*chos-chung brgya-rtsa*, T 4465-567), the *Transmissions of the Vinaya*, and a great many others.

Longcenpa studied many transmitted doctrines under lord Rangjung Dorje, including the *Six-limbed Yoga and its Means to Remove Obstacles* (*sbyor-drug gegs-sel dang bcas-pa*); the *Six Doctrines of Nāropā*, the *Introduction to the Three Bodies* (*sku-gsum ngo-sprod*), *Jinasāgara* (*rgyal-ba rgya-mtsho*), *Avalokiteśvara according to the Tradition of the King* (*spyan-ras-gzigs rgyal-po-lugs*), *Guhyasamāja*, the *Sampuṭa Tantra* (T 381), the *Mahāmāya*, and the forms of *Red* and *Black Yamāri* (T 468-70). Under master Wangtsül he studied the *Six-limbed Yoga*, the *Oḍḍiyāna Tradition of Ritual Service and Attainment* (*bsnyen-sgrub*, i.e. *o-rgyan bsnyen-sgrub*), teachings on vital energy (*rlung-skor*), and many others as well. Under Lama Tampa [Sonam Gyeltsen] of Sakya[658] he studied the many profound doctrines of the Sakyapa, including the *Great Development of the Enlightened Mind* (*sems-bskyed chen-mo*), and the Path and Fruit. Under Zhöndor of Shuksep-ri, a disciple in the line of the three famous gurus of the lineage of Pacification – namely, Ma [Chöki Sherap], So[-cung Gendünbar], and Kam [Yeshe Gyeltsen][659] – he studied the *Three Dohā Cycles* (*do-hā skor-gsum*), the *Three Cycles on Retreat Practice* (*ri-chos skor-gsum*), and the *Hundred Causal Relations* (*rten-'brel brgya-rtsa*).

In short, Longcenpa comprehended most of the philosophical and spiritual systems that were known in the land of snow mountains. He developed an unobstructed facility for explanation, disputation, and composition. Thus, he thoroughly mastered all the branches of conventional science [i.e. grammar, logic, etc.], the textual traditions of the sūtras and of the way of mantras, the cycles of esoteric instruction, and so forth.

Then, because in general he was endowed with boundless sorrow and disillusionment at the condition of the world, he resolved to live in solitude. Seeing the partisan behaviour and misconduct of the Khampa scholars[660] at his college Longcenpa became disgusted and decided to go off to live as a mendicant free from worldly cares. The preceptor and students, who perceived the rare incisiveness of this holy man, could not bear it, and earnestly tried to delay his departure. But he set out undeterred. Near the reliquary of the great translator Ngok,[661] he met an inquisitive monk who sought to delay him further. Longcenpa disclosed the nature of his distress and the monk also complained of the behaviour of the Khampa scholars. The monk encouraged him and said, "Now that you have left the college and there is no limitation on your ability as an author, you should publicise the infamy of the Khampas." For amusement Longcenpa filled a small page, which the monk carried and attached to the throne in the teaching court. When the Khampas noticed it they removed the letter from sight, but the thirty-line alphabetical poem, beginning with the line, "Like the ogres who roam in Kaliṅga...," circulated all over the kingdom.[662]

Longcenpa then wandered about without direction, and devoted himself exclusively to practice. When he had practised yoga in darkness for five months in the Gyamei Cokla Cave, he heard the music of cymbals and melodious song. When a visible manifestation arose, he saw that it was a girl of sixteen years, robed in a train of silk, adorned with gold and turquoise ornaments. She rode upon a horse covered with leather mail that was adorned with bells, and her own face was concealed by a golden veil. He clasped the hem of her dress and prayed, "Please bless me, sublime one!" She removed a crown of precious gems from her head and placed it upon the head of the all-knowing one, saying, "From now on I shall always bless you, and bestow accomplishment on you." Longcenpa remained immersed for a long while in a blissful, radiant, non-discursive contemplation. This was an auspicious sign that he would encounter a doctrine associated with the esoteric instructions of the Great Perfection.

Then, in his twenty-ninth year, he went to meet the genuine guru Kumārādza, who was residing in the uplands of Yartökyam at Samye during the spring and summer seasons. On the way he met Yakde Paṇcen,[663] who urged him to approach His Presence, the Karmapa, but Longcenpa continued his journey without paying attention. In the uplands of Yartökyam he met the awareness-holder Kumārādza, who lived with his group of disciples in about seventy fabric wind-breaks. The master said to them, "Last night I dreamt that a wonderful bird, which announced itself to be a divine bird, came with a large flock in attendance, and carried away my books in all directions. Therefore, someone will come to hold my lineage." He was utterly delighted.

At the same time Longcenpa was abjectly sad, because he had no tribute to offer for the doctrine. He thought, "I should not approach the guru without some tribute for the doctrine. As I have none, I should be ashamed to move on during the daytime, so I will go to the lower part of this valley at dawn tomorrow." But the guru, who knew of his thoughts by supernormal cognitive powers, told [his disciples] that Longcenpa was blameless, for he had offered his tribute inwardly. Two of them repeated this to Longcenpa, who greatly rejoiced.

To arouse disillusionment [towards the world] in his disciples, the awareness-holder Kumārādza had no fixed home. During the spring and summer of that year he wandered nine times from one deserted valley to the next. Because it seemed as if they had to move just as they had made camp, Longcenpa could obtain neither food, nor clothing. With the change of seasons he was completely worn out by the bitter cold and the icy terrain; and he survived for two months on nothing but three measures of flour and twenty-one mercury pills. Then, when the snow fell he lived inside a sack garment which served both as a robe, and as a bed. In these and other ways he endured inconceivable austerity for the sake of the doctrine.

That year he obtained the empowerments, guidance and instructions on the Great Perfection, the secret Innermost Spirituality, and then he meditated upon it.

The next year Kumārādza filled him, as if he were a vase, with higher empowerments and with the tantras, transmissions, and esoteric instructions of the Three Classes of the Great Perfection, along with the rites of the protectors of the doctrine. He was appointed to be the successor to the teaching, and vowed to practise [in retreat] for six years.

In his thirty-first year Longcenpa guided many fortunate beings to spiritual maturation and liberation at Nyipu Shuksep, by means of the Innermost Spirituality. At that time a yogin, Özer Koca, discovered the text of the *Innermost Spirituality of the Ḍākinī* after great trials; and he offered it to Longcenpa to examine. Simultaneously, Longcenpa received the book in a dream from [the protectress] Shenpa Sokdrupma (Butcher Life-grantress).

The following year, his thirty-second, while he was practising at Rimochen in Chimpu, he gave teaching of the Innermost Spirituality to eight fortunate yogins and yoginīs. When he conferred the blessing of the elaborate empowerment one yoginī was possessed by Ekajaṭī, the protectress of mantra; and she began to dance. The other disciples could not bear her radiance, but the guru said, "You need not worry because she is possessed by a ḍākinī. As I am a yogin who has realised that mind and appearances are of the same savour, no obstacles will come of it."

Then the yoginī bowed before the guru. Gazing upon the maṇḍala, she said, "Why is there no peacock quill?"

Longcenpa replied, "I have visualised it mentally."

"In this symbolic doctrine, what has that got to do with it?" With that question, she removed the vase's supporting platform and set down three vases fastened together. The master then performed the ceremony in perfect detail and she clasped her hands together and voiced her approval. When he omitted the final letter *s* from the word *rigs*, and pronounced it as *rik*, she said, "No, no! You should say *rigs*."[664] And while he was reciting the mantra, she said, "You should imitate me," and she sang it in a strange, harmonious melody in the ḍākinīs' language.

During the actual ground or main part of the empowerment, the yoginī sang a song about view and meditation which are beyond the range of intellectual appraisal:

> Mind free from meditation is joyful.
> Mind free from meditation – Oh my! it is happy.

Saying that the offerings were of poor quality and insufficient, she offered, instead, her melodious song. And during the feast offering, when nectar was offered to the guru, she said, "This is a sacrament of the ḍākinīs. You must take it, by all means." And she invited him to drink it all.

At that time, the group of disciples also became exhilarated and they began to sing and to dance. They attained one-pointed absorption in inner radiance, which transcends ordinary sleep,[665] and they could actually see the forms of various warriors, ḍākinīs, and protectors of the doctrine. A black woman appeared and said, "The first fruits of the offering of barley flour have diminished." And the oath-bound Dorje Lekpa appeared in the form of a white man who said, "There is no red ornament [i.e. meat] on my *torma*."

Como Dangla came in the guise of a white man riding on a white horse, desirous of a *torma* offering, but he declined the red *torma* offered to him. A host of ḍākinīs raised a parasol above Longcenpa and circumambulated him uttering such fearsome sounds as HŪṂ and PHAṬ in a tumultuous uproar. And many other inconceivable miracles also took place. One yogin remarked, "Tonight heaven and earth are reversed. No doubt they're after flesh and blood!" And he was terrified.

In the same way, the protectors Ode Kungyel, Nyencen Thangla, and the seven Menmo sisters came to take their *torma* offerings.[666] Then Vajravarāhī actually appeared, her blue body adorned with precious gems and bone ornaments. At that time there was an exchange of questions. She said, "This is a wild night. I have come to spy on the worthy disciples. How is the health of your holy guru [Kumārādza]?"

"This year his health almost failed. Now what will happen?"

Vajravarāhī replied, "How can obstacles come to an emanation of a buddha? The obstacles are the expression of his intention on behalf of his disciples. Do you not know that he is Vimalamitra, returned to Tibet?"

Longcenpa asked, "How long will he live?"

"Until the next year of the sheep. After that, whether he lives or not will depend on his disciples."

"But have I not been urged by guru Kumārādza to help others?"

"Yes, indeed!"

"If I practise the means for attainment in solitude will I achieve the body of light? If I help others instead, then how much will I benefit sentient beings? And how long can I live?"

"Even though you achieve the body of light, you must help sentient beings. Serve others and you can live for thirty more years!"

Then the guru asked, "Who are the protectors of my transmitted precepts?"

"There are a great many. All those of the guru are yours, especially Dorje Yudrönma. Accordingly, the quarter in which you are to serve the world is in the south-west. In your next life your service to the world will be even greater than it is in the present one."[667]

"Well", he asked, "is that owing to the teaching of the *Innermost Spirituality of the Ḍākinī*? Is it all right to confer its empowerment and guidance?"

"Oh, yes indeed, yes indeed! There will be absolutely no error. You are certainly the master of this doctrine."

"But then will people not think that I am a hypocrite [for openly granting the secret teaching]?"

"Why pay attention to slander? I myself will assemble the worthy ones. The unworthy, after all, slander even the Buddha."

Then he asked, "Should I reveal the transmitted doctrines of the Innermost Spirituality in the domain of Dorje Yudrönma?"

"Because the ḍākinīs naturally assemble here, this is where you should reveal the teaching."

Then she made a clear prophetic declaration regarding the treasure troves in Bumthang.[668] Afterwards, he asked, "Will I meet the great master Padmasambhava?"

"In the uplands of three valleys, in the lowlands of three mountains, and in the right-hand corner of a small cave facing west; there you shall meet him."

"When will I meet Vimalamitra?" he asked.

"You have already met him," she answered.[669]

"Is the view that I have realised the ultimate intention of the Innermost Spirituality?"

"There can be no error with respect to the ultimate," she replied.

Then master Rindor [who was one of those present] asked, "Where is Pangangpa Rincen Dorje?"[670]

Vajravarāhī pointed her finger at Longcenpa and said, "Here he is!"

But Longcenpa objected, "His next life was to have been in Bumthang. How can I be he?"

"That is so, but he has not been born thus; for it became necessary for him to explore the field of the buddha-body of perfect rapture in the meantime. After the master Rincen Dorje discovered his treasures he was to practise for some years in secret. Had he done so, he would have mastered, for his own sake, the inner radiance that is the buddha-body of perfect rapture; and he would have been of great service to others. But, because he did not maintain secrecy, he did not live out his full span. Now that he has been born as yourself, the manifestation of inner radiance that you have integrated into your practice of the path *is* that brief exploration of the field of the buddha-body of perfect rapture."

Then Longcenpa asked, "Will my body vanish without a trace?"

"You could achieve that right now if you were to meditate in solitude, but if you serve others you will be liberated during the intermediate state. Your emanation will take birth in Bumthang and will serve others. He, moreover, will journey to the western land of Oḍḍiyāna and reveal the attainment of buddhahood."

"Which tradition", he asked, "will be more beneficial for me to use, the *Innermost Spirituality of Vimalamitra* (*bi-ma'i snying-thig*, NYZ Vols.7-9) or that of the *Ḍākinī*?"

"Both are beneficial. The Vimalamitra tradition will be widespread for a hundred years; and the *Innermost Spirituality of the Ḍākinī* will endure for five hundred years, beginning today."[671]

After that Longcenpa also became exhilarated, and he arose. He sang a song of indestructible reality, which ended as follows:

> This life is bliss and the next will be happy.
> Bliss has arisen from knowing the intermediate state!
> And now, to greater bliss still will I pass.
> I offer this song, O Three Precious Jewels!
> Be delighted! Rejoice! you host of ḍākinīs!

[When he had finished singing] everyone saw an even more inconceivable host of ḍākinīs, all of whom finally dissolved into the guru. They perceived him, then, to be transformed into the buddha-body of perfect rapture for some time.

It was on the twenty-eighth day of the month that the great master Padmasambhava arrived from the south-western frontier. His complexion was white and radiant and he wore a silk cloak and a soft hat made from the hide of a young antelope. He was surrounded by an infinitely large retinue of followers and was seen to vanish into the guru himself. That night ḍākinīs wearing bone ornaments, who were flying to and fro in the sky, honoured him. Three dark brown women began to dance, and they sang:

> Yes, we have arrived, arrived from the land of great bliss.
> We have come to spy on your worthy disciples.
> We have come to inspect the purity of commitments.
> May you benefit the world, O enlightened son!

Then, when Longcenpa was making the inner offering, the great master Padmasambhava appeared, with Vimalamitra to his right, and Vajravārāhī to his left. In front of him there were many ḍākinīs, blowing on thigh-bone trumpets. And behind him were numerous mantra adepts, who were dancing, and ḍākinīs dressed in golden robes, who were singing and dancing. In the midst of the assembly the guru rose and sang songs of indestructible reality:

> Be joyful and happy, all of you yogins.
> Tonight, in the pure Akaniṣṭha realm,
> In my body, a palace of gods peaceful and wrathful,
> The maṇḍala of the conquerors, empty and radiant, unfolds.
> The Buddha dwells not outside, but within!

And:

> O meditator who abides in mind alone,
> Let your mind be at rest, not grasping one point;
> For mind is empty when it proliferates, empty at rest:
> Whatever arises is pristine cognition's play.

At that time the white goddess, Dorje Yudrönma, arrived with her seven sisters and asked him to visit her domain. "I want to live forever in your domain," said Longcenpa.

"I would rejoice if you were to live there forever, but it seems you will not stay beyond mid-winter."

He then asked, "Why have you come to me?"

"I was bound under an oath of allegiance by the guru Padmasambhava. I come in the wake of his treasures."

"But the treasures are yonder, and the adepts who discovered them have passed away. What will you achieve here?"

"The treasures are yonder, but the meaning is here. Though you passed away before, your good fortune did not pass away. Therefore, I have come. The protectors of the transmitted precepts have made a prediction that, because the instructions are very powerful, you are in danger of obstacles to your life. It will be better if you give guidance on them only a little."

He asked, "Will the written texts of the treasures come into my possession?"

"Yes, yes. We will keep it in mind. Do you not remember the accomplishment I bestowed upon you in Uru?"

He recalled the past incident at the Cokla Cave and said, "Then, are you not Dorje Yudrönma?"

"No, no. I am Vajravārāhī. Did you not recognise me? I require two forms, so that I can perform enlightened activities by this mundane body and confer supreme accomplishment in my transcendent form."

Then Longcenpa asked, "Here, where the seminal point is the foremost teaching, the third empowerment is conferred with the assistance of a partner.[672] Why is that?"

"It is necessary for introducing those of great desire to the path. For those without desire it is sufficient to confer it only mentally."

"During the bestowal of the introduction [to reality],[673] what is the significance of the words *absorption of thought in the unborn* and *absorption of intellect in the unaccountable*?"

"What is the use of causing the stabilisation of thought? Introduce the vast and open expanse, which has been liberated from the very beginning."

"Very well, but many expositors of this Innermost Spirituality have appeared. There are those who grant the transmission which is like the handle, for example Karmapa and Rincen Lingpa. Why should I teach it?"

"I am not pleased with their methods of teaching. Even a clay pot has [a handle],[674] but that is not enough. It must also have an owner."

"And what about the treasure discovered by Rincen Lingpa?"

"Oh, that exists, to be sure. But it is not pure [i.e. not the pure Innermost Spirituality]."

"How is it that I have realised you, without meditating upon you?"

"Am I a deity upon whom you must meditate? Have I a mantra you must recite? Am I an object of worship? Do you not know that I am ever present before all yogins who observe their commitments and who have realisation? Throughout all your lives, I have neither been with, nor without you."

Then he asked, "Where are the riches of the Princess,[675] that are said to be concealed in Chimpu?"

"They are on a crag, shaped like an offering of divine foodstuffs, but with the top cut off. The time has not yet come for their revelation."

"When will the treasures of Vimalamitra be discovered?"

"Five years from now they will be discovered and propagated by a mantra adept dressed in white. The four profound volumes will come into your hands."[676]

It was on the eleventh day of the bright half of the month that Longcenpa sent the yogin Özer Koca to bring the books [of the *Innermost Spirituality of the Ḍākinī*]. On his return journey an aura of rainbow light permeated and surrounded them. In particular, during the night of his arrival at Chukpo Trak, near the Stone Stūpas of Zurkardo, all the yogins and yoginīs saw auras of five-coloured rainbow light all the way from there to Rimochen.

Longcenpa performed a feast offering, the rites for the fulfilment of commitments, and so forth, and then opened the door of the esoteric instructions of the *Innermost Spirituality of the Ḍākinī*. The best of gurus, meditational deities and ḍākinīs blessed him so as to disclose fully to his mind the great way in which the [ultimate] essence abides, which cannot be even partially described by the well-known and popular jargon that refers to inner radiance, such as that from the manifestation of that inner radiance by night the intention of the body of reality merges with the primordially pure expanse; that the body of perfect rapture arises as its manifest expression; and that the emanational body and the six realms of existence arise separately from its outward radiance.[677] Thus, the ḍākinīs caused him to see nakedly that which was introduced.

At that time, when the texts for the esoteric instructions of the *Further Innermost Spirituality of the Ḍākinī* (*mkha'-'gro yang-tig*, NYZ Vols. 4-6) were redacted, the master Guru Rinpoche [Padmasambhava] arrived in the guise of Thukdrup (Achievement of Spirituality). One yoginī, who possessed the complete marks and signs of a ḍākinī also saw Tshogyel to his right and Yudrönma to his left, dictating texts. In particular, Yeshe Tshogyel actually remained there for six days.[678] She introduced the master to, and entrusted him with, the symbols, meanings, and texts of the *Innermost Spirituality of the Ḍākinī*. As a result, many of the objects of meditation, systems of introduction, and unique modes of expression – all of which were previously unknown, and unelucidated in writing – spontaneously poured forth from his mind. It is clear that in the land of snow mountains all the other writings on the Innermost Spirituality, those which are considered to be profound, contain not even a fraction of the profound points which are elucidated in this ocean of indestructible reality, the mind treasure of this Second Samantabhadra. Therefore, having realised that that which is found in those texts is like a painted butter lamp [that emits no light] one might well cherish even a single four-line verse of Longcenpa's writings. Most of the germinal instructions originated in this place [Rimochen], but they were systematically arranged in Kangri Thökar, as stated in the author's colophons.

Moreover, for this doctrine, which is like the heart-blood of the ḍākinīs, Kangri Thökar was most blessed: The hosts of the three roots, and of the ḍākinīs who congregated there were endless. They encircled the guru, holding a parasol of peacock feathers, adorned with a pinnacle of precious gems, above his head. When the maṇḍala was laid out, a red woman held the end of the measuring thread; and when the lines were drawn, a woman whose hair was braided with gold and turquoise assisted. Then, during the first empowerment, seven disciples gathered. At that time the guru's nose suddenly started to bleed, and he said, "No more than three can enter this empowerment. This bleeding is due to the excessive number. You four go outside."

The room in which the empowerment was being given was then permeated by an aura of rainbow light. Namdru Remati came in person and said, "Will you not give me an offering? For long I have endured hardship."

She then elucidated the descriptive basis [for the rites][679] of herself and her followers. She also made a prophecy concerning a treasure and displayed a great miracle. But Longcenpa said:

> For myself, having revealed the inner treasure of radiance,
> There is no need for treasure from rocky crags.
> It is fine if there is treasure, it is fine if there is not.
> It is fine if there are any worthy discoverers, fine if not.
> You need not barter your boasts of guarding some treasure
> With a yogin who has exhausted things, exhausted thoughts.

While Longcenpa conferred the background instructions and the precious secret introduction, everyone saw Yeshe Tshogyel take up the vase and grant the empowerment. They all instantly stood up and did homage. Then, when he conferred the introductions to the intermediate state, and to the penetration of the enclosure of inner radiance, the ḍākinīs were delighted. He said, "Non-human beings value this doctrine of mine more highly than do men, and they have greater aspiration and volition. You should keep that in mind!"

When Longcenpa conferred the introduction to the pristine cognition that is the inner radiance, the whole sky was filled with ḍākinīs, their palms pressed together as in prayer. That evening, the protectress of mantra, Ekajaṭī, descended and began to dance. The guru said, "This evening I am teaching the Innermost Spirituality. Are you protectors of the transmitted precepts and ḍākinīs not rejoicing?"

Ekajaṭī answered, "Guru Padmasambhava and Yeshe Tshogyel say just, 'Where is there another so wise as Longcenpa?' It is very wonderful. In general, all the ḍākinīs are rejoicing. Above all, in Orgyen Dzong there is one delighted devotee."

Then the oath-bound protector Kyebuchenpo appeared and urged the master to set out for Orgyen Dzong, saying, "You will have thirty disciples capable of serving the world. Among them, eleven will be great benefactors of living beings, and nine will be exceptional." [And to the disciples themselves] he said, "You disciples are fulfilled by having met this guru."

Afterwards, when Longcenpa granted them the seal of entrustment[680] of the protectors of the doctrine, Shenpa Sokdrupma appeared and said, "Please do not recite my means for attainment."

Similarly, on the evening when he completed all the empowerments and guidance of the *Innermost Spirituality of the Ḍākinī* the master said, "Yesterday the ḍākinīs granted accomplishment. Let us see whether they also come tonight. Mix some water with the ale!"

The disciples strained out the ale and filled a small pot.

"Is this not enough?" they asked.

"That will not suffice. Mix in even more water and strain it again."

They did as they were told, and all that they strained remained potent; so the whole company became intoxicated. The guru said, "This illustrates the reduplication and transformation[681] of a single substance."

After that, Yudrönma urged Longcenpa to set out for her domain once more. When he consented, she said joyfully, "I will go on ahead." But Namdru Remati descended and implored the guru not to go. He said to her, "Though I have given such doctrines to you spirits, you do not understand: Joy and sorrow are the miraculous emanations of mind. You may come wherever I am."

He then gave her an empowerment of contemplation. "I am much obliged," she responded.

"Where did you go yesterday?"

"I went to visit a herd at pasture."

It was well known that at the time the cattle were afflicted with an epidemic.

Then, the yogins and yoginīs also offered a maṇḍala of their own clothes and riches. They promised to practise [the teachings they had received], whereupon Longcenpa said, "Many will endeavour in this doctrine of mine to keep their vows of generosity and of practice." After giving the instructions on entering the enclosure of inner radiance, he said, "These esoteric instructions of mine are rare in Jambudvīpa. The worthy recipient who masters them will quickly achieve the body of light."

When Longcenpa returned from Samye Chimpu, he performed a feast offering at Chukpo Trak, and Yudrönma arrived to welcome him. Then, when he was invited to Shuksep, a ḍākinī possessed a yoginī and asked the guru to set out for Orgyen Dzong. He went to Özer Trin-ki Kyemötsel (Pleasure Garden of Clouds of Light) at Orgyen Dzong in Kangri Thökar, where, in response to the prayers of the yogin Özer Koca, he redacted the *Further Innermost Spirituality of the Ḍākinī*.[682] At that time, the sky was filled with rainbows. Everyone together could see the array of ḍākinīs and endless miracles.

During this period, on various occasions, Longcenpa asked his guru to resolve his doubts regarding the instructions. Wherever he stayed, he planted the banner of practice and so delighted the guru. He was neither attached to, nor fascinated by, appearances; and he was free from both fear of saṃsāra and hope for nirvāṇa. Therefore, he did not involve himself in the affairs of either monastery or household. He honoured his guru five times with offerings that were utterly pure with respect to the three spheres,[683] as well as with two great offerings, and with seven utterly pure acts of worship. He held ceremonies on the eighth, tenth and twenty-fifth days of each month, at which he delighted the warriors and ḍākinīs with bountiful feast offerings and *tormas*.[684]

He reached the citadel of the realised potential of awareness by the passageway of the all-surpassing inner radiance (*'od-gsal thod-rgal*); and thus he entered into continuous yoga. He had visions of countless meditational deities, and, in particular, had a vision of Vimalamitra, who prophetically declared, "Simplify and summarise the meaning of my own Innermost Spirituality, and teach it to your present disciple Zhönu Sangye, who is the emanation of Kumārādza. He will have seven disciples bearing the name Zhönu, all of whom will have the syllable A marked on the tips of their noses. They will preserve and propagate this doctrine."

It was due to this that Longcenpa set forth, in thirty-five sections, the *Further Innermost Spirituality like the Wish-fulfilling Gem* (*yang-tig yid-bzhin-nor-bu*, NYZ Vol.1).[685]

Similarly, Vimala pointed his finger towards Zha in Uru, and declared that Longcenpa should restore the temple there. Accordingly, he went there and began the reconstruction. At that point, many skulls [which had been buried under the ground] in order to supress [evil spirits], leapt into the air. Absorbed in contemplation, Longcenpa recalled them by merely raising his finger in the gesture of menace. Then he extracted a full chest of gold from the back of the upper shrine, and this provided the funds for restoring the temple.

Guru Trakpo

The Oath-bound One [Dorje Lekpa] emanated as a boy wearing a turquoise ear-ring and helped the craftsmen each day. When two memorial pillars toppled over, and no number of assistants could raise them in any way, Longcenpa offered a *torma* to the doctrine protectors and made a solemn declaration of truth. Then, as he impetuously threw off his robe, the pillars could be raised.

Longcenpa restored the damaged charms,[686] which supress the Tamsi demons,[687] in various skulls [that were found at the site]; but when he was at the point of resealing them underground a wild stormy wind blew up, and a hail of earth and stones made the people run away. The skulls leapt up and collided with one another. Owing to the sorcery of the Tamsi demons, the largest of them jumped up into the air, but Longcenpa recalled it by the "contemplation and gaze of blazing wrath", and crushed it under foot. As a clear sign of his championship, he actually appeared to others in the form of Guru Trakpo. Then he buried the skulls beneath the Stūpa of Sorcery (*phra-men mchod-rten*).

During the consecration of the temple, the master wondrously displayed numerous apparitions: Śākyamuni, Maitreya, and the Sixteen Elders appeared with beaming smiles. Maitreya pointed to Longcenpa and prophetically declared, "In your final birth you will become fully awakened as the Tathāgata Sumerudīpadhvaja in the Buddha-field of Padmakūṭa."

When a multitude gathered on both banks of the Kyicu in upper Uru to hear the doctrine, Longcenpa conferred on them the *Guidance of the Unsurpassed Secret* [*Innermost Spirituality*, *gsang-ba bla-na-med-pa'i khrid*]. Again and again, he sponsored bountiful feast offerings for those who congregated about him. Early and late in life he made fine donations to the college of Sangpu as well.

Near Kangpori the master perceived a fearsome apparition and so knew that there would be strife in the world and conflict between the Sakyapa and the Phakmotrupa.[688] Therefore, he went to Bumthang in Bhutan, a land very hard to convert because the light of the teaching was dim, but even there he found a vast field for the propagation of his doctrine. He founded a monastery called Tharpaling, where a multitude of monks gathered. The master Sangye Künga was appointed abbot, and the enlightened activity of the Ancient Translation School in general, and of the Great Perfection in particular, became widespread.

In order to teach by his own example those who practised the way of secret mantra according to their own whim, he received the verbal lineage of the *Innermost Spirituality of the Ḍākinī* from Gyelse Lekpa of Sho, who had been the direct disciple of Cangne Tertön.

When Longcenpa went to Lhasa and saw the image of Lord Śākyamuni Buddha, a ray of light emanated from the circle of hair between the eyebrows of the image, and vanished between his own, whereupon he remembered his previous lives as a scholar at Vulture Peak and in Khotan. He was welcomed here [in Lhasa] by a procession of many monks. Occupying the thrones of religion between Lhasa and Ramoche, Longcenpa extensively turned the wheel of such doctrines as the *Great Development of the Enlightened Mind* (*sems-bskyed chen-mo*). He stifled all the many proud intellectuals who openly and secretly examined his attainments, by means of his "bandit-force" of scripture and logic. Thus, he established them in that faith which gives rise to certainty; and his title "Künkyen Chöje", the "All-Knowing Lord of the Doctrine", rang in all ears.

Another time when Longcenpa saw the image of Lord Śākyamuni, a pure golden light radiated from it. Above the head of Śākyamuni he saw the Seven Generations of Buddhas, as well as Bhaiṣajyaguru, Cakrasaṃvara, Hevajra, Avalokiteśvara [in the form of] the "King of Space", Jinasāgara, and the multitude of the protectors of the teaching.

At such times as these, Longcenpa had visions of the great master Padmasambhava, Guru Trakpo, the Buddhas of the Hundred Authentic Families, the Deities of the Eight Transmitted Precepts of Great Attainment, and other buddhas and bodhisattvas, countless as a mass of sesame seeds; and he obtained their encouragement and permission to compose treatises. His compositions include: the *Seven Great Treasuries* (*mdzod-chen bdun*), which set forth the treasures of his intention in the manner of formal treatises; the *Trilogy of Rest* (*ngal-gso skor-gsum*); the *Trilogy of Natural Liberation* (*rang-grol skor-gsum*); the *Trilogy which Dispels Darkness* (*mun-sel skor-gsum*), which is a commentary on the *Secret Nucleus* that accords with the Innermost Spirituality; the *Twofold Innermost Spirituality* (*snying-tig rnam-pa gnyis*);[689] the *Three Cycles of Further Innermost Spirituality* (*yang-tig skor-gsum*); et cetera. The enumeration of his works, which transcends the imagination, is known from the catalogue entitled the *Repository of Precious Gems* (*dkar-chag rin-po-che'i mdzod-khang*).

Usually, the protectress of mantra Ekajaṭī, the planetary divinity Rāhula, and the oath-bound Dorje Lekpa served and obeyed him. While he was composing the *Seven Treasuries* and other works his attendant actually saw that he had compelled Khyapjuk Chenpo [Rāhula] to mix the ink at Kangri.

The places of practice, where Longcenpa dwelt in total solitude solely for the attainment of the nucleus of the teaching, included Samye Chimpu, Orgyen Dzong, Lharing Trak, Trapu, Shuksep, Kangri Thökar, Zhotö Tidro, Yerpa, Yarlha Shampo, Bumthang, Kyambu Pelgi Geding, Kongpori Lawalung, and Kongpo Tsagongphu. But most of all he stayed in Kangri proper. In Lhodrok, the Yoru region of Central Tibet, and in all the southern regions of Mön [i.e. Bhutan and neighbouring districts], his disciples often gathered in their thousands; and to all of them he displayed boundless compassion. Therefore, Longcenpa accepted no teaching fees, nor did he squander the offerings made by the faithful. He engaged himself only in activities on behalf of his disciples; and he tolerated their faults and tiresome quarrels. Because of his respectful performance of bountiful feast offerings and his intuition of the minds of others, his way of teaching by skilful means and his enlightened activity surpassed the imagination.

There was one Gompa Künrin of Drigung who, being insane with pride in his own power, made ready for war. The great master Padmasambhava had prophesied in his treasures:

> In the land known as Dri
> There will be a son of Māra named Künga,

Whose body will bear a weapon-like mark.
When he dies he will be reborn in hell;
But he will be converted by an emanation
Of Mañjuśrī, who will come from the south.

When Gompa Künrin saw that prediction, he examined his own body, for he still had a grain of past merit, and found that there was a sword-like scar on his back. He knew with certainty that he was the one referred to. Though he had considered waging a great war in Central Tibet and Tsang, he thought little would be achieved by his going to hell, and so he postponed action. He made it known in all quarters that he sought an emanation of Mañjuśrī. At that, all those who were knowledgeable pronounced the same opinion: "In the four regions of Tibet there is, at present, no one more brilliant than the man from Samye." Convinced that Longcenpa was the emanation of Mañjuśrī, Künrin invited him, and honoured him like the crown jewels. The guru uprooted the primary and auxilliary causes and effects of the evil actions, provisional and ultimate, of Künrin and his followers.[690]

About the same time there was, in Central Tibet and Tsang, one Tā'i Situ Cangcup Gyeltsen, who was so arrogant that he found it difficult to show his topknot to anyone [i.e. he did not bow]. He disliked Longcenpa, claiming that he was the "Guru of the Drigungpa" [who were Situ's rivals]. They were reconciled by one whose name Buddhaśrī [Sangyepel] rang in all ears, whose enlightened activity was inspired by limitless, great compassion, and whose exemplary life was that of a scholar and accomplished master. After that, even the "Eight-footed Lion", the Shing-go-chen-pa,[691] who was the king of Tibet [i.e. Situ] bowed his head at Longcenpa's feet.

Similarly, Situ Śākya Zangpo the myriarch of upper Uru, Dorje Gyeltsen the myriarch of Yamdrok, and many other nobles also showed deference to the master. Longcenpa never squandered on impossible schemes even a little of the offerings presented by such devotees, so they revered the Three Precious Jewels even more. He did not consider the things dedicated in the name of the doctrine to be his own property; therefore he could never misuse them. He used to say, "You must have reverence for the Precious Jewels, not for sinful persons." For this reason he never respected or honoured the nobility. "It is the duty of the patron to accumulate merit. Confusion of priest and patron is an evil," he said. And therefore he sealed whatever great offerings were made to him with the dedicatory rites, but gave no other "repayment". He particularly loved the meek, and he ate whatever the humble and indigent served to him as if it were a great treat. Then, he would recite the sūtras and the dedication of merit with exuberance.

Because Longcenpa's enlightened activities, such as those described above, were immeasurable, he could guide not merely those who were visibly taken into his following, but even those who happened [by chance] to see, hear of, come in contact with, or even harm him, to blissful states; and he implanted within them the seed of purity and liberation.

In 1363 (water female hare), during his fifty-sixth year, at a time when he was bestowing on many worthy disciples the attainments of maturation and liberation, he told one Gyelse Zöpa to prepare ink and paper. Then, he composed his testament, the *Taintless Light* (*zhal-chems dri-ma med-pa'i 'od*), which began:

> I have known for sometime saṃsāra's condition;
> Because mundane things are lacking in substance,
> And I must now forsake this changing, apparitional body,
> I will set forth this instruction, alone beneficial: pay it heed!

And it included these verses:

> O Lotus-faced Lord! endowed with compassion,
> Having favoured me today with inspiring deeds,
> It is time I set out, like a traveller, on my road.
> In death I will obtain the profit of joy,
> More by far than the bliss of the merchant who gains
> All he seeks overseas; or that of Devendra,
> Triumphant in battle; or that of an attainer of trance.
> Pema Lendreltsel,[692] without waiting longer,
> Will go now to seize immortality's stronghold, bliss supreme!

When he had revealed this testament, Gyelse Zöpa cried out in tears, "Please do not talk like this!" whereupon the guru discoursed on many doctrines beginning with that of the decay of transient things. Being invited once more to Samye, he travelled to the forests of glorious Chimpu, via Gyama and Samye, turning the wheel of the doctrine on the way there. "This place is just like Śītavana charnel ground in India," he said, "I would rather die here than be born elsewhere. Here I will leave this worn-out, illusory body of mine."

Even though he was ill, he continually taught the doctrine. The disciples thought that he was tired and asked him to stop teaching for a time, but he said, "I have decided to teach this doctrine completely."

Then, on Saturday 23 December 1363 (sixteenth day, twelfth month, water female hare), he delighted the warriors and ḍākinīs with bountiful worship and offerings. He then advised his disciples as follows: "Since everything compounded is insubstantial, you should devote yourselves entirely to the doctrine. In particular, you should concentrate on achieving practical experience of [the esoteric instructions of] Cutting Through Resistance (*khregs-chod*) and All-Surpassing Realisation (*thod-rgal*).[693] If sometimes you do not understand, then examine minutely, and meditate on the *Further Innermost Spirituality like the Wish-fulfilling Gem*, which is like a jewel that grants your desires. Then you will attain nirvāṇa at the level on which [the appearance of] reality is exhausted."

On Monday 25 December 1363 (eighteenth day, twelfth month, water female hare)[694] Longcenpa told his disciples to arrange an altar and to go off to undertake acts of merit, but they begged to remain in his presence. "Very well", he said, "but I am about to leave this worn-out, apparitional body. Be silent and remain absorbed in meditation!"

Then, his precious body assumed the posture of the buddha-body of reality; and he set his intention to rest in the primordial expanse.

At that time, there were limitless miracles, and the whole earth shook and resounded. His body was left undisturbed for twenty-five days, during which time the deities who rejoice in the teaching unfurled a canopy of rainbow light, and caused a shower of flowers to fall. When his intention had thus dissolved in reality, even the four elements departed from the stable order of the four seasons: The earth was warm during the twelfth and first months, the ice melted, and the leaves of the wild rose began to bud. Also, during the funeral ceremony, when the master's body was placed on the pyre, the earth trembled and a mighty thunder resounded seven times. After the cremation his heart, tongue, and eyes – the signs of his having awakened to the essence of the three indestructible realities of body, speech, and mind – fell into the laps of fortunate disciples. Because he had realised all that can be attained with respect to the five bodies [of buddhahood] and the five pristine cognitions, five large remains and countless minor relics were discovered. It is undisputed that the larger relics multiplied by the hundreds and thousands, without limit. And up to the present day, it has been plain to see that those who possess even a tiny fragment of his undamaged remains cannot be afflicted by the "upper demons".[695]

The gurus of the past identified Longcenpa with the grammarian Śrīdhara, who is referred to in a prophecy in the *Great Descent* (*babs-lugs chen-mo*); but according to the sequence fixed therein it would be correct to identify him with Lodröchok.[696] Moreover, the notion that the interval between Kumārādza and this next [emanation of Vimalamitra, i.e. Longcenpa] violates the axiom that "Once every century [an emanation of Vimalamitra will arise]," should not give rise to doubts, because "every century" implies that, in general, when this doctrine [of the Innermost Spirituality] becomes contaminated by sophistry, one will appear to elucidate it. In addition, emanations act, in the manner of apparitions, on behalf of those requiring training, referring solely to the unique circumstances of the situation at hand.

The foremost disciples who tasted the nectar of Longcenpa's teaching were: the three learned and accomplished ones who became famous, namely, Khedrup Delek Gyamtso of Zhoktarling, Khedrup Chöki

Trakpa, and Khedrup Khyapdel Lhündrup; his five spiritual sons, namely, Den-gom Chöki Trakpa of Dokam, Gyelse Zöpa, Lama Pelcokpa, Guru Yeshe Rapjam, and Zhönu Sangye; the four spiritual benefactors who propagated the doctrine, namely, Trülku Peljor Gyamtso, master Sangye Künga, master Lodrö Zangpo, and Tago Cadrel Chöje; and the four accomplished yogins, namely, Phagö Tokden Gyelpo, Neljorpa Özer Koca, Rikdzin Ösel Rangdröl, and Catang Sonam Özer.

Moreover, there were many spiritual benefactors who were holders of his teaching, such as Sangye Pelrin, who had reconciled him with the Lord of Neudong [i.e. Situ], Trakpapel, and Luken Sonam Senge.

At a later date, Longcenpa appeared in a vision to the master of the doctrine Drigung Rincen Phüntsok, and declared that he had been born as [Longcenpa's] son Trülku Dawa, the crown of whose head bore the mark of a horse's head [emblematic of Hayagrīva].[697] Longcenpa's hat was placed on his head and he became a direct disciple through the blessing. He was boundlessly dedicated to maintaining, preserving and propagating the scriptures of Longcenpa. In his lineage Padmasambhava's spiritual successor Śāntapurīpa, otherwise known as the great treasure-finder Sherap Özer, appeared. He established the monastery of Pelri Thekpachok-gi Ling, and persuaded his patron Zhapdrung Chongye to xylograph the *Mind at Rest* and its autocommentary (*sems-nyid ngal-gso rtsa-'grel*). Since they taught the necessity of both studying and practising this teaching, they affirmed themselves to be the genuine holders of the lineage.

So it was that the lineage of the complete cycle of the maturation [i.e. empowerment], liberation [i.e. guidance] and instructions of the Innermost Spirituality, which belongs to the Esoteric Instructional Class [of the Great Perfection] was transmitted in its entirety from the great charioteer, the all-knowing Longcen Rapjampa, by successive stages through:

> Khedrup Khyapdel Lhündrup;
> Trakpa Özer;
> Sangye Önpo;
> Dawa Trakpa;
> Künzang Dorje;
> Gyeltsen Pelzang;
> Natsok Rangdröl;
> Tendzin Trakpa;
> Do-ngak Tendzin;
> Rikdzin Trhinle Lhündrup; to
> the king of the doctrine, Terdak Lingpa.

Later on, in 1759/60 (earth female hare), the great, all-knowing [Longcenpa] thrice revealed the body of his pristine cognition to Rikdzin

Khyentse Özer [Jikme Lingpa] at Womin Pelgi Chimpu.[698] He also entrusted him with a book and said, "All the esoteric instructions which are concealed in the *Great Chariot* and in my other works are clarified herein." When he had transmitted all the instructions and further advice to him, Jikme Lingpa came to comprehend thoroughly the oceanic doctrine, and all the textual traditions and instructions of the All-Knowing Guru in particular. Just as Mātaṅgī had been taken into the following of Āryadeva, so, such an extremely short lineage is permissible.

This completes the general explanation of the descent, in Tibet, of the teaching of the three inner classes of the tantras of the way of secret mantra, and, in particular, the account of the esoteric instructions of the great Innermost Spirituality, the fourth part of this book, *Thunder from the Great Conquering Battle-Drum of Devendra*, which is a history of the precious doctrine of the vehicle of indestructible reality according to the Ancient Translation School.

Part Five
The Distant Lineage of Transmitted Precepts

Introduction

[281.1-2] Now, I should explain in particular the way in which the trilogy of the *Sūtra which Gathers All Intentions*, the *Magical Net*, and the *Mental Class* have come down to us.[699] These teachings are common to all [the Nyingmapa lineages] and have perpetuated, without decline, the river of the transmitted precepts, the "distant lineage" mentioned above. It is said that in [Tibet], the land of snow mountains, the teaching of the vehicle of indestructible reality according to the Ancient Translation School "fell first to Nyak, fell to Nup during the intermediate period, and fell to Zur in the end."

1 *The Lineage of Nyak*

NYAK JÑĀNAKUMĀRA

[281.2-289.4] The first of these, master Nyak Jñānakumāra, was born in Shepa, or Chö, in the district of Yarlung.[700] He was the son of Takdra Lhanang of the Nyak clan, and his wife Suza Drönkyi. When he was born, there was a mole on his neck which resembled a crossed-vajra, and he was given the name Gyelwei Lodrö. The preceptor Bodhisattva [Śāntarakṣita] ordained him as a novice and, later, as a monk with full ordination. He became an inconceivably brilliant translator of many of the doctrines belonging to the sūtras and mantra texts and so became the confluence of the four great rivers of transmitted precepts which were derived from [the teachings of] the great master Padmasambhava, Vimalamitra, Vairocana and Yudra Nyingpo. These "four great rivers" are: (1) the river of conventional textual exegesis, along with the commentaries and lecture notes; (2) the river of instruction of the aural lineage, along with the essential writings and the guidance which lays bare the teaching;[701] (3) the river of blessing and empowerment, along with the means for conferral and the introductions; (4) the river of practical techniques, that of the rites of enlightened activity and attainment, along with the wrathful mantras of the protectors of the teaching.

After the master Padmasambhava had matured Nyak Jñānakumāra in the maṇḍala of [Vajrāmṛta], Nectar the Enlightened Attributes (*bdud-rtsi yon-tan*), Nyak caused the water of accomplishment to spring forth from dry rock in the Crystal Cave of Yarlung. The *Magical Net* also must have been transmitted through his lineage, but he attained the signs of accomplishment primarily from Vajrakīla.

Sometime after the passing of King Trhisong Detsen, one of the queens, Tshepong-za, reviled most of the translators and scholars by her uncivil designs, so Nyak Jñānakumāra went to live at Yamdrok.[702] His own brother, Nyak Getön, became hostile and slandered him, declaring that Nyak was "an adept of extremist mantras". He stole

Nyak's skull-cup, which had been painted red and lacquered on the inside, showed it to foolish people and scratched the inside with the point of his knife, maliciously saying, "This is the work of a charlatan!"

In order to remove widespread doubts, Nyak Jñānakumāra materialised precious gems in the place where he lived. In this way the people learned of his miraculous powers and discounted his brother's words. But even then Nyak knew that his brother was planning many conspiracies and devising various ways to injure him, so he went away.

Nyak Jñānakumāra

When he reached the upper part of Chimyül in Kongpo he found a herd of seven goats wandering through a desolate valley. He ordered his servant Lelmik Woktsen to drive them away, but the latter asked, "What will the owner of these goats say when he arrives?"

Nyak replied, "Where is the owner of the goats to be found in a desolate valley? Drive them away!"

When the owner, Chim Carok (the "Crow of Chim") learned of this he accused Nyak of theft and demanded sevenfold compensation for the goats. Although Nyak gave him sevenfold compensation he remained unsatisfied, destroyed Nyak's hermitage, and pursued him with an iron hammer. Nyak ran away and entered a temple. It is said that as the door closed behind him Chim Carok struck the threshold with his hammer and narrowly missed the head of a young novice.

But Nyak was not even allowed to remain there. He set out for Central Tibet and on the way met one Drosechung, who was chasing a deer. Drosechung's mount was startled, so that the deer escaped. He became enraged and attempted to kill Nyak, but Nyak fled from his sight, longing to escape.

It was at about this time that Queen Margyen had poisoned the crown prince [Mune Tsepo]. The master Vimalamitra had miraculously arrived from China to preside over the funeral ceremony, where Nyak met him and offered him a container[703] full of gold dust. Vimalamitra asked, "Are the translator and his servant well?" To which Nyak replied:

> We were doing well in Yamdrok-gang,
> But Gelatön would not let us be.
> We were doing well in the heart of Chim,
> But hell's own crow would not let us be.
> We were doing well in Central Tibet,
> But Drosechung would not let us be.

Thinking that it was very harmful to the teaching for a translator to be so insulted, Vimalamitra spontaneously taught him the *Perfect Practice of Vajrakīla* (*phur-pa phun-sum-tshogs-pa*, NGB Vol.27), and that of the *Blue-skirted One's Cycle* [*of Vajrakīla, gsham-sngon*].[704] In the Na Cave at Kharcu in Lhodrak the scholar and the translator propitiated Vajrakīla together, using twenty-one kīlas of acacia wood. Such was their accomplishment that the kīlas started knocking against one another. At that point, Nyak, who was absorbed in contemplation, brandished his kīla and said, "This is for the Crow." At once, all the crows in the sky gathered together. Then, he rotated the kīla, saying, "This is for the Crow of Chim." And a pair of crows arrived from Chim. In anger Nyak brandished the kīla at one of the crows and the bird instantly fell dead.[705]

At that Vimalamitra said, "Now you can kill by the power of sorcery, but, I wonder, can you revive by the power of reality? Go ahead and revive it!" But, as had previously occurred in the case of master Jālandharipā and his disciple Kṛṣṇacārin,[706] Nyak could not resurrect the dead. Vimalamitra scattered a handful of sand and instantly the crow came to life and flew away. The master said to Nyak, "When you undertake a wrathful rite without first having attained the realisation to 'liberate' the self [of your victim], then, even if you succeed in the rite, it is a great crime." And then he performed the rite of the "Tie to the Higher Realms" (*gnas-lung*).[707]

Then the deity of Chim appeared in the guise of a white yak, and Nyak "liberated" him first of all. By the power of ritually brandishing his kīla he "liberated" Chim Carok and obtained the superior, middling, and inferior indications that he had destroyed his life-supporting wolf-spirit,[708] along with his servants and slaves, horses and dogs, and kith and kin, and thus put an end to his race.

While inflicting the same punishment on Nyak Getön, his own brother, Nyak developed great compassion, owing to the kindness of master Vimalamitra; for this sort of wrathful rite of occult power is particularly dependent on the coincidence of the indestructible reality of anger.[709]

So his intention turned to reality itself and he was completely unable to perform the rite. Master Vimalamitra said to him, "At this point, if you find an assistant who is endowed with all the signs of a sorcerer, you will be able to perform it." With this, he began to search.

He found a blacksmith called "Pektse the Sogdian" – for at that time blacksmiths were called "Sogdians" – who was wrathful to behold.[710] Nyak perceived that he had all the appropriate physical marks and signs: his head was knotted and the lower part of his body was triangular in shape.[711] Nyak came down behind him and acted as his assistant by operating the bellows. He expounded to him the dialectical doctrines of the causal vehicle, but the blacksmith paid no attention. Then, when Nyak explained the Kriyātantra, Caryātantra, and Yogatantra, he listened occasionally, but otherwise only heard the clanging sound of the hammer as it struck [the anvil]. Finally, when Nyak gave teaching on the three inner classes of tantra and at the same time swallowed the scraps of hot iron that were flying about, the blacksmith was amazed. "How did you acquire such miraculous power?" he asked.

"I acquired it by practising the doctrine I was just explaining."

The blacksmith developed great faith and, making an offering of all of his tools, he became a disciple. His name was changed to Lha Pelgi Yeshe.

Similarly, Nyak discovered that Odren Pelgi Zhönu also possessed the signs of one fit to attain Vajrakīla; so the master and his two disciples propitiated that deity. When Getön heard about it he began a murderous conspiracy. Others restrained him saying that it was not right to blaspheme a venerable monk, but Getön refused to listen. During the night he dreamed that many women encircled him and cut off his head. He told this to his wife, who earnestly tried to restrain him, but without paying attention he rode off on his horse. On the way an enormous bird flew over and startled the horse. Getön's flesh was torn to shreds and his blood was scattered drop by drop. It is said that he was actually "liberated" by the protector. The Sogdian Pelgi Yeshe removed his heart and offered it to the master, who said:

> Let no sin be committed.
> Virtue must be perfectly practised.
> Completely tame your own mind.
> May all sentient beings be happy![712]

In short, Nyak's guardian deity had appeared as a hawk and, having "liberated" Getön along with his life-supporting wolf-spirit, servants and slaves, horses and dogs, and kith and kin, put an end to his race.

In the same way, Nyak summoned the consciousness of Drosechung, who was grazing his herd of horses on the plain of Netang, and completely destroyed him by the ritual thrust of the kīla. He transformed the deity of Dro [Drosechung's clan] into a blue wolf and dealt with his life-supporting wolf-spirit, servants and slaves as before.

This great translator Nyak adhered to learned and accomplished masters who were equal to the Buddha himself, and in this way he acquired very great learning in grammar, logic, dialectics, and the outer and inner mantra texts. Having become a great translator, he interpreted many works on the true doctrine. He became a master of the trilogy of the *Sūtra which Gathers All Intentions*, the *Magical Net* and the *Mental Class* and through his expositions the number of extraordinary disciples multiplied. Thus, his kindness was inconceivable. Finally, he realised the great accomplishment through the *Vajra Bridge of the Aural Lineage* (*snyan-brgyud rdo-rje zam-pa*) and through [teachings belonging to] the Esoteric Instructional Class of the Great Perfection (*man-ngag-sde*).[713] His body vanished in a mass of light, the union of radiance and emptiness.

Nyak Jñānakumāra guided his foremost disciples, until they became the "eight glorious adepts of Vajrakīla". These eight glorious sons were his four earlier disciples – the Sogdian Pelgi Yeshe, Odren Pelgi Zhönu, Nyencen Pelyang, and Thakzang Pelgi Dorje – and his four later disciples – Lamcok Pelgi Dorje, Tarje Pelgi Trakpa, Tra Pelgi Nyingpo, and Lhalung Pelgi Dorje. In addition, there were his nephews Üpa Tosel, Gyepak Sherap and Bhusukuchok, whose lineage gave rise to extensive enlightened activity.

THE SOGDIAN PELGI YESHE

[289.4-290.4] The Sogdian Pelgi Yeshe was a native of Yamdrok. Though he had already attained accomplishment during the time of the great master Padmasambhava, he lived as a blacksmith, so far as ordinary men could see. It is said that the great translator Nyak's life was thrice endangered because, being vastly learned, he had thrice thought himself to be more learned than his masters. For this, he had to show his acceptance of the infallible truth of cause and effect. On one such occasion, one of the three on which Nyak was confronted by mortal enemies, his relative Nyakmar,[714] from a neighbouring district, imprisoned him with homicidal malice. The Sogdian Pelgi Yeshe had

The Sogdian Pelgi Yeshe

previously displayed his courage by seizing a savage beast of prey by the neck, and by other acts associated only with actual accomplishment; so, on this occasion, he fulfilled his solemn, indestructible commitment to risk his life for the guru. He killed two prison guards and pulled the master from the dungeon. In this way, on all three occasions, he destroyed Nyak's mortal enemies and so caught his attention. Owing to this, Nyak actually materialised the maṇḍala of Vajrakīla and took Pelgi Yeshe into his following. Such was the extent to which Pelgi Yeshe abided in authenticity. In his turn, he instructed Nupcen Sangye Yeshe.

2 *The Lineage of Nup*

NUPCEN SANGYE YESHE

[290.4-300.3] "The teachings of the Ancient Translation School fell to Nup during an intermediary period..."

Nupcen Sangye Yeshe was born in the uplands of Dra in the mountains of Central Tibet in February 832 (first month, water male mouse year).[715] His father was Selwa Wangcuk of the Nup clan, and his mother was Chimo Trashi-tsho. At the ancestral charnel ground, on Mount Dra Riwoche, a sandal tree had sprung up. A Chinese monk examined it, said that it portended the birth of an emanation, and showed how to cultivate the tree.[716] In accordance with this early prophecy Nup was born. His secular name was Dorje Trhitsuk, his religious name was Sangye Yeshe, and his secret name was Dorje Yangwangter. In his seventh year, Nup entered the following of Odren Pelgi Zhönu and studied all the sciences.

There was a prophecy in the *Root Tantra of the Gathering of Awareness-holders* (*rig-'dzin 'dus-pa rtsa-ba'i rgyud*, NGB Vol.32), as follows:

> In particular, the secrets of buddha-body will be revealed
> By the precious jewel, Buddhajñāna [i.e. Sangye Yeshe].

Accordingly, in his youth, when Nup received the empowerment of the Eight Transmitted Precepts from the great master Padmasambhava, his flower alighted upon the maṇḍala of Mañjuśrī, representing buddha-body. By propitiating that meditational deity, Nup actualised the signs of accomplishment. Later he also received many tantras and esoteric instructions [from master Padmasambhava] in the Dorje Tse-nga Cave, which lies on the frontier of India and Nepal. Moreover, he attended on such scholars and translators of India, Nepal, and Bru-sha [i.e. Gilgit] as Śrī Siṃha, Vimalamitra, Kamalaśīla, Dhanadhala, Trhaktung Nakpo, Śāntigarbha, Dhanasaṃskṛta, Śākyadeva, Dhanarakṣita, the brahman Prakāśālaṃkāra [i.e. Sukhodyotaka], Dharmabodhi, Dharmarāja, Tsuklak Pelge, Vasudhara, and Chetsenkye; as well as on the learned Tibetan translator Nyak Jñānakumāra and all his eight glorious disciples. Among them, in particular, he attended on the Sogdian Pelgi Yeshe and Zhang Gyelwei Yönten, who had been a disciple of both Ma Rincen-chok and Nyak. Under all of those gurus Nup studied and

Nupcen Sangye Yeshe

mastered all the sūtras, as well as the outer and inner tantras of the mantra vehicle, along with their esoteric instructions. He travelled to India and Nepal seven times and translated many tantras, esoteric instructions, and ritual texts, along with [the rites of] the protectors of the doctrine.

In particular, in 885 (wood snake year), his fifty-fourth year, Nup went to Nepal, where he requested numberless empowerments and instructions from Vasudhara. For the sake of the doctrine he pleased that guru with offerings and faithful devotion. Then the preceptor[717] [Vasudhara] said, "In India lives my master Prakāśālaṃkāra. He is one thousand and six hundred years old. Go to him and request the doctrine."

Nup set out for India as instructed and met the master Prakāśālaṃkāra in Vārāṇasī. He asked for many teachings. In particular, he received the complete empowerment of the [Anuyoga] sūtras along with the instructions of the *Sūtra which Gathers All Intentions*. According to Rok Tsöndrü Senge, this master [Prakāśālaṃkāra] is identical to Sukhodyotaka.

Nup later asked Prakāśālaṃkāra for the textual exegesis of the *Sūtra which Gathers All Intentions*, but the master said, "Dhanarakṣita, Dharmabodhi, and Dharmarāja have been invited to Bru-sha by Chetsenkye. Go there and request the exegesis from them."

Accordingly, Nup went to Bru-sha where, under those four translators and scholars, he made a critical study primarily of that textual exegesis but also of the essential instructions concerning its transmitted empowerment, the subtleties of its practical techniques, and so forth. Thus, he extracted the essence of their spirituality.

Concerning the way in which Nup attained accomplishment: During the nine months [spent in retreat] at Zhugi Dorje Gombu, his mind was liberated and he established [the realisation of] the abiding nature of reality. In Vajrāsana and in Yungdrung Rincen Terne, the Lord of Secrets (Guhyapati) revealed his visage to him. His emblematic vajra fell into Nup's hands and he conferred on Nup the empowerment of the name. Then, in Ölmotshel, the child of a gandhārva conferred on Nup the name Sangye. In Kangzang he was honoured by a yakṣa, and on the shore of the Nine-Island Lake of Yamdrok *(gling dgu'i mtsho)* by three young nāga brothers. In the charnel ground of Lhe the child of a tormented spirit bowed before his feet. In Ömeitshel, Yamāntaka appeared in a vision to confer empowerment and accomplishment upon him.

After achieving dominion over gods and demons, Nup was empowered as a master of secret mantra. The guardians of the *Mātaraḥ* and *Yamāntaka (ma-gshin)* cycles, lords of the ḍākinīs, were appointed to be his protectors. Then, as Mañjuśrī had prophesied, Ekajaṭī presented Nup with the sacraments of accomplishment in the Sanglung Nakpo charnel ground in India.

Thus, his pristine cognition illuminated the expanse [of reality], and the realisations of the great levels were actualised. He beheld in visions the entire maṇḍalas of Padmanarteśvara and of Yamāntaka, and he obtained their empowerments and accomplishments. Moreover, he possessed unobstructed supernormal cognitive powers – clairvoyance and so forth. The wonderful accounts of his career, [which describe him] floating on water, passing through mountains of solid rock, and performing other miracles, surpass the imagination.

Nup founded his foremost hermitage at the pilgrimage place of Yangdzong, in Dra, Central Tibet; and he intended to remain there in total solitude. But he and his disciples faced great hardship because, generally, the laws of the land disintegrated at about that time [owing to the collapse of the dynasty in the wake of the reign of Langdarma]; and there followed a period of increasingly partisan conflict. In particular, he had to train completely all within his sphere of influence who remained from a past life in India where he had taken birth as the butcher Marutse, and had worked on behalf of living beings.[718] Moreover, because here in Tibet the teaching of the royal grandson [Relpacen] had declined and there arose many who did harm to his early and later teaching, Nupcen became inspired by the enlightened activity of the Conqueror to eliminate these by wrathful mantras and so to protect the teaching. Above and beyond that, there were the circumstances created by the murder of his own two sons during the early, middle or later local rebellions.

As Nup himself said:

> Trouble arose in Central Tibet;
> The people deprived me of sustenance.

And:

> Though a minor ascetic of Nup, like myself, sincerely
> Developed an enlightened attitude in accord with the doctrine,
> Hateful enemies would not permit me to practise.
> In order to protect the Buddha's teaching
> I cultivated hatred thereafter.
> Thinking to expose the greatness of the good,
> I studied various malevolent mantra texts.

So it was that Nup introduced the wrathful mantras of the oceanic cycle of Yamāntaka from India and Nepal:

> I went before the feet of eleven gurus,
> But I met with four who were learned:
> These were the master Śrī Siṃha,
> Trhaktung Nakpo of India,
> Śāntigarbha the destroyer,
> And Vasudhara of Nepal.
> Penetrating the spirituality of these four learned masters,
> I fixed their profound esoteric instructions in my heart.

But Nup obtained the very quintessence of their teaching from his Nepali master. As he himself said:

> My master, the king of Nepal,
> Said, "O minor ascetic of Nup!
> Come here to this Yangleshö Cave!"
> He conferred the empowerment of the corpse of
> the great charnel ground[719]
> And entrusted me with the deity Mañjuśrī, Lord
> of Life.

Moreover:

> I, Sangye Yeshe, constructed
> My hermitage at Khar, in Yama.
> On the summit of the Black Pass of Dra
> I set a tornado in motion.
> It demolished thirty-seven hamlets of Dra.

That is to say, when the rebellions reached Dra, during Nup's sixty-first year, he destroyed many towns, using the sharp, wrathful mantra of Yamāntaka. Then, he escaped to Nup Yülrong, but he was not allowed to stay there. He seized Ce Fortress in Nyemo, but there, too, he was surrounded by armed brigands who put his life in peril. From the top of the fortress he called on the fierce gods and demons to bear him witness. After making a truthful declaration in verse,[720] he folded up his religious robes. At that moment the oath-bound protectors of the doctrine became visible, and said, "By our power we can crush Mount Sumeru to powder, we can strike the sun and moon together like cymbals and turn heaven and earth topsy-

Yamāntaka

turvy. But because the retribution for your actions in previous lives was unfolding we were unable to help you before. Now, we will obey your commands."

Nup extracted his acacia-wood kīla from the seam[721] of his robe and drew out the vital heart-mantras of the oath-bound deities. Rolling the kīla in his hands, he pointed it towards the mountain where the armed men were staying. An enormous fire blazed up on the mountain and burned the whole army to ashes. After subduing his enemies so, Nup lived in poverty for three years.

During the reign of King Relpacen, Nup had been in the habit of travelling between India and Tibet. On the other hand, when King Langdarma persecuted the teaching, he asked Nup, "What power do you have?"

Nup replied, "Behold this power of mine, which comes from the recitation of a mere mantra!"

With his index finger he pointed to the sky, and the king saw a black iron scorpion as large as a yak, sitting nine storeys above Nup's pointed finger.

The king was terrified and said, "By all that is precious, I will not harm this mantrin. Go practise your doctrine!"

Then Nup said, "Behold this power yet again!" And with his index finger he hurled a thunderbolt, which pierced the rock on the mountain opposite and smashed it to pieces.

Now the king was extremely terrified and afraid. He said to Nup, "I will harm neither you, nor your attendants." And then he dismissed him. Thus it was by Nup's kindness that the mantra adepts who wore the white robe and long, braided hair were unharmed [during Langdarma's persecution].[722]

Nup could not endure the supression of the teaching by Langdarma, so, having collected many razor-sharp, wrathful mantras, he resolved to bring him to an end by means of the compassionate application of sorcery. But when the evil king was "liberated" by Lhalung Pelgi Dorje,[723] Nup concealed the wrathful mantras as treasures, lest they be misused.

Nup Sangye Yeshe composed treatises, including the following: the *Armour Against Darkness*, which is a vast commentary on the *Sūtra which Gathers All Intentions* (*mdo'i 'grel-chen mun-pa'i go-cha*); the *Disputant's Sword which Cuts through Difficulties* (*dka'-gcod smra-ba'i mtshon-cha*); the *Commentary on the Realisation of the Eighty-Chapter Magical Net* (*sgyu-'phrul brgyad-cu-pa'i mngon-rtogs 'grel*); and the *Lamp for the Eye of Contemplation, which is an Esoteric Instruction of the Great Perfection.*

By the enlightened activities of exegesis and attainment, he covered the earth with the teaching of the three aspects of creation and perfection. While he had many disciples, there were five particularly sublime ones, namely, his four spiritual sons and the one most authentic son. It says in one of the master's own songs:

> In the forest of discriminative awareness
> That is Yangwangter, the ascetic of Nup,
> The divine tree of enlightened attributes grew.
> With it, I filled five supreme vessels:
> There was one who carried off the roots;
> That was Löncen Phakpa.
> There was one who carried off the leaves;
> That was Lekpei Drönme.
> There was one who carried off the flowers;
> That was Tengi Yöntenchok.
> There was one who carried off the fruits;
> That was Yeshe Wangcuk.
> But one alone took the whole tree;
> That was Yönten Gyamtso.

Thus, the four sons were: Pagor Löncen Phakpa, who was learned in the tantras, which are the roots; Sutön Lekpei Drönme, who was learned in [the texts of] deathless nectar,[724] which are the leaves; Tengi Yöntenchok, who was learned in answering objections, which is the flower; and So Yeshe Wangcuk, who was learned in the essential doctrines of view and intention, which are like fruits. The one most authentic son was Khulung Yönten Gyamtso, who was learned in all four subjects.

Moreover, in the history of the empowerment of the *Sūtra which Gathers All Intentions* in particular it says:

> The transmitted precepts of the empowerment, tantra, and instructions fell to Khulungpa [Yönten Gyamtso]. The transmitted precepts of the stream of the four empowerments fell to Su[tön Lekpei Drönme].

In the sūtras, Nupcen Sangye Yeshe is hailed as a bodhisattva of the fourth level. While there was a prophecy that he would be born two thousand years after the Teacher's nirvāṇa, this was an approximation, for it was close to two thousand years. If we make an accurate calculation, following the chronology of the *Kālacakra Tantra*, which is well known today, Nup was born one thousand seven hundred and thirteen years after the Teacher's nirvāṇa. This is because it is calculated from the iron dragon year of the Teacher's passing (881 BC).[725] Twenty-eight years later, in the earth monkey year (853 BC), the secret mantra texts fell onto the roof of the palace of King Ja. One thousand six hundred and eighty-five years after that in the water mouse year 832, Nup was born. This same water mouse year was the forty-third year of King Trhisong, who had been born in the iron horse year 790; and it was the sixth after the ordination of the "seven men who were tested", which had occurred in the fire sheep year 827. In the earth tiger year 858, when Nupcen was in his twenty-seventh year, King Trhisong died. Eighty-five years later, in the water tiger year 943, Nupcen passed away. Therefore, it is clear that he lived for about thirty-seven years after the persecution of the teaching by Langdarma.

Nup passed away in his one hundred and eleventh year in the district of Khyönmi. Finally, he entered nirvāṇa in a mass of light, spontaneously accomplished by means of the path of the natural Great Perfection.

KHULUNG YÖNTEN GYAMTSO

[300.3-302.1] Nup's most authentic son was Yönten Gyamtso. He and Nup had been associated as master and disciple during previous lives. He was born in the district of Nup Khulung.

The Indian Dhanadhala, who had been Yönten Gyamtso's elder brother during a previous life, had attained the accomplishment of the "swift feet of the yakṣiṇī" *(gnod-sbyin-mo'i rkang-mgyogs)*.[726] None the less, he could not perform it successfully, because of a broken wing. Again, having practised the other [means for the attainment of] "swift feet", a yakṣa carried him in the flap of his robe, and in a single night they reached Yönten Gyamtso at Khulung. There, Dhanadhala lovingly empowered the younger brother of his previous life. It is said that because he gave the common accomplishments to his patron, [the latter's descendants] flourished for seven generations.

Dhanadhala advised Yönten Gyamtso not to build his hermitage in the village and revealed to him the geomantic centre of Tsukrum Tawu in Khardong Yönmo.[727] He conferred the *Red* and *Black Yamāri*, who protect the teaching, the cycles of *Mātaraḥ* and *Yamāntaka*, et cetera. Then, he departed for India.

When Yönten Gyamtso was in his thirtieth year he went on a hunting expedition and met the master Sangye Yeshe at Shukla Nakpo in Nar. Recognising Yönten Gyamtso to be a kinsman and a worthy disciple, Nup caused him to enter the doctrine, and took him into his following. Because Nup gave him all the empowerments, tantras, and esoteric instructions, together with the rituals of the protectors of the teaching, in their entirety, the essence of Nup's transmitted precepts and the heart of his spirituality were transmitted to him. So it is known that he completely received all the instructions.

When persecuted by the rebellions and surrounded by a hundred assassins Yönten Gyamtso, who had actually achieved the miraculous power of the "burning gaze", magically caused fire to blaze from his right eye and water to pour forth from his left. The assassins found no opportunity to harm him, and, abandoning their weapons, they had to escape.

Generally speaking, Yönten Gyamtso had visions of many meditational deities, and he developed the supernormal cognitive power of freedom from corruption. He gained control over the elements and was served by oath-bound deities. He acquired both of the great accomplishments, for the truth of reality had become apparent to him.[728] His life story may be known in detail from the texts of the So tradition.

YESHE GYAMTSO, PEMA WANGYEL AND THE LATER SUCCESSORS IN THE LINEAGE OF NUP

[302.1-304.3] Yönten Gyamtso had two sons: Yeshe Gyamtso and Pema Wangyel. Yeshe Gyamtso was the elder. He had accumulated the provisions and practised patience in his previous life. Therefore, he was endowed with a handsome physical appearance. His humility delighted the hearts of all. With supreme devotion he rendered whatever services of body, speech, and mind were pleasing to his guru. Because his discriminative awareness and his conduct of faith and perseverance were perfect, he realised the spiritual intention [of the lineage].

He was empowered as a master of all the tantras, transmissions, and esoteric instructions. The essence of the entire store of empowerment trickled down to him, so he became the full vessel of all his father's teachings. He realised the significance of the abiding nature of reality, which is the supreme accomplishment, by completing the practices of ritual service and attainment. He had visions of many meditational deities and he was able to reveal his body to others in the form of the divine maṇḍala. Oath-bound deities served him and all spirits offered up their vital heart-mantras to him. Because he swiftly manifested the signs of success at whatever rites of sorcery [he undertook], he was adept at occult powers.

His younger brother, Pema Wangyel, realised Yamāri. The active protectors of the *Yamāri* cycle offered up their vital heart-mantras to him. When he struck the water of a flooding river in Central Tibet with his kīla of acacia wood, in a single day the floodwaters receded by about the distance of an arrow shot. Once he "liberated" nine Pönpo sorcerers simultaneously. It is known that no one could rival his unobstructed powers in such wrathful rites of sorcery.

The son of Yeshe Gyamtso was Lharje Hūṃcung. It was he who taught the wrathful mantras to the venerable Milarepa, who then became renowned as a powerful sorcerer.[729] Lharje Hūṃcung had many disciples, but supreme among them was Nyang Sherapchok. Nyang was renowned for his learning in the three aspects of creation and perfection. He also built the temple of Toklashong. When he practised meditation at Haogöl Rock he had a vision of the maṇḍala of Vajrakīla. When he struck a rock with his vajra, the vajra penetrated it like clay and dissolved into it. There are many such accounts of his accomplishments.

His disciple was Nyang Yeshe Jungne of Chölung,[730] who also grasped the spirituality of his guru and became renowned for his learning in the three aspects of creation and perfection.

Most of the lineage descended from the masters just mentioned are called the tradition of Rong, or else the tradition of Nyang, after their clan name.[731]

Again, [Nupcen's disciple] So Yeshe Wangcuk had these disciples: Ngentung Cangcup Gyeltsen, Kongtsün Sherap Yeshe, and Ratung Sherap Tshültrim. Because all three were Yeshe Wangcuk's disciples Gölo Zhönupel maintains that they do not form a linear succession.[732] [The same source states that] Nyang Sherapchok was the common disciple of Yönten Gyamtso and his son, and of So Yeshe Wangcuk. Nyang's disciple was Yeshe Jungne; and the latter's disciple was Lharje Zurpoche, who also received teaching directly from Tongtsap Phakpa Rinpoche [Pagor Löncen Phakpa]. Therefore, between Nupcen and Zurpoche there was only one guru [i.e. Tongtsap Phakpa Rinpoche].

3 *The Lineage of the Zur Family*

[304.3-4] Now, I must describe how [the tradition] "fell to Zur in the end". During the later period of the teaching's expansion, it was Zurpoche Śākya Jungne who planted the roots of the teaching of the Ancient Translation School, Zurcungpa Sherap-tra who extended its branches, and Zur Śākya Senge who cultivated its leaves and fruit. Therefore, they are known as the three generations in the line of Zur.

LHARJE ZURPOCHE ŚĀKYA JUNGNE

[304.5-339.4] In general, this family called Zur had originated in India: Ösel Lhawang Zhönu Tsuktorcen was born in the sublime land of India. He had a son called Manda Zangzhücen, whose son, Zur Gyelwa Sumdra, was born in Dokam [far eastern Tibet]. His son was Zurpa Shenyen Takdracen, and his, Rincen Gyamtso. He had a son called Tshozang Mikpoche. In the *Blue Annals (deb-ther sngon-po)*, Lharje Zurpoche is described as the son of this last mentioned, but elsewhere he is held to have been the son of one Atsara.[733] Here, I regard as reliable a genealogy of the Zur family through to the twenty-seventh generation, which I have seen.[734] According to this, Mikpoche had three sons: Zur Atsara, Zur Khacenlakcen, and Zurzang Sherap Jungne. Of them, the youngest, Sherap Jungne, had four sons: Lharje Zurpoche, Zurtön Lama, Zurgom Dorje Jungne, and Zur Gomcung. The elder brother, Atsara, went to India where he had a son named Nyimei Nyingpo, and, when he returned to Tibet and dwelt at Thaklungpa, one named Zur Thakpa Gomcen. The son of the latter was Zurcung Sherap Trakpa.

Lharje Zurpoche was the visible presence in the world of the Great Glorious One [Yangdak Heruka]. He was born in the district of Yardzong, or Sarma, in Dokam as the son of the benefactress Dewacam. When he entered her womb, his father dreamt that a thousand-spoked golden wheel appeared in his hand, that the sublime Avalokiteśvara

Lharje Zurpoche Śākya Jungne

vanished into his consort's body, and so forth. So he knew his son to be an emanation and gave him the name Śākya Jungne.

The boy learned to read and write from his father. He received the cycle of the *Magical Net*, along with the minor esoteric instructions. Gradually, he received the three stages of ordination from Lacen Gongpa Rapsel, and, in time, was fully ordained. Lacen said that since Zurpoche was an emanation, there was no need to change his name. Under his grandfather, Rincen Gyamtso, he became learned in the Three Classes of Dialectics (*mtshan-nyid sde-gsum*), the Kriyātantra, *Vajravidāraṇa*, *Vairocana*, the *Magical Net* and the *Glorious Paramādya*, and also in the path of skilful means and other esoteric instructions belonging to the inner way of secret mantra. Zurpoche himself said, "Riding on the horse of the channels and currents of vital energy, wearing the robe of the inner heat, taking the instructions as my consoling companion, and guided by faith, I traversed the province of Dokam and approached Dam [to the north of Lhasa]."[735] So it was that when he arrived in Dam from Kham two sons of the gods pointed out the way from the midst of the clouds, and he proceeded towards Central Tibet, without having had to ask for directions.

While practising the Kriyātantra at Namolung, in Yarlung, Zurpoche's [affinity with] the unsurpassedly secret family of the greater vehicle was awakened. He thought to himself, "This exhausting path of renunciation and obligatory undertaking is the cause of bondage. May I find a path belonging to the unsurpassed way of secret mantra, which is easy to pursue and free from difficulty!" That same night he heard a voice telling him to meditate in a mountain forest.

Then, travelling up the Tsangpo River valley, he set out for Tsang. "Is there anyone learned and accomplished in the doctrine of the way of secret mantra?" he asked.

To this someone replied, "There is such a person living in a wood called Naktsel Sumdril."

Zurpoche remembered his former dream, went there, and received teaching on the attainment of nectar elixir (*bdud-rtsi sman-sgrub*) and so forth from Ceshak-chok of Gegong.

Generally speaking, Zurpoche lived with many gurus. But, in particular, he obtained the *Magical Net* and the Mental Class, which were the doctrines on which his flower had alighted, from Nyang Yeshe Jungne of Chölung. At first, he studied the *Sūtra which Gathers All Intentions* and the *Parkap Commentary on the Secret Nucleus*, and the esoteric instructions of the Great Perfection under Namkade; the secret empowerment and the path of skilful means under Nyenak Wangdrak of Yülser and Ce Śākya Gyeltsen; [the teachings on] primordial purity and spontaneous presence (*ka-dag-dang lhun-grub*) and also the *Sequence of the Path of the Magical Net* under Dre Trhocung of upper Nyang; [the cycle devoted to] Yangdak Heruka under Rok Śākya Jungne of Chimpu and Sherap Tshültrim of Denma; and the entire *Sūtra which Gathers All Intentions* under Zhutön Sonam Śākya. He also received the transmission of the *Sūtra which Gathers All Intentions* (*mdo-lung*), its empowerment and means for attainment (*dbang-sgrub*), and the commentary on this tantra along with its rituals (*rgyud-'grel phrin-las-dang-bcas*) from Tongtsap Cangcup, Gyatön Lodrö, and Kadö Yeshe Nyingpo. Zurpoche presented many kinds of wealth, including horses, as offerings to those same gurus; and he only delighted them with worship that was utterly pure in the three spheres.

So it was that Zurpoche received the esoteric instructions of many learned men. He comprehended the nature of their intention and became learned and adept in all the philosophical systems of the Tripiṭaka, as well as those of the tantrapiṭaka. He brought together the root tantras and the exegetical tantras; the root texts and their commentaries; the tantras and their means for attainment; and the means for attainment with their ritual texts and so forth; and he applied them in practice. Dwelling in a mountain forest, he propitiated glorious Yangdak Heruka with one-pointed diligence, and so he became a powerful master of the profound depths of the three aspects of creation and perfection. He unknotted the energy channels of the centre of perfect rapture, which is situated in the throat, and his discriminative awareness grew boundless.[736] He also taught the *Sūtra which Gathers All Intentions* and the *Tantra of the Magical Net* to a large congregation of disciples.

Zurpoche always renounced all those actions which cause agitation, and he cut off pride and social diversions. Without hoping for enlightenment in the future, he practised with intense perseverance fixed in his mind, in order to disclose it in the present.

On one occasion, someone who had the appearance of being a yogin went to receive alms from him. He was offered only a small portion but he took all that there was, and left the door saying, "This Zurpoche is famous and accomplished, but this does not nearly equal the regular offerings of Rok Śākya Jungne." An attendant overheard this and informed the guru. At the guru's bidding he went to extend an invitation to the yogin, and found him in a cave eating porridge which was overflowing from a skull-cup. Although the servant encouraged him to accept the invitation, the yogin declined and said, "Rok Śākya Jungne dwells at Chimpu, having attained power over the duration of his life. Dispatch someone who will bring his doctrine to Zurpoche." And he departed, his feet not touching the ground.

Zurpoche then sent Zangom Sherap Gyelpo with a mule-load [of offerings] to obtain Rok's doctrine. When Zangom reached Samye and asked for directions, no one could give them to him. Then an old woman said, "At first Rok used to live on this mountain at Chimpu." A shepherd also said, "It seems he is living on the mountain just now. Sometimes I even hear the sound of his drum and of the *rulu mantra*."[737] Zangom deposited his load in a place where there were clumps of grass and prayed with faithful devotion. Then with a loud noise the door of a rock cave opened. Zangom passed straight through owing to his great devotion, which caused the Eighteen "Secret Liberators" (*gsang-ba'i sgrol-ging*) to declare, "We must 'liberate' this bringer of disorder!" But Rok Śākya Jungne said to them, "That would be inappropriate, for this one is worthy."

After asking Zangom why he had come, the guru said, "It is an auspicious coincidence that I, Rok Śākya Jungne, should encounter the disciple Zur Śākya Jungne, and that his envoy is Sherap Gyelpo (King of Discriminative Awareness)." Rok granted him the empowerments of sixty-two maṇḍalas, including those of the *Buddhasamāyoga*; the twelve intrinsic and extrinsic maṇḍalas of Yangdak Heruka (*yang-dag-gi bdag-gzhan dkyil-'khor bcu-gnyis*); and Yangdak combined with Vajrakīla.

When Zangom had obtained all the books, transmissions and further advice, and was returning via Samye, he saw a boy wearing a silk turban sitting on top of his mule-load. He returned and asked Rok about the boy. "It is Tshangpa Tungtö" said Rok, "Brahmā wearing a crown of conch shells."[738] Then he granted Zangom [that protector's] offering rite. Later, the instructions were secretly offered to Lama Zurpoche.

Lama Zurpoche meditated with all his disciples for many years; and by maintaining teaching and study he greatly benefitted the world. None the less, he still longed to live in total solitude. He said, "Because I am distracted here by the performance of virtuous deeds, I am going to Ngadak Rock in Podong." He entered into solitary meditative practice there and his disciples also followed behind. He said to them, "If the aspiration for enlightenment is your motivation in coming to see me, there is no remedy except meditative practice. Leave worldly distractions behind you and devote yourselves to practice. I, too, will only practice." So, the master and his disciples practised individually.

Then, on one occasion, the ḍākinīs inspired him by declaring prophetically that he would benefit the world more by going to the lowlands. He proceeded to the valley of Tanak, where, in a cave facing east, which contained an owl's nest, he performed the means for the attainment of the nine-deity maṇḍala of Yangdak Heruka. He actually beheld the visage of the Great Glorious One there. Thus, it was owing to the name of his dwelling that he became famed everywhere as Lama Ukpalungpa, the "Guru of Owl Valley".

Because the provisions for practice were in meagre supply there, and because he had also received a prophetic declaration telling him to move on, he set out in the direction of the lowlands. The local divinity, who was named Zere Zetsen, showed himself and implored Zurpoche to stay. But the master said, "I have received a prophetic declaration telling me to go elsewhere. And, besides, there are no provisions here; so I will go."

The divinity replied, "I shall provide sustenance for you and your disciples. By all means stay!"

Zurpoche agreed to remain for some time.

Then, in Tanak, a rich man became seriously ill. An oracle declared that he should make feast and *torma* offerings, and seek the blessing of Lama Ukpalungpa. When the invalid approached the guru he felt better just by seeing him and asked for a blessing. As soon as the feast offerings had been made he was freed from his ailment. Similarly, Zurpoche had infinite blessings for those who were afflicted by sickness and by evil spirits. The people had faith in him and his merits grew vast. But the guru realised that this common merit was a great obstacle to the attainment of supreme accomplishment; and he decided to go to meditate on the slopes of Riwo Gudü. When he set out, the same local divinity said, "I have given provisions for your practice. Please stay."

Zurpoche answered, "It is very difficult [for you to provide] sustenance that has a pure basis. Because its accumulation is a source of distraction, this time I am going away."

With tearful countenance the divinity said, "If you will not stay under any circumstances, then please regard me with compassion." And he offered up his vital heart-mantra to Zurpoche.

The guru gave him layman's instruction and ordered him to protect the teaching. On his descent from that place, Zurpoche also bound [the local divinity] Como Namar under an oath of allegiance. Then he proceeded to Yesuthar. He said to Zurcungpa, "This rock of Gyawo seems to be the same Riwo Gudü where it was declared I should meditate." The master and all of his disciples remained there engaged in practice.

At that time Lharje Zurpoche's disciples included four "summits", who with the "summit-ridge" were five, as well as another one hundred and eight great meditators. Among them the four "summits" were: Zurcung Sherap-tra, who had arrived at the summit of the view and intention; Menyak Khyungdra, who had arrived at the summit of the exegesis of the *Tantra of the Magical Net*; Zhang Göcung, who had arrived at the summit of vast knowledge; and Zangom Sherap Gyelpo, who had arrived at the summit of meditative practice.

The "summit-ridge" was Tsak Lama, who, above and beyond the doctrine, had arrived at the summit of artistic prowess. Moreover, there are some works which speak of eight "summit-ridges".

In the same way, there were one hundred and eight who were adept in meditation. They include: Dru Gomgying, Yülgom Nakmo, Cegom Śākyagyel, Zurgom Dorjung, Yugom Cobar, and Gompa Sonam Nyingpo. It is said that all of them obtained miraculous powers including celestial travel.

On one occasion three women approached the guru and made this prophetic declaration: "In the lower valley of Shang in Yeru, to the east of the Shang River, lies a valley shaped like the half-moon. In its uplands there is a rock shaped like a heart. In its lowlands there is a plain which resembles the skin of Matram after he was 'liberated'.[739] On a mountain shaped like the trunk of an elephant is a rock which resembles the forehead of a lion. Three rivers flow from three mountain springs, symbolising the three buddha-bodies. If you meditate there you will attain buddhahood in this life and will serve the world for a long time."

At this, the guru bequeathed his hermitage at Trak Gyawo to Zurcungpa as his inheritance and went down [to Shang] with his followers. After he had surveyed the land there, Zhangmo Yöntengyen became his patron and donated a cave, in which the master took up residence. Zurcungpa and more than a hundred great meditators practised throughout the upper and lower reaches of the valley, living in thatched huts, under overhanging rocks, and in wind-breaks. Seven local tribes served the guru and Trampa Pöndrongpa became his main patron. They all held the guru to be the very presence of the Buddha.

Zurpoche practised there for many years. He had visions of the Forty-two Peaceful Deities and of the Fifty[-eight] Blood-drinkers. In particular, he beheld the deities of the maṇḍala of Yangdak Heruka and conversed with them as with other men. He made the Eight Gaurī and others his servants, and spirits attended to the tasks with which he entrusted them. The guru himself said, "I perceive all the earth, stones, mountains and rocks of Ukpalung to be the host of peaceful and wrathful deities. But in particular, I always see this southern peak of Ensermo as the Buddhas of the Five Enlightened Families. Therefore, I shall build a temple of the peaceful deities."

He then made preparations: After surveying the land he exorcised the hostile and evil earth spirits. In the col between the two peaks of the southern mountain, which resembled the claws of a black scorpion running downhill, he assumed the form of the Great Glorious One, Yangdak Heruka. He even left behind a footprint in the place where he stamped down with his right foot. There, he constructed a stūpa containing one hundred thousand images of Heruka; and in each of the four directions and at the centre the four "summits" and the "summit ridge" built a stūpa.

Zurpoche covered a spring, which was the residence of the nāga Tungkyong, with a sheet of copper. Upon it he laid the foundation of a temple. It is said that it was designed to equal the temple of Nyangtötsi in its dimensions, but that the stonemasons slightly reduced it. In the same way, most of the artisans were overcome by unmeritorious thoughts, and only wasted their materials by cutting all of the wooden planks unevenly, and of various lengths, et cetera. But a bodhisattva who has the courage of one who has practised generosity cannot be led astray by miserly and covetous thoughts, and so sees that wealth and property are dream-like and apparitional. Thus, when one of the great pillars had been cut short, and unevenly, Zurpoche, displaying the signs of his accomplishment, rolled the pillar with his foot until it was of the same length as the others. And on that pillar he left the imprint of his vajra. Similarly, he made all the crooked pillars straight as arrows by rolling them with his feet. When the artisans saw this, his patience in the face of their abuses, and other signs of his boundless compassion and power, they became exceeding remorseful. Using the wood that was left over from the temple, they built an exceptional, open portico, supported by four pillars. It became known as the Gyötsang Gyapup, the "Pavilion of Pure Remorse".[740] Later, it was made into the shrine of the protectors of the doctrine.

Zurpoche installed images of the peaceful deities, of whom Vairocana-Samantamukha (*kun-tu-zhal*)[741] was foremost, in the four-pillared upper shrine of the temple; images of Hayagrīva and Amṛtakuṇḍalin as the door-keepers of the upper court, which had eight pillars; and in the shrines of the north and south wings, he installed images of the Great

Mother [Prajñāpāramitā] and Dīpaṃkara, each surrounded by four offering goddesses. In the protectors' shrine, he made relief images[742] of Bhagavat, Śrīdevī, Brahmā, and Śakra. Frescoes of the gurus of the lineage were painted in the eight-pillared upper court, and those of twenty-three maṇḍalas, such as the "Hundred-petalled Lotus", on its surrounding wall. In the lower court, which had twenty pillars, there were frescoes of the Thousand Buddhas; the Buddhas of the Ten Directions; Amitāyus surrounded by the [Eight] "Closest Sons"; the Seven Generations of Buddhas; the twelve deeds; the bodhisattva Dharmodgata; Tārā, who protects from the eight fears; the Lords of the Three Families; the Malaya Buddha-field; the wheel of life; et cetera.

When the building had been completed in this way Zurpoche thought, "Now, I shall cover my temple with gold right up to the roof; and I shall extract the gold from Mount Drong-ri Chukpo."

At midnight the local divinity, a Tsen spirit, came in the form of a black horseman. He bowed before Zurpoche and circumambulated him, saying, "If I were to cover the temple with gold right up to the roof, my gold would be exhausted. I shall offer gold enough to cover completely the images of the deities." And so he did.

During the consecration both the conqueror Zurpoche and Zurcungpa displayed an endless array of miraculous powers: They entered the heart of the image of Sarvavid-Vairocana[743] via the crown, and the crown via the heart. As a result all the artisans developed sincere faith and said, "The guru's temple is like Mount Sumeru. Let us build a stūpa to accompany it." In faith they offered a stūpa modelled on the Blue Stūpa at Samye, which they built to the north of the Trashi Gomang Temple.

The guru's seat became universally renowned as glorious Ukpalung, after his own name. It is said that it was founded in the time of Lharje Zurpoche; that its traditions were established by Zurcungpa; and that Zur Śākya Senge made them widespread. This describes the great service to the teaching of the vehicle of indestructible reality of the Ancient Translation School that was effected by this abbatial succession.

By his teaching and other activities Zurpoche greatly benefitted the world. Once, when the master and all his disciples were performing, at Yang-en Sermo, a year-long retreat devoted to Yangdak Heruka, no lamps could be offered owing to the shortage of butter. By his blessing Zurpoche transformed the spring into a fountain of clarified butter for a week. Thus, they were able to obtain an unending supply of ghee.

At first, the teacher and his students there mainly devoted themselves to study; so there were few who were adept at the rites of enlightened activity. When discussions were held in the teaching court, those who did know the rites were seated among the ignorant, who did not participate in the discussions. [In retaliation] the ritualists would not allow the others to chant when they assembled for the daily *torma* offerings. At this Lama

Zurpoche said, "One may be liberated by arriving at the culmination of any subject. It is not right to scorn one another. Each philosophical and spiritual system among the nine vehicles has its own scope. There is no prejudice towards any one vehicle." An extraordinary understanding of his meaning dawned in them all and they became humble.

At that time the guru said to his four disciples who were like summits, "Each of you four must articulate what you understand to be most important in experientially cultivating the path."

Zurcungpa said, "If one does not meditate, the multitudinous propensities of former desires will never end. Therefore, it is essential to be decisive with respect to experiential cultivation.

"Because we must purify the ephemeral obscurations, which are like pollution, here and now, it is essential to perform acts of virtue, day and night.

"Because we must gather the provision of merit until the abiding nature of reality is disclosed, it is essential to practise virtues energetically, however small."

So it was that, when the other three had also articulated their own understandings, the guru, in delight, sang a song about the incorporation of view, meditation and conduct on the path. It began:

> In practising the true divine doctrine,
> The path is threefold: view, meditation and conduct.
> That which is labelled the "view"
> Is no view when there is something to look for.
> Look to the meaning of freedom from things to view!
> And bring ineffable reality on to your path!

This caused the devotion of all his disciples to increase vastly. Afterwards, Lama Zurpoche maintained the congregation in Ukpalung and built a great tantric college and meditation centre.

While Zurcungpa was propitiating Yangdak Heruka at Yang-en Ngönmo he beheld the causal Heruka[744] with one face and two hands standing erect in front of his hermitage at Shang. He left his retreat and told Lama Zurpoche what had taken place. The guru said "Zurcungpa, you have achieved the accomplishment of the Great Glorious Heruka. The awareness-holder Namkei Nyingpo prophesied that I would construct an image of Heruka and, having subdued the powerful demons which afflict the Tibetan people, would benefit the world. Now, I am going to achieve this."

Then, he said to his attendants, "Gather materials for building a temple. We will exorcise the site!" He sat on Trak Sengei Yatö (Lion-Skull Rock), arranged the *torma* offerings, entered the contemplation of the Great Glorious Heruka, and assumed the appropriate posture. Those who had the good fortune to behold a buddha really saw the guru in that form.

While the foundation-stones were being laid, Zurcungpa was scorned by some because his body was lean and his appearance lustreless. They insulted him saying, "All the others have a large foundation-stone in place. Now, it is time for Zurcungpa to set a strongman's boulder in position!"

To which Zurcungpa replied, "The master and disciples should go for lunch. I will be coming presently." But he did not leave.

When the others had eaten and returned they saw that eight enormous boulders, which no one could budge, even by heroic efforts, had been set up at the four sides and four corners of the foundation. Upon them were chalked the following words:

THESE ARE ZURCUNGPA'S STRONGMAN STONES[745]

When they saw this, the monks were humbled; and those who were fair-minded became devoted to him. It is well known, too, that after Zurcungpa had set his "strongman stones" in position, the evil designs of the wild demons and spirits of darkness, who wished to obstruct the building of the temple, were pacified.

When the time came to join the wood, four pillars were crooked. The guru said, "You straighten them, Zurcungpa!" And in a single breath Zurcungpa twisted and bent them until they were as straight as arrows.

As the roof was approaching completion the guru said, "I have [spiritually] summoned the sculptors. They are on their way." The very next day certain persons familiar with image-making arrived to ask for doctrinal instruction. Zurpoche feigned ignorance and said, "Are you skilled in any trades?"

To which they replied, "We are image-makers who have come to request doctrinal instruction from you."

"That is an auspicious coincidence. You shall indeed receive the doctrine you desire. I am erecting an image of the Great Glorious One, for it will be of great benefit to the world in this degenerate age. I request that you make it."

The sculptors displayed great devotion, so first of all the master gave them the vase empowerment of the glorious Yangdak Heruka. They prepared a mixture which combined relics from the Tathāgata's remains; the flesh of one who had been born as a brahman seven times;[746] earth, stone, water, and wood from the eight charnel grounds; a variety of precious gems; and sacramental medicine refined by the awareness-holders of India and Tibet.

The sculptors asked Zurpoche how large the image should be and he replied, "Make it as high as the roof." They made an appropriate image of the fruitional Heruka, who has three faces, awesome, wrathful, and laughing, and six arms, but the guru said, "It does not resemble my vision. Make it again."

Yangdak Heruka

He had them repeat the work many times and eventually said, "Can you make an image of me?"

"Yes, we can do that."

"Perform supplications tonight, and come to see me tomorrow."

The next day, accompanied by Zurcungpa, the sculptors went to meet the master. He told his attendant Tönyö Dorje to arrange *torma* offerings and feast offerings. Then he propitiated Yangdak Heruka and performed the feast offerings. "Now look!" he said, and as he adopted the gaze [of the deity] he actually became Heruka, a fearsome and wrathful apparition, with one face, two arms, gnashing teeth, and twisted tongue, his head resplendent among the clouds and mist, his right foot resting upon the face of Heruka Rock in Ukpalung, his left foot upon the summit of Mount Tsepo Purkang. His indestructible wings filled the sky. The sculptors could not endure his radiance and lapsed into unconsciousness. When they awoke, the guru eased his intention and, with a brilliant smile, said, "Now, do you understand?"

"Now", they asked, "please show us a Heruka with three faces and six arms, so that we may recreate it."

Zurpoche said, "That is too profound. Owing to the needs of those requiring training, it was the Heruka with one face and two arms that appeared."

While they were making the image according to his orders, they were able to fashion it from the navel downwards just as they had seen it before. But Zurpoche said, "You will have to do the upper section once again." He had them repeat it many times, but then said, "Your obscurations have not been purified. Knead the clay well and leave it here. Bathe in yonder fountain; for it is the water of accomplishment that arose when I scattered a skull-cup full of nectar. Circumambulate the temple seven times and come in. Until then no one should enter. I shall pray to the Great Glorious One."

As they were doing this, a continual buzzing was heard coming from within. When they had finished bathing and circumambulating they went inside; no one at all was near the master. He was absorbed in contemplation. But the clay had been used up and an image of the Great Glorious One, from the navel upwards, had spontaneously appeared. All the disciples and sculptors were absolutely astonished. They bowed before Zurpoche and said, "If the guru himself knew how to make it, then surely he was only testing us by not doing this earlier!"

At that Zurpoche make this declaration, which foretold the future:

> An image resembling me
> Has come to a man like me.
> It will guide the world in the degenerate age;
> It will be a remedy for sickness and demons.
> At first, by depending on Heruka, [this image of] Heruka
> Himself arose. But now that same Heruka
> Will be absorbed into this [image of] Heruka.

In the past, the great accomplished masters were completely mindful of preserving secrecy. Therefore, Zurpoche said that it was improper to make images according to the secret means for attainment in places where many people would congregate. "You must make the images of the Eight Wrathful Goddesses according to the tradition of the tantras," he said.[747] And so they did. The frescoes painted to the right were of the peaceful deities of the *Magical Net*, and those on the left were of the blazing wrathful deities. In front were frescoes of the deities of the entire *Sūtra which Gathers All Intentions*. Painted above were three maṇḍalas; and in the vestibule the glorious Mahākāla according to the tradition of wrathful Yamāntaka, together with the eightfold group of the Mönpa, mounted on tigers.

Then the time came for the consecration. They made preparations for the consecratory feast, saying, "Whom shall we commission to make the ale? Whence shall we get the meat?" An attendant said, "There were great expenses in connection with the craftsmen, labourers, and guests, so our wealth is all but exhausted. Now we must await donations and even take loans from our benefactors. Let us postpone the consecration."

But Zurcungpa said, "We will perform the consecration on time. However there is no way we will find sufficient barley for the ale; there are not even enough clay jars. So let us commission the nāgas to make ale. It is also difficult to find meat; and even if we do find it we cannot pay the price. So let us use Trampa Pöndrongpa's oxen for meat. By petitioning the spirits we will get enough *tsampa* [i.e. parched barley flour]. If we do this nothing at all will be lacking."

Then Lama Zurpoche said, "We will require at least one thousand loads of barley for the ale![748] You are to ferment six measures of barley. Act as if there is more ale for the consecration when you are in public. Zurcungpa, summon a nāginī!"

At that, Zurcungpa intentionally summoned the sister of the nāga demon who dwelt on the rock at Yaze Trakdong. A thin snake appeared, which Zurcungpa turned into a fair lady by means of his gaze. At that Zurpoche said, "I want you to make the ale for the consecration of my temple."

But she replied, "I am of the pure nāga race, which fears defilement. We abstain from alcohol. At the same time, I cannot endure the guru's radiance. So, while there is no way for me to produce ale, I beg that you commission my elder brother. I will offer all necessary help."

Then the guru said, "Now then, Zurcungpa, will you summon and transform her elder brother?"

"I will try to summon him."

He adopted a gaze and a scorpion appeared, the size of a young goat. When overpowered by Zurcungpa's contemplation he revealed his true form. Zurcungpa ordered him to make ale, but he said, "I belong to the race of gods and demons. I require many gifts and favours. I have no time to make ale, yet I am unable to transgress the guru's command."

Zurpoche took both their vital heart-mantras and bound them under oaths of allegiance. The nāgas said, "We will arrive the day after tomorrow. Make preparations! Our nāga race is above defilement. Please arrange a pure and safe environment for our dwelling."

At this Lama Zurpoche said, "I shall bless the environment."

He had three clay jars with stoppers[749] washed with fragrant water and also collected things agreeable to demons and nāgas. The six measures of barley mash were poured into the jars and topped with pure white barley. Then the two nāga demons, brother and sister, were placed inside. The mouths of the jars were fastened with the guru's ceremonial blouse, and the flow of the fluid could be controlled through its sleeves. Zurpoche sealed the jars with an indestructible knot and the nāgas proceeded to gather the essence of ale from all directions, so that the ale was never-ending.

Then an attendant said, "There is now enough ale. But what will we do for *tsampa*?"

The guru replied, "Borrow many sacks." He made a *torma* offering and said, "Pour a handful of *tsampa* into each sack." The attendant did as he was told. The next day all the sacks were full of *tsampa*.

Again, the guru said, "Send a monk to Trampa Pöndrongpa. Tell him that we have disposed of this refuse mash from the ale for the consecration in the forest, and that he should send his oxen to eat it."

When that was done many oxen were sent. The guru said, "Zurcungpa, will you kill and resurrect them?"

Zurcungpa replied, "I shall obey my guru's command."

Zurpoche adopted an enlightened intention and hurled enchanted objects[750] at each of the oxen, whereby they all fell into a coma and died. "Flay the oxen," he said. "Do not break the bones. Keep the joints intact. Leave the internal organs in their proper positions and carve out the muscle meat."

His attendants were terrified and thought, "This master and his disciple are in the sway of evil. They have ordered the oxen to be fed on the mash, and then they have killed them all. Now what will happen when the oxherds arrive?"

With their minds utterly confounded they prepared the meat-feast for the consecration. After the feast the oxherds did arrive. The guru commanded that they be served, too, which perplexed the attendants. Then he said, "Let Zurcungpa convey the oxen to their owner."

At that, Zurcungpa folded the bones in their wrappings of hide. He inserted the internal organs as well, covered them with his robe, and, at the snap of a finger, the oxen trembled and stood up. It is said that [earlier], when an old woman had been carving the meat, she scraped a rib of one of the oxen. After [being revived] that ox had a deformed rib. The display of this miraculous ability to kill and to resurrect caused all those assembled to develop great faith.

Lama Zurpoche, too, looked delightedly upon [the image of] the Great Glorious One, and said, "I pray that you serve the world greatly."

"Hey, hey, need you even ask?" replied the image, rejoicing in the nine dramatic airs.[751] At first the image had a wrathful countenance, but thereafter its appearance became one of laughter.

The guru said, "Now, we should propitiate Yangdak Heruka for one year."

The attendants replied, "The provisions are not sufficient."

Zurcungpa countered, "If the ale is not enough, it will be all right to return to the nāga demon. There is also a little meat and *tsampa* in reserve. If the commitments of yoga are not left to decline, the mundane gods and demons will provide our sustenance. The local divinity will also make offerings. So it will be fine to practice for one year."

About one hundred yogins and yoginīs assembled there. The master ordered each of the practitioners to be provided with a skull-cup full of ale, a duck's egg-sized ball of gruel, and a little meat to observe the commitments. Then the one-year retreat commenced.

During the retreat the guru said, "You, the four summits, are to hold a contest of [contemplative] intention." It is said that when they all had entered a meditative equipoise, three of them attained an immovable intention, one that was mountain-like, not to be destroyed by mere circumstances. But because Zurcungpa had arrived at the abode of supreme, unbiased equanimity, he ascended in the air to the height of a wagon to illustrate the superiority of his view. Then the guru said, "Now, go outside and listen while Zurcungpa recites the *rulu mantra*." One yoginī went outside and listened, but the volume did not decrease. Having crossed over a ridge, she continued to listen, but still the volume did not decrease. At that, the guru praised Zurcungpa highly, saying, "You are all equally spiritual brethren, but you others should not even cross Zurcungpa's shadow."

When they were released from the retreat, the master and his disciples went to Trokpöi Sumdo. The guru became exhilarated and stamped out a dance to the *rulu mantra* on the rock called the "Vajra Bolt" (*brag rdo-rje gtan-pa*). His foot penetrated the rock up to the ankle, as if he were treading on mud. Zurcungpa said, "My guru is a manifest buddha. I shall prostrate my head at his feet." He touched the footprints with his head and left behind a clear impression of his topknot and dangling ear-rings.

At that, Zangom Sherap Gyelpo said, "Wonderfully sublime are the signs of accomplishment which my two gurus, uncle and nephew, possess. It will be a sin for man or beast to tread upon this stone." He transformed his five fingers into five powerful athletes, who raised the Vajra Bolt Rock and set it upright. Then Zhang Göcungwa and Menyak Khyungdra also said, "It is up to us to support it." [They emanated] many powerful athletes who each raised an unshakable boulder to support the rock on each side, and so made its foundation secure. Even today these stones can really be seen.

Then Lama Zurpoche decided to make an image of the fruitional Great Glorious One in Ukpalung.[752] He told all of his disciples to go there. Zurcungpa flew into the sky, saying, "I shall go to serve my guru," and landed on Trak Gyawo. The other disciples travelled there in coracles. The two nāga demons, brother and sister, said, "It is improper for us to be associated with the defiled persons in the coracle. Please take us over the river where it can be forded."[753]

The guru assented to this and delivered the clay pot to his attendant, to whom it seemed to weigh less than a feather. When they reached the riverbank, the guru said to the attendant, "Hold onto me and come without hesitation."

But the attendant's mind was unworthy and he thought, "I'll probably be thrown into the river."

Knowing his anxiety, the guru said, "Now you cannot cross with me. Come via coracle. I am going on ahead." And he went off without his feet touching the water.

The attendant went by coracle and reached the slope on the opposite bank. While waiting there for a long time he grew thirsty, so he drank all the ale he could strain from the pot. Then the thought occurred, "One year and four months have passed since making this ale. What did the guru put in the jar for so much to be produced?"

He broke the seal of the jar and two serpents, white and black, as large as yaks, uncoiled themselves and vanished into the sky. Scorpions, frogs, tadpoles and other creatures followed in their wake and also went snapping and croaking into the sky. At once the sediment became green and rotten and the liquid became pale and sour. The attendant disposed of the mash and carried the jar to the riverbank, where he poured out the liquid. Then he smashed the jar.

When this took place, the guru said, "The auspicious coincidence is lost. If you had not released the two nāga demons of Wokdong, brother and sister, the monastery of Ukpalung would have become the greatest in Tibet; and the hermitage at Trampa, too, would have expanded without decline. None the less, since you poured the liquid towards the south, some centres and monasteries will arise [in that direction]." He appointed the nāga demons, brother and sister, to be the protectors of the transmitted precepts at the hermitage of Trampa. But, due to these circumstances, the image of the fruitional Great Glorious Heruka was never made.

Afterwards, the college and the hermitage became extensive. At that time, in Nyari, there lived a man named Mama Yungdrung Trashi and his wife. They were endowed with riches, but had no children or heirs. Wishing to build a religious centre, they assembled all the local people together and asked, "Who are the best teachers?"

Some claimed that the adepts of mantra were the best, others favoured the venerable monks [of the Buddhist *saṃgha*], while yet others supported the followers of the Pön religion. Because they all disagreed, they advised the couple to follow their own inclinations. The wife said, "Since our resources are adequate, let us invite all three."

The mantra adept of Ukpalung [Zurpoche], Laketsewa the Pönpo, and a venerable monk from Chumik Ringmo were invited. When the three recipients of worship had assembled, they considered building a temple together, but disagreed over which should be the central image. The mantrin insisted upon Vajrasattva, the monk upon Śākyamuni, and the Pönpo upon Shenrap Miwoche;[754] so they decided to build separate temples. Lharje Ukpalungpa joined with the Pönpo to build a temple below Dropuk. The Pönpo said, "Even now, when we make the temple, our deity will have to be subservient if yours occupies the central position. And your deity will have to be subservient if ours occupies the central position."

Zurpoche realised that no good would come of either arrangement; so he gave the temple to the Pönpo. Then, one Drotönpa offered him the place called Dropuk and Zurpoche built a temple there. At that time three related families who were patrons said, "We will take a collection for whoever covers his temple with an ornamental roof." The mantrin and the Pönpo both accomplished the task, but the monk was unsuccessful. The patrons took up a collection for the mantrin and the Pönpo on alternative years, at which the monk said, "Please gather one for us too!" The monk was given one year's collection and thereafter the collection was made on behalf of the three orders during alternate years.

At the temple of Dropuk eight shrines, large and small, were built. Of these the foremost was that of the buddhas of the three times. The upper hall was supported by twenty pillars and the lower hall by sixty pillars. In this place a great seminary was established.

Moreover, one time, when it was well known that the conqueror Zurpoche was propitiating Yangdak Heruka at Gyawo, in Thak, and that his merits were most extensive, the translator Drokmi, who required gold to offer as a parting gift to his paṇḍita [Gayadhara], said to him, "Bring a lot of gold. I shall give you profound instructions."[755]

In order to exemplify [the conduct of] a great person, whose vows to benefit others are firm, and whose conduct with respect to the four attractive qualities of a bodhisattva is flawless, the conqueror Zurpoche – like Karma Pakshi, who to test [his disciples ordered them to build] an ornamental roof for the temple at Tshurpu high enough to be seen from the Damcoktse Pass[756] – said with a concealed intention, "I shall build two golden monuments to dominate the defiles of Lharidong in Dropuk and Thangi Yangdong; and I shall connect them in the middle with an iron chain."

His students make a pledge. "Very well", they said, "we shall each contribute a copper dish, a bell, and a length of iron chain."[757]

The great commotion which ensued alarmed two local divinities. They offered an ingot of gold, the size of a goat's liver, and asked the master not to build the golden monuments. Then they offered a gold mine and said, "You may enjoy it so long as no gold in the shape of a living creature is discovered." After mining an abundance of gold from one pit, an ingot of gold shaped like a frog was discovered. Zurpoche halted the excavation and offered one hundred ounces of gold to the translator in Mugulung.[758] That autumn he even performed humble tasks for Drokmi like carrying briarwood on his back. When he had become consummately learned in the *Three Continua* and their ancillary texts, as well as in the *Indestructible Tent*, he said:

> By the kindness of the great guru,
> I have learned that our Mental Class is our wealth!

Thus, after savouring the doctrine of the new translation schools Zurpoche again maintained that our [Nyingmapa] Mental Class is wealth, like unto the wish-fulfilling gem. His statement is one giving rise to the highest certainty.

In his sixty-first year, when he had almost finished building the temple at Dropuk, that great man, an undeniable emanation who lived on the level of a holder of the awareness of spontaneous presence,[759] having fully realised the attributes of the five paths, resolved to transform his coarse body into its pure essential substance.[760] He said, "Summon Zurcungpa from Trak Gyawo."

When Zurcungpa arrived the master said, "I entrust this centre of mine to you, Zurcungpa. You must benefit the host of disciples by means of the doctrine. Grant it to them according to their intellectual capacities. Protect them as I have done.

"You disciples, too, must attend carefully to whatever Zurcungpa does. Do not disobey his word. Do not even step on his shadow, footprints or robe; for this one has attained the accomplishment of the body, speech, and mind of the Great Glorious One. Therefore, he is even higher than I. Because he will protect you as I have done, practise respectful devotion perfectly."

Then Zurpoche went off to his hermitage at Trampa. One day he said to his attendant, "Prepare a meal this morning before the heat." At sunrise, when the attendant came into his presence, the great guru was sitting on his bed, getting all dressed up. The attendant asked, "Now, where are you off to, that you are getting dressed up?"

> I am going to Sukhāvatī Buddha-field.
> Address your prayers to the meditational deity,
> For the Great Glorious One and I are no different.

So saying, the master took up his vajra and rang his bell. As he did so his body was transformed into light; and he vanished into the heart of the image of the Great Glorious Heruka.

At exactly the same time, a Khampa, who was coming to make offerings to Zurpoche, met the guru on the road. The guru blessed the Khampa's perception, and, accepting the offerings in an emanational palace, distributed the merit. Then, just as if he had awakened from a dream, the Khampa saw nothing at all. Proceeding onwards hesitantly, he heard along the way that the guru had vanished into the heart of the image of the Great Glorious One.

Because the blessing of this image of the Great Glorious One was exceedingly great, sometime later the image itself told the officiating priest to welcome one Gyatön Śāk-ye. At the time of his reception Gyatön appeared riding on a white cow and wearing a wolf-skin hat.[761] In the presence of the image of the Great Glorious Heruka he was transformed into white light. The priest, Majo Tönden, actually saw him perform three counter-clockwise circumambulations and vanish, in fact, into the image. Similarly, one Tshenden Zurmo Öbum is reputed to have vanished into that same image.

ZURCUNG SHERAP-TRA

[339.4-359.6] Among the four "summits", Deshek Gyawopa, or Zurcung Sherap-tra, like the bell-ringer among the bulls, was the prime successor of the mantra-holder Ukpalungpa. He was born in Yeru, Tsang in 1014 (wood male tiger year) to the accompaniment of wonderful omens. His father was Thakpa Gomcen, who sometimes lived as a mendicant; and his mother was Majo Sherap-kyi. In his seventh year he learnt to read and write, and in his ninth he learnt to chant the rite of the peaceful and wrathful deities.

Once, in his thirteenth year, while he was sitting in bed reading a book, his betrothed ran to him and said, "The field is flooded! How can you lie there?"

Wearing his new trousers, Zurcungpa crossed the flooding waters[762] and he began to divert the water from the house. But she scolded him, saying, "You did not even change out of the clothes which were made by my labour. They're ruined!"

Zurcungpa replied, "If you care more about the cloth than about me, have it!" And he threw the trousers away.

She became angry and said, "This is an insult!" And she ran away to her native place.

Zurcungpa was utterly disillusioned with the world. He took her spindle down from a rafter and shouted after her. He remained suspended between hope and doubt, [not knowing] whether to call her back, but [in the end] he handed her the spindle saying, "It is said that a man must have the male wealth, and a woman the female wealth.[763] Take your spindle." She returned to her own land in despair.

Then, without consulting his father, without taking provisions from his mother, and without seeking the approval of friends,[764] Zurcungpa set out, carrying only his wolf-skin coat, to meet Zurpoche. On the way he joined company with two nomads from Tanak, who were bringing turquoise and copper, and a native of Shang, who bore armour. When they arrived there, Zurcungpa had only the wolf-skin coat to offer. While the other three offered their grand presents, the guru said, "Let us see whether or not they are disgusted with the world. Bring each of them some ale-stew and vegetable soup." The two nomads had no desire to eat, the Shangpa ate a little, but Zurcungpa ate the lot. At this the guru said, "Put aside the wolf-skin coat and the armour. But return the turquoise and copper to their owners!" The nomads went away displeased, saying, "The return of our presents is a sign that he

Zurcung Sherap-tra

will not teach us the doctrine." Consequently, they abused Zurpoche's teaching.

The master asked Zurcungpa, "What is your clan?"

Zurcungpa feared that it would be contentious to say that he was of the same clan as the guru, so he said, "I am just a very small Zur (Zurcung)." The nickname stuck. Knowing him to be worthy, Zurpoche made him study. He developed supreme intellectual brilliance.

At first, because of extreme poverty, he subsisted by gathering up the *tormas* scattered by the guru, and making ale-stew of them. But the other students complained to the master. "The sour smell of ale", they said, "lingers on his breath. Neither does he offer ale to the guru, nor does he give any to his spiritual brothers."

Therefore, the guru said, "Zurcungpa, today you are to go and collect wood."

In Zurcungpa's absence he had them search the cottage, but it is said that all they found was a skull-cup full of ale-stew underneath a tattered blanket. At this the guru said, "Zurcungpa, if you have nothing to eat, come to my own hearth."

"I would defile the guru's property," he answered. So it was that he bore the burden of constant austerity.

One day the guru brought a rosewood bowl, which could hold nine handfuls, and said, "Do you have anything to drink?" When offered ale-stew, Zurpoche drank two bowls full.

"Bring more," he said, and continued to drink. Then he said, "Is there anymore?"

"There is about one quart," answered Zurcungpa.

"Now that is not enough. If it were enough, your merit would be the greatest in Tibet. None the less, because of your veneration of me, your merits will still be great." He gave Zurcungpa three loads of barley and said, "When this barley is finished you will not be without necessities."

Zurcungpa persevered day and night in all of his studies and in meditation. Because he was an emanation the expanse of his discriminative awareness unfolded. But although he had inconceivable spiritual experiences and realisations, Zurcungpa could not even afford the supplies for copying books. At that point, Lharje Zurpoche said, "In the place called Phen-gi Khangön lives a wealthy lady meditator named Como Yumo and her daughter. You should stay with them."

"I will not be a householder," replied Zurcungpa.

"Do not be narrow-minded," said the master. "I know the divisions between what the Teacher permitted and what he forbade. If you use the resources of those two, you can ask for empowerments, copy books, and receive the entire doctrine, without remainder. They will both acquire merit for it, and you will accomplish your own purpose. That would be best."

Zurcungpa obeyed and all his wishes were fulfilled. Then, the guru said, "Now, don't stay there anymore. Bring your books and other necessities of worship here gradually and then come to me."

"But is it right to do so?" asked Zurcungpa. "Those two have been very kind."

"Do not be small-minded! You will have the power to benefit the world. In this degenerate age you must propagate the teaching of the Buddha and benefit many beings. How could you be more grateful to them? But if you just hide out there, you will succeed in helping neither yourself, nor others."

Zurcungpa obeyed the command exactly, and the guru's intention was precisely fulfilled.

On one occasion Lharje Zurpoche saw Zurcungpa circumambulate a stūpa near his residence. His feet were moving one cubit above the ground. The guru realised that he was an emanation and thought, "It is a great wonder." He was highly delighted.

So it was that when Zurcungpa wandered afar and was tormented by intense heat in a desolate valley, he was offered a refreshing drink [by the local deities]. When he went to meditate on a lonely mountain peak and grew hungry, he was offered food. So he easily achieved whatever his heart desired, and thought, "Now, if I act on behalf of the world, I will succeed." Lama Zurpoche, too, said, "Now, you must teach." Zurcungpa taught the *Sūtra which Gathers All Intentions* and could gather at once three hundred disciples displaying the text.[765]

At the time the guru praised Zurcungpa greatly, but certain people were somewhat disrespectful and said, "The guru praises his own nephew too highly!"[766] Zurpoche knew that they would incur great demerit by slandering a guru.

It so happened that on one occasion the master and all his disciples went to attend a religious festival[767] in a place called Emar Dorjepo. In a gully, there was a vermin-infested bitch and her puppies. Lama Zurpoche only petted the bitch, but Zurcungpa killed her and the puppies, and then swallowed the vermin. The others said, "Such a lunatic as this Zurcungpa has been appointed to explain the doctrine! Even our benefactors will lose their devotion."

But the guru replied, "Even I knew the dogs were bound for the evil destinies,[768] but I could not 'liberate' them. Zurcungpa has done so, and it is a great wonder."

At that, Zurcungpa adopted a gaze and the dead dogs were turned into offering goddesses. He vomited up the vermin and they flew off into the sky. Zurpoche said, "Now, are you not astonished?"

But they replied, "It is merely an optical illusion."

Afterwards, they came to the Shang River, which was flooding. By his miraculous powers, Zurpoche threw a skull-cup to the slope of the opposite bank and said, "I shall entrust my college to whoever retrieves it." The other three "summits" could not reach it, but Zurcungpa walked across, his feet not touching the water, and retrieved the skull-cup.

Zurpoche urged them to compete in the power of levitation. Among the other teachers and meditators, including the four "summits", there were those who could travel without their feet touching the ground. But Zurcungpa ascended into the air as high as a palmyra tree and was the first to reach the hermitage at Trampa. At that, the other three "summits" began to believe in him and then served the guru completely by obeying each of his commands.

Once Zurcungpa received a prophecy in three stages concerning a sacred location; but because that yogin who had realised emptiness was free from deliberate grasping, he dismissed it all as delusion. Finally, five sixteen-year-old girls, adorned with bone ornaments, appeared. They were playing *ḍāmaru* and dancing. They said to him, "Brother, if you meditate at Riwo Gudü you will accomplish the goals of yourself and of others." Then, they pointed to Trak Gyawo with their fingers.

[Seeing that] there were nine peaks, nine rivers, and nine meadows Zurcungpa knew it to be a sign of the completeness of the nine successive vehicles. "That Trak Gyawo", he said, "resembles the transcendent lord, the Great Glorious Heruka, surrounded by the Eight Gaurī.[769] Therefore, if I practise there, accomplishment will come swiftly, and the blessing will be great. Moreover, since the nature of saṃsāra is suffering, I must cut off worldly entanglements. To achieve the goal of future lives, social diversions and fame are useless. In the short-run it is difficult to save face, and ultimately it is worthless to do so. Therefore, I will meditate in solitude." Entrusting his disciples to the care of the three "useless men"[770] and commanding them to preserve the exegetical teaching of the doctrine, he went off to Trak Gyawo.

Arriving there, Zurcungpa entered exclusively into practice. So, the danger of the local divinity's magical power became very great. However, to such great bulls among accomplished masters both dream and the waking state have the same savour, in that they are fictitious. One night Zurcungpa dreamt that a black man appeared on the peak of Trak Gyawo, grabbed his two feet together, whirled him overhead and threw him. He landed in a wide plain in the river valley of Thak. When Zurcungpa awoke he really found himself in the midst of the plain and had to climb back up. Despite this great magical display he remained undeterred.

Again, when a scorpion the size of a young goat filled his hermitage, Zurcungpa's decisive realisation of cause and effect became manifest. He seized the scorpion by the claws and tore it in half, saying:

> Repenting of each non-virtuous sin,
> I tear the evil scorpion asunder![771]

In this way he mocked those who rely on the words, rather than the meaning.[772] He threw the scorpion away, whereupon all the pieces were transformed into Vairocana Buddha and dissolved into space.

On another occasion, when Zurcungpa was invaded by an army of ants, he told his attendant to bring a mallet;[773] and with it he crushed the ants. The attendant felt disgusted and said, "Think of the sin!"

Zurcungpa replied, "If you had no faith in that, I'll do it this way." And he popped the ants into his mouth and blew out, whereupon all of them arose in the form of Vajrasattva and departed into the sky. At that, the attendant developed great faith.

By his inconceivable miraculous abilities to kill and resurrect, Zurcungpa bound three local divinities, who were siblings, under an oath of allegiance. They actually revealed their forms and prostrated at his feet. Even today there exists a spring which arose where Zurcungpa pierced a rock with his kīla. And when he performed the practice of the meditative absorption of the "seals",[774] according to the *Secret Magical Net*, he had a vision of Vajrasattva, who filled the valley of Thak.

Because Zurcungpa had attained the activity field in which appearances are exhausted,[775] he could transform his body into a storm of fire, water, wind, or earth. All appearances radiantly and resplendently partook of the nature of Vajrasattva; and the power of his positive realisations increasingly developed. But he realised that, in fact, they were not reliable. Appearances, mind and reality merged into a single savour and he reached the level on which his intentions were exhausted. He could move unobstructed through earth, stone, mountain, and rock; fly like a bird in the sky; and so forth. So it was that Zurcungpa obtained independence with respect to the five elements.

On one occasion he said, "One month from today a worthy disciple will arrive." Then, later on, a spiritual benefactor,[776] named Ba Getong, who was an adherent of the dialectical school, came to a religious festival in Thak. He sent an intelligent student to debate with Zurcungpa. The student pointed at a pillar and said, "Let the pillar be the topic."

Zurcungpa said, "The pillar is the topic. To the deluded perceptions of worldlings who are discrete entities, such as yourself, the pillar appears as a discrete entity. But I [am an adept of] the Great Perfection, which concerns what is manifest in and of itself and impartial. [According to this] there can be no ontological verification of the pillar." So saying, he waved his hand and it passed through the pillar without obstruction.

The student was unable to speak for astonishment. He acquired exceptional faith and became Zurcungpa's disciple, Matok Jangbar.

Concerning Zurcungpa's disciples, there were: four "pillars"; eight "rafters"; sixteen "beams"; thirty-two "planks"; two "great meditators"; one "great boaster"; two "simple ones"; two "venerable ones";[777] three "useless men"; and many others.

The four "pillars" were originally students of the spiritual benefactor Khyungpo Trase,[778] who were great dialecticians and intellectually very sharp. When Deshek Gyawopa [i.e. Zurcungpa] and the spiritual benefactor Khyungpo met in Nyangru at the invitation of a patron, Khyungpo sent the four, commanding them to go and refute Zurcungpa, who, he said, was a proponent of erroneous doctrines. When the four entered the presence of the master, he happened to be wearing a fur coat turned inside out. At this one of them said, "Which doctrinal tradition has the custom of wearing an inverted hide?"

"The hide is just as it has always been, so it is not inverted. It is your dogma which confounds inside and outside."

One of the other students said, "Very well, but let us discuss the doctrine."

To which Zurcungpa replied, "The essence of the doctrine is inexpressible and limitless. How can one discuss doctrine?"

At that Kyotön asked, "Well then, according to your tradition of the Great Perfection, is not meditation most important?"

"To what object do I adhere?" Zurcungpa asked in response.

"All right then, but is it non-meditation ?"

"Is there anything that distracts me?" was Zurcungpa's reply. And Kyotön, despite his brilliance, could make no further response.

Again, Lentön Śākya Zangpo asked, "According to the tradition of the *Secret Magical Net*, do you maintain that all appearances are male and female deities?"

"Who would refute", answered Zurcungpa, "the validity of direct perception, to which discrete, inanimate objects appear?"

"Very well, then you do not maintain [that they are deities]?"

"Who can contradict the intention of the sūtras and tantras concerning the purification of discrete, impure, delusory appearances [which are perceived by] sentient beings?"

Thus, Zurcungpa eclipsed the sharp, verbal arguments of the four students with his truly powerful answers, just as Rāhu eclipses [the sun and moon] with his hands; and he grasped them with the claws of his great compassion, which was wholly other-oriented. In this way, the propensities of [the four students'] past deeds were aroused, just as when master Śūra became the disciple of Āryadeva.[779] They said, "Alas! It is hard to find such a spiritual benefactor as this, who possesses an unerring realisation of the meaning of the greater vehicle, and is endowed with the brilliance that comes of awareness and liberation. And yet, if we go openly to him at this time our master will be displeased. So, let us take a solemn vow to abandon that master of false sophistry by some means next year, and to associate with this mighty lord of yoga, who is like the point of a sharp sword cutting through the net of saṃsāra."

After swearing this oath they went away. Then, as bees fly to lotus gardens, just so, when the next year came, they spread the wings of their past propensities and positive aspirations and flew, as if to a vast sandalwood forest, to the college of Deshek Gyawo. There, they became renowned as the four "pillars".

But in the meantime, the four had to return to Khyungpo, who said, "Did you refute Zurcungpa?"

"We could not refute him," they replied.

At that, the fierce windstorm of jealousy agitated Khyungpo's mind, and he announced, "Anyone who kills one like Zurcungpa, who harbours perverse opinions and leads everyone astray, will certainly attain buddhahood!"

The disciples of Zurcungpa heard about this and went to inform the master. But since a naturally liberated bodhisattva has no thought of anger, Zurcungpa answered them with silence. In the morning, he sat upon his teaching throne, smiling.

"What amuses the guru?" asked the disciples.

"As for doctrines", he answered, "this, my secret mantra tradition of the greater vehicle, is it! For it is the tradition of secret mantra that maintains that buddhahood may be attained by 'liberation';[780] the dialecticians do not think so. Now, even such a great dialectician as Khyungpo Trase has said that anyone who kills one like Zurcungpa will attain buddhahood. So, in his innermost heart, he has turned to my doctrine. Therefore, I am delighted!"

[Among the four "pillars":] Kyotön Śāk-ye of Kungbu was the pillar of the Mental Class; Yangkeng Lama of Kyonglung was the pillar of the *Sūtra which Gathers All Intentions*; Len Śākya Zangpo of Chuwar was the pillar of the *Magical Net*; and Datik Co-śāk of Nakmore was the pillar of ritual and means for attainment. With the addition of Matok Cangbar they are also known as the five lineage-holders.

The eight "rafters" were: Matokpa, Kyotön Chöseng, Lenśāk Cangcup, Tsak Śākring, Nuptön Pakma, Üpa Sator, Shütön Dadra, and Tsetrom Cangpel. Sometimes Lala Zicen, Nelba Nyingpo, and Ngamtön Gyelwa are also counted with them. The two "great meditators" were Bagom Tikma and Pöngom Topa. The one "great boaster" was Zitön Sogyel of Latö. The two "venerable ones" were Zhangtön Ngase and Khyungpo Trase. I shall not enumerate the names of the "beams", "planks", and other ordinary disciples. The three "useless men" were Gocatsha, Mikcung Wangseng, and Gocung Wange.

Lama Zurcungpa resolved to remain absorbed in practice for twenty-four continuous years on Mount Trak Gyawo, and so to pass away in the rainbow body. But because he had to break his retreat for two reasons, he remained there for thirteen whole years and one part-year, fourteen in all. At one point he spent a long period without even his attendant coming to serve him. Eventually, when no trace of smoke or noise emerged from his hermitage, the attendant, fearing that some illness had befallen the master, went to investigate. He found the guru with his mouth and nose covered with cobwebs. Thinking that he had passed away, he cried out loud. The master's concentration was disturbed and he said, "If I had remained in that state I would have become free from this burdensome skull! Now I shall have to take birth once more." It is said that [this was fulfilled when] he was reborn as the Great Translator of Sakya.[781]

It appears that this [account refers to] the indication of success on the path, whereby the body becomes many particles of the pure essence [i.e. light] alone, [which takes place] when [clinging to] reality is exhausted all at once.[782]

Again, one morning Zurcungpa said, "Prepare lunch. Let's cook green vegetables this time."

The attendant had not yet boiled the water when the guru arrived, carrying fresh vegetables, and said, "I have circumambulated Ukpalung. Why have you not boiled the water?"

The attendant exclaimed, "Surely you are joking!"

Zurcungpa gave him a present which Zurpoche had given him that morning. Then, with great conviction, the attendant thought, "My guru has undoubtedly attained independence with respect to vital energy and mind!" And thus he developed devotion.

The other reason that Zurcungpa had to leave his hermitage was that the three "useless men" could not uphold the teaching: Gocatsha went to Gö Khukpa [Lhetse][783] saying that he needed the Mother tantras as the background for the path of skilful means. Mikcung Wangseng went to Sumpa Yebar saying that he needed the Yoga [tantras] as the background for the projection of the maṇḍala.[784] Gocung Wange went to Pangka Tarcungwa saying that he needed logic as the background for the philosophy of the ground and path.

Among them, [the first did not realise that] because the paths of skilful means and of liberation[785] are both contained in the *Secret Nucleus*, this fulfils the definition of a Mother Tantra; [the second] had "twisted his eyes backwards in their sockets"[786] because [he did not realise that] the maṇḍala is [already] projected in the natural disposition [of reality]; and the third did not understand that logic, as a verbal philosophy, does not get to the point of the ground and path. Therefore, these three useless men could not preserve the college; and consequently Zurcungpa had to break his retreat.

Still another reason was that the conqueror Zurpoche desired to arrive at the conclusion of coalescence[787] without abandoning his body, even before he had completed the final construction and consecration of the Dropuk Temple. Zurcungpa arrived to comply with the order of the guru, who said, "You must preserve my legacy."

It also happened that when the enlightened activity of Deshek Zurcungpa had become extensive, and there were no mantrins in Tibet who did not make obeisance to him, or who dared sit in a superior position, the translator Gö [Khukpa Lhetse] decreed that the followers of the new translation schools should neither make obeisance to him, nor accept an inferior seat. One day, when all had assembled for a great festival in Shang, the translator Gö arrived after Zurcungpa, who was seated at the head of the row. Then, because the minds of great, spiritual benefactors who are clever with words, but engaged in defilements, cannot endure the splendour of mighty yogins, who equal the Buddha, [Gö and his disciples] – in the manner of [the Buddha's] five noble companions, who could not keep their agreement – were startled, and all evidence of the promise not to prostrate was erased. They all became like five-branched vines, clinging to the ground, and began to make obeisance. Then, when the festival was over, the others asked Gö, "We all promised not to prostrate before Zurcungpa, but were you not the first to do so?"

He replied, "When I came before him I could not tell whether he was the transcendent lord, Great Glorious Heruka, or just Zurcungpa. But, otherwise, I could not conceive of him as a man."

Lekden Degü

Again, because Zurcungpa's magical powers were most vast, he is famed for having travelled to and fro on the rays of the sun. He could teach the doctrine three times in a single day in very remote places: a morning session in Ukpalung, a midday session at Dropuk, and an evening session at Trak Gyawo. Similarly, because he saw the ḍākinīs dancing at Lhazermo, they entered his service and built a shrine with nine supports: seven pillars and two especially lofty columns. It became well known as the Khandro Lhakang, the "Ḍākinīs' Shrine". Images of the Forty-two [Peaceful] Buddhas and of Lekden Degü, the protector of the transmitted precepts, were constructed; and frescoes of both the expanded and condensed maṇḍalas [of the *Magical Net*] were painted on the walls. During the consecration Zurcungpa whipped the image of Lekden with his sleeve and said, "Will you protect the teaching of the Buddha?" At that, the image bowed its head. Then, Zurcungpa asked, "Will you exalt the Precious Jewels?" And the lips of the image trembled.

In the same way, when Zurcungpa had a vision of the Great Glorious One he built a shrine to Yangdak Heruka on the very spot where the Heruka's left foot had rested. Matok Jangbar had a diseased tree, from which the sap was oozing, which he cut down and sanctified for the construction of the shrine. When he offered the first fruits of the tree to the guru, the local divinity Trhengwa sent a tamarisk pillar, which had been left behind, down the Tsangpo River. But the pillar sank for five days at Ngamongtrhang, and so it did not arrive. Zurcungpa sent two disciples there with this command: "Put this white *torma* on the rock; throw this red *torma* into the water; and tell them to bring Lama Zurcungpa's wood immediately!"

When threatened in this way the lord of the waters took fright and sent the wood on at once. Other spirits also obeyed Zurcungpa's command.

As the time approached for Lharje Zurcungpa, the possessor of such magnificent attributes, to enter nirvāṇa, the disciples implored him to beget a son and heir. Zurcungpa invited the Lord of Secrets, Vajrapāṇi, into the womb of his consort by means of the contemplation of the five awakenings. [His heir,] Zur Śākya Senge, was thus clearly endowed with the wonderful marks and signs [of a buddha].

Zurcungpa then delivered [his testament] which is well known as the *Eighty Oral Instructions* (*zhal-gyi gdams-pa brgyad-cu-pa*), and which begins:

> Be a child of the mountains.
> Wear ragged clothes.
> Eat plain food.
> Ignore your enemies.
> Leave your fields untilled.
> Be decisive about the doctrine...

In his sixty-first year, 1074 (wood male tiger), while dwelling at Trak Gyawo, Zurcungpa, accompanied by light and earthquakes, departed for Akaniṣṭha, the Citadel of the Indestructible Array.

ZUR DROPUKPA ŚĀKYA SENGE

[360.1-367.3] Zurcungpa's son, the great Lord of Secrets of Dropuk, Zur Śākya Senge, was like the fountain-head of the exegesis of the *Secret Nucleus* in Tibet.

Zurcungpa had a female disciple named Cosemo Damo Tsuktorcam, in whose womb, he realised, an emanation could be conceived. He asked her brother, Datik Cośāk, who was one of the four "pillars", if he could have his sister; and Datik replied, "Just as you command." Datik placed a vajra and bell in her hands and told her to present them to the guru personally, rather than through an intermediary, and so created a most auspicious coincidence. But because the guru did not marry her, the host of his students became very hostile and proposed to banish her. Kyotön Śāk-ye then said, "I dreamt that a master of the doctrine sat upon her ring-finger. If [her child] is seen as the master's heir, it may possibly benefit the teaching. Let her remain."

Similarly, the other "pillars" dreamt that images of the Buddha and golden vajras dissolved into the lady's body. Hence, she was allowed to stay.

Zur Dropukpa Śākya Senge

In 1074 (wood male tiger year), when the great translator Ngok [Loden Sherap] was in his sixteenth year, Dropukpa was born. The guru said, "When this son of mine entered her womb I had an intimation that Vajrapāṇi had dissolved into her. Therefore, he will come to benefit the world." He named the boy Śākya Senge.

The father renounced absolutely everything and became utterly possessionless. His consort said to him, "Just the other day you were considerate of our son's birth. Now, you have not even provided butter paste to moisten his palate."

Zurcungpa replied, "If he has merits the necessities will arrive, even without my providing them. If not, there will be no advantage in my providing for him anyway." Then, he sat down on the roof of the house.[788]

Just then, a wealthy nun came to offer many loads of barley and a great quantity of butter. A benefactor also arrived from Dokam to make offerings. Zurcungpa exclaimed, "The butter paste to moisten his palate has arrived. This one has merits! He will even serve the world!" Thus he rejoiced.

When the child was eight months old his father passed away. He was brought up by his mother and maternal uncle, and lived for fifteen years in the upper valley of Da. Then he approached Len Śākya Zangpo in Chuwar, where he received the tantra of the *Secret Magical Net*. He also went to Yangkeng in Kyonglung to study the doctrine. In his nineteenth year, he had his investiture[789] and his enlightened activity became quite extensive; so he was distracted from his studies. Subsequently, he found the opportunity to spend one year with Kyotön in Kongbu, but afterwards his enlightened activity once more increased and he had no chance to travel anywhere. He invited a host of learned and accomplished gurus to his home and completed his studies.

From the four "pillars" he received, completely and perfectly, the doctrines of his father, including: the trilogy of the *Sūtra which Gathers All Intentions*, the *Magical Net* and the *Mental Class*; and the tantras, esoterics instructions, rites, means for attainment, practical techniques, and empowerments [belonging to that cycle of doctrines]. In particular, he obtained the cycle of the *Sūtra which Gathers All Intentions* in detail from his uncle Datik; the Great Perfection according to the tradition of the cycles (*rdzogs-chen skor-lugs*)[790] from Len Śākya Cangcup; the final lineage of the Great Perfection (*rdzogs-chen brgyud-pa tha-ma*) from Lharje Shangnak; et cetera. In short, he resolved his doubts by studying and reflecting under [the guidance of] many gurus. He presented [manuscripts of] the long, medium and short versions of the *Mother* [i.e. the *Transcendental Perfection of Discriminative Awareness*], and other bountiful offerings to all those gurus under whom he studied his own spiritual tradition, so that he gained their favour.

After practising for a long time at Dropuk in Nyari, he "hammered home the four nails",[791] as described in the esoteric instructional tantras with reference to the stages of creation and perfection. After blending inseparably with the body, speech and mind of his meditational deity he acquired, even during his youth, great radiance, and could overcome everyone with his charisma.

On one occasion Dropukpa went with four disciples to meet Phadampa Sangye, who was then living in Tingri. The day he was to arrive Phadampa said, "Today an emanation of Vajrapāṇi will arrive. We must welcome him."

After they had arranged the silks, parasols[792] and other paraphernalia, and the day was growing old, five mantrins, a master and his disciples, arrived. Phadampa's disciples said to him, "There is no one else it could be."

And he said, "Welcome them."

At the same time, Lharje Dropukpa said [to his own disciples], "I must test whether Phadampa possesses supernormal cognitive powers." He sent one disciple ahead disguised as himself, while he followed behind like a common servant. Phadampa saw there was a goitre on Dropukpa's throat, and said, "Let the one who has the goitre lead the way. It would be best if master and disciple were not out of order!" Dropukpa became most devoted to him and received Phadampa's nectar-like doctrine. And Phadampa inspired Dropukpa saying, "He will become the great glory of [the Buddha's] teaching in general."

On another occasion, when he was having a painting of Vajrapāṇi designed, Dropukpa told the artist, "Draw it thus!" And he clearly appeared in the form of Vajrapāṇi. For these and many other reasons it was well known that he was the glorious Lord of Secrets, who had come to extend the teaching of secret mantra in this northern land [of Tibet].

Generally speaking, the host of Dropukpa's disciples was countless; but, in particular, he produced a thousand disciples who merited parasols. They were great spiritual benefactors, who upheld the seminaries and protected the teaching. As a result, his enlightened activity over a long period was inconceivable.

Once, when he was teaching the doctrine in Dropuk, he sat on a backless teaching throne, and students surrounded him on all sides. He appeared to be facing his audience in all directions. Therefore, they were convinced that he was actually the representative of the lord of the maṇḍala of the *Magical Net of Vajrasattva* and he became renowned as an undisputed emanation.

When Dropukpa taught the doctrine there were about five hundred who displayed the texts during the summer and winter sessions, and about three hundred during the autumn and spring. Generally speaking, he had over ten thousand students; so people would often resort to paying a gold coin for a suitable little spot within earshot of his teaching court.

Dropukpa was perfectly endowed with the attributes of knowledge, love and power. He acquired the eye of the doctrine, having thoroughly mastered the meaning of the *Glorious Tantra of the Secret Nucleus, which is Definitive with Respect to the Real* (*Śrīguhyagarbhatattvaviniś-cayamahātantra*, T 832). In consequence, the so-called teaching tradition of the Lord of Secrets, Dropukpa, has continued to be discussed even up to the present day, and is renowned like the sun and moon.

Dropukpa had twelve disciples who gained his favour: four "black ones"; four "teachers"; and four "grandfathers". The four "black ones" [*nag-po*, so called because their names all contained the element *nag*, "black"] were Cetön Gyanak, Zurnak Khorlo, Nyangnak Dowo, and Danak Tsuktor Wangcuk. The four "teachers" [*ston-pa*, whose names all contained *ston*, "to teach"] were Nyetön Chöseng, Gyaptön Dorje Gönpo, Zhangtön, and Gyatön. The four "grandfathers" [*mes-po*, unexplained] were Tsangpa Citön, Yutön Horpo, Bangtön Cakyu, and Üpa Chöseng. This enumeration is renowned as the "Upper [Tibetan] Tradition of Zur"; but in the "Lower [or Khampa] Tradition" there is a different lineage.[793]

When the time came for the great Lord of Secrets, Dropukpa, to perform his final deed, he said to the four "teachers", "Bring the supplies for a feast offering. I shall also make a collection." The four "teachers" fulfilled his command and they went to the summit of Takla Ridong in Dropuk, where they held a bountiful feast offering. Dropukpa instructed them in many secret teachings and said, "Do not mourn my absence. Now, without relinquishing my body, I shall go to the level of the awareness-holders. Therefore, you will prosper hereafter. Your lineage and the teaching will flourish."

Dropukpa sang a song of indestructible reality in his glorious voice, and singing different hymns, he rose higher and higher into the sky. Finally, he vanished altogether. The four "teachers" were tormented by heart-breaking grief and wailed with lament. They wallowed on the ground and called out his name, until he descended again like a bird and said, "You ought not to behave like this. I gave you good advice before, but you have disregarded it. Now, my lineage will not have even a little prosperity."

Then, in the next year, 1135 (wood male tiger), which was his sixty-first, Dropukpa passed into the citadel of Akaniṣṭha, the Gathering Place of the Great Assembly. During the cremation, a handsome young mantrin offered a light bay horse harnessed with a wonderful, self-fitting saddle of conch. Since no one knew whence he came, or where he went, it was said that a deity had brought the offering. Similarly, the Tsen spirits, Mātaraḥ, and nāgas also brought offerings.[794] So, there were four kinds of wealth not existing among men.

Dropukpa was eighteen years older than Sakyapa Künga Nyingpo.[795] Thus, Takpo Lharje, Lama Zhang, and Co-se Dzeng were roughly his contemporaries. Moreover, there were only three gurus between Vimalamitra and Dropukpa; for the nun Tremo of Rong Hot Springs (*rong chu-tshan*) was a disciple of Vimalamitra. Her disciple was Marpa Sherap-ö of Caze in Lhodrak. His disciple was Langtön Tarma Sonam of Shang Lhabu, and his disciple was Lharje Horpo Dropukpa.

4 *Biographies of the Rong Tradition*

CETÖN GYANAK

[367.3-369.4] Now, the disciple of Dropukpa was Cetön Gyanak. He was born in the region of Upper Nyang in 1094 (wood male dog year). He used to bring provisions for his two elder brothers who studied in a school of dialectics. He listened incidentally and surpassed them both in what they had been studying deliberately. At that, he said, "Though you have both listened for three years you have understood nothing. If I were to listen I would understand."

The two elder brothers replied, "Nothing more occurred to us two. Whoever knows the doctrine, it is much the same. So, if you understand, you yourself should listen! We will bring the provisions."

Lharje Gyanak remained there and studied Transcendental Perfection under Khyungpo Trase; Abhidharma under Ben; and Madhyamaka and logic under Takpa Khace. He also studied under Sonam Yeshe of Gar. After nine years of study he had reached the furthest limits of learning.

When Gyanak was in his thirtieth year he came to study the way of mantras under the Lord of Secrets, Dropukpa. He stayed with him for eleven years. For three years the guru did not converse with him in any detail, except to call him "Co-se of upper Nyang".[796] Once, when the master Gya Tsönseng and his servants were attending a religious festival at which Lharje was present, they instigated a debate, but were refuted by Lharje Gyanak. Dropukpa was delighted that their pride had been shattered, and he took note of Gyanak. Then, in addition, Dropukpa became overjoyed at the intellectual progress of his son, Cotsün Dorjetra [who was being tutored by Gyanak]. He bestowed upon Gyanak the fundamental texts and instructions of the three aspects of creation and perfection, and also the special esoteric instructions, along with concise notes. For this reason, Je Lhakangpa [i.e. Gyanak] came to possess more complete doctrines and more profound esoteric instructions than the other followers of Zur. At the age of forty he became a monk to avert death.[797] Then the following year Dropukpa passed away.

Gyanak also studied the *Amṛta Tantra* (T 841) under Gyatsang Korwa of upper Nyang; and the *Vajravidāraṇa* and the *Basic Root Tantra of Vajrakīla* (*Vajrakīlayamūlatantrakhāṇḍa*, T 439) under Dro Tarseng of lower Nyang. He also studied various traditions of Vajrakīla, including that of Kyi (*phur-pa skyi-lugs*) and also the Por tradition of the Great Perfection (*rdzogs-chen spor-lugs*) under Tampa Pormang; and the Kham tradition of the Great Perfection, that is, the *Essential Spirituality of Aro* (*aro'i thugs-bcud*) under Como Nyangmo. Similarly, he studied other doctrines, such as the *Brahman's Cycle of the Great Perfection* (*rdzogs-chen bram-ze'i skor*, NGB Vol.7) and the *Ketsangma* (*ke-tshang-ma*). Thus, because of his very great learning, Gyanak became the master of all [the teachings of] the way of mantras and dialectics, as well as of all the tantras and their means for attainment.

When Gyanak manufactured elixir everyone saw the goddess actually emerge from her palace of medicine, circumambulate the maṇḍala three times, and vanish. He worked extensively for the welfare of others and passed away in 1149 (earth female snake), which was his fifty-sixth year.

YÖNTENZUNG

[369.4-6] Lharje Gyanak's nephew was the great guru Yöntenzung. He was born in 1126 (fire male horse year). In his eleventh year he began his studies. For thirteen years he was befriended by his uncle, under whom he completed studies of all the tantras, transmissions, and esoteric instructions concerning the three aspects of creation and perfection. When he reached his twenty-fourth year, his uncle Gyanak passed away and he became the successor to his seat. He resolved all his doubts under Tön-śāk and Zhikpo, both of Central Tibet and others. Then, he continued to work for the welfare of himself and others.

TAMPA SEDRAKPA

[369.6-370.5] Now, Tön-śāk of Central Tibet, who was also known as Tampa Sedrakpa, was a descendant of Cerpa Wangtung of Ze. Having gone to learn to write at the college of Dropukpa, he acquired faith and pursued his studies. Then, he became a follower of Lharje Gyanak after the latter had become a monk to avert death and he received from him all the tantras and instructions in their entirety.

Then Tön-śāk thought that he should practise meditation exclusively. He went in search of a solitary place in the northern mountains, and at Yöla Rock he met one Tampa Yölcungwa, who was carving away at the rock. "Are you building a hermitage here?" he asked.

"Yes, I am."

"Is there no place else to do so?"

To this he received the response, "There is a place over there where there is a forked rosebush. But I shall build here, because this site is more secure."

Then, when Tampa Tön-śāk approached the rock where the forked rosebush was growing, he found some morsels of food beside a spring, and he took this to be a good omen. He stayed there and practised meditation until he had developed extraordinary realisation. Gods and demons obeyed his command. He acquired the ability to benefit many who required instruction and became known as Tampa Sedrakpa, the "Holy Man of the Forked Rose".

ZHIKPO OF CENTRAL TIBET

[370.5-373.1] Zhikpo of Central Tibet was a native of Ce in Yarlung. He was a secretary who was converted to the doctrine at the residence of Dropukpa, and became a follower of Lharje Gyanak. He became proficient in the three aspects of creation and perfection. Then, he decided to return home to celebrate his investiture.

Thinking that he would require a parasol, conch shell, offering utensils and other suitable requisites, he set out to bring them from Nepal. On the way he chanced to think, "Although I know so much doctrine, I have nothing to cultivate experientially. If I die now, nothing will help. I must secure my mind in the instructions alone." With this in mind, he returned, went into the guru's presence and made a request. He was given the instructions of the precious aural lineage, and, applying them experientially, he went on his way.

On reaching Kungtang in Mangyül the ineffable, pristine cognition of the Great Perfection arose within him for seven days. Then, he went to obtain his offering utensils from a Newar. Returning to Kungtang in Mangyül he contracted fever and was laid up. He thought, "Now, what is the use of being unhappy about it?" and composed his mind. Leaving the utensils in the village, Zhikpo went into the mountains, where he experientially cultivated [the teachings] until he could unimpededly traverse earth, stones, mountains and rocks. He then knew that his former ideas were totally unnecessary and decided to abandon the utensils for his investiture. But when he saw the altar-stand and the set of seven offering bowls he remembered his guru's kindness and thought, "This understanding came to me only through the compassion of my guru. I should offer these to him." So he carried the stand and the bowls along, but on the way, because he had put an end to desire, the desire to abandon these things, too, came to him. Once more he thought of his guru's kindness and, still carrying the utensils, he continued his journey. As soon as he reached the temple and placed them before the guru he exclaimed, "Oh, bowls! How long you have fettered me!"

Afterwards, Zhikpo dwelt only in mountain solitudes and undertook to achieve experiential cultivation until he comprehended all things. Because, for him, appearances had dissolved into fictions, he went unharmed by an avalanche of rocks. When he stayed in the upper valley of Pagor in Yeru a thunderbolt crashed down on his bed, but he was unharmed. Others asked, "Was there some lightning here?"

"Must have been lightning or something," he replied.

"But were you not injured?" they asked.

"All sound is inseparable from emptiness," answered Zhikpo. "Where is there the independent existence of a thunderbolt?"

So it was that Zhikpo of Central Tibet lived as a great and mighty lord of yoga. Below the hermitage where he continued to meditate he managed a college for eighteen years. Then, in his seventieth year, he passed away.

This holy person had many disciples who were learned in the textual traditions: Zhikpo Dütsi, Tönpa Lakyap, Cosö of Central Tibet, and Nyetön Nyima Dorje, to name just a few. Moreover, Metön Gönpo of Latö, Cel Künga Dorje and others also received teaching at his feet.

ZHIKPO DÜTSI

[373.1-380.2] Zhikpo Dütsi was the spiritual son of Zhikpo of Central Tibet. His father, Sangye Takcung, was descended from a family which had continually produced learned and accomplished "warriors" ever since the time of their paternal ancestors. Sangye Takcung was renowned as Takcungwa because he was a follower of Takpo Gyare. He went to Lhodrak and worked for the welfare of beings in the monastery of Phurmongang in upper Lho. During his stay there he was invited to Ze by benefactors from that region. They offered him Lhadong Monastery, Uke Monastery and others in Ze, so he took up residence there. The number of his disciples multiplied.

Sangye Takcung had a consort named Como Wangmo, and in 1143 (wood male mouse year) a son was born to them at the monastery of Dong in Ze. A rainbow hung over the infant when he was sleeping inside his cradle. During approximately his second year his father had a wonderful dream and said, "Now I am to die. After my death I am going to the land of awareness-holders. But this son of ours will also benefit others!" With these words he passed away.

When his son, Zhikpo Dütsi, grew up he had much compassion. Once, he gave away all his clothes and so forth to a wretched beggar, without heeding his mother, who had tried to dissuade him. At that, a keen oracle said, "What will become of your son? All the gods and demons of the world circumambulate him *en masse* and worship him!"

One autumn, when harvest time arrived, his mother said, "Everyone is offering *tormas* for the harvest festival.[798] Idiot! even you should offer a water *torma* or something! Each one of us should observe the harvest festival."

The boy went to where the harvest was to take place and called out, "Gods and demons of Ze! Gods and demons of Nyangnak Ölpo! Black Gyelpo of Trangpo Ulu! Don't go anywhere else this morning. This is the festival of old lady Wangmo's harvest! So assist her with the harvest work!" So saying, he scattered the offerings.

His mother was furious and scolded him. She had a field called "Sixty-four". During a very good year it yielded no more than forty bushels, but that year it yielded over fifty, though there was not much corn. So, it was said that the boy might be an emanation. He was sent, therefore, to study under his uncle, Tampa Sedrakpa. For three years he listened carefully to the Great Perfection of the Rong tradition (*rdzogs-chen rong-lugs*), the *Full Summation* (*sgang-dril*), the *Disclosure of the Hidden* (*gab-phyung*) and other teachings. He [later] said, "When the guru passed away my eyes were flooded with tears and I became unconscious."

In his sixteenth year Zhikpo studied at the feet of Yöntenzung of Kyilkar Lhakang. He remained with that master for many years and trained his mind in the three aspects of creation and perfection. But his main practice, and all of his studies, focused on the Mental Class. As Zhikpo himself said, "I have practised only the Mental Class." He studied the *Twenty-four Great Tantras of the Mental Class*, including the *All-Accomplishing King* and the *Ten Sūtras* (*mdo-bcu*, NGB Vol.1), He also studied fourteen different exegetical traditions of the basic cycle of the Mental Class, including the tradition of its cycles (*skor-lugs*), and those of Rong (*rong-lugs*), and of Kham (*khams-lugs*).[799]Among the great treatises on meditation associated with our tradition, he received the *Sun of Yogic Awareness*, and the *Lamp for the Eye of Contemplation*, the *Sun of the Heart of Contemplation* (*bsam-gtan snying-gi nyi-ma*), the *Doubts* (*gdar-sha*) and the *Nails* (*gzer-bu*), the *Answers to Questions which Refer to the Sources* (*zhu-len khung-gdab*), the *Questions and Answers of Vajrasattva* (*Vajrasattvapraśnottara*, P 5082) and most of the others as well. In the cycles of the aural lineages he studied an inconceivable [number of teachings]. They included instruction in the traditions of the cycles, and of Rong and Kham (*skor-rong-khams-gsum*); the aural lineage of the *Brahman's Cycle*; the aural lineages of *Ketsang* and of the *Narrow Path to the Fortress* (*ke-tshang dang rdzong-'phrang snyan-brgyud*); and the Spatial Class. He thoroughly removed his doubts by listening to and pondering over these cycles of the Great Perfection.

Zhikpo Dütsi had begun to teach while in his sixteenth year. He certainly must have reached the summit of learning, for he expounded the *Lecture Notes on the Tradition of the Cycles* (*skor-lugs-kyi stong-thun*). At that time one Lharje Nupme said to him, "O Co-se of Central Tibet! you are like my horse Khyung-truk Khace."[800] And it is said he gave him a remuneration of eleven measures of barley.

Zhikpo remained in the presence of Lama Lhakangpa [i.e. Yöntenzung] for fourteen years. He passed all his vacations at his uncle's seat in Sedrak, where he practised meditation and gave a few explanations. Then, when he had completed his studies, he proceeded to Ze on the invitation of Ladö, one of his father's disciples; and there he took over the monastery of Uke. He also took over Sedrak in Tsang and Chöding, which had been built when four disciples of Tampa Sedrakpa, including Goma Neljorma and Śāknyen, said, "Since we are unable to reach Sedrak, let us make a resting-place in this mountain hollow."

When a disciple of Zhang Tshelpa called Tsangom Hrülpo related the life story of his master to Zhikpo, he developed faith and invited Lama Zhang to come.[801] Zhikpo held a religious assembly and served Lama Zhang with great devotion; for he said, "Though I did not form a doctrinal connection with him [by formally seeking instruction] he is the guru who blessed my mind." Lama Zhang told him that, although water and wood were scarce at the monastery, he should name it Chöding (Vale of Doctrine), for then the assembly would grow there and beings would be benefitted.

Concerning all this people would say, "He studied the doctrine with Lhakangpa [Yöntenzung], but serves Zhang Tshelpa." Lama Lhakangpa was totally free from jealousy, so he sent them about twenty measures of *tsampa*, along with meat and butter, saying, "You should invite a good guru and hold a religious assembly. I will take responsibility for the arrangements, but I have no more than this." At that the foolish people ceased to insult [Zhikpo] and said, "Now we have found a new veneration for our old guru!"

When the time came for Zhikpo to extend his enlightened activity, he gathered an immeasurable number of disciples and worked extensively for the welfare of living creatures. With utmost devotion he used to attend on his guru in accord with the three means to delight him. Of this, he himself said, "Whenever I left his presence, I never departed without placing my head at his feet." He performed inconceivable acts of spiritual and material service for him: for instance, seventeen times he offered extensive sūtras, such as the *Long, Medium and Short Versions of the [Sūtras of] Transcendental Perfection*, written in gold. Because the guru's blessing had penetrated him, he properly apprehended his intention. Having simultaneously attained realisation and liberation, he acquired the power to traverse earth, stones, mountains and rocks without impediment, and he was surrounded by spiritual beings.

There are many stories concerning Zhikpo's possession of the supernormal cognitive powers. While staying at the monastery of Talung in the upper valley of Ze, his body vanished into a boulder and passed without impediment through a clay wall on Sinpo Mountain. He possessed many other miraculous abilities, too.

Zhikpo Dütsi travelled in all parts of the Land of Snows, and secured many beings on the path to liberation. To serve the teaching he built shrines symbolising the buddha-body, speech and mind; he repaired shrines that had deteriorated; and he donated materials for the building projects of others. In these and other ways he applied in practice the meaning of all six transcendental perfections. He attended all the learned translators and scholars who came from India, and followed in the footsteps of the great spiritual benefactors who were holders of the piṭaka. Without ever occupying his mind in worldly affairs, Zhikpo only practised meditation. He was one in whom the enlightened family of the greater vehicle was especially awakened, for he was charitable to all poor and destitute creatures. Therefore, people even gathered from India, China, Nepal and other countries, all speaking different languages.

Three times he sent offerings to the Indestructible Seat in Magadha. Four times he did homage to the two images of Lord Śākyamuni in Lhasa, which are unique ornaments of the world. Four times, too, he rebuilt the stone dikes [of Lhasa].[802] Subsequently, innumerable spiritual benefactors also continued his enlightened activity; so he was a great man, famous beyond dispute in this land of snow mountains.

Through such perfect deeds as these Zhikpo Dütsi only acted to heal others, both directly and indirectly. None the less, during the farewell party after he had rebuilt the stone dikes at Lhasa for the last time, some ill-starred attendants started a drunken brawl. At this, Zhikpo spoke of being disillusioned. He passed away in 1199 (earth female sheep), which was his fifty-sixth year, at the monastery of Gyar Kelok in Sangpu.

Zhikpo's remains were transported by river and preserved for four months at the monastery of Uke in Ze. Then, the king, the officials, and Zhikpo's disciples brought the remains to the temple of Thangkya in Ze, which they had built intending it to be the guru's seat. On that day the earth shook. A lotus grew out of an offering bowl filled with water and other amazing omens occurred. On the morning that his remains were cremated sound, light, rainbows, relics in the forms of stūpas and letters, and countless other signs appeared. Today, only the ruins of that temple remain to be seen.

TATÖN CO-YE

[380.2-385.5] Six disciples became Zhikpo Dütsi's spiritual sons, namely, Tatön Co-ye, Mahā Lhünpo, Khepa Conam, Co-sö of

Central Tibet, Zangtön Hordra, and Nyertön Lama. Tatön Co-ye was foremost among them. His father, Tatön Cobum, was the lord of upper Yoru. He was rich in serfs and estates, but he became disillusioned with the world. Taking four servants with him, he made his escape. He went before Nyö Chuworipa, a spiritual son of Lharje Len Nyatselpa, and all five of them, master and servants, entered the doctrine together. Tatön Cobum thoroughly mastered the Nyingma mantra tradition in general, and, in particular, the texts and instructions of the tradition of the cycles according to the Great Perfection (*rdzogs-chen skor-lugs*). Under Phakmotrupa he studied the Path and Fruit[803] and the Great Seal; under Urtön Lama Tshartön the *Dohā according to the Gang Tradition of the Great Seal* (*phyag-chen sgang-lugs-kyi dohā*); under Zang-ri Drore the *Doctrinal Cycle of Recungpa* (*ras-chung-pa'i chos-skor*);[804] under Nangtön Gönpo the *Vajravidāraṇā* and the *Vajrakīla* cycles; et cetera. In short, he studied the doctrine impartially under many gurus. He took Nyö Chuworipa and Phakmotrupa as his root gurus. After practising at Chuwori he collected many disciples.

His son, Tatön Co-ye, was born in 1163 (water female sheep year). During his fourth year his younger brother, Co-sö, was born. In his childhood Co-sö visited Zhikpo Dütsi and won the master's attention. When Tatön Co-ye was in his twelfth year, he received the cycles of *Cakrasaṃvara* and *Vajrapāṇi the Nectar Drop* (*phyag-rdor bdud-rtsi thigs-pa*) from Lama Martön. He performed the ritual service, reciting the long dhāraṇī for a period of two years. Along with his father, he received one hundred and eight empowerments of *Cakrasaṃvara*. For two years he studied the *Magical Net* at the residence of Kharak Tönying. From both Lama Tsak and Sedur Lungpa he received the texts and instructions of the tradition of the cycles according to the Great Perfection (*rdzogs-chen skor-lugs*). During his sixteenth year he taught *Vajrasattva the Great Space*. Then, in the latter part of his sixteenth year he travelled to lower Ngamshö. Under his father's disciple, Jetsün Hak, he studied the *Gang Tradition of the Great Seal* (*phyag-chen sgang-lugs*). From Zang-ri Gyare he received the *Doctrinal Cycle of [Loro] Recungpa*, the *Me Tradition of Hevajra* (*dgyes-rdor mes-lugs*), *Esoteric Mañjuśrī* (*Mañjuśrī-guhyaka*, T 2584), the *Lūipā Tradition of Cakrasaṃvara* (T 1427), Saroruhavajra's *Means for the Attainment of Hevajra* (*sgrub-thabs mtsho-skyes*, T 1218), the *Zhama Tradition of the Path and Fruit* (*lam-'bras zha-ma lugs*), and all *Three Traditions of Pacification* (*zhi-byed lugs gsum-ka*). In short, he became very learned in [the mantra teachings of] both the ancient and new traditions, without partiality. At some point, too, he studied *Vajrakīla* under Nangtön Cokyam; and he practised it at Chuwori.

In his twenty-fifth year Co-ye came before Zhikpo Dütsi. At first he did not intend to request doctrinal instruction and thought, "In the doctrine I myself am learned. Even in the instructions I am great. But he has a great reputation and fame; and he is my younger brother's guru. Therefore, I should arrange some sort of interview with him." He proceeded on his way and met Zhikpo Dütsi, who was staying at Uke Monastery. By merely beholding the guru's visage he was overcome with devotion. When he was about to leave the next morning he went before the master and asked to be accepted as a disciple.

"Do you have devotion?" the guru asked.

"I have found great devotion."

"Well then, stay from now on, for it is the propensity of past deeds. If saṃsāra is characterised as impermanent one can have no certain knowledge of the future."

"But I did not bring provisions this time."

"No one who comes here brings provisions. What provisions do you alone require?"

At that, Tatön Co-ye attended on Zhikpo for seven years without missing a single day; and he served him with the three means to delight the guru.

He studied the *Triple Cycle of the Mother and Sons, [which comprises] the All-Accomplishing King* (*kun-byed rgyal-po ma-bu skor-sum*), the *Ten Sūtras* which are its exegetical tantras, and the four groups of exegetical tantras pertaining to the *Tantra which Uproots Saṃsāra* (*'khor-ba rtsad-gcod-kyi rgyud-la bshad-rgyud-sde-bzhi*, NGB Vol.1); along with the root texts, commentaries, background doctrines, and esoteric instructions. He also studied the profound fundamental texts concerning the exegetical tradition of the *Eighteen Roots* (*rtsa-ba bco-brgyad-kyi bshad-srol*) and the *Disclosure of the Hidden*, with explanations of the esoteric instructions in relation to meditation, and the commentaries on the meditation of those [just mentioned]: the *Six Suns of the Heart* (*snying-gi nyi-ma drug*), the *Further Heart entitled Six Suns of Awareness* (*yang-snying rig-pa'i nyi-ma drug*), the *Aural Lineage according to the Cycle of the Black Chest* (*snyan-brgyud sgro-ba nag-po'i skor*), the *Great Document on Meditation* (*sgom-yig chen-mo*), the *Sun of Yogic Awareness*, the *Lamp for the Eye of Contemplation*, the *Doubts* and the *Nails*. Among the cycles of the aural lineage, he greatly persevered [in the study of] the traditions of the cycles and of Rong and Kham, along with their instructions and guidebooks.

By drinking profusely from this stream of discourse, he was penetrated spontaneously by its blessing. Having developed an all-surpassing realisation, Co-ye was unconcerned with worldly exaggeration and depreciation. He kept his conduct free from hypocrisy. He had great respect for his guru, and by undertaking to carry out his commands, his intention merged with the master's. Three times he was heard to say, "May I do whatever pleases the guru, and whatever accomplishes his wishes!"

Generally speaking, there was no guru Tatön Co-ye did not serve, but in particular, he sold all his estates and held four religious assemblies at which he renounced everything on behalf of Zhikpo Dütsi. At one time or another, all told, he is said to have offered seventy-four excellent horses to him.

Co-ye committed to writing all of Zhikpo's verbal instructions; and thus he was most kind to the succeeding generations. With inconceivable courage he thought that when he had finished seeking doctrinal instruction he would depart to a forest hermitage, or a wild mountain retreat, where neither the voices of men, nor the songs of birds might be heard; where no one would know he had gone, or know he stayed. For this reason, he copied the books only in the form of terse notes. But he could not bring himself to violate his guru's command that he take on the responsibilities of the teaching master, at the guru's seat. None the less, just by labouring in the service of the guru, the great multitude of his obscurations were removed, and his contemplation also continued to improve, whereupon he said, "[Staying on] proved to be more decisive than retreat."

In consequence of this, when Tatön Co-ye was erecting an image of the Great Compassionate One at Thangkya and so spent eighteen months at Zungkar smelting copper, he developed extraordinary realisation. When King Phodrak[805] took away the emanated master's riding horse, he propitiated the protector of the doctrine [for the purpose of retrieving his guru's mount] at Nangsel Rock in the upper valley of Dorte and had a vision of Mahākāla. When he went to Tölung begging for alms, he met the guru in a dream, and his sufferings vanished by themselves. Thereafter, he said that he never experienced personal sorrow.

In order to manage the affairs of [Zhikpo Dütsi's] seat and carry out his enlightened activities, Co-ye worked extensively for the benefit of beings throughout the kingdom. For six years he attended on the two images of Lord Śākyamuni in Lhasa. Then he passed away in 1230 (iron male tiger), which was his sixty-eighth year, the same year in which Orgyenpa was born. Many remains and relics were left behind.

TATÖN CO-SÖ

[385.5-386.1] Co-ye's younger brother Co-sö was born in 1167 (fire dog year). In his youth he visited Zhikpo Dütsi, who took note of him and granted him the entire Mental Class. Then the master said, "Because you are one who perseveres in the doctrine, you should go to study under my own guru." Co-sö was entrusted to the great Lhakangpa [Yöntenzung] and obtained the complete trilogy of the *Sūtra which Gathers All Intentions*, the *Magical Net*, and the *Mental Class*. He became exceptionally learned, but, because he passed into nirvāṇa in his thirty-first year, 1197 (fire dragon), his enlightened activity did not ripen greatly.

TATÖN ZIJI

[386.1-3] Tatön Ziji was the disciple of one Sangye Öntön.[806] He became quite learned and composed an extensive commentary on the *Secret Nucleus*. It appears that he also composed most of the life stories [of the gurus] of this lineage. But in the *Disclosure of the Contents of Yungtönpa's Commentary* (*gYung-ston-pa'i khog-dbub*) there is a slightly different account. Up to Tatön Ziji [the lineage] was famous for its learning in the entire *Magical Net* and the Mental Class.

PAKSHI ŚĀKYA-Ö

[386.3-392.6] Again, in *Yungtönpa's Commentary* (*gYung-'grel*), where, among many significant digressions, the origins of the continuous exegetical lineage of the *Parkap Commentary* are given, it says that both Cingtön of Tsang and Nyetön Chöki Senge of Gongdring were disciples of the Lord of Secrets, Dropukpa. They both taught Tsangnak Öbar. He taught Metön Gönpo; he, Lama Song; and he, Pakshi Śākya-ö.

Pakshi Śākya-ö was a descendant of the Zur clan. His father, Zur Wangcen Öpoche, was a lord among accomplished masters, who clearly remembered his successive lives. As he had only five daughters and the family was without a son, he became despondent. He invited the great paṇḍita Śākyaśrī to Ukpalung, immediately after the latter's visit to Trhopu in 1204 (wood male mouse year).[807] There, the great paṇḍita said, "This Ukpalung is a domain of secret mantra, adorned with many attributes. The mountain to the north appears as the Conquerors of the Five Families. The birds, wildlife, and so forth are also sublime emanations. In each generation one of your clan comes forth to expound the doctrine of secret mantra. Now, two sons will soon be born to you. Name them after me. They will benefit the doctrine and living creatures."

It happened just as he had said. The elder son was given the name Śākyagön, and the younger Śākya-ö. While the elder brother proved to be a wonderful person, too, it was the younger brother, Śākya-ö, who spoke from childhood like one who spontaneously possessed supernormal cognitive powers. He knew how to teach all the doctrines by means of symbols, such was his discipline. Relying on Lama Gyakap Kongpa, he studied his entire ancestral doctrine. He actually saw [beings in] the intermediate state, so when others came to perform the rite of the "Tie to the Higher Realms",[808] he would say, "You have not freed the deceased from Yama! There is no point to a ritual that is divorced from an enlightened attitude." And they would have to repeat the rite.

One day he said, "I feel regret."

"Whatever for?" he was asked.

"I was to enter the assembly of the awareness-holders forever, but I abused my elder brother, Śākyagön. Henceforth, I am a violator of commitments and cannot enter the assembly of awareness-holders." And he performed a repentance.

There was one Ghare of Minyak who became engulfed in a blood feud with his own relatives. He inquired as to who was the most powerful sorcerer in Tibet and heard that there was one named Śākya-ö, the great. Ghare sent many presents to him, though he lived at a distance of eight months' journey, with a request that he exercise sorcery [to eliminate Ghare's enemies]. But Śākya-ö said, "I have no sorcery. If you want this staff of mine, take it!" And he did not even answer the letter.

When the messenger related what had taken place, Ghare was furious and said, "He has taken my possessions and not given me the instructions!" He grasped the staff with his hand and from within it Dorje Lekpa emerged with four deities in attendance. Ghare joyfully propitiated them and annihilated many of his paternal relatives. Then, to purify himself of this sin, and to accumulate merit, he built a temple and a stūpa.

Ghare of Minyak even came in person to express his gratitude to Zur Śākya-ö; and he brought many offerings. He met the master and undertook to cultivate experientially many doctrines, such as the *Secret Nucleus*. The two then joined company and proceeded to Kharcu in Lhodrak. They meditated and dwelt at Khoting Temple, Paro and elsewhere; and at that time they met Lord Nyang, father and son.[809] From them they received most of the Nyang tradition, including the *Gathering of the Sugatas of the Eight Transmitted Precepts*. Then, they returned to their respective homes. Ghare said, "The guru has been most gracious. I beg that you send one person with me, since I am going to Mongolia. I will make offerings through that person to express my gratitude." Then he set out.

At that time in Mongolia the throne had been seized by the king's younger brother Ariboga.[810] Because the king, Qubilai Qan, had not obtained sovereignty, he prepared for war. He asked Ghare of Minyak, "They say that there is powerful sorcery in Tibet. Do you know anything about it?"

"Yes," replied Ghare, "I know. Which of these three do you require: slaughter, expulsion, or capture?"

To that Qubilai Qan responded, "If [my brother's] death were to occur in association with his karma, I would doubt he would have been slaughtered [by sorcery]. If it so happened that he desired to travel, I would be sceptical of his being expelled. So capture him; for he certainly has no desire to come to this camp of mine, except if he be captured."

At that Ghare made the precious Lama Phakpa his witness.[811] He applied himself to the production of a whirlwind, and the younger brother Ariboga arrived, powerless to do otherwise. But still [the emperor] was not convinced. "Bring down thunderbolts in the middle of this lake and this plain," he commanded. When Ghare brought down thunderbolts in both places the emperor was convinced. He became terrified of the mantrins and gave them great rewards.

It is also said that Ghare was a disciple of one Patsel, who achieved the power of sorcery on the basis of Yamāntaka. He may well have been his disciple, but he obtained the ultimate applications of the wrathful mantras from Zurpa [Śākya-ö].

Pakshi Śākya-ö had dispatched one Tönpa Rāhu, who met with Ghare and was given fine presents. Tönpa Rāhu was presented with [a document] which explained that according to the inventory of Lord Nyang's treasure texts, a treasure containing the water of life was to be found at Dorje Tsheten in Tsang. He was sent to offer [the document] to Lama Śākya-ö. Together with that was the emperor Qubilai Qan's decree:

> A summons to Śākya Öpo and Śākya Gönpo: Perform whatever ceremonies are necessary; but extract the water of life and send it to me! It may well be beneficial. I know what is pleasing and what is sorrowful to you. This is accompanied by a measure of silver mixed with flour for *tormas*.[812]

When this imperial order arrived they performed a great ceremony. Because the emperor was most insistent and the envoy short-tempered, they experienced some difficulty. But the very evening when they recited the prayer to the lineage of the *Magical Net*, which begins "Trio of sound, light, and rays..." (*sgyu-'phrul-gyi brgyud-pa-la sgra-'od-zer gsum-ma'i gsol-'debs*)[813] they obtained a clear prediction concerning the entrance to the treasure.

After that, Zur Śākya-ö, Guru Khyungdra, the governor Śākzang, and the envoy Agayana joined together to make a "public [discovery of] treasure". At first they were powerless to pass beyond the revolving wheel of sharp-edged razors at the gate to the treasures. Zur Śākya-ö then worshipped the lord of the treasure, imploring him to be a fair witness. At that, all were amazed to see the razor blades grind to a halt, just where they were. The master stirred the charcoal that filled the treasure hollow, from the centre of which the mouth and eyes of a frog then emerged. As soon as they saw its limb rise a whirlwind blew up, surprising everyone. When the guru subdued it, performing recitations on his *rudrākṣa* rosary[814] and making a declaration of truth, the whirlwind then subsided. He removed a veil of Chinese silk (*chu-dar*) and [found] two skulls, one male and one female, which were sealed together within three successive copper amulet-boxes, one within the other. He began to reach inside and these objects disintegrated into dust just as he touched them. Wrapped in many embroidered silks were images of Hayagrīva and Varāhī in union, Vajrasattva with his consort, and thirteen paper scrolls containing the means for attainment. In the midst of these, there was a lapis (*mu-men*) flask,[815] about the size of a large inkpot, which contained the water of life. Everyone was astonished.

If the guru had consumed the first fruits he could have lived for a hundred years. But the spoon did not reach the tip of his tongue, so the auspicious opportunity was lost. [The envoy] wrapped the vase up in cloth and carried it to China, striving never to fall asleep. By drinking the water of life Emperor Qubilai Qan is said to have lived for a hundred years. As a reward he issued an edict exempting all the mantrins of Central Tibet and Tsang from taxation and military service.[816] In order to make Śākya-ö equal in rank to the imperial preceptors, the title *Pakshi* was conferred on him.[817] In return for having offered the water of life he was granted lands supporting forty-five households in Mongolia.

Śākya-ö wished to build a great monastery on Mount Medril, but, because there was already a great nāga city in that place, the nāgas asked him [not to do so]. In return they offered him substitute land which they had in the swamp of Gyagen. The nāgas miraculously drained the area and there Śākya-ö built a great centre for the way of mantras. He himself practised one-pointedly in the heart of Khar Dorje Trak, and he passed away in his sixty-third year. By touching his corpse people were cured of leprosy.[818]

ZUR CAMPA SENGE

[392.6-396.3] Pakshi Śākya-ö's disciple was Tanak Düdül, who transmitted the teaching to Da Śākyaphel, under whom Zur Campa Senge studied. Campa Senge's father was the son of Mepo Pakshi[819] and was called Zur Nyima Senge. He was ordained at Trhopu and named [Nyima Senge] by Campapel, the translator of Trhopu.[820] Nyima Senge possessed many enlightened attributes. In particular, he was firmly rooted in the enlightened attitude. Therefore, during the Mongol wars,[821] when he was offered much gold by Sambhata, an aristocrat, who said, "I do not need gold. But please grant me the gift of fearlessness!" Nyima Senge was able [to use the gold] to protect the lives of many beings. And once, while the Great Stūpa (*'bum-chen*) of Trhopu was being constructed and there was a severe drought, he caused a great downpour by exercising his powers of sorcery.

Zur Campa Senge

When the Upper Mongols [*stod-hor*, i.e. Hülegü and the Ilkhans] began to grow exceedingly hostile to the Sakyapa teaching, Nyima Senge, at the order of his imperial benefactors [the Yüan rulers] and with the support (*bca'-rgyu*) of the governor Künzhön, used his wrathful powers of sorcery to massacre three armies, each with ten thousand men, in a glacial crevasse. Therefore, his legacy to the Sakyapa teaching was especially great.[822]

From time to time Zur Nyima Senge constructed temples, complete with their [symbols of] buddha-body, speech, and mind [i.e. images, books, and stūpas]. This illustrates his vast enlightened activity on behalf of the teaching and of living beings.

His son, Zur Campa Senge, was one who had awakened to the enlightened family of the greater vehicle, so he possessed great compassion even from his childhood. If he saw another injuring animals, his heart would be heavily burdened. He was ordained at Trhopu and named [Campa Senge]. He became a learned scholar of Trhopu. Then, in his fourteenth year, he began to teach and he acquired a reputation as a scholar. Yungtön Dorjepel, too, said of him, "My guru was the all-knowing Zur." This was certainly the case, for Campa Senge actually gave discourses to the students from the teaching throne of Trhopu.

In his fifteenth year, at Ukjalung [i.e. Ukpalung], he studied and trained himself in the *Secret Nucleus* under Da Śākyaphel. Thus, he became a lord among scholars. In his seventeenth year he composed the *Definitive Presentation of the Tantras* (*rgyud-kyi rnam-bzhag*) and took over [the administration of] a religious endowment. He studied the *Sequence of the Path of the Magical Net* and the Great Perfection under Cetön Drupabum during his nineteenth year; and he developed an all-surpassing realisation. In his twentieth year he invited Tatön Ziji from Latö and requested the empowerments of beneficence, ability, and profundity[823] according to the Zur tradition of the *Magical Net* (*sgyu-'phrul zur-lugs-kyi phan-nus-zab-gsum-gyi dbang*), and the cycle of transmitted root texts of the *Sūtra which Gathers All Intentions*. From Zurlungpa Druptop Shenyen he received the empowerment of the *Sūtra which Gathers All Intentions*, and the *Long, Medium, and Short [teachings on the] Peaceful and Wrathful Deities according to the Se Tradition* (*se-lugs-kyi zhi-khro rgyas-'bring-bsdus-gsum*). He studied grammar and logic under Tharpa Lotsāwa Nyima Gyeltsen.[824] His study of the *Vajra Garland* under master Pelcok of Trhopu indicates the great extent of [his studies of] the new translations. Campa Senge also learned the *Path and Fruit* from Samding Trupapel; *Vajrapāṇi* and *Vajravidāraṇa* from Lama Yöntengön; the rituals of the protectors of the teaching, medicine, astrology and rites to ensure martial victory from Pön Pelcengön; and the *Red* and *Black Yamāri*, and the cycle of the Spatial Class (*klong-sde'i skor*) from Kangpa Śākbum. In short, he studied the inner and outer sciences, the piṭaka, and numberless tantras under many gurus.

After training himself decisively [in all of these teachings], Zur Campa Senge remained totally absorbed in meditation. He had visions of many meditational deities. It is said that anyone who came into his presence found appearances to be naturally transformed, and was spontaneously overcome with renunciation, faith, and compassion. None the less, this holy person did not remain in the world after his twenty-seventh year, because his food was poisoned by a Pönpo.

Campa Senge's enlightened attributes of knowledge, love, and power were hard to measure, so he was believed to have been an emanation. The number of his disciples was inconceivable: He trained about sixteen spiritual benefactors who had fully mastered the *Sequence of the Path of the Magical Net*, the *Secret Nucleus*, and the *Parkap Commentary*, together with the *Sūtra which Gathers All Intentions*. They acted extensively for the benefit of others and obtained fame in their own right. Foremost among them were Yungtön Dorjepel, the senior disciple of his early years, and Tanak Drölmawa Samdrup Dorje, the foremost disciple of his later years.

YUNGTÖN DORJEPEL

[396.3-398.6] Yungtönpa belonged to the Len clan. He was born in Tshongdü in 1284 (wood male monkey year). From his youth he was endowed with perfect discernment. In general, he knew all the dialectical teachings, and was particularly learned in the *Compendium of the Abhidharma*. He had a most powerful command of all the mantra traditions, ancient and new. Above all, he became the genuine spiritual son of Karmapa Rangjung Dorje. From Zur Campa Senge he obtained the esoteric instructions of the *Trio of the Sūtra which Gathers All Intentions, the Magical Net and the Mental Class* in their entirety; and he became a great master among their proponents. He composed the *Illuminating Mirror (gsal-byed me-long)*, a commentary on the *Tantra of the Secret Nucleus* which came to surpass those of the other exegetical traditions in popularity. Then, when Zur Campa Senge went to study the *Yamāntaka Cycle (gshed-skor)* under Kangpa Śākbum, Yungtönpa accompanied him and studied it as well. He became a very learned and powerful [adept of] the yogic exercises, their functional applications, et cetera. So, when Lhakü Pönpo poisoned Zur Campa Senge, cutting off his life, Yungtönpa turned the wheel of Yamāntaka against him, which caused him, along with his property, fields and household to be swept away by a river and thereby utterly destroyed. At that time, Yungtönpa composed a verse which began:

> I am merely the subduer of my guru's mortal foe...

During his youth Yungtönpa went to China by imperial command. He performed thread-cross and *torma* rites *(mdos-gtor)* which previously had been quite unknown in the world at large.[825] In some regions there had been severe drought, but at the order of the emperor, Yungtönpa caused rain to fall. The emperor was delighted by this revelation of his power. Returning to Tibet, laden with great rewards and riches, Yungtönpa gave nothing to his acquaintances and friends, but offered everything to his guru and to the monastic community, so that the merit might benefit his mother.

Yungtönpa also became a disciple of Putön Rinpoche and acquired great learning in the *Kālacakra*.[826] Moreover, he knew many quirks of causality:[827] When he pierced a skin water-bag with a vulture's quill, the water did not leak. When he touched red-hot iron with his bare flesh, he was unburnt. And when he plastered a wall with a cement made from six kinds of stone, the wall was transformed into a great rock.

Above all, Yungtönpa experientially cultivated the esoteric instructions, in general, and the Great Perfection, in particular, owing to the great inspiration of Karmapa Rangjung Dorje. He obtained the eight great treasures that are described in the *Sūtra of Extensive Play* and thereby unlocked the vast treasure of brilliance, so that he satisfied

Yungtön Dorjepel

living beings with his eloquence. When Yakde Paṇcen saw his *Treatise on the Difference between [the Descriptions of] Buddhahood according to the Sūtra and Mantra Traditions* (*mdo-sngags-kyi sangs-rgyas-la khyad-par-phye-ba'i bstan-bcos*) he developed great faith and, with fourteen disciples, went to meet him and become a supplicant at his feet.

In later life Yungtönpa received complete monastic ordination from Tshokpa Chölungpa. His name, Dorjebum, was changed to Dorjepel. He resided in places like Paro in Bhutan, Phungpo Riwoche, and Ratum Trak; and by his teaching he extensively benefitted others. He passed away in his eighty-second year, 1365 (wood female snake).

TANAK DRÖLMAWA SAMDRUP DORJE

[398.6-400.1] Tanak Drölmawa Samdrup Dorje was born at Tanak Nesar in 1295 (wood female sheep year) as the son of a family which, in each generation, had obtained accomplishment through the Nyingma mantra tradition. He studied extensively under Zur Campa Senge and became particularly learned in the *Magical Net*. He received the empowerment of the *Magical Net* from Len Nyatselpa Sonam Gönpo.

Samdrup Dorje's knowledge and enlightened activity are difficult to estimate: He meditated in total solitude, and in Cema Senge he meditated one-pointedly on the Innermost Spirituality of the Great Perfection (*rdzogs-chen snying-thig*). He reached the limits of awareness, and savoured the entire ocean of buddha-fields equally.

Zur Śākya Jungne of Yang-en and Lama Sengepa of Ukpalung were left in Samdrup Dorje's care from childhood; and they came to respect, above all, their commitments to this guru, who raised them so well. Thus, he was most kind to the lineage of Zur. Len Selwa, too, who became famed as the "All-Knowing Master from Shang", received many empowerments and was blessed by this guru during childhood, and so became greatly learned. In these and other ways Samdrup Dorje's blessings were inconceivable.

At the time of his death, in his eighty-second year, 1376 (fire male dragon), he said to his son, "I am going to Sukhāvatī. You will also live to my age. Then, come to Sukhāvatī!" With these words he passed away.

Tanak Drölmawa Samdrup Dorje

ZUR ZANGPOPEL AND ZUR HAM ŚĀKYA JUNGNE

[400.1-405.6] Two lineages issued from Tanak Drölmawa Samdrup Dorje: the "Zur lineage" (*zur-brgyud*) and the "son's lineage" (*sras-brgyud*). The "Zur lineage" was that of Zur Ham Śākya Jungne.

This Śākya Jungne was the son of Zur Zangpopel, who, during his lifetime, received commissions and gifts from the emperor Buyantu.[828] Once, he had to travel to China by imperial command. Because he had very great occult skills and powers he acted, at first, in the service of the royal emperor by providing protection from crop-failure and suppressing rebellion by means of thread-crosses, malign *torma* (*zor*),[829] lightning, and hail. On one occasion, in particular, an ominous, black cloud in the form of a scorpion appeared in the sky above the royal palace of Tā'i-tu;[830] and no one was able to banish it. At that time, Zur Zangpopel was commissioned by the emperor. He trapped the cloud in eighteen houses made of silk, following the thread-cross rites of the "Mātaraḥs' Vengeance" (*ma-mo 'khang-phab-kyi mdos*). He then performed a *torma* offering dance (*gtor-'chams*) and the black cloud was dispersed. Many such revelations of the greatness of the true doctrine in the land beyond the pale [Tibet] caused the emperor to acquire faith. He requested the empowerment of the nine deities of [the maṇḍala of] Yangdak Heruka and an empowerment of longevity; and he presented Zangpopel with offerings of a silver seal, thirteen measures of silver, and sufficient dress-silk for two hundred shirts. He established a congregation of mantrins in the Tā'i-tu palace: It is well known that kīlas for the four rites were kept in the palace at that time.

From the material resources which Zangpopel thus collected he had printing-blocks made for twenty-eight doctrinal collections of the Ancient Translation School, including the *Root Tantra of the Secret Nucleus*, the *Parkap Commentary*, the *Sequence of the Path of Secret Mantra* (*gsang-sngags lam-rim*), and many esoteric instructions (*man-ngag dgu*). He printed a thousand copies of each and distributed them to students. He contributed many of the materials needed to produce [a copy of] the *Collected Tantras* (*rgyud-'bum*). So, through these and other activities he benefitted the teaching most extensively.

Sometime thereafter the emperor Buyantu passed away, after a medication for fever had been applied to an ailment that was affecting the vital energies.

During this period the Sakyapa and the Zurs enjoyed a most profound intimacy, for, at heart, their philosophies were identical. Therefore, when the news of Zur Campa Senge's death reached Sakya, they said, "This is not good. Now, let us summon Zur Zangpopel from China." Others also conferred, and, finally, they sent the attendant Jamyang to invite him [back to Tibet]. But when Jamyang reached China, Zur Zangpopel was laid up with a fever and was approaching death. Then, owing to the blessings of the ḍākinīs and protectors of the doctrine, he began to show a slight recovery. At that very time, the emperor Buyantu appeared to him in a vision and said, "When you were [preparing] to leave for Tibet, what gifts were you given?"

Zangpopel answered in detail.

"Then you have been given nothing at all," said the emperor and vanished.

When the royal lady Thabula heard the story, she exclaimed, "Seeing you reminds me of the emperor!" and wept. She again offered the master ten measures of silver.

Zangpopel then commissioned an image of Vajrasattva in Chinese bronze[831] and dance masks of a doctrine protector and his lady (*chos-skyong lcam-dral*) and proceeded to Tibet with these. When the protector gazed on Tibet, it ascended seven steps, and so became renowned as the Sebak Komdünma, the "Leather Mask of the Seven Steps".[832]

Having reached Tibet, Zur Zangpopel produced [the aforementioned copy of] the *Collected Tantras* as a service to the teaching. He engaged the protectors of the doctrine as his servants and clearly predicted the future. Later, when he again had to depart for China at the imperial

Zur Ham Śākya Jungne

command, he was not inclined to set out. He made offerings, such as a measure of silver, to the emperor's messenger Themurdar and to Ghare, but they would not go, saying that if they were to return [without Zangpopel] they would be punished. At that he set out for China, having first composed some instructions, which began:

> All independence is bliss,
> And all dependence is sorrow...

Zur Zangpopel lived for no more than about thirty-eight years.

Zur Ham Śākya Jungne was his son. As a child he studied the doctrines of his paternal ancestors; and the propensities of his past deeds were awakened. In his fifth year he stood up in the midst of the noblemen who were escorting his father on the journey to China and delivered a short exegesis of the *Root Tantra* [i.e. the *Secret Nucleus*], which astonished everyone. From his seventh year on he was raised at the college. He was ordained as a novice by Lama Künpangpa, received full ordination from the doctrine master Sonam Trakpa, and became well known under his ordination name, Śākya Jungne. In a decree of the emperor Guluk[833] he was referred to as "Zur Śākya Jungne, son of Zur Pakshi", and he was presented with four large, sixty-ounce measures of gold, twenty large measures of pure silver, and two hundred silk outer robes and linings. The royal lady Tha'u and others also offered vast wealth to him; and so they bountifully benefitted the spiritual and temporal domains of the Zurs.

In particular, Zur Ham Śākya Jungne built a most wonderful, golden image of Mañjughoṣa, which contained fragments of the conqueror Zurpoche's robes. He installed it as the foremost receptacle of worship at glorious Ukjalung. And he completed great rectifications (*tshugs-kha*) [of the customs] at the college and retreat centre. Without sparing his wealth he undertook to serve the doctrine. His radiance, pleasing to behold, even inspired faith in the Mongolian nobleman Themurdar, who then requested an empowerment of longevity. Thus, Śākya Jungne lived as a great spiritual warrior, who could inspire confidence in others.

He met all the learned, noble, and excellent teachers of Central Tibet and Tsang, including the great translator Sazang [Mati Paṇcen],[834] the conqueror Yungtönpa, Jamyang Samdrup Dorje, the heir to the Sakyapa lineage (*sa-skya-pa'i gdung-brgyud*),[835] and all the most famous leaders of the Zur tradition. He became well trained in the Three Classes of Dialectics (*mtshan-nyid sde-gsum*), and in the fundamental texts and esoteric instructions of all schools, ancient and new, of the way of secret mantra. In particular, he diligently trained himself in the *Ornament of Emergent Realisation*, the *Introduction to the Conduct of a Bodhisattva*, the *Kālacakra*, the *Tantra of the All-Accomplishing King*, the *Sequence of the Path of the Magical Net*, the *Secret Nucleus*, and the *Parkap Commentary*; and so he became renowned as a great scholar and accomplished master.

During this later period Zur Ham Śākya Jungne was the sole master of the teaching on the empowerment of the *Sūtra which Gathers All Intentions* according to the tradition of Zur. When he himself received that empowerment from the great Drölmawa Samdrup Dorje, he made offerings headed by Chinese and Tibetan robes, cooking utensils, and fifty loads of barley. He mastered all the transmissions, practical applications and techniques [of that sūtra]. For the sake of the seal of entrustment (*gtad-rgya*)[836] alone, he delighted the guru with offerings of large silks and gold. He had extremely clear visions of Śākyamuni and of the Herukas of the Five Enlightened Families. Also, he composed many works, such as the *Commentary of the Seal of Entrustment, a Memorial of the Deities of the Sūtra which Gathers All Intentions* (*'dus-pa mdo'i lha-thems gtad-rgya'i 'grel-pa*). His actions on behalf of the trilogy of the *Sūtra which Gathers All Intentions*, the *Magical Net*, and the *Mental Class*, were most extensive. Śākya Jungne produced many disciples who clarified the teachings: Drölmawa Samdrup Dorje's son Sangye Rincen, and Nyelpa Delekpa, among others. He passed away in his thirty-eighth year. There is also a "ritual guide" (*chog-khrid*) composed by [his disciple] Nyelpa Delek.

SANGYE RINCEN

[405.6-409.1] Again, there was the lineage of the great Drölmawa Samdrup Dorje's son, known as Sangye Rincen Gyeltsen Pelzangpo, who was born at Nesar in 1350 (iron male tiger) when his father was in his fifty-sixth year. People would say, "This son of yours is no use! Why should you cherish him so?"

To which he replied, "My son will be of benefit to living creatures."

In his sixth year Sangye Rincen mastered the *Tantra of the Secret Nucleus*. Then, he went before Zur Śākya Jungne, who, calling him "my guru's son", raised him as a favourite, but he was too distracted to retain this tantra. Then, in his eighth year he repeated [the course] and retained it. His father taught him the ceremonies and rites of enlightened activity, whereby in his fourteenth year he became a capable master who conferred empowerment on others. Under his father he also mastered the doctrinal cycles of the *Magical Net*.

On one occasion, Sangye Rincen said, "Now, I will become ordained as a monk and train myself in dialectics. I will also study the tantras of the new translation schools."

But his father responded, "For the time being, that would be inappropriate. But you may be ordained later on."

At that, he took a consort and she gave birth to some sons. As a layman he completed his studies and training. Afterwards he received, all at once, the complete ordination at Chökorgang. He remained extremely dignified in his conduct. Having become learned in the *Magical Net*, Sangye Rincen composed a *Great Commentary on the Secret Nucleus (gsang-snying 'grel-chen)*, and a *Detailed Exposition of the Array of the Path of the Magical Net (lam rnam-bkod-la rnam-bzhag)* when he was about forty. Similarly, he composed an *Extensive Descriptive Basis [for the Rites] of the Wrathful Deities (khro-bo-la mngon-par-rtogs-pa rgyas-pa)* and also a *Detailed Ceremony for the Rite of the Tie to the Higher Realms (gnas-lung-la'ang cho-ga rgyas-pa)*, both of these being derived from the eight arisings of enlightened activity *(phrin-las shar-ba brgyad)*. Sangye Rincen received many esoteric instructions from his father and his father's spiritual son, Thupa Dorje; and he applied these in practical experience.

In his seventieth year[837] he accepted Gölo Yezang Tsepa [i.e. Gölo Zhönupel] as a disciple and granted him the empowerment of the peaceful and wrathful deities according to the *Magical Net (sgyu-'phrul zhi-khro'i dbang)*; the longevity empowerment of the *Magical Net (sgyu-'phrul-gyi tshe-dbang)*; the empowerment of the *Churner of the Depths of Hell (dong-sprugs-kyi dbang)*, the empowerments of *[Yamāntaka,] Lord of Life*, and of *Yangdak Mecik (tshe-bdag-dang yang-dag me-gcig-gi dbang)*; the permissory initiations[838] for the *Hayagrīva Traditions of Nawopa and Dagyelma (sna-bo-pa'i lugs-kyi rta-mgrin-dang zla-rgyal-ma'i lugs-kyi rjes-gnang)*; the empowerment of the *Khön Tradition of Vajrakīla*, along with the permissory initiation for the wrathful rites *(phur-pa-'khon-lugs-kyi dbang drag-po rjes-gnang-dang bcas-pa)*; the empowerments of the expressive play of awareness for the *Eighteen Teachings of the Mental Class (sems-sde bco-brgyad-kyi rig-pa'i rtsal dbang)*; the exegesis of the *Tantra of the Secret Nucleus* and its commentary; and an extensive exegesis of the *Array of the Path of the Magical Net* according to his own commentary. In addition, he bestowed on him the transmissions of about forty opuscules, including the *Illuminating Lamp of the Fundamental Text*; the *Forty-Chapter Magical Net (sgyu-'phrul bzhi-bcu-pa*, NGB Vol.14); those of the *Sūtra which Gathers All Intentions*, its root tantra, the *All-Gathering Awareness*, and its commentary by Nupcen Sangye Yeshe, the *Armour Against Darkness*; and those of both the *Eighty-Chapter Magical Net* and the *Superior Magical Net*, and the *Root Text of Yangdak (yang-dag rtsa-ba)*.[839]

Sangye Rincen also gave him the four empowerments of the Innermost Spirituality, beginning with the elaborate one, and guidance [on meditation] according to a guidebook *(khrid-yig)* based on the writings of Melong Dorje, and following, too, the *Esoteric Instructions of the Great Perfection according to Aro (rdzogs-chen a-ro'i man-ngag)*. Similarly, he gave him the *Guidance which Lays Bare the Teaching of the Great Compassionate One (thugs-rje-chen-po'i smar-khrid)* following the lineage of the bodhisattva Yegyelwa. Because of all this, it appears, Gölo Yezang Tsepa himself made this decisive affirmation, "I crossed to the furthest shores of the ocean of learning, and so achieved what is meaningful."

Then, in 1421 (iron female ox), his seventy-second year, the doctrine master Sangye Rincen travelled to Central Tibet. At the monastery of Samtenling in Kangpori he was attended by Wangdrakpa Gyeltsen. The guru gave many empowerments, including those of the *Sūtra which Gathers All Intentions*, and many exegeses and transmissions, including those of the *Secret Nucleus*. Then, in 1431 (iron female pig), his eighty-second year, he passed away in Tsang. From the birth of Zurcungpa until this date four hundred and seventeen years appear to have passed.

GÖLO ZHÖNUPEL (YEZANG TSEPA)

[409.1-411.4] Now, the great man Gö Zhönupel was born in 1392 (water monkey year). His father was called Götön Jungne Dorje, and his mother Sitarkyi. He was ordained by the great preceptor Cenye. From Karmapa V, Tezhinshekpa, he received the bodhisattva vow and the *Six Doctrines*. From Ngok Cangcupel he heard the doctrines of Ngok. But, in particular, it was from the great paṇḍita Vanaratna[840] that he received most of the empowerments of the Unsurpassed tantras. He corrected and translated the *Litany of the Names of Mañjuśrī*, the *Point of Spring* (*Vasantatilaka*, T 1448), the *Brief Teaching of Empowerment* (*Sekoddeśa*, T 361), and Anupamarakṣita's *Commentary on the Six-limbed Yoga* (*Kālacakraṣaḍaṅgayoga*, T 1367).

When Drölcen Sangye Rincen was in his seventieth year, 1419 (earth female pig), this master received from him all the transmitted empowerments of the tantrapiṭaka of the Ancient Translation School in their entirety: the empowerment of the peaceful and wrathful deities according to the *Magical Net* and its longevity empowerment; the *Churner of the Depths of Hell*; the *Lord of Life*; *Yangdak Mecik*; the *Hayagrīva Traditions of Nawopa and Dagyelma*; the *Khön Tradition of Vajrakīla*; and the empowerments of the expressive play of awareness for the *Eighteen Teachings of the Mental Class*. Among exegetical transmissions he received the *Tantra of the Secret Nucleus* with its commentary, and the commentary on the *Array of the Path of the Magical Net* which Sangye Rincen had himself composed. Moreover, he received the explanatory transmissions of about forty opuscules, Indian and Tibetan, including the *Illuminating Lamp of the Fundamental Text* and the *Forty-Chapter Magical Net*; the transmissions of the *Sūtra which Gathers All Intentions*, its root tantra, the *All-Gathering Awareness*, and its commentary by Nup Sangye Yeshe, the *Armour Against Darkness*; and those of both the *Eighty-Chapter Magical Net* and the *Superior Magical Net*, and the *Root Text of Yangdak*. He received, too, the four root empowerments, elaborate and unelaborate, of the Innermost Spirituality, its guidance according to the guidebook of the accomplished master Melong Dorje, and guidance on the *Esoteric Instructions of the Great Perfection according to the Tradition of Aro*. In short, Gö Zhönupel became as a lord of secret mantra teaching according to the Ancient Translation School.

This master himself said, "I acquired exceptional devotion towards the tradition renowned as the Nyingmapa school of secret mantra. So, I was never polluted by the defilement of rejecting [true] doctrine."[841] Such words were intended for those pseudo-scholars of Tibet who were sectarian bigots. In fact, this master was more sublime than other philosophically unbiased spiritual benefactors; this is clearly demonstrated by his own treatises, which are reliable and also vastly eloquent.[842]

This master offered many doctrinal transmissions, empowerments, and much guidance to Karmapa Chödrak Gyamtso, including the *Trilogy of Commentaries by Bodhisattvas* (*sems-'grel skor-gsum*). He acted as the preceptor who gave complete ordination to Zhamarpa IV, Chöki Trakpa; and he gave him an inconceivable number of transmitted empowerments and exegetical transmissions, as well as the guidance of esoteric instruction, for an ocean of tantrapiṭaka, both ancient and new, of which the foremost was the *Magical Net*. The venerable Zhamarpa, too, considered Gö to be his sole, most gracious guru.

Thus, having by many means expanded the teaching of the transmitted precepts and treasures, Gö Zhönupel passed away in his ninetieth year, 1481 (iron ox).

CE-NGA RINPOCHE, ZHAMARPA IV

[411.4-413.2] Now, Zhamarpa IV, Ce-nga Rinpoche, was born in Treshö Khangmar in 1453 (water female bird year). His father was Dong Gönpakyap, and his mother Hraza Sonam Drölma. At Zurmang Monastery[843] he met Karmapa VII, Chödrak Gyamtso, and on receiving ordination from him was given the name Chöki Trakpa Yeshe Pelzangpo. He received the doctrine also from the preceptor Gushri Trakpelpa and from Pengarpa.[844] In his twenty-fourth year he was completely ordained as a monk, under the great translator of Gö, Yezang Tsepa, who acted as preceptor. At one time or another he studied numberless teachings: tantrapiṭaka of the new translation schools, such as *Kālacakra*, *Cakrasaṃvara*, *Hevajra*, *Guhyasamāja*, and *Bhairava*; and the transmitted empowerment and exegetical transmission of the *Secret Nucleus of the Magical Net*, among others [of the Ancient Translation School]. He also received many doctrines of the ancient and new traditions from the great translator Sonam Gyamtso, who was descended from the family of Gyelwa Choyang of Ngenlam.

When Ce-nga Rinpoche received the empowerment of *Vajrakīla* from the master Gö [Zhönupel], he had a vision of master Padmasambhava in a dream, and was even given instructions. He yielded up his physical body during his seventy-third year, 1525 (wood bird), while still occupied with teaching all the various doctrines, ancient and new, to his disciples.

In short, by extensive study this master purified himself. Although he composed a great many means for attainment, exegetical commentaries, maṇḍala rites, dialogues, and other treatises, Zhamarpa's works are all superior to others, because they are refined in word and meaning, of suitable length, conclusive, and fair. His *Guidance on the View of the Great Middle Way, which Definitively Reveals the Absolute* (*don-dam nges-'byed dbu-ma-chen-po'i lta-khrid*) is based on the *Five Doctrines* of the great regent [Maitreya]. Therefore, in adhering above all to the infallible diction of the ultimate doctrinal language this master accords with the great, all-knowing Longcenpa, Karmapa VII, and the all-knowing, great Tölbupa.[845]

DRIGUNG ZURPA RINCEN PHÜNTSOK

[413.2-414.5] The Zhamarpa conferred the teachings on Zurpa Rincen Phüntsok of Drigung. He was born into the Kyura family in Drigung Kunyergang in upper Uru. After his eighth year he was ordained as a novice by Ce-nga Rinpoche, Chöki Trakpa. At thirteen, when he was invited to the consecration of the Trhadruk Temple at Tsitang Samtenling, which had been restored by Karpopa,[846] all sorts of wonderful miracles took place. He set his heart on attainment in such great places of pilgrimage as Yangpacen, Lungshö, and Zhotö Tidro. Once, while he was staying at Tidro, Vajranātha, an accomplished master from India, arrived and gave him the esoteric instructions on vital energy by Javāripā (*dza-bi-ra'i bhū rlung*), and other, further advice. Following a prophetic declaration of the ḍākinīs he changed his dress to white [i.e. became a mantrin free from monastic vows]. In Yangpacen a treasure inventory came into his possession, following which he extracted the yellow scrolls of the five families [which contained] the *True Doctrine of the Most Profound Intention, the Essence of the Body, Speech and Mind of Guru Rinpoche* (*gu-ru rin-po-che'i sku-gsung-thugs-bcud dam-chos dgongs-pa yang-zab shog-ser rigs-lnga*) from the great assembly hall of the ḍākinīs at Tidro.

On another occasion he journeyed to the glorious Copper-coloured Mountain, where he met Guru Rinpoche in the form of a heruka and participated in a feast offering. He was given an empowerment based on the maṇḍala of the three roots, and also all the instructions and further advice. Then, the body of the heruka turned into that of master

Padmasambhava, who orally bestowed on Rincen Phüntsok many esoteric instructions. After that, he returned to his own abode.

Rincen Phüntsok became a master of both the transmitted precepts and the treasures. Having thoroughly mastered the extraordinary exegetical tradition of the trilogy of the *Sūtra which Gathers All Intentions*, the *Magical Net*, and the *Mental Class*, many traditions of the *Eight Transmitted Precepts* (*bka'-brgyad lugs-dgu*), the *Four-Part Innermost Spirituality* (*snying-thig ya-bzhi*), the *Earlier and Later Treasure Troves* (*gter-kha gong-'og*),[847] and so forth, his teaching activity became most extensive. In accord with the tradition of the precious Ngari Paṇcen,[848] his custom was to disclose the central points by means of the transmitted precepts, and to adorn them with the esoteric instructions of the treasures.

KHÖNTÖN PELJOR LHÜNDRUP

[414.5-418.4] Rincen Phüntsok taught the cycles of the *Magical Net* to Rangdröl Nyinda Sangye, who expounded it to Tshewang Norgye, a master of the Khön family. He, in turn, expounded it to his own son, Khöntön Peljor Lhündrup. This master was born in 1561 (iron bird year). The name of his mother was Gyelmodzom.

From childhood the propensities of a holy person were aroused within him, and he truly developed the attitude of a renunciate. During his tenth year he was ordained as a novice by the all-knowing Sonam Gyamtso.[849] He also received [the vows of] refuge and of the creation of the enlightened attitude, as well as the transmission for the meditation of the Great Compassionate One. In addition, he received all kinds of doctrines from several gurus of both the ancient and new traditions. He completed studies of [Sanskrit] grammatical tables,[850] poetics, [Tibetan] grammar,[851] medicine, and the other sciences. But above all, under the tutelage of his father, who was a holder of indestructible reality, he became trained in the *Secret Nucleus of the Magical Net*, in its commentary composed by Yungtönpa, and in the other commentaries of the *Magical Net* cycle, such as the all-knowing Longcenpa's *Dispelling Darkness in the Ten Directions*. It was then that the propensities of [his past life as] the great Dropukpa were aroused, and he became an incomparably learned and accomplished adherent of this path.

In his eighteenth year Peljor Lhündrup received the empowerment, guidance and esoteric instructions of the Great Perfection according to the *Innermost Spirituality of Radiant Space* (*rdzogs-chen klong-gsal snying-thig*) from the great awareness-holder Nyinda Sangye, an emanation of Nup Namkei Nyingpo. Peljor Lhündrup was introduced to the abiding nature of all things, the Great Perfection, the buddha-body of reality that is intrinsically aware; and thus he arrived at what is most profound.

Moreover, he received a great many doctrines belonging to both the transmitted precepts and the treasures, and, in particular, the *Innermost Meaning, the Liberation of All Beings* (*don-tig 'gro-ba kun-grol*), together with the exegetical transmission of the *Precious Treasury of the Supreme Vehicle* (*theg-mchog rin-po-che'i mdzod*). He also reached the limits of study and reflection on all the great textual traditions of the sūtras, and became an itinerant scholar at the great seminary of Tsetang, propounding widespread textual traditions.[852]

Under Tragön Ce-nga Zhönu Chöpel he studied extensively the doctrines of the ancient and new traditions, such as the *Vajra Garland*. In his thirty-fourth year Peljor Lhündrup received complete ordination from Gyelkangtsewa Peljor Gyamtso and the doctrine master Gendün Gyeltsen, who acted as preceptor and master of ceremonies, respectively. It was then that he received the name Peljor Lhündrup. He also studied the mantra cycles of the Gelukpa tradition, and he acted, too, as a teaching master at [the colleges of] Sangpu and Sera Ce.[853]

Although the exegetical tradition of the *Tantra of the Secret Nucleus* had been widely propagated in the past, subsequently it had declined. Therefore, because this master was renowned for his great learning [in it], Orgyen Tendzin, the doctrine master of Trakna, deliberately went before him. He received [the *Secret Nucleus*] in detail following *Yungtönpa's Commentary* (*gYung-'grel*), and even composed a memorandum on it through to the fifth chapter.

Peljor Lhündrup favoured Zur Chöying Rangdröl, in particular, and granted him two daily sessions of instruction on *Yungtönpa's Commentary on the Secret Nucleus*, as well as on the cycle of the Innermost Spirituality (*snying-thig-gi skor*) and numberless other teachings. In accord with the teaching of this master, Zurcen Chöying Rangdröl definitively established the teaching as an itinerant scholar at the great seminary of Tsetang; and thus he silenced those who jealously thought that the Ancient Translation School had no exegesis of the tantras. At about that time, Peljor Lhündrup abandoned the diversions of society and lived in the solitude of Devīkoṭi, the forest of Phawangkha. Padmapāṇi, the Great Fifth [Dalai Lama] supplicated his feet and received from him limitless systems of empowerment, transmission, guidance, and esoteric instruction derived from the ancient and new traditions.

Like some great gurus, Peljor Lhündrup remained aloof to the company of dry dialecticians who concerned themselves with the purity of their philosophical systems. It could be said of him that he bore the stamp of one who had been a disciple of exemplary spiritual benefactors.

When he was in his seventy-sixth year the Great Fifth offered prayers for Peljor Lhündrup's continued longevity (*zhabs-brtan-gyi gsol-'debs*); but saying, "Now, I do not know if I will live much longer," the master declined, and then added, "I must go to the Palace of Lotus Light in Cāmaradvīpa!"

On Sunday 30 August 1637 (eleventh day, eighth month, fire ox year)[854] his physical body vanished into the expanse of reality, accompanied by wondrous omens.

Among the treatises composed by this master, there are: the *Guidebook which Introduces the View Common to the Great Seal, Great Perfection, and Great Madhyamaka* (*phyag-rdzogs-dbu-gsum-gyi lta-ba spyi-khyab-tu ngo-sprod-pa'i khrid-yig*); the *Guidance on the View of Madhyamaka* (*dbu-ma'i lta khrid*); and many works on the conventional sciences [*tha-snyad rig-pa*; e.g. logic, grammar, etc.].

ZURCEN CHÖYING RANGDRÖL

[418.4-424.6] The spiritual son of that master was Zurcen Chöying Rangdröl. He was born in 1604 (wood dragon year). His father was Zurcen Zhönu Töndrup, an emanation of the great awareness-holder Kumārādza, and a direct descendant of the Zur lineage of awareness-holders. His mother was Tshenden Yidzin, who hailed from a family of ḍākinīs. Chöying Rangdröl was recognised as the reincarnation of Trungpa Köncok Rincenpa. Gradually, he learned to read and to write, and he also learned the scripts of India without regard for the difficulty. Under his father he studied the essential cycles of means for attainment (*nyer-mkho'i sgrub-skor*).[855] In his ninth year he met Cangpa Rikdzin Ngagiwangpo,[856] who prophetically declared him to be an incarnation who would greatly benefit the teaching of the Ancient Translation School.

Chöying Rangdröl also studied iconographic drawing, astrological systems, and some cycles of wrathful mantras. At about the age of twelve he sat at the feet of Nangsel Rinpoche Ngawang Yeshe Trupa, and fully received the empowerments, transmissions, and experiential guidance for the cycle of the *Gathering of the Sugatas of the Eight Transmitted Precepts*; the *Innermost Spirituality of the Ḍākinī* according to both the transmitted precepts and the treasures (*mkha'-'gro snying-thig bka'-gter gnyis*); the *Guru, an Ocean of Gems* (*bla-ma nor-bu rgya-mtsho*); and Karma Lingpa's *Natural Liberation of Intention: [A Cycle devoted to] the Peaceful and Wrathful Deities* (*kar-gling zhi-khro dgongs-pa rang-grol*). He received the secret name "Chöying Rangdröl" in connection with the conferral of the empowerment of the peaceful and wrathful deities. And he heard many other treasure doctrines, too.

Chöying Rangdröl experientially cultivated [such teachings as] the *Fivefold Great Seal* (*phyag-chen lnga-ldan*) and the *Guidance on Cutting* (*gcod-khrid*). In Zingpa Tago he performed the three-year, three-fortnight retreat (*lo-gsum phyogs-gsum*)[857] and, by emphasising primarily the [teachings of] primordial purity and spontaneous presence[858] according to the *Innermost Spirituality of the Ḍākinī*, [a doctrine of] the Great Perfec-

Zurcen Chöying Rangdröl

tion (*rdzogs-chen mkha'-'gro snying-thig*), he exploded the ultimate fictitious nature of all things. Obtaining the realisation in which intrinsic awareness, the natural face of [Samantabhadra] the original lord, is disclosed, he became adept at roaming, in the inner radiance, through the fields of the buddha-body of perfect rapture.

In his seventeenth year Chöying Rangdröl went into the presence of the notable Peljor [Lhündrup], the vajra-holder of Phawangkha. He attended upon that guru until his passing, serving him with the three means to delight the guru. The guru, too, rejoiced at heart and took care of him. He poured into him the ocean of doctrines belonging to the transmitted precepts and treasures, as if filling a vase to the brim. In particular, Peljor Lhündrup granted him exegetical teaching during two sessions each day, combining the glorious *Root Tantra of the Secret Nucleus*, the *Parkap Commentary*, and *Yungtönpa's Commentary* in Tibetan. Chöying Rangdröl requested permission to set down a memorandum touching on the points that were hard to remember, but the master said, "If you take notes before a sufficient segment [of the text] has been covered, nothing much will be settled [in your mind]. Therefore, after some time, I shall make an estimate [of how much need be covered first]."

On the roof of his apartment Chöying Rangdröl then practised repeating the text. When about thirty folios had been covered [in the lectures] he received his master's permission to set down a memorandum. He completed it through to the fifth chapter, but the remainder was left to be continued.

In his twentieth year, 1622 (water dog), Chöying Rangdröl repeated the ordinations from that of a novice to that of a fully-ordained monk. He investigated the commentary on the *Secret Nucleus* [by Longcenpa] called *Dispelling Darkness in the Ten Directions* and others; and he requested the exegeses of the four subcommentaries on the *Commentary on the Guhyasamāja Tantra called the Clarifying Lamp*, the *Clarifying Lamp of the Five Stages* (*rim-lnga gsal-sgron*), the *Complete Elucidation of the Hidden Meaning of the Cakrasaṃvara* (*bde-mchog sbas-don kun-gsal*), Norzang's *General Exposition of the Kālacakra* (*nor-bzang-gi dus-'khor spyi-don*), the stages of creation and perfection of the *Guhyasamāja Tantra* (*gsang-'dus bskyed-rdzogs*), and other exegetical traditions. He established a decisive understanding of them all.

In 1624 (wood mouse year) he expounded the *Tantra of the Secret Nucleus* at the beginning of the extensive winter seminar at the great seminary of glorious Tsetang. At that time, he overcame the brilliance of those great teachers who relied on words [rather than on meaning] and thus he vastly served the innermost teaching. Those who remained unbiased praised him; and the great Cangpa Rikdzin [Ngagiwangpo], too, draped a silk scarf around his neck.

From master Phawangkhapa [Peljor Lhündrup] he also received in detail the empowerments, transmissions and esoteric instructions of the *Innermost Spirituality of Radiant Space*. Meditating upon it, Chöying Rangdröl profited through experiences and realisations that were greater than those he had had before. He also received many wrathful mantras of the new translation schools, such as the *Yogic Exercises of Bhairava* (*bhairava'i 'phrul-'khor*).

During the great dispute between the Gelukpa and Drigungpa[859] the venerable Drigung Zurpa Ratna [Rincen Phüntsok] and others had performed the applied sorcery of Rāhula, with the result that many throne-holders of Ganden died of stroke or epilepsy.[860] But now, this master [Chöying Rangdröl] made a protective circle to liberate Köncok Chöpel[861] from the fear of Khyapjuk [i.e. Rāhula].

When Takla Padmamati of Katok journeyed to Lhasa, he received from Chöying Rangdröl the commentary on the *Secret Nucleus* entitled *Dispelling Darkness in the Ten Directions*, among other teachings. Padmamati, in turn, offered this exegetical transmission to Lhodrak Sungtrül,[862] thereby ensuring that this doctrinal succession continued uninterruptedly.

In return [for the teachings he had given], Chöying Rangdröl received from Katokpa [Padmamati] the transmissions and empowerments of the volumes of the *Gathering of Intentions*, along with the means for holding all the tantras (*dgongs-'dus po-ti'i lung-dbang rgyud-dgu bcangs-thabs-dang-bcas-pa*), as well as other teachings, including the ritual manual entitled *Beauteous Flower Garland* (*las-byang me-tog phreng-mdzes*). Above all, they performed the means for the attainment of alchemy on the basis of the maṇḍala of the *Gathering of the Sugatas of the Eight Transmitted Precepts*.

Rāhula

From about this time the Great Fifth [Dalai Lama], the supreme conqueror, began to honour Chöying Rangdröl as his guru and received from him the *Vanquisher* (*zil-gnon*) and other doctrinal transmissions. The Great Fifth experientially cultivated all the transmissions and practical guidance for widespread rites of pacification, enrichment, subjugation, and wrath, including the cycle of wrathful mantras, which Chöying Randgröl offered to him.

During that era, the lords of Tsang and their priests, the Karmapa, harboured great hatred towards the Gelukpa in general, and the Ganden Palace in particular; and they performed numberless rites of sorcery when they were hard pressed during the civil war.[863] But because of the timely activity of the Fifth Dalai Lama and the exceedingly efficacious blessings of Chöying Rangdröl, it so happened that this verse, composed by the Great Fifth, could be spread throughout Tibet and Kham, at the order of the Ganden Palace:

> In the dense wood around the oil-spent town,
> The moisture of risk quenched urgency's blaze;
> Then the conflagration of karma descended and dried
> The river of Karmapa and Tsangpa dominion – that,
> indeed, did amaze!

In this way he affirmed that there was no reason for the partisans of the Gelukpa not to utilise sorcery, and that this master, Chöying Rangdröl, had had a most remedial effect on the teaching in general.

Moreover, the Great Fifth received from Chöying Rangdröl experiential guidance on three traditions of *Vajrakīla* (*phur-ba lugs-gsum*), three traditions of the *Eight Transmitted Precepts* (*bka'-brgyad lugs-gsum*), [the doctrine of] the Great Perfection called the *Innermost Spirituality of Radiant Space*, and so forth; and he undertook to master them. Thus, he maintained, the infallible experience of the Great Perfection arose in his mind, and a confidence that was free from the hopes and fears of saṃsāra and nirvāṇa was born within him.

Chöying Rangdröl also enjoyed a mutual exchange of doctrinal feasts with Gönpo Sonam Chokden of Nesar. He recognised Rikdzin Pema Trhinle, the sun of the teaching of the Ancient Translation School, to be the emanation of Cangpa Rikdzin Ngagiwangpo; and he installed him at the seat of Thupten Dorje Trak.[864] Chöying Rangdröl bestowed all the doctrines of the transmitted precepts and treasures upon him, and enthroned him as a lord of the teaching.

Towards the end of his life Chöying Rangdröl lived in Kungtang, which had been the seat of the lord of beings, the "Unborn" Zhang [Tshelpa].[865] There, he granted the exegesis of the *Tantra of the Secret Nucleus* to Trhinle Lhündrup, the great awareness-holder of Tarding,[866] and received, in return, many empowerments and transmissions, such as those of the *Eight Transmitted Precepts*. He protected all who persevered in the doctrine, including gurus, incarnations and emanations from China, Tibet and Mongolia, by whatever pertains to the path of liberation, whether transmitted precepts or treasures, of the ancient or new traditions. Then, during his sixty-sixth year, 1669 (earth bird), he journeyed to the realm of Lotus Light, accompanied by wondrous omens.

THE FIFTH DALAI LAMA

[424.6-425.5] Although it is impossible to count the host of students who were the spiritual sons of this master [Chöying Rangdröl], the foremost among them was the supreme conqueror, the Great Fifth Dalai Lama. Even when Chöying Rangdröl had journeyed to another realm, it is said, the Great Fifth was taken into his following by the body of his pristine cognition. This is illustrated by the following passage from the supreme conqueror's *Biography of Chöying Rangdröl* (*rnam-thar rgyal-ba-mchog-gi zhal-gsung-ma*):

> Until I have encountered directly
> The expressive play of awareness that is Samantabhadra,
> By the power of these good deeds may I be favoured in all lives
> By you, O lord! my inseparable spiritual benefactor.

The Great Fifth bestowed the exegetical tradition of the *Secret Nucleus*, according to both the *Parkap Commentary* and *Yungtönpa's Commentary*, on the great Nyötön Trhinle Lhündrup, an emanation of Nupcen Sangye Yeshe. From his time until the present day the lineage has continued without interruption owing to the kindness of the great treasure-finder, Rikdzin Gyurme Dorje, and his brother [Locen Dharmaśrī], the two of whom appeared as the timely fruition of the enlightened aspirations of Vairocana and of Yudra Nyingpo.[867]

5 *Dotokpa's Lineage of the Zur Tradition*

DOTOKPA SANGYE-TRA AND KYI CHÖKI SENGE

[425.5-427.3] Moreover, in the lineage of the disciples of the great Dropukpa, there was one called Sangye-tra of Gyamen in Chongye. He was born into the Nya family in the district of Gyamen Taktsepa. In his youth he propitiated Jambhala and a small field which he owned was swept away by a flood. He then went off [as an ascetic], free from worldly cares. In Puguto there was a rich man who had died of leprosy, so no one would come to carry away the corpse. Sangye-tra, moved by fervent compassion, did the funerary work without thinking about it. By the side of the bier a large quantity of gold appeared. *That* was the accomplishment conferred on him by Jambhala.

On his return Sangye-tra met Khyungpo Trhowo at Traci Khangmar. Acting as the attendant while Khyungpo propitiated Yangdak, Sangye-tra also practised the means for attainment and had a vision of the "Nine-lamp Yangdak" (*yang-dag mar-me dgu*). Then, he went to Tsang. He studied the *Sūtra which Gathers All Intentions*, the *Magical Net*, and other texts under a nephew of Ca Chenpo, who had been a student of the lord of secrets, Dropukpa. At that time a rich man offered him one hundred loads of barley. Consequently, free from impediments, he studied the *Magical Net* under Dropukpa's student Nyangnak Dopo and his student, Lharje Da Senge. Having become a great scholar, Sangye-tra founded Dotokthel in his homeland. Gyacing Rupa, a disciple of Nyelwa Zhikpo, also became a supplicant at the feet of Dotokpa [Sangye-tra] and studied much under him.

In particular, this Dotokpa had a student called Kyi Chöki Senge, a learned and accomplished "warrior". He went into the presence of the emperor Qubilai Qan. In order to examine Chöki Senge's powers the emperor rashly had him placed inside a stūpa, and then sealed up the entrance for a year. When the year ended the stūpa was opened. Seeing that Chöki Senge had turned into an image of Vajrakīla, the emperor was most astonished. He sent a great variety of things, including a long roll of silk,[868] as gifts to Dotokpa. Dotokpa also had many monastic estates allotted to him by imperial edict, so [his domains] were exceedingly developed. But this is remembered only in name. Such fluctuations in the teaching naturally inspire world-weariness!

MENLUNGPA ŚĀKYA-Ö

[427.3-429.1] The disciple of Chöki Senge was Menlungpa Śākya-ö. He was the eldest of five sons born to Nyangtön Chenpo of Chongpo Kharu, who became famed as the "five emanational brothers of Yarlung". The eldest was referred to as "Menlungpa" after Menlung, a monastery in Yarlung. The seat of the second brother, Chödenpa, was the monastery that is now the ruin called "Chöden".[869] Chödenpa's real name was Gönpo Dorje. Because he became quite accomplished he left the imprint of his back on a wall, which he had struck and passed through. This imprint exists even now. In the past it seems that there was a great seminary at this place; for a great many fragments of the *Collected Tantras* (*rgyud-'bum*) are still to be seen there. It is said that because Chödenpa performed the means for the attainment of elixir, scorpions and ants became quite rare in this region. The ruins of the monastery appear to be protected even today, for its protectors are most powerful. It is a place where the gods and demons abide in accord with their commitments.

The three younger brothers were known as Keldenpa, Turtröpa, and Wangyelwa. Among the five, it is the eldest, Menlungpa Śākya-ö, who is considered here. He studied the *Sūtra which Gathers All Intentions* and the *Magical Net* thoroughly under Kyi Chöki Senge. Later, he also studied under Sonamgyel, the scholar of Len, who was the son of Len Śākya Öpo. He composed many works, including the *Disclosure of the Contents of the Secret Nucleus* (*gsang-ba snying-po'i khog-dbub*), and a commentary entitled the *Ascertainment of the Meaning of the Tantra* (*ṭī-kā rgyud-don rnam-nges*). His disciple was Sangye Konglawa of Takpo, who produced many disciples in Takpo proper, such as Lama Nyen. Above all, because he was the guru of Konjo Dakpo, [the doctrine] was much propagated in Kham.[870]

In addition, Ön Śākya Bumpa became learned in the exegesis of the *Secret Nucleus* under Menlungpa. Under him Khedrup Chöpel and his son thoroughly received the exegesis of the *Secret Nucleus*. Those in the lineage of Menlungpa were also, in their own place and time, the masters of the doctrines of the *Earlier and Later Treasure Troves*.

DORJE GYELTSEN AND HIS SUCCESSORS

[429.1-6] Gya Yeshe Gönpo, who held the seat of Kyi Chöki Senge, also became thoroughly learned in the *Sūtra which Gathers All Intentions* and the *Magical Net*, under the tutelage of both Kyi Chöki Senge and Len Chögyel. His nephew, Dorje Gyeltsen, went to Sangpu in his youth and became learned in the *Ascertainment of Valid Cognition*. Then, having thoroughly learned the *Sūtra which Gathers All Intentions* and the *Magical Net* under Phungpo Gya Yeshe Gönpo, he composed the *Commentary based on the Text of the Parkap Commentary* (*'grel-pa spar-khab gzhung-du byas-pa'i ṭī-kā*), a *Ritual for Empowerment* (*dbang-gi cho-ga*), and other works. He taught them to his own nephew Lama Tshül Gyelwa. Ridongpa Sherap Gyeltsen studied under him, in turn, and he is said to have propagated the teaching in the vicinity of Takpo for a while, having expounded it in Takpo to Lord Kurap and his servants, as well as to the mantra adepts. The disciple of Sherap Gyeltsen was Sonam Zangpo of Zhangkar. His disciple was master Trashi Gyamtso, from whom Gö Zhönupel received the exegetical transmission of Dorje Gyeltsen's *Commentary on the Secret Nucleus* (*rdo-rje rgyal-mtshan-pa'i snying-ṭīk*), the *Black Deity Vajrakīla* (*phur-pa lha-nag*), and other teachings.

6 *Biographies of the Kham Tradition*

KATOKPA TAMPA DESHEK

[430.1-434.5] Concerning the renowned Kham tradition:[871] Vairocana translated master Sūryaprabhāsiṃha's *Commentary on the Secret Nucleus* (*Śrīguhyagarbhatattvaviniścayavyākhyānaṭīkā*, P 4719) at the Camgön Temple of Odu in Kham and expounded it, too. But it was Katokpa in particular who originally made the teaching of the Ancient Translation School well known in that region. He is known by the names Tampa Dewarshekpa of Katok, Lama Sharwa Popathaye, and Sherap Senge.

Katokpa was the maternal cousin of the venerable Phakmotrupa. He was born by the banks of the Yangtze River (*'bri-chu*) in Puburgang in Dokam during the year 1122 (water male tiger). His father was Tsangpa Peldra of the Ga clan, and his mother Tsangmo Rincengyen. This water tiger year was master Phakmotrupa's thirteenth.

When Katokpa was in his seventeenth year he went to Central Tibet and was ordained as a novice at Phenyül by Lama Cangcup Senge. The name Sherap Senge was conferred upon him. He received full ordination in the Lower Tibetan Vinaya Lineage under the great preceptor of Nak;[872] and he trained himself until he was learned in the Vinaya. He studied the cycle of the *Secret Nucleus of the Magical Net*, the Mental Class, and so on, under a spiritual son of the great Zur Dropukpa named Dzamtön Drowei Gönpo; and he became consummately learned in these very teachings. Dzamtön was the one guru intervening between the venerable Dropukpa and Katokpa, although the Great Fifth's *Record of Teachings Received* (*lnga-pa chen-po'i gsan-yig*) says that Katokpa met Dropukpa in person.

Katokpa also studied ten great tantras of *Cakrasaṃvara* (*bde-mchog rgyud-chen bcu*) under Ra Lotsāwa's disciple, Kam Lotsāwa; the *Subsequent Tantra of Varāhī* (*Akhyātatantrottaravajravarāhyabhidhānād Varāhyabhibodhana*, T 379), and the *Tantra of the Emergence of Cakrasaṃvara* under Cokro Lotsāwa; the cycle of *Hevajra* under Kam Chöki

Katokpa Tampa Deshek

Yeshe; the *Guhyasamāja* under both Dongtön Dorje Nyingpo, a disciple of Gö Lotsāwa [Khukpa Lhetse], and Bodhi Zhangtön; the exegesis of the *[Commentary on the Guhyasamāja Tantra called the] Clarifying Lamp* and the *Yamāri* cycle under Pelgi Wangcuk of Latö, who was the disciple of both [Dongtön and Zhangtön]; the sequence of the empowerment of *Cakrasaṃvara ('khor-lo bde-mchog-gi dbang-bskur-gyi rim-pa)*, the Great Seal, and the esoteric instructions for the *Six Doctrines of Nāropā* under the venerable Tüsum Khyenpa [Karmapa I];[873] et cetera. He became the supreme spiritual son of the venerable Use [Tüsum Khyenpa], and under him he studied and considered, without exception, the sūtra and mantra traditions in general, and, in particular, the ancient and recent Tibetan translations, pertaining to the vehicle of indestructible reality.

Once the precious Dzamtön said to Katokpa, "If you go to the land of Kampo and diligently practise the means for attainment, your body will dissolve into light. But if you go to Katok you will greatly extend the teaching." With his heart set on the teaching alone he went in search of a place called Katok. At first, he arrived at Katil. There, he met some children who were grazing cattle, and asked them, "Where is Katok?"

Śrīdevī

"Up that valley," they replied.

He realised the cattle to be an auspicious sign that there would be persons requiring training, and the cowherds a sign that there would be disciples. Therefore, on that site, which resembled the letter KA, he founded a temple in 1159 (earth female hare year).

At just that time Donyen Menbu [a local divinity], who maintained the vows of Pön, actually revealed his form and created obstacles in various ways. When the venerable master and two students pursued him he dissolved into a boulder.[874] The doctrine master Tsangtön tied it up with his robes and pulled it along, while Tampa [Katokpa] drove it on with a switch. They brought it down to the bank of the river at the bottom of the valley, where it can still be seen today. And once, when eight Pönpo began to practise wrathful mantras [against Katokpa], Śrīdevī[875] brought down the rock-face on which their hermitage was situated. Tampa himself drew a crossed-vajra over it; and the site became known as Phawang Gyelep, "Eight Boulders' Landing". With these and other inconceivable signs of accomplishment Katokpa laid a foundation for the doctrine, and remained there.

To students assembled from as far as Amdo country in the east, to Tshawarong, Lo [Mustang], and Mön in the south, he skilfully revealed various teachings, among which the foremost were the Great Perfection and the exegetical transmission, transmitted empowerment, means for attainment, and so on, of the *Secret Nucleus of the Magical Net*, including all its major and minor Indian and Tibetan commentaries and texts, all according to the continuous tradition of the glorious Zurs, and the *Sūtra which Gathers All Intentions*. In addition, he expounded a great many works including the *Magical Net of Mañjuśrī* and other tantras, and, with regard to the system of the sūtras, the great texts of the conqueror Maitreya, the *Introduction to the Conduct of a Bodhisattva*, et cetera. In short, he laid the foundation for the teaching of the secret mantra in the province of Dokam. Finally, in his seventy-first year, in September/October 1192 (ninth month, water male mouse year), he demonstrated the conquest of his physical body.

In general, the sublime Mañjughoṣa conversed with this great person at all times, just as with another man, and prophesied his every deed. Katokpa could always gaze on the Buddha-field of Akṣobhya, Sukhāvatī, the Buddha-field of Bhaiṣajyaguru, and others. He could also behold, whenever he wished, the peaceful and wrathful deities of the *Magical Net*, the sixty-two deities of the Cakrasaṃvara maṇḍala, and the maṇḍala of Glorious Heruka. He could study the doctrine under the Tathāgatas of the Five Families and discuss it with bodhisattvas. He obtained the prophecy that in his following life he would dwell in Sukhāvatī as the bodhisattva Matisāra (*blo-gros snying-po*) and obtain the actual realisation of the eighth level;[876] and that then, in the future, in the aeon called "Star-like Array", he would become the sugata Amitāyus.

TSANGTÖNPA

[434.5-437.6] Katokpa's regent was Tsangtönpa. He was born in 1126 (fire male horse year) in Tsangzhel, which is a part of Puburgang. In his seventeenth year he met Lama Dewarshekpa [Katokpa] and studied the doctrine under him. The master and student proceeded together to Minyak, where he was given all the esoteric instructions. In his twenty-first year he went to the monastery of Dri Tiramdo and lived there. In his twenty-third he set out for Katok and practised meditation.

Once, in a vision, Lama Dewarshekpa saw a great light in a wide, flooded valley, at which he could not bear to look. When he asked what it was, a voice said, "Great being! it is the seat of your disciple, who resides on the eleventh level, Universal Light."[877] [Approaching Tsangtönpa] the master said, "You are the one!" and at that moment Tsangtönpa beheld the maṇḍalas of Glorious Heruka and of the Forty-two Peaceful Deities. Also, he always saw Śrīdevī and Mahākāla, and

Tsangtönpa

remembered his previous lives as the translator Yeshe-chok, the Indian Vajrapāṇi[878] and others.

In his fifty-sixth year Tsangtönpa ascended to the seat of Katok, where he maintained the trilogy of the *Sūtra which Gathers All Intentions*, the *Magical Net*, and the *Mental Class* according to the tradition of his guru. Once, about this time, the great spiritual warrior Pomdrakpa[879] was wondering why this Tsangtönpa of Katok had such a high reputation. Immediately, he had a vision in which there appeared a great celestial palace of blue light, like a cloudless sky, which housed a great host of the deities of perfect rapture. In front sat the precious Tsangtönpa, surrounded by an inconceivable mass of multicoloured rainbow light. Pomdrakpa realised him to be a buddha and performed a feast offering that evening at which he had visions of many herukas of the Nyingma tradition of secret mantra. In a dream he saw an immeasurable, great mountain composed of precious gems, on the slopes of which various medicinal plants were growing. Many people were gathering these plants. On the summit of the mountain, in the midst of a great palace of blue light, Lama Katokpa [i.e. Tsangtönpa] was seated, [his body] of the nature of light. From a great white conch known to sound by itself with no one to blow on it innumerable conches issued forth, all of them sounding by themselves. They filled all quarters, sounding *ti-ri-ri*... Pomdrakpa said that this indicated the limitless spread of Tsangtönpa's reputation. Later Pomdrakpa travelled to Katok, where he requested the empowerment of the *Magical Net* from the precious Tsangtönpa, with the result that [all-]knowing, pristine cognition was limitlessly awakened within him.

When Tsangtönpa of Katok was equipoised in the contemplation of the Great Perfection inconceivable pure visions arose. [He experienced] the sky-like appearance of nothing at all, he beheld an innumerable host of peaceful and wrathful deities for three evenings, and so forth. Moreover, once in a vision of Akṣobhya's buddha-field all the bodhisattvas in the retinue were buzzing with the news that this doctrine master was the bodhisattva Maṇigarbha (*nor-bu'i snying-po*), in which form he would be reborn in Sukhāvatī in his next life. Again, one time, when he had a vision of that same buddha-field, he heard the teacher Akṣobhya prophetically declare, "O Maṇigarbha, son of the enlightened family, in a future age you will become the tathāgata Özer Raptutrhowa."

Tsangtönpa withdrew from the array of his physical body in 1216 (fire male mouse), his ninetieth year.

CAMPABUM

[437.6-439.5] Tsangtönpa's regent was Campabum. In a previous life, he had been Cārīndra [Kṛṣṇacārin], the spiritual son of the great accomplished master of India, Jālandharipā; for the venerable Mitrayogī had said to his disciple Somayogī, "If you go to Tibet, [you can meet] the masters Śāntideva and Vajrapāṇi, who have taken birth in Tibet at a place called Katok, where they have benefitted numberless disciples. At that seat, too, master Kaṇhapā [Kṛṣṇacārin] the great has taken birth. He remains there even now to benefit his disciples." Moreover, this same one had acted in the service of the teaching during lifetimes spent as the son of an Indian king, as a monk of a brahman family, and so on. Afterwards he was born as the venerable Campa the great. The year of his birth was 1179 (earth pig).

Under the guidance of both Katok Tampa Rinpoche and the doctrine master Tsangtönpa, Campabum studied, reflected and meditated upon the whole ocean of doctrinal traditions of the sūtras and mantras, but he completed his studies under the doctrine master. After Tsangtönpa passed away, Campabum, then in his forty-eighth year, ascended to the seat. He spread out a joyous feast of the ocean of doctrinal traditions of the sūtras and mantras, emphasising the *Magical Net* and the Great Perfection.

Campabum

The great Karmapa [Karmapa II, Pakshi] who was born at Drigyel Tampa Chöcuk, went to Katok at the advice of the bodhisattva Pomdrakpa, whom he first met in Shabam. Under Campa Rinpoche, who acted as the preceptor, and Ce-nga Mangpuwa Sonam Bumpa, who was the master of ceremonies, the Karmapa received full ordination. Becoming thus a *bhikṣu*, he was enthroned as the regent of the Sage. The name Chöki Lama was conferred upon him and he received the empowerments and instructions of the *Magical Net* and the Great Perfection.[880]

Campabum continued to act on behalf of the teaching and living creatures through to his seventy-fourth year, 1252 (water mouse), when he withdrew from the array of his physical body.

THE SUCCESSIVE REGENTS OF KATOK

[439.5-443.3] Campabum's regent, the great Ce-ngawa Sonam Bumpa, was born in 1223 (water sheep year). In his thirtieth year he ascended to the seat and, emphasising the *Sūtra which Gathers All Intentions*, the

Magical Net, and the Great Perfection, he maintained the teaching. He passed away in his sixty-first year.

His regent, Uwö Yeshebum, was born in 1254 (wood male tiger year). He ascended to the seat in his twenty-ninth year, and turned extensively the doctrinal wheel of the sūtras and mantras, with emphasis on the trilogy of the *Sūtra which Gathers All Intentions*, the *Magical Net*, and the *Mental Class*.

During this period the doctrine master Sakya Paṇḍita and his nephew Phakpa Rinpoche went to Mongolia at the invitation of the king. On the way they built the Namgyel Temple in Dzing. Katokpa [Campabum] also went there. Now, all the domains of the Sakyapa naturally became hoards of silver property and objects, but others [such as the Katokpa] were without these [resources]. On this particular occasion, so that they could consecrate the temple [according to the rites of] both the ancient and new traditions simultaneously, Katokpa said, "We Nyingmapa will perform the exorcism at the beginning of the consecration. But I will ask you adherents of the new translation schools to perform the actual ground of the consecration, the invocation of the Beings of Pristine Cognition and so forth." Katokpa then entered into the contemplation of exorcism and turned the temple inside out. When the Sakyapa called down the Beings of Pristine Cognition the temple was restored to its natural condition. Such were the wonders displayed there. Katokpa conferred the empowerment of the peaceful and wrathful deities of the *Magical Net* on Phakpa Rinpoche, who then proceeded to Mongolia. The doctrine master [Sakya Paṇḍita] withdrew from his physical body while he was visiting the Mongol domains. When Phakpa returned to Tibet, he offered a three-storey stūpa of bronze, seven great altar bowls and other items to Katok as gifts, which exist even today.[881]

Cangcup Pelwa, the regent of master Uwöpa Yeshebum, ascended to the seat in his forty-fourth year. In his time there were many at [the hermitages of] Partrö, Pangtrö and Tampuk whose bodies dissolved in the buddha-body of light. Once, while he was constructing a temple, the workers slaughtered many cattle and sheep. They had just separated the meat and the hides when the master approached. It is said that with a snap of his fingers the beasts rose with a roar and disappeared into the sky. In his sixty-fourth year he passed away to benefit another realm.

Sonam Zangpo, who was his regent, ascended to the seat in his fifty-third year. He grounded [his teaching] in the *Magical Net* and the Great Perfection. But also, from about this time, the older treasures, including those of Nyang-rel [Nyima Özer] and Guru Chöwang, began to spread somewhat. In his sixty-third year he passed away to benefit another realm.

The regent Künga Bumpa protected the doctrine as before. Then Wangcuk Pelwa ascended to the seat during his thirty-eighth year.

Though some exegesis was given at this time, he emphasised meditative attainments above all, and dwelt in one-pointed contemplation. On one occasion the king of Jang mustered a great army [and prepared to sack the monastery].[882] The master's servant asked, "What shall we do in the face of this army?"

"Pour a lot of *tsampa* on me!" he replied.

When this was done, there was a great blizzard and the army withdrew. Later, [the king of Jang] bowed at the master's feet and offered a golden image of Śākyamuni, an ivory model of the temple at Vajrāsana, and the great spire which today is on top of the monastery. Wangcuk Pelwa withdrew from his physical body during his fifty-third year.

His regent, Lodrö Bumpa, ascended to the seat in his forty-third year. He had many disciples who attained accomplishment, such as Chusor Namkabum. In the period between [the greatness of] Ukpalung [the seat of] the Zurs, and [the rise of the later] monastic centres of the secret mantra tradition (*gsang-sngags-gling-rnams*)[883] the teaching became sparse, but this master propagated the *Sūtra which Gathers All Intentions*, the *Magical Net*, and others. So his legacy to the teaching in Central Tibet, Tsang and Kham was great. In his sixty-fifth year he passed away to benefit another realm.

The regent Lodrö Senge ascended to the seat in his thirty-sixth year. He grounded [his teaching] in the transmitted precepts of the ancient propagation, but from this time the treasure cycles were extensively promulgated as well. He passed away at sixty.

The regent Cangcup Lodrö continued the tradition of his predecessors and, in particular, expounded the *Four Sections of the Magical Net* (*sgyu-'phrul sde-bzhi*) and the *Array of the Path of the Magical Net*. He also greatly increased the congregations of renunciate meditators at the Ritsip and Partrö [hermitages]. His regent, Cangcup Senge, and his, Cangcup Gyeltsen, both greatly extended teaching, study and meditation on the transmitted precepts and treasures.

KHEDRUP YESHE GYELTSEN

[443.3-445.6] Cangcup Gyeltsen's disciple was Jñānaketu [Yeshe Gyeltsen], the learned and accomplished master of Pubor. There was a prophecy stating him to be the emanation of Jñānakumāra, the translator of Nyak; and he became learned in all the sequences of the path, according to the sūtras and mantras in general. In particular, he studied all the empowerments, exegeses, and means for attainment of the *Sūtra which Gathers All Intentions* and of the peaceful and wrathful deities of the *Magical Net* under the great learned and accomplished master Trao Chöbum. Moktön Dorje Pelzang, in turn, received the *Sūtra which Gathers All Intentions* from this guru; and from him it was received by the great spiritual warrior Dorje Namgyel of Tarlung. From his lineage the renowned Kham tradition of the *Sūtra which Gathers All Intentions* (*dgongs-'dus khams-lugs*) descended to Central Tibet, as explained below.[884]

Khedrup Yeshe Gyeltsen reclarified the root text and commentaries of the *Secret Nucleus*, the *Sūtra which Gathers All Intentions*, and the root texts of the three traditions of the Great Perfection – those of the Mental, Spatial, and Esoteric Instructional Classes, respectively – until they shone like the sun. And he spread the teachings all-pervasively by means of exegesis and attainment.

He composed a great many treatises: the *Commentary on the Peaceful and Wrathful Deities [of the Magical Net]* and the *Commentary on Vajrakīla according to the Transmitted Precepts* (*zhi-khro-dang phur-ba bka'-ma'i 'grel-pa*); a commentary, outline and synopsis of the *Secret Nucleus* (*gsang-ba snying-po-la 'grel-pa/sa-bcad/bsdus-don*); the *Commentary and Annotations on the Array of the Path of the Magical Net* (*lam rnam-bkod-la ṭī-kā-dang mchan-bu*); *Annotations on the Parkap Commentary and the Innermost Point* (*spar-khab-dang thugs-thig-la mchan-bu*); the *Commentary on the Clarification of Commitments entitled the Clear Mirror* (*dam-tshig gsal-bkra-la 'grel-pa gsal-ba'i me-long*); the *Text on the Means for Assuming the Mudrā of the Peaceful and Wrathful Deities* (*zhi-khro'i phyag-rgya bcings-thabs-kyi yi-ge*); the *Commentary on Tampa Rinpoche's General Exposition of the Vehicles* (*dam-pa rin-po-che'i theg-pa spyi-bcing-gi 'grel-pa*); and the *Detailed Exposition of the Feast Offering* (*tshogs-kyi 'khor-lo'i rnam-bshad*); to name but a few.

Yeshe Gyeltsen produced many learned students who attained accomplishment, such as Khawa Karpowa Namka Gyamtso, Künga Dawa, Chokme Cangsem, and Laptön Namka Rincen. Among them, Khawa Karpowa composed a general dissertation, outline, and synopsis on the *Secret Nucleus* (*gsang-snying spyi-don-dang/sa-bcad/bsdus-don*); a *Commentary on the Array of the Path of the Magical Net* (*lam rnam-bkod-la ṭī-kā*); and so forth.

At the end of his life this great learned and accomplished master remained at the hermitage of Phaktso, diligently striving only for attainment. He benefitted innumerable disciples from as far away as Pubor, Khawa Karpo[885] and Jang. He also received a prophecy from the ḍākinī Mahākarmeṇdrāṇi: "Departing from this life in your sixty-fourth year you will extensively benefit living creatures in the northern direction. Then, in Sukhāvatī Buddha-field, as the bodhisattva Sukhāṅkuśa (*bde-ba'i myu-gu*) you will purify [the universe] into buddha-fields; and then during a pure aeon called 'Array of Attributes' you will attain buddhahood as Sukhasāra (*bde-ba'i snying-po*)."

There are inconceivable stories of Yeshe Gyeltsen's learning and accomplishment. He had visions of hosts of buddhas and bodhisattvas and could hang his robes on the rays of the sun, even in the presence of common folk.

THE LINEAGES OF KATOK

[445.5-449.1] The so-called "thirteen generations of the gurus of Katok", of whom Yeshe Gyeltsen was the last, were successive emanations of the Lords of the Three Families [Mañjuśrī, Avalokiteśvara, and Vajrapāṇi]. They maintained [the seat] by means of the exegesis and attainment associated with the teaching of the Ancient Translation School.

Again, there were the disciples of Tampa Deshek who were renowned as the "three from Gyelmorong who just had to listen". These were Sherap Gyeltsen, Sherap Pelwa, and Sherap Dorje. The three had acute minds and were certainly fit to be taught in an instant. Just by hearing the sound of Tampa Rinpoche's voice as he taught the doctrine they became lords among accomplished masters, who reached the profoundest depths of all doctrines. So it is that from that time, when those three spread the teaching in the eastern district of Gyelmorong, until the present day, this precious teaching has not declined.

Moreover, there were the four supreme students of Katok Tampa Deshek who were renowned as the "four sons who were prophesied". Among them, Drutsagangpa was famed for having founded one hundred and eight places of retreat throughout the region from the three districts of Pum, Rong and Zhak all the way to Khawa Karpo; and his legacy as one who spread the teaching profusely was great. Tsade Ce-nga Namka Dorje founded the monastery of Konjo Tsade. Through his students Trung Thuje Yeshe, Tönpa Wangjor and others, the cycles of the *Magical Net* and the Great Perfection came to Central Tibet, where they became known as the "Kham tradition". Moktön Jampel Senge built a monastery in the Dri region and vastly benefitted the teaching and living creatures. From him there originated the lineage renowned as the "thirteen generations of accomplished masters in the line of Mok". Finally, the accomplished master Maṇi Rincen was recognised by Guru Chöki Wangcuk to be the fundamental master of the doctrine of the *Quintessential Gathering of the Great Compassionate One* (*thugs-rje chen-po yang-snying 'dus-pa*). At Katok, Chöki Wangcuk made a prophetic declaration that he should become a mantrin and that his own daughter Kündrölbum and Maṇi Rincen should live together; but the auspicious opportunity was lost because Maṇi Rincen would not transgress the discipline of a renunciate. Even so, as soon as he had finished building the reliquaries of the three superiors (*gong-ma gsum*)[886] and other acts of service, he flapped his robes like wings and flew like a bird into the sky, landing on the summit of the mountain opposite. He also left a footprint there. Then he dwelt in Rakcok, where, after not very long, his body vanished in a mass of light.

Following the "thirteen generations of gurus" there were the "thirteen generations of Trung",[887] who successively maintained the teaching of the transmitted precepts and treasures. In the time of the aforementioned "generations of gurus" the teaching was so widely propagated that there were as many as one hundred and eighty thousand monks [affiliated with Katok]. There was also a dialectical college and a course of study. Academies, retreat centres and so forth were developed separately. In short, both the exegesis and attainment of the teaching of the Ancient Translation School became widespread throughout the area from Gyelmorong in the east, Tshawarong and Mön in the south, and Kongpo in the west, all the way up to Central Tibet and Tsang. Therefore, when, during that intervening period, the teachings of the *Sūtra which Gathers All Intentions*, the *Magical Net*, the *Mental Class* and so on had become rare in Central Tibet and Tsang, it was this tradition that kept them alive. And up to the present it has maintained, without interruption, the stream of empowerment, the exegetical tradition, the continuity of esoteric instruction, and the lineage of transmission.

Again, there is one tradition according to which this river of empowerments, transmissions, and esoteric instructions of both the *Sūtra which Gathers All Intentions* and the *Magical Net* also descended in a lineage from Tampa Deshek, Tsangtönpa, and Campabum, through:

Tsade Ce-ngawa Namka Dorje;
Trung Thuje Yeshe;
Tönpa Wangjor;
the venerable Pelbarwa Namka Dorje;
Tönpa Göngyel;
Yangtrö Tshültrim Gyeltsen;
Trao Chöki Bumpa;
Puborwa Khedrup Yeshe Gyeltsen;
Zhakla Khedrup Yeshe Bumpa;
Mön Katokpa Sonam Gyeltsen;
Katokpa Namdröl Zangpo;
Katokpa Chöki Senge; and
Lhadrowa Chöki Wangpo.

From this last mentioned the lineage gradually descended to the venerable Menlungpa Locok Dorje, whence it has continued without interruption until today.

7 *Miscellaneous Lineages of the Zur and Kham Traditions*

THE EMPOWERMENT OF THE *SŪTRA WHICH GATHERS ALL INTENTIONS* IN KHAM

[449.1-452.4] Moreover, concerning that which is called the "Kham tradition" of the empowerment of the *Sūtra which Gathers All Intentions*: During that aforementioned intervening period, Drölcen Samdrup Dorje conferred this empowerment on both Zur Śākya Jungne of Yang-en and his sister, and the lineage passed to the latter. Her name was Zurmo Gendünbum. In reality, she was a natural yoginī, who from her youth onwards was dignified, even in appearance, and free from the defects of saṃsāra. Training herself in the three aspects of creation and perfection, she attained their limits, realised the abiding nature of reality, and mastered many approaches to contemplation. Thus she became a great learned and accomplished woman. Living in the hermitage of Tsegyel in lower Nyang, she acted on behalf of living creatures. It was she who conferred the empowerment on Zurtön Śākya Shenyen of Yang-en Sangakling. He empowered Trao Chöbum, the learned and accomplished master of Katok. The latter empowered Shenyen Köncok Zangpo, who, in turn, empowered Katokpa Moktön Dorje Pelzangpo.

This Dorje Pelzangpo composed the *Empowerment Ceremony entitled the River of Honey* (*dbang-chog sbrang-rtsi'i chu-rgyun*), which he based on the empowerment ritual of the Len tradition, where the various stages [of empowerment] were properly arranged, and then adorned with the practical techniques of Gö Tsilungpa and the ceremonial arrangements of Trotön Pelden-tra. Moreover, he combined in it the peaceful and wrathful deities of the *Magical Net* and the special transmitted precepts of the Mental Class known as the *Eighteen Significations of the Syllable* A (*sems-sde* A*-don bco-brgyad-kyi sgos-bka'*). This author, Dorje Pelzangpo, was renowned as an awareness-holder who had attained the level of deathlessness, so he was certainly a supreme, holy individual. Above and beyond that, his work was composed at the behest of many incomparable spiritual benefactors. Therefore, it was invaluable, and became the source for the empowerments of the "fifteen ordinary sacraments" (*sgrub-rdzas thun-mong bco-lnga'i dbang*),[888] which had been left out of the *Ceremonial Arrangements of Nyelpa* (*gnyal-ba'i chog-khrigs*). He also revived the transmission of the three profound empowerments of the peaceful deities of the *Magical Net* (*sgyu-'phrul zhi-ba'i zab-dbang-gsum*) which had been lost in Central Tibet and Tsang during this intervening period, but which had been preserved here in the Katok tradition. Because he also maintained the continuous lineage of empowerment for the *Eighteen Significations of the Syllable* A in the Mental Class, he became a most beneficial gateway to the continuity of the teaching.

The empowerment was transmitted from Moktön Dorje Pelzangpo through:

Dorje Namgyel, the bodhisattva of Tarlung;
Khyungtsangpa Trhüzhi Lodrö Pelden;
Pangtön Karma Guru;
Künzang Peljor, the holder of mantras;
Sangdak Trhinle Lhündrup; and
Taktön Chögyel Tendzin.

From this last mentioned the river which had flowed through the Kham tradition descended to the great treasure-finder, the king of the doctrine, [Rikdzin] Gyurme Dorje.

THE LINEAGE OF ROK SHERAP-Ö

Again, Rok Sherap-ö also greatly propagated the exegetical transmissions of the *Sūtra which Gathers All Intentions* and the *Magical Net*. This Sherap-ö first studied the trilogy of the *Sūtra which Gathers All Intentions*, the *Magical Net*, and the *Mental Class* according to the So tradition under Roktön Tsenpo. He also studied the *Sūtra which Gathers All Intentions* and the *Magical Net* according to the Kyo tradition under Lhapdrema Kongpa. Lhap had received the Zur tradition of the *Sūtra which Gathers All Intentions* and the *Magical Net* from master Yamcö Ngödrup, who belonged to the Zur lineage. Also, Dropukpa's disciple Nuptön taught them to Kharak Nyingpo, who taught them to Yamshü. Kharak Nyingpo, moreover, taught his own son, Pemabar, who instructed Rok Sherap-ö [as did Yamshü]. Furthermore, under So Tarma Senge, Rok studied an ancient tradition of teaching using an annotated commentary called the *Profusely Annotated Magical Net* (*sgyu-'phrul mchan-mang*). He also received a lineage derived from Len Śākya Zangpo of Chuwar and another derived from Nyangnak Dopa, who was a student of Lharje Nyariwa. In short, this guru Rok studied many different traditions.

Rok composed the *Lecture Notes on the Ground, Path and Result according to the Magical Net* (*sgyu-'phrul gzhi-lam-'bras-gsum stong-thun*) and a *Commentary on the Array of the Path of the Magical Net* (*lam-rnam-bkod-kyi ṭīkā*). He granted teaching to one known as the "All-Seeing of Nyemdo", who, in turn, composed *Detailed Annotations on the Commentary on the Secret Nucleus and the Array of the Path of the Magical Net* (*snying-ṭīk-dang lam-rnam-bkod-la mchan-bu*). He also greatly propagated the empowerment and exegesis of this tantra among the descendants of Rok.

THE LINEAGE OF YATÖ ZURPA

Similarly, in Tsangtön Mangkar a succession known as the "Yatö Zurpa" emerged, which was well practised in exegesis and attainment. That lineage spread like fire throughout the southern and northern districts of Latö. In the north a few explanations were given by Metön Jungne-ö, Nartön Senge-ö, Yönten Wangcuk of Catarlamo and others; and an exegesis of the *Magical Net* was continued in the succession at Tenpak as well, where the conqueror Longcenpa studied it.

8 *Rongzom Chöki Zangpo*

[452.4-465.1] Chöki Zangpo of Rong,[889] who was renowned as the supreme *mahāpaṇḍita* of [Tibet], the land of snow mountains, took birth in Narlung-rong, a subdistrict of Rulak in lower Tsang. [In order for him to do so,] the rite of the five awakenings of the causal phase[890] was first performed by [his father] Rongben Rincen Tshültrim, the son of Rongben Pelgi Rinpoche. Consequently, [during his lifetime] he was to demonstrate an enlightenment exemplifying five excellences: Dignāga's discriminative awareness, Vasubandhu's learning, Candragomin's expressive style, Dharmakīrti's analytical acumen, and master Āryaśūra's poetic composition.

It is said that Rongzompa was the immediate reincarnation of a paṇḍita called master Smṛtijñānakīrti, who had come [to Tibet] towards the end of the early propagation of the teaching. In the province of Dokam he corrected the translations of some of the tantras, and translated commentaries on the way of secret mantra, including the *Commentary on the Litany of the Names of Mañjuśrī* (*Tha-ga-na'i mtshan-brjod-kyi 'grel-pa,* T 2538) by Thagana, and many means for attainment, such as that of *Esoteric Mañjuśrī.* He also composed some treatises on grammar. Later, he passed into nirvāṇa [while still in Tibet]. But in the lineage of the *Anthologised Sūtras* (*mdo-mang*, T 846-1108), [a section] of the *Kangyur*, Rongzompa follows immediately after Smṛtijñānakīrti, a point which requires consideration [for it would be impossible for one to be the immediate reincarnation of the other if they were master and disciple]. Still, others maintain that a paṇḍita called Ācārya Trhalaringmo came to Kham, and that there he translated and taught the *Extensive Commentary on the Guhyasamāja Tantra* (*gsang-ba 'dus-pa rgya-cher 'grel-pa*) and so forth. When he passed away he reportedly reincarnated [as Rongzompa].

From his youth Rongzompa spontaneously possessed great discriminative awareness, and so studied under Gartön Tshültrim Zangpo in lower Nyang. Once, when his father came to bring him provisions, his fellow students said, "This son of yours has a wild disposition. As we have grown tired of his noisy chattering, it would be best to take him away now." The father asked the master whether he should take the boy away as they had suggested, but the great Gartön replied, "Do not speak of it. He already understands the entire doctrine!"

Rongzom Chöki Zangpo

In his eleventh year Rongzompa studied the dialectical philosophy. Between teaching sessions he used to repeat all his master's words even in the children's playground. Because he mastered all doctrines after hearing them just once, without mistaking even a single word, he became known as an emanation of Mañjuśrī. When he was in his thirteenth year he seemed to have completed his studies and to have become free from ignorance with respect to all that can be known.

He himself was to say, "My learning was not insignificant: There was no doctrine I did not study. But neither were my studies great, for I did not need to review any doctrine more than once."

This great man's discriminative awareness was both quick and profound. It is said that because he possessed vast and taintless brilliance that was supremely wholesome, he obtained infallible retention, keeping in his mind all the words and meanings of all the difficult Indian texts

– sūtras, tantras, and treatises – which he had not previously seen, having perused them only once or twice. From the very outset and without great efforts, he was free from ignorance with respect to Sanskrit and many other languages as well. And because his intellect, unobstructed in all the inner and outer sciences and scriptures, was like a sharp thorn, he was vastly superior to others in indicating subtle distinctions, even in Tibetan, whereby a given word might apply to a given shade of meaning.

Rongzompa knew the significance of many, extensive textual systems teaching such sciences as those of the logical treatises, aphoristic verses, poetics and so forth, without referring merely to [a single authority, for instance,] the treatise of Daṇḍin [the *Mirror of Poetics*].[891] In childhood he delighted in the company of every Indian master, and comprehended their statements. Thus, he found no difficulty in learning [to read] a volume in the Vivarta script,[892] just by glancing over it. It is said that he even learned the languages and sounds of animals. He also composed many commentaries and treatises like [his commentary on] the *Gateway to Language* (*smra-sgo mtshon-cha*). With inconceivable intellectual power he was endowed with a profound intention to serve all men devoted to the doctrine and religious persons in general, and, in particular, those who had entered into the vehicle of indestructible reality and who desired to attain the rites and accomplishments of the secret mantra. So it was that he earnestly advised them with infallible instruction, and thus served them. Since he was endowed with some of the supernormal cognitive powers, he knew the right times and situations for training sentient beings, and so changed the attitudes of most living creatures. In order to turn those who entered the doctrine away from its opponents, well-prepared and methodical treatises would flow forth from his lotus mouth. And he never regretted giving this aid.

Abandoning avarice, Rongzompa renounced possessions for, and tolerated the incompetence of, ordinary persons whose minds were not inclined to the doctrine.[893] Making them the objects of his compassion, he established them in happiness and peace. He cherished sacred matters and meditative resolve like wish-fulfilling gems, or vital forces; and he inspired others to follow suit.

While composing [works concerning] the true doctrine, Rongzompa did not have to hesitate in order to collect and study source-books or make other such investigations, for the eight great treasures of brilliance were liberated [within him], whereby he could penetrate the words and meanings of the doctrine without impediment. Since all his treatises are refined in meaning, verbally refined and of unadulterated expressive style,[894] they are in harmony with the mysteries of the speech of the Teacher, the great Sage. For this reason, others who are known for their learning cannot refute them. It is said that individuals in the lineage of those who have studied his esoteric instructions concerning the way of secret mantra cannot but receive his blessing by following [the texts] literally, even if they have not obtained the transmissions.

When the master Atiśa met this great being, he declared him to be infallible, saying, "This master is, in fact, the deceased master Kṛṣṇācārin of India. How could I be able to discuss the doctrine with him?"

In general, it was said [of him]:

> In Vinaya, Tshurtön Yige was learned.
> In correct ritual practice, Yedrak was skilled.
> Rongpa was learned in grammar and logic.
> But father Chödrak himself gathered all![895]

While, generally speaking, Rongzompa continued unbroken lineages of the sūtra and mantra traditions derived from many gurus, in particular, [he figures in many lineages of] the doctrinal cycles of the vehicle of indestructible reality according to the Ancient Translation School, for example:

(i) The lineage of the instructions of the great master Padmasambhava [passed from that master through]:

> Nanam Dorje Düjom;
> Kharcen Pelgi Wangcuk;
> Tom Atsara Pel Metok;
> Dra Dorje Zhönu;
> Zhangzhang Yönten-tra;
> Rongben Yönten; and
> Rongben Tshültrim Rinpoche [Rongzompa's father].

Rongzompa received them from this last figure in the lineage.

(ii) The lineage of Vairocana's esoteric instructions [which passed from that master through]:

> Yudra Nyingpo;
> Lacen Gongpa Rapsel;
> Trum Shinglakcen;
> Nup Paten; and
> Yazi Pöntön.

The latter expounded them to the all-knowing Rongzompa. This is one lineage of the Mental Class.

(iii) There was also an accomplished individual in Longtang Drölma named Aro Yeshe Jungne.[896] He possessed both the instructions of seven successive masters of India and those of seven successive masters of China. [From him the lineage was transmitted through:]

> Cokro Zangkar Dzökur;
> Yazi Pöntön;[897] to
> Rongzompa.

This is called the Kham tradition of the Great Perfection.

(iv) Again, there were the esoteric instructions given by Vimalamitra to Nyang Tingdzin Zangpo, and those which he taught to Ma Rincen-chok and Nyak Jñānakumāra. Both were transmitted through Khu Cangcup-ö to Khyungpo Yik-ö, and by stages came down to Rongzompa.

Thus, Rongzompa was an unrivalled master of the teaching of the Ancient Translation School of the secret mantra, in whom was found one of the fountain-heads of the teaching.

At the beginning of this master's *Commentary on the Tantra of the Secret Nucleus (gsang-snying 'grel-pa)* it says:

> The nature of the Three Precious Jewels
> Is enlightened mind.

For this reason it is called the *Precious Jewel Commentary (dkon-mchog 'grel)*. The commentary by the great, all-knowing Longcenpa, entitled *Dispelling Darkness in the Ten Directions*, clearly elucidates [the *Secret Nucleus*], commenting on it according to the tradition of the king of vehicles [Atiyoga]. On the other hand, this commentary by the all-knowing Rongzompa appears like a great chest that is sealed tight, vastly commenting on the expanse [of reality]. Knowing that these two are the main Tibetan commentaries [on the *Secret Nucleus*] provides the intellect with [the potential for] great power.

When Rongzompa was young, while studying the teachings of the Ancient Translation School under one Dotön Senge, he once dreamed that he was eating a porridge he had prepared of the *Secret Nucleus*, with a vegetable broth made of the *Buddhasamāyoga*. He told this to his master, who said, "How wonderful! It is a sign that you have completely internalised those doctrines. You should compose a commentary on each."

Therefore, to fulfil his guru's intention, Rongzompa composed three esoteric instructions based on the three precious trainings. These are the *Extensive Sūtra of the Commitments*, which gives definitive expression to the training of superior moral discipline; the *Four Modes and Fifteen Aspects Commentary ('grel-pa tshul-bzhi yan-lag bco-lnga-pa)*, which sets forth the training of superior contemplation; and the *Commentary on the Buddhasamāyoga (mnyam-sbyor-gyi 'grel-pa)*, which consists of esoteric instructions on the view and meditation of the Great Perfection, and which teaches the training of superior discriminative awareness.

Similarly, he composed many commentaries and esoteric instructions, such as those on the *Tantra of the Purification of All Evil Destinies (Sarvadurgatipariśodhanatantra*, T 483), and on the *Bhairava Tantra*. Among them are texts that are inexpressibly profound, and of vast significance, such as the *Introduction to the Way of the Greater Vehicle (theg-pa chen-po'i tshul-la 'jug-pa)*, and so forth. In short, Rongzompa made the abode of omniscience his own; for, with respect to the different sūtras, tantras, and treatises, he mastered all those which are knowable. He even went so far as to write treatises on such worldly occupations as agriculture, animal husbandry, and dairy farming.

Therefore, when at first all the scholars of the four Tibetan provinces assembled with the intention of debating him, it was an occasion for Rongzompa to prune the vines of their brilliance and to flatten the cobra's hood of their pride. So it was that all those scholars, including Yangkye Lama of Shap, Marpa Topa, Uyukpa Datön, Dö Khyungpo Hūṃ-nying, Setrom Gyamtsobar, Tshamtön Koca, Pangka Tarcung, Gö Lhetse, and Gya Gyeltsül had thought to refute Rongzompa by criticising his treatises as being merely the inventions of a native Tibetan. But when they confronted the great man in person they found that he adhered to the scriptural authorities, could bear logical examination, and that he contradicted neither syllogistic proof nor the teachings of their gurus. Thus, he refuted them through the brilliance of his intellect, which was free from all the verbal and substantial faults asserted by his opponents. As they inspected each of his treatises and savoured its meaning, they were all astonished; and every one of them honoured him and made him their guru. So it is said.

So too, the translator of Korup, a monk named Chöki Sherap, who had the guise of one who was much learned, also slandered Rongzompa at first. But on seeing the volume entitled *Introduction to the Way of the Greater Vehicle*, which Rongzompa had composed, he felt great respect. Finally, he honoured Rongzompa with many presents, confessed his fault, and prayed to be accepted as a disciple. Then he studied the *Secret Tantra of [Wrathful] Mañjuśrī*, and many other doctrines.

During his discourses on that *Secret Tantra*, the great paṇḍita declared, "If we had a Sanskrit manuscript, [the tantra] would read like this, but since there is none, we cannot now correct it."

Korup Lotsāwa retained his words and later obtained a Sanskrit manuscript from a paṇḍita called lord Kṛṣṇa, which he studied under him. He found it agreed with the words of Rongzom Paṇḍita and felt great devotion. It is said that he offered to Rongzompa the Sanskrit manuscript which Kṛṣṇapā had provided, and studied it once more under him. In the same way, many translators such as Marpa Chöki Wangcuk[898] and intellectuals who were renowned for their learning bowed before his feet.

Rongzompa adhered to many paṇḍitas including the Indian preceptors Mañjuśrīvarman, Mañjuśrījñāna, Upāyaśrīmitra, Buddhākarabhadra, Devākaracandra, Parameśvara, and Amoghavajra. He acted as their interpreter and translated many texts, including the *Vajrabhairava Tantra*, the tantra of *Black Yamāri*, the *Esoteric Mañjuśrī*,[899] and the *Root Tantra of Cakrasaṃvara*. They are most excellent translations and are thus worthy exemplars of the new translation schools. All of Rongzompa's Indian paṇḍitas used to say to him, "Dharmabhadra!

You should compose many doctrines and protect many living creatures. Not to mention your other attributes, in India men compose without having a third of your knowledge of grammar and logic. So, why don't you write?"

Though endowed with such perfect attributes, Rongzompa persevered in reducing pride and smothering arrogance. If we consider the accounts of his liberated accomplishments, there are many concerning, for example, how he crossed the mirror-like surface of a great cliff through magical abilities, or how he pierced rock with his kīla, flew into the sky, and possessed supernormal cognitive powers, through which he comprehended the domains and conduct of most Tibetan gods and demons. So it was that this great paṇḍita, such an undisputed emanation, was manifestly praised and venerated by all the scholars who lived during his age. He lived for one hundred and nineteen years and is said to have passed away without physical illness. Even the great Gö Lotsāwa [Zhönupel] has praised him saying, "In this snowland of Tibet no scholar has appeared who has been his equal."[900] This is universally known.

Among the students who followed him, there were two lineages: the lineage of his sons, and that of his disciples. First, the lineage which issued from his two sons, Zijibar and Bumbar, lasted for a long time, and everyone who appeared in it attained accomplishment through the practice of Vajrakīla. In the lineage of his disciples, there were seventeen great translators including Korup Lotsāwa, Marpa Topa, and Gö [Khukpa Lhetse]; thirty-five great accomplished masters including Yak Dorje Dzinpa; one hundred and eighty great meditators, masters of yoga, including the venerable Khurbupa, the brother of Macik Zhama;[901] and about five hundred others who upheld the umbrella of his doctrine, including Dorje Wangcuk, the layman of Yölcak, and Yangkye Lama.

9 *The Traditions of Vajrakīla*

THE TRANSMISSIONS OF VAJRAKĪLA

[465.1-475.3] As has already been described, the foremost meditational deities of the ancient masters were Yangdak Heruka and Vajrakīla. Since [the tradition of] the *Yangdak* cycle is already known [pp. 617-45], the propagation of Vajrakīla [will now be discussed].[902] There are, indeed, many different versions [of the means for the attainment of Vajrakīla] to be found among the lineages descended from Padmasambhava, the preceptor of Oḍḍiyāna. They include the *King's Tradition of Vajrakīla (phur-pa rgyal-po lugs)*, the *Venerable Lady's Tradition (jo-mo lugs)*, the *Royal Lady's Tradition* (*lcam-lugs*), also, the *Nanam* or *Rong Tradition* (*sna-nam-mam rong-lugs*), and the *Black Deity* (*lha-nag*) and *Variegated Deity* (*lha-khra*), these [last two] taking their names from the colour of the deities' bodies. Though all of these traditions have the same essential nature, they are known as this or that by their distinctive esoteric instructions and by the descent of their particular transmitted precepts.

(i) Concerning the *King's Tradition*: After the great master [Padmasambhava] had consecrated Samye he is said to have granted [the Vajrakīla teachings] to three persons, namely, King Trhisong Detsen, the venerable lady Kharcenza [Yeshe Tshogyel], and Cendrenpa.

(ii) Concerning the *Venerable Lady's Tradition*: At the time of his departure from Tibet, the master Padmasambhava taught the venerable lady Kharcenza the concise and complete *Root Fragment of Vajrakīla*, the higher rites of which essentially subsume the means for the attainment of enlightenment, and the lower rites of which essentially subsume the integration of sorcery with the path. Then, in the rock cavern of Naring Sengedzong in Mönka [present-day Bhutan], in the south, she opened up the maṇḍala of material symbols and entered into practice.[903] On the twenty-first day all the kīlas [of which the material maṇḍala was composed] laughed, emitted light, and began to jump and shake. The venerable lady thought to herself, "It is said, *If kīla be accomplished, perform the ritual stab*... But in fact, I have no object to stab. Oh well, I shall stab the *zandre* demon of my ancestors."[904] So thinking, the venerable lady rotated the kīla of ritual service. It vanished into the sky and crashed down onto a barberry bush behind her ancestral home, this being the abode of the *zandre* demon of her ancestors. The barberry bush was burnt to a crisp and the *zandre* was "liberated" in the spatial expanse of equanimity.

Afterwards, the descendants of that venerable lady's family kept the kīla. Because it sufficed just to brandish it, the lineage became renowned as "Kharcenza's *zandre*-subduing lineage". The venerable lady expounded this doctrine to her own brother, Kharcen Pelgi Wangcuk, and it was gradually propagated.

(iii) Concerning the *Royal Lady's Tradition*: Cokroza met master Padmasambhava in person, but she requested empowerment from the meditational deity and not from the guru. Therefore, the deity vanished into the guru's heart and she lost the good fortune of receiving empowerment.[905] But the venerable lady Yeshe Tshogyel transmitted it to

Yeshe Tshogyel

Cokroza, with the permission of Padmasambhava, and another lineage thence sprang forth.

(iv) Again, there is the *Nanam Tradition*: This is simply the tradition of the lineage of the great Rongzompa, which has just been explained above. Concerning it, some say that the grandfather of the great Rongzompa, Rongben Yönten Rincen, or Pelgi Rincen, met master Padmasambhava in person, and lived for three hundred years. He taught his son, the father of Rongzom Paṇḍita, who was named Rincen Tshültrim and lived for one hundred and fifty years. From him the lineage known as the *Rong Tradition* emerged.

(v) Concerning the *Black Deity Vajrakīla*: Padmasambhava of Oḍḍiyāna and his consort both instructed Dre Atsara Sale. He taught Langlap Cangcup Dorje, from whom the lineage gradually descended to one Kurup Yangdak of Yamdrok, who made all the deities [of the maṇḍala] black on the basis of the *Nirvāṇa Tantra of Vajrakīla* (*phur-pa mya-ngan-las 'das-pa'i rgyud*, NGB Vol.28). Hence the name [of this tradition].

If this account indeed refers to Atsara Sale, the lineage could not have been direct because there was a great span of time between him and Langlap. However, there was also a certain Dre Atsara Nuru who is said to have attained the accomplishment of longevity. Despite the difference of their names, there is little contradiction [if these two are identified as one and the same].

When the precious lama Phakpa was unable to find a continuous lineage for the "liberating" empowerment of the lower rite (*smad-las sgrol-dbang*), he searched for it saying that he would request it even from a beggar. He heard that there was one Atsara Nuru who had been a personal disciple of Yeshe Tshogyel, and who, having become an awareness-holder controlling the duration of his own life, wandered about with no certain destination in such places as Śītavana. At that, the precious Phakpa sent much gold with Lowo Lotsāwa and thus obtained the continuous lineage of the "liberating" empowerment. So it is said.

(vi) Concerning the *Sakya Tradition of Vajrakīla* (*phur-pa sa-lugs*):[906] This lineage was transmitted in a succession beginning with Khön Lüiwangpo, a disciple of the great master Padmasambhava. An unbroken lineage was well known in both the doctrinal and familial lines of the Sakyapa, hence the name [of this tradition].

(vii) Moreover, the *Perfect Practice of Vajrakīla* based on the *Secret Tantra of Vajrakīla* (*phur-ba gsang-rgyud*, NGB Vol.27), the *Six Secret Tantras* (*gsang-ba'i rgyud drug*, NGB Vols. 28-9), and the *Blue-skirted One's Cycle*, which was abridged from the *Twelve-Section Kīlaya Tantra* (*ki-la-ya tantra bcu-gnyis*, NGB Vol.19), were transmitted in the lineage of Nyak Jñānakumāra, which has been described above [pp. 601-6].

LANGLAP CANGCUP DORJE AND OTHER MASTERS OF VAJRAKĪLA

There were an inconceivable number of individuals who obtained manifest signs of accomplishment from this meditational deity, so it will not be possible to mention them all. None the less, there was one in particular, called Langlap Cangcup Dorje. During his childhood he was separated from his parents, and, like the venerable Milarepa, suffered greatly at the hands of his paternal relations. This was unbearable to Dre Atsara, who gave him a cycle that was profound and to the point, derived from the esoteric instructions of *Vajrakīla*. Langlap practised it and thereby put an end to his paternal family. Although the great fame he achieved in this way increased, he had to live as a shepherd in Khore, for he lacked the fruit of generosity practised in past lives. At the same time, there was one spiritual benefactor, Ra Lotsāwa, whose dominion and fortune were quite vast.[907] Many of the great gurus and noblemen of Tibet, powerless to do otherwise, had to prostrate before him. It is said that if they did not comply Ra Lotsāwa would "liberate" them with the wrathful mantras of Yamāntaka.

About that [wrathful teaching of his]: A whole clay barrel, containing a *Yamāntaka* cycle, had been discovered as treasure by one Tumpa Gya Zhangtrom.[908] Having copied out about half of the *Lord of Life, Evil and Mean-hearted* (*tshe-bdag sdig-pa snying-'dzings*), he went before Ra Lotsāwa, who appended [that teaching] to his own *Yamāntaka* cycle and invented an Indian origin, with the pretense that he had translated it [from Sanskrit]. Similarly, from among the many treasure troves of Bumthang, he discovered numerous esoteric instructions concerning sorcery, exorcism, and hail, Vaiśravaṇa, Jambhala, Gaṇapati, and so forth. So it was that the *Yamāntaka* cycle of the new translation schools came to have many efficacious rites.

When that mantra preceptor [Ra Lotsāwa], who had "liberated" thirteen bodhisattvas, including Marpa's son Tarma Dode,[909] and thirteen translators who were his own equals, including Nyen Lotsāwa, arrived at a religious festival in Khore, Langlap Cangcup Dorje did not prostrate before him. Ra Lotsāwa thought that he was just a fool, but on hearing a description of him, said, "Very well! He will not live beyond this evening. Just wait!" He began to perform the wrathful rite, but during the first declaration of truth [for the purpose] of capturing and summoning [the consciousness of the victim] a shower of briarwood kīlas rained down on him and his disciples, wounding all the ordinary students outside.[910] During the second declaration a rain of iron kīlas fell from the maṇḍalas of the wrathful deities of the ten directions [with their retinues] including the Devourers and the Slaughterers (*za-gsod*).[911] And during the final declaration, Ra Lotsāwa saw the sky fill with fire and droning sounds, and there appeared the Indestructible Youth (*Vajrakumāra*), like a red-hot iron almost cleaving the mountains in two, ravenously grimacing above him. At that, Ra Lotsāwa was terrified. He begged forgiveness and venerated Langlap with prostrations and offerings. This is the origin of the saying that, "The preceptor of Yamāntaka was ruined by Kīla."

It is said that while many obtained accomplishment through the higher rites of Vajrakīla, in the lower rites none revealed a more powerful force than did this Langlap Cangcup Dorje. His main disciples were Nanam Sherap Tshültrim, Kyi Kyangyel of Mongu, Trang Phurbugo of Rong,[912] and Nyang Nak of Uyuk Rölpo.

Among them, Kyi Kyangyel, who was also called Kyiben Cangcup Rincen, had his house, fields and wealth stolen by his paternal relations. He became exceedingly disgusted and requested the [empowerment of] Vajrakīla from Langlap, who said, "Perform the ritual service of the deity for nine months. Then practise the rites of the trio of Se, Cak, and Shel[913] for two months. Your aim will be achieved!"

Doing just that he reached the limits of power. Then, noticing many people in front of an earthen wall, warming themselves in the sun, he saw that all were his enemies. He brandished his kīla in the direction of the wall and the wall collapsed. All his enemies were thus set on the path of the hereafter. For this he became known as Kyi Kyangyel, "Kyi who Brought Down the Wall". All [of this lineage] possessed such occult power, so it will not be possible to write it all down here.

Again, this Vajrakīla tradition is famous for its utterly vast occult power. By brandishing the kīla at a brushfire in a sandalwood forest, the great master Padmasambhava restored the forest. By brandishing it at the flooding waters of the Ganges, Vimalamitra fixed the river's course. By brandishing it at Mount Trakar Kongcen, the Newar Śīlamañju made the rock-face crumble to pieces. By thrusting it at the tracks of a wolf, the venerable lady Kharcenza caused the wolf to be swept away in an avalanche. By raising it against the crow which had carried off his rosary, Menu Gyelwei Nyingpo made the bird fall to earth. And by inflicting it upon the yak-hair tents of the Mön army, Lo Pelgi Lodrö overpowered them. In these and other instances, these masters, thrusting the kīla at both enemies and obstacles, were invincible, even in the face of powerful magic. And by thrusting it inwardly at the five poisonous conflicting emotions, numberless masters obtained supreme accomplishment.

DARCARUPA AND THE TERMA TRADITION OF VAJRAKĪLA

Moreover, there is the tradition of the treasure, through which the manifest signs [of accomplishment] were exceedingly clear. The great master [Padmasambhava] conferred the empowerment, tantra and instructions [of Vajrakīla] on the king [Trhisong], and then secured it in the form of a treasure, along with the *Doctrinal Cycle of the Utterly Secret Hayagrīva (rta-mgrin yang-gsang-gi chos-skor)*, at the rock of Sewalung in Yerpa. When Darcarupa, a lord among accomplished masters, performed the means for attainment in the upper cave of Como Nagyel he met the great master Padmasambhava in person, who said, "Practice in the Moon Cave (Dawa Phuk) at Yerpa!" He did accordingly. There, the great master arrived by horse on the rays of the sun every morning and taught the doctrine to him. Every evening he departed on the sun's rays, saying that he was off to tame the ogres. At that time Darcarupa discovered the kīla, which was a material symbol, at its place of concealment in Sewalung at Yerpa.

When Darcarupa went to Lhasa at market-time he devastated the bazaar with a whirlwind. Then he proceeded to Tsang and met Sakya Paṇḍita, who was on his way to Kyirong, and they stayed in the same house. Since Darca's speech was defective,[914] he counted the mantra, saying "OṂ VAJRAKYILI KYILAYA..." But Sakya Paṇḍita said, "That is wrong. One should say, 'VAJRAKĪLI KĪLAYA...!'"

At this, Darca's heart was swollen with pride. "Even though the mantra is wrong I can still do this!" he said, and forcefully jammed his kīla into a rock as if it were clay. When he pulled out the kīla with a twist, the point was slightly cracked. Sakya Paṇḍita knew him to be an accomplished master and said, "I am on my way to debate with some extremists. You must come as my assistant."

"Okay," he said, and they set out together.

When they reached Kyirong [it was decided that], in accord with the Indian custom, the banner of whichever doctrine prevailed would be raised aloft [i.e. the loser would embrace the victor's doctrine]. Sakya Paṇḍita and Haranandin engaged in the battle of debate for thirteen days, and finally Sakya Paṇḍita was victorious. None the less, Haranandin would not permit [the Indians] to enter the Buddhist teaching, saying, "Let us compete in signs of accomplishment!" At this, the extremist threw back his matted hair and, flapping his hands like wings, flew into the sky. Sakya Paṇḍita saw that he could only be tamed by the power of gnostic mantras and called out to Darca, "Hey! Vajrakyili Kyila! Get over here!"

At once the great lord of yoga stabbed his kīla into the heart of the extremist's shadow, exclaiming, "OṂ VAJRAKYILI KYILAYA HŪṂ PHAṬ!" and the extremist fell to earth like a bird struck by a stone. Then Sakya Paṇḍita, as a heroic sign of his victory in debate, led Haranandin along, so long as he still refused ordination. But since the great master Padmasambhava had ordered the Twelve Goddesses of the Earth to protect the doctrine in Tibet from extemists, they inflicted their punishment: At the Tibetan border near Kyirong the extremist vomited blood from his mouth and was sent down the fifth path.[915] Subsequently, upholders of the non-Buddhist philosophies were not to be seen in Tibet. Some may well have arrived, but no one with the intellectual power capable of really disputing the Buddha's teaching.

Darca himself proceeded to Müse, where he enshrined his kīla as the center-piece of the temple's shrine. Thereafter, it changed hands several times and today is reported to be on display at Sera Monastery.[916]

Vajrakīla

10 *The Lineages of the Empowerment of the "Sūtra which Gathers All Intentions"*

[475.3-5] Again, there were some holy individuals who especially served the teachings associated with the three aspects of creation and perfection, and who stood in the successive lineage of the great empowerment of the *Sūtra which Gathers All Intentions*.

After Drölcen Samdrup Dorje had empowered Zur Ham [Śākya Jungne] and his sister [pp. 700-1] two distinct lineages developed. Including the lineage of Drölcen's own son, there were thus three lineages altogether.

THE LINEAGE OF ZUR HAM ŚĀKYA JUNGNE

[475.5-477.4] At the seat of Yang-en, Nyibukpa Langdro Tshewang Gyelpo received the empowerment of the *Sūtra* from Zur Ham himself. From Nyibukpa, it was received in Chuwar by Lekpa Pelzang, the holder of the Nyibukpa lineage; and from him, Utsewa Jamyang Rincen Gyeltsen of Ngari received it. During the hare year (1497) in Lowo Matang in Ngari [present-day Mustang in Nepal] the latter empowered his own sons, the great paṇḍita [Ngari Pema Wangyel] and his brother, who both became lords among learned and accomplished masters.[917]

The younger brother, Rikdzin Lekdenje, in particular, was in his eighth year when he received the empowerment of the *Sūtra*. Because he lived for one hundred and thirteen years in all he benefitted the teaching and living creatures with the bountiful enlightened activity of his exegeses and attainments. At the behest of Jamyang Khyentse Wangcuk[918] and his nephew, he granted the empowerments of the four rivers of the *Sūtra which Gathers All Intentions* in their entirety, together with the seal of entrustment (*gtad-rgya*),[919] in the palace of Nyuk. At that same time, Kyitön Tshering Wangpo also received it; and he later gave the empowerment of the *Sūtra*, along with its seal of entrustment, at Pelkar in Samdruptse in Tsang.

On that occasion, the great guru Treshongpa Nyaktön Chögyel Dorje, who was a child at the time, was taken there by his father, Mang-rawa

Rikdzin Lekdenje

Pema Düdül; and so he received the complete [empowerment of the *Sūtra*] from Kyitön Tshering Wangpo. Later, at Kong-ra Lhündrupding, Treshongpa also received it from Locen Zhenpen Dorje, and at Thekcokling in Tsang from Namka Drukdra Zangpo, an adept of the Great Perfection, along with a congregation.[920] Treshongpa held Öselchok of Ngari, Kong-ra Locen, and Lhatsün Namka Jikme to be his three root gurus.[921] Relying on them and many other genuine gurus he became vastly learned. He was a great lord among accomplished masters, and his disposition was that of a celibate monk. At Shambhara in Rongmu he remained in strict retreat, but, under the pretext of conferring guidance on the *Black Further Innermost Spirituality* (*yang-tig nag-po*), he granted the empowerment of the *Sūtra*, together with the seal of entrustment, in a unique lineage to the great Menlungpa Nyangtön Locok Dorje [by instructing him] through a secret passageway.[922]

This Nyangtön Locok Dorje had previously received this empowerment in the maṇḍala constructed of coloured powders during the rites of great attainment from Locen Zhenpen Dorje as well; and he held the latter to be his supreme root guru. In general, Nyangtön knew the sūtras, mantras, and sciences, but, in particular, he was learned in the treasure doctrines of Guru Chöwang.[923] He was honoured with the title of *ti-shih* by the supreme conqueror, the Great Fifth Dalai Lama, and became the crown ornament [i.e. guru] of many learned and accomplished masters.[924]

Dorje Trak Rikdzin Pema Trhinle

Dorje Trak Rikdzin Pema Trhinle

[477.5-479.4] Nyangtön Locok Dorje elaborately bestowed the empowerment of the *Sūtra*, along with its seal of entrustment, esoteric instructions, and practical techniques, on Dorje Trak Rikdzin, a supreme emanation, who was a lord of the teaching of the Ancient Translation School. This holy individual was the emanation of Rikdzinje, the reincarnation of Nanam Dorje Düjom. He was born in 1641 (iron female snake year) at Namseling in Mönkar, as the son of the nobleman Karma Phüntsok Wangpo, who belonged to the Canak clan. Since he clearly remembered his past life as Cangpa Rikdzin Ngagiwangpo, he was invited to the seat of his predecessor during his sixth year.[925] Beginning with reading, writing, and the essential rites and means for attainment, he easily learned the textual traditions. He offered a lock from the crown of his head to the supreme conqueror, the all-knowing Great Fifth Dalai Lama [i.e. he took the vows of refuge under him], and the name Künzang Pema Trhinle was conferred upon him. Later, he was fully ordained in the presence of the Dalai Lama and received many profound doctrines from him. In addition, he attended on many learned and accomplished gurus such as Zurcen Chöying Rangdröl and Gönpo Sonam Chokden; and he studied insatiably numberless doctrinal transmissions under them, including the empowerments, guidance, exegeses, transmissions, and esoteric instructions of the ancient and new traditions.

Pema Trhinle established [the meaning of all he had studied through discriminative awareness] born of thought, and his learning grew without obstruction. At Dra Yangdzong, Chuwori, his seat at Dorje Trak, and elsewhere, he cultivated practical experience through discriminative awareness born of meditation. So it was that he obtained stability in the stage of creation and mastery of the pristine cognition of the stage of perfection. Thus, he became a great learned and accomplished master. His enlightened activity, endowed with knowledge, love and power, never strayed from the three spheres of exegesis, attainment and work.

In particular, inspired by the command of the supreme conqueror, the all-knowing Great Fifth, he composed the work entitled *Embarking on the Ocean of Maṇḍalas: The Empowerment Ceremonies of the Sūtra which Gathers All Intentions* (*'dus-pa mdo'i dbang-chog dkyil-'khor rgya-mtsho'i 'jug-ngogs*); and he conferred the empowerment of the *Sūtra* on numerous occasions. Thus, he greatly advanced the teaching of the *Sūtra which Gathers All Intentions*.

Pema Trhinle continued to work extensively on behalf of the teaching and living creatures through to his seventy-seventh year. His written works, in about thirteen volumes, have had a most remedial effect on the teachings of both the transmitted precepts and the treasures.

THE LINEAGE OF ZUR HAM'S SISTER, ZURMO

[479.4-5] This is the Kham tradition, which has already been described following the section on Katok [pp. 700-1].

THE LINEAGE OF THE SON, SANGYE RINCEN

Zhangtön Namka Dorje

[479.5-480.6] Drölcen Samdrup Dorje's son, Sangye Rincen, transmitted the lineage to Zhangtön Namka Dorje. He was a learned student who completed his studies under both Drölcen and his son. In the biography,[926] it says:

> At the funeral service for Jamyang Samdrup Dorje, the major disciples who were invited included about fourteen monks who performed the ceremonies, headed by the gurus who were supreme even among the major disciples. At that time [they included] Lama Zurcenpa, Lama Namdingpa...[927]

Zhangtön is this last mentioned. Particularly, he received the empowerment of the *Sūtra*, together with its seal of entrustment, exegesis and instructions, from the son, Sangye Rincen, at Decen Drölma. He became learned in all the tantras, transmissions and esoteric instructions, along with their means for attainment. In the hermitage of Tanak Namding he became intent on experiential cultivation above all else; and he attained the stability of vital energy and mind. He disclosed the intentions of the stages of creation and perfection, and mastered the four rites of enlightened activity, whereby he acted on behalf of those requiring training.

Zhangtön conferred the empowerment on the learned and accomplished Shami Dorje Gyeltsen in the glorious hermitage at Namding, and granted the exegesis and instructions as well. The latter remained in practice at the hermitage of Decen and acquired stability in the stage of creation, whereby he accomplished the four rites without obstruction. He reached the limits of experience and realisation in the stage of perfection and benefitted the teaching by both exegesis and attainment.

Rikdzin Yudruk Dorje

[480.6-481.4] In the hermitage at Decen, Shami Dorje Gyeltsen conferred on Rikdzin Yudruk Dorje the entire empowerment of the *Sūtra which Gathers All Intentions*, together with its seal of entrustment. He also granted to him the exegesis and instructions. This Yudruk Dorje remained wholly immersed in experiential cultivation in the solitary hermitages of the Central Tibetan mountains, such as Ön and Do, and above all in the hermitage of Lagu-ngö in Tanak, Yeru. This was why he became known as Lama Drupcenpa, "Guru of Great Attainment". He attained the limits of experience and realisation. Just by conferring his blessing, he could liberate people from disease and evil spirits. In these and other ways the expression of his occult and spiritual powers was revealed. He lived to an extremely ripe old age, and this, combined with his solitary cultivation of experience, enabled him to establish those fortunate disciples who yearned for freedom in maturation [through empowerment] and liberation [through his guidance].

Khedrup Lodrö Gyeltsen Pelzangpo (Sodokpa)

[481.4-483.6] Yudruk Dorje bestowed the empowerments of the four rivers of the *Sūtra which Gathers All Intentions* in their entirety, together with its seal of entrustment, exegesis, instructions, and practical techniques on the learned and accomplished Lodrö Gyeltsen Pelzangpo, an emanation of Nyak Jñānakumāra. He was born into the family of Dong at Thak Dongkar in Yeru, Tsang. From his childhood he learned all the conventional sciences without difficulty. In particular, he became adept at the science of medicine. Since he passed his youth in the service of the aristocrat Dongkarwa, he became known as Dongkar Tshoje, the "Physician of Dongkar". During adolescence he awoke to the enlightened family and was ordained as a novice. He was a suppliant at the feet of many learned and accomplished genuine gurus, such as Lacen Dorjechang Trakpa Rincen, Yongdzin Ngawang Trakpa, Dawa Gyeltsen, the spiritual son of Pema Lingpa,[928] the treasure-finder Zhikpo Lingpa,[929] and Dorje Senge, who passed away as a sky-farer without relinquishing his body. Under them, he insatiably studied an infinite number of approaches to the doctrine. Not merely leaving those teachings to be something he had once heard, he removed his doubts. Undistracted by social diversions he persevered in experiential cultivation and accomplished all at once [the three kinds of discriminative awareness, born of] study, thought and meditation.

By virtue of that, the spatial expanse of experience, realisation, and knowledge grew from within him. His knowledge of the textual traditions of the sūtras and mantras in general, and of the doctrines belonging to the transmitted precepts and treasures of the Ancient Translation School, in particular, developed without impediment. And the naturally manifest, unbiased intention of the Great Perfection arose within him. The pulses of the energy channels, currents and seminal points dissolved into the central channel.[930] By mastering the refinement, multiplication, emanation and transformation of dreams,[931] he journeyed to pure lands and met face to face with many buddhas and bodhisattvas, and obtained prophecies from them. By his occult power he destroyed the ruinous demons of Tibet, and the hostile armies on the frontiers. Since he could immediately actualise the signs of [one who can successfully] protect and obstruct, he became universally renowned.

During the early part of his life Lodrö Gyeltsen lived at Kyibuk in lower Nyang. Without straying from the intention of the Indestructible Nucleus of Inner Radiance[932] he continuously propagated the doctrines of the transmitted empowerments, exegeses, transmissions, and profound guidance in whatever manner was suited to the abilities of his disciples. In this way, he fulfilled the hopes of each. He composed detailed expositions, texts concerning the means for attainment, ceremonies and rites, works on practical technique, histories of the doctrine, answers to critics and so forth. He produced golden copies of the *Seventeen Tantras*, the *Innermost Spirituality of Vimalamitra*, the *Gathering of the Sugatas*, et cetera; and he published many volumes of transmitted precepts and treasures. Thus, by vast enlightened activity involving exegesis, attainment, and work, he clarified and spread the teaching of the Ancient Translation School.

Lodrö Gyeltsen's *Notes on the Indications and Avoidance of Death* (*'chi-ba brtags-bslu'i yi-ge*) was clearly composed during his seventy-third year. Therefore, he certainly lived a long life.

Kong-ra Locen Zhenpen Dorje

[483.6-486.2] Lodrö Gyeltsen gave the empowerments of the four rivers of the *Sūtra which Gathers All Intentions* in their entirety, along with its seal of entrustment, exegesis, instructions and practical techniques to Kong-ra Locen Zhenpen Dorje. This holy individual was born in Trashiling, Sikkim, in 1594 (wood male horse year). He was a son of one Öncen, who was the younger brother of Locen Ngagiwangpo, the grandnephew of Tokden Chönyi Rangdröl. Their family was Nup Thropupa. As a boy Zhenpen Dorje was wild-tempered, but highly disciplined. So he was fearlessly brilliant and haughty towards everyone. From childhood, too, he seemed to yearn for a support free from desire, owing to which, during his twelfth year he received the ordination of a novice, and during his twenty-first year the complete ordination in the presence of Zhamar Chöki Wangcuk; and he became supremely dignified in his conduct.

His uncle, Locen Ngagiwangpo, had been invited to tutor the Zhamarpa in the sciences, and so Zhenpen Dorje followed as his servant. He became learned in all the branches of linguistic science, including the *Kalāpasūtra*, the *Mirror of Poetics*, prosody, astrology, and various Indian and Tibetan scripts. Under that doctrine master [the Zhamarpa] and Rinpoche Maseng, among others, he learned all kinds of dialectical texts, and incidentally attended the doctrinal discourses they delivered. Above and beyond that, he attended on many great individuals, including his uncle Locen Ngagiwangpo, Khedrup Lodrö Gyeltsen, Sungtrül Tshültrim Dorje, Nyipuwa Rikdzin Nyingpo, Tsele Pema Lekdrup, Katokpa Pema Lodrö, and Yöndopa Trashi Lhündrup. Under them he studied innumerable doctrines belonging to the transmitted precepts and treasures of the Ancient Translation School, until his doubts were removed. By perseverance in the meditation and attainment of the stages of creation and perfection, he arrived at the limits of experience and realisation. Because he was unsullied by the social diversions of the eight worldly concerns, all who followed him naturally behaved in accordance with the true doctrine.

He prepared copies of the *Collected Tantras of the Nyingmapa* (*rnying-ma rgyud-'bum*) on three occasions. The first two times, in consideration of the continuity of the teaching, he sent those copies to Kham and Kongpo. As this illustrates, whatever he had, whether books or other possessions, he gave away that they might benefit living creatures; and even if he had none, he provided liberal sustenance for those who were engaged in practice. From this master, Zhenpen Dorje, a continuous transmission of the *Collected Tantras of the Nyingmapa* pervaded Kham and Central Tibet. Therefore, his kindness to the teaching was great. By perpetuating the enlightened activity of teaching the sūtras, mantras, and sciences, he fulfilled the hopes of his disciples. He always maintained all those who studied the doctrine by providing sustenance. In short, he was exalted by the enlightened attributes of learning, dignity, and excellence; and his enlightened activities in the three [spheres of] exegesis, attainment, and work were as extensive as space. He passed away into the expanse of peace during his sixty-first year, which was an inauspicious one astrologically.[933]

Sangdak Trhinle Lhündrup

[486.2-489.5] From Kong-ra Locen, the lineage was transmitted to Sangdak Trhinle Lhündrup, the reincarnation of Nupcen Sangye Yeshe. He was born at Chak Cangcupling in 1611 (iron female pig year) as the son of Do-nga Tendzin, a great learned and accomplished teacher of the Nyö clan. From his fifth year he fully mastered both reading and writing. In his eighth year he received the vows of a layman in the presence of his venerable father, and the name Orgyen Tshepel was conferred upon him. Beginning then, he learned the cycle of rites, means for attainment, and practical techniques. By training himself in all the scriptures of the great, all-knowing Longcenpa, and in the conventional sciences like grammar and astrology, he acquired intellectual power. Under his venerable father, in particular, he received many empowerments, exegeses, transmissions and much guidance on the transmitted precepts and treasures; for instance, the means for attainment of the trio of the *Guru, Great Perfection and Great Compassionate One* (*bla-rdzogs-thugs-gsum*).[934] Then, through reflection and meditation he established them [in his mind].

When he was ordained as a novice by the great Tsuklak Gyamtso, the name Trhinle Lhündrup Pelzangpo was conferred upon him, and he received all kinds of doctrinal discourses. Moreover, he attended on more than thirty genuine gurus of the ancient and new traditions, including Nyingmapa [teachers], such as Sungtrül Tshültrim Dorje, Locen Zhenpen Dorje, Lhatsün Künzang Namgyel, Dzokcenpa Drukdra Zangpo, Pönlungpa Tshültrim Gyeltsen, Zur Chöying Rangdröl, and Trhüzhi Norbu Chöten, and other [teachers] of the new translation schools, such as Gyeltsap Trakpa Chöyang, and Gönpo

Sangdak Trhinle Lhündrup

Sonam Chokden. Under them, he insatiably studied innumerable doctrines of the sūtra and mantra traditions.

Concerning the empowerment of the *Sūtra which Gathers All Intentions*, in particular: In his eighth year, Trhinle Lhündrup, in the company of his father, received both the Zur and Kham traditions when the mantra adept Künzang Peljor was invited to Cangcupling. In his twenty-first year he studied the writings of the Kham tradition under Lhatsün Künzang Namgyel. Then, in his twenty-ninth year, in May 1639 (fourth month, earth hare year), at Kong-ra Lhündrupding, in the presence of the great translator Zhenpen Dorje, who had constructed all the root and branch maṇḍalas of the *Sūtra which Gathers All Intentions* with coloured powders, he received the empowerments of its four rivers in their entirety over a period of seventeen days, along with its seal of entrustment and esoteric instructions on the sequence of meditation. [This was] all [given] according to the writings of Nyelpa Delekpa,[935] and in conjunction with the steps of the rite of great attainment.

That same Kong-ra Locen bestowed alms munificently on those who were his fortunate disciples. Beyond that, he would refuse whatever tribute was offered to him for the doctrine and return it, saying, "Our doctrine is not for sale." None the less, it is said that when this master, Trhinle Lhündrup, offered him nine empowerment vases for the corners [of the maṇḍala],[936] Kong-ra Locen was delighted and accepted them. That was certainly a symbolic way of indicating that he regarded Trhinle Lhündrup as a fit vessel for the river of empowerment, and that, hence, he had arranged the auspicious occasion for the teaching to increase.

So it was that Trhinle Lhündrup removed all the doubts associated with study and thought in the appropriate fashion. In many solitary hermitages, he properly applied himself to the experiential cultivation of the essential path. In the visionary clarity of the stage of creation, through which he could eliminate the impure appearances [of the everyday world] he obtained signs which could be tangibly perceived. Thus, he accomplished unimpededly whatever rites he undertook.

By realising, through the stage of perfection, the primordially pure ground, perfect and free from change and transformation, which is the abiding nature of reality as it is, he cut through the entanglements which grasp saṃsāra and nirvāṇa as true. Having dissolved all phenomenal appearances in the space of spontaneously present inner radiance, he had visions of many meditational deities and obtained prophecies. Since he had destroyed selfish mental grasping, an all-embracing compassion for the sake of others effortlessly and powerfully arose, whereby he constantly turned the doctrinal wheels of exegesis and attainment for many fortunate persons, high and low, who aspired to freedom. Thus, he extended the spiritual and temporal well-being of the teaching and living creatures.

In particular, Sangdak Trhinle Lhündrup bestowed all his profound and vast doctrines in their entirety on the supreme spiritual son of his body, speech and mind, the great treasure-finder Gyurme Dorje;[937] and he empowered him as his regent. Then, during his fifty-second year, on Sunday 9 April 1662 (twenty-second day, second month, water tiger year)[938] a protuberance suddenly arose on the crown of his head, from which a vapour, like pale dew by moonlight, or incense smoke, was expelled;[939] and he withdrew from the array of his physical body into the expanse of reality.

Locen Chögyel Tendzin

[489.5-492.5] Trhinle Lhündrup favoured Locen Chögyel Tendzin as his disciple. He was born in the lower village of Edam Ngönpo in 1631 (iron sheep year). Because the propensities of his previous life were clearly manifest, he was recognised as master of his [former] monks and invited to Taktöling, and the other monasteries of his predecessor. Without difficulty he mastered writing, reading, ceremonies and rituals. Having done so, he went to the college of Chongye Pelri to pursue his education. He was ordained as a novice by Sonam Rincen, who occupied that seat, and the name Chögyel Tendzin was conferred upon him. He received all kinds of empowerments and transmissions. Then, beginning with the memorisation of the ceremonial texts for the *Gathering of Intentions* (*dgongs-'dus*) and so forth, and their iconography, iconometry, *torma* sculpture,[940] and chants, he trained himself in all [subjects of study] as far as the great, all-knowing Longcenpa's treatise, *Mind at Rest*, including both the root text and commentary. Afterwards, he also studied, under Nuptön Trakpa Wangpo, the practical applications of such wrathful mantras as those of *Yangdok* (*yang-bzlog*) and *Loktri*,[941] along with Indian and Chinese astrology and divination (*rtsis-dkar-nag*).[942]

In 1648 (earth male mouse), his eighteenth year, Chögyel Tendzin was made disciplinarian of the college, where his strictness set an example. In that same year Rikdzin Trhinle Lhündrup was invited to Chongye Pelri. With the supreme emanation Trhinle Namgyel in the midst [of the assembly], Trhinle Lhündrup conferred on the whole college the empowerment of the *Sūtra which Gathers All Intentions* according to the Zur tradition, in the maṇḍala of coloured powders, along with its instructions and seal of entrustment, and in connection with the rite of great attainment. Subsequently, to a small company of masters and students, he conferred this empowerment according to the Kham tradition, using the maṇḍalas drawn on cloth. At this time, Chögyel Tendzin received both traditions.

Later, at various times and places, he studied many teachings including the *Gathering of the Sugatas of the Eight Transmitted Precepts*, the *Gathering of Intentions*, the *Innermost Spirituality of Vimalamitra*, and the treasure doctrines of Zhikpo Lingpa (*zhig-gling-gi gter-chos*). Moreover, he attended on many genuine learned and accomplished gurus, including Lhatsün Namka Jikme and Sungtrül Tshültrim Dorje, and received from them many empowerments, transmissions, and much guidance on the transmitted precepts and treasures. Then, summoned by the command of the minister Gyari, he proceeded to Kong-ra, where, under Nyangtön Locok Dorje, he studied and mastered the *Kalāpasūtra*, poetics, prosody, and the other branches of linguistic science.

After completing his studies in this way, Chögyel Tendzin lived for sometime at Etongmen and Tshometeng. But, above all, he established his residence at the monastery of Taktöling. He persevered secretly in rites of service and attainment[943] and thereby developed excellent experiences and realisations. Powerful signs that the protectors worked in his service constantly occurred, so even the villagers of those districts were afraid to contradict the order of "Lama Lingpa" [i.e. the guru of Taktöling, Chögyel Tendzin] lest the punishments of the doctrine protectors be forthcoming.

In 1662 (water tiger), his thirty-second year, in particular, he went to Tarling and received some of the treasure doctrines of Pema Lingpa from the great treasure-finder Gyurme Dorje. At that time Gyurme Dorje learned that the continuous lineage of the empowerment of the *Sūtra* and its practical techniques, which he had [formerly] received from his venerable father [Trhinle Lhündrup], were purely held [by Chögyel Tendzin]. Later, therefore, Chögyel Tendzin was invited to [Mindröling,] the seat of that precious, great treasure-finder, where he offered him that empowerment of the *Sūtra*.[944] Thus, Chögyel Tendzin unsurpassably benefitted the teaching of the Ancient Translation School. During his seventy-eighth year, in May/June 1708 (fourth month, earth mouse), he passed away at the monastery of Taktöling.

So it was that, with regard to the transmitted precepts, the number of disciples of the three ancestral Zurs directly multiplied, and countless [lineages] spread forth from them. It is therefore truly said that the great lord of secrets, Dropukpa, in whose lifetime these teachings became widely propagated, was the Lord of Secrets [Guhyapati Vajrapāṇi] himself, born in [Tibet], the land of snow mountains, for the purpose of increasing the teaching of the mantras.

Later, as the result of the increasing degeneration [of the age], the teaching of the Ancient Translation School gradually became sparse, until it was no more visible than the streams of autumn. At this juncture, the great treasure-finder and king of the doctrine, Gyurme Dorje, and the all-knowing, great translator Ngawang Chöpel [i.e. Dharmaśrī, who were spiritual] father and son, along with the host of their disciples, assumed responsibility for the aspirations of the great master Padmasambhava, who had been the crown ornament of the whole populace of the Land of Snows, and for those of Vairocana and Yudra Nyingpo. They united all the fragile streams of instruction from all quarters and made them flow together into an inexhaustible, vast reservoir of teaching; and thus they raised anew the great, unfailing banner of the trilogy of the *Sūtra which Gathers All Intentions*, the *Magical Net*, and the *Mental Class*. A brief biography of the supreme, great treasure-finder will be found below [pp. 825-34].

Locen Dharmaśrī

[492.5-498.6] Now, the great translator Dharmaśrī, the sun of the teaching, was born in 1654 (wood male horse year) as the younger brother of the precious, great treasure-finder Gyurme Dorje. He received the vows of a layman adhering to the threefold refuge from that venerable, treasure-finding guru, who named him Tendzin Jamyang Wangpo. In his fifteenth year he was ordained by the all-knowing Great Fifth Dalai Lama and the name Ngawang Chöpel was conferred upon him along with the vows of a novice. Then, in his twentieth year, he was fully ordained by that same preceptor. Later, complying with his royal order,

Locen Dharmaśrī

he again received the pure lineage of the vows according to the Lower Tibetan Vinaya of the Ancient Translation School from Kharap Zhelngane Köncok Tendzin.

From his guru [Gyurme Dorje], the venerable and great treasure-finder, Dharmaśrī received the vows of a bodhisattva according to the three traditions and so cultivated an enlightened aspiration. His spirituality had matured because, previously, during his twelfth year he had received from him the empowerment of the *Innermost Spirituality of the Awareness-holder* (*rig-'dzin thugs-thig*) in conjunction with the maṇḍala of coloured powders. Both the *prātimokṣa* and bodhisattva vows which he received thereafter arose within him as the essence of the corresponding vows derived from his moral discipline in the mantras; so his mind was well bound.[945]

Dharmaśrī fully mastered reading, writing, ceremonies and rituals. In his sixteenth year he attended Kungtang Paṇcen Shenyen Namgyel's expositions of the *Kalāpasūtra* and prosody in their entirety, his expositions of the Rañjanā, Vivarta (*Vartula*)[946] and other scripts, and those of the *Thirty Verses and Introduction to Gender* (*sum-rtags*, T 4348-9), and of all other branches of linguistic science. Under Dumpa Töndrup

Wangyel he studied Indian and Chinese astrology and divination, the *Svarodaya* (*dbyangs-'char*, T 4326-7)[947] and so forth. He heard Taklung Trapa's explanations of the grammatical tables of the *Sārasvata Grammar* (T 4423), of *sandhi* and verbal derivation according to the *Grammar of Candragomin* and of the prosody of light metrical feet [*yang-pa'i bya-ba*; from the *Precious Source of Prosody*, T 4303-4]. He attended the great treasure-finding guru's expositions of the *Mirror of Poetics*, and of dance, iconometry, and chant according to the unique tradition of the Ancient Translation School. And all of these he mastered thoroughly.

Under his elder brother Gyelse Tenpei Nyima, Dharmaśrī became learned in the practical application and technical jargon of the Vinaya. Just by receiving [the transmission] of most texts, including *Mind at Rest* and the *Treasury of the Scriptural and Logical [Background for] the Vinaya* (*'dul-ba lung-rigs gter-mdzod*), an unimpeded understanding arose. From the spiritual benefactor Sangye Chödar he received the exegeses of the Vinaya, Abhidharma, and Transcendental Perfection. From Kungtang Paṇcen he received the exegeses of the *Lecture Notes on the Middle Way* (*dbu-ma'i stong-thun*) and of the *Three Hundred Verses on the Vinaya* (*Śrāmaṇerakārikā*, T 4124). He studied the exegesis of the *Profound Inner Meaning* under Khedrup Chökyong Gyeltsen. And in the presence of the venerable guru Gyurme Dorje he studied many scriptures of the great, all-knowing doctrine master, Longcenpa; of the masters of the Zur lineage; and of the great Rongzompa. Thus, his mind was liberated, so whatever he studied or considered he did not treat superficially but was able to apply directly to his own mind. This, he said, was owing to the kindness [of his brother, the great treasure-finder].

When, in particular, Dharmaśrī heard the great treasure-finding guru deliver an oral exegesis of the *Secret Nucleus* which combined the *Parkap Commentary* and *Yungtönpa's Commentary*, he plumbed the depths of all the overt and hidden meanings of that tantra. He studied, in the manner of a vase being filled to the brim, all the existing transmitted empowerments, exegetical transmissions, and transmitted esoteric instructions of the classes of the tantras and means for attainment of the Ancient Translation School, including the trilogy of the *Sūtra which Gathers All Intentions*, the *Magical Net*, and the *Mental Class*. Among the treasures he received the empowerments, transmissions, and esoteric instructions for all the treasure doctrines of most of the famous treasure-finders, of which the foremost were the *Earlier and Later Treasure Troves*. And he received, too, the entire transmission of the *Collected Tantras of the Nyingmapa*, which is the root of all [the teachings mentioned here]. Moreover, from Rikdzin Pema Trhinle, Dharmaśrī received the empowerment of the complete *Kālacakra* and the empowerment of the peaceful and wrathful deities of the *Magical Net*.

These must suffice as illustrations: It is impossible to describe the extent to which Dharmaśrī studied, considered, and meditated upon an ocean of doctrinal systems, belonging to various traditions, under some twenty tutors of the ancient and new translation schools, without partiality.

For the sake of the teaching, Locen Dharmaśrī gave the vows of complete ordination to four hundred and forty-seven monks, and those of the novitiate to one thousand two hundred and ninety-eight. From his forty-eighth year to his sixty-fourth, during both the summer and winter sessions, he continuously turned the doctrinal wheel of the *Tantra of the Secret Nucleus* on behalf of about sixty members of the community of awareness-holders, who were intelligent and endowed with supreme good fortune. He also taught many great texts, including the *Ascertainment of the Three Vows*,[948] Transcendental Perfection, and the Vinaya. Eight times he conferred solely the empowerment of the peaceful and wrathful deities of the *Magical Net*, thrice that of the *Sūtra which Gathers All Intentions* and five times that of the *Churner of the Depths of Hell* (*na-rak dong-sprugs*), et cetera. In this way, it seems, he taught all the empowerments, transmissions, and [systems of] experiential guidance of the transmitted precepts and treasures of the ancient and new translation schools, which he had himself received, not less than three or four times each.

In particular, he conferred on Ngawang Künga Trashi, the great lord of the glorious Sakyapa, a great many doctrines and transmissions including the complete empowerments and transmissions of the *New Treasures* [*gter-gsar*, i.e. those of Gyurme Dorje],[949] the *Guidance which Lays Bare the Teaching on the Great Compassionate One* (*thugs-rje-chen-po'i smar-khrid*), and the empowerment of the *Razor Kīla* (*phur-pa spu-gri*). In his fifty-ninth year, 1712 (water dragon), Dharmaśrī was invited to Chamdo in Dokam, where he matured and liberated the minds of Phakpalha Gyelwa Gyamtso, Zhiwa Zangpo and Ngawang Trülku by means of many nectar-like empowerments, transmissions, and esoteric instructions of the ancient and new traditions, without bias. These included the entire cycle of the *New Treasures* (*gter-gsar-skor yongs-rdzogs*), the *Guru as the Gathering of Secrets* (*bla-ma gsang-'dus*), the *Red Wrathful Guru according to the Treasure of Nyang* (*nyang-gter drag-dmar*), the *Razor Kīla*, the *Churner of the Depths of Hell*, and the *Great Compassionate One according to the Tradition of the King* (*thugs-rje chen-po rgyal-po lugs*).

Dharmaśrī even taught the conventional sciences, like grammar, prosody and poetics, not less than five or six times each, according to the intellectual capabilities of particular aspirants. In short, this holy individual lived out his entire life performing bountiful acts in the service of the teaching, in accord with the three ways of the wise [i.e. teaching, debate, and composition]; and in so doing he disclosed the naturally manifest, impartial intention of the Great Perfection. Thus, he was indisputably one who dwelt on the great level of a sublime [bodhisattva].

In order that the teaching might endure for a long time, Locen Dharmaśrī composed the texts making up his eighteen-volume *Collected Works* (*bka'-bum*), beginning with his unprecedented writings on the intentional meaning of the *Sūtra which Gathers All Intentions* and the *Magical Net*, which are in the form of great commentarial vehicles, and continuing through to his works on the conventional sciences. It is manifestly a great treasure trove of perfect treatises and eloquence.

Concerning the sons who were born from his speech: Among most of the great individuals who maintained the doctrine during that epoch, it seems that there were none who failed to bow at his feet. Moreover, the host of his disciples who were learned in scripture and logic, and who were endowed with experiential accomplishment, cannot be enumerated.

11 *Later Lineages of the Transmitted Precepts*

THE MINDRÖLING LINEAGE OF THE TRANSMITTED PRECEPTS

[498.6-506.5] So it was that the transmitted precepts of [the empowerments which cause] maturation and [the guidance which causes] liberation, along with the exegetical transmissions, instructions and practical guidance of the transmitted precepts of the Ancient Translation School, in general, as well as the trilogy of the *Sūtra which Gathers All Intentions*, the *Magical Net*, and the *Mental Class*, in particular, fell to the great treasure-finder, Rikdzin Gyurme Dorje. He bestowed them on his younger brother, the great translator Dharmaśrī, an emanation of Yudra Nyingpo, who gave them to Gyelse Rincen Namgyel, an emanation of Vimalamitra. He, in turn, gave them to the great translator's reincarnation, the great preceptor Orgyen Tendzin Dorje. From those two, master and disciple, the lineage divided into many streams, extending all the way from [the monasteries of] Katok, Pelyül, Zhecen,[950] and Dzokcen in Kham, to Gyelmorong in the far east and to the Golok region of Amdo. In these districts the enlightened activities of exegesis and attainment have extensively and uninterruptedly continued until the present day.

It is not possible to describe all the lineage-holders individually, but here, for example, is one major lineage [of the transmitted precepts]: From the great preceptor Oḍḍiyāna [Orgyen Tendzin Dorje], they were transmitted through:

Trhicen Trhinle Namgyel, who was an emanation of Trhinle Lhündrup;
Trhi Pema Wangyel, the emanation of the great treasure-finder [Rikdzin Gyurme Dorje];
Trhi Sangye Künga, an emanation of Yudra Nyingpo.

From the great treasure-finder to this [last-mentioned] master the lineage represents the continuous family line of the Nyö clan,[951] who were holders of indestructible reality.

Then, the lineage continued through:

Do-nga Tendzin Norbu, the Dokam Kyangkar Trülku, who was supreme for his learning, dignity and accomplishment;
the lord of the circle, Gyurme Phendei Özer,[952] or Jampel Dewei Nyima, the emanation of Vajrapāṇi, the Lord of Secrets.

[This last master] took me personally into his following and I obtained the liberating inspiration of the seal of entrustment.

THE MINDRÖLING LINEAGE OF ATIYOGA

Moreover, there is the special lineage of the Great Perfection [which has transmitted] the cycles of the Mental and Spatial classes, as well as the great Innermost Spirituality. Rikdzin Terdak Lingpa [Gyurme Dorje] transmitted this to Gyelse Rincen Namgyel and to the venerable lady Mingyur Peldrön, an emanation of Yeshe Tshogyel.[953] From these two, it was transmitted successively through:

the great preceptor Orgyen Tendzin Dorje;
Trhicen Trhinle Namgyel;
the venerable lady Trhinle Chödrön;
the all-knowing Dorje Ziji, or Jamyang Khyentse Wangpo, who was the combined emanation of the great paṇḍita Vimalamitra and the sovereign, or religious king, Trhisong Detsen;
Jedrung Trhinle Campei Jungne, an emanation of Langdro, and to the all-pervading lord Gyurme Ngedön Wangpo, the magical emanation of Vairocana.[954]

In the presence of these [last] two lords of the circle, I received the entire maturing [empowerment], liberating [guidance], and esoteric instructions, and thus was favoured with the blessing that transferred to me the intention of the true lineage.

THE LINEAGE OF THE *COLLECTED TANTRAS*

Again, one may refer illustratively to the successive lineage of the transmission of the *Collected Tantras* in their entirety. As will be explained below [pp. 793-5], the rivers of the transmitted precepts of the secret tantras, without exception, converged in the great treasure-finder Ratna Lingpa. From him the lineage continued through:

Tshewang Trakpa, his son and heir, who lived to the age of one hundred and ten;
Ngawang Trakpa, [Tshewang Trakpa's] younger brother;
Ngawang Norbu, [the latter's] son;
Norbu Yongdrak, an emanation of Vimalamitra;
Gyelse Norbu Wangyel;
the all-knowing Tshültrim Dorje, the third speech emanation of Pema Lingpa;[955]
Karwang Tshültrim Gyeltsen of Pönlung;
Tendzin Gyurme Dorje, the fourth successive reincarnation of Pema Lingpa's spiritual son Dawa Gyeltsen, and Rikdzin Terdak Lingpa [Gyurme Dorje] of Mindröling.

The lineage of the former [i.e. Tendzin Gyurme Dorje] continued through:

Ngawang Künzang Dorje, the fourth speech emanation of Pema Lingpa;
Gyurme Chokdrup Pelbar, the fifth successive spiritual son;
Pema Töndrup Trakpa, a holder of indestructible reality;
Künzang Tenpei Gyeltsen, the sixth speech emanation of Pema Lingpa;
Baka Künzang Rikdzin Dorje;
Künzang Tenpei Nyima, the eighth speech emanation of Pema Lingpa;
Baka Rikdzin Khamsum Yongdröl;
Orgyen Namdröl Gyamtso, a holder of indestructible reality;
Gendün Gyamtso, a lord of yoga who had renounced everything.

[Gendün Gyamtso] embraced me with his great kindness.

LINEAGES IN KHAM

The stream of the lineage which descended through Rikdzin Terdak Lingpa was also vastly increased by Jamgön Lodrö Thaye.[956] Therefore, as it is explained here, the genuine teaching of the trilogy of the *Sūtra which Gathers All Intentions*, the *Magical Net*, and the *Mental Class* has continued without decline through to the present day.

The following passage appears in Thuken's *Crystal Mirror of Philosophical Systems* (*thu'u-bkvan-gyi grub-mtha' shel-dkar me-long*):

> A long time has passed since all the essential doctrines of the trilogy of the *Sūtra which Gathers All Intentions*, the *Magical Net*, and the *Mental Class* and so forth vanished into the primordial purity of original space. The Nyingmapa

> of today merely treat as essential such mimicry as the chanting of ritual manuals, the material elaboration of feast offerings, and the rites of suppression, burnt offerings, casting out *tormas*, et cetera...[957]

Such uncritical prattle is exceedingly false. Since a great scholar like Thuken, who bears up to examination, would never present a corrupt account, we think that this statement was undoubtedly an interpolation made later on by some foolish fanatic.[958]

KATOK

To continue: As has already been described, the seminary of the Vajra Seat at Katok was a unique fountain-head of the teaching of the Ancient Translation School. At a later date its enlightened activity was increased by Rikdzin Düdül Dorje[959] and Longsel Nyingpo. None the less, during the intervening period [which followed] the transmitted precepts gradually became rare there. Sonam Detsen, the reincarnation of Düdül Dorje and the spiritual son of Longsel Nyingpo received them at the feet of the great treasure-finder [Terdak Lingpa] of Mindröling,[960] and restored the teaching of the transmitted precepts from its very foundations. Beginning with his reincarnation, Trime Zhingkyong Gönpo, and the others forming the [incarnate] succession of great individuals who maintained the seat of Katok, as well as with Rikdzin Tshewang Norbu,[961] an emanation of Namkei Nyingpo, and Gyurme Tshewang Chokdrup, a great paṇḍita who was an emanation of the great Nyak Jñānakumāra, [this transmission has continued] through to such teachers of more recent times as Situ Künzi Chöki Gyamtso, and the great preceptor Rikdzin Ngawang Pelzang, a subsequent emanation of Vimalamitra. The teaching of the Conqueror in general, and, in particular, the teaching of the transmitted precepts and treasures of the Ancient Translation School, have been rendered as clear as sunshine by these supreme teachers of living beings, whose learned and accomplished lives and enlightened activities, belonging to the three spheres [of exegesis, attainment, and work], have been utterly amazing and totally without rival.

DZOKCEN

Moreover, there was the lord among accomplished masters, Pema Rikdzin of Dzokcen, who is renowned as the combined emanation of master Kukkurāja and Vimalamitra, and whose life was one of inconceivable learning, dignity, and accomplishment. He went to Dokam at the order, issued with foresight, of the supreme conqueror, the Great

Dzokcen Pema Rikdzin

Fifth [Dalai Lama]. There, he founded the retreat centre of Samten Chöling at Rudam Kyitram,[962] and so became a unique benefactor to the teaching of the Ancient Translation School. His successive incarnations, and his spiritual sons, such as the great treasure-finder Nyima Trakpa, Pönlop Namka Ösel, and Zhecen Rapjam Tenpei Gyeltsen, gave rise to a succession of supreme individuals who, like a chain of golden mountains, maintained the teaching through enlightened activity as expansive as the sky.

Above and beyond that, during the period of the fourth Dzokcen emanation Mingyur Namkei Dorje, Gyelse Zhenpen Thaye, the emanation of the great treasure-finder of Mindröling [Rikdzin Terdak Lingpa], made vast spiritual efforts on behalf of the exegesis and attainment of many textual traditions of the sūtras and mantras, and especially on behalf of the transmitted precepts of the Ancient Translation School. Therefore, he sought out and greatly propagated manuscripts of them, and their continuous empowerments, transmissions, and esoteric instructions. He published some ten volumes of ceremonial arrangements for the *Sūtra which Gathers All Intentions*, the *Magical Net*, and so forth. Thus, his kindness and legacy to the continuous teaching surpass the imagination.

Rikdzin Künzang Sherap

PELYÜL

Similarly, Rikdzin Künzang Sherap, an emanation of Lasum Gyelwa Cangcup, founded the doctrinal centre of Namgyel Cangcup Ling at Pelyül.[963] He gave rise to a great family of learned and accomplished individuals who upheld the teaching, including his spiritual sons, and the play of his successive emanations. Thus, he vastly increased the enlightened activities of exegesis, attainment and work.

At a later date, inspired by both Jamgön Khyentse Wangpo and the great treasure-finder Chogyur Lingpa,[964] Gyatrül Pema Do-nga Tendzin instituted, at that very seat, the annual attainment and worship of the twenty-seven great maṇḍalas of the transmitted precepts of the Ancient Translation School, which are all those of which the continuous empowerment and transmission exists at present;[965] and he newly founded Tartang Do-nga Shedrup Ling. In these and in other ways his enlightened activity in the three spheres was most amazing.

Above and beyond that, by the power of his undeviating enlightened aspiration, Orgyen Do-nga Chöki Nyima published, in about twenty volumes, all the texts which constitute the doctrinal treasury of the transmitted precepts. I have had the good fortune to obtain a set of these books of the transmitted precepts of the Ancient Translation School, of which the foremost is the trilogy of the *Sūtra which Gathers All Intentions*, the *Magical Net*, and the *Mental Class*. On the basis of these, at this juncture when the unbearable twists of time in this unfortunate age have turned Tibet and Kham into wild and savage lands, the dying embers of the teaching have spread in this direction [i.e. India].[966] Thus, it is the amazing mass of the kindness of that master alone, such as can never be repaid, that the life of the teaching has ripened into an unending harvest.

This completes the exposition of the descent of the teaching of the trilogy of the *Sūtra which Gathers All Intentions*, the *Magical Net*, and the *Mental Class*, belonging to the extensive, distant lineage of the transmitted precepts, the fifth part of this book, *Thunder from the Great Conquering Battle-Drum of Devendra*, a history of the precious teaching of the vehicle of indestructible reality according to the Ancient Translation School.

Part Six
The Close Lineages of the Treasures

1 *The Nature, Purpose and Kinds of Treasure*

[511.1-523.2] Now, I shall briefly describe the history of the treasures, [which constitute] extremely profound, close lineages.[967]

THE NATURE OF THE TREASURES

The nature or essence of [teachings discovered as] treasure is indicated by the following passage from the *Sūtra of the Dialogue with the Nāga King* (*Nāgarājaparipṛcchāsūtra*, T 153-5):

> These four are the great treasures, which are inexhaustible: (i) The inexhaustible, great treasure of the unbroken line of the Three Precious Jewels; (ii) the inexhaustible, great treasure of immeasurable and supreme realisation of the doctrine; (iii) the inexhaustible, great treasure of bringing delight to sentient beings; and (iv) the inexhaustible, great treasure which is like the sky.

Similarly, it says in the *Sublime Sūtra of Contemplation which Subsumes All Merits* [*Āryasarvapuṇyasamuccayasamādhisūtra*, T 134, quoted in *Śikṣāsamuccaya*, p.105]:

> O Vimalatejas! the doctrinal treasures of bodhisattvas, great spiritual warriors who desire the doctrine, have been inserted in mountains, ravines, and woods. Dhāraṇīs and limitless approaches to the doctrine, which are set down in books, will also come into their hands.

This explains well the [existence of] treasure doctrines, treasure sites, and the individuals who discover them; and [in that same sūtra] one finds the following passage, indicating the [presence of] celestial doctrines, and so forth:

> For one whose aspiration is perfect the doctrine will emerge from the midst of the sky, and from walls and trees, even though no buddha be present.

Moreover, in various well-known sūtras and tantras the essence, formal definition, enumerations, and purposes of treasures are repeatedly indicated; and these have been renowned in both India and Tibet. The treasures, therefore, have not been invented by specific individuals, such as the Tibetans.

THE PURPOSE OF THE TREASURES

As to the reason for concealing these treasures, it says in the *Sūtra of the River's Play* (*chu-klung rol-pa'i mdo*, DZ Vol.9):

> Conceal the doctrinal texts of my teaching,
> As treasures of mind, [emerging] from mind,
> Or make them cores of the earth:
> Though extremists with wild thoughts
> Will certainly confound the definitive meaning,
> The flow of the river will not be cut off!

And in the words of a treasure discovered by the doctrinal king, Ratna Lingpa:[968]

> Because, generally, I harbour great compassion
> For the Tibetans, who love what is new,
> And for the creatures of this defiled age,
> I have filled the frontiers and the centre with treasures,
> Focal points which are the culmination of utter profundity;
> And I have prayed that these be found by my worthy sons.
> In the future, sophists, verbally skilled,
> Anchorites and others who are biased, inflated with
> prejudice,
> Will promote themselves and dispute my treasures.
> But most religious persons in the defiled age will be
> guided by treasures.
> They are profound and complete, unobscured,
> comprehensive:
> Each instruction will certainly liberate someone.
> Therefore, O worthy and well-trained ones, whose
> propensities have awakened,
> If you remember death, then experience these
> treasure doctrines!
> You will obtain liberation's path in one lifetime,
> O my followers!
> In the defiled age all worthy devotees of treasure
> Will be those who now have beheld the guru's visage
> and formed an aspiration.

Since you all have such propensities, cultivate joy!
These words of mine are more rare than gold, or jewels!

Such statements may be found in other treasure texts, too, without limit. Accordingly, concerning the transmitted precepts [of the distant lineage]: During this defiled age their transmitted empowerments and instructions have become adulterated like milk in the market-place. Because [their lineages] have been interrupted by many lineage-holders, the fresh descent of their blessing has been weakened by many violations of the commitments, as well as by pollution [of the teachings] due to interpolations. But, regarding the contents of the treasures: The discoverers of treasure were emanations who had been taken into the following of the great Padmasambhava of Oḍḍiyāna himself, and had thus obtained complete transmission of the empowerments and instructions, which bring about maturation and liberation. By bringing forth in this way profound doctrines which embody the unfading, moist breath of the ḍākinīs, they form close lineages, unequalled in the splendour of their blessings.

THE LINEAGES OF THE TREASURES

It is well known that [the teachings discovered as] treasure have six lineages, because they possess three special lineages over and above the intentional, symbolic and aural lineages which have already been described.[969] These comprise: [the lineage empowered by enlightened aspiration, the lineage of prophetically declared spiritual succession, and the lineage of the ḍākinīs' seal of entrustment].

In the *lineage empowered by enlightened aspiration* the concealer has sealed [the treasure doctrines] with the following statement of aspiration embodying a declaration of truth: "May the individual who has power over such and such a treasure trove come to reveal it!"

In the *lineage of prophetically declared spiritual succession* the person destined to reveal the treasure has been entrusted with the central intention, namely, the genuine pristine cognition that is the object of illustration, and has also received encouragement through a prophetic declaration of future events.

In the *lineage of the ḍākinīs' seal of entrustment* illustrations [of that intention] are verbally arranged in symbolic writing and then invisibly sealed in indestructible rocks, wealth-filled lakes, and immutable chests, their identifying inventories having first been entrusted to their respective treasure lords.[970] When the predicted time arrives, the power of [the concealer's] aspiration matures, the propensities [of the discoverer] awaken, and the lord of the treasure offers encouragement. The appropriate chest, containing all kinds of profound treasure, with or without an inventory, then comes into the hands of the treasure-finder.

THE CONCEALMENT OF THE EARTH TREASURES

In particular, most of the profound doctrines contained in the treasures were encoded in the symbolic script of the ḍākinīs. They cannot be deciphered by any other than the person who has the right fortune; and because that person must encounter the actual inscribed seal indicative of the transmitted precepts of the great Orgyen [Padmasambhava], the lineage is therefore uninterrupted by ordinary people. Its source is venerable, its symbolic conventions uncontrived, its words unconfounded, and its meaning unerring. Since [such treasures] were translated from the secret symbols of the ḍākinīs, the texts are profound and their blessing great. The unworthy, no matter how keen their intelligence, are like blind men examining an elephant and cannot appraise even a portion of them. The revealers of treasure are genuinely beyond the perceptual range of ordinary beings.

In this country of Tibet the one who instructed numberless persons in need of training by enlightened activities associated with the nucleus of the teaching, the vehicle of indestructible reality in general, and the profound treasures in particular, was the Second Buddha, Padmasambhava.[971] In the *Sūtra of Final Nirvāṇa* the Buddha prophesied:

> After my nirvāṇa,
> When about twelve years have passed,
> An individual greater than myself will appear
> On the lake isle of Dhanakośa.

This great master was not merely an individual who traversed the sequence of the path, or a sublime [bodhisattva] abiding on [any of the ten] levels. Indeed, he was the emanational body of Buddha Amitābha, the peerless Śākya King, and others, made manifest in order to train, by various means, those beings, human and non-human, who are difficult to train. It is thus impossible, even for great sublime beings, to describe just an aspect of his career. None the less, a brief outline has already been given above. It was his particularly great enlightened activity to conceal uncountable treasure troves containing doctrines, wealth, medicines, astrological calculations, images, sacramental substances and so forth in the lands of India, Nepal, and Tibet, with the intention of providing a harvest for future disciples and for the teaching.

Above all, skilfully teaching each according to his needs here in Tibet, Guru Rinpoche taught approaches to the doctrine in general, and, in particular, an infinite mass of tantras, transmissions, esoteric instructions and rites associated with the three classes of yoga [Mahāyoga, Anuyoga, and Atiyoga]. All of those transmitted precepts were compiled by the mistress of secrets, the queen of the expanse, Yeshe Tshogyel, who retained them in her infallible memory. She arranged them on five kinds of yellow scroll [symbolising the five families] in the symbolic script of the ḍākinīs and, inserting them in various treasure chests, sealed them to be indestructible. Guru Padmasambhava and his consort, alone or in the company of the king and his subjects, concealed them in different locations and entrusted them to their respective treasure protectors. Yeshe Tshogyel, in particular, lived for more than a hundred years after the guru's departure for Cāmaradvīpa and concealed an inconceivable number of treasure troves in upper, middle and lower Tibet.[972] In this way she fulfilled her service to the treasures.

Moreover, the great paṇḍita Vimalamitra, the generations of the religious kings, the great translator Vairocana, Nup Saṅgye Yeshe, Namkei Nyingpo, Nyak Jñānakumāra, Nanam Dorje Düjom, and Nyangben Tingdzin Zangpo and others also concealed many profound treasures. They consecrated these so that later, when the time was ripe for disciples to be trained, the treasures would be practised, and so benefit living beings. In accord with their prophecies and prayers, the king and his subjects have appeared as an ongoing, magical play of fortunate individuals and emanations, of varied social class and life-style, who have acted on behalf of the teaching and of living beings.

PURE VISIONS AND TREASURES OF INTENTION

All the above refers primarily to the appearance of the earth treasures. As for the origins of the profound pure visions and treasures of intention, however, there is a particular aspiration of the bodhisattvas [*Introduction to the Conduct of a Bodhisattva,* Ch.10, v.37] which says:

> May all corporeal beings continually hear
> The sounds of the doctrine
> From birds and from trees,
> From all the light rays and even from the sky.

It is said that owing to the power of such aspirations, and also because bodhisattvas have no reason to be destitute of the doctrine, they continually hear the sound of the doctrine, even in the sounds of the elements and wild animals. Buddhas and bodhisattvas indeed reveal themselves in visions and teach the doctrine, as it says in the *Sūtra of Contemplation which Subsumes All Merits*:

> O Vimalatejas! the great bodhisattvas who are desirous of the doctrine and who are endowed with perfect aspiration and reverence, will behold the visage of the Transcendent Lord Buddha and hear his doctrine even though they reside in another region of the universe.

Particularly, in the perception of great sublime beings there is only a pure vision [of reality]; impure vision does not occur. Through the perpetual round of the three times they continuously engage in many wonderful doctrinal discussions with their myriad favoured deities of the three roots; and thence there emerge limitless, profound instructions. These are the pure visionary doctrines, which, in accord with the devoted attitudes of specific individuals, have been suitable for propagation amongst the fortunate. Their appearance within the perceptual range of all may be known from the lives of many learned and accomplished masters of India and from those of the spiritual benefactors, treasure-finders, and accomplished masters of the ancient and new traditions of Tibet, impartially.

In the same way there are those [teachings] known as the treasures of intention, on which a sūtra says:

> O Mañjuśrī! know that just as the four elements originate from the treasure of space, so do all doctrines originate from the treasure of the Conqueror's mind. Thereby one should relish the significance of this treasure.

Accordingly, it is said that the treasure troves of the doctrine pour forth from the spatial expanse of the intention of all sublime individuals.

The following passage also occurs in the *Sūtra which Genuinely Comprises the Entire Doctrine*:

> To the bodhisattva whose aspiration is pure all appropriate instructions and teachings come forth just as he wishes.

And again, there is a sūtra which says:

> If you have the confidence of certainty with respect to
> ultimate meaning,
> One hundred thousand doctrinal treasures will pour
> forth from your mind.

Just so, up to the present day, in all the lands of India, Nepal and Tibet, an infinite number of profound instructions have emerged from the profound intentions of great learned and accomplished masters.[973] In brief, these masters have opened at will the doors of doctrines, wealth, sacramental substances,[974] et cetera; and by wonderful enlightened activity, the four ways of liberation,[975] they will maintain the true doctrine, down to the end of this evil age. Even in places where the teachings of the Vinaya and the sūtras do not exist, the teaching of the vehicle of indestructible reality, which is that of the secret mantra, spreads little by little, and expands, without decline. Such is the extensive and continuous enlightened activity [of the treasures] which liberates all beings who are hard to train. Guru [Padmasambhava] himself has asserted:

> In the defiled age the teaching's limits
> Will be preserved by treasures.

Accordingly, until the teaching of the Fifth Guide [Maitreya] arises, the activity of the profound treasures will never decline.

2 *Biographies of the Treasure-finders*

[523.2-523.6] Having thus explained the treasures in general, it will not be possible here to elaborate specifically and at length on the lives of the hosts of accomplished awareness-holders who have revealed the treasures. Included among them are those treasure-finders who have been roughly prophesied, along with their eras and characteristics, in [the various recensions of] the *Injunctions of Padma* (*padma bka'i thang-yig-rnams*),[976] as well as those who have appeared without being clearly referred to therein, but are none the less universally renowned as valid. [All their lives] can be learned from the earlier and later versions of the *Biographies of the Hundred Treasure-finders* (*gter-ston brgya-rtsa'i rnam-thar snga-phyi*)[977] and elsewhere. I have already described the lives of a few supreme, accomplished masters who were successors to the treasure doctrines in the course of several of the foregoing lineages. Here, I shall give only the essential accounts of a few of the most important proven promulgators of the Ancient Translation School in general, with respect to both the transmitted precepts and the treasures.

3 *Sangye Lama*

[523.6-525.5] The earliest of all treasure-finders was Sangye Lama. He was the first of the thirteen incarnations of Gyelse Lharje, during which he was always a treasure-finder. He was born at Tshowar in Latö, approximately during the early part of the life of the great translator Rincen Zangpo,[978] and lived as a shaven-headed monk who was an adherent of the mantra tradition. From a cross-beam in the temple of Lowo Gekar in Ngari he brought forth the *Trio of the Guru, Great Perfection, and Great Compassionate One* (*bla-rdzogs-thugs-gsum*); from the nearby rock of Tamdringül the *Combined Means for Attainment of the Three Roots called "Perpetual Vision of Accomplishment"* (*rtsa-gsum dril-sgrub dngos-grub brtan-gzigs*); and from Thangwar, Khoklang Rock and elsewhere the *Hayagrīva who Overpowers Arrogant Spirits* (*rta-mgrin dregs-pa zil-gnon*), many rituals of the sūtra tradition which had been translated from Chinese, notes on their ritual variants (*kha-bsgyur*), et cetera. He travelled throughout Central Tibet and Tsang, benefitted living creatures to the utmost, and lived until about the age of eighty. It is said that, later, Chöje Lingpa[979] also saw a kīla preserved at Tsāri Tshokar, which had come from Sangye Lama's treasures. The family of that treasure-finder continued until a later time in the region of Latö; and it seems that the treasure-finder called Sangye Bar, too, was born into this same family.

Because of their extreme antiquity, the empowerments, transmissions and texts of Sangye Lama's treasures did not continue later on, excepting the continuous transmission of a few minor sūtras. However, the vision of pristine cognition of the great Orgyen, the knower of the three times, and his spiritual sons, as well as their compassion, have no need for writing. With special consideration for the subjects of Tibet during the extremes of this defiled age, they inspired Pema Ösel Do-nga Lingpa [Jamyang Khyentse Wangpo], a unique charioteer of the ocean of profound treasures who had arisen as the unimpeded, magical emanation of the compassion of Vimalamitra and of the ancestral kings Trhisong Detsen and Relpacen, to be the master of seven successions of transmitted precepts. Thus, all the profound treasures of the hundred treasure-finders directly and indirectly came into his hands, and indestructible prophecies repeatedly disclosed to him the true significance of these opportune occasions. So it was that the yellow scroll of the *Twenty-onefold Dialogue concerning the Combined Means for the Attainment of the Three Roots* (*rtsa-gsum dril-sgrub zhu-lan nyer-gcig-pa*), which was the essence of the profound treasures of this great emanational treasure-finder Sangye Lama, fell into Khyentse Rinpoche's hands.[980] The root text of the treasure could not be established, but Khyentse Rinpoche arranged the ceremonies for the rites and for the *torma* empowerment[981] in accordance with the intention of the text and propagated them. They are found in the *Great Store of Precious Treasures* (*rin-chen gter-gyi mdzod chen-po*).

Sangye Lama

4 *Trapa Ngönshe*

[525.5-527.3] Trapa Ngönshe, a simultaneous emanation of Shüpu Pelgi Senge and the great translator Vairocana, was born in 1012 (water male mouse year preceding the first cycle), into a family descended from Chim Dorje Peucung, at Kyi in Tra, Yoru. As a youth he awoke to the family of the true doctrine and entered the seminary of Samye. He was ordained as a novice by Yamshü Gyelwa-ö, a preceptor who had been Lume's disciple. He became known as Trapa because he was a native of Tra, and Ngönshe because his learning in the Abhidharma was extensive.[982] His ordination name was Wangcuk Bar. From above the door of the central shrine [at Samye] he extracted the *Secret Means for the Attainment of Red Jambhala* (*dzam-dmar gsang-sgrub*) and the *Tantra of the Yakṣa Vajra Mārajit* (*gnod-sbyin rdo-rje bdud-'dul-gyi rgyud*) along with its means for attainment.[983] In particular, as had been prophesied by Zhanglön,[984] he brought forth the master copies[985] of the *Four Glorious Tantras of Medical Science* (*gso-ba rig-pa dpal-ldan rgyud-bzhi'i bla-dpe*),[986] which had been translated by the great translator Vairocana, from the "Vase Pillar" in the middle storey of the innermost shrine at Samye, at three *chutsö* past midnight [approximately 1.12 a.m.] on Wednesday 19 July 1038 (fifteenth day, seventh month, earth male tiger year). He copied the books and returned the originals to their proper resting place. Then he concealed the copies for about one year. Afterwards, he gave them to Khutön Tarma-tra, the spiritual benefactor from Yarlung. The transmitted precepts fell to Yutok Yönten Gönpo, the second king of physicians in [Tibet] the range of snow mountains, who maintained the enlightened activity [of this medical tradition]. Thus, the enlightened activity and wonderful achievements of this master alone have been inconceivable.

By propitiating Jambhala, Trapa Ngönshe was granted the accomplishment of an abundance of gold. On that basis, he founded the great seminary of glorious Tratang[987] in the lower valley of Tranang, and built many similar establishments. Since he acted as master of all those, and of the seminary at Samye as well, he seems to have been a great spiritual benefactor. Various streams of empowerment and transmission connected with the two aforementioned yakṣas [*Red Jambhala* and *Vajra Mārajit*], and the lineage of the exegetical transmission of the *Four Tantras of Medical Science* (*gso-dpyad rgyud-bzhi*), have continued without interruption.

Trapa Ngönshe

5 *Nyang-rel Nyima Özer*

[527.3-533.5] The first of those who were famed as the five kingly treasure-finders and the three supreme emanations was Nyang-rel Nyima Özer, the deliberate reincarnation of the religious king Tshangpa Lhei Metok [i.e. Trhisong Detsen].[988] He was born at Sergön in Dzesa, a part of Tamshül in Lhodrak, in 1136 (fire male dragon year, second cycle).[989] His father was Nyangtön Chöki Khorlo, and his mother Pema Dewatsel. From his childhood onwards there were limitless wonderful signs: In his eighth year he had many pure visions of the Transcendent Lord Śākyendra,[990] the Great Compassionate One, Guru Rinpoche and others, and he was exhilarated for a whole month. In particular, one evening he envisaged Guru Rinpoche riding upon a white horse, the hoofs of which were supported by the ḍākinīs of the four classes. Guru Rinpoche gave him the four empowerments with nectar from his vase, as a result of which Nyang-rel had three experiences, which were like the sky being rent open, the earth shaking, and mountains moving. Consequently, his conduct underwent various changes and everyone held him to be insane. He received the empowerment of Hayagrīva from his father and after propitiating that deity at Dzepu Kang-ra had a vision of him. The neighing of a horse resounded from his copper kīla and Nyang-rel left the impressions of his hands and feet in rock. In accord with a prophetic declaration of the ḍākinīs he went to the base of Mawocok Rock, where a ḍākinī of pristine cognition conferred upon him the name Nyima Özer. He became known thus thereafter.

Guru Rinpoche emanated as a yogin called Wangcuk Dorje, who granted Nyang-rel essential documents containing an inventory [of treasures] and gave him lessons. Also, the inventories of Trapa Ngönshe and the Rashak Treasure-finder,[991] with their supplements, came into his hands. In accordance with them he proceeded to the treasure site at the base of Sinmo Parje Rock. He stayed the night there and on the following day a woman who was an emanation of Yeshe Tshogyel came bringing two antelope-skin chests loaded on a white mule. From within one of them she brought out a tiger-skin casket and offered it to Nyang-rel. He also found the entrance to the treasures and discovered a copper casket, a clay vase, images, sacramental objects, and many other riches. From the copper casket there came forth [the doctrinal cycles of] the *Great Compassionate One* (*thugs-rje chen-po*) and the *Peaceful and Wrathful Aspects of the Guru* (*gu-ru zhi-drag*); from the clay vase the *Cycle of Mahākāla and Malevolent Mantras* (*mgon-po dang ngan-sngags-kyi skor*); and from the tiger-skin casket many doctrinal cycles of the ḍākinīs (*mkha'-'gro'i chos-skor*).

Nyang-rel Nyima Özer

Sometime thereafter a broken finger from an image was given to him by a merchant. Inside of it Nyang-rel found an inventory, following which he discovered two treasure chests, one brownish and the other pale gray, behind an image of Vairocana at Khoting. From inside the brownish chest there came forth the *Tantra of the Gathering of the Sugatas of the Eight Transmitted Precepts*, along with its transmissions and esoteric instructions, arranged in one hundred and thirty doctrinal topics (*bka'-brgyad bde-gshegs 'dus-pa'i rgyud-lung-man-ngag-dang-bcas-pa'i chos-tshan brgya-dang sum-cur bkod-pa*), written in the handwriting of Vairocana and that of Denma Tsemang for use as the religious king Trhisong Detsen's personal copies. Within the pale gray chest he found [images, books, and stūpas] representing respectively the body, speech and mind of Hayagrīva, plus sacraments and much else besides. Moreover, from Samye Chimpu, Sinca Rock in Namkecen, the shrine of Enetrakri, and elsewhere, he also brought forth many treasure troves.

Nyang-rel Nyima Özer attended on numerous gurus including his father, the great Nyangtön; Gyanyönpa Tönden; Zhikpo Nyima Senge; Mel Kawacenpa; and Tönpa Khace.[992] Under [these masters] he studied mantras and dialectics extensively. He practised the attainment of the *Guru as the Gathering of the Three Bodies* (*bla-ma sku-gsum 'dus-pa*) for three years, whereupon he met the master Padmasambhava in person and obtained many oral authorisations. While experientially cultivating the *Guru as the Attainment of Mind* (*bla-ma thugs-sgrub*) at Mutik Shelgi Pagong, Yeshe Tshogyel actually arrived and bestowed on him the text of the *Hundredfold Dialogue of the Ḍākinī* (*mkha'-'gro'i zhu-lan brgya-rtsa*). She led Nyang-rel to the Śītavana charnel ground, where the master Guru Rinpoche and the eight awareness-holders who were successors to the transmitted precepts gave him, separately, the empowerments of the *Eight Transmitted Precepts* (*bka'-brgyad*), in general and in particular. They also gave him the tantras and the esoteric instructions in their entirety.

Nyang-rel took Cobuma, an emanation of Yeshe Tshogyel, to be his wife, and she bore him two sons, Drogön Namka Özer and Namka Pelwa, an emanation of Avalokiteśvara. Once, when the accomplished master Ngödrup arrived, Nyang-rel volunteered that he possessed the treasure troves of the *Eight Transmitted Precepts*. Ngödrup then stated that he had preserved the related *Transmitted Precepts of the Narrow Path to the Fortress* (*rdzong-'phrang bka'-ma*). Nyang-rel therefore studied them as well and blended together, into one stream, the transmitted precepts and the treasures. The accomplished master Ngödrup also gave him the *Five Scrolls of the Doctrinal Cycle of the Great Compassionate One* (*thugs-rje chen-po'i chos-skor shog-dril lnga*) which he had discovered in Lhasa, saying, "Now, you are their master."[993]

Once, while Nyang-rel was performing the means for the attainment of elixir (*sman-sgrub*) the elixir goddess personally offered moist myrobalan to him, together with the leaves.[994] He could ascend, cross-legged, into the sky, travel without his feet touching the ground, and display countless other miraculous abilities. He devoted his whole life to meditative attainment and the advancement of education together. Later, his enlightened activity became as vast as space; so his legacy to the teaching was inconceivable.

In his sixty-ninth year, 1204 (wood male mouse),[995] Nyang-rel Nyima Özer displayed vast wondrous omens. Above all, a white syllable HRĪḤ emerged from his heart and went off to Sukhāvatī. In this way did he withdraw from the array of his body. He had predicted that three emanations of his body, speech, and mind would arise simultaneously.

When Chak Lotsāwa went to cremate the master's remains, he failed to start a fire. Then the pyre ignited all by itself and everyone saw a young boy in the crematorium, surrounded by ḍākinīs, and chanting HA RI ṆI SA with them, as well as many other omens. Many extraordinary relics were left behind as objects of veneration.

During the actual funeral ceremonies, the great paṇḍita Śākyaśrī and his followers were invited to attend, and they were delighted with vast offerings of gold. Nyang-rel's son, thinking he should be ordained as a novice asked Śākyaśrī, who refused to grant his request, saying, "Both of you, father and son, have been great bodhisattvas; and I cannot interrupt a family line of bodhisattvas. Maintaining your present lifestyle you will be of great benefit to living creatures."

Śākyaśrī's extensive praise of both the doctrine and the man shows that, from the start, Nyang-rel was universally renowned as a great indisputable and authentic treasure-finder. Moreover, even biased partisans of the new translation schools are free from the taint of having harboured perverse notions [about Nyang-rel], and he became as famous in the Land of Snows as the sun and moon.

Nyang-rel's son and main disciple, Drogön Namka Pelwa, was the master of his teaching, to whom the succession of the transmitted precepts of maturation and liberation was entrusted in its entirety. A prophetic declaration states him to have been the emanation of Avalokiteśvara. Thinking to fulfil [his father's] intention, through his exceedingly great miraculous abilities he drove the stones in front of Mount Shampo into the sky, as if they were herds of sheep. Others never knew where they came from, but they all landed in a grey mass on the banks of the Kyicu in Lhasa, where they were used for [the reconstruction of] the dike[996] [which protected the image of] Lord [Śākyamuni in Lhasa]. It is said that in past times those stones could be distinguished without error.

Drogön Namka Pelwa also commissioned one hundred and eight wall-sized paintings in the Nepali style. He possessed exceedingly great occult powers and abilities and was served by the protectors of the doctrine. Therefore, he could destroy all his enemies with lightning, hail and so forth, by sheer force at any time of the day, disregarding the season or month.[997] There are many stories which illustrate this. Because of his inconceivable compassion Guru Chöwang and many other emanations became his disciples.

His son, Ngadak Loden, was an emanation of Mañjuśrī, and his son Ngadak Düdül, in turn, an emanation of Vajrapāṇi. Thus, from these emanations of [the Lords of] the Three Families, who are praised in scripture, there developed successively the "lineage of the sons". There were also the lineages of Nyang-rel Nyima Özer's disciples, the foremost of whom were the five "sons who were successors to the transmitted precepts", including Nyö Tragyel, Zhikpo Dütsi, and Menlungpa Mikyö Dorje. Up to the present day these lineages have all-pervasively increased his doctrinal activity throughout Tibet, both on the frontiers, and in central districts.

6 *Guru Chöki Wangcuk*

[533.5-552.3] The second of the famed five kingly treasure-finders and the three supreme emanations was the precious Guru Chöki Wangcuk. The religious king Trhisong Detsen reached the highest fruition in the form of the precious Ngadak Nyang[-rel Nyima Özer] and had attained buddhahood on [the level called] Unattached Lotus Endowed.[998] Guru Chöki Wangcuk was then revealed as an emanation of his buddha-speech.

Moreover, during the ancient propagation of the teaching a Pönpo named Nyaring had vowed to kill King Trhisong by bringing down a thunderbolt. At that, a powerful mantra adept called Pangje Tsentram, who was a disciple of master Padmasambhava, Vimalamitra, and Vairocana, raised his index finger menacingly, and the five thunderbolts which the Pönpo brought down simultaneously were returned to be his own executioners. The Pönpo's village was devastated. The king conferred great rewards on the mantra adept, whose son, Pang Rikdzin Nyingpo, was appointed to be the officiating priest of the four Further Taming temples.[999] Once a year he would visit Khoting to conduct the rites of worship there, and on one such occasion he met the great minister of Layak Dzawar, who presented him with many riches and estates. He accepted them, saying, "This was my land during a previous life."

From Pang's son, Künkyen Sherap Gyelpo, there descended an unbroken line of sagacious and powerful masters; and in that line there arose one Pangtön Trupei Nyingpo. He asked Lama Sangye Nyigom to grant him the vows of celibacy, but was told, "One [married] bodhisattva can benefit living creatures more than an assembly of eight monks. So, I will not break a line of bodhisattvas."

While Pangtön was living at home, he received a prophetic declaration telling him to take the ḍākinī Kargi Wangmo to be his wife. Knowing that this referred to one Karza Gönkyi, who was descended from a family of accomplished masters who could roam through the sky, he married her.

When he was studying the *Root Fragment of Vajrakīla* under Drigung Kyopa,[1000] the latter said to him, "Instruct your youngest son in the doctrine. He will undertake enlightened activity." Zhang Rinpoche had also said to him, "Geshe Locungpa! maybe I will be reborn as your son! That's a joke. But you *will* have a son like me." Pangtön obtained many other prophecies in the same vein.

Guru Chöki Wangcuk

When [the son who had been thus prophesied] entered his mother's womb, there were wonderful omens: The sun and moon were conjoined and vanished into the crown of her head; from her womb there resounded the sound of the unborn syllable A; verses were heard when she was handed a ceremonial silk arrow;[1001] and so forth. Then, at sunrise on Thursday 19 January 1212 (fifteenth day, first month, water male monkey year, fourth cycle)[1002] the boy was born. At the time, his father was making a gold copy of the *Litany of the Names of Mañjuśrī* and, to check the coincidence, noted that he had just reached the words,

> Lord of doctrine, king of doctrine...[1003]

Therefore, the child was named Chöki Wangcuk, "Lord of Doctrine". Seers declared, too, that the infant was worshipped by gods and demons.

Beginning in his fourth year Chöwang learned writing and reading from his father. He studied thirteen treatises on grammar, including the *Sword at the Gateway to Language* (*smra-sgo mtshon-cha*, T 4295), *Five Texts on the Recitation of Sanskrit Formulae* (*rig-klag sde-lnga*), and the *Great Vivarta* (*bi-barta chen-mo*); ten treatises on the principles of behaviour, including the *Point of Human Sustenance*; Chinese divination; the transmitted precepts and treasures on medical science; seven texts on royal genealogy (*rgyal-rabs sde-bdun*); one hundred and four treatises on music and drama, including the *Collected Stories of the Great Lineage of Riddles* (*lde-brgyud chen-po'i sgrung-'bum*);[1004] seventy-five great texts of Pön; one hundred great texts on rites of thread-cross exorcism; much iconometry of the inner and outer traditions of secret mantra; four great volumes of the *Vajrakīla* cycle (*phur-pa'i skor pod-chen bzhi*); and many others. In his tenth year he studied six traditions of Vajrapāṇi according to the new translation schools; and when he propitiated that deity the water in his ritual vase began to boil. He performed the ritual services of Yamāntaka and Vajrakīla to their full measure. In his eleventh year he completed [the study of] the empowerments, tantras, and esoteric instructions of the *Magical Net*. At twelve he learned the *Kaṅkaṇi Dhāraṇī* (*ka-ka-ni*) and the *Five Protective Dhāraṇī* (*Pañcarakṣā*, T558-9 & 561-3), and the *Hundred Means for Attainment*; and he performed the practice of the Hundred-Syllable Mantra (*yig-brgya*). In his thirteenth year he received many traditions of the ancient and new translation schools, including *Yangdak Heruka, Mātaraḥ* and *Yamāntaka*, two traditions of the *Great Compassionate One*, and *Hayagrīva*; and he propitiated them.

During his thirteenth year, too. Chöwang experienced a vision in which the lady Tārā led him to the top of a crystal castle where he met Vajrasattva. There was a four-faced ḍākinī there, whose white face in front said, "You will maintain the teaching of the Buddha"; her yellow face to the right, "You must propagate the true doctrine"; her red face to the rear, "You will exalt the station of the *saṃgha*"; and her blue face to the left, "You must tame those who are hard to train in this evil age". With these words she handed him a white arrow with five quills.[1005]

In his fourteenth year Guru Chöwang studied logic, the *Compendium of the Abhidharma*, the *Introduction to the Conduct of a Bodhisattva*, the *Hevajra Tantra*, and other great texts under Tise Trogyang Sarwa. He also received esoteric instructions such as those of the Great Seal, Great Perfection, Pacification, and Six Doctrines. He studied the *Brief Account of the Truths according to the Madhyamaka* (*dbu-ma bden-chung*, T 3902 & 4467) under Thakorwa; the exegesis and attainment of the cycle of Atiyoga, and other sūtras and mantras of the ancient and new traditions under Tshurtön, father and son; and Pacification, the Great Seal, Great Perfection, Object of Cutting, an introduction to the instructions (*gdams-*

ngag ngo-sprad), and all the wrathful mantras of the protectors of the teaching under his father. And he experientially mastered them all.

In his seventeenth year he met Ngadak Drogön and became the master of the infinite treasure doctrines of the precious Nyang-rel Nyima Özer. When he was eighteen he received [the vows of] the cultivation of the enlightened attitude from Sakya Paṇḍita at Nezhi Gangpo, a doctrinal connection at Kyangsar, and attended the consecration at the Stūpa of Lhalung. That night, in a dream, he went in search of an *udumbara* flower on Mount Wu-t'ai-shan in China, where, seated atop a blue lotus, the sublime Mañjuśrī declared:

> *Jñānakāya Dharmadhātu*! [Body of pristine cognition, expanse of reality!] I am the lord of the doctrine. I know your mind. Knowing the mind is an inconceivable approach to the doctrine. The meaning of this inconceivable approach to the doctrine is naturally present, pristine cognition, the sole seminal point. Now, I have explained to you the meaning of the eighty-four thousand doctrinal components. Examine the significance of it!

At that, Chöwang awoke from his sleep with the conviction that he had obtained the entire doctrine.

When he was in his thirteenth year an inventory on yellow paper, which had been discovered at Samye by Trapa Ngönshe and gradually passed on, came into his possession. In the meantime, many foolish charlatans had tried to find treasure by relying on that inventory. Some had lost their lives and others had to escape from thunderbolts and hailstorms. If anyone kept that inventory at home, its magic became intolerable. And if anyone disposed of it in an abyss, at a crossroad, in a whirlpool, or underground, it remained undamaged by the elements. Since no one could handle it, it became known as the "Yellow Scroll of Devastation". Guru Chöwang's father said, "What will you do with that Yellow Scroll of Devastation, which destroys everything? Can you bribe death?" So he stole the inventory and hid it elsewhere.

Afterwards, in his twenty-second year, Guru Chöwang furtively recovered it and befriended a realised practitioner of the Object of Cutting. With the latter's help, he found a supplementary inventory in the valley of Namkecen in Layak Nyin. He was entrusted with the key by the nine-headed nāga demon who guarded the treasure and by a ḍākinī of pristine cognition, who appeared in the guise of a consort. When he opened the door of the cavern he discovered that the essence of the treasure was a vulture as large as a garuḍa. Riding upon it, he flew over the thirteen stages of the heavens and met the buddha Vajrasattva surrounded by a canopy of rainbow light. He obtained the empowerment of the expressive play of awareness[1006] and was given a vase of nectar. Returning, he opened the door as described in the treasure inventory and extracted a cubit-tall image of a nine-headed nāga in bronze, and two copper amulet-boxes. Inside the nāga image he discovered four instructional cycles and within the amulet-boxes one hundred and eight esoteric instructions.

This was the first of the eighteen great treasure troves, nineteen with the addition of the mind treasure, which he obtained, and which are set forth in this mnemonic:

> Namkecen (i), and Trakmar (ii), Tamdrinzhap (iii),
> Mönkateng (iv), and Tamdrin (v), Entseigo (vi),
> Khoyishinmar (vii), Tamdrin (viii), Dromcöla (ix),
> Sekar (x), Kyawophukring (xi), Caktepma (xii),
> Samye Ārya (xiii), Cakpur (xiv), Mön Bumthang (xv),
> Tsiki Temple (xvi), Rong Rock (xvii), Hawo Kang (xviii),
> And the self-concealed, genuine treasure (xix)
> Came to me, Chöwang, by the power of propensities.

Furthermore, when he brought out those treasures there were most wondrous apparitions, which were witnessed by fortunate persons. Generally, he imposed oaths of allegiance on the lords of the treasures. Otherwise, he commissioned fortunate and worthy persons to do so. Therefore, all his revelations were indisputable.

His father heard of this and said, "Bring out whatever treasures you are said to have discovered."

When Guru Chöwang handed over the copper amulet-boxes, his father said, "Read the catalogue of contents aloud."

He read it and, again, his father said, "Wasn't there a book called the *Buddhasamāyoga Tantra which, Known Alone, Liberates All* (*sangs-rgyas mnyam-sbyor-gyi rgyud gcig-shes kun-grol*)? Read that to me."

When he had read the tantra from the beginning, his father declared, "Now I understand. That's enough. Previously, I have given you not just a little advice. Even if there are additional disputes later on, no more dead words will come of it. Now, that treasure of yours brings an end to any expectations of ruin or fulfilment. It is undisputably a transmitted precept of the great Orgyen, the knower of the three times. I do not need to hope now for other treasure doctrines, however profound.

"The advice I have for you [comes from] forty years, during which I have gathered the intentions of all the learned and accomplished gurus in the four quarters of Tibet, cut through conceptual elaborations, and determined that this mind alone is the ground and root of saṃsāra and nirvāṇa. Now, if you listen to my words, you will by all means emphasise the *Trio of the Guru, Great Perfection, and Great Compassionate One* above all else. Besides that, do not pay even a bit of attention to sorcery and malign mantras, catapults and explosive weapons, hexes and magic or to any of the other crooked crafts,[1007] until you have emphasised this doctrine above all else. He who does not master it, though he has learned much else, dies a beggar.

"In general, I am by no means opposed to the treasure doctrines. The Buddha made prophetic declarations concerning treasures in all the sūtras and tantras. They were the practices attained by awareness-holders of the past. But previously, there were some small-minded treasure-finders who did not reveal the doctrines in their pure form. They indulged in favouritism and flattery and did not achieve much of benefit to living creatures. By propagating malign mantras before all else Gya Zhangtrom[1008] obstructed the welfare of living creatures. Doctor Kutsa, owing to his medical practice, neglected to serve living beings through the doctrine. By practising rites of thread-cross exorcism, the Rashak Treasure-finder later became merely an exorcist. And Pönpo Traksel propitiated Pehar first and foremost, and so became no more than a sorcerer. Such examples are endless.

"Though the conquerors of the past intended to benefit others, these treasure-finders became useless because, without straightening out the root doctrinal texts, they proceeded to act in the name of enlightened activity. But if you practise the doctrine, the protectors of doctrine will incidentally arrive. Even if you do not practise sorcery it will come, for such is the pledge of the doctrinal protectors themselves. Devote yourself to the experiential cultivation of the *Trio of the Guru, Great Perfection, and Great Compassionate One* without many capricious thoughts. Ngadak Nyang and his son are revered by men because of their propitiation of the Great Compassionate One. They are the only treasure-finders who have not come to ruin.

"Six years ago, I intimated that I was to pass away. Now, that time will come in about two months. Men will come saying yours is a false treasure. Disregard them. Before me thirteen generations of the Pang family have passed, and among them there has been no one who did not acquire signs of accomplishment. And I have by no means been the weakest of them."

Ngadak Drogön examined Guru Chöwang's discoveries, saying, "I have had great experience of treasures"; and he was highly delighted. But the master Thakorwa saw a prophecy among them which spoke of an impending invasion of Tibet by the Mongolian army, and he ridiculed it, saying, "Nowadays there are no Mongols in our country." Guru Chöwang was heart-broken and inclined to reconceal the instructions, but two girls helped him to mount a white, winged horse and led him to the glorious [Copper-coloured] Mountain on Cāmaradvīpa. The great Orgyen gave him the complete empowerment of the *Consummation of Secrets (gsang-ba yongs-rdzogs)* and inspired him with instructions and advice, saying:

The highest path of all is service to others.
Whoever grows weary of this
Lengthens the path to enlightenment.

Then Guru Rinpoche said to him, "Do not hanker after this place. If you do, there is a danger that you will transfer from one lifetime to the next." At that moment Guru Chöwang was raised by what seemed to be a globe of light and arrived back home in an instant. In 1240 (iron male mouse year) the army of the Mongol Dorta the Black arrived, and the future was clearly established.[1009]

The truest of Guru Chöwang's disciples was one Bharo Tsukdzin from Kathmandu in Nepal.[1010] On his way to Tibet in search of gold he had received a prophetic declaration from a ḍākinī saying that he would meet the Guru himself. For seven days he actually perceived Guru Chöwang to be Orgyen. Just by hearing the master's speech realisation arose. One evening, while giving an empowerment, Guru Chöwang said to him, "How do you see me?"

"I actually see the meditational deity," replied Bharo.

"Well then, there is no other to whom to offer the feast and the *tormas*!" So saying, Chöwang consumed the offerings for the feast, which included half the carcass of a Bharal sheep,[1011] in an instant. "Now, how do you see me?" he asked.

"The Buddha is actually present," was Bharo's answer.

"Well then, I shall empower you!" At that, he gathered up the implements of worship, broke up the maṇḍala, and began to dance in the place it had been. Knowing that the constitution and attitudes of his worthy disciple were those of one whose conduct was free from acceptance and rejection, and who was fearless with respect to the great commitments of indestructible reality, Guru Chöwang sent forth Vairocana from the great maṇḍala of his indestructible body, from the divine gateway, in the form of great fragrance [excrement] and gave Bharo the empowerment. Bharo's experience was like that of a snake casting off its slough. Similarly, from the swift, secret path of his vajra, Chöwang poured Amoghasiddhi onto the tip of Bharo's tongue in the form of perfume [urine] and Bharo blazed with the all-surpassing, pristine cognition of incorruptible, supreme bliss.[1012]

The master then poked Bharo's heart with his finger, and said, "Recognise this so-called 'I'."

Bharo's clinging to objects vanished like mist.

"Do not deviate from the significance of seeing this 'I'. There is not so much as a hair there on which to meditate!"

When the master said that, Bharo developed an especially great realisation of the Great Perfection, free from activity and impartial. Extraordinary certainty was born within him. "Now", he said, "I would not think to request empowerment even if the buddhas of the three times appeared. Should I also cancel this business of going to India?"

Guru Chöwang replied, "If a buddha were to arise who did not wander in saṃsāra he would be an extremist! Go to India. If you find a guru, serve the guru. If you find disciples, educate the disciples." To Bharo it seemed that this advice was exceedingly fine.

Again, this Newar, Bharo, was a person of very great faith whose propensities had awakened: Looking at the guru's hips he saw the eyes of a wrathful deity; he saw him discuss the doctrine with ḍākinīs and so on. Thus, he only saw the guru in pure visions. Once he asked the master, "Have you realised the signs of accomplishment in the practices of sorcery?"

"I have reached the real point of their practical application, but because I devote myself to reciting the mantra OṂ MAṆI PADME HŪṂ I have no leisure to practise them."[1013]

At that the Newar requested him to demonstrate the occult power of "liberation". Guru Chöwang approached a rabbit. He drew the shape of a rabbit on the ground, repeated a mantra seven times over a needle, and stabbed the drawing. At that instant the rabbit tumbled over. Chöwang said, "Now, we must purify its obscurations. Bring the rabbit." He fastened to it a liberating diagram[1014] and took [the rabbit's consciousness] into his following by offering *tormas* and a dedication of merit. Then Bharo asked, "If such sorcery were used on men, would it not be terrible?"

"Men and marmots are similar," answered the guru, and he performed the same action as before, but with a drawing of a marmot. Consequently, they recovered a corpse from a marmot's burrow. "This is the outcome of such practice. I will teach no one, because it is harmful to sentient beings. Even against an enemy one should not utilise any power that does not conduce to buddhahood. Since these two creatures were animals, I have 'liberated' them. Otherwise, [remember that] it is exceedingly hard to obtain a human body. The sin of taking life is infinite. It is not limited to one death, but all those who are related or associated suffer as well. Occult power should not be used even against an enemy. Rather, we should cultivate compassion."

Thus, Guru Chöwang was one who especially undertook to practise the conduct of a bodhisattva. His vows not to use occult power and sorcery for his own sake were exceedingly firm; and because the compassionate aspect [of such rites] reached its mark, this great guru actualised [the meaning of the phrase] "To liberate even the three evil destinies through compassion." He killed the body of past deeds, a mass composed of the five poisons, and resurrected the consciousness in the expanse of reality. In this way, he brought saṃsāra to its end, and so achieved that which is most wonderful among [acts of] killing and resurrection.

At the time of his departure, the Newar, Bharo, offered sixty *zho*[1015] of gold and requested Guru Chöwang to prevent obstacles from arising on his return journey to India and Nepal. The guru mixed the gold with flour and performed a burnt offering, whereby the knot of Bharo's avarice was completely released. Moreover, this was a wondrous deed which demonstrated his conviction in the Precious Jewels; for, having taken the Precious Jewels as their objects of reference, those who have accustomed themselves to the practice of liberality do not manifestly act as do those who harbour doubts when they renounce material things as being insubstantial, but, none the less, their display of delight over merits which appear as substantial objects may arouse the scrutiny of small-minded persons.

Afterwards, the guru said to Bharo, "Dispose of the ashes from the burnt offering by scattering them in the water, without any reservation. On the way someone will come to give you food. Accept it!"

Bharo did as he was told and was offered a turnip by a girl. He presented it to the guru, who said, "Cook it covered with a cloth."[1016] Then, when Guru Chöwang escorted him a short distance on his journey to India, Bharo once more offered him three *zho* of gold. The guru said, "If we delighted the ḍākinīs by burning gold in fire, they will rejoice even more if we throw this gold into water." And he cast the gold into a river.

Guru Chöwang could reveal himself in six bodily forms simultaneously. He flew in the sky and left countless impressions of his hands and feet in stone, and displayed many other miraculous feats. For this reason he was praised not only by the Nyingmapa, but also by such [adherents of the new translation schools] as the all-knowing Phak-ö and Putön Rinpoche, who praised Guru Chöki Wangcuk as an incomparably great accomplished master. Chöwang clearly remembered thirteen lives beginning with the religious king Trhisong's immediate reincarnation, Ö Thaye, the son of the gods, through to Ngadak Nyang-rel Nyima Özer. Even Śakra and sons of the gods offered him worship and praise. All the gurus of Tibet revered him as their own guru and his reputation shook the earth.

Guru Chöwang built the two temples of Tshongdü Gurmo and Samdrup Dewachenpo. This great treasure-finder discovered an image of the Lord of Sages that was similar to the image of Lord Śākyamuni in Lhasa, and which had been recovered from Mount Mucilinda by the sublime Nāgārjuna and concealed on the snowpeak of Hawo by the great Padmasambhava of Oḍḍiyāna. He enshrined it in the Guru Temple in Layak, which became his main seat. During that era the great gurus and aristocrats of Tibet, without distinction, all came before his feet.

Having served living creatures by such inconceivable compassion and enlightened activity, the time for Guru Chöwang to consummate his deeds drew near. He said:

Concerning me, Chöki Wangcuk,
Sentient beings have diverse thoughts.
Some delight if Chöwang is happy,
Others fear the happiness of Chöwang.

And he continued:

Chöwang's mind knows neither hope, nor fear:
Chöwang's mind knows not pain;
May those who delight in his happiness rejoice!
Chöwang has not abandoned pain;
May those who delight in his suffering rejoice!
Chöwang's mind knows neither birth, nor death;
May those who fear he might die rejoice!
Chöwang's mind has died in the expanse of reality;
May those who fear he might not die rejoice!
Chöwang's mind knows neither change, nor transformation;
May those who hope for eternity rejoice!
Chöwang's mind knows not substantial existence;
May those who fear eternity rejoice!

Thus, he lived as a great master of yoga who had totally uprooted hope and fear.

So that his efforts spent in constructing his temples should prove worthwhile, he gave this advice about the necessary service:

If one harms what is sacred, though he be your own son, throw him out!
But if even a beggar does a service for the temple, do him honour!

Moreover, he said:

To the celestial palace of reality's expanse, all-positive, supreme bliss,
The illusory person who is Chöwang, will now withdraw.
It seems that this body has finished training all of those whom it must.
The signs that my past evil deeds are exhausted have also ripened in this body.
Chöwang's human form, like one in a dream, now will vanish and go.
I dreamt that the gathering, the master and all his disciples, found a pile of gems:
It is a sign that all associated with me will obtain supreme bliss.

Also, he declared:

> Everyone who eats a single fragment of my flesh, or bones,
> As small as a pea, or a mustard seed, traversing the path, will reach supreme bliss.

Guru Chöwang inspired his disciples with these and other similar oral instructions. Then, in his fifty-ninth year, displaying inconceivable signs and miracles, Guru Chöwang departed for the great Palace of Lotus Light.

During that era, when two mantra adepts would meet on the road, they would ask, "Which is your tradition, that of the Earlier or Later Treasure Troves?"[1017] Accordingly, Guru Chöwang was known as a great promulgator of profound treasures.

Among his descendants there was a continuous lineage of sons, consisting of extraordinary individuals such as Pema Wangcen, who was an emanation of Langdro, and Nyel Nyima Özer. In particular, foremost among the lineage of his disciples were Menlungpa Mikyö Dorje,[1018] who was vastly learned in all the transmitted precepts and treasures of the Ancient Translation School, the Newar Bharo Tsukdzin, the nine "worthy sons" and Maṇi Rincen of Katok,[1019] who passed away into a pure realm without relinquishing his body. These and others in the lineage of disciples, who reached high stages of accomplishment, extensively propagated the profound doctrines of Guru Chöwang, of which the foremost were the rites of the enlightened activity of the Great Compassionate One, throughout India, Nepal and the frontier and central districts of Tibet and Kham. The stream has continued until the present day without interruption.

7 Como Menmo

[552.3-557.5] Of the two characteristic ḍākinīs, who were the real presence of Yeshe Tshogyel,[1020] compiler of the most secret transmitted precepts, the first is well known to have been the great emanational treasure-finder Como Menmo. In the prophetic text of her own treasure, the *Gathering of All the Secrets of the Ḍākinīs* (*mkha'-'gro gsang-ba kun-'dus*) it says:

> At sometime the ḍākinīs will entrust this doctrine
> To a girl of enlightened family,
> Blessed by the ḍākinīs, and born in a monkey year.
> Her conduct will be secret, her name Como.
> By realising its blessing she will be naturally liberated,
> But at that time it will not much benefit others.
> Still, all her associates will be conveyed to the level of supreme bliss,
> And will obtain enlightenment, not leaving a trace of their bodies.[1021]

Thus, it was clearly prophesied that she would be truly liberated.

She emanated forth, like a blossoming lotus, in 1248 (earth male monkey year, fourth cycle),[1022] near the Guru's meditation cave at Zarmolung in Eyül, the birthplace of awareness. Her father was a mantrin of a Takpo family named Dorje Gyelpo, and her mother, Pema Peldzom, was descended from the ḍākinīs. Her parents named her Pema Tshokyi. Because her father was a landowner who had not fallen into the extremes of either wealth or poverty, the infant girl was nursed tenderly, but her mother died when she was in her fifth year and her father remarried. Then, she was sent to graze cattle and forced to do all sorts of menial chores. So, she experienced a little hardship.

During this period, when she was in her thirteenth year, she was grazing the cattle during the springtime near the Secret Cave of Supreme Bliss, one of Guru Padmasambhava's places of attainment, at Khyungcen Dingwei Trak in Zarmolung in E. She had dozed off there

Como Menmo

for a short while when a melodious voice coming from the rock roused her from sleep. She saw the entrance of the secret cave open abruptly and her mood changed. Entering the cave without hesitation, she came upon a group of ḍākinīs in the midst of a terrifying charnel ground. The leader of the host actually appeared as Vajravarāhī, and inspired her, saying, "Welcome! girl of our enlightened family." Vajravarāhī took a small volume from the rock behind her and laid it on the crown of Como's head, thus conferring on her the entire maturation [of its empowerment] and liberation [of its guidance] all at once. Then she entrusted her with the book, saying, "This contains the instructions of the *Gathering of All the Secrets of the Ḍākinīs*. If you experientially cultivate it in utmost secrecy, you will obtain the supreme accomplishment." Receiving this prophetic declaration, the girl became a great, native yoginī, who knew all things to be naturally liberated. When they had enjoyed the feast offerings, the emanated maṇḍala became invisible and the ḍākinīs departed for their own domain.

The nectar of the Vajra Queen's blessing matured in Como's mind, and at all times, day and night, she spontaneously poured forth many doctrinal expressions. Some people had faith in her, because of the songs and dances of indestructible reality and her unimpeded telepathic statements. But the majority gave her the nickname Como Menmo, saying, "Having fallen asleep on the mountainside, she has been possessed by a Menmo spirit."[1023] For this reason, she became distressed and decided to leave her own country and travel about with no fixed destination.

She went to Layak Pangdrong in west Lhodrak. Just by meeting Guru Chöki Wangcuk there co-emergent, pristine cognition was effortlessly born within her. The precious Chöwang, too, realised that she was one of the five characteristic consorts prophesied by Guru Padmasambhava, and took her as his secret seal of action.[1024] She unravelled the knots of his energy channels, whereby he realised all the symbols and meanings of the *Great Esoteric Instructional Tantra of the Eight Transmitted Precepts, the Consummation of Secrets* (*bka'-brgyad gsang-ba yongs-rdzogs man-ngag-gi rgyud chen-po*), which he had not been able to establish previously; and he translated it into Tibetan. Consequently their union, which was one of mutual advantage, came to be unsurpassedly beneficial.

Having stayed there for only a short period of time, Como Menmo received all sorts of essential [teachings on] maturation, liberation, and the instructions. Finally, the great treasure-finder said to her, "It seems that your profound doctrine, the *Ḍākinī* volume, is the most wonderful essence of the meditative commitment of your previous life as the ḍākinī Yeshe Tshogyel. But now is not the time to propagate it on behalf of living creatures. Experientially cultivate it in utmost secrecy. Wander throughout the provinces of Central Tibet and Tsang, and benefit living creatures in a secret manner, which will convey all your associates to the level of supreme bliss. In the end you will attain the accomplishment of the sky-farers, without relinquishing your body."

Obeying his earnest admonition Como Menmo, accompanied by two worthy yoginīs, travelled to all the districts and sub-districts as far as Tingri in Latö. Once, she met Lingje Repa and, relying on symbolic means, opened the energy channel of his discriminative awareness, whereby an all-surpassing realisation was born within him. In this way, he became famous all the way to the River Ganges for his lofty realisation.[1025]

So it was that in the end, having spontaneously benefitted living creatures in a secret manner, Como Menmo, then in her thirty-sixth year, went to the summit of Trak Lhari in Central Tibet. It was Wednesday 4 August 1283 (tenth day, seventh month).[1026] The mistress and her two servants performed a feast offering and then the three of them flew off into the sky, like the king of birds, garuḍa. Without relinquishing their bodies they rose higher and higher in the expanse of space and journeyed unimpededly to the assembly of ḍākinīs on the glorious Copper-coloured Mountain of Orgyen. When this occurred, they were actually seen by the local cowherds, who, on arrival there, ate some of the scattered offerings, and so became naturally absorbed in contemplation.

This great secret, which is so amazing, renowned as the *Gathering of All the Secrets of the Ḍākinīs*, remained in the possession of the ḍākinīs for some time, and was beyond the reach and range of ordinary persons. The time to train beings by means of it came later in this age of strife, when, by the power of compassion and enlightened aspirations, the transmission of its words and meaning fell to the emanational treaure-finder, the great awareness-holder, Pema Ösel Do-nga Lingpa. This is because, first and foremost, during his past life as the precious Chöwang, Como Menmo had been his secret friend, and also because he was blessed by the ḍākinīs of pristine cognition. By the great, magical display of his recollection he established the text, which is preserved in the *Great Store of Precious Treasure*.

1 *Samanthabhadra with consort*

2 *The peaceful and wrathful deities*

3 *Vajrasattva*

4 *Mahottara Heruka*

5 *Padmasambhava, his two foremost consorts, and eight manifestations*

6 *Maṇḍalas of the Eight Transmitted Precepts*

7 *The three ancestral religious kings*

8 *Jowo Rinpoche, the famous image of Lord Śākyamuni in the Jokhang*

9 *King Songtsen Gampo, flanked by his Nepalese and Chinese queens*

10 *Gilded roofs of the Jokhang, the first temple of Lhasa*

11 *The stone-lion emblem of the Yarlung dynasty in the Chongye valley*

12 *The central shrine at Samye, Tibet's first monastery*

13 *A realistic representation of Longen Rapjampa*

14 *Remains of the sacred juniper tree at Kangri Thökar*

15 *Tharpaling in Bumthang, Bhutan, founded by Longcen Rapjampa*

16 *Katok Dorjeden Monastery in Kham*

17 *The imposing facade of Mindröling Monastery in Central Tibet*

18 *The hidden valley of Rudam Kyitram behind Dzokcen Monastery*

19 *Pel Tshering-jong, the retreat of Jikme Lingpa near Chongye*

20 *Pelyül Namgyel Cangcup Ling Monastery*

21 *The monastery of Dorje Trak,*
where the Northern Treasures tradition was preserved

22 *The deities of the "Combined Means for Attainment of the Three Roots"*

23 *Painted scroll depicting Terdak Lingpa, with his handprints and footprints in gold*

24 *Dudjom Rinpoche (centre) surrounded by his previous emanations*

8 *Orgyen Lingpa*

[557.5-563.5] Orgyen Lingpa of Yarje[1027] was the seventh incarnation of Lhase Chokdrup Gyelpo.[1028] He was born at Yarje in Tranang in Yoru in 1323 (water female pig year, fifth cycle) into an extraordinary family of mantra adepts. He lived as a venerable monk who upheld the mantra tradition, and was deeply learned in sorcery, medicine, astrology, and so forth.

In his twenty-third year he found an inventory of treasures in the Red Stūpa at Samye. Behind Crystal Rock (*shel-brag*) in Yarlung there was a wonderful crystal cave at the Pema Tsekpa Rock, where the great Orgyen had performed the means for the attainment of nectar-elixir (*bdud-rtsi sman-sgrub*), and where there were natural stone images of the host of peaceful and wrathful deities, of which the guardian of the gate was Khyapjuk Chenpo [i.e. Rāhula]. From the upper heads [of that image of Khyapjuk Chenpo] Orgyen Lingpa extracted the *Trio of the Guru, Great Perfection and Great Compassionate One* (*bla-rdzogs-thugs-gsum*) consisting of the *Stage of Creation for the Peaceful and Wrathful Guru, Three Cycles on the Two Teachings* (*bskyed-rim gu-ru bstan-gnyis skor-gsum zhi-drag*), the *Great Compassionate One, the Innermost Spirituality of Padma* (*thugs-rje chen-po padma'i snying-thig*), and a cycle of the Great Perfection, which included the *Means for the Attainment of Longevity according to the Great Perfection* (*rdzogs-chen tshe-sgrub*), and the *Ati, Citi, Yangti,*[1029] and so forth (*a-ti spyi-ti yang-ti-la-sogs*); from the three lower heads, the *Great Ocean of Doctrine, the Gathering of the Transmitted Precepts of the Meditational Deities* (*yi-dam bka'-'dus chos-kyi rgya-mtsho chen-po*) in one hundred and thirty-two doctrinal topics; from the throat, the *Gathering of the Transmitted Precepts of the Peaceful and Wrathful Deities* (*zhi-khro bka'-'dus*), *Cycle of Krodhakālī* and *Cycle of the Neuter Lord* (*mgon-po ma-ning*);[1030] from the heart, the *Great Injunction of Padma* (*padma bka'-yi thang-yig chen-mo*);[1031] from the lower serpentine tail, the tantra, means for attainment, and rites of the *Lord of Pristine Cognition with Many Deities* (*ye-shes mgon-po lha-mang*),[1032] a medical treatise, and profound instructions concerning the protectors of the teaching; and from the hands and the tip of the serpentine tail, Orgyen Lingpa recovered the *Methods for Beneficial and Injurious Rites* (*phan-gnod-kyi las-thabs*), and manuals for arts and crafts (*bzo-rig patra*). Thus, having brought forth these and others, without limit, Orgyen Lingpa revealed a vast store of profound treasure.

Orgyen Lingpa

Moreover, from Yugong Rock in Tra he retrieved the *Great Sequence of the Path of Secret Mantra* (*gsang-sngags lam-rim chen-mo*), the *Short Biography of Padmasambhava* (*padma'i rnam-thar chung-ba*), the *Testament which Elucidates the Significance of Pacification* (*zhi-byed bka'-chems don-gsal*), and the *Gathering of the Quintessence of Auspicious Coincidence* (*rten-'brel yang-snying 'dus-pa*); from the various treasure sites at Samye, the *Fivefold Group of Injunctions* (*bka'-thang sde-lnga*);[1033] from the Stūpas of Zurkardo, the *Great Compassionate One, the Supreme Light of Pristine Cognition* (*thugs-rje chen-po ye-shes 'od-mchog*), and the *Glorious Tiger-riding Lord* (*dpal-mgon stag-zhon*);[1034] from the "tiger den" at Önpuk the *Cycles of the Wrathful Guru and the Protectors of the Teaching* (*gu-ru drag-po dang bstan-srung skor*); and from Trakpoche in Traci, the *Cycle of Yamāntaka, Lord of Life* (*gshin-rje tshe-bdag-gi skor*). Counting these and others, Orgyen Lingpa found more than one hundred volumes of treasure doctrines; and it is said that the *Gathering of Transmitted Precepts* (*bka'-'dus*) alone comprised some thirty or so. However, because he was unable to establish their texts on the basis of the yellow scrolls, it is well known that he reconcealed them as treasures.

In short, Orgyen Lingpa discovered twenty-eight great treasure troves, along with related materials, as illustrated by an infinite number of images, sacramental objects, riches and treasures. None the less, having opened the gateway of this doctrine for the first time at Trhadruk Khyamtö, during the performance of the great preparation for the empowerment of the *Gathering of Transmitted Precepts* (*bka'-'dus-kyi dbang-sgrub chen-mo*), he was harshly rebuked by Tā'i Situ Cangcup Gyeltsen of Neudongtse, because of a prophecy which contained an insinuation.[1035] For this reason, the rest of the auspicious coincidence was lost and the treasure-finder himself had to flee to the districts of E and Takpo. Not long afterwards, he passed away at Locung in the vicinity of E. His remains were transported to Takpo and placed whole into an earthen reliquary at the monastery of Zhapje.

Later, the worthy aristocrat Kurap heard the well-known [assertion that the flesh of] one born seven times [as a brahman] grants liberation when tasted. He asked for a tiny morsel of the flesh and, tasting it, blazed with mystical experience. He was able to move about one cubit above the ground and fly from one valley to another. Therefore, Orgyen Lingpa's mummified corpse became most valuable.

At a later date, Jamyang Khyentse Wangpo dispatched the preceptor Lama Trashi Özer from Dokam as a messenger to request some of the flesh; and he greatly multiplied it [by using it as] a continuous catalyst for sacramental substances which liberate when tasted. Afterwards, Temo Rinpoche, the regent of Tibet,[1036] had the mummified corpse transported to Pentsang Monastery in Neudong, and enshrined in a wooden reliquary. He kept twenty measures of pills made from the flesh in the Norbu Lingka [i.e. the summer palace in Lhasa].

Subsequently, the supreme conqueror, the Great Thirteenth [Dalai Lama] realised that the body would be excessively harmed by the plunder of its flesh, and that this would be detrimental to the merits of Tibet in general. He wanted to enshrine the precious mummified remains in the Tse Palace [i.e. the Potala in Lhasa], and sent Drön Kungtangpa to transfer the body. But the Great Protector of the Doctrine at Samye unexpectedly possessed [his oracle] and swore that it would be improper to transfer the corpse from that southern region to another place.[1037] Consequently, it was left where it was.

While travelling in the southern districts, Dalai Lama XIII purposely visited Pentsang Monastery and, for the benefit of living creatures, gave to that monastery about four measures of the pills which had previously been compounded from the flesh. All that remained was mixed with medicinal powder and, assisted by his tutor, Camgön Rinpoche of Phurbucok, the supreme conqueror used it to completely restore [the mummified remains] with his own hands. He enshrined it in a reliquary of fine wood which was covered with gilded copper from the base of the spire upwards. Between the spire and the dome he inserted the remains inside a lattice window and personally sealed the lattices.[1038] Later, he sent a letter to the residents of Neudong Fort and the monastic college of Pentsang, containing an enumeration of the various duties to be performed carefully and equally by those who supervised and venerated [the reliquary]. This letter, marked with the Dalai Lama's personal seal, consisted of seventeen pages in the form of a booklet folded back and forth, with each page sealed individually. I have had the good fortune to have actually seen that letter in the archives of the college at Pentsang. At some later time, when the relic-box containing the pills made of the flesh which the Dalai Lama had given to the monastery was opened, [it was found that] they had multiplied by four.

It is said that because Tā'i Situ had disturbed the auspicious coincidence, the dominion of the Phakmotrupa and their followers began to dwindle, like floodwaters at the end of autumn.[1039]

The family of this treasure-finder, Orgyen Lingpa, lived in Trap Tsangka and its environs. Although it is not clear how they served the doctrine it appears that they were a wonderful lineage of awareness-holders, all of whom could display various signs of accomplishment.

It is clear that among the cycles of his treasure doctrines the continuous lineages of empowerment and transmission belonging to the cycles of the *Supreme Light of Pristine Cognition* (*ye-shes 'od-mchog*), the *Wrathful Guru* (*gur-drag*), the *Means for the Attainment of Longevity* (*tshe-sgrub*), and the *Tiger-riding Lord* alone were preserved until the time of Rikdzin Terdak Lingpa.[1040] Still, they are not to be seen today. The continuous transmissions of the *Injunction of Padma which was Discovered at Crystal Rock* (*padma bka'-thang shel-brag-ma*), the *Fivefold Group of Injunctions* (*sde-lnga*), and the *Gathering of the Quintessence of Auspicious Coincidence* do still exist. In particular, as had been clearly prophesied in Orgyen Lingpa's own treasures, an ancient manuscript, containing a cycle summarising the essence of the *Great Gathering of Transmitted Precepts* (*bka'-'dus chen-mo'i snying-po mdor-bsdus skor*) actually came into the hands of the venerable Pema Ösel Do-nga Lingpa. On the basis of some [of the text], which appeared in the symbolic script of the ḍākinīs, he established the continuous transmission of its maturation and liberation, and this, together with the necessary texts, is preserved in the *Great Store of Precious Treasure*. As it is made clear in the *Great Biography* (*rnam-thar chen-mo*)[1041] and elsewhere, this is not merely a means for the attainment of the Guru (*bla-sgrub*) or [a teaching of] the *Eight Transmitted Precepts* (*bka'-brgyad*) to which the name *Gathering of Transmitted Precepts* has been affixed. Rather, it sets forth the twenty-one maṇḍala clusters of the *Gathering of Transmitted Precepts* in direct language. Hence, it is established as an object of great conviction and wonder, and has rekindled the dying embers of the teaching.

9 *Ngödrup Gyeltsen, or Rikdzin Gödemcen*

[563.5-567.6] Ngödrup Gyeltsen, the great awareness-holder and treasure-finder, was the reincarnation of Nanam Dorje Düjom and one of the three supreme emanations. He was born, attended by extraordinary omens, on Tuesday 11 February 1337 (tenth day, month of miracles, fire female ox year, sixth cycle),[1042] into the household of Namolung, which hailed from the district of Thoyor Nakpo, to the north-east of Mount Trazang. He was the son of the master Düdül, who belonged to an unbroken lineage of accomplished masters of Vajrakīla, descended from the clan of the Horpa king Kurser.[1043] In accordance with a prophecy, when Ngödrup Gyeltsen was in his twelfth year three vulture feathers grew from the crown of his head, and five when he was at the age of twenty-four. Therefore, he became universally known as Rikdzin Gödemcen, the "Vulture-quilled Awareness-holder". During his youth he attained the limits of study, reflection, and meditation upon all the Nyingmapa doctrinal cycles which were the doctrines of his forefathers.

There was one Zangpo Trakpa of Manglam who had discovered, in Gyang Yönpolung, eight doctrinal topics, including the *Essential Inventory which Treats the Essence of the Esoteric Instructions in Seven Sections* (*snying-byang man-ngag gnad-kyi don bdun-ma*). He realised that these were required as ancillary texts for the treasures to be revealed at Lhadrak, and for this reason he offered them to the great awareness-holder Gödemcen, sending them through Tönpa Sonam Wangcuk. Accordingly, on Sunday 19 April 1366 (eighth day, snake month, fire horse year),[1044] on the summit of Mount Trazang, at the three stone pillars of Dzengdrak Karpo, Rikdzin Gödemcen found the key to three great treasures and one hundred minor treasures, and at that place he concealed a substitute treasure. That treasure ground, which was then left as it was, is known today as Lungseng, "Windy Hollow". Even at present, new shoots sprout there at the beginning of each new year.

At dusk on Sunday 14 June (fourth day, sheep month) of that same year [1366], in the cave of Zangzang Lhadrak, on the slopes of the rock mountain of Tukdrül Pungdra, Rikdzin Gödemcen discovered a great,

Rikdzin Gödemcen

profound treasure containing five treasure chambers in separate compartments inside a square, blue treasure chest. From the maroon core treasure chamber in the centre he extracted three paper scrolls and three kīlas wrapped in maroon silk; from the white conch treasure chamber to the east, the *Doctrine which Ascertains the Causal and Fruitional Aspects of Deeds, of which the Intention is Vast as Space* (*las rgyu-'bras la-zlo-ba'i chos dgongs-pa nam-mkha' dang mnyam-pa*); from the yellow gold treasure chamber to the south, the *Doctrinal Cycle of the Four Aspects of Ritual Service and Attainment which is Luminous like the Sun and Moon* (*bsnyen-sgrub rnam-pa bzhi'i chos-skor nyi-zla-ltar gsal-ba*); from the red copper treasure chamber to the west, the *Doctrine of Auspicious Coincidence which is like a Sandalwood Tree* (*rten-'brel-can-gyi chos tsan-dan-gyi sdong-po lta-bu*); and from the black iron treasure chamber to the north, the *Doctrine which Pulverises Enemies and Obstacles, and which is like a Poisonous Plant* (*dgra-bgegs thal-bar rlog-pa'i chos dug-gi sdong-po lta-bu*). In short, he found countless doctrines, the *Penetration of Samantabhadra's Intention* (*kun-bzang dgongs-pa zang-thal*) foremost among them, and sacramental objects. Because each of the five treasure chambers held one hundred doctrinal topics, there were five hundred in all. He established their yellow scrolls, and those of their branches, and propagated them amongst worthy recipients. In this way, his doctrinal teaching pervaded all the regions of Tibet.

Generally speaking, all the profound treasures exist only as means to increase the happiness and felicity of [the people of] Tibet and Kham during this and future lives; but, in particular, this Northern Treasure (*byang-gter*) contains, without omission, everything that anyone might require for increasing the teaching, turning back invading armies, terminating infectious disease, the pacification of civil war, exorcism of Gongpo spirits,[1045] restoration of governmental authority, and the control of epidemics and plagues. It contains various ways to promote the happiness of Tibet, in general and in particular, from Khyunglung Ngülkar in Tö [western Tibet] to Longtang Drölma in Mekam [far eastern Tibet], and also the notices and keys for many sacred places and lands, foremost among which were seven great hidden lands. Therefore, this single treasure is universally known to resemble a minister who beneficially serves all Tibet and Kham.

In later life Gödemcen went to Sikkim and opened the gate to that sacred land. Chokdrupde, the king of Kungtang, revered him as his

Rikdzin III, Ngagiwangpo

guru and by doing so promoted the happiness and felicity of Tibet. When Gödemcen had arrived at the completion of such deeds, in his seventy-second year [1408], his intention dissolved into the expanse of reality, accompanied by many wondrous omens.

The doctrinal streams which came through the lineages of his sons, consort and disciples have continued until the present day without decline. Among these doctrinal lineages there were many who passed away in the rainbow body and many who became accomplished masters. During the time of Rikdzin II, Lekdenje, who was the second Gödemcen, and of Trashi Topgyel Wangpöide, the master of the Northern Treasure, who was the reincarnation of Ngari Paṇcen, the entire monastic community of their seminary became a wandering encampment, as a result of the depredations of Zhingshakpa, the governor of Tsang.[1046] Therefore, [its members] became known as Evaṃcokgarwa, the "Camp Troops of Evaṃ Tower". During the lifetime of Rikdzin III, Ngagiwangpo, who was the son of that master of the Northern Treasure, the seat was re-established in Central Tibet and became universally renowned as Thupten Dorje Trak. Rikdzin IV, Zhapdrung Pema Trhinle, greatly increased the enlightened activity of the three spheres [exegesis, attainment, and work] there, so that it became a fountain-head of the teaching of the Ancient Translation School. Up to the present day, the seat of Thubten Dorje Trak has been maintained by the successive emanations of Rikdzin Gödemcen and others. Accordingly, from Ladak in Tö Ngari, all the way to Dartsedo in lower Gyelmorong, there have been a great many centres of the doctrine which adhere to this doctrinal lineage.

10 *Sangye Lingpa*

[567.6-575.3] The great treasure-finder Sangye Lingpa, who was the emanation of Lhase Tamdzin Rölpa Yeshetsel,[1047] was born, attended by wondrous omens, in 1340 (iron male dragon year, sixth cycle) at Traksum Dorje Trak, above the cultivated valley of Kyingpu Yulung, one of Orgyen's places of attainment, in the Nyangpo district of Kongpo. His father, Khamzhik Taklung Nyönpa, was an emanation of Hayagrīva, and his mother, A-Hūṃ Gyen, had the marks of one who had been blessed by Vajravarāhī. The boy was given the name of Rikdzin. In his fifth year he received the vows of a layman from the preceptor Zhönupel,[1048] and had a pure vision of the Great Compassionate One. He learned to read and write the letters just by being shown the script and was quite clever; but his father passed away, his mother remarried, and, disliked by his stepfather, the boy experienced hardship.

During that time he received a prophetic declaration from a red woman, in compliance with which he went to meet the lord among conquerors, Rölpei Dorje [Karmapa IV], in the valley below Longpo Trongsar. At Cangcupling, a monastery near Tsāri, he was ordained as a novice by the preceptor Cangcup Dorje and the master Śākya Yeshe. The name Sangye Zangpo was conferred upon him. Therefore, when later he had discovered profound treasures, he became universally known as Sangye Lingpa. From those two, preceptor and master, he received many transmitted doctrines. Then, when the venerable Rölpei Dorje returned from Central Tibet, he said to Lama Cangcup Dorje, "Give this nephew of yours to me." He complied and the Karmapa, greatly delighted, prophesied that the boy would guide many living creatures.

When Sangye Lingpa arrived in Lhasa, he had visions of Avalokiteśvara, and, above all, of the precious master Padmasambhava. Starting then, he had repeated visions and vowed to practise [in retreat] for three years. After the death of the lama Cangcup Dorje, Sangye Lingpa proceeded into the presence of the lama Chöki Lodrö, a learned and accomplished master at Tsāri, and became his spiritual son. At that time, while that guru went to Central Tibet, he remained behind in solitary retreat in the upper valley of Lhündrup Teng.

One night the treasure protector Tsengö Chenpo actually presented him with three paper scrolls. They contained an inventory of treasures, prophecies, and instructions on the way to attain the treasures. Accordingly, Sangye Lingpa's guru offered provisions so that he could perform the means to attain the treasures in the prescribed manner. Then, Padmasambhava of Oḍḍiyāna, along with a host of ḍākinīs, gave him

Sangye Lingpa

empowerment and permission to fulfil the prophecies. On Friday 23 August 1364 (twenty-fifth day, seventh month, wood male dragon year),[1049] from the great cavern of Puri he extracted the texts and esoteric instructions of the *Intermediate Gathering of Transmitted Precepts, the Gathering of the Guru's Intention* (*bka'-'dus bar-ba bla-ma dgongs-pa 'dus-pa*), which is unique among all the subterranean treasures of Tibet, together with the *Doctrinal Cycle of the Great Compassionate One* (*thugs-rje chen-po'i chos-skor*). Sangye Lingpa showed these books to his guru, who was much delighted. He then studied and and cultivated them experientially, and so became the first master of these doctrines.

Then, beginning that year, Sangye Lingpa gradually discovered treasures at Karzuk Trhang, Jeworong, Tsecen Trak, Longpo Cangde Bumpa, Longpo Kada Trhang, and Kyengi Karteng Trhang. In these locations he found the *Heart Essence of the Attainment of Kīla (phur-sgrub thugs-kyi nying-khu)*, the *Black Tortoise Divination Chart (gtad-khram rus-sbal nag-po)*, *Black Hayagrīva (rta-mgrin nag-po)*, and also the *Great Compassionate One, Utterly Secret and Unsurpassed (thugs-rje chen-po yang-gsang bla-med)*. Further, he discovered material treasures, including sacramental objects and pills, a mask of Orgyen, a gold-filled copper vase, an iron kīla, and twenty-one multiplying remains of the Tathāgata.

When Sangye Lingpa discovered the treasures at Kongpo Chimyül, the treasure-finder Trime Lhünpo was also summoned there by a prophetic declaration of the ḍākinīs. Together, they extracted the *Blue-robed Vajrapāṇi (phyag-rdor gos-sngon-can)*, the *Wrathful Mantra which Halts All the Mönpa Spirits (ngan-sngags mon-pa dgu-rdug)*, the *Enlightened Mind of Orgyen and His Consort (o-rgyan yab-yum-gyi byang-sems)*, et cetera. At Puri Rincen Barwa he discovered the *Doctrinal Cycle of Sublime Avalokiteśvara ('phags-pa spyan-ras-gzigs-kyi chos-skor)*; and at Cagöshong, the *Great Compassionate One (thugs-chen)*, the *Alchemy Cycle (bcud-len skor)*, and the *Wind-Lasso of Īśvara (dbang-phyug rlung-zhags)*. In this last treasure trove he also found the *Prophecy of Cangcup Lingpa Pelgi Gyeltsen (byang-chub gling-pa dpal-gyi rgyal-mtshan-gyi lung-bstan)*. A person who was sent to investigate in Latö, met the treasure-finder [prophesied therein], and became convinced. Moreover, from Tsāri, Sangye Lingpa extracted the *Means for the Attainment of the Nāga King Sugrīva (klu-rgyal mgrin-bzang sgrub-thabs)*; and from Gyer Cemakarpo, the *Means for the Attainment of Longevity which Conjoins the Sun and Moon (tshe-sgrub nyi-zla kha-sbyor)*, among others. And from Gyala Shinjei Badong he brought forth the *Yamāntaka, Lord of Life (gshin-rje tshe-bdag)*, the *Charm which Overthrows when Hurled (thun-phog 'gyel)*, and the *Ceremony for Brandishing the Ritual Kīla of Orgyen (o-rgyan-gyi las-phur gdengs-chog)*, and so forth, in co-operation with the treasure-finder Trime Lhünpo.

Furthermore, in a retreat cave of Orgyen, Sangye Lingpa found the *Essential Epitome of the Great Perfection (rdzogs-chen snying-po bsdus-pa)*. At Kongpo Tamrül he discovered the *Six Root Tantras of the Gathering of Intentions (dgongs-'dus rtsa-ba'i rgyud-drug)*; in Samye Chimpu an especially sublime image of Orgyen; and in Orshö Lungdrom a jewel called "Tiger-Meat God", a ḍākinī's body ornament, and so on. In this way, Sangye Lingpa found eighteen great treasure troves between his twenty-fifth and thirty-second year. In addition, it is not possible to describe the countless minor treasures he discovered.

Those occasions were constantly marked by rains of flowers, canopies of rainbow light, sounds of music, or the appearance of ḍākinīs. In accord with the prophetic declaration of Vajravarāhī and the twelve ḍākinīs [of her circle], Sangye Lingpa divided the *Gathering of Intentions* precisely into thirteen volumes with the edges dyed red, a custom that has been maintained down to the present day.[1050]

It says in a *Prophetic Declaration* (*lung-bstan*):

> One hundred billion will become firm in the stage of creation.
> Eight hundred thousand will actually reveal signs of accomplishment.
> Ninety thousand will be liberated in the incorruptible apparitional body.
> Ten billion will obtain sundry accomplishments.
> Those in whom the seed of liberation is planted will be countless.
> Not confined to one age, this will occur in a gradual lineage.

Exactly so, it is well known that there were, above all, twenty great streams which continued the succession of the *Gathering of Intentions* alone. There were countless masters of the various other treasure doctrines of Sangye Lingpa. The foremost among them were the lord among conquerors, Karmapa IV, Rölpei Dorje; Zhamarpa Khacö Wangpo; the great lord of Neudong [Tā'i Situ Cangcup [Gyeltsen]; the Sakyapa lama Tampa Sonam Gyeltsen; Yakde Paṇcen; the great preceptor of Coten, Sonam Zangpo; and Drigung Chöki Gyelpo. The other aristocrats, great gurus, and important men who followed him were countless.

Particularly, when the Great Ming emperor of China invited Karmapa V, Tezhinshekpa,[1051] he made the following written request: "Please bring with you an immaculate treasure doctrine of Padmākara, the accomplished master from Oḍḍiyāna." The doctrine master Tezhinshekpa brought the profound doctrine of the *Gathering of Intentions*, a miraculous, dark-blue vase, and a golden vajra [emblematic] of the commitments, which he presented to the emperor, who rejoiced and, as is well known, offered the Karmapa a privy seal[1052] and special robes.

Sangye Lingpa founded the monastery of Decen Samdrup in Nyipu and made it his principle seat. When he performed the attainment of nectar-elixir (*bdud-rtsi sman-gyi sgrub-pa*), the signs and miracles which actually appeared were more sublime than those of others. The catalyst [which he compounded at that time] has remained potent to the present day.[1053]

After infinitely benefitting the teaching and living creatures in these ways, on Saturday 8 April 1396 (thirtieth day, third month, fire male mouse),[1054] during his fifty-seventh year, while he was residing at Cangcupling, Sangye Lingpa's intention dissolved into the expanse of reality.

The second incarnation of Sangye Lingpa took birth in Nelpa Meu as the son of Töndrup Gyelpo, but passed away in childhood. The third incarnation was born in Longpo Kying. Trülku Sangye Pelden [as he was known] returned to his predecessor's seat and is known for having widely served the teaching and living creatures.

Afterwards, there was no clear lineage of incarnations, but the lineage of Sangye Lingpa's descendants continued until later times. From his son Yeshe Dorje and Cakyungpa Pelden Senge, who was foremost among the disciples who were the masters of his doctrine, lineages of descendants and disciples, in which there were successive learned and accomplished masters, emerged. The lineage was also transmitted through [the hierarchs of] the earlier and later Tsele,[1055] the elder and younger Tabla,[1056] et cetera. Thus, the profound treasures of Sangye Lingpa, and the *Gathering of Intentions* above all, were extensively propagated throughout Tibet in general, and in the districts of Dokam in particular.

At a later date, Zhapdrung Thucen Ngawang Namgyel of Bhutan[1057] became the master of the doctrine of the entire maturation and liberation of the *Gathering of the Guru's Intention*, which he had received from Kong Rikdzin Nyingpo, the seventh generation descendant of Sangye Lingpa. In the monastic communities of the forts [of Bhutan] of which the foremost was his own seat of Dewachenpo in Punakha, he established the elaborate practice of worship on the tenth day [of each lunar month],[1058] in connection with the great attainment of the *Gathering of Intentions*. This enlightened activity of the ceremony for the fulfilment [of commitments, *skong-chog*],[1059] and so forth, has continued to spread throughout the southern districts [of Bhutan and Sikkim].

11 *Dorje Lingpa*

[575.3-580.3] Dorje Lingpa was the third kingly treasure-finder and the actual presence of the great translator Vairocana. He was born in 1346 (fire male dog year, sixth cycle) at a place called Tranang Entsa in Central Tibet. His father was Khutön Sonam Gyeltsen, who came from a line of mantrins who were holders of indestructible reality, and his mother was Karmogyen. They gave him the name Orgyen Zangpo. The signs and wonders associated with his awakening to the genuine enlightened family were inconceivable. In his seventh year he received the vows of a novice from one known as the all-knowing Trhapa Śākya at Pangshong Lharika. Under that guru, and others as well, he completed the study of sūtra and mantra doctrines, ancient and new.

In his thirteenth year he had seven visions of the precious Orgyen. Then, following an inventory, which had been discovered in the treasures of Guru Chöwang, he found his first treasure trove behind the image of Como [Tārā] at Trhadruk.[1060] It included the *Means for the Attainment of the Three Roots (rtsa-gsum sgrub-thabs)*, minor means for attainment, inventories and their supplements, wrathful mantras, and instructions on alchemy, there being one hundred and eight of each, along with their particular prophecies. In his fifteenth year Dorje Lingpa opened the way to the treasures of Ökar Rock in the lower valley of Cing. Guru Rinpoche actually arrived inside that most spacious cave of attainment, constructed a maṇḍala and gave him empowerment. Preceding each separate scroll of yellow paper, he gave him the transmission and sacraments consecrated as treasures. Moreover, Dorje Lingpa also brought forth an image of Guru Rinpoche, four volumes that had been the King's,[1061] a hundred paper scrolls, four vases containing the water of life, amulets containing sacramental substances, et cetera. Among the treasures, he discovered such doctrinal works as the *Biographical Injunction in Eight Chapters (rnam-thar thang-yig le'u brgyad-pa)*, the *Vast Expanse of the View, a Father Tantra of the Great Perfection (rdzogs-chen pha-rgyud lta-ba klong-yangs)*, the *Sun which Illumines the Expanse, a Mother Tantra (ma-rgyud klong-gsal nyi-ma)*, the *Further*

Innermost Spirituality of the Ḍākinī, the Conjunction of Sun and Moon (*mkha'-'gro yang-tig nyi-zla kha-sbyor*), the *Ten Father Tantra Cycles of the Innermost Spirituality* (*pha-rgyud snying-thig skor bcu*), the *Four Cycles of the Gathering* (*'dus-pa skor bzhi*), the *Eight Appendices* (*zur-pa brgyad*), et cetera.

Dorje Lingpa

Then, gradually, Dorje Lingpa discovered forty-three great treasure troves at their respective treasure sites – one hundred and eight altogether if one counts the minor ones, subsections, and the subdivisions of the treasure sites. This began with his discovery of the *Ten Cycles of Experiential Guidance* (*nyams-khrid skor bcu*) and other texts at Mutik Shelgi Bamgong, and [continued] up to the time when Yeshe Tshogyel actually arrived in Longevity Cave at Campa Temple in Bumthang and gave him the water of life, spiritual elixir which had been produced at Yangleshö, the life-supporting turquoise ornaments of the religious king Trhisong and of Yeshe Tshogyel herself, a wish-fulfilling gem, doctrinal cycles, and many wrathful mantras. When he discovered treasure at Chimpu, he met Orgyen thirteen times. At Chuwori he emanated two bodies and, having publicly extracted treasure from two places at once, left behind impressions of his feet one cubit deep.

In the cave of Metsornyen at Zaplung, Dorje Lingpa received donations from both Thangla and Kangkar Shame [two protective divinities]. He assembled the many great gods and demons of the Land of Snows and undertook the great attainment of the *Eight Transmitted Precepts* (*bka'-brgyad sgrub-chen*). To all of them he gave empowerment. He travelled emanationally to the eight great charnel grounds, where he met the eight awareness-holders, and received the *Instructions of the Eight Confidences* (*gding-brgyad-kyi gdams-pa*). When he discovered the treasure troves, Guru Rinpoche, Yeshe Tshogyel, Vairocana, and others actually appeared and bestowed empowerments and instructions upon him. By displaying a wonderful array of miraculous abilities he loosened all fetters of doubt and secured others in irreversible faith. He also left behind many impressions of his body, hands, and feet. In Zaplung, Kharcu, and Zhotö Tidro, respectively, he found one hundred and eight [rites for] empowerment, consecration, fulfilment [of commitments] and repentance, burnt offerings, and subjugation. Such are the examples of his extensive service on behalf of the happiness of Tibet.

The foremost among Dorje Lingpa's profound, vast and limitless doctrinal treasures was the *Trio of the Guru, Great Perfection, and Great Compassionate One* (*bla-rdzogs-thugs-gsum*). He found wonderful images such as that of Vajrasattva, which he discovered at Phungpo Riwoche, and the eleven-faced Avalokiteśvara and the sandalwood image of Tārā which he discovered in the "Vase Pillar" of Lhasa [i.e. in the Jokhang].[1062] He also discovered sacramental objects, such as [the flesh of one] born [as a brahman] seven times, and spiritual elixir; treasures of wealth, including the wish-fulfilling gem; such Pön works as the *Golden Surgical Needle of the Great Perfection* (*rdzogs-chen gser-thur*), and the *Greater, Medium and Lesser Aural Lineages of Tavihṛca* (*ta-bi-hri-tsa'i snyan-brgyud che-'bring-chung-gsum*). In addition, he profusely discovered texts on medical science and astrology, and his enlightened activity was extensive.

The family lineage descended from his son Chöyingpa, an emanation of Nupcen Sangye Yeshe, has existed up to the present day in the region of Mön.[1063] It is also said that Dorje Lingpa offered the *Cycle of Yamāntaka* (*gshed-skor*) and the *Cycle of the Jambhalas of the Five Families* (*Dzam-lha rigs-lnga'i skor*) to the lord among conquerors, Karmapa IV, Rölpei Dorje. He made his principle seat at Lingmokha. Also, he took charge of the monasteries of Lhodrak, Paro in Mön, Uke in Ze, and others, and so widely benefitted living beings. The name under which he is best known is Dorje Lingpa, but he is also called Pema Lingpa, Künkyong Lingpa, Yungdrung Lingpa, and Jampel Chöki Shenyen. When he had completed his service to the teaching and to living creatures, in his sixtieth year [1405] he delivered his testament, the *Great Prophetic Declaration* (*zhal-chems lung-bstan chen-mo*) and, accompanied by wondrous omens, he passed away at Traklong.

His corpse remained for three years [without decay], during which time it sometimes continued to benefit beings by speaking and reciting four-line dedications of merit. When Dorje Lingpa's remains were finally offered on the funeral pyre many divine images and relics appeared. With a roar of the flames his right foot flew from the crematorium to his spiritual son Trashi Jungne, and his left to Thokme Gyagarwa, as their shares of the remains. The relics from these multiplied many times, and it appears that they lasted until later times.

The lineage of Dorje Lingpa's descendants persisted until later with its seat at Orgyen Chöling in Mön Bumthang. The river of his profound doctrine has continued as a distant lineage until the present day without decline. Moreover, some [of his teachings] have been well preserved by the blessing of a close lineage, the succession of which fell to the venerable Khyentse Wangpo.

12 *Ratna Lingpa*

[580.3-583.4] The great emanational treasure-finder Ratna Lingpa was the reincarnation of Langdro Köncok Jungne. He was born on Thursday 2 August 1403 (fifteenth day, seventh month, water sheep year, seventh cycle)[1064] at Trushül in Lhodrak. His father was a wealthy man named Dode Tar, and his mother Sitar Men. From childhood he learned to read and write without difficulty. From about his tenth year onwards he had many pure visions. By the power of his training during past lives, he learned all the sciences easily and also studied the doctrine extensively.

When Ratna Lingpa was in his twenty-seventh year Guru Rinpoche emanated as an ascetic from Kham, wearing a yellow hat and robe. He actually gave him an inventory of treasures and instructed him. Accordingly, in his thirtieth year he extracted his first treasure trove from Khyungcen Rock. It consisted of the *Cycle of the Means for the Attainment of the Three Roots* (*rtsa-gsum sgrub-skor*), et cetera. From then on, he gradually discovered twenty-five treasure troves, of which the foremost were the *Attainment of Hayagrīva and Vajravārāhī as Consorts in Coalescent Union* (*rta-phag yab-yum zung-'jug-tu sgrub-pa*), found at Dritang Koro Trak; and the *Four Cycles of the Gathering* (*'dus-pa skor-bzhi*), the *Peaceful and Wrathful Guru* (*gu-ru zhi-drag*), the *Great Compassionate One as the Gathering of Secrets* (*thugs-chen gsang-'dus*), and the *Sun which Illuminates the Expanse of the Great Perfection* (*rdzogs-chen klong-gsal nyi-ma*), which were discovered at Namkecen in Lhodrak.

When Ratna Lingpa discovered the treasure at glorious Phukring in Kharcu he displayed inconceivable supernormal cognitive powers and miracles, including a wonderful array of magical feats. He met Orgyen Rinpoche [in visions] twenty-five times, visited the Copper-coloured Mountain in a vision, and so forth, as it is related in his *Biography of the Thirteen Stores* (*mdzod-khang bcu-gsum-gyi rnam-thar*). He often performed the *Attainment of Elixir [according to] the Attainment of Mind* (*thugs-sgrub sman-sgrub*) and the *Attainment of Medicinal Pills [from the Flesh of One] Born [as a Brahman] Seven Times* (*skye-bdun ril-sgrub*),

Ratna Lingpa

and when he granted them, or empowerments, guidance, and instruction, there were inexpressible wonders: rainbow lights shone, rains of flowers fell, and all was pervaded by the fragrance of incense. On none of these occasions was there even the slightest kind of obstacle.

Since the auspicious coincidence was utterly perfect, Ratna Lingpa found in a single [lifetime] the destined treasures of three lifetimes, and hence became known under three names: Zhikpo Lingpa, Drodül Lingpa, and Ratna Lingpa. From Mount Kailash to Gyelmorong in Kham he established innumerable living creatures in maturation and liberation.

Above all, during that era, the tantras of the Nyingmapa, the Ancient Translation School, were not included in the *Kangyur* owing to the following statement which is found in the *Denkarma Catalogue of the Kangyur* (*bka'-'gyur dkar-chag ldan-dkar-ma*, T 4364):

> Because of their great strictness the inner tantras of the secret mantras are not set forth here.[1065]

For this reason continuous lineages of both the texts and their transmissions had become exceedingly rare. Ratna Lingpa made great efforts to collect textual traditions from all quarters, including the abbreviated set of the *Collected Tantras* which was preserved at Ukpalung. Realising that the complete, continuous lineage of their transmission was not to be found anywhere in Kham or in Tibet, except with Megom Samten Zangpo of Tsang, his heart could not bear the approaching end of the continuous line of transmission. Although the venerable Megom was exceedingly aged, the master and disciple both made great efforts over a long period of time and thus he received it. Later, Ratna Lingpa arranged the *Collected Tantras* altogether at Lhündrup Palace in Trushül, and had new copies prepared, the earlier ones in ink, and the later ones in gold. In connection with this he propagated the continuous transmission many times. Therefore, it is certainly only by the compassion of this great treasure-finder that today we can still enjoy these secret tantras, which are like wish-fulfilling gems. Thus, he was uniquely most propitious to the teaching of the Ancient Translation School, in general.

After bringing such deeds to completion, Ratna Lingpa, then in his seventy-sixth year [1478], passed away into the Palace of Lotus Light, accompanied by the most wonderful miracles. Many fine lineages of his sons and disciples, including those of the four spiritual sons dear to his heart, have continued until the present day, and the enlightened activity of his profound doctrine has been preserved without decline.

13 *Pema Lingpa*

[583.4-588.2] Orgyen Pema Lingpa,[1066] who was hailed as the fourth of the five kingly treasure-finders, was the last of the five pure incarnations of the royal princess Pemasel.[1067] His birth at Mön Bumthang in 1450 (iron male horse year, eighth cycle) was attended by many omens. His father was Töndrup Zangpo of the Nyö clan, and his mother Trongma Peldzom. Since, in his previous life, he had been the all-knowing Trime Özer [Longcenpa], he awoke to the genuine enlightened family during his childhood. He learned several scripts, the crafts, and so forth, without having been taught.

In particular, on Wednesday 31 July 1476 (tenth day, seventh month, monkey year),[1068] in the place called Yige Trukma, Pema Lingpa actually beheld the visage of Orgyen Rinpoche, who blessed him and placed in his hands an inventory of one hundred and eight great treasure troves. Accordingly, in his twenty-seventh year he brought forth the first of all his profound treasures, namely, the *Cycles of the Luminous Expanse of the Great Perfection* (*rdzogs-chen klong-gsal-gyi skor-rnams*), from the famous Lake Mebar, where the Tang River meanders in the form of a knot near Naring Trak. Surrounded by a multitude of people he entered the lake without hesitation, holding a burning lamp in his hand. Then, when he re-emerged, the lamp in his hand was unextinguished, and he carried under his arm a great treasure chest, about the size of a clay pot. Everyone was amazed and became established in the faith of conviction. Consequently, Pema Lingpa's indisputable reputation covered the land like the sun and moon.

In the same way, he discovered the *Great Perfection, the Gathering of Samantabhadra's Intention* (*rdzogs-chen kun-bzang dgongs-'dus*) at Samye Chimpu. Moreover, from their respective treasure sites he brought forth the *Cycle of the Small Son which is a Non-Dual Tantra of the Great Perfection* (*rdzogs-chen gnyis-med-rgyud bu-chung-gi skor*); the *Guru, an Ocean of Gems*; the *Great Compassionate One, the Lamp which Dispels Darkness* (*thugs-rje chen-po mun-sel sgron-me*); the *Eight Transmitted Precepts, the Mirror of Mind* (*bka'-brgyad thugs-kyi me-long*), the *Kīla which is the Utterly Secret Vital Razor* (*phur-pa yang-gsang srog-gi spu-gri*), the *Cycle of the Attainment of Nectar-Elixir* (*bdud-rtsi sman-sgrub-kyi skor*), [which three cycles together constitute] the *Trio of the Transmitted Precepts, Kīla, and Elixir* (*bka'-phur-sman-gsum*); [the teachings of] *Vajrapāṇi as the Subduer of the Arrogant and as Slight Rage* (*phyag-rdor dregs-'dul dang gtum-chung*); the *Greater, Medium, and Lesser [Teachings of] the Wrathful [Guru]* (*drag-po che-'bring-chung-gsum*); the *Guidance on Longevity, the Vajra Garland* (*tshe-khrid rdo-rje phreng-ba*); the *Attainment of Longevity, Integrating Gems with the Path* (*tshe-sgrub nor-bu lam-khyer*); the *Black Trilogy* (*nag-po skor-gsum*); the *Cycle of Minor Rites* (*las phran-gyi skor*); and many others. Likewise, the profusion of sacramental objects, and of images, books and stūpas, including [the flesh of one] born seven times [as a brahman] which liberates when tasted, and representative images of Guru Padmasambhava [that he discovered], surpasses the imagination.

In particular, in a ravine this treasure-finder unearthed the temple of Lho Kyercu, which had not previously been visible, and which was similar to the temple of Peltsap Sumpa [at Samye].[1069] That temple may be visited by everyone at the present day. Among the riches Pema

Pema Lingpa

Lingpa discovered as treasures were the life-supporting turquoise gems of the religious king Trhisong Detsen called "Blazing Light", "Blazing Light of a Thousand Mountains", and "Red House Snowpeak"; the seamless robes of the Princess;[1070] a clairvoyant mirror; and many other especially sublime riches of the royal dynasty.

Although an inventory of one hundred and eight treasure troves had come into Pema Lingpa's hands, he could not discover more than half of them. Later, when the treasure-finder was approaching death, his son asked for permission to find the others, but the master said, "It will be hard for you to find the treasure doctrines. But if you purely guard your commitments and pray to me, you may possibly find some minor ones." Accordingly, his spiritual son Dawa is known to have brought forth some treasure troves, too.[1071]

Moreover, the vastly wonderful deeds of Pema Lingpa were inconceivable. He prophesied that in the future he would become the buddha named Vajragarbha in the Buddha-field of the Lotus Array, and said that all those presently associated with him, as well, would be reborn in that realm and become the disciples of that buddha.

Concerning the host of disciples who were his spiritual sons, there is a prophetic declaration among his treasures:

> Ten thousand will be associated by [the force of] past deeds.
> One thousand and two will be associated by aspiration.
> Those associated through the profound essential point
> will be eleven.
> Seven will be maṇḍala-holders.
> And three will be spiritual sons, dear to his heart.

In conformity with this prophecy, an inconceivable number of disciples appeared. Among them, the foremost were the six emanational treasure-finders; the six great accomplished masters; the six great sons who had manifestly disclosed the signs of accomplishment; Tshültrim Peljor, the great preceptor of the Conangpa residence [Phüntsoling], Nangso Gyelwa Töndrup, and Trülku Chokden Gönpo, who were the three spiritual sons whose intention was the same as that of the treasure-finder himself; and his four physical sons, who were emanations of the Lords of the Three Families. Of these, his spiritual son Dawa, who was the emanation of Avalokiteśvara, had inconceivable, expressive powers of blessing. He realised the intention of his father and as a result his enlightened activity became extensive. He was praised as a great, holy individual and revered as a guru by Sakya Dakcen, Drigung Rincen Phüntsok, Zhamarpa Köncok Yenlak, Pawo Chögyel Töndrup, and others. He was also supplicated by all sorts of important persons from Central Tibet, Tsang, and Mön in the south, and his enlightened activity in the service of others became inconceivable. None the less, he practised the way of yoga in secret.

The transmission of Pema Lingpa's profound doctrines was gradually passed down and propagated by Trülku Natsok Rangdröl and Umdze Töndrup Pelbar, who were renowned as the two incomparable doctrine-masters, as well as by his own speech emanations and the emanations of his spiritual son [Dawa], who occupied the seat at Lhalung in Lho-drak. Up to the present day the lineage has been spread throughout the regions of Mön in the south, Central Tibet, Tsang and Dokam. The entire stream of its empowerments, transmissions, and guidance continues without decline.

14 *Karma Lingpa*

[588.3-589.4] The treasure-finder Karma Lingpa, an emanation of the translator Cokro Lüi Gyeltsen, was born sometime during the sixth cycle [24 January 1327 to 20 January 1387] at Khyerdrup, above Takpo.

Karma Lingpa

He was the eldest son of the great accomplished master Nyinda Sangye, and he lived as an upholder of the mantra tradition. Karma Lingpa was endowed with innumerable attributes and dwelt as the very embodiment of unimpeded supernormal cognitive power and enlightened activity.

In his fifteenth year, the prophetic declaration and the auspicious coincidence came together. From Mount Gampodar, which resembles a dancing god, he extracted the *Peaceful and Wrathful Deities, the Natural Liberation of Intention* (*zhi-khro dgongs-pa rang-grol*); the *Great Compassionate One, the Peaceful and Wrathful Deities of Padma* (*thugs-rje chen-po padma zhi-khro*); and other treasures. He gave the complete doctrinal cycle of the *Peaceful and Wrathful Deities of Padma* (*padma zhi-khro'i chos-skor*) to fourteen great disciples, who were the masters of his doctrine. But he gave the doctrinal cycles of the *Natural Liberation of Intention* to his son, Nyinda Chöje alone; and he sealed the lineage with an injunction that for three generations it should be transmitted to only a single person. Because he did not form the auspicious connection with the consort prophesied for him, Karma Lingpa passed into another realm after not very long.

The *Peaceful and Wrathful Deities, the Natural Liberation of Intention* was vastly propagated by Namka Chöki Gyamtso, the third generation successor. The continuous lineage of its empowerment, transmission and guidance is found throughout Central Tibet, Tsang and Kham, and, in particular, in the southern and northern districts of Dokam. The enlightened activity of the *Great Liberation by Hearing during the Intermediate State* [*bar-do thos-grol chen-po*, i.e. the so-called "Tibetan Book of the Dead"] continues to be extensively propagated in most places up to the present.[1072]

15 *Thangtong Gyelpo*

[589.4-593.1] The mighty lord among accomplished masters, Thangtong Gyelpo,[1073] was the combined emanation of Avalokiteśvara and the glorious Hayagrīva, who came forth as if Guru Padmasambhava had taken birth from the womb. He incarnated at Ölpa Lhartse in upper Tsang in 1385 (wood ox year, sixth cycle). Adhering to more than five hundred tutors, he pursued study and reflection without limit. Although he was a naturally arisen, mighty lord among accomplished masters, by virtue of necessity he received the Northern Treasures in their entirety from Künpang Tönyö Gyeltsen and the Shangpa doctrines from the lama Dorje Zhönu;[1074] and he revealed the attainment of accomplishment in both of these traditions. Through the disciplined conduct [of an adherent of the secret mantra] he journeyed to all parts of Jambudvīpa and its subcontinents and, in particular, to such places as the Lotus Light Palace on Cāmaradvīpa, where he heard the doctrine from Guru Rinpoche and numberless accomplished masters; and the ḍākinīs and doctrine protectors did him obeisance.

Thangtong Gyelpo built many temples at geomantic focal points, which repelled invading armies from Tibet.[1075] He bound all the venomous gods and demons under oaths of allegiance. From Samye Chimpu he extracted five paper scrolls, including the *Attainment of Longevity, the Giver of the Glory of Immortality* (*tshe-sgrub 'chi-med dpal-ster*). From Trampagyang he brought forth the *Attainment of Mind, Utterly Secret and Unsurpassed* (*thugs-sgrub yang-gsang bla-med*); from Druptso Pemaling, the *Jewel Hoard of Esoteric Instruction* (*man-ngag rin-chen gter-spungs*); from Taktsang (the "tiger den") at Paro in Mön, a ten-span-long paper scroll which combined the profound, essential points of all the sūtras and tantras; from the Palace of Secret Mantra in Tsāri, the *Cycle of Profound Doctrines which are Mind Treasures* (*zab-chos thugs-gter skor*); and from Zilcen Phuk in Tsāri, the *Illuminating Lamp which Contains the Prophecy of the Great Accomplished Master Himself* (*grub-chen-nyid-kyi lung-bstan gsal-ba'i sgron-me*) and the *Means for the Attainment of Kṣetrapāla* (*zhing-skyong-gi sgrub-thabs*). He discovered many other profound treasures as well, and, in exchange, he concealed many treasure troves [at those sites].

Thangtong Gyelpo subdued an evil extremist king, who resided at Kamata in India, and barbarian tribes on the borders of Tibet; and he introduced them to the doctrine. The array of such miraculous abilities was immeasurable. He produced uncountable [images, books, and stūpas] representing the buddha-body, speech and mind, surpassing the range of the intellect. He built fifty-eight iron suspension bridges and established one hundred and eighteen ferry-crossings.[1076] These and other inconceivable deeds are universally renowned. Above and beyond that, on these occasions, in order to encourage virtuous conduct, he depicted the lives of the past bodhisattvas, religious kings, and others in dramatic performances. This theatrical tradition, which today is known as *Ace Lhamo*, originated as [an aspect of Thangtong Gyelpo's] perfectly wonderful, enlightened activity, so meaningful to behold.[1077]

Thangtong Gyelpo

Finally, when the master reached his one hundred and twenty-fifth year [1509], he passed away bodily, in the way of a sky-farer. At that time his spiritual son Nyima Zangpo sang a lament, at which he returned and conferred his extensive testament. Then he passed away at glorious Riwoche.[1078]

There was one Tshültrim Zangpo, a great accomplished master from Ngari who lived to the age of one hundred and thirty and whose body, in the end, passed away in a mass of light.[1079] He and the accomplished master called Char Thülcen of Dokam seem to have been physical projections of this great accomplished master Thangtong Gyelpo.

Until the present day, many worthy persons have been favoured by the body of his pristine cognition. The host of his disciples was infinite, and, in particular, owing to the auspicious circumstance of this great accomplished master's attainment of the state of a deathless awareness-holder, who could control the duration of his own life, there were many holders of his lineage who attained the accomplishment of longevity.

It appears that the continuous transmission of the profound doctrine, the *Great Aural Lineage of Thangtong* (*zab-chos thang-stong snyan-brgyud chen-mo*) has persisted and the *Attainment of Longevity, the Giver of the Glory of Immortality* pervades all schools, ancient and new. Later on, the venerable Pema Ösel Do-nga Lingpa was repeatedly favoured by the body of Thangtong Gyelpo's pristine cognition and blessed by him. Relying on that, he established an amazing group of doctrines, the *Innermost Spirituality of the Accomplished Master* (*grub-thob snying-thig*), a mind treasure which poured forth from the expanse of his intention and which includes: the *Profound and Vast Creation and Perfection of the Cycle of the Means for the Attainment of the Guru*, which is the root (*rtsa-ba bla-sgrub-kyi skor bskyed-rdzogs zab-rgyas*); and, as branches, the *Five Cycles of the Means for Attainment*, which are in harmony with the path of the *Magical Net*, belonging to the class of tantras (*rgyud-sde sgyu-'phrul-gyi lam dang mthun-pa'i sgrub-thabs skor-lnga*); and the *Essential Summarisation of the Tantras, Transmissions, and Esoteric Instructions of the Class of Means for Attainment, the Eight Transmitted Precepts* (*sgrub-sde bka'-brgyad-kyi rgyud lung man-ngag snying-por dril-ba*). These are preserved in the *Store of Precious Treasure* (*rin-chen gter-mdzod*).

16 *Ngari Paṇcen Pema Wangyel*

[593.1-598.3] The great paṇḍita of Ngari, Pema Wangyel Dorje, was a mind emanation of the religious king Trhisong, and the ninth reincarnation of Gyelse Lharje. He was born in 1487 (fire female sheep year, eighth cycle) in the district of Lowo Matang [present-day Mustang, Nepal].[1080] His father, Jamyang Rincen Gyeltsen, a great learned and accomplished master, hailed from a divine clan and was a later incarnation of lord Marpa, and his mother was Drocam Trhompagyen. He was named Pema Wangyel.

In his eighth year Pema Wangyel became a layman.[1081] From his father he obtained [the vow of] the cultivation of the enlightened attitude and studied fully, and trained himself in, the cycles of the transmitted precepts of the Ancient Translation School, the foremost being the trilogy of the *Sūtra which Gathers All Intentions*, the *Magical Net*, and the *Mental Class*. He practised many rites of service and attainment to the point of realising the signs [of success]. From master Norten Zangpo he received the Vinaya, sūtras, Kadampa cycles (*bka'-gdams-pa'i skor*), and so forth. Starting in his twentieth year, Pema Wangyel thoroughly mastered a hundred great textual traditions, of which the foremost were those of the Madhyamaka, logic, and Transcendental Perfection. Thus, he became meaningfully well known as a "spiritual benefactor".

In his twenty-first year he received the [empowerments which bring about] maturation and [the guidance which brings about] liberation for the *Red Yamāri* and so on, from Jamyang Chökyong, Tshültrim Pel, and others. Performing the rites of service and attainment, he actually beheld the visage of the wrathful Mañjuśrī. In particular, in his twenty-second year, he thoroughly resolved his doubts regarding the transmitted precepts and treasures of the Ancient Translation School under the tutelage of his holy, venerable father.[1082] When he performed the attainment of the *Eight Transmitted Precepts*, his father was inspired by extraordinary pure visions, and so praised him. Later, [the attributes praised by his father] became manifest.

Ngari Paṇcen Pema Wangyel

During the early and later part of his twenty-third year, Pema Wangyel twice received the Path and Fruit from Lowo Lotsāwa. In his twenty-fifth year he received complete ordination at the seminary of Samdrupling from Sonam Lhündrup, the great preceptor of Lowo,[1083] who was the emanation of Jamyang Sakya Paṇḍita, and who officiated as both preceptor and master of ceremonies. From then on Pema Wangyel adhered to the discipline of a total renunciate who remained on one seat.[1084] He properly mastered the practical applications of the Vinaya of the true doctrine, and consequently he became foremost among all those who held the Vinaya during that age. Moreover, under that great preceptor, Namgyel Pelzang, the great paṇḍita of Kuge, and Jamyang Lodröpel he studied grammar, logic, and many empowerments and tantras of the new translation schools of the secret mantra. Training himself in these, he came to be honoured with the crowning title of *Mahāpaṇḍita*.

Pema Wangyel also studied many of the Northern Treasures under Śākya Zangpo, the treasure-finder of Trangpo. In short, as illustrated above, he made efforts to study and to practise the rites of service and attainment for most of the extant traditions of the empowerments, tantras, and esoteric instructions of secret mantra belonging to the new and ancient traditions. He also travelled to the Kathmandu Valley, where he attended on many Newari and Tibetan gurus. Due to his connection with the places of pilgrimage and his practice of contemplation, pure visions arose without limit.

Starting from his thirty-eighth year, Pema Wangyel brought down a great shower of doctrine, ancient and new, without bias: He decided to restore the doctrinal lineages of the ancient and new traditions which had deteriorated in Central Tibet and Tsang. Having obtained the permission of his father and all the lords of Lowo, he proceeded to Central Tibet via Zangzang Lhadrak, together with his younger brother, Lekden Dorje.[1085] On reaching the Emanational Temple of Lhasa [i.e. the Jokhang], he obtained a prophetic declaration.

At Zhungtrezhing, Pema Wangyel received the Maṇḍalas of Ngok (*rngog-dkyil*) and the cycle of *Red Yamāri* from Ngoktön Sonam Tendzin and Zhalu Locen of Tratang. Then he went to Samye and the propensities of [his previous life as] the religious king Trhisong were manifestly aroused. He performed the great attainment of the *Gathering of the Sugatas of the Eight Transmitted Precepts* in the middle shrine, and was favoured by Lhodrak Guru and others. From Trhengso Orgyen Chözang and Kongcen Namka Pelden he received the *Gathering of the Guru's Intention*. When he practised contemplation at Dra Yangdzong and Chimpu he had visions of many deities. Pema Wangyel was invited to Lhodrak by an eighth generation descendant of Guru Chöwang. He restored the deteriorating doctrinal tradition there and performed other acts of great kindness.

This master studied the *Gathering of the Sugatas of the Eight Transmitted Precepts* alone twenty-five times, of which the last, which he received at Lhodrak Gönkar from the peerless, great, accomplished master Namkei Neljor of the Jeu clan, had a genuine and reliable origin. In this way his intention was totally fulfilled.

In particular, concerning his discovery of profound treasures: In his forty-sixth year, from a secret chest lodged in the back of the image of Vairocana with four bodies [facing in four directions, *rnam-snang mi-bzhi*] in the upper hall at Samye, Pema Wangyel brought forth the *Final Gathering of the Transmitted Precepts which is the Doctrinal Cycle of the Entire Gathering of Awareness-holders, the Means for the Attainment of the Seven-Chapter Supplication* (*bka'-'dus phyi-ma rig-'dzin yongs-'dus-kyi chos-skor gsol-'debs le'u-bdun-ma'i sgrub-thabs*). He established most of it and it remains widely propagated even today.

He invited Drigung Rincen Phüntsok – Rikdzin Lekdenje having brought them together – and the three of them, master and disciples, reconsecrated Samye. This greatly aided the temporal and spiritual well-being of Tibet and Kham. After Pema Wangyel had thus limitlessly benefitted the teaching and living creatures in Central Tibet, he departed, in his fifty-sixth year, from Ön Möntang for the great, glorious Copper-coloured Mountain.

Generally speaking, this holy individual's inconceivably learned, dignified and accomplished career is elucidated in his own verse autobiography. Furthermore, he composed the terse but profusely meaningful *Treatise which Ascertains the Three Vows (sdom-gsum rnam-par nges-pa'i bstan-bcos)*. The kindness of this act alone was inconceivable. Up to the present day this work has been the necklace of those who hold the teachings of the Ancient Translation School.

So it was that Pema Wangyel became well known as a great promulgator who, directly and indirectly, clarified the teachings of the transmitted precepts and treasures of the Ancient Translation School. In the lifetime immediately following he returned as the master of the Northern Treasures, Trashi Topgyel, or Chögyel Wangpöide, whose career as an accomplished treasure-finder surpasses the imagination.[1086] The transmission of Pema Wangyel's profound doctrine, too, has continued without decline.

17 *Rikdzin Jatsön Nyingpo*

[598.3-604.3] The great holder of indestructible reality, a monk renowned in one body under three names – those of the treasure-finder Letro Lingpa, the awareness-holder Jatsön Nyingpo, and the mantra adept Hūṃnak Mebar – appeared as an emanation from above of the compassion of Nyangben Tingdzin Zangpo. Nyangben had completely realised the fruit and was supreme among the one hundred and eight disciples of the great master Orgyen who had attained the incorruptible body of light.[1087]

Jatsön Nyingpo was born in 1585 (wood female bird year, tenth cycle) as the sun entered into the constellation Puṣyā,[1088] at Waru Namtsül in Kongpo. His father was Chökyong Gönpo, and his mother Namlung Putri. From childhood he was endowed with the propensities of the doctrine. From his third year he learnt to read just by being shown the script. Many times, too, he left impressions of his hands and feet in stone. From his twelfth year until his twentieth he studied general subjects, medical science in particular, and so reached the summit of scholarship.

During that period Jatsön Nyingpo repeatedly met Orgyen Rinpoche in reality, visions, and dreams. Inspired with renunciation and intense disgust at the world he fixed his mind one-pointedly on the true doctrine. He looked upon all saṃsāric states and associations as fire pits, and so, for the sake of the doctrine, escaped into the presence of the doctrine master Mipham Trashi Lodrö. That master had a dream in which some women brought him an old stūpa that had been built by the master Padmasambhava, saying, "It has to be reconsecrated." When he performed the consecration, the stūpa blazed into light. So, he realised that [his new disciple] was fortunate. Jatsön Nyingpo was ordained as a novice and given the name Ngawang Chögyel Wangpo. He received numberless instructions, including the empowerments, guidance, and transmission of the way of secret mantra, and he passed the time exclusively in one-pointed practice. Moreover, he received all the sūtra and mantra transmissions of the ancient and new traditions from Zhapdrung Norbu Gyenpa, the all-knowing Drukpa, Nyame Lhatsewa, and others, until it was as if there was nothing he had not studied. In particular, he received full ordination from Lhatsewa, and thus attained to the status of a monk.

Rikdzin Jatsön Nyingpo

Jatsön Nyingpo spent seventeen years in a clay-sealed hermitage, and thus hoisted up the banner of attainment. At that time he obtained many prophetic declarations concerning treasure, but he disregarded them. When he had recited the ritual service of Vajrapāṇi one hundred million times, he once more received a prophetic declaration, and was encouraged by the most precious doctrine master Mipham Trashi Lodrö, whereupon on Thursday 13 February 1620 (tenth day, first month, iron male monkey year) he found a treasure inventory, written in the hand of Yeshe Tshogyel, inside a chick-sized garuḍa image of cast iron. It concerned the first of the treasures he was to discover. Accordingly, from the iron gate of Homtrang in Traklung he extracted the *Utterly Profound Gathering of All Precious Jewels* (*yang-zab dkon-mchog spyi-'dus*) and others as secret treasures; and he completely fulfilled the attainment of his treasures and their secret seals.[1089]

Then, successively, from Pucu in Kongpo, the entrance to the pilgrimage place of Jönpalung which is called Cang Trhengdze, Nyemo

Lhari, Kongtrang Gendüne, Zha Temple in Uru, and from elsewhere, Jatsön Nyingpo brought forth many profound treasures, including the *Great Compassionate One* (*thugs-rje chen-po*), *Hayagrīva and Varāhī, the Wish-fulfilling Gem* (*rta-phag yid-bzhin nor-bu*), the *Peaceful and Wrathful Deities, the Nucleus of Definitive Meaning* (*zhi-khro nges-don snying po*), the *Attainment of Longevity, the Thunderbolt Vajra* (*tshe-sgrub gnam-lcags rdo-rje*), *Dorje Trolö* (*rdo-rje gro-lod*), the *Cycle of the Glorious Neuter Lord* (*dpal-mgon ma-ning skor*), and the *Guidebook to the Pilgrimage Place of Pemakö* (*padma-bkod-kyi gnas-kyi lam-yig*). Some of his treasures, such as the *Gathering of All Precious Jewels* were secret treasures, but most were discovered in public.

Jatsön Nyingpo developed boundless supernormal cognitive and miraculous powers. He discerned concealed facts without obscuration, and he could even traverse waters and ravines without impediment. When he discovered the treasure on Mount Nyemo Lhari, in particular, Tratiwa of Kongpo and other irrational persons feared that the essences of the earth would be diminished.[1090] They tried to guard the treasure site with an army, but the treasure-finder became exhilarated and rode on his horse at a gallop right over the great rock abyss. Its faces were mirror-like, such as might allow none but a bird to escape, but Jatsön's horse left a hoofprint on the stone surface. The master extracted the treasure in an instant and departed displaying his discipline and great miraculous abilities. The soldiers were terrified. They all became confused, but then he established them on the level of the faithful. By his inconceivable occult power and force he could subdue Tamsi spirits, repel armies, and so forth.

So it was that Jatsön Nyingpo's manifold enlightened activities increased the [temporal and spiritual] well-being of Tibet, both in general and in particular. He favoured many fortunate disciples and bestowed on them the nectar of maturation and liberation according to the many doctrinal traditions belonging to the transmitted precepts and treasures of the ancient and new traditions. The master himself was dignified and maintained the conduct of total renunciation without transgressing his status as a monk. He also guided those he trained in such manners, so that they remained absorbed in the genuine path and established upon it.

At the isolated and lofty place called Pangri Jokpo, a location which he had opened up himself, he founded a retreat centre. It has been maintained and preserved, without decline, until the present day by the lineage of his successors, emanations, and others.

The first master of Jatsön's doctrine was Gampo Zhapdrung Norbu Gyenpa, who opened the way for the enlightened activity [of those treasures]. From then on, Jatsön Nyingpo extensively gathered [disciples] from Central Tibet, Tsang, and Kham, among whom were the black-hat and red-hat Karmapa [i.e. the Karmapa and the Zhamarpa],

Gyeltsap Trakpa Töndrup,[1091] Drigung Chöki Trakpa,[1092] Drukpa Paksam Wangpo,[1093] Dorje Trak Rikdzin Ngagiwangpo, Tsele Natsok Rangdröl,[1094] Lhatsün Namka Jikme, Rikdzin Trhinle Lhündrup, Kangyurwa Gönpo Sonam Chokden, Puwo Baka Trülku Rikdzin Chöki Gyamtso, Künga Gyamtso the accomplished master of Derge, the great treasure-finder Düdül Dorje, and Tabla Padmamati. He bestowed on them the nectar of his profound doctrine in its entirety, and so formed the auspicious circumstances for the enlightened activity [of his treasures] to spread throughout all quarters.

When Jatsön Nyingpo had reached the limits of such deeds he overtly displayed, during his seventy-second year [1656], signs and miracles at Pangri Jokpo and, as befitted his supernormal cognitive powers, revealed his passage to a great pure land. In his doctrinal lineage there were many, earlier and later on, who accomplished the body of light, such as the two who did so at Takpo solely during the time of Miwang Sonam Topgyel.[1095]

In brief, although this emanational treasure-finder possessed the last of the four kinds of auspicious coincidence – superior, middling, inferior, and most inferior – which are spoken of in the prophetic declarations, none the less, because his enlightened aspiration and the force of his training were especially sublime, he reached the limits of the experiential cultivation of his own profound treasures. On the basis of this, the enlightened activity of his treasure doctrines was propagated and spread throughout the area from India and Nepal in the west to the shores of the ocean in the east; and so it has remained, without decline, down to the present day.[1096]

18 *Rikdzin Düdül Dorje*

[604.3-610.6] The great treasure-finder and awareness-holder Düdül Dorje, a later incarnation of Drokben Khyeucung Lotsāwa, was quite clearly prophesied in about thirteen ancient treasures. Accordingly, he was born in 1615 (wood female hare year, tenth cycle) on the shady side of the well-known [valley of] Ngülpunang, in the Derge district of Dokam. His father was a learned physician of the Ling clan named Ludrup, and his mother was called Poluma. He studied writing, reading, and medical diagnosis under his father, and from his sixth year on experienced many pure visions. He spent his childhood at the seminary of glorious Lhündrup Teng, where he offered a lock from his crown to Künga Gyamtso, the accomplished master of Derge who was an emanation of Rikdzin Gödemcen; and he received the name Künga Sonam Chöpak. He left his footprint on a boulder which even today rests behind the eastern door of the great assembly hall.

Then, while learning, training himself in, studying, and reflecting upon all sorts of texts of the glorious Sakyapa, Düdül Dorje searched for the nucleus, the meaning of pristine cognition, like a thirsty man craving water. As a result, he proceeded to the hermitage of Muksang, where he studied the Great Perfection and many other profound doctrines under Drenpa Köncok Gyeltsen. By cultivating them experientially, the spacious expanse of realisation poured open. Then he travelled to the Central Tibetan districts. At Nyangpo he met the great accomplished master Trashi Tsheten, and received many maturational and liberating instructions. At Trakar Lhacu he abandoned food and, relying on alchemy alone, perfected himself in the profound path of yoga associated with the energy channels, currents, and seminal points. By virtue of the auspicious connection made when he first entered the doctrine, he went to the monasteries of Sakya and Ngor in Tsang, where he received the *Oral Transmission of the Path and Fruit* (*gsung-ngag lam-'bras*), and so forth. Then, during the return journey, he supplicated the great awareness-holder Jatsön Nyingpo at Pangri, and received, in their entirety, many empowerments, esoteric instructions, and much guidance, Jatsön's own profound treasures first and foremost among them.

Above all, during this period Düdül Dorje received a prophecy declaring him to be fortunate with regard to treasure. Complying with it, he proceeded to Puwo, where, at Phodrang Yutso, he persevered in the attainment of Ratna Lingpa's *Utterly Secret and Unsurpassed Kīla* (*rat-gling phur-pa yang-gsang bla-med*). At that time ḍākinīs transported him in a dream to the glorious Copper-coloured Mountain, where, as he experienced it, he remained for twenty-eight days. He received the maturational [empowerment] and liberating [guidance] from Guru Rinpoche in their entirety, and was given prophetic declarations concerning

Rikdzin Düdül Dorje

treasure. This and more is elucidated in the master's own *Mighty King of Pure Vision* (*dag-snang dbang-gi rgyal-po*). Düdül Dorje then went to meet the glorious Orgyen Tendzin, who, reflecting on that dream, was utterly delighted and had Düdül Dorje enthroned as a master of indestructible reality with perfect honours. Thereafter, he lived as a great mantra adept and holder of indestructible reality.

His first profound treasure was in conformity with the inventory which had come into his possession. In his twenty-ninth year he took

Pemakyi, who was of the enlightened family, to be his seal of action (*karmamudrā*), and then, from Yutso Rincen Trak he brought forth an inventory, and from the Decen Sangwa Cave at the Dongcu in Puwo, the cycles of the *Gathering of the Entire Intention of the True Doctrine* (*dam-chos dgongs-pa yongs-'dus*). These were foremost among his profound treasures. He himself said that all those he discovered later were its supplements.

Then, gradually, Düdül Dorje found the *True Doctrine, the Innermost Spirituality of the Body of Emanation*, together with [the rites of] the protector of this transmitted precept, *Kṣetrapāla* (*dam-chos sprul-sku'i snying-thig bka'-srung zhing-skyong dang-bcas-pa*), at Tshawa Drodrak; the *Profoundly Significant, Secret Innermost Spirituality* (*zab-don gsang-ba snying-thig*) and the *Cycle of Glorious Cakrasaṃvara and the Four-armed Protector of Transmitted Precepts* (*dpal bde-mchog bka'-srung phyag-bzhi-pa'i skor*) at Puri Takdzong; the *Innermost Spirituality, the Trio of Amitāyus, Yangdak Heruka, and Vajrakīla, with the Cycle of Its Protectress, Ekajaṭī, the Self-Arisen Queen* (*snying-thig tshe-yang-phur-gsum srung-ma e-ka-dza-ti rang-byung rgyal-mo'i skor*) at Puri Shelgi Yangdrom; the *Guidebook to the Secret Land of Pemakö* (*sbas-yul padma bkod-pa'i gnas-yig*) at the rock on the north bank of the Dongcu in Puwo; and the cycles of the *Trio of Meditational Deities: Red Yamāri, Black Yamāri, and Bhairava* (*yi-dam dmar-nag-'jigs-gsum-gyi skor*) at Trhomzil Trhomkaryak in the Derge district of Dokam. But, except for the *Cycles of the Attainment of Peaceful Mañjuśrī* (*'jam-dpal-zhi-sgrub-kyi skor-rnams*), he does not appear to have established the others. Although Düdül Dorje also discovered the *Cycle of the Attainment of the Glorious Four-faced Protector and of Mahādeva* (*dpal-mgon gdong-bzhi-pa dang lha-chen sgrub-skor*) at Capu Cakpurcen; the *Guru as the Gathering of Awareness-holders* (*bla-ma rig-'dzin 'dus-pa*), the *Attainment of Longevity, the Hot Sunbeam* (*tshe-sgrub tsha-ba dmar-thag*) and the *Cycle of Zhanglön and Pomra, Protectors of the Transmitted Precepts* (*bka'-srung zhang-blon dang spom-ra'i skor*) in the central shrine of Samye; and the *Crown Ornament of the Aural Lineage, the Cycles of the Wish-fulfilling Gem* (*snyan-brgyud gtsug-rgyan yid-bzhin nor-bu'i skor-rnams*) in the upper shrine in the west wing of the Rasa Trhülnang Temple [the Jokhang in Lhasa], it is certain that he did not establish them.

From Düri Namcak Barwa in Puwo the yogin Tungtrengcen brought forth the cycles of the *Peaceful and Wrathful Deities of the Magical Net* and of the *Eight Transmitted Precepts* along with the protectors of these transmitted precepts (*sgyu-'phrul zhi-khro dang bka'-brgyad skor bka'-srung bcas*), and from the Stone Stūpa of Ratsak he brought forth the *Cycle of the Glorious Tiger-riding Lord* (*dpal-mgon stag-zhon skor*); and these he offered to Düdül Dorje. Moreover, it is clearly stated in his *History of the Treasures* (*gter-'byung*) that he discovered many profound treasures, sooner or later, at Shinje Dongka in Yutso, Rikdzin Sangpuk,

Serakcok, Nabün Dzong, Tashö Kyilkor Thang, and elsewhere. He opened up many great pilgrimage places in Central Tibet and the frontier regions, the foremost of them being the secret land of Pemakö. Together with the aforementioned treasure troves he extracted an inconceivable number of images, symbolic objects, and sacramental substances. In short, just as it was said that he would be the successor to a hundred sites and their treasures, as well as to a thousand substances which liberate when tasted, he disclosed the majority of them.

In his forty-second year Düdül Dorje was invited by the lama of Derge, Campa Phüntsok, and his nephew. In the former monastic residence of that master he built the famous Düdül Shrine and fulfilled, thereby, a prophecy of benefit to both the teaching and the state. He visited all the seats of the Nyingmapa, the Ancient Translation School, as far as Katok Dorjeden; and he favoured many fortunate disciples. The cottage where he stayed for a long time practising contemplation at Nopki Phutak Phudrak-ring, near Dzing Namgyel, exists even today.

Düdül Dorje travelled to the residence of the royal house of Ling (*gling-tshang*) and established an excellent patron-priest relationship with the king of Ling.[1097] When he manufactured [sacramental substances by means of] the vase attainment of the *Great Compassionate One as the King of Space* (*thugs-rje chen-po nam-mkha'i rgyal-po'i bum-sgrub*),[1098] there were wonderful signs which surpassed the imagination. [Sacraments] derived from those manufactured then continue to exist at the present day.

The master was gradually invited to Parkam, Putö,[1099] Parma Lhateng, Riwoche, and so on, where he infinitely benefitted the teaching and living creatures. In particular, at Pornetrak he met with Namcö Mingyur Dorje.[1100] They exchanged doctrines and otherwise formed an auspicious connection. The encounter had been arranged by the great accomplished master Karma Chakme,[1101] who scattered flowers of praise on Düdül Dorje.

Düdül Dorje established his seats at Decen Thang in Putö and at Yuri Gango, and he dwelt in these places for a long time. He clarified, in a general way, the gateway to the pilgrimage centre of the secret land of Pemakö. Afterwards, when he had completed his personal deeds, he departed for the great Palace of Lotus Light during his fifty-eighth year, in 1672 (water male mouse). At that time there were sounds, lights, rains of flowers, and numberless other wonderful miracles. Particularly, most of his corpse dissolved into light. What remained, which was about one cubit in length, was offered to the flames, from which a mass consisting of five great remains and many relics was recovered.

This master's foremost personal disciples, who became the masters of his teaching, were Lhatsün Namka Jikme, Rikdzin Longsel

Nyingpo,[1102] Baka Trülku Chöki Gyamtso, Dzokcen Pema Rikdzin,[1103] Künzang Khyapdel Lhündrup, the great accomplished master Pema Norbu and many other holders of indestructible reality in the vicinity of Tawu. Thus, his disciples were numberless. The enlightened activity of Düdül Dorje's doctrinal lineage was preserved without decline, in particular, by Gyelse Norbu Yongdra and others who successively appeared in the lineage of his descendants.

19 *Lhatsün Namka Jikme*

[610.6-614.2] Lhatsün Namka Jikme was simultaneously the embodiment of the compassion of the great paṇḍita Vimalamitra and of the all-knowing Trime Özer [Longcenpa]. He was born in 1597 (fire female bird year, tenth cycle) into the family of Lha Tsepo in the district of Caryül, in the south. He possessed many wonderful features; for example, the space between his eyebrows, his tongue, and the tip of his nose were all very clearly marked with the syllable A.[1104] He was ordained as a novice by Trülku Orgyen Peljor at the hermitage of Sungnyen, and the name Künzang Namgyel was conferred upon him. At first, Lhatsün pursued varied study and reflection at the college of Thangdrok. From many holders of indestructible reality he gradually received the maturational [empowerments] and liberating [guidance] of many profound instructions, including such transmitted precepts and treasures as the *Eight Transmitted Precepts* and the *Gathering of Intentions* (*bka'-dgongs*). Having perfected the practice of the rites of service and attainment of his favoured deity, Lhatsün mastered the accomplishments and enlightened activities. In particular, he attended on Sonam Wangpo, an adept of the Great Perfection, for seventeen years and received the entire cycle of the instructions of the *Innermost Spirituality* (*snying-thig-gi gdams-skor*). He experientially cultivated it and so plumbed the depths of realisation.

To derive the full profit [from his practice] Lhatsün received all the esoteric instructions of the path of desire (*chags-lam-gyi man-ngag*) from the venerable Ngawang Mikyö Dorje. He trained himself until he mastered the pristine cognition of bliss and emptiness [by means of] the yogas of "one's own body as the means" (*rang-lus thabs-ldan*) and "another's body as the seal" (*gzhan-lus phyag-rgya*), whereby his recognition of the four delights dissolved as it arose, and all things seen and heard matured into the inner radiance of co-emergent delight.[1105] Lhatsün practised the disciplined conduct of awareness[1106] in all the great pilgrimage centres of Tibet, such as Caryül, Takpo and Kongpo, and Uru, Yoru and Tsang, and thus he reached a high level of accomplishment. He unravelled the knot of the energy channels in the throat centre, so that everything he said was always refined in word and meaning.

Lhatsün subdued an extremist king in India and established him in the Buddhist teaching. In Tibet, he encouraged all the gods and demons to assist him, and made them restore Samye Monastery. He was endowed with mastery over inconceivable miraculous powers: At Tsāri, for instance, he reversed a great mountain avalanche by exercising his gaze and the gesture of menace.

Lhatsün Namka Jikme

When Lhatsün was absorbed in contemplation at such great pilgrimage places as those of Zabulung, Rincen Shelri Mukpöi Gatsel, Pema Ja-ö Sheldzong, and Shelri Lhei Dingkang in Yarlung, he experienced inconceivable pure visions. Consequently, the spacious store of his intention poured open and there emerged the *Doctrinal Cycle of the Spontaneous Song of the Clouds, the Nucleus of Indestructible Reality* (*rdo-rje snying-po sprin-gyi thol-glu'i chos-skor*), which is praised as the further innermost spirituality of all treasure troves, the essential point of the aural lineages, and [the cause of] liberation when seen, heard, thought of, or encountered. He established the text and bestowed its aural lineage on a few disciples of extraordinary fortune.

Encouraged by the injunctions of the awareness-holder Jatsön Nyingpo, the great treasure-finder Düdül Dorje, and others, and as a means to secure the happiness of all Tibet and Kham, Lhatsün proceeded on foot to Lhari Ösel Nyingpo in Sikkim in 1646 (fire dog), his fiftieth year. He opened up that place of pilgrimage and, complying with a prophecy, founded a temple and a hermitage. While residing, in accord with a prophetic declaration of the ḍākinīs, in the Dhāki-nying Cavern at Trakar Trashiding, the *Doctrinal Cycles of the Vital Attainment of the Awareness-holder* (*rig-'dzin srog-sgrub-kyi chos-skor-rnams*), which are the extraordinary instructions of Ati, the unsurpassed Innermost Spirituality, emerged in a pure vision. He established the text and bestowed the nectar of its maturation and liberation on fortunate disciples.

Moreover, Lhatsün maintained bountiful, enlightened activity which increased the teaching of the Great Perfection, until the reputation of the Sikkimese tradition of the Great Perfection (*'bras-ljongs rdzogs-chen-pa'i ring-lugs*) spread throughout all quarters. It is said that during this later age no one has subsequently surpassed this accomplished master in his attainment of the limits of disciplined conduct. The empowerments, transmissions, and esoteric instructions of the profound doctrine of the *Vital Attainment of the Awareness-holder* and the *Spontaneous Song of the Clouds* have been continually transmitted until the present day without decline. The enlightened activity of their doctrinal lineages has been propagated in most districts of Tibet and Kham and, particularly, in the secret land of Sikkim.

20 *The Fifth Dalai Lama*

[614.3-620.2] The Fifth Dalai Lama, a supreme conqueror renowned under the secret name Dorje Thokmetsel, who was prophesied in many old and new treasure troves as an emanation of the enlightened activity of the religious king Trhisong Detsen, was the actual embodiment of the compassion of Avalokiteśvara, the Lord of the Land of Snows. He was born with wondrous omens in 1617 (fire female snake year, tenth cycle). His father, who hailed from Chongye Taktse, was Miwang Düdül Rapten, a descendant of the royal line of Sahor, and his mother, Künga Lhadze, was the daughter of the myriarch of Yamdrok. In the year of his birth Cangpa Rikdzin Ngagiwangpo conferred on him the transmitted empowerment of the *Tent of Longevity* (*tshe-gur-gyi dbang-bka'*) in order to remove danger.[1107] This was the first auspicious occurrence [during his life]. The Paṇcen Lama, Lozang Chöki Gyeltsen,[1108] recognised him to be the reincarnation of the conqueror Yönten Gyamtso [Dalai Lama IV], and invited him to the great doctrinal centre of glorious Drepung. He offered the lock from the crown of his head, received the name Lozang Gyamtso, and was installed upon the lion throne.

Starting with the *Abbreviated Logic Course* (*bsdus-tshad*),[1109] the Dalai Lama studied all the great textual volumes under Köncok Chöpel of Lingme, whom the great master Padmasambhava had prophesied to be the emanation of the translator Ngok. He learned them all without difficulty. From the Paṇcen Rinpoche he received many empowerments, transmissions, and esoteric instructions. Under Möndro Paṇḍita and his son[1110] he studied poetics, grammar, prosody, synonymics, et cetera; and astrology and divination, the *Svarodaya* and many other works without limit, under Dumpopa and Zurcen Chöying Rangdröl. Thus, the Dalai Lama became a great *mahāpaṇḍita*, fully cognisant of the ten sciences. In his twenty-second year he received complete ordination according to the continuous lineage of vows stemming from Lacen Gongpa Rapsel from the Paṇcen Rinpoche, and was given the new name Ngagi Wangcuk.

The Fifth Dalai Lama

The Dalai Lama attended on many extraordinary learned and accomplished tutors, such as Khöntön Peljor Lhündrup of Phabongkha, Zhalu Sonam Chokdrup, Zurcen Chöying Rangdröl, Menlungpa Locok Dorje, and the king of the doctrine Terdak Lingpa. His own *Record of Teachings Received (gsan-yig)*, which fills four volumes and is held by all to be authoritative, describes how he completed study and reflection on most exegeses of the sūtras and mantras, and the empowerments, transmissions, and esoteric instructions of the mantra tradition, that continued to survive in Tibet during that period, of which the foremost were those of the Sakyapa, Gelukpa, and Nyingmapa. Through contemplation and experiential cultivation he perfected the skills of renunciation and realisation. At some point, too, he performed various wrathful rites of sorcery and the signs [of success] were made manifest.

In particular, his succession to the transmitted precepts of profound, pure visions [was foretold] in a prophecy from the treasures of the glorious Trashi Topgyel:

> Twenty-five [treasures] and five special treasures of mind
> Will be revealed, through pure aspirations,

By your fifth incarnation,
O present king of the black-headed race.

Accordingly, when the Fifth Dalai Lama went to glorious Samye the auspicious circumstances [for the discovery of] actual treasures arose, but, due to the time, place, and situation, he did not take possession of them. Later, when the myriad conquerors belonging to the three roots were actually revealed to him in a vision, he obtained a prophetic declaration and empowerment, in conformity with which he wrote down [the treasures forming] *Twenty-five Doctrinal Groups Sealed to be Kept Secret (gsang-ba rgya-can-du gsol-ba'i chos-sde nyi-shu rtsa-lnga)*. Together with his orally composed supplement, they fill two volumes. He bestowed their maturation and liberation, in their entirety, on a supreme gathering, consisting mainly of holders of the tradition of the Ancient Translation School, such as the king of the doctrine Terdak Lingpa and Rikdzin Pema Trhinle. Therefore, his treasures came to be very widely propagated. Their lineage has continued until the present day without decline.

On the political front: When the Dalai Lama was in his twenty-fifth year [1641] the Mongolian Gushri Tendzin Chögyel captured the three provinces of Tibet through his military might. He offered all the religious and civil properties to the Dalai Lama as the subjects of his dominion. Afterwards, the Dalai Lama was invited to Peking by the great emperor of the east, and presented with, among other things, an imperial edict which proclaimed him the "Dalai Lama, Vajra-holding Master of the Teaching..." The emperor also venerated him as a *ti-shih*, or imperial preceptor, and established a patron-priest relationship.[1111]

The Dalai Lama built the great Potala Palace on Marpo Hill [in Lhasa]. As a king adhering to the vows of a monk, [an emanation of Avalokiteśvara], the sublime lord of the world, and of Trhisong Detsen, [the embodiment of] Mañjuśrī, he governed Tibet and Kham during the degenerate age as had been foretold in infallible indestructible prophecies. In this way, he was a great master who maintained, even down to the present day, the happiness of the whole kingdom of Tibet, by means of the two traditions [i.e. spiritual and temporal law].[1112]

On the doctrinal front: The Dalai Lama turned the infinite doctrinal wheel of the transmitted precepts and treasures of the ancient and new traditions of sūtra and mantra. His disciples included most of the holders of the teaching in Tibet, beginning with such great gurus as the glorious [hierarch of] Sakya and his disciples, [the hierarchs of] the Drigungpa, Taklungpa and Drukpa [Kagyüpa subsects], the supreme emanation of the Paṇcen Rinpoche, and the acting and retired throne-holders of Ganden. In particular, many extraordinary individuals, great promulgators of the Ancient Translation School who could uphold its philosophy, such as the king of the doctrine Terdak Lingpa, Rikdzin

Pema Trhinle, and Lhodrak-se Tendzin Gyurme Dorje, came before him; and so, directly and indirectly, the Fifth Dalai Lama was incomparably gracious to the teaching of the Ancient Translation School.

Moreover, among most of the great gurus and aristocrats from the River Ganges in India all the way to the land of Tongku [i.e. Tonkin] in the east, there was hardly anyone who did not become the Dalai Lama's personal disciple. In Central Tibet, Tsang and Kham, and as far as the lands of China and Mongolia, he founded countless new doctrinal centres. His eloquent and wonderful *Inner and Outer Collected Works* (*gsung-'bum phyi-nang*), exemplified by his commentaries on the texts of the sciences, contain more than thirty large volumes. Among the partisans of the new translation schools, he cherished above all the tradition of Jamyang Khyentse Wangcuk,[1113] and among those of the Nyingmapa, only that of Cangpa Trashi Topgyel. In particular, as had been prophesied, he made good the auspicious connection of priest and patron that existed between the great treasure-finder and the master of the doctrine of Mindröling [i.e. Terdak Lingpa and Locen Dharmaśrī] and himself. In these ways, he planted the roots of continuity for the government of the Ganden Palace.[1114]

Such was the legacy, in the three spheres, of the Fifth Dalai Lama, who, having brought to completion the inconceivable deeds of his outer, inner, and secret careers, became absorbed, during his sixty-sixth year, on Saturday 2 May 1682 (twenty-fifth day, third month, water dog year), in the contemplation of the transcendent lady Vidyā [Kurukullā] as an auspicious token of the enlightened activity of his future dominion[1115] and, in the great palace of the Potala, he passed into bliss.

The emanation immediately following, the awareness-holder Tshangyang Gyamtso,[1116] took birth in the family descended from Pema Lingpa of Mön. From that time until the present day, when the Great Fourteenth in this successive line of incarnations lives as a sovereign lord of the entire teaching of the Conqueror upon the earth, the succession of Dalai Lamas has been famed throughout the world.

21 *Rikdzin Terdak Lingpa, the Great Treasure-finder of Mindröling*

[620.2-636.6] Rikdzin Terdak Lingpa, or Pema Karwang Gyurme Dorje, was the speech emanation of the great translator Vairocana. When, at the time of his death, he had withdrawn from the body of his previous lifetime[1117] into the expanse of inner radiance, he was inspired to serve others by the ḍākinīs' song that is the pure melody of awareness. Consequently, the body of his pristine cognition assumed the form of a heruka and entered the womb. When he took birth at Targye Chöling in Tranang,[1118] on Monday 26 March 1646 (tenth day, second month, fire dog year, eleventh cycle), the earth shook, rainbow auras sparkled, and other wondrous omens occurred. His father was Nyötön Sangdak Trhinle Lhündrup, and his mother Lhandzin Yangcen Drölma of a noble family.

As soon as he was born he was blessed by his venerable father with an empowerment as an auspicious token of keen intellect, and for protection from obstacles. Even later, he would recall with extraordinary clarity of mind the surroundings and happenings at that time, as well as the yogin with a bluish complexion and topknot and the two beautiful women who continually served him from then up to his third year.

Even from the time he was being nursed Terdak Lingpa's expressions revealed him to be adept at contemplation; and during childish play, too, he had the virtuous manner of one in whom the genuine enlightened family had awakened. Thus, he inspired confidence in intelligent persons. At the beginning of his fourth year he received the empowerment of the *Eight Transmitted Precepts, the Consummation of Secrets* from his venerable father; and at that time all objective appearances were sealed with the maṇḍala circle, so that he perceived the foremost [figure of the maṇḍala] and the guru to be no different, and the seed of the four empowerments was sown in the stream of his mind. During the autumn of his tenth year, 1655 (wood sheep), while receiving the empowerment of the *Gathering of the Sugatas*, he was empowered and blessed by the great master Padmasambhava during a vision of inner radiance. Owing to this, [the aforementioned seed] grew, and he experienced [the fruit of] the vase empowerment, whereby he established objective appearances to be apparitional.

Up to that time Terdak Lingpa easily mastered writing and reading, the memorisation of the ceremonies and rites, including the means for attainment, maṇḍala ceremonies, empowerments, permissory initiations, and consecrations belonging to his own tradition, and all their practical techniques. From then on, he became the regent of his venerable father, and maintained all kinds of enlightened activity.

In his eleventh year Terdak Lingpa offered a lock from the crown of his head to the all-knowing conqueror, the Fifth Dalai Lama, at glorious Drepung. The name Ngawang Pema Tendzin was conferred upon him. Because this coincided with the initial arrival of the natural image of the Sublime One of Kyirong,[1119] the Dalai Lama was delighted, and inspired him, saying, "This is an auspicious coincidence!" At that time, light rays emanated from the heart of the image of the Sublime One, which was clearly peaceful, smiling, and passionately engaged, and were absorbed into Terdak Lingpa's body. And when, in his seventeenth year, he met the venerable lord of conquerors, the Great Fifth, at Samye, he saw him in the form of Avalokiteśvara.

Rikdzin Terdak Lingpa

Successively, the all-knowing Great Fifth and his own venerable father, Sangdak Trhinle Lhündrup, had the perfect kindness to favour Terdak Lingpa as their personal disciple. Above and beyond that, he would later [i.e. after their deaths] be blessed by the bodies of their pristine cognition. For this crucial reason, they were his two incomparably gracious root gurus. Moreover, there were sixteen great holders of the teaching under whom he studied the profound paths of maturation and liberation, and thirty-five tutors from whom he received various profound doctrines. Attending on these, Terdak Lingpa, at various places and times, received the complete vows of a layman, the bodhisattva vows according to the three traditions, and, as stated above, the empowerment and introduction to the symbolic significance of the *Eight Transmitted Precepts, the Consummation of Secrets* which had been the first catalyst of his maturation [i.e. his first empowerment]. In this way, he grounded himself in the three vows.

Terdak Lingpa's studies of the doctrinal transmissions were infinite. It would be difficult to grasp even the titles, but they included all the transmitted precepts of the Ancient Translation School for which there exists a continuous lineage nowadays, such as the *Sūtra which Gathers All Intentions*, the *Magical Net*, the *Three Traditions of the Mental Class* (*sems-sde lugs-gsum*), the *Buddhasamāyoga* and the cycles of *Yangdak Heruka*, *Vajrakīla* and *Yamāntaka*; most of the well-known treasures, as exemplified by the varied transmitted precepts of the class of means for attainment, the *Trio of the Guru, Great Perfection, and Great Compassionate One*, in general and in particular; the general transmitted precepts of the new translation schools, such as the *Vajra Garland* and the *Hundred Means for Attainment*, as well as such particular transmitted precepts as those of *Cakrasaṃvara*, *Hevajra*, *Kālacakra*, *Guhyasamāja*, *Yamāntaka*, and the Kriyā and Yoga empowerments, guidance, and exegetical transmissions, along with many works of the sūtra tradition; and the transmission of the entire *Kangyur*, which is the root of them all.

Starting in his thirteenth year, Terdak Lingpa memorised the *Root Tantra of the Secret Nucleus*, the *Supreme Continuum of the Greater Vehicle*, the *Mind at Rest*, and the root text and commentary of the *Wish-fulfilling Treasury*; and from his venerable father he gradually received their oral exegeses. Later, he mastered the scriptures of the Nup tradition, the Zur tradition and of Rongzom Paṇḍita; Sakya Paṇḍita's *Analysis of the Three Vows* (*sa-skya paṇḍi-ta'i rab-dbye*); Comden Rikpei Reldri's *Definitive Order of the Tantrapiṭaka* (*bcom-ldan ral-gri'i spyi-rnam*); and the *Profound Inner Meaning* by Karmapa III, Rangjung Dorje (*rang-byung-zhabs-kyi nang-don*). In particular, by diligently investigating the scriptures of the great, all-knowing Longcenpa he obtained unimpeded powers of intellectual analysis, and thereby resolved his doubts about all things that there are.

He received the empowerments, instructions, and exegetical transmissions of the four rivers [of the *Sūtra which Gathers All Intentions*] in their entirety, including the seal of entrustment and the longevity empowerment for final support from Taktön Chögyel Tendzin who had opened forty-five maṇḍalas on the basis of the *Empowerment Ceremony of the Sūtra which Gathers All Intentions [entitled] the Jewel Rosary* (*'dus-pa mdo'i dbang-chog rin-chen phreng-ba*). Moreover, on the basis of the *Empowerment Ceremony [entitled] the River of Honey* (*dbang-chog sbrang-rtsi'i chu-rgyun*) he received [from the same guru] the complete empowerments, transmissions, and instructions, relying on twenty-one maṇḍalas painted on cloth. Again, from Rikdzin Pema Trhinle of Dorje Trak he received the full empowerments, instructions, and exegetical transmissions, based on the *Empowerment Ceremony [entitled] the Jewel Rosary*, relying on a condensed version [which utilised] twenty-seven maṇḍalas, of which the root maṇḍala was painted on cloth, and the surrounding ones laid out schematically.[1120] Both of these masters conferred on him the secret name Gyurme Dorjetsel.

The connection formed by his aspirations being awakened, the transmitted precepts of the profound treasures fell to Terdak Lingpa as follows. He discovered the treasures of the *Innermost Spirituality of the Awareness-holder* at Yamalung during his eighteenth year, on Friday 15 June 1663 (tenth day, fifth month, water hare); of *Yamāntaka, the Destroyer of Arrogance* (*gshin-rje-gshed dregs-'joms*) at Sheldrak, having displayed his miraculous powers, during his twenty-second year, on Saturday 24 September 1667 (eighth day, *khrums* month, fire sheep); of the *Wrathful Guru* (*gur-drag*) and the *Atiyoga and Vajrasattva Cycles* (*rdor-sems a-ti'i skor*) at Ökar Rock during his thirty-first year on Saturday 19 December 1676 (full moon day, tiger month, fire dragon); and of the *Doctrinal Cycle of the Great Compassionate One as the Universal Gathering of the Sugatas* (*thugs-rje chen-po bde-gshegs kun-'dus-kyi chos-skor*) in public at Shawuk Tago during his thirty-fifth year, on Friday 23 August 1680 (twenty-ninth day, sixth month, iron monkey).

On various different occasions, both before and after those just mentioned, Terdak Lingpa remained in retreat for periods of one year, six months, three months, or one month, at Trakmar Chimpu, Yamalung and other wonderful and great centres of accomplishment, and in the solitudes of such hermitages as his quarters at the old and new seats,[1121] and his cottages at Öseltse and Samtentse. There, he performed the rites of service and attainment for about thirty-five meditational deities, including the peaceful and wrathful Guru [Padmasambhava], Vajrasattva, the Eight Transmitted Precepts, the Great Compassionate One, Yangdak Heruka and Vajrakīla, Yamāntaka, Hayagrīva, and Khecarī. Taking the experiential cultivation of Cutting Through Resistance in the Great Perfection (*rdzogs-pa chen-po khregs-chod*) as the very heart [of the teaching], he also experientially cultivated All-Surpassing Realisation (*thod-rgal*),[1122] the yogas of the energy currents, et cetera, during the appropriate crucial times [to practice those teachings].[1123] In this way, he attained stability in the stage of creation, which eradicates impure vision, and so accomplished all the four rites without any obstruction. As for the stage of perfection: The pulses or rhythms of the energy channels, currents, and seminal points having become purified in the *dhūti* [the central energy channel],[1124] the pristine cognition of the "bliss of melting" blazed as his seal.[1125] The naturally manifest and impartial intention of the Great Perfection being born within him, every trace of subjective grasping dissolved as it arose. He mastered the contemplation in which the inner radiance is continuously present, without differentiation, during both meditative equipoise and its aftermath.[1126]

All appearance and conduct having arisen as the play of pristine cognition, many paṇḍitas and accomplished masters of India and Tibet, such as the great master Padmasambhava, Vimalamitra, Hūṃkara, Buddhaguhya, Vairocana, Yeshe Tshogyel, Nyang-rel Nyima Özer, and the all-knowing lord of the doctrine [Longcenpa] actually appeared in the bodies of their pristine cognition. They created emanational maṇḍalas and empowered Terdak Lingpa in many transmitted precepts and treasures, as exemplified by his own treasures; and they amply commented upon and taught all the essential instructions of the profound path. He also beheld in visions, and was empowered and blessed by, many meditational deities including Vajrakumāra, Vajrasattva, Yangdak Heruka, the Great Compassionate One, the peaceful and wrathful deities, and Vajrayoginī. He traversed many pure lands, such as Sukhāvatī and the glorious Copper-coloured Mountain on Cāmaradvīpa, and so mastered the contemplation of the total purification of the realms. All his acts were unimpededly accomplished by the ḍākinīs and doctrine protectors, and they made prophetic declarations to him. Thus, he had limitless wonderful visions. Since he was endowed with unhindered and unimpeded supernormal cognitive powers, his prophecies regarding the changing patterns of time later turned out exactly as he had foretold them. There appear to be many convincing proofs of this, but I will not elaborate here.

Up to his thirty-first year, the seed of maturation which had been planted in Terdak Lingpa's mind-stream gradually grew, so that his experience of the vase empowerment was such that he established all objective appearances to be radiant and empty, like apparitions.[1127] Therefore, this was the time to act on behalf of living creatures preeminently by means of buddha-body. He travelled to many different districts, north and south, such as Shöcen and Kyilung, where, planting the seed of liberation, without bias, in the minds of numberless persons requiring training, who merely beheld the maṇḍala [of his person] he made an end to saṃsāra.

In his thirty-second year, beginning in March 1677 (second month, fire snake),[1128] his experience of the secret empowerment arose as the radiance and emptiness of intrinsic awareness, whereby subject and object dissolved in the expanse [of reality]. Therefore, this was the time to act on behalf of living creatures pre-eminently by means of buddha-speech. So he continually turned the profound and vast wheel of the doctrine for a host of disciples of superior, moderate and inferior fortune.

Starting in September/October 1683 (*khrums* month, water pig year),[1129] Terdak Lingpa's thirty-eighth, the experience which was born in his mind of the real pristine cognition, exemplified by the "bliss of melting" and of the four delights associated with awareness and emptiness, supreme bliss, co-emergence, and immutability, steadily increased by means of the path of a messenger.[1130] Therefore, it was the time to act on behalf of living creatures by means of buddha-mind. Despite the fact that henceforth he would continue to teach the doctrinal transmissions in general, without bias, he especially assumed responsibility for, above all, guiding fortunate disciples by forcible means to behold the face of naturally present, pristine cognition, having implanted directly within their minds instructions for whatever profound guidance would mature them.

In these ways, he came to embody the savour which is identical for the three indestructible realities of all buddhas.[1131] Therefore, it was the time to act all-pervasively, through enlightened activity on behalf of living creatures equally. In all his actions, he became utterly free from the entanglements of self-interested thought and passed the time engaged in the wholly positive activities of exegesis, attainment and work, with great courage. He held in his heart only the temporal and spiritual well-being of the teaching and living creatures.

Concerning that exegetical activity: The all-knowing supreme conqueror, the Great Fifth Dalai Lama, pre-eminently studied all sorts of profound and extensive doctrinal cycles under Terdak Lingpa, including the *Precious Collected Tantras of the Ancient Translation School* (*snga-'gyur rgyud-'bum rin-po-che*), and conferred on him the title of *Ti-shih*. Exemplified by this, Terdak Lingpa's teaching activity was such that he continuously conferred many approaches to the doctrine, including the empowerments, guidance, and exegetical transmissions of the transmitted precepts and treasures of the Ancient Translation School, the mantras of the new translation schools, and the cycles belonging to the sūtras. [He did so] in accord with the respective intellectual needs of his fortunate disciples, high and low, who faithfully gathered from Central Tibet, Tsang, Kham, Kongpo, Mön to the south, Ngari and elsewhere, without number. Among them were many great individuals, who occupied the high positions of Sakya, Phakmotru, Drigung, Taklung, and so forth; aristocrats, including governors and district administrators;[1132] and the sons of his body and the many holy sons of his speech, who were spiritual benefactors elucidating the teaching. Thus, he clarified and extended the teaching that is without peer. In order that it might endure for a long time he also composed wonderful treatises of unprecedented eloquence, which include the means for attainment, maṇḍala rites, empowerment ceremonies, and so on, for the cycle of transmitted precepts, and the ceremonial arrangements and so forth for the exceptional older treasures, the *Earlier and Later Treasure Troves* foremost among them. These works occupy some thirteen volumes.

Concerning his activity in connection with attainment: As the master himself never strayed from continuous contemplation, both in meditative equipoise and its aftermath, he directly introduced those to whom he gave meditational guidance to awareness itself, not leaving them with a merely academic understanding. When he granted empowerment, the blessing of his pristine cognition actually penetrated the minds of his disciples; and he caused all the myriad rites of service and attainment to be applied practically, not left to be merely exegetical.

Concerning his activity belonging to the sphere of deeds and work: Terdak Lingpa did not lock up in a treasury all the things bestowed upon him from above by His Holiness [the Fifth Dalai Lama] and others, or offered up by the faithful. At the monastic centre of Orgyen Mindröling he newly gathered some three hundred members of the *saṃgha* who, binding themselves to the three vows, spent the time engaged in exegesis and attainment. He continuously ensured that they would not be bereft of the appropriate requisites and so [provided them with] their quarters, images, books, stūpas and other items of worship, and the supplies and provisions required for the rites of attainment and worship during the four seasons. Moreover, he commissioned many paintings and sculptures; more than five hundred volumes in gold and silver, including the *Kangyur*; numerous xylographs for the commentaries, exegeses, ceremonies, rites, et cetera, of the Ancient Translation School; and many stūpas, of which the foremost was the "Great Shrine of a Hundred Thousand Images which Liberates when Seen" (*sku-'bum mthong-grol chen-mo*). Because Terdak Lingpa was endowed with perfect liberality, he gave generously so that those who received his impartial worship and charity might amass the two provisions. In these and other ways, his was a wonderful, marvellous career, during which he undertook only those great deeds which increase the spiritual and temporal well-being of the teaching and of living creatures.

When Terdak Lingpa had, for the while, completed such deeds that are associated with inconceivably secret [activity], in February/March 1714 (first month, wood horse), during his sixty-ninth year, he seemed to become somewhat ill. Beginning on Sunday 11 March (twenty-fifth day), in particular, he bestowed his final instructions on his immediate family members. From that time onwards, those who remained to serve him constantly heard the extremely harmonious sound of a shawm,[1133] which seemed to come from the western side of the outer wall. Simultaneously, the scent of camphor completely pervaded his bedroom, inside and out. Then, on the morning of Saturday 17 March (second day, second month), he said, "I must take seven steps toward the east." He rose and, after moving seven steps, sat down cross-legged and, as his *Dying Testament* (*'da'-ka'i zhal-chems*), said:

> Sights, sounds and awareness are deities, mantras,
> and the disposition of the body of reality,
> Spreading forth infinitely as the play of buddha-body
> and pristine cognition.
> In the experiential cultivation of the great, profound
> and secret yoga,
> May they become indivisible, of one savour in the
> innermost point of mind!

Afterwards, he said, "Now the ḍākinīs have arrived to usher me on!" He moved his hands in the gesture of playing the hand-drum and bell, and adopted a [contemplative] gaze. At that moment, he manifestly revealed wondrous omens and great miracles, and so demonstrated his passage to the great terrestrial pure land of Lotus Light.[1134]

Terdak Lingpa's disciples, exemplified by his spiritual sons and the sons of his speech, are described in a prophetic declaration from a treasure (*gter-lung*):

> As for the disciples of the doctrine master
> Who will maintain their commitments:
> They will include later incarnations of the king
> And his subjects who have attained the levels,
> Such as the present sovereign and his son.[1135]
> Thirty-five will have the power to benefit living
> creatures.
> One hundred and eight will benefit themselves.
> Two thousand will form doctrinal connections.
> Fifty thousand will have connections through his
> aspiration.
> Sixty-seven will be connected through deeds.
> Seven meriting parasols will be found in his
> following.
> Three aristocrats will increase his sphere of
> influence.

Accordingly, the foremost of the personal disciples who drank the nectar of his speech were: the supreme conqueror, the precious Fifth

Dalai Lama, and his regent Sangye Gyamtso,[1136] who were the sun and moon [among those with whom he enjoyed] a patron-priest relationship; Rikdzin Pema Trhinle of Dorje Trak; Sakya Trhicen Künga Trashi; the Zhapdrung along with his successor and the other great personages at the earlier and later seats of Tsedong [i.e. Tsetang and Neudong]; the Tshurpu Gyeltsap and the Trehor Choktrül, among holders of the Kamtsang [i.e. Karma Kagyü] teaching; Drigung Köncok Trhinle Zangpo; Taklungpa Tendzin Sizhi Namgyel; [the rebirth of] the all-knowing Drukpa Paksam Wangpo; the Gampo Choktrul Zangpo Dorje, and his descendants; Chamdo Gyelwa Phakpa Lha; Ngawang Chöki Trülku; Ngawang Künga Tendzin of Dokam; the former and later Tabla; the Katok Gyelse [Sonam Detsen]; and the second Dzokcen Pema Rikdzin Gyurme Thekcok Tendzin. As exemplified by these, among the majority of great famous gurus who were holders of the teaching, there seem to have been none who did not supplicate him.

Terdak Lingpa's sole, inner spiritual son was his younger brother Locen Dharmaśrī, an emanation of Yudra Nyingpo. The offsprings of his body were his sons Pema Gyurme Gyamtso, Zhapdrung Yizhin Lekdrup, Trincen Rincen Namgyel, and his daughter, the venerable lady Mingyur Peldrön.[1137] Furthermore, his attendants Gejong Losel Gyamtso, Ngak Rapjampa Orgyen Chödra, and Bumrampa Orgyen Kelzang and others were disciples who could uphold the great pillar of the teaching. These and the great perfect gathering [which assembled around Terdak Lingpa] vastly increased the enlightened activities of exegesis and attainment.

This great treasure-finder, directly and indirectly, was most gracious to the entire teaching, ancient and new. More than that, he maintained the vitality of the instructions of the minor doctrinal traditions, such as the Conangpa, Shangpa, Pacification and Object of Cutting (*zhi-gcod*), and Podongpa, both through his own powers and by encouraging others.

In particular, at that time the exegesis and attainment of the wonderful traditions which were the legacy of Trhisong Detsen and the priests he patronised, namely, the transmitted precepts of the Nyingmapa, the Ancient Translation School, of which the foremost is the trilogy of the *Sūtra which Gathers All Intentions*, the *Magical Net*, and the *Mental Class*, had almost become like a lamp that had run out of oil. Terdak Lingpa, with courageous and untiring great perseverance, sought out [those traditions], and restored the deteriorated teaching from its very foundations by means of exegesis, attainment, and work. In point of fact, because of the kindness of this most venerable master, his brother, disciples, and descendants, the *Sa-nga Nyingmapa*, or the "ancient school of secret mantra", has been equal to the meaning of its name, and its genuine, authoritative continuous lineage has increased, without decline, down to the present day. Therefore, none can match Terdak

Lingpa's wonderful kindness and legacy. For these reasons, we later Nyingmapa do not merely rely on ephemeral ceremonies and rites which are referred to as profound doctrines, but extensively maintain this tradition, which is a great treasure chest of teaching; and it is appropriate for us to make great efforts to spread it as well.

22 *Jikme Lingpa*

[636.6-646.1] The all-knowing Jikme Lingpa[1138] was the combined emanation of the great paṇḍita Vimalamitra, the religious king Trhisong Detsen and Gyelse Lharje. He was the immediate rebirth of Rikdzin Chöje Lingpa. As had been clearly prophesied in the treasures of Guru Chöwang, Sangye Lingpa, Chöje Lingpa and his disciple Ratön, and others, Jikme Lingpa was born on the morning of Monday 6 February 1730, the anniversary of Longcenpa's death (eighteenth day, twelfth month, earth female bird year, twelfth cycle) near Pelri Monastery in the district of Chongye, to the south of the Red Mausoleum of King Songtsen Gampo (*srong-btsan bang-so dmar-po*).[1139] His family was that of the heirs of Gyadrakpa, one of the six great spiritual sons of Chöje Drukpa.

From childhood he clearly remembered his previous lives as the great treasure-finders Sangye Lama and Chöje Lingpa. In this and other ways he awoke to the genuine enlightened family. During his sixth year, he entered the college of Pelgi Riwo [i.e. Pelri], where the venerable Prajñāraśmi's unblemished legacy in the three spheres was preserved.[1140] He offered a lock from the crown of his head to Ngawang Lozang Pema, an incarnation of Yeshe Tshogyel, and the name Pema Khyentse Özer was conferred on him in the presence of Nesarwa Ngawang Künga Lekpei Jungne.

Jikme Lingpa received the empowerments and transmissions of the *Point of Liberation* and the *Gathering of the Guru's Intention* from Neten Künzang Özer. In particular, in his thirteenth year he met Rikdzin Thukcok Dorje and received the *Great Seal, Liberation through the Vision of Pristine Cognition* (*phyag-rgya chen-po ye-shes mthong-grol*) among other teachings. This was the first cause of his spiritual maturation. Because he adopted Rikdzin Thukcok Dorje as his sole, supreme root guru, he later was taken into the following of the body of his pristine cognition as well. Furthermore, at various times Jikme Lingpa received all kinds of [empowerments, which bring about] maturation, and [guidance, which brings about] liberation, including the most important transmitted precepts and treasures of the Ancient Translation School. These included the foremost teachings of the transmitted precepts and of the *Earlier and Later Treasure Troves*, as well as those of the new translation schools. The many tutors from whom he received them included the great treasure-finder Trime Lingpa, Zhangom Dharmakīrti, Trupwang Śrīnātha of Mindröling, Tendzin Yeshe Lhündrup, Thangdrok-ön Pema Chokdrup, and Mön Dzakar Lama Targye. Incidentally, he studied some of the conventional sciences, including astrology.

Jikme Lingpa

His own writings demonstrate that his mind was bent on the attainment of the essential, and that he eschewed efforts to master the literary conventions, except in so much as he was naturally endowed from birth with talent for the hidden essentials of the great textual traditions of the sūtras and mantras, and for perfect poetic composition.[1141]

In his twenty-eighth year, starting in February/March 1757 (month of miracles, fire ox year) he firmly vowed to pass three years in the seclusion of the Gokang Tikle Nyakcik [Hermitage], which was connected with his own monastery of Pelri. Above all, Jikme Lingpa exclusively practised there the stages of creation and perfection of the

Point of Liberation, the Natural Liberation of Intention (*grol-tig dgongs-pa rang-grol*), a profound treasure of the great treasure-finder Sherap Özer, the succession of which had fallen to him through both close and distant lineages; and he obtained the special signs of "warmth".[1142]

Moreover, having completed the rites of service and attainment associated with myriad deities of many profound treasures, including both the *Earlier and Later Treasure Troves*, he measurably attained the condition of a holder of the awareness of maturation. When he mastered the yogas of the energy channels, currents and seminal points, the energy channels of the centre of rapture, situated in the throat, dissolved in a mass of syllables.[1143] He perceived all appearances as a book and the great treasury of the doctrine spilled open [in the form of] songs of indestructible reality and so forth, which were perfect in word and meaning. When he performed the rites of service and attainment for the *Gathering of the Guru's Intention*, the sound of a horse neighing burst forth from the crown of his head[1144] and the great Orgyen crowned him with the name "Pema Wangcen the Glorious". Through the power of being actually blessed by the master Mañjuśrīmitra he fully comprehended the pristine cognition which may be exemplified.[1145] Thereafter, he maintained in conduct the great discipline of a resplendently attired heruka.

In particular, during a vision of the inner radiance, the ḍākinī of the pristine cognition of the body of reality actually bestowed on him the inventory for the *Innermost Spirituality of Longcenpa* (*klong-byang*) in the symbolic script of the ḍākinīs at the Carung Khashor Stūpa [i.e. the Great Stūpa of Bodhnāth] in Nepal.[1146] Consequently, he reached an exalted level of learning and accomplishment, and became master of the great treasury of doctrine that is widely renowned as the *Great Perfection, the Innermost Spirituality of Longcenpa* (*rdzogs-pa chen-po klong-chen snying-gi thig-le*). But still he was not satisfied, and so, immediately after completing the three years [of retreat] in that place [Pelri], he proceeded to glorious Samye Chimpu. With great austerity he once more concentrated one-pointedly upon the essential attainment for three years in the cave of Sangcen Metok, at which time, in general, he had numberless pure visions, and, in particular, met three times with the body of pristine cognition of the all-knowing king of the doctrine, Longcen Rapjam Zangpo. The blessing of Longcenpa's body, speech and mind being actually transferred to him, Jikme Lingpa acquired his supreme authorisation and beheld the truth of the Great Perfection, the real pristine cognition of the sublime path. At the same location [Samye] he revealed, for the first time, the maturation and liberation of that great treasure of his mind to fifteen fortunate disciples. From then on, he widely propagated its profound meanings, so that he became the unique promulgator of the Innermost Spirituality of the Great Perfection (*rdzogs-pa chen-po snying-thig*).

After Jikme Lingpa had fulfilled his vow to remain in retreat for three years, the true meaning of the indestructible prophetic declaration made in the *Dialogue of Sky and Mountain* (*mkha'-ri zhu-lan*), a profound treasure of Chöwang Rinpoche, was revealed, for there it says:

> In Chongye my emanation will come to serve the world.
> Though no one will know who it is,
> He will teach in a forthright manner.[1147]
> At Chingwardo, or to the south of the Red Mausoleum,
> He may found a monastery at the Lhabap Stūpa.

The body of the pristine cognition of Tsele Natsok Rangdröl actually entrusted this purpose to Jikme Lingpa. Relying upon many auspicious coincidences, such as his symbolic revelations, he then returned to his homeland. In the uplands of Tönkar Valley, in a hidden ravine to the south of the mausoleum of Songtsen Gampo in Chongye, he re-established the mountain hermitage of Pel Tshering-jong Pema Ösel Thekcokling, including both the physical buildings and their contents. Thereafter, he lived out his life as a hidden yogin, free from activities, with his seat established there. To numberless worthy disciples from all quarters of the Land of Snows, as far as Bhutan and India, he skilfully revealed the transmitted precepts and treasures of the Nyingmapa tradition in general. In particular, he taught the instructions of the Innermost Spirituality in its ancient and new recensions.[1148] So it was that his doctrinal activity was wondrous.

Jikme Lingpa profusely gave the gift of the doctrine without hoping for return or [profitable] fruition: He performed many myriad offerings to the three doctrinal centres[1149] and he ransomed countless living creatures from certain death.[1150] He presented a wheel of fine gold to the great temple of Samye and erected a silver image of the Conqueror Ajita [Maitreya]. He repeated the consecration of Samye and when the great Gurkha army, which was hostile to the teaching, advanced upon Tibet, he successfully performed the rites for the aversion of war.[1151] This illustrates his activities in the sphere of work and his wondrous deeds which ensured the well-being of the teaching and the world, for which even the Tibetan government granted him great esteem and veneration.

Above all, during that age the teaching of the Ancient Translation School had everywhere become sparse. Jikme Lingpa could not bear in his heart that the enlightened activity of the vast aspirations of the emanational religious kings, translators, and scholars should become fruitless and that their indescribable legacy should nearly disappear. He had copies made, using the finest supplies and materials, of all the precious tantras of the Nyingmapa tradition which were to be found at Mindröling, some twenty-five volumes, and had the first five pages [of each volume] written in [ink made of] the five precious substances, and the remainder in black ink on a white background (*skya-chos*). Previously, there had been neither a detailed catalogue, nor a verified history, compiled on this topic, but, because his brilliance was profound and vast in connection with the three logical axioms (*gtan-tshigs-gsum*), this venerable master composed the *Narrative History of the Precious Collected Tantras of the Ancient Translation School, the Ornament Covering All Jambudvīpa* (*snga-'gyur rgyud-'bum rin-po-che'i rtogs-pa brjod-pa 'dzam-gling tha-grur khyab-pa'i rgyan*). The fine light of scriptural authority and logic which shines therein totally uproots all the confusions which arise from the darkness of perverted opinion and doubt.

Jikme Lingpa's collected works, which amount to nine volumes, include the basic root texts and elucidations of his mind treasure, the *Innermost Spirituality of Longcenpa* (*thugs-gter klong-chen snying-thig gzhung-rtsa-ba gsal-byed dang bcas-pa*); the *Vajrakīla according to the Tradition of the Tantra* (*phur-pa rgyud-lugs*) – a new redaction of the [Vajrakīla] transmitted precept based on the empowerment which had been conferred on him by Langcen Pelgi Senge[1152] in an emanational maṇḍala and the instructions which followed; and the root text and commentary of the *Precious Treasury of Enlightened Attributes*, which provides the sequential path for the entire teaching. This last composition was a treasure of intention given to him in the form of a treatise by the blessing of the all-knowing, great Longcenpa.

The disciples who attended directly on Jikme Lingpa's discourses included such great gurus and powerful nobles as Sakya Trhicen Ngawang Pelden Chökyong and his brother; the two Drigungpa emanations; the Supreme Emanation of the Dorje Trak Rikdzin; the Speech Emanation of Lhodrak and the Spiritual Son; Jora Trülku, the holder of the Podongpa teaching; the abbots of both the Shartse and Cangtse colleges of Ganden, who were holders of the tradition of Riwo Ganden [i.e. the Gelukpa tradition]; and Göntse Trülku of Tshona in Mön. There can be no counting, to their full limits, his disciples who were detached yogins, meditators, and monks. Also, most of the Nyingmapa gurus and emanations from the province of Kham came before his feet.

Jikme Lingpa's own enlightened activity, which embraced all quarters from the frontiers of India in the south, to China and Mongolia in the east, with the light of the doctrine, has been unrivalled during this late age. This, in particular, was due to the enlightened activity of his sole innermost spiritual son, Trupwang Jikme Trhinle Özer, an emanation of Prince Murup Tsepo,[1153] and also [to the activity] of Jikme Gyelwei Nyugu, a great bodhisattva,[1154] Jikme Kündröl, the learned and accomplished master of Mön, and others.

The master himself asserted that if he were to cultivate one-pointedly the enlightened mind for seven years in mountain retreat, the teaching would be increased and propagated. The truth of that prophecy has been realised in the present day, for the maturing empowerments, liberating guidance, and experiential cultivation of the Innermost Spirituality appears to be spreading, as if to cover all directions.

When he had completed such actions associated with the three spheres, on Friday 12 October 1798 (third day, ninth month, earth horse), during his seventieth year, Jikme Lingpa passed away at his own seat, the hermitage of Namdröl Yangtse in Tshering Valley. The actual demonstration of signs and miracles indicated his passage to the great realm of Lotus Light. Previously, he had bestowed in detail the wonderful, indestructible words of his final testament. Accordingly, his last rites were undertaken by Ön Özer Trhinle and others, who completed extensive ceremonies to fulfil the master's final intentions.

23 *Chogyur Decen Lingpa*

[646.1-658.6] The great treasure-finder Chogyur Decen Zhikpo Lingpa[1155] was an emanation of Murup Tsepo or Yeshe Rölpatsel, who was the son of glorious King [Trhisong] and a holder of commitments. He was born on Monday 10 August 1829 (tenth day, sixth month, earth female ox year, fourteenth cycle)[1156] at Gomde Tranang in Yertö, southern Dokam. His father was Pema Wangcuk, the mantra adept of Gom, who belonged to the family of Acadru, the minister of Nangcen Chinghu.[1157] His mother was Tshering Yangtso. His birth was accompanied by rainbow light and other auspicious omens. From childhood he displayed the wonderful conduct of a holy person; and he learnt to read and write with little difficulty. For this reason he was nicknamed Norbu Tendzin, "Jewel, Holder of the Teaching". He also practised many contemplative sequences unprompted by others.

Once, when he was in his thirteenth year, he went to play at a place called Maṇikha ("Entrance to Jewels", or "Entrance to the Six-Syllable Mantra of Avalokiteśvara"). On that occasion, Orgyen Rinpoche actually appeared to him and pretended to ask the name of the place and so on. After he had answered each question, Guru Rinpoche prophetically declared, "Since the place is called Maṇikha, you Norbu Tendzin, and this country Ārya-Nang (Sublime and Inner), you will be especially sublime in the world!" So saying, he vanished like a rainbow. At about this time, he received the vows of a novice from Taklung Ma Rinpoche.

Pawo VIII, Tsuklak Chöki Gyelpo, made great efforts to confer on him the texts, transmissions, and blessings of the *Warm Sunbeam of the Attainment of Mind* (*thugs-sgrub tsha-ba dmar-thag*) and the *Beauteous Flower Garland Ritual Manual*, both from the *Gathering of the Guru's Intention*. He was advised that it would be well if he were to cultivate experience of them and was thus entrusted with the actual lineage of the treasures. At one point or another, under many tutors, including the hierarchs of the Karma and Drukpa Kagyü sects and their disciples, the supreme emanations of Drigung, and the preceptors and master of

Chogyur Decen Lingpa

the Zurmang seat, he received endless empowerments, transmissions, and esoteric instructions of the sūtra and mantra traditions, ancient and new, as well as their exegetical traditions and ritual practices. He also studied the arts of dance, iconometry, chant and instrumental music. With little difficulty, he showed himself to be extremely skilled in all of them.

In conformity with the inspiration of Guru Rinpoche's prophecy, in his twenty-fifth year Chogyur Lingpa proceeded to the seat of Pelpung, where he met Situ Pema Nyinje Wangpo.[1158] He offered [the kīla known as] the "Laughter of Kīla's Great Power" (*phur-pa dbang-chen bzhad-pa*) and other gifts, which Situ delightedly accepted, so that obstacles were removed and the auspicious circumstances for his continued longevity were established. Situ also gave him confidential advice concerning the need to complete the attainment of his treasures and their secret seals. Then, gradually, Chogyur Lingpa received some profound doctrines, such as concern the cultivation of an enlightened aspiration, from the great preceptor and bodhisattva Dapzang Trülku. From Jamgön Lodrö Thaye he heard most of the transmitted precepts of the Nyingmapa, of which the foremost was the empowerment and exegetical transmission of the peaceful and wrathful deities of the *Magical Net*, and many treasure doctrines, beginning with the *Great Compassionate One as the Universal Gathering of the Sugatas*.

Chogyur Lingpa was most clearly foretold in many outer, inner, and secret prophetic inventories. Among these, the *Established Confluence of Auspicious Coincidences* (*rten-'brel mdo-chings*), in particular, declared:

> An aspiring individual, who will reveal, not leave,
> The profound treasures concealed in the Store of the Sky,[1159]
> Will be your later incarnation, O royal son.[1160]
> In that age most of the translators and scholars,
> And the king and his subjects will assemble together.
> In particular, when the sovereign and his sons reunite,
> Assisting one another, their propensities will gradually awaken,
> And they will encounter my ultimate instructions.
> In pure visions you will meet me in person,
> And effortlessly attain accomplishment
> By experiential cultivation
> Of my guidance which lays bare the practical application
> Of the instructions of secret mantra.
> Many disciples will emerge,
> Who will obtain the accomplishments!

Accordingly, during the ninth month of that year [October 1853] Chogyur Lingpa went to meet the venerable Jamyang Khyentse Wangpo. At that time the master [Khyentse Rinpoche] realised that he possessed a connection with the successive line of the incarnations of the sovereign Trhisong Detsen. Therefore, he initially bestowed on him the *Utterly Secret Razor Kīla* (*phur-pa yang-gsang spu-gri*), and, later, the great empowerment of *Vajrakīla according to the Khön Tradition* (*'khon-lugs phur-pa'i dbang-chen*). As a result, the outer, inner, and secret obstacles of Chogyur Lingpa were removed. During the empowerment of the *Further Innermost Spirituality like the Wish-fulfilling Gem*, he actually perceived the guru to be the great paṇḍita Vimalamitra. He experienced other extraordinary pure visions too, and thus was introduced to naked awareness. Then, when Chogyur Lingpa was entrusted with the vital heart-mantra of the protectress Ekajaṭī, he experienced a vast magnificence, reminiscent of an earthquake, and actually beheld her. She said, "If you, master and disciple, perform the three-year retreat together I shall grant you great accomplishment!" This presaged the later discovery of the *Three Classes of the Great Perfection* (*rdzogs-chen sde-gsum*).

In his twenty-seventh year, when he received the great empowerment of the *Nine-Deity Maṇḍala of Yangdak Heruka* (*yang-dag lha-dgu'i dbang-chen*), he felt that the guru [in the form of] Heruka dissolved into the crown of his own head. As a result, the knots in the energy channels in his heart were unravelled, and from that time onwards songs of indestructible reality poured forth without impediment. He understood without difficulty the symbolic script of the *Attainment of Mind, the Dispeller of All Obstacles* (*thugs-sgrub bar-chad kun-sel*), which he could not properly decipher before. This teaching agrees not only in meaning, but also for the most part in language, with the *Attainment of Mind, the Gathering of the Sugatas* (*thugs-sgrub bde-gshegs 'dus-pa*), a profound treasure of the venerable Khyentse Rinpoche. Therefore, they established the two together without obstacle, just as a mother and child are united. They also performed the treasure attainment (*gter-sgrub*)[1161] together, whereby they experienced numberless pure visions, including one in which they were actually favoured by Guru Padmasambhava and his consort. They obtained the inventories of many treasure troves, and many other auspicious coincidences were established. Since they had confidence in one another, the venerable Khyentse, too, enjoyed the maturational and liberating nectar of these new treasures and authorised them. In this way, the two became like the sun and moon among treasure-finders, universally renowned and indisputable.

In the isolated hermitage of Yangkyil, Chogyur Lingpa remained absorbed in the rites of service and attainment for the *Utterly Profound Gathering of All Precious Jewels*. From then on, in accord with Guru Padmasambhava's prophetic declarations, he persevered in the contemplative sequences, above all, during three years of solitary retreat at Wokmin Karma. Arriving experientially at the culmination of creation, perfection, and Great Perfection, infinite signs and marks of accomplishment were disclosed. It was thus proven by direct perception that he was a great being who had mastery over the four rites of enlightened activity.

CHOGYUR LINGPA'S SEVEN SUCCESSIONS TO THE TRANSMITTED PRECEPTS

In particular, in the *Prophetic Declaration of the Three Classes of the Great Perfection* (*rdzogs-chen sde-gsum-gyi lung-bstan*) it says:

> The streams of seven successions of transmitted precepts
> Will fall to the sovereign and his son as their fortune.
> These are the unbroken lineage, transmitted from
> one to the next (i),
> The substantial profound treasures (ii), those of
> intention (iv),
> Reconcealed treasures (iii), treasures of recollection (v),
> Pure visions (vi), and the aural lineages (vii).

They will reap a great doctrinal harvest in this
degenerate age.
Profound and vast, they will outshine the sun.

In conformity with this, both of the two great treasure-finders, emanations of the sovereign and his son, were endowed with seven successions of the transmitted precepts of the profound doctrine, which were subdivisions of the three [basic types of transmission], namely, the transmitted precepts, treasures, and pure visions.

(i) [Concerning the transmitted precepts]: Chogyur Lingpa received most of the distant lineage of the transmitted precepts in existence nowadays. He taught and propagated the trilogy of the *Sūtra which Gathers All Intentions*, the *Magical Net*, and the *Mental Class* many times. Furthermore, among his profound treasures, there are those which uphold the doctrinal language and philosophical systems, just as they are found in the *Sūtra which Gathers All Intentions*, the *Magical Net*, and other texts of the transmitted precepts. These unprecedented and wonderful discoveries constitute his real succession to the transmitted precepts.

(ii) Concerning the earth treasures, which were his own fortune: In his thirteenth year Chogyur Lingpa began by discovering the *Twenty-four Means for Attainment which were the Prince's Contemplations* (*lha-sras thugs-dam sgrub-thabs nyer-bzhi*), and the *Skull-Mirror of Indestructible Reality, which is Indicative of the Transmitted Precepts of the Gathering of Intentions* (*dgongs-'dus bka'-rtags rdo-rje thod-pa me-long*) at Trakar Dzongcung. In his thirty-ninth year, after his venerable guru [Khyentse Rinpoche] had offered him an inventory and inspiration, he discovered, at Tsike Norbu Pünsum, the *Thirty-seven Supreme Treasures* (*mchog-gter sum-cu-rtsa-bdun*), which included the *Seven Cycles of the Jewel of True Doctrine* (*dam-chos nor-bu skor-bdun*), as well as a representative figure of Guru Rinpoche and the body ornaments of Senge Dradrok. At Dra Yangdzong he discovered the *Seven Cycles of Pacification* (*zhi-byed skor-bdun*), together with their inventories, supplementary inventories, essential inventories, quintessential inventories, et cetera, and also many minor material treasures.

Concerning Chogyur Lingpa's foremost treasures: He brought forth the *Attainment of Mind, the Dispeller of All Obstacles* from Danyin Khala Rongo; the *Great Compassionate One, Lotus Crowned* (*thugs-rje chen-po padma gtsug-tor*) from Nabün Dzong; the *Seven Cycles of Profound Contemplation* (*thugs-dam zab-pa skor-bdun*) from the area behind Wokmin Karma; the cycles of the tantras and transmissions which are its supplements, and also the *Root Attainment of Mind, the Gathering of All Intentions* (*rtsa-ba'i thugs-sgrub dgongs-pa kun-'dus*), along with two representative images from Yegyel Namkadzö; the *True Doctrine, Three Classes of the Great Perfection* (*dam-chos rdzogs-pa chen-po sde-gsum*) from the

Pemashel Cave in Marshödzam; the *Six Scrolls of True Doctrine* (*dam-chos shog-sde drug-pa*) from Mount Kongmo Wokma at Sengcen Namdrak; the *Great Compassionate One, the Magical Net of the Lotus* (*thugs-rje chen-po padma sgyu-'phrul drva-ba*) and the *Churner of Saṃsāra's Depths* (*'khor-ba dong-sprugs*) from Khandro Bumdzong; the *General Summary of Mātaraḥ* (*ma-mo spyi-bsdus*) from Karmei Peldeu; the *Attainment of Mind, the Wish-fulfilling Gem* (*thugs-sgrub yid-bzhin nor-bu*) from Kela Norbu Pünsum, in conformity with the prophetic declaration of the venerable Khyentse; the *Eight Transmitted Precepts, the Universal Gathering of the Sugatas* (*bka'-brgyad bde-gshegs kun-'dus*) and the *Refined Gold of the Profound Great Perfection* (*zab-pa rdzogs-chen gser-zhun*) from Yubel Rock, south of Yegyel; the *Attainment of Mind, the Expressive Play of Indestructible Wrath* (*thugs-sgrub rdo-rje drag-rtsal*) and the *Five Innermost Cycles* (*snying-po skor-lnga*) from the "tiger den" of Rongme Karmo; and the *Saṃvara Buddhasamāyoga* (*bde-mchog sangs-rgyas mnyam-sbyor*) from Rudam Kangtrö.

All those are merely illustrative: From each treasure site there came forth an exceedingly large number of doctrines, sacramental substances, images and symbolic objects. Since most of them were found in public, they were visible to everyone's senses and hence indisputable. In short, just as it had been clearly prophesied that the succession of the transmitted precepts of a hundred treasures from the sites of buddha-body, speech, mind, attributes, and activities would fall to him, along with those of a hundred [doctrines of] Innermost Spirituality and many [substances providing] liberation when tasted, just so, Chogyur Lingpa discovered the *Dokam Inventory of the Twenty-five Great Pilgrimage Places of Dokam* (*mdo-khams gnas-chen nyer-lnga'i mdo-byang*) at the rock of Pawo Wangcen. In this way he made newly manifest many sites, their roots and branches. His wonderful miracles were also inconceivable; for instance, he discovered as treasure about three grades of material for representative images of Guru Rinpoche, but he multiplied the copies [of those images] many times.

(iii) Concerning the reconcealed treasures[1162] which supplement these: These were the *Wrathful Guru, the Innermost Spirituality of the Red HŪṂ* (*gur-drag hūṃ-dmar snying-thig*), a treasure of his own previous incarnation as the great treasure-finder Sangye Lingpa, which fell to him through the power of blessing; and the *Mother Tantra which Integrates the Secret onto the Path* (*ma-rgyud gsang-ba lam-khyer*) of the ḍākinī Künga Bumpa, which fell to him through a close lineage.

(iv) Concerning the profound treasures of intention: Relying upon the inspiration derived from the venerable Tārā's saying to him "It is good!" three times, Chogyur Lingpa established the *Innermost Profundity of Tārā* (*sgrol-ma'i zab-tig*).

(v) Concerning the recollections which supplement them: The master, having remembered his former life as Nup Khulungpa Yönten

Gyamtso, briefly set down in writing the *Transmitted Instructions of the Indestructible Array, which Nupcen [Sangye Yeshe] Conferred as his Final Testament (gnubs-chen 'da'-ka'i zhal-chems lung rdo-rje bkod-pa'i gdams-pa gnang-ba)*, together with *Nup's Boast* (*gnubs-kyi kha-pho*), and he also recalled a way of reciting the *rulu mantra* and limitless choreographic arrangements. Relying on the recollection of his previous life as Sangye Lingpa he established, in detail, the step-by-step guidance for the *Yogic Exercises of the Nine Vigorous Skills according to the Gathering of Intentions* (*dgongs-'dus rtsal-sprugs rnam-dgu'i 'khrul-'khor*).

(vi) Concerning the pure visions: When he opened the entrance to the treasures situated at Riwo Wangzhu, he saw, in Vimalamitra's cave of attainment, the great paṇḍita himself, who gave him instructions. These are preserved as the *Innermost Profundity of Vimalamitra* (*bi-ma-la'i zab-tig*) and so forth.

(vii) Concerning the aural lineage: In a pure vision Chogyur Lingpa went to the glorious Copper-coloured Mountain, where he received from Orgyen Rinpoche the *Instructions of the Innermost Spirituality Concerning the Profound Significance of Ati* (*a-ti zab-don snying-thig-gi gdams-pa*), which he set down in writing, et cetera.

Such is the brief account of Chogyur Lingpa's liberating endowment of seven successions of transmitted precepts. In both early and later life he beheld the deities of the three roots and received their prophetic declarations; the protectors undertook to perform his enlightened activities; and he experienced many pure visions, long and short, in which he journeyed to the glorious mountain on Cāmaradvīpa. This much must suffice for illustrative purposes.

Chogyur Lingpa performed the great attainment,[1163] with the four branches of ritual service and attainment, about thirty-three times, including those which he undertook himself and the occasions on which he proceeded to act as "master of indestructible reality" (*vajrācārya*) at the assemblies of others. By his magnificent, overpowering commands [to the local deities] at the geomantic centres of Tibet and Dokam, including Samye Hepori and Pel Chuwori, and by his many invocations of blessing at the great places of pilgrimage, Chogyur Lingpa pacified the turbulence of military invasion, and so forth. He increased the prosperity of the kingdom and widely attained enlightened activities, just as had been predicted of him.

To the Kagyüpa, of whom the foremost were the Karmapa, Drukpa, Drigungpa, and Taklungpa [subsects]; to the Nyingmapa, of whom the foremost were the Mindröling, Katok, Pelyül, Zhecen, and Dzokcen [monasteries and their adherents]; and to the Sakyapa and other holders of the teaching, without bias, Chogyur Lingpa directly and indirectly conferred the maturation and liberation of the profound doctrine. His gifts of [medicinal] substances which liberate when tasted covered all of Tibet and Kham, the centre and frontiers. In particular, there were ten root masters of his doctrine, most of whom had auspicious connections, so that the enlightened activity of his treasure doctrines, the *Attainment of Mind, the Dispeller of All Obstacles* foremost among them, was widely propagated. At Wokmin Tshurpu [the seat of the Karmapa] he instituted the annual performance of the *Great Attainment of Kīla [according to] the Seven [Cycles of] Profound [Contemplation]* (*zab-bdun phur-pa'i sgrub-chen*), along with the fundamental middle-length dances. As exemplified by this, he established rites of attainment and offering ceremonies, associated with the great and small doctrinal transmissions of his new treasures, at many monasteries.

Among the *Ten Doctrines which Secure the Happiness of Tibet and Kham* (*bod-khams bde-thabs chos-bcu*), Chogyur Lingpa established the *Doctrinal Cycle of Auspicious Coincidence* (*rten-'brel-gyi chos-skor*); and, in accord with its meaning, the wonderful ceremonies for the spread of exegesis, attainment, and work which are associated with the twofold teaching of sūtra and mantra as taught during the age of the preceptor [Śāntarakṣita], the master [Padmasambhava], and the religious king [Trhisong Detsen] were successively instituted at Pelpung, Katok and Dzokcen.[1164] At his own seats of Karmari, Neten Gang and Tsike Düdo, he founded temples, including the buildings themselves and the objects they housed. At the last two centres mentioned he established monastic communities and the continuous exegesis and attainment of the sūtras and mantras.

After bringing such actions to completion, Chogyur Lingpa's intention turned for the while to another great purpose, and in his forty-second year, 1870 (iron male horse), he seemed to fall ill. He had a pure vision in which he went to an utterly pure buddha-field. Then, on Wednesday 29 June 1870 (first day, fifth month),[1165] while demonstrating such wonderful miracles as earthquakes and rainbows, he became equipoised in the expanse of peace.

On Wednesday 7 December (fifteenth day, tenth month), during that same year, the venerable Khyentse Wangpo had a pure vision in which he met the great treasure-finder in the form of the bodhisattva Padmāṅkuśa, in the Lotus-covered Pure Land to the west. Khyentse Rinpoche received the bountiful nectar of his means for attainment, empowerment, and instructions, and concealed them for one month under a pledge of secrecy.[1166] Then, on Sunday 1 January 1871 (tenth day, eleventh month), when, in connection with a feast offering, he established them, a warmth suddenly descended on the land, turning the ice into streams. This auspicious omen appears to have been an extraordinary sign of blessing, made directly manifest to the senses.

24 *Jamyang Khyentse Wangpo*

[658.6-676.5] Jamyang Khyentse Wangpo, or Pema Ösel Do-nga Lingpa, the fifth kingly treasure-finder,[1167] was the coalescent play of the great paṇḍita Vimalamitra and the religious king Trhisong Detsen. He was the thirteenth of Gyelse Lharje's incarnations, during which he was always a treasure-finder. Khyentse Rinpoche was born, with many wondrous omens, on Saturday 15 July 1820 (fifth day, sixth month, iron dragon year, fourteenth cycle), near Yaru Khyungcen Rock in the village of Terlung Tingo, Derge district, Dokam. His father was Trungcen Rincen Wangyel of the Nyö clan, and his mother was Sokza Sonamtsho.

From his very earliest memories, Khyentse Rinpoche was lovingly cared for repeatedly by the six-armed Lord of Pristine Cognition (*Jñānanātha*) and the mantra protectress Ekajaṭī. He had irregular recollections of many of his past lives. From childhood he awoke to the enlightened family of the greater vehicle and, in particular, his heart longed only for ordination. Endowed with incomparable intelligence and discrimination he learnt to read and write and so forth without difficulty. Just by seeing most books only once he mastered both the words and the meaning.

In his twenty-first year he was fully ordained by Rikdzin Zangpo, the preceptor of Orgyen Mindröling. From the Sakyapa Dorje Rincen and others he received [the vows of] the cultivation of the enlightened attitude, in connection with the traditions of the two promulgators [Nāgārjuna and Asaṅga]. He received *Cakrasaṃvara* and *Hevajra* from the brother of Thartse Khen Rinpoche;[1168] *Yangdak Heruka according to the So Tradition* (*so-lugs yang-dag*) and the *Innermost Spirituality of the Awareness-holder* from Gyurme Sangye Künga, the Trhicen of Mindröling; and the peaceful and wrathful deities of the *Magical Net*, along with its empowerment, from Gyurme Thutop Namgyel of Zhecen.[1169] In this way, the roots of the mantra tradition's vows were established.

Khyentse Rinpoche had completely uprooted arrogance in connection with his incarnate status and his noble and wealthy ancestry, and endured great hardships. With tremendous perseverance and endeavour he attended on almost one hundred and fifty tutors from Central Tibet, Tsang, and Kham, amongst whom were included gurus who were holders of indestructible reality, as well as spiritual benefactors and learned masters of the sciences. He completed study and training in the exegeses of the well-known "ten sciences", which include art, medicine, grammar, logic and their branches; and in those of the dialectical texts, as exemplified by the Vinaya, the *Treasury of the Abhidharma*, Madhyamaka, and Transcendental Perfection. He received, in their

Jamyang Khyentse Wangpo

entirety, the maturational [empowerments] and liberating [guidance] of all the traditions of the past which had survived without decline, such as the transmitted precepts and treasures of the Nyingmapa; and also [the teaching of] the ancient and new Kadampa schools; the Sakyapa, Ngorpa and Tsharpa;[1170] the Kagyüpa subsects of Kamtsang, Drigung, Taklung and Drukpa; as well as the Conangpa, Zhalupa[1171] and Podongpa. He also received the existing exegetical traditions for tantras and treatises including the *Secret Nucleus of the Magical Net*, the *Kālacakra Tantra*, and the trio of the *Cakrasaṃvara*, *Hevajra* and *Guhyasamāja* tantras, et cetera; and the transmissions of about seven hundred volumes, comprising all the treatises of the Tibetan philosophical systems, without bias. Foremost among these were the *Precious Translations of the Transmitted Precepts of the Conqueror* (*rgyal-ba'i bka'-'gyur rin-po-che*), the *Collected Tantras of the Nyingmapa*, and the surviving continuous transmission of the *Tangyur* (*bstan-'gyur*).[1172] In short, Khyentse Rinpoche pursued study exclusively for about thirteen years. He heard most of the traditions renowned among those of the "Ten Great Pillars who Supported the Exegetical Lineages" (*bshad-brgyud 'degs-pa'i ka-chen bcu*).[1173] Just by glancing at a volume this master understood the depths of its meaning, and he possessed unfailing retention.

In order to reveal the career of one who did not belittle the doctrine, Khyentse Rinpoche did not abandon [all these doctrines] having merely studied them, but trained and cultivated himself in them to the limits, whereby he came to possess the unclouded eye of the doctrine. So it was that he knew in detail, and without adulteration, the essential points of the view, conduct and assertions of each philosophical system, whether or not their respective traditions and customs were free from deviation, and so forth. During the present day there is no one, high or low, with whom he might be compared.

Khyentse Rinpoche also expounded most of the sūtras, tantras, and treatises which he himself had studied, along with their maturation, liberation and supporting transmissions,[1174] many times each. There was nothing he did not teach at least once, whereby he fulfilled the hopes of each aspirant, from great, holy individuals down to common beggars, by his doctrinal gifts, which were free from materialism. He never amassed property by the perverse livelihood of performing household ceremonies which claim to benefit disciples and living creatures, or by begging for alms. Because the three blazes and the three gatherings shone outwardly, material wealth came to him without effort, and he did not squander any at all on impossible schemes. Instead, he commissioned about two thousand gold and copper images representing the buddha-body; published nearly forty volumes of texts, and had printed, or copied, some two thousand volumes in all, representing the buddha-speech; and as representatives of the buddha-mind, built more than one hundred stūpas of gold and copper, the foremost of which was the great Stūpa of Lhündrup Teng. To house them all he erected a fine array of some thirteen temples, large and small, and in these he established the periodic and daily ceremonies. He did not much concern himself with the difficulties of establishing [monastic and ritual] propriety in the new centres, owing to the adverse circumstances and time, but to those monasteries and centres which had been badly damaged during the later civil disturbances in upper and lower [Dokam] he offered more than three thousand bricks of tea, in accord with the size of the monasteries.[1175] He advised the officials of China and Tibet, as well as the religious king and royal ministers of Derge, of the great importance of adequate support, owing to which monasteries which had declined were restored to their former condition and the appropriate ceremonies were sponsored. And through his admonishments, which conformed to traditional and local custom, he greatly increased them. Such was the great kindness which Khyentse Rinpoche conferred.

To the doctrinal centres, large and small, in the neighbouring districts, he annually provided donations to support [the rites connected with] dhāraṇīs, mantras, and dedications of merit. All told, at various times, his offerings for this purpose totalled some four thousand bricks of tea in value.

In general, because Khyentse Rinpoche had acquired firmness in the twofold precious enlightened attitude,[1176] and especially, because he was endowed with the vast power of pure vision and devotion towards all the philosophical systems, and was otherwise totally without bias and bigotry,[1177] his students were countless. They included all the well-known holders of the teaching, and great individuals among the Sakyapa, Kagyüpa, Nyingmapa, and Gelukpa, as well as spiritual benefactors, practitioners of retreat, poor mendicants, and adherents of the Yungdrung Pön tradition,[1178] without partiality. Among those who assembled continually everyday, without number, headed by the many great officials of China and Tibet, it was as if there was no one who did not obtain, in accord with his or her devotion, a connection [with the master], whether through the gift of the doctrine, the removal of misfortune, empowerment, or blessing. Free from the fetters of the eight worldly concerns, Khyentse Rinpoche eradicated the roots of such human behaviour as saving face and hope and fear, whether found in persons of high or low status. Thus, his career was that of a king among those who had renounced worldly activity and the cares of this life.

Khyentse Rinpoche spent about thirteen years, altogether, performing the rites of service and attainment for many of the favoured deities of the tantrapiṭaka of the ancient and new traditions. He experientially cultivated each and every one of the profound [systems of] guidance, and, above all, those of the *Hundred Systems of Guidance* (*khrid-brgya*)[1179] composed by Jetsün [Künga] Drölcok. The fact that he undertook to accomplish whatever commitments he had assumed alone renders his career incomparable with that of any other.

The foregoing remarks constitute but a brief summary of Khyentse Rinpoche's outer career, which deals with the three spheres of renunciation, study, and work.

In the Land of Snows, it is well known that there are eight lineages of attainment or great conveyances:

(i) The Nyingmapa, or Ancient Translation School, which orginated through the kindness of the preceptor [Śāntarakṣita], the master [Padmasambhava], and the religious king [Trhisong Detsen];

(ii) The Kadampa, which is the tradition of the venerable master, glorious Atiśa, and is endowed with seven divine doctrines;

(iii) The instructions of the Path and Fruit, which are the essential spirituality of the great accomplished master Virūpa, and have been transmitted through the glorious Sakyapa and their disciples;

(iv) The four great and eight minor subsects of the Kagyü, which are descended from Marpa, Milarepa, and Takpo Lharje, and have passed down instructions from the lineage of four transmitted precepts;[1180]

(v) The glorious Shangpa Kagyü [which maintains] the golden doctrines of the learned and accomplished Khyungpo Neljorpa;

(vi) The Six-limbed Yoga, which emphasises above all the yoga of indestructible reality, and which is the stage of perfection of the king of all tantras, the glorious *Kālacakra*;

(vii) The true doctrine of the Pacification of suffering, along with its branch, the Object of Cutting, which is the tradition of the great accomplished master Phadampa Sangye; and

(viii) The Service and Attainment of the Three Indestructible Realities, which the Vajra Queen actually bestowed on the great accomplished master Orgyenpa.

Khyentse Rinpoche had immeasurable faith and devotion towards each of these systems, of which the past traditions have been preserved in unbroken lineages. Therefore, scorning physical fatigue, and with fervent perseverance, he received in full, and without error, all their sequences of maturation and liberation from tutors connected with the sources of each tradition. By reflecting upon them he cleared his doubts; and while experientially cultivating them through meditation he received the blessings of the three secrets and the instructions of close lineages, both in reality and during various visions and dreams, from the learned and accomplished masters of India and Tibet, the peaceful and wrathful meditational deities and conquerors, and the host of ḍākinīs of the three abodes. In these and other ways he had limitless pure visions at each and every instant. But all this is just vaguely illustrative; for, in fact, Khyentse Rinpoche never proclaimed his visions and supernormal cognitive powers, or made other statements about supposed spiritual attainments. For this reason only so much may be known. Above all, having thoroughly mastered the two stages according to those eight conveyances, he became unimpeded in teaching, debate, and composition, and free from the taints of bewilderment; and thus he made fortunate disciples enter his following. This is merely the kernel of his inner career.

In particular, it says in an indestructible prophetic declaration of the great accomplished master Thangtong Gyelpo:[1181]

> Seven hundred years from now,
> In the middle of Dokam, during a dragon year,

A yogin no different from me,
Endowed with five characteristics,
Will emerge as an apparitional person.
He will be the son of Ga, an awareness-holder of Nyö.
His element will be iron. He will have a warrior's signs.[1182]
Being blessed by Pema Gyelpo, he will be Do-nga Lingpa,
Endowed with seven successions of transmitted precepts.
Being blessed by Vimalamitra,
He will be Ösel Trülpei Dorje.
Being blessed by the sovereign, Mañjuśrī's emanation,
He will be Chöki Shenyen.

In accordance with this, as well as with the *Prophetic Inventory of the Three Classes of the Great Perfection* (*rdzogs-chen sde-gsum lung-byang*), which was cited above [p. 844], and others, Khyentse Rinpoche was repeatedly heralded by indestructible prophetic declarations as one who, having mastered seven successions of transmitted precepts, would greatly benefit the teaching and living creatures; and so he manifestly did.

When he was in his eighth year he fell gravely ill and was painfully afflicted. At that time Guru Rinpoche and Yeshe Tshogyel both revealed themselves, empowering and consecrating him in the maṇḍala of Vajrakīla. Having received their further advice he was victorious in the battle with his obstacles. In his fifteenth year, in a pure vision, he approached the Nine-Storey Pagoda at the Indestructible Seat in India. He climbed it storey-by-storey and, in the eighth, he met the great master Mañjuśrīmitra in the guise of a paṇḍita, surrounded by piles of books to the left and right. Khyentse Rinpoche bowed with great devotion and prayed, whereupon Mañjuśrīmitra took a volume from his left and showed it to him. It was a Sanskrit manuscript of the *Verse Summation of the Transcendental Perfection of Discriminative Awareness*. He placed it on the crown of Khyentse's head and transmitted its intention, saying, "This is the complete transmission of all the dialectical doctrines." Then, he took a volume from his right and showed it to him. It appeared to be entitled the *Great Perfection, the Tantra of the Mirror of Vajrasattva's Heart* (*rdzogs-pa chen-po rdor-sems snying-gi me-long-gi rgyud*). He placed it upon the crown of his head and transmitted its intention, saying, "This is the complete [transmission of] the words, meanings, and blessings of the secret mantra vehicle of indestructible reality in general, and of the three classes of the Great Perfection in particular." Then, after making some prophecies, Mañjuśrīmitra joyfully dissolved into light and vanished into the master himself. For a moment Khyentse Rinpoche expansively entered a non-conceptual contemplation. Having roused himself from it, he proceeded outside [the temple], at which point there was a great fire blazing in front of the door. Powerless to do otherwise he entered it and his gross, material body was burnt to nothing. He was transformed into a radiant body of light, thinking, "I am Vimalamitra."

Moreover, during that same period, the mighty lord among accomplished masters, Thangtong Gyelpo, revealed himself in a dream, blessed Khyentse Rinpoche, and conferred on him instructions and further advice; but the master only wrote down the *Means for the Attainment of the Guru* (*bla-sgrub*). Later, he unsealed these transmitted precepts and gradually established the *Cycles of the Innermost Spirituality of the Accomplished Master* (*grub-thob thugs-tig-gi skor-rnams*), including the *Root Verses of the Six Stages of Perfection* (*rdzogs-rim drug-gi rtsa-tshig*), the *Five Cycles of Attainment* (*sgrub-skor lnga*), and the *Gathering of the Blood-drinking Sugatas* (*khrag-'thung bde-gshegs 'dus-pa*). He also had a vision and was blessed by the Lord of Immortality [Amitāyus] and his consort, whereby he received their extraordinary means for attainment. Among them, he established the *Root Text of Caṇḍālī, Mother of Life* (*tshe-yum tsaṇḍa-lī'i rtsa-ba*). Although he experienced these and countless other visions of the myriad deities of the three roots, he profoundly intended to preserve their secrecy. Therefore, others did not know even a bit about them.

In particular, though there appear to be many prophetic declarations among Khyentse Rinpoche's earlier and later [treasures], he himself stated:

> It is said that: "Treasure-finders are ruined by their prophecies..." Just so, once a so-called prophetic declaration is written down it becomes necessary to put its stipulations into practice. But no one at all puts them into practice, because of which [the prophecies] never exactly strike the mark. Too much prattle about them is an ingress for demons!

Therefore, he neither made prophetic declarations, nor delighted in those made by others. This appears to be a point of great consequence.

JAMYANG KHYENTSE WANGPO'S SEVEN SUCCESSIONS TO THE TRANSMITTED PRECEPTS

(i) Concerning Khyentse Rinpoche's succession to the transmitted precepts [of the distant lineage]: In his sixteenth year, at dawn on Saturday 6 May 1835 (tenth day, fourth month), he went to the Lotus Light Palace on Cāmaradvīpa in a pure vision. There, in a magnificent mountain range, in the midst of especially white clouds, he met Guru Saroruhavajra, surrounded by a host of ḍākinīs. The Guru intentionally blessed him, conferred symbolic empowerment, and greatly inspired him by foretelling his seven successions to the transmitted precepts. Finally, adopting a gaze, he said:

Untainted by graspable objects,
Untarnished by grasping thoughts,
Maintaining naked awareness and emptiness –
This is the intention of all buddhas!

Then, together with his retinue he vanished into the master himself, who consequently felt that the spirituality of the Guru had merged indivisibly with his mind. Henceforth, he acquired a natural security in the abiding nature of primordial purity. He became utterly enthusiastic and prayed one-pointedly to Guru Rinpoche, owing to which he effortlessly obtained all the transmitted precepts and treasures of the ancient and new traditions of the sūtras and tantras, along with their maturation, liberation, and supporting transmissions, as well as exceedingly rare continuous lineages. Through his experiential cultivation, teaching and propagation of them, he rekindled the dying embers of the teaching.

(ii) Concerning his earth treasures: In his twentieth year, when Khyentse Rinpoche went to Trakmar Drinzang, the ḍākinī of pristine cognition actually offered him a treasure chest. From it he extracted the *Doctrinal Cycle of the Great Compassionate One as Mind at Rest* (*thugs-rje chen-po sems-nyid ngal-gso'i chos-skor*) and the remains of twenty-one brahmans. From Damshö Nyingdrung he brought forth the *Cycle of the Means for the Attainment of the Guru's Four Bodies* (*bla-ma sku-bzhi'i sgrub-thabs-kyi skor*) and relics emanated from a tooth of Guru Rinpoche. These were brought out and offered to him by [the protector] Nyencen Thangla. At Singu Yutso he discovered the *Cycle of the Magical Net of the Three Roots* (*rtsa-gsum sgyu-'phrul drva-ba'i skor*); and at Terlung Pemei Shelri the *Cycle of the Universal Gathering of the Three Roots* (*rtsa-gsum spyi-'dus-kyi skor*), which was brought out by the magical power of the ḍākinīs and offered to him. In addition to these there were many others, but except for some of the root texts he was not permitted to establish them. As for the *Cycle of the Attainment of Mind as the Wish-fulfilling Gem* (*thugs-sgrub yid-bzhin nor-bu'i skor*) and the representative image [of Padmasambhava, called] "Blazing with the Glory of Accomplishment", which rested at Tsike Norbu Pünsum, he exhorted Chogyur Lingpa to extract and establish them.

In general, the *Four Cycles of the Means for the Attainment of the Guru* (*bla-sgrub skor bzhi-ka*), the *Three Classes of the Great Perfection which are the Innermost Spirituality of Vairocana* (*bai-ro'i thugs-tig rdzogs-chen sde-gsum*), et cetera, appear to have also been the combined treasure troves of this master and Chogyur Lingpa, [which they discovered] in common.

(iii) Concerning the reconcealed treasures which supplement them: In 1859 (*don-grub*, earth sheep year) Guru Rinpoche appeared to Khyentse Rinpoche in the form of the great treasure-finder Sangye

Lingpa, gave him a volume, and blessed him. With that extraordinary, pure vision as the inception, the careers of the treasure-finders and all their extant treasure doctrines shone clearly in Khyentse Rinpoche's mind; and he was authorised to be the successor to their transmitted precepts. In this way, most of the yellow scrolls which had been reconcealed as treasures by their respective previous discoverers were brought forth by the ḍākinīs of pristine cognition and handed down to him, whereupon he deciphered them. Some he established by glancing at the symbolic script, or because, without efforts, they were self-clarifying in the expanse of his intention. During these occasions Guru Rinpoche appeared in person, or in the forms of the various treasure-finders, and bestowed upon him the maturation and liberation [of the treasures] in their entirety, all at once. With most wonderful perseverance, his eminence Jamgön Lodrö Thaye implored Khyentse Rinpoche again and again to rediscover even a portion of the ancient treasures of which the lineages had been broken altogether. Accordingly, he found a great many close lineages of reconcealed treasure. These are preserved in the *Store of Precious Treasure*.

(iv) Concerning his profound treasures of intention: In 1848 (earth monkey), his twenty-ninth year, while *en route* to Central Tibet, Khyentse Rinpoche performed the feast offering of the tenth day at Cangdrok Gegyel. Guru Rinpoche actually revealed himself to him and gave his blessing. When Khyentse Rinpoche offered worship before the representative image of Saroruhavajra at Samye, which had been discovered among the treasures of Nyang-rel Nyima Özer, the image actually turned into Saroruhavajra and gave him blessing and instruction, on the basis of which he brought forth the *Doctrinal Cycle of the Innermost Spirituality of Saroruha, which is the Secret Attainment, among the Three Cycles of the Means for the Attainment of the Guru* (*bla-sgrub skor-gsum-gyi gsang-sgrub mtsho-skyes snying-thig-gi chos-skor*). In January/February 1855 (*rgyal zla-ba*, wood tiger), during his thirty-fifth year, when he performed the rites of the service and attainment of the Immortal Wish-granting Wheel [*'chi-med yid-bzhin 'khor-lo*, the name of a form of White Tārā] he actually beheld the visage of the sublime Tārā, who harmoniously chanted her ten-syllable mantra and blessed him.[1183] Later, when he had also been blessed by three masters who had accomplished immortality,[1184] he brought forth the *Doctrinal Cycle of the Innermost Spirituality of the Sublime Lady* (*'phags-ma'i snying-thig-gi chos-skor*). The origins of the *Cycle of the Innermost Spirituality of the Accomplished Master* have already been described [p. 804]. These treasures of Khyentse Rinpoche are supreme among the treasures of intention, for they comprise verses of indestructible reality which are no different from the tantras, and are beyond the conceptions of ordinary people.

(v) Concerning Khyentse Rinpoche's recollections: Once, while travelling in Tibet, when he passed through the lower valley of Uyuk in Tsang, he remembered precisely the place and time at which, formerly, as the great Cetsün, he had passed away in the body of light. On the basis of this, he established the *Innermost Spirituality of Cetsün (lce-btsun snying-thig)*.[1185] Then, when he remembered his previous life as Langdro Könjung, he brought to light the *Attainment of Longevity, the Innermost Spirituality of Vairocana* (*tshe-sgrub bai-ro'i thugs-tig*), the *Alchemy of White Siṃhavaktrā* (*seng-gdong dkar-mo'i bcud-len*), et cetera.

(vi) Concerning his pure visions: As exemplified by the aforementioned *Cycle of Instructions on Caṇḍālī, Mother of Life, from the Innermost Spirituality of Immortality* (*'chi-med thugs-tig-gi tshe-yum tsaṇḍa-lī'i gdams-skor*), a recension of the *Means for the Attainment of the Guru according to the Innermost Spirituality of Longcenpa, [entitled] "Sealed with the Seminal Point"* (*klong-chen snying-thig-gi bla-sgrub thig-le'i rgya-can-gyi yig-cha*),[1186] and the *Means for the Attainment of the Guru Chogyur Lingpa, the Gathering of the Families of the Three Bodies* (*mchog-gling bla-sgrub sku-gsum rigs-'dus*),[1187] there were undoubtedly many, but he confined the actual propagation to those alone.

(vii) Concerning the aural lineage: While Khyentse Rinpoche was residing in the great pilgrimage centre of Dzongshö Deshek Düpa, he had a pure vision in which he approached the Śaṅkarakūṭa Caitya. There, in each of the eight directions there were arrayed the Eight Emanations of the Guru, and, at the centre, all of them gathered together as Guru Rinpoche. They bestowed upon him, as an aural lineage, the heart of the maturation and liberation of the *Eight Transmitted Precepts of Great Attainment*, the *Peaceful and Wrathful Deities of the Magical Net*, and so forth; and he established them.

All the above constitutes merely the essence of Khyentse Rinpoche's secret career.

In his seventy-third year, after completing, for the while, such marvellous and wonderful deeds, on the morning of Monday 18 April 1892 (twenty-first day, second month, water male dragon year),[1188] Khyentse Rinpoche scattered some flowers and gave many benedictions, after which, equipoised in contemplation, he withdrew from the array of his physical body into the expanse of the great master Vimalamitra's intention. Thereafter, just as had been prophesied, his emanational basis at Mount Wu-t'ai-shan made simultaneously manifest the array of five emanational bodies.[1189] So it is that [as the several Khyentse Rinpoches] he has performed, and continues to perform, inconceivable acts on behalf of the teaching and living creatures.

25 *Jamgön Kongtrül Lodrö Thaye*

[676.5-693.6] Jamgön Yönten Gyamtso Lodrö Thaye[1190] was the actual presence of the great translator Vairocana. The Buddha himself clearly prophesied him in both name and deed, as it is said in the *Sūtra of the King of Contemplation*:

> I prophesy one Lodrö Thaye,
> Who will do much to benefit sentient beings,
> Like the conqueror Maitreya, of infinite fame,
> In whose hand rests supreme contemplation.

Also, it says in the *Sūtra of the Descent to Laṅkā* (Ch.10, v.803):

> In the period following that,
> A guide who is called Lodrö
> Will teach five knowledges
> And come forth as a great warrior.

Moreover, he was clearly and genuinely heralded by Orgyen, the king of the doctrine, in the indestructible prophecies found in many ancient and new treasure troves. In conformity with these [it is known that in the past this master] had arisen as the play of many great learned and accomplished promulgators of India and Tibet, including the Teacher's attendant Ānanda and the great translator Vairocana, who was the emanation of [the Buddha] Vairocana; and thus he had elucidated the teaching of the Conqueror.

Then, this magical emanation took birth, as had been indicated, in the hidden valley of Rongyap at the approach to Pema Lhartse in Drida Zelmogang, Dokam, at sunrise on Thursday 2 December 1813 (tenth day, tenth month, water bird year, fourteenth cycle).[1191] His father was Tendzin Yungdrung of the kingly Khyung clan of accomplished masters, and his mother was the yoginī Trashi Tsho. He had wondrous abilities beyond the range of ordinary persons, and many supreme and holy visionaries prophetically declared that he would become a great man, who would maintain the teaching. All his childhood games reflected only such refined actions as conferring empowerment, teaching the doctrine, and reciting mantras. From his fifth year he mastered the alphabet, among other [topics for] study and reflection, by just being shown the script. Undivided regard for Orgyen Rinpoche was effortlessly born within him, and, in reality, contemplative experiences, and dreams he had only pure vision.

From about his tenth year, Jamgön Kongtrül awoke to the propensities of his previous training, and, with a firm resolve to enter the true doctrine, he learned art, medicine, and the other sciences at just a glance. His temperament was straightforward and gentle, and he did not transgress his vows. The expressive power of his knowledge expanded boundlessly. In these and other ways, he clearly revealed the attributes of a holy individual within the perceptual range of all. Without striving after necessities, he accumulated them through the power of great merit.

Under many learned and accomplished tutors, such as Gyurme Thutop Namgyel of Zecen, a paṇḍita who knew the five sciences, Jamgön Kongtrül's studies surpassed the ten common sciences. Among the uncommon, inner sciences, he studied many transmitted precepts

Jamgön Kongtrül Lodrö Thaye

and commentaries on the intention of the dialectical vehicle, of which the foremost were the Madhyamaka, Transcendental Perfection, Vinaya, the *Treasury of the Abhidharma*, and the *[Five] Doctrines of Maitreya*. He also studied all the utterly uncommon transmitted precepts and treasures, which are the great tantrapiṭaka of the ancient and new traditions. His learning, which was not dependent on others, became like the expanse of sky, whereby he obtained the exalted level to which the renowned title of *Sarvajñānamahāpaṇḍita*[1192] is meaningfully applied.

Jamgön Kongtrül took the revered Camgön Tā'i Situ Pema Nyinje Wangpo as the crown of his enlightened family [i.e. as his root guru]. It was this Situ Rinpoche who disclosed to him the ultimate and definitively secret pristine cognition of co-emergent supreme bliss, as exemplified by the nectar of the three vows; and, in doing so, granted him dominion over the essential true lineage.

In particular, in the presence of more than fifty spiritual benefactors,[1193] without partiality, the foremost of them being Khyentse Wangpo, the embodiment of Mañjuśrīghoṣa, Jamgön Kongtrül pursued all the traditions of the paths of the eight conveyances, the lineages of attainment, which had survived in the Land of Snows; and he completely received the entire profound essence of their maturation, liberation, and instructions. Not leaving any of these as subjects to be studied once, he experientially cultivated each of them and so, with fervent perseverance, raised the banner of attainment until he had accomplished the attributes which are signs of [success on] the path, just as they are described in the texts. In this way he fully mastered the two accomplishments.

When the vase of Jamgön Kongtrül's mind had been filled with textual exegeses and oral explanations of the transmitted precepts, treatises, tantras, transmissions and esoteric instructions, along with their rituals, practical techniques, and fine points, he too composed treatises. These form the wonderful legacy of his studies, reflections, and meditations:

(i) The *Store which Embraces All Knowledge* (*shes-bya kun-la khyab-pa'i mdzod*) excellently presents the entire corpus of the sūtra and mantra traditions, from the paths of the common sciences all the way up to the uncommon Great Perfection, or Atiyoga, which is the culmination of the nine vehicles.

(ii) The *Store of Precious Instructions* (*gdams-ngag rin-po-che'i mdzod*) brings together the essential roots of the eight great conveyances, which are lineages of attainment, and the utterly profound essences of their maturation and liberation.

(iii) The *Mantra Store of the Lineages of Transmitted Precepts* (*bka'-brgyud sngags-kyi mdzod*) gathers together the means for attainment and maṇḍala ceremonies, and the maturation and liberation, of the trio of

Yangdak, *Kīla*, and *Yamāntaka* (*yang-phur-gshin-gsum*) and other transmitted precepts of the vehicle of indestructible reality according to the Ancient Translation School, and those of the tantrapiṭaka cycles of the new translation school of Marpa and Ngok.

(iv) The *Store of Precious Treasure* distils the elixir or refined essence of the ocean of profound treasures derived from the sixfold lineage of the Ancient Translation School.

(v.a) The *Uncommon Store* (*thun-mong ma-yin-pa'i mdzod*) forms the secret, special wealth of Jamgön Kongtrül's own profound treasures, including the yellow scrolls and sacraments, which will be explained below.

(v.b) The *Extensive Store of Transmitted Precepts* (*rgya-chen bka'-mdzod*) compiles the various opuscules which he composed, and which are connected with [the other *Stores*] mentioned above.

In this way Jamgön Kongtrül newly brought forth five great stores or conveyances, which were unprecedented in the world. These are not merely the so-called "collected works" of one who, having obtained some general understanding derived from study and thought in each field, was urged on by the desire to be a writer and the desire to compose, and so authored a few texts devoid of praiseworthy merits. Rather, it is as if they have prolonged the vitality of all continuous transmissions of the teaching, without bias, as their death approached. So if we examine Jamgön Kongtrül's career, which produced over ninety volumes of wonderful scripture, it is as if he spent his whole life as an author.

None the less, if one thinks of his teaching and propagation of the empowerments, guidance, esoteric instructions, recitational transmissions, and so forth, of the ancient and new sūtras and tantras, and transmitted precepts and treasures, without bias, it is as if he spent his whole life teaching and propagating. And, if one investigates how, beginning with the preliminary yogas of accumulation and purification, he experientially cultivated the stages of creation and perfection associated with inconceivable myriads of maṇḍalas, it seems as if he passed the length of his life in a retreat house sealed up with mud.

Likewise, if one considers how Jamgön Kongtrül expanded the new monastic communities at the places of attainment in Tsandra Rincen Trak[1194] and Dzongshö Deshek Düpa, and how he renovated many old establishments, commissioned inconceivable numbers of new representations of the buddha-body, speech, and mind, performed more than one hundred and fifty rites of great attainment involving maṇḍala clusters, offered worship to the Three Precious Jewels and venerated the monastic community – in short, his legacy in connection with the ten modes of doctrinal conduct – it is as if he passed his whole life diligently engaged in the sphere of work and activity. In these ways [his career] was inconceivable, within only the reach of those who are truly sublime.

Above all, concerning Jamgön Kongtrül's succession to the transmitted precepts of profound treasures: When the master was in his fifteenth year he met Guru Rinpoche in a pure vision and received his blessing. On that basis many profound, pure visionary doctrines and numerous successions to the transmitted precepts of the earth treasures came to him, but he remained indifferent to them. Hence, for the time being, the auspicious coincidence was lost, owing to which it so happened that inwardly there were signs of the ḍākinīs' agitation, and outwardly, too, he appeared to be extremely ill. At that time [his consciousness] transferred out of his body, whether in reality or in a dream he could not tell. He met Guru Rinpoche and his consort and conversed with them a great deal. Finally, they advised him to retake his incarnate existence, at which he experienced himself to be back in his own physical frame. Encouraged by that dream omen, and by the venerable Jamyang Khyentse Wangpo, he established the *Prayerful Offering to the Gracious Goddess* (*bka'-drin lha-mo'i gsol-kha*), whereupon a most radiant spherical canopy of rainbows arose in the cloudless sky, and his physical constitution, too, became clear [i.e. free from ailment].

When Jamgön Kongtrül was performing the rites of service and attainment for the *Gathering of the Guru's Intention*, in a dream he met Guru Rinpoche who conferred on him the blessing of the four empowerments, along with the syllables of the mantra, saying "This will remove obstacles to your life during this [astrologically inauspicious] year. Later, in a few years, we shall meet in reality and my instructions and advice will come forth gradually." [How] the meaning intended [came to pass will be revealed below].

During his fortieth year Jamgön Kongtrül met the great treasure-finder Chogyur Lingpa for the first time, and their minds were merged together. He applied in practice the special prophetic inventories which he was given. Furthermore, when they opened the place of pilgrimage at Dzongshö Deshek Düpa, the all-seeing Khyentse Rinpoche and the great treasure-finder Chogyur Lingpa together requested the master to be seated upon the lofty throne of the doctrine in Citta Sangpuk (Secret Cave of Mind). There, they presented him with great offerings as an auspicious token, in connection with which they rang the great bell proclaiming his enthronement under the title Chime Tenyi Yungdrung Lingpa, which had been conferred upon him by Orgyen, the knower of the three times. Afterwards, they offered him fervent requests, in connection with prayers for his continuing longevity, concerning the need to restore the auspicious circumstance [for the discovery] of profound treasure, which previously had declined. In this way, the door of good auspices was opened wide.

Then, gradually, as had been predicted by the venerable Khyentse Rinpoche, the inventory of treasure at Lhamdo Burmo Trak came into Jamgön Kongtrül's possession and the master himself developed extraordinary clear visions. In his fifty-eighth year he extracted the doctrines of the *Gathering of the Three Roots' Intention* (*rtsa-gsum dgongs-pa 'dus-pa*) from Decen Pemakö in Lhamdo Burmo. From Kumcok Decen Cave he brought forth the yellow scroll of the *Doctrinal Background for the Gathering of the Three Roots' Intention* (*rtsa-gsum dgongs-'dus-kyi rgyab-chos shog-ser*), the secret robe of Hūṃkara, et cetera; from Üri Jetsün Cave in Pema Lhartse, a representative image of Guru Padmasambhava called "Blazing with Good Fortune's Glory", longevity pills which Guru Rinpoche had compounded at Māratika, the great preceptor Śāntarakṣita's robe, the religious king Trhisong Detsen's sash and so forth; from Marong Trugu Trashi Terdzong, the *Doctrinal Background for the Ḍākinī Section of the Gathering of the Three Roots' Intention* (*rtsa-gsum dgongs-'dus mkha'-'gro'i rgyab-chos*), the *Cycle of the Means for the Attainment of Caṇḍālī, Mother of Life* (*tshe-yum tsaṇḍa-lī'i sgrub-skor*), among others; from Ronka Sheldrak Ödzong, the yellow scrolls of the *Cycles of the Means for the Attainment of Amitāyus and Hayagrīva* (*tshe-dpag-med dang rta-mgrin sgrub-skor-gyi shog-ser*), the longevity pills of Mandāravā, et cetera; from Tsang-rok Trashi Tsekdzong the sacraments and yellow scrolls of the *Means for the Attainment of the Eight Closest Sons* (*nye-sras-brgyad-kyi dam-rdzas dang sgrub-thabs shog-ser*); and from the Secret Cave of Yeshe Tshogyel at Tsandra Rincen Trak, he brought forth the yellow scroll of the cycles of the means for attainment belonging to the *Transmitted Precepts of the Father Consort and the Transmitted Precepts of the Mother Consort of the Secret Innermost Spirituality* (*gsang-thig yab-bka' yum-bka'i sgrub-skor shog-ser*), the longevity pills of thirteen immortal awareness-holders,[1195] and so on. Together with each treasure trove he also found an indescribable number of exceedingly sublime sacramental objects.

Moreover, there were still certain treasures which did not come into the master's possession by dint of time and circumstance, though they were within his dominion. But due to the venerable Khyentse Rinpoche's proclamation of commitments to the treasure guardians, the treasure-finder Lerap Lingpa[1196] was commissioned and discovered some; and others, too, were extracted by the great treasure-finder Chogyur Lingpa. These were then handed over to the master [Jamgön Kongtrül] himself.

On such occasions as these, at the outset, in conformity with the prophetic inventories, the two Jamgöns would begin by collaborating in the performance of various rites to clear the way. When the profound treasures came into his possession, Jamgön Kongtrül gave them all to the venerable Khyentse Wangpo to inspect. The latter, too, before and after, arrayed many ceremonial feast offerings and maṇḍalas of material offering. In particular, when Jamgön Kongtrül was bringing forth the great doctrinal treasure of the *Gathering of the Three Roots' Intention* Khyentse Rinpoche made profuse offerings of gifts. Previously, when

Chogyur Lingpa had unearthed the doctrinal treasure of the *Attainment of Mind, the Dispeller of All Obstacles*, but had not been able to establish its yellow scroll, Khyentse Rinpoche had helped by assisting with the establishment. So, on this particular occasion, too, he promised to help Jamgön Kongtrül with the establishment of the *Gathering of the Three Roots' Intention, the Group of Doctrines which Gather Together the Five Great Stores in their Entirety* (*rtsa-gsum dgongs-'dus mdzod-chen rnam-lnga yongs-'dus-kyi chos-sde*). Then, gradually, the mantra protectress Ekajaṭī clearly revealed in visions on two occasions the decipherment of the symbolic scripts, the time to release the sealed transmitted precepts, and so forth.

Once, especially, during the evening of the twenty-ninth, [month and year unspecified], the venerable Khyentse Rinpoche experienced a pure vision of the guru, Jamgön Kongtrül himself, manifested in the form of the accomplished awareness-holder Hūṃkara, whereupon there arose within him a visionary clarity in which he was given the empowerments, guidance, and esoteric instructions of the *Gathering of the Three Roots' Intention*. He said that owing to this the entire significance of the yellow scroll clearly emerged from his mind.

Also, among [the texts of] the *Gathering of the Three Roots' Intention*, the two Jamgöns together catalogued the *Group of Doctrines of the Supreme Attainment of the Guru, the Awareness-holder* (*bla-ma rig-'dzin mchog-sgrub-kyi chos-sde*). It appears that if they had followed the great decipherment of the symbolic script of the ḍākinīs this text would have turned out as long as Sangye Lingpa's *Gathering of the Guru's Intention*. None the less, they agreed that if they were to follow the medium decipherment it would be of a suitable intermediate length, and that this would be best. They had established only about six chapters when they were interrupted by the visit of certain aristocrats and the venerable Khyentse Wangpo fell ill. That the time to discover the remaining portion was lost appears to have been the fault of the feeble merits of the world at large.[1197]

During that period, whatever first arose in the venerable Jamgön Kongtrül's mind subsequently developed effortlessly, like the flow of a river. Ḍākinīs congregated and many other extraordinary omens occurred. Once, at dawn, he experienced a clear vision in which there appeared a perfectly arrayed temple. Inside of it sat one who, he thought, was Guru Rinpoche in essence, but the venerable Khyentse Rinpoche in form, and whose body of light, [the coalescence of] appearance and emptiness, revealed no definite form. Jamgön Kongtrül bowed down in reverence and repeated after Khyentse Rinpoche the refuge, cultivation of the enlightened attitude, and sevenfold service according to the *Daily Yoga of the Awareness-holder* (*rig-'dzin rgyun-gyi rnal-'byor*). Khyentse Rinpoche, having performed the creation of the deity and the invocation of blessing, then took up a vase and placed it on the crown of Jamgön Kongtrül's head. He conferred on him the secret empowerment consisting of the "enlightened mind" [produced] in union with a consort. In the empowerment of discerning pristine cognition, he entrusted him with awareness in the form of a woman. Then, Khyentse Rinpoche projected forth from his heart a crystal and showed it to Jamgön Kongtrül, saying, "All things are primordially pure, clear from the depths, like a piece of crystal. Whatever arises is the expression of luminosity, spontaneously present, just like the luminous glow of a crystal radiating outwards." Having conferred introduction on him that way,[1198] his body vanished. Then, reappearing in the form of an active heruka, he instantly summoned the protectors of the transmitted precepts and treasures, so that it was as if [the place] was seething with their presence. At Khyentse Rinpoche's order Jamgön Kongtrül was entrusted with their transmitted precepts. Then, after Khyentse Rinpoche had granted permissory initiation and the entrustment of his instructions, Jamgön Kongtrül heard many verses, which seemed like prophetic inventories, at the end of which he was roused from this spiritual experience. During the song of indestructible reality at [a subsequent] feast offering blissful heat forcefully arose within him and he grew exhilarated. Other signs marking the great descent of blessing also emerged.

The yellow scroll of the *Father Consort and Mother Consort, [Transmitted Precepts] of the Secret Innermost Spirituality* (*gsang-thig yab-yum*) was also established with the venerable Khyentse Rinpoche. Jamgön Kongtrül himself established the *Seven Chapters on the Profound Path* (*lam-zab le'u-bdun-ma*) and had a pure vision of one Pema Rikdzin, in the guise of Guru Padmasambhava, who thrice conferred on him its recitational transmission.

When Jamgön Kongtrül reported to the venerable guru [Khyentse Rinpoche] that he had reason to discover, at Dagam Wangpuk, the *Doctrinal Cycle of the Means for the Attainment of the Seven Lines* (*tshig-bdun sgrub-thabs-kyi chos-skor*) in the form of a pure vision and aural lineage, he was offered representative symbols of the five wheels of inexhaustible ornament, as well as writing materials, and was encouraged to establish it. Accordingly, when he had mostly completed its establishment the two masters together performed the feast offering of the emanational body, Saroruhavajra, and the venerable Khyentse Rinpoche experienced extraordinary visions.

When he established the *Means for the Attainment of Trolö* (*gro-lod sgrub-thabs*) at the "tiger den" of Rongme Karmo, the two masters performed feast offerings together, at which time the venerable Khyentse Rinpoche had a vision of two huge scorpions, white and black. He said that it was a portent of great severity.[1199]

Clear visions arose in which the "palaces" of both Tsandra Rincen Trak and Dzongshö Deshek Düpa appeared to be great places of pilgrimage, and, in conformity with them, Chogyur Lingpa was encouraged [to discover] the guidebooks to these pilgrimage places and to open their gates. Hence, at Padrak he discovered the *Dokam Inventory of the Twenty-five Great Pilgrimage Places*, due to which he was able to open the gates to those places of pilgrimage, and so forth. Moreover, following the orders of the venerable Khyentse Rinpoche, all the conditions of the places of pilgrimage at Alöi Peldeu and the great place of pilgrimage of Pewar, which is an adjunct of Tsandra, were indicated by the supreme Jamgön Kongtrül.

The empowerments and transmissions of the doctrinal collections established by Jamgön Kongtrül spread far and wide among all his worthy disciples, who were headed by the supreme individuals [in the lineages of] Katok, Pelyül, Zhecen and Dzokcen, along with adherents of the Sakyapa, Gelukpa, Drigungpa, Taklungpa and Karma Kamtsang schools. Directly and indirectly, his service to living beings, by that kindness and by means of the sacramental substances [he manufactured], expanded in all directions so that his enlightened activity opened wide the door for all connections with him to be meaningful.

During his empowerments, rites of great attainment, feast offerings, and so forth, there were various amazing omens which all could perceive in common: nectar boiled; *rakta*[1200] overflowed; the fragrance of elixir could be sensed at a great distance; there were canopies of rainbow clouds, showers of flowers, et cetera. In addition, he passed unobstructedly through the walls of houses and left impressions of his hands and feet in stone. Because he did not grasp appearances as truly existent, he lived as a destroyer of bewilderment. In particular, although it had been clearly stated in the prophetic inventory of his profound treasures that his life would be only a short one, by means of the yoga of indestructible reality and the powers of his energy channels and currents, he prolonged the duration of his life, so that when he reached his eighty-seventh year his complexion none the less became youthful and his eyesight grew clear again. In such ways, the signs of his accomplishment, his inner greatness, were manifestly proven.

In this manner Jamgön Kongtrül completed, for the while, his personal deeds. In his eighty-seventh year, on Thursday 28 December 1899 (twenty-sixth day, eleventh month, earth pig year),[1201] accompanied by many wonderful miracles, he withdrew from his bodily array into the expanse of the mind of the spiritual warrior Thöpei Tumbutsel in the western Citadel of Śāntapurī.[1202]

The number of disciples who issued from the speech and mind of this great master was inconceivable, but among them the foremost was the fearless master Jamyang Khyentse Wangpo. Since they both were as guru and disciple to one another, the harmonious reputation of

"Khyentse and Kongtrül who were both Jamgöns"[1203] has been as well known up to the present day as the wind, to everyone from learned scholars to simple cowherds, throughout the districts of Tibet and Kham.

Jamgön Kongtrül also entrusted his entire teachings to others who became his true regents, namely, to the holders of the Kagyüpa teaching, including [the masters of] the Karmapa, Drukpa, Drigungpa, and Taklungpa subsects, foremost among them being the fourteenth and fifteenth successive incarnations of the Karmapa, and the tenth and eleventh Tā'i Situ; to the holders of the Sakyapa and Ngorpa teaching, including Thartse Pönlop Jamyang Loter Wangpo[1204] and Dzongsar Ngari Chöje Künga Jamyang; to the great holders of the teaching of the Ancient Translation School, such as Mipham Jamyang Namgyel, the treasure-finder Lerap Lingpa, and the lords of my own enlightened family [i.e. my own root gurus] – the venerable Gyurme Ngedön Wangpo and Jedrung Trhinle Campei Jungne; and also to many supreme individuals among the Riwo Gedenpa [Gelukpa school], including Yeshe Kongpel, the preceptor of Gyüme, and Trayap Dongtrül Khecok Ngawang Tamcö Gyamtso. In short, among all the innumerable major and minor learned scholars, realised and experienced masters, and spiritual benefactors during that era, throughout the region from Central Tibet and Tsang to the upper, lower and middle districts of Dokam, it appears that there was no one who did not become his personal disciple.

26 *Mipham Jamyang Namgyel Gyamtso*

[693.6-713.5] Mipham Jamyang Namgyel Gyamtso,[1205] the great promulgator of the teaching of the Ancient Translation School was born in 1846 (fire horse year, fourteenth cycle) at a place well known as Yacu Tingcung, on the banks of the slow-flowing [Yalung] River in Dokam. His father was Gönpo Targye of the Lha clan of Ju, and his mother was Mukpodongza Singcungma. His paternal uncle, Ön Lama Pema Targye, conferred the name Mipham Gyamtso as a crown upon him.

From his childhood he naturally possessed all the powers of the enlightened family of the greater vehicle, such as faith, renunciation, discriminative awareness, and compassion. From his sixth or seventh year he memorised the *Ascertainment of the Three Vows* and studied the preliminaries of astrology and divination. From about his tenth year on, he had an unobstructed command of reading and writing, and so he began to make all kinds of oral compositions. From the beginning of his twelfth year, he lived as an ordinary student and monk at Mehor Sa-nga Chöling in Ju, which was a branch monastery of Zecen [Zhecen] Tenyi Targye Ling, in the doctrinal lineage of Orgyen Mindröling. At that time he was praised by all as a learned young monk.

In his fifteenth year Mipham studied for some days an ancient text of the *Svarodaya* and he learned it completely after praying to Mañjuśrī. He propitiated Mañjuśrī in the form of Vādīsiṃha for eighteen months at the hermitage of Junyung and, by performing the pill rites *(ril-bu'i las-sbyor)*,[1206] he obtained extraordinary signs [of accomplishment]. From then on he did not fail to master whatever texts he chanced to examine, including those concerning sūtras, mantras, and sciences. Therefore, he said that he did not have to study anything apart from simple exegetical transmissions.[1207]

When he was in his seventeenth year disturbances in Nyarong caused all the nomadic herdsmen to migrate to Golok, and the venerable Mipham went there, too.[1208] From about this time he became known for his great skill in arithmetic *(sa-ris)*.[1209]

In his eighteenth year Mipham accompanied his maternal uncle Gyurzang on a pilgrimage to Central Tibet during which he attended a monastic college at Ganden Monastery for about one month. Then, when he went to Kharcu in Lhodrak, while on a side-trip during which he travelled to many of the pilgrimage places in the south, ordinary appearances were transformed and whatever appeared arose as the union of bliss and emptiness. For several days he experienced the warmth of bliss. He maintained that this seemed to be the blessing of that locale. On the road back north he had a pure vision in which a volume entitled the *Crystal Mirror of the Great All-Seeing Svarodaya* (*kun-gzigs dbyangs-'char chen-mo shel-gyi me-long*) came into his hands. How this took place is clearly stated at the end of that work.

Mipham Jamyang Namgyel Gyamtso

On his return he received the permissory initiation of *White Mañjuśrī according to the System of Mati* (*ma-ti 'jam-dkar-gyi rjes-gnang*) from Lapkyapgön Wangcen Gyerap Dorje. The signs of accomplishment which are described in that text actually arose, during both the conferral of the empowerment and the performance of the subsequent "bean-sprout rites" (*makṣa'i las-sbyor*).[1210] In this way the lotus of Mipham's discernment blossomed.

From Peltrül Orgyen Jikme Chöki Wangpo, Mipham received the discriminative awareness chapter of the *Introduction to the Conduct of a Bodhisattva* (Ch.9) in five days, whereupon he totally mastered the words and meaning of the text in its entirety. Later, he also composed the *Commentary on the Discriminative Awareness Chapter* (*sher-ṭīk*), and so forth.[1211]

In particular, practising the three means to delight the guru, he attended on the lotus feet of Pema Ösel Do-nga Lingpa, or Jamyang Khyentse Wangpo, who was the lord of his enlightened family [i.e. his root guru] owing to connections established through the deeds of his former lives. This master regarded Mipham as his unique inner spiritual son; so, having first given him the permissory initiation of *White Mañjuśrī according to the System of Mati*, he opened for him the gateways of the doctrine. From that time onwards, as if filling a pot to the brim, Khyentse Rinpoche bestowed on Mipham many approaches to the ordinary and special textual traditions, the especially sublime texts of the sūtras and of the mantras which had come down through his close lineages, and all the maturation, liberation, supporting transmissions, esoteric instructions, practical techniques, and guidance which lays bare the teaching, for all transmitted precepts, treasures, and pure visions belonging to the most secret vehicle of indestructible reality.

Moreover, at one time or another, he received the ordinary sciences from Jamgön Lodrö Thaye, including the *Grammar of Candragomin* and the methods for refining mercury, as well as such special maturing empowerments and liberating instructions as those of *Mañjuśrī, Lord of Life, Iron-like and Iron-evil* (*'jam-dpal tshe-bdag lcags-'dra lcags-sdig*).[1212] From many spiritual benefactors, including Padmavajra, the preceptor of Dzokcen Monastery, he received limitless cycles of teaching concerning the sūtras, mantras, and sciences. He did not just receive these teachings and leave it at that, but he truly cultivated them experientially. Primarily because Mipham had trained himself well during innumerable lives and so possessed the cultivated potential of the positive enlightened family, and secondly, since [that potential] had been totally aroused by the guru's compassion and power to transfer the blessing of his intention, Mipham thoroughly mastered all the profound and vast topics of the Sugata's scriptures, by means of the four modes of genuine individual awareness, and without contradicting the four kinds of reliance. Thus, he mastered the vision of naturally present pristine cognition, which is extensive as the sky, and liberated the eight great treasures of brilliance.

From the spiritual benefactor Ju-ön Jikme Dorje, Mipham received the transmission of the root text of the *Verse Summation of the Transcendental Perfection of Discriminative Awareness*, and immediately afterwards he discoursed upon it for one month. Then, when he studied the

Introduction to the Madhyamaka under Ngawang Jungne, the spiritual benefactor of Bumsar, he requested only the exegetical transmission, so as not to trouble that master. On the very day the master completed the exegetical transmission, he ordered Mipham to sit for an examination. Starting from the very beginning, Mipham explained the *Introduction to the Madhyamaka* with the result that the spiritual benefactor praised him in the midst of the assembly, saying, "Though I have obtained the title 'spiritual benefactor', I do not even possess a fraction of his intellect!"

In the presence of Pönlop Loter Wangpo he studied the *Treasury of Logical Reason* (*tshad-ma rigs-gter*); and from Sölpön Pema he received the exegetical transmissions of varied texts, including the *Doctrines of Maitreya* and the *Bodhisattva Level*, through their continuous lineages alone. Immediately afterwards, Mipham gave extensive discourses upon them. Illustrated in this way, all the meanings of the sūtras, tantras, and the commentaries on their intention poured forth spontaneously from his mind. He roamed freely, like a fearless lion, in the midst of the multitudes who propounded myriad textual traditions. That he was unimpeded in teaching, discourse, composition of textual commentaries, and so forth, was demonstrably visible to all. No one at all could deny it.

The master himself said:

> During my childhood there were many excellent spiritual benefactors of the ancient and new traditions alive, so it was like an era in which the wheel of the doctrine was turned. None the less, I did not study much apart from, in Peltrül Rinpoche's presence, the discriminative awareness chapter of the *Introduction to the Conduct of a Bodhisattva*. Later, by the kindness of my guru and that of my favoured deity, the hard points of texts would become unravelled without great difficulty when I merely read over them. Moreover, during the beginning of my studies I found it easier to learn the works of the new schools and the texts of the ancient schools seemed hard to understand. Still, this being solely due to my own lack of understanding, I thought that these profound texts of the lineage of awareness-holders certainly harboured great essential points of true understanding. Apart from that, I did not experience the arising of doubts even for a moment. In consequence, my own discriminative awareness came to be fully mature. Later, when I looked at them, I saw that all the profound essential points were only to be found in the doctrinal traditions which had been transmitted through the precious lineages of the Ancient Translation School; so especially great certainty was born within me.

During that same period, the lord of refuges and holder of indestructible reality, Khyentse Rinpoche, commanded me to compose some textbooks according to our own tradition. To comply with the guru's order, and to enrich my own intellect, holding only the precious teaching of the conquerors in my heart, I composed some textbooks on the sūtra cycles and so forth. While I was so doing, I emphasised the tenets of our own tradition, and expounded them to some extent. But [the adherents of] the other philosophical systems took them to be refutations and later many critical essays and so forth arrived from all quarters. Yet, in fact, I had been motivated to write in order to fulfil my guru's command, and with the hope of there being some benefit. During the present day the teaching of the Ancient Translation School has almost become like a painted butter lamp [which emits no light], and there are few who even consider and inquire as to just what are the essential points of our tradition's philosophical system; rather, most simply imitate other traditions. Apart from that, I never felt, even in dreams, such motivations as hostility towards other traditions, or self-congratulatory pride [in my own] – if even those who possess the eye of pristine cognition gaze upon me, I have nothing of which to be ashamed!

As for what I have written in response to my critics and so forth: Since I have not obtained the attributes of those who are sublime, how could I ever understand all the profundities of knowledge? None the less, if I state what may be proven, or disproven, by relying upon the immaculate transmitted precepts of the Sugata and the commentaries on their intention, which are the lamp-like words of the great promulgators of India and Tibet, and by examining for myself, too, what is reasonable, and what unreasonable, it may still be of some benefit to others, though I have no idea who can benefit whom. If I were to corrupt the profound transmitted precepts and the commentaries on their intention because of my own lack of understanding and wrong understanding, I would be closing the door to the path of my own liberation; and, because many others would be misled, I would only bring eternal ruin on them. There can be no greater fault that that. Therefore, if those who possess the eye of the doctrine refute me in accord with correct scriptural authority and logic, I should rely upon them like doctors. Such persons must never be refuted out of hostility. For these reasons, it is with a fair mind that I have sometimes entered into debate.

Therefore, when those who are most sublime repudiate the wrong understandings of others and so forth, in order to preserve perfectly the treasury of the true doctrine, it is done in association with a great purpose. Just so, after the debate between the supreme scholar Lozang Rapsel and this master, in which they had alternately sent one another refined gifts of eloquence, their minds merged, and they scattered the flowers of mutual praise.[1213]

When Mipham Rinpoche was looking over the *Exposition of Valid Cognition* he had a dream in which one who was Sakya Paṇḍita in essence appeared to him in the guise of a learned and accomplished master from India, the tip of his nose slightly crooked, and said, "What is there that you do not understand in the *Exposition of Valid Cognition*? It has two parts, refutation and proof." Then, he divided a volume of the *Exposition of Valid Cognition* into two parts and handed it to Mipham, saying, "Combine these two together!" No sooner had he combined them than they turned into a sword, and all things that may be known appeared before him. Swinging that sword once, it clearly appeared to Mipham that he cut through them all in an instant, without impediment. Consequently, he said, there was not a single word in the *Exposition of Valid Cognition* which he did not understand.

On perusing the *Root Text of the Vinaya Sūtra* for the first time, Mipham found it a little hard to understand. Later, when he was reading once over the books of the *Kangyur*, he read the thirteen volumes of the Vinaya one time, owing to which, he said, there was nothing at all which he did not understand in the *Root Text of the Vinaya Sūtra*.

Moreover, regarding such uncommon, profound points as the distinctions between the older and later [schools of] Tibet, without poring over books, and so forth, the channels of his awareness opened up when he was absorbed in the rites of service and attainment, and he was blessed by the guru and his favoured deity, owing to which [the knowledge of those topics] naturally arose in his mind. Therefore, he said that there was no way whatsoever for him not to write.

Once, on an auspicious day, the venerable Khyentse Rinpoche had volumes containing the fine texts of the sūtras, mantras, and sciences, of which the continuous transmissions were rare, and the subject-matter important, arranged on the altar; and then he made vast offerings. He had the venerable Mipham sit before them on top of a high throne covered with a *kaptse*[1214] and empowered him as master of the doctrine, saying, "I am entrusting the transmitted precepts of these books to you. Hereafter, you must preserve them without decline by means of teaching, debate, and composition. You must clarify the precious teaching of the Conqueror in this world system for a long time!" Then, he was given valuable offerings representing the buddha-body, speech and mind, including a scroll-painting of White Tārā and a handwritten prayer for his continuing longevity, which was based on his various names; and, as a sign of this empowerment, the master himself gave him the long-eared paṇḍita hat which he personally wore, and so enthroned him as his true regent and praised him. Even afterwards, while speaking to others, the venerable Khyentse Rinpoche said, "At the present time there is no one on the earth more learned than Lama Mipham. If one wrote of the greatness of his successive lives and his attributes a text the size of the entire *Transcendental Perfection of Discriminative Awareness* would not suffice for it. But even though I could write it, he would be displeased by it now." This last story I heard from a reliable source.

Peltrül Rinpoche

Jamgön Yönten Gyamtso [Kongtrül Rinpoche] also spoke of him as the *mahāpaṇḍita* Mipham Gyamtso and received the exegetical transmissions of Mipham's own *Detailed Exegesis of the Exposition of Valid Cognition* (*tshad-ma rnam-'grel-gyi rnam-bshad*), the *Detailed Exegesis of the Eight Transmitted Precepts* (*bka'-brgyad rnam-bshad*), and so forth.

On one occasion Japa Do-nga, a great scholar of the new traditions,[1215] expressed the opinion that there were some invalid arguments in Mipham's *Commentary on the Discriminative Awareness Chapter of the "Introduction to the Conduct of a Bodhisattva"* (*spyod-'jug sher-le'i 'grel-*

pa). The best of learned, dignified and accomplished masters, Peltrül Rinpoche, was secured as a witness and they debated for many days. Ordinary persons could not tell who was the victor and who the loser, except to say which arguments agreed with their own opinions. At that point one Lama Rikcok asked Peltrül Rinpoche which of the two was victorious. He answered, "I neither know how to decide it, nor how to conclude it. There is a worldly proverb which goes, 'A son is not praised by his father, but by his enemy. A daughter is not praised by her mother, but by the neighbourhood.' Just so, during the early part of the dispute Do-nga's monks told me that they clearly saw a ray of light emanate from the heart of Lama Mipham's image of Mañjuśrī-ghoṣa, which is the representation of his meditational deity, and vanish into the lama's heart. That sums it all up."

At that time, too, Peltrül Rinpoche gave them this command, "Japa Do-nga has written a commentary on [the line]: *Great Perfection is the matrix of all pristine cognition.*[1216] It seems that some consider it to be refutable and others provable. Therefore, conduct a direct exchange on it."

The venerable Mipham was victorious, whereupon Peltrül Rinpoche authorised him to compose exegetical commentaries on the tantras, transmissions, and esoteric instructions. I actually heard this story from the lord of my own enlightened family, Ling Lama Chöjor Gyamtso, who was the personal disciple of both these masters [Peltrül Rinpoche and Mipham Rinpoche].

Later, at the king among places of attainment, the "tiger den" of Karmo, Mipham Rinpoche planted the banner of attainment for a period of thirteen years. Above all, when he performed the ritual service of Mañjuśrī-Yamāntaka, Lord of Life, the deity on whom, in accord with his fortune, his flower had alighted, it is said that there arose, without exception, all the signs which are described in the texts. Moreover, when he passed many years in retreat he never recited, he said, a single rosary mechanically, or with eyes distracted, but [remained absorbed] one-pointedly in the yogas of creation and perfection, as they are explained in the texts.

One time, Mipham went into Khyentse Rinpoche's presence. "How did you apply yourself to experiential cultivation when you stayed in retreat?" he was asked.

"While pursuing my studies", Mipham answered, "I made conclusive investigations, and while performing the ritual service of the meditational deity in retreat I have taken care to see that I have reached the limits of the stage of creation."

"Those are difficult. The great all-knowing Longcenpa said, 'Not doing anything, you must come to rest right where you are.' I have done just that. By so resting I have not seen anything with white flesh and a ruddy complexion that can be called the 'face of mind'. None the less, if I were to die now it would be all right. I do not have even a grain of trepidation." So saying, Khyentse Rinpoche laughed aloud. Mipham [later] said that he understood that to be the guru's instruction.

By emphasising [the yogas of] the indestructible body, during the stage of perfection, the pulses of his active energy currents were, by and large, purified in the expanse of the central energy channel. Thereupon Mipham experienced the true inner radiance – the natural, co-emergent, pristine cognition that is supreme bliss – which is illustrated at its inception by the four delights and the four modes of emptiness [in which] bliss and emptiness [have coalesced]. Most of all, by relying upon the yogas of the Great Perfection, [namely,] Cutting Through Resistance in primordial purity (*ka-dag khregs-chod*) and the All-Surpassing Realisation of spontaneous presence (*lhun-grub thod-rgal*), he visibly reached the limits of reality, without leaving it to be an intellectual investigation. Thereby he came to hold sway over appearance and conduct as the play of buddha-body and pristine cognition.[1217] By the power of totally refining the internal structure of his energy channels into the "cloud-mass wheel of syllables" the discernment that is born of meditation burst forth from the expanse,[1218] and Mipham arrayed all that is profoundly significant, the treasures of his intention, in the form of treatises: the *Cycle of Eulogies and Narratives* (*bstod-tshogs dang rtogs-brjod-kyi skor*), which gives rise to faith, the entrance-way to blessing; the *Cycle of Common Sciences* (*thun-mong rig-gnas-kyi skor*), which removes doubts about knowledge in general; the *Cycle of the Sciences of Inner Meaning* (*nang-don rig-pa'i skor*), which is the profound and vast embarkation point on the path to liberation; and the *Cycle of Dedicatory Prayers and Benedictions* (*bsngo-smon shis-brjod-kyi skor*), which supports the prolonged existence of the teaching, and the permanence, pervasiveness, and spontaneous presence of all that is good.

The thirty-two volumes in which these four general topics, with their many subdivisions, are preserved – their number being equal to that of the excellent major marks – have, as it were, granted vital force to the teaching of the Conqueror, in general, and to the teaching of the Ancient Translation School, in particular, at the very point of death.

So it was that Mipham dwelt, above all, cultivating the two stages experientially, and, between sessions of practice, bestowing all sorts of esoteric instructions in the form of treatises. Then, on Friday 1 March 1912 (thirteenth day, first month, water mouse year), he left his retreat. Beginning on about 6 March (eighteenth day of that same month), he grew weary owing to certain unpleasant visitors, and, on the morning of Saturday 9 March (twenty-first day), he spontaneously wrote the following:

Namo Mañjuśrīsattvāya!
[Homage to Mañjuśrī, the spiritual warrior!]

Having mastered the oceanic conduct
Of the conquerors' sons
In Abhirati[1219] and other pure lands
I vow to maintain a compassionate mind
For living beings throughout space,
While space itself endures.
As a propounder of doctrine in this degenerate age,
Afflicted by deeds,
I have been sorely oppressed for seventeen years,
without respite,
By a severe ailment of the inner energy channels.
Up to now I have dwelt in this world,
By relying on this wickerwork basket,
The body of apparition.
But now I perceive that it will be joyful to die,
So I will set my last discourse down as a letter...

Thus, he wrote out his testament and left it in concealment. Then, during March/May 1912 (second/third month, same year), Mipham recited the dhāraṇī of Akṣobhya about two hundred thousand times.[1220] He imparted some oral instructions to his attendant, Lama Ösel, and on one of these occasions said:

> Nowadays, if one speaks the truth, there is no one to listen. If one speaks falsely everyone holds it to be true. Therefore, I have not disclosed this to anyone before: I am no ordinary person. I am a bodhisattva who has taken birth by the power of his aspiration. In this present body I ought to have greatly benefitted the teaching and living creatures in general, and the teaching of the Ancient Translation School of the secret mantra in particular. But, because the merits of the Nyingmapa are feeble, as a rule, we are much afflicted by obstacles, and, owing to some critical circumstances, I have been greatly ailing, and so forth. Under such conditions, I have hardly thought to do anything beneficial. None the less, I have completed various commentaries, expositions, and so on. Though I would have liked to have written a clear and detailed general introduction to the Madhyamaka, I have not achieved it. But, none the less, it makes no great difference. If it had been possible ever to complete the *Cycle of Mind in its Natural State* (*gnyug-sems skor*) it would have been of great, vital significance, enlivening the entire teaching, without partiality. Although I thought I might achieve it, still it is not finished. Now, in this final age, the barbarians beyond the pale are close to undermining the teaching. For this and other reasons, there is no point whatsoever in my

> actually taking rebirth. If this were a past age, approximating that in which the brothers from Mindröling [Terdak Lingpa and Locen Dharmaśrī] were alive, I might well benefit the teaching and living creatures in all sorts of ways. But now, by dint of time, such things are difficult; so, after this, I have no reason to take birth in impure realms ever again. Remaining only in pure lands it is the nature of reality that, by the power of aspirations, sublime ones eternally and incessantly give rise to the dramatic play of emanation, which trains each in accord with his needs...

On about Wednesday 9 May (twenty-second day), he said, "Now that I have finally recovered from my nervous ailment I never have sensations of pain. Each day and night there only arise the visions of All-Surpassing Realisation – rainbows, light rays and points, and the manifestations of the bodies and realms [of the buddhas]."[1221]

He gave audience to his faithful disciples and benefactors, who had gathered from all directions, and said prayers. They asked him to prolong his life for the sake of the teaching and living creatures, but he replied, "Now, I certainly shall not stay, and I will not be born again. I have reason to go to Shambhala in the north."[1222]

On Friday 14 June 1912 (twenty-ninth day, fourth month, water mouse), during his sixty-seventh year, Mipham Rinpoche assumed the posture of a bodhisattva, with his left hand evenly placed in his lap and his right in the gesture of teaching; and his mind became meditatively equipoised in the expanse of the original ground, free from corruption. Afterwards, when his precious remains were offered up on the pyre, tents of rainbow light and other wonderful and excellent omens appeared to all those gathered, in common. Lama Ösel earnestly strove to perform the funeral rites following the master's demise in such a way as to fulfil all of his intentions.

Among the personal disciples of this master the foremost were Dodrup Jikme Tenpei Nyima, the treasure-finder Sogyel [Lerap Lingpa], Dzokcen Trülku V and the Dzokcen Gemang, Zhecen Rapjam and Zhecen Gyeltsap,[1223] Katok Situ,[1224] Pelyül Gyatrül, Andzom Drukpa,[1225] Trupwang Śākyaśrī,[1226] and the Ngor Pönlop, et cetera. In short, there were countless sons of his speech who included the emanations and great personages of the Sakyapa, Gelukpa, Kagyüpa, and Nyingmapa traditions from [the monasteries of] Katok, Pelyül, Zhecen, Dzokcen, Pelpung, Derge Göncen [and others] all the way up to Repkong;[1227] as well as their scholars who propounded myriad textual traditions, preceptors endowed with the three trainings, mantrins who were confident in the two stages, and ascetics who were free from activity, having deliberately abandoned the cares of this life. The great personages among the guru's spiritual sons have continued to make great endeavours to propagate his enlightened activity.

Although this master actually made no attempt to discover earth treasures, many unprecedented works including esoteric instructions and ritual collections concerning the stages of creation and perfection, which were especially necessary, poured forth as the treasures of his intention, and he propagated them as treatises. Therefore, he was a supremely accomplished king among treasure-finders, one who held dominion over what is, in truth, the king of all treasures, the expansive store of profound intention.

Conclusion

So it is that the doctrinal collections of the close lineages of profound treasures preserve an inconceivable number [of teachings]. These are exemplified by the treasure troves, the foremost of which contain the *Eight Transmitted Precepts*, the *Gathering of Intentions*, and *Vajrakīla* (*bka'-dgongs-phur-gsum*), and each of which also includes [its own versions of] the *Trio of the Guru, Great Perfection and Great Compassionate One*. Because the accounts of the descent of so many lineages are indeed limitless, it is not possible to describe them here. If the reader wishes to know of them in detail, they may be learned from the histories of each respective treasure, from the records of the teachings received by their respective [masters], and so forth.

This completes the brief exposition of the accounts of the exceedingly profound, close lineages of the treasures, the sixth part of this book, *Thunder from the Great Conquering Battle-Drum of Devendra*, which is a history of the precious teaching of the vehicle of indestructible reality according to the Ancient Translation School.

Part Seven
A Rectification of Misconceptions Concerning the Nyingma School

Introduction

[719.1-2] Now, the errors of those partisans who, in the past, have wrongly viewed the teaching of the vehicle of indestructible reality according to the Ancient Translation School must be refuted.

1 *General Reply to Criticisms of the Nyingmapa Tantras*

[719.2-736.1] There were a multitude of utterly profound tantrapiṭaka which arose in Tibet, in proportion to the authentic merits of those to be trained in that glacial land. They did so because of the extraordinary enlightened aspiration of Trhisong Detsen, the divine king of the Land of Snows who was an emanation of sublime Mañjuśrīghoṣa, and due to the blessings of the great accomplished master Padmasambhava, Vimalamitra and others. Among them were the unsurpassed secret mantra derived from the three lineages, including [those derived from] the Indestructible Nucleus of Inner Radiance,[1228] which are the essence of the spirituality of many ḍākinīs and holders of awareness, and which are beyond the range of ordinary persons. Therefore, those [teachings] are worthy of approval, and the biographies of the ancient religious kings and of the great emanational translators and scholars ought to be respected.

So it was that [Trhisong Detsen], the emanational king, sought to kindle the lamp of the doctrine when Tibet was an abode of darkness, occupied by barbarians who did not possess even a reflection of the teaching, and who were miserable because, to their misfortune, they had to seek lasting refuge in those who preached a violent religion, granting only occasional, ephemeral happiness. Even then, the irresistible hurricane of strife's machinations, [instigated by] pernicious and unworthy beings, almost brought other forces into power. But at that time all the venomous deities and ogres were subdued by the compassion of the great master Padmasambhava who enabled the Tibetans to practise the doctrine as they liked. Temples were built, doctrinal centres were established, and with great endeavour the ways of the doctrine were instituted amongst the Tibetans, who had little aptitude even for learning the doctrinal terminology, which previously had been unknown.

At the outset [these masters] began by examining whether or not [the Tibetans] could maintain monastic vows, and they laid a firm foundation for the Buddha's precious teaching, the path of omniscience.

They translated an oceanic corpus of doctrines belonging to the Tripiṭaka and to the secret mantra. They collected fragments, corrected defective texts, established the ground, experientially mastered the path, and caused [the doctrine] to spread throughout the kingdom by means of study, exegesis, and meditation. This opportunity to practise freely the path to liberation and omniscience was due to the kindness of the ancient preceptor [Śāntarakṣita], the master [Padmasambhava], the religious king [Trhisong Detsen], and the emanational translators and scholars.

The Author, Dudjom Rinpoche

For this reason it is no wonder that the learned proponents of philosophical systems and the translators of the later period also managed to follow, without difficulty, the path whose tradition had been established by those great ones of the past, and to contribute to it by means of their own intellects. None the less, some jealous persons created discord by, for example, declaring that certain of the ancient tantras had been composed in Tibet because they did not exist in India. However, the non-existence of those tantras in India did not prove them to be unauthentic. Even the tantras which did exist in India did not originate there: they were brought forth by great accomplished masters from the domains of the gods, nāgas, yakṣas, ḍākinīs and so on, as well as from various great places of pilgrimage including the Sahor and Shambhala regions of Jambudvīpa, Mount Malaya in Laṅkā, Oḍḍiyāna, and the Drāviḍa country; and later they were introduced to India. Therefore, tantras are not unauthentic by definition merely because they did not exist in India. Even though some [of the ancient tantras] might have been found [in India], they would not have been seen by someone making just an occasional journey there [as the later translators did]. For, while the emanational translators and scholars of the past who were abiding on the sublime levels voyaged throughout the twenty-four lands[1229] and elsewhere by means of miraculous abilities, ordinary persons could not travel to them. This is why the great scholar Rongzompa, with whom even the great lord Atiśa had declared himself unable to discuss the doctrine, said that the ancient translations of the secret mantra were superior to the later translations in six ways:[1230]

> First, concerning the greatness of the benefactors who introduced them: Since the benefactors of the ancient translation period were the three ancestral religious kings, who were the sublime Lords of the Three Families in kingly guise, they were unlike the benefactors of the later translation period.
>
> Second, concerning the locations in which they were translated and established: Since the ancient translations were accomplished in such emanated temples as Samye and the other doctrinal centres of the past, high and low,[1231] they are unlike those translated in the monastic grottoes of today.
>
> Third, concerning the distinctions of the translators: Those doctrines were translated by emanational translators, the translators of the past such as Vairocana, Kawa Peltsek, Cokro Lüi Gyeltsen, Zhang Yeshe De, Ma Rincen-chok, and Nyak Jñānakumāra. Thus, they are unlike the translations made by the translators of today, who pass the summer in Mangyül and travel to India and Nepal for a short time during the winter.
>
> Fourth, concerning the distinctions of the scholars [who supervised the ancient translations]: Those doctrines were introduced by buddhas and sublime bodhisattvas abiding on the great levels, [namely,] the scholars of the past such as the preceptor Śāntarakṣita, Buddhaguhya, the great master Padmākara and the great paṇḍita Vimalamitra. Thus, they were unlike the scholars of today who wander about in search of gold.
>
> Fifth, concerning the distinctions of the blossoms [offered] as the basis for commissioning [the translations]: In the past the doctrines were requested with offerings of gold weighed

> out in deerskin pouches, or by the measure. Thus, they were unlike the requests made [by disciples of] the present day with one or two gold bits drawn from under their own arms.[1232]
>
> Sixth, concerning the distinctions of the doctrine itself: The translations of the past were completed at a time when the doctrine of the Buddha had reached its zenith in India. Furthermore, there were tantras which did not even exist in India proper, which were retained by bodhisattvas, accomplished masters, awareness-holders and ḍākinīs who had obtained their empowerments. They were taken from pure lands, and from regions of Jambudvīpa such as Siṅghala and Oḍḍiyāna in the west, through the arrayed miraculous powers of the great master Padmasambhava, Vimalamitra and others, and then translated [in Tibet]. Thus, many [doctrines] which were completely unknown to the scholars and accomplished masters of India arrived to become the meritorious fortune of Tibet.
>
> Furthermore, concerning the translations themselves: Since the translators of the past were emanations, they established the meanings correctly. For this reason their works are easy to understand and, on plumbing their depths, the blessing is great. But the translators of the later period were unable to render the meaning and made lexical translations following [merely] the arrangement of the Sanskrit texts. Consequently, their forced terminology is hard to understand, and on plumbing the depths the blessing is slight. Therefore, they are dissimilar.

During the later expansion of the teaching in Tibet, it became the fashion for everyone who possessed the intellectual skill and a little gold to travel to India and Nepal. If they had gone exclusively for the sake of the teaching and sentient beings it would have been admirable, but most of them were jealous men who set their feet in motion because they desired to become scholars, hankered after the possessions of others, sought to win fame, or were jealously competing with their own gurus, or with spiritual benefactors of similar fortune. This can be ascertained from the incident during Marpa's travels, when a companion threw all his books into the river.[1233] For these reasons, the all-knowing Rongzompa said:

> When the doctrine of the Buddha was at its zenith, the emanational translators established [the texts of] the transmitted precepts without error. Then, they adorned those doctrines in many ways which served to complete them, and which established the actual condition of the knowable. But

> the charlatan translators of the present day made various reforms in the ancient translations, saying, "I am the better translator. My sources are more venerable!" And so, misrepresenting the transmitted precepts of the Buddha and the teachings of their gurus, they all compose their own doctrines. They heap abuse upon one another for their faults. Their doctrines are such that those of the father do not suit the son. [In all of this] they are unlike [the ancient translations].

These words of his are completely true. Orgyenpa Rincenpel,[1234] who attained accomplishment, also said:

> Some Tibetan translators claim that the Nyingma translations had no origin in India. Among them Chak Lotsāwa,[1235] a guru from whom I personally received empowerment, also said that the Nyingma tantras had no origin in India. Such was his small-minded opinion! How could that translator, who travelled for only a short time in East India, be certain of all the texts that existed in India? Above and beyond that, he could not even have been certain about which of them existed in Tibet! Moreover, because India is, in general, a very hot country, many books decay, and so the extent of the Buddha's transmitted precepts cannot be ascertained. How, then, can the translators of Tibet be certain of [all] the sources? Even though I journeyed to the land of Oḍḍiyāna in the west, I could not ascertain even the size of that land.[1236] Furthermore, in later times original Sanskrit manuscripts were mostly preserved in Nepal. Among them, an inconceivable number of different Nyingma tantras were preserved in one of the temples of a Newari *bahal*.[1237] I said to the Nyingmapa of Tibet that I would bring the paṇḍitas here along with the Sanskrit manuscripts of the Nyingmapa tradition, and that they should come to Kyirong to translate, using my services as a translator, but this did not come to pass. Even now it would be well to translate those Nyingmapa texts. Again, some inquisitive Tibetans also say that the Nyingmapa tradition's *Sūtra which Gathers All Intentions* is corrupt, having been composed by some old Tibetan mantrins.[1238] Such words are unworthy! If you were so knowledgeable, then each one of you should also compose such doctrines; the Buddha's transmitted precepts contain nothing better.

Similarly, it says in the *Biography of Lord Atiśa (jo-bo'i rnam-thar)*:[1239]

> Then, it occurred to the lord Atiśa that no one was more learned than he in the traditions of the way of secret mantra

> that were preserved in the human world; and this thought made him proud. But later, when he came to Tibet and opened the treasury of Pehar Ling [at Samye], he saw the Sanskrit manuscripts there, many of which he had neither heard of, nor seen before. His pride was shattered and he said, "I thought there was nothing I did not know in the secret mantra tradition of the greater vehicle. The ḍākinīs had even shown me countless celestial palaces and taught me many tantras, but these texts were not among them. There is no end to this secret mantra tradition of the greater vehicle!" He offered many praises to the [ancient] kings of Tibet, and said, "It appears that the teaching had been propagated in Tibet as it had not been even in India."

And [in the same biography it says]:

> By the kindness of that second Vajradhara, the master Padmasambhava, many secret stores of the ḍākinīs which were unknown in India were translated; and they were preserved in the treasury of Pehar at Samye.

The venerable Tāranātha said:

> In the Drāviḍa country the teaching was not actually present in former times. It was first established there by master Padmākara. Dīpaṃkarabhadra also went there and from that time, for a period of about one hundred years, it was visited by many holders of indestructible reality from Magadha, Oḍḍiyāna, Kashmir, and elsewhere. They made the mantra vehicle especially widespread. There are tantras such as those which, having been concealed in the past, during the reign of Dharmapāla, have declined in India, as well as those which had been brought forth from Oḍḍiyāna. There are many such tantras in Drāviḍa that are not to be found in India.[1240]

These well-stated arguments of fair-minded men expose at once all the defects of the false rhetoric and pious lies of those who claim that [the ancient translations] are not authentic and did not exist in India. By speaking in anger they themselves abandon the doctrine and consequently cause other dull-witted creatures of little merit to harbour doubts. Therefore, they tend only to bring schism to the teaching by acting in the way of the monk Mahādeva.[1241] Beyond that, their ideas are not conducive to the ultimate path.

Moreover, the later scholar Putön, who was disposed to maintain the tradition of the Ancient Translation School, practised the *Four-armed Lord according to the Treasures of Nyang (nyang-gter mgon-po phyag-*

bzhi) and other [Nyingmapa teachings]; and he had a vision of Guru Padmasambhava's eight emanations in which he received a prophetic declaration. It clearly follows from these and other actual reports that by advising equanimity towards the Nyingmapa tantras Putön intended to address the other partisan philosophers of that age. When Tshelpa Situ Mönlam Dorje prepared a set of all the scriptures translated in the Land of Snows and invited Putön to correct it, he inserted the Nyingmapa trilogy of the *Sūtra which Gathers All Intentions*, the *Magical Net*, and the *Mental Class*, along with the [main] cycles belonging to the class of means for attainment into the collected tantras of the *Kangyur* (*bka'-'gyur*). He allowed them to remain there because he had validly proven them to be original texts of the tantras, but he removed many new tantras, including the whole [collection of] *Thirty-two Rali Cakrasaṃvara Tantras* (*ra-li so-gnyis*, T 383-414), and the *Non-Dual Victor* (*Advayasamatāvijayanāmavajraśrīvaramahākalpādi*, T 453), having contended that they were not the transmitted precepts of the Buddha.[1242]

When Śākya Chokden, the great paṇḍita of Zilung,[1243] taught in his *Golden Surgical Needle* (*gser-gyi thur-ma*) that the explicit intention of the *Analysis of the Three Vows* was of provisional meaning, some individuals with untrained intellects doubted him, and foolish bigots took [his work] as a support [for their own prejudices]. None the less, the great paṇḍita did make the following assertion:

> In general, if you presume to consider the Nyingmapa doctrine to be not authentic, it follows that you must consider everything translated before the time of the great translator Rincen Zangpo to be not authentic, including the texts of the Tripiṭaka, and the Kriyā, Caryā, and Yoga tantras which were translated by Kawa Peltsek, Cokro Lüi Gyeltsen, and Zhang Yeshe De. In particular, if you presume to consider the Nyingmapa Unsurpassed tantras of the way of secret mantra to be not authentic, you must also consider the glorious *Guhyasamāja*, the *Hidden Point of the Moon*, and the *Buddhasamāyoga* to be not authentic, for those three are foremost among the so-called *Eighteen Tantrapiṭaka* of the Nyingmapa tradition, and because the great figures of the past taught that by relying on those three roots the so-called Nyingmapa tradition arose in Tibet. In particular, too, even if you consider [merely] the *Yangdak* and *Vajrakīla* tantras to be not authentic, those tantras have been proven genuine by [the existence of] Sanskrit texts, the fact that they were translated by proven translators, and so forth.[1244] Especially, the great men who included various others that are known as Nyingmapa tantras in the *Catalogues of the Collected Tantras* (*rgyud-'bum-gyi dkar-chag*) have also proven that the

Yangdak and *Vajrakīla* tantras are indubitable. This is claimed, for example, in the doctrinal histories of [Comden Rikpei] Reldri and Putön Rinpoche.[1245]

Having roughly stated the opinions of others, the essence of my own tenet is as follows. The master of this teaching, the Teacher and Lord of Sages [Śākyamuni Buddha], delivered [the doctrine], whether in the passionless form [of a monk], or in the guise of a universal monarch, for both are acceptable. By experientially cultivating the sequences of deities and mantras [taught by] that unique Teacher, master Padmasambhava obtained accomplishment, and with his disciples, who attained stability in the two stages and so reached the level of accomplishment, he subdued the venomous gods and demons who obstructed the growth of the true doctrine in Tibet. They taught the appropriate sequences of [practice associated with] the deities, mantras, and view in order that worthy recipients of the vehicle of indestructible reality might be secured on the level of the awareness-holders. Their disciples experientially cultivated the significance [of those teachings] correctly, and there appeared many awareness-holders who attained the level of accomplishment through them. They set down in writing the aural lineages and intentions that were in harmony with them, based on which this utterly pure doctrine renowned as the Nyingmapa developed. As for their authenticity: they do fulfil the definition of treatises which is stated in the *Supreme Continuum of the Greater Vehicle*, (Ch.5, v.19ab):

> There are some which are taught by undistracted minds,
> Referring solely to the Conqueror, the Teacher...

Because they fulfil that definition, the treatises delivered by master Padmasambhava are no different from the transmitted precepts of the Buddha, for it says in the *Supreme Continuum of the Greater Vehicle* (Ch.5, v.19cd):

> Conforming to the path which attains to liberation,
> Let them be reverently accepted in the manner of
> the Sage's transmitted precepts.

Thus, they are similar to the *Five Doctrines of Venerable Maitreya*, the *Abridged Tantra of Kālacakra*,[1246] and its commentary, the *Taintless Light*.

Moreover, some reject the doctrinal terminology of the Anuyoga and Atiyoga for the reason that it is not found in the tantrapiṭaka of the new translation schools. This is praise from those whose reproaches are unskilled, because, generally, it is the custom that the doctrinal terminology and exegeses of the higher scriptures do not occur in lower ones, the Conqueror having distinguished their superiority and inferiority for the sake of those to be trained. Thus, for example, the doctrinal terminology of the vehicle of transcendental perfection is not found in the piṭaka of the pious attendants; that of the outer mantras is not found in the vehicle of transcendental perfection; and that of such Unsurpassed tantras as the *Guhyasamāja*, and *Cakrasaṃvara* is not found in the outer mantras. For this reason, the fact that the doctrinal terminology and exegeses of the Anuyoga and Atiyoga do not much occur in the *Guhyasamāja* and *Cakrasaṃvara*, and so forth, is a proof that the Great Perfection is the pinnacle of all vehicles. It will suffice [to say] that this may be elaborated in detail.

2 *On the View of the Great Perfection*

[736.1-758.2] Again, in the Great Perfection, a philosophy of freedom from deeds with respect to the disposition of reality, when the ultimate, definitive meaning of pristine cognition, which does not rest in the sphere of causal conditioning, is indicated directly, it is explained that there is no need to orient oneself to contrived doctrines that require efforts associated with the causes and effects of good and evil. Certain Tibetans have with some astonishment criticised [that view], saying that it implicitly agrees with Hoshang Mo-ho-yen's philosophy by its indifference to conduct.[1247]

None the less, the Sugata turned the doctrinal wheel three times. In the first turning he taught the infallibility of cause and effect with regard to virtuous and unvirtuous deeds. That promulgation has been established to be of provisional meaning because it was taught with reference to worldly needs. Both the intermediate and final promulgations are truly in agreement with one another concerning the characteristics of the three approaches to liberation. They are merely distinguished insomuch as they are [respectively] profound and exceedingly profound teachings of the abiding nature of reality, which is of profound, definitive meaning. It is well known amongst learned scholars, and has been proven, that the provisional and the definitive are distinguished with reference to the conditioned and the unconditioned, and that the expressed meanings [of the three promulgations] may be differentiated on the basis of the relative strength of those.[1248] For such reasons, the intermediate transmitted precepts temporarily assert that all things subsumed in consciousness are devoid of substantial existence, and, when the definitive significance is revealed, [it is maintained]:

> ...free from all referential activity with respect to anything, all discursive thought is abandoned. Nothing is referred to that is to be accepted, or rejected...

In short, because the characteristics of the three approaches to liberation are found in the abiding nature of reality, which is unconditioned

Acintyaprabhāsa

and genuinely transcends the phenomena of subject and object, the adherent of the Great Perfection, during the phase of the ground, views saṃsāra and nirvāṇa as the same, and does not distinguish cause and effect. During the phase of the path he does not engage in discursive thoughts and so does not conduct himself with reference to the extremes of acceptance and rejection. And, during the phase of the result, with confidence that is free from hope and fear about the goal, he reaches the level on which all things are exhausted. Such is the nucleus of this philosophy. As it says in the *All-Accomplishing King:*

> If one maintains that there is cause and effect
> For Atiyoga, the yoga of the Great Perfection,
> One has not realised the meaning of Great Perfection.
> If one maintains the ultimate and relative to be two,
> One's statements exaggerate and depreciate;
> One has not realised that there are not two.
> The realisation of the buddhas of the three times
> Is gained in the sole determination that two are not seen.

This sort of great philosophical assertion is, in reality, also found to be the intention of the profound, definitively significant sūtras of the Buddha, the Transcendent Lord, who speaks not of twofold divisions. It says in the *Sūtra of the Dialogue with Brahmaviśeṣacinti*:

> What, one might ask, is it that is the nature of all things? The nature of all things is emptiness; they are without objective referent. The nature of all things is signlessness; they are free from idea and concept. The nature of all things is aspirationlessness; there is no acceptance, no rejection, no thought, no force, and total absence of substantial existence. It is naturally radiant. Whatever is the nature of saṃsāra is the nature of nirvāṇa. Whatever is the nature of nirvāṇa is the nature of all things. So it is that mind is naturally radiant.

Therefore, the view is free from assertions, meditation from deliberations, conduct from acceptance and rejection, and the result from hope and fear. But for those four, how else might one establish nakedly the experiential cultivation which is characterised by the three approaches to liberation? If you do not recognise this to be the "philosophy of the indivisibility of saṃsāra and nirvāṇa" which is taught by means of the esoteric instructions of the stage of perfection in many of the tantrapiṭaka which you [adherents of the new translation schools] yourselves accept to be valid, then there can be no occasion for bringing this [philosophy] together with the philosophy established by dialectical deliberations.[1249]

None the less, one might object by saying that while the above may be true from the perspective (*ldog-pa*) of the view, [the Great Perfection is still at fault], for it rejects the area of conduct. But, having established the view on the basis of seeing the undeluded abiding nature of ultimate truth, one transcends the bondage and liberation of contrived doctrines, whether good or evil, concerning the conditioned fundamental virtues, such as those of the three trainings, which depend upon mind and mental events. Therefore, freedom from acceptance and rejection is proven; and that remains the characteristic of aspirationlessness. As it says in the *Sūtra of the Dialogue with Kāśyapa, from the Sublime Pagoda of Precious Jewels*:

> That which is uncompounded is the enlightened family of the sublime ones. That which is the enlightened family of the sublime ones neither adheres to the training, nor transcends the training. That which neither adheres to the training, nor transcends the training neither moves, nor rests, nor rushes. That which neither moves, nor rests, nor rushes has neither mind, nor the properties which emerge from mind. That which has neither mind, nor the properties which emerge from mind possesses neither deeds, nor the ripening

> of deeds. That which possesses neither deeds, nor the ripening of deeds knows neither pleasure nor pain. That which knows neither pleasure, nor pain is the enlightened family of the sublime ones. That which is the enlightened family of the sublime ones possesses neither deeds, nor deed-forming volition.

And:

> There, virtue is empty; and nonvirtue, too, is empty. Virtue is void; and nonvirtue, too, is void. Virtue is unadulterated by nonvirtue; and nonvirtue, too, is unadulterated by virtue. There is neither basis, nor cause, for hankering after virtue and nonvirtue.

It says, too, in the *Hevajra Tantra* (Pt.1, Ch.5, v.11):

> There is no meditation, nor meditator.
> There is no deity, nor mantra.

Now, think as to whether this proclamation of the marvellous teaching, in such passages as these, is, in fact, the tradition of Hoshang Mo-ho-yen![1250]

In general, having realised discriminative awareness without error, skilful means becomes merely an aspect of discriminative awareness. This is the infallible intention of the buddhas. As the master Āryadeva has said [in the *Four Hundred Verses*, Ch.12, v.11]:

> Better that moral discipline may decline,
> Than should the view.

Having correctly realised the view which is here expounded, not only is one not fettered, regardless of conduct, but also one remains on the great highway of the conquerors' sons and obtains the fruit of liberation. Moreover, on this path of the Great Perfection, having established that there is nothing to accept, or to reject in the expanse of the great sameness of reality, one accomplishes one's purpose, but is not obscured by subjective conduct. This is a distinctive doctrine. As it says in the *Authentic Conduct of a Bodhisattva*:

> Ratnadatta declared:
>
> Do not abandon desire.
> Subdue not hatred.
> Don't think about ignorance.
> Do not behave so as to surpass your own body.
> Practice vice.
> Do not eliminate opinion.
> Don't teach about the entanglements.
> Grasp the components as whole.

Combine the psychophysical bases into one entity.
Indulge in the sensory activity fields.
Do not progress beyond an infantile level.
Think unvirtuously.
Renounce virtue.
Do not pay attention to the Buddha.
Do not reflect upon the doctrine.
Worship not the *saṃgha*.
Do not properly undertake the trainings.
Try not to pacify worldly existence.
Do not cross the river [of suffering].

Such are the instructions with which a novice bodhisattva should be instructed and advised. Why so? Because it is this abiding condition of the reality of things that alone abides.

Similarly, it says in the *Tantra of the Great Natural Arising of Awareness*:

Because you yourself are the divine maṇḍala,
naturally manifest to yourself,
Do not offer worship to the deity,
for if you worship you will be fettered by it.
By worship, gestures, and so forth,
the body [of the deity] is obscured.
Do not perform gestures, for if you perform them
a precious jewel will be destroyed.
Do not renounce saṃsāra, for if you renounce it
you will not attain buddhahood.
Because the Buddha is not elsewhere,
he is naught but awareness itself.
Saṃsāra is not elsewhere;
all is gathered within your own mind.
Do not practise conditioned fundamental virtues,
for if you do you will be fettered by them.
Renounce conditioned fundamental virtues,
such as [building] stūpas and temples.
There is no end to contrived doctrines,
but by leaving them be they will end.
Not renouncing the yoga of abandoning deeds,
should you renounce [deeds], you will become a tathāgata.
So it is that you must know the path
of the authentic buddhas in everything.

Thus, when one is grasped by the view, which establishes itself in the significance of the great sameness of reality, of which the disposition is free from all activity, then conditioned good and evil deeds, too, are literally revealed to be the same. The aforementioned tantra says:

> Virtue is not to be practised,
> nor sin to be renounced;
> Awareness free from both virtue and sin
> is the buddha-body of reality.
> Virtue is not to be practised;
> if practised there is no buddhahood.
> Neither is sin to be renounced;
> if renounced, buddhahood is not achieved.

Nowadays, in the Land of Snows, there are many who vehemently reject that tradition when they hear it. However, it is of no importance that the nature of these [teachings] has not penetrated their minds through lack of comprehension. As it says in the *Sublime Sūtra which Reveals the Relative and Ultimate Truth* (*Āryasaṃvṛtiparamārthasatya-nirdeśasūtra*, T 179):

> Mañjuśrī declared: "O son of the gods, that which is just what is, the expanse of reality, and the utterly unborn are ultimately equivalent; ultimately, they are even equivalent to the five inexpiable sins. That which is just what is, the expanse of reality, and the utterly unborn are ultimately equivalent; ultimately, they are even equivalent to opinionatedness."

It is not proven, merely by this teaching, that the area of conduct is left to fade away. In the *Refinement of Gold from Ore, a Great Tantra of the Mental Class* (*sems-sde rgyud chen-po rdo-la gser-zhun*, NGB Vol.1, ll.7-8), which is peculiar to our tradition, it says:

> Since she is the mother of the sugatas, none excepted,
> She is the sole path of all the conquerors,
> The foundation of the oceanic conduct
> Of moral discipline and the other transcendental
> perfections.

Accordingly, this great philosophy does not reject the area of methodical conduct as an aspect of discriminative awareness, and the relative truth is *not* provisionally rejected; for one is to be skilful with respect to means. But when one realises directly the proper essence of reality that is free from delusion and is the abiding truth, then all the doctrines pertaining to the truth of the path, which are allied with enlightenment, such as the ten transcendental perfections, are united herein, without falling into the alternate application of the two truths. This is taught in the *Tantra of the Great Natural Arising of Awareness*:

The spontaneously present buddha-body of reality is free
From the darkness in which clarity and obscuration appear.
It transcends both permanence and annihilation's limits,
Cannot be grasped by either darkness, or light,
Transcends uniqueness and plurality,
Transcends apparent, as well as invisible, things,
Is free from the terms of birth and death.
Where are deviation,[1251] obscuration, and egotism?
In thought itself they are unthinkable!
The ends of the perfection of discriminative awareness
Are subsumed in the body of reality, awareness and radiance.
The ends of the perfection of concentration
Are subsumed in the lamp's total presence.[1252]
The ends of the perfection of perseverance
Are subsumed in non-discursive, naturally present significance.
The ends of the perfection of patience
Are subsumed in cutting straight through appearances.
The ends of the perfection of moral discipline
Are subsumed in companionless solitary retreat.
The ends of the perfection of liberality
Are subsumed in the abandonment of saṃsāra's grasping attachments.
The ends of the perfection of aspiration
Are subsumed in neither hope for, nor fear of, appearances.
The ends of the perfection of means
Are subsumed in awareness' total presence.
The ends of the perfection of power
Are subsumed in sealing delusion's apparitions.
The ends of the perfection of pristine cognition
Are subsumed in its causeless appearance.
So it is that the meaning of the perfections
Is natural, all-pervasive, pristine cognition.

Equally, the *Sūtra of the Dialogue with Brahmaviśeṣacinti* says:

Not to grasp anything is liberality.
Non-rigidity is moral discipline.
Not to protect anything is patience.
Not to endeavour is perseverance.
Not to cogitate is concentration.
Non-referentiality is discriminative awareness.

It says, too, in the *All-Accomplishing King*:

> With respect to the genuine meaningful nucleus about
> which there is nothing to do,
> What great yogins see
> Is a divine maṇḍala resulting from its basis
> In the primordially pure maṇḍala of mind.
> Perfecting it by means of the four branches of service
> and attainment,
> It abides, spontaneously present, embodying emanation
> and absorption.

Now, one might say, if the abiding nature of all things is such that they do not abide in the sphere of the conditioned, and so transcend virtue and sin, bondage and liberation, then the discourses on good and evil deeds and the infallibility of cause and effect are unnecessary. However, those discourses were given with an intention directed to consciousness [rather than pristine cognition]. Thus, for example, with an intention directed to whatever good or bad appears in dreams, which, while true during dreams, seems fictitious on waking, [the Buddha] spoke of all things as dream-like and apparitional, to exemplify their fictitiousness. Just so, until the deluded appearances subsumed by consciousness are exhausted there is still acceptance and rejection, and the infallible ripening of good and evil deeds in accord with cause and effect. But when that delusion is exhausted those things do not appear to the pristinely cognitive aspect [of mind-as-such] which beholds the truth. Because there is then no subjective cognition engaged in the subject-object dichotomy, relative objects do not appear. This is certainly the stated intention of the buddhas and their sons. The intention of the great promulgators who, as prophesied, commented upon the profound definitive meaning also conforms with this, for it resides naturally in the minds of all who perceive what is supreme. The sublime Nāgārjuna says:[1253]

> Just as, for example, on falling asleep,
> A man sees by the power of dreams
> His son, wife, mansion and lands,
> But sees them not upon awakening,
> So it is that when those who know relative
> appearance
> Open the eyes of intelligence,
> Part from the sleep of unknowing,
> And wake up they no longer perceive it.
> Similarly, when those of genuine learning
> Overcome all propensities to unknowing,
> By means of the sunlight of knowledge,

They perceive neither mind, nor mental events, nor objects.

The same is expressed in the *Introduction to the Madhyamaka* (Ch.6, v.27):

Just as what is perceived by an eye that is dim
Impairs not an undimmed cognition,
Just so the mind that's forsaken taintless pristine cognition
Impairs not the taintless mind.

Śāntideva also says [in the *Introduction to the Conduct of a Bodhisattva*, Ch.9, vv.10ab & 15]:

As long as causes are accumulated,
So long does apparition arise.
If the causal stream be broken,
Even relatively it will not arise.
When no delusion is present,
What refers itself to relative appearance as an object?

Akṣobhyaprabha

As proof of that, let us now refer to the decisive resolution of view and conduct in the disposition of the great pristine cognition of sameness, where the multiplicity [of phenomena] is of a single savour, and which occurs here, in the Great Perfection. During the phase of the ground one does not exaggerate discriminative awareness, for one harbours no hopes with reference to conditioned fundamental virtues, having realised through pristine cognition that relative appearance is a fiction; but one does not depreciate means, because, from the standpoint of consciousness, there is still acceptance and rejection. During the phase of the path, because no deliberations transcend discursive thought, there is not even so much as an atom upon which to meditate. Finally, during the phase of the result, if the stream of mind and all that emerges from mind be shut off, where can there be relative appearance? This essential point, which is the ultimate, innermost intention of the last two wheels of the transmitted precepts, is the unblemished, eloquent tradition of those who have undeludedly adhered to the Sugata's teaching in India and here in the Land of Snows. Therefore, it has been reiterated in the writings of all the literary scholars and undeluded contemplatives, from the great translator Ngok Loden Sherap to Conang Sherap Gyeltsen and Putön Rincentrup of Zhalu.

In general, with an intention directed to consciousness, our Teacher revealed the structure of acceptance and rejection, and of cause and effect, that is valid in much the same manner as is the cause and effect [operating] in the world of dreams. But there are those who passionately cling to an understanding that relative appearance is proven to be valid, even within the pristine cognition of the buddhas. For that reason their clinging to the area of conduct becomes hard and fast, until they tear into patches sublime discriminative awareness and the buddhas' pristine cognition. In this way, it is hard for them to find conviction in the philosophy which does not err with respect to profundity. They even carry off the wondrous enlightened activity of the Sugatas on the stretcher of doubt.

Now, the total freedom from deliberations during periods of meditative equipoise may well be the meditation of Hoshang Mo-ho-yen, but even the *Jewel Lamp of the Madhyamaka*, composed by master Bhavya, which you[1254] esteem as a masterpiece of the Madhyamaka, says:

> Not dwelling on any cognition, not conceiving anything, directing no attention to anything...

Furthermore, Atiśa's comments on the sublime Nāgārjuna's intention explain the period during which one abides in the tranquillity of meditative equipoise that is free from ideation and scrutiny, and also in higher insight, by using the example of fire produced by rubbing two sticks forcefully together. He then gives a detailed explanation, beginning:

> One does not form conceptions about any cognition, nor does one grasp any. One abandons all recollections and deliberations...[1255]

Similar expositions are also found in the three *Meditational Sequences* (*Bhāvanākrama*, T 3915-17) of Kamalaśīla, so it certainly must have been a well-known position among the proponents of the Svātantrika-Madhyamaka.[1256] As these assertions all agree, it hardly matters whether or not they agree with Hoshang Mo-ho-yen, as well.

According to the Great Perfection the naturally present awareness that is the essence of higher insight is itself ascertained to be the pristine cognition of discernment.[1257] Therefore, taking that to be the support for meditation, and having become equipoised in reality, which is free from ideation and scrutiny, one abides in that non-discursive state, the unerring abiding nature which is a "great liberation from limits".[1258] As it says in the *Penetration of Sound*:

> The limit of the natural Great Perfection
> Leaves all things where they arise.
> Because appearance and consciousness are coalescent in reality,
> It reaches the total presence of primordial liberation.
> Its intention transcends the intellect,
> Distinctive phenomena are pure where they arise,
> It is free from the extremes of emptiness and substance,
> Movement has ceased, there are no conceptions,
> And, thoughts exhausted, the intellect is transcended.

Not having realised this, the ebb and flow of ideation and scrutiny does not, by itself, reach the reality of higher insight. Thus, the obscuration which results from subjective intellectual adherences, which refer only to a counterfeit emptiness established by mind and mental events, becomes merely a vastly inflated opinion, the nature of which is never-ending and [a cause for] rebirth. The Teacher himself clearly said this in his *Nirvāṇa Sūtra*:

> O Kāśyapa! whoever, referring to emptiness, relies upon emptiness, deviates greatly from this discourse of mine... O Kāśyapa! it is better to abide in a view [which clings to] individual existence to the extent of Mount Sumeru, than with manifest egotism to adopt a view to emptiness.

Some object to such a viewpoint, saying that Nāgārjuna has said:[1259]

> Not relying upon conventions,
> One will not realise the ultimate.

Hence, [they claim that] realisation must depend on arguments involving refutation and proof. But this quotation simply implies that, initially, ultimate truth should be realised by relying on expressed meaning and expression;[1260] Nāgārjuna did not say that it must be realised one-sidedly through sophistic examination. He put that down many times:

> Therefore, that is scrutinised
> By a corpse-like sophistry...

Just so, having entered on the precipitous trail of ideation and scrutiny, [the sophists] circumambulate the crags of refutation and proof, and let the pristine cognition which abides in themselves fly off on the path of exaggeration and depreciation. Arrogantly thinking to remove the two extremes through intellectual contrivances, they become like insects entangled in [cocoons spun from] their own saliva. It is extremely difficult for them to arrive at reality as it is. Since reality is inconceivable it cannot be exemplified through conventions, for conventions remain, essentially, discursive labels. It says in the *Sūtra which Decisively Reveals the Intention*:

> Though in the range of particular discrete characteristics,
> It is inexpressible, completely divorced from conventions:
> Ultimate reality is indisputable;
> Its characteristics transcend all sophistry.

Here, in the natural Great Perfection, three postures hammer in the nail, three gazes take aim at the essence, and, traversing the path of the six lamps, reality is seen directly, without intellectual scrutiny.[1261] Therefore, the difference between this path [and that of dialectics] is like that of heaven and earth. As it says in the *Penetration of Sound*:

> As for the ultimate: having parted from intellect,
> The faculties are naturally liberated at once,
> And one perceives it directly.
> This essential point destroys philosophising,
> And, without clinging or grasping at anything,
> Genuine reality is tasted.
> Then, with no support for three-realmed saṃsāra,
> As when space dissolves into space,
> Just so is this supreme yoga.

For much the same reason, Sakya Paṇḍita said [in the *Analysis of the Three Vows*, Ch.3]:

> The view of the Atiyoga
> Is pristine cognition, but not a vehicle.[1262]

Considering that aspect [of the Great Perfection] which verifies, without delusion, the abiding nature of the profound view, it may be well to describe it as pristine cognition, but his assertion that it is not validly a vehicle is an intentional one. It is because the pristine cognition subsumed by the levels of pious attendants and self-centred buddhas, bodhisattvas, and buddhas is, respectively, incomplete, partially complete, and entirely complete that the definitive order of these four classes of sublime beings and the sequence of the vehicles have been established. It says in the *Supreme Continuum of the Greater Vehicle* (Ch.1, v.50cd):

> Just like space with reference to
> Inferior, middling, or superior forms...

So, exemplified by space which is without qualitative distinctions whether it occupies good or bad vessels, the pristine cognition, disclosed by the greater or lesser power of freedom from obscuration, is [primordially] present as the basis. With an intention directed to this, there is not the slightest contradiction in establishing it to be a vehicle. If one were to maintain that there is no pristine cognition in the minds of the three sublime types of sentient being apart from the buddhas, then [the discussion] would end there. But it is the profound intention of the sūtras and tantras that the vehicles are established because the structure of the levels and paths is based on pristine cognition alone, from the slight vision of it, up to the complete vision of it. Therefore, it says in the *Great Bounteousness of the Buddhas*:

> With mind engaged in the vehicle of pristine cognition and
> the greater vehicle,
> One dedicates [the merits of] those fundamental virtues.

And in the *Dialogue with Suvikrāntavikrami* (*Suvikrāntavikramiparipṛcchā*, T 14) it says:

> The greater vehicle is the pristine cognition of the buddhas.

Those who, not having conviction in the primordial philosophy of the Great Perfection, grasp as supreme those philosophies which have been established on behalf of neophytes, and so push aside the significance of the three approaches to liberation – they are like shadows that have abandoned their form!

Similarly, there are those who even say that because the word "Great Seal", is not taught in the causal vehicle, Gampopa alone contrived to do so.[1263] In this and other ways they insist that his teaching is incorrect. None the less, the utterly unconditioned expanse is termed a "seal",[1264] for instance in the *Sūtra of the Adornment of Pristine Cognition's Appearance which Penetrates the Scope of All Buddhas*, where it says:

> O Ānanda! the seal of the doctrine is the seal of all things. It is the absence of seal, the uncreated seal, the undivided seal. O Ānanda! those who are sealed by that are great bodhisattvas. They are of the dignified family of enlightenment. They are lions among men...

Pel Jikpa Kyopei Yi

The master Jñānakīrti also offers a detailed exposition in his *Introduction to the Real*, beginning:

> The other name for the Mother, the transcendental perfection
> Of discriminative awareness, is the Great Seal,
> For it is the essential nature of undivided pristine cognition...

Therefore, in the actual teaching of the sūtras, the transcendental perfection of discriminative awareness is sometimes referred to as the Great Seal. In the mantras, one who becomes accomplished by means of supreme bliss resorts to the Great Seal [or coalesence of] bliss and emptiness. So, except for the difference between the sūtras and mantras, it is somewhat incorrect to say that the Great Seal is never expounded in the vehicle of the sūtras. Similarly, while the nucleus of the sugata[1265] is taught in a cursory manner on the path of the sūtras, it is in the teaching of the mantras that it is greatly elaborated.

So it is that those who have clung only to the side of provisional meaning, who have taken interest merely in the structure of conventions, and who have been guided by words [alone] have broadcast those scriptural authorities [which confirm] their own biased positions; but their strongholds are torn down by numerous transmitted precepts and treatises which comment on the [Buddha's] intention. There have been many such blind arrows of speculation, which did not get so far as they were aimed, and which totally lack the power to refute by means of valid reasoning. This much will have sufficed as an example.

3 *Response to Critics of the "Sūtra which Gathers All Intentions"*

[758.2-764.2] Now, [while some object] to the empowerment of the *Sūtra which Gathers All Intentions*, which belongs to the transmitted precepts of the Nyingmapa (*rnying-ma bka'-ma mdo-dbang*), and reveals empowerment ceremonies for the three causal vehicles,[1266] the *Hevajra Tantra* (Pt.2, Ch.8, vv.9-10c) says:

> First you should grant the *poṣadha* vow;
> Then, teach the Vaibhāṣika philosophy,
> And likewise the Sautrāntika philosophy;
> Later teach the Yogācāra itself,
> And afterwards the Madhyamaka philosophy.
> Then, after the entire sequence of the mantras is known,
> One should teach Hevajra.

In accord with this exposition, which conforms to a sequential progression through the vehicles, and because the central path of all vehicles is revealed in full here in the mantra path, the three causal vehicles are seized by the skilful means of the mantras. At that time they sublimely surpass the attributes of their own levels and indeed become the swift path, just as the attitudes and applications of the *prātimokṣa* vows of the lesser vehicle, when seized by an enlightened attitude, are transformed into the *prātimokṣa* vows of the greater vehicle, the attributes of which sublimely surpass those of the lower ones. Therefore, this is the special real reason [for the empowerments of the causal vehicles in connection with the *Sūtra which Gathers All Intentions*].

Moreover, the term "empowerment" is actually revealed [in the causal vehicles]; for in the *Three Hundred Verses [on the Vinaya]* the vows of the novitiate are termed "empowerment":

> The moral discipline of renunciation removes suffering,
> Destroys the real roots of viewing the perishable as self,
> And vanquishes mundane glory and flower-arrowed Kāma.
> It is the empowerment granting the glory of perfect
> enlightenment.

In general, empowerment is understood in this way: When universal monarchs are crowned, they are anointed with water from a jewelled vase and given benedictions by the brahmans, whereby they are empowered with dominion over the realm with its seven precious things and so forth. Similarly, when a bodhisattva who has arrived at the end of the stream of the tenth level on the path of sūtras is about to become a buddha,[1267] then light rays emanate from the *ūrṇakeśa*[1268] of the tathāgatas of the ten directions and vanish into the crown of that spiritual warrior. This is termed the "empowerment of light rays".[1269] In fact, no matter what path one enters, the consecration of the buddhas is the means by which one is empowered in its view, meditation, conduct, and result, and so is denoted as an "empowerment". It says in the *Sūtra of the Descent to Laṅkā* (Ch.2, XL):

> Mahāmati! moreover, bodhisattvas who have been blessed with two blessings come before the feet of the tathāgatas, arhats, utterly perfect buddhas and ask all their questions. With which two blessings, one might ask, are they blessed? It is so that they are blessed with the blessing of balanced contemplative absorption and with the blessing of the empowerments conferred by all the bodies, faces, and arms [of the buddhas].
>
> Thereat, Mahāmati! bodhisattvas, great spiritual warriors are blessed with the blessing of the buddhas from [the time of their attainment of] the first level,[1270] and become equipoised in the contemplation of the bodhisattvas, which is called "Illumination of the Greater Vehicle". As soon as those bodhisattvas, great spiritual warriors become equipoised in the bodhisattvas' contemplation of the "Illumination of the Greater Vehicle", the tathāgatas, arhats, utterly perfect buddhas who reside in the ten directions of the universe reveal themselves. They genuinely reveal all their bodies, faces, and discourses. In this way, Mahāmati! they appropriately bless the bodhisattva, great spiritual warrior Vajragarbha and other great bodhisattvas endowed with similar characteristics.
>
> So it is, Mahāmati! that the bodhisattvas, great spiritual warriors on the first level attain the blessing to become equipoised in contemplation. Through the fundamental virtues accumulated during all of a hundred thousand aeons, they finally thoroughly realise the characteristics that are allied to the levels, or opposed to them. Then, on the bodhisattva level called "Cloud of Doctrine", the hands of the conquerors extend from the ten directions of the universe towards those bodhisattvas, great spiritual warriors who,

seated in the Great Lotus Palace, wearing crowns adorned with all the most precious ornaments, are completely surrounded by bodhisattvas, great spiritual warriors like themselves. With [hands whose touch is] like orpiment,[1271] gold, *campaka* flowers, moonlight, and lotuses, the conquerors empower those bodhisattvas, great spiritual warriors, all of whom reside in the Great Lotus Palace, on the crowns of their heads, in the manner of lords, universal monarchs, or Indrarāja. Because they are empowered by all the bodies, faces, and hands of the buddhas, that bodhisattva and these bodhisattvas are said to be blessed by the blessing of the hand empowerment.

And:

For the following reasons, Mahāmati! do the tathāgatas, arhats, utterly perfect buddhas bless bodhisattvas, great spiritual warriors with their blessing: in order that they not be disturbed by the defilements and deeds of Māra; not slide back into the contemplation and level of the pious attendants; become aware, for themselves, individually, of the level of the tathāgatas; and so that their acquired doctrines and masteries increase. Mahāmati! bodhisattvas, great spiritual warriors who are not so blessed slide back into the attitudes of extremists, pious attendants and Māra. They do not attain the unsurpassed and authentic, perfect enlightenment of buddhahood. For reasons such as these, the bodhisattvas, great spiritual warriors are favoured by the tathāgatas, arhats, utterly perfect buddhas.

As has been stated abundantly in such passages, it is indisputable that a bodhisattva who has attained the end of the stream [of the tenth level] must attain buddhahood by relying upon empowerment. Therefore, provisionally, the pious attendants, self-centred buddhas, and bodhisattvas are empowered to cultivate meditatively their respective paths; and because, ultimately, they are [all] seized by the enlightened attitude of the greater vehicle, even [the vehicles of] the pious attendants and self-centred buddhas become swift paths to the attainment of omniscience. For this especially crucial reason Vajradhara, skilled in means and all-knowing, has given such teaching. Moreover, when it is taught that, without relying on the three higher empowerments of the Unsurpassed [Yogatantra],[1272] the level of Vajradhara cannot be attained merely by means of the tantras of the outer way of mantras, what is meant is, in point of fact, much the same as this, for, on the path of the sūtras those [empowerments] are concealed, and only the empowerment, or blessing, of great light rays is spoken of.

4 *Response to Critics of the "Root Tantra of the Secret Nucleus"*

[764.2-770.6] Moreover, because Gö Lhetse did not receive the teachings he had requested from the lord of the doctrine, Zurpoche, he nursed a grudge, due to which, after travelling to India, he reported that the Nyingmapa tantras were not to be found in India.[1273] He censured the glorious *Secret Nucleus* for four faults, et cetera, which were occasionally repeated by some Tibetans.[1274] None the less, just going to India [and finding that] they were unknown in a few districts does not disprove the ancient translations. The Great Perfection and other exceedingly profound tantrapiṭaka were only transmitted through unique lineages directly from mouth to ear. Beyond that, not even written texts were made. As nothing at all of those instructions remained behind, it may well be true that he neither saw, nor heard of them; for India was without this sort of Tibetan custom, whereby the doctrines of the secret mantra are given publicly, even to dogs and mice. Nevertheless, when one such as the "sole divine master" Dīpaṃkara [Atiśa], who was renowned for his great learning in the mantras throughout India, saw the Indian manuscripts at the Pehar Kordzöling [at Samye] in Tibet, his scholarly arrogance was shattered because many tantrapiṭaka were preserved there which he had never heard of or seen before. As that story is clearly set forth in the biography of master Atiśa himself, it is of no importance that an ordinary person such as Lhetse did not see those [tantras in India]. As a further illustration, one may note that one Orgyenpa Rincenpel, who meandered like a river all the way to Oḍḍiyāna in the west, and who could powerfully transform the vision of others, said that he did not see an end to the mantras which appeared in the human world.[1275]

Likewise, the lie that the *Secret Nucleus* had been composed in Tibet was betrayed by an actual Indian manuscript, which came into the possession of Comden Rikpei Reldri, the great paṇḍita Śākyaśrī, Tharpa Lotsāwa, Gölo Zhönupel, Shage Lotsāwa, et cetera. Rikpei Reldri, in particular, who was supremely learned in the later translations and was a great rectifier of the teaching, said in his *Proof of the Secret Nucleus* (*gsang-snying sgrub-pa*):[1276]

This tantra is genuine for the following reasons: In the *Great Commentary on the Glorious Guhyasamāja* (*dpal gsang-ba 'dus-pa'i 'grel-chen*, T 1844) composed by the master Viśvamitra, in the course of his comments on the passage "How far does the Being of Pristine Cognition reach...?" the *Secret Nucleus* is cited as follows (Ch.1, v.3):

> *In the abode of Akaniṣṭha without extremes or centre, in the limitless ground which is the radiant wheel of pristine cognition, there is the celestial palace blazing forth with the jewels of pristine cognition, completely uninterrupted throughout the ten directions...*

And also (Ch.1, v.6):

> *In every inconceivable [world], he appears universally as the diverse buddha-body, speech and mind.*

Then, in commenting on the passage, "The stūpa should be known to be the palatial abode of all buddhas...," he cites it as follows (Ch.1, v.3):

> *The spire is the pristine cognition central to all, in which all maṇḍalas of the buddhas of the ten directions and four times without exception are not distinct from one another, and are of a single essence.*

Then, commenting on the passage, "Substantial existence is based on insubstantiality...," he gives (Ch.2, v.6):

> *Emaho! This wonderful marvellous reality*
> *Is the secret of all perfect buddhas.*
> *All is created from the uncreated.*
> *At creation itself there is no creation.*

Then, while explaining the meaning of "secret" he says, "The *Secret Nucleus* speaks of five empowerments."[1277] Moreover, he quotes the passage beginning (Ch.6, vv.9-11):

> *Their [colours] are blue, white, yellow, scarlet ...*
>
> up to:
>
> *[Pervasive] without extremes or centre,*
> *[It is an unthinkable] spontaneously present*
> *[maṇḍala].*

And he says, "According to the *Secret Nucleus*, there are three realities."

In these and all other such instances Viśvamitra begins by mentioning the title *Secret Nucleus*.

The four perverse faults, et cetera, [criticised by Gö Lhetse], are also to be rejected: [When texts begin with the words] *Thus I have expounded*, it is traditionally held to mean that they were compiled by the buddhas themselves, for it is impossible for even the tenth level bodhisattvas to compile all the teachings of the buddhas. As it says in the *Verification of Secrets*, composed by master Saroruha as a commentary on the *Guhyasamāja*:

> Most masters claim
> That the most radiant tantra,
> The glorious *Guhyasamāja*,
> Had as its compiler
> The warrior called Lokeśvara.
> But by the kindness of my venerable guru
> I know that the compiler of the glorious
> *Guhyasamāja*
> Could not have been any other;
> And so the being who propounded it
> Was that tantra's author,
> The indestructible reality of mind.

In accord with this explanation, there is a tradition whereby the exponent himself is the compiler.

As for the "immeasurable ground" the Abhidharma, too, explains that Akaniṣṭha is immeasurable.

Concerning the *four times*: Viśvamitra's *Great Commentary [on the Glorious Guhyasamāja]* says: "Thus, the fourth time should be known to be sameness..." Moreover, the phrase, *By all the lords of the ten directions and four times* is also found in the new translations. Buddhaguhya explains that it refers to the four aeons.

Regarding Vajrasattva's appearance at the centre [of the maṇḍala]: even the new translations explain that the foremost figure in the maṇḍala may change positions.[1278]

Concerning the passage, *The* visarga *or final punctuation marks* (tig) *are the discriminative awareness through which names are applied* (Ch.4, v.15), the Indian manuscript of the *Secret Nucleus* reads *sūtri prajñātiṣyati*.[1279] *Sūtri* (thread) is the Sanskrit word for *thig* (measuring line). Sūryaprabhāsiṃha's *Commentary [on the Secret Nucleus]* explains [*tig* as being equivalent] to *thig*. *Tig* is an archaicism.

As for the reference to other tantras [which is found in the *Secret Nucleus*]: all the tantras expounded later on, such as the *Hevajra*, also refer to the *Summation of the Real* which had been delivered first.

With such well-wrought arguments, [Rikpei Reldri's work] establishes, in the manner of a teaching dialogue, [the authenticity of the *Secret Nucleus*], having cited quotations from this tantra in the great treatises that were famed in India, along with many commentaries by the masters mentioned above. You should examine it, for it is clearly valid!

For such reasons, the great paṇḍita Śākya Chokden has said:[1280]

> It is not necessary to prove laboriously that
> The Nyingmapa doctrines were translated from Indian originals.
> It is enough that they are proven to be
> The teaching of the emanational master [Padmasambhava].
> Although they do not conform with the mantras and symbols
> Of those translated from India later on,
> The proof of their validity is infallible accomplishment
> Through their supreme and common attainment.
> They may be compared with the doctrines taken
> By supreme accomplished masters from various great lands,
> And which were not translated in India
> From their respective volumes;
> For it is said that with Vajrasattva's consent
> The compilers of those transmitted precepts
> Were themselves permitted to teach them
> In the language of each different country.
> The Nyingmapa doctrinal traditions that definitely were
> Translated from India require no proof.
> Having formulated arguments one might prove
> The indefinite ones to be treatises,[1281]
> But the great ones who came before in Tibet,
> Discovering this to be an artificial, conceptual path,
> Have avoided wandering upon it,
> As they themselves have explained.

This reasoned argument appears to be a learned axiom, when scrutinised fairly. In general, a doctrine is no more important merely because it originated in India. A distinction of good and bad treatises on the basis of country is not known in learned circles. If the author was one who was abiding on the level of accomplishment, the treatises composed by him should be valid. So, it is proven that whether they originated in India or Tibet makes no difference. Sometimes, too, Tibetan treatises are better than Indian treatises. One should regard as reliable those composed by accomplished Tibetans, whose pristine cognition was manifest, rather than those written by ordinary Indian scholars, who based themselves on learning in grammar and logic.

5 *The Continuity of the Nyingmapa Tradition, and its Impact on the Other Schools*

[771.1-786.4] Furthermore, in the period following the persecution of the teaching by Langdarma, one called the "Red Master" and another called the "Blue-skirted Paṇḍita" came from India to Tibet, where, for the sake of riches and honour, they propagated practices involving public orgies and slaughter in the villages.[1282] Because many Tibetans entered their following, Lha Lama, uncle and nephew, as well as the translator Rincen Zangpo and others explained, in the epistles of refutation which they authored in order to prevent harm to the teaching, that these were perversions of the mantra tradition.[1283] The translators of the new schools repeatedly declared, in order to prove the greatness of their own doctrines, that the transmitted precepts of the way of the secret mantra according to the Ancient Translation School had been polluted, owing to which ill-informed persons were carried off on the stretcher of doubt. But, in fact, it may be known from the preceding history how the continuous blessings of this succession of tantras, transmissions, and esoteric instructions have been preserved without decline.

In brief, when the doctrine was persecuted by Langdarma all the dialectical seminaries were destroyed, but the hermitages of the mantra tradition survived somewhat in mountainous ravines, caves, and so forth. For that reason, and in accord with the promise which Langdarma himself made to Nupcen [p. 612], the mantrins were never harmed at all. During those times a multitude of excellent awareness-holders, who had mastery over the two accomplishments, continued to maintain the teaching of the three inner classes of tantra. Their number included Nyangben Tingdzin Zangpo, Ngenlam Cangcup Gyeltsen, most of the eight glorious disciples of Nyak Jñānakumāra, Nupcen and his disciples, Rok Śākya Jungne, and Deshek Zurpoche.

As for how the supreme and common accomplishments were visibly disclosed, without fail, by those who experientially cultivated the tantras of the Ancient Translation School and the esoteric instructions composed by those who dwelt on the great level of the awareness-holders:

there were seven successive generations of disciples beginning with Pang Mipham Gönpo, who did so by means of the instructions of the Spatial Class of the Great Perfection. There were seven generations in the lineage which passed from Nyang Tingdzin Zangpo to Dangma, and so on, whose physical bodies dissolved into the rainbow body, the supreme transformation, by means of the path of the esoteric instructions on inner radiance, the Innermost Spirituality;[1284] as well as many who emerged successively, such as the three ancestral Zurs, who had the discipline to resurrect the dead, and who bodily vanished into space.

It is impossible, too, to enumerate all those who passed into the rainbow body by the paths of the profound treasures of the Great Perfection, as exemplified by the Southern [Treasures of Pema Lingpa] and the Northern [Treasures of Rikdzin Gödemcen]. Even during this late age, this may still be illustrated. For example, in 1883/4 (water sheep year, fifteenth cycle) the lord among accomplished masters, Rikdzin Pema Düdül, vanished in the body of light.[1285] Afterwards, when his personal disciple, the treasure-finder Rangrik Dorje, passed away at Mindröling, his remains vanished into light. What was left behind, which was about six inches in size, was taken to Dokam, where it can still be seen today. During that same period, there were thirteen disciples of the great treasure-finder Düjom Lingpa who attained the rainbow body.[1286] Furthermore, very close to the present day, there have been many whom I remember, who were manifestly perceived to have dissolved into the rainbow body without leaving even a trace of their bodies behind: Lingtsang Dzapa Trashi Özer of Dokam in 1935/6 (wood pig year, sixteenth cycle);[1287] followed by his regent, Lodrö Gyeltsen, in 1937/8 (fire ox year);[1288] followed by Derge Yilungpa Sonam Namgyel in 1952/3 (water dragon year).[1289]

In addition, one cannot number those like Trime Özer, the son of the treasure-finder Düjom Lingpa; Ḍāki Künzang Chönyi Dekyong Wangmo; the Zhecen Gyeltsap, Gyurme Pema Namgyel; the great preceptor of Dzokcen, Zhenpen Chöki Nangwa; Gemang II, Thupwang Tenpei Nyima; Cadrel Künga Pelden; Lingter III, Gyurme Pema Tendzin; the great preceptor of Dzokcen, Pema Thekcok Loden; and my own supreme guides, the great treasure-finder Zilnön Namkei Dorje; Khyapdak Gyurme Ngedön Wangpo; and the lord of the circle, Jampel Dewei Nyima. Their physical bodies mostly vanished into light, accompanied by sound, light, earthquakes and various other miracles. What was left behind, no larger than a cubit, became [after cremation] masses consisting of the five remains and relics.

There were also very many [Nyingmapa masters] who traversed the ocean of learning, such as Rongzom Chöki Zangpo and the all-knowing king of the doctrine, Longcen Rapjampa, who planted their feet on a level such as that of Nāgārjuna and Asaṅga, the supreme adornments

Düjom Lingpa

beautifying Jambudvīpa, whose sublime intellects were fearless in the encounter with the profundities of the Sugata's doctrinal tradition. In the ordinary [sciences], as well, the *Four Medical Tantras* (*gso-dpyad rgyud-bzhi*), translated by the emanational translator Vairocana, have provided great sustenance for numberless living creatures.

Moreover, [the Nyingmapa tradition has been endowed with] profound means for the attainment of myriad deeds by means of the four rites of enlightened activity: pacification, enrichment, subjugation, and wrath. Therefore, when some of those who have been famed for their greatness throughout the Land of Snows have been afflicted with most fearsome circumstances, they have had to seek refuge, directly or indirectly, with the followers of the Ancient Translation School. This is verified by direct evidence: for instance, though Sakya Paṇḍita could defeat Haranandin through reason, when the latter began to fly into the sky it was Darcarwa who bound him with the gnostic mantra of Vajrakīla.[1290] This being so, one should think how far-reaching is that teaching, which is possessed of enlightened activity associated with the manifestly elevated [higher realms of existence] and the definitively good [liberation].[1291] The buddhas and bodhisattvas have acted solely as physicians on behalf of other sentient beings. With this intention the supremely learned Gö Lotsāwa Zhönupel has said [in the *Blue Annals*, p.203]:

> In general, after the persecution of the teaching by Langdarma, there was not a single ordained monk in Central Tibet and Tsang for more than seventy years. However, there were many Nyingmapa mantra adepts who blessed their respective homelands with their distinctive practices. The householders had faith in them, delighted them with food and clothing, et cetera, and occasionally received the vase empowerment alone, whereby their minds gradually matured. Consequently, when those known as the six or eight men from Central Tibet and Tsang, [namely,] Lume and the others, arrived, countless temples and monastic communities were founded in every province and district. It became possible to enjoy, without decline, the transmitted precepts and treatises which had been translated in the past, during the time of the king and his ministers. Moreover, most of the many learned and accomplished individuals who appeared originated from the lineages of the Nyingmapa accomplished masters.

Just so, apart from some esoteric instructions of the Great Perfection which were composed by Indian masters such as Indrabhūti, Buddhajñānapāda, and Nāropā, and which were dispersed throughout Tibet, most of the treatises, and so forth, composed by other accomplished masters were not even translated into Tibetan. These masters, being determined to preserve secrecy, would not leave even a trace of their supremely profound, esoteric instructions behind. So, let alone the issue of public teaching, because even the books were by and large sealed to be kept invisible, they could only be revealed in utter secrecy to one sole supremely fortunate disciple. So it was that, for example, Phamthingpa was familiar with *Nāropā's Sky-farer* (*nā-ro mkha'-spyod*), the mere name of which Marpa had never heard. Likewise, there are accounts [which hold that] the great paṇḍita Śākyaśrī received Vajrakīla from the great master Padmasambhava himself, and that Phadampa Sangye maintained the Great Perfection as his profoundest commitment. At a later date, the great accomplished master Śāntigupta received the transmitted exegeses, empowerments, and esoteric intructions of many tantrapiṭaka from master Padmasambhava in person. Śāntigupta's disciples who came to Tibet related that he also propagated them in Drāviḍa and other countries.[1292] In addition, there was the Great Perfection which Zhang Yudrakpa received directly from the master Padmasambhava, the bodhisattva Śāntarakṣita, and Vimalamitra.

When the venerable Milarepa first received the Mental Class of the Great Perfection from Nup Khulungpa he could not become equipoised in awareness itself, and for the time being the doctrine and the individual seemed to go their own ways.[1293] Finally, on the basis of the venerable Marpa of Lhodrak's [teaching of the] inner heat, he attained accomplishment on the path of the Great Perfection, whereby all thoughts, all things are exhausted. This can be demonstrated by one of his own songs of indestructible reality, in which he says:

> Stabbed in front by the Great Perfection,
> Stabbed in the back by the Great Seal,
> I vomit the blood of instruction...

The venerable Karma Pakshi [Karmapa II], who had been Garap Dorje's disciple Toktsewa, remembered that previous life in which he had comprehended the six million four hundred thousand verses of the Great Perfection. Owing to this, and to his study of the Great Perfection under Katokpa Campabum, and so on, he obtained accomplishment. The all-knowing Rangjung Dorje [Karmapa III] asserted himself to be the emanation of Vimalamitra and, having become the master of the teaching of the Innermost Spirituality, brought forth treasures of intention as well. The great accomplished master Orgyenpa, the venerable Götsangpa, Yang-gönpa and others who realised saṃsāra and nirvāṇa to be of the same savour [i.e. the adherents of the Drukpa Kagyü tradition] obtained accomplishment in the expanse of the Great Perfection, no matter upon which path they provisionally relied. [To affirm this] one should examine the innermost assertions of their respective intentions.

The glorious Sakyapa all attained accomplishment by relying upon the tradition of the ancient translations that was derived from the lineage of Khön Lüiwangpo,[1294] a direct disciple of master Padmasambhava; and Yangdak and Vajrakīla were both adopted as the vital meditational deities of the Sakyapa. During that age, when those Tibetans with arrogant presumptions to scholarship sought to smear the ancient translations, *Yangdak* and *Vajrakīla* were effulgently protected by their [Sakyapa] doctrine masters, who revered them for their purity and so had occasion to cause [their critics] to erase what they had written. The doctrine master Lama Tampa [Sonam Gyeltsen] attained manifest signs [of accomplishment] by relying on *Vajrakīlā*, and he composed a recension of it. In particular, the supreme holders of the Sakyapa teaching tradition, from Dakcen Lodrö Gyeltsen to Künpang Doringpa, Chöje Tsharpa, Jamyang Khyentse Wangcuk, et cetera, were directly or indirectly favoured and blessed by the great master Padmasambhava. Consequently, there were many who obtained accomplishment by the paths of the Ancient Translation School, including the Great Perfection. They can be known from their individual biographies and so forth, but it will not be possible to mention them [all] here.

Moreover, even the instructions of the precious oral teaching of the Path and Fruit which stem from the traditions of that lineage, are, in fact, the exegesis of the stage of perfection found in the Ancient Translation School's *Heruka Galpo*, a tantra of the cycle of *Yangdak, the Mind*, which actually sets forth the structure of the four empowerments, four obscurations, four paths, four philosophical systems, four deceases, four pulses, and four bodies. Because that is demonstrably so, valid evidence has proven [the Path and Fruit] to be an esoteric instruction connected with this tantra.

Again, there was the great accomplished master of Lhodrak renowned as Namka Gyeltsen, or Leki Dorje, who could receive prophetic declarations directly from the Lord of Secrets and so make predictions about whatever had to be done. The esoteric instructions on the two stages which Vajrapāṇi conferred on him as an aural lineage uphold the true path of the Great Perfection. The venerable Tsongkapa implored that great accomplished master to remove his doubts on the genuine, profound view. The master asked the Lord of Secrets, who delivered the *Supreme Nectar-Elixir Dialogue* (*zhus-lan bdud-rtsi sman-mchog*), which says:

> In order to attain the supreme elixir, which is the intention of father Samantabhadra, the heartfelt advice of mother Samantabhadrī, my – the vajra-holder's – own secret injunction, and the highest pinnacle of the vehicles, then cut through to the roots of mind's inner radiance...

And also:

> O Leki Dorje! this, the empty essence of awareness, was not fabricated by anyone. It is without basis, uncaused, abiding from the very beginning... Without constructions and contrivances about it, let it be right where it is. Deviation then attains buddhahood in the primordially pure expanse...

Likewise:

> This natural inner radiance is inseparable from original emptiness, and yet spontaneously present. Its radiant aspect is unobstructed spirituality. Know, too, that whatever arises, without attaining to substantial existence, is that great coalescence. In its inseparability [from emptiness] buddhahood is attained...

It says in the *Elixir Drops of the Creation and Perfection of Vajrapāṇi* (*phyag-na-rdo-rje'i bskyed-rdzogs bdud-rtsi'i thig-pa*):

> The deity of pristine cognition declared:
> The unborn, inconceivable expanse of reality
> Is unimpeded, unelaborate, and it appears as anything.

Saṃsāra and nirvāṇa, no different, are primordially pure.
Whatever is manifest in and of itself dissolves in the unborn expanse.

Moreover:

If delusion's apparitions which grasp two be not destroyed,
One will deviate from the meditative cultivation of emptiness.
If emptiness be not freed from intellect,
Doctrines appearing dualistically cannot liberate you.
Assertions that the five buddha-bodies are to be attained,
The five poisons to be abandoned,
Buddhahood to be obtained,
And saṃsāra to be renounced,
Are attachments to refutation and proof:
If they're not cut off, you'll not obtain the value of the genuine nucleus.
Like a blind man seeking the horizon,
You will wander forever in saṃsāra's abodes.

Though you mentally hanker for that which surpasses the intellect,
Mentally created doctrines cannot liberate you.
"The ultimate is not within intellect's reach and range."[1295]
The pinnacle of vehicles is to be finished with thoughts and finished with things.
Do not apply even the term "awareness"
To your own mind, the buddha-body of reality,
Which is no substance.
Be absorbed in the indiscernible enlightened mind,
Whose nucleus is emptiness and compassion,
The transcendence of utterance, thought, and expression.
Be absorbed in the transcendence of the intellect.
Be totally absorbed in freedom from deeds.

But "be absorbed" is the intellect's phrase:
Without the conventions "absorbed", or "unabsorbed",
Without words, or expressions, free from analytical grounds,
The analytical, apparent intellect is stilled in the expanse.
Refutation, proof, acceptance, and rejection vanish in space,
Like clouds that dissolve in the sky.
Not renouncing discursive thoughts,
They are pure where they arise.

As for view, meditation, conduct and result:
Make freedom from aversion and attraction your view;
Destruction of subjective intellectualising your meditation;

Let freedom from deeds and craving be your conduct;
And your result the abandonment of the wish to attain
extrinsically
The buddha-body of reality, which is naturally within.

The eighty-four thousand doctrines of the vehicles,
Their tantras, commentaries, and esoteric instructions
Transcend what may be expressed;
But this drop of the nectar of esoteric instruction,
Like refined and clarified butter,
Is the quintessence of all together.
As if it were lion's milk, the supreme essence,
I offer it to you, Leki Dorje,
A supreme vessel, like a vase of gold...

This presents the doctrinal terminology of the Great Perfection without adulterating it with other philosophical systems. Hence, it was by this path that Leki Dorje obtained accomplishment. Above and beyond that, Je Guru [Tsongkapa himself], Tokden Jampel Gyamtso and others have explained that, except in the course of his presentations of the Madhyamaka and logical philosophies, the venerable Tsongkapa conformed to the experiential cultivation of the Great Seal and Great Perfection. This, in fact, can be learned by studying the *Supreme Nectar-Elixir Dialogue*, whereby his doubts on the view were resolved [when he queried] the great accomplished master Leki Dorje. This *Dialogue* by and large merits comparison with the *Golden Rosary Dialogue from* the *Innermost Spirituality of the Ḍākinī* (*mkha'-'gro snying-thig-gi-zhus-lan gser-phreng*). Had it been otherwise, Tsongkapa would not have had to rely upon that great accomplished master for merely the view that is an object of [intellectual] understanding, because his discernment with respect to conventional topics was as vast as the illumination of the sun and moon. Therefore, Jamgön Tsongkapa himself said:

> In particular, when I received permission to write down the *Supreme Elixir Dialogue, a Nectar Rosary*, an esoteric instruction which summarises the essence of the intention of the Conqueror and his sons, and which is the secret injunction of the sublime Vajrapāṇi, without interpolation, omission, or error, just as it was orally conferred by the Lord of Secrets, then:
>
> The nectar-like speech of the Lord of Secrets
> Fulfilled the hopes of my mind.
> I overcame the sickness of defilement,
> And thought I had reached Alakāvatī.[1296]

Similarly, Paṇcen Lozang Chöki Gyeltsen wrote in his *Guidebook to the Great Seal* (*phyag-chen-gyi khrid-yig*):

Although many different names have been given –
Great Perfection, Great Seal, and Madhyamaka,
Path and Fruit, Object of Cutting, and Pacification –
When they are investigated by a yogin
Who has cultivated them experientially,
He arrives at just one intention.[1297]

Such a statement, made in general from the perspective of experiential cultivation, gives rise to rejoicing.

Concerning the venerable Phawangkhapa Peljor Lhündrup: It was by relying upon his own father Rikdzin Tshewang Norgye and upon Rangdröl Nyinda Sangye that he became a great lord of yoga, who attained stability on the path of the Innermost Spirituality of the Great Perfection. He composed the *Guidebook which Introduces the View Common to the Great Seal, Great Perfection and Great Madhyamaka*, et cetera, and also some notes clarifying the Innermost Spirituality (*snying-thig-la gsal-byed-kyi yi-ge*). The Great Fifth Dalai Lama received the esoteric instructions of the Great Perfection from this master.

In general, the religious king Trhisong Detsen had returned as the Great Fifth, owing to the timely maturation of his enlightened aspiration to increase the happiness of his Tibetan subjects. He enhanced, here in the Land of Snows, respect for the teaching and doctrinal assemblies, without bias. In particular, his acute, reasoned knowledge of the Ancient Translation School of the secret mantra pursued the doctrine [to such an extent that] the simple enumeration of the transmitted precepts and treasures which he studied fill some three volumes. It is clear from the section concerning the Nyingmapa tantras, found in the fourth volume of his *Record of Teachings Received, the Flow of the Ganges* (*gsan-yig gang-gā'i chu-rgyun*), that he undertook to cut off, by logical proofs and refutations, those who espoused perverse notions [regarding the Nyingmapa tantras].

6 *On the Validity of the Treasures*

[786.4-790.3] Similarly, concerning the Nyingmapa treasures, [it may be said that] all the tantrapiṭaka which were reportedly discovered in ancient India by the great accomplished master Sarahapāda, Garap Dorje, Virūpa, Aśvottama,[1298] Nāgārjuna, Padmākara, Saroruha, Lalitavajra, Cārīndra, and so forth, were, in fact, treasure doctrines; for "treasure" is explained to mean something hidden, that is invisible to direct sensory perception for some time. Therefore, when, for the time being, no worthy recipients to whom the illustrative written tantras [could be transmitted] were found, they were sealed in the invisible expanse, where they were guarded and preserved by the ḍākinīs. Then, those accomplished individuals were given prophetic declarations by their favoured deities and, when the time arrived, they were given permission and empowered by the host of ḍākinīs in the great palaces of mantra, such as the Dharmagañji in Oḍḍiyāna. Having released the seal of entrustment, they were given the volumes of the tantras, experientially cultivated them for themselves, and taught them somewhat to other worthy disciples.

In the same way, with reference to Tibet, the all-seeing master Padmasambhava composed, on the basis of the profound and vast tantrapiṭaka, each requisite for the path in its entirety, including means for attainment, ritual collections and esoteric instructions, for he knew the manner in which those requiring training would appear in the future. He arranged them in yellow scrolls as verbal tantras and entrusted them to their respective non-human treasure lords in mountain ravines, rock-chests, wealth-filled lakes, and elsewhere. He then concealed them to be invisible along with their seals of entrustment which were in the form of prayerful aspirations that they be discovered in the future by the worthy and fortunate individuals who were empowered to do so. At a later date, the power of those prayerful aspirations would awaken in the individuals endowed with suitable fortune. The indications of the appropriate times and the prophetic declarations would come together, whereupon the great master would actually reveal his visage, confer empowerment, and inspire [the treasure-finders] with the seals of entrustment and prophetic declarations. Consequently, having overwhelmed the treasure lords and the protectors of transmitted precepts with their commitments and discipline, all sorts of treasures, those of doctrine and of riches, would come into the possession of the treasure-finders, whereby they would bountifully serve the teaching and sentient beings. This constitutes one aspect of the great enlightened activity of the conquerors. As it says in the *Sublime Sūtra of Contemplation which Subsumes All Merits*, [quoted in *Śikṣāsamuccaya*, p.105]:

> O Vimalatejas! the treasures of bodhisattvas, great spiritual warriors who desire the doctrine, have been inserted in mountains, ravines, and woods. Dhāraṇīs and limitless approaches to the doctrine, which are set down in books, will also come into their hands. O Vimalatejas! deities who formerly beheld the Buddha will encourage the brilliance of all the bodhisattvas, great spiritual warriors who desire the doctrine. O Vimalatejas! even if the lives of those bodhisattvas, great spiritual warriors who desire the doctrine, should expire, they will be revitalised and strengthened by all the buddhas, transcendental lords, and by the deities. By the blessing of the buddhas and the blessing of the deities they will endure, if they so wish, for a thousand years.

In the *Sūtra which Genuinely Comprises the Entire Doctrine*, too, it says:

> Ānanda! whoever writes down these diverse doctrines in books, conceals them as treasures, and worships them, so that the doctrine might be completely preserved, will obtain ten true acquisitions. Ānanda! these are: the treasure of beholding a buddha, for he acquires the eye which does so; the treasure of hearing the doctrine, for he acquires the divine ear; the treasure of seeing the *saṃgha*, for by not regressing he acquires [membership in] the *saṃgha*; the treasure which is inexhaustible, for he has acquired the hand of wealth; the treasure of form, for the major and minor marks are perfected; the treasure of service, for his servants will not part from him; the treasure of holiness, for he has acquired brilliance; the treasure of fearlessness, for he has eliminated his adversaries; and the treasure of sustaining merit, for he sustains sentient beings.[1299]

As the Sugata has made such proclamations in his indisputable lion's roar, one ought well to comprehend them.

7 *The Shortcomings of Refutation and Proof*

[790.3-798.6] In general, as long as one has not examined in detail the distinctions of the objects of refutation, and the refutations, found in the past in the catalogues and broadsides which were famed as *Rejections of Perverse Doctrines* (*chos-log sun-'byin*), it is difficult [to maintain cogently] that they tend only to refute the Nyingmapa. When fair-minded persons examine them in detail many appear to have been composed in order to see just how much it was possible to get away with. If all the doctrines refuted by learned and accomplished Tibetans were false, no authentic doctrine at all would be found.

For instance, in his *Treatise which Analyses the Three Vows* (*rab-dbye'i bstan-bcos*), Sakya Paṇḍita refuted a great many Takpo Kagyü [teachings], such as the *Six Doctrines* and the Great Seal.[1300] In his *Answers to the Questions of the Kadampa Spiritual Benefactor Namkabum* (*bka'-gdams-pa'i dge-bshes nam-mkha'-'bum-gyi dris-lan*, SK Vol.5, no.96) he severely refutes the Kagyü adherents, saying:

> The doctrinal tradition of the Great Seal according to Drigungpa and Taklungpa does not agree with any of the tantrapiṭaka. I think that it is not a genuine path. But do not repeat this to others!

The Kadampa were themselves refuted by Phadampa and others, and the venerable Milarepa criticised Takpo Lharje for adhering to the career of a Kadampa.[1301] The esoteric instructions of Phadampa's Pacification were said by Zhikpo Nyiseng, Co-se Temdrel and others to be fanciful doctrines. They also said that the Object of Cutting was a "doctrine leaked out by a mad nun" [i.e. Macik Lapdrön]. Some said that even the Five Golden Doctrines of the Shangpas had been composed by Khyungpo Tshültrim Gönpo,[1302] and so would not include them in the *Tangyur*. The Sakyapa duo, Yakde Paṇcen and Rongtön Sheja Künzi, and the trio of Korampa Sonam Senge, Śākya Chokden, and Taklung Lotsāwa severely refuted the view and philosophy of the venerable Tsongkapa and maintained that even his visions of Mañjughoṣa were not genuine.[1303] The supremely learned Rikpei Reldri said that the *Kālacakra* was not a genuine tantra because it states that the planets and stars move toward the east, that China lies to the north of Tibet, and so forth. Moreover, the venerable Remdawa said:[1304]

> Although it is said that *Kālacakra* and others
> Were composed by the mighty lords of the tenth level,
> If intellects which discriminate valid from invalid arguments
> Examine them, that is not seen to be proven.
> In the root tantra the two syllables E-VAṂ are not found;
> In the abridged tantra one sees many contradictions.
> Can one trust it any more than a prostitute's son?

With these and many other arguments he refuted the *Kālacakra*. In addition, Gö Lhetse refuted the Path and Fruit saying:

> The golden doctrines of Gayadhara originated
> From the deranged transmission of the *Mātaraḥ Tantra*.[1305]

But he is well known to have been jealous of its propagator, the translator Drokmi.

For all these arguments there was certainly a basic intention and special need; but, for example, on the other hand, the peerless Takpo Kagyü tradition did produce a host of accomplished masters, and it is well established that Jamgön Tsongkapa's enlightened activity on behalf of the Buddhist teaching was that of a "Second Teacher". If the doctrines, which were well expounded by such great persons as these, who were praised in the indestructible prophecies of the Buddha himself and those of the great master [Padmasambhava], and which explicitly abide in what is meaningful, are impure, it would seem that most Tibetans ought to be excommunicated from the teaching of the Conqueror!

In short, the structure of the vehicles and philosophical systems, which is the object of the buddhas' great enlightened activity, and which is a profound secret of inconceivable reality, is not at all similar to the counterfeit ideas and scrutinies associated with the acute investigations of study and reflection which are pondered through the knowable. Because the sugatas, who are all-knowing, have taught [those vehicles and philosophies] we should recognise that the unerring excellent philosophy of the buddhas is characterised as that in which saṃsāra is abandoned, and liberation and nirvāṇa are entered. The venerable Ajita [Maitreya] has accordingly said [in the *Supreme Continuum of the Greater Vehicle*, Ch.5, v.18]:

> Speech which inspires rejection of
> The conflicting emotions of the three world realms,
> And which expresses the attributes of peace,
> Is the word of the Sage;
> Its opposites are otherwise.

Without being mindful of this, how might the profoundest depths of the oceanic realm of the doctrine be within the range of those bigoted Tibetans who harbour pretensions to learning, when, except for being the object of the buddhas alone, they cannot be realised even by sublime beings?[1306] Those who blaspheme [the doctrine] will not even minutely reach what is truly significant, whether they are motivated by the lack of proper realisation, attachment to only provisional meaning, bigoted tendencies, jealousy towards their own equals, or the mere desire for acquisition, honour, and fame.

Just so, when the greater vehicle was expounded by master Nāgārjuna, the pious attendants invented negative prophecies about lord Nāgārjuna and, having inserted them in the scriptures, proclaimed that [the sūtras of] the greater vehicle were not the transmitted precepts [of the Buddha]. When the sublime Asaṅga commented upon the final transmitted precepts in accord with the intention of the great regent [Maitreya], he and his followers were expelled from the greater vehicle. During the reign of King Dharmapāla, adherents of the lesser vehicle destroyed and plundered a silver image of Heruka, burned up volumes of mantras, and proclaimed that the greater vehicle and the way of secret mantra had been created by Māra. The account maintains that they were saved from royal punishment by master Buddhajñānapāda.[1307]

In Tibet as well, when the venerable Daö Zhönu [Gampopa] taught that the abiding nature of reality, as it is explained in the sūtras, is the Great Seal, [his critics] maintained that this was not at all the teaching of the Buddha, saying it was "Takpo's fanciful doctrine". The all-knowing Rangjung Dorje [Karmapa III] and Chödrak Gyamtso [Karmapa VII] expounded [the teaching] in accord with the intention of the final transmitted precepts, but later Mikyö Dorje [Karmapa VIII] and others did not adhere to their view.[1308] When master Tölpopa declared that the ultimate truth was permanent and stable, the Tibetans considered him to be merely a Sāṃkhya extremist.[1309] After the venerable Tsongkapa had explained relative appearance to be logically verifiable later scholars assaulted him with HŪṂ! and PHAṬ! [i.e. showered him with derision]. The great paṇḍita Zilungpa [Śākya Chokden] had to be ejected from the Sakyapa ranks for explaining that the *Analysis of the Three Vows* was of provisional meaning.[1310] Moreover, the all-knowing Great Fifth, having studied and meditated upon the authentic teaching impartially, was very nearly excluded from the Gedenpa [i.e. Gelukpa] order. The obscuration of those who believe such perverse accusations and, having regarded [these pure masters] perversely, so come to abandon the doctrine, is immeasurable.

Even a householder who has not entered the teaching and who performs intolerable, sinful deeds has the opportunity to become tranquil by merely turning to the profound abode [i.e. emptiness], but this is not so for those who blaspheme or abandon the doctrine. As it says in the *Nirvāṇa Sūtra*:

> O Kāśyapa! in the world three kinds of diseased individuals are extremely difficult to cure. What are their diseases? To revile the greater vehicle, to commit the five inexpiable sins, and to harbour perverse attitudes – these three kinds of disease are extremely difficult to cure in the world. Even the pious attendants, self-centred buddhas, and bodhisattvas cannot cure them.

This is elaborated in the *Sūtra of the Dialogue with Sāgaramati*:

> Those who know not the things which make up the world,
> And abide in two perceptions,
> Saying, "this is true, that is false"–
> Such ignoramuses make disputations.
> Because I know the genuine reality
> Of the things which make up the world,
> I never enter into dispute
> With worldly people at all.
> This doctrine, which is free from dispute,
> Has been expounded by all of the buddhas.
> If one knows the world to be sameness,
> There is neither truth, nor falsehood in it.
> If any truth, or falsehood,
> Were to be found in this teaching,
> I would be an adherent of extremes,
> And so be no different from an extremist.
> Because things are not genuine,
> There is no truth and no falsehood.
> Therefore, I explain the doctrine
> Which transcends the world
> To be free from these two.
> Those sages who know this world,
> In accord with the world's reality,
> Do not adhere to views of truth, or falsehood.
> Those who know this world
> To be utterly pure, like the sky,
> Have great reputations
> Which illuminate the world.

Moreover, the great regent Ajita [Maitreya] has said:[1311]

> The learned should not fear,
> as they should the profound doctrine's decline,
> Fire, unbearable venomous snakes,
> murderers, or even thunderbolts.

Fire, snakes, enemies, and the thunderbolt's blaze
just deprive them of their lives,
But beyond that do not convey them
into the utterly terrifying destiny of Avīci hell.
Anyone who, relying on evil companions,
thinks maliciously of a buddha,
Kills his father, mother, or an arhat,
or splits the undivided supreme community;
That person, too, will swiftly be freed from those sins
by definitively thinking on reality.
But where can there be freedom for one
whose mind is hostile to the doctrine?

And it says in the *Pagoda of Precious Jewels*:

> O Kāśyapa! it is right for me, or one like me, to judge doctrines and individuals; but not so others, for they would fall into perverse opinion.

We should reflect upon the meaning of such words, which the Buddha expressed in many ways. As long as we have not acquired the pure eye of the doctrine, whereby the truth about doctrines and individuals is seen, it is an unbearably terrible deed to analyse things through exaggeration and depreciation, saying this is perverse, this impure, and that artificial.

8 *On the Prophecies Found in the Treasures*

[798.6-801.2] Again, let us consider the prophetic declarations which appear in the treasures. Though a proven treasure-finder, who is free from selfish desires, may have prophecies in his or her treasure-doctrines, such prophecies must be ascertained by those who know their intentional basis and reason, and who will not misrepresent them.[1312] Otherwise, one must not one-sidedly grasp as true the meaning of a prophecy, having taken only the words at face value, without distinguishing provisional from definitive meaning. This is because even if one knows [those things], a prophecy about future good or evil times and so forth may be transformed owing to circumstantial causes, conditions, and coincidences, so that it seems that the prophecy is not precisely fulfilled.

As the meanings of prophecies have rarely been completely fulfilled, except by the three supreme emanations and a few of the great Lingpas, among those who appeared in the past, and because nowadays we are greatly burdened by the degenerations of an age in which the merits of sentient beings are steadily declining, it seems to be extremely difficult for perfectly auspicious conditions to occur. None the less, the compassion and blessing of the great master [Padmasambhava] proceed ever more swiftly. As he has said in his own indestructible speech:

> So that the gift of doctrine might be inexhaustible
>   for future living creatures,
> The entire world has been filled
>   with the treasures of Padma.
> All of their discoverers
>   will be my emanations.
> They will adopt all sorts of uncertain
>   guises and ways of conduct,
> But each encounter with them will not but change
>   the vision of those who have faith.
> Still, it will be most difficult
>   for everyone to appraise them.

And also:

> All the discoverers and disciples of treasure,
> who hold the lineage of Padma,
> Will be worthy ones,
> though they act like dogs and pigs.
> They will be especially sublime,
> unlike other common folk.
> All such buddhas in disguise
> will drift about aimlessly;
> But there will be charlatans and con-men,
> who are most hypocritical.
> So do not equate the gold
> with the ore, O living beings!

It also says in a prophecy from the treasures of Trime Künga (*dri-med kun-dga'i gter-lung*):

> Treasure-finders of all sorts will appear continuously,
> And treasure-doctrines will pour forth like spores from
> mushrooms.
> None of them will fail to bear fruit;
> They will be reminders of me, Orgyen.

In a prophecy from the treasures of Ratna Lingpa (*ratna gling-pa'i gter-lung*), too, it says:

> Each great land will have a great treasure;
> That, too, will be a reminder of Orgyen.
> Each minor land will have a minor treasure;
> That, too, will be a reminder of Orgyen.

Moreover:

> When bad times blaze like fire,
> The power of secret mantra will blaze like fire.

Because this is certain, it is vastly important to open wide the eye of pure vision, without clinging to unfounded prattle and to the extremes of one-sided self-interest. In this way, one becomes undeluded about which path to enter, and which to avoid.

9 *On the Relationship between the Nyingmapa and Pönpo Traditions*

[801.2-803.1] Again, some say that the Pön tradition and the Great Perfection seem to be intimately connected because the diction of the Nyingmapa and Pönpo is similar.[1313] There are indeed many similarities in their doctrinal terminology and so forth, but since these [Pön works] were written so as to resemble the Buddhist doctrine how could they be dissimilar? For example, it is taught that in India there were ten conventional [non-Buddhist schools] which paralleled the pious attendants, and, in the same manner, the self-centred buddhas, Mind Only, Madhyamaka, Kriyā, Caryā, Yoga, Father Tantra, Mother Tantra, and Non-Dual Tantra. Likewise, in Tibet as well, Buddhist doctrines including all the texts of the Madhyamaka, Transcendental Perfection, Vinaya, *Treasury of Abhidharma*, and mantras; [means for attainment] of deities such as Cakrasaṃvara, Bhairava, and Vajrakīla; and [the instructions of] the inner heat, Great Seal, Great Perfection, and so forth, have all had their Pönpo imitations. Those, however, are not original. So, how can one begin to refute such limitless, adventitious fantasies?

None the less, the priests of good fortune,[1314] [Pön] mantras, and so forth, which appear to be immediately beneficial, may well have been revealed by the enlightened activities and emanations of the buddhas and bodhisattvas, because the range of the skilful means of the conquerors and their sons is inconceivable, as exemplified by the career of the "Truth-speaking Mendicant".[1315] In general, there are a great many [teachings] which, except for being merely called "Pön", in fact manifestly belong to the Buddhist doctrine.[1316] It is not right to pass final judgement as to whether they may be proven or not, for that merely generates misology.

Moreover, it has been said that there was a causal basis for the origination in pairs of Hinduism and Buddhism in India; Buddhist monks and Pönpos in Tibet, though there were no actual [Indian] extremist schools there; and Buddhists and Taoists in China.[1317] Therefore, so long as other traditions do not harm the teaching, we should just let them be. As it says in the *Sūtra of Candrapradīpa* [i.e. the *Sūtra of the King of Contemplation*, Ch.7, v.6]:

> Do not think hatefully of those
> Extremists who inhabit the world.
> Establishing compassion for them
> Is a special feature of a beginner's patience.

10 *On the "Bad Luck of the Nyingmapa"*

[803.1-807.1] Furthermore, during later times there have been some who have said that if one were to practise the Nyingmapa doctrinal tradition one would be luckless, owing to which one sees many who have alternatively taken it up and then abandoned it as their continuous object of refuge. None the less, no one who understands the reasons, and so has firm conviction at heart, will be at all concerned with the presence or absence of mere temporary luck. Even if a thousand buddhas were to appear in a vision and say to such a person, "Your doctrinal tradition is wrong. Abandon it and practise another!" not even the tips of that one's hairs would waver. While it is of no importance that ordinary persons, who have not been freed from the snare of desire, hatred, and delusion, harbour hopes and doubts, still, for the reasons given below, it would seem to be correct to state that the Nyingmapa are somewhat unlucky.

In antiquity the whole of Tibet was the dominion of evil incorporeal gods and demons. The great master [Padmasambhava] rendered them powerless by the force of his wrathful discipline. He took the vital heart-mantras of those who obeyed the oaths he dictated and appointed them to be protectors. All those who did not keep the vows he "liberated", and thus eradicated. Similarly, in the case of corporeal human beings, the minister Mazhang was buried alive because he obstructed the entry of the doctrine, and many other Pön ministers were also punished. It says in the *Injunction of Padma*:

> The doctrine and Pön met together like murderers.
> As they did not regard one another purely,
> Many learned translators had to be banished.[1318]

Thus, the introduction of the teaching, which was exemplified in the translation and exegesis of the true doctrine according to the wishes of the venerable king [Trhisong], faced much difficulty. Finally, the preceptor Śāntarakṣita and the master Padmasambhava both rejected the view and conduct of the Pönpo, and defeated them with miraculous displays of their signs of accomplishment. The sovereign ordered the Pönpo to observe the true doctrine, but except for a few they disobeyed and transformed many [Buddhist] scriptures into Pön [scriptures]. When the king heard of this he had most of the Pönpo decapitated, but Guru Rinpoche said that the gods and demons of Tibet liked Pön and so allowed oracles and astrology, propitiation of divinities, and rites which summon wealth to remain as they were. He subdued all the others and banished those Pönpo from the realm to the frontiers, along with their tambourines for drums, *shang* for instruments,[1319] fox-skin caps for hats, "Phajo" for a name,[1320] and donkeys for transport.

Afterwards, in the reign of the sovereign Trhi Relpacen, the religious law became extremely severe and the evil ministers suffered. Those who looked askance, or pointed threateningly, at the monastic communities had their eyes gouged out, hands cut off, and so forth. Many were thus punished; and because of the evil ministers, the oath of allegiance could not be given to the gods and nāgas successfully for a third time.[1321] Guru Rinpoche declared:

> In the future, mankind will be possessed by malignant gods, ogres, and Gongpo spirits. By conduct which denies the commitments, vows, and fruition of deeds, they will destroy the spiritual and temporal laws. These evil Pönpo ministers of the present day will assume all sorts of corporeal and incorporeal forms, and will obstruct the teaching in Tibet by various means.

Moreover, the acute and concise antidotes for the demons, Gongpo, and Tamsi spirits of this degenerate age, including [the means for] exorcising Gongpo and Tamsi spirits, for eradicating the Gyelpo and Senmo demons,[1322] and for averting military invasion and rebellion, have emerged exclusively among the profound treasures of the Ancient Translation School. Therefore, all kinds of demons surely harbour unbearable hatred towards the adherents of that tradition. For this they will enjoy whatever fruits accord with the powers and deeds associated with their respective perverse aspirations, for such is the reality of the principle of cause and effect. Therefore, holding them as objects of compassion we should make them the basis for the practice of patience. Apart from that it is improper to cultivate hatred for even an instant, for that would impair the bodhisattva discipline. This I say by way of digression.

In particular, there may be some who, far from remembering the kindness of one such as the great master [Padmasambhava], the sole refuge of the Tibetans, revile him with their perverse opinions. All they achieve is temporal demerit for themselves, but they can never obstruct the career of Guru Rinpoche, which is an ocean of enlightened activity. In addition, it is certainly a special attribute of sublime bodhisattvas that they even cause those with bad connections to terminate saṃsāra.[1323] Therefore, I, Padmasambhava's messenger, prophesy that even these disrespectful critics will at some time undoubtedly become the Guru's disciples and experience the good fortune of eternal bliss.

This completes the refutation of some of the errors of those partisans who in the past have wrongly viewed [the Nyingmapa tradition], the seventh part of this book, *Thunder from the Great Conquering Battle-Drum of Devendra*, which is a history of the precious teaching of the vehicle of indestructible reality according to the Ancient Translation School.

Part Eight
The Chronology of the Doctrine

1 *The Duration of the Doctrine*

[811.1-815.5] Now, the various chronological determinations which have been made in connection with the descent of the [Buddhist] teaching and so on are to be somewhat examined, and the duration of the teaching's existence is to be set forth. In this respect, the written assertions of Indian and Tibetan scholars are often in disagreement because the determination of the years in which [the Buddha], the incomparable Fourth Guide who taught this teaching of the Auspicious Aeon,[1324] took birth, manifestly attained enlightenment, and entered final nirvāṇa, as perceived by ordinary persons requiring training, is within the domain of the inconceivable. It appears to be equally uncertain how much time has elapsed since the Buddha's final nirvāṇa; and, similarly, there are many different [opinions] about the future duration of the teaching of the Conqueror, owing to the various intentions [with which predictions have been made].

The *Minor Transmission of the Vinaya*, the *Narrative of Suvarṇa* (*Suvarṇāvadāna*), the *Auspicious Aeon Sūtra* (*Bhadrakalpikasūtra*, T 94), the *Great Cloud Sūtra* (*Mahāmeghasūtra*, T 658), the *Commentary on the Sūtra of the Teaching Delivered by Akṣayamati* (*Akṣayamatinirdeśasūtravṛtti*, T 3994), and the *Commentaries on the Treasury of the Abhidharma* (*Abhidharmakośabhāṣya*, T 4090-6) unanimously state that the doctrine will endure for one thousand years: five hundred for the actual teaching and five hundred for the nominal teaching. The *Sūtra of Compassion's White Lotus* (*Karuṇāpuṇḍarīkasūtra*, T 111-12) says that the actual teaching will last for one thousand years and the nominal for five hundred years. The *Sūtra of Reality which Appears Variously without Straying from its Essence* (*Dharmatāsvabhāvaśūnyatācalapratisarvālokasūtra*, T 128) speaks of two thousand five hundred years, and, though many extant texts of the *Sūtra of the Dialogue with the Bodhisattva Candragarbha* (*Bodhisattvacandragarbhaparipṛcchāsūtra*, T 356) speak of two thousand years, supreme holy beings have made it out to be three thousand years and so are probably correct. A period of five thousand years has also been expounded in the *Prophetic Sūtra of*

Maitreya (*Maitreyavyākaraṇasūtra*, P 1011) translated by Tharpa Lotsāwa, in Vasubandhu's *Conquest of Objections* (*gnod-'joms*), in Daṃṣṭrasena's *Commentary on the Hundred Thousand Line Transcendental Perfection* (T 3807-8) and elsewhere.[1325] Such are the statements primarily intended for human beings who require training, in general, and for ordinary non-human beings.

Elsewhere, in the residences of such great non-human beings as the nāga king Sāgara, as well as in Trayatriṃśa and Tuṣita, the teaching of the Thousand Buddhas will not decline until the completion of this great aeon.[1326] This is illustrated by statements found in the *Sūtra of the Dialogue with the Nāga King Sāgara* (*Nāgarājasāgaraparipṛcchāsūtra*, T 153-5) and others. In the lord of sūtras, the *Supreme Golden Light* (*Suvarṇaprabhāsottama*, T 555-7), which belongs to the third wheel and expounds the definitive meaning of the greater vehicle,[1327] and in the *Magical Net of Vajrasattva* (NGB Vols. 14-16) which is among the mantras of Unsurpassed [Yogatantra], it says:

> Buddhas never enter final nirvāṇa.
> The doctrine, too, will not decline.

It says also in the *Tantra of the Wish-fulfilling Array* (*yid-bzhin rnam-par bkod-pa'i rgyud*):

> As long as the great host
> Of all beings remains,
> Buddhas will emanate unceasingly,
> And the doctrine of liberation will not decline.

Thus, in the tantrapiṭaka of the way of mantras there are many statements which maintain that the duration of the doctrine is either determined, indeterminate, or never-ending. Here I will not enlarge upon these prophetic declarations.

Similarly, if we consider, in addition to the duration of the teaching, how much time has already passed since it began, many different opinions are found. Among them, I shall rely here upon the determinations of months and years which have been clearly revealed by the perfect Buddha, the Transcendent Lord himself, in the transmissions of the Vinaya, the sūtras, the *Tantra of Kālacakra, the Glorious and Supreme Original Buddha* (*Paramādibuddhoddhṛtaśrīkālacakratantrarāja*, T 362), and in other particularly sublime and immaculate tantras of the way of mantras. I shall also rely on the extraordinary and taintless statements made by the great master Padmākara of Oḍḍiyāna, who is the indestructible reality of buddha-speech, and on those of the great paṇḍita Vimalamitra and the translator Vairocana. If these are considered in accordance with the correct application of astrological charts, they are found mostly to concur with the assertions of Tibetan *Kālacakra* scholars in general, and, in particular, with those of the great promulgators who had been prophesied by the Conqueror. I shall, therefore, at the present juncture, state these appropriate dates because others have little doubt in them, and because that system [of calculation] is well understood.

2 *A Chronology of the Buddha's Life*[1328]

[815.6-819.2] Our Teacher, Siddhārtha, entered the womb at midnight on the fifteenth day of the month of Āṣāḍha[1329] in 962 BC (*don-grub*, earth female sheep)[1330] just as the constellation Puṣya was setting, and while his mother, Māyādevī, was observing a purificatory fast. Then, when nine months and twenty-three days, or ten months, roundly speaking, had passed, at dawn on the seventh day of the waxing half of the month of Vaiśākha[1331] in 961 BC (*drag-po*, iron monkey),[1332] he took birth in the Lumbinī Grove, as Puṣya was in the first stage of its ascent, and when Puṣya was the constellation through which the moon was passing.[1333] In his twenty-ninth year, during the first half of the night on the eighth day of the month of Kārttika[1334] in 933 BC (*kun-'dzin*, earth mouse),[1335] he sowed the seed of his line in Yaśodharā and, at midnight, when he saw the constellation Puṣya rise, he renounced the household life in favour of homelessness, whereupon he practised austerity for six years. In his thirty-fifth year, on the full moon of the month of Vaiśākha in 927 BC (wood horse), he reached the Bodhi Tree and subdued Māra that evening. As midnight passed, the indestructible reality [of the Buddha's mind] became absorbed in contemplation and the moon was eclipsed by Rāhu. A moment before the moon was released from Rāhu's grasp, as the dawn rose and the time approached to beat the victory drum, he became the manifestly perfect Buddha. His son Rāhula, who had remained in his mother's womb for six years, was born at the same time; and while everyone rejoiced at the festival of his birth, Ānanda (All-Rejoicing) was also born.

Immediately after midnight during this eclipse of the moon, early in the hour of the ox,[1336] the moon was obscured from its north-eastern sector by Rāhu's fiery tail, except for one-sixth of the lunar disc. When released from this oppressive obscuration, the moon swelled up to its fullest for something more than thirteen *ghaṭikā* [about five hours and fifteen minutes].[1337]

When seven weeks had passed after this attainment of buddhahood, the Buddha turned the first doctrinal wheel, that of the four truths, in

Vārāṇasī. Then, gradually, he revealed the intermediate transmitted precepts, which concern the transcendent perfection of discriminative awareness and signlessness, on Vulture Peak, and the irreversible vehicle which concerns the nucleus of definitive meaning on Mount Malaya, in the Malla country, and in various other places. Thus he taught three successive doctrinal wheels in conformity with the capacities of those to be trained. Although the exact years in which he taught these wheels have been calculated by some holy beings, they are merely approximations, for beyond that it is difficult to estimate them correctly.[1338] It is also generally impossible to maintain that the establishment of the sequence of vehicles followed a chronological order.

The Tathāgata lived for eighty-one whole years. Then, in the forty-seventh year following his attainment of buddhahood, during the afternoon of the fifteenth day of the mid-spring month of Caitra[1339] in 881 BC (*rnam-gnon*, iron dragon)[1340] he delivered limitless teachings on the vehicle of the Unsurpassed [Yoga]tantra, including the *Glorious and Supreme Original Buddha* [i.e. the *Kālacakra Tantra*], at the Śrī Dhānyakaṭaka Stūpa in South India. This was astrologically conjoined with the time of his [former] victory over the three worlds, that is, the subjugation of Māra. At the beginning of the last watch of the night on the fifteenth day of the following month, Vaiśākha, at Kuśinagara in the Malla country, his physical body passed away into the expanse of reality, without remainder. The Indian master Śīlapālita and the great paṇḍita Śākyaśrī, however, held that he passed into the buddha-body of reality at midnight on the eighth day of Kārttika. The supremely learned Putön of Tibet, and others, have professed the same view.[1341] Again, some have claimed that he passed into nirvāṇa on the fifteenth day of the mid-spring month,[1342] and others hold that it was on the fifteenth day of Āṣāḍha.

3 *From the Buddha's Final Nirvāṇa to the Beginning of the First Tibetan Sexagenary Cycle*

[819.2-823.4] Some astrologers have calculated the chronology of the teaching up to the present beginning from the year following the Buddha's nirvāṇa [i.e. 880 BC, iron snake], but all the great scholars have calculated it beginning from the year of the nirvāṇa itself, as these words prove:

> The year of the Conqueror's nirvāṇa
> Is the first "year of the decease".

Thus, counting from 881 BC (iron dragon), the year of the Buddha's nirvāṇa, through to the present year, 1962 (*dge-byed*, water tiger, sixteenth cycle), 2843 years have passed. The definitive ordering of all other years of the decease must be calculated on this basis. It would be appropriate to explain in detail the chronology of the teaching associated with the succession of the Kulikas, the religious kings of Shambhala, but for fear of verbosity here I shall explain only a few relevant points, little by little:

877 BC In the 5th year of the Conqueror's decease, at sunrise on the 10th day of the month of Jyaiṣṭha[1343] in the wood monkey year, the Second Buddha, Padmākara was born from a lotus bud on an isle in the Sindhu Lake. From that time until the present [1962], 2839 years have passed.[1344]

853 BC In the 29th year of the decease, that of the earth monkey, 2815 years ago, the heroic Lord of Secrets turned the doctrinal wheel for the five noble ones of the genuine enlightened family, on the meteoric summit of Mount Malaya, and the volume containing the tantras fell onto the palace of King Ja of Sahor.

782 BC At the end of the first century, in the earth sheep year, 2744 years ago, the religious king Aśoka was born.[1345]

781 BC In the iron monkey year following the passage of the first century, 2743 years ago, the lake in the Land of Snows had

receded, and the inanimate vessel, including a Sāl forest, and its animate contents evolved there.

771 BC In the 111th year of the decease, that of the iron horse, 2733 years ago, the second council was held.

716 BC In the 166th year of the decease, that of the wood ox, 2678 years ago, Garap Dorje, the teacher of the supreme vehicle, was born.

481 BC In the 401st year of the decease, that of the iron monkey, 2443 years ago, the sublime Nāgārjuna was born.[1346]

After the inanimate vessel and the animate contents had [begun to] evolve in the Land of Snows, during that aforementioned iron monkey year (781 BC), Tibet was governed for 534 years by the nine Masang brothers, [twelve] minor kingdoms and forty principalities, and others. Then,
247 BC in the wood tiger year, 2209 years ago, the lord Nyatrhi Tsenpo emerged as ruler with power over all Tibet.

1 BC The 881st year of the Buddha's decease, that of the iron monkey, 1963 years ago, was the first year prior to the birth of the foreign teacher, Jesus Christ.[1347]

Henceforth [the years] may be easily computed in sequence:

After 621 years[1348] had passed in the course of the dynastic rule of twenty-seven kings of Tibet, reckoned from the
374 CE accession of Nyatrhi Tsenpo in the wood tiger year (247 BC), Lha Thotori Nyentsen was born during the wood dog year.

433 During his sixtieth year, that of the water bird, the Awesome Secret fell onto his palace, and the true doctrine thus emerged in Tibet for the first time.

620 In the iron dragon year which followed the passage of 1500 years of the Buddha's decease, the three 500-year periods of the Age of Fruition, which are first among the ten 500-year divisions of the Conqueror's teaching, had come to an end, and the Age of Attainment began.[1349]

617 In the year of the fire ox, the 185th after the true doctrine emerged in Tibet during the water bird year (433), the religious king Songtsen Gampo was born.[1350]

641 In the 25th year thereafter, that of the iron ox, he founded the Rasa Trhülnang [the Jokhang in Lhasa], et cetera, and introduced the true doctrine and a system of writing.

790 In the 150th year thereafter,[1351] that of the iron horse, the religious king Trhisong Detsen was born.

810 In the 21st year thereafter, that of the iron tiger, the great master [Padmasambhava] came to Tibet, and the doctrinal assembly of glorious Samye was founded.

827 In the 18th year thereafter, that of the fire sheep, the seven trial monks [i.e. the "seven men who were tested"] were ordained as novices, so that the ground for the teaching of the translation, exegesis, and attainment of the true doctrines of the sūtras and mantras was established.

864 In the 38th year thereafter, that of the wood monkey, the great master [Padmasambhava] departed for the island of Cāmara.

866 In the 3rd year thereafter, that of the fire dog, the sovereign Trhi Relpacen was born.

892 In the 27th year thereafter, that of the water mouse, Lacen Gongpa Rapsel was born.

901 In the 10th year thereafter, that of the iron bird, the teaching was persecuted in Central Tibet and Tsang by Langdarma.

906 In the 6th year thereafter, that of the fire tiger, Langdarma was "liberated" by Lhalung Pelgi Dorje.

929 In the 24th year thereafter, that of the earth ox, the kingdom of Tibet disintegrated owing to internal rebellions.

953 In the 25th year thereafter, that of the water ox, Lacen and the ten men from Central Tibet and Tsang began the later propagation of the teaching in Central Tibet from Kham.[1352]

958 In the 6th year thereafter, that of the earth horse, the great translator Rincen Zangpo, the first of all the new translators, was born.

978 In the 21st year thereafter, that of the earth tiger, the learned and accomplished scholar Khyungpo Neljor Tshültrim Gönpo was born.[1353]

982 In the 5th year thereafter, that of the water horse, the glorious lord Atiśa was born.

1004 In the 23rd year thereafter, that of the wood dragon, Dromtön Gyelwei Jungne was born.

1012 In the 9th year thereafter, that of the water mouse, the translator Marpa and the treasure-finder Trapa Ngönshe were born.

1014 In the 3rd year thereafter, that of the wood tiger, Zurcungpa was born.

1027 In the 14th year thereafter, that of the fire hare, the *Commentary on the Kālacakra Tantra*, [the *Taintless Light*,] reached Tibet for the first time. The first sexagenary cycle is counted from this year onwards.

4 *From the Beginning of the First Sexagenary Cycle to the Present*

[823.4-832.4] Henceforth, it will be readily understandable if, in each sexagenary cycle down to the present, the ages of a few of the most well known and great personages be set forth conjoined with an account of the greatest historical changes.

FIRST CYCLE [1027-1087]

When the first cycle began [Wednesday 11 January 1027]:

Rincen Zangpo, the great translator, was in his 70th year	[958-1055]
Khyungpo Neljor was in his 50th year	[978- ?]
Lord Atiśa was in his 46th year	[982-1054]
Dromtön was in his 24th year	[1004-1063]
Marpa was in his 16th year	[1012-1097]
Trapa Ngönshe was in his 16th year	[1012-1090]
Zurcungpa was in his 14th year	[1014-1074]

During this first cycle, the tradition derived from the doctrinal lineage of lord Atiśa and his disciples first originated. Its adherents were called "Kadampa" after the name of their doctrine [*bka'-gdams*, "transmitted precepts and instructions"].

In addition, though the descendants of Khön Lüiwangpo Sungwa,[1354] who had been the direct disciple of the great master [Padmasambhava], had been adherents of the Nyingmapa mantras for about ten generations down to Khönrok Sherap Tshültrim, none the less, Khön Köncok Gyelpo received many doctrines from such new translators as Drokmi Śākya Yeshe and was thus converted to the mantras of the new translation schools. He built the temple of Gorum in 1073 (water ox year, first cycle) on a slope of Mount Pangpo, where the earth was white in the centre. So emerged the tradition called Sakyapa (Pale Earth) from then on, the doctrine having been named after the location.

During the same period, the learned and accomplished Khyungpo Neljor introduced to Tibet the golden doctrines of the Shangpa, and the translator Marpa introduced the sources of the Kagyü teaching.

SECOND CYCLE [1087-1147]

When the second cycle began [Friday 8 January 1087]:

Macik Lapdrön, born iron sheep, was in her 57th year [1031-1126]
Lingje Kesar,[1355] born earth tiger, was in his 50th year [1038-1124]
Venerable Milarepa, born iron dragon, was in his 48th year [1040-1123]
Ngok Lotsāwa, born earth pig,[1356] was in his 29th year [1059-1109]
Dropukpa, lord of secrets, born wood tiger, was in his 14th year [1074-1135]
Takpo Daö Zhönu, born earth sheep, was in his 9th year [1079-1153]

[During this cycle] the Kagyü tradition gradually divided into four great and eight minor subsects, derived from Takpo's disciples, including the "three men from Kham", and these were propagated extensively.

THIRD CYCLE [1147-1207]

When the third cycle began [Saturday 4 January 1147]:

Ca Düldzin Chenpo, born iron sheep, was in his 57th year [1091-1166]
That same year [1091] Phadampa Sangye went to Tingri.
Sacen Künga Nyingpo, born water monkey, was in his 56th year [1092-1158]
Phakmotrupa, born iron tiger, was in his 38th year [1110-1170]
Karmapa Tüsum Khyenpa, born iron tiger, was in his 38th year [1110-1193]
Katok Tampa Deshek, born water tiger, was in his 26th year [1122-1192]
Zhang Tarmatra, born water tiger, was in his 26th year [1122-1193]
Lingje Repa Pema Dorje,[1357] born earth monkey, was in his 20th year [1128-1188]
Ngadak Nyang-rel,[1358] born iron dragon, was in his 12th year [1136-1204]
Jetsün Sonam Tsemo of Sakya, born water dog, was in his 6th year [1142-1182]
Pel Taklung Thangpa, born water dog, was in his 6th year [1142-1210]
Drigung Kyopa, born water pig, was in his 5th year [1143-1217]

FOURTH CYCLE [1207-1267]

When the fourth cycle began [Tuesday 30 January 1207]:

Nyibum the scholar, born earth tiger, was in his 50th year [1158-1213]
Tsangpa Gyare,[1359] born iron snake, was in his 47th year [1161-1211]
Sakya Paṇcen, born water tiger, was in his 26th year [1182-1251]
Taklung Sangye Yarjön, born water pig, was in his 5th year [1203-1272]

After the kingdom of Tibet had disintegrated in the aforementioned year 929 (earth ox), the government was partially preserved in Ngari by minor descendants of the royal family. After remaining thus for 311 years, the army of Dorta the Black arrived in Tibet from China in 1240 (iron mouse year, fourth cycle), and Tibet, the Land of Snows, was brought under China.[1360]

From 1253 (water ox year, fourth cycle), the great lamas of the Sakyapa school held power over all three provinces of Tibet.[1361]

FIFTH CYCLE [1267-1327]

When the fifth cycle began [Thursday 27 January 1267]:

Guru Chöwang, born water monkey, was in his 56th year [1212-1270]
Orgyenpa, the great accomplished master, born iron tiger, was in his 38th year [1230-1309]
Chögyel Phakpa, the lord of living creatures, born wood sheep, was in his 33rd year [1235-1280]
Melong Dorje, the great accomplished master, born wood hare, was in his 25th year [1243-1303]
Como Menmo, born earth monkey, was in her 20th year [1248-1283]
Rikdzin Kumārādza, born fire tiger, was in his 2nd year [1266-1343]

SIXTH CYCLE [1327-1387]

When the sixth cycle began [Saturday 24 January 1327]:

Karmapa Rangjung Dorje, born wood monkey, was in his 44th year [1284-1339]
Yungtön Dorjepel, born wood monkey, was in his 44th year [1284-1365]
Putön, the all-knowing, born iron tiger, was in his 38th year [1290-1364]
Conang Künzi Tölpopa, born water dragon, was in his 36th year [1292-1361]

Longcen Rapjampa, the all-knowing, born earth monkey, was in his 20th year [1308-1363]

From 1349 (earth ox year, sixth cycle), Tā'i Situ Cangcup Gyeltsen of Phakmotru held power over Tibet and Kham.[1362]

SEVENTH CYCLE [1387-1447]

When the seventh cycle began [Monday 21 January 1387]:

Sangye Lingpa, the great treasure-finder, born iron dragon, was in his 48th year [1340-1396]
Dorje Lingpa, born fire dog, was in his 42nd year [1346-1405]
Jamgön Lozang Trakpa, born fire bird, was in his 31st year [1357-1419]
Podong Künkyen Jikdrel, born wood hare, was in his 13th year [1375-1451]
Karmapa V, Tezhinshekpa, born wood mouse, was in his 4th year [1384-1415]
Thangtong Gyelpo,[1363] the great accomplished master, born wood ox, was in his 3rd year [1385-1509]

From 1435 (wood hare year, seventh cycle), Tibet and Kham were governed by the Rinpungpa administration.[1364]

The venerable Tsongkapa [Jamgön Lozang Trakpa] vastly increased the enlightened activities of exegesis and attainment, combining the Kadampa textual tradition with the tantras of the way of the mantra according to the new translations. In 1409 (earth ox year, seventh cycle), he founded the doctrinal centre of Drok Riwo Ganden, whence originated the tradition known as the Geluk, the doctrinal lineage of which [Gandenpa] was named after its seat.

EIGHTH CYCLE [1447-1507]

When the eighth cycle began [Tuesday 17 January 1447], the astrological treatise entitled the *Oral Transmission of Puṇḍarīka* (*skar-rtsis-kyi bstan-bcos pad-dkar zhal-lung*) was composed by those renowned as the "Three Gyamtsos".[1365]

Gendün Trupa [Dalai Lama I], the great paṇḍita, born iron sheep, was in his 57th year [1391-1474]
Gölo Zhönupel, born water monkey, was in his 56th year [1392-1481]
Ratna Lingpa, the great treasure-finder, born water sheep, was in his 45th year [1403-1478]
Karmapa VI, Thongwa Tönden, born fire monkey, was in his 32nd year [1416-1453]

Śākya Chokden, the great paṇḍita, born earth monkey, was in his 20th year [1428-1507]
Korampa, the doctrine master, born earth bird, was in his 19th year [1429-1489]
Chökyong Zangpo, the great translator of Zhalu, born iron bird, was in his 7th year [1441-1538]

NINTH CYCLE [1507-1567]

When the ninth cycle began [Thursday 14 January 1507]:

Pema Lingpa, the great treasure-finder, born iron horse, was in his 58th year [1450-1521]
Sangye Tshencen, the madman of Tsang, born water monkey, was in his 56th year [1452-1507]
Künga Lekpa, the Drukpa madman, born wood pig, was in his 53rd year [1455-1529]
Künga Zangpo,[1366] the madman of Central Tibet, born earth tiger, was in his 50th year [1458- ?]
Gendün Gyamtso [Dalai Lama II], the great paṇḍita, born fire monkey, was in his 32nd year [1476-1542]
Pawo II, Tsuklak Trhengwa,[1367] born wood dog, was in his 4th year [1504-1566]
Karmapa VIII, Mikyö Dorje, was born in this fire hare year [first of the cycle] [1507-1554]
Jetsün Künga Drölcok was also born in this fire hare year [1507-1566]

From 1565 (wood ox year, ninth cycle), the Tsangpa governors ruled Tibet and Kham.[1368]

TENTH CYCLE [1567-1627]

When the tenth cycle began [Saturday 11 January 1567] :

Lodrö Gyamtso, the physician of Zurkar, born earth dragon, was in his 60th year [1508- ?]
Gampopa Trashi Namgyel, born water monkey, was in his 56th year [1512-1587]
Sherap Özer, the great treasure-finder, born fire ox, was in his 51st year [1517-1584]
Pema Karpo, the all-knowing Drukpa, born fire pig, was in his 41st year [1527-1592]
Sodokpa Lodrö Gyeltsen, born water mouse, was in his 16th year [1552-1624?]

Karmapa IX, Wangcuk Dorje, born wood tiger, was in his 14th year [1554-1603]

ELEVENTH CYCLE [1627-1687]

When the eleventh cycle began [Monday 18 January 1627]:

Jetsün Tāranātha, born wood pig, was in his 53rd year [1575-1634]
Rikdzin Jatsön Nyingpo, born wood bird, was in his 43rd year [1585-1656]
Lhodruk Zhapdrung Ngawang Namgyel,[1369] born wood horse, was in his 34th year [1594-1651]
Lhatsün Namka Jikme, born fire bird, was in his 31st year [1597-1650]
Sungtrül III, Tshültrim Dorje, born earth dog, was in his 30th year [1598-1669]
Gampopa Norbu Gyenpa, born earth pig, was in his 29th year [1599-1633]
Karmapa X, Chöying Dorje, born wood snake, was in his 23rd year [1605-1674]
Sangdak Trhinle Lhündrup, born iron pig, was in his 17th year [1611-1662]
Düdül Dorje, the great treasure-finder, born wood hare, was in his 13th year [1615-1672]
Dalai Lama V, Lozang Gyamtso, born fire snake, was in his 11th year [1617-1682]

In 1641 (iron snake year, eleventh cycle), the Mongolian army inflicted great damage on the spiritual and temporal domains of the Karmapa-Tsangpa government.[1370]

From 1642 (water horse year), the Ganden Palace held dominion over the whole of Tibet and Kham.

TWELFTH CYCLE [1687-1747]

When the twelfth cycle began [Thursday 13 February 1687]:

Cangdak Pema Trhinle, born iron snake, was in his 47th year [1641-1717]
Peling Thukse Tendzin Gyurme Dorje, born iron snake, was in his 47th year [1641- ?]
Gyurme Dorje, the great treasure-finder of Mindröling, born fire dog, was in his 42nd year [1646-1714]

Locen Dharmaśrī, born wood horse, was in his 34th year [1654-1717]
Karmapa XI, Yeshe Dorje, born fire dragon, was in his 12th year [1676-1702]
Khamtrül III, Ngawang Künga Tendzin, born iron monkey, was in his 8th year [1680-1728]

In 1717 (fire bird year, twelfth cycle) the Dzungar army severely persecuted the Nyingmapa teaching and monasteries.[1371]

THIRTEENTH CYCLE [1747-1807]

When the thirteenth cycle began [Friday 10 February 1747]:

Rikdzin Tshewang Norbu, born earth tiger, was in his 50th year [1698-1755]
Situ Chöki Jungne, born iron dragon, was in his 48th year [1700-1774]
Dalai Lama VII, Kelzang Gyamtso, the supreme conqueror, born earth mouse, was in his 40th year [1708-1757]
Rikdzin Jikme Lingpa, born earth bird, was in his 19th year [1730-1798]
Karmapa XIII, Düdül Dorje, born water ox, was in his 15th year [1733-1797]
Dodrup Jikme Trhinle Özer, born wood ox, was in his 3rd year [1745-1821]

FOURTEENTH CYCLE [1807-1867]

When the fourteenth cycle began [Sunday 8 February 1807]:

Chöling Karwang Chime Dorje, born water sheep, was in his 45th year [1763- ?]

Gampopa Orgyen Drodül Lingpa [born 1757] and Rikdzin Dorje Thokme [1746-1797] were both his contemporaries. These are renowned as the "three emanational awareness-holders who opened the secret land of Pemakö as a place of pilgrimage".[1372]

Gyelse Zhenpen Thaye of Dzokcen,[1373] born iron monkey, was in his 8th year [1800- ?]
Dalai Lama IX, Lungtok Gyamtso, the supreme conqueror, born wood ox, was in his 3rd year [1805-1815]

In 1855 (wood hare year, fourteenth cycle) the Gurkha army attacked Tibet.[1374]

FIFTEENTH CYCLE [1867-1927]

When the fifteenth cycle began [Tuesday 5 February 1867]:

Peltrül Orgyen Jikme Chöki Wangpo, born earth dragon, was in his 60th year [1808-1887]
Jamgön Lodrö Thaye,[1375] born water bird, was in his 55th year [1813-1899]
Jamyang Khyentse Wangpo, born iron dragon, was in his 48th year [1820-1892]
Chogyur Decen Lingpa, born earth ox, was in his 39th year [1829-1870]
Düjom Lingpa, the great treasure-finder, born wood sheep, was in his 33rd year [1835-1904]
Mipham Namgyel Gyamtso, born fire horse, was in his 22nd year [1846-1912]
Trupwang Śākyaśrī, born water ox, was in his 15th year [1853-1919]
Lerap Lingpa, the great treasure-finder, born fire dragon, was in his 12th year [1856-1926]
Karmapa XV, Khakyap Dorje, was born four years after the inception of this cycle [1871-1922]

In 1888 (earth mouse year, fifteenth cycle), the British arrived in Tibet for the first time.[1376]

In 1904 (wood dragon year), there was a conflict between Britain and Tibet.

In 1910 (iron dog year), the Chinese army invaded.[1377]

In 1914 (wood tiger year), the First World War began.

SIXTEENTH CYCLE [1927-1987]

When the sixteenth cycle began [Friday 4 March 1927]:

Dzokcen Trülku V, Thupten Chöki Dorje, born water monkey, was in his 56th year [1872-1935]
Dalai Lama XIII, Thupten Gyamtso, the supreme conqueror, born fire mouse, was in his 52nd year [1876-1933]
Katok Situ Chöki Gyamtso, born iron dragon, would have been in his 48th year [1880-1925]
Paṇcen Chöki Nyima, born water sheep, was in his 45th year [1883-1937]
Karmapa XVI, Rikpei Dorje, born wood mouse, was in his 4th year [1924-1981]

In 1939 (earth hare year, sixteenth cycle), the Second World War began.

In 1950 (iron tiger year), the turmoil of the Chinese Communist hostility in Tibet began.

SEVENTEENTH CYCLE [1987-2047]

When the twenty-four years from the next one, 1963 (*mdzes-byed*, water hare), through to 1986 (*zad-pa*, fire tiger) have passed,[1378] the seventeenth cycle [1987-2047] will start. At that time:

Künzang Wangyel, the ancestral throne-holder of Mindröling, born in the iron sheep year (1931) will be in his 57th year.

Dalai Lama XIV, Tendzin Gyamtso, the supreme conqueror Padmapāṇi, the crown jewel of us all, born in the wood pig year (1935), will be in his 53rd year.

Künga Trhinle Wangyel, the lord and throne-holder of the Drölma Palace of Sakya, born in the wood bird year (1945), will be in his 43rd year.

I pray that the lotus feet of those great individuals survive for an ocean of aeons, and that their great enlightened activities on behalf of the teaching and living creatures be everlasting, all-pervasive, and spontaneously accomplished!

There are all kinds of disagreements regarding the year-signs and elements from the time when Nyatrhi Tsenpo emerged as the lord of Tibet until the later propagation of the teaching, owing to erroneous records in some of the past doctrinal histories and chronologies of the teaching, or negligence which allowed for discrepancies in temporal sequence, or whatever other reasons. Here, counting from the year of the Buddha's decease and checking against the original sources for Tibetan royal genealogy and doctrinal history, I have set down the exact determination which has thus been obtained.

Although, in general, there have been many changes in the political life of Tibet during the past, as far as the doctrine is concerned, the veracity of the Teacher's own prophetic declaration that his teaching would increasingly spread northwards has been actualised. Due to the merits of those to be trained in Tibet, and by the power of the timely penetration of [the world by] the Conquerors' compassion, individuals who have held the teaching and have shown mastery in inconceivable careers of learning, dignity and accomplishment, have successively appeared from the time of the teaching's inception in the past down to the present day. Because they preserved the most precious teaching and continue to preserve it, the continuity of the doctrine in Tibet has never been impaired. Therefore, there is no reason for errors to have crept into these enumerations of years past.

5 *Some Prophecies*

[833.5-835.4] In the future, when four hundred and sixty-three years have passed counting from the present one, 1962 (water tiger), then at the beginning of the wood male monkey year (2424/5) Rudrakulika, the "Iron Cakravartin" will invade our realm from Shambhala with his emanational armies and destroy all traces of the barbarian forces, none excepted.[1379] Then the *kṛtayuga* of the next four ages will begin.[1380]

Now there are predictions concerning the duration of the secret mantra traditions of the vehicle of indestructible reality in general, and of the teaching of the Great Perfection with its secret transmitted precepts in particular. In general, it is said that the time for teaching through buddha-body begins when [sentient beings] have an infinite life-span and lasts until the life-span is one thousand years; the time for teaching through buddha-speech lasts from then until the life-span is seventy years; and the time for teaching through buddha-mind lasts from then until there is a ten-year life-span. But that is a general statement. As for the duration of the actual teaching [of the Great Perfection] in particular, it is said that the teaching through buddha-body lasts for fifteen thousand periods of five hundred years, and the teachings through buddha-speech and mind for one thousand periods of five hundred years each.[1381]

Concerning the holders of this illuminating doctrine [of the Great Perfection] during this present late age, it says in the *Root Tantra of the Penetration of Sound* (*sgra thal-'gyur rtsa-ba'i rgyud*, NGB Vol.10):

> After I have passed into nirvāṇa,
> In the western land of Oḍḍiyāna,
> The divine lady of Dhanakośa
> Will bear a fatherless son, Vajra-He,
> Who will uphold the genuine teaching.

Beginning thus with Garap Dorje, the last of these successive prophecies reads as follows:

Rudrakulika

Then, the ḍākinī Śrīdharā
Will maintain this teaching and propagate it
During the age when life lasts ten years.
Thereafter it will not endure, but subside whence it arose.

Just so, after the age when life lasts only ten years the disciples of this [Śrīdharā] will have reached perfection and, with the harvest of her teaching, will gradually fly off to the Beauteously Arrayed realm, the realm of Vast Conduct, and the realm of the Melodious Crown. When the teaching has also been brought to perfection seven times in each of those realms, then the world system or field of the emanational body, situated directly in front of the heart orb of [Vairocana] the Great Glacial Lake, will be emptied, and the deeds of the great Vajradhara will have completed one cycle.[1382] Thereafter, in the world system which follows, the doctrine will remain without increase or decline for six hundred billion aeons. In such ways, it is said, enlightened activity is incessant, lasting just as long as does space. Indeed, its manner is not contrary to that of a sky which is without creation and cessation despite the presence of clouds, which are created and cease.

This provisionally ends my exegesis which comprises a brief examination of the various chronological determinations associated with the descent of the vehicles and so forth, and a statement of the teaching's duration, [the eighth part of this book], *Thunder from the Great Conquering Battle-Drum of Devendra*, which is a history of the precious teaching of the vehicle of indestructible reality according to the Ancient Translation School.

Closing Statements

1 *Primary Sources*

[835.6-837.1] The sources for what is expounded herein have been well-gathered from reliable documents including most of the histories of the *Transmitted Precepts of the Nyingmapa* (*rnying-ma bka'-ma*) in general and, in particular, the following:

(i) The all-knowing Longcenpa's *Great Lecture on the History of the Innermost Spirituality, Mother and Son* (*snying-thig ma-bu'i lo-rgyus gtong-thun chen-mo*).

(ii) Locen Dharmaśrī's *Lamp which Illuminates the Essence of Tantra, Transmission, and Esoteric Instruction: a General Exposition of the Empowerment of the Sūtra which Gathers All Intentions* (*'dus-pa mdo'i dbang-gi spyi-don rgyud-lung man-ngag-gi gnad sel-byed sgron-me*).

(iii) Yakde Düldzin Khyenrap Gyamtso's *Answers to Queries on Doctrinal History, a Storehouse of Gems* (*chos-'byung dris-lan nor-bu'i bang-mdzod*).

(iv) Khecok Ngawang Lodrö's *Origin of the Doctrines of the Ancient Translation School, a Scholar's Delight* (*snga-'gyur chos-kyi byung-khungs mkhas-pa dga'-byed*).

(v) The chapter on the Nyingmapa found in Gölo Zhönupel's *Blue Annals* (*deb-ther sngon-po*).

(vi) The chapter on the Nyingmapa found in Pawo Tsuklak Trhengwa's *Scholar's Feast of Doctrinal History* (*chos-'byung mkhas-pa'i dga'-ston*).

(vii) The all-knowing Drukpa Pema Karpo's *Doctrinal History which is Sunlight Extending the Teaching* (*chos-'byung bstan-pa rgyas-pa'i nyin-byed*).

(viii) Jetsün Tāranātha's *Life of Orgyen with Three Reasons for Confidence* (*o-rgyan rnam-thar yid-ches gsum-ldan*).

(ix) The all-knowing Jikme Lingpa's *Narrative History of the Precious Collected Tantras of the Ancient Translation School, the Ornament Covering All Jambudvīpa* (*rnying-rgyud dkar-chag 'dzam-gling tha-grur khyab-pa'i rgyan*).

(x) Katok Paṇḍita Gyurme Tshewang Chokdrup's *Catalogue of the Collected Tantras, a Discourse Resembling a Great Divine Drum* (*rgyud-'bum dkar-chag lha'i rnga-bo-che lta-bu'i gtam*).

(xi) Jamgön Lodrö Thaye's *Lives of the Hundred Treasure-finders, a Beauteous Rosary of Precious Beryl* (*gter-ston brgya-rtsa'i rnam-thar rin-chen bai-ḍūrya'i phreng-mdzes*).

(xii) Excerpts from the oceanic eloquence of Mipham Namgyel [i.e. from his *Collected Works*].

Among other works which I have also considered in detail are:

(xiii) The *Great Record of Teachings Received* (*gsan-yig chen-mo*) of the all-seeing Great Fifth Dalai Lama.

(xiv) The *Record of Teachings Received* (*gsan-yig*) of [Gyurme Dorje], the precious, great treasure-finder of Mindröling.

(xv) Rikdzin Tshewang Norbu's *Definitive Order of the Chronology of the Teaching* (*bstan-rtsis-kyi rnam-bzhag*).

2 *Concluding Benedictions*

[837.1-845.4] Totally unadulterated by rough conjectures, egotistical fancies, and other stains of exaggeration and depreciation, I have long abandoned the base-mindedness of such impure motivations as the desire to seem learned, or to achieve fame. Nowadays, owing to the exigencies of place and time, it is difficult to obtain the texts of all the doctrinal histories of the past, and even the accounts [of events] up to the present day have not been clearly compiled. Therefore, I have been motivated only by the hope that this may benefit those seekers who follow the doctrine, without its vanishing like the tracks of a bird in the sky, as well as by the higher aspiration embodied in the thought that there would be no harm if, during this final age, just an account of the origins of the most secret teaching were to be preserved in writing so as to remain on earth. So, I have written this book during my sojourn in the southern land of India, following my expulsion as a refugee from the Land of Snows to the north. Composed with great endeavour and sincere mind, it boasts of purity, conciseness, and clarity. Hence, it merits the confidence of all.

Again, may it be said:[1383]

> Praised as the summit of the Conqueror's whole doctrinal store, appearing with difficulty in this world, but famed in an ocean of world systems,
> The jewel-like teaching of the definitively secret supreme vehicle is so wondrously and perfectly illuminated that it vies with the *udumbara*.
> Covered over with numberless attributes as stems and leaves, it is entwined by millions of vines of maturation and liberation, and is laden with the two accomplishments' fine fruits.
> To sustain those to be trained, the cool land obtained a pleasure garden of marvellous, holy wish-granting trees.
> E MA! What abundant, meritorious fortune!

After the heavenly stream
of the most secret awareness-holders' piṭaka
Had curled up in the locks
of the three ancestral lineages,[1384]
It was conducted to the Land of Snows,
to become good fortune's nectar stream,
By a hundred aspiration-born labours
of the preceptor, master, and religious king.

Who would surpass the kindness,
which extends to the very horizon,
Of the promulgators who've revealed
the sun of the supreme doctrine,
Blazing with accomplishment's thousand rays,
born of the true lineage,
Disclosed on the wondrous highway
of exegesis and attainment?

It is said that all those who have good fortune
and so have enjoyed
The essential elixir-like savour
of esoteric instruction,
That is brewed with the yeast of the lineage
whose intention is directly perceived,
Become drunk with experience and realisation,
and delight in supreme transformation's
dance.[1385]

The teachings of the Ancient Translation School
are not just empty expressions,
Broadcast by the prattle of fools,
who think only their fathers' bowls clean.[1386]
They are excellent and complete, undeluded
essentials of the sūtra and mantra paths,
Taught by those who've appeared in the wake
of millions of learned and accomplished masters.

Water-lilies blemished
by dark ignorance fold themselves up
In that garden, when they are struck
by the necklace of illumination;
But from the reservoir
of the three faiths,
Certainty's white lotus
has blossomed.

Behold the good fortune
of the ear which receives
Even part of the nectar
of this discourse on doctrinal history,
And so is embraced by one hundred thousand
attributes of excellence.
This is a priceless item,
not subject to devaluation.

Now that this unbearable storm,
the degenerate age's depredation,
Has driven the craft of the Conqueror's teaching
right to the perilous brink,
As its unknowledgeable captain
I've done what I have here,
With a high aspiration to promote
skilful means' artistry.

Though in the cool land
the heavenly Sage's teaching
Has been beautified by a million constellations,
learned and accomplished in the ancient translations,
Still, to raise the horizons
of this most degenerate age,
A sole naked star remains wishing to speak:
I am he.

Though she be no wondrous beauty,
no figure of literary form,
This seductress, brimming
with fine meaning's youthful vigour,
May well steal the thoughts
of lucid young scholars,
When she flashes the bright smile
of deceitless utterance.

This way is a seeing eye
for those with devotion,
An ornament for the throats
of the learned and holy,
And, for those who hold the true lineage,
it is the nectar of my heart.
I think it may well be
a wish-fulfilling gem.

Though the burden of many years
weighs on this physical frame,

The youthful power of intelligence
remains undiminished.
So now it is my heartfelt desire
to play at skilful teaching and composition
In that pleasure grove
in which supreme doctrine appears.

The wish-fulfilling gem of the supreme vehicle's
definitively secret tradition
Was well sought with a hundred efforts
by the host of our forebearers.
Now the burden falls to us followers
to worship it as the pinnacle
Of the banner of exegesis and attainment.
Of this I pray you be knowing!

The good that has come from this little endeavour is like the Manasarovar Lake:[1387] May limitless merits arise from its depths as masses of clouds and fill the entire extent of the celestial expanse of reality!
Let there be brought down a wondrous, plentiful rain of temporal and spiritual well-being, to moisten the hard soil of the world's depredations and give rise to a heavenly, medicinal grove of perfect glory and wealth.
There, may the joyful perfume of the dense groves of pure white-anthered, pollen-drenched lotuses of holiness, which float on the authentic view's lotus pools, waft in a hundred directions.
So that, nurtured by the sunlight of the Three Precious Jewels, the re-emergence of worldly auspices and those of peace, like heavy golden corn, might sustain the *kṛtayuga's* feast.

By wielding the vajra of threefold reason[1388] as their great weapon, the lords among divine promulgators, the proponents of the taintless tradition of the Guide, Supreme Sage, Man-lion,
Have at once crushed the brains of barbarians, who harbour perverse notions, wrong views; with the staff of the view that is free from extremes, they have vanquished flower-arrowed Kāma with his army,
And beat the drum of profoundly significant doctrine. May all of the many creatures who grope in the great darkness of thick ignorant slumber be wakened!

Just hearing the divine melody of the thunder of scripture,
and having abandoned that endless state, may they obtain
the joy of great intelligence, discerning reality.

May this transformation of the expression of the most secret
oceanic doctrinal tradition's origins into written form,
from the lute of my throat, which plays indestructible
reality's tune,
Not decline until that time when the Fifth Guide's doctrinal
drum[1389] resounds in this realm to remove limitless beings'
afflictions; but may the glory of its enlightened activity
blaze everlastingly and all-pervasively.
And may the golden wheel of the indestructible nucleus –
whose celestial axis consists of four visionary appearances,
spontaneously present through the effortless king of
vehicles, whose thousand resplendent spokes are
unelaborate primordial purity, whose all-embracing rim
is the conduct of transcendental perfections –
Ascend through the skies above the four continents of the
Sage's teaching,[1390] so that all that is auspicious, blissful
and fine within the three spheres become like unwavering
Mount Meru!

3 *Colophon*

Thus this work called *Thunder from the Great Conquering Battle-Drum of Devendra* gives clear and lucid expression to the history of the precious teaching of the vehicle of indestructible reality according to the Ancient Translation School, the first of all of the teachings of the Conqueror in the Land of Snows.

It was composed by Śākyamuni's lay disciple, the holder of gnostic mantras Jikdrel Yeshe Dorje Gelek Nampar Gyelweide (Fearless Indestructible Reality of Pristine Cognition, the Victorious Army of All that is Good), or, to use my name as a grammarian, Tshojung Gyepei Langtso Tsuklak Mawei Nyima (Joyous Youth of the Lake-born Lotus, the Sun amongst Proponents of Scripture), though my countrymen in the village lanes universally know me as Düjom Trülku. I was conceived in the taintless family line descended from the religious king of Kanam, the lord of the realm of Puworong, who became so known because Catri Tsenpo, a deity of the Radiant Heaven, had taken possession of that land;[1391] but my umbilical cord was cut in the secret land of Pemakö. The sunlight of [Padmasambhava] the great master of Oḍḍiyāna's compassion having penetrated my heart, I may boast that the lotus of my intellect did blossom a little.

After being greeted by the onset of my fifty-eighth year, I began this work on Saturday 19 May 1962 (full moon day, *Caitra*, *dge-byed* water male tiger year, sixteenth cycle),[1392] which has the good fortune of being the anniversary of the original reception of [the *Kālacakra Tantra*], that king of Non-Dual tantras and nectar of secret injunctions. It was entirely completed on the most powerful tenth day of the waxing half of the monkey month [i.e. the anniversary of Guru Rinpoche's birth, which in 1962 fell on Thursday 12 July],[1393] sustained by that season in which mobile and motionless creatures enjoy the summer's perfect feast and fruits swell with sap, in the city of Ratnapurī, Sahor, India, a supreme location.[1394] It was there that Padmasambhava, as Dewachenpo, the embodiment of great bliss, had conferred maturation on King Ārṣadhara in the maṇḍala of the glorious *Ocean of Doctrine, the*

Gathering of Transmitted Precepts complete with its maṇḍala clusters, and played out the apparitional drama of pristine cognition, or the Great Seal, so as to embrace all of space.

The scribe who set down the original copy was Chödrak Gyamtso, a logician and teacher of mantras from Shinglotsel, the southern district of Mön,[1395] who well accomplished this task with his offering of devotion and diligence.

May this cause the precious teaching of the Conqueror in general, and the taintless tradition of its most secret nucleus in particular, to spread without decline, and to survive perpetually, in all places, times and circumstances; and may it be the basis for all living beings to be sustained throughout all times by the fine feast of perfect auspices, bliss and goodness!

May the great tradition of the preceptor,
  the master and the religious king
Increase until it pervades
  the three spheres of Jambudvīpa!
And throughout the three times may there be
  the virtue and goodness whereby
The minds of creatures are never without
  the appearance of the Three Precious Jewels!

Jayantu! May they be victorious!

Mawocok in east Lhodrak, residence of Nyang-rel Nyima Özer

Sinmo Parje Rock, a treasure site of Nyang-rel Nyima Özer

The Guru Temple in Layak, west Lhodrak, founded by Guru Chöwang

Lhalung, residence of the Peling Sungtrül

The Nyingma School of Tibetan Buddhism

Section Two: Reference Material

The Nyingma School of Tibetan Buddhism
Its Fundamentals and History

Volume Two: Reference Material

Gyurme Dorje and Matthew Kapstein

WISDOM PUBLICATIONS Boston

First Edition 1991

WISDOM PUBLICATIONS
361 Newbury Street
Boston, Massachusetts 02115

Library of Congress Cataloging-in-Publication Data

Bdud-'joms 'Jigs-bral-ye-śes-rdo-rje, 1904–87.
[Bstan-pa'i rnam-gzhag'. English]
The Nyingma School of Tibetan Buddhism:
Its Fundamentals and History/Dudjom Rinpoche:
translated and edited by Gyurme Dorje
in collaboration with Matthew Kapstein.
p. cm.—(Wisdom Advanced Book Blue Series)
Translation of: Bstan-pa'i rnam-gzhag' and 'Chos-byung.
Includes bibliographical references and index.
ISBN 0-86171-087-8
1. Rñiṅ-ma-pa (Sect) I. Title. II. Series. III. Series:
Bdud-'joms 'Jigs-bral-ye-śes-rdo-rje, 1904–87. 'Chos-byung.
English.
BQ7662.2.B3913 1990
294.3'923—dc20 89-4053
CIP

Text set in Plantin Light by Character Graphics of Somerset, England; and Bothwin Promotion Ltd of Hong Kong.

Contents

INDEX OF PERSONAL NAMES

Introduction 391
Index of Personal Names 393

INDEX OF LOCATIONS

Introduction 453
Index of Locations 455

MAPS

Introduction 489
1 Buddhist India and Adjacent Regions 490
2 North-Central India 492
3 Tibet 494
4 Western Tibet and Nepal 496
5 North-Central Tibet 498
6 South-Central Tibet and Bhutan 500
7 North-West Kham 502
8 South-West Kham 506
9 Amdo 508
10 North-East Kham 510
11 South-East Kham 512

Introduction

This book contains a variety of reference material compiled to assist the reader in understanding the many unexplained references, allusions and enumerations found in the treatises in Volume One, and thus to give access to the vast wealth of information which these contain. The need for such a volume emerged during our discussions of technical problems with His Holiness Dudjom Rinpoche and with the other scholars mentioned in the Preface, who then encouraged its compilation. It consists of eight parts: Notes, Glossary of Enumerations, Bibliography, Artifacts and Material Treasures, Index of Technical Terms, Index of Personal Names, Index of Locations and Maps.

The Notes supply brief glosses on occasional obscure points, and direct the reader either to relevant explanatory passages found in the present texts themselves, or to significant discussions found in other works. Since they are not exclusively for the use of experts in Tibetan studies, we have sought to emphasise authoritative western language works. Where reference is made to primary sources of Tibetan or Sanskrit origin, the titles of these texts are untranslated unless they have already appeared in translation in Volume One, in which case this translated title is retained. Points of interest mainly to specialists will be our notes on the use of unusual terminology, the problems of dating, citations from Sanskrit or Tibetan sources, and so forth.

Enumerated categories appear in the Glossary of Enumerations. This lists in numerical order categories such as the "two truths", "four rites", "twenty-five great pilgrimage places of Kham and Amdo", and so forth, detailing the specific elements of each – many of which have never before been defined in western works on Buddhism – using information derived from the *Mahāvyutpatti* and other multilingual Buddhist glossaries.

The Bibliography is divided into two parts. The many Indian and Tibetan texts and teaching cycles mentioned by the Author have been researched and documented in Part One. The complexity of categorising much of this literature and the associated problems entailed in identifying specific texts within such categories are explained in the Introduction to the Bibliography. The accurate identification of texts mentioned in Tibetan historical and doctrinal literature is a necessary step towards acquiring an understanding of Tibetan literary history, and we hope our research will contribute to this little explored field. The second part of the Bibliography details the specific editions of Indian and Tibetan texts to which we have referred in locating quotations found in Volume One. It also lists Indian, Tibetan and secondary language sources consulted for the purpose of annotation.

The list of Artifacts and Material Treasures serves as an index to the many sacred objects mentioned in the text – images, paintings, gemstones, ritual implements, and so forth – and complements the series of treasure doctrines (*gter-chos*) documented in the Bibliography.

The Index of Technical Terms is in effect a trilingual glossary of Buddhist philosophy according to the diverse schools or traditions comprised by the nine vehicles, and also of the "outer sciences" – art, medicine, grammar, logic, and so forth.

The Index of Personal Names has been compiled in an extensive way for the benefit of those unfamiliar with the many epithets by which a single personality can be known, particularly in the narrative context of the *History*. The many variations of these names have been listed individually and also collectively under one main entry, to which the reader is referred.

In the Index of Locations particular attention has been given to the actual identification of the places mentioned, and the reader has frequently been referred to available secondary sources which document the sites in question. In addition, precise grid references have been given wherever possible and these are correlated to a series of accurate, newly prepared, computer-generated maps, which form the concluding section of this volume.

With the exception of the Notes and the Bibliography of Works Referred to by the Translators, entries in Volume Two have generally been followed by their exact Tibetan transliteration as this appears in the original treatises of Dudjom Rinpoche and/or by their Sanskrit equivalent. In listing entries, we have used the following conventions: Parentheses indicate elements commonly omitted in abbreviated references. An oblique dash separates variant forms or spelling. Square brackets have been avoided, or replaced by parentheses. Given the complexity of the material, however, it has not been possible to apply these distinctions exhaustively.

The Notes are numbered consecutively and are therefore easily cross-referenced against the texts. Other entries have been followed by the page numbers on which they appear in Section One. For references to illustrations, plate numbers always precede page numbers and line drawings are indicated by a page number in bold face. Page references for primary or secondary sources are enclosed in parentheses whenever there could be some confusion between these and the regular index numbers. Note numbers are rarely included in the indexes and so this section should be consulted separately.

Readers are also referred to the Guide to Pronunciation for clarification of our use of Tibetan and Sanskrit in romanisation and transliteration, and to the expanded list of abbreviations. An explanation of the conventions used within the translations themselves is given in the Technical Note to Section One.

We are aware that, in the absence of a further set of indexes in which all of these materials are listed following their proper Tibetan orthography, the usefulness of this material for scholars of Tibetan is restricted. A separate Tibetan-English index to meet specialists' requirements will be completed shortly.

Finally, it should be said that our attempt to standardise the English usage for the translations in no way represents a proposed standard vocabulary for Buddhism in English – though it may indeed contribute. The creation of such a vocabulary, if it is ever to emerge, will be the result of an ongoing process of experimentation, dialogue and debate – as was the case when the technical terminology of Buddhism was first formulated in the Tibetan language from the Sanskrit.

Guide to Pronunciation

Readers should familiarise themselves at the outset with the following four rules of pronunciation for Tibetan and Sanskrit:

(1) A final *e* is never silent, but is always pronounced in the manner of the French *é*. Thus, Sanskrit *vane* is pronounced *vané*, and the Tibetan *Ghare*, *Kore* and *Dorje* are pronounced, respectively, *Gharé*, *Koré* and *Dorjé*.

(2) *C* is pronounced somewhat like the English *ch*, but without aspiration. Sanskrit *cakra* and *citta* thus resemble *chakra* and *chitta*, and Tibetan *Co-se*, *Campa* and *Koca* are rather like *Cho-sé*, *Champa* and *Kocha*.

(3) *Ph* is never pronounced like an English *f*, but like a *p* with strong aspiration, for example in Sanskrit *phala* and Tibetan *photrang*.

(4) *Th* is never pronounced like the English *th* in *think* or *that*, but always resembling a *t* with strong aspiration, for example in Sanskrit *tathāgata* and Tibetan *thuk*.

The following remarks explain the conventions adopted for the transcription of Sanskrit and Tibetan in greater detail:

SANSKRIT

The Sanskrit vowels in actual use here are as follows:

a, ā, i, ī, u, ū, ṛ, e, ai, o, au

A, *i*, *u*, *e* and *o* are pronounced as in Italian. *Ā*, *ī* and *ū* are not to be pronounced like the so-called "long vowels" in English, but like the *a* in *father*, the *ea* in *seat* and the *oo* in *boot* respectively. *Ai* is similar to the *y*-sound of English *by*, and *au* to the *ow* of *now*. *Ṛ* resembles the *ri*-sound of *brick*. Vowels may be followed by *ṃ* and *ḥ*, which respectively indicate the nasalisation and aspiration of the vowel to which they are affixed.

The transcribed Sanskrit consonants are:

k, kh, g, gh, ṅ
c, ch, j, jh, ñ
ṭ, ṭh, ḍ, ḍh, ṇ
t, th, d, dh, n
p, ph, b, bh, m
y, r, l, v
ś, ṣ, s, h

Of these, *k, ch, j, t, d, n, p, b, m, y, r, l, v, s*, and *h* indicate roughly the same sounds as they do in English, and *c, ph* and *th* have been explained above. The series *t, th, d, dh, n* is distinguished from the series *ṭ, ṭh, ḍ, ḍh, ṇ* in that the latter or "retroflex" series is pronounced with the tongue striking the roof of the mouth, and the former or "dental" series, with the tongue striking the upper incisors. *Kh, gh, jh, dh, ḍh* and *bh* are similar to *k, g, j, d, ḍ* and *b* respectively, but with strong aspiration. *Ṅ* resembles the *ng* in English *sing*, and *ñ* the *ny* in *canyon*. *Ṣ* and *ś* are both similar to the English *sh*-sound, but the tongue is positioned further back when pronouncing the former.

TIBETAN

The transcription of Tibetan in English introduces special problems owing to the fact that the pronunciation of the spoken language does not closely correspond to the orthography of the literary language. For this reason a transliteration of the Tibetan spellings is of little use to the ordinary reader, who will have no way of knowing that, for example, *bsgrubs* and *dbyings* are currently pronounced as *drup* and *ying* respectively. On the other hand, students of the classical Tibetan language usually prefer the literal transcriptions to simplified phonetic schemes. The solution adopted in the present work has been to give all Tibetan personal and place names occurring in the text in just such a simplified system, relegating the precise transliterations to the indexes. At the same time, book titles, technical terms and peculiarities of language which are given parenthetically or discussed in the annotations have been given in a formal transliteration of the classical Tibetan, the system used being based upon that of the late Turrell V. Wylie, which will be familiar to specialists.

Our simplified phonetic transcription approximates the pronunciation of modern Central Tibetan, but without the subtlety or precision of a formal phonetic transcription, such as that developed by Chang and Shefts. Our intention here is merely to minimise the difficulties with which Tibetan names confront the reader.

In addition to the five vowels *a*, *i*, *u*, *e* and *o*, which have the same values here that they do in Sanskrit, Tibetan introduces two more – *ö* and *ü* – which are pronounced as in German.

The following additional consonants are used, along with those also found in Sanskrit: *ng*, *ny*, *tr*, *trh*, *dr*, *ts*, *tsh*, *dz*, *w*, *sh*, *z*, *zh*. Of these, *ng*, *ny*, *tr*, *dr*, *w*, *sh* and *z* are similar to their English values. *Trh* is like *tr*, but with strong aspiration. *Ts* resembles the *ts*-sound in English *bets*, and *dz* the sound in *adze*. *Tsh* is the strongly aspirated version of *ts*. *Zh* is similar to the *s* in leisure, or the *j* of French words such as *jamais*.

Specialists will note that this system does not reflect tone, an important feature of modern spoken Tibetan, and that we have dropped the aspirate in cases where it is not usually pronounced, even if it occurs in the classical orthography. Following a vowel, *l* is often silent, the preceding vowel being lengthened by way of compensation.

Abbreviations for Section Two

Auth.	Author
BB	Bauddha Bhāratī Series. Varanasi.
B.Budh.	Bibliotheca Buddhica. St. Petersburg/Leningrad, 1897-1936.
BIT	Bibliotheca Indo-Tibetica. Sarnath, UP: Central Institute of Higher Tibetan Studies.
Blue Annals	G. N. Roerich (trans.), *The Blue Annals*. 2nd edn. Delhi: Motilal Banarsidass, 1976. Translation of 'Gos Lo-tsā-ba Gzhon-nu-dpal, *deb-ther sngon-po*.
BMGD	*Bla-ma dgongs-'dus*. Disc. Sangs-rgyas gling-pa. 13 vols. NNS 44-56 (1972 onwards). I(Sik)-Tib 72-903387. A more recent edition, not consulted here, has appeared in 18 volumes. Paro: Lama Ngodup and Sherab Drimey, 1981. Bhu-Tib 81-901820.
BST	Buddhist Sanskrit Texts. Darbhaṅga, Bihar: Mithila Institute of Post-Graduate Studies and Research in Sanskrit Learning.
CLTC	*Mchog-gling gter-chos*. The collected rediscovered teachings of Gter-chen Mchog-gyur-gliṅ-pa. New Delhi: Patshang Lama Sonam Gyaltsen, 1975. 30 vols. I-Tib 75-903248. Those who are particularly interested in the works of Mchog-gyur gling-pa, should also be aware of the following collection, which, however, was not consulted here: *The treasury of revelations and teachings of Gter-chen Mchog-gyur-bde-chen-gliṅ-pa*. Paro: Lama Pema Tashi, 1982. Bhu-Tib 82-906203.
Disc.	"Discovered by": in the case of treasures (*gter-ma*).
DDTC	*Bdud-'dul rdo-rje'i gter-chos*. The collected rediscovered teachings of Spo-bo Gter-chen Bdud-'dul-rdo-rje. 8 vols. Darjeeling: Bairo Trulku, 1976. I-Tib 76-901008.

DLTC — *Rdor-gling gter-chos.* The collected *gter-ma* rediscoveries of Gter-chen Rdo-rje-gliṅ-pa. 4 vols. Paro: Dodrup Sangye Lama, 1976. I(Bhu)-Tib 76-901752.

DZ — *Gdams-ngag mdzod. Store of Precious Instructions.* 12 vols. Delhi: N. Lungtok and N. Gyaltsan, 1971.

EIPRB — K. Potter, *Encyclopedia of Indian Philosophies.* Vol. 1, Bibliography (rev. edn.). Princeton: Princeton University Press, 1983. References give the entry numbers for works cited.

Fundamentals — Dudjom Rinpoche, Jikdrel Yeshe Dorje, *The Nyingma School of Tibetan Buddhism: Its Fundamentals and History*, Vol. 1, Bk. 1.

GCD — *Rñiṅ ma'i rgyud bcu bdun.* 3 vols. New Delhi: Sanje Dorje, 1973-7. I-Tib 73-906438.

GCKZ — *Rgya-chen bka'-mdzod.* Auth. 'Jam-mgon Kong-sprul Blo-gros mtha'-yas. 20 vols. Paro: Ngodup, 1975. I(Bhu)-Tib 75-903141. The last four volumes (17-20) constitute the *Store which Embraces All Knowledge (shes-bya kun-khyab mdzod)*, which does not, however, properly belong to GCKZ. For considerable information on Kong-sprul's writing, the reader is referred to D. Schuh, *Tibetische Handschriften und Blockdrucke*: *Gesammelte Werken des Koṅ-sprul Blo-gros mtha'-yas.* Verzeichnis der Orientalischen Handschriften in Deutschland, XI, VI. Wiesbaden: Franz Steiner Verlag, 1976.

GDKT — *Rgyud-sde kun-btus.* Compiled by 'Jam-dbyangs Blo-gter dbang-po. 30 vols. Delhi: N. Lungtok and N. Gyaltsan, 1971 onwards. I-Tib 70-919390.

GGFTC — G. Dorje, *The Guhyagarbhatattvaviniścayamahātantra and its XIVth Century Tibetan Commentary: Phyogs-bcu mun-sel.* 3 vols. Unpublished Ph.D. thesis. University of London, 1987.

GOS — Gaekwad's Oriental Series. Baroda: Oriental Institute.

GT — T. V. Wylie, *The Geography of Tibet according to the 'Dzam-gling rgyas-bshad.* SOR 25 (1962).

GTKT — *Sgrub-thabs kun-btus.* Compiled by 'Jam-dbyangs Blo-gter dbang-po. 14 vols. Dehra Dun: G. T. K. Lodoy, N. Lungtok and N. Gyaltsan, 1970. I-Tib 70-912479.

HBI — É. Lamotte, *Histoire du Bouddhisme Indien.* Bibliothèque du Muséon, Vol. 43. Louvain: Publications Universitaires, 1958. English trans. S.

	Webb-Boin, 1988. The French page numbers given in our notes are correlated in the margins of the English version.
HIL	*History of Indian Literature*. Ed. J. Gonda. Wiesbaden: Otto Harrassowitz.
HIL 1.1	J. Gonda, *Vedic Literature*. HIL Vol. 1, fascicule 1 (1975).
HIL 5.2	H. Scharfe, *Grammatical Literature*. HIL Vol. 5, fascicule 2 (1977).
HIL 5.3	E. Gerow, *Indian Poetics*. HIL Vol. 5, fascicule 3 (1977).
HIL 5.4	C. Vogel, *Indian Lexicography*. HIL Vol. 5, fascicule 4 (1979).
HIL 6.2	B. K. Matilal, *Nyāya-Vaiśeṣika*. HIL Vol. 6, fascicule 2 (1977).
HIL 6.4	D. Pingree, *Jyotiḥśāstra: Astral and Mathematical Literature*. HIL Vol. 6, fascicule 4 (1981).
HIL 7.1	D. S. Ruegg, *The Literature of the Madhyamaka School of Philosophy in India*. HIL Vol. 7, fascicule 1 (1981).
HIL 9.3	D. Zbavitel, *Bengali Literature*. HIL Vol. 9, fascicule 3 (1976).
History	Dudjom Rinpoche, Jikdrel Yeshe Dorje, *The Nyingma School of Tibetan Buddhism: Its Fundamentals and History*, Vol. 1, Bk. 2.
HOS	Harvard Oriental Series. Cambridge, MA: Harvard University Press.
JIP	*Journal of Indian Philosophy*.
JLSB	*'Jigs-med gling-pa'i gsung-'bum*. The collected works of Kun-mkhyen 'Jigs-med-gliṅ-pa. 9 vols. NNS 29-37 (1970 onwards). I(Sik)-Tib 74-917093. The Sde-dge xylo., which is still available, has not been consulted here.
JTPD	*'Ja'-tshon pod-drug*. Disc. 'Ja'-tshon snying-po. 7 vols. Darjeeling: Taklung Tsetrul Pema Wangyal, 1979-82. I-Tib 79-905783.
KCST	*Klong-chen gsung thor-bu*. Miscellaneous Writings of Kun-mkhyen Kloṅ-chen-pa Dri-med 'od-zer. 2 vols. Delhi: Sanje Dorje, 1973.
KCZD	*Klong-chen mdzod-bdun*. Sde-dge edn. 6 vols. Gangtok: Sherab Gyaltsen and Khyentse Labrang, 1983. I-Tib 83-905058.
KGDD	*Bka'-brgyad bde-gshegs 'dus-pa'i chos-skor*. Disc. Nyang-ral Nyi-ma 'od-zer. 13 vols. NNS 75-87 (1978). I-Tib 78-905643. Several other versions of

this cycle, which we have not referred to here, have been published in India and Bhutan, the most important of these being the Mtshams-brag manuscript in 13 vols. Paro: Ngodrup, 1979-80. I(Bhu)-Tib 79-903504.

KGHP — A. Ferrari, *mK'yen brtse's Guide to the Holy Places of Central Tibet*. Ed. L. Petech. SOR 16 (1958).

KGNZ — *Bka'-brgyud sngags-mdzod*. Compiled by 'Jam-mgon Kong-sprul Blo-gros mtha'-yas. 8 vols. Paro: Dilgo Khyentsey Rinpoche, 1982. Bhu-Tib 82-901827. An earlier edition of the same collection, which we have not consulted here, was published by SNGP in 6 volumes in 1974. I-Tib 75-900393. The addition of two volumes to the Paro edn. is explained by the inclusion of a manuscript version of a very rare Vajrapāṇi cycle, which, however, does not properly belong to the KGNZ.

LCSB — *Lo-chen gsung-'bum*. Collected works of Smin-gliṅ Lo-chen Dharma-śrī. 19 vols. Dehra Dun: D. G. Khochhen Trulku, 1975. I-Tib 75-904278.

Litho. — Lithographic edition. Used in the case of certain Tibetan works only.

LTWA — Library of Tibetan Works and Archives. Dharamsala, HP.

MCB — *Mélanges Chinois et Bouddhiques*. Institut Belge des Hautes Études Chinoises, Brussels.

MPSB — *Mi-pham gsung-'bum*. No complete edition of Mi-pham's works is yet available, nor was any ever published in Tibet. The most complete traditional edition was prepared in Sde-dge and is still available. This has been partially reproduced in India: Collected Writings of 'Jam-mgon 'Ju Mi-pham-rgya-mtsho. 15 vols. NNS 60-74 (1972 onwards). I(Sik)-Tib 72-906838. In this bibliography MPSB will signify the latter edition. For much valuable information on Mi-pham's writings, refer to D. Schuh, *Tibetische Handschriften und Blockdrucke sowie Tonbandaufnahmen Tibetischer Erzählungen*. Teil 5. Wiesbaden: Franz Steiner Verlag, 1973, pp. 63-266. A new edition of Mi-pham's collected works, incorporating all that is available at the present time, has been published under the direction of Dilgo Khyentsey Rinpoche: *Sde-dge par-ma*. 25 vols. Paro: Dilgo Khyentsey Rinpoche, 1982-.

MTTWL P. Pfandt, *Mahāyāna Texts Translated into Western Languages*. Cologne: In Kommission bei E. J. Brill, 1983.

Mvt. *Mahāvyutpatti*. Ed. R. Sakaki, Kyoto, 1916-25.

NA Not available. Used when the mass of evidence suggests that the text or teaching in question is simply not extant at the present time.

NGB *Rnying-ma'i rgyud-'bum. Collected Tantras of the Nyingmapa*. Thimpu: Jamyang Khyentse Rinpoche, 1973, 36 vols. Catalogue by E. Kaneko, Tokyo, 1982. The Sde-dge xylo., which is still available, has not been consulted here.

NL Not located. Used when there is not sufficient evidence to apply the label NA, but we none the less have no certain knowledge of available editions or manuscripts.

NMKMG *Rnying-ma bka'-ma rgyas-pa. Collected Transmitted Precepts of the Nyingmapa*. Ed. Dudjom Rinpoche. 55 vols. Kalimpong, WB: Dubjung Lama, 1982. I-Tib 82-900981. Vols. 21-55 consist of commentarial and other ancillary material newly incorporated into the *Bka'-ma* collection by the editor. An earlier edition, to which we do not refer here, comprises 14 vols.: NNS 7-20 (1969 onwards). I(Sik)-Tib 71-908710.

NNS Ngagyur Nyingmay Sungrab. Published by Sonam T. Kazi, Gangtok, Sikkim.

NYZ *Snying-thig ya-bzhi. Four-Part Innermost Spirituality*. 11 vols. New Delhi: Trulku Tsewang, Jamyang and L. Tashi, 1970. The Sde-dge xylo., which is still available, has not been consulted here.

P *The Tibetan Tripiṭaka, Peking Edition*. 168 vols. Tokyo-Kyoto: Suzuki Research Foundation, 1955-61.

Pl. Plate. See Volume One, pp. xv-xxi.

PLTC *Pad-gling gter-chos*. The rediscovered teachings of the great Padma-gliṅ-pa. 22 vols. Thimphu: Kunsang Tobgay, 1975. I(Bhu)-Tib 75-903254.

PPCT K. Dowman, *The Power Places of Central Tibet*. London/New York: Routledge and Kegan Paul, 1988.

PRS L. Lancaster (ed.), *Prajñāpāramitā and Related Systems*. Berkeley Buddhist Studies Series, Vol. 1. Berkeley: Asian Humanities Press, 1977.

Pub. Photo-mechanical publication. Used only of editions which reproduce, by such means as photo-

	offset, older Tibetan manuscripts or xylographic editions, but omitted in connection with the Tibetan collections referred to by abbreviation (BMGD, CLTC, DZ, etc.), which are all reproductions of this sort. Where no title is specified following "pub." the work in question was published under the Tibetan title of the entry following which it is here listed.
Redisc.	"Rediscovered by": in the case of treasures that had been reconcealed after their original discovery (*yang-gter*).
RLTC	*Rat-gling gter-chos.* Collected rediscovered teachings of Ratna-gliṅ-pa. 19 vols. Darjeeling: Taklung Tsetrul Pema Wangyal, 1977. I-Tib 77-901310.
RTD	*Rin-chen gter-mdzod. Store of Precious Treasure.* 111 vols. Paro: Ngodrup and Sherap Drimey, 1976. Index compiled by Sik K. Yeshe Zangmo, 1984.
SBE	F. Max Müller (ed.), *Sacred Books of the East.* Oxford University Press. Reprinted, Delhi: Motilal Banarsidass.
SK	*Sa-skya bka'-'bum. The Complete Works of the Great Masters of the Sa Skya Pa Sect of Tibetan Buddhism.* 15 vols. Tokyo: Tokyo Bunko, 1968.
Skt.	Sanskrit
SNGP	Sungrab Nyamso Gyunphel Parkhang. Palampur, HP: Tibetan Craft Community.
SOR	Serie Orientale Roma. Published by the Instituto Italiano per il Medio ed Estremo Oriente (Is.M.E.O.).
SP	*Śatapiṭaka Series.* Sarasvati Vihar, New Delhi.
SSS	Smanrtsis shesrig spendzod. Leh, Ladakh: S. W. Tashigangpa.
STC	B. N. Aziz and M. Kapstein (eds.), *Soundings in Tibetan Civilization.* New Delhi: Manohar, 1985.
T	*A Complete Catalogue of the Tibetan Buddhist Canon.* (Tōhoku University catalogue of the Sde-dge edition of the Canon.) Ed. H. Ui et al. Sendai, 1934.
Taishō	*Taishō shinshū daizōkyō.* J. Takakusu, K. Watanabe, et al. (eds.), Tokyo: Taishō Issaikyō Kankō Kai, 1924-32. We refer to this, the Chinese Buddhist Tripiṭaka, only in those instances where the text in question is not available in either an Indic version or in Tibetan.
TG	*The Tibet Guide.* Lhasa, Central Tibet and Tsang by S. Batchelor; Western Tibet by B. Beresford

	and S. Jones; Eastern Tibet by G. Dorje. 2nd rev. edn., Boston: Wisdom Publications, 1991.
TH	Gyurme Dorje, *Tibet Handbook*. Chicago, Ill: Passport books: 1996, 1999, 2002.
Tib.	Tibetan
TMS	G.C.C. Chang (ed.), *A Treasury of Mahāyāna Sutras: Selections from the Mahāratnakūṭa*. University Park, PA: The Pennsylvania State University Press, 1983.
TSHR	M. Aris and Aung San Suu Kyi (eds.), *Tibetan Studies in Honour of Hugh Richardson*. Warminster: Aris and Phillips, 1980.
TSWS	Tibetan Sanskrit Works Series. Patna, Bihar: Kashi Prasad Jayaswal Research Institute.
TWB	Prof. Yensho Kanakure et al. (ed.), *A Catalogue of the Tōhoku University Collection of Tibetan Works on Buddhism*. Sendai: Tōhoku Imperial University, 1953.
TWPS	L. Chandra, *Tibetan Works Printed by the Shoparkang of the Potala*. SP 38 (1959), pp. 120-32. Note that most of the texts listed herein are now available again in Lhasa. Enquiries must be directed to the *Dang'anju*, which is the restored *Zhol parkhang*.
Xylo.	Xylographic edition.
ZGSB	*Zhe-chen rgyal-tshab-kyi gsung-'bum*. The collected works of Źe-chen Rgyal-tshab Padma rnam-rgyal. 18 vols. Paro: Ngodup, 1975 onwards. I(Bhu)-Tib 75-903143.

Notes

Note

On occasions when the translations in Books One and Two are cross-referenced against each other, page numbers are preceded by the short-title of the relevant book, i.e. either Fundamentals *or* History. *In cases where references are given to passages within the same text, however, only the page numbers are given.*

Readers are referred to the Bibliography whenever full information on primary and secondary sources does not appear in the relevant note.

1 *Fundamentals*

FUNDAMENTALS: TRANSLATOR'S INTRODUCTION

1 These and all subsequent enumerations are to be found in the Glossary of Enumerations in Volume Two.

2 In this traditional enumeration, the antigods were not given a class status distinct from that of the Four Great Kings (*Caturmahārāja-kāyika*).

3 Refer to pp. 162-9, where Madhyamaka philosophy is discussed.

4 These are explained on pp. 162-9.

5 For works of Sanskrit origin, wherever possible the formal Sanskrit titles are given in parentheses at the first mention of each text. The English rendering, however, follows the Tibetan, which often refers to texts by secondary or abridged titles. Further details for all texts mentioned can be found in the first part of the Bibliography in Volume Two.

6 An asterisk (*) has been used to indicate hypothetical reconstructions of Sanskrit technical terms not presently documented in available Sanskrit texts. Please note, however, that although many Sanskrit personal and place names used in these translations are similarly hypothetical, an asterisk has *not* been used to indicate these for purely aesthetic reasons.

7 I.e. those works contained in his *Collection of Eulogies* (*Stavakāya*, T 1118-36).

8 The distinction between these views and their integration from the standpoint of experience are the subject-matter of Pt. 3.

9 See H. V. Guenther, *Buddhist Philosophy in Theory and Practice*.

FUNDAMENTALS: PART ONE

10 I.e. Vajradhara of Oḍḍiyāna, a form of the great master Padmasambhava; see *History*, pp. 468-74, 512-20 and 533-7.

11 See *History*, Pt. 3.

12 Lokeśvara or Lokanātha (*'jig-rten-gyi mgon-po*) is more commonly known as Avalokiteśvara (*spyan-ras-gzigs-kyi dbang-phyug*). He is the bodhisattva who protects Tibet and whose blessing is said to have given rise to the Tibetan race. See *History*, p. 510.

13 Their biographies are included in the *History*: see pp. 607-16 for Nupcen Sangye Yeshe, Nup Khulungpa Yönten Gyamtso and the Zur family; pp. 755-9 for Nyang-rel Nyima Özer; pp. 701-2 for Rok Sherap-ö; pp. 703-9 for Rongzompa Chöki Zangpo; and pp. 575-96 for Longcen Rapjampa.

14 The text gives the root in the "coded" form *ḍudhṛñ* according to the tradition of the Pāṇinian *Dhātupāṭhas*. See G. B. Palsule, *The Sanskrit Dhātupāṭhas*, Ch. 3, p. 59, for an analysis of "the wonderful system of the Anubandhas [code letters] invented by the ancient Hindu grammarians".

15 Cf. Paṇḍit Śivadatta (ed.), *The Nāmaliṅgānuśāsana of Amarasinha*, p. 73: "Dharma is that which upholds the world or is upheld by persons."

16 *dge-sbyong-gi chos-bzhi*. The text wrongly reads *dge-slong-gi chos-bzhi* (Khenpo Palden Sherap).

17 Tib. *dbyer-med*. This reading is preferred by the Author to *byed-med*, which is given in the text.

18 *ma-rig-pa zhes-pa ni gzhi 'khrul-rtog-gi cha 'dzin-pa*. The phrase is omitted in the text, but included in the primary source: Longcenpa, *Treasury of the Supreme Vehicle (theg-mchog rin-po-che'i mdzod)*, p. 84.

19 For the relationship of hatred to the creation phase of meditation, refer to p. 359.

20 I.e. the five sensory perceptions and the consciousness of the intellect.

21 See the Glossary of Enumerations. Six of these are objective, six are subjective and six are sensory.

22 *rig-cing yul-du byed-pa rnam-par shes-pa'i phung-po*. This phrase is omitted in the text, but found in the primary source: Longcenpa, *Treasury of the Supreme Vehicle*, p. 79.

23 These subjective modes of the activity fields are not referred to as the consciousness of the eye (*mig-gi rnam-par shes-pa'i skye-mched*) and so forth in the Abhidharma. They are simply known as the activity field of the eye (*mig-gi skye-mched*), etc. Refer to the Glossary of Enumerations under *twelve activity fields*.

24 The neutral deeds are those connected with the experiences of meditative absorption and the like. See below, pp. 61-4.

25 See the chart of the three world systems or realms of saṃsāra, pp. 14-15. Mount Sumeru is held to be the central axis of the world of Patient Endurance (*mi-mjed 'jig-rten-gyi khams*, Skt. *Sahalokadhātu*) within the desire realm. See also n. 376.

26 See the chart above, pp. 14-15. The extraordinary form realms (*khyad-par-can*) are the Five Pure Abodes (*gtsang-gnas lnga*), which are contrasted with the twelve ordinary form realms (*tsam-po*).

27 This quotation is also cited by the author of the *gzhung-lugs legs-bshad*, p. 62. Both this and the following quotation are given in DZ Vol. 1, pp. 113-14; and in Jamgön Kongtrül, *shes-bya kun-khyab mdzod*, Vol. 2, p. 351.

28 On Buddhaguhya, refer to *History*, pp. 464-5.

29 See the chart on pp. 14-15.

30 See the chart, pp. 14-15, for this Brahmakāyika realm, and for those other god realms such as Avṛha which are mentioned in the following pages.

31 The vehicle of Brahmā (*tshangs-pa'i theg-pa*) surpasses the vehicle of gods and humans because it reaches the summit of cyclical existence, as described below.

32 The summit of existence refers to the highest possible mode of being within cyclical existence or saṃsāra. It is contrasted with the nirvāṇa of the buddha levels.

33 These four formless absorptions are said to be endowed with the four nominal or mental components, but not the component of form.

34 See *History*, p. 688.

35 Līlāvajra's brief biography is given in the *History*, pp. 463-4.

36 For Vimalamitra's biography, see *History*, pp. 480-1, 497-501, 555-6, 601 and *passim*.

37 For the background to this debate, refer to sGam-po-pa, *The Jewel Ornament of Liberation*, translated by H. V. Guenther, pp. 3-4; and to Sakya Paṇḍita, *thub-pa dgongs-gsal*, p. 2.1-2.

38 The former are the Outsiders or adherents of non-Buddhist traditions and the latter, the Insiders, are the followers of Buddhism.

39 The traditional Indian and Buddhist system of cosmology holds that the span of life is gradually reduced during the course of a single aeon, from an indefinitely long period to ten years.

40 An Indian source for this quotation preserved in Sanskrit is Kamalaśīla, *Tattvasaṃgrahapañjikā*, Vol. 1, p. 52. See also *Nyāyavārttika*, 4.1.21.

41 According to Longcenpa, *Wish-fulfilling Treasury* (*yid-bzhin rin-po-che'i mdzod*), p. 396, the Followers of the Owl are identical to the Vaiśeṣika. They are so called because when Kaṇāda attained the accomplishment of Īśvara, the deity alighted on a stone *liṅgam* within his meditation cave in the form of an owl (*ulūka*). There is also a tradition which claims Kaṇāda was known as the "Owl" after the name of his clan.

42 The origin of this fivefold classification, and the precise identities of several of the subjects, persons and texts here listed remain problematic. The grammatical tradition is listed among the six topics associated with Vedic study (*vedāṅga*), but usually traces itself to the *ṛṣi* Pāṇini, who is said to have been inspired by the god Śiva. The earliest logical method developed in India is that referred to as *ānvīkṣikī*, "inquiry", on which see S. C. Vidyabhusana, *A History of Indian Logic*, Sect. I. The Followers of Satyavacas (*bden-smras*) are probably the adherents of the Upanishads. The Mīmāṃsaka (*spyod/dpyod-pa-ba*), whose sūtra is probably referred to here, are not usually associated with the legendary *ṛṣi* Bhṛgu (*ngan-spong*), on whom see R. Goldman, *Gods, Priests and Warriors*, but rather with Jaimini. On the *Anthology of Caraka* (*Carakasaṃhitā*) and its traditions, refer to A. L. Basham (ed.), *A Cultural History of India*, Ch. XII.

43 Aviddhakarṇa (*rna ma-phug-pa*) was a Nyāya-vaiśeṣika philosopher who flourished some time before Śāntarakṣita, as he is frequently criticised in the latter's *Tattvasaṃgrahakārikā*. None of his works survive today. For a summary of research on this thinker to date, see K. H. Potter (ed.), *Encylopedia of Indian Philosophies: Indian Metaphysics and Epistemology*, pp. 338-40. See also Longcenpa, *Treasury of the Supreme Vehicle*, p. 98. The text wrongly reads *rnam-phug-pa* (Khenpo Palden Sherap).

44 Unidentified, but possibly this refers to Deva Sūri *Pramāṇa-*

nayatattvālokālaṃkāra, a major Jain philosophical text. The nine categories are also authoritatively given in, e.g., the *Navatattvasūtra* and the *Pañcāstikāya* of the Jains.

45 Tib. *zad-pa*.

46 This appears to be the non-extant *Bṛhaspatisūtra*, the views of which are reported in Indian philosophical works such as: Bhāvaviveka, *Tarkajvāla*; Śāntarakṣita, *Tattvasaṃgraha*; Jayarāśi, *Tattvopaplavasiṃha*; Haribhadrasūri, *Ṣaḍdarśanasamuccaya*; Mādhava, *Sarvadarśanasaṃgraha*; and in such later Tibetan treatises as Longcenpa, *Treasury of Spiritual and Philosophical Systems (grub-mtha' mdzod)*.

47 Tib. *tshu-rol mdzes-pa-ba* is a rendering for Skt. *Cārvāka*, which is interpreted in Tibetan to mean "adherents of pleasures at hand", i.e. hedonists.

48 The Outsiders *(phyi-rol-pa)* or non-Buddhists are here divided into those who follow a course independent of Buddhism and those who overtly teach a non-Buddhist doctrine, but are in fact emanations of the buddhas.

49 For some interesting observations on the relationship between the scepticism of the Lokāyata and the Prāsaṅgika dialectic, refer to D. Chattopadhyāya, *Indian Philosophy, a popular introduction*, pp. 186ff.

50 Tib. *myang-'das*, literally meaning "gone beyond sorrow".

51 Superior mind *(lhag-pa'i sems*, Skt. *adhicitta)* is that which develops experience in meditation.

52 The Sage *(drang-srong*, Skt. *ṛṣi)* in this case refers to Śākyamuni Buddha.

53 For a different interpretation of this passage, see E. Obermiller, *History of Buddhism by Bu-ston*, p. 25.

54 See pp. 153-5; also *History*, pp. 423-5.

55 Darbhaṅga edn., BST 4, p. 286.

56 For Nartön Senge-ö, see *Blue Annals*, p. 157.

57 *Innermost Spirituality of Vimalamitra (bi-ma snying-thig)*, Pt. 2, Vol. *Cha*, pp. 1-159.

58 Unidentified.

59 For Śāntipā or Ratnākaraśānti, see *Blue Annals*, pp. 206, 634-8; Tāranātha, *History of Buddhism in India*, translated by Lama Chimpa and A. Chattopadhyaya, p. 295, n. 12; and HIL 7.1, pp. 122-4.

60 I.e. the Nyingma tradition.

61 The primary source for this section is Vasubandhu, *Commentary on the Ornament of the Sūtras of the Greater Vehicle (Mahāyānasūtrālaṃkāravyākhyā*, Darbhaṅga edn., BST 13), p. 55.

62 The Sanskrit version (Darbhaṅga edn., p. 56) of the *Ornament of the Sutras of the Greater Vehicle* reads *āpatti*, although the Tibetan clearly gives *vipatti* in keeping with the content of the passage.

63 The distinction between the causal aspect of the vehicle or the bodhisattva vehicle and the six resultant vehicles of tantra is explored in great detail in Pt. 2, pp. 139-48; in Pt. 3 which deals with the nature of the causal aspects; and in Pt. 4 which focuses on the resultant aspects.

64 The eleventh level is held by bodhisattvas to be the buddha level. For these *eleven levels*, and the subsequent buddha levels until the sixteenth, Unsurpassed Pristine Cognition *(ye-shes bla-ma)*, which are described below, see the Glossary of Enumerations; and Longcenpa, *Dispelling*

Darkness in the Ten Directions (*phyogs-bcu mun-sel*), pp. 428-35 (GGFTC, pp. 967-76).

65 This text is among those translated into Tibetan from the Chinese.

66 This is one of only a few verses from this text extant in Sanskrit. It is interpolated in Candrakīrti's *Clearly Worded Commentary* (*Prasannapadā*, Darbhaṅga edn., BST 10), p.1.

67 A Buddhist source for this well-known Indian cliché is Kamalaśīla, *Tattvasaṃgrahapañjikā*, Vol. 1, p. 2. Many other treatises that were studied in Tibet also refer to it.

68 Vajradharma is the peaceful aspect of Vajrapāṇi. See *History*, p. 451.

69 The passage quoted here is not found in Vasubandhu's work. There is, however, a parallel passage in Yaśomitra, *Abhidharmakośavyākhyā* (T 4092), Vol. 1, p. 15.

70 A brief account of the lives of Śāriputra and Maudgalyāyana is given in the *History*, pp. 425-6. For a more detailed study of these texts and the tradition which holds the Abhidharma to have been compiled by arhats, refer to HBI, pp. 198-210.

71 On Vasubandhu, see S. Anacker, *Seven Works of Vasubandhu*; Tāranātha, *History of Buddhism in India*, pp. 167-75; also Obermiller, *History of Buddhism by Bu-ston*, pp. 136-47; and E. Frauwallner, *On the Date of the Buddhist Master of the Law Vasubandhu*, and the sources cited therein. Frauwallner's hypothesis, however, that there were two important Vasubandhus, has not met with general scholarly acceptance.

72 Refer to the first part of the Bibliography under *Yogācāra Level*. These treatises are the *Bhūmivastu* (T 4035-7), the *Vastusaṃgrahaṇī* (T 4039-40), the *Paryāyasaṃgrahaṇī* (T 4041), the *Vivaraṇasaṃgrahaṇī* (T 4042) and the *Viniścayasaṃgrahaṇī* (T 4038).

73 On Asaṅga, see Tāranātha, *History of Buddhism in India*, pp. 154-67; also Obermiller, *History of Buddhism by Bu-ston*, pp. 136-47; and W. Rahula's introduction to *Le Compendium de la Super-Doctrine d'Asaṅga*. The third level of bodhisattva realisation is known as the Illuminating (*'od-byed*, Skt. *Prabhākarī*). See the Glossary of Enumerations under *ten levels*.

74 On Dignāga, refer to Tāranātha, *History of Buddhism in India*, pp. 181-5; Obermiller, *History of Buddhism by Bu-ston*, pp. 149-52; and to M. Hattori, *Dignāga on Perception*.

75 Refer to the first part of the Bibliography, under *Eight Dissertations*. They are the *Commentary on the Ornament of the Sūtras of the Greater Vehicle* (*Sūtrālaṃkāravṛtti*, T 4062), the *Commentary on the Analysis of the Middle and Extremes* (*Madhyāntavibhaṅgavṛtti*, T 4027), the *Commentary on the Analysis of Phenomena and Reality* (*Dharmadharmatāvibhaṅgavṛtti*, T 4028), the *Rational System of Exposition* (*Vyākhyāyukti*, T 4061), the *Dissertation on the Proof of Deeds* (*Karmasiddhiprakaraṇa*, T 4062), the *Dissertation on the Five Components* (*Pañcaskandhaprakaraṇa*, T 4059), the *Twenty Verses* (*Viṃśatikā*, T 4055) and the *Thirty Verses* (*Triṃśikā*, T 4055).

76 On Śāntideva, see Tāranātha, *History of Buddhism in India*, pp. 215-20; Obermiller, *History of Buddhism by Bu-ston*, pp. 161-6; and HIL 7.1.

77 On Jikme Lingpa, see *History*, pp. 835-40; Gyatso, *Apparitions*.

78 On Dharmakīrti, see Tāranātha, *History of Buddhism in India*, pp.

228-40; and Obermiller, *History of Buddhism by Bu-ston*, pp. 152-5. Bibliographies documenting recent research on the works of Dharmakīrti will be found in the sources listed under *Pramāṇaviniścaya* in the second part of the Bibliography.

79 On the patriarch Upagupta, see *History*, p. 436; Strong, *The Legend*. An account of Yaśaḥ's involvement in the second council is provided in *History*, p. 429. It is based on the *Minor Transmissions* (*Kṣudrāgama*, T 6). For a more detailed account of this period and its personalities, such as Yaśaḥ, Sarvakāmin and Kubjita, refer to HBI, pp. 134ff.

80 On Nāgārjuna, refer to Obermiller, *History of Buddhism by Bu-ston*, pp. 122-30; Tāranātha, *bka'-babs bdun-ldan-gyi rnam-thar* (translated in D. Templeman, *The Seven Instruction Lineages*, pp.4-8); E. Lamotte, *Traité de la Grande Vertu de Sagesse*; and M. Walleser, "The Life of Nāgārjuna from Tibetan and Chinese Sources" *Asia Major* 1 (1923), pp. 421-55. Research to date is surveyed in HIL 7.1.

81 Because the *Vindication of Conventional Truth* does not exist in a Tibetan translation, Tibetan authorities often count Nāgārjuna's *Jewel Garland* (*Ratnāvalī*) as the sixth collection of reasoning.

82 The term "reality" in this Buddhist usage refers to the abiding emptiness of all things (*chos-nyid*, Skt. *dharmatā*) and "apparitional reality" to their manifestation (*chos-can*, Skt. *dharmin*). See p. 19.

83 On Kawa Peltsek, see *History*, pp. 515 and 522.

84 The text reads instead *lam rnam-bkod* (P 4737), which was composed by King Ja.

85 Refer to L. Sternbach, "Les Aphorismes dits de Cāṇakya dans les textes bouddhiques du Tibet et du Turkestan Oriental" *Journal Asiatique* 259 (1971), pp. 71-82, for remarks on the extant Tibetan redaction of this work.

86 An oral attribution made by Lama Sonam Topgyel. However the precise source is unidentified.

87 These are, respectively, Mvt. 4972-5006, 5007-26, 5027-34 and 5035-45.

88 Here the text reads *shes-rig* for *shes-rab*.

89 Yutokpa is briefly mentioned in *History*, p. 753. See also Rechung Rinpoche, *Tibetan Medicine*, pp. 147-327, for a detailed biography; and F. Meyer, *Gso-ba rig-pa: le système médical tibétain*, pp. 80, 91-2.

90 According to the Indian tradition, this treatise is attributed to Vāgbhaṭa. Tibetans have identified Śūra with both Aśvaghoṣa and Vāgbhaṭa. See Tāranātha, *History of Buddhism in India*, pp. 130-6; also F. Lessing and A. Wayman, *Mkhas Grub Rje's Fundamentals of the Buddhist Tantras*, p. 78n.; and C. Vogel, *Vāgbhaṭa's Aṣṭāṅgahṛdaya*.

91 All inflected nouns and conjugated verbs are subsumed within these two classes. "Gender" (*rtags*, Skt. *liṅga*), as used here, should be taken to refer to nominal stems of determinate gender, in contrast to, e.g., adjectival or pronominal stems, whose gender must be fixed.

92 These subdivisions are represented by a series of grammatical texts (T 4422-8) in the *Tangyur* (*bstan-'gyur*).

93 This is not precisely the form in which this verse is given in the *Compendium of Valid Cognition*. It corresponds exactly, however, to Śaṅkarasvāmin, *Nyāyapraveśa*, v. 1.

94 This line actually corresponds to Dharmakīrti, *Exposition of Valid*

Cognition (*Pramāṇavārttika*), Ch. 1, v. 3.

95 Briefly, the axiom of the result (*'bras-rtags*, Skt. *kāryahetu*) governs causal inferences; the axiom of identity (*rang-bzhin-rtags*, Skt. *svabhāvahetu*) governs inferences determined by the internal relations among a subject of phenomena (*chos-can*, Skt. *dharmin*) and its phenomena (*chos*, Skt. *dharma*); and the axiom of the absence of the objective referent (*mi-dmigs-pa'i rtags*, Skt. *anupalabdhihetu*) governs negative inferences, such as the *modus tollens* of classical western logic.

96 For the history of this debate in Tibet, refer to D. S. Ruegg, *The Life of Bu ston Rinpoche*, pp. 37-8, n. 1.

97 Tib. *go-la* refers to the twenty-eight constellations (*rgyu-skar nyer-brgyad*) and the twelve lunar mansions (*khyim bcu-gnyis*). See D. Schuh, *Untersuchungen zur Geschichte der Tibetischen Kalenderrechnung*, pp. 147-8.

98 The twelve two-hour periods are named after the twelve animals, which follow the same sequential order as the twelve months and twelve years. See n. 1330.

99 The nine numbers (*sme-ba dgu*) and the trigrams (*spar-kha*) are explained in W. A. Sherrill and W. K. Chu, *Anthology of the I Ching*. For indications concerning their roles in Tibetan astrology and divination, see G. Dorje, *Tibetan Elemental Divination Paintings*, pp. 92-108; and the articles by S. Hummel and D. Schuh listed in the final section of the Bibliography.

100 Refer to the fifteenth-century Tibetan compendium of knowledge, *bshad-mdzod yid-bzhin nor-bu*, pp. 428-32.

101 On Daṇḍin, see D. K. Gupta, *A Critical Study of Daṇḍin and his Works*; and S. K. De, *History of Sanskrit Poetics*.

102 See Jamgön Kongtrül, *shes-bya kun-khyab mdzod*, Vol. 2, p. 324, for a discussion on the Gauḍa style of East India and the Vaidarbha style of the south, as understood in Tibet.

103 Geometric poetry refers to verses which can be read in any direction. It includes acrostic verse (*ardhabhrama* or *sarvatobhadra*), and zigzagging (*gomūtrikā*). See Gupta, *A Critical Study of Daṇḍin and his Works*, pp. 238-9.

104 The modern study of Sakya Paṇḍita's life and works is thoroughly surveyed in D. P. Jackson, *The Entrance Gate for the Wise (Section III)*.

105 On the South Indian (Vaidarbha) tradition of verse, refer to M. Winternitz, *History of Indian Literature*, Vol. III, p. 15

106 On Candragomin, see Tāranātha, *History of Buddhism in India*, pp. 199-209; Obermiller, *History of Buddhism by Bu-ston*, pp. 132-4; and M. Tatz, "The Life of Candragomin in Tibetan Historical Tradition" *The Tibet Journal* VII, 3 (1982), pp. 3-22.

107 On Śrīgupta, see Tāranātha, *History of Buddhism in India*, pp. 225 and 252; and on Śākyamati, ibid., p. 260.

FUNDAMENTALS: PART TWO

108 See below, p. 131.

109 A "countless" aeon (*grangs-med bskal-pa*) refers not to infinity but to a specific span of time defined in the *Treasury of the Abhidharma*

(*Abhidharmakośa*) as 10^{59} aeons. Refer to R. Kloetzli, *Buddhist Cosmology*, pp. 113ff.

110 The Point of Enlightenment (*byang-chub snying-po*, Skt. *bodhimaṇḍa*) refers to the *outer* place and time at which Śākyamuni and other buddhas attain manifest enlightenment, i.e. Vajrāsana, the Indestructible Seat, at Bodh Gayā; to the *inner* Point of Enlightenment which is the Akaniṣṭha realm; and to the *secret* Point of Enlightenment which is the buddha-body of indestructible reality (*vajrakāya*). For the specific enlightenment of Śākyamuni and his encounter with Māra, see *History*, pp. 419-21.

111 *History*, pp. 423ff.

112 See p. 118 below. The Indestructible Nucleus of Inner Radiance (*'od-gsal rdo-rje snying-po*, Skt. **Prabhāsvaravajragarbha*) is the dimension or buddha-field of the buddha-body of reality, Samantabhadra, which cannot be limited in space and time. The teachings of the Great Perfection which pertain to this level are referred to as the vehicle of the Indestructible Nucleus of Inner Radiance.

113 I.e. it is without the subject-object dichotomy and without the threefold distinctions of beginning, middle and end.

114 See below, p. 140. It is contrasted with the "pristine cognition which quantitatively knows [phenomena]" (*ji-snyed-pa mkhyen-pa'i ye-shes*).

115 This is a synonym for the supreme buddha-body of reality (*chos-sku chen-po*, Skt. *mahādharmakāya*). See p. 342.

116 The tenth level of bodhisattva realisation is known as the Cloud of Doctrine (*chos-kyi sprin-pa*, Skt. *Dharmameghā*). See n. 385.

117 There is an extensive account of this cosmological formation at the beginning of Longcenpa's *Wish-fulfilling Treasury*, pp. 28-31. See also the Glossary of Enumerations for the *twenty-five world systems* said to be situated upon the equipoised hands of Vairocana in the form of *ye-shes gangs-chen mtsho* (Skt. **Jñānamahāhimasāgara*); and also *History*, pp. 409 and 961. Our world realm is situated at the heart of Vairocana and is representative of the mind aspect of his buddha-mind (*thugs-kyi thugs*). See also Jamgon Kongtrul, *Myriad Worlds*.

118 The reference for the past lives of Vajradhara is Longcenpa, *Treasury of the Supreme Vehicle*, pp. 12-14.

119 The major and minor marks of the buddha-body of perfect rapture are detailed below on p. 124 in terms of their outer, inner, secret and most secret appearances. See the Glossary of Enumerations for the outer category of the *thirty-two major marks* and the *eighty minor marks*.

120 For the Innermost Spirituality, refer to *History*, pp. 554-96.

121 During the creation stage of meditative experience (*bskyed-rim*, Skt. *utpattikrama*) the visualisation requires the meditator to invite the appropriate maṇḍala of deities from the expanse of reality, and then to make offerings and recite their mantras. The accomplishments which are attained thereby vary according to the nature of the maṇḍala.

122 This quotation occurs in the *Bhadracaryāpraṇidhānarāja* section of the *Sūtra of the Great Bounteousness of the Buddhas* (*Avataṃsakasūtra*), v. 3a.

123 The major and minor marks described here, which accord with the view of the Great Perfection, are considered to be the fourth or most secret kind of pristine cognition. Refer to p. 342.

124 The twofold bliss is that of the sixteen vowels which symbolise dis-

criminative awareness (*shes-rab*, Skt. *prajñā*) and the sixteen consonants which symbolise skilful means (*thabs*, Skt. *upāya*). During the perfection stage of contemplation (*rdzogs-rim*, Skt. *sampannakrama*) these seed-syllables of light occupy the right and left channels in the body respectively, but they intermingle in the central channel. (Our text here reads *phan-tshun ma-'dres...* instead of *phan-tshun 'dres-shing...*) Then, generating the coalescent bliss of discriminative awareness, or emptiness, and skilful means, or compassion, they give rise to the sixteen delights (*dga'-ba bcu-drug*). This experience is duplicated in accordance with the upward and downward movement of the vital energy (*rlung*, Skt. *vāyu*), and so these sixteen delights come to possess the thirty-two major marks of the buddha-body of perfect rapture. Each of the sixteen delights experienced in series by the male consort is also endowed with the five pristine cognitions, making a total of eighty minor marks. This is the resultant and primordial buddha-body, which is not created by an accumulation of causes and provisions. The feeling of receptiveness, which this surpasses, is an experience belonging to the path of connection (*sbyor-lam*, Skt. *prayogamārga*) in the causal phase of the vehicle (Khenpo Palden Sherap). See also Longcenpa, *Dispelling Darkness in the Ten Directions*, p. 460 (GGFTC, pp. 1015-17).

125 *rnam-pa mchog-dang ldan-pa'i stong-pa-nyid* is the emptiness in which the pure appearances of the buddha-body and pristine cognition are coalesced. See pp. 282-3.

126 See Pl. 2 for the maṇḍala of peaceful and wrathful deities.

127 *rdo-rje btsun-mo* (Skt. *Vajrayoṣit*) is the ḍākinī or female consort who embodies emptiness and the expanse of reality. Refer to Jamgön Kongtrül's discussion in *shes-bya kun-khyab mdzod*, Vol. 4, p. 411, in which the womb of the Vajra Queen is identified with emptiness free from conceptual elaboration and the buddha level itself.

128 Surendra or Devendra is the form assumed by the Buddha among the gods and Munīndra is his form as Śākyamuni among human beings. For the precise identification of *vaiḍūrya* as beryl and aquamarine, see Meyer, *Gso-ba rig-pa: le système médical tibétain*, p. 177. The English word beryl in fact shares a common origin with the Tamil *vēḷūr/bēlūr* and the Prakrit *veḷūriya* (Skt. *vaiḍūrya*). The terrain of beryl is the Trayatriṃśa heaven.

129 Vairocana is so called because he is the pure, enlightened nature of the component of form. Similarly, Akṣobhya-Vajrasattva is the king of consciousness, Ratnasambhava is the king of feeling, Amitābha is the king of discernment and Amoghasiddhi is the king of habitual tendencies.

130 The extraordinary Akaniṣṭha of the body of perfect rapture is perceived only by buddhas and tenth level bodhisattvas and is contrasted with the lower Akaniṣṭha realms of the emanational body which are visible to bodhisattvas below the tenth level. However the natural body of perfect rapture is strictly described as being manifest only to itself and not in an extraneous manner. The interpretation of this terse passage follows the oral commentary of Tülku Pema Wangyel.

131 Or "the lord of Yama's functionaries" (*las-kyi gshin-rje mgon*).

132 Tib. *rlung-dkyil* is the maṇḍala of wind, on which, according to the

Abhidharma, the physical universe is based.

133 Īśvara refers in this context not to Śiva but to Indra. Refer to Śūra, *Jātakamālā*, Peking *Tangyur*, Vol. 128, p. 21; and for Brahmā, ibid., pp. 21-2. Also see the Sanskrit version of the *Jātakamālā* (Darbhaṅga edn., BST 21); and its English translation by P. Khoroche, *Once the Buddha Was a Monkey*, Chs. 11, 17 and 29.

134 On Vemacitra, see the *Divyāvadāna*, 182.13; the *Sūtra of Extensive Play* (*Lalitavistara*), 241.3; and the *Mahāvastu*, 3.138.2.

135 The tale of the woodpecker is related by Śūra in the *Jātakamālā*, Ch. 34. For an English translation, see Āryaśūra, *The Marvelous Companion*, pp. 349-53; Khoroche, *Once the Buddha*, pp. 249-53.

136 For the tale of Dṛḍhasamādāna, see *Sūtra of the Wise and Foolish* (*mdo-mdzangs-blun*, T 341), Ch. 49.

137 Tib. *mu-ge'i tshe nya-bo-che*.

138 The noble creature (*srog-chags des-pa*) is the rohita fish. This is recounted by Peltrül Rinpoche in *The Words of My Perfect Teacher*, pp. 230-31.

139 For the horse Ājāneyabalaha, see the Pali *Valahassa Jātaka*, no. 196; and also R.A. Stein, *Recherches sur l'épopée et le barde au tibet*, pp. 426, 510-11, where *cang-shes balaha* is identified with Hayagrīva on the basis of the *bka'-gdams pha-chos bu-chos*, and as the mount of Ling Kesar.

140 The golden bee was an emanation of Avalokiteśvara. Refer to *Karaṇḍavyūhasūtra*, pp. 47ff., as cited in H. Dayal's *Bodhisattva Doctrine in Sanskrit Buddhist Literature*, p. 49.

141 The primary source for this section is Longcenpa, *Treasury of the Supreme Vehicle*, pp. 20-6.

142 I.e. the Indestructible Seat at Bodh Gayā. See p. 115 above and *History*, p. 409.

143 Tib. *sangs-rgyas stong-rtsa gcig* is interpreted by the Author in this context to mean the Thousand Buddhas. Longcenpa in the *Treasury of the Supreme Vehicle*, p. 24, reads *sangs-rgyas stong-dang rtsa gnyis*. In his *Dispelling Darkness in the Ten Directions*, p. 131, he explains the added two to be Vajrapāṇi and Mañjuśrī. Pawo Tsuklak Trhengwa in the *Scholar's Feast of Doctrinal History* (*dpa'-bo chos-'byung*), p. 200, maintains that in the *Penetration of Sound* (*sgra thal-'gyur*) the additional two are asserted to be *lha'i bu nyi-ma rab-tu snang-ba* and *dga'-byed dbang-phyug*.

144 Vajradhara is known as the sixth teacher because he presides over the maṇḍala of the Conquerors of the Five Enlightened Families: Vairocana, Akṣobhya, Ratnasambhava, Amitābha and Amoghasiddhi.

145 This is, of course, quite distinct from the Bodhi Tree at Vajrāsana (Author).

146 The eighth level experienced by bodhisattvas is known as the Immovable (*mi-gYo-ba*, Skt. *Acalā*) because there is no possibility of regression for one who reaches it.

147 I.e. the Bodhi Tree which subsequently became the location or Point of Enlightenment for Śākyamuni Buddha at Vajrāsana.

148 Refer to *History*, pp. 617-84.

149 For the views of the main proponents of the later Tibetan schools, refer to pp. 197-205.

150 The correspondence of the Tibetan to the Sanskrit is not precise for this particular verse.

151 Seminal point (*thig-le*, Skt. *bindu*) is the nucleus or seed of the enlightened mind which comprises a range of meanings, from the white and red seminal fluids of the physical body to the seminal points of light which appear during All-Surpassing Realisation. In this context, the white and red seminal points (*thig-le dkar-dmar*) are the sperm and ovum which, in union with vital energy (*rlung*), create the three world realms along with their appearances, and become the source of rebirth in saṃsāra. According to the resultant phase of the greater vehicle, these propensities are purified by the *empowerment of supreme desire* (*'dod-chags chen-po'i dbang-bskur*), whereas the *empowerment of great light rays* (*'od-zer chen-po'i dbang-bskur*) given in the causal phase of the greater vehicle merely purifies the two obscurations in a gradual way. For the distinctions between these two, see p. 247; *History*, pp. 912-13; and also Longcenpa, *Treasury of the Supreme Vehicle*, pp. 663-4.

152 Tib. *dam-pa'i bdag* is equivalent to Skt. *paramātmā*. It is explained in the *Supreme Continuum of the Greater Vehicle* that the true self is revealed when the dichotomy of self and non-self has been transcended (Ch. 1, v. 37): "It is true self owing to the quiescence of all conceptual elaboration with reference to self and non-self."

FUNDAMENTALS: PART THREE

153 The third promulgation is called irreversible because there is no possibility of its revelations being qualified or reversed, as is the case with the previous promulgations (Lama Sonam Topgyel).

154 I.e. Vajrāsana. See above, n. 110.

155 These three essential natures are explained below in accordance with Vijñānavāda, pp. 160-2; and according to Great Madhyamaka, pp. 169-77.

156 These behaviour patterns, which are mentally imposed, are held to be form by the Vaibhāṣika. Refer to the discussion in Mipham Rinpoche, *mkhas-pa'i tshul-la 'jug-pa'i sgo*, fols. 4a.3-4b.4.

157 See pp. 226-7 below; and the Glossary of Enumerations under *sixteen minor truths*.

158 Refer to the *Abhidharmakośavyākhyā*, Vol. 2, pp. 966-70, in which Yaśomitra compares this contemplation to a diamond drill which pierces all, because it pierces all dispositions.

159 See below, pp. 160-2, for the basic tenets of Mind Only.

160 The self-centred buddhas are said to be rhinoceros-like because they adhere to a course of solitary realisation, in which their meditation depends on the subtle subjective aspect of phenomena. See below, pp. 227-31.

161 For the background relevant to this quotation, refer to S. Lévi, *Matériaux pour l'étude du système Vijñaptimātrā*, p. 43, n. 1.

162 These are explained in Longcenpa, *Wish-fulfilling Treasury*, pp. 617-18. The third category holds sensa and consciousness to be mental attributes which are the two parts of one essential consciousness, in the manner of the white and the yolk of an egg.

163 The Vijñānavāda are still trapped within the subject-object dichotomy because they hold intrinsic awareness to exist in an absolute sense. They do not understand the coalescence of awareness and emptiness which is basic to the higher vehicles from Great Madhyamaka to the Great Perfection of Atiyoga (Tülku Pema Wangyel).

164 For the five axioms (*gtan-tshig lnga*), refer to Longcenpa, *Treasury of Spiritual and Philosophical Systems*, pp. 118ff.; and HIL 7.1, p. 112.

165 Tib. *yongs-gcod* is equivalent to Skt. *pariccheda*. The text wrongly reads *yongs-dpyod*.

166 Tib. *rnam-bcad*, Skt. *vyavaccheda*. The text reads *rnam-dpyad*.

167 These impure levels of realisation are the first seven attained by bodhisattvas. Refer to the Glossary of Enumerations under *ten levels*.

168 This text is by Āryadeva, yet may be attributed to Nāgārjuna in the sense that it was he who imparted the Madhyamaka teachings to Āryadeva (Khenpo Palden Sherap).

169 The Great Madhyamaka (*dbu-ma chen-po*) is also known as Yogācāra-Madhyamaka. As such it is not to be confused with the Yogācāra-Svātantrika school. It integrates the view that all things of saṃsāra are intrinsically empty (*rang-stong*) of their own inherent substantiality with the view that all enlightened attributes are empty of those extraneous phenomena (*gzhan-stong*). See below, pp. 183-6. The quotation given here does not occur in the extant Tibetan text of Bhavya's *Madhyamakaratnapradīpa*, rather it paraphrases passages found on fols. 280-1 of the Derge canonical edn. of the text: *dbu-ma*, Vol. *Tsha*.

170 This verse also occurs in the *Ornament of Emergent Realisation*, Ch. 5, v. 21.

171 Refer to D. T. Suzuki, *The Laṅkāvatāra Sūtra*, p. 136. A variant reading would be "the subject, object and sensations". See above, p. 55.

172 These are exemplified by the *Five Doctrines of Maitreya* (*byams-chos sde-lnga*), and the *Trilogy of Commentaries by Bodhisattvas* (*byang-chub sems-'grel-gyi skor-gsum*). Refer to the first part of the Bibliography.

173 Tib. *sbyang-bzhi*, Skt. **caturdhā vyavadāna*, is unidentified. Perhaps the purification of the *four perverted views* (see Glossary of Enumerations) is intended.

174 The Guru of Suvarṇadvīpa (*gser-gling-pa*) or Sumatra was also known as Dharmakīrti and Dharmapāla. He was Atiśa's teacher. See Tāranātha, *History of Buddhism in India*, p. 213n.

175 The third level of bodhisattva realisation is known as the Illuminating (*'od-byed*, Skt. *Prabhākarī*).

176 The Vaibhāṣika, Sautrāntika and Vijñānavāda systems.

177 This refers to the tendency to miss the experience of reality (*chos-nyid*) or emptiness, and to reduce the apparitional reality (*chos-can*) into categories which are then invested with substantial existence. This occurs in the Vaibhāṣika, Sautrāntika and Vijñānavāda systems.

178 These three kinds of tantra or continuum are explained below, pp. 263-7.

179 These are held to be the four attributes of absolute reality, according to the *Supreme Continuum of the Greater Vehicle*.

180 This quotation is from the *Sūtra of Queen Śrīmālā* (*Śrīmālādevīsūtra*). Cf. A. and H. Wayman (trans.), *The Lion's Roar of Queen Śrīmālā*, p. 106.

181 Tib. *gzhung-lam*, Skt. *granthamārga*, refers to the texts and path of the teaching on the Transcendental Perfection of Discriminative Awareness (*Prajñāpāramitā*), which is central to the bodhisattva vehicle.

182 Through their methodical order and planning such activities are said to be indicative of the transmitted precepts taught by Śākyamuni Buddha.

183 This nature is respectively the buddha-body of form (*gzugs-sku*, Skt. *rūpakāya*) and the buddha-body of reality (*chos-sku*, Skt. *dharmakāya*).

184 The paths of learning (*slob-pa'i lam*, Skt. *śaikṣamārga*) are the first four gradual paths traversed by bodhisattvas, i.e. those of provisions, connection, insight and meditation. The fifth path is that of no-more-learning, or the final path (*aśaikṣamārga/niṣṭhamārga*). See also n. 382.

185 There is an account of this incident during a past life of Śākyamuni in Peltrül Rinpoche, *kun-bzang bla-ma'i zhal-lung*, pp. 192bff.

186 This Tathāgata Śākyamuni was the first teacher of Śākyamuni Buddha.

187 Refer to the section on nihilism, pp. 66-7.

188 The Archer is Saraha.

189 For Terdak Lingpa's biography, see *History*, pp. 825-9; and for his brother, Locen Dharmaśrī, pp. 728-32.

190 On Mipham Rinpoche, who is known as Mipham Namgyel Gyamtso or Mipham Jampel Gyepa, see *History*, pp. 869-80.

191 On Atiśa, the founder of the Kadampa tradition, see *Blue Annals*, pp. 242ff.; A. Chattopadhyaya, *Atiśa and Tibet*; and H. Eimer's works on Atiśa which are detailed in the final section of the Bibliography.

192 On Tilopā, refer to Tāranātha, *History of Buddhism in India*, p. 299n.; and to H. V. Guenther (trans.), *The Life and Teaching of Nāropā*. For the lives of Tilopā and the other great accomplished masters mentioned in the following pages, see J. Robinson, *Buddha's Lions*; and K. Dowman, *Masters of Mahāmudrā*.

193 See Guenther, *The Life and Teaching of Nāropā*.

194 On Advayavajra or Maitripā, see *Blue Annals*, p. 731; and *Advayavajrasaṃgraha*.

195 On Saraha, refer to H. V. Guenther (trans.), *The Royal Song of Saraha*; and to M. Shahidullah, *Les Chants Mystiques de Kanḥa et de Saraha*.

196 Saraha appeared in a dream to Marpa Lotsāwa and this song is a recollection of the teaching he received. See Nalanda Translation Committee, *The Life of Marpa*, p. 46.

197 On Milarepa, refer to L. Lhalungpa (trans.), *The Life of Milarepa*; G. C. C. Chang (trans.), *The Hundred Thousand Songs of Milarepa*; and *Blue Annals*, pp. 427-37.

198 On Gampopa or Takpo Lharje, see sGam-po-pa, *The Jewel Ornament of Liberation*; also *Blue Annals*, pp. 451-62.

199 Ngamdzong Tönpa was one of Marpa's four main students who transmitted the Kagyü tradition. See *Blue Annals*, pp. 435-7, 449.

200 On Zhang Rinpoche, see *Blue Annals*, pp. 711ff.; also *History*, pp. 655 and 921.

201 On Karmapa III, Rangjung Dorje, refer to *History*, pp. 572-4 and 666; also refer to Karma Thinley, *The History of the Sixteen Karmapas of Tibet*, pp. 55-8.

202 On Karmapa VII, Chödrak Gyamtso, see Thinley, *The History of the Sixteen Karmapas of Tibet*, pp. 83-7.

203 For Situ VIII, Dharmākara, refer to E. G. Smith's introduction to *The Autobiography and Diaries of Situ Paṇ-chen*.

204 This is the *dri-ma med-pa zhes-bya-ba'i-cher 'grel-pa* which is contained in the *sa-skya bka'-'bum*, Vol. 5, no. 65.

205 This work is no. 98 in the *sa-skya bka'-'bum*, Vol. 5. Our text wrongly reads *snye-mo sgom-chen-gyis dris-lan*.

206 On the life of Tsongkapa, see *Blue Annals*, pp. 1073-9; R. Kaschewsky, *Das Leben des lamaistischen Heiligen Tsoṅ-kha-pa Blo-bzaṅ grags-pa*; and R. A. F. Thurman (ed.), *The Life and Teachings of Tsong Khapa*.

207 On Tölpopa Sangye or Sherap Gyeltsen, see n. 1309; *Blue Annals*, pp. 775-7; and C. Stearns, *Buddha from Dolpo*.

208 Tib. *gsang-mdzad*. This reading is recommended by Lama Sonam Topgyel in preference to that given in the text, which would read "secret repositories" or "treasuries" (*gsang-mdzod*).

209 These three synonyms for ultimate reality in the outer tantras are respectively derived from Kriyātantra, Ubhayatantra and Yogatantra. See pp. 269-73.

210 See D. S. Ruegg, "Le Dharmadhātustava de Nāgārjuna" in *Études tibetaines dediées à la memoire de Marcelle Lalou*, p. 466.

211 Cf. Nāgārjuna, *Root Stanzas on the Madhyamaka entitled Discriminative Awareness* (*Mūlamadhyamakakārikā*), Ch. 18, v. 6.

212 Tib. *bde-chen-zhing*. As cited above on p. 127, this is the preferred reading. Here, however, our text gives *bde-gshegs-zhing*.

213 This incident occurs at the end of the first chapter of the *Vimalakīrtinirdeśasūtra*, in which Brahmā Śikhin considered the buddha-fields to be pure and Śāriputra held them to be impure. After their debate, the Buddha intervened to say that the buddha-fields are always pure when seen with pure vision, whereas Śāriputra could not actually see this purity. This is also recounted elsewhere, e.g. by Mipham Rinpoche in his *spyi-don 'od-gsal snying-po*, p. 78.

214 Tib. *ri-dvags me'i gtsang-sbra-can* is a legendary species of wildlife which holds fire to be not hot but purificatory. It is referred to in the texts of Madhyamaka (Khenpo Tsewang Dongyel).

215 This verse is also given in Ch. 10, v. 638.

216 Tib. *gang-zag*. The text reads *gang-dag*.

217 Tib. *bram-ze'i 'jig-tshogs-kyi lta-ba* refers to the view of the eternalistic extremists, which is said to have twenty aspects. See Mipham Rinpoche, *grub-mtha'i mdzod bsdus-pa*, p. 71; and S. Collins, *Selfless Persons*, pp. 118-19.

218 On Ngok Loden Sherap, refer to *Blue Annals*, pp. 328ff.

219 Tib. *ma bral-bas*. The text wrongly reads *bral-bas*.

220 The text ascribes this treatise to Nāgārjuna, although in the colophon of the Peking edn., Vol. 83, p. 90, 5.5, it clearly states that Vimalamitra entrusted it to Nyak Jñānakumāra in Phenyül.

221 The theory of atomism developed in the Vaibhāṣika school was decisively rejected by the Vijñānavāda, and probably also by the Sautrāntika. See M. Kapstein "Mereological Considerations in Vasubandhu's 'Proof of Idealism'" in *Reason's Traces*.

222 Refer to the Glossary of Enumerations under *eight vows of the prātimokṣa*.

223 These are referred to in the Glossary of Enumerations under *five, eight,*

ten and all things to be renounced.

224 See below, p. 229.

225 This is a meditative experience occurring on the path of connection (*sbyor-lam*). See below, p. 236; also Longcenpa, *Treasury of Spiritual and Philosophical Systems*, pp. 142-6.

226 I.e. they are superior to the pious attendants.

227 Although the ignorance which gives rise to the three poisons is reversed by the self-centred buddhas, the subject is not yet realised to be empty of the three interrelated aspects of ignorance. Refer to p. 54.

228 These first four paths are identical to the four paths of learning outlined above on p. 175, namely, the paths of provision, connection, insight and meditation. The three paths referred to are the first three of these.

229 This verse is probably derived from the *theg-chen rnal-'byor-la 'jug-pa*, which has only recently become available. Refer to nn. 608, 896 below; and to *Blue Annals*, pp. 999-1001, for Aro Yeshe Jungne.

230 This rendering follows the meaning of the Tibetan. For a detailed discussion of the Indian origins of the term *bodhisattva*, refer to A. L. Basham's contribution to L. Kawamura (ed.), *The Bodhisattva in Asian Culture*.

231 In this classification of seven *prātimokṣa* vows, the lay vows for men (*upāsaka*) and the lay vows for women (*upāsikā*) are combined so that the generally known eight vows of the *prātimokṣa* become seven. See the quotation cited above on p. 226 from the *Treasury of the Abhidharma*.

232 These meditative experiences on the path of connection, known as the feeling of warmth (*drod*), its climax (*rtse-mo*), the feeling of receptiveness (*bzod*) and the supreme phenomenon (*chos-mchog*) are explained in Longcenpa, *Treasury of Spiritual and Philosophical Systems*, pp. 142-6. For an overall account of the bodhisattva path, refer to Dayal, *The Bodhisattva Doctrine in Sanskrit Buddhist Literature*, Ch. 4.

233 The ninth level of bodhisattva realisation is known as Excellent Intelligence (*legs-pa'i blo-gros*, Skt. *Sādhumatī*).

FUNDAMENTALS: PART FOUR

234 It is the bodhisattva vehicle, among the causal vehicles of dialectics, which is also known as the vehicle of transcendental perfection.

235 The unsurpassed vehicle of the tantras in general is here contrasted with the higher view of the tantras belonging to the vehicle of skilful means. "Purity and suffering" (*rnam-par byang-ba-dang sdug-bsngal*) refer respectively to the last two and the first two sublime truths.

236 The maṇḍala of seals (*phyag-rgya'i dkyil-'khor*) refers to the seals of the deity's body, speech and mind.

237 The abiding nature of inconceivable reality is held to be vast because it contains manifold skilful means, and profound because it is essentially discriminative awareness and emptiness.

238 Refer, e.g., to Jamgön Kongtrül, *shes-bya kun-khyab mdzod*, Vol. 2, pp. 656-82; and to Mipham Rinpoche, *spyi-don 'od-gsal snying-po*, pp. 146-8. The vehicle of indestructible reality employs a series of four empowerments which enable one's awareness of pure enlightened

attributes to ripen. The four are known as the vase empowerment (*bum-dbang*), the secret empowerment (*gsang-dbang*), the empowerment of discriminating pristine cognition (*shes-rab ye-shes-kyi dbang*) and the empowerment of word and meaning (*tshig-don-gi dbang*); see also below, p. 360. Among them, the third empowerment reveals the secret appearance of the deity and emphasises meditation on the perfection stage, leading to the eventual realisation of the body of reality through union with the ḍākinī, embodiment of emptiness.

239 During empowerment, when creatively visualised as the deity, the meditator is known as the Being of Commitment (*dam-tshig sems-dpa'*, Skt. *samayasattva*). Subsequently, the entry of the actual deity into this Being of Commitment is referred to as the "descent of the Being of Pristine Cognition" (*ye-shes sems-dpa'i dbab-pa*, Skt. *jñānasattva-patana*). This is also known as the "irresistible descent of pristine cognition" (*ye-shes btsan-thabs-su dbab-pa*).

240 These seven aspects of spiritual wealth according to ultimate truth are therefore the ultimate truth of the expanse, the ultimate truth of pristine cognition, and the ultimate truth of original natural cessation which has five aspects corresponding to the buddha-body, speech, mind, enlightened attributes and activities.

241 It is said that the gods perceive water as nectar, humans and animals perceive it as a drink, tormented spirits perceive it as pus and blood, and the denizens of hell see it as molten lava, whereas the buddhas perceive it as the divine consort Māmakī.

242 Tib. *'gyur ma-yin*. Our text reads *'gyur-ba-yin*; refer to the Peking *Tangyur*: *rgyud-'grel*, Vol. 81, p. 297.4.1.

243 It is the causal buddha-body of form (*rgyu'i gzugs-sku*) which is visualised on the path, in contrast to the resultant buddha-body of form (*'bras-bu'i gzugs-sku*) described above, pp. 123ff.

244 The desired qualities (*'dod-yon*, Skt. *kāmaguṇa*) are the pleasurable enjoyments of the five senses.

245 Tib. *don-dam-du ni mnyam-rdzogs-la*. Compare the alternative reading for this line on p. 245 above (i.e. *don-dam-du ni dbyer-med-la*).

246 The three maṇḍalas here refer to the view, commitment and conduct of secret mantra (Lama Sonam Topgyel).

247 See the quotation from *Tantra of the Inconceivable Rali Cakrasaṃvara* on p. 248 above.

248 Each of the levels is simultaneously the renunciation of an obscuration and the application of an appropriate antidote. See the Glossary of Enumerations for the *ten*, *eleven* or *sixteen levels*.

249 The deity's seal which secures all appearances within the maṇḍala of buddha-body is known as the great seal (*phyag-rgya chen-po*, Skt. *Mahāmudrā*). See below, p. 258.

250 In order for all appearances to be secured by the great seal of the deity's form, a melting bliss is generated within the energy channels by the fusion and melting of the seed syllables E and VAṂ, symbolising the coalescence of emptiness (E) and bliss (VAṂ). It is said that this coalescence is a prerequisite for all buddhas who become enlightened. The co-emergent bliss (*sahajasukha*) is the transmuted sexual energy issuing from the pulse of the seminal point of desire within the central channel of the body. Through this transmutation the propensities

which lead to rebirth in saṃsāra are reversed.

251 Among these, medicinal pills extracted from herbal and mineral essences promote longevity, eye-salve promotes supernormal vision, and the enchanted sword cuts through obscuration. On the accomplishment of "swift feet", refer to *History*, p. 614.

252 Tib. *lta-ba'i lung*. Our text wrongly reads *rlung* for *lung*.

253 On these four attributes, see Jamgön Kongtrül, *shes-bya kun-khyab mdzod*, Peking edn., Vol. 2, pp. 611ff.

254 Concerning the meditations on the presence of the buddha-body of reality in the heart centre: in the context of the Mahāyoga path of skilful means, see Longcenpa, *Dispelling Darkness in the Ten Directions*, p. 455 (GGFTC, p. 1010); and in the context of Atiyoga meditation, ibid., pp. 463ff. (GGFTC, pp.1022ff.) On the pure and impure expressions of the seed-syllables in the body which give rise to buddhahood or saṃsāra, see the same source, pp. 172ff. (GGFTC, pp. 552ff.)

255 For the tradition of the Zur family, refer to *History*, pp. 617-49.

256 Tib. *bya-min* literally means "non-Kriyā", i.e. the Caryātantra or Ubhayatantra.

257 Quoted by Longcenpa in his *sngags-kyi spyi-don tshangs-dbyangs 'brug-sgra*, p. 52.

258 See n. 1380 below.

259 This point is explained in the Glossary of Enumerations under *four kinds of desire*. Refer also to *History*, p. 413.

260 These six modes indicate the gradual appearance of the deity out of emptiness. See also below, p. 351.

261 For the distinction between the higher secret mantra (*gsang-sngags*), and the lower gnostic mantras (*rig-sngags*), see the Glossary of Enumerations under *three kinds of mantra*.

262 Syllables conjoined with syllables form mantra chains such as the Hundred-Syllable Mantra of Vajrasattva (*yig-brgya*).

263 These four yogas are generally known as the four miracles (*cho-'phrul bzhi*). Refer to p. 356 below.

264 See p. 255, n. 249.

265 For the historical background to the origin of these tantras and their means for attainment, the *sādhana* classes of Mahāyoga, see *History*, pp. 458-83.

266 Tib. *mnyam-gnyis*. Refer, e.g., to Mipham Rinpoche, *spyi-don 'od-gsal snying-po*, pp. 99-100. Our text reads *mnyam-nyid*.

267 Skt. *mākṣika*. This is a specific kind of mercury which is reputedly employed as a catalyst for the transmutation of iron into gold. Refer to Mipham Rinpoche, *spyi-don 'od-gsal snying-po*, pp. 48-9.

268 The upper and lower doors refer respectively to the higher centres and the secret or sexual centre, either in one's own body or in that of one's partner. See also Longcenpa, *Dispelling Darkness in the Ten Directions*, pp. 453ff. (GGFTC, pp. 1006ff.); and the Glossary of Enumerations under *six centres forming the "upper door" of the body*.

269 These occur during the practice of the inner heat (*gtum-mo*).

270 Refer to the Glossary of Enumerations under *four branches of ritual service and attainment*.

271 Tib. *rin-po-che kaustubha* according to Mipham Rinpoche, *spyi-don 'od-gsal snying-po*, pp. 48-9, is applied to the base metal which extracts

gold. In classical Indian mythology Kaustubha is the name of Viṣṇu's gem, which was obtained during the churning of the primeval ocean.

272 This refers to the dissolution of the physical elements and the mental faculties at death.

273 The mental body (*yid-kyi lus*) is the form assumed by consciousness during the intermediate state of reality (*chos-nyid bar-do*) and the intermediate state of rebirth (*srid-pa bar-do*), i.e. after death and before rebirth. See W. Y. Evans-Wentz (ed.), *The Tibetan Book of the Dead*, pp. 85ff.; or F. Fremantle and C. Trungpa, *The Tibetan Book of the Dead*, pp. 33ff.

274 On melting bliss (*zhu-bde*), see n. 250 above.

275 The male and female yogins (*rnal-'byor pho-mo*) are peripheral in the maṇḍala, and so form the retinue of the central or foremost divine consorts (*gtso-bo yab-yum*).

276 For a discussion on this verse and the empowered awareness (*dbang-bsgyur rigs*), or that awareness which has power over the life-span, refer to Longcenpa, *Dispelling Darkness in the Ten Directions*, pp. 361-3, 466 (GGFTC, pp. 852, 1027). Other passages in the literature of the *Sequence of the Path of the Magical Net*, however, suggest "empowered family" as an alternative rendering of this phrase. See, e.g., the *Litany of the Names of Mañjuśrī* (*Mañjuśrīnāmasaṃgīti*), vv. 23-4, and Mañjuśrīmitra's comments as given in R.M. Davidson's translation of the text in MCB 20 (1981), n. 62.

277 As explained above in n. 144, Vajradhara is known as the sixth regent (*rgyal-tshab drug-pa*) because he is the spontaneous presence of the Five Conquerors and the five buddha-bodies.

278 For the origins of the *Eighteen Great Tantrapiṭaka* of Mahāyoga and the eight classes of means for attainment, refer to *History*, pp. 458ff.

279 These eight classes each represent a large number of tantra texts, as found in the *Collected Tantras of the Nyingmapa*. A principle tantra of each is also contained in the *Kangyur* (*bka'-'gyur*), T 838-44 and 439.

280 For the classification of *Kālacakra* as Mother Tantra, see Jamgön Kongtrül, *shes-bya kun-khyab mdzod*, Vol. 3, p. 232.

281 The *General Sūtra which Gathers All Intentions* is the exegesis of the *Root Tantra of All-Gathering Awareness*.

282 Tib. *kara* is a corrupt form of Skt. *ākara*, meaning "source". The source of all display (*rol-pa'i kara*) is the sexual centre of the consort.

283 These include the axioms of Madhyamaka outlined in pp. 163-4; and the axioms of Mahāyoga, pp. 275-6.

284 Tib. *gzhag-nas*. Our text reads *gzhag-na* in accordance with the Peking *Kangyur*, Vol. 9. However, the preferred reading is cited below on p. 368.

285 I.e. in an immediate manner without requiring the gradual creation of the visualisation as in Mahāyoga.

286 The following *ten levels* and *five paths* known to Anuyoga correspond to those of the causal vehicles discussed in Pt. 3. Refer also to the Glossary of Enumerations.

287 When a bodhisattva has advanced on the path of meditation he receives a prophetic declaration from the buddhas in which the time and circumstances for his own future buddhahood are revealed. See, e.g., the life of Tsangtönpa in *History*, pp. 691-3.

288 For the path of great desire, refer to the discussion on the necessity of the empowerment into this path on p. 152.

289 This refinement ends the cycle of rebirth in saṃsāra.

290 *srog-chen-po'i rlung* is a synonym for egotism and ignorance. Tib. *srog-chags*, which means living creatures or insects in this context, is a code standing for the "vital energy of great life-breath".

291 These rites of sexual union (*sbyor*) and "liberation" (*sgrol*) are referred to in *History*, pp. 617-49 and 660-70. For a detailed discussion, refer to Longcenpa, *Dispelling Darkness in the Ten Directions*, pp. 386-402 (GGFTC, pp. 899-922). For their abuse during the tenth century, refer to R. A. Stein, *Tibetan Civilization*, pp. 71-2; and S. G. Karmay, "The Ordinance of Lha Bla-ma Ye-shes 'od" in TSHR, pp. 150-62. Here "liberation" means the forceful removal of consciousness from the body of another and its transference to a higher level of rebirth.

292 Tib. *mi-nag mdung-thung-can bsod-pa*. In a previous life, Śākyamuni Buddha "liberated" an assailant who almost murdered five hundred merchants, in order to release him from rebirth in the hells. See Peltrül Rinpoche, *The Words of My Perfect Teacher*, p. 125, and the *theg-chen gsang-ba chen-po thabs-la mkhas-pa'i mdo* referred to in that text.

293 Tib. *ded-dpon-gyi bu-mo-la bsgrod-pa*. This is an incident recounted in Peltrül Rinpoche, *The Words of My Perfect Teacher*, pp. 125-6, which describes the compassionate association of Karma, a celibate young brāhman, with a brāhman girl.

294 The text here reads *nye-ba'i rnal-'byor*, i.e. Upayoga, the "approximate yoga".

295 Tib. *mtshan-ma yod-med* refers to the symbolic and non-symbolic methods of meditation which correspond respectively to the relative and ultimate truths.

296 I.e. Nāgārjuna and Asaṅga.

297 These are the Unsurpassed tantras according to the new translation schools. See Lessing and Wayman, *Mkhas Grub Rje's Fundamentals of the Buddhist Tantras*, pp. 250ff.

298 The black outline (*re-kha nag-po*) is the form assumed by the central channel as a mark of success in the practices of vital energy according to the *Kālacakra Tantra*. Although all the pure appearances of the deities are reflected within it, the body of rainbow light cannot be obtained. Refer to Jamgön Kongtrül, *shes-bya kun-khyab mdzod*, Vol. 4, p. 185.

299 Through the action seal (*las-rgya*, Skt. *karmamudrā*), the result of an awareness-holder of the desire realm is attained. It is the yoga pertaining to the sexual centre of one's partner. The result of an awareness-holder of the form realm is secured by the seal of pristine cognition (*ye-shes-kyi phyag-rgya*, Skt. *jñānamudrā*).

300 Refer to p. 247, n. 238 above.

301 Refer to p. 288 for the path of desire (*chags-lam*).

302 The vajra and bell are ritual implements which respectively symbolise skilful means and discriminative awareness.

303 I.e. the non-Buddhist schools and systems.

304 Tib. *thig-le chen-po* is a synonym for the buddha-body of reality. See the Index of Technical Terms under *seminal point*.

305 Tib. *mi-'jig-pa*. The text wrongly reads *mi-'jigs-pa*. Compare the same

quotation as cited on p. 181.

306 For an explanation of this verse, see Guenther, *Buddhist Philosophy in Theory and Practice*, pp. 200-2.

307 The "second stage which is the essence" refers to the perfection stage (*rdzogs-rim*). The second stage of this second stage is known as the Great Perfection (*rdzogs-chen*) because the perfection stage can be either symbolic (*mtshan-yod rdzogs-rim*) or non-symbolic (*mtshan-med rdzogs-rim*), and it is the latter which is referred to as the Great Perfection.

308 Refer to the Glossary of Enumerations under *ten levels*. The first is known as the Joyful (*rab-tu dga'-ba*, Skt. *Pramuditā*). The seventh is known as the Far-Reaching (*ring-du song-ba*, Skt. *Dūraṅgamā*). The eighth and tenth levels are mentioned in nn. 116, 146 and 385.

309 The buddhas of the surpassed levels are those who have accomplished the respective realisations of the systems just mentioned.

310 I.e. the single essence is not obtained through the subject-object dichotomy.

311 Tib. *gti-mug ma-gsal cig*. The same quotation cited on p. 899 of the *History*, reads *gti-mug ma-bsam cig*. Similarly the following line reads *rang-gi lus-las gyen-du ma-bskyod cig*, whereas the equivalent line cited in the *History* reads *rang-gi lus-las gyen-du ma-spyod cig*.

312 This interpretation follows the oral commentary of Lama Sonam Topgyel.

313 These are spontaneous axioms which arise internally and replace the lower axioms of Madhyamaka and Mahāyoga which are contrived by the intellect.

314 The text reads *yin-tu smra-ba*, after the reading in Longcenpa, *Treasury of Spiritual and Philosophical Systems*, p. 337. An alternative suggested tentatively by Khenpo Palden Sherap would read "freely" (*yan-tu*) for *yin-tu*.

315 This and the subsequent divisions and cycles of the Esoteric Instructional Class are indicated in terms of their essence (*ngo-bo*, i.e. "essentially"), their natural expression (*rang-bzhin*, i.e. "naturally") and their character (*mtshan-nyid*, i.e. "characteristically"), which correspond respectively to the buddha-bodies of reality, perfect rapture and emanation.

316 In other words, the moment of death and liberation are simultaneous.

317 Tib. *rtog-pa* means thought. Our text erroneously reads *rtogs-pa*, i.e. realisation.

318 Interpreted according to the oral commentary of Tülku Pema Wangyel.

319 The nucleus or awareness which is reality's expanse arises as a series of seminal points of light which are known as indestructible chains (of light). When this expanse is fully mature, the three world realms dissolve into inner radiance.

320 For the channels and vital energy within the body, see the Glossary of Enumerations under *ten kinds of vital energy* and *six centres forming the "upper door" of the body*. See also the disussion in Longcenpa, *Dispelling Darkness in the Ten Directions*, pp. 453ff. (GGFTC, pp. 1006ff.); and in Jamgön Kongtrül, *shes-bya kun-khyab mdzod*, Vol. 2, pp. 631-45.

321 See n. 151 above.

322 The forehead centre corresponds to the god realms, the throat centre

to the antigods, the heart centre to human beings, the navel centre to animals, the secret centre to tormented spirits and the soles of the feet to the denizens of the hot and cold hells. Through these practices of the perfection stage (*rdzogs-rim*), the vital energy and mind remain in these centres, saṃsāra is not transcended, and rebirth consequently occurs.

323 Whereas in the perfection stage the vital energy and mind remain in the centres after entering from the left and right channels in the form of the white and red seminal points and releasing the knots in the central channel, in All-Surpassing Realisation this purification is not required because the vital energy of pristine cognition naturally causes the channels to vanish into light. According to Longcenpa, *Wish-fulfilling Treasury*, pp. 851-8, there are twenty-one knots altogether, twenty of which are divided into pairs corresponding to their location in the right and left channels. Their vanishing in ten pairs also corresponds to the renunciation and realisation of the ten levels.

324 These particular appearances of the hundred buddha-fields and contemplations correspond to the realisation of the first level, through the vanishing of the first pair of knotted channels into light.

325 This text belongs to the *Great Perfection endowed with Conch-Syllables* (*dung-yig-can*) from the *Innermost Spirituality of Vimalamitra*, Pt. 2, Vol. *Cha*, pp. 1-159.

326 The biographies of Zurcungpa Sherap-tra and his son Dropukpa are presented in the *History*, pp. 635-49. For the four "pillars", see pp. 640ff. The source for the material found in the recapitulations of this and the previous chapter is Locen Dharmaśrī, *gsang-bdag zhal-lung*.

327 I.e. the Kriyātantra which realises the three enlightened families and the Yogatantra which realises the five enlightened families are here said to be equivalent to the common vehicles of the bodhisattvas and so forth because their realisation is incomplete.

328 Refer to *History*, p. 701.

329 *History*, p. 653.

330 *History*, pp. 667-8.

331 *History*, pp. 666-7.

332 Tib. *ye-shes yon-tan kun-rdzob lha*. Compare the identical passage cited above on p. 270. Here, our text gives *ye-shes bzhi-yon kun-rdzob lha* in conformity with the Peking *Tangyur* (P 3736), Vol. 83, p. 106.4.2. The Author and Khenpo Palden Sherap prefer the former reading.

333 For a detailed account of these and the succeeding empowerments, refer to Longcenpa, *Dispelling Darkness in the Ten Directions*, pp. 370-9, (GGFTC, pp. 369-81); and to Jamgön Kongtrül, *shes-bya kun-khyab mdzod*, Vol. 2, pp. 656-82, 737-9. See also the Glossary of Enumerations under *fifteen ordinary sacraments (of empowerment)*. The water and crown empowerments employ their appropriate symbolic implements to purify obscurations respectively into the mirror-like pristine cognition and the pristine cognition of sameness.

334 These sublime, gentle and rough appearances are purified when they are seen respectively as Mañjuśrī who is sublime in discriminative awareness, Avalokiteśvara who is gentle in compassion, and Vajrapāṇi who is rough in power. These are the Lords of the Three Enlightened Families (*rigs-gsum mgon-po*) which pertain to Kriyātantra, and on

whom see also *History*, pp. 452-4.

335 Tib. *yig*. The text wrongly reads *yid*.

336 On the distinction between the Being of Commitment and the Being of Pristine Cognition, see n. 239 above.

337 Tib. *sangs-rgyas sa*. Compare the identical passage above on p. 270. At this point, our text reads *sangs-rgyas-pa*. The former, however, is preferred by the Author.

338 The symbolic implements of these three empowerments are employed to purify obscurations respectively into Amitābha's pristine cognition of discernment, Amoghasiddhi's pristine cognition of accomplishment and Vairocana's pristine cognition of reality's expanse. These and the preceding two are all aspects of the outer vase empowerment (*phyi bum-pa'i dbang*). See also n. 333 above.

339 Tib. *rdo-rje 'chang-sar*. Compare the same verse cited above on p. 272. Here the text reads *rdo-rje 'chang-bar*.

340 The sixth empowerment is known as that of the master or that of the irreversible vase, which seals the previous five and so confers the ability to transmit the teaching. Refer also to n. 333 above.

341 Unidentified. Perhaps he is Lentön Śākya Zangpo. Refer to *History*, p. 640.

342 Garap Dorje was the first human preceptor of the Great Perfection. See *History*, pp. 490-3. The prefix *ru* means "first" or "predecessor", and in this case indicates his primacy in the lineage (Khenpo Palden Sherap).

343 These are two of the four "pillars" who were students of Zurcungpa. See *History*, pp. 640ff.

344 Kyo Kongbupa was also among the four "pillars"; *History*, pp. 640ff.

345 *History*, p. 622.

346 See n. 333 above. The conferral of these four empowerments, beginning with the common vase empowerment, is held to result in the maturation respectively of the emanational body, the body of perfect rapture, the body of reality and the essential body.

347 These include ten aspects of beneficence and five of ability. See Longcenpa, *Dispelling Darkness in the Ten Directions*, pp. 372-9 (GGFTC, pp. 871-81); and the Glossary of Enumerations under *fifteen ordinary sacraments (of empowerment)*.

348 Tib. *grol-phyir-du*. Compare the same passage above on p. 249. Here the text reads *grol-phyir las*, but the former reading is preferred.

349 See the Glossary of Enumerations under *twenty-eight commitments of Mahāyoga*.

350 This is Vimalamitra's commentary on the *Root Tantra of the Secret Nucleus*.

351 Examples of such practices are the ceremonies for the commemoration of Padmasambhava on the tenth day (*tshes-bcu*), and for the commemoration of the ḍākinīs on the twenty-fifth day (*nyer-lnga*).

352 Tib. *sgrol*, Skt. *tana*, according to the intentional language (Skt. *sandhyābhāṣā*), refers to the rites of forceful "liberation". Tib. *sbyor*, Skt. *gaṇa*, according to the secret language, refers to sexual practices. See above, pp. 292-3.

353 Tib. *brgyad-brgya so-gcig*. The text wrongly reads *brgyad-brgya-po-gcig*. See Jamgön Kongtrül, *shes-bya kun-khyab mdzod*, Vol. 2, pp. 748-9.

354 The seals connected with the deity in Yogatantra and Mahāyoga are here contrasted with those of Anuyoga, which take immediate effect.

355 This empowerment is the initial entrance into the Great Perfection. For its subdivisions, refer to Longcenpa, *Treasury of Spiritual and Philosophical Systems*, pp. 370-2; and to *History*, p. 501.

356 These terms have a specific meaning in the context of Atiyoga, as elaborated by Longcenpa in *The Treasury of the Abiding Nature of Reality* (*gnas-lugs rin-po-che'i mdzod*), and are, of course, unconnected with the mundane views of apathy and nihilism, for which the same terms are applied in Tibetan (i.e. *phyal-pa* and *med-pa*).

FUNDAMENTALS: CONCLUSION

357 On Locen Dharmaśrī, see *History*, pp. 728-31; on Gyurme Tshewang Chokdrup, p. 736; on Jamgön Kongtrül, pp. 859-68; on Dodrup Jikme Tenpei Nyima, p. 879; and on Zhecen Gyeltsap, pp. 879 and 919.

358 These scriptures are partly enumerated in *History*, p. 591. For an enumeration of the *Seven [Great] Treasuries* (*mdzod-bdun*) of Longcenpa, refer to the first part of the Bibliography.

359 This is the *Four-Part Innermost Spirituality* (*snying-thig ya-bzhi*) which was redacted by Longcenpa. See *History*, pp. 554-96, for the background to this tradition.

360 This is a metaphor for the violation of the commitment not to divulge the secret teachings to an unsuitable recipient.

361 The personal names of the Author which are built into the structure of the verse introduce the Colophon.

362 The sponsor was one Ngawang Samdrup of Tingri who received the name Pelhün Yülgyel in a dream (Lama Sonam Topgyel).

2 *History*

HISTORY: INTRODUCTORY VERSES

363 This refers to the fundamental Buddhist view of dependent origination (*rten-cing 'brel-bar 'byung-ba*, Skt. *pratītyasamutpāda*), the Nyingmapa interpretation of which is summarised in *Fundamentals*, pp. 54-7. The verse as a whole is addressed to the Buddha, the first of the Three Precious Jewels.

364 Concerning the transmission or scriptural authorisation (*lung*, Skt. *āgama*) of the true doctrine and its realisation (*rtogs-pa*, Skt. *adhigama*), the *Treasury of the Abhidharma* (Ch. 8, v. 39cd) says:

> The two kinds of the Teacher's true doctrine
> Are transmission and realisation.

For their divisions and subdivisions, see *Fundamentals*, pp. 72ff.

365 I.e. the *saṃgha*, the spiritual community which maintains the Buddha's teaching.

366 The intricate metaphysical and cosmological doctrine upon which this verse is based is discussed at length in *Fundamentals*, Pt. 2. For the various lineages referred to in the last line, see below, pp. 447-57 and 775.

367 For the various divine manifestations of the Teacher alluded to here, see below, pp. 447-50.

368 The epithet "Lord of the World" or Lokeśvara (*'jigs-rten dbang-phyug*) is here a title indicating that Songtsen Gampo is the emanation of the bodhisattva Avalokiteśvara. See also n. 12.

369 The Land of Snows is Tibet, which is referred to as a frontier, or land beyond the pale (*mtha'-khob*), in its relation to Buddhist India prior to the beginnings of Buddhism in Tibet.

370 The Lord of Sukhāvatī Field is Buddha Amitābha. His special realm, the "Pure Land" revered in East Asian Buddhism, is richly described in the Sanskrit *Sukhāvatīvyūhasūtra*, for an English translation of which, see SBE, Vol. 49, Pt. 2, pp. 1-107. According to the teachings of the vehicle of indestructible reality (*Vajrayāna*), Amitābha's seed-syllable is HRĪḤ.

371 "Skull-garlanded Master" refers to Padmasambhava in the form of Pema Thötrengtsel (*padma thod-phreng-rtsal*).

372 The Śākya King is Śākyamuni Buddha.

373 The Lord of Secrets is Vajrapāṇi in the form of Guhyapati. See pp. 451-7. Śāntarakṣita is regarded as his emanation.

374 The sceptre is the sword symbolising discriminative awareness which is held by the bodhisattva Mañjuśrī. His emanation was Trhisong Detsen.

375 The indestructible lineage of supreme transformation refers to the supreme masters who become accomplished in the rainbow body through the esoteric instructions of All-Surpassing Realisation (*thod-rgal*) according to the Great Perfection. See *Fundamentals*, pp. 337-45.

HISTORY: PART ONE

376 The world of Patient Endurance (*mi-mjed 'jig-rten-gyi khams*, Skt. *Sahalokadhātu*), is the thirteenth among twenty-five world systems said to be resting one above the other on the palms of Vairocana Buddha; there are five world realms focused in each of his five centres representing buddha-body, speech, mind, enlightened attributes and activities. Counting upwards from Vairocana's secret centre the thirteenth or world of Patient Endurance lies at the heart of Vairocana's mind (*thugs-kyi thugs*). It contains the four continents of Videha in the east, Jambudvīpa in the south, Godānīya in the west and Uttarakuru in the north, all together multiplied one billion times (1000^3), in three phases which are known respectively as the chiliocosm (*stong spyi-phud-kyi 'jig-rten-gyi khams*), the dichiliocosm (*stong-gnyis-pa bar-ma'i 'jig-rten-gyi khams*) and the great trichiliocosm (*stong-gsum-gyi stong chen-po'i 'jig-rten-gyi khams*, Skt. *trisahasramahāsahasralokadhātu*). See *Fundamentals*, pp. 130-1; and Kloetzli, *Buddhist Cosmology*, Chs. 2-4.

377 The Jambu or rose-apple tree (*Eugenia Jambolana*) is unique to this continent according to all major Indian religious traditions. See W. Kirfel, *Symbolik des Hinduismus und des Jinismus*, pp. 81 and 130.

378 For a general account of the Buddhist concept of cosmic aeons (*bskal-pa*, Skt. *kalpa*), see Kloetzli, *Buddhist Cosmology*, pp. 73-6. Most aeons are not graced by the presence of even a single buddha and so are "dark ages" (*mun-bskal*). Ours, however, with its thousand buddhas is so fortunate as to have been named the "Auspicious Aeon" (*bskal-pa bzang-po*, Skt. *Bhadrakalpa*) by the gods themselves. Cf. Peltrül Rinpoche, *The Words of My Perfect Teacher*, pp. 25-8.

379 Śākyamuni Buddha is the fourth supreme emanational body to appear during this aeon. The previous three were Buddhas Krakucchandra, Kanaka and Kāśyapa.

380 The basic doctrines of this school are described in *Fundamentals*, pp. 156-7. For a historical survey, see A. K. Warder, *Indian Buddhism*, pp. 341-7 and *passim*.

381 See n. 109 above.

382 The path of provisions (*tshogs-lam*, Skt. *sambhāramārga*) is first among the five paths of a bodhisattva's progress towards enlightenment. The others are the paths of connection (*sbyor-lam*, Skt. *prayogamārga*), insight (*mthong-lam*, Skt. *darśanamārga*), meditation (*bsgom-lam*, Skt.

bhāvanāmarga) and no-more-learning (*mi-slob-pa'i lam*, Skt. *aśaikṣamārga*). For their relationship to the ten levels according to the tantras, see *Fundamentals*, pp. 281-3; and for their distinctive attributes, p. 236.

383 For a different reading of this verse, which better agrees with the extant Sanskrit text, see *Fundamentals*, p. 231. Refer, too, to R. Kloppenborg, *The Paccekabuddha*, for a detailed study of the self-centred buddha based pre-eminently on the texts of the Theravādin tradition.

384 A detailed explanation of this phrase may be found in L. de La Vallée Poussin, *L'Abhidharmakośa de Vasubandhu*, Vol. III, pp. 252-3.

385 The tenth level, Cloud of Doctrine, is the highest traversed by bodhisattvas. See Glossary of Enumerations under *ten levels*; and also Dayal, *The Bodhisattva Doctrine in Sanskrit Buddhist Literature*, pp. 270-91.

386 On the Akaniṣṭha heaven, see pp. 447-9; also *Fundamentals*, p. 129; and the chart on pp. 14-15.

387 On the contemplation of nothing at all, see *Fundamentals*, p. 62.

388 The expression "non-dual" (*gnyis-med*, Skt. *advaya*) in this context should be understood to refer to the absence of the subject-object dichotomy characteristic of mundane consciousness. It is not, however, synonymous with the Vedantic term *advaita*, which refers to an absolute monism, i.e. the doctrine that there is but a single substance. Alternatively, it may refer here to the non-duality of the experiences of profundity and clarity.

389 Concerning the Point of Enlightenment (*bodhimaṇḍa*), refer to *Fundamentals*, p. 115 and n. 110, for an explanation of its outer, inner and secret meanings.

390 The Pure Abode (*śuddhanivāsa*) comprises the five highest form realms, known in ascending order as Avṛha, Atapa, Sudṛśa, Sudarśana and Akaniṣṭha. For their position within the whole structure of the three world realms of saṃsāra and the realisation attained by their occupants, see *Fundamentals*, p. 62; and the chart on pp. 14-15.

391 *'du-'bral-med-pa*. This phrase denotes an identity relation, its terms being neither united through artificial conjunction, nor capable of separation.

392 Further information on the *Six Sages Embodying Awareness* will be found in *Fundamentals*, pp. 129ff.; and in the Glossary of Enumerations.

393 "Both goals" are the two kinds of benefit, i.e. to oneself and to others (*rang-don* and *gzhan-don*).

394 Among these forms of the emanational buddha-body (*nirmāṇakāya*), those of artistry comprise created emanations (*bzo-ba'i sprul-sku*) which manifest as images, books and other beneficial objects; those of birth (*skye-ba'i sprul-sku*) include sentient beings of all types who work for the benefit of others; and the supreme emanations (*mchog-gi sprul-sku*) are Śākyamuni and other buddhas who perform the twelve deeds for the sake of living creatures.

395 The following account is ultimately derived from canonical sources, the first and foremost being the *Sūtra of Extensive Play*. Contemporary discussions of the Buddha's life, based on both literary and archaeological evidence, are too numerous to survey here. See HBI, pp.13-25 and the sources mentioned therein. Chief among the post-1958 re-

searches are the several volumes of A. Bareau's *Recherches sur la Biographie du Buddha*.

396 On the purificatory fast, see *Fundamentals*, p. 226.

397 Buddha Akṣobhyavajra, according to the traditions of the vehicle of indestructible reality, is particularly associated with the vase empowerment, for which reason he is especially referred to here on the occasion of the Bodhisattva's consecratory bath. Some of the symbolic significance of this consecration for practitioners of the vehicle of indestructible reality has been indicated in R. A. F. Thurman's article, "Tsoṅ-kha-pa's Integration of Sūtra and Tantra" in STC, pp. 372-82.

398 The sūtras of the greater vehicle frequently give the name in this form instead of the more familiar "Siddhārtha".

399 The suffering of change, the all-pervading suffering of conditioned existence and the suffering of pain itself are the three kinds of suffering to which all saṃsāra is subject. For a detailed discussion, see, e.g., sGam-po-pa, *The Jewel Ornament of Liberation*, pp. 55ff.

400 According to HBI, p. 346, this incident occurred near Rāmagrāma, east of Kapilavastu. Khetsun Zangpo Rinpoche however informs us of a contemporary Indian view that the Sacred Stūpa (*mchod-rten rnam-dag*) was situated near Mankapur in Uttar Pradesh.

401 The pinnacle or summit of existence is explained in *Fundamentals*, p. 62.

402 The realm of desire (*'dod-pa'i khams*, Skt. *kāmadhātu*) is that which comprises the five lower classes of sentient beings and the lowest levels of the gods known in ascending order as the realms of the Four Great Kings (*Caturmahārājakāyika*), the heaven of Thirty-three Gods (*Trayatriṃśa*), the Strifeless (*Yāma*), the Joyful (*Tuṣita*), Delighting in Emanation (*Nirmāṇarati*) and Mastery over Transformations (*Paranirmitavaśavartin*). For their position within the three world realms of saṃsāra and the realisation acquired by their inhabitants, see *Fundamentals*, pp. 61-2; and the chart on pp. 14-15.

403 On great loving kindness (*byams-pa chen-po*), see *Fundamentals*, p. 88.

404 "Five-arrowed One" (*mda'-lnga*, Skt. Pañcaśara) and Smara (*dran-pa*, lit. "Memory") are both epithets of Kāmadeva or Māra, the lord of the desire realm. His emblem is the crocodile banner.

405 Puṇḍarīkā (*pad-dkar-ma*), Menakā (*me-na-kā*), Subhūṣaṇā (*legs-brgyan-ma*) and Keśamiśrā (*skra-'dres-ma*) are four of the thirteen celestial courtesans (*lha'i smad-'tshong-ma bcu-gsum*), also known as offering goddesses (*mchod-pa'i lha-mo*). Others are *dga'-ba'i shing-rta-ma, glog-'od-can, chu-shing bri-can, thig-le mchog-ma* or Tilottamā, *legs-bzang-ma, ma-nyang skyes-ma, a-lam bu-sha* or Alambuṣā, *skad-legs-ma* and *rab-myos-ma* or Pramodā.

406 The fourth meditative concentration (*bsam-gtan bzhi-pa*) is described in the quotation cited in *Fundamentals*, p. 61. See also the Glossary of Enumerations under *four (meditative) concentrations*.

407 "Middle way" here refers to the central channel (*rtsa-dbu-ma*, Skt. *avadhūti*) within the body. All impure psychophysical bases bound within the subject-object dichotomy were transformed here into pristine cognition and the enlightened attributes of the buddhas; see *Fundamentals*, p. 341.

408 On Rāhu, the eclipser of the moon, see Nebesky-Wojkowitz, *Oracles and Demons of Tibet*, pp. 259-63; and A. L. Basham, *The Wonder that was India*, p. 491.

409 The "impure religion of Magadha" is, of course, the Brāhmaṇism of the Buddha's day. While maintaining that this religion does not provide an ultimately salvific vehicle, Buddhists do not deny its many positive teachings. See, e.g., *Fundamentals*, pp. 57-62.

410 Corruptions (*zag-pa*, Skt. *āsrava*) comprise all those propensities which serve to sustain the round of saṃsāra. In attaining nirvāṇa, these are exhausted (*zad*); but, in addition, the Buddha knows directly that they have been completely exhausted.

411 "Long-living" (*tshe-dang ldan-pa*, Skt. *āyuṣmān*) implies that one is still bound to the cyclical existence of saṃsāra and so is not a realised buddha.

412 Refer here to the Glossary of Enumerations under *four truths*.

413 For a more detailed account of the subject-matter of the three wheels of the doctrine than will be found in the present summary, see *Fundamentals*, Pt. 3. See also Lessing and Wayman, *Mkhas grub rje's Fundamentals of the Buddhist Tantras*, pp. 43-53.

414 Vulture Peak is Gṛdhrakūṭa, near Rājagṛha (modern Rajgir) in Bihar, north India.

415 The teaching of path and result is that which leads out of cyclical existence or saṃsāra. It refers to the five paths (see n. 382 above) and the corresponding results which are attained by arhats, self-centred buddhas or bodhisattvas; see *Fundamentals*, pp. 223ff.

416 These are, primarily, the *eight great fears*, on which see the Glossary of Enumerations.

417 Kuśinagarī, in the Buddha's day within the domains of the Mallas, is identified with modern Kasiā, about thirty-five miles to the east of Gorakhpur in north India.

418 The so-called extremist (*mu-stegs*) or non-Buddhist doctrines are dealt with generally in *Fundamentals*, pp. 62-9.

419 Avīci is held to be the lowest and most unbearable of the hellish domains, occupied by sentient beings at the bottom of saṃsāra. See the chart on pp. 14-15; also sGam-po-pa, *The Jewel Ornament of Liberation*, p. 58.

420 *Udumbara* here refers to a large and rare mythical lotus, which blossoms only once in an age.

421 On the traditions relative to these original reliquaries, refer to HBI, pp. 24-5; and Bareau, *Recherches sur la Biographie du Buddha*, II.II, pp. 308-23.

422 These three councils are considered in HBI, pp. 136-54 and 297-319. For the first council in particular, the standard work is J. Przyluski, *Le Concile de Rājagṛha*; and, for the second, M. Hofinger, *Étude sur le Concile de Vaiśālī*. Cf. also Lessing and Wayman, *Mkhas grub rje's Fundamentals of the Buddhist Tantras*, pp. 59-69; and J. Nattier and C. Prebish, "Mahāsaṅghika Orgins: The Beginnings of Buddhist Sectarianism" in *History of Religions*, Vol. 16, no. 3 (1977).

423 Our interpretation of the terse mnemonic given here is based on the discussion of the heresy found in *Minor Transmissions* (*Kṣudrāgama*, T 6), in the Derge *Kangyur*, Vol. *Da*, pp. 646-63. We are indebted

to Lama Sonam Topgyel for locating this valuable passage.

424 Cf. Tāranātha, *History of Buddhism in India*, p. 94.

425 The major traditions relative to the origins and development of the eighteen schools of the lesser vehicle (*Hīnayāna*) are summarised in HBI, pp. 571-606. The divisions reported in our present text agree with those listed in Sarvāstivādin sources.

426 See Obermiller, *History of Buddhism by Bu-ston*, Pt. 2, p. 98. According to the Tibetan Vinaya tradition there were one hundred kings in the dynasty of Nāgapāla, son of King Gaganapati in Vārāṇasī. The last of these was King Kṛkī.

427 The elder Vātsīputra is held to have been a founder of the Ārya-sammitīya order. The Kashmiri schools referred to are the branches of the Mūlasarvāstivāda.

428 Theravādin sources usually date the third council two hundred and thirty-six years after the Buddha's nirvāṇa. But on this, see HBI, p. 298.

429 Cf. Lessing and Wayman, *Mkhas grub rje's Fundamentals of the Buddhist Tantras*, pp. 69-71; Tāranātha, *History of Buddhism in India*, pp. 96ff.; and Obermiller, *History of Buddhism by Bu-ston*, Pt. 2, pp. 101ff.

430 *rnam-mchan rnying-pa*. Rikdzin Lhündrup in the Hindi version of the *History*, p. 22, has suggested that this refers to an ancient annotation on the *Exposition of Valid Cognition* (*rnam-'grel-gyi mchan-bu rnying-pa*).

431 Concerning the parallel division of the treatises according to the "profound view" (*zab-mo lta-ba*) and "extensive conduct" (*rgya-chen spyod-pa*), refer to *Fundamentals*, pp. 94-5.

432 Cf. the traditions reported in HBI, pp. 226-36.

433 "Nirgrantha" originally referred to Jain ascetics in general, but later is used of the Digambara or "sky-clad" sect in particular. An excellent introduction to their religious life will be found in P. S. Jaini, *The Jaina Path of Purification*, pp. 4-6ff.

434 There are *twelve ascetic virtues*; see the Glossary of Enumerations.

435 The Teacher's descent from the realm of the gods (*lha-babs dus-chen*) refers to the events following the period of a rain retreat passed by Śākyamuni Buddha in the Trayatriṃśa heaven, where he taught his late mother. The location of his descent is traditionally held to have been Laṅkā; hence the title of the *Sūtra of the Descent to Laṅkā*. This event is commemorated annually by Tibetans on the twenty-second of the ninth month.

436 It is said that humans in our own era are physically small relative to those of such golden ages as that in which Maitreya will make his appearance.

437 The current rite of ordination (*lta-da'i cho-ga*) is graded through the levels of a renunciate (*rab-'byung*, Skt. *pravrajya*), novitiate (*dge-tshul*, Skt. *śramaṇera*) and complete monkhood (*bsnyen-rdzogs*, Skt. *upasampadā*). This is contrasted with the ancient and sudden method of ordination (*sngon-chog*) through which Śāriputra, Kāśyapa and others were instantly ordained by Śākyamuni Buddha.

438 Aśoka is commonly associated with the prolific building and veneration of stūpas. See, J. Przyluski, *La Légende de l'Empereur Aśoka*; and J. Strong, *The Legend of King Aśoka*.

439 I.e. he would become not a buddha, but an arhat. The marks of

a buddha refer to the *thirty-two major* and *eighty minor marks*. These are listed in, e.g., Mvt. 236-67, 269-349; the *Ornament of Emergent Realisation* (*Abhisamayālaṃkāra*), vv. 13-32; and Longcenpa, *Dispelling Darkness in the Ten Directions*, pp. 73-6 (GGFTC, pp. 406-9). See also *Fundamentals*, p. 124; and the Glossary of Enumerations.

440 Cf. Tāranātha, *History of Buddhism in India*, p. 33.

441 On the Trayatriṃśa heaven in relation to other divine realms, see n. 402 above.

442 The great Sixteen Elders, and many of the literary and artistic traditions associated with them, are considered extensively in M.W. de Visser, *The Arhats in China and Japan*; and J. Tate, *The Sixteen Elders*. While their divine intercession in Chinese life is detailed therein, the basis for associating them with the emperors here mentioned remains obscure. But cf. L. S. Dagyab, *Tibetan Religious Art*, Pt. I, Sect. IV.

443 Cf. Tāranātha, *History of Buddhism in India*, pp. 29-33.

444 The basic philosophical tenets of this school are summarised in *Fundamentals*, p. 158. For further background, see also Warder, *Indian Buddhism*, pp. 345-6, 421-2, 472-3.

445 The *Great Treasury of Detailed Exposition* (*Mahāvibhāṣa*), which today survives only in its Chinese translation (Taishō 1545), is assigned by Étienne Lamotte to the second century AD; see HBI, pp. 303-5, 424-5, etc. The prolific writings of Nāgārjuna are usually assigned to about AD 200, though they may have been composed slightly earlier. The treatises of Maitreyanātha are said to have been introduced into our world by Asaṅga, who was probably active during the fourth century. For the lives and works of these authors and others mentioned in the succeeding paragraphs, see *Fundamentals*, pp. 88-96; Tāranātha, *History of Buddhism in India*, Chs. 15-28; and Obermiller, *History of Buddhism by Bu-ston*.

446 For the description of the "six adornments" and "two supreme ones" in Tibetan painting, see Namgyal Institute, *Rgyan drug mchog gnyis*. On the doctrinal developments of the Mahāyāna sūtra and *śāstra* tradition in general from ancient India through to China, Japan and Tibet, see P. Williams, *Mahāyāna Buddhism*.

447 Cf. HBI, pp. 648-9.

448 The Ancient Translation School or *snga-'gyur rnying-ma* tradition refers to the cycles of teaching current in Tibet prior to the death of Smṛtijñānakīrti, and to their subsequent propagation; the new traditions are those which arrived in Tibet during the later spread of the doctrine, from the time of Rincen Zangpo onwards.

449 The most popular account of these masters in Tibetan has been translated into English by J. B. Robinson as *Buddha's Lions*, and by K. Dowman in *Masters of Mahāmudra*. Their iconographic representation is detailed in T. Schmid, *The Eighty-five Siddhas*. For related traditions, see also S. Dasgupta, *Obscure Religious Cults*, Chs. 1-9 and especially Ch. 8, pp. 202ff.

450 Spiritual maturity and liberation (*smin-grol*) are catalysed by the guru's empowerment (*dbang*) and guidance (*khrid*) respectively. See *Fundamentals*, pp. 346-71.

HISTORY: PART TWO

451 The sixth enlightened or buddha family is that of the body of reality, Samantabhadra, in the form of Vajradhara, who embodies the Conquerors of the Five Enlightened Families (*rgyal-ba rigs-lnga*). See *Fundamentals*, pp. 120-2.

452 The Great Akaniṣṭha realm (*'og-min chen-po*, Skt. *Mahākaniṣṭha*) is the abode manifest in and of itself (*rang-snang*), in which Samantabhadra transmits realisation to the Conquerors of the Five Enlightened Families and the maṇḍalas of peaceful and wrathful deities by the blessing of the buddha-body of reality's intention. On its significance, see *Fundamentals*, pp. 129ff. and n. 130.

453 The All-Pervader (*khyab-'jug*) here refers to Samantabhadra.

454 The Indestructible Nucleus of Inner Radiance (*'od-gsal rdo-rje snying-po*) is the dimension of the body of reality; see *Fundamentals*, p. 118 and n. 112.

455 The "special" or "extraordinary" Akaniṣṭha realm (*khyad-par-can-gyi 'og-min*, Skt. *Viśiṣṭākaniṣṭha*) which manifests extraneously (*gzhan-snang*) is the abode in which Vajradhara and the Conquerors of the Five Enlightened Families transmit the teaching of Unsurpassed Yogatantra to tenth level bodhisattvas by the intentional symbols of the buddha-body of perfect rapture.

456 Cf. *Fundamentals*, p. 125.

457 See above, p. 413; and *Fundamentals*, p. 62.

458 The ordinary Akaniṣṭha (*'og-min tsam-po*, Skt. **Gauṇākaniṣṭha*) and the imputed Akaniṣṭha realm (*btags-pa'i 'og-min*, Skt. **Aupacārikākaniṣṭha*) are the extraneous realms within the Pure Abodes in which the Unsurpassed Yoga tantras are transmitted respectively to ninth and eighth level bodhisattvas by the buddhas in the form of wrathful and peaceful meditational deities. See also Fundamentals, pp. 128-9.

459 On the Vajra Queen, see *Fundamentals*, p. 125, n. 127.

460 In the Hindu traditions Rudra is typically an epithet of Śiva, but for Tibetan Buddhists he is a wrathful embodiment of ego which has run wild. For a traditional and elaborate presentation of the myth of Rudra, see *The Life and Liberation of Padmasambhava*, Pt. I, pp. 26-46; and Longcenpa, *Dispelling Darkness in the Ten Directions*, Ch. 15, pp. 488ff. (GGFTC, pp. 1075ff.).

461 Vajradharma is the peaceful aspect of the Lord of Secrets: Guhyapati or Vajrapāṇi.

462 In the lineages which follow, Sanskrit names have been given in most cases following the standard conventions for Tibetan-Sanskrit translation. However, we know of no extant Sanskrit source for these lineages. It should be noted also that there are sometimes variants in the way in which different Tibetan sources report these names, e.g. that of the yakṣa Yaśasvī Varapāla below.

463 Yaśasvī Varapāla (*grags-ldan mchog-skyong*) is the yakṣa's name; the old edition of this text wrongly reads *phyogs-skyong*. See *Scholar's Feast of Doctrinal History*, p. 236. This observation has been confirmed by the Author.

464 On this empowerment, see *Fundamentals*, p. 345.

465 Cf. *Fundamentals*, pp. 81-6.

466 Vimalakīrti is best known to the Buddhist world through the magnificent sūtra of the greater vehicle bearing his name, i.e. the *Vimalakīrtinirdeśasūtra* (T 176), on which see E. Lamotte, *L'Enseignement de Vimalakīrti*; R. A. F. Thurman, *The Holy Teaching of Vimalakīrti*; and the translation from the Chinese by C. Luk.

467 Various versions of the legend of the ascendancy of the lion clan (Siṅghala) in Śrī Laṅkā are known. Cf. E. F. C. Ludowyk, *The Footprint of the Buddha*, pp. 14-15; and HBI, pp. 129-35.

468 Sumana or Sumanakūṭa is Adam's Peak, a place revered by Śrī Laṅkan adherents of all the major religions. The "king of powerful craft" referred to in the verse below is probably Saman, the local god who is identified with the Vedic Yama, lord of the dead. Refer to S. Paranavitana, *The God of Adam's Peak*.

469 This would appear to be none other than the footprint on Adam's Peak, locally called Siripāda (Skt. *Śrīpāda*). For a description of this and of the pilgrimage to it, see Ludowyk, *The Footprint of the Buddha*, pp. 16ff.; and R. F. Gombrich, *Precept and Practice*, pp. 108-12 and 178-9.

470 The traditions concerning this figure have been studied in S. G. Karmay, "King Tsa/Dza and Vajrayāna" in M. Strickmann (ed.), *Tantric and Taoist Studies in Honour of R. A. Stein*, pp. 192-211. Y. Imaeda, "Un Extrait Tibétain du *Mañjuśrīmūlakalpa* dans les Manuscripts de Touen-Houang" in *Nouvelles Contributions aux Études de Touen-Houang*, pp. 306, 311, records the occurrence of Ca/Tsa as a royal name in the early ninth-century document considered therein; but Karmay, p. 195, n. 10, discounts the possibility of this being associated with the personage here discussed.

471 On this verse, see Karmay, "King Tsa/Dza and Vajrayāna", pp. 197-9.

472 Intermediate (*bar-pa*) here means later or second, i.e. coming between King Indrabhūti and later lineage-holders. For other references to this intermediate Indrabhūti, see Tāranātha, *History of Buddhism in India*, p. 241, n. 68 and p. 410; and especially, Karmay, "King Tsa/Dza and Vajrayāna", pp. 205-6.

473 This system is examined in detail in *Fundamentals*, pp. 275-83.

474 For the tantrapiṭaka here enumerated, refer to the first part of the Bibliography under the *Eighteen Great Tantrapiṭaka (of the Mahāyoga)*.

475 On Tilopā and Nāropā in particular, see Guenther, *The Life and Teaching of Nāropā*.

476 In rendering the name *sgeg-pa'i rdo-rje* as Līlāvajra the translators are bowing to an established convention which has recently been justifiably challenged by Davidson in "The Litany of Names of Mañjuśrī", p. 6, n. 18, where he argues that Vilāsavajra is the correct Sanskrit name.

477 The term *spar-khab*, from which this work takes its abbreviated title, is found in the dedicatory final verse of that text, the Peking *Tangyur*, Vol. 83; and in the *Commentaries on the Guhyagarbhatantra and Other Rare Nyingma Texts from the Library of Dudjom Rinpoche*, Vol. 1, p. 222. Its precise interpretation, however, is at the present time uncertain.

478 The *Garland of Activity* was omitted in the published text, but was

inserted subsequently by the Author before the *Hidden Point of the Moon* (*zla-gsang thig-le*). An alternative reading would be *Buddhasamāyoga* (the mind of body), *Hidden Point of the Moon* (the mind of speech), *Guhyasamāja* (the mind of mind), *Paramādya* (the mind of enlightened attributes) and *Garland of Activity* (the mind of enlightened activities). In this instance, however, the *Magical Net* (the general tantra of mind) is included instead of the *Paramādya*. See also Jikme Lingpa, *Narrative History of the Precious Collected Tantras* (*rnying-ma'i rgyud-'bum-gyi rtogs-brjod*), p. 466.

479 The outcaste boy is Mātaṅgīpā; see Tāranātha, *History of Buddhism in India*, p. 129, n. 139 and p. 273.

480 The great accomplished master Nāgabodhi was the first to propagate the tradition of Saraha and Nāgārjuna; see Tāranātha, *History of Buddhism in India*, pp. 126-7, 152 and 273.

481 For the background to the *Ārya* tradition of the *Guhyasamāja*, which is that of Nāgārjuna, refer to A. Wayman, *The Buddhist Tantras: New Light on Indo-Tibetan Esotericism*, Ch. 2; also idem, *Yoga of the Guhyasamājatantra*, pp. 91-4.

482 See below, p. 533.

483 The "Zombie" Sukhasiddhi is Garap Dorje; see pp. 490-3.

484 A survey of the different types of biography of Padmasambhava will be found in A.-M. Blondeau, "Analysis of the Biographies of Padmasambhava according to Tibetan Tradition: Classification of Sources" in TSHR, pp. 45-52.

485 *kṛṣṇa-'dzin*. Often one sees this name spelt according to its Tibetan pronunciation, i.e. *trig-na-'dzin*.

486 As explained in n. 291 above, to "liberate" in this context means to forcefully transfer the consciousness of a sentient being permanently from the body in order to remove obstacles, and, out of compassion, to establish that being in a higher rebirth. Refer to the biographies of Nyak Jñānakumāra, pp. 601-4; and Guru Chöwang, pp. 760-70.

487 This means that, having been absorbed into the very heart of pristine cognition, he was fully empowered and so reborn, free of all obscuration. The symbolism of a passage such as the present one operates on several levels, however, so that a single fixed interpretation is not possible.

488 Tibetan Buddhist pilgrims hold the Māratika Cave to be the cave of Haileshi, in Nepal's Sagarmatha district, south of the Mount Everest region, near the town of Rumjitar.

489 Amitāyus is here an aspect of Buddha Amitābha as the body of perfect rapture, who is particularly the patron of longevity.

490 I.e., the level of no return to the cyclical existence of saṃsāra.

491 On Aśoka, see above, p. 453.

492 The actual site of pilgrimage at the present day is a cave located on the slope behind the Vajreśvarī Temple in Pharping, Nepal.

493 The Tibetan term *ma-mo* is used to translate the "Sanskrit" *mātarī* in the *Hevajra Tantra* (e.g. Pt. 1, Ch. 1, v. 16) where a specific channel is intended. It should be noted, however, that *ma-mo* is used to translate the term *mātṛkā*, as well, and that this latter term is used to denote a group of goddesses widely worshipped in the Kathmandu Valley, and throughout northern India. See A. W. Macdonald and A. V. Stahl,

Newar Art, pp. 83-8.

494 This is the aural lineage of Zhang-Zhung, the Pönpo tradition of the Great Perfection. On Tavihṛca in particular, see L. Chandra (ed.), *The History and Doctrine of the Bon-po Niṣpanna-yoga*, pp. 15.5-6 and 26.5-27.4. See also S. G. Karmay, "Origin and Development of the Tibetan Religious Traditions of the Great Perfection."

495 See below, pp. 519-20.

496 The distinctions between the outer and inner classes are considered in *Fundamentals*, pp. 273-4.

497 During the empowerment ceremony, the initiate casts a flower offering onto the symbolic maṇḍala. The direction in which the flower falls – east, south, west, north or centre – holds particular significance, and one has a special affinity with the deity located there.

498 On the enlightened family of indestructible reality (Skt. *vajrakula*), that of Akṣobhya, see *Fundamentals*, p. 274.

499 Ritual service (*bsnyen-pa*, Skt. *sevā*) entails the recitation of mantra combined with one-pointed prayerful devotion to a deity externally visualised; further ritual service (*nye-bar bsnyen-pa*, Skt. *upasevā*) entails the prayer to receive the consecration which will transform the mundane body, speech and mind into the three seed-syllables of indestructible reality; the rite or means for attainment (*sgrub-pa*, Skt. *sādhana*) entails accomplishment in the form of light rays which are absorbed from the sugatas of the ten directions into the deity and thence into oneself, in actuality, meditation or dreams; then, the rite of great attainment (*sgrub-chen*, Skt. *mahāsādhana*) entails ultimate realisation of beginningless primordial purity, the naturally present pristine cognition experienced when body, speech and mind are coalesced with the deity. This is the inner significance of the ritual ceremonies and elaborate dances contained within the "drupchen". See Mipham Rinpoche, *tshig-bdun rnam-bshad padma dkar-po*, pp. 22-3.

500 Garuḍa is a gigantic and divine bird and, according to Hindu mythology, the mount of the god Viṣṇu. He is a divinity in his own right and is worshipped as such by both Hindus and Buddhists.

501 For a summary of available information on this figure, see *Niṣpannayogāvalī*, pp. 9-12; and HIL 7.1, pp. 114-15.

502 Davidson, "The Litany of Names of Mañjuśrī", p. 5, holds Mañjuśrīmitra to have been a Śrī Laṅkan.

503 These are the emanations of the deity which actually accomplish the four kinds of enlightened activity on behalf of the adept.

504 Jetāri is known for his contributions to the science of logic. See Vidyabhusana, *A History of Indian Logic*, pp. 136-7, 140, 151; and G. Tucci, *Minor Buddhist Texts*, Pt. 1, pp. 249-74.

505 See Tāranātha, *History of Buddhism in India*, p. 432. The younger Amoghavajra visited Tibet in 1086.

506 "Sublime" (*'phags-pa*, Skt. *ārya*) refers to those who have sublimated the cyclical existence of saṃsāra.

507 Some of the sources associating this mountain with Nāgārjuna are discussed by Karmay in "King Tsa/Dza and Vajrayāna", p. 197, n. 16.

508 Vajrakumāra, the "Indestructible Youth", is an epithet of Vajrakīla, or of his "offspring".

509 The Śaṅkarakūṭa Caitya was situated in the Śītavana charnel ground in Magadha. Originally the *Gathering of the Sugatas of the Eight Transmitted Precepts* (*bka'-brgyad bder-'dus*) was concealed there, along with the *Eight Sections of the Magical Net* in the stūpa's base, the *Gathering of the Sugatas* in the vase-shaped dome with the special tantras in its four cardinal directions, the *Consummation of Secrets* (*gsang-ba yongs-rdzogs*) in the flute, the *rgyud rang-byung rang-shar* in the rim of the spire, and the *yang-gsang bla-med yang-ti nag-po* in the point of the spire. See E. Dargyay, *The Rise of Esoteric Buddhism in Tibet*, p. 15, whose account is derived from the treasure of Nyang-rel Nyima Özer entitled *Gathering of the Sugatas*.

510 The Mahottara casket was gold (*gser*), not *bse*-stone as the text mistakenly reads. See the *Scholar's Feast of Doctrinal History*, p. 243. Note that the catalogue numbers given for this series of tantras are those corresponding to the extant texts of the eight cycles in NGB and the *Kangyur*.

511 *gzi*. A peculiar black-and-white-striped agate, beads of which are highly prized by Tibetans for their talismanic value.

512 This location in South India is revered by Vajrayāna Buddhists as the site where the Buddha taught the *Kālacakra Tantra*.

513 Communal feast offerings (*tshogs-kyi 'khor-lo*, Skt. *gaṇacakra*), in contrast to other forms of contemplative activity, involve much ritual and material elaboration. Cf. Longcenpa, *Dispelling Darkness in the Ten Directions*, pp. 402ff. (GGFTC, pp. 922ff.); and Gonpo Tsetan, *The Udumbara Bouquet*.

514 "Exercises which circulate the lamp-like vital energy" are, according to Khetsun Zangpo Rinpoche, a cycle of teachings based on Indian haṭha yoga.

515 The lower method grants supernormal cognitive powers such as invisibility, but not the ability to transcend saṃsāra, which is the feature of the higher methods of Mahāyoga and Anuyoga, or the great transformation into the rainbow body – the highest attainment of the buddha level according to the Great Perfection of Atiyoga. See *Fundamentals*, pp. 337-45.

516 Sthiramati comes between Dhanarakṣita and Sukhodyotaka in the Anuyoga lineage. See *Scholar's Feast of Doctrinal History*, p. 239. His writings on Anuyoga are represented by P 4752-4.

517 R. A. Stein, "Étude du monde chinoise: institutions et concepts" *L'Annuaire du Collège de France* 72 (1972), pp. 502-3, maintains that Chetsenkye may perhaps be identified with the Pönpo translator Tshotsenkye (*mtsho-btsan-skyes*), who appears to have flourished about the year 1000.

518 The *yojana*, an ancient Indian unit of length, is generally held by Buddhists to be four thousand arm-spans, i.e. about eight thousand yards. It is defined as follows in the *Treasury of the Abhidharma* (Ch.3, vv. 87-8):

> Twenty-four inches equal one cubit.
> Four cubits equal one bow-span.
> Five hundred bow-spans equal one "range of hearing".
> Eight "ranges of hearing" are said to equal one *yojana*.

519 The syllables mentioned confer respectively the blessings of buddha-body (OṂ), speech (ĀḤ), mind (HŪṂ), attributes (SVĀ) and activities (HĀ).

520 On these classes of spirits, see Nebesky-Wojkowitz, *Oracles and Demons of Tibet*, Ch. VII, Ch. XII, pp. 281-2 and *passim*.

521 This verse is explained in detail in *Fundamentals*, pp. 319ff.

522 For the "Establishment of the Intrinsic Essential of the Innermost Spirituality" (*thig-le rang-gnad-du dbab-pa*), see *Fundamentals*, p. 333. It is the essence of the Esoteric Instructional Class of the Great Perfection.

523 Jambhala and Vasudharā are two of the most popular wealth-granting deities. For further information, refer to Nebesky-Wojkowitz, *Oracles and Demons of Tibet*, pp. 73-81.

524 These "rites for deriving the most success" (*'bogs-chog*) transfer the ability to fulfil and restore the commitments of the secret mantra.

525 Mañjuvajra is a form of Guhyasamāja, whose tradition in Tibet originates from master Buddhajñānapāda. See Dudjom Rinpoche, *rgyal-rabs*, pp. 198-218. The maṇḍala is detailed in *Niṣpannayogāvalī*, pp. 1-4.

526 The "practice which divides saṃsāra and nirvāṇa" (*'khor-'das ru-shan*), as explained in texts such as Jikme Lingpa's *khrid-yig ye-shes bla-ma*, is a meditation leading to the rejection of saṃsāra, enabling one to undertake the preliminaries and main practice of Atiyoga.

527 Khotan in Chinese Turkestan was one of the greatest of Buddhist centres during the first millenium AD. For an introduction to the extensive literature on Buddhism in that region, see, e.g., K. Saha, *Buddhism in Central Asia*, pp. 33-4 and *passim*; also M. A. Stein, *Ancient Khotan: detailed report of archaeological explorations in Chinese Turkestan*, 2 vols.; and R. E. Emmerick (ed. & trans.), *The Book of Zambasta: A Khotanese Poem on Buddhism*. A useful synthesis of research to date is D. L. Snellgrove, *Indo-Tibetan Buddhism*, Pt. 4.

528 The body of supreme transformation (*'pho-ba chen-po'i ku*) is the rainbow body (*'ja'-lus*) attainment of All-Surpassing Realisation (*thod-rgal*). The higher rainbow body transmutes all psychophysical components into the light of buddhahood, so that no outward change is visible. This is why Padmasambhava, Vimalamitra, Vairocana and so forth can pass into other buddha-fields in the same forms. The lower rainbow body attainment transmutes consciousness, feeling, perception and habitual tendencies into the light of buddhahood, but the component of form shrinks in size until only fingernails, tooth-enamel, hair or relics remain. See also *Fundamentals*, pp. 337-45; and Mipham's discussion, cited in n. 1285 below.

529 India here refers only to Madhyadeśa, the heartland of Central India.

530 The Kokī countries are situated in the area from north-east India towards Burma and Cambodia; see Tāranātha, *History of Buddhism in India*, pp. 330-1.

531 The "present time" refers to the era of Tāranātha; this passage is derived from his *History of Buddhism in India*, pp. 320, 332-3.

532 On the tradition of Gorakṣanātha, refer to G. W. Briggs, *Gorakhnāth and the Kānphaṭa Yogīs*; and to Dasgupta, *Obscure Religious Cults*, Ch. 8, pp. 206-9 and *passim*. For the Nāthapaṇthas, see Chs. 8-9 of the latter work. The Hindu traditions here mentioned stem

from masters who, like Gorakṣanātha, are equally claimed by the Buddhists. The association of Śāntigupta with the Naṭeśvaras is due to Tāranātha, *bka'-babs bdun-ldan-gyi rnam-thar*. See the translation in Templeman, *The Seven Instruction Lineages*, pp. 75ff.

HISTORY: PART THREE

533 As explained by Dudjom Rinpoche, *rgyal-rabs*, pp. 8-14, Tibet was initially under the sway of ten successive classes of non-human or spiritual beings, namely, the *gnod-sbyin nag-po*, *re-ti mgo-gYag bdud*, *srin-bu skye-rengs khrag-mig*, *dmar-'jam lha*, *rmu-rgyal kho-rje*, *krog-krog 'dre*, *ma-sengs rus-dgu*, *klu*, *rgyal-po* and *'gong-po spun-dgu*. Subsequently, when human beings settled there, the country was divided between the following twelve minor kingdoms: *mchims-yul gru-shul* ruled by *mchims-rje gu-yod*; *zhang-zhang* ruled by King *lig snya-shur*; *myang-do phyong-dkar* ruled by King *gtsang-rje thod-dkar*; *gnubs-yul gling-dgu* ruled by King *gnubs-rje dmigs-pa*; *nyang-ro sham-bod* ruled by King *rngam-rje 'brom*; *gyi-ri ljongs-sdon* ruled by King *gyi-rje rman-po*; *ngam-shod khra-snar* ruled by King *zing-rje khri 'phrang-sum*; *'ol-phu spang-mkhar* ruled by King *zing-rje thon-greng*; *srin-rong la-mo gong* ruled by King *brang-rje gong-nam*; *kong-yul bre-snu* ruled by King *kong-rje dar-po tug-dang*; *nyang-yul-rnams gsum* ruled by *nyang-btsun glang-rgyal*; and *dvags-yul gru-bzhi* ruled by King *dvags-rje mang-po rgyal*.

As a result of constant warfare between these twelve kingdoms, power devolved into the hands of forty principalities (*sil-ma bzhi-bcu*). Apart from *'brog-mo rnam-gsum* ruled by the lord *rgyal-po se-mi ra-khrid*, *gye-mo yul-drug* ruled by the lord *gye-rje mkhar-ba*, and *se-mo gru-bzhi* ruled by the lord *gnyags-gru 'brang*, their names and localities are unknown at the present day.

534 The various traditions concerning Nyatrhi Tsenpo have been summarised and compared by E. Haarh in *The Yar-luṅ Dynasty*, Chs. 10-11, pp. 168-270.

535 The kings in the ancient royal dynasties of Tibet can be enumerated as follows:

The seven heavenly kings called *Trhi* (*gnam-gyi khri-bdun*) were *gnya'-khri btsan-po*, *mu-khri btsan-po*, *ding-khri btsan-po*, *so-khri btsan-po*, *mar-khri btsan-po*, *gdags-khri btsan-po*, and *sribs-khri btsan-po*. All of these are said to have been immortal beings who ascended to the heavens after fulfilling their reigns. Their succession was matriarchal.

The two celestial kings called *Teng* (*stod-kyi steng-gnyis*) were *gri-gum btsan-po* and *spu-de gung-rgyal*. The former is said to have been assassinated and so became the first mortal king of Tibet. *spu-de gung-rgyal* or *bya-khri btsan-po* of Kanam was the culture hero who discovered basic metals, agriculture and founded Yarlung.

The six earthly kings called *Lek* (*sa-yi legs-drug*) were *e-sho legs*, *de-sho legs*, *thi-sho legs*, *gong-ru legs*, *'brong-gzher legs*, and *i-sho legs*.

The eight middle kings called *De* (*bar-gyi lde-brgyad*) were *za-nam zin-lde*, *lde-'phrul nam-gzhung btsan*, *se-snol gnam-lde*, *se-snol-po lde*, *lde snol-nam*, *lde snol-po*, *lde rgyal-po*, and *lde sprin-btsan*.

The five linking kings called *Tsen* (*tshigs-la btsan-lnga*) were *rgyal to-re long-btsan*, *khri btsan-gnam*, *khri sgra-spungs btsan*, *khri thog-rje thog-btsan*, and *lha tho-tho ri gnyan-btsan* who discovered the "Awesome Secret".

The ancestors of the religious kings (*chos-rgyal-rnams-kyi mes*) were *khri-gnyan gzungs-btsan*, *'brong-gnyan lde'u*, *stug-ri gnyan-gzigs*, and *gnam-ri srong-btsan* who was the father of Songtsen Gampo.

Then the religious kings (*chos-rgyal rnams*) were *srong-btsan sgam-po*, *gung-ri gung-btsan*, *mang-srong mang-btsan*, *'dus-srong mang-po rje klung-nam-'phrul-gyi rgyal-po*, *khri-lde gtsug-brtan*, *khri-srong lde'u btsan*, *mu-ne btsad-po*, Prince *mu-rab btsad-po*, *mu-tig btsad-po* who was also known as *sad-na legs-mjing*, and *khri ral-pa-can*. Politically Tibet was at the zenith of its political power during this period. The conquest of the Chinese capital Chang-'an (modern Xi'an) was effected briefly in October 763.

Finally, King *glang-dar-ma* (b. 817), the apostate who ruled from 841 to 846 (or 838 to 842) was the last of the ancient line to govern the whole country. The dates given here are those of modern historians, based upon the records of Chinese, Tun-huang and Arabic origin, which for reasons stated on p. 399, are at variance by as much as sixty years with the traditional Tibetan dating for the royal dynasty between the reign of Songtsen Gampo and the restoration of the doctrine. For a synopsis of this problem, refer to Roerich's introduction to the *Blue Annals*; and for a detailed comparison of the various enumerations of the ancient kings, see Haarh, *The Yar-luṅ Dynasty*, Chs. 1-2, pp. 33-71. In chapter eight of the present work these divergencies have been noted in the course of nn. 1350-3 below.

536 According to Khetsun Zangpo Rinpoche, this version of the prophecy belongs to an early sūtra translation no longer extant.

537 Cf. Haarh, *The Yar-luṅ Dynasty*, p. 85. The Six-Syllable Mantra is that of the bodhisattva Avalokiteśvara: OṂ MAṆI PADME HŪṂ.

538 The "pure" *Testament of Ba* (*sba-bzhed gtsang-ma*), was composed probably in the late eight or early ninth century. Until recently only an annotated version (*zhabs-brtags-ma*), dating from perhaps the fourteenth century, was known to exist. See R. A. Stein, *Une Chronique Ancienne de bSam-yas*. In 1980, however, an unsupplemented version was published in Peking by Gönpo Gyeltsen, on which see D. S. Ruegg, "The Great Debate between Gradualists and Simultaneists in Eighth Century Tibet".

539 Considerable research has been devoted to the life and reign of this monarch. See especially: Haarh, *The Yar-luṅ Dynasty*, p. 62 and *passim*; A. Macdonald, "Une lecture des Pelliot tibétaine 1286, 1287, 1038, 1047 et 1290. Essai sur le formation et l'emploi des mythes politiques dans la religion royale de Sroṅ-bcan sgam-po" in *Études tibétaines dédiées à la memoire de Marcelles Lalou*, pp.90-391; H. E. Richardson, "The Dharma that came down from Heaven" in *Buddhist Thought and Asian Civilization*; and G. Tucci, *The Tombs of the Tibetan Kings*.

540 On this verse, refer to *Blue Annals*, pp. 44-5 and n. 33.

541 A traditional and popular romanticised account of the king's marriage may be found in J. Bacot, "Le marriage chinois du roi tibétain Sroṅ bcan sgam po" MCB 3 (1935).

542 For a detailed description of these two images, see KGHP, p. 86.

543 These are discussed in detail in M. Aris, *Bhutan*, pp. 5-33. Through the influence of Songtsen Gampo's Chinese consort Wen-ch'eng K'ong-jo, divination techniques based on *kaptse* or elemental charts (see *Fundamentals*, p. 104) and geomancy were introduced to Tibet. The supine ogress (*brag srin-mo*) or demoness represents the natural energies of the Tibetan landscape, the harnessing and protection of which was effected by the construction of temples at geomantic sites or focal points (*me-btsa'*) on the ogress' body. At the geomantic centre, the Trhülnang Temple was constructed at Lhasa, representing the heart-blood of the ogress. Four District Controlling temples (*ru-gnon-gi lha-khang*) were then erected around it. They were located in Trhadruk (*khra-'brug*) in Yoru upon her left shoulder, Ka-tshel in Uru upon the right shoulder, Drompagyel in Rulak upon her left hip and Tsangtram in Yeru upon the right hip. Surrounding these concentrically, the four Border Taming temples (*mtha'-'dul-gi lha-khang*) were built in Khoting in Lhodrak upon the ogress' left elbow, Pucu in Kongpo upon her right elbow, Bumthang in Mön upon her left knee and Tradüntse in the north (*byang*) upon her right knee. An outer series of Further Taming temples (*yang-'dul-gi lha-khang*) was also constructed beyond them. These were in Lungngen in Cangtshel upon the ogress' left hand, Langtang Drölma in Dokam upon her right hand, Kyercu in Paro upon her left foot and Camtrin in Mangyül upon her right foot. Other enumerations are also given in Aris' work cited above.

544 Nothing is known of this brāhman Śaṅkara. He is certainly not to be identified with the Hindu Vedantist philosopher of the same name.

545 On this work, see Aris, *Bhutan*, pp. 8ff.; and M. Kapstein, "Remarks on the *Maṇi bKa'-'bum* and the Cult of Avalokiteśvara in Tibet" in S. D. Goodman and R. M. Davidson (eds.), *Tibetan Buddhism: Reason and Revelation*.

546 Among the eight treatises composed by Thönmi Sambhoṭa only two are extant and contained in the *Tangyur*, namely, the *lung-ston-pa-la rtsa-ba sum-cu-pa* (T 4348) and the *rtags-kyi 'jug-pa* (T 4349). The titles of the other six are now unknown.

547 See *Fundamentals*, pp. 59-60.

548 The source of this tradition of the copper-plate inscription is the annotated *Testament of Ba*. See Stein, *Une Chronique Ancienne de bSam-yas*.

549 All these spiritual beings were bound under oath by Guru Padmasambhava to guard the transmitted precepts and treasures, and to protect the sites of monasteries, hermitages and sacred places. See *The Life and Liberation of Padmasambhava*, Pt. 2, pp. 370-5; and also the Glossary of Enumerations for a full list.

550 The oracular mirror is employed for the divination of past, present and future events. Cf. Rikdzin Lhündrup's Hindi version of the *History*, Ch. 3, n. 17; and G. Tucci, *The Religions of Tibet*, pp. 202-4.

551 Odantapurī Monastery was founded at the site of present-day Bihar Sharif in Patna district, probably during the reign of Gopāla I of the Pāla dynasty, who flourished in the mid- or late eighth century.

552 I.e. Samye was built to resemble our world realm, the world of Patient Endurance. The three shrines of the three queens are described in

KGHP, p. 114.

553 The Sarvāstivāda order has always been the Hīnayāna school to which the Tibetans have adhered for their Vinaya.

554 Vaiśravaṇa is an important wealth-granting deity, for whose rites in Tibet, see Nebesky-Wojkowitz, *Oracles and Demons of Tibet*, Ch. IV.

555 The doctrine according to which contradiction is here avoided is elaborated above, pp. 473-4.

556 Cf. *The Life and Liberation of Padmasambhava*, Ch. 107.

557 See *Sūtra of the Wise and the Foolish*, Ch. 13.

558 The *twenty mountain caves of Ngari* have been listed in the Glossary of Enumerations. We have been unable to identify a precise enumeration of twenty-one places of attainment in Central Tibet and Tsang although there are indeed many sacred sites there (see KGHP). The *twenty-five great pilgrimage places of Kham and Amdo* (see Glossary of Enumerations) are well known from the rediscovered teachings of Chogyur Lingpa, on whom see pp. 844-8. His guidebooks to these pilgrimage places are to be found in Vol. 30 of his *Collected Rediscovered Teachings*. The five valleys are *shangs-kyi zab-bu lung* in the centre, *kong-gi ljongs-pa lung* in the east, *mon-gyi srib-btsan lung* in the south, *'gos-kyi phag-ri lung* in the west and *skyid-kyi gro-ma-lung* in the north. The one parkland is *padma gling* on the south-east border, the three districts are Sikkim (*'bras-mo ljongs*) on the south-west border, *mkhan-pa ljongs* on the north-west border and *lung-gsum ljongs* on the north-east border. See also *The Life and Liberation of Padmasambhava*, Pt. 2, pp. 644-6.

559 According to Dudjom Rinpoche, *rgyal-rabs*, pp. 228-34, Murup Tsepo led an expeditionary force against the Bhaṭa Hor, setting out for the north in 827 (*me-lugs*, *rgyal-rabs* dating) and returning in 836 (*me-'brug*).

560 The Gyelpo Shingjachen would here appear to be none other than the great protector Pehar. Usually he is regarded as the latter's emanation, see Nebesky-Wojkowitz, *Oracles and Demons of Tibet*, pp. 97-100 and 111-15; and Dudjom Rinpoche, *rgyal-rabs*, pp. 207, 228-34.

561 On the inscriptions of the ancient kings of Tibet, see especially H. E. Richardson, *Ancient Historical Edicts at Lhasa*; and Tucci, *The Tombs of the Tibetan Kings*. Complete texts of the extant inscriptions may be found in *bod-kyi rdo-ring-dang dril-bu'i kha-byang*. Richardson has recently re-edited all of this material, with new translations and extensive commentary, in *A Corpus of Early Tibetan Inscriptions*.

562 The source of this quotation is the *sgra sbyor bam gnyis* (T 347), pp. 2-3, a summary of Buddhist lexicography and translation conventions compiled under imperial order.

563 See below, p. 794 and n. 1065, for the relevant ancient quotation.

564 According to the traditional account Pelgi Dorje gained access to the royal presence disguised as a Pönpo sorceror, and then used his ritual bow and arrow to slay the evil monarch. Also see below, p. 524.

565 On these two kings, see Stein, *Tibetan Civilization*, p. 70. Pelkortsen's death at the hands of his rebellious subjects ended the dynasty which had begun with Nyatrhi Tsenpo.

566 I.e. the far north-east of Tibet, in the direction of Mongolia.

567 The three levels of ordination were normally given over a ten-year period.

568 The Lower Tibetan Lineage of the Vinaya (*smad-'dul*) is contrasted with the Upper Lineage introduced into Tibet by Dharmapāla, and the Sakya Lineage which was transmitted from Nāgārjuna through Guṇamati and eventually descended to Tsongkapa. Cf. *Blue Annals*, pp. 34-5.

569 For Dharmaśrī and the seminary of Mindröling, see below, pp. 728-31. The entire lineage down to Dharmaśrī's age is surveyed in Zhecen Gyeltsap, *źe-chen chos-'byuṅ*, pp. 63-100.

570 This Abhidharma lineage was codified in the fourteenth century by Sazang Mati Paṇcen in his great *Abhidharmasamuccaya Commentary*. He discusses the lineage briefly there, Vol. 2, p. 520.

571 The Author has provided a compilation of material from these histories in his *rgyal-rabs*. His own sources, as listed in the bibliography of that work, p. 391, are: the *bka'-chems skor* of Songtsen Gampo; the *gter-ma ka-bkol-ma* of Jowoje Atiśa; the *bsam-yas-kyi dkar-chag chen-mo*, which is also known as *sba-bzhed che-'bring*; the *Early and Later Injunctions of Padma* (*thang-yig snga-phyi*); the *Biography of Vairocana* (*bai-ro'i 'dra-'bag*); the *Great Account* (*lo-rgyus chen-mo*) of Khutön; the *Royal History* (*rgyal-rabs*) of Yarlung Jowo; the *Red Annals* (*deb-dmar*) of Tshelpa; the *Royal History which is a Clear Mirror* (*rgyal-rabs gsal-ba'i me-long*) of Sakya; the *Blue Annals* (*deb-sngon*) of Gölo Zhönupel; the *Scholar's Feast of Doctrinal History* (*chos-'byung mkhas-pa'i dga'-ston*) of Pawo Tsuklak Trhengwa; the *Annals entitled the Delight of the Youthful Perfect Age* (*rdzogs-ldan gzhon-nu'i dga'-ston*) of the Dalai Lama V; and the *Genealogy of the Divine Kings entitled Mirror for the Mind which is Brief in Word but Clear in Meaning (lha'i btsan-po'i gdung-rabs tshig-nyung don-gsal yid-kyi me-long)* of Katok Tshewang Norbu.

HISTORY: PART FOUR

572 On the distinction between the stages of creation (*bskyed-rim*), perfection (*rdzogs-rim*) and Great Perfection (*rdzogs-pa chen-po*), see *Fundamentals*, pp. 358-9.

573 See below, pp. 607-13.

574 See above, p. 462, n. 497.

575 On this work, unfortunately little studied as yet, see R. A. Stein, "Une Mention du Manichéisme dans le Choix du Bouddhisme comme religion d'état par le roi Tibétain Khri-sroṅ lde-bcan" in *Indianisme et Bouddhisme, Mélanges offerts à Mgr. Etienne Lamotte*, (1980), pp. 329-37; and G. Tucci, *Minor Buddhist Texts*, Pt. 2, pp. 122-5.

576 Tib. *mkha'-spyod-pa* or sky-farer indicates the accomplishment of celestial travel, on which see *Fundamentals*, p. 259. It is also the name given to one of the *four ways of death*, which are listed in the Glossary of Enumerations.

577 This is none other than Pelgi Yeshe, on whom see below, pp. 605-6.

578 The accomplishment of transforming a zombie or *ro-langs* (lit. standing corpse) into gold is achieved by the yogin in the context of particular cremation-ground rituals. See A. David-Neel, *Magic and Mystery in Tibet*, pp. 134-7. The corpse is resurrected, its tongue tenaciously bitten by the yogin, and then the transformation is said to occur.

579 The vital energy (*rlung*, Skt. *vāyu*) and mind (*sems*, Skt. *citta*) operate respectively in the right and left channels of the body in the form of the white and red seminal points. During the unenlightened state the vital energies cling and differentiate through their five functions of life-breath, secretion, speech, digestion and metabolism, and so pervade all major and minor channels within the body. Maturation occurs when these "active vital energies" (*las-kyi rlung*) and the mind are reunited in the central channel as the vital energy of pristine cognition (*ye-shes-kyi rlung*) and the enlightened mind. See Longcenpa, *Dispelling Darkness in the Ten Directions*, pp. 453ff. (GGFTC, pp. 1006ff.).

580 On the state of coalescence, see *Fundamentals*, p. 259.

581 The twenty-five great accomplished masters of Chimpu (*rje-'bangs nyer-lnga*) are enumerated above on pp. 534-6.The precise enumerations of the others are unknown (Khetsun Zangpo Rinpoche).

582 See below, pp. 607-15.

583 The effortless vehicle is Atiyoga, the highest.

584 For the distinctions between the White, Black and Variegated branches of the Spatial Class, see *Fundamentals*, pp. 326-8; and the detailed explanation in Longcenpa, *Treasury of Spiritual and Philosophical Systems*, pp. 339-48.

585 On the accomplishment of swift-footedness, see *Fundamentals*, p. 259. It is conferred by yakṣa and yakṣiṇī spirits and classed among the mundane accomplishments which do not transcend the cycle of existence.

586 Of the *Eighteen Esoteric Instructions of the Mental Class* which are listed in the Bibliography, the first five were those translated by Vairocana; the remaining thirteen were subsequently translated by Vimalamitra with the assistance of Nyak Jñānakumāra and Yudra Nyingpo.

587 On the reasons for the exile of Vairocana to Kham, see *The Life and Liberation of Padmasambhava*, Pt. 2, pp. 450-70; the *Scholar's Feast of Doctrinal History*, pp. 225-9; and P. Kvaerne, "A Preliminary Study of Ch. VI of the *Gzer-mig*" in TSHR, pp. 185-91. A major source to be explored in depth is the *Biography of Vairocana* (*rje-btsun thams-cad mkhyen-pa bai-ro-tsa-na'i rnam-thar 'dra-'bag chen-mo*), Ch. 11.

588 The lineages indicated in this paragraph are detailed in Pt. 5.

589 The *four ways of death* are listed in the Glossary of Enumerations.

590 Phadampa is revered in Tibet as the founder of the tradition known as Pacification (*zhi-byed*). For his life and deeds, refer to B. N. Aziz, "Indian Philosopher as Tibetan Folk Hero" *Central Asiatic Journal* 23, 1-2 (1979), pp. 19-37; and idem, "The Work of Pha-dam-pa Sangs-rgyas as Revealed in Ding-ri Folklore" in TSHR, pp. 21-9. Cf. also *Blue Annals*, Book XII.

591 The *Vajra Bridge* is a teaching according to the Spatial Class of the Great Perfection. It is known as such because its practice leads to the attainment of the rainbow body in one lifetime. See *Fundamentals*, pp. 326-8.

592 On the Six-Syllable Mantra, see n. 537.

593 This master appears to have played a major role in the transmission of the *Supreme Continuum of the Greater Vehicle* in Tibet. See, e.g., Jamgön Kongtrül, *rgyud bla-ma'i 'grel-pa*, introduction; and Jetsün Künga Drölcok, *khrid-brgya lo-rgyus*. His tradition did much to inspire

the elaboration of the teaching of extrinsic emptiness (*gzhan-stong*), on which see *Fundamentals*, pp. 169ff.

594 See *Fundamentals*, p. 370, n. 355.

595 "Water-stone" (*chu-rdo*) refers to a type of soft, porous rock.

596 Atiśa's direct and circuitous paths of Transcendental Perfection are exemplified in his *Lamp for the Path to Enlightenment* (*Bodhipathapradīpa*) and the many brief precepts anthologised in, e.g., DZ Vols. 2-3.

597 For a useful introduction to the life and teachings of this great woman, see *Blue Annals*, pp. 982-4; and J. Gyatso, "A Preliminary Study of the *Gcod* Tradition" in STC, pp. 320-41.

598 The available data on this master is summarised in B. N. Aziz's introduction to *The Traditions of Pha-dam-pa Saṅs-rgyas*.

599 Refer to sGam-po-pa, *The Jewel Ornament of Liberation*.

600 Four Syllables: In the practice of *gtum-mo* when the inner heat blazes upward from the syllable VAṂ to melt the seminal point in the crown centre, the seed-syllables of body, speech and mind (OṂ ĀḤ HŪṂ) then lose their stability in the crown, throat and heart centres respectively (Khetsun Zangpo Rinpoche.)

601 The text erroneously reads *zla-bzhi* for *brda-bzhi*.

602 Deathless nectar (*'chi-med bdud-rtsi*) is a purificatory means of subsistence on alchemical and herbal essences and so forth.

603 As above, n. 600, the three movements are the destabilisation of the syllables OṂ ĀḤ HŪṂ effected by the syllable VAṂ when it generates the heat to melt the seminal point of the crown centre.

604 *thugs-pa lcags-bsregs*. The red-hot image that emerges when the mould used in iron-casting is broken.

605 Vajrapāṇi is frequently invoked to deal with skin diseases such as leprosy which are said to be caused by malign nāgas or water spirits.

606 There are *four kinds of relics*, on which see *Fundamentals*, p. 337; and the Glossary of Enumerations. They are generally the small indestructible particles among the larger bone remains left behind after the cremation of an enlightened master.

607 On this renowned logician, see L. W. J. van der Kuijp, "Phya-pa Chos-kyi Seng-ge's Impact on Tibetan Epistemological Theory" JIP 5 (1977), pp. 355-69.

608 The *Seven Sessions of Aro* (*a-ro thun-bdun*), also known as *Aro khrid-mo-che*, is the system of the Mental Class which was formulated by Aro Yeshe Jungne in Kham (*khams-lugs*). It was so called because he held both the Indian and Chinese lineages during the seventh generation of their transmission. See DZ Vol. 1; and Karmay, "Origin and Early Development of the Tibetan Religious Traditions of the Great Perfection", pp. 181-2, n. 41.

609 Phakmotrupa (1110-70) was one of the four greatest disciples of Gampopa. The tradition named after him was for some centuries one of the most influential Kagyü subsects, and came to wield great temporal power as well. His own disciples went on to found eight independent subsects of their own. See *Blue Annals*, pp. 552-63; Stein, *Tibetan Civilization*, pp. 74-81; and Tucci, *The Religions of Tibet*, pp. 26, 36, 40-1.

610 On this figure, see below, pp. 674-5.

611 See below, pp. 825-34.

612 Her father was King Trhisong Detsen.

613 The seed-syllable NṚ focused in the heart centre of the body is the source of human existence. In Sanskrit it is the root indicating "human existence", "mankind" or "man".

614 Pema Lendreltsel was the reincarnation of the princess Pemasel. According to the *Scholar's Feast of Doctrinal History*, p. 213, he was also known as Pangangpa Rincen Dorje (see below, p. 582). Other sources, however, hold Rincen Dorje to have been his reincarnation. He, in turn, was succeeded by Longcen Rapjampa, and he, by Pema Lingpa. See pp. 796-9.

615 See n. 586 above; and Longcenpa, *Treasury of Spiritual and Philosophical Systems*, pp. 357-61.

616 Mount Wu-t'ai-shan (*ri-bo rtse-lnga*) is a mountain sacred to Mañjuśrī and located in Shanxi province. See also p. 495. For much useful background on Wu-t'ai-shan as a place of Chinese Buddhist pilgrimage, see R. Birnbaum, *Studies on the Mysteries of Mañjuśrī*.

617 For a description of this important temple, see H. E. Richardson, "Tibetan inscriptions at Źva-ḥi Lha Khaṅ" *Journal of the Royal Asiatic Society* (1952), pp. 133-54, and (1953), pp. 1-12; also KGHP, pp. 37-9, 110, etc.

618 Elder (*gnas-brtan*) is usually equivalent to Skt. *sthavira*. Zhecen Gyeltsap, *źe-chen, chos-'byung*, p. 208, however, glosses *gnas-brtan* in this instance with the words *dkon-gnyer dkun-ma*, "ordinary temple attendant", which refers, he maintains, to Dangma's long-held position in the Zha Temple in Uru.

619 On this renowned ascetic, see Nālandā Translation Committee, *The Rain of Wisdom*, pp. 256-8.

620 Uttaraphalgunī (*khra'i zla-ba*) is the latter half of the second Tibetan month (March/April). It is also known as *dbo zla-ba*. The earlier half, Pūrvaphalgunī, is known in Tibetan as *gre-zla-ba* or *rta-chung zla-ba*.

621 The Tibetan *kha-byang* means an inventory to concealed treasure doctrines. In this context however it equally refers to the cave facing (*kha*) north (*byang*), which is symbolic of the inventory Zhangtönpa was to discover.

622 Physical refinement: this is *shin-tu sbyangs-pa yang-dag byang-chub-kyi yan-lag*, Skt. *praśrabdhi*, one of the seven limbs of enlightenment (*byang-chub-kyi yan-lag bdun*, Skt. *saptabodhyaṅga*) cultivated by a bodhisattva.

623 The western chronology giving precise days and months from this point onwards is calculated according to the tables appended to Schuh's *Untersuchungen zur Geschichte der Tibetischen Kalenderrechnung*. Refer to pp. 399-400, for guidelines on our usage of Schuh's tables.

624 I.e. white representing Vairocana, blue representing Akṣobhya-Vajrasattva, yellow representing Ratnasambhava, red representing Amitābha, and green representing Amoghasiddhi. See *Fundamentals*, pp. 125-7.

625 The *Seventeen Tantras of the Esoteric Instructional Class* are listed in the first part of the Bibliography. See also Longcenpa, *Treasury of Spiritual and Philosophical Systems*, pp. 390ff.

626 The aftermath of meditative absorption (*rjes-thob*, Skt. *pṛṣthalabdha*) refers to the experiences which occur during the intervals between

specific periods of meditative absorption (*snyoms-'jug*, Skt. *samāhita*).

627 On this Kagyü master, see *Blue Annals*, pp. 403-7.

628 Trakpa Gyeltsen (1147-1216) was the third of the five great masters of the early Sakyapa school. See *Blue Annals*, pp. 194, 211, 217.

629 The three continua in general are the tantras of ground, path and result, on which see *Fundamentals*, pp. 263-7. Here, however, they refer to such instructions specifically within the Sakya tradition.

630 The Protector of Pristine Cognition (*ye-shes mgon-po*, Skt. Jñānanātha) is a form of Mahākāla. See Nebesky-Wojkowitz, *Oracles and Demons of Tibet*, pp. 44-8.

631 See *Blue Annals*, pp. 711-15. Zhang (1122-93) was the founder of the Tshelpa Kagyü tradition.

632 The *khukcö* flower (*khug-chos me-tog*), also known as *ug-chos*, is said by Kalön Jigme Taring and Hugh Richardson to be *Incarvillea Delavayi*. It is a pink trumpet-shaped flower on a short stalk blossoming between May and July.

633 See *Scholar's Feast of Doctrinal History*, p. 198, for this prediction which is derived from the *Penetration of Sound*, pp. 40-1.

634 According to *Blue Annals*, p. 195, this occurred in the year 1214 when Guru Cober was nineteen. In that source the Translator of Sakya is clearly stated to be Sa-skya Paṇ-chen, i.e. Sakya Paṇḍita.

635 On the Mitrayogī tradition, see *Blue Annals*, pp. 1031-4.

636 See Guenther, *The Royal Song of Saraha*, Pt. 1.

637 This is of course the famed image in the Lhasa Jokhang. See Pl. 8.

638 The actual ground of the practice (*dngos-gzhi*) is preceded by the preliminaries (*sngon-'gro*), on which see Jamgön Kongtrül, *The Torch of Certainty*, and *The Words of My Perfect Teacher.*

639 "Secret vajra" (*gsang-ba rdo-rje*) is here a mystical metaphor for penis.

640 These are famed as "secret lands" (*sbas-yul*), on which see E. Bernbaum, *The Way to Shambhala*, pp. 53-77.

641 Orgyenpa Rincenpel, p. 891, played a dominant role in the transmission of the Drukpa Kagyü and Karma Kagyü traditions during the latter part of the thirteenth century. In addition, he founded his own teaching system known as the *Oḍḍiyāna Tradition of Ritual Service and Attainment* (*o-rgyan bsnyen-bsgrub*), which was connected with the *Kālacakra Tantra*. See *Blue Annals*, pp. 696-702; G. Tucci, *Travels of Tibetan Pilgrims in the Swat Vally*, pp. 41-64; and the Glossary of Enumerations under *three indestructible realities*.

642 Kumārādza, the name by which this figure is best known, is a Tibetanised form of the Sanskrit name Kumārarāja.

643 *spyan-ras-gzigs na-rag dong-sprugs*, an aspect of Avalokiteśvara particularly favoured among the Nyingmapa.

644 This quotation occurs in a biography of Drigung Rincen Phüntsok, on whom, see below, pp. 595 and 676-7.

645 This is a valuable assertion that must be seriously considered in studying the evolution of the doctrines of the Great Perfection. In particular, the diction of early authors such as Nupcen Sangye Yeshe and Rongzom Chöki Zangpo should be closely compared to that of Kumārādza's leading disciples Longcen Rapjampa and Karmapa Rangjung Dorje and their successors.

646 *gza'-sngags-dam-gsum*. See, in particular, Nebesky-Wojkowitz, *Oracles*

and Demons of Tibet, Ch. X, pp. 185-6, 259-64. Nebesky-Wojkowitz, however, does not seem to have been aware of their occurrence as a trio in the tradition of the Great Perfection.

647 See *Scholar's Feast of Doctrinal History*, p. 198, and the *Penetration of Sound*, pp. 40-1.

648 All the major chronological schools agree on the date for Kumārādza's passing.

649 The Chinese emperor was Toghan Timur (reigned 1332-68). See Karma Thinley, *The History of the Sixteen Karmapas of Tibet*, pp. 57-8.

650 See below, pp. 666-7.

651 The *Scholar's Feast of Doctrinal History*, p. 198, states the source to be the *Innermost Spirituality of the Ḍākinī* (*mkha'-'gro snying-thig*).

652 See above, p. 515.

653 Dromtön (1004-64) was one of the three leading disciples of Atiśa and a founder of the Kadampa tradition. Refer to *Blue Annals*, pp. 251-67.

654 The date of Longcenpa's birth is calculated according to the old Phukpa school. The Tshurpu system omits from its reckoning the eighteenth day on which he passed away, while Phakpa omits the sixteenth day preceding his demise, which is also mentioned in the biography. Hence only Phukpa includes all of these three days, although it is a system of calculation adopted after the death of Longcenpa.

655 Namdru Remati, the protectress from the Mātaraḥ maṇḍala, is the embodiment of the constellation Andromeda. See also Nebesky-Wojkowitz, *Oracles and Demons of Tibet*, p. 33.

656 On the seminary of Sangpu Neutok, see *Blue Annals*, pp. 328ff.

657 Note also that this epithet echoes the name of a group of profound scriptures of the Great Perfection, the *Tantras of the Extent of Vast Space* (*klong-chen rab-'byams-kyi rgyud-rnams*, NGB Vol. 3).

658 Sonam Gyeltsen (1312-75) is best known to western scholars as the possible author of a popular history of the ancient Tibetan kings, the *rgyal-rabs gsal-ba'i me-long*. That Longcenpa regarded him as an important philosophical thinker is revealed by his letter to Sonam Gyeltsen in *Kloṅ-chen gSuṅ thor-bu*, Vol. 1, pp. 360-3.

659 The traditions of these masters, and their positions in the lineage of Pacification are detailed in *Blue Annals*, pp. 872ff.

660 Regional factionalism seems to have been endemic in the Tibetan monastic colleges from an early date. For an example belonging to the twelfth century, see M. Kapstein, "The Shangs-pa bKa'-brgyud: an unknown tradition of Tibetan Buddhism" in TSHR, pp. 138-44.

661 I.e. Ngok Loden Sherap the great translator. See *Blue Annals*, especially pp. 328ff.

662 The entire text of this satirical poem is preserved in the *Kloṅ-chen gSuṅ thor-bu*, Vol. 1, pp. 268-70.

663 This great scholar contributed vastly to the exegesis of the Transcendental Perfection of Discriminative Awareness, and to other traditions as well. See *Blue Annals*, pp. 532-6; and the English introduction to Yakde Paṇcen, *phar-phyin 'phrul-gyi bang-mdzod*, Vol. 1.

664 In modern Central Tibetan the final "*-s*" is never pronounced, though it is still written in words in which it once occurred. In Longcenpa's day it had probably only recently passed out of the vernacular. The ḍākinī is here a champion of the older pronunciation! The usage of

rigs for *rig-pa* or awareness is prevalent in works such as Longcenpa, *Dispelling Darkness in the Ten Directions*, e.g. pp. 361-3, 466 (GGFTC, pp. 852, 1027). The tradition of the *Tantra of the Secret Nucleus* (*rgyud gsang-ba'i snying-po*) itself adopts the former in the well-known verse cited above, p. 281, n. 276.

665 Contemplative experience correlates in various ways with ordinary mental states. Thus ordinary waking consciousness corresponds to the experience of the "body of illusion" (*sgyu-lus*, Skt. *māyākāya*), mundane dreaming to the yoga of the dream state (*rmi-lam*, Skt. *svapna*), and deep dreamless sleep to inner radiance (*'od-gsal*, Skt. *prabhāsvara*). Hence, there is the reference to sleep at this juncture.

666 The deity Ode Kungyel is held to be the protector of a mountain range in Nyangpo which bears the same name; see Nebesky-Wojkowitz, *Oracles and Demons of Tibet*, pp. 206, 227. For Nyencen Thangla, ibid., pp. 205-10. The seven Menmo sisters (*sman-mo mched-bdun*) were subdued at Silma in Tsang by the master Padmasambhava: ibid., pp. 198-202; and *The Life and Liberation of Padmasambhava*, Pt. 2, p. 373.

667 The prophecy is referring to Longcenpa's subsequent incarnation as the treasure-finder Pema Lingpa in Bhutan to the south-west of Tibet.

668 The treasure troves in Bumthang are those which he later discovered as Pema Lingpa.

669 Kumārādza, the teacher of Longcenpa, was of course the emanation of Vimalamitra.

670 Longcenpa was the reincarnation of Pangangpa Rincen Dorje who, according to different traditions, is held to have been either identical to, or the reincarnation of, Pema Lendreltsel, the discoverer of the *Innermost Spirituality of the Ḍākinī*. See above, p. 555, n. 614.

671 The point is that the widespread propagation of the *Innermost Spirituality of Vimalamitra* continued for one hundred years and the *Innermost Spirituality of the Ḍākinī* for five hundred years. Although both lineages are preserved at the present time, there are few who actively practise their teachings. And yet they are treasured for providing the essential background to many cycles which are currently practised.

672 On the third empowerment and its related teachings, see *Fundamentals*, pp. 301-2, n. 238.

673 *ngo-sprod*. This is the formal introduction to the experience of reality itself, which is conferred from master to student in a direct manner.

674 "Even a clay pot has a handle" – this is a pun on the Tibetan word *lung* which means either "transmission" or "the handle of a vase".

675 This is the princess Pematsel mentioned above on p. 554.

676 I.e. the four profound volumes of the *Innermost Spirituality of Vimalamitra*.

677 On "the manifestation of inner radiance by night", see *Fundamentals*, p. 280.

678 According to H. V. Guenther in the introduction to *Kindly Bent to Ease Us*, Vol. 1, p. xiv, it was on this occasion that he was given the name Dorje Ziji by Yeshe Tshogyel. Previously Guru Rinpoche had named him Trime Özer.

679 *mngon-rtogs*. The text in which the visualisation and ritual of the deity is described.

680 It is by conferring the seal of entrustment (*gtad-rgya*) that the continuity of transmitted doctrines is maintained.

681 *sprul-bsgyur*. This compound belongs to the technical terminology of the yoga of the dream state, but is also applied to the manufacture of sacramental substances.

682 Longcenpa developed the *Innermost Spirituality of the Ḍākinī* into his own mind treasure, the *Further Innermost Spirituality of the Ḍākinī*. Later he condensed it along with the *Further Innermost Spirituality of the Guru* (*bla-ma yang-tig*, NYZ Vol. 1) into the *Profound Further Innermost Spirituality* (*zab-mo yang-tig*, NYZ Vols. 10-11).

683 "Offerings pure in respect of the three spheres" are those purely given without trace of attachment in the giver, the giving or to the gift itself.

684 Ceremonies of the eighth, tenth and twenty-fifth days respectively commemorate the medicine buddhas, Guru Padmasambhava in his various manifestations and the ḍākinīs.

685 This is the *Further Innermost Spirituality of the Guru* or the *Further Innermost Spirituality like the Wish-fulfilling Gem* (*yang-tig yid-bzhin nor-bu*) which Longcenpa developed from the *Innermost Spirituality of Vimalamitra*.

686 *bca'-ka*.

687 On Tamsi demons, see Nebesky-Wojkowitz, *Oracles and Demons of Tibet*, pp. 517-18, 119, 284.

688 On the conflict between Sakya and Drigung, see, e.g., D. Snellgrove and H. Richardson, *A Cultural History of Tibet*, pp.144-5, 152; and *Blue Annals*, pp. 217-18. This led eventually to the formal assumption of power in 1349 of Tā'i Situ Cangcup Gyeltsen of Phakmotru (1302-64). Longcenpa moved to Bhutan in consequence of a dispute with this new potentate of Tibet, which endured for some ten years. See below, pp. 591-2; and for an enumeration of the eight monasteries which he founded or developed there, see Aris, *Bhutan*, pp. 155, 315.

689 Our text erroneously reads *gsum* (three) for *gnyis* (two). For a highly useful anthology of Longcenpa's writings, drawn from many of the texts mentioned in this paragraph, see Tulku Thondup Rinpoche, *Buddha Mind*.

690 This incident is recounted by Guenther in his introduction to *Kindly Bent to Ease Us*, Vol. 1, p. xv. Tā'i Situ Cangcup Gyeltsen was unfortunately provoked into believing Longcenpa to be an ally of his opponent Drigung Gompa Künrin. Shortly after the former assumed power, Künrin organised a revolt. Longcenpa tried to mediate, but his actions were misinterpreted and in consequence he was forced into exile in Bhutan where he remained at the monastery of Tharpaling near Bumthang (see n. 688 above). Eventually he was reconciled with Tā'i Situ (the "Eight-footed Lion" or "Shing-go-chen-pa") through the efforts of his lay patrons Prince Situ Śākya Zangpo of upper Ü and Dorje Gyeltsen of Yamdrok.

691 *shing-sgo chen-pa*: "King of the Land of Wooden Doors" was a title adopted by Tā'i Situ Cangcup Gyeltsen. Tibet is called the land of wooden doors because (according to Nyoshul Khen Rinpoche) a wooden gateway was erected on the Amdo frontier with China to mark a peace treaty during the reign of Relpacen. According to Khenpo Palden Sherap the significance is that in antiquity the first Tibetans

to build houses constructed their doors of plentiful forest wood. The Author recommends both views should be recorded here. T. V. Wylie in GT, p. 155, n. 373, maintains the latter view on the basis of G. Tucci's *Tibetan Painted Scrolls*, p. 698, n. 486: "This expression becomes synonymous with the areas of Dbus and gTsang, where the population is largely sedentary as opposed to the nomadic peoples of other areas." The former lived in permanent houses while the latter lived in tents.

692 In this instance Longcenpa refers to himself by this name, not to his previous incarnation.

693 See *Fundamentals*, pp. 335-45.

694 The date of Longcenpa's death is here calculated according to the old Phukpa school, on which see p. 400. The Tshurpu calendar omits the eighteenth day of this particular month on which he passed away, and the Phakpa school omits the sixteenth day which is mentioned in this biography. Cf. n. 654 above.

695 "Upper demons" (*steng-gdon*) afflict the brain causing epilepsy, stroke and nervous disorders.

696 See the *Scholar's Feast of Doctrinal History*, p. 198, and the *Penetration of Sound*, pp. 40-1, where the prediction concerning Lodröchok clearly intervenes between those of Gelong Pelden (i.e. Kumārādza) and the ḍākinī Śrīdharā.

697 See below, pp. 676-7.

698 See below, pp. 835-40.

HISTORY: PART FIVE

699 On the trilogy of the *Sūtra which Gathers All Intentions*, the *Magical Net* and the *Mental Class* (*mdo-sgyu-sems-gsum*), see p. 396. The term *Mental Class* in this context specifically refers to the cycle of teachings associated with the *All-Accomplishing King* (*chos thams-cad rdzogs-pa chen-po byang-chub-kyi sems kun-byed rgyal-po*, T 828), which exemplifies the Mental Class of the Great Perfection.

700 See p. 533 above.

701 *dmar-khrid*.

702 See Dudjom Rinpoche, *rgyal-rabs*, p. 313. Queen Margyen, also known as Queen Tshepong-za, was the senior consort of King Trhisong, and a partisan of the Pön tradition. When the crown-prince Mune Tsepo came to power in 796 (*rgyal-rabs* dating), he married his father's younger consort Phoyongza and in direct consequence was poisoned to death by his own mother out of jealousy in 798, shortly before his father's demise. The queen then became openly hostile to Buddhist teachers such as Nyak. Cf. also Kvaerne, "A Preliminary Study of Chapter VI of the *gZer-mig*".

703 *long-mo*.

704 The *Perfect Practice of Vajrakīla* is a means for attainment derived from the *Vajrakīlaguhyatantra* (NGB Vol. 27). The *Blue-skirted One's Cycle* (*gsham-sngon*) is another tradition derived from the *Twelve-Section Kīlaya Tantra* (*kilaya tan-tra bcu-gnyis*, NGB Vols. 19, 29). Together with the *Six Secret Tantras* (NGB Vols. 28-9) they were passed down

in the lineage of Nyak Jñānakumāra. See p. 712 below.

705 The "Crow of Chim" or Chim Carok, one of Nyak's enemies, was unfortunately named. Nyak's careless invocation of the rite brought death to an innocent crow (*bya-rog*).

706 It is not clear to us exactly which tale this refers to. But compare this with the story of Jālandharipā's disciple Kaṇhapā (who is often identified with Kṛṣṇacārin) in Robinson, *Buddha's Lions*, pp. 81-5.

707 The rite of the "Tie to the Higher Realms" (*gnas-lung*) is a funeral ceremony in which the consciousness of the deceased is actually transferred to a higher level of existence. The rite of "liberation" (*sgrol*) is one aspect of the fourth rite (*drag-po'i phrin-las*) through which the consciousness of a sentient being trapped in the unfavourable conditions of bad karma can be transferred forcefully to the favourable conditions of a buddha-field by great mantra adepts acting out of compassion. Obstacles to oneself and to others are said to be thereby removed. Such is the purpose of all the wrathful actions which are described in this and subsequent passages. Refer to Longcenpa, *Dispelling Darkness in the Ten Directions* pp. 396-402 (GGFTC, pp. 914-22).

708 Life-supporting wolf-spirits (*bla-spyang*) are one manifestation of the life-supporting talisman (*bla-gnas*) which was generally adopted by Tibetan potentates as a magical means of personal protection. The ancient kings are said to have possessed turquoise crown ornaments (*bla-gYu*) which were empowered in this way. The power traditionally ascribed to a life-supporting talisman is illustrated by an incident from the *Epic of Ling Kesar* in which the hostile king Sa-tham proves to be invincible until the moment when Kesar kills the seven bears which were his life-support. See also Nebesky-Wojkowitz, *Oracles and Demons of Tibet*, pp. 481-3.

709 All that arises in the mind is ultimately grounded in the very nature of mind itself, and thus, if used skilfully, provides a path leading to the realisation of that nature. Vimalamitra guided Nyak's wrath in such a way that realisation emerged from wrath itself, which was then transmuted into great compassion.

710 The Sogdians and related peoples of Central Asia, such as the Scythians, were renowned metal-workers. The name *sog-po* (originally referring to the Sogdians) was later applied to the Mongols when they overran the whole of Central Asia. See Stein, *Tibetan Civilization*, p. 34; and G. Uray, "The Four Horns of Tibet according to the Royal Annals" *Acta Orientalia Hungarica* X, 1 (1960), pp. 31-57, n. 34.

711 I.e. Pektse's body was similar to a kīla or ritual dagger – the symbolic implement of Vajrakīla through which wrathful rites of "liberation" are performed.

712 This is a variant on one of the most famous and ancient summations of the teaching, which is found in, e.g., *Dhammapāda*, v. 183, and other canonical texts. See N.S. Shukla, *The Buddhist Hybrid Sanskrit Dharmapāda*, p. 62, no. 357.

713 See p. 540.

714 Nyakmar and Getön are apparently one and the same.

715 As noted briefly in the Translators' Introduction and in n. 535 above, there are many discrepancies in the dating of the imperial period of Tibetan history which come to light when the various available sources

are compared. One of the problems centres on whether Songtsen Gampo died in 649/50 as stated by Chinese and early Tibetan sources (Tun Huang, *T'ang Annals*), or whether he lived until 718 as claimed by some Tibetan sources (cf. Dudjom Rinpoche, *rgyal-rabs*, pp. 137ff.). In addition, Tibetan historians disagree as to the length of time that elapsed between Langdarma's persecution and the restoration of Buddhism in Central Tibet. Nupcen's birth according to the tradition which asserts Songtsen Gampo's longevity and a late date for the Langdarma persecution would be February 832, whereas the dating based on the early annals would place his birth in 772 (*chu-pho-byi lo*). Our present *History* assumes that the dates associated with the life of Nupcen, which are given below on p. 613, follow the former tradition. See also pp. 948-50; and, for further information, Karmay, "Origin and Early Development of the Tibetan Religious Traditions of the Great Perfection", pp. 170-1, 187.

716 Chinese preceptors (Ch. *Ho-shang*, Tib. *Hva-shang*) were active in Central Tibet until their defeat in the great debate at Samye by Kamalaśīla who represented the orthodox Indian philosophical tradition of Svātantrika-Madhyamaka. They later continued to teach their sūtra-based tradition in the Gyelmorong area of Kham where the Great Perfection was also transmitted by Vairocana during his exile. See also pp. 896ff. Some of their texts are said to be among the concealed treasures which were subsequently rediscovered by Ratna Lingpa and others. That Nupcen Sangye Yeshe was himself much influenced by Chinese Ch'an Buddhism is made abundantly clear by his *Lamp for the Eye of Contemplation*, Ch. 5. Cf. Jeffrey Broughton, "Early Ch'an in Tibet" in R. Gimello and P. N. Gregory (eds.), *Studies in Ch'an and Hua-yen*; Karmay, "Origin and Early Development of the Tibetan Religious Traditions of the Great Perfection", *passim*; and Ruegg, "The Great Debate between Gradualists and Simultaneists in Eighth-Century Tibet".

717 Preceptor here, following the oral interpretation of Khenpo Palden Sherap, corresponds closely to the archaic Tibetan word *ru*, which also means superior, primordial, or precursor. See also n. 342.

718 On Marutse the butcher (*gshan-pa ma-ru-rtse*), see Nebesky-Wojkowitz, *Oracles and Demons of Tibet*, p. 92.

719 I.e. the empowerment for the zombie or *vetāla* ritual. See n. 578 above.

720 Running throughout Indo-Tibetan religious culture is a profound belief in the power of truth and the truthful utterance, which when properly applied can work wonders. See, e.g., H. Zimmer, *Philosophies of India*, pp. 160-9.

721 *cha-ga*.

722 That the persecution was directed primarily at the monastic establishment and not at the Buddhist laity is indicated by S. G. Karmay, "The Rdzogs-chen in its Earliest Text" in STC, pp. 272-82. Nup's own survival of the persecution is indicated in his *Lamp for the Eye of Contemplation*. Langdarma, in his decision to supress the Buddhist monasteries, may have been following the lead of the T'ang emperor Wu-tsung, who suppressed Buddhism in 845, as well as responding to reactionary forces in Tibetan society.

723 See above, pp. 523-4.

724 The texts of deathless nectar are exemplified by the *Eight Volumes of*

Nectar (*bdud-rtsi bam-brgyad*, T 841 and NGB Vol. 26).

725 Regarding the traditional Tibetan dating of Buddha Śākyamuni's final nirvāṇa, see p. 948.

726 On the accomplishment of the "swift feet of the yakṣiṇī" (*gnod-sbyin-mo'i rkang-mgyogs*), see *Fundamentals*, p. 259. The *Scholar's Feast of Doctrinal History*, p. 225, speaks of two kinds of swift-footedness, one of which was conferred by Rematī, the yakṣiṇī.

727 For an explanation of the geomantic centres, see n. 543; also Aris, *Bhutan*, pp. 5-33.

728 "Both of the great accomplishments" acquired by Yönten Gyamtso refers to the supreme accomplishment of enlightenment and the mundane accomplishment of special powers, on which see, e.g., *Fundamentals*, pp. 259-60.

729 For the standard account of Milarepa's apprenticeship under this master, see Lhalungpa, *The Life of Milarepa*, pp. 27ff; and D. Martin "The Teachers of Mi-la-ras-pa" *The Journal of the Tibet Society* 2 (1982).

730 Nyang Yeshe Jungne of Chölung – the text wrongly reads Nyang *Sherap* Jungne.

731 The principle division in the lineage of the transmitted precepts is a geographical one between the tradition of Rong in Central Tibet and the tradition of Kham in the east. The Rong tradition will be described first.

732 See *Blue Annals*, p. 109.

733 Atsara is a Tibetan corruption of Skt. *ācārya*, "master" or "teacher".

734 "I" probably refers here to an earlier historian rather than to the present Author.

735 Zurpoche's outward journey from Kham to Central Tibet is paralleled by his inward meditative experience. The robe worn by adepts of the inner heat (*gtum-mo*) is one of thin, white linen.

736 On the centre of perfect rapture (*sambhogacakra*), which is the centre of buddha-speech located in the throat, see pp. 818-19, 837 and n. 1143.

737 The *rulu mantra* is that of Yangdak Heruka.

738 This may well refer to a form of Pehar. See Nebesky-Wojkowitz, *Oracles and Demons of Tibet*, pp. 97, 99 and 145ff.

739 Matram is Rudra, the matricide who is said to have been subdued by Hayagrīva. See, e.g., *The Life and Liberation of Padmasambhava*, Pt. 1, pp. 26-46.

740 *rgya-phubs/phibs*. On this characteristic motif in Tibetan architecture, see A. Chayet, "The Jehol Temples and their Tibetan Models" in STC, pp. 65-72; and idem, *Les Temples de Jehol et leurs modèles tibétaines*.

741 I.e. Vairocana with four faces facing in the four cardinal directions.

742 *glo-'bur*.

743 This is Vairocana in the form of Samantamukha. See n. 741 above.

744 The causal Heruka (*rgyu'i he-ru-ka*) is the simple form with one face and two hands visualised through the stage of creation. It is contrasted with the maturational Heruka (*'bras-bu'i he-ru-ka*) which is the multi-armed deity spontaneously appearing through the stage of perfection. See below, pp. 627-8; also the sections on Mahāyoga and Anuyoga in *Fundamentals*, pp. 275-89 and 359-69.

745 Cf. Lhalungpa, *The Life of Milarepa*, pp. 52-3.

746 The flesh of one born a brahman or vegetarian over seven successive lifetimes is regarded traditionally as having miraculous properties. See, e.g., the account of the life of Orgyen Lingpa, pp. 775-89.

747 As explained on p. 462, Mahāyoga is divided into the section of tantra texts and the section of means for attainment derived from the former. The first is, relatively speaking, exoteric and the second esoteric. See also *Fundamentals*, p. 283.

748 According to the Tibetan system of weights and measures, one load (*khal gcig*) comprises twenty measures (*'bre nyi-shu*), a measure being about four pints.

749 *them-bu*.

750 *thun*.

751 Cf. *Hevajra Tantra*, Pt. 2, Ch. 5, v. 26:

> Flirtatious, heroic and fearsome,
> Mirthful, stern and terrific,
> Compassionate, awed and at peace,
> He is endowed with the nine flavours of drama.

752 On the fruitional or maturational Heruka, see n. 744 above.

753 *chu-rab*.

754 Shenrap Miwoche is regarded by the Pönpo as the founder of their religion. See S. G. Karmay, *The Treasury of Good Sayings*, intro., pp. xviii-xx, 23-4 and *passim*; D. L. Snellgrove, *The Nine Ways of Bon*, intro.; and Tucci, *The Religions of Tibet*, Ch. 7.

755 Drokmi Lotsāwa (993-1050), the student of the Indian Gayadhara, was responsible for introducing into Tibet the tradition of the Path and Fruit (*lam-'bras*), which was to become the foremost teaching of the Sakyapa lineage. His requirements for gold were notorious; see, e.g., Nālandā Translation Committee, *The Life of Marpa the Translator*, pp. 6-8.

756 Name of a pass leading into the valley in which Tshurpu is situated.

757 The bells and dishes would have been attached to the chain as decorations.

758 This is Myu-gu-lung, in Tsangtön Mangkar Valley, situated to the immediate west of Sakya. See *Blue Annals*, pp. 207-8; and KGHP, pp. 64-5.

759 On "holder of the awareness of spontaneous presence" (*lhun-grub rig-'dzin*), see *Fundamentals*, p. 282.

760 The essential substances are pure essences or particles of rainbow light. See *Fundamentals*, p. 340.

761 The wolf-skin hat (*spyang-zhva*) is a garment typically worn by the Pönpo, see below, p. 939. Similarly, the practice of counter-clockwise circumambulation is characteristic of the Pönpo. Cf. D.L. Snellgrove, *Himalayan Pilgrimage*, pp. 42-3.

762 The text erroneously reads *rung-chu* instead of *rud-chu*, "flooding waters" (Khenpo Palden Sherap).

763 "Male wealth" is a family's land and house, and "female wealth" its utensils and valuables. Cf. Stein, *Tibetan Civilization*, p. 109.

764 These first three clauses represent a common formula expressive of unalterable determination in spiritual practice. See Künzang Pelden,

byang-chub sems-dpa'i spyod-pa-la 'jug-pa'i tshig-'grel, fol. 21b.

765 *dpe-'grems*.

766 Zurcungpa is here referred to as Zurpoche's nephew simply because he hails from the same clan, though the genealogy given on p. 617 makes him Zurpoche's grandnephew.

767 *chos-'khor*.

768 The evil destinies (*ngan-'gro*) are those which entail birth as animals, tortured spirits or denizens of hell.

769 For the *Eight Gaurī* in the retinue of Yangdak Heruka, see the Glossary of Enumerations.

770 How they came to be so called is explained below, p. 643.

771 *sdig-pa mi-dge so-sor bshags*. Zurcungpa is here punning on the word *sdig-pa*, which means both "sin" and "scorpion", as well as on the word *bshags*, which means "to repent" and also "to cleave" or "to split".

772 For the full implications of this phrase, see *Fundamentals*, pp. 215-16.

773 *tsong-ge*.

774 These seals or mudrā (*phyag-rgya*) are the seals of the body, speech and mind of the peaceful and wrathful deities (Khenpo Palden Sherap).

775 "The activity field in which appearances are exhausted" (*chos-zad-pa'i skye-mched*) refers to the experience of Cutting Through Resistance (*khregs-chod*). See *Fundamentals*, pp. 334-7.

776 Tib. *dge-ba'i bshes-gnyen*, Skt. *Kalyāṇamitra*. In essence this term refers to one who benefits others by means of the teachings of the greater vehicle. It was taken over by the Kadampa school at an early date as a title for their masters and gradually came to be used to describe those who had passed the scholastic curriculum of the dialectical colleges. Later the Gelukpa school formalised this usage so that in their colleges it became roughly the equivalent of the western Doctor of Divinity or Doctor of Theology degree.

777 *sta-gu-ra mi-gnyis*. According to *Blue Annals*, p. 119, and the Hindi translation of the present text by Rikdzin Lhündrup, p. 186, this term means the "two honourables" (*ādāraṇīya*). Khenpo Palden Sherap speculates that it may mean "two who lived in tents". However the precise derivation of the word is uncertain.

778 This figure played a major role in the diffusion of Buddhist formal logic in Tibet. See *Blue Annals*, pp. 70-1.

779 See Tāranātha, *History of Buddhism in India*, pp. 124-5 and 131-2, for this account of Śūra's meeting with Āryadeva.

780 As pointed out above, nn. 291 and 486, "liberation" refers to the forceful transference of consciousness to a higher level.

781 The identity of the Great Translator of Sakya (*sa-lo-chen-po*) referred to here is unclear. According to Khetsun Zangpo Rinpoche he may possibly have been Sakya Locen Jinpei Dorje. Alternatively, Sakya Lotsāwa Jamyang Künga Zangpo and even Sakya Paṇḍita have been suggested.

782 Regarding the four visionary appearances, of which this is the fourth, it says in the *Penetration of Sound*, p. 91:

> Then turning from that to the four visionary appearances: by the visionary appearance of the direct perception of reality (*chos-nyid mngon-sum-gyi snang-ba*) the terms which

> rely on ideas and scrutiny are transcended; by the visionary appearance of ever increasing contemplative experience (*nyams gong-'phel-ba'i snang-ba*) bewildering appearances decrease and the pristine cognition of the *bardo* is manifested; by the visionary appearance of reaching the limit of awareness (*rig-pa tshad-phebs-kyi snang-ba*) the appearances on the path to realisation of the three bodies are transcended; and by the visionary appearance in which reality is exhausted (*chos-nyid zad-pa'i snang-ba*) the continuity of the three realms of saṃsāra is broken.

See also *Fundamentals*, pp. 337-45 and 371. During these four successive visions it is said that the four empowerments of the Great Perfection are received. For the latter, see pp. 498-501.

783 This translator did much to advance the teaching of the *Guhyasamāja Tantra* in Tibet. See *Blue Annals*, pp. 359ff. He was a vociferous opponent of the Ancient Translation School, on which see below, pp. 914ff.

784 *phyir-'don-pa*.

785 The paths of skilful means (*thabs-lam*) and liberation (*grol-lam*) are explained in *Fundamentals*, pp. 279-81 (under Mahāyoga); and pp. 286-7 (under Anuyoga).

786 *mig-ltag khung-du 'chus*.

787 Coalescence (*zung-'jug*, Skt. *yuganaddha*) is conceived variously according to the different vehicles of the secret mantra, e.g. as that of appearance and emptiness, bliss and emptiness, awareness and emptiness, the expanse of reality and pristine cognition, or buddha-body and pristine cognition. See *Fundamentals*, pp. 206ff. and 245ff. According to the higher vehicles coalescence is said to occur primordially and not causally.

788 Tibetan houses usually have flat roofs, used for threshing grain and as a place to catch the sun on warm days.

789 *che-'don* or investiture is a ceremony marking the maturity of a young hierarch, elevating him or her to precedence in a particular spiritual community and conferring temporal power over the monastic estates. *Blue Annals*, p. 124, reads "coming of age ceremony".

790 *rdzogs-chen skor-lugs*. *skor*, or "cycle", refers here to the four cycles of the Esoteric Instructional Class, on which see *Fundamentals*, pp. 332, 333.

791 On the *four nails*, see the Glossary of Enumerations.

792 The parasol is a symbol of power or authority, here displayed out of respect for Phadampa's illustrious guest.

793 It is after Dropukpa that the Central Tibetan tradition or *rong-lugs* and the Eastern tradition or *khams-lugs* of the transmitted precepts began to diverge.

794 For Tsen spirits, see Nebesky-Wojkowitz, *Oracles and Demons of Tibet*, pp. 12-15, etc.; and for the Mātaraḥ (*ma-mo*), ibid., pp. 267-73.

795 Sacen Küñga Nyingpo (1092-1158) was the first of the "five superiors" (*gong-ma lnga*) of the Sakyapa school.

796 *jo-sras*. This title was used to address the son of a priestly family.

797 *gshegs-btsun-mdzad*: our interpretation of this obscure phrase follows

the oral commentary of Khenpo Palden Sherap.

798 *'ongs-'don* means a public gathering according to Khenpo Palden Sherap; in this particular case it would seem to refer to a harvest festival or thanksgiving ceremony. Cf. *Blue Annals*, p. 134.

799 For the tradition of the cyles of the Great Perfection, see above n. 790. For the Rong and Kham traditions, see nn. 731 and 793 above.

800 The comparison with a horse, traditionally held to be a noble animal, is complimentary. The horse was known as "Loud-voiced Garuḍa-nestling" (*khyung-phrug kha-che*).

801 Lama Zhang was a Kagyü master who, to judge from the many references to him one finds in the literature of the period, was much beloved by adherents of all schools. He was the founder of the Tshelpa Kagyü order. See *Blue Annals*, pp. 711-15; and Stein, *Tibetan Civilization*, p. 76.

802 The Indestructible Seat is the Vajrāsana at Bodh Gayā in Bihar. The images of Śākyamuni are in the Lhasa Trhülnang and Ramoche temples; see p. 510 and Pl. 37. The stone dikes of Lhasa are said to have been first constructed during the reign of Songtsen Gampo; see A. Grünwedel, *Die Tempel von Lhasa*, pp. 21ff., which is based on Dalai Lama V, *Guide to the Cathedral of Lhasa*.

803 Phakmotrupa (1110-70), though famed primarily as a Kagyüpa master, studied also under Sacen Künga Nyingpo. Hence, his involvement in the transmission of the Path and Fruit, a pre-eminently Sakyapa instruction. See *Blue Annals*, p. 556.

804 Recung Dorje-tra was one of Milarepa's leading disciples. His life is summarised in *Blue Annals*, pp. 436ff. In the well-known *Life of Milarepa*, he plays the role of interlocutor, but he was not the author of that work as is asserted in the Evans-Wentz edition. For a convenient summary of the contributions of the actual author, Tsangnyön Heruka (1452-1507), see Nālandā Translation Committee, *The Life of Marpa the Translator*, pp. xix-xxi. Recung is also referred to as "Loro Recungpa", after the name of his favourite dwelling-place.

805 This appears to be the name of a malicious spirit.

806 According to *Blue Annals*, p. 133, Sangye Öntön was a relative of Zhikpo Dütsi.

807 The Kashmiri scholar Śākyaśrī spent the years from 1204 to 1213 in Tibet, during which time he taught extensively to adherents of all the major Tibetan schools. His close ties to Trhopu (*khro-phu*) are evidenced in *Blue Annals*, pp. 599, 710, 1063. It was Campapel, the translator of Trhopu, who invited him to Tibet, served as his interpreter, and eventually became his biographer. He is said to have died in Kashmir in 1225.

808 For this ritual, see n. 707 above.

809 Nyang-rel Nyima Özer (see pp. 755-9) passed away in 1192 or 1204. This must then either refer to his son and grandson, or be an erroneous reference to his son alone.

810 The struggle between Qubilai and Ariboga for the throne occurred in 1260. See Stein, *Tibetan Civilization*, pp. 77-8.

811 Phakpa (1235-80) was made the effective ruler of Tibet by Qubilai in 1253, his power being enhanced in 1260. He held the rank of "Imperial Preceptor" (*ti-shih*), on which see nn. 817 and 924 below.

812 Cf. the texts of other letters from Mongol Qans to Tibetan lamas, e.g. in Tsepon W. D. Shakabpa, *Tibet: A Political History*, pp. 61-6.

813 The complete text of this prayer does not seem to be known at the present time.

814 *Rudrākṣa* is the berry of a tree (*Elaeocarpus Ganitrus*). Rosaries made from these berries are favoured for use in connection with wrathful rites of subjugation.

815 *mu-men* according to S. C. Das, *Tibetan-English Dictionary*, p. 968, is sapphire. According to Nyoshul Khenpo it is a non-crystalline precious stone, probably lapis. For its medical usage in the treatment of leprosy, skin ailments and as an antidote for poisoning see, e.g., *gso-rig snying-bsdus skya-rengs gsar-pa*, p. 243.

816 This edict does not appear to be otherwise known, but would be consistent with Qubilai's attitude towards Tibetan practitioners of the vehicle of indestructible reality. Cf. Tsepon W.D. Shakabpa, *Bod kyi srid don rgyal rabs*, Vol. 1, pp. 289-301.

817 Pakshi (Chinese *po-shih* and Mongolian *baγši*) was a title which was interpreted in Tibet to imply spiritual equality with the imperial preceptors of China (*ti-shih* or *gong-ma'i bla-ma*). From the time of Chögyel Phakpa the latter were appointed from the Sakya tradition which was predominantly patronised by the Yüan dynasty.

818 Leprosy is held to originate from the nāga or water spirits. Through their favours, the lama's flesh would have granted immunity from the disease.

819 Possibly to be identified with Pakshi Śākya-ö, though this is uncertain.

820 On Campapel, the translator of Trhopu (b. 1172/3), see n. 807 above; and *Blue Annals*, pp. 708ff.

821 These were the Mongol incursions during the year 1285. See Stein, *Tibetan Civilization*, p. 78.

822 Qubilai Qan's elder brother Hülegü founded the Ilkhan dynasty in Iran in 1258, and as early as 1267 began to challenge Qubilai's authority in Tibet by extending his patronage to the Drigungpa sect, which rivalled the Sakyapa. From 1285 onwards the Ilkhans lent military support to Drigung, but Sakya, with the help of an army dispatched by Qubilai, was ultimately victorious, Drigung Monastery being sacked in 1290. Cf. Stein, *Tibetan Civilization*, pp. 78-9; and Shakabpa, *Tibet: A Political History*, p. 70.

823 These Mahāyoga empowerments, numbering eighteen altogether, are listed in the Glossary of Enumerations under *fifteen ordinary sacraments (of empowerment)*. See also *Fundamentals*, p. 360; and Longcenpa, *Dispelling Darkness in the Ten Directions*, pp. 370-9 (GGFTC, pp. 869-81).

824 This translator was also the tutor of Putön Rinpoche. Refer to *Blue Annals*, p. 793; and Ruegg, *The Life of Bu ston Rin po che*, pp. 80-1.

825 A *mdos* or thread-cross is a wooden-framed structure crossed with many layers of thread or silk. Used as a device for the trapping and exorcising of evil forces, its structure varies in size and appearance depending upon the deity invoked and the function of the rite. See Nebesky-Wojkowitz, *Oracles and Demons of Tibet*, pp. 369-97; and Tucci, *The Religions of Tibet*, pp. 181ff.

826 This great scholar (1290-1364) has long been well known to western students of Buddhism in Tibet. The following works are the most

significant contributions to the study of his life and works published to date: Obermiller, *History of Buddhism by Bu-ston*; Ruegg, *The Life of Bu ston rin po che*; idem, *La théorie du tathāgatagarbha et du gotra*; idem, *Le traité du tathāgatagarbha du Bu ston Rin chen grub*. For Putön's view of the ancient translations, see below, pp. 892-3 .

827 *rten-'brel.*

828 Buyantu was emperor from 1311 to 1320.

829 On these magical weapons, see Nebesky-Wojkowitz, *Oracles and Demons of Tibet*, pp. 354ff. and 496ff.

830 Tā'i-tu is the name usually given by Tibetan sources for the Yüan Imperial Palace. Cf. *Blue Annals*, pp. 500-1. It corresponds to Chinese *ta-tu*, the Yüan period name of Peking (modern Beijing), constructed by Qubilai between the years 1267 to 1274.

831 Chinese bronze (*li-ma*).

832 "Leather Mask of the Seven Steps" (*bse-'bag goms-bdun-ma*): for leather mask (*bse-'bag*) in general, see Nebesky-Wojkowitz, *Oracles and Demons of Tibet*, pp. 102-4. Stein, however, has argued that *bse* in this instance means not "leather", but refers rather to the *bse*-spirits, and that the mask is thus a representation of such a *bse*.

833 Guluk, the third Yüan emperor, reigned from 1307 to 1311.

834 Mati Paṇcen was a leading Sanskritist, who made the final revisions of the *Kālacakra Tantra*. He also authored several influential commentaries on philosophical works. See n. 570 above; and *Blue Annals*, pp. 776, 1045-6.

835 Probably Danyi Chenpo Zangpopel (*bdag-nyid chen-po bzang-po dpal*), 1262-1322, or one of his sons.

836 The seal of entrustment or succession (*gtad-rgya*) refers to the approval granted by a preceptor to a student, thereby authorising the latter to become a lineage-holder and transmitter of the transmitted precepts. For its function within the close lineage of the treasures (*gter-ma*), see below, p. 745.

837 Our text erroneously reads *bcu-bdun* for *bdun-cu*.

838 A permissory initiation (*rjes-snang*) refers to the blessing of the buddhas or meditational deities which, when conferred by one's guru, authorises one to practise the visualization and mantra of the buddha or deity in question. Compare the usage of this term here with its usage in relation to the causal vehicles, where it is translated as the Buddha's mandate, see *Fundamentals*, pp. 75-6.

839 Compare this with an identical passage on p. 674 where the *Forty-Chapter Magical Net* has been inserted after the *Eighty-Chapter Magical Net* instead of after the *Illuminating Lamp of the Fundamental Text*.

840 This Bengali master of the *Kālacakra* tradition was one of the last great Indian Buddhist scholars to visit Tibet. His unusual career is treated in *Blue Annals*, pp. 797ff.

841 *Blue Annals*, p. 153.

842 Cf. *Blue Annals*, p. 171:

> I [Gölo] have given a brief description of the greatness of these teachers belonging to this lineage, in order to remove the great sin committed by fools who wrongly understood the Doctrine [i.e. attacked the rÑiṅ-ma-pa].

843 The history and status of this major Karma Kagyü establishment is surveyed in the autobiography of its late hierarch, Chögyam Trungpa Rinpoche, *Born in Tibet*, especially Ch. 2.

844 I.e. Pengar Jampel Zangpo (*ban-sgar 'jam-dpal bzang-po*), on whom see Nālandā Translation Committee, *The Rain of Wisdom*, pp. 123-5, 324.

845 The "ultimate doctrinal language" is that of the subtle, inner Great Madhyamaka. See *Fundamentals*, pp. 169-216; and for Tölbupa in particular, p. 204 and n. 1309.

846 On Karpopa, see below, p. 697.

847 The *Earlier and Later Treasure Troves* (*gter-kha gong-'og*) are respectively those discovered by Nyang-rel Nyima Özer and Guru Chöwang. See pp. 755-70.

848 See below, pp. 805-8.

849 This is Dalai Lama III, under whom many of the Mongol tribes were converted to Buddhism. See, e.g., Stein, *Tibetan Civilization*, pp. 81, 82.

850 *sgra'i ri-mo*.

851 *sum-rtags*, i.e. the study of the *sum-cu-pa* and *rtags-kyi 'jug-pa* attributed to Thönmi Sambhoṭa, on whom see p. 512 and n. 546.

852 Advanced philosophy students in Tibet would customarily spend some period as visiting scholars at institutions with which they were otherwise unaffiliated. Exposed thus to divergent approaches to the teaching, they would hone their intellectual skills by engaging in debate with any who would challenge them.

853 Sera Ce (*se-ra byes*) is one of the colleges of Sera Monastery, near Lhasa. Its curriculum is surveyed in L. Candra (ed.), *Materials for a History of Tibetan Literature*, Pt. 3, pp. 666-7; and Geshe Lhundup Sopa, *Lectures on Tibetan Religious Culture*, Ch. 2.

854 The date of Peljor Lhündrup's death is calculated according to the old Phukpa school. According to Schuh, *Untersuchungen zur Geschichte der Tibetischen Kalenderrechnung*, p. 139, Dalai Lama V used old Phukpa, and his successor, the regent Sangye Gyamtso, was the first to employ the new Phukpa calculations from 1696 onwards. Refer to p. 400.

855 I.e. those cycles of teaching which are considered essential to the Zur tradition.

856 On this figure, see p. 783.

857 This is undertaken by advanced students of the vehicle of indestructible reality in order to perfect the techniques of yoga and meditation. See, e.g., Ngawang Zangpo, *Jamgon Kongtrul's Retreat Manual.*

858 See *Fundamentals*, pp. 335-45.

859 For details of this dispute, see Stein, *Tibetan Civilization*, p. 81. The Drigungpa formed an alliance with the Zhamarpa and the king of Tsang against the Gelukpa and the Ganden Palace in 1537. See also n. 1114.

860 On the induction of epilepsy and stroke by means of sorcery, see n. 695 above.

861 Köncok Chöpel was a teacher of Dalai Lama V. See p. 821.

862 The Lhodrak Sungtrül is the incarnation of the great treasure-finder Pema Lingpa, associated with Nenang Monastery near Truptso Pema-

ling in Lhodrak; see below, p. 799. Tabla (or Takla) Padmamati was particularly influential in connection with the lineage of Zhikpo Lingpa, on whom see n. 929 below.

863 The lords of Tsang and the Karmapa assumed control over most of Central Tibet in 1565. Established by Karma Tsheten of Tsang and continued by his successor Karma Tenkyong (1599-1641), their administration was finally ended by the Qōśot Mongols under Guśrī Khan who duly enthroned Dalai Lama V in 1642. Cf. Stein, *Tibetan Civilization*, pp. 82-3; Snellgrove and Richardson, *A Cultural History of Tibet*, pp. 194-5; and Z. Ahmad, *Sino-Tibetan Relations in the Seventeenth Century*.

864 On this monastic establishment and its hierarch Pema Trhinle, see below, pp. 736-7.

865 A brief reference to Zhang as the "Unborn" may be found in *Blue Annals*, p. 900. See also n. 801 above.

866 See below, pp. 724-6.

867 On Rikdzin Gyurme Dorje or Terdak Lingpa, see pp. 825-34; and on Locen Dharmaśrī, pp. 728-32.

868 *dar-ring-chen-mo*.

869 Unidentified.

870 For a later Menlungpa's connection with the Kham tradition, see below, p. 699.

871 For the lineage of Katok Monastery in general, see H. Eimer and P. Tsering, "Äbte und Lehrer von Kaḥ-thog" *Zentralasiatische Studien* 13 (1979), pp. 457-509; and idem, "A List of Abbots of Kaḥ-thog Monastery" *The Journal of the Tibet Society* 1 (1981).

872 For the Lower Tibetan Vinaya lineage, see pp. 525-6 and n. 568.

873 On the first Karmapa hierarch and Gampopa's greatest disciple, see *Blue Annals*, pp. 473ff.; and Karma Thinley, *The History of the Sixteen Karmapas of Tibet*, pp. 41-5.

874 *pha-vang*. But this word may mean "bat" (the animal) as well as "boulder".

875 On this wrathful protectress, see Nebesky-Wojkowitz, *Oracles and Demons of Tibet*, Ch. II.

876 The eighth level of realisation attained by a bodhisattva is known as the Unmoving (*mi-gYo-ba*, Skt. *Acalā*). See *Fundamentals*, p. 137 and n. 146.

877 For the eleventh level, Universal Light (*kun-tu 'od*, Skt. *Samantaprabhā*), which is that of buddhas rather than bodhisattvas, see *Fundamentals*, p. 237.

878 On this figure, who was instrumental in transmitting the *Dohā* in Tibet, see Guenther, *The Royal Song of Saraha*, pp. 16-17.

879 Pomdrakpa was the spiritual heir of the first Karmapa's leading disciple, Sangye Recen. In his turn he became the tutor of Tüsum Khyenpa's reincarnation, Karma Pakshi. See *Blue Annals*, pp. 483ff.

880 On Karma Pakshi's affiliation with and contribution to the Nyingma tradition, see M. Kapstein, "Religious Syncretism in 13th century Tibet: *The Limitless Ocean Cycle*" in STC, pp. 358-71.

881 Sakya Paṇḍita and Chögyel Phakpa journeyed to visit the Mongol prince Godan in Gansu in 1246. When Phakpa was seventeen (1251) Sakya Paṇḍita passed away. At nineteen (1253), Phakpa became advisor

to Qubilai Qan and returned to Tibet in 1265. His second visit to China for seven years began in 1268. After his return in 1276 he held the conclave at Chumik and died, perhaps poisoned, at Sakya in 1280. See *Blue Annals*, pp. 211-12; and Shakabpa, *Tibet: A Political History*, pp. 62-9. The Author and Khenpo Palden Sherap have agreed with the hypothesis that the consecration of Dzing Namgyel was performed by Katokpa Campabum, who was still officiating until 1251 when Sakya Paṇḍita passed away.

882 Jang was one of the principalities of far south-eastern Tibet, centered on Lijiang in Yunnan. On the patronage of Buddhism by its kings, see Y. Imaeda, *The 'Jang Sa-tham Edition of the Tibetan Buddhist Canon.*

883 This refers to the great Nyingma centres founded or restored from the seventeenth century onwards, such as Mindröling and Dorje Trak. See below, pp. 733-9.

884 See pp. 700-1.

885 The sacred mountain of far south-eastern Tibet and the surrounding region, presently in north-western Yunnan. See TH, pp. 417-9.

886 The "three superiors" of Katok (*gong-ma gsum*) were, of course, Katokpa Tampa Deshek, Tsangtönpa and Campabum.

887 *drung* means "attendant". The title *drung(-pa)* or *zhabs-drung* is given to the attendant of a hierarch. In cases in which the attendant himself rises to assume a major position in a given lineage he and his successors often maintain the original title as an indication of their continuing service to the lineage itself.

888 See the Glossary of Enumerations for the *fifteen ordinary sacraments (of empowerment)*; also *Fundamentals*, p. 360. Together with the three empowerments of profundity (*zab-dbang gsum*) they form the eighteen empowerments of Mahāyoga. Altogether, they comprise ten outer empowerments of beneficence (*phyi phan-pa'i dbang bcu*), five inner empowerments of ability (*nang nus-pa'i dbang lnga*) and the three secret empowerments of profundity (*gsang-ba zab-mo'i dbang gsum*). Cf. Longcenpa, *Dispelling Darkness in the Ten Directions*, pp. 370-9 (GGFTC, pp. 869-81).

889 The account given here may be compared with that found in *Blue Annals*, pp. 160-7.

890 See the Glossary of Enumerations for the *five awakenings*. Their generation at the birth of an emanational master has also been referred to in the account of Dropukpa's life, p. 645 above. At the time of enlightenment they bring about five resultant excellences (*'bras-bu'i phun-sum-tshogs-pa lnga*) associated with the buddha-body of perfect rapture, namely, those of teacher (Samantabhadra in the form of Vajradhara), place (Akaniṣṭha), retinue (Conquerors of the Five Enlightened Families and tenth level bodhisattvas), time (unbroken timeless continuity of the experience) and teaching (ultimate truth in which saṃsāra and nirvāṇa are identical). Here five parallel accomplishments are poetically ascribed to Rongzompa.

891 The point of this example is that Daṇḍin's treatise, on which see *Fundamentals*, pp. 104-5, was virtually the only work on classical Indian poetics studied in Tibet. Only a real savant would have been familiar with, e.g., Maṃmata.

892 For contemporary Tibetan views on the Vivarta or Vartula script, see

Narkyid, "In Defence of Amdo Gendun Chompel's Theory of the Origin of the Tibetan Script" *Tibet Journal* VII, 3 (1982), pp. 23-34; and Namkai Norbu, *The Necklace of Gzi*, pp. 7-13.

893 *chos-la blo ma-sgyur*. The text erroneously reads *chos-kyi bla-mar sgyur*.

894 These three qualities are usually ascribed to the transmitted precepts of the Buddha himself. See *Fundamentals*, pp. 73-4.

895 Rongzompa himself is "father Chödrak".

896 The teachings of this obscure figure, who is perhaps to be assigned to the tenth century, have played a profound role in the tradition of the Great Perfection. For a brief biographical reference, see *Blue Annals*, pp. 999-1001. Also, see n. 608 above.

897 Our text erroneously reads *zi* for *ya-zi*.

898 The founder of the Kagyü lineage in Tibet. His traditional biography has been translated into English: Nālandā Translation Committee, *The Life of Marpa the Translator*. Marpa's dates are usually given as 1012-96, but see ibid., p. 199n.

899 *Esoteric Mañjuśrī*, as indicated above on p. 702, was composed and translated by Smṛtijñānakīrti. The commentary by Rongzompa is contained in *Selected Writings of Roṅ-zom Chos-kyi bzaṅ-po*. Refer to *Esoteric Mañjuśrī* in the first part of the Bibliography.

900 *Blue Annals*, p. 166.

901 On Macik Zhama (b. 1062) and her brother Khurbupa or Khönpupa (*'khon-phu-ba*, b. 1069), see *Blue Annals*, pp. 220ff. It appears that Macik Zhama is therein confused with the founder of the tradition of the Object of Cutting (*gcod-yul*), Macik Lapdrön. Cf. Gyatso, "A Preliminary Study of the *Gcod* Tradition".

902 For the iconography of the kīla, the foremost ritual emblem of this tradition, see J. Huntington, *The Phur-pa, Tibetan Ritual Daggers*. Evidence for the antiquity of kīla practice in Tibet and India is surveyed in R. A. Stein "A propos des documents anciens relatifs au *phur-bu*" in *Csoma de Koros Symposium*; and in R. Mayer "Tibetan Phur-bas and Indian Kīlas" in *The Buddhist Forum*.

903 The maṇḍala of material symbols here would entail the use of the symbolic kīla implement (*rdzas-phur*).

904 *Zandre* (*za-'dre*) are a class of malicious spirits who haunt fixed locations and require propitiation with offerings of foodstuffs.

905 Cf. p. 496.

906 Concerning the importance of Vajrakīla for the Sakyapa, refer to E. G. Smith's introduction to *Kongtrul's Encyclopedia of Indo-Tibetan Culture*, p. 8, n. 17. Sakya Paṇḍita himself was responsible for locating a Sanskrit manuscript of the *Root Fragment of Vajrakīla* (T 439) and redacting its Tibetan translation.

907 A summary of his life may be found in *Blue Annals*, pp. 374-80.

908 On this figure (b. 1016), see p. 765; and R. Prats, *Contributo allo Studio Biografico dei primi Gter-ston*, pp. 25-8.

909 On the death of Tarma Dode, see Nalanda Translation Committee, *The Life of Marpa the Translator*, pp. 156-73; and Lhalungpa, *The Life of Milarepa*, pp. 82-3. These sources, however, do not specifically mention Ra Lotsāwa.

910 *tha-phyi'i grva-pa*.

911 The Devourers (*za*) and Slaughterers (*gsod*) are protectors associated

with Vajrakīla.

912 Our text erroneously reads *rang* for *rong*.

913 The trio of Se (*bse*), Cak (*lcags*) and Shel (*shel*) are protective deities associated with Vajrakīla, and named according to three different kinds of material kīla – briar, iron and crystal.

914 *zhal 'chos-pa*.

915 The fifth path or death follows upon the four modes of life (*āśrama*) prevalent in traditional Indian culture. These are the way of the celibate student (*brahmacarī*), the way of the householder (*gṛhasthī*), the way of the forest-dweller (*āraṇyavāsī*) and the way of the homeless mendicant (*sannyāsī*).

916 *se-ra phur-mjal*. See KGHP, pp. 100-1. The kīla itself is only seen publicly once each year, during a special empowerment conferred by the abbot of Sera Ce College on the seventeenth of the twelfth month as a prelude to the New Year celebrations. The annual ceremony has been maintained by the Sera Monastery community in exile in Mysore, India, but the actual kīla remains in the shrine of the secret attainment of Hayagrīva (*rta-mgrin gsang-sgrub*) in Sera itself. Since 1980, with the partial relaxation of Chinese restrictions on the practice of religion in Tibet, the shrine has again become an important pilgrimage site. The translators were able to visit it during separate journeys from 1984 onwards, but, unfortunately, were not permitted to photograph the exquisitely embossed brass reliquary, which shows the figures of Padmasambhava, Darca and Sakya Paṇḍita and in which the kīla is kept.

917 On Ngari Paṇcen, see below, pp. 805-8.

918 This figure (b. 1524) was one of the leading Sakyapa scholars of the period.

919 For these four rivers, see p. 601. The seal of entrustment (*gtad-rgya*) has been explained above in this chapter, n. 836.

920 *'dus-pa-dang lhan-cig*.

921 On Kong-ra Locen Zhenpen Dorje, see below, pp. 723-4; and for Lhatsün Namka Jikme, pp. 818-20.

922 The practice of the *Black Further Innermost Spirituality* requires solitary retreat in total darkness in order to simulate the experiences which follow death. A "secret passageway" is utilised to provide the practitioner with food, and also serves as the channel through which he or she can occasionally converse with the meditation master.

923 See below, pp. 760-70.

924 *ti-shih*, "Teacher of the Emperor" – this form of Chinese honour was adopted and conferred by Dalai Lama V. See also nn. 811, 817 above.

925 See p. 783.

926 Presumably that of Drölcen Samdrup Dorje.

927 Lama Namdingpa is Zhangtön Namka Dorje. The identification of Lama Zurcenpa is uncertain.

928 See pp. 681 and 799.

929 A brief biography of this treasure-finder (1584-1643) may be found in Jamgön Kongtrül, *Lives of the Hundred Treasure-finders* (*gter-ston brgya-rtsa*), fols. 91b-93b.

930 On energy channels, currents and seminal points (*rtsa-rlung-thig-le*), see *Fundamentals*, pp. 279-87 and 341; also Longcenpa, *Dispelling Darkness in the Ten Directions*, pp. 453ff. (GGFTC, pp. 1006ff.).

931 These are aspects of dream yoga (*rmi-lam*), for a general introduction to which see, e.g., W. Y. Evans-Wentz, *Tibetan Yoga and Secret Doctrines*, pp. 215ff.

932 The Indestructible Nucleus of Inner Radiance is the dimension of the buddha-body of reality (*dharmakāya*); see *Fundamentals*, p. 115.

933 *dgung-keg*. This refers to any year, i.e. one's thirteenth, twenty-fifth, thirty-seventh and so on, in which the animal sign is the same as that under which one was born. See G. Dorje, *Tibetan Elemental Divination Paintings*, pp. 229-31.

934 Jamyang Khyentse Wangpo, *Mkhyen-brtse on the History of the Dharma*, pp. 40-1, defines the trio of *Guru, Great Perfection and Great Compassionate One* as follows:

> The blessed cycles of the peaceful and wrathful Guru...; the cycles of the Great Perfection, the consummation of all profound paths...; and the cycles for the attainment of the Great Compassionate One, the divine fortune of Tibet, the Land of Snows...

935 See above, p. 701.

936 *grva'i-dbang-bum*. We follow here the explanation of Khetsun Zangpo Rinpoche.

937 See pp. 825-34.

938 The date of Sangdak Trhinle Lhündrup's death is calculated according to the new Phukpa school since it has been recorded by his son Dharmaśrī. The date according to the old Phukpa school would have read Sunday 2 March 1662.

939 This is a sign of proficiency in the transference of consciousness (*'pho-ba*) through which, at the moment of death, one can take rebirth in a pure land or buddha-field such as Sukhāvatī.

940 *bca'*.

941 Yangdok (*yang-bzlog*) is propitiated as a means of averting war and other unfavourable conditions; it derives from the maṇḍala of Yangdak Heruka. Drangsong Loktri is a sage and protector from the maṇḍala of Yamāntaka (Khetsun Zangpo Rinpoche).

942 As stated in the *Fundamentals*, p. 104, *rtsis dkar-nag* refers to Indian astronomy (*dkar-rtsis*) and Chinese divination (*nag-rtsis* or *'byung-rtsis*).

943 On the rites of service, further service, attainment and great attainment, see n. 499 above.

944 See p. 828.

945 The conferral of every empowerment of the way of secret mantra must include the disciple's affirmation of the vows of refuge and of the cultivation of the enlightened attitude, in addition to the specific commitments associated with the empowerment. Often the layman's *prātimokṣa* vows must be affirmed as well. Cf. the quotation from the *Hevajra Tantra* given on p. 911.

946 See n. 892 above.

947 *Svarodaya* is a profound branch of Indian divination and numerology ascribed to Īśvara in its origin. Refer to the life of Mipham Rinpoche on p. 890; and also to *Fundamentals*, p. 104.

948 His own extensive commentary on this text, called *dpag-bsam snye-ma*, is doubtlessly the most influential one amongst modern Nyingmapa. On the *Ascertainment of the Three Vows* itself, see p. 808.

949 Treasure doctrines (*gter-chos*) discovered since the time of Terdak Lingpa have been known as new treasures (*gter-gsar*) in contrast to those which were discovered earlier (*gter-rnying*).

950 Zhecen Monastery was founded in 1735 (wood tiger year) by Rapjam II, Gyurme Künzang Namgyel (b. 1713). Its history is detailed in Zhecen Gyeltsap, *źe-chen chos-'byuṅ*. For a modern description in English, see TH, pp. 473-4. With the exception of Zhecen, the monasteries mentioned here are discussed in the pages that follow.

951 I.e. the linear descendants of Terdak Lingpa.

952 See the biographical sketch of the Author in the Foreword.

953 See p. 833, n. 1137.

954 Again, see the Author's biographical sketch in the Foreword.

955 In general, Tshültrim Dorje is known as Sungtrül II. See Aris, *Bhutan*, p. 318, n. 70; and the *Collected Works of Pema Lingpa* (*pad-gling 'khrungs-rabs-kyi rtogs-brjod nyung-gsal dad-pa'i me-tog*), Vol. *Pha*.

956 See below, pp. 859-68.

957 Thu'u-bkvan, *Crystal Mirror of Philosophical Systems* (*grub-mtha' shel-gyi me-long*), p. 80.

958 On Thuken's view of the Nyingma tradition in general and the background for this assertion, see M. Kapstein, "The Purificatory Gem and its Cleansing: A Late Tibetan Polemical Discussion of Apocryphal texts" in *The Tibetan Assimilation of Buddhism*.

959 See pp. 813-17.

960 Mindröling was constructed at Traci in 1676 by Terdak Lingpa. For a description, see TH, pp. 169-71; and PPCT, pp. 164-7.

961 Katok Rikdzin Tshewang Norbu was a master of extremely eclectic interests who played an instrumental role in the preservation of the then-suppressed Conangpa tradition. A great traveller, he visited Nepal on at least three occasions during which he restored the stūpas of Bodhnāth and Svayambhūnāth. As a skilled political negotiator he journeyed as far as Ladakh.

962 Dzokcen (Rudam Samten Chöling) Monastery was founded in the year 1685 by Pema Rikdzin. For a description, see TH, pp. 471-3.

963 Pelyül Monastery (Pelyül Namgyel Cangcup Chöling) was founded in 1665 by Pelyül Rikdzin Künzang Sherap. On the history of this monastery and its influence in both Kham and Amdo, see Ven. Lama Jampal Zangpo, *A Garland of Immortal, Wish-fulfilling Trees*; and TH, pp. 463-4.

964 See pp. 841-7.

965 These twenty-seven maṇḍalas of the long lineage of transmitted precepts (*bka'-ma*) are also known as *tshogs-chen 'dus-pa'i dkyil-'khor*. They comprise all levels of teaching referred to within the nine vehicles, as stated on pp. 911-13; and in *Fundamentals*, pp. 364-5.

966 According to the Author's oral communication, the edition of the *Transmitted Precepts* (*rnying-ma bka'-ma*) referred to here was published xylographically at Pelyül Monastery in Kham.

HISTORY: PART SIX

967 The close lineage of treasures (*nye-brgyud gter-ma*) is so called because the teachings formerly concealed by Guru Padmasambhava and others

were subsequently discovered and propagated in more recent times. The line of their transmission is therefore short or close when contrasted with the distant or long lineage of the transmitted precepts (*ring-brgyud bka'-ma*), by which teachings were passed down from earliest times through an unbroken chain of accomplished masters.

968 This prophetic declaration is attributed to Ratna Ḷingpa, *tshes-bcu bskul-thabs*.

969 See pp. 447-57, for an account of these lineages.

970 The treasure lords (*gter-bdag*, Skt. *nidhipati*) are spiritual beings bound under oath of allegiance by Guru Padmasambhava to protect and guard his treasures.

971 See pp. 468-74 and 512-20, for the traditions concerning his career in India and Tibet in general.

972 I.e. the western Tibetan districts of Ngari and Tö, the central districts of Ü and Tsang, and the eastern districts of Kham and Amdo respectively.

973 According to Sangye Lingpa, *bka'-thang gser-phreng*, Ch. 48, pp. 319ff.:

> Treasures are divided into eighteen types, namely, the fourfold group of secret treasures (*gsang*), profound treasures (*zab*), mind treasures (*thugs*) and intentional treasures (*dgongs*); the fourfold group of material treasures (*rdzas*), life-supporting treasures (*bla*) minor treasures (*phran*) and treasures which liberate by taste (*myong*); the fourfold group of Indian treasures (*rgya*), Tibetan treasures (*bod*), lordly treasures (*rje*) and father treasures (*yab*); the threefold group of mother treasures (*yum*), neuter treasures (*ma-ning*) and outer treasures (*phyi*); and lastly the threefold group of inner treasures (*nang*), middling treasures (*bar*) and treasures of wealth (*nor-gter*).

974 *dam-rdzas*.

975 The "four ways of liberation" are: liberation by sight (*mthong-grol*), which comes through seeing the objects which represent the buddha-body, speech and mind; liberation by hearing (*thos-grol*), when a description of the *bardo* is narrated in the presence of a recently deceased person; liberation by wearing (*btags-grol*), when a circular diagram or yantra is worn or attached to the shoulders, head and heart at the moment of death (in life the diagram is worn around the neck in a cloth pouch or in the case of mantrins it is sealed within a golden casket and tied in the topknots of their braided hair); and liberation by taste (*myang-grol*), when the flesh of one who has been born a brāhman or vegetarian over seven successive lives, or some other sacramental substance, is consumed.

976 On these prophecies, see R. Prats, "Some Preliminary Considerations Arising from a Biographical Study of the Early *gTer-ston*" in TSHR, pp. 256-60.

977 Representative of these are the early biographies composed by Cangdak Trashi Topgyel and the later ones by Jamgön Kongtrül. For full details of these, refer to the first part of the Bibliography under *Earlier and Later Versions of the Biographies of the Hundred Treasure-Finders*.

978 On this figure, see in particular D. L. Snellgrove and T. Skorupski, *The Cultural Heritage of Ladakh*, Vol. 2, Pt. III.

979 Chöje Lingpa was an emanation of Sangye Lama. See the Glossary of Enumerations under *thirteen incarnations of Gyelse Lharje*.

980 See below, pp. 855-8.

981 I.e. an abbreviated empowerment ritual in which a *torma* sculpture functions as the maṇḍala into which the disciple is empowered.

982 Ostensibly the name Trapa Ngönshe (spelt in Tibetan *gra-pa mngon-shes*) could be taken to mean "monk endowed with supernormal cognitive powers". The explanation given in the text, however, precludes this interpretation.

983 On the yakṣa Vajra Mārajit (*gnod-sbyin rdo-rje bdud-'dul*), see Nebesky-Wojkowitz, *Oracles and Demons of Tibet*, pp. 77-8.

984 Minister Zhang or Zhanglön (*zhang-blon*) is an epithet of the yakṣa Vajra Mārajit. See Nebesky-Wojkowitz, *Oracles and Demons of Tibet*, pp. 77-8, where he is referred to as *gnod-sbyin zhang-blon rdo-rje bdud-'dul*.

985 These books were formerly the property or "master copy" (*bla-dpe*) of King Trhisong.

986 Refer to *Fundamentals*, p. 99 and n. 89. See also Meyer, *Gso-ba rig-pa: Le système médical tibétain*, pp. 85ff.

987 See *Blue Annals*, pp. 94-7, on the founding of Tratang in 1081.

988 Tshangpa Lhei Metok is the secret name which Trhisong Detsen received when empowered into the Vajradhātu maṇḍala at Chimpu by Guru Padmasambhava. See pp. 534-5. For the *five kingly treasure-finders* and *three supreme emanations*, see the Glossary of Enumerations.

989 According to our text the birth of Nyang-rel would have occurred in 1124 (wood dragon year). However, Stein, *Tibetan Civilization*, p. 74, gives 1136 (fire dragon year). Since Nyang-rel lived until the age of 69; this date would be preferred, assuming his death occured in 1204. But see n. 995 below.

990 I.e. Buddha Śākyamuni.

991 The Rashak Treasure-finder (i.e. *ra-shag chos-'bar*) was a contemporary of Milarepa and Ngok Lotsāwa. See Jamgön Kongtrül, *Lives of the Hundred Treasure-finders*, pp. 46b.5-47a.6.

992 According to *Blue Annals*, pp. 888-90, Mel Kawacen lived from 1126 to 1211. Zhikpo Nyima Senge is referred to as an adept of Phadampa's Pacification, in the same source, p. 937.

993 See above, p. 511 and n. 545. This is the core of the *Collected Works of the King concerning the Mantra "Oṃ Maṇi Padme Hūṃ"*, attributed to King Songtsen Gampo.

994 Myrobalan (*a-ru-ra*) is specifically *Terminalia chebula*. Its uses and properties according to the Tibetan medical system are described in T. Clifford, *The Diamond Healing: Tibetan Buddhist Medicine and Psychiatry*, p. 119.

995 Our text gives 1192 (water mouse) for Nyang-rel's death. Chak Lotsāwa Chöjepel is reported in *Blue Annals*, pp. 1057-9, to have lived from 1197 to 1264. So it is possible that the person referred to below should be identified with his uncle, Chak Dracom, to whom *Blue Annals*, pp. 1054-6, assigns the dates 1153-1216. None the less, it is clear from the same source, p. 1064, that Śākyaśrī (1127-1225) travelled in Tibet

only from 1204 to 1213. Pawo Tsuklak Trhengwa, *mkhas-pa'i dga'-ston*, p. 260, and Jamgöng Kongtrül, *Lives of the Hundred Treasure-finders*, fol. 49a.5, concluded therefore that Nyang-rel passed away in 1204. Nevertheless, see now the arguments of van der Kuijp, "On the *Lives*" (1994).

996 On this dike, see p. 656 and n. 802. Zhikpo Dütsi who restored the dike was a disciple of Nyang-rel, as indicated below.

997 Lesser adepts would be obliged to perform such wrathful rites of sorcery only on certain astrologically propitious days of the month.

998 Unattached Lotus Endowed (*ma-chags padma-can*) is the twelfth level of realisation. See *Fundamentals*, p. 254; and Longcenpa, *Dispelling Darkness in the Ten Directions*, p. 430 (GGFTC, p. 975).

999 On these *four Further Taming temples*, see the Glossary of Enumerations; also, p. 510 and n. 543.

1000 This was Jikten Gönpo (1143-1217), Phakmotrupa's foremost disciple and the founder of the Drigung Kagyü school. He was widely renowned as an incarnation of Nāgārjuna. See *Blue Annals*, pp. 596ff.

1001 The ceremonial silk arrow (*mda'-dar*) is the emblem of Amitāyus, symbolic of longevity. It is draped with five-coloured veils and brandished with a circular movement of the right hand.

1002 This calculation accords with the old Phukpa, Tshurpu and Phakpa schools. The year of Chöwang's birth, 1212, falls within the fourth sexagenary cycle. Some sources say he was born in the water monkey year of the third cycle, but this is inconsistent with him meeting Sakya Paṇḍita at the age of eighteen.

1003 The *Litany of the Names of Mañjuśrī*, v. 55c.

1004 According to Khenpo Palden Sherap, this is the preferred reading. Our text wrongly reads *sde-brgyud chen-po'i sgrung-'bum*.

1005 The ḍākinī's four faces symbolise the four rites of enlightened activity: peaceful (white), expansive (yellow), overpowering (red) and wrathful (blue). The five-quilled arrow is indicative of the five pristine cognitions, but also prophetically symbolises Chöwang's future mastery of certain treasure-troves.

1006 On this empowerment, see *Fundamentals*, p. 370.

1007 In Tibetan this verse reads:

> *sgyogs-dang dpag-chen*
> *than-dang cho-'phrul*
> *bzo-sna kyag-kyog rnams...*

The early association of the treasure-finders with the military arts requires careful study. Perhaps, in this respect, they are to be compared with the sorcerers and alchemists of other medieval civilisations.

1008 See above, p. 713 and n. 908.

1009 According to Mongolian sources, Tibet was first contacted by the emissaries of Chinggis Qan in 1206. But on this tradition, see L. Kwanten, "Chingis Khan's Conquest of Tibet: Myth or Reality" *Journal of Asian History* 8 (1974), pp. 1-20; and T. V. Wylie, "The First Mongol Conquest of Tibet Reinterpreted" *Harvard Journal of Asiatic Studies* 37 (1977), pp. 103-33. Then, in 1239 (earth pig) Godan, the second son of Ogodai, sent an army into Tibet under the general Dorta the Black and Gyelmen. That the force reached as far as Reting (*rva-sgrengs*) and Gyel Lhakang is undisputed; however there are varying accounts of the date on which this incursion took place. Our present text gives in its two editions 1204 (wood mouse, third cycle) and 1264 (wood mouse, fourth cycle). The Author has agreed, however, that the element should be iron rather than wood, giving us the year 1240 (iron mouse), which is sufficiently close to the Chinese records. See also Stein, *Tibetan Civilization*, pp. 77-80; and Shakabpa, *Tibet: A Political History*, p. 61.

1010 The name Bharo (Newar *bāḍe*) refers to the Buddhist priestly caste among the Newars, which in later times had exclusive rights to gold- and silver-work. See Snellgrove and Richardson, *A Cultural History of Tibet*, p. 202 and 274n.; also, Macdonald and Stahl, *Newar Art*, p. 73.

1011 Bharal Sheep (*gna'-ba*) or *Ovis Nahar*.

1012 The divine gateway (*lha'i sgo*) and the vajra (*rdo-rje*) are the secret names respectively for the rectum and the penis. Since Bharo was an adept of the Great Perfection he perceived Guru Chöwang's body of indestructible reality (*vajrakāya*) in its true divine nature without the slightest trace of impurity.

1013 OṂ MAṆI PADME HŪṂ is the mantra of Avalokiteśvara's compassion. Chöwang's point is that there are peaceful applications of this mantra which generate compassion for all sentient beings, and that this motivation must preside over any application of wrathful sorcery.

1014 On the liberating diagram, see n. 975 above.

1015 The *zho* is a weight measure, being equivalent to one-tenth of the Tibetan ounce (*srang*).

1016 Our version is incomplete. For the significance of the turnip here, see the *Scholar's Feast of Doctrinal History*, p. 275, which states that the turnip which was cooked in secrecy turned into a strong and pleasant tasting meat. This indicated that Bharo's success would be assured and that he should not divulge Chöwang's enlightened attributes to anyone. The turnip is often associated with the activity of ḍākinīs in Tibet.

1017 See n. 847 above.

1018 On p. 759 above, this figure is also listed as a disciple of Nyang-rel Nyima Özer. Possibly this presents a problem, but again, it is not unknown in Tibet for one whose life overlaps with successive emanations of a single master to consider himself to be the disciple in youth of the one and in old age of the other.

1019 See p. 698.

1020 The second real presence of Yeshe Tshogyel was the ḍākinī Künga Bumpa (*mkha'-'gro-ma kun-dga' 'bum-pa*), who can perhaps be assigned to the early fourteenth century. See Jamgön Kongtrül, *Lives of the Hundred Treasure-finders*, pp. 113b.4-114b.4.

1021 See Jamyang Khyentse Wangpo, *Mkha' 'gro gsaṅ ba kun 'dus kyi chos skor*, p. 276, ll. 3-4.

1022 Como Menmo's birth must have occurred in 1248 (earth monkey year, fourth cycle), and not in the same year of the third cycle (1188) as our text claims, because she was a disciple of Guru Chöwang. See n. 1002 above.

1023 On the Menmo (*sman-mo*), see Nebesky-Wojkowitz, *Oracles and Demons of Tibet*, pp. 198ff.

1024 On the "seal of action" or action seal (*las-rgya*, Skt. *karmamudrā*), see p. 475; *Fundamentals*, pp. 277ff.; and Longcenpa, *Dispelling Darkness in the Ten Directions*, pp. 386-96 (GGFTC, pp. 899-914).

1025 Since Como Menmo was born in 1248, it would seem unlikely that she could have met Lingje Repa who, according to *Blue Annals*, pp. 660-4, lived from 1128 to 1188 and founded the monastery of Ralung in 1180. According to the same source, p. 660, a certain Menmo with whom "he had a karmic link" married him and became his yogic partner. Her life story could well have been woven together with that of Como Menmo. The Author also accepts the divergence of dating between Como Menmo and Lingje Repa, and maintains that she may have emanated during an earlier age with the sole intention of benefitting him.

1026 This calculation agrees with all the calendrical systems. The year of her death, at the age of thirty-six, would fall within the fourth cycle, as pointed out above.

1027 For contemporary research on this figure, see A.-M. Blondeau, "Le Lha-'dre bka'-thaṅ" in *Études tibétains dédiées à la mémoire de Marcelle Lalou*, pp. 29-126, and the sources cited therein.

1028 Lhase Chokdrup Gyelpo is another name for Gyelse Lharje; see the Glossary of Enumerations under *thirteen incarnations of Gyelse Lharje*.

1029 As stated in Dudjom Rinpoche's *gter-mdzod thob-yig*, pp. 147-52, Ati, Citi and Yangti are three subdivisions of the Esoteric Instructional Class of Atiyoga, successively more profound. Ati means the Innermost Spirituality belonging to the Esoteric Instructional Class of Atiyoga (*atiyoga man-ngag snying-thig*). Citi reveals the essential points in general of the profound tantras of the Esoteric Instructional Class (*man-ngag-sde'i rgyud-don zab-mo spyi-gnad ston-pa spyi-ti yo-gar grags-pa*). Yangti reveals the aural lineage which is most secret and uncommon (*yang-gsang thun-mong ma-yin-pa'i snyan-rgyud ston-pas yang-ti yo-gar grags-pa*). They are exemplified respectively by NGB Vols. 7, 6 and 8.

1030 The Neuter Lord (*mgon-po ma-ning*) is a form of Mahākāla.

1031 On the relationship of this work to other recensions of Padmasambhava's biography, see Blondeau, "Analysis of the Biographies of Padmasambhava according to Tibetan Tradition: Classification of Sources". For the western language renditions, refer to the Bibliography.

1032 On the Lord of Pristine Cognition (*ye-shes-mgon-po*), see Nebesky-Wojkowitz, *Oracles and Demons of Tibet*, pp. 44-8.

1033 On this collection, see Blondeau, "Le Lha-'dre bka'-thaṅ", and the sources cited therein.

1034 For the Glorious Tiger-riding Lord (*dpal-mgon stag-zhon*), see Nebesky-Wojkowitz, *Oracles and Demons in Tibet*, pp. 34, 52.

1035 This prophecy made by Orgyen Lingpa is to be found in the *Injunction of Padma Discovered at Crystal Rock* (*padma bka'-thang*), Ch. 92, pp. 564ff. It contains the cryptic statement: "The pig will uproot the soil," which was interpreted to mean that Tā'i Situ Cangcup Gyeltsen of Phakmotru (the pig) would politically uproot Sakya (the soil). Cf. also, pp. 590-2.

1036 Temo Rinpoche was regent from 1886 until 1895, when the Thirteenth Dalai Lama compelled his resignation. In 1899 he was implicated in a plot to overthrow the Dalai Lama by means of sorcery. See Shakabpa,

Tibet: A Political History, pp. 198-9; and L. Petech, *Aristocracy and Government in Tibet 1728-1959*, pp. 5 and 62.

1037 The sudden and unexpected possession (*thog-babs*) of an oracle is a most ominous portent (Lama Sonam Topgyel). The Great Protector of the Doctrine at Samye is Pehar, on whom see Nebesky-Wojkowitz, *Oracles and Demons of Tibet*, pp. 94-133.

1038 The reliquary of Orgyen Lingpa resembled other tombs in the stūpa design – with its base in the shape of the bulbous dome (*bum-pa*), a window of lattice-work (*'phrul-mig*) in front and surmounted by a spire (*bre*).

1039 In 1435 the dynasty of Phakmotru conceded power to the princes of Rinpung who were lay patrons of the Karmapa. See p. 954 and n. 1364; Snellgrove and Richardson, *A Cultural History of Tibet*, pp. 154, 180; and Shakabpa, *Tibet: A Political History*, pp. 86-90.

1040 Terdak Lingpa himself reports only the last two mentioned, in his *Record of Teachings Received*, pp. 423-5.

1041 This is the biography of Khyentse Rinpoche by Jamgön Kongtrül. See the first part of the Bibliography for publication details.

1042 The dating given here for Rikdzin Gödemcen follows the Tshurpu school. The other possibility according to the calculation of the Phakpa school would be Sunday 12 January 1337.

1043 Kurser is a legendary Horpa king who figures prominently in the Kesar Epic. See Stein, *Recherches sur l'épopée et le barde au tibet*, index, p. 600, under "Gur-ser (E), roi des Hor".

1044 Tshurpu calculation, as explained above. According to both the Tshurpu and the Phakpa schools the snake month is the fourth (whereas it is the second according to the Phukpa schools); similarly the sheep month is the sixth according to Tshurpu and Phakpa, but the fourth in Phukpa. See Schuh, *Untersuchungen zur Geschichte der Tibetischen Kalenderrechnung*, p. 146.

1045 On the Gongpo (*'gong-po*), see especially Nebesky-Wojkowitz, *Oracles and Demons of Tibet*, pp. 283-5.

1046 The governor of Tsang, Zhingshakpa Tsheten Dorje, actively supported the Karmapa and persecuted the adherents of the Northern Treasures (*byang-gter*). Consequently, he was "liberated" to a higher level of existence by Cangdak Trashi Topgyel. See Dudjom Rinpoche, *rgyal-rabs*, pp. 492-3.

1047 Lhase Tamdzin Rölpa Yeshetsel was Murup Tsepo, the son of Trhisong Detsen.

1048 Not to be identified with Gö Lotsāwa, pp. 674-5 above.

1049 This calculation is made according to all the four major calendrical schools.

1050 The Nyingmapa in general prefer to dye the edges of their books red, rather than yellow as is sometimes done by the other traditions.

1051 The Great Ming emperor of China who invited Karmapa V Tezhinshekpa to Peking was Yung-lo (reigned 1403-24); see E. Sperling, "The 5th Karma-pa and some aspects of the relationship between Tibet and the early Ming" in TSHR, pp. 280-9. According to the Karma Kagyü tradition, Yung-lo sponsored and requested the manufacture of the actual Black Crown (*dbu-zhva nag-po*) of the Karmapa which is worn for only special ceremonial and ritual occasions.

1052 *sgal-tshig-gi dam* (Mongolian *tamaγa*) is the name of the privy seal which is the property of dignitaries such as the Dalai Lamas.

1053 Such catalysts are medicinal compounds of nectar-like substance (*bdud-rtsi sman*). They are employed to multiply the original quantity when blended with other medicinal substances.

1054 This calculation accords with all schools except the new Phukpa, which was not in existence when the biography of Sangye Lingpa was originally redacted.

1055 The earlier and later Tsele (*rtse-le gong-'og*) refer to Tsele Monastery in Takpo, founded by Künkyen Chöku Özer, and the nearby New Tsele Monastery (*rtse-le dgon-gsar*), founded by Rikdzin Sonam Namgyel. Cf. Jamyang Khyentse Wangpo, *Mkhyen-brtse on the History of Dharma in Tibet*, p. 18. Tsele Natshok Rangdröl (seventeenth century) is the best known of their hierarchs. See also n. 1094 below.

1056 The elder and younger Tabla (*ta-bla snga-phyi*) are Tabla Padmamati of Katok and one whom we are unable to identify.

1057 On Zhapdrung Ngawang Namgyel (1594-1651) and his role in the political and spiritual life of Bhutan, see Aris, *Bhutan*, Pt. 3, "The Zhabs-drung and the Creation of Bhutan".

1058 For the importance of the tenth-day ceremony (*tshes-bcu*) which commemorates the twelve manifestations of Guru Padmasambhava respectively on the tenth day of each month, see Ratna Lingpa, *tshes-bcu bskul-thabs*; Tucci, *The Religions of Tibet*, p. 148; and Gonpo Tseten, *The Udumbara Bouquet*, pp. 11-18. The *eight emanations* of Padmasambhava are given in the Glossary of Enumerations. The twelve manifestations are given in the Index of Personal Names under *Guru Rinpoche*.

1059 The ceremony for the fulfilment of commitments (*skong-chog*) invokes the protectors of the doctrine and employs confession as a means of restoring violations of the commitments assumed by those who enter the tantra vehicles.

1060 The Como of Trhadruk (*khra-'brug jo-mo*) is a miracle-performing image of Tārā in the temple of Trhadruk which was founded by King Songtsen Gampo. See KGHP, pp. 50, 125; PPCT, pp. 177-9; and TG, pp. 250-1.

1061 I.e. King Trhisong Detsen's.

1062 The "Vase Pillar" (*ka-ba bum-pa-can*), adjacent to the shrine of the great image of Śākyamuni brought to Tibet by Princess Wen-ch'eng K'ong-jo, has been the site of several treasure discoveries. See Tsepon W. D. Shakabpa, *Guide to the Central Temple of Lhasa*, p. 47.

1063 "Mön" is frequently used to refer to Bhutan and neighbouring districts in Tibet. On this term in general, see Aris, *Bhutan*, intro., p. xvi.

1064 All the four major calendrical schools arrive at this calculation, except the Phukpa in which the day of his birth (fifteenth) is omitted for the seventh month.

1065 The *Denkarma Catalogue of the Kangyur* is the oldest of its kind in Tibet, dating back to the early ninth century; see M. Lalou, "Les Textes Bouddhiques au temps du Roi Khri-sroṅ-lde-bcan" *Journal Asiatique* CCXLI (1953), pp. 313-53. Lalou assigns that work to the year 812. The present quotation, however, is not found therein. It occurs, rather, in the nearly contemporaneous *sgra sbyor bam gnyis* (T 4347), pp. 6-7.

1066 For much useful information on Pema Lingpa, see Aris, *Bhutan*, pp. 158-65 and *passim*; idem, *Hidden Treasures and Secret Lives*, pp. 13-106; and Padma Tshewang, *The Treasure Revealer of Bhutan*.

1067 See p. 554 above; the Glossary of Enumerations under *five pure incarnations of the royal princess Pemasel*; and KGHP, p. 45.

1068 This calculation accords with all four schools except Phakpa, which would give us instead Thursday 1 August 1476.

1069 According to the Author, this temple was one branch or *gling-phran* of Samye Monastery. See TH, pp. 178-9; and PPCT, pp. 216-32.

1070 I.e. Princess Pemasel.

1071 On Dawa (b.1499), see Aris, *Hidden Treasures and Secret Lives*, pp. 91, 95-6, 105-6.

1072 For the various English language translations of this work, see the first part of the Bibliography. The traditions associated with it are considered at length by D. I. Lauf in *Secret Doctrines of the Tibetan Books of the Dead*.

1073 For much useful material on this great saint, see J. Gyatso, "The Teachings of Thang-stong rgyal-po" in TSHR, pp. 111-19; idem, *The Literary Transmission of the Traditions of Thang-stong rgyal-po*, unpublished Ph.D. thesis; C. R. Stearns, "The Life and Teachings of the Tibetan Saint Thang-stong rgyal-po", unpublished MA thesis; and Aris, *Bhutan*, pp. 185-90 and *passim*.

1074 On Thangtong Gyelpo's position in the Shangpa tradition, see Kapstein, "The Shangs-pa bKa'-brgyud: an unknown tradition of Tibetan Buddhism", pp. 141-2.

1075 See p. 511; also Aris, *Bhutan*, pp. 5-33.

1076 Parts of the bridges are still in existence. It has recently been demonstrated that they were constructed of a specially alloyed, non-corrosive iron. See Aris, *Bhutan*, pp. 185-90.

1077 On Thangtong Gyelpo's contribution to Tibetan theatre, see Stein, *Tibetan Civilization*, pp. 276-7; and Wang Yao, "Tibetan Operatic Themes" in STC, pp. 186-96.

1078 Aris, *Bhutan*, pp. 185, 321, disputes the date of Thangtong Gyelpo's death, following Stein, *Recherches sur l'épopée et le barde au tibet*, p. 238, n. 17, who gives 1385-1464 instead of 1509. J. Gyatso and C. R. Stearns argue in favour of the dates 1361-1485, as given in the standard biography.

1079 This figure is associated with a popular rite for the propitiation of Avalokiteśvara, entitled *yi-ge drug-pa'i sgrub-thabs*, rediscovered in the last century by Jamyang Khyentse Wangpo. Through the efforts of the recent abbots of Dzarong-phu, near Mount Everest, it has become particularly popular among the Sherpa and Tibetan populations of northern Nepal.

1080 The condition of this region in recent years has been described in G. Tucci, *Preliminary Report on Two Scientific Expeditions in Nepal*, pp. 15-25; Snellgrove, *Himalayan Pilgrimage*, pp. 188-99; M. Peissel, *Mustang, The Forbidden Kingdom*; and D. Jackson, *The Mollas of Mustang*.

1081 I.e. he received the five vows of an *upāsaka*.

1082 This incident is alluded to on p. 717.

1083 On this learned master (1456-1532), see E. G. Smith's introduction to Glo-bo mKhan-chen, *Tshad-ma rigs-pa'i gter-gyi rnam-par bshad-pa*.

1084 I.e. he never left his place of meditation.

1085 This is the very Lekdenje, on whom see above, p. 717.

1086 For Cangdak Trashi Topgyel, see pp. 783 and 824.

1087 See pp. 555-6.

1088 The constellation Puṣya (Cancer γ, δ, θ) is auspiciously associated with the birth of the Buddha Śākyamuni. See below, p. 946; and Przyluski, *Le Concile de Rājagṛha*, p. 88.

1089 The term "secret seal" is equivalent to the seal of concealment (*sbas-rgya*) by which the treasures were originally hidden. According to the treasure (*gter-ma*) tradition, there are four kinds of seal connected with the transmission of the teachings, namely, the seal of commitment (*samaya-rgya*), the seal of treasures (*gter-rgya*), the seal of concealment (*sbas-rgya*), and the seal of entrustment or succession (*gtad-rgya*) through which the most secret teachings are transmitted. Treasures discovered in secret (*gsang-gter*) are contrasted with those discovered in public (*khrom-gter*).

1090 The essences of the earth (*sa-bcud*) are minerals such as sulphur, and precious gemstones.

1091 The Gyeltsaps are the regents of Tshurpu, the Central Tibetan seat of the Karmapa. Trakpa Töndrup, the fourth, lived *c.* 1550 to *c.* 1617.

1092 Chöki Trakpa (b.1595) was a renowned exponent of the Drigung Kagyüpa system of the yogas of Nāropā.

1093 Paksam Wangpo (1593-1641), the fifth in the line of Drukcen incarnations, was the immediate successor of the great Pema Karpo (1527-92).

1094 Tsele (fl. mid-seventeenth century) was one of the most influential exponents of the vehicle of indestructible reality within the Drukpa Kagyü and Nyingma traditions. His works are even now regarded as authoritative guides to the resolution of philosophical difficulties. See, e.g., E. Schmidt (trans.), *The Mirror of Mindfulness*.

1095 The career of this great political leader (1689-1747) has been the subject of detailed study by L. Petech in *China and Tibet in the Early 18th Century*; and Shakabpa, *Tibet: A Political History*, pp. 143-7. See also S. Jagchid, "A Mongol Text Letter from a Tibetan Leader" *Central Asiatic Journal* 17 (1973), pp. 150-63. An account of this figure is also found in the writings of the Italian Capuchin Cassiano Beligatti de Macerata, who knew him personally. See J. Macgregor, *Tibet: A Chronicle of Exploration*, pp. 105-7.

1096 For some indications concerning the practice of Jatsön Nyingpo's *Gathering of All Precious Jewels* in modern Nepal, see D. L. Snellgrove, *Buddhist Himalaya*, pp. 228ff.

1097 On this aristocratic household, see Stein, *Recherches sur l'épopée et le barde au tibet*, Ch. 5.

1098 In the vase attainment (*bum-sgrub*), the ritual vase (*bum-pa*) becomes a container for sacramental substances known as nectar-elixir (*bdud-rtsi sman*).

1099 *spu-stod*. Our text erroneously reads *spa-stod*.

1100 This prodigy, whose floruit may be assigned to the mid-seventeenth century, received the revelations known as "celestial doctrines" (*gnam-chos*), from his twelfth year onwards. He passed away in his twenty-fourth, leaving as his legacy some fifteen volumes of collected visionary teachings. See Tsering Lama, *A Garland of Immortal, Wish-fulfilling Trees*, pp. 45-52.

1101 Karma Chakme (1613-78) was the tutor of Namcö Mingyur Dorje and the redactor of his teachings. A prolific author in his own right, he was considered to be an emanation of Karmapa VIII, Mikyö Dorje. See Tsering Lama, *A Garland of Immortal, Wish-fulfilling Trees*, pp. 35-44.

1102 See above, p. 736.

1103 See above, p. 736.

1104 A is the seed-syllable which is symbolic of emptiness.

1105 The practices of Mahāyoga and Anuyoga are applied in accordance with either of two paths – the path of skilful means (*thabs-lam*) and the path of liberation (*grol-lam*), on which see *Fundamentals*, pp. 279-81 and 286-7. The path of skilful means is also known as the path of desire (*chags-lam*) – for its object is the coalescence of bliss and emptiness achieved by relying on "one's own body as the means" (*rang-lus thabs-ldan*) and "one's consort's or partner's body as the seal" (*gzhan-lus phyag-rgya*), i.e. the "action seal". The practices associated with this path of skilful means are discussed in Longcenpa, *Dispelling Darkness in the Ten Directions*, pp. 453ff. (GGFTC, pp. 1006ff.).

The coalescence of the four delights with the four modes of emptiness which is referred to here and in the passage below, p. 830, is also illustrated by the following account derived from the *gtum-mo 'bar-'dzag yig-chung*, *snying-thig rtsa-pod*, Vol. 3, pp. 23-6:

> Through the practice of the inner heat (*gtum-mo*) the blissful warmth (*bde-drod*) descends through the central channel, giving rise to the four successive delights (*dga'-ba bzhi*). In the crown centre, it gives rise to Vairocana's pristine cognition of delight (*dga'-ba'i ye-shes*) and the vase empowerment is received through which this delight is united or coalesced with emptiness (*stong-pa*). In the throat centre it gives rise to Amitābha's pristine cognition of supreme delight (*mchog-dga'i ye-shes*) and the secret empowerment is received through which this supreme delight is coalesced with great emptiness (*stong-pa chen-po*). In the heart centre it gives rise to Akṣobhya's pristine cognition free from delight (*dga'-bral ye-shes*) and the empowerment of discerning pristine cognition is received, through which this absence of delight is coalesced with extreme emptiness (*shin-tu stong-pa*). And in the navel centre it gives rise to Ratnasambhava's pristine cognition of co-emergent delight (*lhan-skyes dga'-ba'i ye-shes*) and the empowerment of word and meaning is received through which this co-emergent delight is coalesced with total emptiness (*thams-cad stong-pa*). Therein the recognition of the four delights dissolve as they arise. Finally, the blissful warmth gives rise, in the secret centre, to Amoghasiddhi's inconceivable pristine cognition (*bsam-gyi mi-khyab-pa'i ye-shes*) and the empowerment of the expressive power of awareness is received.

1106 The disciplined conduct of awareness (*rig-pa brtul-zhugs-kyi spyod-pa*) is that which corresponds to the path of skilful means. See *Fundamentals*, p. 281.

1107 According to Khetsun Zangpo Rinpoche, the *Tent of Longevity* is a practice belonging to the Northern Treasures (*byang-gter*) tradition, which combines *Yamāntaka, Lord of Life* (*gshin-rje tshe-bdag*) with Mahākāla in the form of "Lord of the Tent" (*mgon-po gur* or *gur-gyi mgon-po*), i.e. the form of Mahākāla associated especially with the *Vajrapañjara Tantra* (T 419).

1108 This was the first Paṇcen Rinpoche, 1570-1662.

1109 This refers to the systematic teaching of logic instituted by Chapa Chöki Senge (1109-69), on whom see L.W.J. van der Kuijp, *Contributions to the Development of Tibetan Buddhist Epistemology*, pp. 59-96. Chapa's own writings have fallen out of use, but later textbooks adhere pedagogically to his system, for a sample of which, see D. Perdue, *Debate in Tibetan Buddhist Education*.

1110 See E. G. Smith's introduction to *Kongtrul's Encyclopaedia*, p. 20, n. 40.

1111 The Qōśot Mongols under Guśrī Qan subdued the king of Tsang, Karma Tenkyong, in the year 1642, two years before the Manchus overthrew the Ming dynasty in China. It was K'anghsi, the second emperor of the Ch'ing Dynasty who invited Dalai Lama V to Peking. See Stein, *Tibetan Civilization*, pp. 82-3; Snellgrove and Richardson, *A Cultural History of Tibet*, p. 198; and also Dawa Norbu, "An Analysis of Sino-Tibetan Relationships" in STC, pp. 176-95.

1112 The internal administration of Tibet under the Dalai Lamas was characteristically held to insist upon the integration of religious and temporal traditions (*chos-srid lugs-gnyis*). A detailed historical analysis of this theme is found in Dongar Lobzang Chinlei, *bod-kyi chos-srid zung-'brel skor bshad-pa*. For a useful introduction to the practical implications of this system for the actual organisation of the Tibetan government, see H. E. Richardson, *A Short History of Tibet*, pp. 18-27.

1113 A treasure-discoverer of the Sakyapa school, Khyentse Wangcuk was born in 1524.

1114 Ganden Palace (*dga'-ldan-gyi pho-brang*) was the name of office of the Dalai Lama which ruled Tibet from the time of Dalai Lama V until 1959. The name is derived from that of the Great Fifth's residence at Drepung Monastery prior to the construction of the Potala Palace; see TH, pp. 134-40.

1115 "Enlightened activity of his future dominion" (*'byung-'gyur dbang-gi phrin-las*). This activity forms one aspect of the third of the four rites (*las-bzhi*), that of subjugation, which is the special accomplishment achieved through the rites of Kurukullā.

1116 Dalai Lama VI is best known for his free-wheeling life-style and beautiful songs. See Yu Dawchyuan, *Love-songs of the Sixth Dalai Lama Tshangs-dbyangs-rgya-mthso*; and Aris, *Hidden Treasures and Secret Lives*, pp. 107-212. One version of his eccentric life story has been translated by P. Klafkowski as *The Secret Liberation of the Sixth Dalai Lama*. On this, however, see the reviews by J. W. de Jong in the *Indo-Iranian Journal* 24 (1982), pp. 223-5; and by P. Denwood in the *Bulletin of SOAS* 45 (1982), pp. 381-3.

1117 His previous embodiment was named Sinpo Chöki Koca.

1118 Targye Chöling in Tranang was the ancestral seat of Mindröling in

Central Tibet. See PPCT, p. 170.

1119 *skyid-rong rang-byung 'phags-pa*. This is the "Kyirong Wati" mentioned in GT, p.129; and known in *Blue Annals*, p. 528, as *'phags-pa wa-ti*. It was brought to the Potala via Drepung in 1656 when rumours of an impending war with Nepal were widespread.

1120 All maṇḍalas referred to in this section are derived from the *tshogs-chen 'dus-pa* of Anuyoga. See *Fundamentals*, pp. 284-9. Anuyoga includes empowerments associated with the nine vehicles, on which see pp. 911-13.

1121 I.e. the old seat of Targye Chöling and the new seat of Orgyan Mindröling which was founded by Terdak Lingpa in 1676.

1122 On these practices of Cutting Through Resistance and All-Surpassing Realisation, see *Fundamentals*, pp. 335-45.

1123 The crucial times and duration for such practices are given in the appropriate texts for each.

1124 *Dhūti* or *avadhūti* is the central energy channel. See *Fundamentals*, pp. 340-1; and also Longcenpa, *Dispelling Darkness in the Ten Directions*, pp. 453ff. (GGFTC, pp. 1006ff.).

1125 On this bliss of melting (*zhu-bde*), see nn. 250 and 1105 above.

1126 On the relation between meditative equipoise and its aftermath, see especially *Fundamentals*, p. 206.

1127 For the *four empowerments*: the vase, secret empowerment, empowerment of discerning pristine cognition and the empowerment of word and meaning, see n. 1198 below; *Fundamentals*, p. 360; and the Glossary of Enumerations.

1128 According to the new Phukpa system, the second month corresponds to March/April.

1129 According to the new Phukpa calendar, *khrums zla-ba* corresponds to September/October.

1130 The messenger (*pho-nya*) is the consort or partner who acts as an intermediary, bringing to the practitioner the pristine cognition of co-emergent bliss. See n. 1105 above.

1131 I.e. the three indestructible realities of buddha-body, speech and mind.

1132 Governor (*dpon-chen*) and district administrator (*dpon-skya*). For an account of these offices during the Sakya administration of Tibet, see Tucci, *Tibetan Painted Scrolls*, pp. 33-5, where *dpon-chen* is explained to mean "myriarch" (*khri-chen*) and *dpon-skya* to mean "minister of transport".

1133 The Tibetan shawm (*rgya-gling*) is similar to the Persian *shanā'ī*, to which it perhaps owes its origins. Curiously, the very name in Tibetan may have originated as a translation from the Persian word, which means "royal flute", for in some old texts one sees the spelling *rgyal-gling*, with precisely the same significance. For this suggestion we are indebted to Mme Mireille Helffer.

1134 Terrestrial pure lands (*sa'i zhing-khams*) within the sphere of the emanational body are contrasted with celestial pure lands (*mkha'-spyod-kyi zhing-khams*) which are frequented by the buddha-body of perfect rapture; see *Fundamentals*, pp. 123ff.

1135 I.e. King Trhisong and his twenty-four main subjects. The "present sovereign" referred to in the prophecy is King Trhisong, and "his son" is Murup Tsepo. The prophecy is addressed by Padmasambhava to

King Trhisong.

1136 Sangye Gyamtso became the regent of Tibet in 1682 after the death of Dalai Lama V. He was killed in 1705 by Lhazang Qan, leader of the Qōśot Mongols. See Stein, *Tibetan Civilization*, p. 85; and, for more details, the works of Z. Ahmad, L. Petech and Tsepon W. D. Shakabpa listed in the final section of the Bibliography.

1137 Mingyur Peldrön was largely responsible for the restoration of Mindröling following the Dzungar invasion of 1717. A brilliant teacher, she authored several important meditation manuals.

1138 For detailed information on many points dealt with in the present account, see S. D. Goodman, "Rig-'dzin 'Jigs-med gling-pa and the *Klong-Chen sNying-Thig*" in Goodman and R. M. Davidson (eds.), *Tibetan Buddhism: Reason and Revelation*.

1139 For an account of this and the surrounding royal tombs, see Tucci, *The Tombs of the Tibetan Kings*.

1140 Prajñāraśmi was the treasure-finder Sherap Özer. See Jamgön Kongtrül, *Lives of the Hundred Treasure-finders*, pp. 135a.6-137a.6.

1141 The root text of Jikme Lingpa's doctrinal masterpiece, the *Precious Treasury of Enlightened Attributes*, is renowned among Tibetan literati for its poetic beauty. See Blankleder and Fletcher, trans.

1142 "Warmth" (*drod*): see n. 1105 above.

1143 The throat centre of buddha-speech is known as the centre of perfect rapture (*long-spyod rdzogs-pa'i 'khor-lo*, Skt. *sambhogacakra*). This dissolution into a mass of seed-syllables indicates that Jikme Lingpa attained accomplishments associated with buddha-speech.

1144 The horse is, of course, symbolic of Hayagrīva.

1145 *mtshon-byed dpe'i ye-shes*. This is the pristine cognition which arises in consequence of instruction and empowerment. It forms the basis for the realisation of the "genuine pristine cognition which is the object of exemplification" (*mtshon-bya don-gyi ye-shes*).

1146 For the traditional account of the construction of this monument and pilgrimage centre, see Keith Dowman, *The Legend of the Great Stūpa*.

1147 *gcig-car smra-ba 'byung*. Our interpretation of this phrase follows the Author's oral explanation. *gcig-car* here has nothing to do with the teaching of instantaneous enlightenment (as it often does), but rather suggests forthrightness or spontaneity.

1148 The ancient recensions are those redacted by Longcenpa in the *Fourfold Innermost Spirituality* (*snying-thig ya-bzhi*) and the new recension is Jikme Lingpa's own *Innermost Spirituality of Longcenpa* (*klong-chen snying-thig*).

1149 I.e. the three doctrinal centres of Samye, Trhadruk and the Jokhang at Lhasa.

1150 The ransom of animals (*tshe-thar/srog-blu*) due to be slaughtered was widely practised in Tibet for the sake of accumulating the provision of merit (*bsod-nams-kyi tshogs*).

1151 This was the Gurkha incursion in the years from 1788 to 1792, on which see Stein, *Tibetan Civilization*, p. 88; Snellgrove and Richardson, *A Cultural History of Tibet*, pp. 226-7; and Shakabpa, *Tibet: A Political History*, pp. 156ff.

1152 For Langcen Pelgi Senge, see p. 535.

1153 Jikma Trhinle Özer (1745-1821) was the first Dodrup Rinpoche. He gathered disciples from throughout eastern Tibet and thus greatly promoted the rediscovered teachings of his master. As preceptor to the queen of Derge, Tshewang Lhamo, he gained for his efforts the royal support of her household. For the account of his life, see Tulku Thondup, *Masters of Meditation and Miracles*, pp. 136-162. His relations with the Derge kingdom are discussed on p. 155.

1154 An important teacher in his own right, Jikme Gyelwei Nyugu is remembered above all through the beautiful record of his oral instructions set down by his disciple Dza Peltrül Rinpoche (1808-87), i.e. the *kun-bzang bla-ma'i zhal-lung*, which remains a most popular teaching manual of the Nyingma tradition. See S. T. Kazi (trans.), *Kun Zang La May Zhal Lung*; and Padmakara Translation Committee, *The Words of My Perfect Teacher.*

1155 For the remaining four treasure-finders discussed in this part and, in particular, their role in the spiritual eclecticism of nineteenth-century Kham, see Smith's introduction to *Kongtrul's Encyclopedia*.

1156 This is a new Phukpa calculation; the Tshurpu calculation would read 11 July 1829.

1157 A brief introduction to the Nangcen district may be found in Karma Thinley, *Important events and places in the history of Nangchin Kham and E. Tibet*. See also Trungpa Rinpoche, *Born in Tibet*, which refers to many locations in Nangcen, though this is seldom made explicit.

1158 This figure (1774-1853?), the ninth in the line of Situ incarnations, was a leading master of the Karma Kagyü tradition, and also revered as a treasure-finder.

1159 "Store of the Sky" (*nam-mkha'i mdzod*) is the name of one particular treasure trove in Kham, see the Index of Locations under *Yegyel Namkadzö*.

1160 I.e. Murup Tsepo. The meeting of Chogyur Lingpa with Jamyang Khyentse Wangpo was, in effect, the reunion of Murup Tsepo with his father, the sovereign Trhisong Detsen.

1161 "Treasure attainment" (*gter-sgrub*) is the means of performing and attaining accomplishment in accordance with any teaching discovered as treasure, which must be performed by the treasure-finder in connection with his or her discovery.

1162 Reconcealed treasures (*yang-gter*) are those which were discovered and then reconcealed by an earlier treasure-finder, to be found again in the future.

1163 The great attainment (*bsgrub-chen*), the fourth category of the four branches of ritual service and attainment, may include an elaborate dramatic and choreographic performance directed by the *vajrācārya* (*rdo-rje slob-dpon*). See n. 499 above.

1164 These dramatic ceremonies, enacting the lives of the preceptor Śāntarakṣita, the great master Padmasambhava and the religious king Trhisong Detsen (*mkhan-slob-chos gsum*), continue to be performed at the present day.

1165 This is a new Phukpa calculation; Tshurpu would read Tuesday 31 May 1870.

1166 This pure vision was the *Means for the Attainment of the Guru Chogyur*

Lingpa, the Gathering of the Families of the Three Bodies (*mchog-gling bla-sgrub sku-gsum rigs-'dus*), referred to on p. 858 below.

1167 See the Glossary of Enumerations under *five kingly treasure-finders*.

1168 The Thartse Khen Rinpoche is one of four preceptors in the Ngorpa subsect of the Sakya tradition; two of these are hereditary positions and the others, including that of Thartse, rotate every four years. Since no one can hold the office twice, it often would pass into the hands of the brother of the previous preceptor. The Sakyapa recognised Khyentse Rinpoche himself to be the emanation of an eighteenth-century Thartse Khen Rinpoche, named Campa Namka Chime.

1169 On this figure, see Smith's introduction to *Kongtrul's Encyclopedia*, p. 30.

1170 A good introduction to the subsects of the Sakyapa tradition is given by R. M. Davidson in, "The Ṅor-pa Tradition" *Wind Horse* 1, pp. 79-98.

1171 Losel Tenkyong of Zhalu (b. 1804) was a particularly close associate of Khyentse and Kongtrül, who played an instrumental role in connection with their efforts to revive rare lineages. See Smith's introduction to *Kongtrul's Encyclopedia*, pp. 34-5; and Kapstein, "The Shangs-pa bKa'-brgyud: an unknown tradition of Tibetan Buddhism".

1172 According to the venerable Dezhung Rinpoche, the continuous transmission survives for not more than about forty volumes, i.e. less than one-fifth of the *Tangyur*.

1173 These "Ten Great Pillars" were Thönmi Sambhoṭa, Vairocana, Kawa Peltsek, Cokro Lüi Gyeltsen, Zhang Yeshe De, Rincen Zangpo, Dromtön Gyelwei Jungne, Ngok Lotsāwa Loden Sherap, Sakya Paṇḍita and Gö Khukpa Lhetse. They are contrasted with the Eight Pillars who Supported the Lineages of Means for Attainment (Khetsun Zangpo Rinpoche).

1174 I.e. *smin, grol, rgyab-chos lung*. See p. 733, in relation to the lineage of transmitted precepts.

1175 On the political upheavals of the period, refer to T. Tsering, "Ñag-roṅ mgon-po rnam-rgyal: A 19th century Khams-pa Warrior" in STC, pp. 196-214. Bricks of dried tea were frequently used as currency in traditional Tibet.

1176 The *twofold precious enlightened attitude* refers to the relative (*kun-rdzob*) enlightened attitude which requires the generation of the four immeasurables, namely, loving kindness, compassion, sympathetic joy and equanimity; and the ultimate (*don-dam*) enlightened attitude which affirms the liberation of all sentient beings in the primordially pure nature of fundamental reality. Alternatively the term may refer to the two aspects of the relative enlightened attitude, namely, aspiration (*smon-pa*) and undertaking or entrance (*'jug-pa*). See also the Glossary of Enumerations.

1177 The emphasis on freedom from sectarian bigotry upon which Khyentse and his followers insisted, has led some scholars to speak of an impartial or eclectic (*ris-med*) movement in nineteenth-century Tibetan Buddhism. See especially Smith's introduction to *Kongtrul's Encyclopaedia*.

1178 I.e. the "auspicious" tradition of the Pönpo, whose ascetic teachings are represented primarily by the sixth of the nine Pönpo vehicles. See Tucci, *The Religions of Tibet*, p. 229.

1179 The text incorrectly reads *khrid-rgya*.
1180 These are to be found in the Glossary of Enumerations.
1181 This prophecy is found in the *Innermost Spirituality of the Accomplished Master (grub-thob thugs-thig)*, which was rediscovered by Khyentse Rinpoche.
1182 Khyentse Rinpoche was born in the district of Ga, within the clan of Nyö, during an iron dragon year.
1183 The ten-syllable mantra of White Tārā is OṂ TĀRE TUTTARE TURE SVĀHĀ. See S. Beyer, *The Cult of Tārā*, index, p. 533, under "Mantra, 10-syllable, of Tārā".
1184 As communicated by the Author, the three masters who had accomplished immortality were Guru Padmasambhava, Vimalamitra and the Newar Śīlamañju.
1185 For the life of Cetsün, see pp. 557-9.
1186 This is Khyentse Rinpoche's recension of a treasure discovered by Jikme Lingpa – the *bla-sgrub thig-le rgya-can* – from the *Innermost Spirituality of Longcenpa*.
1187 See above, p. 848.
1188 This is a new Phukpa calculation; the other schools would read Saturday 19 March 1892.
1189 On the various enumerations of Khyentse Rinpoche's emanations, see A. Macdonald, *Le Maṇḍala du Mañjuśrīmūlakalpa*, pp. 91-5; and Smith's introduction to *Kongtrul's Encyclopedia*, pp. 73-4.
1190 In addition to Smith's introduction to *Kongtrul's Encyclopedia*, already referred to, see Jamgön Kongtrül, *The Torch of Certainty*, translated by Hanson.
1191 Schuh, *Untersuchungen zur Geschichte der Tibetischen Kalenderrechnung*, p. 80, affirms that the dating for Jamgön Kongtrül's life is to be calculated according to the Tshurpu calendrical system. According to new Phukpa his birth would have occurred on Friday 3 December 1813.
1192 I.e. "omniscient great paṇḍita".
1193 Jamgön Kongtrül has left us a brief account of the names of these masters and the studies which he undertook under their guidance in the *mos-gus rab-byed* in nineteen folios.
1194 Tsandra Rincen Trak was Kongtrül's own main seat. He wrote an exceptionally detailed descriptive guide to it entitled *dpal-spungs yang-khrod tsā-'dra rin-chen brag-gi sgrub-sde'i dkar-chag* in one hundred and twenty-seven folios.
1195 According to Khetsun Zangpo Rinpoche, the "thirteen immortal awareness-holders" are probably deities in the maṇḍala of Amitāyus.
1196 Lerap Lingpa or Tertön Sogyel (1856-1926) is mentioned, along with others, as a master of the author of the Ling xylographic recension of the Kesar Epic: R.A. Stein, *L'épopée tibétaine de Gesar dans sa version lamaïque de Ling*, p. 8. According to Lama Sonam Topgyel, he was also responsible for uncovering the 1899 plot against the Thirteenth Dalai Lama, on which see n. 1036 above; and Shakabpa, *Tibet: A Political History*, p. 195.
1197 The visit of those aristocrats was ill-timed. The secrecy of the decipherment was interrupted, the commitments were violated and Khyentse Rinpoche fell ill in consequence.

1198 On the *four empowerments*, see the Glossary of Enumerations; and *Fundamentals*, p. 360. The vase empowerment (*bum-dbang*) reveals the emanational buddha-body. The secret empowerment (*gsang-dbang*) reveals the buddha-body of perfect rapture through practices associated with the energy channels, currents and seminal points, the latter of which are also known as "enlightened mind" (*byang-sems*). The empowerment of discerning pristine cognition (*shes-rab ye-shes-kyi dbang*) reveals the buddha-body of reality through awareness symbolised by the ḍākinī. The fourth empowerment of word and meaning (*tshig-don-gyi dbang*) reveals the essential buddha-body through the meditative practices of the Great Perfection.

1199 The scorpions are the emblem of Dorje Trolö.

1200 *Rakta*, "blood", is a sacramental substance symbolic of passion transmuted into enlightened involvement in the world. Its miraculous overflow is a portent of boundless enlightened activity.

1201 Again this is a Tshurpu calculation; according to new Phukpa, Jamgön Kongtrül would have passed away on Saturday 27 January 1900. Schuh, *Untersuchungen zur Geschichte der Tibetischen Kalenderrechung*, p. 80, gives 29 December 1899 but this is equivalent to the twenty-seventh day of the eleventh Tibetan month; our text has the twenty-sixth of the eleventh month. Smith gives 1899 in *Kongtrul's Encyclopedia*, p. 2.

1202 A synonym for the western Buddha-field of Sukhāvatī, or a metaphor for the peace of enlightenment that is great bliss. See Jikme Lingpa, *Narrative History of the Precious Collected Tantras of the Ancient Translation School* (*rnying-ma rgyud-'bum-gyi rtogs-brjod*), p. 364: *bde-ba chen-po shanti-pu-ri grong-khyer*.

1203 I.e. emanations of Mañjunātha (Mañjuśrī): *'jam-mgon mkhyen-kong rnam-gnyis*.

1204 Loter Wangpo (1847-1914), a leading Sakyapa disciple of Khyentse Rinpoche, played a major role in the redaction and publication of GDKT and the *Exposition of the Path and Fruit on Behalf of the Closest Students* (*lam-'bras slob-bshad*), encyclopaedic compilations of teachings belonging to the vehicle of indestructible reality as preserved by the new translation schools, with the Sakyapa foremost among them.

1205 For much valuable data, refer to S. D. Goodman, "Mi-pham rgya-mtsho: an account of his life, the printing of his works, and the structure of his treatise entitled *Mkhas pa'i tshul la 'jug pa'i sgo*" *Wind Horse* 1, pp. 58-78. Aspects of his philosophical thought are discussed in M. Kapstein, "Mi-pham's Theory of Interpretation" in *Reason's Traces*; and in J. Pettit, *The Beacon of Certainty*.

1206 The pill rites (*ril-bu'i las-sbyor*) performed by Mipham Rinpoche in connection with the propitiation of Mañjuśrī are practised so as to realise the ordinary accomplishments, e.g. during times of eclipse. These practices are described in detail in GTKT, Vol. II, pp. 70-137.

1207 "Exegetical transmission" (*bshad-lung*). This refers to the initiation into the study of a text by hearing the master recite it, along with occasional explanation of particular points of difficulty.

1208 On the Nyarong disturbances of the 1860s, see GT, p. 183, n. 627; E. Teichman, *Travels of a Consular Officer in East Tibet*, p. 5; and Tsering, "Ñag-roṅ mgon-po rnam-rgyal: A 19th Century Khams-pa

Warrior", pp. 196-214. The five clans of Nyarong were unified after 1837 by Gönpo Namgyel. In 1860 they invaded and conquered Derge and Hor-khog. In 1862 the rebellion was suppressed by Lhasa.

1209 *sa-ris* is an arithmetical calculation performed, not with the aid of an abacus, but traced in sand.

1210 "Bean-sprout rites" (*makṣa'i las-sbyor*) are those in which the mantra of White Mañjuśrī is recited while a dark-brown *makṣaka* bean is held in the mouth. If the bean sprouts, this is a sign of successful accomplishment.

1211 On Mipham's association with Peltrül Rinpoche, and his contribution to the study of the ninth chapter of the *Introduction to the Conduct of a Bodhisattva*, see E. G. Smith's introduction to *Mi-pham's Brgal-lan*. Cf. also, K. Lipman, "A Controversial Topic from Mipham's Analysis of Śāntarakṣita's *Madhyamakālaṃkāra*" *Windhorse* 1 (1981), pp. 40-57.

1212 Teachings based on Mañjuśrī in the forms of Lord of Life, Iron-like and Iron-evil are common to various means for attainment. But see also the entry under *Mañjuśrī Lord of Life, Iron-like and Iron-evil*, in the first part of the Bibliography.

1213 The basic documents for the study of their dispute have been published in *Mi-pham's Rablan*; and Pari Rapsel, *'ju-lan ga-bur chu-rgyun*. The former has an excellent introduction by Smith.

1214 For the *kaptse* (*gab-rtse*) diagrams, derived from Chinese geomancy, see *Fundamentals*, p. 104; and G. Dorje, *Tibetan Elemental Divination Paintings*, pp. 63-4.

1215 I.e. he was a Nyingmapa who was learned in the new traditions, but not an adherent of these traditions himself (Tulku Thondup Rinpoche).

1216 This quotation is derived from both the *Oral Transmission of Mañjuśrī*, and Ngari Paṇcen, *Ascertainment of the Three Vows*. See listed in the first part of the Biblography.

1217 See *Fundamentals*, pp. 335-45.

1218 On the "cloud-mass wheel of syllables" (*yi-ge 'khor-lo tshogs*), see n. 1143 above. For an explanation and discussion of the significance of syllables in the vehicle of indestructible reality, see Longcenpa, *Dispelling Darkness in the Ten Directions*, Chs. 4-5, pp. 170-224 (GGFTC, pp. 550-631).

1219 Abhirati (*mngon-dga'*) is the eastern Buddha-field of Akṣobhya; see *Fundamentals*, p. 128.

1220 As stated below, Mipham suffered from a violent nervous ailment (*'khrugs-nad*). Indeed, extant samples of his handwriting reveal a deterioration until, in his last year, they become entirely illegible (Khenpo Sangye Tenzin). Akṣobhya, the "unshakeable", was invoked to counteract this malady.

1221 On the appearance of seminal points of rainbow light through the practice of All-Surpassing Realisation, see *Fundamentals*, pp. 337-45.

1222 In connection with Shambhala, see the prophetic declarations cited by the Author, p. 960. On Shambhala in general, refer to Bernbaum, *The Way to Shambhala*.

1223 Zhecen Gyeltsap (d. *c.* 1926) was with Khencen Künzang Pelden (*c.* 1870 - *c.* 1940) largely responsible for continuing Mipham's teaching tradition. His collected works occupied thirteen volumes.

1224 I.e. Katok Situ Chöki Gyamtso, the author of *An Account of a Pilgrimage to Central Tibet During the Years 1918 to 1920*.

1225 Andzom Drukpa, a leading adept of the Great Perfection, was the publisher of very fine blockprint editions of the works of Longcenpa and many other major Nyingmapa texts.

1226 Trupwang Śākyaśrī (1853-1919), an adherent of both the Nyingmapa and Drukpa Kagyüpa traditions, was one of the most influential treasure-finders during the early decades of the present century.

1227 Repkong district in the province of Amdo has long enjoyed the reputation of a major centre of Nyingma practice. See TH, pp. 570-5.

HISTORY: PART SEVEN

1228 On the Indestructible Nucleus of Inner Radiance (*'od-gsal rdo-rje snying-po*), see p. 448, and *Fundamentals*, p. 115, where it is explained as the dimension of the buddha-body of reality (*chos-sku*).

1229 The *twenty-four lands* are those enumerated in the *Hevajra Tantra*, Pt. 1, Ch. 7, vv. 12-17. See the Glossary of Enumerations for their exact names.

1230 This and the following quotations from Rongzompa are said to be taken from his *Commentary on the Secret Nucleus* (*dkon-mchog 'grel*).

1231 The expression "high and low" doctrinal centres refers respectively to those at Lhasa and Samye (Lama Sonam Topgyel).

1232 Literally drawn from the under-arm pocket of the Tibetan garment.

1233 Nālandā Translation Committee, *The Life of Marpa the Translator*, p. 37, provides the standard account of this incident.

1234 Orgyenpa Rincenpel (1230-1309) is renowned as a master of the Nyingma, Kagyü and *Kālacakra* traditions. The precise source of the following quotation remains unidentified.

1235 On this figure, see p. 758, n. 995 above; and G. Roerich, *Biography of Dharmasvāmin*.

1236 Concerning Orgyenpa's journey to Oḍḍiyāna, consult Tucci, *Travels of Tibetan Pilgrims in the Swat Valley*.

1237 The text reads *bhe-ha-ra* (Skt. *vihāra*). For an introduction to the Newar Buddhist establishments of the Kathmandu Valley, see Macdonald and Stahl, *Newar Art*, pp. 71ff.

1238 These charges appear to have originated as early as the eleventh century, i.e. in the polemics of the Guge prince Photrang Zhiwa-ö. See Karmay, "King Tsa/Dza and Vajrayāna", p. 204. For the detailed Nyingma response, see below, pp. 911-13.

1239 The following two quotations correspond closely to passage 076 of Atiśa's biography, as edited in Eimer, *Rnam thar rgyas pa*, Vol. 2, p. 53.

1240 Tāranātha, *History of Buddhism in India*, p. 332. India here refers only to the Magadha heartland.

1241 On Mahādeva, see p. 429.

1242 Concerning the dispute about the *Non-Dual Victor*, see *Blue Annals*, p. 417, n. 4.

1243 On Śākya Chokden (1428-1507) and his many contributions to philosophical controversy in Tibet, see Kuijp, *Contributions to the Development of Tibetan Buddhist Epistemology*, pp. 10-22.

1244 This refers to Sakya Paṇḍita's confirmation of the authenticity of these tantras, on which see pp. 710-16.

1245 The *rgyud-sde spyi-rnam* and other major works of Comden Rikpei Reldri have only recently been located. Putön does list Sakya Paṇḍita's translation of the *Root Fragment of Vajrakīla* (*rdo-rje phur-ba rtsa-ba'i dum-bu*) in his *rgyud-'bum-gyi dkar-chag*, p. 373, l. 4.

1246 The *Kālacakra Tantra* is here referred to as the abridged version because it is traditionally held that the longer unabridged version was not transmitted in Jambudvīpa. Putön holds that the long version had twelve thousand verses; see Obermiller, *History of Buddhism by Bu-ston*, Pt. 2, p. 170.

1247 A standard account of Hoshang Mo-ho-yen's view of conduct is that of Obermiller, *History of Buddhism by Bu-ston*, Pt. 2, p. 193: "if one commits virtues or sinful deeds, one comes to blissful or evil births (respectively). In such a way the deliverance from Saṁsāra is impossible, and there will be always impediments to the attainment of Buddhahood."

1248 On the three turnings or promulgations of the doctrinal wheel, see pp. 423-5. For a detailed discussion, see *Fundamentals*, pp. 76 and 153-5. On provisional and definitive significance, see *Fundamentals*, pp. 187-90.

1249 The view held by adherents of the new translation schools is traditionally one in which the philosophies of tantra and the dialectics are integrated. The Author here asserts that the view of the Great Perfection is central to this integration.

1250 The texts which have just been quoted are common to all the Buddhist traditions in Tibet. They are not the exclusive property of the tradition of Chinese Ch'an Buddhism attributed to Hoshang Mo-ho-yen, and their view is identical to that of the Great Perfection. Hence the convergence of the various traditions concerned on this point cannot be taken as evidence of error on the part of any of them.

1251 I.e. deviation (*gol-sa*) from the true view of the Great Perfection into that of the lower vehicles, or into the "four experiences" (*nyams-bzhi*) of bliss, emptiness, radiance and non-conceptualisation, which can mislead meditation. See *Fundamentals*, pp. 294-310.

1252 This refers to the meditative practices of All-Surpassing Realisation. See *Fundamentals*, pp. 337-45.

1253 Unidentified. This passage is also cited in *Fundamentals*, p. 164.

1254 I.e. the adherents of the new translation schools.

1255 This quotation is drawn from Atiśa, *Bodhimārgapradīpapañjikā*, which comments on the *Bodhipathapradīpa*, vv. 56-8. See R. Sherburne, SJ (trans.), *A Lamp for the Path and Commentary*, p. 151.

1256 On the view of the Svātantrika-Madhyamaka as interpreted by the Nyingma tradition, see *Fundamentals*, pp. 162-4.

1257 On the pristine cognition of discernment (*sor-rtogs ye-shes*), see *Fundamentals*, p. 141.

1258 "Great liberation from limits" or "great liberation from extremes" (*mtha'-grol chen-po*): see *Fundamentals*, p. 334.

1259 Quoted by Nāgārjuna in *Vigrahavyāvartanīsvavṛttiḥ*, as a comment on v. 28.

1260 On "expressed meaning and expression", see *Fundamentals*, pp. 71-2.

1261 These categories from the Great Perfection are given in the Glossary of Enumerations.

1262 Sakya Paṇḍita, *Analysis of the Three Vows (sdom-gsum-gyi rab-tu dbye-ba'i bstan-bcos*, Gangtok edn.), fol. 62b6.

1263 Refer to sGam-po-pa, *The Jewel Ornament of Liberation*, p. 216. Though Gampopa did indeed introduce material from the Great Seal tradition in the context of the transcendental perfection of discriminative awareness, he never maintained that the two could be fully assimilated one to the other, as his critics sometimes claim.

1264 On "seals", see *Fundamentals*, p. 356.

1265 On the term "nucleus of the sugata", see *Fundamentals*, pp. 169ff.

1266 On the empowerments according to the Anuyoga teachings, see *Fundamentals*, pp. 364-5.

1267 On the tenth level, Cloud of Doctrine, see *Fundamentals*, p. 117.

1268 *Ūrṇakeśa (mdzod-spu)* is the circle of hair between the eyes of a buddha, from which rays of light emanate.

1269 The "empowerment of great light rays" is discussed in *Fundamentals*, p. 142.

1270 On the first level, the Joyful (*rab-tu dga'-ba*, Skt. *Pramodā*), see *Fundamentals*, pp. 281-2; and sGam-po-pa, *The Jewel Ornament of Liberation*, pp. 240-2.

1271 Orpiment is "yellow arsenic powder" (*ba-bla*). According to *gso-rig snying-bsdud skya-rengs gsar-pa*, p. 251, this substance is medically applied for the prevention of decay and epidemics. It can be taken as a treatment for anything from a swelling goitre to a festering wound, and is even nowadays used as an antidote for mercury poisoning.

1272 On the *three higher empowerments*, see the Glossary of Enumerations; and *Fundamentals*, p. 360.

1273 On this rivalry, see p. 643.

1274 The *four faults attributed to the "Secret Nucleus"* are listed in the Glossary of Enumerations. Gö Lhetse probably published this critique in his oft-mentioned *Broadside ('byams-yig)*, on which see *sngags log sun-'byin-gyi skor*, pp. 18-25. The traditional refutations of Lhetse's charges are given below. Cf. also *Scholar's Feast of Doctrinal History*, pp. 179ff; Jikme Lingpa, *rgyud-'bum 'dri-lan*, pp. 281ff.; and Sodokpa Lodrö Gyeltsen, *rgyal-dbang karma-pa mi-bskyod rdo-rjes gsang-sngags rnying-ma-ba-rnams-la dri-ba'i chab-shog gnang-ba'i dris-lan lung-dang rig-pa'i 'brug-sgra*, in *Collected Writings of Sog-bzlog-pa*, Vol 2, p. 33.

1275 See above, p. 891.

1276 The following reproduces almost the entire text of this short work, as preserved in the *Collected Writings of Sog-bzlog-pa*, Vol. 1, pp. 524-6. To help clarify the complex embedding of quotations found here, all passages from the *Tantra of the Secret Nucleus* itself are in italics.

1277 For the *five empowerments* and *three realities* which are referred to in the context of the *Secret Nucleus*, see the Glossary of Enumerations.

1278 *dkyil-'khor-gyi gtso-bo 'pho-bar bya-ba.*

1279 The *Scholar's Feast of Doctrinal History*, p. 180, cites this as *Prajñāsūtraṃ trikrasyati*.

1280 The passage which follows is cited, too, in the *Collected Writings of Sog-bzlog-pa*, Vol. 1, pp. 519-20. Sodokpa however rejects the possibility of treating the Nyingmapa tantras as treatises.

1281 I.e. even if their Indian origins are suspect, they can be held to be authoritative treatises so long as they are shown to conform to normal doctrinal criteria. The problem here alluded to is discussed in some detail in the contribution of Davidson to Buswell, *Buddhist Apocryphya*; and in Kapstein, "The Purificatory Gem and Its Cleansing: A Late Tibetan Polemical Discussion of Apocryphal Texts".

1282 According to Tāranātha, *History of Buddhism in India*, p. 302, the Red Master (*atsara dmar-po*) was a student of Ratnavajra named Guhyaprajñā. The Blue-skirted Paṇḍita is mentioned in *Blue Annals*, p. 697.

1283 Refer to Karmay, "The Ordinance of Lha Bla-ma Ye-shes-'od", pp. 150-62; idem, "An Open Letter by Pho-brang Zhi-ba-'od to the Buddhists of Tibet" *The Tibet Journal* V, 3 (1980), pp. 3-28; and idem, "A Discussion on the Doctrinal Position of rDzogs-chen from the 10th to the 13th centuries" *Journal Asiatique* (1975), pp. 147-56.

1284 On the rainbow body, see n. 528; and *Fundamentals*, pp. 336-7, 341-2.

1285 This occurrence aroused considerable controversy in Tibet at the time, and receives detailed discussion in Mipham Rinpoche, *gzhan-stong khas-len seng-ge'i nga-ro*, fols. 18b3ff.

1286 Düjom Lingpa (1835-1904) was the Author's previous incarnation. He was one of the most prolific treasure-finders of nineteenth-century Kham. See his biography in Pema Lungtok Gyatso et al., *gter-chen chos-kyi rgyal-po khrag-'thung bdud-'joms gling-pa'i rnam-thar zhal-gsungs-ma*.

1287 This is the great Pönpo scholar, Shardza Trashi Gyeltsen (1859-1935), on whom see Karmay, *The Treasury of Good Sayings*, especially pp. xv-xvi; Shardza, *Heart Drops of the Dharmakaya*.

1288 Probably this is Köpo Kelzang Gyeltsen, mentioned by Karmay, *The Treasury of Good Sayings*, p. xvi.

1289 This was the father of the late lama Jurme Drakpa (d. 1975) of Jore Bungalow, Darjeeling, who was a well-known meditation master. For an account of the father's miraculous death, see Trungpa Rinpoche, *Born in Tibet*, pp. 95-6.

1290 See pp. 714-16.

1291 *mtho-ris dang nges-legs*.

1292 Śāntigupta (late fifteenth to early sixteenth century) was a South Indian yogin who preserved and transmitted the surviving precepts of seven successive lineages. These traditions and Śāntigupta's own life form the subject-matter of Tāranātha's *bka'-babs bdun-ldan-gyi rgyud-pa'i rnam-thar*, translated by Templeman in *The Seven Instruction Lineages*. See also p. 504 and n. 532.

1293 According to the standard traditional account, Nup was Milarepa's master only in sorcery. His master in the Great Perfection was Rongtön Lhaga. See Lhalungpa, *The Life of Milarepa*, p. 42; and Martin, "The Teachers of Mi-la-ras-pa".

1294 The text erroneously reads Ba Selnang for Khön Lüiwangpo.

1295 Śāntideva, *Introduction to the Conduct of a Bodhisattva*, Ch. 9, v. 2c.

1296 Alakāvatī (*lcang-lo-can*) is the abode of yakṣas presided over by the Lord of Secrets, Vajrapāṇi in the form of Vaiśravaṇa or Kubera.

1297 Paṇcen Lozang Chöki Gyeltsen, *dge-ldan bka'-brgyud rin-po-che'i phyag-chen rtsa-ba rgyal-ba'i gzhung-lam*, fol. 2a4-5.

1298 Aśvottama (*rta-mchog*) or Aśvavarapāda in *Pag Sam Jon Zang*, p. 93, is said to have been the teacher of Viṇapā from Oḍḍiyāna.

1299 One treasure has perhaps been omitted in this quotation, which is in any case unlocatable in the extant *Sūtra which Genuinely Comprises the Entire Doctrine* (*Dharmasaṃgītisūtra*, P 904, Vol. 36, pp. 1-45). Alternatively, the totality of the list may be counted as its tenth member.

1300 Sakya Paṇḍita's principle targets were the "heresies" of the Drigung Kagyü and Tshelpa Kagyü, both of which sought to resolve the complexities of the doctrine by insisting on a single quintessential metaphor: the "single intention" (*dgongs-pa gcig*) in the case of the former, and the "one purity that achieves all" (*dkar-po gcig-thub*) in the case of the latter.

1301 This refers to Milarepa's insistence that Gampopa, during their first meeting, abandon monastic rules by partaking of ale. See Chang, *The Hundred Thousand Songs of Milarepa*, Vol. 2, p. 473.

1302 The text erroneously reads "four golden doctrines" (*gser-chos bzhi*), though five are properly enumerated. See the Glossary of Enumerations; and Kapstein, "The Shangs-pa bKa'-brgyud: an unknown tradition of Tibetan Buddhism", pp. 138-44. The basic Shangpa texts are found in the Peking edition of the *Tangyur*, but not in the Derge edition.

1303 On Yakde Paṇcen (1299-1378) and Rongtön Sheja Künzi (1367-1449), see *Blue Annals*, pp. 339-40, 532-6, 1080-1. It is clear that Yakde Paṇcen, who predeceased the publication of Tsongkapa's (1357-1419) major works, cannot be counted as a critic of the latter. Most likely he is listed here owing to his association with the tradition of Tölpopa (see n. 1309 below), whom Tsongkapa vehemently opposed, and because Rongtön, who was Tsongkapa's first great critic, was educated in his school. The attacks on Tsongkapa launched by Korampa Sonam Senge (1429-89) and Śākya Chokden (1428-1507) were, on the other hand, so threatening to the Gelukpa establishment that their writings were banned in Central Tibet. The works of Korampa were eventually re-assembled and published in Derge during the eighteenth century, while those of Śākya Chokden were preserved only in Bhutan. Taklung Lotsāwa, the last named critic of Tsongkapa, is Taktsang Lotsāwa Sherap Rincen (b. 1405), who has been the target of particularly rigorous refutation by later Gelukpa masters. See Kuijp, *Contributions to the Development of Tibetan Buddhist Epistemology*, p. 16, n. 46; and J. Hopkins, *Meditation on Emptiness*, *passim*.

1304 The source of the quotation is unidentified. Remdawa Zhönu Lodrö (1349-1412), a Sakyapa, was a foremost teacher of Tsongkapa. See *Blue Annals*, pp. 339-40, 349, 1075.

1305 This quotation is attributed to the *Broadside* of Gö Lhetse. See n. 1274 above.

1306 I.e. by sublime bodhisattvas who have yet to realise the buddha level.

1307 This incident connected with Buddhajñānapāda is mentioned in Tāranātha, *History of Buddhism in India*, p. 279.

1308 Karmapa VIII, Mikyö Dorje's (1507-54) disagreements with earlier Karma Kagyü masters have not yet received scholarly attention. On his disputes with the Gelukpa school, see P. Williams, "A Note on Some Aspects of Mi Bskyod Rdo Rje's Critique of Dge Lugs Pa Madhyamaka" JIP 11 (1983), pp. 124-45; and on those with the Nyingmapa, see Kapstein, "The Purificatory Gem and Its Cleansing: A late Tibetan Polemical Discussion of Apocryphal Texts", n. 39.

1309 On Tölpopa Sherap Gyeltsen (1292-1361) and his doctrine of "extrinsic emptiness" (*gzhan-stong*), see especially D.S. Ruegg, "The Jo Naṅ pas: A School of Buddhist Ontologists according to the Grub mtha' śel gyi me loṅ" *Journal of the American Oriental Society* 83 (1963), pp. 73-91; S. Hookham, *The Buddha Within*; and C. Stearns, *The Buddha from Dolpo*. Cf. also *Fundamentals*, pp. 169ff. Tsongkapa's critique of Tölpopa receives detailed treatment in R.A.F. Thurman, *Tsong Khapa's Speech of Gold in the Essence of True Eloquence*.

1310 See Kuijp, *Contributions to the Development of Tibetan Buddhist Epistemology*, pp. 15-16.

1311 Unidentified.

1312 Prophecies concerning the discovery of the treasures are found in *The Life and Liberation of Padmasambhava*, Pt. II, pp. 619ff. See also, Prats, "Some Preliminary Considerations Arising from a Bibliographical Study of the Early *Gter-ston*", pp. 256-60; and Tulku Thondup Rinpoche, *Hidden Teachings of Tibet*.

1313 For a good example of this, see Karmay, "The Rdzogs-chen in its Earliest Text".

1314 *Phyva-gshen*. This refers to the adepts of the first way of Pön, who, according to Tucci, *The Religions of Tibet*, p. 228: "were able to distinguish the profitable from the dangerous, and therefore to function as diviners or augurs." Cf. also Snellgrove, *The Nine Ways of Bon*, pp. 24-41.

1315 This perhaps refers to the *nirgrantha* ascetic Satyaka-Mahāvādin, who was brought into the fold with six thousand of his followers through the Buddha's skilful means. See *Sūtra of the Arrayed Bouquet*, p. 277, ll. 10-16.

1316 Cf. Karmay, "The Rdzogs-chen in its earliest Text"; and idem,"Origin and Early Development of the Tibetan Religious Traditions of the Great Perfection". Stein in *Tibetan Civilization*, p. 241, also remarks that the Pönpo have modelled their monasteries, and the technical vocabulary for their philosophy and meditation on those of Buddhism. Some Pönpo works which, according to Nyingma tradition, were permitted by Padmasambhava are also represented in the *Store of Precious Treasures*; for there were certain treasure-finders who recovered both Pön and Buddhist treasures, e.g. Dorje Lingpa. See p. 791 above. For accounts of some of the treasure-finders common to the two traditions, see also Prats, *Contributo allo studio biografico dei primi gter-ston*.

1317 *rgya-nag-na ha-shang-dang ho-shang*. This passage in general merits comparison with Karma Chakme, *ri-chos mtshams-kyi zhal-gdams*, fol. 23a2-6, especially l. 5: "In India they say 'Outsider' and 'Insider', in China 'Taoist' (*ha-shang*) and 'Buddhist' (*ho-shang*), and in Tibet 'Buddhist' and 'Pönpo'. All of these are causally connected."

1318 *The Life and Liberation of Padmasambhava*, Pt. II, Canto 82, p. 489.

1319 The *shang* instrument is a Pönpo religious hand-bell made of bronze, with a wooden chime. See M. Helffer, "Note à propos d'une clochette *gshang*" *Objets et Mondes* 21, 3 (1981), pp. 129-34.

1320 The title "Phajo" indicates the head of a family: Stein, *Tibetan Civilization*, p. 95, translates it "father-lord". It was also a term of respect applied to the old Pön priests, the prophets who knew the origin of the three worlds, ibid., p. 231.

1321 See pp. 512-16.

1322 On Gongpo (*'gong-po*) spirits, see Nebesky-Wojkowitz, *Oracles and Demons of Tibet*, pp. 168-70. For Tamsi (*dam-sri*) demons, ibid., pp. 119, 284, 300-1, 469, 577-8. On Gyelpo (*rgyal-po*) and Senmo (*bsen-mo*) spirits who respectively manifest through anger and attachment, refer to the same source, pp. 233-6 for the former, and pp. 385, 396 for the latter.

1323 Cf. Śāntideva, *Introduction to the Conduct of a Bodhisattva*, Ch. 1, vv. 35-6.

HISTORY: PART EIGHT

1324 On the Auspicious Aeon (*bskal-pa bzang-po*, Skt. *Bhadrakalpa*) and the reason why the Teacher, Śākyamuni Buddha, is referred to as the Fourth Guide, see p. 409 and nn. 378-9 above.

1325 The Gelukpa tradition identifies Vasubandhu's *Conquest of Objections* with Daṃṣṭrasena's *Commentary on the Hundred Thousand Line Transcendental Perfection*, and maintains that the author of this work was solely Daṃṣṭrasena. Cf. Lessing and Wayman, *Mkhas Grub Rje's Fundamentals of the Buddhist Tantras*, p. 97. In the Nyingmapa view these are regarded as two separate treatises (Nyoshul Khenpo).

1326 One great aeon is said to contain eighty smaller aeons. See also n. 1380 below.

1327 The "third wheel of definitive significance" is explained at length in *Fundamentals*, pp. 169-217.

1328 The dating given here for Śākyamuni Buddha and all dates from the Indian period follow the *Kālacakra* reckoning which is based on scriptural authority and prophetic declaration. Thus there is a divergence of approximately four hundred years between this traditional dating of the Buddha's life and that favoured by modern historical scholars, i.e. *c.* 563 to 483 BC. A. Bareau, "La Date du Nirvāṇa" *Journal Asiatique* (1953), pp. 27-52, tabulates over fifty traditional calculations of the year of the Buddha's nirvāṇa, ranging from about 2100 BC to 265 BC.

1329 Āṣāḍha (*chu-stod*) is the sixth month of the Tibetan year, corresponding to July/August.

1330 According to the *Kālacakra* system of astrological calculation, earth-time is divided into cycles of sixty years known as *rab-byung*. Each of the sixty years within a single cycle has a distinctive name, but may also be referred to by a combination of twelve animals (hare, dragon, snake, horse, sheep, monkey, bird, dog, pig, mouse, ox and tiger) with the five elements (fire, earth, iron, water and wood). This latter system accords with elemental divination (*'byung-rtsis*) derived from Chinese traditions. Thus *don-drub* or the earth sheep year is the fifty-third within the sexagenary cycle. See Schuh, *Untersuchungen zur Geschichte der Tibetischen Kalenderrechnung*, pp. 144-5.

1331 The month of Vaiśākha (*sa-ga*) is the fourth month of the Tibetan year, corresponding to May/June.

1332 *drag-po* or the iron monkey year is the fifty-fourth in the sexagenary cycle. See Schuh, *Untersuchungen zur Geschichte der Tibetischen Kalenderrechnung*, pp. 144-5.

1333 On the constellation Puṣya, see n. 1088.

1334 Kārttika (*smin-drug*) is the tenth month, corresponding to November/December.

1335 *kun-'dzin*, or the earth mouse year, is the twenty-second year in the sexagenary cycle.

1336 The days are further divided into twelve two-hour periods, known as *khyim* or *dus-tshad*, and named after the twelve animals in the aforementioned sequence. The hour of the ox would fall approximately between midnight and 2 a.m. See chart in G. Dorje, *Tibetan Elemental Divination Paintings*, p. 89.

1337 A *ghaṭikā* (*chu-tshad*) is one-fifth of a two-hour period, i.e. twenty-four minutes.

1338 For various attempts to calculate the precise duration of each promulgation or turning of the doctrinal wheel, see Obermiller, *History of Buddhism by Bu-ston*, Pt. 2, pp. 46-52. Putön himself rejects all such efforts as lacking any authoritative source.

1339 Caitra (*nag*) is the third month of the Tibetan year, corresponding to April/May. It is also known as the mid-spring month (*dpyid-zla 'bring-po*) according to the Phukpa system of calculation. The chart of the twelve months in Schuh, *Untersuchungen zur Geschichte der Tibetischen Kalenderrechnung*, p. 146, shows the correspondences between their seasonal names, the animals and the constellations.

1340 The iron dragon year (*rnam-gnon*) is the fourteenth in the sexagenary cycle; see Schuh, *Untersuchungen zur Geschichte der Tibetischen Kalenderrechnung*, p. 144.

1341 Obermiller, *History of Buddhism by Bu-ston*, Pt. 2, p. 107.

1342 On the mid-spring month, see n. 1339 above.

1343 Jyaiṣṭha (*snron*) is the fifth month of the Tibetan year, corresponding to June/July.

1344 The Author concurs that the calculations of 2839, 2815, 2744 and 2743 given here and in the following paragraphs are accurate and that the calculations given in the Tibetan text, i.e. 2838, 2814, 2743 and 2742 years, are at fault.

1345 According to recent estimates, Aśoka came to the throne in about 269 BC. See Basham, *The Wonder that was India*, p. 53. The most thorough treatment of the question remains that of P. H. L. Eggermont, *The Chronology of the Reign of Asoka Moriya*, where the period of Aśoka's rule is given as 268-233 BC. As stated in n. 1328 above, the dating given in our text is based on traditional sources.

1346 The Author concurs that the text should read 401st year (not 400th). Nāgārjuna's floruit is considered by most modern historians to have occurred during the second century CE.

1347 1 BC is, of course, the year traditionally held to precede the birth of Jesus, not that of his death. The Tibetan text, assimilating the Christian calendrical convention to the Tibetan emphasis on the date of death, erroneously reads *'das-lo* for *'khrungs-lo*.

1348 The text erroneously reads 619 years. Corrected with the Author's approval.

1349 According to this calculation, the duration of Śākyamuni Buddha's teaching is held to be five thousand years, divided into ten periods of five hundred years each. In the first period there was a profusion of arhats, so it was called the period of arhats. The second is called the period of non-returners and the third, the period of stream-entry. Those three periods together are called the Age of Fruition or enlightenment. In the fourth period there is a predominance of discriminative awareness, therefore it is so called. The fifth is called the period of contemplation and the sixth, that of moral discipline. Those three periods together are called the Age of Attainment. The next three periods of Abhidharma, Sūtra and Vinaya are collectively known as the Age of Transmission. The tenth and final period is called the Age of Convention or symbols because at that point the actual practice of the path will be lost, and only conventional tokens of the renunciate ordination (*pravajyā*) will remain. See Rikdzin Lhündrup's Hindi translation of the *History*, Ch. 8, n. 21; HBI, pp. 210-22; and Obermiller, *History of Buddhism by Bu-ston*, Pt. 2, pp. 102-5.

1350 There is much disagreement in Tibetan and other sources concerning the year of birth and life-span of King Songtsen Gampo. A fine survey of the problem is given by H. E. Richardson in "How old was Srong btsan sgam po?" *Bulletin of Tibetology* 2, 1 (1965). Richardson concludes that the king was born in the period from 609 to 613 and died in 650. For the traditional account of his longevity, see also Dudjom Rinpoche, *rgyal-rabs*, pp. 129-51.

1351 As stated below by the Author, p. 959, the absence of systematic accounts of the period between the fall of the dynasty (846) and the revitalisation of the teaching in the late tenth century has led to considerable confusion in Tibetan dating of the imperial period. In essence, the problem consists in determining just how many sixty-year cycles elapsed during the Age of Fragmentation. To compensate for past miscalculations, one must subtract sixty years from each of the dates given for the period from 790 to 953. Thus, Trhisong was born not in 790 but in 730, i.e. 90 and not 150 years after Songtsen Gampo had founded the Jokhang. In 750 Samye was founded. In 767 the "seven who were tested" were initiated. In 804 Guru Padmasambhava left Tibet. In 806 Trhi Relpacen was born. In 832 Lacen Gongpa Rapsel was born. In 841 the persecution began. In 846 Langdarma was assassinated. In 869 the kingdom disintegrated; and in 893 Lume returned to Central Tibet. The Author concurs in this respect with Shakabpa and other modern Tibetan historians who have made this adjustment. Even with this adjustment, however, the dating for the period remains problematic – e.g. Stein, *Tibetan Civilization*, p. 60, gives 775 as the foundation of Samye; and Richardson assigns the reign of Langdarma to the period from 836 to 842. For a compendium of the traditional chronologies, see Tshe-brtan Zhabs-drung, *bstan-rtsis kun-las btus-pa*.

1352 Cf. *Blue Annals*, pp. 60-7. It is clear that Lacen did not visit Central Tibet in person, and that Lume is intended. Six men of Central Tibet and Tsang are usually spoken of, rather than ten. As Roerich indicates in the same source, p. xviii, the date, whether calculated as 893 or 953 is problematic.

1353 The Shangpa Kagyü historical tradition maintains that Khyungpo Neljor was born in a tiger year and lived for 150 years. The tiger year in question is usually said to be 978 or 990. In any case, Khyungpo was certainly active as late as the early twelfth century. See Kapstein, "The

Shangs-pa bKa'-brgyud: an Unknown Tradition of Tibetan Buddhism".

1354 On Khön Lüiwangpo (i.e. Luwangsungwa), see also pp. 515 and 712.

1355 Kesar of Ling is the legendary hero of the Tibetan epic. See especially A. David-Neel, *The Superhuman Life of Gesar of Ling*; Stein, *Recherches sur l'épopée et le barde au Tibet*; and idem, *L'épopée tibètaine de Gesar dans sa version lamaïque de Ling*.

1356 The birth of Ngok Lotsāwa occurred not in 1071 (iron pig) but in 1059 (earth pig). This is correctly stated in *Blue Annals*, p. 328, and in the old Kalimpong edition of the present *History*, p. 795. Furthermore, on p. 646, it is stated that Dropukpa was sixteen years younger than Ngok.

1357 Lingje Repa Pema Dorje lived from 1128 to 1188, on which see *Blue Annals*, pp. 659-64 and n. 1025. Our text here places him in the fourth cycle; see also n. 1359 below.

1358 Nyang-rel's dates are either 1124-96 or 1136-1204; see n. 995 for an explanation.

1359 Our text wrongly includes Guru Chöwang and Como Menmo here in the fourth cycle; they should be included in the fifth, as explained in nn. 1002 and 1022. Similarly Lingje Repa has been reassigned to the third cycle, while Tsangpa Gyare, who lived from 1161 to 1211 belongs here, instead of in the fifth cycle where he has been mistakenly assigned. See *Blue Annals*, pp. 664-70; and Aris, *Bhutan*, p. 165. The latter was a teacher of Götsangpa (1189-1258), who, in turn, taught Orgyenpa (1230-1309).

1360 The episode of Dorta Nakpo's invasion, given erroneously in the third cycle, should be transferred to the fourth cycle; see n. 1009. This of course refers to Mongol rather than Chinese rule.

1361 The Sakya ascendancy endured from 1235 to 1349. See Snellgrove and Richardson, *A Cultural History of Tibet*, pp. 148-9; C.W. Cassinelli and R.B. Ekvall, *A Tibetan Principality, The Political System of Sa sKya*; and Shakabpa, *Tibet: A Political History*, pp. 61-72. For the chronology of the period in particular, see Wylie, "The First Mongol Conquest of Tibet Reinterpreted"; H. Franke, "Tibetans in Yüan China" in J. D. Langlois (ed.), *China under Mongol Rule*; and Shoju Inaba, "The Lineage of the Sa skya pa, A Chapter of the Red Annals" in *Memoirs of the Research Department of Toyo Bunko* 22 (1963), pp. 150-63 .

1362 Eleven hierarchs of Phakmotru successively governed Tibet and Kham from 1349 to 1435. See the accounts in Shakabpa, *Tibet: A Political History*, pp. 73-90; and G. Tucci, *Deb t'er dmar po gsar ma*, pp. 203-19.

1363 Concerning the problems involved in the dating of Thangtong Gyelpo, refer to n. 1078.

1364 Four kings of the Rinpung administration successively governed Tibet from 1435 to 1565. See Shakabpa, *Tibet: A Political History*, pp. 86-90.

1365 The Three Gyamtsos were Phukpa Lhündrup Gyamtso, the founder of the old Phukpa school, Khedrup Gyamtso and Sangye Gyamtso. See Schuh, *Untersuchungen zur Geschichte der Tibetischen Kalenderrechnung*, pp. 81, 83, 86.

1366 E. G. Smith in his introduction to L. Chandra (ed.), *The Life of the Saint of Gtsaṅ*, p. 3, provides no date for the death of Künga Zangpo, the madman of Central Tibet (b. 1458). For the madman of Tsang, Sangye Tshencen's death, however, he suggests 1495 in *Śaṅs-pa gser-'phreṅ*, p. 6.

1367 Pawo II, Tshuklak Trhengwa lived not from 1454 as stated in our text, but from 1504 to 1566. Hence he was in his 4th year (not 54th) when the ninth cycle began in 1507. Correction made with the Author's approval.

1368 On the kings of the Tsang administration (1565-1641) in Tibet, see pp. 682-3, 783; and Shakabpa, *Tibet: A Political History*, pp. 89-113.

1369 The date for Lhodruk Zhapdrung Ngawang Namgyel's death is usually given as 1651. His death was originally concealed until 1705 approximately with the pretense that he remained in a secret retreat. See Aris, *Bhutan*, pp. 233-42.

1370 The role played by the Qōśot Mongols under Guśri Qan in the establishment of the Dalai Lama's temporal power is alluded to on pp. 682-3 and 823. See also Ahmad, *Sino-Tibetan Relations in the Seventeenth Century*; and Shakabpa, *Tibet: A Political History*, pp. 131-7.

1371 In 1717 the Dzungars occupied Lhasa and killed Lhazang, the leader of the Qōśot Mongols who had previously murdered the regent Sangye Gyamtso and helped the Chinese to remove Dalai Lama VI in 1706. A great persecution of Nyingmapa monasteries followed, resulting in the deaths of Locen Dharmaśrī, Cangdak Pema Trhinle and others. This is certainly one reason for the subsequent shift in Nyingmapa activity to East Tibet from the eighteenth century onwards. See especially Petech, *China and Tibet in the Early XVIIIth Century*.

1372 On the setting of Pemakö, the Author's native place, see J. Bacot, *Le Tibet Révolté: Vers Népémakö, la terre promise des Tibetains*, pp. 10-12; also TH, pp. 407-8. Rikdzin Dorje Thokme is probably to be indentified with Bacot's "grand lama nommé Song-gye Tho-med."

1373 Gyelse Zhenpen Thaye of Dzokcen was born not in 1740, as the original text states, but in 1800. The date of his death is presently unidentified. See Tulku Thondup Rinpoche, *The Tantric Tradition of the Nyingmapa*, p. 95.

1374 On the Gurkha invasion of 1855, see Shakabpa, *Tibet: A Political History*, pp. 156-66. This was their second attack upon Tibet. On the first, see p. 838. The 1846 Tibet-Nepal Treaty is given in Richardson, *A Short History of Tibet*, pp. 247-9.

1375 Jamgön Kongtrül passed away either in 1899 or 1900 according to different systems of calculation; see nn. 1191 and 1201 for an explanation.

1376 1888 marks the Tibeto-British conflict over the boundaries of Sikkim, at which time the British invaded the Chumbi valley. It was a confrontation which led to the Younghusband expedition and treaty of 1904, the year of the Author's birth. For a detailed study of these events, see, e.g., P. Mehra, *The Younghusband Expedition*. Many useful references and a good overview of the conflict in its wider historical contexts may be gathered from D. Woodman, *Himalayan Frontiers*; and A. K. Jasbir Singh, *Himalayan Triangle*.

1377 In 1910 the troops of Chao Erh-feng occupied Lhasa, and Dalai Lama XIII was temporarily driven to seek refuge in India. See Shakabpa, *Tibet: A Political History*, pp. 225ff.

1378 *mdzes-byed* or the water hare year is the thirty-seventh year in the sexagenary cycle; *zad-pa* or fire tiger is the sixtieth.

1379 It is recorded that the Rudrakulika will be a future emanation of the Author. The wheel (*cakra*) of power, or force, turned by Rudrakulika is of iron. It symbolises the authority of a universal monarch (*cakravartī*), and may also be fashioned of gold, silver or copper (Khetsun Zangpo Rinpoche). According to Longdöl Lama, *Collected Works*, Vol. *Ja*, fol. 12a, and Stein, *Recherches sur l'épopée et le barde au Tibet*, pp. 525-6: "he was invested as a universal monarch by a sign which fell from the sky, viz. a wheel of iron." Cf. also Bernbaum, *The Way to Shambhala*, pp. 238ff.

1380 On Buddhist cosmology in general, see Kloetzli, *Buddhist Cosmology*. The temporal scheme of the universe presupposed here is similar, though in specifics not identical, to that of the Hindu Puranas, according to which, as summarised by Basham, *The Wonder that was India*, pp. 320-1, each aeon (kalpa) is divided into:

> . . . fourteen *manvantara*, or secondary cycles, each lasting 306,720,000 years, with long intervals between them... Each *manvantara* contains seventy-one *Mahāyuga*, or aeons [great ages], of which a thousand form the kalpa. Each mahāyuga is further divided into four *yugas* or ages, called *Kṛta* [*rdzogs-ldan*], *Tretā* [*gsum-ldan*], *Dvāpara* [*gnyis-ldan*] and *Kali* [*rtsod-ldan*]. The lengths of these ages are respectively 4800, 3600, 2400, and 1200 Brahmā-years of the gods; each of which equals 360 human years.

These four successive ages represent a gradual decline in positive attributes. For the special meditative practices and vehicles associated with these particular ages, see *Fundamentals*, p. 268.

1381 See Longcen Rapjampa, *Treasury of the Supreme Vehicle*, Chs. 1-2, for a thorough survey of cosmology according to the Great Perfection.

1382 The realms in which the emanational buddha-body operates are those of the world of Patient Endurance. See *Fundamentals*, p. 130. This world is held to be situated at the heart centre of Vairocana in the form of the Great Glacial Lake (Skt. *Mahāhimasāgara*); see p. 409. The heart-orb (*dpal be'u*, Skt. *śrīvatsa*) symbolised by the auspicious eternal knot is itself indicative of the world system of Patient Endurance.

HISTORY: CLOSING STATEMENTS

1383 The verses that follow are composed in an extremely ornate style of Tibetan ornamented verse (*snyan-ngag*, Skt. *kāvya*) which reflects the conventions of Indian courtly poetry, both by displaying much metrical variation, and by the employment of varied and sometimes complex tropes, including simile (*dpe-rgyan*, Skt. *upamā*) and extended metaphor (*gzugs-ldan*, Skt. *rūpaka*). Unfortunately, the intricate characteristics of this verse-genre do not run as well in English as the more simple and direct aspects of many other types of Tibetan verse. Useful background reading on the main features of classical Sanskrit poetics is M. van Buitenen et. al, *The Literatures of India*. See also *Fundamentals*, pp. 104-6.

1384 This metaphor is based on the legend of the goddess Gaṅgā, who embodies the River Ganges, becoming entwined in the locks of Maheś-vara (lord Śiva) and so conducted on her steady course to the ocean. It is said of Śiva in this connection that "holding the Ganges on his head, he brought into his power the means of the liberation of the world." Quoted in A. Daniélou, *Hindu Polytheism*, p. 215. Cf. also Basham, *The Wonder that was India*, p. 374. On the term "awareness-holders' piṭaka", see *Fundamentals*, p. 78.

1385 The term "supreme transformation" or "great transformation" (*'pho-ba chen-po*) is explained in *Fundamentals*, pp. 241-2.

1386 I.e. those who indulge in parochialism.

1387 Lake Manasarovar situated near Kailash is renowned as a sacred pilgrimage place of vast riches and blessings. For a fine description, see Lama Anagarika Govinda, *The Way of the White Clouds*, pp. 197-211.

1388 For the "threefold reason" see the Glossary of Enumerations under *three kinds of valid cognition*.

1389 The Fifth Guide will be the next buddha, Maitreya.

1390 This metaphor compares the *cakravartin*'s wheel of gold with the indestructible nucleus of the teaching. Its axis is the teaching of All-Surpassing Realisation (*thod-rgal*), its spokes are Cutting Through Resistance (*khregs-chod*) and its rim is Transcendental Perfection (*pha-rol-tu phyin-pa*). These teachings are explained in depth in *Fundamentals*, Pts. 3-4.

1391 Catri Tsenpo (*bya-khri btsan-po*) was the middle son of King Drigum Tsenpo (*gri-gum btsan-po*) who fled to Mount Kanam in Puwo after his father's assassination, and established a residence there. He is known as a "deity of the Radiant Heaven" since he was a close descendant of the divine kings of Tibet who, after fulfilling their purpose, were said to ascend to the heavens on a sky-cord. Catri Tsenpo's father is said to have been the first mortal king of Tibet.

1392 The water tiger year (*dge-byed*) is the thirty-sixth in the sexagenary cycle. This is a new Phukpa calculation.

1393 Some traditions ascribe the birth of Guru Padmasambhava to the sixth Tibetan month. However according to the new Phukpa calendar of the Mindröling tradition, the monkey month is the fifth, and the older Tshurpu and Phakpa systems enumerate it as the seventh. The present calculation is based on the new Phukpa system.

1394 Ratnapurī is, in this case, the town of Mandi in Himachal Pradesh. It is held by Tibetans to be the ancient kingdom of Sahor; see pp. 470-1.

1395 I.e. Shinglotsel in Bhutan.

Glossary of Enumerations

Introduction

Numeric categorisation, though common to many cultures, is particularly developed in Tibetan Buddhism, and in its Indian antecedents, where it is employed in part as a mnemonic device, enabling a vast amount of information to be retained and transmitted in oral tradition.

This glossary was originally conceived to reduce the number of annotations needed to explain the frequently recurring numerical categories in the translations, and grew to become the beginning of a dictionary of Tibetan Buddhist enumerations. In compiling it, we have drawn upon extant traditional dictionaries of enumerated categories, such as the *Mahāvyutpatti* (Mvt.), the great Tibetan-Sanskrit lexicon compiled in the ninth century under royal decree by the Tibetan translation committees to help standardise their work, and upon various encyclopaedia from the writings of Buddhist scholars both inside and outside the Nyingma tradition, including the works of Locen Dharmaśrī, Jikme Lingpa, Kongtrül Rinpoche and Longdöl Lama. We have also consulted work carried out in this field by contemporary scholars such as Edward Conze, Har Dayal, Robert Thurman and others, who published short lists of enumerations to accompany their translations of specific Mahāyāna texts, and such recent works as Gönpo Wangyal's Tibetan lexicon, *chos-kyi rnam-grangs shes-bya'i nor-gling 'jug-pa'i gru-gzings*.

Most of the enumerations mentioned in the treatises are listed here. The main exceptions are those concerning texts, which have been assigned to the Bibliography, and a few which we have been unable to identify. Page numbers follow each entry. These generally refer the reader only to the specific mention of the enumeration in the translations. Oblique references, references to sections dealing with the actual concept or meaning of an enumerated term, and references to the individual elements of an enumeration, are to be found in the indexes.

Glossary of Enumerations

TWO

TWO ACCOMPLISHMENTS *grub gnyis*

The supreme and common accomplishments (*mchog-dang thun-mong-gi dngos-grub*). 404, 861, 918, 967

TWO ASPECTS OF RELATIVE APPEARANCE *kun-rdzob gnyis*

The correct relative appearance (*yang-dag-pa'i kun-rdzob*, Skt. *tathyāsaṃvṛti*) and the incorrect relative appearance (*log-pa'i kun-rdzob*, Skt. *mithyāsaṃvṛti*). 166

TWO BENEFITS *don gnyis*

Benefit for oneself (*rang-don*, Skt. *svārtha/ātmahita*) and benefit for others (*gzhan-don*, Skt. *parārtha/parahita*). 171, 379

TWO BUDDHA-BODIES *sku gnyis*

The body of reality (*chos-sku*, Skt. *dharmakāya*) and the body of form (*gzugs-sku*, Skt. *rūpakāya*). 18, 26, 169, 379

TWO BUDDHA-BODIES OF FORM *gzugs-sku gnyis*

The body of perfect rapture (*longs-spyod rdzogs-pa'i sku*, Skt. *sambhogakāya*) and the emanational body (*sprul-pa'i sku*, Skt. *nirmāṇakāya*). 113, 168, 195-6, 237, 251, 342

TWO CELESTIAL KINGS CALLED "TENG" *stod-kyi steng gnyis*

Drigum Tsenpo and Pude Kungyel. 507, n. 535

TWO CONCEPTS OF SELFHOOD *bdag gnyis*, Skt. *ātmadvaya*

The concept of a self of individuals (*gang-zag-gi bdag-nyid*, Skt. *pudgalātma*) and the concept of the substantial reality of phenomena (*chos-kyi bdag-nyid*, Skt. *dharmātma*). 184

TWO DIVISIONS OF MAHĀYOGA *ma-hā-yo-ga'i sde gnyis*

The class of tantra (*rgyud-sde*, Skt. **tantravarga*) and the class of means for attainment (*sgrub-sde*, Skt. **sādhanavarga*). 462

TWO EXTREMES *mtha' gnyis*, Skt. *antadvaya*

Being and non-being (*yod-med*), or subject and object (*gzung-'dzin*). 79, 82, 162, 907

TWOFOLD BUDDHA/ENLIGHTENED FAMILY *rigs rnam gnyis*

The buddha or enlightened family which naturally abides (*rang-bzhin gnas-pa'i rigs*, Skt. *prakṛtiṣṭhagotra*) and the buddha or enlightened family of inner growth (*rgyas-'gyur-gyi rigs*, Skt. *samudānītagotra*). 191, 196-7

TWOFOLD ENLIGHTENED FAMILY (WHICH NATURALLY ABIDES) (*rang-bzhin gnas-pa'i*) *rigs-de gnyis-po*

The body of reality as the enlightened family which naturally abides as reality (*chos-nyid rang-bzhin gnas-pa'i rigs*) and the body of form as the enlightened family which naturally abides as the apparition of reality (*chos-can rang-bzhin gnas-pa'i rigs*). 191-4

TWOFOLD PRECIOUS ENLIGHTENED ATTITUDE *rin-chen sems-bskyed gnyis*

The attitude of aspiration (*smon-pa'i sems-bskyed*, Skt. *praṇidhicittotpāda*) and the attitude of engagement or entrance (*'jug-pa'i sems-bskyed*, Skt. *prasthānacittotpāda*). Alternatively, the absolute enlightened attitude (*don-dam byang-chub-sems*, Skt. *pāramārthikabodhicitta*) and the relative enlightened attitude (*kun-rdzob byang-chub-sems*, Skt. *sāṃketikabodhicitta*). The former division represents the two aspects of the relative enlightened attitude. For a comparative analysis of these classifications according to the major traditions of Buddhism in Tibet, refer to L. Dargyay, "The View of Bodhicitta in Tibet" in L. Kawamura (ed.), *The Bodhisattva in Asian Culture*, (pp. 95-109). 852, n. 1176

TWOFOLD PRISTINE COGNITION (OF ARHATS) *ye-shes gnyis*

The pristine cognition which perceives the cessation of corruption or defilements (*zad-pa shes-pa'i ye-shes*) and the pristine cognition which perceives that corruption is not recreated (*mi-skye-ba shes-pa'i ye-shes*). 227

TWO IMAGES OF LORD ŚĀKYAMUNI/THE TEACHER (IN LHASA) *jo-śāk rnam/ston-pa'i sku gnyis*

Jowo Rinpoche in the Jokhang and Jowo Mikyö Dorje in the Ramoche Temple. Pl. 8; 51, 656, 659

TWO KINDS OF MADHYAMAKA *dbu-ma phyi-nang phra-rags gnyis*

The coarse Outer Madhyamaka of the Svātantrika and the Prāsaṅgika, and the subtle Inner Madhyamaka also known as Yogācāra-Madhyamaka. 208-9

TWO KINDS OF REALISATION *rtogs-pa gnyis*

The realisation which is primordially acquired (*ye-nas chos-nyid rang-gi rig-pas rtogs-pa*) and the realisation resulting from attainments acquired on the path (*lam-bsgom stobs-kyis rtogs-pa*). 27, 71-2, 176-7

TWO KINDS OF RENUNCIATION *spang-ba rnam gnyis*

Renunciation due to natural purity (*rang-bzhin dag-pa'i spang-ba*) and renunciation applied as an antidote in order to remove obscurations which suddenly arise (*glo-bur dri-ma bral-ba'i spang-ba*). 27, 175-7

TWO KINDS OF SELFLESSNESS *bdag-med-kyi don rnam gnyis*, Skt. *ubhayanairātmya*

The twofold truth of selflessness: the selflessness of individuals (*gang-zag-gi bdag-med*, Skt. *pudgalanairātmya*) and the selflessness of phenomena (*chos-kyi bdag-med*, Skt. *dharmanairātmya*). 108, 208, 216, 231, 234, 237

TWO KINDS OF SUDDENLY ARISEN OBSCURATION *glo-bur-pa'i sgrib gnyis*

These are the TWO OBSCURATIONS. 116, 139

TWO MARVELLOUS MASTERS *rmad-byung-gi slob-dpon gnyis*

Śāntideva and Candragomin. 441

TWO METHODS OF ABSORPTION *'jog-thabs gnyis-po*

In the perfection stage of Mahāyoga, these are the immediacy of total awareness (*rig-pa spyi-blugs*) and the meditative absorption which follows after insight (*mthong-ba'i rjes-la 'jog-pa*). 280

TWO MODES OF EMPTINESS *stong-lugs gnyis-ka*

Intrinsic emptiness (*rang-stong*), according to which all things of saṃsāra are empty of their own inherent essence, and extrinsic emptiness (*gzhan-stong*), according to which all the realities of nirvāṇa are empty of extraneous phenomena. 184

TWO MODES OF THE PATH OF LIBERATION *grol-lam rnam gnyis*

According to Mahāyoga, these are the immediately attained path to liberation (*cig-car-pa*) and the gradually attained path to liberation (*rim-gyis-pa*). 277-8

TWO MODES OF PURIFICATION *sbyong-tshul gnyis*

According to Mahāyoga, these are purification through the coarse creation stage (*rags-pa bskyed-rim*) and through the subtle perfection stage (*phra-ba rdzogs-rim*). 279

TWO OBSCURATIONS *sgrib gnyis*

The obscuration of conflicting emotions (*nyon-mongs-pa'i sgrib-ma*, Skt. *kleśāvaraṇa*) and the obscuration concerning the knowable (*shes-bya'i sgrib-ma*, Skt. *jñeyāvaraṇa*). Also referred to as the TWO KINDS OF SUDDENLY ARISEN OBSCURATION. 51, 142, 159, 167, 175, 379

TWO ORDERS *sde gnyis*

Those of the sūtra and mantra traditions. 522

TWO PATHS (OF THE GREAT PERFECTION) *(rdzogs-chen-gyi) lam gnyis*

Cutting Through Resistance (*khregs-chod*) and All-Surpassing Realisation (*thod-rgal*). 334-45

TWO PATHS OF SKILFUL MEANS *thabs-lam gnyis*

According to Mahāyoga, these are esoteric instructions associated respectively with the upper doors or centres of the body (*steng-sgo*) and the lower door or secret centre of the body (*'og-sgo*). 277

TWO PROMULGATORS *shing-rta gnyis*

Nāgārjuna and Asaṅga. Also known as the TWO SUPREME ONES. 180, 300-1, 849

TWO PROVISIONS *tshogs gnyis*, Skt. *sambhāradvaya*

The provision of merit (*bsod-nams-kyi tshogs*, Skt. *puṇyasambhāra*) and the provision of pristine cognition (*ye-shes-kyi tshogs*, Skt. *jñānasambhāra*). 26,

30, 175, 194-5, 197, 235, 244, 266, 332, 335, 379, 420, 462, 831

TWO PROVISIONS OF SKILFUL MEANS AND DISCRIMINATIVE AWARENESS *thabs-shes tshogs gnyis*

An alternative expression for the preceeding entry. 192

TWO PURITIES *dag-pa gnyis*

The purities resulting from the removal of the obscuration of conflicting emotions and of the obscuration covering the knowable (*nyon-mong-gi sgrib-dang shes-bya'i sgrib-kyis dag-pa*). Alternatively, the primordial purity of emptiness and the purity which results from abandoning obscuration. 139-40

TWO SECRET CENTRES *mkha'-gsang gnyis*

The secret or sexual centres of the father consort (*yab*) and the mother consort (*yum*). 277, 368

TWO STAGES *rim gnyis*, Skt. *dvikrama*

According to the vehicles of tantra, these are the creation stage (*bskyed-rim*, Skt. *utpattikrama*) and the perfection stage (*rdzogs-rim*, Skt. *sampannakrama*) of meditation. 204, 254, 320, 475, 476, 496, 853, 877, 879, 923

TWO STAGES OF THE PATH *rim-pa gnyis*

According to Mahāyoga, these are the path of skilful means (*thabs-lam*) and the path of liberation (*grol-lam*). 34, 276-81

TWO SUBDIVISIONS OF THE ORAL TRADITION CATEGORY (OF THE ESOTERIC INSTRUCTIONAL CLASS) *kha-gtam gnyis*

The Oral Tradition which Permeates All Discourses (*gleng-ba yongs-la bor-ba'i kha-gtam*) and the Oral Tradition which is Divulged in Speech at No Fixed Time (*khar-phog dus-med-pa'i kha-gtam*). 331

TWO SUBDIVISIONS OF THE RANDOM CATEGORY (OF THE ESOTERIC INSTRUCTIONAL CLASS) *kha-'thor-gyi man-ngag gnyis*

With reference to the establishment of reality there are the Esoteric Instructions which Conclude the Path (*bzhag-pa lam-gyi mtha' gcod-pa'i man-ngag*) and with reference to liberation there are the Esoteric Instructions of Pure Power which Disclose the Path (*grol-ba stobs dag-pa lam mngon-gyur-gyi man-ngag*). 331

TWO SUPREME ONES *mchog gnyis*

Nāgārjuna and Asaṅga. Also known as the TWO PROMULGATORS. 441

TWO TRADITIONS *lugs gnyis*

The temporal and spiritual traditions (*chos-srid gnyis-ldan*) established by Dalai Lama V. 823

TWO TRUTHS *bden-pa gnyis*, Skt. *satyadvaya*

Relative truth (*kun-rdzob-kyi bden-pa*, Skt. *saṃvṛtisatya*) and ultimate truth (*don-dam bden-pa*, Skt. *paramārthasatya*). 26, 29, 32, 34, 35, 76, 162, 168, 200, 204, 206-16, 232, 245, 248, 293, 294, 296, 303, 320, 349, 351, 354, 901

TWO VEHICLES *theg-pa gnyis*

The Greater (*Mahāyāna*) and Lesser (*Hīnayāna*) vehicles. 17, 81, 83

THREE

THREE ABODES *gnas gsum*

The abodes of the ḍākinīs and warriors of body, speech and mind. 469, 853

THREE ANCESTRAL RELIGIOUS KINGS *chos-rgyal mes-dbon rnam gsum*

Songtsen Gampo, Trhisong Detsen and Trhi Relpacen. 47, 510-22, 523, 889

THREE ANCESTRAL ZURS *zur mes-dbon gsum*

Zurpoche, Zurcungpa and Zur Dropukpa. 728, 919

THREE APPEARANCES *snang gsum*

In general, these are the object (*gzung-bya'i yul*), the subjective consciousness (*'dzin-pa'i sems*) and the body (*'gro-ba'i lus*). In particular, these refer to: (1) the desire realm which is the variable coarse appearance of body (*lus rags-pa'i snang-ba 'dod-khams*); (2) the form realm which is the blissful semi-appearance of speech (*ngag phyed-snang-ba gzugs-khams*); and (3) the formless realm which is the intangible appearance of mind (*sems-kyi snang-ba ma-myong-ba gzugs-med khams*). Alternatively, the three appearances may be: the impure appearance, which appears to sentient beings (*sems-can-la ma-dag-par snang-ba*); the pure appearance, which appears to bodhisattvas on the path (*lam-skabs byang-sems-la dag-par snang-ba*); and the utterly pure appearance, which is apparent to buddhas alone (*sangs-rgyas-la shin-tu dag-par snang-ba*). 142, 288

THREE APPROACHES TO LIBERATION *rnam-thar sgo gsum*

Emptiness (*stong-pa-nyid*, Skt. *śūnyatā*), aspirationlessness (*smon-pa med-pa*, Skt. *apraṇihita*) and attributelessness (*mtshan-ma med-pa*, Skt. *animitta*). 28, 187, 335, 896, 898, 908

THREE ASPECTS OF CREATION AND PERFECTION *bskyed-rdzogs gsum*

The creation stage (*bskyed-rim*), the perfection stage (*rdzogs-rim*), and their coalescence (*zung-'jug*). 83, 358, 476, 612, 615, 616, 619, 650, 651, 652, 654, 700, 717

THREE ASPECTS OF THE GRADUAL PATH OF LIBERATION *rim-gyis-pa'i grol-lam gsum*

According to Mahāyoga, the basis characterised as knowledge or (discriminative) awareness is the view (*rgyu shes-pa'i mtshan-nyid lta-ba*), the conditions characterised as the entrance are contemplation (*rkyen 'jug-pa'i mtshan-nyid ting-nge-'dzin*) and the result brought about by the path is the awareness-holder (*lam-gyur-gyi 'bras-bu rig-'dzin*). 278-81

THREE ASPECTS OF MORAL DISCIPLINE *tshul-khrims gsum*

According to the bodhisattva vehicle, these involve gathering virtues (*dge-ba chos-sdud*), acting on behalf of sentient beings (*sems-can don-byed*) and controlling malpractices (*nyes-spyod sdom-pa'i tshul-khrims*). 235, 355

THREE ASPECTS OF THE REALITY OF MEDITATIVE CONCENTRATION *bsam-gtan-gyi de-nyid gsum*

According to Kriyātantra, by abiding in the flame of secret mantra accomplishment is conferred (*gsang-sngags mer-gnas dngos-grub ster*), by abiding in their sound yoga is conferred (*sgrar-gnas rnal-'byor ster-bar byed*) and at the limit of their sound freedom is granted (*sgra-mthas thar-pa sbyin-par byed*). 270

THREE ATTAINMENTS *thob-pa gsum*

According to Jikme Lingpa, *khrid-yig ye-shes bla-ma*, pp. 52b-53a, the three attainments are the third of the esoteric instructions of the Great Perfection contained in the FOUR CONSOLIDATIONS. They are (1) the condition under which appearances arise as buddha-fields by the attainment of power over external appearances (*phyi snang-ba-la dbang thob-pas rkyen snang zhing-khams-su 'char*); (2) the condition under which matter is purified into inner radiance by the attainment of power over the internal illusory body (*nang sgyu-lus-la dbang thob-pas gdos-bcas 'od-gsal-du dag*); and (3) the condition under which even the consciousness endowed with the five inexpiable sins is entrusted to awareness by the attainment of power over the secret vital energy and mind (*gsang-ba rlung-sems-la dbang thob-pas mtshams-med lnga-dang ldan-pa'i rnam-par shes-pa yang rig-pa gtang-bas 'drongs-pa'o*). 343

THREE ATTRIBUTES *yon-tan gsum*, Skt. *triguṇa*

According to Sāṃkhya philosophy, these are spirit (*snying-thobs*, Skt. *sattva*), energy (*rdul*, Skt. *rajas*) and inertia (*mun-pa*, Skt. *tamas*). 65

THREE AUTHORS OF FUNDAMENTAL TEXTS *gzhung-byed-pa-po gsum*

Nāgārjuna, Asaṅga and Dignāga. 440

THREE BLAZES *'bar-ba gsum*

The blazing of blissful warmth in the body (*lus-la bde-drod 'bar-ba*), the blazing of potency in speech (*ngag-la nus-pa 'bar-ba*) and the blazing of realisation in the mind (*sems-la rtogs-pa 'bar-ba*). 851

THREE BRANCHES OF THE SPATIAL CLASS *klong-gi sde dkar-nag-khra gsum*

These are included in the FOUR CATEGORIES OF THE SPATIAL CLASS, as enumerated in *Fundamentals*, (pp. 326-7). 539

THREE BUDDHA-BODIES *sku gsum*, Skt. *trikāya*

The body of reality (*chos-sku*, Skt. *dharmakāya*), the body of perfect rapture (*longs-spyod rdzogs-pa'i sku*, Skt. *sambhogakāya*) and the emanational body (*sprul-pa'i sku*, Skt. *nirmāṇakāya*). 12, 18, 19, 22, 23, 29, 113, 115, 118, 139, 142, 148, 151, 183, 184, 191, 194, 196, 251, 280, 306, 352, 357, 363, 404, 448, 503, 554, 622

THREE BUDDHAS OF THE PAST *'das-pa'i sangs-rgyas gsum*

Krakucchanda, Kanakamuni and Kāśyapa. 423

THREE CATEGORIES (OF BEINGS) *gnas-skabs gsum*

In relation to the nucleus of the tathāgata (*tathāgatagarbha*), these are sentient beings who are impure (*ma-dag-pa'i sems-can*), bodhisattvas who are in the course of purification (*dag-pa byed-pa'i byang-chub sems-dpa'*) and tathāgatas who are utterly pure (*shin-tu dag-pa'i de-bzhin gshegs-pa*). 173

THREE CATEGORIES OF THE ESOTERIC INSTRUCTIONAL CLASS *man-ngag-gi sde'i dbye-ba gsum*

The Random (*kha-'thor*) category, the category of the Oral Tradition (*kha-gtam*) and the category of the Teaching according to its Own Textual Tradition of Tantras (*rgyud rang-gzhung-du bstan-pa*). See also Longcenpa, *Treasury of Spiritual and Philosophical Systems*, pp. 348ff.; and idem, *Treasury of the Supreme Vehicle*, (pp. 157ff.). 37, 331

THREE CATEGORIES OF THE SPATIAL CLASS *klong-sde gsum-du 'dus-pa*

Liberation from activity (*byas-grol*), liberation in the establishment of the abiding nature (*bzhag-grol*) and direct liberation (*cer-grol*). 329

THREE CAUSAL VEHICLES *rgyu'i theg-pa gsum*

See THREE OUTER VEHICLES OF DIALECTICS

THREE CHARACTERISTICS (OF THE CONTINUUM OF THE PATH) *mtshan-nyid gsum*

Awareness in the manner of the FOUR KINDS OF REALISATION is characteristic of knowledge (*rtogs-pa rnam-pa bzhi'i tshul rig-pa-ni shes-pa'i mtshan-nyid*); repeated experience of it is characteristic of the entrance (*yang-nas yang-du-goms-par byed-pa-ni 'jug-pa'i mtshan-nyid*); and actualisation of it by the power of experience is the characteristic of the result (*goms-pa'i mthus mngon-du gyur-ba-ni 'bras-bu'i mtshan-nyid*). 265

THREE CLASSES OF DIALECTICS *mtshan-nyid sde gsum*

The classes of dialectics of the pious attendants, self-centred buddhas and bodhisattvas. See THREE OUTER VEHICLES OF DIALECTICS

THREE CLASSES OF THE GREAT PERFECTION *rdzogs-chen sde gsum*

The Mental Class (*sems-kyi sde*), the Spatial Class (*klong-gi sde*) and the Esoteric Instructional Class (*man-ngag-gi sde*). 36-9, 319-45, 494, 538-96, 854

THREE CLASSES OF YOGA *yoga'i sde gsum*

These are the same as the THREE INNER CLASSES OF TANTRA. 746

THREE COMMENTATORS *'grel-pa byed-pa-po gsum*

Āryadeva, Vasubandhu and Dharmakīrti. 440

THREE COMMON CLASSES OF MEANS FOR ATTAINMENT *thun-mong-gi sgrub-sde gsum*

According to Mahāyoga, these are Mātaraḥ the Liberating Sorcery (*ma-mo rbod-gtong*), Mundane Praise (*'jig-rten mchod-bstod*) and Malign Mantra (*drag-sngags dmod-pa*). 362

THREE CONFLICTING EMOTIONS *nyon-mongs gsum*

See THREE POISONS

THREE CONTEMPLATIONS *ting-nge-'dzin gsum*

According to Mahāyoga, these are the yoga of great emptiness which is discriminative awareness (*shes-rab stong-pa chen-po'i rnal-'byor*), the apparitional display of compassion which is skilful means (*thabs snying-rje sgyu-ma*) and the seals which are subtle and coarse (*phyag-rgya phra-rags*). They are also enumerated under the FIVE PATHS OF MAHĀYOGA. 358, 360, 362-3

THREE CONTINUA (KINDS OF TANTRA COMPRISING THE ACTUAL MEANING) *(brjod-bya) rgyud gsum*

According to the vehicles of the secret mantra, these are the continua of the ground, path and result (*gzhi-lam-'bras gsum*). 32, 185-6, 263-7

THREE (CORRECT) TRAININGS *(yang-dag-pa'i) bslab-pa gsum*, Skt. *triśikṣā*

Moral discipline (*tshul-khrims*, Skt. *śīla*), discriminative awareness (*shes-rab*, Skt. *prajñā*) and mind, i.e. meditation (*sems*, Skt. *citta*). 70-1, 73, 79, 88, 322, 403, 707, 879, 898

THREE CORRUPTIONS *zag-pa gsum*

The corruption of desire (*'dod-pa'i zag-pa*), the corruption of rebirth (*srid-pa'i zag-pa*) and the corruption of view (*lta-ba'i zag-pa*). 472

THREE COUNCILS *bka'-bsdu-ba gsum*, Skt. *tisraḥ saṃgītayaḥ*

According to the Tibetan tradition, the first was convened in Rājagṛha in the year following the Buddha's final nirvāṇa; the second was convened at Vaiśālī during the reign of Vigataśoka; and the third was convened during the reign of Kaniṣka. 428-30

THREE DEGREES OF ENLIGHTENMENT *byang-chub gsum*, Skt. *bodhitraya*

The level of enlightenment attained by the pious attendants, self-centred buddhas and bodhisattvas. 414

THREE DISTRICTS *ljongs gsum*

Sikkim (i.e. Dremojong), Khenpajong and Lungsumjong. 518

THREE DIVINE REALMS *lha-gnas gsum*

As outlined in the chart on pp. 14-15, these are the FIVE PURE ABODES OF THE FORM REALMS, the TWELVE ORDINARY FORM REALMS and the realms of the SIX SPECIES OF KĀMA DIVINITIES. 458

THREE DOCTRINAL CENTRES *chos-'khor gnas gsum*

Samye, Lhasa Jokhang and Trhadruk. Pls. 38, 40, 100-1; 838

THREE ENLIGHTENED FAMILIES (OF PURE DEITIES OF RELATIVE APPEARANCE) *(kun-rdzob dag-pa'i lha) rigs gsum*

According to Kriyātantra, these are the Tathāgata family (*de-bzhin gshegs-pa'i rigs*), the Lotus family (*padma'i rigs*) and the Vajra family or family of Indestructible Reality (*rdo-rje'i rigs*). 270, 346, 349-50

THREE ESSENCELESS NATURES *ngo-bo-nyid-med-pa gsum*, Skt. *trividhā niḥsvabhāvatā*

These are the lack of inherent existence of the THREE ESSENTIAL NATURES, namely, absence of substantial existence with respect to characteristic (*lakṣaṇa*), production (*utpāda*) and the absolute (*paramārtha*). 219-20

THREE ESSENTIAL NATURES *mtshan-nyid gsum/ngo-bo-nyid gsum/rang-bzhin gsum*, Skt. *trilakṣaṇa/trisvabhāva*

The imaginary (*kun-brtags*, Skt. *parikalpita*), the dependent (*gzhan-dbang*, Skt. *paratantra*) and the absolute (*yongs-grub*, Skt. *pariniṣpanna*). See, e.g., D. T. Suzuki, *Studies in the Laṅkāvatāra Sūtra*, (pp. 154-63). 24-6, 28, 154, 160-1, 170-2, 182-3, 216

THREE ESSENTIALS WHICH GUIDE (THE EYES) TOWARDS THE EXPANSE *'khrid-pa dbyings-kyi gnad gsum*

These are the THREE GAZES – upwards, sideways and downwards – which direct the eyes towards the expanse of the buddha-body of reality, the buddha-body of perfect rapture and the emanational body respectively. Refer to Longcenpa, *Treasury of the Supreme Vehicle*, Vol. 2, (p. 282). 338

THREE ESSENTIALS OF OBJECTIVE APPEARANCE *snang-ba yul-gyi gnad gsum*

According to Longcenpa, *Treasury of the Supreme Vehicle*, Vol. 2, p. 282, in the path of All-Surpassing Realisation these are: (1) the essential which swiftly intensifies the appearance of awareness, which is partially pure, just as it is, by focusing on an outer object, such as the vanishing of clouds in the sky (*phyi'i yul nam-mkha' sprin-dengs-la gtad-pas rig-pa rang-sa sangs-phyed-la snang-ba'i 'bel-myur*); (2) the essential which unites the mother and offspring inner radiance by focusing on the inner object which is the lamp of the expanse (*nang-gi yul dbyings-kyi sgron-ma-la gtad-pas 'od-gsal ma-bu 'brel*); and (3) the essential which clarifies the primordially pure intention, just as it is, wherein all things have ceased, by focusing on the secret object which is awareness just as it is (*gsang-ba'i yul rig-pa rang-sa-la gtad-pas ka-dag chos-zad-kyi dgongs-pa rang-sa-na gsal-ba'i gnad*). 338

THREE EVIL DESTINIES/EXISTENCES *ngan-'gro/-song gsum*, Skt. *tisro durgatayaḥ*

The denizens of hell (*dmyal-ba*, Skt. *naraka*), the tormented spirits (*yi-dvags*, Skt. *preta*) and the animals (*dud-'gro*, Skt. *tiryak*). 58, 767

THREE FAITHS *dad-pa gsum*, Skt. *trividhā śraddhā*

Confidence (*dang-ba*), aspiration (*'dod-pa*) and conviction (*yid-ches-pa*). Irreversible faith (*phyir mi-ldog-pa'i dad-pa*) is sometimes added to these as a fourth or as an intensification of the preceding three. 968

THREE FAMILIES, LORDS OF *rigs-gsum mgon-po*, Skt. *trikulanātha*

Mañjuśrī, the lord of the Tathāgata family; Avalokiteśvara, the lord of the Lotus family; and Vajrapāṇi, the lord of the Vajra family. 137, 270, 352, 453, 624, 698, 758, 798, 889

THREEFOLD REFUGE *skyabs-gsum*, Skt. *triśaraṇa*

This refers to refuge in the THREE PRECIOUS JEWELS. 69, 728

THREE GATHERINGS *'du-ba gsum*

The gathering of people during the day (*nyin-mor mi 'du-ba*), the gathering of ḍākinīs by night (*mtshan-mor mkha'-'gro 'du-ba*) and the gathering of material resources at all times (*rtag-tu zas-nor 'du-ba*). 851

THREE GAZES *lta-stangs gsum*

By gazing upwards at the *ūrṇakeśa*, the eye of reality perceives the buddha-body of reality and propensities are removed. By gazing sideways, the eye of pristine cognition perceives the buddha-body of perfect rapture and so saṃsāra and nirvāṇa are blended in a common savour. By gazing downwards, the eye of discriminative awareness perceives the emanational body and so arrives at the appearance of pristine cognition. 907

THREE GENERAL COMMITMENTS *spyi'i dam-tshig gsum*

According to Kriyātantra, in the *Secret Tantra of General Rites*, these are the commitments of taking refuge (*skyabs-su 'gro-ba*), generating the enlightened mind of aspiration (*smon-pa'i sems bskyed*) and the bodhisattva vow (*byang-*

chub sems-dpa'i sdom-pa) which is the enlightened mind of engagement or entrance (*'jug-pa'i sems-bskyed*). 350

THREE GENERAL STYLES OF EXEGESIS *spyi-don rnam gsum*

This is the second of the FOUR STYLES of appraisal of the secret mantra texts which (1) counters regret for entering into the sūtras, etc. (*mdo-sogs-la zhugs-pa'i 'gyod-pa zlog-pa*); (2) counters regret for entering the inner mantras, etc. (*sngags-nang-pa-la zhugs-pa'i 'gyod-zlog*); and (3) conveys the general meaning of the creation stage (*bskyed-rim-pa'i spyi-don*). 292-3

THREE GREAT DESCENTS *babs-lugs chen-po gsum*

See THREE LINEAGES

THREE GREAT EMANATIONAL TEACHINGS *sprul-pa'i bstan-pa chen-po gsum*

According to the Great Perfection, these are buddha-body (*sku*), speech (*gsung*) and mind (*thugs*). 134-8

THREE GUIDING VEHICLES *'dren-pa'i theg-pa gsum*

See THREE OUTER VEHICLES OF DIALECTICS

THREE GYAMTSOS *rgya-mtsho rnam-gsum-du grags-pa*

The authors of the astrological treatise entitled *pad-dkar zhal-lung*, namely, Phukpa Lhündrup Gyamtso, Khedrup Gyamtso and Sangye Gyamtso. 954

THREE HIGHER (SUPREME UNCOMMON) EMPOWERMENTS *(thun-min mchog-) dbang gong-ma gsum*

The secret empowerment (*gsang-dbang*, Skt. *guhyābhiṣeka*); the empowerment of discriminating pristine cognition (*shes-rab ye-shes-kyi dbang*, Skt. *prajñājñānābhiṣeka*), or third empowerment (*dbang gsum-pa*); and the empowerment of word and meaning (*tshig-don-gyi dbang*), also known as the fourth empowerment (*dbang bzhi-pa*, Skt. *caturtha*). The secret one is associated with the commitments such as enjoying the five meats and five nectars without concepts of purity or impurity; the third is associated with conduct which concerns the consort embodying awareness (*rig-ma*, Skt. *vidyā*); and the fourth is associated with the sameness of all things. See, e.g., Mipham Rinpoche, *spyi-don 'od-gsal snying-po*, p. 146; and Jamgön Kongtrül, *shes-bya kun-khyab mdzod*, Vol. 2, pp. 656-82. These empowerments are called "uncommon" because they are revealed solely in the Unsurpassed Yogatantra. They are also referred to as the THREE PROFOUND EMPOWERMENTS. 347, 360, 913

THREE (IMPERISHABLE) INDESTRUCTIBLE REALITIES *rdo-rje (mi-shigs-pa) gsum* Skt. *trivajra*

The indestructible reality of the buddha-body, speech and mind, which each comprise two of the SIX PURE ESSENCES – the body being identified with earth and water, speech with fire and air, and mind with space and pristine cognition. Also known as the THREE SECRETS. 264, 594, 830, 853

THREE INDESTRUCTIBLE REALITIES, SERVICE AND ATTAINMENT OF *rdo-rje gsum-gyi bsnyen-sgrub*

According to the system of Orgyenpa, these are explained as follows: (1) training the body through the indestructible reality of the buddha-body, there is the branch of ritual service which develops composure (*sku rdo-rjes lus-la sbyang-ste sor-sdud bsnyen-pa'i yan-lag*); (2) training the speech through the indestructible reality of the buddha-speech, there is the branch of attainment associated with breath control (*gsungs rdo-rjes ngag-la sbyang-ste srog-'dzin sgrub-pa'i yan-lag*); and (3) training the mind through the indestructible reality of the buddha-mind, there is the branch of great attainment associated with recollection and contemplation (*thugs rdo-rjes yid-la sbyang-ste dran-ting sgrub-chen-gyi yan-lag*). 853

THREE INNER CLASSES OF TANTRA/TANTRAPIṬAKA *nang-pa rgyud-sde (rnam-pa) gsum*

Mahāyoga, Anuyoga and Atiyoga. Also referred to as the THREE CLASSES OF YOGA and the THREE VEHICLES OF INNER TANTRAS OF SKILFUL MEANS. 396-7, 529-96, 604, 918

THREE INTERRELATED ASPECTS OF IGNORANCE *ma-rig-pa gsum*

The ignorance of belief in individual selfhood (*bdag-nyid gcig-pu'i ma-rig-pa*), the co-emergent ignorance (*lhan-cig skyes-pa'i ma-rig-pa*) and the ignorance of the imaginary (*kun-tu brtags-pa'i ma-rig-pa*). 12, 54

THREE KINDS OF CONDUCT *spyod-pa gsum*

According to Anuyoga, these are consecration or blessing (*byin-gyis rlob*), the overpowering of mundane appearances (*dbang-bsgyur*) and the conduct of skilful means (*thabs-kyi spyod-pa*). 369

THREE KINDS OF DIRECT PERCEPTION *mngon-sum gsum*

Direct sensory perception (*dbang-po'i mngon-sum*, Skt. *indriyapratyakṣa*), the direct perception of intrinsic awareness, i.e. of one's own mental states (*rang-rig mngon-sum*, Skt. *svasaṃvedanapratyakṣa*) and the direct perception (of emptiness) by the yogin (*rnal-'byor mngon-sum*, Skt. *yogipratyakṣa*). Note that canonical sources usually list four kinds of direct perception, adding to these three intellectual direct perception (*blo'i mngon-sum*, Skt. *manaḥ-pratyakṣa*). 102

THREE KINDS OF DISCRIMINATIVE AWARENESS *shes-rab gsum*, Skt. *trividhā prajñā*

Discriminative awareness born of study (*thos-pa-las byung-ba'i shes-rab*, Skt. *śrutamayīprajñā*), discriminative awareness born of thought (*bsam-pa-las byung-ba'i shes-rab*, Skt. *cintāmayīprajñā*) and discriminative awareness born of meditation (*bsgoms-pa-las byung-ba'i shes-rab*, Skt. *bhāvanāmayīprajñā*). 277, 332, 722

THREE KINDS OF LAYMAN *dge-bsnyen gsum*

The layman who takes one vow (i.e. not to kill), the layman who takes several vows (i.e. not to kill, steal or commit falsehood) and the layman who takes full vows (i.e. not to kill, steal, lie, commit sexual misconduct or be intoxicated). 70

THREE KINDS OF MAṆḌALA *dkyil-'khor rnam-pa gsum*

According to Anuyoga, these are the primordial maṇḍala of Samantabhadrī (*ye ji-bzhin-pa'i dkyil-'khor*); the natural and spontaneously present maṇḍala of Samantabhadra (*rang-bzhin lhun-grub-kyi dkyil-'khor*); and the fundamental maṇḍala of enlightened mind which is their offspring (*rtsa-ba byang-chub sems-kyi dkyil-'khor*). 34, 284-6, 365-7

THREE KINDS OF MANTRA *sngags gsum*

Gnostic mantra (*rig-sngags*, Skt. *vidyāmantra*), dhāraṇī mantra (*gzungs-sngags*, Skt. *dhāraṇīmantra*) and secret mantra (*gsang-sngags*, Skt. *guhyamantra*). The *dgongs-pa grub-pa'i rgyud* says: "One should know that all mantra are divided into three classes: gnostic mantra which are the essence of skilful means, dhāraṇīs which are the essence of discriminative awareness and secret mantra which are the non-dual pristine cognition." Thus dhāraṇīs are said to originate from the teachings of the Transcendent Perfection of Discriminative Awareness, gnostic mantra from the Kriyātantra and secret mantra from Mahāyoga, Anuyoga and Atiyoga. 257

THREE KINDS OF (MUNDANE) AWARENESS-HOLDER *rig-pa 'dzin-pa rnam gsum*

These are the lesser awareness-holder of the eight common accomplishments (*las-chen brgyad grub-pa rig-pa 'dzin-pa chung-ngu*); the middling common awareness-holder of the desire realm (*'bring-ni 'dod-pa'i rig-pa 'dzin-pa phal-pa*); and the greater awareness-holder of the desire and form realms (*chen-po-ni 'dod-pa-dang gzugs-kyi rig-pa 'dzin-pa*). 31, 259

THREE KINDS OF PRISTINE COGNITION *ye-shes rnam gsum*, Skt. *jñānalakṣaṇa-traya*

According to the *Sūtra of the Descent to Laṅkā*, Ch. 3, these are the mundane (*'jig-rten-pa'i ye-shes*), supramundane (*'jig-rten-las 'das-pa'i ye-shes*) and most supramundane (*shin-tu 'jig-rten-las 'das-pa'i ye-shes*) pristine cognitions. An alternative enumeration given in Ch. 2 of the same work refers to the following three characteristics of the pristine cognition of those who are sublime: (1) freedom from appearance (Skt. *nirābhāsalakṣaṇa*); (2) sustaining power (Skt. *adhiṣṭhānalakṣaṇa*); and (3) realisation of one's own sublime pristine cognition (Skt. *pratyātmāryajñānagatilakṣaṇa*). 180-1

THREE KINDS OF RITE *cho-ga gsum*

According to Mahāyoga, these are the body (of the deity) in its entirety (*sku yongs-rdzogs*), the speech in the form of seed-syllables (*gsung yig-'bru*) and the buddha-mind of concentration (*thugs bsam-gtan*). 279

THREE KINDS OF TANTRA *rgyud rnam-pa gsum*

These are the THREE CONTINUA as enumerated in the exegetical tradition of the *Guhyasamāja Tantra*: the ground (*gzhi*), the nature (*rang-bzhin*) of the path and the inalienableness (*mi-'phrog-pa*) of the result. 262

THREE KINDS OF TANTRA (BELONGING TO UNSURPASSED YOGATANTRA) *(bla-med) rgyud gsum*

Father Tantra (*pha-rgyud*), Mother Tantra (*ma-rgyud*) and Non-Dual Tantra (*gnyis-med rgyud*). 362

THREE KINDS OF TRANSMITTED PRECEPT *bka' gsum*

Transmitted precepts given as oral teaching (*gsungs-pa*), given by consecration or blessing (*byin-gyis brlabs-pa*) and given by mandate (*rjes-su gnang-ba*). 74

THREE KINDS OF VALID COGNITION *tshad-ma gsum*

Direct perception (*mngon-sum tshad-ma*, Skt. *pratyakṣapramāṇa*), implicit inference (*dngos-stobs rjes-dpag-gi tshad-ma*, Skt. *anumānapramāṇa*) and scriptural authority (*lung/shin-tu lkog-gyur-gyi tshad-ma*, Skt. *āgamapramāṇa*). 73, 275, 970

THREE LEVELS OF ORDINATION *so-thar rnam-pa gsum*

The renunciate (*rab-byung*, Skt. *pravrajyā*), the novitiate (*dge-tshul*, Skt. *śramaṇera*) and the complete monk or nun (*bsnyen-rdzogs*, Skt. *upasampadā*). Also referred to as the THREE STAGES OF ORDINATION. 524

THREE LINEAGES *brgyud-pa gsum*

The intentional lineage of buddhas, symbolic lineage of awareness-holders and aural lineage of mundane individuals. Referred to poetically as the THREE GREAT DESCENTS. 397, 406, 447, 887, 968

THREE LOGICAL AXIOMS (OF IMPLICIT INFERENCE) *(dngos-stobs rjes-dpag-gi) gtan-tshigs gsum*, Skt. *trīṇi liṅgāni*

The axiom of the result (*'bras-bu'i gtan-tshigs*, Skt. *kāryahetu*), the axiom of identity (*rang-bzhin-gi gtan-tshigs*, Skt. *svabhāvahetu*) and the axiom of the absence of the objective referent (*ma-dmigs-pa'i gtan-tshigs*, Skt. *anupalabdhihetu*). 102, 839

THREE LOWER CLASSES OF TANTRA/TANTRAPIṬAKA *rgyud-sde 'og-ma gsum*

Kriyātantra (*bya-ba'i rgyud*), Ubhayatantra or Caryātantra (*upa'i rgyud* or *spyod-pa'i rgyud*) and Yogatantra (*rnal-'byor-gyi rgyud*). Also known as the THREE OUTER TANTRAPIṬAKA. 83, 268-73, 348-57

THREE LOWER KINDS OF SUBLIME BEING *'phags-pa 'og-ma gsum*

Pious attendants (*nyan-thos*, Skt. *śrāvaka*), self-centred buddhas (*rang-rgyal*, Skt. *pratyekabuddha*) and bodhisattvas (*byang-chub sems-dpa'*). 175

THREE LOWER PIṬAKA *sde-snod 'og-ma gsum*

See THREE PIṬAKA

THREE MAṆḌALAS (OF THE MANTRAS) *dkyil-'khor gsum*

As expounded in Ratnākaraśānti, *Definitive Order of the Three Vehicles*, mantras are endowed with: the purity of their visualisation (*dmigs-pa rnam-par dag-pa*), the power of their assistance (*grogs-kyi mthu*) and the level of their conduct (*spyod-pa'i sa*). 253

THREE MEANS TO DELIGHT THE GURU *mnyes-pa gsum*

Through accomplishment in meditative practices, through service by means of body and speech, and through material offerings. 655, 658, 680, 871

THREE MEDIA *sgo gsum*

The ordinary body (*lus*, Skt. *kāya/śarīra*), speech (*ngag*, Skt. *vāk*) and mind (*yid*, Skt. *manas*). 264, 304, 367

THREE MEN FROM KHAM *khams-pa mi gsum*

Phakmotrupa, Karmapa Tüsum Khyenpa and Seltong Shogom, who were all students of Gampopa. 952

THREE MOVEMENTS WITH REFERENCE TO THE FOUR SYLLABLES *yi-ge bzhi-la mi-sdad-pa gsum*

According to Khetsun Zangpo Rinpoche, this refers to the destabilisation of the three syllables OṂ, ĀḤ and HŪṂ within the central channel of the body when the inner heat rises from the syllable VAṂ during the practice of inner heat (*gtum-mo*). 548

THREE NEIGHS OF HAYAGRĪVA *rta-mgrin-gyi rta-skad thengs gsum*

These are the THREE CONTINUA of ground, path and result. Alternatively: (1) the neigh which arouses the world to the unborn identity of saṃsāra and nirvāṇa; (2) the neigh which offers animate and inanimate worlds as a feast offering to repay karmic debts (*gsob*); and (3) the neigh which then enlists the support of beings and binds them under an oath of allegiance. 361

THREE OBSCURATIONS *sgrib-pa gsum*, Skt. *trīṇy āvaraṇāni*

The obscurations of the knowable, of conflicting emotions and of propensities. Alternatively, the third may be absorption in trance. 469

THREE OUTER TANTRAPIṬAKA *phyi rgyud-sde gsum*

These are the THREE LOWER CLASSES OF TANTRA. 273

THREE OUTER VEHICLES OF DIALECTICS *phyi mtshan-nyid theg-pa gsum*

The vehicles of pious attendants (*nyan-thos-kyi theg-pa*, Skt. *śrāvakayāna*), self-centred buddhas (*rang-rgyal-gyi theg-pa*, Skt. *pratyekabuddhayāna*) and bodhisattvas (*byang-chub sems-dpa'i theg-pa*, Skt. *bodhisattvayāna*). Also referred to as the THREE CAUSAL VEHICLES, the THREE CLASSES OF DIALECTICS, the THREE VEHICLES and poetically as the THREE GUIDING VEHICLES, they are explained in *Fundamentals*, (pp. 151-237). 83, 454, 618, 671, 911

THREE PHASES OF LIFE *skye-ba rim-pa gsum*

These are the phases from conception in the womb to the moment of birth (*mngal-du skye-ba bzung-pa-nas btsas-pa'i bar*), from the moment of birth to adult maturity (*btsas-nas nar-son-pa'i bar*) and from adult maturity to old age (*nar-son-nas rgan-po'i bar*). 34, 278-81

THREE PIṬAKA/TRIPIṬAKA *sde-snod gsum*, Skt. *tripiṭaka*

The Vinayapiṭaka (*'dul-ba'i sde-snod*), Sūtrapiṭaka (*mdo'i sde-snod*) and Abhidharmapiṭaka (*chos mngon-pa'i sde-snod*). Also referred to as the THREE LOWER PIṬAKA. 76, 78-80, 203, 259, 405, 428, 429, 436, 437, 441, 468, 511, 560, 619, 888

THREE POISONS *dug gsum*

These are the THREE CONFLICTING EMOTIONS of desire (*'dod-chags*, Skt. *rāga*), hatred (*zhe-sdang*, Skt. *dveṣa*) and delusion (*gti-mug*, Skt. *moha*). 18, 24, 33, 34, 55, 77, 88, 159, 229, 273, 277

THREE POSTURES *'dug-stangs gsum*

According to the *Penetration of Sound*: (1) the posture of the lion which rests in the buddha-body of reality frees one from all fears of bewilderment and enables one to see with eyes of indestructible reality; (2) the posture of the elephant which rests in the buddha-body of perfect rapture brings about the experience of reality and enables one to see with lotus eyes; (3) the crouching posture of a sage which rests in the emanational body emanates reality as appearances, and enables one to see with the eyes of reality. 907

THREE PRECIOUS JEWELS *dkon-mchog gsum*, Skt. *triratna*

Buddha (*sangs-rgyas*), the doctrine (*chos*, Skt. *dharma*) and the community (*dge-'dun*, Skt. *saṃgha*). 59, 69-70, 95, 203, 350, 468, 523, 583, 592, 707, 743, 862, 970, 973

THREE PRESENCES *sdod-pa gsum*

This, the second of the FOUR CONSOLIDATIONS according to the esoteric instructions on All-Surpassing Realisation, is explained as follows in Jikme Lingpa, *khrid-yig ye-shes bla-ma*, pp. 49a-b: (1) the bewildering thoughts of saṃsāra are purified by presence in which there is no bodily activity (*lus bya-ba-la mi-gnas-par sdod-pas 'khor-ba'i 'khrul-rtog dag*); (2) the conditions of fluctuating thought cease by means of presence in which there is no increase in vital energy (*rlung 'phel-med-du sdod-pas rnam-rtog gYo-ba'i rkyen zad*); (3) the extent of the buddha-fields is reached by means of presence in which there is no hesitation or doubt regarding appearances (*snang-ba 'dar-'phrigs-med-par sdod-pas zhing-khams tshad-la phebs-par-byed*). 343

THREE PROFOUND EMPOWERMENTS *zab-dbang gsum*

These are the THREE HIGHER SUPREME UNCOMMON EMPOWERMENTS. 347, 701

THREE PROMULGATIONS OF THE DOCTRINAL WHEEL *chos-'khor gsum*

See THREE (SUCCESSIVE) PROMULGATIONS/TURNINGS OF THE DOCTRINAL WHEEL

THREE PROVINCES OF TIBET *bod 'chol-ka gsum*

The three districts of Ngari in Upper Tibet, Central Tibet including Tsang, and Amdo and Kham in Lower Tibet. 823, 953

THREE PURITIES (OF KRIYĀTANTRA) *dag-pa gsum*

The purity of deity and mantra; the purity of substances and rapture; and the purity of mantra and contemplation. 35, 295-6, 349

THREE PURITIES (OF MAHĀYOGA) *dag-pa gsum*

One of the FOUR AXIOMS OF MAHĀYOGA consisting of the purity of the outer world (*snod dag-pa*), the purity of its inner contents, i.e. living creatures (*bcud dag-pa*) and the purity of the components, bases and activity fields forming the mind-stream (*rgyud-rnams dag-pa*). 275-6

THREE REALITIES *de-kho-na-nyid gsum*

According to the *Tantra of the Secret Nucleus*, as explained in Sūryaprabhāsiṃha's *Commentary on the Secret Nucleus*, pp. 2-3, these are the uncreated reality which is the causal basis of the maṇḍala, the resultant reality which is the spontaneous Samantabhadra and the reality which appears as a chain of seed-syllables and is the causal basis of the secret enlightened mind. 915

THREE REALMS *khams gsum*, Skt. *tridhātu*.

See THREE (WORLD) REALMS

THREE REALMS BEGINNING WITH BRAHMAKĀYIKA *tshangs-ris-la-sogs-pa gsum*

The Brahmakāyika or Stratum of Brahmā (*tshangs-ris-pa*), Brahmapurohita or Priest Brahmā (*tshangs-pa mdun-na 'don*) and Mahābrahmā or Great Brahmā (*tshangs-pa chen-po*), all of which are the levels realised through the first concentration (*bsam-gtan dang-po*). 14, 61

THREE ROOTS *rtsa-ba gsum*

The guru (*bla-ma*), meditational deity (*yi-dam*, Skt. *devatā*) and ḍākinī (*mkha'-'gro-ma*). 376, 555, 586, 676, 748, 823, 847, 855

THREE SEALS *phyag-rgya gsum*

Either impurity, impermanence and suffering; or the FOUR SEALS INDICATIVE OF THE TRANSMITTED PRECEPTS, in which the third (selflessness) and the fourth (nirvāṇa is peace) are combined. 71

THREE SECRETS *gsang-ba gsum*

These are the THREE IMPERISHABLE INDESTRUCTIBLE REALITIES of buddha-body, speech and mind. 853

THREE SPHERES *'khor gsum*, Skt. *trimaṇḍala*

The subject, object and their interaction. 316, 588, 619

THREE SPHERES (OF ACTIVITY ON THE PART OF MEMBERS OF THE *SAṂGHA*) *'khor-lo gsum*

Exegesis (*bshad-pa*), attainment (*sgrub-pa*) and work (*las*); or alternatively renunciation (*spang-ba*), study (*slob-pa*) and work. 720, 724, 736, 738, 783, 824, 835, 840, 852

THREE SPHERES (OF EXISTENCE) *srid/sa gsum*, Skt. *tribhava/tribhuvana*

The nether world of the nāgas (*sa-'og klu'i srid-pa*), the surface world of humans (*sa'i steng mi'i srid-pa*) and the upper world of gods (*gnam-steng lha'i srid-pa*). 45, 212, 301, 405, 971, 973

THREE STAGES OF ORDINATION *tshig(s)-gsum rim nod-pa*

These are the THREE LEVELS OF ORDINATION. 618

THREE SUBTLE PRISTINE COGNITIONS *ye-shes phra-ba gsum*

The subtle pristine cognition of appearances (*snang-ba*), emptiness (*stong-pa*) and their coalescence (*zung-'jug*). Refer to Mipham Rinpoche, *spyi-don 'od-gsal snying-po*, (p. 194). 342

THREE (SUCCESSIVE) PROMULGATIONS/TURNINGS OF THE DOCTRINAL WHEEL *chos-'khor (rim-pa) gsum*, Skt. *triparivartadharmacakrapravartana*

The first promulgation at Vārāṇasī (*chos-'khor dang-po*), the intermediate promulgation at Vulture Peak (*bar-ma'i chos-'khor*) and the final promulgation in indefinite realms (*chos-'khor tha-ma*). 17, 23-4, 28, 76, 151-5, 187, 425, 896

THREE SUCCESSIVE PROMULGATIONS OF THE TRANSMITTED PRECEPTS *bka'i rim-pa gsum*

The teachings which correspond to the THREE SUCCESSIVE PROMULGATIONS OF THE DOCTRINAL WHEEL, namely, the first transmitted precepts (*bka' dang-po*), the intermediate transmitted precepts (*bka' bar-ma*) and the final transmitted precepts (*bka' tha-ma*). 18, 188

THREE SUFFERINGS *sdug-bsngal gsum*, Skt. *triduḥkhatā*

The suffering of change (*'gyur-ba'i sdug-bsngal*, Skt. *vipariṇāmaduḥkhatā*), the suffering of propensities (*'du-byed-kyi sdug-bsngal*, Skt. *saṃskāra-duḥkhatā*) and the suffering of suffering or pain itself (*sdug-bsngal-gi sdug-bsngal*, Skt. *duḥkhaduḥkhatā*). 419

THREE SUPERIORS (OF KATOK) (*kaḥ-thog*) *gong-ma gsum*

Katokpa Tampa Deshek, Tsangtönpa and Campabum. 698

THREE SUPPORTIVE ESSENTIALS OF THE BODY *bca'-ba lus-kyi gnad gsum*

According to All-Surpassing Realisation, these are the THREE POSTURES of lion, elephant and sage. Refer to Longcenpa, *Treasury of the Supreme Vehicle*, Vol. 2, (p. 280). 338

THREE SUPREME EMANATIONS *mchog-gi sprul-sku gsum*

Nyang-rel Nyima Özer, Guru Chöwang and Rikdzin Gödemcen. Refer to Jamyang Khyentse, *Mkhyen brtse on the History of the Dharma*, (pp. 41-2). 755, 760, 780, 934

THREE TIMES *dus gsum*, Skt. *trikāla*

The past (*'das-pa*, Skt. *atīta*), present (*da-lta-ba*, Skt. *vartamāna*) and future (*ma-'ongs-pa*, Skt. *anāgata*). 157-8, 276, 308, 316, 320, 334, 414, 453, 633

THREE TRADITIONS OF BODHISATTVA VOW *bka'-srol gsum-pa'i byang-sems-kyi sdom-rgyun*

According to Terdak Lingpa's *Record of Teachings Received*, pp. 15-16, these are the tradition of Mañjuśrī via Nāgārjuna and Candrakīrti; the tradition of Maitreya via Asaṅga and Vasubandhu; and the tradition of Mañjuśrī via Śāntideva. All three were gathered together by Longcenpa. 729, 827

THREE TRADITIONS OF THE MENTAL CLASS *sems-sde lugs gsum*

The Rong tradition in Central Tibet, the Kham tradition in East Tibet and the original cycles (*skor*) of the Mental Class. 827

THREE TRADITIONS OF PACIFICATION *zhi-byed lugs-gsum*

The Ma, So and Kham traditions. Refer to *Blue Annals*, (pp. 867-979). 657

THREE TRAININGS *bslab-pa gsum*, Skt. *triśikṣā*

See THREE (CORRECT) TRAININGS

THREE TURNINGS OF THE DOCTRINAL WHEEL (OF THE CAUSAL VEHICLES) *rgyu'i chos-'khor gsum*

See THREE (SUCCESSIVE) PROMULGATIONS/TURNINGS OF THE DOCTRINAL WHEEL

THREE TYPES OF DEEDS *las gsum-po*, Skt. *trīṇi karmāṇi*

Virtuous (*bsod-nams*, Skt. *kuśala*), unvirtuous (*bsod-nams ma-yin-pa*, Skt. *akuśala*) and indeterminate (*lung ma-bstan*, Skt. *avyākṛta*). 56

THREE TYPES OF EMANATIONAL BODY *sprul-sku rnam gsum*

Emanations of natural expression (*rang-bzhin sprul-pa*), emanations which train living beings (*'gro-'dul sprul-pa*) and diversified emanations (*sna-tshogs sprul-pa*). 21, 128

THREE TYPES OF SCRUTINY (OF PURE SCRIPTURAL AUTHORITY) *(dag-pa'i lung-gi) dpyad gsum*

As impurities are ascertained by the process of burning, cutting and polishing, so too are the scriptures to be critically investigated. Refer to Śāntarakṣita's *Tattvasaṃgraha*, vv. 3340-4, which compares the study of the Buddha's words by means of inference, scriptural authority and example to the purification of gold by burning, cutting and polishing. 102

THREE UNCOMPOUNDED ENTITIES *'dus-ma-byas gsum*, Skt. *trividham asaṃskṛtam*

According to the Vaibhāṣika, these are space (*nam-mkha'*, Skt. *ākāśa*), the cessation of corruption due to individual scrutiny (*so-sor brtags-pas 'gog-pa*, Skt. *pratisaṃkhyānirodha*) and the cessation (of the future arising of any object) independent of individual scrutiny (*brtags-min-gyi 'gog-pa*, Skt. *apratisaṃkhyānirodha*). 157

THREE UNCORRUPTED PATHS *zag-pa med-pa'i lam gsum*, Skt. *traya anāsrava-mārgāḥ*

The path of insight (*mthong-lam*, Skt. *darśanamārga*), the path of meditation (*bsgom-lam*, Skt. *bhāvanāmārga*) and the final path (*mthar-lam*, Skt. *niṣṭha-mārga*). 281

THREE UNMOVING STATES *mi-'gul-ba gsum*

These are the first of the FOUR CONSOLIDATIONS of All-Surpassing Realisation. They are described in Jikme Lingpa, *khrid-yig ye-shes bla-ma*, p. 49a, as follows: (1) without moving from the postures of the body, the energy channels and currents are relaxed of their own accord (*lus bzhag-stang-las mi-'gul-bas rtsa-rlung rang-dal*); (2) without moving from the gazes of the eyes, appearances are enhanced (*mig gzigs-stangs-las mi-'gul-bas snang-ba'i 'phel-'dzin*); and (3) without moving from the state of the unfabricating mind, the expanse and awareness are integrated (*sems bzo-med-las mi-'gul-bas dbyings-rig zung-du chud-par-byed*). 343

THREE VEHICLES *theg-pa gsum*, Skt. *triyāna*

These refer either to the THREE OUTER VEHICLES OF DIALECTICS of the pious attendants, self-centred buddhas and bodhisattvas, or to the vehicle which directs (or uproots) the cause of suffering (*kun-'byung 'dren-pa*), the vehicle of austere awareness (*dka'-thub rig-pa*) and the vehicle of overpowering means (*dbang-bsgyur thabs-kyi theg-pa*). 17, 81-3, 174, 190, 197, 285, 425

THREE VEHICLES OF INNER TANTRAS OF SKILFUL MEANS *nang-rgyud thabs-kyi theg-pa gsum*

These are the THREE INNER CLASSES OF TANTRA. 84

THREE VEHICLES OF THE OUTER TANTRAS OF AUSTERE AWARENESS *phyi thub-pa rgyud-kyi theg-pa gsum*

The Kriyātantra, Ubhayatantra or Caryātantra, and Yogatantra vehicles. 81, 84, 269, 286, 346, 348-57

THREE VOWS *sdom-pa gsum*, Skt. *trisaṃvara*

The *prātimokṣa* (*so-thar*), bodhisattva vows (*byang-sems-kyi sdom-pa*, Skt. *bodhisattvasaṃvara*) and mantra vows (*gsang-sngags-kyi dam-tshig*, Skt. *samaya*). 78, 300, 302, 827, 831, 861

THREE WAYS TO BRING FORTH THE FRUIT OF THE INSTRUCTIONS *btsa'-lugs gsum*

According to Pawo Tsuklak Trhengwa, *Scholar's Feast of Doctrinal History*, pp. 223-4, based on the *Biography of Vairocana*, these are: (1) to bring forth the harvest that is like the eyeball in order to clarify all saṃsāra and nirvāṇa; (2) to bring forth the harvest that is like the heart because it is the essence of all vehicles; (3) and to bring forth the harvest that is like life itself because it is the root of all things. 539

THREE WAYS OF ENTERING (THE LIBERATING PATH OF DISCIMINATIVE AWARENESS) *'jug-pa rnam gsum*

According to Anuyoga, these are the mind which enters into the pursuit of ideas and scrutiny (*rtog-dpyod-kyi rjes-su 'jug-pa'i yid*), the mind which enters into the pursuit of truth (*don-gyi rjes-su 'jug-pa'i yid*) and the mind which enters into the pursuit of seed-syllables (*yi-ge'i rjes-su 'jug-pa'i yid*). 286-7

THREE WAYS OF THE WISE *mkhas-tshul gsum*

Teaching (*'chad-pa*), debate (*rtsod-pa*) and composition (*rtsom-pa*). 731

THREE WHEELS OF THE DOCTRINE *chos-kyi 'khor-lo gsum*

The doctrines which respectively concern the middle way and the four truths, the absence of characteristics and the definitive meaning. See THREE (SUCCESSIVE) PROMULGATIONS/TURNINGS OF THE DOCTRINAL WHEEL

THREE (WORLD) REALMS *('jig-rten-gyi) khams gsum*, Skt. *tri(loka)dhātu*

The desire realm (*'dod-pa'i khams*, Skt. *kāmadhātu*), form realm (*gzugs-khams*, Skt. *rūpadhātu*) and formless realm (*gzugs-med-kyi khams*, Skt. *ārūpyadhātu*). 13, 31, 38, 51, 56, 73, 202, 259, 302, 321, 337, 339-40, 363, 418, 490, 491, 575, 907, 930

THREE YOGAS (OF ANUYOGA) *rnal-'byor gsum*

These are explained in *Fundamentals*, pp. 285-6.

TRIO OF THE GURU, GREAT PERFECTION AND GREAT COMPASSIONATE ONE *bla-rdzogs-thugs gsum*

Refer to *History*, (p. 396 and n. 934). 724, 764, 765, 791, 821, 827, 881

FOUR

FOUR ACTIVITY FIELDS *skye-mched bzhi*, Skt. *catvāry āyatanāni*

See FOUR FORMLESS REALMS

FOUR ASPECTS OF TRAINING IN THE ELABORATE SEAL (OF MAHĀYOGA MEDITATION) *phyag-rgya spros-bcas-la bslab-pa bzhi*

The visualisation of maṇḍalas (*dkyil-'khor*), clusters of deities (*tshom-bu*), numbers of deities (*grangs*) and the faces and arms of the deities (*zhal-phyag*). 279-80

FOUR ASSEMBLIES *'khor-bzhi-po*, Skt. *catuḥpariṣad*

Monks (*dge-slong*, Skt. *bhikṣu*) or arhats (*dgra-bcom-pa*), nuns (*dge-slong-ma*, Skt. *bhikṣuṇī*), laymen (*dge-bsnyen*, Skt. *upāsaka*) and laywomen (*dge-bsnyen-ma*, Skt. *upāsikā*). Also referred to as the FOUR ORDERS. 74, 423, 426

FOUR ASSURANCES *gdeng bzhi*

According to Jikme Lingpa's *khrid-yig ye-shes bla-ma*, pp. 53a-b, this, the fourth and last of the FOUR CONSOLIDATIONS of All-Surpassing Realisation, consists of: (1) the assurance that, though one has heard of the suffering of beings in the three evil existences, the duration of their lives therein and so forth, one is unafraid of these evil existences because one has directly determined that bewilderment is unknown from the beginning in the intrinsic nature, without the possibility of joyful or sorrowful experiences (*ngan-song gsum-gyi sdug-bsngal-dang tshe-tshad la-sogs-pa thos-kyang rang-ngo gdod-nas 'khrul mi-shes-pa'i thog-tu bde-sdug shes-bya-la mi-srid-par thag-chod-pas ngan-song-la bag mi-tsha-ba'i gdeng*); (2) the assurance that one does not have to aspire towards the maturation of the cause and result in that one has directly reached the ground of awareness, whereupon even the mere name of saṃsāra does not exist (*rig-pa gzhi thog-tu phebs-pa-la 'khor-ba ming-tsam-du'ang ma-grub-pas rgyu-'bras rnam-smin-la ma-re-ba'i gdeng*); (3) the assurance that, having been so liberated in the ground of reality, there is no need to aspire towards the object of attainment because the nirvāṇa wherein mere bliss is experienced is without individual characteristics (*chos-nyid gzhi-la 'di-ltar grol-nas 'di-tsam-du bde'o snyam-pa'i myang-'das rang-mtshan-pa med-pas thob-bya-la re-ba med-pa'i gdeng*); and (4) the assurance that, though one has heard that the enlightened attributes in the fields of the conquerors are limitless, one's delight is purified in sameness because one has reached the ground in which the buddhas are no different, by even a hair's breadth, from the awareness that is one's own essence (*rgyal-ba'i khams-la yon-tan tshad-med-par thos-kyang rang-ngo rig-pa-las tha-dad-pa'i sangs-rgyas rgyu spu'i rtse-mo tsam-du'ang med-pa gzhi thog-tu phebs-bas dga'-brod mnyam-pa-nyid-du dag-pa'i gdeng*). 343, 372

FOUR ATTRACTIVE QUALITIES OF A BODHISATTVA *bsdu-dngos bzhi*, Skt. *catuḥ-saṃgrahavastu*

These are liberality (*sbyin-pa*, Skt. *dāna*), pleasant speech (*snyan-par smra-ba*, Skt. *priyavacana*), purposeful activity (*don-spyod-pa*, Skt. *arthacaryā*) and harmony (*don mthun-pa*, Skt. *samānavihāra*). 633

FOUR AWAKENINGS *mngon-byang bzhi*, Skt. *caturabhisambodhi*

These are similar to the FIVE AWAKENINGS, omitting the first, i.e. emptiness. They are the lunar throne (*zla-gdan*), the seed-syllables of speech (*gsung yig-'bru*), the symbolic implements of mind (*thugs phyag-mtshan*) and the perfect body of the deity (*sku yongs-rdzogs*). 279

FOUR AXIOMS (OF MAHĀYOGA) *gtan-tshigs bzhi*

The FOUR KINDS OF REALISATION, the THREE PURITIES OF MAHĀYOGA, the FOUR MODES OF SAMENESS and supreme identity (*bdag-nyid chen-po*). 34, 275-6

FOUR BASIC SCHOOLS *rtsa-ba'i sde-pa bzhi*

The Mahāsaṅghika, Sthavira, Sammitīya and Mūlasarvāstivādin. 429

FOUR BRANCHES OF RITUAL SERVICE AND ATTAINMENT *bsnyen-sgrub yan-lag bzhi*, Skt. *caturaṅgasevāsādhana*

Ritual service (*bsnyen-pa*, Skt. *sevā*) entails the recitation of mantra and one-pointed prayerful devotion to a deity that is visualised; further ritual service (*nye-bar bsnyen-pa*, Skt. *upasevā*) entails the prayer that the deity's blessings will descend, transforming the mundane body, speech and mind into the three syllables of indestructible reality; attainment (*sgrub-pa*, Skt. *sādhana*) entails that accomplishments are absorbed from the sugatas of the ten directions into the deity and thence into oneself, either in actuality, meditation or dreams; and great attainment (*sgrub-chen*, Skt. *mahāsādhana*) is the ultimate realisation of beginningless primordial purity which is experienced when body, speech and mind are identical to the deity. This is the inner significance of the ritual ceremonies and elaborate dance routines contained within the *sgrub-chen*. Also referred to as the FOUR UNIONS. 280, 297, 494, 847, 903

FOUR BUDDHA-BODIES *sku bzhi*, Skt. *catuḥkāya*

The body of reality (*chos-sku*, Skt. *dharmakāya*), the body of perfect rapture (*longs-spyod rdzogs-pa'i sku*, Skt. *sambhogakāya*), the emanational body (*sprul-pa'i sku*, Skt. *nirmāṇakāya*) and the body of their essentiality (*ngo-bo-nyid-kyi sku*, Skt. *svābhāvikakāya*). 19, 288, 369, 923

FOUR CASES WHEN THE TEACHING SHOULD BE GRANTED *sbyin-pa'i gnas bzhi*

According to Pawo Tsuklak Trhengwa, *Scholar's Feast of Doctrinal History*, pp. 223-4, which quotes the *Biography of Vairocana*: (1) the texts, commentaries and esoteric instructions should be given to one who is faithful, gentle, even-tempered and steadfast; (2) teaching should be given completely and openly to a recipient who is noble and of long standing; (3) teaching should be given and entrusted earnestly to the faithful who request it; and (4) teaching should be given with enthusiasm to those of faith who have little discriminative awareness. 539

FOUR CASES WHEN THE TEACHING SHOULD NOT BE GRANTED *mi-sbyin-pa'i gnas bzhi*

According to the same text cited above: (1) teaching should not be given to those who are extremely aggressive, faithless or loquacious; (2) teaching should not be given to those who have little faith, perseverance and discriminative awareness, or who are partial in their desire for long exegeses and commentaries; (3) teaching should not be given to those who diminish other doctrines by making long notations and not meditating; and (4) the faithless who seek the doctrine for the sake of wealth should be investigated from the position of the faithful and then abandoned. 539

FOUR CATEGORIES OF THE SPATIAL CLASS *klong-sde bzhi*

These are: (1) the Black Space propounded as the Absence of Causes (*klong nag-po rgyu-med-du smra-ba*); (2) the Variegated Space propounded as Diversity (*klong khra-bo sna-tshogs-su smra-ba*); (3) the White Space propounded as the Mind (*klong dkar-po sems-su smra-ba*); (4) and the Infinite Space in which Cause and Result are Determined (*klong rab-'byams rgyu-'bras la-bzla-ba*). 326-7

FOUR CENTRES *'khor-lo bzhi*, Skt. *catvāri cakrāṇi*

The forehead centre of great bliss (*spyi bde-chen-gi 'khor-lo*, Skt. *mahāsukhacakra*); the throat centre of perfect rapture (*mgrin-pa longs-spyod-kyi 'khor-lo*, Skt. *sambhogacakra*); the heart centre of the doctrine (*snying-ka chos-kyi 'khor-lo*, Skt. *dharmacakra*); and the navel centre of emanation (*lte-ba sprul-pa'i 'khor-lo*, Skt. *nirmāṇacakra*). 286, 368

FOUR CENTRES OF MAÑJUŚRĪ THE BODY *'jam-dpal-gyi sku 'khor-lo bzhi*

These are the secret centre of the abiding nature of mind (*gnas-kyi 'khor-lo*); the centre of existence connected with the navel (*srid-pa'i 'khor-lo*); the cutting centre connected with the arms of the deity (*gcod-pa'i 'khor-lo*); and the centre of emanation connected with the legs and feet of the deity (*sprul-pa'i 'khor-lo*). 361

FOUR CLASSES OF ḌĀKINĪS *rigs-bzhi mkha'-'gro-ma*

In this context, the term may refer to ḍākinīs of the four peripheral enlightened families, i.e. the Jewel, Lotus, Action, and Buddha or Vajra families; or to ḍākinīs belonging to four of the six classes, i.e. *Padminī, Śaṅkhinī, Mṛginī, Hastinī, Varṇinī* and *Citriṇī*. See GGFTC (pp. 961-7 and n. 14). 755

FOUR CLASSES OF SUBLIME BEING *'phags bzhi*, Skt. *āryāś catvāraḥ*

The arhats among the pious attendants (*nyan-thos*), the self-centred buddhas (*rang-rgyal*), bodhisattvas (*byang-chub sems-dpa'*) and buddhas (*sangs-rgyas*). 72, 908

FOUR CLASSES OF TANTRA *rgyud-sde bzhi*

These are the FOUR TANTRAPIṬAKA. 96, 473

FOUR COMMITMENTS (OF ANUYOGA) DEFINITIVE TO THE IMPORTANT SŪTRAS *gal-mdo nges-pa'i dam-tshig bzhi*

According to Jamgön Kongtrül, *shes-bya kun-khyab mdzod*, Vol. 2, pp. 188ff., these are the commitments of utter purity in relation to the body, speech, mind and entire perceptual range. 367

FOUR COMMITMENTS RELATING TO CONTINUITY OF THE PATH OF CONDUCT *spyod-lam rgyun-gyi dam-tshig bzhi*

According to Jamgön Kongtrül, *shes-bya kun-khyab mdzod*, Vol. 2, p. 192, these are to abandon sleep which cuts off the life of concentration, to abandon alcohol, to propound the symbolic language of secret mantra and to destroy idleness. 367

FOUR COMMON SCIENCES *thun-mong-gi rig-gnas bzhi*

The arts (*bzo-rig-gnas*, Skt. *śilpavidyā*), grammar (*sgra'i rig-gnas*, Skt. *śabdavidyā*), medicine (*gso-ba'i rig-gnas*, Skt. *cikitsāvidyā*) and logic (*gtan-tshigs-kyi rig-gnas*, Skt. *hetuvidyā*). 89, 97-103

FOUR CONCENTRATIONS *bsam-gtan bzhi*, Skt. *caturdhyāna*

See FOUR (MEDITATIVE) CONCENTRATIONS

FOUR CONDITIONS OF BEWILDERMENT *rkyen bzhi'i 'khrul-pa/'khrul-pa'i rkyen bzhi*

The causal condition (*rgyu'i rkyen*, Skt. *hetupratyaya*) which is the THREE INTERRELATED ASPECTS OF IGNORANCE, the referential condition (*dmigs-pa'i rkyen*, Skt. *ālambanapratyaya*) which is the appearances, the possessive condition (*bdag-po'i rkyen*, Skt. *adhipatipratyaya*) which is the ego, and the immediate condition (*de-ma-thag-pa'i rkyen*, Skt. *samanantarapratyaya*) which is their present conjunction. 54-5

FOUR CONDITIONS OF SAṂSĀRA *'khor-ba'i rkyen bzhi*

See preceding entry

FOUR CONSOLIDATIONS *mtha'-rten bzhi*

According to All-Surpassing Realisation, these are the THREE UNMOVING STATES, the THREE PRESENCES, the THREE ATTAINMENTS and the FOUR ASSURANCES. 343

FOUR CONTINENTS *gling bzhi*, Skt. *caturdvīpa*

Surpassing the Body (*lus-'phags*, Skt. *Pūrvavideha*) in the east, Rose-Apple Continent (*'dzam-bu-gling*, Skt. *Jambudvīpa*) in the south, Enjoyer of Cattle (*ba-glang spyod*, Skt. *Aparagodanīya*) in the west and Unpleasant Sound (*sgra mi-snyan*, Skt. *Uttarakuru*) in the north. 14, 56, 60, 131, 409, 438, 515, 577

FOUR CORRECT TRAININGS *yang-dag spong bzhi*, Skt. *catuḥsamyakprahāṇa*

The aspiration that sinful, non-virtuous attributes, which have not arisen, may not be developed; the aspiration that sinful, non-virtuous attributes which have arisen may be renounced; the aspiration that virtuous attributes which have not arisen may be developed; and the aspiration that virtuous attributes which have arisen may remain and be unchanging and entirely perfect in the future; Mvt. (958-61). 236

FOUR CREATIVE STAGES (OF THE PATH OF CUTTING THROUGH RESISTANCE) *(khregs-chod) lam-gyi bskyed-rim bzhi*

The abiding state (*gnas*), the unwavering state (*mi-gYo*), sameness (*mnyam-nyid*) and spontaneous presence (*lhun-gyis grub*). 371

FOUR CYCLES (OF THE GREAT PERFECTION) *rdzogs-chen (skor bzhi)*

The Outer, Inner, Secret and Unsurpassedly Secret cycles of the Esoteric Instructional Class. 332, 498, 501

FOUR DECEASES *'da'-ka-ma bzhi*

According to Khetsün Zangpo Rinpoche, these are the decease in which appearances have been transformed according to the vase empowerment (*bum-dbang-gi snang-ba 'da'-ka-ma*); the decease that is the yoga of the seminal point according to the secret empowerment (*gsang-dbang thig-le rnal-'byor 'da'-ka-ma*); the decease that is the mode of the body's death according to the discriminating awareness empowerment (*lus-kyi 'chi-lugs sher-dbang 'da'-ka-ma*); and the decease according to the fourth empowerment (*dbang bzhi-pa'i 'da'-ka-ma*). 923

FOUR DELIGHTS *dga'-ba bzhi*

On the path of desire (*chags-lam*) or skilful means (*thabs-lam*), the practice of inner heat (*gtum-mo*) is activated, giving rise to the experience of blissful warmth in the body (*bde-drod*). The melting bliss then descending through the central channel from the crown centre, gives rise to the pristine cognition of delight (*dga'-ba'i ye-shes*) and the vase empowerment is received through which this delight is united with emptiness (*stong-pa*); in the throat centre it gives rise to the pristine cognition of supreme delight (*mchog-dga'i ye-shes*) and the secret empowerment is received through which this supreme delight is united with great emptiness (*stong-pa chen-po*); then in the heart centre it gives rise to the pristine cognition that is free from delight (*dga'-bral ye-shes*) and the empowerment of discriminating pristine cognition is received through which this absence of delight is united with extreme emptiness (*shin-tu stong-pa*); then in the navel centre it gives rise to the pristine cognition of co-emergent delight (*lhan-skyes dga'i ye-shes*) and the empowerment of word and meaning is received through which this co-emergent delight is united with total emptiness (*thams-cad stong-pa*); and finally, after the four delights have been thus realised, in the secret centre it gives rise to the inconceivable pristine cognition (*bsam-gyis mi-khyab-pa'i ye-shes*) and the skilful empowerment of awareness is received. In this way the path of desire unites the four delights with the FOUR MODES OF EMPTINESS. Refer to Longcenpa, *Dispelling Darkness in the Ten Directions*, pp. 386-96. (GGFTC, pp. 900-14). 818, 830, 877

FOUR DISTINCTIVE FEATURES OF THE MANTRAS *sngags-kyi khyad-par bzhi*

Mantras are unobscured in the area of skilful means (*thabs-kyi cha-la ma-rmongs-pa*), they have manifold means (*thabs mang-ba*), they are without difficulty (*dka'-ba med-pa*) and they are intended for those of highest acumen (*dbang-po rnon-po'i dbang-byas-pa*). 246

FOUR DOCTRINES OF A SPIRITUAL ASCETIC *dge-sbyong-gi chos bzhi*, Skt. *catvāraḥ śramaṇadharmāḥ*

Not to hate others despite being the object of their hatred; not to retaliate in anger even when angry; not to injure others even when injured; and not to beat others even when one is beaten by them. 52

FOUR DRAMATIC MANNERS *tshig-ldan-sogs (zlos-gar-gi tshul) bzhi*

Dialogue (*bhāratī*), conflict (*ārabhaṭī*), grandure (*sātvatī*) and grace (*kaiśikī*). 107

FOUR ELEMENTS *'byung-ba bzhi*, Skt. *caturbhūta*

Earth, water, fire and air. 38, 53, 117-8, 328, 336, 542, 543, 594, 748

FOUR EMPOWERMENTS *dbang bzhi*, Skt. *caturabhiṣeka*

The common vase empowerment (*thun-mong-pa bum-dbang*) and the THREE HIGHER SUPREME UNCOMMON EMPOWERMENTS. 360, 546, 613, 755, 825, 863, 923

FOUR EMPOWERMENTS OF THE INNERMOST SPIRITUALITY *snying-thig-gi (rtsa) dbang bzhi*

As described in *History*, pp. 499-501, these are the outer empowerment of conceptual elaboration (*phyi spros-bcas-kyi dbang*); the inner empowerment which is free from conceptual elaboration (*nang spros-bral-gi dbang*); the secret empowerment that is very unelaborate (*gsang-ba shin-tu spros-bral-gi dbang*); and the most secret empowerment which is extremely unelaborate (*gsang-chen rab-tu spros-bral-gi dbang*). The distinctions between these are explained in Longcenpa, *Treasury of Spiritual and Philosophical Systems*, pp. 370-2. Briefly, the first employs a multiplicity of ritual objects and ideas, the second is free from both ritual objects and ideas, the third is beyond conception and description, while the fourth is the empowerment into the nature of the body of reality. 673, 674-5

FOUR EMPOWERMENTS OF THE PATH OF LIBERATION *grol-lam-gyi dbang bzhi*

See FOUR EMPOWERMENTS

FOUR ENEMIES TO BE DESTROYED *dgra-bzhi gzhom-pa*

According to the commitments of Anuyoga, these are the enemy of wilful artificiality with respect to view, meditation and conduct; the enemy of prattle about coarse training in a lower view; the enemy of violating the basic and ancillary commitments; and the enemy which steals the result through speculation and idleness. Refer to Jamgön Kongtrül, *shes-bya kun-khyab mdzod*, Vol. 2, (p. 192). 367

FOUR ENLIGHTENED ATTRIBUTES *yon-tan bzhi*, Skt. *catasras tathāgataguṇa-pāramitāḥ*

Purity (*dag-pa*, Skt. *śuddhā*), permanence (*rtag-pa*, Skt. *nitya*), bliss (*bde-ba*, Skt. *sukha*) and true self (*dam-pa'i bdag*, Skt. *paramātmā*). 212

FOUR ENLIGHTENED FAMILIES *rigs-bzhi*, Skt. *catuṣkula*

Ubhayatantra adds to the THREE ENLIGHTENED FAMILIES, a fourth which combines the Action family (*las-kyi rigs*, Skt. *karmakula*) with the Jewel family (*rin-chen rigs*, Skt. *ratnakula*). 271-2, 353

FOUR ESSENTIAL RECOLLECTIONS *dran-pa nyer-gzhag bzhi*, Skt. *catuḥsmṛtyupa-sthāna*

The recollection of the body (*lus dran-pa nyer-gzhag*, Skt. *kāyasmṛtyupa-sthāna*), the recollection of feeling (*tshor-ba dran-pa nyer-gzhag*, Skt. *vedanā-smṛtyupasthāna*), the recollection of mind (*sems dran-pa nyer-gzhag*, Skt. *cittasmṛtyupasthāna*) and the recollection of phenomena (*chos dran-pa nyer-gzhag*, Skt. *dharmasmṛtyupasthāna*); Mvt. (953-6). 236

FOUR ETERNALISTIC SCHOOLS *rtag-lta sde bzhi*

The Sāṃkhya (*grangs-can-pa*), Aiśvara (*dbang-phyug-pa*), Vaiṣṇava (*khyab-'jug-pa*) and Jaina (*rgyal-ba-pa*). 16, 64-6

FOUR EXTRAORDINARY ATTRIBUTES (OF THE GROUND) *yon-tan khyad-par-can bzhi*

Corresponding to the FOUR ENLIGHTENED ATTRIBUTES, these are: harmony with the buddha-fields, buddha-bodies and so forth; supreme bliss; non-interruption of enlightened experience; and attainment through the nature of reality. 263

FOUR EXTREMES *mtha' bzhi*, Skt. *caturanta*

Being (*yod*), non-being (*med*), both being and non-being (*yod-med*) and neither being nor non-being (*yod-med min*). 26, 126, 162, 184, 233, 269, 348, 350-1

FOUR FAULTS (ATTRIBUTED TO THE *SECRET NUCLEUS*) *skyon bzhi*

Different enumerations of these have been given. For example, Sodokpa Lodrö Gyeltsen, *dris-lan lung-dang rigs-pa'i 'brug-sgra*, p. 33, reports them to be that this tantra is flawed in word (*sgra-skyon*), flawed in meaning (*don-skyon*), flawed by contradiction (*'gal-skyon*) and flawed by disconnection (*ma-'brel-ba'i skyon*). According to the *Scholar's Feast of Doctrinal History*, p. 179, they are the error of the introductory statement "At the time I gave this explanation" (*'di-skad bdag-gis bshad-pa ces mi-rigs-pa*), the error of the maṇḍala having an immeasurable ground (*gzhi tshad-med mi-rigs-pa*), the error of explaining the three times as four times (*dus-gsum-la dus-bzhir bshad-pa mi-rigs-pa*) and the error of Vajrasattva being the central deity of the maṇḍala (*dkyil-'khor-gyi gtso-bo rdo-rje sems-dpas byas-pa mi-rigs-pa*). Similarly, Gö Khukpa Lhetse in his *Broadside* is said to have criticised the fault of the introduction (*klong-log*) which claims that the *Secret Nucleus* has no audience of bodhisattvas who requested and received it, unlike the other tantras; the fault of time (*dus-log*) which claims the *Secret Nucleus* speaks of four times instead of three; the fault of the maṇḍala (*dkyil-'khor log*) which claims that Vajrasattva appears at the centre of the maṇḍala instead of Vairocana; and the fault of the tantra itself (*rgyud-log*) which claims that the *Secret Nucleus* refers to other tantras when indicating the auspicious times and days for its practice. These four faults, which have many aspects, have been refuted by Rikpei Reldri, Sodokpa Lodrö Gyeltsen, Jikme Lingpa and others. See GGFTC (pp. 61-72). 914, 916

FOUR FEARLESSNESSES *mi-'jigs-pa bzhi*, Skt. *caturvaiśāradya*

Fearlessness in the knowledge of all things (*chos thams-cad mkhyen-pa-la mi-'jigs-pa*, Skt. *sarvadharmābhisambodhivaiśāradya*); fearlessness in the knowledge of the cessation of all corruption (*zag-pa zad-pa thams-cad mkhyen-pa-la mi-'jigs-pa*, Skt. *sarvāsravakṣayajñānavaiśāradya*); fearlessness to declare definitively that phenomena which obstruct the path do not become anything else (*bar-du gcod-pa'i chos-rnams gzhan-du mi-'gyur-bar nges-pa'i lung-bstan-pa-la mi-'jigs-pa*, Skt. *antarāyikadharmānanyathātvaniścitavyākaraṇa-vaiśāradya*); and the fearlessness that the path of renunciation through which all excellent attributes are to be obtained, has been just so realised (*phun-sum tshogs-pa thams-cad thob-par 'gyur-bar nges-par 'byung-ba'i lam de-bzhin-du gyur-ba-la mi-'jigs-pa*, Skt. *sarvasampadadhigamāya nairyāṇikapratipattathā-tvavaiśāradya*); Mvt. (130-4). 22, 140, 171, 266

FOUR FEMALE EARTH SPIRITS *sa'i bdag-mo bzhi*

The four guardians of Yangleshö who confronted Padmasambhava at Chumik Cangcup in Nepal. Their names are Dorje Yacin (*rdo-rje ya-byin*), the daughter of a Māra demon; Decen Decin (*bde-can de-byin*), the daughter of Rāhu; Secin (*bse-byin*), the daughter of a Tsen spirit; and Phakcin (*phag-byin*), the daughter of a nāga spirit. See, e.g., Jikme Lingpa, *Vajrakīla according to the Tradition of the Tantra*, (p. 460). 481

FOUR FORMLESS ABSORPTIONS *gzugs-med-pa'i snyoms-'jug bzhi*, Skt. *catuḥ-samāpatti*

These correspond respectively to the FOUR FORMLESS REALMS at the summit of existence in saṃsāra; Mvt. (1492-5). 13, 61-2

FOUR FORMLESS REALMS *gzugs-med khams-pa'i gnas bzhi*, Skt. *caturārūpya-dhātu*

The activity field infinite as the sky (*nam-mkha' mtha'-yas skye-mched*, Skt. *ākāśānantyāyatana*); the activity field of infinite consciousness (*rnam-shes mtha'-yas skye-mched*, Skt. *vijñānānantyāyatana*); the activity field of nothing at all (*ci-yang med-pa'i skye-mched*, Skt. *akiṃcanyāyatana*); and the activity field where there is neither perception nor non-perception (*'du-shes-med 'du-shes med-min skye-mched*, Skt. *naivasaṃjñānāsaṃjñāyatana*); Mvt. (3110-13). 13, 15, 61-2

FOUR FOUNDATIONS OF MINDFULNESS *dran-pa nyer-bzhag bzhi*

See FOUR ESSENTIAL RECOLLECTIONS

FOUR FURTHER TAMING TEMPLES *yang-'dul lha-khang bzhi*

Lungngen in Cangtshel, Langtang Drölma in Dokam, Kyercu in Paro and Camtrin in Mangyül. For a detailed account, refer to M. Aris, *Bhutan*, pp. 5-33, where alternative enumerations are also given. N. 543, 760

FOUR GREAT AXIOMS (OF MADHYAMAKA) *gtan-tshig chen-po bzhi*

The vajra fragments (*rdo-rje gzegs-ma*), the refutation of the four limits of production (*mu-bzhi skye-'gog*), the supreme relativity (*rten-'brel chen-po*) and the absence of the singular and the multiple (*gcig-dang du-bral*). 35, 294

FOUR GREAT CYCLES OF WORSHIP *mchod-pa chen-po bzhi*

According to Dudjom Rinpoche, *rgyal-rabs*, p. 312, these cycles introduced by King Mune Tsepo concerned the Vinaya and Abhidharma at Lhasa and Trhadruk and those of the Sūtras and Abhisambodhi (i.e. the *Vairocana Tantra*) at Samye. 521

FOUR GREAT MODES OF LIBERATION *grol-lugs chen-po bzhi*

Primordial liberation (*ye-grol*), natural liberation (*rang-grol*), direct liberation (*cer-grol*) and liberation from extremes (*mtha'-grol*). 334

FOUR GREAT RIVERS OF THE TRANSMITTED PRECEPTS *bka'i chu-babs chen-po bzhi*

The river of conventional textual exegeses with commentaries and lecture notes; the river of instructions of the aural lineage with their essential writings and guidance which lays bare the teaching; the river of blessing and empowerment with the means for its conferral and the introductions to reality; and the river of practical techniques with the rites of enlightened activity, attainment and the protectors. 601

FOUR GREAT SUBSECTS OF THE KAGYÜ TRADITION *bka'-brgyud che bzhi*

The Karmapa school founded by Tüsum Khyenpa, the Barampa school founded by Tarma Wangcuk, the Tshelpa school founded by Zhang Tshelpa Tsöndru Trakpa and the Phakmotrupa school founded by Phakmotrupa Dorje Gyelpo. 395, 853, 952

FOUR GUARDIAN KINGS *rgyal-chen bzhi*, Skt. *Caturmahārājika*

Dhṛtarāṣṭra in the east, Virūḍhaka in the south, Virūpākṣa in the west and Vaiśravaṇa in the north. 419

FOUR IMMEASURABLES *tshad-med bzhi*, Skt. *caturaprameya*

Loving kindness (*byams-pa*, Skt. *maitrī*), compassion (*snying-rje*, Skt. *karuṇā*), sympathetic joy (*dga'-ba*, Skt. *muditā*) and equanimity (*btang-snyoms*, Skt. *upekṣā*). 13, 61-2, 417

FOUR INEXHAUSTIBLE GREAT TREASURES *gter-chen mi-zad-pa bzhi*

The unbroken lineage of the THREE PRECIOUS JEWELS, the immeasurable great realisation of the doctrine, the treasure which brings delight to sentient beings and the treasure which is like the sky. 743

FOUR INTERMEDIATE STATES *bar-do rnam bzhi*

The intermediate state of the birthplace (*skye-gnas-kyi bar-do*), the intermediate state of the moment of death (*'chi-kha'i bar-do*), the intermediate state of reality (*chos-nyid bar-do*) and the intermediate state of rebirth (*srid-pa bar-do*). 39, 344-5

FOUR KAPTSE *ga-rtse bzhi*

The schemata of elemental divination representing: the discrete elements (*'byung-ba rang-rgyud*), apparent sense objects (*snang-ba yul*), the intellect which analyses these elemental relationships (*spyod-byed yid*) and the mind that apprehends positive and negative consequences (*'dzin-pa sems*). 104

FOUR KINDS OF AWARENESS-HOLDER *rig-'dzin rnam bzhi*

The awareness-holder of maturation (*rnam-smin rig-'dzin*), the awareness-holder of power over the life-span (*tshe-dbang rig-'dzin*), the awareness-holder of the great seal (*phyag-chen rig-'dzin*) and the awareness-holder of spontaneous presence (*lhun-grub rig-'dzin*). 31, 260, 281-2, 363

FOUR KINDS OF BIRTHPLACE *skye-gnas rigs bzhi*, Skt. *caturyoni*

Birth from the womb (*mngal-nas skye-ba*, Skt. *jārāyuja*), birth from an egg (*sgo-nga-las skye-ba*, Skt. *aṇḍaja*), birth from heat and moisture (*drod-sher-las skye-ba*, Skt. *saṃsvedaja*) and miraculous birth (*brdzus-te skye-ba*, Skt. *upapāduka*). 279

FOUR KINDS OF COVERT INTENTION *ldem-por dgongs-pa rnam bzhi*

The covert intention in respect of entry into the teaching (*gzhugs-pa-la ldem-por dgongs-pa*, Skt. *avatārābhisandhi*), the covert intention in respect of characteristics (*mtshan-nyid-la ldem-por dgongs-pa*, Skt. *lakṣaṇābhisandhi*), the covert intention in respect of antidotes (*gnyen-po-la ldem-por dgongs-pa*, Skt. *pratipakṣābhisandhi*) and the covert intention in respect of interpretation (*bsgyur-ba-la ldem-por dgongs-pa*, Skt. *pariṇāmanābhisandhi*). 30, 220-2

FOUR KINDS OF DESIRE *'dod-chags tshul/rigs bzhi*

Desires which are engendered through exchange of glances, laughter, embrace and sexual union are respectively transformed by Kriyātantra in which the deities regard each other, Ubhayatantra in which the deities smile at each other, Yogatantra in which they embrace and Unsurpassed Yogatantra in which they are in sexual union. Refer to Longcenpa, *Treasury of Spiritual and Philosophical Systems*, (pp. 292-4). 269, 413

FOUR KINDS OF ENLIGHTENED ACTIVITY *phrin-las rnam bzhi*, Skt. *catuṣkarman*

These are the FOUR RITES. 146

FOUR KINDS OF INDIVIDUALS *gang-zag bzhi*, Skt. *catvāraḥ pudgalāḥ*

Ordinary persons (*so-so skye-bo*, Skt. *pṛthagjana*), pious attendants (*nyan-thos*, Skt. *śrāvaka*), self-centred buddhas (*rang-rgyal*, Skt. *pratyekabuddha*) and bodhisattvas (*byang-chub sems-dpa'*). 186

FOUR KINDS OF INSTRUCTION (OF THE SUPREME EMANATIONAL BODY) *'dul-ba rnam-par bzhi*

Instruction by the great merit of the buddha-body (*sku bsod-nams chen-pos 'dul-ba*); instruction by the direct perception of buddha-mind (*thugs mngon-sum-pas 'dul-ba*); instruction by inconceivable miraculous abilities (*rdzu-'phrul bsam-gyis mi-khyab-pas 'dul-ba*); and instruction by knowledge conveyed in speech (*gsung rig-pas 'dul-ba*). 21, 131-2, 146, 414, 415

FOUR KINDS OF INTENTION *dgongs-pa rnam bzhi*, Skt. *caturabhiprāya*

The intention directed towards sameness (*mnyam-pa-nyid-la dgongs-pa*, Skt. *samatābhiprāya*), the intention directed towards other meanings (*don-gzhan-la dgongs-pa*, Skt. *arthāntarābhiprāya*), the intention directed towards other times (*dus-gzhan-la dgongs-pa*, Skt. *kālāntarābhiprāya*) and the intention directed towards other individuals (*gang-zag gzhan-la dgongs-pa*, Skt. *pudgalāntarābhiprāya*); Mvt. (1667-70). 30, 218-20

FOUR KINDS OF PRISTINE COGNITION *ye-shes bzhi*

The outer, inner and secret pristine cognitions which pertain respectively to the outer, inner and secret major and minor marks; and the pristine cognition of reality (*de-kho-na-nyid ye-shes*) which pertains to the supreme marks of the Great Perfection. 124, 251

FOUR KINDS OF REALISATION *rtogs bzhi*

First of the FOUR AXIOMS OF MAHĀYOGA, consisting of the single basis (*rgyu gcig-pa*), manner of the seed-syllables (*yig-'bru'i tshul*), consecration or blessing (*byin-gyis-rlabs-pa*) and direct perception (*mngon-sum-pa*). 265, 275

FOUR KINDS OF RELIANCE *rton-pa bzhi*, Skt. *catuḥpratiśaraṇa*

Reliance on meaning rather than on words, reliance on the doctrine rather than on individuals, reliance on pristine cognition rather than on consciousness, and reliance on the definitive rather than on the provisional meaning; Mvt. (1546-9). 186, 871

FOUR KINDS OF RELICS *ring-bsrel rnam bzhi*

Relics of the body of reality (*chos-sku'i ring-bsrel*), relics of bone remains (*sku-gdung ring-bsrel*), relics of clothing (*sku-bal ring-bsrel*) and relics of miniature size (*nyung-ngu lta-bu'i ring-bsrel*). 38, 337

FOUR KINDS OF TREATISE *bstan-bcos rnam-pa bzhi*

The meaningless, low in meaning, erroneous and meaningful. 89

FOUR LAMPS *sgron-ma bzhi*

The watery lamp of the far-sighted eyes (*rgyangs-zhag chu'i sgron-ma*), the lamp of emptiness which is the seminal point (*thig-le stong-pa'i sgron-ma*), the lamp of the expanse of awareness (*rig-pa dbyings-kyi sgron-ma*) and the lamp of discriminative awareness which is naturally present (*shes-rab rang-byung-gi sgron-ma*). 338-9

FOUR LANGUAGES *skad-rigs bzhi*, Skt. *caturbhāṣā*

Sanskrit (*legs-sbyar*), Prakrit (*phal-pa*), Apabhraṃśa (*zur-chags*) and Paiśācī (*sha-za*). 107

FOUR LIMITS *mu bzhi*, Skt. *catuṣkoṭi*

This can refer to the FOUR EXTREMES, to the four pairs constituting the EIGHT EXTREMES or to: the limits of birth and death or production and cessation (*skye-'gog*); the limits of eternalism and nihilism (*rtag-chad*); the limits of being and non-being (*yod-med*); and the limits of appearance and emptiness (*snang-stong*). 163-4

FOUR MAHĀKRODHA DEITIES *khro-bo chen-po bzhi*, Skt. **caturmahākrodha*

Yamāntaka, Mahābala, Hayagrīva and Amṛtakuṇḍalin. 125-6

FOUR MAHĀKRODHĪ DEITIES *khro-mo chen-mo bzhi*, Skt. **caturmahākrodhī*

Aṅkuśā, Pāśā, Sphoṭā and Gaṇṭhā. 126

FOUR (MEDITATIVE) CONCENTRATIONS *bsam-gtan bzhi*, Skt. *caturdhyāna*

The first is the meditative concentration which possesses both ideas and scrutiny (*rtog-pa-dang bcas-shing dpyod-pa-dang bcas-pa'i bsam-gtan dang-po*), the second is the meditative concentration which possesses no ideas but scrutiny alone (*rtog-pa med-la dpyod-pa tsam-dang bcas-pa bsam-gtan gnyis-pa*), the third is the meditative concentration of mental action which is devoid of ideas and scrutiny (*rtog-pa-dang dpyod-pa yang-med-pa yid-la byed-pa bsam-gtan gsum-pa*) and the fourth is the meditative concentration of mental action which is united with delight (*dga'-ba sdud-pa yid-la byed-pa'i bsam-gtan bzhi-pa*); Mvt. (1477-81). 13, 14-15, 61-2, 115

FOUR MIRACLES *cho-'phrul bzhi*

Contemplation (*ting-'dzin*), consecration or blessing (*byin-rlabs*), empowerment (*dbang-bskur*) and offering (*mchod-pa*). In Yogatantra these are known as the FOUR YOGAS. 355-6

FOUR MODES OF EMPTINESS *stong bzhi*

Emptiness (*stong-pa*), great emptiness (*stong-pa chen-po*), extreme emptiness (*shin-tu stong-pa*) and total emptiness (*thams-cad stong-pa*). For an explanation of these, refer to the FOUR DELIGHTS. 877

FOUR MODES OF GENUINE INDIVIDUAL AWARENESS *so-so yang-dag-pa rang-gi rig-pa bzhi*, Skt. *catuḥpratisaṃvid*

The genuine awareness of the doctrine (*chos-kyi so-so yang-dag-pa rang-gi rig-pa*, Skt. *dharmapratisaṃvid*), the genuine awareness of meaning (*don-gyi so-so yang-dag-pa rang-gi rig-pa*, Skt. *arthapratisaṃvid*), the genuine awareness of definitions (*nges-pa'i tshig-kyi so-so yang-dag-pa rang-gi rig-pa*, Skt. *niruktapratisaṃvid*) and the genuine awareness of brilliance (*spobs-pa-kyi so-so yang-dag-pa rang-gi rig-pa*, Skt. *pratibhānapratisaṃvid*). 871

FOUR MODES OF SAMENESS *mnyam-pa bzhi*

One of the FOUR AXIOMS OF MAHĀYOGA consisting of the sameness of emptiness (*stong-pa*), the sameness of the coalescence of appearances and emptiness (*snang-stong zung-'jug*), the sameness of freedom from conceptual elaboration (*spros-bral*) and sameness itself (*mnyam-nyid*). 275-6

FOUR MOMENTS AS THEY APPLY TO EACH OF THE FOUR TRUTHS *bden-bzhi'i skad-cig-ma bzhi*

An explanation of these and their aspects is given under SIXTEEN MOMENTS OF PRISTINE COGNITION. 158, 230

FOUR NAILS *gzer bzhi*

These are the four nails which control life-breath (*srog-sdom gzer-bzhi*) according to Yogatantra, namely, the nail of unchanging intention (*mi-'gyur dgongs-pa'i gzer*), the divine nail of contemplation (*ting-'dzin lha'i gzer*), the nail of mantra which is the nucleus (*snying-po sngags-kyi gzer*) and the nail of activity which is the emanation and absorption of light rays (*'phro-'du phrin-las-kyi gzer*). 647

FOUR NEGATIVE DOCTRINES *nag-po'i chos bzhi*, Skt. *catuḥkṛṣṇadharma*

According to the *Pagoda of Precious Jewels* as quoted in Longcenpa, *Treasury of Spiritual and Philosophical Systems*, p. 201, these are: to deceive the teacher and others who are worthy of reverence (*bla-ma-dang mchod-par 'os-pa bslus-pa*); to have a bad conscience with respect to what, on behalf of others, is no cause for regret, i.e. regret for entering the Greater Vehicle (*gzhan 'gyod-pa'i gnas ma-yin-pa-la 'gyod-pa bskyed-pa*); to disparage those bodhisattvas who have cultivated an enlightened attitude (*sems-bskyed-pa'i byang-chub sems-dpa'-la bsngags-pa ma-yin-pa'i mi-snyan-pa*); and to act towards others without higher motivation but with unworthy speech, deceit and guile (*brjod-pa ma-yin-pa'i sgras tshigs-su bcad-pa brjod-pa-dang sgyu-dang gYos gzhan-la nye-bar spyod-kyis lhag-pa'i bsam-pas ma-yin-pa*). 236

FOUR NOMINAL COMPONENTS, CONTEMPLATION ENDOWED WITH *ming-bzhi-la ldan-pa'i ting-nge-'dzin*

These are the four mental components of feeling, perception, habitual tendencies and consciousness which are separated from the fifth component, form, during the FOUR FORMLESS ABSORPTIONS at the summit of existence in saṃsāra. 62

FOUR OBSCURATIONS *sgrib bzhi*

Conflicting emotions, world-forming deeds, obscuration with respect to knowable phenomena, and propensities. 923

FOUR OMENS *mtshan-ma bzhi*, Skt. *caturnimitta*

The omens perceived by Śākyamuni, which prompted his renunciation of the household life, namely, old age, sickness, death and a wandering ascetic. 418-19

FOUR ORDERS *tshogs rnam-pa bzhi*, Skt. *catuḥpariṣad*

These are the FOUR ASSEMBLIES. 137, 226

FOUR ORDINARY ASSEMBLIES *thun-mong-gi 'khor rnam-pa bzhi*

See FOUR ASSEMBLIES

FOUR PAIRS OF SACRED BEINGS *skyes-bu zung bzhi*

The pair which enters and becomes established in the stream to nirvāṇa (*rgyun-zhugs-kyi 'bras-bu-la zhugs-gnas gnyis*); the pair which enters and becomes established in a single rebirth (*lan-cig phyir 'ong-ba-la zhugs-gnas gnyis*); the pair which enters and becomes established in not returning to saṃsāra (*phyir mi-'ong-ba-la zhugs-gnas gnyis*); and the pair which enters and becomes established as arhats (*dgra-bcom-pa-la zhugs-gnas gnyis*). Also referred to as the EIGHT KINDS OF INDIVIDUAL (AMONGST PIOUS ATTENDANTS), they achieve the FOUR RESULTS. 227

FOUR PATHS (OF LEARNING) *(slob-pa'i) lam bzhi*, Skt. *(śaikṣa)mārgāś catvāraḥ*

According to the vehicle of bodhisattvas, these are the paths of accumulation (*tshogs-lam*, Skt. *sambhāramārga*), connection (*sbyor-lam*, Skt. *prayogamārga*), insight (*mthong-lam*, Skt. *darśanamārga*) and meditation (*sgom-lam*, Skt. *bhāvanāmārga*). 192, 196-7, 231, 236, 259, 287, 923

FOUR PERVERTED VIEWS *phyin-ci-log bzhi*, Skt. *caturviparyāsa*

To view what is impermanent as permanent, what is painful as blissful, what is tainted as pure and what is non-self as self. n. 173

FOUR PHILOSOPHICAL SYSTEMS *grub-mtha' bzhi*, Skt. *catvāraḥ siddhāntabhedāḥ*

Those of the Vaibhāṣika (*bye-brag-tu smra-ba*), Sautrāntika (*mdo-sde-pa*), Vijñānavāda (*rnam-shes-su smra-ba* or *sems-tsam-pa*) and Mādhyamika (*dbu-ma-pa*). 178, 184, 923

FOUR PILLARS *ka-ba bzhi*

The four main students of Zurcungpa Sherap-tra, namely, Kyotön Śākye of Kungbu, Yangkeng Lama of Kyonglung, Len Śākya Zangpo of Chuwar and Datik Cośāk of Nakmore. 346, 640-2, 645, 647

FOUR POSITIVE DOCTRINES *dkar-chos bzhi*, Skt. *catuḥśukladharma*

According to the *Pagoda of Precious Jewels*, these are: not to speak falsely (*rdzun-tshig mi-smra-ba*); to abide on behalf of all sentient beings with higher motivation and without deceit or guile (*sgyu-dang gYo-med-par sems-can thams-cad-kyi drung-na lhag-bsam-gyis gnas-pa*); to regard bodhisattvas as one's teachers (*byang-chub sems-dpa'-la ston-pa'i 'du-shes bskyed*); and to inspire those sentient beings, whom one totally matures, to grasp the genuine, unsurpassed perfect enlightenment (*sems-can gang-rnams yongs-su smin-byed yang-dag-par bla-med yang-dag rdzogs-pa'i byang-chub 'dzin-du 'jug-pa*). 236

FOUR PULSES *'gros bzhi*

The energy channels, currents and seminal points, along with consciousness. 923

FOUR RESULTS *'bras-bu bzhi*, Skt. *catuḥphala*

Entering the stream to nirvāṇa (*rgyun-du zhugs-pa*, Skt. *śrota'āpanna*), being tied to a single rebirth (*lan-cig phyir 'ong-ba*, Skt. *sakṛdāgāmī*), not returning to saṃsāra (*phyir mi-'ong-ba*, Skt. *anāgāmī*) and attaining the status of an arhat or slayer of the foe of conflicting emotion (*dgra-bcom-pa*); Mvt. (5132-6). 227

FOUR RITES *las-bzhi*

Pacification (*zhi-ba*, Skt. *śānti*), enrichment (*rgyas-pa*, Skt. *puṣṭi*), overpowering (*dbang*, Skt. *vaśa*) and forceful rites of "liberation" which compassionately sever consciousness from the body and transfer it to a higher level of existence (*drag-po mngon-spyod*, Skt. *abhicāra*). Also referred to as the FOUR KINDS OF ENLIGHTENED ACTIVITY. 478, 669, 721, 829, 844, 920

FOUR RIVERS OF THE *SŪTRA WHICH GATHERS ALL INTENTIONS mdo'i chu-babs bzhi rdzogs*

These are explained under the FOUR GREAT RIVERS OF THE TRANSMITTED PRECEPTS. 717, 722, 723, 828

FOUR ROOT DOWNFALLS *rtsa-ltung bzhi*, Skt. *caturmūlāpatti*

These are cited in accord with the *Twenty Verses on the Bodhisattva Vow* in *Fundamentals*, (p. 235). 95

FOUR ROOT EMPOWERMENTS OF THE INNERMOST SPIRITUALITY *snying-thig-gi rtsa-dbang bzhi*

See FOUR EMPOWERMENTS OF THE INNERMOST SPIRITUALITY

FOUR SEALS *phyag-rgya bzhi*, Skt. *caturmudrā*

The seal of commitment (*dam-tshig-gi phyag-rgya*. Skt. *samayamudrā*), the doctrinal seal (*chos-kyi phyag-rgya*, Skt. *dharmamudrā*), the seal of action (*las-kyi phyag-rgya*, Skt. *karmamudrā*) and the great seal (*phyag-rgya chen-po*, Skt. *mahāmudrā*). 33, 35, 272, 295-6, 301, 355-6

FOUR SEALS INDICATIVE OF THE TRANSMITTED PRECEPTS *bka'-rtags-kyi phyag-rgya bzhi*

All that is compounded is impermanent (*'dus-byas thams-cad mi-rtag-pa*), all that is corrupt is suffering (*zag-bcas thams-cad sdug-bsngal-ba*), all things are without self (*chos thams-cad bdag-med-pa*) and nirvāṇa is peace (*mya-ngan-las 'das-pa zhi-ba*). 16, 70-1

FOUR SENSATIONS *nyams bzhi*

These are the sensations of seeing (*mthong-ba*), hearing (*thos-pa*), smelling (*snom-pa*) and tasting (*myong-ba*). 20, 125

FOUR SENSE OBJECTS *yul bzhi*, Skt. *caturviṣaya*

Form (*gzugs*, Skt. *rūpa*), sound (*sgra*, Skt. *śabda*), smell (*dri*, Skt. *gandha*) and taste (*ro*, Skt. *rasa*). 20, 125, 257

FOUR SENSE ORGANS *dbang-po bzhi*, Skt. *caturindriya*

The eye (*mig-gi dbang-po*, Skt. *cakṣurindriya*), ear (*rna-ba'i dbang-po*, Skt. *śrotrendriya*), nose (*sna'i dbang-po*, Skt. *ghrāṇendriya*) and tongue (*lce'i dbang-po*, Skt. *jihvendriya*); Mvt. (1853-6). 20, 125

FOUR SPECIAL ATTRIBUTES (OF THE TREATISES) *(bstan-bcos-kyi) khyad-chos bzhi*

The attribute of motivation (*kun-slong-gi khyad-par*), the attribute of expressive words (*brjod-bya tshig-gyi khyad-par*), the attribute of expressed meaning (*rjod-byed don-gyi khyad-par*) and the attribute of purposeful composition (*dgos-pa byed-las-kyi khyad-par*). 18, 88

FOUR SPECIAL QUALITIES OF THE TRANSMITTED PRECEPTS *bka'i khyad-par bzhi*

The possession of expressed meaning (*brjod-bya don-dang ldan-pa*), immaculate words of expression (*rjod-byed tshig dri-ma med-pa*), the renunciation of conflicting emotions (*byed-las khams-gsum-gyi nyon-mongs-pa spong-ba*) and teaching the benefits of peace as the result (*'bras-bu zhi-ba'i phan-yon ston-pa*). 73

FOUR STYLES *tshul bzhi*

The lexical (*yi-ge*), general (*spyi*), concealed (*sbas-pa*) and conclusive (*mthar-thug*) styles for the appraisal or exegesis of secret mantra texts. 35, 292-3

FOUR SUBDIVISIONS OF THE THIRD CATEGORY OF THE ESOTERIC INSTRUCTIONAL CLASS *gsum-pa rgyud rang-gzhung-du bstan-pa'i tshul bzhi*

Instructions given in the manner of the Full Summation of the View (*lta-ba sgang dril-ba*); those given in the manner of Blood-letting which Removes Obstacles (*rtar-ga gegs-sel*); those given in a manner which Reveals the Hidden (*gab-pa mngon-phyung*); and those given in the manner of Exegeses which are Naturally Clear (*bshad-pa rang-gsal-gyi tshul*). 331

FOUR SUPERIOR COMMITMENTS *lhag-pa'i dam-tshig bzhi*

According to Anuyoga, there are no limits to guard because the essence of the ultimate commitment is free from transgressions and violations; there is exclusive plainness and evenness because the forms of the subject-object dichotomy have been transcended; these are gathered in the single expanse of the mind-as-such; and there is the commitment of reality itself. Refer to Jamgön Kongtrül, *shes-bya kun-khyab mdzod*, Vol. 2, (p. 189). 367

FOUR SUPPORTS FOR MIRACULOUS ABILITY *rdzu-'phrul rkang bzhi*, Skt. *catvāra ṛddhipādāḥ*

The support for miraculous ability which combines the contemplation of aspiration with the volition to renounce (*'dun-pa'i ting-nge-'dzin spang-ba'i 'du-byed-dang ldan-pa'i rdzu-'phrul-gyi rkang-pa*, Skt. *chandasamādhiprahāṇasaṃskārasamanvāgatarddhipāda*); the support for miraculous ability which combines the contemplation of the mind with the volition to renounce (*sems-kyi ting-nge-'dzin spang-ba'i 'du-byed-dang ldan-pa'i rdzu-'phrul-gyi rkang-pa,* Skt. *cittasamādhiprahāṇasaṃskārasamanvāgatarddhipāda*); the support for miraculous ability which combines the contemplation of perseverance with the volition to renounce (*brtson-'grus-kyi ting-nge-'dzin spang-ba'i 'du-byed-dang ldan-pa'i rdzu-'phrul-gyi rkang-pa,* Skt. *vīryasamādhiprahāṇasaṃskārasamanvāgatarddhipāda*); and the support for miraculous ability which combines the contemplation of scrutiny with the volition to renounce (*dpyod-pa'i ting-nge-'dzin spang-ba'i 'du-byed-dang ldan-pa'i rdzu-'phrul-gyi rkang-pa,* Skt. *mīmāṃṣāsamādhiprahāṇasaṃskārasamanvāgatarddhipāda*). 236

FOUR SYLLABLES *yi-ge bzhi-pa*

See THREE MOVEMENTS WITH REFERENCE TO THE FOUR SYLLABLES

FOUR TANTRAPIṬAKA *rgyud-sde bzhi*

Kriyātantra, Ubhayatantra or Caryātantra, Yogatantra and Unsurpassed Yogatantra. Also referred to as the FOUR CLASSES OF TANTRA. 32-4, 203, 263, 268-74

FOUR TEMPORAL AGES *dus bzhi*, Skt. *caturyuga*

The perfect age (*rdzogs-ldan*, Skt. *kṛtayuga*), the age of "threes" (*gsum-ldan*, Skt. *tretāyuga*), the age of "twos" (*gnyis-ldan*, Skt. *dvāparayuga*) and the age of degeneration (*rtsod-ldan*, Skt. *kaliyuga*). The names are derived from the ancient Indian game of four-sided dice, "perfection" being the score of four, second-place a three, third-place a two, and *kali* being the name for the lowest score, a one. 268-9

FOUR TEMPORAL DIMENSIONS *dus bzhi*

The past (*'das-pa*), present (*da-lta-ba*), future (*ma-'ongs-pa*) and indefinite time (*ma-nges-pa'i dus*). Also referred to as the FOUR TIMES. 125

FOUR TIBETAN PROVINCES *bod ru bzhi*

Uru and Yoru in Central Tibet, with Yeru and Rulak in Tsang. 708

FOUR TIMES *dus bzhi*

The FOUR TEMPORAL DIMENSIONS. 244, 307, 633, 915, 916

FOUR TRANSMITTED PRECEPTS, LINEAGE OF *bka'-bzhi brgyud-pa*

The transmitted precepts of the Great Seal which descended through Vajrapāṇi, Saraha, Lohipā, Dārikapā, Diṅgīpā and Tilopā; the transmitted precepts of the Father tantras which descended through Guhyapati, Sa-bcu dbang-phyug blo-gros rin-chen, Nāgārjuna, Mātaṅgīpā and Tilopā; the transmitted precepts of the Mother tantras which descended through Sumati Samantabhadrī, Thang-lo-pa, Shing-lo-pa, Karṇaripā and Tilopā; and the transmitted precepts of inner radiance which descended through Vajrapāṇi, Ḍombī Heruka, Bi-na-sa, Kambalapāda, Indrabhūti and Tilopā. Refer to E. G. Smith's introduction to *Bka'-brgyud Gser-phreṅ*, (p. 3n.). 853

FOUR TRUTHS *bden-pa rnam bzhi*, Skt. *caturāryasatya*

The truth of suffering (*sdug-bsngal-gyi bden-pa*, Skt. *duḥkhasatya*), the truth of the origin of suffering (*kun-'byung-gi bden-pa*, Skt. *samudayasatya*), the truth of its cessation (*'gog-pa'i bden-pa*, Skt. *nirodhasatya*) and the truth of the path (*lam-gyi bden-pa*, Skt. *mārgasatya*). The three times to which they pertain are the present, future and past. The twelve ways in which they are taught are as follows: Suffering is this, it can be diagnosed, it has been diagnosed; the origin of suffering is this, it can be abandoned, it has been abandoned; the cessation of suffering is this, it can be verified, it has been verified; the path to the cessation of suffering is this, it can be developed and it has been developed. 23-4, 137, 153, 188, 224-7, 230, 421, 423, 946

FOUR UNIONS *sbyor-ba bzhi*, Skt. *caturyoga*

These are the FOUR BRANCHES OF RITUAL SERVICE AND ATTAINMENT. 277

FOUR VISIONARY APPEARANCES *snang-ba bzhi*

The visionary appearance of the direct perception of reality (*chos-nyid mngon-sum-gi snang-ba*), the visionary appearance of increasing contemplative experience (*nyams gong-'phel-ba'i snang-ba*), the visionary appearance of reaching the limit of awareness (*rig-pa tshad-phebs-kyi snang-ba*) and the visionary appearance of the cessation of clinging to reality (*chos-nyid-du 'dzin-pa zad-pa'i snang-ba*). 38, 332, 339, 341, 343, 371, 971

FOUR WAYS OF DEATH *'chi-lugs bzhi*

Those of dissolving into space (*nam-mkha'*), cremation (*me-dpung*), death in the manner of an awareness-holder (*rig-'dzin*) and celestial flight (*mkha'-'gro*). According to Tsele Natsok Rangdröl, *bar-do'i spyi-don*, fol. 8b.1-3, these are described respectively as follows: (1) body and mind dissolve in the emptiness of the buddha-body of reality, as the space within and without a vase merge when the vase breaks; (2) one passes away like a fire with no more fuel; (3) space is filled with light and one dies like an awareness-holder; and (4) even though one dies, one need not relinquish the body and so one dies as a sky-farer. 543

FOUR WAYS OF LIBERATION *grol bzhi*

Liberation by seeing (*mthong-grol*) objects which represent the buddhas' body, speech and mind; liberation by hearing (*thos-grol*) the nature of the intermediate state of reality at the time of death; liberation by wearing (*brtags-grol*) a diagram or yantra which is attached to the shoulders, head and heart at the moment of death, or worn by mantrins in the topknot of their braided hair; and liberation by tasting (*myang-grol*) when the flesh of one who has been born a brahman (i.e. a vegetarian) or a bodhisattva over seven successive lives is consumed. 748

FOUR YOGAS *rnal-'byor bzhi*

These are explained in the context of Yogatantra under the FOUR MIRACLES. 33, 272

FIVE

FIVE ASPECTS OF THE ENTRANCE (TO MAHĀYOGA) *'jug-pa'i yan-lag lnga*

Death (*'chi-ba*), the intermediate state before birth (*skye-ba bar-ma*) and the THREE PHASES OF LIFE. 278-9

FIVE AWAKENINGS *mngon-par byang-chub-pa lnga*, Skt. *pañcābhisambodhi*

According to Yogatantra, the sequence of visualisation through the creation stage is as follows: emptiness (*stong-pa-nyid*), the lunar throne (*zla-gdan*), the seed-syllables of buddha-speech (*gsung yig-'bru*), the hand implements symbolic of buddha-mind (*thugs phyag-mtshan*) and the complete body of the deity (*sku yongs-rdzogs*). 33, 272-3, 355-6, 412, 645, 703

FIVE (BASIC) CATEGORIES (OF THE KNOWABLE) *shes-bya thams-cad gzhi lnga*, Skt. *jñeyāni pañca*

According to the Vaibhāṣika, these are the forms that appear (*snang-ba gzugs*, Skt. *rūpa*), the dominant mind (*gtso-bo sems*, Skt. *citta*), the concomitant mental events (*'khor-du sems-byung*, Skt. *caitasika*), disjunct conditions (*mi-ldan-pa'i 'du-byed*, Skt. *cittaviprayuktasaṃskāra*) and the uncompounded entities (*'dus-ma-byas-pa*, Skt. *asaṃskṛta*). 24, 156-7

FIVE BASIC COMMITMENTS *rtsa-ba dam-tshig lnga*

According to Kriyātantra, these are not to sleep on a high bed or meditation throne (*khri-la nyal-bar mi-bya*), not to eat meat (*sha mi-za*), not to drink ale, i.e. alcohol (*chang mi-btung*) and not to eat garlic (*sgog-pa mi-za*), or radishes (*la-phug mi-za*). 350

FIVE BASIC PHILOSOPHICAL VIEWS OF OUTSIDERS *phyi-rol lta-ba log-pa'i rtsa-ba'i grub-mtha' lnga*

The views of the FIVE SOPHISTIC SCHOOLS OF THE EXTREMIST MASTERS. 82

FIVE BASIC POINTS *gzhi lnga*

These five points proclaimed by Mahādeva were: that arhats were in a position to answer others (*gzhan-la gdab*, Skt. *pratyuttara*), that they had ignorance (*mi shes-pa*, Skt. *ajñānatā*), doubt (*yid-gnyis*, Skt. *vimati*), imagination (*yongs-su brtags-pa*, Skt. *parikalpa*) and were able to maintain themselves (*bdag-nyid gso-bar byed-pa*, Skt. *ātmapoṣaṇa*). The enumeration given here follows *Blue Annals*, pp. 28-9; and Tāranātha, *History of Buddhism in India*, pp. 80-1. However, cf. HBI, pp. 300ff., for variant lists derived from other traditions. 429

FIVE BUDDHA-BODIES *sku lnga*, Skt. *pañcakāya*

The body of reality (*chos-sku*, Skt. *dharmakāya*), the body of perfect rapture (*longs-spyod rdzogs-pa'i sku*, Skt. *sambhogakāya*), the emanational body (*sprul-pa'i sku*, Skt. *nirmāṇakāya*), the body of awakening (*mngon-byang-gi sku*, Skt. *abhisambodhikāya*) and the body of indestructible reality (*rdo-rje sku*, Skt. *vajrakāya*). 18, 19, 128, 139-40, 282, 363, 568, 594, 924

FIVE BUDDHA FAMILIES *rigs lnga*

See FIVE ENLIGHTENED/BUDDHA FAMILIES

FIVE CERTAINTIES *nges-pa lnga*

These are the attributes of the body of perfect rapture, namely, those of the perfected teacher (*ston-pa*), teaching (*bstan-pa*), retinue (*'khor*), place (*gnas*) and time (*dus*). Also known as the FIVE EXCELLENCES. 117, 123, 145

FIVE CHARACTERISTIC CONSORTS PROPHESIED BY PADMASAMBHAVA *mtshan-ldan gzungs-ma lnga*

Mandāravā, Kālasiddhi, Yeshe Tshogyel, Śākyadevī of Nepal and Trashi Khyedren, the princess of Mön. 773

FIVE CLASSES OF BEINGS *'gro-ba lnga*, Skt. *pañcagati*

Gods, humans, animals, tormented spirits and denizens of hell. 414

FIVE CLASSES OF MEANS FOR ATTAINMENT OF THE DEITIES OF PRISTINE COGNITION *ye-shes lha'i sgrub-sde lnga*

Those of the deities Yamāntaka, Hayagrīva, Śrīheruka, Vajrāmṛta or Mahottara, and Vajrakīla. 361-2

FIVE COMPONENTS *phung-po lnga*, Skt. *pañcaskandha*

Form (*gzugs-kyi phung-po*, Skt. *rūpaskandha*), feelings (*tshor-ba'i phung-po*, Skt. *vedanāskandha*), perceptions (*'du-shes-kyi phung-po*, Skt. *saṃjñā-skandha*), habitual tendencies (*'du-byed-kyi phung-po*, Skt. *saṃskāraskandha*), and consciousness (*rnam-shes-kyi phung-po*, Skt. *vijñānaskandha*). 13, 20, 25, 55-6, 160-1, 170, 213

FIVE COMPONENTS (OF THE ENLIGHTENED ONES) *(mi-mnyam-pa dang mnyam-pa'i) phung-po lnga*, Skt. *asamasamapañcaskandha*

The component of moral discipline (*tshul-khrims-kyi phung-po*, Skt. *śīla-skandha*), the component of contemplation (*ting-'dzin-gyi phung-po*, Skt. *samādhiskandha*), the component of discriminative awareness (*shes-rab-kyi phung-po*, Skt. *prajñāskandha*), the component of liberation (*rnam-par grol-ba'i phung-po*, Skt. *vimuktiskandha*) and the component of the vision of the liberated pristine cognition (*rnam-par grol-ba'i ye-shes mthong-ba'i phung-po*, Skt. *vimuktijñānadarśanaskandha*); Mvt. (104-8). 125

FIVE CONFLICTING EMOTIONS *nyon-mongs lnga*, Skt. *pañcakleśa*

Desire (*'dod-chags*, Skt. *rāga*), hatred (*zhe-sdang*, Skt. *dveṣa*), delusion (*gti-mug*, Skt. *moha*), pride (*nga-rgyal*, Skt. *māna*) and envy (*phra-dog*, Skt. *īrsyā*). Also known as the FIVE POISONS. 128, 714

FIVE CONQUERORS *rgyal-ba lnga*

These are the FIVE TEACHERS. 125

FIVE CONTEMPLATIVE EXPERIENCES *ting-nge-'dzin nyams lnga*

According to Mahāyoga, these five experiences relating to the creation and perfection stages are: wavering (*gYo*), attainment (*thob*), skill (*goms*), firmness (*brtan*) and conclusion (*mthar-phyin*). 34, 278

FIVE DEFECTS OF WOMANKIND *bud-med-kyi skyon lnga*

According to Longdöl Lama, *The Collected Works of Longdöl Lama*, p. 1455, these are to desire other men (*skyes-pa gzhan-la sems-pa*), to harbour great jealousy for other women (*bud-med gzhan-la phrag-dog-che*), to have ill will (*sems-pa ngan*), to be very stingy (*ser-sna-che*) and to be perpetually ignorant (*rtag-tu ma-rig bya-byed*). 418

FIVE DISTINCTIONS (BETWEEN THE OUTER AND INNER TANTRAS) *(rgyud phyi-nang-gi) khyad-par lnga*

According to Dropukpa, these are the distinctions of view (*lta-ba*), the mode of acquiring accomplishment (*dngos-grub len-pa*), empowerment (*dbang*), conduct (*spyod-pa*) and result (*'bras-bu*). 346-8

FIVE DOCTRINES *chos lnga*

In the context in which this appears in *Fundamentals*, p. 128, the precise enumeration has not been identified.

FIVE DOCTRINES (OF THE *SŪTRA OF THE DESCENT TO LAṄKĀ*) *chos lnga*, Skt. *pañcadharma*

Following Suzuki's *Studies in the Laṅkāvatāra Sūtra*, pp. 154-63, these are name (*ming*, Skt. *nāma*), causal characteristics (*rgyu-mtshan*, Skt. *nimitta*), thoughts (*rnam-rtog*, Skt. *vikalpa*), the genuine pristine cognition (*yang dag-pa'i ye-shes*, Skt. *samyagjñāna*) and the absolute (*de-bzhin-nyid*, Skt. *tathatā*). 216

FIVE, EIGHT, TEN AND ALL THINGS TO BE RENOUNCED *spang-bya lnga-brgyad-bcu-dang thams-cad*

The five to be renounced for laymen (*dge-bsnyen*, Skt. *upāsaka*) are killing, stealing, falsehood, sexual misconduct and alcohol; the eight to be renounced by observers of the purificatory fast (*bsnyen-gnas*, Skt. *upavāsa*) are those five with the addition of afternoon food, singing and the wearing of ornaments; the ten to be renounced by novices (*dge-tshul*, Skt. *śramaṇera*) are the above eight with the addition of precious gems and high thrones or beds; and all things which are to be renounced by monks (*dge-slong*, Skt. *bhikṣu*) are the two hundred and fifty-three vows described in the *Bhikṣuvibhaṅga*, and in the other transmissions of the Vinaya. 226

FIVE ELEMENTAL PROPERTIES *khams lnga*, Skt. *pañcadhātu*

There are five properties compounding external objects through the five elements, namely, the property of space which embraces the sense organs, the property of cohesion which embraces names, the property of solidity which produces the basis of the body, the property of heat which brings objects to maturity and the property of movement which supports all moving worlds. Refer to Longcenpa, *Treasury of the Supreme Vehicle*, p. 75. Alternatively, this expression may be synonymous with the FIVE ELEMENTS. 20, 125

FIVE ELEMENTS *'byung-ba lnga*

See FIVE (GROSS) ELEMENTS

FIVE EMPOWERMENTS OF AWARENESS *rig-pa'i dbang lnga*

The common empowerments of water, crown, vajra, bell and name, the first two of which are conferred in Kriyātantra and the last three in Ubhayatantra. 354

FIVE EMPOWERMENTS (OF THE *SECRET NUCLEUS*) *(gsang-snying-gi) dbang lnga*

These are also known as the five empowerments of ability (*nus-pa'i dbang lnga*), which are included among the FIFTEEN ORDINARY SACRAMENTS OF EMPOWERMENT, namely, the empowerment of the listener (*nyan-pa'i dbang*) which is that of Ratnasambhava, the empowerment of the meditator (*bsgom-pa'i dbang*) which is that of Akṣobhya, the empowerment of the expositor (*'chad-pa'i dbang*) which is that of Amitābha, the empowerment of enlightened activity (*phrin-las-kyi dbang*) which is that of Amoghasiddhi and the empowerment of the king of indestructible reality (*rdo-rje rgyal-po'i dbang*) which is that of the FIVE ENLIGHTENED FAMILIES. Refer to Longcenpa, *Dispelling Darkness in the Ten Directions*, pp. 372-6 (GGFTC, pp. 871-7). 915

FIVE ENLIGHTENED ACTIVITIES *phrin-las lnga*

Pacification of suffering and its causes (*sdug-bsngal rgyu-bcas zhi-ba*), enrichment of excellent provisions (*legs-tshogs rgyas-pa*), overpowering those who require training (*gdul-bya dbang-du mdzad*), wrathfully uprooting those who are difficult to train (*gdul-dka'-rnams drag-pos tshar-bcad-pa*) and spontaneously accomplishing whatever emerges without effort (*rtsol-med-du 'byung-ba lhun-grub*). 283

FIVE ENLIGHTENED ATTRIBUTES *yon-tan lnga*

Pure buddha-fields (*rnam-par dag-pa'i zhing-khams*), immeasurable celestial palaces (*rgya-tshad-bral-ba'i gzhal-yas khang*), radiant and pure rays of light (*gsal-zhing dag-pa'i 'od-zer*), exalted thrones (*khyad-par 'phags-pa'i gdan-khri*) and the rapturous enjoyment of acting as desired (*dgyes-mgur spyod-pa'i longs-spyod*). 283

FIVE ENLIGHTENED/BUDDHA FAMILIES *rigs lnga*, Skt. *pañcakula*

The Tathāgata or Buddha family (*buddha rigs* or *de-bzhin gshegs-pa'i rigs*, Skt. *tathāgatakula*), the Vajra family or family of Indestructible Reality (*rdo-rje'i rigs*, Skt. *vajrakula*), the Jewel family (*rin-chen rigs*, Skt. *ratnakula*), the Lotus family (*padma rigs*, Skt. *padmakula*) and the Action family (*las-kyi rigs*, Skt. *karmakula*). 11, 21, 33, 273, 343, 346, 355, 357, 447, 453, 561, 563, 623, 660, 672, 691, 746-7

FIVE EXCELLENCES *phun-sum tshogs-pa lnga*

These are the FIVE CERTAINTIES. 22, 137, 280, 703

FIVE FACULTIES *dbang-po lnga*, Skt. *pañcendriya*

Faith (*dad-pa*, Skt. *śraddhā*), perseverance (*brtson-'grus*, Skt. *vīrya*), recollection or mindfulness (*dran-pa*, Skt. *smṛti*), contemplation (*ting-nge-'dzin*, Skt. *samādhi*) and discriminative awareness (*shes-rab*, Skt. *prajñā*); Mvt. (977-81). 236

FIVE FAMILIES *rigs-can lnga*, Skt. *pañcagotra*

The five types of beings are: those who aspire to the vehicle of pious attendants (*nyan-thos-kyi theg-pa mngon-par rtogs-pa'i rigs*, Skt. *śrāvakayānābhisamayagotra*); those who aspire to the vehicle of self-centred buddhas (*rang-rgyal theg-pa mngon-par rtogs-pa'i rigs*, Skt. *pratyekabuddhayānabhisamayagotra*); those who aspire to the vehicle of tathāgatas (*de-bzhin gshegs-pa theg-pa mngon-par rtogs-pa'i rigs*, Skt. *tathāgatayānābhisamayagotra*); the dubious family (*ma-nges-pa'i rigs*, Skt. *aniyatagotra*); and the cut-off family (*rigs-med-pa*, Skt. *agotraka*); Mvt. 1260-5. Refer to sGampopa, *The Jewel Ornament of Liberation*, translated by H.V. Guenther, (Ch. 1). 133

FIVE FIELDS OF THE EMANATIONAL BODY OF NATURAL EXPRESSION *rang-bzhin sprul-pa'i sku'i zhing-khams lnga*

These are listed in *Fundamentals*, p. 128.

FIVE GOLDEN DOCTRINES OF THE SHANGPAS *shangs-pa'i gser-chos lnga*

The root is the *Six Doctrines of Niguma* (*rtsa-ba ni-gu chos-drug*); the trunk is the *Amulet-Box Precept of the Great Seal* (*sdong-po phyag-chen ga'u-ma*); the branches are the *Three Ways of Carrying Realisation on the Path* (*yal-kha lam-khyer rnam-gsum*); the flowers are the *Red and White Khecarī* (*me-tog mkha'-spyod dkar-dmar*); and the fruit is *Deathlessness and Non-Deviation* (*'bras-bu 'chi-med chugs-med*). Refer also to first part of the Bibliography under *Five Golden Doctrines of the Shangpa*. 929

FIVE (GROSS) ELEMENTS *'byung-ba (chen-po) lnga*, Skt. *pañca(mahā)bhūta*

Earth, water, fire, air and space. 13, 56, 104, 264, 640

FIVE IMPURITIES *snyigs-ma lnga*, Skt. *pañcakaṣāya*

The impurity of life-span, i.e. beings are short-lived (*tshe'i snyigs-ma*, Skt. *ayuḥkaṣāya*), the impurity of view (*lta-ba'i snyigs-ma*, Skt. *dṛṣṭikaṣāya*), the impurity of conflicting emotions (*nyon-mongs-kyi snyigs-ma*, Skt. *kleśakaṣāya*), the impurity of sentient beings (*sems-can-gyi snyigs-ma*, Skt. *sattvakaṣāya*) and the impurity of our present age (*dus-kyi snyigs-ma*, Skt. *kalpakaṣāya*); Mvt. (2335-40). 212

FIVE INEXPIABLE SINS *mtshams-med-pa lnga*, Skt. *pañcānantarīya*

Matricide (*ma gsod-pa*, Skt. *mātṛghāta*), arhaticide (*dgra-bcom-pa gsod-pa*, Skt. *arhadghāta*), patricide (*pha gsod-pa*, Skt. *pitṛghāta*), creating schism in the community (*dge-'dun-gyi dbyen-byas-ba*, Skt. *saṅghabheda*) and maliciously to draw blood from a tathāgata's body (*de-bzhin gshegs-pa'i sku-la ngan-sems-kyis khrag 'byin-pa*, Skt. *tathāgatasyāntike duṣṭacittarudhirotpādanam*); Mvt. (2323-8). 320, 901, 932

FIVE KINDS OF AWARENESS-HOLDER OF THE GREAT SEAL *phyag-chen rig-'dzin rnam lnga*

The awareness-holder of indestructible reality (*rdo-rje'i rig-'dzin*, Skt. **vajravidyādhara*), the awareness-holder of the doctrinal wheel (*chos-'khor-gyi rig-'dzin*, Skt. **dharmacakravidyādhara*), the awareness-holder of precious gemstones (*rin-chen-gyi rig-'dzin*, Skt. **ratnavidyādhara*), the awareness-holder of the lotus (*padma'i rig-'dzin*, Skt. **padmavidyādhara*) and the awareness-holder of the sword (*ral-gri'i rig-'dzin*, Skt. **khaḍgavidyādhara*). 282

FIVE KINDS OF BUDDHA-MIND *thugs lnga*

These are the FIVE PRISTINE COGNITIONS. 283

FIVE KINDS OF LOGICAL AXIOM *gtan-tshigs lnga*

According to Madhyamaka, these are the vajra fragments (*rdo-rje gzegs-ma*), the negation of production from existence or non-existence (*yod-med skye-'gog*), the refutation of the four limits of production (*mu-bzhi skye-'gog*), the supreme relativity (*rten-'brel chen-po*) and the absence of the singular and the multiple (*gcig-dang du-bral*). Refer also to Longcenpa, *Treasury of Spiritual and Philosophical Systems*, (pp. 118ff). 26

FIVE KINDS OF SEAL *phyag-rgya rigs lnga*, Skt. *pañcamudrā*

The enlightened or buddha-body, speech, mind, attributes and activities which are symbolised respectively by the five seals or hand gestures, namely, the seal of the doctrinal wheel (*chos-kyi 'khor-lo'i phyag-rgya*, Skt. *dharmacakramudrā*), the earth-touching seal (*sa-reg-gi phyag-rgya*, Skt. *bhūmisparśamudrā*), the seal of liberality (*sbyin-pa'i phyag-rgya*, Skt. *dānamudrā*), the seal of concentration (*bsam-gtan-gyi phyag-rgya*, Skt. *dhyānamudrā*) and the seal of fearlessness (*'jigs-med-kyi phyag-rgya*, Skt. *abhayamudrā*). 357

FIVE KINDS OF YELLOW SCROLL *shog-ser rigs lnga*

Those scrolls in which earth treasures or their inventories were concealed are held to be of five kinds, symbolising the FIVE ENLIGHTENED FAMILIES. 746

FIVE KINGLY TREASURE-FINDERS *gter-ston rgyal-po lnga*

These are the following among the emanations of King Trhisong Detsen: Nyang-rel Nyima Özer, Guru Chöwang, Dorje Lingpa, Orgyen Pema Lingpa and Jamyang Khyentse Wangpo. Refer to Jamyang Khyentse, *Mkhyen brtse on the History of the Dharma*, (p. 41). 755, 760, 789, 796, 849

FIVE KNOWLEDGES *shes-bya lnga*

In the context of the prophecy concerning Jamgön Kongtrül (*History*, p. 859), these are either the FIVE DOCTRINES OF THE *SŪTRA OF THE DESCENT TO LAṄKĀ*, the *Five Great Stores* which he compiled, or the FIVE SCIENCES in general. 859

FIVE LINKING KINGS CALLED *TSEN* *tshigs-la btsan lnga*

Gyel Tore Longtsen, Trhi Tsen-nam, Trhi Drapungtsen, Trhi Thokje

Thoktsen and Lha Thotori Nyentsen, in whose reign the "Awesome Secret" was revealed. 508, n. 535

FIVE MĀRAS TO BE RENOUNCED *bdud-lnga spang-ba*

According to Anuyoga, these are the demon which causes insecurity through divisive thoughts; the demon which is laziness with respect to the equanimity of the real; the demon which is capricious with respect to pleasure and social diversions; the demon of the sharp sword of harsh speech; and the demon which causes disturbances in a wrathful, fierce manner. Refer to Jamgön Kongtrül, *shes-bya kun-khyab mdzod*, Vol. 2, (p. 192). 367

FIVE MEATS *sha lnga*, Skt. *pañcamaṃsa*

Those of human flesh, elephant, horse, dog and cow (or, in other traditions, lion and peacock), which are considered taboo by mundane beings. 274

FIVE MINOR FAMILIES *rigs-chung lnga*

According to Yogatantra, there are five minor families corresponding to the five major families, namely, the Tathāgata, Vajra, Jewel, Lotus and Activity. 273

FIVE MINOR SCIENCES *rig-pa'i gnas chung-ba lnga*

Astrology (*rtsis*, Skt. *jyotiḥśāstra*), poetics (*snyan-ngag*, Skt. *kāvya*), prosody (*sdeb-sbyor*, Skt. *chandas*), synonymics (*mngon-brjod*, Skt. *abhidhāna*) and drama (*zlos-gar*, Skt. *nāṭya*). 103-7

FIVE MODES OF BUDDHA-SPEECH *gsung lnga*

Uncreated meaning (*skye-med don-gyi gsung*), intentional symbols (*dgongs-pa brda'i gsung*), expressive words (*brjod-pa tshigs-gi gsung*), the speech of indestructible, indivisible reality (*dbyer-med rdo-rje'i gsung*) and the speech of the blessing of awareness (*rig-pa byin-rlabs-kyi gsung*). 282-3

FIVE MUNDANE SUPERNORMAL COGNITIVE POWERS *'jig-rten-pa'i mngon-shes lnga*

See FIVE SUPERNORMAL COGNITIVE POWERS

FIVE NECTARS *bdud-rtsi lnga*, Skt. *pañcāmṛta*

Semen, blood, urine, excrement and flesh. As it is said in Mipham Rinpoche, *spyi-don 'od-gsal snying-po*, (p. 166): "One does not abandon white elixir [semen; *dkar-rtsi*], red elixir [blood; *dmar-rtsi*], great fragrance and meat [urine and faeces; *dri-sha-chen*], or the pure vessel and contents [flesh; *dag-pa'i snod-bcud*]." Also referred to as the FIVE SACRAMENTAL SUBSTANCES. 274, 348, 361

FIVE (NOBLE) COMPANIONS *bzang-po sde lnga*, Skt. *pañcakabhadravargīya*

Ājñātakauṇḍinya (*kun-shes kauṇḍinya*), Aśvajit (*rta-thul*), Bāṣpa (*rlangs-pa*), Mahānāma (*ming-chen*) and Bhadrika (*bzang-ldan*). 153, 419, 422, 423, 643

FIVE NOBLE ONES *rigs-can lnga*

The god Yaśasvī Varapāla, the nāga king Takṣaka, the yakṣa Ulkāmukha, the ogre Matyaupāyika and the human awareness-holder Vimalakīrti the Licchavi. 454-5, 458, 948

FIVE OUTER AND INNER AWAKENINGS *phyi-nang-gi mngon-byang lnga*

These are the outer and inner aspects of the FIVE AWAKENINGS. According to Āryadeva, *Lamp which Subsumes Conduct*, the outer awakenings are the attainment of buddhahood by way of desirelessness through the bodhisattva vehicle and the inner awakenings are the attainment of the body of coalescence where the body of reality, which is inner radiance, is made manifest by four kinds of desire (through the third empowerment of mantras). 115

FIVE PATHS (OF ANUYOGA) *lam lnga*

These correspond to the FIVE PATHS OF THE CAUSAL VEHICLES. They are the yoga of the spiritual warrior who aspires on the path of provisions (*tshogs-lam 'dun-pa sems-dpa'i rnal-'byor*), the yoga which reveals the great awareness (or family) of the path of connection (*sbyor-lam rigs-chen 'byed-pa'i rnal-'byor*), the yoga which confers the great liberating inspiration of the path of insight (*mthong-lam dbugs-chen 'byin-pa'i rnal-'byor*), the yoga which obtains the great prophetic declaration of the path of meditation (*sgom-lam lung-chen thob-pa'i rnal-'byor*) and the yoga which perfects the great expressive power of the final path (*mthar-lam rtsal-chen rdzogs-pa'i rnal-'byor*). 34, 288, 369

FIVE PATHS (OF THE CAUSAL VEHICLES) *lam lnga*, Skt. *pañcamārga*

The path of provisions (*tshogs-lam*, Skt. *sambhāramārga*), the path of connection (*sbyor-lam*, Skt. *prayogamārga*), the path of insight (*mthong-lam*, Skt. *darśanamārga*), the path of meditation (*bsgom-lam*, Skt. *bhāvanāmārga*) and the path of no-more-learning (*mi-slob-pa'i lam*, Skt. *aśaikṣamārga*). 30, 142, 155, 159, 174, 230, 237, 634

FIVE PATHS (OF MAHĀYOGA) *lam lnga*

Great emptiness (*stong-pa chen-po*), great compassion (*snying-rje chen-po*), the single seal (*phyag-rgya gcig-pa*), the elaborate seal (*phyag-rgya spros-bcas*) and the attainment of the maṇḍala clusters (*tshom-bu tshogs-sgrub*). 278-81

FIVE POISONS *dug lnga*

The FIVE CONFLICTING EMOTIONS. 253, 332, 767, 924

FIVE POWERS *stobs lnga*, Skt. *pañcabala*

Faith (*dad-pa'i stobs*, Skt. *śraddhābala*), perseverance (*brtson-'grus-kyi stobs*, Skt. *vīryabala*), recollection or mindfulness (*dran-pa'i stobs*, Skt. *smṛtibala*), contemplation (*ting-'dzin-gyi stobs*, Skt. *samādhibala*) and discriminative awareness (*shes-rab-kyi stobs*, Skt. *prajñābala*); Mvt. 983-7. These are intensifications of the FIVE FACULTIES. 236

FIVE PRECIOUS SUBSTANCES *rin-chen lnga*

Gold, silver, turquoise, coral and pearl; or gold, silver, copper, iron and lead. 838

FIVE PRISTINE COGNITIONS *ye-shes lnga*, Skt. *pañcajñāna*

The pristine cognition of the expanse of reality (*chos-dbyings-kyi ye-shes*, Skt. *dharmadhātujñāna*), the mirror-like pristine cognition (*me-long-gi ye-shes*, Skt. *ādarśajñāna*), the pristine cognition of discernment (*so-sor-rtog-pa'i ye-shes*, Skt. *pratyavekṣaṇajñāna*), the pristine cognition of sameness (*mnyam-nyid-kyi ye-shes*, Skt. *samatājñāna*) and the pristine cognition of accomplishment (*bya-ba grub-pa'i ye-shes*, Skt. *kṛtyānuṣṭhānajñāna*). Also referred to as the FIVE KINDS OF BUDDHA-MIND. 22-3, 117, 125, 128, 142, 273, 288, 338, 342, 352, 357, 594

FIVE PROPENSITIES OF THE SUBJECT-OBJECT DICHOTOMY *bag-chags lnga*, Skt. **pañcavāsanā*

Those of the mundane body (*lus*), speech (*ngag*), mind (*yid*), social class (*rigs*) and duties (*bya-ba*). 357

FIVE PURE ABODES (OF THE FORM REALMS) *gtsang-gnas lnga*, Skt. *pañcaśuddhanivāsa*

Avṛha (*mi-che-ba*), Atapa (*mi-gdung-ba*), Sudṛśa (*gya-nom snang-ba*), Sudarśana (*shin-tu mthong*) and Akaniṣṭha (*'og-min*). 15, 62

FIVE PURE INCARNATIONS OF THE ROYAL PRINCESS PEMASEL *lha-lcam padma gsal-gyi dag-pa'i skye-ba lnga*

Pemasel, Pema Lendreltsel, Pangangpa Rincen Dorje, Longcenpa and Pema Lingpa. According to the *Scholar's Feast of Doctrinal History*, p. 213, Pema Lendreltsel was the secret name of Pangangpa Rincen Dorje. 796

FIVE SACRAMENTAL SUBSTANCES *dam-rdzas lnga*

These are the FIVE NECTARS. 348

FIVE SCIENCES *rig-pa lnga*, Skt. *pañcavidyā*

These are the FOUR COMMON SCIENCES with the addition of the inner science of Buddhism (*nang-don rig-pa*, Skt. *adhyātmavidyā*). 98, 108, 860

FIVE SENSES *sgo lnga*, Skt. **pañcadvāra*

Seeing, hearing, smelling, tasting and touching. 156, 158, 340, 356

FIVE SENSE ORGANS *dbang-po lnga*, Skt. *pañcendriya*

The FOUR SENSE ORGANS, with the addition of the body (*lus-kyi dbang-po*, Skt. *kāyendriya*). 56, 463

FIVE SENSUAL RAPTURES *'dod-pa'i longs-spyod lnga*

The raptures of seeing, hearing, smelling, tasting and touching. 258

FIVE SENSORY PERCEPTIONS *sgo lnga'i shes-pa*, Skt. *pañcadvārajñāna*

The consciousnesses corresponding to the FIVE SENSES. 55

FIVE SEQUENCES OF DRAMATIC JUNCTURE *mtsham-sbyor-gi yan-lag lnga*, Skt. *pañcasaṃdhyaṅga*

According to Bharata, *Dramatical Treatise*, Ch. 19, pp. 37-67, these are the introduction (*mukha*), progression (*pratimukha*), development (*garbha*), plot-crisis (*vimarśa*) and conclusion (*nirvahaṇa*). 107

FIVE SOPHISTIC SCHOOLS OF THE EXTREMIST MASTERS *rtog-ge sde lnga*

These are the Sāṃkhya (*grangs-can-pa*), Aiśvara (*dbang-phyug-pa*), Vaiṣṇava (*khyab-'jug-pa*), Jaina (*rgyal-ba-pa*) and Nihilists (*chad-pa'i lta-ba*). 64

FIVE SPECIAL CONSIDERATIONS *gzigs-pa lnga*

Those which Śākyamuni made before taking birth in Jambudvīpa, namely, the special considerations of continent, family, father, mother and time. 416

FIVE SUPERNORMAL COGNITIVE POWERS *mngon-shes lnga*, Skt. *pañcābhijñā*

These are clairvoyance (*lha'i mig-gi mngon-shes*, Skt. *divyacakṣurabhijñā*); clairaudience (*lha'i rna-ba'i mngon-shes*, Skt. *divyaśrotrābhijñā*); knowledge of the minds of others (*pha-rol-gyi sems shes-pa'i mngon-shes*, Skt. *paracittābhijñā*); miraculous abilities (*rdzu-'phrul-gyi bya-ba shes-pa'i mngon-shes*, Skt. *ṛddhyabhijñā*); and knowledge of past lives (*sngon-gyi gnas rjes-su dran-pa'i mngon-shes*, Skt. *pūrvanivāsānusmṛtyabhijñā*). 61, 259, 515

FIVE TEACHERS *ston-pa lnga*

These are Vairocana, the king of form; Akṣobhya, the king of consciousness; Ratnasambhava, the king of feelings; Amitābha, the king of perception; and Amoghasiddhi, the king of habitual tendencies. Refer to the *Tantra of the Secret Nucleus*, Ch. 1. Also known as the FIVE CONQUERORS, they preside over the FIVE ENLIGHTENED FAMILIES. 128

FIVE VALLEYS *lung lnga*

Zabulung in Shang is in the centre of Tibet, Jongpalung in Kongpo is in the east, Siptenlung in Mön is in the south, Phakrilung in Gö is in the west and Dronalung in Kyi is in the north. 518

FIVE VEHICLES *theg-pa lnga*

The vehicles of gods and humans (*lha-mi'i theg-pa*), pious attendants (*nyan-thos-kyi theg-pa*), self-centred buddhas (*rang-sangs-rgyas-kyi theg-pa*), bodhisattvas (*byang-chub sems-dpa'i theg-pa*) and of the result (*'bras-bu'i theg-pa*). 17, 81-2, 133

FIVE WHEELS OF INEXHAUSTIBLE ORNAMENT *mi-zad rgyan-gyi 'khor-lo lnga*

Buddha-body, speech, mind, enlightened attributes and activities. 866

FIVE YOGAS (OF ANUYOGA) *rnal-'byor lnga*

The meditative practices associated with the FIVE PATHS OF ANUYOGA. 288, 369

FIVE YOGAS (OF MAHĀYOGA) *rnal-'byor lnga*

These comprise one yoga of the creation stage belonging to the path of provisions (*tshogs-lam*) and four yogas of the perfection stage belonging to the phases of the path of connection (*sbyor-lam*). See Mipham Rinpoche, *spyi-don 'od-gsal snying-po*, pp. 54-5. The four correspond to the experiences of warmth (*drod*), climax (*rtse-mo*), receptivity (*bzod-pa*) and supreme phenomenon (*chos-mchog*), which characterise the path of connection. 363

SIX

SIX ACTIVITIES *bya-ba drug*

According to Kriyātantra, these are the time for entering (*'jug-pa'i dus*), food (*zas*), attire (*gos*), ritual cleansing (*gtsang-sbra*), visualisation supports (*dmigs-rten*) and mantras for recitation (*bzlas-brjod sngags*). 351

SIX ADORNMENTS OF JAMBUDVĪPA *'dzam-bu-gling mdzes-pa'i rgyan drug*

Nāgārjuna, Asaṅga, Dignāga, Āryadeva, Vasubandhu and Dharmakīrti. 440-1

SIX AGGREGATES OF CONSCIOUSNESS *rnam-shes tshogs drug*, Skt. *ṣaḍvijñānakāya*

The consciousness of the eye (*mig-gi rnam-shes*, Skt. *cakṣurvijñāna*), the consciousness of the ear (*rna-ba'i rnam-shes*, Skt. *śrotravijñāna*), the consciousness of the nose (*sna'i rnam-shes*, Skt. *ghrāṇavijñāna*), the consciousness of the tongue (*lce'i rnam-shes*, Skt. *jihvāvijñāna*), the consciousness of the body (*lus-kyi rnam-shes*, Skt. *kāyavijñāna*) and the consciousness of the intellect (*yid-kyi rnam-shes*, Skt. *manovijñāna*). 162, 166.

SIX CATEGORIES *tshig-don drug*, Skt. *ṣaṭpadārtha*

According to the Vaiśeṣika, these are substance (*rdzas*, Skt. *dravya*), attribute (*yon-tan*, Skt. *guṇa*), action (*las*, Skt. *karman*), universal (*spyi*, Skt. *sāmānya*), particular (*bye-brag*, Skt. *viśeṣa*) and inherence (*'du-ba*, Skt. *samavāya*). See also Longcenpa, *Wish-fulfilling Treasury*, (pp. 400-27). 65

SIX CENTRES FORMING THE UPPER DOOR OF THE BODY *rang-lus steng-sgo 'khor-lo drug*

These energy points situated within the meditator's own body are: the crown centre (*gtsug-tor nam-mkha'i 'khor-lo*), forehead centre (*spyi-bo bde-chen-gi 'khor-lo*), throat centre (*mgrin-pa longs-spyod-kyi 'khor-lo*), heart centre (*snying-ka chos-kyi 'khor-lo*), navel centre (*lte-ba sprul-pa'i 'khor-lo*) and secret centre (*gsang-chen bde-skyong-gi 'khor-lo*). 368

SIX CLASSES OF LIVING BEINGS/CREATURES *'gro-ba rigs drug*, Skt. *ṣaḍgati*

Gods (*lha*, Skt. *deva*), antigods (*lha-ma-yin*, Skt. *asura*), human beings (*mi*, Skt. *manuṣya*), tormented spirits (*yi-dvags*, Skt. *preta*), animals (*dud-'gro*, Skt. *tiryak*) and denizens of hell (*dmyal-ba*, Skt. *naraka*). 14-15, 21, 99, 166, 250, 312, 341, 357

SIX CLASSES OF TANTRA *rgyud-sde drug*

Kriyā, Caryā or Ubhaya, Yoga, Mahāyoga, Anuyoga and Atiyoga. 96

SIX CONFLICTING EMOTIONS *nyon-mongs-pa drug*, Skt. *ṣaṭkleśa*

Delusion (*gti-mug*, Skt. *moha*), desire (*'dod-chags*, Skt. *rāga*), hatred (*zhe-sdang*, Skt. *dveṣa*), pride (*nga-rgyal*, Skt. *abhimāna*), envy (*phrag-dog*, Skt. *īrṣyā*) and the ignorance (Skt. *avidyā*) on which basis there is subjective grasping of bewildering thoughts (*ma-rig-pa zhes-pa-ni gzhi 'khrul-rtog-gi cha 'dzin-pa*). 12, 55

SIX DOCTRINES *chos drug*, Skt. *ṣaḍdharma*

Inner heat (*gtum-mo*), the apparitional body (*sgyu-lus*), dream (*rmi-lam*), inner radiance (*'od-gsal*), transference of consciousness (*'pho-ba*) and the intermediate state (*bar-do*). 547, 549, 569, 577-8, 674, 689, 930

SIX EARTHLY KINGS CALLED *LEK* *sa-yi legs drug*

Esho Lek, Desho Lek, Thisho Lek, Gongru Lek, Drongzher Lek and Isho Lek. 507-8, n. 535

SIX EMPOWERMENTS (OF YOGATANTRA) *dbang drug*

These are the FIVE EMPOWERMENTS OF AWARENESS with the addition of the irreversible empowerment of the vase (*phyir mi-ldog-pa bum-pa'i dbang*), also known as the empowerment of the master of indestructible reality (*rdo-rje slob-dpon-gyi dbang*). 354

SIX ENLIGHTENED FAMILIES (OF FATHER TANTRA) *(pha-rgyud) rigs drug*

Akṣobhya (*mi-bskyod-pa*), Vairocana (*rnam-snang*), Ratnasambhava (*rin-'byung*), Amitābha (*'od-dpag-med*), Amoghasiddhi (*don-grub*) and Vajradhara (*rdo-rje 'chang*). 274

SIX ENLIGHTENED FAMILIES (OF KRIYĀTANTRA) *rigs drug*, Skt. *ṣaṭkula*

The Tathāgata (*de-bzhin gshegs-pa'i rigs*, Skt. *tathāgatakula*), Lotus (*padma'i rigs*, Skt. *padmakula*), Indestructible Reality (*rdo-rje'i rigs*, Skt. *vajrakula*), Wealth (*nor-bu'i rigs*, Skt. *maṇikula*), Enrichment (*rgyas-pa'i rigs*, Skt. *pauṣṭikakula*) and Mundane (*'jig-rten-gyi rigs*, Skt. *laukikakula*) families. 271

SIX ENLIGHTENED FAMILIES (OF MOTHER TANTRA) *(ma-rgyud) rigs drug*

Vajrasattva (*rdo-rje sems-dpa'*), Vairocana (*rnam-snang*), Vajrāditya (*rdo-rje nyi-ma*), Padmanarteśvara (*padma gar-dbang*), Aśvottama (*rta-mchog*) and Heruka (*he-ru-ka*). 274

SIX ESSENTIALS *gnad drug*

According to All-Surpassing Realisation, these are the THREE SUPPORTIVE ESSENTIALS OF THE BODY and the THREE ESSENTIALS WHICH GUIDE THE EYES TOWARDS THE EXPANSE. 371

SIX GREAT COUNTRIES WHERE THE TRUE DOCTRINE WAS PROPAGATED *dam-pa'i chos dar-ba'i yul-chen-po drug*

India, China, Tibet, Khotan, Shambhala and Kailash. 507

SIX LAMPS *sgron-ma drug*

Certain teaching cycles of All-Surpassing Realisation emphasise that there are six lamps rather than the basic FOUR LAMPS enumerated in *Fundamentals*, pp. 338-9. They are described as follows: the lamp of naturally present discriminative awareness is the basis of the arising (of apparitional reality) (*shes-rab rang-byung-gi sgron-mas 'char-ba'i gzhi byas-so*); the lamp of the far-sighted watery eyes senses that arising apparition (*rgyang-zhags chu'i sgron-mas 'char-byed-kyi sgo-byas-so*); the lamp of the pure expanse of awareness is the ornament of that arising apparition (*rig-pa dbyings-kyi sgron-mas shar-ba'i rgyan byas-so*); the lamp of emptiness which is the seminal point is the characteristic of that arising apparition (*thig-le stong-pa'i sgron-mas shar-ba'i mtshan-nyid byas-so*); the lamp of the flesh, i.e. the heart (*citta sha'i sgron-ma*); and the lamp of the soft white channels which connect the heart to the eyes (*dkar-'jam rtsa'i sgron-ma*). As explained by Khetsun Zangpo Rinpoche, the last two lamps are inherently related to the lamp of the far-sighted watery eyes. 907

SIX-LIMBED YOGA (OF THE KĀLACAKRA) *sbyor drug*, Skt. *ṣaḍaṅgayoga*

Composure (*sor-sdud*), concentration (*bsam-gtan*), breath-control (*srog-'dzin*), apprehension of the complete deity (*sku ril-bur 'dzin-pa*), subsequent recollection of this (*rjes-su dran-pa*) and contemplation (*ting-nge-'dzin*). 301, 546, 577-8, 674, 853

SIX LIMITS *mtha' drug*

These are the parameters for the appraisal of the scriptures or texts of secret mantra. They comprise those which employ the language of (hidden) intention (*dgongs-pa'i skad*), those which do not (*de-bzhin-min*), those which are literal (*sgra ji-bzhin-pa*), those which are not (*de-bzhin-min*), those of provisional meaning (*drang-ba'i don*, Skt. *neyārtha*) and those of definitive meaning (*nges-don*, Skt. *nītārtha*). 35, 290-2

SIX LINEAGES *brgyud drug/drug-ldan brgyud*

The intentional lineage of the conquerors (*rgyal-ba'i dgongs-pa'i brgyud-pa*), the symbolic lineage of awareness-holders (*rig-'dzin brda'i brgyud-pa*), the aural lineage of mundane individuals (*gang-zag-snyan-khung-gi brgyud-pa*), the lineage empowered by enlightened aspiration (*smon-lam dbang-bskur-ba'i brgyud-pa*), the lineage of prophetically declared spiritual succession (*bka'-babs lung-bstan-gyi brgyud-pa*) and the lineage of the ḍākinīs' seal of entrustment (*mkha'-'gro gtad-rgya'i brgyud-pa*). 404, 745, 862

SIX MODES OF THE DEITY *lha drug*

According to Kriyātantra, these are the deity of emptiness (*stong-pa'i lha*), the deity of seed-syllables (*yi-ge'i lha*), the deity of sound (*sgra'i lha*), the deity of form (*gzugs-kyi lha*), the deity of seals (*phyag-rgya'i lha*) and the deity of symbols (*mtshan-ma'i lha*). 270, 350-1

SIX PAṆḌITAS OF THE GATES *mkhas-pa sgo drug*, Skt. *ṣaḍdvārapaṇḍita*

The six paṇḍitas installed at Nālandā during the reign of King Canaka of the Pāla dynasty were: Ratnākaraśānti at the eastern gate; Prajñākaramati at the southern gate (according to Tāranātha, *History of Buddhism in India*) or the western gate (according to *Blue Annals*); Vagīśvarakīrti at the western gate (according to Tāranātha) or the southern gate (according to *Blue Annals*); Nāropā at the northern gate (succeeded by Bodhibhadra); while Ratnavajra and Jñānaśrīmitra occupied the centre of the teaching maṇḍala at Nālandā. 442

SIX PURE ESSENCES *dvangs-ma drug*

Those of the FIVE ELEMENTS and the mind in their refined states. Their relationship to the buddha-body, speech and mind is explained under the THREE IMPERISHABLE INDESTRUCTIBLE REALITIES. 264

SIX REALMS OF EXISTENCE *'jig-rten-gyi khams drug*

The realms of the SIX CLASSES OF LIVING BEINGS. 585

SIX SAGES EMBODYING AWARENESS *rig-pa'i skyes-bu thub-pa drug*

Śakra among the gods, Vemacitra among the antigods, Śākyamuni among humans, Jvālamukha among tormented spirits, Siṃha among animals and Yama among the hells. 129-30, 414

SIX SENSE ORGANS *dbang-po drug*, Skt. *ṣaḍindriya*

The FIVE SENSE ORGANS with the addition of the sense organ of the intellect (*yid-kyi dbang-po*, Skt. *mana' indriya*). 55-6

SIX SPECIES OF KĀMA DIVINITIES *'dod-lha rigs-drug*

These are the realms of the Four Great Kings (*rgyal-chen bzhi'i ris*, Skt. *Caturmahārājakāyika*), the Heaven of Thirty-three Gods (*sum-cu rtsa-gsum-pa*, Skt. *Trayatriṃśa*), the Strifeless (*'thab-bral*, Skt. *Yāma*), the Joyful (*dga'-ldan*, Skt. *Tuṣita*), the Delighting in Emanation (*'phrul-dga'*, Skt. *Nirmāṇarati*) and the Mastery over Transformations (*gzhan-'phrul dbang-byed*, Skt. *Paranirmitavaśavartin*). 14, 60

SIX SUPERIORITIES OF THE ANCIENT TRANSLATIONS *snga-'gyur che-ba drug*

According to Rongzompa (cited in *History*, pp. 889-90), the ancient translations are superior through their benefactors (the THREE ANCESTRAL RELIGIOUS KINGS), their locations (Samye, etc.), their translators (Vairocana, etc.), their scholars (Padmasambhava, etc.), their large offerings and their very doctrines. 375

SIX SUPERNORMAL COGNITIVE POWERS *mngon-shes drug*, Skt. *ṣaḍabhijñā*
These are the FIVE SUPERNORMAL COGNITIVE POWERS with the addition of the supernormal power over the cessation of corruption (*zag-pa zad-pa'i mngon-shes*, Skt. *āsravakṣayābhijñā*). 21, 132, 415

SIX-SYLLABLE MANTRA *yi-ge drug-pa*, Skt. *ṣaḍakṣara*
The mantra of Avalokiteśvara, OṂ MA ṆI PAD ME HŪṂ, each syllable of which purifies one of the SIX CLASSES OF LIVING BEINGS. 508, 545, 569, 841

SIX TRANSCENDENTAL PERFECTIONS *pha-rol-tu phyin-pa drug*, Skt. *ṣaṭpāramitā*
Liberality (*sbyin-pa*, Skt. *dāna*), moral discipline (*tshul-khrims*, Skt. *śīla*), patience (*bzod-pa*, Skt. *kṣānti*), perseverance (*brtson-'grus*, Skt. *vīrya*), concentration (*bsam-gtan*, Skt. *dhyāna*) and discriminative awareness (*shes-rab*, Skt. *prajñā*). 36, 235-6, 255, 260, 300, 302, 306, 308, 320, 656

SIX VEHICLES OF DEFINITIVE ATTAINMENT *nges-pa thob-pa theg-pa drug*
The vehicles of the bodhisattvas, Kriyātantra, Ubhayatantra, Yogatantra, Mahāyoga and Anuyoga. 295

SIX WORLDS *'jig-rten drug*
Those of the four directions, zenith and nadir. 414

SEVEN

SEVEN ASPECTS OF SPIRITUAL WEALTH (OF THE ULTIMATE TRUTH) *don-dam bden-pa dkor bdun*
These are the ultimate truth of the expanse (*dbyings don-dam*), the ultimate truth of pristine cognition (*ye-shes don-dam*) and the fivefold ultimate truth of the result, i.e. the great mystery of the buddha-body, speech, mind, attributes and activities (*'bras-bu don-dam*). 248-9

SEVEN ASPECTS OF SUBLIME WEALTH *'phags-pa'i nor bdun*
Faith (*dad-pa*), moral discipline (*tshul-khrims*), generosity (*gtong-ba*), study (*thos-pa*), conscience (*ngo-tsha shes-pa*), shame (*khrel-yod-pa*) and discriminative awareness (*shes-rab*). 568, 575

SEVEN BRANCHES OF ENLIGHTENMENT *byang-chub yan-lag bdun*, Skt. *saptabodhyaṅga*
These are recollection or mindfulness (*dran-pa yang-dag byang-chub-kyi yan-lag*, Skt. *smṛtisambodhyaṅga*), doctrinal analysis (*chos rab-tu rnam-par 'byed-pa*, Skt. *dharmapravicaya*), perseverance (*brtson-'grus*, Skt. *vīrya*), delight (*dga'-ba*, Skt. *prīti*), mental and physical refinement (*shin-tu sbyangs-pa*, Skt. *praśrabdhi*), contemplation (*ting-'dzin*, Skt. *samādhi*) and equanimity (*btang-snyoms*, Skt. *upekṣā*); Mvt. (988-95). 236

SEVEN BRANCHES OF UNION *kha-sbyor bdun*, Skt. *saptasampuṭa*
Non-substantiality (*rang-bzhin med*), union with awareness in the form of

the consort (*rig-ma*), supreme bliss (*bde-chen*), the body of perfect rapture (*longs-spyod rdzogs-pa'i sku*), no cessation of the experience (*'gog-pa med*), total compassion (*snying-rje yongs*) and no interruption of the experience (*rgyun mi-chad*). Refer to Khyentse Rinpoche's definition cited in Nālandā Translation Committee, *The Rain of Wisdom*, (pp. 341-2). 266

SEVEN CATEGORIES OF THE MENTAL CLASS *sems-phyogs bdun*

These are enumerated in *Fundamentals*, (pp. 323-5). 37

SEVEN CYCLES OF THE GREAT PERFECTION WHICH ARE NATURALLY PRESENT *rdzogs-chen skor-bdun rang-chas*

According to Khetsun Zangpo Rinpoche, these are probably to be identified with the seven precious cycles (*nor-bu skor-bdun*), namely, inner heat (*gtum-mo*), dream yoga (*rmi-lam*), illusory body (*sgyu-lus*), transference of consciousness (*'pho-ba*), intermediate state (*bar-do*), inner radiance (*'od-gsal*) and light rays (*'od-zer*). Alternatively the expression may refer to the SEVEN CATEGORIES OF THE MENTAL CLASS. 545

SEVEN DISTINCTIONS OF ENLIGHTENED ATTRIBUTES *yon-tan-gyi khyad-par bdun*

According to the *Buddhasamāyoga*, awareness-holders abide in contemplation (*ting-nge-'dzin-la gnas-pa*), possess the five supernormal cognitive powers (*mngon-shes lnga-dang ldan-pa*), act on behalf of beings in various fields (*zhing sna-tshogs-su 'gro-ba'i don spyod-pa*), lack desire and envy (*'dod-cing 'chums-pa med-pa*), enjoy limitless desires as supreme bliss (*'dod-pa mtha'-yas-pa-la bde-ba chen-por longs-spyod-pa*), transcend the span of life (*tshe-tshad-las brgal-ba*) and abide in the mental body (*yid-kyi lus-su gnas-pa*). 259

SEVEN DIVINE DOCTRINES (OF ATIŚA) *lha-chos bdun*

The THREE PIṬAKA and the teaching cycles connected with Śākyamuni, Avalokiteśvara, Tārā and Acala. 853

SEVENFOLD SERVICE *yan-lag bdun-pa*, Skt. *saptāṅga*

Prostration, offering, confession and repentance, sympathetic joy, prayer that the wheel of the doctrine be turned, prayer that buddhas and bodhisattvas remain active in the world, and dedication of merit. 865

SEVEN GENERATIONS OF BUDDHAS *sangs-rgyas rabs bdun*

Vipaśyin (*rnam-gzigs*), Śikhin (*gtsug-tor-can*), Viśvabhuk (*kun-skyobs*), Krakucchanda (*log-pa dang-sel*), Kakutsunda (*'khor-ba 'jig*), Kanakamuni (*gser-thub*) and Kāśyapa (*'od-srung*); Mvt. (87-93). 136, 591, 624

SEVEN HARMONIOUS TONES *glu-dbyangs-kyi nges-pa bdun*, Skt. *saptasvara*

Corresponding to the musical scale, these are the crane-like middle tone (*bar-ma-pa*, Skt. *madhyama*), the ox-like sage tone (*drang-srong-ba*, Skt. *ṛṣabha*), the goat-like third tone (*sa-'dzin-pa*, Skt. *gandhāra*), the peacock-like sixth tone (*drug-ldan*, Skt. *ṣadja*), the cuckoo-like fifth tone (*lnga-ba*, Skt. *pañcama*), the horse-like clear tone (*blo-gsal*, Skt. *dhaivata*) and the elephantine base tone (*'khor-nyan*, Skt. *niṣāda*); Mvt. (5027-34). 98, 107

SEVEN HEAVENLY KINGS CALLED *TRHI gnam-gyi khri bdun*

Nyatrhi Tsenpo, Mutrhi Tsenpo, Dingtrhi Tsenpo, Sotrhi Tsenpo, Mertrhi Tsenpo, Daktrhi Tsenpo and Siptrhi Tsenpo. All are said to have been immortal beings who ascended to the heavens on sky-cords having fulfilled the purpose of their reigns. 507, n. 535

SEVEN KINDS OF AWARENESS-HOLDER *rig-'dzin rnam-pa bdun*

Those who possess the SEVEN DISTINCTIONS OF ENLIGHTENED ATTRIBUTES. 31, 259-60

SEVEN MEN WHO WERE TESTED *sad-mi mi bdun*

These were the first monks of Tibet: Ba Trhizi (*sba khri-gzigs*), ordained as Śrīghoṣa (*dpal-dbyangs*); Ba Selnang (*sba gsal-snang*), ordained as Jñānendra (*ye-shes dbang-po*); Ba Trhizher (*sba khri-bzher/-gzhir*); Pagor (*spa-gor*) Vairocana, or Vairocanarakṣita; Ma Rincen-chok (*rma rin-chen-mchog*); Gyelwa Choyang (*rgyal-ba mchog-dbyangs*); and Khön Lüiwangpo Sungwa (*'khon klu'i dbang-po srung-ba*), or Nāgendrarakṣita. Alternate listings often include Tsang Lekdrup (*rtsang legs-grub*) or Lasum Gyelwei Cangcup (*la-sum rgyal-ba'i byang-chub*). 511, 515, 575, 950

SEVEN MENMO SISTERS *sman-mo mched bdun*

The precise enumeration is unidentified. They were subdued by Padmasambhava at Silma in Tsang. Refer to R. de Nebesky-Wojkowitz, *Oracles and Demons of Tibet*, (pp. 198-202). 581

SEVEN PARTICULAR ATTRIBUTES OF NATURAL EXPRESSION (OF THE BODY OF PERFECT RAPTURE) *rang-bzhin bdun*

The natural expression which is fully mature in the nature of just what is (*de-bzhin-nyid-du nar-son-pa'i rang-bzhin*); the natural expression which is the spontaneous presence of enlightened attributes without their being sought (*yon-tan ma-btsal-bar lhun-gyis grub-pa'i rang-bzhin*); the natural expression which is pristine cognition without extremes or centre (*ye-shes mtha'-dbus dang bral-ba'i rang-bzhin*); the natural expression whose true essence cannot be pointed out (*rang-gi ngo-bo bstan-du med-pa'i rang-bzhin*); the natural expression which remains free from the range of objective qualification, even having disclosed sameness (*mnyam-nyid mngon-du mdzad-kyang spyod-yul dang bral-ba'i rang-bzhin*); the natural expression which is liberated from concepts of one and many (*gcig-dang du-ma-las grol-ba'i rang-bzhin*); and the natural expression which is without conjunction and disjunction throughout the three times (*dus-gsum 'du-bral med-pa'i rang-bzhin*). 20, 124, 251

SEVEN PATRIARCHS *bstan-pa'i gtad-rabs bdun*

Mahākāśyapa, Ānanda, Śāṇavāsika, Upagupta, Dhītika, Kṛṣṇa and Sudarśana. Their life stories are given in *History*, pp. 432-9.

SEVEN POWERS OF INTENTION *dgongs-pa'i rtsal bdun*

These powers of intention associated with King Ja are directed towards: excellent gold plates as a writing material (*gser-gyi byang-bu 'bri gzhi phun-sum-tshogs-pa-la dgongs-pa*), excellent molten beryl as the substance in which one writes (*bai-ḍūrya'i zhun-ma rgyu phun-sum-tshogs-pa-la dgongs-pa*), excellent treasure chests of various precious gems (*rin-chen sna-tshogs-kyi sgrom-bu snod-la dgongs-pa*), celestial abodes which cannot be destroyed by the four elements (*nam-mkha' 'byung-bzhis mi-'jig-pa gnas-la dgongs-pa*), the special treasure guardians who possess the eye of pristine cognition (*ye-shes spyan-*

ldan rnams gter-srung khyad-par-can-la dgongs-pa), the keenest faculties possessed by King Ja (*chos-bdag rgyal-po dza dbang-po yang-rab-la dgongs-pa*) and towards the spread and propagation of (the doctrine by) ordinary and sublime beings, bodhisattvas and other such lineage-holders (*skye-'phags byang-sems sogs brgyud-'dzin dar-rgyas-la dgongs-pa*). 455

SEVEN PRECIOUS STONES *rin-po-che sna bdun*

Gold, silver, turquoise, coral, pearl, emerald, and sapphire. 435

SEVEN PRECIOUS THINGS *rin-chen bdun*, Skt. *saptaratna*

The wheel, gem, queen, minister, elephant, general and horse. 912

SEVEN SISTERS OF DORJE YUDRÖNMA *rdo-rje gYu-sgron-ma dkar-mo mched bdun*

Unidentified. Refer to Nebesky-Wojkowitz, *Oracles and Demons of Tibet*, pp. 190-2, where Dorje Yudrönma is described as an important member of the TWELVE GODDESSES OF THE EARTH. 584

SEVEN SUCCESSIONS OF THE TRANSMITTED PRECEPTS *bka'-babs bdun*

Those which descended to Chogyur Lingpa and Jamyang Khyentse Wangpo, namely, the transmitted precepts (*bka'*), earth treasures (*sa-gter*), reconcealed treasures (*yang-gter*), intentional treasures (*dgongs-gter*), recollected treasures (*rjes-su dran-pa'i gter*), pure visions (*dag-snang*) and aural transmissions (*snyan-brgyud*). 751-2, 844-7, 854, 855-8

SEVEN TOPICS OF INDESTRUCTIBLE REALITY *rdo-rje'i gnas bdun*, Skt. *sapta vajrapadāni*

According to the *Supreme Continuum of the Greater Vehicle*, these are the buddha (*sangs-rgyas*), doctrine (*chos*, Skt. *dharma*), community (*tshogs*, Skt. *gaṇa*, i.e. *saṃgha*) and seed of enlightenment (*khams*, Skt. *dhātu*) which form the subject-matter of the first chapter, pertaining to the nucleus of the tathāgata (*Tathāgatādhikāra*); enlightenment (*byang-chub*, Skt. *bodhi*) which is the topic of the second (*Bodhyadhikāra*); the enlightened attributes (*yon-tan*, Skt. *guṇa*) which are the topic of the third (*Guṇādhikāra*); and the enlightened activities (*phrin-las*, Skt. *kṛtyakriyā*) which are the topic of the fourth (*Tathāgatakṛtyakriyādhikāra*). 95

SEVEN TRIAL MONKS *sad-mi mi bdun*

See SEVEN MEN WHO WERE TESTED

SEVEN WONDERFUL EPISODES (IN THE LIFE OF ŚĀNTIDEVA) *ngo-mtshar-gyi gtam bdun*

According to Tāranātha, *History of Buddhism in India*, p. 220, these refer to his vision of the meditational deity, his bringing of prosperity to Nālandā, his silencing others in debate and converting heretics, beggars, the king, and extremists. 441

EIGHT

EIGHT AGGREGATES OF CONSCIOUSNESS *rnam-shes tshogs brgyad*, Skt. *aṣṭa-vijñānakāya*

The SIX AGGREGATES OF CONSCIOUSNESS with the addition of the consciousness of the ground-of-all (*kun-gzhi'i rnam-shes*, Skt. *ālayavijñāna*) and the consciousness of the intellect endowed with conflicting emotions (*nyon-mongs-pa-can-gyi yid-kyi rnam-shes*, Skt. *kliṣṭamanovijñāna*) from which the other six arise. 162, 202, 216, 221, 297, 309, 333-4, 341

EIGHT ARISINGS OF ENLIGHTENED ACTIVITY *phrin-las shar-ba brgyad*

According to Locen Dharmaśrī, *gsang-bdag zhal-lung*, p. 109, these concern the peaceful and wrathful deities (*zhi-khro gnyis*), the assembled offerings of mother and offspring (*tshogs ma-bu gnyis*), empowerment and its integration (*dbang bsre-ba gnyis*), cremation and burnt offerings (*ro-sreg-dang sbyin-sreg gnyis*). 673

EIGHT AWARENESS-HOLDERS *rig-'dzin brgyad*

See EIGHT (GREAT) AWARENESS-HOLDERS

EIGHT CATEGORIES OF DIALECTICAL SOPHISTRY *rtog-ge'i tshig-don brgyad*

Direct perception (*mngon-sum*), inference (*rjes-dpag*), proof (*sgrub-ngag*) and refutation (*thal-'gyur*), each of which is either valid (*yang-dag*) or invalid (*ltar-snang*), making eight categories. 101

EIGHT CHARNEL GROUNDS *dur-khrod brgyad*

The Most Fierce (*gtum-drag*), Dense Thicket (*tshang-tshing 'khrigs-pa*), Dense Blaze (*'bar 'khrigs-pa*), Endowed with Skeletons (*keng-rus-can*), Cool Forest, (*bsil-bu tshal*, Skt. *Śītavana*), Black Darkness (*mun-pa nag-po*), Resonant with "Kilikili" (*ki-li ki-lir sgra-sgrog-pa*) and Wild Cries of "Ha-ha" (*ha-ha rgod-pa*). 626, 791

EIGHT CLASSES OF MEANS FOR ATTAINMENT *sgrub-sde brgyad*

According to Mahāyoga, these are the classes of Yamāntaka, Hayagrīva, Śrīheruka, Vajrāmṛta, Vajrakīla, Mātaraḥ, Mundane Praise and Malign Mantra. 283, 361-2, 475-83, 521, 534, 805, 828

EIGHT CLOSEST SONS *nye-sras brgyad*

The bodhisattvas Mañjuśrī, Vajrapāṇi, Avalokiteśvara, Kṣitigarbha, Sarvanivāraṇaviṣkambhin, Ākāśagarbha, Maitreya and Samantabhadra. 624, 864

EIGHT CONVEYANCES *shing-rta brgyad*

See EIGHT (GREAT) CONVEYANCES, OR LINEAGES OF ATTAINMENT

EIGHT COMMON ACCOMPLISHMENTS *thun-mong-gi dngos-grub brgyad*, Skt. *aṣṭasādhāraṇasiddhi*

Medicinal pills (*ril-bu*), eye-salve (*mig-sman*), swift feet (*rkang-mgyogs*), penetration of matter (*sa-'og*), accomplishment of the enchanted sword (*ral-gri'i dngos-grub*), sky-faring (*mkha'-la phur*), invisibility (*mi-snang-ba*) and immortality along with the suppression of disease (*shi-ba med-dang nad-'joms*). Also referred to as the EIGHT GREAT ACTIVITIES. 247, 480

EIGHT DIMENSIONS OF RADIANCE AND CONSTANCY (OF THE SEED-SYLLABLES) (*yig-'bru'i*) *gsal-brtan-gyi tshad brgyad*

The four of radiance are luminosity (*gsal-le*), pristine purity (*sing-nge*), intensity (*lhag-ge*) and brilliance (*lhang-nge-ba*). The four of constancy are immovability (*mi-gYo*), unchangeability (*mi-'gyur*), manifest unchangeability (*mngon-*

par mi-'gyur) and ability to transform into anything (*cir-yang bsgyur-du btub-pa*). Refer to Jamgön Kongtrül, *lam-rim ye-shes snying-po'i 'grel-pa*, (p. 90a). 279

EIGHT DIVISIONS (OF THE CONDUCT OF SELF-RESTRAINT ON THE PATH OF LIBERATION) (*grol-lam bag-yod-kyi spyod-pa*) *brgyad*

According to Mahāyoga, these are the conduct of faithful perseverance (*dad-brtson-gyi spyod-pa*), the conduct which is in harmony with discriminative awareness (*shes-rab-dang mthun-pa'i spyod-pa*), the conduct which is in harmony with compassion (*snying-rje-dang mthun-pa'i spyod-pa*), the conduct which is one-sided (*phyogs-gcig-pa'i spyod-pa*), the conduct which is elaborate (*spros-bcas-kyi spyod-pa*), the conduct which concerns the provisions (*tshogs-kyi spyod-pa*), the conduct which concerns miraculous abilities (*rdzu-'phrul-gyi spyod-pa*) and the conduct which is immediate (*cig-car-ba'i spyod-pa*). 281

EIGHT EMANATIONS (OF THE GURU) (*gu-ru*) *mtshan brgyad*

These are Padmasambhava's eight manifestations: Padmākara, Padmasambhava, Loden Chokse, Śākya Senge, Senge Dradrok, Pema Gyelpo, Dorje Trolö and Nyima Özer. Refer also to the Index of Personal Names under *Guru Rinpoche*. Pl. 5; 520, 858, 893

EIGHT EXTREMES *mtha' brgyad*, Skt. **aṣṭānta*

Creation (*skye-ba*), cessation (*'gog-pa*), nihilism (*chad-pa*), eternalism (*rtag-pa*), coming (*'ong-ba*), going (*'gro-ba*), diversity (*tha-dad*) and identity (*don-gcig*). 233

EIGHT FEARS *'jigs-pa brgyad*

See EIGHT (GREAT) FEARS

EIGHTFOLD GROUP OF THE MÖNPA, MOUNTED ON TIGERS *stag-zhon mon-pa sde brgyad*

These are the eight groups of protectors in the retinue of the Tiger-riding Mahākāla (*mgon-po stag-zhon*). The precise enumeration has not been identified. Often associated with the southern regions around Bhutan which are traditionally known as Mön. 628

EIGHTFOLD GROUPS OF SPIRITS *sde brgyad*

According to Nupcen Sangye Yeshe, *sde-brgyad gser-skyems*, there are six series of eightfold groups of spirits as follows:

(1) the outer eightfold group (*phyi-yi sde-brgyad*) consisting of *lha-yi dbang-po brgya-byin*, *lha-min dbang-po thags-bzang-ris*, *mi'am-ci ljon-rta-mgo-can*, *gnod-sbyin gang-ba bzang-po*, *mkha'-lding gser-mig 'khyil-ba*, *srin-po lang-ka mgrin-bcu*, *chos-skyong Mahākāla* and *dri-za zur-phud lnga-pa*;

(2) the inner eightfold group (*nang-gi sde-brgyad*) consisting of *yab-gcig bdud-rje nag-po*, *btsan-rgyal yam-shud dmar-po*, *yul-lha phya-sangs klu-sras*, *srog-bdag rgyal-po snying-'byin*, *chos-skyong gnod-sbyin dmar-po*, *lha-mo 'jigs-pa'i glog-'byin*, *dge-bsnyen rdo-rje legs-pa* and *dkar-mo nyi-zla thos-phreng*;

(3) the secret eightfold group (*gsang-ba'i sde-brgyad*) consisting of *bdud-po kha-thun rakṣa*, *gshin-rje gshed-po dmar-nag*, *klu-bdud Nāgarāja*, *gnod-sbyin shan-pa gri-thogs*, *ma-mo srid-pa khroms-'debs*, *btsan-po yam-shud srog-len*, *bdud-po re-te 'go-yag* and *srog-bdag dung-gi thor-tshugs*;

(4) the supreme eightfold group (*mchog-gi sde-brgyad*) consisting of *gza'-mchog rgyal-po Rāhula, dkar-mchog khram-shing kha-thor, bdud-mchog Manurakṣa, btsan-mchog gri-btsan 'thum-po, ma-mchog lce-spyang mdung-'dzin, klu-mchog klu-rgyal dung-skyong, mgon-mchog nag-po lte-dkar* and *rgyal-mchog li-byin hara*;
(5) the emanational eightfold group (*sprul-pa'i sde-brgyad*) consisting of *dpung-gYas dgra-lhar sprul-pa, dpung-gYon ma-mor sprul-pa, chu-so bdud-du sprul-pa, mgo-bo srin-por sprul-pa, mjug-ma dmu-ru sprul-pa, lag-gYas gshin-rjes sprul-pa, lag-gYon klu-btsan sprul-pa* and *mig-dang snying-dang mtshan-ma gsum gza'-bdud nyid-du sprul-pa*;
(6) the eightfold group of phenomenal existence (*snang-srid sde-brgyad*) consisting of *sa-bdag hal-khyi nag-po, klu-bdud gdol-ba nag-po, sa-yi lha-mo brtan-ma, phyogs-skyong rgyal-chen sde-bzhi, mgon-po bdun-cu-rtsa-lnga, yul-'di'i gzhi-bdag thams-cad, pho-lha dgra-lha srog-lha* and *mo-lha mo-sman*. 535

EIGHTFOLD PATH *('phags-)lam (yan-lag) brgyad*, Skt. *aṣṭāṅgamārga*

Correct view (*yang-dag-pa'i lta-ba*, Skt. *samyagdṛṣṭi*), correct thought (*yang-dag-pa'i rtog-pa*, Skt. *samyaksaṃkalpa*), correct speech (*yang-dag-pa'i ngag*, Skt. *samyagvāk*), correct limits to activity (*yang-dag-pa'i las-kyi mtha'*, Skt. *samyakkarmānta*), correct livelihood (*yang-dag-pa'i 'tsho-ba*, Skt. *samyagājīva*), correct effort (*yang-dag-pa'i rtsol-ba*, Skt. *samyagvyāyāma*), correct recollection or mindfulness (*yang-dag-pa'i dran-pa*, Skt. *samyaksmṛti*) and correct contemplation (*yang-dag-pa'i ting-nge-'dzin*, Skt. *samyaksamādhi*); Mvt. (996-1004). 236

EIGHT GAURĪ *gau-rī brgyad*

These are listed under the NINE-DEITY MAṆḌALA OF YANGDAK. 623, 639

EIGHT GREAT ACCOMPLISHED MASTERS *grub-pa'i slob-dpon chen-po brgyad*

Vimalamitra, Hūṃkara, Mañjuśrīmitra, Nāgārjuna, Padmasambhava, Dhanasaṃskṛta, Rambuguhya-Devacandra and Śāntigarbha. Also referred to as the EIGHT GREAT AWARENESS-HOLDERS, their stories are given in *History*, pp. 475-83.

EIGHT GREAT ACTIVITIES *las-chen brgyad*

These are the EIGHT COMMON ACCOMPLISHMENTS. 259

EIGHT (GREAT) AWARENESS-HOLDERS *rig-'dzin (chen-po) brgyad*

The EIGHT GREAT ACCOMPLISHED MASTERS. 470, 757, 791

EIGHT (GREAT) CONVEYANCES, OR LINEAGES OF ATTAINMENT *sgrub-brgyud shing-rta (chen-po) brgyad*

The Nyingmapa, Kadampa, Path and Fruit, Marpa Kagyüpa, Shangpa Kagyüpa, Kālacakra, Pacification and Object of Cutting, and the Oḍḍiyāna Tradition of Service and Attainment. 852-3, 861

EIGHT (GREAT) FEARS *'jigs-pa (chen-po) brgyad*

The fears of fire, water, earth, air, elephants, snakes, thieves and kings. 538, 624

EIGHT GREAT GRAMMATICAL SŪTRAS *sgra-mdo chen-po brgyad*

Those of Indra, Candra, Kāśakṛtsna, Āpiśali, Śākaṭāyana, Pāṇini, Amara, and Jinendra. Refer to Vopadeva's *Dhātupāṭha*, Intro. (śl. 2). 99

EIGHT GREAT TREASURES (OF BRILLIANCE) *(spobs-pa'i) gter chen-po brgyad*

According to the *Sūtra of Extensive Play*, these are the treasure of recollection which overcomes forgetfulness (*dran-pa'i gter*), the treasure of intellect which develops the mind (*blo-gros-kyi gter*), the treasure of realisation which completely grasps the meaning of all sūtras (*rtogs-pa'i gter*), the treasure of the retention of all that one has heard (*gzungs-kyi gter*), the treasure of brilliance which delights all sentient beings with excellent exegeses (*spobs-pa'i gter*), the treasure of doctrine which well preserves the sacred teachings (*chos-kyi gter*), the treasure of enlightenment which never breaks its relationship with the THREE PRECIOUS JEWELS (*byang-sems-kyi gter*), and the treasure of accomplishment which is receptive to the uncreated reality of emptiness (*sgrub-pa'i gter*). 666, 705, 871

EIGHT KINDS OF INDIVIDUAL (AMONG PIOUS ATTENDANTS) *gang-zag brgyad*

These are the FOUR PAIRS OF SACRED BEINGS. 227

EIGHT KINDS OF PRECIOUS GEMS *rin-po-che sna-brgyad*

The caskets discovered by the EIGHT GREAT ACCOMPLISHED MASTERS were made of gold, silver, iron, copper, turquoise, *bse*-stone, agate and *gzi*-stone. 482-3

EIGHT LIBERTIES *dal-ba brgyad*, Skt. *aṣṭakṣaṇa*

Freedom from birth in the hells, among tormented spirits, among animals, as savages, extremists, or long-living gods, birth in a land where there is no doctrine, or as a dumb imbecile. 573

EIGHT MIDDLE KINGS CALLED *DE bar-gyi lde brgyad*

Zanam Zinde, Detrhül Namzhungtsen, Senöl Namde, Senöl Pode, Denölnam, Denölpo, De Gyelpo and Detrin Tsen. 508, n. 535

EIGHT MINOR SUBSECTS OF THE KAGYÜ SCHOOL *bka'-brgyud chung brgyad*

These are the traditions following Phakmotrupa, namely, the Drigungpa which was founded by Drigung Kyopa Jiktensumgön (1143-1217); the Taklungpa founded by Taklung Thangpa Trashipel (1142-1210); the Trhopupa founded by Campapel (1173-1228); the Ling-re founded by Lingje Repa (1128-88); the Martshang founded by Marpa Druptop Sherap Senge; the Yelpa founded by Yeshe Tsekpa; the Gyazang founded by Zarwa Kelden Yeshe; and the Shukseb founded by Kyergom Chenpo. 395, 853, 952

EIGHT OFFERING GODDESSES *mchod-pa'i lha-mo brgyad*

Lāsyā, Gītā, Nartī (or Naivedyā), Mālā, Dhūpī, Puṣpā, Ālokā and Gandhā. 624

EIGHT PILLARS WHO SUPPORTED THE LINEAGES OF THE MEANS FOR ATTAINMENT *sgrub-brgyud 'degs-pa'i ka-chen brgyad*

Pagor Vairocana, Dromtön, Khyungpo Neljor, Drokmi Lotsāwa, Marpa Lotsāwa, Phadampa Sangye, Kyijo Lotsāwa and Orgyenpa. n. 1173

EIGHT QUALITIES OF PURE WATER *yan-lag brgyad-dang ldan-pa'i chu*

Coolness, sweetness, lightness, softness, clearness, soothing quality, pleasantness and wholesomeness. 418

EIGHT RESULTS *'bras-bu brgyad*, Skt. *aṣṭaphala*

In this enumeration pious attendants are distinguished by their entrance into (*zhugs-pa*) and establishment in (*gnas*) the FOUR RESULTS, making a total of eight. 227

EIGHT SIMILIES OF ILLUSION *sgyu-ma'i dpe brgyad*, Skt. *aṣṭamāyopamā*

Dream (*rmi-lam*, Skt. *svapna*), illusion (*sgyu-ma*, Skt. *māyā*), optical illusion (*mig-yor*, Skt. *pratibhāsa*), mirage (*smig-rgyu*, Skt. *marīci*), reflection of the moon in water (*chu-zla*, Skt. *udakacandra*), echo (*brag-cha*, Skt. *pratiśrutkā*), castle in the sky (*dri-za'i grong-khyer*, Skt. *gandharvanagara*) and emanation or phantom (*sprul-pa*, Skt. *nirmita*). These traditional examples are given a detailed interpretation from the Nyingma perspective in Longcenpa, *sgyu-ma ngal-gso*, translated in H.V. Guenther, *Kindly Bent to Ease Us*, (Vol. 3). 236

EIGHT STŪPAS *mchod-rten brgyad*, Skt. *aṣṭastūpa*

Those holding the original remains of Śākyamuni Buddha, which were retained by the Mallas of Kuśinagara, Ajātaśatru of Magadha, the Licchavis of Vaiśālī, the Śākyas of Kapilavastu, the Bulakas of Calakalpā, the Krauḍyas of Rāmagrāma, the Brahmans of Viṣṇudvīpa and the Mallas of Pāpā. See also HBI (pp. 24-5). 427

EIGHT SUBJECTS OF SCRUTINY *brtag-pa brgyad*

The scrutiny of precious gems (*rin-chen*), land (*gzhi*), garments (*gos*), trees (*ljon-shing*), horses (*rta*), elephants (*glang*), men (*pho*) and women (*mo*). Refer to Longcenpa, *Treasury of Spiritual and Philosophical Systems*, (p. 40). 97, 99

EIGHT TOPICS (OF THE *ORNAMENT OF EMERGENT REALISATION*) *(mngon-rtogs rgyan-gi) dngos brgyad*

Understanding all forms (*rnam-mkhyen*, Skt. *sarvākārajñāna*), understanding of the path (*lam-shes-nyid*, Skt. *mārgajñatā*), understanding of everything (*thams-cad shes-pa-nyid*, Skt. *sarvajñatā*), the manifestly perfect realisation of all forms (*rnam-kun mngon-rdzogs rtogs-pa*, Skt. *sarvākārābhisambodha*), reaching the climax of existence (*rtse-mor phyin-pa*, Skt. *murdhābhisamaya*), culminating realisation (*mthar-gyis-pa*, Skt. *anupurvābhisamaya*), the instantaneous perfect enlightenment (*skad-cig-ma gcig-gis mngon-par rdzogs-par byang-chub-pa'i sbyor-ba*, Skt. *ekakṣaṇābhisamaya*) and the buddha-body of reality (*chos-sku*, Skt. *dharmakāya*). 94-5

EIGHT TRANSMITTED PRECEPTS *bka' brgyad*

The deities associated with the EIGHT CLASSES OF MEANS FOR ATTAINMENT. Pl. 4; 521, 591, 606, 805, 828

EIGHT VIRTUES (OF WOMANKIND) *yon-tan brgyad*

According to Longdöl Lama, *The Collected Works of Longdöl Lama*, p. 1456, these are: not to be under the sway of desires when one does not even have a spouse, not to be jealous when thinking of others, not to chatter, to speak the truth, to have sympathy, to have few wrong views, to have suitable intelligence and to have most illustrious sons. 418

EIGHT VOWS OF THE *PRĀTIMOKṢA* *so-thar sdom brgyad*, Skt. **aṣṭaprātimokṣa-saṃvara*

Those of laymen and laywomen (*dge-bsnyen* and *dge-bsnyen-ma*, Skt. *upāsaka* and *upāsikā*), male and female practitioners of the purificatory fast (*bsnyen-gnas*, Skt. *upavāsa* and *upavāsī*), male and female novices (*dge-tshul* and *dge-tshul-ma*, Skt. *śrāmaṇera* and *śrāmaṇerikā*) and monks and nuns (*dge-slong* and *dge-slong-ma*, Skt. *bhikṣu* and *bhikṣuṇī*). Canonical sources, however, usually speak of seven such vows, grouping the second pair together as one. 158, 226

EIGHT VOWS (OF THE PURIFICATORY FAST) *(gso-sbyong) yan-lag brgyad(-pa'i khrims)*, Skt. *astāṅgaśīla*

Abstinence from murder, theft, deceit and sexual misconduct are the four basic vows; while abstinence from alcohol, dancing and decoration, high expensive seats or beds and food in the afternoon are the four branches. 58, 226, 513

EIGHT WORLDLY CONCERNS *'jigs-rten chos brgyad*, Skt. *aṣṭa lokadharmāḥ*

Profit, loss, pleasure, pain, fame, defamation, praise and blame. 723, 852

EIGHT WRATHFUL GODDESSES *khros-ma brgyad*

These are the EIGHT GAURĪ in the maṇḍala of Yangdak Heruka, listed under the NINE-DEITY MAṆḌALA OF YANGDAK. 628

NINE

NINE BASIC CONDITIONS (OF THE PIṬAKA) *rgyu dgu*, Skt. *navakāraṇa*

These are defined in *Fundamentals*, pp. 78-9.

NINE BRANCHES OF THE SCRIPTURES *gsung-rab yan-lag dgu*, Skt. **navāṅga-pravacana*

The sūtras (*mdo-sde*), aphorisms in prose and verse (*dbyangs-bsnyad*, Skt. *geya*), prophetic declarations (*lung-bstan*, Skt. *vyākaraṇa*), verses (*tshig-bcad*, Skt. *gāthā*), meaningful or purposeful expressions (*ched-brjod*, Skt. *udāna*), legends or frame-stories (*gleng-gzhi*, Skt. *nidāna*), extensive teachings (*shin-tu rgyas-pa*, Skt. *vaipulya*), tales of past lives (*skyes-rabs*, Skt. *jātaka*) and marvellous events (*rmad-du byung*, Skt. *adbhutadharma*). 76

NINE CATEGORIES (OF JAINISM) *shes-bya tshig-gi don dgu*, Skt. *navapadārtha*

Animate substance (*srog*, Skt. *jīva*), inanimate substance (*zag-pa*, Skt. *ajīva*), commitments (*sdom-pa*, Skt. *saṃvara*), rejuvination, i.e. purgation of past deeds (*nges-par rga-ba*, Skt. *nirjara*), bondage (*'ching*, Skt. *bandha*), deeds (*las*, Skt. *karmāsrava*), evil (*sdig-pa*, Skt. *pāpa*), virtue (*bsod-nams*, Skt. *puṇya*) and liberation (*thar-pa*, Skt. *mokṣa*). 16, 66

NINE-DEITY MAṆḌALA OF YANGDAK *yang-dag lha dgu*

These are Yangdak Śrīheruka surrounded by the EIGHT GAURĪ, namely, the blue Gaurī in the east, the yellow Caurī in the south, the red Pramohā in the west, the black Vetālī in the north, the orange Pukkasī in the south-east, the dark-yellow Ghasmarī in the south-west, the dark-blue Śmaśānī in the north-west and the pale-yellow Caṇḍālī in the north-east. They are also known as *Nine-Lamp Yangdak* (*yang-dag mar-me dgu*). The same deities appear in many other wrathful maṇḍalas, e.g. the *Secret Nucleus* and *Hevajra*, but in the latter, Pramohā and Śmaśānī are represented by Ḍombī and Śavarī, respectively. 621, 669

NINE DRAMATIC AIRS *gar-gyi cha-byed dgu*, Skt. *navanāṭyarasa*
The playful air of grace (*sgeg-pa*, Skt. *śṛṅgāra*), the heroic (*dpa'-bo*, Skt. *vīra*), the ugly (*mi-sdug-pa*, Skt. *bībhatsa*), the fierce (*drag-shul*, Skt. *raudra*), the laughing (*gad*, Skt. *hāsya*), the terrifying (*'jigs-su rung-ba*, Skt. *bhayānaka*), the compassionate (*snying-rje*, Skt. *karuṇa*), the awesome (*rngoms-pa*, Skt. *adbhuta*) and the peaceful (*zhi-ba*, Skt. *śānta*). 98, 630, n. 751

NINE ENUMERATIONS (OF ANUYOGA COMMITMENTS) *rnam-grangs dgu*
These are listed according to the *General Sūtra which Gathers All Intentions*, Ch. 66, in *Fundamentals*, p. 367.

NINE KINDS OF TREATISE *bstan-bcos rnam dgu*
According to the *Yogācāra Level*, these are the meaningless (*don-med*), the erroneous (*don-log*), the meaningful (*don-ldan*), the hypocritical or deceitful (*ngan-gYo*), the merciless (*brtse-bral*), those which cause renunciation of suffering (*sdug-bsngal spong*), those devoted to worldly study (*thos*), to polemics (*rtsod*) and to attainment (*sgrub-pa*). 89

NINE MASANG BROTHERS *ma-sang dpun dgu*
This is the seventh group of spirits who took possession of Tibet in archaic times. Their names are Nyenya Pangkye (*gnyan-gYa' spang-skyes*), Karting Namtsho (*gar-ting nam-tsho*), Lenglen Lamtsangkye (*gleng-lan lam-tsang-skyes*), Rutho Karkye (*ru-tho gar-skyes*), Shedo Kartingne (*she-do kar-ting-nas*), Me Pemakye (*me padma skyes*), Sange Trhülpoche (*gsang-ge 'phrul-po-che*), Trangwa Trangmagur (*drang-ba drang-ma-mgur*) and Kötong Namtsha (*bkod-stong nam-tsha*). 949

NINE SEQUENCES OF THE VEHICLE *theg-pa'i rim-pa dgu*
See NINE VEHICLES

NINE SIMILIES (FOR THE PRESENCE OF THE NUCLEUS OF THE TATHĀGATA IN BEINGS) *dpe dgu*, Skt. *navodāharaṇāni*
According to the *Supreme Continuum of the Greater Vehicle*,(pp. 59-60, vv. 96-7) the nucleus of the tathāgata is present: "Like (a statue of) the buddha in a soiled lotus (*buddhaḥ kupadme*), like honey in beehives (*madhu makṣikāsu*), like kernels in husks (*tuṣeṣu sārāṇi*), like gold in alluvium (*aśucau suvarṇam*), treasure in the earth (*nidhīḥ kṣitau*), the stages beginning with the sprout in a tiny seed (*alpaphale 'ṅkurādi*), a conqueror's body in sodden clothes (*praklinnavastreṣu jinātmabhāvaḥ*), royalty in the womb of a common woman (*jaghanyanārījaṭhare nṛpatvam*) and a precious image in clods of earth (*bhaven mṛtsu ca ratnabimbam*)." 197

NINE SUCCESSIVE VEHICLES *theg-pa'i rim-pa dgu*
See NINE VEHICLES

NINE TOPICS (OF CHINESE DIVINATION) (*'byung-rtsis-kyi*) *don rnam-pa dgu*
Elemental bases (*khams*), years (*lo*), numbers (*sme-ba*), trigrams (*spar-kha*),

months (*zla-ba*), days (*nyi-ma*), two-hour periods (*dus-tshod*), planets (*gza'*) and stars (*skar-ma*). 104

NINE VEHICLES *theg-pa('i rim-pa) dgu*

Those of the pious attendants (*nyan-thos-kyi theg-pa*, Skt. *śrāvakayāna*), self-centred buddhas (*rang-rgyal-ba'i theg-pa*, Skt. *pratyekabuddhayāna*), bodhisattvas (*byang-chub sems-dpa'i theg-pa*, Skt. *bodhisattvayāna*), Kriyātantra (*bya-ba'i rgyud-kyi theg-pa*), Ubhayatantra (*upa'i rgyud-kyi theg-pa*) or Caryātantra (*spyod-pa'i rgyud-kyi theg-pa*), Yogatantra (*rnal-'byor-gyi rgyud-kyi theg-pa*), Mahāyoga (*rnal-'byor chen-po'i theg-pa*), Anuyoga (*rjes-su rnal-'byor-gyi theg-pa*) and Atiyoga, the Great Perfection (*rdzogs-pa chen-po shin-tu rnal-'byor-gyi theg-pa*). 12, 13, 17, 28, 30, 34, 35, 40, 41, 81, 86, 364-5, 625, 638-9, 861

TEN

TEN ASPECTS (OF THE EXCELLENT TEACHINGS) *(legs-gsung-gi) rnam-pa bcu*

According to the *Rational Exposition*, these are the nature of their genuine source (*yang-dag-par bslang-ba-nyid*), their scope (*dbang-du mdzad-pa-nyid*), their approach (*'jug-pa-nyid*), sound teaching (*rab-tu bstan-pa-nyid*), classification (*rab-tu dbye-ba-nyid*), support (*rten-nyid*), causing comprehension (*go-bar mdzad-pa-nyid*), title (*gdags-pa-nyid*), time (*dus-nyid*) and complete grasp of enlightened attributes (*yon-tan yongs-su 'dzin-pa-nyid*). 74

TEN CATEGORIES OF THE (OUTER AND INNER) MANTRAS *sngags (phyi-nang-)gi de-nyid bcu*, Skt. *daśatattva*

As stated in A. Wayman and F. Lessing, *Mkhas Grub Rje's Fundamentals of the Buddhist Tantras*, pp. 272-3, the outer ten are the maṇḍala, contemplation, seal, stance, seated posture, recitation, burnt offerings, offerings, rites of enlightened activity and concluding acts (*slar-sdud*); while the ten inner categories are the two reversals through creative visualisation and sealing (*phyir-zlog-pa gnyis*), the second and third empowerments, wrathful rites which break the resolve of hostile forces, *torma* offerings, recitation of verses of indestructible reality, wrathful subjugation by means of the kīla, consecration and attainment of the maṇḍala. 303, 304

TEN CATEGORIES OF (THE SUBJECT-MATTER OF) TANTRA *rgyud-don-gyi dngos-po bye-brag-tu phye-nas bcu* or *rgyud-kyi de-nyid bcu*

A view of the real (*de-kho-na-nyid lta-ba*), determinate conduct (*la-dor-ba spyod-pa*), maṇḍala array (*bkod-pa dkyil-'khor*), successive gradation of empowerment (*rim-par bgrod-pa dbang*), commitment which is not to be transgressed (*mi-'da'-ba dam-tshig*), enlightened activity which is displayed (*rol-pa phrin-las*), fulfilment of aspiration (*don-du gnyer-ba sgrub-pa*), offerings which bring the goal to fruition (*gnas-su stobs-pa mchod-pa*), unwavering contemplation (*mi-gYo-ba ting-nge-'dzin*) and mantra recitation (*zlos-pa sngags*), accompanied by the seal which binds the practitioner to realisation (*'ching-ba phyag-rgya*). 266, 347, 358

TEN CHAPTERS (OF THE *INTRODUCTION TO THE CONDUCT OF A BODHISATTVA*) *(spyod-'jug-gi) le'u bcu*, Skt. *(Bodhicaryāvatārasya) daśa paricchedāḥ*

The beneficial attributes of enlightened mind (*byang-sems-kyi phan-yon bshad-*

pa, Skt. *bodhicittānuśaṃsā*), repentance of sins (*sdig-pa bshags-pa*, Skt. *pāpadeśanā*), seizing the enlightened mind (*byang-sems yongs-bzung*, Skt. *bodhicittaparigraha*), vigilance with respect to enlightened mind (*bag-yod bstan-pa*, Skt. *bodhicittāpramāda*), the guarding of awareness (*shes-bzhin bsrung-ba*, Skt. *saṃprajanyarakṣaṇa*), the transcendental perfection of patience (*bzod-pa bstan-pa*, Skt. *kṣāntipāramitā*), the transcendental perfection of perseverance (*brtson-'grus bstan-pa*, Skt. *vīryapāramitā*), the transcendental perfection of concentration (*bsam-gtan bstan-pa*, Skt. *dhyānapāramitā*), the transcendental perfection of discriminative awareness (*shes-rab bstan-pa*, Skt. *prajñāpāramitā*) and the dedication of merit (*bsngo-ba*, Skt. *pariṇāmanā*). 94

TEN DIRECTIONS *phyogs bcu*, Skt. *daśadik*

East, south-east, south, south-west, west, north-west, north, north-east, zenith and nadir. 307, 412, 414, 419, 453, 624, 713, 915, 916

TEN DIVINE VIRTUES *lha-chos dge-ba bcu*

These are the TEN VIRTUES. 512

TEN ENDOWMENTS *'byor-ba bcu*

The five which concern oneself are a human birth, in a land where the doctrine prevails, with pure sense faculties, having committed no extremely negative action and having faith. The five which concern others are that the Buddha has appeared, that he has taught the doctrine, that this continues to exist, that it has followers and that they lovingly act on behalf of others. 573

TEN GREAT PILLARS WHO SUPPORTED THE EXEGETICAL LINEAGES *bshad-brgyud 'degs-pa'i ka-chen bcu*

Thönmi Sambhoṭa, Vairocana, Kawa Peltsek, Chokro Lüi Gyeltsen, Zhang Yeshede, Rincen Zangpo, Dromtön Gyelwa Jungne, Ngok Lotsāwa Loden Sherap, Sakya Paṇḍita and Gö Khukpa Lhetse. These ten complement the EIGHT PILLARS WHO SUPPORTED THE LINEAGES OF THE MEANS FOR ATTAINMENT. 851

TEN HIGHER LEVELS OF THE DESIRE REALM *'dod-khams-kyi mtho-ris gnas bcu*

The human beings of the FOUR CONTINENTS and the SIX SPECIES OF KĀMA DIVINITIES. 14, 60

TEN KINDS OF VITAL ENERGY *rlung bcu*, Skt. *daśavāyu*

These are the five basic energies (*rtsa-ba rlung lnga*) of breath (*srog-'dzin*, Skt. *prāṇa*), excretion/reproduction (*thur-sel*, Skt. *apāna*), speech (*rgyen-rgyu*, Skt. *udāna*), digestion (*mnyam-rgyu*, Skt. *samāna*) and metabolism/circulation/muscular movement (*khyab-byed*, Skt. *vyāna*). Then the five ancillary energies (*yan-lag-gi rlung lnga*) are those of the nāgas (*klu'i rlung*, Skt. *nāga*), connecting with the eyes; of the tortoise (*ru-sbal-gi rlung*, Skt. *kūrma*), connecting with the heart; of Brahmā (*tshang-pa'i rlung*, Skt. *brahmā/kṛkila*), connecting with the nose; of Devadatta (*lhas-sbyin-gyi-rlung*, Skt. *devadatta*), connecting with the tongue; and of the King of Wealth (*nor-lha rgyal-gi rlung*, Skt. *dhanañjaya*), connecting with the whole body. 292

TEN LEVELS (OF ANUYOGA) *sa bcu*

These correspond to the TEN LEVELS OF BODHISATTVAS. They are the levels of Indefinite Transformation (*'gyur-ba ma-nges-pa*), Basis of Reliance (*brten-pa gzhi'i sa*), Important Purification (*gal-chen sbyong-ba'i sa*), Continuity of Training (*bslab-pa rgyun-gyi sa*), Supporting Merit (*bsod-nams rten-gyi sa*), Superior Progress through Reliance (*brten-pas khyad-par-du 'gro-ba'i sa*), the level which Gives Birth to the Result with respect to the Aftermath of Inner Radiance on the Path of Insight (*mthong-lam 'od-gsal-las langs-pa'i rjes-la dmigs-pa 'bras-bu skye-ba'i sa*), Unchanging Abidance (*gnas-pa mi-'gyur-ba'i sa*), Expanding Reality (*bdal-ba chos-nyid*) and Riding on Perfection (*rdzogs-pa ci-chibs-kyi sa*). 34, 287-8

TEN LEVELS (OF BODHISATTVAS) *sa bcu*, Skt. *daśabhūmi*

The Joyful (*rab-tu dga'-ba*, Skt. *Pramuditā*), the Immaculate (*dri-ma med-pa*, Skt. *Vimalā*), the Illuminating (*'od-byed*, Skt. *Prabhākarī*), the Flaming (*'od-'phro-ba*, Skt. *Arciṣmatī*), the Hard to Conquer (*sbyang dka'-ba*, Skt. *Sudurjayā*), the Manifest (*mngon-du byed-pa*, Skt. *Abhimukhī*), the Far-Reaching (*ring-du song-ba*, Skt. *Duraṅgamā*), the Unmoving (*mi-gYo-ba*, Skt. *Acalā*), the Excellent Intelligence (*legs-pa'i blo-gros*, Skt. *Sādhumatī*) and the Cloud of Doctrine (*chos-kyi sprin-pa*, Skt. *Dharmameghā*). 30, 142, 174, 237, 281-2, 341, 416, 574, 746

TEN MEANINGS OF THE WORD *DHARMA* *chos-kyi don bcu*

The knowable (*shes-bya*), the path (*lam*), nirvāṇa (*mya-ngan-las 'das*), objects of mind (*yid-kyi yul*), merit (*bsod-nams*), life-span (*tshe*), the scriptures (*gsung-rab*), emergent objects (*'byung-'gyur*), regulations (*nges-pa*), and religious traditions (*chos-lugs*). 51-3

TEN MODES OF DOCTRINAL CONDUCT *chos-spyod bcu*, Skt. *daśadhā dharmacaritam*

According to the *Analysis of the Middle and Extremes*, Ch. 5, vv. 9-10, these are writing, worship, charity, listening, retention, reading, exegesis, daily recitation, thought and meditation. 60, 862

TEN NON-VIRTUES *mi dge-ba bcu*, Skt. *daśākuśala*

Murder (*srog-gcod-pa*, Skt. *prāṇātighāta*), theft (*ma-byin-par len-pa*, Skt. *adattādāna*), sexual misconduct (*'dod-pas log-par gYem-pa*, Skt. *kāmamithyācāra*), falsehood (*rdzun-du smra-ba*, Skt. *mṛṣāvāda*), slander (*phra-ma*, Skt. *paiśunya*), irresponsible chatter (*ngag-bkyal-ba*, Skt. *abaddhapralāpa*), verbal abuse (*tshig-rtsub-mo*, Skt. *pāruṣya*), covetousness (*brnab-sems*, Skt. *abhidhyā*), vindictiveness (*gnod-sems*, Skt. *vyāpāda*) and holding wrong views (*log-lta*, Skt. *mithyādṛṣṭi*). 13, 58, 60-1, 64

TEN PLANETS *gza' bcu*, Skt. *daśagraha*

The Sun (*nyi-ma*, Skt. *āditya*), Moon (*zla-ba*, Skt. *candra*), Mars (*mig-dmar*, Skt. *aṅgāraka*), Mercury (*lhag-pa*, Skt. *budha*), Jupiter (*phur-bu*, Skt. *bṛhaspati*), Venus (*pa-sangs*, Skt. *śukra*), Saturn (*spen-ba*, Skt. *śanaiścara*), the ascending and descending nodes of the Moon (*sgra-can*, Skt. *rāhu* and *mjug-ring*, Skt. *ketu*) and the comet Encke (*du-ba mjug-ring*). 104, 351

TEN POWERS *dbang bcu*, Skt. *daśavaśitā*

The power or dominion over life (*tshe*, Skt. *āyuḥ*), deeds (*las*, Skt. *karman*), necessities (*yo-byad*, Skt. *pariṣkāra*), devotion (*mos-pa*, Skt. *adhimukti*), prayer or aspiration (*smon-lam*, Skt. *praṇidhāna*), miraculous abilities (*rdzu-

'phrul, Skt. *ṛddhi*), birth (*skye-ba*, Skt. *upapatti*), doctrine (*chos*, Skt. *dharma*), mind (*sems*, Skt. *citta*) and pristine cognition (*ye-shes*, Skt. *jñāna*); Mvt. (771-80). 405

TEN POWERS (OF BODHISATTVAS) *stobs bcu*, Skt. *daśabala*

These powers developed by bodhisattvas are reflection (*bsam-pa'i stobs*, Skt. *āśayabala*), superior aspiration (*lhag-bsam*, Skt. *adhyāśaya*), application (*sbyor-ba*, Skt. *prayoga*), discriminative awareness (*shes-rab*, Skt. *prajñā*), prayer or aspiration (*smon-lam*, Skt. *praṇidhāna*), vehicle (*theg-pa*, Skt. *yāna*), conduct (*spyod-pa*, Skt. *caryā*), transformation (*rnam-par 'phrul-pa*, Skt. *vikurvaṇa*), enlightenment (*byang-chub*, Skt. *bodhi*) and turning the doctrinal wheel (*chos-kyi 'khor-lo bskor-ba*, Skt. *dharmacakrapravartana*); Mvt. (760-9). 435

TEN POWERS (OF A BUDDHA) *yon-tan stobs bcu*, Skt. *daśatathāgatabala*

The power of knowing the positive and negative contingencies of things (*gnas-dang gnas ma-yin-pa mkhyen-pa'i stobs*, Skt. *sthānāsthānajñānabala*), the power of knowing the maturation of deeds (*las-kyi rnam-smin mkhyen-pa'i stobs*, Skt. *karmavipākajñānabala*), the power of knowing diverse volitions (*mos-pa sna-tshogs mkhyen-pa'i stobs*, Skt. *nānādhimuktijñānabala*), the power of knowing diverse sensory bases (*khams sna-tshogs mkhyen-pa'i stobs*, Skt. *nānadhātujñānabala*), the power of knowing those who are of supreme acumen and those who are not (*dbang-po mchog-dang mchog ma-yin-pa mkhyen-pa'i stobs*, Skt. *indriyavarāvarajñānabala*), the power of knowing the paths going everywhere (*thams-cad-du 'gro-ba'i lam mkhyen-pa'i stobs*, Skt. *sarvatragāmanīpratipajjñānabala*), the power of knowing concentration, liberation, contemplation, absorption, conflicting emotion, purification and acquisition (*bsam-gtan-dang rnam-thar-dang ting-'dzin-dang snyoms-'jug-dang kun-nas nyon-mongs-pa-dang rnam-par byang-ba-dang ldan-pa thams-cad mkhyen-pa'i stobs*, Skt. *sarvadhyānavimokṣasamādhisamāpattisaṃkleśavyavadānavyutthānajñānabala*), the power of recollecting past abodes (*sngon-gyi gnas rjes-su dran-pa mkhyen-pa'i stobs*, Skt. *pūrvanivāsānusmṛtijñānabala*), the power of knowing the transference of consciousness at death and birth (*'chi-'pho-ba dang skye-ba mkhyen-pa'i stobs*, Skt. *cyutyutpattijñānabala*) and the power of knowing the cessation of corruption (*zag-pa zad-pa mkhyen-pa'i stobs*, Skt. *āsravakṣayajñānabala*); Mvt. (119-29). 22, 171, 266

TEN SCIENCES *rig-pa'i gnas bcu*, Skt. *daśavidyā*

The arts, grammar, medicine, logic, inner science (i.e. religious theory and practice), astrology, poetics, prosody, synonymics and drama. 821, 850, 860

TEN SIGNS OF INNER RADIANCE *'od-gsal rtags bcu*

These are enumerated in Longcenpa, *Dispelling Darkness in the Ten Directions*, p. 344, as smoke (*du-ba*), mirage (*smig-rgyu*), clouds (*sprin*), fire-flies (*me-khyer*), sunlight (*nyi-ma*), moonlight (*zla-ba*), the blazing of gemstones (*rin-po-che 'bar-ba*), eclipse (*sgra-gcan*), starlight (*skar-ma*) and rays of light (*'od-zer*). 301

TEN TRANSCENDENTAL PERFECTIONS *pha-rol-tu phyin-pa bcu*, Skt. *daśapāramitā*

The SIX TRANSCENDENTAL PERFECTIONS with the addition of skilful means (*thabs*, Skt. *upāya*), prayer or aspiration (*smon-lam*, Skt. *praṇidhāna*), power (*stobs*, Skt. *bala*) and pristine cognition (*ye-shes*, Skt. *jñāna*); Mvt. (913-23). 236, 901-2

TEN TRANSGRESSIONS *rung-ba ma-yin-pa'i gzhi bcu*, Skt. *daśaniṣiddha*

As stated in the *Minor Transmissions* (*bka'-'gyur*, Vol. *Da*, pp. 646-63), the following ten transgressions were the issue of the second council at Vaiśālī: exclamations of "alas" (*hu-lu hu-lu*), celebrating the arhats (*yi-rangs*), the deliberate practice of agriculture (*kun-spyod*), sipping medicine from a pot of ale (*snod*), the misuse of the sacred stored salt (*lan-tsha*), eating while on the road (*lam*), desecration of offerings with two fingers (*sor-gnyis*), stirring curd and milk together as an afternoon beverage (*dkrug*), using a new mat without an old patch (*gding*) and begging for gold or silver (*gser*). Other sources include Tāranātha, Bu-ston, Hsüan Tsang, as well as Sinhalese works such as the *Cullavagga*, *Mahāvaṃsa* and *Dīpavaṃsa*. 429

TEN VIRTUES *dge-ba bcu*, Skt. *daśakuśala*

The renunciation of the TEN NON-VIRTUES and the practice of their opposites; Mvt. 1687-98. They are also referred to as the TEN DIVINE VIRTUES. 56, 59, 60, 61, 513

ELEVEN

ELEVEN COMMITMENTS (OF KRIYĀTANTRA) *dam-tshig bcu-gcig*

Not to abandon the THREE PRECIOUS JEWELS (*dkon mchog-gsum*), the enlightened mind (*byang-chub-sems*), the mantras (*sngags*), the seals (*phyag-rgya*), the vajra and bell (*rdo-rje dril-bu*), the deity and guru (*lha dang bla-ma*); and not to sleep on a throne (*khri-la mi-nyal-ba*), not to eat meat (*sha mi-za*), not to drink ale (*chang mi-btung*) and not to eat garlic (*sgog-pa*) or radishes (*la-phug bza' mi-bya*). 350, 355

ELEVEN LEVELS (OF A BUDDHA) *sa bcu-gcig*

According to the causal vehicles, a buddha attains eleven levels, namely, the TEN LEVELS OF BODHISATTVAS with the addition of the level of Universal Light (*kun-tu-'od*, Skt. *Samantaprabhā*). 237

TWELVE

TWELVE ACTIVITY FIELDS *skye-mched bcu-gnyis*, Skt. *dvādaśāyatana*

The activity field of the eye (*mig-gi skye-mched*, Skt. *cakṣurāyatana*), of form (*gzugs-kyi skye-mched*, Skt. *rūpāyatana*), of the ear (*rna-ba'i skye-mched*, Skt. *śrotrāyatana*), of sound (*sgra'i skye-mched*, Skt. *śabdāyatana*), of the nose (*sna'i skye-mched*, Skt. *ghrāṇāyatana*), of smell (*dri'i skye-mched*, Skt. *gandhāyatana*), of the tongue (*lce'i skye-mched*, Skt. *jihvāyatana*), of taste (*ro'i skye-mched*, Skt. *rasāyatana*), of the body (*lus-kyi skye-mched*, Skt. *kāyāyatana*), of touch (*reg-bya'i skye-mched*, Skt. *spraṣṭavyāyatana*), of the intellect (*yid-kyi skye-mched*, Skt. *manaāyatana*) and of mental objects (*chos-kyi skye-mched*, Skt. *dharmāyatana*); Mvt. (2027-39). 13, 55-6

TWELVE ANTIDOTES/EMPTINESSES REVERSING DEPENDENT ORIGINATION *lugs-ldog stong-pa bcu-gnyis*

The antidote for the TWELVE MODES OF DEPENDENT ORIGINATION

namely, the realisation of the emptiness of each. 230

TWELVE ASCETIC VIRTUES *sbyangs-pa'i yon-tan bcu-gnyis*, Skt. *dvādaśadhūtaguṇa*

Wearing clothing found in a dust-heap (*phyag-dar khrod-pa*, Skt. *pāṃśukūlika*), owning only three robes (*chos-gos gsum-pa*, Skt. *traicīvarika*), wearing felt or woollen clothes (*phyings-pa-can*, Skt. *nāmantika*), begging for food (*bsod-snyoms-pa*, Skt. *paiṇḍapātika*), eating one's meal at a single sitting (*stan-gcig-pa*, Skt. *aikāsanika*), restricting the quantity of food (*zas-phyis mi-len-pa*, Skt. *khalu paścād bhaktika*), staying in isolation (*dgon-pa-ba*, Skt. *āraṇyaka*), sitting under trees (*shing-drung-pa*, Skt. *vṛkṣamūlika*), sitting in exposed places (*bla-gab med-pa*, Skt. *ābhyavakāśika*), sitting in charnel grounds (*dur-khrod-pa*, Skt. *śmāśānika*), sitting even during sleep (*cog-bu-pa*, Skt. *naiṣadika*) and staying wherever one happens to be (*gzhi ji-bzhin-pa*, Skt. *yathā saṃstarika*); Mvt. (1127-39). 227

TWELVE BRANCHES OF THE SCRIPTURES *gsung-rab yan-lag bcu-gnyis*, Skt. **dvādaśāṅgapravacana*

The NINE BRANCHES OF THE SCRIPTURES with the addition of the narratives (*rtogs-pa brjod-pa*, Skt. *avadāna*), fables (*de-lta-bu byung-ba*, Skt. *itivṛttaka*) and established instructions (*gtan-phab*, Skt. *upadeśa*). 17, 76

TWELVE DEEDS (OF THE SUPREME EMANATIONAL BODY) *mdzad-pa bcu-gnyis*

Remaining in Tuṣita, descent and entry into the womb, taking birth, proficiency in the arts, enjoyment of consorts, renouncing the world, practising asceticism, reaching the point of enlightenment, vanquishing Māra's host, attaining perfect enlightenment, turning the doctrinal wheel and passing into the final nirvāṇa. Various enumerations of the twelve are given. Cf. Longcenpa, *Treasury of the Supreme Vehicle* (p. 271). 21, 129, 137, 415-16, 624

TWELVE DIFFERENT INTENTIONS (OF BUDDHA-MIND) *dgongs-pa mi-'dra-ba bcu-gnyis*

The four outer contemplations – the progress of a spiritual warrior (*dpa'-bar-'gro-ba*), the precious crown (*rin-po-che'i tog*), emanation (*rnam-par rol-pa*) and the basket of plenty (*za-ma-tog*); the four inner contemplations – penetrating all objects (*yul-kun-la 'jug-pa*), manifestation (*mngon-par snang-ba*), the crown-jewel (*gtsug-gi nor-bu*) and arraying the summit of the victory banner (*rgyal-mtshan rtse-mo yongs-su bkod-pa*); and the four secret contemplations – purity of the movement of subtle energies (*'gyu-ba dag-pa*), profound appearance (*zab-mo snang-ba*), jewel lamp (*rin-chen sgron-me*) and excellence (*legs-pa*). Refer to Longcenpa, *Treasury of the Supreme Vehicle*, (p. 28). 137

TWELVE DIFFERENT REALMS (OF THE EMANATIONAL BODY) *gnas-ris bcu-gnyis*

These are enumerated in *Fundamentals*, pp. 134-7.

TWELVE DIFFERENT DOCTRINAL WHEELS OF BUDDHA-SPEECH *gsung chos-kyi 'khor-lo mi-'dra-ba bcu-gnyis*

These are equivalent to the TWELVE BRANCHES OF THE SCRIPTURES. As enumerated in Longcenpa, *Treasury of the Supreme Vehicle*, pp. 28ff., they comprise the four outer wheels of the sūtras, aphorisms in prose and verse, prophetic declarations and verse; the four inner wheels of extensive teachings, tales of past lives, legends and parables; and the four secret wheels of meaningful expressions, narratives, established instructions and marvellous events. 137

TWELVE EXCELLENT DIVISIONS OF THE UNSURPASSED TANTRA *rgyud-kyi rab-tu dbye-ba bcu-gnyis*

The SIX ENLIGHTENED FAMILIES OF FATHER TANTRA and the SIX ENLIGHTENED FAMILIES OF MOTHER TANTRA. 274

TWELVE GODDESSES OF THE EARTH *brtan-ma bcu-gnyis*

The TWELVE MĀTARAḤ. Various enumerations are given in Nebesky-Wojkowitz, *Oracles and Demons of Tibet*, (pp. 181-98). 481, 513, 537, 715

TWELVE MASTERS WHO WERE RENOWNED AT VIKRAMAŚĪLA *rnam-gnon tshul-gyis bsngags-pa'i slob-dpon bcu-gnyis*

These were Jñānapāda, Dīpaṃkarabhadra, Laṅkājayabhadra, Śrīdhara, Bhavabhadra, Bhavyakīrti, Līlāvajra, Durjayacandra, Samayavajra, Tathāgatarakṣita, Bodhibhadra and Kamalarakṣita. 442

TWELVE MĀTARAḤ *ma-mo bcu-gnyis*

See TWELVE GODDESSES OF THE EARTH

TWELVE MINOR KINGDOMS *rgyal-phran bcu-gnyis*

When living beings first settled in Tibet, the country was divided into twelve kingdoms, namely, *mchims-yul gru-shul* ruled by *mchims-rje gu-yod*; *zhang-zhung* ruled by the king *lig-snya shur*; *myang-do phyong-dkar* ruled by *gtsang-rje thod-dkar*; *gnubs-yul gling-dgu* ruled by the king *gnubs-rje dmigs-pa*; *nyang-ro sham-bod* ruled by the king *rngam-rje 'brom*; *gyi-ri ljongs-sdon* ruled by the king *gyi-rje rman-po*; *ngam-shod khra-snar* ruled by the king *zing-rje khri-'phrang gsum*; *'ol-phu spang-mkhar* ruled by the king *zing-rje thon-greng*; *srim-rong la-mo-gong* ruled by the king *brang-rje gong-nam*; *kong-yul bre-sna* ruled by the king *kong-rje dar-po tug-dang*; *nyang-yul rnams-gsum* ruled by *nyang-btsun glang-rgyal*; and *dvags-yul gru-bzhi* which was ruled by the king *dvags-rje mang-po rgyal*. 507, 949

TWELVE MODES OF DEPENDENT ORIGINATION *rten-cing 'brel-bar 'byung-ba'i tshul bcu-gnyis*, Skt. *dvādaśāṅgapratītyasamutpāda*

These are ignorance (*ma-rig-pa*, Skt. *avidyā*), habitual tendencies (*'du-byed*, Skt. *saṃskāra*), consciousness (*rnam-shes*, Skt. *vijñāna*), name and form (*ming-dang gzugs*, Skt. *nāmarūpa*), the six activity fields of the eye, ear, nose, tongue, body and intellect (*skye-mched drug*, Skt. *ṣaḍāyatana*), contact (*reg-pa*, Skt. *sparśa*), feeling (*tshor-ba*, Skt. *vedanā*), craving (*sred-pa*, Skt. *tṛṣṇa*), the FIVE COMPONENTS (*nye-bar len-pa'i phung-po lnga*, Skt. *upādānaskandha*), rebirth (*srid-pa*, Skt. *bhava*), birth (*skye-ba*, Skt. *jāti*) and old age and death (*rga-shi*, Skt. *jarāmaraṇa*); Mvt. (2241-58). 25, 159, 228

TWELVE ORDINARY (FORM) REALMS *so-skye'i gnas bcu-gnyis*

Refer to the chart on pp. 14-15, for their enumeration in accordance with Mvt. 3085-100, and for their correspondence to the FOUR MEDITATIVE CONCENTRATIONS. 62

TWELVE TEACHERS OF THE EMANATIONAL BODY *sprul-pa'i sku ston-pa bcu-gnyis*

These are enumerated in *Fundamentals*, (pp. 134-8). 22

THIRTEEN

THIRTEEN COMMITMENTS (OF YOGATANTRA) *dam-tshig bcu-gsum*

These are equivalent to the ELEVEN COMMITMENTS OF KRIYĀTANTRA with the addition of the commitments not to drink water in a locality inhabited by violators of commitments (*lung-gcig chu-la mi-btung*) and not to converse with such violators (*nyams-dang kha mi-bsre-ba bsrung*). 355

THIRTEEN GENERATIONS OF THE GURUS OF KATOK *kaḥ-thog bla-rabs bcu-gsum*

According to Jamyang Khyentse Wangpo, *gsung-rtsom gces-sgrig*, pp. 22-3, the thirteen generations of lamas who established Katok are the successive regents of Katokpa Tampa Deshek, namely, Tsangtönpa Dorje Gyeltsen, Campabum, Ce-nga Mangpuwa Sonam Bumpa, Uwöpa Yeshebum, Cangcup Pelwa, Sonam Zangpo, Künga Bumpa, Lodrö Bumpa, Lodrö Senge, Cangcup Lodrö, Cangcup Senge, Cangcup Gyeltsen and Khedrup Yeshe Gyeltsen. This enumeration omits Katokpa Wangcuk Pelwa after Künga Bumpa. Another list given in Gönpo Wangyal, *chos-kyi rnam-grangs*, p. 378, counts Katokpa Tampa Deshek as the first of the thirteen, and instead omits Cangcup Senge and Khedrup Yeshe Gyeltsen, as follows: Katok Tampa Deshek, Tsangtönpa, Campabum, Sonam Bumpa, Uwöpa Yeshebumpa, Cangcup Pelwa, Sonam Zangpo, Künga Bumpa, Wangcuk Pelwa, Lodrö Bumpa, Lodrö Senge, Cangcup Lodrö and Cangcup Gyeltsen. 688-99

THIRTEEN HUNTING GODS *mgur-lha bcu-gsum*

These are *thang-lha yar-zhur*, *yar-lha sham-po*, *gtsang-lha byol-yug*, *srog-lha gangs-tar*, *rgyogs-chen sdong-ra*, *dog-lha byang-rtse*, *lcogs-lha mtshal-rtse*, *gangs-dkar gYu-rtse*, *sum-ri gnyen-po*, *'dzum-chen stong-phron*, *dbyi-chen rab-rngo*, *'bri-chen sdong-du* and *bod-kyi ba-ru*. 513

THIRTEEN INCARNATIONS OF GYELSE LHARJE *rgyal-sras lha-rje'i yang-srid bcu-gsum*

Gyelse Lharje Chokdrup Gyelpo was the son of Prince Mutik Tsepo and the immediate reincarnation of King Trhisong Detsen. According to Jamgön Kongtrül, *Great Biography of Khyentse Rinpoche*, fols. 6b-7a, his incarnations were: Sangye Lama; Gya Lotsā Dorje Zangpo; Nyima Senge; Kusa Menpa Pemakyap, alias Khutsa Da-ö; Doben Gyamtso-ö and, simultaneously, Zur Pakshi Śākya-ö; Tragom Chöki Dorje and, simultaneously, Khyung-nak Śākya-dar; Yarje Orgyen Lingpa; Töl Ngakcang Letro Lingpa; Nesar Khyentsei Wangcuk and, simultaneously, Ngari Paṇcen; Ebecok Karwang Letro Lingpa; Puwo Razhi Tertön Pema Rikdzin, alias Pema Tshewang-tsel; Orgyen Chöje Lingpa Dewei Dorje-tsel; and Khyentse Rinpoche, i.e. Pema Ösel Do-nga Lingpa. 751

THIRTEEN PARTICULAR COMMITMENTS (OF KRIYĀTANTRA) *bye-brag-gi dam-tshig bcu-gsum*

These are equivalent to the THIRTEEN COMMITMENTS OF YOGATANTRA. 350

FOURTEEN

FOURTEEN BASIC VIOLATIONS OF THE COMMITMENTS *bsrung-bya'i dam-tshig rtsa-ltung bcu-bzhi*, Skt. *caturdaśamūlāpatti*

To disparage the master; to transgress the three levels of vows; to be hostile to vajra brothers and sisters; to forsake loving kindness on behalf of sentient beings; to abandon the enlightened mind; to disparage one's own doctrine or that of others; to divulge secrets to the immature; to abuse the FIVE COMPONENTS which are primordially pure; to be prejudiced about phenomena which are in any case intrinsically pure; to lack compassion for evil beings, especially those who harm the doctrine; to apply conceptualisation to ineffable nature; to belittle those who have faith; to violate the commitments that have been undertaken; and to disparage women, the source of discriminative awareness. The source is Aśvaghoṣa's *Mūlāpattisaṃgraha*, as quoted by Lessing and Wayman, *Mkhas Grub Rje's Fundamentals of the Buddhist Tantras*, (p. 328). 361

FOURTEEN PARTICULAR COMMITMENTS (OF YOGATANTRA) *dam-tshig bcu-bzhi*

These are identical to the preceding entry. 355

FIFTEEN

FIFTEEN ORDINARY SACRAMENTS (OF EMPOWERMENT) *sgrub-rdzas thun-mong bco-lnga*

The fifteen ordinary sacraments and the THREE PROFOUND EMPOWERMENTS together form the eighteen empowerments of Mahāyoga. Of these the former include ten outer empowerments of beneficence (*phyi-phan-pa'i dbang-bcu*) and five inner empowerments of ability (*nang nus-pa'i dbang-lnga*), while the latter includes the THREE PROFOUND EMPOWERMENTS that are secret (*gsang-ba zab-mo'i dbang-gsum*). The ten empowerments of beneficence are those of crown ornament, diadem, rosary, armour, victory-banner, seals, parasol, vase, food and drink, and the five essences. For their significance, see Longcenpa, *Dispelling Darkness in the Ten Directions*, pp. 376-9 (GGFTC, pp. 878-9). The five empowerments of ability are listed under the FIVE EMPOWERMENTS OF THE *SECRET NUCLEUS*. 701

SIXTEEN

SIXTEEN ASPECTS (OF THE FOUR DRAMATIC MANNERS) *tshul bzhi'i yan-lag bco-drug*, Skt. *ṣoḍaśavṛttyaṅga*

As enumerated in A. B. Keith, *Sanskrit Drama*, pp. 298-300, these are: dialogue (*bhāratī*) which includes elucidation (*prarocanā*, Tib. *rab-tu snang-ba*), prelude (*āmukha*), one-act drama (*vīthī*) and comedy (*prahasana*); grandure (*sātvatī*) which includes haughty provocation (*utthāpaka*), change (*parivartaka*), dialogue with or without threats (*saṃlāpa*) and the end of an alliance (*sāṅghātya*); grace (*kaiśikī*) which includes amorous play (*narman*), the partial expression of love combined with other emotions such as fear (*narmasphoṭa*), the disguise of a lover (*narmagarbha*) and ecstatic union with a lover which has troublesome consequences (*narmasphūrja*); and conflict or horror (*ārabhaṭī*) which includes the sudden change of characters (*saṃkṣip-taka*), or of mood (*avapāta*), the intrusion of the supernatural (*vastūtthāpana*) and tumultuous situations (*sampheṭa*). 107

SIXTEEN ASPECTS OF THE FOUR TRUTHS *bden-bzhi'i rnam-pa bcu-drug*

These are the SIXTEEN MINOR TRUTHS. 24

SIXTEEN DELIGHTS *dga'-ba bcu-drug*

Delight (*dga-'ba*), supreme delight (*dga'-mchog*), absence of delight (*dga-'bral*) and co-emergent delight (*lhan-cig skyes-pa'i dga'-ba*), each of which has four aspects through its conjunction with the same four, making sixteen in all. Cf. Longcenpa, *Dispelling Darkness in the Ten Directions*, pp. 386-96 (GGFTC, pp. 900-14). 125

SIXTEEN ELDERS *gnas-brtan bcu-drug*, Skt. *ṣoḍaśa sthavirāḥ*

These were Panthaka (*lam-pa*) in Trayatriṃśa; Abhedya (*mi-phyed-pa*) in the Himalayas; Kanaka (*gser-can*) in the western continent of Godānīya; Bakkula (*bakkula*) in the northern continent of Uttarakuru; Bhāradvāja in the eastern continent of Videha; Mahākālika (*dus-ldan chen-po*) in Tāmradvīpa; Vajrīputra (*rdo-rje-mo'i bu*) in Siṃhaladvīpa; Rāhula (*sgra-gcan 'dzin*) in Priyaṅgudvīpa; Śrībhadra (*dpal-bzang*) in Yamunādvīpa; Gopaka (*sbed-byed*) on Mount Bihula; Nāgasena (*klu-sde*) on Mount Urumuṇḍa; Vanavāsin (*nags-gnas*) on Mount Saptaparṇa; Kṣudrapanthaka (*lam-phran*) on Mount Gṛdhrakūṭa; Kanakavatsa (*gser-gyi be'u*) in Kashmir; Aṅgiraja (*yan-lag 'byung*) on Mount Kailash; and Ajita (*ma-pham-pa*) on the Crystal Slope of Sage Mountain. 432, 438, 590

SIXTEEN GREAT CITIES OF JAMBUDVĪPA *'dzam-bu'i gling-gi grong-khyer chen-po bcu-drug*

These are the spheres of activity of the SIXTEEN ELDERS. An alternative listing refers to the sixteen great countries of India: Aṅga, Magadha, Kāśī, Kosala, Vṛji, Malla, Ceḍi, Vatsa, Kuru, Pañcāla, Matsya, Śūrasena, Aśmaka, Avanti, Gandhāra and Kamboja. 438

SIXTEEN LEVELS *sa bcu-drug*

The ELEVEN LEVELS OF A BUDDHA, to which are added the following: (12) Unattached Lotus Endowed (*ma-chags padma-can-gyi sa*); (13) Great Cloud Mass of Rotating Syllables (*yi-ge 'khor-lo tshogs-chen-gyi sa*); (14) Great Contemplation (*ting-nge-'dzin chen-po*); (15) Holder of Indestructible Reality (*rdo-rje-'dzin-gyi sa*); (16) Unsurpassed Pristine Cognition (*ye-shes bla-ma'i sa*). 84

SIXTEEN MINOR TRUTHS *bden-chung bcu-drug*, Skt. *ṣoḍaśākāravisāritacatur-āryasatya*

Suffering (*sdug-bsngal*, Skt. *duḥkha*), impermanence (*mi-rtag-pa*, Skt. *anitya*), emptiness (*stong-pa*, Skt. *śūnyata*), selflessness (*bdag-med-pa*, Skt. *anā-tmaka*); the origin of suffering (*kun-'byung-ba*, Skt. *samudaya*), production (*rab-tu skye-ba*, Skt. *prabhava*), causal basis (*rgyu*, Skt. *hetu*), condition (*rkyen*, Skt. *pratyaya*); cessation (*'gog-pa*, Skt. *nirodha*), quiescence (*zhi-ba*, Skt. *śānta*), excellence (*gya-nom-pa*, Skt. *praṇīta*), disillusionment with saṃsāra (*nges-par 'byung-ba*, Skt. *niḥsaraṇa*); path (*lam*, Skt. *mārga*), reason (*rigs-pa*,

Skt. *nyāya*), attainment (*sgrub-pa*, Skt. *pratipatti*) and the act of becoming disillusioned with saṃsāra (*nges-par 'byin-ba*, Skt. *nairyāṇika*); Mvt. 1189-209. Also referred to as the SIXTEEN ASPECTS OF THE FOUR TRUTHS. 226

SIXTEEN MOMENTS OF PRISTINE COGNITION *ye-shes bcu-drug*, Skt. *ṣoḍaśacittakṣaṇa*

The perception of the doctrine of the truth of suffering (*sdug-bsngal-la chos-shes-pa*, Skt. *duḥkhadharmajñāna*), receptiveness to the perception of the doctrine of suffering (*sdug-bsngal-la chos shes-pa'i bzod-pa*, Skt. *duḥkhadharmajñānakṣānti*), the after-effect of the perception of the doctrine of the truth of suffering (*sdug-bsngal-la rjes-su rtogs-pa'i shes-pa*, Skt. *duḥkhānvayajñāna*) and receptiveness to the after-effect of the perception of the doctrine of the truth of suffering (*sdug-bsngal-la rjes-su rtogs-pa'i shes-pa'i bzod-pa*, Skt. *duḥkhānvayajñānakṣānti*). These four moments are then applied in the same order to the truth of the origin of suffering, to the truth of its cessation and to the truth of the path, making sixteen moments in all; Mvt. (1216-32). 226-7, 230

SIXTEEN ORNAMENTS OF ENIGMATIC INNUENDO *gab-tshig-gi rgyan bcu-drug*, Skt. *ṣoḍaśaprahelikā*

According to Daṇḍin's *Mirror of Poetics*, Ch. III, vv. 96-124, and D. K. Gupta, *A Critical Study of Daṇḍin and his Works*, pp. 230-9, these are as follows: meaning concealed by a concentration of words, the real meaning lost in the apparent, the use of semantically connected words at a great distance from each other, contrived meaning, harmonious or derivative meaning, coarse meaning, enumeration, assumed meaning, abbreviation, hidden meaning, confusing use of synonyms, vexing or foolish use of words, stealthy meaning, obscurity in a single respect (i.e. of the container), obscurity in both respects (i.e. of the container and content) and a combination of various forms of the above. 105

SIXTEEN PURE HUMAN LAWS *mi-chos gtsang-ma bcu-drug*

Refer to the quotation in *Fundamentals*, (pp. 59-60). 512

SEVENTEEN

SEVENTEEN FORM REALMS *lha-gzugs-khams gnas-ris bcu-bdun*

The TWELVE ORDINARY FORM REALMS and the FIVE PURE ABODES OF THE FORM REALMS. 13, 15, 61

EIGHTEEN

EIGHTEEN APPENDAGES OF MUSIC *rol-mo'i bye-brag bco-brgyad*

The dancer, dance, large drum, kettledrum, tambour, large kettledrum, gong, lute, one-sided kettledrum, bell-metal cymbals, bell, three-string lute, mukuṇḍa drum, cymbals, chorus, tabor, instrumentation and flute; Mvt. (5007-26). 98

EIGHTEEN DISTINCT ATTRIBUTES OF THE BUDDHAS *sangs-rgyas-kyi chos ma-'dres-pa bco-brgyad*, Skt. *aṣṭadaśāveṇikabuddhadharma*

(1) The tathāgatas are without bewilderment (*'khrul-pa med-pa*, Skt. *nāsti*

skhalitam); (2) they are not noisy (*ca-co med-pa*, Skt. *nāsti ravitam*); (3) they are without false memories (*bsnyel-ba med-pa*, Skt. *nāsti muṣitasmṛtitā*); (4) they are without unabsorbed minds (*sems mnyam-par ma-gzhag-pa med-pa*, Skt. *nāsty asamāhitacitta*); (5) they are without various perceptions (*tha-dad-pa'i 'du-shes med-pa*, Skt. *nāsti nānātvasaṃjñā*); (6) they are without equanimity which does not make distinctions (*so-sor ma-rtogs-pa'i btang-snyoms med-pa*, Skt. *nāsty apratisaṃkhyāyopekṣā*); (7) they do not degenerate in their devotion (*'dun-pa nyams-pa med-pa*, Skt. *nāsti cchandasya hāniḥ*); (8) they do not degenerate in their perseverance (*brtson-'grus nyams-pa med-pa*, Skt. *nāsti vīryasya hāniḥ*); (9) they do not degenerate in their recollection (*dran-pa nyams-pa med-pa*, Skt. *nāsti smṛtihāniḥ*); (10) they do not degenerate in their contemplation (*ting-'dzin nyams-pa med-pa*, Skt. *nāsti samādhihāniḥ*); (11) they do not degenerate in their discriminative awareness (*shes-rab nyams-pa med-pa*, Skt. *nāsti prajñāhāniḥ*); (12) they do not degenerate in their liberation (*rnam-grol nyams-pa med-pa*, Skt. *nāsti vimuktihāniḥ*); (13) all the activities of their bodies are preceded by pristine cognition and are followed by pristine cognition (*lus-kyi las thams-cad ye-shes-kyi sngon-du 'gro-shing ye-shes-kyi rjes-su 'brang-ba*, Skt. *sarvakāyakarmajñānapūrvagamaṃ jñānānuparivarti*); (14) all the activities of their speech are preceded by pristine cognition and are followed by pristine cognition (*ngag-gi las thams-cad ye-shes-kyi sngon-du 'gro-shing ye-shes-kyi rjes-su 'brang-ba*, Skt. *sarvavākkarmajñānapūrvagamaṃ jñānānuparivarti*); (15) all the activities of their minds are preceded by pristine cognition and are followed by pristine cognition (*yid-kyi las thams-cad ye-shes-kyi sngon-du 'gro-shing ye-shes-kyi rjes-su 'brang-ba*, Skt. *sarvamanaḥkarma jñānapūrvagamaṃ jñānānuparivarti*); (16) they enter into the perception of the pristine cognition which is unobstructed and unimpeded in respect of the past (*'das-pa'i dus-la ma-chags ma-thogs-pa'i ye-shes gzigs-par 'jug-go*, Skt. *atīte 'dhvany asaṅgam apratihataṃ jñānadarśanaṃ pravartate*); (17) they enter into the perception of the pristine cognition which is unobstructed and unimpeded in respect of the future (*ma-'ongs-pa'i dus-la ma-chags ma-thogs-pa'i ye-shes gzigs-par 'jug-go*, Skt. *anāgate 'dhvany asaṅgam apratihataṃ jñānadarśanaṃ pravartate*); and (18) they enter into the perception of the pristine cognition which is unobstructed and unimpeded in respect of the present (*da-ltar-gyi dus-la ma-chags ma-thogs-pa'i ye-shes gzigs-par 'jug-go*, Skt. *pratyutpanne 'dhvany asaṅgam apratihataṃ jñānadarśanaṃ pravartate*); Mvt. (135-53). 22, 140

EIGHTEEN PSYCHOPHYSICAL BASES *khams bco-brgyad*, Skt. *aṣṭadaśadhātu*

The sensory bases of the eye, form and the consciousness of the eye; those of the ear, sound and the consciousness of the ear; those of the nose, smell and the consciousness of the nose; those of the tongue, taste and the consciousness of the tongue; those of the body, touch and the consciousness of the body; and those of the intellect, phenomena and the consciousness of the intellect; Mvt. (2040-58). 13, 55, 513

EIGHTEEN SCHOOLS *sde-pa bco-brgyad*, Skt. *aṣṭadaśanikāya*

These are: the Āryasarvāstivāda who subdivided into the Kāśyapīya, Mahiśāsaka, Dharmaguptaka, Bahuśrūtīya, Tāmraśāṭīya, Vibhajyavāda and Mūlasarvāstivādin; the Āryasaṃmitīya who subdivided into the Kaurukullika, Avantaka and Vātsīputrīya; the Āryamahāsaṃghika who subdivided into the Pūrvaśaila, Uttaraśaila, Haimavata, Lokottaravāda and Prajñaptivāda; and the Āryasthavira sect who subdivided into the Mahāvihāravādin, Jetavanīya and Abhayagirivāsin. Refer to *Blue Annals*, pp. 27-33. There are, however, many conflicting accounts, on which see HBI (Ch. VI). 429

EIGHTEEN SECRET LIBERATORS *gsang-ba'i sgrol-ging bco-brgyad*

As listed in Nebesky-Wojkowitz, *Oracles and Demons of Tibet*, pp. 278-9, these comprise nine male spirits (*pho-dgu*), namely, *vajra ging-ka-ra*, *rdo-rje gnod-sbyin*, *rdo-rje srin-po*, *rdo-rje 'byung-po*, *rdo-rje spyang-khyi*, *rdo-rje gshin-rje*, *rdo-rje ro-langs*, *rdo-rje 'chi-bdag* and *rdo-rje dus-'tshams*; and nine female spirits (*mo-dgu*), namely, *khams-gsum dbugs sdud-ma*, *dbang-sdud lcags-kyus 'dren-ma*, *khams-gsum rgyas-'debs-ma*, *gzugs-med rlung-ltar 'du-ma*, *gar-gyi glog-ltar 'du-ma*, *rbod-ltong lam-ltar byad-ma*, *rna-nyan phra-ma zer-ma*, *khams-gsum snying-gsod-ma* and *tshogs-kyi phyag-tshangs chen-mo*. 620

NINETEEN

NINETEEN-DEITY MAṆḌALA OF MAÑJUVAJRA *'jam-dpal rdo-rje lha bcu-dgu*

As listed in Ngor Thartse Khenpo Sonam Gyatso et al., *Tibetan Maṇḍalas: The Ngor Collection*, 44:3, the dieties are: Mañjuśrīvajra (Guhyasamāja), Vairocana, Ratnasambhava, Amitābha, Amoghasiddhi, Locanā, Māmakī, Pāṇḍaravāsinī, Tārā, *gzugs rdo-rje-ma*, *sgra rdo-rje-ma*, *dri rdo-rje-ma*, *ro rdo-rje-ma*, *reg-bya rdo-rje-ma*, *chos-dbyings rdo-rje-ma*, *gshin-rje gshed*, *shes-rab mthar-byed*, *padma mthar-byed* and *bgegs mthar-byed*. 496, n. 525

NINETEEN ROOT DOWNFALLS *rtsa-ltung bcu-dgu*, Skt. **ekonaviṃśatimūlāpatti*

There are five root downfalls certain for kings, five for councillors, eight for ordinary persons and one which is common to all. These are enumerated as follows in Longcenpa, *Treasury of Spiritual and Philosophical Systems*, p. 200: The five certain for kings are to steal the wealth of the THREE PRECIOUS JEWELS, to punish disciplined monks, to direct a renunciate away from his or her training, to commit the five inexpiable sins and to hold wrong views. The five certain for councillors are to subjugate towns, the countryside, citadels, cities and provinces. The eight certain for ordinary persons are to teach emptiness to those of unrefined intelligence, to oppose those who enter into the greater vehicle, to join the greater vehicle having rejected the *prātimokṣa* vows, to uphold or cause one to uphold the vehicles of pious attendants and self-centred buddhas, to praise oneself and depreciate others, to speak of one's own receptivity as profound, to misappropriate the wealth of the Precious Jewels and to cause others to abandon the riches of tranquillity. That which is common to all is to abandon the enlightened attitude of aspiration. The foremost canonical source is the *Sūtra of Ākāśagarbha*, as summarised in Śāntideva's *Compendium of Lessons*, (Ch. 4). 235

TWENTY

TWENTY COMMITMENTS CONCERNING ATTAINMENT *sgrub-pa'i nyi-shu*

These Anuyoga commitments are listed by Jamgön Kongtrül, *shes-bya kun-khyab mdzod*, Vol. 2, pp. 185-6, as follows: one should not injure the body of or disobey the commands of one's vajra master; one should not enjoy one's teacher's consort; one should not squander the feast offerings of the faithful; one should neither defile the wealth of the precious jewels and the learned, nor drink ale to the point of intoxication; one should not enjoy the female consort of a vajra brother; one should not adhere to a consort who lacks the appropriate signs; one should not adhere to sacramental substances which lack the appropriate signs; one should not depreciate the attributes of the learned; one should not teach the secret doctrines to unworthy recipients; one should not abandon a consort who has the appropriate signs or a student who is a worthy recipient; one should separate neither the genuine bliss and emptiness, nor the symbolic male and female deities; one should not quarrel at home even with one's siblings or spouse; one should not enjoy that which has been enjoyed and left over by others; one should not covet the teacher's seat; one should not break one's natural retreat; one should not abandon contemplation out of indolence; one should not interrupt recitation and rituals with the words of men; one should not transgress the seals which symbolise empowerment, nor should one forget their symbolism; one should not disturb the maṇḍala of yogins, nor divert the strength of living beings; and one should continuously bear one's master upon the crown of one's head. 367

TWENTY ELEMENTS OF SAṂSĀRA *'khor-ba'i chos nyi-shu*

To regard form as self, as a possession of self, as in the self, or as that in which the self is; and analogously for the remaining four components of feeling, perception, habitual tendencies and consciousness. 347

TWENTY MOUNTAIN CAVES OF NGARI *mnga'-ris skor-du gangs-brag nyi-shu*

The twenty snow mountains of Ngari are *thang-lha gangs*, *ma-mkhar gangs*, *ti-se gangs*, *bu-le gangs*, *'o-de gung-rgyal gangs*, *sham-po gangs*, *mkhar-ri gangs*, *lha-rgod gangs*, *pho-ma gangs*, *rdo-rje gangs*, *jo-mo kha-rag gangs*, *ha'o gang-bzang gangs*, *rtse-'dud gangs*, *la-phyi gangs*, *tshe-ring gangs*, *ti-sgro gangs*, *gsal-rje gangs*, *lha-ri gangs*, *tsā-ri gangs* and *nga-la gangs*. Not all of these mountain ranges, however, are in the Ngari province of Tibet. 518

TWENTY ROOT DOWNFALLS *rtsa-ltung nyi-shu*, Skt. **viṃśatimūlāpatti*

According to the *Pagoda of Precious Jewels*, these comprise the NINETEEN ROOT DOWNFALLS, with the addition of the downfall which occurs when the enlightened mind of engagement or entrance is abandoned. 235

TWENTY WAYS (IN WHICH THE BODHISATTVA'S BODY IS ENLIGHTENED) *rnam-pa nyi-shu byang-chub-pa*

According to Nyoshul Khen Rinpoche, this refers to the ten aspects of renunciation and the ten aspects of realisation which pertain to the TEN LEVELS OF BODHISATTVAS. The term may also refer in Madhyamaka to the purification of the fourfold view of self (*bdag-lta bzhi*) which applies to each of the FIVE COMPONENTS of form, feeling, perception, habitual tendencies and consciousness (see TWENTY ELEMENTS OF SAṂSĀRA); and in the context of the vehicles of secret mantra, it may refer to the accomplishment of twenty specific exercises pertaining to the experiential cultivation of the energy channels, currents and seminal points within the body. 416

TWENTY-ONE

TWENTY-ONE *GENYEN dge-bsnyen nyer-gcig*

According to Nebesky-Wojkowitz, *Oracles and Demons of Tibet*, pp. 222-3, these are named after the mountains or valleys which are their residences, namely, *tsha-ri gangs*, *bar-yul gangs*, *la-phyi gangs*, *gnod-sbyin gangs*, *rgyal-gyi mkhan-pa-lung*, *dpal-gyi gra-bu-lung*, *dpal-gyi 'jag-ma-lung*, *skyid-kyi gro-ma-lung*, *spang-phung gangs*, *gsal-ja gangs*, *gYu-lung gangs*, *'brong-rdza gangs*, *bal-yul gangs*, *jo-mo gangs*, *rnye-bo gangs*, *rdza-yul gangs*, *rna-nam gangs*, *shel-bzang gangs*, *rong-btsan gangs*, *sgam-po gangs* and *lho-rong gangs*. Alternatively, in the various recensions of the *Injunctions of Padma*, it is recounted that, at *dam-snying grongs-ngos* in Kham, Padmasambhava subdued Nyencen Thangla with his retinue of twenty-one demons (four *rgyal-po* spirits, four *sde-dpon*, four *dmag-dpon*, four *bdud-po* and five *las-mkhan*) and having bound them to the *dge-gnyen* (Skt. *upāsaka*) vows renamed them as *mchog-rag-rtsal*, the "Protector of Marpori" and the "twenty-one *genyen*". 513

TWENTY-ONE HIGHER REALMS *khams gong-ma nyi-shu-rtsa-gcig*

The SEVENTEEN FORM REALMS together with the FOUR FORMLESS REALMS. 14-15, 61

TWENTY-ONE MAṆḌALA CLUSTERS OF THE *GATHERING OF THE TRANSMITTED PRECEPTS bka'-'dus tshom-bu nyer-gcig*

As enumerated in *Ocean of Doctrines, the Gathering of Transmitted Precepts*, these are: Glorious Mahottara Heruka in the centre; Yangdak Heruka, Vajrāvali, Vajrapāṇi and *rdo-rje rtsal-rdzogs* in the east; Vajrakapālamāla, Cakrasaṃvara, Yamāntaka and *ratna rtsal-rdzogs* in the south; Hayagrīva, Hevajra, Guhyasamāja and *padma rtsal-rdzogs* in the west; Chemcok, Kālacakra, *mkha'-klong 'khyil-ba* and *karma rtsal-rdzogs* in the north; *mngon-rdzogs rgyal-po* in the south-east; Vajrakumāra in the south-west; *dregs-'dul* in the north-west; and *stobs-ldan nag-po* in the north-east. 779

TWENTY-THREE

TWENTY-THREE COMMITMENTS RELATING TO DISCIPLINE *brtul-zhugs-kyi nyer-gsum*

These Anuyoga commitments are enumerated in Jamgön Kongtrül, *shes-bya kun-khyab mdzod*, Vol. 2, p. 189-92, as follows: (1) In the manner of a fox who has been trapped, and turns away without regard for life itself, having had a limb torn off, the yogin guards the commitments even at the cost of life itself. This is the skilful means which destroys disharmonious aspects and enters into the power of the commitments (*va*). (2) In the manner of the all-knowing horse who knows and swiftly encircles everything in a moment, discriminative awareness is the unimpeded discipline regarding all individual and general characteristics that can be known (*cang-shes*). (3) In the manner of a Gyiling steed which roams anywhere with great expressive power, the respectful body enacts the discipline which perseveres in the dance, mudrās and exercises, and destroys idleness (*gyi-ling*). (4) In the manner of a rutting elephant who, incensed, destroys whatever enemies appear without investigating them, one who knows saṃsāra and nirvāṇa to be indivisible performs conduct which destroys the four enemies of view and conduct (*glang-chen spyod*). (5) In the manner of a tiger whose aggressive spirit is fierce, overbearing and hostile, the powerful discipline of heroic contemplation which realises the abiding nature performs rites of "liberation" and transference of consciousness for those students who are aggressive (*stag*). (6) In the manner of a great garuḍa who glides effortlessly through the sky and discerns all without special regard, the view is one of effortless conduct through realisation of the indivisibility of the expanse and pristine cognition (*khyung-chen*). (7) In the manner of a bear who terrifies and crushes whatever it focuses upon without hesitation, one who has plumbed the depths of the view and conduct of yoga is disciplined in the rites of sorcery and sexual union without hesitation (*dom*). (8) In the manner of an ocean whose golden depths are unmoved is the discipline of firm unchanging mind which is able (to understand) the profound secret meaning and experiential cultivation (*rgya-mtsho*). (9) In the manner of a dumb mute who neither accepts nor rejects is the discipline which reaches the limit of discriminative awareness, realising selflessness by impartial meditative absorption (*lkug-pa gti-mug-can*). (10) In the manner of unmoving Mount Sumeru is the discipline of skilful means which depends on the unwavering antidote of unchanging loyalty to teacher and friends, and on the sinking into and grasping of contemplation (*ri-rab mi-gYo-ba*). (11) In the manner of the vast and extensive sky which accomodates everything without acceptance and rejection is the discipline which is warm and hospitable to fraternal yogins and the conduct which does not lapse from the vehicle of saṃsāra and nirvāṇa but remains within this view and conduct of supreme identity (*nam-mkha'*). (12) In the manner of a thunderbolt which falls and destroys is the discipline which unimpededly destroys all enemies and obstacles by forceful contemplation (*thog*). (13) In the manner of Vajrapāṇi who destroys all who hold erroneous views, the yogin performs the discipline through which, having meditated on the wrathful deity, one cuts through and destroys these views without hesitation (*lag-na-rdo-rje*). (14) In the manner of a crow who looks out for both enemies and plunder at the same time, is the discipline of skilful means which perseveres simultaneously in constant renunciation and enterprise (*bya-rog*). (15) In the manner of an elephant who plunges into water without regard for being soaked or unsoaked, one who has plumbed the depths of the view and conduct of supreme identity practises without the duality of renunciation and acceptance, and practises the discipline of the four rites of enlightened activity without discriminating among those who require training (*glang-chen*). (16) In the manner of a friendless lion who sits alone is the discipline which sustains the view and meditation by abiding in solitude after renouncing those disharmonious associations of view and conduct (*seng-ge*). (17) In the manner of a duck who easily associates without marriage, so is the discipline which associates without ties and the skilful means which cause sentient beings to reach the happiness of liberation through compassion and loving kindness (*ngang-pa*). (18) In the manner of a magician who constructs illusions, one who meditates and teaches having understood components and activity fields to be the apparitional maṇḍala of the conquerors enacts discipline through skilful means (*sgyu-ma-mkhan*). (19) In the manner of a pig who eats everything without discerning purity and impurity are the discipline and conduct of sameness, without accepting and rejecting the five sacramental substances (*phag*). (20) In the manner of a jackal who likes to kill without impediment is the discipline of skilful means which "liberates" heretical thoughts through compassion experienced in view and conduct, arrays such consciousness in an uncorrupted (realm), and thus perfects the provisions (*ce-spyang*). (21) In the manner of lightning which illuminates everything swiftly and simultaneously is the discipline which perseveres so that one's own benefit be attained and others' benefit be swiftly attained through experiential cultivation of the path (*glog*). (22) In the manner of a vulture who avoids the taking of life as a moral discipline is the discipline which delights in and sustains commitments associated with supreme identity but appears not to indulge in other vehicles connected with disciplinary conduct (*bya-rgod*). (23) In the manner of a modest king who rules the kingdom and dearly protects his retinue rather than himself, the yogin performs acts of pure delightful discipline, protects living beings by realising all things not on behalf of himself but for others, and overpowers the kingdom by the discipline which strives through skilful means to experience and realise the indivisibility of the expanse and pristine cognition as supreme bliss (*rgyal-po bag-ldan*). 367

TWENTY-FOUR

TWENTY-FOUR LANDS *gyul nyer-bzhi*

According to D. L. Snellgrove, *The Hevajra Tantra*, Vol. 1, p. 70, these are Jālandhara, Oḍḍiyāna, Paurṇagiri, Kāmarūpa, Mālava, Sindhu, Nagara, Munmuni, Kāruṇyapāṭaka, Devīkoṭa, Karmārapāṭaka, Kulatā, Arbuda, Godāvarī, Himādri, Harikela, Lampāka, Kāñci, Saurāṣṭra, Kaliṅga, Kokaṇa, Caritra, Kośala and Vindhyākaumārapaurikā. 889

TWENTY-FIVE

TWENTY-FIVE CATEGORIES (OF THE SĀṂKHYA) *shes-bya thams-cad grangs nyi-shu rtsa-lnga*, Skt. *pañcaviṃśatitattva*

The self (*puruṣa*) and the twenty-four aspects of "nature" (*prakṛti*): prime matter (*pradhāna*); intellect (*buddhi* or *mahat*); ego (*ahaṃkāra*); the five quiddities (*pañcatanmātra*) which are the objects of the FIVE SENSES; the eleven faculties (*ekādaśendriya*) which are the FIVE SENSE ORGANS with the addition of speech, hand, foot, the organs of excretion and generation, and mind; and the FIVE ELEMENTS. 16, 64

TWENTY-FIVE FIELDS/WORLD SYSTEMS (ON VAIROCANA'S HANDS) *(zhing-) khams nyi-shu-rtsa-lnga*

These are structured vertically upon the hands of Buddha Vairocana, corresponding successively to his body, speech, mind, attributes and activities. According to Longcenpa, *Wish-fulfilling Treasury*, pp. 28-31, they are *dpal-'byung 'od-zer rnam-snang* (representing body of body), *padma dpal-gyis brgyan* (body of speech), *rin-chen rgyan snang-bkod* (body of mind), *me-tog sil-ma bkram-pa* (body of attributes), *dge-ba sna-tshogs dag-pa'i zhing* (body of activities); *me-tog shin-tu rgyas-pa* (speech of body), *yang-dag 'byung-ba'i gzi-brjid dbyangs* (speech of speech), *sgra-dbyangs mi-zad sgrogs-po'i zhing* (speech of mind), *rdo-rje rgyal-mtshan* (speech of attributes), *rnam-par snang* (speech of activities); *snang-ba'i mdog* (mind of body), *rnam-snang dang-ba* (mind of speech), *mi-mjed 'jig-rten-gyi khams* (mind of mind), *'od-'phro dri-med* (mind of attributes), *rin-chen brgyan-pa'i zhing* (mind of activities); *rdul-bral* (attributes of body), *dag-par snang* (attributes of speech), *rin-chen 'od-'phro* (attributes of mind), *rab-snang* (attributes of attributes), *snang-byed* (attributes of activity); *'od-byed* (activity of body), *'od-'phro bkod-pa* (activity of speech), *snang-ldan* (activity of mind), *rab-mdzes* (activity of attributes) and *rab-tu dga'-ba* (activity of activity). 123, 130, 409

TWENTY-FIVE GREAT ACCOMPLISHED MASTERS OF CHIMPU *mchims-phu'i grub-chen nyer-lnga*

Otherwise known as *rje-'bangs nyer-lnga* (the "king and his twenty-five subjects"), they are enumerated in *History*, pp. 534-6. The exact enumerations of the fifty-five realised ones of Yangdzong, the one hundred and eight accomplished masters of Yerpa and Chuwori and the thirty mantra adepts of Sheldrak are unknown. Of the twenty-five ḍākinīs, seventeen are enumerated. 537

TWENTY-FIVE GREAT PILGRIMAGE PLACES OF KHAM AND AMDO *mdo-khams gnas-chen nyer-lnga*

A) *skyo-brag seng-ge rdzong* in *rdza-chu* (main pilgrimage place of buddha-body); (1) *spyi-'byams nyi-zla-phug* in *rdza-chu* (body aspect of buddha-body); (2) *glo-thu karma* (speech aspect of buddha-body); (3) *mnyan* in *'bri-klung* (mind aspect of buddha-body); (4) *kha-la rong-sgo* in Nangcen (attribute aspect of buddha-body); (5) *he brag-dkar* (activity aspect of buddha-body);
B) *spu-bo dga'-ba-lung* (main pilgrimage place of buddha-speech); (6) *padma shel-ri* (speech aspect of buddha-speech); (7) *kha-ba dkar-po* in Tshawarong (body aspect of buddha-speech); (8) *na-bun rdzong* in Nangcen (mind aspect of buddha-speech); (9) *ye-rgyal nam-mkha' rdzong* (attribute aspect of buddha-speech); (10) *hor tre-shod* or *lcags-mdud kha-ba lung-ring* (activity aspect of buddha-speech);
C) *dan-ti shel-gyi brag* in *rma-khog* (main pilgrimage place of buddha-mind); (11) *rma-smad rdo-rje'i brag* (mind aspect of buddha-mind); (12) *me-nyag bzhag-ra lha-rtse* (body aspect of buddha-mind); (13) *war-ti'i brag* (speech aspect of buddha-mind); (14) *mkha'-'gro 'bum-rdzong* in lower Nangcen (attribute aspect of buddha-mind); (15) *spo-ne brag-dkar* (activity aspect of buddha-mind);
D) *ru-dam gangs-kyi ra-ba*, otherwise called *khro-ri rdo-rje zil-khrom* (main pilgrimage place of buddha-attributes); (16) *rdzong-shod bde-gshegs 'dus-pa'i pho-brang* in *'dzings* (attribute aspect of buddha-attributes); (17) *rngul-mda' pho-brang* in front of Lhündrup Teng Temple in Derge (body aspect of buddha-attributes); (18) *padma shel-phug* in the lower valley of *rme-shod 'dzom-nang* (speech aspect of buddha-attributes); (19) *tsā-'dra rin-chen brag* (mind aspect of buddha-attributes); (20) *'dzom-thog phu-seng gnam-brag* in *'bri-chu* (activity aspect of buddha-attributes);
E) *kaḥ-thog rdo-rje gdan* (main pilgrimage place of buddha-activity); (21) *brag-ri rdo-rje spungs-pa* (activity aspect of buddha-activity); (22) *gtsang-gshis rdo-rje gro-lod* (speech aspect of buddha-activity); (23) *rngu* (body aspect of buddha-activity); (24) *bkra-shis*, perhaps *kam-po gangs-ra* (mind aspect of

buddha-activity); (25) *hyal-gyi brag* (attribute aspect of buddha-activity). 518, 867

TWENTY-FIVE (GREAT PROFOUND) TREASURES *(zab-pa'i) gter(-chen) nyer-lnga*

According to Dalai Lama V, *Record of Teachings Received*, Vol. 2, pp. 476ff.: "The profound treasures of Orgyen Rinpoche consist of central treasures which penetrate like roots (*dbus-gter 'jug-pa rtsa-ba lta-bu*), southern treasures concentrated like stalks (*lho-gter dril-ba sdong-po lta-bu*), western treasures radiating like flowers (*nub-gter gsal-ba me-tog lta-bu*), northern treasures expanding like branches (*byang-gter rgyas-pa yal-ga lta-bu*) and eastern treasures maturing like fruits (*shar-gter smin-pa 'bras-bu lta-bu*)." Since each category has subdivisions resembling roots, stalks, flowers, branches and fruits there are said to be twenty-five great profound treasures altogether. Refer to Tulku Thondup Rinpoche, *Hidden Teachings of Tibet*, p. 115 and notes. 518, 822

TWENTY-FIVE RESULTANT REALITIES *'bras-chos nyer-lnga*

These are the FIVE BUDDHA-BODIES, the FIVE MODES OF BUDDHA-SPEECH, the FIVE KINDS OF BUDDHA-MIND, the FIVE ENLIGHTENED ATTRIBUTES and the FIVE ENLIGHTENED ACTIVITIES. 34, 35, 267, 282-3, 288-9, 369

TWENTY-FIVE WORLD SYSTEMS *khams nyer-lnga*

See TWENTY-FIVE FIELDS/WORLD SYSTEMS (ON VAIROCANA'S HANDS)

TWENTY-EIGHT

TWENTY-EIGHT COMMITMENTS (OF MAHĀYOGA) *(rnal-'byor chen-po'i) dam-tshig nyi-shu-rtsa-brgyad*

According to the *Miraculous Key of Further Discernment*, these are the three basic commitments of body, speech and mind (*sku-gsung-thugs-kyi rtsa-ba'i dam-tshig gsum*) and the twenty-five ancillary ones, five of which are to be practised (*spyad-par bya-ba*), namely, five kinds of rites of "liberation" and sexual practices; five not to be renounced (*spang-bar mi-bya-ba*), namely, the FIVE CONFLICTING EMOTIONS; five to be adopted (*blang-bar bya-ba*), namely, the FIVE NECTARS; five to be known (*shes-par bya-ba*), namely, the FIVE COMPONENTS, FIVE ELEMENTS, FIVE SENSE OBJECTS, sacraments of meat and propensities in their pure nature; and five to be attained (*bsgrub-par bya-ba*), namely, the buddha-body, speech, mind, attributes and activities. Cf. Līlāvajra, *Clarification of Commitments*, pp. 147-8; and Jamgön Kongtrül, *shes-bya kun-khyab-mdzod*, Vol. 2, (pp. 182-5). 361

TWENTY-EIGHT COMMON COMMITMENTS (OF ANUYOGA) *thun-mongs-gi nyi-shu-rtsa-brgyad*

These are equivalent to the TWENTY-EIGHT COMMITMENTS OF MAHĀYOGA. 367

THIRTIES

THIRTY DESIGNATED ARTS *bzor-btags-pa sum-cu*

These include creative techniques, writing, drawing, arithmetic, wrestling, hair-styling, deportment, elephant-riding, sword-fencing, javelin-throwing, archery and so forth; Mvt. (4972-5006). 98

THIRTY-TWO MAJOR MARKS *mtshan-bzang so-gnyis*, Skt. *dvātriṃśanmahāpuruṣalakṣaṇa*

According to the *Ornament of Emergent Realisation*, Ch. 8, vv. 13-17, these are palms and soles marked with doctrinal wheels, feet firm like those of a tortoise, webbed fingers and toes, soft and supple hands and feet, a body with seven well-proportioned parts, long toes and fingers, broad arches, a tall and straight body, inconspicuous ankles, body-hairs which curl upwards, antelope-like calves, long and beautiful arms, a supremely contracted sexual organ, a golden complexion and delicate skin, well-grown body hairs which curl distinctly to the right, a hair-ringlet (*ūrṇakeśa*) between the eyebrows, a lion-like chest, well-rounded shoulders, a broad back, a supreme sense of taste, a symmetrical body like a banyan tree, the *uṣṇīṣa* proturberance on the head, a long and beautiful tongue, a Brahmā-like voice, lion-like jaws, teeth which are pure white, equal in size, close-fitting, and forty in number, sapphire blue eyes, and bovine eyelashes; Mvt. 235-67. See also R. Thurman, *The Holy Teaching of Vimalakīrti*, p. 156; and H. Dayal, *The Bodhisattva Doctrine in Sanskrit Buddhist Literature*, (pp. 300-5). 20, 124-5

THIRTY-FIVE ORNAMENTS OF SENSE *don-rgyan sum-cu so-lnga*, Skt. *arthālaṃkāra*

According to Daṇḍin's *Mirror of Poetics*, Ch. 2, and Gupta, *A Critical Study of Daṇḍin and his Works*, these are: natural description (*svabhāvokti*), simile (*upamā*), metaphor (*rūpaka*), poetic association (*dīpaka*), repetition (*āvṛtti*), denial (*ākṣepa*), corroboration (*arthāntaranyāsa*), contrast (*vyatireka*), peculiar causation (*vibhāvanā*), concise suggestion (*samāsokti*), hyperbole (*atiśayokti*), poetic fancy (*utprekṣā*), cause (*hetu*), misrepresentation (*leśa*), subtlety (*sūkṣma*), relative order (*yathāsaṃkhya*), flattery (*preyas*), demeanour (*rasavat*), coincidence (*samāhita*), vigour (*ūrjasvi*), periphrastic speech (*paryāyokta*), exaltation (*udātta*), obfuscation (*apahnuti*), double entendre (*śliṣṭa*), statement of difference (*viśeṣokti*), equal pairing (*tulyayogitā*), incongruity (*virodha*), artful praise (*vyā-jastuti*), damning with faint praise (*aprastutapraśaṃsā*), co-mention (*sahokti*), illustrative simile (*nidarśana*), benediction (*āśis*), barter (*parivṛtti*), description of the past or future as if it were the present (*bhāvika*) and a conjunction of poetic figures (*saṃkirṇa*). 105

THIRTY-SIX ACTIONS OF THE WHEEL OF THE INEXHAUSTIBLE ORNAMENTS OF BUDDHA-BODY, SPEECH AND MIND *sku-gsung-thugs mi-zad-pa rgyan-gyi 'khor-lo'i mdzad-pa sum-cu-rtsa-drug*

These are the TWELVE DEEDS OF THE SUPREME EMANATIONAL BODY, the TWELVE DIFFERENT DOCTRINAL WHEELS OF BUDDHA-SPEECH and the TWELVE DIFFERENT INTENTIONS OF BUDDHA-MIND. 121

THIRTY-SIX CHARACTERISTICS (OF DRAMA) *mtshan-nyid sum-cu-so-drug*

According to Bharata, *Dramatical Treatise*, Ch. 17, these are embellishment (*bhūṣaṇa*), abbreviation (*akṣarasaṃghāta*), fortune/prosperity (*śobhā*), declaration (*udāharaṇa*), cause (*hetu*), doubt (*saṃśaya*), illustration (*dṛṣṭānta*), attainment (*prāpti*), intention (*abhiprāya*), evidence (*nidarśana*), explanation (*nirūkta*), accomplishment (*siddhi*), distinction (*viśeṣana*), lack of qualities (*guṇātipāta*), hyperbole (*atiśaya*), equal scrutiny (*tulyatarka*), versification (*padoccaya*), perception (*dṛṣṭa*), indication (*upadiṣṭa*), ideas (*vicāra*), opposition (*tadviparyāya*), slips of the tongue (*bhraṃśa*), conciliation (*anunaya*), garlands (*mālā*), concord (*dākṣiṇya*), reproach (*garhaṇa*), presumption (*arthāpatti*), proof (*prasiddhi*), question (*pṛcchā*), beauty (*sārūpya*), imagination (*manoratha*), disparagement (*leśa*), agitation (*kṣobha*), enumeration of qualities (*guṇakīrtana*), unmentioned accomplishment (*anuktasiddhi*) and words of affection (*priyavacana*). 107

THIRTY-SIX EMPOWERMENTS/CEREMONIES (OF ANUYOGA) *dbang-chog so-drug*

The ten outer empowerments (*phyi-yi dbang bcu*), eleven inner empowerments (*nang-gi dbang bcu-gcig*), thirteen empowerments of attainment (*sgrub-pa'i dbang bcu-gsum*) and two secret empowerments (*gsang-ba'i dbang gnyis*). Refer to Jamgön Kongtrül, *shes-bya kun-khyab mdzod*, Vol. 2, pp. 748-9; and to the Peking *Kangyur*, Vol. 9, (pp. 276-7). 364-5

THIRTY-SEVEN ASPECTS OF ENLIGHTENMENT *byang-chub-kyi chos sum-cu-rtsa-bdun*, Skt. *saptatriṃśadbodhipakṣadharma*

These are the FOUR ESSENTIAL RECOLLECTIONS, the FOUR CORRECT TRAININGS, the FOUR SUPPORTS FOR MIRACULOUS ABILITY, the FIVE FACULTIES, the FIVE POWERS, the SEVEN BRANCHES OF ENLIGHTENMENT and the EIGHTFOLD PATH. 236

FORTIES

FORTY PRINCIPALITIES *sil-ma bzhi-bcu*

As a result of constant warfare between the TWELVE MINOR KINGDOMS, power devolved into the hands of forty principalities ruled by forty minor feudal kings. Apart from *'brog-mo rnam-gsum* ruled by the lord *rgyal-po se-mi ra-khrid*, *gye-mo yul-drug* ruled by the lord *gye-rje mkhar-ba* and *se-mo gru-bzhi* ruled by the lord *gnyags-gru 'brang*, their names and localities are unknown at the present day. Refer to Dudjom Rinpoche, *rgyal-rabs*, (pp. 13-14). 507, 949

FORTY-TWO PEACEFUL DEITIES *zhi-ba'i lha zhe-gnyis*

According to the *Tantra of the Secret Nucleus* and related works, such as the so-called *Tibetan Book of the Dead*, these are Samantabhadra, Samantabhadrī, Vairocana, Akṣobhya, Ratnasambhava, Amitābha, Amoghasiddhi, Ākāśadhātvīśvarī, Buddhalocanā, Māmakī, Paṇḍaravāsinī, Samayatārā, Kṣitigarbha, Vajrapāṇi, Ākāśagarbha, Avalokiteśvara, Lāsyā, Mālyā, Gītā, Nartī, Maitreya, Nivaraṇaviṣkambhin, Samantabhadra, Mañjuśrī, Dhūpā, Puṣpā, Ālokā, Gandhā, Amṛtakuṇḍalin, Hayagrīva, Mahābala, Yamāntaka, Aṅkuśā, Pāśā, Sphoṭā, Ghaṇṭā, Munīndra, Vemacitra, Śākyamuni, Siṃha, Jvālamukha and Yamarāja. 125-6, 623, 644, 691

FORTY-SIX TRANSGRESSIONS *nyes-byas zhe-drug*, Skt. *ṣaṭcatvāriṃśadduṣkṛta*

Refer to the *Twenty Verses on the Bodhisattva Vow*, translated in M. Tatz, *Difficult Beginnings*. These are also cited in Jamgön Kongtrül, *shes-bya kun-khyab mdzod*, Vol. 2, pp. 114-17, where they are explained to include thirty-four transgressions which contradict the gathering of virtuous doctrines and twelve which contradict activity on behalf of others. The former comprise seven contradicting liberality, nine contradicting moral discipline, four contradicting patience, three contradicting perseverance, three contradicting concentration and eight contradicting discriminative awareness. The latter comprise those transgressions which separate one from general acts of benefit and those which separate one from particular acts of benefit. 95

FIFTIES

FIFTY-ONE MENTAL EVENTS *sems-byung lnga-bcu-rtsa-gcig*, Skt. *ekapañcāśac-caitasika*

The five ever-present ones (*kun-'gro lnga*) of contact, attention, feeling, cognition and motivation; the five which determine objects (*yul so-sor nges-pa lnga*) of adherence, inclination, recollection, contemplation and discriminative awareness; the eleven attendant functions of every positive attitude (*bcu-gcig dge-sems kun-gyi 'khor-du 'byung-ba*) of faith, carefulness, lucidity, equanimity, decency, decorum, detachment, non-hatred, non-delusion, non-violence and perseverance; the six root conflicting emotions (*rtsa-ba'i nyon-mongs-pa drug*) of hatred, desire, arrogance, ignorance, view of mundane aggregates and doubt; and the twenty subsidiary conflicting emotions (*nye-bar nyon-mongs-pa nyi-shu*) of anger, hostility, dissimulation, malice, jealousy, miserliness, deception, dishonesty, spitefulness, pride, contempt, indecorum, dullness, over-exuberance, distrust, laziness, carelessness, forgetfulness, excitability and inattentiveness; and the four variables (*'gyur-ba bzhi*) of drowsiness, regret, ideas and scrutiny. Refer to H.V. Guenther, *Buddhist Philosophy in Theory and Practice*, pp. 63-4, which is based on Mipham Rinpoche, *yid-bzhin mdzod-kyi grub-mtha' bsdus-pa*, (pp. 13ff). 156

FIFTY-EIGHT BLOOD-DRINKERS/WRATHFUL DEITIES *khrag-thung/khro-bo lnga-bcu lnga-brgyad*

According to the *Tantra of the Secret Nucleus* and works such as the so-called *Tibetan Book of the Dead*, these comprise the Buddha, Vajra, Ratna, Padma and Karma Heruka, along with their respective Krodhīśvarī, the EIGHT GAURĪ or Mātaraḥ, the eight Piśācī, the twenty-eight Īśvarī and the four female gatekeepers. 623

SIXTIES

SIXTY DOCTRINES *chos-kyi rnam-grangs drug-cu*

The TWELVE DEEDS OF THE SUPREME EMANATIONAL BODY in the twelve realms, each of which possesses the FIVE EXCELLENCES of place, teacher, retinue, doctrine and time. 137

SIXTY-FOUR CRAFTS *sgyu-rtsal drug-cu rtsa-bzhi*

According to the *Sūtra of Extensive Play*, Ch. 10 (*Lipiśālāsaṃdarśana-parivarto daśamaḥ*), these include such crafts as flower-arranging, hunting and knowledge of the languages of many races including those of spiritual beings. 98, 418

SIXTY-FOUR ENLIGHTENED ATTRIBUTES *yon-tan-gyi chos drug-cu-rtsa-bzhi*, Skt. *catuḥṣaṣṭir guṇāh*

Refer to Ch. 3 (*Guṇādhikāra*) of the *Supreme Continuum of the Greater Vehicle* by Maitreya. These are the TEN POWERS OF A BUDDHA, the FOUR FEARLESSNESSES, the EIGHTEEN DISTINCT ATTRIBUTES OF THE BUDDHAS and the THIRTY-TWO MAJOR MARKS. 95, 203

SEVENTIES

SEVENTY POINTS OF THE *ORNAMENT OF EMERGENT REALISATION* *mngon-rtogs-rgyan-gyi don bdun-cu*

These represent the subdivisions of the EIGHT TOPICS OF THE *ORNAMENT OF EMERGENT REALISATION*. Refer to E. Conze, *Abhisamayālaṁkāra*, for detailed discussions. 95

EIGHTIES

EIGHTY MINOR MARKS *dpe-byad brgyad-cu*, Skt. *aśītyānuvyañjana*

These are enumerated in Mvt. 268-349; and refer to Thurman, *The Holy Teaching of Vimalakīrti*, (pp. 156-7). 20, 124-5

EIGHTY-FOUR ACCOMPLISHED MASTERS *grub-thob brgyad-cu rtsa-bzhi*, Skt. *caturaśītisiddha*

Refer to J. Robinson, *Buddha's Lions*, for their enumeration and life stories. 442

NINETIES

NINETY-SIX DOCTRINES (OF A SINGLE EMANATIONAL BODY) *chos dgu-bcu go-drug*

Refer to Jamgön Kongtrül, *shes-bya kun-khyab mdzod*, Vol. 1, (p. 327). 22, 138

HUNDREDS

HUNDRED AUTHENTIC FAMILIES OF BUDDHAS *sangs-rgyas rigs-brgya*

Those of the FORTY-TWO PEACEFUL DEITIES and the FIFTY-EIGHT BLOOD-DRINKERS. 591

HUNDRED TREASURE-FINDERS *gter-ston brgya-rtsa*

Refer to Tulku Thondup Rinpoche, *Hidden Teachings of Tibet*, pp. 189-201, for the traditional enumerations of the treasure-finders. 752

HUNDRED TREASURES WHICH WERE THE MASTER COPIES OF KING TRHISONG *rgyal-po'i bla-gter brgya*

These are not enumerated and are only known from a few colophons. 518

TWO HUNDRED AND FIFTY DISCIPLINES OF THE VINAYA *nyi-brgya lnga-bcu'i 'dul-khrims*

The vows of a fully-ordained monk (*dge-slong*, Skt. *bhikṣu*) which are explained in the *Transmissions of the Vinaya*. Refer also to C. S. Prebish, *Buddhist Monastic Discipline*, which describes these in detail. 230

EIGHT HUNDRED AND THIRTY-ONE ANCILLARY EMPOWERMENTS (OF ANUYOGA) *(anu-yo-ga'i) yan-lag-gi dbang brgyad-brgya so-gcig*

Refer to the discussion in Jamgön Kongtrül, *shes-bya kun-khyab mdzod*, Vol. 2, (p. 748). 364

THOUSANDS

THOUSAND BUDDHAS *sangs-rgyas stong-rtsa gcig*

Also known as the THOUSAND SUPREME EMANATIONAL BODIES, they are enumerated in detail in the *Auspicious Aeon Sūtra*. 136, 431, 624, 938, 944

THOUSAND SUPREME EMANATIONAL BODIES *mchog-gi sprul-sku stong-rtsa*

Refer to the *Sūtra of Inconceivable Secrets* as cited in Obermiller, *History of Buddhism*, Pt. 2, pp. 91ff.; and see the preceeding entry. 409

TWENTY-ONE THOUSAND (DOCTRINAL) COMPONENTS *(chos-kyi) phung-po nyis-khri chig-stong*

Those components of doctrine forming the Mantrapiṭaka of the Awareness-holders. 77-8

TWENTY-ONE THOUSAND PHENOMENA/KINDS (OF DESIRE, HATRED, DELUSION AND THEIR COMBINATION) *dug-gsum-ka cha-mnyam-pa-la nyi-khri chig-stong*

The four groups of conflicting emotions arising from the ramification of dispositions grounded in ignorance. Cf. the discussion in Longcenpa, *Treasury of Spiritual and Philosophical Systems*, (p. 37). 55

EIGHTY-FOUR THOUSAND CONFLICTING EMOTIONS/PHENOMENA *nyon-mong/chos brgyad-khri bzhi-stong*

The amalgam of the four groups of conflicting emotions referred to in the preceeding entry. 55, 133

EIGHTY-FOUR THOUSAND (DOCTRINAL) COMPONENTS *(chos-kyi) phung-po brgyad-khri bzhi-stong*

The antidotes corresponding to the EIGHTY-FOUR THOUSAND CONFLICTING EMOTIONS. Cf. also the *Treasury of Abhidharma*, Ch. 1, (v. 25). 17, 77, 86, 133, 763, 925

EIGHTY-FOUR THOUSAND DOCTRINES OF THE VEHICLES *brgyad-khri bzhi-stong theg-pa'i chos*

The EIGHTY-FOUR THOUSAND DOCTRINAL COMPONENTS. 925.

MILLIONS

SIX MILLION FOUR HUNDRED THOUSAND VERSES (OF THE NATURAL GREAT PERFECTION) *rang-bzhin rdzogs-pa chen-po ślo-ka 'bum-phrag drug-cu rtsa-bzhi*

The traditional enumeration of the volume of texts of the Great Perfection, as represented by the Atiyoga sections of the *Collected Tantras of the Nyingmapa*. 332, 493, 539, 922

Bibliography

Introduction

This bibliography is divided into two parts. The first lists all those works mentioned in the texts of His Holiness Dudjom Rinpoche's *Fundamentals* and *History* according to the English titles given in the translations in Volume One, and provides whatever information the translators have had at their disposal regarding the actual identity of the works in question. The second gives detailed information on the specific texts and editions to which the translators have themselves referred.

The vast literature of Tibetan Buddhism remains mostly unknown to contemporary scholarship, although Tibetan language publishers in South Asia, Tibet and mainland China have reproduced thousands of manuscripts and printed texts during the last thirty years. The student of Tibetan religious history and doctrine is therefore confronted at the outset with the methodological difficulty of establishing the precise relationship between the literature to which reference is made in any given work, and the actual Tibetan literature to which we have real access at the present time. Here, we set forth the tentative results of our researches to date, certain that much emendation and revision will be called for. We have also included general titles for traditions of meditational and ritual practice which, properly speaking, do not belong in a bibliography as they are not the titles of texts. Our regret is that it has not been possible to provide the reader with a Tibetan-English index at this time, however our intention is to make this material available in the future. The remarks which follow explain our treatment of the main classes of literary materials with which we are concerned in Part One.

SŪTRAS AND TREATISES (*ŚĀSTRA*) OF INDIAN ORIGIN

Of the several bodies of literature to which our texts refer, it is the Indian works which, excepting the tantras, are the best known to contemporary scholarship. Indian sūtras and treatises translated into Tibetan are usually cited by Tibetan authors by means of abbreviated rather than full titles, but this is only occasionally a source of confusion. A more common difficulty is that quotations taken from one text come to be attributed to another when citations are given from memory, as is usually the case in traditional Tibetan scholarship.

In this bibliography, we have generally avoided providing detailed information on the available editions and translations of Indian Buddhist sūtras and treatises, and instead adopted the expedient of referring the reader to recent bibliographies, especially Karl Potter's revised bibliography to the *Encyclopedia of Indian Philosophy* (EIPRB), Peter Pfandt's *Mahāyāna Texts Translated into Western Languages* (MTTWL), and several of the volumes of the new *History of Indian Literature* (HIL), appearing under the general editorship of Jan Gonda. In addition, we give references to the publication of relevant works in important Indological and Buddhological Series, and to some very recent contributions that are not noted in the aforementioned bibliographies.

THE TANTRAS, THEIR COMMENTARIES AND THE LITERATURE DERIVED FROM THEM

The tantras, including both those which are adhered to by all schools of Tibetan Buddhism in common, and those which are peculiar to the Nyingma tradition, present the student of Tibetan literature with a special set of problems; for abbreviated titles are very frequently applied to several tantras and, moreover, are equally applied to the entire system of Vajrayāna practice stemming from the tantras in question. Thus, for instance, *dus-'khor* (*Kālacakra*) may refer not only to the *Kālacakra Tantra* in its various longer and shorter versions, but equally to any of the means for attainment, instruction manuals, empowerment ceremonies, etc., whether composed in India or Tibet, that are related to the theory and practice of the *Kālacakra Tantra*. These remarks apply equally to, for example, *gsang-'dus* (*Guhyasamāja*), *bde-mchog* (*Saṃvara*), *kye-rdor* (*Hevajra*), *phur-pa* (*Vajrakīla*), *bka'-brgyad* (*Eight Transmitted Precepts*), and so forth. It is therefore often not possible to establish the precise connection between any such abbreviated reference to a Vajrayāna system of practice and the known textual corpus associated with that system. Of course, when a fuller title is given, or when a textual passage is actually quoted, the situation is quite different and it may then become possible to establish the precise identification of the text cited. Similarly, comparison with accounts given in parallel source materials may help to establish the likelihood, at least, of a given abbreviated citation's exact identification.

Given these particular difficulties, we have provided, in the cases of the general titles such as those mentioned above, references which will serve to introduce some of the most important sources for the study of the Vajrayāna systems in question, at least so far as concerns the Nyingma tradition and those other schools with which it has historically been most closely associated. Thus, in any such case, the reader will find references to the foremost tantra or tantras of the system, as found in the *Kangyur* (T or P), and/or the *Collected Tantras of the Nyingmapa* (NGB). In addition, she or he will find references to several of the most important collections of Tibetan Vajrayāna materials, in which major redactions of the relevant means for attainment, etc., are given. Scholars undertaking research in this field must exercise care to determine whether or not such references may have any bearing in any given case. Those who wish to determine the general correspondences which hold between a given tantra or group of tantras in the *Kangyur* and the ancillary texts found in the *Tangyur*, are referred to A. Wayman, *The Buddhist Tantras: New Light on Indo-Tibetan Esotericism*, pp. 233-9.

The reader should note that the references we have given to NGB include, in addition to citation by volume, the precise index number which is assigned to each tantra included in NGB in the catalogue of that collection by Prof. Eiichi Kaneko, the *Ko-tantura Zenshū Kaidai Mokuroku*. This work, with Prof. Kaneko's learned introduction surveying the overall structure of Nyingmapa literature, represents the first major systematic contribution to the analysis of the tremendous body of extant Nyingma tantras.

WORKS ATTRIBUTED TO KNOWN TIBETAN AUTHORS, EXCLUDING TREASURES (*gter-ma*)

Here, as everywhere else, texts are usually cited by abbreviated rather than full titles, and these may sometimes refer not to single texts, but to whole groups of related works by a single author. These problems are compounded by the absence of any comprehensive inventory of extant and available Tibetan literature. In general, we have attempted to locate Tibetan works among the Tibetan language publications of the past decades. Inevitably, our occasional failure to locate a given work is not, in the absence of other evidence, proof that the work in question is unavailable. Since the only fully comprehensive collection of South Asian Tibetan language publications is that acquired by the United States Library of Congress under the conditions of Public Law 480, and its successor programmes for the acquisition of books and periodicals, we have provided, along with the standard bibliographical data for such publications, the Library of Congress

Accessions Lists' temporary catalogue numbers. Scholars wishing to locate, in American library collections, texts so listed will find that this will greatly facilitate the search.

Note that when a given text has been published many times, we do not always list all editions. With a very few exceptions we have ignored the numerous Tibetan editions of popular works from the *Kangyur* and *Tangyur*.

TREASURES (*gter-ma*)

It is this genre, of those with which we have been concerned, that is the least known and most troublesome to the bibliographer. The brief titles of treasures, like those of tantras, are used to refer to whole classes of literature rather than to single texts, so that in many cases it is impossible to determine with certainty the specific text to which a given citation applies. Moreover, there are instances in which different cycles revealed by altogether different treasure-finders share precisely the same title, and this, compounded with the fact that many of the treasure-finders are themselves known by a variety of names, further frustrates the effort to establish precise textual identifications. In all such instances, we can do no more than provide references to published editions of the cycle or cycles which appear to be in question, leaving it to future researchers to achieve greater precision.

The treasures that have come down to us can be divided according to the different ways in which they are arranged. Four types of collection are particularly noteworthy in the present context: (i) collections of single cycles, or of several very closely related cycles, which attempt to incorporate all the literature belonging to the cycle or cycles concerned. Examples would be the most complete editions of the *Innermost Spirituality of Longcenpa* (*klong-chen snying-thig*), the *Gathering of the Guru's Intention* (*bla-ma dgongs-'dus*), or the *Four-Part Innermost Spirituality* (*snying-thig ya-bzhi*). (ii) Smaller collections also based upon single cycles, but incorporating only the liturgical texts actually utilised by the tradition, or monastic establishment, responsible for publishing the collection. Examples are the innumerable local redactions of the *Peaceful and Wrathful Deities, the Natural Liberation of Intention* (*zhi-khro dgongs-pa rang-grol*), or of the *Consummation of All that is Precious* (*dkon-mchog spyi-'dus*), that are found throughout the Tibetan-speaking regions of the Himalayas. (iii) Collections of the "complete" treasures of a single treasure-finder. For examples, see CLTC, JTPD, PLTC and RLTC in the list of Abbreviations for Volume Two. (iv) In a class by itself is the *Store of Precious Treasure* (*rin-chen gter-mdzod*), which anthologises an extraordinary quantity of material, drawn from hundreds of treasure cycles.

In our references to treasure cycles, we generally attempt to provide substantial data on cycles which have appeared in publications representing types (i) and (iii). Smaller liturgical collections of type (ii) are usually omitted. References to the *Store of Precious Treasure* (RTD) have been provided selectively, in accord with the following guidelines: (1) where RTD appears to include a substantial redaction of a given cycle, we have referred to it, though fragments separated from the main body of the cycle as it occurs in RTD may be omitted; (2) where a major cycle is incorporated in RTD only in the form of many small selections scattered throughout, we have indicated that fact without providing precise citations; (3) where a very well known cycle is represented in RTD only by a few small selections, it may be ignored altogether; and (4) very rare cycles occurring in RTD are cited wherever we have been able to establish their identity.

ACKNOWLEDGEMENTS

A number of individuals and institutions generously shared materials with us specifically in connection with the compilation of this bibliography. The following remarks we hope will convey our grateful indebtedness to them.

Dr Helmut Eimer's researches into several of the main areas of Tibetan Buddhist history provide rich stores of documentation. In addition, Dr Eimer kindly called our attention to MTTWL. Dr Eiichi Kaneko's catalogue of the *Collected Tantras of the Nyingmapa* has been mentioned above. Without it, our references to the Nyingma tantras would undoubtably be much poorer. The task of surveying published Pönpo literature was much assisted by Dr Samten G. Karmay, whose *A Catalogue of Bonpo Publications*, is a mine of information on that tradition. Dr Steven D. Goodman provided us at an early stage with his catalogue of the *Four-Part Innermost Spirituality* (NYZ), which has not yet been published, and which has facilitated our work with that great collection. Our references to materials associated with the tradition of Thangtong Gyelpo are primarily due to Dr Janet Gyatso, of the Department of Religion, Amherst College. For much valuable data on Tibetan doxographical literature we thank Dr Katsumi Mimaki, whose *Blo gsal grub mtha'* provides a richly informative study of that genre. Mrs Hannah Robinson, of the former Institute for Advanced Studies of World Religions (IASWR) Library, Stony Brook, New York, kindly made portions of her catalogue of that library's Tibetan holdings available to us. The hard task of locating relevant material in the *Store of Precious Treasure* was much eased for us by Bhikkhuṇi Sik K. Yeshe Zangmo's *An Index of the Rinchen Gter*

Mdzod Chenmo, kept in the library of Cambridge University. Also, thanks are due to the Interlibrary Loan Office of the Rockefeller Library, Brown University, for procuring for us a great many works not available at Brown, to Mudd Library, Yale University, for rare permission to enter their stacks to consult the PL480 Tibetan collection which is housed there, and to the library of the School of Oriental and African Studies in London.

Finally, something must be said of our gratitude to Mr E. Gene Smith, of the US Library of Congress. Without his more than twenty years of labour on behalf of Tibetan literature, very little of the rich body of material that is now available to us would ever have seen the light of day. For scholars, Gene Smith has opened up a previously uncharted continent, and for those practising within the Tibetan religious tradition, he has insured that the textual resources, on which the survival of the living tradition to a very great extent depends, will be available to be transmitted to a new generation of men and women of the Buddhist community.

Part One
Works Cited by the Author

Note

Titles of texts generally appear in italics in the translations. Those of rites and teachings are mostly unemphasised.

Page numbers for the appearance of each entry in Volume One have been given in italic type within square brackets. Abbreviated and alternative titles have generally been listed individually and cross-referenced to a main entry where more information and a complete listing of page references can be found. Elements commonly omitted in abbreviation are indicated in the main entry by parentheses, and alternative titles are listed before the page numbers.

Works Cited by the Author

Abbreviated Logic Course. *bsdus-tshad*. Refer to n. 1109. The most ancient text of this genre presently available appears to be the *Ra-ba stod-pa'i bsdus-grva*. Pub. Dharamsala: Damchoe Sangpo, 1980. I-Tib 80-901211. [*821*]

Abridged Commentary on the Eighty-Chapter Magical Net. *brgyad-cu-pa'i bsdus-'grel*. Auth. Vimalamitra. NL. [*481*]

Abridged Commentary on the Tantra of the Awakening of the Great Vairocana. *rnam-snang mngon-byang-gi bsdus-'grel*. Skt. *Vairocanābhisambodhitantrapiṇḍārtha*. Auth. Buddhaguhya. T 2662. [*466*]

Abridged Tantra of Kālacakra. *dus-kyi 'khor-lo bsdus-pa*. [*894*] See *Kālacakra Tantra*

Ace Lhamo. *A-lce lha-mo*. Theatrical tradition ascribed to Thang-stong rgyal-po. Refer to n. 1077. [*803*]

Alchemical Transmutation into Gold. *gser-'gyur(-gyi bstan-bcos bsdus-pa)*. Skt. *Rasāyanaśāstroddhṛti*. T 4314. Concerning this work, see E. T. Fenner, "*Rasāyana* in the *Tantras*—What is it?" *Wind Horse* 1 (1981), pp. 99-111. [99]

Alchemy Cycle. *bcud-len skor*. Disc. Sangs-rgyas gling-pa. Possibly to be identified with the alchemical texts in BMGD Vol. 7. [*786*]

Alchemy of White Siṃhavaktrā. *seng-gdong dkar-mo'i bcud-len*. Disc. 'Jam-dbyangs mkhyen-brtse'i dbang-po. RTD Vol. 48, pp. 331-5. [*858*]

All-Accomplishing King. *kun-byed (rgyal-po)*. See *(Tantra of the) All-Accomplishing King*

All-Gathering Awareness. *kun-'dus rig-pa*. See *(Root Tantra of) All-Gathering Awareness*

Amṛta Tantra. *bdud-rtsi'i rgyud*. Possibly to be identified with the *Eight Volumes of Nectar*. But cf. T 401, 435 and 645. [*651*] See also *Nectar the Enlightened Attributes* and *Vajrāmṛta Cycle*

Analysis of the Meaning of Empowerment. *dbang-don rnam-par 'byed-pa*. Unidentified. Quoted in Lo-chen Dharmaśrī, *gsang-bdag zhal-lung*. [*364*]

Analysis of the Middle and Extremes. *dbus-mtha' (rnam-'byed)*. Skt. *Madhyāntavibhāga* or *Madhyāntavibhaṅga*. Auth. Maitreyanātha. T 4021.

B.Budh. 30 (1936). EIPRB 1241-9. MTTWL 112. TSWS 10 (1967). One of the *Five Doctrines of Venerable Maitreya*. [*95*, *202*] See also *Eight Dissertations*

Analysis of Phenomena and Reality. *chos dang chos-nyid rnam-'byed*. Skt. *Dharmadharmatāvibhāga* or *Dharmadharmatāvibhaṅga*. Auth. Maitreyanātha. T 4022-3. One of the *Five Doctrines of Venerable Maitreya*. [*95*]

Analysis of the Sugata's Texts. *bde-bar gshegs-pa'i gzhung rnam-par 'byed-pa*. Skt. *Sugatamatavibhaṅgakārikā*. Auth. Jetāri. T 3899. HIL 7.1, p. 100. The Sanskrit text has been recovered and edited by J. Newman on the basis of its inclusion in the commentary on the *Kālacakra Tantra* called *Taintless Light*. [*233*]

Analysis of the Three Vows. *sdom-gsum rab-dbye* or *sa-skya paṇḍita'i rab-dbye*. Auth. Sa-skya Paṇḍita. SK Vol. 5, no. 24. See Jared Rhoton, trans., *Sakya Paṇḍita's Treatise on the Three Codes*. Albany: SUNY Press, 2002. Also referred to as the *Treatise which Analyses the Three Vows*. [*827, 893, 907, 929, 931*] *Analyses the Three Vows*. [*827*, *893*, *907*, *929*, *931*]

Analysis of the Two Truths. *bden-gnyis rnam-'byed*. Skt. *Satyadvayavibhaṅgakārikā*. Auth. Jñānagarbha. T 3881. HIL 7.1, pp. 68-71. Ed. and trans. D. M. Eckel, *Jñānagarbha's Commentary on the Distinction between the Two Truths*. Albany, New York: SUNY Press, 1986. [*233*]

Analytical Commentary on the Tantra of the Secret Nucleus. *gsang-ba snying-po-la 'grel-pa rnam-bshad-kyi 'grel*. Auth. Buddhaguhya. NL. Stated by Lo-chen Dharmaśrī, *gsang-bdag zhal-lung*, p. 107, to be one of the five main Indian commentaries on this tantra. [*466*]

Ancient Annotation. *rnam-mchan rnying-pa*. Refer to n. 430. [*431*]

Annotations on the Parkap Commentary and the Innermost Point. *spar-khab-dang thugs-thig-la mchan-bu*. Auth. Mkhas-grub ye-shes rgyal-mtshan. NL. [*697*]

Answers to Queries on Doctrinal History, a Storehouse of Gems. *chos-'byung dris-lan nor-bu'i bang-mdzod*. Auth. gYag-sde 'dul-'dzin Mkhyen-rab rgya-mtsho. Probably this is the *Saṅs rgyas bstan pa'i chos 'byuṅ dris lan nor bu'i phreṅ ba*. Pub. Gangtok, Sikkim: Dzongsar Chhentse Labrang, 1981. I-Tib 81-902988. [*965*]

Answers to the Questions of the Kadampa Spiritual Benefactor Namkabum. *bka'-gdams-pa'i dge-bshes nam-mkha'-'bum-gyi dris-lan*. Auth. Sa-skya Paṇḍita. SK Vol. 5, no. 96. [*929*]

Answers to the Questions of Nyemo Gomcen. *snyi-mo sgom-chen-gyi dris-lan*. Auth. Sa-skya Paṇḍita. SK Vol. 5, no. 98. [*203*]

Answers to Questions which Refer to the Sources. *zhus-len* [*sic*] *khung-gdab*. NL. [*654*]

Anthologised Sūtras. *mdo-mang*. T 846-1108 (i.e. *gzungs-'dus*). [*703*]

Anthology of Caraka. *tsa-ra-ka 'bum-sde*. Skt. *Carakasaṃhitā*. Auth. Caraka (but in our text attributed to Ātreya). Skt. edn. with Hindi, Gujarati and English trans. Shree Gulabkunverba, Ayurvedic Society. 6 vols. Jamnagar: Gulabkunverba, 1949. [*65-6*]

Anthology of Vedic Treatises. *rig-byed-kyi bstan-bcos 'bum-sde.* [65] See *Four Veda*

Apprehending the Entire Intention, a Commentary on the Guhyasamāja. *'dus-pa-la'ang 'grel-pa dgongs-pa thams-cad nye-bar len-pa.* Skt. *Śrīguhyasamājaṭīkā.* Auth. Vajrahāsya. T 1909. [*466*]

Armour Against Darkness, a Commentary on the Sūtra which Gathers All Intentions. *mdo'i 'grel-chen* (or *mdo-'grel*) *mun-pa'i go-cha.* Auth. Gnubs-chen Sangs-rgyas Ye-shes. NMKMG Vols. 50-1. A commentary based upon it is composed by Kaḥ-thog mkhan-po Nus-ldan, *Dpal spyi mdo dgoṅs pa 'dus pa'i 'grel pa.* Kalimpong: Dupjung Lama, 1983. I-Tib 83-903671. [*612, 673, 674*]

Array of the Path of the Magical Net. *sgyu-'phrul (lam) rnam-bkod* or *lam rnam-bkod.* Skt. *Māyāpathavyavasthāpana.* Auth. Indrabhūti. P 4737. [*346, 360-1, 460, 462, 533, 673, 674, 696*]

Ārya Cycle of Guhyasamāja. *'phags-skor-gyi 'dus-pa.* This is Guhyasamāja according to the tradition of Nāgārjuna, Āryadeva and Candrakīrti. Refer to A. Wayman, *The Buddhist Tantras: New Light on Indo-Tibetan Esotericism.* London: Routledge and Kegan Paul, 1973, Ch. 2. Idem, *Yoga of the Guhyasamājatantra.* Delhi: Motilal Banarsidass, 1980. Also referred to as *Nāgārjuna's Cycle of Teachings on the Guhyasamāja.* [*464, 502-3*]

Ascertainment of the Meaning of the Tantra. *ṭī-kā rgyud-don rnam-nges.* Auth. Sman-lung-pa Shākya-'od. NL. [*686*]

Ascertainment of the Three Vows. *sdom-gsum rnam-(par) nges-(pa'i) bstan-bcos.* Auth. Mnga'-ris Paṇ-chen Padma dbang-rgyal. NMKMG Vol. 37. Xylo. Stengs-po-che Monastery, Nepal. N-Tib 78-914802. Also referred to as the *Treatise which Ascertains the Three Vows.* [*731, 808, 869*]

Ascertainment of Valid Cognition. *tshad-ma rnam-nges.* Skt. *Pramāṇaviniścaya.* Auth. Dharmakīrti. T 4211. EIPRB 2128-30. MTTWL 170. See also C. Lindtner, "Marginalia to Dharmakīrti's Pramāṇaviniścaya I-II" *Wiener Zeitschrift für die Kunde Südasiens* 28 (1984), pp. 149-75. [*102, 158, 687*]

Aspiration of Good Conduct. *bzang(-po) spyod(-pa'i smon-lam-gyi rgyal-po).* Skt. *Bhadracaryāpraṇidhānarāja.* T 44, 1095 and 4377. Part of the *Sūtra of the Arrayed Bouquet.* MTTWL 25. Skt. and Tib. edn. S. K. Pathak, *Śrīḥ Āryabhadracaripraṇidhānarāja.* Gangtok, Sikkim: Namgyal Institute of Tibetology, 1961. [*119*]

Astrological Treatise entitled Martial Conquest. *gYul-las rnam-rgyal.* Skt. *Yuddhajayanāmatantrarājasvarodaya.* T 4322. HIL 6.4, pp. 77-8. [*104*]

Atharvaveda. *srid-bsrung.* The second of the *Four Veda.* HIL 1.1, Ch. 6. [65]

Ati, Citi, Yangti. *ati spyi-ti yang-ti.* Disc. O-rgyan gling-pa. NA. Refer to n. 1029. [775]

Atiyoga and Vajrasattva Cycles. *rdor-sems a-ti'i skor.* Disc. Gter-bdag gling-pa. (1) *Atiyoga Cycle*: *Rdzogs pa chen po A ti zab don sñiṅ po'i chos skor.* Pub. Dehra Dun: D. G. Khochhen Trulku, 1977. I-Tib 77-903287.

(2) *Vajrasattva Cycle*: *Rdo rje sems dpa' thugs kyi sgrub pa*. Pub. Dehra Dun: D. G. Khochhen Trulku, 1976. I-Tib 77-900724. RTD Vol. 3, pp. 231-566. [*828*]

Attainment of Alchemy on the Basis of the Maṇḍala of the Gathering of the Sugatas of the Eight Transmitted Precepts. *bka'-brgyad bde-gshegs 'dus-pa'i dkyil-'khor-la brten-pa'i ra-sa-ya-na'i sgrub-pa*. NL. [*682*]

Attainment of Elixir (according to) the Attainment of Mind. *thugs-sgrub sman-sgrub*. Disc. Ratna gling-pa. RLTC Vol. 3, pp. 411-32 and 445-91. [*793*]

Attainment of Hayagrīva and Vajravarāhī as Consorts in Coalescent Union. *rta-phag yab-yum zung-'jug-tu sgrub-pa*. Disc. Ratna gling-pa. NL. [*793*]

Attainment of Longevity, the Giver of the Glory of Immortality. *tshe-sgrub 'chi-med dpal-ster*. Disc. Thang-stong rgyal-po. In: *The collected works of Thaṅ-stoṅ-rgyal-po*, Thimphu: Kunzang Tobgey, 1976. I(Bhu)-Tib 77-900723; Vol. 4, pp. 629-51. GTKT Vol. 1, pp. 427-80; Vol. 13, pp. 592-622. [*802*, *804*]

Attainment of Longevity, the Hot Sunbeam. *tshe-sgrub tsha-ba dmar-thag*. Disc. Bdud-'dul rdo-rje. RTD Vol. 31, pp. 1-42. [*815*]

Attainment of Longevity, the Innermost Spirituality of Vairocana. *tshe-sgrub bai-ro'i thugs-tig*. Disc. 'Jam-dbyangs mkhyen-brtse'i dbang-po. RTD Vol. 63, pp. 489-524. [*858*]

Attainment of Longevity, Integrating Gems with the Path. *tshe-sgrub nor-bu lam-khyer*. Disc. Padma gling-pa. PLTC Vol. 12, pp. 3-168. [*797*]

Attainment of Longevity, the Thunderbolt Vajra. *tshe-sgrub gnam-lcags rdo-rje*. Disc. Rig-'dzin 'Ja'-tshon snying-po. JTPD Vol. 2. RTD Vol. 24, pp. 19-39; Vol. 30, pp. 387-506. SSS 14 (1972). I-Tib 75-928501. Pub. Tezu, Arunachal Pradesh: Ngawang Sonam, 1979. I-Tib 79-903494. [*811*]

Attainment of Medicinal Pills (from the Flesh of One) Born (as a Brahman) Seven Times. *skye-bdun ril-sgrub*. Disc. Ratna gling-pa. NL. [*793*]

Attainment of Mind, the Dispeller of All Obstacles. *thugs-sgrub bar-chad kun-sel*. Disc. Mchog-gyur bde-chen gling-pa. CLTC Vols. 1-9, *passim*. RTD *passim*. Pub. New Delhi: Karma Chhophel, 1973. I-Tib 74-900028. [*844*, *845*, 848, 865]

Attainment of Mind, the Expressive Play of Indestructible Wrath. *thugs-sgrub rdo-rje drag-rtsal*. Disc. Mchog-gyur bde-chen gling-pa. CLTC Vol. 2. [*846*]

Attainment of Mind, the Gathering of the Sugatas. *thugs-sgrub bde-gshegs 'dus-pa*. Disc. Mchog-gyur bde-chen gling-pa. RTD Vols. 7-8, *passim*. [*844*]

Attainment of Mind, Utterly Secret and Unsurpassed. *thugs-sgrub yang-gsang bla-med*. Disc. Thang-stong rgyal-po. NL. [*802*]

Attainment of Mind, the Wish-fulfilling Gem. *thugs-sgrub yid-bzhin nor-bu*. Disc. Mchog-gyur bde-chen gling-pa. CLTC Vols. 9-10. RTD Vol. 15, pp. 141-345. Also referred to as the *Cycle of the Attainment of Mind as the Wish-fulfilling Gem*. [*846*, *856*]

Aural Lineage according to the Cycle of the Black Chest. *snyan-brgyud sgro-ba nag-po'i skor*. NL. Roerich in *Blue Annals*, p. 145, takes *sgro-ba nag-po* to be the name of a person rather than an object. [*658*]

Aural Lineage of the Vajra Bridge. *snyan-brgyud rdo-rje zam-pa*. See *Vajra Bridge*

Aural Lineages of Ketsang and of the Narrow Path to the Fortress. *ke-tshang dang rdzong-'phrang snyan-brgyud*. Listed separately as the *Ketsangma* (*Tradition of the Great Perfection*) and *Transmitted Precepts of the Narrow Path to the Fortress*.

Auspicious Aeon Sūtra. *mdo-sde bskal-po bzang-po*. Skt. *Bhadrakalpikasūtra*. T 94. MTTWL 26. [*943*]

Authentic Conduct of a Bodhisattva. *byang-chub sems-dpa'i spyod-pa dam-pa*. Skt. *Āryabodhisattvacaryānirdeśasūtra*. T 184. MTTWL 42. [*322*, *899*]

Autocommentary on the Mind at Rest. *sems-nyid ngal-gso rtsa-'grel* [*595*] See *Great Chariot*

Avalokiteśvara, the Churner of Saṃsāra's Hellish Depths. *spyan-ras-gzigs na-rag dong-sprugs*. Disc. Guru Chos-dbang. RTD Vol. 76, pp. 497-626. [*569*]

Avalokiteśvara according to the Tradition of the King. *spyan-ras-gzigs rgyal-po lugs*. This refers to the empowerments and means for attainment derived from the *Collected Works of the King concerning the Mantra "Oṃ Maṇi Padme Hūṃ"*. DZ Vol. 11, pp. 598-617. GDKT Vol. 22, no. 130. RTD Vol. 33, pp. 1-237. [*578*]

(Awakening of Great) Vairocana. *rnam(-par) snang(-mdzad) mngon(-par) byang(-chub-pa)*. Skt. *Mahāvairocanābhisaṃbodhitantra*. T 494. MTTWL 124. GDKT Vol. 3, no. 20. [*271*, *272*, *618*]

Basic Root Tantra of Vajrakīla. *phur-pa rtsa-ba sor-bzhag*. Perhaps to be identified with the *Root Fragment of Vajrakīla*. Skt. *Vajrakīlayamūlatantrakhāṇḍa*. T 439. GCKZ Vol. 3. NMKMG Vol. 10. [*651*]

Bean-Sprout Rites (belonging to the Cycle of White Mañjuśrī according to the System of Mati). *makṣa'i las-sbyor*. GTKT Vol. 2, pp. 124-6. [*870*]

Beauteous Flower Garland Ritual Manual. *las-byang me-tog phreng-mdzes*. Disc. Sangs-rgyas gling-pa. BMGD Vol. 1. RTD Vol. 9, pp. 387-416. [*682*, *841*]

Bhairava (Cycle/Tantra). *'jigs-byed*. T 468 and 470. GDKT Vols. 9-10, nos. 54-9. KGNZ Vol. 5, pp. 85-177. Also referred to as the *Vajrabhairava Tantra*. [*283*, *442*, *477*, *675*, *707*, *708*] See also *Yamāntaka (Cycle/Tantra)*, *Yamāri (Cycle/Tantra)* and *Yamāntaka and Yamāri: Introductory Note*

Bhaṭṭārikā according to the Tradition of Ra Lotsāwa. *rje-btsun-ma rva-lugs*. Possibly to be identified with the tradition represented by GDKT Vol. 12, no. 69. [*562*]

Billion Lines on the Transcendental Perfection of Discriminative Awareness. *shes-phyin bye-ba-phrag-brgya-pa*. Skt. **Śatakoṭiprajñāpāramitā*. NA. [*154*]

Billion Verses of the Great Collection of Most Extensive Sūtras according to the Greater Vehicle. *shin-tu rgyas-pa chen-po'i mdo-sde theg-chen-gyi 'dus-pa chen-po bye-ba-phrag-brgya-pa*. Skt. **Mahāvaipulyamahāyānasūtrāntamahāsaṃgraha*. NA. [*154*]

Binding of the Chapters of the Gathering of the Sugatas. *bde-'dus-kyi sa-gcod tshoms-kyi chings*. NL. [*89*]

Biographical Injunction in Eight Chapters. *rnam-thar thang-yig le'u brgyad-pa*. Disc. Rdo-rje gling-pa. NL. [*789*]

Biographies of the Hundred Treasure-finders. See *Earlier and Later Versions of the Biographies of the Hundred Treasure-finders*

Biography of Chöying Rangdröl. *rnam-thar rgyal-ba-mchog-gi zhal-gsung-ma*. Auth. Dalai Lama V, Ngag-dbang blo-bzang rgya-mtsho. TWB 5597. [*684*]

Biography of Lord Atiśa. *jo-bo'i rnam-thar*. See H. Eimer, *Rnam thar rgyas pa, Materialen zu einer Biographie des Atiśa*. Asiatische Forschungen 67. Wiesbaden: Otto Harrassowitz, 1979. [*891*]

Biography of the Thirteen Stores. *mdzod-khang bcu-gsum-gyi rnam-thar*. Auth. Ratna gling-pa. RLTC Vol. 13, pp. 39-236. [*793*]

Black Deity Vajrakīla. *phur-pa lha-nag*. [*687*, *710*, *712*]

Black Further Innermost Spirituality. *yang-tig nag-po*. Disc. Dung-mtsho ras-pa. Published in 3 vols. Dalhousie: Damchoe Sangpo, 1979. I-Tib 79-906946. RTD Vol. 91, pp. 1-299. SSS 41 (1972). I-Tib 72-908332. [*718*]

Black Hayagrīva. *rta-mgrin nag-po*. Disc. Sangs-rgyas gling-pa. NL. [*786*]

Black Tortoise Divination Chart. *gtad-khram rus-sbal nag-po*. Disc. Sangs-rgyas gling-pa. NL. [*786*]

Black Trilogy. *nag-po skor-gsum*. Disc. Padma gling-pa. PLTC Vol. 11, pp. 445-521. The three black-coloured protective deities whose rites are contained here are *gshin-rje kha-thun nag-po*, *phra-men phag-sha nag-po* and *mu-stegs gu-lang nag-po*. [*797*]

Black Yamāri. *gshin-rje dgra-nag*. Skt. *Kṛṣṇayamāri*. T 469, 473. NGB Vols. 20-2. GDKT Vol. 8, no. 52. NMKMG Vol. 4. Also referred to as the *Black Tantra of Yamāntaka*. [*283*, *477*, *571*, *578*, *614*, *665*, *708*] See also *Yamāri (Cycle/Tantra)* and *Yamāntaka and Yamāri: Introductory Note*

Blossom of Esoteric Instructions. *man-ngag snye-ma*. Skt. *Śrīsaṃpuṭatantrarājaṭīkāmnāyamañjarī*. Auth. Abhayakāragupta. T 1198. [*264-5*]

Blue Annals. *deb(-ther) sngon(-po)*. Auth. 'Gos Lo-tsā-ba Gzhon-nu-dpal. Trans. G. N. Roerich, *The Blue Annals*. 2nd edn., Delhi: Motilal Banarsidass, 1976. Pub. Lokesh Chandra, SP 212 (1974). I-Tib 75-900107. Typeset edn., Chengdu: Sichuan Minorities Press, 1984. 2 vols. [*398*, *617*, *921*, *965*]

Blue-robed Vajrapāṇi. *phyag-rdor gos-sngon-can*. Disc. Sangs-rgyas gling-pa and Dri-med lhun-po. NL. [*786*]

Blue-skirted One's Cycle (of Vajrakīla). *gsham-sngon-can-gyi skor*. Refer to n. 704. [*603*, *712*]

Bodhisattva Level. *byang-sa*. Skt. *Bodhisattvabhūmi*. Auth. Asaṅga. T 4037. Part of the *Yogācāra Level*. MTTWL 41. TSWS 7 (1978). See also M. Tatz, *Asaṅga's Chapter on Ethics*. Lewiston, New York: The Edwin Mellen Press, 1986. [*108*, *872*]

Bodhisattva Vows according to Three Traditions. *byang-sdom bka'-srol gsum*. See the Glossary of Enumerations under *three traditions of bodhisattva vow*. The current rites for the conferral of these vows, as transmitted within the Nyingma tradition, are found in: DZ Vol. 2, pp. 387-486. NMKMG Vol. 1. [*729*, *827*]

Body of Consciousness. *rnam-shes tshogs*. Skt. *Vijñānakāya*. Auth. Devaśarman. Only extant in Chinese: Taishō 1539. EIPRB 86. One of the *Seven Sections of the Abhidharma*. See also L. de La Vallée Poussin (trans.) in *Études Asiatiques*, *Publications de l'École Française d'Extrême-Orient*, Vol. 19 (1925), pp. 343-76. Idem, *L'Abhidharmakośa du Vasubandhu*. Paris: Paul Geuthner, 1923-36, Vol. 1, pp. xxxiii-xxxvi. Fumimaro Watanabe, *Philosophy and its Development in the Nikāyas and Abhidharma*. Delhi: Motilal Banarsidass, 1983, Ch. 11. [*90*]

Body of the Elemental Bases. *khams-kyi tshogs*. Skt. *Dhātukāya*. Auth. Pūrṇa (or, according to other sources, Vasumitra). Only extant in Chinese: Taishō 1540. EIPRB 85. One of the *Seven Sections of the Abhidharma*. See also L. de La Vallée Poussin, *L'Abhidharmakośa du Vasubandhu*. Paris: Paul Geuthner, 1923-36, Vol. 1, pp. xli-xlii. [*90*]

Brahman's Cycle (of the Great Perfection). *(rdzogs-chen) bram-ze'i skor*. NGB Vol. 7. [*651*]

Brief Account of the Truths according to the Madhyamaka. *dbu-ma bden-chung*. Skt. *Satyadvayāvatāra*. Auth. Atiśa. T 3902 and 4467. HIL 7.1, p. 113. MTTWL 210. [*762*]

Brief Teaching of Empowerment. *dbang mdor-bstan*. Skt. *Sekoddeśa*. T 361. GOS 90 (1941). SP 18 (*c.* 1963). SP 69 (1966). [*674*]

Brief Teaching on the Tenets of the View. *lta-'dod mdor-bstan*. Skt. *Pradarśanānumatoddeśaparīkṣā*. Auth. Narendrakīrti. P 4610. [*250*]

Buddhakapāla. *sangs-rgyas thod-pa*. T 424. GDKT Vol. 15, no. 86. KGNZ Vol. 3, pp. 203-92. [*503*, *576*]

Buddhasamāyoga (Tantra). *sangs-rgyas mnyam-sbyor*. T 366-7. NGB Vol. 16, nos. 206-8. GDKT Vol. 10, nos. 61-2. NMKMG Vol. 3. SP 70 (1966). [*258*, *260*, *459*, *461*, *464*, *477*, *533*, *620*, *707*, *827*, *893*]

Buddhasamāyoga Tantra which, Known Alone, Liberates All. *sangs-rgyas mnyam-sbyor-gyi rgyud gcig-shes kun-grol*. Disc. Guru Chos-dbang. Perhaps to be identified with the *Saṅs-rgyas mñam-sbyor lcags-sñug-ma*. 2 vols. Paro: Ugyen Tempai Gyaltsen, 1980. I(Bhu)-Tib 80-901439. [*764*]

Cakrasaṃvara. *'khor-lo sdom-pa* or *bde-mchog*. T 368. GDKT Vols. 11-12, nos. 63-7; Vols. 13-14, nos. 71-80. KGNZ Vol. 3, pp. 3-202. An indigenous Tibetan work representing the Cakrasaṃvara cycle is translated in Kazi Dawa-Samdup, *Shrī Sambhāra, a Buddhist Tantra* in A. Avalon (ed.), *Tantrik Texts*, Vol. 7. London: Luzac and Co., 1919. [*283*, *362*, *467*, *485*, *562*, *568*, *657*, *675*, *827*, *849*, *850*, *895*]

Cakrasaṃvara and Hevajra. *bde-dgyes*. Listed separately.

Cakrasaṃvara according to the Tradition of Ghaṇṭāpāda. *bde-mchog dril-bu-pa*. Skt. *Śrīcakrasaṃvarasādhana*. Auth. (Vajra)ghaṇṭāpāda. T 1432. GDKT Vols. 11-12, no. 65. [*576*]

Catalogue of the Collected Tantras, a Discourse Resembling a Great Divine Drum. *rgyud-'bum dkar-chag lha'i rnga-bo-che lta-bu'i gtam*. Auth. Kaḥ-thog Paṇḍita 'Gyur-med tshe-dbang mchog-grub. NGB Vols. 35-6. [*41*, *398*, *966*]

Catalogues of the Collected Tantras. *rgyud-'bum-gyi dkar-chag*. Refer to preceding entry, the *Narrative History of the Precious Collected Tantras* and n. 1245. Note also in this context Chos-rgyal 'Phags-pa, *Rgyud-sde'i dkar-chag*, in *Sa-skya bka'-'bum*, Vol. 7, pp. 136.3-138.2.6. [*893*]

Ceremonial Arrangements of the Empowerment for the Sūtra (which Gathers All Intentions). *mdo-dbang-gi chog-khrigs*. Auth. Dro-ston Dpal-ldan-grags. NL. Apparently incorporated into the tradition of the *Empowerment Ceremony (entitled) the River of Honey*. [*700*]

Ceremonial Arrangements of Nyelpa. *gnyal-pa'i chog-khrigs*. Auth. Gnyal-pa Bde-legs. NL. [*701*]

Ceremonial Arrangements for the Sūtra which Gathers All Intentions, the Magical Net, and so forth, (published in ten volumes). *mdo-sgyu sogs-kyi chog-khrigs glegs-bam bcu*. Redacted by Rgyal-sras Gzhan-phan mtha'-yas. NL in this form, but largely preserved in NMKMG. [*737*]

Ceremony for Brandishing the Ritual Kīla of Orgyen. *o-rgyan-gyi las-phur gdengs-chog*. Disc. Sangs-rgyas gling-pa and Dri-med lhun-po. NL. [*786*]

Chapter on Discriminative Awareness from the Introduction to the Conduct of a Bodhisattva. *spyod-'jug shes-rab le'u*. The ninth chapter of the *Introduction to the Conduct of a Bodhisattva*. [*875*]

Chapterless Commentary on the Supplementary Magical Net. *le-lag-gi sa-ma 'grel*. Auth. Rong-zom Chos-kyi bzang-po. NL. [*92*]

Chapter on Light Feet. *sdeb-sbyor yang-pa'i bya-ba*. Probably to be identified with the introductory sections of the *Precious Source of Prosody*. Lo-chen Dharmaśrī's own commentary on this may be found in: LCSB Vol. 3. SK Vol. 8, no. 1. TWPS 80. [*730*]

Chapter entitled the Vision of Vajrasattva. *rdor-sems zhal-mthong-gi le'u*. Chapter seventy-four of the *Eighty-Chapter Magical Net*. [*459-60*]

Charm which Overthrows when Hurled. *thun-phog 'gyel*. Disc. Sangs-rgyas gling-pa and Dri-med lhun-po. NL. [*786*]

Churner of the Depths of Hell. *(na-rag) dong-sprugs*. A rite of Vajrasattva belonging to the Transmitted Precepts of the Nyingma tradition. DZ Vol. 1, pp. 144-58. LCSB Vol. 13. NMKMG Vol. 13. Alternatively, the Avalokiteśvara cycle called the *na-rag dong-sprugs*, discovered by Guru Chos-dbang: RTD Vol. 76, pp. 497-626. [*673*, *674*, *731*]

Churner of Saṃsāra's Depths. *'khor-ba dong-sprugs*. [*136*]

Churner of Saṃsāra's Depths. *'khor-ba dong-sprugs*. Disc. Mchog-gyur bde-chen gling-pa. CLTC Vol. 10. [*846*]

Clarification of Commitments. *dam-tshig gsal-bkra*. Skt. *Samayavivyakti*. Auth. Līlāvajra (Vilāsavajra). P 4744. [*96*, *464*]

Clarifying Lamp. *sgron-gsal*. Skt. *Pradīpodyotana*. Auth. Candrakīrti. T 1785. Skt. edn. Pradhan, TSWS Vol. 25 (1985). Also referred to as the *Commentary on the Guhyasamāja Tantra called the Clarifying Lamp*. [*109*, *260-1*, *464*, *502*, *681*, *689*]

Clarifying Lamp of the Five Stages. *rim-lnga gsal-sgron*. Auth. Tsong-kha-pa. Typeset edn.: Varanasi, 1969. I-Tib 79-905623. [*681*]

Clear Distinction. *bye-brag gsal-ba*. Skt. *Vaiśeṣikadarśana/sūtra*. Auth. Kaṇāda (Ulūka). EIPRB 479-532. HIL 6.2, pp. 53-9. [*65*]

Clear Judgement. *rnam-dpyod gsal-ba*. Skt. *Mīmāṃsādarśana*. Auth. Jaimini (but in our text attributed to Bhṛgu). EIPRB 136-212. [*65*]

Clear Nucleus Grammar. *brda-sprod snying-po gsal-ba*. Auth. Dpang Lo-tsā-ba Blo-gros brtan-pa. TWPS 78. [*100*]

Clearly Worded Commentary. *tshig-gsal*. Skt. *Mūlamadhyamakavṛttiprasannapadā*. Auth. Candrakīrti. T 3860. B.Budh. 4 (1903-13). BST 10 (1960). EIPRB 451, 645, 647-8, 655-7, 659, 662-5, 747, 2019, 2027, 2084-92. HIL 7.1, pp. 74-81, 126, 129. MTTWL 139. [*76*, *94*, *577*]

Clearly Worded Commentary and Introduction to the Madhyamaka. *tshig-'jug*. Listed separately.

Clear Word. *tshig-gsal*. Skt. *Prasphuṭapadā*. Auth. Dharmamitra. T 3796. [*128-9*]

Collected Stories of the Great Lineage of Riddles. *lde-brgyud chen-po'i sgrung-'bum*. Refer to n. 1004. [*762*]

Collected Tantras. *rgyud-'bum*. An early edition of the following entry. [*669*, *670*]

Collected Tantras (of the Nyingmapa). *rnying(-ma'i) rgyud(-'bum)*. NGB. Note that there appear to be considerable variations among the different editions, of which, besides NGB, two have been published to date: (1) The Mtshams-brag manuscript. Thimphu, Bhutan: National Library, Royal Government of Bhutan, 1982. 46 vols. Bhu-Tib 82-902165. (2) The Rgyud-'bum of Vairocana. 8 vols. SSS 16-23 (1971). I-Tib 70-924557. In addition, the India Office Library, London, houses a manuscript set probably based on the Sde-dge xylo., which is still available in Kham. Also referred to as the *Precious Collected Tantras of the Ancient Translation School*. [*40*, *41*, *577*, *686*, *723-4*, *730*, *734*, *795*, *830*, *851*]

Collected Works of Jikme Lingpa (in nine volumes). *gsung-'bum glegs-bam dgu*. JLSB. [*41*]

Collected Works of the King concerning the Mantra "Oṃ Maṇi Padme Hūṃ." *ma-ṇi bka'-'bum*. Disc. Grub-thob Dngos-grub, Mnga'-bdag Nyang and Ston-pa Shākya-'od. Pub. New Delhi: Trayang and Jamyang Samten, 1975. 2 vols. I-Tib 75-901057. Besides this, numerous smaller editions have appeared. The secondary literature is surveyed in A.-M. Blondeau, "Le 'Découvreur' du *Maṇi bka'-'bum* — était-il Bon-po?" in L. Ligeti (ed.), *Tibetan and Buddhist Studies*. Budapest: Akadémiai

Kiadó, 1984, Vol. 1, pp. 77-123. [*511*] See also *Avalokiteśvara according to the Tradition of the King*

Collected Works of Locen Dharmaśrī (in eighteen volumes). *bka'-'bum pustaka bco-brgyad*. Auth. Lo-chen Dharmaśrī. Pub. in 19 vols. LCSB. [*41*, *732*]

Collected Works of Mipham Rinpoche. *mi-pham rin-po-che'i legs-bshad rgya-mtsho*. MPSB. [*41*, *966*]

Collected Works of Pema Trhinle (in thirteen volumes). *padma phrin-las-kyi bka'-'bum pod bcu-gsum*. No complete edition has yet become available. [*41*]

Collected Works of Terdak Lingpa (in thirteen volumes). *gter-bdag gling-pa'i gsung-'bum po-ti bcu-gsum*. No complete edition has been published to date. The best editions of his writings and treasures to appear so far are those published by D. G. Khochhen Trulku, to which we refer wherever possible throughout this bibliography. [*831*]

Collection of Eulogies. *bstod-tshogs*. Skt. *Stavakāya*. Auth. Nāgārjuna. T 1118-36. EIPRB 633-7. HIL 7.1, pp. 31-2. MTTWL 55. See also F. Tola and C. Dragonetti, "Nāgārjuna's Catuḥstava" JIP 13 (1985), pp. 1-54. [*203*, *207*, *216*, *301*] See also *Eulogy to the Expanse of Reality* and *Eulogy to the Inconceivable Madhyamaka*

Collection of the Greater Vehicle. *(theg-pa chen-po) bsdus-pa*. Skt. *Mahāyānasaṃgraha*. Auth. Asaṅga. T 4048. EIPRB 1250-2. MTTWL 125. [*91*, *202*, *214*]

Collection of Madhyamaka Reasoning. *(dbu-ma) rigs-tshogs*. Skt. *Yuktikāya*. Auth. Nāgārjuna. T 3824-8. HIL 7.1, pp. 4-23. Tib. edn. L. P. Lhalungpa. *Dbuma* [*sic*] *rigs tshogs drug*. Delhi, 1970. The five (or six) collections of reasoning are enumerated in *Fundamentals*, p. 94. *Ratnāvalī* replaces the now unavailable *Vyavahārasiddhi* in this and other Tibetan editions. [*94*, *203*, *206*, *301*]

Collection of Meaningful Expressions. *ched-du brjod-pa'i tshoms*. Skt. *Udānavarga*. Auth. Dharmatrāta. T 326. Tib. edn. H. Beckh. *Udānavarga: eine Sammlung Buddhistischer Spruche in Tibetischer Sprache*. Berlin, 1911. Skt. edn. F. Bernhard. *Udānavarga*. 2 vols. Göttingen: Vandenhoeck & Ruprecht, 1965-8. Trans. G. Sparham, *The Tibetan Dhammapada*. London: Wisdom Publications, 1986. [*58*, *90*, *221*]

Collection of Prosody. *sdeb-sbyor-gyi tshoms*. Auth. Sa-skya Paṇḍita. SK Vol. 5, no. 15: *sdeb-sbyor sna-tshogs me-tog-gi chun-po*. [*105*]

Collection of Realisation. *rtog-bsdus/-'dus*. Skt. *Sarvakalpasamuccayasarvabuddhasamāyogottaratantra*. T 367. NGB Vol. 16, no. 208. [*122*]

Combined Means for Attainment of the Three Roots called "Perpetual Vision of Accomplishment". *rtsa-gsum dril-sgrub dngos-grub brtan-gzigs*. Disc. Sangs-rgyas bla-ma. NA. [*751*] See also *Twenty-onefold Dialogue concerning the Combined Means for Attainment of the Three Roots*

Commentaries on the Kālacakra Tantra and the Vajracatuḥpīṭha Tantra. *dus-gdan-gyi 'grel-pa*. Listed separately as *Taintless Light* (*the Great Commentary on the Kālacakra*) and *Commentary on the Four Seats*.

Commentaries on the Ornament of Emergent Realisation. *rgyan-'grel-rnams*. T 3787-9, 3791, 3793-6. [*230*]

Commentaries on the Treasury of the Abhidharma. *mdzod-'grel rnams*. T 4090-6, 4421. [*90, 943*] See also *Treasury of the Abhidharma*

Commentary and Annotations on the Array of the Path of the Magical Net. *lam rnam-bkod-la ṭī-kā-dang mchan-bu*. Auth. Mkhas-grub Ye-shes rgyal-mtshan. NL. [*697*]

Commentary on the Array of the Path of the Magical Net. *lam rnam-bkod-la ṭī-kā*. Auth. Kha-ba dkar-po-ba Nam-mkha' rgyal-mtshan. NL. [*697*]

Commentary on the Array of the Path of the Magical Net. *lam rnam-bkod-kyi ṭī-kā*. Auth. Rog Shes-rab-'od. NL. [*702*]

Commentary based on the Text of the Parkap Commentary. *'grel-pa spar-khab gzhung-du byas-pa'i ṭī-kā*. Auth. Rdo-rje rgyal-mtshan. NL. [*687*]

Commentary on the Bhairava Tantra. *'jigs-byed rgyud-kyi 'grel-pa*. Auth. Rong-zom Chos-kyi bzang-po. NL. [*707*]

Commentary on the Buddhasamāyoga. *mnyam-sbyor 'grel-pa*. Auth. Hūṃkara. [*533*] See *Elucidation of the Significance of the Four Limbs*

Commentary on the Buddhasamāyoga. *mnyam-sbyor 'grel-pa*. Auth. Kukkurāja. See *Six Arrays of Esoteric Meaning*

Commentary on the Buddhasamāyoga. *mnyam-sbyor-gyi 'grel-pa*. Auth. Rong-zom Chos-kyi bzang-po. NL. [*707*]

Commentary on the Clarification of Commitments entitled the Clear Mirror. *dam-tshig gsal-bkra-la 'grel-pa gsal-ba'i me-long*. Auth. Mkhas-grub Ye-shes rgyal-mtshan. NL. [*697*]

Commentary on the Collection of Meaningful Expressions. *ched-du brjod-pa'i tshoms-kyi 'grel-pa*. Skt. *Udānavargavṛtti*. Auth. Prajñāvarman. T 4100. Tib. edn. M. Balk, *Prajñāvarman's Udānavargavivaraṇa*. Bonn: Indica et Tibetica Verlag, 1984. 2 vols. [*92*]

Commentary on Difficulties entitled Endowed with Pristine Cognition *dka'-'grel ye-shes-ldan*. Skt. *Śrībuddhakapālatantrapañjikā Jñānavatī*. Auth. Saraha. T 1652. [*261*]

Commentary on the Discriminative Awareness Chapter (of the Introduction to the Conduct of a Bodhisattva). *spyod-'jug sher-le'i 'grel-pa* or *sher-ṭīk*. Auth. 'Jam-mgon Mi-pham rgya-mtsho. Refer to n. 1211. Pub. Gangtok: Sherab Gyaltsen, 1979. I-Tib 79-903492. MPSB Vol. 13. [*871, 875*]

Commentary on Enlightened Mind. *byang-chub sems-'grel*. Skt. *Bodhicittavivaraṇa*. Auth. Nāgārjuna. T 1800-1. HIL 7.1, pp. 104-5. MTTWL 36. Ed. and trans. in C. Lindtner, *Nagarjuniana*. Indiske Studier IV. Copenhagen: Akademisk Verlag, 1982, pp. 180-217. [*234*]

Commentary which Epitomises the Hevajra (Tantra). *don-bsdus-kyi 'grel-pa*. Skt. *Hevajrapiṇḍārthaṭīkā*. Auth. Vajragarbha. T 1180. [*269*] See also *Trilogy of Commentaries by Bodhisattvas*

Commentary on the Eulogy (entitled Taintless Gem Rosary). *bstod-'grel*. Auth. Sa-skya Paṇḍita. SK Vol. 5, no. 65: *dri-ma med-pa zhes-bya-ba'i rgya-cher 'grel-pa*. [*203*]

Commentary on the Final Meditation. *bsam-gtan phyi-ma'i 'grel-pa*. Skt. *Dhyānottarapaṭalaṭīkā*. Auth. Buddhaguhya. T 2670. [*349*]

Commentary on the Four Hundred Verses. *dbu-ma bzhi-brgya-pa'i 'grel-pa*. Skt. *Bodhisattvayogācāracatuḥśatakaṭīkā*. Auth. Candrakīrti. T 3865. EIPRB 2080. MTTWL 54. [*309*] See also *Four Hundred Verses*.

Commentary on the Four Seats. *gdan(-bzhi) 'grel(-pa)*. Skt. *Catuḥpīṭhatantrarājasmṛtinibandha*. Auth. Bhavabhadra. T 1607. [*104*]

Commentary on the General Sūtra which Gathers All Intentions. *spyi-mdo (dgongs-pa 'dus-pa)'i 'grel-pa*. Auth. Indrabhūti (King Ja). NL. [*485*]

Commentary on the Guhyasamāja Tantra, based on the Guru's Instruction. *'dus-pa-la rgyud-kyi bshad-pa*. Skt. *Śrīguhyasamājatantranidānagurūpadeśanavyākhyāna*. Auth. Līlāvajra (Vilāsavajra). T 1910. [*464*]

Commentary on the Guhyasamāja Tantra called the Clarifying Lamp. *'dus-pa'i rgyud-'grel gsal-sgron*. See *Clarifying Lamp* and *Four Subcommentaries on the Commentary on the Guhyasamāja Tantra called the Clarifying Lamp*

Commentary on the Hundred Thousand Line Transcendental Perfection. *'bum-ṭīk*. Auth. Daṃṣṭrasena. T 3807. Refer to n. 1325. [*944*]

Commentary on the Intention of the Four Glorious Tantras of Medical Science. *dpal-ldan rgyud-bzhi'i dgongs-pa (gYu-thog-pas) bkral-pa*. [*99*] See *Four Glorious Tantras of Medical Science*

Commentary on the Introduction to the Three Bodies. *sku gsum-la 'jug-pa'i sgo'i 'grel-pa*. Skt. *Kāyatrayavṛtti*. Auth. Jñānacandra. T 3891. [*183*]

Commentary on the Kālacakra Tantra (entitled Taintless Light). *dus-'khor rgyud-'grel (dri-med 'od)*. See *Taintless Light (the Great Commentary on the Kālacakra)*

Commentary on the Litany of the Names of Mañjuśrī. *'jam-dpal-gyi mtshan yang-dag-par brjod-pa bla-med rgyud-tu bkral-ba'i ṭī-kā* or *'jam-dpal mtshan-brjod-kyi 'grel-pa*. Auth. Līlāvajra (Vilāsavajra). T 2533. [*464*]

Commentary on the Litany of the Names of Mañjuśrī. *Tha-ga-na'i mtshan-brjod-kyi 'grel-pa*. Auth. Thagana. None of the commentaries on the *Litany of the Names of Mañjuśrī* available in the *Tangyur* is attributed to this author. Tibetan authorities sometimes identify it with T 2538 by Smṛtijñānakīrti. [*703*]

Commentary on the Magical Net of Mañjuśrī. *'phags-pa 'jam-dpal-gyi mtshan yang-dag-par brjod-pa'i rgya-cher bshad-pa*. Skt. *Mañjuśrīnāmasaṃgītiṭīkā*. Auth. Mañjuśrīkīrti. T 2534. [*305*]

Commentary on the Nucleus of Indestructible Reality. *rdo-rje snying(-po'i rgyud-kyi) 'grel-(pa)*. Skt. *Vajrahṛdayālaṃkāratantrapañjikā*. Auth. Rab-tu zhi-ba'i bshes-gnyen. T 2515. Alternatively, the text referred to may be the *Commentary which Epitomises the Hevajra Tantra*. [*82, 211*]

Commentary on the Oral Instructions of Sublime Mañjuśrī. *'phags-pa 'jam-dpal dbyangs-kyi zhal-lung-gi 'grel-pa*. Skt. *Sukusumanāmamukhāgamavṛtti*. Auth. Vitapāda. T 1866. [*313*]

Commentary, Outline and Synopsis of the Secret Nucleus. *gsang-ba snying-po-la 'grel-pa sa-bcad bsdus-don*. Auth. Mkhas-grub Ye-shes rgyal-mtshan. NL. [*697*]

Commentary on the Peaceful and Wrathful Deities (of the Magical Net) and on Vajrakīla according to the Transmitted Precepts. *zhi-khro-dang phur-pa bka'-ma'i 'grel-pa*. Auth. Mkhas-grub Ye-shes rgyal-mtshan. NL. [*697*]

Commentary of Pāṇini. *pā-ṇi-pa'i 'grel-pa*. Skt. *Pāṇinivyākaraṇasūtra*. Auth. Pāṇini. T 4420. HIL 5.2, Ch. 2. [*99-100*]

Commentary on the Prātimokṣa Sūtra in Fifty Sections. *so-thar-gyi mdo'i 'grel-pa bam-po lnga-bcu-pa*. Skt. *Prātimokṣasūtraṭīkāvinayasamuccaya*. Auth. Vimalamitra. T 4106. [*92*]

Commentary on the Realisation of the Eighty-Chapter Magical Net. *sgyu-'phrul brgyad-cu-pa'i mngon-rtogs 'grel*. Auth. Gnubs-chen Sangs-rgyas ye-shes. NL. [*612*]

Commentary on the Root Tantra of Cakrasaṃvara. *bde-mchog rtsa-rgyud-kyi 'grel-pa*. Skt. *Śrīcakrasaṃvaratantrarājasaṃvarasamuccayanāmavṛtti*. Auth. Indrabhūti. T 1413. [*462*]

Commentary on the Root Tantra entitled Seven Seals. *rtsa-rgyud-la 'grel-pa rgya-bdun-ma*. Auth. Hūṃkara. NL. [*489*]

Commentary of the Seal of Entrustment, a Memorial of the Deities of the Sūtra which Gathers All Intentions. *'dus-pa mdo'i lha-thems gtad-rgya'i 'grel-pa*. Auth. Zur-ham Shākya 'byung-gnas. NL. [*672*]

(Commentary on the Secret Nucleus entitled) Dispelling Darkness in the Ten Directions. *snying-'grel phyogs-bcu mun-sel*. Auth. Klong-chen rab-'byams-pa. Refer to *Trilogy which Dispels Darkness* for publication details. Trans. GGFTC. Another recent study which draws extensively on this work is: H. V. Guenther, *Matrix of Mystery*. Boulder/London: Shambhala, 1985. [*92*, *677*, *681*, *707*]

Commentary on the Secret Nucleus. *gsang-ba snying-po-la ṭīkā rgyas-pa*. Auth. Rta-ston Gzi-brjid. NL. [*660*]

Commentary on the Secret Nucleus. *snying-'grel*. Not precisely identified. It should be noted that the abbreviation *snying-'grel* is also used to refer to Vajragarbha's *Commentary which Epitomises the Hevajra (Tantra)*. [*477-8*]

Commentary on the Secret Nucleus entitled (Illuminating Lamp of the) Fundamental Text. *snying-po'i 'grel-pa (khog-gzhung) gsal-sgron*. Auth. Vimalamitra. P 4739. [*266*] See *Illuminating Lamp of the Fundamental Text*

Commentary on the Secret Nucleus (by Sūryaprabhāsiṃha). *nyi-'od seng-ge'i 'grel-pa*. Skt. *Śrīguhyagarbhatattvaviniścayavyākhyānaṭīkā*. Auth. Sūryaprabhāsiṃha. P 4719. Pub. Gangtok: Dodrup Sangye, 1976. I-Tib 76-902441. [*40*, *688*, *916*]

Commentary on the Six-limbed Yoga. *sbyor-drug 'grel-pa*. Skt. *Ṣaḍaṅgayogaṭīkā*. Auth. Anupamarakṣita. T 1367. [*674*]

Commentary on the Sublime Seal of Great Realisation. *'phags-pa rtogs-chen phyag-rgya'i 'grel-pa*. NL. Cf. T 4524. [*85*]

Commentary on the Supreme Continuum of the Greater Vehicle. *rgyud bla-ma'i 'grel-pa*. Skt. *Mahāyānottaratantraśāstravyākhyā*. Auth. Asaṅga. T 4025. [*170*, *174*, *175*, *186*] See also *Supreme Continuum of the Greater Vehicle*

Commentary on the Sūtra of the Teaching Delivered by Akṣayamati. *blo-gros mi-zad-pas bstan-pa'i mdo-'grel*. Skt. *Akṣayamatinirdeśasūtravṛtti*. Auth. Vasubandhu. T 3994. [*943*]

Commentary on Tampa Rinpoche's General Exposition of the Vehicles. *dam-pa rin-po-che'i theg-pa spyi-bcing-gi 'grel-pa*. Auth. Mkhas-grub Ye-shes rgyal-mtshan. NL. [*697*]

Commentary on the Tantra of the Awakening of Great Vairocana. *rnam-snang mngon-byang-gi 'grel-pa*. Skt. *Mahāvairocanābhisaṃbodhitantraṭīkā*. Auth. Buddhaguhya. T 2663. [*269*]

Commentary on the Tantra of the Dialogue with Subāhu. *dpung-bzang-gi rgyud-kyi 'grel-pa*. Skt. *Subāhuparipṛcchānāmatantrapiṇḍārtha*. Auth. Buddhaguhya. T 2671. Cf. T 2672-3. [*260*]

Commentary on the Tantra of the Purification of All Evil Destinies. *ngan-song sbyong-rgyud-kyi 'grel-pa*. Auth. Rong-zom Chos-kyi bzang-po. NL. [*707*]

Commentary on the Tantra of the Secret Nucleus. *gsang-snying 'grel-pa*. Auth. Rong-zom Chos-kyi bzang-po. NMKMG Vol. 25. Pub. Gangtok: Dodrup Sangyay Lama, 1976. I-Tib 76-902140. Also referred to as the *Four Modes and Fifteen Aspects Commentary* and the *Precious Jewel Commentary*. [*707*]

Commentary on Vajrakīla according to the Transmitted Precepts. See *Commentary on the Peaceful and Wrathful Deities (of the Magical Net) and the Commentary on Vajrakīla according to the Transmitted Precepts*

Commentary on the Verification of Co-emergence. *lhan-cig skyes-grub-kyi gzhung-'grel*. Skt. *Sahajasiddhipaddhati*. Auth. Ma Dpal-mo (Śrī). T 2261. [*485*]

Commentary on the Verse Summation of the Transcendental Perfection of Discriminative Awareness. *sdud-pa'i 'grel-pa*. Skt. *Sañcayagāthāpañjikā*. To be identified with either T 3792 by Haribhadra, or T 3798 by Buddhaśrījñāna. [*92*]

Common Savour. *ro-snyoms*. An essential precept of the Great Seal according to the 'Brug-pa bka'-brgyud tradition. The fundamental texts are given in DZ Vol. 7, pp. 59-88. [*549*]

Compendium of the Abhidharma. *mngon-pa kun-las-btus-pa*. Skt. *Abhidharmasamuccaya*. Auth. Asaṅga. T 4049. EIPRB 1212-23. MTTWL 1. [*90*, *91*, *526*, *666*, *762*]

Compendium of the Abhidharma and Treasury of the Abhidharma. *mngon-pa gong-'og rnams*. Listed separately.

Compendium of Lessons. *bslab-btus*. Skt. *Śikṣāsamuccaya*. Auth. Śāntideva. T 3939-40. B.Budh. 1 (1897-1902). BST 11 (1961). EIPRB 3444-50. HIL 7.1, pp. 83-5, 128. MTTWL 211. See also J. Hedinger, *Aspekte der Schulung in der Laufbahn eines Bodhisattva*. Wiesbaden: Otto Harrassowitz, 1984. [*92*, *235*, *577*]

Compendium of the Nucleus of Pristine Cognition. *ye-shes snying-po kun-las btus-pa*. Skt. *Jñānasārasamuccaya*. Auth. Āryadeva. T 3851. HIL 7.1, p. 106. MTTWL 88. See also K. Mimaki, "Le commentaire de Mi pham sur le *Jñānasārasamuccaya*" in *Mélanges offerts au Professeur J. W. de Jong*. Canberra, 1982. [*65*]

Compendium of the Sūtra's Meaning. *mdo'i don bsdu-ba*. Skt. *Guhyārthasūtra-piṇḍārtha*. Auth. Dharmabodhi. P 4751. [*489*]

Compendium of Valid Cognition. *tshad-ma kun(-las) btus(-pa)*. Skt. *Pramāṇa-samuccaya*. And its commentary, *Pramāṇasamuccayavṛtti*. Auth. Dignāga. T 4203-4. EIPRB 519, 846, 1774-93. MTTWL 166. HOS 47 (1968). [*91*, *92*, *101*, *102*, *103*, *564*]

Complete Elucidation of the Hidden Meaning of the Cakrasaṃvara. *bde-mchog sbas-don kun-gsal*. Auth. Tsong-kha-pa. TWB 5316. [*681*]

Components of the Doctrine. *chos-kyi phung-po*. Skt. *Dharmaskandha*. Auth. Śāriputra (according to the Tibetan tradition, but elsewhere attributed to Maudgalyāyana). At present extant only in Chinese: Taishō 1537. EIPRB 13. L. de La Vallée Poussin, *L'Abhidharmakośa de Vasubandhu*. Paris: Paul Geuthner, 1923-36, Vol. 1, p. xxxvii. One of the *Seven Sections of the Abhidharma*. [*90*]

Condensed Commentary on the Secret Nucleus. *snying-'grel piṇḍārtha*. Skt. *Guhyagarbhapiṇḍārtha*. Auth. Vimalamitra. P 4755. [*92*]

Conquest of Objections. *gnod-'joms*. Auth. Vasubandu. Refer to n. 1325. [*944*]

Consummation of Secrets. *gsang-ba yongs-rdzogs*. See *(Eight Transmitted Precepts, the) Consummation of Secrets*

Cremation Ritual. *ro-sreg-gi las*. Skt. *Māyājālalaghudṛṣṭāntasvāśrayakrama*. Auth. Vimalamitra. P 4747. [*481*]

Crest of Indestructible Reality. *rdo-rje gtsug-tor*. Skt. *Vajroṣṇīṣakriyātantra*. See F. Lessing and A. Wayman, *Mkhas Grub Rje's Fundamentals of the Buddhist Tantras*. The Hague/Paris: Mouton, 1968, p. 137. The only section of this tantra presently available is T 808, *Dhyānottarapaṭala*. [*305*]

Crossing the Lion's Neck. *seng-ge mjing-bsnol*. NL. [*565*]

Crossing the Peacock's Neck. *rma-bya mjing-bsnol*. NGB Vol. 2, nos. 36-7. [*136*]

Crown Ornament of the Aural Lineage, the Cycles of the Wish-fulfilling Gem. *snyan-brgyud gtsug-rgyan yid-bzhin nor-bu'i skor-rnams*. Disc. Bdud-'dul rdo-rje. NA. [*815*]

Crystal Mirror of the Great All-Seeing Svarodaya. *kun-gzigs dbyangs-'char chen-mo shel-gyi me-long*. Auth. 'Jam-mgon Mi-pham rgya-mtsho. Pub. Sataun, HP: Getse Tulku Kunga Lodoy, Kham Kathok Tibetan Society, 1969. I-Tib 77-910110. [*870*]

Crystal Mirror of Philosophical Systems. *thu'u-bkvan-gyi grub-mtha' shel-dkar me-long*. Auth. Thu'u-bkvan Blo-bzang Chos-kyi nyi-ma. Pub. in *Collected Works of Thu'u-bkwan blo-bzaṅ chos-kyi-ñi-ma*, Vol. 2. Delhi: Ngawang Gelek Demo, 1969. I-Tib 73-902408. Typeset edn.: Gansu:

Minorities Press, 1984. For translated selections, see S. C. Das, *Studies in the History and Religion of Tibet*. Delhi: Mañjuśrī, 1971. D. S. Ruegg, "The Jo naṅ pas: A School of Buddhist Ontologists according to the *Grub mtha' śel gyi me loṅ*" *Journal of the American Oriental Society* 83 (1963), pp. 73-91. [*755-6*]

Culmination of the Supreme Path. *lam-mchog mthar-thug*. Auth. Zhang Rin-po-che. DZ Vol. 5, pp. 744-77. [*201-2*]

Cycle of the Attainment of the Glorious Four-faced Protector and of Mahādeva. *dpal-mgon gdong-bzhi-pa dang lha-chen sgrub-skor*. Disc. Bdud-'dul rdo-rje. NA. [*815*]

Cycle of the Attainment of Mind as the Wish-fulfilling Gem. See *Attainment of Mind, the Wish-fulfilling Gem*

Cycle of the Attainment of Nectar-Elixir. *bdud-rtsi sman-sgrub-kyi skor*. Disc. Padma gling-pa. PLTC Vol. 9, pp. 383-539. [*797*]

Cycle of Common Sciences. *thun-mong rig-gnas-kyi skor*. Auth. 'Jam-mgon Mi-pham rgya-mtsho. Refers to those works in MPSB which concern the four common sciences and the five minor sciences. [*877*]

Cycle of Dedicatory Prayers and Benedictions. *bsngo-smon shis-brjod-kyi skor*. Auth. 'Jam-mgon Mi-pham rgya-mtsho. Refers to the many such works found throughout MPSB. [*877*]

Cycle of Eulogies and Narratives. *bstod-tshogs-dang rtogs-brjod-kyi skor*. Auth. 'Jam-mgon Mi-pham rgya-mtsho. Refers to the eulogies, etc. found throughout MPSB. [*877*]

Cycle of Glorious Cakrasaṃvara and the Four-armed Protector of Transmitted Precepts. *dpal bde-mchog bka'-srung phyag-bzhi-pa'i skor*. Disc. Bdud-'dul rdo-rje. NA. [*815*]

Cycle of the Glorious Neuter Lord. *dpal-mgon ma-ning skor*. Disc. Rig-'dzin 'Ja'-tshon snying-po. JTPD Vols. 6-7. Also pub. Tezu, Arunachal Pradesh: Ngawang Sonam, 1979. I-Tib 79-903471. [*811*]

Cycle of the Glorious Tiger-riding Lord. *dpal-mgon stag-zhon skor*. Disc. Dung-'phreng-can, and offered to Bdud-'dul rdo-rje. NA. [*815*]

Cycle of Götsangpa's Guidance *or* Guidance on the Path according to Götsangpa. *rgod-tshang-pa'i khrid-kyi skor* or *rgod-tshang-pa'i lam-khrid*. Auth. Rgod-tshang-pa Mgon-po rdo-rje. This material is found scattered throughout the known works of the author: *The Collected Works of Rgod-tshaṅ-pa Mgon-po-rdo-rje*. 2 vols. Pub. SNGP, 1972. I-Tib 72-906726. 3 vols. Pub. Thimphu: Kunzang Tobgey, 1976. I(Bhu)-Tib 76-902028. 5 vols. Pub. Thimphu: Tango Monastic Community, 1981. Bhu-Tib 81-901041. [*571*, *576*]

Cycle of Hevajra. *dgyes-pa rdo-rje'i skor*. See *Hevajra (Cycle/Tantra)*

Cycle of Innermost Spirituality. *snying-thig-gi skor*. See *Four-Part Innermost Spirituality*

Cycle of Instructions on Caṇḍālī, Mother of Life, from the Innermost Spirituality of Immortality. *'chi-med thugs-tig-gi tshe-yum tsaṇḍa-lī'i gdams-skor*. Disc. 'Jam-dbyangs mkhyen-brtse'i dbang-po. Redacted by 'Jam-mgon Kong-sprul Blo-gros mtha'-yas. RTD Vol. 77, pp. 389-414.

[*858*] See also *Cycle of the Means for the Attainment of Caṇḍālī, Mother of Life* and the *Root Text of Caṇḍālī, Mother of Life*

Cycle of Instructions of Zhang Tshelpa. *zhang tshal-pa'i gdams-skor*. See, e.g., *Źaṅ tshal pa'i bka' thor bu*. SNGP 1972. I-Tib 72-900813. Cf. also *Culmination of the Supreme Path*. [*576*]

Cycle of the Jambhalas of the Five Families. *Dzam-lha rigs-lnga'i skor*. Disc. Rdo-rje gling-pa. NL. [*791*]

Cycle of Krodhakālī. *khros-ma nag-mo'i skor*. Disc. O-rgyan gling-pa. NA. [*775*]

Cycle of the Magical Net of the Three Roots. *rtsa-gsum sgyu-'phrul drva-ba'i skor*. Disc. 'Jam-dbyangs mkhyen-brtse'i dbang-po. Possibly to be identified with RTD Vol. 7, pp. 49-90. [*856*]

Cycle of Mahākāla and Malevolent Mantras. *mgon-po-dang ngan-sngags-kyi skor*. Disc. Nyang-ral Nyi-ma 'od-zer. NL. However, cf. the cycle of the *Four-armed Lord according to the Treasures of Nyang*. [*756*]

Cycle of Meaning, which is Aro's Great System of Guidance. *a-ro'i khrid-mo-che don-skor*. [*571*] See *Seven Sessions of Aro (Yeshe Jungne)*

Cycle of the Means for the Attainment of Caṇḍālī, Mother of Life. *tshe-yum tsaṇḍā-lī'i sgrub-skor*. Disc. 'Jam-mgon Kong-sprul Blo-gros mtha'-yas. [*864*] See *Cycle of Instructions on Caṇḍālī, Mother of Life, from the Innermost Spirituality of Immortality*

Cycle of the Means for the Attainment of the Guru's Four Bodies. *bla-ma sku-bzhi'i sgrub-thabs-kyi skor*. Disc. 'Jam-dbyangs mkhyen-brtse'i dbang-po. NL. However, cf. *Four Cycles of the Means for the Attainment of the Guru*. [*856*]

Cycle of the Means for the Attainment of the Three Roots. *rtsa-gsum sgrub-skor*. Disc. Ratna gling-pa. RLTC Vol. 16. RTD Vol. 5, p. 507 to Vol. 6, p. 121. [*793*]

Cycle of the Meditational Deities of Atiśa. *jo-bo'i yi-dam skor*. To be identified with the *Snar-thang brgya-rtsa*, GDKT Vol. 13. [*577*]

Cycle of Mind in its Natural State. *gnyug-sems skor*. Auth. 'Jam-mgon Mi-pham rgya-mtsho. NNS 57 (1972). I(Sik)-Tib 72-903167. ZGSB Vol. 1. Litho. Varanasi: Tarthang Tulku, 1965. I-Tib-76. [*878*]

Cycle of Minor Rites. *las-phran-gyi skor*. Disc. Padma gling-pa. PLTC Vol. 11, pp. 522-603. [*797*]

Cycle of the Neuter Lord. *mgon-po ma-ning-gi skor*. Disc. O-rgyan gling-pa. NA. [*775*]

Cycle of Profound Doctrines which are Mind Treasures. *zab-chos thugs-gter skor*. Disc. Thang-stong rgyal-po. NL. [*802*]

Cycle of the Sciences of Inner Meaning. *nang-don rig-pa'i skor*. Auth. 'Jam-mgon Mi-pham rgya-mtsho. This refers to the majority of works in MPSB, including philosophical treatises and commentaries, and texts on all aspects of Buddhist practice. [*877*]

Cycle of the Small Son which is a Non-Dual Tantra of the Great Perfection. *rdzogs-chen gnyis-med rgyud bu-chung-gi skor*. Disc. Padma gling-pa. PLTC Vol. 6. [*796*]

Cycle Summarising the Essence of the Great Gathering of Transmitted Precepts. *bka'-'dus chen-mo'i snying-po mdor-bsdus skor.* See *(Ocean of Doctrine, the Great) Gathering of Transmitted Precepts*

Cycle of the Tantra of the Magical Net. *sgyu-'phrul skor-gyi yig-cha.* Auth. Lo-chen Dharmaśrī. LCSB Vols. 6-7, 12. NMKMG Vols. 11-12, 32-4. SSS 36 (1972). I-Tib 72-903163. [*375*]

Cycle of Trhopupa. *khro-phu-pa'i skor.* Transmitted in the lineage of Khro-phu lo-tsā-ba Byams-pa-dpal. DZ Vol. 5, pp. 530-7. GDKT Vol. 11. [*577*]

Cycle of the Universal Gathering of the Three Roots. *rtsa-gsum spyi-'dus-kyi skor.* Disc. Jam-dbyangs mkhyen-brtse'i dbang-po. RTD Vol. 7, pp. 49-90. [*856*]

Cycle of Yamāntaka. *gshed-skor.* Disc. Rdo-rje gling-pa. NL. [*791*]

Cycle of Yamāntaka, Lord of Life. *gshin-rje tshe-bdag-gi skor.* Disc. O-rgyan gling-pa. NA. [*776*]

Cycle of Zhanglön and Pomra, Protectors of the Transmitted Precepts. *bka'-srung zhang-blon-dang spom-ra'i skor.* Disc. Bdud-'dul rdo-rje. NA. [*815*]

Cycles of the Attainment of Peaceful Mañjuśrī. *'jam-dpal zhi-sgrub-kyi skor-rnams.* Disc. Bdud-'dul rdo-rje. RTD Vol. 25, pp. 425-517. [*815*]

Cycles of the Innermost Spirituality of the Accomplished Master. *grub-thob thugs-tig-gi skor-rnams.* See *Innermost Spirituality of the Accomplished Master*

Cycles of the Luminous Expanse of the Great Perfection. *rdzogs-chen klong-gsal-gyi skor-rnams.* Disc. Padma gling-pa. PLTC Vols. 5 and 17. [*796*]

Cycles of the Means for the Attainment of Amitāyus and Hayagrīva. *tshe-dpag-med-dang rta-mgrin sgrub-skor-gyi shog-ser.* Disc. 'Jam-mgon Kong-sprul Blo-gros mtha'-yas. NL. [*864*]

Cycles of the Wrathful Guru and Protectors of the Teaching. *gu-ru drag-po dang bstan-srung skor.* Disc. O-rgyan gling-pa. NA. [*776*]

Daily Yoga of the Awareness-holder. *rig-'dzin rgyun-gyi rnal-'byor.* Disc. 'Jam-mgon Kong-sprul Blo-gros mtha'-yas. RTD Vol. 15, pp. 415-22. [*865*]

Decree of Emperor Qubilai Qan. *se-chen-gan-gyi lung.* Refer to n. 812. [*662*]

Definitive Order of the Chronology of the Teaching. *bstan-rtsis-kyi rnam-bzhag.* Auth. Kaḥ-thog Rig-'dzin Tshe-dbang nor-bu. Pub. in *The Collected Works (Gsuṅ 'bum) of Kaḥ-thog Rig-'dzin Tshe-dbaṅ-nor-bu.* Dalhousie, HP: Damchoe Sangpo, 1976. Vol. 4, pp. 103-61. I-Tib 76-905079. See also R. Prats, "Tshe-dbaṅ-nor-bu's Chronological Notes on the Early Transmission of the *Bi ma sñiṅ thig*" in L. Ligeti (ed.), *Tibetan and Buddhist Studies.* Budapest, 1984, Vol. 2, pp. 197-209. [*966*]

Definitive Order of the Tantrapiṭaka. *bcom-ldan ral-gri'i spyi-rnam.* Auth. Bcom-ldan Rig-pa'i ral-gri. NL. [*827*]

Definitive Order of the Three Vehicles. *theg-pa gsum rnam-par gzhag-pa.* Skt. *Triyānavyavasthāna.* Auth. Ratnākaraśānti. T 3712. [*253*]

Definitive Presentation of the Tantras. *rgyud-kyi rnam-bzhag*. Auth. Zur Byams-pa Seng-ge. NL. [*665*]

Definitive Verification of the Means for the Attainment of the Great Heruka. *khrag-'thung chen-po'i sgrub-thabs yang-dag-par grub-pa*. Skt. *Saṃsiddhimahāśrīherukasādhana*. Auth. Hūṃkara. T 1678. [*477*]

Denkarma Catalogue of the Kangyur. *bka'-'gyur dkar-chag ldan-dkar-ma*. Auth. Ska-ba Dpal-brtsegs and Nam-mkha'i snying-po. T 4364. Ed. M. Lalou, "Les Textes Bouddhiques au Temps du Roi Khri-sroṅ-lde-bcan" *Journal Asiatique* CCXLI-3 (1953), pp. 313-53. [*794*]

Destruction of Bewilderment. *dbu-ma 'khrul-'joms*. Skt. *Madhyamakabhramaghāta*. Auth. Āryadeva. T 3850. HIL 7.1, pp. 54, 112. [*167*]

Detailed Annotations on the Commentary on the Secret Nucleus and the Array of the Path of the Magical Net. *snying-ṭīk-dang lam-rnam-bkod-la mchan-bu*. Auth. Snye-mdo Kun-gzigs. NL. [*702*]

Detailed Ceremony for the Rite of the Tie to the Higher Realms. *gnas-lung-la'ang cho-ga rgyas-pa*. Auth. Sangs-rgyas rin-chen. NL. [*673*]

Detailed Commentary on the Heart Sūtra of Discriminative Awareness. *shes-rab snying-po'i rgya-cher 'grel-pa*. Skt. *Āryaprajñāpāramitāhṛdayaṭīkā*. Auth. Praśastrasena. T 3821. MTTWL 158. See also D. Lopez, *The Heart Sūtra Explained*. Albany, NY: SUNY Press, 1987. [*577*]

Detailed Exegesis of the Eight Transmitted Precepts. *bka'-brgyad rnam-bshad*. Auth. 'Jam-mgon Mi-pham rgya-mtsho. Pub. in *Rare Writings of 'Jam-mgon 'Ju Mi-pham rgya-mtsho*. Paro: Lama Dodrup Sangyay, 1977. I(Bhu)-Tib 77-902412. [*875*]

Detailed Exegesis of the Exposition of Valid Cognition. *tshad-ma rnam-'grel-gyi rnam-bshad*. Auth. 'Jam-mgon Mi-pham rgya-mtsho. Litho. Clement Town, UP: Nyingma Lamas College, n.d. [*875*]

Detailed Exposition of the Array of the Path of the Magical Net. *lam rnam-bkod-la rnam-bzhag*. Auth. Sangs-rgyas rin-chen. NL. [*673*]

Detailed Exposition of the Feast Offering. *tshogs-kyi 'khor-lo'i rnam-bshad*. Auth. Mkhas-grub Ye-shes rgyal-mtshan. NL. [*697*]

Determination and Distinction. *la-shan (lta-ba'i sgron-me)*. Auth. Bzhad-pa'i rdo-rje (i.e. Dga'-rab rdo-rje). P 4727. [*350*, *351*]

Dhāraṇī of the Wish-fulfilling Gem. *tsindha-ma-ṇi'i gzungs*. Skt. *Cintāmaṇidhāraṇī*. Name of a formula recited in connection with the rites of Avalokiteśvara according to the Kriyā tantras. [*508*]

Dialogue with the Four Goddesses. *lha-mo bzhis zhus-pa*. Skt. *Caturdevīparipṛcchā*. T 446. [*77*]

Dialogue with Maitreya. *byams-pas zhus-pa*. Skt. *Maitreyaparipṛcchā*. T 85-6. [*234*]

Dialogue of Sky and Mountain. *mkha'-ri'i zhu-lan*. Disc. Guru Chos-dbang. NL. [*838*]

Dialogue with Suvikrāntavikrami. *rab-rtsal rnam-gnon-gyis zhus-pa*. Skt. *Suvikrāntavikramiparipṛcchā*. T 14. EIPRB 1822-4. MTTWL 227. BST 17 (1961). [*908*]

Diamond Cutter. *rdo-rje gcod-pa*. Skt. *Vajracchedikā Prajñāpāramitā*. T 16. EIPRB 1020-45. MTTWL 244. BST 17 (1961). SOR 13 (1957). Gilgit version ed. G. Schopen, in L. O. Gómez (ed.), *The Mahāyāna Path*. Ann Arbor, Michigan, 1989. [*336*]

Direct and Circuitous Paths of Transcendental Perfection according to the System of Atiśa. *jo-bo-rje'i pha-rol-tu phyin-pa'i lam rkyang-khug*. The precise teachings of Atiśa with which these are to be identified remain uncertain. It is also possible that the phrase has only a general denotation. [*546*]

Disclosure of the Contents of the Secret Nucleus. *gsang-ba snying-po'i khog-dbub*. Auth. Sman-lung-pa Shākya-'od. NL. [*686*]

Disclosure of the Contents of Yungtönpa's Commentary. *gYung-ston-pa'i khog-dbub*. Auth. Sgrol-ma-ba Bsam-grub rdo-rje. NMKMG Vol. 28. [*660*]

Disclosure of the Hidden. *gab(-pa) mngon(-phyung)*. Name of a classification of teaching according to the Great Perfection. It is often found in the titles of books of both the Great Perfection and Great Seal traditions. Also referred to as *Transmitted Precepts given in a manner which Reveals the Hidden*. [*331*, *654*, *658*]

Dispelling Darkness in the Ten Directions (a Commentary on the Secret Nucleus). *(snying-'grel) phyogs-bcu mun-sel*. See *(Commentary on the Secret Nucleus entitled) Dispelling Darkness in the Ten Directions*

Disputant's Sword which Cuts through Difficulties. *dka'-gcod smra-ba'i mtshon-cha*. Auth. Gnubs-chen Sangs-rgyas ye-shes. NL. [*612*]

Dissertation. *rab-tu byed-pa*. Skt. *Prakaraṇapāda*. Auth. Vasumitra. Extant only in Chinese: Taishō 1541-2. EIPRB 84. L. de La Vallée Poussin, *L'Abhidharmakośa de Vasubandhu*. Paris: Paul Guethner, 1923-36, Vol. 1, pp. xxxii-xxxiii. One of the *Seven Sections of the Abhidharma*. [*90*]

Doctrinal Background for the Ḍākinī Section of Gathering of the Three Roots' Intention. *rtsa-gsum dgongs-'dus mkha'-'gro'i rgyab-chos*. Disc. 'Jam-mgon Kong-sprul Blo-gros mtha'-yas. [*864*] See *Gathering of the Three Roots' Intention*

Doctrinal Background for the Gathering of the Three Roots' Intention. *rtsa-gsum dgongs-'dus-kyi rgyab-chos shog-ser*. Disc. 'Jam-mgon Kong-sprul Blo-gros mtha'-yas. [*864*] See *Gathering of the Three Roots' Intention*

Doctrinal Cycle of Auspicious Coincidence. *rten-'brel-gyi chos-skor*. Disc. Mchog-gyur bde-chen gling-pa. CLTC Vol. 19. [*848*]

Doctrinal Cycle of the Four Aspects of Ritual Service and Attainment which is Luminous like the Sun and Moon. *bsnyen-sgrub rnam-pa bzhi'i chos-skor nyi-zla-ltar gsal-ba*. Disc. Rig-'dzin Rgod-kyi ldem-'phru-can. The identification of this amongst available Northern Treasures (*byang-gter*) texts is uncertain. [*781*]

(Doctrinal Cycle of the) Great Compassionate One. *thugs-rje chen-po'i chos-skor*. Disc. Sangs-rgyas gling-pa. RTD Vol. 35, pp. 331-527. Also referred to as the *Doctrinal Cycle of Sublime Avalokiteśvara*. [*785-6*]

Doctrinal Cycle of the Great Compassionate One as Mind at Rest. *thugs-rje chen-po sems-nyid ngal-gso'i chos-skor*. Disc. 'Jam-dbyangs mkhyen-brtse'i dbang-po. NL. [*856*]

(Doctrinal Cycle of the) Great Compassionate One as the Universal Gathering of the Sugatas. *thugs-rje chen-po bde-gshegs kun-'dus-kyi chos-skor*. Disc. Gter-bdag gling-pa. RTD Vol. 38, pp. 67-405. Pub. Dehra Dun: D. G. Khochhen Trulku, 1975. I-Tib 75-906625. [*828, 843*]

Doctrinal Cycle of the Innermost Spirituality of Saroruha, which is the Secret Attainment, among the Three Cycles of the Means for the Attainment of the Guru. *bla-sgrub skor-gsum-gyi gsang-sgrub mtsho-skyes snying-thig-gi chos-skor*. Disc. 'Jam-dbyangs mkhyen-brtse'i dbang-po. RTD Vol. 15, pp. 347-95. [*857*]

Doctrinal Cycle of the Innermost Spirituality of the Sublime Lady. *'phags-ma'i snying-thig-gi chos-skor*. Disc. 'Jam-dbyangs mkhyen-brtse'i dbang-po. RTD Vol. 46, pp. 247-444; Vol. 57, pp. 271-392; Vol. 99, pp. 191-7, 329-83. [*857*]

Doctrinal Cycle of Kharak. *kha-rag chos-skor*. NL. See *Blue Annals*, pp. 999-1005. [*578*]

Doctrinal Cycle of (Loro) Recungpa. *(lo-ro) ras-chung-pa'i chos-skor*. Perhaps to be identified with the *ras-chung snyan-brgyud* cycle, sections of which may be found in DZ Vol. 5, pp. 251-455. See also: Gtsaṅ-smyon Heruka, *Bde mchog mkha' 'gro sñan rgyud*. 2 vols. SSS 11-12 (1971). I-Tib 76-924556. Byaṅ-chub bzaṅ-po, *Bde mchog mkha' 'gro sñan rgyud*. 2 vols. New Delhi, 1973. I-Tib 73-902914. [*657*]

Doctrinal Cycle of the Means for the Attainment of the Seven Lines. *tshig-bdun sgrub-thabs-kyi chos-skor*. Disc. 'Jam-mgon Kong-sprul Blo-gros mtha'-yas. RTD Vol. 16, pp. 301-631. [*866*]

(Doctrinal Cycle of the) Spontaneous Song of the Clouds, the Nucleus of Indestructible Reality. *rdo-rje snying-po sprin-gyi thol-glu'i chos-skor*. Disc. Lha-btsun Nam-mkha' 'jigs-med. Xylo. Gangtok, 1978. I-Tib 82-906676. [*819-20*]

Doctrinal Cycle of Sublime Avalokiteśvara. *'phags-pa spyan-ras-gzigs-kyi chos-skor*. Disc. Sangs-rgyas gling-pa. See *Doctrinal Cycle of the Great Compassionate One*

Doctrinal Cycle of the Utterly Secret Hayagrīva. *rta-mgrin yang-gsang-gi chos-skor*. Disc. 'Dar-phya rū-pa, with successive additions by later treasure-finders. RTD Vol. 39, p. 359 to Vol. 40, p. 85. [*715*]

Doctrinal Cycles of the Ḍākinīs. *mkha'-'gro'i chos-skor*. Disc. Nyang-ral Nyi-ma 'od-zer. Perhaps this is RTD Vol. 54, pp. 285-540. [*756*]

Doctrinal Cycles of the Vital Attainment of the Awareness-holder. *rig-'dzin srog-sgrub-kyi chos-skor rnams*. Disc. Lha-btsun Nam-mkha' 'jigs-med. RTD *passim*. Xylo. *srog-sgrub rgyab-chos*. Palace Monastery, Gangtok. I(Sik)-Tib 74-900111. Pub. in 2 vols. Gangtok: Dzongsar Chhentse Labrang, 1980. I-Tib 80-900958. [*820*]

Doctrinal History which is Sunlight Extending the Teaching. *chos-'byung bstan-pa rgyas-pa'i nyin-byed*. Auth. 'Brug-chen Padma dkar-po. SP 75

(1968). Also pub. in *Collected Works of Kun-mkhyen Padma dkar-po*, Vol. 2. Darjeeling: Kargyud Sungrab Nyamso Khang, 1973. I-Tib 73-902758. [*965*]

Doctrinal Treasury of the Transmitted Precepts in Twenty Volumes. *bka'-ma'i chos-mdzod gzhung-pod yongs-rdzogs glegs-bam nyi-shu*. Pub. by O-rgyan mdo-sngags chos-kyi nyi-ma at Dpal-yul. NMKMG Vols. 1-20 are based on this edition. [*739*]

Doctrine which Ascertains the Causal and Fruitional Aspects of Deeds, of which the Intention is Vast as Space. *las-rgyu-'bras la-zlo-ba'i chos dgongs-pa nam-mkha'-dang mnyam-pa*. Disc. Rig-'dzin Rgod-kyi ldem-'phru-can. The identification of this, and of the two entries which follow, amongst available Northern Treasure (*byang-gter*) texts is uncertain. [*781*]

Doctrine of Auspicious Coincidence which is like a Sandalwood Tree. *rten-'brel-can-gyi chos tsan-dan-gyi sdong-po lta-bu*. Disc. Rig-'dzin Rgod-kyi ldem-'phru-can. NL. [*781*]

Doctrine which Pulverises Enemies and Obstacles, and which is like a Poisonous Plant. *dgra-bgegs thal-bar rlog-pa'i chos dug-gi sdong-po lta-bu*. Disc. Rig-'dzin Rgod-kyi ldem-'phru-can. NL. [*781*]

Doctrines of Maitreya. See *Five Doctrines of (Venerable) Maitreya*

Dohā (of Saraha). *do-hā*. Skt. *Dohākośa*. T 2245, 2251, 2263-4, 2266, 2273. HIL 9.3, pp. 124-33. P. C. Bagchi, *Dohākośa*, Pt. I. Calcutta Sanskrit Series, no. 25C. Calcutta, 1938. Trans. H. V. Guenther, *The Royal Song of Saraha*. Seattle: University of Washington Press, 1968. M. Shahidullah, *Les Chants Mystiques de Kāṇha et de Saraha*. Paris: A. Maisonneuve, 1928. D. L. Snellgrove (trans.), in E. Conze (ed.), *Buddhist Texts through the Ages*. New York: Philosophical Library, 1954, pp. 224-39. See further the bibliography given in P. Kvaerne, *An Anthology of Buddhist Tantric Songs*. Oslo: Universitetsforlaget, 1977. [*197*, *546*, *564*]

Dohā according to the Gang Tradition of the Great Seal. *phyag-chen sgang-lugs-kyi do-hā*. NL. [*657*]

Dohā Composed by Lord Maitripā. *mnga'-bdag mai-tri-pas bsdebs-pa'i do-hā*. Skt. *Mahāmudrākanakamālā*. T 2454. [*329*]

Dokam Inventory of the Twenty-five Great Pilgrimage Places of Dokam. *mdo-khams gnas-chen nyer-lnga'i mdo-byang*. Disc. Mchog-gyur bde-chen gling-pa. CLTC Vol. 30. Note: our interpretation of the term *mdo-byang* as referring to the province of *mdo-khams* is uncertain. An alternative rendering would take the syllable *mdo* in its meanings of "confluence" or "sūtra", so that the expression as a whole might be taken to mean "synoptic inventory". [*846*, *867*]

Dorje Trolö. *rdo-rje gro-lod*. Disc. Rig-'dzin 'Ja'-tshon snying-po. RTD Vol. 19, pp. 105-21. [*811*]

Doubts. *gdar-sha*. Unidentified. But note that the phrase *gdar-sha gcod* is commonly used in connection with orally transmitted meditation instruction to mean "resolution of doubts". [*654*, *658*]

Dramatical Treatise. *bha-ra-ta*. Skt. *Nāṭyaśāstra*. Auth. Bharata. GOS 36 (1926), 68 (1934), 124 (1954), 145 (1964). Known in Tibet only through secondary references. Skt. version ed. and trans. M. Ghosh. Calcutta: Manisha Granthalaya, 1956 and 1967; and Asiatic Society, 1961. HIL 5.3, pp. 245-50. [*106*]

Dying Testament. *'da'-ka'i zhal-chems*. Auth. Gter-bdag gling-pa. Text given in *History*, p. 832. Pub., with the commentary of Padma 'gyur-med rgya-mtsho, Clement Town, UP: Nyingma Lamas' College, n.d. [*832*]

Earlier and Later Treasure Troves. *gter-kha gong-'og*. General term for the treasures of Nyang-ral Nyi-ma 'od-zer (*gter-kha gong-ma*) and those of Guru Chos-dbang (*gter-kha 'og-ma*). [*677, 686, 730, 831, 836, 837*]

Earlier and Later Versions of the Biographies of the Hundred Treasure-finders. *gter-ston brgya-rtsa'i rnam-thar snga-phyi*. The earlier version is the *gter-brgya'i rnam-thar don-bsdus gsol-'debs*. Auth. Byang-bdag Bkra-shis stobs-rgyal. RTD Vol. 2, pp. 1-31. Also pub. with a detailed commentary by Karma Mi-'gyur-dbaṅ-rgyal in *Gter ton brgya rtsa'i mtshan sdom gsol 'debs*. Darjeeling: Taklung Tsetrul Pema Wangyal, 1978. I-Tib 79-903886. The later version is *Lives of the Hundred Treasure-finders, a Beauteous Rosary of Precious Beryl*. [*750*]

Eight Appendices. *zur-pa brgyad*. Disc. Rdo-rje gling-pa. NL. [*790*]

Eight Dissertations. *pra-ka-ra-ṇa sde-brgyad*. Skt. *Aṣṭaprakaraṇa*. Auth. Vasubandhu. Refer to n. 75 for their identification. S. Anacker, *Seven Works of Vasubandhu* (Delhi: Motilal Banarsidass, 1984), translates the following five among the eight: *Commentary on the Analysis of the Middle and Extremes*, *Dissertation on the Proof of Deeds*, *Dissertation on the Five Components*, *Twenty Verses* and *Thirty Verses*. See *Ornament of the Sūtras of the Greater Vehicle* for references to works that involve Vasubandhu's commentary on that text. The remaining two of the *Eight Dissertations*—the *Commentary on the Analysis of Phenomena and Reality* and the *Rational System of Exposition*—have yet to be systematically studied by contemporary western scholars. [*91*]

Eight Divisions of Medical Science. *yan-lag brgyad*. Skt. *Aṣṭāṅgahṛdayasaṃhitā*. Auth. Vāgbhaṭa (but in our text attributed to Śūra). T 4310. Ed. and trans. C. Vogel, *Vāgbhaṭa's Aṣṭāṅgahṛdaya*. Deutsche Morgenländische Gesellschaft XXXVII, 2. Wiesbaden: Franz Steiner Verlag, 1965. [*99*]

Eighteen Esoteric Instructions of the Mental Class. *sems-sde bco-brgyad*. DZ Vol. 1, pp. 159-371. NMKMG Vol. 17. Longcenpa, *Treasury of Spiritual and Philosophical Systems*, pp. 357-8, lists the tantras from which they are derived as: *rig-pa'i khu-byug, rtsal-chen 'brug-pa, khyung-chen lding-ba, rdo-la gser-zhun, mi-nub rgyal-mtshan nam-mkha' che* (which five constitute the earlier translations made by Vairocana), *rtse-mo byung-rgyal, nam-mkha'i rgyal-po, bde-ba 'phrul-bkod, rdzogs-pa spyi-chings, byang-chub sems-tig, bde-ba rab-'byams, srog-gi 'khor-lo, thig-le drug-pa, rdzogs-pa spyi-spyod, yid-bzhin nor-bu, kun-tu rig-pa, rje-btsun dam-pa* and *sgom-pa don-grub* (which thirteen constitute the later translations made by Vimalamitra, Nyak Jñānakumāra and Yudra Nyingpo). Also referred to as the *Eighteen Teachings of the Mental Class*. [*538, 673-4*]

Eighteen Great Tantrapiṭaka (of the Mahāyoga). *tantra (chen-po) sde bco-brgyad* or *rgyud-sde chen-po bco-brgyad.* Zhecen Gyeltsap Pema Namgyel, *sgrub-brgyud shing-rta brgyad-kyi byung-ba brjod-pa'i gtam mdor-bsdus legs-bshad padma dkar-po'i rdzing-bu*, p. 29, lists these as: the five great tantras of buddha-body, speech, mind, attributes and activities—*Buddhasamāyoga*, *Candraguhyatilaka*, *Guhyasamāja*, *Śrīparamādya* and *Karmamāla*; the five tantras concerned with means for attainment—*heruka rol-pa*, *rta-mchog rol-pa*, *snying-rje rol-pa*, *bdud-rtsi rol-pa* and *phur-pa bcu-gnyis-pa*; the five tantras concerned with conduct—*ri-bo brtsegs-pa*, *ye-shes ngam-glog*, *dam-tshig bkod-pa*, *ting-'dzin rtse-gcig* and *glang-chen rab-'bog*; the two supplementary tantras—*rnam-snang sgyu-'phrul drva-ba* and *thabs-kyi zhags-pa*; and the single tantra which summarises all the others—*Guhyagarbha*. For other enumerations, see Longcenpa, *sngags-kyi spyi-don tshangs-dbyangs 'brug-sgra*, pp. 27-8. E. Kaneko, *Ko-Tantora Zenshū Kaidai Mokuroku*. Tokyo: Kokusho Kankōkai, 1982, pp. 65-6. GGFTC, pp. 33-6. [*460-1*, *464*, *533*, *893*]

Eighteen Notes on the Sūtra. *mdo'i yig-sna bco-brgyad*. Auth. Sukhodyotaka. NL. [*489*]

Eighteen Roots. *rtsa-ba bco-brgyad*. See *(Exegetical Tradition of the) Eighteen Roots*

Eighteen Significations of the Syllable A. *a-don bco-brgyad*. [*700*, *701*] See *Eighteen Esoteric Instructions of the Mental Class*

Eighteen Teachings of the Mental Class. See *Eighteen Esoteric Instructions of the Mental Class*

Eighteen-Volume Collected Works. *bka'-'bum pusta-ka bco-brgyad*. Auth. Lochen Dharmaśrī. [*732*] See *Collected Works of Locen Dharmaśrī*

Eight General and Particular Classes of Means for Attainment (according to Mahayoga). *sgrub-sde brgyad spyi be-brag rnams*. NGB Vols. 20-33, 283, 361-2. [*283*, *361-2*]

Eight Mahākāla Tantras. *ma-hā-kā-la'i rgyud brgyad*. Disc. Nāgārjuna. NL. Perhaps associated with T 667-9. [*480*]

Eight Sections of the Magical Net. *sgyu-'phrul sde-brgyad*. There exist different enumerations of these eight, all of which are comprised in NGB Vols. 14-15. For a discussion of these traditions, see GGFTC, pp. 37-49. [*283*]

Eight-Session Practice. *thun-brgyad-ma*. A teaching in the tradition of Atiśa, transmitted through his disciple Kham-pa lung-pa. DZ Vol. 3, pp. 52-66. [*546*]

Eight Transmitted Precepts. *bka'-brgyad*. Disc. Nyang-ral Nyi-ma 'od-zer. [*677*, *756*, *757*] See *Gathering of the Sugatas (of the Eight Transmitted Precepts)*

(Eight Transmitted Precepts, the) Consummation of Secrets. *bka'-brgyad yongs-rdzogs*, *bka'-brgyad gsang-ba yongs-rdzogs* or *bka'-brgyad gsang-rdzogs*. Disc. Guru Chos-dbang. RTD Vol. 22, p. 369 to Vol. 23, p. 5; and *passim*. Pub. Paro: Sherab Drimey, 1983. Bhu-Tib 83-905925. [*765*, *773*, *825*, *827*]

Eight Transmitted Precepts, the Mirror of Mind. *bka'-brgyad thugs-kyi me-long*. Disc. Padma gling-pa. PLTC Vol. 10. RTD Vol. 23, pp. 431-501. Also pub. Thimphu: Kunsang Topgyel and Mani Dorji, 1979. I(Bhu)-Tib 79-906030. [*796*]

Eight Transmitted Precepts, the Universal Gathering of Sugatas. *bka'-brgyad bde-gshegs kun-'dus*. Disc. Mchog-gyur bde-chen gling-pa. CLTC Vol. 22. RTD Vol. 25, pp. 165-210. [*846*]

Eight Volumes of Nectar. *bdud-rtsi bam-brgyad*. Skt. *Sarvapañcāmṛtasārasiddhimahodgatahṛdayaparivartāṣṭaka*. T 841. NGB Vol. 26, no. 302. [*480*] See also *Amṛta Tantra*, *Nectar the Enlightened Attributes* and *Vajrāmṛta Cycle*

Eighty-Chapter Magical Net. *sgyu-'phrul brgyad-cu-pa*. T 834. NGB Vol. 14, no. 189. Full title: *gsang-ba'i snying-po de-kho-na-nyid nges-pa*. [*673*, *674*] See also *Chapter entitled the Vision of Vajrasattva*

Eighty Oral Instructions. *zhal-gyi gdams-pa brgyad-cu-pa*. Auth. Zur-chung Shes-rab-grags. Pub., with the annotations of Zhe-chen rgyal-tshab Padma rnam-rgyal, in ZGSB Vol. 5. [*645*]

Elixir Drops of the Creation and Perfection of Vajrapāṇi. *phyag-na rdo-rje bskyed-rdzogs bdud-rtsi'i thig-pa*. Auth. Tsong-kha-pa. TWB 5268. [*923*]

Elucidation of the Significance of the Four Limbs: the Esoteric Instructions of the Buddhasamāyoga. *sangs-rgyas mnyam-sbyor-gyi man-ngag yan-lag bzhi'i don snang-bar byed-pa*. Skt. *Caturaṅgārthālokanāma*. Auth. Hūṃkara. T 1676. [*477*, *533*]

Emanation of the Lamp. *sgron-sp(b)rul*. NL. [*546*]

Embarking on the Ocean of Maṇḍalas: the Empowerment Ceremonies of the Sūtra which Gathers All Intentions. *'dus-pa mdo'i dbang-chog dkyil-'khor rgya-mtsho'i 'jug-ngogs*. Auth. Rig-'dzin Padma 'phrin-las. Pub. Dalhousie, HP: Damchoe Sangpo, 1979. 3 Vols. I-Tib 79-901767. [*720*]

Emergence of Cakrasaṃvara. *sdom-'byung*. Skt. *Śrīmahāsaṃvarodayatantrarāja*. T 373. Partially ed. and trans. Shiníchi Tsuda, *The Saṃvarodaya Tantra: Selected Chapters*. Tokyo: The Hokuseido Press, 1974. Also referred to as the *Tantra of the Emergence of Cakrasaṃvara*. [*99*, *451*, *503*, *688*]

Emergence of Indestructible Reality. *rdo-rje 'byung-ba*. Skt. *Vajrodaya*. Auth. Ānandagarbha. T 2516. [*356-7*]

Empowerment Ceremony (entitled) the Jewel Rosary. *dbang-chog rin-chen phreng-ba*. [*828*] See *Empowerment Ceremony of the Sūtra which Gathers All Intentions (entitled) the Jewel Rosary*

Empowerment Ceremony (entitled) the River of Honey. *dbang-chog sbrang-rtsi'i chu-rgyun*. Auth. Rdo-rje dpal-bzang-po. NL. However, at least one of the available redactions of the empowerment for the *Sūtra which Gathers All Intentions* is clearly derived from the *River of Honey*, and may well include substantial portions of that text: *mdo-dbaṅ-gi skor*. Paro: Lama Ngodup, 1979. 3 vols. I(Bhu)-Tib 79-902891. [*700*, *828*]

Empowerment Ceremony of the Sūtra which Gathers All Intentions (entitled) the Jewel Rosary. *'dus-pa mdo'i dbang-chog rin-chen phreng-ba*. NL. [*828*]

Empowerment Ritual of the Len Tradition. *glen-lugs-kyi dbang-chog*. NL. Apparently incorporated into the tradition of the *Empowerment Ceremony (entitled) the River of Honey*. [*700*]

Empowerment of Vajrapāṇi. *phyag-na rdo-rje dbang-bskur*. Skt. *Vajrapāṇyabhiṣekamahātantra*. T 496. [*272*]

Empowerments of Beneficence, Ability, and Profundity according to the Zur Tradition of the Magical Net. *sgyu-'phrul zur-lugs-kyi phan-nus-zab gsum-gyi dbang*. Refer to n. 823. [*665*]

Empowerments of the Expressive Play of Awareness for the Eighteen Teachings of the Mental Class. *sems-sde bco-brgyad-kyi rig-pa'i rtsal-dbang*. [*673*] See *Eighteen Esoteric Instructions of the Mental Class*

Enlightened Mind of Orgyen and His Consort. *o-rgyan yab-yum byang-sems*. Disc. Sangs-rgyas gling-pa and Dri-med lhun-po. NL. Probably it is a sacramental substance, rather than a text, that is referred to in this instance. [*786*]

Entire Sūtra which Gathers All Intentions. *mdo yongs-rdzogs*. See *Sūtra which Gathers All Intentions*

Entrance to Knowledge. *ye-shes-la 'jug-pa*. Skt. *Jñānaprasthāna*. Auth. Kātyāyanīputra (or, according to other traditions, Vasumitra). Extant only in Chinese: Taishō 1543-4. EIPRB 21-6. L. de la Vallée Poussin, *L'Abhidharmakośa de Vasubandhu*. Paris: Paul Geuthner, 1923-36, Vol. 1, pp. xxix-xxxii. One of the *Seven Sections of the Abhidharma*. [*90*]

Enumeration of Classes. *yang-dag 'gro-ba'i rnam-grangs*. Skt. *Saṃgītiparyāya*. Auth. Mahākauṣṭhila (or, according to other traditions, Śāriputra). Extant only in Chinese: Taishō 1536. EIPRB 28-9. L. de La Vallée Poussin, *L'Abhidharmakośa de Vasubandhu*. Paris: Paul Geuthner, 1923-36, Vol. 1, p. xlii. One of the *Seven Sections of the Abhidharma*. [*90*]

Enumeration of Doctrines which is the Great Pagoda of Precious Jewels. *dkon-mchog brtsegs-pa chen-po'i chos-kyi rnam-grangs*. [*340*] See *Pagoda of Precious Jewels*

Epitome of the Illumination of the Real. *de-kho-na-nyid snang-ba'i don-bsdus*. Probably to be identified with Skt. *Tattvālokāvyākhyā*. Auth. Ānandagarbha. T 2510. [*272*]

Epitome of the Transcendental Perfection of Discriminative Awareness (in Eight Thousand Lines). *brgyad-stong don-bsdus*. Skt. *Prajñāpāramitāpiṇḍārtha* or *Prajñāpāramitāsaṃgrahakārikā*. Auth. Dignāga. T 3809. EIPRB 1235, 1772-3. MTTWL 160. BST 4 (1960). [*182-3*, *189*]

Esoteric Instructions of the Dohā. *do-ha'i man-ngag*. See *Dohā (of Saraha)*

Esoteric Instructions on the Empowerment Circle. *dbang-bskur-gyi 'khor-lo'i man-ngag*. Skt. *Ratnacakrābhiṣekopadeśakrama*. Auth. Indrabhūti. T 2472. [*300*]

Esoteric Instructions on the Great Perfection according to (the Tradition of) Aro. *rdzogs-chen a-ro-lugs-kyi man-ngag*. [*673*, *675*] See *Seven Sessions of Aro (Yeshe Jungne)*

Esoteric Instructions of the Path of Desire. *chags-lam-gyi man-ngag*. Transmitted by Karma-pa VIII, Mi-bskyod rdo-rje. The reference in *History* is not sufficiently precise to permit identification with any given text. Representative works in the Karmapa's tradition may be found in DZ Vol. 6, pp. 1-291. [*818*]

Esoteric Instructions on the Symbolism of the Great Seal. *phyag-rgya chen-po brda'i man-ngag*. Identification uncertain. Note that there is a work in the *Tangyur* by this title: *Mahāmudrāratnābhigītyupadeśa*. T 2445. Auth. Mkha'-'gro-ma. The reference in *History*, however, is probably to the *Phyag rgya chen po brda'i skor gsum* of Pha-dam-pa Sangs-rgyas. Pub. National Library of Bhutan, 1985. Bhu-Tib 85-902604. [*545*]

Esoteric Mañjuśrī. *'jam-dpal gsang-ldan*. Skt. *Mañjuśrīguhyaka*. The transmission of this cycle in Tibet is traditionally associated with Smṛtijñānakīrti, whose major work on it is T 2584. GDKT Vol. 10, no. 60. KGNZ Vol. 4, pp. 375-504. The commentary by Rong-zom Chos-kyi bzang-po is preserved in *Selected Writings of Roṅ-zom Chos-kyi-bzaṅ-po*. SSS 73 (1973). I-Tib 74-902673. [*657*, *703*, *708*]

Essence of the View which Negates Everything. *thams-cad-la skur-ba 'debs-pa'i lta-ba'i snying-po*. Apparently to be identified with the *Bṛhaspatisūtra*. NA. [*66*]

Essential Epitome of the Great Perfection. *rdzogs-chen snying-po bsdus-pa*. Disc. Sangs-rgyas gling-pa. Perhaps to be identified with BMGD Vol. 9. [*786*]

Essential Inventory which Treats the Essence of the Esoteric Instructions in Seven Sections. *snying-byang man-ngag gnad-kyi don-bdun-ma*. Disc. Bzang-po grags-pa. NL. [*780*]

Essential Spirituality of Aro. *a-ro'i thugs-bcud*. [*651*] See *Seven Sessions of Aro (Yeshe Jungne)*

Essential Summarisation of the Tantras, Transmissions, and Esoteric Instructions of the Class of Means for Attainment, the Eight Transmitted Precepts. *sgrub-sde bka'-brgyad-kyi rgyud-lung man-ngag snying-por dril-ba*. Disc. 'Jam-dbyangs mkhyen-brtse'i dbang-po. RTD Vol. 24, p. 261 to Vol. 25, p. 91. The third part of the *Innermost Spirituality of the Accomplished Master*. [*804*]

Established Confluence of Auspicious Coincidences. *rten-'brel mdo-chings*. NL. [*843*]

Establishment of the Intrinsic Essential of the Innermost Spirituality. *bsdus-pa thig-le rang-gnad-du dbab-pa*. Refer to n. 522. [*494*]

Eulogy to the Expanse of Reality. *chos-dbyings bstod-pa*. Skt. *Dharmadhātustava*. Auth. Nāgārjuna. T 1118. EIPRB 633-4, 637. MTTWL 55. HIL 7.1, pp. 31-2, 126. One of the *Collection of Eulogies*. See also F. Tola and C. Dragonetti, "Catuḥstava" JIP 13 (1985), pp. 1-54. [*173*, *196*, *211*, *265*, *301*]

Eulogy to the Inconceivable Madhyamaka. *dbu-ma bsam-gyis mi-khyab-par bstod-pa*. Skt. *Acintyastava*. Auth. Nāgārjuna. T 1128. EIPRB 636. MTTWL 55. HIL 7.1, pp. 31, 126, 131. See also F. Tola and C. Dragonetti, "Catuḥstava" JIP 13 (1985), pp. 1-54. [*217-18*]

Exegesis of the Glorious Guhyasamāja. *gsang-'dus rdo-rje bzhad-pa'i bshad-lugs*. Skt. *Tantrarājaśrīguhyasamājaṭīkā*. Auth. Vajrahāsya. T 1909. [*533*]

Exegetical Commentary on the Collection of the Greater Vehicle. *theg-bsdus-kyi 'grel-pa bshad-sbyar*. Skt. *Mahāyānasaṃgrahopanibandhana*. Auth. Asvabhāva. T 4051. EIPRB 1250, 1867. MTTWL 127. [*222*]

Exegetical Tantra on the Eight Divisions of Medicine. *yan-lag bshad-brgyud*. Second of the *Four Glorious Tantras of Medical Science*. [99]

Exegetical Tantra of the Oceanic Magical Net. *bshad-rgyud rgya-mtsho*. [*447*] See *Oceanic Magical Net*

(Exegetical Tradition of the) Eighteen Roots. *rtsa-ba bco-brgyad-kyi bshad-srol*. NL. Possibly, this simply refers to the *Eighteen Esoteric Instructions of the Mental Class*. [*658*]

Exegetical Treatise on the Vajra Bridge. *rdo-rje zam-pa'i gzhung-bshad*. NL. Several works so described are mentioned in *History*. [*552*]

Expanded Commentary on the Later Stages of Meditation. *bsam-gtan phyi-ma'i rgyas-'grel*. Skt. *Dhyānottarapaṭalaṭīkā*. Auth. Buddhaguhya. T 2670. [*466*]

Exposition of Valid Cognition. *tshad-ma rnam-'grel*. Skt. *Pramāṇavārttika*. Auth. Dharmakīrti. T 4210. EIPRB 1249, 2113-27. MTTWL 168. BB 3 (1968). SOR 23 (1960). TSWS 1 (1954). [*68*, *102*, *874*]

Extensive Commentary on the Guhyasamāja Tantra. *gsang-ba 'dus-pa rgya-cher 'grel-pa*. Reported in *History*, to have been translated by Ācārya Phra-la-ring-mo. [*703*]

Extensive Descriptive Basis (for the Rites) of the Wrathful Deities. *khro-bo-la mngon-par rtogs-pa rgyas-pa*. Auth. Sangs-rgyas rin-chen. NL. [*673*]

Extensive Magical Net. *sgyu-'phrul rgyas-pa*. The texts comprising NGB Vol. 14. Also referred to as the *Tantra of the Extensive Magical Net*. Note that the quotations given here are from the *Supplementary Magical Net* (*sgyu-'phrul le-lag*). [*20-1*, 60, *62*, *127*, *144*, *145*, *147*, *213*, *227*, *231*, *237*, *245-6*, *259*]

Extensive Store of Transmitted Precepts. *rgya-chen bka'-mdzod*. Auth. 'Jam-mgon Kong-sprul Blo-gros mtha'-yas. GCKZ. [*862*] See also *Five Great Stores*

Extensive Sūtra of the Commitments. *dam-tshig mdo-rgyas*. Auth. Rong-zom Chos-kyi bzang-po. NL. [*198*, *707*]

Eye-opening Commentary on the Supplementary Magical Net. *le-lag-gi spyan-'grel*. Skt. *Vajrasattvamāyājālatantraśrīguhyagarbhanāmacakṣuṣ-ṭīkā*. Auth. Vimalamitra. P 4756. [*481*]

Father Consort and Mother Consort, (transmitted precepts) of the Secret Innermost Spirituality. *gsang-thig yab-yum*. See *Transmitted Precepts of the Father Consort and Transmitted Precepts of the Mother Consort of the Secret Innermost Spirituality*

Fifteen Doctrines on the Kriyātantra according to the System of Pari. *ba-ri-pa'i kriya'i chos bco-lnga*. Auth. Ba-ri Lo-tsā-wa. NL. [*547*]

Final Gathering of the Transmitted Precepts which is the Doctrinal Cycle of the Entire Gathering of Awareness-holders, the Means for the Attainment of the Seven-Chapter Supplication. *bka'-'dus phyi-ma rig-'dzin yongs-'dus-kyi chos-skor gsol-'debs le'u bdun-ma'i sgrub-thabs*. Disc. Mnga'-ris Paṇ-chen Padma dbang-rgyal. RTD Vol. 6, pp. 123-40; Vol. 11, pp. 1-112; Vol. 30, pp. 61-227. [*807*]

Final Lineage of the Great Perfection. *rdzogs-chen brgyud-pa tha-ma*. NL. [*647*]

Five Anthologies (by Jamgön Kongtrül). *kong-sprul mdzod-lnga*. See *Five Great Stores*

Five Basic Tantras and Six Branch Tantras of the Mental Class. *sems-sde rtsa-ba'i rgyud-lnga dang yan-lag-gi rgyud drug*. [*136*]

Five Collections of (Madhyamaka) Reasoning. *dbu-ma rigs-tshogs*. See *Collection of Madhyamaka Reasoning*

Five Cycles of (the Means for) Attainment, (which are in harmony with the Path of the Magical Net). *yan-lag rgyud-sde sgyu-'phrul-gyi lam-dang mthun-pa'i sgrub-thabs skor-lnga* or *sgrub-skor lnga*. Disc. 'Jam-dbyangs mkhyen-brtse'i dbang-po. RTD Vol. 4, pp. 449-612. The second part of the *Innermost Spirituality of the Accomplished Master*. [*804*, *855*]

Five Doctrines of (Venerable) Maitreya. *rje-btsun byams-pa chos-lnga* or *rgyal-tshab chen-po'i chos-lnga*. Listed separately as the *Analysis of the Middle and Extremes*, *Analysis of Phenomena and Reality*, *Ornament of Emergent Realisation*, *Ornament of the Sūtras of the Greater Vehicle* and *Supreme Continuum of the Greater Vehicle*. Also referred to as the *Texts of Maitreya*. [*90*, *205*, *207*, *213*, *577*, *676*, *691*, *861*, *872*, *894*]

Fivefold Great Seal. *phyag-chen lnga-ldan*. An important system of *mahāmudrā* practice, which became a particular specialty of the 'Bri-gung Bka'-brgyud tradition. Major redactions are: DZ Vol. 6, pp. 418-55. *Instructions on the Phyag chen lṅa ldan*. 2 vols. Bir, HP: D. Tsondu Senghe, 1980. I-Tib 80-904070. *'Bri-guṅ Bka'-brgyud-pa exegesis of Mahāmudrā*. Bir, HP: D. Tsondu Senghe, 1980. I-Tib 82-901895. Other versions of this teaching were also transmitted by the different Bka'-brgyud lineages, e.g. by the Khro-phu Bka'-brgyud: DZ Vol. 6, pp. 530-2. See also Khenpo Könchog Gyaltsen and K. Rogers, *The Garland of Mahamudra Practices*. Ithaca, NY: Snow Lion, 1986. [*679*]

Fivefold Group of Injunctions. *(bka'-thang) sde-lnga*. Disc. O-rgyan gling-pa. SP 307-8 (1982). I-Tib 82-905496/7. Xylo. Lhasa. I-Tib X9-913564. Xylo. Kalimpong. N-Tib 80-905397. Pub. Paro: Ngodup, 1976. I(Bhu)-Tib 76-901404. Concerning the secondary literature, see A.-M. Blondeau, "Le Lha-'dre bka'-thaṅ" in *Études tibétaines dédiées à la mémoire de Marcelle Lalou*. Paris: A. Maisonneuve, 1971, pp. 29-126. [*776*, *778*]

Fivefold Rite for Entering into All Maṇḍalas. *dkyil-'khor thams-cad-kyi rjes-su 'jug-pa'i cho-ga lnga-pa*. Skt. *Sarvamaṇḍalānuvartipañcavidhi*. Auth. Kukkurāja. T 1670. [*461*]

Five General and Ten Special Tantras of the Eight Transmitted Precepts. *sgrub-pa bka'-brgyad-kyi spyi-rgyud lnga dang sgos-rgyud bcu-rnams*. To be identified among the tantras given in KGDD Vols. 1-3. Fourteen may be found in NGB Vols. 31-2, nos. 375-88. [*482-3*]

Five Golden Doctrines of the Shangpas. *shangs-pa'i gser-chos lnga*. Refer to n. 1302 and to the Glossary of Enumerations. The teachings themselves are redacted in DZ Vol. 8. See also G. H. Mullin, *Selected Works of the Dalai Lama II: The Tantric Yogas of Sister Niguma*. Ithaca: Gabriel/Snow Lion, 1985. Further information will be found in *Shanpa Kargyu* [*sic*] *Golden Dharmas*. Pts. 1 and 2. Chenian Booklet Series 125-6. Berkeley: C. M. Chen, 1982. [*929*] See also *Shangpa Doctrines*

Five Great Mind Treasures. *thugs-gter chen-po lnga*. Unidentified. [*518*, *822*]

Five Great Stores. *mdzod-chen rnam-pa lnga*. Auth. 'Jam-mgon Kong-sprul Blo-gros mtha'-yas. Listed separately as *Extensive Store of Transmitted Precepts*, *Great Store of Precious Treasure*, *Mantra Store of the Lineages of Transmitted Precepts*, *Store which Embraces All Knowledge*, *Store of Precious Instructions* and *Uncommon Store*. Also referred to as the *Five Anthologies*. [*41*, *861-2*]

Five Innermost Cycles. *snying-po skor lnga*. Disc. Mchog-gyur bde-chen gling-pa. CLTC Vols. 20-1. In RTD they are arranged as follows: Vol. 14, pp. 375-427 (*bla ma dgongs 'dus snying po*); Vol. 25, pp. 211-47 (*yi dam bka' 'dus snying po*); Vol. 57, pp. 405-29 (*mkha' 'gro dgongs 'dus snying po*); Vol. 60, pp. 443-64 (*chos skyong dgongs 'dus snying po*); and Vol. 92, pp. 713-27 (*zhal gdams snying po 'dus pa*). [*846*]

Five Inner (Unsurpassed) Tantrapiṭaka. *(bla-med) nang-rgyud sde-lnga*. Listed separately as *Guhyasamāja (Tantra)*, *Tantra of the Hidden Point of the Moon*, *Buddhasamāyoga (Tantra)*, *Glorious Paramādya* and *Garland of Activity*. [*461*, *464-5*]

Five Profound Sūtras. *zab-chos mdo lnga*. Listed separately as *Sūtra of the King of Contemplation*, *Sūtra (of the Greater Vehicle) which Decisively Reveals the Intention*, *Sūtra of the Descent to Laṅkā*, *Sūtra of the Bounteous Array*. The fifth may be either the *Sūtra of the Great Bounteousness of the Buddhas* or the *Sūtra of the Nucleus of the Tathāgata*. [*577*]

Five Protective Dhāraṇī. *grva-lnga*. Skt. *Pañcarakṣā*. T 558-9 and 561-3. GDKT Vol. 1, no. 5. For the history of modern researches on the texts, see P. Aalto, *Prolegomena to an Edition of the Pañcarakṣā*. Studia Orientalia, XIX:12. Helsinki, 1954. Mongolian version ed. P. Aalto in Asiatische Forschungen 10. Wiesbaden: Otto Harrassowitz, 1961. [*762*]

Five Scrolls of the Doctrinal Cycle of the Great Compassionate One. *thugs-rje chen-po'i chos-skor shog-dril lnga*. Disc. Grub-thob Dngos-grub. Incorporated into the *Collected Works of the King concerning the Mantra "Oṃ Maṇi Padme Hūṃ"*. [*757*]

Five Sections of the Levels. *sa-sde lnga*. [*91*] See *Yogācāra Level*

Five Stages. *rim-pa lnga*. Skt. *Pañcakrama*. Auth. Nāgārjuna. T 1802. KGNZ Vol. 4, pp. 219-374. Skt. edn. L. de La Vallée-Poussin, *Études et Textes Tantriques: Pañcakrama*. Université de Gand, Receuil de Travaux publiées par la faculté de Philosophie et Lettres, fascicule 16. Gand: H. Engelcke, 1896. [*301*, *549*]

Five Tantras of Buddha-body, Speech, Mind, Enlightened Attributes and Activities. *sku-gsung-thugs yon-tan phrin-las-kyi rgyud lnga*. [*136*]

Five Texts of the Mental Class which were the Earliest Translated (by Vairocana). *sems-sde snga-'gyur lnga*. [*540*] See *Eighteen Esoteric Instructions of the Mental Class*

Five Texts on the Recitation of Sanskrit Formulae. *rig-klag sde-lnga*. NL. [*762*]

Five Transmissions of the Gathering of the Sugatas. *bde-'dus-kyi lung-lnga*. Auth. Vajradharma. Probably to be identified among the texts found in KGDD Vol. 4. [*90*]

Flame of Dialectics. *rtog-ge 'bar-ba*. Skt. *Tarkajvālā*. Auth. Bhavya (Bhāvaviveka). T 3856. EIPRB 2005-15. MTTWL 104-5. HIL 7.1, pp. 63-5, 127-8, 131. [*430*]

Flash of Splendour. *rngam-glog*. Skt. *Jñānāścaryadyuticakrasūtra*. T 830. NGB Vol. 12, no. 163. [*276*]

Flower Garland of the Vinaya. *me-tog phreng-rgyud*. Skt. *Vinayapuṣpamālā*. Identified as *Vinayakārikā*, Auth. Viśākhadeva, T 4123. See E. Obermiller, *History of Buddhism by Bu-ston*. Tokyo: Suzuki Research Foundation, 1964, Pt. 1, n. 495. [*93*]

Forty-Chapter Magical Net. *(sgyu-'phrul) bzhi-bcu-pa*. NGB Vol. 14, no. 190. Full title: *dpal gsang ba'i snying po de kho na nyid nges pa*. [*673*, *674*]

Four-armed Lord according to the Treasures of Nyang. *nyang-gter mgon-po phyag-bzhi*. Disc. Nyang-ral Nyi-ma 'od-zer. RTD Vol. 59, pp. 173-552. [*892*]

Four Cycles of the Esoteric Instructional Class. *man-ngag-sde'i skor-bzhi*. The Outer, Inner, Secret and Unsurpassedly Secret cycles. [*332*]

Four Cycles of the Gathering. *'dus-pa skor-bzhi*. Disc. Rdo-rje gling-pa. Referred to in DLTC Vol. 2, pp. 49 and 58. Partially preserved in RTD Vol. 10, pp. 1-115. [*790*]

Four Cycles of the Gathering. *'dus-pa skor-bzhi*. Disc. Ratna gling-pa. RLTC Vols. 3-4 and 6-8. [*793*]

Four Cycles of the Means for the Attainment of the Guru. *bla-sgrub skor-bzhi-ka*. Disc. Mchog-gyur bde-chen gling-pa and 'Jam-dbyangs mkhyen-brtse'i dbang-po. NL. Cf. *Cycle of the Means for the Attainment of the Guru's Four Bodies* and the *Doctrinal Cycle of the Innermost Spirituality of Saroruha*. [*856*]

Four Glorious Tantras of Medical Science. *dpal-ldan rgyud-bzhi*, *gso-dpyad rgyud-bzhi* or *sman-gyi rgyud-bzhi*. And their master copies: *gso-ba rig-pa dpal-ldan rgyud-bzhi'i bla-dpe*. Disc. Grva-pa mngon-shes. Sometimes attributed to the authorship of gYu-thog Yon-tan mgon-po (ninth century). See Rechung Rinpoche, *Tibetan Medicine*. Berkeley/Los Angeles: University of California Press, 1976, pp. 255-7. The Four Tantras are: (i) the *Root Tantra (rtsa-rgyud)*, (ii) the *Exegetical Tantra (bshad-rgyud)*, (iii) the *Tantra of Esoteric Instructions (man-ngag-gi rgyud)* and (iv) the *Subsequent Tantra (phyi-ma'i rgyud)*. SSS 68 (1975). A good modern typeset edn. is: *Bdud-rtsi snying-po yan-lag brgyad-pa gsang-ba man-*

ngag-gi rgyud. Lhasa: Tibetan People's Publishing House, 1982. See also F. Meyer, *Gso ba rig pa: le système médical tibétain*. Paris: Éditions du Centre National de la Recherche Scientifique, 1981; and Parfionovich, Dorje, and Meyer, *Tibetan Medical Paintings*. Also referred to as the *Four Medical Tantras*. [*99, 753, 754, 920*]

Four Great Volumes of the Vajrakīla Cycle. *phur-pa'i skor pod-chen bzhi*. NL. [*762*]

Four Groups of Exegetical Tantras Pertaining to the Tantra which Uproots Saṃsāra. *'khor-ba rtsad-gcod-kyi rgyud-la bshad-rgyud sde-bzhi*. NGB Vol. 1, nos. 4-7. [*658*]

Four Hundred Verses. *bzhi-brgya-pa*. Skt. *Catuḥśataka*. Auth. Āryadeva. T 3846. EIPRB 358-68. MTTWL 53. Trans. K. Lang, *Āryadeva's Catuḥśataka: On the Bodhisattva's Cultivation of Merit and Knowledge*. Indiske Studier VII. Copenhagen: Akademisk Forlag, 1986. See also K. Lang, "Āryadeva on the Career of a Bodhisattva" in TSHR, pp. 192-8. J. May, "Āryadeva et Candrakīrti sur la permanence". Pt. I in *Indianisme et Bouddhisme, Mélanges offerts à Mgr. Étienne Lamotte*. Louvain-la-Neuve, 1980. Pt. II in *Bulletin de l'École Française d'Extrême-Orient* LXIX (1981), pp. 75-96. [*168, 309, 899*]

Four Instructional Cycles. *gdams-ngag skor-bzhi*. Disc. Guru Chos-dbang. NL. [*764*]

Four Medical Tantras. See *Four Glorious Tantras of Medical Science*

Four Methods of Establishment. *bzhag-thabs bzhi*. Auth. Jñānasūtra. NYZ *bi-ma snying-thig*, Pt. 1, Vol. *Ga*, pp. 325-31. DZ Vol. 1, pp. 480-2. [*501*]

Four Modes and Fifteen Aspects Commentary. *'grel-pa tshul-bzhi yan-lag bco-lnga-pa*. Auth. Rong-zom Chos-kyi bzang-po. Alternative title for the *Commentary on the Tantra of the Secret Nucleus* or *Precious Jewel Commentary*. [*707*]

Four-Part Innermost Spirituality. *snying-thig ya-bzhi*. NYZ. A second edition has also been published in 13 vols. Delhi: Sherab Gyaltsen Lama, 1975. I-Tib 75-903140. In this version the main sections are arranged as follows: Vols. 1-2, *bla ma yang thig*; Vols. 3-6, *bi ma snying thig*; Vols. 7-9, *mkha' 'gro yang tig*; Vols. 10-11, *mkha' 'gro snying tig*; Vols. 12-13, *zab mo yang tig*. An older version of NYZ is still available in Sde-dge. Also referred as the *Mother and Son Cycles of Innermost Spirituality*. [*375, 677*]

Four Root Sūtras (of Anuyoga). *rtsa-ba'i mdo bzhi*. NGB Vols. 11-12. Listed separately as *Root Tantra of All-Gathering Awareness*, *Flash of Splendour* and *Sūtra which Gathers All Intentions*. The fourth is the *Play of the Cuckoo in the Charnel Ground* (*dur-khrod khu-byug rol-pa*), NGB Vol. 11, no. 161. [*289*]

Four Sections of the Magical Net. *sgyu-'phrul sde-bzhi*. There are different enumerations of these, contained in NGB Vols. 14-15 and 19. See GGFTC, pp. 37-41. [*696*]

Four Subcommentaries on the Commentary on the Guhyasamāja Tantra called the Clarifying Lamp, (exegesis on). *'dus-pa'i 'grel-pa sgron-gsal-la bzhi sbrags-kyi bshad-pa*. Auth. Dbyangs-can dga'-ba'i blo-gros. TWB 6599. [*681*]

Four Syllables. *yi-ge bzhi*. Refer to n. 600. [*547*]

Four Symbols. *brda'-bzhi*. NL. [*548*]

Four Transmissions of the Piṭaka. *sde-snod lung-sde bzhi*. These are probably the transmissions of the four anthologies of the Hīnayāna sūtras according to the Sarvāstivādin tradition, namely, *Dīrghāgama*, *Madhyamāgama*, *Saṃyuktāgama* and *Ekottarāgama*. Refer to HBI, pp. 167-81. [*153*]

Four Veda. *rigs-byed chen-po bzhi*. HIL 1.1 *passim*. Listed separately as *Ṛgveda*, *Atharvaveda*, *Sāmaveda* and *Yajurveda*. [*65*]

Full Summation. *sgang-dril*. NL. Note that this phrase is frequently met in connection with the precepts of the Great Seal and Great Perfection traditions, e.g. *Fundamentals*, p. 331. [*654*]

Further Heart entitled Six Suns of Awareness. *yang-snying rig-pa'i nyi-ma drug*. NL. [*658*]

Further Innermost Spirituality of the Ḍākinī. *man-ngag mkha'-'gro yang-tig*. Redacted by Klong-chen Rab-'byams-pa. NYZ Vols. 4-6. The relationship between this text and the *Innermost Spirituality of the Ḍākinī* is explained in n. 682. [*585, 588*]

Further Innermost Spirituality of the Ḍākinī, the Conjunction of Sun and Moon. *mkha'-'gro yang-tig nyi-zla kha-sbyor*. Disc. Rdo-rje gling-pa. NL. However, referred to in DLTC Vol. 2, p. 56. [*789-90*]

Further Innermost Spirituality like the Wish-fulfilling Gem. *yang-tig yid-bzhin nor-bu*. Redacted by Klong-chen Rab-'byams-pa. NYZ Vol. 1. Refer to n. 685. [*588, 593, 843*]

Gaṇapati (according to the New Yamāntaka Cycle of Ra Lotsāwa). *(rva-lugs) tshogs-bdag*. NL. [*713*]

Gang Tradition of the Great Seal. See *Dohā according to the Gang Tradition of the Great Seal*

Ganges Great Seal. *phyag-chen gang-gā-ma*. Skt. *Mahāmudropadeśa*. Auth. Tilopa. T 2303. DZ Vol. 6, pp. 33-6. Trans. G. C. C. Chang in *Teachings of Tibetan Yoga*. Citadel Press, 1974. [*199-200*]

Garland of Activity. *las-kyi phreng-ba* or *karma-mā-le*. Skt. *Karmamāla*. NGB Vol. 17, no. 215. [*464*]

Garland of Views: A Collection of Esoteric Instructions. *man-ngag lta(-ba'i) phreng(-ba)*. Skt. *Upadeśadarśanamālā*. Auth. Padmasambhava. P 4726. DZ Vol. 1, pp. 16-26. NMKMG Vol. 23. MPSB Vol. 12. Archaic edn. in *Selected Writings of Roṅ-zom Chos-kyi-bzaṅ-po*. SSS Vol. 73 (1973), pp. 1-18. I-Tib 74-902673. [*40, 63, 67, 96, 224, 234, 265, 352, 354, 355, 516, 533*]

Gateway to Language. *smra-sgo*. Auth. Rong-zom Chos-kyi bzang-po. This work is sometimes identified with the *Sword at the Gateway to Language*. [*705*]

Gathering of All Precious Jewels. *dkon-mchog spyi-'dus*. See *(Utterly Profound) Gathering of All Precious Jewels*

Gathering of All the Secrets of the Ḍākinīs. *mkha'-'gro gsang-ba kun-'dus*. Disc. Jo-mo sman-mo. Redisc. 'Jam-dbyangs mkhyen-brtse'i dbang-po. RTD Vol. 55, pp. 1-340. Pub. Gangtok: Gonpo Tsetan Lama, 1976. I-Tib 76-903111. [*771-4*]

Gathering of the Blood-drinking Sugatas. *khrag-'thung bde-gshegs 'dus-pa*. An alternative title for the third part of the *Innermost Spirituality of the Accomplished Master*. [*855*]

Gathering of the Entire Intention of the True Doctrine. *dam-chos dgongs-pa yongs-'dus*. Disc. Bdud-'dul rdo-rje. DDTC Vols. 1-2. Pub. in 2 vols. Dalhousie: Damchoe Sangpo, 1980. I-Tib 80-902333. [*815*]

Gathering of the Guru's Intention. *bla-ma dgongs-'dus*. Disc. Sangs-rgyas gling-pa. BMGD, RTD *passim*. [*785*, *807*, *835*, *837*, *841*, *863*, *865*] See also following entry

Gathering of Intentions (along with the means for holding all the textual transmissions, empowerments and tantras). *(zab-chos) dgongs-'dus (po-ti'i lung-dbang-rgyud-dgu bcangs-thabs-dang bcas-pa)*. [*682*, *727*] See preceding entry

Gathering of the Quintessence of Auspicious Coincidence. *rten-'brel yang-snying 'dus-pa*. Disc. O-rgyan gling-pa. NL. [*776*, *778*]

Gathering of the Sugatas (of the Eight Transmitted Precepts). *(bka'-brgyad) bde-gshegs-'dus-pa/(bka'-brgyad) bder-'dus*. The main tantras of this extensive body of material are found in NGB Vols. 31-2, nos. 375-88. The treasures of Nyang-ral Nyi-ma 'od-zer, listed here as the *Tantra of the Gathering of the Sugatas of the Eight Transmitted Precepts*, are redacted in KGDD. See also RTD Vol. 21, p. 183 to Vol. 22, p. 367. [*483*, *575*, *661*, *679*, *682*, *723*, *727*, *807*, *825*]

Gathering of the Three Roots' Intention, (the Group of Doctrines which Gather together the Five Great Stores in their Entirety). *rtsa-gsum dgongs-'dus (mdzod-chen rnam-lnga yongs-'dus-kyi chos-sde)*. Disc. 'Jam-mgon Kong-sprul Blo-gros mtha'-yas, aided by 'Jam-dbyangs mkhyen-brtse'i dbang-po. RTD Vol. 7, pp. 439-60; Vol. 15, pp. 399-461; Vol. 98, pp. 119-283. [*864-5*]

Gathering of Transmitted Precepts, (twenty-one maṇḍala clusters of). See *(Ocean of Doctrine, the Great) Gathering of Transmitted Precepts*

Gathering of the Transmitted Precepts of Peaceful and Wrathful Deities. *zhi-khro bka'-'dus*. Disc. O-rgyan gling-pa. NA. [*775*]

General Dissertation, Outline and Synopsis on the Secret Nucleus. *gsang-snying spyi-don, sa-bcad, bsdus-don*. Auth. Kha-ba dkar-po-ba Nam-mkha' rgyal-mtshan. NL. [*697*]

General Exposition of the Kālacakra. *nor-bzang-gi dus-'khor spyi-don*. Auth. Nor-bzang rgya-mtsho. NL. [*681*]

General Summary of Mātaraḥ. *ma-mo spyi-bsdus*. Disc. Mchog-gyur bde-chen gling-pa. CLTC Vol. 21. [*846*]

General Sūtra which Gathers All Intentions. *spyi-mdo dgongs(-pa) 'dus(-pa)*. See *Sūtra which Gathers All Intentions*

Glorious Kālacakra. [*264*] See *Kālacakra Tantra*

Glorious Paramādya. *dpal mchog dang-po*. Skt. *Śrīparamādya*. T 487-8. NGB Vol. 17, nos. 213-14. GDKT Vol. 5, no. 25. [*273*, *618*]

Glorious (Root) Tantra of the Secret Nucleus which is Definitive with respect to Reality. *dpal gsang-ba('i) snying-po (de-kho-na-nyid nges-pa'i rgyud (rtsa-ba))*. See *Tantra of the Secret Nucleus*

Glorious Seminal Point of Embrace. *dpal kha-sbyor thig-le*. Skt. *Śrīsaṃpuṭa-tilaka*. T 382. GDKT Vol. 20, nos. 111-12. KGNZ Vol. 2, pp. 359-468. [*258*] See also *Sampuṭa Tantra*

Glorious Tantra of the Cessation of the Four Elements. *dpal 'byung-bzhi zad-pa'i rgyud*. NL. [*136*]

Glorious Tiger-riding Lord. *dpal-mgon stag-zhon*. See *Tiger-riding Lord*

Golden Rosary Dialogue from the Innermost Spirituality of the Ḍākinī. *mkha'-'gro snying-thig-gi zhus-lan gser-phreng*. NYZ *mkha'-'gro snying-thig*, Pt. *Waṃ*, pp. 1-34. [*925*]

Golden Surgical Needle. *gser-gyi thur-ma*. Auth. Zi-lung Paṇ-chen (i.e. Gser-mdog Paṇ-chen) Shākya mchog-ldan. In *The Collected Works of Gser-mdog Paṇ-chen*, Vol. 6. Thimphu: Kunzang Tobgey, 1975. I(Bhu)-Tib 75-908629. [*893*]

Golden Surgical Needle of the Great Perfection. *rdzogs-chen gser-thur*. Disc. Rdo-rje gling-pa. Referred to in DLTC Vol. 2, p. 58; Vol. 4, pp. 58-9, 232-7, 322. Pub. Dolanji, HP: Tshul-khrims-bkra-śis, 1977. I-Tib 78-900967. The text is here ascribed to Bon-źig G'yuṅ-druṅ-gliṅ-pa, (b. 1228). This name is, of course, one of Rdo-rje gling-pa's epithets, but the date of birth is in error. S. G. Karmay, *A Catalogue of Bon-po Publications* (Tokyo: The Tokyo Bunko, 1977) pp. 84-5, suggests that the two are perhaps different treasure-finders, who were conflated at some later date. The evidence of DLTC, however, supports their identification. [*791*]

Grammar of Candragomin. *sgra tsandra-pa*. Skt. *Candravyākaraṇasūtra*. Auth. Candragomin. T 4269. HIL 5.2, pp. 164-7 Ed. B. Liebich. Leipzig, 1902. Repr. Wiesbaden, 1966. [*92*, *100*, *730*, *871*]

Grammar of Candragomin, (sandhi and verbal derivation from). *tsandra-pa'i yi-ge bsdu-ba-dang ting-mtha'*. See preceding entry

Great All-Radiating Seminal Point which is an Ancient Translation. *snga-'gyur thig-le kun-gsal chen-po*. NGB Vol. 5, no. 81. [*257*]

Great Array (of the Highest). *(a-ti) bkod-pa chen-po*. This designation refers to materials contained in the *bi ma snying thig*, NYZ, vols. 7-9. [*55, 87, 138, 319, 330, 359, 370-1*]

Great Assembly of Vajrapāṇi. *phyag-rdor 'khor-chen*. GDKT Vol. 8, no. 46. [*576*]

Great Attainment of Kīla (according to) the Seven (Cycles of) Profound (Contemplation). *zab-bdun phur-pa'i sgrub-chen*. Disc. Mchog-gyur bde-chen gling-pa. RTD Vol. 50, pp. 511-656. The cycle in general may be found in CLTC Vol. 15. The liturgical arrangement for use in connection with the *Great Attainment* rites has been published xylographically: Rum-btegs, Sikkim, *c*. 1972. I(Sik)-Tib 72-906295. [*848*]

Great Aural Lineage of Thangtong. *zab-chos thang-stong snyan-brgyud chen-mo*. Disc. Thang-stong rgyal-po. *Thang-stong snyan-brgyud*, 2 vols. New Delhi: Trayang, 1973. I-Tib 73-903240. *The collected works of Thaṅ-stoṅ-rgyal-po*, Vols. 1-4. Thimphu: Kunzang Tobgey, 1976. I(Bhu)-Tib 77-900723. [*804*]

Great Biography. *rnam-thar chen-mo*. The biography of 'Jam-dbyangs mkhyen-brtse'i dbang-po (1820-92). Auth. 'Jam-mgon Kong-sprul Blo-gros mtha'-yas. GCKZ Vol. 14. RTD Vol. 95. [*778*]

Great Bounteousness (of the Buddhas). *('phags-pa sangs-rgyas) phal-po-che'i mdo* or *phal-chen*. See *Sūtra of the Great Bounteousness of the Buddhas*

Great Chariot. *shing-rta chen-mo*. Auth. Klong-chen Rab-'byams-pa. Auto-commentary on the *Mind at Rest*. For translated selections, see Tulku Thondup Rinpoche, *Buddha Mind*. Ithaca, NY: Snow Lion, 1989. [*196*, *197-8*, *359*, *595*, *596*]

Great Cloud Sūtra. *sprin chen-po'i mdo*. Skt. *Mahāmeghasūtra*. T 232-5, 657-8. MTTWL 117. [*943*]

Great Commentary on the Buddhasamāyoga. *mnyam-sbyor 'grel-chen*. Skt. *Śrīsarvabuddhasamāyogaḍākinīmāyāsaṃvaratantrārthodaraṭīkā*. Auth. Indranāla. T 1659. [*343*, *534*]

Great Commentary on the Glorious Guhyasamāja. *dpal gsang-ba 'dus-pa'i 'grel-chen*. Auth. Viśvamitra. T 1844. [*914*, *916*]

Great Commentary on the Secret Nucleus. *gsang-snying 'grel-chen*. Auth. Sangs-rgyas rin-chen. NL. [*673*]

Great Commentary on the Transcendental Perfection of Discriminative Awareness in Eight Thousand Lines. *brgyad-stong 'grel-chen*. Skt. *Aṣṭa-sāhasrikāprajñāpāramitāvyākhyābhisamayālaṃkārāloka*. Auth. Haribha-dra. T 3791. EIPRB 98, 117, 123, 1226, 1228, 1235, 3670-6. MTTWL 4. BST 4 (1960). GOS 62 (1932). [*76*]

Great Compassionate One. *thugs-rje chen-po*. Disc. Nyang-ral Nyi-ma 'od-zer. RTD Vol. 33, pp. 277-387. [*756*]

Great Compassionate One. *thugs-chen*. Disc. Sangs-rgyas gling-pa. See *(Doctrinal Cycle of the) Great Compassionate One*

Great Compassionate One. *thugs-rje chen-po*. Disc. Rig-'dzin 'Ja'-tshon snying-po. JTPD Vol. 5. RTD Vol. 37, pp. 253-371. SSS 13 (1972). I-Tib 79-928502. Also pub. Tezu, Arunachal Pradesh: Ngawang Sonam, 1979. I-Tib 79-903500. [*811*]

Great Compassionate One as the Gathering of Secrets. *thugs-chen gsang-'dus*. Disc. Ratna gling-pa. RLTC Vols. 6-7. RTD Vol. 36, pp. 197-381. Pub. Bir, HP: Kandro, 1976. I-Tib 76-901400. [*793*]

Great Compassionate One, the Innermost Spirituality of Padma. *thugs-rje chen-po padma'i snying-thig*. Disc. O-rgyan gling-pa. NA. [*775*]

Great Compassionate One as the King of Space, vase attainment of. *thugs-rje chen-po nam-mkha'i rgyal-po'i bum-sgrub*. Disc. *Bdud-'dul rdo-rje*. RTD Vol. 37, pp. 373, 465. [*816*]

Great Compassionate One, the Lamp which Dispels Darkness. *thugs-rje chen-po mun-sel sgron-me*. Disc. Padma gling-pa. PLTC Vol. 7. RTD Vol. 36, pp. 383-450. [*796*]

Great Compassionate One, Lotus Crowned. *thugs-rje chen-po padma gtsug-tor*. Disc. Mchog-gyur bde-chen gling-pa. CLTC Vols. 12-13. RTD Vol. 39, pp. 129-65. [*845*]

Great Compassionate One, the Magical Net of the Lotus. *thugs-rje chen-po padma sgyu-'phrul drva-ba*. Disc. Mchog-gyur bde-chen gling-pa. CLTC Vols. 11-12. RTD Vol. 39, pp. 63-128. [*846*]

Great Compassionate One, the Peaceful and Wrathful Deities of Padma. *thugs-rje chen-po padma zhi-khro*. Disc. Karma gling-pa. NA. However, there is a rediscovered version (*yang-gter*) of a treasure by this name, the original discoverer of which is supposed to have been Karma gling-pa's descendant Nyi-ma seng-ge. The rediscoverer was 'Jam-dbyangs mkhyen-brtse'i dbang-po: RTD Vol. 34, pp. 235-432. [*801*]

Great Compassionate One, the Supreme Light of Pristine Cognition. *thugs-rje chen-po ye-shes 'od-mchog*. See *Supreme Light of Pristine Cognition*

Great Compassionate One according to the Tradition of the King. *rgyal-po-lugs-kyi thugs-rje chen-po*. See *Avalokiteśvara according to the Tradition of the King*

Great Compassionate One as the Universal Gathering of the Sugatas. *thugs-rje chen-po bde-gshegs kun-'dus*. See *(Doctrinal Cycle of the) Great Compassionate One as the Universal Gathering of the Sugatas*

Great Compassionate One, Utterly Secret and Unsurpassed. *thugs-rje chen-po yang-gsang bla-med*. Disc. Sangs-rgyas gling-pa. NL. [*786*]

Great Descent. *babs-lugs chen-mo*. Said to be the prophetic section of the *Penetration of Sound*. [*594*]

Great Development of the Enlightened Mind. *sems-bskyed chen-mo*. NL. [*578*, *590*]

Great Document on Meditation. *sgom-yig chen-mo*. NL. [*658*]

Great Empowerment of Vajrakīla according to the Khön tradition. *'khon-lugs phur-pa'i dbang-chen*. See *Khön Tradition of Vajrakīla*

Greater, Medium and Lesser Aural Lineages of Tavihṛca. *ta-bi-hri-tsa'i snyan-brgyud che-'bring-chung gsum*. Disc. Rdo-rje gling-pa. NL. See, however, the *Zhang-zhung snyan-brgyud* in *The History and Doctrine of the Bon-po Niṣpanna Yoga*. SP 73 (1968), pp. 145ff. S. G. Karmay, *A Catalogue of Bonpo Publications* (Tokyo: The Tokyo Bunko, 1977), pp. 94-7, makes it clear that tradition attributes the redaction of the *Zhang-zhung snyan-brgyud* primarily to Tavihṛca. Nevertheless, the relationship between these two traditions, if indeed there is any relationship, remains to be established. [*791*]

Greater, Medium and Lesser (Teachings of) the Wrathful (Guru). *drag-po che-'bring-chung gsum*. Disc. Padma gling-pa. PLTC Vol. 2. [*797*]

Greater Net. *drva-chen*. Auth. Buddhaguhya. P 4736. NMKMG Vol. 23. [*466*]

Greater Sequence of the Path and Lesser Sequence of the Path. *lam-rim che-chung gnyis*. [*466*] See *Sequence of the Path (of the Magical Net)*

Great Esoteric Instructional Tantra of the Eight Transmitted Precepts, the Consummation of Secrets. *bka'-brgyad gsang-ba yongs-rdzogs man-ngag-gi rgyud chen-po*. Disc. Guru Chos-dbang. See *Eight Transmitted Precepts, the Consummation of Secrets*

Great Exposition of Word and Meaning. *tshig-don chen-mo*. Auth. Nyi-'bum. NL. [*563*]

Great Garuḍa. *khyung-chen*. NGB Vol. 1, no. 8. Refer to S. G. Karmay, "The Rdzogs-chen in its Earliest Text" in STC, pp. 272-82. [*370, 371*]

(Great) Gathering of Transmitted Precepts. *bka'-'dus chen-mo'i snying-po mdor-bsdus skor*. Disc. O-rgyan gling-pa. Available to 'Jam-dbyangs mkhyen-brtse'i dbang-po. [*778-9*] See also *(Ocean of Doctrine, the) Great Gathering of Transmitted Precepts*

Great Injunction of Padma. *padma bka'-yi thang-yig chen-mo*. [*775*] See *Injunction of Padma (which was Discovered at Crystal Rock)*

Great Lecture on the History of the Innermost Spirituality, Mother and Son. *snying-thig ma-bu'i lo-rgyus gtong-thun chen-mo*. Auth. Klong-chen Rab-'byams-pa. NYZ, *bi-ma snying-thig*, Pt. 3, Vol. *Tha*, pp. 1-179. [*965*]

Great Liberation by Hearing during the Intermediate State. *bar-do thos-grol chen-po*. Disc. Karma gling-pa. For editions of the Tibetan text, see *Peaceful and Wrathful Deities, the Natural Liberation of Intention*. Trans. Kazi Dawa-Samdup, in W. Y. Evans-Wentz (ed.), *The Tibetan Book of the Dead*. London/Oxford/New York: Oxford University Press, 1927. F. Freemantle and C. Trungpa, *The Tibetan Book of the Dead*. Berkeley/London: Shambhala, 1975. See also D. I. Lauf, *Secret Doctrines of the Tibetan Books of the Dead*. Boulder/London: Shambhala, 1977. D. M. Back, *Eine Buddhistische Jenseitsreise*. Wiesbaden: Otto Harrassowitz, 1979. Dorje and Coleman, forthcoming. [*801*]

Great Means for Attaining the Empowerment of (the Ocean of Doctrines) which Gather the Transmitted Precepts. *bka'-'dus-kyi dbang-sgrub chen-mo*. See *Great Ocean of Doctrine, the Gathering of the Transmitted Precepts of the Meditational Deities*

Great Mother. *yum rgyas-pa*. See *Transcendental Perfection of Discriminative Awareness in One Hundred Thousand Lines*

Great Ocean of Doctrine, the Gathering of the Transmitted Precepts of the Meditational Deities. *yi-dam bka'-'dus chos-kyi rgya-mtsho chen-po*. Disc. O-rgyan gling-pa. NA. The rediscovered version is the *Ocean of Doctrine, the Great Gathering of Transmitted Precepts*. [775]

Great Perfection according to Aro. *a-ro'i lugs-kyi rdzogs-chen man-ngag-gi khrid* or *rdzogs-chen a-ro'i man-ngag*. See *Seven Sessions of Aro (Yeshe Jungne)*

Great Perfection endowed with Conch-Syllables. *rdzogs-pa chen-po dung-yig-can*. Auth. Vimalamitra. NYZ *Bi-ma snying-thig*, Pt. 2, Vol. *Cha*, 1-159. [77] See also *Illuminating of the Lamp*

Great Perfection, Exegetical Tradition of the Esoteric Instructional Class. *(rdzogs-chen man-ngag sde'i) bshad-rgyud*. Redacted by Mañjuśrīmitra. Not precisely identified, but probably represented by materials to be found in NYZ. [*494*]

Great Perfection, the Gathering of Samantabhadra's Intention. *rdzogs-chen kun-bzang dgongs-'dus*. Disc. Padma gling-pa. PLTC Vols. 4 and 15. [*796*]

(Great Perfection, the) Innermost Spirituality of Longcenpa. *(rdzogs-pa chen-po) klong-chen snying-gi thig-le*. Disc. 'Jigs-med gling-pa. JLSB Vols. 7-8. RTD Vols. 106-9. Pub. in 3 vols. New Delhi: Ngawang Sopa, 1973. I-Tib 73-904268. Trans. (selections), Tulku Thondup, *The assemblage of the knowledge-holders*. Santiniketan, WB: T. Thondup, 1980. I-Tib 82-900323. Idem, *The queen of great bliss*. Gangtok, Sikkim: Dodrup Chen Rinpoche, 1982. I-Tib 83-907620. See also S. D. Goodman, "The *Klong-chen snying-thig*: An Eighteenth Century Tibetan Revelation". Unpublished Ph.D. dissertation, University of Saskatchewan, 1983. [*837*, *839*]

Great Perfection of the Kham Tradition. *rdzogs-chen khams-lugs*. DZ Vol. 1, pp. 305-55. NMKMG Vol. 17. [*651*, *654*, *658*]

Great Perfection of the Rong Tradition. *rdzogs-chen rong-lugs*. DZ Vol. 1, pp. 270-95. NMKMG Vol. 17. [*654*, *658*]

Great Perfection, the Tantra of the Mirror of Vajrasattva's Heart. *rdzogs-pa chen-po rdor-sems snying-gi me-long-gi rgyud*. A text seen in a vision by 'Jam-dbyangs mkhyen-brtse'i dbang-po. Note that there does exist a tantra called *Mirror of the Heart of Vajrasattva*. [*854*]

Great Perfection according to the Tradition of the Cycles. *rdzogs-chen skor-lugs*. The cycles referred to are the four of the esoteric instructional class, on which see *Fundamentals*, p. 332. [*647*, *654*, *657-8*]

Great Prophetic Declaration. *zhal-chems lung-bstan chen-mo*. Auth. Rdo-rje gling-pa. NL. [*791*]

Great Record of Teachings Received (in four volumes). *gsan-yig (chen-mo glegs-bam bzhi)*. See *Record of Teachings Received*

Great Seal, Liberation through the Vision of Pristine Cognition. *phyag-rgya chen-po ye-shes mthong-grol*. Granted to 'Jigs-med gling-pa by Rig-'dzin Thugs-mchog rdo-rje. NL. Perhaps this is the *yang-ti ye-shes mthong-grol*, Disc. Bstan-gnyis gling-pa. [*835*]

Great Seal Opuscules. *phyag-chen kha-'thor*. NL. [*564*]

Great Sequence of the Path of Secret Mantra. *gsang-sngags lam-rim chen-mo*. Disc. O-rgyan gling-pa. NA. [*776*]

(Great) Store of Precious Treasure. *rin-chen gter-gyi mdzod chen-po*. Compiled by 'Jam-mgon Kong-sprul Blo-gros mtha'-yas. RTD. This edition reproduces the xylo. of Mtshur-phu, Central Tibet, in its first 96 vols. The remaining 15 vols. constitute a new supplement arranged under the direction of Dilgo Khyentsey Rinpoche. In Tibet there was also a second xylo. published at Dpal-spungs, in the Sde-dge district of Khams, a complete set of which is preserved in the library of the

Namgyal Institute of Tibetology, Gangtok, Sikkim. New woodblocks for this edition are currently being made in Sde-dge. A catalogue of the Dpal-spungs edn. has recently been published: *Rin chen gter mdzod kyi dkar chag*. Paro: Dilgo Khyentsey Rinpoche, 1982. Bhu-Tib 82-900630. [*752*, *774*, *778*, *804*, *857*, *862*] See also *Five Great Stores*

Great Sūtra of Final Nirvāṇa. See *Sūtra of Final Nirvāṇa*

Great Torma Offering of Jvālamukhī. *kha-'bar-ma'i gtor-chen*. The version of this rite that is known to us was discovered by Guru Chos-dbang: RTD Vol. 69, pp. 423-595. This, however, cannot be what is referred to in the *History*, since the events described predate Guru Chos-dbang. [*545*]

Great Treasury of Detailed Exposition. *bye-brag bshad-mdzod (chen-mo)* or *bye-brag-tu bshad-pa*. See *Treasury of Detailed Exposition*

Great Vivarta. *bi-barta chen-mo*. Name of a grammatical text, or a type of script, studied by Guru Chos-dbang. NL. As an example of work of the genre to which the *Great Vivarta* presumably belonged, see 'Gos Khug-pa Lhas-btsas, *Rgya-gar-gyi lañtsa-yi skad-gnyis*. Delhi: Sherab Gyeltsen, 1976. I-Tib 76-905317. [*762*]

Group of Doctrines of the Supreme Attainment of the Guru, the Awareness-holder. *bla-ma rig-'dzin mchog-sgrub-kyi chos-sde*. Disc. 'Jam-mgon Kong-sprul Blo-gros mtha'-yas, assisted by 'Jam-dbyangs mkhyen-brtse'i dbang-po. RTD Vol. 15, pp. 399-461. [*865*]

Guhyasamāja and Bhairava. *gsang-'jigs*. Listed separately.

Guhyasamāja and Cakrasaṃvara. *gsang-bde*. Listed separately.

Guhyasamāja (Tantra). *(dpal-ldan) 'dus-pa('i rgyud)*, *gsang-ba 'dus-pa*, *gsang-'dus(-kyi rgyud)*. T 442-3. NGB Vol. 17, nos. 211-12. BST 9 (1965). GOS 53 (1931). KGNZ Vol. 4, pp. 86-374. GDKT Vol. 7, nos. 42-5. Trans. F. Fremantle in *A Critical Study of the Guhyasamāja Tantra*. Unpublished Ph.D. thesis, London University. [*257*, *262*, *274*, *283*, *322-3*, *362*, *363*, *442*, *464*, *466-7*, *494-6*, *502*, *533*, *578*, *675*, *681*, *689*, *827*, *850*, *893*, *895*, *916*]

Guidance on Cutting. *gcod-khrid*. [679] See *Object of Cutting*

Guidance which Lays Bare the Teaching of the Great Compassionate One (according to the Tradition of Yegyelwa). *thugs-rje chen-po dmar-khrid (ye-rgyal lugs)*. NL. Ye-rgyal-ba was a leading disciple of Karma-pa III, Rang-byung rdo-rje and tutor of Karma-pa IV, Rol-pa'i rdo-rje. Refer to *Blue Annals*, pp. 497, 517. [*673-4*]

Guidance which Lays Bare the Teaching on the Great Compassionate One. *thugs-rje chen-po'i smar-khrid*. For works representing this genre in general, see DZ Vol. 11, pp. 429-617. [*731*]

Guidance on Longevity, the Vajra Garland. *tshe-khrid rdo-rje phreng-ba*. Disc. Padma gling-pa. PLTC Vol. 8. [797]

Guidance on the Path according to Götsangpa. *rgod-tshang-pa'i lam-khrid*. [576] See *Cycle of Götsangpa's Guidance*

Guidance of the Unsurpassed Secret (Innermost Spirituality). *gsang-ba bla-na med-pa'i khrid*. Not identified with a particular text. [*590*]

Guidance on the View of the Great Middle Way, which Definitively Reveals the Absolute. *don-dam nges-'byed dbu-ma chen-po'i lta-khrid*. Auth. Zhva-dmar-pa IV, Chos-kyi grags-pa. NL. [*676*]

Guidance on the View of Madhyamaka. *dbu-ma'i lta-khrid*. Auth. 'Khon-ston Dpal-'byor lhun-grub. NL. [*679*]

Guidebook of the Accomplished Master Melong Dorje. *me-long rdo-rjes mdzad-pa'i khrid-yig*. Auth. Me-long rdo-rje. NL. [*675*]

Guidebook to the Great Seal. *phyag-chen-gyi khrid-yig*. Auth. Paṇ-chen Blo-bzang chos-kyi rgyal-mtshan. DZ Vol. 3, pp. 421-30. [*925-6*]

Guidebook which Introduces the View Common to the Great Seal, Great Perfection and Great Madhyamaka. *phyag-rdzogs-dbu gsum-gyi lta-ba spyi-khyab-tu ngo-sprod-pa'i khrid-yig*. Auth. 'Khon-ston Dpal-'byor lhun-grub. NL. [*679, 926*]

Guidebook to the Pilgrimage Place of Pemakö. *padma-bkod-kyi gnas-kyi lam-yig*. Disc. Rig-'dzin 'Ja'-tshon snying-po. A portion of this work appears to be preserved in RTD Vol. 19, pp. 105-21. [*811*]

Guidebook to the Secret Land of Pemakö. *sbas-yul padma bkod-pa'i gnas-yig*. Disc. Bdud-'dul rdo-rje. NL. [*815*]

Guru as the Attainment of Mind. *bla-ma thugs-sgrub*. NL. [*757*]

Guru as the Gathering of Awareness-holders. *bla-ma rig-'dzin 'dus-pa*. Disc. Bdud-'dul rdo-rje. NL. [*815*]

Guru as the Gathering of Secrets. *bla-ma gsang-'dus*. Disc. Guru Chos-dbang. RTD Vol. 7, pp. 461-614. Pub. Paro: Ugyen Tempai Gyaltsen, 1979. I(Bhu)-Tib 80-900644. [*731*]

Guru as the Gathering of the Three Bodies. *bla-ma sku-gsum 'dus-pa*. Mentioned in the biography of Nyang-ral Nyi-ma 'od-zer. NL. [*757*]

Guru, an Ocean of Gems. *bla-ma nor-bu rgya-mtsho*. Disc. Padma-gling-pa. PLTC Vols. 1 and 20. RTD Vol. 10, pp. 307-52. [*679, 796*]

Hayagrīva (Cycle/Tantra). *rta-mgrin*. T 839. NGB Vols. 23-4. Cf. *Hayagrīvadhāraṇī*, T 733. When the context is that of the *Eight Transmitted Precepts* (*bka'-brgyad*), the tantra that this is to be identified with is: KGDD Vol. 3. NGB Vol. 32, no. 383. Also referred to as *Lotus the Speech* and *(Play of the) Supreme Horse*. [*283, 361, 473, 479, 483, 575, 762*]

Hayagrīva who Overpowers Arrogant Spirits. *rta-mgrin dregs-pa zil-gnon*. Disc. Sangs-rgyas bla-ma. NA. [*751*]

Hayagrīva Traditions of Nawopa and Dagyelma. *sna/rna-bo-pa'i lugs-kyi rta-mgrin-dang zla-rgyal-ma'i lugs*. NL. [*673, 674*] See also *Permissory Initiation of Hayagrīva according to the Tradition of Dagyelma*

Hayagrīva and Varāhī, the Wish-fulfilling Gem. *rta-phag yid-bzhin nor-bu*. Disc. Rig-'dzin 'Ja'-tshon snying-po. JTPD Vol. 3. RTD Vol. 41, pp. 213-43; Vol. 76, pp. 347-84. Pub. Tezu, Arunachal Pradesh: Ngawang Sonam, 1979. I-Tib 79-903466. [*811*]

Heart Essence of the Attainment of Kīla. *phur-sgrub thugs-kyi nying-khu*. Disc. Sangs-rgyas gling-pa. RTD Vol. 49, pp. 363-501. [*786*]

Heart Sūtra of Discriminative Awareness. *sher-snying*. Skt. *Bhagavatīprajñāpāramitāhṛdayasūtra*. T 21, 531. EIPRB 1046-68. MTTWL 85. BST 17 (1961). See also D. Lopez, *The Heart Sūtra Explained*. Albany: State University of New York Press, 1988. [*75*]

Heruka. *khrag-'thung*. The term is used to refer to any of a very large number of wrathful male meditational deities. In the Nyingmapa tradition it refers in particular, though not exclusively, to *Mahottara* (*Chemcok*) or to *Yangdak*.

Heruka Galpo (Tantra). *(rgyud) he-ru-ka gal-po*. NGB Vol. 25, nos. 289-92. [*58*, *60*, *68*, *228*, *232-3*, *244*, *270*, *271-2*, *292*, *350-3*, *354*, *356*, *475*, *923*]

Hevajra (Cycle/Tantra). *brtag-gnyis*, *dgyes-rdor*, *he-badzra* or *kye-yi rdo-rje*. Skt. *Hevajratantrarāja*. T 417-18. Ed. and trans. D. L. Snellgrove. *The Hevajra Tantra*, Pts. 1 and 2. London Oriental Series, Vol. 6. London: Oxford University Press, 1959; repr. 1964, 1971. SP 70 (1966). GDKT Vol. 18, nos. 99-110. KGNZ Vol. 2, pp. 3-350. [*61*, *260*, *291*, *304*, *308*, *345*, *362*, *442*, *449*, *451*, *471*, *473*, *550*, *568-9*, *675*, *688*, *762*, *827*, *849*, *850*, *899*, *911*]

Hidden Point of the Moon. *zla-gsang thig-le*. Skt. *Candraguhyatilakatantra*. T 477. NGB Vol. 16, no. 210. [*283*, *464*, *893*] See also *Tantra of the Hidden Point of the Moon*

Higher Rites of Vajrakīla. *phur-pa stod-las*. General term for those among the rites of service and attainment of Vajrakīla whereby enlightenment is to be achieved without recourse to the wrathful activity of sorcery. [*714*]

History of Buddhism in India. *rgya-dkar chos-'byung*. Auth. Tāranātha. Typeset edn. Sarnath, UP: Pleasure of Elegant Sayings Printing Press, 1972. I-Tib 73-900134. Pub. in *Five historical works of Tāranātha*. Tezu, Arunachal Pradesh: Tibetan Nyingmapa Monastery, 1974. I-Tib 74-901746. Trans. Lama Chimpa and A. Chattopadhyaya. Calcutta: K. P. Bagchi and Co., 1970. Refer to n. 1240. [*892*]

History of the Empowerment for the Sūtra which Gathers All Intentions. *mdo-dbang rang-gi lo-rgyus*. Two such works are to be noted in particular: (1) Auth. Rig-'dzin Padma 'phrin-las. SSS 37 (1972). I-Tib 72-903251. (2) Auth. Lo-chen Dharmaśrī. LCSB Vol. 12. [*613*]

History by Nelpa Paṇḍita. *nel-pa paṇḍita'i chos-'byung*. Pub. in *Rare Tibetan Historical and Literary Texts from the Library of Tsepon W. D. Shakabpa*, Series I. New Delhi, 1974. I-Tib 75-900392. See also H. Uebach, "Zur Identifizierung des Nel-pa'i čos-'byuṅ" in *Tibetan Studies Presented at the Seminar of Young Tibetologists*. Zurich, 1978, pp. 219-30. Idem, "An 8th Century List of Thousand-Districts" in STC, pp. 147-51. [*509*]

History of the Treasures (of Düdül Dorje). *gter-'byung*. NL. [*815*]

Holy Ornament. *dam-pa rgyan*. Skt. *Tattvālokaparamālaṃkāra*. Auth. Buddhaguhya. P 4735. [*466*]

Hundred Brief Doctrines. *chos-chung brgya-rtsa*. This is the *jo-bo'i chos-chung*. T 4465-567. [*578*]

Hundred Causal Relations. *rten-'brel brgya-rtsa*. Mentioned in *History*, p. 578, in apparent connection with the tradition of Pacification. See DZ Vol. 9, pp. 136-44

Hundred and Eight Esoteric Instructions. *man-ngag rgya-rtsa brgyad*. Disc. Guru Chos-dbang. NL. [*764*]

Hundred and Fifty Verses on the Modes of Discriminative Awareness. *shes-phyin tshul brgya-lnga-bcu-pa*. Skt. *Prajñāpāramitānayaśatapañcaśatikā*. T 17. [*273*]

Hundredfold Dialogue of the Ḍākinī. *mkha'-'gro zhu-lan brgya-rtsa*. Disc. Nyang-ral Nyi-ma 'od-zer. Pub. as *Jo mo la gdams pa'i chos skor*. Paro, 1983. I(Bhu)-Tib 84-900517. Selections trans. E. P. Kunsang, *Dakini Teachings*. Boston: Shambhala, 1990. [*757*]

Hundred Means for Attainment. *sgrub-thabs brgya-rtsa*. T 3143-304 and 3306-99. GTKT Vols. 11-13. [*762*, *827*]

Hundred Parables on Deeds. *mdo-sde las brgya-pa*. Skt. *Karmaśataka*. T 340. [57, *147*]

Hundred Systems of Guidance. *rje-btsun grol-mchog-gi gsung khrid-brgya*. Auth. Jo-nang rje-btsun Kun-dga' grol-mchog. DZ Vol. 12, pp. 245-620. [*852*]

Hundred Thousand Verses of the Vajrakīla Tantra. See following entry

Hundred Thousand Verse Tantra of Supreme Awareness *or* Hundred Thousand Verses of the Vajrakīla Tantra. *bityottama-la*, *'bum sde'i rgyud* or *phur-pa 'bum-sde*. Apparently not preserved in its entirety at the present time. NGB Vols. 19 and 27-9, no. 353, represents a major fragment. [*481*, *516*]

Hundred Verses on Discriminative Awareness. *shes-rab brgya-pa*. Skt. *Prajñāśatakanāmaprakaraṇa*. Auth. Nāgārjuna. T 4328. [97]

Illuminating of the Lamp. *sgron-ma snang-byed*. Alternative title for the *Great Perfection endowed with Conch-Syllables*. [*343*]

Illuminating Lamp which Contains the Prophecy of the Great Accomplished Master Himself. *grub-chen-nyid-kyi lung-bstan gsal-ba'i sgron-me*. Disc. Thang-stong rgyal-po. NL. [*802*]

Illuminating Lamp of the Fundamental Text. *khog-gzhung gsal-sgron*. Auth. Vimalamitra. P 4739. [*126*, *266*, *481*, *673*, *674*]

Illuminating Mirror, a Commentary on the Tantra of the Secret Nucleus. *gsang-ba snying-po-la ṭīkā gsal-byed me-long*. Auth. gYung-ston Rdo-rje-dpal. NMKMG Vol. 28. Also referred to as *Yungtönpa's Commentary on the Secret Nucleus*. [*660*, *666*, *678*, *680*, *684*, *730*]

Illuminating the Substance of the Aural Lineage. *snyan-brgyud dngos-po gsal-byed*. Auth. Mi-la-ras-pa. DZ Vol. 5, pp. 443-55. [*200*]

Immortal Wish-granting Wheel. *'chi-med yid-bzhin 'khor-lo*. See *Rites of the Service and Attainment of the Immortal Wish-granting Wheel*

Imperial Edict. *'ja'-sa gser-yig*. NL. [*663*]

Indestructible Peak. *(rdo-rje) rtse-mo*. Skt. *Vajraśekharamahāguhyayogatantra*. T 480. GDKT Vol. 5, no. 24. [*78*, *258*, *357*]

Indestructible Prophetic Declaration of Thangtong Gyelpo. *grub-chen thang-stong rgyal-po'i rdo-rje'i lung*. NL. [*853*]

(Indestructible) Tent. *(rdo-rje) gur*. Skt. *Vajrapañjaratantra*. T 419. KGNZ Vol. 2, pp. 351-8. GDKT Vol. 20, nos. 109-10. [*268, 576, 633*]

Injunction of Padma (which was Discovered at Crystal Rock). *padma bka'-thang (shel-brag-ma)*. Disc. O-rgyan gling-pa. Xylo. Leh, Ladakh. I-Tib-430. Xylo. Snyi-shang Brag-dkar-shar Monastery, Manang, Nepal. N-Tib 73-906442. Trans. G.-C. Toussaint, *Le Dict de Padma, Padma thang yig, Ms. de Lithang*. Bibliothéque de l'Institut de Hautes Études Chinoises, Vol. 3. Paris: Librairie Ernest Leroux, 1933. Trans. from the French of G.-C. Toussaint by K. Douglas and G. Bays, *The Life and Liberation of Padmasambhava*. 2 vols. Emeryville, California: Dharma Publications, 1978. Also referred to as the *Great Injuction of Padma*. [*775, 778, 938*]

Injunctions of Padma. *(padma bka'-yi) thang-yig(-rnams)*. For a general survey of the texts with this title, refer to A.-M. Blondeau, "Analysis of the Biographies of Padmasambhava according to Tibetan Tradition: Classification of Sources" in TSHR, pp. 45-52. The texts of this genre which are mentioned in the present work are the *Injunction of Padma which was Discovered at Crystal Rock*, the *Short Biography of Padmasambhava* and the *Life of Orgyen (Padmasambhava) with Three Reasons for Confidence*. Refer also to n. 976. [*750*]

Inner and Outer Collected Works (of Dalai Lama V, in thirty volumes). *gsung-'bum phyi-nang (pod-chen sum-cu)*. Auth. Dalai Lama V, Ngag-dbang blo-bzang rgya-mtsho. TWB 5587-822. [*824*]

Innermost Meaning, the Liberation of All Beings. *don-tig 'gro-ba kun-grol*. Disc. Dri-med lhun-po. RTD Vol. 35, pp. 1-53. [*678*]

Innermost Point. *thugs-thig*. Skt. *Cittabindu*. Auth. Līlāvajra (Vilāsavajra). P 4723. [*464*]

Innermost Profundity of Tārā. *sgrol-ma'i zab-tig*. Disc. Mchog-gyur bde-chen gling-pa. CLTC Vol. 26. RTD Vol. 58, pp. 1-193. [*846*]

Innermost Profundity of Vimalamitra. *bi-ma-la'i zab-tig*. Disc. Mchog-gyur bde-chen gling-pa. CLTC Vol. 26. [*847*]

Innermost Spirituality of the Accomplished Master. *grub-thob thugs-thig*. Disc. 'Jam-dbyangs mkhyen-brtse'i dbang-po, inspired by the vision of Thang-stong rgyal-po. Its main divisions are listed separately as (1) *Profound and Vast Creation and Perfection of the Cycle of Means for the Attainment of the Guru*, (2) *Five Cycles of (the Means for) Attainment (which are in harmony with the Path of the Magical Net)* and (3) *Essential Summarisation of the Tantras, Transmissions, and Esoteric Instructions of the Class of Means for Attainment, the Eight Transmitted Precepts*. Also referred to as the *Cycles of the Innermost Spirituality of the Accomplished Master*. [*804, 855, 857*]

Innermost Spirituality of the Awareness-holder. *rig-'dzin thugs-thig*. Disc. Gter-bdag gling-pa. RTD Vol. 13, pp. 61-197. Pub. Dehra Dun: D. G. Khochhen Trulku, 1975. I-Tib 75-904946. [*729, 828, 849*]

Innermost Spirituality of Cetsün. *lce-btsun snying-thig*. Disc. 'Jam-dbyangs mkhyen-brtse'i dbang-po. RTD Vol. 87, pp. 259-350. In addition, there has been a reproduction of the A-'dzom 'Brug-pa redaction. Delhi: Dam-chos-smon-lam, 1975. I-Tib 75-900761. [*858*]

Innermost Spirituality of the Ḍākinī. *(man-ngag) mkha'-'gro snying-tig*. Disc. Padma Las-'brel-rtsal. Redacted by Klong-chen Rab-'byams-pa. NYZ Vols. 2-3. See also *Four-Part Innermost Spirituality*. In addition, a manuscript of considerable antiquity from the Lahoul-Spiti region of Himachal Pradesh has been reproduced in 2 vols. Sumra, HP: Orgyan Dorji, 1978. I-Tib 78-906099. [*554-5*, *580*, *582*, *583*, *585*, *586*, *587*, *679*]

Innermost Spirituality of Karmapa. *karma snying-tig*. Disc. Karma-pa III, Rang-byung rdo-rje. RTD Vol. 86, pp. 423-70. [*574*]

Innermost Spirituality of Longcenpa, including the basic root texts and elucidations. *thugs-gter klong-chen snying-thig gzhung-rtsa-ba gsal-byed-dang bcas-pa*. See *(Great Perfection, the) Innermost Spirituality of Longcenpa*

Innermost Spirituality of Radiant Space. *(rdzogs-chen) klong-gsal snying-thig*. Disc. Ratna gling-pa. RLTC Vols. 11, 12, 19. RTD Vol. 88, pp. 447-652. Note that this should not be confused with the *klong-gsal rdo-rje snying-po*. Disc. Klong-gsal snying-po. [*677*, *681*, *683*]

Innermost Spirituality, Transmitted Precepts of the Exegetical Tradition of the Esoteric Instructional Class. *bshad-rgyud snying-thig-gi bka'-rnams*. See *Four-Part Innermost Spirituality*

Innermost Spirituality: the Trio of Amitāyus, Yangdak Heruka, and Vajrakīla, with the Cycle of its Protectress, Ekajaṭī, the Self-Arisen Queen. *snying-thig tshe-yang-phur gsum srung-ma e-ka-dza-ṭi rang-byung rgyal-mo'i skor*. Disc. Bdud-'dul rdo-rje. DDTC Vol. 6. RTD Vol. 50, pp. 101-213. Pub. New Delhi: Sanje Dorje, 1973. I-Tib 73-906926. [*815*]

Innermost Spirituality of Vimalamitra. *bi-ma'i snying-tig*. Redacted by Klong-chen rab-'byams-pa. NYZ Vols. 7-9. [*583*, *585*, *723*, *727*] See also *Four-Part Innermost Spirituality*

Inquiry into Relations. *'brel(-ba) brtag(-pa)*. Skt. *Sambandhaparīkṣā*. Auth. Dharmakīrti. T 4214. EIPRB 2116. MTTWL 195. BB 8 (1972). [*102*]

Instructions of the Eight Confidences. *gding-brgyad-kyi gdams-pa*. Disc. Rdo-rje gling-pa. NL. [*791*]

Instructions of the Innermost Spirituality concerning the Profound Significance of Ati. *a-ti zab-don snying-thig-gi gdams-pa*. Disc. Mchog-gyur bde-chen gling-pa. CLTC Vol. 26. [*847*]

Intermediate Gathering of Transmitted Precepts, the Gathering of the Guru's Intention. *bka'-'dus bar-ba bla-ma dgongs-pa 'dus-pa*. See *Gathering of the Guru's Intention*

Intermediate Mother. *yum bar-ma*. See *Transcendental Perfection of Discriminative Awareness in Twenty-five Thousand Lines*

Introduction to the Conduct of a Bodhisattva. *(byang-chub sems-dpa'i) spyod(-pa-la) 'jug(-pa)*. Skt. *Bodhisattvacaryāvatāra*. Auth. Śāntideva.

T 3871. EIPRB 3412-43. MTTWL 34. HIL 7.1, pp. 82-3, 128, 131. B.Budh. 28 (1929). BST 12 (1960). Trans. S. Batchelor, *A Guide to the Bodhisattva's Way of Life*. LTWA, 1979. [*94*, *108*, *214*, *235-6*, *300*, *323*, *577*, *671*, *691*, *747*, *762*, *871-2*, *904*]

Introduction to the Essence of the Secret Cycle. *gsang-skor gnad-kyi ngo-sprod*. NL. Certainly to be identified among the traditions preserved in the *Four-Part Innermost Spirituality*, though the precise textual identifications remain to be established. [*569*]

Introduction to the Madhyamaka. *(dbu-ma-la) 'jug-pa*. Skt. *Madhyamakāvatāra*. Auth. Candrakīrti. T 3861. EIPRB 2081-3. MTTWL 109. HIL 7.1, pp. 71-4, 130. B.Budh. 9 (1907-12). Trans. C. W. Huntington and Geshé Namgyal Wangchen, *The Emptiness of Emptiness*. Honolulu: University of Hawaii Press, 1989. [*57*, *144*, *147-8*, *164-6*, *168*, *192-3*, *577*, *872*, *904*]

Introduction to the Real. *de-kho-na-nyid 'jug-pa*. Skt. *Tattvāvatāra*. Auth. Jñānakīrti. T 3709. [*305*, *909*]

Introduction to the Three Bodies. *sku-gsum ngo-sprod*. Auth. Karma Pakshi. Expanded by later Karma-pa hierarchs. DZ Vol. 6, pp. 225-46. [*578*]

Introduction to the Three Bodies. *sku-gsum-la 'jug-pa*. Skt. *Kāyatrayāvatāramukha*. Auth. Nāgārjuna. T 3890. HIL 7.1, p. 56. [*183*]

Introduction to the Way of the Greater Vehicle. *theg-pa chen-po'i tshul-la 'jug-pa*. Auth. Rong-zom Chos-kyi bzang-po. Reproduced in *Commentaries on the Guhyagarbha Tantra and other rare Nyingma Texts from the Library of Dudjom Rinpoche*. Vol. 1. New Delhi: Sanje Dorje, 1974. I-Tib 74-900928. Also in *Roṅ zom bka' 'bum*. Thimphu: Kunzang Tobgay, 1976. I(Bhu)-Tib 77-902743. [*707-8*]

Introduction to Yoga. *rnal-'byor rgyud-la'ang rdo-rje dbyings-kyi sgrub-thabs yo-ga-la 'jug-pa*. Skt. *Tantrārthāvatāra*. Auth. Buddhaguhya. T 2501. [*466*]

Inventory for the Innermost Spirituality of Longcenpa. *klong-byang*. Disc. 'Jigs-med gling-pa. See *(Great Perfection, the) Innermost Spirituality of Longcenpa*

Inventory of Lord Nyang's Treasure Texts. *mnga'-bdag nyang-gi gter-yig kha-byang*. NL. [*662*]

Jambhala (according to the New Yamāntaka Cycle of Ra Lotsāwa). *(rva-lugs) dzam-bha-la*. NL. [*713*]

Javāripā's Esoteric Instructions on Vital Energy. *dza-ba-ri'i bhū-rlung-gi man-ngag*. Redacted by 'Bri-gung-pa Rin-chen phun-tshogs. RTD Vol. 48, pp. 337-414. [*676*]

Jewel Garland. *rin-chen phreng-ba*. Skt. *Ratnāvalī*. Auth. Nāgārjuna. T 4158. BST 10 (1960). EIPRB 686-9. MTTWL 189. A number of newly recovered Sanskrit fragments have been published by S. Dietz, *Journal of the Nepal Research Centre* IV, pp. 189-220. See also C. Lindtner, *Nagarjuniana*. Indiske Studier IV. Copenhagen: Akademisk Forlag, 1982, pp. 163-9. M. Hahn, *Nāgārjuna's Ratnāvalī*. Bonn: Indica et Tibetica Verlag, 1982. [*168*, *205*]

Jewel Hoard of Esoteric Instructions. *man-ngag rin-chen gter-spungs*. Disc. Thang-stong rgyal-po. NL. [*802*]

Jewel Lamp of the Madhyamaka. *dbu-ma rin-chen sgron-ma*. Skt. *Madhyamakaratnapradīpa*. Auth. Bhavya (Bhāvaviveka). T 3854. EIPRB 2020. MTTWL 106. HIL 7.1, p. 66. [*168*, *169*, *905*]

Jewel Ornament of Liberation. *dvags-po thar-rgyan*. Auth. Sgam-po-pa. Xylo. Rum-btegs, Sikkim. I(Sik)-Tib 72-905370. Trans. H. V. Guenther, *The Jewel Ornament of Liberation*. Berkeley: Shambhala, 1971. Refer to n. 1263. [*908*]

Jinasāgara. *rgyal-ba rgya-mtsho*. RTD Vol. 33, pp. 389-522. GDKT Vol. 16, nos. 90-1. GTKT Vol. 4. Pub. in *Rare Karma-pa Texts on the Practice of Mahāmudrā*. Bir, HP: Kandro, 1974. I-Tib 74-901395. The great commentary on this cycle appears in *The collected works of Karma Chags-med*, Vol. 5. Bir, HP: Kandro, 1974. I-Tib 74-900426. [*578*]

Kadampa Tradition endowed with Seven Divine Doctrines. *lha-chos bdun-ldan bka'-gdams*. These are the *seven divine doctrines of Atiśa* listed in the Glossary of Enumerations. Representative texts may be found in DZ Vols. 2-3. [*853*]

Kālacakra Tantra. *dus(-kyi) 'khor(-lo)* Skt. *Paramādibuddhoddhṛtaśrīkālacakranāmatantrarāja*. T 362. Tib., Skt. and Mongolian edn. R. Vira and L. Chandra, *The Kālacakra Tantra and Other Texts*. SP Vols. 69-70 (1966). DZ Vol 10. GDKT Vol. 17, nos. 97-8. See J. Newman, "The *Paramādibuddha* and its Relation to the Early Kālacakra Literature" *Indo-Iranian Journal* 30 (1987), pp. 93-102. Also referred to as the *Abridged Tantra of Kālacakra*, the *Glorious Kālacakra* and the *Root Tantra of the Kālacakra*. The foremost commentary on this tantra is the *Taintless Light*. [*99*, *126*, *212*, *258*, *264*, *283*, *290*, *339-40*, *395*, *399*, *442*, *451*, *576*, *613*, *666*, *671*, *827*, *850*, *894*, *930*, *944*, *947*, *972*]

Kalāpasūtra. *sgra ka-lā-pa*. Auth. Rgyal-po'i lha (Rājadeva) or, according to Tāranātha, Saptavarman. T 4282. HIL 5.2, pp. 162-3. [*92*, *100*, *723*, *727*, *729*]

Kangyur. *bka'-'gyur*. For a useful survey of the various editions and the current state of research about them, see H. Eimer, "Some results of recent Kanjur research" *Archiv für Zentralasiatische Geschichtsforschung*, 1. Sankt Augustin: VGH Wissenschaftsverlag, 1983, pp. 3-21. Also referred to as the *Precious Translations of the Transmitted Precepts of the Conqueror*. [*40*, *703*, *794*, *827*, *831*, *851*, *874*, *893*]

Kaṅkaṇi Dhāraṇī. *ka-ka-ni*. The *dhāraṇī* of Akṣobhya Buddha. [*762*]

Ketsangma (Tradition of the Great Perfection). *(rdzogs-chen) ke-tshang-ma*. NL. [*651*]

Kham Tradition of the Great Perfection. *rdzogs-chen khams-lugs*. See *Great Perfection of the Kham Tradition*

Khön Tradition of Vajrakīla. *phur-pa 'khon-lugs*. GDKT Vol. 16, no. 96. GCKZ Vols. 3-4. GTKT Vol. 13. And see *The Vajrakīla rites as practised by the 'Khon lineage of Sa-skya*. New Delhi: Ngawang Sopa, 1973. I-Tib 73-905479. Also referred to as the *Sakya Tradition of Vajrakīla*. [*673*, *674*, *712*]

Kīla which is the Utterly Secret Vital Razor. *phur-pa yang-gsang srog-gi spu-gri*. Disc. Padma gling-pa. PLTC Vol. 16. RTD Vol. 50, pp. 37-100. [*796-7*]

King's Tradition of Vajrakīla. *phur-pa rgyal-po lugs*. [*710*]

King of the Three Commitments. *dam-tshig gsum-rgyal*. Skt. *Trisamayavyūha-rājatantra*. T 502. GDKT Vol. 1, no. 2. GTKT Vol. 5. [*271*]

Kor Tradition. *skor-lugs*. See *Great Perfection according to the Tradition of the Cycles*

Kṛṣṇayamāri. See *Black Yamāri*

Kyi Tradition of Vajrakīla. *phur-pa skyi-lugs*. NL. [*651*]

Kyo Tradition of the Sūtra which Gathers All Intentions and the Magical Net. *mdo-dang sgyu-'phrul skyo-lugs*. NL. [*701*]

Lamp of Discriminative Awareness. *shes-rab sgron-ma*. Auth. Dharmabodhi NL. [*489*]

Lamp for the Eye of Contemplation (which is an Esoteric Instruction of the Great Perfection). *(rdzogs-chen-gyi man-ngag) bsam-gtan mig(-gi) sgron (-me)* or *mig-sgron*. Auth. Gnubs-chen Sangs-rgyas ye-shes. SSS 74 (1974). I-Tib 74-902536. See also J. Broughton, "Early Ch'an in Tibet" in R. M. Gimello and P. N. Gregory (eds.), *Studies in Ch'an and Hua-yen*. Honolulu: University of Hawaii Press, 1983. And S. G. Karmay, *The Great Perfection*. Leiden: E. J. Brill, 1988. [*570-1*, *612*, *654*, *658*]

Lamp which Illuminates the Essence of Tantra, Transmission, and Esoteric Instruction: a General Exposition of the Empowerment of the Sūtra which Gathers All Intentions. *'dus-pa mdo'i dbang-gi spyi-don rgyud-lung man-ngag-gi gnad sel-byed sgron-me*. Auth. Lo-chen Dharmaśrī. LCSB Vol. 12, pp. 1-259. NMKMG Vol. 14. [*965*]

Lamp on the Levels of Yoga. *rnal-'byor sa'i sgron-ma*. Auth. Hūṃkara. NL. [*489*]

Lamp which Subsumes Conduct. *spyod-pa bsdus-pa'i sgron-ma*. Skt. *Caryā-melāpakapradīpa*. Auth. Āryadeva. T 1803. Manuscript version pub. Dolanji, HP: Tashi Dorji, 1976. I-Tib 76-903112. [*413*]

Lamp of the Three Modes. *tshul-gsum sgron-ma*. Skt. *Nayatrayapradīpa*. Auth. Tripiṭakamāla. T 3707. [*246*]

Lecture Notes on the Ground, Path and Result according to the Magical Net. *sgyu-'phrul gzhi-lam-'bras gsum stong-thun*. Auth. Rog Shes-rab-'od. NL. [*702*]

Lecture Notes on the Middle Way. *dbu-ma'i stong-thun*. Transmitted by Gung-thang Paṇ-chen. NL. [*730*]

Lecture Notes on the Nucleus of the Sugata. *bde-gshegs snying-po'i stong-thun*. Auth. 'Jam-mgon Mi-pham rgya-mtsho. MPSB Vol. 3. Litho edn. Steng-po-che, Nepal, *c*. 1974. [*198*]

Lecture Notes on the Tradition of the Cycles. *skor-lugs-kyi stong-thun*. NL. [*655*]

Lesser Net. *drva-chung*. Skt. *Sūkṣmajāla*. Auth. Buddhaguhya. P 4734. NMKMG Vol. 23. [*466*]

Lesser (Sequence of the) Path. *(sgyu-'phrul drva-ba) lam(-gyi rnam-bshad) chung(-ba)*. Auth. Buddhaguhya. DZ Vol. 1, pp. 1-15. NMKMG Vol. 23. [*282*, *466*]

Letter to a Friend. *bshes(-pa'i) spring(-yig)*. Skt. *Suhṛllekha*. Auth. Nāgārjuna. T 4182. EIPRB 690-3. MTTWL 218. HIL 7.1, pp. 26-7. Trans. Geshe Lobsang Tharchin and A. B. Engle, *Nāgārjuna's Letter*. LTWA 1979. [*58*]

Liberating Empowerment of the Lower Rite (of Vajrakīla). *phur-pa smad-las sgrol-dbang*. The empowerment associated with the wrathful activity of sorcery in the Vajrakīla traditions. [*712*]

Life of Orgyen (Padmasambhava) with Three Reasons for Confidence. *o-rgyan rnam-thar yid-ches gsum-ldan*. Auth. Tāranātha. RTD Vol. 1, pp. 245-89. Pub. in *Accounts of the lives of manifestations of Guru Rin-po-che*. Tezu, Arunachal Pradesh: Tseten Dorji, Tibetan Nyingmapa Monastery, 1973. I-Tib 74-900059. Also in *Five historical works of Tāranātha*. Tezu, Arunachal Pradesh: Tseten Dorji, Tibetan Nyingmapa Monastery, 1974. I-Tib 74-901746. [*965*]

Light Rays of Grammatical Speech. *bstan-bcos brda-sprod ngag-gi 'od-zer*. Auth. Viṣṇu. NL. [*65*]

Limitless Choreographic Arrangements. *gar-gyi rnam-'gyur mtha'-klas-pa*. Disc. Mchog-gyur bde-chen gling-pa. It is unlikely that this is to be identified with a particular text. [*847*]

Lion's Perfect Expressive Power. *seng-ge rtsal-rdzogs (chen-po'i rgyud)*. NGB Vol. 9, no. 144. GCD Vol. 2. [*126*, *333*]

Lion's Roar in Affirmation of Extrinsic Emptiness. *gzhan-stong khas-len seng-ge'i nga-ro*. Auth. 'Jam-mgon Mi-pham rgya-mtsho. MPSB Vol. 11. Xylo. Ser-lo Monastery, Nepal. N-Tib 72-902223. [*198*]

Litany of the Names of Mañjuśrī. *('phags-pa) 'jam-dpal-gyi mtshan (yang-dag-par) brjod(-pa)*. Skt. *Mañjuśrīnāmasaṃgīti*. T 360. NGB Vol. 15, no. 196. SP 18 (*c*. 1963). SP 69 (1966). Ed. and trans. R. M. Davidson, "The Litany of Names of Mañjuśrī" MCB 20 (1981), pp. 1-69. A. Wayman, *Chanting the Names of Mañjuśrī*. Boulder/London: Shambhala, 1985. GDKT Vol. 6, no. 41; Vol. 10, no. 60. GTKT Vol. 2. KGNZ Vol. 4, pp. 375-504. NMKMG Vol. 22. Also referred to as the *Magical Net of Mañjuśrī* and the *Sublime Litany of the Names of Mañjuśrī*. [*74-5*, *77*, *81*, *82*, *116*, *142*, *177*, *212*, *291*, *305-6*, *463*, *468*, *550*, *674*, *691*, *761*]

Lives of the Hundred Treasure-finders, a Beauteous Rosary of Precious Beryl. *gter-ston brgya-rtsa'i rnam-thar rin-chen bai-ḍūrya'i phreng-mdzes*. Auth. 'Jam-mgon Kong-sprul Blo-gros mtha'-yas. RTD Vol. 1, pp. 291-759. Pub. Tezu, Arunachal Pradesh: Tseten Dorji, Tibetan Nyingmapa Monastery, 1973. I-Tib 74-900058. [*966*]

Lock of the Heart. *thugs-kyi sgo-lcags*. Skt. *Cittatālaka*. Auth. Śrī Siṃha. P 4758. [*40*, *357*, *365*]

Loktri (the Sage). *(drang-srong) lok-tri*. The reference to this in *History* does not specify the redaction concerned. Selections of Nyingmapa rites focusing upon this deity are found in RTD Vol. 54. [*727*]

Longevity Empowerment of the Magical Net. *sgyu-'phrul-gyi tshe-dbang*. [*673, 674*]

Long, Medium and Short (teachings on the) Peaceful and Wrathful Deities according to the Se tradition. *se-lugs-kyi zhi-khro rgyas-'bring-bsdus gsum*. Absorbed into the traditions preserved in NMKMG Vols. 11-12. [*665*]

Long, Medium and Short Versions of the Mother *or* Long, Medium, and Short Versions of the Sūtras of Transcendental Perfection. *yum rgyas-'bring-bsdus gsum* or *(sher-phyin) rgyas-'bring-bsdus gsum*. Listed separately as the *Transcendental Perfection of Discriminative Awareness in Eight Thousand Lines*, *Transcendental Perfection of Discriminative Awareness in Twenty-five Thousand Lines* and *Transcendental Perfection of Discriminative Awareness in One Hundred Thousand Lines*. [*566, 647, 655*]

Lord of Life, Evil and Mean-hearted. *tshe-bdag sdig-pa snying-'dzings*. Disc. Dum-pa rgya zhang-khrom. [*713*] See *Yamāntaka Cycle*

Lord of Life (Yamāntaka). *tshe-bdag*. See *Yamāntaka (Cycle/Tantra)*

Lord of Pristine Cognition with Many Deities (the tantra, means for attainment and rites of). *ye-shes mgon-po lha-mang-gi rgyud sgrub-thabs las-tshogs*. Disc. O-rgyan gling-pa. NA. [*775*]

Lotus Peak. *padma rtse-mo*. Skt. *Padmaśekhara*. NL. [*251*]

Lotus the Speech. *padma gsung*. NGB Vols. 23-4. [*283*] See also *Transmitted Precepts of the Lotus Speech Tantras* and *Hayagrīva (Cycle/Tantra)*

Lotus Sūtra. *dam-chos pad-dkar*. Skt. *Saddharmapuṇḍarīkasūtra*. T 113. EIPRB 556-601. MTTWL 191. B.Budh. 10 (1908-12). BST 6 (1960). SBE 21. Akira Yuyama, *A Bibliography of the Sanskrit Texts of the Saddharmapuṇḍarīkasūtra*. Canberra: Australian National University Press, 1970. [*80, 83, 414*]

Lower Tibetan Lineage of the Vinaya (Vows). *snga-'gyur smad-'dul-gyi sdom-rgyun*. NMKMG Vol. 1. Refer to n. 568. [*525-6*]

Lūipā Tradition of Cakrasaṃvara. *bde-mchog lū'i-pa*. Skt. *Bhagavadabhisamayanāma*. Auth. Lūipā. T 1427. GDKT Vol. 11, no. 63. [*657*]

Magical Net. *sgyu(-'phrul) drva(-ba)*. The main tantras of this system are collected together in NGB Vols. 14-16 and 19. The rites are to be found in NMKMG Vols. 11-12. Refer also to GGFTC, pp. 37ff. The history of these lineages are described throughout *History*, Pt. 5. [*362, 396, 460, 462-70, 533, 550, 762, 804, 827, 833, 843, 845, 849, 858, 893*]

Magical Net of Indestructible Reality. *sgyu-'phrul rdo-rje*. To be identified with the *Exegetical Tantras of the Magical Net*. NGB Vol. 15. [*449*]

Magical Net of Mañjuśrī. *'jam-dpal sgyu-'phrul drva-ba*. See *Litany of the Names of Mañjuśrī*

Magical Net of Vajrasattva. *rdo-rje sems-dpa' sgyu-'phrul drva-ba* or *sgyu-'phrul rdo-rje sems-dpa'*. To be identified in general with the root texts of the cycle, contained in NGB Vol. 14, and specifically with the *Tantra of the Secret Nucleus*. [*283, 533, 648, 944*]

Mahāmāya (Tantra). *Mahāmāya* or *sgyu-'phrul chen-po*. T 425. GDKT Vol. 15, no. 87. KGNZ Vol. 3, pp. 293-412. [*257-8*, *291*, *442*, *578*]

Mahāvyutpatti. *bye-brag rtogs-byed*. T 4346. B.Budh. 13 (1911). Ed. R. Sakaki, Kyoto, 1916-25; repr. Tokyo, 1965. Ed. and trans. in *Collected Works of Alexander Csoma de Körös*, Vol. 3. Budapest: Akadémiai Kiadó, 1984 (originally published in three parts in 1910, 1916 and 1944). [*98-9*]

Mahottara (Tantra). *che-mchog(-gi rgyud)*. Depending upon the context to be identified either with *dpal heruka rol-pa'i rgyud*, T 840. NGB Vol. 18, nos. 216 and 218, or with *dpal che-mchog 'dus-pa rtsa-ba'i rgyud*, NGB Vol. 32, no. 380. KGDD Vol. 2. The latter is the text intended in connection with the *Eight Transmitted Precepts*. Chemcok also occurs as an epithet of Vajrāmṛta, the foremost deity of the cycle of *Nectar the Enlightened Attributes*. [*362*]

Malign Mantra. *drag-sngags dmod-pa*. Skt. **Vajramantrabhīru*. T 843. NGB Vol. 32, no. 388. KGDD Vol. 3. [*283*, *362*, *483*]

Maṇḍalas of the Ngok (Tradition). *rngog-dkyil*. The traditional classification of the maṇḍalas transmitted through the family of Mar-pa's disciple Rngog Chos-sku rdo-rje lists seven: (1) The nine-deity maṇḍala of Hevajra. *dgyes-rdor lha-dgu*. GDKT Vol. 19, no. 107. KGNZ Vol. 2, pp. 1-188. (2) The fifteen-deity maṇḍala of Nairātmyā. *bdag-med lha-mo bco-lnga*. GDKT Vol. 19, no. 108. KGNZ Vol. 2, pp. 189-240. (3) The many deity maṇḍala of the transmitted precepts of Vajracatuḥpīṭha, the father consort. *gdan-bzhi yab-bka' lha-mang*. (4) The transmitted precepts of the mother consort Jñāneśvarī. *yum-bka' ye-shes dbang-phyug*. GDKT Vol. 15, nos. 88-9. KGNZ Vol. 3, pp. 413-580. (5) The five-deity maṇḍala of Mahāmāya. *mahāmāya lha-lnga*. GDKT Vol. 15, no. 87. KGNZ Vol. 3, pp. 293-412. (6) The five-ḍākinī maṇḍala of the consummation of the families (of the Hevajra maṇḍala), according to the *Vajrapañjara Tantra*. *gur rigs-bsdus mkha'-'gro lnga*. GDKT Vol. 20, no. 110. KGNZ Vol. 2, pp. 241-358. (7) Esoteric Mañjuśrī. *'jam-dpal gsang-ldan*. GDKT Vol. 10, no. 60. KGNZ Vol. 4, pp. 375-504. The maṇḍalas of Ngok form the essential framework of KGNZ. [*807*]

Mañjuśrī the Body. *'jam-dpal sku*. NGB 21-2. NMKMG Vols. 4-6. Where the reference is to the tradition of the *Eight Transmitted Precepts* in particular, the tantra in question is probably T 838. NGB Vol. 32, no. 382. KGDD Vol. 3. [*283*, *361*] See also *Yamāntaka (Cycle/Tantra)*

Mañjuśrī Lord of Life, Iron-like and Iron-evil. *'jam-dpal tshe-bdag lcags-'dra lcags-sdig*. In the context of *History*, p. 871, where this phrase is used, it almost certainly refers to two cycles found in RTD: (1) *'jam-dpal tshe-bdag lcags-'dra*. Disc. Dum-pa rgya zhang-khrom. RTD Vol. 26, pp. 1-417. (2) *'jam-dpal tshe-bdag lcags-sdig*. Disc. Mchog-gyur bde-chen gling-pa. RTD Vol. 27, pp. 165-318. Also referred to as *Mañjuśrī-Yamāntaka, Lord of Life*. [*871*, *876*]

Mantra Store of the Lineages of Transmitted Precepts. *bka'-brgyud sngags-kyi mdzod*. Compiled by 'Jam-mgon Kong-sprul Blo-gros mtha'-yas. KGNZ. [*861*] See also *Maṇḍalas of the Ngok (Tradition)* and *Five Great Stores*

Manuals for Arts and Crafts. *bzo-rig patra*. Disc. O-rgyan gling-pa. NA. [*776*]

Mātaraḥ the Liberating Sorcery. *ma-mo rbod-gtong*. See *Mātaraḥ (Cycle/Tantra)*

Mātaraḥ and Yamāntaka. *ma-gshin*. Listed separately.

Mātaraḥ (Cycle/Tantra). *ma-mo('i rgyud)*. T 842. NGB Vols. 30-1 and 33. Where the context is particularly that of the *Eight Transmitted Precepts*, the main text is NGB Vol. 32, no. 385. KGDD Vol. 3. On the term "Mātaraḥ", refer to n. 493. [*283*, *362*, *473*, *483*, *609*, *614*, *762*, *930*]

Me Tradition of Hevajra. *dgyes-rdor mes-lugs*. The tradition of Mar-pa's disciple Mes-tshon-pa Bsod-nams rgyal-mtshan. Refer to *Blue Annals*, p. 405. NL. [*657*]

Means for Attaining the Real. *de-kho-na-nyid sgrub-pa'i thabs (zhes-bya-ba rdzogs-pa chen-po'i lam-gyi rim-pa)*. Auth. Nāropā. Unidentified. [*299*, *302*, *308*, *312*, *317*, *326*, *333-4*, *337*]

Means for the Attainment of Co-Emergence. *lhan-skyes sgrub-thabs*. Skt. *Śrīguhyasamājasahajasādhana*. Auth. Līlāvajra (Vilāsavajra). T 1913. [*464*]

Means for the Attainment of Garuḍa. *khyung sgrub-thabs*. There are, of course, a great many works of this type available. The reference found in *History* is not sufficiently specific to permit any identification of the precise tradition involved. [*545*]

Means for the Attainment of the Guru (belonging to the Innermost Spirituality of the Accomplished Master). *grub-thob bla-sgrub*. Disc. 'Jam-dbyangs mkhyen-brtse'i dbang-po. The first part of the *Innermost Spirituality of the Accomplished Master*. [*855*]

Means for the Attainment of the Guru Chogyur Lingpa, the Gathering of the Families of the Three Bodies. *mchog-gling bla-sgrub sku-gsum rigs-'dus*. Disc. 'Jam-dbyangs mkhyen-brtse'i dbang-po. RTD Vol. 17, pp. 233-70. [*858*]

Means for the Attainment of the Guru according to the Innermost Spirituality of Longcenpa, (entitled) "Sealed with the Seminal Point", a recension of. *klong-chen snying-thig-gi bla-sgrub thig-le'i rgya-can-gyi yig-cha*. Disc. 'Jam-dbyangs mkhyen-brtse'i dbang-po. RTD Vol. 17, pp. 105-64. [*858*]

Means for the Attainment of Hevajra. *sgrub-thabs mtsho-skyes*. Skt. *Śrīhevajrasādhana*. Auth. Saroruhavajra. T 1218. GDKT Vol. 18, no. 100. [*657*]

Means for the Attainment of Kṣetrapāla. *zhing-skyong-gi sgrub-thabs*. Disc. Thang-stong rgyal-po. NL. [*802*]

Means for the Attainment of Longevity which Conjoins the Sun and Moon. *tshe-sgrub nyi-zla kha-sbyor*. Disc. Sangs-rgyas gling-pa. RTD. vol. 29, pp. 337-381. [*786*]

Means for the Attainment of Longevity (according to the Great Perfection). *(rdzogs-chen) tshe-sgrub*. Disc. O-rgyan gling-pa. Available through the seventeenth century, but now perhaps NA. [*775*, *778*]

Means for the Attainment of Mañjuśrī. *'jam-dpal sgrub-thabs*. The reference found in *History* is not sufficiently specific for precise identification. [*545*]

Means for the Attainment of the Nāga King Sugrīva. *klu(-yi) rgyal(-po) mgrin-bzang sgrub-thabs*. Disc. Sangs-rgyas gling-pa. NL. [*786*]

Means for Attainment entitled Samantabhadra. *sgrub-thabs kun-bzang*. Skt. *Samantabhadranāmasādhana*. Auth. Buddhajñāna. T 1855. [*496*]

Means for the Attainment of Supreme Bliss. *bde-ba chen-po'i sgrub-thabs*. Skt. *Mahāsukhasādhana*. Auth. Vajrahāsya. T 1911. [*466*]

Means for the Attainment of the Three Roots. *rtsa-gsum sgrub-thabs*. Disc. Rdo-rje gling-pa. NL but referred to in DLTC Vol. 4, p. 19. [*789*]

Means for the Attainment of Trolö. *gro-lod sgrub-thabs*. Disc. 'Jam-mgon Kong-sprul Blo-gros mtha'-yas. RTD Vol. 21, pp. 147-82. [*866*]

Means for Meditation on Atiyoga. *ati rnal-'byor-gyi sgom-thabs*. Skt. *Atiyogabhāvanānāma*. Auth. Nāgabodhi. T 2417. [*317-18*]

Medical Treatise. *sman-dpyad*. Disc. O-rgyan gling-pa. NA. [*775*]

Meditational Sequences. *sgom-rim*. See *Three Meditational Sequences*

Meditative Absorption in the Mudrā. *phyag-rgya bsam-gtan*. Skt. *Māyājālamudrādhyāna*. Auth. Vimalamitra. P 4732. [*278*, *481*]

Melgyo Tradition of the Cakrasaṃvara. *bde-mchog mal-gyo lugs*. The tradition of Mal-gyo Lo-tsā-ba Blo-gros-grags. Refer to *Blue Annals*, pp. 380-2. NL. [*562*, *564*]

Memorandum on Yungtönpa's Commentary (through to the fifth chapter). *gYung-'grel-gi le'u lnga-pa yan-gyi zin-bris*. Auth. Chos-rje O-rgyan bstan-'dzin. NL. [*678*]

Memorandum on Yungtönpa's Commentary, the Parkap Commentary and the Secret Nucleus (through to the Fifth Chapter). *gYung-ston-pa spar-khab gsang-snying-gi 'grel-gyi le'u lnga-pa yan-gyi zin-bris*. Auth. Zur Chos-dbyings rang-grol. NL. [*680-1*]

Methods for Beneficial and Injurious Rites. *phan-gnod-kyi las-thabs*. Disc. O-rgyan gling-pa. NA. [*776*]

Methods for Refining Mercury. *dngul-chu btso-bkru'i lag-len*. The reference found in *History* is probably to praxis rather than to a particular text. The canonical work on the subject, however, is *Rasasiddhiśāstra*. Auth. Vyāḍipāda. T 4313. [*871*]

Mighty King of Pure Vision. *dag-snang dbang-gi rgyal-po*. Auth. or Disc. Bdud-'dul rdo-rje. NL. [*814*]

Mind at Rest. *sems-nyid ngal-gso*. Auth. Klong-chen Rab-'byams-pa. The first part of the *Trilogy of Rest*. [*359*, *595*, *727*, *730*, *827*]

Minor Transmissions (of the Vinaya). *('dul-ba) lung phran-tshegs*. Skt. *Vinayakṣudrāgama*. T 6. HBI, pp. 181-97. [76-7, *93*, *98*, *428-30*, *436*, *943*]

Miraculous Key of Further Discernment. *yang-'byed 'phrul(-gyi) lde(-mig)*. NGB Vol. 2, no. 26. [*230*, *350*, *355*, *360*, *361*, *370*, *372*]

Miraculous Key to the Storehouse. *bang-mdzod 'phrul(-gyi) lde(-mig)*. NGB Vol. 2, no. 24. [*40, 246, 363, 367, 368, 369, 372*]

Mirror Commentary on the Ornament of Emergent Realisation. *mngon-rtogs rgyan-gyi snang-ba*. Skt. *Abhisamayālaṃkārāloka*. Auth. Haribhadra. T 3791. BST 4 (1960). [*184*]

Mirror of the Heart of Vajrasattva. *rdo-rje sems-dpa' snying-gi me-long*. NGB Vol. 10, no. 156. [*344*]

Mirror of Poetics. *snyan-ngag me-long dbyug-pa-can-gyi gzhung*. Skt. *Kāvyādarśa*. Auth. Daṇḍin. T 4301. TWPS 62. Ed. Skt. and Tib. A. C. Banerjee, *Kāvyādarśa*. University of Calcutta, 1939. HIL 5.3, pp. 226-33. Refer also to n. 101. [*104-6, 705, 723, 730*]

Mother and Son of the Clarifying Lamp. *gsal-sgron ma-bu*. Refer to n. 100. [*104*]

Mother and Son Cycles of Innermost Spirituality. *snying-thig ma-bu'i skor*. Alternative title of NYZ. [*375*] See *Four-Part Innermost Spirituality*

Mother Tantra which Integrates the Secret onto the Path. *ma-rgyud gsang-ba lam-khyer*. Disc. Kun-dga' 'bum-pa. Redisc. Mchog-gyur bde-chen gling-pa. CLTC Vol. 25. RTD Vol. 85, pp. 203-416. [*846*]

Mundane Praise. *'jig-rten mchod-bstod*. Skt. *Lokastotrapūja*. T 844. NGB Vol. 32, no. 387. KGDD Vol. 3. [*283, 362, 483*]

Nāgārjuna's Cycle of Teachings on the Guhyasamāja. See *Ārya Cycle of Guhyasamāja*

Nails. *gzer-bu*. NL. However, cf. the various classifications so called in *Fundamentals*, pp. 325, 329, 333. [*654, 658*]

Nanam Tradition (of Vajrakīla) *or* Rong Tradition (of Vajrakīla). *(phur-pa) sna-nam-mam rong-lugs*. NMKMG Vol. 8. [*712*]

Nāropā's Sky-farer. *nā-ro mkha'-spyod*. GDKT Vol. 12, no. 70. GTKT Vol. 4. [*921*]

Narrative History of the Precious Collected Tantras of the Ancient Translation School, the Ornament Covering All Jambudvīpa. *rnying-rgyud dkar-chag 'dzam-gling tha-grur khyab-pa'i rgyan* or *snga-'gyur rgyud-'bum rin-po-che'i rtogs-pa brjod-pa 'dzam-gling tha-grur khyab-pa'i rgyan*. Auth. 'Jigs-med gling-pa. NGB Vol. 34, no. 407. JLSB Vol. 3. [*839, 965*]

Narrative of Suvarṇa. *gser-can-gyi rtogs-brjod*. Skt. *Suvarṇāvadāna*. NL. See, however, Obermiller, *History of Buddhism by Bu-ston* (Tokyo: Suzuki Research Foundation, 1964), Pt. 2, p. 102, where it is said to be drawn from a commentary on the now lost *Abhidharmasūtra*. [*943*]

Narrow Path to the Fortress. *rdzong-'phrang snyan-brgyud*. Probably not to be identified with the *Transmitted Precepts of the Narrow Path to the Fortress*. [*654*]

Natural Liberation of Intention: (A Cycle devoted to) the Peaceful and Wrathful Deities. *dgongs-pa rang-grol-gyi chos-skor rnams* or *kar-gling zhi-khro dgongs-pa rang-grol*. See *Peaceful and Wrathful Deities, the Natural Liberation of Intention*

Nectar the Enlightened Attributes. *bdud-rtsi yon-tan*. NGB Vol. 26. NMKMG Vol. 3. Also referred to as the *Transmitted Precepts of Vajrāmṛta* and the *Vajrāmṛta Cycle*. [*283*, *362*, *480*, *481*, *534*, *601*] See also *Eight Volumes of Nectar*

Net of Pristine Cognition. *ye-shes drva-ba*, i.e. *dpal sgyu-'phrul dr(v)a-ba ye-shes-kyi snying-po'i rgyud*. NGB Vol. 15, no. 198. [*139-40*]

New Treasures. *gter-gsar*. In the biography of Lo-chen Dharmaśrī, *History*, pp. 728-32, this term refers in particular to the treasures of his brother, Gter-bdag gling-pa. More generally, however, one sees it used to refer to any of the treasures discovered from the time of Gter-bdag gling-pa down to the present day. [*731*]

Nine Cycles of the Meditational Sequence. *bsgom-rim skor-dgu*. Auth. Satya-(vacas), Tib. Bden-smras. Not precisely identified, but apparently an Upanishadic teaching. [*65*]

Nine-Deity Maṇḍala of Yangdak Heruka. *yang-dag lha-dgu('i dkyil-'khor)*. GDKT Vol. 15, no. 85. NMKMG Vol. 3. Also referred to as *Nine-Lamp Yangdak*. [*621*, *685*, *843*]

Nine-Lamp Yangdak. *yang-dag mar-me dgu*. See previous entry

Nineteen Treasure Troves of Chöwang. *chos-dbang-gi gter bcu-dgu*. [*764*]

Ninety Volumes of Scripture. *gsung-rab glegs-bam dgu-bcu*. Auth. 'Jam-mgon Kong-sprul Blo-gros mtha'-yas. These contain the *Five Great Stores*. In the original Tibetan xylographic editions they amounted to some ninety volumes altogether, but in the smaller volumes in which they have been reprinted in India, they come to about 150. [*862*]

Nirvāṇa Sūtra. *mya-ngan-las 'das-pa'i mdo*. See *Sūtra of Final Nirvāṇa*

Nirvāṇa Tantra of Vajrakīla. *phur-pa mya-ngan-las-'das-pa'i rgyud*. NGB Vol. 28, no. 336. [*712*]

Non-Dual Victor. *gnyis-med rnam-rgyal*. Skt. *Advayasamatāvijayanāmava-jraśrīvaramahākalpādi*. T 453. Refer to n. 1242. [*893*]

Northern (Treasures of Rikdzin Gödemcen). See *Southern (Treasures of Pema Lingpa) and the Northern (Treasures of Rikdzin Gödemcen)*

Notebook on Iconometry. *cha-tshad-kyi yi-ge*. Skt. *Pratibimbamānalakṣaṇanā-ma*. Auth. Ātreya. T 4316. [*99*]

Notes Clarifying the Innermost Spirituality. *snying-thig-la gsal-byed-kyi yi-ge*. Auth. 'Khon-ston Dpal-'byor lhun-grub. NL. [*926*]

Notes on the Indications and Avoidance of Death. *'chi-ba brtags-bslu'i yi-ge*. Auth. Mkhas-grub Blo-gros rgyal-mtshan. NL. [*723*]

Notes on Ritual Variants. *kha-bsgyur*. Disc. Sangs-rgyas bla-ma. NA. [*751*]

Nup's Boast. *gnubs-kyi kha-pho*. Disc. Mchog-gyur bde-chen gling-pa. CLTC Vol. 26. [*847*]

Nupcen's Final Testament. *gnubs-chen 'da'-ka'i zhal-chems*. See *Transmitted Instructions of the Indestructible Array, which Nupcen conferred as his Final Testament*

Nyang Tradition. *nyang-lugs*. See *Great Perfection of the Rong Tradition*

Object of Cutting. *gcod-yul*. For a general survey of the available literature, refer to J. Gyatso, "A Preliminary Study of the *Gcod* Tradition" in STC, pp. 320-41. [*395*, *546*, *549*, *565*, *577*, *679*, *762*, *833*, *929*]

Ocean of Ḍākas. *mkha'-'gro rgya-mtsho*. Skt. *Ḍākārṇavatantra*. T 372. Apabhraṃśa edn. N. N. Chaudhuri. Calcutta, 1935. [*576*]

Ocean of Definitive Meaning on Retreat Practice. *ri-chos nges-don rgya-mtsho*. Auth. Dol-po-pa Shes-rab rgya-mtsho. Pub. Gangtok: Dodrup Sangyey Lama, 1976. I-Tib 76-901146. [*204*]

(Ocean of Doctrine, the Great) Gathering of Transmitted Precepts. *bka'-'dus (chos-kyi rgya-mtsho)* Disc. O-rgyan gling-pa. Redisc. 'Jam-dbyangs mkhyen-brtse'i dbang-po. RTD Vol. 23, pp. 209-429. Xylo. Zangs-mdog dpal-ri, Kalimpong, WB, n.d. [*471*, *778-9*, *972-3*]

Oceanic Magical Net. *sgyu-'phrul rgya-mtsho*. NGB Vol. 15, no. 199. Also referred to as the *Exegetical Tantra of the Oceanic Magical Net*. [*124-5*, *276-7*, *447*]

Ocean of Means for Attainment. *sgrub-thabs rgya-mtsho*. [*578*] See *Hundred Means for Attainment*

Oḍḍiyāna Tradition of Ritual Service and Attainment. *o-rgyan bsnyen-sgrub*. Originating with O-rgyan-pa Rin-chen-dpal. DZ Vol. 10. [*578*]

Opening the Eye of Discriminative Awareness. *shes-rab spyan-'byed*. Skt. *Mahāyogaprajñāpraveśacakṣurupadeśanāma*. Auth. Vimalamitra. P 4725. [*481*]

Oral Instructions of (Sublime) Mañjuśrī (for Attaining the Real). *('phags-pa) 'jam-dpal(-gyi de-kho-na-nyid sgrub-pa'i) zhal-lung* or *zhal-gyi lung*. Skt. *Dvikramatattvabhāvanānāmamukhāgama*, and its shorter version, *Mañjuśrīmukhāgama*. Auth. Buddhaśrījñāna. T 1853-4. [*57*, *313*, *315*, *464*, *496*]

Oral Transmission of the Path and Fruit. *gsung-ngag lam-'bras*. See *Path and Fruit*

Oral Transmission of Puṇḍarīka. *skar-rtsis-kyi bstan-bcos pad-dkar zhal-lung*. Auth. the Three Gyamtsos: Phug-pa Lhun-grub rgya-mtsho, Mkhas-grub rgya-mtsho, and Sangs-rgyas rgya-mtsho. A copy of this rare astrological treatise is available in the Theos Bernard Collection, Yale University. We thank Ms Amy Heller for calling our attention to it. [*954*]

Origin of the Doctrines of the Ancient Translation School, a Scholar's Delight. *snga-'gyur chos-kyi byung-khungs mkhas-pa dga'-byed*. Auth. Mkhas-mchog Ngag-dbang blo-gros. NL. [*965*]

Ornamental Flower of Speech. *smra-ba rgyan-gyi me-tog*. NL. [*100*]

Ornamental Mirror of Categories. *tshig-don rgyan-gyi snang-ba*. Apparently a Jaina work. NL. It may be Deva Sūri, *Pramāṇanayatattvālokālaṃkāra*. On this and other Jaina texts, see S. Dasgupta, *A History of Indian Philosophy*. Delhi: Motilal Banarsidass, 1975, Vol. 1, pp. 171-2. [66]

Ornament of Emergent Realisation. *mngon-rtogs rgyan*. Skt. *Abhisamayālaṃkāra*. Auth. Maitreyanātha. T 3786. EIPRB 1224-40. MTTWL 2-5. B.Budh. 23 (1929). BST 4 (1960). SOR 6 (1954). SOR 37 (1967). See also Lati Rinbochay et al., *Meditative States in Tibetan Buddhism*. London: Wisdom, 1982. One of the *Five Doctrines of Venerable Maitreya*. [*92, 94, 117, 159, 184, 229, 230, 671*]

Ornament of Kosala. *de-kho-na-nyid bsdus-pa'i 'grel-pa ko-sa-la'i rgyan*. Skt. *Kosalālaṃkāra*. Auth. Śākyamitra. T 2503. [*468, 488*]

Ornament of the Madhyamaka. *dbu-ma rgyan*. Skt. *Madhyamakālaṃkārakārikā*. Auth. Śāntarakṣita. T 3884. EIPRB 3487. HIL 7.1, 90-2. Ed. and trans. Masamichi Ichigō, *Madhyamakālaṃkāra*. Kyoto: Kyoto Sangyo University, 1985. [*302*]

Ornament of the Sūtras of the Greater Vehicle. *(theg-pa chen-po) mdo-sde rgyan*. Skt. *Mahāyānasūtrālaṃkārakārikā*. Auth. Maitreyanātha. T 4020. EIPRB 1253-66. MTTWL 129. BST 13 (1970). Trans. R. A. F. Thurman, *Ornament of the Scriptures of the Universal Vehicle*. Forthcoming. One of the *Five Doctrines of Venerable Maitreya*. [*78, 79-80, 95, 98, 140-1, 173, 177, 193, 219, 220*]

Pacification. *zhi-byed*. A major teaching tradition stemming from Pha-dam-pa Sangs-rgyas. Representative texts may be found in DZ Vol. 9. Refer also to the articles by B. N. Aziz listed in the final section of the Bibliography. [*395, 551, 565, 577, 578, 762, 833, 929*] See also *Three Traditions of Pacification*

Pacification according to the Early, Middle and Later Traditions. *zhi-byed snga-phyi-bar gsum*. Refer to the preceding entry; and, for the history of these traditions, to *Blue Annals*, Ch. 12.

Pacification and Object of Cutting. *zhi-gcod*. Listed separately.

Pagoda of Precious Jewels. *dkon-mchog brtsegs-pa*. Skt. *Mahāratnakūṭa*. T 45-93. EIPRB 127-35. MTTWL 122. Extensive selections trans. in TMS. Also referred to as the *Sublime Pagoda of Precious Jewels*. [*83, 235, 302-3, 334, 340, 933*]

Parkap Commentary (on the Secret Nucleus). *(gsang-ba snying-po'i ('grel-pa)) spar-khab*. Skt. *Guhyagarbhamahātantrarājaṭīkā*. Auth. Līlāvajra (Vilāsavajra). P 4718. NMKMG Vol. 23. Pub. in *Commentaries on the Guhyagarbha Tantra and other Rare Nyingma Texts from the Library of Dudjom Rinpoche*. Vol. 1. New Delhi: Sanje Dorje, 1974. I-Tib 74-900928. Zhe-chen xylo. pub. Gangtok: Dodrup Sangyey Lama, 1976. I-Tib 76-902711. [*40, 63, 464, 619, 660, 665, 669, 672, 680, 684, 730*]

Path and Fruit. *(gsung-sngags rin-po-che) lam-'bras(-dang bcas-pa'i gdams-ngag)*. Selections representing these teachings may be found in DZ Vol. 4. The most extensive redaction will be completed in about 25 vols.: *lam-'bras slob-bśad*. Dehra Dun: Sakya Centre, 1983 onwards. I-Tib 83-905043. See also *Virūpa: Rdo rje'i tshig rkang*. SSS 7 (1970). I-Tib 72-918340. [*395, 576, 578, 657, 665, 923*]

Path of Skilful Means according to Nāropā. *nā-ro'i thabs-lam*. [*546*] See *Six Doctrines of Nāropā*

Peaceful and Wrathful Aspects of the Guru. *gu-ru zhi-drag*. Disc. Nyang-ral Nyi-ma 'od-zer. See RTD Vol. 8, pp. 457-537. KCST Vol. 2, pp. 395-514. [*756*]

Peaceful and Wrathful Deities of the Magical Net. *sgyu-'phrul zhi-khro*. [*858*] See *Magical Net*

Peaceful and Wrathful Deities of the Magical Net and of the Eight Transmitted Precepts, along with the Protectors of these Transmitted Precepts. *sgyu-'phrul zhi-khro-dang bka'-brgyad skor bka'-srung bcas*. Disc. Dung-'phreng-can, and offered by him to Bdud-'dul rdo-rje. NL. [*815*]

Peaceful and Wrathful Deities, the Natural Liberation of Intention. *zhi-khro dgongs-pa rang-grol*. Disc. Karma gling-pa. RTD Vol. 4, pp. 1-281. The most comprehensive edition to appear to date has been published in 3 vols.: Delhi: Sherab Lama, 1975-6. I-Tib 75-903780. See also *Great Liberation by Hearing during the Intermediate State*. Additional selections are translated in W. Y. Evans-Wentz (ed.), *The Tibetan Book of the Great Liberation*. Oxford: Oxford University Press, 1954, pp. 195-239. [*679*, *801*]

Peaceful and Wrathful Deities, the Nucleus of Definitive Meaning. *zhi-khro nges-don snying-po*. Disc. Rig-'dzin 'Ja'-tshon snying-po. JTPD Vol. 4. Pub. Tezu, Arunachal Pradesh: Ngawang Sonam, 1979. I-Tib 79-903489. [*811*]

Peaceful and Wrathful Deities of Padma. *padma zhi-khro'i chos-skor*. See *Great Compassionate One, the Peaceful and Wrathful Deities of Padma*

Peaceful and Wrathful Guru. *gu-ru zhi-drag*. Disc. Ratna gling-pa. RLTC Vols. 3-5. [*793*]

Pearl Necklace. *mu-tig phreng-ba*. NGB Vol. 9, no. 149. GCD Vol. 2. [*56-7*, *371*]

Pehar. *pe-har*. The reference in *History* does not permit the precise identification of any given textual tradition. [*545*]

Penetrating Exegetical Tantra of the Magical Net. *bshad-rgyud thal-ba*. NGB Vol. 15, nos. 200-1. [*277*]

Penetration of Samantabhadra's Intention. *kun-bzang dgongs-pa zang-thal*. Disc. Rig-'dzin Rgod-kyi ldem-'phru-can. RTD *passim*. SSS 60-4 (1973). I-Tib 73-902355. SSS 93-6 (1979). I-Tib 79-901828. [*781*]

Penetration of Sound. *(sgra) thal-'gyur (rtsa-ba'i rgyud)*. NGB Vol. 10, no. 155. [*54-5*, *136*, *141*, *337*, *339*, *447*, *563*, *572*, *906-7*, *960-1*]

Perfect Practice of Vajrakīla. *phur-pa phun-sum tshogs-pa*. Refer to n. 704; and to the *'phrin las phun sum tshogs pa'i rgyud*. NGB Vol. 27, no. 332. [*603*, *712*]

Permissory Initiation of Hayagrīva according to the Tradition of Dagyelma. *rta-mgrin zla-rgyal-ma'i lugs-kyi rjes-gnang*. GTKT Vol. 7. [*673*, *674*]

Permissory Initiation of White Mañjuśrī according to the System of Mati. *ma-ti 'jam-dkar-gyi rjes-gnang*. GTKT Vol. 2. [*870-1*]

Pill Rites for Mañjuśrī. *ril-bu'i las-sbyor*. Refer to n. 1206. [*869*]

Piṭaka of the Bodhisattva. *byang-chub sems-dpa'i sde-snod*. Skt. *Bodhisattvapiṭaka*. T 56. MTTWL 44. [*316*]

Play of Mañjuśrī. *'jam-dpal rnam-par rol-pa*. Skt. *Mañjuśrīvikrīḍitamahāyānasūtra*. T 96. MTTWL 133. [*171*]

(Play of the) Supreme Horse. *rta-mchog rol-pa*. Skt. *Aśvottamavīṇāsamatamahātantra*. T 839. NGB Vol. 23, nos. 265-6. [*479, 534*] See also *Hayagrīva (Cycle/Tantra)*

Point of the Axioms. *gtan-tshigs thig-pa*. Skt. *Hetubindu*. Auth. Dharmakīrti. T 4213. NGB Vol. 18. EIPRB 2093-4. MTTWL 83. GOS 113 (1949). [*102*]

Point of Human Sustenance. *lugs-kyi bstan-bcos skye-bo gso-ba'i thig-pa*. Skt. *Nītiśāstrajantupoṣaṇabindu*. Auth. Nāgārjuna. T 4330. Trans. from the Mongolian by S. Frye, *Nāgārjuna's A Drop of Nourishment for the People*. LTWA, 1981. [*97, 762*]

Point of Liberation. *grol(-ba'i) thig(-le)*. Skt. *Muktitilaka*. Auth. Buddhajñānapāda. T 1859. [*252-3, 412, 453, 496*]

Point of Liberation: (the Natural Liberation of Intention). *grol-tig (dgongs-pa rang-grol)*. Disc. Shes-rab 'od-zer. RTD Vols. 4, pp. 283-337; Vol. 11, pp. 187-263; Vol. 30, pp. 347-89; Vol. 37, pp. 221-52; Vol. 41, pp. 179-211; Vol. 43, pp. 373-87; Vol. 61, pp. 97-131. [*835, 837*]

Point of Reason. *rigs-thigs*. Skt. *Nyāyabindu*. Auth. Dharmakīrti. T 4212. EIPRB 2095-112. MTTWL 147. B.Budh. 7 (1918), 24-5 (1927-8), 26 (1930-2). TSWS 2 (1955). [*102*]

Point of Spring. *dpyid-thig*. Skt. *Vasantatilaka*. Auth. Kṛṣṇācārin. T 1448. [*674*]

Por Tradition of the Great Perfection. *rdzogs-chen spor-lugs*. NL. [*651*]

Practical Techniques of Gö Tsilungpa. *'gos-rtsi-lung-pa'i phyag-bzhes*. NL. Apparently incorporated into the tradition of the *Empowerment Ceremony entitled River of Honey*. [*700*]

Praise of the Mother. *yum-la bstod-pa*. Skt. *Prajñāpāramitāstotra*. Auth. Rāhulabhadra. T 1127 (where it is attributed to Nāgārjuna). MTTWL 162. HIL 7.1, pp. 54-6, 128. BST 4 (1960). [*185*]

Prātimokṣa Sūtra. *so-thar-gyi mdo*. T 2. See C. S. Prebish, *Buddhist Monastic Discipline*. University Park/London: The Pennsylvania State University Press, 1975. [*429*]

Prayerful Offering to the Gracious Goddess. *bka'-drin lha-mo'i gsol-kha*. Disc. 'Jam-mgon Kong-sprul Blo-gros mtha'-yas. NL. [*863*]

Prayer to the Lineage of the Magical Net which begins "Trio of Sound, Light and Rays . . .". *sgyu-'phrul-gyi brgyud-pa-la sgra-'od-zer gsum-ma'i gsol-'debs*. NL. [*662*]

Precious Collected Tantras of the Ancient Translation School. *snga-'gyur rgyud-'bum rin-po-che*. See *Collected Tantras (of the Nyingmapa)*

Precious Jewel Commentary. *dkon-mchog-'grel*. See *Commentary on the Tantra of the Secret Nucleus*

Precious Source of Prosody. *(sdeb-sbyor) rin-chen 'byung-gnas*. Skt. *Chandoratnākara*. Auth. Ratnākaraśānti. T 4303-4, 4439. Refer to M. Hahn, *Ratnākaraśānti's Chandoratnākara*. Nepal Research Centre, Miscellaneous Papers, no. 34. Kathmandu, 1982. Also referred to as the *Prosody of Ratnākara*. [*105-6, 730*]

Precious Translations of the Transmitted Precepts of the Conqueror. *rgyal-ba'i bka'-'gyur rin-po-che*. [*851*] See *Kangyur*

Precious Treasury of Enlightened Attributes, (its root text and commentary). *yon-tan (rin-po-che'i) mdzod (rtsa-'grel)*. Auth. 'Jigs-med gling-pa. JLSB Vols. 1-2. NMKMG Vol. 38. Pub. Bodhnath, Nepal: Ngagyur Dojod Ling, 1981. N-Tib 82-902339. The root text alone pub. Thimphu: Kunzang Tobgey, 1975. I(Bhu)-Tib 76-900257. [*92*, *839*]

Precious Treasury of the Supreme Vehicle. *theg-mchog rin-po-che'i mdzod*. See *Treasury of the Supreme Vehicle*

Precious Wish-fulfilling Treasury. See *Wish-fulfilling Treasury*

Profound Inner Meaning. *rang-byung zhabs-kyi nang-don* or *zab-mo nang-don*. Auth. Karma-pa III, Rang-byung rdo-rje. Xylo. Rum-btegs, Sikkim. I(Sik)-Tib 76-921408. [*202*, *730*, *827*] See also *Two Short Treatises*

Profound Instruction concerning the Protectors of the Teaching. *bstan-pa srung-ba'i gdams-zab*. Disc. O-rgyan gling-pa. NA.

Profoundly Significant, Secret Innermost Spirituality. *zab-don gsang-ba snying-thig*. Disc. Bdud-'dul rdo-rje. NA. [*815*]

Profound and Vast Creation and Perfection of the Cycle of Means for the Attainment of the Guru. *rtsa-ba bla-sgrub-kyi skor bskyed-rdzogs zab-rgyas*. Disc. 'Jam-dbyangs mkhyen-brtse'i dbang-po. RTD Vol. 17, pp. 165-231. The first part of the *Innermost Spirituality of the Accomplished Master*. [*804*]

Profusely Annotated Magical Net. *sgyu-'phrul mchan-mang*. NL. [*701*]

Proof of Mind in its Natural State (along with its Branches). *gnyugs-sems sgrub-pa (yan-lag dang-bcas-pa)*. [*198*] See *Cycle of Mind in its Natural State*

Proof of Other Minds. *rgyud-gzhan grub-pa*. Skt. *Saṃtānāntarasiddhi*. Auth. Dharmakīrti. T 4219. EIPRB 2132-4. B.Budh. 19 (1916). MTTWL 200. [*102*]

Proof of the Secret Nucleus. *gsang-snying sgrub-pa (rgyan-gyi me-tog)*. Auth. Bcom-ldan Rig-pa'i ral-gri. Refer to n. 1276. [*914-16*]

Propensity for the Commitments. *dam-tshig phra-rgyas*. Skt. *Samayānuśa-yanirdeśa*. Auth. Līlāvajra (Vilāsavajra). P 4745. [*464*]

Prophecy Addressed to Vimaladevī. *lha-mo dri-ma med-pa lung bstan-pa*. Unidentified. [*508*]

Prophecy of Cangcup Lingpa Pelgi Gyeltsen. *byang-chub gling-pa dpal-gyi rgyal-mtshan-gyi lung-bstan*. Disc. Sangs-rgyas gling-pa. NL. [*786*]

Prophecy from the Treasure of Ratna Lingpa. *ratna gling-pa'i gter-lung*. Disc. Ratna gling-pa. The passage quoted in *History* is attributed to the *tshes-bcu bskul-thabs*. RTD Vol. 16, pp. 121-7. [*744-5*, *935*]

Prophecy from the Treasures of Glorious Trashi Topgyel. *dpal bkra-shis stobs-rgyal-gyi gter-lung*. NL. [*822*]

Prophecy from the Treasures of Trime Künga. *dri-med kun-dga'i gter-lung*. Disc. Dri-med kun-dga'. NL. [*935*]

Prophetic Declaration of Intention. *dgongs-pa lung-ston*. Skt. *Sandhivyākaraṇatantra*. T 444. [*256*]

Prophetic Declaration (about Sangye Lingpa). *sangs-rgyas gling-pa'i lung-bstan*. NL. [*787*]

Prophetic Declaration of the Three Classes of the Great Perfection. *rdzogs-chen sde-gsum-gyi lung-bstan*. Disc. Mchog-gyur bde-chen gling-pa. NL. Perhaps to be found among the available texts of the *Three Classes of the Great Perfection*. Also referred to as the *Prophetic Inventory of the Three Classes of the Great Perfection*. [*844*, *854*]

Prophetic Inventory of the Three Classes of the Great Perfection. See preceding entry

Prophetic Sūtra of Maitreya. *byams-pa lung-bstan-gyi mdo*. Skt. *Maitreyavyākaraṇasūtra*. P 1011. Skt. and Tib. edn. Prabhas Chandra Majumder, *Ārya Maitreyavyākaraṇam*. Calcutta: Firma K. L. Mukhopadhyay, 1959. [*943-4*]

Prosody of Ratnākara. *rin-chen 'byung-gnas-kyi sdeb-sbyor*. See *Precious Source of Prosody*

Protective Cover. *rgyab-sha*. NL. [*546*]

Protector of Pristine Cognition. *ye-shes mgon-po*. Refer to n. 630. [*562*]

Questions and Answers of Vajrasattva. *rdo-rje sems-dpa'i zhu-len* [*sic*]. Skt. *Vajrasattvapraśnottara*. P 5082. [*347*, *654*]

Quintessential Gathering of the Great Compassionate One. *thugs-rje chen-po yang-snying 'dus-pa*. Disc. Guru Chos-dbang. RTD Vol. 34, pp. 1-234. [*698*]

Rational System of Exposition. *rnam(-par) bshad(-pa'i) rigs-pa*. Skt. *Vyākhyāyukti*. Auth. Vasubandhu. T 4061. [*51*, *74*, *89*, *108*]

Razor Kīla. *phur-pa spu-gri*. Disc. Gter-bdag gling-pa. See *(Utterly Secret) Razor Kīla*

Realisation of Kurukullā. *ku-ru-kulle'i rtogs-pa*. Skt. *Muktakenatārodbhavakurukullesādhana*. Auth. Nāgārjuna. T 3562. [*480*]

Reasoning of Polemics. *rtsod-pa'i rigs-pa*. Skt. *Vādanyāya*. Auth. Dharmakīrti. T 4218. EIPRB 2069, 2135. BB 8 (1972). [*102*]

Recension of Vajrakīla. *rdo-rje phur-pa'i yig-cha*. Auth. Bla-ma dam-pa Bsod-nams rgyal-mtshan. NL. [*922*]

Record of Teachings Received. *gsan-yig*. Auth. Gter-bdag gling-pa. Pub. New Delhi: Sanje Dorje, 1974. I-Tib 74-900490. [*966*]

Record of Teachings Received *or* Record of Teachings Received, the Flow of the Ganges. *gsan-yig* or *gsan-yig gang-gā'i chu-rgyun*. Auth. Dalai Lama V, Ngag-dbang blo-bzang rgya-mtsho. Pub. Delhi: Nechung and Lhakhar, 1970. 4 vols. I-Tib 78-918067. Also referred to as the *Great Record of Teachings Received*. [*688*, *822*, *926*, *966*]

Red, Black and Bhairava Tantras of Yamāntaka. *gshin-rje-gshed dmar-nag-'jigs gsum*. T 468-70, 473-5, 478. NMKMG Vols. 4-6. Listed separately as *Red Yamāri (Cycle/Tantra)*, *Black Yamāri* and *Bhairava (Cycle/Tantra)*. [*283*]

Red and Black Yamāri. *gshin-rje dmar-nag*. Listed separately as *Red Yamāri (Cycle/Tantra)* and *Black Yamāri*.

Red Wrathful Guru according to the Treasure of Nyang. *nyang-gter drag-dmar*. Disc. Nyang-ral Nyi-ma 'od-zer. RTD Vol. 17, pp. 271-413. [*731*]

Red Yamāri (Cycle/Tantra). *gshin-rje-gshed dmar* or *gshed-dmar skor*. T 474-5. GDKT Vol. 8, nos. 50-1. KGNZ Vol. 5, pp. 3-83. NMKMG Vols. 5-6. Also referred to as the *Red Tantra of Yamāntaka*. [*283, 546, 578, 614, 665, 805, 807*] See also *Yamāri (Cycle/Tantra)* and *Yamāntaka and Yamāri: Introductory Note*

Refined Gold of the Profound Great Perfection. *zab-pa rdzogs-chen gser-zhun*. Disc. Mchog-gyur bde-chen gling-pa. CLTC Vols. 24 and 30. [*846*]

Refinement of Gold from Ore, a Great Tantra of the Mental Class. *sems-sde rgyud chen-po rdo-la gser-zhun*. NGB Vol. 1, no. 14. MPSB Vol. 11. Trans. Namkai Norbu and K. Lipman, *Primordial Experience*. Boston: Shambhala, 1987. [*901*]

Refutation of Disputed Topics. *dbu-ma rtsod-bzlog*. Skt. *Vigrahavyāvartanī*. Auth. Nāgārjuna. T 3828. EIPRB 669, 699-707. MTTWL 248. HIL 7.1, pp. 21-3, 127, 130. BST 10 (1960). GOS 49 (1929). MCB 9 (1951). [*94, 167*]

Rejections of Perverse Doctrines. *chos-log sun-'byin*. General designation for Tibetan polemical writings on texts and practices held to be inauthentic. A representative collection is *Sṅags log sun 'byin gyi skor*. Thimphu: Kunsang Topgyel and Mani Dorji, 1979. Bhu-Tib 81-901052. See also *Collected Writings of Sog-bzlog-pa Blo-gros-rgyal-mtshan*. 2 vols. New Delhi: Sanje Dorje, 1975. I-Tib 75-900763. [*929*]

Removal of Darkness: A Commentary on the Superior Magical Net. *sgyu-'phrul bla-ma'i 'grel-pa mun-sel*. Auth. Vimalamitra. NL. [*481*]

Repository of Precious Gems. *dkar-chag rin-po-che'i mdzod-khang*. Auth. Chos-grags bzang-po. Included in the same author's biography of Klong-chen Rab-'byams-pa: *kun-mkhyen dri-med 'od-zer-gyi rnam-thar mthong-ba don-ldan*. NYZ, *bi-ma snying-thig*, Pt. 3, Vol. *Tsha*. [*591*]

Revelation of Endless Treasure. *mi-zad-pa'i gter bstan-pa*. NL. [*77*]

Ṛgveda. *snyan-ngag*. The first of the *Four Veda*. HIL 1.1, especially Chs. 3-6. [*65*]

Rites of the Service and Attainment of the Immortal Wish-granting Wheel. *'chi-med yid-bzhin 'khor-lo'i bsnyen-sgrub*. GTKT Vol. 1. KGNZ Vol. 1, pp. 55-206. [*857*]

Rite which Ties by the Rope of the Compassion of the Gathering of the Sugatas. *bde-'dus-kyi thugs-rje dpyang-thag gnas-kyi-lung*. Auth. Vajradharma. P 4781. [*68*]

Ritual for Burnt Offerings. *sbyin-sreg*. Skt. *Māyājālahomasaṃkṣiptakrama*. Auth. Vimalamitra. P 4746. [*481*]

Ritual for Empowerment. *dbang-gi cho-ga*. Auth. Rdo-rje rgyal-mtshan. NL. [*687*]

Ritual Geometry. *thig-rim*. Auth. Vimalamitra. NL. [*481*]

Ritual Guide. *chog-khrid*. Auth. Gnyal-pa Bde-legs. NL. [*672*]

Root Attainment of Mind, the Gathering of All Intentions. *rtsa-ba'i thugs-sgrub dgongs-pa kun-'dus*. Disc. Mchog-gyur bde-chen gling-pa. CLTC Vol. 2. [*845*]

Root Fragment of Vajrakīla. *phur-pa rtsa-ba'i dum-bu*. [*710*, *761*] See also *Basic Root Tantra of Vajrakīla*

Root Stanzas on the Madhyamaka entitled Discriminative Awareness. *dbu-ma rtsa-ba shes-rab*. Skt. *Prajñānāmamūlamadhyamakakārikā*. Auth. Nāgārjuna. T 3824. EIPRB 644-78. MTTWL 135. HIL 7.1, pp. 9-18, 126-7, 130. BBud. 4 (1903-13). BST 10 (1960). V. Fatone, *The Philosophy of Nāgārjuna*. Delhi: Motilal Banarsidass, 1981. D. Kalupahana (trans.), *Mūlamadhyamakakārikās*. Albany: SUNY Press, 1986. [*94*, *167*, *228*, *299*, *321*]

Root Sūtra of the Vinaya. *'dul-ba mdo rtsa-ba*. Skt. *Vinayamūlasūtra*. Auth. Guṇaprabha. T 4117. Ed. Jha. TSWS (1982). [*90*, *92*, *93*, *874*]

(Root Tantra of) All-Gathering Awareness. *(rtsa-rgyud) kun-'dus rig-pa*. T 831. NGB Vol. 12, no. 162. [*285*, *289*, *364*, *366-7*, *368-9*, *673*, *674*]

Root Tantra of Cakrasaṃvara. *bde-mchog rtsa-rgyud*. See *Short Tantra of Cakrasaṃvara*

Root Tantra of the Gathering of Awareness-holders. *rig-'dzin 'dus-pa rtsa-ba'i rgyud*. NGB Vol. 32, no. 386. KGDD Vol. 2. [*607*]

Root Tantra of the Gathering of the Sugatas. *bder-'dus rtsa-rgyud*. NGB Vol. 31, no. 375. KGDD Vol. 2. [*449*]

Root Tantra of the Kālacakra. *dus-'khor rtsa-rgyud*. Skt. *Kālacakranāmatantrarāja*. T 362. See *Kālacakra Tantra*

Root Tantra of the Magical Net. *sgyu-'phrul rtsa-rgyud*. See *Tantra of the Secret Nucleus*

Root Tantra of Mañjuśrī. *'jam-dpal rtsa-rgyud*. Skt. *Mañjuśrīmūlatantra*. T 543. BST 18 (1964). A. Macdonald, *Le Maṇḍala du Mañjuśrīmūlakalpa*. Paris: A. Maisonneuve, 1962. Macdonald's bibliography, pp. 177-81, thoroughly documents earlier studies of this tantra. [*435*, *507*, *510*]

Root Tantra of the Penetration of Sound. *sgra thal-'gyur rtsa-ba'i rgyud*. [*960-1*] See *Penetration of Sound*

Root Tantra (of the Secret Nucleus). *rtsa-rgyud (gsang(-ba) snying(-po))*. See *Tantra of the Secret Nucleus*

Root Tantra of Vajrakīla. *rdo-rje phur-pa'i rtsa-rgyud*. See *Vajrakīla (Cycle/Tantra)*

Root Text of Caṇḍālī, Mother of Life. *tshe-yum tsaṇḍā-lī'i rtsa-ba*. Disc. 'Jam-dbyangs mkhyen-brtse'i dbang-po. RTD Vol. 77, pp. 389-400. [*855*] See also *Cycle of Instructions on Caṇḍālī, Mother of Life, from the Innermost Spirituality of Immortality*

Root Text of the Vinaya Sūtra. *'dul-ba mdo-rtsa*. See *Root Sūtra of the Vinaya*

Root Text of Yangdak. *yang-dag rtsa-ba*. See *Yangdak Heruka (Cycle/Tantra)*

Root Verses of the Six Stages of Perfection. *rdzogs-rim drug-gi rtsa-tshigs*. Disc. 'Jam-dbyangs mkhyen-brtse'i dbang-po. Part of the *Innermost Spirituality of the Accomplished Master*. [*855*]

Royal Lady's Tradition of Vajrakīla. *phur-pa lcam-lugs*. [*710-12*]

Sakya Tradition of Vajrakīla. *phur-pa sa-lugs*. [*712*] See *Khön Tradition of Vajrakīla*

Sāmaveda. *nges-brjod*. The third of the *Four Veda*. HIL 1.1, Ch. 7, pp. 313-22. [*65*]

Sampuṭa Tantra. *sam-pu-ṭa, yang-dag-pa sbyor-ba* or *kha-sbyor*. T 381-2. KGNZ Vol. 2, pp. 359-468. [*578*] See also *Glorious Seminal Point of Embrace*

Saṃvara Buddhasamāyoga. *bde-mchog sangs-rgyas mnyam-sbyor*. Disc. Mchog-gyur bde-chen gling-pa. CLTC Vol. 24. RTD Vol. 5, pp. 281-403. [*846*]

Sārasvata Grammar. *sara-sva-sti* [*sic*] or *dbyangs-can sgra mdo*. Skt. *Sārasvatavyākaraṇa*. Auth. Anubhūtisvarūpācārya. T 4423. TWPS 75. HIL 5.2, pp. 189-90. Skt. edn. Nava Kishora Kara Śarma. Varanasi, 1935-6. [*730*]

Scholar's Feast of Doctrinal History. *chos-'byung mkhas-pa'i dga'-ston*. Auth. Dpa'-bo Gtsug-lag 'phreng-ba. Delhi: Delhi Karmapae Chodey Gyalwae Sungrab Partun Khang, 1980. I-Tib 81-900485. SP 9 (1961). [*965*]

Secret Cycles. *gsang-skor*. A classification of the Great Perfection. [*332, 570-1*]

Secret Innermost Spirituality of the Great Perfection. *rdzogs-pa chen-po gsang-ba snying-tig*. Refers generally to the Esoteric Instructional Class of the Great Perfection, on which see *Fundamentals*, pp. 329-45; and in particular the *Four-Part Innermost Spirituality*. [*329-45*]

Secret Magical Net. *gsang-ba sgyu-'phrul*. See *Tantra of the Secret Nucleus*

Secret Means for the Attainment of Red Jambhala. *dzam-dmar gsang-sgrub*. Disc. Grva-pa mngon-shes. RTD Vol. 79, pp. 271-331. [*753*]

Secret Mirror of the Essence. *gsang-ba gnad-kyi me-long*. Unidentified. [*569*]

Secret Nucleus (of the Magical Net). *((sgyu-'phrul) gsang-ba) snying-po*. See *Tantra of the Secret Nucleus*

Secret Tantra of General Rites. *gsang-ba spyi-rgyud*. Skt. *Sarvamaṇḍalasāmānyavidhīnāṃ guhyatantra*. T 806. GDKT Vol. 1, no. 1. GTKT Vol. 2. Note that where the context suggests that the tantra referred to under this title is a tantra of the Great Perfection, it is to be identified not with T 806, but with NGB Vol. 3, no. 48. [*350*]

Secret Tantra of Vajrakīla. *phur-pa gsang-rgyud*. NGB Vol. 27, no. 315. [*712*]

Secret Tantra of (Wrathful) Mañjuśrī. *'jam-dpal gsang-ba'i rgyud* or *'jam-dpal khros-pa gsang-rgyud*. Skt. *Mañjuśrīkarmacatuścakraguhyatantra*. T 838. NGB Vols. 20-2. [*477, 708*]

Secret Treasury of the Ḍākinī. *mkha'-'gro-ma'i gsang-mdzod*. NL. [*304*]

Seminal Point of Pristine Cognition. *ye-shes thig-le*. Skt. *Jñānatilakatantra*. T 422. [*349*, *352*, *354*, *363*]

Sequence of the Activity of Indestructible Reality. *rdo-rje las-rim*. Skt. *Vajrakarmakrama*. P 4761. [*360*]

Sequence of the Empowerment of Cakrasaṃvara. *'khor-lo bde-mchog-gi dbang-bskur-gyi rim-pa*. The tradition transmitted through the lineage of the Karma-pa is represented by GDKT Vol. 12, no. 67. KGNZ Vol. 3, pp. 3-202. [*689*]

Sequence of Indestructible Activity. *sgyu-'phrul rdo-rje las-rim*. Skt. *Māyājālavajrakarmakrama*. Auth. Buddhaguhya. P 4720. [*466*]

Sequence of the Path (of the Magical Net). *(sgyu-'phrul) lam-rim*. Skt. *Māyājālapathakrama*. Auth. Buddhaguhya. P 4736. NMKMG Vol. 23. The shorter version, listed here as the *Lesser (Sequence of the) Path*, is given in DZ Vol. 1, pp. 1-15. [*24*, *40*, *60*, *62*, *68*, *92*, *96*, *123*, *225*, *229*, *234-5*, *243*, *245*, *249*, *251-2*, *270*, *279*, *348-9*, *353*, *361*, *462*, *466*, *476*, *619*, *665*, *672*]

Sequence of the Path of Secret Mantra. *gsang-sngags lam-rim*. This perhaps refers to the treasure of this title discovered by Nyang-ral Nyi-ma 'od-zer. Pub., with an extensive commentary, in SSS 35 (1972). I-Tib 72-903208. [*669*]

Sequence of the Supreme Point concerning the Stage of Perfection of Hevajra. *dgyes-pa rdo-rje'i rdzogs-rim thig-le chen-po'i rim-pa*. Skt. *Mahātilakakrama*. Auth. Līlāvajra (Vilāsavajra). T 1290. [*464*]

Sequence of the View. *lta-rim*. Skt. *Dṛṣṭikramanirdeśa*. See *(Seventeenfold Appearance of the) Sequence of the View*

Service and Attainment of the Three Indestructible Realities. *rdo-rje gsum-gyi bsnyen-sgrub*. See *Oḍḍiyāna Tradition of Ritual Service and Attainment*

Seven Chapters on the Profound Path. *lam-zab le'u bdun-ma*. Disc. 'Jam-mgon Kong-sprul Blo-gros mtha'-yas. RTD Vol. 7, pp. 439-60. [*866*]

Seven Cycles. *sde-skor bdun-pa*. Transmitted in the lineage of Gyelwa Potön. Possibly to be identified with the Taoist inspired lineage of the *rDe'u skor bdun-pa*, Auth. Bla-ma Sro-ba. See S. G. Karmay, *The Origin and Early Development of the Tibetan Religious Traditions of the Great Perfection*. Ph.D. thesis. University of London, 1976, pp. 362, 376, n. 2. [*547*]

Seven Cycles of the Great Perfection which are Naturally Present. *rdzogs-pa chen-po skor-bdun rang-chas*. Listed in the Glossary of Enumerations. [*545*]

Seven Cycles of the Jewel of True Doctrine. *dam-chos nor-bu skor-bdun*. Disc. Mchog-gyur bde-chen gling-pa. Not yet precisely identified among the works preserved in CLTC. [*845*]

Seven Cycles of Pacification. *zhi-byed skor-bdun*. Disc. Mchog-gyur bde-chen gling-pa. CLTC Vol. 24. RTD Vol. 72, pp. 435-541. [*845*]

Seven Cycles of the Peaceful Guru. *gu-ru zhi-ba sde-skor bdun-pa*. NL. Alternatively, this may be a compound meaning "Peaceful Guru and Seven Cycles", for the second of which see *Seven Cycles* above. [*548*]

Seven Cycles of Profound Contemplation. *thugs-dam zab-pa skor-bdun*. Disc. Mchog-gyur bde-chen gling-pa. CLTC Vols. 14-19. RTD *passim*. [*845*]

Seven Great Treasuries. *mdzod-chen bdun*. Auth. Klong-chen Rab-'byams-pa. Listed separately as *Treasury of the Abiding Nature of Reality*, *Treasury of Esoteric Instructions*, *Treasury of the Expanse of Reality*, *Treasury of Spiritual and Philosophical Systems*, *Treasury of the Supreme Vehicle*, *Treasury of Word and Meaning* and *Wish-fulfilling Treasury*. For translated selections, see Tulku Thondup Rinpoche, *Buddha Mind*. Ithaca, NY: Snow Lion, 1989. Also referred to as the *Seven Treasuries (of the Scriptures)*. [*40*, *91*, *591*]

Seven Nails. *gzer-bu bdun*. Auth. Śrīsiṃha. NYZ, *bi-ma snying-thig*, Pt. 1, Vol. *Ga*, pp. 318-25. DZ Vol. 1, pp. 474-6. [*500*]

Seven Sections of the Abhidharma. *mngon-pa sde-bdun*. Listed separately as *Body of Consciousness*, *Body of the Elemental Bases*, *Components of the Doctrine*, *Dissertation*, *Entrance to Knowledge*, *Enumeration of Classes*, and *Treatise on Description*. Concerning this classification scheme in general, see L. de La Vallée Poussin, *L'Abhidharmakośa de Vasubandhu*. Paris: Paul Geuthner, 1923-36, Vol. 1, pp. xxix-xlii. HBI, pp. 197-210. [*90-1*]

Seven Sections of Valid Cognition. *(tshad-ma) sde-bdun*. Auth. Dharmakīrti. Listed separately as *Ascertainment of Valid Cognition*, *Exposition of Valid Cognition*, *Inquiry into Relations*, *Point of the Axioms*, *Point of Reason*, *Proof of Other Minds* and *Reasoning of Polemics*. Also referred to as the *Seven Treatises on Valid Cognition*. [92, *102*, *577*]

Seven Sessions of Aro (Yeshe Jungne). *a-ro thun-bdun*. DZ Vol. 1, pp. 356-71. NMKMG Vol. 17. Refer to n. 608. Also referred to as the *Essential Spirituality of Aro* and the *Esoteric Instructions of the Great Perfection according to Aro*. [*550*, *651*, *673*, *675*] See also *Cycle of Meaning, which is Aro's Great System of Guidance*

Seven Tantras of Subtle Meaning. *phra-ba rgyud-bdun*. [*137*]

(Seventeenfold Appearance of the) Sequence of the View. *lta-rim (snang-ba bcu-bdun-pa)*. Auth. Ska-ba Dpal-brtsegs. T 4356. NMKMG Vol. 23. On this text, see K. Mimaki, *Blo gsal grub mtha'*. Kyoto: Zinbun Kagaku Kenkyusyo, 1982, pp. 41-2. [*40*, *96*, *224-5*, *229*, *349*, *353*, *354-5*]

Seventeen Tantras (of the Esoteric Instructional Class). *(man-ngag sde'i) rgyud bcu-bdun*. GCD. NGB Vols. 9-10, nos. 143-59. These are the *Natural Arising of Awareness* (*rig-pa rang-shar*), *Mirror of the Heart of Vajrasattva* (*rdo-rje sems-dpa' snying-gi me-long*), *Lion's Perfect Expressive Power* (*seng-ge rtsal-rdzogs*), *Absence of Syllables* (*yi-ge med-pa*), *Beauteous Good Auspices* (*bkra-shis mdzes-ldan*), *Penetration of Sound* (*sgra thal-'gyur*), *Mirror of the Heart of Samantabhadra* (*kun-tu bzang-po thugs-kyi me-long*), *Blazing Lamp* (*sgron-ma 'bar-ba*), *Array of Fine Gemstones* (*nor-bu 'phra-bkod*), *Coalescence of Sun and Moon* (*nyi-zla kha-sbyor*), *Pearl Necklace* (*mu-tig phreng-ba*), the *Natural Liberation of Awareness* (*rig-pa rang-grol*), *Sixfold Expanse* (*klong drug-pa*), *Naturally Born Perfection* (*rdzogs-pa rang-byung*), *Black Wrathful Goddess* (*nag-mo khros-ma*),

Blazing Relics of Buddha-body (*sku-gdung 'bar-ba*) and *Mound of Gemstones* (*rin-chen spungs*). The empowerment rites associated with the collection are found in NMKMG Vol. 20. An antique manuscript redaction, unfortunately incomplete, has also appeared: Sumra, HP: Orgyan Dorji, 1977. I-Tib 78-906111. [*37*, *562*, *723*]

Seven Texts on Royal Geneology. *rgyal-rabs sde-bdun*. NA. [*762*]

Seven Treasuries (of the Scriptures). *(gsung-rab) mdzod-bdun*. [*40*, *91*] See *Seven Great Treasuries*

Seventy Literary Transmissions (of Anuyoga). *lung-gi yi-ge bdun-cu*. These are to be identified with the enumeration of *lung-phran bdun-cu rtsa-lnga* mentioned in Sog-zlog-pa blo-gros rgyal-mtshan, *rnam-thar yid-kyi mun-sel*, pp. 134-5. [*289*]

Seventy Verses on Emptiness. *stong-nyid bdun-cu-pa*. Skt. *Śūnyatāsaptati*. Auth. Nāgārjuna. T 3827. MTTWL 222. HIL 7.1, pp. 20-1. BIT 8 (1985). Trans. D. R. Komito, *Nāgārjuna's "Seventy Stanzas"*. Ithaca, NY: Snow Lion, 1987. For references to several recent contributions to the study of this work, see idem, "Insight and Liberation in Nāgārjuna's *Seventy Stanzas on Emptiness*" in STC, pp. 342-57. [*94*]

Seventy Verses on Going for Refuge. *skyabs-'gro bdun-cu-pa*. Skt. *Triśaraṇasaptati*. Auth. Candrakīrti. T 3971. [*70*]

Shangpa Doctrines. *shangs-chos*. DZ Vol. 8. GDKT Vol. 21, nos. 120-2. GTKT Vols. 5, 9, 11. Bo-doṅ paṇ-chen Phyogs-las-rnam-rgyal, *Encyclopedia Tibetica*, Vols. 86, 93, 103. New Delhi: Tibet House, 1969 onwards. I-Tib 78-905620. [*802*] See also *Five Golden Doctrines of the Shangpas*

Short Biography of Padmasambhava. *padma'i rnam-thar chung-ba*. Disc. O-rgyan gling-pa. Xylo. Lcem-re Monastery, Ladakh. I-Tib-384. Xylo. Enchay Monastery, Gangtok, Sikkim. I(Sik)-Tib 72-906714. [*776*]

Short Chapter on Discrimination. *'byed-pa le'u-chung*. NL. [*59-60*]

Short Commentary. *'grel-chung*. Skt. *Abhisamayālaṃkāranāmaprajñāpāramitopadeśaśāstravṛtti* or *Sphuṭārtha*. Auth. Haribhadra. T 3793. Ed. Hirofusa Amano, *A Study on the Abhisamaya-Alaṃkāra-Kārikā-Śāstra-Vṛtti*. Tokyo: Japan Science Press, 1975. [*163*, *546*]

Short Commentary on the Secret Nucleus. *snying-po'i 'grel-chung*. Skt. *Śrīguhyagarbhapiṇḍārthaṭīkā*. Auth. Vimalamitra. P 4755. [*131*, *481*]

Short Tantra of Cakrasaṃvara. *bde-mchog nyung-ngu'i rgyud*. Skt. *Tantrarājaśrīlaghusaṃvara*. T 368. Also referred to as the *Root Tantra of Cakrasaṃvara*. [*205*, *451*, *708*]

Significance of the Maṇḍala Doctrine. *dkyil-'khor chos-don*. Skt. *Dharmamaṇḍalasūtra*. Auth. Buddhaguhya. T 3705. [*466*]

Sikkimese Tradition of the Great Perfection. *'bras-ljongs rdzogs-chen-pa'i ring-lugs*. This is the tradition of Lha-btsun Nam-mkha' 'jigs-med, who travelled to Sikkim in 1646. [*818-20*]

Six Arrays of Esoteric Meaning. *gsang-don rnam-par bkod-pa drug*. Skt. *Ṣaḍguhyārthadharavyūha*. Auth. Kukkurāja. T 1664-9. [*461*, *533*]

Six Doctrines (of Nāropā). *nā-ro chos-drug-gi man-ngag*. The *locus classicus* is T 2330, *Ṣaḍdharmopadeśa*. Auth. Tilopā. For their elaboration within the various Mar-pa Bka'-brgyud lineages, see DZ Vols. 5-7. Refer also to H. V. Guenther, *The Life and Teaching of Nāropā*. Oxford: Clarendon Press, 1963. On their formulation within the Dge-lugs-pa tradition, see G. C. C. Chang (trans.), *Esoteric Teachings of the Tibetan Tantras*. Ed. C. A. Muses. York Beach, Maine: Samuel Weiser, 1983. [*547*, *549*, *569*, *577*, *578*, *674*, *689*, *929*]

Six Doctrines of Varāhī. *phag-mo'i chos-drug*. Identified in *Blue Annals* as T 1551-6. [*576*]

Six Experiences of Meditation. *sgom-nyams drug-pa*. Auth. Mañjuśrīmitra. NYZ, *bi-ma snying-thig*, Pt. 1, Vol. *Ga*, pp. 304-31. DZ Vol. 1, pp. 476-8. [*498*]

Six-faced One. *gdong-drug*. Skt. *Ṣaḍānana*. Auth. Devākaracandra. T 2015. [*477*]

Sixfold Sequence. *rim-pa drug-pa*. Skt. *Kramaṣaṭka*. Auth. Līlāvajra (Vilāsavajra). P 4741. [*464*]

Six-limbed Yoga (of the Kālacakra). *sbyor-drug* or *(dus-kyi 'khor-lo'i) sbyor-ba yan-lag drug*. Skt. *Ṣaḍaṅgayoga*. Auth. Anupamarakṣita. T 1367. DZ Vol. 10. [*301*, *546*, *577*, *578*, *674*]

Six-limbed Yoga and its Means to Remove Obstacles. *sbyor-drug gegs-sel-dang bcas-pa*. As above. Tāranātha's redaction of the *Means to Remove Obstacles* is preserved in DZ Vol. 10, pp. 266-310. [*578*]

Six Million Four Hundred Thousand Verses (of the Great Perfection). *(rdzogs-chen) śva-lo-ka 'bum-phrag drug-cu-rtsa-bzhi*. Traditional enumeration of the volume of the *rdzogs-chen* tantras. [*332*, *493*, *539*, *922*]

Six Root Tantras of the Gathering of Intentions. *dgongs-'dus rtsa-ba'i rgyud drug*. Disc. Sangs-rgyas gling-pa. Perhaps to be identified with the six tantras given in BMGD Vol. 3. [*786*]

Six Scrolls of True Doctrine. *dam-chos shog-sde drug-pa*. Disc. Mchog-gyur bde-chen gling-pa. CLTC Vol. 20. RTD Vol. 42, pp. 433-67. [*846*]

Six Secret Tantras (of Vajrakīla). *(phur-pa) gsang-ba'i rgyud drug*. Their precise identification remains somewhat unclear: several of the tantras in NGB Vols. 27-9 are (sub)titled *Secret Tantra of Vajrakīla*. [*712*]

Six Suns of the Heart. *snying-gi nyi-ma drug*. NL. [*658*] See also *Sun of the Heart of Contemplation*

Six Tantras which Clarify the Six Limits (of Anuyoga). *mtha'-drug gsal-bar byed-pa'i rgyud drug*. These are: *kun-tu bzang-po che-ba rang-la gnas-pa'i rgyud*, NGB Vol. 12, no. 164; *dbang bskur rgyal-po*, NGB Vol. 12, no. 165; *ting-'dzin mchog*, NGB Vol. 12, no. 166; *skabs sbyor bdun-pa*, NGB Vol. 12, no. 168; *brtson-pa don-bden*, NGB Vol. 12, no. 169; *dam-tshig bkod-pa*, NGB Vol. 12, no. 167. [*289*]

Sixty Verses on Reason. *rigs-pa drug-cu-pa*. Skt. *Yuktiṣaṣṭikā*. Auth. Nāgārjuna. T 3825. EIPRB 708-9. MTTWL 262. HIL 7.1, pp. 19-20. [*94*]

Skull-Mirror of Indestructible Reality, which is Indicative of the Transmitted Precepts of the Gathering of Intentions. *dgongs-'dus bka'-rtags rdo-rje thod-pa me-long*. Disc. Mchog-gyur bde-chen gling-pa. NL. It is possible that this is to be interpreted as referring to ritual objects rather than to a text, i.e. "a vajra, a skull and a mirror, which are (symbolic) indications of the transmitted precepts of the *Gathering of Intentions*." [*845*]

So Tradition of the Sūtra, the Magical Net and the Mental Class. *so-lugs-kyi mdo-dang sgyu-'phrul-dang sems-phyogs*. NL. [*701*]

Song of Esoteric Instruction: An Inexhaustible Treasure Store. *mi-zad-pa'i gter-mdzod man-ngag-gi glu*. Skt. *Dohākośopadeśagīti*. Auth. Saraha. T 2264. [*335*] See also *Dohā (of Saraha)*

Song of Indestructible Reality in Answer to Questions Posed in a Trilogy by the Goddess of Longevity, which is the Root of the Aural Lineage of Ngamdzong. *ngam-rdzong snyan-brgyud rtsa-ba tshe-ring skor-gsum-gyi zhus-lan rdo-rje'i mgur*. Auth. Mi-la-ras-pa. See G. C. C. Chang (trans.), *The Hundred Thousand Songs of Milarepa*. New Hyde Park, New York: University Books, 1962, Sect. 29. [*200-1*]

Song of Instruction Given to Lord Marpa. *mnga'-bdag mar-pa-la gdams-pa'i mgur*. Refer to n. 196. DZ Vol. 5, pp. 63-6. [*200*]

Song with a View to the Expanse of Reality. *chos-dbyings-la lta-ba'i glu*. Skt. *Dharmadhātudarśanagīti*. Auth. Dīpaṃkara (Atiśa). T 2314. [*198-9*]

Southern (Treasures of Pema Lingpa) and the Northern (Treasures of Rikdzin Gödemcen). *lho-byang-gis mtshon-pa'i rdzogs-chen zab-gter*. The "Southern Treasures" are chiefly those of Padma gling-pa, though in certain contexts this may also refer to the "New Treasures" (*gter-gsar*) of Gter-bdag gling-pa. The "Northern Treasures" are generally the discoveries of Rig-'dzin Rgod-kyi ldem-'phru-can and his successors. [*919*]

Special Transmitted Precepts of the Mental Class known as the Eighteen Significations of the syllable A. *sems-sde a-don bco-brgyad-kyi sgos-bka'*. See *Eighteen Esoteric Instructions of the Mental Class*

Spontaneous Song of the Clouds. *sprin-gyi thol-glu*. See *(Doctrinal Cycle of the) Spontaneous Song of the Clouds*

Śrīheruka. See *Heruka*

Stage of Creation for the Peaceful and Wrathful Guru, Three Cycles on the Two Teachings. *bskyed-rim gu-ru bstan-gnyis skor-gsum zhi-drag*. Disc. O-rgyan gling-pa. NA. [*775*]

Stages of the Realisation of the Peaceful and Wrathful Deities. *zhi(-ba-dang) khro(-ba'i) mngon(-par) rtogs(-pa'i) rim-pa*. Auth. Buddhaguhya. NL. [*466*]

Stanzas on the Novitiate. *dge-tshul-gyi kā-ri-kā*. Skt. *Āryamūlasarvāstivādiśrāmaṇerakārikā*. Either T 4124 by Śākyaprabha, or T 4127 by Nāgārjuna. The latter, which is generally more popular for use in elementary instruction in Tibet, ed. and trans. in Lobsang Dagpa et al., *The Discipline of the Novice Monk*. Mussoorie, UP: Sakya College, 1975. The former is also referred to as the *Three Hundred Verses on the Vinaya*. [*92, 730, 911*]

Store which Embraces All Knowledge. *shes-bya kun-la khyab-pa'i mdzod*. Auth. 'Jam-mgon Kong-sprul Blo-gros mtha'-yas. SP 80 (1970). I-Tib

77-913514. GCKZ Vols. 17-20. Typeset edn. in 3 vols. Beijing: Minorities Press, 1982. [*861*] See also *Five Great Stores*

Store of Precious Instructions. *gdams-ngag rin-po-che'i mdzod*. Auth. 'Jam-mgon kong-sprul Blo-gros mtha'-yas. DZ. Besides this, a second edition has appeared in 17 vols. Paro: Lama Ngodrup and Sherab Drimey, 1979. I(Bhu)-Tib 79-906514. [*861*] See also *Five Great Stores*

Store of Precious Treasure. *rin-chen gter-mdzod*. See *(Great) Store of Precious Treasure*

Subjugation of Demons. *'byung-po 'dul-byed*. Skt. *Bhūtaḍāmaratantra*. T 747. GTKT Vol. 3. [*271*]

Sublime Great Bounteousness of the Buddhas. See *Sūtra of the Great Bounteousness of the Buddhas*

Sublime Lasso of Skilful Means. *'phags-pa thabs-kyi zhags-pa*. T 835. [*253*]

Sublime Litany of the Names of Mañjuśrī. *('phags-pa) 'jam-dpal-gyi mtshan (yang-dag-par) brjod(-pa)*. Skt. *Mañjuśrīnāmasaṃgīti*. [*463*] See *Litany of the Names of Mañjuśrī*

Sublime Pagoda of Precious Jewels. See *Pagoda of Precious Jewels*

Sublime Seal of Great Realisation. *'phags-pa rtogs-chen phyag-rgya*. T 265. [*85*]

Sublime Sūtra of Clouds of Precious Jewels. *'phags-pa dkon-mchog sprin-gyi mdo*. Skt. *Āryaratnameghasūtra*. T 231. MTTWL 187. [*181*, *309-10*]

Sublime Sūtra of Contemplation which Subsumes All Merits. See *Sūtra of Contemplation which Subsumes All Merits*

Sublime Sūtra of the Descent to Laṅkā. See *Sūtra of the Descent to Laṅkā*

Sublime Sūtra which Genuinely Comprises the Entire Doctrine. See *Sūtra which (Genuinely) Comprises the Entire Doctrine*

Sublime Sūtra of the King of Contemplation. See *Sūtra of the King of Contemplation*

Sublime Sūtra Revealed by Akṣayamati. See *Sūtra Revealed by Akṣayamati*

Sublime Sūtra which Reveals the Relative and Ultimate. *'phags-pa kun-rdzob-dang don-dam-gyi bden-pa bstan-pa'i mdo*. Skt. *Āryasaṃvṛtiparamārtha-satyanirdeśasūtra*. T 179 [*320-1*, *901*]

Sublime Sūtra of the Teaching Given in a Dream. See *Sūtra of the Teaching Given in a Dream*

Sublime Tantra of the Summation of the Real. See *Tantra of the Summation of the Real*

Subsequent Root Tantra of the Magical Net. *sgyu-'phrul rtsa-rgyud phyi-ma*. [*360*] See *Subsequent Tantra of the Secret Nucleus*

Subsequent Tantra of the Emergence of Cakrasaṃvara. *bde-mchog sdom-'byung-gi rgyud phyi-ma*. Skt. *Saṃvarodayottaratantra*. NA. Refer to n. 471. [*458*]

Subsequent Tantra of Kālacakra. *dpal dus-kyi 'khor-lo'i rgyud phyi-ma*. Skt. *Śrīkālacakratantrottaratantrahṛdaya*. T 363. SP 69-70 (1966). [*478*]

Subsequent Tantra of the Secret Nucleus. *snying-po'i rgyud phyi-ma*. NGB Vol. 14, no. 188. [*262*]

Subsequent Tantra of Varāhī. *phag-mo phyi-ma*. Skt. *Ākhyātatantrottaravajra-varāhī varāhyabhidhānād Varāhyabhibodhana*. T 377-9. [*688*]

Summation of the Meaning of Empowerment. *dbang-don bsdus-pa*. NL. Quoted by Lo-chen Dharmaśrī, *gsang-bdag zhal-lung*. [*364*]

Summation of the Meaning (of the Secret Sūtra). *don-bsdus*. Skt. *Guhyasūtra-piṇḍartha*. P 4751. [*285-6*, *288-9*, *367*, *368*]

Summation of the Real. See *(Tantra of the) Summation of the Real*

Summation of the Real. *de-kho-na-nyid bsdus-pa*. Skt. *Tattvasaṃgraha*. Auth. Śantarakṣita. T 4266. [*67*]

Sun Commentary. *'od-ldan*. Skt. *Śrāmaṇerakārikāvṛttiprabhāvatī*. Auth. Śāk-yaprabha. T 4125. [*71*]

Sun of the Heart of Comtemplation. *bsam-gtan snying-gi nyi-ma*. Probably to be identified with the *Pan-sgrub rnams-kyi thugs-bcud snying-gi nyi-ma* in *The rgyud 'bum of Vairocana*. SSS 16 (1971). Vol. 1. I-Tib 70-924557. [*654*]

Sun which Illuminates the Expanse of the Great Perfection. *rdzogs-chen klong-gsal nyi-ma*. Disc. Ratna gling-pa. NL unless the work referred to is to be identified with the *rdzogs-chen klong-gsal snying-thig*, Disc. Ratna gling-pa. RLTC Vols. 11, 12, 19. RTD Vol. 88, pp. 447-652. [*793*]

Sun which Illumines the Expanse, a Mother Tantra. *ma-rgyud klong-gsal-nyi-ma*. Disc. Rdo-rje gling-pa. NL. Referred to, however, in DLTC Vol. 2, p. 56. [*789*]

Sun of Yogic Awareness. *(rnal-'byor) rig(-pa'i) nyi(-ma)*. Auth. Vajrahāsya. NL. [*488*, *654*, *658*]

Superior Magical Net. *(sgyu-'phrul) bla-ma*. T 837. NGB Vol. 14, no. 193. [*130*, *324*, *673*, *674*]

Supreme Continuum of the Greater Vehicle. *(theg-chen) rgyud bla(-ma)*. Skt. *Mahāyānottaratantraśāstra*. Auth. Maitreyanātha. T 4024. EIPRB 932-44. MTTWL 181-2. SOR 33 (1966). Tib. edn. Zuiryu Nakamura, *Zō-wa-taishō, Kukyō-ichijō-hōshōron-kenkyū*. Tokyo: Suzuki Gakujutsu Zai-dan (Suzuki Research Foundation), 1967. One of the *Five Doctrines of Venerable Maitreya*. Also referred to as the *Treatise on the Supreme Continuum of the Greater Vehicle*. [*27*, *69*, *72*, *73-4*, *88*, *90*, *95*, *116*, *127*, *128*, *129*, *140*, *146*, *147*, *170*, *171*, *173-5*, *177*, *191*, *192*, *194-6*, *202*, *212*, *216*, *298*, *415*, *827*, *894*, *908*, *930*]

Supreme Elixir Dialogue, a Nectar Rosary. *zhus-lan sman-mchog bdud-rtsi phreng-ba*. See *Supreme Nectar-Elixir Dialogue*

Supreme Golden Light, the Lord of Sūtras. *gser-'od dam-pa mdo-sde'i dbang-po*. Skt. *Suvarṇaprabhāsottama*. T 555-7. EIPRB 984-96. MTTWL 226. BST 8 (1967). [*944*]

Supreme Horse. *rta-mchog*. See *(Play of the) Supreme Horse*

Supreme Light of Pristine Cognition. *ye-shes 'od-mchog*. Disc. O-rgyan gling-pa. NL now, but available at least until the seventeenth century. [*776*, *778*]

Supreme Nectar-Elixir Dialogue. *zhus-lan bdud-rtsi sman-mchog*. Auth. Tsong-kha-pa. TWB 5268. [*923*, *925*]

Supreme Text. *gzhung dam-pa*. Skt. *Vinaya-uttaragrantha*. T 7. HBI, pp. 181-97. [*93*]

Sūtra of the Adornment of Pristine Cognition's Appearance (which Penetrates the Scope of All Buddhas). *sangs-rgyas thams-cad-kyi yul-la 'jug-pa ye-shes snang-ba rgyan-gyi mdo*. Skt. *Sarvabuddhaviṣayāvatārajñānālokālaṃkārasūtra*. T 100. [*176*, *178*, *219*, *297-8*, *908*]

Sūtra of Ākāśagarbha. *nam-mkha'i snying-po'i mdo*. Skt. *Ākāśagarbhasūtra*. T 260. MTTWL 8. [*235*]

Sūtra of the Array of Attributes (in the Buddhafield of Mañjuśrī). *mdo-sde yon-tan bkod-pa* or *yon-tan yongs-su bkod-pa'i mdo*. Skt. *Āryamañjuśrībuddhakṣetraguṇavyūhasūtra*. T 59. MTTWL 132. Trans. in TMS, pp. 164-88. [*412*, *423*, *424*]

Sūtra of the Arrayed Bouquet. *sdong-po bkod-pa'i mdo*. Skt. *Gaṇḍavyūhasūtra*. Part of the *Sūtra of the Great Bounteousness of the Buddhas*. T 44. MTTWL 76. BST 5 (1960). [*117*, *118*, *192*, *211*, *212*]

Sūtra of the Auspicious Aeon. See *Auspicious Aeon Sūtra*

Sūtra of the Bounteous Array. *rgyan stug-po bkod-pa'i mdo*. Skt. *Ghanavyūhasūtra*. T 110. [*154*, *161*, *413*]

Sūtra of Candrapradīpa. *zla-ba sgron-me'i mdo*. Alternative title for the *Sūtra of the King of Contemplation*. [*318*, *937*]

Sūtra of Compassion's White Lotus. *snying-rje pad-dkar*. Skt. *Karuṇāpuṇḍarīkasūtra*. T 111-12. MTTWL 93. Skt. edn. Isshi Yamada. 2 vols. London: School of Oriental and African Studies, 1968. [*943*]

Sūtra which Comprises the Entire Doctrine. See *Sūtra which (Genuinely) Comprises the Entire Doctrine*

Sūtra of Contemplation which Subsumes All Merits. *(phags-pa) bsod-nams thams-cad sdud-pa'i ting-nge-'dzin-gyi mdo*. Skt. *Āryasarvapuṇyasamuccayasamādhisūtra*. T 134. Also referred to as the *Sublime Sūtra of Contemplation which Subsumes All Merits*. [*743*, *747*, *928*]

Sūtra of the Cornucopia of Avalokiteśvara's Attributes. *mdo-sde za-ma-tog (bkod-pa)*. Skt. *Āryakāraṇḍavyūhanāmamahāyānasūtra*. T 116. MTTWL 90. BST 17 (1961). See also C. Régamey, "Motifs vichnouites et śivaïtes dans le Kāraṇḍavyūha" in *Études tibétaines dédiées à la mémoire de Marcelle Lalou*. Paris: A. Maisonneuve, 1971. [*508*]

Sūtra which Decisively Reveals the Intention. See *Sūtra (of the Greater Vehicle) which Decisively Reveals the Intention*

Sūtra of the Declaration of Enlightened Intention. *dgongs-pa lung bstan-pa'i mdo*. Skt. *Sandhivyākaraṇatantra*. T 444. [*454*]

Sūtra of the Descent to Laṅkā. *mdo lang-kār gshegs-pa* or *('phags-pa) lang-kār gshegs-pa('i mdo-sde)*. Skt. *Laṅkāvatārasūtra*. T 107. EIPRB 946-66. MTTWL 103. BST 3 (1963). Also referred to as the *Sublime Sūtra of the Descent to Laṅkā*. [*17-18*, *60-1*, *80*, *81*, *82*, *83*, *84*, *86*, *129*, *154*, *172*, *179-84*, *216*, *314*, *413*, *455*, *859*, *912-13*]

Sūtra of the Dialogue with the Bodhisattva Candragarbha. *byang-chub sems-dpa' zla-ba'i snying-pos zhus-pa'i mdo*. Skt. *Candragarbhaparipṛcchā*. T 356. [*943*]

Sūtra of the Dialogue with Brahmaviśeṣacinti. See *Sūtra of the (Greater Vehicle which is a) Dialogue with Brahmaviśeṣacinti*

Sūtra of the Dialogue with Kāśyapa from the Sublime Pagoda of Precious Jewels. *'phags-pa dkon-mchog brtsegs-pa-las 'od-srung-gis zhus-pa'i mdo*. Skt. *Kāśyapaparivartanāmamahāyānasūtra*. T 87. EIPRB 127-35. MTTWL 95. Trans. TMS, pp. 387-414. [*172*, *298*, *898*]

Sūtra of the Dialogue with King Dhāraṇīśvara. *gzungs-kyi dbang-phyug rgyal-pos zhus-pa'i mdo*. Skt. *Dhāraṇīśvararājaparipṛcchāsūtra*. To be identified with the *Tathāgatamahākaruṇānirdeśasūtra*. T 147. Several passages from the original Sanskrit are preserved in the *Supreme Continuum of the Greater Vehicle* and its commentary by Asaṅga. [*187-8*]

Sūtra of the Dialogue with the Nāga King. *klu'i rgyal-pos zhus-pa'i mdo*. To be identified with the following entry, or with the *Anavataptanāgarāja-paripṛcchāsūtra*, T 156. [*743*]

Sūtra of the Dialogue with the Nāga King Sāgara. *klu'i rgyal-po rgya-mtshos zhus-pa'i mdo*. Skt. *Sāgaranāgarājaparipṛcchāsūtra*. T 153-5. MTTWL 193. [*944*]

Sūtra of the Dialogue with Sāgaramati. *blo-gros rgya-mtshos zhus-pa'i mdo*. Skt. *Sāgaramatiparipṛcchāsūtra*. T 152. MTTWL 192. [*311*, *932*]

Sūtra which Dispels the Grief of Ajātaśātru. *ma-skyes-dgra'i 'gyod-pa bsal-ba'i mdo*. Skt. *Ajātaśatrukaukṛtyavinodanasūtra*. T 216. [*230*]

Sūtra which Encourages Superior Aspiration. *lhag-bsam bskul-ba'i mdo*. Skt. *Adhyāśayasañcodanasūtra*. T 69. MTTWL 7. [*73*]

Sūtra Excerpts. *bkol-mdo rnams*. Auth. Dharmabodhi. NA. [*489*]

Sūtra of Extensive Play. *rgya-cher rol-pa*. Skt. *Lalitavistarasūtra*. T 95. MTTWL 102. BST 1 (1958). Trans. (from Foucaux's French version) by G. Bays, *Voice of the Buddha*. 2 vols. Emeryville, CA: Dharma Press, 1983. [*98*, *185*, *419-23*, *666*]

Sūtra of Final Nirvāṇa. *myang-'das-kyi mdo* or *mya-ngan-las 'das-pa'i mdo chen-po*. Skt. *Mahāparinirvāṇasūtra*. T 119-21. MTTWL 118. Also referred to as the *Great Sūtra of Final Nirvāṇa* and the *Nirvāṇa Sūtra*. [*75-6*, *154-5*, *191*, *311-12*, *746*, *906*, *932*]

Sūtra of the Gathering of Intentions. See following entry

Sūtra which Gathers All Intentions. *(mdo) dgongs(-pa) 'dus(-pa)* or *'dus-pa mdo*. T 829. NGB Vol. 11, no. 160. NMKMG Vols. 14-16. The story of its transmission is given throughout *History*, Pt. 5. Also referred to as the *Great Sūtra which Gathers All Intentions*. [*40*, *41*, *81*, *284*, *285*, *287*, *292*, *365-6*, *367*, *369*, *396*, *458*, *488*, *489*, *537*, *805*, *827-8*, *833*, *845*, *891*, *893*, *911-13*]

Sūtra which Gathers All Intentions, writings about it by Lo-chen Dharmaśrī. *'dus-pa mdo-skor-gyi yig-cha*. LCSB Vols. 10-12. NMKMG Vols. 14-16. [*41*, *375*]

Sūtra which Gathers All Intentions and the Tantra of the Magical Net. *mdo-sgyu*. Listed separately.

Sūtra which (Genuinely) Comprises the Entire Doctrine. *('phags-pa) chos yang-dag-par sdud-pa'i mdo*. Skt. *Āryadharmasaṃgītisūtra*. T 238. MTTWL 69. Also referred to as the *Sublime Sūtra which Genuinely Comprises the Entire Doctrine*. [*138*, *473-4*, *748*, *928*]

Sūtra of the Great Bounteousness of the Buddhas. *('phags-pa sangs-rgyas) phal-po-che('i mdo)*. Skt. *Buddhāvataṃsakasūtra*. T 44. EIPRB 967-83. MTTWL 24. Trans. T. Cleary, *The Flower Ornament Scripture*. 3 vols. Boulder: Shambhala, 1984 onwards. Also referred to as the *Sublime Great Bounteousness of the Buddhas*. [*20*, *85*, *119*, *120*, *124*, *130-1*, *132*, *154*, *908*] See also *Aspiration of Good Conduct*, *Sūtra of the Arrayed Bouquet* and *Sūtra of the Ten Levels*

Sūtra (of the Greater Vehicle) which Decisively Reveals the Intention. *dgongs-pa nges(-par) 'grel(-pa) (theg-pa chen-po'i mdo)*. Skt. *Saṃdhinirmocana-sūtra*. T 106. EIPRB 929-31. MTTWL 197. Also referred to as the *Sublime Sūtra which Decisively Reveals the Intention*. [*155*, *188*, *219-20*, *299*, *314*, *907*]

Sūtra of the (Greater Vehicle which is a) Dialogue with Brahmaviśeṣacinti. *tshangs-pa khyad-par sems-kyis zhus-pa'i mdo*. Skt. *Brahmaviśeṣacinti-paripṛcchāsūtra*. T 160. [*316-7, 898*]

Sūtra of the Greater Vehicle Requested by Sublime Mañjuśrī. *'phags-pa 'jam-dpal-gyis zhus-pa'i theg-pa chen-po'i mdo*. Perhaps to be identified with T 90, trans. in TMS, pp. 100-14. [*748*]

Sūtra of Inconceivable Secrets. *gsang-ba bsam-gyis mi-khyab-pa'i mdo*. Skt. *Tathāgatācintyaguhyanirdeśasūtra*. T 47. MTTWL 232. [*118*, *431*]

Sūtra of the Introduction to the Development of the Power of Faith. *dad-pa'i stobs bskyed-pa 'jug-pa'i mdo*. Skt. *Śraddhābalādhānāvatāramudrāsūtra*. T 201. MTTWL 214. [*146*]

Sūtra of the Irreversible Wheel. *phyir mi-bzlog-pa 'khor-lo'i mdo*. Skt. *Avai-vartacakrasūtra*. T 240. [*190*]

Sūtra of the King of Contemplation. *ting-nge-'dzin rgyal-po'i mdo* or *mdo ting-'dzin rgyal-po*. Skt. *Samādhirājasūtra*. T 127. EIPRB 997-1000. BST 2 (1961). Also referred to as the *Sūtra of Candrapradipa* and the *Sublime Sūtra of the King of Contemplation*. [*160*, *168*, *173*, *218*, *318*, *577*, *859*, *937*]

Sūtra of the Lamp of Precious Jewels. *dkon-mchog sgron-me'i mdo* or *dkon-mchog ta-la-la*. Skt. *Ratnolkānāmadhāraṇīmahāyānasūtra*. T 145, 847. MTTWL 190. [*133-4*]

Sūtra of Magical Transformation of the Scope of Activity. *spyod-yul rnam-par 'phrul-pa'i mdo*. Skt. *Bodhisattvagocaropāyaviṣayavikurvāṇanirdeśasūtra*. T 146. [*471*]

Sūtra of the Meeting of Father and Son. *yab-sras mjal-ba'i mdo*. Skt. *Pitā-putrasamāgamanasūtra*. T 60. MTTWL 156. [*120*, *414*]

Sūtra of the Nucleus of the Buddha. *sangs-rgyas-kyi snying-po'i mdo*. See following entry

Sūtra of the Nucleus of the Tathāgata. *de-bzhin gshegs-pa'i snying-po'i mdo*. Skt. *Tathāgatagarbhasūtra*. T 258. MTTWL 231. [*194*, *295*, *315*]

Sūtra of Queen Śrīmālā. *dpal-phreng*. Skt. *Śrīmālādevīsiṃhanādasūtra*. T 92. MTTWL 215. Trans. TMS, pp. 363-86. [*194*]

Sūtra of Reality which Appears Variously Without Straying from its Essence. *chos-nyid rang-ngo mi-gYo-ba tha-dad snang-ba'i mdo*. Skt. *Dharmatāsvabhāvaśūnyatācalapratisarvālokasūtra*. T 128. [*943*]

Sūtra Repaid with Gratitude. *drin-lan bsab-pa'i mdo*. T 353. [*97-8*]

Sūtra Requested by the Devaputra Suvikrāntacinta. *lha'i bu rab-rtsal-sems-kyis zhus-pa'i mdo*. Skt. *Suvikrāntacintadevaputraparipṛcchāsūtra*. T 161. [*85*]

Sūtra Requested by Jñānottara according to the Piṭaka of the Greater Vehicle. *theg-pa chen-po'i sde-snod ye-shes dam-pa'i mdo*. Skt. *Jñānottarabodhisattvaparipṛcchāsutrā*. T 82. Trans. TMS, pp. 427-68. [*303*]

Sūtra Requested by Śāriputra. *sha-ri'i bus zhus-pa'i mdo*. Skt. *Śāriputrāṣṭaka*. P 5812. [*99*]

Sūtra which Resembles the Elephant's Expressive Power. *glang-po'i rtsal lta-bu'i mdo*. Skt. *Hastikaksyasūtra*. T 207. MTTWL 82. [*129-30*]

Sūtra Revealed by Akṣayamati. *('phags-pa) blo-gros mi-zad-pa (bstan-pa)'i mdo*. Skt. *Akṣayamatinirdeśasūtra*. T 175. MTTWL 10. Also referred to as the *Sublime Sūtra Revealed by Akṣayamati*. [*211*, *218*]

Sūtra of the Rites of Renunciation and Fulfilment. *dpang-skong phyag-(b)rgya-pa'i mdo*. T 267. [*508*]

Sūtra of the River's Play. *chu-klung rol-pa'i mdo*. DZ Vol. 9, pp. 2-16. [*744*]

Sūtra of the Teaching Given in a Dream. *rgyal-po kri-kri'i rmi-lam lung-bstan-pa'i mdo*. Skt. *Āryasvapnanirdeśasūtra*. T 48. [*430*]

Sūtra of the Ten Levels. *mdo-sde sa-bcu-pa*. Skt. *Daśabhūmikasūtra*. Part of the *Sūtra of the Great Bounteousness of the Buddhas*. T 44. EIPRB 967-70, 974, 977. MTTWL 61. BST 7 (1967). Trans. M. Honda, SP 74, pp. 115-276. [*75*]

Sūtra of Valid Cognition. *tshad-ma mdo*. See *Compendium of Valid Cognition*

Sūtra of the Wise and the Foolish. *mdo mdzangs-blun*. Skt. *Damomūrkhasūtra*. T 341. Typeset edn. Dharmsala, HP: Council of Cultural and Religious Affairs of His Holiness the Dalai Lama, 1968. I-Tib 77-921896. Qinghai: Minorities Press, 1984. Trans., from the Mongolian, S. Frye, *Sutra of the Wise and the Foolish*. LTWA, 1981. [*518*]

Svarodaya. *dbyangs-'char*. T 4326-7. HIL 6.4, pp. 77-8. [*730*, *821*, *869*]

Sword at the Gateway to Language. *smra-sgo mtshon-cha*. Skt. *Vacanamukhāyudhopamanāma*. Auth. Smṛtijñānakīrti. T 4295-6. Ed. Beijing: Minorities Press, 1980. [*762*] See also *Gateway to Language*

Taintless Light (the Great Commentary on the Kālacakra). *(dus-'khor 'grel-chen) dri-ma med pa'i 'od*. Skt. *Vimalaprabhā*. Auth. Puṇḍarīka. T 845. Skt. edn. Jagannath Upadhyaya, BIT 11, 12, 13. Tib. manuscript version pub. Bir, HP: Tsondu Senghe, 1976. I-Tib 76-902672. For much useful information, see J. Newman, *The Outer Kālacakra*. Ann

Arbor: University Microfilms, 1987. Also M. Broido, "Killing, Lying, Stealing, and Adultery" in D. Lopez (ed.), *Buddhist Hermeneutics*. Honolulu: University of Hawaii Press, 1988. [*92*, *104*, *250*, *261*, *894*, *950*] See also *Trilogy of Commentaries by Bodhisattvas*

Taintless Light. *zhal-chems dri-ma med-pa'i 'od*. Auth. Klong-chen Rab-'byams-pa. NYZ, *mkha'-'gro yang-tig*, Pt. *Hūṃ*, pp. 266-81. Trans. H. V. Guenther, *Crystal Mirror* 5 (1977), pp. 331-43. [*593*]

Tangyur. *bstan-'gyur*. The collection of translations of the commentarial treatises. For a useful survey of the various editions and the current state of research about them, see C. Vogel, *Vāgbhaṭa's Aṣṭāṅgahṛdaya*. Deutsche Morgenländische Gesellschaft XXXVII, 2. Wiesbaden: Franz Steiner Verlag, 1965, pp. 21-33. [*851*, *929*]

Tantra which Acquires the Accomplishment of All Families. *rigs thams-cad-pa'i dngos-grub len-pa'i rgyud*. NL. [*351*]

(Tantra of the) All-Accomplishing King. *kun-byed rgyal-po'i rgyud*. T 828. NGB Vol. 1, no. 1. NMKMG Vol. 17. Refer to E. K. Dargyay, "A Rñiṅ-ma Text: The *Kun byed rgyal po'i mdo*" in STC, pp. 282-93. Also referred to as the *Triple Cycle of the Mother and Sons (which comprises) the All-Accomplishing King*. [*17*, *36*, *40*, *78*, *81*, *273*, *295-7*, *303-4*, *307-8*, *311*, *317*, *320*, *325*, *353*, *354*, *357*, *365*, *370*, *524*, *654*, *658*, *671*, *897*, *903*]

Tantra of the Array of the Nucleus of Indestructible Reality. *rdo-rje snying-po bkod-pa'i rgyud*. Not identified with certainty. However, note that this closely approximates one of the subtitles of the *Sūtra which Gathers All Intentions*, i.e. *don-gyi snying-po rdo-rje bkod-pa'i rgyud (Tantra of the Array of Indestructible Reality, the Nucleus of Meaning)*. [*268*]

Tantra of the Array of Pristine Cognition. *ye-shes rnam-par bkod-pa'i rgyud*. NL. [*231*]

Tantra of the Array of Wish-granting Gems. *yid-bzhin rin-po-che bkod-pa'i rgyud*. Possibly to be identified with NGB Vol, 2, no. 39. [*414*] See also *Tantra of the Wish-fulfilling Array*

Tantra of the Compendium of the Indestructible Reality of Pristine Cognition. *ye-shes rdo-rje kun-las btus-pa'i rgyud*. Skt. *Vajrajñānasamuccaya-tantra*. T 447. [*292*]

Tantra which Comprises the Supreme Path of the Means which Clearly Reveal All-Positive Pristine Cognition (*or* the Pristine Cogntion of Samantabhadra). *kun-bzang ye-shes gsal-bar ston-pa'i thabs-kyi lam-mchog 'dus-pa'i rgyud*. NGB Vol. 3, no. 46. [*460*]

Tantra of the Dialogue with Subāhu. *dpung-bzang-gi rgyud*. Skt. *Subāhupari-pṛcchānāmatantra*. T 805. [*78*, *270*]

Tantra of the Emergence of Cakrasaṃvara. *bde-mchog sdom-pa 'byung-ba'i rgyud*. See *Emergence of Cakrasaṃvara*

Tantra of the Emergence of Tārā. *sgrol-ma 'byung-ba*. Skt. *Sarvatathāgata-mātṛtārāviśvakarmabhavatantra*. T 726. [*270-1*]

Tantra of the Extensive Magical Net. See *Extensive Magical Net*

Tantra of the Gathering of the Sugatas of the Eight Transmitted Precepts (along with its transmissions and esoteric instructions, arranged in one hundred and thirty doctrinal topics). *bka'-brgyad bde-gshegs 'dus-pa'i rgyud-lung-man-ngag-dang-bcas-pa'i chos-tshan brgya-dang sum-cur bkod-pa*. Disc. Nyang-ral Nyi-ma 'od-zer. KGDD. [*756*]

Tantra which Genuinely Gathers All the Deities. *lha thams-cad yang-dag-par 'dus-pa'i rgyud*. NL. [*268-9*]

Tantra of the Goddess Kālī. *lha-mo nag-mo'i rgyud*. Skt. *Śrīdevīkālīpraśaṃsā-rājatantra*. Disc. Nāgārjuna. T 671. [*480*]

Tantra of the Great Coalescence of Sun and Moon. *nyi-ma-dang zla-ba kha-sbyor-ba chen-po'i rgyud*. NGB Vol. 9, no. 146. GCD Vol. 3. [*128*]

Tantra of the Great Natural Arising of Awareness. *rig-pa rang-shar chen-po'i rgyud*. NGB Vol. 10, no. 153. [*40*, *86-7*, *224*, *227-8*, *232*, *270*, *271*, *336*, *338-9*, *348*, *349*, *351*, *352*, *356*, *357-8*, *360*, *900*, *901-2*]

Tantra of the Hidden Point of the Moon. *zla-gsang thig-le*. Skt. *Śrīcandra-guhyatilakanāmamahātantrarāja*. T 477. NGB Vol. 16, n. 210. [*461*] See also *Hidden Point of the Moon* and *Tantra of the Supreme Seminal Point*

Tantra of the Inconceivable Rali Cakrasaṃvara. *ra-li bsam-gyi mi-khyab-pa'i rgyud*. Skt. *Śrīcakrasaṃvaraguhyācintyatantrarāja*. T 385. Part of the *Thirty-two Rali Cakrasaṃvara Tantras*. [*31*, *248*]

Tantra of Kālacakra, the Glorious and Supreme Original Buddha. *dpal-mchog dang-po'i sangs-rgyas*. See *Kālacakra Tantra*

Tantra of the Magical Net. (*spyi-rgyud/rgyud-chen*) *sgyu-'phrul drva-ba*. NGB Vols. 14-16. [*275*, *620*, *622*]

Tantra of the Magical Net of Vajrasattva. *rdo-rje sems-dpa' sgyu-'phrul drva-ba*. T 833. NGB Vol. 15, no. 197. This title refers generally to the root texts of the cycle contained in NGB Vol. 14. [*283*, *460*]

Tantra of the Purification of All Evil Destinies. *ngan-song sbyong-rgyud*. Skt. *Sarvadurgatipariśodhanatantra*. T 483, 485. GDKT Vol. 6, nos. 27-38. Skt. and Tib. ed. and trans. T. Skorupski, *The Sarvadurgatipariśodhana Tantra: Elimination of All Evil Destinies*. Delhi: Motilal Banarsidass, 1983. See also, idem, "Tibetan Homa Rites" in J. F. Staal, *Agni: the Vedic Ritual of the Fire Altar*. Berkeley: Asian Humanities Press, 1983, Vol. 2, pp. 403-17. [*707*]

Tantra of the Secret Nucleus. *rgyud gsang-ba snying-po* or *snying-po'i rgyud*. Skt. *Guhyagarbhatattvaviniścayamahātantra*. T 832. NGB Vol. 14, no. 187. Ed. and trans. in GGFTC. Also refer to H. V. Guenther, *Matrix of Mystery*. Boulder/London: Shambhala, 1984. The history of its transmission is given throughout *History*, Pt. 5. It is also referred to as the *Root Tantra of the Secret Nucleus*, the *Root Tantra of the Magical Net* and the *Secret Nucleus of the Magical Net*. [*40*, *81*, *124*, *126*, *212-13*, *223*, *244*, *267*, *275-6*, *278*, *292*, *300*, *307*, *347*, *362*, *414*, *415*, *499*, *450*, *451*, *481*, *533*, *591*, *827*, *850*, *914-17*]

(Tantra of the) Summation of the Real. (*'phags-pa) de(-kho-na)-nyid bsdus-pa('i rgyud)* or *saṃ-gra-ha*. Skt. *Sarvatathāgatatattvasaṃgrahanāmama-hāyānasūtra*. T 479. Ed. Isshi Yamada, *Sarva-tathāgata-tattva-saṅgraha-*

nāma Mahāyāna-sūtra. SP 262 (1981). L. Chandra and D. Snellgrove, *Sarva-tathāgata-tattva-saṅgraha—Facsimile Reproduction of a Tenth Century Manuscript from Nepal.* SP 269 (1981). F. Lessing and A. Wayman *Mkhas Grub Rje's Fundamentals of the Buddhist Tantras.* The Hague/Paris: Mouton, 1968, pp. 214-17. Also referred to as the *Sublime Tantra of the Summation of the Real.* [*78, 269, 273, 354, 441, 468, 488, 916*]

Tantra of the Supreme Radiance of Truth without Conceptual Elaborations. *spros-bral don-gsal chen-po'i rgyud.* NGB Vol. 6, no. 110. [*211*]

Tantra of the Supreme Seminal Point. *thig-le mchog-gi rgyud.* Possibly to be identified with the *Tantra of the Hidden Point of the Moon.* [*369*]

Tantra which Uproots Saṃsāra. *'khor-ba rtsad-gcod-kyi rgyud.* See *Four Groups of Exegetical Tantras Pertaining to the Tantra which Uproots Saṃsāra*

Tantra of the Wish-fulfilling Array. *yid-bzhin rnam-par bkod-pa'i rgyud.* Cf. *Tantra of the Array of Wish-granting Gems.* [*944*]

Tantra of the Yakṣa Vajra Mārajit. *gnod-sbyin rdo-rje bdud-'dul-gyi rgyud.* Disc. Grva-pa mngon-shes. NL. [*753*]

Teaching Cycle of Lord Maitripā. *mnga'-bdag mai-tri-pa'i gdams-skor.* It is not clear which texts in particular this refers to. Surviving works by Maitripā are found in the Skt. edn. *Advayavajrasaṃgraha.* GOS 40 (1927). [*200*]

Teachings for Retreat. *yang-dgon-pa'i ri-chos-rnams.* Auth. Yang-dgon-pa Rgyal-mtshan-dpal. Refer to *The Collected Works of Yaṅ-dgon-pa.* 3 vols. Thimphu: Kunsang Topgey, 1976. I(Bhu)-Tib 76-901006. *Collected Writings of Rgyal-ba Yaṅ-dgon-pa.* 3 vols. Thimphu: Tango Monastic Community, 1982. Bhu-Tib 82-902180. Selections from the *Teachings for Retreat* have also appeared in *Yaṅ-dgon-pa'i ri-chos.* Gangtok: Dzongsar Jamyang Khyentsey Labrang, 1979. I-Tib 80-902344. Also referred to as the *Three Cycles on Retreat Practice.* [*571, 578*]

Teachings on Vital Energy. *rlung-skor.* NL. [*578*]

Technique of Pulverisation. *zhib-mo rnam-'thag.* Skt. *Vaidalyasūtra.* Auth. Nāgārjuna. T 3826. EIPRB 698. HIL 7.1, pp. 21, 130. See also C. Lindtner, *Nagarjuniana.* Indiske Studier IV. Copenhagen: Akademisk Forlag, 1982; pp. 87-93. [*94*]

Ten Cycles of Experiential Guidance. *nyams-khrid skor-bcu.* Disc. Rdo-rje gling-pa. NL. Referred to, however, in DLTC Vol. 4, pp. 20 and 57. [*790*]

Ten Doctrines which Secure the Happiness of Tibet and Kham. *bod-khams bde-thabs chos-bcu.* Disc. Mchog-gyur bde-chen gling-pa. CLTC Vol. 19. RTD Vol. 39, pp. 195-6; Vol. 83, pp. 427-77. [*848*]

Ten Father Tantra Cycles of the Innermost Spirituality. *pha-rgyud snying-thig skor-bcu.* Disc. Rdo-rje gling-pa. NL. Referred to, however, in DLTC Vol. 4, pp. 20 and 57. [*790*]

Ten Great Tantras of Cakrasaṃvara. *bde-mchog rgyud-chen bcu.* Their precise enumeration remains uncertain. *Blue Annals,* p. 377, mentions "eight chief Tantras of Saṃvara", though the attempt to identify them among the *Thirty-Two Rali Tantras* is doubtful. Cf. also the list of texts on p. 375 of the same work, the first nine of which belong to the Saṃvara cycle. [*688*]

Ten-span-long Paper Scroll which combined the Profound, Essential Points of All the Sūtras and Tantras. *mdo-rgyud thams-cad-kyi zab-gnad phyogs gcig-tu dril-ba'i shog-dril 'dom-bcu*. Disc. Thang-stong rgyal-po. NL. [*802*]

Ten Sūtras (of the Exegetical Tantra). *(bshad-rgyud) mdo-bcu*. NGB Vol. 1, no. 2. [*654, 658*]

Ten Tantras on the Discipline of Coarse (Defilements). *rags-pa 'dul-ba'i rgyud-bcu*. [*136*]

Tent of Longevity, (the transmitted empowerment of). *tshe-gur-gyi dbang-bka'*. NL. Apparently belongs to the Northern Treasure (*byang-gter*) tradition. [*821*]

Ten Verses on the Real. *de-kho-na-nyid bcu-pa*. Skt. *Tattvadaśaka*. Auth. Advayavajra (Maitripā). T 2236. DZ Vol. 5, pp. 21-33. [*200*]

Ten Volumes of Ceremonial Arrangements for the Sūtra which Gathers All Intentions, the Magical Net, and so forth. *mdo-sgyu sogs-kyi chog-khrigs glegs-bam bcu*. Redacted by Rgyal-sras Gzhan-phan mtha'-yas. NL in this form, but largely preserved in NMKMG. [*737*]

Testament of Ba. *rba/sba-bzhed*. Auth. traditionally ascribed to Sba Gsal-snang. The "pure" version (*rba/sba-bzhed gtsang-ma*), referred to in *History* has not recently been available, but may possibly be identified with the unsupplemented edition published in Beijing in 1980 by Gönpo Gyeltsen, on which refer to n. 538. The annotated version (*sba-bzhed zhabs-btags-ma*), however, has been published at least twice in recent years: (1) R. A. Stein, *Une Chronique Ancienne de bSam-yas*. Paris: Institut des Hautes Études Chinoises, 1961. (2) Dharamsala, HP: Tibetan Educational Printing Press, 1968. I-Tib-464. This typeset edn. is based entirely on the Stein-Richardson text. [*509, 517*]

Testament which Elucidates the Significance of Pacification. *zhi-byed bka'-chems don-gsal*. Disc. O-rgyan gling-pa. NA. [*776*]

Text on the Means for Assuming the Mudrā of the Peaceful and Wrathful Deities. *zhi-khro'i phyag-rgya bcings-thabs-kyi yi-ge*. Auth. Mkhas-grub ye-shes. NL. [*697*]

Text on the Rites of the Guru. *bla-ma'i las-gzhung*. NL. [*575*]

Texts of Maitreya. *byams-gzhung*. See *Five Doctrines of (Venerable) Maitreya*

Texts of the So Tradition. *so-lugs-kyi yig-cha*. NL. [*615*]

Texts and Teaching Cycles of the Esoteric Instructional Class. [*322-3, 554-96*]

Texts and Teaching Cycles of the Mental Class. [*325, 538-53*]

Texts and Teaching Cycles of the Spatial Class. [*329, 538-53*]

Thirteen Later Translations of the Mental Class (by Vimalamitra). *sems-sde phyi-'gyur bcu-gsum*. [*555*] See *Eighteen Great Tantrapiṭaka (according to Mahāyoga)*

Thirteen Paper Scrolls containing Means for Attainment. *sgrub-thabs-gyi shog-dril bcu-gsum*. Disc. Pakshi Shākya-'od. NA. [*663*]

Thirteen Volumes of the Vinaya. *'dul-pod bcu-gsum*. The first thirteen volumes of the *Kangyur* (Vols. *Ka-Pa*) in the Sde-dge edition. [*874*]

Thirty-Line Alphabetical Poem. *ka-kha sum-cu-pa*. Auth. Klong-chen Rab-'byams-pa. KCST Vol. 1, pp. 268-70. [*578-9*]

Thirty-seven Supreme Treasures. *mchog-gter sum-cu-rtsa-bdun*. Disc. Mchog-gyur bde-chen gling-pa. The identification of these among the works preserved in CLTC is not yet certain. [*845*]

Thirty-two Rali Cakrasaṃvara Tantras. *ra-li so-gnyis (yongs-rdzogs)*. T 383-414. [*893*] See also *Tantra of the Inconceivable Rali-Cakrasaṃvara*

Thirty Verses. *sum-cu-pa*. Skt. *Triṃśikākārikā*. Auth. Vasubandhu. T 4055. EIPRB 1447-66. MTTWL 236. Tib. edn. Enga Teramoto. Kyoto: Otani Daigaku, 1933. Trans. S. Anacker, *Seven Works of Vasubandhu*. Delhi: Motilal Banarsidass, 1984. T. Kochumuttom, *A Buddhist Doctrine of Experience*. Delhi: Motilal Banarsidass, 1982. [*229*]

Thirty Verses and Introduction to Gender. *sum-rtags*. Auth. Anu or Thon-mi Saṃbhoṭa. T 4348-9. TWPS 93. Concerning the secondary literature, refer to R. A. Miller, *Studies in the Grammatical Tradition in Tibet*. Amsterdam Studies in the Theory and History of Linguistic Science III, 6. Amsterdam: John Benjamins BV, 1976. [*729*]

Thread-cross Rites of the Mātaraḥs' Vengeance. *ma-mo 'khang-phab-kyi mdos*. NL. [*669*]

Three Classes of the Great Perfection. *rdzogs-chen sde-gsum*. Disc. Mchog-gyur bde-chen gling-pa. CLTC Vol. 23 (incomplete redaction). RTD Vol. 86, pp. 333-46; Vol. 89, pp. 569-613; Vol. 91, pp. 301-643; Vol. 110-11, complete. Pub. Bir, HP: Tulku Ugyen Topgyal, Tibetan Khampa Industrial Society, 1974. I-Tib 74-900601. Also referred to as the *True Doctrine*, *Three Classes of the Great Perfection*. [*843*, *845*, *856*] See also *Prophetic Declaration of the Three Classes of the Great Perfection*

Three Classes of the Great Perfection which are the Innermost Spirituality of Vairocana. *bai-ro'i thugs-tig rdzogs-chen sde gsum*. Disc. Mchog-gyur bde-chen gling-pa and 'Jam-dbyangs mkhyen-brtse'i dbang-po. To be identified with the preceding entry. [*856*]

Three Continua. *rgyud gsum*. Refer to n. 629. For examples of redactions of this teaching that enjoy popularity at the present time, see: Ṅor-chen Dkon-mchog lhun-grub, *lam 'bras dṅos gźi'i khrid yig rgyud gsum mdzes rgyan*. Delhi: Phan-khaṅ zhabs-druṅ, 1966 or 1967. I-Tib-168. Ṅag-dbaṅ-chos-grags, *Gsuṅ ṅag lam 'bras sñan gsum rgyud gsum sñiṅ po'i legs bśad*. Dolanji Village, HP: Tashi Dorji, 1976. I-Tib 76-902699. [*562*, *564*, *633*]

Three Cycles of Further Innermost Spirituality. *yang-tig skor-gsum*. Redacted by Klong-chen Rab-'byams-pa. (1) *mkha' 'gro yang tig*. (2) *bla ma yang tig*. (3) *yang tig yid bzhin nor bu*. [*591*] See also *Four-Part Innermost Spirituality*

Three Cycles of the Intentional Object. *dmigs-pa skor-gsum*. NL. [*546*]

Three Cycles on Retreat Practice. *ri-chos skor-gsum*. [*578*] See *Teachings for Retreat*

Three Dohā Cycles. *do-hā skor gsum*. Auth. Saraha. *King Dohā, Queen Dohā, People Dohā*. Refer to H. V. Guenther (trans.), *The Royal Song of Saraha*. Berkeley/London: Shambhala, 1973. See also Karma 'Phrin-las-pa, *Do-ha skor-gsum-gyi ṭī-ka*. Thimphu, 1984. I(Bhu)-Tib 84-902937. [*578*]

Three Drops of Nectar. *bdud-rtsi thigs-gsum*. NL. [*546*]

Three Emphases of the Path. *lam-gyi gtso-bo rnam-gsum*. Auth. Tsong-kha-pa. P 6087. DZ Vol. 3, pp. 368-71. TWB 5275 (67). Geshe Lhundup Sopa and J. Hopkins, *Cutting Through Appearances: Practice and Theory of Tibetan Buddhism*. Ithaca, NY: Snow Lion, 1989. [*204*]

Three Hundred Verses (on the Vinaya). *('dul-ba) sum-brgya-pa*. Auth. Śākyaprabha. [*730, 911*] See *Stanzas on the Novitiate*

Three Meditational Sequences. *sgom-rim gsum-ka*. Skt. *Bhāvanākrama*. Auth. Kamalaśīla. T 3915-17. MTTWL 29. SOR 9 (1956-8). HIL 7.1, pp. 96-9, 125-6, 129. [*906*]

Three Phrases which Penetrate the Essential. *tshig-gsum gnad-du brdeg-pa*. Auth. Dga'-rab rdo-rje. NYZ, *bi-ma snying-thig*, Pt. 1, Vol. *Ga*, pp. 304-18. [*494*]

Three Stages. *rim-pa gsum*. Skt. *Māyājālopadeśakramatraya*. Auth. Vimalamitra. P 4742. [*362-3, 481*]

Three Traditions of the Eight Transmitted Precepts. *bka'-brgyad lugs-gsum*. NL. [*683*]

Three Traditions of the Mental Class. *sems-sde lugs-gsum*. Listed separately as *Great Perfection of the Kham Tradition*, *Great Perfection of the Rong Tradition* (i.e. the Nyang Tradition) and *Seven Sessions of Aro (Yeshe Jungne)*. Very often, however, the last mentioned is treated as a special subdivision of the Kham Tradition. [*827*]

Three Traditions of Pacification. *zhi-byed lugs gsum-ka*. [*657*] See *Pacification according to the Early, Middle and Later Traditions*

Three Traditions of Vajrakīla. *phur-ba lugs-gsum*. NL. [*683*]

Three Verses on the Aural Lineage. *rna-brgyud tshigs-gsum*. NL. [*546*]

Tiger-riding Lord. *(dpal-mgon) stag-zhon*. Disc. O-rgyan gling-pa. A rite of Mahākāla. NA now, but available through the seventeenth century. [*776, 778*]

Transcendence of Existence according to the Madhyamaka. *dbu-ma srid-pa 'pho-ba*. Skt. *Bhavasaṃkrānti*. Auth. Nāgārjuna. T 3840, 4152 and 4558. EIPRB 628-32. MTTWL 30. HIL 7.1, pp. 28-9. [*321-2*]

Transcendental Perfection of Discriminative Awareness in Eight Thousand Lines. *(sher-phyin) brgyad-stong-pa*. Skt. *Aṣṭasāhasrikāprajñāpāramitā*. T 12. EIPRB. 108-126. MTTWL 22. BST 4 (1960). Also referred to as the *Short Mother* and the *Sublime Transcendental Perfection of Discriminative Awareness in Eight Thousand Lines*. [*75, 154, 334, 441, 566, 575-6*]

Transcendental Perfection of Discriminative Awareness in One Hundred Thousand Lines. *sher-phyin stong-phrag brgya-pa* or *'bum*. Skt. *Śatasāhasrikāprajñāpāramitā*. T 8. EIPRB 93-7. MTTWL 208. Also referred to as the *Great Mother* and the *Long Mother*. [*53*, *154*, *183*, *522*, *526*, *566*]

Transcendental Perfection of Discriminative Awareness in Twenty-five Thousand Lines. *shes-rab-kyi pha-rol-tu phyin-pa stong-phrag nyi-shu-rtsa-lnga-pa*. Skt. *Pañcaviṃśatisāhasrikāprajñāpāramitā*. T 9. EIPRB 98-9. MTTWL 154. See also N. R. Lethcoe, "The Bodhisattva Ideal in the *Aṣṭa*. and *Pañca*. *Prajñāpāramitā Sūtras*" in PRS. Also referred to as the *Intermediate Mother*. [*61*, *85*, *154*, *172*, *176*, *182*, *216*, *307*]

Transmissions of the Vinaya. *'dul-ba'i sde-snod*. T 1-7. Refer also to HBI, pp. 181-97. [*423*, *518*, *578*] See also *Vinayapiṭaka*

Transmitted Instructions of the Indestructible Array, which Nupcen Conferred as his Final Testament. *gnubs-chen 'da'-ka'i zhal-chems lung rdo-rje bkod-pa'i gdams-pa gnang-ba*. Disc. Mchog-gyur bde-chen gling-pa. CLTC Vols. 22-3. RTD Vol. 86, pp. 1-171. [*847*]

Transmitted Precepts of the Enlightened Activity of Vajrakīla. *phrin-las phur-pa'i bka'-rnams*. See *Vajrakīla (Cycle/Tantra)*

Transmitted Precepts of the Father Consort and Transmitted Precepts of the Mother Consort of the Secret Innermost Spirituality. *gsang-thig yab-bka' yum-bka'i sgrub-skor shog-ser*. Disc. 'Jam-mgon Kong-sprul Blo-gros mtha'-yas, assisted by 'Jam-dbyangs mkhyen-brtse'i dbang-po. RTD Vol. 16, pp. 1-300. Also referred to as the *Father Consort and Mother Consort*, *(Transmitted Precepts) of the Secret Innermost Spirituality*. [*864*, *866*]

Transmitted Precepts given in a manner which Reveals the Hidden. See *Disclosure of the Hidden*

Transmitted Precepts of the Lotus Speech Tantras. *padma gsung-gi tantra-rnams-kyi bka'-babs*. [*479*] See *Hayagrīva (Cycle/Tantra)*

Transmitted Precepts of the Narrow Path to the Fortress. *rdzong-'phrang bka'-ma*. NMKMG Vol. 13. [*757*]

Transmitted Precepts of the Vajrakīla Tantras. *phur-pa'i rgyud rnams-kyi bka'-rnams*. See *Vajrakīla (Cycle/Tantra)*

Transmitted Precepts of Vajrāmṛta. *rdo-rje bdud-rtsi'i bka'-rnams*. [*480*] See *Nectar the Enlightened Attributes*

Treasure Doctrines of Pema Lingpa. *pad-gling-gi chos-bka'*. PLTC. [*727*]

Treasure Doctrines of Zhikpo Lingpa. *zhig-gling-gi gter-chos*. RTD, *passim*. No complete edition of this treasure-finder's discoveries appears to have come to light so far. One major cycle that has appeared is the *Thugs rje chen po 'khor ba las grol gyi chos skor*. 2 vols. Gangtok: Sherab Gyaltsen Lama, 1976. I-Tib 76-902130. [*727*]

Treasury of the Abhidharma. *(chos mngon-pa) mdzod*. Skt. *Abhidharmakośa*. Auth. Vasubandhu. T 4089. EIPRB 1395-430. BB 5-8 (1970-2). B.Budh. 20 (1917, 1930) and 21 (1918-31). MCB 16 (1971). TSWS 8 (1967, 1975). [*71*, *93*, *156*, *221*, *226*, *231*, *411*, *526*, *552*, *850*, *861*, *936*]

Treasury of the Abiding Nature of Reality. *gnas-lugs (rin-po-che'i) mdzod*. Auth. Klong-chen Rab-'byams-pa. Ed. Dodrup Chen Rinpoche. Gangtok, Sikkim, *c*. 1966. I-Tib-140. KCZD Vol. 5

Treasury of Amarasiṃha. *'chi-med mdzod*. Skt. *Amarakośa*. Auth. Amarasiṃha. T 4299. HIL 5.4, pp. 309-13. [*106*] See also *Wish-fulfiller*

Treasury of Detailed Exposition. *bye-brag bshad-mdzod (chen-mo)*. Skt. *Vibhāṣākośa*. Auth. Vasumitra. Now extant only in Chinese: Taishō 1545. EIPRB 459-63. L. de La Vallée-Poussin, *L'Abhidharmakośa de Vasubandhu*. Paris: Paul Geuthner, 1923-36, Vol. 1, pp. xliii-lix. HBI, pp. 197-209 and *passim*. Also referred to as the *Great Treasury of Detailed Exposition*. [*90*, *93*, *427*, *440*]

Treasury of Esoteric Instructions. *man-ngag (rin-po-che'i) mdzod*. Auth. Klong-chen Rab-'byams-pa. Ed. Dodrup Chen Rinpoche. Gangtok, Sikkim, *c*. 1969. I(Sik)-Tib 74-909428. KCZD Vol. 6.

Treasury of the Expanse of Reality. *chos-dbyings (rin-po-che'i) mdzod*. Auth. Klong-chen Rab-'byams-pa. Ed. Dodrup Chen Rinpoche. Gangtok, Sikkim, 1964. I-Tib-20. KCZD Vol. 2

Treasury of Logical Reason. *tshad-ma rigs-gter*. Auth. Sa-skya Paṇḍita. SK Vol. 5, no. 19. Xylo. Gangtok, Sikkim: Sa-ngor Monastery. Xylo. Simtokha, Bhutan. I(Bhu)-Tib 76-905037. See also L. W. J. van der Kuijp, *Contributions to the Development of Tibetan Buddhist Epistemology*. Wiesbaden: Franz Steiner Verlag, 1983. [*872*]

Treasury of the Scriptural and Logical (Background for) the Vinaya. *'dul-ba lung-rigs gter-mdzod*. Auth. Skyed-tshal mkhan-po 'Jam-dbyangs kun-dga' chos-bzang (fifteenth century). New Delhi: Ngawang Topgay, 1974. I-Tib 74-903076. [*730*]

Treasury of (Spiritual and) Philosophical Systems. *grub-mtha' (rin-po-che'i) mdzod*. Auth. Klong-chen Rab-'byams-pa. Ed. Dodrup Chen Rinpoche. Gangtok, Sikkim, *c*. 1969. I(Sik)-Tib 78-909429. KCZD Vol. 6. [*40*, *196*]

Treasury of the Supreme Vehicle. *theg-mchog (rin-po-che'i) mdzod*. Auth. Klong-chen Rab-'byams-pa. Ed. Dodrup Chen Rinpoche. 2 vols. Gangtok, Sikkim, *c*. 1969. I(Sik)-Tib 72-909430. KCZD Vols. 3-4. Also referred to as the *Precious Treasury of the Supreme Vehicle*. [*678*]

Treasury of Word and Meaning. *tshig-don (rin-po-che'i) mdzod*. Auth. Klong-chen Rab-'byams-pa. Ed. Dodrup Chen Rinpoche. Gangtok, Sikkim, *c*. 1969. I(Sik)-Tib 76-909431. KCZD Vol. 5

Treatise which Analyses the Three Vows. *rab-dbye'i bstan-bcos*. See *Analysis of the Three Vows*

Treatise which Ascertains the Three Vows. *sdom-gsum rnam-par nges-pa'i bstan-bcos*. Auth. Mnga'-ris Paṇ-chen Padma dbang-rgyal. See *Ascertainment of the Three Vows*

Treatise on Behaviour entitled the Holy Ornament. *lugs-kyi bstan-bcos dam-pa'i rgyan*. NL. Refer to n. 27. [59]

Treatise on the Behaviour of Kings. *tsa-ṇa-ka'i rgyal-po lugs-kyi bstan-bcos*. Skt. *Cāṇakyarājanītiśāstra*. T 4334. Refer to n. 85. [97]

Treatise on Description. *gdags-pa'i bstan-bcos*. Skt. *Prajñaptiśāstra*. Auth. Maudgalyāyana (or, according to other traditions, Kātyāyana). T 4086-8. Chinese version: Taishō 1538. EIPRB 27. L. de La Vallée Poussin, *L'Abhidharmakośa de Vasubandhu*. Paul Geuthner, 1923-36, Vol. 1, pp. xxxvii-xli. One of the *Seven Sections of the Abhidharma*. [*90*]

Treatise on the Difference between (the descriptions of) Buddhahood according to the Sūtra and Mantra Traditions. *mdo-sngags-kyi sangs-rgyas-la khyad-par phye-ba'i bstan-bcos*. Auth. gYung-ston Rdo-rje-dpal. NL. [*667*]

Treatise explaining the Enumerations found in the Sūtra which Gathers All Intentions. *mdo'i rnam-grangs 'chad-pa'i bstan-bcos*. Auth. Dhanarakṣita. NL. [*488-9*]

Treatise on the Proof of Authentic Transmitted Precepts. *bka' yang-dag-pa'i tshad-ma'i bstan-bcos*. Auth. Khri Srong-lde-btsan. T 4352. Refer to n. 575. [*535*]

Treatise on the Supreme Continuum of the Greater Vehicle. *rgyud bla-ma'i bstan-bcos*. See *Supreme Continuum of the Greater Vehicle*

Trilogy of Commentaries by Bodhisattvas. *sems-'grel skor-gsum*. The first two are listed separately as *Taintless Light (the Great Commentary on the Kālacakra)* and the *Commentary which Epitomises the Hevajra (Tantra)*. The third is the *Commentary which Epitomises the Short Tantra of Cakrasaṃvara*. Skt. *Laghutantrapiṇḍārthavivaraṇa*. Auth. Vajrapāṇi. T 1402. Tibetan authors usually refer to it as *phyag-rdor stod-'grel*. [*675*]

Trilogy which Dispels Darkness. *mun-sel skor-gsum*. Auth. Klong-chen Rab-'byams-pa. (1) *bsdus-don ma-rig mun-pa thams-cad sel-ba*. NMKMG Vol. 27. Xylo. Sonam Kazi, Sikkim, 1973. I(Sik)-Tib 73-905823. (2) *spyi-don legs-bshad snang-bas yid-kyi mun-pa thams-cad sel-ba*. NMKMG Vol. 27. Xylo. Sonam Kazi, Sikkim, 1973. I(Sik)-Tib 73-905821. (3) *gsang-snying 'grel-chen phyogs-bcu'i mun-sel*. The last mentioned is listed separately as the *(Commentary on the Secret Nucleus entitled) Dispelling Darkness in the Ten Directions*. NMKMG Vol. 26. Pub. Varanasi: Tarthang Tulku, *c*. 1967. I-Tib-248. Paro: Ngodup, 1975. I(Bhu)-Tib 75-903142. Trans. in GGFTC. [*591*]

Trilogy of Natural Liberation. *rang-grol skor-gsum*. Auth. Klong-chen Rab-'byams-pa. DZ Vol. 1, pp. 744-888. KLST Vol. 2, pp. 178-318. NNS. 4 (1969) I(Sik)-Tib 72-908484. Pub. Dodrup Chen Rinpoche, in the fourth vol. of his edition of the *Trilogy of Rest*. Partially trans. H. V. Guenther in *Crystal Mirror* 4 (1975), pp. 113-46. Also in Tulku Thondup Rinpoche, *Buddha Mind*. Ithaca, NY: Snow Lion, 1989. [*591*]

Trilogy of Rest. *ngal-gso skor gsum*. Auth. Klong-chen Rab-'byams-pa. Pub. in *Ṅal gso skor gsum, Raṅ grol skor gsum and Sṅags kyi spyi don*. Gangtok, Sikkim: Dodrup Chen Rinpoche, 1973. 4 vols. I(Sik)-Tib 73-903533. The root texts are translated in H. V. Guenther, *Kindly Bent to Ease Us*. 3 vols. Emeryville, California: Dharma Publications, 1975-6. [*591*]

Trio of the Cakrasaṃvara Tantra, Hevajra Tantra and Guhyasamāja Tantra. *bde-dgyes-gsang gsum*. Listed separately.

Trio of the Gathering of Transmitted Precepts, the Gathering of Intentions and Vajrakīla. *bka'-dgongs-phur gsum*. This refers in general to the treasures pertaining to the cycles of the *Eight Transmitted Precepts (bka'-brgyad)*, especially as redacted by Nyang-ral Nyi-ma 'od-zer, Guru Chos-dbang and Rig-'dzin Rgod-kyi ldem-'phru-can, the *Gathering of Intentions (dgongs-'dus)*, especially as redacted by Sangs-rgyas gling-pa and Mnga'-ris paṇ-chen, and *Vajrakīla (rdo-rje phur-pa)*, especially as redacted by Ratna gling-pa. [*881*]

Trio of the Guru, Great Perfection and Great Compassionate One. *bla-rdzogs-thugs gsum*. For its use as a general classification, refer to n. 934. [*396, 724, 764-5, 827, 881*]

Trio of the Guru, Great Perfection and Great Compassionate One. *bla-rdzogs-thugs gsum*. Disc. Sangs-rgyas bla-ma. NA. [*751*]

Trio of the Guru, Great Perfection and Great Compassionate One. *bla-rdzogs-thugs gsum*. Disc. O-rgyan gling-pa. NA. [*775*]

Trio of the Guru, Great Perfection and Great Compassionate One. *bla-rdzogs-thugs gsum*. Disc. Rdo-rje gling-pa. NA. [*791*]

Trio of Meditational Deities: Red Yamāri, Black Yamāri and Bhairava. *yi-dam dmar-nag-'jigs-gsum-gyi skor*. Disc. Bdud-'dul rdo-rje. DDTC Vol. 8. RTD Vol. 25, pp. 425-517. [*815*]

Trio of the Sūtra which Gathers All Intentions, the Tantra of the Magical Net, and the Mental Class of the Great Perfection. *mdo-sgyu-sems gsum*. The lineage of their transmission is mentioned throughout *History*, Pt. 5.

Trio of the Transmitted Precepts *(bka'-brgyad)*, Kīla *(phur-ba)* and Elixir *(sman-sgrub)*. *bka'-phur-sman gsum*. Disc. Padma gling-pa. Listed separately as the *Eight Transmitted Precepts, the Mirror of Mind*, the *Kīla which is the Utterly Secret Vital Razor* and the *Cycle of the Attainment of Nectar-Elixir*. [*797*]

Trio of Yangdak, Kīla and Yamāntaka. *yang-phur-gshin gsum*. Auth. 'Jam-mgon Kong-sprul Blo-gros mtha'-yas. Though the catalogues of Kong-sprul's work traditionally locate this "trio" in KGNZ, it has never been included as such in any edition thereof. The three are to be identified as follows: (1) *Yangdak according to the Khön tradition ('khon-lugs yang-dag)*. GCKZ Vol. 4. (2) *Vajrakīla according to the Khön tradition ('khon-lugs phur-pa)*. GCKZ Vols. 3-4. (3) *Red Yamāri (gshin-rje gshed dmar)*. KGNZ Vol. 5, pp. 3-83. [*861-2*]

Triple Cycle of the Mother and Sons, (which comprises) the All-Accomplishing King. *kun-byed rgyal-po ma-bu skor-sum*. See *Tantra of the All-Accomplishing King*, which is called a "Triple Cycle" owing to its division into three main parts: Chs. 1-57, 58-69 and 70-84. [*658*]

True Doctrine, the Innermost Spirituality of the Body of Emanation, together with (the Rites of) the Protector of this Transmitted Precept, Kṣetrapāla. *dam-chos sprul-sku'i snying-thig bka'-srung zhing-skyong-dang bcas-pa*. Disc. Bdud-'dul rdo-rje. DDTC Vols. 3-4. RTD Vol. 12, pp. 381-434. [*815*]

True Doctrine of the Most Profound Intention, the Essence of the Body, Speech and Mind of Guru Rinpoche, Yellow scrolls of the five families (which contained). *gu-ru rin-po-che'i sku-gsung-thugs-bcud dam-chos dgongs-pa yang-zab shog-ser rigs-lnga.* Disc. 'Bri-gung-pa Rin-chen phun-tshogs. RTD Vol. 6, pp. 141-76; Vol. 19, pp. 21-33; Vol. 30, pp. 229-92. Pub. Bir, HP: Tsondu Senghe, 1975. 4 vols. I-Tib 75-905229. [*676*]

True Doctrine, Three Classes of the Great Perfection. *dam-chos rdzogs-pa chen-po sde-gsum.* See *Three Classes of the Great Perfection*

Turquoise Display. *gYu-thang(-ma kras-dgu).* Auth. Nāgārjuna. P 4729. Refer to n. 220. [*40, 225, 227, 230, 352-3, 355, 366*]

Twelve Intrinsic and Extrinsic Maṇḍalas of Yangdak Heruka. *yang-dag-gi bdag-gzhan dkyil-'khor bcu-gnyis.* NL. [*620*]

Twelve Rare Tantras (of Anuyoga). *(anu-yoga'i) dkon rgyud bcu-gnyis.* The texts of Anuyoga contained in NGB Vol. 13. As stated in 'Jigs-med gling-pa, *rgyud-'bum rin-po-che'i rtogs-brjod*, p. 146, these are *zhi-ba lha-rgyud; chos-nyid zhi-ba'i lha-rgyud*; *khro-bo'i lha-rgyud chen-mo*; *khro-bo'i lha-rgyud rtogs-pa chen-po*; *thugs-rje chen-po'i gtor-rgyud*; *rnal-'byor nang-pa'i tshogs-rgyud chen-po*; *dpal-'bar khro-mo*; *rakta dmar-gyi rgyud*; *me-lha zhi-bar kyur-ba 'bar-ba'i rgyud*; *khro-bo'i sbyin-bsregs rdo-rje'i ngur-mo*; *hūṃ-mdzad chen-mo*; and *zla-gsang chen-mo*. [*283*]

Twelve-Section Kīlaya Tantra. *ki-la-ya tantra bcu-gnyis.* NGB Vol. 29, nos. 351-2. [*712*] See also *Blue-skirted One's Cycle (of Vajrakīla)*

Twenty-five Doctrinal Groups Sealed to be Kept Secret. *gsang-ba rgya-can-du gsol-ba'i chos-sde nyi-shu rtsa-lnga.* Disc. Dalai Lama V Ngag-dbang blo-bzang rgya-mtsho. TWB 5672-822. RTD *passim.* Selected texts related to this cycle pub. *Gsaṅ ba'i rnam thar rgya can ma.* SSS 42 (1972). I-Tib 72-908270. See also Samten Karmay, *Secret Visions of the Fifth Dalai Lama.* London: Serindia, 1988. [*823*]

Twenty-five (Great Profound) Treasures. *zab-pa'i gter-chen nyer-lnga.* Refer to the Glossary of Enumerations. [*518, 822*]

Twenty-four Means for Attainment which were the Prince's Contemplations. *lha-sras thugs-dam sgrub-thabs nyer-bzhi.* Disc. Mchog-gyur bde-chen gling-pa. Not yet identified among the works preserved in CLTC. [*845*]

Twenty-four Great Tantras of the Mental Class. *sems-phyogs-kyi rgyud-sde chen-po nyi-shu rtsa-bzhi.* As enumerated in Longcenpa, *Treasury of Spiritual and Philosophical Systems*, pp. 258-60, these are as follows: *sems-nyid bya-rtsol las-'das-pa nam-mkha'-che rtsa-ba'i rgyud-dang phyi-ma'i rgyud, nam-mkha-che phyi-ma phyi-ma'i rgyud, sems-nyid 'pho-'gyur med-pa chos-nyid rgyal-po'i rgyud, sems-nyid thig-le nyag-gcig-tu ston-pa byang-chub-kyi sems thig-le'i rgyud, sems-nyid rang-byung-gi ye-shes-su bstan-pa ye-shes thig-le'i rgyud, sems-nyid thams-cad-kyi rtsa-bar bstan-pa man-ngag phreng-ba'i rgyud, sems-nyid kun-khyab chen-por bstan-pa gsang-ba rgyal-po'i rgyud, sems-nyid rang-rig-tu bstan-pa ye-shes dam-pa'i rgyud, sems-nyid kun-tu bzang-po'i rol-par ston-pa mkha'-dbyings rnam-dag-gi rgyud, sems-nyid kun-gyi snying-po ston-pa man-ngag snying-po'i rgyud, sems-nyid rang-rig-tu yid-ches-pa snying-po gsang-ba'i rgyud, sems-nyid kun-gyi rtsa-ba nam-mkha' che rtsa-ba-can-gyi rgyud, sems-nyid gcig-tu 'dus-pa nyag-gcig dgongs-pa'i rgyud, sems-nyid ji-bzhin-par bzhag-pa bsam-*

gtan chen-po'i rgyud, sems-nyid rgyun-chags-su goms-pa bsam-gtan rgyun-chags-kyi rgyud, sems-nyid thams-cad-du gsungs-pa sgo-mang mdo'i rgyud, sems-nyid dbang-dang sbyar-ba nam-mkha' che dbang-gi rgyud, sems-nyid sgra-tshig las-'das-pa nam-mkha'-che yi-ge med-pa'i rgyud, sems-nyid gdod-ma'i gnas-su bstan-pa nam-mkha'-che gzhi'i rgyud, sems-nyid 'od-gsal-du bstan-pa rin-chen 'bar-ba'i rgyud, sems-nyid yon-tan lhun-grub-tu bstan-pa rin-po-che phreng-ba'i rgyud, sems-nyid khams-gsum-la gsal-ba khams-gsum sgron-ma'i rgyud, sems-nyid spang-blang las-'das-par ston-pa nges-pa snying-po'i rgyud and *sems-nyid 'pho-'gyur med-par ston-pa rdo-rje gsang-ba'i rgyud*. [*654*]

Twenty-onefold Dialogue concerning the Combined Means for the Attainment of the Three Roots. *rsta-gsum dril-sgrub zhu-lan nyer-gcig-pa*. Disc. Sangs-rgyas bla-ma. Redisc. 'Jam-dbyangs mkhyen-brtse'i dbang-po. Partially preserved in RTD Vol. 5, pp. 405-61. [*752*]

Twenty Thousand Tantras of Expressive Words. *rjod-byed tshig-gi rgyud khri-phrag gnyis*. Texts of the Esoteric Instructional Class. [*332*]

Twenty Verses on the Bodhisattva Vow. *sdom-pa nyi-shu-pa*. Skt. *Bodhisattvasaṃvaraviṃśaka*. Auth. Candragomin. T 4081. MTTWL 45. Trans. M. Tatz, *Candragomin's Twenty Verses on the Bodhisattva Vow*. LTWA. Idem, *Difficult Beginnings*. Boulder/London: Shambhala, 1985. [*95, 235*]

Two Analyses. *rnam-'byed gnyis*. Listed separately as *Analysis of the Middle and Extremes* and *Analysis of Phenomena and Reality*. [*95*]

Two Analyses. *'byed gnyis*. Skt. *Vinayavibhaṅga* ("Analysis of the Vows of a Monk"), T 3, and *Bhikṣuṇīvibhaṅga* ("Analysis of the Vows of a Nun"), T 5. HBI, pp. 181-97. [*93*]

Two Exegetical Treatises, Long and Short, on the Vajra Bridge. *rdo-rje zam-pa'i gzhung-bshad che-chung gnyis*. See *Exegetical Treatise on the Vajra Bridge*

Twofold Innermost Spirituality. *snying-tig rnam-pa gnyis*. Refer to n. 689, to the *Innermost Spirituality of the Ḍākinī* and to the *Innermost Spirituality of Vimalamitra*. [*591*]

Two Short Treatises. *gzhung-chung gnyis*. Auth. Karma-pa III, Rang-byung rdo-rje. These are the *rnam-shes ye-shes 'byed pa'i bstan-bcos* and *bde-gshegs snying-po bstan-pa'i bstan-bcos*. Xylo. Rum-btegs, Sikkim. I-(Sik)-Tib 72-905547. Pub. with the annotations of Karma-pa XV, Mkha'-khyab rdo-rje in *Three important verse treatises on aspects of Mahāyāna and Vajrayāna Buddhism*. New Delhi: Karmapae Chodhey Gyalwae Sungrab Partun Khang, 1976. I-Tib 76-902728. [*202*]

Two Stages. *rim-pa gnyis*. Skt. *Śrīguhyagarbhakramadvayoddeśa*. Auth. King Ja (Indrabhūti). P 4771. [*462*]

Two Summations. *bsdus-pa'i bstan-bcos sdom rnam-gnyis*. Listed separately as *Compendium of the Abhidharma* and *Collection of the Greater Vehicle*. [*91*]

Two Systems of the Six Doctrines. *chos-drug gnyis*. Probably this refers to the systems of Nāropā and Niguma, though it may also refer to two redactions of the system of Nāropā alone. Refer to the Glossary of

Enumerations under *Six Doctrines* and *Five Golden Doctrines of the Shangpas*, within which the position of the *Six Doctrines of Niguma* may be gathered. [*576*]

Uncommon Store. *thun-mong ma-yin-pa'i mdzod*. Disc. 'Jam-mgon Kong-sprul Blo-gros mtha'-yas. This, the collection of Kong-sprul's treasures, was never published independently. The available works making up the *Uncommon Store* are those among Kong-sprul's treasures that have been preserved in RTD. [*862*] See also *Five Great Stores*

Unsurpassedly Secret Cycle (of the Esoteric Instructional Class of the Great Perfection). *gsang-ba bla-na med-pa'i skor*. This classification, identified with the *Innermost Spirituality*, is discussed in *Fundamentals*, p. 332.

Utter Delight of the Nāgas. *klu kun-tu dga'-bo*. Skt. *Nāgānandanāṭaka*. Auth. Harṣadeva. T 4154. Tib. and Skt. edn. Vidhushekhara Bhattacharya, *Nāgānanda*. Calcutta: Asiatic Society, 1957. Ed. and trans. Bak Kun Bae, *Śrī Harṣa's Plays*. London: Asia Publishing House, 1964, pp. 49-223. Trans. A. Daniélou, *Trois Pièces de Théâtre de Harsha*. Paris: Éditions Buchet/Chastel, 1977, pp. 67-146. [*106-7*]

(Utterly Profound) Gathering of All Precious Jewels. *yang-zab dkon-mchog spyi-'dus*. Disc. Rig-'dzin 'Ja'-tshon snying-po. JTPD Vol. 1. RTD Vol. 12, pp. 1-380. Pub. 2 vols. Tezu, Arunachal Pradesh: Ngawang Sonam, 1979. I-Tib 79-903476 and I-Tib 79-903483. The many editions of liturgical texts associated with this cycle are too numerous to detail here. [*810, 811, 844*]

(Utterly Secret) Razor Kīla. *phur-pa yang-gsang spu-gri*. Disc. Gter-bdag gling-pa. Xylo. Dalhousie, HP: Phun-gling gsung-rab nyams-gso rgyun-spel par-khang, 1967. I-Tib-191. [*731, 843*]

Utterly Secret and Unsurpassed Kīla. *rat-gling phur-pa yang-gsang bla-med*. Disc. Ratna gling-pa. RLTC Vols. 10 and 18. RTD Vol. 49, p. 503 to Vol. 50, p. 36. Pub. 2 vols. Tezu, Arunachal Pradesh, 1974. I-Tib 74-901177. In addition, many editions. of liturgical texts belonging to this cycle have appeared. Some selections have been translated by A. Heller in T. Marcotty (ed.), *Dagger Blessing*. Delhi: B. R. Publishing, 1987. [*814*]

Vairocana (Tantra). *rnam-snang*. See *(Awakening of Great) Vairocana*

Vaiśravaṇa (according to the New Yamāntaka Cycle of Ra Lotsāwa). *(rwa-lugs) rnam-sras*. NL. [*713*]

Vajrabhairava Tantra. *rdo-rje 'jigs-byed*. See *Bhairava (Cycle/Tantra)*

Vajra Bridge (of the Aural Lineage). *(man-ngag) rdo-rje zam-pa*. DZ Vol. 1, pp. 372-467. NMKMG Vols. 18-19. [*544-53, 605*]

Vajraḍāka. *rdo-rje mkha'-'gro*. T 370-1. [*451*]

Vajra Garland. *rdo-rje phreng-ba*. Skt. *Vajrāvali*. Auth. Abhayākaragupta. T 3140. GDKT Vol. 22, pp. 262-660. This may also refer to the *Tantra of the Vajra Garland* (*Vajramālā*, T 445). [*264, 576, 665, 678, 824*]

Vajrakīla (Cycle/Tantra). *rdo-rje phur-pa*, *phur-pa'i rgyud* or *kīla'i rgyud*. T 439. KGDD Vol. 3. NGB Vols. 19, 27-9; and Vol. 32, no. 384 (the tantra associated with the *Eight Transmitted Precepts*). NMKMG Vols.

7-8. Also referred to as *Vajrakīla the Enlightened Activity*. [*283*, *362*, *472-3*, *481*, *483*, *575*, *657*, *676*, *710-16*, *828*, *893-4*, *922*]

Vajrakīla the Enlightened Activity. *phur-pa phrin-las*. See *Vajrakīla (Cycle/Tantra)*

Vajrakīla according to the Khön Tradition. *'khon-lugs phur-pa*. See *Khön Tradition of Vajrakīla*

Vajrakīla according to the Tradition of the Tantra. *phur-pa rgyud-lugs*. Auth. 'Jigs-med gling-pa. JLSB 6. NMKMG Vol. 7. [*839*]

Vajrāmṛta Cycle. *bdud-rtsi'i skor*. [*534*] See also *Amṛta Tantra*, *Eight Volumes of Nectar* and *Nectar the Enlightened Attributes*

Vajrapāṇi the Nectar Drop. *phyag-rdor bdud-rtsi thigs-pa'i skor*. NL. [*657*]

Vajrapāṇi as the Subduer of the Arrogant and as Slight Rage. *phyag-rdor dregs-'dul dang gtum-chung*. Disc. Padma gling-pa. PLTC Vol. 9, pp. 5-381. RTD Vol. 45, pp. 249-305. [*797*]

Vajrapāṇi (Tantras). *phyag-rdor*. T 454-64. GDKT Vol. 2, no. 19; Vol. 8, nos. 46, 49. GTKT Vol. 3. [*665*]

Vajrasattva the Great Space. *rdo-rje sems-dpa' nam-mkha'-che*. NGB Vol. 1, nos. 9, 13, 19; Vol. 2, nos. 31-2. [*370*, *372*, *657*]

Vajravidāraṇa Tantra. *(rdo-rje) rnam-'joms*. Skt. *Vajravidāraṇanāmadhāraṇī*. T 750. GDKT Vol. 2, nos. 16-18; Vol. 8, no. 47. GTKT Vol. 7. NMKMG Vol. 2. [*78*, *351*, *618*, *651*, *657*, *665*]

Valid Cognition of the Transmitted Precepts, (the Esoteric Instructions of the Ḍākinī). *bka' yang-dag-pa'i tshad-ma (zhes-bya-ba (mkha'-'gro-ma)'i man-ngag)*. Skt. *Ājñāsamyakpramāṇa*. Auth. Tilopā. T 2331. [*199*]

Vanquisher. *zil-gnon*. Disc. 'Bri-gung-pa Chos-dbyings rang-grol. NL. [*682*]

Variegated Deity Vajrakīla. *phur-pa lha-khra*. [*710*]

Vast Expanse of the View, a Father Tantra of the Great Perfection. *rdzogs-chen pha-rgyud lta-ba klong-yangs*. Disc. Rdo-rje gling-pa. Referred to in DLTC, Vol. 2, p. 56. Partially preserved in RTD Vol. 88, pp. 63-85. [*789*]

Veda. *rig-byed*. See *Four Veda*

Venerable Lady's Tradition of Vajrakīla. *phur-pa jo-mo lugs*. [*710*]

Verification of Co-emergence. *lhan-cig skyes-grub*. Skt. *Sahajasiddhi*. Auth. Indrabhūti. T 2260. Skt. and Tib. edn. in *Guhyādi-aṣṭasiddhi saṃgraha*. Sarnath: Rare Buddhist Text Project, 1987. [*462*]

Verification of Pristine Cognition. *ye-shes grub-pa*. Skt. *Jñānasiddhi*. Auth. Indrabhūti. T 2219. GOS 44. Skt. and Tib. edn. in *Guhyādi-aṣṭasiddhi saṃgraha*. Sarnath: Rare Buddhist Text Project, 1987. [*462*]

Verification of Secrets. *gsang-ba grub-pa*. Skt. *Sakalatantrasambhavasañcodanīśrīguhyasiddhināma* or *Guhyasiddhi*. Auth. Saroruha (Padmavajra). T 2217. Skt. and Tib. edn. in *Guhyādi-aṣṭasiddhi saṃgraha*. Sarnath: Rare Buddhist Text Project, 1987. [*916*]

Verse Summation of the Transcendental Perfection of Discriminative Awareness. *mdo sdud-pa* or *sher-phyin sdud-pa*. Skt. *Prajñāpāramitāsaṃcayagā-*

thā or *Ratnaguṇasaṃcayagāthā*. T 13. EIPRB 445-54. MTTWL 183. B.Budh. 29. BST 17 (1961). See also Akira Yuyama, "The First Two Chapters of the *Prajñā-pāramitā-ratna-guṇa-saṃcaya-gāthā*" in PRS, pp. 203-18. [*74*, *80*, *232*, *343*, *854*, *871*]

View of Reason. *rigs-pa'i lta-ba*. Skt. *Nyāyadarśana* or *Nyāyasūtra*. Auth. Akṣapāda (Gautama). EIPRB 775-853. HIL 6.2, pp. 76-80. [*65*]

Vinayapiṭaka. *'dul-ba'i sde-snod rnams*. T 1-7. Refer to E. Frauwallner, *The Earliest Vinaya and the Beginnings of Buddhist Literature*. SOR 8 (1956). [*80*, *423*, *663*] See also *Transmissions of the Vinaya*

Vinayavastu. *'dul-ba'i gzhi*. T 1. HBI pp. 181-97. See also Jampa Panglung, "Preliminary Remarks on the Uddānas in the Vinaya of the Mūlasarvāstivādin" in TSHR, pp. 226-32. Idem, *Die Erzählstoffe des Mūlasarvāstivādin-Vinaya*. Tokyo: Reyukai Library, 1983. F.-R. Hamm, *Rab tu 'byuṅ ba'i gźi. Die tibetische übersetzung des Pravrajyāvastu im Vinaya des Mūlasarvāstivādins*. Ed. and seen through the press by H. Eimer. 2 vols. Asiatische Forschungen 82. Wiesbaden: Otto Harrassowitz, 1983. [*93*]

Vindication of Conventional Truth. *tha-snyad sgrub-pa*. Skt. *Vyavahārasiddhi*. Auth. Nāgārjuna. Only some fragments (in Tibetan) available. HIL 7.1, pp. 8, 26. MTTWL 258. [*94*]

Warm Sunbeam of the Attainment of Mind. *thugs-sgrub tsha-ba dmar-thag*. Disc. Sangs-rgyas gling-pa. BMGD Vol. 2. [*841*]

Way of Reciting the Rulu Mantra. *ru-lu'i 'dren-stangs*. A recollection of Mchog-gyur bde-chen gling-pa; probably not to be identified with a particular text. [*847*]

Weapons of Expression. *smra-ba'i mtshon-cha*. Auth. Agni. NL. [*65*]

Wind-Lasso of Īśvara. *dbang-phyug rlung-zhags*. Disc. Sangs-rgyas gling-pa. NL. [*786*]

Wish-fulfiller. *'dod-'jo*. Skt. *Amaraṭīkākāmadhenu*. Auth. Subhūticandra. T 4300. Partially ed. S. C. Vidyabhusana, *Amaraṭīkā Kāmadhenuḥ*. Calcutta: Biblia Indica Tibetan Series, 1912. Ed. L. Chandra, *The Amarakoṣa in Tibet*. SP 38 (1965). HIL 5.4, pp. 314-15. [*51*]

Wish-fulfilling Treasury, (root text and commentary). *yid-bzhin (rin-po-che'i) mdzod (rtsa-'grel)*. Auth. Klong-chen Rab-'byams-pa. Pub. Dodrup Chen Rimpoche, Gangtok, Sikkim. 2 vols. I-Tib-143. KCZD Vol. 1. Ch. 1 trans. K. Lipman in *Crystal Mirror* 5 (1977), pp. 344-64. Also referred to as the *Precious Wish-fulfilling Treasury*. [*41*, *197*, *209-10*, *827*]

Wrathful Guru. *gur-drag*. Disc. O-rgyan gling-pa. Available through the seventeenth century, but now NA. [*778*]

Wrathful Guru. *gur-drag*. Disc. Gter-bdag gling-pa. RTD Vol. 19, pp. 343-441. [*828*]

Wrathful Guru, the Innermost Spirituality of the Red HŪṂ. *gur-drag hūṃ-dmar snying-thig*. Disc. Sangs-rgyas gling-pa. Redisc. Mchog-gyur bde-chen gling-pa. CLTC Vol. 26. [*846*]

Wrathful Mantra which Halts All the Mönpa Spirits. *ngan-sngags mon-pa dgu-rdug*. Disc. Sangs-rgyas gling-pa and Dri-med lhun-po. NL. [*786*]

Wrathful Mantras of the Oceanic Cycle of Yamāntaka. *gshed-skor rgya-mtsho'i drag-sngags*. Introduced by Gnubs-chen Sangs-rgyas ye-shes. Cf. the *Zla gsaṅ be'u bum*. Dehra Dun: D. G. Khochhen Trulku, 1975. I-Tib 75-904324. [*610*]

Yajurveda. *mchod-sbyin*. The fourth of the *Four Veda*. HIL 1.1, Ch. 7, pp. 323-37. [*65*]

Yamāntaka and Yamāri: Introductory Note. The great proliferation, particularly in the Nyingma tradition, of meditational and ritual cycles focusing upon a great many aspects of the wrathful forms of Mañjuśrī—Yamāntaka, Yamāri, and Bhairava—makes the exact identification of texts especially difficult here. Following are some main collections of relevant texts: T 467-75 and 478. NGB Vols. 20-2. GDKT Vols. 8-10, nos. 52-9. KGDD Vol. 3 (NGB Vol. 32, no. 382). KGNZ Vol. 5, pp. 3-177. NMKMG Vols. 4-6

Yamāntaka Cycle. *gshin-rje'i skor*. Disc. Dum-pa rgya zhang-khrom. Pub. 3 vols. Tashi Jong, HP: Khampa Gar Monastery, 1981. I-Tib 81-901503/901710. Pub. 2 vols. *'Jam dpal gśin rje'i gśed khro chu dug sdoṅ nag po'i chos skor*. Bir, HP: Pema Lodoe and Zogyam, 1978-80. I-Tib 78-906117. Pub. 2 vols. *'Jam dpal khro chu dug gdoṅ nag po'i sgrub skor*. Thimphu: Ugyen Tempai Gyaltsen, 1981. Bhu-Tib 81-901844. [*713*]

Yamāntaka (Cycle/Tantra). *gshin-rje*. Where the context involves the revealed treasures of the *Eight Transmitted Precepts* (*bka'-brgyad*) in particular, the reference is to NGB Vol. 32, no. 382. KGDD Vol. 3. Also referred to as the *Lord of Life*. [*477-9*, *483*, *535*, *609-11*, *614*, *666*, *673*, *674*, *762*, *827*] See also *Bhairava (Cycle/Tantra)*, *Yamāntaka and Yamāri: Introductory Note* and *Yamāri (Cycle/Tantra)*

Yamāntaka, the Destroyer of Arrogance. *gshin-rje-gshed dregs-'joms*. Disc. Gter-bdag gling-pa. Pub. Dehra Dun: D. G. Khochhen Tulku, 1976. I-Tib 77-900730. [*828*]

Yamāntaka, Lord of Life. *gshin-rje tshe-bdag*. Disc. Sangs-rgyas gling-pa and Dri-med lhun-po. NL. [*786*]

Yamāri (Cycle/Tantra). *gshed (skors/rgyud)*. [*534*, *615*, *689*] See also *Black Yamāri*, *Red Yamāri (Cycle/Tantra)* and *Yamāntaka and Yamāri: Introductory Note*

Yamari: Red and Black. *gshin-rje dmar-nag*. See *Black Yaṃāri* and *Red Yamāri (Cycle/Tantra)*

Yangdak Heruka according to the So tradition. *yang-dag so-lugs*. NL. [*849*]

Yangdak Heruka (Cycle/Tantra) *or* Yangdak, the Mind. *yang-dag* or *yang-dag thugs(-kyi bka'-babs)*. Where the context suggests that it is a tantra belonging to the *Eight Transmitted Precepts* to which reference is made, the text in question is probably to be identified with NGB Vol. 32, no. 381. NMKMG Vol. 3. More generally, the tantras focusing on Yangdak are collected in NGB Vol. 25. [*283*, *361*, *362*, *472*, *473*, *475-7*, *483*, *673-4*, *710*, *762*, *827*, *893-4*, *922-3*] See also *Heruka Galpo (Cycle/Tantra)*

Yangdak Mecik ("Yangdag the Single Flame"). *yang-dag me-gcig*. Incorporated into NMKMG Vol. 3. [*673-4*] See also *Yangdak Heruka (Cycle/Tantra)*

Yangdak, the Mind. See *Yangdak Heruka (Cycle/Tantra)*

Yangdak Rulu Golden Rosary. *yang-dag ru-lu gser-phreng*. Auth. Hūṃkara. NL. [*476*]

Yangdak combined with Vajrakīla. *yang-phur sbrags-ma*. General term for meditational and ritual cycles in which the practices of these two deities are found together. [*472*]

Yangdok. *yang-bzlog*. Name of an aspect of wrathful Mañjuśrī propitiated to avert the calamities brought about by violent enemies. [*727*]

Yellow Scrolls of the Means for Attainment and Sacraments of the Eight Closest Sons. *nye-sras-brgyad-kyi dam-rdzas dang sgrub-thabs shog-ser*. Disc. 'Jam-mgon Kong-sprul Blo-gros mtha'-yas. NA. Kong-sprul's redaction of the means for attainment based upon this, however, has been published xylographically at Rum-btegs, Sikkim. [*864*]

Yoga of Co-emergence. *lhan-skyes rnal-'byor*. For examples representing the tradition of Sgam-po-pa, see DZ Vols. 5-7. [*547*]

Yogācāra Level. *rnal-'byor spyod-pa'i sa* or *sa-sde*. Skt. *Yogācārabhūmiśāstra*. Auth. Asaṅga. T 4035-42. EIPRB 1268-87. MTTWL 258. TSWS 7 (1978) and 14 (1973). See n. 72 for their identification. Also referred to as the *Five Sections of the Levels*. [*89*, *91*, *98*, *230*]

Yogic Exercises of Bhairava. *bhairava'i 'phrul-'khor*. In the context in which this reference occurs, it is almost certainly a teaching of the Dge-lugs-pa tradition. Representative Dge-lugs-pa manuals on the yogas of Bhairava will be found listed in L. Chandra (ed.), *Materials for a History of Tibetan Literature*, Vol. 3, SP 30 (1963), pp. 729-39. [*681*]

Yogic Exercises of the Nine Vigorous Skills according to the Gathering of Intentions. *dgongs-'dus rtsal-sprugs rnam-dgu'i 'khrul-'khor*. Disc. Mchog-gyur bde-chen gling-pa. NL. [*847*]

Yogic Sequence which is a Lamp on the Greater Vehicle. *rnal-'byor-gyi rim-pa theg-chen sgron-ma*. Auth. Sukhodyotaka. NL. [*489*]

Yungtönpa's Commentary on the Secret Nucleus. *bod-'grel gYung-ṭīk*. See *Illuminating Mirror, a Commentary on the Tantra of the Secret Nucleus*

Zhama Tradition of the Path and Fruit. *lam-'bras zha-ma lugs*. Refer to *Blue Annals*, pp. 218ff. [*657*]

Zur Tradition of (the Empowerment for) the Sūtra which Gathers All Intentions. *mdo-(dbang) zur-lugs*. This tradition is partially preserved in NMKMG. See also *Zur lugs gsaṅ sñiṅ yig cha'i skor*. 4 vols. Dalhousie, HP: Damchoe Sangpo, 1980-1. I-Tib 80-902507. [*672*, *727*]

Part Two
Works Referred to by the Translators

1 *Indic Texts*

Acintyastava. Auth. Nāgārjuna. Ed. C. Lindtner, *Nagarjuniana*. Indiske Studier IV. Copenhagen: Akademisk Forlag, 1982, pp. 140-61.

Advayavajrasaṃgraha. Auth. Advayavajra (i.e. Maitripā). Ed. H. Sastri, GOS 40 (1927).

Abhidharmakośakārikā and *Bhāṣya*. Auth. Vasubandhu. Ed. D. Shastri, BB 5-8 (1970-2). Trans. L. de La Vallée-Poussin, *L'Abhidharmakośa de Vasubandhu*. 6 vols. Paris: Paul Guethner, 1923-36. Repr. MCB 16 (1971).

Abhidharmakośavyākhyā. Auth. Yaśomitra. Ed. D. Shastri, BB 5-8 (1970-2).

Abhisamayālaṃkāra. Auth. Maitreyanātha. Ed. P. L. Vaidya, BST 4 (1960).

Abhisamayālaṃkārāloka. Auth. Haribhadra. Ed. P. L. Vaidya, BST 4 (1960).

Udānavarga. Auth. Dharmatrāta. Tib. edn. H. Beckh, *Udānavarga: eine Sammlung buddhistischer Spruche in tibetischer Sprache*. Berlin, 1911. Skt. edn. F. Bernhard, *Udānavarga*. 2 vols. Göttingen: Vandenhoeck & Ruprecht, 1965-8.

Karaṇḍavyūhasūtra. Ed. P. L. Vaidya, BST 17 (1961).

Gaṇḍavyūhasūtra. Ed. P. L. Vaidya, BST 5 (1960).

Guhyasamājatantra. Ed. S. Bagchi, BST 9 (1965). Ed. B. Bhattacharya, GOS 53 (1967).

Catuḥśataka. Auth. Āryadeva. Chs. 8-16 ed. and trans. in P. L. Vaidya, *Études sur Āryadeva et son Catuḥśataka*. Paris: Paul Guethner, 1923. Ed. with Hindi trans., Bhāgcandra Jain Bhāskar, *Catuḥśatakam*. Nagpur: Ālok Prakāśan, 1971.

Cullavagga. The lesser section of the Khaṇḍaka of the Vinayapiṭaka. Ed. H. Oldenberg. Pali Text Society, 1880. Trans. I. B. Horner, *The Book of Discipline*, Vol. V, 1952.

Jātakamālā. Auth. Āryaśūra. Ed. P. L. Vaidya, BST 21 (1959). Trans. J. S. Speyer, *The Jātakamālā of Āryaśūra*. London: Pali Text Society, 1895.

Tattvasaṃgrahakārikā. Auth. Śāntarakṣita. Ed. D. Shastri, BB 1-2 (1968). Trans. G. Jha, GOS 80 (1937), 83 (1939).

Tattvasaṃgrahapañjikā. Auth. Kamalaśīla. Ed. and trans. together with *Tattvasaṃgrahakārikā*.

Tattvopaplavasiṃha. Auth. Jayarāśi. Ed. S. Sanghavi and R. C. Parikh, GOS 87 (1940).

Tarkajvāla. Auth. Bhāvaviveka. P 5256. Ch. 3, 1-136, ed. and trans. in Shotaro Iida, *Reason and Emptiness: A Study in Logic and Mysticism*. Tokyo: The Hokuseido Press, 1980.

Triṃśikā. Auth. Vasubandhu. Ed. S. Lévi, *Vijñaptimātratāsiddhī*. Paris: Librairie Ancienne Honoré Champion, 1925. Trans. S. Lévi, *Materiaux pour l'étude du système Vijñaptimātra*. Paris: Librairie Ancienne Honoré Champion, 1932.

Dīpavaṃsa. Ed. and trans. Oldenberg. London: Williams and Norgate, 1879.

Divyāvadāna. Ed. P. L. Vaidya. BST 18 (1959).

Dhammapāda. Ed. and trans. S. Radhakrishnan. London: Oxford University Press, 1950.

Dharmadhātustava. Auth. Nāgārjuna. Fragments collected by D. S. Ruegg in *Études tibétaines dédiées à la mémoire de Marcelle Lalou*. Paris: A. Maisonneuve, 1971, pp. 448-71.

Navatattvasūtra. Trans. J. Stevenson, 1848. Repr. Varanasi: Bharat-Bharati, 1972.

Niṣpannayogāvalī. Ed. B. Bhattacharya, GOS 109 (1972).

Nyāyavārttika. Auth. Uddyotakara. Ed. in *Nyāyadarśanam*. Kyoto: Rinsen Book Company, 1982.

Nyāyapraveśa. Śaṅkarasvāmin. Ed. A. B. Dhruva, GOS 38 (1930), 39 (1927). Ed. and trans. Musashi Tachikawa, "A Sixth Century Manual of Indian Logic" JIP 1 (1971), pp. 111-45.

Pañcāstikāya. Ed. and trans. A. Chakravartinayanar, *The Sacred Books of the Jains*, Vol. 3. Arrah, India, 1920. Repr. New York: AMS Press, 1974.

Prajñāpāramitāpiṇḍārtha. Auth. Dignāga. Ed. P. L. Vaidya, BST 4 (1960).

Prajñāpāramitāsañcayagāthā (i.e. *Ratnaguṇasañcayagāthā*). Ed. P. L. Vaidya, BST 17 (1961).

Pramāṇanayatattvālokālaṃkāra. Auth. Deva Sūri. See *Ornamental Mirror of Categories*

Pramāṇavārttika. Auth. Dharmakīrti. Ed. D. Shastri, BB 3 (1968). *Svārthānumāna* chapter ed. R. Gnoli, SOR 23 (1960).

Pramāṇaviniścaya. Auth. Dharmakīrti. T 4211. T. Vetter, *Dharmakīrti's Pramāṇaviniścayaḥ*, I. Österreichische Akademie der Wissenschaften. Philosophisch-Historische Klasse. Sitzungsberichte 250, Band 3. Vienna, 1966. E. Steinkellner, *Dharmakīrti's Pramāṇaviniścayaḥ*, II.1. Sitzungsberichte 287, Band 4. Vienna, 1973. E. Steinkellner, *Dharmakīrti's Pramāṇaviniścayaḥ*, II.2. Sitzungsberichte 358. Vienna, 1979.

Pramāṇasamuccayakārikā and *Vṛtti*. Auth. Dignāga. T 4203-4. Partially ed. and trans. in M. Hattori, *Dignāga on Perception*. HOS 47 (1968).

Prasannapadā. Auth. Candrakīrti. Ed. P. L. Vaidya, BST 10 (1960). Partially trans. M. Sprung, *Lucid Exposition of the Middle Way*. Boulder: Prajñā Press, 1979.

Buddhacarita. Auth. Aśvaghoṣa. Ed. and trans. E. H. Johnston. Delhi: Motilal Banarsidass, 1972.

Bodhicittavivaraṇa. Auth. Nāgārjuna. Ed. C. Lindtner, *Nagarjuniana*. Indiske Studier IV. Copenhagen: Akademisk Forlag, 1982, pp. 180-217.

Bodhisattvacaryāvatāra. Auth. Śāntideva. Ed. P. L. Vaidya, BST 12 (1960). Trans. S. Batchelor, *A Guide to the Bodhisattva's Way of Life*. LTWA, 1979.

Bodhisattvacaryāvatārapañjikā. Auth. Prajñākaramati. Ed. P. L. Vaidya, BST 12 (1960).

Bhadrakalpikasūtra. T 94. MTTWL 26. See *Auspicious Aeon Sūtra*

Bhadracaryāpraṇidhānarāja. Skt. and Tib. edn. S. K. Pathak, *Śrīḥ Āryabhadracaripraṇidhānarāja*. Gangtok, Sikkim: Namgyal Institute of Tibetology, 1961.

Bhikṣuvibhaṅga. T 3. See *Two Analyses*

Mañjuśrīnāmasaṃgīti. Ed. and trans. R. M. Davidson, "The Litany of Names of Mañjuśrī" MCB 20 (1981), pp. 1-69.

Madhyāntavibhāga. Auth. Maitreyanātha. TSWS 10 (1967).

Mahāyānasaṃgraha. Auth. Asaṅga. Ed. and trans. É. Lamotte, *La Somme du Grand Véhicule d'Asaṅga*. 2 vols. Louvain: Institut Orientaliste, 1973.

Mahāyānasūtrālaṃkāra. Auth. Maitreyanātha. Ed. S. Bagchi, BST 13 (1970).

Mahāyānasūtrālaṃkāravyākhyā. Auth. Vasubandhu. Ed. together with the preceding.

Mahāyānottaratantraśāstra. Auth. Maitreyanātha. Skt. edn. E. H. Johnston, *Ratnagotravibhāga Mahāyānottaratantraśāstra*. Patna: Bihar Research Society, 1950. Tib. edn. Zuiryu Nakamura, *Zō-wa-taishō, Kukyō-ichijō-hōshōron-kenkyū*. Tokyo: Suzuki Gakujutsu Zaidan (Suzuki Research Foundation), 1967. Trans. Jikido Takasaki, *A Study on the Ratnagotravibhāga*, SOR 33 (1966).

Mahāyānottaratantraśāstravyākhyā. Auth. Asaṅga. Ed. together with the preceding.

Mahāvaṃsa. Auth. Mahānāma. Ed. W. Geiger. Pali Text Society, 1908; repr. 1958. Trans. Geiger. Colombo: Govt. of Ceylon, 1912; repr. 1980.

Mahāvastu. Trans. J. J. Jones. 3 vols. Sacred Books of the Buddhists 16, 18, 19. London: Luzac and Co., 1949-56.

Mahāvyutpatti. Ed. R. Sakaki, Kyoto, 1916-25; repr. Tokyo, 1965.

Mūlamadhyamakakārikā. Auth. Nāgārjuna. Ed. P. L. Vaidya, BST 10 (1960). Trans. in F. J. Streng, *Emptiness: A Study in Religious Meaning*. Nashville/New York: Abingdon, 1967, pp. 183-220.

Mūlāpattisaṃgraha. Auth. Aśvaghoṣa. T 5270. Ed. and trans. S. Lévi, *Journal Asiatique*, Oct.-Dec. 1929, pp. 266-7.

Ratnāvali. Auth. Nāgārjuna. Skt. fragments ed. P. L. Vaidya, BST 10 (1960). Tib. edn. L. P. Lhalungpa. *Dbuma [sic] rigs tshogs drug*. Delhi, 1970. Trans. J. Hopkins, *The Precious Garland and the Song of the Four Mindfulnesses*. London: Allen and Unwin, 1975.

Laṅkāvatārasūtra. Ed. P. L. Vaidya, BST 3 (1963). Trans. D. T. Suzuki, *The Laṅkāvatāra Sūtra*. London: Routledge and Kegan Paul, 1932, 1956, etc.

Lalitavistarasūtra. Ed. P. L. Vaidya, BST 1 (1958).

Vajracchedikā. Ed. P. L. Vaidya, BST 17 (1961). Ed. and trans. E. Conze, *Vajracchedikā Prajñāpāramitā*, SOR 13 (1957).

Vigrahavyāvartanī. Auth. Nāgārjuna. Ed. P. L. Vaidya, BST 10 (1960). Ed. and trans. K. Bhattacharya, *The Dialectical Method of Nāgārjuna*. Delhi: Motilal Banarsidass, 1978. Root text ed. C. Lindtner, *Nagarjuniana*. Indiske Studier IV. Copenhagen: Akademisk Forlag, 1982, pp. 70-86.

Vimalakīrtinirdeśasūtra. Tib. edn. Jisshu Oshika, *Acta Indologica* 1 (1970), pp. 137-240. Translations by É. Lamotte, C. Luk and R. A. F. Thurman are listed separately in the final section of the Bibliography.

Vyavahārasiddhi. Auth. Nāgārjuna. Fragments ed. C. Lindtner, *Nagarjuniana*. Indiske Studier IV. Copenhagen: Akademisk Forlag, 1982, pp. 94-9.

Śikṣāsamuccaya. Ed. P. L. Vaidya, BST 11 (1961).

Śrīmālādevīsūtra. Trans. A. and H. Wayman, *The Lion's Roar of Queen Śrīmālā*. New York/London: Columbia University Press, 1974.

Ṣaḍdarśanasamuccaya. Auth. Haribhadrasūri. Ed. K. N. Mishra. Chowkhamba Sanskrit Series 95. Varanasi, 1979.

Satyadvayavibhaṅga. Auth. Jñānagarbha. Ed. and trans. M. D. Eckel, *Jñānagarbha's Commentary on the Distinction between the Two Truths*. Albany, NY: SUNY Press, 1986.

Saddharmapuṇḍarīkasūtra. Ed. P. L. Vaidya, BST 6 (1960). Trans. L. Hurvitz, *Scripture of the Lotus Blossom of the Fine Dharma*. New York: Columbia University Press, 1976.

Samādhirājasūtra. Ed. P. L. Vaidya, BST 2 (1961).

Sarvadarśanasaṃgraha. Auth. Sāyaṇa Mādhava. Ed. V. Abhyankar. Poona: Bhandarkar Oriental Research Institute, 1978.

Sukhāvatīvyūhasūtra. Ed. P. L. Vaidya, BST 17 (1961). Trans. F. Max Müller, SBE 49.

Suhṛllekha. Auth. Nāgārjuna. Ed. A. Sonam. Sarnath, UP: Rin-chen dongrub, 1971. I-Tib 72-924259. Trans. P. D. Santina et al., *Nāgārjuna's Letter to King Gautamīputra*. Delhi: Motilal Banarsidass, 1976.

Stavakāya. Auth. Nāgārjuna. See *Collection of Eulogies*

Hevajratantra. Ed. and trans. D. L. Snellgrove. *The Hevajra Tantra*, Pts. 1 and 2. London Oriental Series, Vol. 6. London: Oxford University Press, 1959; repr. 1964, 1971.

2 *Tibetan Texts*

kun-bzang bla-ma'i zhal-lung. Auth. Rdza Dpal-sprul O-rgyan 'jigs-med chos-kyi dbang-po. Xylo. Rum-btegs, Sikkim, *c.* 1968. I(Sik)-Tib 76-903001.

kloṅ-chen gsuṅ-thor-bu. Auth. Klong-chen Rab-'byams-pa. KCST.

bka'-thang gser-phreng. Disc. Sangs-rgyas gling-pa. Kalimpong: Dudjom Rinpoche, 1970. I-Tib 79-922880.

bka'-gdams pha-chos bu-chos. Litho. 2 vols. Varanasi: Kalsang Lhundup, 1973. I-Tib 73-906437.

bka'-babs bdun-ldan-gyi rnam-thar. Auth. Tāranātha. Reproduced in *Two Sources for the History of Buddhist Tantricism in India*. SNGP, 1970. I-Tib 73-913513.

mkha' 'gro gsaṅ ba kun 'dus kyi chos skor. Disc. 'Jam-dbyang mkhyen-brtse'i dbang-po. Gangtok: Gonpo Tsetan Lama, 1976. I-Tib 76-903111.

mkhas-pa'i tshul-la 'jug-pa'i sgo. Auth. 'Jam-mgon Mi-pham rgya-mtsho. Xylo. SNGP, n.d.

khrid-brgya lo-rgyus. Auth. Jo-nang rje-btsun Kun-dga' grol-mchog, completed by Tāranātha. DZ Vol. 12, pp. 309-58.

khrid-yig ye-shes bla-ma. Auth. 'Jigs-med gling-pa. Xylo. SNGP, n.d.

grub-mtha' bsdus-pa. Auth. 'Jam-mgon Mi-pham rnam-rgyal. Pub. in Vol. 2 of Dodrup Chen Rinpoche's edn. of the *Wish-fulfilling Treasury*, listed in the first part of the Bibliography.

grub-mtha' shel-gyi me-long. Auth. Thu'u-bkvan chos-kyi rdo-rje. See *Crystal Mirror of Philosophical Systems*

dge-ldan bka'-brgyud rin-po-che'i phyag-chen rtsa-ba rgyal-ba'i gzhung-lam. Auth. Paṇ-chen blo-bzang chos-kyi rgyal-mtshan. DZ Vol. 3, pp. 421-30.

dgongs-pa grub-pa'i rgyud. NL. Quoted in the *sngags-kyi spyi-don tshangs-dbyangs 'brug-sgra* of Klong-chen Rab-'byams-pa. Varanasi: Tarthang Tulku, *c.* 1968.

rgyal-rabs. Auth. Bdud-'joms Rin-po-che. Full title: *gangs chen bod chen po'i rgyal rabs 'dus gsal du bkod pa sngon med dvangs shel 'phrul gyi me long*. In *The Collected Works of H. H. Bdud-'joms Rin-po-che*, Vol. 3.

rgyal-rabs gsal-ba'i me-long. Auth. Bla-ma dam-pa Bsod-nams rgyal-mtshan. Ed. Kuznetsov. Leiden: E. J. Brill, 1966.

rgyud rang-byung rang-shar. NGB Vol. 10.

rgyud bla-ma'i 'grel-pa. Auth. 'Jam-mgon Kong-sprul Blo-gros mtha'-yas. Xylo. Rum-btegs Monastery, Sikkim, n.d.

rgyud-'bum dris-lan. Auth. 'Jigs-med gling-pa. JLSB Vol. 3.

rgyud-'bum-gyi dkar-chag. Auth. Bu-ston Rin-chen-grub. *The Collected Works of Bu-ston Rin-chen-grub*, Vol. 24. SP 64. I-Tib-49.

rgyud gsang-ba snying-po'i 'grel-chen gsang-bdag zhal-lung. Auth. Lo-chen Dharmaśrī. NMKMG Vol. 32. SSS 36 (1972). I-Tib 72-903163.

sgra-sbyor bam-gnyis. T 4347. Ed. Sonam Angdu, in *Tibeto-Sanskrit Lexicographical Materials*. Leh: Rinchen Tondup Tongspon, 1973. I-Tib 76-901144.

sngags-kyi spyi-don tshangs-dbyangs 'brug-sgra. Auth. Klong-chen Rab-'byams-pa. Varanasi: Tarthang Tulku, *c*. 1968. Also pub. in Vol. 4 of Dodrup Chen Rinpoche's edn. of the *Trilogy of Rest*, listed in the first part of the Bibliography.

sngags-log sun-'byin-gyi skor. Auth. 'Gos Khug-pa Lhas-btas et al. See *Rejections of Perverse Doctrines*

rje-btsun thams-cad mkhyen-pa bai-ro-tsa-na'i rnam-thar 'dra-'bag chen-mo. Biography of Vairocana. Xylo. Lhasa.

'jam-dbyangs mkhyen-brtse'i dbang-po'i gsung-rtsom gces-sgrig. Auth. 'Jam-dbyangs Mkhyen-brtse'i dbang-po. Chengdu: Sichuan Minorities Press, 1989.

'ju-lan ga-bur chu-rgyun. Auth. Pa-ri rab-gsal. Litho. Delhi: Byams-pa chos-rgyal, 1969.

chos-kyi rnam-grangs. Auth. Dgon-po dbang-rgyal. Chengdu: Sichuan Minorities Press, 1986.

rnying-ma'i rgyud-'bum-gyi rtogs-brjod. Auth. 'Jigs-med gling-pa. See *Narrative History of the Precious Collected Tantras of the Ancient Translation School, the Ornament Covering All Jambudvīpa*

snying-thig rtsa-pod. Disc. 'Jigs-med gling-pa. 3 vols. Paro: Ngodrup, 1976

gter-chen chos-kyi rgyal-po khrag-'thung bdud-'joms gling-pa'i rnam-thar zhal-gsung-ma. Xylo. Lhasa, n.d. Also pub. Dehra Dun: G. T. K. Lodoy and N. Gyaltsen, 1970.

gter-ston brgya-rtsa. Auth. 'Jam-mgon Kong-sprul Blo-gros mtha'-yas. See *Lives of the Hundred Treasure-finders, a Beauteous Rosary of Precious Beryl*

gter-mdzod thob-yig. Auth. Bdud-'joms Rin-po-che. Litho. *po-ti* format, n.d.

gtum-mo 'bar-'dzag yig-chung. In *snying-thig rtsa-pod*, Vol. 3, pp. 23-6.

bstan-rtsis kun-las btus-pa. Auth. Tshe-brtan zhabs-drung. Xining: Qinghai Minorities Press, 1982.

theg-mchog rin-po-che'i mdzod. Auth. Klong-chen Rab-'byams-pa. See *Treasury of the Supreme Vehicle thub-pa dgongs-gsal*. Auth. Sa-skya Paṇḍita. SK Vol. 5, no. 1.

deb-ther sngon-po. See *Blue Annals*

dris-lan lung-dang rigs-pa'i 'brug-sgra. Auth. Sog-bzlog-pa Blo-gros Rgyal-mtshan. In *Collected Writings of Sog-bzlog-pa Blo-gros-rgyal-mtshan*. 2 vols. New Delhi: Sanje Dorje, 1975. I-Tib 75-900763.

sde-brgyad gser-skyems. Auth. Gnubs-chen Sangs-rgyas ye-shes. Xylo. Mtho-mthong Monastery, Nepal. N-Tib 72-902832.

sdom-gsum-gyi rab-tu dbye-ba'i bstan-bcos. Auth. Sa-skya Paṇḍita. SK Vol. 5, no. 24. See *Analysis of the Three Vows*

mdo mdzangs-blun. T 341. Typeset edn. Dharmsala, HP: Council of Cultural and Religious Affairs of His Holiness the Dalai Lama, 1968. I-Tib 77-921896. Xining: Qinghai Minorities Press, 1984. Trans., from the Mongolian, S. Frye, *Sutra of the Wise and the Foolish*. LTWA, 1981. See *Sūtra of the Wise and Foolish*

gnas-lugs rin-po-che'i mdzod. Auth. Klong-chen Rab-'byams-pa. See *Treasury of the Abiding Nature of Reality*

rnam thar rgyas pa. See H. Eimer, *Rnam thar rgyas pa: Materialen zu einer Biographie des Atiśa*, in the following section.

pad-gling 'khrungs-rabs-kyi rtogs-brjod nyung-gsal dad-pa'i me-tog. PLTC Vol. 14, pp. 511-600.

padma bka'-thang. Disc. O-rgyan gling-pa. Listed as the *Injunction of Padma (which was Discovered at Crystal Rock)* in the first part of the Bibliography; and as *The Life and Liberation of Padmasambhava*, in the final part.

dpag bsam ljon bzang. Auth. Sum-pa mkhan-po Ye-shes dpal-'byor. Ed. S. C. Das, *Pag Sam Jon Zang*. Calcutta: Presidency Jail Press, 1908.

dpag-bsam snye-ma. Auth. Lo-chen Dharmaśrī. NMKMG Vol. 37. Tibetan xylo. Rdza-rong-phu Monastery. N-Tib 71-914803.

dpa'-bo chos-'byung. Auth. Dpa'-bo Gtsug-lag 'phreng-ba. See *Scholar's Feast of Doctrinal History*

dpal-spungs yang-khrod tsā-'dra rin-chen brag-gi sgrub-sde'i dkar-chag. Auth. 'Jam-mgon Kong-sprul Blo-gros mtha'-yas. GCKZ Vol. 11, pp. 477-545.

spyi-don 'od-gsal snying-po. Auth. 'Jam-mgon Mi-pham rgya-mtsho. NMKMG Vol. 27.

spyi-don legs-bshad snang-bas yid-kyi mun-pa thams-cad sel-ba. Auth. Klong-chen Rab-'byams-pa. See *Trilogy which Dispels Darkness*

phar-phyin 'phrul-gyi bang-mdzod. Auth. gYag-sde Paṇ-chen. Pub. 2 vols. New Delhi: Ngawang Topgay, 1975.

phyogs-bcu mun-sel. Auth. Klong-chen Rab-'byams-pa. See *Trilogy which Dispels Darkness*

bairo 'dra-'bag. See *rje-btsun thams-cad mkhyen-pa bai-ro-tsa-na'i rnam-thar 'dra-'bag chen-mo*

bar-do'i spyi-don. Auth. Rtse-le Sna-tshogs rang-grol. Typeset, *po-ti* format. Kalimpong: Mani Printing, n.d.

bi-ma snying-thig. Redacted by Klong-chen Rab-'byams-pa. See *Innermost Spirituality of Vimalamitra*

bod-kyi chos-srid zung-'brel skor bshad-pa. Auth. Dongar Luosang Chinlei [Dung-dkar blo-bzang phrin-las]. Beijing: Minorities Press, 1981.

bod-kyi rdo-ring-dang dril-bu'i kha-byang. Beijing: Minorities Press, 1984.

bod-kyi srid-don rgyal-rabs. Auth. Rtsis-dpon Zhva-sgab-pa Dbang-phyug bde-ldan [Tsepon W. D. Shakabpa]. 2 vols. Kalimpong: Shakabpa House, 1976.

byang-chub sems-dpa'i spyod-pa-la 'jug-pa'i tshig-'grel. Auth. Mkhan-chen Kun-bzang dpal-ldan. Xylo. Ser-lo Monastery, Nepal. N-Tib 74-923789.

mos-gus rab-byed. Auth. 'Jam-mgon Kong-sprul Blo-gros mtha'-yas. GCKZ Vol. 2, pp. 45-82.

tshes-bcu bskul-thabs. Disc. Ratna gling-pa. RTD Vol. 16, pp. 121-7.

tshig-bdun rnam-bshad padma dkar-po. Auth. 'Jam-mgon Mi-pham rgya-mtsho. Varanasi: Snyi-lcang Thub-bstan chos-grags rgya-mtsho, 1971.

tshogs-chen 'dus-pa. Auth. Gter-bdag gling-pa. NMKMG Vol. 16.

gzhan-stong khas-len seng-ge'i nga-ro. Auth. 'Jam-mgon Mi-pham rgya-mtsho. Xylo. Ser-lo Monastery, Nepal. N-Tib 72-902223.

gzhung-lugs legs-bshad. Auth. Sa-skya Paṇḍita. SK Vol. 5, no. 3. This work is now generally considered to be a forgery. The scholarship on it is surveyed in D. P. Jackson, *The Entrance Gate for the Wise (Section III)*. Vienna, 1987, Vol. 1, pp. 48-9.

źe-chen chos-'byuṅ. Auth. Zhe-chen rgyal-tshab Padma rnam-rgyal. SSS 10 (1971). I-Tib 79-925448.

yid-bzhin rin-po-che'i mdzod. See *Wish-fulfilling Treasury*

yon-tan rin-po-che'i mdzod. See *Precious Treasury of Enlightened Attributes*

ri-chos mtshams-kyi zhal-gdams. Auth. Karma chags-med. Tib. xylo. Rtsib-ri. N-Tib 72-914960.

lam-rim ye-shes snying-po'i 'grel-pa. Auth. 'Jam-mgon Kong-sprul Blos-gros mtha'-yas. Xylo. Mtho-mthong, Nepal.

shes-bya kun-khyab mdzod. Auth. 'Jam-mgon Kong-sprul Blo-gros mtha'-yas. GCKZ 17-20; and Beijing: Minorities Press, 1982. 3 vols.

bshad-mdzod yid-bzhin nor-bu. A 15th Century Tibetan Compendium of Knowledge. SP 78 (1969).

gsang-bdag zhal-lung. See *rgyud gsang-ba snying-po'i 'grel-chen gsang-bdag zhal-lung*

gso-rig snying-bsdus skya-rengs gsar-pa. Lhasa: Tibet Minorities Press, 1978.

3 *Secondary Literature*

Ahmad, Z. *Sino-Tibetan Relations in the Seventeenth Century*. SOR 40 (1970).

Anacker, S. *Seven Works of Vasubandhu*. Delhi: Motilal Banarsidass, 1984.

Aris, M. *Bhutan*. Warminster: Aris and Phillips, 1979.

——. *Hidden Teachings and Secret Lives*. London: RKP International, 1988.

Aris, M. and Aung San Suu Kyi (eds.). *Tibetan Studies in Honour of Hugh Richardson*. TSHR.

Āryaśūra. *The Marvelous Companion*. Berkeley: Dharma Publishing, 1983.

Atiśa. *A Lamp for the Path and Commentary*. Trans. R. Sherburne, SJ. London: George Allen and Unwin, 1983.

Aziz, B. N. "Indian Philosopher as Tibetan Folk Hero." *Central Asiatic Journal* 23, 1-2 (1979), pp. 19-37.

——. Introduction to *The Traditions of Pha-dam-pa Sangs-rgyas*. 5 vols. Thimphu: Druk Sherik Parkhang, 1979. Bhu-Tib 80-904347.

——. "The Work of Pha-dam-pa Sangs-rgyas as revealed in Ding-ri Folklore." In TSHR, pp. 21-9.

Aziz, B. Nimri and Kapstein, M. (eds.). *Soundings in Tibetan Civilization*. STC.

Bacot, J. "Le marriage chinois du roi tibétain Sroṅ bcan sgam po." MCB 3 (1935).

——. *Le Tibet Révolté: Vers Népémakö, la terre promise des Tibétains*. Paris: Hachette, 1912.

Bareau, A. "La Date du Nirvāṇa." *Journal Asiatique* (1953), pp. 27-52.

——. *Recherches sur la Biographie du Buddha*. Paris: École Française d'Extrême-Orient, Vols. 53 (1963) and 77 (1970-1).

Basham, A. L. (ed.). *A Cultural History of India*. Oxford: Clarendon Press, 1975.

——. "The Evolution of the Concept of the Bodhisattva." In L. Kawamura (ed.), *The Bodhisattva in Asian Culture*, pp. 19-59.

——. *The Wonder that was India*. New York: Grove Press, 1959.

Batchelor, S. et al. *The Tibet Guide*. TG.

Bernbaum, E. *The Way to Shambhala*. Garden City, New York: Anchor Books, 1980.

Beyer, S. *The Cult of Tārā*. Berkeley/Los Angeles/London: University of California Press, 1978.

Birnbaum, R. *Studies on the Mysteries of Mañjuśrī*. Society for the Study of Chinese Religion Monograph Series, 1983.

Blondeau, A.-M. "Analysis of the Biographies of Padmasambhava according to Tibetan Tradition: Classification of Sources." In TSHR, pp. 45-52.

——. "Le Lha-'dre bka'-thaṅ." In *Études tibétaines dédiées à la mémoire de Marcelle Lalou*. Paris: A. Maisonneuve, 1971, pp. 29-126.

Bosson, J. *Treasury of Aphoristic Jewels*. Indiana University Uralic and Altaic Series, Vol. 92. Bloomington, Indiana: Indiana University Press, 1969.

Briggs, G. W. *Gorakhnāth and the Kānphaṭa Yogīs*. Delhi: Motilal Banarsidass, 1973.

Broughton, J. "Early Ch'an in Tibet." In R. M. Gimello and P. N. Gregory (eds.), *Studies in Ch'an and Hua-yen*. Hawaii: University of Hawaii Press, 1983.

Bruyat, C. et al. (trans.). *Le Chemin de la grande perfection*. Padmākara, 1987.

van Buitenen, H., Dimock, E., Gerow, E., Naim, C. M. and Ramanujan, A. K. *The Literatures of India*. Chicago: University of Chicago Press, 1976.

Buswell, Robert (ed.). *Buddhist Apocrypha*. Honolulu: University of Hawaii Press, 1990.

Cassinelli, C. W. and Ekvall, R. B. *A Tibetan Principality, The Political System of Sa sKya*. New York: Cornell University Press, 1969.

Chandra, L. *Buddhist Iconography of Tibet*. 2 vols. Kyoto: Rinsen Book Company, 1986.

—— (ed.). *The History and Doctrine of the Bon-po Niṣpanna-yoga*. [In Tibetan.] SP 73 (1968).

—— (ed.). *Materials for a History of Tibetan Literature*. 3 vols. SP 28-30 (1963).

Chang, G. C. C. (trans.). *The Hundred Thousand Songs of Milarepa*. 2 vols. New Hyde Park, New York: University Books, 1962.

Chang, K. and Shefts, B. *A Manual of Spoken Tibetan (Lhasa Dialect)*. Seattle: University of Washington Press, 1964.

Chattopadhyāya, A. *Atiśa and Tibet*. 2nd edn. Delhi: Motilal Banarsidass, 1981.

Chattopadhyāya, D. *Indian Philosophy, a popular introduction*. 4th rev. edn. Delhi: People's Publishing House, 1979.

Chayet, A. "The Jehol Temples and their Tibetan Models." In STC, pp. 65-72.

——. *Les Temples de Jehol et leurs modèles tibétaines*. Paris: Éditions Recherche sur les Civilizations, 1985.

Clifford, T. *The Diamond Healing: Tibetan Buddhist Medicine and Psychiatry*. Wellingborough, Northamptonshire: The Aquarian Press, 1984.

Collected Works of Dudjom Rinpoche. Published as *The collected writings and revelations of H. H. Bdud-'joms Rin-po-che 'Jigs-bral ye-śes rdo-rje*. 19 vols. Kalimpong: Dupjung Lama, 1979. I-Tib 79-901972.

Collected Writings of Sog-bzlog-pa Blo-gros-rgyal-mtshan. [In Tibetan.] 2 vols. New Delhi: Sanje Dorje, 1975. I-Tib 75-900763.

Collection of All Means for Attainment. GTKT.

Collection of All Tantras. GDKT.

Collins, S. *Selfless Persons*. Cambridge: Cambridge University Press, 1982.

Commentaries on the Guhyagarbha Tantra and other Rare Nyingma Texts from the Library of Dudjom Rinpoche. Vol. 1. [In Tibetan.] New Delhi: Sanje Dorje, 1974. I-Tib 74-900928.

Conze, E. *Abhisamayālaṃkāra*. Rome: Is.M.E.O., 1954.

Dagyab, L. S. *Tibetan Religious Art*. Asiatische Forschungen 52. Wiesbaden: Otto Harrassowitz, 1977.

Dalai Lama V, Ngag-dbang blo-gros rgya-mtsho. *Guide to the Cathedral of Lhasa*. [In Tibetan.] In Ngawang Gelek Demo (ed.), *Three Kachacks*. New Delhi, 1970. I-Tib 70-917195. Litho. Rajpur, UP: K. Lhundup, 1974. I-Tib 75-900792.

Daniélou, A. *Hindu Polytheism*. Bollingen Series 73. New York: Pantheon Books, 1964.

Dargyay, E. *The Rise of Esoteric Buddhism in Tibet*. Delhi: Motilal Banarsidass, 1977.

Dargyay, L. "The View of Bodhicitta in Tibet." In L. Kawamura (ed.), *The Bodhisattva in Asian Culture*, pp. 95-109.

Das, S. C. *A Tibetan-English Dictionary with Sanskrit Synonyms*. Calcutta: Bengal Secretariat Book Depot, 1902. Rev. edn. Delhi: Motilal Banarsidass, 1970.

Dasgupta, S. *Obscure Religious Cults*. Calcutta: University of Calcutta, 1946.

David-Neel, A. *Magic and Mystery in Tibet*. New York: Penguin, 1971.

——. *The Superhuman Life of Gesar of Ling*. Boulder: Prajñā Press, 1981.

Davidson, R. M. "The Litany of Names of Mañjuśrī." MCB 20 (1981), pp. 1-69.

——. "The Ṅor-pa Tradition." *Wind Horse* 1, pp. 79-98.

—— (ed.). *Wind Horse*, 1. Berkeley: Asian Humanities Press, 1981.

Dayal, H. *The Bodhisattva Doctrine in Sanskrit Buddhist Literature*. London: Kegan Paul, Trench, Trubner and Co., 1932.

De, S. K. *History of Sanskrit Poetics*. Calcutta: Firma K. L. Mukhopadhyay, 1960.

Denwood, P. Review of P. Klafkowski, *The Secret Liberation of the Sixth Dalai Lama*. Bulletin of SOAS 45 (1982), pp. 381-3.

Dorje, G. *The Guhyagarbhatattvaviniścayamahātantra and its XIVth Century Tibetan Commentary: Phyogs-bcu mun-sel*. GGFTC.

Dowman, K. *The Legend of the Great Stūpa*. Berkeley: Dharma Publications, 1973.

——. *Masters of Mahāmudrā*. Albany, NY: SUNY Press, 1986.

——. *Power Places of Central Tibet*. PPCT.

Eggermont, P. H. L. *The Chronology of the Reign of Asoka Moriya*. Leiden: E. J. Brill, 1956.

Eimer, H. *Berichte über das Leben des Atiśa*. Asiatische Forschungen 51. Wiesbaden: Otto Harrassowitz, 1977.

——. *Bodhipathapradīpa*. Asiatische Forschungen 59. Wiesbaden: Otto Harrassowitz, 1979.

——. "The Development of the Biographical Tradition concerning Atiśa." *The Journal of the Tibet Society* 2 (1982), pp. 41-51.

——. "The Hymn of Praise in Eighty Verses. The Earliest Source for the Life of Atiśa." In *Atish Dipankar Millenium Birth Commemoration Volume. Jagajjoti* Sept. 1982 – Jan. 1983. Calcutta, 1983, pp. 1-8.

——. *Rnam thar rgyas pa, Materialen zu einer Biographie des Atiśa*. Asiatische Forschungen 67. Wiesbaden: Otto Harrassowitz, 1979.

Eimer, H. and Tsering, P. "Abte und Lehrer von Kaḥ-thog." *Zentralasiatische Studien* 13 (1979), pp. 457-509.

——. "A List of Abbots of Kaḥ-thog Monastery." *The Journal of the Tibet Society* 1 (1981).

Emmerick, R. E. (ed. and trans.). *The Book of Zambasta: A Khotanese Poem on Buddhism*. London: Oxford University Press, 1968.

Evans-Wentz, W. Y. (ed.) *Milarepa*. Trans. Kazi Dawa-Samdup. London/Oxford/New York: Oxford University Press, 1928.

—— (ed.). *The Tibetan Book of the Dead*. Trans. Kazi Dawa-Samdup. London/Oxford/New York: Oxford University Press, 1927.

—— (ed.). *The Tibetan Book of the Great Liberation*. Trans. Kazi Dawa-Samdup. London/Oxford/New York: Oxford University Press, 1977.

—— (ed.). *Tibetan Yoga and Secret Doctrines*. Trans. Kazi Dawa-Samdup. London/Oxford/New York: Oxford University Press, 1958.

Ferrari, A. *mK'yen brtse's Guide to the Holy Places of Central Tibet*. KGHP.

Franke, H. "Tibetans in Yüan China." In J. D. Langlois (ed.), *China under Mongol Rule*. Princeton: Princeton University Press, 1981.

Frauwallner, E. *On the Date of the Buddhist Master of the Law Vasubandhu*. SOR 3 (1951).

Fremantle, F. and Trungpa, C. *The Tibetan Book of the Dead*. Berkeley/London: Shambhala, 1975.

Frye, S. (trans.). *Sutra of the Wise and the Foolish*. LTWA, 1981.

sGam-po-pa. *The Jewel Ornament of Liberation*. Trans. H. V. Guenther. Berkeley: Shambhala, 1971.

Gard, R. A. (ed.). *Buddhism*. New York: George Braziller, 1961.

Goldman, R. *Gods, Priests and Warriors*. New York: Columbia University Press, 1977.

Gombrich, R. F. *Precept and Practice*. Oxford: Clarendon Press, 1971.

Gonpo Tsetan [Mgon-po Tshe-brtan]. *The Udumbara Bouquet*. Santa Cruz, California: Ngagyur Nyingma Foundation, 1982.

Goodman, S. D. "Mi-pham rgya-mtsho: an account of his life, the printing of his works, and the structure of his treatise entitled *Mkhas-pa'i tshul la 'jug pa'i sgo*." *Wind Horse* 1, pp. 58-78.

——. "The Klong-chen snying-thig: An Eighteenth Century Tibetan Revelation." Forthcoming.

——. "Rig-'dzin 'Jigs-med gling-pa and the *Klong-chen sNying-thig*." In S. D. Goodman and R. M. Davidson (eds.), *Tibetan Buddhism: Reason and Revelation*. Albany, NY: SUNY Press, 1992.

——. *Snying thig ya bzhi'i dkar chag*. In "The Klong-chen snying-thig: An Eighteenth Century Tibetan Revelation", Appendix B.

Govinda, Lama A. *The Way of the White Clouds*. London: Hutchinson, 1966.

Grünwedel, A. *Tāranātha's Edelsteinmine*. Petrograd: B.Budh. XVIII, 1914.

——. *Die Tempel von Lhasa*. Heidelberg: Carl Winter's Universitätsbuchhandlung, 1919.

Guenther, H. V. *Buddhist Philosophy in Theory and Practice*. Baltimore: Pelican, 1972.

—— (trans.). sGam-po-pa. *The Jewel Ornament of Liberation*. Berkeley: Shambhala, 1971.

—— (trans.). *Kindly Bent to Ease Us*. 3 vols. Emeryville, California: Dharma Publications, 1975-6.

—— (trans.). *The Life and Teaching of Nāropā*. Oxford: Clarendon Press, 1963.

—— (trans.). *The Royal Song of Saraha*. Berkeley/London: Shambhala, 1973.

Gupta, D. K. *A Critical Study of Daṇḍin and his Works*. Delhi: Meharchand Lachhmandas, 1970.

Gyatso, J. *The Literary Transmission of the Traditions of Thang-stong rgyal-po*. Unpublished Ph.D. dissertation. The University of California at Berkeley, 1981.

——. "A Preliminary Study of the *Gcod* Tradition." In STC, pp. 320-41.

——. "The Teachings of Thang-stong rgyal-po." In TSHR, pp. 111-19.

Haarh, E. *The Yar-luṅ Dynasty*. Copenhagen: G. E. C. Gad's Forlag, 1969.

Hanson, J. (trans.). Jamgön Kongtrül, *The Torch of Certainty*. Boulder: Shambhala, 1977.

Hattori, M. *Dignāga on Perception*. HOS 47 (1968).

Helffer, M. "Note à propos d'une clochette *gshang.*" *Objets et Mondes* 21, 3 (1981), pp. 129-34.

Henss, M. *Tibet: Die Kulturdenkmäler.* Zurich: Atlantis, 1981.

Hofinger, M. *Étude sur le Concile de Vaiśālī.* Bibliothèque du *Muséon*, Vol. 20. Louvain, 1946.

Hookham, S. *Tathāgatagarbha Doctrine according to the Gzhan Stong Interpretation of the Ratnagotravibhāga.* Ph.D. thesis. University of Oxford, 1986. [Revised version forthcoming from SUNY Press, Albany, NY.]

Hopkins, J. *Meditation on Emptiness.* London: Wisdom Publications, 1983.

Hummel, S. "The sMe-ba-dgu, the Magic Square of the Tibetans." *East and West* XIX, 1-2 (Rome 1969), pp. 139-46.

Huntington, J. *The Phur-pa, Tibetan Ritual Daggers.* Artibus Asiae Supplementum 33. Ascona, 1975.

Imaeda, Y. "Un Extrait Tibétain du *Mañjuśrīmūlakalpa* dans les Manuscripts de Touen-Houang." In *Nouvelles Contributions aux Études de Touen-Houang.* Geneva: Librairie Droz, 1981, pp. 303-20.

——. *The 'Jang Sa-tham Edition of the Tibetan Kanjur.* Tokyo, 1983.

Inaba, Shoju. "The Lineage of the Sa skya pa, A Chapter of the Red Annals." In *Memoirs of the Research Department of the Toyo Bunko* 22 (1963), pp. 106-23.

Jackson, D. P. *The Entrance Gate for the Wise (Section III).* Vienna, 1987.

——. *The Mollas of Mustang.* LTWA, 1983.

Jagchid, S. "A Mongol Text Letter from a Tibetan Leader." *Central Asiatic Journal* 17 (1973), pp. 150-63.

Jaini, P. S. *The Jaina Path of Purification.* Berkeley/Los Angeles/London: University of California Press, 1979.

——. "On the Theory of the Two Vasubandhus." *Bulletin of the School of Oriental and African Studies* 21 (1958), pp. 48-53.

Jamyang Khyentse Wangpo ['Jam-dbyangs mkhyen-brtse'i dbang-po], *Mkhyen-brtse on the History of the Dharma.* [In Tibetan.] SSS 39 (1972). I-Tib 72-904179.

Jasbar Singh, A. K. *Himalayan Triangle.* London: The British Library, 1988.

Jong, J. W. de. Review of P. Klafkowski, *The Secret Liberation of the Sixth Dalai Lama. Indo-Iranian Journal* 24 (1982), pp. 223-5.

Kaneko, Eiichi. *Ko-Tantora Zenshū Kaidai Mokuroku.* Tokyo: Kokusho Kankōkai, 1982.

Kapstein, M. "Mereological Considerations in Vasubandhu's 'Proof of Idealism.'" In *Idealistic Studies*, Vol. XVIII, no. 1 (1988), pp. 32-54.

——. "Mi-pham's Theory of Interpretation." In D. Lopez (ed.), *Buddhist Hermeneutics.* Honolulu: University of Hawaii Press, 1987.

——. "The Purificatory Gem and Its Cleansing: A Late Tibetan Polemical Discussion of Apocryphal Texts." In *History of Religions*, Vol. 28, no. 3 (1989), pp. 217-24.

——. "Religious Syncretism in 13th Century Tibet: *The Limitless Ocean Cycle*." In STC, pp. 358-371.

——. "Remarks on the *Maṇi bKa'-'bum* and the Cult of Avalokiteśvara in Tibet." In S. D. Goodman and R. M. Davidson (eds.), *Tibetan Buddhism: Reason and Revelation*. Albany, NY: SUNY Press. Forthcoming.

——. "The Shangs-pa bKa'-brgyud: an unknown tradition of Tibetan Buddhism." In TSHR, pp. 138-44.

Karma Thinley [Karma phrin-las]. *Important events and places in the history of Nangchin Kham and E. Tibet*. [In Tibetan.] Delhi, 1968. I-Tib-465.

——. *The History of the Sixteen Karmapas of Tibet*. Boulder: Shambhala, 1978.

Karmay, S. G. *A Catalogue of Bonpo Publications*. Tokyo: The Toyo Bunko, 1977.

——. "A Discussion on the Doctrinal Position of rDzogs-chen from the 10th to the 13th centuries." *Journal Asiatique* (1975), pp. 147-56.

——. "King Tsa/Dza and Vajrayāna." In M. Strickmann (ed.), *Tantric and Taoist Studies in Honour of R. A. Stein*, MCB 20 (1981), pp. 192-211.

——. "An Open Letter by Pho-brang Zhi-ba-'od to the Buddhists of Tibet." *The Tibet Journal* 5, 3 (1980), pp. 3-28.

——. "The Ordinance of Lha Bla-ma Ye-shes 'od." In TSHR, pp. 150-62.

——. *Origin and Early Development of the Tibetan Religious Traditions of the Great Perfection*. Ph.D. thesis. University of London, 1986. [Now published as *The Great Perfection* by E. J. Brill, Leiden, but page references in the present work are to the thesis.]

——. "The Rdzogs-chen in its Earliest Text." In STC, pp. 272-82.

——. *The Treasury of Good Sayings*. London Oriental Series 26. London: Oxford University Press, 1972.

Kaschewsky, R. *Das Leben des lamaistischen Heiligen Tsoṅ-kha-pa Blo-bzaṅ grags-pa*. Wiesbaden: Otto Harrassowitz, 1971.

Katok Situ Chöki Gyamtso [Kaḥ-thog Si-tu Chos-kyi rgya-mtsho]. *An Account of a Pilgrimage to Central Tibet during the years 1918 to 1920*. [In Tibetan.] SNGP 1972. I-Tib 72-901801.

Kawamura, L. (ed.). *The Bodhisattva in Asian Culture*. Waterloo, Ontario: Wilfrid Laurier University Press, 1981.

Kazi, Sonam T. (trans.). *Kun Zang La May Zhal Lung*. Englewood Cliffs, New Jersey: Diamond Lotus Publications, 1989.

Keith, A. B. *Sanskrit Drama*. Oxford, 1924.

Khenpo Sangay Tenzin and Gomchen Oleshey. "The Nyingma Icons: a collection of line drawings of 94 deities and divinities of Tibet." *Kailash*, Vol. III, no. 4 (1975), pp. 319-416.

Kirfel, W. *Symbolik des Hinduismus und des Jinismus*. Hiersemann: Stuttgart, 1959.

Klafkowski, P. *The Secret Liberation of the Sixth Dalai Lama*. Wiener Studien zur Tibetologie und Buddhismuskunde 3. Vienna, 1979.

Kloppenborg, R. *The Paccekabuddha*. Leiden: E. J. Brill, 1974.

Kloetzli, R. *Buddhist Cosmology*. Delhi: Motilal Banarsidass, 1983.

Kongtrül, Jamgön. *The Torch of Certainty*. Trans. J. Hanson. Boulder/ London: Shambhala, 1977.

van der Kuijp, L. W. J. *Contributions to the Development of Tibetan Buddhist Epistemology*. Wiesbaden: Franz Steiner Verlag, 1983.

———. "Phya-pa Chos-kyi Seng-ge's Impact on Tibetan Epistemological Theory." JIP 5 (1978), pp. 355-69.

Kunsang, E. P. (trans.). Tsele Natsok Rangdröl, *The Mirror of Mindfulness*. Boston: Shambhala, 1989.

Kvaerne, P . "A Preliminary Study of Ch. VI of the *Gzer-mig*." In TSHR, pp.185-91.

Kwanten, L . "Chingis Khan's Conquest of Tibet: Myth or Reality?" *Journal of Asian History* 8 (1974), pp. 1-20.

Lalou, M. "Les Textes Bouddhiques au temps du Roi Khri-sroṅ-lde-bcan." *Journal Asiatique* CCXLI-3 (1953), pp. 313-53.

Lamotte, E. *L'Enseignement de Vimalakīrti*. Louvain: Institut Orientaliste, 1962. [Trans. English S. Webb-Boin. London: Pali Text Society, 1976.]

———. *Histoire du Bouddhisme Indien*. HBI.

———. *Traité de la Grande Vertu de Sagesse*. 5 vols. Louvain: Institut Orientaliste, 1949, 1970, etc.

La Vallée Poussin, L. de. *L'Abhidharmakośa de Vasubandhu*. 6 vols. Paris: Paul Guethner, 1923-36. Repr. MCB 16 (1971). [An English translation by Leo Pruden has now been published by Asian Humanities Press.]

Lauf, D. I. *Secret Doctrines of the Tibetan Books of the Dead*. Boulder/ London: Shambhala, 1977.

Lessing, F. and Wayman, A. *Mkhas Grub Rje's Fundamentals of the Buddhist Tantras*. The Hague/Paris: Mouton, 1968.

Lévi, S. *Matériaux pour l'étude du système Vijñaptimātratā*. Paris: Librairie Ancienne Honoré Champion, 1932.

Lhalungpa, L. *The Life of Milarepa*. New York: E. P. Dutton, 1977.

Lindtner, C. *Nagarjuniana*. Indiske Studier IV. Copenhagen: Akademisk Forlag, 1982.

The Life and Liberation of Padmasambhava. Trans. from the French of G.-C. Toussaint by K. Douglas and G. Bays. 2 vols. Emeryville, California: Dharma Publications, 1978.

Lipman, K. "A Controversial Topic from Mipham's Analysis of Śāntarakṣita's *Madhyamakālaṃkāra*." *Wind Horse* 1 (1981), pp. 40-57.

Longdöl Lama [Klong-rdol bla-ma]. *The Collected Works of Longdöl Lama*. SP 100 (1973).

Ludowyk, E. F. C. *The Footprint of the Buddha*. London: George Allen and Unwin, 1958.

Luk, C. (trans.). *Vimalakīrtinirdeśasūtra*. Berkeley/London: Shambhala, 1972.

Macdonald, A. W. and Stahl, A. V. *Newar Art*. Warminster: Aris and Phillips, 1979.

Macdonald, A. "Une lecture des Pelliot tibétaine 1286, 1287, 1038, 1047 et 1290. Essai sur le formation et l'emploi des mythes politiques dans la religion royale de Sroṅ-bcan sgam-po." In *Études tibétaines dédiées à la mémoire de Marcelle Lalou*. Paris: A. Maisonneuve, 1971, pp. 90-391.

——. *Le Maṇḍala du Mañjuśrīmūlakalpa*. Paris: A. Maisonneuve, 1962.

Macgregor, J. *Tibet: A Chronicle of Exploration*. New York: Praeger Publishers, 1970.

Martin, D. "The Teachers of Mi-la-ras-pa." *The Journal of the Tibet Society* 2 (1982).

Mayer, R. "Tibetan Phur-bas and Indian Kīlas." In *The Buddhist Forum*. London: SOAS, 1990.

Mehra, P. *The Younghusband Expedition*. London: Asia Publishing House, 1968.

Meyer, F. *Gso-ba rig-pa: Le système médical tibétain*. Paris: Éditions du Centre National de la Recherche Scientifique, 1981.

Mimaki, K. *Blo gsal grub mtha'*. Kyoto: Zinbun Kagaku Kenkyusyo, 1982.

Mitra, D. *Buddhist Monuments*. Calcutta: Sahitya Samsad, 1971, 1980.

Müller, F. M. (ed.). *Sacred Books of the East*. SBE.

Nālandā Translation Committee. *The Life of Marpa the Translator*. Boulder: Prajñā Press, 1982.

——. *The Rain of Wisdom*. Boulder: Shambhala, 1980.

Namgyal Institute of Tibetology. *Rgyan drug mchog gnyis*. Gangtok, Sikkim, 1968.

Narkyid, Ngawang Thondup. "In Defence of Amdo Gendun Chompel's Theory of the Origin of the Tibetan Script." *Tibet Journal* VII, 3 (1982), pp. 23-34.

Nattier, J. and Prebish, C. "Mahāsaṅghika Origins: The Beginnings of Buddhist Sectarianism." In *History of Religions*, Vol. 16, no. 3, 1977.

Nebesky-Wojkowitz, R. de. *Oracles and Demons of Tibet*. London/The Hague: Mouton and Co., 1956.

Ngor Thartse Khenpo Sonam Gyatso [Ngor thar-rtse mkhan-po bsod-nams rgya-mtsho] et al. (eds.). *Tibetan Maṇḍalas: The Ngor Collection*. Tokyo: Kodansha Ltd., 1983.

Norbu, Dawa. "An Analysis of Sino-Tibetan Relationships." In STC, pp. 176-95.

Norbu, Namkai [Nam-mkha'i Nor-bu]. *The Necklace of Gzi*. Dharamsala: Information Office of His Holiness the Dalai Lama, 1981.

Obermiller, E. *History of Buddhism by Bu-ston*. Tokyo: Suzuki Research Foundation (reprint series, 5), 1964.

Pag Sam Jon Zang. [*dpag bsam ljon bzang*] By Sum-pa mkhan-po Ye-shes dpal-'byor. Ed. S. C. Das. Calcutta: Presidency Jail Press, 1908.

Palsule, G. B. *The Sanskrit Dhātupāṭhas*. Poona: University of Poona, 1961.

Paranavitana, S. *The God of Adam's Peak*. Artibus Asiae Supplementum 18. Ascona, 1963.

Peissel, M. *Mustang, The Forbidden Kingdom*. New York: E. P. Dutton, 1967.

Perdue, D. *Debate in Tibetan Buddhist Education*. LTWA, 1976.

Petech, L. *Aristocracy and Government in Tibet*, 1728-1959. SOR 45 (1973).

——. *China and Tibet in the Early 18th Century*. 2nd edn. Leiden: E. J. Brill, 1972.

Potter, K. *Encyclopedia of Indian Philosophies; Indian Metaphysics and Epistemology: The Tradition of Nyāya-Vaiśeṣika up to Gaṅgeśa*. Princeton: Princeton University Press, 1977.

Prats, R. *Contributo allo Studia Biografico dei primi Gter-ston*. Naples: Istituto Universitario Orientale, 1982.

——. "Some Preliminary Considerations Arising from a Bibliographical Study of the Early *gTer-ston*." In TSHR, pp. 256-60.

Prebish, C. S. *Buddhist Monastic Discipline*. University Park/London: The Pennsylvannia State University Press, 1975.

Przyluski, J. *Le Concile de Rājagṛha*. Paris: P. Guethner, 1926.

——. *La Légende de l'Empereur Aśoka*. Paris: Annales du Musée Guimet Bibliothèque d'Études, 1923.

Putön. *History of Buddhism*. See E. Obermiller. *History of Buddhism by Bu-ston*.

Rahula, W. *Le Compendium de la Super-Doctrine d'Asaṅga*. Paris: École Française d'Extrême Orient, 1971.

Rechung Rinpoche. *Tibetan Medicine*. Berkeley/Los Angeles: University of California Press, 1976.

Richardson, H. *Ancient Tibetan Historical Edicts at Lhasa*. London: The Royal Asiatic Society of Great Britain and Ireland, 1952.

——. *A Corpus of Early Tibetan Inscriptions*. London: Royal Asiatic Society, 1983.

——. "The Dharma that came down from Heaven." In *Buddhist Thought and Asian Civilization*. Emeryville, California: Dharma Publications, 1977.

——. "How old was Srong brtsan sgam po?" *Bulletin of Tibetology* 2, 1 (1965).

——. *A Short History of Tibet*. New York: E. P. Dutton and Co., 1962.

——. "Tibetan Inscriptions at Źva-ḥi Lha Khaṅ." *Journal of the Royal Asiatic Society* (1952), pp. 133-54; (1953), pp. 1-12.

Rikdzin Lhündrup [Rig-'dzin lhun-grub]. *Tibbat meṃ pracīna bauddhadharma-kā itihāsa.* [Hindi translation of the *History.*] Madhav Nikunj, Kalimpong: Dudjom Rinpoche, 1972.

Robinson, H. G. (compiler). *First Cumulative Dictionary Catalogue of Tibetan Works in the Library of the Institute for Advanced Studies of World Religions.* Stony Brook, New York: The Institute for Advanced Studies of World Religions, 1985.

Robinson, J. B. (trans.). *Buddha's Lions.* Emeryville, California: Dharma Publications, 1979.

Rock, J. F. *The Amnye Ma-cchen Range and Adjacent Regions.* SOR 12 (1956).

Roerich, G. *Biography of Dharmasvāmin.* Patna: K. P. Jayaswal Research Institute, 1959.

——— (trans.). *The Blue Annals.* Referred to in this volume as *Blue Annals.*

Ruegg, D. S. "Le Dharmadhātustava de Nāgārjuna." *Études tibétaines dédiées à la mémoire de Marcelle Lalou.* Paris: A. Maisonneuve, 1971, pp. 446-71.

———. "The Great Debate between Gradualists and Simultaneists in Eighth-Century Tibet." In *Buddha-nature, Mind and the Problem of Gradualism in a Comparative Perspective.* SOAS, University of London, 1989.

———. "The Jo naṅ pas: A School of Buddhist Ontologists according to the *Grub mtha' śel gyi me loṅ*". *Journal of the American Oriental Society* 83 (1963), pp. 73-91.

———. *The Life of Bu ston Rin po che.* SOR 34 (1966).

———. *The Literature of the Madhyamaka School of Philosophy in India.* HIL 7.1.

———. *La théorie du tathāgatagarbha et du gotra.* Paris: École Française d'Extrême-Orient, 1969, Vol. 70.

———. *Le traité du tathāgatagarbha du Bu ston Rin chen grub.* Paris: École Française d'Extrême Orient, 1973.

Sabzang Mati Paṇcen [Sa-bzang Ma-ti Paṇ-chen], *Abhidharmasamuccaya Commentary.* Full title: *dam pa'i chos mngon pa kun las btus pa'i 'grel pa shes bya rab gsal snang ba.* [In Tibetan.] 2 vols. Gangtok: Gonpo Tseten, 1977. I-Tib 77-905312.

Saha, K. *Buddhism in Central Asia.* Calcutta: Firma K. L. Mukhopadhyay, 1970.

Schmid, T. *The Eighty-Five Siddhas.* Sino-Swedish Expedition Publication 42. Stockholm: Statens Etnografiska Museum, 1958.

Schuh, D. "Über die Möglichkeit der identifizierung tibetischer Jahresangaben anhand der sme-ba dgu." *Zentralasiatischer Studien* 6 (1972), pp. 485-504.

———. *Untersuchungen zur Geschichte der Tibetischen Kalenderrechnung.* Verzeichnis der Orientalischen Handschriften in Deutschland, Supplementband 16. Wiesbaden: Franz Steiner Verlag, 1973.

Shahidullah, M. *Les Chants Mystiques de Kāṇha et de Saraha*. Paris: A. Maisonneuve, 1928.

Shakabpa, Tsepon W. D. *Guide to the Central Temple of Lhasa*. [In Tibetan.] Full title: *lha ldan rva sa 'phrul snang gtsug lag khang gi dkar chag*. Kalimpong: Shakabpa House, 1982. I-Tib 82-901896.

——. *Tibet: A Political History*. New Haven/London: Yale University Press, 1973. Expanded Tib. edn. in 2 vols.: *bod kyi srid don rgyal rabs*. Kalimpong: Shakabpa House, 1976.

Sherriland, W. A. and Chu, W. K. *Anthology of the I Ching*. London: Routledge and Kegan Paul, 1978.

Shukla, N. S. (ed.). *The Buddhist Hybrid Sanskrit Dharmapāda*. TSWS 19 (1979).

Situ VIII, Chöki Jungne [Si-tu Chos-kyi 'byung-gnas]. *The Autobiography and Diaries of Situ Paṇchen*. [In Tibetan.] With an introduction by E. G. Smith. SP 77 (1968). I-Tib-458.

Śivadatta, Paṇḍit (ed.). *The Nāmaliṅgānuśāsana of Amarasinha*. [In Sanskrit]. Bombay, 1915.

Smith, E. G. Introduction to Glo-bo mKhan-chen, *Tshad-ma rigs-pa'i gter-gyi rnam-par bshad-pa*. NNS 25 (1970). I(Sik)-Tib 79-913063.

——. Introduction to *Bka' brgyud gser 'phreṅ*. Vol. 1. Delhi, 1975. I-Tib 75-903778.

——. Introduction to *Kongtrul's Encyclopedia of Indo-Tibetan Culture*. SP 80 (1970). I-Tib 77-913514.

——. Introduction to *The Life of the Saint of Gtsaṅ*. SP 79 (1969). I-Tib 77-908709.

——. Introduction to *Mi-pham's Rablan*. NNS 5 (1969). I(Sik)-Tib 75-908711.

——. Introduction to *Śaṅs-pa gser-'phreṅ*. SSS 15 (1970). I-Tib 74-913670.

Snellgrove, D. L. *Buddhist Himālaya*. Oxford: Oxford University Press, 1975.

——. *The Hevajra Tantra*. Pts. 1 and 2. London Oriental Series, Vol. 6. London: Oxford University Press, 1959; repr. 1964, 1971.

——. *Himalayan Pilgrimage*. Oxford: Oxford University Press, 1961.

——. *Indo-Tibetan Buddhism*. Boston: Shambhala, 1987.

——. *The Nine Ways of Bon*. London Oriental Series 18. London: Oxford University Press, 1967.

Snellgrove, D. L. and Richardson, H. *A Cultural History of Tibet*. New York/Washington: Frederick A. Praeger, 1968.

Snellgrove, D. and Skorupski, T. *A Cultural History of Ladakh*. 2 vols. Boulder: Shambhala, 1977-80.

Sopa, Geshe Lhundup. *Lectures on Tibetan Religious Culture*. 2 vols. LTWA 1983.

Sperling, E. "The 5th Karma-pa and some aspects of the relationship between Tibet and the early Ming." In TSHR, pp. 280-9.

Speyer, J. S. (trans.). *The Jātakamālā of Āryaśūra*. London: The Pali Text Society, 1895.

Staal, J. F. *Agni: the Vedic Ritual of the Fire Altar*. 2 Vols. Berkeley: Asian Humanities Press, 1983.

Stearns, C. R. "The Life and Teachings of the Tibetan Saint Thang-stong rgyal-po." Unpublished MA thesis. Seattle: University of Washington, 1979.

Stein, M. A. *Ancient Khotan: detailed report of archaeological explorations in Chinese Turkestan*. Oxford: Clarendon Press, 1907.

Stein, R. A. *Une Chronique Ancienne de bSam-yas*. Paris: Institut des Hautes Études Chinoises, 1961.

——. *L'épopée tibétaine de Gesar dans sa version lamaïque de Ling*. Paris: Presses Universitaires de France, 1956.

——. "Étude du monde chinoise: institutions et concepts." *L'Annuaire du Collège de France* 72 (1971-2), pp. 489-510.

——. "Une mention de Manichéisme dans le choix de Bouddhisme comme religion d'état par le roi Tibétain Khri-sroṅ lde-bcan." In *Indianisme et Bouddhisme, Mélanges offerts à Mgr. Étienne Lamotte*. Louvain: Institut Orientaliste, 1980, pp. 329-37.

——. "À propos des documents anciens relatifs au *phur-bu*." In L. Ligeti (ed.), *Proceedings of the Csoma de Körös Memorial Symposium*. Budapest: Akadémiai Kiadó, 1978, pp. 427-44.

——. *Recherches sur l'épopée et le barde au Tibet*. Paris: Presses Universitaires de France, 1959.

——. *Tibetan Civilization*. Stanford: Stanford University Press, 1972.

——. *Les tribus anciennes des marches Sino-tibétaines*. Paris: Presses Universitaires de France, 1961.

Sternbach, L. "Les Aphorismes dits de Cāṇakya dans les textes bouddhiques du Tibet et du Turkestan Oriental." *Journal Asiatique* 259 (1971), pp. 71-82.

Strong, J. *The Legend of King Aśoka*. Princeton, NJ: Princeton University Press, 1983.

Suzuki, D. T. (trans.). *The Laṅkāvatāra Sūtra*. London: Routledge and Kegan Paul, 1932, 1956, etc.

——. *Studies in the Laṅkāvatāra Sūtra*. London: George Routledge and Sons, 1930.

Tāranātha. *History of Buddhism in India*. Trans. Lama Chimpa and A. Chattopadhyaya. Calcutta: K. P. Bagchi and Co., 1970.

Tate, J. "The Sixteen Arhats in Tibetan Painting." *Oriental Art* 35, 4 (1989/90), pp. 196-206.

Tatz, M. "The Life of Candragomin in Tibetan Historical Tradition." *Tibet Journal* VII, 3 (1982), pp. 3-22.

Teichman, E. *Travels of a Consular Officer in East Tibet*. Cambridge: University Press, 1922.

Templeman, D. (trans.). *The Seven Instruction Lineages (bka'-babs bdun-ldan)*. LTWA, 1983.

Terdak Lingpa [Gter-bdag gling-pa]. *Record of Teachings Received*. [In Tibetan.] New Delhi: Sanje Dorje, 1974. I-Tib 74-900490.

Thondup Rinpoche, Tulku [Sprul-sku don-grub]. *Buddha Mind*. Ithaca, NY: Snow Lion, 1989.

——. *Hidden Teachings of Tibet*. London: Wisdom Publications, 1986.

——. *The Tantric Tradition of the Nyingmapa*. Marion, MA: Buddhayana, 1984.

Thurman, R. A. F. *The Holy Teaching of Vimalakīrti*. University Park/London: The Pennsylvania State University Press, 1976.

—— (ed.). *Life and Teachings of Tsong Khapa*. LTWA, 1982.

——. "Tsoṅ-kha-pa's Integration of Sūtra and Tantra." In STC, pp. 372-82.

——. *Tsong Khapa's Speech of Gold in the Essence of True Eloquence*. Princeton, NJ: Princeton University Press, 1984.

Toussaint, G.-C. (trans.). *Le Dict de Padma, Padma thang yig, Ms. de Lithang*. Bibliothèque de l'Institut de Hautes Études Chinoises, Vol. 3. Paris: Librairie Ernest Leroux, 1933.

Trungpa Rinpoche, Chögyam. *Born in Tibet*. 3rd edn. Boulder: Shambhala, 1977.

Tsering Lama Jampal Zangpo. *A Garland of Immortal Wish-fulfilling Trees*. Trans. Sangye Khandro. Ithaca, NY: Snow Lion, 1988.

Tsering, Tashi. "Ñag-roṅ mgon-po rnam-rgyal: A 19th Century Khams-pa Warrior." In STC, pp. 196-214.

Tucci, G. *Deb t'er dmar po gsar ma*. SOR 24 (1971).

——. *Indo-Tibetica*. 7 vols. Rome, 1932-41.

——. *To Lhasa and Beyond*. Rome: Instituto Poligrafico dello Stato, 1956.

——. *Minor Buddhist Texts*. Pts. 1 and 2. SOR 9 (1956 and 1958). Repr. Kyoto: Rinsen Book Company, 1978.

——. *Preliminary Report on Two Scientific Expeditions in Nepal*. SOR 10.1. (1956).

——. *The Religions of Tibet*. Berkeley/Los Angeles: University of California Press, 1980.

——. *Tibetan Painted Scrolls*. 3 vols. Rome: Libreria dello Stato, 1949.

——. *The Tombs of the Tibetan Kings*. SOR 1 (1950).

——. *Travels of Tibetan Pilgrims in the Swat Valley*. Calcutta, 1940.

Uray, G. "The Four Horns of Tibet according to the Royal Annals." *Acta Orientalia Hungarica* X, 1 (1960), pp. 31-57.

Vidyabhusana, S. C. *A History of Indian Logic*. Delhi: Motilal Banarsidass, 1971, 1978.

Visser, M. W. de. *The Arhats in China and Japan*. Berlin: Oesterheld and Co., 1923.

Vogel, C. *Vāgbhaṭa's Aṣṭāṅgahṛdaya*. Deutsche Morgenländische Gesellschaft XXXVII, 2. Wiesbaden: Franz Steiner Verlag, 1965.

Walleser, M. "The Life of Nāgārjuna from Tibetan and Chinese Sources." *Asia Major* 1 (1923), pp. 421-55.

Wang Yao. "Tibetan Operatic Themes." In STC, pp. 186-96.

Warder, A. K. *Indian Buddhism*. Delhi: Motilal Banarsidass, 1970.

Wayman, A. *The Buddhist Tantras: New Light on Indo-Tibetan Esotericism*. London: Routledge and Kegan Paul, 1973.

——. *Yoga of the Guhyasamājatantra*. Delhi: Motilal Banarsidass, 1980.

Wayman, A. and H. (trans.). *The Lion's Roar of Queen Śrīmālā*. New York/London: Columbia University Press, 1974.

Williams, P. "A Note on Some Aspects of Mi Bskyod Rdo Rje's Critique of Dge Lugs Pa Madhyamaka." JIP 11 (1983), pp. 125-45.

——. *Mahāyāna Buddhism*. London/New York: Routledge, 1989.

Winternitz, M. *History of Indian Literature*. Vol. III. Delhi: Motilal Banarsidass, 1985.

Woodman, D. *Himalayan Frontiers*. New York/Washington: Frederick A. Praeger, 1969.

Wylie, T. V. "The First Mongol Conquest of Tibet Reinterpreted." *Harvard Journal of Asiatic Studies* 37 (1977), pp. 103-33.

——. *The Geography of Tibet according to the 'Dzam-gling rgyas-bshad*. GT.

——. *A Place Name Index to George N. Roerich's Translation of the Blue Annals*. SOR 15 (1957).

——. "A standard system of Tibetan transcription." *Harvard Journal of Asiatic Studies* 22 (1959), pp. 261-7.

Yu Dawchyuan. *Love-songs of the Sixth Dalai Lama Tshangs-dbyangs-rgya-mtsho*. Peking: Academia Sinica, 1930. See also K. Dhondup, *Songs of the Sixth Dalai Lama*. LTWA, 1981.

Zangmo, Bhikkhuni Sik K. Yeshe. *An Index of the Rinchen Gter Mdzod Chenmo*. Unpublished. Library of Cambridge University.

Zimmer, H. *Philosophies of India*. Bollingen Series 26. Princeton: Princeton University Press, 1969.

4 *Addenda to the Bibliography*

Achard, Jean-Luc. *L'Essence Perlée du Secret. Recherches philologiques et historiques sur l'origine de la Grande Perfection dans la tradition rNying ma pa.* Turnhout: Brepols, 1999.

Barron, Richard, trans. *The Precious Treasury of the Way of Abiding.* Padma Publishing, 1998.

Barron, Richard, trans. *The Precious Treasury of the Basic Space.* Padma Publishing, 2001.

Barron, Richard, trans. A *Treasure Trove of Scriptural Transmission.* Padma Publishing, 2001.

Blezer, Hank. *Kar gliṅ źi khro: A Tantric Buddhist Concept.* Leiden: Research School CNWS, 1997.

Boord, Martin J. *The Cult of the Deity Vajrakīla,* Buddhica Britannica Series Continua IV. Tring, U.K.: The Institute of Buddhist Studies, 1993.

Dorje, Gyurme. *Tibet Handbook.* Chicago, Ill: Passport Books, 1st ed. 1996, 2nd ed. 1999, 3rd ed. 2002.

Dorje, Gyurme. *Tibetan Elemental Divination Paintings.* London: Eskenazi & Fogg, 2001.

Dorje, Gyurme, with G. Coleman. *The Complete Tibetan Book of the Dead.* Forthcoming.

Dreyfus, Georges. *Recognizing Reality.* Albany, NY: State University of New York Press, 1997.

Dudjom Lingpa. *Buddhahood Without Meditation,* trans. Richard Barron. Padma Publishing, 1997.

Edou, Jérôme. *Machig Labdrön and the Foundations of Chöd.* Ithaca: Snow Lion, 1996.

Ehrhard, Franz-Karl. *"Flügelschäge des Garuḍa": Literar- und ideengeschichtliche Bemerkungen zu einer Liedersammlung des rDzogs-chen.* Tibetan and Indo-Tibetan Studies 3. Stuttgart: Franz Steiner Verlag, 1990.

Germano, David. "Architecture and Absence in the Secret Tantric History of rDzogs Chen," *Journal of the International Association for Buddhist Studies,* 17/2 (1994): 203–335.

Goldstein, Melvyn C., and Matthew T. Kapstein, eds. *Buddhism in Contemporary Tibet: Religious Revival and Cultural Identity.* Berkeley: University of California Press, 1998.

Goodman, Steven D., and Ronald M. Davidson, eds. *Tibetan Buddhism: Reason and Revelation.* Albany: SUNY Press, 1992.

Guenther, Herbert V. *Wholeness Lost and Wholeness Regained: Forgotten Tales of Individuation from Ancient Tibet.* Albany: State University of New York Press, 1994.

Guenther, Herbert V. *The Teachings of Padmasambhava.* Leiden: Brill, 1996.

Gyatso, Janet, ed. *In the Mirror of Memory.* Albany: State University of New York Press, 1992.

Gyatso, Janet. *Apparitions of the Self.* Princeton: Princeton University Press, 1998.

Hookham, S.K. *The Buddha Within.* Albany: State University of New York Press, 1991.

Huber, Toni. *The Cult of Pure Crystal Mountain.* New York: Oxford University Press, 1999.

Huntington, C.W., Jr., with Geshé Namgyal Wangchen. *The Emptiness of Emptiness: An Introduction to Early Indian Mādhyamika.* Honolulu: University of Hawai'i Press, 1989.

Jackson, David. *Enlightenment by a Single Means.* Vienna: Verlag der Österreichischen Akademie der Wissenschaften, 1994.

Jackson, Roger, and José Cabezón, eds. *Tibetan Literature: Studies in Genre.* Ithaca: Snow Lion Publications, 1995.

Jamgon Kongtrul Lodro Thaye. *Myriad Worlds: Buddhist Cosmology in Abhidharma, Kalacakra, and Dzog-chen,* trans. Tibet Sonada Translation Committee. Ithaca, NY: Snow Lion, 1995.

Kapstein, Matthew T. *The Tibetan Assimilation of Buddhism: Conversion, Contestation, and Memory.* New York: Oxford University Press, 2000.

Kapstein, Matthew T. *Reason's Traces: Identity and Interpretation in Indian and Tibetan Buddhism.* Boston: Wisdom Publications, 2001.

Karmay, Samten Gyaltsen. *Secret Visions of the Fifth Dalai Lama: The Gold Manuscript in the Fournier Collection.* London: Serindia Publications, 1988.

Khoroche, Peter, trans. *Once the Buddha Was a Monkey.* Chicago/London: University of Chicago Press, 1989.

Kohn, Richard. *Lord of the Dance: The Mani Rimdu Festival in Nepal and Tibet.* Albany, NY: State University of New York Press, 2001.

Könchog Gyaltsen, Khenpo. *The Great Kagyu Masters: The Golden Lineage Treasury,* ed. Victoria Huckenpahler. Ithaca: Snow Lion Publications, 1990.

van der Kuijp, Leonard W. J. "On the *Lives* of Śākyaśrībhadra (?–1225)," *Journal of the American Oriental Society* 114.4 (1994): 599–616.

Kunsang, Eric Pema, trans. *Dakini Teachings: Padma Sambhava's Oral Instructions to Lady Tsogyal.* Boston/London: Shambhala, 1990.

Kunsang, Eric Pema, trans. *The Lotus-Born: The Life of Padmasambhava.* Boston/London: Shambhala, 1993.

Kværne, Per. *The Bon Religion of Tibet.* London: Serindia Publications, 1995.

Longchen Yeshe Dorje, Kangyur Rinpoche. *Treasury of Precious Qualities,* trans. Padmakara Translation Group. Boston: Shambhala, 2001.

Lopez, Donald Jr., ed. *Tibetan Religions in Practice.* Princeton: Princeton University Press, 1997.

Martin, Dan. *Tibetan Histories:A Bibliography of Tibetan-Language Historical Works.* London: Serindia Publications, 1997.

Mayer, Robert. *A Scripture of the Ancient Tantra Collection:The Phur-pa bcu-gnyis.* Oxford: Kiscadale Publications, 1996.

Mimaki, Katsumi. "Doxographie tibétaine et classifications indiennes," in Fukui Fumimasa and Gérard Fussman, eds., *Bouddhisme et cultures locales: Quelques cas de réciproques adaptations.* Études thématiques 2. Paris: École Française d'Extrême-Orient, 1994, pp. 115–36.

Ngawang Zangpo, trans. *Jamgon Kongtrul's Retreat Manual.* Ithaca, NY: Snow Lion, 1994.

Orgyan Topgyal. *The Life and Teaching of Chokgyur Lingpa.* Rangjung Yeshe Publications, 1988.

Padma Tshewang, Khenpo Phuntshok Tashi, Chris Butters, and Sigmund K. Sætreng. *The Treasure Revealer of Bhutan: Pemalingpa, the Terma Tradition, and Its Critics.* Bibliotheca Himalayica III, 8. Kathmandu: EMR Publishing House, 1995.

Padmakara Translation Committee. *The Words of My Perfect Teacher.* San Francisco: Harper Collins, 1994.

Parfionovitch, Yuri, Gyurme Dorje, and Fernand Meyer. *Tibetan Medical Paintings.* London: Serindia, 1992.

Pettit, John. *Mipham's Beacon of Certainty.* Boston: Wisdom Publications, 1999.

Ricard, Matthieu et al., trans. *The Life of Shabkar: The Autobiography of a Tibetan Yogin.* Albany, NY: State University of New York Press, 1994.

Richardson, Hugh E. *Ceremonies of the Lhasa Year.* London: Serindia Publications, 1993.

Richardson, Hugh E. *High Peaks, Pure Earth: Collected Writings on Tibetan History and Culture.* Edited by Michael Aris. London: Serindia Publications, 1998.

Samuel, Geoffrey. *Civilized Shamans: Buddhism in Tibetan Societies.* Washington/London: Smithsonian Institution Press, 1993.

Shardza Tashi Gyaltsen. *Heart Drops of the Dharmakaya,* commentary by Lopon Tenin Namdak. Ithaca, NY: Snow Lion, 1993.

Smith, E. Gene. *Among Tibetan Texts.* Boston: Wisdom Publications, 2001.

Sørensen, Per K. *Tibetan Buddhist Historiography: The Mirror Illuminating the Royal Genealogies.* Wiesbaden: Harrassowitz Verlag, 1994.

Stearns, Cyrus. *Buddha from Dolpo.* Albany: State University of New York Press, 1999.

Srong, John S. *The Legend and Cult of Upagupta.* Princeton: Princeton University Press, 1992.

Tulku Thondup. *Masters of Meditation and Miracles: Lives of the Great Buddhist Masters of India and Tibet,* ed. Harold Talbot. Boston: Shambhala, 1999.

Wallace, Vesna A. *The Inner Kālacakratantra: A Buddhist Tantric View of the Individual.* New York: Oxford University Press, 2001.

Wangdu, Pasang, and Hildegard Diemberger. *dBa' bzhed: The Royal Narrative Concerning the Bringing of the Buddha's Doctrine to Tibet.* Vienna: Austrian Academy of Sciences, 2000.

Williams, Paul. *Altruism and Reality: Studies in the Philosophy of the Bodhicaryāvatāra.* Surrey: Curzon, 1998.

———. *The Reflexive Nature of Awareness: A Tibetan Madhyamaka Defence.* Surrey, England: Curzon, 1998.

Artifacts and Material Treasures

Introduction

The objects listed here for the most part complement the texts detailed in the first part of the Bibliography. This is most obvious in the case of the treasures (*gter-ma*), since the treasure-finders (*gter-ston*) revealed both doctrinal treasures (*gter-chos*) and material treausures (*rdzas-gter*), such as kīlas and sacred images. Most entries have not been identified, but occasionally additional information has been given in the Notes, which should be consulted separately. Readers are also referred to Tulku Thondup Rinpoche's *Hidden Teachings of Tibet*, for illustrations of several of the Padmasambhava images mentioned in the *History*, namely, those discovered by Sangye Lingpa, Pema Lingpa and Chogyur Lingpa.

Items have been entered in thematic sequence and in the order of their occurence in the text.

Note

Plate numbers from the first edition are cited in the reference material that follows. The first edition contained 110 plates, which were later reduced to 24 in number, however, the original numbering system for plates has been retained so that interested readers may refer back to the first edition. The key below summarizes the renumbering of the remaining color plates so the reader can make the conversion for the present edition.

First edition:	This edition:	First edition:	This edition:
1	1	66	13
2	2	67	14
3	3	68	15
5	4	70	16
16	5	72	18
25	6	74	20
37	8	75	21
39	9	76	22
40	10	88	17
52	11	89	23
53	12	90	19
60	7	99	24

Artifacts and Material Treasures

AMULETS (*ga'u*)

Amulets containing sacramental substances (*dam-rdzas-kyi gva'u*), discovered by Dorje Lingpa, 789

BRIDGES (*zam-pa*)

Fifty-eight iron suspension bridges (*lcags-zam lnga-bcu-rtsa-brgyad*), built by Thangtong Gyelpo, 803

ENGRAVINGS (*brkos-phor*)

Mould engraved with the *Dhāraṇī of the Wish-fulfilling Gem* (*tsinta-maṇi'i gzungs-kyi brkos-phor*, Skt. *Cintāmaṇidhāraṇī*), 508

FERRY-CROSSINGS (*gru-shan*)

One hundred and eighteen ferry-crossings (*gru-shan brgya-dang bco-brgyad*), established by Thangtong Gyelpo, 803

FRESCOES (*gyang-gi ri-mo*)

Frescoes in Ukpalung Monastery: the gurus of the lineage (*bla-ma brgyud-pa*); twenty-three maṇḍalas (*dkyil-'khor nyer-gsum*), such as the "Hundred-petalled Lotus" (*padma brgya-ldan*); the Thousand Buddhas (*sangs-rgyas stong-rtsa*); Buddhas of the Ten Directions (*phyogs-bcu'i sangs-rgyas*); Amitāyus surrounded by the [Eight] "Closest Sons" (*tshe-dpag-med nye-sras-kyis bskor-ba*); Seven Generations of Buddhas (*sangs-rgyas rabs-bdun*); the twelve deeds (*mdzad-pa bcu-gnyis*); the bodhisattva Dharmodgata (*byang-chub sems-dpa' chos-'phags*); Tārā, who protects from the eight fears (*sgrol-ma 'jigs-pa brgyad-skyobs*); the Lords of the Three Families (*rigs-gsum mgon-po*); the Malaya Buddha-field (*ma-la-ya'i zhing-bkod*); the wheel of life (*srid-pa'i tsa-kra*), 624

Frescoes at Trampa Hermitage: the peaceful deities according to the *Magical Net* (*sgyu-'phrul zhi-ba*); the blazing wrathful deities (*'bar-ba khro-bo'i lha-tshogs*); the deities of the entire *Sūtra which Gathers All Intentions* (*mdo yongs-rdzogs*); three maṇḍalas (*dkyil-'khor gsum*); glorious Mahākāla according to the tradition of Wrathful Yamāntaka (*dpal-mgon mahākāla drag-po gshin-rje ltar*); the eightfold group of the Mönpa, mounted on tigers (*stag-zhon mon-pa sde-brgyad*), 628

Frescoes of the expanded and condensed maṇḍalas [of the *Magical Net*, *dkyil-'khor rgyas-bsdus*], in the Khandro Lhakang, 644

IMAGES (*sku-rten sna-tshogs-pa*)

One-cubit-tall image of the Lord of Secrets, Vajrapāṇi (*gsang-ba'i bdag-po'i sku khru-gang*), revealed to King Ja, 459

Self-created image of the Sublime One [Avalokiteśvara, *rang-byon 'phags-pa*], given to King Songtsen Gampo by Ā-kar Matiśīla, still preserved as the most sacred image in the Potala, 510

Two images of the Teacher, representative of the Buddha himself, the size of an eight-year-old and that of a twelve-year-old (*ston-pa dgung-lo brgyad-pa-dang bcu-gnyis-pa'i sku-tshad*), still preserved in the Jokhang and Ramoche temples, Pls. 37, 41; 510

(Two) image(s) of Lord Śākyamuni in Lhasa (*jo-śāk rnam gnyis*), Pls. 37, 41; 564, 590, 656, 659, 758, 768

Images of deities at Drinzang Temple in Trakmar (*brag-dmar mgrin-bzang-gi lha-khang-la . . . lha-sku-rnams*), 513-14

Stone image in the meadow of Trikmo-lha (*krig-mo-lha'i ne'u sing-gi rdo-sku*), in Tsāri, 570

Blue-coloured image of Bhaṭṭārikā (*rje-btsun-ma mthing-tshon gang-ba*), 572

Images at Ukpalung: Vairocana-Samantamukha (*rnam-snang kun-tu-zhal*), Hayagrīva (*rta-mgrin*), Amṛtakuṇḍalin (*bdud-rtsi 'khyil*), the Great Mother (*yum chen-mo*), Dīpaṃkara (*mar-me mdzad*); relief images of Bhagavat (*mgon-po legs-ldan*), Śrīdevī (*dpal-ldan lha-mo*), Brahmā (*tshangs-pa*) and Śakra (*brgya-byin*), 623-4

Image of Sarvavid-Vairocana (*kun-rig*), at Ukpalung, 624

Images at Trampa Hermitage: the Great Glorious One (*dpal chen-po'i sku*); the Eight Wrathful Goddesses according to the tradition of the tantras (*khro-mo brgyad-pa rgyud-lugs ltar*), 626-8, 630, 634-5

Buddhas of the three times (*dus-gsum sangs-rgyas*), at the Temple of Dropuk, 633

Images of the Forty-two [Peaceful] Buddhas and of Lekden Degü, the protector of the transmitted precepts (*sangs-rgyas bzhi-bcu-rtsa-gnyis-dang bka'-srung legs-ldan lde-gus*), in the Khandro Lhakang, 644

Image of the Great Compassionate One at Thangkya (*thang-skya'i thugs-rje chen-po*), 659

Images of Hayagrīva and Varāhī in union (*rta-phag zhal-sbyor*), discovered by Pakshi Śākya-ö, 663

Image of Vajrasattva with his consort (*rdor-sems yab-yum*), discovered by Pakshi Śākya-ö, 663

Image of Vajrasattva in Chinese bronze (*rdo-rje sems-dpa'i sku rgya-nag li-ma*), commissioned by Zur Zangpopel, 670

Golden image of Mañjughoṣa which contained fragments of the conqueror Zurpoche's robes (*rgyal-ba zur-po-che'i sku-chos-kyi dum-bu bzhugs-pa'i 'jam-dbyangs-kyi gser-sku*), built at Ukpalung by Zur Ham Śākya Jungne, 671

Image of Vajrakīla (*rdo-rje phur-pa'i sku*), the transfiguration of Kyi Chöki Senge, 685

Golden image of Śākyamuni (*gser-gyi thub-pa'i sku*), at Katok offered by the king of Jang, 696

Image of Vairocana at Khoting (*mkho-mthing rnam-snang-gi sku*), 756

Image of Hayagrīva (*rta-mgrin-gyi sku-rten*), discovered by Nyang-rel Nyima Özer, 757

Cubit-tall image of a nine-headed nāga in bronze (*khro-chu'i klu-bdud mgo-dgu-pa*), discovered by Guru Chöwang, 764

Image of the Lord of Sages (*thub-pa'i dbang-po'i snang-brnyan*) similar to the Lord Śākyamuni image in Lhasa, discovered by Nāgārjuna and rediscovered by Guru Chöwang, 768

Natural stone images of the host of peaceful and wrathful deities guarded by Khyapjuk Chenpo (*zhi-khro'i lha-tshogs rang-byung-du bzhugs-pa'i sgo-srung khyab-'jug chen-po*), 775

Especially sublime image of Orgyen (*o-rgyan-gyi sku-tshabs khyad-'phags*), discovered at Samye Chimpu by Sangye Lingpa, 786

Image of Como [Tārā] at Trhadruk (*khra-'brug jo-mo'i sku*), Pl. 43; 789

Image of Guru Rinpoche (*sku-tshab*), discovered by Dorje Lingpa, 789

Image of Vajrasattva (*rdo-rje sems-dpa'i sku*), discovered at Phungpo Riwoche by Dorje Lingpa, 791

Eleven-faced Avalokiteśvara (*bcu-gcig zhal-gyi sku-rten*), discovered in the "Vase Pillar" of Lhasa by Dorje Lingpa, 791

Sandalwood image of Tārā (*tsan-dan-gyi sgrol-ma*) discovered in the "Vase Pillar" of Lhasa by Dorje Lingpa, 791

Representative images of Guru Padmasambhava (*sku-tshab padma gu-ru*), discovered by Pema Lingpa, 797

Image of Vairocana with four bodies (*rnam-snang mi-bzhi*), in the upper hall at Samye, 807

Chick-sized garuḍa image of cast iron (*lcags-khro'i bya-khyung bye'u-phrug-tsam*), discovered by Rikdzin Jatsön Nyingpo, 810

Natural image of the Sublime One of Kyirong (*skyid-grong-gi rang-byung 'phags-pa*), 826

Silver image of the Conqueror Ajita (*rin-chen gnyis-pa'i rgyal-ba ma-pham-pa'i snang-brnyan*), erected by Jikme Lingpa, 838

Representative figure of Guru Rinpoche (*gu-ru'i sku-tshab*), discovered by Chogyur Lingpa at Tsike Norbu Pünsum, 845

Two representative images (*sku-tshab rnam-gnyis*), discovered by Chogyur Lingpa at Yegyel Namkadzö, 845

Representative image [of Padmasambhava called] "Blazing with the Glory of Accomplishment" (*dngos-grub dpal-'bar*), discovered by Jamyang Khyentse Wangpo, 856

Representative image of Saroruhavajra (*mtsho-skyes rdo-rje'i sku-tshab*), discovered at Samye by Nyang-rel Nyima Özer, 857

Representative image of Guru Padmasambhava called "Blazing with Good Fortune's Glory" (*bkra-shis dpal-'bar*), discovered by Jamgön Kongtrül, 864

Lama Mipham's image of Mañjuśrīghoṣa (*'jam-dpal dbyangs-kyi sku*), 876

JEWELS (*nor-bu*)

Kaustubha gemstone (*rin-po-che kau-stu-bha*), 277

Jewel called Tiger-Meat God (*nor-bu stag-sha de-ba*), discovered by Sangye Lingpa at Orshö Lungdrom, 786

Life-supporting turquoise ornaments of the religious king Trhisong and of Yeshe Tshogyel herself (*chos-rgyal-dang mtsho-rgyal-nyid-kyi bla-gYu*), discovered by Dorje Lingpa, 790

Wish-fulfilling gem (*yid-bzhin nor-bu*), discovered by Dorje Lingpa, 790

Wish-fulfilling gem (*nor-bu bsam-'phel*), discovered by Dorje Lingpa, 791

Life-supporting turquoise gems of the religious king Trhisong Detsen called "Blazing Light" (*rin-po-che 'od-'bar*), "Blazing Light of a Thousand Mountains" (*stong-ri 'od-'bar*) and "Red House Snowpeak" (*gangs-ri khang-dmar*), discovered by Pema Lingpa, 798

KĪLAS (*phur-pa*)

Kīla (*phur-pa*) of the venerable lady Kharcenza, Yeshe Tshogyel, 710-11

Kīla of Darcarupa preserved at Sera Monastery (*sera phur-mjal*), 714-16, n. 916

Kīla (*gter-phur*) preserved at Tsāri Tshokar, from the treasures of Sangye Lingpa, 751

Three kīlas wrapped in maroon silk (*phur-pa gsum chu-dar smug-pos dril-ba*), discovered in the cave of Zangzang Lhadrak by Rikdzin Gödemcen, 781

Iron kīla (*lcags-phur*), discovered by Sangye Lingpa, 786

"Laughter of Kīla's Great Power" (*phur-pa dbang-chen bzhad-pa*), offered by Chogyur Lingpa to Situ Pema Nyinje Wangpo, 842

LONGEVITY PILLS (*tshe-ril*)

Longevity pills of Mandāravā (*man-dā-ra-ba'i tshe-ril*), discovered by Jamgön Kongtrül, 864

Longevity pills which Guru Rinpoche compounded at Māratika (*mā-ra-ti-kar gu-ru'i phyag-sgril tshe-ril*), discovered by Jamgön Kongtrül, 864

Longevity pills of thirteen immortal awareness-holders (*'chi-med rig-'dzin bcu-gsum-gyi tshe-ril*), discovered by Jamgön Kongtrül, 864

MASKS (*'bag-ma*)

Dance masks of a doctrine protector and his lady (*chos-skyong lcam-dral-gyi 'chams-sku*), commissioned by Zur Zangpopel, 670

Sebak Komdünma, the "Leather Mask of the Seven Steps", or "Mask of the *Se*-spirit" (*se-'bag goms-bdun-ma*), commissioned by Zur Zangpopel, 670

Mask of Orgyen (*o-rgyan-gyi 'dra-'bag*), discovered by Sangye Lingpa, 786

OFFERING-BOWLS (*ting*)

Seven great altar bowls (*ting chen-po bdun*), offered to Katok by Phakpa Rinpoche, 695

ORNAMENTS AND OTHER OBJETS D'ART (*rgyan-cha-sogs*)

Ivory model of the temple at Vajrāsana (*ba-so-las bcos-pa'i gan-dho-la*), at Katok, offered by the king of Jang, 696

Ḍākinī's body ornament (*mkha'-'gro'i sku-rgyan*), discovered at Orshö Lung-drom by Sangye Lingpa, 786

Gold-filled copper vase (*zangs-bum gser-gyis bkang-ba*), discovered by Sangye Lingpa, 786

Clairvoyant mirror (*me-long rgyang-gsal*), discovered by Pema Lingpa, 798

Wheel of fine gold (*gser-sbyang-kyi 'khor-lo*), presented to the great temple of Samye by Jikme Lingpa, 838

Body ornaments of Senge Dradok (*seng-sgrogs sku-rgyan*), discovered at Tsike Norbu Pünsum by Chogyur Lingpa, 845

PAINTINGS (*ri-mo, bris-sku*)

Painting of Mañjuśrī (*'jam-dpal-gyi bris-sku*), 463

Picture of Mañjuśrī (*'jam-dpal-gyi bris-sku*), 465

One hundred and eight wall-sized paintings in the Nepali style (*bal-ris-kyi thang-ka thog-tshad-ma brgya-dang brgyad*), commissioned by Drogön Namka Pelwa, 758

Scroll-painting of White Tārā (*sgrol-dkar-gyi zhal-thang*), given to Mipham Rinpoche by Khyentse Rinpoche, 874

PILLARS (*ka-ba*)

"Vase Pillar" in the middle storey of the innermost shrine at Samye (*bsam-yas dbu-rtse'i bar-khang ka-ba bum-pa-can*), 753

"Vase Pillar" of Lhasa (*lha-sa'i ka-ba bum-pa-can*), 791

PRINTS (*lag-rjes zhabs-rjes-la-sogs-pa*)

Śrīpāduka (*shrī-pā-du-ka*), an enormous footprint of the Buddha, in Śrī Laṅkā, 456

Body imprint of Guru Rinpoche at Dorje Tsekpa in Bumthang (*bum-thang rdo-rje brtegs-pa-la sku-rjes*), Pl. 50; 519

Handprint of Guru Rinpoche at Namtso Chukmo (*gnam-mtsho phyug-mo-la phyas-rjes*), 519

Footprint of Guru Rinpoche on the White Rock in Paro (*spa-gro'i brag-dkar-la zhabs-rjes*), 519

RELICS (*ring-bsrel*)

Relics (*gdung-dang ring-bsrel*) of the Tathāgata Śākyamuni, 427, 433, 435, 626, 786; see also *relics* in the Index of Technical Terms

Maṇḍala of the Conquerors of the Five Families (*rgyal-ba rigs lnga'i dkyil-'khor*), from the remains of Kumārādza, 527

Remains (*sku-gdung/skyes-bdun*) of Orgyen Lingpa, 777-8

Twenty-one multiplying remains of the Tathāgata (*de-bzhin gshegs-pa'i 'phel-gdung nyer-gcig*), discovered by Sangye Lingpa, 786

Remains of twenty-one brahmans (*bram-ze nyer-gcig*), discovered by Khyentse Rinpoche, 856

Relics emanated from a tooth of Guru Rinpoche (*gu-ru rin-po-che'i tshems-las sprul-pa'i ring-bsrel*), discovered at Damshö Nyingdrung by Khyentse Rinpoche, 856

ROBES (*gos-chas*)

Seamless robes of the Princess (*lha-lcam-gyi na-bza' srub-med*), discovered by Pema Lingpa, 798

Secret robe of Hūṃkara (*hūṃ-ka-ra'i gsang-gos*), discovered at the Kumcok Decen Cave by Jamgön Kongtrül, 864

The great preceptor Śāntarakṣita's robe (*mkhan-chen zhi-'tsho'i sku-chos*), discovered at the Üri Jetsün Cave in Pema Lhartse by Jamgön Kongtrül, 864

The religious king Trhisong Detsen's sash (*chos-rgyal khri-lde'i sku-rag*), discovered at the Üri Jetsün Cave in Pema Lhartse by Jamgön Kongtrül, 864

SPIRES (*ganydzi-ra*)

The great spire (*gtsug-lag-gi rtse'i ganydzi-ra che-ba*) on top of Katok Monastery, offered by the king of Jang, 696

STŪPAS (*mchod-rten*)

Seven stūpas holding the Buddha's remains (*sku-gdung-gi mchod-rten bdun*), 435-6

Golden stūpa (*gser-gyi mchod-rten*), of the "Awesome Secret", 508

Three-storey stūpa of bronze (*mchod-rten li-ma thog-tshad gsum-pa*), offered to Katok by Phakpa Rinpoche, 695

Reliquary (*gdung-rten*) of Orgyen Lingpa at Pentsang Monastery, 777-8

WATER OF LIFE (*tshe-chu*)

Lapis flask, about the size of large inkpot, containing water of life (*tshe-chu'i snod mu-men-gyi bum-pa*), discovered by Pakshi Śākya-ö, 663

Four vases containing the water of life (*tshe-chu bum-pa bzhi*), discovered at the Longevity Cave at Campa Temple in Bumthang by Dorje Lingpa, 789

Water of life (*tshe-chu*), discovered by Dorje Lingpa, 790

Spiritual elixir produced at Yangleshö (*yang-le-shod-du bsgrub-pa'i chos-sman*), discovered by Dorje Lingpa, 790

Index of Technical Terms

Introduction

This index of technical terms has also been given the function of a trilingual glossary of terminology for Buddhism and the outer sciences. The traditional sources consulted in compiling it include the *Seven Great Treasuries* of Longcen Rapjampa and Jamgön Kongtrül Rinpoche's *Store which Embraces All Knowledge*, as well as the primary Indian treatises studied in Tibet. Reference has also been made to such recent lexicographical works as the *bod-rgya tshig-mdzod chen-mo* and the ongoing compilation of Tibetan Buddhist terminology by Erik Pema Kunsang.

Readers are referred to the Glossary of Enumerations for more information on numerical categories and to the Notes for occasional more detailed explanation of terms; neither of these two sections have been cross-referenced here. Where an entry is followed by "*passim*", it may be useful to consult the detailed contents lists for Books One and Two appearing in Section One, which outline the structure and subject-matter of each.

Note

To avoid unnecessary repetition, master terms have been omitted in sub-entries, or replaced by a comma. Sub-sub-entries run on.

Index of Technical Terms

Abhidharma *chos mngon-pa*: see under *piṭaka*
seven sections of *mngon-pa sde-bdun*, 90-1
abiding mode (of reality) *gnas-tshul*, 32, 210, 212-13, 215-16, 232, 234, 249, 314
abiding nature (of reality) *gnas-lugs*: the primordial emptiness or nature of the buddha-body of reality, 23, 36, 85-6, 122, 141-2, 154, 161, 167-8, 177, 183-5, 206, 217, 220, 232, 234, 247, 249, 251-2, 257, 259-60, 263, 273, 275-6, 285, 287, 291, 295, 297-300, 302, 307-8, 310, 312-13, 315, 321, 323, 327, 335-6, 338, 342-5, 447, 566, 609, 615, 625, 677, 700, 726, 856, 896, 898, 900, 901, 903, 906, 907, 931
harmony and disharmony of the apparitional and *gnas-snang mthun mi-mthun*, 206, 210-11
absolute (nature/reality) *(chos-nyid) yongs-grub-kyi mtshan-nyid*, Skt. *pari-niṣpannalakṣaṇa*, 24, 25, 26, 27, 154, 161-2, 170-1, 173, 176, 178, 182; see also *essential natures, three*
absorption *snyoms-'jug*, Skt. *samāpatti*: see *meditative absorption(s)*
acacia wood *seng(-ldeng)*, Skt. *khadira*, 603, 612, 615
ācārya *slob-dpon*: a master or teacher, 558; see also *master*
accomplished master *grub-pa/grub-thob*, Skt. *siddha*, *passim*
accomplishment(s) *dngos-grub*, Skt. *siddhi*, *passim*
common *thun-mong-gi dngos-grub*, Skt. *sādhāraṇasiddhi*, 260, 477, 480, 487, 614, 787, 918; eight *thun-mong-gi dngos-grub brgyad*, 247, 259
of the divine body in which bliss and emptiness are coalesced in inner radiance *bde-stong 'od-gsal-gyi lha-sku 'grub*, 288
of the divine body which coalesces vital energy and mind *rlung-sems-kyi lha-sku 'grub*, 288
of the divine body of devoted conduct *mos-spyod-kyi lha-sku 'grub*, 288
of the divine body in which pristine cognition and the pure (path of) learning are coalesced *ye-shes-dang dag-pa'i slob-pa'i zung-'jug-gi lha-sku 'grub*: i.e. prior to the attainment of the path of no-more-learning, 288
great/supreme/uncommon *mchog-gi dngos-grub*, Skt. *paramasiddhi*, 45, 247, 260, 281, 404, 472, 473, 476, 481, 488, 536, 584, 605, 615, 621, 714, 772, 843, 918
level of *dngos-grub-kyi sa*, 894, 917
signs of *dngos-grub-kyi rtags-mtshan/grub-rtags*, 601, 607, 631, 690, 713, 714, 715, 765, 767, 778, 787, 798, 844, 866, 869, 870, 939; see also *signs of success*
of the sky-farer *mkha'-spyod-pa'i dngos-grub*, 773
of the "swift feet of the yakṣiṇī" *gnod-sbyin-mo'i rkang-mgyogs-kyi dngos-grub*, 614
of swift-footedness *rkang-mgyogs-kyi dngos-grub*, 540

two *dngos-grub gnyis*, 404, 861, 918, 967
water of *grub-chu*, 601, 628
action seal *las-kyi phyag-rgya*, Skt. *karmamudrā*: see under *seal(s)*
activity field(s) *skye-mched*, Skt. *āyatana*, 93, 170, 212, 217, 221, 224, 247, 251, 259, 276, 322, 367, 424, 543, 900
in which appearances are exhausted *chos zad-pa'i skye-mched*, 639; see also under *visionary appearance(s)*
four *skye-mched bzhi*: the four formless realms, 15, 62
infinite as the sky *nam-mkha' mtha'-yas skye-mched*, 15, 62
of infinite consciousness *rnam-shes mtha'-yas skye-mched*, 15, 62
of nothing at all *ci-yang med-pa'i skye-mched*, 15, 62
of phenomena *chos-kyi skye-mched*, Skt. *dharmāyatana*, 52
twelve *skye-mched bcu-gnyis*, 13, 55-6
where there is neither perception nor non-perception *'du-shes med 'du-shes med-min skye-mched*, 15, 62
Adherents of the Nine Categories *don-dgu-pa*, 66; see also *Jaina*
Adherents of the Six Categories *don-drug-pa*, Skt. *ṣaḍpadārtha*, 65; see also *Vaiśeṣika*
Adherents of the Three Attributes *yon-tan gsum-pa*, Skt. *Traiguṇya*, 65; see also *Sāṃkhya*
aeon(s) *bskal-pa*, Skt. *kalpa*, 121, 138, 200-1, 247, 256, 258-9, 271, 292, 313, 420, 474, 691, 697, 916
auspicious *bskal-pa bzang-po*, Skt. *Bhadrakalpa*, 409, 414, 943-4
"countless" *grangs-med bskal-pa*, 115, 246, 251, 254, 258, 411, 412
affixation *rkyen*, Skt. *pratyaya*: in grammar, 100
Aiśvara *dbang-phyug-pa*, Skt. *Aiśvara*: the Followers of Shaivism or Followers of Īśvara, 16, 65
Akaniṣṭha *'og-min*: see Index of Locations
alchemy *bcud-len*, Skt. *rasāyana*: a means of extracting elixir from minerals of the earth or herbs and plant substances, and subsisting upon it, 549, 550, 575, 682, 789
ālikāli: literally refers to the vowels and consonants of the Sanskrit language, but secretly to the rites of wrathful "liberation" and sexual union, 292
all-positive king *kun-bzang rgyal-po*: an epithet of Samantabhadra, the buddha-body of reality, 317
All-Surpassing Realisation *thod-rgal*, Skt. *vyutkrāntaka*, 38-9, 334, 337-45, 371, 456, 540, 552, 565, 588, 593, 658, 665, 773, 828-9, 879; see also *lamps* and *visionary appearance(s)*
four assurances *gdeng-bzhi*, 372
four consolidations *mtha'-rten bzhi*, 343
six essentials *gnad-drug*, 371
of spontaneous presence *lhun-grub thod-rgal*, 877
three attainments *thob-pa gsum*, 343
three essentials which guide (the eyes) towards the expanse *'khrid-pa dbyings-kyi gnad gsum*, 338; see also *gazes, three*
three essentials of objective appearance *snang-ba yul-gyi gnad gsum*, 338
three presences *sdod-pa gsum*, 343
three supportive essentials of the body *bca'-ba lus-kyi gnad gsum*, 338; see also *postures, three*
three unmoving states *mi-'gul-ba gsum*, 343
Ancient Translations *snga-'gyur*: the teachings of the Nyingma tradition which were translated in Tibet up to the time of Smṛtijñānakīrti, 40, 376, 396, 522, 523, 545, 666, 671, 696, 720, 724, 922, 969
Ancient Translation School *snga-'gyur rnying-ma*: adherents of the above tradition, 11, 41, 47, 109, 148, 198, 237, 372, 378, 394, 400, 401, 441, 442, 461, 504, 523, 526, 527, 560, 565, 569, 577, 590, 596, 599, 607, 617, 624, 657, 669, 674, 675, 677, 678, 679, 683, 688, 698, 699, 706, 707, 719, 722, 723, 728, 729, 730, 731, 733, 736, 737, 738, 739, 747, 750, 762, 770, 783, 789, 794, 795, 805, 807, 808, 809, 811, 816, 823, 824, 827, 830, 831, 833, 836, 838, 842, 852, 856, 861, 862, 868, 869, 872, 873, 877, 878, 881, 883-940, 962, 968, 972; see also *Nyingma*
relationship to the New Translation School, 918-25

six superiorities of *snga-'gyur che-ba drug*, 375, 889-90
antigods *lha-ma-yin*, Skt. *asura*, 14, 66, 130-2, 466, 491
Anuyoga *rjes-su rnal-'byor*: see under *piṭaka* and *vehicle(s)*
Apabhraṃśa *zur-chags*, 107
Apathetic *phyal-ba*, 16, 63, 67
aphorisms in prose and verse *dbyangs-bsnyad*, Skt. *geya*, 76
aphoristic verses *don-du 'gyur-ba'i tshigs-bcad*, 705
apparitional mode/nature (of reality) *snang-tshul*, 13, 56-7, 203, 210-13, 217, 232, 250-1, 260, 562
apparition of/apparitional reality *chos-can*, Skt. *dharmin*: lit. "possessor of *dharma*", this term refers to the concrete reality of apparent objects, which is contrasted, in works such as the *Analysis of Phenomena and Reality (Dharmadharmatāvibhāga)*, with actual reality (*chos-nyid*, Skt. *dharmatā*) or emptiness. In logical treatises, it refers to the topic to be analysed. For the specific Nyingma interpretation, see Longcenpa, *Treasury of the Supreme Vehicle*, (p. 82), 37, 38, 95, 191-2, 201, 211, 215, 287, 319, 325-6, 330
appearance(s) *snang-ba*, *passim*; see also *form* and *visionary appearance(s)*
pure appearance/vision *dag-snang*, 249, 564, 747-8, 755, 767, 784, 793, 805, 807, 813, 819, 837, 843, 844, 845, 847, 848, 852, 853-4, 855, 857, 858, 860, 865, 866, 871, 935
three *snang-ba gsum*, 142, 258, 288
appraisal of textual traditions *gzhung-lugs 'jal-byed*
key to the appraisal of causal vehicle texts *'jal-byed lde-mig*, 30, 217-22
key to the appraisal of secret mantra texts *sngags-gzhung 'jal-byed*, 35, 290-3
Arabic chronicles, 399
arhat *dgra-bcom-pa*: one who has slain the foe of conflicting emotion and reached the highest result of the vehicles of pious attendants. Buddhas and self-centred buddhas may be referred to as arhats insomuch as they have also realised nirvāṇa, 18, 83, 90-1, 93, 159, 174, 231, 423, 425, 426, 428, 429, 430, 434, 435, 436, 437, 438, 439, 440, 912, 913, 933
arithmetic *sa-ris*: arithmetical calculations traced in sand, which are then easily erased, 869
arts *bzo'i rig-gnas*, Skt. *śilpavidyā*, 18, 59, 98-9, 103, 418, 860; see also *crafts, sixty-four*
thirty designated *bzor btags-pa sum-cu*, 98
artistic techniques, eighteen *bzo-sbyangs bco-brgyad*, 99
āryā metre *'phags-pa*: in prosody, a stanza comprising two half-verses, the first of which contains eight feet of thirty *mātrā (morae)* and the second eight feet of twenty-seven *mātrā*, 106
Āṣāḍha *chu-stod*: July to August, 947
ascendant conjunction *'char-rtsis*: a calculation in astrology, 104
ascetic *dge-sbyong*, Skt. *śramaṇa*, 422, 551
contemplation *dka'-thub-kyi ting-nge-'dzin*, 419
discipline/practice *brtul-zhugs-kyi spyod-pa*, 221, 270, 501
four doctrines of a spiritual *dge-sbyong-gi chos-bzhi*, Skt. *catvāraḥ śramaṇa-dharmāḥ*, 52
virtues *sbyangs-pa'i yon-tan*, Skt. *dhūtaguṇa*, 432, 434, 497; twelve *sbyangs-pa'i yon-tan bcu-gnyis*, Skt. *dvādaśadhūtaguṇa*, 227
asceticism *brtul-zhugs*, Skt. *vrata*, 304
aspects *rkang-pa*: the mathematical calculations in astrology of the lunar path, on which see D. Schuh, *Untersuchungen zur Tibetischen Kalenderrechnung*, (p. 124), 104
aspiration *smon-lam*, Skt. *praṇidhāna*, 47, 82, 118-19, 122, 127, 129, 146-7, 194-6, 228, 235-6, 266, 422, 552, 587, 641, 728, 743, 744, 745, 747, 748, 774, 798, 812, 822, 828, 832, 838, 842, 878, 879, 927, 967, 968, 969
enlightened *thugs-bskyed*, 729, 738, 887, 926
perfection of *smon-lam-gyi pha-rol-tu phyin-pa*, Skt. *praṇidhānapāramitā*, 902
superior *lhag-bsam*, Skt. *adhyāśaya*, 376, 403

aspirationlessness *smon-pa med-pa*, Skt. *apraṇihitam*, 24, 154, 218, 316-17, 898
assembly(ies) *tshogs*, 448, 449; see also *community*
four (ordinary/monastic) *'khor-bzhi-po*, 74, 423, 426; see also *orders, four*
astrology *skar-rtsis*: i.e. that which is Indian in origin, in contrast to the Chinese tradition of divination (*nag-rtsis*), 18, 103-4, 575, 665, 679, 723, 724, 727, 730, 746, 775, 791, 821, 836, 869, 939, 946-8, 954
astrological charts *skar-rtsis-kyi ri-mo*, 944
Atiyoga *shin-tu rnal-'byor*: see *Great Perfection* and under *piṭaka* and *vehicle(s)*
atom *rdul-phra-rab*, Skt. *paramāṇu*: i.e. an indivisible atomic particle, 19, 20, 24, 25, 38, 117, 156, 159, 215, 224-5, 229
atomic matter *rdul-rdzas*, 35, 294, 336-7, 341
attainment *sgrub-pa*, *passim*
of elixir *sman-sgrub*, 686, 757
great *sgrub-chen*, Skt. *mahāsādhana*, 807
means for *sgrub-thabs*, Skt. *sādhana*: see *means for attainment*
of medicinal pills from the flesh of one born as a brahman seven times *skye-bdun (ril-sgrub)*, 791, 793, 797
place of *sgrub-gnas*, 518, 519, 862, 876
supreme and common *mchog-dang thun-mong-gi sgrub-pa*, 917
auspicious coincidence *rten-'brel*, *passim*; for the philosophical implications of this term, see *dependent origination*
austerity *dka'-thub*, Skt. *tapas*, 64, 270, 351, 427, 548, 569, 580, 946
awakening(s) *mngon-byang*, Skt. *abhi-sambodhi*, 113
five *mngon-byang lnga*, Skt. *pañcābhi-sambodhi*: according to Yogatantra, 33, 272-3, 355-6, 412, 645, 703
four *mngon-byang bzhi*, Skt. *caturabhi-sambodhi*, 279
outer and inner *phyi-nang-gi mngon-byang*, 413; five *phyi-nang-gi mngon-byang lnga*, 115
awareness *rig-pa*, Skt. *vidyā*, 21, 38, 53, 123, 162, 171, 177, 201, 204, 252, 276, 280, 297, 308-9, 311-12, 325, 327, 329, 332-41, 350, 358, 360, 365-6, 371, 403, 448, 449, 476, 588, 641, 771, 818, 825, 830, 832, 843, 900, 901, 906, 922, 923, 924
channels of *rig-pa'i rtsa*, 874
empowered *dbang-bsgyur rig-pa*, 281
expressive play of *rig-pa'i rtsal*, 684
in the form of a woman *rig-ma*, 866
immediacy of total *rig-pa spyi-blugs*, 280
intrinsic *rang-rig*, Skt. *svasaṃvittiḥ*, 17, 21, 24, 25, 36, 38, 102, 127, 158, 162, 172, 176, 181, 201, 213, 231, 234, 259, 263, 275-6, 278, 299-300, 316, 318, 333-4, 349, 355, 358, 680, 830; four modes of genuine individual *so-so yang-dag-pa rang-gi rig-pa bzhi*, Skt. *catuḥpratisaṃvid*, 871; individual or (intuitive) *so-so rang-gi rig-pa*, Skt. *pratisaṃvid*, 104, 176, 180-1, 185, 208, 272, 309, 333, 342; see also *pristine cognition of intrinsic awareness*
limit of *rig-pa'i tshad*, 343, 668
naked *rig-pa rjen-pa*, 856
of the present *shes-bzhin*, Skt. *saṃ-prajanya*, 94, 236
and radiance *rig-gsal*, 902
total presence of *rig-pa cog-bzhag ngang*, 902
awareness-holder(s) *rig-'dzin*, Skt. *vidyā-dhara*, 31, 34, 45, 47, 259-60, 271, 278, 280-2, 306, 375, 397, 406, 483, 485, 487, 489, 490, 498, 543, 568, 573, 579, 625, 626, 649, 653, 661, 677, 679, 683, 700, 731, 750, 765, 774, 778, 780, 809, 813, 820, 824, 854, 864, 865, 872, 887, 890, 894, 918, 957
body of pristine cognition of *ye-shes-kyi sku-ste rig-pa 'dzin-pa*, 259-60
controlling the duration of life/with power over the life-span *tshe-dbang rig-'dzin*, 260, 281-2, 470, 472, 712, 804
of the desire realm *'dod-pa'i rig-'dzin*, 301
eight *rig-'dzin brgyad*, 757, 791
of the form realm *gzugs-kyi rig-'dzin*, 301
four kinds of *rig-'dzin rnam-bzhi*, 31, 260, 281-2, 363
of the great seal *phyag-rgya chen-po'i rig-'dzin*, 260, 282, 467, 472; five kinds of *phyag-rgya chen-po'i rig-'dzin lnga*, 282

human and non-human *rig-'dzin mi-dang mi-ma-yin*, 452-6
Mantrapiṭaka of *rig-'dzin-gyi sde-snod*: see under *piṭaka*
seven kinds of *rig-'dzin rnam-bdun*, 31, 259-60
sky-faring *mkha'-spyod-pa'i rig-'dzin*, 270, 272, 301
of (spiritual) maturation *rnam-smin rig-'dzin*, 260, 281, 470, 837
of spontaneous presence *lhun-grub rig-'dzin*, 260, 266, 282, 521, 634
supramundane *'jig-rten-las 'das-pa'i rig-'dzin*, 31, 259
three kinds of (mundane) *('jig-rten-pa'i) rig-'dzin rnam gsum*, 31, 259
Awesome Secret *gnyan-pa gsang-ba*, 508-9, 949
axioms *gtan-tshigs*: see *(logical) axioms*
bahal *ba-hal/be-hār*: a Newari *vihāra*, 891
balimācārya: a master of *torma* offerings, 479
bardo *bar-do*, Skt. *antarābhava*: see *intermediate state*
Being of Commitment *dam-tshig sems-dpa'*, Skt. *samayasattva*: the deity which is creatively visualised, 351, 355
Being of Pristine Cognition *ye-shes sems-dpa'*, Skt. *jñānasattva*: the real deity who enters into the creatively visualised Being of Commitment, 270, 351, 355, 695, 915
benefits, two *don-gnyis*, 171, 379
bewilderment *'khrul-pa*, Skt. *bhrānti*, 12, 26, 53-5, 117, 218, 330, 333, 349, 355, 853, 866
four conditions of *'khrul-pa'i rkyen-bzhi*, 54-5
bhikṣu *dge-slong*: see *monk*
birth *skye-ba*, Skt. *jāti*: see under *intermediate state*
birthplace *skye-gnas*, Skt. *yoni*
four kinds of *skye-gnas rigs-bzhi*, 279
purification of *skye-gnas sbyang-ba*, 416
blazes, three *'bar-ba gsum*, 851
blessing(s)/consecration *byin-gyis brlabs-pa*, Skt. *adhiṣṭhāna*, 17, 35, 45, 74-5, 117, 133-5, 144-5, 196, 255, 275, 293, 295, 343, 345, 353, 355-6, 369, 414, 468, 469, 546, 551, 552, 555, 564, 595, 601, 621, 624, 634, 639, 655, 658, 706, 721, 734, 745, 746, 771, 792, 798, 839, 841, 846, 848, 852, 853, 854, 857, 863, 865, 866, 871, 877, 890, 918, 928, 934
of pristine cognition *ye-shes-kyi byin-brlabs*, 272, 353, 831
two *byin-brlabs gnyis*, 912-13
which is the ultimate truth without symbols, *don-dam mtshan-ma med-pa'i byin-brlabs*: according to Ubhayatantra, 32, 33, 207, 264
bliss *bde-ba*, Skt. *sukha*, *passim*; see also under *coalescence/union*
co-emergent *lhan-cig-skyes-pa'i bde-ba*, Skt. *sahajasukha*, 258, 830, 861
great/supreme *bde-ba chen-po*, Skt. *mahāsukha*, 20, 45, 124-5, 145, 185, 202, 250, 258-9, 263-4, 273, 277, 281, 284, 286, 296-7, 302, 313, 329, 343, 365-6, 377, 406, 462, 536, 583, 593, 766, 769, 770, 771, 830, 861, 877, 909, 972; of purpose *yid-bzhin bde-ba-mchog*, 230-1; indestructible discipline of *bde-chen rdo-rje'i brtul-zhugs*, 405
melting *zhu-bde*, 34, 258, 280-1, 829, 830
Blood-drinkers, fifty-eight *khrag-'thung nga-bcu lnga-brgyad*: see under *deities/conquerors, peaceful and wrathful*
bodhisattva(s) *byang-chub sems-dpa'*, 18, 20, 27, 30, 47, 68, 78, 82, 91, 95, 98, 118-19, 129-30, 136, 138, 142, 154, 164, 167, 173-5, 180, 182, 186, 190, 232, 315, 322, 393, 423, 424, 430, 447, 449, 451, 452, 474, 524, 571, 574, 575, 613, 633, 641, 674, 691, 693, 694, 697, 701, 722, 732, 743, 746, 747, 758, 760, 767, 803, 842, 878, 889, 890, 900, 908, 909, 912-13, 921, 928, 932, 936
eighth level *sa-brgyad-pa'i byang-chub sems-dpa'*, 137, 449
male and female *sems-dpa'-dang sems-ma*, 125
ninth level *sa-dgu-pa'i byang-chub sems-dpa'*, 449
tenth level *sa-bcu-pa'i byang-chub sems-dpa'*, 912, 913, 916
third level *sa-gsum-pa'i byang-chub sems-dpa'*, 184
Bodhi Tree *byang-chub shing-sdong*, Skt. *bodhivṛkṣa*: i.e. at Vajrāsana (Bodh Gaya) in India, 417

body *sku*, Skt. *kāya*: i.e. of a buddha, see *buddha-body(ies)*
body *lus*
conventional *brtags-pa'i lus*, 412
corrupt *zag-pa'i lus*, 498
rainbow *'ja'-lus*, 259, 441, 540, 550, 556, 642, 783; see also *buddha-body of great/supreme transformation*
body-colours *sku-mdog*: i.e. of the different deities, 125, 137, 915
book, four-inch: a symbol of buddha-speech according to the Great Perfection, 134-5
brahman *bram-dze*, 121, 440, 475, 478, 485, 511, 607, 693, 856, 912
seven times born as *skye-bdun*, 626, 777, 791
Brāhmaṇa view of mundane aggregates *bram-dze'i 'jig-tshogs-kyi lta-ba*, Skt. *satkāyadṛṣṭi*: the view of the eternalistic extremists such as the Sāṃkhya, 221
brilliance *spobs-pa*, Skt. *pratibhāna*, 405, 493, 577, 636, 641, 666, 681, 704, 705, 708, 797, 839, 928
eight great treasures of *spobs-pa'i gter chen-po brgyad*, 666, 705, 871
bse-stone *bse*, 666, 705, 871
Buddha *sangs-rgyas*: defined as one, such as Śākyamuni, who has utterly purified obscurations (*sangs*) and developed pristine cognition (*rgyas*); defined, 18; *passim*
perfectly realised *yang-dag-par rdzogs-pa'i sangs-rgyas*, Skt. *Samyaksam-buddha*, 421
buddha-body(ies) *sku*, Skt. *kāya*, 17, 18-23, 25, 26, 31, 75, 111-48, 161, 171, 184, 186, 191-5, 203, 207, 209-10, 212-14, 244, 246, 249, 251, 255, 259, 263, 267, 289, 313, 341-2, 356, 404, 413, 458, 462, 477, 594, 607, 634, 656, 664, 803, 829, 832, 846, 851, 862, 874, 877, 879, 915, 960
of awakening *mngon-byang sku*, Skt. *abhisambodhikāya*, 19, 22, 139-40, 282
of coalescence *zung-'jug-gi sku*, Skt. *yuganaddhakāya*, 413, 467, 487, 540
emanational *sprul-pa'i sku*, Skt. *nirmāṇakāya*, 11, 12, 19, 21-2, 23, 115, 118, 123, 127-38, 139, 145, 153, 191-2, 196, 282, 299, 337, 339, 343, 409, 414, 415-16, 454, 585, 746, 866, 961; four kinds of instruction of the supreme *'dul-ba rnam-bzhi*, 21, 131-2, 146, 414, 415; three types of *sprul-sku rnam-gsum*, 21, 128-34, 415-16; twelve deeds of the supreme *mchog-gi sprul-sku'i mdzad-pa bcu-gnyis*, Pls. 6-8; 21, 129, 137, 415-16, 624; twelve teachers of *sprul-pa'i sku ston-pa bcu-gnyis*, 22, 134-8
essential *ngo-bo-nyid sku*, Skt. *svā-bhāvikakāya*, 115, 184-5, 191-5
five *sku-lnga*, Skt. *pañcakāya*, 18, 19, 128, 139-40, 282, 363, 568, 594, 924
of form *gzugs-sku*, Skt. *rūpakāya*, 18, 19, 26, 30, 38, 115, 117, 168, 193-4, 221, 259, 263, 335, 341-2, 355; nine similes for *dpe-dgu*, 197; two *gzugs-sku gnyis*, 113, 168, 195-6, 237, 251, 342
four *sku-bzhi*, Skt. *catuḥkāya*, 19, 191-2, 288, 923
(great), of reality *chos-sku (chen-po)*, Skt. (*mahā*)*dharmakāya*, 11, 12, 18, 19-20, 22, 26, 27, 30, 31, 32, 34, 38, 95, 113, 115-23, 127, 134, 139, 144-5, 165, 168, 171, 184-5, 192-8, 201-2, 219, 221, 237, 245-7, 250, 263-4, 279, 282, 309, 329, 339, 342-3, 357, 403, 413, 415, 421, 447, 448, 572, 585, 677, 832, 837, 901, 902, 924, 925, 947
of great/supreme transformation *'pho-ba chen-po'i sku*, Skt. **mahāsaṅkrānti-kāya*, 38, 342, 501; see also *body, rainbow*, *buddha-body of light* and *supreme transformation*
of indestructible reality *rdo-rje'i sku*, Skt. *vajrakāya*, 19, 22, 139-40, 197, 282, 301, 341, 414, 464, 471, 480, 877
of light *'od-kyi sku*, 473, 537, 567, 581, 588, 695, 809, 812, 855, 858, 919; see also *buddha-body of great/supreme transformation*
of perfect rapture *longs-spyod-rdzogs-pa'i sku*, Skt. *sambhogakāya*, 11, 12, 19, 20-1, 22, 23, 115, 117-18, 122-9, 134, 139, 145-6, 196-7, 282, 340, 342-3, 409, 582, 583, 585, 680
of pristine cognition *ye-shes-kyi sku*, Skt. *jñānakāya*, 259-60, 350, 412, 502, 595, 684, 763, 804, 825, 827, 829, 835, 837, 838

of reality: see *buddha-body, (great) of reality*
of supreme bliss *bde-ba chen-po'i sku*, Skt. *mahāsukhakāya*, 369
three *sku-gsum*, Skt. *trikāya*, 12, 18, 19, 22, 23, 29, 113, 115, 118, 139, 142, 148, 151, 183-4, 191, 194, 196, 251, 280, 306, 352, 357, 363, 404, 448, 503, 554, 622
two *sku-gnyis*, 18, 26, 169, 379
youthful vase *gzhon-nu bum-pa'i sku*: a synonym for the great buddha-body of reality, 19, 38, 117, 342
buddha family(ies) *rigs*, Skt. *kula*, 448, 561, 563; see also *enlightened family(ies)*
five *sangs-rgyas rigs-lnga*, 453, 572; see also *enlightened families, five*
sixth *rigs drug-pa*, 447, 448
(buddha-)field *(sangs-rgyas-kyi) zhing-khams*, Skt. *(buddha)kṣetra*, 19, 117-20, 123-4, 127-31, 145, 161, 171, 212, 214, 247-8, 253, 259, 263, 283, 307, 339, 341, 343, 518, 582, 668, 693, 697, 848, 879
five, of the emanational body of natural expression *rang-bzhin sprul-pa'i sku'i zhing-khams lnga*, 128
buddhahood/buddha nature *sangs-rgyas-nyid*, Skt. *buddhatva*, 17, 19, 27, 29, 30, 36, 67, 115-17, 120-1, 129-31, 141-2, 200, 203, 220, 244, 264-6, 273, 284, 289, 291, 297-8, 306, 332, 357, 366, 369, 411, 412, 413, 420, 421, 423, 432, 433, 434, 447, 458, 545, 568, 582, 594, 622, 641, 642, 697, 760, 767, 900, 901, 913, 923, 924, 946, 947
buddha-mind *thugs*, Skt. *citta*, 17, 21, 22, 31, 75, 115, 124-5, 132, 135-8, 147, 171, 181, 186, 246, 249, 255, 261, 270, 334, 338, 340, 350, 356, 404, 414, 451, 458, 462, 475, 594, 634, 656, 664, 803, 830, 846, 851, 862, 874, 915, 960; see also *intention(s)* and *pristine cognition(s)*
five kinds of *thugs-kyi rnam-pa lnga*, 283
innermost point of *thugs-kyi thig-le*, 832; see also *seminal point, sole/unique*
buddha nature: see *buddhahood/buddha nature*
buddha-speech *gsung*, Skt. *vāk*, 17, 21, 22, 31, 45, 71, 75, 115, 117, 124-5, 132, 135-8, 147, 186, 246, 249, 255, 289, 356, 404, 414, 425, 447, 458, 462, 479, 594, 634, 656, 664, 760, 803, 830, 846, 851, 862, 874, 915, 944, 960; see also under *indestructible reality*
five modes of *gsung-lnga*, 282-3
Buddhism, 11, 16, 19, 39, 41, 47, 393, 394, 396, 397; see also *teaching*
Buddhist *nang-pa*, 11, 12, 16, 18, 23, 36, 40, 41, 82, 89, 185, 393, 394, 395, 398, 463, 471, 472, 485, 493, 503, 632, 715, 936, 943; see also *Insiders*
burnt offerings *sbyin-sregs*, Skt. *homa*: refer to J. F. Staal, *Agni: the Vedic Ritual of the Fire Altar*, for abundant material on the background and development of these rites, 290, 292, 304, 514, 516, 736, 768, 791
Burushaski *bru-sha*: an archaic language of Gilgit, 11, 489
Caitra *nag*: April to May, 947
campaka flowers *me-tog tsam-pa-ka*: *michelia champaca*, 913
Caryātantra *spyod-pa'i rgyud*: see *vehicle of Ubhayatantra/Caryātantra*
causal basis/cause *rgyu*, Skt. *hetu*, *passim*
of separation from defilements *bral-rgyu*, 191-4, 197, 254
causality *rten-'brel*, 666; see also *dependent origination*
cause: see *causal basis*
celestial mansion/palace *gzhal-yas khang*, Skt. *vimāna*: residence of the deities, 123, 126, 171, 247, 255, 283, 287, 293, 416, 692, 769, 892, 915
centre(s) *rtsa-'dab/rtsa-'khor*, Skt. *cakra*: a focal point of energy within the central channel of the body, 124; see also *door*
four *'khor-lo bzhi*, Skt. *catvāri cakrāṇi*, 286, 368
heart-centre *snying-gi 'khor-lo*, 264
(of perfect rapture) in the throat *mgrin-pa (longs-spyod-rdzogs-pa'i) 'khor-lo*, Skt. *sambhogacakra*, 620, 819, 837
secret (or sexual) *mkha'-gsang*, 286; two *mkha'-gsang gnyis*, 277, 368
six *'khor-lo drug*, 368
throat: see *centre (of perfect rapture) in the throat*
certainty(ies) *nges-shes*, 872, 968
five *nges-pa lnga*, 117, 123, 145; see also *excellences, five*

cessation *'gog-pa/zad-pa*, Skt. *nirodha/kṣaya*, *passim*
of all phenomena/things *chos-zad*, 84, 334
of (apparitional) reality *chos-nyid zad-pa*, 335; see also under *visionary appearance(s)*
of breathing *dbugs chad-pa*, 332
of corruption *zag-pa zad-pa*, Skt. *āsravakṣaya*: according to the vehicle of pious attendants, 203, 226, 227, 229, 231
due to individual scrutiny *so-sor brtags-pas 'gog-pa*, Skt. *pratisaṃkhyā-nirodha*, 157
independent of individual scrutiny *brtag-min-gyi 'gog-pa*, Skt. *apratisaṃkhyānirodha*, 157
of intellect/mind *blo-zad*, 84, 144, 165
of quiescence *zhi-ba'i 'gog-pa*, 342
channel *rtsa*, Skt. *nāḍī*: see *energy channel/pathway*
charnel ground *dur-khrod*, Skt. *śmaśāna*, 460, 469, 471, 482, 490, 493, 494, 497, 567, 609, 610, 618, 626, 757, 772, 791
chiliocosm *stong dang-po'i 'jig-rten-gyi khams*, 131, 212
Chinese chronicles, 399
Chinese silk *chu-dar*, 663
clairaudience *lha-snyan*, Skt. *divyaśrotra*, 132; see also *divine ear*
clairvoyance *lha-mig*, Skt. *divyacakṣuḥ*, 132, 548, 609; see also *divine eye*
classes of (living) beings *'gro-ba'i rigs*
five *'gro-ba rigs lnga*, 414
six *'gro-ba rigs drug*, 14-15, 99, 166, 250, 312, 341, 357, 414
twelve dissimilar classes or types of living beings to be trained *gdul-bya rigs mi-mthun-pa bcu-gnyis*, 137
twelve thought patterns of living beings *'gro-ba'i rigs mi-'dra-ba-rnams-kyi rtog-pa bcu-gnyis*, 137
coalescence/union *zung-'jug*, Skt. *yuga-naddha*, 33, 201, 208, 232, 254, 269, 274, 537, 605, 643, 923
of appearance and emptiness *snang-stong zung-'jug*, 29, 31, 144-5, 192, 198, 204, 207, 209, 245, 865
of awareness and emptiness *rig-stong zung-'jug*, 34, 203-4, 273
of bliss and emptiness *bde-stong zung-'jug*, 33, 125, 204, 251, 255, 273, 277, 281, 288, 301, 362, 870, 877, 909
of the expanse of reality and pristine cognition *dbyings-dang ye-shes-kyi zung-'jug*: in Anuyoga, 284-5, 354-6
level of *zung-'jug-gi sa*, 477
of radiance and emptiness *gsal-stong zung-'jug*, 33-4, 273, 350, 362
coalescent being *zung-'jug-gi sems-dpa*, Skt. *yuganaddhasattva*, 259
co-emergence *lhan-skyes*, Skt. *sahaja*, 404, 830
colleges and meditation centres/hermitages/retreats *bshad-grva-dang sgrub-khang*, 519, 625, 632, 671
commentary *'grel-pa*, Skt. *vṛtti*, 30, 39-41, 90-2, 99, 102, 142, 182, 186, 230, 301, 393, 405, 533, 658, 673, 674, 676, 677, 681, 691, 697, 701, 703, 705, 767, 831, 861, 872, 873, 876, 878, 894, 925
on the final promulgation, 95
on the first promulgation, 93
on the Fourth Piṭaka, 96
on the intermediate promulgation, 94-5
commentators *'grel-pa byed-pa-po*, 90-1, 440
commitment(s) *dam-tshig*, Skt. *samaya*, 16, 58, 63, 252-4, 266, 303, 305, 308, 320, 546, 567, 583, 585, 630, 661, 668, 686, 787, 798, 832, 852, 864, 921, 928, 939; see also *vows* for those of the lower vehicles and *oath of allegiance* for those observed by doctrinal protectors
of Atiyoga, 370
ceremony for the fulfilment of *skong-chog*: this expiates any violations, 585, 745, 788, 791
five basic *rtsa-ba dam-tshig lnga*: according to Kriyātantra, 350
fourteen basic violations of *bsrung-bya'i dam-tshig rtsa-ltung bcu-bzhi*: according to Yogatantra, 361
fourteen particular *dam-tshig bcu-bzhi*: according to Yogatantra, 355
holder of *dam-tshig 'dzin-pa*, 841
nine enumerations of *dam-tshig rnam-grangs dgu*: according to Anuyoga, 367
of the sacramental substances: see *sacrament/sacramental objects/substances*

thirteen *bye-brag-gi dam-tshig bcu-gsum*: according to Yogatantra, 350, 355
thirteen particular *bye-brag-gi dam-tshig bcu-gsum*: according to Kriyātantra, 350
three general *spyi'i dam-tshig gsum*: according to Kriyātantra, 350
twenty, concerning attainment *sgrub-pa'i nyi-shu*: according to Anuyoga, 367
twenty-eight *dam-tshig nyer-brgyad*: according to Mahāyoga, 361
twenty-eight common *thun-mong-gi nyi-shu rtsa-brgyad*: according to Anuyoga, 367
twenty-three, relating to discipline *brtul-zhugs-kyi nyer-gsum*: according to Anuyoga, 367
of Ubhayatantra, 353
commitment seal of buddha-mind which secures the mind of conflicting emotions in the pristine cognition of sameness *mnyam-nyid nyon-yid thugs-dam-rgya*, 356
common savour *ro-snyams*, Skt. *samarasa*, 260-1, 305, 322, 404, 571
community *dge-'dun*, Skt. *saṃgha*, 16, 95, 394, 403, 519, 731, 933; see also *monastic community* and *saṃgha*
compassion *snying-rje*, Skt. *karuṇā*, 13, 18, 19, 22, 23, 61, 68, 88, 117, 140, 146-7, 168, 193-4, 200-1, 231-2, 249, 251, 281, 322, 393, 403, 409, 425, 564, 568, 571, 575, 591, 592, 593, 604, 622, 623, 641, 652, 653, 664, 665, 705, 726, 744, 751, 758, 767, 768, 774, 795, 809, 818, 821, 869, 871, 887, 924, 934, 937, 939, 959
great *snying-rje chen-po*, Skt. *mahā-karuṇā*: as a stage of Mahāyoga, 278-9, 281, 360
component(s) *phung-po*, Skt. *skandha/upādānaskandha*, 59, 93, 170, 212, 217, 224, 247, 250, 251, 259-60, 276, 315, 333-4, 367, 424, 899
of consciousness *rnam-shes-kyi phung-po*, Skt. *vijñānaskandha*, 56, 176, 212, 224; see also under *consciousness*
eighty-four thousand (doctrinal) *(chos-kyi) phung-po brgyad-khri bzhi-stong*, 17, 77, 86, 133, 763, 925; see also *extensive teachings, extremely*
of feelings *tshor-ba'i phung-po*, Skt. *vedanāskandha*, 55-6, 176, 212
five *phung-po lnga*, Skt. *pañcaskandha*, 13, 20, 25, 55-6, 160-1
five *phung-po lnga*, Skt. *(asamāsama)-pañcaskandha*: i.e. of the enlightened ones, 125
of form *gzugs-kyi phung-po*, Skt. *rūpa-skandha*, 55, 176, 212, 214-15
four nominal *ming-bzhi-la ldan-pa*, 62
of habitual tendencies *'du-byed-kyi phung-po*, Skt. *saṃskāraskandha*, 56, 176, 212
of perceptions *'du-shes-kyi phung-po*, Skt. *saṃjñāskandha*, 56, 176, 212
compounded entities *'du-byas*, Skt. *saṃskṛta*, 52-3, 70-1, 93, 197, 211, 225, 297, 319, 321, 426
Conangpa *jo-nang-pa*, 833, 850
concentration *bsam-gtan*, Skt. *dhyāna*: see *meditative concentration(s)*
conceptual elaboration *spros-pa*, Skt. *pra-pañca*, 19, 22, 24, 26, 28, 29, 31, 35, 38, 154, 162, 164, 167, 184-5, 196, 203-4, 208-9, 215, 219, 232, 234, 250, 252, 269, 272, 284, 295, 304-6, 308-9, 312, 314-15, 317, 320-1, 324, 330, 336, 342, 354, 360, 362, 365, 368, 764
conceptualising/discursive thought *rnam-rtog*, Skt. *vikalpa*, *passim*
condition(s) *rkyen*, Skt. *pratyaya*, 93, 118, 145-6 and *passim*
four, of saṃsāra *'khor-ba'i rkyen-bzhi*, 54-5
conduct *spyod-pa*, Skt. *caryā*, *passim*
of Atiyoga, 372
of the bodhisattvas, 94-5, 236
disciplined, (of awareness) *rig-pa'i dka'-thub-kyi spyod-pa*, 818, 820
extensive *spyod-pa rgyas-pa*, 431, 440
according to Kriyātantra, 270, 351-2
according to Mahāyoga, 277, 363
in the mundane vehicle, 60
of overpowering discipline *brtul-bzhugs-kyi spyod-pa*: in Mahāyoga, 281
of the pious attendants, 93, 227
of the self-centred buddhas, 230
of self-restraint in Mahāyoga, the eight divisions *grol-lam bag-yod-kyi spyod-pa brgyad*, 281
ten modes of doctrinal *chos-spyod bcu*, 60, 862
three kinds of *spyod-pa gsum*: according to Anuyoga, 369

according to Ubhayatantra, 271, 352
in the vehicle of Brahmā, 61
according to Yogatantra, 357
conflicting emotions *nyon-mongs*, Skt. *kleśa*, 23, 25, 61, 73, 79, 89, 93, 130, 159, 171, 174, 195, 198-9, 227, 229, 236, 255, 265, 292, 302, 309, 311, 321, 332, 341, 420, 424, 930; see also *defilements*
all-conflicting emotions *kun-nas nyon-mongs*, Skt. *saṃkleśa*, 57, 73, 170-1, 176, 234
eighty-four thousand *nyon-mongs brgyad-khri bzhi-stong*, 133
five *nyon-mongs-pa lnga*, 128, 714
six *nyon-mongs-pa drug*, 12, 55
subsidiary *nye-bar nyon-mongs*, Skt. *upakleśa*, 176
three *nyong-mongs-pa gsum*, 88; see also *poisons, three*
conqueror(s) *rgyal-ba*, Skt. *jina*: an epithet for the buddhas, who are conquerors of Māra, *passim*
consciousness *rnam-par shes-pa*, Skt. *vijñāna*, 24, 25, 27, 28, 29, 35, 36, 54-6, 156-205, 250-1, 257, 265, 294, 424, 863, 896, 903, 905, 906 and *passim*; see also *mind*
apperceptive *rnam-par rig-byed*, Skt. *vijñapti*, 56
as a component, 56, 176, 212, 224, 294
of conflicting emotions *nyong-mongs-pa-can yid-kyi rnam-shes*, Skt. *kliṣṭa-manovijñāna*, 340; see also *mind which apprehends emotionally conflicted thoughts*
contrasted with pristine cognition, 180-4, 201, 203, 210-11, 215-16
eight aggregates of *rnam-shes tshogs brgyad*, Skt. *aṣṭavijñānakāya*, 162, 202, 216, 221, 297, 309, 333-4, 341
of the eye *mig-gi rnam-shes*, Skt. *cakṣurvijñāna*, 56
of the five senses *sgo-lnga'i rnam-shes*, 156, 158, 340, 356; see also *sensory perceptions, five*
of the ground-of-all *kun-gzhi'i rnam-shes*, Skt. *ālayavijñāna*, 12, 27, 55, 178, 340
of the intellect/mental faculty *yid-kyi rnam-shes*, Skt. *manovijñāna*, 55, 156-7, 178-9, 257, 340, 356
proponents of: see *Vijñānavādin*
six aggregates of *rnam-shes tshogs drug*, Skt. *ṣaḍvijñānakāya*, 162, 166
consecration *rab-gnas*: a ceremony of inauguration, 629, 630, 643, 644, 676, 695, 791, 809, 826, 838, 912
consort(s), 470, 489, 562, 663, 673; see also under *deity(ies)*
father/male *yab*: male deities or yogins, 125, 273, 281
father and mother *yab-yum*, 369; deities *yab-yum-gyi lha*, 274
five characteristic *mtshan-ldan gzungs-ma lnga*, 773
male and female *yab-yum*, 277
mother/female *yum*: the female adepts and deities, 125, 273, 281, 284
constellations and lunar mansions, the moving band of *skar-khyim-gyi go-la*: in astrology, 104, 946, 969
contemplation(s) *ting-nge-'dzin*, Skt. *samādhi*, 23, 34, 75, 117, 121, 125, 141, 248, 253-6, 259-61, 265-6, 272, 278, 281, 312, 334, 340-1, 348-9, 356-7, 412, 421, 423, 424, 456, 475, 482, 486, 493, 494, 498, 513, 514, 535, 554, 555, 562, 587, 590, 603, 625, 629, 659, 695, 696, 700, 774, 819, 822, 824, 825, 831, 858, 859, 913
on all that appears *kun-snang-gi ting-nge-'dzin*, 279
blissful, radiant and non-discursive *bde-gsal mi-rtog-pa'i ting-nge-'dzin*, 579
of the causal basis *rgyu'i ting-nge-'dzin*, 279
formless *gzugs-med-kyi ting-nge-'dzin*, 486
endowed with four nominal components *ming-bzhi-la ldan-pa'i ting-nge-'dzin*, 62
named "Great Lotus" *padma chen-po zhes-pa ting-nge-'dzin*, 130
of the Great Perfection *rdzogs-pa chen-po'i ting-nge-'dzin*, 693
of the "Illumination of the Greater Vehicle" *theg-pa chen-po rab-tu snang-ba*, 912
of just what is *de-bzhin-nyid-kyi ting-nge-'dzin*, 279; see also *contemplation of reality, just as it is*
non-conceptual *mi-rtog-pa'i ting-nge-'dzin*, Skt. *nirvikalpasamādhi*, 280, 287, 368, 854

non-symbolic *mtshan-med ting-nge-'dzin*, 34, 248, 354
of nothing at all *ci-yang-med-pa'i ting-nge-'dzin*; 412, 419, 693; see also *meditative absorption(s)*
of the pinnacle/summit of existence *srid-rtse'i ting-nge-'dzin*, 56, 419
profound and vast *zab-rgyas ting-'dzin*, 75, 247, 423
of reality, just as it is *chos-nyid de-bzhin-nyid-kyi ting-nge-'dzin*, 363; see also *contemplation of just what is*
of the summit of existence: see *contemplation of the pinnacle/summit of existence*
symbolic *mtshan-bcas ting-nge-'dzin*, 34, 248, 354
three *ting-nge-'dzin gsum*: according to Mahāyoga, 278-81, 358, 360, 362-3
two kinds of *ting-'dzin-la mos-bsgom-dang nges-rdzogs gnyis*: according to Mahāyoga, the meditation of devotion as in the performance of daily ceremonies (*mos-bsgom*) and the definitive perfection of perpetual contemplation (*nges-rdzogs*), 278, 363
contemplative experiences, five *ting-'dzin nyams lnga*: according to Mahāyoga, 34, 278
continents, four *gling-bzhi*, Skt. *caturdvīpa*, 14, 56, 60, 131, 409, 438, 515, 555, 577
continuum/continua *rgyud*, Skt. *tantra*, 12, 51, 142, 147, 197, 275, 971
of the basis/ground *gzhi'i rgyud*, 32, 34, 154, 169, 247, 253-5, 276, 291, 348, 897, 905
of the path *lam-gyi rgyud-rnams*, 32, 34, 154, 169, 247, 265-6, 348, 897, 905; three characteristics of *lam-rgyud-kyi mtshan-nyid gsum*, 265
of the result *'bras-bu'i rgyud*, 32, 154, 169, 247, 266-7, 348, 897, 905
three (comprising the actual or expressed meaning) *(brjod-bya) rgyud-gsum*, 32, 185-6, 196-8, 208, 244, 262-7
core-penetrating *zang-thal/zang-ka-ma dang thal-du byung-ba*: in the Great Perfection, the penetrating openness of the very core of reality, which is the nucleus of pristine cognition, 335, 337, 344
corruption(s) *zag-pa*, Skt. *āsrava*: the flux of world-forming deeds caused by ignorance, 132, 157, 227, 319, 330, 423, 615, 879
three *zag-pa gsum*, 472
councils *bsdu-ba*, Skt. *saṃgīti*, 75, 410, 428-31, 441, 456, 949
covert intention *ldem-dgongs*, Skt. *abhisandhi*, 30, 218-22
four kinds of *ldem-dgongs bzhi*, 30, 220-2
crafts, sixty-four *sgyu-rtsal re-bzhi*, 98, 418
creation and perfection, three aspects of *bskyed-rdzogs gsum*, 83, 358, 476, 612, 615, 616, 619, 650, 651, 652, 654, 700, 717
creation stage *bskyed-rim*, Skt. *utpattikrama*: the elaborate gradual phase of creative visualisation according to the tantra vehicles, 34, 35, 36, 85, 87, 204, 251, 274, 278-81, 284, 290-1, 293, 300-2, 305, 335-6, 358-60, 362-3, 365, 370, 458-83, 486, 496, 523, 531, 647, 681, 720, 721, 723, 726, 787, 829, 836, 844, 862, 865, 876-7, 880
Cutting Through Resistance *khregs-chod*, 38, 334-7, 341, 371, 593
four creative stages of the path of *khregs-chod lam-gyi bskyed-rim bzhi*, 371
in the Great Perfection *rdzogs-pa chen-po khregs-chod*, 828
in primordial purity *ka-dag khregs-chod*, 877
cyclical existence *'khor-ba*: see *saṃsāra*
ḍāka *mkha'-'gro*: male space-farers who embody awareness, 442, 451, 490, 492; see also *warrior*
ḍākinīs *mkha'-'gro-ma*: female space-farers who embody emptiness, 135-6, 199, 406, 442, 451, 468, 469, 470, 471, 472, 482, 485, 486, 490, 492, 493, 494, 498, 499, 501, 503, 593, 567, 580, 581, 582, 583, 585, 587, 588, 609, 621, 644, 670, 676, 679, 697, 745, 756, 757, 760, 762, 766, 767, 771, 772, 773, 774, 785, 786, 787, 802, 814, 820, 825, 829, 832, 846, 855, 856, 863, 865, 887, 889, 890, 892, 927, 961
of the four classes *rigs-bzhi'i mkha'-'gro-ma*, 755
of pristine cognition *ye-shes mkha'-'gro*, Skt. *jñānaḍākinī*, 469, 480, 502, 572, 755, 763, 774, 837, 857

of the three abodes *gnas-gsum-gyi mkha'-'gro-ma*, 469, 853
script/symbolic language of *mkha'-'gro brda'-yig*, 469, 580, 745-6, 747, 778, 837, 844, 857, 865
ḍāmaru *ḍa-ma-ru*: a skull-drum, 638
death *'chi-ba*, Skt. *maraṇa*, 278-9; see also under *intermediate state*
four ways of *'chi-lugs bzhi*, 543, 547
deceases, four *'da'-ka-ma bzhi*, 923
declension *rnam-dbye*, Skt. *vibhakti*: in grammar, 100
deeds *mdzad-pa*: i.e. those of a buddha, 137-8, 146, 221, 253, 415-16, 436, 812; see also *enlightened activity(ies)*
deeds, world-forming *las*, Skt. *karman*, 13, 16, 51, 55-61, 63, 76, 93, 118-19, 130, 161, 198, 214, 229, 260, 277, 298, 321, 409, 414, 450, 641, 658, 671, 767, 769, 798, 832, 878, 896, 898-9, 903, 913; see also *karma*
freedom from *bya-bral*, 896
three types of *las gsum-po*, 56
defilements *nyon-mongs*, Skt. *kleśa*, 913; see also *conflicting emotions*
definitive meaning *nges-don*, Skt. *nītārtha*: see under *meaning*
deity(ies) *lha*, Skt. *devatā*, *passim*; see also *consort(s)*
body of *lha'i sku*, 255, 281, 356, 900
body, speech and mind of *lha'i sku-gsung-thugs*, 31, 246, 575, 647
central *gtso-bo'i lha*, 271, 281
of the expanse of indestructible reality *rdo-rje dbyings-kyi lha*: according to Yogatantra, 32, 33, 207, 264, 272, 353, 355; see also *maṇḍala of indestructible (reality's) expanse*
favoured *lhag-pa'i lha*, Skt. *iṣṭadevatā*, 747, 818, 852, 872, 874, 927
guardian *srung-ma*, 605
local *gzhi bdag*, 847; see also *local divinity*
male and female *lha-dang lha-mo*, 304, 348, 355, 367-8, 641; wrathful *khro-bo khro-mo*, 125; see also *deities/conquerors, peaceful and wrathful*
meditational *yi-dam*, 91, 108, 510, 534, 537, 564, 585, 588, 607, 615, 634, 647, 665, 710, 711, 713, 726, 766, 828, 829, 853, 876, 922
of perfect rapture *longs-spyod-rdzogs-pa'i lha*, 692
of pristine cognition *ye-shes-kyi lha*, 347, 923
of relative appearance *kun-rdzob-kyi lha*, 349
six modes of *lha drug*: according to Kriyātantra, 270, 350-1
symbolic *mtshan-bcas lha*, 287, 350-1
of the three roots *rtsa-gsum-pa'i lha*: the guru, meditational deity and ḍākinī, 376, 555, 586, 676, 748, 823, 847, 855
wrathful *khro-bo lha*, 713, 767; male and female *khro-bo khro-mo*, 125; see also following entry
deities/conquerors, peaceful and wrathful *zhi-khro lha/rgyal-ba*, 132, 279-80, 447, 511, 583, 635, 679, 693, 775, 853; see also preceding entry
(Fifty-eight) Blood-drinkers/wrathful *khrag-'thung/khro-bo lha (nga-brgyad)*, 280, 623, 713, 767
(Forty-two) Peaceful *zhi-ba'i lha (zhe-gnyis)*, 125-6, 280, 623, 644, 691, 701
of the *Magical Net sgyu-'phrul zhi-khro*, 628, 673, 674, 691, 695, 696, 700-1, 730, 731, 843, 849
delight(s) *dga'-ba*, Skt. *ānanda*, 301
co-emergent *lhan-skyes dga'-ba*, 818
four *dga'-ba bzhi*, 818, 830, 877
sixteen *dga'-ba bcu-drug*, 125
supreme *mchog-gi dga'-ba*, 125, 376
delusion *gti-mug*, Skt. *moha*, 12, 18, 34, 55, 130, 403, 547, 638, 901, 902, 903, 904, 924, 938
twenty-one thousand kinds of *gti-mug-gi cha nyis-khri chig-stong*, 77
dependent (nature) *gzhan-dbang-gi mtshan-nyid*, Skt. *paratantralakṣaṇa*, 24, 25, 26, 154, 160-1, 170-2, 182, 219-20; see also *essential natures, three*
dependent origination *rten-'brel*, Skt. *pratītyasamutpāda*, 227-31, 403; see also *auspicious coincidence* and *causality*
inward *nang-gi rten-'brel*, 208
outward *phyi'i rten-'brel*, 208
twelve antidotes/emptinesses belonging to the trend in which it is reversed *rten-'brel lugs-ldog stong-pa bcu-gnyis*, 230
twelve modes of *rten-'brel bcu-gnyis*, 25, 159, 228

desire *'dod-chags*, Skt. *rāga*, 12, 18, 33, 55-6, 61, 64, 72, 129, 130, 273, 302, 306, 317, 322, 340, 412, 584, 625, 652, 653, 899, 938
four kinds of *'dod-chags tshul/rigs bzhi*, 269, 413
realms *'dod-pa'i khams*, Skt. *kāmadhātu*, 13, 56, 129, 142, 258-9
twenty-one thousand kinds of *'dod-chags-kyi cha rnam-pa nyis-khri chig-stong*, 77
desired qualities *'dod-yon*, Skt. *kāmaguṇa*: the five sensual pleasures, 251, 254; see also *sensual raptures, five*
determination *la-bzla-ba*: i.e. that made by the view of the Great Perfection which transcends or has transcended the subject-object dichotomy, 37, 320
deva *lha*: gods within the three realms of saṃsāra, 451, 452; see also *gods*
deviation *gol-sa*: i.e. from the view of the Great Perfection, 36, 37, 295-7, 302, 323, 330, 340-1, 353, 851, 902, 923
dhāraṇī *gzungs*: a mantra-like formula or incantation which serves a mnemonic function, promoting retention of extensive bodies of doctrine, 23, 141, 657, 743, 852, 878, 928
dharma *chos*: defined, 51-3; *passim*; see also *doctrine(s)*
dhūti *dhū-ti*, Skt. *avadhūti*: see *energy channel/pathway, central*
dialectical doctrines (of the causal vehicles) *rgyu mtshan-nyid-kyi chos*, 854; see also under *vehicle(s)*
dialectical sophistry, eight categories of *rtog-ge'i tshig-don brgyad*, 101
dialectician *mtshan-nyid-pa*, 642, 678
dialectics *mtshan-nyid*, 26, 605, 650, 651, 672, 704, 723, 757, 850, 898, 907
three classes of *mtshan-nyid sde-gsum*: the three causal vehicles, 618, 671
dichiliocosm *stong gnyis-pa'i 'jigs-rten-gyi khams*: a universe of 1000^2 world realms, 131
direct perception *mngon-sum*, Skt. *pratyakṣa*, 21, 275-6, 300, 318, 340, 415, 641, 844, 920
three kinds of *mngon-sum gsum*, 102
directions, ten *phyogs-bcu*, Skt. *daśadik*, 412
discrete entities *rang-rgyud-pa'i chos-rnams*, 104, 640, 641
discriminative awareness *shes-rab*, Skt. *prajñā*, 18, 28, 33, 34, 45, 55, 62, 79, 88, 94, 99, 117, 125, 168, 181, 184, 185, 192, 231-2, 244-5, 247-9, 260, 269, 273-4, 278, 281, 286, 293, 296, 300, 302-3, 306, 313, 343-4, 359-60, 362, 364, 368, 422, 543, 560, 563, 568, 570, 613, 615, 620, 637, 703, 704, 773, 869, 871, 872, 877, 899, 901, 902, 905, 916
born of meditation *bsgoms-pa-las byung-ba'i shes-rab*, Skt. *bhāvanāmayī-prajñā*, 535, 720, 877
born of thought *bsam-pa-las byung-ba'i shes-rab*, Skt. *cintāmayīprajñā*, 720
perfection of *shes-rab-kyi pha-rol-tu phyin-ma/pa*, Skt. *prajñāpāramitā*, 23, 74-5, 182-3, 185, 188-9, 208, 236, 300, 308, 901, 902, 909, 947
superior *lhag-pa'i shes-rab*, Skt. *adhi-prajñā*, 71, 424, 707
three kinds of *shes-rab gsum*, 185, 277, 332, 722
discursive/conceptualising thought *rnam-rtog*, Skt. *vikalpa*, *passim*
disjunct conditions *ldan-min 'du-byed*, Skt. *viprayuktasaṃskāra*: in Abhidharma, those conditions, such as linguistic phenomena, cessation of consciousness in meditative absorption and relations, which are not reducible to the categories of form and mind, 24, 156-8
display *rol-pa*, Skt. *lalita*, 324, 326-8, 363, 365-6, 368, 372; see also *expressive play/power* and *play*
disposition (of reality) *ngang*, 251, 287, 311-12, 315-16, 323, 325, 328, 337, 340, 342-4, 351, 357, 368, 371, 571, 643, 832, 896, 900
dissertation *rab-tu byed-pa/pra-ka-ra-ṇa*, Skt. *prakaraṇa*, 102
distinct attributes of the buddhas, eighteen *sangs-rgyas-kyi chos ma-'dres-pa bco-brgyad*, Skt. *aṣṭadaśāvenika-buddhadharma*, 22, 140
divination *nag-rtsis*: i.e. Chinese divination, in contrast to the Indian tradition of astrology (*skar-rtsis*), 104, 727, 730, 762, 821, 869; see also *elemental divination*

divination chart *gtad-khram*: a divination device which determines malign forces — *gtad* means entrusting and *khram* the crossing or sealing of malign forces, 786
divine ear *lha-snyan*, Skt. *divyaśrotra*, 928; see also *clairaudience*
divine eye *lha-mig*, Skt. *divyacakṣuḥ*, 928; see also *clairvoyance*
(doctrinal) components *(chos-kyi) phung-po*
eighty-four thousand *phung-po brgyad-khri bzhi-stong*, 17, 77, 86, 133, 763, 925
twenty-one thousand *phung-po nyis-khri chig-stong*, 77-8
doctrinal seal of buddha-speech which secures the mental faculty as the pristine cognition of discernment *sor-rtog yid gsung chos-rgya*, 356
doctrinal terminology *chos-skad*, 887, 894-5, 925, 936
doctrinal tradition *chos-lugs*, 51-2, 917, 920
doctrinal wheel(s) *chos-kyi 'khor-lo*, Skt. *dharmacakra*, 28, 73, 76, 128-9, 131, 151-5, 188, 409, 412, 416, 421, 427, 590, 593, 695, 726, 731, 823, 830, 872, 948; see also *transmitted precepts*
first promulgation/turning, of the middle way which abandons both extremes concerning the four truths *dbu-ma'i lam-gyi bden-pa bzhi'i chos-'khor*, 23, 27, 28, 76, 93, 137, 153, 186-8, 423, 896, 946
second/intermediate promulgation/turning, concerning signlessness *mtshan-med 'bar-ma'i chos-'khor*, 23-4, 27, 28, 76, 94-5, 153-4, 172, 178, 184-8, 206, 216, 423-4, 526, 896, 905
of the secret mantra *gsang-sngags-kyi chos-'khor*, 95-6, 445-50, 458
(third/final) promulgation/turning, of definitive meaning *nges-don-gyi chos-'khor (phyi-ma/gsum-pa)*, 24, 27, 28, 30, 36, 76, 95, 153-4, 160, 170, 178, 185-8, 190, 206, 216, 236, 300-1, 424, 527, 896, 905, 944; see also *promulgation of the doctrinal wheel, irreversible*
three promulgations/turnings *chos-kyi 'khor-lo gsum*, 17, 23-4, 27, 76, 151-5, 187, 425, 896, 946-7
twelve different, of speech *gsung-chos-kyi 'khor-lo mi-'dra-ba bcu-gnyis*, 137
doctrine(s) *chos*, Skt. *dharma*, defined, 51-3; *passim*; see also under *treasure(s)*
ages of, 949
background *rgyab-chos*, 658
of cause and effect *rgyu-'bras-kyi chos*, 538, 540
chronology of, 941-62
duration of, 943-5
eye of *chos-kyi spyan*, 933
five *chos-lnga*: i.e. of the *Sūtra of the Descent to Laṅkā*, 128
four negative *nag-po'i chos bzhi*, Skt. *catuḥkṛṣṇadharma*, 236
four positive *dkar-chos bzhi*, Skt. *catuḥśukladharma*, 236
four, of a spiritual ascetic *dge-sbyong-gi chos bzhi*, 52
genuine/true *dam-pa'i chos*, Skt. *sad-dharma*: the Buddha's teaching, 51, 59, 68, 70-2, 102, 113, 137, 195, 217, 235, 393, 403, 422, 428, 498, 504, 508, 509, 512, 513, 515, 516, 527, 575, 669, 675, 705, 723, 748, 753, 762, 806, 809, 874, 894, 938, 939, 949
lord of *chos-kyi bdag-po*, 761
mundane *'jig-rten-gyi chos*, Skt. *laukikadharma*, 12, 16, 51
nectar-like *bdud-rtsi lta-bu'i*, 421, 423, 648; see also *nectar(-like instruction)*
ninety-six, of a single emanational body *mchog-sprul-gyi chos dgu-bcu dgu-drug*, 22, 138
of nirvāṇa *mya-ngan-las 'das-pa'i chos*, 12, 16-18, 53, 70-2
perception of *chos-shes*, Skt. *dharma-jñāna*, 226; after-effect of *chos-kyi rjes-su shes-pa*, Skt. *dharmānvaya-jñāna*, 227
of the purification of the birthplace *skye-gnas sbyang-ba'i chos*, 416
of realisation *rtogs-pa'i chos*, Skt. *adhigamadharma*, 16, 17, 71-2, 403
of saṃsāra *'khor-ba'i chos*, 12-16, 53, 54-69
seven divine *lha-chos bdun*: of Atiśa and the Kadampa tradition, 853
sixty *chos-kyi rnam-grangs drug-tu*, 137
supramundane *'jig-rten-las-'das-pa'i chos*, Skt. *lokottaradharma*, 12, 51
ten meanings of *chos-kyi don bcu*, 51-3
thirty-seven aspects of enlightenment *byang-chub-kyi chos sum-cu-rtsa-bdun*,

Skt. *saptatriṃśadbodhipakṣadharma*, 236

of transmission *lung-gi chos*, Skt. *āgamadharma*, 16-17, 403, 582

door *sgo*, Skt. *dvāra*: in general this term indicates the apertures of the physical body and the gates of the five senses. In the context of the path of skilful means, it specifically refers to the energy centres in the body; see also *centre(s)*

lower, of one's partner's body *gzhan-lus 'og-sgo*: the secret centre of the partner, embodying awareness and emptiness, 277, 363, 368

lower, of skilful means *thabs 'og-sgo*, 286

upper, of one's own body *rang-lus steng-sgo*, 277, 363, 368

upper, of skilful means *thabs steng-sgo*, 286

drama *zlos-gar*, Skt. *nāṭya*, 18, 98, 103, 106-7, 577, 762, 803

thirty-six characteristics of *zlos-gar-gi mtshan-nyid sum-bcu-so-drug*, 107

dramatic airs, nine *gar-gyi cha-byad dgu*, 98, 630

dramatic juncture, five sequences of *mtsham-sbyor-gi yan-lag lnga*, 107

dramatic manners, four *zlos-gar-gi tshul bzhi*, 107

sixteen aspects of *tshul bzhi'i yan-lag bco-drug*, 107

Drigungpa *'bri-gung-pa*, 592, 681, 823, 830, 839, 841, 847, 850, 867, 868, 929

Drukpa Kagyüpa *'brug-pa bka'-brgyud-pa*, 823, 841, 847, 850, 868, 922

Dvāparayuga *gnyis-ldan*: the third age of the aeon, which is particularly suited to the practice of Yogatantra, 268

elaboration *spros-pa*, Skt. *prapañca*, 302, 344, 403, 498; see also *conceptual elaboration*

elder *gnas-brtan*, Skt. *sthavira*, 93, 137, 429, 430, 438-9, 556, 557, 558

element(s) *'byung-ba*, Skt. *(mahā)bhūta*, 53, 104, 301, 321, 368, 615, 747, 763

five (gross) *'byung-ba (chen-po) lnga*, Skt. *pañca(mahā)bhūta*, 13, 56, 104, 264, 640

four *'byung-ba bzhi*, Skt. *caturbhūta*, 38, 53, 117-18, 328, 336, 542, 543, 594, 748

elemental divination *'byung-rtsis*: Chinese divination or geomancy, 104; see also *divination*

nine topics of *'byung-rtsis-kyi don rnam-pa dgu*, 104

elemental properties, five *khams-lnga*, Skt. *pañcadhātu*, 20, 125

elemental components *'byung-'gyur*, 368

elixir *sman*: spiritual medicine, 867; see also *nectar(s)*

attainment of *sman-sgrub*, 686, 757

elixir/water of life *tshe-chu*, 573, 662-3, 789, 790

nectar-elixir *bdud-rtsi sman*, 619, 651, 775

spiritual *chos-sman*: i.e. the doctrine, 791

emaho *e-ma-ho*: an exclamation of wonder, 915

emanation(s) *sprul-pa/sku*, Skt. *nirmāṇa-(kāya)*, 68, 113, 118-20, 122, 124, 127, 129-30, 214, 342, 413, 415, 468, 478, 492, 496, 526, 555, 556, 592, 594, 560, 572, 582, 587, 607, 618, 634, 637, 645, 648, 654, 665, 677, 683, 698, 704, 719, 727, 733, 734, 735, 736, 738, 745, 747, 751, 753, 755, 757, 758, 760, 780, 791, 809, 813, 821, 823, 825, 833, 835, 839, 841, 854, 859, 922, 934, 936; see also under *buddha-body(ies)*

of artistry and birth *bzo-ba-dang skye-ba-dang*, 133, 415

supreme *mchog-gi sprul-sku*, 415; see also under *buddha-body(ies)*

emanational teachings of buddha-body, speech and mind, three great *sprul-pa'i bstan-pa chen-po gsum*: according to the Great Perfection, 134-8

emotional defilement *nyon-mongs*, Skt. *kleśa*: see *conflicting emotions*

empowerment(s) *dbang-bskur*, Skt. *abhiṣeka*: the required entrance for the tantra vehicles, *passim*; see also *maturation*

of awareness' expressive play/power *rig-pa'i rtsal-dbang*: according to Atiyoga, 370, 673, 674, 763-4

of beneficence, ability and profundity *phan-nus-zab-gsum-gyi dbang*, 360, 665

(common) vase *thun-mong-pa'i bum-dbang*: according to Kriyātantra and Ubhayatantra, 360, 626, 825-6, 829, 921

of the corpse of the great charnel ground *bam-chen ro-yi dbang-bskur*, 610
of discerning/discriminating pristine cognition *shes-rab ye-shes-kyi dbang*: see *empowerment, third*
eight hundred and thirty-one ancillary *yan-lag-gi dbang brgyad-brgya so-cig*: according to Anuyoga, 364
extremely unelaborate *rab-tu spros-med dbang-bskur*: according to Atiyoga, 500, 501
of the fifteen ordinary sacraments *sgrub-rdzas thun-mong bco-lnga'i dbang*: according to Mahāyoga, 700-1
five *dbang-lnga*: according to the *Secret Nucleus*, i.e. those of beneficence, 915
five, of awareness *rig-pa'i dbang-lnga*: according to Kriyātantra and Ubhayatantra, i.e. those of ability, 354; see also *empowerment, (common) vase*
four *snying-thig-gi dbang-bzhi*: according to Innermost Spirituality, 499-501, 673, 674-5
four *dbang-bzhi*: according to Mahāyoga 360, 546, 613, 755, 825, 863, 923
fourth *dbang bzhi-pa*, Skt. *caturtha*: according to Mahāyoga, also called the empowerment of word and meaning. Refer to Mipham Rinpoche, *spyi-don 'od-gsal snying-po*, (pp. 149 ff.), 360
of great light rays *'od-zer chen-po'i dbang*: according to the sūtras. This is contrasted with the empowerment of supreme desire, 142, 912-13
of the Great Perfection *rdzogs-chen-gyi dbang-bskur*, 370, 677; see also *empowerment of awareness' expressive play/power*
inner unelaborate *nang spros-med dbang-bskur*: according to Atiyoga, 500, 501, 675
of the irreversible vase *phyir mi-zlog-pa'i bum-dbang*: according to Yogatantra, 354; see also *empowerment of the master of indestructible reality*
"liberating", of the lower rite of Vajrakīla *smad-las sgrol-dbang*, 712
of longevity *tshe-dbang*, 669, 673, 674; for final support *mtha'-rten tshe-dbang*, 828
of the master of indestructible reality *rdo-rje'i slob-dpon-gyi dbang*, Skt. *vajrācāryābhiṣeka*: according to Yogatantra, 354
means for the conferral of *bskur-thabs*, 601
of the Mental Class *sems-sde (A-don bco-brgyad-kyi) dbang*, 700, 701
of the nine vehicles *theg-pa dgu'i dbang*: according to Anuyoga, 364-5, 910-12
outer elaborate *phyi spros-pa'i dbang-bskur*: according to Atiyoga, 499-500, 501, 580, 586, 673, 675
outer, inner and secret *phyi-nang-gsang-gi dbang-bskur*, 469
secret *gsang-dbang*, Skt. *guhyābhiṣeka*, 360, 619, 830, 866
six *dbang-drug*: according to Yogatantra, 354
of supreme desire *'dod-chags chen-po'i dbang*: according to Unsurpassed Tantra. It is contrasted with the empowerment of great light rays, 142
of the *Sūtra which Gathers All Intentions mdo-dbang*, 911-13
symbolic *brda'i dbang-bskur*, 855
third *dbang gsum-pa*: also known as the empowerment of discriminating pristine cognition. Refer to Mipham Rinpoche, *spyi-don 'od-gsal snying-po*, (pp. 146-8), 247, 301, 360, 584, 866
thirty-six, ceremonies *dbang-chog so-drug*: according to Anuyoga, 364-5
three higher (supreme, uncommon) *(thin-min mchog-)dbang gong-ma gsum*, 347, 360, 913; see also following entry
three profound *zab-dbang gsum*: according to Mahāyoga, i.e. those of profundity, 347, 701
vajra, bell and name *rdor-dril-ming-gsum-gyi dbang*: according to Ubhaya-tantra, 352
vase, of awareness *rig-pa spyi-blugs-kyi dbang*, 493; see also following entry
vase, that is the conqueror's means/which pours out all the conquerors' means *rgyal-thabs bum-dbang/rgyal-thabs spyi-blugs-kyi dbang-chen*: according to Atiyoga. On this, Longcenpa, *Treasury of the Supreme Vehicle*, p. 291, says *'khor-'das gnyis-*

ka'i dbang-bskur, phyi rgyal-thabs spyi-blugs-su bskur-bas stong-gsum-gyi 'jig-rten gling-bzhi ri-rab-dang-bcas-pa-la dbang thob: "Having conferred the empowerment of both saṃsāra and nirvāṇa, outwardly as a pouring out of all the conquerors' means, one obtains the empowerment of the trichiliocosm, together with the four continents and Mount Meru", 345, 453
vases for the corners (of the maṇḍala) *dbang-gi bum-grva*, 726
very unelaborate *shin-tu spros-med dbang-bskur*: according to Atiyoga, 500, 501
water and crown *chu-dang cod-pan-gyi dbang*: according to Kriyātantra, 349, 352
of word and meaning *tshig-don-gyi dbang*: see *empowerment, fourth*
emptiness *stong-pa nyid*, Skt. *śūnyatā*, 23, 29, 31, 35, 37, 38, 45, 55, 144-5, 154, 168, 170-3, 178, 184-6, 188-9, 191-3, 196-214, 206, 209, 217-18, 220, 226, 230, 234, 236, 250, 263-4, 272, 274, 280, 294-5, 304-5, 314, 316-18, 321-4, 330-2, 335, 339, 342, 351, 354, 356, 359-60, 365, 371, 403, 404, 583, 638, 653, 818, 830, 856, 877, 898, 906, 923, 924, 931; see also under *coalescence/union*
emptiness of *stong-pa nyid-kyi stong-nyid*, 309
endowed with all supreme aspects *rnam-pa kun-gyi mchog dang-ldan-pa'i stong-pa-nyid*, Skt. *sarvākāra-guṇopetaśūnyatā*, 125, 185, 203, 250, 255, 281, 291
extrinsic *gzhan-stong*: i.e. the absolute's emptiness of extraneous entities or other substances, 27, 28, 41, 170-2, 188; adherents of/apologists for *gzhan-stong-pa*, 207-8
form of, within a black outline *re-kha nag-po'i nang-la stong-pa-nyid*, 301
four modes of *stong-nyid tshul-bzhi*, 877
great *stong-pa chen-po*: according to Mahāyoga, 278-9, 309
intrinsic *rang-stong*, 27, 28, 41, 171, 188, 307; adherents/proponents of *rang-stong-pa*, 171, 186
two modes of *stong-pa-nyid-kyi lugs gnyis*, 184
enclosure *sbubs-ma*, 448, 587, 588
endowments, ten *'byor-ba bcu*, 573
energy channel(s)/pathway(s) *rtsa*, Skt. *nāḍī*, 20, 115, 124, 620, 773, 837, 877, 878
central *dbu-ma*, Skt. *avadhūti*, 341, 722, 829, 877
and currents *rtsa-rlung*, 867; and seminal points *rtsa-rlung thig-le gsum*, 20, 34, 36, 214, 247, 251, 290, 293, 295, 301, 304, 362-3, 722, 813, 837
knotted *rtsa-mdud*, 341, 773, 819, 844
left *rkyang-ma*, Skt. *lalanā*, 341
of light *'od-kyi rtsa*, 341
right *ro-ma*, Skt. *rasanā*, 341
energy field below the earth *rlung-dkyil*, Skt. *vāyumaṇḍala*, 131
enlightened activity(ies) *phrin-las*, Skt. *karman*, 22, 47, 68, 95, 116, 125, 135, 137-8, 143, 146-8, 196, 249, 266-7, 288-9, 342-3, 414, 425, 462, 481, 524, 584, 590, 591, 592, 601, 605, 610, 612, 643, 647, 648, 655, 656, 660, 664, 668, 672, 717, 720, 721, 723, 724, 733, 736, 737, 738, 746, 748, 757, 765, 768, 770, 783, 788, 798-9, 801, 803, 811, 812, 817, 818, 820, 821, 824, 826, 830, 838, 839, 844, 846, 847, 848, 867, 880, 905, 920, 928, 930, 936, 939, 954, 959, 961; see also *deeds* and *rites*
eight arisings of *phrin-las shar-ba brgyad*, 673
five *phrin-las lnga*, 283
four kinds of *phrin-las rnam-bzhi*, 146; see also *rites, four*
enlightened attitude *byang-chub sems*, Skt. *bodhicitta*: see *enlightened mind/attitude*
enlightened attributes *yon-tan*, Skt. *guṇa*, 18, 23, 26, 27, 28, 61, 74, 95, 124-5, 140-1, 144-8, 170-1, 174-6, 184, 188, 191, 195, 197-9, 249-50, 263, 266, 269-70, 289, 297, 306, 341, 342, 345, 349-50, 376, 462, 480, 613, 663, 665, 724, 846
five *yon-tan lnga*, 283
four *yon-tan bzhi*, 186, 212; see also *transcendental perfection of enlightened attributes*
of pristine cognition *ye-shes-kyi yon-tan*, 349

seven distinctions of *yon-tan-gyi khyad-par bdun*, 259
sixty-four *yon-tan-gyi chos drug-cu-rtsa-bzhi*, 95, 203
enlightened family(ies) *rigs*, Skt. *kula/gotra*, 29, 130, 189, 191-205, 236, 298, 364, 416, 454, 493, 498, 564, 569, 619, 656, 664, 693, 722, 753, 771, 772, 796, 815, 835, 849, 861, 868, 869, 871, 876, 898, 899, 908, 948; see also *buddha-family(ies)*
of activity *las-kyi rigs*, Skt. *karmakula*, 353
which is attained *sgrub-pa'i rigs*: i.e. that of inner growth, 29, 191-2
five *rigs-lnga*, Skt. *pañcakula*: according to Yogatantra, 11, 21, 33, 273, 343, 346, 355, 357, 447, 453, 561, 563, 623, 660, 672, 676, 691, 746-7
four *rigs-bzhi*, Skt. *catuṣkula*: according to Ubhayatantra, 271-2, 353
five minor *rigs-chung lnga*: according to Yogatantra, 273
of inner growth *rgyas-'gyur-gyi rigs*, Skt. *samudānītagotra*, 196, 198, 202
intermediaries, male and female *pho-nya-dang pho-nya-mo*: according to Kriyātantra, 271
which naturally abides: see *enlightened family, (twofold) which naturally abides*
of precious gems *rin-chen rigs*, Skt. *ratnakula*, 353
six *rigs-drug*: according to Kriyātantra, 271
six, (of the Father tantras) *(pha-rgyud) rigs-drug*, 274
six, (of the Mother tantras) *(ma-rgyud) rigs-drug*, 274
sixth *drug-pa*, 447
three (of pure deities of relative appearance) *(kun-rdzob dag-pa'i lha) rigs-gsum*, Skt. *trikula*: according to Kriyātantra, 270, 346, 349-50
twofold buddha/enlightened family *rigs-rnam-gnyis*, 191, 196-7
(twofold), which naturally abides *rang-bzhin gnas-pa'i rigs (gnyis)*, Skt. *prakṛtiṣṭhagotra*, 29, 32, 191-2, 194, 196, 198, 202, 263
vajra *rdo-rje'i rigs*, Skt. *vajrakula*, 475
enlightened mind/attitude *byang-chub sems*, Skt. *bodhicitta*: *byang* meaning pure of obscurations and *chub* meaning perfect in enlightened attributes, 94, 118, 120, 122, 138, 197, 232, 249, 251, 261, 263, 285, 296-7, 308, 311, 320, 323, 325-6, 333, 350, 355, 661, 663, 707, 839, 865, 911, 913, 924
of aspiration *smon-pa'i sems-bskyed*, Skt. *praṇidhicittotpāda*, 235, 842
cultivation/development/generation of *sems-bskyed*, Skt. *bodhicittotpāda*, 192, 194, 235, 251, 395, 411, 412, 610, 677, 763, 805, 849
of engagement *'jug-pa'i sems-bskyed*, Skt. *prasthānacittotpāda*, 235
twofold precious *rin-chen sems-bskyed gnyis*, 852
"enlightened mind" *byang-sems*: a synonym for *thig-le* or seminal point, 290, 866
enlightenment *byang-chub*, Skt. *bodhi*, 12, 29, 32, 45, 83, 95, 98, 120, 129, 147, 193, 227-8, 232, 235-6, 246-7, 256, 258, 266, 292, 307, 313, 335, 342-3, 372, 411, 412, 413, 414, 415, 416, 420, 497, 498, 577, 620, 703, 710, 766, 771, 901, 911, 913, 943
aspect of, called physical refinement *shin-tu sbyangs-ba*, Skt. *praśrabdhi*, 561
seven branches of *byang-chub yan-lag bdun*, Skt. *saptabodhyaṅga*, 236
three degrees of *byang-chub gsum*, Skt. *bodhitraya*, 414
entrance *'jug-pa*, *passim*; see also *empowerment(s)*
to the Brahmā vehicle, 61
to the vehicle of Anuyoga, 354-5
to the vehicle of Atiyoga, 370
to the vehicle of bodhisattvas, 232-4
to the vehicle of Kriyātantra, 349
to the vehicle of Mahāyoga, 278, 360
to the mundane vehicle, 58
to the vehicle of pious attendants, 223-4
to the vehicle of self-centred buddhas, 227-8
to the vehicle of Ubhayatantra, 352
to the vehicle of Yogatantra, 354
envy *phra-dog*, Skt. *īrṣyā*, 12, 55
equanimity *btang-snyoms*, Skt. *upekṣā*, 13, 61, 631, 893
erotic grace *sgeg-pa*, Skt. *līlā*: i.e. graceful song and dance, 98, 107
esoteric instructions *man-ngag*, Skt. *āmnāya*, 18, 39, 104, 108, 199, 216,

248, 286, 290, 293, 300, 306, 319, 344, 369, 375, 406, 453, 477, 478, 483, 489, 496, 500, 535, 538, 539, 545, 546, 562, 563, 569, 573, 578, 608, 610, 614, 615, 618, 619, 647, 650, 651, 658, 666, 669, 671, 673, 675, 677, 678, 681, 689, 691, 699, 705, 706, 707, 710, 713, 719, 720, 721, 725, 730, 734, 737, 757, 762, 764, 807, 813, 820, 821, 822, 842, 861, 862, 865, 871, 876, 877, 880, 918, 919, 921, 925, 968
of the Great Perfection *rdzogs-chen man-ngag*, 921
of the path of desire *chags-lam-gyi man-ngag*, 818
Esoteric Instructional Class *man-ngag-gi sde*: of the Great Perfection, 37-8, 319, 327, 329-45, 371, 494, 498, 538, 554-96, 697; see also *All-Surpassing Realisation* and *Cutting Through Resistance*
four cycles of *(man-ngag-sde'i) skor bzhi*, 332, 498, 501, 654
Inner Cycle (which Resembles the Eyes) *(mig-dang 'dra-ba) nang-skor*, 332, 498, 499
Outer Cycle (which Resembles the Body) *(lus-dang 'dra-ba) phyi-skor*, 332, 498, 499
Secret Cycle(s) (which Resemble(s) the Heart) *(snying-dang 'dra-ba) gsang-skor*, 332, 498, 499, 569, 570, 657, 658
three categories of *man-ngag sde'i dbye-ba gsum*, 37, 331
Unsurpassedly Secret Cycle (which Resembles the Perfection of All) *(thams-cad rdzogs-pa-dang 'dra-ba) yang-gsang bla-na med-pa'i skor*, 332, 498, 500; see also *Innermost Spirituality*
view and path of *man-ngag-sde'i lta-ba-dang lam*, 333
essence *ngo-bo(-nyid)*, Skt. *svabhāva*: in general this term refers to the essence of anything, as opposed to its superficial attributes or characteristics. In particular it indicates the nature of the buddha-body of reality, 22, 32, 54-5, 57, 68, 71-2, 87, 116, 139, 146, 167, 175, 184, 189, 197-8, 211, 243, 245, 248-9, 251, 264, 302, 307, 309, 311-13, 317, 320, 324, 330, 335, 343, 357-8, 403, 494, 594, 887, 907, 923
essenceless natures, three *ngo-bo-nyid med-pa gsum*, Skt. *trividhā niḥsvabhāvatā*, 219-20
essential natures, three *mtshan-nyid gsum/ngo-bo-nyid gsum/rang-bzhin gsum*, Skt. *trilakṣaṇa/trisvabhāva*, 24, 25, 26, 28, 154, 160-1, 170-2, 182-3, 216; see *absolute (nature/reality)*, *imaginary (nature)* and *dependent (nature)*
establishment (of reality) *bzhag-thabs*, 37, 331, 336
eternalism and nihilism *rtag-chad*, 82, 95, 144, 164, 252, 324; see also *extreme(s)*, *extremist(s)* and *nihilism*
four eternalistic schools *rtag-lta sde-bzhi*, 16, 64-6
evil destinies/existences *ngan-song/-'gro*, Skt. *durgati*, 21, 53, 56, 65, 88, 127, 147, 193, 213, 277, 303, 638
three *ngan-song/-'gro gsum*, Skt. *tisro durgatayaḥ*, 58, 767
excellences, five *phun-sum tshogs-pa lnga*, 22, 137, 280, 703; see also *certainties, five*
excellent teaching, ten aspects of *legs-gsung-gi rnam-pa bcu*, 74
exegesis *bshad-pa*, Skt. *ākhyā*, 47, 65, 104, 290-3, 376, 403, 489, 523, 526, 527, 535, 601, 609, 612, 645, 673, 674, 678, 683, 689, 696, 698, 699, 702, 717, 720, 721, 722, 723, 724, 726, 730, 733, 737, 738, 762, 822, 827, 830, 831, 848, 861, 888, 895, 921, 938, 950, 954, 962, 968
three general styles of *spyi-don rnam-gsum*, 206, 292-3
Exegetical Lineages, Ten Great Pillars who Supported *bshad-brgyud 'degs-pa'i ka-chen bcu*, 851
exegetical tradition *bshad-lugs*, 41, 139, 678, 684, 842, 850
exegetical transmission *bshad-lung*, 674, 675, 682, 687, 691, 701, 730, 733, 754, 827, 828, 842, 869, 872
existence and quiescence *srid-zhi*: a synonym for saṃsāra and nirvāṇa, *passim*; see also *quiescence*
exorcism *gtad*, 695, 713
expanse of peace *zhi-ba'i dbyings*, 848

expanse (of reality) (*chos-kyi*) *dbyings*, Skt. (*dharma*)*dhātu*, 20, 22, 27, 29, 32, 34, 35, 36, 37, 38, 71, 116-17, 119, 124, 126-8, 139, 144-5, 161, 164-5, 167, 172-5, 180-1, 183-5, 189, 191-2, 195-9, 201-3, 206-7, 209, 231, 234, 247, 250-2, 258, 284-5, 288, 294-5, 297, 306-7, 310, 315, 320-1, 323, 325, 330, 332, 337-8, 342, 354-5, 358, 365, 368-9, 376, 403, 413, 447, 448, 449, 494, 539, 574, 584, 585, 594, 609, 637, 679, 707, 711, 726, 748, 763, 767, 769, 773, 787, 804, 813, 825, 830, 857, 858, 867, 877, 879, 899, 901, 908, 922, 923, 924, 927, 947, 970

experiential cultivation *nyams-len*, *passim*

exposer of secrets *gsang-ston*, Skt. *raho 'nuśāsaka*: functionary at an ordination ceremony, 515

expression/expressive words/style *brjod-byed tshig/brjod-pa*, 71-3, 88, 703, 907

expressive play/power *rtsal*: the spontaneous activity of enlightenment or energy of mind-as-such, 37, 55, 117, 124, 126, 147, 201, 204, 249, 284, 316, 324-6, 328-30, 332, 357-8, 360, 366, 403, 684, 860; see also *display* and *play*

extensive teachings *rgyas-pa*

- extremely *shin-tu rgyas-pa chen-po*, 86; see also *components, eighty-four thousand (doctrinal)*
- as the nine vehicles *rgyas-pa chen-po*, 86
- as one of the twelve branches of the scriptures *shin-tu rgyas-pa*, 76-7

external perception *gzhan-snang*: the condition under which the emanational body is perceived, 139, 145

extreme(s) *mtha'*, Skt. *anta*, 94, 116, 119, 144, 209, 236, 248, 284, 295, 302, 324, 328, 423, 751, 932, 935

- eight *mtha'-brgyad*, 233
- eternalistic and nihilistic *rtag-pa'i mtha'-dang chad-pa'i mtha'*, 16, 252, 324
- four *mtha'-bzhi*, 26, 126, 162, 184, 233, 269, 348, 350-1
- two *mtha'-gnyis*, 79, 82, 95, 162, 252, 907

extremist(s) *mu-stegs-pa*, Skt. *tīrthika*, 103, 146, 425, 471, 472, 478, 486, 493, 715, 767, 803, 819, 913, 932, 936, 937; see also *eternalism and nihilism* and *nihilism*

- eternalistic *mu-stegs-pa*, Skt. *tīrthika*, 16, 63-8, 89, 184, 224, 318
- nihilistic *mur-stug-pa*, 16, 27, 63, 66-9, 224, 318

faculties, five *dbang-po lnga*, Skt. *pañcendriya*: attributes of the bodhisattva path among the thirty-seven aspects of enlightenment, not to be confused with the five sense organs, 236

families *rigs*, Skt. *gotra*: i.e. the families or types of sentient beings in contrast to the buddha or enlightened families, 95

- cut-off *rigs-med-pa*, Skt. *agotraka*, 64, 194
- dubious *ma-nges-pa'i rigs*, Skt. *aniyata-gotra*, 63
- five *rigs-can lnga*, Skt. *pañcagotra*, 133

faith(s) *dad-pa*, Skt. *śraddhā*, 59, 568, 575, 604, 615, 618, 639, 655, 665, 669, 853, 869

- three *dad-pa gsum*, 968

fearlessnesses *mi-'jigs-pa*, Skt. *abhaya*, 201, 663, 928

- four *mi-'jigs-pa bzhi*, Skt. *caturvaiśā-radya*, 22, 140, 171, 266

feast offering *tshogs(-kyi 'khor-lo)*, Skt. *gaṇacakra*: an assembly or congregation in which elaborate feast offerings are consumed according to the teaching of the three highest vehicles. See Gonpo Tsetan, *The Udumbara Bouquet*; also GGFTC (pp. 923-31), 255, 281, 290, 460, 487, 561, 580, 585, 588, 590, 591, 621, 627, 649, 676, 692, 736, 766, 772, 773, 848, 857, 864, 866, 867

field *zhing-khams*, Skt. *kṣetra*: see *(buddha-) field*

Followers of Brahmā *tshangs-pa-ba*, Skt. *Brāhmaṇa*, 66

Followers of Bṛhaspati *phur-bu-pa*, Skt. *Bārhaspatya*, 16, 67, 197

Followers of the Conqueror *rgyal-ba-pa*: see *Jaina*

Followers of Īśvara *dbang-phyug-pa*: see *Aiśvara*

Followers of Kapila *ser-skya-pa*, Skt. *Kāpila*: the Sāṃkhya School of Hinduism, 64-5

Followers of the Owl *'ug-phrug-pa*, Skt. *Aulūkya*, 65; see also *Vaiśeṣika*
Followers of the Veda *rig-byed-pa*, Skt. *Vaidika*, 66
form *gzugs*, Skt. *rūpa*: in Abhidharma, this term indicates the apparent or sensible forms which comprise the objective aspect of phenomena, 156, 158 and *passim*; see also under *component(s)*
physical *sku-gzugs*: i.e. as the emanational teaching of the Great Perfection, 115, 135
form realms *gzugs-kyi khams*, Skt. *rūpadhātu*, 13, 56, 62, 129, 142, 258-9, 301, 340
extraordinary *khyad-par-can*, 58, 60, 62
ordinary *tsam-po*, 58-60, 62
formless realms *gzugs-med khams*, Skt. *ārūpyadhātu*, 13, 15, 56, 61-2, 129, 142, 146, 165, 176, 340; see also *meditative absorption(s)*
four *gzugs-med khams-pa'i gnas-bzhi*, Skt. *caturārūpyadhātu*, 13, 15, 61-2
fundamental nature/reality *gshis(-lugs)*, 38, 146, 165, 176, 211, 217-18, 232, 249, 294, 297-300, 303, 305, 314, 316-17, 320, 324, 335-7, 377
gandharva *dri-za*: denizens of the sky, who subsist on odours, 423, 425, 609
garuḍa *mkha'-lding*, 477, 763, 773, 810
gatherings, three *'du-ba gsum*, 851
Gaurī, Eight *gau-rī brgyad*, 623, 629
gaze(s) *lta-stangs*, 614, 819
three *lta-stangs gsum*, 907; see also *three essentials which guide (the eyes) towards the expanse* under *All-Surpassing Realisation*
of the buddha-body of reality *chos-sku'i lta-stangs*, 572
Gedenpa *dge-ldan-pa*: i.e. Gelukpa, 931
Riwo *ri-bo dge-ldan-pa*, 868
Gelukpa *dge-lugs-pa*, 29, 395, 678, 681, 682, 683, 822, 852, 867, 868, 879, 923-6, 954; see also preceding entry
genyen, twenty-one *dge-bsnyen nyer-gcig*, 513
geomantic centre/focal point/site *me-btsa'*: focal points of power on the surface of the earth, and especially on the body of the supine ogress which represents the Tibetan landscape, 330, 510, 614, 802, 847
geometric poetry *zung-ldan bya-dka'*: comprising alliteration, lines read in two directions (*ardhabhrama*), zigzagging (*gomūtrika*) and lines read in all directions (*sarvatobhadra*), 105
gesture *phyag-rgya*, Skt. *mudrā*, 900; see also *hand-gesture* and under *seal(s)*
of menace *sdigs-mdzub*, 819
symbolic *brda'*, 230
of teaching *chos-'chad-kyi phyag-rgya*, 879
ghandhola spire *ghan-dho-la*, Skt. *gandhālaya*: an offering-shrine, usually in the form of a stūpa, 133
ghaṭikā *chu-tshod*: a period of twenty-four minutes, 946
ghee *mar(-gyi nying)-khu*, Skt. *ghṛta*, 465, 624
gnostic mantras/spells *rig-sngags*, Skt. *vidyāmantra*: the mantras of the outer tantras, 260, 271, 273, 468, 478, 489, 503, 504, 715, 920, 972; see also *mantra(s)* and *mantra syllables*
gods *lha*, Skt. *deva*: sentient beings of the higher realms, 11, 13, 14-15, 57-8, 60, 65-6, 130, 132, 303, 416, 419, 422, 423, 424, 425, 432, 433, 441, 454, 468, 491, 492, 889, 939; see also *deva*
and demons *lha-'dre*, 609, 654, 686, 709, 761, 802, 819, 894, 938, 939
goddess *lha-mo*, Skt. *devī*, 651, 715
goddesses of the earth, twelve *brtan-ma bcu-gnyis*, 513
Gongpo spirits *'gong-po*: bewitching demons, 782, 939
grammar *sgra'i rig(-gnas)*, Skt. *śabdavidyā*, 18, 65, 98, 99-101, 103, 292, 512, 577, 578, 605, 665, 677, 679, 703, 706, 709, 724, 730, 731, 762, 806, 821, 850, 917; see also *science, linguistic*
Great Madhyamaka, subtle and inner *phra-ba nang-gi dbu-ma chen-po*, 25-8, 29-30, 32, 161-216; see also under *Madhyamaka*
Great Perfection *rdzogs-pa chen-po*, Skt. **mahāsandhi*: the vehicle of Atiyoga, and the ground, path and result taught therein; defined, 311-18; 11, 17, 19, 20, 35-9, 85-7, 124, 134-8, 207, 274, 294-345, 347, 358-9, 397,

451, 453-4, 461, 490-504, 524, 531, 538-96, 614, 619, 646, 647, 651, 652, 654, 665, 666, 668, 677, 679, 680, 683, 691, 693, 694, 695, 698, 707, 718, 722, 732, 734, 762, 766, 813, 818, 820, 828, 837-8, 844, 861, 876, 877, 895-910, 914, 919, 921, 922, 923, 925, 926, 936, 960-1; see also under *piṭaka* and *vehicle(s)*

aural lineage of *snyan-brgyud*, 473, 494, 499, 503, 550, 556, 570, 652, 658

cycles of *rdzogs-chen skor-rnams*: see *Esoteric Instructional Class*

exegetical tradition of *bshad-brgyud*, 494, 556

Kham tradition of *rdzogs-chen khams-lugs*, 706

three classes/traditions of *rdzogs-chen sde/lugs-gsum*, 36-9, 319-45, 538-96, 697, 854

two paths of *rdzogs-chen-gyi lam gnyis*, 334-45

the verbal lineage/tantras of *tshig-rgyud*, 493, 556, 574, 590

Great Seal *phyag-rgya chen-po*, Skt. *Mahāmudrā*: see under *seal(s)*

ground *gzhi*, Skt. *āśraya*: the abiding nature of reality, on which basis buddhahood may be realised, 36, 54-5, 115-17, 127, 141, 145, 170-1, 178, 192, 196, 207, 250, 252, 254, 257, 264-5, 270-1, 323-4, 338, 342-3, 413, 643, 897, 916; see also under *continuum/continua*

actual *dngos-gzhi*: the main body of practice or empowerment, 567, 580

original *gdod-ma'i gzhi*, 879

ground-of-all *kun-gzhi*, Skt. *ālaya*: the substratum or buddha-body of reality as the unactualised ground of saṃsāra and nirvāṇa alike. It is contrasted with the consciousness of the ground-of-all (*kun-gzhi rnam-par shes-pa*, Skt. *ālayavijñāna*), which is the foundation of all consciousness actualised in saṃsāra, 32, 55, 161, 221, 263, 312, 314, 340-1, 356

guidance *khrid*, *passim*; see also *liberation*

which lays bare the teaching *smar/dmar-khrid*: teachings which expose the nature of reality nakedly as if revealing the red (*dmar*) blood of the heart; or alternatively, teaching which is abundantly rich (*smar*) and detailed, 601, 843, 871

guru *bla-ma*: a supreme spiritual teacher, *passim*

root *rtsa-ba'i bla-ma*, 657, 718, 719, 835, 861, 868, 871

three means to delight *mnyes-pa gsum*, 658, 680, 871

Gyelpo spirits *rgyal-po*: "king" spirits who manifest through anger and hatred, 491, 516, 519, 565, 939

habitual tendencies *'du-byed*, Skt. *saṃskāra*: see under *component(s)*

hand gesture *lag-pa'i phyag-rgya*, Skt. *mudrā*, 117, 290; see also *gesture* and under *seal(s)*

five kinds of seal *phyag-rgya rigs-lnga*, 357

harmonious tones, seven *glu-dbyangs-kyi nges-pa bdun*, 98, 107

hatred *zhe-sdang*, Skt. *dveṣa*, 12, 18, 33, 130, 273, 306, 322, 340, 899, 938, 939

twenty-one thousand kinds of *zhe-sdang-gi cha nyis-khri chig-stong*, 77

heart-orb of Vairocana *thugs dpal be'u*, Skt. **cittaśrīvatsa*, 961

hedonists *tshu-rol mdzes-pa-ba*, Skt. *Cārvāka*, 67

hells *dmyal-ba*, Skt. *naraka*: the lowest level of cyclical existence occupied by sentient beings, 14, 130, 214

Śāriputra's visit to, 592

heruka *he-ru-ka*: the wrathful meditational deity, 45, 404, 449, 623, 676, 692, 837; see also *supreme identity*

active *las-kyi he-ru-ka*, 866

causal *rgyu'i he-ru-ka*, 625

fruitional *'bras-bu'i he-ru-ka*, 626, 631, 632

higher insight *lhag-mthong*, Skt. *vipaśyana*, 13, 61-2, 79, 167, 226, 236, 247, 254-5, 338-9, 906

higher realms *mtho-ris*, Skt. *svarga*, 14-15, 56, 61, 65, 81, 97, 920; see also Index of Locations

Hindu/Hinduism *phyi-pa*: lit. "outsider"—the term may be used to refer to any doctrines or adherent of doctrines "outside" those taught by the buddhas, 394, 503, 936; see also *Outsiders*

homonym *sgra-gcig-la don du-ma*, 106

ideas/ideation and scrutiny *rtog-dpyod*, 61, 117, 247, 287, 293, 295-6, 302, 314-15, 329, 905, 906, 907, 930
ignorance *ma-rig-pa*, Skt. *avidyā*, 12, 24, 32, 54-5, 67, 69, 104, 159, 161, 166-7, 175, 195, 228-9, 309, 423, 704, 899, 968
  co-emergent *lhan-cig skyes-pa'i ma-rig-pa*, 54
  of the imaginary *kun-tu-brtags-pa'i ma-rig-pa*, 54
  of individual selfhood *bdag-nyid gcig-pu'i ma-rig-pa*, 54
  three interrelated aspects of *ma-rig-pa gsum*, 12, 54
illusion, eight similes of *sgyu-ma'i dpe-brgyad*, 236
imaginary (nature) *kun-brtags-kyi mtshan-nyid*, Skt. *parikalpitalakṣaṇa*, 24, 25, 26, 154, 160, 170, 182, 216, 219-20; see also *essential natures, three*
immeasurables, four *tshad-med bzhi*, 13, 61-2, 417
impermanence *mi-rtag-pa*, Skt. *anitya*, 16, 28, 53, 70-1, 153, 158-9, 186-7, 197, 199, 211, 226, 230, 400, 419, 571
impurity(ies) *ma-dag-pa*, Skt. *aśuddhi*, 199, 273, 326 and *passim*
  five *snyigs-ma lnga*, Skt. *pañcakaṣāya*, 212
independent/inherent existence *rang-bzhin*, Skt. *svabhāva*, 26, 57, 94, 128, 154, 158, 164, 167, 171-2, 184, 190, 195, 206, 214-16, 224, 229, 234, 255, 299, 314, 317, 335, 653; see also *substantial existence*
indestructible chain (of light) *rdo-rje lu-gu-rgyud*, 38, 337-9
Indestructible Nucleus of Inner Radiance *'od-gsal rdo-rje snying-po*: the dimension of the buddha-body of reality, 19, 115, 118, 122, 448, 722, 887, 971; see also under *vehicle(s)*
indestructible reality *rdo-rje*, Skt. *vajra*: defined, 260-1; 45, 95, 122, 211, 260-1, 339, 404, 451, 586, 853, 867, 971; see also *vajra*
  of anger *zhe-sdang rdo-rje*, 604
  dance of *rdo-rje'i gar*, 514, 773
  embodiment of *rdo-rje'i bdag*, 185; see also *supreme identity* and *self, true*
  expanse of *rdo-rje dbyings*, Skt. *vajradhātu*, 353-4
  holder of *rdo-rje 'dzin-pa*, Skt. *vajradhṛk*: an exponent of the vehicle of indestructible reality, not to be confused with the thirteenth buddha level, which is also called Holder of Indestructible Reality, 33, 115, 264, 296, 330, 481, 515, 733, 735, 809, 814, 817, 850, 873, 892; see also *vajra-holder*
  knot of *rdo-rje mdud*, 629
  line/phrase/verse of *rdo-rje tshig*, Skt. *vajrapāda*, 35, 290-3, 376, 857
  master of *rdo-rje slob-dpon*, Skt. *vajrācārya*, *passim*
  of mind *thugs-kyi rdo-rje*, 916, 946; see also *buddha-mind*
  song of *rdo-rje glu*, Skt. *vajragītā*, 572, 583, 773, 837, 844, 866, 927
  speech *rdo-rje'i gsung*, 468, 934, 944: see also *buddha-speech*
  three (imperishable) *rdo-rje (mi-shigs-pa) gsum*, 264, 594, 830, 853
  Twelve Great Laughs of *rdo-rje'i gad-mo chen-po bcu-gnyis*, 336
  wings of *rdo-rje gshog-pa*, 627
individual *gang-zag*, Skt. *pudgala*: mundane beings, 93, 158, 215, 218-20, 312, 396, 397, 398, 411, 440, 933
  eight kinds of *gang-zag brgyad*: the four pairs of sacred beings, 227
  four kinds of *gang-zag bzhi*, 186
  three kinds of *gang-zag gsum*, 932
inexpiable sins, five *mtshams-med-pa lnga*, Skt. *pañcānantarīya*, 320, 901, 932
inference *rjes-dpag*, Skt. *anumāna*, 101
  three logical axioms (of implicit) *(dgnos-stobs rjes-dpag-gi) gtan-tshigs gsum*, 102, 839
inherent existence *rang-bzhin*, Skt. *svabhāva*: see *independent/inherent existence*
inner heat *gtum-mo*, Skt. *caṇḍāli*, 547, 548, 922, 936
Innermost Spirituality *snying-thig*, Skt. **cittatilaka*: the tradition of the unsurpassedly secret cycle of the Esoteric Instructional Class of the Great Perfection, 122, 332, 494, 500, 501, 554-96, 668, 678, 734, 820, 837, 840, 846, 919, 922, 926; see also *Unsurpassedly Secret Cycle (which Resembles the Perfection of All)* under *Esoteric Instructional Class*

ancient and new *snying-thig gsar-rnying*, 838

inner radiance *'od-gsal*, Skt. *ābhāsvara/prabhāsvara*: the radiance or luminosity of mind-as-such, particuarly as realised between the waking and dream states, 38, 71, 142, 145, 161, 171, 174, 183, 189, 191-2, 195, 198, 200-1, 211, 247, 252, 272, 278, 280, 288, 293-4, 297, 300, 302, 311, 329, 333-5, 337, 340, 354, 362, 369, 413, 421, 462, 581, 582, 585, 587, 588, 618, 680, 726, 818, 825, 838, 877, 919, 923

ten signs of *'od-gsal rtags-bcu*, 301

Insiders *nang-pa*: i.e. Buddhists, 69

instruction(s) *gdams-pa*, *passim*; see also *nectar-like (instruction)*

established *gtan-la phab-pa*, 76-7

four, of the supreme emanational body *'dul-ba rnam-bzhi*, 21, 131-2, 146, 414, 415; see also *Vinaya*

further advice/instruction *rjes-su gdams-pa*, *passim*

oral advice/instruction *gdams-ngag*, *passim*

seven, of Upagupta *nyer-sbas-kyi gdams-ngag bdun*, 437

insubstantiality *rang-bzhin med-pa*, Skt. *niḥsvabhāvatā*: i.e. lack of independent or substantial existence, 421

intellect/intelligence *blo-gros*, Skt. *mati*, *passim*

intention(s) *dgongs-pa*, Skt. *abhiprāya*: i.e. of buddha-mind, 30, 72, 88, 94-6, 102, 121, 143, 154, 170, 178, 182, 184, 186, 188, 197, 203, 207-8, 214, 216-22, 246, 248, 255, 282, 290-1, 293, 300-1, 312, 317, 326, 342, 397, 403, 404, 406, 413, 426, 447, 573, 574, 582, 585, 604, 613, 615, 619, 627, 630, 640, 707, 722, 732, 783, 804, 807, 819, 829, 840, 848, 854, 856, 858, 861, 871, 879, 880, 894, 899, 903, 905, 908, 910, 926, 930, 943; see also *buddha-mind*

four kinds of *dgongs-pa rnam-bzhi*, Skt. *caturabhiprāya*, 30, 218-20

seven powers of *dgongs-pa'i rtsal bdun*, 455

twelve different, of buddha-mind *dgongs-pa mi-'dra-ba bcu-gnyis*, 137

intentional symbols *dgongs-pa brda'*: i.e. symbols indicative of buddha-mind, 448; see also *symbols/symbolic convention/symbolism*

intermediary(ies) *pho-nya*, Skt. *dūta*, 645

male and female, of the enlightened family *pho-nya-dang pho-nya-mo*: according to Kriyātantra, 271

intermediate state *bar-do*, Skt. *antarābhava*, 34, 39, 278-9, 339, 363, 496, 582, 583, 587, 660

before birth *skye-ba bar-ma*, 278

between the intermediate states of reality and rebirth *srid-pa bar-ma*, 379

of the birthplace *skyes-gnas bar-do*, 279, 344

of existence *rang-bzhin bar-do*, 278-80

four *bar-do rnam bzhi*, 39, 344-5

of the moment of death *'chi-ka'i bar-do*, 278-9, 344

of reality *chos-nyid bar-do*, 279, 344-5

of rebirth *srid-pa bar-do*, 279, 345

introduction *ngo-sprod*: i.e. to the face of reality, 332, 584, 586, 601, 866

to the instructions *gdams-ngag ngo-sprod*, 762-3

inventory of treasure doctrines *kha-byang*, 561, 662, 676, 745, 755, 756, 763, 764, 775, 785, 789, 793, 796, 810, 814, 815, 837, 843, 845, 863, 864

essential *gnad-byang*, 845

prophetic *lung-byang*, 863, 864, 866, 867

quintessential *snying-byang*, 845

supplementary *yang-byang*, 763, 789, 845

Jaina *rgyal-ba-pa*: followers of Śākyamuni's contemporary, the conqueror Mahāvīra, and of the *tīrthaṅkara* who preceded him, 16, 66

Jainism *rgyal-ba-pa*, 16, 66

Jambu tree *shing dzam-bu bri-ksha'i ljon-pa*, Skt. *jambuvṛkṣa*: the rose-apple tree, 409

just what is, the nature of *de-bzhin-nyid*, Skt. *tathatā*, 31, 79, 124, 154, 172-3, 183-5, 200, 217, 279, 300, 307-8, 313, 320, 334, 362, 403, 412, 447, 539, 901

Jyaiṣṭha *snron zla-ba*: June to July, 948

Kadampa *bka'-gdams-pa*, 11, 29, 198-9, 395, 548, 805, 853

schools, ancient and new *bka'-gdams gsar-rnying*: the ancient school is that

of Atiśa and his followers, while the new one is the Gelukpa school of Je Tsongkapa, 526, 850, 929, 951, 954
Kagyü school *bka'-brgyud*, 395, 952
  eight minor subsects of *bka'-brgyud chung brgyad*, 395, 853, 952
  four great subsects of *bka'-brgyud che bzhi*, 395, 853, 952
Kagyüpa *bka'-brgyud-pa*, 11, 29, 199-203, 823, 847, 850, 852, 868, 879, 922, 931
Kalantaka bird *ka-lanta-ka*, 455
Kaliyuga *snyigs-ma'i dus*: the fourth or degenerate age of the aeon, which is suited for the practice of the Unsurpassed Yogatantra, 268
Kāma divinities, six species of *'dod-lha rigs-drug*, 60
Kamtsang *kaṃ-tshang*: the Karmapa or Karma Kamtsang school, 833, 850
kaptse, (four) *gab-rtse (bzhi)*: diagrams of cyclical existence based on the Chinese tradition of divination, 104, 874
karma *las*, 13, 55-7, 661, 683; see also *deeds*, *world-forming*
Karma Kamtsang *karma kaṃ-tshang*: the Karmapa or Kamtsang school, 841, 867
Karmapa *karma-pa*, 569, 584, 682, 683, 812, 841, 847, 848, 868, 956; see preceding entry
Kārttika *smin-drug*: November to December, 946-7
Katokpa *kaḥ-thog-pa*: the tradition of Katok Monastery, 695
Kham tradition *khams-lugs*: see under *transmitted precepts*
khukcö flowers *khug-chos me-tog*, 563
kīla *phur-ba/phur-bu*: a three-bladed ritual dagger or spike, 535, 537, 603, 605, 612, 615, 639, 669, 709, 710, 711, 713, 714, 715, 716, 751, 755, 781, 786, 842
  which is a material symbol *rdzas-phur*, 715
koṣa: a bear-like creature, 490
knowledge, love and power, *mkhyen-brtse-nus gsum*, 648, 665, 720
Kriyātantra *bya-ba'i rgyud*: see under *vehicle(s)*
Kṛtayuga *rdzogs-ldan*: the first of the four ages of the aeon, which is suited ideally for the practice of Kriyātantra, 268, 960, 970
lama *bla-ma*: see *guru*
lamps *sgron-ma*: according to All-Surpassing Realisation
  four *sgron-ma bzhi*, 338-9
  six *sgron-ma drug*, 907
languages, four *skad-rigs bzhi*, 107
lapis lazuli *mu-men*, 663
layman *dge-bsnyen*, Skt. *upāsaka*, 394, 423, 543, 568, 622, 673, 709, 724, 728, 805
  three kinds of *dge-bsnyen gsum*, 70
laywoman *dge-bsnyen-ma*, Skt. *upāsikā*, 423
learning, dignity and excellence *mkhas-btsun-bzang*, 724, 734, 736
lecture notes *stong-thun*, 601
legend *de-lta-bu byung-ba*, Skt. *itivṛttaka*, 76
level(s) *sa*, Skt. *bhūmi*, 142, 248, 304, 315, 320, 335, 423, 424, 594, 609, 732, 832
  of the awareness-holders *rig-pa 'dzin-pa'i sa*: the attainment of the buddha-body of supreme transformation, 649, 918
  of the Bounteous Array (of Five Enlightened Families) *(rigs-lnga) stug-po bkod-pa'i sa*: according to Yogatantra, 84, 273, 296
  buddha, 34, 35, 36, 38, 82-3, 204, 207, 214-15, 237, 270, 352, 369
  of deathlessness *'chi-med sa*, 700
  eighth, (Unmoving) *sa brgyad-pa (mi-gYo-ba)*, 282, 449, 691
  eleventh, (Universal Light) *sa bcu-gcig-pa (kun-tu 'od)*, 30, 84, 237, 295, 691
  fifteenth (Great/Supreme Bliss) *sa bcu-lnga-pa (bde-ba chen-po)*, 84, 771
  first, (Joyful) *sa dang-po (rab-tu dga'-ba)*, 281-2, 912
  fourteenth, (Great (Cloud) Mass of Rotating Syllables) *sa bcu-bzhi-pa (yi-ge (sprin-gyi) 'khor-lo tshogs-chen)*, 84
  fourth, (Flaming) *sa bzhi-pa ('od-'phro-ba)*, 613
  of a Holder of Indestructible Reality (Vajradhara) *rdo-rje 'dzin-pa*: the thirteenth buddha-level, 254, 462, 496; of Four Enlightened Families *rigs-bzhi rdo-rje 'dzin-pa'i sa*, 84, 271, 353; of Three Enlightened Families *rigs-gsum rdo-rje 'dzin-pa'i sa*, 270, 352

indestructible *rdo-rje sa*: i.e. the resultant or buddha levels rather than the causal levels, 404
ninth, (Excellent Intelligence) *sa dgu-pa (legs-pa'i blo-gros)*, 449
of no-return *phyir mi-ldog-pa'i sa*: the penultimate result according to the vehicle of pious attendants, 471
sixteenth, (Unsurpassed Pristine Cognition) *sa bcu-drug-pa (ye-shes bla-ma)*, 84
of a Sky-farer (of Four Enlightened Families) *(rigs-bzhi) mkha'-spyod-pa'i sa*, 84, 272; see also *level of a Holder of Indestructible Reality*
ten *sa-bcu*: according to Anuyoga, 34, 287-8
ten *sa-bcu*, Skt. *daśabhūmi*: of bodhisattvas, 30, 142, 174, 237, 281-2, 341, 416, 574, 746
tenth, (Cloud of Doctrine) *sa bcu-pa (chos-kyi sprin-pa)*, 282, 412, 448, 912, 930
third, (Illuminating) *sa gsum-pa ('od-byed)*, 91, 184
thirteenth, (Holder of Indestructible Reality/Vajradhara) *sa bcu-gsum-pa (rdo-rje 'dzin-pa)*: see *level of a Holder of Indestructible Reality*
twelfth, (Unattached Lotus Endowed) *sa bcu-gnyis-pa (ma-chags padma-can)*, 254, 757
liberality *sbyin-pa*, Skt. *dāna*, 220, 255, 303, 305-6, 313, 768, 831, 902
perfection of *sbyin-pa'i pha-rol-tu phyin-pa*, Skt. *dānapāramitā*, 902
"liberate"/"liberation" *sgrol-ba*: to transfer forcefully and compassionately the consciousness of a sentient being to a higher level of existence, thus benefitting that being and removing obstacles caused by his or her evil karma, 469, 535, 603, 604, 605, 612, 615, 620, 622, 642, 711, 713, 767, 938, 950
liberated careers *rnam-thar*: the lives of those who attained liberation both for themselves and others, 406, 442
liberating diagram *btags-grol*, 767
liberation *grol-ba/thar-pa*, Skt. *mokṣa/mukti*, 16, 18, 19, 21, 27, 28, 30, 37, 38, 64-7, 69, 84, 88, 96-7, 108, 115, 125, 139, 147, 192-3, 223, 228, 259, 261, 264, 282, 305, 323-4, 326, 331-2, 335-6, 342, 345, 359, 364, 370, 411, 415, 416, 425, 430, 432, 449, 540, 547, 557, 571, 593, 595, 641, 642, 655, 656, 744, 787, 788, 819, 873, 877, 888, 894, 898, 899, 903, 930, 944,
definitely good *nges-legs*, Skt. *niḥśreyasa*, 920
four great modes of *grol-lugs chen-po bzhi*, 38, 334
four ways of *grol bzhi*, 748
from limits *mtha'-grol*, 906
maturation and *smin-sgrol*: in this context liberation refers to the guidance which confers liberation, see under *maturation*
path of *grol-lam*, 643, 683; two modes of *grol-lam rnam-gnyis*: according to Mahāyoga, 277-8; three aspects of the gradual *rim-gyis-pa'i grol-lam rnam-gsum*: according to Mahāyoga 34, 278-81
primordial *ye-grol*, 906
three approaches to *rnam-thar sgo-gsum*, Skt. *trīṇi vimokṣamukhāni*, 28, 154, 187, 316-17, 335, 896, 898, 908
liberators, eighteen secret *gsang-ba'i sgrol-ging bco-brgyad*, 620
liberties, eight *dal-ba brgyad*, 573
life, three phases of *skye-ba'i rim-gsum* 34, 278-81
life-support *bla-gnas*: a sympathetic energy force, either in living or talismanic form, adopted to sustain a person's life, 605, 790
life-supporting wolf-spirit *bla-spyang*, 604, 605
limits, four *mu-bzhi*, Skt. *catuṣkoṭi*, 163-4
limits, six *mtha'-drug*: parameters of the scriptures, 35, 290-2
lineage(s) *brgyud-pa*, Skt. *paramparā*, *passim*
of Anuyoga, 485-9, 537, 700, 717-32
of Atiyoga, 413-14, 490-501; Mental and Spatial Classes, 538-53; Esoteric Instructional Class, 538, 554-96
aural, of mundane individuals *gang-zag snyan-khung-gi brgyud-pa*, 397, 404, 447, 452, 456-7, 601, 745, 819, 844, 847, 858, 866, 894, 923
close, of treasures *nye-brgyud gter-ma*, 482-4, 741-881
of the ḍākinīs' seal of entrustment *mkha'-'gro gtad-rgya'i brgyud-pa*, 745

distant, of transmitted precepts *ring-brgyud bka'-ma*, 597-740, 792
eight, of attainment or (great) conveyances *sgrub-brgyud shing-rta (chen-po) brgyad*, 852-3, 861
empowered by enlightened aspiration *smon-lam dbang-bskur-gyi brgyud-pa*, 745
indestructible, of supreme transformation *'pho-ba chen-po'i rdo-rje brgyud-pa*, 406
intentional, of the conquerors *rgyal-ba dgongs-pa'i brgyud-pa*, 397, 404, 447-50, 745
lineage-holder *brgyud-'dzin*, 552, 642, 733
of Mahāyoga, 458-84; class of means for attainment *sgrub-sde'i brgyud-pa*, 475-84; class of tantra *rgyud-sde'i brgyud-pa*, 458-74
of the patriarchs of the teachings *bstan-pa'i gtad-rabs*, 432-9
of prophetically declared spiritual succession *bka'-babs lung-bstan-gyi brgyud-pa*, 745
six *brgyud-pa drug*, 404, 745, 862
symbolic, of the awareness-holders *rig-'dzin brda'i brgyud-pa*, 397, 404, 447, 452-6, 745, 872
three *brgyud-pa gsum*, 397, 406, 447, 887, 968
true *dam-pa'i brgyud-pa*, 861, 969
living being/creature *'gro-ba*, Skt. *gati*: see *families*
local divinity *gzhi-bdag*, 571, 621, 622, 624, 630, 633, 638, 639, 645, 690; see also under *deity(ies)*
logic *gtan-tshigs-kyi rig-gnas*, Skt. *hetuvidyā*, 16, 18, 67, 69, 98, 101-3, 292, 313, 440, 564, 577, 578, 590, 605, 642, 650, 665, 679, 705, 706, 709, 732, 805, 806, 850, 873, 917
(logical) axioms *gtan-tshigs*, Skt. *hetu*, 163-4, 167, 247
of awareness *rig-pa'i gtan-tshigs*: in Anuyoga, 287
five kinds of *gtan-tshigs lnga*, 26, 163-4
four *gtan-tshigs bzhi*: of Mahāyoga, 34, 275-6
four great *gtan-tshigs chen-po bzhi*, 35, 294
three *gtan-tshigs gsum*, 102, 839
logical contrareity and inclusion *'gal-khyab*, 314
longevity *tshe-ring/tshe*, Skt. *dīrghāyuḥ*, 99, 470, 550, 564, 671, 678, 712, 804, 842, 863, 874
long-living *tshe-dang ldan-pa*, Skt. *āyuṣmān*, 137, 423
lord *bdag-po/mgon-po/dbang-phyug*, *passim*
of attainment *sgrub-pa'i bdag-po*, 322
of the tenth level *sa-bcu'i bdag-po*, 117, 127-8, 186
loving kindness *byams-pa*, Skt. *maitrī*, 13, 23, 61, 141, 232, 249, 251, 421, 520, 564, 571
Madhyamaka *dbu-ma*, 16, 18, 25-8, 29-30, 41, 108, 128, 160, 162-216, 235-6, 315, 317, 323, 564, 577, 650, 805, 850, 861, 878, 911, 925, 926, 936
coarse and outer *phyi rags-pa'i dbu-ma*, 26, 29, 162-9, 206
five kinds of logical axioms *gtan-tshigs lnga*, 26, 163-4
four great axioms of *gtan-tshigs chen-po bzhi*, 35, 294
subtle and inner *nang phra-ba'i dbu-ma*, 26-8, 169-216
Mādhyamika *dbu-ma-pa*: a follower of the Madhyamaka, 25, 35, 162, 232, 234-5, 294, 342, 350
mahāpaṇḍita: great scholar, 703, 806, 821
Mahāsaṃghika *phal-chen-pa*, 429-30
Mahāvaśavartin, Akaniṣṭha of *gnas dbang-sgyur chen-po'i 'og-min*: the deities or inhabitants of Akaniṣṭha, 449
Mahāyoga *rnal-'byor chen-po*: see under *vehicle(s)*
class of means for attainment *mahāyoga'i sgrub-sde*, 275, 283, 361-2, 461, 475-83, 533, 534-7, 730, 804
class of tantras *mahāyoga'i rgyud-sde*, 275, 283, 361-2, 458-74, 533-4, 730, 804
five aspects of the entrance to *'jug-pa'i yan-lag lnga*, 278-81
four axioms of *gtan-tshigs bzhi*, 34, 275
two divisions of *sde-gnyis*, 462
maṇḍala *dkyil-'khor*: a cosmogram of deities or enlightened attributes, 20, 34, 36, 117, 122, 124-6, 132, 247, 249, 251-3, 255-6, 266, 276, 279-81, 287, 291, 295, 297, 304, 306, 308, 320, 324, 338-9, 349-50, 362, 366-8, 404, 406, 447, 449, 462, 475, 476, 481, 485,

494, 499, 538, 572, 580, 583, 586, 588, 601, 606, 607, 609, 615, 616, 620, 621, 623, 628, 643, 644, 648, 651, 669, 676, 682, 691, 712, 713, 726, 738, 766, 772, 789, 798, 825, 828, 829, 854, 862, 900, 903, 915, 972

attainment of the maṇḍala clusters *tshom-bu tshogs-sgrub*: in Mahāyoga, 279

of buddha-body and pristine cognition *sku-dang ye-shes-kyi dkyil-'khor*, 347, 360

of buddha-body, speech and mind *sku-gsung-thugs-kyi dkyil-'khor*, 31, 246

centre *dkyil*: the principal deity or attribute, 125-6, 281, 916

ceremony/rite *dkyil-'khor-gyi cho-ga*, Skt. *maṇḍalavidhi*, 826, 831, 861

of cloth *ras-kyi dkyil-'khor*, 727, 828

cluster of deities *tshom-bu*, 125, 279-81, 779, 862, 973

of coloured powders *rdul-tshon-gyi dkyil-'khor*: a symbolic representation of deities, 829, 839

emanated *sprul-pa'i dkyil-'khor*, 290, 718, 727, 729

fundamental (offspring), of enlightened mind *byang-sems rtsa-ba'i sras-kyi dkyil-'khor*: according to Anuyoga, 32, 34, 264, 284-5, 366

of the indestructible body *rdo-rje'i sku'i dkyil-'khor*, 766

of indestructible (reality's) expanse *rdo-rje dbyings-kyi dkyil-'khor*, Skt. *vajradhātumaṇḍala*, 354, 466, 538; see also *deities of the expanse of indestructible reality*

material *rdzas-kyi dkyil-'khor*, 710, 864

outer, inner and secret *phyi-nang-gsang-gi dkyil-'khor*, 534

periphery *'khor*: the surrounding deities, 125-6, 281

primordial *ye-nas dkyil-'khor*: according to Anuyoga, 34, 284, 365

of the seals *phyas-rgya'i dkyil-'khor*, 246

spontaneously present, of natural expression *rang-bzhin lhun-grub-kyi dkyil-'khor*: according to Anuyoga, 34, 284, 366

three kinds of *dkyil-'khor gsum*: according to Anuyoga, 34, 284-6, 365-7

three *dkyil-'khor gsum*: according to Ratnākaraśānti, *Definitive Order of the Three Vehicles*, 253

mandate *rjes-su gnang-ba*: in this context it refers to one kind of the Buddha's transmitted precepts, 17, 74-6; for its sense in the vehicle of indestructible reality, see *permissory initiation*

manifest in and of itself/self-manifesting *rang-snang*: the perceptual status of the buddha-bodies of reality and perfect rapture, in contrast to that of the emanational body which is extraneously manifest (*gzhan-snang*), 115, 117, 122-7, 132, 139, 145, 194, 249, 284, 326, 330, 341-3, 345, 358, 360, 447, 448, 640, 924

mantra(s) *sngags*: defined, 31, 257; *passim*; see also *gnostic mantra(s)/spells*, *mantra syllables*, *piṭaka*, *secret mantra*, *seed-syllables*, *tantra(s)* and *vehicle(s)*

combined with sūtras *mdo-sngags*, 693, 695, 696, 706, 722, 724, 725, 737, 789

contrasted with deities, 185, 306

contrasted with sūtras, 142-8

fifteen distinctive features (of the superiority of the inner mantra to the outer sūtra vehicle) *sngags-kyi khyad-par bco-lnga*, 248-55

four distinctive features of *sngags-kyi khyad-par bzhi*, 246

malevolent/malign *drag-sngags*, 610, 764, 765

outer and inner *phyi-nang-gi sngags*, 477, 498, see also under *secret mantra* and *vehicle(s)*; ten categories of *sngags-phyi-nang-gi de-nyid bcu*, Skt. *daśa-tattva*, 303-5, 308, 349-50, see also *tantra, ten categories of*

teaching/tradition: see under *vehicle(s)*

text *sngags(-gzhung)*, *passim*

three kinds of *sngags-gsum*, 257; see also *secret mantra*, *gnostic mantras/spells* and *dhāraṇī*

vital-heart *srog-snying*, 471, 478, 513, 514, 612, 615, 622, 629, 843, 938; see also *seed-syllables*

wrathful *drag-sngags*, 516, 601, 610, 612, 615, 662, 679, 682, 690, 713, 727, 763, 789, 790

mantra adept *sngags-'chang*, Skt. *mantra-dhṛk*, *passim*
mantra syllables *'bru-yig*, 75, 549, 585, 852, 863, 894, 917; see also *recitation*, *seed-syllables* and *syllables*
  A, 501, 572, 588, 761, 818, 860
  EVAṂ: lit. "thus" in Sanskrit. According to the teachings of the Vajrayāna, E symbolises emptiness and VAṂ symbolises coalescent bliss, 31, 207, 258, 930
  four *yi-ge bzhi-pa*, 547, 548
  HA-RI-ṆI-SA, 758
  HRĪḤ, 405, 468, 757
  HŪṂ, 135, 469, 476, 581, 931
  hundred *yig-brgya*, Skt. *śatākṣara*, 762
  KA, 690
  NṚ, 554
  OṂ ĀḤ HŪṂ, 564
  OṂ ĀḤ HŪṂ SVĀHĀ, 490
  OṂ MAṆI PADME HŪṂ, the six-syllable mantra *yi-ge drug-pa*, Skt. *ṣaḍakṣarī*, 508, 545, 569, 767, 841
  OṂ VAJRA KĪLI KĪLAYA, 715
  PHAṬ, 581, 931
  rulu mantra *ru-lu sngags*: this refers to any of the several mantras of the wrathful herukas which include the syllables *ru-lu*, 620, 631, 847
  ten, of Tārā *yi-ge bcu-pa*, 857
mantrin *sngags-pa*, *passim*
marks *mtshan-dpe*
  eighty minor *dpe-byad brgyad-cu*, Skt. *aśītyanuvyañjana*, 20, 124-5
  major and minor *mtshan-dang dpe-byad*, Skt. *lakṣaṇa* and *anuvyañjana*, 122-4, 128, 135, 191, 405, 436, 447, 468, 645, 928
  thirty-two major *mtshan-bzang so-gnyis*, Skt. *dvātriṃśanmahāpuruṣalakṣaṇa*, 20, 124-5, 877
marvellous events *rmad-du byung*, Skt. *adbhūtadharma*, 76-7
master *slob-dpon*, Skt. *ācārya*, *passim*
  of ceremonies *las-kyi slob-spon*, Skt. *karmācārya*, 515, 525, 551, 678, 694, 806
  of indestructible reality *rdo-rje slob-dpon*, Skt. *vajrācārya*, *passim*
materialist *rgyang-'phen-pa*, Skt. *lokāyata*, 16, 63-4, 67
mātrā metre *phyi-mo*: the many variations of Sanskrit metre based on *pāda* (metrical lines) which consist of a determined number of morae or light syllables, 106
maturation *smin-pa*, Skt. *vipāka*: a synonym for empowerment, 972
  and liberation *smin-sgrol*, 471, 566, 580, 593, 595, 721, 733, 745, 758, 772, 773, 778, 788, 794, 805, 811, 813, 814, 818, 820, 823, 827, 835, 837, 844, 847, 850, 853, 857, 858, 861, 871, 967; and supporting transmission *smin-sgrol rgyab-chos gsum*: these are empowerment, guidance and transmission respectively, 442, 851, 856, 871
  seed of *smin-pa'i sa-bon*, 829
meaning *don*, Skt. *artha*: i.e. truth, object, purpose, significance, topic or concept, *passim*
  definitive *nges-don*, Skt. *nītārtha*, 28-9, 137, 142-3, 148, 162, 164, 169, 173, 182, 184, 187-90, 201, 208, 216-18, 236, 276, 290, 413, 424, 453, 744, 896, 903, 934, 944, 947; sūtras of *nges-don-gyi mdo-sde-rnams*, 154-5, 187-90, 898
  expressed *brjod-bya'i don*, 71, 73, 88, 907
  provisional *drang-don*, Skt. *neyārtha*, 28-9, 187-90, 216-18, 290, 301, 893, 896, 909, 931, 934; sūtras of *drang-don-gyi mdo-sde*, 187-90
meaningful expression *ched-du brjod-pa*, Skt. *udāna*, 76
means: see *skilful means*
means for attainment *sgrub-thabs*, Skt. *sādhana*, 283, 462, 470, 472, 475, 480, 481, 482, 483, 489, 498, 535, 564, 576, 587, 619, 621, 628, 642, 647, 651, 663, 676, 679, 682, 686, 691, 696, 703, 710, 715, 719, 722, 724, 757, 775, 826, 827, 831, 848, 861, 893, 920, 927; see also under *Mahāyoga* and *piṭaka*
  eight classes of *sgrub-sde brgyad*, 283, 361-2, 475-83, 521, 534
  five classes of means for attainment of deities of pristine cognition *ye-shes lha'i sgrub-sde lnga*: according to Mahāyoga, 361-2; see also under *lineage(s)*
  general and special classes of *sgrub-sde spyi bye-brag*, 482

of the guru *bla-sgrub*, Skt. *gurusādhana*, 779
of longevity *tshe-sgrub*, Skt. *āyuḥsādhana*, 470
three common classes of *thun-mong-gi sgrub-sde gsum*: according to Mahāyoga, 362; see also under *lineage(s)*
meats, five *sha-lnga*, Skt. *pañcamaṃsa*: commitments of Unsurpassed Yogatantra, 274
media, three *sgo-gsum*, the sensory gates of body, speech and mind, 264, 304, 367; see also *door*
medicine/medical science *gso-ba'i rig-gnas*, Skt. *cikitsāvidyā*, 18, 65, 98-9, 575, 651, 665, 677, 722, 746, 762, 775, 791, 809, 850, 860
meditation *sgom-pa*, Skt. *bhāvanā*, *passim*
aftermath of *rjes-thob*, Skt. *pṛṣthalabdha*, 147, 168
of Anuyoga *anuyoga'i sgom-pa*, 286-7, 368-9
as an aspect of discriminative awareness *bsgom-pa-las 'byung-ba'i shes-rab*, 71, 99, 276
of Atiyoga *atiyoga'i sgom-pa*, 334-45, 370-1
belt *sgom-thag*, 540
of the bodhisattvas *byang-chub sems-dpa'i sgom-pa*, 236
according to the Brahmā vehicle *bram-ze theg-pa'i sgom-pa*, 61-2
of definitive perfection *nges-rdzogs*: in Mahāyoga, 278, 363
devotional *mos-bsgom*: in Mahāyoga, 278, 363
of Great Madhyamaka *dbu-ma chen-po'i bsgom-pa*, 184-5
of Kriyātantra *bya-ba'i rgyud-kyi sgom-pa*, 270, 350-1
of Mahāyoga *ma-hā-yo-ga'i sgom-pa*, 278-81, 301, 361-3
according to the mundane vehicle *'jig-rten theg-pa'i sgom-pa*, 60
non-meditation *sgom-med*, 304-5, 317, 543, 548, 580, 641
as one of the transcendental perfections *bsam-gtan phar-phyin*, 94
of the outer tantras *phyi-rgyud-kyi sgom-pa*, 348
of the pious attendants *nyan-thos-pa'i sgom-pa*, 226-7
of the self-centred buddhas *rang-rgyal theg-pa'i sgom-pa*, 230
of Ubhayatantra *upa rgyud-kyi sgom-pa*, 33, 271, 352
of Yogatantra *rnal-'byor rgyud-kyi sgom-pa*, 33, 272, 355-7
meditational deities *yi-dam*, Skt. *iṣṭadevatā*: deities who are the focus of meditation and means for attainment, and who confer supreme accomplishments: see *deity(ies)*
meditative absorption(s) *snyoms-'jug*, Skt. *samāpatti*, 29, 93, 157, 164, 206, 254-6, 286, 293, 302, 314, 342, 356, 368, 454, 549, 561, 581, 584, 639, 912
aftermath of *rjes-thob*, Skt. *pṛṣṭhalabdhajñāna*, 166-7, 177, 206, 562
four formless *gzugs-med bzhi*, 13, 15, 61-2
two methods of *'jog-thabs gnyis-po*, 280
meditative commitment *thugs-dam*, 773
meditative concentration(s) *bsam-gtan*, Skt. *dhyāna*, 61-2, 71, 270, 302, 306, 902
four *bsam-gtan bzhi*, Skt. *caturdhyāna*, 13, 14-15, 61-2, 115
fourth *bsam-gtan bzhi-pa*, 421
perfection of *bsam-gtan-gyi pha-rol-tu phyin-pa*, Skt. *dhyānapāramitā*, 902
three aspects of the reality of *bsam-gtan-gyi de-nyid gsum*: according to Kriyātantra, 270
meditative equipoise and its aftermath *mnyam-bzhag-dang rjes-thob*, Skt. *samāhita* and *pṛṣṭhalabdha*, 75, 125, 147, 166-8, 177, 194-5, 208-9, 236, 272, 274, 315-16, 336, 631, 829, 831, 905; see also under *meditation* and *meditative absorption(s)*
meditator, great *sgom-chen*, 622, 709
Menmo sisters, seven *sman-mo mched bdun*, 581
Menmo spirit *sman-mo*: a female demon inhabiting the countryside, 773
mental body *yid-lus*: the insubstantial body assumed by the mind during the intermediate state after death, 178, 260
Mental Class of the Great Perfection *sems-kyi sde*, 37, 319-26, 327, 370-1, 494, 496, 524, 538-53, 554, 619, 633, 642, 654, 660, 688, 697, 700, 701, 706, 734, 833, 845, 922

seven categories of *sems-phyogs bdun*, 37, 323-5
mental events *sems-byung*, Skt. *caitasika*, 24, 35, 156-8, 164, 166-7, 183, 252, 294, 314-15, 329, 334, 340, 898, 904, 906
fifty-one *sems-byung lnga-bcu-rtsa-gcig*, 156
merit *bsod-nams*, Skt. *kuśala/puṇya*, 23, 51-3, 85, 94, 131, 247, 323, 345, 376, 378, 412, 415, 416, 419, 421, 550, 592, 594, 621, 633, 634, 637, 647, 661, 666, 768, 928, 934; see also under *provisions*
dedication of *bsngo-ba*, Skt. *pariṇāmanā*, 592, 767, 792, 852
metaphor *gzugs*, Skt. *rūpaka*: in poetics, 105
metrical feet *dzā-ti*, Skt. *jāti*, 106, 730
metrical lines: see *pāda*
middle path/way *dbu-ma'i lam*, Skt. *madhyamapratipad*, 95, 162, 182, 311-12, 421, 423
mind *sems*, Skt. *citta*: i.e. of an ordinary being, *passim*; see also under *component(s)* and *consciousness*
in Abhidharma: this refers in particular to the dominant mind, i.e. consciousness, which is contrasted with peripheral mental events, 24, 35, 156-8, 164, 166-7, 224-5, 229, 252, 294, 314-15, 334, 340, 898, 904, 906
which apprehends emotionally conflicted thoughts *nyong-mongs-pa-can yid-kyi rnam-shes*, Skt. *kliṣṭamanovijñāna*, 55; see also *consciousness of conflicting emotions*
of inner radiance *'od-gsal-gyi sems*, Skt. *prabhāsvaracitta*, 189
in its natural state *gnyug-ma'i sems*, 41, 200
superior *lhag-pa'i sems*, Skt. *adhicitta*, 71, 79, 423, 707; see also *meditation*
supreme *sems chen-po*, 116
those holding the mind to emerge from space *nam-mkha' yid-can-pa*, 67, 197
vital energy and *rlung-sems*, 536
mind *thugs*, Skt. *citta*: see *buddha-mind*, *mind-as-such* and *pristine cognition(s)*
mind-as-such *sems-nyid*: i.e. the fundamental reality of buddha-mind, 30, 31, 36, 37, 87, 183, 197, 202, 214, 217, 244, 248-9, 260, 264, 276, 284, 297, 307, 319-20, 324-6, 328, 334, 346, 350, 358, 369, 903
Mind Only *sems-tsam*, Skt. *Cittamātra*: Vijñānavāda, 25, 27, 28, 159, 161-2, 170, 178-86, 235, 936
mindfulness *dran-pa*, Skt. *smṛti*, 236; see also *recollection(s)*
mind-stream *rgyud*, Skt. *santāna*, 276; see also *continuum/continua*
miracle(s) *cho-'phrul*, Skt. *prātihārya*, 131, 358, 433, 434, 469
four *cho-'phrul bzhi*: according to Mahāyoga—also known as the four yogas, 355-6
miraculous ability/power *rdzu-'phrul*, Skt. *ṛddhi*, 21, 132, 135, 137-8, 230, 248, 281, 425, 456, 471, 473, 474, 513, 538, 622, 624, 630, 639, 757, 758, 791, 803, 811, 889
four supports for *rdzu-'phrul rkang-bzhi*, Skt. *catvāra ṛddhipādāḥ*, 236
monastic community *dge-'dun*, Skt. *saṃgha*, 423, 666, 783, 848, 862, 921, 939; see also *community* and *saṃgha*
monk *dge-slong*, Skt. *bhikṣu*: i.e. fully-ordained, holding two hundred and fifty-three vows, 226, 393, 394, 423, 424, 426, 429, 430, 440, 450, 515, 520, 521, 523, 524, 526, 541, 547, 548, 575, 578, 590, 601, 604, 607, 626, 630, 632, 633, 672, 675, 694, 775, 809, 810, 921, 936, 950; see also under *ordination* and *vows*
morae, Skt. *laghumātrā*: light syllables in prosody, two of which are equivalent to one heavy syllable (Skt. *guru-mātrā*), 106
moral discipline *tshul-khrims*, Skt. *śīla*, 12, 30, 58, 117, 125, 220-1, 248, 253, 306, 729, 899, 901, 902; see also under *commitment(s)* and *vows*
of Anuyoga, 367
of Atiyoga, 370
of the bodhisattvas, 235-6
of the Brahmā vehicle, 61
of Kriyātantra, 350
of Mahāyoga, 361
of the mundane vehicle, 58-60
perfection of *tshul-khrims-kyi pha-rol-tu phyin-pa*, Skt. *śīlapāramitā*, 902
of the pious attendants, 226
of the self-centred buddhas, 230

superior *lhag-pa'i tshul-khrims*, Skt. *adhiśīla*, 71, 79, 423, 707
three aspects of *tshul-khrims gsum*: according to the bodhisattva vehicle, 235, 355
of Ubhayatantra, 352
of Yogatantra, 355
morphological change *rnam-'gyur*, Skt. *vikāra*, 100
Mu spirits *dmu*: malignant spirits causing dropsy, 491
mudrā *phyag-rgya*: see *gesture*, *hand gesture* and *seal(s)*
mudrā *(las-kyi) phyag-rgya*, Skt. *(karma-) mudrā*: see *seal*, *action*
Mūlasarvāstivāda tradition *gzhi thams-cad yod-par smra-ba*, 429-30; see also *Sarvāstivāda order*
music, eighteen appendages of *rol-mo'i bye-brag bco-brgyad*, 98
nāga *klu*: spirits of the water and subterranean regions, usually depicted as serpents, 132, 423, 424, 427, 438-9, 441-2, 451, 452, 454, 466, 481, 492, 514, 516, 609, 623, 629, 630, 631, 632, 649, 663, 763, 764, 889, 939
nāginī *klu-mo*: a female nāga, 452, 629
nails, four *gzer-bzhi*, 647
Naiyāyika *rigs-pa-can*: an adherent of the Nyāya tradition of logic, 16, 65
naked ascetic *gcer-bu-pa*, Skt. *nirgrantha*: followers of Jainism in the Digambara tradition, 66; see also *Jaina*
narrative *rtogs-pa brjod-pa*, Skt. *avadāna*, 76
Naṭeśvara suborder of the Nāthapaṇṭhas *na-tha-partha'i nang-tshan naḍeshva-ra'i sde*, 504
natural descriptions *rang-bzhin brjod-pa*, Skt. *svabhavokti*: in poetics, the first ornament of sense (Skt. *arthā-laṃkāra*), 105
natural expression *rang-bzhin*: an attribute of the buddha-body of perfect rapture, according to the Great Perfection, 20, 32, 72, 128-9, 135, 144, 146, 161, 171, 174-5, 197, 199, 215, 246, 255, 257, 264, 294, 300, 302, 304, 308, 315, 317, 338, 341, 359, 403
according to the four cycles of the Esoteric Instructional Class of Atiyoga, 332
seven particular attributes of *rang-bzhin bdun*, 20, 124, 251
natural stems *rang-bzhin,* Skt. *prakṛti*: in grammar, i.e. stems, 100
natural nouns *ming*, Skt. *nāman*: i.e. nominal stems, 100
natural roots *byings*, Skt. *dhātu*, 100
natures, three *rang-bzhin gsum*, Skt. *tris-vabhāva*: see *essential natures, three*
nectar(s) *bdud-rtsi*, Skt. *amṛta*, 581, 755, 811, 820, 844, 848, 861, 867; see also *elixir*
deathless *'chi-med bdud-rtsi*, 548, 575, 613
five *bdud-rtsi lnga*, Skt. *pañcāmṛta*: sacramental substances, a commitment of Unsurpassed Yogatantra, 274
nectar-elixir *bdud-rtsi sman*, 619, 651, 775
nectar(-like instruction) *bdud-rtsi*, 422, 432, 577, 594; see also under *doctrine*
of esoteric instruction *man-ngag-gi bdud-rtsi*, 925
profound *bdud-rtsi zab-mo*, 416, 421
of secret injunctions *gsung-tshig bdud-rtsi*, 972
negation *dgag-pa*, Skt. *pratiṣedha*
explicit *med-dgag*, Skt. *prasajya-pratiṣedha*, 28, 164, 184, 196, 206, 208, 250, 326
implicitly affirmative *ma-yin dgag*, Skt. *paryudāsapratiṣedha*, 164, 208, 326
new translation school(s) *gsar-'gyur/gsar-ma-pa*: the teaching tradition(s) based on texts translated into Tibetan after the time of Smṛtijñānakīrti, 11, 198-205, 441-2, 550, 560, 565, 633, 643, 657, 665, 666, 671, 672, 675, 677, 683, 695, 708, 713, 720, 724, 731, 748, 758, 762, 768, 789, 806, 807, 809, 811, 823, 824, 827, 833, 836, 842, 852, 856, 861, 862, 872, 894, 898, 950, 954
in relation to the Ancient Translation School, 918-26
Ngorpa *ngor-pa*: a subsect of the Sakyapa school, 850, 868
nihilism *chad-lta*, 66-8, 197, 343; see also *eternalism and nihilism*, *extreme(s)* and *extremist(s)*

Nirākāravādin *rnam-rdzun-pa*: adherents of Vijñānavāda who hold sensa to be false, 25, 161-2
Nirgrantha Jain *gcer-bu-pa*: the Digambara or naked ascetics within the Jain tradition, 432; see also *Jaina*
nirvāṇa *mya-ngan-las 'das*: the literal meaning in Tibetan is "gone beyond the sorrows of saṃsāra", 16, 19, 23, 29, 30, 32, 36, 37, 39, 49, 51-3, 70-2, 80, 84, 95, 109, 116, 118, 127, 170, 173-4, 183, 187, 194, 200, 202, 206, 213, 225, 229, 244, 248-9, 260, 263, 284, 303, 305-7, 312, 317, 319, 321, 324-5, 329, 331-2, 340, 344, 372, 415, 426, 428, 432, 433, 435, 436, 437, 447, 494, 500, 502, 550, 588, 594, 614, 645, 660, 683, 726, 746, 764, 897, 898, 922, 924, 930, 947, 948; see also *quiescence*
  final *yongs-su mya-ngan-las 'das*, Skt. *parinirvāṇa*: the final passing away of buddhas such as Śākyamuni, 75, 129, 131, 416, 426, 427, 428, 430, 435, 437, 438, 440, 441, 454, 508, 613, 943, 944, 948
non-Buddhist *phyi-pa*, 440, 471, 475, 485, 715, 936; see also *Hindu/Hinduism* and *Outsiders*
non-virtues, (ten) *mi-dge-ba (bcu)*, Skt. *(daśā)kuśala*, 13, 56, 58, 60-1, 64, 302-3
no understanding, those of *ma-rtogs-pa*, Skt. *apratipanna*, 13-16, 54, 62-4, 67, 873
nouns, table of *ming-gi kun-bshad*: in grammar, 101
Northern Treasures *byang-gter*: those discovered by Rikdzin Gödemcen, 782, 783, 802, 806, 808, 919
novice/novitiate *dge-tshul*, Skt. *śrāmaṇera*: a novice monk in the monastic tradition, 545, 566, 569, 676, 722, 723, 724, 726, 728, 731, 753, 758, 950; see also under *ordination* and *vows*
nucleus *snying-po*, Skt. *garbha*: the nucleus of reality, 27, 29, 31, 36, 71, 115, 154, 161, 174, 190, 192, 197, 199-201, 213, 216, 247, 268, 284, 299-302, 308, 326, 330, 333, 337, 345, 351, 366, 368, 372, 376, 378, 403, 409, 591, 746, 813, 897, 903, 924, 947, 973; see also *seed*
  of indestructible reality *rdo-rje snying-po*, Skt. *vajragarbha*, 336
  of the sugata *bde-gshegs snying-po*, Skt. *sugatagarbha*: the nucleus of enlightenment present in all sentient beings, 27, 116, 127, 146, 171, 173, 178, 189, 194, 263, 909
  of the tathāgata *de-gshegs snying-po*, Skt. *tathāgatagarbha*: the nucleus of enlightenment present in all sentient beings, 20, 27, 29, 32, 95, 147, 154, 171, 173-7, 186-7, 194, 198, 236, 291, 424
nun *dge-slong-ma*, Skt. *bhikṣuṇī*: i.e. fully-ordained, 424, 490, 546, 547, 647; see also under *ordination* and *vow(s)*
Nyang/Rong tradition *nyang/rong-lugs*, 397, 616, 617-87; see also *Zur tradition*
Nyingma (tradition/school) *rnying-ma*, 11, 12, 17, 22, 28, 32-3, 35, 36, 39, 40, 47, 208, 247, 394, 395, 396, 397, 399, 413-4, 550, 657, 667, 675, 692, 883-940; see also *Ancient Translation School*
Nyingmapa *rnying-ma-pa*: an adherent of the Nyingma or Ancient Translation School, 19, 29, 39, 86, 115, 378, 394, 396, 397, 599, 633, 695, 724, 735-6, 768, 780, 794, 816, 822, 824, 833, 834, 838, 839, 842, 847, 850, 852, 879, 883-940, 951, 957, 965
oath of allegiance, to bind under *dam-la btags-pa*, 469, 472, 481, 513, 514, 519, 584, 622, 629, 639, 764, 802, 939; see also *commitment(s)*
Object of Cutting *gcod-yul*, 395, 546, 577, 762, 763, 833, 853, 926, 929
obscuration(s) *sgrib(-pa)*, Skt. *āvaraṇa*, 17, 20, 23, 24, 27, 29, 32, 72, 127, 132, 140, 159, 171, 175-7, 191-2, 210, 212-13, 248, 323, 336, 345, 449, 573, 625, 628, 659, 767, 811, 902, 906, 908
  four *sgrib-bzhi*, 923
  three *sgrib-gsum*, 469
  two *sgrib-gnyis*, 51, 142, 159, 167, 175, 378
  two kinds of suddenly arisen *glo-bur-pa'i sgrib gnyis*, 116, 139
Oḍḍiyāna Tradition of Ritual Service and Attainment *o-rgyan bsnyen-sgrub*, 578; see also *rites of/ritual service and*

attainment of the three indestructible realities
offering *mchod-pa*, Skt. *pūjā*, 53, 60, 99, 122, 124, 248, 253, 255, 266, 290, 350, 356-7, 420, 422, 429, 499, 546, 561, 565, 583, 588, 591, 593, 619, 620, 630, 652, 656, 714, 758, 766, 848, 863, 864; see also *torma*
goddesses *mchod-pa'i lha-mo*, 624, 638,
water *yon-chab*, 543
ogre *srin-po*, Skt. *rākṣasa*: a cannibalistic demon, 136, 454, 455, 516, 520, 715, 887, 939
ogress *srin-mo*, Skt. *rākṣasī*, 133, 455, 507
supine *srin-mo gan-rkyal-du bskyel-ba*, 510
omniscience *thams-cad mkhyen-pa-nyid*, Skt. *sarvajñatā*, 24, 82, 96, 108, 154, 176, 289, 298, 305, 342, 425, 707, 887, 888, 913
openness, vast *rgya-yan chen-po*, 305, 324
oracular mirror *pra-sen*: employed in divination to detect past, present and future events, 514
orders, four *tshogs rnam-pa bzhi*, 137, 226; see also *assemblies, four (ordinary/ monastic)*
ordination *rab-tu byung-ba*, Skt. *pravajyā*: i.e. as a renunciate, 93, 436, 464, 469, 488, 515, 524, 525, 552, 667, 673, 675, 681, 715, 731, 753, 849; see also *vows*
complete/full, of a monk/nun *bsnyen-rdzogs*, Skt. *upasampadā*, 226, 250, 524, 601, 676, 678, 681, 688, 694, 723, 806, 821, 823
according to the current rite *lta-da'i cho-ga*, 435
novitiate *dge-tshul*, Skt. *śrāmaṇera*, 226, 524, 681, 723, 841
three levels/stages of *(so-thar) rnam-pa gsum/tshig(s)-gsum rim-nod-pa*, 524, 618
ornaments *rgyan*, Skt. *alaṃkāra*
body *sku-rgyan*, 786, 845
bone *rus-pa'i rgyan*, 581, 583, 638
five wheels of inexhaustible *mi-zad-pa'i rgyan-gyi 'khor-lo lnga*, 866
in poetics, 105; of enigmatic innuendo *gab-tshig-gi rgyan*, Skt. *prahelikā*, 105; phonetic *sgra'i rgyan*, Skt. *śabdālaṃkāra*, 105; of sense *don-rgyan*, Skt. *arthālaṃkāra*, 105
Outsiders *phyi-rol-pa*: i.e. non-Buddhists, 68-70, 82, 89, 104, 169
Pacification *zhi-byed*: the tradition of Padampa Sangye, 395, 657, 762, 833, 853, 926, 929; see also listed in the first section of the Bibliography
pāda *rkang-pa*: a metrical line (lit. "foot") of verse, 93, 105-6
Paiśācī *sha-za'i skad*, 107
paṇḍita *mkhas-pa*, Skt. *paṇḍita*: a scholar or expert, *passim*; see also *scholar*
long-eared hat of *paṇ-zhva rna-ring*, 875
parable *gleng-gzhi*, Skt. *nidāna*, 76-7
paradigms of the roots *byings-mdo*, Skt. *dhātupāṭha*: in grammar, 100-1
path(s) *lam*, Skt. *mārga/patha*, *passim*; see also under *continuum/continua* and *truth(s)*
of Atiyoga: see *meditation of Atiyoga*
of conclusion: see *path, final/of conclusion*
of connection/connecting *sbyor-lam*, Skt. *prayogamārga*, 115, 175, 236, 288, 363, 411; receptiveness on *sbyor-lam bzod-pa*, Skt. *kṣānti*: on this, see Longcenpa, *Treasury of Spiritual and Philosophical Systems*, (pp. 143-6), 125; middling degree of receptiveness on *bzod-'bring*, 228; supreme phenomenon on *chos-mchog*, Skt. *agradharma*, 236; feeling of warmth on *sbyor-lam drod*, Skt. *uṣmagata*, 159, 236; climax/summit on *rtse-mo*, Skt. *mūrdhāna*, 236
definitive, of skilful means *thabs-kyi nges-pa'i lam*: according to Anuyoga, 34, 286, 368-9
final/of conclusion *mthar-lam*, Skt. *niṣṭhamārga*, 266, 281, 288, 312, 521
five *lam lnga*, Skt. *pañcamārga*: of bodhisattvas, 30, 142, 155, 159, 174, 230, 237, 634
five *lam-lnga*: according to Anuyoga, 34, 288, 369
five *lam lnga*: according to Mahāyoga, 278-81
four: see *paths of learning, four*
of (great) desire *'dod-chags (chen-po'i) lam*, 288, 364, 818; esoteric instructions of *chags-lam-gyi man-ngag*, 818
indestructible *rdo-rje lam*, Skt. *vajra-mārga*, 404

of insight *mthong-lam*, Skt. *darśana-mārga*, 129, 155, 175, 228, 236, 247, 259, 281, 288, 411, 489
of learning *slob-pa'i lam*, 192, 196-7, 259; four *slob-pa'i lam bzhi*, 231, 236, 287, 923
liberating, of discriminative awareness *shes-rab-kyi rnam-grol lam*: according to Anuyoga, 34, 286-7, 368-9; three ways of entering *rnam-grol lam-gyi 'jug-pa rnam gsum*, 286-7
of liberation *grol-lam*, 643, 683; two modes of *grol-lam rnam-gnyis*: according to Mahāyoga, 277-8; three aspects of the gradual *rim-gyis-pa grol-lam rnam-gsum*: according to Mahāyoga 34, 278-81
of meditation *bsgom-lam*, Skt. *bhāvanāmārga*, 155, 159, 175, 236, 281, 288, 411
of a messenger (or intermediary in the sexual practices) *pho-nya'i lam*, 830
of no-more-learning *mi-slob-pa'i lam*, Skt. *aśaikṣamārga*, 155, 159, 237, 247, 282, 287-8, 411, 493
of provisions *tshogs-lam*, Skt. *sambhāramārga*, 159, 175, 228, 236, 288, 363, 441
of skilful means *thabs-lam*, 618, 619, 643; two *thabs-lam rnam-gnyis*: according to Mahāyoga, 277; two esoteric instructions of *thabs-lam-gyi man-ngag gnyis*: according to Anuyoga, 34, 286, 368
sublime eightfold *'phags lam yan-lag brgyad*, Skt. *aṣṭāṅgamārga*, 236
two *lam gnyis*: according to Anuyoga, the definitive path of skilful means and liberating path of discriminative awareness *(thabs-kyi nges-pa'i lam-dang shes-rab rnam-par grol-ba'i lam)*, 286-7, 368-9
two stages of *lam-gyi rim-gnyis*: according to Mahāyoga, 34, 276-81
Path and Fruit *lam-'bras*: the esoteric instructions of Virūpa primarily preserved within the Sakyapa tradition, 395, 576, 578, 657, 806, 813, 853, 923, 926, 930
patience *bzod-pa*, Skt. *kṣānti*, 94, 193, 306, 902; see also *receptiveness*
perfection of *bzod-pa'i pha-rol-tu phyin-pa*, Skt. *kṣāntipāramitā*, 902
patriarchs, line of *gtad-rabs*, 396, 410, 432-9
(perfect) rapture *longs-spyod (rdzogs-pa)*, Skt. *sambhoga*, 123-4, 141, 145, 254-5, 349, 357
perfection stage *rdzogs-rim*, Skt. *sampanna-krama*: the subtle phase of creative visualisation in the vehicles of tantra, which may be either elaborate, involving yogic exercises, or unelaborate, involving meditation on emptiness, 34, 36, 85, 87, 204, 251, 274, 278-81, 284, 291, 293, 295, 300-2, 305, 312-13, 320, 335, 350, 359, 362-5, 367, 370, 461, 464, 485-9, 496, 523, 531, 537, 571-2, 647, 681, 720, 721, 723, 726, 829, 836, 844, 853, 862, 876, 877, 880, 898, 923
permanence *rtag-pa*, Skt. *nitya*, 20, 186, 211-12, 877, 902
permissory initiation *rjes-gnang*, 673, 826, 866, 870; see also *mandate*
perseverance *brtson-'grus*, Skt. *vīrya*: 94, 153-4, 272, 281, 286, 297, 304, 306, 353, 615, 620, 723, 833, 850, 853, 857, 861, 902
perfection of *brtson-'grus-kyi pha-rol-tu phyins-pa*, Skt. *vīryapāramitā*, 902
Phakmotrupa *phag-mo-gru-pa*: the followers of the Kagyü tradition of Phakmotrupa, 590, 778
Phakpa calendrical system *'phags-lugs*: the system established by Chögyel Phakpa, 400
phenomena *chos*, *passim*; see also *dharma*
eighty-four thousand *chos brgyad-khri bzhi-stong*, 55; see also *conflicting emotions*
twenty-one thousand *(dug gsum-ka cha-mnyam-pa-la) nyis-khri chig-stong*, 55; see also *desire*, *delusion* and *hatred*
philosophical (and spiritual) system(s)/ tenets *grub-mtha'*, Skt. *siddhānta*: 11, 16, 23, 26, 30, 37, 63-4, 67-8, 88, 91, 162, 167-8, 176, 184-5, 190, 204, 208-9, 216, 249, 260, 287, 324, 340, 404, 411, 463, 572, 578, 619, 625, 669, 678, 845, 851, 873, 888, 925, 930
four *grub-mtha' bzhi*, 178, 184, 923
five basic, of wrong view held by Outsiders *phyi-rol lta-ba log-pa'i rtsa-ba'i grub-mtha' lnga*, 82; see also *five*

sophistic schools of the extremist masters under *sophistry*
Phukpa calendrical systems, old and new *phug-lugs gsar-rnying*, 400
pilgrimage place *gnas(-chen)*, 567, 609, 676, 807, 819, 820, 847, 863, 866-7, 889, 957
pinnacle/summit of existence *srid-pa'i rtse(-mo)*, Skt. *bhavāgra*, 62, 69-71, 94, 197
pious attendants *nyan-thos*, Skt. *śrāvaka*: defined, 223; 24, 25, 35, 75, 78, 82, 90-1, 137, 153, 156, 158-9, 174, 179, 180, 186, 196, 203, 220, 230, 248, 294, 302, 315, 411, 432, 434, 440, 908, 913, 931, 932
piśācī *phra-men*: female animal-headed, cannibalistic deities of the wrathful maṇḍala, 132
piṭaka *sde-snod*: this comprises all the textual traditions of the diverse vehicles of the transmitted precepts; defined, 78-80; 259, 481, 498, 515, 665; see also *appraisal of textual traditions*
  Abhidharmapiṭaka *chos mngon-pa'i sde-snod*, 17, 77-9, 91, 102, 424, 428, 430, 431, 650, 730, 753
  of Anuyoga *anu-yo-ga'i sde-snod rnams*, 289
  bodhisattvapiṭaka of extensive teaching *shin-tu rgyas-pa chen-po byang-chub sems-dpa'i sde-snod*, Skt. **mahā-vaipulyabodhisattvapiṭaka*, 77-8, 154
  of the Esoteric Instructional Class *man-ngag-sde'i sde-snod*, 332-3
  of the final transmitted precepts *bka' tha-ma'i sde-snod*, 178
  Fourth *sde-snod bzhi-pa*: the Mantrapiṭaka of the Awareness-holders, 78, 95-6
  of the greater vehicle *theg-pa chen-po'i sde-snod-rnams*, 78, 266, 431, 456
  holder of *sde-snod 'dzin-pa*, Skt. *piṭaka-dhara*, 656
  of Kriyātantra, 270-1
  of Mahāyoga, 283
  Mantrapiṭaka of the Awareness-holders *rig-'dzin sngags-kyi sde-snod*: the Fourth Piṭaka, 17, 31, 77-8, 95-6, 257, 968; see also *piṭaka of the resultant secret mantra* and *of the vehicle of indestructible reality*
  of the Mental Class *sems-sde'i sde-snod*, 325-6
  of the pious attendants *nyan-thos-kyi sde-snod*, 78, 226, 230, 895
  of prose and verse combined *dbyangs-bsnyad-pa'i sde*, 52
  of the resultant secret mantra *'bras-bu gsang-sngags-kyi sde-snod*: the Mantrapiṭaka of the Awareness-holders, 241
  of the self-centred buddhas *rang-rgyal-gyi sde-snod*, 230
  of the Spatial Class *klong-sde'i sde-snod*, 329
  Sūtrapiṭaka *mdo-sde'i sde-snod*, 17, 52, 73, 76-9, 423-4, 428, 430
  tantrapiṭaka *rgyud-sde*: see under *tantra(s)*
  three/Tripiṭaka *sde-snod gsum*, 76, 78-80, 203, 405, 428, 429, 436, 437, 441, 468, 511, 560, 619, 888, 893
  three lower *sde-snod 'og-ma gsum*, 259
  of Ubhayatantra, 272
  of the vehicle of indestructible reality: the Mantrapiṭaka of the Awareness-holders, 259
  Vinayapiṭaka *'dul-ba'i sde-snod*, 17, 77-80, 423, 428, 430, 431, 730
  of Yogatantra, 273
plainness *phyal-ba*, 370
planets, (ten) *gza'(-bcu)*, 104, 351, 469, 930
play *rtsal*, 584, 829, 832, 849; see also *display* and *expressive play/power*
Podongpa *bo-dong-pa*, 833, 839, 850
poetics *snyan-ngag(-gi rig-gnas)*, Skt. *kāvyavidyā*, 18, 103-5, 577, 677, 705, 727, 731, 821
Point of Enlightenment *byang-chub snying-po*, Skt. *bodhimaṇḍa*, 115, 129, 412, 416, 419
poison(s) *dug*, Skt. *viṣa*: i.e. the conflicting emotions
  five *dug-lnga*, 253, 332, 767, 924
  three *dug-gsum*, 18, 24, 33-4, 55, 77, 88, 159, 229, 273, 277
Pön *bon*, 690, 936-7, 938-40
Pönpo *bon-po*, 508, 509, 632-3, 665, 690, 760, 762, 765, 791, 936-40
posture(s) *'dug-stangs*
  of a bodhisattva *sems-dkyil*, 879
  of the buddha-body of reality *chos-sku'i 'dug-stangs*, 594
  dramatic *stangs-stabs*, 304

lotus *pad-ma dkyil-krung*, Skt. *paryaṅka*, 190
of a ṛṣi *drang-srong-gi 'dug-stang*, 572
sedentary vajra-like *rdo-rje skyil-mo-krung*, 304
three *'dug-stangs gsum*: according to Atiyoga, 907; see also *three supportive essentials of the body* under *All-Surpassing Realisation*
power(s) *stobs*, Skt. *bala*, 201, 236, 902
five *stobs-lnga*, Skt. *pañcabala*, 236
occult *nus-pa/mthu*, *passim*
perfection of *stobs-kyi pha-rol-tu phyin-pa*, Skt. *balapāramitā*, 902
ten *yon-tan stobs-bcu*, Skt. *daśa-tathāgatabala*: of the tathāgatas, 22, 171, 188, 266
ten *dbang bcu*, Skt. *daśavaśitā*, 405
ten *stobs-bcu*, Skt. *daśabala*: those cultivated by arhats and bodhisattvas, 435
practice which divides saṃsāra from nirvāṇa *'khor-'das ru-shan*, 500
Prakrit *phal-skad*, Skt. *prākṛta*, 107
Prāsaṅgika-Madhyamaka *dbu-ma thal-'gyur*, 26, 28, 162, 164-9, 185, 206-8; see also *Madhyamaka*
dialectic *thal-'gyur*, Skt. *prasaṅga*: the *reductio ad absurdum* in Buddhist logic, 69
Prāsaṅgika-Mādhyamika *dbu-ma thal-'gyur-ba*: an adherent of the Prāsaṅgika dialectic as the appropriate form of argument for the Madhyamaka school, 164
prātimokṣa *so-thar*: see under *vows*
preceptor *mkhan-po*, Skt. *upādhyāya*, 47, 425, 509, 513, 514, 515, 522, 524, 552, 565, 566, 568, 569, 601, 675, 678, 688, 694, 708, 714, 728, 734, 736, 753, 777, 784, 798, 806, 842, 868, 871, 879, 888
Precious Jewels, Three *dkon-mchog gsum*, Skt. *triratna*, 59, 69-70, 95, 203, 350, 468, 523, 583, 592, 644, 707, 743, 768, 862, 970, 973
predictions/prophecies/prophetic declarations *lung-bstan*, Skt. *vyākaraṇa*, 76, 91, 397, 416, 438, 440, 498, 577, 584, 586, 621, 638, 676, 698, 722, 726, 745, 747, 755, 765, 766, 772, 784, 785, 786, 807, 810, 812, 814, 820, 829, 832, 839, 842, 844, 846, 847, 855, 893, 923, 927, 934-5, 944, 959, 960-1; see also under *inventory of treasure doctrines*
indestructible *rdo-rje lung-bstan*, 801, 823, 838, 853, 854, 859, 930
preliminary practice *sngon-'gro*, 567; see also *ground, actual* and under *yoga(s)*
prepositional prefixes *nye-bsgyur*, Skt. *upasarga*: in grammar, 101
pride *nga-rgyal*, Skt. *abhimāna*, 12, 55
primordial purity *ka-dag*: in Cutting Through Resistance, 139, 176, 342, 403, 550, 566, 585, 619, 679, 726, 856, 971
original ground in which primordial purity and spontaneous presence are coalesced *ka-dag lhun-grub zung-'jug gdod-ma'i gzhi*: according to Atiyoga, 207
pristine cognition(s) *ye-shes*, Skt. *jñāna*, *passim*; see also *buddha-mind*
of accomplishment *bya-ba (grub-pa)'i ye-shes*, Skt. *kṛtyānusthānajñāna*, 23, 141, 283, 356
blissful, radiant and non-conceptual *bde-gsal mi-rtog-pa*, 340-1, 362
blessing/consecration of *ye-shes-kyi byin-brlabs*, 272, 353, 831
coalescence/indivisibility of pristine cognition and reality's expanse *dbying-ye dbyer-med*: according to Anuyoga, 207; see also *coalescence of the expanse of reality and pristine cognition*
co-emergent *lhan-cig skyes-pa'i ye-shes*, Skt. *sahajajñāna*, 34, 286, 335, 340, 345, 368, 773, 877
contrasted with consciousness, 180-2
of discernment *sor-rtog ye-shes*, Skt. *pratyavekṣaṇajñāna*, 23, 117, 283, 356, 906
of the expanse of reality *chos-dbyings ye-shes*, Skt. *dharmadhātujñāna*, 19, 22, 117, 140, 283, 356
eye of *ye-shes-kyi spyan*, Skt. *jñāna-cakṣuh*, 535, 873
five *ye-shes lnga*, Skt. *pañcajñāna*, 22-3, 125, 128, 140-2, 273, 288, 342, 352, 357, 594
four kinds of *ye-shes bzhi*, 124, 251
genuine/real *don-gyi ye-shes*, 745, 830, 837

of intuitive awareness/that is intuitively aware *rang-rig-pa'i ye-shes*, 115, 198, 326, 413
irresistible descent of *ye-shes btsan-thabs-su dbab-pa*, 39, 247
matrix of *ye-shes spyi-gzugs*, 309, 313, 876
which may be exemplified *dpe'i ye-shes*, 837
mirror-like *me-long (lta-bu'i) ye-shes*, Skt. *ādarśajñāna*, 22, 140-1, 283, 313, 356
perfection of *ye-shes-kyi pha-rol-tu phyin-pa*, Skt. *jñānapāramitā*, 902
which qualitatively knows (the view) *ji-lta-ba mkhyen-pa'i ye-shes*, 117, 127, 140, 141
which quantitatively knows (phenomena) *ji-snyed-pa mkhyen-pa'i ye-shes*, 127, 140-2
of sameness *mnyam-nyid ye-shes*, Skt. *samatājñāna*, 19, 22, 117, 141, 192, 283, 356, 905
sixteen moments of *ye-shes bcu-drug* (i.e. *sems-kyi skad-cig bcu-drug*, Skt. *ṣodaśacittakṣaṇa*), 226-7
three kinds of *ye-shes rnam-gsum*: according to the *Sūtra of the Descent to Laṅkā*, 180-1
three subtle *ye-shes phra-ba gsum*, 342
twofold *ye-shes gnyis*: of arhats, 227
wheel of *ye-shes-kyi 'khor-lo*, 915
privy seal *rgal-tshig/sgar-tshig*, 787
profound/profundity *zab*: the quality of discriminative awareness which is contrasted with vast or extensive (*rgyas*) skilful means, 28, 37, 75, 78, 84, 184, 247, 305, 321, 329, 331, 335, 344, 393, 412, 416, 440, 448, 468, 488, 677, 707, 726, 744, 830, 839, 845, 871, 907, 920, 923, 927, 931
promulgation of the doctrinal wheel *chos-'khor bskor-ba*, Skt. *dharmacakra-pravartana*: see *doctrinal wheel(s)*
irreversible *phyir mi-ldog-pa*: the third turning of the wheel, 154, 187-8, 190, see also under *doctrinal wheel(s)*; vehicle of the *phyir mi-ldog pa'i theg-pa*, 947
promulgators who were masters of the greater vehicle, two *theg-chen-gyi slob-dpon shing-rta gnyis*: Nāgārjuna and Asaṅga, 180, 182, 184, 300-1, 440-1, 849, 903
promulgators of India and Tibet *'phags-bod-kyi shing-rta (chen-po)*, 859, 873
proof *sgrub-pa*: in logic, 101-2, 209, 327, 874, 895, 907, 917, 924, 926, 929-33
syllogistic *gtan-tshigs*, 708; see also *(logical) axioms*
propensities *bag-chags*, Skt. *vāsanā*: residual tendencies established in the consciousness of the ground-of-all by past actions, 35, 55-6, 79, 116, 127, 161, 167, 172, 183, 195, 207, 209, 214-15, 221, 228, 258, 279-80, 288, 324, 333, 416, 641, 658, 671, 677, 726, 744-5, 764, 767, 807, 809, 843, 860, 903
five *bag-chags lnga*: of the subject-object dichotomy, 357
prophecies/prophetic declarations *lung-bstan*, Skt. *vyākaraṇa*: see *predictions/prophecies/prophetic declarations*
prose *lhug-pa*, Skt. *gadya*: in poetics, 105, 107
prosody *sdeb-sbyor*, Skt. *chandovidyā*, 18, 103, 105-6, 577, 723, 727, 729, 730, 731, 821
protector(s) of the doctrine/teaching *chos-skyong/bstan-srung*, Skt. *dharmapāla*, 406, 580, 581, 587, 589, 591, 601, 608, 614, 621, 623, 659, 665, 670, 727, 758, 760, 763, 765, 775-6, 777, 802, 829, 847
"active", of Yamāri *las-gshin*, 615
of the transmitted precepts *bka'-srung*, 581, 584, 587, 632, 644, 815, 866, 928
protectress (of mantra) *sngags-srung-ma*, 580, 587, 815, 843, 849, 865
provisions *tshogs*, Skt. *sambhāra*, 29, 36, 168-9, 171, 220-1, 228, 247-8, 251, 253-5, 258, 288, 292, 297, 345, 411, 412, 492, 621, 630, 658
of merit *bsod-nams-kyi tshogs*, Skt. *puṇyasambhāra*, 26, 29, 115, 146, 168, 177, 192, 255, 303, 305, 411, 420, 462, 625
of pristine cognition *ye-shes-kyi tshogs*, Skt. *jñānasambhāra*, 26, 29, 115, 147, 168, 177, 192, 255, 302-3, 411, 420, 462
two *tshogs-gnyis*, 26, 30, 175, 194-5, 197, 235, 244, 266, 332, 335, 379, 420, 462, 831

two, of skilful means and discriminative awareness *thabs-shes tshogs-gnyis*, 192

provisional meaning *drang-don*, Skt. *neyārtha*: see under *meaning*

psychophysical bases *khams*, Skt. *dhātu*, 21, 93, 131, 170, 212, 217, 224, 247, 251, 259, 276, 322, 334, 367, 421, 424, 900

eighteen *khams bco-brgyad*, Skt. *aṣṭadaśadhātu*, 13, 55, 513

pulse(s) *'gros*, 258

of the active energy currents *las-rlung-gi rgyu-ba*, 877; see also *vital energy*

of the energy channels, currents and seminal points *rtsa-rlung thig-le'i 'gros*, 829; see also under *energy channels(s)/pathway(s)*

four *'gros-bzhi*, 923

Pure Abodes *gtsang-ris gnas*, Skt. *śuddhādhivāsa*, 15, 62, 413, 449

pure essence(s)/essential substance(s) *dvangs-ma*: the elements in their refined state, 264, 281-2, 338, 340, 543, 634, 642

six *dvangs-ma drug*, 264

pure human laws, sixteen *mi-chos gtsang-ma bcu-drug*, 59-60, 512

pure land *(sangs-rgyas-kyi) zhing-khams*, Skt. *buddhakṣetra*, 722, 812, 890; see also *buddha-field*

terrestrial *sa'i zhing-khams*, 832

purification *sbyong-ba*, 265, 304 and *passim*

two modes of *sbyong-tshul gnyis*: according to Mahāyoga, the creation and perfection stages, 279

purificatory fast *bsnyen-gnas*, Skt. *upavāsa/poṣadha*, 58, 416, 429, 946; see also under *vows*

purity(ies) *dag-pa*, Skt. *śuddhi*, 37, 154, 170, 186, 212, 251-3, 272-3, 293, 298, 306, 313, 316, 320, 324, 326, 348, 354, 518

three *dag-pa gsum*: according to Kriyātantra, 35, 295-6, 349

three *dag-pa gsum*: an axiom of Mahāyoga, 275-6

two *dag-pa gnyis*, 139-40

Puṣya *rgyal*: January to February, 809, 946

quiescence *zhi-ba*: i.e. nirvāṇa, 113, 116, 164, 167, 175, 188, 199, 226, 234, 314, 340-2; see also *nirvāṇa*

rājā *rā-dza*: an Indian prince or petty king *(rgyal-po)*, 538

rakta *rak-ta*: blood or a sacramental substance representing it, 867

Rañjana *lanytsha*: an ornamental Indian script, widely used among Newari Buddhists, 729

real nature *de-kho-na-nyid*, Skt. *tattva*: a synonym for reality *(chos-nyid*, Skt. *dharmatā)*, 305-6 and *passim*

one's own *bdag-gi de-kho-na-nyid*: according to Kriyātantra, 32, 33, 207, 263-4

realisation *rtogs-pa*, Skt. *adhigama*, 16-17, 31, 33, 36, 71-2, 79, 85, 94, 116, 153, 159, 165, 180, 195-6, 201, 215, 223, 227, 229, 234, 243, 263, 266, 277, 287, 293, 295, 305-6, 318, 320, 322, 330, 332, 338, 341, 343, 345-7, 350, 404, 406, 412, 420, 440, 442, 447, 460, 481, 540, 543, 547, 585, 603, 609, 637, 639, 640, 641, 652, 655, 659, 680, 691, 721, 722, 723, 727, 743, 766, 773, 813, 818, 822, 897, 931, 968

emergent *mngon-rtogs*, Skt. *abhisamaya*, 341

four kinds of *rtogs-bzhi*: according to Mahāyoga, 275

supreme *rtogs-pa chen-po*, 116

two kinds of *rtogs-pa gnyis*, 16-17, 27, 71-2, 176-7

realities

twenty-five resultant *'bras-chos nyer-lnga*, 34, 35, 267, 288-9, 369

three *de-kho-na-nyid gsum*: of the *Tantra of the Secret Nucleus*, 915

reality *chos-nyid*, Skt. *dharmatā*: the great emptiness of all things, defined in Longcenpa, *Treasury of the Supreme Vehicle*, (p. 82), 19, 20, 33, 37, 52, 68, 95, 103, 108, 116, 118-19, 123, 127, 139, 142, 154, 168, 172-3, 175, 177, 180, 182, 184-5, 191-2, 194, 198-9, 201-6, 209, 211, 214-15, 217, 236, 245, 251-2, 254-6, 258, 260-1, 263-5, 270-2, 277, 285, 287-8, 293, 295, 299, 301-2, 305-6, 308-9, 311, 317, 319, 322-30, 332-3, 338, 340-1, 344, 349-50, 354, 359, 366-8, 398, 413, 424, 448, 501, 540, 548, 556, 569, 571, 594, 603, 604, 615, 625, 640, 642, 879, 900, 901, 906, 907, 930, 932, 933, 971; see also *absolute (nature/reality)* and *abiding nature (of reality)*

excellent analysis of *legs-pa rnam-par phye-ba*, 153-4
modes of *yin-lugs*: the specific attributes of the abiding nature of reality, 37, 319, 336
natural sound of *chos-nyid rang-sgra*, 134-5
realms *khams*, Skt. *dhātu*: see *(world) realms*
reason/reasoning *rigs-pa*, Skt. *yukti*, 53, 94, 127, 163-4, 169, 216, 226, 275, 920
threefold *tshad-ma gsum*: the three kinds of valid cognition, 970
receptiveness *bzod-pa*, Skt. *kṣānti*, 125, 227; see also *path of connection* and *patience*
to the after-effect of the perception of the doctrine *rjes-shes bzod-pa*, Skt. *anvayajñānakṣānti*, 227
to the perception of the doctrine *chos-shes bzod-pa*, Skt. *dharmajñānakṣānti*, 226
recitation *bzlas-brjod*, Skt. *jāpa*: i.e. of mantras, 246, 266, 270-2, 287, 304, 320, 351, 356, 368, 548, 662
recollection(s) *dran-pa*, Skt. *smṛti*, 255, 302, 308, 324, 368, 573, 774, 906
four essential recollections *dran-pa nyer-gzhag bzhi*, Skt. *catuḥsmṛtyupasthāna*: often referred to as the "four foundations of mindfulness", 236
refuge(s) *skyabs-'gro*, Skt. *śaraṇagamana*, 16, 70, 865
lord of *skyabs-rje*, 873
threefold *skyabs-gsum*, Skt. *triśaraṇa*, 69, 728
refutation *'gag-pa*, 101, 163, 170, 209, 873, 874, 907, 924, 926, 929-33, 940; see also *negation*
regulation *nges-pa*, 51-3; see also *vows*
relative appearance *kun-rdzob*, Skt. *saṃvṛti*, 20, 26, 28, 31, 33, 94, 119, 140, 162-3, 166-8, 171, 178, 206, 208, 210, 225, 233, 245, 247, 249, 251, 264, 270, 278, 320, 350, 903, 904, 905, 931
two aspects of *kun-rdzob gnyis*, 166
relative truth *kun-rdzob-kyi bden-pa*, Skt. *saṃvṛtisatya*: see under *truth(s)*
reliance, four kinds of *rton-pa bzhi*, Skt. *catuḥpratiśaraṇa*, 186, 215-16, 871
relics *ring-bsrel*, 435, 550, 553, 561, 564, 572, 594, 758, 792; see also *reliquary* and *remains*
in the form of letters and stūpas, 656
four kinds of *ring-bsrel rnam-bzhi*, 38, 337
of Śākyamuni/the tathāgata(s), 427, 456, 471, 626; see also *remains of Śākyamuni*
tooth relics of the Buddha *mtshems*, 433
reliquary *gdung-rten*, 777-8; see also *stūpa(s)*
remains *gdung*, 656, 758, 777-8, 792; see also *relics*
five (large) *gdung (chen) lnga*, 561, 572, 594
in the form of the syllables OṂ ĀḤ HŪṂ, 564
and relics *gdung-dang ring-bsrel*, 557, 572
representing the five buddha families, 563
of Śākyamuni, 435, 626, 786
renunciate *rab-byung*, Skt. *pravrājaka*: one who has assumed the preliminary monastic vows, 93, 421, 519, 677, 696, 698, 806; see also under *vows*
renunciation *spang-ba*, Skt. *prahāṇa*, 16, 24, 37, 63, 72, 80, 116, 158, 184, 225-6, 251, 254, 273, 302-3, 316, 319, 331, 341, 370-1, 418, 422, 426, 550, 619, 665, 809, 811, 822, 869, 911; see also *trainings, four correct*
five, eight, ten and all things to be renounced *spang-bya lnga-brgyad-bcu-dang thams-cad*, 226
supreme *spang-ba chen-po*, 116
two kinds of *spang-ba rnam-gnyis*, 27, 175-7
result(s) *'bras-bu*, Skt. *phala*: this term indicates above all the resultant attainment of buddhahood, *passim*; see also under *continuum/continua*
of Anuyoga, 287-9, 369
of an arhat *dgra-bcom-pa*, 227
of Atiyoga, 372
according to the bodhisattvas, 237
according to the Brahmā vehicle, 62
eight *'bras-bu brgyad*, 227
entering the stream to nirvāṇa *rgyun-du zhugs-pa*, Skt. *srota'āpanna*, 227
four *'bras-bu bzhi*, 227
of Kriyātantra, 270, 352
of Mahāyoga, 281-3, 363
according to the mundane vehicle, 60-1
not returning to saṃsāra *phyir mi-'ong-ba*, Skt. *anāgāmi*, 227
according to the pious attendants, 93, 227

according to the self-centred buddhas, 230-1
of separation from obscuration *bral-'bras*, 192, 194-5
tied to a single rebirth *lan-gcig phyir 'ong-ba*, Skt. *sakṛdāgāmi*, 227
of Ubhayatantra, 271-2, 353
of Yogatantra, 272-3, 357
retention *gzungs*, Skt. *dhāraṇī*, 201, 278, 405, 424, 435, 535, 704, 851; see also *dhāraṇī*
Rinpungpa *rin-spung-pa*, 954
rites *las*, 770, 831, 842; see also *enlightened activity(ies)*
of enrichment *rgyas*, Skt. *puṣṭi*, 283, 682, 920
four *las-bzhi*, 283, 478, 669, 721, 829, 844, 920; see also *enlightened activities, four kinds of*
of pacification *zhi*, Skt. *śānti*, 283, 682, 920
of sexual union and "liberation" *sbyor-sgrol*, 292-3, 363; see also *"liberate"/ "liberation"*
of subjugation or dominion *dbang*, Skt. *vaśa*, 283, 682, 920
of wrath *drag(-po mngon-spyod)*, Skt. *abhicāra*, 283, 398, 603, 673, 682, 713, 822, 920; see also *sorcery*
rite(s)/ritual(s) *cho-ga*, Skt. *vidhi*, 248, 608, 642, 676, 713, 729, 861, 864
bean-sprout *makṣa'i las-sbyor*, 870
descriptive basis for *mngon-rtogs*, 586
to ensure martial victory *gYul-rgyal-gyi cho-ga*, 665
pill *ril-bu'i las-sbyor*, 869
three kinds of *cho-ga gsum*: according to Mahāyoga, 279; see also *contemplations, three*
of the "Tie to the Higher Realms" *gnas-lung-gi cho-ga*, 603, 660-1
rites of/ritual service and attainment *bsnyen-sgrub*, Skt. *sevāsādhana*, 727, 805, 806-7, 810, 818, 828, 831, 837, 844, 852, 857, 863, 874
four branches of *bsnyen-sgrub yan-lag bzhi*, 280, 297, 494, 847, 903
four unions of *sbyor-ba bzhi*, 277; see also preceding entry
rite of attainment *sgrub-pa*, Skt. *sādhana*, 277, 476, 615, 738, 831, 848
rite of great attainment *sgrub-chen*, Skt. *mahāsādhana*, 277, 476, 718, 725, 727, 788, 791, 867
ritual service *bsnyen-pa*, Skt. *sevā*, 277, 476, 569, 615, 657, 711, 714, 762, 876; further *nye-bar bsnyen-pa*, Skt. *upasevā*, 277, 476
of the three indestructible realities *rdo-rje gsum-gyi bsnyen-sgrub*: the tradition of Orgyenpa Rincenpel, 853
Rong tradition of transmitted precepts *rong-lugs*: see *Nyang/Rong tradition*
root downfalls *rtsa-ltung*, Skt. *mūlāpatti*
four *rtsa-ltung bzhi*, 95, 235
nineteen *rtsa-ltung bcu-dgu*, 235
twenty *rtsa-ltung nyi-shu*, 235
rosary *phreng-ba*, Skt. *mālā*, 542
bodhi seed *bo-dhi-tse'i phreng-ba*, 543
rudrākṣa, 662
ṛṣi *drang-srong*: a saint or sage, 65, 99, 137, 435, 467
posture of *drang-srong-gi 'dug-stangs*, 572
rules: in grammar
for euphonic conjunction *mtsham-sbyor*, Skt. *sandhi*, 100-1, 730
for syllabic quantity, Skt. *vṛtta*, 101, 106
sacrament/sacramental objects/substances *dam-rdzas*, 363, 463, 581, 620, 631, 746, 748, 756, 757, 777, 781, 786, 789, 791, 797, 816, 846, 862, 864, 867
of accomplishment *grub-rdzas*, 609
five *dam-rdzas lnga*, 348; see also *nectars, five*
sacramental medicine *chos-sman*, 626; see also *elixir, spiritual*
Sage *thub-pa*, Skt. *muni*: lit. "one who is capable", used as an epithet of the buddhas, 73, 77, 88, 103, 153, 184, 200-1, 214, 300, 414
Sākāravādin *rnam-bden-pa*: Vijñānavādin who holds sensa to be veridical, 25, 161-2
Sakya *sa-skya*: the school, 395, 823
Sakyapa *sa-skya-pa*: the tradition founded at Sakya by Khön Köncok Gyelpo, which emphasises the teachings of the Path and Fruit, 11, 29, 203-4, 395, 578, 590, 664, 671, 695, 712, 731, 813, 822, 847, 850, 852, 853, 867, 868, 879, 922-3, 929, 931, 951, 953
sal forest/tree *shing sā-la*, Skt *sāla*, 426, 949

sameness *mnyam-nyid*, Skt. *samatā*, 31, 36, 37, 60, 62, 124, 208-9, 212, 215, 219, 229, 234, 245, 249, 251-3, 259, 306, 308, 316, 320, 322, 324, 360, 371, 899, 900, 916, 932

four modes of *mnyam-pa bzhi*: according to Mahāyoga, 275-6

saṃgha *dge-'dun*, 322, 429, 632, 762, 900, 928; see also *community* and *monastic community*

Sāṃkhya *grangs-can-pa*, 16, 64-5, 931

twenty-five categories of *shes-bya'i grangs nyi-shu rtsa-lnga*, 16, 64

Sammitīya *mang-pos bkur-ba*, 429-30

saṃsāra *'khor-ba*: the cyclical existence of sentient beings who suffer through the round of rebirth, 11, 14-16, 18, 19, 20, 23, 26, 27, 28, 29, 30, 31, 32, 35, 36, 37, 38, 39, 49, 51, 53-69, 75, 81-2, 94-5, 109, 116, 127, 146, 153, 166, 170, 173-4, 179, 183, 187, 193, 200, 202, 210, 213-14, 221, 223-6, 228-9, 237, 249, 253, 257, 260, 263, 265, 277, 280, 284, 302-3, 305-8, 312, 317, 321, 323-5, 329, 331-2, 334, 337, 339-41, 344, 363, 370, 372, 405, 447, 471, 571, 588, 593, 639, 641, 658, 683, 700, 726, 764, 767, 809, 897, 898, 900, 902, 907, 922, 924, 930, 940

four conditions of *'khor-ba'i rkyen bzhi*, 54-5

twenty elements of *'khor-ba'i chos nyi-shu*, 347

sandhi *mtsham-sbyor*: see *rules for euphonic conjunction*

Sanskrit *legs-sbyar*, 11, 107, 312, 515, 526, 705, 708, 713, 854, 891, 892, 893

sarvajñānamahāpaṇḍita: lit. "great paṇḍita of universal learning"—a title of Jamgön Kongtrül, 861

Sarvāstivāda order *thams-cad yod-par smra-ba*, 515; see also *Mūlasarvāstivāda tradition*

Sautrāntika *mdo-sde-pa*, 24-5, 90-1, 155, 158, 160, 162, 225, 440, 911

science(s) *rig-gnas*, Skt. *vidyā*, 59, 97-109, 441, 470, 481, 564, 575, 577, 578, 677, 719, 723, 724, 824, 850, 860, 869, 871, 874

common/ordinary/outer, (four) *thun-mong/phyi'i rig-gnas (bzhi)*, 89, 97-103, 463, 665, 705, 861, 871, 920

conventional *tha-snyad rig-gnas*, 679, 722, 731, 732, 836; see also preceding entry

five minor *rig-gnas chung lnga*, 103-7

five *rig-gnas lnga*, 98, 108, 860

inner *nang-pa'i rig-gnas*, Skt. *adhyātmavidyā*: i.e. Buddhist teaching, 89, 98, 102-3, 108-9, 665, 705, 860

linguistic *sgra'i rig-gnas*, Skt. *śabdavidyā*, 723, 727, 729; see also *grammar*

ten *rig-gnas bcu*, 821, 850, 860

scholar *paṇḍita*, 102, 144, 167, 249, 404, 405, 430, 441, 463, 492, 493, 498, 509, 515, 522, 526, 538, 578, 590, 592, 601, 603, 607, 609, 656, 664, 671, 708, 709, 736, 838, 874, 887, 888, 889-95

schools, eighteen *sde-pa bco-brgyad*, 429

scripture *gsung-rab*, Skt. *pravacana*, 51-3, 60, 69, 73, 99, 216, 221-2, 393, 429, 441, 493, 522, 537, 564, 577, 590, 595, 705, 730, 732, 827, 862, 871, 893, 931, 939, 971; see also *piṭaka*

nine branches of *gsung-rab-kyi yan-lag dgu*, 76

twelve branches of *gsung-rab-kyi yan-lag bcu-gnyis*, 17, 76

scriptural authority/transmission and logical/theoretical reasoning *lung-rigs*, 102, 189, 216, 290, 577, 708, 839, 873

scrutiny *dpyad-pa/brtag-pa*, 37, 214, 305, 314-15, 330, 332, 339, 344

eight subjects of *brtag-pa brgyad*, 97, 99

three types of *dpyad-gsum*, Skt. *triparīkṣā*: in logic, 102

seal(s) *phyag-rgya*, Skt. *mudrā*, 33, 255, 266, 271, 290, 308, 350, 377, 639, 829, 908-9; see also *gesture*, *hand-gesture* and *symbolic hand implements*

action *las-kyi phyag-rgya*, Skt. *karma-mudrā*: the mudrā or seal of action, who is the female consort, 293, 301, 356, 449, 462, 475, 476, 773, 815; embodying the enlightened activity which secures the five senses as the pristine cognition of accomplishment *bya-ba sgo-lnga phrin-las las-rgya*, 356

commitment *dam-tshig phyag-rgya*, Skt. *samayamudrā*, 356; of buddha-mind which secures the mind of conflicting emotions in the pristine

cognition of sameness *mnyam-nyid nyon-yid thugs-dam-rgya*, 356
doctrinal *chos-kyi phyag-rgya*, Skt. *dharmamudrā*, 356; of buddha-speech which secures the mental faculty as the pristine cognition of discernment *sor-rtog yid gsung chos-rgya*, 356
elaborate *phyag-rgya spros-bcas*: according to Mahāyoga, 279-80
of entrustment *gtad-rgya*, 587, 672, 717, 719, 721, 722, 723, 725, 727, 734, 828, 927, 928
five kinds of *phyag-rgya rigs-lnga*, 357
four *phyag-rgya bzhi*, 33, 35, 272, 295-6, 301, 355-6
four, indicative of the transmitted precepts *bka'-rtags-kyi phyag-rgya bzhi*, 16, 70-1
Great *phyag-rgya chen-po*, Skt. *mahāmudrā*, 258, 272, 291, 356, 365, 461, 476, 481, 545, 547, 564, 569, 689, 762, 908-9, 922, 925, 926, 929, 931, 936, 973; of buddha-body which secures the ground-of-all as the mirror-like pristine cognition *me-long kun-gzhi sku phyag-chen*, 356
of pristine cognition *ye-shes phyag-rgya*, Skt. *jñānamudrā*, 301
secret *gsang-rgya*, 810, 842
single *phyag-rgya gcig-pa*: according to Mahāyoga, 278-81
subtle and coarse *phyag-rgya phra-rags*: according to Mahāyoga, 360
three *phyag-rgya gsum*: impurity, impermanence and suffering, or the four seals indicative of the transmitted precepts with the exception of nirvāṇa, 71
secret mantra *gsang-sngags*, Skt. *guhya-mantra*: defined, 257-62; 47, 75, 77, 82, 122, 185-6, 257-62; 271, 273, 302, 454, 609, 613; see also *gnostic mantras/spells*, *lineage(s)*, *mantra(s)*, *mantra syllables*, *piṭaka*, *tantra(s)* and *vehicle(s)*
ancient tradition of *gsang-sngags rnying-ma*, 441; see also *Ancient Translation School*
contrasted with causal vehicles, 243-56
inner and outer classes/traditions of *gsang-sngags-kyi phyi-nang lugs*, 475, 762; see also under *mantra(s)* and *vehicle(s)*
new tradition of *gsar-lugs/gsar-ma*: see *new translation school(s)*
origin of, 443-504
seed *khams*, Skt. *dhātu*, 27, 29, 82-3, 153, 159, 174, 180, 192, 199; see also *nucleus* and *seminal point(s)*
of buddhahood *sangs-rgyas-kyi khams*, 203; see also *seed, virtuous of beginningless reality*
that is enlightened mind *khams byang-chub sems*, 20, 124, 362
of enlightenment *byang-chub-kyi khams*, 64
in the form of nectar *khams bdud-rtsi*, 115
of liberation *thar-pa'i sa-bon*, 787, 829
virtuous, of beginningless reality *thog-med-nas chos-nyid-kyi khams dge-ba*, 194, 197-8; see also *seed of buddhahood*
seed-syllables *'bru-yig*, Skt. *bījākṣara*, 33, 275, 287, 351, 356; see also *mantra(s)*, *mantra syllables*, *recitation* and *syllables*
which have eight dimensions of radiance and constancy *yig-'bru'i gsal-brtan-gyi tshad brgyad*, 279
self *bdag*, Skt. *ātmā*, 16, 20, 25, 53, 68, 71, 158-9, 187, 199, 212-13, 218,
true *bdag-nyid chen-po*, Skt. *paramātmā*: the transcendence of the dichotomy of self and non-self, 142, 186, 212; for the significance of this term in the vehicle of indestructible reality, see also *indestructible reality, embodiment of* and *supreme identity*
self-centred buddha *rang-rgyal/rang sangs-rgyas*, Skt. *pratyekabuddha*: defined, 227; 24-5, 35, 82-3, 153, 159, 174, 180, 186, 227, 294, 302, 315, 411, 908, 913, 932
selfhood *bdag-nyid*, Skt. *ātmā*, 28, 62, 229
two concepts of *bdag-gnyis*, 184
selflessness *bdag-med*, Skt. *nairātmya*, 35, 153, 159, 180, 185-6, 212-13, 218, 226-7, 294
two kinds of *bdag-med don rnam-gnyis*, 108, 208, 216, 231, 234, 237
of the individual *gang-zag-gi bdag-med*, Skt. *pudgalanairātmya*, 18, 25, 223-4, 229, 234
of phenomena *chos-kyi bdag-med*, Skt. *dharmanairātmya*, 18, 181, 224-5, 234

self-manifesting *rang-snang*: see *manifest in and of itself*
seminal fluids, male and female *khu-rdul*: *khu* meaning sperm and *rdul* meaning ovum, 279
seminal point(s) *thig-le*, Skt. *bindu*: the nucleus or seed of the enlightened mind, which comprises a range of meanings, from the white and red seminal fluids of the physical body to the seminal points of light which appear during All-Surpassing Realisation, 20, 38, 186, 264, 277, 290, 302, 312, 337, 339-40, 362, 584
  blazing and secretion of *thig-le'i 'bar-'dzag*, 277
  great *thig-le chen-po*: the great buddha-body of reality, 306, 337, 339, 370
  pulse of the seminal point of great desire *'dod-chags chen-po'i thig-le'i 'gros*, 258
  sole/unique *thig-le nyag-gcig*, 763; see also *buddha-body, (great) of reality* and *seminal point, great*
  white and red *thig-le dkar-dmar*, 142, 341
seminal retention *thig-le dbab-bzung*, 489
Senmo spirits *bsen-mo*: female spirits who manifest through lust and attachment, 565, 939
sensations, four *nyams-bzhi*: the consciousnesses of the four senses—seeing, hearing, smelling and tasting—excluding the fifth, i.e. touch, 20, 125
sense objects, (four) *yul(-bzhi)*, 20, 125, 257, 449
sense (organs) *dbang-po*, Skt. *indriya*., 21, 93, 102, 126, 131, 156, 257, 309, 423, 424, 449
  five *dbang-po lnga/sgo lnga*, Skt. *pañcadvāra*: lit. "five gates", 56, 463
  four *dbang-po bzhi*, 20, 125
  of the intellect *yid-kyi dbang-po*, 56
  six *dbang-po drug*, 55-6
sensory perceptions, five *sgo-lnga'i shes-pa*, Skt. *pañcadvārajñāna*, 12, 55; see also *consciousness of the five senses*
sensual raptures, five *'dod-pa'i longs-spyod lnga*, 258: see also *desired qualities* and *(perfect) rapture*
sensum *rnam-pa*, Skt. *ākāra*, 25, 158, 225
sentient beings *sems-can*, Skt. *sattva*: these are of six classes, *passim*; see also *families*
sevenfold service *yan-lag bdun-pa*, 865
shang *gshang*: a Pönpo musical instrument, 939
Shangpa Kagyü *shangs-pa bka'-brgyud*, 395, 802, 833, 853, 929, 952
Shing-go-chen-pa *shing-sgo chen-pa*: lord of the land of wooden doors (Tibet), an epithet for Tā'i Situ Cangcup Gyeltsen, 592
signs *mtshan/rtags*, *passim*
  of success, 822, 861; see also *accomplishment, signs of*
  ten, of inner radiance *'od-gsal rtags-bcu*, 301
signlessness *mtshan-ma med-pa-nyid*, Skt. *animittam*: one of the three approaches to liberation, 23, 153-4, 218, 316-17, 423, 898, 947
simile *dpe*, Skt. *upamā*: in poetics, 105
skilful means *thabs*, Skt. *upāya*, 22, 31, 32, 33, 45, 69, 84, 120, 122, 129, 143, 168, 192, 232, 236, 245-8, 253, 258-60, 262, 269-70, 273-4, 276-7, 286, 290, 292, 296, 302, 306, 313, 321, 323, 347-8, 352, 359-60, 362-3, 368-70, 414, 425, 571, 591, 618, 905, 911, 936, 969
  perfection of *thabs-kyi pha-rol-tu phyin-pa*, Skt. *upāyapāramitā*, 902
sky-cord *dmu-thag*, 507
sky-farer *mkha'-spyod-pa*, Skt. *khecara*, 535, 536, 543, 547, 803; see also under *awareness-holder*
sophist *rtog-ge-ba*, Skt. *tārkika*, 94, 314, 416, 421, 744
sophistry *rtog-ge*, Skt. *tarka*, 103, 181, 275, 309, 314, 594, 641, 907
  eight categories of dialectical *rtog-ge'i tshig-don brgyad*, 101
  five sophistic schools of the extremist masters *rtog-ge sde-lnga*, 64
sorcerer *nus-pa-can/mngon-spyod-pa*, Skt. *abhicārin*, 604, 615
sorceress (spirit) *phra-men-ma*: a demoness in human form with prophetic powers, sometimes equated with the *piśācī* class of deities, 486-7
sorcery *mngon-spyod-kyi las*, Skt. *abhicāra*, 603, 612, 615, 661, 662, 663, 664, 681, 682, 710, 713, 764, 767, 775, 822; see also *rites of wrath*
Southern Treasures *lho-gter*: especially those discovered by Pema Lingpa, 919

Spatial Class of the Great Perfection *klong-gi sde*, 37, 326-9, 371, 494, 538-53, 665, 697, 734, 919
four categories of *klong-sde bzhi*, 37, 326-7
three branches of *klong-sde dkar-nag-khra gsum*, 539
speech *ngag*, Skt. *vāk*: especially of a mundane being, *passim*
twelve different fetters of *('gro-ba'i) ngag-gi bcings-pa mi-'dra-ba bcu-gnyis*, 137
speech *gsung*, Skt. *vāk*: especially of a buddha, see *buddha-speech*
spheres (of existence), three *srid-pa/sa gsum*, Skt. *tribhuvana/tribhava*, 45, 212, 301, 405, 971
spheres, three *'khor-gsum*, Skt. *trimaṇḍala*: those of the subject, object and their interaction, 316, 588, 619
spheres, three *'khor-lo gsum*: those of exegesis, attainment and work, or of renunciation, study and work, 720, 724, 736, 738, 783, 824, 830, 833, 835, 840, 848, 852
spiritual ascetic *dge-sbyong*, Skt. *śramaṇa*: see *ascetic*
spiritual benefactor *dge(-ba'i) bshes(-gnyen)*, Skt. *kalyāṇamitra*, 59, 147, 226, 231, 525, 526, 545, 571, 595, 640, 641, 643, 648, 656, 665, 675, 678, 684, 700, 713, 730, 748, 753, 754, 805, 831, 850, 852, 861, 868, 871, 872, 879, 890
spirituality *thugs-rje*: the counterpart in buddhahood to compassion (*snying-rje*), which is similar to the quality cultivated on the path by bodhisattvas. In the Great Perfection, this is the dynamic aspect of primordial enlightenment giving rise to the emanational body, 32, 75, 127, 141, 264, 299, 332, 342, 403, 414, 610, 616, 856, 887, 923
spiritual maturation/maturity and liberation *smin-sgrol*: see *maturation and liberation*
spiritual and philosophical system *grub-mtha'*, Skt. *siddhānta*: see *philosophical (and spiritual) system(s)/tenets*
spiritual son *thugs-sras*, *passim*
spiritual and temporal laws *chos-khrims-dang rgyal-khrims*, 939
spiritual and temporal well-being *phan-bde*, Skt. *hitasukha*, 403, 405, 726, 811, 830, 831, 970
spiritual warrior *sems-dpa'*, Skt. *sattva*, 75, 122, 376, 671, 692, 696, 743, 867, 877, 912, 913, 928
spontaneous presence *lhun-grub*, Skt. *anābhoga*: an attribute in particular of All-Surpassing Realisation, 55, 116-17, 124, 146, 184, 252, 282, 317, 342-3, 370-1, 454, 550, 619, 679, 877
stages, two *rim-gnyis*, 204, 254, 320, 475, 476, 496, 877, 879, 923; see also *creation stage* and *perfection stage*
Sthavira *gnas-brtan-pa*, 429-30
stūpa(s) *mchod-rten*: a reliquary symbolic of buddha-mind, 99, 433, 434, 435, 436, 456, 471, 493, 508, 549, 550, 623, 624, 637, 661, 685, 757, 797, 809, 815, 831, 851, 900, 915; see also *reliquary*
eight *mchod-rten brgyad*, 427
styles of appraisal/exegesis of the scriptures, four *'jal-byed tshul-bzhi*, 35, 206, 292-3
subject-object dichotomy *gzung-'dzin*, Skt. *grahyagrahaka*, 24, 25, 26, 27, 28, 29, 33, 37, 56, 127, 158, 181, 206, 215, 221, 224-5, 236, 295-6, 309, 320, 336, 343-4, 357, 421, 903
sublime (being) *'phags-pa*, Skt. *ārya*: this term generally indicates one who has attained the path of seeing, whether as a pious attendant, self-centred buddha, or bodhisattva, *passim*
four classes of *'phags-bzhi*, 72, 908
three lower kinds of *'phags-pa 'og-ma gsum*, 175
sublime wealth *'phags-pa'i nor*: its seven aspects are listed in the Glossary of Enumerations, 568, 575
Subsequent Yoga *rjes-su rnal-'byor*: see *Anuyoga*
substance *dngos-po*, Skt. *vastu*, 16, 52, 156, 158, 163, 168, 201, 214, 225, 264, 314, 322-3, 337, 349, 906
substantial existence *rang-bzhin*, Skt. *svabhāva*, 769, 896, 915; see also *independent/inherent existence*
suffering *sdug-bsngal*, Skt. *duḥkha*, 12, 13, 16, 18, 23, 51, 53, 57-8, 69, 70-1, 88, 117-18, 133, 153, 186-7, 193-4,

199, 213, 224, 226, 252, 303, 322-4, 419, 571, 639, 659, 769, 900, 911, 923; see also under *truth(s)*
of change *'gyur-ba'i sdug-bsngal*, Skt. *vipariṇāmaduḥkhatā*, 197, 419
embraced by conditions of mundane existence *'du-byed-kyi sdug-bsngal*, Skt. *saṃskāraduḥkhatā*, 419
of pain itself *sdug-bsngal-gyi sdug-bsngal*, Skt. *duḥkhaduḥkhatā*, 419
suffixes *uṇā*, Skt. *uṇādi*: in grammar, 101
sugata *bde-bar gshegs-pa*: lit. "one who has gone to bliss", i.e. a buddha, *passim*
nucleus of *bde-gshegs snying-po*, Skt. *sugatagarbha*: the nucleus of enlightenment present in all sentient beings, 27, 116, 127, 146, 171, 173, 178, 189, 194, 263, 909
supernormal cognitive power(s) *mngon-shes*, Skt. *abhijñā*, 288, 465, 473, 516, 548, 567, 572, 579, 609, 615, 648, 656, 660, 709, 793, 801, 811, 812, 829, 853
of clairvoyance and exhaustion of corruption *lha'i mig-dang zag-pa zad-pa'i mngon-shes*, 421, 454, 705
five (mundane) *mngon-shes lnga*, Skt. *pañcābhijñā*, 61, 259, 515
six *mngon-shes drug*, Skt. *ṣaḍabhijñā*, 21, 132, 415
supreme identity *bdag-nyid chen-po*, Skt. *mahātmā*, 322, 346-7; see also *heruka* and *deities, meditational*; for the significance of this term in the sūtra tradition, see *self, true*
axiom of *gtan-tshigs bdag-nyid chen-po*: according to Mahāyoga, 275-6
supreme transformation *'pho-ba chen-po*, Skt. **mahāsaṅkrānti*, 919, 968; see also under *buddha-body(ies)* and *transference of consciousness*
sūtra(s) *mdo*: defined, 79; *passim*; see also under *piṭaka* and *vehicle(s)*
profounder *zab-mo'i mdo-sde*: those of the Greater Vehicle which focus on buddha-attributes, 414
contrasted with tantra, 142-8, 243-56, 441, 909
and mantra/tantra, *passim*
tradition/transmission, 153-237, 689, 693, 809, 822, 823, 827, 836, 842, 848
Svātantrika-Madhyamaka *dbu-ma rang-rgyud*, 26, 28, 162-4, 167, 169, 906
Svātantrika-Mādhyamika *dbu-ma rang-rgyud-pa*, 164, 206, 234
syllables *yi-ge*, Skt, *akṣara*, 271, 287, 368, 837; see also *mantra(s)*, *mantra syllables* and *seed-syllables*
symbols/symbolic convention/symbolism *brda'*, Skt. *saṃketa*, 290, 393, 460, 545, 660, 664, 917; see also *intentional symbols*
symbolic hand implements *phyag-mtshan*: the emblems held by the deities which symbolise their buddha-mind, 137, 352, 356
symbolic script *brda'-yig*: see under *ḍākinīs*
sympathetic joy *dga'-ba*, Skt. *muditā*: one of the four immeasurables cultivated by a bodhisattva, 13, 106
synonym *don-gcig-la ming du-ma*, 106
synonymics *mngon-brjod*, Skt. *abhidhāna-vidyā*, 18, 103, 106, 821
Taklungpa *stag-lung-pa*, 823, 830, 847, 850, 867, 868, 929
Takpo Kagyü *dvags-po bka'-brgyud*, 929, 930
Taming temples: see n. 543
Border *mtha'-'dul lha-khang*, Pls. 45, 47, 102; 510
Further *yang-'dul lha-khang*, Pl. 44; 510, 760
District Controlling temples *ru-gnon lha-khang*, Pls. 38, 46; 510
Tamsi demons/spirits *dam-sri*: nine sibling spirits who violated their commitments, said to pose a particular danger to infant children, 589, 590, 811, 939
tantra(s) *rgyud*: see also *continuum/continua*, *lineage(s)*, *mantra(s)*, *piṭaka* and *vehicle(s)*
Anuyoga *anu-yo-ga'i rgyud-rnams*: see under *vehicle(s)*
Atiyoga *ati-yo-ga'i rgyud-rnams*: see under *vehicle(s)*
Caryātantra *spyod-pa'i rgyud*: see under *vehicle(s)*
contrasted with sūtra, 142-8, 243-56, 441, 909
distinctions between the inner tantras, 358-9
exegetical *bshad-rgyud*, Skt. *ākhyātantra*, 619, 658 and *passim*

Father *pha-rgyud*, Skt. *yogitantra*: a class of Unsurpassed Yogatantra, 136, 274, 358, 362, 936
five distinctions between the outer and inner *phyi-rgyud-dang nang-rgyud-kyi khyad-par lnga*, 346-8
four tantrapiṭaka/classes of tantra *rgyud-sde bzhi*, 32-4, 96, 203, 263, 268-74, 473
inner *nang-rgyud*: Mahāyoga, Anuyoga and Atiyoga, 207, 461, 522, 608, 794
Kriyātantra *bya-ba'i rgyud/kriyā*: see under *vehicle(s)*
Mahāyoga *ma-hā-yo-ga'i rgyud-rnams*: see under *vehicle(s)*
Mother *ma-rgyud*, Skt. *yoginītantra*: a class of Unsurpassed Yogatantra, 136, 274, 643, 936
new *rgyud gsar-ma*, 562; see also *new translation school(s)*
Non-Dual *gnyis-med rgyud*, Skt. *advayatantra*, 274, 936, 972
outer/lower *phyi-rgyud*: i.e. Kriyātantra, Ubhayatantra and Yogatantra, 207, 348, 458, 459, 608
response to criticisms of the Nyingma, 887-95
root *rtsa-rgyud*, *passim*
six classes of *rgyud-sde drug*: the three outer tantras—Kriyātantra, Ubhayatantra and Yogatantra—and the three inner tantras—Mahāyoga, Anuyoga and Atiyoga, 96
of skilful means *thabs-kyi rgyud*, 273
and sūtra, *passim*
tantrapiṭaka *rgyud-sde*, 65, 73, 78, 136, 186, 214, 246, 261, 441-2, 462, 463, 619, 674, 675, 852, 861, 862, 887, 894, 898, 914, 927, 944
ten categories of tantra/outer and inner mantras *rgyud-don-gyi dngos-po bcu/ sngags phyi-nang-gi de-nyid bcu*, 266, 303-5, 308, 347, 349-50, 358
text *rgyud*, *passim*; see also *piṭaka*
three inner classes of tantra/tantrapiṭaka *nang rgyud-sde gsum*, 396-7, 529-96, 604, 918
three kinds of *rgyud-gsum*: according to the *Guhyasamāja Tantra*, 262
three outer/lower classes of tantra/ tantrapiṭaka *phyi rgyud-sde ('og-ma) gsum*: Kriyātantra, Ubhayatantra and Yogatantra, 83-4, 268-73, 348-57
Ubhayatantra *gnyis-ka'i rgyud*: see under *vehicle(s)*
Unsurpassed Yogatantra *bla-med rnal-'byor-gyi rgyud*, Skt. *Anuttarayoga-tantra*: see under *vehicle(s)*
verbal, of the Great Perfection *rdzogs-chen tshig-rgyud*: those concealed by Garap Dorje, 493, 927; see also *Great Perfection*
Yogatantra *rnal-'byor-gyi rgyud*: see under *vehicle(s)*
Yoginī *rnal-'byor-ma'i rgyud*, 503
Taoist *ha-shang*, 936
tathāgata(s) *de-bzhin gshegs-pa*: lit. "one who has gone thus to nirvāṇa", i.e. a buddha, *passim*
male and female *de-bzhin gshegs-pa-dang gshegs-ma*, 125
nucleus of *de-gshegs snying-po*, Skt. *tathāgatagarbha*: the nucleus of enlightenment present in all sentient beings, 20, 27, 29, 32, 95, 147, 154, 171, 173-7, 186-7, 194, 198, 236, 291, 424
Teacher *ston-pa*, Skt. *śāstṛ*: in general this refers to those teachers endowed with the three buddha-bodies, specifically it refers to Śākyamuni Buddha, 111-48 and *passim*
teaching *bstan-pa*, Skt. *śāsana*: i.e. Buddhism, *passim*
duration of, 134-5
temporal ages, four *dus-bzhi*, Skt. *caturyuga*, 268-9
temporal dimensions/times, four *dus-bzhi*: the three times with the addition of indefinite time, 20, 125
thread-cross *mdos*: a ritual utilising a wooden-framed structure crossed with many layers of thread or silk as a device for trapping and exorcising evil forces. This implement is also called *nam-mkha'*, 666, 669, 762, 765
rites of the Mātaraḥs' vengeance *ma-mo 'khang-phab-kyi mdos*, 669
Tibetan *bod-skad*: i.e. the language, 11, 393, 496, 515, 522, 526, 705, 773, 917, 921
ti-shih *ti-shri*: an imperial preceptor, 719, 823, 830
time moment, indivisible *dus-kyi skad-cig-ma*, Skt. *kṣaṇa*, 24, 25, 224-5

times
four *dus-bzhi*: see *temporal dimensions/ times, four*
three *dus-gsum*, Skt. *trikāla*, 157-8, 633
torma *gtor-ma* Skt. *naivedya/bali*: offering cakes ceremonially presented to deities or spiritual beings for diverse purposes connected with rites of service and attainment, 292, 304, 545, 546, 581, 588, 589, 621, 624, 625, 627, 630, 636, 645, 654, 662, 666, 736, 766, 767
empowerment *gtor-dbang*, 752
malign *zor*: a form of sorcery in which the *torma* itself becomes the instrument of wrathful action, 669
offering dance *gtor-'chams*, 581, 669
sculpture *bca'*, 727
water *chu-gtor*: an offering of water specifically consecrated to the tormented spirits, who would otherwise suffer from thirst, 545, 654
tormented spirits *yi-dvags*, Skt. *preta*, 14, 130, 609
total presence *cog-bzhag*: the immovable presence of fundamental reality in Cutting Through Resistance, 902; see also *Cutting Through Resistance*
tradition *lugs*, *passim*
doctrinal *chos-lugs*: in this context the term has the sense of behaviour or conduct, 51-3
trainings *spong-ba/bslab-pa*
four correct *yang-dag spong-bzhi*, Skt. *catvāri prahāṇāni*: among the thirty-seven branches of enlightenment, these concern the renunciation and acceptance in which a bodhisattva must correctly train, 236
three (precious) correct *(yang-dag-pa'i) bslab-pa gsum*, Skt. *triśikṣā*, 70-1, 73, 79, 88, 322, 403, 423, 707, 879, 898, 900
tranquillity *zhi-gnas*, Skt. *śamatha*, 13, 23, 61, 79, 226, 236, 247, 254-5, 286, 359, 905
Transcendent Lady *bcom-ldan-'das-ma*, Skt. *Bhagavatī*: used here as a title for Kurukullā, 824
Transcendent Lord *bcom-ldan-'das*, Skt. *bhagavān*: a buddha such as Śākyamuni; lit. one who has *subdued* obscurations (*bcom*), *possesses* the enlightened attributes (*ldan*), and has *passed* into nirvāṇa (*'das*), *passim*
transcendental perfection(s) *pha-rol-tu phyin-pa*, Skt. *pāramitā*, 94, 237, 245, 249, 261, 266, 441, 475, 524, 546, 577, 650, 730, 731, 805, 850, 861, 901, 936, 971
of enlightened attributes *yon-tan-gyi pha-rol-tu phyin-pa*, Skt. *guṇapāramitā*, 212; see also *enlightened attributes, four*
six *phar-phyin drug*, Skt. *ṣaṭpāramitā*, 36, 235-6, 255, 260, 300, 302, 306, 308, 320, 656
ten *phar-phyin bcu*, Skt. *daśapāramitā*, 236, 901-2
transference of consciousness *'pho-ba*, Skt. **saṅkrānti*: the transference at death into a higher realm of existence, 306, 473; see also under *buddha-body of great/supreme transformation* and *supreme transformation*
transgressions *nyes-byas*, Skt. *duṣkṛta*
forty-six *nyes-byas zhe-drug*, 95
and natural offences *bcas-pa-dang rang-bzhin(-gyi ltung-ba)*, Skt. *prajñapti-sāvadya* and *prakṛtisāvadya*: the former are evil deeds caused by the transgression of vows, and the latter are natural evils such as the ten non-virtues and the five inexpiable sins, 423
ten *rung-ba ma-yin-pa'i gzhi bcu*, 429
translation *sgra-bsgyur*: see *Ancient Translation School* and *new translation school(s)*
translator(s) *lo-tsā-ba*: the Tibetan term is said to be derived from Skt. *loka-cakṣuḥ*, lit. "eye of the world", 22, 47, 393, 405, 509, 515, 522, 526, 547, 601, 603, 605, 607, 609, 633, 643, 671, 675, 696, 708, 709, 725, 728, 733, 821, 838, 859, 887, 889-90, 938, 950
transmission(s) *lung*, Skt. *āgama*, 39, 71-2, 155, 211, 375, 442, 564, 577, 580, 584, 619, 620, 651, 656, 672, 673, 674, 675, 677, 678, 679, 681, 682, 683, 699, 701, 706, 720, 721, 723, 724, 727, 730, 731, 734, 736, 737, 738, 751, 778, 789, 794, 795, 799, 808, 809, 821, 827, 828, 835, 841,

850, 854, 861, 862, 866, 867, 874, 876, 918, 930
exegetical *bshad-lung*: see *exegesis*
literary *lung*, 16, 208, 290, 305
two methods of, in the Nyingma school: the distant lineage of transmitted precepts *(ring-brgud bka'-ma)* and close lineage of the treasures *(nye-brgyud gter-ma)*, 396, 397 and *passim*
transmitted precepts *bka'*, Skt. *subhāṣita/pravacana*, 12, 16, 17-18, 37, 68, 72-93, 186, 216-17, 259, 300, 331, 395, 409-10, 428-31, 432, 441, 451, 460, 462, 468, 475-81, 537, 554, 675, 678, 679, 680, 683, 696, 699, 710, 720, 722, 723, 724, 727, 728, 731, 733-9, 746, 750, 757-9, 762, 764, 770, 805, 808, 811, 818, 822, 823, 827, 828, 829, 830, 831, 835, 836, 838, 842, 845, 850, 856, 860, 861, 862, 863, 871, 873, 874, 890-1, 893, 894, 910, 921, 926, 931, 965; see also *doctrinal wheel(s)*
compilation of *bka' bsdu-ba*, 153-5, 428-31, 451-7; in Tibet, 515, 523, 917
distant lineage of *ring-brgyud bka'-ma*, 39, 41, 396, 397, 398, 597-739, 745, 845
final *bka' tha-ma*, 182, 186, 189, 424, 905, 931
five classifications of *bka'-la dbye-ba lnga*, 74-87
four great rivers of *bka'i chu-babs chen-po bzhi*, 601
four *bka' bzhi*: of the Kagyüpa, 853
four special qualities of *bka'i khyad-par bzhi*, 73
given in oral teaching *zhal-nas gsungs-ba'i bka'*, 17, 74-5
intermediate *bka' bar-ma*, 182, 189, 423, 896, 905, 947
Kham tradition of *khams-lugs*, 397, 649, 654, 658, 688-701, 706, 725, 727
Nyang/Rong tradition of *nyang/rong-lugs*, 397, 616, 617-87; see also *Zur tradition*
sealed *bka'-rgya(-ma)*, 865
of secret mantra, 445, 451; see also *vehicle(s)*
seven successions of *bka'-babs bdun*, 751-2, 844-7, 854, 855-8
succession to *bka'-babs*, 863
three kinds of *bka' gsum*, 74; see also *doctrinal wheel(s)*
three successive promulgations of *bka' rim-pa gsum*, 18, 188; see also *doctrinal wheel(s)*
treasure(s) *gter-ma*: teachings which have been concealed and rediscovered: defined, 743-9; 396, 397, 475, 476, 482-3, 498, 511, 516, 518, 519, 556, 558, 573, 584, 585, 586, 612, 662, 675, 677, 678, 679, 680, 683, 695, 696, 699, 713, 714, 720, 722, 723, 724, 727, 731, 736, 741-881, 926, 927-8, 934-5
attainment of *gter-sgrub*, 810, 842, 844
chest *gter-sgrom*, 747, 756, 781, 796, 834, 856
close lineage of *nye-brgyud gter-ma*, 39, 396, 397, 741-881
doctrine/doctrinal *gter-chos*, 561, 567, 679, 719, 727, 730, 743, 744, 745, 750, 763, 764, 765, 777, 778, 787, 791, 798, 812, 848, 857, 927; see also *inventory of treasure doctrines*
earth *sa-gter*, 744, 746-7, 845-6, 856-63
eight great, (of brilliance) *(spobs-pa'i) gter chen-po brgyad*, 666, 705, 871
four inexhaustible great *gter-chen mi-zad-pa bzhi*, 743
guardian/protector *gter-srung*, 747, 785, 864, 866
of intention/mind *dgongs-gter*, 574, 586, 744, 747-8, 764, 822, 839, 844, 846, 857, 877, 880, 922
lord of *gter-bdag*, Skt. *nidhipati*, 662, 745, 764, 927-8
material *rdzas-gter*, 786
profound *zab-gter*, 744, 746, 747, 749, 751, 752, 770, 776, 781, 782, 784, 814, 815, 838, 843, 844, 845, 862, 863, 867, 919
protector *gter-srung*: see *treasure guardian/protector*
public *khrom-gter*, 662, 811, 328, 846
of recollection *rjes-dran-gyi gter*, 844, 846-7, 857-8
reconcealed *yang-gter*, 844, 846, 856-7
secret *gsang-gter*, 810, 811
site *gter-kha*, 743, 755, 786, 789, 790, 811, 864; see also *treasure troves*
treasure-finder *gter-ston*, 397, 482-3, 554-61, 580-90, 684, 701, 726, 728,

730, 733, 734, 736, 737, 745, 748, 749-881, 928, 934-5, 950
troves *gter-kha*, 582, 732, 745, 746, 747, 748, 757, 764, 777, 790, 793, 796, 798, 816, 819, 821, 844, 881, see also *treasure site*; ancient and new *gter-kha gsar-rnying*, 859
treatise(s) *bstan-bcos*, Skt. *śāstra*, 17, 18, 39, 40-1, 64, 66, 72, 88-119, 169, 184, 186, 217, 292, 440, 461, 464, 476-7, 484, 488, 496, 502, 515, 523, 537, 552, 591, 612, 675, 676, 679, 703, 705, 708, 727, 732, 775, 850, 851, 861, 894, 910, 917, 921
exegetical *gzhung-bshad*, 552, 666, 681
four kinds of *bstan-bcos rnam-pa bzhi*, 89
four special attributes of *bstan-bcos-kyi khyad-chos bzhi*, 18, 88
nine kinds of *bstan-bcos rnam-dgu*, 89
quantitative *ji-snyed-pa ston-pa'i bstan-bcos*, 18, 97-107
qualitative *ji-lta-ba ston-pa'i bstan-bcos*, 18, 108
teaching liberation and omniscience *thar-pa-dang thams-cad mkhyen-pa (thob-pa'i thabs) ston-pa'i bstan bcos*, 108-9
treasures in the form of *dgongs-gter bstan-bcos-su bkod-pa*, 877, 880
Tretāyuga *gsum-ldan*: the second age of the aeon, which is ideally suited to the practice of Ubhayatantra, 268
trichiliocosm *stong-gsum-gyi stong chen-po*, Skt. *trisahasramahāsahasra*: one billion worlds, 113, 120, 124, 131, 409, 414
Tripiṭaka/three piṭaka *sde-snod gsum*, 76, 78-80, 203, 259, 405, 428, 429, 436, 437, 441, 468, 511, 560, 619, 888, 893
troll *grul-bum*, Skt. *kumbhāṇḍa/kuṣmāṇḍa*, 132
true acquisitions, ten *de-nyid thob-pa bcu*, 928
truth(s) *bden-pa*, Skt. *satya*, *passim*
of cessation *'gog-pa'i bden-pa*, Skt. *nirodhasatya*, 16, 27, 29, 32, 35, 71-2, 153, 192, 196, 224, 226, 257, 294
conventional *tha-snyad(-kyi bden-pa)*, Skt. *vyavahārasatya*, 207, 209-10, 906, 907, 909
declaration of *bden-tshig*, 589, 611, 662, 713, 745
four *bden-pa bzhi*, 23-4, 137, 153, 188, 224-7, 230, 421, 423, 946-7; four moments as they apply to *bden-bzhi'i rnam-pa bzhi*, 158, 230
indivisible *gnyis-med bden-pa*: according to Mahāyoga, 32, 34, 207, 209, 249, 359-61
of the origin of suffering *kun-byung bden-pa*, Skt. *samudayasatya*, 32, 93, 153, 213, 224, 226, 257, 303
of the path *lam-gyi bden-pa*, Skt. *mārga-satya*, 17, 27, 29, 32, 36, 37, 71-2, 85, 93, 153, 157, 224, 226, 257, 302, 307, 319, 901
relative *kun-rdzob bden-pa*, Skt. *saṃvṛtisatya*, 26, 29, 57, 162-3, 166, 178, 200, 206, 209, 215, 217-18, 232, 234, 247, 249-51, 354, 897, 901; correct *yang-dag-pa'i kun-rdzob bden-pa*, Skt. *tathyāsaṃvṛtisatya*, 162, 166, 233, 350, 354; erroneous/incorrect *log-pa'i kun-rdzob bden-pa*, Skt. *mithyāsaṃvṛtisatya*, 162, 166, 233, 350, 354
sixteen minor *bden-chung bcu-drug*, 24, 226
of suffering *sdug-bsngal-gyi bden-pa*, Skt. *duḥkhasatya*, 32, 93, 153, 213, 224, 226, 257, 303
two *bden-pa gnyis*, Skt. *satyadvaya*: relative and ultimate, 26, 29-30, 32, 34, 35, 76, 162, 168, 200, 204, 206-16, 232, 245, 248, 294, 296, 303, 320, 349, 351, 354, 897, 901
ultimate *don-dam bden-pa*, Skt. *para-mārthasatya*, 25, 26, 27, 28, 29, 33, 57, 153, 162-5, 167, 174-6, 178-9, 185, 193, 206, 208, 215, 217, 232-4, 247, 250, 270, 278, 309, 314, 320-1, 349-50, 354, 360, 897, 898, 901, 906, 924, 931, see also *ultimate reality*; which employs synonyms *rnam-grangs-dang ldan-pa'i don-dam bden-pa*, Skt. *paryāyaparamārtha-satya*, 24, 162, 200, 208, 233; seven aspects of the spiritual wealth of *don-dam bden-pa dkor-bdun*, 153, 248-9; without synonyms *rnam-grangs min-pa'i don-dam bden-pa*, Skt. *aparyāyaparamārthasatya*, 24, 154, 162, 201, 204, 206-9, 233
tsampa *rtsam-pa*: parched barley flour, 629, 630, 655, 696

Tsangpa (dominion/governors) *gtsang-pa*, 955, 956
Tsen spirits *btsan*: a group of demons headed by *tsi'u dmar-po*. See R. de Nebesky-Wojkowitz, *Oracles and Demons of Tibet*, (pp. 166ff.), 491, 694
Tsharpa *tshar-pa*: a division of the Sakyapa school, 850
Tshurpu calendrical system, 400
Ubhayatantra *upa'i rgyud*: see under *vehicle(s)*
udumbara *u-dum-va-ra*: a mythical lotus of a huge size, blooming once in five hundred years, 426, 763, 967
ultimate reality *don-dam*, Skt. *paramārtha*, 28, 33, 35, 76, 127, 140, 159, 171-2, 177, 179, 188, 197, 201, 207-8, 210, 215-16, 219-20, 224-5, 233-4, 245, 249, 252, 254, 271, 294-5, 309, 314, 322, 355-6, 582, 907; see also *truth, ultimate*
  definitive vehicles of *don-dam nges-pa'i theg-pa*: the vehicles from that of the bodhisattva upwards, 285, 454
ultimate truth *don-dam bden-pa*, Skt. *paramārthasatya*: see under *truth(s)*
uncompounded (nature) *'dus-ma-byas*, Skt. *asaṃskṛta*, 51, 139, 146, 156-8, 196-8, 206-7, 302, 321, 328, 898
union *zung-'jug*, Skt. *yuganaddha*: see *coalescence*
union, seven branches of *kha-sbyor yan-lag bdun*, Skt. *saptasampuṭa*, 266
universal emperor/monarch *'khor-lo bsgyur-ba*, Skt. *cakravartin*, 60, 132, 191, 196, 417, 450, 894, 913
Unsurpassed (Yoga)tantra *bla-na med-pa'i (rnal-'byor-gyi) rgyud*, Skt. *Anuttarayogatantra*: see under *vehicle(s)*
  twelve excellent divisions of *bla-med rgyud-kyi rab-tu dbye-ba bcu-gnyis*, 274
Upayogatantra *upa-yoga*: see *Ubhayatantra*
upper demons *steng-gdon*, 594
ūrṇakeśa *mdzod-spu*: the hair ringlet between eyebrows of a buddha—one of the thirty-two major marks, 912
uṣṇīṣa *gtsug-tor*: the protuberance on the head of a buddha—one of the thirty-two major marks, 271
Uttaraphālgunī *khre'u zla-ba*: early April, 557
Vaibhāṣika *bye-brag-tu smra-ba*, 24, 25, 90-1, 93, 155-8, 160, 162, 225, 411, 911
Vaiśākha *sa-ga zla-ba*: May to June, 946-7
Vaiśeṣika *bye-brag-pa*, 16, 65
Vaiṣṇava *khyab-'jug-pa*, 16, 65-6
vajra *rdo-rje*: see also *indestructible reality*
  and bell *rdo-rje dril-bu*, Skt. *vajraghaṇṭa*, 305, 350, 634, 645
  crossed-vajra *rdo-rje rgya-gram*, Skt. *viśvavajra*, 494, 601, 690
  (emblem) *(mtshan-pa'i) rdo-rje*, 120-2, 198, 340, 356, 468, 535, 609, 616, 623, 646, 787
  hand-sized *rdo-rje phyag gang-ba*: the emanational teaching of the Great Perfection, 134-5
  master *rdo-rje slob-dpon*, Skt. *vajrācārya*, 494; see also *master of indestructible reality*
  secret *gsang-ba'i rdo-rje*: the penis, 567, 766
  vajra-holder *rdo-rje 'dzin-pa*, Skt. *vajradhṛk*: an exponent of the vehicle of indestructible reality, 680, 823, 923; see also *indestructible reality, holder of*
  vajra-like contemplation *rdo-rje lta-bu'i ting-nge-'dzin*, Skt. *vajropama-samādhi*, 159, 198
Vajra Queen *rdo-rje btsun-mo*, Skt. *vajra-yoṣit*, 125, 404, 449
valid cognition *tshad-ma*, Skt. *pramāṇa*
  of inference, 312; see also *inference*
  three kinds of (all-embracing) *(kun-khyab) tshad-ma gsum*, 73, 275, 970
vast/vastness *rgyas*: the attribute of skilful means in contrast to profound/profundity (*zab*) which is the attribute of discriminative awareness, 28, 170, 247, 331, 344, 584, 707, 726, 830, 839, 845, 871
vehicle(s) *theg-pa*, Skt. *yāna*: defined, 80-7; *passim*
  of Anuyoga *rjes-su rnal-'byor-gyi theg-pa*, 17, 32, 34-5, 36, 40, 81, 86-7, 137, 264, 284-9, 294, 297, 358-9, 363-9, 396, 397, 460, 461, 485-9, 531, 537, 746
  of Atiyoga *shin-tu rnal-'byor-gyi theg-pa*: defined, 311-18; 17, 19, 29, 32, 34, 35-9, 40, 81, 86-7, 264, 274, 284,

294-345, 347, 358-9, 365, 369-72, 396, 397, 461, 490-504, 531, 537, 558-96, 707, 746, 762, 820, 861, 897, 907, 923; see also *Great Perfection*
of the awareness-holders *rig-'dzin theg-pa*, Skt. **vidyādharayāna*: the vehicle of indestructible reality/secret mantra, 81, 248
basic, of gods and humans *sor-bzhag lha-mi'i theg-pa*, 57-61, 69, 81-2, 86, 97
of bodhisattvas *byang-chub sems-dpa'i theg-pa*, Skt. *bodhisattvayāna*, 17, 30, 81-3, 85-7, 155, 172, 223, 231-7, 286, 295
of Brahmā *tshangs-pa'i theg-pa*, Skt. *Brahmayāna*, 13, 54, 57, 61-2, 82, 86
of Caryatantra: see *vehicle of Ubhayatantra/Caryātantra*
(causal/outer), of dialectics *rgyu mtshan-nyid/phyi'i theg-pa*, Skt. **hetulakṣanayāna*, 12, 23-30, 36, 41, 81, 144-5, 151-237, 243-56, 273, 282, 285-6, 292, 348, 425, 441, 577, 604, 861, 908; three *rgyu mtshan-nyid/phyi'i theg-pa gsum*, 81, 83, 911
definitive, of ultimate reality *don-dam nges-pa'i theg-pa*: the vehicles from that of the bodhisattva upwards, 285, 454
of dialectics/dialectical *mtshan-nyid theg-pa*: see *vehicles, (causal/outer) of dialectics*
of direction from the cause of suffering *kun-'byung 'dren-pa'i theg-pa*: the three causal vehicles of dialectics, 81
effortless, *bya-rtsol med-pa'i theg-pa*: Atiyoga, 538, 971
of extremists *mu-stegs-pa'i theg-pa*: non-Buddhist traditions, 261
five *theg-pa lnga*, 17, 81-2, 133
greater *theg-pa chen-po*, Skt. *mahāyāna*, 23, 24, 25-30, 64, 73, 81-5, 95, 115, 131, 153-5, 160-222, 231-7, 243-4, 395, 396, 410, 412-13, 415, 430-1, 440, 441, 442, 449, 455, 456, 481, 503, 504, 522, 564, 619, 641-2, 656, 664, 849, 869, 892, 908, 912, 913, 931, 944; causal *rgyu'i theg-pa chen-po*: i.e. the vehicle of bodhisattvas, 82, 84, 113, 142-4, 305
of the Indestructible Nucleus of Inner Radiance *'od-gsal rdo-rje snying-po'i theg-pa*: the All-Surpassing Realisation of the Great Perfection, 115
of indestructible reality *rdo-rje theg-pa*, Skt. *vajrayāna*: defined, 260-1; 12, 31, 83, 85, 109, 148, 189, 223, 237, 241, 244, 246, 249, 260-1, 293, 305-6, 372, 400, 401, 409, 442, 445, 454, 504, 527, 577, 596, 599, 624, 689, 705, 706, 739, 746, 748, 854, 862, 871, 881, 885, 894, 940
of (the inner tantras of) skilful means *nang-pa thabs-kyi rgyud-kyi theg-pa*: Mahāyoga, Anuyoga and Atiyoga, 84, 245-6, 252, 286, 346, 357-72, 493; see also *vehicles of overpowering (skilful) means*
irreversible *phyir mi-zlog-pa'i theg-pa*: the vehicle of the final promulgation of the sūtras, 947
of Kriyātantra *bya-ba'i rgyud-kyi theg-pa*, 17, 29, 31, 32, 33, 35, 81, 86-7, 137, 245-6, 252, 264, 268-71, 292, 295-6, 305, 348-52, 353, 449, 456, 502, 531, 604, 618, 619, 827, 893, 936
lesser *theg-pa chung-ba/theg-dman*, Skt. *hīnayāna*, 23, 24-5, 81, 83, 153, 155-9, 223-31, 248, 411-56, 481, 504, 522, 911, 931
of Mahāyoga *rnal-'byor chen-po'i theg-pa*, 17, 32, 34, 35-6, 40, 77, 81, 86-7, 264, 274-83, 294-7, 358-63, 396, 397, 458-83, 531, 533-7, 746
mundane *'jig-rten-pa'i theg-pa*, Skt. *laukikayāna*: the vehicle of Brahmā and the basic vehicles of gods and humans, 13, 54, 57-61
nine (sequences of) *theg-pa('i rim-pa) dgu*, 12, 13, 17, 28, 30, 34, 35, 40, 41, 81, 86, 364-5, 625, 638-9, 861
outer, of dialectics: see *vehicles, (causal/outer) of dialectics*
of the outer tantras/mantras of austere awareness *phyi dka'-thub rig-pa'i rgyud-kyi theg-pa*: Kriyātantra, Ubhayatantra and Yogatantra, 32-3, 81, 286, 346-57, 493, 895, 913; three *phyi dka'-thub rig-pa'i rgyud-kyi theg-pa gsum*, 84, 269, see also *dialectics, three classes of*
of Outsiders *phyi-rol-pa'i theg-pa*: the vehicles of non-Buddhists, 306
of overpowering (skilful) means *dbang-bsgyur thabs-kyi theg-pa*: the vehicles

of the inner tantras of skilful means, Mahāyoga, Anuyoga and Atiyoga, 33, 81, 245, 269, 273-4
of pious attendants *nyan-thos theg-pa*, Skt. *śrāvakayāna*, 17, 24, 30, 81-7, 155, 161, 190, 227-31, 261, 286, 306, 913
of pristine cognition *ye-shes-kyi theg-pa*: Atiyoga, 85
resultant, (of secret mantra) *(gsang-sngags) 'bras-bu theg-pa*, Skt. **phalayāna*: the vehicle of indestructible reality, 12, 23, 29, 30-9, 81, 85, 113, 142, 171, 185, 203, 239-372, 412-13, 442
of secret mantra *gsang-sngags-kyi theg-pa*, Skt. *guhyamantrayāna*: the vehicle of indestructible reality, 28, 83-4, 243-372, 412, 443-504, 531-95, 608, 618, 619, 641, 648, 651, 671, 689, 691, 692, 703, 706, 707, 728, 748, 757, 794, 800, 802, 809, 822, 823, 836, 842, 843, 848, 854, 878, 887, 888, 891, 892-3, 911, 914, 926, 931, 935, 944, 954, 960, 962, 972
of self-centred buddhas *rang sangs-rgyas-kyi theg-pa*, Skt. *pratyekabuddhayāna*, 17, 24-5, 30, 81-7, 155, 161, 261, 286, 306, 913
of skilful means: see *vehicles of (the inner tantras of) skilful means*
single *theg-pa gcig*, Skt. *ekayāna*, 80-3, 85-6, 143, 188, 207, 320
six, of definitive attainment *nges-pa thob-pa'i theg-pa drug*: the greater vehicle, 295
supramundane *'jig-rten-las 'das-pa'i theg-pa*, Skt. *lokottarayāna*: the Buddhist vehicles, 68, 70-2
supreme *theg-mchog*: Atiyoga, 404, 406, 413-14, 566, 908, 949, 967, 970
of the tathāgatas *de-bzhin gshegs-pa'i theg-pa*: the vehicle of bodhisattvas, whose result is Buddhahood, 82
three *theg-pa gsum*, Skt. *triyāna*, 17, 81-3, 174, 190, 197, 285, 425
three, of inner tantras of skilful means *nang-rgyud thabs-kyi theg-pa gsum*: Mahāyoga, Anuyoga and Atiyoga, 84
three, of the outer tantras of austere awareness *phyi dka'-thub rig-pa'i rgyud-kyi theg-pa gsum*: see *vehicles of the outer tantras/mantras of austere awareness*
of transcendental perfection *pha-rol-tu phyin-pa'i theg-pa*, Skt. *pāramitāyāna*: the vehicle of bodhisattvas, 243, 249, 306, 503, 895
two *theg-pa gnyis*, 17, 81, 83
of Ubhayatantra/Caryātantra *upa'i/gnyis-ka'i/spyod-pa'i rgyud-kyi theg-pa*, 17, 31, 32, 33, 35, 81, 86-7, 246, 264, 268-9, 271-2, 292, 295-6, 305, 348, 352-3, 449, 456, 502, 531, 604, 893, 936
of Unsurpassed (Yoga)tantra *bla-na med-pa'i (rgyud-kyi) theg-pa*, Skt. *anuttaratantrayāna*, 32, 33-4, 81, 83-4, 142, 214, 252, 266, 268-9, 273-4, 301, 340, 376, 448, 451, 456-7, 502, 516, 531, 674, 893, 895, 913, 944, 947
of Yogatantra *rnal-'byor-gyi rgyud-kyi theg-pa*, Skt. *yogatantrayāna*, 17, 31, 32, 33, 35, 81, 86-7, 252, 264, 268, 271-3, 295-6, 348, 352-7, 364, 450, 465, 468, 469, 488, 502, 503, 531, 604, 643, 827, 893, 936
verse *tshig-bcad*, Skt. *padya*: in poetics, 76, 105-7
mixed, and prose *spel-ma*, Skt. *miśra*, 105
vibhaṅga *rnam-par 'byed-pa*: here, the analytical texts of Maitreya, 95
view *lta-ba*, Skt. *dṛṣṭi*, *passim*
of Anuyoga, 284-6, 365-7
of Atiyoga, 294-345, 370
of the bodhisattvas, 95, 234-5
of the Brahmā vehicle, 61
of the Great Madhyamaka, 169-216, 234
of Kriyātantra, 269-70, 349-50
of Mahāyoga, 275-6, 360-1
of the Mind-Only/Vijñānavāda School, 160-2, 234
of the mundane vehicle, 58
of the pious attendants, 158-9, 224-5
of the Prāsaṅgika-Mādhyamika, 164-9, 234
profound *zab-mo lta-ba*, 431
of the Sautrāntika, 158, 225
of the self-centred buddhas, 159, 229
of the Svātantrika-Mādhyamika, 162-4, 234
of Ubhayatantra, 271, 352
of the Vaibhāṣika, 156-7, 225

of Yogatantra, 272, 354-5
Vijñānavāda *rnam-rig smra-ba*, 25, 27, 30, 160-3, 178, 189, 234, 301
Vijñānavādin *rnam-rig smra-ba*, 35, 160, 294
Vinaya *'dul-ba*: defined, 80; 93, 137, 187, 429, 498, 524, 526, 552, 569, 576, 688, 730, 731, 748, 805, 806, 850, 861, 874; see also under *instruction(s)*, *ordination*, *piṭaka* and *vows*
 Lower Tibetan Lineage of *smad-'dul-gyi brgyud-pa*, 525, 688, 729
 piṭaka *'dul-ba'i sde-snod*: see under *piṭaka*
virtue(s) *dge-ba*, Skt. *kuśala*, 56, 193, 199, 214, 302-3, 320, 322, 604, 625, 899, 900, 901, 903, 944
 fundamental *dge-ba'i rtsa-ba*, Skt. *kuśalamūla*, 85, 302, 307, 898, 900, 905, 908, 912
 ten (divine) *dge-ba bcu*, Skt. *daśakuśala*, 13, 56, 59, 60, 61, 512, 513
 ten, "endowed with corruption" *zag-bcas-kyi dge-ba bcu*, 60
visarga: usually the sign of final aspiration but here it refers to final punctuation marks (*tig*), 916
vision, pure *dag-snang*: see under *appearance(s)*
visionary appearance(s) *snang-ba*: in All-Surpassing Realisation, 337, 339
 of the cessation of clinging to reality *or* of the cessation/exhaustion of (apparitional) reality *chos-nyid-du 'dzin-pa'i zad-pa/chos-nyid zad-pa'i snang-ba*, 337, 339, 371, 594; see also under *cessation*
 of the direct perception of reality *chos-nyid mngon-sum*, 339, 371
 four *snang-ba bzhi*, 38, 332, 341, 343, 371, 971
 of increasing contemplative experience *nyams gong-'phel-ba*, 339, 371
 of reaching the limit of awareness *rig-pa tshad-phebs*, 339, 371
vital energy *rlung*, Skt. *vāyu*, 24, 115, 362, 489, 536, 578, 618, 669, 676; see also *energy channels, currents and seminal points*
 active *las-kyi rlung*, 877; see also *pulse of the active energy currents*
 of great life-breath *srog chen-po'i rlung*: ignorance, 291
 koṭākhyā, 292
 and mind *rlung-sems*, 288, 341, 643, 721
 of pristine cognition *ye-shes-kyi rlung*, 115, 341
 ten kinds of *rlung bcu*, 292
Vivarta script *bi-barta*, 705, 729
vows *sdom-pa*, Skt. *saṃvara*, 70, 80, 729 and *passim*; see also *commitment(s)*, *moral discipline* and *ordination*
 bodhisattva *byang-chub sems-dpa'i sdom-pa*, Skt. *bodhisattvasaṃvara*, 78, 423, 674, 729, 805, 827, 849, 939
 of celibacy *tshangs-spyod*, Skt. *brahma-carya*, 422, 760
 inner, of the awareness-holders *rig-'dzin nang-gi sdom-pa*, 78, 729; see also *commitment(s)*
 lay-vows *dge-bsnyen*, Skt. *upāsaka*, 70, 226, 784, 827, 911; see also *layman*
 mantra *sngags-kyi sdom-pa*, 849; see also *commitment(s)*
 monastic *sdom-brtson/rab-byung*, 526, 887; see also *ordination*
 novitiate *dge-tshul*, Skt. *śrāmaṇera*: see under *ordination*
 of Pön *bon-gyi sdom-pa*, 690
 pōṣadha, 911
 prātimokṣa *so-thar sdom-pa*: the vows of pious attendants and self-centred buddhas, 78, 235, 729, eight *so-thar sdom-brgyad*, 158, 226
 of the purificatory fast *bsnyen-gnas*, Skt. *upavāsa*, 58, 226; eight *gso-sbyong/yan-lag brgyad(-pa'i khrims)*, 513
 three *sdom-pa gsum*, Skt. *trisaṃvara*, 78, 300, 302, 827, 831, 861
 two hundred and fifty disciplines of the Vinaya *nyi-brgya lnga-bcu'i 'dul-khrims*: the vows of a fully-ordained monk, 230; see also under *ordination*
warrior *dpa'-bo*, Skt. *vīra*: an heroic being in terms of spiritual commitment, 404, 460, 469, 581, 588, 593, 653; see also *ḍāka*
water of life *tshe-chu*: see under *elixir*
wheel(s) *'khor-lo*, Skt. *cakra*: see *centre(s)*
 cloud-mass, of syllables *yi-ge'i sprin-gyi 'khor-lo*, 877
 of the doctrine *chos-kyi 'khor-lo*, Skt. *dharmacakra*: see *doctrinal wheel(s)* and *promulgation of the doctrinal wheel*

of inexhaustible ornament *mi-zad-pa'i rgyan-gyi 'khor-lo*, 126; five *mi-zad-pa'i rgyan-gyi 'khor-lo lnga*, 866
thirty-six actions of the wheels of the inexhaustible ornaments of body, speech and mind *sku-gsung-thugs mi-zad-pa rgyan-gyi 'khor-lo'i mdzad-pa sum-cu-rtsa-drug*, 121
Wish-fulfilling Gem *yid-bzhin nor-bu*, Skt. *Cintāmāṇi*, 133, 147, 195, 198, 468-9
Wishing Tree *dpag-bsam-gyi shing*, Skt. *kalpavṛkṣa*, 133, 148, 198
(world) realms *('jig-rten-gyi) khams*, Skt. *(loka)dhātu*, *passim*
six, of existence *'jig-rten-gyi khams drug*, 585
three *khams-gsum*, 13, 31, 38, 51, 56, 73, 202, 259, 302, 321, 337, 339-40, 363, 418, 458, 490, 491, 575, 907, 930
worldly concerns, eight *'jig-rten chos brgyad*, 723, 852
wrong understanding, those of *log-par rtogs-pa*, Skt. *vipratipanna*, 13, 16, 54, 62-7, 873
yakṣa *gnod-sbyin*: a very large class of nature spirits, many of which are associated with mountains, trees, forests, rocks, abandoned buildings, etc. In India they are frequently related to vegetation, 75, 132, 135-6, 433, 435, 451, 452-3, 454, 466, 492, 609, 614, 754, 889
yakṣiṇī *gnod-sbyin-mo*: a female yakṣa, 465, 480, 481
year signs and elements *lo-rtags-dang khams*: the twelve animals and five elements marking the years of a sexagenary cycle, 959, n. 1330
yoga(s) *rnal-'byor*: lit. "union in fundamental reality", 35, 39, 102, 184, 248, 254, 256, 270, 276, 295, 312, 320, 343-5, 357, 360, 368, 413, 423, 459, 490, 547, 579, 588, 630, 653, 709, 715, 735, 769, 813, 829, 832, 853, 867, 876, 877, 897, 900, 907, 926
of another's body as the seal *gzhan-lus phyag-rgya*, 818; see also under *seal(s)* and *door*
daytime *nyin-gyi rnal-'byor*, 280
dream *rmi-lam*, 548
five *rnal-'byor lnga*: according to Mahāyoga, 363
five *rnal-'byor lnga*: i.e. the five paths of Anuyoga, 288, 369
four *rnal-'byor bzhi*, 33, 272; see also *miracles, four*
of one's own body as the means *rang-lus thabs-ldan*, 818; see also under *door*
preliminary, of accumulation and purification *sngon-'gro bsags-sbyong-gi rnal-'byor*, 862; see also *preliminary practice*
Six-limbed *sbyor-ba yan-lag drug-pa*: of the *Kālacakra Tantra*, 301, 546, 577-8, 674, 853
three *rnal-'byor gsum*: according to Anuyoga, 285-6
three classes of *yo-ga'i sde gsum*: the vehicles of the inner tantras of skilful means, 746
Yogācāra *rnal-'byor spyod-pa*: this term may originally refer to the conduct of the bodhisattva path in general, rather than to the mentalist school alone, 315, 911; see also *Mind Only* and *Vijñānavāda*
Yogācāra-Madhyamaka *rnal-'byor spyod-pa'i dbu-ma*: Great Madhyamaka, 169
Yogatantra *rnal-'byor-gyi rgyud*: see under *piṭaka* and *vehicle(s)*
yogic exercises *'phrul-'khor*, Skt. *yantra*, 606
yogin *rnal-'byor-pa*: a male practitioner of yoga, 115, 184, 195, 201, 270, 281, 304, 313, 335, 344, 353, 356, 394, 447, 473, 504, 511, 545, 547, 566, 573, 575, 580, 581, 583, 585, 586, 588, 630, 638, 641, 643, 755, 839, 854, 903, 926
twelve orders of *dzo-ki sde-tshan bcu-gnyis*: followers of Gorakṣanātha, 504
yoginī *rnal-'byor-ma*: a female practitioner of yoga, 460, 494, 538, 547, 573, 580, 585, 586, 588, 620, 630, 631, 700, 772, 773, 859
Yoginī tantras *rnal-'byor-ma'i rgyud*, 503
yojana *dpag-tshad*: a measurement of distance; defined, n. 518; 490
youthful vase body *gzhon-nu bum-pa'i sku*: the great buddha-body of reality: see under *buddha-body(ies)*
Yungdrung Pön tradition *gYung-drung bon-lugs*, 852; see also *Pön*
zandre *za-'dre*: a vampire demon, 711

Zhalupa *zhva-lu-pa*, 850
zho *zho*: a half tola of gold (approximately 5.85g.), ten of which equal one *srang*, 768
zi-stone *gzi*: a species of etched agate, highly valued in Tibet, 483
zombie *ro-langs*, Skt. *vetāla*: lit. "standing corpse", 535
Zur tradition *zur-lugs*, 139, 266, 617-49, 665, 668, 671, 672, 679, 691, 700-2, 725, 727, 730; see also *Nyang/Rong tradition*

Index of Personal Names

Introduction

In Indian and Tibetan Buddhist literature, great historical figures are often referred to by a diversity of names and epithets. This partly reflects the tendency of Buddhist masters to extend their sphere of activity through diverse geographical regions, where they are then known by diverse names (Padmsambhava being a notable example), and partly also the custom of receiving new names to mark increasingly advanced stages of meditative attainment or ordination: *prātimokṣa*, bodhisattva and mantra. In the case of Dalai Lama V, for example: Dalai Lama V refers to his position in the line of incarnations to which he belongs; Padmapāṇi indicates his status as an incarnation of Avalokiteśvara; Lozang Gyamtso and Ngagi Wangcuk indicate his gradual acceptance of monastic ordination; Dorje Thokmetsel indicates his prowess as a treasure-finder and mantra adept; and popularly he is referred to as the Great Fifth (*lnga-pa chen-po*) on account of his supremacy as a spiritual and temporal leader. This custom of conferring names and titles continues to the present day.

The word order in Tibetan and Sanskrit names is important. Titles, such as scholar (*paṇḍita*), master (*slob-dpon*, Skt. *ācārya*), lord of accomplished masters (*grub-dbang*, Skt. *siddheśvara*), lord of doctrine (*chos-rje*, Skt. *dharmasvāmin*), treasure-finder (*gter-ston*) and so forth, often precede the personal name. Epithets or titles indicative of clan, lineage, place of birth or residence, or incarnation line, may also be conjoined with personal names, or replace them altogether.

In this index, for the benefit of those unfamiliar with Tibetan conventions, we have listed most of the variations that occur in the text separately and referred the reader to one main entry (usually the most well-known form) where all these variations appear as sub-entries along with their page references.

Names are listed in English alphabetical order and letter by letter, except on those occasions when we have attempted to list diverse incarnations within their proper numerical sequences. Entries beginning with "Śākya" follow those beginning with "Sakya". Parentheses have generally been used to indicate elements omitted in shortened forms of a name, however it has not been possible to apply this convention exhaustively.

Dates have been supplied utilising information given in the body of the text or gathered from other Tibetan historical sources: it is hoped that further research will succeed in resolving many of the chronological uncertainties. Where enumerated categories of names occur, these are cross-referenced against the Glossary of Enumerations whenever more information is to be found there. Readers should also consult the Notes for occasional biographical information, which has not been cross-referenced here.

Sanskrit names have been restored with reference to original extant texts and dictionaries. In the case of a few deities, entered under their Sanskrit names — for example Guhyasamāja, Cakrasamvara and Kālacakra — it is not always clear from the context whether these refer to actual deities or to texts/teaching cycles. In such cases, readers should also consult the first part of the Bibliography.

Finally, line drawings illustrating many of the major figures described in the *History* appear throughout Volume One, and page references for these are listed in bold face.

Index of Personal Names

Abhayākaragupta (*c.* 1100) *'jigs-med 'byung-gnas sbas-pa*, 477
Acadru family *a-lcags 'gru'i rigs*, 841
Acala *mi-gYo-ba*, 577
Acintyaprabhāsa *ston-pa khye'u snang-ba dam-pa bsam-gyis mi-khyab-pa*: the first emanational teacher according to the Great Perfection, 136, **897**
Adhicitta, the deva *sems-lhag-can/lhag-sems-can*, 453, 490
Advayavajra *gnyis-med rdo-rje*, 200; see *Maitripā*
Agayana, the envoy *gser-yig-pa a-ga-ya-na*, 662
Agni, ṛṣi *drang-srong agni*, 65
Agniśuci, the deer *ri-dvags me'i gtsang-sbra-can*, 214
A-Hūṃ Gyen *a-hūṃ rgyan*, 784
Ājāneyabalaha *cang-shes bha-la-ha*, 133
Ajātaśatru, king *ma-skyes-dgra*, 428, 433, 435
Ajita, (conqueror/regent) *(rgyal-ba/rgyal-tshab) ma-pham-pa*, 98, 128, 129, 170-1, 838, 930, 932; see *Maitreya*
Ājñātakauṇḍinya *kun-shes*, 115
Ā-kar Matiśīla *ā-dkar mati-shi-la*, 510
Ākāśagarbha *nam(-mkha'i) snying(-po)*, 125
Akhu Pelbar *a-khu dpal-'bar*, 545
Akṣapāda *rkang-mig*, 65
Akṣobhya *mi-bskyod-pa/mi-'khrugs-pa*, 20, 125, 274, 355, 477, 690, 878
  Akṣobhyaprabha *ston-pa khye'u 'od mi-'khrugs-pa*: the second emanational teacher according to the Great Perfection, 136, **904**
  Akṣobhyavajra *mi-bskyod rdo-rje*, 416
All-Positive King *kun-bzang rgyal-po*, 317; see *Samantabhadra*
Ālokā *mar-me-ma*, 125
Ālokabhāsvatī, queen of Oḍḍiyāna *snang-ba gsal-ba'i 'od-ldan-ma*, 490
Amarasiṃha *'chi-med seng-ge*, 106
Amitābha (Buddha) *(sangs-rgyas) 'od-dpag(-tu) med(-pa)/snang-ba mtha'-yas*, Pl. 11; 20, 125, 274, 355, 468, 479, 746
Amitāyus *tshe-dpag-med*, 470, 549, 564, 624
  Lord of Immortality and his consort *'chi-med mgon-po yab-yum*, 855
  sugata Amitāyus *bde-bar gshegs-pa tshe-dpag-med*, 691
Amoghasiddhi *don(-yod) grub(-pa)*, 20, 125, 274, 355, 481, 766
Amoghavajra, the elder *don-yod rdo-rje che-ba*, 479
Amoghavajra, the younger *don-yod rdo-rje chung-ba/a-mo-gha-badzra*, 479, 708
Amṛtabhaiṣajya *bdud-rtsi sman(-lha)*, 452; see also *Avalokiteśvara*
  Bhaiṣajyaguru *sman-bla/sman-gyi bla-ma*, 591, 691
Amṛtakuṇḍalin *bdud-rtsi 'khyil*, 548, 623
Amṛtodana *bdud-rtsi zas*, 434
Ānanda *kun-dga'-bo*, 75, 421, 428, 432, 433, **434**, 434-5, 438, 859, 908, 928, 946
Ānandā, the nun *kun-dga'-mo*: a teacher of Vimalamitra (see *bairo 'dra-'bag*, Ch. 5), 469
Ānandagarbha *kun-dga' snying-po*, 272
Anantaguṇā ḍākinī (the Ḍākinī of Limitless Virtues) *yon-tan mtha'-yas-pa'i mkha'-'gro-ma*, 493
Anāthapiṇḍada *mgon-med zas-sbyin*, 137, 423
Andzom Drukpa (1842-1924) *a-'dzom 'brug-pa*, 879

Anupamarakṣita *dpe-med 'tsho*, 674
Aparājita *a-dzi*, 548
Ārāḍa(kālāma) *ring-'phur*, 419, 422
Archer *mda'-ba/mda'-bsnun*, 197; see *Saraha*
Arhat Suvarṇaprabhāsa *dgra-bcom-pa gser-'od dam-pa*: the eighth emanational teacher according to the Great Perfection, 136
Ariboga (or Arikbugha) *a-re-bho-ga*: the younger brother of Qubilai Qan, to whom in 1264 he conceded defeat, 661, 662
Aro (Yeshe Jungne) *a-ro (ye-shes 'byung-gnas)*, 231-2, 571, 673, 675, 706
Ārṣadhara, king (of Sahor) *rgyal-po gtsug-lag 'dzin*, 470, 972
Āryadeva *'phags-pa lha/arya de-ba*, **165**, 167, 309, 413, 440, 464, 498, 502, 596, 641, 899
Āryaśūra *dpa'-bo*, 703; see *Śūra*
Ārya Tārā *'phags-ma sgrol-ma*, 466; see *Tārā*
Asaṅga *thogs(-med)*, 18, 28, 91, 108, **169**, 182, 184, 189, 300-1, 404, 440, 441, 463, 849, 919, 931
"Ashen Zombie" *ro-langs thal-mdog*, Skt. *Vetala Bhasmavarṇa, 477, 493; see *Garap Dorje*
Aśoka, the religious king *chos-rgyal mya-ngan med*, 429, 435, 948
  Dharmāśoka, king *rgyal-po dharma sva-ka*, 429
Aśvottama (or Aśvavarapāda) *rta-mchog*: teacher of Viṇāpā, 927
Aśvottama/Supreme Horse *rta-mchog*, 274, 534; see *Hayagrīva*
Atiśa, (lord/master) (982-1054) *(jo-bo-rje/slob-dpon) a-ti-sha*, 184, 198, 205, 395, 546, 548, 550, 706, 853, 889, 891-2, 905-6, 914, 950, 951
  Dīpaṃkara *di-paṃ-ka-ra*, 914
Ātmaprakāśā *bdag-nyid gsal-rigs-ma*, 498
Ātreya, ṛṣi *drang-srong rgyun-shes-kyi bu/e-tra'i bu*, 66, 99
Avadhūti *a-ba-dhu-ti-pa*, 477
Avalokiteśvara *spyan-ras-gzigs*, Pl. 12; 75, 125, 261, 393, 449, 451, 452, **453**, 466, 497, 498, 507, 510, 564, 567, 572, 617, 698, 757, 758, 784, 791, 798, 802, 821, 823, 826, 841; see also *Amṛtabhaiṣajya* and *Lords of the Three (Enlightened) Families*
  Avalokiteśvara in the form of the "King of Space" *spyan-ras gzigs nam-mkha' rgyal-po*, Skt. Gaganarāja, 591
  eleven-faced Avalokiteśvara *zhal-bcu-gcig-pa*, 791
  Great Compassionate One *thugs-rje chen-po*, Skt. Mahākāruṇika, 507, 511, 560, 564, 565, 569, 659, 677, 755, 762, 765, 770, 784, 828, 829
  Lokeśvara/Lord of the World *(dpa'-bo) 'jigs-rten dbang-phyug*, 47, 404, 916
  Padmapāṇi *lag-na padma*, 564
  Sublime One *'phags-pa*, 510
Aviddhakarṇa *rna ma-phug-pa*, 65
Ba Getong, spiritual benefactor *dge-bshes sba dge-mthong*, 640
Bagom Tikma *'ba'-sgom dig-ma*, 642
Bagom (Yeshe Cangcup) *sba-sgom (ye-shes byang-chub)*, 542-3, 545-6, 548
Baka Künzang Rikdzin Dorje *rba-kha kun-bzang rig-'dzin rdo-rje*, 735
Baka Rikdzin Khamsum Yongdröl *rba-kha rig-'dzin khams-gsum yongs-grol*, 735
Baka Trülku Chöki Gyamtso *rba-kha sprul-sku chos-kyi rgya-mtsho*, 817
  Puwo Baka Trülku Rikdzin Chöki Gyamtso *spu-bo rba-kha sprul-sku rig-'dzin chos-kyi rgya-mtsho*, 812
Balabhadra, king of Bhaṃdva *rgyal-po ba-la bha-dra*, 504
Balāhaka, bodhisattva *byang-chub sems-dpa' sprin-gyi shugs-can*, 136
Bālapāda *byis-pa'i zhabs*, 462; see *Jālandharipā*
Bangtön Cakyu *sbangs-ston lcags-kyu*, 649
Ba-ratna *rba rat-na*, 515, 524; see *Ba Trhizi of the Zhang family*
Bartön *'bar-ston*, 549
Barza Lhayang *'bar-bza' lha-dbyangs*, 537
Ba Selnang *sba gsal-snang*, 509, 515
  Yeshe Wangpo *ye-shes dbang-po*, 515
Ba Trhizi of the Zhang family *zhang-blon dad-pa-can rba khri-gzigs*, 515
  Ba-ratna *rba ratna*, 515, 524
  Pelyang *dpal-dbyangs*, 515
Ben *'ban*, 650
Bhadra *bzang-po*, 429
Bhadrapāla, bodhisattva *bzang-skyong*, 423
Bhadrapāla, the deva *de-ba bzang-skyong*, 463
Bhadrika *rab-bzang*, 115
Bhagavat *(mgon-po) legs-ldan*, 624; see *Lekden Degü*

Bhairava *'jigs-byed*, 449, 936

Bhaiṣajyaguru *sman-bla/sman-gyi bla-ma*, 591, 691; see *Amṛtabhaiṣajya*

Bhallika *bzang-skyong*, 421

Bhaṇṭa (or Bhaṭa) *bhaṇṭa*, 435

Bharadvāja *bha-ra-dva-dza*, 64

Bharata *bha-ra-ta*, 106

Bharo Tsukdzin, the Newar *bha-ro gtsug-'dzin*, 766-8, 780

Bhāṣita, ṛṣi *drang-srong bha-shi-ta*, 466, 467

Bhāskara, the boy *khye'u snang-byed*, 193

Bhaṭa Hor *bhaṭa-hor*, 519

Bhaṭṭārikā *rje-btsun-ma*, 572

Bhavya, master *slob-dpon bha-vya* or *skal-ldan/legs-ldan*, 169, 184, 905

Bhelakīrti *bhe-la kirti*, 497

Bhṛgu, ṛṣi *drang-srong ngan-spong*, 65

Bhṛkuṭī *khro-gnyer-can-ma*, 466, 510

Bhusukuchok *bhu-su-ku mchog*, 605

black-hat Karmapa *zhva-nag karma-pa*, 811; see *Karmapa X*

"Blue-skirted Paṇḍita" *paṇḍita sham-thabs sngon-po-can*, 918

Bodhisattva *byang-chub sems-dpa'*, 416-21; see *Buddha*

Bodhisattva *(mkhan-po) bo-dhi sa-tva*, 405, 513-15, 601; see *Śāntarakṣita*

Bodhivajra *byang-chub rdo-rje*, 478

Bodhi Zhangtön *bo-dhi zhang-ston*, 689

Brahmā *tshang-pa*, 16, 66, 132, 417, 422, 624

  four-faced Brahmā *tshang-pa gdong bzhi-pa*, 65

Brahmaratnaprabha *tshang-pa rin-chen 'od*, 452

Brahmasarvatāra *tshang-pa kun-sgrol*, 452

Brahmaśikhandara *tshang-pa gtsug-phung 'dzin*, 452

Brahma Śikhin *tshang-pa ral-pa-can*, 214

Bṛhaspati (Guru of the Gods) *phur-bu*, 66-7, 197

British *dbyin-ji*, 958

Buddha *sangs-rgyas*: Śākyamuni, Pls. 37, 41; 16, 23, 47, 71, 72, 73, 74, 75, 80, 83, 91, 120, 129, 138, 147, 154, 190, 195, 196-7, 199, 212, 213, 226, 244, 289, 295, 299, 307, 313, 315, 318, 322, 336, 393, 394, 400, 409, **417**, 411-27, 430, 433, 435, 440, 441, 454, 456, 472, 504, 518, 583, 605, 610, 622, 643, 644, 646, 648, 716, 747, 762, 837, 859, 890-1, 893, 898, 900, 910, 931, 933, 943-8, 944, 949, 959

  Bodhisattva *byang-chub sems-dpa'*, 416-21

  Conqueror *rgyal-ba*, Skt. Jina, 47, 68, 73, 88, 113, 120, 127-8, 143, 146, 151, 278, 307, 308, 312, 315, 324, 376, 404, 405, 406, 409, 427, 431, 442, 507, 522, 527, 610, 736, 748, 824, 859, 874, 877, 894, 930, 943, 945, 948, 967, 969, 972

  Fourth Guide *rnam-'dren bzhi-pa*, 409, 943

  Gautama *gau-ta-ma*, 422-3

  Lord of Sages/Munīndra *thub-pa'i dbang-po*, 11, 128, 503, 768, 894

  Lord of the Śākyas *śā-kya'i mgon*, 130

  Sage *thub-pa*, Skt. Muni, 73, 77, 103, 184, 200, 204, 300, 422, 427, 555, 705, 894, 969, 971

  Śākya King *śā-kya'i rgyal-po*, 405, 746

  Śākyamuni (Buddha) *śā-kya thub-pa*, 11, 17, 26, 36, 115, 137, 153, 193, 221, 312, 396, 411-27, 430, 434, 454, 564, 573, 590, 656, 659, 672, 696, 768, 894, 946-8, 972

  Śākyendra, the Transcendent Lord *śā-kya dbang-po*, 755

  Sarvārthasiddha *don-thams-cad grub-pa*, 417

  Siddhārtha, (prince) *(rgyal-bu) don-grub*, 412, 575, 946

  Sugata *bde-bar gshegs-pa*, 22, 138, 186, 218, 268, 300, 409, 871, 873, 896, 928

  Śvetaketu, holy *dam-pa tog-dkar*, 412, 416

  Tathāgata *de-bzhin gshegs-pa*, 99, 103, 146, 153-5, 172, 179-80, 189, 192, 195, 216, 253, 292, 316, 334, 340, 393, 414, 422, 423, 425, 426, 456, 471, 626, 786, 947

  Teacher *ston-pa*, Skt. Śāstṛ, 47, 68, 71, 73-6, 78, 88, 90-1, 104, 109, 113-48, 153-5, 193, 218, 231, 409, 411, 413, 428, 429, 430, 432, 434, 435, 436, 437, 438, 439, 440, 441, 452, 454, 458, 613, 637, 705, 894, 906, 946

  Transcendent Lord (Buddha) *bcom-ldan-'das*, Skt. Bhagavān, 75-6, 175, 186, 188, 190, 215, 303, 312, 363, 428, 433, 454, 455, 747, 898, 944, 945

Buddhaguhya *sangs-rgyas gsang-ba*, 39, 40, 92, 96, 123, 249, 270, 462, **465**, 464-66, 468, 470, 481, 533, 829, 889, 916
Buddhajñāna *(ratna) buddha dznya-na*, 607; see *Nup(cen) Sangye Yeshe*
Buddhajñānapāda *(sangs-rgyas) ye-shes zhabs*, 252, 313, 412, 442, 453, 464, 465, 475, **495**, 494-6, 497, 921, 931
Buddha Kalyāṇamati *sangs-rgyas dge-ba'i blo-gros*, 121
Buddhākarabhadra *bu-ddha ā-ka-ra bha-dra*, 708
Buddha Kāśyapa *sangs-rgyas 'od-srungs*, 430, 509
  Kāśyapa, the teacher, the elder *ston-pa 'od-srung bgres-po*: the tenth emanational teacher according to the Great Perfection, 137
Buddha Puṣpamahāroca *sangs-rgyas me-tog mdzes-pa chen-po*, 120
Buddhaśānti *sangs-rgyas zhi-ba*, 464, 465
Buddhas of the Five Enlightened Families *rgyal-ba rigs-lnga*, 11, 123, 623
  Conquerors of the Five (Enlightened) Families *rgyal-ba rigs lnga*, 122, 561, 572, 660
  Five Conquerors/Teachers *rgyal-ba/ston-pa lnga*, 125, 128
  Herukas of the Five Enlightened Families *he-ru-ka rigs-lnga*, 672
  Tathāgatas of the Five (Enlightened) Families *de-bzhin gshegs-pa rigs-lnga*, 343, 691
  Teachers of the Five Buddha/ Enlightened Families *rigs-lnga'i ston-pa rnams*, 19, 21, 117, 448
Buddhas of the Hundred Authentic Families *dam-pa rigs-brgya*, 591
Buddhas of the Past, Three *'das-pa'i sangs-rgyas gsum*, 423
Buddhaśrī (Sangyepel) *bu-ddha shri (sangs-rgyas dpal)*, 592; see *Sangye Pelrin*
Buddhaśrīśānti of Oḍḍiyāna *sangs-rgyas dpal zhi-ba*, 477
Buddha Sucaritacakra *sangs-rgyas 'khor-lo legs-par spyod-pa*, 120
Buddhas, the Thousand *sangs-rgyas stong-rtsa*: the thousand supreme emanational bodies, 136, 409, 624, 938, 944
Buddhirakṣita *blo-sems 'tsho*, 509
Bumbar *'bum-'bar*, 709
Bumrampa Orgyen Kelzang *'bum-ram-pa o-rgyan skal-bzang*, 833
Buyantu, the emperor (reigned 1311-20) *gong-ma bu-yan-thu gan*, 669
Ca Chenpo: see *Ca Düldzin Chenpo*
Cadrel Künga Pelden *bya-bral kun-dga' dpal-ldan*, 919
Ca Düldzin Chenpo (1091-1166) *bya 'dul-'dzin chen-po*, 952
  Ca Chenpo *bya chen-po*, 685
Cakrasaṃvara *tsa-kra sambara/'khor-lo bde-mchog/bde-mchog*, 449, 549, 591, 936; see also Bibliography
  sixty-two deities of the Cakrasaṃvara maṇḍala *bde-mchog drug-cu rtsa-gnyis*, 691
Cakyungpa Pelden Senge *bya-khyung-pa dpal-ldan seng-ge*, 788
Camgön Rinpoche of Phurbucok *phur-lcogs byams-mgon rin-po-che*, 778
(Camgön Tā'i) Situ Pema Nyinje Wangpo (1774-1853) *(byams-mgon tā'i) si-tu padma nyin-byed dbang-po*: i.e. Tā'i Situ IX, 842, 861
Campabum (1179-1252) *byams-pa 'bum*: i.e. Katokpa Gyeltsap II, 693-4, **694**, 695, 699
  Campa Rinpoche *byams-pa rin-po-che*, 694
Campapel, the translator of Trhopu (b. 1172/3) *khro-lo byams-pa dpal*, 663
  Trhopu Lotsāwa *khro-phu lo-tsa-ba*, 564
Campa Phüntsok, lama of Derge *sde-dge bla-ma byams-pa phun-tshogs*, 816
Campa Rinpoche *byams-pa rin-po-che*, 694; see *Campabum*
Campa Senge *byams-pa seng-ge*, 663-5; see *(Zur) Campa Senge*
Canak clan *bya-nag-gi rigs*, 719
Cāṇakya *tsa-ṇa-ka*, 97
Candragomin *tsa-ndra go-mi*, 92, 100, 108, 441, 455, 703, 730, 871
Candrakīrti *zla(-ba) grags(-pa)*, 164-5, 309, 464, 577
Candrarakṣita, the king of Oḍiviśa *zla-ba srung*, 441
Cangcup Dorje, the preceptor/lama *mkhan-po/bla-ma byang-chub rdo-rje*, 784
Cangcup Gyeltsen *byang-chub rgyal-mtshan*: i.e. Katokpa Gyeltsap XII, 696
Cangcup Lodrö *byang-chub blo-gros*: i.e. Katokpa Gyeltsap X, 696

Cangcupmen of the Drom family, the royal consort *btsun-mo 'brom-bza' byang-chub sman*, 554
Cangcup Pelwa *byang-chub dpal-ba*: i.e. Katokpa Gyeltsap V, 695
Cangcup Senge *byang-chub seng-ge*: i.e. Katokpa Gyeltsap IX, 696
Cangcup Senge, lama *bla-ma byang-chub seng-ge*, 688
(Cangdak) Pema Trhinle *(byang-bdag) padma phrin-las*, 41, 956; see *Dorje Trak Rikdzin IV*
Cangne Tertön *byang-nas gter-ston*, 590
Cangpa Rikdzin Ngagiwangpo *byang-pa rig-'dzin ngag-gi dbang-po*, 679, 681, 683, 719, 821; see *Dorje Trak Rikdzin III*
Cangpa Trashi Topgyel (1550-1602) *byang-pa bkra-shis stobs-rgyal*, 824
  Chögyel Wangpöide *chos-rgyal dbang-po'i sde*, 808
  Trashi Topgyel (Wangpöide, the master of the Northern Treasure) *(byang-bdag) bkra-shis stobs-rgyal (dbang-po'i sde)*, 783, 808, 822
Caraka *tsa-ra-ka*, 65
Cārīndra *spyod-'chang dbang-po*, 693, 927; see *Kṛṣṇacārin*
Carme Tshülrin *byar-med tshul-rin*, 552
Catang Sonam Özer *bya-btang bsod-nams 'od-zer*, 595
Catri Tsenpo *bya-khri btsan-po*: the middle son of Drigum Tsenpo who fled to Puworong, 972
Cegom, lama *bla-ma lce-sgom*, 559; see *Rongnangda Cegom Nakpo*
Cegom Nakpo *lce-sgom nag-po*, 571; see *Rongnangda Cegom Nakpo*
Cegom Śākyagyel *lce-sgom śākya-rgyal*, 622
Cel (Lotsāwa) Künga Dorje *dpyal (lo-tsā-ba) kun-dga' rdo-rje*, 359, 653
  Lharje Celpa *lha-rje dpyal-pa*, 348
Celuka *tsi-lu-pa*, 442
Cendrenpa *spyan-'dren-pa*, 710
Ce-nga Chöki Trakpa *spyan-snga chos-kyi grags-pa*, 553; see *Zhamarpa IV*
Ce-nga (Mangpu)wa Sonam Bumpa *spyan-snga (mang-phu-)ba bsod-nams 'bum-pa*: i.e. Katokpa Gyeltsap III, 694-5
Ce-nga Neljor *spyan-snga rnal-'byor*, 547
Ce-nga Rinpoche *spyan-snga rin-po-che*, 675-6; see *Zhamarpa IV*
Cenye, the great preceptor *spyan-gYas mkhan-chen*, 674
Cerpa Wangtung of Ze *gzad-kyi gcer-pa wang-thung*, 651
Ce Śākya Gyeltsen *lce śā-kya rgyal-mtshan*, 619
Ceshak-chok of Gegong *dge-gong-gi lce-shag-mchog*, 619
Ce Thupei Wangpo of Nyangro Nyentso *nyang-ro gnyan-tsho lce thub-pa'i dbang-po*, 557
Cetön Drupabum *lce-ston grub-pa 'bum*, 665
Cetön Gyanak (1094-1148) *lce-ston rgya-nag*, 648, 650-1
  Co-se of upper Nyang *jo-sras nyang-stod-pa*, 650
  Je Lhakangpa *rje lha-khang-pa*, 650
  Lharje Gyanak *lha-rje rgya-nag*, 650, 651, 652
Cetsün Senge Wangcuk *lce-btsun seng-ge dbang-phyug*, Pl. 29; 556, **558**, 557-9
  Cetsün, the great *lce-btsun chen-po*, 561, 858
Chak Lotsāwa (Dracom) (1153-1216) *chags lo-tsā-ba (dgra-bcom)*: uncle of the following, 758
Chak Lotsāwa (Chöje Pel) (1197-1264) *chag lo-tsā-ba (chos-rje dpal)*, 758, 891
Chale *jo-mo phya-le*: consort of Dzeng Dharmabodhi, 549
Chamdo Gyelwa Phakpa Lha *chab-mdo rgyal-ba 'phags-pa lha*, 833
Chandaka *'dun-pa*, 417, 418
Chapa Chöki Senge (1109-69) *phya-pa chos-kyi seng-ge*, 550
Char Thülcen, the accomplished master of Dokam *grub-thob phyar-thul-can*, 804
Chetsenkye of Bru-sha *bru-sha'i che-btsan skyes*, 489, 537, 607, 609
Chim Carok, the "Crow of Chim" *mchims bya-rog*, 602, 603
Chim, the deity of *mchims-lha*, 603
Chim Dorje Peucung *mchims rdo-rje spre'u chung*, 753
Chime Tenyi Yungdrung Lingpa *'chi-med bstan-gnyis gYung-drung gling-pa*, 863; see *Jamgön Kongtrül (Lodrö Thaye)*
Chimo Trashi-tsho *mchims-mo bkra-shis mtsho*, 607
Chödenpa Gönpo Dorje *chos-ldan-pa mgon-po rdo-rje*, 686
Chödrak, father *a-pha chos-grags*, 706; see *Rongzompa (Chöki Zangpo)*

Chödrak Gyamtso *chos-grags rgya-mtsho*, 973

Chögyel Phakpa (1235-80) *chos-rgyal 'phags-pa*, 953

Phakpa (Rinpoche, lama) *(bla-ma) 'phags-pa (rin-po-che)*, 662, 695, 712

Chögyel Tendzin *chos-rgyal bstan-'dzin*, 727-8; see *(Locen) Chögyel Tendzin*

Chögyel Wangpöide *chos-rgyal dbang-po'i sde*, 808; see *Cangpa Trashi Topgyel*

Chogyur (Decen Zhikpo) Lingpa, the great treasure finder (1829-70) *gter-chen mchog-gyur (bde-chen zhig-po) gling-pa*, 738, **842**, 841-8, 856, 863, 864-5, 867, 958

Norbu Tendzin *nor-bu bstan-'dzin*, 841

Padmāṅkuśa, bodhisattva *byang-chub sems-dpa' padma'i myu-gu*, 848

Chöje Drukpa *chos-rje 'brug-pa*: the first Drukcen, 835; see *Tsangpa Gyare*

Chöje Lingpa *chos-rje 'gling-pa*, 751, 835; see *(Rikdzin) Chöje Lingpa*

Chöje Tsharpa (1502-66/7) *chos-rje tshar-pa*: i.e. Lodrö Gyeltsen (*blo-gros rgyal-mtshan*), 922

Chokdrupde, the king of Kungtang *gung-thang rgyal-po mchog-grub sde*, 782

Chöki Lama *chos-kyi bla-ma*, 694; see *Karmapa II*

Chöki Lodrö, lama *bla-ma chos-kyi blo-gros*, 784

Chöki Lodrö of Sheldrak *shel-brag chos-kyi blo-gros*, 553

Chöki Shenyen *chos-kyi bshes-gnyen*, 854; see *(Jamyang) Khyentse Wangpo*

Chöki Sherap, the translator of Korup *go-rub lo-tsā-ba dge-slong chos-kyi shes-rab*, 708; see *Korup Lotsāwa*

Chöki Trakpa Yeshe Pelzangpo *chos-kyi grags-pa ye-shes dpal-bzang-po*, 675; see *Zhamarpa IV*

Chokme Cangsem *phyogs-med byang-sems*, 697

Chökyong Gönpo *chos-skyong mgon-po*, 809

Chökyong Zangpo, great translator of Zhalu (1441-1527) *zha-lu chos-skyong bzang-po*, 955

Chöling Karwang Chime Dorje (b. 1763) *chos-gling gar-dbang 'chi-med rdo-rje*, 957

Chörin *sras-po chos-rin*, 552

Chöwang Künzang *chos-dbang kun-bzang*, 553

Chöwang Rinpoche *chos-dbang rin-po-che*, 838; see *Guru Chöwang*

Chöyingpa *chos-dbyings-pa*, 791

Chöying Rangdröl (*chos-dbyings rang-grol*), 679-83, 684; see *(Zurcen) Chöying Rangdröl*

Chumikpa *chu-mig-pa*, 564

Chusor Namkabum *chu-gsor nam-mkha' 'bum*, 696

Cingtön of Tsang *gtsang-pa bying-ston*, 660

Cobuma *jo-'bum-ma*, 757

Cogön *jo-mgon*, 552

Cokro Lotsāwa *cog-ro lo-tsā-ba*, 688

Cokro Lüi Gyeltsen *lcog-ro klu'i rgyal-mtshan*, 515, 522, 527, 555, 800, 889, 893

Cokro Pucungmen *cog-ro bu-chung sman*, 514

Cokroza (Cangcupmen) *cog-ro-bza' (byang-chub sman)*, 537, 711-12

Cokro Zangkar Dzökur *cog-ro zangs-dkar mdzod-khur*, 706

(Comden) Rikpei Reldri *(bcom-ldan) rig-pa'i ral-gri/rig-ral*, 827, 894, 914-17, 930

Como Dangla *jo-mo mdangs-lha*: the protector, 581

Como Gyagar *jo-mo rgya-gar*, 562

Como Kangmo *jo-mo gang-mo*, 543

Como Menmo (1248-83) *jo-mo sman-mo*, **772**, 771-4, 953

Pema Tshokyi *padma mtsho-skyid*, 771

Como Namar *jo-mo sna-dmar*: a local divinity, 622

Como Nyangmo *jo-mo nyang-mo*, 651

Como(wa) *jo-mo(-ba)*, 545, 546

Como Wangmo *jo-mo wang-mo*, 653

Como Yumo *jo-mo gYu-mo*, 637

Conang Künzi Tölpopa *jo-nang kun-gzigs dol-bo-pa*, 953; see *Tölbupa/Tölpopa (Sherap Gyeltsen)*

Conang Sherap Gyeltsen *jo(-nang shes-rab rgyal-mtshan)*, 905; see *Tölbupa/ Tölpopa (Sherap Gyeltsen)*

Conqueror *rgyal-ba*, Skt. Jina: Śākyamuni Buddha, 47, 68, 73, 88, 113, 120, 127-8, 143, 146, 151, 278, 307, 308, 312, 315, 324, 376, 404, 405, 406, 409, 427, 431, 442, 507, 522, 527, 610, 736, 748, 824, 859, 874, 877, 894, 930, 943, 945, 948, 967, 969, 972; see *Buddha*

Conquerors of the Five Enlightened Families *rgyal-ba rigs lnga*, 122, 561,

572, 660; see *Buddhas of the Five Enlightened Families*
Co-se (Dzeng) *jo-sras*, 549, 565, 649; see *Dzeng Co-se*
Cosema Dorjekyi *jo-sras-ma rdo-rje skyid*, 548
Cosemo Damo Tsuktorcam *jo-sras-mo mda'-mo gtsug-tor-lcam*, 645
Co-se Temdrel *jo-sras rten-'brel*, 929
Co-se of upper Nyang *jo-sras nyang-stod-pa*, 650; see *Cetön Gyanak*
Co-se Zhanglakyap of Traci *gra-phyi'i jo-sras zhang-la-skyabs*, 551
Co-sö of Central Tibet (b. 1168) *dbus-pa jo-bsod*, 656, 657
Cotsün Dorjetra *sras-jo-btsun rdo-rje grags*: son of Dropukpa, 650
Dakcen Lodrö Gyeltsen (1444-95) *bdag-chen blo-gros rgyal-mtshan*, 922
Ḍāki Künzang Chönyi Dekyong Wangmo *ḍā-ki kun-bzang chos-nyid bde-skyong dbang-mo*, 919
(Dalai Lama I,) Gendün Trupa (1391-1474) *dge-'dun grub-pa*, 954
(Dalai Lama II,) Gendün Gyamtso (1476-1542) *dge-'dun rgya-mtsho*, 955
(Dalai Lama IV,) Yönten Gyamtso (1589-1617) *yon-tan rgya-mtsho*, 821
Dalai Lama V, Lozang Gyamtso (1617-82) *blo-bzang rgya-mtsho*, **822**, 956
  Dorje Thokmetsel *rdo-rje thogs-med rtsal*, 821
  (Great) Fifth (Dalai Lama) *lnga-pa (chen-po)*, 682-4, 688, 719, 720, 728, 736-7, 821-4, 826, 830, 831, 832-3, 926, 931, 966
  Lozang Gyamtso *blo-bzang rgya-mtsho*, 821
  Ngagi Wangcuk *ngag-gi dbang-phyug*, 821
  Padmapāṇi, the Great Fifth Dalai Lama *phyag-na padma lnga-pa chen-po*, 678
(Dalai Lama VI,) Tshangyang Gyamtso (1683-1706) *tshangs-dbyangs rgya-mtsho*, 824
Dalai Lama VII, Kelzang Gyamtso (1708-57) *skal-bzang rgya-mtsho*, 957
Dalai Lama IX, Lungtok Gyamtso (1805-15) *lung-rtogs rgya-mtsho*, 957
Dalai Lama XIII, Thupten Gyamtso (1876-1933) *thub-bstan rgya-mtsho*, 958
  Great Thirteenth (Dalai Lama) *bcu-gsum-pa chen-po*, 777-8
Dalai Lama XIV, Tendzin Gyamtso (b. 6 July 1935) *mnga'-bdag sku-phreng bcu-bzhi-pa chen-po bstan-'dzin rgya-mtsho*, 959
  Great Fourteenth *bcu-bzhi-pa chen-po*, 824
Daṃṣṭrasena *mche-sde*, 944
Danak Tsuktor Wangcuk *mda'-nag gtsug-tor dbang-phyug*, 648
Dānaśīla *dā-na-shi-la*, 515, 522
Daṇḍapāṇi *lag-na be-con*, 418
Daṇḍin *dbyug-pa-can/daṇḍi*, 104, 705
Dangma (Lhündrup Gyeltsen, the elder) *(gnas-brtan) ldang-ma (lhun-grub rgyal-mtshan)*, 556-7, **557**, 558, 919
Daö Zhönu *zla-'od gzhon-nu*, 931; see *Gampopa*
Dapzang Trülku, the great preceptor and bodhisattva *mkhan-chen byang-sems zla-bzang sprul-pa'i sku*, 842
Darcarupa/Darcarwa *'dar-phya-ru-ba/'dar-phyar-ba*, 714-16, 920
Da Śākyaphel *mda' śākya 'phel*, 663, 665
Datik (Co-śāk of Nakmore) *(nag-mo-re'i) mda'-tig (jo-śak)/mdal-tig (jo-śāk)*, 358, 642, 645, **647**
Dawabum *gcung-po zla-ba 'bum*, 563
Dawa (Gyeltsen) *zla-ba (rgyal-mtshan)*: the spiritual son of Pema Lingpa, 722, 735, 798, 799
Dawa Trakpa *zla-ba grags-pa*, 595
De, eight middle kings called *bar-gyi lde brgyad*: listed in the Glossary of Enumerations, 508, n. 535
(Deities of the) Eight Transmitted Precepts (of Great Attainment) *(sgrub-chen) bka'-brgyad(-kyi lha-tshogs)*, Pls. 5, 17-24; 591, 828; see also listed separately as *Hayagrīva*, *Malign Mantra*, *Mātaraḥ*, *Mundane Praise*, *Vajrakīla*, *Vajrāmṛta*, *Yamāntaka*, *Yangdak Heruka* and as the deity which consumes all these *Mahottara*
deities, peaceful and wrathful *zhi-khro*: see *peaceful and wrathful deities*
Den-gom Chöki Trakpa of Dokam *mdo-khams-pa 'dan-sgom chos-kyi grags-pa*, 595
Denma Tsemang *ldan-ma rtse-mang*, 535, 756
Derge Yilungpa Sonam Namgyel (d. 1952) *sde-dge yid-lhung-pa bsod-nams rnam-rgyal*, 919

Deshek Gyawo(pa) *bde-gshegs rgya-bo(-pa)*, 635, 641; see *Zurcung(pa Sherap-tra)*
Deshek Zurcungpa *bde-gshegs zur-chung-pa*, 643; see *Zurcung(pa Sherap-tra)*
Deshek Zurpoche *bde-gshegs zur-po-che*, 918; see *(Zurpoche) Śākya Jungne*
Deu Gangpa, the preceptor *mkhan-po lde'u sgang-pa*, 565
Devadatta *lhas-byin*, 418, 420
Devākaracandra *de-ba-ga-ra tsa-ntra*, 708
Devaśarman *lha-skyid*, 90
Devendra *lha-yi dbang-po/lha-dbang*, 400, 401, 575, 593
Indra *brgya-byin*: i.e. Śatakratu, 417, 422
Indrarāja *dbang-po'i rgyal-po*, 913
Indraśakra *dbang-po brgya-byin*, 452
Śakra, (lord) *(dbang-po) brgya-byin*: i.e. Śatakratu, 130, 624, 768
Surendra *lha-dbang*, 128
Devourers and Slaughterers *za-gsod*: protectors associated with Vajrakīla, 713
Dewacam, the benefactress *yon-bdag-mo bde-ba-lcam*, 617
Dewachenpo *bde-ba-chen-po*, 972; see *Guru Rinpoche*
Dewarshekpa, lama *bla-ma bde-bar gshegs-pa*, 691; see *Katok(pa) Tampa Deshek*
Dhanadhala *dha-na-dha-la*, 607, 614
Dhanarakṣita *dha-na-rakṣita/dharmarakṣita*, 488-9, 607, 609
Dhanasaṃskṛta *dha-na-saṃ-skri-ta*, 483, 607
Dharmabhadra *dharma bha-dra*, 708; see *Rongzompa (Chöki Zangpo)*
Dharmabodhi (of Magadha) *dhar-ma bo-dhi*, 489, 537, 607, 609
Dharmakīrti *chos-grags*, 92, 102, **103**, 440, 703
Dharmamitra *chos-kyi bshes-gnyen*, 128
Dharmapāla, king (reigned *c.* 770-810) *rgyal-po dharma pā-la*, 478, 501, 892, 931
Dharmarāja(pāla) *dharma rā-dza (pā-la)*, 489, 607, 609
Dharmāśoka, king *rgyal-po dharma sva-ka*, 429; see *Aśoka*
Dharmaśrī, the great translator *lo-chen dharma-shri* 526, 733; see *Locen Dharmaśrī*
Dharmatāśīla *dharma-ta shi-la*, 522
Dharmodgata, bodhisattva *byang-chub sems-dpa' chos-'phags*, 624
Dhātvīśvarī *dbyings-kyi dbang-phyug-ma*, 20, 125
Dhītika *dhi-dhi-ka*, 437
Dhūpā *bdug-spos-ma*, 125
Dignāga *phyogs-kyi glang-po*, 91, 92, **101**, 102, 108, 189, 440, 703
Dīpaṃkara *di-paṃ-ka-ra*, 914; see *Atiśa*
Dīpaṃkarabhadra *mar-me mdzad bzang-po*, 892
Dīpaṃkara (Buddha) *(sangs-rgyas) mar-me mdzad*, 416, 624
Dode Tar *mdo-sde dar*, 793
Dodrup I, Jikme Trhinle Özer (1745-1821) *rdo-grub 'jigs-med phrin-las 'od-zer*, 957
Trupwang Jikme Trhinle Özer *grub-dbang 'jigs-med phrin-las 'od-zer*, 839
Dodrup III, Jikme Tenpei Nyima (1865-1926) *rdo-grub 'jigs-med bstan-pa'i nyi-ma*, 375, 879
Dö Khyungpo Hūṃ-nying *mdo'i khyung-po hūṃ-snying*, 708
Ḍombī Heruka *ḍombi he-ru-ka*, 253, 471
Do-nga Lingpa *mdo-sngags gling-pa*, 854; see *(Jamyang) Khyentse Wangpo*
Do-nga Tendzin *mdo-sngags bstan-'dzin*, 595, 724
Do-nga Tendzin Norbu, the Dokam Kyangkar Trülku *mdo-khams gyang-mkhar sprul-sku mdo-sngags bstan-'dzin nor-bu*, 734
Dong, family of *ldong-gi rigs*, 722
Dong Gönpakyap *ldong dgon-pa skyabs*, 675
Dongkar Tshoje (Physician of Dongkar) *gdong-khar 'tsho-byed*, 722; see *Sodokpa Lodrö Gyeltsen*
Dongkarwa, the aristocrat *sde-pa gdong-khar-ba*, 722
Dongtön Dorje Nyingpo *ldong-ston rdo-rje snying-po*, 689
Donyen Menbu *rdo-gnyan rman-bu*: a local divinity, 690
Dorjebum *rdo-rje 'bum*, 667; see *Yungtön(pa) Dorjepel*
Dorje Gyelpo *rdo-rje rgyal-po*, 771
Dorje Gyeltsen, myriarch of Yamdrok *yar-'brog khri-dpon rdo-rje rgyal-mtshan*, 592
Dorje Gyeltsen *rdo-rje rgyal-mtshan*, 686-7
Dorje Lekpa, (the Oath-bound One/protector) *rdo-rje legs-pa/dam-can (rdo-rje legs-pa)*, Skt. Vajrasādhu,

555, 556, **560**, 560-1, 572, 581, 589, 591, 661
Dorje Lingpa *rdo-rje gling-pa* (1346-1405), **790**, 789-92, 954
Jampel Chöki Shenyen *'jam-dpal chos-kyi bshes-gnyen*, 791
Künkyong Lingpa *kun-skyong gling-pa*, 791
Orgyen Zangpo *o-rgyan bzang-po*, 789
Pema Lingpa *padma gling-pa*, 791
Yungdrung Lingpa *yung-drung gling-pa*, 791
Dorje Namgyel, the great spiritual warrior/ bodhisattva of Tarlung *sems-dpa' chen-po/byang-chub sems-dpa' dar-lung-pa rdo-rje rnam-rgyal*, 697, 701
Dorje Senge *rdo-rje seng-ge*, 722
Dorje Thokmetsel *rdo-rje thogs-med rtsal*, 821; see *Dalai Lama V*
Dorje Trakpotsel (Expression of the Ferocious Vajra) *rdo-rje drag-po rtsal*: Guru Rinpoche's wrathful manifestation during the fourth month, also known as Pema Dorje Trakpotsel, 469; see *Guru Rinpoche*
Dorje Trak Rikdzin I, Gödemcen (1337-1409) *rdo-rje brag rig-'dzin rgod-ldem-can*, **781**
Ngödrup Gyeltsen *dngos-grub rgyal-mtshan*, 780-3
Rikdzin Gödemcen *rig-'dzin rgod-ldem-can*, 780-3, 813, 919
Rikdzinje *rig-'dzin-rje*, 719
Dorje Trak Rikdzin II, Lekdenje (1488-1569) *rdo-rje brag rig-'dzin legs-ldan-rje*, **718**
Lekden Dorje *legs-ldan rdo-rje*, 807
Rikdzin II, Lekdenje *rig-'dzin legs-ldan-rje*, 717, 783, 807
Dorje Trak Rikdzin III, Ngagiwangpo (1580-1639) *rdor-brag rig-'dzin ngag-gi dbang-po*, **782**, 812
Cangpa Rikdzin Ngagiwangpo *byang-pa rig-'dzin ngag-gi dbang-po*, 679, 681, 683, 719, 821
Rikdzin III, Ngagiwangpo *rig-'dzin ngag-gi dbang-po*, 783
Dorje Trak Rikdzin IV, Pema Trhinle (1641-1717) *rdor-brag rig-'dzin padma phrin-las*, **719**, 719-20
(Cangdak) Pema Trhinle *(byang-bdag) padma phrin-las*, 41, 956
Künzang Pema Trhinle *kun-bzang padma phrin-las*, 720
Rikdzin Pema Trhinle *rig-'dzin padma phrin-las*, 398, 683, 730, 823, 824, 828, 833
Rikdzin IV, Zhapdrung Pema Trhinle *rig-'dzin bzhi-pa zhabs-drung padma phrin-las*, 783
Dorje Trak Rikdzin V, Kelzang Pema Wangcuk (1719/20-70) *rdo-rje brag rig-'dzin skal-bzang padma dbang-phyug*: see *Supreme Emanation of the Dorje Trak Rikdzin*
Dorje Trhitsuk *rdo-rje khri-gtsug*, 607; see *Nup(cen) Sangye Yeshe*
Dorje Trolö (Vajra Pot-belly) *rdo-rje gro-(bo-)lod*: Guru Rinpoche's manifestation during the eleventh month, 519, **519**; see *Guru Rinpöche*
Dorje Wangcuk, the layman of Yölcak *yol-lcags dge-bsnyen rdo-rje dbang-phyug*, 709
(Dorje) Yangwangter *(rdo-rje) yang-dbang gter*, 607, 613; see *Nup(cen) Sangye Yeshe*
(Dorje) Yudrönma *(rdo-rje) gYu-sgron-ma*: her "seven sisters" are unidentified, 581-2, 584, 586, 587, 588
Dorje Zhönu, lama *bla-ma rdo-rje gzhon-nu*, 802
Dorje Ziji, the all-knowing *kun-mkhyen rdo-rje gzi-brjid*, 734; see *(Jamyang) Khyentse Wangpo*
Dorta the Black, (the Mongol) *(hor/rgya) do-rta nag-po*, 766, 953
Dotokpa Sangye-tra *rdo-thogs-pa sangs-rgyas grags*, 685-6
Dotön Senge *mdo-ston seng-ge*, 707
Dra Dorje Zhönu *sgra rdo-rje gzhon-nu*, 706
Drangsong Trhöpei Gyelpo *drang-srong khros-pa'i rgyal-po*: the seventh emanational teacher according to the Great Perfection, 136
Dṛḍhasamādāna, the king of lions *yi-dam brtan-pa*, 132
Dre Atsara (Nuru) *'bre a-tsa-ra (nu-ru)*, 712, 713
Dre Atsara Sale *'bre a-tsa-ra sa-le*, 712
Dre Gyelwei Lodrö *'bre rgyal-ba'i blo-gros*, 535
Drenpa Köncok Gyeltsen *'dren-pa dkon-mchog rgyal-mtshan*, 813
Dre Trhocung of upper Nyang *nyang-stod-kyi 'bre khro-chung*, 619

Drigung Chöki Gyelpo (b. 1335) *'bri-gung chos-kyi rgyal-po*, 787

Drigung Chöki Trakpa (b. 1595) *'bri-gung chos-kyi grags-pa*: the twenty-first *gdan-rabs* of Drigung, 812

Drigung Köncok Trhinle Zangpo *'bri-gung dkon-mchog phrin-las bzang-po*, 833

Drigung Kyopa (1143-1219) *'bri-gung skyob-pa*, 761, 952

Drigungpa emanations, the two *'bri-gung sprul-sku gnyis*: i.e. Chetsang and Chungtsang (*'bri-gung che-tshang chung-tshang*), 839

Drigung (Zurpa) Rincen Phüntsok (1509-57) *'bri-gung-pa chos-rgyal (zur-pa) rin-chen phun-tshogs*: the sixteenth *gdan-rabs* of Drigung, 571, 595, 676-7, 681, 798, 807

Drigung Zurpa Ratna *'bri-gung zur-pa rat-na*, 681

Drocam Trhompagyen *'bro-lcam khrom-pa rgyan*, 805

Dro, the deity of *'gro-lha*, 605

Drodül Lingpa *'gro-'dul gling-pa*, 794; see *Ratna Lingpa*

Drogön Namka Özer *'gro-mgon nam-mkha' 'od-zer*, 757

(Drogön) Namka Pelwa (*'gro-mgon) nam-mkha' dpal-ba*, 757, 758

Ngadak Drogön *mnga'-bdag 'gro-mgon*, 763, 765

Drokben Khyeucung Lotsāwa *'brog-ban khye'u chung lo-tsā-ba*, 535, 813

Drokmi (Śākya Yeshe), the translator (993-1050) *'brog-mi lo-tsā-ba (śā-kya ye-shes)*, 395, 633, 930, 951

Drölcen/Drölmawa Samdrup Dorje (1295-1376) *sgrol-chen/sgrol-ma-ba bsam-'grub rdo-rje*, 348, 672, 700, 717, 720, 721; see *Tanak Drölmawa Samdrup Dorje*

(Drölcen) Sangye Rincen (1350-1431) *(sgrol-chen) sangs-rgyas rin-chen*, 672-4, 720-1

Sangye Rincen Gyeltsen Pelzangpo *sangs-rgyas rin-chen rgyal-mtshan dpal-bzang-po*, 672

Drölgom, the spiritual benefactor *dge-bshes sgrol-sgom*, 546

Drölmawa Samdrup Dorje *sgrol-ma-ba bsam-'grub rdo-rje*, 672; see *Tanak Drölmawa Samdrup Dorje*

Dromtön (Gyelwei Jungne) (1004-64) *'brom-ston rgyal-ba'i 'byung-gnas*, 550, 575, 950, 951

Dromza Pamti Chenmo *'brom-bza' spam-ti chen-mo*, 537

Dromza Sonamgyen *'brom-bza' bsod-nams rgyan*, 575

Drön Kungtangpa *mgron gung-thang-pa*, 777

Dropukpa, (the lord of secrets) *(gsang-bdag) sgro-phug-pa*, 346, 646-9, 650, 651, 660, 677, 685, 701, 728, 952; see *Zur (Dropukpa) Śākya Senge*

Dro Rincen Barwa *'bro rin-chen 'bar-ba*, 556

Drosechung *'gro-sras chung*, 603, 605

Dro Tarseng of lower Nyang *nyang-smad sgro-dar-seng*, 651

Drotönpa *sgro-ston-pa*, 632

Dru Gomgying *gru sgom-'gying*, 622

Drukpa (Paksam Wangpo), the all-knowing (1593-1641) *'brug-pa (thams-cad mkhyen-pa) dpag-bsam dbang-po*: the fifth Drukcen, 809, 812, 833

Druktön Trakpa of Kharak *kha-rag 'brug-ston grags-pa*, 562

Drupcenpa, lama *bla-ma sgrub-chen-pa*, 721; see *(Rikdzin) Yudruk Dorje*

Drutsagangpa *'bru-tsha sgang-pa*, 698

Dudjom Rinpoche, (His Holiness) (1904-87), Pl. 99; 11, 35, 39, 41-2, 394, 398, 400, **888**

Düjom Trülku *bdud-'joms sprul-sku*, 972

Jikdrel Yeshe Dorje (Gelek Nampar Gyelweide) (Fearless Indestructible Reality of Pristine Cognition, the Victorious Army of All that is Good) *'jigs-'bral ye-shes rdo-rje (dge-legs rnam-par rgyal-ba'i sde)*, 377-8, 379, 400, 972

Tshojung Gyepei Langtso Tsuklak Mawei Nyima (Joyous Youth of the Lake-born Lotus, the Sun amongst Proponents of Scripture) *mtsho-byung dgyes-pa'i lang-tsho gtsug-lag smra-ba'i nyi-ma*, 972

Düdül Dorje, (the great treasure-finder) (1615-72) *(gter-chen) bdud-'dul rdo-rje*, 812, 956; see *Rikdzin Düdül Dorje*

Düdül, master *slob-dpon bdud-'dul*, 780

Düjom Lingpa, the great treasure-finder (1835-1904) *gter-chen bdud-'joms gling-pa*, 919, **920**, 958

Düjom Trülku *bdud-'joms sprul-sku*, 972; see *Dudjom Rinpoche*
Dültsangma, the nāginī *klu-mo 'dul-tshang-ma*, 452
Dumpa Töndrup Wangyel *ldum-pa don-grub dbang-rgyal*, 729-30
Dumpopa *ldum-po-ba*, 821
Dzaborwa *rdza-bor-ba*, 546
Dzamtön (Drowei Gönpo) *'dzam-ston ('gro-ba'i mgon-po)*, 688, 689
Dzemza Lhamo *'dzem-bza' lha-mo*, 537
Dzeng Co-se *'dzeng jo-sras*, 550-1, 552
Co-se (Dzeng) *jo-sras*, 549, 565, 649
"Mad" Co-se, the younger Dzeng *jo-sras 'dzeng-chung smyon-pa*, 551
Dzeng (Dharmabodhi) (1052-1136) *'dzeng (dha-rma bo-dhi)*, **544**, 543-50, 551, 552
Pawo Dzengcung *dpa'-bo 'dzeng-chung*, 547
Dzokcen Gemang *rdzogs-chen dge-mang*, 879; see *Gyelse Zhenpen Thaye (of Dzokcen)*
Dzokcenpa Drukdra Zangpo *rdzogs-chen-pa 'brug-sgra bzang-po*, 724
Dzokcen I, Pema Rikdzin (1625-97) *rdzogs-chen-pa padma rig-'dzin*, 817, **737**
Pema Rikdzin of Dzokcen *rdzogs-chen padma rig-'dzin*, 736-7
Dzokcen Pema Rikdzin II, Gyurme Thekcok Tendzin *rdzogs-chen gnyis-pa 'gyur-med theg-mchog bstan-'dzin*, 833
Dzokcen IV, Mingyur Namkei Dorje (b. 1793) *rdzogs-chen sprul-sku bzhi-pa mi-'gyur nam-mkha'i rdo-rje*, 737
Dzokcen Trülku V, Thupten Chöki Dorje (1872-1935) *rdzogs-chen lnga-pa thub-bstan chos-kyi rdo-rje*, 879, 958
Dzongsar Ngari Chöje Künga Jamyang *rdzong-gsar mnga'-ris chos-rje kun-dga' 'jam-dbyangs*, 868
Dzungar(s) *jun-gar-pa*, 957
(Eight) Closest Sons *nye-sras (brgyad)*: listed in the Glossary of Enumerations, 624, 864
Eighteen "Secret Liberators" *gsang-ba'i sgrol-ging bco-brgyad*: listed in the Glossary of Enumerations, 620
Eight Emanations of the Guru/Guru Padmasambhava's Eight Emanations *gu-ru mtshan brgyad*: listed in the Glossary of Enumerations under *Eight Emanations (of Padmasambhava)*, Pl. 16; 858, 893; see *Guru Rinpoche*
eightfold group of the Mönpa, mounted on tigers *stag-zhon mon-pa sde-brgyad*, 628
"Eight-footed Lion", the Shing-go-chen-pa *shing-sgo chen-pa seng-ge rkang-pa brgyad-pa*, 592; see *Tā'i Situ (Cangcup Gyeltsen)*
Eight Gaurī *gau-rī brgyad*: listed in the Glossary of Enumerations, 623, 639
"eight glorious adepts of Vajrakīla" *phur-pa mkhan-po-dag dpal brgyad*, 605
eight glorious disciples (of Nyak Jñānakumāra) *(gnyag dznya-na kumāra'i) slob-ma dpal brgyad*, 608, 918
eight great accomplished masters *grub-pa'i slob-dpon chen-po brgyad*: listed in the Glossary of Enumerations, 482-3; see also following entry
eight (great) awareness-holders *rig-'dzin (chen-po) brgyad*, 470, 757, 791; see also preceding entry
eight "rafters" *gding-ma brgyad*: students of Zurcungpa, 640, 642
Eight Transmitted Precepts *bka-'brgyad*, 828; see *(Deities of the) Eight Transmitted Precepts (of Great Attainment)*
Eight Wrathful Goddesses *khro-mo brgyad*, 628
eighty-four accomplished masters *grub-thob brgyad-cu rtsa-bzhi*, 442
Ekajaṭī, (the mantra protectress) *e-ka-dza-ṭi (sngags-bdag/sngags-srung-ma)*, 561, 570, **570**, 572, 580, 587, 591, 609, 843, 849, 865
elixir goddess *sman-gyi lha-mo*, 757
E Yeshe Gyelwa *dbas ye-shes rgyal-ba*, 526
Fifth Dalai Lama *rgyal-mchog lnga-pa*: see *Dalai Lama V*
Fifth Guide *rnam-'dren lnga-pa*, 749, 971; see *Maitreya*
Fifty-eight Blood-drinkers *khrag-thung/khro-bo lnga-bcu nga-brgyad*: listed in the Glossary of Enumerations, 623; see also *peaceful and wrathful deities*
fifty-five realised ones of Yangdzong *yang-rdzong-gi rtogs-ldan nga-lnga*, 537
Five-arrowed One *mda'-lnga*, Skt. Pañcaśara, 421; see *Kāma*

Five Conquerors/Teachers *rgyal-ba/ston-pa lnga*: listed in the Glossary of Enumerations under *Five Teachers*, 125; see *Buddhas of the Five Enlightened Families*

five emanational brothers of Yarlung *yar-klung sprul-sku mched-lnga*, 686

five kingly treasure-finders *gter-ston rgyal-po lnga*: listed in the Glossary of Enumerations, 755, 760, 789, 796, 849

five (noble) companions *lnga-sde bzang-po*: listed in the Glossary of Enumerations, 153, 419, 422, 423, 643

five noble ones *rigs-can lnga*: listed in the Glossary of Enumerations, 454-5, 458, 948

five sons who were successors to the transmitted precepts *bka'-babs-kyi bu-lnga*: students of Nyang-rel Nyima Özer, 759

Forty-two (Peaceful) Buddhas/Deities *(zhi-ba'i) sangs-rgyas/lha zhe-gnyis*: listed in the Glossary of Enumerations, 125-6, 623, 644, 691; see also *peaceful and wrathful deities*

four "black ones" *nag-po bzhi*: students of Dropukpa, 648

four female earth spirits *sa-bdag-mo bzhi*: listed in the Glossary of Enumerations, 481

four "grandfathers" *mes-po bzhi*: students of Dropukpa, 648-9

four guardian kings *rgyal-chen bzhi*, Skt. Caturmahārājika: listed in the Glossary of Enumerations, 419

  great kings of the four directions *phyogs-bzhi'i rgyal-chen*, 421

Four Mahākrodha *khro-bo chen-po bzhi*: wrathful male deities, listed in the Glossary of Enumerations, 125-6

Four Mahākrodhī *khro-mo bzhi*: wrathful female deities, listed in the Glossary of Enumerations, 126

four "pillars" *ka-ba bzhi*: students of Zurcungpa, 346, 640-2, 645, 647

four sons who were prophesied *lung-bstan bu-bzhi*: students of Katokpa Tampa Deshek, 698

four "summits" *rtse-mo bzhi*: students of Zurpoche, 622, 623, 625, 631, 635, 638

four "teachers" *ston-pa bzhi*: students of Dropukpa, 648-9

Fourth Guide *rnam-'dren bzhi-pa*, 409, 943; see *Buddha*

Ga, the awareness-holder of Nyö *gnyos-kyi rig-'dzin sga*: the father of Khyentse Rinpoche, 854

Gagasiddhi *ga-ga si-ddhi*, 489

Gaje Wangcuk, son of the gods *lha'i bu dga'-byed dbang-phyug*, 136

Gampo Choktrül Zangpo Dorje *sgam-po mchog-sprul bzang-po rdo-rje*, 833

Gampopa Orgyen Drodül Lingpa *sgam-po-pa o-rgyan 'gro-'dul gling-pa*, 957

Gampopa, (the physician of Takpo) (1079-1153) *sgam-po-pa (dvags-po lha-rje)*: his emanations who were hierachs of Taklha Gampo (*dvags-lha sgam-po*) in chronological order include: Gampo Trashi Namgyel, Gampopa Zhapdrung Norbu Gyenpa, Gampo Choktrül Zangpo Dorje, Gampopa Orgyen Drodül Lingpa, 200, 547, 908

  Daö Zhönu *zla-'od gzhon-nu*, 931

  Nyiwa Rincen *snyi-ba rin-chen*, 200

  Takpo (Daö Zhönu) *dvags-po (zla-'od gzhon-nu)*, 931, 952

  Takpo Lharje *dvags-po lha-rje*, 649, 853, 929

Gampopa Trashi Namgyel (1512/13-87) *sgam-po-pa bkra-shis rnam-rgyal*, 955

Gampopa (Zhapdrung) Norbu Gyenpa (1588/99-1633) *sgam-po-pa (zhabs-drung) nor-bu rgyan-pa*, 809, 811, 956

Gaṇapati *tshogs-bdag*, 713

Gandhā *dri-chab-ma*, 125

Gar, the religious minister *chos-blon mgar*, 510

Garap Dorje, (the emanation) *(sprul-sku) dga'-rab rdo-rje*, Skt. *Pramodavajra, 39, 358, 371, 451, 477, 487, **491**, 490-4, 503, 539, 922, 927, 949, 960

  "Ashen Zombie" *ro-langs thal-mdog*, Skt. *Vetala Bhasmavarṇa, 477, 493

  Prajñābhava *shes-rab 'byung-gnas/pra-dzya-bha-ba*, 493

  Sukha the "Zombie" *ro-langs bde-ba*, 487-8, 493

  "Zombie" Sukhasiddhi *ro-langs bde-ba'i dngos-grub*, 466

Gartön Tshültrim Zangpo *'gar-ston tshul-khrims bzang-po*, 703

Garuḍa *khyung-po*, 545
Gautama *gau-ta-ma*, 422-3; see *Buddha*
Gayadhara, (the paṇḍita) *(paṇḍita) ga-ya-dha-ra*, 633, 930
Gejong Losel Gyamtso *dge-sbyong blo-gsal rgya-mtsho*, 833
Gelatön *dge-la-ston*, 603; see *(Nyak) Getön*
Gelong Pelden *dge-slong dpal-ldan*, 572; see *Kumārādza*
Gemang II, Thupwang Tenpei Nyima *dge-mang gnyis-pa thub-dbang bstan-pa'i nyi-ma*: the second Dzokcen Gemang, 919
Gendün Gyamtso (1476-1542) *dge-'dun rgya-mtsho*: i.e. Dalai Lama II, 955
Gendün Gyeltsen, the doctrine master *chos-rje dge-'dun rgyal-mtshan*, 678
Gendün Trupa (1391-1474) *dge-'dun grub-pa*: i.e. Dalai Lama I, 954
Geshe Locungpa *dge-bshes lo-chung-ba*, 761; see *Pangtön Trupei Nyingpo*
Geshe Po *dge-bshes spo*, 545
Gewei Yicen (Virtuous-minded), the householder *dge-ba'i yid-can*: father of Śrī Siṃha, 497
Ghaṇṭāpāda *dril(-bu-pa)*, 404
Ghare (of Minyak) *(mi-nyag) gha-ras*, 661-2, 671
Gītā *glu-ma*, 125
Glorious Heruka/Śrīheruka *dpal he-ru-ka*, 475-7, 534, 691; see *Yangdak Heruka*
Gocatsha *'go-bya-tsha*, 642, 643
Gocung Wange *'go-chung dbang-nge*, 642, 643
Gö (Khukpa Lhetse, the translator) *gos(-lo khug-pa lhas-btsas)*, 643, 709
  Gö Lhetse *'gos lhas-btsas*, 708, 914, 916, 930
  Gö Lotsāwa *'gos lo-tsā-ba*, 689
Gö Lotsāwa: see preceding entry
Gölo Yezang Tsepa: see following entry
Gölo(tsāwa) Zhönupel (1392-1481) *'gos-lo gzhon-nu dpal/'gos lo-tsā-ba*, 398, 553, 616, 673, 674-5, 676, 709, 914, 921, 954, 965
  (Gölo) Yezang Tsepa *('gos-lo) ye-bzang rtse-pa*, 673-4, 675
  Gö Zhönupel *'gos gzhon-nu-dpal*, 687
Gomadevī, daughter *sras-mo go-ma-de-bi*, 462
Goma Neljorma *sgom-ma rnal-'byor-ma*, 655
Gomdar, attendant *nye-gnas sgom-dar*, 572
Gompa, master *slob-dpon sgom-pa*, 571
Gompa Künrin of Drigung *'bri-gung sgom-pa kun-rin*, 591-2
  Künga *kun-dga'*, 591
Gompa Sonam Nyingpo *sgom-pa bsod-nams snying-po*, 622
Gönkyap, master *slob-dpon mgon-skyabs*, 552
Gönpo Sonam Chokden (of Nesar) (1603-59) *(gnas-gsar-ba) mgon-po bsod-nams mchog-ldan*, 683, 720, 724-5
  Kangyurwa Gönpo Sonam Chokden *bka'-'gyur-ba mgon-po bsod-nams mchog-ldan*, 812
Gönpo Targye of the Lha clan of Ju *'ju lha-rigs mgon-po dar-rgyas*, 869
Göntse Trülku of Tshona in Mön *mon mtsho-sna dgon-rtse sprul-sku*, 839
Gopā *sa-'tsho-ma*, 418
Gorakṣanātha *go-rakṣa*, 504
Goriwa, master *slob-dpon go-ri-ba*, 552
Götön Jungne Dorje *'gos-ston 'byung-gnas rdo-rje*, 674
Götsangpa (1189-1258) *rgod-tshang-pa*: i.e. Gönpo Dorje *(mgon-po rdo-rje)*, 922
Gö Tsilungpa *'gos rtsi-lung-pa*, 700
Gö Zhönupel *'gos gzhon-nu-dpal*, 687; see *Gölo(tsāwa) Zhönupel*
Great All-Pervader *khyab-'jug chen-po*, Skt. Mahāviṣṇu, 447; see *Samantabhadra*
Great Compassionate One *thugs-rje chen-po*, Skt. Mahākāruṇika, 507, 511, 560, 564, 565, 569, 677, 659, 755, 762, 765, 770, 784, 828, 829; see *Avalokiteśvara*
(Great) Fifth (Dalai Lama) *lnga-pa (chen-po)*, 682-4, 688, 719, 720, 728, 736-7, 821-4, 830, 831, 832-3, 926, 931, 966; see *Dalai Lama V*
Great Glorious (Yangdak Heruka) *dpal-chen-po (yang-dag he-ru-ka)*, 617, 621, 623, 625-8, 630, 631-2, 634-5, 639, 643, 644; see *Yangdak Heruka*
great kings of the four directions *phyogs-bzhi'i rgyal-chen*, 421; see *four guardian kings*
Great Mother *yum-chen-mo*: Prajñāpāramitā, 623-4
Great Thirteenth (Dalai Lama) *bcu-gsum-pa chen-po*, 777-8; see *Dalai Lama XIII*
Great Translator of Sakya *sa-lo chen-po*, 642, n. 781
Guhyajñānā, the ḍākinī of pristine cognition *ye-shes mkha'-'gro-ma gsang-ba ye-shes*, 469

Guhyapati/Lord of Secrets *gsang(-ba'i) bdag(-po)*, 282, 377, 405, 430, 441, 451, 454, 458, 459, 460, 485, 490, 609, 645, 648, 734, 728, 923, 925, 948; see *Vajrapāṇi*

Guhyaputra *gu-hya-pu-tri*: the son of King Ja, 485

Guhyasamāja *gsang(-ba) 'dus(-pa)*: see Bibliography

nineteen-deity maṇḍala of Mañjuvajra *'jam-pa'i rdo-rje lha bcu-dgu'i dkyil-'khor*: listed in the Glossary of Enumerations, 496

Guluk, emperor *go-lug rgyal-po*, 671

Guṇaprabha *yon-tan 'od*, 441

Gunirū, the yoginī *rnal-'byor-ma gu-ni-ru*, 494

Gupta *sbas*, 435, 436

Gurkha(s) *go-rṣa*, 838, 957

(Guru) Chöwang *or* Chöki Wangcuk (1212-70) *(gu-ru) chos(-kyi) dbang(-phyug)*, 695, 719, 758, **761**, 760-70, 773, 789, 807, 698, 835, 953

Chöwang Rinpoche *chos-dbang rin-po-che*, 838

Guru Cober (1172-1231) *gu-ru jo-'ber*, **563**, 563-4, 565

Guru Khyungdra *gu-ru khyung-grags*, 662

Guru Rinpoche *gu-ru rin-po-che*: Padmasambhava, Pls. 16, 26, 58, 78; 468-74, **470**, 512-21, 585, 676, 746, 755, 757, 766, 789, 791, 793, 814, 841, 842, 845, 846, 854, 856, 857, 858, 863, 864, 865, 939-40, 972

Eight Emanations of the Guru/Guru Padmasambhava's Eight Emanations *gu-ru mtshan brgyad*: listed in the Glossary of Enumerations, Pl. 16; 858, 893

The twelve manifestations of Guru Rinpoche which correspond to the twelve months are:

1) Śāntarakṣita (Preserver of Peace) *sha-nta-rakṣita*, 469

2) Loden Chokse (Intelligent Boon-seeker) *blo-ldan mchog-sred*, 470 and

2) Śākyasiṃha (Lion of the Śākyas) *śā-kya seng-ge*, 469, 488

3) Padmākara (Lotus-origin) *padma 'byung-gnas*, 469, **517**, 787, 889, 892, 927, 944, 948

4) (Pema) Dorje Trakpotsel (Expression of the Ferocious Vajra) *rdo-rje drag-po rtsal*, 469

5) Siṃhanāda/Senge Dradrok (Lion's Roar) *seng-ge sgra-sgrog*, 472, 845

6) (Guru) Saroruhavajra (Vajra of the Lake-born Lotus) *mtsho-skyes rdo-rje*, 469, 857, 855-6, 866

7) Khyeucung Khadingtsel (Youth who Flies like Garuḍa) *khye'u chung mkha'-lding rtsal*, 471

8) Sūryaraśmi (Sunbeam) *nyi-ma 'od-zer*, 471

9) Pema (Dorje) Thötrengtsel (Lotus whose Expression is a Garland of Skulls) *padma thod-phreng-rtsal*, 471

10) Padmasambhava, (the great master) *(slob-dpon chen-po) padma (sam-bha-ba)*: also used as a general name for Guru Rinpoche, 38, 39, 40, 63, 96, 265, 342, 394, 396, 397, 455, **470**, 468-74, 481, 483, 488, 498, 504, 512-21, 522, 532, 533, 534, 535, 554-5, 568, 569, 573, 575, 582, 583, 584, 585, 587, 591, 595, 601, 605, 607, 676, 677, 706, 710, 711, 712, 714, 715, 728, 745, 746, 747, 749, 757, 760, 768, 771, 773, 784, 785, 797, 802, 809, 821, 825, 828, 829, 844, 848, 852, 856, 864, 866, 887, 888, 890, 892, 893, 894, 917, 921, 922, 927, 930, 934-5, 938-40, 949-50, 951, 972

11) Dorje Trolö (Vajra Pot-belly) *rdo-rje gro-(bo-)lod*, 519, **519**

12) Pema Gyelpo/Padmarāja (Lotus King) *padma rgyal-po*, 471, 854

Other manifestations/names include:

Dewachenpo *bde-ba-chen-po*, 972

Guru Trakpo *gu-ru drag-po*, 519, **589**, 590, 591

King Śikhin (Crested King) *rgyal-po thor-cog-can*, 469

master *slob*, 968, 973

Orgyen Dorje Chang *o-rgyan rdo-rje 'chang*, 45

Orgyen (Rinpoche/the precious) *o-rgyan (rin-po-che)*: Guru Rinpoche of Oḍḍiyāna, 557, 746, 751, 764, 765, 766, 774, 775, 784, 786, 789, 790, 793, 796, 809, 837, 841, 847, 859, 860, 863, 935

peaceful and wrathful Guru *bla-ma zhi-drag*, 828
Pema Rikdzin *padma rig-'dzin*, 866
Tavihṛca *ta-bi-hri-tsa*: a Pönpo teacher identified as a form of Guru Rinpoche, 473
Thukdrup *thugs-sgrub*, 586
Wangcuk Dorje *dbang-phyug rdo-rje*, 755
Guru of Suvarṇadvīpa *gser-gling-pa*: Dharmapāla, the guru of Atiśa, 184, n. 174
Guru Trakpo *gu-ru drag-po*, 519, **589**, 590, 591; see *Guru Rinpoche*
Guru Yeshe Rapjam *gu-ru ye-shes rab-'byams*, 595
Gushri Tendzin Chögyel, the Mongolian (b. 1582) *sog-po gu-shri bstan-'dzin chos-rgyal*, 823
Gushri Trakpelpa, the preceptor *mkhan-po gu-shri grags-dpal-pa*, 675
Gyacing Rupa *rgya-'chings ru-ba*, 685
Gyadrakpa *rgya-brag-pa*, 835
Gya Gyeltsül *rgya rgyal-tshul*, 708
Gyakap Kongpa, lama *bla-ma rgya-khab gong-pa*, 660
Gyanyönpa Tönden *rgya-smyon-pa don-ldan*, 757
Gyaptön Dorje Gönpo *rgyab-ston rdo-rje mgon-po*, 649
Gyare *rgya-ras*, 547
Gyari, the minister *rgya-ri dpon-sa*, 727
Gyatön *rgya-ston*, 649
Gyatön Lodrö *rgya-ston blo-gros*, 619
Gyatön Śāk-ye *rgya-ston śāk-ye*, 634
Gyatrül Pema Do-nga Tendzin *rgya-sprul padma mdo-sngags bstan-'dzin*, 738
Gyatsang Korwa of upper Nyang *nyang-stod-kyi rgya-rtsang skor-ba*, 651
Gya Tsönseng *rgya brtson-seng*, 650
Gya Yeshe Gönpo *rgya ye-shes mgon-po*, 686; see *(Phungpo) Gya Yeshe Gönpo*
Gya Zhangtrom *rgya zhang-khrom*, 765; see *(Tumpa) Gya Zhangtrom*
Gyedor, lama *bla-ma dgyes-rdor*, 568
Gyelkangtsewa Peljor Gyamtso *rgyal-khang rtse-ba dpal-'byor rgya-mtsho*, 678
Gyelmodzom *rgyal-mo 'dzom*, 677
Gyelmoyang *rgyal-mo gYang*, 561
Gyelmo Yudra Nyingpo *rgyal-mo(-rong-gi) gYu-grags snying-po*, 535; see *Yudra Nyingpo*
Gyelse Lekpa of Sho (b. 1290) *sho'i rgyal-sras legs-pa*, 574, 590
Gyelse Lharje *rgyal-sras lha-rje*: the second son of Mutik Tsepo, refer to the Glossary of Enumerations for his *thirteen incarnations*, 751, 805, 835, 849
Lhase Chokdrup Gyelpo *lha-sras mchog-grub rgyal-po*, 775
Gyelse Norbu Wangyel *rgyal-sras nor-bu dbang-rgyal*, 735
Gyelse Norbu Yongdra *rgyal-sras nor-bu yongs-grags*, 817
Gyelse Rincen Namgyel *rgyal-sras rin-chen rnam-rgyal*: i.e. Minling Trhicen III, 733, 734
Trincen Rincen Namgyel *drin-chen rin-chen rnam-rgyal*, 833
Gyelse Tenpei Nyima *rgyal-sras bstan-pa'i nyi-ma*: Dharmaśrī's elder brother, 730
Gyelse Zhenpen Thaye (of Dzokcen) (b. 1800 or 1740) *(rdzogs-chen) rgyal-sras gzhan-phan mtha'-yas*: founder of Śrī Siṃha College at Dzokcen, 737, 957
Dzokcen Gemang *rdzogs-chen dge-mang*, 879
Gyelse Zöpa *rgyal-sras bzod-pa*, 593, 595
Gyeltsap IV, Trakpa Töndrup (of Tshurpu) (*c.* 1550-1617) *rgyal-tshab grags-pa don-grub*, 812
Gyeltsap V, Trakpa Chöyang (of Tshurpu) (1618-58) *rgyal-tshab grags-pa mchog-dbyangs*, 724
Gyeltsen Pelzang *rgyal-mtshan dpal-bzang*, 595
Gyelwa Choyang *rgyal-ba mchog-dbyangs*, 535, **536**, 575, 675
Jñānendrarakṣita *dznya-na-indra-rakshi-ta*, 575
Ngenlam Gyelwa Choyang *ngan-lam rgyal-ba mchog-dbyangs*, 515
Yeshe Wangposung *ye-shes dbang-po srung*, 575
Gyelwa Potön *rgyal-ba spo-ston*, 547
Gyelwei Lodrö *rgyal-ba'i blo-gros*, 601; see also *Nyak Jñānakumāra*
Gyepak Sherap *dgyes-'phags shes-rab*, 605
Gyi-phan *gyi-phan*, 524
Gyurme Chokdrup Pelbar *'gyur-med mchog-grub dpal-'bar*: i.e. Lhodrak Thukse Dawa Gyeltsen V, 735
Spiritual Son *thug-sras*, 839
Gyurme Dorje, (the great treasure-finder of Mindröling) *(smin-gling gter-chen)*

'gyur-med rdo-rje, 726, 728, 729, 730, 731, 734, 735, 956, 966; see *(Rikdzin) Terdak Lingpa*
Gyurme Dorjetsel *'gyur-med rdo-rje rtsal*: see *(Rikdzin) Terdak Lingpa*, 828
Gyurme Ngedön Wangpo, (Khyapdak/all-pervading lord) *(khyab-bdag) 'gyur-med nges-don dbang-po*, 734, 868, 919
Gyurme Phendei Özer *'khor-lo'i mgon-po 'gyur-med phan-bde'i 'od-zer*: one of the Minling Trhicens and a teacher of the Author, 734
Jampel Dewei Nyima, (lord of the maṇḍala circle) *('khor-lo'i mgon-po) 'jam-dpal bde-ba'i nyi-ma*, 734, 919
Gyurme Sangye Künga, the Trhicen of Mindröling *smin-gling khri-chen sangs-rgyas kun-dga'*: i.e. Minling Trhicen VII, 849
Trhi Sangye Künga *khri sangs-rgyas kun-dga'*, 733
Gyurme Thutop Namgyel of Zhecen *zhe-chen-pa/ze-chen 'gyur-med mthu-stobs rnam-rgyal*, 849, 860
Gyurme Tshewang Chokdrup (1761-1829) (paṇḍita of Katok) *(kaḥ-thog paṇḍita) 'gyur-med tshe-dbang mchog-grub*, 41, 375, 398, 736
Katok Paṇḍita Gyurme Tshewang Chokdrup *kaḥ-thog paṇḍita 'gyur-med tshe-dbang mchog-grub*, 966
Gyurzang *'gyur-bzang*: the maternal uncle of Mipham Rinpoche, 870
Haranandin *'phrog-byed dga'-bo*, 715, 920
Haribhadra *seng-ge bzang-po*, 184
Haribhadra, king *rgyal-po seng-ge bzang-po*, 501
Haribhala, master *slob-dpon ha-ri-bha-la*, 497
Hayagrīva *rta-mgrin*, Pl. 18; 473, **479**, 535, 567, 595, 623, 663, 755, 757, 762, 784, 802, 828; see also Bibliography
Aśvottama/Supreme Horse *rta-mchog*, 274, 534
Maheśvara *dbang-chen*, 535
Heruka *he-ru-ka*, 274, 404, 442, 534, 545, 626, 628, 893, 931; see *Yangdak Heruka*
Herukas of the Five Enlightened Families *he-ru-ka rigs-lnga*, 672; see *Buddhas of the Five Enlightened Families*
Hevajra *he-badzra/kye-rdo-rje/dgyes-pa rdo-rje*, 449, 464, 473, 568, 591, 911
His Presence, the Karmapa *sku-mdun karma-pa*, 579; see *Karmapa III*
Ho-shang Mo-ho-yen *ho/hva-shang mahāyāna*, 511, 896, 899, 905, 906
Hraza Sonam Drölma *dbra-bza' bsod-nams sgrol-ma*, 675
Hülegü *hu-le-gu*: the brother of Qubilai and founder of the Ilkhan dynasty in Persia, 664
Hūṃkara *hūṃ-ka-ra/hūṃ-mdzad*, 475-7, **476**, 483, 489, 516, 533, 829, 864, 865
Hūṃkara, the wrathful deity *khro-bo hūṃ-mdzad*, 475
Hūṃnak Mebar, the mantra adept *hūṃ-nag me-'bar*, 809; see *(Rikdzin) Jatsön Nyingpo*
Ilkhan(s) *stod-hor*, 664; see *Upper Mongol(s)*
Immortal Wish-granting Wheel *'chi-med yid-bzhin 'khor-lo*: a form of White Tārā, 857; see *Tārā*
Indra *brgya-byin*: i.e. Śatakratu, 417, 422; see *Devendra*
Indrabhūti *indra bhu-ti*, 252, 277, 300, 346, 460, 462, 485, 487, 921; see *Ja*
Indrabhūti, (the Great) *indra bhu-ti (chen-po)*: the king of Oḍḍiyāna, perhaps to be identified with *Ja*, 441, 458-9, 468, 503
Indrabhūti, the intermediate *indra bhu-ti bar-pa*, 459, n. 472, 502; see *Ja*
Indrabhūti, the Younger *indra bhu-ti chung-ba/chen-po'i sras*, 462, 485-7; see *Kambalapāda*
Indranāla *brgya-byin sdong-po*, 534
Indrarāja *dbang-po'i rgyal-po*, 913; see *Devendra*
Indraśakra *dbang-po brgya-byin*: Indra, 452; see *Devendra*
Indrasena *dbang-po'i sde*, 471
Īśvara *dbang-phyug*: Śiva, 16, 65, 132
Īśvarasena *dbang-phyug sde*, 440
Ja, king (of Sahor) *(za-hor) rgyal-po dza*, 39, 458, **459**, 460, 462, 466, 485, 487, 502, 613, 948; see also *Indrabhūti, (the Great)*
Indrabhūti *indra bhu-ti*, 252, 277, 300, 346, 460, 462, 485, 487, 921
Indrabhūti, the intermediate *indra bhu-ti bar-pa*, 459, 502
Vyākaraṇavajra *lung-bstan rdo-rje*, 485
Jāladatta *drva-ba sbyin*, 423

Jālandharipā *dza-lan-dha-ri-pa*, 459, 462, 473, 494, 603, 693
Bālapāda *byis-pa'i zhabs*, 462
Jambhala *rmugs-'dzin/dzam-bha-la*, 494, 571, 685, 713, 753
Jamgön Khyentse Wangpo *'jam-mgon mkhyen-brtse'i dbang-po*, 738; see *(Jamyang) Khyentse Wangpo*
Jamgön Kongtrül (Lodrö Thaye) (1813-99) *'jam-mgon kong-sprul (blo-gros mtha'-yas)*, 41, 375, 398, 735, 842, 857, **860**, 859-68, 871, 958
Chime Tenyi Yungdrung Lingpa *'chi-med bstan-gnyis gYung-drung gling-pa*, 863
Jamgön Yönten Gyamtso (Lodrö Thaye) *'jam-mgon yon-tan rgya-mtsho (blo-gros mtha'-yas)*, 859, 875, 966
Jamgön Lozang Trakpa *'jam-mgon blo-bzang grags-pa*, 954; see *Tsongkapa*
Jamgön Mipham Mawei Senge (1846-1912) *'jam-mgon mi-pham smra-ba'i seng-ge*, 375; see *Mipham Gyamtso*
Jamgön Tsongkapa *'jam-mgon tsong-kha-pa*, 925, 930; see *Tsongkapa*
Jamgön Yönten Gyamtso (Lodrö Thaye) *'jam-mgon yon-tan rgya-mtsho (blo-gros mtha'-yas)*, 859, 875, 966; see *Jamgön Kongtrül (Lodrö Thaye)*
Jampel Chöki Shenyen *'jam-dpal chos-kyi bshes-gnyen*, 791; see *Dorje Lingpa*
Jampel Dewei Nyima, (lord of the maṇḍala circle) *('khor-lo'i mgon-po) 'jam-dpal bde-ba'i nyi-ma*, 734, 919; see *Gyurme Phendei Özer*
Jamyang, the attendant *nye-gnas 'jam-dbyangs*, 669
Jamyang Chökyong *'jam-dbyangs chos-skyong*, 805
Jamyang Khyentse Wangcuk (b. 1524) *'jam-dbyangs mkhyen-brtse dbang-phyug*, 717, 824, 922
(Jamyang) Khyentse Wangpo (1820-92) *'jam-dbyangs mkhyen-brtse'i dbang-po*, Pl. 32; 41, 734, 751, 777, 792, 843, 848, **850**, 849-58, 861, 863, 864, 865, 867-8, 871, 958
Chöki Shenyen *chos-kyi bshes-gnyen*, 854
Do-nga Lingpa *mdo-sngags gling-pa*, 854
Dorje Ziji, the all-knowing *kun-mkhyen rdo-rje gzi-brjid*, 734
Jamgön Khyentse Wangpo *'jam-mgon mkhyen-brtse'i dbang-po*, 738
Khyentse Rinpoche *mkhyen-brtse rin-po-che*, 752, 844, 845, 846, 848, 849-58, 863-6, 871, 873, 874-5, 876-7
Ösel Trülpei Dorje *'od-gsal sprul-pa'i rdo-rje*, 854
Pema Ösel Do-nga Lingpa *padma 'od-gsal mdo-sngags gling-pa*, 751, 774, 778, 804, 849-58, 871
Jamyang Lodröpel *'jam-dbyangs blo-gros dpal*, 806
Jamyang Rincen Gyeltsen *'jam-dbyangs rin-chen rgyal-mtshan*, 805
Utsewa Jamyang Rincen Gyeltsen (of Ngari) *dbu-rtse-ba'i 'jam-dbyangs rin-chen rgyal-mtshan*, 717
Jamyang Sakya Paṇḍita *'jam-dbyangs sa-skya paṇḍita*, 806; see *Sakya Paṇḍita*
Jamyang Samdrup Dorje *'jam-dbyangs bsam-grub rdo-rje*, 671, 721; see *Tanak Drölmawa Samdrup Dorje*
Jang, the king of *'jang rgyal-po*, 696
Japa Do-nga *'ja'-pa mdo-sngags*, 875-6
Jatsön Nyingpo *'ja'-tshon snying-po*, 813, 814, 820; see *(Rikdzin) Jatsön Nyingpo*
Javāripā *dza-bi-ra*, 676
Jedrung Trhinle Campei Jungne *rje-drung phrin-las byams-pa'i 'byung-gnas*, 734, 868
Je Guru *rje gu-ru*, 925; see *Tsongkapa*
Je Lhakangpa *rje lha-khang-pa*, 650; see *Cetön Gyanak*
Jesus Christ *phyi-gling-pa'i ston-pa ye-shu ma-shi-ka*, 949
Jetāri *dze-ta-ri*, 233, 478
Je Tsongkapa *rje tsong-kha-pa*, 395; see *Tsongkapa*
Jetsün Hak *rje-btsun hags*, 657
Jetsün (Künga) Drölcok (1507-66) *rje-btsun (kun-dga') grol-mchog*, 852, 955
Jetsün Sonam Tsemo of Sakya (1142-82) *sa-skya-pa rje-btsun bsod-nams rtse-mo*, 952
(Jetsün) Tāranātha (1575-1634) *(rje-btsun) tā-ra-nā-tha*, 892, 956, 965
Jikdrel Yeshe Dorje (Gelek Nampar Gyelweide) (Fearless Indestructible Reality of Pristine Cognition, the Victorious Army of All that is Good) *'jigs-'bral ye-shes rdo-rje (dge-legs rnam-par rgyal-ba'i sde)*, 377-8, 379, 400, 972; see *Dudjom Rinpoche*

Jikme Gyelwei Nyugu *'jigs-med rgyal-ba'i myu-gu*, 839

Jikme Kündröl, the learned and accomplished master of Mön *mon mkhas-grub 'jigs-med kun-grol*, 839

Jikme Lingpa *jigs-med gling-pa*, 41, 92, 835-40, 965; see *(Rikdzin) Jikme Lingpa*

Jinamitra *dzi-na-mi-tra*, 515, 526

Jinasāgara *rgyal-ba rgya-mtsho*, 591

Jñānacandra *ye-shes zla-ba*, 183

Jñānaketu *dznya-na ke-tu*, 303

Jñānaketu *(mkhas-grub) dznya-na ke-tu*, 696; see *(Khedrup) Yeshe Gyeltsen (of Pubor)*

Jñānakīrti, master *slob-dpon ye-shes grags-pa*, 909

Jñānakumāra, the translator of Nyak *gnyags-lo dznyāna ku-mā-ra*, 696; see *Nyak Jñānakumāra*

Jñānanātha *ye-shes mgon-po*, 849; see *Lord of Pristine Cognition*

Jñānasena, the translator *lo-tsā-wa dznya-na se-na*, 522; see *Zhang Yeshe De*

Jñānasūtra *ye-shes mdo*, 39, 497-501, **499**

Jñānavajra *bram-ze ye-shes rdo-rje*, 478

Jñānendrarakṣita *dznya-na-indra-rakshi-ta*, 575; see *Gyelwa Choyang*

Jora Trülku, holder of the Podongpa teaching *bo-dong-pa'i bstan-'dzin sbyor-ra sprul-sku*, 839

Ju-ön Jikme Dorje, the spiritual benefactor *dge-bshes 'ju-dbon jigs-med rdo-rje*, 871

Jvālamukha *kha(-la) (me-)'bar*, 130

Kadö Yeshe Nyingpo *bka'-sdod ye-shes snying-po*, 619

Kālacakra *dus-kyi 'khor-lo*, 449; see also Bibliography

Kālacakrapāda, the elder and younger *dus-'khor zhabs-pa che-chung*, 442

Kālagrīva, the nāga king *klu-rgyal mgrin-pa nag-po*, 452

Kalantaka *ka-lanta-ka*: a bird, 455

Kalyāṇa *dge-ba*, 440

Kalyāṇacittā *dge-ba'i sems-can ma*, 498

Kāma, flower-arrowed *me-tog mda'-can*, 911, 970

  Five-arrowed One *mda'-lnga*, Skt. Pañcaśara, 421

  Smara *dran-pa*, 421

Kamalaśīla *ka-ma-la-shi-la*, 607, 906

Kambalapāda *lva-ba zhabs*, 459, 485-7, **486**

  Indrabhūti, the Younger *indra bhu-ti chung-ba/chen-po'i sras*, 462, 485-7

  Śakraputra *śa-kra/tra-putri*, 462, 485

Kam Chöki Yeshe *kam chos-kyi ye-shes*, 688-9

Kam Lotsāwa (b. 1119) *kam lo-tsā-ba*, 688

Kam Yeshe Gyeltsen *kam ye-shes rgyal-mtshan*, 578

Kaṇāda *gzeg-zan*, 65

Kangkar Shame *gangs-dkar sha-me*: a protector, 791

Kangpa Śākbum *gangs-pa śāk-'bum*, 665, 666

Kangyurwa Gönpo Sonam Chokden *bka'-'gyur-ba mgon-po bsod-nams mchog-ldan*, 812; see *Gönpo Sonam Chokden (of Nesar)*

Kaṇhapā(da) *ka-ṇha-pa*, 455, 693; see *Kṛṣṇacārin*

Kaniṣka, king *ka-ni-ṣka*, 429, 430, 456

Kaṇṭhaka *bsngags-ldan*, 417, 419

Kapila, the ṛṣi *drang-srong ser-skya*, 64-5

Kapilabhadrī *ser-skya bzang-mo*, 432

Kargi Wangmo, the ḍākinī *mkha'-'gro gar-gyi dbang-mo*, 760

Karma Chakme (c. 1605-70) *karma chags-med*, 816

Karma Lingpa *karma gling-pa/kar-gling*, 679, **800**, 800-1

Karmapa I, Tüsum Khyenpa (1110-93) *rje dus-gsum mkhyen-pa*, 689, 952

  Use, the venerable *rje dbu-se*, 689

Karmapa II, Karma Pakshi (1204-83) *karma pak-shi*, 633, 694, 922

  Chöki Lama *chos-kyi bla-ma*, 694

Karmapa III, Rangjung Dorje (1284-1339) *(rje-drung/chos-rje) rang-byung rdo-rje*, 569, 570, 571, **573**, 572-4, 578, 584, 666, 827, 922, 931, 953

  His Presence, the Karmapa *sku-mdun karma-pa*, 579

Karmapa IV, Rölpei Dorje (1340-83) *rgyal-dbang rol-pa'i rdo-rje*, 784, 787, 791

Karmapa V, Tezhinshekpa (1384-1415) *karma-pa de-bzhin gshegs-pa*, 674, 787, 954

Karmapa VI, Thongwa Tönden (1416-53) *karma-pa mthong-ba don-ldan*, 954

Karmapa VII, Chödrak Gyamtso (1454-1506) *(rje bdun-pa/karma-pa) chos-grags rgya-mtsho*, 203, 675, 676, 931

Karmapa VIII, Mikyö Dorje (1507-54) *mi-bskyod rdo-rje*, 931, 955

Karmapa IX, Wangcuk Dorje (1554-1603) *karma dbang-phyug rdo-rje*, 956
Karmapa X, Chöying Dorje (1605-74) *karma-pa chos-dbyings rdo-rje*, 956
black-hat Karmapa *zhva-nag karma-pa*, 811
Karmapa XI, Yeshe Dorje (1676-1702) *karma-pa ye-shes rdo-rje*, 957
Karmapa XIII, Düdül Dorje (1734-97) *karma-pa bdud-'dul rdo-rje*, 957
Karmapa XIV, Thekcok Dorje (1797-1867) *karma-pa bcu-bzhi-pa theg-mchog rdo-rje*, 868
Karmapa XV, Khakyap Dorje (1871-1922) *karma-pa bco-lnga-pa mkha'-khyab rdo-rje*, 868, 958
Karmapa XVI, Rikpei Dorje (1924-81) *rig-pa'i rdo-rje*, 958
Karma Phüntsok Wangpo, the nobleman *sde-pa karma phun-tshogs dbangs-po*, 719
Karmogyen *dkar-mo rgyan*, 789
Karpopa *dkar-po-pa*, 676; see *Khawa Karpowa Namka Gyamtso*
Karwang Tshültrim Gyeltsen of Pönlung *bon-lung-pa gar-dbang tshul-khrims rgyal-mtshan*, 735
Karza Gönkyi *dkar-bza' mgon-skyid*, 760
Kāśyapa *'od-srung*, 83, 172, 432-4, 435, 906, 932; see *Mahākāśyapa*
Kāśyapa, the teacher, the elder *ston-pa 'od-srungs bgres-po*: the tenth emanational teacher according to the Great Perfection, 137; see *Buddha Kāśyapa*
Kāśyapa, the monk *dge-slong 'od-srung*, 440
(Katok Gyelse) Sonam Detsen *(kaḥ-thog rgyal-sras) bsod-nams lde'u-btsan*, 736, 833
Katokpa Chöki Senge *kaḥ-thog-pa chos-kyi seng-ge*, 699
Katokpa Gyeltsap I, Tsangtönpa Dorje Gyeltsen (1126-1216) *kaḥ-thog-pa rgyal-tshab gtsang-ston-pa rdo-rje rgyal-mtshan*: see *Tsangtönpa*
Katokpa Gyeltsap II, Campabum (1179-1252) *kaḥ-thog-pa rgyal-tshab byams-pa 'bum*: see *Campabum*
Katokpa Gyaltsap III, Ce-nga Mangpuwa Sonam Bumpa (b. 1223) *kaḥ-thog-pa rgyal-tshab spyan-snga mang-phu-ba bsod-nams 'bum-pa*: see *Ce-nga (Mangpu)wa Sonam Bumpa*
Katokpa Gyeltsap IV, Uwöpa Yeshebum (b. 1254) *kaḥ-thog-pa rgyal-tshab dbu-'od-pa ye-shes 'bum*: see *Uwöpa Yeshebum*
Katokpa Gyeltsap V, Cangcup Pelwa *kaḥ-thog-pa rgyal-tshab byang-chub dpal-ba*: see *Cangcup Pelwa*
Katokpa Gyeltsap VI, Sonam Zangpo *kaḥ-thog-pa rgyal-tshab bsod-nams bzang-po*: see *Sonam Zangpo*
Katokpa Gyeltsap VII, Künga Bumpa *kaḥ-thog-pa rgyal-tshab kun-dga' 'bum-pa*: see *Künga Bumpa*
Katokpa Wangcuk Pelwa *kaḥ-thog-pa dbang-phyug dpal-ba*: see *Wangcuk Pelwa* and Glossary of Enumerations under *thirteen generations of the gurus of Katok* for an explanation of this listing
Katokpa Gyeltsap VIII, Lodrö Bumpa *kaḥ-thog-pa rgyal-tshab blo-gros 'bum-pa*: see *Lodrö Bumpa*
Katokpa Gyeltsap IX, Lodrö Senge *kaḥ-thog-pa rgyal-tshab blo-gros seng-ge*: see *Lodrö Senge*
Katokpa Gyeltsap X, Cangcup Lodrö *kaḥ-thog-pa rgyal-tshab byang-chub blo-gros*: see *Cangcup Lodrö*
Katokpa Gyeltsap XI, Cangcup Senge *kaḥ-thog-pa rgyal-tshab byang-chub seng-ge*: see *Cangcup Senge*
Katokpa Gyeltsap XII, Cangcup Gyeltsen *kaḥ-thog-pa rgyal-tshab byang-chub rgyal-mtshan*: see *Cangcup Gyeltsen*
Katokpa Gyeltsap XIII, Yeshe Gyeltsen *kaḥ-thog-pa rgyal-tshab ye-shes rgyal-mtshan*: see *(Khedrup) Yeshe Gyeltsen (of Pubor)*
(Katokpa) Moktön Dorje Pelzang(po) *(kaḥ-thog-pa) rmog-ston rdo-rje dpal-bzang(-po)*, 696, 700-1
Katokpa Namdröl Zangpo *kaḥ-thog-pa rnam-grol bzang-po*, 699
Katok Paṇḍita Gyurme Tshewang Chokdrup *kaḥ-thog paṇḍita 'gyur-med tshe-dbang mchog-grub*, 966; see *Gyurme Tshewang Chokdrup*
Katokpa Pema Lodrö *kaḥ-thog-pa padma blo-gros*, 723; see *Tabla Padmamati*
Katok(pa) Tampa Deshek (1122-92) *kaḥ-thog(-pa) dam-pa bde-gshegs*, **689**, 688-91, 693, 698, 952

Dewarshekpa, lama *bla-ma bde-bar gshegs-pa*, 691
Matisāra, the bodhisattva *byang-chub sems-dpa' blo-gros snying-po*, 691
Sharwa Popathaye, lama *bla-ma shar-ba spobs-pa mtha'-yas*, 688
Sherap Senge *shes-rab seng-ge*, 688
Tampa Deshek *dam-pa bde-gshegs*, 698, 699
Tampa Dewarshekpa of Katok *kaḥ-thog-pa dam-pa bde-bar gshegs-pa*, 688
Tampa Rinpoche *dam-pa rin-po-che*, 698
Katok Situ (Chöki Gyamtso) (1880-1925) *kaḥ-thog si-tu (chos-kyi rgya-mtsho)*: a nephew of Khyentse Rinpoche, 879, 958
Situ Künzi Chöki Gyamtso *si-tu kun-gzigs chos-kyi rgya-mtsho*, 736
Kātyāyanaputra *ka-tya'i bu*, 90
Kauśika *kau-shi-ka*, 176
Kawa Ö-chokdra *ka-ba 'od-mchog-grags*, 524
Kawa Peltsek *ska-ba dpal-brtsegs*, 40, 96, 224-5, 515, 522, 526, 527, 535, 555, 889, 893
Keldenpa *skal-ldan-pa*, 686
Keldenpa Chöki Senge *skal-ldan-pa chos-kyi seng-ge*, 569
Keśamiśrā *skra-'dres-ma*, 421
Ke-wang *hva-shang ke-wang*, 524
Khampalungpa (b. 1025) *khams-pa lung-pa*: a disciple of Atiśa, 546
Khamtrül III, Ngawang Künga Tendzin (1680-1728) *khams-sprul gsum-pa ngag-dbang kun-dga' bstan-'dzin*, 957
Ngawang Künga Tendzin of Dokam *mdo-khams-pa ngag-dbang kun-dga' bstan-'dzin*, 833
Khamzhik Taklung Nyönpa *khams-zhig stag-lung smyon-pa*, 784
Khandro Yeshe Tshogyel *mkha'-'gro ye-shes mtsho-rgyal*, 554; see *(Yeshe) Tshogyel*
Khandülma, the nāginī *klu-mo kha-'dul-ma*, 452
Kharak Gomcung *kha-rag sgom-chung*, 557, 558
Kharak Nyingpo *kha-rag snying-po*, 701
Lharje Kharakpa *lha-rje kha-rag-pa*, 347
Kharak Tönying *kha-rag ston-snying*, 657
Kharap Zhelngane Köncok Tendzin *kha-rab zhal-snga-nas dkon-mchog bstan-'dzin*, 729
Kharcen Pelgi Wangcuk *mkhar-chen dpal-gyi dbang-phyug*, 535, 706, 711
Kharcen(-za) Yeshe Tshogyel *mkhar-chen(-bza') ye-shes mtsho-rgyal*, 535, 536, 710-11, 714; see *(Yeshe) Tshogyel*
Khawa Karpowa Namka Gyamtso *kha-ba dkar-po-ba nam-mkha' rgya-mtsho*, 697
Karpopa *dkar-po-pa*, 676
Khecarī *mkha'-spyod-ma*, 828
Khecok Ngawang Lodrö *mkhas-mchog ngag-dbang blo-gros*, 965
Khedrup Chöki Trakpa *mkhas-grub chos-kyi grags-pa*, 594-5
Khedrup Chökyong Gyeltsen *mkhas-grub chos-skyong rgyal-mtshan*, 730
Khedrup Chöpel *mkhas-grub chos-dpal*, 686
Khedrup Delek Gyamtso of Zhoktarling *zhog-thar gling mkhas-grub bde-legs rgya-mtsho*, 594
Khedrup Lodrö Gyeltsen Pelzangpo *mkhas-grub blo-gros rgyal-mtshan dpal bzang-po*, 722-3; see *Sodokpa Lodrö Gyeltsen*
Khedrup Khyapdel Lhündrup *mkhas-grub khyab-brdal lhun-grub*, 595
(Khedrup) Yeshe Gyeltsen (of Pubor) *(spu-bor-ba mkhas-grub) ye-shes rgyal-mtshan*: i.e. Katokpa Gyeltsap XIII, 696-7, 698
Jñānaketu *mkhas-grub dznya-na ke-tu*, 696
Puborwa Khedrup Yeshe Gyeltsen *spu-bor-ba mkhas-grub ye-shes rgyal-mtshan*, 699
Sukhāṅkuśa, the bodhisattva *byang-sems bde-ba'i smyu-gu*, 697
Sukhasāra *bde-ba'i snying-po*, 697
Khenpo Lhakawa *mkhan-po la-kha-ba*, 552
Khepa Conam *mkhas-pa jo-nam*, 656
Khön family *'khon-rigs*, 395
Khön Köncok Gyelpo (1034-1102) *'khon dkon-mchog rgyal-po*, 951
Khön Lüiwangpo (Sungwa) *'khon klu'i dbang-po (srung-ba)*, 515, 712, 922, 951
Khönrok Sherap Tshültrim *'khon-rog shes-rab tshul-khrims*, 951
(Khöntön) Peljor Lhündrup (1561-1637) *('khon-ston) dpal-'byor lhun-grub*, 677-80, 822
Phawangkhapa (Peljor Lhündrup) *pha-wang-kha-pa (dpal-'byor lhun-grub)*, 681, 926

Khön Trakpa Gyeltsen (1147-1216) *'khon-grags-pa rgyal-mtshan*, 562
Khu Cangcup-ö *khu byang-chub 'od*, 707
Khugyur Selweichok *khu-'gyur gsal-ba'i mchog*, 541-2
Khulung Yönten Gyamtso *khu-lung-pa yon-tan rgya-mtsho*, 613, 614-15; see *Nup Khulungpa (Yönten Gyamtso)*
Khurbupa, venerable *rje 'khur-bu-pa*, 709
Khutön Sonam Gyeltsen *khu-ston bsod-nams rgyal-mtshan*, 789
Khutön Tarma-tra *yar-lung-gi dge-bshes khu-ston dar-ma grags*, 753
Khuwo Phajo *khu-bo pha-jo*, 551
Khuza Peltsünma *khu-bza' dpal-btsun-ma*, 537
Khyapdak Gyurme Ngedön Wangpo *khyab-bdag 'gyur-med nges-don dbang-po*, 919; see *Gyurme Ngedön Wangpo*
Khyapjuk (Chenpo) *khyab-'jug (chen-po)*, 591, 681, 775; see *Rāhula*
Khyentse Rinpoche *mkhyen-brtse rin-po-che*, 752, 844, 845, 846, 848, 849-58, 863-6, 871, 873, 874-5, 876-7; see *(Jamyang) Khyentse Wangpo*
Khyentse Wangpo *mkhyen-brtse'i dbang-po*: see *(Jamyang) Khyentse Wangpo*
Khyeucung Khadingtsel (Youth who Flies like Garuḍa) *khye'u chung mkha'-lding rtsal*: Guru Rinpoche's manifestation of the seventh month, 471
Khyung clan of accomplished masters *khyung-rgyal grub-rigs*, 859
Khyung Nakshadar *khyung nag-zhag-dar*, 569
Khyungpo Neljor(pa) (Tshültrim Gönpo) *khyung-po rnal-'byor(-pa) (tshul-khrims mgon-po)*, 395, 853, 950, 951, 952
　Khyungpo Tshültrim Gönpo *khyung-po tshul-khrims mgon-po*, 929
Khyungpo Trase *dge-bshes khyung-po grags-se*, 640-2, 650
Khyungpo Trhowo *khyung-po khro-bo*, 685
Khyungpo Tshultrim Gönpo *khyung-po tshul-khrims mgon-po*, 929; see *Khyungpo Neljor(pa)*
Khyungpo Yik-ö *khyung-po dbyig-'od*, 707
Khyung-truk Khace *rta khyung-phrug kha-che*: a horse, 655
Khyungtsangpa/wa (Trhüzhi) Lodrö Pelden *khyung-tshang-pa/ba 'khrul-zhig blo-gros dpal-ldan*, 553, 701
Köncok Chöpel (of Lingme) *(gling-smad-pa) dkon-mchog chos-'phel*, 681, 821
Kongcen Namka Pelden *kong-chen nam-mkha' dpal-ldan*, 807
Kong-ra Locen (Zhenpen Dorje) (1594-1654) *gong-ra lo-chen (gzhan-phan rdo-rje)*, 718, 723-4, 725, 726
　Locen Zhenpen Dorje *lo-chen gzhan-phan rdo-rje*, 718, 724
Kong Rikdzin Nyingpo *kong rig-'dzin snying-po*, 788
Kongtsün Sherap Yeshe *kong-btsun shes-rab ye-shes*, 616
Konjo Dakpo *go-'jo bdag-po*, 686
Korampa (Sonam Senge) (1429-89) *go(-rams-pa bsod-nams seng-ge)*, 929, 955
Kortön Radza *kor-ston ra-dza*, 551
Korup Lotsāwa *go-rub lo-tsā-ba*, 708, 709
　Chöki Sherap, the translator of Korup *go-rub lo-tsā-ba chos-kyi shes-rab*, 708
Koṣa *ko-ṣa*: a bear-like creature, 490
Kṛkī, king *rgyal-po kri-kri*, 430
Kṛmivarman *srin-bu go-cha*, 418
Kṛṣṇa, lord *jo-bo kri-ṣṇa*: a paṇḍita, 708; see *Kṛṣṇapā*
Kṛṣṇa of Pāṭaliputra, the sublime *phags-pa nag-po dmar-bu-can*, 437
Kṛṣṇacārin *nag-po spyod-pa/nag*, 404, 462, 471, 473, 603, 693, 706
　Cārīndra *spyod-'chang dbang-po*, 693, 927
　Kaṇhapā(da) *ka-ṇha-pa*, 455, 693
Kṛṣṇadhara, minister of righteousness *chos-blon kri-ṣṇa-'dzin*, 469
Kṛṣṇapā *kri-ṣṇa-pa*: a paṇḍita, 708
　Kṛṣṇa, lord *jo-bo kri-ṣhna*, 708
Kṣitigarbha *sa-snying*, 125
Kubjita *sgur po*, 93
Kukkurāja *ku-ku-rā-dza*, 39, **461**, 458-62, 466, 533, 736
　Kukkuripā *ku-ku-ri-pa*, 442
　Kuttarāja *ku-ta-rā-dza*, 460
Kukkurāja, the later *ku-ku-rā-dza phyi-ma*, 487
Kukkuripā *ku-ku-ri-pa*, 442; see *Kukkurāja*
Kulikas *rigs-ldan-gyi rabs*: the dynastic kings of Shambhala, 948
Kumārādza (1266-1343) *ku-mā-rā-dza*, 40, **568**, 568-72, 573, 579, 580, 581, 588, 594, 679
　Gelong Pelden *dge-slong dpal-ldan*, 572

Rikdzin Kumārādza *rig-'dzin ku-mā-rā-dza*, 953

Tharpagyen *thar-pa rgyan*, 568

Zhönu Gyelpo *gzhon-nu rgyal-po*, 569

Kumāravīrabalin *gzhon-nu dpa'-bo stobs-ldan*: the sixth emanational teacher according to the Great Perfection, 136, 449

Kündrölbum *sras-mo kun-grol-'bum*, 698

Künga *kun-dga'*, 591; see *Gompa Künrin of Drigung*

Künga Bumpa *kun-dga' 'bum-pa*: i.e. Katokpa Gyeltsap VII, 695

Künga Bumpa, the ḍākinī *mkha-'gro-ma kun-dga' 'bum-pa*, 846

Künga Dawa *kun-dga' zla-ba*, 697

Künga Gyamtso, accomplished master of Derge *sde-dge grub-thob kun-dga' rgya-mtsho*, 812, 813

Künga Lekpa, the Drukpa madman (1455-1529) *'brug-pa smyon-pa kun-dga' legs-pa*, 955

Künga Lhadze *sras-mo kun-dga' lha-mdzes*, 821

Künga, master *slob-dpon kun-dga'*, 567

Künga Özer, master *slob-dpon kun-dga' 'od-zer*, 576

Künga Sonam Chöpak *kun-dga' bsod-nams chos-'phags*, 813; see *Rikdzin Düdül Dorje*

Künga of Tingri (1062-1124) *ding-ri kun-dga'*, 547

Künga Trhinle Wangyel, the lord and throne-holder of the Drölma Palace of Sakya (b. 1945) *sa-skya sgrol-ma-pa'i bdag-khri kun-dga' phrin-las dbang-rgyal*: the Sakya Trhicen, 959

Künga Zangpo, the madman of Central Tibet (b. 1458) *dbus-smyon-pa kun-dga' bzang-po*, 955

Kungtang Paṇcen (Shenyen Namgyel) *gung-thang paṇ-chen (bshes-gnyen rnam-rgyal)*, 729, 730

Künkyen Chöje *kun-mkhyen chos-rje*, 590; see *Longcen Rapjampa*

Künkyen Sherap Gyelpo *kun-mkhyen shes-rab rgyal-po*, 760

Künkyong Lingpa *kun-skyong gling-pa*, 791; see *Dorje Lingpa*

Künpang Doringpa *kun-spangs rdo-ring-pa*, 922

Künpang Tönyö Gyeltsen *kun-spangs don-yod rgyal-mtshan*, 802

Künpangpa, lama *bla-ma kun-spangs-pa*, 671

Künzang, (master) *(slob-dpon) kun-bzang*, 550, 551-2

Künzang Dorje *kun-bzang rdo-rje*, 595

Künzang Khyapdel Lhündrup *kun-bzang khyab-brdal lhun-grub*, 817

Künzang Namgyel *kun-bzang rnam-rgyal*, 818; see *Lhatsün Namka Jikme*

Künzang Peljor, the holder of mantras/mantra adept *sngags-'chang kun-bzang dpal-'byor*, 701, 725

Künzang Pema Trhinle *kun-bzang padma phrin-las*, 720; see *Dorje Trak Rikdzin IV*

Künzang Tenpei Gyeltsen (1763-1817) *kun-bzang bstan-pa'i rgyal-mtshan*: i.e. Lhodrak Sungtrül VI, 735

Speech Emanation of Lhodrak *lho-brag gsung-sprul*, 839

Künzang Tenpei Nyima (1843-91) *kun-bzang bstan-pa'i nyi-ma*: i.e. Lhodrak Sungtrül VIII, 735

Künzang Wangyel, the ancestral throne-holder of Mindröling (b. 1931) *smin-gling khri-chen kun-bzang dbang-rgyal*: the present Minling Trhicen, 959

Künzhön, the governor *dpon-chen kun-gzhon*, 664

Kurap, the aristocrat *sku-rabs sde-pa*, 777

Lord Kurap *sku-rabs sde-dpon*, 687

Kurser, the Horpa King *hor gur-ser rgyal-po*, 780

Kurukullā *rig-byed-ma*, 824

Vidyā, the transcendent lady *bcom-ldan-'das-ma rig-byed-ma*, 824

Kurup Yangdak of Yamdrok *yar-'brog-pa gu-rub yang-dag*, 712

Kusara, master *slob-dpon ku-sa-ra*, 511

Kutsa, doctor *ku-tsha sman-pa*, 765

Kuttarāja *ku-ta-rā-dza*, 460; see *Kukkurāja*

Kyebuchenpo, the oath-bound protector *dam-can skyes-bu chen-po*, 587

Kyere Chokyong *kye-re mchog-skyong*, 533

Kyetse Yeshe Wangcuk *skye-tshe ye-shes dbang-phyug*, 552

Kyiben Cangcup Rincen *skyi-ban byang-chub rin-chen*, 714; see *Kyi Kyangyel (of Mongu)*

Kyi Chöki Senge *skyi chos-kyi seng-ge*, 685-6

Kyi Kyangyel (of Mongu) *(mong-dgu'i) skyi gyang-sgyel*, 714

Kyiben Cangcup Rincen *skyi-ban byang-chub rin-chen*, 714

Kyi Nyima Dorje *skyi nyi-ma rdo-rje*, 77

Kyitön Tshering Wangpo *skyi-ston tshe-ring dbang-po*, 717, 718

Kyo Kongbupa *skyo gong-bu-pa*, 358; see *Kyotön Śāk-ye of Kungbu*

Kyotön *skyo-ston*, 640-1, 647; see *Kyöton Śāk-ye of Kungbu*

Kyotön Chöseng *skyo-ston chos-seng*, 642

Kyotön Śāk-ye of Kungbu/Kongbu *gung-bu/gong-bu skyo-ston śāk-ye*, 358, 640-1, 642, 646

Kyo Kongbupa *skyo gong-bu-pa*, 358

Kyotön *skyo-ston*, 640-1, 647

Kyura family *skyu-ra rigs*, 676

Labrangpa Chöpel Gyeltsen *bla-brang-pa chos-dpal rgyal-mtshan*, 577

Lacen Dorjechang Trakpa Rincen *bla-chen rdo-rje 'chang grags-pa rin-chen*, 722

Lacen (Gongpa Rapsel) *bla-chen (dgongs-pa rab-gsal)*, 524, **526**, 618, 706, 821, 950

Muzu Labar *dmu-gzugs la-'bar*, 524

Śākya Gewarapsel *śā-kya dge-ba rab-gsal*, 524

Ladö *bla-'dos*, 655

Laketsewa the Pönpo *bon-po la-ke-rtse-ba*, 632

Lakṣāśva, king *rgyal-po lakṣa-ashva*, 456

Lala Zicen *la-la gzi-chen*, 642

Lalitavajra *rol-pa'i rdo-rje*, 477, 487

Lamcok Pelgi Dorje *lam-mchog dpal-gyi rdo-rje*, 605

(Langcen) Pelgi Senge *(rlangs-chen) dpal-gyi seng-ge*, 535, 839

Langdarma (Udumtsen), king (b. 817) *glang dar-ma ('u-dum btsan)*, 40, 394, 523, 609, 612, 614, 918, 921, 950

Langdro (Köncok Jungne) *lang-gro dkon-mchog 'byung-gnas/dkon-'byung*, 536, 720, 734, 793,

Langdro Könjung *lang-gro dkon-'byung*, 858

Langdro Könjung: see preceding entry

Lang Khampa Gocha *rlang kham-pa go-cha*, 526

Langlap Cancup Dorje *lang-lab byang-chub rdo-rje*, 712, 713-14

Langtön Tarma Sonam of Shang Lhabu *shangs lha-bu'i langs-ston dar-ma bsod-nams*, 649

Laṅkājayabhadra *laṅkā rgyal-ba bzang-po*, 455

Lapdrönma *lab-sgron-ma*, 546; see *Macik Lapdrön*

Lapkyapgön Wangcen Gyerap Dorje *lab skyabs-mgon dbang-chen dgyes-rab rdo-rje*, 870

Laptön Namka Rincen *lab-ston nam-mkha' rin-chen*, 697

Laru Pende of upper Önak *'on-nag stod-pa gla-ru ban-de*, 552

Lasum Gyelwa Cangcup *la-gsum rgyal-ba byang-chub*, 515, 536, 738

Lāsyā *sgeg-mo*, 125

Layak Dzawar, the great minister of *la-yag rdza-bar-gyi dpon-chen*, 760

Lekden Degü *bka'-srung legs-ldan lde-gus*, 644, **644**

Bhagavat *(mgon-po) legs-ldan*, 624

Lekden Dorje *legs-ldan rdo-rje*, 807; see *Dorje Trak Rikdzin II*

Lek, six earthly kings called *sa'i legs drug*: listed in the Glossary of Enumerations, 507-8, n. 535

Leki Dorje (1326-1401) *las-kyi rdo-rje*, 923, 925

Namka Gyeltsen, accomplished master of Lhodrak *lho-brag grub-thob nam-mkha' rgyal-mtshan*, 923

Lekpa Pelzang *legs-pa dpal-bzang*, 717

Lekpei Drönme *legs-pa'i sgron-me*, 613; see *(Sutön) Lekpei Drönme*

Lelmik Woktsen *glal-mig 'og-btsan*, 602

Lencap Parwa *glan-chab bar-ba*, 358

Len clan *gdung-rus glan*, 666

Len Chögyel *glan chos-rgyal*, 687

Len Nyatselpa Sonam Gönpo *glan nya-tshal-pa bsod-nams mgon-po*, 668

Lharje Len Nyatselpa *lha-rje glan nya-tshal-pa*, 657

Len Śākya Cangcup *glan śā-kya byang-chub*, 647

Lenśāk Cangcup *glan-śāk byang-chub*, 642

Lenśāk Cangcup: see preceding entry

Len Śākya Öpo *glan śā-kya 'od-po*, 686

Len Śākya Zangpo (of Chuwar) *(chu-bar-gyi) glan śā-kya bzang-po*, 358, 642, 647, 701

Lentön Śākya Zangpo *glan-ston śā-kya bzang-po*, 641

Len Selwa *glan gsal-ba*, 668

All-Knowing Master from Shang *shangs-pa kun-mkhyen*, 668

Lentön Śākya Zangpo *glan-ston śā-kya bzang-po*, 641; see *Len Śākya Zangpo (of Chuwar)*

Lerap Lingpa, the treasure-finder (1856-1926) *gter-ston las-rab gling-pa*, 864, 868, 879, 958

Sogyel, the treasure finder *gter-ston bsod-rgyal*, 879

Letro Lingpa, the treasure-finder *gter-ston las-'phro gling-pa*, 809; see *(Rikdzin) Jatsön Nyingpo*

Lha, lama *bla-ma lha*, 552

Lhabumen *lha-bu sman*, 515

Lhadrowa Chöki Wangpo *lha-bro-ba chos-kyi dbang-po*, 699

Lhakangpa, (lama) *(bla-ma) lha-khang-pa*, 655, 659; see *Yöntenzung*

Lhakü Pönpo *lha-khud bon-po*, 666

Lha Lama, uncle and nephew *lha bla-ma khu-dbon*: Yeshe-ö and Cangcup-ö, 918

Lhalung Pelgi Dorje *lha-lung dpal-gyi rdo-rje*, 523, 524, **525**, 526, 536, 540, 612, 950

Lhandzin Yangcen Drölma *lha-'dzin dbyangs-can sgrol-ma*, 825

Lhapdrema Kongpa *lhab-dres-ma gong-pa*, 701

Lha Pelgi Yeshe *lha dpal-gyi ye-shes*, 604; see *Sogdian Pelgi Yeshe*

Lharipel *lha-ri-dpal*, 565

Lharje Celpa *lha-rje dpyal-pa*, 348; see *Cel (Lotsāwa) Künga Dorje*

Lharje Da Senge *lha-rje mda' seng-ge*, 685

Lharje Dropukpa *lha-rje sgro-phug-pa*, 648; see *Zur (Dropukpa) Śākya Senge*

Lharje Gyanak *lha-rje rgya-nag*, 650, 651, 652; see *Cetön Gyanak*

Lharje Horpo Dropukpa *lha-rje hor-po sgro-phug-pa*, 649; see *Zur (Dropukpa) Śākya Senge*

Lharje Hūṃcung *lha-rje hūṃ-chung*, 615

Lharje Kharakpa *lha-rje kha-rag-pa*, 347; see *Kharak Nyingpo*

Lharje Nupme *lha-rje gnubs-smad*, 655

Lharje Nyariwa *lha-rje nya-ri-ba*, 701; see *Zur (Dropukpa) Śākya Senge*

Lharje Len Nyatselpa *lha-rje glan nya-tshal-pa*, 657; see *Len Nyatselpa Sonam Gönpo*

Lharje Rok Sherap-ö *lha-rje rog shes-rab 'od*, 358; see *Rok Sherap-ö*

Lharje Shangnak *lha-rje shangs-nag*, 647

Lharje Ukpalungpa *lha-rje 'ug-pa lung-pa*, 632; see *(Zurpoche) Śakya Jungne*

Lharje Zurpoche (Śākya Jungne) *lha-rje zur-po-che (śā-kya 'byung-gnas)*, 616, 617-35; see *(Zurpoche) Śākya Jungne*

Lhase Chokdrup Gyelpo *lha-sras mchog-grub rgyal-po*, 775; see *Gyelse Lharje*

Lhase Tamdzin Rölpa Yeshetsel *lha-sras dam-'dzin rol-pa ye-shes rtsal*, 784; see *Murup Tsepo (Yeshe Rölpatsel)*

Lhasung *mes-po lha-srung*, 575

Lha Thotori Nyentsen *lha tho-tho-ri gnyan-btsan*, 393, 508, **508**, 949

Lha Tsepo, family of *lha-btsad-po'i rigs*, 818

Lhatsün Künzang Namgyel: see following entry

Lhatsün Namka Jikme (1597-1652) *lha-btsun nam-mkha' 'jigs-med*, 718, 727, 812, 816, **819**, 818-20, 956

(Lhatsün) Künzang Namgyel *(lha-btsun) kun-bzang rnam-rgyal*, 724, 725, 818

Lhodrak Guru *lho-brag gu-ru*, 807

Lhodrak Sungtrül (III, Tshültrim Dorje) (1598-1669) *lho-brag gsung-sprul (tshul-khrims rdo-rje)*, 681

(Sungtrül) Tshültrim Dorje *(gsung-sprul) tshul-khrims rdo-rje*, 723, 724, 727, 735, 956

Lhodrak Sungtrül IV, Ngawang Künzang Dorje (1680-1723) *lho-brag gsung-sprul ngag-dbang kun-bzang rdo-rje*: see *Ngawang Künzang Dorje*

Lhodrak Sungtrül VI, Künzang Tenpei Gyeltsen (1763-1817) *lho-brag gsung-sprul kun-bzang bstan-pa'i rgyal-mtshan*: see *Künzang Tenpei Gyeltsen*

Lhodrak Sungtrül VIII, Künzang Tenpei Nyima (1843-91) *lho-brag gsung-sprul kun-bzang bstan-pa'i nyi-ma*: see *Künzang Tenpei Nyima*

Lhodrak Thukse Dawa Gyeltsen *lho-brag thugs-sras zla-ba rgyal-mtshan*: the spiritual son of Pema Lingpa, see *Dawa (Gyeltsen)*

Lhodrak (Thuk)-se IV, Tendzin Gyurme Dorje (b. 1641) *lho-brag sras bstan-'dzin 'gyur-med rdo-rje*, 824

Peling Thukse Tendzin Gyurme Dorje *pad-gling thugs-sras bstan-'dzin 'gyur-med rdo-rje*, 956

Tendzin Gyurme Dorje *bstan-'dzin 'gyur-med rdo-rje*, 735
Lhodrak Thukse Dawa Gyeltsen V, Gyurme Chokdrup Pelbar *lho-brag sras zla-ba rgyal-mtshan 'gyur-med mchog-grub dpal-'bar*: see *Gyurme Chokdrup Pelbar*
Lhodruk Zhapdrung Ngawang Namgyel *lho-'brug zhabs-drung ngag-dbang rnam-rgyal*, 956; see *Zhapdrung I*
Licchavi *li-tsā-bi*, 454, 460, 485, 507, 510
Līlāvajra *sgeg-pa rdo-rje/sgeg-pa'i zhabs*, 40, 63, 96, 462, **463**, 463-4, 465, 494
  Śrīmad Uttamabodhibhagavat *dpal-ldan byang-chub mchog-gi skal-ba dang-ldan-pa*, 464
  Sūryavat *nyi-ma-dang 'dra-ba*, 463, 464
  Viśvarūpa *sna-tshogs gzugs-can*, 463, 464
Ling clan *gling-gi rigs*, 813
Lingje Kesar (1038-1124) *gling-rje ge-sar*, 952
Lingje Repa (Pema Dorje) (1128-88) *gling-rje ras-pa (padma rdo-rje)*, 773, 952
Ling Lama Chöjor Gyamtso *gling-bla-ma chos-'byor rgya-mtsho*, 876
Lingpas *gling-pa*: the great treasure-finders, 934
Ling, the royal house of *gling-tshang*, 816
Lingter III, Gyurme Pema Tendzin *gling-gter gsum-pa 'gyur-med padma bstan-'dzin*, 919
Lingtsang Dzapa Trashi Özer of Dokam (1859-1935) *mdo-khams gling-tshang rdza-pa bkra-shis 'od-zer*, 919
Locanā *spyan-ma*, 20, 125
(Locen) Chögyel Tendzin (1631-1708) *(lo-chen) chos-rgyal bstan-'dzin*, 726-8
Locen Dharmaśrī, Ngawang Chöpel (Gyamtso) (1654-1717) *lo-chen dharma-shri ngag-dbang chos-'phel (rgya-mtsho)*, 41, 198, 375, 684, **729**, 728-32, 824, 833, 879, 957, 965
  Dharmaśrī, the great translator *lo-chen dharma-shri*, 526, 733
  Ngawang Chöpel *ngag-dbang chos-'phel*, 728
  Tendzin Jamyang Wangpo *bstan-'dzin 'jam-dbyangs dbang-po*, 728
Locen Ngagiwangpo *lo-chen ngag-gi dbang-po*, 723
Locen Rincen Zangpo *lo-chen rin-chen bzang-po*, 11; see *Rincen Zangpo*
Locen Zhenpen Dorje *lo-chen gzhan-phan rdo-rje*, 718, 724; see *Kongra Locen (Zhenpen Dorje)*
Loden Chokse (Intelligent Boon-seeker) *blo-ldan mchog-sred*: one of Guru Rinpoche's manifestations during the second month, 470; see *Guru Rinpoche*
Lodrö Bumpa *blo-gros 'bum-pa*: i.e. Katokpa Gyeltsap VIII, 696
Lodröchok *blo-gros mchog*, 594; see *Longcen Rabjampa*
Lodrö Gyamtso, the physician of Zurkar (b. 1508) *zur-mkhar sman-pa blo-gros rgya-mtsho*, 955
Lodrö Gyeltsen, the regent (d. 1937) *rgyal-tshab blo-gros rgyal-mtshan*, 919
Lodrö Senge *blo-gros seng-ge*: i.e. Katokpa Gyeltsap IX, 696
Lodrö Zangpo, master *slob-dpon blo-gros bzang-po*, 595
Lokeśvara/Lord of the World *(dpa'-bo) 'jigs-rten dbang-phyug*, 47, 404, 916; see *Avalokiteśvara*
Loktön Gendünkyap *klog-ston dge-'dun skyabs*, 552
Lönсen Phakpa *blon-chen 'phags-pa*, 613; see *(Pagor) Lönсen Phakpa*
Longcen Rabjampa/Longcenpa, (the all-knowing) (1308-63) *(kun-mkhyen) klong-chen rab-'byams-pa/klong-chen-pa*, Pls. 30, 66; 18, 29, 40, 41, 47, 91, 139, 141, 196-8, 208-10, 359, 375, 396, 397, 555, 571, 572, **576**, 575-96, 676, 677, 681, 702, 707, 724, 727, 730, 796, 827, 829, 835, 837, 839, 876, 919, 954, 965
  Künkyen Chöje *kun-mkhyen chos-rje*, 590
  Lodröchok *blo-gros mchog*, 594
  Longcen Rabjam Zangpo *klong-chen rab-'byams bzang-po*, 837
  Samye Lungmangwa *bsam-yas lung-mang-ba*, 577
  Second Samantabhadra *kun-tu bzang-po gnyis-pa*, 586
  Tathāgata Sumerudīpadhvaja *de-bzhin gshegs-pa ri-rab mar-me'i rgyal-mtshan*, 590
  Trime Özer *dri-med 'od-zer*, 375, 796, 818
  Tshültrim Lodrö *tshul-khrims blo-gros*, 576

Longcen Rabjam Zangpo: see preceding entry

Longsel Nyingpo *klong-gsal snying-po*, 736; see *(Rikdzin) Longsel Nyingpo*

Lo Pelgi Lodrö *lo dpal-gyi blo-gros*, 714

Lord of Immortality and his consort *'chi-med mgon-po yab-yum*, 855; see *Amitāyus*

Lord Kurap *sku-rabs sde-dpon*, 687; see *Kurap*

lord of Neudong, the great *sne-gdong gong-ma chen-po*: a successor of Tā'i Situ Cangcup Gyeltsen, 787

Lord of Neudong *sne-gdong gong-ma*, 595; see *Tā'i Situ (Cangcup Gyeltsen)*

Lord Nyang *mnga'-bdag nyang*, 511, 661, 662; see *Nyang-rel Nyima Ozer*

Lord Nyang, father and son *mnga'-bdag nyang yab-sras*, 661, n. 809; see *Nyang-rel Nyima Özer*

Lord of Pristine Cognition, six-armed *ye-shes mgon-po phyag-drug-pa*: Jñānanātha, 849

Lord of Sages/Munīndra *thub-pa'i dbang-po*, 11, 128, 503, 768, 894; see *Buddha*

Lord of the Śākyas *śā-kya'i mgon*, 130; see *Buddha*

Lord of Secrets/Guhyapati *gsang(-ba'i) bdag(-po)*, 282, 377, 405, 430, 441, 451, 454, 458, 459, 460, 485, 490, 609, 645, 648, 728, 734, 923, 925, 948; see *Vajrapāṇi*

Lord of the World/Lokeśvara *'jig-rten dbang-phyugs*, 47, 404, 916; see *Avalokiteśvara*

Lords of the Three (Enlightened) Families *rigs-gsum mgon-po*, Skt. *trīkulanātha*, 137, 270, 352, **453**, 624, 698, 758, 798, 889; see also listed separately as *Avalokiteśvara*, *Mañjuśrī* and *Vajrapāṇi*

(Loro) Recungpa (1084-1161) *(lo-ro) ras-chung-pa*: i.e. Recung Dorje-tra *(ras-chung rdo-rje grags)*, 657

Lotön Dorje Wangcuk *lo-ston rdo-rje dbang-phyug*, 524

Lotuses of the Lake *mtsho-nang-gi padma*: the two wives of Songtsen Gampo, Pl. 39; 510

  Trhitsün, the Nepalese princess *bal-mo-bza' khri-btsun*, 510

  Wen-ch'eng K'ong-jo, the Chinese princess *rgya-mo-bza' 'un-shing kong-jo*, 510

Lowo Lotsāwa *glo-bo lo-tsā-ba*, 712, 806

Lozang Gyamtso *blo-bzang rgya-mtsho*, 821; see *Dalai Lama V*

Lozang Rapsel, the supreme scholar *mkhas-mchog blo-bzang rab-gsal*, 874

Ludrup *klu-sgrub*, 813

Lūipā *lū('i-pa)*, 404

Luken Sonam Senge *glu-mkhan bsod-nams seng-ge*, 595

Lume (Tshültrim Sherap) *klu-mes (tshul-khrims shes-rab)*, 524, 525-6, 753, 921

Lung-ham Chenpo *rlung-ham chen-po*, 546

Lungre *rlung-ras*, 547

Ma (Chöki Sherap) *rma (chos-kyi shes-rab)*, 578

Macik Lapdrön (b. 1031, 1049 or 1055; d. 1126, 1129 or 1143) *ma-gcig lab-sgron*, 929, 952

  Lapdrönma *lab-sgron-ma*, 546

Macik Zhama (b. 1062) *ma-gcig zha-ma*, 709

"Mad" Co-se, the Younger Dzeng *jo-sras 'dzeng-chung smyon-pa*, 551; see *Dzeng Co-se*

"Mad" Samdrup, the ascetic woman *ma-jo smyon-ma bsam-'grub*, 551

Madhuranirghoṣa, the great bodhisattva *byang-chub sems-dpa' chen-po sgra-dbyangs snyan-pa*, 190

Madhyāhnika (Midday) *nyi-ma'i gung-pa*, 435, 437, **438**, 438-9

  Madhyāntika (Midway) *chu'i dbus-pa*, 435

Magyapa, king *dmag-brgya-pa*, 507

Mahādeva *lha-chen-po*, 429, 892

Mahākāla *mgon-po (nag-po chen-po)*, 659, 691

  four-armed Mahākāla *mgon-po phyag-bzhi-pa*, 569-70

  glorious Mahākāla according to the tradition of Wrathful Yamāntaka *dpal-mgon mahākāla drag-po gshin-rje*, 628

Mahākarmendrāṇī, the ḍākinī *mkha'-'gro las-kyi dbang-mo*, 482, **483**, 697

Mahākāśyapa *'od-srung chen-po*, 426, 427, 428, 432-4, **433**

  Kāśyapa *'od-srung*, 83, 172, 432-4, 435, 906, 932

  Nyagrodhaja *nya-gro-dha skyes*, 432

Mahākausṭhila *gsus-po-che*, 90
Mahā Lhünpo *ma-hā lhun-po*, 656
Mahāmati *blo-gros chen-po*, 179-80, 455, 912-13
Mahāpadma, king *padma chen-po*, 429, 441
Mahāprajāpati *skye-dgu'i bdag-mo*, 418; see *Prajāpatī*
Mahāsaṅghika(s) *phal-chen-pa*, 429, 430
Maheśvara *dbang-chen*, 535; see *Hayagrīva*
Mahottara (Chemcok) Heruka *che-mchog he-ru-ka*, Pl. 5; 362, 449, 483, **484**, 535
Maitreya, (conqueror/regent/lord) *(rgyal-ba/rgyal-tshab) byams-pa (mgon-po)*, 90, 98, 125, 129, 170, 177, **179**, 182, 205, 207, 212-13, 216, 298, 301, 430-1, 433-4, 440, 577, 590, 676, 691, 749, 838, 859, 930, 931, 932
  Ajita, (conqueror/regent) *(rgyal-ba/rgyal-tshab) ma-pham-pa*, 98, 128, 129, 170-1, 838, 930, 932
  Fifth Guide *rnam-'dren lnga-pa*, 749, 971
  great regent *rgyal-tshab chen-po*, 676, 931
  Maitreyanātha *byams-pa mgon-po*, 440
Maitripā, lord *mnga'-bdag me/mi-tri-pa*, 200, 329, 395
  Advayavajra *gnyis-med rdo-rje*, 200
Majo Dowa *ma-jo bzlo-ba*, 551
Majo Sherap-kyi *ma-jo shes-rab skyid*, 635
Majo Tönden *dkon-gnyer ma-jo don-ldan*, 634
Mālā *phreng-ba-ma*, 125
Malign Mantra *drag-sngags*, 283, 362, 483, 535
Mama Yungdrung Trashi *ma-ma gYung-drung bkra-shis*, 632
Māmakī *mā-ma-kī*, 20, 125, 250
Mandāravā *mandā-ra-bā*, Pl. 16; 470, 536, 864
Manda Zangzhücen *ma-nda zangs-zhus-can*, 617
Mang-rawa Pema Düdül *mang-ra-ba padma bdud-'dul*, 717-18
Maṇigarbha, the bodhisattva *byang-chub sems-dpa' nor-bu snying-po*, 693; see *Tsangtönpa*
Maṇimālya *nor-bu'i phreng-ba*, 120
Maṇi Rincen (the accomplished master of Katok) *(kaḥ-thog grub-thob) ma-ṇi rin-chen*, 698, 770
Mañjughoṣa: see following entry
Mañjuśrī *'jam-dpal*, 125, 130, 146, 176, 219, 298, 304, 320, 330, 344, 430, 431, 441, 449, 451, 452, **453**, 463, 465, 466, 478, 495, 535, 545, 592, 607, 609, 698, 704, 748, 758, 763, 805, 823, 854, 869, 877, 901; see also *Lords of the Three (Enlightened) Families*
  Mañjuśrīghoṣa *jam-dpal dbyangs*, 861, 876, 887
  Mañjughoṣa *'jam-pa'i dbyangs*, 440, 466, 477, 512, 577, 671, 691, 929
  Mañjuśrī the Body *'jam-dpal sku*, 283, 361; see *Yamāntaka*
  Mañjuśrī in the form of Vādīsiṃha *'jam-dpal smra-seng*, 869
  Mañjuśrī, Lord of Life *'jam-dpal tshe-bdag*, 610; see *Yamāntaka*
  (Mañjuśrī)tīkṣṇa(vajra) *('phags-pa 'jam-dpal rdo-rje) rnon-po*, 452, 493
  Mañjuśrī-Yamāntaka (Lord of Life) *'jam-dpal ya-mānta-ka (tshe-bdag)/'jam-dpal gshin-rje*, 478, 876; see *Yamāntaka*
Mañjuśrījñāna *manydzu-shrī dznyā-na*, 708
Mañjuśrīkīrti *'jam-dpal grags-pa*, 305
Mañjuśrīmitra *'jam-dpal bshes-gnyen*, 39, 477-9, 483, 490-4, **492**, 495-6, 498, 837, 854
  Sāra, the venerable brahman *bram-ze snying-po'i zhabs/sa-ra-pa-da*, 478
  Sārasiddhi, the brahman *bram-ze snying-po grub-pa*, 478
Mañjuśrīmitra, the younger *'jam-dpal bshes-gnyen phyi-ma*, 498, 554
Mañjuśrītīkṣṇa *'phags-pa 'jam-dpal rnon-po*, 493; see *Mañjuśrī*
  Tīkṣṇavajra *rdo-rje rnon-po*, 452
Mañjuśrīvarman *mandzyu-shrī varma*, 708
Mañjuvajra, nineteen-deity maṇḍala of *'jam-pa'i rdo-rje lha bcu-dgu'i dkyil-'khor*: listed in the Glossary of Enumerations, 496; see *Guhyasamāja*
Manorathanandin, the nāga *klu yid-'ong dga'-ba*, 452
Māra *bdud*: the Buddha's tempter or demonic forces in general, 71, 115, 129-30, 131, 343, 416, 420, 421, 436, 490, 518, 591, 913, 931, 946, 947
Mārajitā, the ḍākinī *bdud-'dul-ma*, 469, 472
Margyen, queen *btsan-po yum dmar-rgyan*, 603; see *Tshepongza*
Ma Rincen-chok *rma rin-chen mchog*, 515, 533, 535, 608, 707, 889

Marpa Chöki Wangcuk (1012-96) *mar-pa chos-kyi dbang-phyug*, 395, 708
Marpa of Lhodrak *lho-brag mar-pa*, 922
Marpa, lord *mnga'-bdag mar-pa*, 200, 805
Marpa, (the translator) *mar-pa (lo-tsā-ba)*, 713, 853, 862, 890, 921, 950, 951, 952
Marpa Sherap-ö (of Caze in Lhodrak) *(lho-brag bya-ze'i) mar-pa shes-rab 'od*, 540, 649
Marpa Topa (1042-1136) *mar-pa do-pa*, 708, 709
Mar Śākyamuni *smar śā-kya mu-ni*, 524, 525
Martön, lama *bla-ma dmar-ston*, 657
Marutse, the butcher *shan-pa ma-ru-tse*, 610; see *Nup(cen) Sangye Yeshe*
Masang brothers, nine *ma-sangs spun-dgu*: listed in the Glossary of Enumerations, 949
Mātaṅgī(pā) *ma-tanggi(-pa)*, 464, 502, 596
Mātaraḥ *ma-mo*, 283, 362, 483, 535, 649, 669; see also Bibliography
twelve Mātaraḥ *ma-mo bcu-gnyis*, 481; see *twelve goddesses of the earth*
Matisāra, the bodhisattva *byang-chub sems-dpa' blo-gros snying-po*, 691; see *Katok(pa) Tampa Deshek*
Matok Jangbar *ma-thog byang-'bar*, 640, 644
Matokpa *ma-thog-pa*, 642
Matraṃ *ma-traṃ*, 622
Mātulasulabha *zhang-po bzang-len*, 418
Matyaupāyika, the ogre *srin-po blo-gros thabs-ldan*, 454
Maudgalyāyana *maudgal-gyi bu*, 90-1, 423, 425, 426, **426**, 428
Māyādevī *sgyu-'phrul lha-mo*, 416, 946
Mazhang, the minister *ma-zhang*, 938
Megom Samten Zangpo of Tsang *gtsang-gi mes-sgom bsam-gtan bzang-po*, 795
Melgongza Rincentsho *mal-gong-bza' rin-chen mtsho*, 536
Mel Kawacenpa (1163-1220 or 1126-1211) *mal ka-ba-can-pa*, 757
Melong Dorje (1243-1303) *me-long rdo-rje*, **566**, 566-8, 569, 673, 675, 953
Menakā *me-na-kā*, 421
Menlungpa Mikyö Dorje *sman-lung-pa mi-skyod rdo-rje*, 759, 770
Menlungpa (Nyangtön) Locok Dorje (d. 1671) *sman-lung-pa (nyang-ston) blo-mchog rdo-rje*, 699, 718, 822
Nyangtön Locok Dorje *nyang-ston blo-mchog rdo-rje*, 718-19, 727
Menlungpa Śākya-ö (b. 1239) *sman-lung-pa śā-kya 'od*, 686
Menlungpa Śākya Zhönu *sman-lung-pa śā-kya gzhon-nu*, 574
Menmo sisters, seven *sman-mo mched-bdun*, 581
Menu Gyelwei Nyingpo *me-nu rgyal-ba'i snying-po*, 714
Menyak Khyungdra/Jungdra *me-nyags khyung-grags/'jung-grags*, 358-9, 622, 631
Mepo Pakshi *mes-po pak-shi*, 663
Metön Gönpo of Latö *la-stod-kyi mes-ston mgon-po*, 653, 660
Metön Jungne-ö *me-ston 'byung-gnas 'od*, 702
Mikcung Wangseng *mig-chung dbang-seng*, 642, 643
Milarepa, venerable (1040-1123 or 1052-1135) *rje-btsun mi-la ras-pa*, 200-1, 550, 615, 713, 853, 922, 929, 952
Mingyur Namkei Dorje *mi-'gyur nam-mkha'i rdo-rje*, 737; see *Dzokcen IV*
Mingyur Peldrön, the venerable lady *rje-btsun mi-'gyur dpal-sgron*, 734, 833
Minling Trhicen I *smin-gling khri-chen*: see *(Rikdzin) Terdak Lingpa*
Minling Trhicen II, Pema Gyurme Gyatso (1686-1717) *smin-gling khri-chen padma 'gyur-med rgya-mtsho*: the son of Terdak Lingpa, see *Pema Gyurme Gyatso*
Minling Trhicen III, Gyelse Rincen Namgyel *smin-gling khri-chen rgyal-sras rin-chen rnam-rgyal*: see *Gyelse Rincen Namgyel*
Minling Trhicen V, Trhinle Namgyel *smin-gling khri-chen phrin-las rnam-rgyal*: see *Trhicen Trhinle Namgyel*
Minling Trhicen VI, Pema Wangyel *smin-gling khri-chen padma dbang-rgyal*: see *Trhi Pema Wangyel*
Minling Trhicen VII, Gyurme Sangye Künga *smin-gling khri-chen 'gyur-med sangs-rgyas kun-dga'*: see *Gyurme Sangye Künga*
Mipham Jamyang Namgyel (Gyamtso) (1846-1912) *mi-pham 'jam-dbyangs rnam-rgyal (rgya-mtsho)*, 868, **870**, 869-80

Jamgön Mipham Mawei Senge *'jam-mgon mi-pham smra-ba'i seng-ge*, 375
Mipham Gyamtso *mi-pham rgya-mtsho*, 869
Mipham Jampel Gyepa *mi-pham 'jam-dpal dgyes-pa*, 198
Mipham Namgyel (Gyamtso) *mi-pham rnam-rgyal (rgya-mtsho)*, 958, 966
Mipham Rinpoche *mi-pham rin-po-che*, 29, 41, 375, 397
Mipham Trashi Lodrö, the doctrine master *chos-rje mi-pham bkra-shis blo-gros*, 809, 810
Mitrayogī *rje-btsun mi-tra-dzo-gi*, 564, 693
Miwang Düdül Rapten *mi-dbang bdud-'dul rab-brtan*, 821
Miwang Sonam Topgyel (d. 1747) *mi-dbang bsod-nams stobs-rgyal*, 812
Moktön Dorje Pelzang(po) *rmog-ston rdo-rje dpal-bzang(-po)*, 696, 701; see *(Katokpa) Moktön Dorje Pelzang(po)*
Moktön Jampel Senge *rmog-ston 'jam-dpal seng-ge*, 698
Möndro Paṇḍita *smon-'gro paṇḍita*, 821
Mön Dzakar Lama Targye *mon rdza-dkar bla-ma dar-rgyas*, 836
Mön Katokpa Sonam Gyeltsen *mon kaḥ-thog-pa bsod-nams rgyal-mtshan*, 699
Mönpa, eightfold group of *mon-pa sde-brgyad*, 628
Mṛgajā *ri-dvags skyes*, 418
Mukpodongza Singcungma *smug-po gdong-bza' sring-chung-ma*, 869
Mūlasarvāstivāda *gzhi thams-cad yod-par smra-ba*, 429-30
Mundane Praise *'jig-rten mchod-bstod*, 283, 362, 483, 535; see also Bibliography
Mune Tsepo *mu-ne btsad-po*, 521, 603
Mutrhi *mu-khri*, 518
Munīndra/Lord of Sages *thub-pa'i dbang-po*, 11, 128, 503, 768, 894; see *Buddha*
Murup Tsepo (Yeshe Rölpatsel) *mu-rub btsad-po (ye-shes rol-pa rtsal)*, 519, 521, 839, 841
Lhase Tamdzin Rölpa Yeshetsel *lha-sras dam-'dzin rol-pa ye-shes rtsal*, 784
Yeshe Rölpatsel *ye-shes rol-pa rtsal*, 841
Mutik Tsepo *mu-tig btsad-po*, 521
Senalek (Jingyön) *sad-na legs (mjing-yon)*, 22, 521
Mutrhi Tsenpo *mu-khri btsan-po*: the son of Nyatrhi Tsenpo, 507
Mutrhi *mu-khri*, 518; see *Mune Tsepo*
Muzu Labar *dmu-gzugs la-'bar*, 524; see *Lacen Gongpa Rapsel*
Nāga, the elder *gnas-brtan klu*, 429
nāga demon, the nine-headed *(gter-srung) klu-bdud mgo-dgu*: a treasure protector, 763
Nāgabodhi *klu-byang/klu'i byang-chub*, 317-18, 464
Nāgamitra *klu'i bshes-gnyen*, 183
Nāgaputra *nā-ga pu-tri*: the son of King Ja, 485
Nāgārjuna *klu/klu-sgrub*, 18, 28, 40, 83, 94, 108, **163**, 164, 167, 173, 182, 184-5, 196, 211, 216, 225, 265, 300-1, 305, 314, 317, 321, 334, 404, 437, 440, 442, 464, 479-80, 483, 502, 577, 768, 849, 905, 906, 907, 919, 927, 931, 949
Nāgārjunagarbha, the sublime *'phags-pa klu-sgrub snying-po*, 479
Nāgārjunagarbha *klu-sgrub snying-po*, 479
Nāgārjunagarbha, the sublime *'phags-pa klu-sgrub snying-po*, 479; see *Nāgārjuna*
Nak, the great preceptor of *nags-kyi mkhan-chen*, 688
Namcö Mingyur Dorje (fl. *c.* 1660) *gnam-chos mi-'gyur rdo-rje*, 816
Namdingpa, lama *bla-ma gnam-sdings-pa*, 721; see *Zhangtön Namka Dorje*
Namdru Remati *nam-gru re-ma-ti*: the constellation Andromeda, 575, 586, 587
Namgyel Pelzang, the great paṇḍita of Kuge *gu-ge paṇ-chen rnam-rgyal dpal-bzang*, 806
Namkabum, the Kadampa spiritual benefactor *bka'-gdams-pa dge-bshes nam-mkha' 'bum*, 929
Namka Chöki Gyamtso *nam-mkha' chos-kyi rgya-mtsho*, 801
Namkade *nam-mkha' sde*, 619
Namka Drukdra Zangpo *nam-mkha' 'brug-sgra bzang-po*, 718
Namka Gyeltsen, accomplished master of Lhodrak *lho-brag grub-thob nam-mkha' rgyal-mtshan*, 923; see *Leki Dorje*
Namka Pelwa *nam-mkha' dpal-ba*, 757; see *(Drogön) Namka Pelwa*
Namkei Dorje of Gyamen *rgya-sman-pa nam-mkha'i rdo-rje*, 569

Namkei Neljor of the Jeu clan *rje'u rigs-kyi nam-mkha'i rnal-'byor*, 807
Namkei Nyingpo *nam-mkha'i snying-po*, 515, **534**, 535, 625, 736, 747
Nup Namkei Nyingpo *gnubs nam-mkha'i snying-po*, 677
Namlang Putri *nam-langs bu-khrid*, 809
Namolung, household of *sna-mo lung*, 780
Nanam Dawei Dorje *sna-nam zla-ba'i rdo-rje*, 526
Nanam Dorje Düjom *sna-nam rdo-rje bdud-'joms*, 513, 535, 706, 719, 747, 780
Nanam Sherap Tshültrim *sna-nam shes-rab tshul-khrims*, 714
(Nanam) Zhang Yeshe De *(sna-nam-)zhang ye-shes sde*, 535; see *Zhang Yeshe De*
Nanda *gcung dga'-bo*, 417, 418
Nanda, king *dga'-bo*, 429
Nangsel Rinpoche Ngawang Yeshe Trupa *snang-gsal rin-po-che ngag-dbang ye-shes grub-pa*, 679
Nangso Gyelwa Töndrup *nang-so rgyal-ba don-grub*, 798
Nangtön Cokyam *nang-ston jo-'khyams*, 657
Nangtön Gönpo *nang-ston mgon-po*, 657
Nangwa Selwa Raptukhyenma (She who Intuits what is Clearly Manifest) *snang-ba gsal-ba rab-tu mkhyen-ma*: the mother of Śrī Siṃha, 497
Nāropā *na-ro-pa*, 199, 299-300, 301-2, 308, 312, 317, 326, 333-4, 337, 395, 462, 546, 921
Nārotapa *na-ro-ta-pa*, 326
Nārotapa: see preceding entry
Nartī *gar-ma*, 125
Nartön Senge-ö *snar-ston seng-ge 'od*, 77, 78, 702
Naṭa *naṭa*, 435
Natsok Rangdröl *sna-tshogs rang-grol*, 595; see *(Tsele) Natsok Rangdröl*
Nectar, the Enlightened Attributes *bdud-rtsi yon-tan*, 283, 362; see *Vajrāmṛta*
Nelba Nyingpo *rnal-rba snying-po*, 642
Neljorpa Özer Koca *rnal-'byor-pa 'od-zer go-cha*, 595; see *Özer Koca*
Nelpa Paṇḍita (fl. 1283) *nel-pa paṇḍita*, 509
Nesarwa Ngawang Künga Lekpei Jungne (1704-60) *gnas gsar-ba ngag-dbang kun-dga' legs-pa'i 'byung-gnas*, 835
Neten Künzang Özer *gnas-brtan kun-bzang 'od-zer*, 835
Neudong, the great lord of *sne-gdong gong-ma chen-po*: a successor of Tā'i Situ Cangcup Gyeltsen, 787
Neudong, Lord of *sne-gdong gong-ma*, 595; see *Tā'i Situ (Cangcup Gyeltsen)*
Neu Zurpa (1042-1118 or 1062-1138) *sne'u zur-pa*, 546
Newar Śīlamañju *bal-po'i śīla-manydzu*, 714; see *Śīlamañju*
Ngadak Drogön *mnga'-bdag 'gro-mgon*, 763, 765; see *(Drogön) Namka Pelwa*
Ngadak Düdul *mnga'-bdag mdud-'dul*, 758
Ngadak Loden *mnga'-bdag blo-ldan*, 758
Ngadak Nyang(-rel Nyima Özer) *mnga'-bdag nyang(-rel nyi-ma 'od-zer)*, 760, 765, 768, 952; see *Nyang-rel Nyima Özer*
Ngagi Wangcuk *ngag-gi dbang-phyug*, 821; see *Dalai Lama V*
Ngak Rapjampa Orgyen Chödra *ngag-rab-'byams-pa o-rgyan chos-grags*, 833
Ngamdzong (Tönpa) *ngams-rdzong (ston-pa)*, 200
Ngamtön Gyelwa *ngam-ston rgyal-ba*, 642
Ngaripa, master *slob-dpon mnga'-ris-pa*, 569
Ngari Paṇcen Pema Wangyel (1487-1543) *mnga'-ris paṇ-chen padma dbang-rgyal*, 805-8, **806**
Ngari Paṇcen/great paṇḍita (of Ngari) *mnga'-ris paṇ-chen*, 677, 717, 783
Pema Wangyel *padma dbang-rgyal*, 805-8
Ngawang Chögyel Wangpo *ngag-dbang chos-rgyal dbang-po*, 809; see *(Rikdzin) Jatsön Nyingpo*
Ngawang (Chöki) Trülku *ngag-dbang (chos-kyi) sprul-sku*, 731, 833
Ngawang Chöpel *ngag-dbang chos-'phel*, 728; see *Locen Dharmaśrī*
Ngawang Jungne, spiritual benefactor of Bumsar *'bum-gsar dge-bshes ngag-dbang 'byung-gnas*, 872
Ngawang Künga Tendzin of Dokam *mdo-khams-pa ngag-dbang kun-dga' bstan-'dzin*, 833; see *Khamtrül III*
Ngawang Künga Trashi (b. 1517) *dpal-ldan sa-skya-pa bdag-chen ngag-dbang kun-dga' bkra-shis*, 731
Ngawang Künzang Dorje (1680-1723) *ngag-dbang kun-bzang rdo-rje*: i.e. Lhodrak Sungtrül IV, 735
Ngawang Lozang Pema *ngag-dbang blo-bzang padma*, 835

Ngawang Mikyö Dorje *rje ngag-dbang mi-bskyod rdo-rje*, 818
Ngawang Norbu *ngag-dbang nor-bu*, 735
Ngawang Pema Tendzin *ngag-dbang padma bstan-'dzin*, 826; see *(Rikdzin) Terdak Lingpa*
Ngawang Trakpa *ngag-dbang grags-pa*, 735
Ngawang Trülku *ngag-dbang sprul-sku*, 731; see *Ngawang (Chöki) Trülku*
Ngenlam Cangcup Gyeltsen *ngan-lam byang-chub rgyal-mtshan*, 541, 918
Ngenlam Gyelwa Choyang *ngan-lam rgyal-ba mchog-dbyangs*, 515; see *Gyelwa Choyang*
Ngentung Cangcup Gyeltsen *ngan-thung byang-chub rgyal-mtshan*, 616
Ngödrup, the accomplished master *grub-thob dngos-grub*, 511, 757
Ngödrup, brother *a-jo dngos-grub*: the brother of Dzeng, 549
Ngödrup Gyeltsen *dngos-grub rgyal-mtshan*, 780-3; see *Dorje Trak Rikdzin I*
Ngok Cangcupel *rngog byang-chub dpal*, 674
Ngok Dorje Senge of Zhung *gzhung-gi rngog rdo-rje seng-ge*, 562
Ngok, the (great) translator *rngog lo(-chen-po)*, 578, 646, 821; see *Ngok (Loden Sherap)*
Ngok Gyeltse *rngog rgyal-rtse*, 562
Ngok Lekpei Sherap *rngog legs-pa'i shes-rab*, 577
Ngok (Loden Sherap) (1059-1109) *rngog (blo-ldan shes-rab)*, 221, 646, 862, 905
  Ngok Lotsāwa *rngog lo-tsā-ba*, 952
  Ngok, the (great) translator *rngog lo(-chen-po)*, 578, 646, 821
Ngok Lotsāwa: see preceding entry
Ngoktön Sonam Tendzin *rngog-ston bsod-nams bstan-'dzin*, 807
Ngor Pönlop *ngor dpon-slob*, 879
Ngülmo Gyalecam *dngul-mo rgya-le-lcam*, 547
Ngurpa, the great preceptor *mkhan-chen ngur-pa*, 552
Nine-Lamp Yangdak *yang-dag mar-me dgu* 685; see *Yangdak Heruka*
nine Masang brothers *ma-sang dpun-dgu*: listed in the Glossary of Enumerations, 949
nine "worthy sons" *snod-lam-gyi bu-dgu*: students of Guru Chöwang, 770
Nivāraṇaviṣkambhin *sgrib-sel*, 125
Norbu Tendzin *nor-bu bstan-'dzin*, 841; see *Chogyur (Decen Zhikpo) Lingpa*
Norbu Yongdrak *nor-bu yongs-grags*, 735
Norten Zangpo *nor-bstan bzang-po*, 805
Norzang (Gyamtso) *nor-bzang (rgya-mtsho)*, 681
Nup(cen) Sangye Yeshe *gnubs(-chen) sangs-rgyas ye-shes*, 47, 397, 533, 537, 540, 599, 606, **608**, 607-14, 616, 673, 674, 684, 724, 747, 791, 827, 847, 918
  Buddhajñāna *(ratna) buddha dznya-na*, 607
  Dorje Trhitsuk *rdo-rje khri-gtsug*, 607
  (Dorje) Yangwangter *(rdo-rje) yang-dbang gter*, 607, 613
  Marutse, the butcher *shan-pa ma-ru-tse*, 610
  Sangye Yeshe *sangs-rgyas ye-shes*, 535, 607, 614
Nup clan *gnubs-rigs*, 607
Nup Khulungpa (Yönten Gyamtso) *gnubs khu-lung-pa (yon-tan rgya-mtsho)*, 47, 846-7, 922
  Khulung Yönten Gyamtso *khu-lung-pa yon-tan rgya-mtsho*, 613, 614-15
  Yönten Gyamtso *yon-tan rgya-mtsho*, 613, 616
Nup Namkei Nyingpo *gnubs nam-mkha'i snying-po*, 677; see *Namkei Nyingpo*
Nup Paten *gnubs dpa'-brtan*, 706
Nup Shangcen: see following entry
Nup Shangpoche *gnubs shangs-po-che*, 545, 548
  Nup Shangcen *gnubs shangs-chen*, 547
Nuptön *gnubs-ston*, 701
Nuptön Pakma *gnubs-ston bag-ma*, 642
Nuptön Trakpa Wangpo *gnubs-ston grags-pa dbang-po*, 727
Nup Trhopupa, family *gnubs khro-phu-pa'i rigs*, 723
Nya family *rus-gnya'*, 685
Nyagrodhaja *nya-gro-dha skyes*, 432; see *Mahākāśyapa*
Nyagrodhaketu the brahman *bram-ze nya-gro-dha'i tog*, 432
Nyak clan *gnyags(-rus)*, 601
(Nyak) Getön *(gnyags) dge-ston*, 601, 604-5
  Gelatön *dge-la-ston*, 603
  Nyakmar *gnyags-dmar*, 605
Nyak Jñānakumāra *gnyags dznyāna ku-mā-ra*, 397, 398, 533, 534, 535, 540,

602, 599-606, 608, 707, 712, 722, 736, 747, 889, 918

Gyelwei Lodrö *rgyal-ba'i blo-gros*, 601

Jñānakumāra, the translator of Nyak *gnyags-lo dznyāna ku-mā-ra*, 696

Nyakmar *gnyags-dmar*, 605; see *Nyak Getön*

(Nyame) Lhatsewa *(mnyam-med) lha-rtse-ba*, 809, 810

Nyang(ben) Tingdzin Zangpo *nyang(-ban) ting-'dzin bzang-po*, 555-6, **556**, 707, 747, 809, 918, 919

Nyang Cangcup-tra/Trakpa *nyang byang-chub grags(-pa)*, 542, 543

Nyang Shawacen *nyang sha-ba-can*, 542

Nyang clan *nyang-rus*, 616

Nyang Dharmasiṃha of Tsentang *btsan-thang-pa nyang dharma-siṃha*, 552

Tsentangpa Nyang Dharmasiṃha *btsan-thang-pa nyang dharma-siṃha*, 550

Nyang Kadampa of Meldro *mal-dro nyang bka'-gdams-pa*, 557

Nyangmi Tarma *nyang-mi dar-ma*, 556

Nyangnak Dowo/Dopo/Dopa *nyang-nag mdo-bo/mdo-po/mdo-pa* 648, 685, 701

Nyang Nak of Uyuk Rölpo *'u-yug rol-po'i nyang-nag*, 714

Nyang-rel Nyima Özer, lord (1136-1204) *mnga'-bdag nyang-ral nyi-ma 'od-zer*, 47, 695, **756**, 755-9, 763, 829, 857, 892

Lord Nyang *mnga'-bdag nyang*, 511, 661, 662

Lord Nyang, father and son *mnga'-bdag nyang yab-sras*, 661, n. 809

Ngadak Nyang(-rel Nyima Özer) *mnga'-bdag nyang(-ral nyi-ma 'od-zer)*, 760, 765, 768, 952

Nyang Shawacen *nyang sha-ba-can*, 542; see *Nyang Cangcup-tra*

Nyang Sherapchok *nyang shes-rab mchog*, 615, 616

(Nyang) Sherap Jungne *(nyang) shes-rab 'byung-gnas*, 542-3

Nyang Tingdzin Zangpo *nyang ting-'dzin bzang-po*, 555-6, 707, 918, 919; see *Nyang(ben) Tingdzin Zangpo*

Nyangtön Chenpo of Chongpo Kharu *'phyong-po kha-ru'i nyang-ston chen-po*, 686

Nyangtön Chöki Khorlo *nyang-ston chos-kyi 'khor-lo*, 755

Nyangtön, the great *nyang-ston chen-po*, 757

Nyangtön, the great: see preceding entry

Nyangtön Locok Dorje *nyang-ston blo-mchog rdo-rje*, 718-19, 727; see *Menlungpa (Nyangtön) Locok Dorje*

(Nyang) Yeshe Jungne (of Chölung) *(chos-lung-gi nyang) ye-shes 'byung-gnas*, 616, 619

Nyaring, the Pönpo *bon-po gnya'-ring*, 760

Nyatrhi Tsenpo (King of the Shoulder-borne Sedan-chair) *gnya'-khri btsan-po*, 507, 949, 959

Nyel Nyima Özer *gnyal nyi-ma 'od-zer*, 770

Nyelpa Delek(pa) *gnyal-pa bde-legs(-pa)*, 672, 725

Nyelpa *gnyal-pa*, 701

Nyelwa Zhikpo *gnyal-ba zhig-po*, 685

Nyemdo, the All-Seeing of (b. 1263 or 1217-77) *snye-mdo thams-cad gzigs-pa*: i.e. Künga Töndrup (*kun-dga' don-grub*), 702

Nyemo Gomcen *snye-mo sgom-chen*, 203

Nyen, lama *bla-ma gnyen*, 686

Nyenak Wangdrak of Yülser *yul-gser-gyi gnyan-nag dbang-drag*, 619

Nyencen Pelyang *gnyan-chen dpal-dbyangs*, 605

(Nyencen) Thangla *(gnyan-chen) thang-lha*: the protector, 581, 791, 856

Nyen Lotsāwa *gnyan lo-tsā-ba*, 713

Nyenre *gnyan-ras*, 569

Nyertön Lama *gnyer-ston bla-ma*, 657

Nyetön Chöki Senge of Gongdring *sgong-drings-pa nye-ston chos-kyi seng-ge*, 660

Nyetön Chöseng *nye-ston chos-seng*, 649

Nyetön Nyima Dorje *snye-ston nyi-ma rdo-rje*, 653

Nyibukpa (Langdro Tshewang Gyelpo) *nyi-sbug-pa (lang-gro tshe-dbang rgyal-po)*, 717

Nyibum (1158-1213) *nyi-'bum*, **562**, 561-3, 953

Nyima Raptu Nangje, son of the gods *lha'i-bu nyi-ma rab-tu snang-byed*, 136

Nyima Senge *nyi-ma seng-ge*, 663-4; see *(Zur) Nyima Senge*

Nyima Trakpa, the great treasure finder *gter-chen nyi-ma grags-pa*, 737

Nyima Zangpo *nyi-ma bzang-po*, 803

Nyimei Nyingpo *nyi-ma'i snying-po*: a member of the Zur family, 617

Nyinda Chöje *nyi-zla chos-rje*: the son of Karma Lingpa, 801

Nyinda Sangye *nyi-zla sangs-rgyas*: the father of Karma Lingpa, 800

Nyinda Sangye, the great awareness-holder *rig-'dzin chen-po nyi-zla sangs-rgyas*, 677; see *Rangdröl Nyinda Sangye*

Nyipuwa Rikdzin Nyingpo *snyi-phu-ba rig-'dzin snying-po*, 723

Nyiwa Rincen *snyi-ba rin-chen*, 200; see *Gampopa*

Nyö Chuworipa *gnyos chu-bo-ri-pa*, 657

Nyö clan *gnyos-rigs*, 724, 733, 796, 849

Nyötingmawa Sangye Trakpa *myos-mthing-ma-ba sangs-rgyas grags-pa*, 577

Nyötön (Sangdak) Trhinle Lhündrup *gnyos-ston (gsang-bdag) phrin-las lhun-grub*, 684, 825; see *Sangdak Trhinle Lhündrup (Pelzangpo)*

Nyö Tragyel *gnyos grags-rgyal*, 759

Oceza Kargyelma *'o-lce-bza' skar-rgyal-ma*, 537

Oḍḍiyāna, the great preceptor *mkhan-chen oḍḍi-yā-na*, 733; see *Orgyen Tenzin Dorje*

Ode Kungyel *'o-lde gung-rgyal*: the protector, 581

Odren Pelgi Wangcuk *'o-bran dpal-gyi dbang-phyug*, 535

Odren Pelgi Zhönu *'o-bran dpal-gyi gzhon-nu*, 540, 604, 605, 606, 607

offering goddesses *mchod-pa'i lha-mo*: listed in the Glossary of Enumerations under *eight offering goddesses*, 624

Öki Kyinkorcen *'od-kyi dkyil-'khor-can*: ruler of Ngenlam, 575

Ölka, an artist of *'ol-kha'i lha-bris-pa*, 550

Öncen *dbon-chen*, 723

Ön Lama Pema Targye *dbon bla-ma padma dar-rgyas*, 869

Ön Özer Trhinle *dbon 'od-zer phrin-las*, 840

Ön Śākya Bumpa *dbon śā-kya 'bum-pa*, 686

Ön Sangshe *dbon sangs-shes*, 569

Orgyen (Rinpoche/the precious) *o-rgyan rin-po-che*: Guru Rinpoche of Oḍḍiyāna, 554, 746, 751, 764, 765, 766, 774, 775, 784, 786, 789, 790, 793, 796, 809, 837, 841, 847, 859, 860, 863, 935; see *Guru Rinpoche*

Orgyen Do-nga Chöki Nyima *o-rgyan mdo-sngags chos-kyi nyi-ma*, 738

Orgyen Dorje Chang *o-rgyan rdo-rje 'chang*, 45; see *Guru Rinpoche*

Orgyen Lingpa (of Yarje) (*c.* 1323-60) *(yar-rje) o-rgyan gling-pa*, 775-9, **776**

Orgyen Namdröl Gyamtso *o-rgyan rnam-grol rgya-mtsho*, 735

Orgyenpa (Rincenpel) (1230-1309) *o-rgyan-pa (rin-chen dpal)*, 568, 569, 571, 659, 853, 891, 914, 922, 953

Orgyen Pema Lingpa *o-rgyan padma gling-pa*, 796; see *Pema Lingpa*

Orgyen Tendzin Dorje, the great preceptor *o-rgyan bstan-'dzin rdo-rje*, 733, 734

Oḍḍiyāna, the great preceptor *mkhan-chen oḍḍi-ya-na*, 733

Orgyen Tendzin (of Trakna) *o-rgyan bstan-'dzin/brag-sna chos-rje o-rgyan bstan-'dzin*, 678, 814

Orgyen Tshepel *o-rgyan tshe-'phel*, 724; see *Sangdak Trhinle Lhündrup (Pelzangpo)*

Orgyen Zangpo *o-rgyan bzang-po*, 789; see *Dorje Lingpa*

Ösel-chok of Ngari *mnga'-ris-pa 'od-gsal mchog*, 718

Ösel, lama *bla-ma 'od-gsal*, 878, 879

Ösel Lhawang Zhönu Tsuktorcen *'od-gsal lha-dbang gzhon-nu gtsug-tor-can*, 617

Ösel Trülpei Dorje *'od-gsal sprul-pa'i rdo-rje*, 854; see *(Jamyang) Khyentse Wangpo*

Ösung, king *mnga'-bdag 'od-srungs*, 523

Ö Thaye, son of the gods *lha-sras 'od-mtha'-yas*: a previous incarnation of Guru Chöwang, 768

Özer Koca, the yogin *rnal-'byor-pa 'od-zer go-cha*, 580, 585, 588

Neljorpa Özer Koca *rnal-'byor-ba 'od-zer go-cha*, 595

Özer Raptutrhowa, tathāgata *de-bzhin gshegs-pa 'od-zer rab-tu 'phro-ba*, 693; see *Tsangtönpa*

Padmākara (Lotus-origin) *padma 'byung-gnas*: Guru Rinpoche's manifestation during the third month, Pl. 13; 469, **517**, 787, 889, 892, 927, 944, 948; see *Guru Rinpoche*

Padmanarteśvara *padma gar-gyi dbang-phyug/padma gar-dbang*, 274, 449, 609

Padmāṅkuśa, bodhisattva *byang-chub sems-dpa' padma'i myu-gu*, 848; see *Chogyur (Decen Zhikpo) Lingpa*

Padmapāṇi *lag-na padma*, 564; see *Avalokiteśvara*

Padmapāṇi, the Great Fifth Dalai Lama *phyag-na padma lnga-pa chen-po*, 678; see *Dalai Lama V*

Padmarāja/Pema Gyelpo (Lotus King) *padma rgyal-po*: Guru Rinpoche's manifestation during the twelfth month, 471, 854; see *Guru Rinpoche*

Padmasambhava, (the great master) *(slob-dpon chen-po) padma (sam-bha-ba)*: Guru Rinpoche's manifestation during the tenth month, and used also as a general name for Guru Rinpoche, Pls. 16, 26, 58, 78; 38, 39, 40, 63, 96, 265, 342, 394, 396, 397, 455, **470**, 468-74, 481, 483, 488, 498, 504, 512-21, 522, 532, 533, 534, 535, 554-5, 567, 569, 573, 575, 582, 583, 584, 585, 587, 591, 595, 601, 605, 607, 676, 677, 706, 710, 711, 712, 714, 715, 728, 745, 746, 747, 749, 757, 760, 768, 771, 773, 784, 785, 797, 802, 809, 821, 825, 828, 829, 844, 848, 852, 856, 864, 866, 887, 888, 890, 892, 893, 894, 917, 921, 922, 927, 930, 934-5, 938-40, 949-50, 951, 972; see *Guru Rinpoche*

Padmavajra, the preceptor of Dzokcen Monastery *rdzogs-chen mkhan-po padma badzra*, 871

(Pagor) Löncen Phakpa *(spa-gor) blon-chen 'phags-pa*, 613, 616

Tongtsap Phakpa Rinpoche *tong-tshab 'phugs-pa rin-po-che*, 616

Pagor Vairocana *pa-gor bai-ro-tsa-na*, 515

Pakshi Śākya-ö(po) *pak-shi śā-kya 'od(-po)*, 660-3; see *Zurpa Śākya-ö*

Paṇcen Lama IV, Lozang Chöki Gyeltsen (1567-1662) *paṇ-chen bla-ma blo-bzang chos-kyi rgyal-mtshan*, 821, 925

Paṇcen Rinpoche *paṇ-chen rin-po-che*, 821, 823

Paṇcen (Lama) IX, Chöki Nyima (1883-1937) *paṇ-chen chos-kyi nyi-ma*, 958

Paṇcen Rinpoche *paṇ-chen rin-po-che*, 821, 823; see *Paṇcen Lama IV*

Pāṇḍaravāsinī *gos-dkar-mo*, 20, 125

Pangangpa Rincen Dorje *spang-sgang-pa rin-chen rdo-rje*, 582; see *Pema Lendreltsel*

Pang family *spang-mi-rabs*, 765

Pang(-gen) Sangye Gönpo *spang-rgan sangs-rgyas mgon-po*, 540, 541, **541**

Pang Mipham Gönpo *spang mi-pham mgon-po*, 541, 919

Pangka Tarcung(wa) *spang-ka dar-chung(-ba)*, 643, 708

Pangje Tsentram *spang-rje btsan-khram*, 760

Pang Lo Lodrö Tenpa: see following entry

Pang Lotsāwa (Lodrö Tenpa) (1276-1342) *dpang-lo chen-po (blo-gros brtan-pa)*, 100

Pang Lo Lodrö Tenpa *dpang-lo blo-gros brtan-pa*, 577

Pang Mipham Gönpo *spang mi-pham mgon-po*, 541, 919; see *Pang(-gen) Sangye Gönpo*

Pang Rakṣita *spang rakṣita*, 540

Pang Rikdzin Nyingpo *spang rig-'dzin snying-po*, 760

Pangtön Chöwang Lhündrup *dpang-ston chos-dbang lhun-grub*, 553

Pangtön Karma Guru(pa) *dpang-ston karma gu-ru-pa*, 553, 701

Pangtön Künzang Chögyel *dpang-ston kun-bzang chos-rgyal*, 553

Pangtön Trupei Nyingpo *spang-ston grub-pa'i snying-po*: the father of Guru Chöki Wangcuk, 760-5

Geshe Locungpa *dge-bshes lo-chung-ba*, 761

Pāṇini *pāṇi-pa*, 99

Parameśvara *pa-ra-me-shva-ra*, 708

Pari, lama (b. 1040) *bla-ma ba-ri-pa*, 545

Pārśva *rtsibs-legs*, 430

Patañjali *chur-lhung-gi bu*, 64

Patsel *pa-tshal*, 662

Pawo Chögyel Töndrup *dpa'-bo chos-rgyal don-grub*, 798

Pawo Dzengcung *dpa'-bo 'dzeng-chung*, 547; see *Dzeng (Dharmabodhi)*

Pawo II, Tsuklak Trhengwa (1504-66) *dpa'-bo gtsug-lag phreng-ba*, 955, 965

Pawo III, Tsuklak Gyamtso (1567-1633) *dpa'-bo gtsug-lag rgya-mtsho*

Tsuklak Gyamtso *gtsug-lag rgya-mtsho*, 724

Pawo VIII, Tsuklak Chöki Gyelpo (b. 1781) *dpa'-bo gtsug-lag chos-kyi rgyal-po*, 841

peaceful and wrathful deities *zhi-khro*, Pl. 2; 125-6, 623, 829

Fifty-eight Blood-drinkers *khrag-thung/khro-bo lnga-bcu nga-brgyad*: listed in the Glossary of Enumerations, 623

Forty-two Peaceful Buddhas/Deities *zhi-ba'i sangs-rgyas/lha zhe-gnyis*: listed in the Glossary of Enumerations, 125-6, 623, 644, 691
peaceful deities of the *Magical Net sgyu-'phrul zhi-ba*, 628
peaceful and wrathful deities of the *Magical Net sgyu-'phrul zhi-khro*, 691
wrathful deities, male and female *khro-bo khro-mo*, 125-6, 623
peaceful and wrathful Guru *bla-ma zhi-drag*, 828; see *Guru Rinpoche*
Pehar *pe-har*, **520**, 545
Shingjachen, the Gyelpo spirit *rgyal-po shing-bya-can*, 519
Pektse, the Sogdian *sog-po beg-tse*, 604; see *Sogdian Pelgi Yeshe*
Pelbarwa Namka Dorje, venerable *rje-btsun dpal-'bar-ba nam-mkha' rdo-rje*, 699
Pelbudor *bal-bu-dor*, 549
Pelcok of Trhopu, the master *khro-phu'i slob-dpon dpal-mchog*, 665
Pelcokpa, lama *bla-ma dpal-mchog-pa*, 595
Pelgi Rincen *dpal-gyi rin-chen*, 712; see *Rongben Yönten (Rincen)*
Pelgi Senge *dpal-gyi seng-ge*, 535; see *(Langcen) Pelgi Senge*
Pelgi Wangcuk of Latö *la-stod dpal-gyi dbang-phyug*, 689
Pelgi Yeshe, the Sogdian *sog-po dpal-gyi ye-shes*: see *Sogdian Pelgi Yeshe*
Pelhün Yülgyel of Tingri *ding-ri dpal-lhun gYul-rgyal*: i.e. Ngawang Samdrup (*ngag-dbang bsam-sgrub*), 378
Peling Thukse Tendzin Gyurme Dorje *pad-gling thugs-sras bstan-'dzin 'gyur-med rdo-rje*, 956; see *Lhodrak (Thuk-)se IV*
Pel Jikpa Kyopei Yi *dpal 'jigs-pa'i skyobs-pa'i yid*: the third emanational teacher according to the Great Perfection, 136, **909**
Peljor Lhündrup *dpal-'byor lhun-grub*, 680; see *(Khönton) Peljor Lhündrup*
Pelkortsen, king (d. 983 or 985) *dpal-'khor-btsan*, 523
Pel Taklung Thangpa *dpal stag-lung thang-pa*, 952; see *Taklung Thangpa Trashipel*
Peltrül Orgyen Jikme Chöki Wangpo (1808-87) *dpal-sprul o-rgyan 'jigs-med chos-kyi dbang-po*, 871, **875**, 958
Peltrül Rinpoche *dpal-sprul rin-po-che*, 872, 876
Peltrül Rinpoche: see preceding entry
Pelyang *dpal-dbyangs*, 515; see *Ba Trhizi of the Zhang family*
Pelyül Gyatrül *dpal-yul rgya-sprul*, 879
Pemabar *padma 'bar*, 701
Pema Dewatsel *padma bde-ba rtsal*, 755
Pema Gyelpo/Padmarāja (Lotus King) *padma rgyal-po*: Guru Rinpoche's manifestation during the twelfth month, 471, 854; see *Guru Rinpoche*
Pema Gyurme Gyamtso (1686-1717) *padma 'gyur-med rgya-mtsho*: i.e. Minling Trhicen II, the son of Terdak Lingpa, 833
Pema Karpo, the all-knowing Drukpa (1527-92) *'brug-pa kun-mkhyen padma dkar-po*, 955, 965
Pema Karwang Gyurme Dorje *padma gar-dbang 'gyur-med rdo-rje*, 825; see *(Rikdzin) Terdak Lingpa*
Pema Khyentse Özer *padma mkhyen-brtse'i 'od-zer*, 835; see *(Rikdzin) Jikme Lingpa*
Pemakyi *rigs-ldan padma skyid*, 815
Pema Lendreltsel (1292-1316) *padma las-'brel rtsal*, 555, 593
Pangangpa Rincen Dorje *spang-sgang-pa rin-chen rdo-rje*, 582
Pema Lingpa (1450-1521) *padma gling-pa*: for the incarnations of his speech and spiritual son, see *Lhodrak Sungtrül* and *Lhodrak (Thuk-)se*, 722, 727, 735, 796-8, **797**, 824, 919, 955
Orgyen Pema Lingpa *o-rgyan padma gling-pa*, 796
Vajragarbha Buddha *rdo-rje snying-po*, 798
Pema Lingpa *padma gling-pa*, 791; see *Dorje Lingpa*
Pema Norbu, the great accomplished master *grub-chen padma nor-bu*, 817
Pema Ösel Do-nga Lingpa *padma 'od-gsal mdo-sngags gling-pa*, 751, 774, 778, 804, 849-58, 871; see *(Jamyang) Khyentse Wangpo*
Pema Peldzom *padma dpal-'dzom*, 771
Pema Rikdzin *padma rig-'dzin*: a form of Guru Rinpoche, 866; see *Guru Rinpoche*
Pema Rikdzin of Dzokcen *rdzogs-chen padma rig-'dzin*, 736-7; see *Dzokcen I*

Pemasel, princess *lha-lcam padma gsal*: see the Glossary of Enumerations for her *five pure incarnations*, 554-5, 796

Pema Thekcok Loden, the great preceptor of Dzokcen *rdzogs-chen mkhan-chen padma theg-mchog blo-ldan*, 919

Pema Thötrengtsel (Lotus whose Expression is a Garland of Skulls) *padma thod-phreng-rtsal*: Guru Rinpoche's manifestation during the ninth month, 471; see *Guru Rinpoche*

Pema Töndrup Trakpa *padma don-grub grags-pa*, 735

Pema Tshokyi *padma mtsho-skyid*, 771; see *Como Menmo*

Pema Wangcen *padma dbang-chen*, 770

Pema Wangcen the Glorious *dpal padma dbang-chen*, 837; see *(Rikdzin) Jikme Lingpa*

Pema Wangcuk, the mantra adept of Gom *sgom-pa sngags-'chang padma dbang-phyug*, 841

Pema Wangyel *padma dbang-rgyal*, 615-16

Pema Wangyel *padma dbang-rgyal*, 805-8; see *Ngari Paṇcen Pema Wangyel*

Pengarpa (Jampel Zangpo) (fl. mid fifteenth century) *ban-sgar-pa ('jam-dpal bzang-po)*, 675

Phadampa (Sangye) (fl. *c.* 11th-12th centuries) *(grub-chen) pha-dam-pa (sangs-rgyas)*, 395, 544-5, 548, 549, 647-8, 853, 921, 929, 952

Phagö Tokden Gyelpo *pha-rgod rtogs-ldan rgyal-po*, 595

Phakmotrupa, (the Central Tibetan) (1110-70) *(dbus-pa) phag-mo gru-pa*, 551, 567, 590, 657, 688

Phak-ö, the all-knowing *kun-mkhyen 'phags-'od*, 768

Phakpalha Gyelwa Gyamtso *'phags-pa lha rgyal-ba rgya-mtsho*, 731

Phakpa (Rinpoche, lama) *(bla-ma) 'phags-pa (rin-po-che)*, 662, 695, 712; see *Chögyel Phakpa*

Phamtingpa *pham-mthing-pa*, 921

Phawangkhapa (Peljor Lhündrup) *pha-wang-kha-pa (dpal-'byor lhun-grub)*, 681, 926; see *(Khöntön) Peljor Lhündrup*

Phodrak, king *pho-brag btsad-po*, 659

(Phungpo) Gya Yeshe Gönpo *(phung-po) rgya ye-shes mgon-po*, 686-7

Pītaśaṅkarā ḍākinī (the Yellow Bliss-giving Ḍākinī) *bde-byed ser-mo mkha'-'gro-ma*, 493

Podong Künkyen Jikdrel (1375-1451) *bo-gdong kun-mkhyen 'jigs-bral*, 954

Poluma *bo-lu-ma*, 813

Pomdrakpa, (the great spiritual warrior) (1170-1249) *(sems-dpa' chen-po) spom-brag-pa*, 692-3, 694

Pöngom Topa *bon-sgom do-pa*, 642

Pönlop Loter Wangpo (1847-1914) *dpon-slob blo-gter dbang-po*, 872

  Thartse Pönlop Jamyang Loter Wangpo *thar-rtse dpon-slob 'jam-dbyangs blo-gter dbang-po*, 868

Pönlop Namka Ösel *dpon-slob nam-mkha' 'od-gsal*, 737

Pönlungpa Tshültrim Gyeltsen *bon-lung-pa tshul-khrims rgyal-mtshan*, 724

Pön Pelcengön *dpon dpal-chen mgon*, 665

Pönpo Cangdrup *dpon-po byang-sgrub*, 571

Pönpo Traktsel *bon-po drag-rtsal*, 765

Prabhāhasti *pra-bha-ha-sti*, **467**, 467-8, 469, 481, 488

  Śākyaprabha *śā-kya 'od*, 467-8, 488

Prabhāvatī, the ḍākinī *mkha'-'gro 'od-'chang-ma*, 469

Pradīpālokā *snang-ba sgron-me*, 477

Prajāpati *skye-dgu'i bdag-mo*, 423, 425

  Mahāprajāpati *skye-dgu'i bdag-mo*, 418

Prajāpatibrahmā *skye-dgu'i bdag-po tshang-pa*, 452

Prajñābhava *shes-rab 'byung-gnas/pra-dznya-bha-ba*, 493; see *Garap Dorje*

Prajñāpāramitā *shes-rab-kyi pha-rol-tu phyin-ma*, 291

Prajñāraśmi *pra-dznya rasmi*, 835; see *Sherap Özer*

Prakāśālaṃkāra, (the brahman) *(bram-ze) gsal-ba'i rgyan*, 607, 608-9; see *Sukhoddyotaka*

Pramoda, the gandharva *dri-za rab-dga'*, 425

Puborwa Khedrup Yeshe Gyaltsen, 699; see *(Khedrup) Yeshe Gyaltsen (of Pubor)*

Puṇḍarīkā *pad-dkar-ma*, 421

Puṇyadhara, king of Nepal *dge-'dzin*, 472

Puṇyakīrti of Maru *bsod-nams grags-pa*, 467

Pūrṇa *gang-po*, 90

Pūrṇopaśānti, the ḍākini *mkha'-'gro-ma purṇa-nye-bar zhi-ba*, 451

Puṣpā *me-tog-ma*, 125

Putön (Rincentrup of Zhalu) (1290-1364) *(zhal-lu-pa) bu-ston (rin-chen grub)*, 892, 905, 947, 953
Putön Rinpoche *bu-ston rin-po-che*, 666, 768, 894
Puwo Baka Trülku Rikdzin Chöki Gyamtso *spu-bo rba-kha sprul-sku rig-'dzin chos-kyi rgya-mtsho*, 812; see *Baka Trülku Chöki Gyamtso*
Qarloq *gar-log*, 524
Qubilai Qan (reigned 1260-94) *se-chen gan*: the first Yüan emperor, 438, 661-3, 685-6
Rāhu: see following entry
Rāhula *gza'/ra-hu-la*, 572, 591, 681, **682**, 775
Khyapjuk (Chenpo) *khyab-'jug (chen-po)*, 591, 681, 775
Rāhu *gza'/dus-me*, 422, 946
Rāhula *sgra-gcan 'dzin*: the son of Śākyamuni, 421, 434, 946
Rāhula *sgra-gcan-'dzin*, 185, 464; see *Saraha*
Rāhulabhadra, the scholar *paṇḍita sgra-gcan-'dzin bzang-po*, 475; see *Saraha*
Rakṣitapāda (of Koṅkana) *(koṅkana-ru) srung-ba'i zhabs*, 464, 494, 496, 502
Ra Lotsāwa (Dorje-tra) (b. 1016) *rva lo-tsā-ba (rdo-rje grags)*, 688, 713-14
Rāma, king *rgyal-po ra-ma-ṇa*, 455
Rambuguhya *ram-bu gu-hya*: i.e. Rambuguhya Devacandra *(devatsandra)*, 483
Rangdröl *slob-dpon rang-grol*, 552
Rangdröl Nyinda Sangye *rang-grol nyi-zla sangs-rgyas*, 677, 926
Nyinda Sangye, the great awareness-holder *rig-'dzin chen-po nyi-zla sangs-rgyas*, 677
Rangjung Dorje *rang-byung rdo-rje*: see *Karmapa III*
Rangrik Dorje, the treasure-finder *gter-ston rang-rig rdo-rje*, 919
Rashak Treasure-finder *ra-shag gter-ston*, 755, 765
Ratha, the yakṣa *gnod-sbyin shing-rta*, 435
Ratnadatta *rin-byin*, 322, 899
Ratna Lingpa, (the great treasure-finder) (1403-79) *(gter-chen) ratna gling-pa*, 734, 744, 793-5, **794**, 814, 935, 954
Drodül Lingpa *'gro-'dul gling-pa*, 794
Zhikpo Lingpa *zhig-po gling-pa*, 794
Ratnākaraśānti *rin-chen 'byung-gnas zhi-ba*, 105, 184
Śāntipā, (master) *(slob-dpon) śa-nti-pa*, 77, 105, 455
Ratnarakṣita *ratna ra-kṣi-ta*, 522
Ratnasambhava, the bodhisattva *rin-chen 'byung-gnas*, 423
Ratnasambhava, the Conqueror *rgyal-ba rin-'byung/rin-chen 'byung-gnas*, 20, 125, 274, 355, 480
Ratnavajra, the brahman *bram-ze rin-chen rdo-rje*, 485
Ratön *rva-ston*, 835
Ratung Sherap Tshültrim *ra-thung shes-rab tshul-khrims*, 616
Rāvaṇa *sgra-sgrogs(-kyi-bu)*, 455
"Red Master" *a-tsa-ra dmar-po*: Guhyaprajñā, 918
Red Yamāri *(gshin-rje-)gshed dmar*, Skt. Raktayamāri, 546; see also Bibliography
Relpacen, king *khri ral-pa-can*, 393, 394, 521-2, 610, 612, 751
Trhi Detsukten *khri lde-gtsug-brtan*, 521
Trhi Relpacen *khri ral-pa-can*, 397, 521, 523, 939, 950
Remdawa (1349-1412) *rje-btsun red-mda'-ba*: i.e. Remdawa Zhönu Lodrö, 930
Repa Gomtak *ras-pa sgom-thag*, 547
Repa Trimeö *ras-pa dri-med 'od*, 565
Ridongpa Sherap Gyeltsen *ri-gdong-pa shes-rab rgyal-mtshan*, 687
Rikcok, lama *bla-ma rig-mchog*, 876
Rikdzin *rig-'dzin*, 784; see *Sangye Lingpa*
(Rikdzin) Chöje Lingpa *(rig-'dzin) chos-rje gling-pa*: the twelfth emanation of Gyelse Lharje, 751, 835
Rikdzin Dorje, the scribe *rig-'dzin rdo-rje*, 378
Rikdzin Dorje Thokme *rig-'dzin rdo-rje thogs-med*, 957
Rikdzin Düdül Dorje (1615-72) *rig-'dzin bdud-'dul rdo-rje*, 736, 813-17, **814**
Düdül Dorje, (the great treasure-finder) *(gter-chen) bdud-'dul rdo-rje*, 736, 812, 820, 956
Künga Sonam Chöpak *kun-dga' bsod-nams chos-'phags*, 813
Rikdzin Gödemcen *rig-'dzin rgod-ldem-can*, 780-3, **781**, 813, 919; see *Dorje Trak Rikdzin I*
Rikdzin Gyurme Dorje *rig-'dzin 'gyur-med rdo-rje*, 684, 701, 733; see *(Rikdzin) Terdak Lingpa*

(Rikdzin) Jatsön Nyingpo (1585-1656) *(rig-'dzin) 'ja'-tshon snying-po*, 809-12, **810**, 813, 814, 820, 956
Hūṃnak Mebar, the mantra adept *hūṃ-nag me-'bar*, 809
Letro Lingpa, the treasure-finder *gter-ston las-'phro gling-pa*, 809
Ngawang Chögyel Wangpo *ngag-dbang chos-rgyal dbang-po*, 809
Rikdzinje *rig-'dzin-rje*, 719; see *Dorje Trak Rikdzin I*
(Rikdzin) Jikme Lingpa (1730-98) *(rig-'dzin) 'jigs-med gling-pa*, Pl. 31; 41, 92, 835-40, **836**, 957, 965
Pema Khyentse Özer *padma mkhyen-brtse'i 'od-zer*, 835
Pema Wangcen the Glorious *dpal padma dbang-chen*, 837
Rikdzin Khyentse Özer *rig-'dzin mkhyen-brtse'i 'od-zer*, 595-6
Rikdzin Khyentse Özer: see preceding entry
Rikdzin Kumārādza *rig-'dzin ku-mā-rā-dza*, 953; see *Kumārādza*
Rikdzin Künzang Sherap (1636-98) *rig-'dzin kun-bzang shes-rab*, 738, **738**
Rikdzin II, Lekdenje *rig-'dzin legs-ldan rje*, 717, 807; see *Dorje Trak Rikdzin II*
(Rikdzin) Longsel Nyingpo (1625-1682) *(rig-'dzin) klong-gsal snying-po*, 736, 816-17
Rikdzin III, Ngagiwangpo *rig-'dzin ngag-gi dbang-po*, 783; see *Dorje Trak Rikdzin III*
Rikdzin Ngawang Pelzang (1879-1941) *rig-'dzin ngag-dbang dpal-bzang*: i.e. Khenpo Ngaga (*mkhan-po ngag-dga'*), 736
Rikdzin Ösel Rangdröl *rig-'dzin 'od-gsal rang-grol*, 595
Rikdzin Pema Düdül (d. 1883) *rig-'dzin padma bdud-'dul*, 919
Rikdzin Pema Trhinle *rig-'dzin padma phrin-las*, 398, 683, 730, 823, 824, 828, 833; see *Dorje Trak Rikdzin IV*
(Rikdzin) Terdak Lingpa (1646-1714) *(rig-'dzin) gter-bdag gling-pa*: the successive throne-holders of Mindröling who followed Terdak Lingpa are cross-referenced under *Minling Trhicen*, Pl. 89; 29, 198, 365, 375, 396, 397, 398, 553, 595, 734, 735, 736, 737, 778, 822, 823, 824, **826**, 825-34, 879
Gyurme Dorje, (the great treasure-finder of Mindröling) *(smin-gling gter-chen) 'gyur-med rdo-rje*, 726, 728, 729, 730, 731, 734, 735, 956, 966
Gyurme Dorjetsel *'gyur-med rdo-rje rtsal*, 828
Ngawang Pema Tendzin *ngag-dbang padma bstan-'dzin*, 826
Pema Karwang Gyurme Dorje *padma gar-dbang 'gyur-med rdo-rje*, 825
Rikdzin Gyurme Dorje *rig-'dzin 'gyur-med rdo-rje*, 684, 701, 733
Rikdzin Thukcok Dorje *rig-'dzin thugs-mchog rdo-rje*, 835
Rikdzin Trhinle Lhündrup *rig-'dzin phrin-las lhun-grub*, 595, 727, 812; see *Sangdak Trhinle Lhündrup (Pelzangpo)*
Rikdzin Tshewang Norbu (1698-1755) *rig-'dzin tshe-dbang nor-bu*, 736, 957, 966
Rikdzin Tshewang Norgye *rig-'dzin tshe-dbang nor-rgyas*, 926; see *Tshewang Norgye*
(Rikdzin) Yudruk Dorje *(rig-'dzin) gYu-'brug rdo-rje*, 721, 722
Drupcenpa, lama *bla-ma sgrub-chen-pa*, 721
Rikdzin Zangpo, the preceptor of Orgyen Mindröling *o-rgyan smin-grol-gling-gi mkhan-po rig-'dzin bzang-po*, 849
Rikdzin IV, Zhapdrung Pema Trhinle *rig-'dzin bzhi-pa zhabs-drung padma phrin-las*, 783; see *Dorje Trak Rikdzin IV*
Rikpei Reldri *rig(-pa'i) ral(-gri)*, 827, 894, 914-17, 930; see *(Comden) Rikpei Reldri*
Rincen Gyamtso *rin-chen rgya-mtsho*: the grandfather of Zurpoche Śākya Jungne, 617, 618
Rincen Lingpa *rin-chen gling-pa*, 584, 585
Rincen Tshültrim *rin-chen tshul-khrims*, 712; see *Rongben (Rincen) Tshültrim (Rinpoche)*
Rincen Zangpo, the (great) translator (958-1055) *lotsāba/lo(-chen) rin-chen bzang-po*, 751, 893, 918, 950, 951
Locen Rincen Zangpo *lo-chen rin-chen bzang-po*, 11
Rindor, master *slob-dpon rin-rdor*, 582
Rinpungpa administration (1435-1565) *sde-srid rin-spungs-pa*, 954

Rinpoche Maseng *rin-po-che smra-seng*, 723
Rinpoche Trak-ye *rin-po-che grags-ye*, 569
Ritrö Lungcung *ri-khrod rlung-chung*, 546, 547
Rok clan *rog-rus*, 575
Rokpoga, the lama of Thöpa *thod-pa'i bla-ma rog-po-dga'*, 551
Rok Śākya Jungne *rog śā-kya 'byung-gnas*, 619, 620-1, 918
Rok Sherap-ö *rog shes-rab 'od*, 47, 347, 701-2
  Lharje Rok Sherap-ö *lha-rje rog shes-rab 'od*, 358
Roktön Tsenpo *rog-ston btsan-po*, 701
Rok Tsöndrü Senge *rog brtson-'grus seng-ge*, 609
Rongben Pelgi Rinpoche *rong-ban dpal-gyi rin-po-che*: see *Rongben Yönten (Rincen)*
Rongben (Rincen) Tshültrim (Rinpoche) *rong-ban (rin-chen) tshul-khrims (rin-po-che)*: the father of Rongzompa Chöki Zangpo, 703, 706, 712
Rongben Yönten (Rincen) *rong-ban yon-tan (rin-chen)*, 706, 712
  Pelgi Rincen *dpal-gyi rin-chen*, 712
  Rongben Pelgi Rinpoche *rong-ban dpal-gyi rin-po-che*, 703
Rongmenza Tshültrim-drön *rong-sman-bza' tshul-khrims sgron*, 537
Rongnangda Cegom Nakpo *rong-snang-mda' lce-sgom nag-po*, 559
  Cegom Nakpo *lce-sgom nag-po*, 571
  Lama Cegom *bla-ma lce-sgom*, 559
Rongpa *rong-pa*, 706
Rongtön Sheja Künzi (1367-1449) *rong(-ston shes-bya kun-gzigs)*, 929
Rongzompa (Chöki Zangpo) (11th century) *rong-zom-pa (chos-kyi bzang-po)*, 29, 47, 92, 97, 198, 396, 703-9, **704**, 712, 730, 889-91, 919
  Dharmabhadra *dharma bha-dra*, 708
  father Chödrak *a-pha chos-grags*, 706
  Rongzom Paṇḍita *rong-zom paṇḍita*, 40, 712, 827
Rongzom Paṇḍita: see preceding entry
Ṛṣabha *rgyal-ba dam-pa*, 66
Rudra *drag-po*, 449
Rudrakulika (or Rudracakrin) *rigs-ldan drag-po lcags-'khor-can*: the future king of Shambhala, 960, **961**
Rüza Töndrupma *rus-bza' don-grub-ma*, 537
Sacen Künga Nyingpo (1092-1158) *sa-chen kun-dga' snying-po*, 952
  Sakyapa Künga Nyingpo *sa-skya-pa kun-dga' snying-po*, 649
Sādhuśāstrī *sā-dhu-sā-stri*, 477
Sāgara, the nāga king *klu'i rgyal-po rgya-mtsho*, 944
Sage *thub-pa*, Skt. Muni, 73, 77, 103, 184, 200, 204, 300, 422, 427, 555, 705, 894, 969, 971; see *Buddha*
Śāknyen *śāk-gnyen*, 655
Śakra, (lord) *(dbang-po) brgya-byin*: i.e. Śatakratu, 130, 624, 768; see *Devendra*
Śakrabhūti *śa-kra-bu-ti*, 462; see *Uparāja*
Śakraputra *śa-kra/tra-putri*, 462, 485; see *Kambalapāda*
Sakya Dakcen *sa-skya bdag-chen*, 798
Sakya, the Great Translator of *sa-lo chen-po*, 642, n. 781
Sakya Paṇḍita/Paṇcen, (the doctrine master) (1182-1251) *(chos-rje) sa-skya paṇḍita/paṇ-chen*, 105, 203-4, 564, 695, 715, 763, 827, 874, 907, 920, 929, 953
  Jamyang Sakya Paṇḍita *'jam-dbyangs sa-skya paṇḍita*, 806
Sakyapa Dorje Rincen *sa-skya-pa rdo-rje rin-chen*, 849
Sakyapa Künga Nyingpo *sa-skya-pa kun-dga' snying-po*, 649; see *Sacen Künga Nyingpo*
Sakya Trhicen Künga Trashi *sa-skya khri-chen kun-dga' bkra-shis*, 833
Sakya Trhicen Ngawang Pelden Chökyong *sa-skya khri-chen ngag-dbang dpal-ldan chos-skyong*, 839
Śākya Chokden, (the great paṇḍita of Zilung) (1428-1507) *(zi-lung-pa paṇ-chen) śā-kya mchog-ldan*, 893-4, 917, 929, 955
  Zilungpa (Śākya Chokden), the great paṇḍita *paṇ-cen zi-lung-pa (śā-kya mchog-ldan)*, 931
Śākyadeva *śā-kya de-ba*, 607
Śākyadevī *śā-kya de-bi*, 472
Śākya (clan) *śā-kya('i rigs)*, 417, 418, 420
Śākya Gewarapsel *śā-kya dge-ba rab-gsal*, 524; see *Lacen Gongpa Rapsel*
Śākyagön/Gön(po) *śā-kya mgon(-po)*, 660, 661, 662
Śākya Gyelpo (1384-1474) *(slob-dpon) śā-kya rgyal-po*, 552-3

Śākya Jungne *śā-kya 'byung-gnas*, 671-2; see *(Zur Ham) Śākya Jungne*

Śākya Jungne *śā-kya 'byung-gnas*, 618; see *(Zurpoche) Śākya Jungne*

Śākya King *śā-kya'i rgyal-po*, 405, 746; see *Buddha*

Śākyamati *śā-kya blo-gros*, 108

Śākyamitra *śā-kya bshes-gnyen*, 468, 488, **488**

Śākyamuni (Buddha) *śā-kya thub-pa*, 11, 17, 26, 36, 115, 137, 153, 193, 221, 312, 396, 411-27, **417**, 430, 434, 454, 564, 573, 590, 656, 659, 672, 696, 768, 894, 946-8, 972; see *Buddha*

Śākya-ö/Öpo, the teacher *ston-pa śā-kya 'od(-po)*, 660, 662-3; see *Zur(pa) Śākya-ö*

Śākyaprabha *śā-kya 'od*, 441

Śākyaprabha *śā-kya 'od*, 467-8, 488; see *Prabhāhasti*

Śākyaprabha, the younger *śā-kya 'od chung-ba*, 488

Śākya Senge *śā-kya seng-ge*, 646; see *Zur (Dropukpa) Śākya Senge*

Śākyasiṃha (Lion of the Śākyas) *śā-kya seng-ge*: one of Guru Rinpoche's manifestations during the second month, 469, 488; see *Guru Rinpoche*

Śākyaśrī, the great paṇḍita (1127-1225) *paṇ-chen śā-kya shri*, 660, 758, 914, 921, 947

  Tönpa Khace *ston-pa kha-che*, 757

Śākyendra, the transcendent lord *śā-kya dbang-po*, 755

Śākya Yeshe, master *slob-dpon śā-kya ye-shes*, 784

Śākzang, the governor *dpon-chen śāk-bzang*, 662

Śākya Zangpo, the treasure-finder of Trangpo *drang-po gter-ston śā-kya bzang-po*, 806

Samantabhadra *kun-tu bzang-po*: the primordial buddha-body of reality, Pl. 1; 11, 19, 21, 34, 35, 113, 115-19, **116**, 120, 122, 126, 135, 183, 198, 212, 276, 284, 297, 342, 366, 372, 397, 403, 430, 447-8, **448**, 567, 574, 680, 923

  All-Positive King *kun-bzang rgyal-po*, 317

  Great All-Pervader *khyab-'jug chen-po*, Skt. Mahāviṣṇu, 447

Samantabhadra, the bodhisattva *byang-sems kun-tu bzang-po*, 125, 508

Samantabhadra, Second *kun-tu bzang-po gnyis-pa*, 586; see *Longcen Rabjampa*

Samantabhadra, the yakṣa *gnod-sbyin kun-tu bzang-po*, 452

Samantabhadrī *kun-tu bzang-mo*, Pl. 1; 34, 37, **116**, 284, 319, 365, 366, **448**, 923

Samayatārā *dam-tshig sgrol-ma*, 20, 125; see *Tārā*

Sambhata, aristocrat *mi-chen sam-bha-ta*, 663

Samding Trupapel *bsam-sdings grub-pa dpal*, 665

Samdrup Rincen, preceptor of Samye *bsam-yas mkhan-po bsam-grub rin-chen*, 576

Sammitīya(s) *mang-pos bkur-ba*, 429

Samye Lungmangwa *bsam-yas lung-mang-ba*, 577; see *Longcen Rabjampa*

Samye, the yogin *yo-gi bsam-yas*, 566

Śāṇavāsika *śa-ṇa'i gos-can*, 433, 435-6, **436**

Sangdak Trhinle Lhündrup (Pelzangpo) (1611-62) *gsang-bdag phrin-las lhun-grub (dpal-bzang-po)*, 701, 724-6, **725**, 827, 956

  Nyötön (Sangdak) Trhinle Lhündrup *gnyos-ston (gsang-bdag) phrin-las lhun-grub*, 684, 825

  Orgyen Tshepel *o-rgyan tshe-'phel*, 724

  Rikdzin Trhinle Lhündrup *rig-'dzin phrin-las lhun-grub*, 595, 727, 812

  Trhinle Lhündrup (Pelzangpo, the great awareness-holder of Tarding) *(dar-lding rig-'dzin chen-po) phrin-las lhun-grub (dpal-bzang-po)*, 683, 724, 728, 733

Sangtön Yeshe Lama *gsang-ston ye-shes bla-ma*, 540

Sangye Bar *sangs-rgyas 'bar*, 751

Sangye Chödar, the spiritual benefactor *dge-bshes sangs-rgyas chos-dar*, 730

Sangye Gyamtso, regent (1655-1705) *rgyal-tshab sangs-rgyas rgya-mtsho*, 833

Sangye Konglawa of Takpo *dvags-po'i sangs-rgyas gong-la-ba*, 686

Sangye Künga, master *slob-dpon sangs-rgyas kun-dga'*, 590, 595

Sangye Lama (*c.* 990-1070) *sangs-rgyas bla-ma*, 751-2, **752**, 835

Sangye Lingpa, (the great treasure-finder) (1340-96) *(gter-chen) sangs-rgyas*

gling-pa, 784-8, **785**, 835, 847, 856-7, 865, 954
Rikdzin *rig-'dzin*, 784
Sangye Zangpo *sangs-rgyas bzang-po*, 784
Sangye Lingpa III: see *Trülku Sangye Pelden*
Sangye Nyigom, lama *bla-ma sangs-rgyas nyi-sgom*, 760
Sangye Önpo *sangs-rgyas dbon-po*, 595
Sangye Önpo of Sengegyap *seng-ge rgyab-pa sangs-rgyas dbon-po*, 567; see *Trhüzhi Sengegyap*
Sangye Öntön *sangs-rgyas dbon-ston*, 660
Sangye Pelrin *sangs-rgyas dpal-rin*, 595
Buddhaśrī (Sangyepel) *bu-ddha shri (sangs-rgyas dpal)*, 592
Sangye Repa *sangs-rgyas ras-pa*, 567
Sangye Rincen Gyeltsen Pelzangpo *sangs-rgyas rin-chen rgyal-mtshan dpal-bzang-po*, 672; see *(Drölcen) Sangye Rincen*
Sangye Takcung *sangs-rgyas dvags-chung*, 653
Sangye Tshencen, the madman of Tsang (1452-1507) *gtsang-smyon sangs-rgyas mtshan-can*, 955
Sangye Yeshe *sangs-rgyas ye-shes*, 535, 607, 614; see *Nup(cen) Sangye Yeshe*
Sangye Zangpo, the great preceptor *mkhan-chen sangs-rgyas bzang-po*, 552
Sangye Zangpo *sangs-rgyas bzang-po*, 784; see *Sangye Lingpa*
Śaṅkara, the brahman *bram-ze shaṃ-ka-ra*, 511
Śāntamati *zhi-ba'i blo-gros*, 340
Śāntapurīpa *sha-nta-pu-ri-pa*, 595; see *Sherap Özer*
Śāntarakṣita *zhi-ba 'tsho*, Pl. 14; 394, 397, 405, 509, 513, **514**, 515, 522, 601, 848, 852, 864, 888, 889, 921, 938
Bodhisattva *(mkhan-po) bo-dhi sa-tva*, 405, 513-15, 601
preceptor *mkhan*, 968, 973
Śāntarakṣita (Preserver of Peace) *sha-nta-rakṣita*: Guru Rinpoche's manifestation during the first month, 469; see *Guru Rinpoche*
Śāntarakṣitā, the ḍākinī *mkha'-'gro-ma zhi-ba'i 'tsho*, 469
Śāntideva *zhi-ba lha*, 92, 94, 300, 441, 693, 904
Śāntigarbha *zhi-ba'i snying-po*, 483, 515, 534, 607, 610
Śāntigupta *rdo-rje slob-dpon chen-po sha-nta-gu-pta*, 504, 921
Śāntihasta *zhi-ba'i lag-pa*, 498
Śāntipā, (master) *(slob-dpon) sha-nti-pa*, 77, 105, 455; see *Ratnākaraśānti*
Śāntiprabha *zhi-ba 'od*, 467
Sāra, the venerable brahman *bram-ze snying-po'i zhabs/sa-ra-pa-da*, 478; see *Mañjuśrīmitra*
Śāradvatīputra *sha-ra-dva-ti'i bu*, 178; see *Śāriputra*
Saraha, (the great brahman) *(bram-ze chen-po) sa-ra-ha*, 200, 335, 345, 404, 440, 442
Archer *mda'-ba/mda'-bsnun*, 197
Rāhula *sgra-can-'dzin*, 185, 464
Rāhulabhadra, the scholar *paṇḍita sgra-gcan-'dzin bzang-po*, 475
Sarahapāda, (the brahman) *(bram-ze) sa-ra-ha zhabs*, 471, 927
Sarahapāda, (the brahman): see preceding entry
Sārasiddhi, the brahman *bram-ze snying-po grub-pa*, 478; see *Mañjuśrīmitra*
Sarasvatī *dbyangs-can-ma/mtsho-ldan-ma*, 577
Śāriputra *sha-ri'i bu*, 75, 90-1, 214, 423, **424**, 425-6, 428
Śāradvatīputra *sha-ra-dva-ti'i bu*, 178
Saroruha *mtsho-skyes*, 459, 471, 916, 927
Saroruhavajra (Vajra of the Lake-born Lotus) *mtsho-skyes rdo-rje*: Guru Rinpoche's manifestation during the sixth month, 469, 857, 855-6, 866; see *Guru Rinpoche*
Sarvajñādeva *thams-cad mkhyen-pa'i lha*, 515
Sarvakāmin *thams-cad 'dod*, 93
Sarvamitra *kun-gyi bshes-gnyen*, 418
Sarvārthasiddha *don-thams-cad grub-pa*, 417; see *Buddha*
Sarvavid-Vairocana *kun-rig(s) rnam-snang*, 624; see *Vairocana (Buddha)*
Satya(vācas), the ṛṣi *drang-srong bden(-smras)*, 65
Sauripāda of Vajrāsana *sau-ri-pa*, 477
Sazang (Mati Paṇcen), the great translator (1294-1376) *sa-bzang lo-chen (ma-ti paṇ-chen)*, 671
"Sebak Komdünma" *se-'bag goms-bdun-ma*, 670
Sedur Lungpa *se-dur lung-pa*, 657

Selungpa, the preceptor *mkhan-po se-lung-pa*, 566
Selwa Wangcuk *gsal-ba dbang-phyug*, 607
Senalek (Jingyön) *sad-na legs (mjing-yon)*, 22, 521; see *Mutik Tsepo*
Senge Dradok/Siṃhanāda (Lion's Roar) *seng-ge sgra-sgrogs*: Guru Rinpoche's manifestation during the fifth month, 472, 845; see *Guru Rinpoche*
Sengegyapa, the middle *seng-ge rgyab-pa bar-pa*, 565
Sengepa of Ukpalung, lama *'ug-pa-lung-pa'i bla-ma seng-ge-pa*, 668
Senge Trak of Korong *go-rong-pa seng-ge brag*, 524
Serlungpa *gser-lung-pa*, 550, 552, 566
Setrom Gyamtsobar *se-khrom rgya-mtsho 'bar*, 708
Seven Generations of Buddhas *sangs-rgyas rabs-bdun*: listed in the Glossary of Enumerations, 136, 591, 624
seven men who were tested *sad-mi mi-bdun*: the "seven trial monks", listed in the Glossary of Enumerations, 511, 515, 575, 950
Shage Lotsāwa *sha-gad lo-tsā-ba*, 914
Shami Dorje Gyeltsen *sha-mi rdo-rje rgyal-mtshan*, 721
Shang, the All-Knowing Master from *shangs-pa kun-mkhyen*, 668; see *Len Selwa*
Shangparepa *shangs-pa ras-pa*, 559
Sharwa Popathaye, lama *bla-ma shar-ba spobs-pa mtha'-yas*, 688; see *Katok(pa) Tampa Deshek*
Shekar Dorjetsho *shel-dkar rdo-rje mtsho*, 536
Shenpa Sokdrupma *shan-pa srog-sgrub-ma*: the protectress, 580, 587
Shenrap Miwoche *gshen-rab mi-bo-che*, 632
Shenyen Köncok Zangpo *bshes-gnyen dkon-mchog bzang-po*, 700
Sherap Dorje *shes-rab rdo-rje*, 698
Sherap Drönma, the Khotanese lady *li-yul-bza' shes-rab sgron-ma*, 540
Sherap Gyeltsen *shes-rab rgyal-mtshan*, 687, 698
Sherap Jungne *shes-rab 'byung-nas*, 543; see *(Nyang) Sherap Jungne*
Sherap Özer, the great treasure-finder (1517-84) *gter-chen shes-rab 'od-zer*, 595, 837, 955
  Prajñāraśmi *pra-dznya rasmi*, 835
Śāntapurīpa *sha-nta-pu-ri-pa*, 595
Sherap Pelwa *shes-rab dpal-ba*, 698
Sherap Senge *shes-rab seng-ge*, 688; see *Katok(pa) Tampa Deshek*
Sherap-tra *shes-rab grags*, 549
Sherap Tshültrim of Denma *ldan-ma shes-rab tshul-khrims*, 619
Shing-go-chen-pa *shing-sgo chen-pa*, 592; see *Tā'i Situ (Cangcup Gyeltsen)*
Shingjachen, the Gyelpo spirit *rgyal-po shing-bya-can*, 519; see *Pehar*
Shongbu, the translator *shong-bu lo-tsā-ba*, 546
Shore *sho-ras*, 547
Shübuza Sherapma *shud-bu-bza' shes-rab-ma*, 537
Shüpu Pelgi Senge *shud-bu dpal-gyi seng-ge*, 535, 753
Shütön Dadra *shud-ston zla-grags*, 642
Siddhārtha, (prince) *(rgyal-bu) don-grub*, 412, 575, 946; see *Buddha*
Śikhin, king *rgyal-po thor-cog-can*: an emanation of Guru Rinpoche, 469; see *Guru Rinpoche*
Śīlamañju (from Nepal/the Newar, master) *(bal-po'i slob-dpon) śīla-manydzu*, 38, 511, 714
Śīlapālita, master *slob-dpon tshul-khrims bskyang*, 947
Śīlendrabodhi *shi-lendra bo-dhi*, 522
Siṃha, the merchant *ded-dpon seng-ge*, 455
Siṃha *seng-ge*: the leonine form in which the Buddha appears to animals, 130
Siṃhanāda/Senge Dradok (Lion's Roar) *seng-ge sgra-sgrogs*: Guru Rinpoche's manifestation during the fifth month, 472, 845; see *Guru Rinpoche*
Siṃhaputra *seng-he/sing-ha putra*, 487
Siṃharāja *seng-ha/sing-ha ra-dza*, 462
Sitarkyi *srid-thar skyid*, 674
Sitar Men *srid-thar sman*, 793
Situ, the All-Knowing (Dharmākara): see following entry
Situ VIII, Chöki Jungne *si-tu chos-kyi 'byung-gnas*: i.e. Tā'i Situ VIII, 957
  All-knowing Situ (Dharmākara) *si-tu kun-mkhyen*, 203
Situ Künzi Chöki Gyamtso *si-tu kun-gzigs chos-kyi rgya-mtsho*, 736; see *Katok Situ (Chöki Gyamtso)*
Situ Pema Nyinje Wangpo *si-tu padma nyin-byed dbang-po*, 842; see *(Camgön Tā'i) Situ Pema Nyinje Wangpo*

Situ Śākya Zangpo, the myriarch of upper Uru *dbur-stod khri-dpon si-tu śā-kya bzang-po*, 592
six adornments of Jambudvīpa *'dzam-bu-gling mdzes-pa'i rgyan-drug*: listed in the Glossary of Enumerations, 440-1
six emanational treasure-finders *sprul-pa'i gter-ston drug*: disciples of Pema Lingpa, 798
six great accomplished masters *grub-thob chen-po drug*: disciples of Pema Lingpa, 798
six great sons who manifestly disclosed signs of accomplishment *grub-rtags mngon-sum thon-pa'i bu-chen-drug*: disciples of Pema Lingpa, 798
six paṇḍitas of the gates *mkhas-pa sgo-drug*, Skt. *ṣaḍdvārapaṇḍita*: listed in the Glossary of Enumerations, 442
Six Sages (Embodying Awareness) *(rig-pa'i skyes-bu) thub-pa drug*: listed in the Glossary of Enumerations, 129-30, 414
six species of Kāma divinities *'dod-lha rigs-drug*: listed in the Glossary of Enumerations, 60
sixteen "beams" *phyam bcu-drug*, 640
Sixteen Elders *gnas-brtan chen-po bcu-drug*: listed in the Glossary of Enumerations, Pls. 9-10; 432, 438, 590
Smara *dran-pa*, 421; see *Kāma*
Smṛtijñānakīrti *slob-dpon smri-ti dznyā-na ki-rti*, 11, 703
Socung Gendünbar *so(-cung) dge-'dun 'bar*, 578
Sodokpa Lodrö Gyeltsen (1552-*c*.1624) *sog-bzlog-pa blo-gros rgyal-mtshan*, 722-3, 955
  Dongkar Tshoje (Physician of Dongkar) *gdong-khar 'tsho byed*, 722
  Khedrup Lodrö Gyeltsen Pelzangpo *mkhas-grub blo-gros rgyal-mtshan dpal bzang-po*, 722-3
Sogdian Lhapel: see following entry
Sogdian Pelgi Yeshe *sog-po dpal-gyi ye-shes*, 533, 540, 604-6, **606**, 608
  Lha Pelgi Yeshe *lha dpal-gyi ye-shes*, 604
  Pektse, the Sogdian *sog-po beg-tse*, 604
  Sogdian Lhapel *sog-po lha-dpal*, 535
Sogyel, the treasure-finder *gter-ston bsod-rgyal*, 879; see *Lerap Lingpa*
Sokza Sonamtsho *sog-bza' bsod-nams mtsho*, 849
Sölpön Pema *gsol-dpon padma*, 872
So Mangtsen *so-mang-btsan*, 547
Somayogī *slob-ma so-ma dzo-gi*, 693
Sonam Detsen *bsod-nams lde'u btsan*, 736; see *(Katok Gyelse) Sonam Detsen*
Sonam Gyamtso, the all-knowing (great translator) *(lo-chen) thams-cad mkhyen-pa bsod-nams rgya-mtsho*, 675, 677
Sonamgyel, the scholar of Len *glan-mkhas bsod-nams rgyal*, 686
Sonam Gyeltsen, the great preceptor *mkhan-chen bsod-nams rgyal-mtshan*, 552
Sonam Lhündrup, the great preceptor of Lowo (1420-89) *glo-bo mkhan-chen bsod-nams lhun-grub*, 806
Sonam Rincen *bsod-nams rin-chen*, 726
Sonam Trakpa, the doctrine master *chos-rje bsod-nams grags-pa*, 671
Sonam Wangpo, an adept of the Great Perfection *rdzogs-pa chen-po bsod-nams dbang-po*, 818
Sonam Yeshe of Gar *'gar bsod-nams ye-shes*, 650
Sonam Zangpo, the great preceptor of Coten *jo-bstan mkhan-chen bsod-nams bzang-po*, 787
Sonam Zangpo *bsod-nams bzang-po*: i.e. Katokpa Gyeltsap VI, 695
Sonam Zangpo of Zhangkar *zhang-mkhar bsod-nams bzang-po*, 687
Song, lama *bla-ma srong*, 660
Songtsen Gampo, king *srong-btsan sgam-po*, Pls. 39, 60; 393, 397, 404, 510-12, **511**, 522, 835, 838, 949
So-nyün Dang *so-snyun gdangs*, 546
So Tarma Senge *so dar-ma seng-ge*, 701
Sotön *so-ston*, 552
(So) Yeshe Wangcuk *(so) ye-shes dbang-phyug*, 613, 616
Speech Emanation of Lhodrak and the Spiritual Son, 839; see *Lhodrak Sungtrül IV* and *Lhodrak Thukse Dawa Gyeltsen V*
Śrīdevī *dpal-ldan lha-mo*, 624, 690, **690**, 691
Śrīdhara, the grammarian *sgra-mkhas dpal-'dzin*, 594
Śrīdharā, the ḍākinī *mkha'-'gro dpal-'dzin-ma*, 961
Śrīgupta, master *slob-dpon dpal-sbas*, 108
Śrīheruka *(dpal) yang-dag he-ru-ka*, 475-7, 534; see *Yangdak Heruka*

Śrīmad Uttamabodhibhagavat *dpal-ldan byang-chub mchog-gi skal-ba dang-ldan-pa*, 464; see *Līlāvajra*

Śrī Siṃha *shri sing-ha*, 40, 470, 496, **497**, 497-501, 515, 538, 539, 554, 607, 610

Sthāvarā *sa'i lha-mo brtan-ma*, 420

Sthavira(s) *gnas-brtan-pa*, 429-30

Sthiramati *blo-brtan*, 429, 489

Subhadra, the mendicant *kun-tu-rgyu rab-bzang*, 425

Subhūṣaṇā *legs-rgyan-ma*, 421

Subhūti *rab-'byor*, 75, 172, 176, 183, 307

Sublime One *'phags-pa*, 510; see *Avalokiteśvara*

Sucandra *zla-ba bzang-po*, 451

Sudāna, a householder *legs-sbyin*, 120

Sudarśana *legs-mthong*, 437

Sudatta, the brahman youth *bram-ze'i khye'u legs-byin*, 121

Śuddhodana, king *rgyal-po zas-gtsang-ma*, 417, 419

Sudharmā *su-dharma*, 490

Sugata *bde-bar gshegs-pa*, 22, 138, 186, 218, 268, 300, 409, 871, 873, 896, 928; see *Buddha*

Sujātā *legs-skyes-ma*, 419

Sujaya, king *rgyal-po legs-rgyal*, 440

Sukhacakra *bde-ldan 'khor-lo*, 498

Sukhāṅkuśa, the bodhisattva *byang-sems bde-ba'i smyu-gu*, 697; see *(Khedrup) Yeshe Gyeltsen (of Pubor)*

Sukhasāra *bde-ba'i snying-po*, 697; see *(Khedrup) Yeshe Gyeltsen (of Pubor)*

Sukhasāravatī *bde-ba'i snying-ldan-ma*, 490

Sukha the "Zombie" *ro-langs bde-ba*, 487-8, 493; see *Garap Dorje*

Sukhoddyotaka *bde-ba gsal-mdzad*, 489, 607, 609

  Prakāśālaṃkāra, (the brahman) *(bram-ze) gsal-ba'i rgyan*, 607, 608-9

"summit ridge" *rtse-lkog*, 622, 623; see *Tsak Lama*

Sumpa Yebar *sum-pa ye-'bar*, 643

(Sungtrül) Tshültrim Dorje *(gsung-sprul) tshul-khrims rdo-rje*, 723, 724, 727, 735, 956; see *Lhodrak Sungtrül III*

Supreme Emanation of the Dorje Trak Rikdzin (1719/20-70) *rdo-rje rig-'dzin mchog-gi sprul-sku*: i.e. Dorje Trak Rikdzin V, 839

Supreme Horse/Aśvottama *rta-mchog*, 274, 534; see *Hayagrīva*

Supreme Pair *mchog-zung*: i.e. Buddha Śākyamuni's disciples Śāriputra and Maudgalyāyana, 91

Śūra, (master) *(slob-dpon) dpa'-bo*, 69, 71, 99, 641

  Āryaśūra *'phags-pa dpa'-bo*, 703

Surendra *lha-dbang*, 128; see *Devendra*

Surendrabodhi *su-rendra-bodhi*, 522

Sūryakiraṇā, the ḍākinī *mkha'-'gro-ma nyi-ma 'od-zer*, 493

Sūryaprabhāsiṃha *slob-dpon nyi-'od seng-ge*, 40, 63, 688, 916

Sūryaraśmi (Sunbeam) *nyi-ma 'od-zer*: Guru Rinpoche's manifestation during the eighth month, 471; see *Guru Rinpoche*

Sūryavat *nyi-ma-dang 'dra-ba*, 463, 464; see *Līlāvajra*

(Sutön) Lekpei Drönme *(sru-ston) legs-pa'i sgron-me*, 613

Suza Drönkyi *sru-bza' sgron-skyid*, 601

Svāstika *bkra-shis*, 419

Śvetaketu, holy *dam-pa tog-dkar*, 412, 416; see *Buddha*

Tabla, the former and later/elder and younger *ta-bla(-ma) snga-phyi*, 788, 833

Tabla Padmamati *ta-bla padma-ma-ti*, 812

  Katokpa Pema Lodrö *kaḥ-thog-pa padma blo-gros*, 723

  Takla Padmamati of Katok *kaḥ-thog stag-bla padma-mati*, 681

Tago Cadrel Chöje *stag-mgo bya-bral chos-rje*, 595

Tā'i Situ (Cangcup Gyeltsen) (1302-73) *tā'i si-tu (byang-chub rgyal-mtshan)*, 592, 777, 778, 954

  "Eight-footed Lion", the Shing-go-chen-pa *shing-sgo chen-pa seng-ge rkang-pa brgyad-pa*, 592

  Lord of Neudong *sne-gdong gong-ma*, 595

Tā'i Situ VIII, Chöki Jungne (1700-74) *tā'i si-tu chos-kyi 'byung-gnas*: see *Situ VIII, Chöki Jungne*

Tā'i Situ IX, Pema Nyinje Wangpo (1774-1853) *tā'i si-tu padma nyin-byed dbang-po*: see *(Camgön Tā'i) Situ Pema Nyinje Wangpo*

Tā'i Situ X, (Pema Künzang Chögyel) (1854-85) *tā'i si-tu bcu-pa*: alias *si-rgod-ma*, 868

Tā'i Situ XI, (Pema Wangcuk Gyelpo) (1886-1952) *tā'i si-tu bcu-gcig-pa*, 868
Takdra Lhanang *stag-sgra lha-nang*, 601
Takla Padmamati of Katok *kaḥ-thog stag-bla padma-mati*, 681; see *Tabla Padmamati*
Taklung Lotsāwa *stag-lung lo-tsā-ba*: see *Taktsang Lotsāwa Sherap Rincen*
Taklung Ma Rinpoche *stag-lung ma rin-po-che*, 841
Taklungpa Tendzin Sizhi Namgyel *stag-lung-pa bstan-'dzin srid-zhi rnam-rgyal*, 833
Taklung Trapa *stag-lung grva-pa*, 730
Taklung Sangye Yarjön (1203-72) *stag-lung sangs-rgyas yar-byong*, 953
Taklung Thangpa Trashipel (1142-1210) *stag-lung thang-pa bkra-shis dpal*
  Pel Taklung Thangpa *dpal stag-lung thang-pa*, 952
Takpa Khace *stags-pa kha-che*, 650
Takpo (Daö Zhönu) *dvags-po (zla-'od gzhon-nu)*, 931, 952; see *Gampopa*
Takpo Gyare *dvags-po rgya-ras*, 653
Takpo Lharje *dvags-po lha-rje*, 649, 853, 929; see *Gampopa*
Takṣaka, the nāga king *klu-rgyal 'jog-po*, 452, 454
Takshamcen *stag-sham-can*, 547
Taksowa, lama *bla-ma stag-so-ba*, 562
Taktön Chögyel Tendzin *dvags-ston chos-rgyal bstan-'dzin*, 701, 828
Taktsang Lotsāwa Sherap Rincen (b. 1405) *stag-tshang lo-tsā-ba shes-rab rin-chen*, 929-30, n. 1303
Tampa Deshek *dam-pa bde-gshegs*, 698, 699; see *Katok(pa) Tampa Deshek*
Tampa Dewarshekpa of Katok *kaḥ-thog-pa dam-pa bde-bar gshegs-pa*, 688; see *Katok(pa) Tampa Deshek*
Tampa Pormang *dam-pa spor-mang*, 651
Tampa Rinpoche *dam-pa rin-po-che*, 698; see *Katok(pa) Tampa Deshek*
Tampa Sedrakpa *dam-pa se-sbrag-pa*, 651-2, 654, 655
  Tön-śāk of Central Tibet *dbus-pa ston-śāk*, 651
Tampa (Sonam Gyeltsen of Sakya), lama (1312-75) *(sa-skya-pa) bla-ma dam-pa (bsod-nams rgyal-mtshan)*, 578, 787, 922
Tampa Yölcungwa *dam-pa yol-chung-ba*, 652
Tanak Drölmawa Samdrup Dorje (1295-1376) *rta-nag sgrol-ma-ba bsam-grub rdo-rje*, 665, 667-8, **668**, 669
  Drölcen/Drölmawa Samdrup Dorje *sgrol-chen/sgrol-ma-ba bsam-'grub rdo-rje*, 348, 672, 700, 717, 720, 721
  Jamyang Samdrup Dorje *'jam-dbyangs bsam-grub rdo-rje*, 671, 721
Tanak Düdül *rta-nag bdud-'dul*, 663
T'ang T'ai-tsung (reigned 626-49) *thung spyi'u*: father of Wen-ch'eng K'ong-jo, 438
Tārā *sgrol-ma*, Pl. 43; 510, 560, 567, 762, 789, 791, 857
  Ārya Tārā *'phags-ma sgrol-ma*, 466
  Immortal Wish-granting Wheel *'chi-med yid-bzhin 'khor-lo*: a form of White Tārā, 857
  Samayatārā *dam-tshig sgrol-ma*, 20, 125
  Tārā, who protects from the eight fears *sgrol-ma 'jigs-pa brgyad-skyobs*, 624
  White Tārā *sgrol-dkar*, 857, 874
Tāranātha *tā-ra-nā-tha*, 892; see *(Jetsün) Tāranātha*
Tarje Pelgi Trakpa *dar-rje dpal-gyi grags-pa*, 533, 605
Tarma Dode *dar-ma mdo-sde*, 713
Tarma Gönpo *dar-ma mgon-po*, 569
Tathāgata *de-bzhin gshegs-pa*, 99, 103, 146, 153-5, 172, 179-80, 189, 192, 195, 216, 253, 292, 316, 334, 340, 393, 414, 422, 423, 425, 426, 456, 471, 626, 786, 947; see *Buddha*
Tathāgata Özer Raptutrhowa *de-bzhin gshegs-pa 'od-zer rab-tu 'phro-ba*, 693; see *Tsangtönpa*
Tathāgata Śākyamuni *de-bzhin gshegs-pa śā-kya mu-ni*, 190, 193
Tathāgata Sumerudīpadhvaja *de-bzhin gshegs-pa ri-rab mar-me'i rgyal-mtshan*, 590; see *Longcen Rabjampa*
Tathāgatas of the Five (Enlightened) Families *de-bzhin gshegs-pa rigs-lnga*, 343, 691; see *Buddhas of the Five Enlightened Families*
Tathāgata Vairocana, king of form *de-bzhin gshegs-pa gzugs-kyi rgyal-po*, 128, 221; see *Vairocana (Buddha)*
Tathāgata Vimalacandraprabha *de-bzhin gshegs-pa dri-med zla-'od*, 220
Tathāgata Vipaśyin *de-bzhin gshegs-pa rnam-par gzigs*, 219
Tatön Cobum (b. 1174) *rta-ston jo-'bum*, 657

(Tatön) Co-sö (1167-97 or 1168-98) *(rta-ston) jo-bsod*, 657, 659-60
Tatön Co-ye (1163-1230) *rta-ston jo-ye*, 656-9
Tatön Ziji *rta-ston gzi-brjid*, 660, 665
Tavihṛca *ta-bi-hri-tsa*: Pönpo teacher identified as a form of Guru Rinpoche, 473; see *Guru Rinpoche*
Teacher *ston-pa*, Skt. Śāstṛ, 47, 68, 71, 73-6, 78, 88, 90-1, 104, 109, 113-48, 153-5, 193, 218, 231, 409, 411, 413, 428, 429, 430, 432, 434, 435, 436, 437, 438, 439, 440, 441, 452, 454, 458, 613, 637, 705, 894, 906, 946; see *Buddha*
Teachers of the Five Buddha/Enlightened Families *rigs-lnga'i ston-pa rnams*, 19, 21, 117, 448; see *Buddhas of the Enlightened Families*
Teachers/Conquerors, Five *ston-pa/rgyal-ba lnga*: listed in the Glossary of Enumerations, 125, 128; see *Buddhas of the Enlightened Families*
Temo Rinpoche *srid-skyong de-mo rin-po-che*: from 1886 to 1895 the regent of Tibet, 777, n. 1036
Tendzin Gyurme Dorje *bstan-'dzin 'gyur-med rdo-rje*, 735; see *Lhodrak (Thuk-)se IV*
Tendzin Jamyang Wangpo *bstan-'dzin 'jam-dbyangs dbang-po*, 728; see *Locen Dharmaśrī*
Tendzin Trakpa *bstan-'dzin grags-pa*, 595
Tendzin Yeshe Lhündrup *bstan-'dzin ye-shes lhun-grub*, 836
Tendzin Yungdrung *bstan-'dzin gYung-drung*, 859
Teng, two celestial kings called *stod-kyi ltengs gnyis*: listed in the Glossary of Enumerations, 507, n. 535
Tengi Yöntenchok *dan-gyi yon-tan mchog*, 613
Ten Great Pillars who Supported the Exegetical Lineages *bshad-brgyud 'degs-pa'i ka-chen bcu*: listed in the Glossary of Enumerations, 851
Tenpasung, master *slob-dpon bstan-pa srung*, 575
Ten Phakpa, master *slob-dpon dan-'phags-pa*, 577
Terdak Lingpa *gter-bdag gling-pa*, 29, 198, 365, 375, 396, 397, 595, 736, 822, 823, 824, 825-34, 879; see *(Rikdzin) Terdak Lingpa*
Thabula, the royal lady *dpon-mo tha-bu-la*, 670
Thagana *tha-ga-na*, 703
Thakorwa *mtha'-skor-ba*, 762, 765
Thakpa Gomcen *thags-pa sgom-chen*, 635; see *(Zur) Thakpa Gomcen*
Thakzang Pelgi Dorje *thag-bzang dpal-gyi rdo-rje*, 605
Thangdrok-ön Pema Chokdrup *thang-'brog-dbon padma mchog-grub*, 836
Thangla *thang-lha*: the protector, 791; see *(Nyencen) Thangla*
Thangtong Gyelpo (1385-1464 or 1361-1485) *thang-stong rgyal-po*, 802-4, **803**, 853, 855, 954
Tharpagyen *thar-pa rgyan*, 568; see *Kumārādza*
Tharpa Lotsāwa (Nyima Gyeltsen) *thar-lo(-tsā-ba nyi-ma rgyal-mtshan)*, 665, 914, 944
Thartse Khen Rinpoche *thar-rtse mkhan rin-po-che*, 849
Thartse Pönlop Jamyang Loter Wangpo *thar-rtse dpon-slob 'jam-dbyangs blo-gter dbang-po*, 868; see *Pönlop Loter Wangpo*
Tha'u, the royal lady *dpon-mo tha'u*, 671
Thazhi Trakpa Rincen *mtha'-bzhi grags-pa rin-chen*, 552
Themurdar, (the emperor's messenger) *(rgyal-po'i pho-nya) the-mur-dar*, 671
Thilise, the translator *thi-li-se lo-tsā-ba*, 509
thirteen disciples of the great treasure-finder Düjom Lingpa who attained the rainbow body *bdud-'joms gling-pa'i bu-slob 'ja'-lus thob-pa bcu-gsum*, 919
thirteen generations of accomplished masters in the line of Mok *grub-thob rmog-rabs bcu-gsum*, 698
thirteen generations of the gurus of Katok *kaḥ-thog bla-rabs bcu-gsum*: listed in the Glossary of Enumerations, 688-98
thirteen generations of Trung *drung-rabs bcu-gsum*: i.e. the attendant lamas of Katok Monastery, 698-9, n. 887
thirteen hunting gods *mgur-lha bcu-gsum*: listed in the Glossary of Enumerations, 513
thirty mantra adepts of Sheldrak *shel-brag-gi sngags-pa sum-cu*, 537

Thokme Gyagarwa *thogs-med rgya-gar-ba*, 792
Thönmi Sambhoṭa *thon-mi sam-bho-ṭa*, 512, 522
Thöpei Tumbutsel, the spiritual warrior *dpa'-bo thod-pa'i dum-bu-rtsal*, 867
Thötreng, the king of ogres *srin-po'i rgyal-po rakṣa thod-phreng*, 520
Thousand Buddhas *sangs-rgyas stong-rtsa gcig*: the thousand supreme emanational bodies, 136, 409, 624, 938, 944
three ancestral religious kings *mes-dbon rnam-gsum*: listed in the Glossary of Enumerations, 47, 510-22, 523, 889
three ancestral Zurs *zur mes-dbon gsum*: listed in the Glossary of Enumerations, 617-49, 728
three authors of fundamental texts *gzhung-byed-pa-po gsum*: listed in the Glossary of Enumerations, 440
Three Buddhas of the Past *'das-pa'i sangs-rgyas gsum*: listed in the Glossary of Enumerations, 423
Three Gyamtsos *rgya-mtsho rnam-gsum*: listed in the Glossary of Enumerations, 954
three from Gyelmorong who just had to listen *rong-po thos-chog rnam-gsum*, 698
three men from Kham *khams-pa mi-gsum*: listed in the Glossary of Enumerations, 952
three supreme emanations *mchog-gi sprul-sku gsum*: listed in the Glossary of Enumerations, 755, 760, 780, 934
three "useless men" *go-ma-chod mi-gsum*, 640, 642, 643
Thukdrup *thugs-sgrub*: a form of Guru Rinpoche, 586; see *Guru Rinpoche*
Thuken (Lozang Chöki Nyima) (1737-1802) *thu'u bkvan (blo-bzang chos-kyi nyi-ma)*, 735
Thü Khambar, lama *bla-ma thud kha-'bar*, 547
Thupa Dorje, spiritual son *thugs-sras thub-pa rdo-rje*, 673
Thupwang Tenpei Nyima, Gemang II *dge-mang gnyis-pa thub-dbang bstan-pa'i nyi-ma*: the second Dzokcen Gemang, 919
Tīkṣṇavajra *rdo-rje rnon-po*, 452; see *Mañjuśrītīkṣṇa*
Tilopā *ti-lli-pa/ti-lo-pa*, 199, 462
Tise Trogyang Sarwa *ti-se gro-gyang gsar-ba*, 762
Tokden Chönyi Rangdröl *rtogs-ldan chos-nyid rang-grol*, 723
Tokden Jampel Gyamtso (1365-1428) *rtogs-ldan 'jam-dpal rgya-mtsho*, 925
Toktsewa *tog-rtse-ba*: a student of Garap Dorje, 922
Tölbupa/Tölpopa (Sherap Gyeltsen), the all-knowing (1292-1361) *kun-mkhyen dol-bu-pa (shes-rab rgyal-mtshan)*, 676, 931
  Conang Künzi Tölpopa *jo-nang kun-gzigs dol-bo-pa*, 953
  Conang Sherap Gyeltsen *jo(-nang) shes-rab rgyal-mtshan*, 905
  Tölpa Sangye, the all-knowing *kun-mkhyen dol-pa sangs-rgyas*, 204
Tölpa Sangye, the all-knowing: see preceding entry
Tölpopa: see preceding entry
Tom Atsara Pel Metok *dom a-tsa-ra dpal me-tog*, 706
Töncar Cangyön *ston-'char byang-yon*, 565
Töndrup Gyelpo *don-grub rgyal-po*, 788
Töndrup Zangpo of the Nyo clan *myos-rigs-kyi don-grub bzang-po*, 796
Tongtsap Cangcup *tong-tshab byang-chub*, 619
Tongtsap Phakpa Rinpoche *tong-tshab 'phags-pa rin-po-che*, 616; see *(Pagor) Löncen Phakpa*
Tönpa Göngyel *ston-pa mgon-rgyal*, 699
Tönpa Khace *ston-pa kha-che*, 757; see *Śākyaśrī*
Tönpa Lakyap *ston-pa bla-skyabs*, 653
Tönpa Rāhu *ston-pa rā-hu*, 662
Tönpa Sonam Wangcuk *ston-pa bsod-nams dbang-phyug*, 780
Tönpa Wangjor *ston-pa dbang-'byor*, 698, 699
Tön-śāk of Central Tibet *dbus-pa ston-śāk*, 651; see *Tampa Sedrakpa*
Töntshül *ston-tshul*, 576
Tönyö Dorje *don-yod rdo-rje*, 627
Towarepa of Tshurpu *mtshur-phu'i do-ba-ras-pa*, 567
Tragön Ce-nga Zhönu Chöpel *brag-dgon spyan-snga gzhon-nu chos-dpal*, 678
Trakbum, the Nepali *bal-yul-gyi grags-'bum*, 564
Trakpa Özer *grags-pa 'od-zer*, 595

Trakpapel *grags-pa dpal*, 595
Tralungpa, lama *bla-ma bkra-lung-pa*, 571
Trama, the minister of the Zhang family *zhang-drva-ma*, 515
Trampa Pöndrongpa *sram-pa bon-grong-pa*, 622, 629, 630
Trang Phurbugo of Rong *rong-gi skrang phur-bu mgo*, 714
Transcendent Lord (Buddha) *bcom-ldan-'das*, Skt. Bhagavān, 75-6, 175, 186, 188, 190, 215, 303, 312, 363, 428, 433, 454, 455, 747, 898, 944, 945; see *Buddha*
Trao Chöbum, the great learned and accomplished master *mkhas-grub chen-po bra'o chos-'bum*, 696, 700
 Trao Chöki Bumpa *bra'o chos-kyi 'bum-pa*, 699
Trao Chöki Bumpa: see preceding entry
Trapa Ngönshe (1012-90) *grva-pa mngon-shes*, 753-4, **754**, 755, 763, 950, 951
 Wangcuk Bar *dbang-phyug 'bar*, 753
Tra Pelgi Nyingpo *gra dpal-gyi snying-po*, 540, 605
Trapuṣa *ga-gon*, 421
Trashi Dorje *bkra-shis rdo-rje*, 559; see *Zhangtön (Trashi Dorje)*
Trashi Gyamtso, master *slob-dpon bkra-shis rgya-mtsho*, 687
Trashi Jungne *bkra-shis 'byung-gnas*, 792
Trashi Özer, lama (1836-1910) *bla-ma bkra-shis 'od-zer*, 777
Trashi Rincen, master *slob-dpon bkra-shis rin-chen*, 576
Trashi Topgyel (Wangpöide, the master of the Northern Treasure) *(byang-bdag) bkra-shis stobs-rgyal (dbang-po'i sde)*, 783, 808, 822; see *Cangpa Trashi Topgyel*
Trashi Tsheten, the great accomplished master *grub-chen bkra-shis tshe-brtan*, 813
Trashi Tsho, the yoginī *rnal-'byor-ma bkra-shis mtsho*, 859
Tratiwa of Kongpo *kong-po pra-ti-ba*, 811
Trayap Dongtrül Khecok Ngawang Tamcö Gyamtso *brag-yab gdong-sprul mkhas-mchog ngag-dbang dam-chos rgya-mtsho*, 868
treasure-finders, hundred *gter-ston brgya-rtsa*, 752
Tre Gangpa, master *slob-dpon bkras-sgang-pa*, 565
Trehor Choktrül (Karma Tendzin Targye) *tre-hor mchog-sprul (karma bstan-'dzin dar-rgyas)*, 833
Tremo, the nun *dge-slong-ma bre-mo*, 649
Trenka Mukti *bran-ka mu-kti*, 533
Treshongpa (Nyaktön Chögyel Dorje, the great guru) *(bla-chen) bres-gshongs-pa (gnyags-ston chos-rgyal rdo-rje)*, 717, 718
Trhaktung Nakpo *khrag-'thung nag-po*, 607, 610
Trhalaringmo, ācārya *a-tsa-ra phra-la ring-mo*, 703
Trhapa Śākya, the all-knowing *kun-mkhyen khrab-pa śā-kya*, 789
Trhengso Orgyen Chözang *phreng-so o-rgyan chos-bzang*, 807
Trhengwa, the local divinity *gzhi-bdag phreng-ba*, 645
Trhicen Trhinle Namgyel *khri-chen phrin-las rnam-rgyal*: i.e. Minling Trhicen V, 733, 734
Trhi Detsukten *khri lde-gtsug-brtan*, 521; see *Relpacen, king*
Trhinle Chödrön, the venerable lady *rje-btsun phrin-las chos-sgron*, 734
Trhinle Lhündrup (Pelzangpo, the great awareness-holder of Tarding) *(dar-lding rig-'dzin chen-po) phrin-las lhun-grub (dpal-bzang-po)*, 683, 724, 728, 733; see *Sangdak Trhinle Lhündrup (Pelzangpo)*
Trhinle Namgyel, the supreme emanation *mchog-sprul phrin-las rnam-rgyal*, 727
Trhi Pema Wangyel *khri padma dbang-rgyal*: i.e. Minling Trhicen VI, 733
Trhi Relpacen *khri ral-pa-can*, Pl. 60; 397, 521, **521**, 523, 939, 950; see *Relpacen*
Trhi Sangye Künga *khri sangs-rgyas kun-dga'*: i.e. Minling Trhicen VII, 733; see *Gyurme Sangye Künga*
Trhi, seven heavenly kings called *gnam-gyi khri bdun*: listed in the Glossary of Enumerations, 507, n. 535
Trhisong (Detsen), king *khri-srong (lde-btsan)*, Pls. 15, 60; 393, 394, 397, 405, **512**, 512-21, 522, 531, 534, 535, 538, 555, 601, 613-14, 710, 714, 734, 751, 756, 760, 768, 789, 790, 805, 807, 821, 823, 833, 835, 841, 843, 848, 849, 852, 864, 887, 888, 926, 938, 949

religious king *chos*, 968, 973
Tshangpa Lhei Metok, the religious king *chos-rgyal tshangs-pa lha'i me-tog*, 755
Trhitsün, the Nepalese princess *bal-mo-bza' khri-btsun*, Pl. 37; 510
Trhopu Lotsāwa *khro-phu lo-tsā-ba*, 564; see *Campapel*
Trhopupa *khro-phu-pa*: a teacher of Longcenpa, 576
Trhumza Shelmen *phrum-bza' shel-sman*, 537
Trhüzhi Norbu Chöten *'khrul-zhig nor-bu chos-brtan*, 724
Trhüzhi Sengegyap *'khrul-zhig seng-ge rgyab-pa*, 564-6, **565**, 567
Sangye Önpo of Sengegyap *seng-ge rgyab-pa sangs-rgyas dbon-po*, 567
Trime Künga *dri-med kun-dga'*, 935; see *Trime Lingpa*
Trime Lhünpo, the treasure-finder *gter-ston dri-med lhun-po*, 786
Trime Lingpa, the great treasure-finder *gter-chen dri-med gling-pa*, 836
Trime Künga *dri-med kun-dga'*, 935
Trime Özer *dri-med 'od-zer*, 375, 796, 818; see *Longcen Rabjampa*
Trime Özer, the son of the treasure-finder Düjom Lingpa *bdud-'joms-gter-sras dri-med 'od-zer*, 919
Trime Zhingkyong Gönpo *dri-med zhing-skyong mgon-po*, 736
Trincen Rincen Namgyel *drin-chen rin-chen rnam-rgyal*, 833; see *Gyelse Rincen Namgyel*
trio of Se, Cak and Shel *bse-lcags-shel gsum*: protectors of Vajrakīla, 714
Tröjor, lama *bla-ma drod-'byor*, 547
Trongma Peldzom *grong-ma dpal-'dzom*, 796
Trotön Pelden-tra *gro-ston dpal-ldan-grags*, 700
Trülku Chokden Gönpo *sprul-sku mchog-ldan mgon-po*, 798
Trülku Dawa *sprul-sku zla-ba*, 595
Trülku Natsok Rangdröl *sprul-sku sna-tshogs rang-grol*, 799
Trülku Öbar Senge *sprul-sku 'od-'bar seng-ge*, 552
Trülku Orgyen Peljor *sprul-sku o-rgyan dpal-'byor*, 818
Trülku Peljor Gyamtso *sprul-sku dpal-'byor rgya-mtsho*, 595
Trülku Sangye Pelden *sprul-sku sangs-rgyas dpal-ldan*: the third emanation of Sangye Lingpa, 788
Trülkuwa *sprul-sku-ba*, 574
Trülku Zhangtön *sprul-sku zhang-ston*, 559; see *Zhangtön (Trashi Dorje)*
Trum Shinglakcen *grum shing-glag-can*, 706
Trungcen Rincen Wangyel *drung-chen rin-chen dbang-rgyal*, 849
Trungpa Köncok Rincenpa *drung-pa dkon-mchog rin-chen-pa*, 679
Trung Thuje Yeshe *drung thugs-rje ye-shes*, 698, 699
Trupwang Jikme Trhinle Özer *grub-dbang 'jigs-med phrin-las 'od-zer*, 839; see *Dodrup I*
Trupwang Śākyaśrī (1853-1919) *grub-dbang śā-kya shri*, 879, 958
Trupwang Śrīnātha of Mindröling *smin-gling grub-dbang shri-nā-tha*, 836
Tsade Ce-nga(wa) Namka Dorje *tsa-sde spyan-snga(-ba) nam-mkha' rdo-rje*, 698, 699
Tsak Lama *bla-ma rtsags*, 622
"summit ridge" *rtse-lkog*, 622, 623
Tsak, lama *bla-ma rtsags*, 657
Tsak Śākring *rtsag śāk-rings*, 642
Tsangmo Rincengyen *gtsang-mo rin-chen rgyan*, 688
Tsangnak Öbar *rtsangs-nag 'od-'bar*, 660
Tsangom Hrülpo *gtsang-sgom hrul-po*, 655
Tsangpa governors/dominion *sde-srid gtsang-pa*: this refers in particular to the Tsangpa ruler Karma Tenkyong executed in 1642, but see also *Zhingshakpa (Tsheten Dorje)*, 683, 955, 956
Tsangpa Citön *rtsangs-pa byi-ston*, 649
Tsangpa Gyare (1161-1211) *gtsang-pa rgya-ras*: the first Drukcen, 953
Chöje Drukpa *chos-rje 'brug-pa*, 835
Tsangpa Peldra of the Ga clan *sga-rigs gtsang-pa dpal-sgra*, 688
Tsangpa, the preceptor *mkhan-po gtsang-pa*, 568
Tsang Rapsel *gtsang rab-gsal*, 524, 525
Tsang Śākdor *rtsangs śāk-dor*, 540
Tsangtönpa, the doctrine master (1126-1216) *chos-rje gtsang-ston-pa*: i.e. Katokpa Gyeltsap I, Tsangtönpa Dorje Gyeltsen, **692**, 691-3, 699
Manigarbha, the bodhisattva *byang-chub sems-dpa' nor-bu snying-po*, 693

Tathāgata Özer Raptutrhowa *de-bzhin gshegs-pa 'od-zer rab-tu 'phro-ba*, 693
Tsariwa, lama *bla-ma tsa-ri-ba*, 565
(Tsele) Natsok Rangdröl (b. 1608) *(rtse-le) sna-tshogs rang-grol*, 595, 812, 838
Tsele Pema Lekdrup *rtse-le padma legs-grub*, 723
Tsele Pema Lekdrup: see preceding entry
Tsen, five linking kings called *tshig-la btsan-lnga*: listed in the Glossary of Enumerations, 508, n. 535
Tsen Khawoche, the spiritual benefactor (b. 1011) *dge-bshes btsan kha-bo-che*, 545
Tsengö Chenpo, the treasure protector *gter-srung btsan-rgod chen-po*, 785
Tsengönpa, master *slob-dpon btsan-dgon-pa*, 577
Tsentangpa Nyang Dharmasiṃha *btsan-thang-pa nyang dharma-siṃha*, 550; see *Nyang Dharmasiṃha of Tsentang*
Tsetrom Cangpel *tshe-phrom byang-dpal*, 642
Tsewe Rölpei Lodrö *brtse-bas rol-pa'i blo-gros*: the ninth emanational teacher according to the Great Perfection, 137
Tshamtön Koca *mtshams-ston go-cha*, 708
Tshangpa Lhei Metok, the religious king *chos-rgyal tshangs-pa lha'i me-tog*, 755; see *Trhisong Detsen*
Tshangpa Tungtö (Brahmā Wearing a Crown of Conch Shells) *tshangs-pa dung-thod*: a form of Pehar, protector of the Yangdak maṇḍala, 620-1
Tshangyang Gyamtso, the awareness-holder (1683-1706) *rig-'dzin tshangs-dbyangs rgya-mtsho*: i.e. Dalai Lama VI, 824
Tshargu Kyide *mtshar-dgu skyid-bde*, 543
Tshar Tengpa *mtshar-stengs-pa*, 569
Tshelpa Situ Mönlam Dorje *tshal-pa si-tu smon-lam rdo-rje*, 893
Tshenamza Sangye Tsho *tshe-nam-bza' sangs-rgyas mtsho*, 536
Tshenden Yidzin *mtshan-ldan yid-'dzin*, 679
Tshenden Zurmo Öbum *mtshan-ldan zur-mo 'od-'bum*, 635
Tshepong-za, queen *btsun-mo tshe-spong bza'*, 601
Margyen, queen *btsan-po yum dmar-rgyan*, 603
Tshering Yangtso *tshe-ring gYang-mtsho*, 841
Tshewang Norgye, a master of the Khön family *'khon-rigs slob-dpon tshe-dbang nor-rgyas*, 677
Rikdzin Tshewang Norgye *rig-'dzin tshe-dbang nor-rgyas*, 926
Tshewang Trakpa *tshe-dbang grags-pa*, 735
Tshogyel *mtsho-rgyal*, 518, 586; see *(Yeshe) Tshogyel*
Tshojung Gyepei Langtso Tsuklak Mawei Nyima (Joyous Youth of the Lake-born Lotus, the Sun amongst Proponents of Scripture) *mtsho-byung dgyes-pa'i lang-tsho gtsug-lag smra-ba'i nyi-ma*, 972; see *Dudjom Rinpoche*
Tshokpa Chölungpa *tshogs-pa chos-lung-pa*, 667
Tshombuza Pematsho *tshom-bu-bza' padma mtsho*, 536
Tshozang Mikpoche *mtsho-bzang mig-po-che*, 617
Tshül Gyelwa, lama *bla-ma tshul rgyal-ba*, 687
Tshültrim Dorje *tshul-khrims rdo-rje*, 735, 956; see *Lhodrak Sungtrül III*
Tshültrim Lodrö *tshul-khrims blo-gros*, 576; see *Longcen Rabjampa*
Tshültrim Pel *tshul-khrims dpal*, 805
Tshültrim Peljor, the great preceptor of the Conangpa residence *jo-gdan mkhan-chen tshul-khrims dpal-'byor*, 798
Tshültrim Zangpo *tshul-khrims bzang-po*, 804
Tshurpu Gyeltsap VI, (Norbu Zangpo) (1659-98) *mtshur-phu rgyal-tshab (nor-bu bzang-po)*, 833
Tshurtön, father and son *mtshur-ston yab-sras*, 762
Tshurtön Yige *tshur-ston dbyig-ge*, 706
Tsöndru Wangcuk, lama *bla-ma brtson-'grus dbang-phyug*, 552
Tsongkapa, venerable/Je *rje tsong-kha-pa* (1357-1419), 204, 395, 923, 925, 929, 954
Jamgön Lozang Trakpa *'jam-mgon blo-bzang grags-pa*, 954
Jamgön Tsongkapa *'jam-mgon tsong-kha-pa*, 925, 930
Je Guru *rje gu-ru*, 925
Tsuklak Gyamtso *gtsug-lag rgya-mtsho*: i.e. Pawo III, 724
Tsuklak Pelge *gtsug-lag dpal-dge*, 489, 607
Tsukru Rincen Zhönu *gtsug-ru rin-chen gzhon-nu*, 533

Tu Dorje Gyeltsen, (lama) *(bla-ma) du rdo-rje rgyal-mtshan*, 550, 552
Tuwa, master *slob-dpon du-ba*, 551
(Tumpa) Gya Zhangtrom (b. 1016) *(dum-pa) rgya zhang-khrom*, 713, 765
Tungkyong, the nāga *klu dung-skyong*, 623
Tungtrengcen, the yogin *rnal-'byor-pa dung-phreng-can*, 815
Turtröpa *dur-khrod-pa*, 686
Tutön Tepa Tsöndrü *du-ston dad-pa brtson-'grus*, 552
Tutön Vajreśvara *du-ston badzra-shva-ra*, 552
Tuwa, master *slob-dpon du-ba*, 551; see *Tu Dorje Gyeltsen*
twelve goddesses of the earth *brtan-ma bcu-gnyis*, 513, 537, 715
twelve Mātaraḥ *ma-mo bcu-gnyis*, 481
twelve masters who were renowned at Vikramaśīla *rnam-gnon tshul-gyi bsngags-pa'i slob-dpon bcu-gnyis*: listed in the Glossary of Enumerations, 442
twelve teachers of the emanational body *sprul-sku'i ston-pa bcu-gnyis*, 22, 134-8
twenty-five ḍākinīs who attained bodies of light *'od-skur gshegs-pa'i mkha'-'gro nyer-lnga*, 537
twenty-five great accomplished masters of Chimpu *mchims-phu'i grub-chen nyer-lnga*, Pl. 26; 534-7
twenty-one genyen *dge-bsnyen nyer-gcig*: listed in the Glossary of Enumerations, 513
two "great meditators" *sgom-chen mi gnyis*, 640, 642
two "Jamgons" *'jam-mgon rnam gnyis*: i.e. Jamyang Khyentse Wangpo and Jamgön Kongtrül, 864, 868
two marvellous masters *rmad-byung-gi slob-dpon gnyis*: i.e. Śāntideva and Candragomin, 441
two nāga demons of Wokdong, brother and sister *'og-gdong klu-bdud ming-sring gnyis*, 632
two promulgators *shing-rta gnyis*: i.e. Nāgārjuna and Asaṅga, 180, 300-1, 849; see also *two supreme ones*
two "simple ones" *dkyus-pa gnyis*, 640
two supreme ones *mchog-gnyis*: i.e. Nāgārjuna and Asaṅga, 441; see also *two promulgators*
two "venerable ones" *sta-gu-ra mi gnyis*, 640, 642
Udraka *lhag-spyod*, 419, 422
Udrenpa, lama *bla-ma dbu-'dren-pa*, 547
Uighur *hor*, 524
Ukpalungpa, lama/lharje *bla-ma/lha-rje 'ug-pa lung-pa*, 621, 632, 635; see *(Zurpoche) Śākya Jungne*
Ulkāmukha, the yakṣa *gnod-sbyin skar-mda' gdong*, 453, 454
Umdze Töndrup Pelbar *dbu-mdzad don-grub dpal-'bar*, 799
Üpa Chöseng *dbus-pa chos-seng*, 649
Upagupta *nyer-sbas*, 93, 435, 436-7, **437**
Upajīvaka *nye-bar 'tsho*, 422
Upāli *nye-bar-'khor*, 428
Uparāja *nye-bar rgyal-po/upa-rā-dza*, 460, 462, 485
Śakrabhūti *śa-kra-bu-ti*, 462
Uparāja, king *u-pa-rā-dza*, 490, 492
Üpa Sator *dbus-pa sa-'thor*, 642
Üpa Tosel *dbus-pa do-gsal*, 605
Upāyaśrīmitra *u-pa-ya shri mi-tra*, 708
Upper Mongols *stod-hor*: the Ilkhan dynasty, 664
Ilkhans *stod-hor*, 664
Urtön Lama Tshartön *dbur-ston bla-ma mtshar-ston*, 657
Uru Zhölma Gecok *dbu-ru gzhol-ma dge-mchog*, 556
Use, the venerable *rje dbu-se*, 689; see *Karmapa I*
Utsewa Jamyang Rincen Gyeltsen *dbu-rtse-ba 'jam-dbyangs rin-chen rgyal-mtshan*, 717
Uttara *bla-ma*, 440
Uwö(pa) Yeshebum (b. 1254) *dbu-'od(-pa) ye-shes 'bum*: i.e. Katokpa Gyeltsap IV, 695
Uyukpa Datön *u-yug-pa mda'-ston*, 708
Vādīsiṃha *smra(-ba'i) seng(-ge)*, 869; see *Mañjuśrī in the form of Vādīsiṃha*
Vāgbhaṭa, 99
Vāgīśvarakīrti *ngag-gi dbang-phyug grags-pa*, 467
Vairocana (Buddha) *(sangs-rgyas) rnam-par snang-mdzad*, Pl. 4; 19, 20, 117, 125, 215, 274, 355, 409, 449, 477, 639, 756, 766, 859
Sarvavid-Vairocana *kun-rig(s) rnam-snang*, 624
Tathāgata Vairocana, king of form *de-bzhin gshegs-pa gzugs-kyi rgyal-po*, 128, 221

Vairocana the Great Glacial Lake (of Pristine Cognition) *rnam-par snang-mdzad (ye-shes) gangs-chen mtsho*, Skt. Vairocana *Jñānamahāhimasāgara, 118, 123, 130, 409, 961

Vairocana-Samantamukha *rnam-par kun-tu zhal*, 623

Vairocana, (the translator) *bai-ro-tsa-na*, Pl. 28; 394, 397, 515, 522, 527, 533, 535, **539**, 538-40, 554, 601, 684, 688, 706, 747, 728, 734, 753, 756, 760, 789, 791, 825, 829, 859, 889, 920, 944

Vaiśravaṇa *bai-sra-ma-ṇa/rnam-thos-sras*, 516, 713

Vajradhara *rdo-rje 'dzin*, 75, 313, 403, 453, 462

Vajradhara, (the Sixth Conqueror/teacher) *(drug-pa) rdo-rje 'chang*, 113, **121**, 120-2, 136, 257, 274, 282, 404, 414, 447, 448, 503, 521, 892, 913, 961

Vajradharma *rdo-rje chos*: a peaceful form of Vajrapāṇi, 68, 90, **450**, 451, 482; see *Vajrapāṇi*

Vajradhātu ḍākinī (the Ḍākinī of the Indestructible Expanse) *rdo-rje dbyings-kyi mkha'-'gro-ma*, 493

Vajrāditya *rdo-rje nyi-ma*, 274

Vajragarbha *rdo-rje snying-po*: author of the *Commentary which Epitomises the Hevajra Tantra*, 451

Vajragarbha *rdo-rje snying-po*: the bodhisattva, 75, 451, 912

Vajragarbha Buddha *rdo-rje snying-po*, 798; see *Pema Lingpa*

Vajrahāsya *rdo-rje bzhad-pa/ba-dzra hasya*, 466-7, 468, 488, 533

Vajra Heruka *badzra he-ru-ka*, 476; see *Yangdak Heruka*

Vajrakīla *rdo-rje phur-pa*, 283, 362, 468, 472, 481, **482**, 535, 548, 601, 603, 604, 606, 616, 620, 685, 709, 710-16, **716**, 762, 780, 828, 839, 854, 920, 922, 936; see also Bibliography

  Vajrakumāra *rdo-rje gzhon-nu*, 481, 713, 829

Vajrakumāra: see preceding entry

Vajrāmṛta *rdo-rje bdud-rtsi*: the embodiment of enlightened attributes, **480**, 480-1, 601

  Nectar the Enlightened Attributes *bdud-rtsi yon-tan*, 283, 362; see also Bibliography

Vajranātha *rdo-rje mgon-po*, 676

Vajrapāṇi *phyag-na rdo-rje/phyag-rdor/rdo-rje 'dzin-pa*, 125, 135, 282, 306, 431, 441, 449, 452, **453**, 454, 459-60, 490, 510, 521, 549, 563, 564, 646, 647, 648, 693, 698, 728, 734, 758, 762, 810, 923, 925; see also *Lords of the Three (Enlightened) Families*

  Guhyapati/Lord of Secrets *gsang(-ba'i) bdag(-po)*, 282, 377, 405, 430, 441, 451, 454, 458, 459, 460, 485, 490, 609, 645, 648, 734, 728, 923, 925, 948

  Vajradharma *rdo-rje chos*: a peaceful form of Vajrapāṇi, 68, 90, **450**, 451, 482

Vajrapāṇi *badzra pa-ṇi*: disciple of Nyang Dharmasiṃha, 552

Vajrapāṇi, the Indian (b. 1017) *rgya-gar phyag-na*, 692

Vajrapāṇi, the yakṣa *gnod-sbyin lag-na rdo-rje*, 453

Vajraphala *badzra pha-la*, 563

Vajra Queen *rdo-rje btsun-mo*, Skt. Vajrayoṣit, 125, 404, 449, 772

Vajrasattva *rdo-rje sems-dpa'*: the buddha-body of perfect rapture, Pl. 3; 122, **256**, 258, 261, 274, 403, 453, 459, 460, 490, 493, 498, 567, 632, 639, 640, 648, 663, 670, 762, 763, 791, 829, 916, 917

Vajravarāhī *rdo-rje phag-mo*, 469, 536, 548, 569, 570, 581-3, 584, 772, 784, 786

  red Varāhī *phag-dmar*, 567

  Varāhī *phag-mo*, 451, 567, 663

  white Varāhī *phag-dkar*, 577

Vajrayoginī *rdo-rje rnal-'byor-ma*, 829

Vālmīki *grogs-mkhar*, 66

Vanaratna, the great scholar/paṇḍita (1384-1468) *paṇ-chen nags-kyi rin-chen/paṇ-chen ba-na ratna*, 455, 674

Varāhī *phag-mo*, 451, 567, 663; see *Vajravarāhī*

Varāhī, red *phag-dmar*, 567; see *Vajravarāhī*

Varāhī, white *phag-dkar*, 577; see *Vajravarāhī*

Vasubandhu *dbyig-gnyen*, 71, 91, **157**, 301, 440, 703, 944

Vasudhara, (king of Nepal) *(bal-po'i rgyal-po) ba-su-dha-ra*, 489, 537, 607, 608, 610

Vasudharā *nor-rgyun-ma*, 494

Vasukalpa, king *rgyal-po ba-su kalpa*, 442

Vasumitra *ba-su mi-tra/dbyigs-bshes*, 90, 430
Vātsīputra, the elder *gnas-brtan ma'i bu*, 430
Vemacitra *thag-bzang-ris*, 130, 132
Vidyā, the transcendent lady *bcom-ldan-'das-ma rig-byed-ma*, 824; see *Kurukullā*
Vidyāvajra *rig-pa'i rdo-rje*, 459
Vidyutprabha *glog-gi 'od*, 121
Vigataśoka *mya-ngan-bral*, 429
Vimalakīrti the Licchavi *li-tsā-bi dri-ma med-par grags-pa*, 454, 460, 485
Vimala(mitra) *bi-ma-la (mi-tra)/dri-med bshes-gnyen*, 38, 39, 63, 77, 92, 278, 342, 394, 480-1, 483, 497-501, **500**, 515, 533, 534, 554, 555-6, 558, 559, 561, 567, 572, 573, 581, 582, 583, 585, 588-9, 594, 601, 603, 604, 607, 649, 707, 714, 733, 734, 735, 736, 747, 751, 760, 818, 829, 835, 843, 847, 849, 854, 855, 858, 887, 889, 890, 921, 922, 944
Vimalatejas *dri-med gzi-brjid*, 743, 747, 928
Vimukticandra *rnam-grol zla-ba*, 75
Vīrasena, king *dpa'-bo'i sde*, 429
Virūpa *bi-ru-pa*, 395, 471, 473, 853, 927
Viśākhā, the laywoman *dge-bsnyen-ma sa-ga*, 423
Viṣṇu *khyab-'jug*, 16, 65-6
Viśvamitra *bi-shva mi-tra*, 533, 915, 916
Viśvarūpa *sna-tshogs gzugs-can*, 463, 464; see *Līlāvajra*
Viśvarūpī, a great ogress *srin-mo chen-mo vishva-ru-pī*, 455
Vitapāda, 313
Vyākaraṇavajra *lung-bstan rdo-rje*, 485; see *Ja*
Wangcuk Bar *dbang-phyug 'bar*, 753; see *Trapa Ngönshe*
Wangcuk Dorje *dbang-phyug rdo-rje*: a form of Guru Rinpoche, 755; see *Guru Rinpoche*
Wangcuk Pelwa *dbang-phyug dpal-ba*: one of the Katokpa Gyeltsaps, refer to the Glossary of Enumerations under *thirteen generations of the gurus of Katok*, 695
Wangdrakpa Gyeltsen *dbang-grags-pa rgyal-mtshan*, 674
Wangtsül, master *slob-dpon dbang-tshul*, 578
Wang-ye, master *slob-dpon dbang-ye*, 576
Wangyelwa *dbang rgyal-ba*, 686
We Jampel *dbas 'jam-dpal*, 533
We Lodrö *dbas blo-gros*, 556
Wen-ch'eng K'ong-jo, the Chinese princess *rgya-mo-bza' 'un-shing kong-jo*, Pl. 39; 510
White Tārā *sgrol-dkar*, 857, 874; see *Tārā*
wrathful deities, male and female *khro-bo khro-mo*, 125-6, 623; see also *peaceful and wrathful deities*
Yab Ngöndzok Gyelpo *yab mngon-rdzogs rgyal-po*: the eleventh emanational teacher according to the Great Perfection, 137
Yakde Düldzin Khyenrap Gyamtso *gYag-sde 'dul-'dzin mkhyen-rab rgya-mtsho*, 965
Yakde Paṇcen (1299-1378) *gYag-sde paṇ-chen*, 579, 667, 787, 929
Yak Dorje Dzinpa *gYag rdo-rje 'dzin-pa*, 709
Yaktön Dawa Özer of Pung-ring *spung-ring gYag-ston zla-ba 'od-zer*, 550, 552
Yama *gshin-rje/gshin-po-gshed*, 130, 661
Yamāntaka *gshin-rje gshed*, Pl. 17; 477-8, **478**, 483, 609, 610, 611, **611**, 614, 662, 666, 713-14, 762, 828
  Mañjuśrī the Body *'jam-dpal sku*, 283, 361
  Mañjuśrī, Lord of Life *'jam-dpal tshe-bdag*, 610
  Mañjuśrī-Yamāntaka (Lord of Life) *'jam-dpal ya-mānta-ka (tshe-bdag)/ 'jam-dpal gshin-rje*, 478, 876
Yamāri, (black and red) *gshin-rje (dmar-nag)*, 614, 615; see also Bibliography
Yamcö Ngödrup, master *slob-dpon yam-chos dngos-grub*, 701
Yamdrok, the myriarch of *yar-'brog khri-dpon*, 821
Yamdrokza Chöki Drönma *yar-'brog-bza' chos kyi sgron-ma*, 537
Yamshü *yam-shud*, 701
Yamshü Gyelwa-ö *yam-shud rgyal-ba 'od*, 753
Yangdak Heruka *yang-dag he-ru-ka*, Skt. Śrīheruka, Pl. 19; 472, 473, 475-7, 481, 516, 534, 535, 617, 619, 620, 623, 624, 625, 626-8, **627**, 630, 633, 710, 828, 829, 922
  Glorious Heruka/Śrīheruka *dpal he-ru-ka*, 475-7, 691
  Great Glorious (Yangdak Heruka) *dpal-chen-po (yang-dag he-ru-ka)*, 617, 621, 623, 625-8, 630, 631-2, 634-5, 639, 643, 644

Heruka *he-ru-ka*, 274, 404, 442, 534, 545, 626, 628, 893, 931
Nine-Lamp Yangdak *yang-dag mar-me-dgu*, 685
Vajra Heruka *badzra he-ru-ka*, 476
Yangdak Heruka, nine-deity maṇḍala of *yang-dag lha-dgu*, 621, 669
Yangdak the Mind *yang-dag thugs*, 283, 361, 475, 923
Yang-gönpa (Gyeltsenpel) (1213-58) *yang-dgon-pa (rgyal-mtshan-dpal)*, 571, 922
Yangkeng (Lama) of Kyonglung *skyong-lung-gi yang-kheng (bla-ma)*, 642, 647
Yangkye Lama (of Shap) *(shab-kyi) yang-khyed bla-ma*, 708, 709
Yangtrö Tshültrim Gyeltsen *yang-khrod tshul-khrim rgyal-mtshan*, 699
Yangwangter *yang-dbang gter*, 613; see *Nup(cen) Sangye Yeshe*
Yaśaḥ *grags(-pa)*, 93, 429, 436, 440
Yaśasvī Varapāla, the deva/god *grags-ldan mchog-skyong*, 452, 454
Yaśasvī Varapāla, the yakṣa *grags-ldan mchog-skyong*, 453
Yaśodharā *grags-'dzin-ma*, 417, 418, 946
Yatri Tarma Sherap *ya-phri dar-ma shes-rab*, 540
(Ya)zi Pöntön *(ya-)zi bon-ston*, 706
Yedrak *ye-grags*, 706
Yegön, master *slob-dpon ye-dgon*, 571
Yegyelwa (the bodhisattva) *(byangs-sems) ye-rgyal-ba*, 574, 674
Yerwapa, the preceptor *mkhan-po yer-ba-pa*, 569
Yeshe-chok, the translator *lo-tsā-ba ye-shes mchog*, 692
Yeshe Dorje *ye-shes rdo-rje*, 788
Yeshe Gyamtso *ye-shes rgya-mtsho*, 615
Yeshe Gyeltsen, king *ye-shes rgyal-mtshan*, 524
Yeshe Gyeltsen *ye-shes rgyal-mtshan*, 698; see *(Khedrup) Yeshe Gyeltsen (of Pubor)*
Yeshe Jungne *ye-shes 'byung-gnas*, 616; see *(Nyang) Yeshe Jungne (of Chölung)*
Yeshe Kongpel, the preceptor of Gyüme *rgyud-smad mkhan-po ye-shes gong-'phel*, 868
Yeshe Rölpatsel *ye-shes rol-pa rtsal*, 841; see *Murup Tsepo (Yeshe Rölpatsel)*
(Yeshe) Tshogyel *(ye-shes) mtsho-rgyal*, Pls. 16, 27; 394, 518, 586, 587, **711**, 710-12, 734, 746-7, 755, 757, 771, 773, 790, 791, 810, 829, 835, 854, 864
Khandro Yeshe Tshogyel *mkha'-'gro ye-shes mtsho-rgyal*, 554
Kharcen(-za) Yeshe Tshogyel *mkhar-chen(-bza') ye-shes mtsho-rgyal*, 535, 536, 710-11, 714
Yeshe Wangcuk *ye-shes dbang-phyug*, 613, 616; see *(So) Yeshe Wangcuk*
Yeshe Wangpo *ye-shes dbang-po*, 515; see *Ba Selnang*
Yeshe Wangposung *ye-shes dbang-po srung*, 575; *Gyelwa Choyang*
Yesheyang, master *slob-dpon ye-shes dbyangs*, 535
Yezang Tsepa *ye-bzang rtse-pa*, 674-5; see *Gölo(tsāwa) Zhönupel*
Yo Gejung *gYo dge-'byung*, 524, 525
Yöndopa Trashi Lhündrup *yon-do-pa bkra-shis lhun-grub*, 723
Yongdzin Ngawang Trakpa *yongs-'dzin ngag-dbang grags-pa*, 722
Yöntengön, lama *bla-ma yon-tan mgon*, 665
Yönten Gyamtso, the conqueror (1589-1617) *rgyal-ba yon-tan rgya-mtsho*: i.e. Dalai Lama IV, 821
Yönten Gyamtso *yon-tan rgya-mtsho*, 613, 616; see *Nup Khulungpa (Yönten Gyamtso)*
Yönten Wangcuk of Catarlamo *bya-tar la-mo pa yon-tan dbang-phyug*, 702
Yöntenzung, (1126-95) *yon-tan gzungs*, 651, 654, 659
(Lama) Lhakangpa *(bla-ma) lha-khang-pa*, 655, 659
Yudra Nyingpo *gYu-sgra snying-po*, 524, 526, 540, 555, 601, 684, 706, 728, 733, 833
Gyelmo Yudra Nyingpo *rgyal-mo(-rong-gi) gYu-grags snying-po*, 535
Yudrönma *gYu-sgron-ma*, 586, 587, 588; see *(Dorje) Yudrönma*
Yudruk Dorje *gYu-'brug rdo-rje*, 722; see *(Rikdzin) Yudruk Dorje*
Yugom Cobar *gYu-sgom jo-'bar*, 622
Yülgom Nakmo *yul-sgom nag-mo*, 622
Yumo *yu-mo*, 546
Yungdrung Lingpa *gYung-drung gling-pa*, 791; see *Dorje Lingpa*
Yung-lo, the emperor (reigned 1403-24) *ye-dbang*: the third Ming emperor (*ta-ming*), 438

Yungtön(pa) Dorjepel (1284-1365) *gYung-ston(pa) rdo-rje dpal*, 40, 348, 574, 664, 665, 666-7, **667**, 671, 677, 680, 684, 730, 953
  Dorjebum *rdo-rje 'bum*, 667
Yutok Yönten Gönpo (1127-1203) *gYu-thog yon-tan mgon-po*, 753
  Yutokpa *gYu-thog-pa*, 99
Yutön Horpo *gYu-ston hor-po*, 649
Zadam Rincen-yik *za-dam rin-chen dbyig*, 541
Zalungpa, (the accomplished master) *(grub-thob) za-lung-pa*, 566, 567, 576
Zam, master *slob-dpon zam*, 550
Zangom Sherap Gyelpo *bzang-sgom shes-rab rgyal-po*, 620, 622, 631
Zangpo Trakpa of Manglam *mang-lam bzang-po grags-pa*, 780
Zang-ri Drore *zangs-ri 'bro-ras*, 657
Zang-ri Gyare *zangs-ri rgya-ras*, 657
Zangtön Hordra *bzang-ston hor-grags*, 657
Zere Zetsen, the local divinity *gzhi-bdag ze-re ze-btsan*, 621
Zermo Gelong *zer-mo dge-slong*, 540
Zhakla Khedrup Yeshe Bumpa *bzhag-bla mkhas-grub ye-shes 'bum-pa*, 699
Zhalu Locen of Tratang *gra-thang-pa'i zhva-lu lo-chen*, 807
Zhalu Sonam Chokdrup (1602-81) *zhva-lu bsod-nams mchog-grub*, 822
Zhamarpa II, Khacö Wangpo (1350-1405) *zhva-dmar-pa mkha'-spyod dbang-po*, 787
Zhamarpa IV, Chöki Trakpa (1453-1524) *zhva-dmar bzhi-pa chos-kyi grags-pa*, 675-6
  Ce-nga Chöki Trakpa *spyan-snga chos-kyi grags-pa*, 553
  Ce-nga Rinpoche *spyan-snga rin-po-che*, 675-6
  Chöki Trakpa Yeshe Pelzangpo *chos-kyi grags-pa ye-shes dpal-bzang-po*, 675
Zhamarpa V, Köncok Yenlak (1525-83) *zhva-dmar-pa dkon-mchog yan-lag*, 798
Zhamar VI, Chöki Wangcuk (1584-1635) *zhva-dmar chos-kyi dbang-phyug/kar-ma-pa zhva-dmar*, 723, 811
Zhang Dronyön *zhang 'gro-smyon*, 547
Zhang family *zhang-rigs*, 515
Zhang Göcung(wa) *zhang 'gos-chung(-ba)*, 622, 631
Zhang Gyelwei Yönten *zhang rgyal-ba'i yon-tan*, 533, 608
Zhanglön *zhang-blon*: i.e. the yakṣa Zhanglön Dorje Düdül, 753
Zhangmo Yöntengyen *zhang-mo yon-tan rgyan*, 622
Zhangom Dharmakīrti *zhang-sgom dharma ki-rti*, 836
Zhang Tarmatra *zhang dar-ma grags*, 952; see *Zhang (Tshelpa Rinpoche)*
Zhangtön *zhang-ston*, 649
Zhangtön Namka Dorje *zhang-ston nam-mkha' rdo-rje*, 720-1
  Namdingpa, lama *bla-ma gnam-sdings-pa*, 721
Zhangtön Ngase *zhang-ston sngags-se*, 642
Zhangtön (Trashi Dorje) (1097-1167) *zhang-ston (bkra-shis rdo-rje)*, **559**, 559-61
  Trashi Dorje *bra-shis rdo-rje*, 559
  Trülku Zhangtön *sprul-sku zhang-ston*, 559
Zhang (Tshelpa Rinpoche), lama (1122/3-93) *bla-ma zhang (tshal-pa rin-po-che)*, 201-2, 576, 649, 655, 683, 761
  Zhang Tarmatra *zhang dar-ma grags*, 952
  Zhang, the "Unborn" *'gro-mgon skye-med zhang*, 683
  Zhang Yudrakpa *zhang gYu-brag-pa*, 562, 921
Zhang, the "Unborn": see preceding entry
Zhang Yeshe De *zhang ye-shes sde*, 515, 522, 889, 893
  Jñānasena, the translator *lo-tsā-ba dznya-na se-na*, 522
  (Nanam) Zhang Yeshe De *(sna-nam-)zhang ye-shes sde*, 535
Zhang Yudrakpa *zhang gYu-brag-pa*, 562, 921; see *Zhang (Tshelpa Rinpoche)*
Zhangzhang Yönten-tra *zhang-zhang yon-tan grags*, 706
Zhapdrung Chongye *zhabs-drung 'phyong-rgyas*, 595
Zhapdrung Norbu Gyenpa *zhabs-drung nor-bu rgyan-pa*, 809; see *Gampopa (Zhapdrung) Norbu Gyenpa*
Zhapdrung I, Thucen Ngawang Namgyel of Bhutan (1594-1651) *lho-'brug zhabs-drung mthu-chen ngag-dbang rnam-rgyal*, 788
  Lhodruk Zhapdrung Ngawang Namgyel *lho-'brug zhabs-drung ngag-dbang rnam-rgyal*, 956

Zhapdrung of Tsedong along with his successor *rtse-gdong zhabs-drung khu-dbon*, 833

Zhapdrung Yizhin Lekdrup *zhabs-drung yid-bzhin legs-grub*, 833

Zhecen Gyeltsap, Gyurme Pema Namgyel (1871-1926) *zhe-chen rgyal-tshab 'gyur-med padma rnam-rgyal*, 41, 375, 879, 919

Zhecen Rapjam I, Tenpei Gyeltsen *zhe-chen rab-'byams bstan-pa'i rgyal-mtshan*, 737

Zhecen Rapjam IV, (Karwang Chöki Gyeltsen) *zhe-chen rab-'byams*, 879

Zheldam, lama *bla-ma zhal-gdams*, 548

Zhenpen Chöki Nangwa, the great preceptor of Dzokcen (1871-1927) *rdzogs-chen mkhan-chen gzhan-phan chos-kyi snang-ba*: i.e. Khenpo Zhe-nga, 919

Zhikpo of Central Tibet *dbus-pa zhig-po*, 651, 652-3

Zhikpo (Dütsi) (d. 1199) *zhig-po (bdud-rtsi)*, 653-6, 657-8, 659, 759

Zhikpo Lingpa, the treasure-finder (1524-83) *gter-ston zhig-po gling-pa*, 722

Zhikpo Lingpa *zhig-po gling-pa*, 794; see *Ratna Lingpa*

Zhikpo Nyima Senge *zhig-po nyi-ma seng-ge*: a student of Padampa Sangye, 757

Zhikpo Nyiseng *zhig-po nyi-seng*, 929

Zhikpo Nyiseng: see preceding entry

Zhingshakpa (Tsheten Dorje), the governor of Tsang *sde-srid gtsang-pa zhing-shag-pa (tshe-brtan rdo-rje)*: rose to power in 1565, 783, n. 1046

Zhiwa Zangpo *zhi-ba bzang-po*, 731

Zhöndor *gzhon-rdor*, 577

Zhöndor of Shuksep-ri *shug-gseb-ri gzhon-rdor*, 578

Zhöngyel, master *slob-dpon gzhon-rgyal*, 577

Zhönubum *gzhon-nu 'bum*, 565

Zhönu Gyelpo *gzhon-nu rgyal-po*, 569; see *Kumārādza*

Zhönu Rölpa Nampar Tsewa *gzhon-nu rol-pa rnam-par brtse-ba*: the fourth emanational teacher according to the Great Perfection, 136

Zhönupel, the preceptor *mkhan-po gzhon-nu dpal*, 784

Zhönu Sangye *gzhon-nu sangs-rgyas*, 588, 595

Zhönu Sherap, the great preceptor *mkhan-chen gzhon-nu shes-rab*, 552

Zhönu Töndrup *gzhon-nu don-grub*, 577

Zhönu Trakpa, master *slob-dpon gzhon-nu grags-pa*, 552

Zhutön Sonam Śākya *zhu-ston bsod-nams śā-kya*, 619

Zicen of Lake Manasarovar, the nāga *klu'i ma-dros gzhi-can*, 514

Zijibar *gzi-brjid 'bar*, 709

Zik Yeshe (Wang)po *gzig ye-shes (dbang-)po*, 550, 552

Zilnön Namkei Dorje, the great treasure-finder *gter-chen zil-gnon nam-mkha'i rdo-rje*, 919

Zilungpa (Śākya Chokden), the great paṇḍita *paṇ-chen zi-lung-pa (śā-kya mchog-ldan)*, 931; see *Śākya Chokden*

Zitön Sogyel of Latö *la-stod zi-ston bsod-rgyal*, 642

Ziza Tecok *zi-bza' des-chog*, 551

"Zombie" Sukhasiddhi *ro-langs bde-ba'i dngos-grub*, 466; see *Garap Dorje*

Zur Atsara *zur atsa-ra*, 617

(Zur) Campa Senge *(zur) byams-pa seng-ge*, 663-5, **664**, 666, 667, 669

(Zurcen) Chöying Rangdröl (1604-57/69) *(zur-chen) chos-dbyings rang-grol*, 678, **680**, 679-83, 684, 720, 724, 821, 822

Zurcen Zhönu Töndrup *zur-chen gzhon-nu don-grub*, 679

Zurcung(pa Sherap-tra/Trakpa) (1014-74) *zur-chung(-pa shes-rab grags-pa)*, 346, 358, 617, 622, 624-31, 634, **636**, 635-45, 646-7, 674, 950, 951

  Deshek Gyawo(pa) *bde-gshegs rgya-bo(-pa)*, 635, 641

  Deshek Zurcungpa *bde-gshegs zur-chung-pa*, 643

Zur (Dropukpa) Śākya Senge (1074-1135) *zur (sgro-phug-pa) śā-kya seng-ge*, 540, 624, 645-9, **646**, 688

  Dropukpa, (lord of secrets) *(gsang-bdag) sgro-phug-pa*, 346, 646-9, 650, 651, 660, 677, 685, 701, 728, 952

  Lharje (Horpo) Dropukpa *lha-rje (hor-po) sgro-phug-pa*, 648, 649

  Lharje Nyariwa *lha-rje nya-ri-ba*, 701

  Śākya Senge *śā-kya seng-ge*, 646

Zur family *zur-rigs*, 47, 139, 266, 397, 599, 617-49, 660-5, 669-72, 676-7, 679-83, 691, 696, 701, 727, 728, 730, 827, 919

Zur Gomcung *zur sgom-chung*, 617

Zurgom Dorje Jungne *zur-sgom rdo-rje 'byung-gnas*, 617
Zurgom Dorjung *zur-sgom rdor-'byung*, 622
Zurgom Dorjung: see preceding entry
Zur Gyelwa Sumdra *zur rgyal-ba gsum-sgrags*, 617
(Zur Ham) Śākya Jungne *(zur-ham) śā-kya 'byung-gnas*, 669, **670**, 671-2, 717, 720
Zur Śākya Jungne of Yangen *yan-dben-pa'i zur śā-kya 'byung-gnas*, 668, 700
Zur Khacenlakcen *zur kha-can lag-can*, 617
Zurlungpa Druptop Shenyen *zur-lung-pa grub-thob bshes-gnyen*, 665
Zurmo (Gendünbum) *zur-mo (dge-'dun 'bum)*, 700, 720
Zurnak Khorlo *zur-nag 'khor-lo*, 648
(Zur) Nyima Senge *(zur) nyi-ma seng-ge*, 663-4
Zur Pakshi *zur pak-shi*, 671; see *Zur Zangpopel*
Zur(pa) Śākya-ö *zur(-pa) śā-kya 'od*, 662
Pakshi Śākya-ö *pak-shi śā-kya 'od*, 660-3
Śakya-ö/Öpo, the teacher *ston-pa śā-kya 'od(-po)*, 660, 662-3
Zurpa Shenyen Takdracen *zur-pa bshes-gnyen stag-sgra-can*, 617
(Zurpoche) Śākya Jungne, (lama/lharje) (10th-11th centuries) *(bla-ma/lha-rje) (zur-po-che) śā-kya 'byung-gnas*, 616, **618**, 617-38, 643, 671, 914
Deshek Zurpoche *bde-gshegs zur-po-che*, 918
Ukpalungpa, lama/lharje *bla-ma/lha-rje 'ug-pa lung-pa*, 621, 632, 635
Zur Śākya Jungne of Yangen *yang-dben-pa'i zur śā-kya 'byung-gnas*, 668, 700; see *(Zur Ham) Śākya Jungne*
Zur Śākya Senge *zur śā-kya seng-ge*: see *Zur (Dropukpa) Śākya Senge*
(Zur) Thakpa Gomcen *(zur) thag-pa sgom-chen*, 617, 635
Zurtön Lama *zur-ston bla-ma*, 617
Zurtön Śākya Shenyen *zur-ston śā-kya bshes-gnyen*, 700
Zur Wangcen Öpoche *zur dbang-chen 'od-po-che*, 660
Zur Zangpopel *zur bzang-po dpal*, 669-71
Zur Pakshi *zur pak-shi*, 671
Zurzang Sherap Jungne *zur-bzang shes-rab 'byung-gnas*, 617

Index of Locations

Introduction

The locations listed in this index include both the Indian and Tibetan geographical sites enumerated in Section One and those buddhafields and non-human realms to which the original texts refer. Since, however, the majority of entries relate to Tibet, the following introduction is intended as a brief explanation of the formation of Tibetan place names, and of our treatment of them here.

The mountainous terrain of Tibet provides the Tibetan language with a number of technical geographical terms usually appended to place names as an affix. For example, *-cu* (*chu*) indicates a river, *-do* (*mdo*) a confluence of rivers, *-tso* (*mtsho*) a lake and *-ka* (*kha*) the region around the source of a river. Similarly, *-ri* (*ri*) means mountain or hill, *-trak/Trak* (*brag*) a rock, *-puk* (*phug*) a cave and *gang/Gang* (*sgang*) a plateau or occasionally a watershed. Valleys are indicated in different ways: *lung* (*lung*) meaning a small valley, *-rong/Rong* (*rong*) referring to the long deep gorges formed by the rivers in Eastern Tibet and *-trhang* (*phrang*) meaning a narrow precipitous gorge. The affix *-pu* (*phu*) indicates the upper part of a valley, while *-tö* (*stod*) and *-me* (*smad*) respectively refer to the upper and lower parts of a valley or region. Flat open plains are known as *-thang* (*thang*), or *-shö* (*shod*) when they lie below a high ridge. The terms *-yül* (*yul*) and *-jong* (*ljongs*) indicate districts or regions, while *dzong* (*rdzong*) indicates a fortress or an administrative district governed by a fortress.

In Tibetan, place names are usually listed in the order of region, place and so forth. Nesting has therefore been utilised in this index to group many, though not all, of the Tibetan place names under local or regional headings. For example, the "Blue Stūpa at Samye" will be found under "Samye", as will its "central shrine", the small hill behind Samye called "(Samye) Hepori" and the "Sangcen Metok" cave located at Chimpu. Alternative names can also appear as subentries, for example "Wokmin Tshurpu" under "Tshurpu". As a general convention, mountains have been grouped together under their prefix "Mount".

Throughout this index we have attempted to identify as accurately as possible the actual location of the places mentioned, both geographically and by giving their modern name. Prior to 1978 Tibet was little known to foreign travellers, but in recent years the country has opened slightly and fieldwork has contributed greatly to our task.

Reference has also been made to secondary works available on Tibet. In particular to George Roerich's translation of the *Blue Annals* (*Blue Annals*); Turrell Wylie's *The Geography of Tibet according to the 'Dzam-gling rgyas-bshad* (GT); Alphonsa Ferrari's translation of *mK'yen brtse's Guide to the Holy Places of Central Tibet* (KGHP) and Keith Dowman's recent reworking of the same text including the excellent results of his fieldwork entitled *The Power Places of Central Tibet* (PPCT); Stephen Batchelor's *The Tibet Guide* (TG) and Gyurme Dorje's *Tibet Handbook with Bhutan* (TH). Page references have been given in parentheses for passages in these and other works describing the places listed in more detail. Further information on geographical data contained in the *Blue Annals* in particular will be found in Turrell Wylie's *A Place Name Index to George N. Roerich's Translation of the Blue Annals*.

Where numerical categories of locations occur, these have been cross-referenced to the Glossary of Enumerations whenever more information is to be found there. Occasional additional information in the Notes, however, has generally not been cross-referenced.

Finally, many of the Indian and Tibetan locations mentioned in Section One have been plotted in the series of specially prepared maps which form the final section of this book, and grid references for the Tibetan locations in particular have been listed following the page numbers. As an aid to the reader, we have included grid references both for those locations which are specifically identified on the maps and for others which cannot be precisly indicated, either because their exact longitude and latitude are unknown or because the scale of the maps renders their inclusion impractical. In the latter cases the index itself often reveals that such locations are in close proximity to more important sites which have been indicated.

Index of Locations

Ābhāsvara (Inner Radiance) *'od-gsal*: the highest realm of form attainable through the second meditative concentration, 15

Abhirati *mngon-dga'*: the eastern buddha-field of Akṣobhya and the eastern buddha-field of Akaniṣṭha, 128, 878; see also *Buddha-field of Akṣobhya*

Aeon of Great Brahmā *tshangs-chen-gyi bskal-pa*: the temporal dimension of the emanational body, 19, 118

Akaniṣṭha (Highest) *'og-min*: highest of the Five Pure Abodes, 15, 21, 126-9, 131, 199, 213, 354, 412, 422, 425, 454, 583

- Akaniṣṭha-Ghanavyūha Realm *'og-min stug-po bkod-pa'i zhing*, 413; see also *Bounteous Array* and *Ghanavyūha Realm*
- Akaniṣṭha of the Mahāvaśavartin *dbang-sgyur chen-po'i 'og-min*, 449
- Citadel of Akaniṣṭha, the Gathering Place of the Great Assembly *'og-min tshogs-chen 'dus-pa'i grong-khyer*, 649
- Citadel of the Indestructible Array *'og-min rdo-rje bkod-pa'i grong-khyer*, 645
- imputed Akaniṣṭha *btags-pa'i 'og-min*, 128-9, 449
- (indestructible) Great Akaniṣṭha *(rdo-rje'i) 'og-min chen-po*, 447, 449
- ordinary Akaniṣṭha *'og-min tsam-po*, 449
- special Akaniṣṭha *khyad-par-can-gyi 'og-min*, 448

Alakāvatī *lcang-po-can*: the abode of yakṣas presided over by Guhyapati Vajrapāṇi in the form of Vaiśravaṇa or Kubera, 925

Alöi Peldeu *a-lo'i dpal de'u*: a treasure site *(gter-kha)* of Kongtrül Rinpoche, possibly Ulakdo north of Zhecen in Dzacukha, 867; Map 10, F23

Amdo *a-mdo*, 513, 690, 733

Anabhraka (Cloudless) *sprin-med*: the lowest realm of form attainable through the fourth meditative concentration, 15

Anavatapta Lake *ma-dros mtsho*: Lama A. Govinda, *The Way of the White Clouds*, (pp. 197-211); M. Henss, *Tibet: Die Kulturdenkmäler*, (Ch. III); Map 4, H06; see *Lake Manasarovar*

Aparagodanīya (Enjoyer of Cattle) *ba-lang spyod*: the western continent inhabited by human beings, 14

Appearance in the Womb of Conception *chags-'byung mngal-du snang-ba*, 136

Apramāṇābha (Immeasurable Radiance) *tshad-med 'od*: the middling realm of form attainable through the second concentration, 15

Apramāṇaśubha (Immeasurable Virtue) *tshad-med dge*: the middling realm of form attainable through the third meditative concentration, 15

Array of Attributes, pure aeon of *bskal-pa yon-tan bkod-pa*, 697

Array of Gem Clusters, mountain of *rin-po-che'i phung-po rnam-par bkod-pa*, 121

Array of Natural Expression, field of *rang-bzhin rnam-par bkod-pa*, 120

Arrow-born Well *mda'-chu khron-pa skyes*: near Kapilavastu, 418

Ārya-Nang (Sublime and Inner) *ārya-nang*: Nangcen, south of Jyekundo and

north of Riwoche in Kham, 841; Map 7, F21 & Map 10, F/G 21/22
Asura Cave *a-su-ra'i brag-phug*: to the north-west of India and not to be confused with the Asura Cave at Yangleshö (mentioned on p. 472), 489
Atapa (Painless) *mi-gdung-pa*: second of the Five Pure Abodes, 15
Aṭavī *'brog*, 427
Auspicious Myriad Gate Temple *bkra-shis khri-sgo*: in China, 498, 500
Avīcī hell *mnar-med-pa'i dmyal-ba*, 425, 933
Avṛha (Slightest) *mi-che-ba*: lowest of the Five Pure Abodes, 15, 62
Bahuputraka Caitya *bu-mangs mchod-rten*: between Rājagṛha and Nālandā, 432
Banyan Cave *nyagrodha'i phug*: at Rājagṛha, 428
Beauteously Arrayed Realm *mdzes-ldan bkod-pa*, Skt. **Prāsādikavyūhakṣetra*, 961
Benares *kā-shi*: Vārāṇasī, 432
Bengal *baṃ-ga-la*, 395
Bhaiṣajyavana *sman-gyi nags*, 427
Bhaṃdva *bhaṃ-dva-kyi yul*: in the Vindhyā Mountains, 504
Bhasing Forest in Nepal *bal-po bha-sing-gi nags*, 500, 501, 540
Bhirya *bhi-rya*, 501
Bhutan *lho-'brug/lho-mon/mon*, 378, 590, 591, 667, 710, 788, 838; Map 6, K/L 14/16; see also *Mön*
Blazing Fire Mountain Charnel Ground (of Most Secret Display) *(gsang-chen rol-pa) dur-khrod me-ri 'bar-ba*, 136, 490
Bodhi Tree *byang-chub-kyi shing*: the Tree of Enlightenment at Vajrāsana, 137, 417, 419, 946
Bodhi Tree Temple *byang-chub shing-gi lha-khang*: in China, 498
Border Taming temples *mtha'-'dul lha-khang*, Pls. 45, 47, 102; 510, n. 543
Bounteous Array *stug-po bkod-pa('i khams)*, Skt. *Ghanavyūha*, 117, 273, 296, 354, 357; see also *Akaniṣṭha-Ghanavyūha Realm* and *Ghanavyūha Realm*
Brahmā's Drumbeat *tshangs-pa rnga-sgra*: see *(Fields of) Brahmā's Drumbeat*
Brahmakāyika (Stratum of Brahmā) *tshangs-ris*: the lowest realm of form attainable through the first meditative concentration, 14, 61, 62
Brahmapurohita (Priest Brahmā) *tshangs-pa mdun-na 'don*: the middling realm of form attainable through the first meditative concentration, 15
Brahmā realms *gtsang-gnas*, 62; see also *higher realms*
Bṛhatphala (Great Fruition) *'bras-bu che*: the highest realm of form attainable through the fourth meditative concentration, 15
Britain *dbyin(-yul)*, 958
Bru-sha *bru-sha'i yul*: Hunza/Gilgit area, 11, 489, 537, 607, 609
Buddha-field of Akṣobhya *sangs-rgyas mi-'khrugs-pa'i zhing/mi-bskyod-pa'i zhing-khams*, 477, 691, 693; see also *Abhirati*
Buddha-field of Bhaiṣajyaguru *sman-gyi bla-ma'i zhing-khams*, 691
Buddha-field whose Foundation and Centre are Adorned with Flowers *gzhi-dang snying-po me-tog-gis brgyan-pa'i zhing*, Skt. *Kusumatalagarbhālaṃkārakṣetra*, 131, 409
Buddha-field of the Lotus Array *padma bkod-pa'i zhing-khams*, 798; see also *Cāmara(dvīpa)* and *Sukhāvatī*
  Great Lotus Palace *pad-ma chen-po'i gzhal-med khang*, 913
  Lotus-covered Pure Land to the west *nub-phyogs zhing-khams pad-mas khebs-pa*, 848
  Lotus Light, (great realm of) *padma-'od(-kyi zhing-khams chen-po)*, 683, 832, 840; see also *Citadel of Lotus Light*
  Palace of Lotus Light (in Cāmara) *pho-brang padma-'od-kyi bkod-pa/padma-'od-kyi gzhal-yas/padma-'od-kyi pho-brang*, 520, 678, 770, 795, 802, 816, 855
  western Citadel of Śāntapurī *nub-phyogs sha-nta pu-ri'i grong-khyer*, 867
(Buddha-field of) Padmakūṭa *padma brtsegs-pa('i zhing)*: the western Buddha-field of Akaniṣṭha, 128, 590
Buddhaśaraṇa *bu-ddha sa-ra-ṇa*: in Śrī Laṅkā, 456
Bumsar *'bum-gsar*: north-east of Sershul in Dzacukha, 872; Maps 9/10, E23
Bumthang *bum-thang*: in Bhutan, 582, 590; Map 6, L15; see also *Mön Bumthang*

Dorje Tsekpa in Bumthang *bum-thang rdo-rje brtsegs-pa*, Pl. 50; 519
Longevity Cave at the Campa Temple in Bumthang *bum-thang byams-pa lha-khang-gi tshe-phug*, Pl. 47; 790
Burma *payigu'i gling*: Payigudvīpa, 455
Cagöshong *bya-rgod gshong*: a Border Taming temple near Podong and treasure site of Sangye Lingpa; KGHP (p. 67, n. 572), 786; Map 6, J12
Cakpur *lcags-phur*: KGHP (pp. 57, 138), TH (pp. 210-11), 764; Map 6, K16
Capu Cakpurcen *bya-phu lcags-phur-can*: in Kharcu; KGHP (pp. 57, 138), 815; Map 6, K16
Caityagiri *mchod-rten ri*: Sāñci in Madhya Pradesh, 427
Caktepma *phyag mtheb-ma*: a treasure site of Guru Chöwang, 764
Cāmara(dvīpa) *rnga-yab gling*, 455, 516, 520, 678, 747, 765, 829, 847, 855, 950; see also *Buddha-field of the Lotus Array* and *Copper-coloured Mountain*
Camgön Temple of Odu/Orngu *'o-rdu/'o-rngu byams-mgon-gyi gtsug-lag-khang*: temple in the Gyelmorong region of Kham, 688
Candradvīpa *tsa-ndra dvipa*: island at the delta of the River Ganges, in the Bay of Bengal, 504
Cangcupling *byang-chub gling*: monastery near Tsāri, south of Takpo, 784, 787; Map 8, K18
Cangdrok Gegyel *byang-'brog dge-rgyal*, 857; Map 7, G17
Cang Trhengdze *byang 'phreng-mdzes*: entrance to Jönpalung, 810
Cangtsik *lcang-tshigs*: near Phukpoche, 545; Map 6, J16
Carung Khashor Stūpa *mchod-rten bya-rung kha-shor*: Bodhnath or Bauddha, Nepal, for the traditional account of which, see K. Dowman, *The Legend of the Great Stūpa*; Pl. 97; 837
Caryül in the south *lho-rgyud byar-yul*: south of Takpo; TH (p.198); 818; Map 8, K17
Catarlamo *bya-tar la-mo*: in north Latö, 702; Map 4, K10/11
Caturmahārājakāyika (Four Great Kings) *rgyal-chen bzhi'i ris*: the lowest of the desire realms inhabited by Kāma divinities, 14
Cave of the Most Wrathful Sage *rab-tu khros-pa drang-srong-gi phug-pa*, 135
Cel, upper valley of *jal-gyi phu*, 558
Cema Senge *bye-ma seng-ge*: near Uyuk, 668; Map 6, J13
Central Asia *hor*, 393, 430, 516; see also *Mongolia* and *Turkestan*
Central India *'phags-yul*, 464, 475, 489, 504
Central Tibet *dbus*, 397, 513, 524-5, 533, 540, 545, 561, 574, 591-2, 603, 607, 609-10, 615, 618, 651-3, 655, 657, 663, 671, 674, 688, 696, 697-9, 721, 724, 751, 773, 784, 785, 798, 799, 801, 807-8, 811, 816, 824, 830, 857, 868, 870, 921, 950, 955; Maps 5 & 6
Ceylon *siṅghalā*, 460; see also *Laṅkā* and *Siṅghala*
(Chak) Cangcupling *(chag) byang-chub gling*, 724-5
Chamdo in Dokam *mdo-khams chab-mdo*: on the Mekong River; TH (pp. 395-401); Map 10, G22
chiliocosm *stong dang-po*, 131, 212
Chimpu *mchims-phu*: KGHP (pp. 45-6, 115); PPCT (pp. 226-32); Pl. 57; 517, 533, 537, 542, 554, 558, 561, 593, 620, 790, 807; Map 6, J16; see also *Samye* and *Trakmar*
Gegong in Chimpu *mchims-phu'i dge-gong*, 555, 619
Rimochen in Chimpu *mchims-phu'i ri-mo-can*: KGHP (p. 117), 580, 585, 586
Tregugeu in glorious Chimpu *dpal-gyi mchims-phu'i bre-gu dge'u*: PPCT (p. 231), 534
Womin Pelgi Chimpu *'og-min dpal-gyi mchims-phu*: Samye, 596
China *rgya-nag/rgya/rgya-yul*, 104, 393, 438, 473, 497-8, 499, 507, 511, 516, 555, 559, 574, 603, 656, 663, 666, 669, 670, 671, 683, 706, 763, 787, 824, 839, 851, 852, 930, 936, 953, 958-9
Chingwardo *'phying bar-mdo*: in Chongye; PPCT (pp. 196-8), 838; Map 6, J16
Chöden *chos-ldan*, 686; Map 6, J16
Chöding *chos-sdings*: Ön River valley; KGHP (pp. 47, 119); PPCT (p. 240), 655; Map 6, J16
Chökorgang *chos-'khor sgang*, 673; Map 8, J17

Chölung *chos-lung*: in Ölka behind Mount Odekungyel; PPCT (pp. 249-50), 616, 619; Map 8, J17
Chongpo Kharu *'phyong-po kha-ru*: in Yarlung, 686; Map 6, J16
Chongye *'phyong-rgyas*; near Yarlung; see Henss, *Tibet: Die Kulturdenkmäler* (Ch. V, Sect. 3-4); TH (pp. 201-6); Pl. 52; 838; Map 6, J16
Chongye Taktse *'phyong-rgyas stag-rtse*: KGHP (pp. 52, 130); PPCT (pp. 198-9), 821; Map 6, J16
Gokang Tikle Nyakcik *sgo-khang thig-le nyag-gcig*: hermitage connected with the monastery of Pelri; PPCT (pp. 202-3), 836; Map 6, J16
Gyamen in Chongye *'phyong-rgyas rgya-sman*, 685; Map 6, K16
Gyamen Taktsepa *rgya-sman stag-rtse-pa*, 685; Map 6, K16
Namdröl Yangtse Hermitage in Tshering valley *tshe-ring-ljongs-kyi yang-dben rnam-grol yang-rtse*, 840; Map 6, J16
Pelgi Riwo College (*dpal-gi ri-bo'i chos-grva*), Pelri Thekpachok-gi Ling (*dpal-ri theg-pa mchog-gi gling)*, Pelri Monastery (*dpal-ri dgon-pa*), Chongye Pelri College (*'phyong-rgyas dpal-ri grva-tshang*): founded by Sherap Özer and restored by Jikme Lingpa; KGHP (pp. 53, 130); PPCT (pp. 202-3); TH (pp. 205-6); 595, 726-7, 835, 836; Map 6, J16
Pel Tshering-jong Pema Ösel Thekcok-ling *dpal tshe-ring ljong padma 'od-gsal theg-mchog gling*: PPCT (p. 202); TH (p. 205); Pl. 90; 838; Map 6, J16
Chukpo Trak *phyug-po brag*: in Zurkardo; KGHP (p. 46, n. 161); PPCT (pp. 219-21), 585, 588; Map 6, J16
Chumik Ringmo *chu-mig ring-mo*: near Narthang; KGHP (pp. 62, 146), 632; Map 6, J13
Chuwar *chu-bar*: south-west of Sakya, 642, 647, 717; Map 6, K12
Chuwori *chu-bo-ri*: a sacred mountain by the Tsangpo River, 32 miles south-west of Lhasa; KGHP (pp. 71, 163); PPCT (pp. 137-8), 657, 720, 790
Pel Chuwori *dpal chu-bo-ri*, 537, 847; Map 6, J15
Citadel of Lotus Light *padma 'od-kyi grong-khyer*, 378; see also *Buddha-field of the Lotus Array*
Citadel of Śāntapurī, western *nub-phyogs sha-nta pu-ri'i grong-khyer*, 867; see also *Buddha-field of the Lotus Array*
Citavara *tsi-ta-ba-ri'i yul*: in Rajasthan, 467
Citta Sangpuk (Secret Cave of Mind) *tsi-tta gsang-phug*: at Dzongshö Deshek Dupa, 863; Map 10, G23
Copper-coloured Mountain, glorious *zangs-mdog dpal-ri*, 520, 676, 765, 774, 793, 808, 814, 829, 847; see also *Buddha-field of the Lotus Array* and *Cāmaradvīpa*
Crystal Retreat in Tentik *dan-tik shel-gyi yang-dgon*: the main pilgrimage place of buddha-mind in East Tibet, on the Huang-ho River in Amdo; TH (pp. 560-1); 524; Map 9, B26
Da, upper valley of *mda'-phu*, 647
Dagam Wangpuk *zla-gam dbang-phug*: a treasure site of Jamgön Kongtrül at Meshö, between Pelpung and Dzongshö, 866; Map 10, G23
Dam *'dam*: north of Lhasa; KGHP (p. 81); PPCT (p. 131), 618; Map 5, H16
Damshö Nyingdrung *'dam-shod snying-drung*: a treasure site of Kongtrül Rinpoche, 856; Map 5, H15
Damcoktse Pass *'dams-cog-rtse-la*: near Tshurpu, 633; Map 6, J15
Ḍāmiḍodvīpa *ḍa-mi-ḍo dvi-pa*: the Dravidian south of India, 504; see also *Drāviḍa*
Danatika, river *chu-bo dan-tik*, 494
Danyin Khala Rongo *zla-nyin kha-la rong-go*: a treasure site of Chogyur Lingpa in Nangcen, representing the attribute of buddha-body, 845; Map 7, F21
Dartsedo in lower Gyelmorong *smad-rgya(l) dar-rtse-mdo*: the former capital of the Chakla kingdom, and present capital of the Kanze Autonomous Prefecture in Sichuan, known also as Kangdin or Tachienlu; TH (pp. 447-51); 783; Map 10, H26
Decen (Drölma), hermitage of *dben-gnas bde-chen/bde-chen-gyi sgrub-khang*: in Tanak, 721; Map 6, J13
Decen Samdrup in Nyipu, monastery of *snyi-phu bde-chen bsam-'grub-kyi*

dgon-pa: the main seat of Sangye Lingpa, 787; Map 8, H18
Deer Park of Ṛṣipatana *drang-srong lhung-ba ri-dvags-kyi nags-tshal*: Sārnāth, near Vārāṇasī, 153
Den *'dan*: Tentik in Amdo, 524; Map 9, B26
Denma *ldan-ma*, 619
Derge *sde-dge*: Henss, *Tibet: Die Kulturdenkmäler* (Ch. XIII, Sect. 3); TH (pp. 467-70); 812, 813, 815, 816, 852; Map 10, G23
  Derge Göncen *sde-dge'i dgon-chen*: TH (pp. 468-9); 879
  Ngülpunang in Derge, valley of *sde-dge dngul-phu nang*: perhaps connected with *rngul-mda' pho-brang* in front of Lhündrup Teng, which represents the body aspect of enlightened attributes, 813
  Terlung Tingo, Derge District, Dokam, village of *mdo-khams sde-dge gter-klung dil-mgo'i grong*: birthplace of Jamyang Khyentse Wangpo, west of Longtang Drölma, 849; Map 10, F22
desire realm *'dod-khams*, Skt. *kāmadhātu*, 13, 56, 60, 129, 142, 258, 301, 340, 420; see also *Kāma divinities*
  ten higher levels of the desire realm *'dod-khams-kyi mtho-ris gnas-bcu*: listed in the Glossary of Enumerations, 14, 60
  three lower levels of the desire realm *ngan-song gsum*, 14
Devīkoṭa *de-bi-ko-ṭa*: in north Bengal; Tāranātha, *History of Buddhism in India*, (p. 214), 473
Devīkoṭi, the forest of Phawangkha *yul devikoṭi'am pha-vang-kha'i nags-khrod*: north-west of Lhasa; KGHP (pp. 42, 102); PPCT (pp. 65-6), 678; Map 6, J16; see also *Phawangkha*
Dewachenpo in Punakha *spung-thang bde-ba chen-po*: the seat of Zhapdrung I, Thucen Ngawang Namgyel in Bhutan, 788; Map 6, L14
Ḍhāki-nying Cavern at Trakar Trashiding *brag-dkar bkra-shis sdings ḍhā-ki snying-gi phug*: in Sikkim, Pl. 85; 820; Map 6, L13
Dhanakośa (Treasury of Wealth) isle *dha-na-ko-sha('i mtsho-gling)*: a district of Oḍḍiyāna, 469, 472, 490, 492, 538, 746, 966
Dhanaśrīdvīpa *dhanaśrī'i gling*: Sumatra; Tāranātha, *History of Buddhism in India*, (p. 332), 455, 504; see also *Suvarṇadvīpa*
Dharmagañji *dharma-ganydzi*: palace in Oḍḍiyāna, 503, 927
Dhūmasthira (Place of Smoke) *dhu-ma sti-ra*: the capital of Oḍḍiyāna, 485, 502, 503
  great charnel ground of Dhūmasthira *du-ba'i gnas-kyi dur-khrod*, 539
dichiliocosm *stong bar-ma*, 131
District Controlling temples *ru-gnon-gyi gtsug-lag-khang*, Pls. 38, 46, 100; 510, n. 543
Do *rdo*: mountain range west of Ön in Central Tibet, 721; Map 6, J16
Dokam *mdo-khams*: i.e. Amdo and Kham, 53, 617-18, 647, 688, 691, 703, 731, 736, 777, 788, 799, 801, 804, 813, 815, 841, 847, 849, 851, 853, 859, 868, 869, 919; Maps 7-11
  lower Dokam *mdo-khams smad*, 851
  upper Dokam *mdo-khams stod*, 851
Dorje Trak *rdo-rje brag*: monastery founded in 1632 by Rikdzin III, Ngagi-wangpo; north of the Tsangpo River, south-west of Öncangdo, north of Cedezhöl and west of Dra; GT (p. 89, n. 485); KGHP (pp. 46, 118); PPCT (pp. 206-9); TH (pp. 162-3); Pl. 75; 720, 812, 828, 833; Map 6, J16; see also *Khar Dorje Trak* and *Thubten Dorje Trak*
Dorje Tse-nga Cave *rdo-rje'i rtse-lnga'i phug*: on the frontier of India and Nepal, 607
Dorje Tsheten in Tsang *gtsang-gi sa-cha'i rdo-rje tshe-brtan*, 662
Dorte, Nangsel Rock in the upper valley of *rdor-thes phu'i snang-gsal brag*, 659; Map 6, J16
Dotokthel *rdo-thogs thel*: monastery at Gyamen in Chongye, 685; Map 6, K16; see also *Chongye*
Dra *sgrags*: west of Zurkar; KGHP (pp. 46, 117); PPCT (pp. 205-15), 611; Map 6, J16; see also *Nup Yülrong*
  Black Pass of Dra *sgrags-la nag-po*, 611
  Dra Yangdzong *sgrags yang-rdzong*: pilgrimage site of buddha-body in

the interior of Dra; KGHP (pp. 117-18); PPCT (pp. 210-13), 537, 542, 609, 720, 807, 845
uplands of Dra in the mountains of Central Tibet *dbus-ri'i brgyud sgrags-kyi phu*, 566, 607
Yangdzong in Dra *sgrags yang-rdzong*: see *Dra Yangdzong*
Zhokteng in the upper valley of Dra *sgrags-kyi phu'i zhogs-steng*, 566
Drāviḍa *'gro-lding-ba'i yul*, 472, 503, 889, 892, 921; see also *Ḍāmiḍodvīpa*
Drepung, glorious *dpal-ldan 'bras-spungs*: monastery west of Lhasa, founded in 1416 by Jamyang Chöje Tashi Palden; KGHP (pp. 41, 96-7); TG (Ch. 6); Henss, *Tibet: Die Kulturdenkmäler*, (Ch. XI, Sect. 2); PPCT (pp. 67-72), 821, 826; Map 6, J16
Ganden Palace *dga'-ldan pho-brang*: residence of the Dalai Lamas in Drepung; PPCT (pp. 70-1); TG (Ch. 6), 682-3, 824, 956
Dri region *'bri-rgyud*, 698; Map 5, H16/17
Drigung *'bri-gung*: monastery founded in 1179 by Menyak Gomring; GT (pp. 87-8, n. 469); KGHP (pp. 44, 111-12); PPCT (pp. 113-16); TG (Ch. 21), 395, 591, 595, 676, 830, 841; Map 5, H17
Drigung Kunyergang in upper Uru *dbur-stod 'bri-gung sku-gnyer sgang*; TH (pp. 150-1); 676; Map 5, H17
Dritang Koro Trak *'bri-thang ko-ro brag*: a treasure site of Ratna Lingpa, 793; Map 5, H16
Dri Tiramdo, monastery of *'bri-ti-ra-mdo'i dgon-pa*: on the Yangtze River, 691
Drida Zelmogang *'bri-zla zal-mo-sgang*: Yangtze area between Derge and Drölma Lhakang; R. A. Stein, *Recherches sur l'épopée et le barde au Tibet*, (p. 225), 859; Map 10, F/G23
Drigyel Tampa Chöcuk *'bri-rgyal dam-pa chos-phyug*: birthplace of Karmapa II, Karma Pakshi, near Derge, 694
Pema Lhartse in Drida Zelmogang *'bri-zla zal-mo-sgang-gi padma lha-rtse*: at Dzongsar, 859; Map 10, G23
Üri Jetsün Cave in Pema Lhartse *padma lha-rtse'i dbus-ri rje-btsun phug*, 864
Dromcöla *sgrom-chos la*: a treasure site of Guru Chöwang, 764
Dropuk in Nyari *nya-ri sgro-phug*, 632-3, 644-5, 647, 648; Map 5, H13
Dropuk (Temple) *sgro-phug (lha-khang)*, 633, 634
Lharidong in Dropuk *sgro-phug-gi lha-ri gdong*, 633
Takla Ridong in Dropuk *sgro-phug-gi stag-lha ri-gdong*, 649
Druptso Pemaling *sgrub-mtsho padma gling*: in Lhodrak; KGHP (pp. 57, 139); TH (p. 212); 802; Map 6, K15
Düdül Shrine *bdud-'dul lha-khang*: in Derge, 816
Dvikrama *rim-pa gnyis-pa*, 477
Dzeng *'dzeng*: in Takpo, 549; Map 8, J17
Dzengdrak Karpo, three stone pillars of *'dzeng-brag dkar-po'i rdo-ring gsum*: on the summit of Mount Trazang, 780; Map 4, J11
Dzepu Kang-ra *'dzed-phu gangs-ra*: in Lhodrak, 755; Map 6, K15
Dzing Namgyel *'dzeng/'dzing rnam-rgyal*: near Dzongshö, 816; Map 10, G23
Namgyel Temple in Dzing *'dzing-du rnam-rgyal lha-khang*, 695
Dzokcen *rdzogs(-chen)*: monastery founded in 1685 by Pema Rikdzin; TH (pp. 471-3); Pls. 71-2; 733, 736-7, 847, 848, 867, 871, 879, 957; Map 10, F23; see also *Rudam Kyitram* and *Samten Chöling*
Dzongshö Deshek Dupa *rdzong-shod bde-gshegs 'dus-pa*: in Dzing, representing the attribute aspect of enlightened attributes, opened by Chogyur Lingpa, 858, 862, 863, 866; Map 10, G23
E *e-yul*: south of Ölka and west of Takpo; TH (p. 220); KGHP (pp. 51, 126); 571, 577, 777; Map 8, J17
Etongmen *e-mthong sman*, 727
Khyungcen Dingwei Trak in Zarmolung in E *e-gzar-mo-lung khyung-chen lding-ba('i brag guru'i sgrub-gnas bde-chen gsang-phug)*: location of the Secret Cave of Supreme Bliss, 771
lower village of Edam Ngönpo *e-'dam sngon-po grong-smad*, 726
Zarmolung in Eyül, the birthplace of awareness *e-yul rig-pa'i 'byung-gnas-kyi (guru'i sgrub-phug) gzar-mo-lung*: KGHP (pp. 51, 126), 771
East Asia, 393

eight charnel grounds *dur-khrod brgyad*: listed in the Glossary of Enumerations, 626, 791
eight ogre islands *srin-po'i gling brgyad*, 520
eight stūpas *mchod-rten brgyad*: listed in the Glossary of Enumerations, 427
Emar Dorjepo *e-dmar rdo-rje spo*: in Shang, 638; Map 6, J14
Enetrakri, shrine of *dben-gnas brag-ri lha-khang*: a treasure site of Nyang-rel Nyima Özer, 757; Map 6, K16
Ensermo, southern peak of *dben ser-mo'i lho-ri*: in Ukpalung, 623; Map 6, J14; see also *Ukpalung*
Entseigo *dben-rtsa'i sgo*: a treasure site of Guru Chöwang, 764
Evaṃcokgarwa (Camp Troops of Evaṃ Tower) *e-vaṃ lcog-sgar-ba*: a name for the community of Dorje Trak before the monastery was re-established in 1672 at its present site, 783
(Fields of) Brahmā's Drumbeat *tshangs-pa rnga-sgra'i zhing*: dimension of the buddha-body of perfect rapture, 19, 118
Field of the Indestructible Nucleus of Inner Radiance *'od-gsal rdo-rje snying-po'i zhing*: dimension of the buddha-body of reality, 19, 118
form realms *gzugs-khams*, 13, 56, 129, 142, 258, 301, 340
  extraordinary form realms *gzugs-khams khyad-par-can*: i.e. the Five Pure Abodes, 58, 60
  ordinary (form) realms *so-skye'i gnas*, 14-15, 58-9, 60
  seventeen realms of form *gzugs-khams gnas-ris bcu-bdun*, 13-15, 61
  twelve ordinary realms of the four concentrations *so-skye'i gnas bcu-gnyis*: the twelve lower Brahmā realms, 14-15, 62
formless realms, (four) *gzugs-med-kyi khams(-pa'i gnas bzhi)*: listed in the Glossary of Enumerations, 13, 15, 56, 61-2, 129, 142, 340
forty principalities *sil-ma bzhi-bcu*, 507, 949
four continents *gling-bzhi*, Skt. *caturdvīpa*: listed in the Glossary of Enumerations, 14, 56, 60, 131, 409, 438, 515, 577
Further Taming temples *yang-'dul-gyi gtsug-lag/lha-khang*, Pl. 44; 510, n. 543, 760
Gajane *gadzane'i yul*: Ghazni?, 488
Ganden *dga'-ldan*: monastery north-east of Lhasa, founded in 1409 by Tsongkapa; KGHP (pp. 42, 98); PPCT (pp. 99-103); Henss, *Tibet: Die Kulturdenkmäler*, (Ch. XI, Sect. 1); TG (Ch.16); PPCT (pp. 99-103), 681, 823, 870; Map 6, J16
  Drok Riwo Ganden *'brog ri-bo dga'-ldan-gyi chos-sde*, 954
  Riwo Ganden *ri-bo dga'-ldan*, 839
  Shartse and Cangtse Colleges of Ganden *dga'-ldan shar-byang rnam-gnyis*: KGHP (p. 107); TG (Ch. 16), 839
Ganden Palace *dga'-ldan pho-brang*: in Drepung: PPCT (pp. 70-1); TG (Ch. 6), 682-3, 824, 956; Map 6, J16
Gandhamādana Mountain *ri-spos-ngad-ldan*: in Kashmir, 439
Ganges, river *(chu-bo) gaṅgā*, 170, 184, 190, 195, 248, 435, 471, 714, 773, 824
Gar *'gar*, 650; Map 4, F05
Garden of Sustaining Youth *'tsho-byed gzhon-nu'i ldum-ra*, 136
Ghanavyūha Realm *stug-po bkod-pa'i zhing*, 19, 413; see also *Akaniṣṭha-Ghanavyūha Realm* and *Bounteous Array*
Gauḍa, 105
god realms *lha'i-yul/gnas*, Skt. *devaloka*, 11, 453; see also *Brahmā realms*, *form realms*, *higher realms* and *Kāma divinities*
Golok (region of Amdo) *(a-mdo) mgo-log-gi (yul)*: the *smar-khog* region; TH (pp. 596-609, 638-40); J. F. Rock, *The Amnye Ma-cchen Range and Adjacent Regions*, (pp. 123ff.), 733, 869; Map 9, D/E 23/27
Gomde Tranang in Yertö *yer-stod-dang 'brel-bar sgom-sde grva-nang*: southern Dokam, birthplace of Chogyur Lingpa in Nangcen; *Blue Annals*, (p. 549), 841
  Gom *sgom*, 841
Gongdring *sgong-drings*, 660
Gorum, temple of *sgo-rum-gyi gtsug-lag khang*: at Sakya, founded in 1073 by Khön Köncok Gyelpo; KGHP (pp. 63, 148); PPCT (pp. 275-6);

TG (Ch. 42), 951; Map 6, K12/13; see also *Sakya*

Great Shrine of a Hundred Thousand Images which Liberates when Seen *sku-'bum mthong-grol chen-mo*: built by Terdak Lingpa at Mindröling, 831; Map 6, J16

Gujarat *gudzi-rath*, 504

Guṇavera, great Caitya of *guṇavera zhes-pa'i mchod-rten*: in Laṅkā, 456

Gurmo *mgur/'gur-mo*: one of six myriarchies in Tsang (*de*) visited by Śākyaśrī; GT (p. 129); KGHP (p. 90), 548

Gyagen, swamp of *rgya-rgan-gyi thang-mtsho*: near Serthar above Gyarong, 663; Map 5, H16

Gyala Shinjei Badong *rgya-la gshin-rje'i rba-dong*: in Powo, north-west of the Namcak Barwa and south of the Gyala Pelri massives; TH (p. 231), 786; Map 8, J19

Gyama *rgya-ma*: birthplace of Songtsen Gampo south-east of Lamo; KGHP (pp. 44, 109); PPCT (pp. 103-5); Pl. 36; 593; Map 6, J16

(Gyamei) Cokla Cave *(rgya-ma'i) cog-la brag-phug*, 579, 584

Gyamnyeduka *rgyam-nye-du-kha*: at Phungpo Riwoche in Tsang, 542; Map 6, J14

Gyang Yönpolung *rgyang yon-po lung*: near Lhartse; KGHP (p. 66, n. 557); PPCT (pp. 278-9), 780; Map 6, J12

Gyang-ro Tshelma *rgyang-ro tshal-ma*, 545

Gyelmorong *(rgyal-mo) rong*: river valley running from the watershed above Serthar and Dzamtang, south-east through Barkham and Dartsedo; east and north-east of Minyak, also known as Gyelmo Tshawarong; TH (pp. 616-24), 698, 699, 733, 794; Map 10, H/G 26/27; see also *Tshawarong*

(Gyelmo) Taktse Castle *(rgyal-mo) stag-rtse mkhar*, 540, 541; Map 10, H27

lower Gyelmorong *smad-rgya(l)*, 783

Rongtrak in Gyelmorong, temple of the protector at *rgyal-rong brag-la mgon-po'i dgon-pa*, 540; Map 10, H26

Gyelpori *rgyal-po ri*, 550; see also *Mount Sumeru*

Gyer Cemakarpo *dgyer bye-ma dkar-po*: a treasure site of Sangye Lingpa, 786

Gyüme *rgyud-smad*: tantric college in Lhasa; PPCT (pp. 61-2); TG (Ch. 9), 868; Map 6, J16

Haogöl Rock *ha'o sgol-gyi brag*, 616

Hastisthala *glang-po'i sgang*: probably to be identified with Hastināpura in modern Himachal Pradesh, 498; see also following entry

Hastivana *glang-po'i tshal*, 481

Hawo Kang *ha-bo gangs*, 764, 768; see *(Samye) Hepori*

hells *dmyal-ba'i gnas/naraka*, 130, 214

Hepori *has-po-ri*: see *(Samye) Hepori*

higher realms, twenty-one *khams gong-ma nyi-shu rtsa-gcig*, 14-15, 56, 61, 65, 97, 661; see also *Brahmā realms*, *Pure Abodes* and *seventeen realms of form* under *form realms*

Himalayas *ri kha-ba-can*, 466

Homtrang in Traklung *brag-lung hom-'phrang*: in Kongpo, 810; Map 8, J19

Hurmudzu *hu-rmu-dzu*: a district of Oḍḍiyāna, possibly Hunza, 472

Indestructible Seat *rdo-rje'i gdan*: at Bodh Gaya, Bihar, Pl. 96; 409, 419, 462, 498, 854; see also *Point of Enlightenment* and *Vajrāsana*

India *'phags-yul/rgya-dkar/-gar*, 16, 39, 100, 103, 393-4, 396, 404, 441-2, 460, 462, 467-8, 470, 472-3, 477, 485, 489, 498-9, 503, 507, 511, 515, 517, 522, 526, 538, 544, 545, 548, 573, 607-8, 609-10, 612, 614, 617, 626, 656, 679, 693, 706, 737, 744, 746, 748, 767, 768, 770, 803, 812, 819, 824, 829, 838, 853, 854, 859, 873-4, 888-9, 890-2, 905, 914, 917-18, 936, 967, 972; Maps 1 & 2

Central India *'phags-yul*, 464, 475, 489, 504

South India *lho-phyogs*, 504, 947

West India *nub-phyogs*, 490, 498

Indus River *chu-klung sindhu*, 488; Map 4, G05/F04

Island of Ogresses *srin-mo'i gling*, 133

Jālandhara *dza-landhā-ra*, 430

Jālandhara Monastery *dza-landhā-ra'i dgon-pa*, 430

Jambudvīpa *'dzam-bu'i gling*: the southern continent inhabited by human beings, 14, 134-5, 193, 409, 412,

415-16, 432, 435, 455, 458, 462, 471, 495, 507, 520, 521, 534, 588, 973; see also *Rose-Apple Continent*
sixteen great cities of Jambudvīpa *'dzam-bu gling-gi grong-khyer chen-po bcu-drug*: listed in the Glossary of Enumerations, 438
Jang *'jang*: currently in north-west Yunnan, 696, 697; Map 11, L25/26
Java *nas-gling*: Yavadvīpa, 455
Jeworong *rje-bo rong*: in the Kongpo area, 786; Map 8, J19
Jokhang *jo-bo*: the main temple in Lhasa, built by Songtsen Gampo's Nepalese queen; KGHP (pp. 73, 86-7); PPCT (pp. 41-8); TG (Ch. 2); Henss, *Tibet: Die Kulturdenkmäler*, (Ch. IV, Sect 2); TH (pp. 78-88), Pl. 40; 510, 758, 791, 807, 815, 949; Map 6, J16; see also *Emanational Temple of Lhasa* under *Lhasa*, and *(Rasa) Trhülnang*
Jönpalung *ljon-pa lung*: in Kongpo, 810; Map 8, J19
Ju *'ju*: a subdistrict of the Dzacukha region, north-west of Dzokcen; GT (pp. 119-230); TH (pp. 475-77), 869; Map 10, F23 & Map 9, E23
Junyung, hermitage of *'ju-nyung ri-khrod*, Pl. 94; 869; Map 9, E23
Mehor Sa-nga Chöling in Ju *'ju me-hor gsang-sngags chos-gling*, 869
Jvālinī Cave *'bar-ba'i phug*: said to be located south of Magadha, in modern Madhya Pradesh; Tāranātha, *History of Buddhism in India*, (pp. 188, 286), 427
Kailash *kailasha*: TG (Ch. 45); TH (pp. 336-49), 507: see also *Mount Kailash*
Kalimpong *ka-(lon-)sbug/-spungs*, 42, 378, 379, 400
Kaliṅga *ka-ling yul*: ancient name for southern Orissa, 579
Kāma divinities, six species of *'dod-lha rigs-drug*, 14, 60; see also *desire realm*
Kamalaśīla, eastern city of *ka-ma-la-shi-la'i shar-gyi grong-khyer*: in East India, 498
Kāmarūpa *kā-ma-ru-pa/kā-ma-ru'i (grong-khyer)*: region and city of Assam, 472, 501
Kamata in India *rgya-gar ka-ma-ta*: M. Aris, *Bhutan*, (p. 174), 803
Kampo *kampo'i gnas*: perhaps this is *skam-po gnas-nang* near Lithang, founded in 1164 by Karmapa I, Tüsum Khyenpa (H. E. Richardson, oral communication); R. de Nebesky-Wojkowitz, *Oracles and Demons of Tibet*, (p. 226), 689; Map 11, J25
Kañcī *kanytsa'i yul*: Conjeevaram/ Kañcipuram, an ancient capital of Drāviḍa, 472
Kaṇḍala, a dense forest *kaṇḍala zhes-pa'i nags*: in Śrī Laṅkā, 456
Kangbar *gangs-bar*, 546, 550
Kangpori *gangs-po-ri*: mountain above Tsetang, legendary birthplace of the Tibetan race; KGHP (pp. 49, 123); Pl. 33; 590; Map 6, J16; see also *Kongpori Lawalung*
Samtenling in Kangpori, monastery of *gangs-po-ri'i bsam-gtan gling*: PPCT (p. 253), 674
Kangri Thökar *gangs-ri thod-dkar*: above Shuksep; PPCT (pp. 143-5); Pls. 37, 105; 586, 591; Map 6, J16
Kangri *gangs-ri*, 591
Orgyen Dzong (in Kangri Thökar) *(gangs-ri thod-dkar) o-rgyan rdzong*: a meditation cave of Longcenpa; PPCT (p. 144), 587, 588, 591
Özer Trin-ki Kyemötsel (Pleasure Garden of Clouds of Light) at Orgyen Dzong in Kangri Thökar *gangs-ri thod-dkar o-rgyan rdzong 'od-zer sprin-gyi skyed-mos tshal*, 588
Kangzang *gang-bzang*: Nöjin Kangzang, mountain range around Karo-la on the Gyaltse-Yamdrok road; TH (pp. 216, 253); Pl. 65; 609; Map 6, K15 K15
Kapilavastu *ser-skya'i gnas/grong*: city-state west of Lumbinī in Nepal, 420, 427
Karcung Temple of the Indestructible Expanse *skar-chung rdo-rje dbyings-kyi gtsug-lag khang*: at *ra-ma sgang* near Lhasa, Pl. 104; 521; Map 6, J16
Kardzuk Trhang *dkar-'dzug 'phrang*: a treasure site of Sangye Lingpa, 786; Map 8, J19
Karmaprasiddhi *las-rab grub-pa*: the northern field of Akaniṣṭha, 128
Karmari *karma-ri*: a seat of Chogyur Lingpa in Nangcen, near Karma Monastery, 848; Map 7, G21

Karma Peldeu *karma'i dpal mde'u*: a treasure site of Chogyur Lingpa, 846

Wokmin Karma *'og-min karma*: here this refers to a retreat of Chogyur Lingpa, 844, 845

Karṇikāvana Temple *rna-rgyan-gyi gtsug-lag khang*: in Kashmir, 430; see also *Kuvana Monastery*

Kashmir *kha-che'i yul/ka-shmi-ra*, 430, 435, 438-9, 468, 488, 501, 862

Kathmandu *bal-yul yam-bu/ne-pā-la'i khul*: city and valley in Nepal, 766, 807; Map 4, L10

Katil *kaḥ-thil*: at Katok, 689; Map 10, G23

Katok (Dorjeden) (Vajra Seat) *kaḥ(-thog rdo-rje'i gdan)*: monastery above Horpo, founded in 1159 by Katokpa Tampa Deshek, and the main pilgrimage place of enlightened activity in East Tibet; GT (p. 103, n. 666); TG (Ch. 52); TH (pp. 513-15); Pl. 70; 375, 681, 688, 701, 720, 733, 736, 770, 816, 847, 848, 867, 879; Map 10, G23

Phaktso *'phag-mtsho*: hermitage, 697

Pangtrö *spang-khrod*: hermitage, 695

Partrö *bar-khrod*: hermitage, 695-6

Ritsip *ri-rtsibs*: hermitage, 696

Tampuk *dam-phugs*: hermitage, 695

Kauśambī *kaushambhi*: Kosam near Allahabad, Uttar Pradesh, 427

Kawacen *ka-ba-can*, 567

Kela Norbu Pünsum *ke-la nor-bu spun-gsum*: a treasure site of Chogyur Lingpa, 846; Map 10, F22; see also *Tsike Norbu Pünsum*

Kham *khams*, 513, 524, 526, 533, 555, 574, 618, 683, 686, 688-701, 703, 706, 724, 733, 735-9, 770, 782, 793-5, 801, 807, 811, 820, 823, 824, 830, 839, 848, 850, 868, 950, 952, 954, 955, 956

Khandro Bumdzong *mkha'-'gro 'bum-rdzong*: a treasure site of Chogyur Lingpa in lower Nangcen, representing the attribute aspect of buddha-mind, 846; Map 7, G21

Kharak *kha-rag*: birthplace of Tāranātha in *rong-mdo*; KGHP (p. 155), 562; Map 6, J15

Kharcu (in Lhodrak) *(lho-brag) mkhar-chu*: see under *Lhodrak*

Khardong Yönmo *mkhar-gdong yon-mo*: location of the geomantic centre *(me-btsa')* of Tsukrum Tawu, 614

Khar Dorje Trak *mkhar-rdo-rje brag*, 663; see *Dorje Trak*

Khar in Yama *ya-ma'i mkhar*, 611

Khawa Karpo *kha-ba dkar-po*: mountain in Tshawarong between the Salween and Mekong rivers, representing the body aspect of buddha-speech; TH (pp. 417-9), 697, n. 885, 698; Map 11, L23

Khenpajong *mkhen-pa ljongs*: in Bhutan; Aris, *Bhutan*, (pp. 45 ff.), 567, n. 640; Map 6, L15/16

Khenpaling *mkhan-pa gling*, 567, n. 640

Khoklang Rock *khog-glang brag*: near Mustang in Ngari, 751

Khore *'khor-re*: the Sakyapa temple of *'khor-'chags* or Kojarnath below Taklakot on the Karnali River; TH (pp. 352-3), 713; Map 4, H06

Khotan *li-yul*, 500, 507, 540, 590

Khoting (Temple) *mkho-mthing (lha-khang)*: Lhodrak Lhakang; TH (pp. 209-10), 661, 756, 760; Map 6, K16

Khoyishinmar *mkho-yi shin-dmar*: a treasure site of Guru Chöwang, 764

Khyönmi *khyon-mi yul*, 614

Khyungcen Rock *khyung-chen brag*: a treasure site of Ratna Lingpa, 793

Khyunglung Ngülkar in Tö *stod khyung-lung dngul-mkhar*: Tralung, the birthplace of Shenrap Miwoche, 782; Map 4, G05

Koki *ko-ki'i yul*: South-East Asian mainland, 504, n. 530

Kongbu/Kungbu *gong-bu/gung-bu*, 642, 647

Kongpo/Kongyül *kong-po/kong-yul*: TH (228-42); KGHP (pp. 48, 122); TG (Ch. 57), 571, 574, 699, 724, 811, 818, 830; Map 8 J19

Kongpo Chimyul *kong-po mchims-yul*: in Gyamda district, 602, 603, 786

Kongpo Tamrül *kong-po dam-rul*, 786

Kongpo Tsagongphu *kong-po tsa-gong-phu*, 591

Lake Castle of Kongpo *kong-po'i mtsho-rdzong*: Traksum Dorje Trak; *Blue Annals*, (p. 874), 547; Map 8, H18

Nyangpo district of Kongpo *nyang-po kong-po'i yul*: GT (p. 96, n. 571);

KGHP (pp. 48, 122); TG (Ch. 57), 784; Map 8, H/J18
Orshö Lungdrom *'or-shod rlung-sgrom*: a treasure site of Sangye Lingpa, 786
Orshö Thoteng Monastery in Kongpo *kong-po 'or-shod mtho-stengs dgon-pa*, 568; Map 8, H18
Pucu in Kongpo *kong-po bu-chu*: TH (p. 233); Pl. 45; 810
Traksum Dorje Trak *brag-gsum rdo-rje brag*: birthplace of Sangye Lingpa; GT (p. 96, n. 575); TH (pp. 240-42); Pl. 79; 784; Map 8, H18
Waru Namtsül in Kongpo *kong-po wa-ru gnam-tshul*, 809
Kongpori Lawalung *gongs-po-ri'i gla-ba-lung*: a seat of Longcenpa at Kangpori, 591
Kong-ra Lhündrupding *gong-ra lhun-grub sding*, 718, 725
Kong-ra *gong-ra*, 727
Kongtrang Gedüne *kong-'phrang dge-'dun gnas*: a treasure site of Jatsön Nyingpo in Kongpo, 811; Map 8, J19
Kongyül/Kongpo *kong-yul/kong-po*: see *Kongpo*
Konjo Tsade, monastery of *go-'jo tsa-sde dgon-pa*: south-west of Pelyül; E. Teichman, *Travels of a Consular Officer in Eastern Tibet*, (pp. 175-7), 698; Map 10, H23
Koṅkana *kongka-na*: northern Karnataka, 464, 494, 502
Korong *go-rong*, 524
Korup *go-rub*, 708; Map 6, J14
Kosala *yul kosala*: either the region around Śrāvastī, or the area once known as Mahākosala between Raipur, Madhya Pradesh, and Orissa, 488
Kṣemākara, city of *grong-khyer skyid-pa'i 'byung-gnas*, 485
Kuge *gu-ge*: in Ngari, north of the Sutlej River; G. Tucci, *Indo-Tibetica*; KGHP (pp. 79, 98, 120); TG (Ch. 47); TH (pp. 353-67); Lama Govinda, *The Way of the White Clouds*, 806; Map 4, G04/05
Kuladzokpa *sku-la rdzogs-pa*: charnel ground, 471
Kumcok Decen Cave *sku-mchog bde-chen phug*: a treasure site of Kongtrül Rinpoche, 864; Map 10, G23
Kungbu/Kongbu *gung-bu/gong-bu*, 642, 647
Kungtang *gung-thang*: i.e. Tshel Kungtang, the location of Tshel Monastery, founded in 1175 by Zhang Tsöndrü Trakpa, 683
Kungtang in Mangyül *mang-yul gung-thang*: KGHP (pp. 66, 154), 518, 520, 652, 782; Map 4, J/K10
Kupavana, a forest behind Vāraṇāsī *ku-pa'i tshal*, 494
Kurelung in Bhutan *mon ku-re-lung*, 378; Map 6, L16
Kuśinagara *grong-khyer rtsa-can*: Kasiā, Deoria District, Uttar Pradesh, 425, 947
Kusumakūṭārāma *gnas me-tog brtsegs-pa'i kun-dga' ra-ba*: in Jālandhara, 430
Kuvana Monastery *ku-bā-na'i dgon-pa*: in Kashmir, 430; see also *Karṇikāvana Temple*
Kuvana Temple of Jālandhara Monastery *ku-bā-na'i gtsug-lag khang*, 430
Kyambu Pelgi Geding *skyam-bu dpal-gyi dge-sdings*, 591
Kyangsar *gyang-gsar*, 763
Kyapne Dzong *skyabs-gnas rdzong*, 567
Kyawophukring *skya-bo phug-ring*: perhaps *skya-bo kha-dong* near Saga; KGHP (p. 65), 764; Map 4, J10
Kyengi Karteng Trhang *rkyen-gyi dkar-steng 'phrang*, 786; Map 8, J19
Kyicu *skyid-shod*: i.e. the river valley, 521, 590, 758; Map 6, J15/16
Kyikung *skyid-khung*: source of the Kyicu River, 548; Map 6, J16
Kyilkar Lhakang *skyil-mkhar lha-khang*: the ancestral residence of Cetön Gyanak; TH (p. 262), 654; Map 6, K14
Kyilung *skyi-lung*: in Shang, 829; Map 6, J14
Kyingpu Yulung, cultivated valley of *gying-phu gYu-lung-gi mda'-gdab*: in the Nyangpo district of Kongpo, 784; Map 8, J18
Kyirong *skyid-grong*: TH (pp. 306-8); 513, 715, 826, 891; Map 4, K10
Kyonglung *skyong-lung*, 642, 647
Kyorlung, college of *skyor-lung grva-tshang*: north of Nyetang, on the north bank of the Kyicu River, founded in 1169 by Belti (*sbal-ti*); KGHP (pp. 73, 167), 552; Map 6, J15

Labar, charnel ground of *dur-khrod la-bar*, 567
Ladak in Tö Ngari *stod-mnga'-ris la-dvags*, 783; Map 4, F03/04
Lake Manasarovar *ma-dros*, 514, 970; Map 4, H06; see also *Anavatapta Lake*
Lake Mebar *me-'bar mtsho*: Tang District of Bhutan; Aris, *Bhutan*, (p. 38), 796; Map 6, L15
Lake Mönka Sermo *mon-kha zer-mo'i mtsho*: in Bhutan, 547
Lamo *la-mo*: east of Lhasa; KGHP (pp. 43, 109), 525; Map 6, J16
Land of Ogres *srin-yul*: near Oḍḍiyāna, 468, 473; see also *eight ogre islands*
Land of Snows/Snow Mountains *gangs-can 'jongs*: see *Tibet*
Langdro Chepa Takdra *lang-gro 'chad-pa stag-'dra*, 558, 559
Laṅkā *laṅka'i yul/singhala*, 454, 455-6, 889; see also *Ceylon* and *Siṅghala*
Latö *la-stod*: east of Mangyül, south of the Tsangpo River; KGHP (pp. 66, 153); PPCT (pp. 280-2); TH (pp. 296-314), 569, 642, 653, 665, 689, 751, 786; Map 4, K11/12; see also *Tingri*
  northern and southern districts of Latö *la-stod byang-dang lho*, 702
  Tshowar in Latö *la-stod mtsho-bar*, 751
Layak *la-yag*: see under *Lhodrak*
Len *glan*, 686
Lhabap Stūpa *lha-babs mchod-rten*: at Chongye; PPCT (pp. 189-90), 838
Lhadrak *lha-brag*: Zangzang Lhadrak, 780; Map 4, J11
Lhamdo Burmo Trak *lha-mdo 'bur-mo brag*: between Bakung and Pelyül; Teichman, *Travels of a Consular Officer in Eastern Tibet*, (pp. 206, 239), 863
  Decen Pemakö in Lhamdo Burmo *lha-mdo 'bur-mo bde-chen padma-bkod*: a treasure site of Kongtrül Rinpoche, 864
Lhari Ösel Nyingpo in Sikkim *'bras-gshongs lha-ri 'od-gsal snying-po*, 820; Map 6, L13
Lhari (in Phukpoche) *(phug-po-che) lha-ri*: mountain in Central Tibet, 542, 543; Map 6, J16; see also *Trak Lhari* and *Phukpoche*
Lharing Trak *lha-ring brag*: a seat of Longcenpa, 591
Lhasa *lha-sa*: KGHP (pp. 39-41); PPCT (pp. 38-72); TG (Chs. 1-15); TH (pp. 65-130), 523, 564, 590, 618, 656, 659, 681, 715, 757, 758, 768, 777, 784, 815, 823, 949; Map 6, J16
  Emanational Temple of Lhasa *lha-ldan sprul-pa'i gtsug-lag khang*: the Jokhang, 807; see also *Jokhang* and *(Rasa) Trhülnang*
  stone dikes (of Lhasa) *rdo-rags/jo-bo'i chu-rags*, 656
  Trak Lhalu Cave at Lhasa *lha-sa brag lha-klu phug*: KGHP (pp. 41, 92); PPCT (pp. 49-50); TG (Ch. 10), 556
Lhazermo *lha-zer-mo*, 644
  Khandro Lhakang (Ḍākinīs' Shrine) *mkha'-'gro lha-khang*, 644
Lhazur (Monastery) *lha-zur (dgon-pa)*, 548, 549; Map 8, K17
Lhe, charnel ground of *dur-khrod lhas*: perhaps in Lhodrak; KGHP (pp. 58, 140), 609; Map 6, K15
Lhodrak *lho-brag*; TH (pp. 208-14), 791, 807, 839, 922-3; Map 6, K15/16
  Caze in Lhodrak *lho-brag bya-ze*, 649
  Dzepu Kang-ra *'dzed-phu gangs-ra*, 755
  Guru Temple in Layak *la-yag guru lha-khang*: in west Lhodrak; KGHP (pp. 58, 140); Pl. 108; 768; Map 6, K15; see also *Samdrup Dewachenpo*
  Kharcu (in Lhodrak) *(lho-brag) mkhar-chu*: pilgrimage site of buddha-mind; TH (pp. 210-11); Pl. 103; 567, 569, 570, 661, 791, 870; Map 6, K16
  Layak Dzawar *la-yag rdza-bar*, 760; Map 6, K15
  Layak Pangdrong in west Lhodrak *lho-brag nub la-yag spang-grong*, 773; Map 6, K15
  Lhalung, stūpa of *lha-lung-gi mchod-rten*, 763; Map 6, K15
  Lhalung in Lhodrak *lho-brag lha-lung(-gi gdan-sa)*: seat of the Peling Sungtrül in west Lhodrak; TH (pp. 213-14); Pl. 140; 799; Map 6, K15
  Lhodrak Gönkar *lho-brag dgon-dkar*, 807
  Lhündrup Palace in Trushül *gru-shul lhun-grub pho-brang*: seat of Ratna Lingpa, 795; Map 6, K16
  Na Cave at Kharcu in Lhodrak *lho-brag mkhar-chu sna'i brag-phug*, 603; Map 6, K16

Namkecen in Layak Nyin, valley of *la-yag nyin-gyi lung-pa gnam-skas-can*, 763; Map 6, K15

Namkecen in Lhodrak *lho-brag gnam-skas-can*, 793; Map 6, K15

Phukring in Kharcu *mkhar-chu dpal-gyi phug-ring*: KGHP (pp. 57, 138), 793; Map 6, K16

Phurmongang in upper Lho *lho-stod phur-mong-sgang bya-ba'i dgon-pa*, 653

Sergön in Dzesa, a part of Tamshül in Lhodrak *lho-brag gtam-shul-gyi bye-brag 'dzed-sa ser-dgon*, 755; Map 6, K16

Sinca Rock in Namkecen *gnam-skas-can-gyi srin-bya brag*, 757; Map 6, K15

Tamshül in Lhodrak *lho-brag gtam-shul*: valley in east Lhodrak, modern Tsho-me Dzong; TH (pp. 206-7), 755; Map 6, K16

Trushül in Lhodrak *lho-brag gru-shul*: between Nyel and Loro; KGHP (pp. 51, 127), 793; Map 6, K16

Lhodrok *lho-'brog*: area south of Yamdrok, 591; Map 6, K15/16

Lho Kyercu, temple of *lho skyer-chu'i lha-khang*: Paro Kyercu in Bhutan; Aris, *Bhutan*, (pp. 3-5ff.); Pl. 44; 797; Map 6, L14

Lhündrup Teng *lhun-grub steng*: the Göncen in Derge, founded in 1616 at a site originally consecrated by Thangtong Gyelpo; TH (pp. 468-69); Map 10, G23

great Stūpa of Lhündrup Teng *lhun-grub steng-gi mchod-sdong chen-mo*: TG (Ch. 51), 851

seminary of glorious Lhündrup Teng *dpal lhun-grub steng-gi chos-grva*, 813

Lhündrup Teng, upper valley of *lhun-grub steng-gi phu*: in Tsāri, 785; Map 8, K18

Lingmokha *gling-mo-kha*: in Bhutan; Aris, *Bhutan*, (p. 158), 791

Ling, residence of the royal house of *gling-tshang*: near Derge, 816; Map 10, F23/24

Lo *glo*: Mustang, Nepal, 690, 805; Map 4, J08

Lowo (Matang) *mnga'-ris glo-bo ma-thang*: Mustang, 717, 805, 806

Locung *lo-chung*, 546

Locung in the vicinity of E *e'i 'dabs blo-chung*, 777; Map 8, J17; see also under *E*

Lomo *yul-lo-mo*, 542, 546

Longpo Cangde Bumpa *long-po byang-sde 'bum-pa*: between Takpo and Kongpo; KGHP (pp. 48, 122), 786; Map 8, J18/19

Longpo Kada Trhang *long-po ka-mda' phrang*, 786

Longpo Kying *long-po gying*, 788

Longpo Trongsar, valley below *long-po grong-gsar mda'*, 784; Map 8, J18

Longtang Drölma (in Mekam) *(smad-khams-kyi) klong-thang sgrol-ma*: the Tārā Temple at Tingo/Denkhok, 706, 782; Map 10, F23

Lowo Gekar in Ngari, temple of *mnga'-ris glo-bo dge-skar-gyi gtsug-lag khang*, 751

Lumbinī Grove *lumbi'i tshal*, 416, 417, 946

Lungseng (Windy Hollow) *rlung-gseng*: at Zangzang Lhadrak, 780; Map 4, J11

Lungshö *klung-shod*: valley of the Kyicu River near Drigung Dzongsar; KGHP (p. 111); PPCT (p. 106), 676; Map 5, H16

Madhima *ma-dhi-ma*: an island in Oḍḍiyāna, 463

Magadha *ma-ga-dha*: the region of southern Bihar, 409, 419, 422, 432, 437, 489, 656, 892

Mahābrahmā (Great Brahmā) *tshangs-pa chen-po*: the highest realm of form attainable through the first meditative concentration, 14

Makkolam *sa-dkar-can*, 427

Malaya Buddha-field *ma-la-ya'i zhing-bkod*, 624

Malayagiri/Malaya Mountain *ri ma-la-ya*, 454, 455, 458; see also *Mount Malaya*

Malla country *gyad-kyi yul*, 947

Malung *rma-lung*: the Huang-ho Valley in Amdo; J. F. Rock, *The Amnye Macchen Range and Adjacent Regions*, (pp. 61ff. and 72ff.); Map 9

Dorjei Trakra Encung Namdzong in Malung *rma-lung rdo-rje'i brag-ra an-chung gnam-rdzong*: near Centsha, also called *rma-smad rdo-rje'i brag*, and rep resenting the mind aspect of buddha-mind; TH (pp. 568-70), 524; Map 9, B27

Manglam *mang-lam*, 780

Mangyül *mang-yul*: west of Latö; KGHP (pp. 66, 154), 889; Map 4, J08/10

Maṇikha (Entrance to Jewels *or* Entrance to the Six-Syllable Mantra of Avalokiteśvara) *ma-ṇi-kha*, 841

Māratika (Cave) *(brag-phug) ma-ra-ti-ka*: at Haileshi, near Rumjitar in Nepal, 470, n. 488, 864

Marong Trugu Trashi Terdzong *rma-rong gru-gu bkra-shis gter-rdzong*: north-west of Dzokcen, 864; Map 10, F23

Marpo Hill/Marpori (Red Mountain) *dmar-po-ri*: site of the present Potala Palace at Lhasa: PPCT (p. 51); TG (Ch. 3), 513, 823; Map 6, J16

Maru *ma-ru'i yul*: an ancient name for Rajasthan; Tāranātha, *History of Buddhism in India*, (p. 253), 467

Maru, palace *pho-brang ma-ru*: at Nyangdren Phawongkha in the valley of the Kyicu; KGHP (pp. 41, 94-5), 510; Map 6, J16

Mathurā *bcom-brlag*: on the Yamunā River in Uttar Pradesh, 435

Mawocok Rock *sma-bo cog-gi brag*: residence of Nyang-rel Nyima Özer in east Lhodrak; TH (pp. 207-8); Pl. 106; 755; Map 6, K16

Meldro *mal-dro*: a river valley south of the Zha Temple, on the main road from Lhasa to Kongpo; KGHP (pp. 44, 108-10), 557; Map 6, J16

Melodious Crown *gtsud-phud dbyangs-ldan*, 961

Mindröling *smin(-grol) gling*: monastery founded in 1670 by Terdak Lingpa; KGHP (pp. 54, 132); PPCT (pp. 165-7); TH (pp. 169-72); Tucci *To Lhasa and Beyond*; Pl. 88; 375, 728, 733-4, 735-7, 824-34, 838, 847, 849, 879, 919, 956, 959; Map 6, J16

  Orgyen Mindröling, (seminary of) *o-rgyan smin-grol-gling(-gi chos-grva)*, 526, 831, 849, 869

Minyak *mi-nyag*: east and north-east of Lithang, across the Nyag-chu River; TH (pp. 443-46), 661, 691; Map 10, H26

Moisture Gathering Light Mass *drod-gsher 'dus-pa 'od-kyis spung-ba*, 136

Mön *(lho-)mon*: Bhutan and surrrounding region, 591, 690, 699, 714, 791, 798-9, 802, 824, 830, 839, 973; Map 6, K/L 14/16; see also *Bhutan*

  Khandroling in Mön *mon-gyi mkha'-'gro'i gling*: a seat of Melong Dorje, 569

  Mön Bumthang *mon bum-thang*, 764, 792, 796; Map 6, L15; see also *Bumthang*

  Möngar, town of *mon-'gar grong-mo-che*: East Bhutan, south-east of Bumthang on the Kuru-chu River, 549; Map 6, L16

  Möngu *mon-dgu*, 714

  Mönkateng *mon-kha steng*: upper Mönkar; KGHP (pp. 56, 136), 764

  Namseling in Mönkar *mon-mkhar rnam-sras gling*, 719

  (Nering) Sengedzong (in Mönka) *(mon-kha ne/sna-ring) senge-rdzong*: north of Lhüntse Dzong in Bhutan, a pilgrimage site of buddha-activity; KGHP (pp. 56, 136), 518, 710; Map 6, L16

Mongolia *hor/sog*, 395, 574, 661, 663, 683, 695, 823-4, 839; see also *Central Asia* and *Turkestan*

Mount Abu *a-bhu zhes-pa'i ri*: in Rajasthan, 456

Mount Bhāskara *ri-bo snang-byed*, 501

Mount Dra Riwoche *sgrags ri-bo-che*, 607; Map 6, J16; see also *uplands of Dra in the mountains of Central Tibet* under *Dra*

Mount Drong-ri Chukpo *'brong-ri chugs-po*: Zurpoche's gold-mine near Drongtse, 624; Map 6, J14

Mount Gampodar *sgam-po gdar-gyi ri*: a treasure site of Karma Lingpa, 801; Map 8, J18

Mount Kailash *gangs/ri ti-se*: Henss, *Tibet: Die Kulturdenkmäler* (Ch. III); TH (pp. 336-49), 466, 533, 794; Map 4, G06; see also *Kailash*

Mount Kangpori *gangs-po-ri*: see *Kangpori*

Mount Khawa Karpo *kha-ba dkar-po*: see *Khawa Karpo*

Mount Kongmo Wokma at Sengcen Namdrak *seng-chen gnam-brag-gi ri gong-mo 'og-ma*: a treasure site of Chogyur Lingpa in the Yangtze valley region at Dzomtö, also called *'dzom-thog phu seng gnam-brag* and representing the activity aspect of

enlightened attributes, 846; Map 10, G23
Mount Kosala *ri-bo kosala*, 500
Mount Kukkuṭapāda *ri-bya rkang*, 433
Mount Lhari Rölpa *lha-ri rol-pa*: perhaps this is to be identified with Lhabapri near Sheldrak; Pl. 34; 507
Mount Malaya *ri ma-la-ya*, 135, 154, 468, 478, 493, 889, 947, 948; see also *Malayagiri* under *Malaya Buddha-field*
Mount Medril *mas-'gril-gyi ri*, 663
Mount Mucilinda *ri btang-bzung*, 768
Mount Muruṇḍaka *mu-ruṇḍaka-la*: near Oḍḍiyāna, 487
Mount Namcak Barwa *gnam-lcags 'bar-ba*: see *Düri Namcak Barwa in Puwo* under *Puwo(rong)*
(Mount) Nyemo Lhari *snye-mo lha-ri*: a treasure site of Jatsön Nyingpo, 810-11
Mount Pangpo *spang-po-ri*: at Sakya, 951; Map 6, K12
Mount Pleasant *yid-bzang brtsegs-pa'i ri-sul*: Sumanakūṭa or Adam's Peak in Śrī Laṅkā, 455
Mount Potalaka *ri po-ta-la/yul gru-'dzin*: the abode of Avalokiteśvara, reputedly in South India, 466, 507
Mount Rincen Pung *ri-bo rin-chen spung*: in Kalimpong, 378; Map 6, L13
Mount Shampo *sham-po ri*: PPCT (pp. 184-5), 758; Map 6, K16; see also *Yarlha Shampo*
Mount Sumeru *ri-rab-kyi rtse/ri-rgyal lhun-po*, 56, 172, 449, 490, 515, 577, 611, 624, 906, 971; see also *Gyelpori*
Mount Trakar Kongcen *ri-bo brag-mkhar gong-can*, 714
(Mount) Trak Gyawo *brag-rgya-bo*, 622, 631, 634, 638-9, 642, 644, 645; see also *Gyawo* and *Thak* under *Riwo Güdu*
Mount Trazang *ri-bo bkra-bzang*: KGHP (pp. 65, 153), 780; Map 4, J11
Mount Tsepo Purkang *ri-bo btsad-po pur-khang*: near Ukpalung, 627; Map 6, J14
Mount Tukdrül Pungdra *brag-ri dug-sbrul spungs-'dra*: at Zangzang Lhadrak, 780; Map 4, J11
Mount Vimalasvabhāva *bi-ma-la-sva-bha-va'i ri*: see *Vimalasvabhāva Mountain*
Mount Wu-t'ai-shan *ri-bo rtse-lnga*: in Shanxi Province, China, Pl. 63; 495, 497, 555, 763, 858
Mugulung/Nyugulung *mu-gu-lung/myu-gu-lung*: in Tsangtön Mangkar, not to be confused with the monastery of the same name in north-central Nepal, founded in 1043 by Drokmi; Aris, *Bhutan*, (pp. 134-5); D. L. Snellgrove, *Himalayan Pilgrimage*; 633; Map 6, K12
Muksang, hermitage of *rmugs-sang-kyi sgrub-gnas*: near Pelyül in Kham, 813; Map 10, G23
Muse *mus-srad*: a temple in the Mu valley; KGHP (pp. 68, 158), 716; Map 6, J13
Mutik Shelgi Pagong/Bamgong *mu-tig shel-gyi spa-gong/sbam-gong*, 757, 790
myriad oceanic world systems *rab-'byams-kyi rgya-mtsho*, 131
myriad world systems *rab-'byams*, 131, 146
series of myriad world systems *rab-'byams rgyud*, 131
Nabün Dzong *na-bun rdzong*: a treasure site of Düdül Dorje, 816, 845; Map 7, F21
nāgas, domain of *klu-yul/gnas*, 452
Nairañjanā River *chu-klung nairañdzana*: Lilajan River in Gaya District, Bihar, 412, 419
Naivedyaśālā Pagoda, nine-storey *lha'i bshos khang-brtsegs-dgu*: at Vajrāsana, 488; see also *Nine-Storey Pagoda*
Nak *nags*, 688
Nakmore *nag-mo-re*, 642
Naktsel Sumdril, a wood *nags-tshal gsum-sgril*, 619
Nālandā, (glorious) *(śrī)nālendra*: seven miles north of Rajgir, Bihar, 426, 464, 467, 475, 489
Namkecen *gnam-skas-can*: see under *Lhodrak*
Namtso Chukmo *gnam-mtsho phyug-mo*: a large lake, 120 miles north of Lhasa; TH (pp. 139-40), 519; Map 5, H15
Nandanavana *dga'-ba'i (tshal)*: charnel ground, 469
Nangcen Chinghu *nang-chen ching-hu*: Nangcen district in Kham, which since 1727 has been associated loosely or otherwise with the Kokonor Territory (Qinghai),

i.e. Chinghu; TH (pp. 485-89), 841; Map 7, F21 & Map 10, F/G 21/22
Naring Trak *sna-ring brag*: near the Tang River in Bhutan; Aris, *Bhutan*, (p. 4), 796; Map 6, L15
Narlung-rong, a subdivision of Rulak in lower Tsang *gtsang-smad ru-lag-gi sa-cha'i snar-lung-rong*, 703; Map 6, J14
Shukla Nakpo in Nar *snar-gyi shug-la nag-po*, 614
Narttaka Vihāra in the Northern Vindhyā Mountains *ri-bo 'bigs-byed gar-mkhan-gyi gtsug-lag-khang*, 93
Nelpa Meu *nel-pa sme'u*, 788
Nepal *bal/bal-yul/bal-po'i yul*, 394, 472, 475, 489, 509, 511, 540, 607, 608, 610, 652, 656, 717, 746, 748, 766, 768, 770, 805, 812, 837, 889, 890, 891
Nesar *gnas-gsar*, 683; Map 6, J13; see also *Tanak Nesar*
Nesar *gnas-gsar*: see *Nyangtötsi* under *Nyangru* and also *Tsiki Temple*
Netang, plain of *ne-thang*: perhaps to be identified with Nyetang, 605; Map 6, J15
Neten Gang *gnas-brtan sgang*: seat of Chogyur Lingpa at Yegyel Namkadzö, 848; Map 7, G21
Neudong *sne'u gdong*: south of Tsetang; KGHP (pp. 49, 123-4); PPCT (pp. 176-7), 595, 787, 833; Map 6, J16
Neudong Fort *sne'u gdong rtse*: PPCT (p. 176), 777, 778; Map 6, J16
Pentsang Monastery/Monastic College (in Neudong) *(sne'u gdong) ban-gtsang dgon/grva-tshang*, 777-8; Map 6, J16
Nezhi Gangpo *gnas-gzhi sgang-po*: in the Tamshül River valley, Lhodrak; TH (p. 208), 763; Map 6, K16
Ngadak Rock in Podong *bo-dong mnga'-bdag brag*: in Tsang; KGHP (pp. 67, 156), 621; Map 6, J13
Ngamongtrhang *rnga-mong phrang*: on the Tsangpo River, 645
Ngamshö *ngam-shod*: above Densathil near Phukpoche, 545; Map 6, J16
lower Ngamshö *ngam-shod smad*, 657
sands of Ngamshö *ngam-shod-kyi bye-ma*, 516
valleys of Ngamshö *ngam-shod lung-po*, 549
Ngarcung *ngar-chung*, 567
Ngari *mnga'-ri(s)*: TG (Chs. 45-7); TH (pp. 325-70), 513, 523, 717-18, 751, 804, 830, 953; Map 4
twenty mountain caves of Ngari *mnga'-ris skor-du gangs-brag nyi-shu*: listed in the Glossary of Enumerations, 518
Ngarpuk *ngar-phug*: at Yangdzong in Dra; KGHP (p. 46), 569; Map 6, J16
Ngenlam *ngan-lam*: in Uru, 541, 575, 675
three-valley district of Ngenlam in Uru *yul-dbu-ru ngan-lam ral gsum*, 541
Ngor *ngor*: monastery south-east of Nartang, founded in 1429 by Künga Zangpo; KGHP (pp. 62-4); PPCT (p. 274), 813; Map 6, J13
Nīla, river *chu-klung nila*, 472
Nine-Island Lake of Yamdrok *yar-'brog gling-dgu'i mtsho*, Pl. 65; 609; Map 6, J/K15; see also *Yamdrok-gang*
Nine-Storey Pagoda at the Indestructible Seat in India *rdo-rje gdan-gyi ke'u tshang rim-pa dgu-pa*: at Vajrāsana, 854; see also *Naivedyaśālā Pagoda*
Nine-Storey Pagoda, the Great *ke'u tshang chen-po dgu-brtsegs*: in the sandal-wood forest of Dhanakośa, 538
Nirmāṇarata (Delighting in Emanation) *'phrul-dga'*: the penultimate desire realm inhabited by Kāma divinities, 14
Nopki Phutak Phudrak-ring near Dzing Namgyel *nobs-kyis phu-stag phu-brag ring*, 816; Map 10, G23
Norbu Lingka *nor-gling (pho-brang)*: the summer palace of the Dalai Lamas in Lhasa; TG (Ch. 4); Henss, *Tibet: Die Kulturdenkmäler*, (Ch. IV, Sect. 5), 777; Map 6, J16
Nup Yülrong *gnubs yul-rong*: in the lower valley of Dra; PPCT (p. 215), 548, 611; Map 6, J16; see also *Dra*
(Nup) Khulung *(gnubs) khu-lung*, 614; Map 6, J14
Nyāgrodhikā in Magadha *nya-gro-dha-can*: near Kapilavastu, 432
Nyangdren Phawongkha (in the Kyicu valley) *nyan-bran pha-bong-kha*, 510, 511; Map 6, J16; see also *Maru*
Nyangpo *nyang-po*, 813; Map 8, J/H18
Nyangru *nyang-ru*: the Nyangcu valley including Gyantse, Tsang: PPCT

(pp. 269-70); TG (Chs. 35-7), 640; Map 6, J/K14
Khüyül in upper Nyang *nyang-stod khu-yul*, 560
Kyibuk in lower Nyang *nyang-smad skyid-sbug*, 722
lower Nyang *nyang-smad*: KGHP (pp. 60, 144); PPCT (pp. 269-73), 651, 703; Map 6, J13/14
Nyangro Nyentso *yul nyang-ro gnyan-tsho*, 557
Nyangnak Ölpo *nyang-nag 'ol-po*, 654
Nyangtötsi, temple of *nyang-stod rtsis-kyi lha-khang*: Border Taming Temple at Tsi Nesar; Aris, *Bhutan*, (p. 25); KGHP (pp. 59, 142); PPCT (p. 271), 623; Map 6, J14; see also *Tsiki Temple*
Patsap in lower Nyang *nyang-smad pa-tshab*, 560
Tsegyel in lower Nyang, hermitage of *nyang-smad rtse-rgyal-gyi sgom-khang*, 700
upper Nyang *nyang-stod*: KGHP (pp. 59, 143); PPCT (pp. 268-9), 556, 619, 650, 651; Map 6, K14
upper Yudruk in Nyang *yul nyang gYu-'brug stod-pa*, 542
Nyari *nya-ri*, 632, 647; Map 5, H13; see also *Dropuk in Nyari*
Nyarong *nyag-rong*: south of Kanze and north-east of Lithang; TH (pp. 498-99), 869; Map 10, G25
Nyemo Cekar *yul snye-mo bye-mkhar*: birthplace of Vairocana, near Uyuk; KGHP (pp. 69, 161-2); PPCT (130-1), 538; Map 6, J15; see also *Pagor in Yeru*
Ce Fortress in Nyemo *snye-mo bye-mkhar*, 611
Nyemo Lhari *snye-mo lha-ri*: see *(Mount) Nyemo Lhari*
Nyetang *snye-thang*: ten miles south-west of Lhasa on the north bank of the Kyicu River, the deathplace of Atiśa; KGHP (pp. 72, 165); PPCT (pp. 134-6); TG (Ch. 22); Henss, *Tibet: Die Kulturdenkmäler*, (Ch. VII), 557, 605; Map 6, J15
Nyingmei Yutso, the Turquoise Lake *rnying-ma'i gYu-mtsho*: at Tsāri Nyingma, 571; Map 8, K18; see also *Tsāri* and *Yutso Rincen Trak*
Nyipu *snyi-phu*; Map 6, J16
(Nyipu) Shuksep *(snyi-phu) shug-gseb*: PPCT (pp. 142-3), 580, 588
Shuksep-ri *shug-gseb-ri*, 578
Nyuk, palace of *gnyug-gi rgyal-khang*, 717; Map 6, J13
Nyuktsel, hollow of *(o-rgyan-gyi sgrub-gnas) gnyugs-tshal sbug*, 570
Odantapurī Monastery *otantapuri'i gtsug-lag khang*: at Bihar Shariff, 515
Oḍḍiyāna *oḍḍiyāna/o-rgyan*, 135, 441-2, 449, 461, 463, 464-5, 468-9, 471-2, 477, 485-7, 490, 494, 501-3, 518, 534, 569-70, 582, 710, 712, 745, 768, 785, 787, 889-92, 914, 927, 944, 960, 972; see also *Dhanakośa*, *Dharmagañji*, *Dhūmasthira*, *Hurmudzu*, *Madhima*, *Rukma*, *Śaṅkarakūṭa*, *Sikhodhara*, *Sindhu Lake* and *Vajra Cavern of Oḍḍiyāna*
Oḍḍiyāna, the Land of the Ḍākinīs *o-rgyan mkha'-'gro'i gling*, 442
self-created temple of Heruka *heruka'i lha-khang-rang-byung*: in Oḍḍiyāna, 442
Oḍiviśa *oḍi-bisha*: Orissa, 441
Ogre Cave endowed with the Sound of the Rulu Mantra *srin-phug ru-lu'i sgra-dang ldan-pa*, 136
Ökar Rock (in the lower valley of Cing) *(bying-mda') o-dkar brag*: KGHP (pp. 54, 132); PPCT (pp. 161-2), 549, 789, 828; Map 6, J16
Ölka *'ol-kha*: on the north bank of the Tsangpo River, east of Zang-ri; KGHP (pp. 48, 121); PPCT (pp. 245-50), 550; Map 8, J17
Ölmotshel *'ol-mo tshal*, 609
Ölpa Lhartse in upper Tsang *gtsang-stod 'ol-pa lha-rtse*: birthplace of Thangtong Gyelpo, currently under the administration of Ngamring Dzong; GT (p. 67, n. 176); PPCT (pp. 276-8), 802; Map 6, J12
Ömeitshel *'od-ma'i tshal*, 609
Ön *'on*: mountain range, and a river flowing south into the Tsangpo beyond Tsetang; KGHP (pp. 47, 119); PPCT (pp. 236-42), 545, 721; Map 6, J16
Önbar Sardzingka in Yoru *gYo-ru 'on-bar gsar-rdzing-kha*, 568

Ön Möntang *'on smon-thang*, 808; Map 6, J16
"tiger den" at Önpuk *'on-phug stag-tshang*: KGHP (pp. 47, 120); PPCT (pp. 241-2), 776; Map 6, J16
upper Önak *'on-nag stod*, 552
Öncangdo Peme Trashi Gepel, temple of *(skyid-smad) 'on-cang rdo dpe-med bkra-shis dge-'phel-gyi gtsug-lag khang*: in the lower Kyicu valley; GT (p. 147); KGHP (pp. 72-3, 166); PPCT (pp. 241-2); Pl. 105; 522; Map 6, J15
ordinary (form) realms *tsam-po*: see under *form realms*
Orgyen Chöling *o-rgyan chos-gling*: at Mön Bumthang; Aris, *Bhutan*, (pp. 40, 158), 792; Map 6, L15
Orgyen Dzong *o-rgyan rdzong*: see under *Kangri Thökar*
Öseltse *'od-gsal rtse*: cottage/hermitage at Mindröling, 828; Map 6, J16
Oyuk river-basin *'o-yug mda'*, 560; Map 6, J14; see also *Uyuk*
Oyuk Chigong *'o-yug phyi-gong*: a retreat of Cetsün Senge Wangcuk, 558, 559; Map 6, J14
Padmakūṭa *padma brtsegs-pa*: see *(Buddha-field of) Padmakūṭa*
Padrak *dpa'-brag*: perhaps the rock of Pawo Wangcen, treasure site of the Dokam Inventory, 867; Map 10, G23
Pagoda of Tuṣita *dga'-ldan brtsegs-pa*, 136; see also *Tuṣita*
Pagor in Yeru, upper valley of *gYas-ru'i ba-gor*: in Nyemo Cekar, 653; Map 6, J15
Pangri (Jokpo) *bang-ri ('jog-po)*: in Kongpo; TH (pp. 239-40), 811, 812, 813; Map 8, J18
Pangshong Lharika *spang-gshong lha-ri-kha*, 789
Pangtrö *spang-khrod*: hermitage at Katok, 695
Pare *ba-red*, 525
Paranirmitavaśavartin (Mastery over Transformation) *lha'i gzhan-'phrul dbang-byed*: highest of the desire realms inhabited by Kāma divinities, 14, 60
Parīttābha (Little Radiance) *'od-chung*: the lowest realm of form attainable through the second meditative concentration, 15
Parīttaśubha (Little Virtue) *dge-chung*: the lowest realm of form attainable through the third meditative concentration, 15
Parkam *bar-khams*, 816
Parma Lhateng *bar-ma lha-steng*: between Puwo and Riwoche in Tshawagang; *Blue Annals*, (p. 550), 816
Paro (in Bhutan/Mön) *(mon-)spa-gro*, 661, 667, 791; Map 6, L14
Taktsang, the "tiger den" at Paro in Mön *mon spa-gro stag-tshang*, Pl. 55; 802
White Rock in Paro *spa-gro'i brag-dkar*, 519
Partrö *bar-khrod*: hermitage at Katok, 695-6; Map 10, G23
Paruṣakavana (Coarse Wood) *rtsub-'gyur tshal*, 469
Pāṭaliputra *skya-nar-bu/dmar-bu-can*: near Patna, Bihar, 435, 437
Pawo Wangcen, rock of *dpa'-bo dbang-chen brag*: a treasure site of Chogyur Lingpa at Dagam Wangpuk, 846; Map 10, G23; see also *Padrak*
Payigudvīpa *payigu'i gling*: Burma, 455
Pehar Kordzöling/treasury of Pehar *dpe-har dkor-mdzod gling*: at Samye: PPCT (pp. 223-4), 892, 914; Map 6, J16
Peking *pe-cing*: modern Beijing, 823
Pelbu, forest of *bal-bu'i nags*: near Phuk-poche, 543; Map 6, J16
Pelkar in Samdruptse in Tsang *gtsang bsam-'grub rtse'i dpal-dkar*: in Shigatse, 717; Map 6, J13
Pelpung, (seat of) *dpal-spung(-kyi gdan-sa)*: south of Derge Göncen, founded in 1727 by Situ VIII, Chöki Jungne; D. Snellgrove and H. Richardson, *A Cultural History of Tibet*, (p. 137); TH (pp. 466-67), 842, 848, 879; Map 10, G23
Peltsap Sumpa, temple of *dpal-tshab gsum-pa'i lha-khang*: at Samye, 797, n. 1069; Map 6, J16
Pel Tshering-jong Pema Ösel Thekcokling *dpal tshe-ring ljongs padma 'od-gsal theg-mchog-gling*: see under *Chongye*
Pelung *dpal-lung*, 551
Pelyül *dpal(-yul)*: TH (pp. 462-64)

Namgyel Cangcup Ling *(dpal-yul) rnam-rgyal byang-chub gling-gi (chos-sde)*: founded in 1665 by Künzang Sherap, Pl. 74; 733, 738-9, 847, 867, 879; Map 10, G23
Pema Ja-ö Sheldzong *padma 'ja'-'od shel-rdzong*: a haunt of Lhatsün Namka Jikme in Sikkim, 819
Pemakö, (secret land of) *(sbas-yul) padma-bkod*: J. Bacot, *Le Tibet Révolté: Vers Népémakö, la terre promise des Tibétains*; TH (pp. 407-8), 811, 816, 957, 972; Map 8, J19/20
Pemashel Cave in Marshödzam *smar-shod-dzam-nang padma shel-phug*: a treasure site of Chogyur Lingpa near Pelpung and Dzongshö, also called *rme-shod padma shel-phug*, representing the speech aspect of enlightened attributes, Pl. 93; 845-6; Map 10, G23; see also *Terlung Pemei Shelri*
Pema Tsekpa Rock, crystal cave *brag padma brtsegs-pa'i shel-phug*: a treasure site of Orgyen Lingpa behind Sheldrak in Yarlung: PPCT (p. 193), 775; Map 6, J16
Persia *ta-sig*: "Persia" here denotes both modern Iran and all the other regions of Inner Asia in which Iranian languages are or once were spoken, 489
Pewar, great pilgrimage place of *(tsa-'dra'i gnas-lag) dpe-war gnas-chen*: an adjunct of Tsandra Rincen Trak, opened by Kongtrül Rinpoche, 867; Map 10, G23
Phakmotru *phag(-mo-gru)*: Densathil in Yarlung, founded in 1158 by Phakmotrupa Dorje Gyelpo; KGHP (pp. 47, 120); PPCT (pp. 242-4), 569, 830, 954; Map 6, J16
Phaktso, hermitage of *'phag-mtsho'i ri-khrod*: a branch of Katok, 697; Map 10, G23
Phangtang, palace at *'phang-thang-gi pho-brang*, 513
Phawang Gyelep (Eight Boulders' Landing) *pha-vang brgyad-sleb*: at Katok, 690; Map 10, G23
Phawangkha *pha-vang-kha*: situated on the hillside behind Sera; KGHP (pp. 42, 101-2); PPCT (pp. 65-6), 680, 822; Map 6, J16; see also *Devīkoṭi*
Phen-gi Khangön *phan-gyi khang-sngon*: second household of Zurcungpa, 637
Phenyül *'phan-yul*: between Taklung and Lamo, site of Nālendra Monastery, founded in 1436 by Rongtön Sheja Künzi; KGHP (p. 39); PPCT (pp. 83-6), 688; Map 6, J16
  Kawa Namoche in Phenyül *'phan-yul ka-ba na-mo-che*, 522
Phodrang Yutso *pho-brang gYu-mtsho*: in Tsāri, 814
Phukcungrong *phug-chung rong*: at Phukpoche, 546; Map 6, J16
Phukpoche *phug-po-che*: near Ngamshö, 542, 545, 548, 549; Map 6, J16; see also *Lhari (in Phukpoche)* and *Trak Lhari*
Phungpo Riwoche in Gyamnyeduka in Tsang *gtsang rgyam nye-du-kha'i phung-po ri-bo-che*: Riwoche on the south bank of the Tsangpo River; KGHP (pp. 70, 162), 542, 667, 791; Map 6, J14
Phüntsoling, the Conangpa residence *jo-gdan phun-tshogs-gling*: founded in 1615 or 1627 by Tāranātha, and forcibly converted to the Gelukpa school in 1650; KGHP (pp. 66-7, 155-6); PPCT (p. 279), 798; Map 6, J12
Phurbucok *phur-lcogs*: hillside north-west of Sera; GT (p. 83); KGHP (pp. 43, 103); PPCT (p. 66), 778; Map 6, J16
Pleasure Grove of Anāthapiṇḍada *mgon-med zas-sbyin-gyi kun-dga' ra-ba*: at Jetavana in Śrāvastī, 137
Point of Enlightenment *byang-chub snying-po*, Skt. *Bodhimaṇḍa*, 115, n. 110, 154, 412, 416, 419; see also *Indestructible Seat* and *Vajrāsana*
Pönlung *bon-lung*, 735
Pornetrak *spor-ne brag*: at Riwoche in Kham, representing the activity aspect of buddha-mind: TG (Ch. 54), 816; Map 7, G21
Potala (Palace) *(pho-brang chen-po) potala*: the winter residence of the Dalai Lamas and seat of the Tibetan Government, situated on Marpori in Lhasa. It was constructed at the order of Dalai Lama V, beginning in 1645-8; KGHP (pp. 40, 88); PPCT

(pp. 51-8); Henss, *Tibet: Die Kulturdenkmäler*, (Ch. IV, Sect. 4); TG (Ch. 3); TH (pp. 96-104); Pl. 86; 513, 777, 823, 824; Map 6, J16
Prabhāskara, great charnel ground of *rab-tu snang-byed ces-pa'i dur-khrod chen-po*, 501
Puburgang in Dokam *mdo-khams bu-'bur sgang*: a plateau lying between the Yangtze and the southern Yalung rivers, 688; Map 10 H24/25
Pubor *bu-'bor*, 696, 697
Tsangzhel, part of Puburgang *bu-'bur sgang-gi bye-brag gtsang-zhal*, 691
Puguto *spu-gu-do*: near Gyamen in Chongye, 685; Map 6, K16
Pum, Rong and Zhak *bum-rong-bzhag*: see *three districts of Pum, Rong and Zhak*
Pung-ring *spung-ring*, 551, 552
Puṇyaprasava (Increasing Merit) *bsod-nams 'phel*: the middling realm of form attainable through the fourth meditative concentration, 15
Purang *spu-'rangs*: in Ngari, south of Lake Manasarovar; GT (p. 61), 569; Map 4, H06
Pure Abode(s) *gtsang-ma'i gnas/ris dag*, Skt. *Śuddhanivāsa*, 413, 449
Five Pure Abodes *gtsang-ma'i gnas lnga*: listed in the Glossary of Enumerations, 15, 62
Pūrvavideha (Surpassing the Body) *lus-'phags*: the eastern continent inhabited by human beings, 14
Puwo(rong) *spu-bo (rong)*: comprising upper Puwo, or the valleys of the Putö and Parlung Tsangpo, and lower Puwo, or the valley of the Yi'ong Tsangpo; TH (pp. 405-7); Map 8, H19/20 & J20
Decen Sangwa Cave at the Dongcu in Puwo *spu-bo 'dong-chu bde-chen gsang-ba phug*, 815; Map 8, H20
Decen Thang in Putö *spu-stod bde-chen thang*: Putö River valley, 816; Map 8, H20
Dongcu in Puwo *spu-bo 'dong-chu*, 815; Map 8, H20
Düri Namcak Barwa in Puwo *spu-bo bdud-ri gnam-lcags 'bar-ba*: Mount Namcak Barwa; TH (pp. 231, 407-8); Pl. 83; 815; Map 8, J20
great cavern of Puri *spu-ri phug-mo-che*: a treasure site of Sangye Lingpa, 785
Kanam in Puworong *spu-bo rong-gi ka-gnam*, 972; Map 8, J20
Puri Rincen Barwa *spu-ri rin-chen 'bar-ba*: a treasure site of Sangye Lingpa; TH (pp. 231, 407-8), 786
Puri Shelgi Yangdrom *spu-ri shel-gyi yang-sgrom*, 815
Puri Takdzong *spu-ri dvags-rdzong*: a treasure site of Düdül Dorje, 815
Putö *spu-stod*: the Putö and Parlung (Po) river valleys; TH (p. 407), 815, 816; Map 8, H20
Qarloq *gar-log*, 524
Ragye *ra-'gyel*: a centre of Lume, 525
Rājagṛha *rgyal-po'i khab*: Rajgir, Bihar, 136, 154, 419, 427, 428, 431, 489
Rakcok *rag-cog*: perhaps near Katok, 698; Map 10, G23
Ramoche *ra-mo-che*: temple in Lhasa built by Songtsen Gampo's Chinese queen; KGHP (pp. 40, 87); PPCT (pp. 59-60); TG (Ch. 8); Henss, *Tibet: Die Kulturdenkmäler*, (Ch. IV, Sect. 3); Pl. 42; 510, 590; Map 6, J16
(Rasa) Trhülnang *(ra-sa) 'phrul-snang*: the Jokhang in Lhasa, 510, 815, 949; see also *Emanational Temple of Lhasa* under *Lhasa*, and *Jokhang*
Ratnapurī *ratna pu-ri*: Tshopema or Rewalsar, in Sahor, modern Mandi District, Himachal Pradesh, Pl. 51; 972
Ratsak, stone stūpa of *ra-tsag-rdo'i mchod-rten*: KGHP (p. 73, n. 693), 815; Map 6, J15
Ratum Trak *ra-tum brag*, 667
"Real Origin of the Ḍākinīs", a cave *mkha'-'gro-ma mngon-par 'byung-ba'i phug*, 493
Realm of the Bounteous Array *stug-po bkod-pa'i khams*: see *Bounteous Array*
realm of desire *'dod-khams*, Skt. *kāmadhātu*: see *desire realm*
Red Mausoleum (of King Songtsen Gampo) *(srong-btsan) bang-so dmar-po*: in Chongye; KGHP (pp. 53, 130); PPCT (pp. 199-201); TG (Ch. 33); TH (p. 204); Tucci, *Tombs of the Tibetan Kings*, 835, 838
reliquary of the great translator Ngok *rngog-lo chen-po'i gdung-rten*: at Sangpu, 578, n. 661; Map 6, J16

Repkong *re-bkong*: modern Tongren, south of the Huang-ho River and Rongpo Göncen; TH (pp. 570-5), 879; Map 9, C26
Rikdzin Sangpuk *rig-'dzin gsang-phug*: a treasure site of Düdül Dorje, 815
Rincen Shelri Mukpöi Gatsel *rin-chen shel-ri smug-po'i dga'-tsal*: a haunt of Lhatsün Namka Jikme, 819
Ritsip *ri-rtsibs*: a branch of Katok, 696
Riwo Gudü *ri-bo dgu-'dus*, 621, 622, 638; Map 6, J14; see also *Gyawo* under *Thak*, and *(Mount) Trak Gyawo*
Riwo Wangzhu *ri-bo dbang-gzhu*: a treasure site of Chogyur Lingpa, 847
Riwoche, glorious *dpal ri-bo-che*: i.e. Cung Riwoche, south-west of Zangzang Lhadrak, 804; Map 4, J11
Riwoche *ri-bo-che*: north-west of Chamdo in Kham: TH (pp. 390-4), 816; Map 7, G21
Rizar Göpo, valley of *ri-gzar rgod-po*, 558
Rong *rong*: river valley in Tsang flowing north into Tsangpo at Rinpung; KGHP (pp. 70, 162), 703; Map 6, J14/15
Rong Hot Springs *rong chu-tshan*: this is *dum-pa chu-tshan-kha*; KGHP (pp. 71, 163), 649; Map 6, J15
Rong Rock *rong-brag*, 764
(Rongme) Karmo, "tiger den" of *rong-me dkar-mo stag-tshang/dkar-mo stag-tshang*: a treasure site of Chogyur Lingpa near Derge, 846, 866, 876; Map 10, G23
Rongyap, hidden valley of *rong-rgyab sbas-pa' ljongs*: birthplace of Kongtrül Rinpoche in Drida Zelmogang, 859; Map 10, G24
Rongka Sheldrak Ödzong *rong-kha shel-brag 'od-rdzong*: a treasure site of Kongtrül Rinpoche, 864; Map 10, G24
Rose-Apple Continent *'dzam-bu'i gling*, Skt. *Jambudvīpa*: the southern continent inhabited by human beings, 409; see also *Jambudvīpa*
Ṛṣipatana, Deer Park of *drang-srong lhung-ba ri-dvags-kyi nags-tshal*: Sārnāth, near Vārāṇasī, 153
Rudam Kyitram *ru-dam skyid-khram (lung)*: valley behind Dzokcen Monastery; TG (Ch. 50); Pl. 72; 737; Map 10, F23; see also *Dzokcen*
Rudam Kangtrö *ru-dam gangs-khrod*: *ru-dam gangs-kyi ra-ba*, the main pilgrimage place of enlightened attributes in East Tibet, 846; Map 10, F23/24
Rukma *ruk-ma*: a district of Oḍḍiyāna, 472
Rulak in lower Tsang *gtsang-smad ru-lag*: i.e. the western region of Tsang; PPCT (p. 286), 703
Sacred Stūpa *mchod-rten rnam-dag*, Skt. *Viśuddha Stūpa*, 419, n. 400
Sahor *sa/za-hor*, 458, 460, 467, 470-1, 513, 821, 889, 948, 972
Sāketa *sar-bcas*: near Ayodhyā in Uttar Pradesh, 427
Sakya *sa(-skya)*: on the "Great Temple" (*lha-khang chen-mo*), founded in 1268 by Pöncen Śākya Yeshe and other older sites at Sakya, refer to PPCT (pp. 275-6); TG (Ch. 42); TH (pp. 279-87); Henss, *Tibet: Die Kulturdenkmäler* (Ch. VIII), 395, 578, 669, 813, 823, 830, 952; Map 6, K12; see also *Gorum*
Drölma Palace of Sakya *sa-skya sgrol-ma pho-brang*, 959; Map 6, K12
Sakyak *sa-skyags*, 570; Map 6, K16
Samdrup Dewachenpo *bsam-'grub bde-ba chen-po('i lha-khang)*: the Guru Temple in Layak, west Lhodrak, built by Guru Chöwang; KGHP (pp. 58, 140); Pl. 108; 768; Map 6, K15
Samdrupling, seminary of *bsam-'grub gling-gi chos-grva*, 806; Map 4, J08
Ṣaṃṣara *ṣaṃ-ṣa-ra*: birthplace of Līlāvajra, 463
Samten Chöling, retreat centre of *sgrub-sde bsam-gtan chos-gling*: Dzokcen Monastery; TH (pp. 471-3), 737; Map 10, F23; see also *Dzokcen*
Samtentse *bsam-gtan rtse*: cottage/hermitage at Mindröling, 828; Map 6, J16
Samye, glorious (Temple of Unchanging Spontaneous Presence) *dpal bsam-yas (mi-'gyur lhun-gyis grub-pa'i gtsug-lag khang)/bsam-yas chos-grva*; KGHP (pp. 44, 113-14); PPCT (pp. 216-25); TH (pp. 172-82); Tucci, *To Lhasa and Beyond*; Henss, *Tibet: Die Kulturdenkmäler*, (Ch. VI); Pl. 101; 514-15, 517, 521, 523, 575, 579,

592-3, 620, 710, 753, 763, 776-7, 807, 819, 823, 837-8, 857, 889, 892, 914, 949; Map 6, J16; see also *Chimpu* and *Trakmar*

Blue Stūpa at Samye *bsam-yas mchod-rten sngon-po*: KGHP (pp. 44, 114); PPCT (p. 221), 624

central shrine *dbu-rtse*: PPCT (pp. 222-4); TG (Ch. 27); TH (pp. 174-8); Pl. 53; 515, 753, 815

Red Stūpa at Samye *bsam-yas mchod-rten dmar-po*: PPCT (p. 221), 775

Samye Ārya *bsam-yas ārya*: the shrine of Āryapālo or Tamdrinling, to the south of the main temple at Samye; PPCT (p. 224); TG (Ch. 27), 764

Samye Chimpu *bsam-yas mchims-phu*: PPCT (pp. 226-32); TH (pp. 180-2); Pl. 57; 542, 573, 588, 591, 757, 786, 796, 802, 837

(Samye) Hepori *(bsam-yas) has-po-ri*: PPCT (p. 225); KGHP (p. 45), 514, 847; see also *Hawo Kang*

Sangcen Metok, cave of *gsang-chen me-tog phug*: KGHP (p. 45); PPCT (p. 228); TH (p. 180), 837

three shrines of the three queens *btsun-mo gsum-gyi gling gsum*: PPCT (p. 221), 515

Sanglung Nakpo charnel ground in India *rgya-gar-dur-khrod gsang-lung nag-po*, 609

Sangpu *gsang-phu*: college founded in 1073 by Ngok Lekpei Sherap on the south bank of the Kyicu River, south of Nyetang and north of Öncangdo; KGHP (pp. 72, 165); PPCT (pp. 140-2), 590, 678, 687; Map 6, J16

Gyar Kelok in Sangpu, monastery of *gsang-phu'i rgyar-gas-logs-kyi dgon-pa*, 656

Lingme *gling-smad*: college at Sangpu; PPCT (p. 141), 821

Lingtö *gling-stod*: college at Sangpu; KGHP (pp. 72, 165); PPCT (p. 141), 577

Sangpu Neutok, seminary of *gsang-phu ne'u thog-gi chos-grva*, 577

Śaṅkarakūṭa Caitya *mchod-rten bde-byed brtsegs-pa*: near Vajrāsana at the Śītavana charnel ground, 482-3, 858

Śaṅkarakūṭa, great temple of *bde-byed brtsegs-pa zhes-bya-ba'i lha-khang chen-po*: in Oḍḍiyāna, 490

secret lands of upper, lower and central Tibet *stod-smad-bar gsum-gyi sbas-yul*, 518, n. 558

Sedrak in Tsang *gtsang-du se-sbrag*, 655

Sekar *sras-mkhar*: Milarepa's tower in Lhodrak; KGHP (pp. 57, 138); TH (pp. 211-12), 764; Map 6, K15

Sengedzong *seng-ge rdzong*: see *(Nering) Sengedzong (in Mönka)* under *Mön*

Sengegyap (in Sizhel) *(sri-zhal-gyi) seng-ge rgyab*, 565, 567

Sera Monastery *se-ra dgon-pa*: due north of Lhasa, founded in 1419 by Camcen Chöje Śākya Yeshe; GT (p. 158, n. 374); KGHP (pp. 42, 99-100); PPCT (pp. 63-5); TG (Ch. 5); Henss, *Tibet: Die Kulturdenkmäler*, (Ch. XI, Sect. 3), 716; Map 6, J16

Sera Ce, college of *se-ra byes grva-tshang*: the largest of the three colleges at Sera; KGHP (p. 100); PPCT (pp. 64-5); TG (Ch. 5), 678

Serakcok *bse-rag cog*, 816

Serlung (Monastery) *gser-lung (dgon-pa)*, 551-2

Shabam *sha-'bam*, 694

Shambhala *shambhala/shambhaka*, 442, 449, 507, 879, 889, 948, 960

Shambhara in Rongmu *rong-smu'i sham-bha-ra*, 718

Shang *shangs*: TH (pp. 250-1), 558, 561, 570, 622, 625, 635, 643, 668; Map 6, J14

lower valley of Shang in Yeru *gYas-ru shangs-kyi mda'*, 622

Shang Lhabu *shangs lha-bu*, 649

Shang River *shang(s)-chu*: KGHP (p. 157), 622, 638

Shang Tanak *shangs rta-nag*: i.e. Shang and Tanak, 561

Shap *shab*: river valley between Trhopu and Nyingri; KGHP (pp. 67-8, 157), 708; Map 6, J13

Shawuk Tago *sha-'ug ltag-sgo*: a treasure site of Terdak Lingpa east of Bhutan and the residence of Karmapa I, Tüsum Khyenpa; Aris, *Bhutan*, (p. 101); *Blue Annals*, (p. 196), 567, 828; Map 6, L16

Sheldrak *shel-brag*: PPCT (pp. 190-3); Pl. 77; 537, 553, 828; Map 6, J16; see also *Crystal Cave* under *Yarlung*

Shinglötsel, the southern district of Mön *lho-mon shing-lo'i tshal*: Bhutan, 973

Shöcen *shod-chen*, 829

Shokyam, city of *grong-khyer sho-khyam*: in China, perhaps to be identified with Khotanese Svahvam, Chinese Suofeng in Ningxia, 497

Sho(kyam) *sho(-skyam)*: the seat of master Tuwa, perhaps Serlung Monastery, 551, 574, 590

Shuksep *shug-gseb*: see *(Nyipu) Shuksep*

Sikkim *'bras-yul/'bras-gshongs/sbas-yul 'bras-mo-ljongs*, 378, 723, 782, 788, 820; Map 6, L13

Sikodhara *si-ko-dha-ra*: a district of Oḍḍiyāna, 492

Siljin charnel ground, great *bsil-byin zhes-pa'i dur-khrod chen-po*: in China, 498, 499

Sindhu Lake *sindhu'i mtsho*: in Oḍḍiyāna, 405, 948

Singu Yutso *si-ngu gYu-mtsho*: a treasure site of Khyentse Rinpoche, near Derge, 856; Map 10, G24

Siṅghala *singhala'i gling*: Śrī Laṅkā, 455, 456, 460, 890; see also *Ceylon* and *Laṅkā*

Sinmo Parje Rock *brag srin-mo spar-rjes*: a treasure site of Nyang-rel Nyima Özer in the Tamshül River valley; KGHP (pp. 56, 136); Pl. 107; 755; Map 6, K16; see also *Sinca Rock* under *Namkecen*

Sinpo Mountain *srin-po-ri*: perhaps this is Sinpori in Yartökhyam, north of Chuwori at the confluence of the Kyicu and Tsangpo rivers, 656; Map 6, J15

Śiśumāra Hill *byis-pa gsod*: at Mathurā; Tāranātha, *History of Buddhism in India*, (p. 34), 427

Śītavana (charnel ground) *(dur-khrod) bsil-ba'i tshal*, 469, 482, 493, 593, 712, 757

six great countries where the true doctrine was propagated *dam-pa'i chos dar-ba'i yul-chen-po drug*: listed in the Glossary of Enumerations, 507

six realms of existence *'jig-rten-gyi khams-drug*, 585

sixteen fields beneath the crossed legs of Vairocana the Great Glacial Lake *rnam-par snang-mdzad gangs-chen mtsho'i zhabs-kyi skyil-krung man-chad-las. . . zhing-khams bcu-drug*, 123

six worlds *'jig-rten drug*: listed in the Glossary of Enumerations, 414

Sosadvīpa, charnel ground of *so-sa gling-gi dur-khrod*, 469, 494, 497-8

Śrāvastī *mnyan-yod*: modern Sahet Mahet, Uttar Pradesh, 427, 430, 518

Śrī Dakṣiṇa, Stūpa/city of *mchod-rten/grong-khyer dpal yon-can*: Śrī Dhānyakaṭaka Caitya, 485, 489

Śrī Dhānyakaṭaka Caitya *shri dhana'i gling/dpal-ldan 'bras-spungs*: on the Kṛṣṇa River in Andhara Pradesh, 485, 947

Śrīmat *dpal-dang ldan-pa*: the southern field of Akaniṣṭha, 128

Śrīpāduka *shri pā-du-ka*: footprint of Śākyamuni Buddha in Śrī Laṅkā, 456, n. 469

Śrīparvata *shri par-va-ta*: Nāgārjunakoṇḍa in Andhara Pradesh, 480, n. 507

Starlike Array, aeon of *bskal-pa skar-ma bkram-pa lta-bu*, 691

Stūpa of Sorcery *phra-men mchod-rten*: at Zha in Uru, 590; Map 6, J16

Sudarśana (Extreme Insight) *shin-tu mthong*: the penultimate level among the Five Pure Abodes, 15

Sudṛśa (Attractive) *gya-nom snang-ba*: the third of the Five Pure Abodes, 15

Sukhāvatī (Buddha-field/paradise) *bde-ba-can/bde-chen zhing/bde-ldan zhing*, 21, 127, 213, 405, 468, 634, 668, 691, 693, 697, 757, 829; see also *Buddha-field of the Lotus Array*

Sumatra: see *Suvarṇadvīpa*

Sungnyen, hermitage of *gsung-snyan ri-khrod*, 818

Sūryaprakāśa, precipice of *ri-bo nyi-ma rab-tu snang-byed*, 493

Suvarṇadvīpa *gser-gling*: the island of Sumatra, 184; see also *Dhanaśrīdvīpa*

Suvarṇadvīpa city/district of Kashmir in West India *grong-khyer gser-gling/gser-gyis brgyan-pa'i gling/kha-che'i yul gser-gling*, 498, 501

Tā'i-tu, royal palace of *pho-brang ta'i tu*: Peking; GT (p. 111, n. 806), 669, n. 830

Taklung *stag-lung*: monastery north of Lhasa, founded in 1178 by Taklung Thangpa Trashipel; PPCT (pp. 88-90); TG (Ch. 19); TH (pp. 145-6), 830; Map 5, H16

Takpo *dvags-po*: region east of Ölka; KGHP (pp. 48, 121); PPCT (pp. 255-63), 544, 547, 550, 551, 686, 687, 771, 777, 812, 818; Map 8, J17/18

- Khyerdrup above Takpo *dvags-po'i yul-gyi stod khyer-grub*, 800
- Takpo Zhu *dvags-po zhu*, 548; Map 8, J18
- Taktöling, (monastery of) *dvags-stod gling(-gi-dgon-pa)*: KGHP (pp. 47, 120), 726, 727, 728

Tamdrin *rta-mgrin*: a treasure site of Guru Chöwang, probably Tamdrinling (Tamdrinzhap) at Samye, 764; Map 6, J16

Tamdringül, rock of *brag rta-mgrin mgul*: in Mustang, 751; Map 4, J08

Tamdrinzhap *rta-mgrin zhabs*: Tamdrinling at Samye; KGHP (p. 45, n. 142); PPCT (p. 224), 764; Map 6, J16

Tampuk *dam-phug*: hermitage at Katok, 695; Map 10, G23

Tāmralipti *zangs-gling*: Tamluk on the Bengal coast, 455

Tanak *rta-nag(-gi lung-pa)*: valley on the north bank of the Tsangpo River, north-west of Shigatse; KGHP (pp. 68, 157), 561, 621, 635; Map 6, J13

- Lagu-ngö in Tanak, Yeru, hermitage of *gYas-ru rta-nag-gi la-rgu-rngos-dgon*, 721; Map 6, J13
- Tanak Namding, hermitage of *rta-nag gnam-sdings/gnam-sdings dpal-gyi sgrub-khang*, 721
- Tanak Nesar *rta-nag gnas-gsar*: i.e. *sgrol-ma phug*; KGHP (p. 68), 667

Tang River *stang-chu*: in Bhutan; M. Aris, *Bhutan*, (pp. 38-40), 796; Map 6, L15

Tarding/Tarling *dar-lding/dar-ling*: see under *Tra*

Tartang Do-nga Shedrup Ling *dar-thang mdo-sngags bshad-sgrub gling*; a branch of Pelyül founded in the mid-nineteenth century by Gyatrül Rinpoche, in the Pema Dzong district of Golok; TH (pp. 605-6), 738; Map 9, E25

Tashö Kyilkor Thang *rta-shod dkyil-'khor thang*: a treasure site of Düdül Dorje, 816

Tawu *rta'u phyogs*: Taofu, between Trehor and Dartsedo in Kham; TH (pp. 501-2), 817; Map 10, H26

Tenpak *dan-phag*: north-west of Lhasa, 702; Map 6, J16

Terlung Pemei Shelri *gter-klung padma'i shel-ri*: a treasure site of Khyentse Rinpoche, Pl. 93; 856; Map 10, G23; see also *Pemashel Cave in Marshödzam*

Thak *thag*, 640; Map 6, J13

- Deshek Gyawo, college of *bde-gshegs rgya-bo'i bshad-gvra*, 641
- Gyawo, rock of *brag rgya-bo*, 622; see also *Riwo Gudü* and *(Mount) Trak Gyawo*
- Gyawo in Thak *thag-gi rgya-bo*, 633
- Thak Dongkar in Yeru, Tsang *gtsang gYas-ru'i thag gdong-khar*, 722; Map 6, J13
- Thak, river valley of *thag-gi mdo*: i.e. *span thag-ma* north of Shigatse; KGHP (p. 70), 639

Thangdrok, college of *thang-'brog grva-tshang*, 818

Thangi Yangdong *thang-gi yang-gdong*: near Dropuk, 633; Map 6, J13

Thangwar *thang-bar*: in Mustang, 751; Map 4, J08

Tharpaling, monastery of *thar-pa gling*: in Bumthang, founded by Longcenpa; Aris, *Bhutan*, (pp. 155, 315); Pl. 68; 590

Tharu kingdoms *tha-ru'i rgyal-khams*: eastern Nepal, 472

Thekcokling in Tsang *gtsang theg-mchog gling*: a small side valley between Drongtse and Nesar, 718; Map 6, J14

Thoyor Nakpo, district of *tho-yor nag-po'i yul*: birthplace of Rikdzin Gödemcen near Mount Trazang, 780; Map 4, J11

three districts *ljongs-gsum*: Sikkim (i.e. Dremojong), Khenpajong and Lungsumjong, 518

three districts of Pum, Rong and Zhak *bum-rong-bzhag gsum*: north-east Kham. Rong may be Rongtrak in Gyel-morong, while Zhak may be *bzhag-*

ra lha-rtse in Minyak, representing the body aspect of buddha-mind, 698; Map 10, H26
three districts of Tra and Töl *gra-dol-yul gsum*: Traci, Tranang and Töl: GT (p. 166); PPCT (pp. 155-70), 516; Map 6, J16
three divine realms *lha-gnas gsum*: listed in the Glossary of Enumerations, 458
three evil destinies/existences *ngan-'gro/-song gsum*: listed in the Glossary of Enumerations, 58, 767
three (world) realms *(jig-rten-gyi) khams gsum*: listed in the Glossary of Enumerations, 13, 31, 38, 51, 56, 73, 202, 259, 302, 321, 337, 339-40, 363, 418, 490, 491, 575, 907, 930
Thubten Dorje Trak *thub-bstan rdo-rje brag*, 683, 783; see *Dorje Trak*
Tibet *bod*, *passim*
four Tibetan provinces *bod ru-bzhi*: Uru and Yoru in Central Tibet with Yeru and Rulak in Tsang, 708
Land of Snows/Snow Mountains *gangs-can 'jongs*, 47, 404-5, 409, 507, 512, 522, 599, 728, 758, 791, 821, 838, 852, 861, 887, 893, 901, 905, 920, 926, 948, 949, 953, 967-8, 972
three provinces of Tibet *bod 'chol-ka gsum*: Ngari in Upper Tibet, Central Tibet including Tsang, and Amdo and Kham in Lower Tibet, 823, 953
upper, middle and lower Tibet *bod stod-dbus-smad gsum*, 747
Tidro *ti-sgro*: see *Zhotö Tidro*
Tingri (in Latö) *ding-ri (la-stod)*: PPCT (p. 281); TH (pp. 296-303); 378, 547, 569, 647, 773, 952; Map 4, K11
Namar in Tingri *ding-ri sna-dmar*, 571
Tīrahuti *ti-ra-hu-ti*: the region of Tirhut around Muzaffarpur in north-east India; Tāranātha, *History of Buddhism in India*, (pp. 133, 210, 314, 318), 472
Toklashong, temple of *dog-la gshongs-kyi gtsug-lag khang*: built by Nyang Sherapchok, 615
Töl *dol*: i.e. Tölpo in north-west Nepal — not to be confused with the valley of the same name above Cedezhöl, 544; Map 4, J08
Dong-na in Töl *dol-gyi gdong-sna*, 543
Tshercung in Töl *dol-gyi 'tsher-chung*, 543
Tölung *stod-lung*: valley of the Tölung River which flows into the Kyicu River, west of Drepung; KGHP (pp. 73, 167); PPCT (pp. 122-31), 572, 659; Map 6, J15
Tongbap, narrow pass of *dong-bab-kyi 'phrang*: at Kungtang in Mangyül, 517
Tongku *(shar-phyogs) tong-ku*: South-East Asia in general, but specifically Tongkin, 824
Tönkar Valley, uplands of *don-mkhar lung-po'i phu*: the location of Tsheringjong in Chongye; PPCT (pp. 201-2); TH (p. 205), 838; Map 6, J16 Map 6, J16
Tra *yul grva*: KGHP (pp. 54-5); PPCT (pp. 157-70), 753; Map 6, J16
Kyi in Tra, Yoru *gYo-ru grva'i skyid*, 753
Phuso Getreng in Tra, Yoru, village of *gYo-ru gra'i phu-so gad-phreng-gi grong*, 564
Tarding/Tarling/Targye Chöling in Tranang *dar-lding/dar-gling grva-nang dar-dgyas chos-gling*: the residence of Sangdak Trhinle Lhündrup; KGHP (pp. 55, 133); PPCT (p. 170), 683, 727, 825
Tödrong in the Tra Valley of Yoru, village of *gYo-ru gra'i cha stod-grong*: birthplace of Longcenpa; PPCT (p. 169), 575
Traci *gra-phyi*: on the south bank of the Tsangpo River opposite Dra; KGHP (pp. 54, 132); PPCT (pp. 160-1, 164-7), 551
Traci Khangmar *gra-phyi khang-dmar*, 685
Trakpoche in Traci *gra-phyi brag-po-che*, 776
Tranang, lower valley of *gra-nang-gi mda'*: KGHP (pp. 54, 132); PPCT (pp. 157-60), 753
Tranang Entsa *gra-nang dben-rtsa*, 789
Trapu *gra-phu*: PPCT (pp. 164-70), 591
Yarje in Tranang, Yoru *gYo-ru gra-nang-gi yar-rje*: KGHP (p. 55); PPCT (pp. 169-70), 775
Yugong Rock in Tra *gra'i gYu-gong brag*: a treasure site of Orgyen Lingpa, 776

Trakar Dzongcung *brag-dkar rdzong-chung*: a treasure site of Chogyur Lingpa, perhaps *he brag-dkar*, which represents the activity of buddha-body, 845
Trakar Lhacu *brag-dkar lha-chu*: perhaps this is Lhacu near Tölung Decen, 813; Map 6, J15
Trak Daweidong *brag zla-ba'i gdong*, 516
Trak Gyawo *brag rgya-bo*: see *(Mount) Trak Gyawo*
Trak Lhari *brag lha-ri*, 773; see also *Lhari (in Phukpoche)*
Traklong *brag-long*, 791
Trakmar *brag-dmar*: three miles north of the Tsangpo River, in the Samye area; KGHP (pp. 44, 113); PPCT (p. 230), 513, 516, 764; Map 6, J16; see also *Chimpu* and *Samye*
"Peacock Lake" of Trakmar *brag-dmar mtsho-mo mgul-sngon*, 516
Trakmar Chimpu *brag-dmar mchims-phu*: KGHP (pp. 44-5); PPCT (p. 230), 828
Trakmar Drinzang, (temple at) *brag-dmar mgrin-bzang(-gi lha-khang)*: north of Samye; KGHP, (pp. 44, 113); PPCT (p. 233), 513, 856
Trakmar Gegong in Chimpu *mchims-phu brag-dmar dge-gong*: the cave of Trakmar Keutsang at Trakmar Chimpu; PPCT (p. 230); Pls. 56, 58, 558
Tamarisk Forest of Trakmar *brag-dmar 'om-bu'i tshal*, 513
Trakmar Göndzong in Tongkungrong *stong-khung-rong-gi brag-dmar dgon-rdzong*: in Kham, 540; Map 11, J23
Trakna *brag-sna*, 678; Map 6, J12
Trak Sengei Yatö (Lion-Skull Rock) *brag seng-ge'i ya-thod*: in Ukpalung, 625; Map 6, J14
Trampagyang *gram-pa rgyangs*: near Lhartse Dzong; KGHP (pp. 66, 154), 802; Map 6, J12
Trampa, hermitage of *sram-pa grub-khang*: at Shangda Pelcen in Shang; KGHP (pp. 69, 159), 632, 634; Map 6, J14
Trangpo *drang-po*, 806
Trangpo Ulu *sprang-po 'u-lu*, 654
Trap Tsangka *grab gtsang-kha*, 778; Map 8, J17
Trashi Gomang Temple *bkra-shis sgo-mangs lha-khang*: in lower Shang, 624; Map 6, J14
Trashiling, Sikkim *'bras-yul bkra-shis gling*, 723; Map 6, L13
Trakar Trashiding *brag-dkar bkra-shis sdings*, Pl. 85; 820
Tratang *gra-thang*: in Tranang; KGHP (p. 54, 132); PPCT (pp. 158-9), 807; Map 6, J16
Tratang, the great seminary of glorious *dpal grva-thang-gi chos-grva chen-po*: founded by Trapa Ngönshe; KGHP (p. 54); PPCT (pp. 158-9), 753
Tra and Töl, three districts of *gra-dol-yul gsum*: see *three districts of Tra and Töl*
Trayatriṃśa (Heaven of the Thirty-three Gods) *sum-cu rtsa-gsum*, 14, 66, 135, 193, 438, 453, 944
Treshö Khangmar *tre-shod khang-dmar*: located in Tre-bo/Trehor in Kham, near *tre-shod lcags-mdud kha-ba lung* which represents the activity aspect of buddha-speech; Stein, *Recherches sur l'épopée et le barde au Tibet*, (pp. 214-16); TG (Ch. 49), 675; Map 10, G24
Trhadruk Temple at Tsitang Samtenling *rtsis-thang bsam-gtan gling-du khra-'brug*: Trhadruk is possibly the oldest of Songtsen Gampo's geomantic temples; PPCT (pp. 177-9); TH (pp. 191-3); Henss, *Tibet: Die Kulturdenkmäler*, (Ch. V, Sect. 5); Pls. 38, 100; 676; Map 6, J16
Como Tārā at Trhadruk, image of *khra-'brug jo-mo'i sku*: KGHP (pp. 50, 125); Pl. 43; 789
Trhadruk Khyamtö *khra-'brug khyams-stod*: KGHP (p. 50, n. 237), 777
Trhap *khrab*: near Phukpoche, 545; Map 6, J16
Trhaplakha *khrab-la-kha*, 552
Trhomzil Trhomkaryak *khrom-zil khrom-dkar-yag*: a treasure site of Düdül Dorje in the district of Derge, perhaps to be identified with *khro-ri rdo-rje zil-khrom* in Rudam, the main pilgrimage place of enlightened attributes, 815; Map 10, F24
Trhopu *khro-phu*: founded in 1171 by Gyeltsa Rincen-gön (*rgyal-tsha rin-*

chen-mgon), 660, 663, 664, 665; Map 6, J13
Great Stūpa of Trhopu *khro-phu'i 'bum-chen*, 663
Trhowoma *khro-bo-ma*, 566
Trhülnang Temple *'phrul-snang-gi gtsug-lag khang*: see *(Rasa) Trhülnang*
Trhün *'phrun*, 546
trichiliocosm, (great) *stong-gsum-gyi stong (chen-po)*, Skt. *trisahasramahā-sahasra*, 113, 120, 124, 131, 409, 414
Trikmo-lha, meadow of *krig-mo-lha'i ne'u-sing*: in Tsāri, 570; Map 8, K18
Trokpöi Sumdo *grogs-po'i sum-mdo*: near Ukpalung, 631; Map 6, J14
Tsandra (Rincen Trak) *tsa-'dra (rin-chen brag)*: at Pelpung, associated with Jamgön Kongtrül and Chogyur Lingpa, 862, 866, 867; Map 10, G23; see also *Pewar*
Secret Cave of Yeshe Tshogyel at Tsandra Rincen Trak *tsa-'dra rin-chen brag-gi mtsho-rgyal gsang-phug*: at Pelpung in Derge district, representing the mind aspect of enlightened attributes; see E. G. Smith, *Shangs-pa bKa'-brgyud*, (p. 1), 864; Map 10, G23
Tsang *gtsang*, 513, 524-5, 533, 544-5, 547-8, 574, 592, 619, 660, 663, 671, 674, 682, 685, 696, 699, 715, 717, 751, 773, 798-9, 801, 807, 811, 813, 818, 824, 830, 850, 858, 868, 921, 950, 955
Tsangpo River *gtsang-po*: the Brahmaputra, 619, 645
Tsang-rok Trashi Tsekdzong *gtsang-rog bkra-shis brtsegs-rdzong*: a treasure site of Kongtrül Rinpoche, 864
Tsangtön Mangkar *gtsang-ston mang-dkar*: gorge between Lhartse and Shekar; KGHP (pp. 64-5, 152); PPCT (pp. 279-80), 702; Map 6, K12
Tsāri *tsā-ri*: south of Takpo; PPCT (p. 263); TH (pp. 224-7), 570, 784, 786, 819; Map 8, K18
New Tsāri Hermitage *tsā-ri dgon-gsar*, 574; Map 8, K18
Palace of Secret Mantra in Tsāri *tsā-ri gsang-sngags pho-brang*, 802; Map 8, K17
Tsāri Sarma *tsā-ri gsar-ma*, 571; Map 8, K18
Tsāri Tshokar *tsā-ri mtsho-dkar*, 751; Map 8, K18
Zilcen Phuk in Tsāri *tsā-ri zil-chen phug*, 802; Map 8, K18
Tse Palace *rtse pho-brang*: the Potala in Lhasa, 777; Map 6, J16
Tsecen Trak *rtse-chen brag*: a treasure site of Sangye Lingpa, 786
Tsedong *rtse-gdong*: i.e. Tsetang and Neudong, 833; Map 6, J16
Tsele, early and later *rtse-le gong-'og*: monasteries in Takpo, 788, n. 1055
Tsetang, great seminary of (glorious) *chos-grva chen-po rtses-thang/dpal-gyi rtses*: founded in 1352 by Lama Tampa Sonam Gyeltsen of Sakya: PPCT (p. 174), 678, 681; Map 6, J16
Tshawa Drodrak *tsha-ba sgro-brag*: a treasure site of Düdül Dorje in Tshawagang; TG (Ch. 56), 815; Map 10, H22
Tshawarong *tsha-ba-rong/(lho) tsha-ba-rong*: lower valley of the Salween River, south of Tshawa Pasho, 690, 699; Map 10, H22
Tshawarong *tsha-ba-rong*: the river valley of Gyelmo Tshawarong in the far east of Kham, 540; Map 10, G/H 26/27; see also *Gyelmorong*
(Gyelmo) Taktse Castle (at Tsharong) *(tsha-rong/rgyal-mo) stag-rtse mkhar*, 540, 541; Map 10, H27
Tshometeng *mtsho-smad steng*, 727; Map 6, K16
Tshona, in Mön *mon mtsho-sna*: TH (pp. 199-201); Aris, *Bhutan* (p. 130), 839
Tshongdü *tshong-'dus*: a centre built by Lume in Traci; PPCT (p. 161), 525, 666; Map 6, J16
Tshongdü Gurmo *tshong-'dus mgur-mo*: a temple built by Guru Chöwang at Gurmo, 768
Tshurpu *mtshur-phu*: north-west of Lhasa, founded in 1189 by Karmapa I, Tüsum Khyenpa; TH (pp. 135-7); KGHP (pp. 69, 162, 168); PPCT (pp. 124-9); TG (Ch. 18), 567, 569, 570, 633; Map 6, J15
Wokmin Tshurpu *'og-min mtshur-phu*, 848
Tsike Düdo *rtsi-ke 'dus-mdo*: a seat of Chogyur Lingpa in Nangcen, 848; Map 10, F22

Tsike Norbu Pünsum *rtsi-ske nor-bu spun-gsum*, 845, 856; see also *Kela Norbu Pünsum*

Tsiki Temple *rtsis-kyi lha-khang*, 764; see *Nyangtötsi* under *Nyangru*

Tsukrum Tawu *gtsug-rum lta-bu*, 614; see also *Khardong Yönmo*

Tukdrül Pungdra, rock mountain of *brag-ri dug-sbrul spungs-'dra*: at Zangzang Lhadrak, 780; Map 4, J11

Tunglung *dung-lung*, 567

Turkestan *hor*, 473; see also *Central Asia*, *Mongolia* and *Uighur*

Turquoise Eyebrow in Mongolia *sog-po gYu'i smin-ma-can*, 137

Turtrö Monastery *dur-khrod dgon-pa*: at Tsetang in Yarlung, 552; Map 6, J16

Tuṣita (Joyful) *dga'-ldan (lha'i) gnas*: the fourth of the desire realms inhabited by Kāma divinities, 14, 21, 127, 129, 213, 416, 449, 944; see also *Pagoda of Tuṣita*

twelve different realms (of the emanational body) *(sprul-pa'i) gnas-ris bcu-gnyis*, 134-7

twelve minor kingdoms *rgyal-phran bcu-gnyis*: listed in the Glossary of Enumerations, 507, 949

twenty-five fields/world systems (on Vairocana's hands) *zhing-khams nyi-shu-rtsa-lnga*: listed in the Glossary of Enumerations, 123, 130, 409

twenty-five great pilgrimage places of Kham and Amdo *mdo-khams-su gnas-chen nyer-lnga*: listed in the Glossary of Enumerations, 518, 846

twenty-five places of attainment in Central Tibet and Tsang *dbus-gtsang-du sgrub-gnas nyer-gcig*, 518

twenty-four lands *gnas nyer-bzhi*: the sacred sites of ancient India, listed in the Glossary of Enumerations, 889

twenty mountain caves of Ngari *mnga'-ris skor-du gangs-brag nyi-shu*: listed in the Glossary of Enumerations, 518

Uighur *hor-yul*, 524; see also *Central Asia* and *Turkestan*

Ukjalung *'ug-bya lung*, 665; see also following entry

Ukpalung *(dpal) 'ug-pa lung*: south of Tsangpo, opposite Shang; KGHP (pp. 70, 162); PPCT (p. 272), 623-6, 631-2, 642, 644, 660, 668, 696, 795; Map 6, J14

- Gyötsang Gyapup, the "Pavillion of Pure Remorse" *'gyod-tshang rgya-phub*: at Ukpalung, 623
- Heruka Rock in Ukpalung *'ug-pa lung-gi heruka'i brag*, 627

Uru *dbu-ru*: the area of Central Tibet north of Lhasa, 584, 818

- upper Uru *dbur-stod*, 590, 592

Urumuṇḍa Mountain *ri mu-ru-ṇḍa*: at Mathurā; Tāranātha, *History of Buddhism in India*, (p. 34), 435

Uttarakuru (Unpleasant Sound) *sgra mi-snyan*: the northern continent inhabited by human beings, 14

Uttarasāra Forest *uttasara'i tshal*, 488

Uyuk *'u-yug*: valley in Tsang, north of Rinpung; KGHP (pp. 69, 160); TH (pp. 248-9); Pl. 61; 558; Map 6, J14; see also *Oyuk river-basin*

- lower valley of Uyuk in Tsang *gtsang 'u-yug-gi mdo*, 857-8
- Uyuk Rölpo *'u-yug rol-po*, 714

Vaiśālī *yangs-pa-can*: near modern Basarh in northern Bihar, 154, 418, 419, 427, 429, 435

"Vajra Bolt" *rdo-rje'i gtan-pa*: at Trokpoi Sumdo in Ukpalung, 631; Map 6, J14

Vajra Cavern of Oḍḍiyāna *rdo-rje'i phug*, 489

Vajrakūṭa *rdo-rje brtsegs-pa*, 460

Vajrāsana *rdo-rje gdan*: Bodh Gaya, Pl. 96; 115, 135, 137, 409, 411-12, 419, 471-2, 477, 478, 488, 493, 494, 609, 696; see also *Indestructible Seat* and *Point of Enlightenment*

Vārāṇasī *vā-rā-ṇa-si/chos-skor gnas*: i.e. Sārnāth in eastern Uttar Pradesh, 153, 422, 423, 427, 465, 466, 608, 947; see also *Benares*

Vast Conduct, realm of *yangs-pa spyod-pa*, Skt. *Vipalacaryākṣetra*, 961

Veṇupura *'od-ma'i grong*: the village of the grove of Veṇuvana near Rājagṛha, 427

Vikramaśīla *rnam-gnon tshul/bi-kra-ma-shī-la*: identified with Sultangañj at Bhagalpur in eastern Bihar, 442, 479

Vimalasvabhāva Mountain *bi-ma-la-sva-bha-va'i ri*, 431

Vindhyā Mountains *'bigs-byed ri-bo'i khong/ ri bhindra*, 504
Vṛkṣaraju, city of *grong-khyer shing-thag-can*, 426
Vulture Peak *bya-rgod phung-po'i ri*: Gṛddhrakūṭa at Rājagṛha, 136, 137, 154, 423, 590, 947
Wa Senge Cavern/Trak *va seng-ge brag*: in Gyelmorong, 541-2; Map 10, H26
Wokdong *'og-gdong*: uphill from Trampa in lower Shang; *Blue Annals*, (p. 111), 632; Map 6, J14
world realm of desire *'dod-pa'i 'jig-rten-gyi khams*: see *desire realm*
world (system) of Patient Endurance *mi-mjed 'jig-rten-gyi khams*, Skt. *Sahalokadhātu*, 21, 130, 136, 151, 190, 214, 409
Yacü Tingcung *ya-chu'i ding-chung*: birthplace of Mipham Rinpoche, 869; Map 10, F24
yakṣas, domain of *gnod-sbyin-gyi gnas*, 452-3
Yalung *rdza-chu*, 869
Yamalung *gYa'-ma lung*: north of Samye, a treasure site of Terdak Lingpa; KGHP (pp. 44, 113); PPCT (p. 233); Pl. 59; 573, 828; Map 6, J16
Yāma (Strifeless) *'thab-bral*: the third realm of desire occupied by Kāma divinities, 14
Yamdrok-gang *yar-'brog sgang*: KGHP (pp. 71, 163); PPCT (pp. 265-8), 603; Map 6, J/K 15; see also *Nine-Island Lake of Yamdrok*
  Yamdrok *yar-'brog*, 592, 601, 605, 712, 821
  Yamdrok Tonang *yul-yar-'brog do-nang*: the main hill complex in the middle of Lake Yamdrok, 559
Yamshü *yam-shud*: a centre built by Lume, identified with Traplakha, 525; Map 6, J16
Yang-en *yang-dben*: in Ukpalung, Shang, 668, 700, 717; Map 6, J14
  Yang-en Ngönmo *yang-dben sngon-mo*, 625
  Yang-en Sangakling *yang-dben gsang-sngags gling*: in Ukpalung between Panam and Shigatse; KGHP (pp. 60, 144); PPCT (p. 272), 700; Map 6, J14
  Yang-en Sermo *yang-dben ser-mo*, 624
Yangkyil, hermitage of *yang-'khyil dben-pa'i gnas*: a retreat of Chogyur Lingpa, 844; Map 10, F22
Yangleshö (Cave) *yang-le-shod(-kyi brag-phug)*: at Pharping, Nepal, 481, 610, 790; Map 4, L10
Yangpacen *yangs-pa-can*: the Zhamarpa residence, north of Tshurpu; GT (p. 78); PPCT (pp. 129-30), 676; Map 5, H15
Yangtze River *'bri-chu/klung dal-'bab*, 688
Yardzong (or Sarmo) in Dokam *mdo-khams-kyi sa-cha yar-rdzong ngam gsar-mo*: birthplace of Zurpoche, 617; Map 7, G21
Yarlha Shampo *yar-lha sham-po*: south of Yarlung; KGHP (pp. 50, 126); PPCT (pp. 184-5), 591; Map 6, K16; see also *Mount Shampo*
  Shampo *sham-po*, 571
Yartökyam, uplands of *yar-stod skyam-kyi phu*: mountains dividing the Kyicu from the Tsangpo River; KGHP (pp. 47, 119), 579; Map 6, J16
Yaru Khyungcen Rock *dbyar-ru khyung-chen brag*: the birthplace of Khyentse Rinpoche west of Longtang Drölma, 849; Map 10, F23
Yarlung *yar-lung*: KGHP (pp. 49-50, 125-6); PPCT (pp. 171-95); TG (Chs. 28-30); TH (pp. 190-1); Henss, *Tibet: Die Kulturdenkmäler* (Ch.V, Sect. 1), 545, 753; Map 6, J16
  Ce in Yarlung *yar-klung byas*, 652
  Chö in Yarlung *yar-klung 'phyos*; KGHP (pp. 53, 131), 541, 599; Map 6, J16
  Crystal Cave/Rock *yar-(k)lung shel-gyi brag(-phug)*: Yarlung Sheldrak/Shepa south-west of Tsetang, north of Chongye; GT (p. 90, n. 506); KGHP (pp. 51, 128); PPCT (pp. 190-3); TH (pp. 190-1); Pl. 77; 601, 775; see also *Sheldrak*
  Menlung, a monastery in Yarlung *yul yar-klung dgon-pa sman-lung*, 686
  Namolung in Yarlung *yar-klung na-mo-lung*, 619
  Shelri Lhei Dingkang in Yarlung *yar-lung shel-ri lha'i lding-khang*: a haunt of Lhatsün Namka Jikme at Sheldrak, 819; Map 6, J16
  Shepa in Yarlung *yar-klung shel-pa*: i.e. Yarlung Sheldrak, 599; see above *Crystal Cave*

Thangcung in Yarlung *yar-lung thang-chung*, 543
Tsentang Gozhi/Tsentang in Yarlung *(yar-klungs) btsan-thang (sgo-bzhi)*: KGHP (pp. 52, 129); PPCT (pp. 190, 195), 507, 552; Map 6, J16
Tsharteng in Yarlung *yar-klungs mtshar-steng*, 570
Yavadvīpa *nas-gling*: Java, 455
Yaze Trakdong, rock at *ya-zad brag-gdong-gi brag*: in Shang, 629; Map 6, J14
Yegyel Namkadzö *ye-rgyal nam-mkha'i mdzod*: a treasure site of Chogyur Lingpa in southern Nangcen, representing the attribute aspect of buddha-speech, 845; Map 7, G21
"Store of the Sky" *nam-mkha' mdzod*, 843
Yubel Rock, south of Yegyel *ye-rgyal lho-phyogs gYu-'bal brag*, 846
Yerpa *yer-pa*: north-east of Lhasa; GT (p. 83); KGHP (pp. 43, 103-4); PPCT (pp. 73-9); TG (Ch. 17); Pl. 49; 525, 537, 591; Map 6, J16
Como Nagyel, upper cave of *jo-mo nags-rgyal-gyi phug-pa*, 715
Moon Cave (Dawa Phuk) at Yerpa *yer-pa zla-ba phug*: KGHP (pp. 43, 104); PPCT (p. 75), 715
Sewalung in Yerpa, rock of *yer-pa se-ba lung-gi brag*, 715
Yeru, Tsang *gYas-ru gtsang*: eastern Tsang, 635, 721
Yesuthar *gYas-su thar*: at Trak Gyawo in Thak, 622; Map 6, J13
Yige Trukma *yi-ge drug-ma*: in Bhutan, 796
Yöla Rock *yol-ba brag*: at Sedrak in the northern mountains of Tsang, 652
Yölcak *yol-lcags*, 709
Yoru *gYo-ru*: area in Central Tibet, south of Lhasa, 591, 753, 818
upper Yoru *gYo-ru stod*, 657
Yülser *yul-gser*, 619
Yumbu Lagang Palace *pho-brang yum-bu gla-sgang*: in Yarlung; KGHP (pp. 49, 124, 125); PPCT (pp. 179-83); TG (Ch. 30); TH (pp. 194-5); Henss, *Tibet: Die Kulturdenkmäler* (Ch. V, Sect. 4); Pl. 35; 508; Map 6, J16
Yungdrung Rincen Terne *gYung-drung rin-chen gter-gnas*: perhaps Yungdrung-ling in Yeru, 609
Yuri Gango *gYu-ri sgang-'go*: the residence of Düdül Dorje in Putö, 816; Map 8, H20
Yutso Rincen Trak *gYu-mtsho rin-chen brag*: at Tsāri Nyingma, 815; Map 8, K18; see also *Nyingmei Yutso* and *Tsāri*
Shinje Donka in Yutso *gYu-mtsho gshin-rje'i dong-kha*: a treasure site of Düdül Dorje, 815; Map 8, K18
Zabulung *zab-bu-lung*: in Shang; KGHP (pp. 69, 160), 819; Map 6, J14
Metsornyen at Zaplung, cave of *zab-lung me-tshor gnyan-gyi phug-pa*, 791
Zaplung *zab-lung*, 791
Zamka *zam-kha*, 561
Zangcen district in Tsang *gtsang-gi gnas-gzhi bzang-can*, 544
Zangdok Pelri, monastery of *zang-mdog dpal-ri dgon-pa*: in Kalimpong, West Bengal, 42, 379; Map 6, L13
Zang-ri *zangs-ri*: north of Tsangpo, east of Densathil; KGHP (pp. 47-8); PPCT (pp. 245-8); TH (pp. 217-20); 545; Map 8, J17
Zangtso *zang-mtsho*, 567
Zangzang Lhadrak *(brag-ri dug-sbrul spung-'dra sked-pa) zang-zang lha-brag(-gi phug-pa)*: the location of a cave on the slopes of Mount Tukdrül Pungdra, near Trazang; KGHP (p. 65, n. 539), 780-1, 807; Map 4, J11
Ze *gzad(-lung)*: valley adjacent to Shuksep and close to the Kyicu River, 651, 653, 654, 655; Map 6, J16
Dong in Ze, monastery of *gzad-kyi gdong dgon-pa*, 653
Lhadong Monastery in Ze *gzad-kyi lha-gdong dgon-pa*, 653
Talung in the upper valley of Ze, monastery of *gzad-phu'i da-lung dgon-pa*, 656
Thangkya in Ze, temple of *gzad thang-skya'i gtsug-lag khang*: not to be confused with Thangkya Lhakhang, on which see PPCT (pp. 109-10), 656, 659
Uke (Monastery in Ze) *(gzad-kyi) 'ug-skad (dgon-pa)*, 653, 655, 656, 658, 791
Zecen *ze-chen*, 860; see *Zhecen*
Zecen Tenyi Targyeling *ze-chen bstan-gnyis dar-rgyas-gling*, 869
Zha in Uru *dbu-ru zha*: KGHP (pp. 44, 110); PPCT (pp. 111-12); TH (pp. 149-50), 542, 589-90; Map 6, J16

Zha Temple in Uru *dbu-ru zha'i lha-khang*, Pl. 64; 556, 589, 811

Zhalu *zha-lu*: in Tsang, founded in 1040; KGHP (pp. 60, 143); PPCT (p. 271); TG (Ch. 39); TH (pp. 271-5), Henss, *Tibet: Die Kulturdenkmäler* (Ch. IX), 905, 955; Map 6, J13

Zhang-Zhung *zhang-zhung yul*: the Kuge region east of Gartok—an important kingdom of western Tibet before the rise of the Yarlung dynasty, 473; Map 4, G/H05

Zhapje, monastery of *zhabs-rjes dgon-pa*: in Takpo, 777; Map 8, J18

Zhecen *zhe(-chen)*: monastery in Derge district between Nangdo and Dzokcen founded in 1735 by Zhecen Rapjam II, Gyurme Künzang Namgyel; TH (pp. 473-4); Teichman, *Travels of a Consular Officer in Eastern Tibet* (pp. 81, 231); Pl. 73; 733, 847, 849, 867, 869, 879; Map 10, F23; see also *Zecen*

Zhoktarling *zhog-thar gling*, 594

Zhöl Pillar *rdo-ring zhol*: at Lhasa, 520

Zhotö Tidro *gzho-stod ti-sgro*: KGHP (pp. 44, 112); PPCT (pp. 117-21); TH (pp. 151-2); Pl. 69, 517, 554, 591, 676, 791; Map 5, H17

Crystal Cave of Zhotö Tidro *gzho-stod ti-sgro'i shel-phug*, 548

great assembly hall of the ḍākinīs at Tidro *ti-sgro'i tshogs-khang chen-mo*: PPCT (p. 119), 676

Tidro Rock in Zho *gzho'i ti-sgro brag*: PPCT (p. 119), 557

Zhugi Dorje Gombu *zhug-gi rdo-rje sgom-bu*, 609

Zhung *gzhung*, 562; Map 6, J16

Zhungtrezhing *gzhung spre-zhing*: the Kagyü residence of Ngok Chöku Dorje, in the Namrap valley, east of Gongkar; KGHP (pp. 55, 134); PPCT (pp. 154-5), 807; Map 6, J16

Zingpa Tago *zing-pa stag-mgo*, 679

Zotang *zo-thang*: a gold-field, 545

Zungkar *zung-mkhar*: near Thangkya, 659; Map 6, J16

Zurkar *zur-mkhar*: KGHP (pp. 46, 117), 516, 955; Map 6, J16

(Stone) Stūpas of Zurkardo *zur mkhar-rdo'i mchod-rten*: five stūpas by the Tsangpo River, west of Samye; KGHP (pp. 46, 117); PPCT (pp. 219-21); Pl. 54; 585, 776

Zurmang Monastery/Seat *zur-mang dgon/gdan-sa*: founded in 1475, north-east of Nangcen on the Dzacu River; TH (pp. 484-87); C. Trungpa, *Born in Tibet* (Chs. 2-3), 675, 842; Map 7, F21

Maps

Introduction

The maps in this section have been specially prepared to illustrate the geographical scope of Indo-Tibetan Buddhism over the centuries from the Nyingma standpoint in particular. Their primary function is to assist the reader in locating the various places mentioned in the *History*, and although current international frontiers including the *de facto* Sino-Indian border are shown as a visual aid, their inclusion should under no circumstances be interpreted as authoritative or as a statement on recent political events.

The geographical areas illustrated here are:

1 Buddhist India and Adjacent Regions
2 North-Central India
3 Tibet
4 Western Tibet and Nepal
5 North-Central Tibet
6 South-Central Tibet and Bhutan
7 North-West Kham
8 South-West Kham
9 Amdo
10 North-East Kham
11 South-East Kham

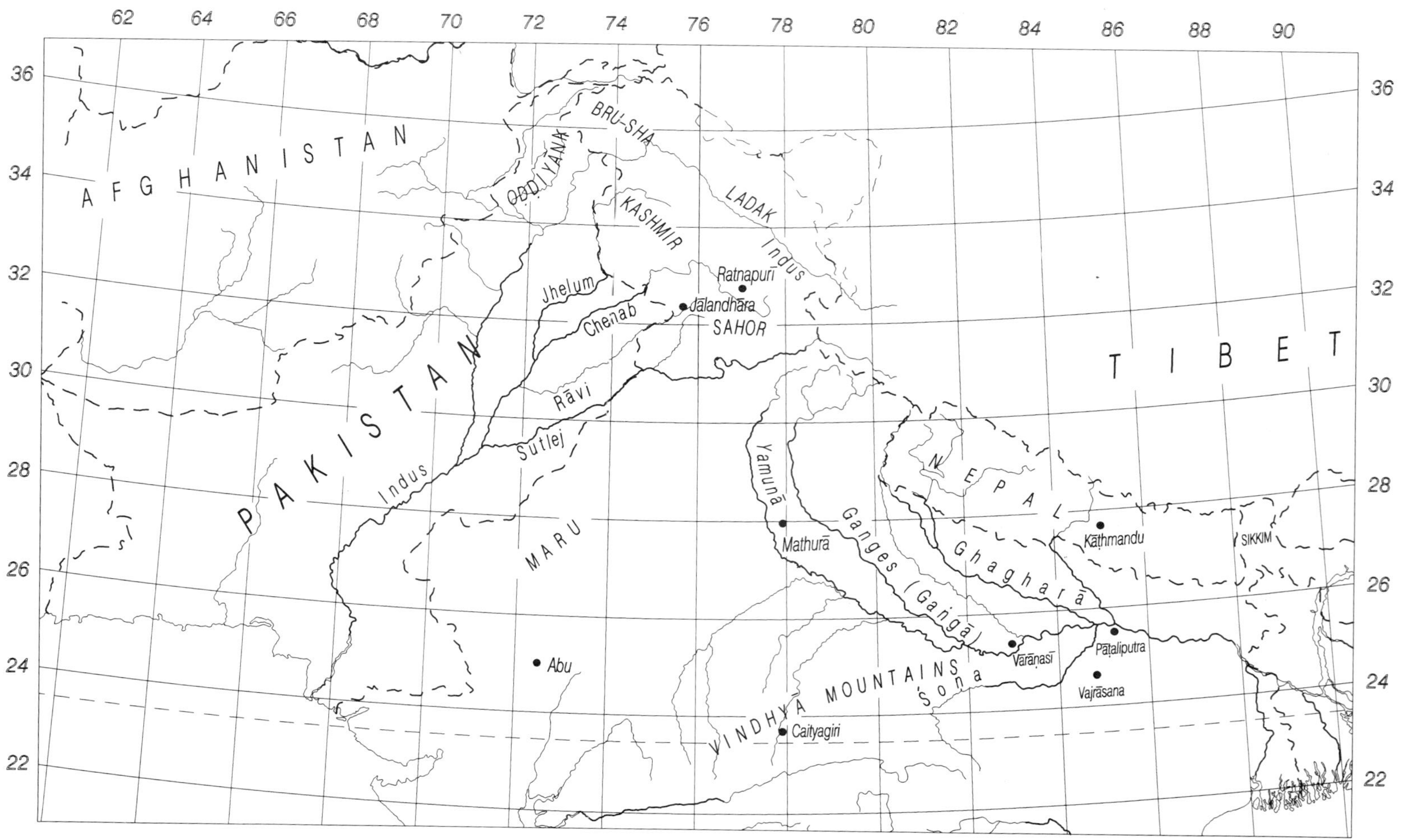
AFGHANISTAN
PAKISTAN
TIBET
NEPAL
SIKKIM
ODDIYANA
BRU-SHA
KASHMIR
LADAK
SAHOR
MARU
VINDHYA MOUNTAINS
Indus
Jhelum
Chenab
Rāvi
Sutlej
Yamunā
Ganges (Gaṅgā)
Ghagharā
Śona
Ratnapurī
Jālandhāra
Mathurā
Vārāṇasī
Pāṭaliputra
Vajrāsana
Kāṭhmandu
Abu
Caityagiri
62
64
66
68
70
72
74
76
78
80
82
84
86
88
90
36
34
32
30
28
26
24
22

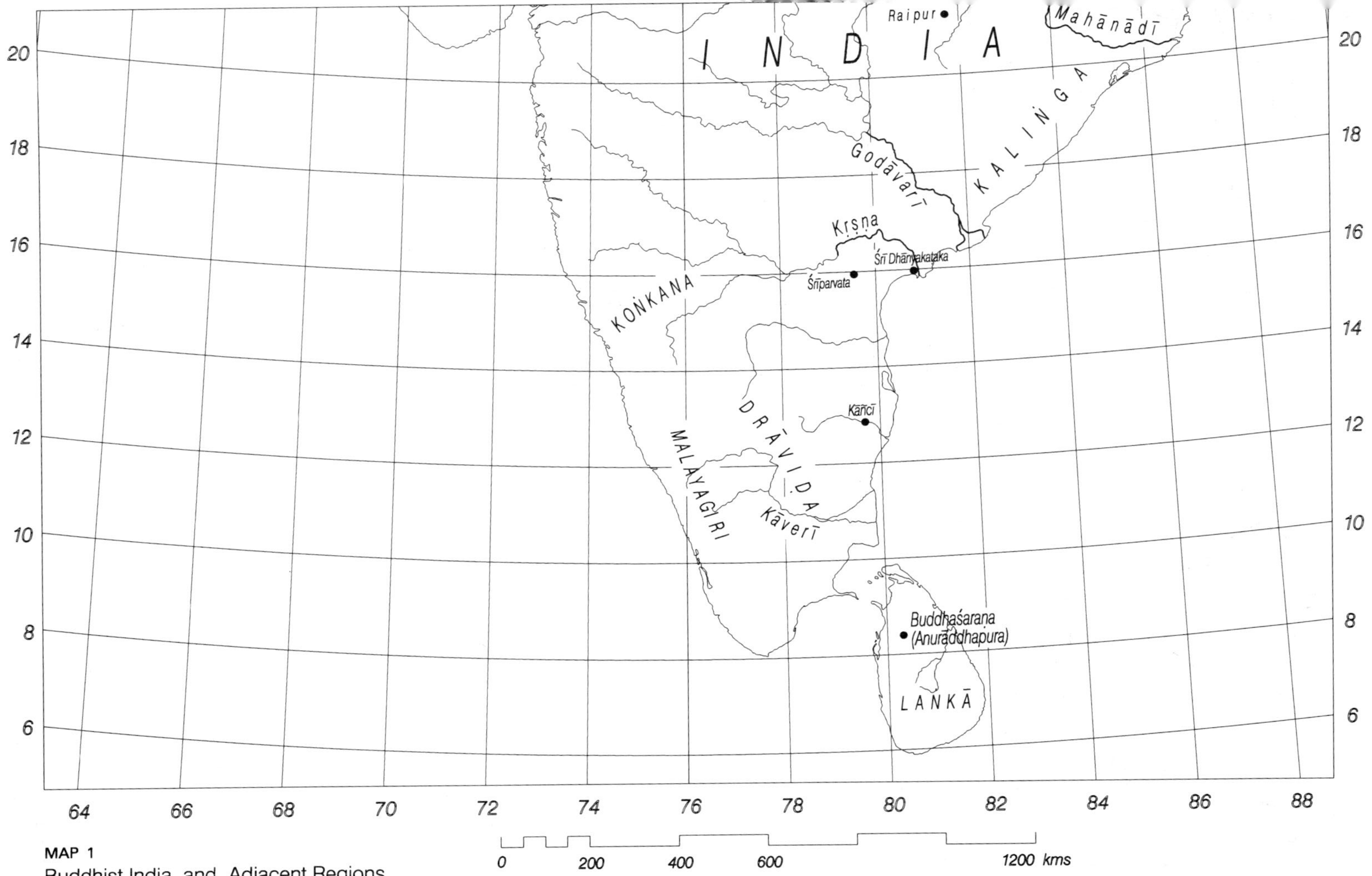

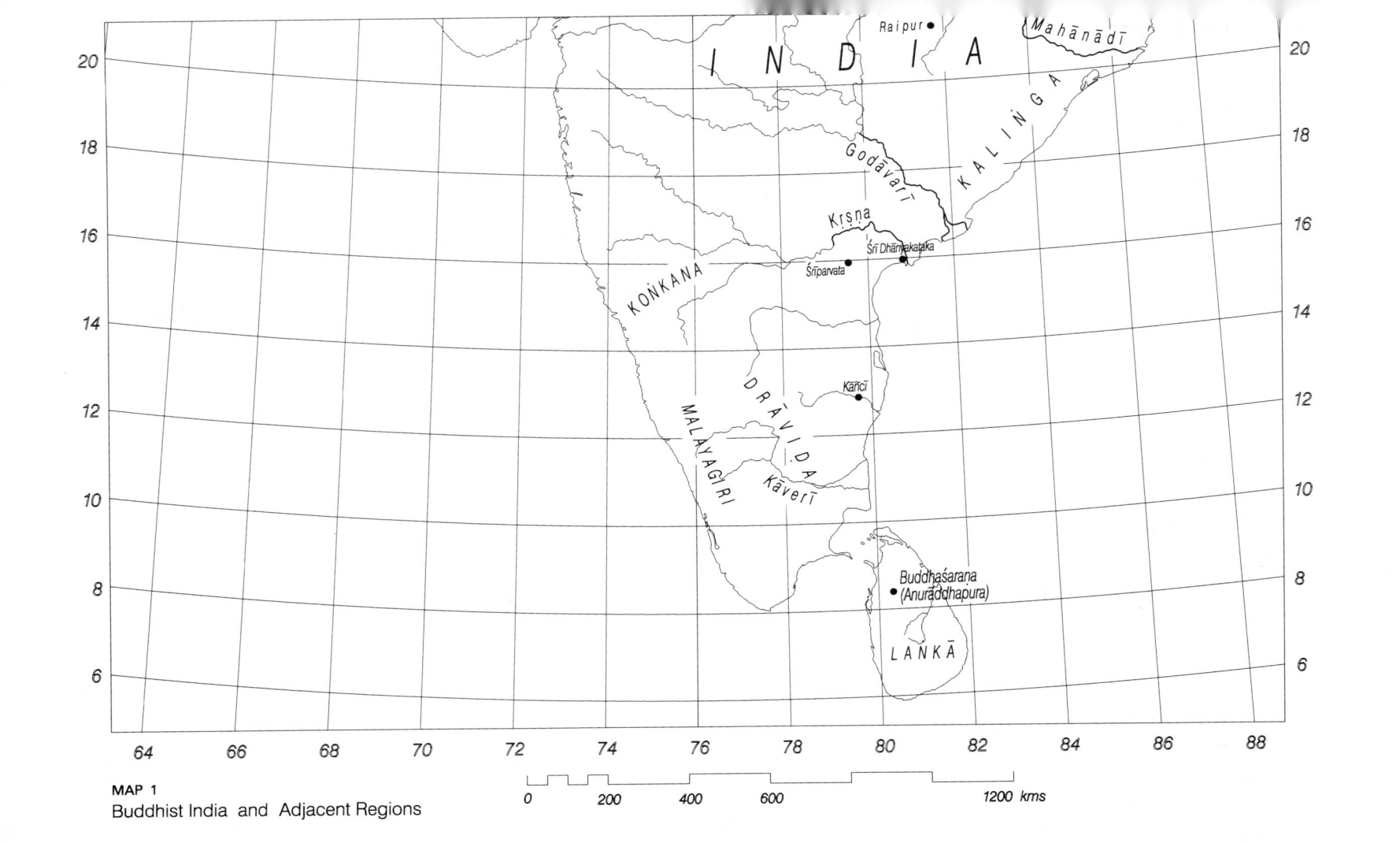

MAP 1
Buddhist India and Adjacent Regions

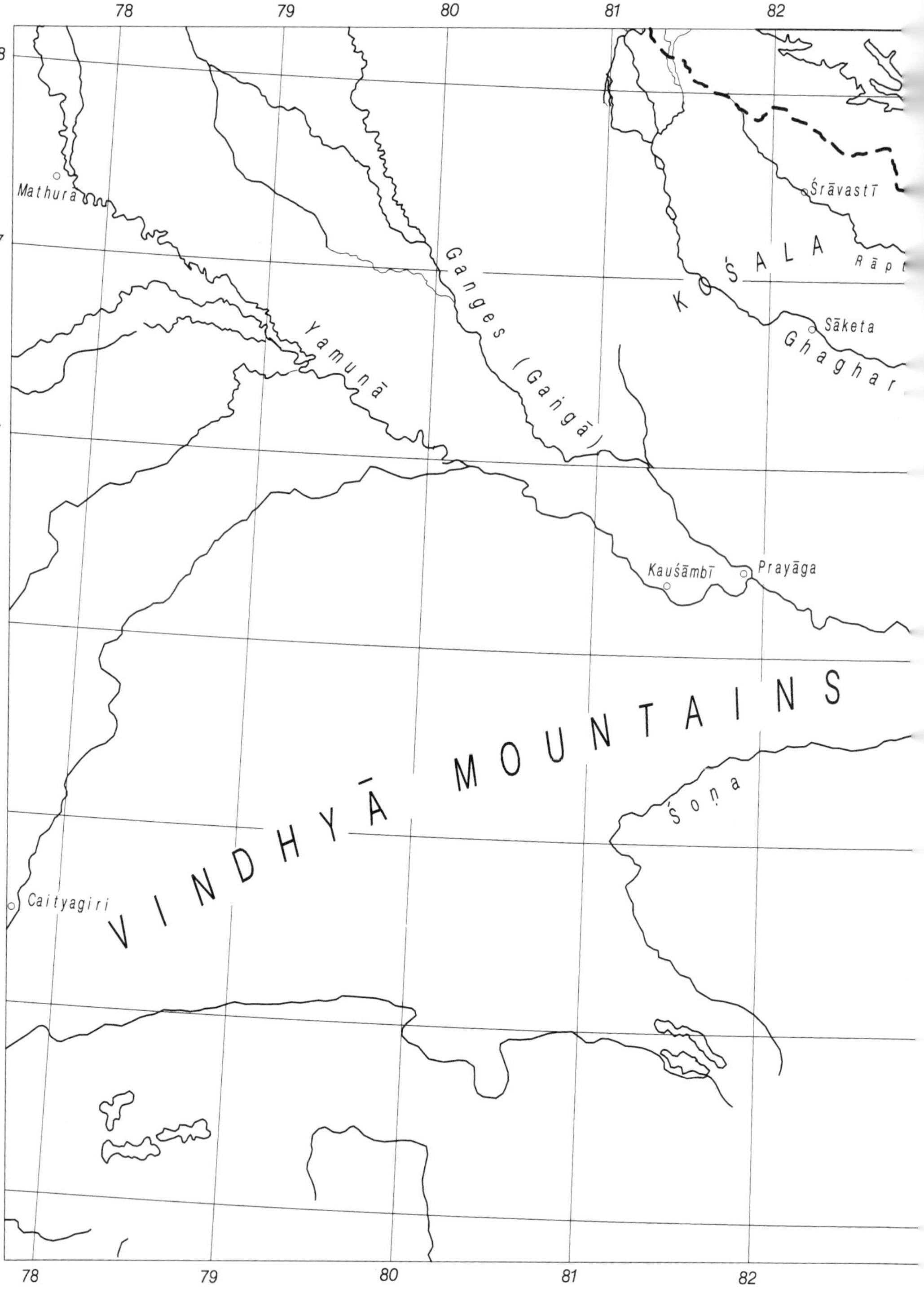

MAP 2
North–Central India

0 50 100 200 kms

Land over 1000 M

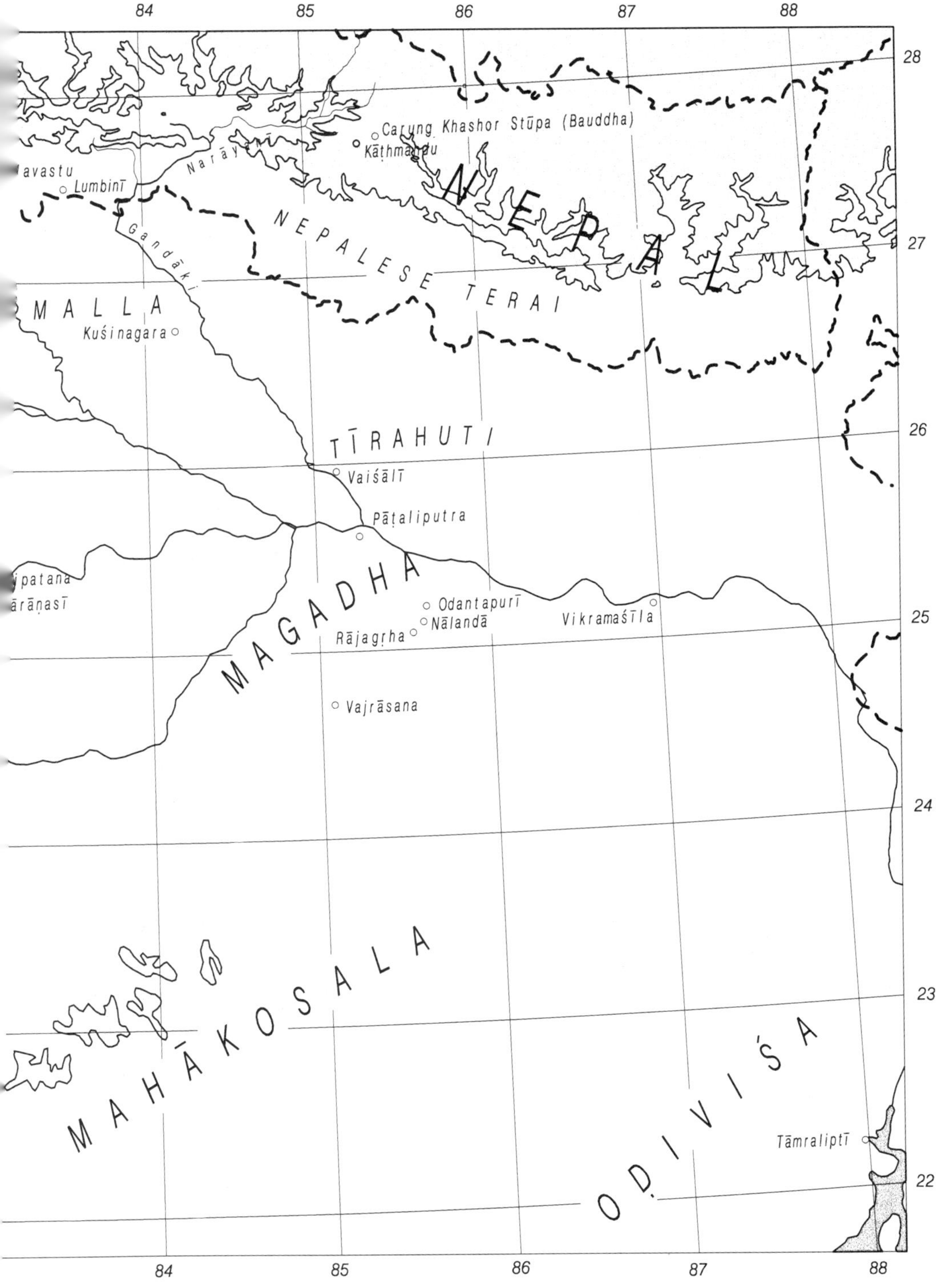

Carung Khashor Stūpa (Bauddha)
Kāṭhmāṇḍu
NEPAL
NEPALESE TERAI
Lumbinī
Gandākī
MALLA
Kuśinagara
TĪRAHUTI
Vaiśālī
Pāṭaliputra
MAGADHA
Odantapurī
Nālandā
Rājagṛha
Vikramaśīla
Vajrāsana
MAHĀKOSALA
ODIVIŚA
Tāmraliptī
84
85
86
87
88
28
27
26
25
24
23
22

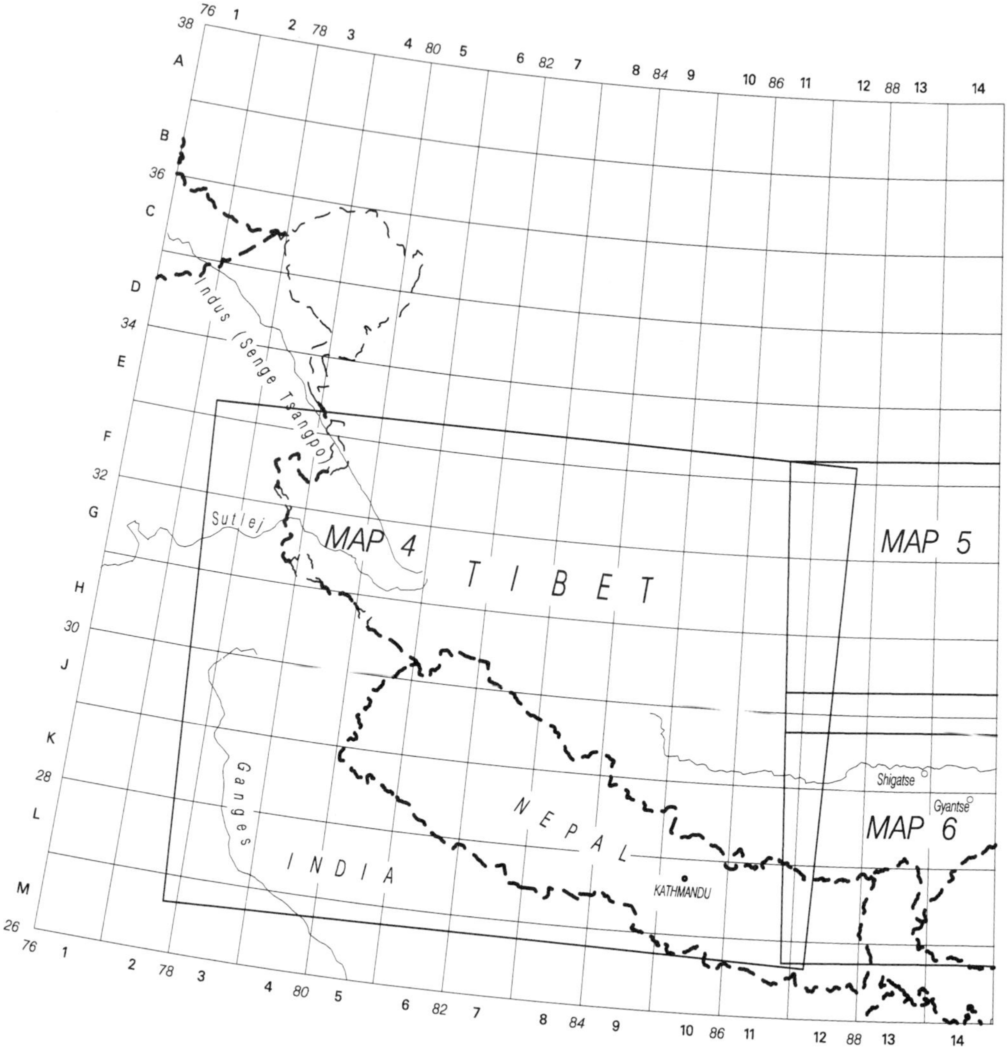

MAP 3
Tibet

0 100 200 300 600 kms

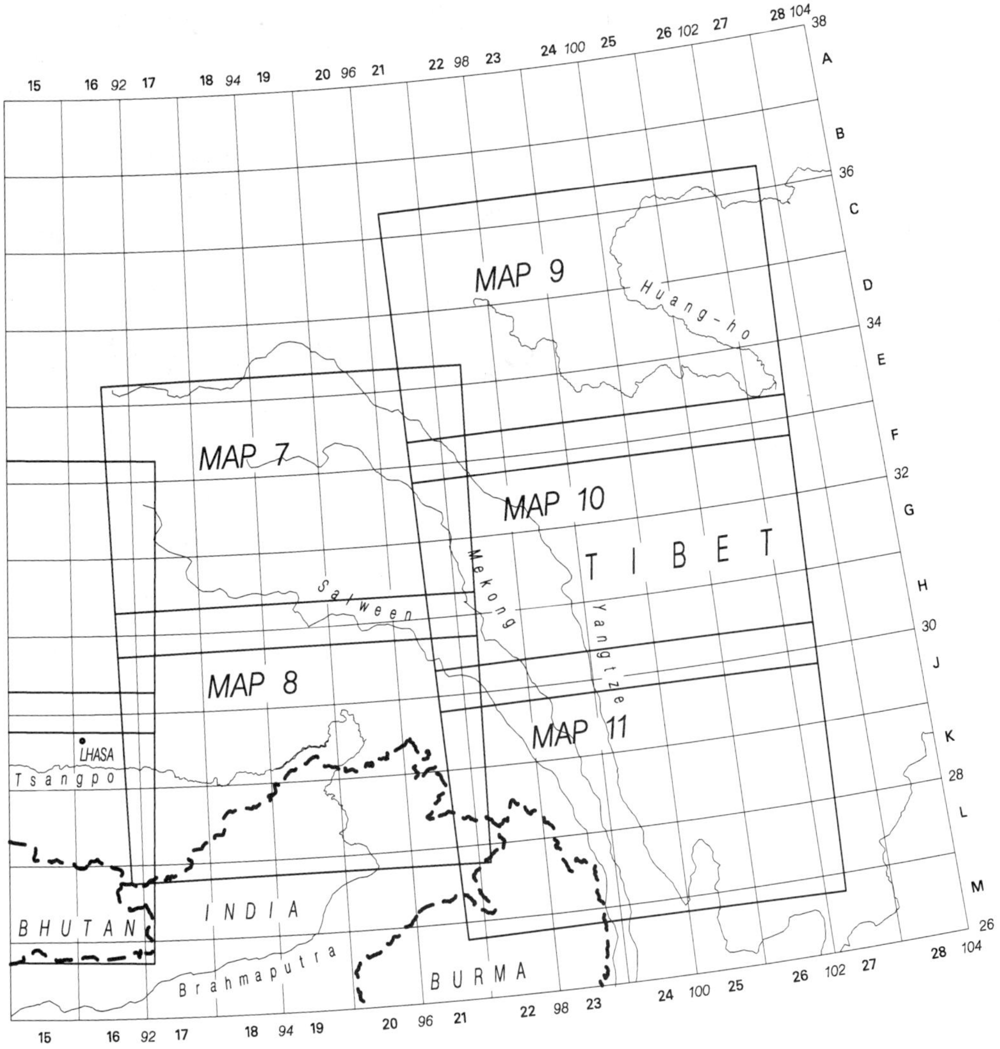
MAP 7
MAP 8
MAP 9
MAP 10
MAP 11
TIBET
INDIA
BHUTAN
BURMA
LHASA
Tsangpo
Brahmaputra
Salween
Mekong
Yangtze
Huang-ho
15
16 92
17
18 94
19
20 96
21
22 98
23
24 100
25
26 102
27
28 104
38
A
B
36
C
D
34
E
F
32
G
H
30
J
K
28
L
M
26

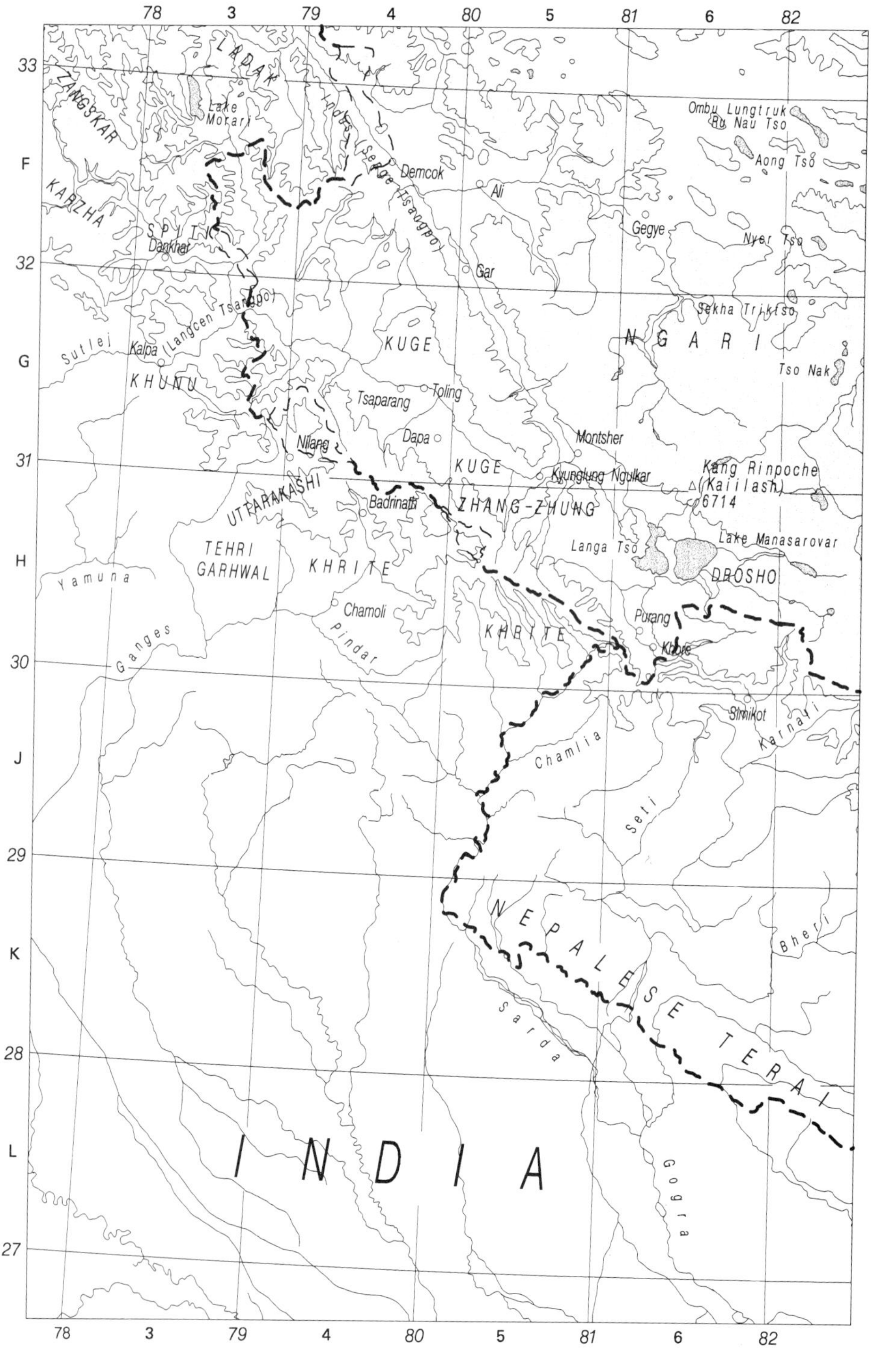

MAP 4
Western Tibet and Nepal

0 50 100 200 kms

Land over 5000 M

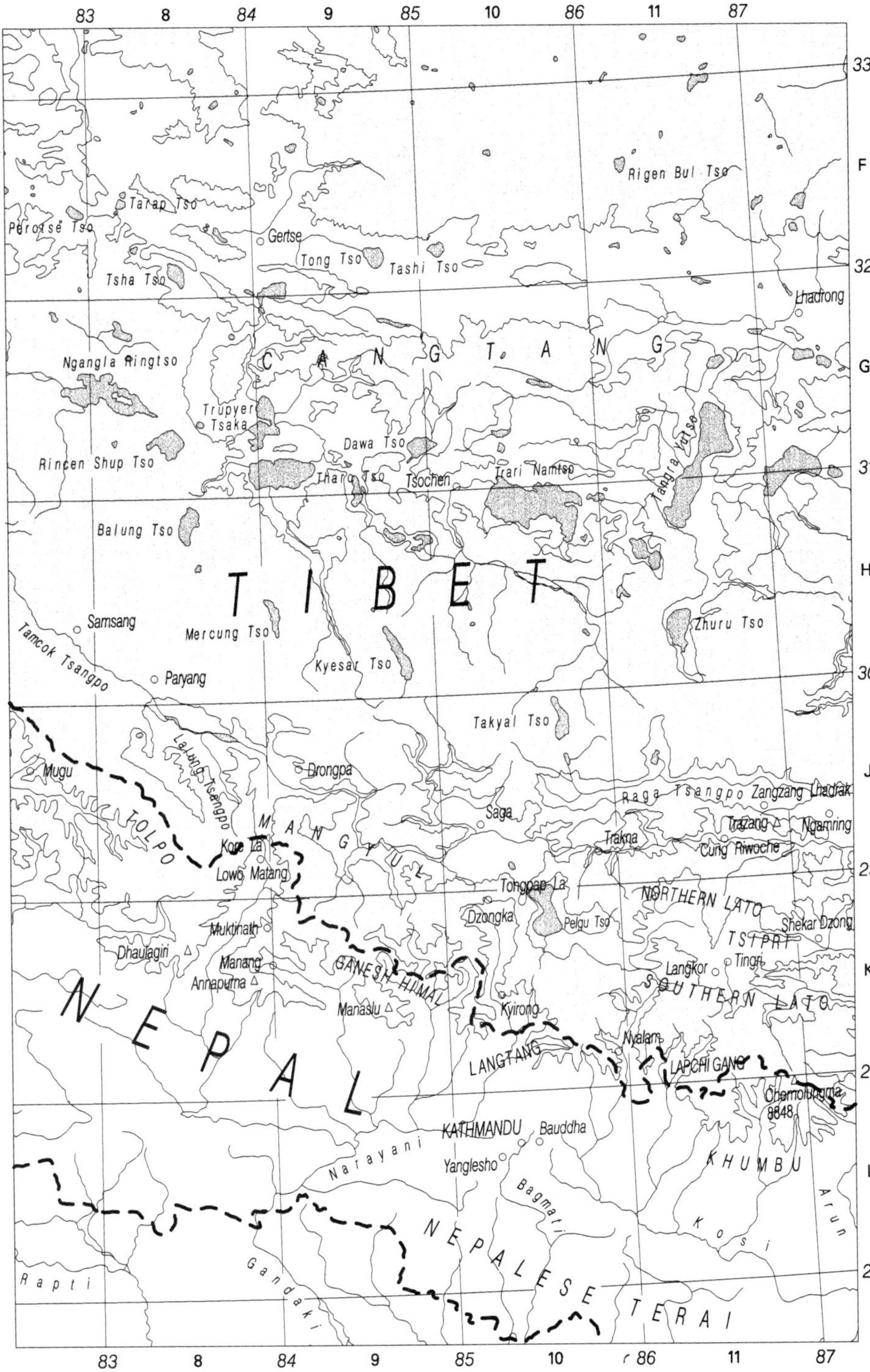
83
8
84
9
85
10
86
11
87
33
F
32
G
31
H
30
J
29
K
28
L
27
Rigen Bul Tso
Tarap Tso
Perotse Tso
Gertse
Tong Tso
Tashi Tso
Tsha Tso
Lhadrong
C A N G T A N G
Ngangla Ringtso
Trupyer Tsaka
Dawa Tso
Rincen Shup Tso
Tharo Tso
Tsochen
Trari Namtso
Tangra Yutso
Balung Tso
TIBET
Samsang
Mercung Tso
Zhuru Tso
Tamcok Tsangpo
Kyesar Tso
Paryang
Takyal Tso
Lalung Tsangpo
Mugu
Drongpa
Raga Tsangpo
Zangzang
Lhadrak
Saga
Trazang
Ngamring
TOLPO
MANGYUL
Kore La
Trakna
Cung Riwoche
Lowo Matang
Tongpap La
NORTHERN LATO
Dzongka
Pelgu Tso
Shekar Dzong
Muktinath
TSIPRI
Dhaulagiri
Manang
GANESH HIMAL
Langkor
Tingri
Annapurna
SOUTHERN LATO
NEPAL
Manaslu
Kyirong
Nyalam
LANGTANG
LAPCHI GANG
Chomolungma
8848
KATHMANDU
Bauddha
Yanglesho
KHUMBU
Narayani
Bagmati
Arun
NEPALESE TERAI
Kosi
Gandaki
Rapti
83
8
84
9
85
10
86
11
87

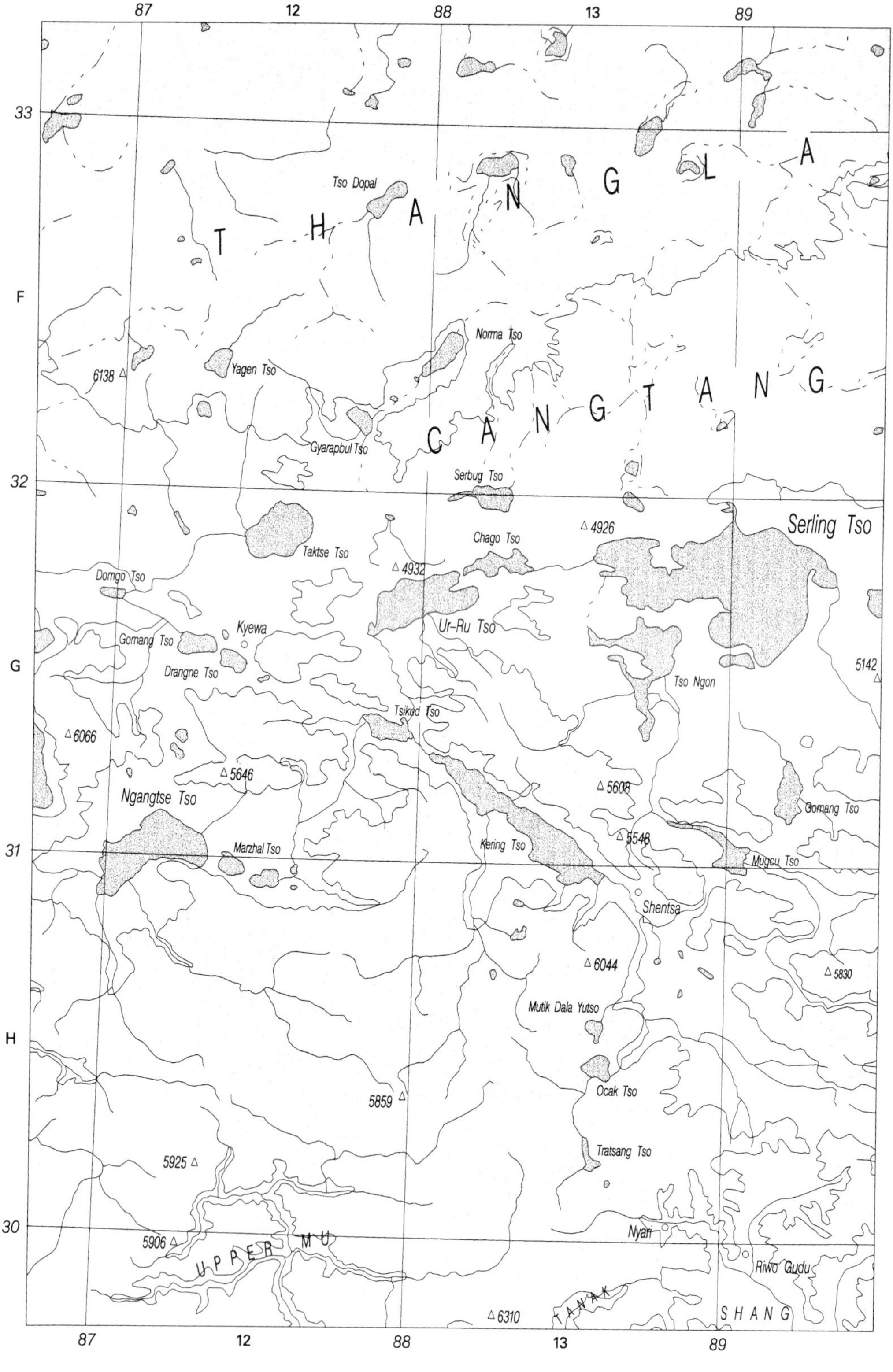

MAP 5
North–Central Tibet

0 50 100 kms

Land over 5000 M

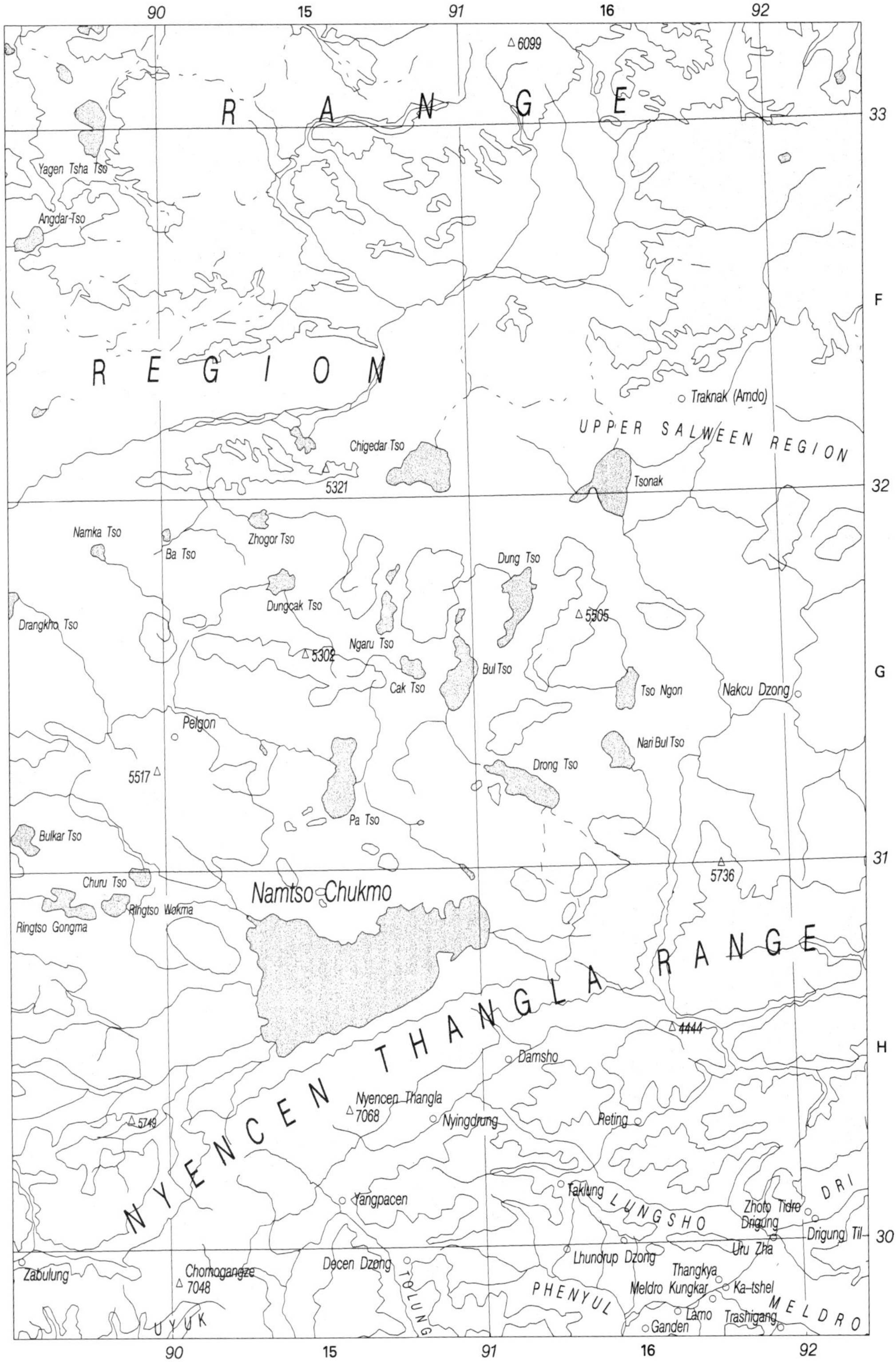
90
15
91
16
92
6099
R A N G E
33
Yagen Tsha Tso
Angdar-Tso
F
R E G I O N
Traknak (Amdo)
UPPER SALWEEN REGION
Chigedar Tso
5321
Tsonak
32
Namka Tso
Ba Tso
Zhogor Tso
Dung Tso
Dungcak Tso
5505
Drangkho Tso
Ngaru Tso
5302
Bul Tso
Cak Tso
Tso Ngon
Nakcu Dzong
G
Pelgon
Nari Bul Tso
Drong Tso
5517
Pa Tso
Bulkar Tso
31
5736
Churu Tso
Namtso Chukmo
Ringtso Wokma
Ringtso Gongma
NYENCEN THANGLA RANGE
4444
H
Damsho
Nyencen Thangla
7068
5749
Nyingdrung
Reting
Yangpacen
Taklung
LUNGSHO
DRI
Zhoto Tidro
Drigung
Drigung Til
30
Uru Zha
Zabulung
Chomogangze
7048
Decen Dzong
TOLUNG
Lhundrup Dzong
Thangkya
PHENYUL
Meldro Kungkar
Ka-tshel
MELDRO
Lamo
Trashigang
UYUK
Ganden
90
15
91
16
92

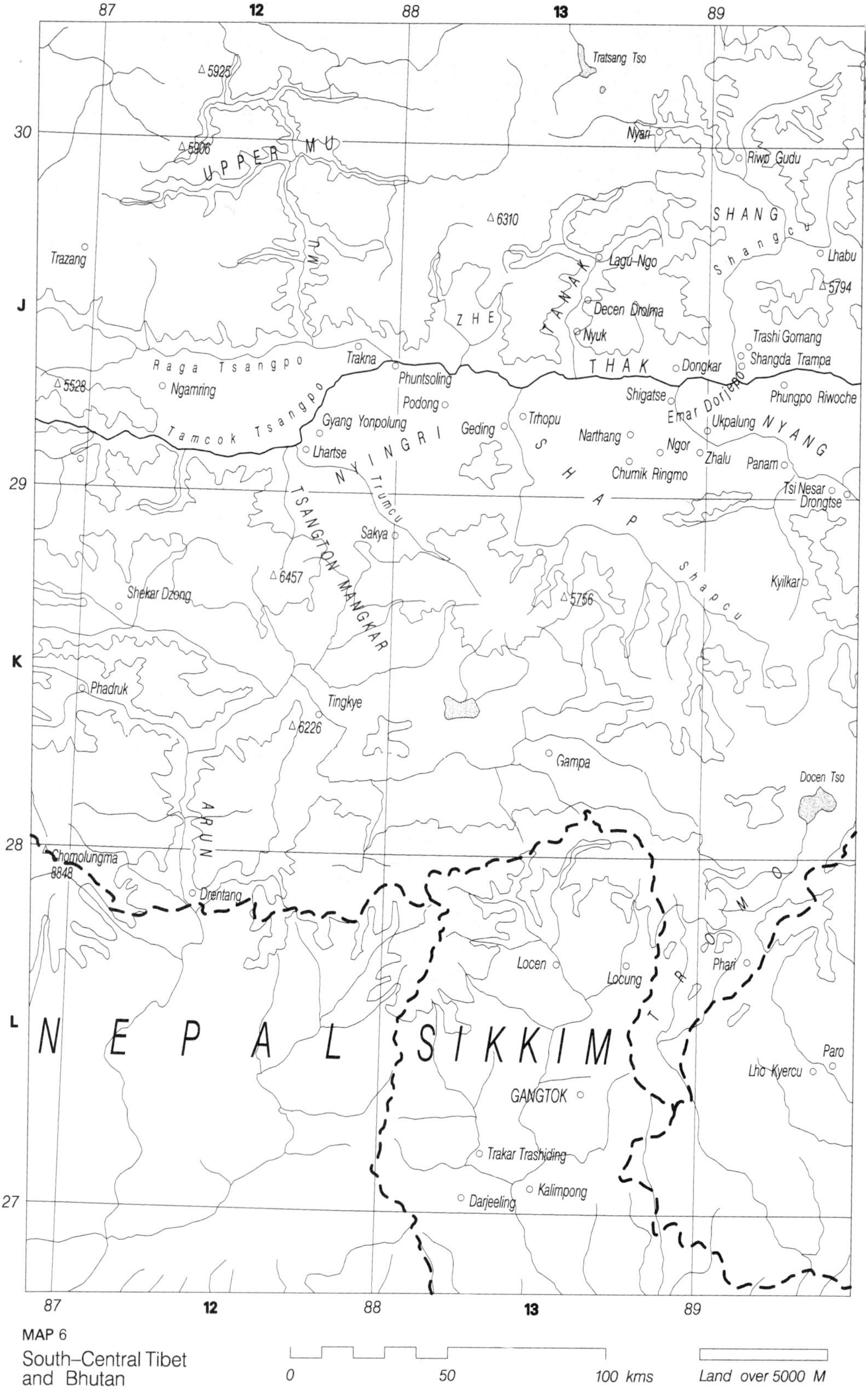

MAP 6
South–Central Tibet and Bhutan

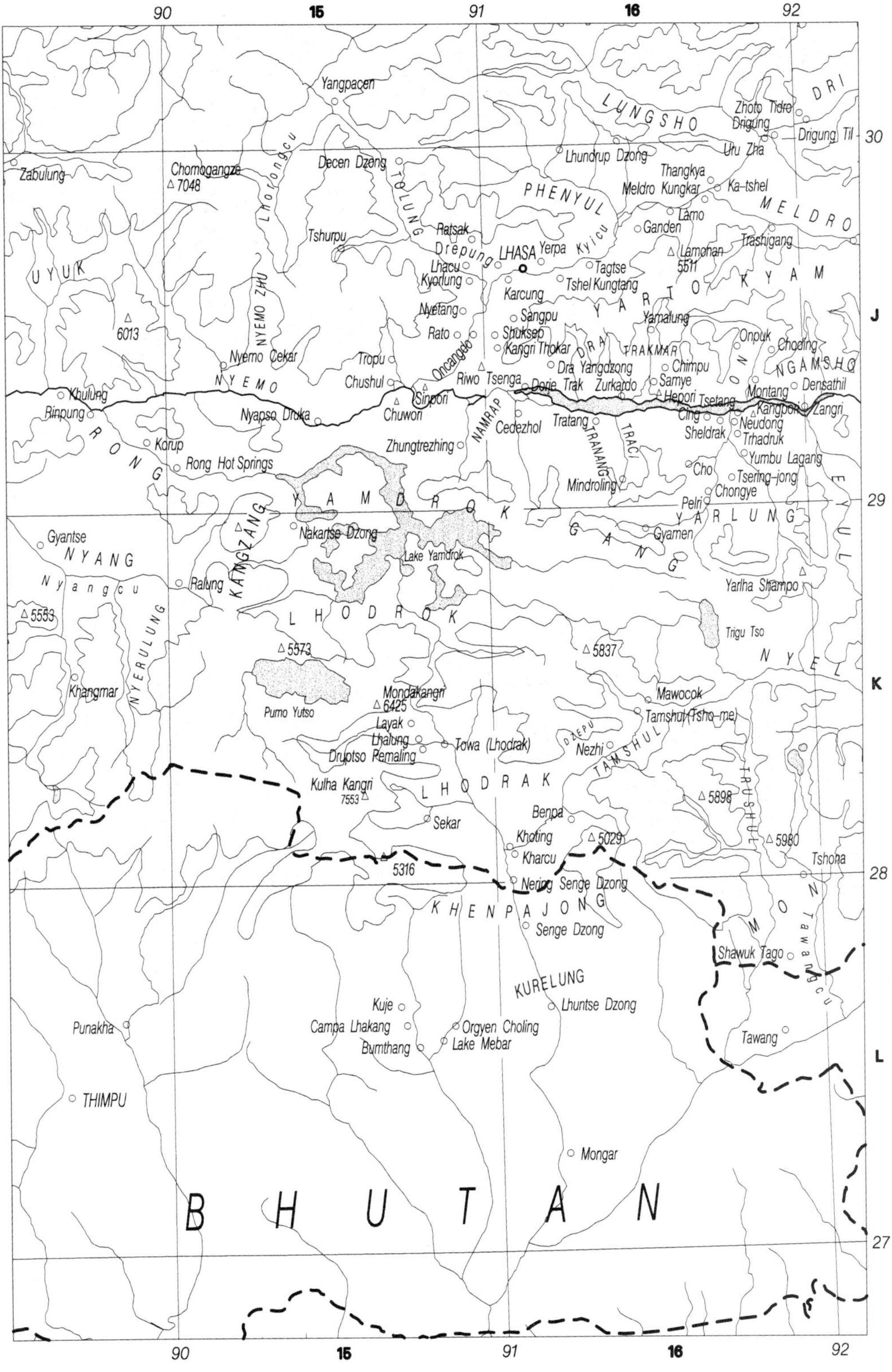

90
15
91
16
92
30
29
28
27
J
K
L
Yangpacen
LUNGSHO
DRI
Zhoto Tidro
Drigung
Drigung Til
Uru Zha
Lhundrup Dzong
Zabulung
Chomogangze
7048
Lhorongcu
Decen Dzong
TOLUNG
PHENYUL
Thangkya
Meldro Kungkar
Ka-tshel
MELDRO
Lamo
Ganden
Tshurpu
Ratsak
Drepung
LHASA
Yerpa
Kyicu
Trashigang
Lamohan
5511
UYUK
NYEMO ZHU
Lhacu
Kyorlung
Tagtse
Tshel Kungtang
YARTO KYAM
Karcung
Nyetang
Sangpu
6013
Rato
Shuksep
Yamalung
Kangri Thokar
DRA
TRAKMAR
Onpuk
Choding
Nyemo Cekar
Oncangdo
Tropu
Dra Yangdzong
Chimpu
NGAMSHO
Chushul
Riwo Tsenga
Dorje Trak
Zurkardo
Samye
Densathil
NYEMO
Khulung
Sinpori
Hepori
Tsetang
Montang
Binpung
Chuwori
NAMRAP
Kangpori
Zangri
Nyapso Druka
Cedezhol
Tratang
Cing
Neudong
RONG
Korup
Zhungtrezhing
TRANANG
TRACI
Sheldrak
Trhadruk
Rong Hot Springs
Yumbu Lagang
Cho
Tsering-jong
Mindroling
Chongye
YAMDROK
Pelri
EYUL
YARLUNG
Gyantse
Nakartse Dzong
GANG
Gyamen
NYANG
KAMGZANG
Lake Yamdrok
Nyangcu
Ralung
Yarlha Shampo
5553
NYERULUNG
LHODROK
Trigu Tso
5573
5837
NYEL
Khangmar
Mondakangri
6425
Mawocok
Pumo Yutso
Tamshul (Tsho-me)
Layak
Lhalung
Towa (Lhodrak)
DZEPU
Druptso Pemaling
Nezhi
TAMSHUL
TRUSHUL
Kulha Kangri
7553
LHODRAK
5898
Benpa
Sekar
Khoting
5029
5980
Kharcu
5316
Tshona
Nering Senge Dzong
KHENPAJONG
MON
Senge Dzong
Tawangcu
Shawuk Tago
KURELUNG
Kuje
Lhuntse Dzong
Punakha
Campa Lhakang
Orgyen Choling
Bumthang
Lake Mebar
Tawang
THIMPU
Mongar
BHUTAN

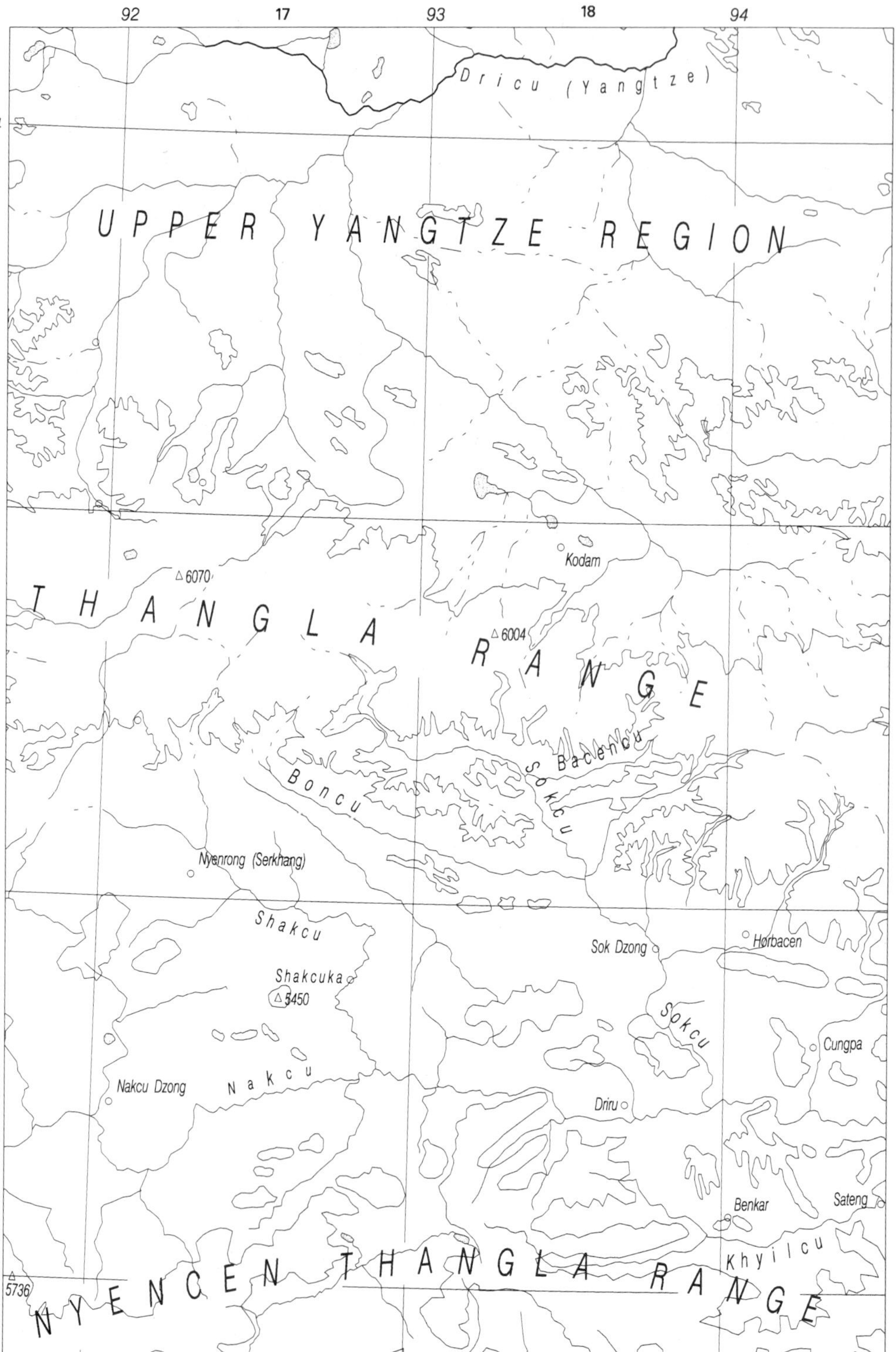

MAP 7
North–West Kham

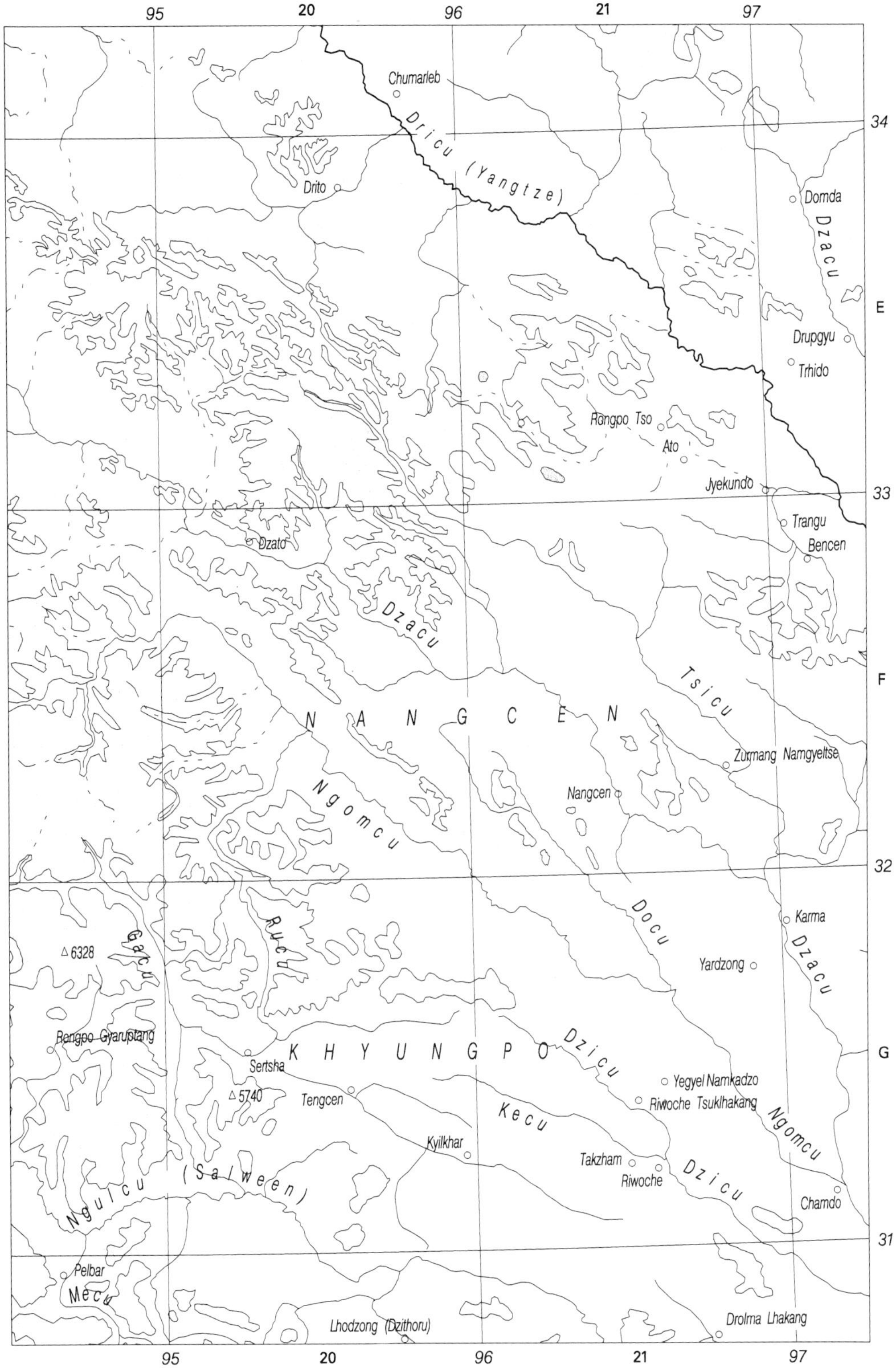

95
20
96
21
97
34
33
32
31
E
F
G
Chumarleb
Dricu (Yangtze)
Drito
Domda
Dzacu
Drupgyu
Trhido
Rongpo Tso
Ato
Jyekundo
Trangu
Bencen
Dzato
Dzacu
Tsicu
N A N G C E N
Zurmang Namgyeltse
Nangcen
Ngomcu
Docu
Karma
Dzacu
Yardzong
△ 6328
Gacu
Rucu
Rongpo Gyaruptang
K H Y U N G P O
Dzicu
Sertsha
Yegyel Namkadzo
△ 5740
Tengcen
Riwoche Tsuklhakang
Kecu
Ngomcu
Kyilkhar
Takzham
Riwoche
Dzicu
Chamdo
Ngulcu (Salween)
Pelbar
Mecu
Lhodzong (Dzithoru)
Drolma Lhakang

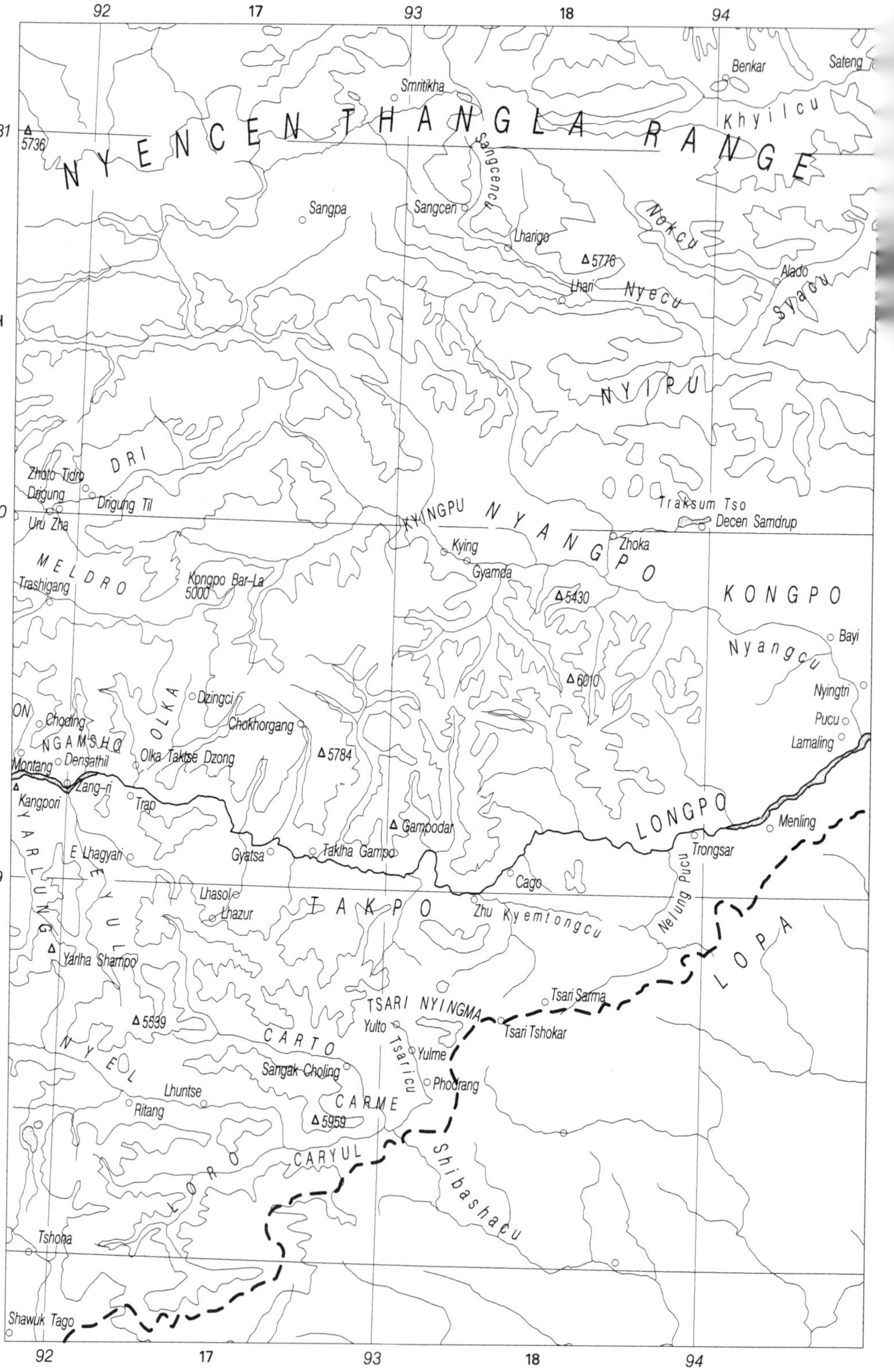

MAP 8
South–West Kham

0 50 100 kms

Land over 5000 M

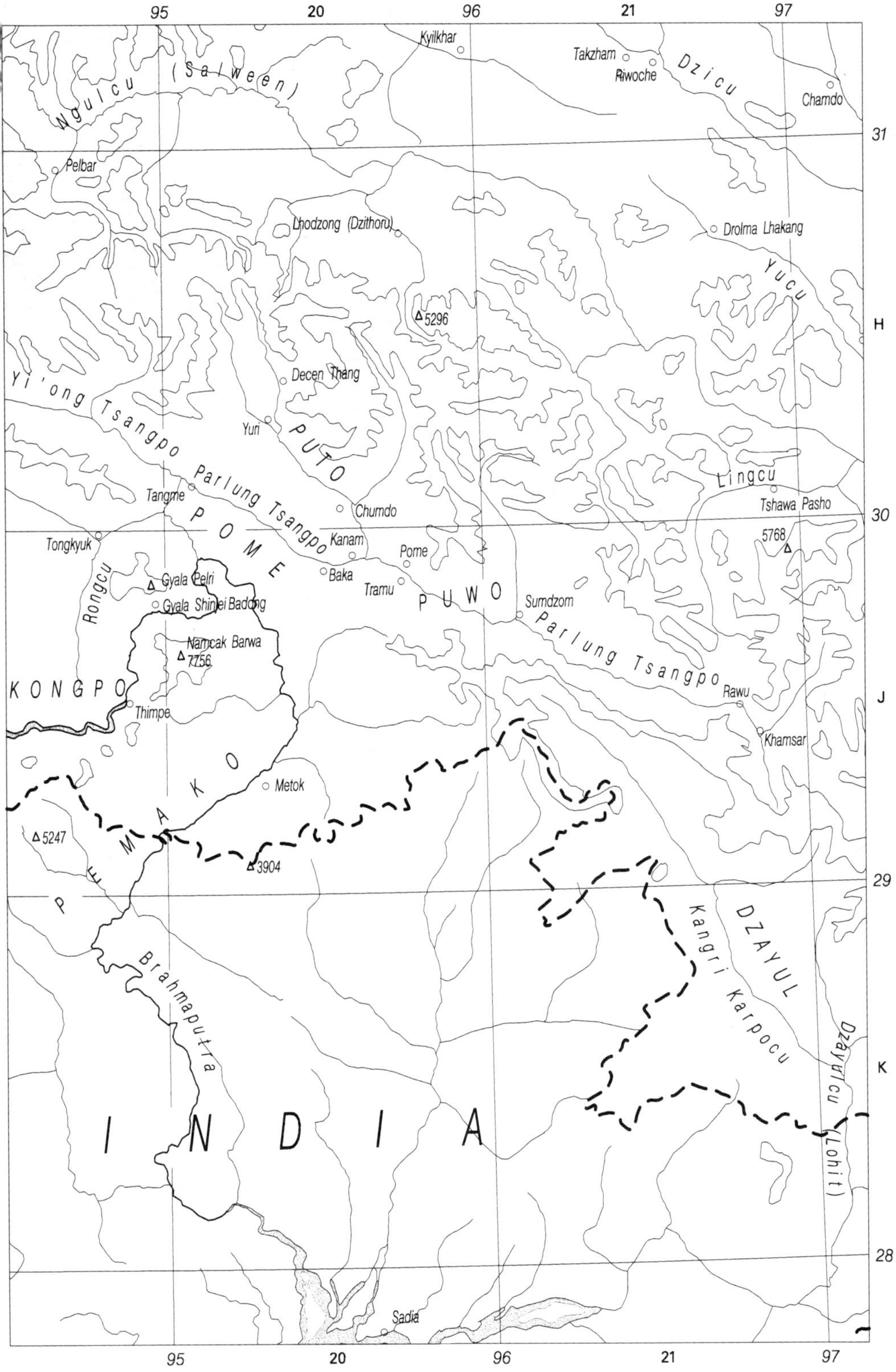

95
20
96
21
97
31
30
29
28
H
J
K
Kyilkhar
Takzham
Riwoche
Dzicu
Chamdo
Ngulcu (Salween)
Pelbar
Lhodzong (Dzithoru)
Drolma Lhakang
Yucu
5296
Decen Thang
Yi'ong Tsangpo
Yuri
PUTO
Parlung Tsangpo
Tangme
Chumdo
Lingcu
Tshawa Pasho
5768
Tongkyuk
POME
Kanam
Pome
Baka
Tramu
PUWO
Sumdzom
Rongcu
Gyala Pelri
Gyala Shinjei Badong
Namcak Barwa
7756
KONGPO
Thimpe
Rawu
Khamsar
Metok
PEMAKO
5247
3904
DZAYUL
Kangri Karpocu
Brahmaputra
Dzayulcu (Lohit)
INDIA
Sadia

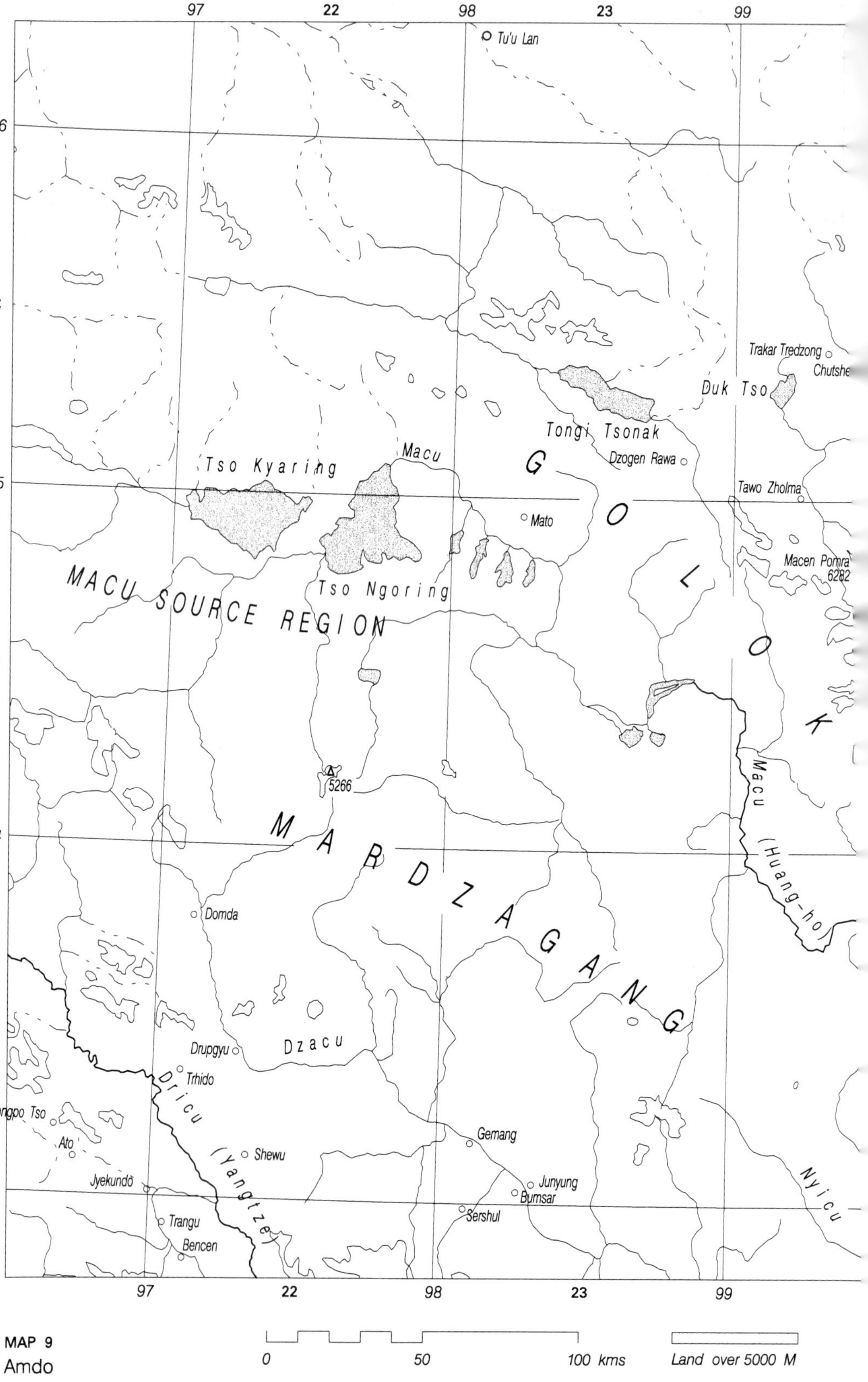
97
22
98
23
99
Tu'u Lan
36
C
Trakar Tredzong
Chutshe
Duk Tso
Tongi Tsonak
Dzogen Rawa
Macu
G
O
L
O
K
Tso Kyaring
35
Tawo Zholma
Mato
Macen Pomra
6282
MACU SOURCE REGION
Tso Ngoring
D
5266
Macu
(Huang-ho)
M
A
R
D
Z
A
G
A
N
G
34
Domda
E
Drupgyu
Dzacu
Trhido
Dricu
(Yangtze)
Rongpo Tso
Ato
Shewu
Gemang
Jyekundo
Junyung
Bumsar
Sershul
33
Trangu
Bencen
Nyicu
97
22
98
23
99
0
50
100 kms
Land over 5000 M

MAP 9
Amdo

26
100
25
101
102
Tentik
4469
4485
Kungho
Dorjei Trakra
Encung Nam Dzong
Trhikhakhar (Ku'e-Te)
36
Hoka
Magithang (Centsha)
Macu (Huang-ho)
REPKONG
Ku'e-Nan
Shing Hae
Rongpo
C
Gucu
Thung-te
Xiahe
Labrang
Tsekho
35
ARIG
Xueshan
Arig Rabgya
Amchok
Lucu Dzong
Lucu
D
Tawo (Macen)
GOLOK
Macu Dzong
34
GOLOK
Bagcen (Gade)
Macu (Huang-ho)
Gyurne (Dalak)
E
Jikdril
Tartang Do-nga
Shedrup Ling
NYENPO YURTSE
Garcu
Dome Gongma
33
Dodrup Chode
Parma
Marcu
Docu
Ngawa
Ngacu
Hongyuan
100
25
101
26
102

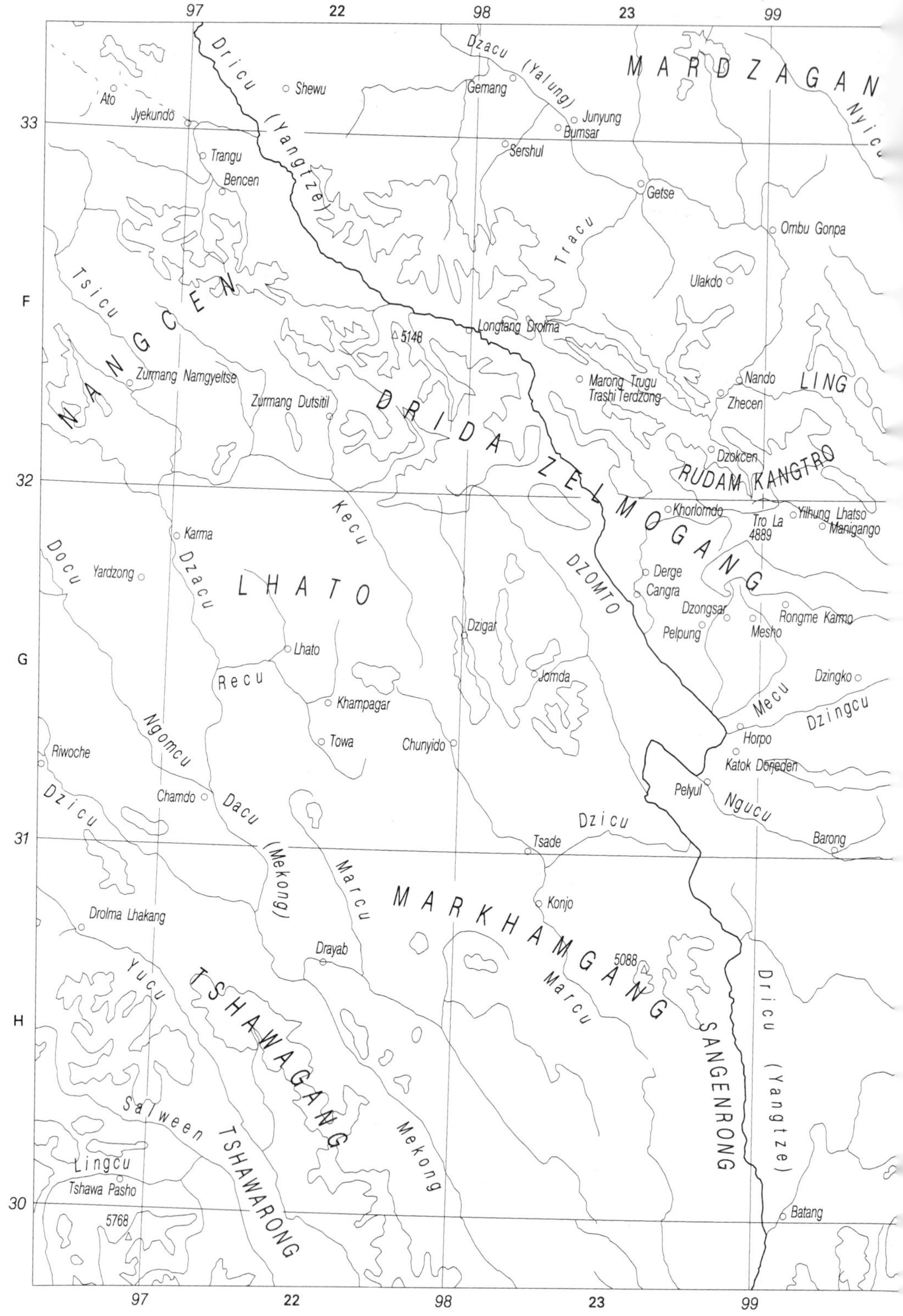

MAP 10
North–East Kham

0 50 100 kms

Land over 5000 M

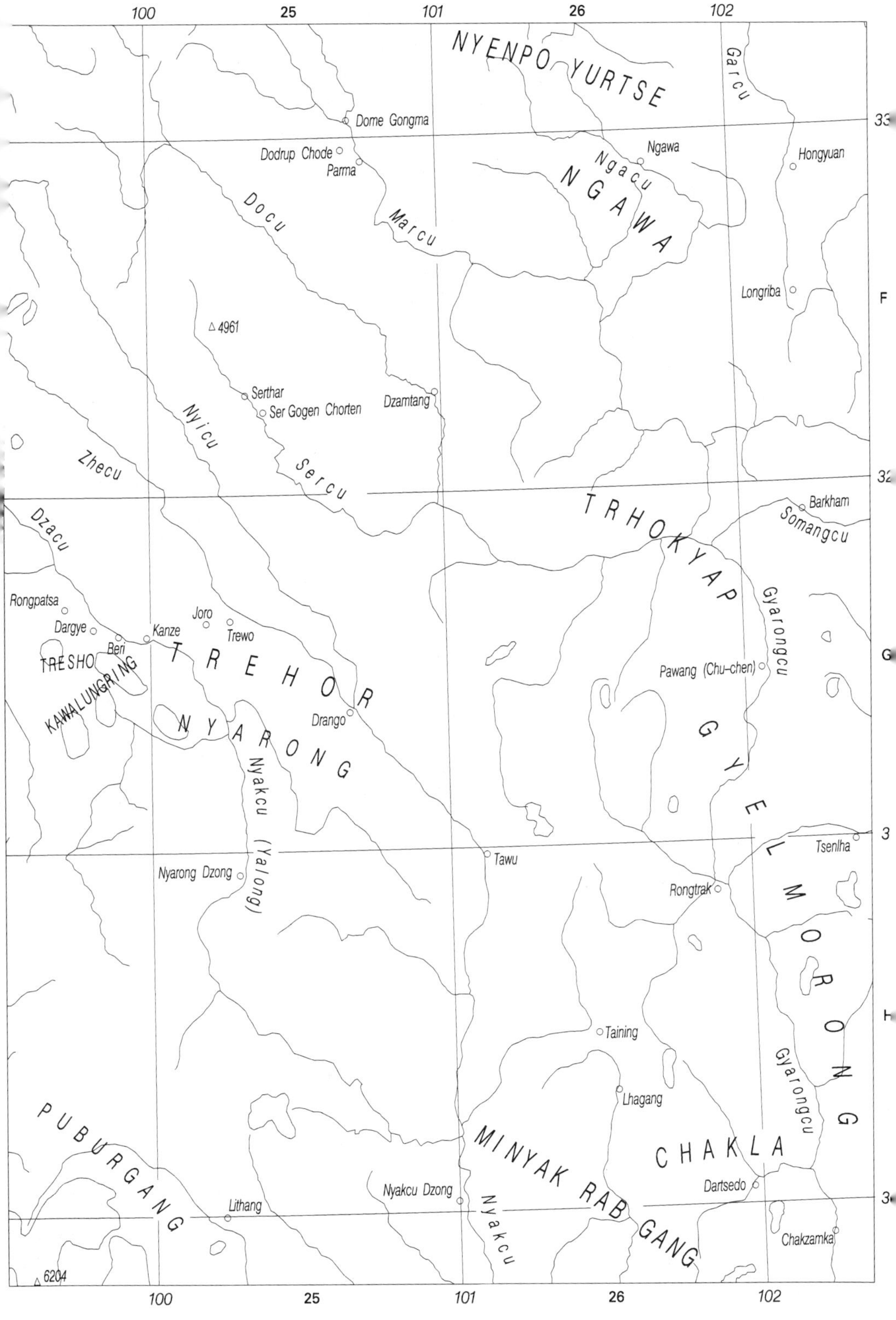

100
25
101
26
102
NYENPO YURTSE
Garcu
Dome Gongma
Dodrup Chode
Parma
Ngawa
Ngacu
NGAWA
Hongyuan
Docu
Marcu
Longriba
4961
Serthar
Ser Gogen Chorten
Dzamtang
Nyicu
Zhecu
Sercu
Dzacu
TRHOKYAP
Barkham
Somangcu
Rongpatsa
Dargye
Joro
Trewo
Kanze
Beri
TRESHO
KAWALUNGRING
TREHOR
NYARONG
Drango
Nyakcu (Yalong)
Gyarongcu
Pawang (Chu-chen)
GYELMORONG
Tawu
Tsenlha
Nyarong Dzong
Rongtrak
Taining
Lhagang
Gyarongcu
PUBURGANG
MINYAK RABGANG
CHAKLA
Dartsedo
Nyakcu Dzong
Nyakcu
Lithang
Chakzamka
6204
F
G
H

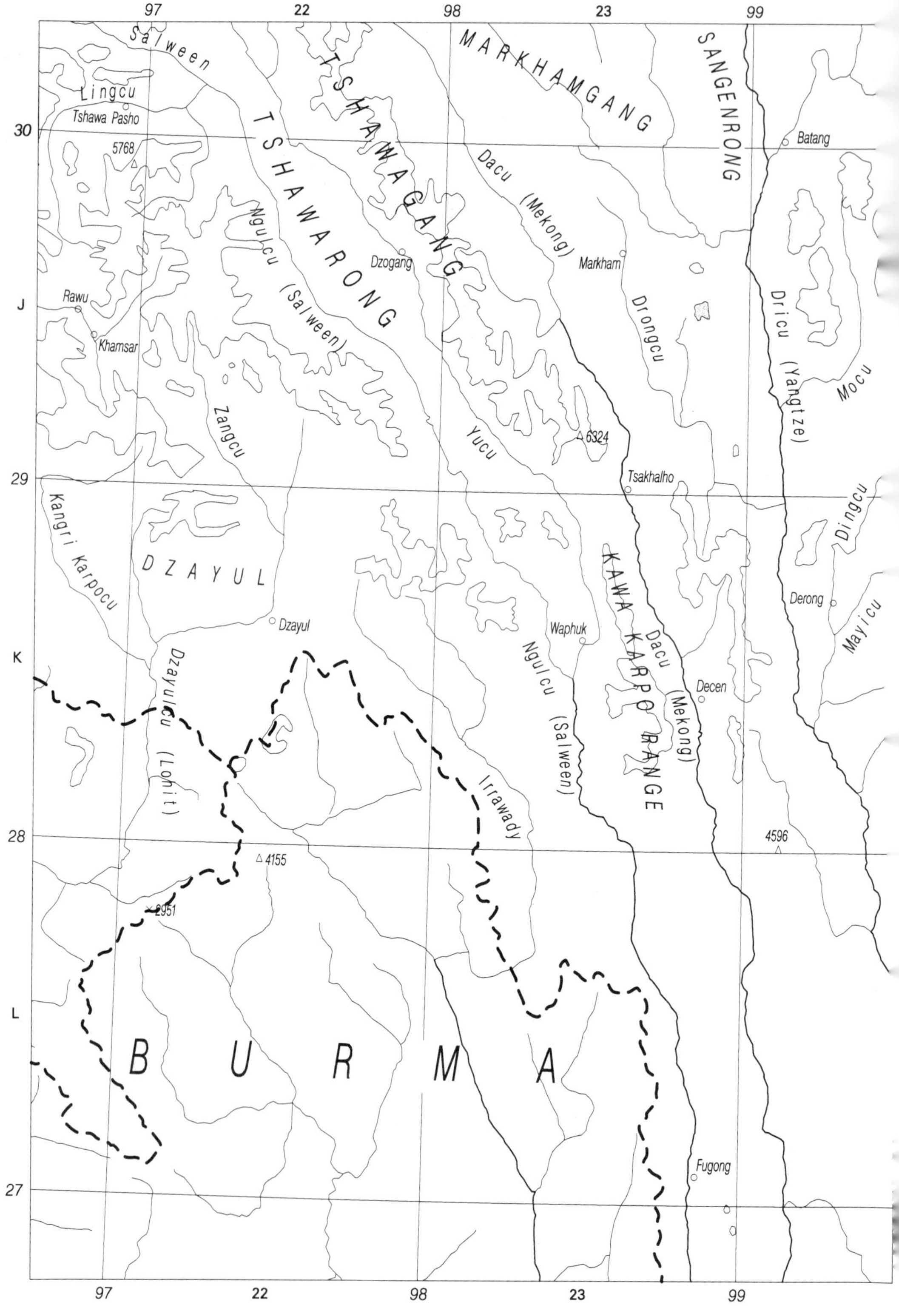

MAP 11
South–East Kham

0 50 100 kms

Land over 5000 M

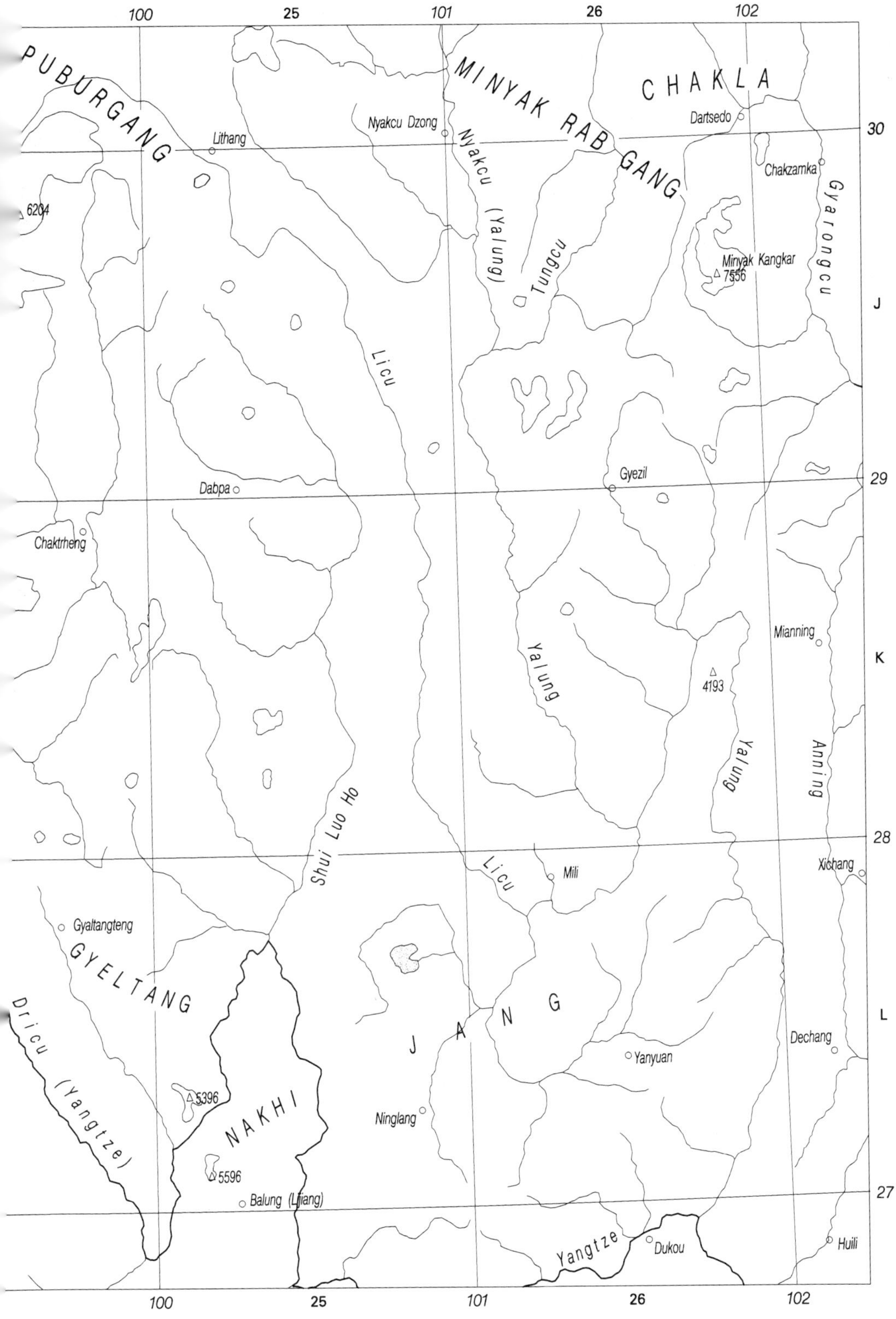

100
25
101
26
102
PUBURGANG
MINYAK RAB GANG
CHAKLA
Nyakcu Dzong
Dartsedo
30
Lithang
Nyakcu (Yalung)
Chakzamka
Gyarongcu
6204
Minyak Kangkar
7556
Tungcu
J
Licu
Gyezil
Dabpa
29
Chaktrheng
Mianning
K
Yalung
4193
Yalung
Anning
Shui Luo Ho
28
Licu
Mili
Xichang
Gyaltangteng
GYELTANG
L
Dricu (Yangtze)
J A N G
Dechang
Yanyuan
5396
NAKHI
Ninglang
5596
Balung (Lijiang)
27
Yangtze
Dukou
Huili
100
25
101
26
102

About the Author

HIS HOLINESS DUDJOM RINPOCHE was born in 1904 in the Puwo region of Tibet. As the supreme head of the Nyingma School, he ranked among the greatest of Tibetan Buddhist practitioners and was a lineage master upholding all the major Nyingma transmissions. He was also a discoverer of concealed treasure teachings (*gter-ston*) who established many teaching cycles widely practised and propagated to this day.

A prodigious and prolific scholar, his extraordinary clarity of mind manifested itself from his earliest years in an ability to communicate the profoundest teachings with a simplicity and grace that made his essential spirit readily available to all. The two treatises translated in *The Nyingma School of Tibetan Buddhism* are foremost among his several great encyclopaedic works. Compiled in exile, they were expressly intended to maintain for future generations the accumulated wealth of the Nyingma teachings within their own philosophical, historical and cultural context at a time when there was a risk of their being lost.

Dudjom Rinpoche's collected writings total some nineteen Tibetan volumes, and as an editor of important Tibetan texts, he was responsible for such vast compilations as the *Transmitted Precepts of the Nyingmapa* in fifty-five volumes. The sphere of his teaching activity spread throughout Tibet and Bhutan; the Tibetan-populated areas of Nepal and India; and in the latter part of his life, to many countries in the West and South-East Asia. He passed away at his home in the Dordogne, France, in 1987.

About the Translators

GYURME DORJE holds a Ph.D. in Tibetan literature (SOAS, 1987), and an M.A. in Sanskrit and Oriental Studies (Edinburgh, 1971). For over thirty years he has been continuously engaged in both classical and modern Tibetan studies, translating primary sources and conducting expeditions throughout the Tibetan plateau. He began translating *The Nyingma School of Tibetan Buddhism* at the suggestion of H.H. Dudjom Rinpoche in 1971. Other published works of which is author, translator, or co-editor include: *Tibetan Medical Paintings*, the *Tibet Handbook with Bhutan* (now in its third edition), and *Tibetan Elemental Divination Paintings*. Forthcoming publications include *The Great Temple of Lhasa, An Encyclopaedic Tibetan-English Dictionary, The Guhyagarbha Tantra: Dispelling the Darkness of the Ten Directions,* and *The Complete Tibetan Book of the Dead.*

MATTHEW KAPSTEIN (Ph.D., Brown University, 1987) is Professor of Tibetan and Buddhist Studies at the University of Chicago. He has studied with and translated for many leading Tibetan teachers, and was invited by H.H. Dudjom Rinpoche to participate in the translation of the present works beginning in 1979. His publications include *The Tibetan Assimilation of Buddhism* (Oxford University Press), *Reason's Traces* (Wisdom Publications), and, in collaboration with the anthropologist Melvyn Goldstein, *Buddhism in Contemporary Tibet* (University of California Press). He is presently working on a multi-volume history of Buddhist thought in Tibet.

Wisdom Publications

WISDOM PUBLICATIONS, a not-for-profit publisher, is dedicated to making available authentic Buddhist works for the benefit of all. We publish translations of the sutras and tantras, commentaries and teachings of past and contemporary Buddhist masters, and original works by the world's leading Buddhist scholars. We publish our titles with the appreciation of Buddhism as a living philosophy and with the special commitment to preserve and transmit important works from all the major Buddhist traditions.

To learn more about Wisdom, or to browse books online, visit our website at wisdompubs.org. You may request a copy of our mail-order catalog online or by writing to:

Wisdom Publications
199 Elm Street
Somerville, Massachusetts 02144 USA
Telephone: (617) 776-7416
Fax: (617) 776-7841
Email: info@wisdompubs.org
www.wisdompubs.org

The Wisdom Trust

As a not-for-profit publisher, Wisdom is dedicated to the publication of fine Dharma books for the benefit of all sentient beings and dependent upon the kindness and generosity of sponsors in order to do so. If you would like to make a donation to Wisdom, please do so through our Somerville office. If you would like to sponsor the publication of a book, please write or email us at the address above.

Thank you.

Wisdom is a nonprofit, charitable 501(c)(3) organization affiliated with the Foundation for the Preservation of the Mahayana Tradition (FPMT).